The **HUTCHINSON**
GUIDE TO THE
WORLD
THIRD EDITION

The HUTCHINSON GUIDE TO THE WORLD

THIRD EDITION

ORYX PRESS

The rare Arabian Oryx is believed to have inspired the myth of the unicorn. This desert antelope became virtually extinct in the early 1960s. At that time several groups of international conservationists arranged to have 9 animals sent to the Phoenix Zoo to be the nucleus of a captive breeding herd. Today the Oryx population is over 1,000 and over 500 have been returned to the Middle East.

Published in the United States in 1998
by The Oryx Press
4041 North Central at Indian School Road
Phoenix, Arizona 85012–3397

© 1998 by Helicon
42 Hythe Bridge Street
Oxford OX1 2EP
England

ISBN 1-57356-220-3
(99458603)

MANAGING EDITOR
Denise Dresner

CONTRIBUTORS
Anne Baker
Anna Farkas
David Munro
David Nash
Matthew Shepherd
Deborah Sporton

ART AND DESIGN
Terence Caven

EDITORS
Jane Anson
Malgorzata Colquhoun
Katie Emblen
Ingrid von Essen
Catherine Thompson

CARTOGRAPHY
Olive Pearson

PRODUCTION
Tony Ballsdon

Contents

Preface

Now in its third edition, the *Hutchinson Guide to the World* has been completely redesigned and expanded to give the reader quick access to facts and figures on the world's countries, places, and population. For ease of use, this edition has been split into three parts: countries of the world, world gazetteer, and appendices.

Countries of the World are arranged alphabetically, with an entry for each of the 192 sovereign nations. Some 50 categories of information are provided for each country, grouped under the general headings of Government, Economy and Resources, Population, Transport, History, and Practical Information.

The **World Gazetteer** includes over 6,500 articles on the world's cities and towns, regions, provinces, and geographical features.

The **Appendices** include tables on world geography, population, and administrative divisions.

Arrangement of entries
Entries are ordered alphabetically, as if there were no spaces between words. Thus, entries for words beginning 'New' follow the order:

New Brunswick
Newbury
New Caledonia
Newcastle

Words beginning 'St' and 'Saint' are both treated as if they were spelt 'Saint'.

Foreign names
Names of foreign places are usually shown in their English form, except where the foreign name is more familiar; thus, there is an entry for Florence, not Firenze, but for Livorno not Leghorn.

Chinese names
Pinyin, the preferred system for transcribing Chinese names of places, is generally used: thus, there is an entry at Beijing, not Peking.

Cross-references
Cross-references are used selectively, principally in entries for former names, foreign names, or alternative spellings that refer the reader directly to a main entry.

Abbreviations and symbols

GDP	–	gross domestic product
GNP	–	gross national product
PPP	–	purchasing power parity
km	–	kilometre
m	–	metre
mi	–	mile
mil	–	million
N, S, E, W	–	north, south, east, west
est	–	estimate.

Countries of the World

Afghanistan Republic of

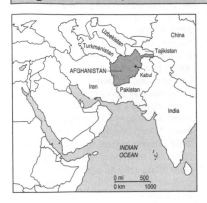

National name *Jamhuria Afghanistan*
Area 652,090 sq km/251,771 sq mi
Capital Kabul
Major towns/cities Kandahar, Herat, Mazar-i-Sharif, Jalalabad
Physical features mountainous in centre and NE (Hindu Kush mountain range; Khyber and Salang passes, Wakhan salient, and Panjshir Valley), plains in N and SW, Amu Darya (Oxus) River, Helmand River, Lake Saberi

Government

Head of state and government Mohammad Rabbani from 1996
Political system transitional
Administrative divisions 32 provinces
Political parties Hezb-i-Islami, Islamic fundamentalist Mujaheddin, anti-Western; Jamiat-i-Islami, Islamic fundamentalist Mujaheddin; National Liberation Front, moderate Mujaheddin
Armed forces approximately 248,000 (1995)
Conscription compulsory for four years, with break of three years after second year (since 1992 conscription has been difficult to enforce and desertion is common)
Death penalty retains and uses the death penalty for ordinary crimes
Defence spend (% GDP) 15.0 (1990); N/A (1995)
Education spend (% GNP) 2.0 (1992); N/A (1993–94)
Health spend (% GDP) 1.6 (1990)

Economy and resources

Currency afgháni
GDP ($ US) 12.8 billion (1995e)
Real GDP per capita (PPP) ($ US) 600 (1995e)

GDP growth rate N/A
Average annual inflation 56.7% (1991)
Foreign debt ($ US) 9.58 billion (1993)
Trading partners former USSR countries, Japan, Singapore, Germany
Resources natural gas, coal, iron ore, barytes, lapis lazuli, salt, talc, copper, chrome, gold, silver, asbestos, small petroleum reserves
Industries food products, cotton textiles, cement, coalmining, chemical fertilizers, small vehicle assembly plants, processed hides and skins, carpetmaking, sugar manufacture, leather and plastic goods
Exports fruit and nuts, carpets, wool, karakul skins, cotton, natural gas. Principal market: Kyrgyzstan 37.3% (1995)
Imports basic manufactured goods and foodstuffs (notably wheat), petroleum products, textiles, fertilizers, vehicles and spare parts. Principal source: Japan 25.6% (1995)
Arable land 12.1% (1993)
Agricultural products wheat, barley, maize, rice; livestock rearing (sheep, goats, cattle, and camels); world's leading opium producer (1995)

Population and society

Population 20,883,000 (1996e)
Population growth rate 5.8% (1990–95); 2.7% (2000–05)
Population density (per sq km) 32 (1996e)
Urban population (% of total) 20 (1995)
Age distribution (% of total population) <15 40.8%, 15–65 56.4%, >65 2.8% (1995)
Ethnic distribution Pathans, or Pushtuns, comprise the largest ethnic group, 54% of the population, followed by the Tajiks (concentrated in the N, 27%), the Uzbeks (8%), and Hazaras (7%)
Languages Pushtu, Dari (Persian), Uzbek, Turkoman, Kirgiz
Religions Muslim (85% Sunni, 15% Shi'ite)
Education (compulsory years) 6
Literacy rate 44% (men); 14% (women) (1995e)
Labour force 41% of population: 61% agriculture, 14% industry, 25% services (1992)
Life expectancy 45 (men); 46 (women) (1995–2000)
Child mortality rate (under 5, per 1,000 live births) 257 (1995)
Physicians 1 per 6,730 people (1990e)

TV sets (per 1,000 people) 10 (1995)
Radios (per 1,000 people) 122 (1995)

Transport

Airports two international airports: Kabul (Khwaja Rawash) and Kandahar; 18 domestic airports; total passenger km: 197 mil (1994)
Railroads none (a trans-Afghan railroad was proposed in an Afghan-Pakistan-Turkmen agreement of 1994)
Roads total road network: 21,000 km/ 13,050 mi, of which 13.3% paved (1995e); passenger cars: 1.5 per 1,000 people (1993e)

Chronology

6th century BC Part of Persian Empire under Cyrus II and Darius I.
329 BC Conquered by Alexander the Great.
323 BC Fell to the Seleucids, who ruled from Babylon.
304 BC Ruled by Mauryan dynasty in S and independent Bactria in N.
135 BC Central Asian tribes established Kusana dynasty.
3rd–7th centuries AD Decline of Kusana dynasty. Emergence of Sassanids as ruling power with Hepthalites (central Asian nomads) and western Turks also fighting for control.
642–11th century First Muslim invasion followed by a succession of Muslim dynasties, including Mahmud of Ghazni 998.
1219–14th century Mongol invasions led by Genghis Khan and Tamerlane.
16th–18th centuries Much of Afghanistan came under the rule of the Mogul Empire under Babur (Zahir) and Nadir Shah.
1747 Afghanistan became an independent emirate under Dost Muhammad.
1838–42 First Afghan War, instigated by Britain to counter the threat to British India from expanding Russian influence in Afghanistan.
1878–80 Second Afghan War.
1919 Afghanistan recovered full independence following Third Afghan War.
1953 Lt-Gen Daud Khan became prime minister and introduced social and economic reform programme.
1963 Daud Khan forced to resign and constitutional monarchy established.
1973 Monarchy overthrown in coup by Daud Khan.

1978 Daud Khan assassinated in coup; Muhammad Taraki and the communist People's Democratic Party of Afghanistan (PDPA) took over. Start of Muslim guerrilla (Mujaheddin) resistance.
1979 Taraki ousted and murdered; replaced by Hafizullah Amin. USSR entered country to prop up government, installing Babrak Karmal in power. Amin executed.
1986 Replacement of Karmal as PDPA leader by Dr Najibullah Ahmadzai. Partial Soviet troop withdrawal.
1988 New non-Marxist constitution adopted.
1989 Withdrawal of Soviet troops; state of emergency imposed as Mujaheddin

continued resistance to PDPA regime and civil war intensified.
1991 US and Soviet military aid withdrawn. Mujaheddin began talks with Russians and Kabul government.
1992 Najibullah government overthrown. Mujaheddin leader Burhanuddin Rabbani elected president. Hezb-i-Islami barred from government.
1993 Intensive fighting around Kabul. Peace agreement between Rabbani and dissident Hezb-i-Islami leader Gulbuddin Hekmatyar made Hekmatyar prime minister.
1994 Continuing rebel attacks on Kabul finally quelled. Hekmatyar dismissed from office.

1995 Talibaan Islamic fundamentalist army claimed town of Herat and advanced on Kabul.
1996 Talibaan controlled two-thirds of country, including Kabul; country split between Talibaan-controlled fundamentalist S and more liberal N; six-member interim council of clerics installed, headed by Mohamad Rabbani; strict Islamic law imposed; new regime not recognized by international community. UN-sponsored peace talks made little progress.
1997 Despite military reverses, Talibaan controlled majority of provinces, and were recognized as legitimate government of Afghanistan by Pakistan and Saudi Arabia.

Practical information

Visa requirements UK: visa required. USA: visa required
Embassy in the UK 31 Prince's Gate, London SW7 1QQ. Tel: (0171) 589 8891; fax: (0171) 581 3452
British embassy Karte Parwan, Kabul. Tel: (93) 30511 (the embassy is closed at present)
Embassy in the USA 2341 Wyoming Avenue NW, Washington, DC 20008. Tel: (202) 234 3770/3771; fax: (202) 328 3516
American embassy the USA does not have an embassy in Afghanistan (embassy closed January 1989)
Chamber of commerce Afghan Chamber of Commerce and Industry, Mohd Jah Khan Wat, Kabul. Tel: (93) 26796; telex: 245

Office hours generally 0800–1200 and 1300–1630 Sat–Wed; 0830–1300 Thu
Banking hours generally 0800–1200 and 1300–1630 Sat–Wed; 0800–1330 Thu
Time difference GMT+4.5
Chief tourist attractions Bamian (with its high statue of Buddha and thousands of painted caves); the Blue Mosque of Mazar; the suspended lakes of Bandi Amir; the Grand Mosque and minarets of Herat; the towns of Kandahar, Girishk, and Baekh (ancient Bactria); the high mountains of the Hindu Kush
Major holidays 27 April, 1 May, 19 August; variable: Eid-ul-Adha, Arafa, Ashora, end of Ramadan, New Year (Hindu), Prophet's Birthday, first day of Ramadan

---

Albania Republic of

National name *Republika e Shqipërisë*
Area 28,748 sq km/11,099 sq mi
Capital Tiranë (Tirana)
Major towns/cities Durrës, Shkodër, Elbasan, Vlorë, Korçë
Major ports Durrës

Physical features mainly mountainous, with rivers flowing E–W, and a narrow coastal plain

Government

Head of state Rexhep Mejdani from 1997
Head of government Fatos Nano from 1997
Political system emergent democracy
Administrative divisions 12 prefectures
Political parties Democratic Party of Albania (PDS; formerly the Democratic Party: DP), moderate, market-oriented; Socialist Party of Albania (PSS), ex-communist; Human Rights Union (HMU), Greek minority party
Armed forces 73,000 (1995)
Conscription compulsory for 15 months
Death penalty retains the death penalty for ordinary crimes, but considered abolitionist in practice; committed 1996 to put into place a moratorium on executions until total abolition
Defence spend (% GDP) 2.8 (1995)

Education spend (% GDP) 3.0 (1993–94)

Economy and resources

Currency lek
GDP ($ US) 2 billion (1994)
Real GDP per capita (PPP) ($ US) 2,788 (1994)
GDP growth rate 7.4% (1994); 1.4% (1990–95)
Average annual inflation 23% (1994)
Foreign debt ($ US) 709 million (1995)
Trading partners Italy, Greece, USA, Germany, Bulgaria
Resources chromite (one of world's largest producers), copper, coal, nickel, petroleum and natural gas
Industries food processing, mining, textiles, oil products, cement, energy generation
Exports chromium and chrome products, processed foodstuffs, plant and animal products, bitumen, electricity, tobacco. Principal market: Italy 52% (1994)

Imports machinery, fuels and minerals, plant and animal raw materials, chemical products. Principal source: Italy 34% (1994)
Arable land 24% (1993)
Agricultural products wheat, sugar beet, maize, potatoes, barley, sorghum, cotton, tobacco

Population and society

Population 3,401,000 (1996e)
Population growth rate 0.9% (1990–95); 1.1% (2000–05)
Population density (per sq km) 118 (1996)
Urban population (% of total) 37 (1995)
Age distribution (% of total population) <15 31.4%, 15–65 63.1%, >65 5.5% (1995)
Ethnic distribution 90% of Albanian, non-Slavic, descent; 8% ethnic Greek (concentrated in the S)
Languages Albanian, Greek
Religions Muslim, Orthodox, Roman Catholic
Education (compulsory years) 8
Literacy rate 85% (men); 85% (women) (1994)
Labour force 48% of population: 55% agriculture, 23% industry, 22% services (1990)
Unemployment 19.8% (1994)
Life expectancy 70 (men); 76 (women) (1995–2000)
Child mortality rate (under 5, per 1,000 live births) 40 (1995)
Physicians 1 per 530 people (1993e)
Hospital beds 1 per 327 people (1995e)
TV sets (per 1,000 people) 103 (1995)
Radios (per 1,000 people) 207 (1995)

Transport

Airports international airport: Tiranë (Rinas); no regular domestic air service; total passenger km: 2 mil (1994)

Railroads total length: around 720 km/ 447 mi (1994); total passenger km: 779 m (1990)
Roads total road network: 15,500 km/963 mi, of which 30% paved (1995); passenger cars: 19.5 per 1,000 people (1995)

Chronology

2000 BC Part of Illyria.
168 BC Illyria conquered by Romans.
AD 395 Became part of Byzantine Empire.
6th–14th centuries Byzantine decline exploited by Serbs, Normans, Slavs, Bulgarians, and Venetians.
1381 Ottoman invasion of Albania followed by years of resistance to Turkish rule.
1468 Resistance led by national hero Skanderbeg (George Kastrioti) largely collapsed, and Albania passed to Ottoman Empire.
15th–16th centuries Thousands fled to S Italy to escape Ottoman rule; over half of the rest of the population converted to Islam.
1878 Foundation of Albanian League promoted emergence of nationalism.
1912 Achieved independence from Turkey as a result of First Balkan War and end of Ottoman Empire in Europe.
1914–20 Occupied by Italy.
1925 Declared itself a republic.
1928–39 Monarchy of King Zog.
1939 Italian occupation led by Benito Mussolini.
1943–44 Under German rule following Italian surrender.
1946 Proclaimed Communist People's Republic of Albania, with Enver Hoxha as premier.
1949 Developed close links with Joseph Stalin in USSR and entered Comecon (Council for Mutual Economic Assistance).
1961 Broke with USSR in wake of Nikita Khrushchev's denunciation of Stalin, and withdrew from Comecon.

1978 Severed diplomatic links with China, choosing isolationism and neutrality.
1982 Hoxha made Ramiz Alia head of state.
1985 Death of Hoxha. Alia became head of the Party of Labour of Albania (PLA).
1987 Normal diplomatic relations restored with Canada, Greece, and West Germany.
1988 Albania attended conference of Balkan states for the first time since the 1930s.
1990 One-party system abandoned in face of popular protest; first opposition party formed.
1991 Communist PLA won first multiparty elections; Alia re-elected president. PLA renamed PSS.
1992 Presidential elections won by Sali Berisha of the Democratic Party (DP). Alia and other former communist officials charged with corruption and abuse of power. Totalitarian and communist parties banned.
1993 Open conflict began between ethnic Greeks and Albanians, followed by a purge of ethnic Greeks from senior positions in the civil service and army. Alia sentenced to eight years' imprisonment. DP renamed the PDS.
1995 Alia released from prison following appeal-court ruling. Communist-era MPs and Communist Party officials banned from national and local elections until 2002.
1996 Ruling PDS accused of ballot-rigging following overwhelming victory in elections.
1997 Antigovernment riots broke out following collapse of bogus 'investment' schemes; police killed demonstrators in southern port of Vlorë. Southern Albania fell under rebel control. General election was won by the PSS; Rexhep Mejdani was elected president and ex-communist Fatos Nano became prime minister at the head of a broad coalition.

Practical information

Visa requirements UK: visa not required. USA: visa not required
Embassy in the UK 4th Floor, 38 Grosvenor Gardens, London SW1W 0EB. Tel: (0171) 730 5709; fax: (0171) 730 5747
British embassy Office of the British Chargé d'Affaires, c/o French Embassy, Rruga Skënderben 14, Tiranë. Tel: (42) 34250; telex: 2150
Embassy in the USA Suite 1000, 1511 K Street NW, Washington, DC 20005.Tel: (202) 223 4942/8187; fax: (202) 628 7342
American embassy Rruga E Labinoti 103, Tiranë.

Tel: (42) 32875, 33520; fax: (42) 32222
Chamber of commerce Chamber of Commerce of the Republic of Albania, Rruga Kavajes 6, Tiranë. Tel/fax: (42) 27997
Office hours 0700–1500 Mon–Fri
Banking hours 0700–1500 Mon–Fri
Time difference GMT +1
Chief tourist attractions main tourist centres include Tiranë, Durrës, and Popgradec. The ancient towns of Apollonia and Butrint are important archaeological sites, and there are many other towns of historic interest
Major holidays 1–2, 11 January, 8 March, 1 May, 28 November, 25 December; variable: end of Ramadan, Easter Monday, Good Friday, Eid-ul-Adha, Orthodox Easter

Algeria Democratic and Popular Republic of

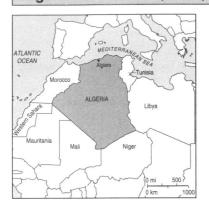

National name *al-Jumhuriya al-Jazairiya ad-Dimuqratiya ash-Shabiya*
Area 2,381,741 sq km/919,590 sq mi
Capital Algiers (al-Jaza'ir)
Major towns/cities Oran, Annaba, Blida, Sétif, Constantine (Qacentina)
Major ports Oran (Ouahran), Annaba (Bône)
Physical features coastal plains backed by mountains in N, Sahara desert in S; Atlas mountains, Barbary Coast, Chott Melrhir depression, Hoggar mountains

Government

Head of state Liamine Zeroual from 1994
Head of government Ahmed Ouyahia from 1995
Political system military rule
Administrative divisions 48 departments
Political parties National Liberation Front (FLN), nationalist, socialist; Socialist Forces Front (FSS), Berber-based, left of centre; Islamic Front for Salvation (FIS), Islamic fundamentalist (banned from 1992); National Democratic Rally (RND), left of centre
Armed forces 121,700 (1995)
Conscription compulsory for 18 months
Death penalty retained and used for ordinary crimes
Defence spend (% GDP) 2.5 (1995)
Education spend (% GNP) 5.6 (1993–94)
Health spend (% GDP) 5.4 (1990)

Economy and resources

Currency Algerian dinar
GDP ($ US) 41.9 billion (1994)
Real GDP per capita (PPP) ($ US) 5,442 (1994)
GDP growth rate 0.1% (1990–95)

Average annual inflation 29% (1994)
Foreign debt ($ US) 32.6 billion (1995)
Trading partners France, Italy, Germany, USA, the Netherlands
Resources natural gas and petroleum, iron ore, phosphates, lead, zinc, mercury, silver, salt, antimony, copper
Industries food processing, machinery and transport equipment, textiles, cement, tobacco
Exports crude oil, gas, vegetables, tobacco, hides, dates. Principal market: Italy 18.8% (1995)
Imports machinery and transportation equipment, food and basic manufactures. Principal source: France 29.6% (1995)
Arable land 3.1% (1993)
Agricultural products wheat, barley, potatoes, citrus fruits, olives, grapes; livestock rearing (sheep and cattle)

Population and society

Population 28,784,000 (1996e)
Population growth rate 2.3% (1990–95); 2% (2000–05)
Population density (per sq km) 12 (1996)
Urban population (% of total) 56 (1995)
Age distribution (% of total population) <15 38.7%, 15–65 57.7%, >65 3.6% (1995)
Ethnic distribution 99% of Arab Berber origin, the remainder of European descent, mainly French
Languages Arabic (official); Berber, French
Religion Sunni Muslim (state religion)
Education (compulsory years) 9
Literacy rate 64% (men); 45% (women) (1995e)
Labour force 28% of population: 26% agriculture, 31% industry, 43% services (1990)
Unemployment 25% (1995)
Life expectancy 67 (men); 70 (women) (1995–2000)
Child mortality rate (under 5, per 1,000 live births) 61 (1995)
Physicians 1 per 1,064 people (1991)
Hospital beds 1 per 415 people (1990)
TV sets (per 1,000 people) 89 (1995)
Radios (per 1,000 people) 238 (1995)

Transport

Airports international airports: Algiers (Houari Boumédienne), Annaba (El Mellah), Oran (Es Senia), Constantine (Ain El Bey); ten domestic airports; total passenger km: 2,706 mil (1994)

Railroads total length: 4,772 km/2,965 mi; total passenger km: 2,524 mil (1994)
Roads total road network: 102,424 km/63,646 mi, of which 68.9% paved (1995); passenger cars: 30.6 per 1,000 people (1995e)

Chronology

9th century BC Part of Carthaginian Empire, centred on Tunisia to the E, with Annaba, Algiers, and Skikda emerging as important trading posts en route to Spain.
146 BC Conquered by Romans, who called the area Numidia.
AD 396 St Augustine, one of the great early Christian leaders, became bishop of Hippo, modern Annaba.
6th century Part of the Byzantine Empire.
late 7th century Conquered by Muslim Arabs, who spread Islam as the basis of a new Berberized Arab-Islamic civilization.
1516 Ottoman Turks expelled recent Christian Spanish invaders. Under Ottoman rule much influence was left to local Arab tribes, Berbers, Barbary pirates, and deys, administrative officers who were elected for life.
1816 Anglo-Dutch forces bombarded Algiers as a reprisal against the Barbary pirates' attacks on Mediterranean shipping.
1830–47 French occupation of Algiers, followed by extension of control to the N, overcoming fierce resistance from Amir Abd al-Qadir, a champion of Arab Algerian nationalism, and from Morocco.
1850–70 Mountainous inland region, inhabited by the Kabyles, occupied by French.
1871 Major rebellion against French rule as French settlers began to immigrate and take over the best agricultural land.
1900–09 Sahara region subdued by France, who kept it under military rule.
1937 Algerian People's Party (PPA) formed by the charismatic separatist Messali Hadj.
1940 Following France's defeat by Nazi Germany, Algeria became allied to the pro-Nazi Vichy regime during World War II.
1945 8,000 died following the ruthless suppression of an abortive PPA-supported uprising against French rule.
1954–62 Battle of Algiers: bitter war of independence fought between the

National Liberation Front (FLN) and the French colonial army.

1958 French inability to resolve the escalating civil war in Algeria, where French settlers had risen in favour of integration with France, toppled the Fourth Republic and brought to power, in Paris, Gen Charles de Gaulle, who accepted the principle of national self-determination.

1962 Independence achieved from France. Republic declared. Ahmed Ben Bella of the FLN elected prime minister; many French settlers fled.

1963 Ben Bella elected Algeria's first president and one-party state established.

1965 Ben Bella deposed by military, led by Col Houari Boumédienne (FLN).

1971 Oil and gas industry nationalized.

1976 New Islamic-socialist constitution approved.

1978 Death of Boumédienne.

1979 Benjedid Chadli (FLN) elected president. Ben Bella freed after 14 years of house arrest.

1981 Algeria helped secure release of US hostages in Iran.

1988 Riots in protest at austerity policies; 170 killed. Reform programme introduced. Diplomatic relations restored with Morocco after a 12-year break.

1989 Constitutional changes introduced limited political pluralism.

1991 Elections cancelled after Islamic fundamentalist Islamic Salvation Front (FIS) won first round of multiparty elections.

1992 Chadli resigned; military took control of government; Muhammad Boudiaf became president. State of emergency declared and FIS ordered to disband. Boudiaf assassinated, allegedly by fundamentalists, and was replaced by Ali Kafi.

1993 Worsening civil strife; assassinations of politicians and other public figures; foreigners murdered.

1994 Gen Lamine Zeroual replaced Kafi as president. Fundamentalists' campaign of violence intensified.

1995 Zeroual won presidential elections.

1996 Constitution amended to increase president's powers and counter religious fundamentalism. Arabic declared the official public language.

1997 Widespread killings by fundamentalists. RND-FLN victory in national assembly elections. Ahmed Ouyuahia reappointed prime minister.

Practical information

Visa requirements UK: visa required. USA visa required

Embassy in the UK 54 Holland Park, London W11 3RS. Tel: (0171) 221 7800; fax: (0171) 221 0448

British embassy BP 43, Résidence Cassiopée, Bâtiment B, 7 chemin des Glycines, 16000 Alger-Gare, Algiers. Tel: (2) 622 411; fax: (2) 692 410

Embassy in the USA 2118 Kalorama Road NW, Washington, DC 20008. Tel: (202) 265 2800

American embassy 4 chemin Cheikh Bachir El-Ibrahimi, Algiers.Tel: (2) 691 186, 691 854, 693 875, 691 255; fax: (2) 693 979

Chamber of commerce Chambre Nationale de Commerce (CNC), BP100, Palais Consulaire, rue Amilcar Cabral, Algiers. Tel: (2) 575 555; fax: (2) 629 991

Office hours generally 0800–1200 and 1300–1700 Sat–Wed

Banking hours 0900–1630 Sun–Thu

Time difference GMT +/–0

Chief tourist attractions include the Mediterranean coast, the Atlas Mountains, and the desert; the Hoggar massif and the Tassili N'Ajjer (Plateau of Chasms) – both important centres of Tuareg culture

Major holidays 1 January, 1 May, 19 June, 5 July, 1 November; variable: Eid-ul-Adha, Ashora, end of Ramadan, New Year (Muslim), Prophet's Birthday

---

Andorra Principality of

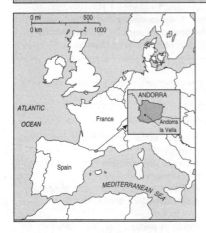

National name *Principat d'Andorra*
Area 468 sq km/180 sq mi
Capital Andorra-la-Vella
Major towns/cities Les Escaldes, Escaldes-Engordany (suburb of capital)

Physical features mountainous, with narrow valleys; the E Pyrenees, Valira River

Government

Heads of state Joan Marti i Alanis (bishop of Urgel, Spain) and Jacques Chirac (president of France)
Head of government Marc Forne from 1994
Political system co-principality
Administrative divisions seven parishes
Political parties National Democratic Grouping (AND; formerly the Democratic Party of Andorra: PDA) moderate, centrist; National Democratic Initiative (IND), left of centre; New Democracy Party (ND), centrist; National Andorran Coalition (CNA), centrist; Liberal Union (UL), right of centre
Armed forces no standing army

Death penalty abolished 1990 (last execution 1943)

Economy and resources

Currency French franc and Spanish peseta
GDP ($ US) 1 billion (1993e)
Real GDP per capita (PPP) ($ US) 16,200 (1993e)
GDP growth rate N/A
Trading partners France, Spain
Resources iron, lead, alum, hydro power
Industries cigar and cigarette manufacturing, textiles, leather goods, wood products, processed foodstuffs, furniture, tourism, banking and financial services
Exports cigars and cigarettes, furniture, electricity. Principal market: France 46.7% (1994)
Imports foodstuffs, electricity, mineral fuels. Principal source: Spain 38.9% (1994)

Arable land 21% (1993)
Agricultural products tobacco, potatoes, rye, barley, oats, vegetables; livestock rearing (mainly sheep) and timber production

Population and society

Population 71,000 (1996e)
Population growth rate 5.5% (1990–95)
Population density (per sq km) 157 (1996)
Urban population (% of toal) 63 (1995)
Age distribution (% of total population) <15 18%, 15–65 72.1%, >65 9.9% (1989)
Ethnic distribution 25% Andorrans, 75% immigrant Spanish workers
Languages Catalan (official); Spanish, French
Religion Roman Catholic
Education (compulsory years) 10
Literacy rate 99% (men); 99% (women) (1995e)
Labour force 4% agriculture, 23% industry, 73% services (1992)
Unemployment 0% (1994)
Life expectancy 70 (men); 73 (women) (1994e)
Physicians 1 per 8 people (1994e)

Hospital beds 1 per 454 people (1994e)
TV sets (per 1,000 people) 368 (1995)
Radios (per 1,000 people) 212 (1995)

Transport

Airports international airports: none; closest airport for Andorran traffic 20 km/ 12.5 mi from Andorra at Seo de Urgel, Spain
Railroads none; there is a connecting bus service to stations in France and Spain
Roads total road network: 220 km/137 mi, of which 55 % paved (1995); passenger cars: 62.1 per 1,000 people (1993)

Chronology

AD 803 *Holy Roman Emperor Charlemagne liberated Andorra from Muslim control.*
819 Louis I, 'the Pious', the son of Charlemagne, granted control over the area to the Spanish bishop of Urgel.
1278 Treaty signed making Spanish bishop and French count joint rulers of Andorra (through marriage the king of France later inherited the count's right).

1806 After temporary suspension during the French Revolution, from 1789 the feudal arrangement of dual allegiance to the co-princes (French and Spanish rulers) was re-established by the French emperor Napoleon Bonaparte.
1970 Extension of franchise to third-generation female and second-generation male Andorrans.
1976 First political organization, Democratic Party of Andorra, formed.
1977 Franchise extended to first-generation Andorrans.
1981 First prime minister appointed by General Council.
1991 Links with European Community formalized.
1993 New constitution legalized political parties and introduced first direct elections, leading to coalition government being formed under acting prime minister, Oscar Ribas Reig. Became member of United Nations.
1994 Reig resigned after coalition lost support and was succeeded by Marc Forne; joined Council of Europe.
1997 Liberal Union (UL) won assembly majority in general election.

Practical information
Visa requirements UK: visa not required. USA: visa not required
Embassy in the UK none; Andorran Trade Delegation, 63 Westover Road, London SW18 2RF. Tel: (0181) 874 4806
British embassy British Consulate (Barcelona), 13th Floor, Edificio Torre de Barcelona, Avenida Diagonal 477, 08036 Barcelona. Tel: (3) 419 9044; fax: (3) 405 2411
Embassy in the USA 2 United Nations Plaza, 25th Floor, New York, NY 10017. Tel: (212) 750 8064; fax: (212) 750 6630
American embassy the USA does not have an embassy in Andorra; US interests in Andorra are represented by the Consulate General's office: Paseo Reina Elisenda 23, 08034 Barcelona, Spain. Tel: (343) 280 2227; fax: (343) 205 7705

Chamber of commerce Sindicat d'Initiativa de las Valls d'Andorra, Carrer Dr Vilanova, Andorra la Vella. Tel: 820 214; fax: 825 823
Office hours vary considerably
Banking hours 0900–1300 and 1500–1700 Mon–Fri; 0900–1200 Sat
Time difference GMT +1
Chief tourist attractions attractive mountain scenery, winter-sports facilities available at five skiing centres; duty-free shopping facilities; the spa town of Les Escaldes
Major holidays 1, 6, January, 19 March, 1 May, 24 June, 15 August, 8 September, 1, 4, November, 8, 25–26 December; variable: Ascension Thursday, Carnival, Corpus Christi, Good Friday, Easter Monday, Whit Monday

Angola People's Republic of

National name *República Popular de Angola*
Area 1,246,700 sq km/481,350 sq mi
Capital Luanda (and chief port)
Major towns/cities Lobito, Benguela, Huambo, Lubango, Malange, Namibe (formerly Moçâmedes)
Major ports Huambo, Lubango, Malange
Physical features narrow coastal plain rises to vast interior plateau with rainforest in NW; desert in S; Cuanza, Cuito, Cubango, and Cunene rivers

Government

Head of state José Eduardo dos Santos from 1979
Head of government Fernando Franca van Dunem from 1996
Political system emergent democracy
Administrative divisions 18 provinces
Political parties People's Movement for the Liberation of Angola–Workers' Party (MPLA–PT), Marxist-Leninist; National Union for the Total Independence of Angola (UNITA); National Front for the Liberation of Angola (FNLA)

Armed forces 82,000 (1995); plus a paramilitary force of approximately 40,000
Conscription military service is compulsory for two years
Death penalty abolished 1992
Defence spend (% GDP) 4.8 (1995)
Education spend (% GNP) 2.8 (1992); N/A (1993–94)
Health spend (% GDP) 1.8 (1990)

Economy and resources

Currency kwanza
GDP ($ US) 3.72 billion (1995)
Real GDP per capita (PPP) ($ US) 1,600 (1994e)
GDP growth rate 8.6% (1994); –4.1% (1990–95)
Average annual inflation 972% (1994)
Foreign debt ($ US) 11.5 billion (1995)
Trading partners Portugal, USA, Germany, France, Japan, Brazil, the Netherlands
Resources petroleum, diamonds, granite, iron ore, marble, salt, phosphates, manganese, copper
Industries mining, petroleum refining, food processing, textiles, construction materials
Exports petroleum and petroleum products, diamonds, gas. Principal market: USA 65.4% (1995)
Imports foodstuffs, transport equipment, base metals, electrical equipment. Principal source: France 23.4% (1995)
Arable land 2.4% (1993)
Agricultural products coffee, sugar cane, bananas, cassava, maize, sweet potatoes

Population and society

Population 11,185,000 (1996e)
Population growth rate 3.7% (1990–95); 3.1% (2000–05)
Population density (per sq km) 9 (1996)
Urban population (% of total) 32 (1995)
Age distribution (% of total population) <15 47.1%, 15–65 50%, >65 2.9% (1995)
Ethnic distribution eight main ethnic groups (Bakonga, Mbunda, Ovimbundu, Lunda-Tchokwe, Nganguela, Nyaneka-Humbe, Hiriro, and Ambo), and about 100 subgroups. A major exodus of Europeans in the 1970s left around

30,000, mainly Portuguese
Languages Portuguese (official); Bantu dialects
Religions Roman Catholic 68%, Protestant 20%, animist 12%
Education (compulsory years) 8
Literacy rate 56%(men); 28% (women) (1995e)
Labour force 68.2% agriculture, 10.5% industry, 21.3% services (1991)
Unemployment 15% (1993)
Life expectancy 47 (men); 51 (women) (1995–2000)
Child mortality rate (under 5, per 1,000 live births) 292 (1995)
Physicians 1 per 13,888 people (1990e)
Hospital beds 1 per 775 people (1990e)
TV sets (per 1,000 people) 7.4 (1995)
Radios (per 1,000 people) 34 (1995)

Transport

Airports international airports: Luanda (4 de Fevereio); domestic services to all major towns; total passenger km: 1,396 mil (1994)
Railroads total length: 2,771 km/ 1,722 mi; total passenger km: 246 mil (1991)
Roads total road network: 72,626 km/ 45,130 mi, of which 25% paved (1995); passenger cars: 17.8 per 1,000 people (1995e)

Chronology

14th century Under Wene, the powerful Kongo kingdom extended control over much of N Angola.
early 16th century The Kongo ruler King Afonso I adopted Christianity and sought constructive relations with Portuguese traders.
1575 and 1617 Portugal secured control over the ports of Luanda and Benguela and began to pentetrate inland, meeting resistance from Queen Nzinga, the Ndonga ruler.
17th–18th centuries Inland, the Lunda peoples established powerful kingdoms which stretched into S Congo; the Portuguese made Angola a key centre for the export of slaves; over one million were shipped to Brazil 1580–1680.
1836 Slave trade officially abolished.
1885–1915 Military campaigns waged by Portugal to conquer the interior.
1926 Modern borders delineated.
1951 Angola became an overseas territory of Portugal.

1956 Formation of People's Movement for the Liberation of Angola (MPLA), a socialist guerrilla independence movement based in the Congo to the N.
1961 50,000 massacred in rebellion on coffee plantations; forced labour abolished, but armed struggle for independence now waged.
1962 Second nationalist guerrilla movement formed, the National Front for the Liberation of Angola (FNLA), based in N.
1966 National Union for the Total Independence of Angola (UNITA) formed in SE Angola as a breakaway from the FNLA.
1975 Independence achieved from Portugal. MPLA (backed mainly by Cuba) proclaimed People's Republic of Angola under the presidency of Dr Agostinho Neto. FNLA and UNITA (backed by South Africa and the USA) proclaimed People's Democratic Republic of Angola.
1976 MPLA gained control of most of the country. South African troops withdrew, but Cuban units remained as civil war continued.
1979 Neto died and was succeeded by José Eduardo dos Santos.
1980 UNITA guerrillas, aided by South Africa, continued raids against the Luanda government and bases of the Namibian South West Africa People's Organization (SWAPO) in Angola.
1988 Peace treaty, providing for the withdrawal of all foreign troops, signed with South Africa and Cuba.
1989 Cease-fire agreed with UNITA broke down and guerrilla activity resumed.
1991 Peace agreement ended civil war. Amnesty for all political prisoners. New multiparty constitution.
1992 MPLA general election victory, led by dos Santos, was fiercely disputed by UNITA, and plunged the country into renewed civil war.
1993 MPLA government recognized by USA. United Nations (UN) sanctions imposed against UNITA.
1994 Peace treaty signed by government and UNITA representatives.
1995 UN peacekeepers drafted in.
1996 UNITA leader Jonas Savimbi rejected offer of vice presidency.
1997 Delay in formation of national unity government. Unity government eventually sworn in but boycotted by Savimbi.

Practical information

Visa requirements UK: visa required. USA: visa required
Embassy in the UK 98 Park Lane, London W1Y 3TA.
Tel: (0171) 495 1752; fax: (0171) 495 1635
British embassy CP 1244, Rua Diogo Cão 4, Luanda.
Tel: (2) 392 991; fax: (2) 333 331
Embassy in the USA 1819 L Street NW, Suite 400,
Washington, DC 20036. Tel: (202) 785 1156;
fax: (202) 785 1258
American embassy No 32 Rua Houari Boumédienne,
Miramar, Luanda. Tel: (2) 345 481, 346 418; fax: (2) 346 924
Chamber of commerce Angolan Chamber of Commerce

and Industry, Largo do Kinaxixi 14, 1° andar, CP 92, Luanda.
Tel: (2) 344 506
Office hours 0730–1230 and 1430–1830 Mon–Thu;
0730–1230 and 1430–1730 Fri
Banking hours 0845–1600 Mon–Fri
Time difference GMT +1
Chief tourist attractions travel within Angola remains unsafe
due to the presence of undisciplined armed troops,
unexploded landmines, hostile actions against aircraft, and
widespread banditry (June 1996)
Major holidays 1 January, 4 February, 27 March, 14 April, 1
May, 1 August, 17 September, 11 November, 1, 10, 25
December

Antigua and Barbuda State of

Area Antigua 280 sq km/108 sq mi,
Barbuda 161 sq km/62 sq mi, plus
Redonda 1 sq km/0.4 sq mi (440 sq km/
169 sq mi altogether)
Capital St John's (on Antigua) (and chief
port)
Major towns/cities Codrington (on
Barbuda)
Physical features low-lying tropical
islands of limestone and coral with some
higher volcanic outcrops; no rivers and
low rainfall result in frequent droughts
and deforestation. Antigua is the largest
of the Leeward Islands; Redonda is an
uninhabited island of volcanic rock rising
to 305 m/1,000 ft

Government

Head of state Elizabeth II from 1981,
represented by governor general James
B Carlisle from 1993
Head of government Lester Bird from
1994
Political system liberal democracy
Administrative divisions six parishes
Political parties Antigua Labour Party

(ALP), moderate left of centre; United
Progressive Party (UPP), centrist;
Barbuda People's Movement (BPM), left
of centre
Armed forces 200 (1995); US
government leases two military bases on
Antigua
Conscription military service is
voluntary
Death penalty retained and used for
ordinary crimes
Defence spend (% GDP) 0.8% (1995)
Education spend (% GNP) 3.7%
(1988); N/A (1993–94)

Economy and resources

Currency Eastern Caribbean dollar
GDP ($ US) 494 million (1994)
Real GDP per capita (PPP) ($ US)
8,977 (1994)
GDP growth rate 5.3% (1994)
Average annual inflation 3.5%
(1994)
Foreign debt ($ US) 327 million
(1994)
Trading partners USA, UK, Canada,
Trinidad and Tobago, Barbados
Industries oil refining, food and
beverage products, paint, bedding,
furniture, electrical components. Tourism
is the main economic activity.
Exports petroleum products, food,
manufactures, machinery and transport
equipment. Principal market: USA
(mainly re-exports)
Imports petroleum, food and live
animals, machinery and transport
equipment, manufactures, chemicals.
Principal source: USA 27% (1994e)
Arable land 18% (1993)
Agricultural products cucumbers,
pumpkins, mangoes, coconuts, limes,
melons, pineapples, cotton; fishing

Population and society

Population 66,000 (1996e)
Population growth rate 0.6% (1990–95)
Population density (per sq km) 150
(1996)
Urban population (% of total) 31 (1992)
Age distribution (% of total population)
<15 38%, 15–65 56.9%, >65 5.1%
(1992)
Ethnic distribution population almost
entirely of black African descent
Language English
Religion Christian (mostly Anglican)
Education (compulsory years) 11
Literacy rate 92% (men); 88% (women)
(1992)
Labour force 11% agriculture, 19.7%
industry, 69.3% services (1991)
Unemployment 3.2% (1990)
Life expectancy 70 (men); 74 (women)
(1994e)
Child mortality rate (under 5, per 1,000
live births) 22 (1995)
Physicians 1 per 3,750 people (1990)
Hospital beds 1 per 364 people (1990)
TV sets (per 1,000 people) 424 (1995)
Radios (per 1,000 people) 439 (1995)

Transport

Airports international airports: St John's
(V C Bird International); one airstrip on
Barbuda; total passenger km: 240 mil
(1994)
Railroads none
Roads total road network: 245 km/
152 mi (1995e); passenger cars: 195 per
1,000 people (1994)

Chronology

1493 Antigua, then peopled by Native
American Caribs, visited by Christopher
Columbus; he named it after a painting in

the Church of Sante Maria la Antigua, in
Seville.
1632 Antigua colonized by British settlers
from St Kitts.
1667 Treaty of Breda formally ceded
Antigua to Britain, ending French claim.
1674 Christopher Codrington, a sugar
planter from Barbados, established sugar
plantations and acquired Barbuda island
on lease from the British monarch in
1685; Africans brought in as slaves.
1834 Antigua's slaves were freed.
1860 Annexation of Barbuda.
1871–1956 Antigua and Barbuda

administered as part of the Leeward
Islands federation.
1946 Antigua Labour Party (ALP) formed
by Vere Bird.
1958–62 Part of the West Indies
Federation.
1967 Antigua and Barbuda became an
associated state within the
Commonwealth, with full internal
independence, but Britain responsible for
defence and foreign affairs.
1969 Separatist movement developed on
Barbuda.
1971 Progressive Labour Movement

(PLM) won the general election,
defeating ALP, and George Walter
replaced Bird as prime minister.
1976 PLM called for early independence,
but ALP urged caution. ALP, led by Bird,
won the general election.
1981 Independence from Britain
achieved.
1983 Assisted US invasion of Grenada,
despite policy on nonalignment.
1991 Bird remained in power despite
calls for his resignation.
1993 Lester Bird succeeded his father as
ALP leader.

Practical information

Visa requirements UK: visa not required. USA: visa not
required
Embassy in the UK 15 Thayer Street, London W1M 5LD.
Tel: (0171) 486 7073/4/5; fax: (0171) 486 9970
British embassy British High Commission, PO Box 483,
Price Waterhouse Centre, 11 Old Parham Road, St John's.
Tel: 462 0008/9; fax: 462 2806
Embassy in the USA 3216 New Mexico Avenue NW,
Washington, DC 20016. Tel: (202) 362 5211, 5166, 5122;
fax: (202) 362 5225
American embassy the USA does not have an embassy in
Antigua and Barbuda (embassy closed 30 June 1994); the
US ambassador to Barbados is accredited to Antigua and
Barbuda

Chamber of commerce Antigua and Barbuda Chamber of
Commerce and Industry Ltd, Redcliffe Street, POB 774,
St John's. Tel: 462 0743; fax: 462 4575
Office hours 0800–1630 Mon–Thu; 0800–1500 Fri
Banking hours 0800–1400 Mon–Thu (Barclays 0800–1400
Mon, Tue, and Wed; 0800–1700 Fri)
Time difference GMT –4
Chief tourist attractions over 300 beaches; the historic
Nelson's Dockyard in English Harbour (a national park);
cruise-ship facilities; Barbuda is less developed, but offers
pink sandy beaches, beauty, and wildlife; animal attractions;
international sailing regatta and carnival week
Major holidays 1 January, 1 July, 1 November, 25–26
December; variable: Good Friday, Easter Monday, Whit
Monday, Labour Day (May), CARICOM (July), Carnival
(August)

Argentina Republic of

National name *República Argentina*
Area 2,780,092 sq km/1,073,393 sq mi
Capital Buenos Aires
Major towns/cities Rosario, Córdoba,
San Miguel de Tucumán, Mendoza,
Santa Fé, La Plata
Major ports La Plata and Bahía Blanca

Physical features mountains in W,
forest and savanna in N, pampas
(treeless plains) in E central area,
Patagonian plateau in S; rivers
Colorado, Salado, Paraná, Uruguay, Río
de La Plata estuary; Andes mountains,
with Aconcagua the highest peak in the
W hemisphere; Iguaçu Falls
Territories claims Falkland Islands (*Islas
Malvinas*), South Georgia, the South
Sandwich Islands, and part of
Antarctica

Government

Head of state Carlos Menem from 1989
Head of government Carlos Menem
from 1989
Political system democratic federal
republic
Administrative divisions 23 provinces
and one federal district (Buenos Aires)
Political parties Radical Civic Union
Party (UCR), moderate centrist;
Justicialist Party (PJ), right-wing
Perónist; Movement for Dignity and

Independence (Modin), right-wing; Front
for a Country in Solidarity (Frepaso),
centre left
Armed forces 67,300 plus paramilitary
gendarmerie of 18,000 run by Ministry of
Defence (June 1995)
Conscription abolished 1995
Death penalty reintroduced 1976
Defence spend (% GDP) 1.7 (1995)
Education spend (% GNP) 3.6
(1993–94)
Health spend (% GDP) 4.2 (1990)

Economy and resources

Currency peso = 10,000 australs (which
it replaced 1992)
GDP ($ US) 281.9 billion (1994)
Real GDP per capita (PPP) ($ US)
8,937 (1994)
GDP growth rate 7.4% (1994); 5.7%
(1990–95)
Average annual inflation 4.2% (1994);
255.4% (1985–95)
Foreign debt ($ US) 89.75 billion
(1995)

Trading partners USA, Brazil, the Netherlands, Germany, Italy, Uruguay, Chile

Resources coal, crude oil, natural gas, iron ore, lead ore, zinc ore, tin, gold, silver, uranium ore, marble, borates, granite

Industries petroleum and petroleum products, primary iron, crude steel, sulphuric acid, synthetic rubber, paper and paper products, crude oil, cement, cigarettes, motor vehicles

Exports meat and meat products, prepared animal fodder, cereals, petroleum and petroleum products, soya beans, vegetable oils and fats. Principal market: Brazil 20.8% (1995)

Imports machinery and transport equipment, chemicals and mineral products. Principal sources: USA 26.2% (1995)

Arable land 9% (1993)

Agricultural products wheat, maize, soya beans, sugar cane, rice, sorghum, potatoes, tobacco, sunflowers, cotton, vine fruits, citrus fruit; livestock production (chiefly cattle)

Population and society

Population 35,219,000 (1996e)

Population growth rate 1.2% (1990–95); 1.1% (2000–05)

Population density (per sq km) 13 (1996)

Urban population (% of total) 88 (1995)

Age distribution (% of total population) <15 28.7%; 15–65 61.8%; >65 9.5% (1995)

Ethnic distribution 85% of European descent, mainly Spanish; 15% mestizo (offspring of Spanish-American and Native American parents)

Languages Spanish 95% (official); Italian 3%

Religion Roman Catholic (state-supported)

Education (compulsory years) 7; age limits 7–16

Literacy rate 95% (men); 95% (women) (1995e)

Labour force 38% of population: 12% agriculture, 32% industry, 55% services

Unemployment 18.6% (May 1995)

Life expectancy 70 (men); 77 (women) (1995–2000)

Child mortality rate (under 5, per 1,000 live births) 27 (1995)

Physicians 1 per 329 people (1991)

Hospital beds 1 per 222 people (1995)

TV sets (per 1,000 people) 219 (1995)

Radios (per 1,000 people) 676 (1995)

Transport

Airports international airports: Buenos Aires, Aeroparque Jorge Newbery, Córdoba, Corrientes, El Plumerillo, Ezeiza, Jujuy, Resistencia, Río Gallegos, Salta, San Carlos de Bariloche; domestic services to all major towns; total passenger km: 11,250 mil (1994)

Railroads total length: 34,115 km/ 21,199 mi; total passenger km: 6,460 mil (1994)

Roads total road network: 216,100 km/ 134,285 mi, of which 28.5% paved (1995e); passenger cars: 135 per 1,000 people (1995e)

Chronology

1516 Spanish navigator Juan Diaz de Solis discovered Río de La Plata.

1536 Buenos Aires founded, but soon abandoned because of attacks by Native Americans.

1580 Buenos Aires re-established as part of Spanish province of Asunción.

1617 Buenos Aires became a separate province within Spanish viceroyalty of Lima.

1776 Spanish South American Empire reorganized: Atlantic regions became viceroyalty of La Plata, with Buenos Aires as capital.

1810 After French conquest of Spain, Buenos Aires junta took over government of viceroyalty.

1816 Independence proclaimed as United Provinces of Río de La Plata, but Bolivia and Uruguay soon seceded; civil war followed between federalists and those who wanted a unitary state.

1835–52 Dictatorship of General Juan Manuel Rosas.

1853 Adoption of federal constitution based on US model; Buenos Aires refused to join confederation.

1861 Buenos Aires incorporated into Argentine confederation by force.

1865–70 Argentina took part in War of Triple Alliance against Paraguay.

late 19th century Large-scale European immigration and rapid economic development; Argentina became a major world supplier of meat and grain.

1880 Buenos Aires became a special federal district and national capital.

1880–1916 Government dominated by oligarchy of conservative landowners; each president effectively chose his own successor.

1916 Following introduction of secret ballot, Radical Party of Hipólito Irigoyen won election victory, beginning a period of 14 years in government.

1930 Military coup ushered in a series of conservative governments sustained by violence and fraud.

1943 Group of pro-German army officers seized power; Colonel Juan Perón emerged as a leading figure.

1946 Perón won free presidential election; he secured working-class support through welfare measures, trade unionism, and the popularity of his wife, Eva Perón (Evita).

1949 New constitution abolished federalism and increased powers of president.

1952 Death of Evita. Support for Perón began to decline.

1955 Perón overthrown; constitution of 1853 restored.

1966–70 Dictatorship of General Juan Carlos Ongania.

1973 Perónist Party won free elections; Perón returned from exile in Spain to become president.

1974 Perón died; succeeded by his third wife, Isabel Perón.

1976 Coup resulted in rule by military junta headed by Lt-Gen Jorge Videla (until 1978; succeeded by General Roberto Viola 1978–81 and General Leopoldo Galtieri 1981–82).

1976–83 Military regime conducted murderous campaign ('Dirty War') against left-wing elements.

1982 Invasion of Falkland Islands by Argentina. Intervention and defeat by UK; Galtieri replaced by General Reynaldo Bignone.

1983 Return to civilian rule under President Raúl Alfonsín; investigation launched into 'disappearance' of more than 8,000 people during 'Dirty War'.

1985 Economic austerity programme failed to halt hyperinflation.

1989 Perónist candidate Carlos Menem won presidential election. Annual inflation rate reached 12,000%.

1990 Full diplomatic relations with UK restored.

1995 President Menem re-elected.

Practical information

Visa requirements UK: visa not required for tourist visits; visa required for business purposes. USA: visa not required for tourist visits; visa required for business purposes
Embassy in the UK 53 Hans Place, London SW1X 0LA. Tel: (0171) 584 6494; fax: (0171) 589 3106
British embassy Casilla de Correo 2050, Dr Luis Agote 2412/52, 1425 Buenos Aires. Tel: (1) 803 7070/1; fax: (1) 803 1731
Embassy in the USA 1600 New Hampshire Avenue NW, Washington, DC 20009. Tel: (202) 939 400/1/2/3
American embassy 4300 Colombia, 1425 Buenos Aires. Tel: (1) 777 4533, 4534

Chamber of commerce Cámara Argentina de Comercio, Avda Leandro N Alem 36, 1003 Buenos Aires. Tel: (1) 331 8051; fax: (1) 331 8055
Office hours 0900–1900 Mon–Fri
Banking hours 1000–1500 Mon–Fri
Time difference GMT –3
Chief tourist attractions include the Andes Mountains; lake district centred on Bariloche; Atlantic beaches; Patagonia; Mar del Plata beaches; Iguaçu Falls; the Pampas; Tierra del Fuego
Major holidays 1 January, 1, 25 May, 10, 20 June, 9 July, 17 August, 12 October, 8, 25, 31 December; variable: Good Friday, Holy Thursday

Armenia Republic of

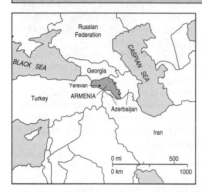

National name *Haikakan Hanrapetoutioun*
Area 29,800 sq km/11,505 sq mi
Capital Yerevan
Major towns/cities Gyumri (formerly Leninakan), Vanadzor (formerly Kirovakan)
Physical features mainly mountainous (including Mount Ararat), wooded

Government

Head of state Levon Ter-Petrossian from 1990
Head of government Robert Kocharyan from 1997
Political system authoritarian nationalist
Administrative divisions 10 regions
Political parties Armenian Pan-National Movement (APM), nationalist, left of centre; Armenian Revolutionary Federation (ARF), centrist (banned 1994); Communist Party of Armenia (banned 1991–92); National Unity, opposition coalition
Armed forces 60,000 (1995)

Conscription compulsory for 18 months
Death penalty retained and used for ordinary crimes
Defence spend (% GDP) 4.4 (1995)
Education spend (% GNP) 3.5 (1993)
Health spend (% GDP) 4.2 (1991)

Economy and resources

Currency dram (replaced Russian rouble 1993)
GDP ($ US) 3 billion (1994)
Real GDP per capita (PPP) ($ US) 1,737 (1994)
GDP growth rate 5.4% (1994); –21.2% (1990–95)
Average annual inflation 179.4% (1985–95)
Foreign debt ($ US) 374 million (1995)
Trading partners Russia, Ukraine, Belarus, Georgia, Kazakhstan, Turkmenistan, USA
Resources copper, zinc, molybdenum, iron, silver, marble, granite
Industries food processing and beverages, fertilizers, synthetic rubber, machinery and metal products, textiles, garments
Exports machinery and metalworking products, chemical and petroleum products. Principal market: Russia 20% (1995)
Imports light industrial products, petroleum and derivatives, industrial raw materials. Principal source: Russia 32.3% (1995)
Arable land 18% (1993)
Agricultural products potatoes, vegetables, fruits, cotton, almonds, olives, figs, cereals; livestock rearing (sheep and cattle)

Population and society

Population 3,638,000 (1996e)
Population growth rate 1.4% (1990–95); 1% (2000–05)
Population density (per sq km) 122 (1996)
Urban population (% of total) 69 (1995)
Age distribution (% of total population) <15 29.6 %, 15–65 63%, >65 7.4% (1995)
Ethnic distribution 91% of Armenian ethnic descent, 5% Azeri, 2% Russian, and 2% Kurdish
Language Armenian
Religion Armenian Christian
Education (compulsory years) 9
Literacy rate 99% (men); 99% (women) (1995)
Labour force 32.2% agriculture, 32.8% industry, 35% services (1993)
Unemployment 9.1% (1996)
Life expectancy 76 (men); 70 (women) (1995–2000)
Child mortality rate (under 5, per 1,000 live births) 31 (1995)
Physicians 1 per 250 people (1994e)
Hospital beds 1 per 111 people (1995e)
TV sets (per 1,000 people) 224 (1995)
Radios (per 1,000 people) 5 (1995)

Transport

Airports international airports Yerevan (Zvarnots); domestic services to most major towns
Railroads total length: 830 km/516 mi; total passenger km: 435 mil (1993)
Roads total road network: 7,720 km/ 4,797 mi, of which 97.1% paved; passenger cars: 0.4 per 1,000 people (1995e)

Chronology

6th century BC Armenian peoples moved into the area, which was then part of the Persian Empire.

c. 94–56 BC Under King Tigranes II 'the Great', Armenia reached height of its power, expanding southwards to become the strongest state in the eastern Roman empire, controlling an area from the Caucasus to the Mediterranean.

c. AD 300 Christianity became the state religion when the local ruler was converted by St Gregory the Illuminator.

c. AD 390 Divided between Byzantine Armenia, which became part of Byzantine Empire, and Persarmenia, under Persian control.

886–1045 Independent under the Bagratid monarchy.

13th century After being overrun by the Mongols, a substantially independent Little Armenia survived until 1375.

early 16th century Conquered by Muslim Ottoman Turks.

1813–28 Russia took control of E Armenia.

late 19th century Revival in Armenian culture and national spirit, provoking Ottoman backlash in W Armenia and international concern at Armenian maltreatment: the 'Armenian Question'.

1894–96 Massacre of Armenians by Turkish soldiers to suppress unrest.

1915 Suspected of pro-Russian sympathies, two-thirds of Armenia's population of 2 million were deported to Syria and Palestine. Around 600,000– 1 million died en route: the survivors contributed towards an Armenian diaspora in Europe and North America.

1916 Conquered by tsarist Russia and became part of a brief 'transcaucasian Alliance' with Georgia and Azerbaijan.

1918 Became an independent republic.

1920 Occupied by Red Army of Soviet Union (USSR), but W Armenia remained part of Turkey and NW Iran.

1936 Became constituent republic of USSR; rapid industrial development.

late 1980s Armenian 'national reawakening', encouraged by *glasnost* (openness) initiative of Soviet leader Mikhail Gorbachev.

1988 Earthquake – around 20,000 people died.

1989 Strife-torn Nagorno-Karabakh placed under direct rule from Moscow; civil war erupted with Azerbaijan over Nagorno-Karabakh and Nakhichevan, an Azerbaijani-peopled enclave in Armenia.

1990 Nationalists secured control of Armenian parliament in elections in May; former dissident Ter-Petrossian indirectly elected president; independence declared, but ignored by Moscow and international community.

1991 After collapse of USSR, Armenia joined new Commonwealth of Independent States. Ter-Petrossian directly elected president. Nagorno-Karabakh declared its independence.

1992 Armenia recognized as independent state by USA and admitted into United Nations.

1993 Armenian forces gained control of more than one-fifth of Azerbaijan, including much of Nagorno-Karabakh.

1994 Nagorno-Karabakh cease-fire ended conflict.

1995 Privatization and price-liberalization programme launched. Ruling APM re-elected, amid reports of intimidation of opposition candidates.

1996 Ter-Petrossian re-elected president. Hrand Bagratian replaced as prime minister by Armen Sarkissian.

1997 Sarkissian resigned for health reasons; replaced by Robert Kocharyan. Border fighting with Azerbaijan. Arkady Gukasyan elected president of Nagorno-Karabakh.

Practical information

Visa requirements UK: visa required. USA: visa required

Embassy in the UK 25A Cheniston Gardens, London W8 6TG. Tel: (0171) 938 5435; fax: (0171) 938 2595

British embassy Armenia Hotel, 1 Vramshapouh Arka Street, Yerevan 375010. Tel: (2) 151 807; fax: (2) 151 803

Embassy in the USA 11th floor, 1660 L Street NW, Washington, DC 20036. Tel: (202) 628 5766; fax: (202) 628 5769

American embassy 18 Gen Bagramian, Yerevan. Tel: (3742) 151 144, 524 661; fax: (3742) 151 138

Chamber of commerce Chamber of Commerce and Industry of the Republic of Armenia, ulitsa Alevardyan 39, Yerevan. Tel: (2) 565 438; fax: (2) 565 071

Time difference GMT +4

Chief tourist attractions Armenian mountains in the Lesser Caucasus; Lake Sevan

Major holidays 1, 6 January, 28–31 March, 24, 28 May, 21 September, 7 December; variable: Good Friday, Easter Monday

Australia Commonwealth of

Area 7,682,300 sq km/2,966,136 sq mi

Capital Canberra

Major towns/cities Adelaide, Alice Springs, Brisbane, Darwin, Melbourne, Perth, Sydney, Hobart, Geelong, Newcastle, Townsville, Wollongong

Physical features Ayers Rock; Arnhem Land; Gulf of Carpentaria; Cape York Peninsula; Great Australian Bight; Great Sandy Desert; Gibson Desert; Great Victoria Desert; Simpson Desert; the Great Barrier Reef; Great Dividing Range and Australian Alps in the E (Mount Kosciusko, 2,229 m/7,136 ft, Australia's highest peak). The fertile SE region is watered by the Darling, Lachlan, Murrumbridgee, and Murray rivers. Lake Eyre basin and Nullarbor Plain in the S

Territories Norfolk Island, Christmas Island, Cocos (Keeling) Islands, Ashmore and Cartier Islands, Coral Sea Islands, Heard Island and McDonald Islands, Australian Antarctic Territory

Government

Head of state Elizabeth II from 1952, represented by governor general William

George Hayden from 1989
Head of government John Howard from 1996
Political system federal constitutional monarchy
Administrative divisions six states and two territories
Political parties Australian Labor Party, moderate left of centre; Liberal Party of Australia, moderate, liberal, free enterprise; National Party of Australia (formerly Country Party), centrist non-metropolitan
Armed forces 56,000 (1995)
Death penalty abolished 1985
Defence spend (%GDP) 2.5 (1995)
Education spend (% GDP) 6% (1993–94)
Health spend (%GNP) 5.8 (1993)

Economy and resources

Currency Australian dollar
GDP ($ US) 392.6 billion (1996)
Real GDP per capita (PPP) ($ US) 20,368 (1996)
GDP growth rate 3% (1996); 3.5% (1990–95)
Average annual inflation 2.9% (1996); 3.7% (1985–95)
Trading partners USA, Japan, UK, New Zealand, Republic of Korea, China, Taiwan, Singapore
Resources coal, iron ore (world's third-largest producer), bauxite, copper, zinc (world's second-largest producer), nickel (world's fifth-largest producer), uranium, gold, diamonds
Industries mining, metal products, textiles, wood and paper products, chemical products, electrical machinery, transport equipment, printing, publishing and recording media, tourism, electronic communications
Exports major world producer of raw materials: iron ore, aluminium, coal, nickel, zinc, lead, gold, tin, tungsten, uranium, crude oil; wool, meat, cereals, fruit, sugar, wine. Principal markets: Japan 22% (1996)
Imports processed industrial supplies, transport equipment and parts, road vehicles, petroleum and petroleum products, medicinal and pharmaceutical products, organic chemicals, consumer goods. Principal source: USA 23% (1996)
Arable land 6%
Agricultural products wheat, barley, oats, rice, sugar cane, fruit, grapes; livestock (cattle and sheep) and dairy products

Population and society

Population 18,057,000 (1996e)
Population growth rate 1.4% (1990–95); 1.1% (2000–05)
Population density (per sq km) 2 (1996)
Urban population (% of total) 85 (1995)
Age distribution (% of total population) <15 21.6%, 15–65 66.8%, >65 11.6% (1995)
Ethnic distribution 99% of European descent; remaining 1% Aborigine or Asian
Languages English, Aboriginal languages
Religions Anglican 26%, other Protestant 17%, Roman Catholic 26%
Education (compulsory years) 10 or 11 (states vary)
Literacy rate 99% (men); 99% (women) (1995e)
Labour force 50% of total population: 6% agriculture, 26% industry, 68% services (1990)
Unemployment 8.6% (1996)
Life expectancy 75 (men); 81 (women) (1995–2000)
Child mortality rate (under 5, per 1,000 live births) 8 (1995)
Physicians 1 per 438 people (1991)
Hospital beds 1 per 222 people (1992)
TV sets (per 1,000 people) 495 (1995)
Radios (per 1,000 people) 1,304 (1995)

Transport

Airports international airports: Sydney (NSW), Melbourne (Victoria), Canberra, Brisbane, Cairns (Queensland), Perth (Western Australia), Adelaide (South Australia), Hobart (Tasmania), Townsville (Quensland), Darwin (Northern Territory); domestic services to all major resorts and cities; total passenger km: 61,124 mil (1994)
Railroads total length: 37,295 km/23,175 mi: passengers carried: 407 mil (1994)
Roads total road network: 895,030 km/556,172 mi, of which 38.6% paved (1995e); passenger cars: 464.7 per 1,000 people (1995e)

Chronology

c. 40,000 BC Aboriginal immigration from S India, Sri Lanka, and SE Asia.
AD 1606 First recorded sightings of Australia by Europeans including discovery of Cape York by Dutch explorer Willem Jansz in *Duyfken.*
1770 Captain James Cook claimed New South Wales for Britain.
1788 Sydney founded as British penal colony.

late 18th–19th centuries Great age of exploration: coastal surveys by George Bass and Matthew Flinders; interior by Charles Sturt, Edward Eyre, Robert Burke and William Wills, John McDouall Stuart, and John Forrest. Overlanders and squatters also opened up new territory, as did bushrangers, including Ned Kelly.
1804 Castle Hill Rising by Irish convicts in New South Wales.
1813 Crossing of Blue Mountains removed major barrier to exploration of interior.
1825 Tasmania seceded from New South Wales.
1829 Western Australia colonized.
1836 South Australia colonized.
1840–68 End of convict transportation.
1850 British Act of Parliament permitted Australian colonies to draft their own constitutions and achieve virtual self-government.
1851–61 Gold rushes contributed to exploration and economic growth.
1851 Victoria seceded from New South Wales.
1855 Victoria achieved self-government.
1856 New South Wales, South Australia, and Tasmania achieved self-government.
1859 Queensland formed from New South Wales and achieved self-government.
1860 (National) Country Party founded.
1890 Western Australia achieved self-government.
1891 Depression gave rise to Australian Labor Party.
1899–1900 South African War – forces offered by individual colonies.
1901 Creation of Commonwealth of Australia.
1902 Immigration Restriction Act introduced language tests for potential settlers; women gained right to vote.
1914–18 World War I: over 300,000 Australian volunteers fought in Middle East and on western front.
1919 Australia given mandates over Papua New Guinea and Solomon Islands.
1927 Seat of federal government moved to Canberra.
1931 Statute of Westminster confirmed Australian independence.
1933 Western Australia's vote to secede was overruled.
1939–45 World War II: Australian troops fought in Greece, N Africa, and SW Pacific.

1941 Curtin's appeal to USA for military help marked shift away from exclusive relationship with Britain.
1944 Liberal Party founded by Menzies.
1948–75 Influx of around 2 million new immigrants, chiefly from continental Europe.
1950–53 Australia contributed troops to United Nations (UN) forces in Korean War.
1951 Australia joined USA and New Zealand in ANZUS Pacific security alliance.
1965–72 Australian troops participated in Vietnam War.

1967 Referendum gave Australian Aborigines full citizenship rights. Australia became a member of the Association of South East Asian Nations (ASEAN).
1973 Britain entered European Economic Community (EEC), and in 1970s Japan became Australia's chief trading partner.
1974 'White Australia' immigration restrictions abolished.
1975 Constitutional crisis: Governor General John Kerr dismissed Prime Minister Gough Whitlam after senate blocked financial legislation. Papua New Guinea became independent.

1978 Northern Territory achieved self-government.
1983 Labor Party returned to power under Bob Hawke.
1986 Australia Act passed by British Parliament eliminating last vestiges of British legal authority in Australia.
1988 Free Trade Agreement signed with New Zealand.
1992 Citizenship Act removed oath of allegiance to British crown.
1993 Labor Party won record fifth election victory.
1996 Liberal-National coalition, headed by John Howard, won general election.

Practical information

Visa requirements UK: visa required. USA: visa required
Embassy in the UK High Commission, Australia House, The Strand, London WC2B 4LA. Tel: (0171) 379 4334; fax: (0171) 240 5333
British embassy British High Commission, Commonwealth Avenue, Yarralumla, Canberra, ACT 2600. Tel: (6) 270 6666; fax: (6)273 3236
Embassy in the USA 1601 Massachusetts Avenue NW, Washington, DC 20036. Tel: (202) 797 3000; fax: (202) 797 3168
American embassy Moonah Place, Yarralumla, Canberra, ACT 2600. Tel: (6) 270 5000; fax: (6) 270 5970
Chamber of commerce International Chamber of Commerce, POB E118, Queen Victoria Terrace, Canberra,

ACT 2600. Tel: (6) 295 1961; fax: (6) 295 0170. Australian Chamber of Commerce and Industry, POB E14, Queen Victoria Terrace, Canberra ACT 2600. Tel: (6) 273 2311; fax: (6) 273 3196
Office hours 0900–1730 Mon–Fri
Banking hours 0930–1600 Mon–Thu; 1930–1700 Fri (hours vary throughout the country)
Time difference GMT +8/10
Chief tourist attractions swimming and surfing on the Pacific beaches; skin-diving along the Great Barrier Reef; sailing from Sydney and other harbours; winter sports in the Australian Alps; summer sports in the Blue Mountains; Alice Springs and Ayers Rock in desert interior; unique wildlife
Major holidays 1 January, 25 April, 25–26 December (except South Australia); variable: Good Friday, Easter Monday, Holy Saturday; additional days vary between states

---

Austria Republic of

National name *Republik Österreich*
Area 83,500 sq km/32,239 sq mi
Capital Vienna
Major towns/cities Graz, Linz, Salzburg, Innsbruck, Klagenfurt
Physical features landlocked mountainous state, with Alps in W and S

(Austrian Alps, including Grossglockner and Brenner and Semmering passes, Lechtaler and Allgauer Alps N of River Inn, Carnic Alps on Italian border) and low relief in E where most of the population is concentrated; River Danube

Government

Head of state Thomas Klestil from 1992
Head of government Franz Vranitzky from 1986
Political system democratic federal republic
Administrative divisions nine provinces
Political parties Social Democratic Party of Austria (SPÖ), democratic socialist; Austrian People's Party (ÖVP), progressive centrist; Freedom (formerly Froodom Party of Austria: FPÖ), right wing; United Green Party of Austria (VGÖ), conservative ecological; Green Alternative Party (ALV), radical ecological
Armed forces 56,000 (1995)
Conscription 6 months

Death penalty abolished 1968
Defence spend (% GDP) 1.0 (1995)
Education spend (% GNP) 5.5 (1993–94)
Health spend (% GDP) 6.0 (1993)

Economy and resources

Currency schilling
GDP ($ US) 226.1 billion (1996)
Real GDP per capita (PPP) ($ US) 21,120 (1996)
GDP growth rate 0.3% (1996); 1.9% (1990–95)
Average annual inflation 1.8% (1996); 3.2% (1985–95)
Trading partners EU, Switzerland, USA, Japan
Resources lignite, iron, kaolin, gypsum, talcum, magnesite, lead, zinc, forests
Industries raw and rolled steel, machinery, cellulose, paper, cardboard, cement, fertilizers, viscose staple yarn, sawn timber, flat glass, salt, sugar, milk, margarine

Exports dairy products, food products, wood and paper products, machinery and transport equipment, metal and metal products, chemical products. Principal market for exports: EU countries 63.6% (1993)

Imports petroleum and petroleum products, food and live animals, chemicals and related products, textiles, clothing. Principal source: EU countries 67% (1993)

Arable land 16.9% (1993)

Agricultural products wheat, barley, rye, oats, potatoes, maize, sugar beet; dairy products

Population and society

Population 8,106,000 (1996e)

Population growth rate 0.7% (1990–95); 0.2% (2000–05)

Population density (per sq km) 97 (1996)

Urban population (% of total) 56 (1995)

Age distribution (% of total population) <15 17.8%, 15–65 67.3%, >65 14.9% (1995)

Ethnic distribution 98% German, 0.7% Croatian, 0.3% Slovene

Language German

Religions Roman Catholic 78%, Protestant 5%

Education (compulsory years) 9

Literacy rate 99% (men); 99% (women) (1995)

Labour force 46% of population: 8% agriculture, 38% industry, 55% services (1990)

Unemployment 4.4% (1996)

Life expectancy 74 (men); 80 (women) (1995–2000)

Child mortality rate (under 5, per 1,000 live births) 7 (1995)

Physicians 1 per 253 people (1996)

Hospital beds 1 per 95 people (1995)

TV sets (per 1,000 people) 497 (1995)

Radios (per 1,000 people) 620 (1995)

Transport

Airports international airports: Vienna (Wien-Schwechat), Graz (Thalerhof), Innsbruck (Kranebitten), Klagenfurt (Wörthersee), Linz (Hörsching), Salzburg (Maxglam); domestic services between the above; total passenger km: 5,933 mil (1994)

Railroads total length: 6,185 km/ 3,843 mi; total passenger km: 9,384 mil (1994)

Roads total road network: 200,000 km/ 124,280 mi, of which 100% paved (1995); passenger cars: 447 per 1,000 people (1995)

Chronology

14 BC Country S of River Danube conquered by Romans.

5th century AD Region occupied by Vandals, Huns, Goths, Lombards, and Avars.

791 Charlemagne conquered Avars and established East Mark, nucleus of future Austrian Empire.

976 Holy Roman Emperor Otto II granted East Mark to House of Babenburg, which ruled until 1246.

1156 Margrave of Austria raised to duke.

1282 Holy Roman Emperor Rudolf of Habsburg seized Austria and invested his son as its duke; for over 500 years most rulers of Austria were elected Holy Roman emperor.

1453 Austria became an archduchy.

1519–56 Emperor Charles V was both archduke of Austria and king of Spain; Habsburgs dominant in Europe.

1526 Bohemia came under Habsburg rule.

1529 Vienna besieged by the Ottoman Turks.

1618–48 Thirty Years' War: Habsburgs weakened by failure to secure control over Germany.

1683 Polish-Austrian force led by Jan Sobieski defeated the Turks at Vienna.

1699 Treaty of Karlowitz: Austrians expelled the Turks from Hungary, which came under Habsburg rule.

1713 By the Treaty of Utrecht, Austria obtained the Spanish Netherlands (Belgium) and political control over most of Italy.

1740–48 War of Austrian Succession: Prussia (supported by France and Spain) attacked Austria (supported by Holland and England) on the pretext of disputing rights of Maria Theresa; Austria lost Silesia to Prussia.

1772 Austria joined in partition of Poland, annexing Galicia.

1780–90 'Enlightened despotism': Joseph II tried to impose radical reforms.

1792 Austria went to war with revolutionary France.

1804 Francis II took the title Emperor of Austria.

1806 Holy Roman Empire abolished.

1809–48 Guided by foreign minister Prince Klemens von Metternich, Austria took a leading role in resisting liberalism and nationalism throughout Europe.

1815 After the Napoleonic Wars, Austria lost its Netherlands but received Lombardy and Venetia.

1848 Outbreak of liberal-nationalist revolts throughout the Austrian Empire; Ferdinand I abdicated in favour of Franz Joseph; revolutions suppressed with difficulty.

1859 France and Sardinia expelled Austrians from Lombardy by force.

1866 Seven Weeks' War: Prussia defeated Austria, which ceded Venetia to Italy.

1867 Austria conceded equality to Hungary within the dual monarchy of Austria-Hungary.

1878 Treaty of Berlin: Austria-Hungary occupied Bosnia-Herzegovina; annexed 1908.

1914 Archduke Franz Ferdinand, the heir to the throne, assassinated by a Serbian nationalist; Austria-Hungary invaded Serbia, precipitating World War I.

1916 Death of Franz Joseph; succeeded by Karl I.

1918 Austria-Hungary collapsed in military defeat; empire dissolved; republic proclaimed.

1919 Treaty of St Germain reduced Austria to its present boundaries and prohibited union with Germany.

1934 Political instability culminated in brief civil war; right-wingers defeated socialists.

1938 The *Anschluss*: Nazi Germany incorporated Austria into the Third Reich.

1945 Following World War II, the victorious Allies divided Austria into four zones of occupation (US, British, French, and Soviet); Second Republic established under Karl Renner.

1955 Austrian State Treaty ended occupation; Austria regained independence on condition of neutrality.

1960–70s Austria experienced rapid industrialization and prosperity under governments dominated by moderate socialists and centrists.

1986 Election of Kurt Waldheim as president, despite allegations of war crimes during World War II, led to a measure of diplomatic isolation until Waldheim's replacement 1992.

1995 Became a full European Union (EU) member.

Practical information

Visa requirements UK: visa not required. USA: visa not required
Embassy in the UK 18 Belgrave Mews West, London SW1X 8HV. Tel: (0171) 235 3731; fax: (0171) 235 8025
British embassy Juarèsgasse 12, 1030 Vienna. Tel: (1) 713 1575; fax: (1) 714 7824
Embassy in the USA 3524 International Court NW, Washington, DC 20008. Tel: (202) 895 6700; fax: (202) 895 6750
American embassy Boltzmanngasse 16, A-1091 Vienna. Tel: (1) 31339; fax: (1) 310 0682
Chamber of commerce Wirtschaftskammer Österreich

(Austrian Economic Chamber), Wiedner Haupstrasse 63, 1045 Vienna. Tel: (1) 50105; fax: (1) 50206
Office hours 0800–1600 Mon–Fri
Banking hours 0800–1230 and 1330–1500 Mon, Tue, Wed, and Fri; 0800–1230 and 1330–1730 Thu (head offices do not close for the break)
Time difference GMT +1
Chief tourist attractions mountain scenery, enjoyed by visitors in both summer and winter; arts festivals at cultural centres of Vienna and Salzburg
Major holidays 1, 6 January, 1 May, 15 August, 26 October, 1 November, 8, 24–26 December; variable: Ascension Thursday, Corpus Christi, Easter Monday, Whit Monday

Azerbaijan Republic of

National name *Azarbaijchan Respublikasy*
Area 86,600 sq km/33,436 sq mi
Capital Baku
Major towns/cities Gyandzha (formerly Kirovabad), Sumgait, Nakhichevan, Stepanakert
Physical features Caspian Sea with rich oil reserves; the country ranges from semidesert to the Caucasus Mountains

Government

Head of state Geidar Aliyev from 1993
Head of government Artur Rasizade from 1996
Political system authoritarian nationalist
Administrative divisions 54 regions, 11 cities, and one autonomous republic (Nakhchyuan)
Political parties Popular Front of Azerbaijan (FPA), democratic nationalist; New Azerbaijan, ex-communist; Communist Party of Azerbaijan (banned 1991–93); Muslim Democratic Party (Musavat), Islamic, pro-Turkic unity
Armed forces 87,000 (1995)
Conscription military service is for 17 months

Death penalty retained and used for ordinary crimes
Defence spend (% GDP) 5 (1995)
Education spend (% GNP) 5.5 (1993–94)
Health spend (% GDP) 4.3 (1991)

Economy and resources

Currency manat (left rouble zone 1993)
GDP ($ US) 4 billion (1994)
Real GDP per capita (PPP) ($ US) 1,670 (1994)
GDP growth rate –21.9% (1994); –20.2 (1990–95)
Average annual inflation 279.3% (1994e)
Foreign debt ($ US) 321 million (1995)
Trading partners Iran, Turkey, former USSR (principally Russia, Ukraine, and Turkmenistan), Greece
Resources petroleum, natural gas, iron ore, aluminium, copper, barytes, cobalt, precious metals, limestone, salt
Industries petroleum extraction and refining, chemicals, petrochemicals, construction, machinery, food processing, textiles, timber
Exports refined petroleum products, machinery, food products, textiles. Principal market: Iran 30% (1995)
Imports industrial raw materials, processed food, machinery. Principal source: Turkey 21.2% (1995)
Arable land 49% (1993)
Agricultural products grain, grapes and other fruit, vegetables, cotton, silk, tobacco; livestock rearing (cattle, sheep, and goats); fisheries (about 10 tonnes of caviar are produced annually); silkworm breeding

Population and society

Population 7,594,000 (1996e)
Population growth rate 1.2% (1990–95); 1% (2000–05)
Population density (per sq km) 88 (1996)
Urban population (% of total) 56 (1995)
Age distribution (% of total population) <15 31.8%, 15–65 62.3%, >65 5.9% (1995)
Ethnic distribution 83% of Azeri descent, 6% Russian, 6% Armenian
Language Azeri
Religions Shi'ite Muslim 62%, Sunni Muslim 26%, Orthodox Christian 12%
Education (compulsory years) 11
Literacy rate 96% (men); 96% (women) (1995e)
Labour force 33.7% agriculture, 24.3% industry, 42% services (1991)
Unemployment 1% (1996)
Life expectancy 68 (men); 75 (women) (1995–2000)
Child mortality rate (under 5, per 1,000 live births) 50 (1995)
Physicians 1 per 278 people (1994e)
Hospital beds 1 per 104 people (1994e)
TV sets (per 1,000 people) 33 (1995)
Radios (per 1,000 people) 20 (1995)

Transport

Airports international airports: Baku; total passenger km: 1,731 mil (1994)
Railroads total length: 2,122 km/1,319 mi
Roads total road network: 57,770 km/ 35,898 mi, of which 93.8% paved (1995e); passenger cars: 38.3 per 1,000 people (1995e)

Chronology

4th century BC Established as an independent state for the first time by

Atrophates, a vassal of Alexander III of Macedon.
7th century Spread of Islam.
11th century Immigration by Oghuz Seljuk peoples, from the steppes to the NE.
13th–14th centuries Incorporated within Mongol Empire; the Mongol ruler Tamorlane had his capital at Samarkand.
16th century Baku besieged and incorporated within Ottoman Empire, before falling under Persian dominance.
1805 Khanates (chieftaincies), including Karabakh and Shirvan, which had won independence from Persia, gradually became Russian protectorates, being confirmed by the Treaty of Gulistan, which concluded the 1804–13 First Russo-Iranian War.
1828 Under Treaty of Turkmenchai, which concluded the Second Russo-Iranian War begun in 1826, Persia was granted control over the S and Russia over N Azerbaijan.
late 19th century Petroleum industry developed, resulting in large influx of Slav immigrants to Baku, which supplied half of Russia's oil needs by 1901.
1906 Himmat ('Effort') Party, linked to the Russian Social-Democrat Labour Party (Bolshevik), founded in Baku.

1912 Himmat Party banned; Islamic nationalist Musavat ('Equality') Party formed in Baku.
1917–18 Member of anti-Bolshevik Transcaucasian Federation.
1918 Became an independent republic.
1920 Occupied by Red Army and subsequently forcibly secularized.
1922–36 Became part of the Transcaucasian Federal Republic with Georgia and Armenia.
early 1930s Peasant uprisings against agricultural collectivization and Stalinist purges of the local Communist Party.
1936 Became a constituent republic of the USSR.
late 1980s Growth in nationalist sentiment, taking advantage of the *glasnost* initiative of the reformist Soviet leader Mikhail Gorbachev.
1988 Riots followed the request of Nagorno-Karabakh, an Armenian-peopled enclave within Azerbaijan, for transfer to Armenia.
1989 Nagorno-Karabakh placed under direct rule from Moscow; civil war broke out with Armenia over Nagorno-Karabakh.
1990 Soviet troops dispatched to Baku to restore order, amid Azeri calls for secession from USSR.

1991 Independence declared after collapse of anti-Gorbachev coup in Moscow, which had been supported by Azeri communist leadership. Joined new Commonwealth of Independent States (CIS); Nagorno-Karabakh declared independence.
1992 Admitted into United Nations and accorded diplomatic recognition by the USA; Albulfaz Elchibey, leader of the nationalist Popular Front, elected president; renewed campaign to capture Nagorno-Karabakh.
1993 Elchibey fled military revolt, replaced in a coup by former Communist Party leader Geidar Aliyev, later elected president. Rebel military leader Surat Huseynov appointed prime minister. Nagorno-Karabakh overtaken by Armenian forces.
1994 Nagorno-Karabakh cease-fire agreed. After coup attempt, Huseynov replaced as premier by Fuad Kuliyev. State of emergency imposed.
1995 Attempted coup foiled. Pro-Aliyev legislature elected and market-centred economic reform programme introduced.
1996 Kuliyev replaced by Artur Rasizade.
1997 Border fighting with Armenia. Arkady Gukasyan elected president of Nagorno-Karabakh.

Practical information

Visa requirements UK: visa required. USA: visa required
Embassy in the UK 4 Kensington Court, London W8 5DL. Tel: (0171) 938 5482; fax: (0171) 937 1783
British embassy c/o Old Intourist Hotel, Room 214, Baku. Tel: (12) 924 813; fax: (12) (873) 144 6456
Embassy in the USA (temporary) Suite 700, 927 15th Street NW, Washington, DC 20005. Tel: (202) 842 0001; fax: (202) 842 0004
American embassy Azadliq Prospekti 83, Baku. Tel: (9412)

960 019, 980 336/7, 936 480, 963 621; fax: (9412) 983 755
Chamber of commerce Chamber of Commerce and Industry, Istiglaliyat Street 31/33, 370001 Baku. Tel: (12) 928 912; fax: (12) 989 324
Banking hours 0930–1730 Mon–Fri (midday closing hours vary)
Time difference GMT +4
Chief tourist attractions resorts on Caspian Sea and on Apsheron peninsula, near Baku
Major holidays 1 January, 8 March, 28 May, 9, 18 October, 17 November, 31 December

Bahamas Commonwealth of the

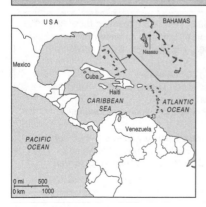

Area 13,864 sq km/5,352 sq mi
Capital Nassau (on New Providence Island)
Major towns/cities Freeport (on Grand Bahama)
Physical features comprises 700 tropical coral islands and about 1,000 cays; the Exumas are a narrow spine of 365 islands; only 30 of the desert islands are inhabited; Blue Holes of Andros, the world's longest and deepest submarine caves
Principal islands Andros, Grand Bahama, Abaco, Eleuthera, New Providence, Berry Islands, Bimini

Islands, Great Inagua, Acklins Island, Exuma Islands, Mayguana, Crooked Island, Long Island, Cat Islands, Rum Cay, Watling (San Salvador) Island, Inagua Islands

Government

Head of state Elizabeth II from 1973, represented by governor general Orville Turnquest from 1995
Head of government Hubert Ingraham from 1992
Political system constitutional monarchy
Administrative divisions 21 districts

Political parties Progressive Liberal Party (PLP), centrist; Free National Movement (FNM), centre left
Armed forces a paramilitary coastguard numbering 900 (1995)
Conscription military service is voluntary
Death penalty retained and used for ordinary crimes
Defence spend (% GDP) 0.6 (1995)
Education spend (% GNP) 3.9 (1993–94)
Health spend (% GDP) 2.5 (1994)

Economy and resources

Currency Bahamian dollar
GDP ($ US) 3.4 billion (1994)
Real GDP per capita (PPP) ($ US) 15,875 (1994)
GDP growth rate 0.3% (1994)
Average annual inflation 3.2% (1985–95)
Foreign debt ($ US) 453.3 million (1994)
Trading partners USA, Aruba, UK, France, Canada
Resources aragonite (extracted from seabed), chalk, salt
Industries pharmaceutical chemicals, salt, rum, beer, cement, shipping, financial services, tourism
Exports foodstuffs (fish), oil products and transhipments, chemicals, rum, salt. Principal market: USA 23.7% (1995)
Imports machinery and transport equipment, basic manufactures, petroleum and products, chemicals. Principal source: USA 29.4% (1995)
Arable land 0.6% (1993)
Agricultural products sugar cane, cucumbers, tomatoes, pineapples, papayas, mangoes, avocados, limes and other citrus fruit; commercial fishing (conches and crustaceans)

Population and society

Population 284,000 (1996e)
Population growth rate 1.5% (1990–95)
Population density (per sq km) 20 (1996)
Urban population (% of total) 66 (1995)
Age distribution (% of total population) <15 30%, 15–65 65%, >65 5% (1994)
Ethnic distribution about 85% of the population is of African origin; remainder is mainly American, Canadian, and British
Languages English and some Creole
Religions Christian 94% (Roman Catholic 26%, Anglican 21%, other Protestant 48%)
Education (compulsory years) 10
Literacy rate 98% (men); 95% (women) (1995e)
Labour force 50% of population: 6.5% agriculture, 12.1% industry, 81.4% services (1993)
Unemployment 13% (1994)
Life expectancy 70 (men); 79 (women) (1995–2000)
Child mortality rate (under 5, per 1,000 live births) 28 (1995)
Physicians 1 per 800 people (1994e)
Hospital beds 1 per 267 people (1993e)
TV sets (per 1,000 people) 229 (1995)
Radios (per 1,000 people) 735 (1995)

Transport

Airports international airports: Nassau, Freeport, Moss Town; four domestic airports serve internal chartered flights; total passenger km: 191 mil (1994)
Railroads none
Roads total road network: 2,450 km/1,522 mi, of which 57% paved (1995e);

passenger cars: 172 per 1,000 people (1993e)

Chronology

8th–9th centuries AD Arawak Indians driven northwards to the islands by the Caribs.
1492 First visited by Christopher Columbus; Arawaks deported to provide cheap labour for the gold and silver mines of Cuba and Hispaniola (Haiti).
1629 The English king Charles I granted the islands to Robert Heath.
1666 Colonization of New Providence island began.
1783 Recovered after brief Spanish occupation and became a British colony, being settled during the American War of Independence, by American loyalists who brought with them black slaves.
1838 Slaves were emancipated.
1940–45 The Duke of Windsor, the former King Edward VIII, was governor of Bahamas.
from 1950s Major development of the tourist trade, especially from the USA.
1964 Became internally self-governing.
1967 First national assembly elections; Lynden Pindling, of the centrist Progressive Liberal Party (PLP), became prime minister.
1973 Full independence achieved, within the British Commonwealth.
1983 Allegations of drug trafficking by government ministers.
1984 Deputy prime minister and two cabinet ministers resigned. Pindling denied any personal involvement and was endorsed as party leader.
1992 Centre-left Free National Movement (FNM) led by Hubert Ingraham won absolute majority in assembly elections, ending 25 years of rule by Pindling.

Practical information

Visa requirements UK: visa not required. USA: visa not required
Embassy in the UK 10 Chesterfield St, London W1X 8AH. Tel: (0171) 408 4488; fax: (0171) 499 9937
British embassy British High Commission, PO Box N-7516, 3rd Floor, Bitco Building, East St, Nassau. Tel: 325 7471/2/3; fax: 323 3871
Embassy in the USA 2220 Massachusetts Avenue NW, Washington, DC 20008. Tel: (202) 319 2660; fax: (202) 319 2668
American embassy Mosmar Building, Queen Street,

Nassau. Tel: (809) 322 1181, 328 2206; fax: (809) 328 7838
Chamber of commerce Bahamas Chamber of Commerce, Shirley St, POB N-665, Nassau. Tel: 322 2145; fax: 322 4649
Office hours 0900–1700 Mon–Fri
Banking hours 0930–1500 Mon–Thu; 0930–1700 Fri
Time difference GMT –5
Chief tourist attractions mild climate and beautiful beaches
Major holidays 1 January, 10 July, 25–26 December; variable: Good Friday, Easter Monday, Whit Monday, Labour Day (June), Emancipation (August), Discovery (October)

Bahrain State of

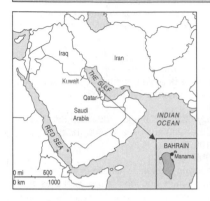

National name *Dawlat al Bahrayn*
Area 688 sq km/265 sq mi
Capital Al Manamah on the largest
island (also called Bahrain)
Major towns/cities Muharraq, Jiddhafs,
Isa Town, Hidd, Rifa'a, Sitra
Major ports Mina Sulman
Physical features archipelago of 35
islands in Arabian Gulf, composed
largely of sand-covered limestone;
generally poor and infertile soil; flat and
hot; causeway linking Bahrain to
mainland Saudi Arabia

Government

Head of state Sheik Isa bin Sulman al-
Khalifa from 1961
Head of government Sheik Khalifa bin
Sulman al-Khalifa from 1970
Political system absolute emirate
Administrative divisions 12 districts
Political parties none
Armed forces 10,700 (1995)
Conscription military service is
voluntary
Death penalty retained and used for
ordinary crimes
Defence spend (% GDP) 5.2 (1995)
Education spend (% GNP) 4.7
(1993–94)
Health spend (% GDP) 3 (1993)

Economy and resources

Currency Bahraini dinar
GDP ($ US) 7.3 billion (1995e)
Real GDP per capita (PPP) ($ US)
12,000 (1994)
GDP growth rate 2.7% (1995e)
Average annual inflation 0.4%
(1985–95)
Foreign debt ($ US) 2.42 billion (1994)
Trading partners USA, UK, Saudi
Arabia, Japan, South Korea, Australia

Resources petroleum and natural gas
Industries petroleum refining, aluminium
smelting, petrochemicals, shipbuilding and
repairs, electronics assembly (banking)
Exports petroleum and petroleum
products, aluminium. Principal market:
India 21.5% (1994)
Imports crude petroleum, machinery and
transport equipment, chemicals, basic
manufactures. Principal source: Saudi
Arabia 40% (1994)
Arable land 1.5% (1993)
Agricultural products dates, tomatoes,
melons, vegetables; poultry products and
fishing

Population and society

Population 570,000 (1996e)
Population growth rate 2.8% (1990–95)
Population density (per sq km) 840
(1996)
Urban population (% of total) 84 (1995)
Age distribution (% of total population)
<15 32%, 15–65 65%, >65 3% (1994)
Ethnic distribution about 73% Arab and
9% Iranian; Pakistani and Indian
minorities
Languages Arabic (official); Farsi,
English, Urdu
Religions 85% Muslim (Shi'ite 60%,
Sunni 40%), Christian; Islam is the state
religion
Education (compulsory years) 12
Literacy rate 89% (men); 79% (women)
(1995e)
Labour force 45% of population: 2%
agriculture, 30% industry, 68% services
(1990)
Unemployment 1.8% (1995 official rate;
Western diplomats estimate 25–30%)
Life expectancy 71 (men); 75 (women)
(1995–2000)
Child mortality rate (under 5, per 1,000
live births) 20 (1995)
Physicians 1 per 775 people (1991)
Hospital beds 1 per 368 people (1991e)
TV sets (per 1,000 people) 467 (1995)
Radios (per 1,000 people) 575 (1995)

Transport

Airports international airports: Muharraq
(Bahrain); total passenger km: 2,439 mil
(1994)
Railroads none
Roads total road network: 2,835 km/
1,722 mi, of which 79% paved (1995);
passenger cars: 251 per 1,000 people
(1995)

Chronology

4th century AD Became part of Persian
(Iranian) Sassanian Empire.
7th century Adopted Islam.
8th century Came under Arab Abbasid
control.
1521 Seized by Portugal and held for
eight decades, despite local unrest.
1602 Fell under the control of a Persian
Shi'ite dynasty.
1783 Overthrew Persian rule and
became a sheikdom under the Sunni
Muslim al-Khalifa dynasty, which
originated from the same tribal
federation, the Anaza, as the al-Saud
family, who now rule Saudi Arabia.
1816–20 Friendship and peace treaties
signed with Britain, which sought to end
piracy in the Gulf.
1861 Became British protectorate,
government shared between the ruling
sheik (Arab leader) and a British adviser.
1923 British influence increased when
Sheik Isa al-Khalifa was deposed and
Charles Belgrave was appointed as the
dominating 'adviser' to the new ruler.
1928 Sovereignty claimed by Persia
(Iran).
1930s Oil discovered, providing
backbone for country's wealth.
1953–56 Council for National Unity was
formed by Arab nationalists, but
suppressed after large demonstrations
against British participation in the Suez
War.
1968 Britain announced its intention to
withdraw its forces. Bahrain formed, with
Qatar and the Trucial States of the
United Arab Emirates, the Federation of
Arab Emirates.
1970 Iran accepted a United Nations
(UN) report showing that Bahrain's
inhabitants preferred independence to
Iranian control.
1971 Qatar and the Trucial States
withdrew from the federation; Bahrain
became an independent state under
Sheik Sulman al-Khalifa.
1973 New constitution adopted, with an
elected national assembly dominated by
left-nationalist Bahrain National
Liberation Front (BNLF).
1975 Prime minister Sheik al-Khalifa
resigned; national assembly dissolved
and political activists driven underground.
Emir and his family assumed virtually
absolute power.
early 1980s Tensions between the Sunni
and Shi'ite Muslim communities

heightened by Iranian Shi'ite Revolution of 1979.
1986 Gulf University established in Bahrain. Causeway opened linking the island with Saudi Arabia.
1991 Bahrain joined UN coalition that

ousted Iraq from its occupation of Kuwait; signed defence cooperation agreement with USA.
1994 Antimonarchy protests by Shi'ite Muslim majority community.
1995 Sheik al-Khalifa reappointed prime

minister. Prodemocracy demonstrations violently suppressed, with 11 deaths.
1996 Emir proposed an expanded consultative assembly in move towards democracy.

Practical information

Visa requirements UK: visa not required. USA: visa required
Embassy in the UK 98 Gloucester Road, London SW7 4AV. Tel: (0171) 370 5132/3; fax: (0171) 370 7773
British embassy PO Box 114, 21 Government Avenue, Manama, 306. Tel: (973) 534 404; fax: (973) 531 273
Embassy in the USA 3502 International Drive NW, Washington, DC 20008. Tel: (202) 342 0741, 342 0742; fax: (202) 362 2192
American embassy Building No. 979, Road 3119 (next to Al-Ahli Sports Club), Zinj District, Manama. Tel: 273 300; fax: 272 594

Chamber of commerce Bahrain Chamber of Commerce and Industry, PO Box 248, Manama. Tel: (973) 233 913; fax: (973) 241 294
Office hours usually 0730–1200 and 1430–1800 Sat–Thu
Banking hours 0800–1200 and usually 1600–1800 Sat–Wed; 0800–1100 Thu
Time difference GMT +3
Chief tourist attractions Bahrain is the site of the ancient trading civilization of Dilmun, and there are several sites of archaeological importance
Major holidays 1 January, 16 December; variable: Eid-ul-Adha, Ashora, end of Ramadan, New Year (Muslim), Prophet's Birthday

Bangladesh People's Republic of (formerly *East Pakistan*)

National name *Gana Prajatantri Bangladesh*
Area 144,000 sq km/55,598 sq mi
Capital Dhaka (formerly Dacca)
Major towns/cities Rajshahi, Khulna, Chittagong, Comilla, Barisal, Sylhet
Major ports Chittagong, Khulna
Physical features flat delta of rivers Ganges (Padma) and Brahmaputra (Jamuna), the largest estuarine delta in the world; annual rainfall of 2,540 mm/100 in; some 75% of the land is less than 3 m/10 ft above sea level; hilly in extreme SE and NE

Government

Head of state Abdur Rahman Biswas from 1991
Head of government Sheikha Hasina Wazed from 1996

Political system emergent democratic republic
Administrative divisions 64 districts within five divisions
Political parties Bangladesh Nationalist Party (BNP), Islamic, right of centre; Awami League (AL), secular, moderate socialist; Jatiya Dal (National Party), Islamic nationalist
Armed forces 115,500 (1995)
Conscription military service is voluntary
Death penalty retained and used for ordinary crimes
Defence spend (% GDP) 1.8 (1995)
Education spend (% GNP) 2.3 (1993–94)
Health spend (% GDP) 1.4 (1990)

Economy and resources

Currency taka
GDP ($ US) 26.2 billion (1994)
Real GDP per capita (PPP) ($ US) 1,330 (1994)
GDP growth rate 4.6% (1994); 4.1% (1990–95)
Average annual inflation 6.4% (1985–95)
Foreign debt ($ US) 16.4 billion (1995)
Trading partners USA, Hong Kong, Japan, Singapore, UK
Resources natural gas, coal, limestone, china clay, glass sand
Industries textiles, food processing, industrial chemicals, petroleum refineries, cement

Exports raw jute and jute goods, tea, clothing, leather and leather products, shrimps and frogs' legs. Principal market: USA 31.5% (1995)
Imports wheat, crude petroleum and petroleum products, pharmaceuticals, cement, raw cotton, machinery and transport equipment. Principal source: India 15.3% (1995)
Arable land 65.6% (1993)
Agricultural products rice, jute, wheat, tobacco, tea; fishing and fish products

Population and society

Population 120,073,000 (1996e)
Population growth rate 2.2% (1990–95); 2% (2000–05)
Population density (per sq km) 834 (1996)
Urban population (% of total) 18 (1995)
Age distribution (% of total population) <15 39.5%, 15–65 57.5%, >65 3.1% (1995)
Ethnic distribution 98% of Bengali descent, half a million Bihari, and around 1 million belonging to 'tribal' communities
Languages Bengali (official); English
Religions Sunni Muslim 85%, Hindu 12%; Islam is the state religion
Education (compulsory years) 5
Literacy rate 57% (men); 22% (women) (1995e)
Labour force 49% of population: 56.5% agriculture, 9.8% industry, 33.7% services (1993)
Unemployment 30% (1991e)

Life expectancy 58 (men); 58 (women)
(1995–2000)
Child mortality rate (under 5, per 1,000
live births) 115 (1995)
Physicians 1 per 5,200 people (1993e)
Hospital beds 1 per 3,302 people
(1993e)
TV sets (per 1,000 people) 5.9 (1995)
Radios (per 1,000 people) 47 (1995)

Transport

Airports international airports: Dhaka
(Zia), Chittagong, Sylhet; seven domestic
airports; total passenger km: 2,936 mil
(1994)
Railroads total length: 2,706 km/1,682
mi; total passenger km: 4,570 mil (1994)
Roads total road network: 168,513 km/
104,714 mi, of which 9.3% paved (1995);
passenger cars: 0.4 per 1,000 people
(1995e)

Chronology

c. 1000 BC Arrival of Bang tribe in lower
Ganges valley, establishing the kingdom
of Banga (Bengal).
8th–12th centuries AD Bengal ruled
successively by the Buddhist Pala and
Hindu Senha dynasties.
1517 Portuguese merchants arrived in
Chittagong.
1576 Bengal conquered by Muslim
Mogul emperor Akbar.
1651 British East India Company
established a commercial factory in
Bengal.
1757 Bengal came under de facto British
rule after Robert Clive defeated the
nawab (ruler) of Bengal at Battle of
Plassey.
1905–12 Bengal briefly partitioned by

the British Raj between a Muslim-
dominated E and Hindu-dominated W.
1906 Muslim League (ML) founded in
Dhaka.
1947 Bengal formed into E province of
Pakistan on partition of British India,
with ML administration in power.
1952 12 students killed by troops in
anti-Urdu and pro-Bengali language
riots in Dhaka.
1954 The opposition United Front,
dominated by the Awami League (AL)
and campaigning for East Bengal's
autonomy, trounced ML in elections.
1955 East Bengal renamed East
Pakistan.
1966 Sheik Mujibur Rahman of AL
announced a Six-Point Programme of
autonomy for East Pakistan.
1970 500,000 people killed in cyclone.
Pro-autonomy AL secured crushing
electoral victory in East Pakistan.
1971 Bangladesh ('land of the Bangla
speakers') emerged as independent
nation, under leadership of Sheik
Mujibur Rahman, after bloody civil war
with Indian military intervention on the
side of East Pakistan; 10 million
refugees fled to India.
1974 Hundreds of thousands died in
famine; state of emergency declared.
1975 Mujibur Rahman assassinated.
Martial law imposed.
1976–77 Maj-Gen Zia ur-Rahman
assumed power as president.
1978–79 Elections held and civilian rule
restored with clear victory for Zia's
BNP.
1981 Maj-Gen Zia assassinated during
attempted military coup. Abdul Sattar
(BNP) elected president.
1982 Lt-Gen Hussain Mohammed
Ershad assumed power in army coup.

Martial law reimposed; market-oriented
economic programme adopted.
1986 Elections held but disputed and
boycotted by BNP. Martial law ended.
1987 State of emergency declared in
response to opposition demonstrations
and violent strikes.
1988 Assembly elections boycotted by
main opposition parties. State of
emergency lifted. Islam made state
religion. Monsoon floods left 30 million
homeless and thousands dead.
1989 Power devolved to Chittagong Hill
Tracts to end 14-year conflict between
local people and army-protected
settlers.
1990 Following mass anti-government
protests, President Ershad resigned;
chief justice Shahabuddin Ahmad
became interim president.
1991 Former president Ershad jailed for
corruption and illegal possession of
arms. Cyclone killed around 139,000
and left up to 10 million homeless.
Elections resulted in coalition
government with BNP dominant.
Parliamentary government restored,
with Abdur Rahman Biswas as
president and Begum Khaleda Zia prime
minister.
1994–95 Opposition boycotted
parliament, charging government with
fraud.
1996 Zia handed over power to neutral
caretaker government. General election
won by AL, led by Sheika Hasina
Wazed, daughter of Sheik Mujibur
Rahman. BNP boycotted parliament.
Agreement with India on sharing of
River Ganges water.
1997 Former president Ershad released
from prison.

Practical information

Visa requirements UK: visa required. USA: visa not required
for a tourist visit of up to 15 days
Embassy in the UK 28 Queen's Gate, London SW7 5JA.
Tel: (0171) 584 0081; fax: (0171) 255 2130
British embassy British High Commission, PO Box 6079,
United Nations Road, Baridhara, Dhaka 12. Tel: (2) 882 705;
fax: (2) 883 437
Embassy in the USA 2201 Wisconsin Avenue NW,
Washington, DC 20007. Tel: (202) 342 8372/3/4/5/6
American embassy Diplomatic Enclave, Madani Avenue,
Baridhara, Dhaka. Tel: (2) 884 700–722; fax: (2) 883 744
Chamber of commerce Federation of Bangladesh
Chambers of Commerce and Industry, Federation Bhaban,

60 Motijheel C/A, 4th Floor, POB 2079, Dhaka 1000.
Tel: (2) 250 566
Office hours 0800–1430 Sat–Thu
Banking hours 0900–1500 Sat–Wed; 0900–1300 Thu
Time difference GMT +6
Chief tourist attractions cities of Dhaka and Chittagong;
Cox's Bazaar on the Bay of Bengal – the world's longest
beach (120 km/74.5 mi); Tekhaf, at the southernmost point of
Bangladesh
Major holidays 21 February, 26 March, 1 May, 1 July,
7 November, 16, 25, 31 December; variable: Eid-ul-Adha,
end of Ramadan, New Year (Bengali), New Year (Muslim),
Prophet's Birthday, Jumat-ul-Wida (May), Shab-e-Barat
(April), Buddah Purnima (April/May), Shab-I-Qadr (May),
Durga-Puza (October)

Barbados

Area 430 sq km/166 sq mi
Capital Bridgetown
Major towns/cities Speightstown, Holetown, Oistins
Physical features most easterly island of the West Indies; surrounded by coral reefs; subject to hurricanes June–November; highest point Mount Hillaby 340 m/1,115 ft

Government

Head of state Elizabeth II from 1966, represented by Denys Williams from 1995
Head of government Owen Arthur from 1994
Political system constitutional monarchy
Administrative divisions 11 parishes
Political parties Barbados Labour Party (BLP), moderate left of centre; Democratic Labour Party (DLP), moderate left of centre; National Democratic Party (NDP), centrist
Armed forces 600 (1995)
Conscription military service is voluntary
Death penalty retained and used for ordinary crimes
Defence spend (% GDP) 0.7 (1995)
Education spend (% GNP) 7.5 (1993–94)
Health spend (% GDP) 10 (1990)

Economy and resources

Currency Barbados dollar
GDP ($ US) 1.7 billion (1994)
Real GDP per capita (PPP) ($ US) 11,051 (1994)
GDP growth rate 4.1% (1994)
Average annual inflation 2.5% (1985–95)

Foreign debt ($ US) 566 million (1993)
Trading partners USA, Trinidad and Tobago, Canada, Jamaica, St Lucia
Resources petroleum and natural gas
Industries sugar refining, food processing, industrial chemicals, beverages, tobacco, household applicances, electrical components, plastic products, electronic parts, tourism
Exports sugar, molasses, syrup-rum, chemicals, electrical components. Principal market: USA 20% (1995)
Imports machinery, foodstuffs, motor cars, construction materials, basic manufactures. Principal source: USA 30% (1995)
Arable land 37.2% (1993)
Agricultural products sugar cane, cotton, sweet potatoes, yams, carrots and other vegetables; fishing (740 fishing vessels employed in 1994)

Population and society

Population 261,000 (1996e)
Population growth rate 0.3% (1990–95)
Population density (per sq km) 608 (1996)
Urban population (% of total) 48% (1995)
Age distribution (% of total population) <15 24%, 15–65 64%, >65 12% (1994)
Ethnic distribution about 80% of African descent, about 16% mixed ethnicity, and 4% of European origin (mostly British)
Languages English and Bajan (Barbadian English dialect)
Religions 33% Anglican, 13% Pentecostalist, 6% Methodist, 4% Roman Catholic
Education (compulsory years) 12
Literacy rate 98% (men); 97% (women) (1995e)
Labour force 5.9% agriculture, 18.7% industry, 65% services (1994)
Unemployment 20.5% (1995e)
Life expectancy 74 (men); 79 (women) (1995–2000)
Child mortality rate (under 5, per 1,000 live births) 10 (1995)
Physicians 1 per 1,100 people (1993)
Hospital beds 1 per 137 people (1993)
TV sets (per 1,000 people) 284 (1995)
Radios (per 1,000 people) 900 (1995)

Transport

Airports international airports: Bridgetown (Grantley Adams)

Railroads none
Roads total road network: 1,610 km/ 1,000 mi, of which 95.8% paved (1995e); passenger cars: 142.8 per 1,000 people (1993e)

Chronology

1536 Visited by Portuguese explorer Pedro a Campos and the name Los Barbados ('The Bearded Ones') given in reference to its 'bearded' fig trees. Indigineous Arawak people was virtually wiped out, via epidemics, after contact with Europeans.
1627 British colony established; developed as a sugar-plantation economy, initially on basis of black slaves brought in from W Africa.
1639 Island's first parliament, the House of Assembly, established.
1816 Last and largest-ever revolt by slaves led by Bussa.
1834 Slaves freed.
1937 Outbreak of riots, followed by the establishment of the Barbados Labour Party (BLP) by Grantley Adams, and moves towards a more independent political system.
1951 Universal adult suffrage introduced. BLP won general election.
1954 Ministerial government established, with BLP leader Adams as first prime minister.
1955 A group broke away from the BLP and formed the Democratic Labour Party (DLP).
1961 Independence achieved from Britain. DLP, led by Errol Barrow, in power.
1966 Barbados achieved full independence within Commonwealth, with Barrow as prime minister.
1967 Became a member of the United Nations.
1972 Diplomatic relations with Cuba established.
1976 BLP, led by Tom Adams, the son of Grantley Adams, returned to power.
1983 Barbados supported US invasion of Grenada.
1985 Adams died; Bernard St John became prime minister.
1986 DLP, led by Barrow, returned to power.
1987 Barrow died; Erskine Lloyd Sandiford became prime minister.
1994 BLP, led by Owen Arthur, won decisive election victory.

Practical information

Visa requirements UK: visa not required (some visitors will require a business visa). USA: visa not required (some visitors will require a business visa)
Embassy in the UK High Commission, 1 Great Russell Street, London WCN 22B 3JY. Tel: (0171) 631 4975; fax: (0171) 323 6872
British embassy British High Commission, PO Box 676, Lower Collymore Rock, St Michael. Tel: 436 6694; fax: 436 5398
Embassy in the USA 2144 Wyoming Avenue NW, Washington, DC 20008. Tel: (202) 939 9218/9; fax: (202) 332 7467
American embassy Canadian Imperial Bank of Commerce

Building, Broad Street, Bridgetown. Tel: (809) 436 4950; fax: (809) 429 5246
Chamber of commerce Barbados Chamber of Commerce Inc, Nemwil House, 1st Floor, Lower Collymore Rock, PO Box 189, St Michael. Tel: 426 2056; fax: 429 2907
Office hours 0800/0830–1600/1630 Mon–Fri
Banking hours generally 0800–1500 Mon–Thu; 0800–1300 and 1500–1700 Fri
Time difference GMT –4
Chief tourist attractions good climate; coral beaches; swimming; outdoor sports
Major holidays 1 January, 30 November, 25–26 December; variable: Good Friday, Easter Monday, Whit Monday, Kadooment (August), May Holiday, United Nations (October)

Belarus Republic of

National name *Respublika Belarus*
Area 207,600 sq km/80,154 sq mi
Capital Minsk (Mensk)
Major towns/cities Gomel, Vitebsk, Mogilev, Bobruisk, Hrodna, Brest
Physical features more than 25% forested; rivers Dvina, Dnieper and its tributaries, including the Pripet and Beresina; the Pripet Marshes in the E; mild and damp climate

Government

Head of state Alexandr Lukashenko from 1994
Head of government Syargey Ling from 1996
Political system emergent democracy
Administrative divisions six regions (oblasts)
Political parties Belarus Communist Party (BCP, banned 1991–92); Belarus Patriotic Movement (BPM), populist; Belarusian Popular Front (BPF; Adradzhenne), moderate nationalist; Christian Democratic Union of Belarus,

centrist; Socialist Party of Belarus, left of centre
Armed forces 98,000 (1995)
Conscription compulsory for 18 months
Death penalty retained and used for ordinary crimes
Defence spend (% GDP) 3.3 (1995)
Education spend (% GNP) 6.1 (1993–94)
Health spend (% GDP) 3.6 (1993)

Economy and resources

Currency rouble and zaichik
GDP ($ US) 20 billion (1994)
Real GDP per capita (PPP) ($ US) 4,713 (1994)
GDP growth rate –10.1% (1995); –9.3% (1990–95)
Average annual inflation 309.4% (1985–95e)
Foreign debt ($ US) 1.65 billion (1995)
Trading partners former USSR (principally Russia, Ukraine, and Kazakhstan), Germany, Poland, USA
Resources petroleum, natural gas, peat, salt, coal, lignite
Industries machine building, metalworking, electronics, chemicals, construction materials, food processing, textiles
Exports machinery, chemicals and petrochemicals, iron and steel, light industrial goods. Principal market: Russia 41.6% (1996)
Imports petroleum, natural gas, chemicals, machinery, processed foods. Principal source: Russia 50.5% (1996)
Arable land 45% (1993)
Agricultural products potatoes, grain, sugar beet; livestock rearing (cattle and pigs) and dairy products. Livestock

sector accounts for approximately 60% of agricultural output

Population and society

Population 10,138,000 (1996e)
Population growth rate –0.1% (1990–95); –0.1% (2000–05)
Population density (per sq km) 88 (1996e)
Urban population (% of total) 71 (1995)
Age distribution (% of total population) <15 21.6%, 15–65 65.8%, >65 12.6% (1995)
Ethnic distribution 75% of Belarusian ('eastern Slav') descent, 13% ethnic Russian, 4% Polish, 3% Ukranian, 1% Jewish
Languages Belarusian (official); Russian, Polish
Religions Russian Orthodox, Roman Catholic; Baptist, Muslim, and Jewish minorities
Education (compulsory years) 11
Literacy rate 98% (men); 98% (women) (1995e)
Labour force 21.2% agriculture, 34.9% industry, 43.9% services (1994)
Unemployment 3.8% (1996)
Life expectancy 68 (men); 75 (women) (1995–2000)
Child mortality rate (under 5, per 1,000 live births) 20 (1995)
Physicians 1 per 243 people (1995)
Hospital beds 1 per 85 people (1995)
TV sets (per 1,000 people) 220 (1995)
Radios (per 1,000 people) 285 (1995)

Transport

Airports international airports: Minsk; total passenger km: 2,604 mil (1994)

Railroads total length: 5,488 km/3,410 mi; total passenger km: 16,063 mil (1994) **Roads** total road network: 51,547 km/ 32,031 mi, of which 98.6% paved; passenger cars: 90 per 1,000 people (1995)

Chronology

5th–8th centuries Settled by East Slavic tribes, ancestors of present-day Belarusians.
11th century Minsk founded.
12th century Part of Kievan Russia, to the S, with independent Belarus state developing around Polotsk, on River Dvina.
14th century Incorporated within Slavonic Grand Duchy of Lithuania, to the W.
1569 Union with Poland.
late 18th century Came under control of tsarist Russia as Belarusia ('White Russia'), following three partitions of Poland in 1772, 1793, and 1795.
1812 Minsk destroyed by French emperor Napoleon Bonaparte during his military campaign against Russia.

1839 Belarusian Catholic Church forcibly abolished.
1914–18 Belarus was the site of fierce fighting between Germany and Russia during World War I.
1918–19 Briefly independent from Russia.
1919–20 Wars between Poland and Soviet Russia over control of Belarus.
1921 West Belarus ruled by Poland; East Belarus became a Soviet republic.
1930s Agriculture collectivized despite peasant resistance; more than 100,000 people, chiefly writers and intellectuals, shot in mass executions ordered by Soviet dictator Joseph Stalin.
1939 West Belarus occupied by Soviet troops.
1941–44 Nazi occupation resulted in the death of 1.3 million people, including many Jews; Minsk destroyed.
1945 Became founding member of the United Nations; much of West Belarus incorporated into the Soviet republic.
1950s–60s Large-scale immigration of ethnic Russians and 'Russification'.
1986 Fallout from the nearby Chernobyl nuclear reactor in Ukraine rendered a fifth of agricultural land unusable.

1989 Belarusian Popular Front established as national identity revived under *glasnost* initiative of Soviet leader Mikhail Gorbachev.
1990 Belarusian established as state language and republican sovereignty declared.
1991 Strikes and unrest in Minsk; BCP suspended following attempted coup against Gorbachev in Moscow; moderate nationalist Stanislav Shushkevich elected president. Independence recognized by USA; Commonwealth of Independent States (CIS) formed in Minsk.
1993 ADP re-established.
1994 President Shushkevich ousted; Alexandre Lukashenko, a pro-Russian populist, elected president.
1995 Friendship and cooperation pact signed with Russia.
1996 Agreement on 'economic union' with Russia. President's referendum for a new constitution popularly endorsed. Prime Minister Mikhas Chygir replaced by Syargey Ling.
1997 Observer status in Council of Europe suspended. Treaty with Russia ratified.

Practical information

Visa requirements UK: visa required. USA: visa required
Embassy in the UK 6 Kensington Court, London W8 5DL. Tel: (0171) 937 3288; fax: (0171) 3361 0005
British embassy Zakharova 26, 220034 Minsk. Tel: (172) 368 687; fax: (172) 144 7226
Embassy in the USA 1619 New Hampshire Avenue NW, Washington, DC 20009. Tel: (202) 986 1604; fax: (202) 986 1805
American embassy Starovilenskaya 46, 220002 Minsk.

Tel: (172) 315 000; fax: (172) 347 853
Chamber of commerce Chamber of Commerce and Industry, Masherava 14, 220600 Minsk. Tel: (172) 269 172; fax: (172) 269 860
Office hours 0900–1800 Mon–Fri
Banking hours 0930–1730 Mon–Fri
Time difference GMT +2
Chief tourist attractions forests; lakes; wildlife
Major holidays 1, 7 January, 8 March, 1, 9 May, 3, 27 July, 2 November, 25 December; variable: Good Friday, Easter Monday

---

Belgium Kingdom of

National name French *Royaume de Belgique*, Flemish *Koninkrijk België*
Area 30,510 sq km/11,779 sq mi
Capital Brussels
Major towns/cities Antwerp, Ghent, Liège, Charleroi, Bruges, Mons, Namur, Leuven
Major ports Antwerp, Ostend, Zeebrugge
Physical features fertile coastal plain in NW, central rolling hills rise eastwards, hills and forest in SE; Ardennes Forest; rivers Schelde and Meuse

Government

Head of state King Albert from 1993

Head of government Jean-Luc Dehaene from 1992
Political system federal constitutional monarchy
Administrative divisions ten provinces within three regions
Political parties Flemish Christian Social Party (CVP), centre left; French Social Christian Party (PSC), centre left; Flemish Socialist Party (SP), left of centre; French Socialist Party (PS), left of centre; Flemish Liberal Party (PVV), moderate centrist; French Liberal Reform Party (PRL), moderate centrist; Flemish People's Party (VU), federalist; Flemish Vlaams Blok, right wing; Flemish Green

Party (Agalev); French Green Party (Ecolo)
Armed forces 47,000 (1995)
Conscription abolished 1995
Death penalty retained for ordinary crimes, but considered abolitionist in practice; last execution 1950
Defence spend (% GDP) 1.7 (1995)
Education spend (% GNP) 5.6 (1993–94)
Health spend (% GDP) 7.3 (1993)

Economy and resources

Currency Belgian franc
GDP ($ US) 264.4 billion (1996)
Real GDP per capita (PPP) ($ US) 21,454 (1996)
GDP growth rate 2.4% (1996); 1.1% (1990–95)
Average annual inflation 1.9% (1996); 3.1% (1985–95)
Trading partners Germany, the Netherlands, Belgium, Luxembourg, France, UK, USA
Resources coal, coke, natural gas, iron
Industries wrought and finished steel, cast iron, sugar refining, glassware, chemicals and related products, beer, textiles, rubber and plastic products
Exports food, livestock and livestock products, gem diamonds, iron and steel manufacturers, machinery and transport equipment, chemicals and related products. Principal market: Germany 20.6% (1996)
Imports food and live animals, machinery and transport equipment, precious metals and stones, mineral fuels and lubricants, chemicals and related products. Principal source: Germany 19.9% (1996)
Arable land 39.6%
Agricultural products wheat, barley, potatoes, beet (sugar and fodder), fruit, tobacco; livestock (pigs and cattle) and dairy products

Population and society

Population 10,159,000 (1996e)
Population growth rate 0.3% (1990–95); 0.1% (2000–05)
Population density (per sq km) 333 (1996e)
Urban population (% of total) 97 (1995)
Age distribution (% of total population) <15 17.8%, 15–65 66.4%, >65 15.8%
Ethnic distribution mainly Flemings in N, Walloons in S
Languages in the N (Flanders) Flemish (a Dutch dialect, known as *Vlaams*) 55%; in the S (Wallonia) Walloon (a French

dialect) 32%; bilingual 11%; German (E border) 0.6%. Dutch is official in the N, French in the S; Brussels is officially bilingual
Religions Roman Catholic 75%, various Protestant denominations
Education (compulsory years) 12
Literacy rate 99% (men); 99% (women) (1995e)
Labour force 41% of population: 3% agriculture, 28% industry, 70% services (1990)
Unemployment 9.8% (1996)
Life expectancy 74 (men); 81 (women) (1995–2000)
Child mortality rate (under 5, per 1,000 live births) 10 (1995)
Physicians 1 per 267 people (1995)
Hospital beds 1 per 124 people (1991)
TV sets (per 1,000 people) 454 (1995)
Radios (per 1,000 people) 790 (1995)

Transport

Airports international airports: Brussels (Zaventem), Antwerp (Deurne), Ostend, Liège, Charleroi; total passenger km: 7,496 mil (1994)
Railroads total length: 3,368 km/2,093 mi; total passenger km: 6,757 mil (1995)
Roads total road network: 142,563 km/ 88,589 mi; passenger cars: 418 per 1,000 people (1995)

Chronology

57 BC Romans conquered the Belgae (the indigenous Celtic people), and formed province of Belgica.
3rd–4th centuries AD Region overrun by Franks and Saxons.
8th–9th centuries Part of Frankish Empire; peace and order fostered growth of Ghent, Bruges, and Brussels.
843 Division of Holy Roman Empire; became part of Lotharingia, but frequent repartitioning followed.
10th–11th centuries Seven feudal states emerged: Flanders, Hainaut, Namur, Brabant, Limburg, and Luxembourg, all nominally subject to French king or Holy Roman emperor, but in practice independent.
12th century Economy began to flourish: textiles in Bruges, Ghent, and Ypres; copper and tin in Dinant and Liège.
15th century One by one, states came under rule of dukes of Burgundy.
1477 Passed into Habsburg dominions through marriage of Mary of Burgundy to Maximilian, archduke of Austria.

1555 Division of Habsburg dominions; Low Countries allotted to Spain.
1648 Independence of Dutch Republic recognized; S retained by Spain.
1713 Treaty of Utrecht transferred Spanish Netherlands to Austrian rule.
1792–97 Austrian Netherlands invaded by revolutionary France and finally annexed.
1815 Congress of Vienna reunited N and S Netherlands as one kingdom under House of Orange.
1830 Largely French-speaking people in S rebelled against union with Holland and declared Belgian independence.
1831 Leopold of Saxe-Coburg-Gotha became first king of Belgium.
1839 Treaty of London recognized independence of Belgium and guaranteed its neutrality.
1847–70 Government dominated by Liberals; growth of heavy industry.
1870–1914 Catholic Party predominant.
1914–18 Invaded and occupied by Germany. Belgian forces under King Albert I fought in conjunction with Allies.
1919 Acquired Eupen-Malmédy region from Germany.
1940 Second invasion by Germany; King Leopold III ordered Belgian army to capitulate.
1944–45 Belgium liberated.
1948 Belgium formed Benelux customs union with Luxembourg and the Netherlands.
1949 Belgium was a founding member of North Atlantic Treaty Organization (NATO).
1951 Leopold III abdicated in favour of his son Baudouin.
1958 Belgium was a founding member of European Economic Community (EEC), which made Brussels its headquarters.
1967 NATO made Brussels its headquarters.
1971 Constitution amended to safeguard cultural rights of Flemish- (in Flanders in N) and French-speaking communities (Walloons in SE) in an effort to ease linguistic dispute.
1974 Separate regional councils and ministerial committees established for Flemings and Walloons.
1980 Open violence over language divisions; regional assemblies for Flanders and Wallonia and three-member executive for Brussels created.
1993 Federal system adopted, based on Flanders, Wallonia, and Brussels. King Baudouin died, succeeded by his brother Albert.
1995 Dehaene-led coalition re-elected.

Practical information

Visa requirements UK: visa not required. USA: visa not required
Embassy in the UK 103–105 Eaton Square, London SW1W 9AB. Tel: (0171) 470 3700; fax: (0171) 259 6213
British embassy 85 rue d'Arlon, B-1040 Brussels. Tel: (2) 287 6211; fax: (2) 287 6355
Embassy in the USA 3330 Garfield Street NW, Washington, DC 20008. Tel: (202) 333 6900; fax: (202) 333 3079
American embassy 27 boulevard du Régent, B-1000 Brussels. Tel: (2) 508 2111; fax: (2) 511 2725
Chamber of commerce Kamer van Koophandel en Nijverheid van Antwerpen, 12 Markgravestraat, B-2000

Antwerp. Tel: (3) 232 2219; fax: (3) 233 6442. Chambre de Commerce et d'Industrie de Bruxelles, 500 ave Louise, 1050 Brussels. Tel: (2) 648 5002; fax: (2) 640 9228
Office hours 0830–1730 Mon–Fri
Banking hours 0900–1200 and 1400–1600 Mon–Fri; some banks open 0900–1200 Sat
Time difference GMT +1
Chief tourist attractions towns of historic and cultural interest include Bruges, Ghent, Antwerp, Liège, Namur, Tournai, and Durbuy; seaside towns; forested Ardennes region
Major holidays 1 January, 30 November, 25–26 December; variable: Ascension Thursday, Easter Monday, Whit Monday, May, August, and November holidays

Belize (formerly *British Honduras*)

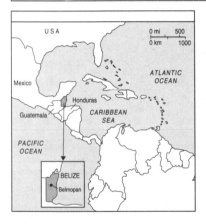

Area 22,963 sq km/8,866 sq mi
Capital Belmopan
Major towns/cities Belize City, Dangriga, Orange Walk, Corozal
Major ports Belize City, Dangriga, Punta Gorda
Physical features tropical swampy coastal plain, Maya Mountains in S; over 90% forested

Government

Head of state Elizabeth II from 1981, represented by governor general Dr Norbert Colville Young from 1993
Head of government Manuel Esquivel from 1993
Political system constitutional monarchy
Administrative divisions six districts
Political parties People's United Party (PUP), left of centre; United Democratic Party (UDP), moderate conservative
Armed forces 1,050 (1995); plus 700 militia reserves
Conscription military service is voluntary

Death penalty retained and used for ordinary crimes
Defence spend (% GDP) 2.6 (1995)
Education spend (% GNP) 5.7 (1993–94)
Health spend (% GDP) 9.6 (1994)

Economy and resources

Currency Belize dollar
GDP ($ US) 552 million (1994)
Real GDP per capita (PPP) ($ US) 5,590 (1994)
GDP growth rate 1.6% (1994)
Average annual inflation 3.5% (1985–95)
Foreign debt ($ US) 175 million (1991–93)
Trading partners USA, UK, Mexico, Canada
Industries clothing, agricultural products (particularly sugar cane for sugar and rum), timber, tobacco
Exports sugar, clothes, citrus products, forestry and fish products, bananas. Principal market: UK 40.2% (1994)
Imports foodstuffs, machinery and transport equipment, mineral fuels, chemicals, basic manufactures. Principal source: USA 53.1% (1994)
Arable land 2% (1993)
Agricultural products sugar cane, citrus fruits, bananas, maize, red kidney beans, rice; livestock rearing (cattle, pigs, and poultry); fishing; timber reserves

Population and society

Population 219,000 (1996e)
Population growth rate 2.6% (1990–95); 2.3% (2000–05)
Population density (per sq km) 10 (1996e)

Urban population (% of total) 47 (1995)
Age distribution (% of total population) <15 42.3%, 15–65 53.5%, >65 4.2% (1995)
Ethnic distribution Creoles, Mestizos, Caribs, East Indians, Canadians and Europeans, including Spanish and British Mennonites
Languages English (official); Spanish (widely spoken), Creole dialects
Religions Roman Catholic 60%, Protestant 35%
Education (compulsory years) 10
Literacy rate 93% (men); 93% (women) (1994)
Labour force 31% of population: 34% agriculture, 19% industry, 48% services (1990)
Unemployment 13.1% (1994)
Life expectancy 73 (men); 76 (women) (1995–2000)
Child mortality rate (under 5, per 1,000 live births) 40 (1995)
Physicians 1 per 2,010 people (1990)
Hospital beds 1 per 360 people (1990)
TV sets (per 1,000 people) 178 (1995)
Radios (per 1,000 people) 587 (1995)

Transport

Airports international airports: Belize City (Philip S W Goldson); domestic air services provide connections to major towns and offshore islands
Railroads none
Roads total road network: 2,770 km/1,721 mi, of which 18.8% paved (1995e)

Chronology

325–925 AD Part of the Native American Maya civilization.

1600s Colonized by British buccaneers and log-cutters
1862 Formally declared a British colony, known as British Honduras.
1893 Mexico renounced its long-standing claim to the territory.
1954 Constitution adopted, providing for limited internal self-government. General election won by PUP led by George Price.
1964 Self-government achieved from the UK. Universal adult suffrage and a two-chamber legislature introduced.

1970 Capital moved from Belize City to new town of Belmopan.
1973 Name changed to Belize.
1975 British troops sent to defend the long-disputed frontier with Guatemala.
1980 United Nations called for full independence.
1981 Full independence achieved, with Price as prime minister.
1984 Price defeated in general election. Manuel Esquivel of the right-of-centre United Democratic Party (UDP) formed

government. The UK reaffirmed its undertaking to defend the frontier.
1989 Price and PUP won general election.
1991 Diplomatic relations re-established with Guatemala, which finally recognized Belize's sovereignty.
1993 UDP defeated PUP in general election; Esquivel returned as prime minister. UK announced intention to withdraw troops following resolution of the border dispute with Guatemala.

Practical information

Visa requirements UK: visa not required. USA: visa not required
Embassy in the UK 22 Harcourt House, 19 Cavendish Square, London W1M 9 AD. Tel: (0171) 499 9728; fax: (0171) 491 4139
British embassy British High Commission, PO Box 91, Embassy Square, Belmopan. Tel: (8) 22146/7; fax: (8) 22761
Embassy in the USA 2535 Massachusetts Avenue NW, Washington, DC 20008. Tel: (202) 332 9636; fax: (202) 332 6888
American embassy Gabourel Lane and Hutson Street, Belize City. Tel: (2) 77161/2/3; fax: (2) 30802

Chamber of commerce Belize Chamber of Commerce and Industry, 63 Regent Street, POB 291, Belize City. Tel: (2) 75924; fax: (2) 74984
Office hours 0800–1200 and 1300–1700 Mon–Thu; 0800–1200 and 1300–1630 Fri
Banking hours 0800–1300 Mon–Thu; 0800–1200 and 1500–1800 Fri
Time difference GMT –6
Chief tourist attractions beaches and barrier reef; hunting and fishing; Mayan remains; nine major wildlife reserves (including the only reserves for jaguar and red-footed booby)
Major holidays 1 January, 9 March, 1, 24 May, 10, 24 September, 12 October, 19 November, 25–26 December; variable: Good Friday, Easter Monday, Holy Saturday

---

Benin People's Republic of (formerly known as *Dahomey* 1904–75)

National name *République Populaire du Bénin*
Area 112,622 sq km/43,483 sq mi
Capital Porto-Novo (official), Cotonou (de facto)
Major towns/cities Abomey, Natitingou, Parakou, Kandi, Ouidah, Djougou, Bohicou
Major ports Cotonou
Physical features flat to undulating terrain; hot and humid in S; semiarid in N; coastal lagoons with fishing villages on stilts; Niger River in NE

Government

Head of state and government Mathieu Kerekou from 1996

Political system socialist pluralist republic
Administrative divisions six provinces
Political parties Union for the Triumph of Democratic Renewal (UTDR); National Party for Democracy and Development (PNDD); Party for Democratic Renewal (PRD); Social Democratic Party (PSD); National Union for Solidarity and Progress (UNSP); National Democratic Rally (RND). The general orientation of most parties is left of centre
Armed forces 4,800 (1995)
Conscription by selective conscription for 18 months
Death penalty retained and used for ordinary crimes
Defence spend (% GDP) 1.3 (1995)
Education spend (% GNP) 5.6 (1990)
Health spend (% GDP) 2.8 (1990)

Economy and resources

Currency franc CFA
GDP ($ US) 1.5 billion (1994)
Real GDP per capita (PPP) ($ US) 1,696 (1994)
GDP growth rate 4.8% (1994)
Average annual inflation 2.9% (1985–95e)
Foreign debt ($ US) 1.7 billion (1995)

Trading partners Morocco, France, USA, Portugal, China, Ghana, Nigeria, Thailand, Côte d'Ivoire, Italy
Resources petroleum, limestone, marble
Industries palm-oil processing, brewing, cement, cotton ginning, sugar refining, textiles
Exports cotton, crude petroleum, palm oil and other palm products. Principal market: Morocco 37.6% (1994)
Imports foodstuffs (particularly cereals), miscellaneous manufactured articles (notably cotton yarn and fabrics), fuels, machinery and transport equipment, chemicals, beverages, tobacco. Principal source: France 24.3% (1994)
Arable land 12.7% (1993)
Agricultural products cotton, maize, yarns, cassava, sorghum, millet; fishing

Population and society

Population 5,563,000 (1996e)
Population growth rate 3.1% (1990–95); 2.8% (2000–05)
Population density (per sq km) 49 (1996e)
Urban population (% of total) 31 (1995)
Age distribution (% of total population) <15 47.4%, 15–65 49.7%, >65 2.8% (1995)

Ethnic distribution 98% indigenous African, distributed among 42 ethnic groups, the largest being the Fon, Adja, Yoruba, and Braiba; small European (mainly French) community
Languages French (official); Fon 47% and Yoruba 9% in S; six major tribal languages in N
Religions animist 60%, Muslim, Roman Catholic
Education (compulsory years) 6
Literacy rate 32% (men); 16% (women) (1995e)
Labour force 46% of population: 64% agriculture, 8% industry, 28% services (1990)
Life expectancy 47 (men); 51 (women) (1995–2000)
Child mortality rate (under 5, per 1,000 live births) 142 (1995)
Physicians 1 per 16,000 people (1994e)
TV sets (per 1,000 people) 5.9 (1995)
Radios (per 1,000 people) 92 (1995)

Transport

Airports international airports: Cotonou (Cotonou-Cadjehoun); four domestic airports; total passenger km: 215 mil (1994)
Railroads total length: 578 km/359 mi (1995); total passenger km: 116 mil (1995)
Roads total road network: 8,460 km/ 5,257 mi, of which 31.4% paved (1995e);

passenger cars: 6.6 per 1,000 people (1995e)

Chronology

12th–13th centuries Settled by Ewe-speaking people, called the Aja, who mixed with local peoples and gradually formed the Fon ethnic group.
16th century Aja kingdom, called Great Ardha, at its peak.
early 17th century Kingdom of Dahomey established in S by Fon peoples, who defeated the neighbouring Dan; following contact with European traders, the kingdom became became an intermediary in the slave trade, which was particularly active along the Bight (Bay) of Benin, between Ghana and Nigeria, during the 16th–19th centuries.
1800–50 King Dezo of Dahomey raised regiments of female soldiers to attack the Yoruba ('land of the big cities') kingdom of E Benin and SW Nigeria to obtain slaves; palm-oil trade developed.
1857 French base established at Grand-Popo.
1892–94 War between the French and Dahomey, after which the victorious French established a protectorate.
1899 Incorporated in federation of French West Africa as Dahomey.
1914 French troops from Dahomey participated in conquest of German-ruled Togoland to W, during World War I.

1940–44 Along with the rest of French West Africa, supported the 'Free French' anti-Nazi resistance cause during World War II.
1960 Independence achieved from France.
1960–72 Acute political instability, with frequent switches from civilian to military rule, and regional ethnic disputes.
1972 Military regime established by Major Mathieu Kerekou.
1974 Kerekou announced that country would follow a path of 'scientific socialism'.
1975 Name of country changed from Dahomey to Benin.
1977 Return to civilian rule under new constitution, but with Kerekou as president.
1989 Army deployed against antigovernment strikers and protesters, inspired by E European revolutions; Marxist-Leninism dropped as official ideology and market-centred economic reform programme adopted.
1990 Referendum backed establishment of multiparty politics.
1991 In multiparty elections, President Kerekou was replaced by the leader of the new Benin Renaissance Party (PRB), Nicéphore Soglo, who formed a ten-party coalition government.
1996 Kerekou defeated Soglo in presidential election run-off despite opposition claims of fraud.

Practical information

Visa requirements UK: visa required. USA: visa required
Embassy in the UK Dolphin House, 16 The Broadway, Stanmore, Middlesex HA7 4DW. Tel: (0181) 954 8800; fax: (0181) 954 8844
British embassy British Consulate, Lot 24, Patte d'Oie, Cotonou. (All staff based in Nigeria.) Tel: 301120
Embassy in the USA 2737 Cathedral Avenue NW, Washington, DC 20008. Tel: (202) 232 6656/7/8; fax: (202) 265 1996
American embassy Rue Caporal Bernard Anani, Cotonou.

Tel: 300 650, 300 513, 301 792; fax:301 439, 301 974
Chamber of commerce Chambre de Commerce, d'Agriculture et d'Industrie de la République du Bénin, ave du Général de Gaulle, BP31, Cotonou. Tel: 313 299
Office hours 0830–1230 and 1500–1830 Mon–Fri
Banking hours 0800–1100 and 1500–1700 Mon–Fri
Time difference GMT +1
Chief tourist attractions national parks; game reserves
Major holidays 1, 16 January, 1 April, 1 May, 26 October, 30 November, 25, 31 December; variable: Eid-ul-Adha, end of Ramadan, Good Friday, Easter Monday, Whit Monday

---

Bhutan Kingdom of

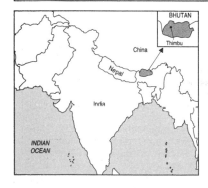

National name *Druk-yul*
Area 46,500 sq km/17,953 sq mi
Capital Thimphu (Thimbu)
Major towns/cities Paro, Punakha, Mongar, P'sholing, W'phodrang, Bumthang
Physical features occupies southern slopes of the Himalayas; Gangkar Punsum (7,529 m/24,700 ft) is one of the world's highest unclimbed peaks; cut by valleys formed by tributaries of the Brahmaputra; thick forests in the S

Government

Head of state and government Jigme Singye Wangchuk from 1972
Political system absolute monarchy
Administrative divisions 20 districts
Political parties none officially; illegal Bhutan People's Party (BPP) and Bhutan National Democratic Party (BNDP), both ethnic Nepali
Armed forces 5,500 (1994)
Conscription military service is voluntary

Death penalty retains the death penalty for ordinary crimes but can be considered abolitionist in practice (date of last known execution 1964)
Education spend (% GNP) 7.9 (1992)
Health spend (% GDP) 4.4 (1992)

Economy and resources

Currency ngultrum; also Indian currency
GDP ($ US) 1.3 billion (1995e)
Real GDP per capita (PPP) ($ US) 730 (1995e)
GDP growth rate 6% (1995e)
Average annual inflation 8.6% (1995e)
Foreign debt ($ US) 85 million (1991–93)
Trading partners India, Middle East, Singapore, Europe
Resources limestone, gypsum, coal, slate, dolomite, lead, talc, copper
Industries food processing, cement, calcium carbide, textiles, tourism, cardamon, gypsum, timber, handicrafts, cement, fruit, electricity (to India), precious stones, spices
Exports cardamon, cement, timber, fruit, electricity (to India), precious stones, spices. Principal market: India 94% (1994)
Imports aircraft, mineral fuels, machinery and transport equipment, rice. Principal source: India 77% (1994)
Arable land 2.4%
Agricultural products potatoes, rice, apples, oranges, cardamoms; timber production

Population and society

Population 1,812,000 (1996e)
Population growth rate 1.2% (1990–95); 2.3% (2000–05)
Population density (per sq km) 39 (1996e)
Urban population (% of total) 6 (1995)

Age distribution (% of total population) <15 41.1%, 15–65 55.5%, >65 3.5% (1995)
Ethnic distribution 54% Bhotia, living principally in the N and E; 32% of Tibetan descent; a substantial Nepali minority lives in the S – they are prohibited from moving into the Bhotia-dominated N
Languages Dzongkha (official, a Tibetan dialect), Sharchop, Bumthap, Nepali, and English
Religions 70% Mahayana Buddhist (state religion), 25% Hindu
Education not compulsory
Literacy rate 51% (men); 25% (women) (1995e)
Labour force 51% of population: 94% agriculture, 1% industry, 5% services (1990)
Life expectancy 52 (men); 55 (women) (1995–2000)
Child mortality rate (under 5, per 1,000 live births) 189 (1995)
Physicians 1 per 6,000 people (1996)
Hospital beds 1 per 688 people (1996)
TV sets (per 1,000 people) 5.9 (1995)
Radios (per 1,000 people) 17 (1995)

Transport

Airports international airports: Paro; total passenger km: 5 mil (1994)
Railroads none
Roads total road network: 2,210 km/ 1,373 mi (1995e)

Chronology

to 8th century Under effective Indian control.
16th century Came under Tibetan rule.
1616–51 Unified by Ngawang Namgyal, leader of the Drukpa Kagyu (Thunder Dragon) Tibetan Buddhist branch.
1720 Came under Chinese rule.

1774 Treaty signed with East India Company.
1865 Trade treaty with Britain signed after invasion.
1907 Ugyen Wangchuk, the governor of Tongsa, became Bhutan's first hereditary monarch.
1910 Anglo-Bhutanese Treaty signed, placing foreign relations under the 'guidance' of the British government in India.
1926 Jigme Wangchuk succeeded to the throne.
1949 Indo-Bhutan Treaty of Friendship signed, giving India continued influence over Bhutan's foreign relations, but returning territory annexed in 1865.
1952 Reformist king Jigme Dorji Wangchuk came to power.
1953 National assembly (Tshogdu) established.
1958 Slavery abolished.
1959 4,000 Tibetan refugees given asylum after Chinese annexation of Tibet.
1968 King established first cabinet.
1972 King died and was succeeded by his Western-educated son Jigme Singye Wangchuk.
1973 Joined the nonaligned movement.
1979 Tibetan refugees told to take Bhutanese citizenship or leave; most stayed.
1983 Bhutan became a founding member of the South Asian Regional Association for Cooperation.
1988 Buddhist Dzongkha Drukpa king imposed 'code of conduct' suppressing the customs of the large Hindu-Nepali community in the S.
1990 Hundreds of people allegedly killed during prodemocracy demonstrations.
1993 Leader of banned Bhutan People's Party (BPP) sentenced to life imprisonment for 'antinational activities'.

Practical information

Visa requirements UK: visa required. USA: visa required
Embassy in the UK no diplomatic representation
British embassy no diplomatic representation
Embassy in the USA no diplomatic representation
American embassy no diplomatic representation
Chamber of commerce Bhutan Chamber of Commerce and

Industry, POB 147, Thimphu. Tel: (2) 23140; fax: (2) 23936
Time difference GMT +6
Chief tourist attractions Bhutan is open only to 'controlled' tourism – many monasteries, mountains, and other holy places remain inaccessible to tourists; wildlife includes snow leopards and musk deer
Major holidays 2 May, 2 June, 21 July, 11–13 November, 17 December

Bolivia Republic of

National name *República de Bolivia*
Area 1,098,581 sq km/424,162 sq mi
Capital La Paz (seat of government),
Sucre (legal capital and seat of
judiciary)
Major towns/cities Santa Cruz,
Cochabamba, Oruro, El Alto, Potosí
Physical features high plateau
(Altiplano) between mountain ridges
(cordilleras); forest and lowlands (llano)
in the E; Andes; lakes Titicaca (the
world's highest navigable lake, 3,800 m/
12,500 ft) and Poopó

Government

Head of state and government Hugo
Banzer Suarez from 1997
Political system emergent democratic
republic
Administrative divisions nine
departments
Political parties National Revolutionary
Movement (MNR), centre right;
Movement of the Revolutionary Left
(MIR), left of centre; Nationalist
Democratic Action Party (ADN), right
wing; Solidarity and Civic Union (UCS),
populist, free market
Armed forces 33,500 (1995)
Conscription selective conscription for
12 months at the age of 18
Death penalty retained and used for
ordinary crimes but can be considered
abolitionist in practice (last execution
1974)
Defence spend (% GDP) 2.6 (1995)
Education spend (% GNP) 5.4
(1993–94)
Health spend (% GDP) 1.9 (1993)

Economy and resources

Currency boliviano
GDP ($ US) 5.5 billion (1994)
Real GDP per capita (PPP) ($ US)
2,598 (1994)
GDP growth rate 4.2% (1994);
3.8%(1990–95)
Average annual inflation 18.5%
(1985–95)
Foreign debt ($ US) 5,266 million (1995)
Trading partners USA, Argentina, UK,
Brazil, Japan, Belgium
Resources petroleum, natural gas, tin
(world's fifth-largest producer), zinc,
silver, gold, lead, antimony, tungsten,
copper
Industries mining, food products,
petroleum refining, tobacco, textiles
Exports metallic minerals, natural gas,
jewellery, soya beans, wood. Principal
market: USA 24.1% (1995). Illegal trade
in coca and its derivatives (mainly
cocaine) was worth approximately $600
million in 1990 – almost equal to annual
earnings from official exports
Imports industrial materials, machinery
and transport equipment, consumer
goods. Principal source: USA 19.4%
(1995)
Arable land 1.9% (1993)
Agricultural products coffee, coca,
soya beans, sugar cane, rice, chestnuts,
maize, potatoes; livestock products (beef
and hides); forest resources

Population and society

Population 7,593,000 (1996e)
Population growth rate 2.4%
(1990–95); 2.2% (2000–05)
Population density (per sq km) 7
(1996e)
Urban population (% of total) 61 (1995)
Age distribution (% of total population)
<15 40.6%, 15–65 55.6%, >65 3.8%
(1995)
Ethnic distribution 30% Quechua
Indians, 25% Aymara Indians, 25–30%
mixed, 5–15% of European descent
Languages Spanish (official); Aymara,
Quechua
Religion Roman Catholic 95% (state-
recognized)
Education (compulsory years) 8
Literacy rate 85% (men); 71% (women)
(1995e)
Labour force 40% of population: 47%
agriculture, 19% industry, 34% services
(1993)

Unemployment 6% (1993e)
Life expectancy 60 (men); 63 (women)
(1995–2000)
Child mortality rate (under 5, per 1,000
live births) 105 (1995)
Physicians 1 per 2,564 people (1991)
Hospital beds 1 per 686 (1987)
TV sets (per 1,000 people) 115 (1995)
Radios (per 1,000 people) 672 (1995)

Transport

Airports international airports: La Paz
(El Alto), Santa Cruz (Viru-Viru); 28
domestic airports; total passenger km:
1,139 mil (1994)
Railroads total length: 3,652 km/2,269
mi; total passenger km: 276 mil (1994)
Roads total road network: 55,487
km/34,480 mi, of which 4.8% paved
(1995e); passenger cars: 31.2 per 1,000
people (1995)

Chronology

c. AD 600 Development of sophisticated
civilization at Tiahuanaco, S of Lake
Titicaca.
c. 1200 Tiahuanaco culture was
succeeded by smaller Aymara-speaking
kingdoms.
16th century Became incorporated
within westerly Quechua-speaking Inca
civilization, centred in Peru.
1538 Conquered by Spanish and, known
as 'Upper Peru', became part of the
Viceroyalty of Peru, whose capital was at
Lima (Peru); Charcas (now Sucre)
became the local capital.
1545 Silver discovered at Potosí in the
SW, which developed into chief silver-
mining town and most important city in
South America in the 17th and 18th
centuries.
1776 Transferred to the Viceroyalty of La
Plata, with its capital in Buenos Aires.
late 18th century Increasing resistance
of Native Americans and mestizos to
Spanish rule; silver production
slumped.
1825 Liberated from Spanish rule by the
Venezuelan freedom fighter Simón
Bolívar, after whom the country was
named, and his general, Antonio José de
Sucre, after battle of Tumulsa; Sucre
became Bolivia's first president.
1836–39 Part of a federation with Peru,
headed by Bolivian president Andres
Santa Cruz, but it dissolved following
defeat in war with Chile.

1879–84 Lost coastal territory in the Atacama, containing valuable minerals, after defeat in war with Chile.
1880 Start of a period of civilian rule which lasted until 1936.
1903 Lost territory to Brazil.
1932–35 Lost further territory after defeated by Paraguay in the Chaco War, tought over control of the Chaco Boreal.
1952 After military regime overthrown by peasants and mineworkers in the Bolivian National Revolution, the formerly exiled Dr Victor Paz Estenssoro of the centrist National Revolutionary Movement (MNR) became president and introduced social and economic reforms, including universal suffrage, nationalization of tin mines, and land redistribution.
1956 Dr Hernán Siles Zuazo (MNR) became president, defeating Paz.
1960 Paz returned to power.

1964 Army coup led by Vice President Gen René Barrientos.
1967 Peasant uprising, led by Ernesto 'Che' Guevara, put down with US help; Guevara was killed.
1969 Barrientos killed in plane crash, replaced by Vice President Siles Salinas, who was soon deposed in army coup.
1971 Col Hugo Banzer Suárez came to power after further military coup.
1974 Attempted coup prompted Banzer to postpone promised elections and ban political and trade-union activity.
1980 Inconclusive elections were followed by the country's 189th coup, led by Gen Luis García. Allegations of corruption and drug trafficking led to cancellation of US and European Community (EC) aid.
1981 García forced to resign. Replaced by Gen Celso Torrelio Villa.

1982 Torrelio resigned and, with economy worsening, junta handed power over to civilian administration headed by Siles Zuazo.
1983 US and EC economic aid resumed as austerity measures introduced.
1985 President Siles resigned after general strike and attempted coup. Election result inconclusive; veteran Dr Paz Estenssoro (MNR) chosen by congress as president. Inflation rate 23,000%.
1989 Jaime Paz Zamora, of the left-wing Movement of Revolutionary Left (MIR) chosen as president in power-sharing arrangement with Banzer.
1993 Gonzalo Sanchez de Lozada (MNR) elected president after Banzer withdrew his candidacy. Foreign investment encouraged as inflation fell to single figures.
1997 Banzer elected president.

Practical information

Visa requirements UK: visa not required for a stay of up to 90 days. USA: visa not required for a stay of up to 90 days
Embassy in the UK Embassy and Consulate, 106 Eaton Square, London SW1W 9AD. Tel: (0171)235 4248; fax: (0171) 235 1286
British embassy Avenida Arce 2732, Casilla 694, La Paz. Tel: (2) 357 424; fax: (2) 391 063
Embassy in the USA 3014 Massachusetts Avenue NW, Washington, DC 20008. Tel: (202) 483 4410/1/2; fax: (202) 328 3712
American embassy Avenida Arce 2780, San Jorge, La Paz. Tel: (2) 430 251; fax: (2) 433 900

Chamber of commerce Cámara Nacional de Comercio, Edificio Cámara Nacional de Comercio, Avda Mariscal Santa Cruz 1392, 1°, Casilla 7, La Paz. Tel: (2) 350 042; fax: (2) 391 004
Office hours 0830–1200 and 1430–1830 Mon–Fri; 0900–1200 some Saturdays
Banking hours 0830–1200 and 1430–1730 Mon–Fri
Time difference GMT –4
Chief tourist attractions Lake Titicaca; pre-Inca ruins at Tiwanaku; Chacaltaga in the Andes Mountains; UNESCO World Cultural Heritage Sites of Potosí and Sucre; skiing in the Andes
Major holidays 1 January, 1 May, 6 August, 1 November, 25 December; variable: Carnival, Corpus Christi, Good Friday

---

Bosnia-Herzegovina Republic of

National name *Republika Bosna i Hercegovina*
Area 51,129 sq km/19,740 sq mi
Capital Sarajevo

Major towns/cities Banja Luka, Mostar, Prijedor, Tuzla, Zenica
Physical features barren, mountainous country, part of the Dinaric Alps; limestone gorges; 20 km/12 mi of coastline with no harbour

Government

Heads of state Alija Izetbegović from 1990, Momcilo Krajisnik and Kerismir Zubak from 1996
Heads of government Haris Silajdzic and Boro Bosnic from 1997
Political system emergent democracy
Political parties Party of Democratic Action (PDA), Muslim-oriented; Serbian Renaissance Movement (SPO), Serbian nationalist; Croatian Christian Democratic Union of Bosnia-Herzegovina

(CDU), Croatian nationalist; League of Communists (LC) and Socialist Alliance (SA), left wing
Armed forces 92,000 (1995)
Death penalty retained and used for ordinary crimes
Defence spend (% GDP) 18.8 (1995)

Economy and resources

Currency dinar
GDP ($ US) 1 billion (1995e)
Real GDP per capita (PPP) ($ US) 300 (1995e)
GDP growth rate N/A
Average annual inflation 120% (1992)
Foreign debt ($ US) 2 billion (1992e)
Resources copper, lead, zinc, iron ore, coal, bauxite, manganese
Industries iron and crude steel,

armaments, cement, textiles, vehicle assembly, wood products, oil refining, electrical appliances, cigarettes; industrial infrastructure virtually destroyed by war

Exports coal, domestic appliances (industrial production and mining remain low). Principal market: Italy 29.4% (1995)

Imports foodstuffs, basic manufactured goods, processed and semiprocessed goods. Principal source: Croatia 44% (1995)

Arable land 50% (1992)

Agricultural products before the war, these were maize, wheat, potatoes, rice, tobacco, fruit, olives, grapes; livestock rearing (sheep and cattle); timber reserves

Population and society

Population 3,628,000 (1996e)

Population growth rate −4.4% (1990–95); 0.2% (2000–05)

Population density (per sq km) 71 (1996e)

Urban population (% of total) 49 (1995)

Age distribution (% of total population) <15 22.2%, 15–65 70%, >65 7.8% (1995)

Ethnic distribution 44% ethnic Muslim, 31% Serb, 17% Croat, 6% 'Yugoslav'. Croats are most thickly settled in SW Bosnia and W Herzegovina, Serbs in eastern and western Bosnia. Since the start of the civil war in 1992 many Croats and Muslims have fled as refugees to neighbouring states

Language Serbian variant of Serbo-Croatian

Religions Sunni Muslim, Serbian Orthodox, Roman Catholic

Education (compulsory years) 8

Literacy rate 90% (men); 90% (women) (1992)

Labour force 2% agriculture, 45% industry, 53% services (1990e)

Unemployment 28% (1992e)

Life expectancy 70 (men); 76 (women) (1995–2000)

Infant mortality rate (per 1,000 live births) 17 (1995)

TV sets (per 1,000 people) 0.2 (1995)

Radios (per 1,000 people) 235 (1995)

Transport

Airports international airport: Sarajevo; two smaller civil airports (civil aviation was severely disrupted by fighting in early 1990s; no air services to Sarajevo since 1992)

Railroads total length: 1,021 km/634 mi; total passenger km: 554 mil (1991)

Roads total road network: 21,168 km/ 13,154 mi (1990)

Chronology

1st century AD Part of Roman province of Illyricum.

395 On division of Roman Empire, stayed in W, along with Croatia and Slovenia, whereas Serbia to E became part of the Byzantine Empire.

7th century Settled by Slav tribes.

12–15th centuries Independent state.

1463 and 1482 Bosnia and Herzegovina, in S, successively conquered by Ottoman Turks; many Slavs were converted to Sunni Islam.

1878 Became an Austrian protectorate, following Bosnian revolt against Turkish rule in 1875–76.

1908 Annexed by Austrian Habsburgs in wake of Turkish Revolution.

1914 Archduke Franz Ferdinand, the Habsburg heir, assassinated in Sarajevo by a Bosnian-Serb extremist, precipitating World War I.

1918 On collapse of Habsburg Empire, became part of Serb-dominated 'Kingdom of Serbs, Croats, and Slovenes', known as Yugoslavia from 1929.

1941 Occupied by Nazi Germany and became 'Greater Croatia' fascist puppet state and scene of fierce fighting.

1943–44 Liberated by the communist Partisans, led by Marshal Tito.

1945 Became republic within Yugoslav Socialist Federation.

1980 Upsurge in Islamic nationalism.

1990 Ethnic violence erupted between Muslims and Serbs. Communists defeated in multiparty elections; coalition formed by Serb, Muslim, and Croatian parties, with a nationalist Muslim, Alija Izetbegovic, as president.

1991 Serb-Croat civil war in Croatia spread disorder into Bosnia. Fears that Serbia aimed to annex Serb-dominated parts of the republic led to 'sovereignty' declaration by parliament. Serbs within Bosnia established own autonomous enclaves.

1992 In a Serb-boycotted referendum, Bosnian Muslims and Croats voted overwhelmingly for independence, which was recognized by USA and European Community (EC); admitted into United Nations (UN). Violent civil war broke out, as independent 'Serbian Republic of Bosnia-Herzegovina', comprising

parts of E and W, proclaimed by Bosnian-Serb militia leader Radovan Karadzic, with Serbian backing. UN forces drafted into Sarajevo to break Serb siege of city; accusations of 'ethnic cleansing', particularly of Muslims, by Bosnian Serbs.

1993 UN–EC peace plan failed. USA began airdrops of food and medical supplies. Six UN 'safe areas' created (Srebrenica, Tuzla, Zepa, Gorazde, Bihac, Sarajevo), intended as havens for Muslim civilians. Croat-Serb partition plan rejected by Muslims.

1994 Serb siege of Sarajevo lifted after UN–NATO ultimatum and Russian diplomatic intervention. Croat-Muslim federation formed after cease-fire in N. Cease-fire negotiated by former US president Jimmy Carter.

1995 Hostilities resumed; 'safe areas' of Srebrenica (where more than 4,000 Muslims were massacred) and Zepa were overrun before the Serbs were halted by Croatians near Bihac. US-sponsored peace accord, providing for two sovereign states (one Muslim-Croat, one Serb) and cease-fire agreed at Dayton, Ohio, USA; peace accord reached; 60,000-strong NATO peacekeeping force deployed.

1996 International Criminal Tribunal for Former Yugoslavia began in the Hague. Arms-control accord signed. Three-person presidency elected, consisting of Alija Izetbegovic (incumbent Muslim president), Momcilo Krajisnik (Serb), and Kresimir Zubak (Croat). Biljana Plavisic elected president of Republika Srpska (Serb-controlled Bosnia). Bosnian Serb prime minister Rajko Kasagic dismissed. Full diplomatic relations established with Yugoslavia. New government formed, with Gojko Klickovic as prime minister. NATO-led Stabilization Force replaced Implementation Force. Herceg-Bosna para-state and the Bosnian Republic replaced by Muslim-Croat Federation, with Edhem Bicakcic as prime minister.

1997 A Muslim, Haris Silajdzic, and a Serb, Boro Bosnic, appointed co-chairs of the all-Bosnian Council of Ministers. Serb-dominated part of Bosnia signed joint customs agreement with Yugoslavia. Croat Vladimir Soljic elected president of Muslim-Croat Federation, with Muslim Ejup Ganic as his deputy. Implementation of Dayton Peace Accord delayed. Municipal elections held after 12-month delay.

Practical information

Visa requirements UK: visa not required. USA: visa not required
Embassy in the UK 40–41 Conduit Street, London W1R 9FB. Tel: (0171) 734 3758; fax: (0171) 734 3760
British embassy 8 Mustafe Golubica, 71000 Sarajevo. Tel: (71) 444 429; fax: (71) 444 429
Embassy in the USA Suite 760, 1707 L Street NW, Washington, DC 20036. Tel: (202) 833 3612, 3613, 3615; fax: (202) 833 2061

American embassy 43 Ul. Djure Djakovica, Sarajevo. Tel: (71) 645 992, 445 700, 659 743
Chamber of commerce Chamber of Economy of Bosnia and Herzegovina, Mis. Irbina 13, 71000 Sarajevo. Tel: (71) 211777
Banking hours normal banking services have broken down
Time difference GMT +1
Major holidays 1–2 January, 1 March, 1–2 May, 27 July, 25 November

Botswana Republic of

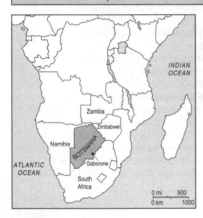

Area 582,000 sq km/224,710 sq mi
Capital Gaborone
Major towns/cities Mahalapye, Serowe, Tutume, Bobonong Francistown, Selebi-Phikwe, Lobatse, Molepolol, Kange
Physical features Kalahari Desert in SW (70–80% of national territory is desert), plains (Makgadikgadi salt pans) in E, fertile lands and Okavango Delta in N

Government

Head of state and government Quett Ketumile Joni Masire from 1980
Political system democratic republic
Administrative divisions ten districts and four town councils
Political parties Botswana Democratic Party (BDP), moderate centrist; Botswana National Front (BNF), moderate left of centre
Armed forces 7,500 (1995)
Conscription military service is voluntary
Death penalty retained and used for ordinary crimes
Defence spend (% GDP) 7.1 (1995)
Education spend (% GNP) 8.5 (1993–94)
Health spend (% GDP) 6.3 (1994)

Economy and resources

Currency franc CFA
GDP ($ US) 4 billion (1994)
Real GDP per capita (PPP) ($ US) 5,367 (1994)
GDP growth rate 4.1% (1994); 4.2% (1990–95)
Average annual inflation 10.6% (1994); 11.6% (1985–95)
Foreign debt ($ US) 699 million (1995)
Trading partners Lesotho, Namibia, South Africa, Swaziland – all fellow SACU (Southern African Customs Union) members; UK and other European countries, USA
Resources diamonds (world's third-largest producer), copper-nickel ore, coal, soda ash, gold, cobalt, salt, plutonium, asbestos, chromite, iron, silver, manganese, talc, uranium
Industries mining, food processing, textiles and clothing, beverages, soap, chemicals, paper, plastics, electrical goods
Exports diamonds, copper and nickel, beef. Principal market: Europe 86.7% (1994)
Imports machinery and transport equipment, food, beverages, tobacco, chemicals and rubber products, textiles and footwear, fuels, wood and paper products. Principal source: SACU 79.6% (1994)
Arable land 0.7% (1993)
Agricultural products sorghum, vegetables, pulses; cattle raising (principally for beef production) is main agricultural activity

Population and society

Population 1,484,000 (1996e)
Population growth rate 3.1% (1990–95); 2.7% (2000–05)
Population density (per sq km) 3 (1996e)

Urban population (% of total) 28% (1995)
Age distribution (% of total population) <15 43.2%, 15–65 54.3%, >65 2.4% (1995)
Ethnic distribution about 90% Tswana and 5% Kung and other hunter-gatherer groups; the remainder is European
Languages English (official), Setswana (national)
Religions Christian 50%, animist, Baha'i, Muslim, Hindu
Education not compulsory
Literacy rate 84% (men); 65% (women) (1995e)
Labour force 44% of population: 46% agriculture, 20% industry, 33% services (1990)
Unemployment approximately 20% (1995)
Life expectancy 65 (men); 69 (women) (1995–2000)
Child mortality rate (under 5, per 1,000 live births) 52 (1995)
Physicians 1 per 4,130 people (1994)
TV sets (per 1,000 people) 19 (1995)
Radios (per 1,000 people) 131 (1995)

Transport

Airports international airports: Gaborone (Sir Seretse Khama), Kasane; six domestic airports; total passenger km: 58 mil (1994)
Railroads total length: 888 km/552 mi (1995); total passenger journeys: 525,000 (1994)
Roads total road network: 11,800 km/7,333 mi, of which 14.2% paved (1995e); passenger cars: 14.1 per 1,000 people (1995e)

Chronology

18th century Formerly inhabited by nomadic hunter-gatherer groups, including the Kung, the area was settled by the Tswana people, from whose eight branches the majority of the people are descended.

1872 Khama III the Great, a converted Christian, became chief of the Bamangwato, the largest Tswana group. He developed a strong army and greater unity among the Botswana peoples.

1885 Became the British protectorate of Bechuanaland at the request of Chief Khama, who feared invasion by Boers from the Transvaal (South Africa) following the discovery of gold.

1895 The southern part of the Bechuanaland Protectorate was annexed by Cape Colony (South Africa).

1960 New constitution created a legislative council controlled (until 1963) by a British High Commissioner.

1965 Capital transferred from Mafeking to Gaborone. Internal self-government achieved, with Seretse Khama, the grandson of Khama III and leader of the centrist Democratic Party (BDP), elected head of government.

1966 Independence achieved from Britain. Name changed to Botswana;

Seretse Khama elected president under new presidentialist constitution.

mid-1970s The economy grew rapidly as diamond mining expanded.

1980 Seretse Khama died, and was succeeded by Vice President Quett Masire (BDP).

1985 South African raid on Gaborone, allegedly in search of African National Congress (ANC) guerrillas.

1993 Relations with South Africa fully normalized following ending of apartheid and establishment of a multiracial government.

Practical information

Visa requirements UK: visa not required. USA: visa not required

Embassy in the UK High Commission, 6 Stratford Place, London W1N 9AE. Tel: (0171) 499 0031; fax: (0171) 495 8595

British embassy British High Commission, Private Bag 0023, Gaborone. Tel: 352 841/2/3; fax: (0171) 356 105

Embassy in the USA Suite 7M, 3400 International Drive NW, Washington, DC 20008. Tel: (202) 244 4990/1; fax: (202) 244 4164

American embassy mailing address: PO Box 90, Gaborone. Tel: 353 982; fax: 356 947

Chamber of commerce Botswana National Chamber of

Commerce and Industry, PO Box 20344, Gaborone. Tel: 52677

Office hours 0800–1700 Mon–Fri, April–October; 0730–1630 Mon–Fri, October–April

Banking hours 0900–1430 Mon, Tue, Thu, and Fri; 0815–1200 Wed; 0815–1045 Sat

Time difference GMT +2

Chief tourist attractions Kalahari Desert; five game reserves and three national parks, including Chobe National Park, Moremi Wildlife Reserve, and Kalahari Gemsbok National Park

Major holidays 1–2 January, 30 September, 25–26 December; variable: Ascension Thursday, Good Friday, Easter Monday, Holy Saturday, President's Day (July), July Holiday, October Holiday

Brazil Federative Republic of

National name *República Federativa do Brasil*

Area 8,511,965 sq km/3,286,469 sq mi

Capital Brasília

Major towns/cities São Paulo, Belo Horizonte, Nova Iguaçu, Rio de Janeiro, Belém, Recife, Pôrto Alegre, Salvador, Curitiba, Manaus, Fortaleza

Major ports Rio de Janeiro, Belém, Recife, Pôrto Alegre, Salvador

Physical features the densely forested Amazon basin covers the northern half of the country with a network of rivers; the S is fertile; enormous energy resources, both hydroelectric (Itaipú Reservoir on the Paraná, and Tucuruí on the Tocantins) and nuclear (uranium ores); mostly tropical climate

Government

Head of state and government Fernando Henrique Cardoso from 1994

Political system democratic federal republic

Administrative divisions 26 states and one federal district

Political parties Workers' Party (PT), left of centre; Social Democratic Party (PSDB), moderate, left of centre; Brazilian Democratic Movement Party (PMDB), centre left; Liberal Front Party (PFL), right wing; National Reconstruction Party (PRN), centre right

Armed forces 295,000; public security forces under army control 385,600 (1995)

Conscription 12 months

Death penalty for exceptional crimes only; last execution 1855

Defence spend (% GDP) 1.5 (1995)

Education spend (% GNP) 1.6 (1993–94)

Health spend (% GDP) 2.8 (1990)

Economy and resources

Currency real

GDP ($ US) 554.6 billion (1994)

Real GDP per capita (PPP) ($ US) 5,362 (1994)

GDP growth rate 5.8% (1994); 2.7% (1990–95)

Average annual inflation 26.4% (1994); 873.8% (1985–95)

Foreign debt ($ US) 159.13 billion (1995)

Trading partners USA, Germany, Japan, Iran, the Netherlands, France, Argentina, UK

Resources iron ore (world's second-largest producer), tin (world's fourth-largest producer), aluminium (world's fourth-largest producer), gold, phosphates, platinum, bauxite, uranium, manganese, coal, copper, petroleum,

natural gas, hydroelectric power, forests
Industries mining, steel, machinery and
transport equipment, food processing,
textiles and clothing, chemicals,
petrochemicals, cement, lumber
Exports steel products, transport
equipment, coffee, iron ore and
concentrates, aluminium, iron, tin, soya
beans, orange juice (85% of world's
concentrates), tobacco, leather footwear,
sugar, beef, textiles. Principal market:
USA 18.9% (1995)
Imports mineral fuels, machinery and
mechanical appliances, chemical
products, foodstuffs, coal, wheat,
fertilizers, cast iron and steel. Principal
source: USA 23.9% (1995)
Arable land 4.9% (1993)
Agricultural products soya beans,
coffee (world's largest producer), tobacco,
sugar cane (world's third-largest
producer), cocoa beans (world's second-
largest producer), maize, rice, cassava,
oranges; livestock (beef and poultry)

Population and society

Population 161,087,000 (1996e)
Population growth rate 1.7% (1990–95);
1.4% (2000–05)
Population density (per sq km) 19
(1996e)
Urban population (% of total) 78 (1995)
Age distribution (% of total population)
<15 32.3%, 15–65 62.5%, >65 5.2%
(1995)
Ethnic distribution wide range of ethnic
groups, including 55% of European origin
(mainly Portuguese, Italian, and German),
38% of mixed parentage, 6% of African
origin, as well as Native Americans and
Japanese
Languages Portuguese (official); 120
Indian languages
Religions Roman Catholic 89%; Indian
faiths
Education (compulsory years) 8
Literacy rate 82% (men); 80% (women)
(1995e)
Labour force 44% of population: 23%
agriculture, 23% industry, 54% services
(1990)
Unemployment 4.9% (1993)
Life expectancy 65 (men); 70 (women)
(1995–2000)
Child mortality rate (under 5, per 1,000
live births) 60 (1995)
Physicians 1 per 847 people (1991)
TV sets (per 1,000 people) 220 (1995)
Radios (per 1,000 people) 399 (1995)

Transport

Airports principal international airports:
Rio de Janeiro (Brasília and Guarulhos),

São Paulo (Guarulhos, Viracopos, and
Congonhas), Manaus (Eduardo Gomes),
Salvador (Dois de Julho); 27 domestic
airports; total passenger km: 32,139 mil
(1994)
Railroads total length: 29,099 km/18,082
mi; total passenger km 14,038 mil (1993)
Roads total road network: 1,939,000 km/
1,204,895 mi, of which 9.2% paved
(1995e); passenger cars: 83.5 per 1,000
people (1993e)

Chronology

1500 Originally inhabited by South
American Indians. Portuguese explorer
Pedro Alvares Cabral sighted and claimed
Brazil for Portugal.
1530 Start of Portuguese colonization;
Portugal monopolized trade but colonial
government was decentralized.
1580–1640 Brazil, with Portugal, came
under Spanish rule.
17th century Huge sugar-cane
plantations established with slave labour
in coastal regions, making Brazil world's
largest supplier of sugar; cattle ranching
developed inland.
1695 Discovery of gold in central
highlands.
1763 Colonial capital moved from Bahia
to Rio de Janeiro.
1770 Brazil's first coffee plantations
established in Rio de Janeiro.
18th century Population 1798 totalled 3.3
million, of which around 1.9 million were
slaves, mainly of African origin; significant
growth of gold-mining industry.
19th century Rapid expansion in coffee
growing.
1808 Following Napoleon's invasion of
Portugal, the Portuguese regent, Prince
John, arrived in Brazil and established his
court at Rio de Janeiro; Brazilian trade
opened to foreign merchants.
1815 United Kingdom of Portugal, Brazil,
and Algarve made Brazil co-equal with
Portugal and Rio de Janeiro as capital.
1821 Political disorder in Portugal forced
King John VI to return to Europe, leaving
government of Brazil to his son, Crown
Prince Pedro.
1822 Pedro defied orders from
Portuguese parliament to return to
Portugal; he declared Brazil's
independence to avoid reversion to
colonial status.
1825 King John VI recognized his son as
Emperor Pedro I of Brazil.
1831 Pedro I abdicated in favour of his
infant son, Pedro II; regency (to 1840)
dominated by Brazilian politicians.
1847 First prime minister appointed, but
emperor retained wide-ranging powers.
1865–70 Brazilian efforts to control

Uruguay led to War of the Triple Alliance
with Paraguay.
1888 Abolition of slavery in Brazil.
1889 Monarch overthrown by liberal
revolt; federal republic established with
central government controlled by coffee
planters; by 1902 Brazil produced 65% of
world's coffee.
1915–19 Lack of European imports
during World War I led to rapid
industrialization, especially in state of
São Paulo.
1930 Revolution against planter oligarchy
placed Getúlio Vargas in power; he
introduced social reforms and economic
planning.
1937 Vargas established authoritarian
corporate state.
1942 Brazil entered World War II as ally
of USA; small fighting force sent to Italy
1944.
1945 Vargas ousted by military coup, but
Gen Eurico Gaspar Dutra soon forced to
abandon free-market policies.
1951 Vargas elected president;
continued to extend state control of
economy.
1954 Vargas committed suicide.
1956–61 Juscelino Kubitschek became
president, pursuing measures geared
towards rapid economic growth.
1960 Capital moved to Brasília.
1961 Janio Quadros elected president,
introducing controversial programme for
radical reform; resigned after seven
months; succeeded by Vice President
João Goulart.
1964 Bloodless coup established
technocratic military regime; free political
parties abolished; intense concentration
on industrial growth aided by foreign
investment and loans.
1970s Economic recession and inflation
undermined public support for military
regime.
1985 After gradual democratization from
1979, Tancredo Neves became first
civilian president in 21 years; on Neves's
death, Vice President José Sarney took
office.
1988 New constitution reduced powers
of president.
1989 Fernando Collor (PRN) elected
president, promising economic
deregulation; Brazil suspended foreign
debt payments.
1992 Collor charged with corruption and
replaced by Vice President Itamar
Franco.
1994 New currency introduced (third in
eight years). Fernando Henrique
Cardoso (PSDB) elected president.
Collor cleared of corruption charges.
1997 Constitution amended to allow
president to seek second term of office.

Practical information

Visa requirements UK: visa not required for tourist visits. USA: visa required
Embassy in the UK 32 Green Street, London W1Y 4AT. Tel: (0171) 499 0877; fax: (0171) 493 5105
British embassy Caixa Postal 07-0586, Setor de Embaixadas Sul, Quadra 801, Conjunto K, 70408-900 Brasília, Distrito Federal. Tel: (61) 225 2710; fax: (61) 225 1777
Embassy in the USA 3006 Massachusetts Avenue NW, Washington, DC 20008. Tel: (202) 745 2700; fax: (202) 745 2827
American embassy Avenida das Nacoes, Lote 3, Brasília, Distrito Federal. Tel: (61) 321 7272; fax: (61) 225 9136

Chamber of commerce Confederaçao Nacional do Comércio, SCS, Edif. Presidente Dutra, 4° andar, Quadra 11, 70327 Brasília, Distrito Federal. Tel: (61) 223 0578
Office hours 0900–1800 Mon–Fri
Banking hours 1000–1630 Mon–Fri
Time difference GMT –2/5
Chief tourist attractions Rio de Janeiro and beaches; Iguaçu Falls; tropical forests of Amazon basin; wildlife of the Pantanal; Mato Grosso
Major holidays 1 January, 21 April, 1 May, 7 September, 12 October, 2, 15 November, 25 December; variable: Carnival (2 days), Corpus Christi, Good Friday, Holy Saturday, Holy Thursday

Brunei State of

National name *Negara Brunei Darussalam*
Area 5,765 sq km/2,225 sq mi
Capital Bandar Seri Begawan
Major towns/cities Seria, Kuala Belait, Bangar
Physical features flat coastal plain with hilly lowland in W and mountains in E (Mount Pagon 1,850 m/6,070 ft); 75% of the area is forested; the Limbang valley splits Brunei in two, and its cession to Sarawak 1890 is disputed by Brunei; tropical climate; Temburong, Tutong, and Belait rivers

Government

Head of state and government HM Muda Hassanal Bolkiah Mu'izzaddin Waddaulah, Sultan of Brunei, from 1967
Political system absolute monarchy
Administrative divisions four districts
Political parties Brunei National Democratic Party (BNDP) and Brunei National United Party (BNUP) (both

banned since 1988); Brunei People's Party (BPP) (banned since 1962)
Armed forces 4,900 (1995); plus paramilitary Gurkha reserve of 2,300
Conscription military service is voluntary
Death penalty retains the death penalty for ordinary crimes but can be considered abolitionist in practice (last execution 1957)
Defence spend (% GDP) 6 (1995)
Education spend (% GNP) 3.6 (1993–94)

Economy and resources

Currency Brunei dollar (ringgit)
GDP ($ US) 6.47 billion (1994)
Real GDP per capita (PPP) ($ US) 30,447 (1994)
GDP growth rate 2% (1995e)
Average annual inflation 0.3% (1985–95)
Trading partners Singapore, Japan, USA, EU countries, Malaysia, South Korea, Thailand
Resources petroleum, natural gas
Industries petroleum refining, textiles, cement, mineral water, canned foods, rubber
Exports crude petroleum and natural gas (accounting for 91.7% of total export earnings 1993). Principal market: Japan 50% (1994)
Imports machinery and transport equipment, basic manufactures, food and live animals, chemicals. Principal source: Singapore 29% (1994)
Arable land 0.5% (1993)
Agricultural products rice, cassava, bananas, pineapples, vegetables; fishing; forest resources

Population and society

Population 300,000 (1996e)
Population growth rate 2.1% (1990–95)
Population density (per sq km) 52 (1996e)
Urban population (% of total) 58 (1995)
Age distribution (% of total population) <15 34%, 15–65 63%, >65 3% (1994)
Ethnic distribution 68% indigenous Malays, predominating in government service and agriculture; more than 20% Chinese, predominating in the commercial sphere
Languages Malay (official), Chinese (Hokkien), English
Religions Muslim 66%, Buddhist 14%, Christian 10%
Education (compulsory years) 12
Literacy rate 93% (men); 83% (women) (1995e)
Labour force 41% of population: 2% agriculture, 24% industry, 74% services (1990)
Unemployment 4.8% (1992)
Life expectancy 73 (men); 77 (women) (1995–2000)
Child mortality rate (under 5, per 1,000 live births) 10 (1995)
Physicians 1 per 1,522 people (1994e)
Hospital beds 1 per 310 people (1994)
TV sets (per 1,000 people) 239 (1995)
Radios (per 1,000 people) 273 (1995)

Transport

Airports international airports: Bandar Seri Begawan (Brunei International); total passenger km: 2,029 mil (1994)
Railroads none
Roads total road network: 1,120 km/ 696 mi, of which 34.6% paved (1995e); passenger cars: 560.3 per 1,000 people (1995e)

Chronology

15th century Islamic monarchy established, ruling Brunei and north Borneo, including Sabah and Sarawak states of Malaysia.
1841 Lost control of Sarawak.
1888 Brunei became a British protoctorate.
1906 Became a dependency when British resident was appointed adviser to the sultan.
1929 Oil was discovered.
1941–45 Occupied by Japan.

1950 Sir Omar became the 28th sultan.
1959 Written constitution made Britain responsible for defence and external affairs.
1962 Sultan began rule by decree after plan to join Federation of Malaysia was opposed by a week-long rebellion organized by the Brunei People's Party (BPP).
1967 Sultan Omar abdicated in favour of his son Hassanal Bolkiah, but remained chief adviser.
1971 Brunei given full internal self-government.

1975 United Nations resolution called for independence for Brunei.
1984 Independence achieved from Britain, with Britain maintaining a small force to protect the oil and gas fields.
1985 A 'loyal and reliable' political party, the Brunei National Democratic Party (BNDP), legalized.
1986 Death of former sultan Omar. Formation of multiethnic Brunei National United Party (BNUP); nonroyals given key cabinet posts for the first time.
1988 BNDP and BNUP banned.
1991 Joined nonaligned movement.

Practical information

Visa requirements UK: visa not required for visits of up to 30 days. USA: visa not required
Embassy in the UK 19/20 Belgrave Square, London SW1X 8PG. Tel: (0171) 581 0521; fax: (0171) 235 9717
British embassy British High Commission, PO Box 2197, 3rd Floor, Hong Kong Bank Chambers, Jalan Pemancha, Bandar Seri Begawan 2085. Tel: (2) 222 231; fax: (2) 226 002
Embassy in the USA Watergate, Suite 300, 3rd floor, 2600 Virginia Avenue NW, Washington, DC 20037. Tel: (202) 342 0159; fax: (202) 342 0158
American embassy Third Floor, Teck Guan Plaza, Jalan Sultan, Bandar Seri Begawan. Tel: (2) 229 670; fax: (2) 225 293

Chamber of commerce Brunei Darussalem International Chamber of Commerce and Industry, POB 2246, Bandar Seri Begawan 1922. Tel: (2) 236 601; fax: (2) 228 389
Office hours 0800–1200 and 1300–1700 Mon–Thu; 0900–1200 Sat
Banking hours 0900–1200 and 1400–1500 Mon–Fri; 0900–110 Sat
Time difference GMT +8
Chief tourist attractions tropical rainforest
Major holidays 1 January, 23 February, 31 May, 15 July, 25 December; variable: Eid-ul-Adha, end of Ramadan, Good Friday, New Year (Chinese), New Year (Muslim), Prophet's Birthday, first day of Ramadan, Meraj (March/April), Revelation of the Koran (May)

Bulgaria Republic of

National name *Republika Bulgaria*
Area 110,912 sq km/42,823 sq mi
Capital Sofia
Major towns/cities Plovdiv, Varna, Ruse, Burgas, Stara Zagora
Major ports Black Sea ports Burgas and Varna
Physical features lowland plains in N and SE separated by mountains (Balkan

and Rhodope) that cover three-quarters of the country; River Danube in N

Government

Head of state Petar Stoyanov from 1997
Head of government Ivan Kostov from 1997
Political system emergent democratic republic
Administrative divisions nine regions
Political parties Union of Democratic Forces (UDF), right of centre; Bulgarian Socialist Party (BSP), left wing, ex-communist; Movement for Rights and Freedoms (MRF), Turkish-oriented, centrist; Civic Alliances for the Republic (CAR), left of centre; Real Reform Movement (DESIR)
Armed forces 102,000 (1995)
Conscription compulsory for 12 months
Death penalty retained and used for ordinary crimes
Defence spend (% GDP) 3.3 (1995)
Education spend (% GNP) 4.5 (1993–94)
Health spend (% GDP) 1.5 (1990)

Economy and resources

Currency lev
GDP ($ US) 10 billion (1994)
Real GDP per capita (PPP) ($ US) 4,533 (1994)
GDP growth rate 2.6% (1995); –4.3 (1990–95)
Average annual inflation 45.3% (1985–95)
Foreign debt ($ US) 10.9 billion (1995)
Trading partners EU countries (principally Germany, Greece, Italy), former USSR (principally Russia), Macedonia, USA
Resources coal, iron ore, manganese, lead, zinc, petroleum
Industries food products, petroleum and coal products, metals, mining, paper, beverages and tobacco, electrical machinery, textiles
Exports base metals, chemical and rubber products, processed food, beverages, tobacco, textiles, footwear. Principal market: EU 38.9% (1995)
Imports mineral products and fuels, chemical and rubber products, textiles, footwear, machinery and transport

equipment, medicines. Principal source: EU 45.2% (1995)
Arable land 55% (1993)
Agricultural products wheat, maize, barley, sunflower seeds, grapes, potatoes, tobacco, roses; viticulture (world's fourth-largest exporter of wine 1989); forest resources

Population and society

Population 8,468,000 (1996e)
Population growth rate 2.8% (1990–95); 2.5% (2000–05)
Population density (per sq km) 76 (1996e)
Urban population (% of total) 71 (1995)
Age distribution (% of total population) <15 18.3%, 15–65 67.1%, >65 14.5% (1995)
Ethnic distribution Southern Slavic Bulgarians constitute around 90% of the population; 9% are ethnic Turks, who during the later 1980s were subjected to government pressure to adopt Slavic names and to resettle elsewhere
Languages Bulgarian, Turkish
Religions Eastern Orthodox Christian, Muslim, Roman Catholic, Protestant
Education (compulsory years) 8
Literacy rate 93% (men); 93% (women) (1995e)
Labour force 22.1% agriculture, 36.6% industry, 41.3% services (1993)
Unemployment 13.8% (1994)
Life expectancy 68 (men); 75 (women) (1995–2000)
Child mortality rate (under 5, per 1,000 live births) 19 (1995)
Physicians 1 per 298 people (1995)
Hospital beds 1 per 102 people (1995)
TV sets (per 1,000 people) 378 (1995)
Radios (per 1,000 people) 471 (1995)

Transport

Airports international airports: Sofia, Varna, Burgas; seven domestic airports; total passenger km: 2,241 mil (1994)
Railroads total length: 4,292 km/2,667 mi; total passenger km: 5,059 mil (1994)
Roads total road network: 36,777 km/22,853 mi, of which 91.9% paved (1995); passenger cars: 196.5 per 1,000 people (1995)

Chronology

c. 3500 BC onwards Settlement of semi-nomadic pastoralists from central Asian steppes, who formed the Thracian community.
mid-5th century BC Thracian state formed, which was to extend over

Bulgaria, N Greece, and N Turkey.
4th century BC Phillip II and Alexander the Great of Macedonia, to the SW, waged largely unsuccessful campaigns against the Thracian Empire.
AD 50 Thracians subdued and incorporated within Roman Empire as the province of Moesia Inferior.
3rd–6th centuries Successively invaded from the N and devastated by the Goths, Huns, Bulgars, and Avars.
681 The Bulgars, an originally Turkic group that had merged with earlier Slav settlers, revolted against the Avars and established, S of the River Danube, the first Bulgarian kingdom, with its capital at Pliska, in the Balkans.
864 Orthodox Christianity adopted by Boris I.
1018 Subjugated by the Byzantines, whose empire had its capital at Constantinople; led to Bulgarian Church breaking with Rome in 1054.
1185 Second independent Bulgarian Kingdom formed.
mid-13th century Bulgarian state destroyed by Mongol incursions.
1396 Bulgaria became the first European state to be absorbed into the Turkish Ottoman Empire; the imposition of a harsh feudal system and the sacking of monasteries followed.
1859 Bulgarian Catholic Church re-established links with Rome.
1876 Bulgarian nationalist revolt against Ottoman rule crushed brutally by Ottomans, with 15,000 massacred at Plovdiv ('Bulgarian Atrocities').
1878 At the Congress of Berlin, concluding a Russo-Turkish war in which Bulgarian volunteers had fought alongside the Russians, the area S of the Balkans, Eastern Rumelia, remained an Ottoman province, but the area to the N became the autonomous Principality of Bulgaria, with a liberal constitution and Alexander Battenberg as prince.
1885 Eastern Rumelia annexed by the Principality; Serbia defeated in war.
1908 Full independence proclaimed from Turkish rule, with Ferdinand I as tsar.
1913 Following defeat in the Second Balkan War, King Ferdinand I abdicated and was replaced by his son Boris III.
1919 Bulgarian Agrarian Union government, led by Alexander Stamboliiski, came to power and redistributed land to poor peasants.
1923 Agrarian government overthrown in right-wing coup and Stamboliiski murdered.
1934 Semifascist dictatorship established

by King Boris III, who sided with Germany during World War II, but died mysteriously in 1943 after a visit to Adolf Hitler.
1944 Soviet invasion of German-occupied Bulgaria.
1946 Monarchy abolished and communist-dominated people's republic proclaimed following plebiscite.
1947 Gained South Dobruja in the NE, along the Black Sea, from Romania; Soviet-style constitution established a one-party state; industries and financial institutions nationalized and cooperative farming introduced.
1949 Death of Georgi Dimitrov, the communist government leader; replaced by Vulko Chervenkov.
1954 Election of Todor Zhivkov as Bulgarian Communist Party (BCP) general secretary; Bulgaria became a loyal and cautious satellite of the USSR.
1968 Participated in the Soviet-led invasion of Czechoslovakia.
1971 Zhivkov became president, under new constitution.
1985–89 Haphazard administrative and economic reforms, known as *preustroistvo* ('restructuring'), introduced under stimulus of reformist Soviet leader Mikhail Gorbachev.
1989 Programme of enforced 'Bulgarianization' resulted in mass exodus of ethnic Turks to Turkey. Zhivkov ousted by foreign minister Petar Mladenov. Opposition parties tolerated.
1990 BCP reformed under new name Bulgarian Socialist Party (BSP). Zhelyu Zhelev of the centre-right Union of Democratic Forces (UDF) indirectly elected president. Following mass demonstrations and general strike, BSP government replaced by coalition.
1991 New liberal-democratic constitution adopted. UDF beat BSP in general election by narrow margin; formation of first noncommunist, UDF-minority government.
1992 Zhelev became Bulgaria's first directly elected president. Following industrial unrest, Lyuben Berov became head of a nonparty government. Zhivkov sentenced to seven years' imprisonment for corruption while in government.
1993 Voucher-based 'mass privatization' programme launched.
1994 Berov resigned; general election won by BSP.
1995 Zhan Videnov (BSP) became prime minister.

1996 Radical economic and industrial reforms imposed. Petar Stoyanov replaced Zhelev as president. Mounting inflation and public protest at the state of the economy.

1997 General strike. Interim government led by Stefan Sofiyanski. UDF leader Ivan Kostov became prime minister. Former communist leader Todor Zhivkov released from house arrest. Bulgarian currency pegged to German mark in return for support from International Monetary Fund. New political group, the Real Reform Movement (DESIR), formed.

Practical information

Visa requirements UK: visa required. USA: visa not required for tourist visits of up to 30 days
Embassy in the UK 186–188 Queen's Gate, London SW7 5HL. Tel: (0171) 584 9400; fax: (0171) 584 4948
British embassy Boulevard Vassil Levski 65–67, Sofia 1000. Tel: (2) 885 361/2; fax: (2) 656 022
Embassy in the USA 1621 22nd Street NW, Washington, DC 20008. Tel: (202) 387 7969; fax: (202) 234 7973
American embassy 1 Saborna Street, Sofia. Tel: (2) 884 801//2/3/4/5; fax: (2) 801 977

Chamber of commerce Bulgarian Chamber of Commerce and Industry, 1040 Sofia, Suborna ST 11A. Tel: (2) 872 631; fax: (2) 873 209
Office hours 0800–1800 Mon–Fri
Banking hours 0800–1130 and 1400–1800 Mon–Fri; 0830–1130 Sat
Time difference GMT +2
Chief tourist attractions Black Sea coastal resorts; mountain scenery; historic towns; skiing resorts
Major holidays 1 January, 3 March, 1, 24 May, 24–25 December; variable: Easter Monday

---

Burkina Faso The People's Democratic Republic of (formerly *Upper Volta*)

National name *République Démocratique Populaire de Burkina Faso*
Area 274,122 sq km/105,838 sq mi
Capital Ouagadougou
Major towns/cities Bobo-Dioulasso, Koudougou
Physical features landlocked plateau with hills in W and SE; headwaters of the River Volta; semiarid in N, forest and farmland in S; linked by rail to Abidjan in Côte d'Ivoire, Burkina Faso's only outlet to the sea

Government

Head of state Blaise Compaoré from 1987
Head of government Kadre Desire Ouedraogo from 1996
Political system emergent democracy
Administrative divisions 30 provinces
Political parties Popular Front (FP), centre-left coalition grouping; National Convention of Progressive Patriots–Democratic Socialist Party (CNPP–PSD), left of centre
Armed forces 5,800 (1995); includes gendarmerie of 4,200
Conscription military service is voluntary
Death penalty retained and used for ordinary crimes
Defence spend (% GDP) 2.4 (1995)
Education spend (% GNP) 3.6 (1993–94)
Health spend (% GDP) 7 (1990)

Economy and resources

Currency franc CFA
GDP ($ US) 1.9 billion (1994)
Real GDP per capita (PPP) ($ US) 796 (1994)
GDP growth rate 1% (1994); 2.6% (1990–95)
Average annual inflation 24.6% (1994); 2.5% (1985–95)
Foreign debt ($ US) 1.26 billion (1995)
Trading partners France, Côte d'Ivoire, Thailand, Italy, Taiwan, Niger, Nigeria
Resources manganese, zinc, limestone, phosphates, diamonds, gold, antimony, marble, silver, lead
Industries food processing, textiles, cotton ginning, brewing, processing of hides and skins
Exports cotton, gold, livestock and livestock products. Principal market: France 13.2% (1994)
Imports machinery and transport equipment, miscellaneous manufactured articles, food products (notably cereals), refined petroleum products, chemicals.

Principal source: Côte d'Ivoire 25.6% (1994)
Arable land 13% (1993)
Agricultural products cotton, sesame seeds, shea nuts (karité nuts), millet, sorghum, maize, sugar cane, rice, groundnuts; livestock rearing (cattle, sheep, and goats)

Population and society

Population 10,780,000 (1996e)
Population growth rate –0.5% (1990–95); –0.4% (2000–05)
Population density (per sq km) 39 (1996e)
Urban population (% of total) 27% (1995)
Age distribution (% of total population) <15 44.9%, 15–65 52%, >65 3.1% (1995)
Ethnic distribution over 50 ethnic groups, including the nomadic Mossi (48%), Fulani (10%), and Gourma (5%). Settled tribes include: in the N the Lobi-Dagari (7%) and the Mande (7%); in the SE the Bobo (7%); and in the SW the Senoufu (6%) and Gourounsi (5%)
Languages French (official); about 50 Sudanic languages spoken by 90% of population
Religions animist 53%, Sunni Muslim 36%, Roman Catholic 11%
Education (compulsory years) 6
Literacy rate 28% (men); 9% (women) (1995e)
Labour force 54% of population: 92% agriculture, 2% industry, 6% services (1990)

Unemployment 8.1% (1994e)
Life expectancy 45 (men); 48 (women)
(1995–2000)
Child mortality rate (under 5, per 1,000
live births) 164 (1995)
Physicians 1 per 28,620 people (1991)
TV sets (per 1,000 people) 5.7 (1995)
Radios (per 1,000 people) 28 (1995)

Transport

Airports international airports:
Ouagadougou, Bobo-Dioulasso; total
passenger km: 239 mil (1994)
Railroads total length: 622 km/389 mi;
total passengers carried: 600,000 (1993)
Roads total road network: 12,506 km/
7,771 mi, of which 16% paved (1995);
passenger cars: 3.5 per 1,000 people
(1995e)

Chronology

13th–14th centuries Formerly settled by
Bobo, Lobi, and Gurunsi peoples, E and
centre were conquered by Mossi and
Gurma peoples, who established
powerful warrior kingdoms, some of
which survived until late 19th century.
1895–1903 France secured protectorates
over the Mossi kingdom of Yatenga and
the Gurma region, and annexed the
Bobo and Lobi lands, meeting armed
resistance.
1904 The French-controlled region,
known as Upper Volta, was attached
administratively to French Sudan; tribal
chiefs were maintained in their traditional
seats and the region was to serve as a
labour reservoir for more developed
colonies to S.
1919 Made a separate French colony.
1932 Partitioned between French Sudan,
Ivory Coast, and Niger.
1947 Became a French overseas territory.
1960 Independence achieved, with
Maurice Yaméogo as the first president.
1966 Military coup led by Lt-Col
Sangoulé Lamizana, and a supreme
council of the armed forces established.
1977 Ban on political activities removed.
Referendum approved a new constitution
based on civilian rule.
1978 Lamizana elected president.
1980 Lamizana overthrown in bloodless
coup led by Col Saye Zerbo as economy
deteriorated.
1982 Zerbo ousted in a coup by junior
officers: Maj Jean-Baptiste Ouedraogo
became president and Capt Thomas
Sankara prime minister.
1983 Sankara seized complete power.
1984 Upper Volta renamed Burkina Faso
('land of upright men') to signify break
with colonial past; literacy and
afforestation campaigns by radical
Sankara, who established links with
Libya, Benin, and Ghana.
1987 Sankara killed in coup led by Capt
Blaise Compaoré.
1991 New constitution approved.
Compaoré re-elected president.
1992 Multiparty elections won by pro-
Compaoré Popular Front (FP), despite
opposition claims of ballot-rigging.
1996 Kadre Desire Ouedraogo appointed
prime minister.
1997 CDP assembly election victory.
Ouedraogo reappointed prime minister.

Practical information

Visa requirements UK: visa required. USA: visa required
Embassy in the UK Honorary Consulate, 5 Cinnamon Row,
Plantation Wharf, London SW11 3TW. Tel: (0171) 738 1800;
fax: (0171) 738 2820
British embassy British Consulate, BP 1918 Ouagadougou.
(All staff based in Abidjan, Côte d'Ivoire.) Tel: (226) 336 363
Embassy in the USA 2340 Massachusetts Avenue NW,
Washington, DC 20008. Tel: (202) 332 5577, 6895
American embassy Avenue Raoul Follerau, Ouagadougou.
Tel: 306723/4/5; fax: 303890
Chamber of commerce Chambre de Commerce, d'Industrie
et d'Artisanat du Burkina, ave Nelson Mandela, 01 BP 502,
Ouagadougou 01. Tel: (226) 306 114; fax: (226) 306 116
Office hours 0700–1230 and 1500–1730 Mon–Fri
Banking hours 0730–1130 and 1500–1600 Mon–Thu;
0730–1130 and 1530–1700 Fri
Time difference GMT+/–0
Chief tourist attractions big-game hunting in east and
southwest, and along banks of Mouhoun (Black Volta) River;
wide variety of wildlife; biennial Ouagadougou film festival
Major holidays 1, 3 January, 1 May, 4, 15 August,
1 November, 25 December; variable: Ascension Thursday,
Eid-ul-Adha, Easter Monday, end of Ramadan, Prophet's
Birthday, Whit Monday

Burundi Republic of

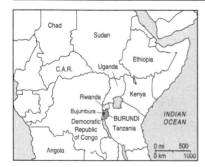

National name *Republika y'Uburundi*
Area 27,834 sq km/10,746 sq mi
Capital Bujumbura

Major towns/cities Kitega, Bururi,
Ngozi, Muhinga, Muramuya
Physical features landlocked grassy
highland straddling watershed of Nile and
Congo; Lake Tanganyika, Great Rift Valley

Government

Head of state Pierre Buyoya from 1996
Head of government Pascal-Firmin
Ndimira from 1996
Political system authoritarian nationalist
Administrative divisions 15 provinces
Political parties Front for Democracy in
Burundi (FRODEBU), left of centre;
Union for National Progress (UPRONA),
nationalist socialist

Armed forces 12,600 (1996); plus a
paramilitary force of 2,000 gendarmes
Conscription military service is
voluntary
Death penalty retains the death penalty
for ordinary crimes but can be
considered abolitionist in practice (last
execution 1982)
Defence spend (% GDP) 5.3 (1995)
Education spend (% GNP) 3.8
(1993–94)
Health spend (% GDP) 1.7 (1990)

Economy and resources

Currency Burundi franc
GDP ($ US) 1 billion (1994)

Real GDP per capita (PPP) ($ US) 698 (1994)
GDP growth rate −18% (1994); −3.1% (1990–95)
Average annual inflation 14.9% (1994); 6.1% (1985–95)
Foreign debt ($ US) 1.1 billion (1995)
Trading partners Belgium, Germany, France, Tanzania, Japan, USA
Resources nickel, gold, tungsten, phosphates, vanadium, uranium, peat, petroleum deposits have been detected
Industries textiles, leather, food and agricultural products
Exports coffee, tea, glass products, hides and skins. Principal market: UK 28.3% (1995)
Imports machinery and transport equipment, petroleum and petroleum products, cement, malt (and malt flour). Principal source: Belgium and Luxembourg 15.4% (1995)
Arable land 40.8%
Agricultural products coffee, tea, cassava, sweet potatoes, bananas, beans; cattle rearing

Population and society

Population 6,221,000 (1996e)
Population growth rate 3% (1990–95); 2.6% (2000–05)
Population density (per sq km) 224 (1996e)
Urban population (% of total) 8% (1995)
Age distribution (% of total population) <15 46.3%, 15–65 50.8%, >65 3% (1995)
Ethnic distribution two main groups: the agriculturalist Hutu, comprising about 85% of the population, and the predominantly pastoralist Tutsi, about 14%. There is a small Pygmy minority, comprising about 1% of the population, and a few Europeans and Asians
Languages Kirundi (a Bantu language) and French (both official), Kiswahili
Religions Roman Catholic 62%, Pentecostalist 5%, Anglican 1%, Muslim 1%, animist
Education (compulsory years) 6
Literacy rate 61% (men); 40% (women) (1995e)
Labour force 54% of population: 92%

agriculture, 3% industry, 6% services (1990)
Unemployment 7.3% (1992)
Life expectancy 50 (men); 53 (women) (1995–2000)
Child mortality rate (under 5, per 1,000 live births) 176 (1995)
Physicians 1 per 16,667 people (1991)
Hospital beds 1 per 1,699 people (1990e)
TV sets (per 1,000 people) 2 (1995)
Radios (per 1,000 people) 68 (1995)

Transport

Airports international airports: Bujumbura; total passenger km: 2 mil (1994)
Railroads none
Roads total road network: 5,162 km/3,207 mi, of which 20% paved (1993); passenger cars: 2.2 per 1,000 people (1994)

Chronology

10th century Originally inhabited by the hunter-gatherer Twa Pygmies. Hutu peoples settled in the region and became peasant farmers.
13th century Taken over by Bantu Hutus.
15th–17th centuries The majority Hutu community came under the dominance of the cattle-owning Tutsi peoples, immigrants from the E, who became a semi-aristocracy; the minority Tutsis developed a feudalistic political system, organized around a nominal king, with royal princes in control of local areas.
1890 Known as Urundi, the Tutsi kingdom, along with neighbouring Rwanda, came under nominal German control as Ruanda-Urundi.
1916 Occupied by Belgium during World War I.
1923 Belgium was granted a League of Nations mandate to administer Ruanda-Urundi; it was to rule 'indirectly' through the Tutsi chiefs.
1962 Separated from Ruanda-Urundi, as Burundi, and given independence as a monarchy under Tutsi King Mwambutsa IV.
1965 King refused to appoint a Hutu

prime minister after an election in which Hutu candidates were victorious; attempted coup by Hutus brutally suppressed.
1966 King deposed by his teenage son Charles, who became Ntare V; he was in turn deposed by his Tutsi prime minister Col Michel Micombero, who declared Burundi a republic; the Tutsi-dominated Union for National Progress (UPRONA) declared only legal political party.
1972 Ntare V killed, allegedly by Hutus, provoking a massacre of 150,000 Hutu by Tutsi soldiers; 100,000 Hutu fled to Tanzania.
1976 Army coup deposed Micombero and appointed the Tutsi Col Jean-Baptiste Bagaza as president, who launched a drive against corruption and a programme of land reforms and economic development.
1987 Bagaza deposed in coup by the Tutsi Maj Pierre Buyoya.
1988 About 24,000 Hutus killed by Tutsis and 60,000 fled as refugees to Rwanda.
1992 New multiparty constitution adopted following referendum.
1993 Melchior Ndadaye, a Hutu, elected president in first-ever democratic contest but later killed in coup by Tutsi-dominated army; massacres followed, claiming 100,000 lives.
1994 Cyprien Ntaryamira, a Hutu, became president but later killed in air crash along with Rwandan president Juvenal Habyarimana. Ethnic violence; 750,000 Hutus fled to Rwanda. Hutu Sylvestre Ntibantunganya became head of state, serving with a Tutsi prime minister, as part of a four-year power-sharing agreement between main political parties.
1995 Renewed ethnic violence in the capital, Bujumbura, following massacre of Hutu refugees.
1996 Former Tutsi president Pierre Buyoya seized power amid renewed ethnic violence; coup provoked economic sanctions by other African countries. 'Government of national unity' appointed, with Pascal-Firmin Ndimira as premier. Bujumbura shelled by Hutu rebels.

Practical information

Visa requirements UK: visa required. USA: visa required
Embassy for the UK Square Marie Louise 46, 1040 Brussels, Belgium. Tel: (2) 230 4535; fax: (2) 230 7883
British embassy British Consulate, 43 Avenue Bubanza, BP 1344, Bujumbura. (All staff based in Kampala, Uganda.) Tel: (2) 23711
Embassy in the USA Suite 212, 2233 Wisconsin Avenue NW, Washington, DC 20007. Tel: (202) 342 2574

American embassy Avenue des Etats-Unis, Bujumbura. Tel: (2) 23454; fax: (2) 22926
Chamber of commerce Chambre de Commerce et de l'Industrie du Burundi, BP 313, Bujumbura. Tel: (2) 22280
Office hours 0730–1200 and 1400–1730 Mon–Fri
Banking hours 0800–1130 Mon–Fri
Time difference GMT +2
Chief tourist attractions tourism is relatively undeveloped
Major holidays 1 January, 1 May, 1 July, 15 August, 18 September, 1 November, 25 December; variable: Ascension Thursday

Cambodia State of (formerly *Khmer Republic* 1970–76, *Democratic Kampuchea* 1976–79, *People's Republic of Kampuchea* 1979–89)

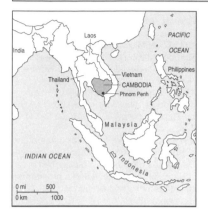

National name *Roat Kampuchea*
Area 181,035 sq km/69,897 sq mi
Capital Phnom Penh
Major towns/cities Battambang, Kompong Cham
Major ports Kompong Cham
Physical features mostly flat, forested plains with mountains in SW and N; Mekong River runs N–S; Lake Tonle Sap

Government

Head of state Prince Norodom Sihanouk from 1991
Head of government joint prime ministers Ung Huot and Hun Sen from 1997
Political system limited constitutional monarchy
Administrative divisions 22 provinces
Political parties United Front for an Independent, Neutral, Peaceful, and Cooperative Cambodia (FUNCINPEC), nationalist, monarchist; Liberal Democratic Party (BLDP), republican, anticommunist (formerly the Khmer People's National Liberation Front (KPNLF)); Cambodian People's Party (CPP), reform socialist (formerly the communist Kampuchean People's Revolutionary Party (KPRP)); Cambodian National Unity Party (CNUP) (political wing of the Khmer Rouge), ultranationalist communist
Armed forces 88,500 (1995)
Conscription military service is compulsory for five years between ages 18 and 35
Death penalty abolished 1989
Defence spend (% GDP) 4.7 (1995)

Economy and resources

Currency Cambodian riel
GDP ($ US) 2.77 billion (1995)
Real GDP per capita (PPP) ($ US) 660 (1995e)
GDP growth rate 7.6% (1995); 6.4% (1990–95)
Average annual inflation 9.1% (1995); 70.3% (1985–95)
Foreign debt ($ US) 2.03 billion (1995)
Trading partners Singapore, Thailand, Vietnam, Japan, Hong Kong, Indonesia, Taiwan
Resources phosphates, iron ore, gemstones, bauxite, silicon, manganese
Industries rubber processing, seafood processing, rice milling, textiles and garments, pharmaceutical products, cigarettes
Exports timber, rubber, fishery products. Principal market: Thailand 41.7% (1995)
Imports cigarettes, construction materials, petroleum products, motor vehicles, alcoholic beverages, consumer electronics. Principal source: Singapore 35.2% (1995)
Arable land 13% (1993)
Agricultural products rice, maize, sugar cane, cassava, bananas; timber and rubber (the two principal export commodities); fishing

Population and society

Population 10,273,000 (1996e)
Population growth rate 3% (1990–95); 2.3% (2000–05)
Population density (per sq km) 57 (1996e)
Urban population (% of total) 21%
Age distribution (% of total population) <15 44.9%, 15–65 52.4%, >65 2.6% (1995)
Ethnic distribution 91% Khmer, 4% Vietnamese, 3% Chinese
Languages Khmer (official), French
Religions Theravāda Buddhist 95%, Muslim, Roman Catholic
Education (compulsory years) 6
Literacy rate 48% (men); 65% (women) (1995e)
Labour force 50% of population: 74% agriculture, 8% industry, 19% services (1990)
Life expectancy 53 (men); 55 (women) (1995–2000)
Child mortality rate (under 5, per 1,000 live births) 174 (1995)

Physicians 1 per 20,230 people (1990e)
Hospital beds 1 per 612 people (1988)
TV sets (per 1,000 people) 8.5 (1995)
Radios (per 1,000 people) 112 (1995)

Transport

Airports international airports: Phnom Penh (Pochentong); five domestic airports
Railroads total length: 1,370 km/851 mi (1994)
Roads total road network: 35,769 km/ 22,227 mi, of which 7.5% paved (1995); passenger cars: 0.1 per 1,000 people (1995)

Chronology

1st century AD Part of the kingdom of Hindu-Buddhist Funan (Fou Nan), centred on Mekong delta region.
6th century Conquered by the Chenla kingdom.
9th century Establishment by Jayavarman II of extensive and sophisticated Khmer Empire, supported by an advanced irrigation system and architectural achievements, with a capital at Angkor in the NW.
14th century Theravāda Buddhism replaced Hinduism.
15th century Came under the control of Siam (Thailand), which made Phnom Penh the capital and, later, Champa (Vietnam).
1863 Became a French protectorate, but traditional political structures left largely intact.
1887 Became part of French Indo-China Union, which included Laos and Vietnam.
1941 Prince Norodom Sihanouk was elected king.
1941–45 Occupied by Japan during World War II.
1946 Recaptured by France; parliamentary constitution adopted.
1949 Guerrilla war for independence secured semi-autonomy within the French Union.
1953 Independence achieved from France as the Kingdom of Cambodia.
1955 Norodom Sihanouk abdicated as king and became prime minister, representing the Popular Socialist Community mass movement.
1960 On the death of his father, Norodom Sihanouk became head of state.

later 1960s Mounting guerrilla insurgency, led by the communist Khmer Rouge, and civil war in neighbouring Vietnam.
1970 Prince Sihanouk overthrown by US-backed Lt-Gen Lon Nol in a right-wing coup; name of Khmer Republic adopted; Sihanouk, exiled in China, formed own guerrilla movement.
1975 Lon Nol overthrown by Khmer Rouge, which was backed by North Vietnam and China; name Kampuchea adopted, with Sihanouk as head of state.
1976–78 Khmer Rouge, led by Pol Pot, introduced an extreme Maoist communist programme, forcing urban groups into rural areas and resulting in over 2.5 million deaths from famine, disease, and maltreatment; Sihanouk removed from power.
1978–79 Vietnamese invasion and installation of government headed by Heng Samrin, an anti-Pol Pot communist.
1980–82 Faced by guerrilla resistance from Pol Pot's Chinese-backed Khmer Rouge and Sihanouk's ASEAN and US-backed nationalists, more than 300,000 Cambodians fled to refugee camps in Thailand and thousands of soldiers were killed.

1985 Reformist Hun Sen appointed prime minister and more moderate economic and cultural policies pursued.
1987–89 Vietnamese troop withdrawal.
1989 Renamed State of Cambodia and Buddhism was re-established as state religion.
1991 Peace agreement signed in Paris provided for a cease-fire and a United Nations Transitional Authority in Cambodia (UNTAC) to administer country in conjunction with all-party Supreme National Council; communism abandoned. Sihanouk returned as head of state.
1992 Political prisoners released; refugees resettled; freedom of speech and party formation restored. Khmer Rouge refused to disarm in accordance with peace process.
1993 Free general elections (boycotted by Khmer Rouge) resulted in surprise win by FUNCINPEC; new constitution adopted. Sihanouk reinstated as constitutional monarch; Prince Norodom Ranariddh, FUNCINPEC leader, appointed executive prime minister, with reform-socialist CPP leader Hun Sen deputy premier. Khmer Rouge continued fighting.

1994 Antigovernment coup foiled. Surrender of 7,000 guerrillas of outlawed Khmer Rouge in response to government amnesty.
1995 Prince Norodom Sirivudh, FUNCINPEC leader and half-brother of King Sihanouk, exiled for allegedly plotting to assassinate Hun Sen and topple government.
1996 Political instability exacerbated by assassination of opposition leader Sam Rainsy. Serious split in Khmer Rouge when its deputy leader Ieng Sary formed new Democratic National United Movement (DNUM) and granted amnesty by Sihanouk. Kov Samuth assassinated. Heightened tensions between Hun Sen's CPP and the royalist FUNCINPEC.
1997 16 killed in street demonstration; opposition blamed supporters of Hun Sen. Relations between joint prime ministers deteriorated. Divisions within Khmer Rouge. Pol Pot sentenced to life imprisonment after trial by Khmer Rouge. FUNCINPEC troops routed by CPP, led by Hun Sen. First prime minister Prince Norodom Ranariddh deposed and replaced by Ung Huot. Peace restored in Phnom Penh.

Practical information

Visa requirements UK: visa required. USA: visa required
Embassy in the UK no diplomatic representation in the UK
British embassy 29 Street 75, Phnom Penh. Tel: (855) 232 7124
Embassy in the USA 4500 16th Street NW, Washington, DC 20011. Tel: (202) 726 7742; fax: (202) 726 8381
American embassy 27 EO Street 240, Phnom Penh. Tel: (23) 426436, 426438; fax: (23) 426 437

Chamber of commerce Council for the Development of Cambodia, Government Palace, quai Sisowath, Wat Phnom, Phnom Penh. Tel: (23) 50428; fax: (23) 61616
Office hours 0700–1130 and 1400–1730 Mon–Fri
Banking hours 0800–1500 Mon–Fri
Time difference GMT +7
Chief tourist attractions ancient Khmer ruins and monuments, including great temples of Angkor Thom and Prasat Lingpoun; tropical vegetation and mangrove forests
Major holidays 9 January, 17 April, 1, 20 May, 22 September; variable: New Year (April)

Cameroon Republic of

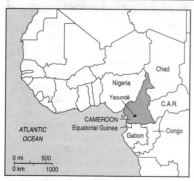

National name *République du Cameroun*
Area 475,440 sq km/183,567 sq mi
Capital Yaoundé
Major towns/cities Garoua, Douala, Nkongsamba, Maroua, Bamenda, Bafoussam
Major ports Douala
Physical features desert in far N in the Lake Chad basin, mountains in W, dry savanna plateau in the intermediate area, and dense tropical rainforest in S; Mount Cameroon 4,070 m/13,358 ft, an active volcano on the coast, W of the Adamawa Mountains

Government

Head of state Paul Biya from 1982
Head of government Simon Achidi Achu from 1992
Political system emergent democratic republic
Administrative divisions ten provinces
Political parties Cameroon People's Democratic Movement (RDPC), nationalist, left of centre; Front of Allies

for Change (FAC), centre left
Armed forces 23,600 (1995); include 9,000 paramilitary forces
Conscription military service is voluntary; paramilitary compulsory training programme in force
Death penalty retained and used for ordinary crimes
Defence spend (% GDP) 1.8 (1995)
Education spend (% GNP) 3.1 (1993–94)
Health spend (% GDP) 1 (1990)

Economy and resources

Currency franc CFA
GDP ($ US) 7.5 billion (1994)
Real GDP per capita (PPP) ($ US) 2,120 (1994)
GDP growth rate 3.2% (1994); −1.8% (1990–95)
Average annual inflation 26.9% (1994); 2% (1985–95)
Foreign debt ($ US) 9.3 billion (1995)
Trading partners France, Spain, Italy, Germany, the Netherlands, Belgium, USA
Resources petroleum, natural gas, tin ore, limestone, bauxite, iron ore, uranium, gold
Industries petroleum refining, aluminium smelting, cement, food processing, footwear, beer, cigarettes
Exports crude petroleum and petroleum products, timber and timber products, coffee, aluminium, cotton, bananas. Principal market: France 22.8% (1995)
Imports machinery and transport equipment, basic manufactures, chemicals, fuel. Principal source: France 38.3% (1995)
Arable land 12.5% (1993)
Agricultural products coffee, cocoa, cotton, cassava, sorghum, millet, maize, plantains, palm (oil and kernels), rubber, bananas; livestock rearing (cattle and sheep); forestry and fishing

Population and society

Population 13,560,000 (1996e)
Population growth rate 2.8% (1990–95); 2.8% (2000–05)
Population density (per sq km) 29 (1996e)
Urban population (% of total) 45 (1995)
Age distribution (% of total population) <15 44%, 15–65 52.4%, >65 3.6% (1995)
Ethnic distribution main groups include the Cameroon Highlanders

(31%), Equatorial Bantu (19%), Kirdi (11%), Fulani (10%), Northwestern Bantu (8%), and Eastern Nigritic (7%)
Languages French and English in pidgin variations (official); there has been some discontent with the emphasis on French – there are 163 indigenous peoples with their own African languages (Sudanic languages in N, Bantu languages elsewhere)
Religions Roman Catholic 35%, animist 25%, Muslim 22%, Protestant 18%
Education (compulsory years) 6 in Eastern Cameroon; 7 in Western Cameroon
Literacy rate 66% (men); 43% (women) (1995e)
Labour force 40% of population: 70% agriculture, 9% industry, 21% services (1990)
Unemployment 25% (1990)
Life expectancy 57 (men); 60 (women) (1995–2000)
Child mortality rate (under 5, per 1,000 live births) 106 (1995)
Physicians 1 per 12,500 people (1991)
Hospital beds 1 per 393 people (1990e)
TV sets (per 1,000 people) 24 (1995)
Radios (per 1,000 people) 152 (1995)

Transport

Airports international airports: Douala, Garoua, Yaoundé; eight domestic airports; total passenger km: 436 mil (1994)
Railroads total length: 1,104 km/686 mi; total passenger km: 352 mil (1993)
Roads total road network: 34,300 km/ 21,314 mi, of which 12.5% paved (1995e); passenger cars: 7.1 per 1,000 people (1995e)

Chronology

1472 First visited by the Portuguese, who named it the Rio dos Camaroes ('River of Prawns') after the giant shrimps they found in the Wouri River estuary, and later introduced slave trading.
early 17th century The Douala people migrated to the coastal region from the E and came to serve as intermediaries between Portuguese, Dutch, and English traders and interior tribes.
1809–48 Northern savannas conquered by the Fulani, Muslim pastoral nomads from S Sahara, forcing forest and upland peoples southwards.
1856 Douala chiefs signed a

commercial treaty with Britain and invited British protection.
1884 Treaty signed establishing German rule as the protectorate of Kamerun; cocoa, coffee, and banana plantations developed.
1916 Captured by Allied forces in World War I.
1919 Divided under League of Nations' mandates between Britain, which administered the SW and N, adjoining Nigeria, and France, which administered the E and S (comprising four-fifths of the area), and developed palm oil and cocoa plantations.
1946 French Cameroon and British Cameroons made UN trust territories.
1955 French crushed a revolt by the Union of the Cameroon Peoples (UPC), southern-based radical nationalists.
1960 French Cameroon became the independent Republic of Cameroon, with Ahmadou Ahidjo, a Muslim from the N, elected president; UPC rebellion in SW crushed, and a state of emergency declared.
1961 Following a UN plebiscite, northern part of British Cameroons merged with Nigeria and southern part joined the Republic of Cameroon to become the Federal Republic of Cameroon, with French and English as official languages.
1966 Autocratic one-party regime introduced; government and opposition parties merged to form Cameroon National Union (UNC).
1970s Petroleum exports made possible successful investment in education and agriculture.
1972 New constitution made Cameroon a unitary state.
1982 President Ahidjo resigned; succeeded by his prime minister Paul Biya, a Christian from the S.
1983 Biya began to remove the northern Muslim political 'barons' close to Ahidjo, who went into exile in France.
1984 Biya defeated a plot by Muslim officers from the N to overthrow him.
1985 UNC adopted the name RDPC.
1990 Widespread public disorder as living standards declined; Biya granted amnesty to political prisoners.
1992 Ruling RDPC won first multiparty elections in 28 years. Biya's presidential victory challenged by opposition, who claimed ballot-rigging.
1995 Cameroon admitted to Commonwealth.
1997 RDPC assembly election victory; President Biya re-elected.

Practical information
Visa requirements UK: visa not required. USA: visa not required
Embassy in the UK 84 Holland Park, London W11 3SB. Tel: (0171) 727 0771/3; fax: (0171) 792 9353
British embassy BP 547, Avenue Winston Churchill, Yaoundé. Tel: (237) 220 545/796; fax: (237) 220 148
Embassy in the USA 2349 Massachusetts Avenue NW, Washington, DC 20008. Tel: (202) 265 8790/1/2/3/4
American embassy Rue Nachtigal, Yaoundé. Tel: 234 014, 230 512; fax: 230 753

Chamber of commerce Chambre de Commerce, d'Industrie et des Mines du Cameroun, BP 4011, Place de Gouvernement, Douala. Tel: (237) 423 690; fax: (237) 425 596
Banking hours 1730–1130 and 1430–1630 Mon–Fri
Time difference GMT +1
Chief tourist attractions national parks; game reserves; sandy beaches
Major holidays 1 January, 11 February, 1, 20 May, 15 August, 25 December; variable: Ascension Thursday, Eid-ul-Adha, end of Ramadan, Good Friday

Canada

Area 9,970,610 sq km/3,849,652 sq mi
Capital Ottawa
Major towns/cities Toronto, Montréal, Vancouver, Edmonton, Calgary, Winnipeg, Québec, Hamilton, Saskatoon, Halifax, Regina, Windsor, Oshawa, London, Kitchener
Physical features mountains in W, with low-lying plains in interior and rolling hills in E; St Lawrence Seaway, Mackenzie River; Great Lakes; Arctic Archipelago; Rocky Mountains; Great Plains or Prairies; Canadian Shield; Niagara Falls; climate varies from temperate in S to arctic in N; 45% of country forested

Government

Head of state Elizabeth II from 1952, represented by governor general Roméo A. LeBlanc from 1995
Head of government Jean Chrétien from 1993
Political system federal constitutional monarchy
Administrative divisions ten provinces and two territories
Political parties Liberal Party,

nationalist, centrist; Bloc Québécois, Québec-based, separatist; Reform Party, populist, right wing; New Democratic Party (NDP), moderate left of centre; Progressive Conservative Party (PCP), free enterprise, right of centre
Armed forces 71,000 (1995)
Death penalty for exceptional crimes only; last execution 1962
Defence spend (% GDP) 1.6 (1995)
Education spend (% GNP) 7.6 (1993–94)
Health spend (% GDP) 7.4 (1993)

Economy and resources

Currency Canadian dollar
GDP ($ US) 579.3 billion (1996)
Real GDP per capita (PPP) ($ US) 21,465 (1996)
GDP growth rate 2.8% (1996); 1.8% (1990–95)
Average annual inflation 2.9% (1985–95)
Major trading partners USA, EU countries, Japan, China, Mexico, South Korea
Resources petroleum, natural gas, coal, copper (world's third-largest producer), nickel (world's second-largest producer), lead (world's fifth-largest producer), zinc (world's largest producer), iron, gold, uranium, timber
Industries transport equipment, food products, paper and related products, wood industries, chemical products, machinery
Exports motor-vehicles and parts, lumber, wood pulp, paper and newsprint, crude petroleum, natural gas, aluminium and alloys, petroleum and coal products. Principal market: USA 81.4% (1996)
Imports motor-vehicle parts, passenger vehicles, computers, foodstuffs, telecommunications equipment. Principal source: USA 75.7% (1996)

Arable land 4.6% (1993)
Agricultural products wheat, barley, maize, oats, rapeseed, linseed; livestock production (cattle and pigs)

Population and society

Population 29,680,000 (1996e)
Population growth rate 1.2% (1990–95); 0.9% (2000–05)
Population density (per sq km) 3 (1996e)
Urban population (% of total) 77% (1995)
Age distribution (% of total population) <15 20.8%, 15–65 67.3%, >65 11.8% (1995)
Ethnic distribution about 45% of British origin, 29% French, 23% of other European descent, and about 3% Native Americans and Inuit
Languages English, French (both official; 60% English mother tongue, 24% French mother tongue); there are also Native American languages and the Inuit Inuktitut
Religions Roman Catholic, various Protestant denominations
Education (compulsory years) 10
Literacy rate 99% (men); 99% (women) (1995e)
Labour force 53% of population: 3% agriculture, 25% industry, 71% services (1990)
Unemployment 9.7% (1996)
Life expectancy 75 (men); 81 (women) (1995–2000)
Child mortality rate (under 5, per 1,000 live births) 8 (1995)
Physicians 1 per 446 people (1991)
TV sets (per 1,000 people) 714 (1995)
Radios (per 1,000 people) 1,053 (1995)

Transport

Airports international airports: Calgary, Edmonton, Gander, Halifax, Hamilton,

Montréal (Dorval, Mirabel), Ottawa (Uplands), St John's, Saskatoon, Toronto (Lester B Pearson), Vancouver, Winnipeg; domestic services to all major cities/towns; total passenger km: 43,490 mil (1994)
Railroads total length: 70,739 km/43,957 mi; total passenger km: 1,440 mil (1994)
Roads total road network: 1,021,000 km/634,449 mi, of which 35.1% paved (1995e); passenger cars: 467 per 1,000 people (1995e)

Chronology

35,000 BC First evidence of people reaching North America from Asia by way of Beringia.
c. 2000 BC Inuit (Eskimos) began settling Arctic coast from Siberia eastwards to Greenland.
c. 1000 AD Vikings, including Leif Ericsson, established Vinland, a settlement in NE America that did not survive.
1497 John Cabot, an Italian navigator in the service of English king Henry VII, landed on Cape Breton Island and claimed the area for England.
1534 French navigator Jacques Cartier reached the Gulf of St Lawrence and claimed the region for France.
1608 Samuel de Champlain, a French explorer, founded Québec; French settlers developed fur trade and fisheries.
1663 French settlements in Canada formed the colony of New France, which expanded southwards.
1670 Hudson's Bay Company established trading posts N of New France, leading to Anglo-French rivalry.
1689–97 King William's War: Anglo-French conflict in North America arising from the 'Glorious Revolution' in Europe.
1702–13 Queen Anne's War: Anglo-French conflict in North America arising from the War of the Spanish Succession in Europe; Britain gained Newfoundland.

1744–48 King George's War: Anglo-French conflict in North America arising from the War of Austrian Succession in Europe.
1756–63 Seven Years' War: James Wolfe captured Québec 1759; France ceded Canada to Britain by the Treaty of Paris.
1775–83 American Revolution caused influx of 40,000 United Empire Loyalists, who formed New Brunswick 1784.
1791 Canada divided into Upper Canada (much of modern Ontario) and Lower Canada (much of modern Québec).
1793 British explorer Alexander Mackenzie crossed the Rocky Mountains to reach the Pacific coast.
1812–14 War of 1812 between Britain and USA; US invasions repelled by both provinces.
1820s Start of large-scale immigration from British Isles caused resentment among French Canadians.
1837 Rebellions led by Louis Joseph Papineau in Lower Canada and William Lyon Mackenzie in Upper Canada.
1841 Upper and Lower Canada united as Province of Canada; achieved internal self-government 1848.
1867 British North America Act united Ontario, Québec, Nova Scotia, and New Brunswick in Dominion of Canada.
1869 Red River Rebellion of Métis (people of mixed French and Native American descent), led by Louis Riel, against British settlers in Rupert's Land.
1870 Manitoba (part of Rupert's Land) formed the fifth province of Canada; British Columbia became the sixth in 1871, and Prince Edward Island became the seventh in 1873.
late 19th century Growth of large-scale wheat farming, mining, and railways.
1885 Northwest Rebellion crushed and Riel hanged; Canadian Pacific Railway completed.
1896 Wilfred Laurier was the first French Canadian to become prime minister.
1905 Alberta and Saskatchewan formed

from Northwest Territories and became provinces of Canada.
1914–18 Half a million Canadian troops fought for the British Empire on the western front in World War I.
1931 Statute of Westminster affirmed equality of status between Britain and Dominions.
1939–45 World War II: Canadian participation in all theatres.
1949 Newfoundland became the tenth province of Canada; Canada was a founding member of the North Atlantic Treaty Organization (NATO).
1950s Postwar boom caused rapid expansion of industry.
1957 Progressive Conservatives returned to power after 22 years in opposition.
1960 Québec Liberal Party of Jean Lesage launched 'Quiet Revolution' to re-assert French-Canadian identity.
1970 Pierre Trudeau invoked War Measures Act to suppress separatist terrorists of the Front de Libération du Québec.
1976 Parti Québécois won control of Québec provincial government; referendum rejected independence 1980.
1982 'Patriation' of constitution removed Britain's last legal control over Canada.
1987 Meech Lake Accord: constitutional amendment proposed to increase provincial powers (to satisfy Québec); failed to be ratified 1990.
1989 Canada and USA agreed to establish free trade by 1999.
1992 Self-governing homeland for Inuit approved; constitutional reform package, the Charlottetown Accord, rejected in national referendum.
1993 Progressive Conservatives reduced to two seats in crushing election defeat.
1994 Canada formed the North American Free Trade Area with USA and Mexico.
1995 Québec referendum narrowly rejected sovereignty proposal.
1997 Liberals re-elected by narrow margin.

Practical information

Visa requirements UK: visa not required. USA: visa not required
Embassy in the UK Macdonald House, 1 Grosvenor Square, London W1X 0AB. Tel: (0171) 258 6600; fax: (0171) 258 6333
British embassy British High Commission, 80 Elgin Street, Ottawa KIP 5K7. Tel: (613) 237 1530; fax: (613) 237 7980
Embassy in the USA 501 Pennsylvania Avenue NW, Washington, DC 20001. Tel: (202) 682 1740; fax: (202) 682 7726
American embassy 100 Wellington Street, K1P 5T1, Ottawa. Tel: (613) 238 5335, 4470; fax: (613) 238 5720
Chamber of commerce Canadian Chamber of Commerce,

55 Metcalfe Street, Suite 1160, Ottawa ON KIP 6N4. Tel: (613) 238 400; fax: (613) 238 7643
Office hours 0900–1700 Mon–Fri
Banking hours 1000–1500 Mon–Fri
Time difference GMT –3.5/9
Chief tourist attractions forests; lakes; rivers; Rockies of British Columbia; St Lawrence Seaway; Niagara Falls; fjords of Newfoundland and Labrador; historic cities of Montréal and Québec; museums and art galleries of Toronto, Vancouver, and Ottawa
Major holidays 1 January, 1 July (except Newfoundland), 11 November, 25–26 December; variable: Good Friday, Easter Monday, Labour Day (September), Thanksgiving (October), Victoria (May), additional days vary between states

Cape Verde Republic of

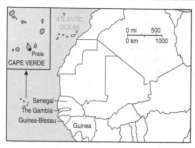

National name *República de Cabo Verde*
Area 4,033 sq km/1,557 sq mi
Capital Praia
Major towns/cities Mindelo
Major ports Mindelo
Physical features archipelago of ten volcanic islands 565 km/350 mi W of Senegal; the windward (Barlavento) group includes Santo Antão, São Vicente, Santa Luzia, São Nicolau, Sal, and Boa Vista; the leeward (Sotovento) group comprises Maio, São Tiago, Fogo, and Brava; all but Santa Luzia are inhabited

Government
Head of state Monteiro Mascarenhas from 1991
Head of government Carlos Viega from 1991
Political system emergent democracy
Administrative divisions 14 districts
Political parties African Party for the Independence of Cape Verde (PAICV), African nationalist; Movement for Democracy (MPD), moderate, centrist
Armed forces 1,100 (1995)
Conscription selective conscription
Death penalty abolished 1981
Defence spend (% GDP) 1.8 (1995)
Education spend (% GNP) 4.4 (1993–94)
Health spend (% GDP) 2 (1993)

Economy and resources
Currency Cape Verde escudo

GDP ($ US) 309.5 million (1994)
Real GDP per capita (PPP) ($ US) 1,862 (1994)
GDP growth rate 4% (1994)
Average annual inflation 4.5% (1995); 7.2 % (1985–95)
Foreign debt ($ US) 157.5 million (1993)
Trading partners Portugal, the Netherlands, Algeria, Italy, Côte d'Ivoire, Spain, USA, Brazil, Japan
Resources salt, pozzolana (volcanic rock), limestone, basalt, kaolin
Industries fish processing, machinery and electrical equipment, transport equipment, textiles, chemicals, rum
Exports fish, shellfish and fish products, salt, bananas. Principal market: Portugal 50% (1995)
Imports food and live animals, machinery and electrical equipment, transport equipment, mineral products, metals. Principal source: Portugal 45% (1995)
Arable land 10.7% (1993)
Agricultural products maize, beans, potatoes, cassava, coconuts, sugar cane, bananas, coffee, groundnuts; fishing (mainly tuna, lobster, shellfish)

Population and society
Population 396,000 (1996e)
Population growth rate 2.8% (1990–95)
Population density (per sq km) 98 (1996e)
Urban population (% of total) 53 (1994)
Age distribution (% of total population) <15 42%, 15–65 54%, >65 4% (1994)
Ethnic distribution about 60% of mixed descent (Portuguese and African), known as *mestiços* or creoles; the remainder is mainly African. The European population is very small
Languages Portuguese (official), Creole
Religions Roman Catholic 93%, Protestant (Nazarene Church)
Education (compulsory years) 6
Literacy rate 80% (men); 60% (women) (1995e)

Labour force 37% of population: 31% agriculture, 30% industry, 40% services (1990)
Unemployment 25.8% (1990e)
Life expectancy 65 (men); 67 (women) (1995–2000)
Child mortality rate (under 5, per 1,000 live births) 73 (1995)
Physicians 1 per 5,280 people (1990e)
Hospital beds 1 per 930 people (1990e)
TV sets (per 1,000 people) 3.6 (1995)
Radios (per 1,000 people) 179 (1995)

Transport
Airports international airports: Sal Island (Amílcar Cabral), São Tiago; eight domestic airports; total passenger km: 173 mil (1994)
Railroads none
Roads total road network: 1,100 km/ 684 mi, of which 78% paved (1995e); passenger cars: 6.9 per 1,000 people (1995e)

Chronology
1462 Originally uninhabited; settled by Portuguese, who brought in slave labour from W Africa.
later 19th century Decline in prosperity as slave trade ended.
1950s Liberation movement developed on the islands and the Portuguese African mainland colony of Guinea-Bissau.
1951 Became an overseas territory of Portugal.
1975 Independence achieved. National people's assembly elected, with Aristides of the PAICV as the first executive president; a policy of nonalignment followed.
1981 Goal of union with Guinea-Bissau abandoned; became one-party state.
1988 Rising unrest and demand for political reforms.
1991 In first multiparty elections, new MPD won majority and Monteiro Mascarenhas became president; market-centred economic reforms introduced.

Practical information

Visa requirements UK: visa required. USA: visa required
Embassy for the UK 44 Konninginnegracht, 2514 AD, The Hague, the Netherlands. Tel: (70) 346 9623; fax: (70) 346 7702
British embassy British Consulate, c/o Shell Cabo Verde, Sarl Ave, Amílcar Cabral CP4, Sarl Vincente. (All staff based in Dakar, Senegal.) Tel: (238) 314 470; fax: (238) 314 755
Embassy in the USA 3415 Massachusetts Avenue NW, Washington, DC 20007. Tel: (202) 965 6820; fax: (202) 965 1207

American embassy Rua Abilio Macedo 81, Praia. Tel: 615 616; fax: 611 355
Chamber of commerce Associaçao Comercial, Industrial e Agricola de Barlavento, CP 62 Mindelo, São Vicente. Tel: (238) 313 281; fax: (238) 317 110
Office hours 0830–1230 and 1430–1800 Mon–Fri
Banking hours 0800–1400 Mon–Fri
Time difference GMT –1
Chief tourist attractions mountain scenery; extensive white sandy beaches on islands of São Tiago, Sal, Boa Vista, Maio
Major holidays 1, 20 January, 8 March, 1 May, 1 June, 12 September, 24–25 December; variable: Good Friday

Central African Republic National name *République Centrafricaine*

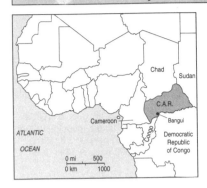

Area 622,436 sq km/240,322 sq mi
Capital Bangui
Major towns/cities Berbérati, Bouar, Bambari, Bossangoa, Carnot
Physical features landlocked flat plateau, with rivers flowing north and south, and hills in NE and SW; dry in N, rainforest in SW; mostly wooded; Kotto and Mbali river falls; the Oubangui River rises 6 m/20 ft at Bangui during the wet season (June–November)

Government

Head of state Ange-Felix Patasse from 1993
Head of government Gabriel Koyambounou from 1995
Political system emergent democratic republic
Administrative divisions 16 prefectures
Political parties Central African People's Liberation Party (MPLC), left of centre; Central African Democratic Rally (RDC), nationalist, right of centre
Armed forces 2,700 (1995); plus 2,300 in paramilitary forces
Conscription selective national service for two-year period
Death penalty retains the death penalty for ordinary crimes but can be considered abolitionist in practice (last execution 1981)
Defence spend (% GDP) 1.8 (1995)
Education spend (% GNP) 2.8 (1993–94)
Health spend (% GDP) 2.6 (1990)

Economy and resources

Currency franc CFA
GDP ($ US) 9 million (1994)
Real GDP per capita (PPP) ($ US) 1,130 (1994)
GDP growth rate 5.8% (1994); 1% (1990–95)

Average annual inflation 3.7% (1985–95)
Foreign debt ($ US) 944 million (1995)
Trading partners France, Belgium, Luxembourg, Cameroon, Germany, Japan, Switzerland, Democratic Republic of Congo
Resources gem diamonds and industrial diamonds, gold, uranium, iron ore, manganese, copper
Industries food processing, beverages, tobacco, furniture, textiles, paper, soap
Exports diamonds, coffee, timber, cotton. Principal market: France 40.1% (1995)
Imports machinery, road vehicles and parts, basic manufactures, food and chemical products. Principal source: France 37% (1995)
Arable land 3.1% (1993)
Agricultural products cassava, coffee, yams, maize, bananas, groundnuts; forestry

Population and society

Population 3,344,000 (1996e)
Population growth rate 2.5% (1990–95); 2.3% (2000–05)
Population density (per sq km) 5 (1996e)
Urban population (% of total) 39 (1995)
Age distribution (% of total population) <15 42.7%, 15–65 53.4%, >65 4% (1995)
Ethnic distribution over 80 ethnic groups, but 66% of the population falls into one of three: the Banda (30%), the Baya-Mandjia (29%), and the Mbaka (7%). There are clearly defined ethnic zones; the forest region, inhabited by Bantu groups, the Mbaka, Lissongo, Mbimu, and Babinga; the river banks, populated by the Sango, Yakoma, Baniri, and Buraka; and the savanna region, where the Banda, Sande, Sara, Ndle, and Bizao live. Europeans number fewer than 7,000, the majority being French
Languages French (official), Sangho (national), Arabic, Hunsa, and Swahili
Religions Protestant, Roman Catholic, Muslim, animist
Education (compulsory years) 8
Literacy rate 52% (men); 25% (women) (1995e)
Labour force 49% of population: 80% agriculture, 4% industry, 16% services (1990)
Unemployment 5.6% (1993)
Life expectancy 48 (men); 53 (women) (1995–2000)

Child mortality rate (under 5, per 1,000 live births) 165 (1995)
Physicians 1 per 17,218 people (1991)
Hospital beds 1 per 710 people (1991)
TV sets (per 1,000 people) 4.9 (1995)
Radios (per 1,000 people) 75 (1995)

Transport

Airports international airports: Bangui-M'Poko; 37 small airports for international chartered services; total passenger km: 227 mil (1994)
Railroads none
Roads total road network: 23,810 km/14,796 mi, of which 1.8% paved (1995e); passenger cars: 0.2 per 1,000 people (1995e)

Chronology

10th century Immigration by peoples from Sudan to E and Cameroon to W.
16th century Part of the Gaoga Empire.
16th–18th centuries Population reduced greatly by slave raids both by coastal traders and Arab empires in Sudan and Chad.
19th century The Zande nation of the Bandia peoples became powerful in E. Bantu speakers immigrated from Zaire and the Baya from N Cameroon.
1889–1903 The French established control over the area, quelling insurrections; a French colony known as Oubangi-Chari was formed and partitioned among commercial concessionaries.
1920–30 Series of rebellions against forced labour on coffee and cotton plantations savagely repressed by French.
1946 Given a territorial assembly and representation in French parliament.
1958 Achieved self-government within French Equatorial Africa, with Barthélémy Boganda, founder of the pro-independence Movement for the Social Evolution of Black Africa (MESAN) prime minister.
1960 Achieved independence as Central African Republic; David Dacko, nephew of the late Boganda, elected president.
1962 The republic made a one-party state, dominated by MESAN and loyal to the French interest.
1965 Dacko ousted in military coup led by Col Jean-Bedel Bokassa as the economy deteriorated.

1972 Bokassa, a violent and eccentric autocrat, declared himself president for life.
1977 Bokassa made himself emperor of the 'Central African Empire'.
1979 Bokassa deposed by Dacko in French-backed bloodless coup, following violent repressive measures including the massacre of 100 children by the emperor, who went into exile.
1981 Dacko deposed in a bloodless coup, led by Gen André Kolingba, and military government established.
1983 Clandestine opposition movement formed.
1984 Amnesty for all political party leaders announced. President Mitterrand of France paid a state visit.
1988 Bokassa, who had returned from exile, found guilty of murder and embezzlement; he received death sentence, later commuted to life imprisonment.
1991 Opposition parties allowed to form.
1992 Multiparty elections promised, but cancelled with Kolingba in last place.
1993 Kolingba released several thousand prisoners, including Bokassa. Ange-Felix Patasse of the leftist African People's Labour Party (MLPC) elected president, ending 12 years of military dictatorship.
1996 Army revolt over pay; Patasse forced into hiding.

Practical information

Visa requirements UK: visa required. USA: visa required
Embassy for the UK 30 rue des Perchamps, 75016, Paris, France. Tel: (1) 4224 4256; fax: (1) 4288 9895
British embassy British Consulate, PO Box 728, Bangui. (All staff based in Yaoundé, Cameroon.) Tel: (236) 610 300; fax: (236) 615 130
Embassy in the USA 1618 22nd Street NW, Washington, DC 20008. Tel: (202) 483 7800/1; fax: (202) 332 9893
American embassy Avenue David Dacko, Bangui. Tel: 610 200/210, 612 578; fax: 614 494

Chamber of commerce Chambre de Commerce, d'Industrie, des Mines et de l'Artisanat, BP 813, Bangui. Tel: (236) 614 255; telex: 5261
Office hours 0630–1330 Mon–Fri; 0700–1200 Sat
Banking hours 0730–1130 Mon–Fri
Time difference GMT +1
Chief tourist attractions waterfalls; forests; wildlife; game reserves; hunting and fishing
Major holidays 1 January, 29 March, 1 May, 1 June, 13, 15 August, 1 September, 1 November, 1, 25 December; variable: Ascension Thursday, Easter Monday, Whit Monday

Chad Republic of

National name *République du Tchad*
Area 1,284,000 sq km/495,752 sq mi
Capital N'djaména (formerly Fort Lamy)
Major towns/cities Sarh, Moundou, Abéché, Bongor, Doba
Physical features landlocked state with mountains (Tibetsi) and part of Sahara Desert in N; moist savanna in S; rivers in S flow NW to Lake Chad

Government

Head of state Idriss Deby from 1990
Head of government Nassour Ouaidou Guelendouksia from 1997
Political system emergent democratic republic

Administrative divisions 14 prefectures
Political parties Patriotic Salvation Movement (MPS), centre left; Alliance for Democracy and Progress (RDP), centre left; Union for Democracy and Progress (UPDT), centre left; Action for Unity and Socialism (ACTUS), centre left; Union for Democracy and the Republic (UDR), centre left
Armed forces 25,400 (1995); plus gendarmerie of 4,500
Conscription conscription is for three years
Death penalty retained and used for ordinary crimes
Defence spend (% GDP) 2.6 (1995)
Education spend (% GNP) 2.2 (1993–94)
Health spend (% GDP) 4.7 (1990)

Economy and resources

Currency franc CFA
GDP ($ US) 9 million (1994)
Real GDP per capita (PPP) ($ US) 700 (1994)
GDP growth rate 4% (1994e); 1.9% (1990–95)
Average annual inflation 3.1% (1985–95)
Foreign debt ($ US) 908 million (1995)

Trading partners France, Portugal, Nigeria, Cameroon, USA, Belgium, Luxembourg, Italy, Germany
Resources petroleum, tungsten, tin ore, bauxite, iron ore, gold, uranium, limestone, kaolin, titanium
Industries cotton processing, sugar refinery, beer, cigarettes, soap, bicycles
Exports cotton, live cattle, meat, hides and skins. Principal market: Portugal 16.3% (1995)
Imports petroleum and petroleum products, cereals, pharmaceuticals, chemicals, machinery and transport equipment, electrical equipment. Principal source: France 39% (1995)
Arable land 2.5% (1993)
Agricultural products cotton, millet, sugar cane, sorghum, groundnuts; livestock rearing (cattle, sheep, and goats)

Population and society

Population 6,515,000 (1996e)
Population growth rate 2.7% (1990–95); 2.5% (2000–05)
Population density (per sq km) 5 (1996e)
Urban population (% of total) 21 (1995)

Age distribution (% of total population) <15 43.4%, 15–65 53%, >65 3.6% (1995)

Ethnic distribution mainly Arabs in the N, and Pagan, or Kirdi, groups in the S. There is no single dominant group in any region, the largest are the Sara, who comprise about a quarter of the total population. Europeans, mainly French, constitute a very small minority

Languages French, Arabic (both official), over 100 African languages spoken

Religions Muslim, Christian, animist

Education (compulsory years) 8

Literacy rate 42% (men); 18% (women) (1995e)

Labour force 49% of population: 83% agriculture, 4% industry, 13% services (1990)

Life expectancy 48 (men); 51 (women) (1995–2000)

Child mortality rate (under 5, per 1,000 live births) 152 (1995)

Physicians 1 per 28,570 people (1994e)

Hospital beds 1 per 1,565 people (1994e)

TV sets (per 1,000 people) 1.4 (1995)

Radios (per 1,000 people) 248 (1995)

Transport

Airports international airports: N'djaména; 12 small airports for domestic services; total passenger km: 222 mil (1994)

Railroads none

Roads total road network: 32,700 km/ 20,320 mi, of which 0.8% paved (1995e); passenger cars: 3 per 1,000 people (1995e)

Chronology

7th–9th centuries Berber pastoral nomads, the Zaghawa, immigrated from north and became ruling aristocracy, dominating the Sao people, sedentary black farmers, and established Kanem state.

9th–19th centuries The Zaghawa's Saifi dynasty formed the kingdom of Bornu, which stretched to the W and S of Lake Chad, and converted to Islam in the 11th century. At its height between the 15th and 18th centuries, it raided the S for slaves, and faced rivalry from the 16th century from the Baguirmi and Ouadai Arab kingdoms.

1820s Visited by British explorers.

1890s–1901 Conquered by France, who ended slave raiding by Arab kingdoms.

1910 Became a colony in French Equatorial Africa and cotton production expanded in the S.

1944 The pro-Nazi Vichy government signed agreement giving Libya rights to the Aouzou Strip in N Chad.

1946 Became overseas territory of French Republic, with its own territorial assembly and representation in the French parliament.

1960 Independence achieved, with François Tombalbaye of the Chadian Progressive Party (CPT), dominated by Sara Christians from the S, as president.

1963 Violent opposition in the Muslim N, led by the Chadian National Liberation Front (Frolinat), backed by Libya following the banning of opposition parties.

1968 Revolt of northern militias quelled with France's help.

1973 Africanization campaign launched

by Tombalbaye, who changed his first name to Ngarta.

1975 Tombalbaye killed in military coup led by southerner Gen Félix Malloum. Frolinat continued its resistance.

1978 Malloum tried to find a political solution by forming a coalition government with former Frolinat leader Hissène Habré, but it soon broke down.

1979 Malloum forced to leave the country; interim government set up under Gen Goukouni Oueddei (Frolinat). Habré continued his opposition with his Army of the North (FAN), and Libya provided support for Goukouni.

1981–82 Habré gained control of half the country. Goukouni fled and set up a 'government in exile'.

1983 Habré's regime recognized by the Organization of African Unity (OAU) and France, but in the N, Goukouni's supporters, with Libya's help, fought on. Eventually a cease-fire was agreed, with latitude 16°N dividing the country.

1987 Chad, France, and Libya agreed on OAU cease-fire to end the civil war between the Muslim Arab N and Christian and animist black African S.

1988 Libya relinquished its claims to the Aouzou Strip.

1990 President Habré ousted after army defeated by Libyan-backed Patriotic Salvation Movement (MPS) rebel troops based in the Sudan and led by Habré's former ally Idriss Deby.

1991–92 Several antigovernment coups foiled.

1993 Transitional charter adopted, as prelude to full democracy at a later date.

1997 Nassour Ouaidou Guelendouksia appointed prime minister.

Practical information

Visa requirements UK: visa required. USA: visa required

Embassy for the UK 65 rue des Belles Feuilles, 75116 Paris, France. Tel: (1) 4553 3675; fax: (1) 4553 1609

British embassy British Consulate, BP 877, avenue Charles de Gaulle, N'djaména. (All staff based in Abuja, Nigeria.) Tel: (235) 513 064; telex: 5234

Embassy in the USA 2002 R Street NW, Washington, DC 20009. Tel: (202) 462 4009; fax: (202) 265 1937

American embassy avenue Félix Eboue, N'djaména. Tel: (51) 7009, 9052, 9233; fax: (51) 5654

Chamber of commerce Chambre de Commerce, Chambre Consulaire, BP 458, N'djaména. Tel: (235) 515 264

Office hours 0700–1400 Mon–Sat; 0700–1200 Fri

Banking hours 0700–1100 Mon–Sat; 0700–1030 Fri

Time difference GMT +1

Chief tourist attractions varied scenery – desert in north, dense forest in south

Major holidays 1 January, 1, 25 May, 7 June, 11 August, 1, 28 November, 25 December; variable: Eid-ul-Adha, Easter Monday, end of Ramadan, Prophet's Birthday

Chile Republic of

National name *República de Chile*
Area 756,950 sq km/292,258 sq mi
Capital Santiago
Major towns/cities Concepción, Viña del Mar, Valparaiso, Talcahuano, San Bernardo, Puente Alto, Chillán, Rancagua, Talca, Temuco
Major ports Valparaíso, Antofagasta, Arica, Iquique, Punta Arenas
Physical features Andes mountains along E border, Atacama Desert in N, fertile central valley, grazing land and forest in S
Territories Easter Island, Juan Fernández Islands, part of Tierra del Fuego, claim to part of Antarctica

Government

Head of state Eduardo Frei from 1993
Head of government Dante Cordova from 1995
Political system emergent democratic republic
Administrative divisions 12 regions and one metropolitan area
Political parties Christian Democratic Party (PDC), moderate centrist; National Renewal Party (RN), right wing; Socialist Party of Chile (PS), left wing; Independent Democratic Union (UDI), right wing; Party for Democracy (PPD), left of centre; Union of the Centre-Centre (UCC), right wing; Radical Party (PR), left of centre
Armed forces 99,000 (1995)
Conscription one year (army) or two years (navy and air force)
Death penalty retained and used for ordinary crimes
Defence spend (% GDP) 3.8 (1995)

Education spend (% GNP) 2.9 (1993–94)
Health spend (% GDP) 3.4 (1990)

Economy and resources

Currency Chilean peso
GDP ($ US) 52 billion (1994)
Real GDP per capita (PPP) ($ US) 9,129 (1994)
GDP growth rate 4.2% (1994); 7.3% (1990–95)
Average annual inflation 17.9% (1985–95)
Foreign debt ($ US) 25.56 billion (1995)
Trading partners USA, Japan, Brazil, Germany, Argentina, UK
Resources copper (world's largest producer), gold, silver, iron ore, molybdenum, cobalt, iodine, saltpetre, coal, natural gas, petroleum, hydroelectric power
Industries nonferrous metals, food processing, petroleum refining, chemicals, paper products (cellulose, newsprint, paper and cardboard), motor tyres, beer, glass sheets, motor vehicles
Exports copper, fruits, timber products, fishmeal, vegetables, manufactured foodstuffs and beverages. Principal market: USA 16.6% (1996)
Imports machinery and transport equipment, wheat, chemical and mineral products, consumer goods, raw materials. Principal source: USA 23.7% (1996)
Arable land 5.3% (1993)
Agricultural products wheat, sugar beet, potatoes, maize, fruit and vegetables; livestock

Population and society

Population 14,421,000 (1996e)
Population growth rate 1.6% (1990–95); 1.2% (2000–05)
Population density (per sq km) 19 (1996e)
Urban population (% of total) 84 (1995)
Age distribution (% of total population) <15 29.5%, 15–65 63.8%, >65 6.6% (1995)
Ethnic distribution 65% mestizo (mixed Native American and Spanish descent), 30% European, remainder mainly Native American
Language Spanish
Religion Roman Catholic
Education (compulsory years) 8
Literacy rate 93% (men); 93% (women) (1995e)

Labour force 38% of population: 19% agriculture, 25% industry, 56% services (1990)
Unemployment 5.1% (1993e)
Life expectancy 71 (men); 78 (women) (1995–2000)
Child mortality rate (under 5, per 1,000 live births) 15 (1995)
Physicians 1 per 943 people (1991)
Hospital beds 1 per 302 people (1991e)
TV sets (per 1,000 people) 215 (1995)
Radios (per 1,000 people) 348 (1995)

Transport

Airports international airports: Santiago (Arturo Merino Benítez), Arica (Chacalluta); domestic services to main towns; total passenger km: 5,398 mil (1994)
Railroads total length: 6,572 km/4,084 mi; total passenger km: 816 mil (1994)
Roads total road network: 79,750 km/49,557 mi, of which 13.8% paved (1995e); passenger cars: 56.8 per 1,000 people (1995e)

Chronology

1535 First Spanish invasion of Chile abandoned in face of fierce resistance from indigenous Araucanian Indians.
1541 Pedro de Valdivia began Spanish conquest and founded Santiago.
1553 Valdivia captured and killed by Araucanian Indians led by Chief Lautaro.
17th century Spanish developed small agricultural settlements ruled by government subordinate to viceroy in Lima, Peru.
1778 King of Spain appointed a separate captain-general to govern Chile.
1810 Santiago junta proclaimed Chilean autonomy after Napoleon dethroned king of Spain.
1814 Spanish viceroy regained control of Chile.
1817 Army of the Andes, led by José de San Martín and Bernardo O'Higgins, defeated the Spanish.
1818 Achieved independence from Spain with O'Higgins as supreme director.
1823–30 O'Higgins forced to resign; civil war between conservative centralists and liberal federalists ended with conservative victory.
1833 Autocratic republican constitution created unitary Roman Catholic state with strong president and limited franchise.

1851–61 President Manuel Montt bowed to pressure to liberalize constitution and reduce privileges of landowners and church. •

1879–84 Chile defeated Peru and Bolivia in War of the Pacific and increased its territory by a third.

late 19th century Mining of nitrate and copper became major industry; large-scale European immigration followed 'pacification' of Araucanian Indians.

1891 Constitutional dispute between president and congress led to civil war; congressional victory reduced president to figurehead status.

1920 Election of liberal president Arturo Alessandri Palma; congress blocked his social reform programme.

1925 New constitution increased presidential powers, separated church and state, and made primary education compulsory.

1927 Military coup led to dictatorship of Gen Carlos Ibáñez del Campo.

1931 Sharp fall in price of copper and nitrate caused dramatic economic and political collapse.

1932 Re-election of President Alessandri, who restored order by harsh measures.

1938 Popular Front of Radicals, Socialists, and Communists took power under Pedro Aguirre Cedra, who introduced economic policies based on US New Deal.

1947 Communists organized violent strikes to exploit discontent over high inflation.

1948–58 Communist Party banned.

1952 General Ibáñez elected president on law-and-order platform; austerity policies reduced inflation to 20%.

1958 Jorge Alessandri (son of former president) succeeded Ibáñez as head of Liberal-Conservative coalition.

1964 Christian Democrat Eduardo Frei Montalva became president; he introduced cautious 'communitarian' social reforms, but failed to combat inflation.

1970 Salvador Allende, leader of Popular Unity coalition, became world's first democratically elected Marxist president; he embarked on an extensive programme of nationalization and radical social reform.

1973 Allende killed in CIA-backed military coup; Gen Augusto Pinochet established dictatorship combining severe political repression with free-market economics.

1981 Pinochet began eight-year term as president under new constitution described as 'transition to democracy'.

1983 Economic recession provoked growing opposition to regime from all sides.

1988 Referendum on whether Pinochet should serve a further term resulted in a clear 'No' vote; he agreed to hold elections in following year.

1990 End of military regime; Christian Democrat Patricio Aylwin became president, with Pinochet as commander in chief of army; investigation into over 2,000 political executions during military regime.

1994 Eduardo Frei (son of former president) succeeded Aylwin as president.

1995 Frei introduced measures to reduce military influence in government.

Practical information

Visa requirements UK: visa not required. USA: visa not required

Embassy in the UK 12 Devonshire Street, London W1N 2DS. Tel: (0171) 580 6392; fax: (0171) 436 5204

British embassy Avenida El Bosque Norte (Casilla 16552), Santiago 9. Tel: (2) 231 3737; fax: (2) 231 9771

Embassy in the USA 1732 Massachusetts Avenue NW, Washington, DC 20036. Tel: (202) 785 1746; fax: (202) 887 5579

American embassy Avenida Andres Bello 2800, Santiago.

Tel: (2) 232 2600; fax: (2) 330 3710

Chamber of commerce Cámara de Comercio de Santiago de Chile, AG, Santa Lucía 302, 3°, Casilla 1297, Santiago. Tel: (2) 632 1232; fax: (2) 633 0962

Office hours 0900–1830 Mon–Fri

Banking hours 0900–1400 Mon–Fri

Time difference GMT –4

Chief tourist attractions beaches; Andean skiing resorts; lakes, rivers, desert scenery; Easter Island Neolithic sites

Major holidays 1 January, 1, 21 May, 29 June, 15 August, 11, 18–19 September, 12 October, 1 November, 8, 25, 31, December; variable: Good Friday, Holy Saturday

---

China People's Republic of

National name *Zhonghua Renmin Gonghe Guo*

Area 9,572,900 sq km/3,696,000 sq mi

Capital Beijing (Peking)

Major towns/cities Shanghai, Hong Kong, Chongqing (Chungking), Tianjin, Guangzhou (Canton), Shenyang (Mukden), Wuhan, Nanjing (Nanking), Harbin, Chengdu, Xiang, Zibo

Major ports Tianjin (Tientsin), Shanghai, Hong Kong, Qingdao (Tsingtao), Guangzhou (Canton)

Physical features two-thirds of China is mountains or desert (N and W); the low-lying E is irrigated by rivers Huang He (Yellow River), Chang Jiang (Yangtze-Kiang), Xi Jiang (Si Kiang)

Government

Head of state Jiang Zemin from 1993

Head of government Li Peng from 1987

Political system communist republic

Administrative divisions 22 provinces, five autonomous regions, and three municipalities

Political party Chinese Communist Party (CCP), Marxist-Leninist-Maoist

Armed forces 2,930,000; reserves approximately 1.2 million (1995)

Conscription selective: 3 years (army and marines), 4 years (air force and navy)

Death penalty retained and used for ordinary crimes

Defence spend (% GDP) 5.7 (1995)
Education spend (% GNP) 2.6
(1993–94)
Health spend (% GDP) 2.1 (1990)

Economy and resources

Currency yuan
GDP ($ US) 522.2 billion (1994)
GDP per capita ($ US) 2,604 (1994)
GDP growth rate 10.2% (1995); 12.8%
(1990–95)
Average annual inflation 14.8% (1995);
9.5% (1985–95)
Foreign debt ($ US) 118.09 billion
(1995)
Trading partners Japan, USA, Taiwan
Resources coal, graphite, tungsten,
molybdenum, antimony, tin (world's
largest producer), lead (world's fifth-
largest producer), mercury, bauxite,
phosphate rock, iron ore (world's largest
producer), diamonds, gold, manganese,
zinc (world's third-largest producer),
petroleum, natural gas, fish
Industries raw cotton and cotton cloth,
cement, paper, sugar, salt, plastics,
aluminium ware, steel, rolled steel,
chemical fertilizers, silk, woollen fabrics,
bicycles, cameras, electrical appliances;
tourism is growing
Exports basic manufactures,
miscellaneous manufactured articles
(particularly clothing and toys), crude
petroleum, machinery and transport
equipment, fishery products, cereals,
canned food, tea, raw silk, cotton cloth.
Principal market: Japan 20.9% (1996)
Imports machinery and transport
equipment, basic manufactures,
chemicals, wheat, rolled steel, fertilizers.
Principal source: Japan 22.1% (1996)
Arable land 9.6% (1993)
Agricultural products sweet potatoes,
wheat, maize, soya beans, rice, sugar
cane, tobacco, cotton, jute; world's largest
fish catch (over 17 tonnes in 1993)

Population and society

Population 1,232,083,000 (1996e)
Population growth rate 1.1% (1990–95);
0.8% (2000–05)
Population density (per sq km) 128
(1996e)
Urban population (% of total) 30 (1995)
Age distribution (% of total population)
<15 26.4%, 15–65 67.5%, >65 6.1%
(1995)
Ethnic distribution 94% Han Chinese,
the remainder being Zhuang, Uygur, Hui
(Muslims), Yi, Tibetan, Miao, Manchu,
Mongol, Buyi, or Korean; numerous

lesser nationalities live mainly in border
regions
Languages Chinese, including Mandarin
(official), Cantonese, Wu, and other
dialects
Religions Taoist, Confucianist, and
Buddhist; Muslim 20 million; Catholic 3–6
million (divided between the 'patriotic'
church established 1958 and the 'loyal'
church subject to Rome); Protestant
3 million
Education (compulsory years) 9
Literacy rate 84% (men); 62% (women)
(1995e)
Labour force 59% of population: 72%
agriculture, 15% industry, 13% services
(1990)
Unemployment 2.3% (1993)
Life expectancy 68 (men); 72 (women)
(1995–2000)
Child mortality rate (under 5, per 1,000
live births) 47 (1995)
Physicians 1 per 636 people (1995e)
Hospital beds 1 per 430 people (1995e)
TV sets (per 1,000 people) 205 (1995)
Radios (per 1,000 people) 185 (1995)

Transport

Airports international airports: Beijing
(Capital International Central), Guangzhou
(Baiyun), Shanghai (Hongqiao), Hong
Kong (Kai Tak International); 59 domestic
airports; total passenger km: 51,395 mil
(1994)
Railroads total length: 54,000 km/
33,556 mi; total passenger km: 363,605
mil (1994)
Roads total road network: 1,110,000
km/689,754 mi, of which 89.7% paved
(1995e); passenger cars: 2.9 per 1,000
people (1995e)

Chronology

c. 3000 BC Yangshao culture reached its
peak in the Huang He Valley; displaced
by Longshan culture in E China.
c. 1766–c. 1122 BC First major dynasty,
the Shang, arose from Longshan culture;
writing and calendar developed.
c. 1122–256 BC Zhou people of W China
overthrew Shang and set up new dynasty;
development of money and written laws.
c. 500 BC Confucius expounded
philosophy which guided Chinese
government and society for the next 2,000
years.
403–221 BC 'Warring States Period': Zhou
Empire broke up into small kingdoms.
221–206 BC Qin kingdom defeated all
rivals and established first empire with
strong central government; emperor Shi

Huangdi built Great Wall of China.
202 BC–AD 220 Han dynasty expanded
empire into central Asia; first overland
trade with Europe; art and literature
flourished; Buddhism introduced from
India.
220–581 Large-scale rebellion destroyed
Han dynasty; empire split into three
competing kingdoms; several short-lived
dynasties ruled parts of China.
581–618 Sui dynasty reunified China and
repelled Tatar invaders.
618–907 Tang dynasty enlarged and
strengthened the empire; great revival of
culture; major rebellion 875–84.
907–60 'Five Dynasties and Ten
Kingdoms': disintegration of empire amid
war and economic decline; development
of printing.
960–1279 Song dynasty reunified China
and restored order; civil service
examinations introduced; population
reached 100 million; Manchurians
occupied northern China 1127.
1279 Mongols conquered all China, which
became part of the vast empire of Kublai
Khan, founder of the Yuan dynasty;
Venetian traveller Marco Polo visited
China 1275–92.
1368 Rebellions drove out the Mongols;
Ming dynasty expanded empire;
architecture flourished in new capital of
Beijing; dislike of Mongols led to contempt
for all things foreign.
1516 Portuguese explorers reached
Macau; other European traders followed;
first Chinese porcelain arrived in Europe
1580.
1644 Manchurian invasion established the
Qing (or Manchu) dynasty; Manchurians
assimilated and Chinese trade and culture
continued to thrive.
1796–1804 Anti-Manchu revolt weakened
Qing dynasty; population increase in
excess of food supplies led to falling living
standards and cultural decline.
1839–42 First Opium War; Britain forced
China to cede Hong Kong and open five
ports to European trade; Second Opium
War extracted further trade concessions
1856–60.
1850–64 Millions died in Taiping
Rebellion; Taipings combined Christian
and Chinese beliefs and demanded land
reform.
1894–95 Sino-Japanese War: Chinese
driven out of Korea.
1897–98 Germany, Russia, France, and
Britain leased ports in China; conquest by
European empires seemed likely.
1898 Hong Kong was secured by Britain
on a 99-year lease.

1900 Anti-Western Boxer Rebellion crushed by foreign intervention; jealousy between Great Powers prevented partition.

1911 Revolution broke out; Republic of China proclaimed by Sun Yat-sen of Guomindang (National People's Party).

1912 Abdication of infant emperor Pu-i; General Yuan Shih-K'ai became dictator.

1916 Power of central government collapsed on death of Yuan Shih-K'ai; N China dominated by local warlords.

1919 Beijing students formed 4 May movement to protest at transfer of German possessions in China to Japan.

1921 Sun Yat-sen elected president of nominal national government; Chinese Communist Party founded; communists worked with Guomindang to reunite China from 1923.

1925 Death of Sun Yat-sen; leadership of Guomindang gradually passed to military commander Chiang Kai-shek.

1926–28 Revolutionary Army of Chiang Kai-shek reunified China; Guomindang broke with communists and tried to suppress them in civil war.

1932 Japan invaded Manchuria and established puppet state of Manchukuo.

1934–35 Communists undertook Long March from Jiangxi and Fujian in S to Yan'an in N to escape encirclement by Guomindang.

1937–45 Japan renewed invasion of China; Chiang Kai-shek received help from USA and Britain from 1941.

1946 Civil war resumed between Guomindang and communists led by Mao Zedong.

1949 Victorious communists proclaimed People's Republic of China under Chairman Mao; Guomindang fled to Taiwan.

1950–53 China intervened heavily in Korean War.

1958 'Great Leap Forward': extremist five-year plan to accelerate output severely weakened economy.

1960 Sino-Soviet split: China accused USSR of betraying communism; USSR withdrew technical advisers; border clashes on Ussuri River 1969.

1962 Economic recovery programme under Liu Shaoqi caused divisions between 'rightists' and 'leftists'; brief border war with India.

1966–69 'Great Proletarian Cultural Revolution'; leftists overthrew Liu Shaoqi with support of Mao; Red Guards disrupted education, government, and daily life in attempt to enforce revolutionary principles.

1970 Mao supported efforts of Prime Minister Zhou Enlai to restore order.

1971 People's Republic of China admitted to United Nations; full diplomatic relations with USA established in 1979.

1976 Deaths of Zhou Enlai and Mao Zedong led to power struggle between rightists and leftists; Hua Guofeng became leader and arrested leftist 'Gang of Four'.

1977–81 Rightist Deng Xiaoping emerged as supreme leader; pragmatic economic policies introduced market incentives and encouraged foreign trade.

1987 Deng Ziaoping retired from Politburo but remained a dominant figure.

1989 Over 2,000 killed when army crushed prodemocracy student demonstrations in Tiananmen Square, Beijing; international sanctions imposed.

1991 China and USSR reached agreement on disputed border.

1996 Reunification with Taiwan declared a priority.

1997 Deng Xiaoping died aged 92. Collective leadership in power. Joint declaration with Russia, opposing the USA as the only superpower. Government reported strong growth in economy. Hong Kong returned to Chinese sovereignty. President Jiang Zemin promised widespread privatization.

Practical information

Visa requirements UK: visa required. USA: visa required

Embassy in the UK 49–51 Portland Place, London W1N 3AH. Tel: (0171) 636 9375/5726; fax: (0171) 636 2981

British embassy 11 Guang Hua Lu, Jian Guo Men Wai, Beijing 100600. Tel: (1) 532 1961/5; fax: (1) 532 1937

Embassy in the USA 2300 Connecticut Avenue NW, Washington, DC 20008. Tel: (202) 328 2500/1/2

American embassy Xiu Shui Bei Jie 3, Beijing 100600. Tel: (10) 532 3831; fax: (10) 532 6422

Chamber of commerce All-China Federation of Industry and Commerce, 93 Beiheyan Dajie, Beijing 100006.

Tel: (1) 513 6677; fax: (1) 512 2631

Office hours 0800–1200 and 1400–1800 Mon–Sat

Banking hours 0930–1200 and 1400–1700 Mon–Fri; 0900–1700 Sat

Time difference GMT +8

Chief tourist attractions scenery; historical sites such as the Great Wall, Temple of Heaven, Forbidden City (Beijing), Ming tombs, terracotta warriors (Xian); Buddhist monasteries and temples in Tibet (Xizang)

Major holidays 1 January, 8 March, 1 May, 1 August, 9 September, 1–2 October; variable: Spring Festival (January/February, 4 days),

---

Colombia Republic of

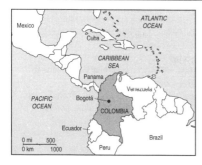

National name *República de Colombia*

Area 1,141,748 sq km/440,828 sq mi

Capital Bogotá

Major towns/cities Medellín, Cali, Barranquilla, Cartagena, Bucaramanga, Buenaventura

Major ports Barranquilla, Cartagena, Buenaventura

Physical features the Andes mountains run N–S; flat coastland in W and plains (llanos) in E; Magdalena River runs N to Caribbean Sea; includes islands of Providencia, San Andrés, and Mapelo; almost half the country is forested

Government

Head of state and government Ernesto Samper Pizano from 1994

Political system democratic republic

Administrative divisions 32 departments and one capital district

Political parties Liberal Party (PL), centrist; Conservative Party (PSC), right

of centre; M-19 Democratic Alliance (ADM-19), left of centre; National Salvation Movement (MSN), right-of-centre coalition grouping
Armed forces 146,400 (1995); plus a paramilitary police force of 87,000
Conscription selective conscription for 1–2 years
Death penalty abolished 1910
Defence spend (% GDP) 2 (1995)
Education spend (% GNP) 3.7 (1993–94)
Health spend (% GDP) 1.8 (1990)

Economy and resources

Currency Colombian peso
GDP ($ US) 67.3 billion (1994)
Real GDP per capita (PPP) ($ US) 6,107 (1994)
GDP growth rate 5.7% (1994); 4.6% (1990–95)
Average annual inflation 25.2% (1985–95)
Foreign debt ($ US) 20.76 billion (1995)
Trading partners USA, EU countries, Argentina, Brazil, Chile, Mexico, Venezuela, Japan
Resources petroleum, natural gas, coal, nickel, emeralds (accounts for about half of world production), gold, manganese, copper, lead, mercury, platinum, limestone, phosphates
Industries food processing, chemical products, textiles, beverages, transport equipment, cement
Exports coffee, petroleum and petroleum products, coal, gold, bananas, cut flowers, cotton, chemicals, textiles, paper. Principal market: USA 33.6% (1995). Illegal trade in cocaine – in 1995 it was estimated that approximately $3.5 billion (equivalent to about 4% of GDP) was entering Colombia as the proceeds of drug-trafficking
Imports machinery and transport equipment, chemicals, minerals, food, metals. Principal source: USA 39% (1995)
Arable land 3.4% (1993)
Agricultural products coffee (world's second-largest producer), cocoa, sugar cane, bananas, tobacco, cotton, cut flowers, rice, potatoes, maize; timber; beef production

Population and society

Population 36,444,000 (1996e)
Population growth rate 1.7% (1990–95); 1.3% (2000–05)
Population density (per sq km) 32 (1996e)

Urban population (% of total) 73 (1995)
Age distribution (% of total population) <15 32.9%, 15–65 62.6%, >65 4.5% (1995)
Ethnic distribution main ethnic groups are of mixed Spanish, Native American, and African descent; Spanish customs and values predominate
Language Spanish
Religion Roman Catholic
Education (compulsory years) 5
Literacy rate 87% (men); 86% (women) (1995e)
Labour force 40% of population: 27% agriculture, 23% industry, 50% services (1990)
Unemployment 7.4% (1994e)
Life expectancy 67 (men); 73 (women) (1995–2000)
Child mortality rate (under 5, per 1,000 live births) 36 (1995)
Physicians 1 per 1,064 (1991)
TV sets (per 1,000 people) 117 (1995)
Radios (per 1,000 people) 564 (1995)

Transport

Airports international airports: Santa Fe de Bogotá, DC (El Dorado International), Medellín, Cali, Barranguilla, Bucaramanga, Cartagena, Cúcuta, Leticia, Pereira, San Andrés, Santa Maria; over 80 smaller airports serving domestic flights; total passenger km: 5,675 mil
Railroads total length: 3,380 km/ 2,100 mi (1995); total passenger km: 16 mil (1992)
Roads total road network: 106,600 km/ 66,241 mi, of which 11.9% paved (1995e); passenger cars: 22.2 per 1,000 people (1993e)

Chronology

late 15th century S Colombia became part of Inca Empire, whose core lay in Peru.
1522 Spanish conquistador Pascual de Andagoya reached San Juan River.
1536–38 Spanish conquest by Jimenez de Quesada overcame powerful Chibcha Indian chiefdom, which had its capital in the uplands at Bogotá and was renowned for its gold crafts; became part of Spanish Viceroyalty of Peru, which covered much of South America.
1717 Bogotá became capital of new Spanish Viceroyalty of Nueva (New) Granada, which also ruled Ecuador and Venezuela.
1809 Struggle for independence from Spain began.

1819 Venezuelan freedom fighter Simón Bolívar, 'the Liberator', who had withdrawn to Colombia 1814, raised a force of 5,000 British mercenaries and defeated Spanish at the battle of Boyaca, establishing Colombia's independence; Gran Colombia formed, also comprising Ecuador, Panama, and Venezuela.
1830 Became separate state, which included Panama, on dissolution of Republic of Gran Colombia.
1863 Became major coffee exporter. Federalizing, anticlerical Liberals came to power, with country divided into nine largely autonomous 'sovereign' states; church disestablished.
1885 Conservatives came to power, beginning 45 years of political dominance; power was recentralized and church restored to influence.
1899–1903 Civil war between Liberals and Conservatives, ended with Panama's separation as an independent state.
1930 Liberals returned to power at the time of the economic depression; social legislation introduced and labour movement encouraged.
1946 Conservatives returned to power after Liberal vote divided between rival candidates.
1948 Left-wing mayor of Bogotá assassinated; widespread outcry.
1949 Start of civil war, 'La Violencia', during which over 250,000 people died.
1957 Hoping to halt violence, Conservatives and Liberals agreed to form National Front, sharing the presidency.
1970 National Popular Alliance (ANAPO) formed as left-wing opposition to National Front.
1974 National Front accord temporarily ended.
1975 Civil unrest due to disillusionment with government.
1978 Liberals, under Julio Turbay, revived the accord and began an intensive fight against drug dealers.
1982 Liberals maintained their control of congress but lost the presidency. Conservative president Belisario Betancur granted guerrillas an amnesty and freed political prisoners.
1984 Minister of justice assassinated by drug dealers; campaign against them stepped up.
1986 Virgilio Barco Vargas, Liberal, elected president by record margin.
1989 Drug cartel assassinated leading presidential candidate; Vargas declared antidrug war; bombing campaign by drug

traffickers killed hundreds; police killed José Rodríguez Gacha, one of the most wanted cartel leaders.

1990 Cesar Gaviria Trujillo elected president. Liberals maintained control of congress.

1991 New constitution prohibited extradition of Colombians wanted for trial in other countries; several leading drug

traffickers arrested. Many guerrillas abandoned the armed struggle, but the Colombian Revolutionary Armed Forces (Farc) and National Liberation Army remained active. Liberals won general election.

1992 Medellín drug-cartel leader Pablo Escobar escaped from prison. State of emergency declared.

1993 Escobar shot while attempting to avoid arrest.

1994 Liberals returned to power, with reduced majority. Ernesto Samper Pizano, Liberal, elected president.

1995 Samper under pressure to resign over corruption allegations; state of emergency declared. Leaders of Cali drug-cartel imprisoned.

Practical information

Visa requirements UK: visa not required for a stay of up to 90 days. USA: visa not required for a stay of up to 90 days
Embassy in the UK Flat 3A, 3 Hans Crescent, London SW1X 0LN. Tel: (0171) 589 9177; fax: (0171) 581 1829
British embassy Apartado Aéreo 4508, Torre Propaganda Sancho, Calle 98, No. 9–03, Piso 4, Santa Fe de Bogotá DC. Tel: (1) 218 5111; fax: (1) 218 2460
Embassy in the USA 2118 Leroy Place NW, Washington, DC 20008. Tel: (202) 387 8338; fax: (202) 232 8643
American embassy Calle 22D-BIS, No. 47–51, Apartado Aéreo 3831. Tel: (1) 315 0811; fax: (1) 315 2197
Chamber of commerce Instituto Colombiano de Comercio

Exterior, Apartado Aéreo 240193, Calle 28, No. 13-A-15, 5° Santa Fe de Bogotá DC. Tel: (1) 283 3284; fax: (1) 281 2560, 283 1953
Office hours 0800–1200 and 1400–1700 Mon–Fri
Banking hours 0900–1500 Mon–Fri
Time difference GMT –5
Chief tourist attractions Caribbean coast; 16th-century walled city of Cartagena; Amazonian town of Leticia; Andes Mountains; forest and rainforest; pre-Columbian relics and colonial architecture
Major holidays 1, 6 January, 29 June, 20 July, 7, 15 August, 12 October, 1, 15 November, 8, 25, 30–31 December; variable: Ascension Thursday, Corpus Christi, Good Friday, Holy Thursday, St Joseph (March), Sacred Heart (June)

Comoros Federal Islamic Republic of

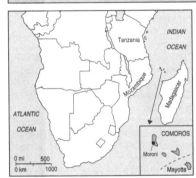

National name *Jumhurīyat al-Qumur al-Itthādīyah al-Islāmīyah* or *République Fédérale Islamique des Comoros*
Area 1,862 sq km/718 sq mi
Capital Moroni
Major towns/cities Mutsamudu, Domoni, Fomboni, Dzaoudzi
Physical features comprises the volcanic islands of Njazídja, Nzwani, and Mwali (formerly Grande Comore, Anjouan, Moheli); at N end of Mozambique Channel in Indian Ocean between Madagascar and coast of Africa

Government

Head of state Muhammad Taki Abdoulkarim from 1996

Head of government Ahmed Abdou from 1996
Political system emergent democracy
Administrative divisions three prefectures (each of the three main islands is a prefecture)
Political parties National Union for Democracy in the Comoros (UNDC), Islamic, nationalist; Rally for Democracy and Renewal (RDR), left of centre
Armed forces 800 (1995)
Conscription military service is voluntary
Death penalty retains the death penalty for ordinary crimes but can be considered abolitionist in practice (no executions since independence)
Education spend (% GNP) 3.7 (1994)
Health spend (% GDP) 3.3 (1990)

Economy and resources

Currency Comorian franc
GDP ($ US) 370 million (1994e)
Real GDP per capita (PPP) ($ US) 700 (1994e)
GDP growth rate 0.9% (1994)
Average annual inflation 31% (1994); 4% (1985–95)
Foreign debt ($ US) 190 million (1994)
Trading partners France, USA, Bahrain, Kenya, Botswana, Brazil, South Africa
Industries sawmilling, processing of

vanilla and copra, printing, soft drinks, plastics
Exports vanilla, cloves, ylang-ylang, essences, copra, coffee. Principal market: France 54.6% (1995)
Imports rice, petroleum products, transport equipment, meat and dairy products, cement, iron and steel, clothing and footwear. Principal source: France 60.1% (1995)
Arable land 35% (1993)
Agricultural products vanilla, ylang-ylang, cloves, basil, cassava, sweet potatoes, rice, maize, pulses, coconuts, bananas

Population and society

Population 632,000 (1996e)
Population growth rate 3.7% (1990–95)
Population density (per sq km) 283 (1996e)
Urban population (% of total) 30 (1994)
Age distribution (% of total population) <15 49%, 15–65 49%, >65 2% (1994)
Ethnic distribution population of mixed origin, with Africans, Arabs, and Malaysians predominating; the principal ethnic group is the Antalaotra
Languages Arabic (official), Comorian (Swahili and Arabic dialect), Makua, French

Religion Muslim; Islam is the state religion

Education (compulsory years) 9

Literacy rate 64% (men); 50% (women) (1995e)

Labour force 44% of population: 77% agriculture, 9% industry, 13% services (1990)

Unemployment 16% (1990)

Life expectancy 58 (men); 59 (women) (1995–2000)

Child mortality rate (under 5, per 1,000 live births) 124 (1995)

Physicians 1 per 7,500 people (1990)

Hospital beds 1 per 342 people (1990)

TV sets (per 1,000 people) 0.7 (1995)

Radios (per 1,000 people) 137 (1995)

Transport

Airports international airport: Moroni-Hahaya, on Njazídja; each of the three other islands has a small airfield; total passenger km: 3 mil (1994)

Railroads none

Roads total road network: 875 km/ 544 mi, of which 76.5% paved (1995e); passenger cars: 10.9 (1995e)

Chronology

5th century AD First settled by Malay-Polynesian immigrants.

7th century Converted to Islam by Arab seafarers and fell under the rule of local sultans.

late 16th century First visited by European navigators.

1886 Moheli island in S became a French protectorate.

1904 Slave trade abolished, ending influx of Africans.

1912 Grande Comore and Anjouan, the main islands, joined Moheli to become a French colony, which was attached to Madagascar from 1914.

1947 Became a French Overseas Territory separate from Madagascar.

1961 Internal self-government achieved.

1975 Independence achieved from France, but island of Mayotte to the SE voted to remain part of France. Joined the United Nations.

1976 President Ahmed Abdallah overthrown in a coup by Ali Soilih; relations deteriorated with France as a Maoist-Islamic socialist programme was pursued.

1978 Soilih killed by French mercenaries led by Bob Denard. Federal Islamic republic proclaimed, with exiled Abdallah restored as president; diplomatic relations re-established with France.

1979 The Comoros became a one-party state; powers of the federal government increased.

1989 Abdallah killed by French mercenaries who, under French and South African pressure, turned authority over to French administration; Said Muhammad Djohar became president in a multiparty democracy.

1990–92 Antigovernment coups foiled.

1993 Djohar's supporters won overall majority in assembly elections.

1995 Djohar overthrown in coup led by Col Denard, who was persuaded to withdraw by French troops.

1996 Djohar allowed to return from exile in a nonpolitical capacity and Muhammad Taki Abdoulkarim elected president. National Rally for Development (RND) virtually unopposed in assembly elections. Ahmed Abdou appointed prime minister.

1997 Secessionist rebels took control of the island of Anjouan.

Practical information

Visa requirements UK: visa required. USA: visa required

Embassy for the UK 20 rue Marbeau, 75016 Paris, France. Tel: (1) 4067 9054; fax: (1) 4067 7296

British embassy British Consulate, Henri Fraise et Fils 38, Co Océan Indien, PO Box 986, Moroni. Tel: (269) 733 182; fax: (269) 733 182. (All staff based in Madagascar.)

Embassy in the USA (temporary) c/o the Permanent Mission of the Federal and Islamic Republic of the Comoros to the United Nations, 336 East 45th Street, 2nd Floor, New York, NY 10017. Tel: (212) 972 8010; fax: (212) 983 4712

American embassy the USA does not have an embassy in Comoros; the ambassador to Mauritius is accredited to Comoros

Chamber of commerce Chambre de Commerce, d'Industrie et d'Agriculture, BP 763, Moroni. Tel: (269) 610 426

Office hours 0730–1430 Mon–Thu; 0730–1100 Fri

Banking hours 0730–1300 Mon–Thu; 0730–1100 Fri

Time difference GMT +3

Chief tourist attractions rich marine life; beaches; underwater fishing; mountain scenery

Major holidays 6 July, 27 November; variable: Eid-ul-Adha, Arafa, Ashora, first day of Ramadan, end of Ramadan, New Year (Muslim), Prophet's Birthday

---

Congo Democratic Republic of (formerly *Zaire*)

National name *République Démocratique du Congo*

Area 2,344,900 sq km/905,366 sq mi

Capital Kinshasa

Major towns/cities Lubumbashi, Kananga, Mbuji-Mayi, Kisangani, Bukavu, Kikwit, Matadi

Major ports Matadi, Kalemie

Physical features Zaïre/Congo River basin has tropical rainforest (second-largest remaining in world) and savanna; mountains in E and W; lakes Tanganyika, Albert, Edward; Ruwenzori Range; Victoria Falls

Government

Head of state and government Laurent Kabila from 1997

Political system transitional

Administrative divisions ten regions

Political parties Popular Movement of the Revolution (MPR), African socialist; Democratic Forces of Congo–Kinshasa (formerly Sacred Union, an alliance of some 130 opposition groups), moderate, centrist; Union for Democracy and Social Progress (UPDS), left of centre; Congolese National Movement–

Lumumba (MNC), left of centre
Armed forces 28,100 (1995); plus
paramilitary forces of 31,000
Conscription military service is
compulsory
Death penalty retained and used for
ordinary crimes
Defence spend (% GDP) 2 (1995)
Education spend (% GNP) 0.9 (1990)
Health spend (% GDP) 0.8 (1990)

Economy and resources

Currency zaïre
GDP ($ US) 7.2 billion (1994e)
Real GDP per capita (PPP) ($ US) 429
(1994)
GDP growth rate –0.6% (1995)
Average annual inflation 542% (1995)
Foreign debt ($ US) 11.3 billion (1993)
Trading partners Belgium and
Luxembourg, USA, France, UK,
Germany, South Africa
Resources petroleum, copper, cobalt
(65% of world's reserves), manganese,
zinc, tin, uranium, silver, gold, diamonds
(one of the world's largest producers of
industrial diamonds)
Industries textiles, cement, food
processing, tobacco, rubber,
engineering, wood products, leather,
metallurgy and metal extraction,
electrical equipment, transport
vehicles
Exports mineral products (mainly
copper, cobalt, industrial diamonds, and
petroleum), agricultural products (chiefly
coffee). Principal market: Belgium and
Luxembourg 37% (1995)
Imports manufactured goods, food and
live animals, machinery and transport
equipment, chemicals, mineral fuels and
lubricants. Principal source: Belgium
and Luxembourg 15% (1995)
Arable land 3.1% (1993)
Agricultural products coffee, palm oil,
palm kernels, sugar cane, cassava,
plantains, maize, groundnuts, bananas,
yams, rice, rubber, seed cotton; forest
resources

Population and society

Population 46,812,000 (1996e)
Population growth rate 3.2%
(1990–95); 3% (2000–05)
Population density (per sq km) 20
(1996e)
Urban population (% of total) 29 (1995)
Age distribution (% of total population)
<15 48%, 15–65 49.1%, >65 2.9%
(1995)
Ethnic distribution almost entirely of

African descent, distributed among over
200 ethnic groups, the most numerous
being the Kongo, Luba, Lunda, Mongo,
and Zande
Languages French (official); Swahili,
Lingala, Kikongo, and Tshiluba are
recognized as national languages; over
200 other languages
Religions Roman Catholic, Protestant,
Kimbanguist; also 0.5 million Muslims
Education (compulsory years) 6
Literacy rate 84% (men); 61% (women)
(1995e)
Labour force 43% of population: 68%
agriculture, 13% industry, 19% services
(1990)
Unemployment 35% (1993e)
Life expectancy 50 (men); 53 (women)
(1995–2000)
Child mortality rate (under 5, per 1,000
live births) 185 (1995)
Physicians 1 per 14,286 people (1991)
Hospital beds 1 per 438 people (1991)
TV sets (per 1,000 people) 2.2 (1995)
Radios (per 1,000 people) 98 (1995)

Transport

Airports international airports:
Kinshasa (N'djili), Luano (near
Lubumbashi), Bukava, Goma,
Kisangani; over 40 domestic airports
and 150 landing strips; total passenger
km: 480 mil (1994)
Railroads total length: 4,772 km/2,965
mi; total passenger km: 469 mil (1990)
Roads total road network: 154,027 km/
95,712 mi (1995e); passenger cars: 17
per 1,000 people (1995e)

Chronology

13th century Rise of Kongo Empire,
centred on banks of River Zaïre/Congo.
1483 First visited by Portuguese, who
named the area Zaire (from Zadi, 'big
water') and converted local rulers to
Christianity.
16th–17th centuries Great
development of slave trade by
Portuguese, Dutch, British, and French
merchants, initially supplied by Kongo
intermediaries.
18th century Rise of Luba state, in
southern copper belt of N Katanga, and
Lunda, in Kasai region in central S.
mid-19th century Eastern Zaire
invaded by Arab slave traders from E
Africa.
1874–77 British explorer Henry Morton
Stanley navigated Congo River to
Atlantic Ocean.

1879–87 Stanley engaged by King
Leopold II of Belgium to sign protection
treaties with local chiefs and 'Congo
Free State' awarded to Leopold by
1884–85 Berlin Conference; great
expansion in rubber export, using forced
labour.
1908 Leopold forced to relinquish
personal control of Congo Free State,
after international condemnation of
human-rights abuses. Became colony of
Belgian Congo and important exporter
of minerals.
1959 Riots in Kinshasa (Leopoldville)
persuaded Belgium to decolonize
rapidly.
1960 Independence achieved as
Republic of the Congo. Civil war broke
out between central government based
in Kinshasa (Leopoldville) with Joseph
Kasavubu as president, and rich mining
province of Katanga.
1961 Former prime minister Patrice
Lumumba murdered in Katanga; fighting
between mercenaries engaged by
Katanga secessionist leader Moise
Tshombe, and United Nations troops;
Kasai and Kivu provinces also sought
(briefly) to secede.
1963 Katanga secessionist war ended;
Tshombe forced into exile.
1964 Tshombe returned from exile to
become prime minister; pro-Marxist
groups took control of E Zaire.
1965 Western-backed Col Sese Seko
Mobutu seized power in coup, ousting
Kasavubu and Tshombe.
1971 Country renamed Republic of
Zaire, with Mobutu as president as
authenticité (Africanization) policy
launched.
1972 Mobutu's Popular Movement of
the Revolution (MPR) became only legal
political party. Katanga province
renamed Shaba.
1974 Foreign-owned businesses and
plantations seized by Mobutu and given
to his political allies.
1977 Original owners of confiscated
properties invited back. Zairean
guerrillas, chiefly Lundas, invaded
Shaba province from Angola, but were
repulsed by Moroccan, French, and
Belgian paratroopers.
1980s International creditors forced
launch of series of austerity
programmes, after level of foreign
indebtedness had mounted with
collapse in world copper prices.
1991 After antigovernment riots,
Mobutu agreed to end ban on multiparty

politics and share power with opposition; Etienne Tshisekedi appointed premier, but soon dismissed.
1992 Tshisekedi reinstated against Mobutu's wishes after renewed rioting.
1993 Rival pro- and anti-Mobutu governments created.

1994 Kengo Wa Dondo elected prime minister by interim parliament, with Mobutu's agreement. Mass influx of Rwandan refugees.
1995 Continuing secessionist activity in Shaba and Kasai provinces and interethnic warfare in Kivu, adjoining Rwanda in E.
1996 Zaire on brink of war with

Rwanda after Rwandan support of Hutu killings by Tutsis in Zaire. Massive Hutu refugee crisis narrowly averted as thousands allowed to return to Rwanda.
1997 Mobutu ousted by rebel forces of Laurent Kabila, who declared himself president and renamed Zaire the Democratic Republic of Congo.

Practical information

Visa requirements UK: visa required. USA: visa required
Embassy in the UK 26 Chesham Place, London SW1X 8HH. Tel: (0171) 235 6137; fax: (0171) 235 9048
British embassy BP 8049, avenue des Trois Z, Kinshasa-Gombe. Tel: (12) 34775/8
Embassy in the USA 1800 New Hampshire Avenue NW, Washington, DC 20009. Tel: (202) 234 7690/1
American embassy 310 avenue des Aviateurs, Kinshasa. Tel: (12) 21533/4/5; fax: (88) 43805, ext. 2308 or 43467

Chamber of commerce Chambre de Commerce, d'Industrie et d'Agriculture, BP 7247, 10 avenue des Aviateurs, Kinshasa. Tel: (12) 22286; telex: 21071
Office hours 0730–1500 Mon–Fri; 0730–1200 Sat
Banking hours 0800–1130 Mon–Fri
Time difference GMT +1/2
Chief tourist attractions lake and mountain scenery; extensive tropical rainforests along Zaïre/Congo River
Major holidays 1, 4 January, 1, 20 May, 24, 30 June, 1 August, 14, 27 October, 17, 24 November, 25 December

---

Congo Republic of

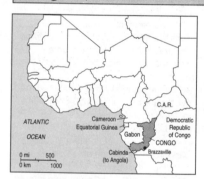

National name *République du Congo*
Area 342,000 sq km/132,046 sq mi
Capital Brazzaville
Major towns/cities Pool, Pointe-Noire, Nkayi, Loubomo, Bouenza, Cuvette, Niari, Plateaux
Major ports Pointe-Noire
Physical features narrow coastal plain rises to central plateau, then falls into northern basin; Zaïre (Congo) River on the border with the Democratic Republic of Congo; half the country is rainforest

Government

Head of state Denis Sassou-Nguessou from 1997
Head of government Charles David Ganao from 1996
Political system emergent democracy
Administrative divisions nine regions

and one capital district
Political parties Pan-African Union for Social Democracy (UPADS), moderate, left of centre; Congolese Movement for Democracy and Integral Development (MCDDI), moderate, left of centre; Congolese Labour Party (PCT), left wing
Armed forces 10,000 (1995); plus a paramilitary force of 5,000
Conscription national service is voluntary
Death penalty retains the death penalty for ordinary crimes but can be considered abolitionist in practice (last execution 1982)
Defence spend (% GDP) 1.7 (1995)
Education spend (% GNP) 8.3 (1993–94)
Health spend (% GDP) 3 (1990)

Economy and resources

Currency franc CFA
GDP ($ US) 1.6 billion (1994)
Real GDP per capita (PPP) ($ US) 2,410 (1994)
GDP growth rate –4.9% (1994); –0.6% (1990–95)
Average annual inflation 2.2% (1985–95)
Foreign debt ($ US) 6.03 billion (1995)
Trading partners France, Belgium, Luxembourg, USA, Italy, Spain, China

Resources petroleum, natural gas, lead, zinc, gold, copper, phosphate, iron ore, potash, bauxite
Industries mining, food processing, textiles, cement, metal goods, chemicals, forest products
Exports petroleum and petroleum products, saw logs and veneer logs, veneer sheets. Principal market: Belgium and Luxembourg 24.3% (1995)
Imports machinery, chemical products, iron and steel, transport equipment, foodstuffs. Principal source: France 31.2% (1995)
Arable land 0.4% (1993)
Agricultural products cassava, plantains, sugar cane, oil palm, maize, coffee, cocoa; forestry

Population and society

Population 2,668,000 (1996e)
Population growth rate 3% (1990–95); 2.6% (2000–05)
Population density (per sq km) 8 (1996e)
Urban population (% of total) 59 (1995)
Age distribution (% of total population) <15 45.6%, 15–65 51%, >65 3.4% (1995)
Ethnic distribution predominantly Bantu; population comprises 15 main ethnic groups and 75 tribes. The Kongo,

or Bakongo, account for about 45% of the population, then come the Bateke, or Teke, at about 20%, and then the Mboshi, or Boubangui, about 16%

Languages French (official); Kongo languages; local patois Monokutuba and Lingala

Religions animist, Christian, Muslim

Education (compulsory years) 10

Literacy rate 70% (men); 44% (women) (1995e)

Labour force 42% of population: 49% agriculture, 15% industry, 37% services (1990)

Life expectancy 48 (men); 52 (women) (1995–2000)

Child mortality rate (under 5, per 1,000 live births) 108 (1995)

Physicians 1 per 3,571 people (1991)

Hospital beds 1 per 282 people (1990e)

TV sets (per 1,000 people) 7.7 (1995)

Radios (per 1,000 people) 116 (1995)

Transport

Airports international airports: Brazzaville (Maya-Maya), Pointe-Noire; six domestic airports; total passenger km: 264 mil (1994)

Railroads total length: 795 km/494 mi; total passenger km: 285 mil (1994)

Roads total road network: 12,760 km/ 7,929 mi, of which 9.7% paved (1995e); passenger cars: 14 per 1,000 people (1995e)

Chronology

late 15th century First visited by Portuguese explorers, at which time the Bakongo (a six-state confederation centred S of the Congo River in Angola)

and Bateke, both Bantu groups, were the chief kingdoms.

16th century Portuguese, in collaboration with coastal peoples, exported slaves from the interior to plantations in Brazil and São Tomé; missionaries spread Roman Catholicism.

1880 French explorer Pierre Savorgnan de Brazza established French claims to coastal region, with the makoko (king) of the Bateke accepting French protection.

1905 International outrage at revelations of the brutalities of forced labour, which decimated the population, as ivory and rubber resources were ruthlessly exploited by private concessionaries.

1910 As Moyen-Congo, became part of French Equatorial Africa, which also comprised Gabon and the Central African Republic, with the capital at Brazzaville.

1920s More than 17,000 were killed as forced labour used to build the Congo-Ocean railroad; first Bakongo political organization founded.

1940–44 Supported the 'Free French' anti-Nazi resistance cause during World War II, Brazzaville serving as capital for Gen Charles de Gaulle's forces.

1946 Became autonomous, with a territorial assembly and representation in French parliament.

1960 Achieved independence from France, with Abbé Fulbert Youlou, a moderate Catholic Bakongo priest, as the first president.

1963 Youlou forced to resign after labour unrest. Alphonse Massamba-Débat became president with Pascal Lissouba as prime minister, and a

single-party state was established under the socialist National Revolutionary Movement (MNR).

1968 Military coup, led by Capt Marien Ngouabi, ousted Massamba-Débat.

1970 A Marxist People's Republic declared, with Ngouabi's PCT the only legal party.

1977 Ngouabi assassinated in a plot by Massamba-Débat, who was executed; Col Joachim Yhombi-Opango became president.

1979 Yhombi-Opango handed over the presidency to the PCT, who chose Col Denis Sassou-Nguessou as his successor.

early 1980s Petroleum production increased fivefold.

1990 With the collapse of Eastern European communism, the PCT abandoned Marxist-Leninism and promised multiparty politics and market-centred reforms in an economy crippled by foreign debt.

1992 Multiparty elections gave the coalition dominated by the Pan-African Union for Social Democracy (UPADS) an assembly majority, with Pascal Lissouba elected president.

1993 Yhombi-Opango appointed prime minister; violent strikes and unrest after opposition disputed election results.

1994 International panel appointed to investigate results; UPADS-dominated coalition declared winner.

1995 New broad-based government formed, including opposition groups; market-centred economic reforms, including privatization.

1996 Charles David Ganao appointed prime minister.

Practical information

Visa requirements UK: visa required. USA: visa required

Embassy in the UK Honorary Consulate of the Republic of the Congo, Alliance House, 12 Caxton Street, London SW1H 0QS. Tel: (0171) 222 7575; fax: (0171) 233 2087

British embassy British Consulate, Côte de l'Hotel Méridien, rue Lyantey 26, Brazzaville. Tel: (242) 838 527; fax: (242) 837 257 (The embassy closed 26 July 1991; diplomatic accreditation has been transferred to the British embassy in Kinshasa on a nonresident basis.)

Embassy in the USA 4891 Colorado Avenue NW, Washington, DC 20011. Tel: (202) 726 0825;

fax: (202) 726 1860

American embassy Avenue Amilcar Cabral, Brazzaville. Tel: 832 070; fax: 836 338

Chamber of commerce Chambre Nationale de Commerce, BP 1438, Brazzaville. Tel: (242) 832 956

Office hours usually 0800–1200 and 1430–1800 Mon–Fri; 0800–1200 Sat

Banking hours 0630–1300 Mon–Fri (counters close at 1130)

Time difference GMT +1

Major holidays 1 January, 18 March, 1 May, 31 July, 13–15 August, 1 November, 25, 31 December; variable: Good Friday, Easter Monday

Costa Rica Republic of

National name *República de Costa Rica*
Area 51,100 sq km/19,729 sq mi
Capital San José
Major towns/cities Alajuela, Cartago, Limón, Puntarenas
Major ports Limón, Puntarenas
Physical features high central plateau and tropical coasts; Costa Rica was once entirely forested, containing an estimated 5% of the Earth's flora and fauna

Government

Head of state and government José Maria Figueres Olsen from 1994
Political system liberal democracy
Administrative divisions seven provinces
Political parties National Liberation Party (PLN), left of centre; Christian Socialist Unity Party (PUSC), centrist coalition; ten minor parties
Armed forces army abolished 1948; 4,300 civil guards and 3,200 rural guards
Death penalty abolished 1887
Defence spend (% GDP) 0.3 (1995)
Education spend (% GNP) 4.7 (1993–94)
Health spend (% GDP) 5.6 (1990)

Economy and resources

Currency colón
GDP ($ US) 8.3 billion (1994)
Real GDP per capita (PPP) ($ US) 5,919 (1994)
GDP growth rate 4.5% (1994); 5.1%(1990–95)
Average annual inflation 9% (1994); 18.5% (1985–95)
Foreign debt ($ US) 3.8 billion (1995)
Trading partners USA, Japan, Venezuela, Germany, Italy, Guatemala
Resources gold, salt, hydro power
Industries food processing, chemical

products, beverages, paper and paper products, textiles and clothing, plastic goods, electrical equipment
Exports bananas, coffee, sugar, cocoa, textiles, seafood, meat, tropical fruit. Principal market: USA 38.6% (1995)
Imports raw materials for industry and agriculture, consumer goods, machinery and transport equipment, construction materials. Principal source: USA 36.4% (1995)
Arable land 5.6% (1993)
Agricultural products bananas, coffee, sugar cane, maize, potatoes, tobacco, tropical fruit; livestock rearing (cattle and pigs); fishing

Population and society

Population 3,500 ,000 (1996e)
Population growth rate 2.4% (1990–95); 1.8% (2000–05)
Population density (per sq km) 68 (1996e)
Urban population (% of total) 50 (1995)
Age distribution (% of total population) <15 35%, 15–65 60.4%, >65 4.7% (1995)
Ethnic distribution about 97% of the population is of European descent, mostly Spanish, and about 2% is of African origin
Language Spanish (official)
Religion Roman Catholic 90%
Education (compulsory years) 9
Literacy rate 93% (men); 93% (women) (1995e)
Labour force 38% of population: 26% agriculture, 27% industry, 47% services (1990)
Unemployment 4.1% (1993)
Life expectancy 76 (men); 79 (women) (1995–2000)
Child mortality rate (under 5, per 1,000 live births) 16 (1995)
Physicians 1 per 1,136 people (1991)
Hospital beds 1 per 464 people (1990)
TV sets (per 1,000 people) 143 (1995)
Radios (per 1,000 people) 263 (1995)

Transport

Airports international airports: San José (Juan Santamaría), Liberia (Daniel Oduber Quirós); 11 domestic airports as well as charter services to provincial towns and villages); total passenger km: 1,611 mil (1994)
Railroads total length: 950 km/590 mi; total passenger journeys: 335,276

(1994); rail system ceased operating 1995
Roads total road network: 35,600 km/ 22,122 mi, of which 16.7% paved (1995e); passenger cars: 80.1 per 1,000 people (1995e)

Chronology

1502 Visited by Christopher Columbus, who named the area Costa Rica (the rich coast), observing the gold decorations worn by the Native Americans Guaymi.
1506 Colonized by Spain, but fierce guerrilla resistance was mounted by the indigenous population, although many later died from exposure to European diseases.
18th century Settlements began to be established in the fertile central highlands, including San José and Alajuela.
1808 Coffee was introduced from Cuba and soon became the staple crop.
1821 Independence achieved from Spain, and was joined initially with Mexico.
1824 Became part of United Provinces (Federation) of Central America, also embracing El Salvador, Guatemala, Honduras, and Nicaragua.
1838 Became fully independent when it seceded from the federation.
1849–59 Under presidency of Juan Rafuel Mora.
1870–82 Period of military dictatorship.
later 19th century Immigration by Europeans to run and work small coffee farms.
1917–19 Brief dictatorship by Frederico Tinoco.
1940–44 Liberal reforms, including recognition of workers' rights and minimum wages, introduced by President Rafael Angel Calderón Guradia, founder of the United Christian Socialist Party (PUSC).
1948 Brief civil war following a disputed presidential election.
1949 New constitution adopted, giving women and blacks the vote. National army abolished and replaced by civil guard. José Figueres Ferrer, cofounder of the PLN, elected president; he embarked on ambitious socialist programme, nationalizing the banks and introducing a social security system.
1958–73 Mainly conservative administrations.

1974 PLN regained the presidency under Daniel Oduber and returned to socialist policies.
1978 Rodrigo Carazo, conservative, elected president. Sharp deterioration in the state of the economy.
1982 Luis Alberto Monge (PLN) elected president. Harsh austerity programme introduced. Pressure from the USA to abandon neutral stance and condemn Sandinista regime in Nicaragua.
1985 Following border clashes with Nicaraguan Sandinista forces, a US-trained antiguerrilla guard formed.
1986 Oscar Arias Sanchez (PLN) won the presidency on a neutralist platform.
1987 Arias won Nobel Prize for Peace for devising a Central American peace plan signed by leaders of Nicaragua, El Salvador, Guatemala, and Honduras.
1990 Rafael Calderón of the centrist PUSC elected president as economy deteriorated.
1994 José Maria Figueres Olsen (PLN), son of José Figueres Ferrer elected president.

Practical information

Visa requirements UK: visa not required. USA: visa not required
Embassy in the UK Embassy and Consulate, Flat 1, 14 Lancaster Gate, London W2 3LH. Tel: (0171) 706 8844; fax: (0171) 706 8655
British embassy Apartado 815, 11th Floor, Edificio Centro Colón, 1007 San José. Tel (506) 221 5566; fax: (506) 233 9938
Embassy in the USA 2114 S Street NW, Washington, DC 20008. Tel: (202) 234 2945; fax: (202) 265 4795
American embassy : Pavas Road, San José. Tel: 220 3939; fax: 220 2305
Chamber of commerce Cámara de Comercio de Costa Rica, Apartado 1114, Urbanización Tournón, 1000 San José. Tel: (506) 221 0005; fax: (506) 233 7091
Office hours 0800–1200 and 1400–1600 Mon–Fri
Banking hours 0900–1500 Mon–Fri
Time difference GMT –6
Chief tourist attractions nature reserves and national parks make up one-third of the country; Irazú and Poás volcanoes; Orosí valley; colonial ruins at Ujarras; railway through rainforest to Limón; San José (the capital); Pacific beaches; Caribbean beaches at Limón
Major holidays 1 January, 19 March, 11 April, 1 May, 29 June, 25 July, 2, 15 August, 15 September, 12 October, 8, 25 December; variable: Corpus Christi, Good Friday, Holy Saturday, Holy Thursday

Côte d'Ivoire Republic of

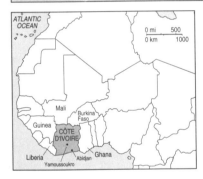

National name *République de la Côte d'Ivoire*
Area 322,463 sq km/124,502 sq mi
Capital Yamoussoukro
Major towns/cities Abidjan, Bouaké, Daloa, Man, Korhogo
Major ports Abidjan, San Pedro
Physical features tropical rainforest (diminishing as exploited) in S; savanna and low mountains in N; coastal plain; Vridi canal, Kossou dam, Monts du Toura

Government

Head of state Henri Konan Bedie from 1993
Head of government Kablan Daniel Duncan from 1993
Political system emergent democratic republic
Administrative divisions 10 regions, comprising 50 departments

Political parties Democratic Party of Côte d'Ivoire (PDCI), nationalist, free enterprise; Rally of Republicans (RDR), nationalist; Ivorian Popular Front (FPI), left of centre; Ivorian Labour Party (PIT), left of centre
Armed forces 8,400 (1995); plus paramilitary forces numbering 7,800
Conscription selective conscription for six months
Death penalty retains the death penalty for ordinary crimes but can be considered abolitionist in practice
Defence spend (% GDP) 1 (1995)
Education spend (% GNP) 5.6 (1994)
Health spend (% GDP) 1.7 (1990)

Economy and resources

Currency franc CFA
GDP ($ US) 6.7 billion (1994)
Real GDP per capita (PPP) ($ US) 1,668 (1994)
GDP growth rate 1.7% (1994); 0.7% (1990–95)
Average annual inflation 11.7% (1995); (2.1% (1985–95)
Foreign debt ($ US) 19 billion (1995)
Trading partners France, Nigeria, Germany, the Netherlands, Italy, USA
Resources petroleum, natural gas, diamonds, gold, nickel, reserves of manganese, iron ore, bauxite
Industries agro-processing (dominated by cocoa, coffee, cotton, palm kernels, pineapples, fish), petroleum refining, tobacco
Exports cocoa beans and products, petroleum products, timber, coffee, cotton, tinned tuna. Principal market: France 16% (1994)
Imports crude petroleum, machinery and vehicles, pharmaceuticals, fresh fish, plastics, cereals. Principal source: France 28% (1994)
Arable land 7.6% (1993)
Agricultural products cocoa (world's largest producer), coffee (world's fifth-largest producer), cotton, rubber, palm kernels, bananas, pineapples, yams, cassava, plantains; fishing; forestry

Population and society

Population 14,015,000 (1996e)
Population growth rate 3.5% (1990–95); 3.2% (2000–05)
Population density (per sq km) 43 (1996e)
Urban population (% of total) 44 (1995)
Age distribution (% of total population) <15 49.1%, 15–65 48.2%, >65 2.6% (1995)
Ethnic distribution no single dominant ethnic group; main groups include the Agni, Baoule, Krou, Senoufou, and Mandingo. There are about 2 million Africans who have settled from neighbouring countries, particularly Burkina Faso. Europeans number about 70,000
Language French (official); over 60 local languages

Religions animist, Muslim (mainly in N), Christian (mainly Roman Catholic in S)
Education (compulsory years) 6
Literacy rate 67% (men); 40% (women) (1995e)
Labour force 37% of population: 60% agriculture, 10% industry, 30% services (1990)
Unemployment 20% (1992e)
Life expectancy 49 (men); 51 (women) (1995–2000)
Child mortality rate (under 5, per 1,000 live births) 150 (1995)
Physicians 1 per 18,000 people (1994e)
Hospital beds 1 per 1,670 people (1994e)
TV sets (per 1,000 people) 62 (1995)
Radios (per 1,000 people) 153 (1995)

Transport

Airports international airports: Abidjan (Port Bouet), Bouaké, Yamoussoukro (San Pedro); domestic services to all major towns; total passenger km: 282 mil (1994)
Railroads total length: 660 km/410 mi; total passenger km: 173 mil (1993)
Roads total road network: 50,160 km/ 31,169 mi, of which 9.6% paved (1995e); passenger cars: 18 per 1,000 people (1995e)

Chronology

1460s Portuguese navigators arrived.
16th century Ivory export trade developed by Europeans and slave trade, though to a lesser extent than neighbouring areas; Krou people migrated from Liberia to the W and Senoufo and Lubi from the N.
late 17th century French coastal trading posts established at Assini and Grand Bassam.
18th–19th centuries Akan peoples, including the Baoulé, immigrated from the E and Malinke from the NW.
1840s French began to conclude commercial treaties with local rulers.
1893 Colony of Côte d'Ivoire created by French, after war with Mandinkas; Baoulé resistance continued until 1917.
1904 Became part of French West Africa; cocoa production encouraged.
1940–42 Under pro-Nazi French Vichy regime.
1946 Became overseas territory in French Union, with own territorial assembly and representation in French parliament: Felix Houphouët-Boigny, a Western-educated Baoulé chief who had formed the Democratic Party (PDCI) to campaign for

autonomy, was elected to the French assembly.
1947 A French-controlled area to the N, which had been added to Côte d'Ivoire in 1932, separated to create new state of Upper Volta (now Burkina Faso).
1950–54 Port of Abidjan constructed.
1958 Achieved internal self-government.
1960 Independence secured, with Houphouët-Boigny as president of a one-party state.
1960s–1980s Political stability, close links maintained with France and economic expansion of 10% per annum, as the country became one of the world's largest coffee producers.
1986 Name changed officially from Ivory Coast to Côte d'Ivoire.
1987–93 Per capita incomes fell by 25% owing to an austerity programme by the International Monetary Fund.
1990 Strikes and student unrest, but Houphouët-Boigny re-elected in a contested presidential election, as multiparty politics re-established.
1993 Houphouët-Boigny died and was succeeded by parliamentary speaker Baoulé Henri Konan Bedie.
1995 Bedie and PDCI re-elected in contest boycotted by opposition.

Practical information

Visa requirements UK: visa required. USA: visa not required for a stay of less than 90 days
Embassy in the UK 2 Upper Belgrave Street, London SW1X 8BJ. Tel: (0171) 235 6991; fax: (0171) 259 5439
British embassy 3rd Floor, Immeuble 'Les Harmonies', Angle boulevard Carde et avenue Dr Jamot, Plateau, Abidjan. Tel: (225) 226850/1/2; fax: (225) 223 221
Embassy in the USA 2424 Massachusetts Avenue NW, Washington, DC 20008. Tel: (202) 797 0300
American embassy 5 rue Jesse Owens, Abidjan. Tel: (225) 210 979; fax: (225) 223 259

Chamber of commerce Chambre de Commerce et d'Industrie de Côte d'Ivoire, 01 BP 1399, 6 avenue Joseph Anoma, Abidjan 01. Tel: (225) 331 600; fax: (225) 323 946
Office hours 0730–1200 and 1430–1730 Mon–Fri; 0800–1200 Sat
Banking hours 0800–1130 and 1430–1630 Mon–Fri
Time difference GMT +/–0
Chief tourist attractions game reserves; lagoons; forests; the lively city of Abidjan
Major holidays 1 January, 1 May, 15 August, 1 November, 7, 24–25, 31 December; variable: Ascension Thursday, Eid-ul-Adha, Good Friday, Easter Monday, Whit Monday, end of Ramadan

Croatia Republic of

National name *Republika Hrvatska*
Area 56,538 sq km/21,829 sq mi
Capital Zagreb
Major towns/cities Osijek, Split, Dubrovnik, Rijeka, Zadar, Pula
Major ports chief port: Rijeka (Fiume); other ports: Zadar, Sibenik, Split, Dubrovnik
Physical features Adriatic coastline with large islands; very mountainous, with part of the Karst region and the Julian and Styrian Alps; some marshland

Government

Head of state Franjo Tudjman from 1990

Head of government Zlatko Matesa from 1995
Political system emergent democracy
Administrative divisions 21 counties
Political parties Croatian Democratic Union (CDU), Christian Democrat, right of centre, nationalist; Croatian Social-Liberal Party (CSLP), centrist; Social Democratic Party of Change (SDP), reform socialist; Croatian Party of Rights (HSP), Croat-oriented, ultranationalist; Croatian Peasant Party (HSS), rural-based; Serbian National Party (SNS), Serb-oriented

Armed forces 105,000 (1995)
Conscription compulsory for ten months
Death penalty abolished 1990
Defence spend (% GDP) 12.6 (1995)
Education spend (% GDP) 3.2 (1994)
Health spend (% GDP) 0.6 (1994)

Economy and resources

Currency kuna
GDP ($ US) 14 billion (1994)
Real GDP per capita (PPP) ($ US)
3,960 (1994)
GDP growth rate 0.8% (1994)
Average annual inflation 107.2%
(1994)
Foreign debt ($ US) 3.7 billion (1995)
Trading partners Germany, Italy,
Slovenia, Austria, Iran, former USSR,
Bosnia-Herzegovina
Resources petroleum, natural gas, coal,
lignite, bauxite, iron ore, salt
Industries food processing, textiles,
chemicals, ship-building, metal
processing, construction materials,
Tourism was virtually eliminated during
hostilities, but a revival began 1992
Exports machinery and transport
equipment, chemicals, foodstuffs,
miscellaneous manufactured items
(mainly clothing). Principal market:
Germany 22.1% (1994)
Imports machinery and transport
equipment, basic manufactures, mineral
fuels, miscellaneous manufactured
articles. Principal source: Germany
21.2% (1994)
Arable land 43% (1993)
Agricultural products wheat, maize,
potatoes, plums, sugar beet; livestock
rearing (cattle and pigs); dairy products

Population and society

Population 4,501,000 (1996e)
Population growth rate −0.1%
(1990–95); −0.1% (2000–05)
Population density (per sq km) 80
(1996e)
Urban population (% of total) 64
(1995)
Age distribution (% of total population)
<15 19.1%, 15–65 68.2%, >65 12.8%
(1995)
Ethnic distribution in 1991, 77% of the
population were ethnic Croats, 12% were
ethnic Serbs, and 1% were Slovenes.
Since the civil war began 1992, more
than 300,000 Croats have been
displaced from Serbian enclaves within
the republic, and there are an estimated
500,000 refugees from Bosnia in the
republic. Serbs are most thickly settled in

areas bordering Bosnia-Herzegovina,
and in Slavonia, although more than
150,000 fled from Krajina to Bosnia-
Herzegovina and Serbia following the
region's recapture by the Croatian army
in August 1995
Language Croatian variant of Serbo-
Croatian (official); Serbian variant of
Serbo-Croatian also widely spoken,
particularly in border areas in E
Religion Roman Catholic (Croats);
Orthodox Christian (Serbs)
Education (compulsory years) 8
Literacy rate 97% (men); 97% (women)
(1995e)
Labour force 5.3% agriculture, 59.4%
industry, 35.3% services (1992)
Unemployment 13% (1994e)
Life expectancy 68 (men); 77 (women)
(1995–2000)
Child mortality rate (under 5, per 1,000
live births) 14 (1995)
Physicians 1 per 518 people (1993e)
Hospital beds 1 per 167 people
(1993e)
TV sets (per 1,000 people) 255 (1995)
Radios (per 1,000 people) 266 (1995)

Transport

Airports international airports: Zagreb
(Pleso), Dubrovnik; three domestic
airports; total passenger km: 405 mil
(1994)
Railroads total length: 2,452 km/1,524
mi; total passenger km: 962 mil (1994)
Roads total road network: 26,929 km/
16,734 mi, of which 81.5% paved
(1995); passenger cars: 149 per 1,000
people (1995)

Chronology

early centuries AD Part of Roman
region of Pannonia.
AD 395 On division of Roman Empire,
stayed in W half, along with Slovenia
and Bosnia.
7th century Settled by Carpathian
Croats, from NE; Christianity adopted.
924 Formed by Tomislav into
independent kingdom, which
incorporated Bosnia from 10th century.
12th–19th centuries Enjoyed autonomy
under Hungarian crown, following
dynastic union in 1102.
1526–1699 Slavonia, in E, held by
Ottoman Turks, while Serbs were invited
by Austria to settle along the border with
Ottoman-ruled Bosnia, in Vojna Krajina
(military frontier).
1797–1815 Dalmatia, in W, ruled by
France.

19th century Part of Austro-Hungarian
Habsburg Empire.
1918 On dissolution of Habsburg Empire,
joined Serbia, Slovenia, and Montenegro
in 'Kingdom of Serbs, Croats, and
Slovenes', under Serbian Karageorgevic
dynasty.
1929 The Kingdom became Yugoslavia.
Croatia continued its campaign for
autonomy.
1930s Ustasa, a Croat terrorist
organization, began a campaign against
dominance of Yugoslavia by the non-
Catholic Serbs.
1941–44 Following German invasion, a
'Greater Croatia' Nazi puppet state,
including most of Bosnia and W Serbia,
formed under Ustasa leader, Ante
Pavelic; more than half a million Serbs,
Jews, and members of the Romany
community were massacred in
extermination camps.
1945 Became constituent republic of
Yugoslavia Socialist Federation after
communist partisans, led by Croat
Marshal Tito, overthrew Pavelic.
1970s Separatist demands resurfaced,
provoking a crackdown.
late 1980s Spiralling inflation and a
deterioration in living standards sparked
industrial unrest and a rise in nationalist
sentiment, which affected the local
communist party.
1989 Formation of opposition parties
permitted.
1990 Communists defeated by
conservative nationalist CDU led by ex-
Partisan Franjo Tudjman in first free
election since 1938. 'Sovereignty'
declared.
1991 Serb-dominated region of Krajina in
SW announced secession from Croatia.
Croatia declared independence, leading
to military conflict with Serbia, and
internal civil war ensued.
1992 United Nations (UN) peace accord
accepted; independence recognized by
European Community and USA; Croatia
entered UN. UN peacekeeping force
stationed in Croatia. Tudjman directly
elected president.
1993 Government offensive launched to
retake parts of Serb-held Krajina,
violating 1992 UN peace accord.
1994 Accord with Muslims and ethnic
Croats within Bosnia, to the E, to link
recently formed Muslim–Croat federation
with Croatia.
1995 Serb-held W Slavonia and Krajina
captured by government forces; mass
exodus of Croatian Serbs. Offensive
extended into Bosnia-Herzegovina to halt

Bosnian Serb assault on Bihac in W Bosnia. Serbia agreed to cede control of E Slavonia to Croatia over a two-year period.

1996 Diplomatic relations between Croatia and Yugoslavia restored. Croatia entered Council of Europe.
1997 Opposition successes in local

elections. Tudjman re-elected despite failing health. Last Serb enclave in E Slavonia reintegrated into Croatia.

Practical information

Visa requirements UK: visa not required. USA: visa required
Embassy in the UK 18–21 Jermyn Street, London SW1Y 6HP. Tel: (0171) 434 2946; fax: (0171) 434 2953
British embassy PO Box 454, 2nd Floor, Astra Tower, Tratinska, 4100 Zagreb. Tel: (1) 334 245; fax: (1) 338 893
Embassy in the USA 2343 Massachusetts Avenue NW, Washington, DC 20008. Tel: (202) 588 5899; fax: (202) 588 8936
American embassy Andrije Hebranga 2, Zagreb. Tel: (41) 455 5500; fax: (41) 455 8585

Chamber of commerce Croatian Chamber of Commerce, Trg. Ruzveltov 1, 41000 Zagreb. Tel: (1) 453 422; fax: (1) 448 618
Office hours 0800–1600 Mon–Fri
Banking hours 0700–1500 Mon–Fri; 0800–1400 Sat
Time difference GMT +1
Chief tourist attractions Adriatic coast with 1,185 islands. Owing to civil conflict which began 1991, tourist activity has been greatly reduced; historic cities, notably Dubrovnik, have been severely damaged
Major holidays 1, 6 January, 1, 30 May, 22 June, 15 August, 1 November, 25–26 December; variable: Good Friday, Easter Monday

Cuba Republic of

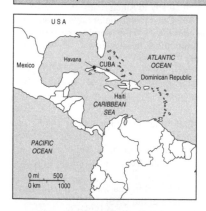

National name *República de Cuba*
Area 110,860 sq km/42,803 sq mi
Capital Havana
Major towns/cities Santiago de Cuba, Camagüey, Holguín, Guantánamo, Santa Clara, Bayamo, Cienfuegos
Physical features comprises Cuba and smaller islands including Isle of Youth; low hills; Sierra Maestra mountains in SE; Cuba has 3,380 km/2,100 mi of coastline, with deep bays, sandy beaches, coral islands and reefs

Government

Head of state and government Fidel Castro Ruz from 1959
Political system communist republic
Administrative divisions 14 provinces and the special municipality of the Isle of Youth (Isla de la Juventud)
Political party Communist Party of Cuba (PCC), Marxist-Leninist
Armed forces 105,000 (1995)
Conscription compulsory for two years

Death penalty retained and used for ordinary crimes
Defence spend (% GDP) 2.8 (1995)
Education spend (% GNP) 6.6 (1993–94)
Health spend (% GDP) 3.4 (1990)

Economy and resources

Currency Cuban peso
GDP ($ US) 11.9 billion (1994)
Real GDP per capita (PPP) ($ US) 3,000 (1994)
GDP growth rate 0.7% (1994)
Average annual inflation 50% (1994e)
Foreign debt ($ US) 9.1 billion (1995); another $20 billion owed to Russia (1995)
Trading partners Canada, Spain, Russia, China, Mexico, Bulgaria
Resources iron ore, copper, chromite, gold, manganese, nickel, cobalt, silver, salt
Industries mining, textiles and footwear, cigarettes, cement, food processing (sugar and its by-products), fertilizers
Exports sugar, minerals, tobacco, citrus fruits, fish products. Principal market: Canada 15.8% (1995e)
Imports mineral fuels, machinery and transport equipment, foodstuffs, beverages. Principal source: Spain 17.3% (1995e)
Arable land 23.5% (1993)
Agricultural products sugar cane (world's fourth-largest producer of sugar), tobacco, rice, citrus fruits, plantains, bananas; forestry; fishing

Population and society

Population 11,018,000 (1996e)

Population growth rate 0.8% (1990–95); 0.5% (2000–05)
Population density (per sq km) 99 (1996e)
Urban population (% of total) 76 (1995)
Age distribution (% of total population) <15 22.9%, 15–65 68.2%, >65 8.9% (1995)
Ethnic distribution predominantly of mixed Spanish and African or Spanish and Native American origin
Language Spanish
Religions Roman Catholic; also Episcopalians and Methodists
Education (compulsory years) 6
Literacy rate 95% (men); 93% (women) (1995e)
Labour force 45% of population: 18% agriculture, 30% industry, 51% services (1990)
Unemployment 17.3% (1994)
Life expectancy 74 (men); 78 (women) (1995–2000)
Child mortality rate (under 5, per 1,000 live births) 10 (1995)
Physicians 1 per 212 people (1993e)
Hospital beds 1 per 165 people (1993e)
TV sets (per 1,000 people) 228 (1995)
Radios (per 1,000 people) 351 (1995)

Transport

Airports international airports: Havana, Santiago de Cuba, Holguín, Camagüey, Varadero; 11 domestic airports; total passenger km: 1,556 mil (1994)
Railroads total length: 4,807 km/ 2,987 mi; total passenger km: 2,346 mil (1994)

Roads total road network: 27,100 km/ 16,840 mi, of which 55.8% paved (1995e); passenger cars: 1.9 per 1,000 people (1993e)

Chronology

3rd century AD The Ciboney, Cuba's earliest known inhabitants, were dislodged by the immigration of Taino, Arawak Indians from Venezuela.

1492 Christopher Columbus landed in Cuba and claimed it for Spain.

1511 Spanish settlement established at Baracoa by Diego Velazquez.

1523 Decline of Native American population and rise of sugar plantations led to import of slaves from Africa.

mid-19th century Cuba produced one-third of the world's sugar.

1868–78 Unsuccessful first war for independence from Spain.

1886 Slavery was abolished.

1895–98 Further uprising against Spanish rule, led by José Martí, who died in combat; 200,000 soldiers deployed by Spain.

1898 USA defeated Spain in Spanish-American War; Spain gave up all claims to Cuba, which was ceded to the USA.

1901 Cuba achieved independence; Tomás Estrada Palma became first president of the Republic of Cuba.

1906–09 Brief period of US administration after Estrada resigned in the face of an armed rebellion by political opponents.

1909 The liberal José Miguel Gomez became president, but soon became tarred by corruption.

1924 Gerado Machado, an admirer of the Italian fascist leader Benito Mussolini, established a brutal dictatorship which lasted nine years.

1925 Socialist Party founded, from which the Communist Party later developed.

1933 Army sergeant Fulgencio Batista seized power.

1934 USA abandoned its right to intervene in Cuba's internal affairs.

1944 Batista retired and was succeeded by the civilian Ramon Gray San Martin.

1952 Batista seized power again to begin an oppressive and corrupt regime.

1953 Fidel Castro Ruz led an unsuccessful coup against Batista on the 100th anniversary of the birth of Martí.

1956 Second unsuccessful coup by Castro.

1959 Batista overthrown by Castro and his 9,000-strong guerrilla army. Constitution of 1940 replaced by a 'Fundamental Law', making Castro prime minister, his brother Raúl Castro his deputy, and Argentinian-born Ernesto 'Che' Guevara third in command.

1960 All US businesses in Cuba appropriated without compensation; USA broke off diplomatic relations.

1961 USA sponsored an unsuccessful invasion by Cuban exiles at the Bay of Pigs. Castro announced that Cuba had become a communist state, with a Marxist-Leninist programme of economic development, and became allied with the USSR.

1962 Cuban missile crisis: Cuba was expelled from the Organization of American States. Castro responded by tightening relations with the USSR, which installed nuclear missiles in Cuba (subsequently removed at US insistence). US trade embargo imposed.

1965 Cuba's sole political party renamed Cuban Communist Party (PCC). With Soviet help, Cuba began to make considerable economic and social progress.

1972 Cuba became a full member of the Moscow-based Council for Mutual Economic Assistance (COMECON).

1976 New socialist constitution approved; Castro elected president.

1976–81 Castro became involved in extensive international commitments, sending troops as Soviet surrogates, particularly to Africa.

1982 Cuba joined other Latin American countries in giving moral support to Argentina in its dispute with Britain over the Falklands.

1984 Castro tried to improve US-Cuban relations by discussing exchange of US prisoners in Cuba for Cuban 'undesirables' in the USA.

1988 Peace accord with South Africa signed, agreeing to withdrawal of Cuban troops from Angola, as part of a reduction in Cuba's overseas military activities.

1991 Soviet troops withdrawn with the collapse of the USSR.

1993 US trade embargo tightened; market-oriented reforms introduced in face of deteriorating economy.

1994 Mass refugee exodus; US policy on Cuban asylum seekers revised.

Practical information

Visa requirements UK: visa required. USA: visa required
Embassy in the UK 167 High Holborn, London WC1V 6PA. Tel: (0171) 240 2488; fax: (0171) 836 2602
British embassy Calle 34, 708 Miramar, Havana. Tel: (7) 331 771; fax: (7) 338 104
Embassy in the USA none. Cuba has an Interests Section in the Swiss embassy; address: Cuban Interests Section, Swiss Embassy, 2639 16th Street NW, Washington, DC 20009. Tel: (202) 797 8518–8520
American embassy none. The USA has an Interests Section in the Swiss embassy; address: USINT, Swiss Embassy, Calzada Entre L Y M, Vedado Seccion, Havana. Tel: (7) 333 551–559, (7) 333 543–547 (operator assistance required); fax: (7) 333 700; the protecting power in Cuba is Switzerland

Chamber of commerce Cámara de Comercio de la República de Cuba, Calle 21, No. 661/701, esq Calle A, Apartado 4237, Vedado, Havana. Tel: (7) 303 356; fax: (7) 333 042
Office hours 0830–1230 and 1330–1630 Mon–Fri; some offices also open 0800–1700 on alternate Saturdays
Banking hours 0830–1200 and 1330–1500 Mon–Fri; 0830–1030 Sat
Time difference GMT –5
Chief tourist attractions sandy beaches; Sierra Maestra range, which encircles the port of Santiago; mountain forest of pine and mahogany; Havana city centre, a UN World Heritage site, with colonial fortresses and castles; Santiago, the former capital, with Museum of Colonial Art and Festival de Carib (April)
Major holidays 1 January, 1 May, 25–26 July, 10 October

Cyprus Greek Republic of Cyprus in S, and Turkish Republic of Northern Cyprus in N

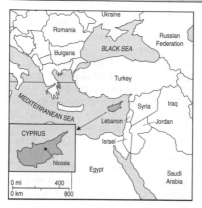

National name *Kypriakí Dimokratía* (S), and *Kibris Cumhuriyeti* (N)
Area 9,251 sq km/3,571 sq mi (3,335 sq km/ 1,287 sq mi is Turkish-occupied)
Capital Nicosia (divided between Greek and Turkish Cypriots)
Major towns/cities Morphou, Limassol, Larnaca, Famagusta, Paphos
Major ports Limassol, Larnaca, and Paphos (Greek); Kyrenia and Famagusta (Turkish)
Physical features central plain between two E–W mountain ranges

Government

Head of state and government Glafkos Clerides (Greek) from 1993, Rauf Denktas (Turkish) from 1976
Political system democratic divided republic
Administrative divisions six districts
Political parties *Greek zone*: Democratic Party (DEKO), federalist, centre left; Progressive Party of the Working People (AKEL), socialist; Democratic Rally (DISY), centrist; Socialist Party–National Democratic Union of Cyprus (SK–EDEK), socialist; *Turkish zone*: National Unity Party (NUP), Communal Liberation Party (CLP), Republican Turkish Party (RTP), New British Party (NBP)
Armed forces National Guard of 10,000 (1995); Turkish Republic of Northern Cyprus (TRNC) 4,000, plus 26,000 reserves (1995)
Conscription is for 26 months
Death penalty laws provide for the death penalty only for exceptional crimes such as under military law or crimes committed in exceptional circumstances such as wartime

Defence spend (% GDP) 4.5 (1995)
Education spend (% GNP) 4 (1992); N/A (1993–94)
Health spend (% GDP) 2.1 (1994)

Economy and resources

Currency Cyprus pound and Turkish lira
GDP ($ US) 7.19 billion (1994)
Real GDP per capita (PPP) ($ US) 13,071 (1994)
GDP growth rate 5.1% (1994)
Average annual inflation 4.9% (1994); 4.3% (1985–95e)
Foreign debt ($ US) 2.1 billion (1993)
Trading partners government-controlled area: UK, USA, Arab countries, France, Germany, Greece, Japan, Italy; TRNC area: Turkey, UK, other EU countries
Resources copper precipitates, beutonite, umber and other ochres
Industries food processing, beverages, textiles, clothing and leather, chemicals and chemical petroleum, metal products, wood and wood products, tourism, financial services (24 offshore banking units in December 1994)
Exports government-controlled area: clothing, potatoes, pharmaceutical products. Principal market: UK 27.1% (1994); TRNC area: citrus fruits, industrial products. Principal market: UK 46.3% (1994)
Imports government-controlled area: mineral fuels, textiles, vehicles, metals, foodstuffs, tobacco. Principal source: UK 11.4% (1994); TRNC area: basic manufactures, machinery and transport equipment, food and live animals. Principal source: Turkey 45.1% (1994)
Arable land 40% (1994)
Agricultural products government-controlled area: barley, potatoes, grapes, citrus fruit, olives; TRNC area: wheat, barley, potatoes, citrus fruit, olives; livestock rearing (sheep and goats)

Population and society

Population 756,800 (1996e)
Population growth rate 1.1% (1990–95)
Population density (per sq km) 82 (1996e)
Urban population (% of total) 56 (1994)
Age distribution (% of total population) <15 26%, 15–65 64%, >65 10% (1994)

Ethnic distribution about 80% of the population is of Greek origin, while about 18% are of Turkish descent, and live in the northern part of the island within the self-styled Turkish Republic of Northern Cyprus
Languages Greek and Turkish (official), English
Religions Greek Orthodox, Sunni Muslim
Education (compulsory years) 9
Literacy rate 94% (men); 94% (women) (1995e)
Labour force 48% of population: 14% agriculture, 30% industry, 56% services (1990)
Unemployment government-controlled area: 2.5% (1994)
Life expectancy 76 (men); 80 (women) (1995–2000)
Child mortality rate (under 5, per 1,000 live births) 10 (1995)
Physicians 1 per 1,000 people (1994e)
Hospital beds 1 per 600 people (1994e)
TV sets (per 1,000 people) 322 (1995)
Radios (per 1,000 people) 309 (1995)

Transport

Airports international airports: Nicosia (Larnaca), Paphos; total passenger km: 2,810 mil (1994)
Railroads none
Roads total road network: 10,150 km/ 6,307 mi, of which 57% paved (1995); passenger cars: 340.5 per 1,000 people (1995)

Chronology

14th–11th centuries BC Colonized by Myceneans and Achaeans from Greece.
9th century BC Phoenicans settled in Cyprus.
7th century BC Several Cypriot kingdoms flourished under Assyrian influence.
414–374 BC Under Evagoras of Salamis (in eastern Cyprus) the island's ten city kingdoms were united into one state and Greek culture, including the Greek alphabet, was promoted.
333–58 BC Became part of the Greek Hellenistic and then, from 294 BC, the Egypt-based Ptolemaic empire.

58 BC Cyprus was annexed by the Roman Empire.

AD 45 Christianity introduced.

AD 395 When the Roman Empire divided, Cyprus was allotted to the Byzantine Empire.

7th–10th centuries Byzantines and Muslim Arabs fought for control of Cyprus.

1191 Richard I of England, 'the Lionheart', conquered Cyprus as a base for Crusades; he later sold it to a French noble, Guy de Lusignan, who established a feudal monarchy which ruled for three centuries.

1498 Venetian Republic took control of Cyprus.

1571 Conquered by Ottoman Turks, who introduced Turkish Muslim settlers, but permitted Christianity to continue in rural areas.

1821–33 Period of unrest, following execution of popular Greek Orthodox archbishop Kyprianos.

1878 Anglo-Turkish Convention: Turkey ceded Cyprus to British administration in return for defensive alliance.

1914 Formally annexed by Britain after Turkey entered World War I as a Central Power.

1915 Greece rejected an offer of Cyprus in return for entry into World War I on Allied side.

1925 Cyprus became a crown colony.

1931 Greek Cypriots rioted in support of demand for union with Greece (*enosis*); legislative council suspended.

1948 Greek Cypriots rejected new constitution because it did not offer links with Greece.

1951 Britain rejected Greek proposals for *enosis*.

1955 National Organization of Cypriot Fighters (EOKA), led by George Grivas, began terrorist campaign for *enosis*.

1956 British authorities deported Archbishop Makarios, head of the Cypriot Orthodox Church, for encouraging EOKA.

1958 Britain proposed autonomy for Greek and Turkish Cypriot communities under British sovereignty; plan accepted by Turks, rejected by Greeks; violence increased.

1959 Britain, Greece, and Turkey agreed to Cypriot independence, with partition and *enosis* both ruled out.

1960 Cyprus became an independent republic with Archbishop Makarios as president; Britain retained two military bases.

1963 Makarios proposed major constitutional reforms; Turkish Cypriots withdrew from government and formed separate enclaves; communal fighting broke out.

1964 United Nations (UN) peacekeeping force installed.

1968 Intercommunal talks made no progress; Turkish Cypriots demanded federalism; Greek Cypriots insisted on unitary state.

1974 Coup by Greek officers in Cypriot National Guard installed Nikos Sampson as president; Turkey, fearing *enosis,* invaded northern Cyprus; Greek Cypriot military regime collapsed; President Makarios restored.

1975 Northern Cyprus declared itself the Turkish Federated State of Cyprus, with Rauf Denktas as president.

1977 Makarios died; succeeded by Spyros Kyprianou.

1983 Denktas proclaimed independent Turkish Republic of Cyprus; recognized only by Turkey.

1985 Summit meeting between Kyprianou and Denktas failed to reach agreement; further peace talks failed 1989 and 1992.

1988 Kyprianou succeeded as Greek Cypriot president by Georgios Vassiliou.

1993 Glafkos Clerides (DISY) replaced Vassiliou.

1994 European Court of Justice declared trade with northern Cyprus illegal.

1996 Further peace talks jeopardized by boundary killing of Turkish Cypriot soldier; mounting tension between N and S.

1997 Decision to purchase Russian anti-aircraft missiles created tension. Richard Holbrooke appointed UN envoy to negotiate peace in Cyprus, but talks later collapsed.

Practical information

Visa requirements UK: visa not required. USA: visa not required

Embassy in the UK 93 Park Street, London W1Y 4ET. Tel: (0171) 499 8272; fax: (0171) 491 0691

British embassy British High Commission, PO Box 1978, Alexander Pallis Street, Nicosia. Tel: (2) 473 131/7; fax: (2) 367 198

Embassy in the USA 2211 R Street NW, Washington, DC 20008. Tel: (202) 462 5772 (The representative of the Turkish area is at 1667 K Street NW, Washington, DC. Tel: (202) 887 6198.)

American embassy corner of Metochiou and Ploutarchou streets, Engomi, Nicosia. Tel: (2) 476 100; fax: (2) 465 944

Chamber of commerce Cyprus Chamber of Commerce and Industry, PO Box 1455, 38 Grivas Dhigenis Avenue, Nicosia. Tel: (2) 449 500; fax: (2) 449 048

Office hours all offices have half-day closing on Wed, otherwise 0800–1300 and 1600–1900 Mon–Fri (summer); 0800–1300 and 1500–1800 Mon–Fri (winter)

Banking hours generally 0815–1230 Mon–Fri; in tourist areas also 1630–1830 (summer, except Tue) and 1530–1730 (winter)

Time difference GMT +2

Chief tourist attractions sandy beaches; forested mountains; winter skiing; archaeological and historic sites; the old city of Nicosia, with its Venetian walls and cathedral (International State Fair and Nicosia Art Festival in May); Limassol, with its 14th-century castle (Spring Carnival, arts festival (July), wine festival (September)

Major holidays 1, 6 January, 25 March, 1 May, 28–29 October, 25–26 December; variable: Eid-ul-Adha, Good Friday, Easter Monday, end of Ramadan, Holy Saturday, Prophet's Birthday

Czech Republic

National name *Česká Republika*
Area 78,864 sq km/30,449 sq mi
Capital Prague
Major towns/cities Brno, Ostrava, Olomouc, Liberec, Plzeň, Ustí nad Labem, Hradec Králové
Physical features mountainous; rivers: Morava, Labe (Elbe), Vltava (Moldau)

Government

Head of state Václav Havel from 1993
Head of government Václav Klaus from 1993
Political system emergent democracy
Administrative divisions eight regions
Political parties Civic Democratic Party (CDP), right of centre, free-market; Civic Democratic Alliance (CDA), right of centre, free-market; Civic Movement (CM), liberal, left of centre; Communist Party of Bohemia and Moravia (KSCM), reform socialist; Agrarian Party, centrist, rural-based; Liberal National Social Party (LNSP; formerly the Czech Socialist Party (SP)), reform socialist; Czech Social Democratic Party (CSDP), moderate left of centre; Christian Democratic Union–Czech People's Party (CDU–CPP), centre right; Movement for Autonomous Democracy of Moravia and Silesia (MADMS), Moravian and Silesian-based, separatist; Czech Republican Party, far right
Armed forces 86,000 (1995)
Conscription compulsory for 12 months
Death penalty abolished 1990
Defence spend (% GDP) 2.8 (1995)
Education spend (% GNP) 5.9 (1993–94)
Health spend (% GDP) 5.9 (1991)

Economy and resources

Currency koruna (based on Czechoslovak koruna)
GDP ($ US) 36 billion (1994)
Real GDP per capita (PPP) ($ US) 9,201 (1994)
GDP growth rate 4.8% (1995); –2.6% (1990–95)
Average annual inflation 9.1% (1995); 12.2% (1985–95e)
Foreign debt ($ US) 16.5 billion (1995)
Trading partners EU countries, Slovak Republic, Poland, Russia, USA
Resources coal, lignite
Industries steel, cement, motor cars, textiles, bicycles, beer, trucks and tractors
Exports basic manufactures, machinery and transport equipment, miscellaneous manufactured articles, beer. Principal market: EU 37.4% (1995)
Imports machinery and transport equipment, basic manufactures, chemicals and chemical products, mineral fuels. Principal source: EU 34.7% (1995)
Arable land 43% (1993)
Agricultural products wheat, barley, sugar beet, potatoes, hops; livestock rearing (cattle, pigs, and poultry); dairy farming

Population and society

Population 10,251,000 (1996e)
Population growth rate 0% (1990–95); –0.1% (2000–05)
Population density (per sq km) 130 (1996e)
Urban population (% of total) 65 (1995)
Age distribution (% of total population) <15 19.4%, 15–65 68.1%, >65 12.5% (1995)
Ethnic distribution predominantly Western Slav Czechs; there is also a sizeable Slovak minority and small Polish, German, and Hungarian minorities
Language Czech (official)
Religions Roman Catholic, Hussite, Presbyterian Evangelical Church of Czech Brethren, Orthodox
Education (compulsory years) 9
Literacy rate 99% (men); 99% (women) (1995e)
Labour force 6.9% agriculture, 44.6% industry, 48.6% services (1993)
Unemployment 3% (1995)
Life expectancy 68 (men); 75 (women) (1995–2000)
Child mortality rate (under 5, per 1,000 live births) 10 (1995)
Physicians 1 per 323 people (1992)
Hospital beds 1 per 121 people (1992)
TV sets (per 1,000 people) 482 (1995)
Radios (per 1,000 people) 638 (1995)

Transport

Airports international airports: Prague (Ruzyně), Brno (Cernovice), Ostrava (International and Mosnov – domestic), Karlovy Vary; total passenger km: 1,976 mil (1994)
Railroads total length: 9,440 km/5,866 mi; total passenger km: 8,481 mil (1994)
Roads total road network: 124,770 km/77,532 mi, of which 13.4% paved (1995); passenger cars: 302 per 1,000 people (1995)

Chronology

5th century Settled by West Slavs.
8th century Part of Charlemagne's Holy Roman Empire.
9th century Kingdom of Greater Moravia, centred around the eastern part of what is now the Czech Republic, founded by the Slavic prince Sviatopluk; Christianity adopted.
906 Moravia conquered by the Magyars (Hungarians).
995 Independent state of Bohemia in the NW, centred around Prague, formed under the Premysl rulers, who had broken away from Moravia; became kingdom in 12th century.
1029 Moravia became a fief of Bohemia.
1355 King Charles IV of Bohemia became Holy Roman emperor.
early 15th century Nationalistic Hussite religion, opposed to German and papal influence, founded in Bohemia by John Huss.
1526 Bohemia came under the control of the Austrian Catholic Habsburgs.
1618 Hussite revolt precipitated the Thirty Years' War, which resulted in the Bohemians' defeat, more direct rule by the Habsburgs, and re-Catholicization.
1867 With creation of dual Austro-Hungarian monarchy, Bohemia was reduced to a province of Austria, leading to a growth in national consciousness.
1918 Austro-Hungarian Empire dismembered; Czechs joined Slovaks in forming Czechoslovakia as independent democratic nation, with Tomas Masaryk president.
1938 Under the Munich Agreement, Czechoslovakia was forced to surrender

the Sudeten German districts in the N to Germany.

1939 The remainder of Czechoslovakia annexed by Germany, Bohemia-Moravia being administered as a 'protectorate'; President Eduard Beneš set up a government-in-exile in London; liquidation campaigns against intelligentsia.

1945 Liberated by Soviet and American troops; communist-dominated government of national unity formed under Beneš; 2 million Sudeten Germans expelled.

1948 Beneš ousted; communists assumed full control under a Soviet-style single-party constitution.

1950s Political opponents purged; nationalization of industries.

1968 'Prague Spring' political liberalization programme, instituted by Communist Party leader Alexander Dubček, crushed by invasion of Warsaw Pact forces to restore the 'orthodox line'.

1969 New federal constitution, creating a separate Czech Socialist Republic;

Gustáv Husák became Communist Party leader.

1977 Formation of the 'Charter '77' human-rights group by intellectuals, including the playwright Václav Havel, encouraged a crackdown against dissidents.

1987 Reformist Miloš Jakeš replaced Husák as communist leader, and introduced a *prestvaba* ('restructuring') reform programme on the Soviet leader Mikhail Gorbachev's *perestroika* model.

1989 Major prodemocracy demonstrations in Prague; new political parties formed and legalized, including Czech-based Civic Forum under Havel; Communist Party stripped of powers. New 'grand coalition' government formed; Havel appointed state president. Amnesty granted to 22,000 prisoners.

1990 Multiparty elections won by Civic Forum.

1991 Civic Forum split into centre-right Civic Democratic Party (CDP) and centre-left Civic Movement (CM); evidence of increasing Czech and Slovak separatism.

1992 Václav Klaus, leader of the Czech-based CDP, became prime minister; Havel resigned following nationalist Slovak gains in assembly elections. Creation of separate Czech and Slovak states and a customs union agreed. Market-centred economic-reform programme launched, including mass privatizations.

1993 Czech Republic became sovereign state within the United Nations, with Klaus as prime minister. Havel elected president.

1994 Joined NATO's 'partnership for peace' programme. Strong economic growth registered.

1996 Applied for EU membership. Klaus-led coalition lost its parliamentary majority after elections but remained in power. Ruling coalition successful in upper-house elections.

1997 Former communist leader Miloš Jakeš charged with treason. Ruling coalition survived a currency crisis and criticism by President Havel. Czech Republic invited to join NATO and to begin EU membership negotiations.

Practical information

Visa requirements UK: visa not required. USA: visa not required
Embassy in the UK 26–30 Kensington Palace Gardens, London W8 4QY. Tel: (0171) 243 1115; fax: (0171) 727 9654
British embassy Thunovská 14, 11 800 Prague 7. Tel: (2) 2451 0439; fax: (2) 539 927
Embassy in the USA 3900 Spring of Freedom Street NW, Washington, DC 20008. Tel: (202) 363 6315, 6316; fax: (202) 966 8540
American embassy Trziste 15, 11801 Prague 1.

Tel: (2) 2451 0847; fax: (2) 2451 1001
Chamber of commerce Czech Chamber of Commerce and Industry, Argentinská 38, 170 05 Prague 7. Tel: (2) 6679 4880; fax: (2) 875 348
Office hours 0800–1600 Mon–Fri
Banking hours generally 0800–1800 Mon–Fri
Time difference GMT +1
Chief tourist attractions scenery; winter-sports facilities; historic towns, including Prague, Karlovy Vary, Olomouc, and Cesky; castles and cathedrals; numerous resorts and spas
Major holidays 1 January, 1 May, 5–6, July, 28 October, 24–26 December; variable: Easter Monday

---

Denmark Kingdom of

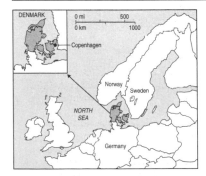

National name *Kongeriget Danmark*
Area 43,075 sq km/16,631 sq mi

Capital Copenhagen
Major towns/cities Århus, Odense, Ålborg, Esbjerg, Randers
Major ports Århus, Odense, Ålborg, Esbjerg
Physical features comprises the Jutland peninsula and about 500 islands (100 inhabited) including Bornholm in the Baltic Sea; the land is flat and cultivated; sand dunes and lagoons on the W coast and long inlets on the E; the main island is Sjælland (Zealand), where most of Copenhagen is located (the rest is on the island of Amager)
Territories the dependencies of Faroe Islands and Greenland

Government

Head of state Queen Margrethe II from 1972
Head of government Poul Nyrup Rasmussen from 1993
Political system liberal democracy
Administrative divisions 14 counties, one city and one borough
Political parties Social Democrats (SD), left of centre; Conservative People's Party (KF), moderate centre right; Liberal Party (V), centre left; Socialist People's Party (SF), moderate left wing; Radical Liberals (RV), radical internationalist, left of centre; Centre Democrats (CD),

moderate centrist; Progress Party (FP), radical antibureaucratic; Christian People's Party (KrF), interdenominational, family values
Armed forces 33,000; 72,200 reservists and volunteer Home Guard of 65,200 (1995)
Conscription 9–12 months (27 months for some ranks)
Death penalty abolished 1978
Defence spend (% GDP) 1.8 (1995)
Education spend (% GNP) 8.5 (1993–94)
Health spend (% GDP) 5.5 (1993)

Economy and resources

Currency Danish krone
GDP ($ US) 174.2 billion (1996)
Real GDP per capita (PPP) ($ US) 22,314 (1996)
GDP growth rate 2.5% (1996); 2% (1990–95)
Average annual inflation 2.3% (1996); 2.8% (1985–95)
Trading partners EU (principally Germany, Sweden, and UK), Norway, USA
Resources crude petroleum, natural gas, salt, limestone
Industries mining, food processing, fisheries, machinery, textiles, furniture, electronic goods and transport equipment, chemicals and pharmaceuticals, printing and publishing
Exports pig meat and pork products, other food products, fish, industrial machinery, chemicals, transport equipment. Principal market: Germany 35.8% (1995)
Imports food and live animals, machinery, transport equipment, iron, steel, electronics, petroleum, cereals, paper. Principal source: Germany 32.4% (1995)
Arable land 58.9% (1993)
Agricultural products wheat, rye, barley, oats, potatoes, sugar beet, dairy products; livestock production (pigs) and dairy products; fishing

Population and society

Population 5,237,000 (1996e)
Population growth rate 0.2% (1990–95); 0% (2000–05)
Population density (per sq km) 122 (1996e)
Urban population (% of total) 85 (1995)
Age distribution (% of total population) <17.2%, 15–65 67.6%, >65 15.2% (1995)
Ethnic distribution all Danes are part of the Scandinavian ethnic group

Languages Danish (official); there is a German-speaking minority
Religion Lutheran 97%
Education (compulsory years) 9
Literacy rate 99% (men); 99% (women) (1995e)
Labour force 57% of population: 6% agriculture, 28% industry, 66% services (1990)
Unemployment 6.9% (1996)
Life expectancy 73 (men); 79 (women) (1995–2000)
Child mortality rate (under 5, per 1,000 live births) 7 (1995)
Physicians 1 per 352 people (1992)
Hospital beds 1 per 236 people (1994)
TV sets (per 1,000 people) 574 (1995)
Radios (per 1,000 people) 1,034 (1995)

Transport

Airports international airports: Copenhagen (Kastrup), Århus; ten major domestic airports; total passenger km: 5,112 mil (1994)
Railroads total length: 3,359 km/2,087 mi; total passenger km: 4,596 mil (1993)
Roads total road network: 71,420 km/44,380 mi, of which 100% paved (1995e); passenger cars: 340 per 1,000 people (1995)

Chronology

5th–6th centuries Danes migrated from Sweden.
8th–10th centuries Viking raids throughout Europe.
c. 940–85 Harald Bluetooth unified Kingdom of Denmark and established Christianity.
1014–35 King Canute I created empire embracing Denmark, Norway, and England; empire collapsed after his death.
12th century Denmark re-emerged as dominant Baltic power.
1340–75 Valdemar IV restored order after period of civil war and anarchy.
1397 Union of Kalmar: Denmark, Sweden, and Norway (with Iceland) united under a single monarch.
1449 Sweden broke away from union.
1460 Christian I secured duchies of Schleswig and Holstein.
1523 Denmark recognized Sweden's independence.
1536 Lutheranism established as official religion of Denmark.
1563–70 Unsuccessful war to recover Sweden.
1625–29 Denmark sided with Protestants in Thirty Years' War.

1643–45 Second attempt to reclaim Sweden ended in failure.
1657–60 Further failed attempt to reclaim Sweden.
1665 Frederick III made himself absolute monarch.
1729 Greenland became Danish province.
1780–81 Denmark, Russia, and Sweden formed 'Armed Neutrality' coalition to protect neutral shipping during War of American Independence.
1788 Serfdom abolished.
1800 France persuaded Denmark to revive Armed Neutrality against British blockade.
1801 First Battle of Copenhagen: much of Danish fleet destroyed by British navy.
1807 Second Battle of Copenhagen: British seized rebuilt fleet to pre-empt Danish entry into Napoleonic War on French side.
1814 Treaty of Kiel: Denmark ceded Norway to Sweden as penalty for supporting France in Napoleonic War; Denmark retained Iceland.
1848–50 Germans of Schleswig-Holstein revolted with Prussian support.
1849 Liberal pressure compelled Frederick VII to grant democratic constitution.
1864 Prussia seized Schleswig-Holstein after short war.
1914–1919 Denmark neutral during World War I.
1918 Iceland achieved full self-government.
1919 Denmark recovered northern Schleswig under peace settlement after World War I.
1929–40 Welfare state established under left-wing coalition government dominated by Social Democrat Party.
1940–45 German occupation.
1944 Iceland declared independence.
1949 Denmark became a founding member of North Atlantic Treaty Organization (NATO).
1960 Denmark joined European Free Trade Association (EFTA).
1973 Withdrew from EFTA and joined European Economic Community (EEC).
1981 Greenland achieved full self-government.
1992 Referendum rejected Maastricht Treaty on European union.
1993 Second referendum approved Maastricht Treaty after government negotiated a series of 'opt-out' clauses.
1996 Centre Democrats withdrew from governing coalition.

Practical information

Visa requirements UK: visa not required. USA: visa not required
Embassy in the UK Royal Danish Embassy, 55 Sloane Street, London SW1X 9SR. Tel: (0171) 333 0200; fax: (0171) 333 0270
British embassy Kastelsvej 36–40, DK-2100 Copenhagen. Tel: (45) 3526 4600; fax: (45) 3332 1501
Embassy in the USA 3200 Whitehaven Street NW, Washington, DC 20008. Tel: (202) 234 4300; fax: (202) 328 1470
American embassy Dag Hammarskjölds Alle 24, 2100 Copenhagen. Tel: (31) 423 144; fax: (35) 430 223
Chamber of commerce Det Danske Handelskammer,

Børsen, DK-1217 Copenhagen K. Tel: (45) 3395 0500; fax: (45) 3332 5216
Office hours 0900–1700 Mon–Fri
Banking hours 0930–1700 Mon, Tue, Wed, and Fri; 0930–1800 Thu
Time difference GMT +1
Chief tourist attractions landscape with woods, small lakes; volcanic Faeroe Islands with ancient culture and customs; Copenhagen, with its Tivoli Amusement Park (May–September), palaces, castle, cathedral, national museum, and Little Mermaid sculpture
Major holidays 1 January, 5 June, 24–26 December; variable: Ascension Thursday, Good Friday, Easter Monday, Holy Thursday, Whit Monday, General Prayer (April/May)

Djibouti Republic of

National name *Jumhouriyya Djibouti*
Area 23,200 sq km/8,957 sq mi
Capital Djibouti (and chief port)
Major towns/cities Tadjoura, Obock, Dikhil, Ali-Sabieh
Physical features mountains divide an inland plateau from a coastal plain; hot and arid

Government

Head of state Hassan Gouled Aptidon from 1977
Head of government Barkat Gourad from 1981
Political system emergent democracy
Administrative divisions five districts
Political parties People's Progress Assembly (RPP), nationalist; Democratic Renewal Party (PRD), moderate left of centre
Armed forces 8,400 (1995); plus 3,900 French troops
Conscription national service is voluntary
Death penalty retains the death penalty

for ordinary crimes but can be considered abolitionist in practice (no executions since independence)
Defence spend (% GDP) 5.3 (1995)
Education spend (% GNP) 3.8 (1993–94)
Health spend (% GDP) 1.3 (1991)

Economy and resources

Currency Djibouti franc
GDP ($ US) 500 million (1994e)
Real GDP per capita (PPP) ($ US) 1,200 (1994e)
GDP growth rate –2.9% (1994)
Average annual inflation 3% (1993)
Foreign debt ($ US) 279 million (1993)
Trading partners Kenya, Thailand, France, Ethiopia, Somalia
Industries mineral-water bottling, dairy products and other small-scale enterprises; an important port serving the regional hinterland
Exports hides, cattle, coffee (exports are largely re-exports). Principal market: Kenya 42% (1995)
Imports vegetable products, foodstuffs, beverages, vinegar, tobacco, machinery and transport equipment, mineral products. Principal source: Thailand 15.4% (1995)
Arable land 2% (1993)
Agricultural products mainly market gardening (for example, tomatoes); livestock rearing (over 50% of the population are pastoral nomads, herding goats, sheep, and camels); fishing

Population and society

Population 617,000 (1996e)
Population growth rate 2.2% (1990–95)

Population density (per sq km) 27 (1996e)
Urban population (% of total) 83 (1994)
Age distribution (% of total population) <15 42%, 15–65 55%, >65 3% (1994)
Ethnic distribution population divided mainly into two Hamitic groups; the Issas (Somalis) in the S, and the minority Afars (or Danakil) in the N and W. There are also minorities of Europeans (mostly French), as well as Arabs, Sudanese, and Indians
Languages French (official), Somali, Afar, Arabic
Religion Sunni Muslim
Education (compulsory years) 6
Literacy rate 60% (men); 33% (women) (1995e)
Unemployment 40% (1995e)
Life expectancy 49 (men); 52 (women) (1995–2000)
Child mortality rate (under 5, per 1,000 live births) 158 (1995)
Physicians 1 per 6,590 people (1993e)
Hospital beds 1 per 3,000 people (1990)
TV sets (per 1,000 people) 43 (1995)
Radios (per 1,000 people) 80 (1995)

Transport

Airports international airport: Djibouti (Ambouli); six domestic airports
Railroads total length: 106 km/67 mi; (part within Djibouti of 781-km/488-mi track linking Djibouti with Addis Ababa, Ethiopia); total passengers: 957,000 (1991)
Roads total road network: 2,890 km/1,796 mi, of which 12.6% paved (1995e); passenger cars: 16.7 per 1,000 people (1995e)

Chronology

3rd century BC The N settled by Able immigrants from Arabia, whose descendants are the Afars (Danakil).
early Christian era Somali Issas settled in coastal areas and S, ousting Afars.
825 Islam introduced by missionaries.
16th century Portuguese arrived to challenge trading monopoly of Arabs.
1862 French acquired a port at Obock.
1888 Annexed by France as part of French Somaliland.
1900s Railroad linked Djibouti port with the Ethiopian hinterland.
1946 Became overseas territory within

French Union, with own assembly and representation in French parliament.
1958 Voted to become overseas territorial member of French Community.
1967 French Somaliland renamed the French Territory of the Afars and the Issas.
early 1970s Issas (Somali) peoples campaigned for independence, but the minority Afars, of Ethiopian descent, and Europeans sought to remain French.
1977 Independence achieved as Djibouti, with Hassan Gouled Aptidon, the leader of the independence movement, elected president.

1981 New constitution made the People's Progress Assembly (RPP) the only legal party. Treaties of friendship signed with Ethiopia, Somalia, Kenya, and Sudan.
1984 Policy of neutrality reaffirmed. Economy undermined by severe drought.
1992 New multiparty constitution adopted; fighting erupted between government forces and Afar Front for Restoration of Unity and Democracy (FRUD) guerrilla movement in the NE.
1993 Opposition parties allowed to operate, but Gouled re-elected president.
1994 Peace agreement reached with Afar FRUD militants, ending civil war.

Practical information

Visa requirements UK: visa required. USA: visa required
Embassy for the UK 26 rue Emile Ménier, 75116 Paris, France. Tel: (1) 4727 4922; fax: (1) 4553 5053
British embassy British Consulate, BP 81 Gellatly Hankey et Cie, Djibouti. Tel: (253) 351 940; fax: (253) 353 294
Embassy in the USA Suite 515, 1156 15th Street NW, Washington, DC 20005. Tel: (202) 331 0270; fax: (202) 331 0302
American embassy Plateau du Serpent, Boulevard Marechal Joffre, Djibouti. Tel: (253) 353 995; fax: (253) 353 940

Chamber of commerce Chambre Internationale de Commerce et d'Industrie, BP 84, Place de Lagarde, Djibouti. Tel: (253) 351 070; fax: (253) 350 096
Office hours 0620–1300 Sat–Thu
Banking hours 0715–1145 Sat–Thu
Time difference GMT +3
Chief tourist attractions desert scenery in interior; watersports facilites on coast
Major holidays 1 January, 1 May, 27 June (2 days), 25 December; variable: Eid-ul-Adha (2 days), end of Ramadan (2 days), New Year (Muslim), Prophet's Birthday, Al-Isra Wal-Mira'age (March–April)

Dominica Commonwealth of

Area 751 sq km/289 sq mi
Capital Roseau, with a deepwater port
Major towns/cities Portsmouth, Berekua, Marigot, Rosalie
Major ports Roseau, Portsmouth, Berekua, Marigot, Rosalie
Physical features second largest of the Windward Islands, mountainous central ridge with tropical rainforest

Government

Head of state Clarence Seignoret from 1983

Head of government Edison James from 1995
Political system liberal democracy
Administrative divisions ten parishes
Political parties Dominica Freedom Party (DFP), centrist; Labour Party of Dominica (LPD), left-of-centre coalition; Dominica United Workers' Party (DUWP), left of centre
Armed forces defence force disbanded 1981; police force of approximately 300
Death penalty retained and used for ordinary crimes
Education spend (% GNP) 5.8 (1992); N/A (1993–94)

Economy and resources

Currency Eastern Caribbean dollar; pound sterling; French franc
GDP ($ US) 207 million (1994)
Real GDP per capita (PPP) ($ US) 6,118 (1994)
GDP growth rate 1% (1994)
Average annual inflation 1.6% (1994); 4.4% (1985–95)
Foreign debt ($ US) 102.3 million (1994)
Trading partners USA, UK, the Netherlands, South Korea, Belgium, Japan, Trinidad and Tobago

Resources pumice, limestone, clay
Industries banana packaging, vegetable oils, soap, canned juice, cigarettes, rum, beer, furniture, paint, cardboard boxes, candles, tourism
Exports bananas, soap, coconuts, grapefruit, galvanized sheets. Principal market: UK 25.3% (1995)
Imports food and live animals, basic manufactures, machinery and transport equipment, mineral fuels. Principal source: USA 13% (1995)
Arable land 9.3% (1993)
Agricultural products bananas, coconuts, mangoes, avocados, papayas, ginger, citrus fruits, vegetables; livestock rearing; fishing

Population and society

Population 71,000 (1996e)
Population growth rate –0.1 (1990–95)
Population density (per sq km) 94 (1996e)
Urban population (% of total) 41 (1993)
Age distribution (% of total population) <15 37.5%, 15–65 54.2%, >65 8.3% (1993)
Ethnic distribution majority descended from African slaves; a small number of the

indigenous Arawaks remain
Languages English (official), but the Dominican patois reflects earlier periods of French rule
Religion Roman Catholic 80%
Education (compulsory years) 10
Literacy rate 94% (men); 94% (women) (1994e)
Labour force 25.8% agriculture, 21.2% industry, 53% services (1990)
Unemployment 23% (1994)
Life expectancy 72 (men); 76 (women) (1994e)
Child mortality rate (under 5, per 1,000 live births) 21 (1995)
Physicians 1 per 2,952 people (1993)
Hospital beds 1 per 320 people (1994)
TV sets (per 1,000 people) 70 (1995)
Radios (per 1,000 people) 634 (1995)

Transport

Airports international airports: Roseau (Canefield), Portsmouth/Marigot (Melville Hall); aircraft arrivals and departures: 16,678 (1993)
Railroads none
Roads total road network: 765 km/ 475 mi, of which 50.3% paved (1995e)

Chronology

1493 Visited by the explorer Christopher Columbus, who named the island Dominica ('Sunday Island').
1627 Presented by the English King Charles I to the Earl of Carlisle, but initial European attempts at colonization were fiercely resisted by the indigenous Carib community.
later 18th century Succession of local British and French conflicts over control of the fertile island.
1763 British given possession of the island by the Treaty of Paris (ending the Seven Years' War), but France continued to challenge this militarily until 1805, when there was formal cession in return for the sum of £12,000.
1834 Slaves, who had been brought in from Africa, were emancipated.
1870 Became part of the British Leeward Islands federation.
1940 Transferred to British Windward Islands federation.
1951 Universal adult suffrage established.
1958–62 Part of the West Indies Federation.
1960 Granted separate, semi-independent status, with a legislative

council and chief minister.
1961 Edward leBlanc, leader of newly formed DLP, became chief minister.
1974 LeBlanc retired; replaced as chief minister by Patrick John (DLP).
1978 Independence achieved as a republic within the Commonwealth, with John as prime minister.
1980 DFP won convincing victory in general election, and Eugenia Charles became Caribbean's first woman prime minister.
1981 John implicated in plot to overthrow government, but subsequently acquitted.
1983 Small force participated in US-backed invasion of Grenada.
1985 John retried, found guilty, and sentenced to 12 years' imprisonment. Regrouping of left-of-centre parties resulted in new Labour Party of Dominica (LPD).
1991 Windward Islands confederation comprising St Lucia, St Vincent, Grenada, and Dominica proposed.
1993 Charles resigned DFP leadership, but continued as prime minister.
1995 DUWP won general election; Edison James appointed prime minister and Eugenia Charles retired from politics.

Practical information

Visa requirements UK: visa not required for stays of up to six months. USA: visa not required for stays of up to six months
Embassy in the UK High Commisssion, 1 Collingham Gardens, London SW5 0HW. Tel: (0171) 370 5194/5; fax: (0171) 373 8743
British embassy British High Commission, British Consulate, Office of the Honorary British Consul, PO Box 6, Roseau. (All staff based in Bridgetown, Barbados.) Tel: (809) 448 1000; fax: (809) 448 1110
Embassy in the USA Dominica does not have an embassy in the USA
American embassy the USA does not have an embassy in Dominica; the ambassador to Dominica lives in Bridgetown

(Barbados), but travels frequently to Dominica
Chamber of commerce Dominica Association of Industry and Commerce, PO Box 85, 111 Bath Road, Roseau. Tel: (809) 448 2874; fax: (809) 448 6868
Office hours 0800–1300 and 1400–1700 Mon; 0800–1300 and 1400–1600 Tue–Fri
Banking hours 0800–1500 Mon–Thu; 0800–1700 Fri
Time difference GMT –4
Chief tourist attractions scenery; nature reserves; marine reserves; rich birdlife, including rare and endangered species such as the imperial parrot
Major holidays 1 January, 1 May, 3–4 November, 25–26 December; variable: Carnival (2 days), Good Friday, Easter Monday, Whit Monday, August Monday

Dominican Republic

National name *República Dominicana*
Area 48,442 sq km/18,703 sq mi
Capital Santo Domingo
Major towns/cities Santiago de los Caballeros, La Romana, San Pedro de Macoris, San Francisco de Macoris, Concepcion de la Vega, San Juan
Physical features comprises eastern two-thirds of island of Hispaniola; central mountain range with fertile valleys; Pico Duarte 3,174 m/10,417 ft, highest point in Caribbean islands

Government

Head of state and government Leoned

Fernandez from 1996
Political system democratic republic
Administrative divisions 29 provinces and a national district (Santo Domingo)
Political parties Dominican Revolutionary Party (PRD), moderate, left of centre; Christian Social Reform Party (PRSC), independent socialist; Dominican Liberation Party (PLD), nationalist
Armed forces 24,500 (1995); plus a paramilitary force of 15,000
Conscription military service is voluntary
Death penalty abolished 1966
Defence spend (% GDP) 1.3 (1995)

Education spend (% GNP) 1.9 (1993–94)
Health spend (% GDP) 2.1 (1990)

Economy and resources

Currency Dominican Republic peso
GDP ($ US) 10.4 billion (1994)
Real GDP per capita (PPP) ($ US) 3,933 (1994)
GDP growth rate 4.3% (1994); 3.9% (1990–95)
Average annual inflation 26.3% (1985–95)
Foreign debt ($ US) 4.26 billion (1995)
Trading partners USA, Venezuela, Mexico, Japan, South Korea, the Netherlands, Belgium
Resources ferro-nickel, gold, silver
Industries food processing (including sugar refining), petroleum refining, beverages, chemicals, cement
Exports raw sugar, molasses, coffee, cocoa, tobacco, ferro-nickel, gold, silver. Principal market: USA 45.1% (1995)
Imports petroleum and petroleum products, coal, foodstuffs, wheat, machinery. Principal source: USA 44.1% (1995)
Arable land 20.5% (1993)
Agricultural products sugar cane, cocoa, coffee, bananas, tobacco, rice, tomatoes

Population and society

Population 7,961,000 (1996e)
Population growth rate 1.9% (1990–95); 1.4% (2000–05)
Population density (per sq km) 163 (1996e)
Urban population (% of total) 65 (1995)
Age distribution (% of total population) <15 35.1%, 15–65 60.9%, >65 4% (1995)
Ethnic distribution about 73% of the population are mulattos, of mixed European and African descent; about 16% are European; 11% African
Language Spanish (official)
Religion Roman Catholic
Education (compulsory years) 8
Literacy rate 85% (men); 82% (women) (1995e)

Labour force 40% of population: 25% agriculture, 29% industry, 46% services (1990)
Unemployment 30% (1990e)
Life expectancy 69 (men); 73 (women) (1995–2000)
Child mortality rate (under 5, per 1,000 live births) 44 (1995)
Physicians 1 per 935 people (1991)
Hospital beds 1 per 510 people (1991)
TV sets (per 1,000 people) 93 (1995)
Radios (per 1,000 people) 176 (1995)

Transport

Airports international airports: Santo Domingo (Internacional de las Americas), Puerto Plata (La Union), Punta Cana, La Romana; most main cities have domestic airports; total passenger km: 234 mil (1994)
Railroads total length: 517 km/321 mi
Roads total road network: 12,300 km/ 7,643 mi of which 49.3% paved (1995e); passenger cars: 25.6 per 1,000 people (1995e)

Chronology

14th century Settled by Carib Indians, who followed an earlier wave of Arawak Indian Immigration.
1492 Visited by Christopher Columbus, who named it Hispaniola ('Little Spain').
1496 At Santo Domingo, the Spanish established the first European settlement in the western hemisphere, which became capital of all Spanish colonies in America.
first half of 16th century One-third of a million Arawaks and Caribs died, as a result of enslavement and exposure to European diseases; black African slaves were consequently brought in to work the island's gold and silver mines, which were swiftly exhausted.
1697 Divided between France, which held the western third (Haiti), and Spain, which held the E (Dominican Republic, or Santo Domingo).
1795 Santo Domingo was ceded to France.
1808 Following a revolt by Spanish Creoles, with British support, Santo

Domingo was retaken by Spain.
1821 Became briefly independent after uprising against Spanish rule, and then fell under the control of Haiti.
1844 Separated from Haiti to form Dominican Republic.
1861–65 Under Spanish protection.
1904 The USA took over the near-bankrupt republic's debts.
1916–24 Temporarily occupied by US forces.
1930 Military coup established personal dictatorship of General Rafael Trujillo Molina after overthrow of president Horacio Vázquez.
1937 Army massacred 19,000–20,000 Haitians living in the Dominican provinces adjoining the frontier.
1961 Trujillo assassinated.
1962 First democratic elections resulted in Juan Bosch, founder of the left-wing Dominican Revolutionary Party (PRD), becoming president.
1963 Bosch overthrown in military coup.
1965 30,000 US marines intervened to restore order and protect foreign nationals after Bosch had attempted to seize power.
1966 New constitution adopted. Joaquín Balaguer, protégé of Trujillo and leader of the centre-right Christian Social Reform Party (PRSC), became president.
1978 PRD returned to power, with Silvestre Antonio Guzmán as president.
1982 PRD re-elected, with Jorge Blanco as president.
1985 Blanco forced by International Monetary Fund to adopt austerity measures to save economy.
1986 PRSC returned to power; Balaguer re-elected president.
1990 Balaguer re-elected by a small majority.
1994 Balaguer re-elected; election results disputed by opposition but eventually declared valid on condition that Balaguer serve reduced two-year term.
1996 Leoned Fernandez of the left-wing Dominican Liberation Party (PLD) was elected president.

Practical information

Visa requirements UK: visa not required for stays of up to 90 days. USA: visa not required for stays of up to 60 days
Embassy in the UK Honorary Consulate of the Dominican Republic, 6 Queen's Mansions, Brook Green, London W6 7EB. Tel: (0171) 602 1885
British embassy Edificio Corominas Pepin, Ave 27 Febrero No. 233, Santo Domingo. Tel: (809) 472 7111; fax: (809) 472 7574
Embassy in the USA 1715 22nd Street NW, Washington, DC 20008. Tel: (202) 332 6280; fax: (202) 265 8057
American embassy corner of Calle Cesar Nicolas Penson

and Calle Leopoldo Navarro, Santo Domingo. Tel: (809) 221 2171/8100; fax: (809) 686 7437
Chamber of commerce Cámara de Comercio y Produccíon del Distrito Nacional, Apartado Postal 815, Arz. Nouel 206, Santo Domingo. Tel: (809) 682 7206; fax: (809) 685 2228
Office hours 0830–1200 and 1400–1800 Mon–Fri
Banking hours 0800–1600 Mon–Fri
Time difference GMT –4
Chief tourist attractions beaches on north, east, and southeast coasts; forested and mountainous landscape
Major holidays 1, 6, 21, 26 January, 27 February, 1 May, 16 August, 24 September, 25 December; variable: Corpus Christi, Good Friday

Ecuador Republic of

National name *República del Ecuador*
Area 270,670 sq km/104,505 sq mi
Capital Quito
Major towns/cities Guayaquil, Cuenca, Machala, Portoviejo, Manta, Ambeto, Esmeraldas
Major ports Guayaquil
Physical features coastal plain rises sharply to Andes Mountains, which are divided into a series of cultivated valleys; flat, low-lying rainforest in the E; Galápagos Islands; Cotopaxi, the world's highest active volcano. Ecuador is crossed by the equator, from which it derives its name

Government

Head of state and government (interim) Fabian Alarcon from 1997
Political system emergent democratic republic
Administrative divisions 21 provinces
Political parties Social Christian Party (PSC), right wing; Ecuadorean Roldosist Party (PRE), populist, centre left; United Republican Party (PUR), right-of-centre coalition; Democratic Left (ID), moderate socialist; Conservative Party (PC), right wing
Armed forces 57,100 (1995)
Conscription military service is selective for one year
Death penalty abolished 1906
Defence spend (% GDP) 3.4 (1995)
Education spend (% GNP) 3 (1993–94)
Health spend (% GDP) 2.6 (1990)

Economy and resources

Currency sucre
GDP ($ US) 16.6 billion (1994)

Real GDP per capita (PPP) ($ US) 4,626 (1994)
GDP growth rate 4% (1994); 3.4% (1990–95)
Average annual inflation 22.9% (1995); 45.5% (1985–95)
Foreign debt ($ US) 14 billion (1995)
Trading partners USA, Colombia, Germany, Chile, Peru, Japan, Italy, Spain
Resources petroleum, natural gas, gold, silver, copper, zinc, antimony, iron, uranium, lead, coal
Industries food processing, petroleum refining, cement, chemicals, textiles
Exports petroleum and petroleum products, bananas, shrimps (a major exporter), coffee, seafood products, cocoa beans and products, cut flowers. Principal market: USA 42.4% (1994)
Imports machinery and transport equipment, basic manufactures, chemicals, consumer goods. Principal source: USA 25.3% (1994)
Arable land 5.7% (1993)
Agricultural products bananas, coffee, cocoa, rice, potatoes, maize, barley, sugar cane; fishing (especially shrimp industry); forestry

Population and society

Population 11,699,000 (1996e)
Population growth rate 2.2% (1990–95); 1.7% (2000–05)
Population density (per sq km) 41 (1996e)
Urban population (% of total) 58 (1995)
Age distribution (% of total population) <15 36.4%, 15–65 59.2%, >65 4.4% (1995)
Ethnic distribution about 55% mestizo (of Spanish-American and Native American parentage), 25% Native American, 10% Spanish, 10% African
Languages Spanish (official), Quechua, Jivaro, and other indigenous languages
Religion Roman Catholic
Education (compulsory years) 6
Literacy rate 88% (men); 84% (women) (1995e)
Labour force 35% of population: 33% agriculture, 19% industry, 48% services (1990)
Unemployment 8.9% (1993)
Life expectancy 67 (men); 73 (women) (1995–2000)
Child mortality rate (under 5, per 1,000 live births) 40 (1995)
Physicians 1 per 918 people (1993)
Hospital beds 1 per 602 people (1993)

TV sets (per 1,000 people) 96 (1995)
Radios (per 1,000 people) 332 (1995)

Transport

Airports international airports: Quito (Mariscal Sucre), Guayaquil (Simón Bolívar); six domestic airports; total passenger km: 1,410 mil (1994)
Railroads total length: 966 km/600 mi; total passenger km: 27 mil (1994)
Roads total road network: 43,106 km/26,786 mi, of which 18.4% paved (1995); passenger cars: 34.5 per 1,000 people (1995e)

Chronology

1450s The Caras people, whose kingdom had its capital at Quito, conquered the Incas of Peru.
1531 Spanish conquistador Francisco Pizarro landed on Ecuadorian coast, en route to Peru, where Incas were defeated.
1534 Conquered by Spanish. Quito, which had been destroyed by Native Americans, was refounded by Sebastian de Belalcazar; the area became part of Spanish Viceroyalty of Peru, which covered much of South America, with its capital at Lima (Peru).
later 16th century Spanish established large agrarian estates, owned by Europeans and worked by Native American peons.
1739 Became part of new Spanish Viceroyalty of Nueva Granada, which included Colombia and Venezuela, with its capital in Bogotá (Colombia).
1809 With the Spanish monarchy having been overthrown by Napoleon Bonaparte, creole middle class began to press for independence.
1822 Spanish Royalists defeated by Field Marshal Antonio José de Sucre, fighting for Simón Bolívar, 'the Liberator', at battle of Pichincha, near Quito; became part of independent Gran Colombia, which also comprised Colombia, Panama, and Venezuela.
1830 Became fully independent state, after leaving Gran Colombia.
1845–60 Political instability, with five presidents holding power, increasing tension between conservative Quito and liberal Guayaquil on the coast, and minor wars with Peru and Colombia.
1860–75 Power held by Gabriel García Moreno, an autocratic theocrat

Conservative who launched education and public-works programmes.
1895–1912 Dominated by Gen Eloy Alfaro, a radical, anticlerical Liberal from the coastal region, who reduced the power of the church.
1925–48 Great political instability; no president completed his term of office.
1941 Lost territory in Amazonia after defeat in war with Peru.
1948–55 Liberals in power.
1956 Camilo Ponce became first conservative president in 60 years.
1960 Liberals in power, with José María Velasco Ibarra returning as president.
1961 Velasco deposed and replaced by the vice president.
1962 Military junta installed.
1968 Velasco returned as president.

1970s Ecuador emerged as a significant oil producer.
1972 A coup put the military back in power.
1979 New democratic constitution; Liberals in power but opposed by right- and left-wing parties.
1981 Border dispute with Peru flared up again.
1982 Deteriorating economy and austerity measures provoked strikes, demonstrations, and a state of emergency.
1984–85 No party with a clear majority in the national congress; León Febres Cordero narrowly won the presidency for the Conservatives.
1988 Rodrigo Borja Cevallos elected president for moderate left-wing coalition and introduced unpopular austerity

measures.
1992 PUR leader Sixto Duran Ballen elected president; PSC became largest party in congress. Ecuador withdrew from OPEC to enable it to increase its oil exports.
1994 Mounting opposition to Duran's economic liberalization and privatization programme.
1995 Parliament dismissed three key ministers, including the finance minister for corruption; long-standing border dispute with Peru resolved.
1996 Abdala Bucaram elected president.
1997 Bucaram removed from office and replaced by vice-president Rosalia Arteaga, but a national referendum later ratified Fabian Alarcon as interim president.

Practical information

Visa requirements UK: visa not required (except for business visits of three–six months). USA: visa not required (except for business visits of three–six months)
Embassy in the UK Flat 3B, 3 Hans Crescent, London SW1X 0LS. Tel: (0171) 584 1367; fax: (0171) 823 9701
British embassy Casilla 314, Calle Gonzáloz Suárez 111, Quito. Tel: (2) 560 669; fax: (2) 560 730
Embassy in the USA 2535 15th Street NW, Washington, DC 20009. Tel: (202) 234 7200
American embassy Avenida 12 de Octubre y Avenida Patria, Quito. Tel: (2) 562 890; fax: (2) 502 052
Chamber of commerce Federación Nacional de Cámaras de Comercio del Ecuador, Avenida Olmedo 414, Casila y Boyacá, Guayaquil. Tel: (4) 323 130; fax: (4) 323 478

Office hours 0800–1230 and 1500–1900 Mon–Fri; 0930–1230 Sat
Banking hours 0900–1330 and 1430–1830 Mon–Fri; some banks are also open 0930–1400 Sat
Time difference GMT –5
Chief tourist attractions Andes Mountains; rainforests of upper Amazon basin; colonial churches and palaces of Guayaquil; Quito, the former Inca capital, with its cathedral, churches, and palaces – the old city is a designated UN World Heritage site; Galápagos Islands, with marine iguanas and giant tortoises
Major holidays 1 January, 1, 24 May, 30 June, 24 July, 10 August, 9, 12 October, 2–3 November, 6, 25, 31 December; variable: Carnival (2 days), Good Friday, Holy Thursday

---

Egypt Arab Republic of

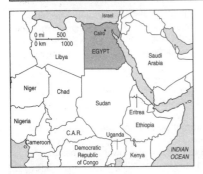

National name *Jumhuriyat Misr al-Arabiya*
Area 1,001,450 sq km/386,659 sq mi
Capital Cairo
Major towns/cities El Gîza, Shubra Al Khayma, Alexandria, Port Said, El-Mahalla el-Koubra, Tauta, El-Mansoura
Major ports Alexandria, Port Said, Suez,

Damietta, Shubra Al Khayma
Physical features mostly desert; hills in E; fertile land along Nile valley and delta; cultivated and settled area is about 35,500 sq km/13,700 sq mi; Aswan High Dam and Lake Nasser; Sinai

Government

Head of state Hosni Mubarak from 1981
Head of government Kamal Ahmed Ganzouri from 1996
Political system democratic republic
Administrative divisions 26 governates
Political parties National Democratic Party (NDP), moderate, left of centre; Socialist Labour Party (SLP), right of centre; Liberal Socialist Party, free enterprise; New Wafd Party, nationalist; National Progressive Unionist Party, left wing
Armed forces 436,000 (1995)

Conscription 3 years (selective)
Death penalty retained and used for ordinary crimes
Defence spend (% GDP) 4.3 (1995)
Education spend (% GNP) 5 (1993–94)
Health spend (% GDP) 1 (1990)

Economy and resources

Currency Egyptian pound
GDP ($ US) 42.9 billion (1994)
Real GDP per capita (PPP) ($ US) 3,846 (1994)
GDP growth rate 2% (1994); 1.3% (1990–95)
Average annual inflation 8.2% (1994); 15.7% (1985–95)
Foreign debt ($ US) 34.11 billion (1995)
Trading partners USA, Italy, Germany, France
Resources petroleum, natural gas,

phosphates, manganese, uranium, coal, iron ore, gold
Industries petroleum and petroleum products, food processing, petroleum refining, textiles, metals, cement, tobacco, sugar crystal and refined sugar, electrical appliances, fertilizers
Exports petroleum and petroleum products, textiles, clothing, food, live animals. Principal market: Italy 18.6% (1995)
Imports wheat, maize, dairy products, machinery and transport equipment, wood and wood products, consumer goods. Principal source: USA 18.9% (1995)
Arable land 2.4% (1993)
Agricultural products wheat, cotton, rice, corn, beans

Population and society

Population 63,271,000 (1996e)
Population growth rate 2.2% (1990–95); 1.7% (2000–05)
Population density (per sq km) 63 (1996e)
Urban population (% of total) 45 (1995)
Age distribution (% of total population) <15 38%, 15–65 57.8%, >65 4.2% (1995)
Ethnic distribution 93% indigenous
Languages Arabic (official); ancient Egyptian survives to some extent in Coptic; English; French
Religions Sunni Muslim 90%, Coptic Christian 7%
Education (compulsory years) 5
Literacy rate 63% (men); 34% (women) (1995e)
Labour force 35% of population: 40% agriculture, 22% industry, 38% services (1990)
Unemployment 13% (1993)
Life expectancy 65 (men); 67 (women) (1995–2000)

Child mortality rate (under 5, per 1,000 live births) 51 (1995)
Physicians 1 per 672 people (1992e)
Hospital beds 1 per 538 people (1994e)
TV sets (per 1,000 people) 110 (1995)
Radios (per 1,000 people) 312 (1995)

Transport

Airports international airports: Cairo (two), Alexandria (El Nouzha), Luxor; eight domestic airports; total passenger km: 6,324 mil (1994)
Railroads total length: 4,751 km/ 2,952 mi; total passenger km: 36,644 mil (1992)
Roads total road network: 58,000 km/ 36,041 mi, of which 78% paved (1995e); passenger cars: 21.2 (1995e)

Chronology

1st century BC–7th century AD Conquered by Augustus AD 30, Egypt passed under rule of Roman, and later Byzantine, governors.
AD 639–42 Arabs conquered Egypt, introducing Islam and Arabic; succession of Arab dynasties followed.
1250 Mamelukes seized power.
1517 Became part of Turkish Ottoman Empire.
1798–1801 Invasion by Napoleon followed by period of French occupation.
1801 Control regained by Turks.
1869 Opening of Suez Canal made Egypt strategically important.
1881–82 Nationalist revolt resulted in British occupation.
1914 Egypt became a British protectorate.
1922 Achieved nominal independence under King Fuad I.
1936 Full independence from Britain achieved. King Fuad succeeded by his son Farouk.
1946 Withdrawal of British troops except

from Suez Canal zone.
1952 Farouk overthrown by army in bloodless coup.
1953 Egypt declared a republic, with Gen Neguib as president.
1956 Neguib replaced by Col Gamal Nasser. Nasser announced nationalization of Suez Canal; Egypt attacked by Britain, France, and Israel. Cease-fire agreed following US intervention.
1958 Short-lived merger of Egypt and Syria as United Arab Republic (UAR).
1967 Six-Day War with Israel ended in Egypt's defeat and Israeli occupation of Sinai and Gaza Strip.
1970 Nasser died suddenly; succeeded by Anwar Sadat.
1973 Attempt to regain territory lost to Israel led to Yom Kippur War; cease-fire arranged by US secretary of state Henry Kissinger.
1978–79 Camp David talks in USA resulted in a peace treaty between Egypt and Israel. Egypt expelled from Arab League.
1981 Sadat assassinated by Muslim fundamentalists, succeeded by Hosni Mubarak.
1983 Improved relations between Egypt and Arab world; only Libya and Syria maintained trade boycott.
1987 Egypt readmitted to Arab League.
1989 Improved relations with Libya; diplomatic relations with Syria restored.
1991 Participation in Gulf War on US-led side. Major force in convening Middle East peace conference in Spain.
1992 Violence between Muslims and Christians.
1994 Government crackdown on Islamic militants.
1995 Abortive attempt to assassinate Mubarak.
1996 Kamal Ahmed Ganzouri appointed prime minister.

Practical information

Visa requirements UK: visa required. USA: visa required
Embassy in the UK 26 South Street, London W1Y 8EL. Tel: (0171) 499 2401; fax: (0171) 355 3568
British embassy 7 Sharia Ahmad Raghab, Garden City, Cairo. Tel: (2) 354 0850; fax: (2) 354 0859
Embassy in the USA 3521 International Court NW, Washington, DC 20008. Tel: (202) 895 5400; fax: (202) 244 4319/5131
American embassy (North Gate) 8, Kamel El-Din Salah Street, Garden City, Cairo. Tel: (2) 355 7371; fax: (2) 357 3200
Chamber of commerce Federation of Chambers of Commerce, 4 el-Falaki Square, Cairo. Tel: (2) 355 1164;

telex: 92645
Government office hours 0900–1400 Sat–Thu
Banking hours 0830–1400 Sat–Thu
Time difference GMT +2
Chief tourist attractions beaches and coral reefs on coast south of Suez; Western Desert, containing the Qattara Depression – the world's largest and lowest depression; ancient pyramids and temples, including those at Saqqara, Gîza, and Karnak
Major holidays 7 January, 25 April, 1 May, 18 June, 1, 23 July, 6 October; variable: Eid-ul-Adha (2 days), Arafa, end of Ramadan (2 days), New Year (Muslim), Prophet's Birthday, Palm Sunday and Easter Sunday (Eastern Orthodox), Sham-el-Nessim (April/May)

El Salvador Republic of

National name *República de El Salvador*
Area 21,393 sq km/8,259 sq mi
Capital San Salvador
Major towns/cities Soyapango, Santa Ana, San Miguel, Nueva San Salvador, Mejicanos
Physical features narrow coastal plain, rising to mountains in N with central plateau

Government

Head of state and government Armando Calderón Sol from 1994
Political system emergent democracy
Administrative divisions 14 departments
Political parties Christian Democrats (PDC), anti-imperialist; Farabundo Martí Liberation Front (FMLN), left wing; National Republican Alliance (ARENA), extreme right wing; National Conciliation Party (PCN), right wing
Armed forces 30,500 (1995); plus a national civilian police force of 8,000
Conscription selective conscription for two years
Death penalty laws provide for the death penalty only for exceptional crimes such as crimes under military law or crimes committed in exceptional circumstances such as wartime (last known execution 1973)
Defence spend (% GDP) 1.8 (1995)
Education spend (% GNP) 1.6 (1993–94)
Health spend (% GDP) 2.6 (1990)

Economy and resources

Currency Salvadorean colón
GDP ($ US) 8.1 billion (1994)
Real GDP per capita (PPP) ($ US) 2,417 (1994)
GDP growth rate 6% (1994); 6.3% (1990–95)

Average annual inflation 10.6% (1994); 14.7% (1985–95)
Foreign debt ($ US) 2.6 billion (1995)
Trading partners USA, Guatemala, Costa Rica, Honduras, Mexico, Japan, Germany, Venezuela
Resources salt, limestone, gypsum
Industries food processing, beverages, petroleum products, textiles, tobacco, paper products, chemical products
Exports coffee, textiles and garments, sugar, shrimp, footwear, pharmaceuticals. Principal market: USA 53.4% (1996)
Imports petroleum and other minerals, cereals, chemicals, iron and steel, machinery and transport equipment, consumer goods. Principal source: USA 49.9% (1996)
Arable land 26.9% (1993)
Agricultural products coffee, sugar cane, cotton, maize, beans, rice, sorghum; fishing (shrimp)

Population and society

Population 5,796,000 (1996e)
Population growth rate 2.2% (1990–95); 2% (2000–05)
Population density (per sq km) 275 (1996e)
Urban population (% of total) 45 (1995)
Age distribution (% of total population) <15 40.7%, 15–65 55.2%, >65 4.1% (1995)
Ethnic distribution about 92% of the population are mestizos, 6% Indians, and 2% of European origin
Languages Spanish, Nahuatl
Religions Roman Catholic, Protestant
Education (compulsory years) 9
Literacy rate 76% (men); 70% (women) (1995e)
Labour force 36% of population: 36% agriculture, 21% industry, 43% services (1990)
Unemployment 9% (1993)
Life expectancy 66 (men); 71 (women) (1995–2000)
Child mortality rate (under 5, per 1,000 live births) 40 (1995)
Physicians 1 per 1,563 people (1991)
Hospital beds 1 per 932 people (1991e)
TV sets (per 1,000 people) 689 (1995)
Radios (per 1,000 people) 459 (1995)

Transport

Airports international airport: San Salvador (El Salvador International); three domestic airports; total passenger km: 1,573 mil (1994)

Railroads total length: 602 km/374 mi; total passenger km: 6 mil (1994)
Roads total road network: 43,106 km/ 26,786 mi, of which 18.4% paved (1995); passenger cars: 18.8 per 1,000 people (1995e)

Chronology

11th century Pipils, descendants of the Nahuatl-speaking Toltec and Aztec people of Mexico, settled in the country and came to dominate El Salvador until the Spanish conquest.
1524 Conquered by the Spanish adventurer Pedro de Alvarado and made a Spanish colony, with resistance being crushed by 1540.
1821 Independence achieved from Spain; briefly joined with Mexico.
1823 Became part of United Provinces (Federation) of Central America, also embracing Costa Rica, Guatemala, Honduras, and Nicaragua.
1833 Unsuccessful rebellion against Spanish control of land led by Anastasio Aquino.
1840 Became fully independent when Federation dissolved.
1859–63 Coffee growing introduced by president Gerardo Barrios.
1932 Peasant uprising, led by Augustín Farabundo Martí, suppressed by military at a cost of the lives of 30,000, virtually eliminating Native American Salvadoreans.
1961 Following a coup, the right-wing National Conciliation Party (PCN) established and in power.
1969 Brief 'Football War' with Honduras, which El Salvador attacked, at the time of a football competition between the two states, following evictions of thousands of Salvadoran illegal immigrants from Honduras.
1977 Allegations of human-rights violations; growth of left-wing Farabundo Martí National Liberation Front (FMLN) guerrilla activities. Gen Carlos Romero elected president.
1979 A coup replaced Romero with a military-civilian junta.
1980 The archbishop of San Salvador and human-rights champion, Oscar Romero, assassinated; country on verge of civil war. José Napoleón Duarte (PDC) became first civilian president since 1931.
1981 Mexico and France recognized the FMLN guerrillas as a legitimate political force, but the USA actively assisted the

government in its battle against them; 30,000 were killed 1979–81 by right-wing death squads.
1982 Assembly elections boycotted by left-wing parties. Held amid considerable violence, they were won by far-right National Republican Alliance (ARENA).
1984 Duarte won presidential election.
1986 Duarte sought a negotiated settlement with the guerrillas.
1989 Alfredo Cristiani (ARENA) became president in rigged elections; rebel attacks intensified.
1991 United Nations-sponsored peace accord signed by representatives of the government and the socialist guerrilla group, the FMLN, which now became a political party.
1993 UN-sponsored commission published report on war atrocities; government amnesty for those implicated; top military leaders officially retired.
1994 Armando Calderón Sol (ARENA) elected president.

Practical information

Visa requirements UK: visa not required for a stay of up to 90 days. USA: visa required (Tourist Card)
Embassy in the UK Tennyson House, 159 Great Portland Street, London W1N 5FD. Tel: (0171) 436 8282; fax: (0171) 436 8181
British embassy PO Box 1591, Paeso General Escalón 4828, San Salvador. Tel: (503) 298 1768/9; fax: (503) 298 3328
Embassy in the USA 2308 California Street NW, Washington, DC 20008. Tel: (202) 265 9671/2
American embassy Final Boulevard Santa Elena, Station Antiguo Cuscatlan, San Salvador. Tel: 278 4444; fax: 278 6011

Chamber of commerce Cámara de Comercio e Industria de El Salvador, Apartado 1640, 9a Avenida Norte y 5a Calle Poniente, San Salvador. Tel: (503) 771 2055; fax: (503) 771 4461
Office hours 0800–1200 and 1430–1730 Mon–Fri
Banking hours 0900–1300 and 1345–1600 Mon–Fri
Time difference GMT –6
Chief tourist attractions Mayan temples and other remains; upland scenery with lakes and volcanoes; Pacific beaches
Major holidays 1 January, 1 May, 29–30 June, 15 September, 12 October, 2, 5 November, 24–25, 30–31 December; variable: Good Friday, Holy Thursday, Ash Wednesday, San Salvador (4 days)

Equatorial Guinea Republic of

National name *República de Guinea Ecuatorial*
Area 28,051 sq km/10,830 sq mi
Capital Malabo
Major towns/cities Bata, Evinayong, Ebebiyin, Mongomo
Physical features comprises mainland Río Muni, plus the small islands of Corisco, Elobey Grande and Elobey Chico, and Bioko (formerly Fernando Po) together with Annobón (formerly Pagalu); nearly half the land is forested; volcanic mountains on Bioko

Government

Head of state Teodoro Obiang Nguema Mbasogo from 1979
Head of government Silvestre Siale Bileka from 1993

Political system emergent democratic republic
Administrative divisions seven provinces
Political parties Democratic Party of Equatorial Guinea (PDGE), nationalist, right of centre, militarily controlled; People's Social Democratic Convention (CSDP), left of centre; Democratic Socialist Union of Equatorial Guinea (UDSGE), left of centre
Armed forces 1,320 (1995)
Conscription military service is voluntary
Death penalty retained and used for ordinary crimes
Defence spend (% GDP) 1.3 (1995)
Education spend (% GNP) 1.8 (1993–94)

Economy and resources

Currency franc CFA
GDP ($ US) 142 million (1994)
Real GDP per capita (PPP) ($ US) 1,673 (1994)
GDP growth rate 8.9% (1994)
Average annual inflation –1.5% (1993); 4.1% (1985–95)
Foreign debt ($ US) 259 million (1991–93)
Trading partners USA, Spain, Italy, the Netherlands, Liberia, France, Nigeria, Cameroon
Resources petroleum, natural gas, gold, uranium, iron ore, tantalum, manganese
Industries wood processing, food processing
Exports timber, re-exported ships and boats, textile fibres and waste, cocoa, coffee. Principal market: USA 34% (1995)
Imports ships and boats, petroleum and related products, food and live animals, machinery and transport equipment, beverages and tobacco, basic manufactures. Principal source: Spain 51% (1995)
Arable land 4.6% (1993)
Agricultural products cocoa, coffee, cassava, sweet potatoes, bananas, palm oil, palm kernels; exploitation of forest resources (principally of *okoumé* and *akoga* timber)

Population and society

Population 410,000 (1995e)
Population growth rate 2.6% (1990–95); 2.4% (2000–05)
Population density (per sq km) 15 (1996e)
Urban population (% of total) 42 (1995)
Age distribution (% of total population) <15 43.3%, 15–65 52.8%, >65 4% (1995)
Ethnic distribution 80–90% of the Fang ethnic group, of Bantu origin; most other groups have been pushed to the coast by Fang expansion

Languages Spanish (official); pidgin English is widely spoken, and on Annobón (whose people were formerly slaves of the Portuguese) a Portuguese patois; Fang and other African patois spoken on Río Muni
Religions Roman Catholic, Protestant, animist
Education (compulsory years) 8
Literacy rate 89% (men); 67% (women) (1995e)
Labour force 77% agriculture, 2% industry, 21% services (1990)
Life expectancy 48 (men); 52 (women) (1995–2000)
Child mortality rate (under 5, per 1,000 live births) 175 (1995)
Physicians 1 per 3,520 people (1991)
Hospital beds 1 per 97 people (1991e)
TV sets (per 1,000 people) 9.6 (1995)
Radios (per 1,000 people) 425 (1995)

Transport

Airports international airports: Malabo, Bata; domestic services operate between major towns; total passenger km: 7 mil (1994)
Railroads none

Roads total road network: 2,820 km/ 1,752 mi (1995e); passenger cars: 3.3 per 1,000 people (1995e)

Chronology

1472 First visited by Portuguese explorers.
1778 Bioko (formerly known as Fernando Po) Island ceded to Spain, which established cocoa plantations there in the late 19th century, importing labour from W Africa.
1885 Mainland territory of Mbini (formerly Río Muni) came under Spanish rule, the whole colony being known as Spanish Guinea, with the capital at Malabu on Bioko Island.
1920s League of Nations special mission sent to investigate the forced, quasi-slave labour conditions on the Bioko cocoa plantations, then the largest in the world.
1959 Became a Spanish Overseas Province; African population finally granted full citizenship.
early 1960s On the mainland, the Fang people spearheaded a nationalist movement directed against Spanish favouritism towards Bioko Island and its

controlling Bubi tribe.
1963 Achieved internal autonomy.
1968 Independence achieved from Spain. Macias Nguema, a nationalist Fang, became first president, discriminating against the Bubi community.
1970s Economy collapsed as Spanish settlers and other minorities fled in the face of intimidation by Nguema's brutal, dictatorial regime, which was marked by the murder, torture, and imprisonment of tens of thousands of political opponents and rivals, as well as the closing of churches.
1979 Nguema overthrown, tried, and executed. He was replaced by his nephew, Teodoro Obiang Nguema Mbasogo, who established a military regime, but released political prisoners and imposed restrictions on the Catholic church.
1992 New pluralist constitution approved by referendum.
1993 Obiang's PDGE won first multiparty elections on low turnout.
1996 Obiang re-elected amid claims of fraud by opponents.

Practical information

Visa requirements UK: visa required. USA: visa required
Embassy for the UK 6 rue Alfred de Vigny, 75008 Paris, France. Tel: (1) 4766 4433; fax: (1) 4764 9452
British embassy British Consulate, Winston Churchill Avenue, BP 547, Yaoundé, Cameroon. Tel: (237) 220 545; fax: (237) 220 148 (All staff based in Yaoundé, Cameroon.)
Embassy in the USA (temporary) 57 Magnolia Avenue, Mount Vernon, NY 10553. Tel: (914) 738 9584, 667 6913; fax: (914) 667 6838
American embassy the USA does not have an embassy in

Equatorial Guinea (embassy closed September 1995); US relations with Equatorial Guinea are handled through the US embassy in Yaoundé, Cameroon
Chamber of commerce Cámara de Comercio Agrícola y Forestal de Malabo, Apartado 51, Malabo. Tel: (240) 151
Office hours 0800–1700 Mon–Fri
Banking hours 0800–1200 Mon–Sat
Time difference GMT +1
Chief tourist attractions beaches around small offshore islands; tourism remains undeveloped
Major holidays 1 January, 1 May, 5 June, 3 August, 12 October, 10, 25 December; variable: Corpus Christi, Good Friday, Constitution (August)

Eritrea State of

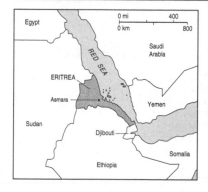

Area 125,000 sq km/48,262 sq mi
Capital Asmara
Major towns/cities Asab, Keren, Massawa, Adigrat
Major ports Asab, Massawa
Physical features coastline along the Red Sea 1,000 km/620 mi; narrow coastal plain that rises to an inland plateau; Dahlak Islands

Government

Head of state and government Issaias Afwerki from 1993
Political system emergent democracy

Administrative divisions ten provinces
Political parties People's Front for Democracy and Justice (PFDJ) (formerly Eritrean People's Liberation Front: EPLF), left of centre; Eritrean National Pact Alliance (ENPA), moderate, centrist
Armed forces 55,000 (1995)
Conscription compulsory for 18 months
Death penalty retained and used for ordinary crimes
Defence spend (% GDP) 5.7 (1995)
Education spend (% GDP) 3.2 (1993)
Health spend (% GDP) 1.8 (1993)

Economy and resources

Currency Ethiopian birr
GDP ($ US) 558 million (1994e)
Real GDP per capita (PPP) ($ US) 960 (1994)
GDP growth rate 9.4% (1994)
Average annual inflation 10% (1995e)
Trading partners Ethiopia, Saudi Arabia, Italy, Sudan, United Arab Emirates
Resources gold, silver, copper, zinc, sulphur, nickel, chrome, potash, basalt, limestone, marble, sand, silicates
Industries food processing, textiles, leatherwear, building materials, glassware, petroleum products
Exports textiles, leather and leather products, beverages, petroleum products, basic household goods. Principal market: Ethiopia 68.7% (1993)
Imports machinery and transport equipment, petroleum, food and live animals, basic manufactures. Principal source: Saudi Arabia 31% (1993)
Arable land 10.6% (1993)
Agricultural products sorghum, teff (an indigenous grain), maize, wheat, millet; livestock rearing (goats and camels); fisheries

Population and society

Population 3,280,000 (1996e)
Population growth rate 2.7% (1990–95); 2.5% (2000–05)
Population density (per sq km) 28 (1996e)
Urban population (% of total) 17 (1995)
Age distribution (% of total population) <15 44%, 15–65 53.1%, >65 2.9% (1995)

Ethnic distribution several ethnic groups, including the Amhara and the Tigrais
Languages Amharic (official), Tigrinya (official), Arabic, Afar, Bilen, Hidareb, Kunama, Nara, Rashaida, Saho, and Tigre
Religions Sunni Muslim, Coptic Christian
Education (compulsory years) 7
Literacy rate 20–25% (men); 5–10% (women) (1995e)
Unemployment 50% (1994e)
Life expectancy 51 (men); 55 (women) (1995–2000)
Child mortality rate (under 5, per 1,000 live births) 195 (1995)
Physicians 1 per 45,588 people (1993e)
TV sets (per 1,000 people) 0.3 (1995)
Radios (per 1,000 people) 98 (1995)

Transport

Airports international airport: Asmara (Yohannes IV); two domestic airports
Railroads none
Roads total road network: 3,930 km/ 2,442 mi, of which 21.4% paved (1995e); passenger cars: 1.5 per 1,000 people (1995e)

Chronology

4th–7th centuries AD Part of Ethiopian Aksum kingdom.
8th century Islam introduced to coastal areas by Arabs.
12th–16th centuries Under the influence of Ethiopian Abyssinian kingdoms.
mid-16th century Came under the control of the Turkish Ottoman Empire.
1882 Occupied by Italy.
1889 Italian colony of Eritrea created out of Ottoman areas and coastal districts of Ethiopia.
1920s Massawa developed into largest port in E Africa.
1935–36 Used as base for Italy's conquest of Ethiopia and became part of Italian East Africa.
1941 Became British protectorate after Italy removed from N Africa.
1952 Federation formed with Ethiopia by United Nations (UN).
1958 Eritrean People's Liberation Front (EPLF) formed to fight for independence after general strike brutally suppressed by Ethiopian rulers.
1962 Annexed by Ethiopia, sparking a secessionist rebellion which was to last 30 years and claim 150,000 lives.
1974 Ethiopian emperor Haile Selassie deposed by military; EPLF continued struggle for independence.
1977–78 EPLF cleared the territory of Ethiopian forces, but position was soon reversed by Marxist Ethipoian government of Col Mengistu Haile Mariam, which had Soviet backing.
mid-1980s Severe famine in Erltrea and refugee crisis as Ethiopian government sought forcible resettlement.
1990 Strategic port of Massawa captured by Eritrean rebel forces.
1991 Ethiopian president Mengistu overthrown. EPLF secured whole of Eritrea and provisional government formed under Issaias Afwerki.
1993 Independence approved in regional referendum and recognized by Ethiopia. Transitional government established for four-year period, with Afwerki elected president; 500,000 refugees outside Eritrea began to return.
1994 EPLF renamed PFDJ.
1997 New constitution adopted.

Practical information

Visa requirements UK: visa required. USA: visa required
Embassy in the UK Eritrean Consulate, 96 White Lion Street, London N1 9PF. Tel: (0171) 713 0096; fax: (0171) 713 0161
British embassy British Consulate, PO Box 5584, c/o Mitchell Gotts Building, Emperor Yohannes Avenue 5, Asmara. Tel: (1) 120 145; fax: (1) 120 104
Embassy in the USA Suite 400, 910 17th Street NW, Washington, DC 20006. Tel: (202) 429 1991; fax: (202) 429 9004
American embassy Franklin D Roosevelt Street, Asmara. Tel: (1) 120 004; fax: (1) 127 584

Chamber of commerce Asmara Chamber of Commerce, PO Box 856, Asmara. Tel: (1) 21388; fax: (1) 20138
Office hours 0800–1200 and 1400–1700 Mon–Fri; 0800–1200 Sat
Banking hours 0800–1200 and 1400–1700 Mon–Fri; 0800–1200 Sat
Time difference GMT +3
Chief tourist attractions tourism remains largely undeveloped; Dahlak Islands (a coral archipelago rich in marine life) near Massawa; unique ecosystem on escarpment that rises from coastal plain
Major holidays 1, 6 January, 24 May, 20 June, 1 September, 25 December; variable: Eid-ul-Adha, Arafa, end of Ramadan

Estonia Republic of

National name *Eesti Vabariik*
Area 45,000 sq km/17,374 sq mi
Capital Tallinn
Major towns/cities Tartu, Narva, Kohtla-
Järve, Pärnu
Physical features lakes and marshes in
a partly forested plain; 774 km/481 mi of
coastline; mild climate; Lake Peipus and
Narva River forming boundary with
Russian Federation; Baltic islands, the
largest of which is Saaremaa

Government

Head of state Lennart Meri from 1992
Head of government Mart Siimann from
1997
Political system emergent democracy
Administrative divisions 15 counties
and six towns
Political parties Coalition Party (KMU),
ex-communist, left of centre, 'social
market'; Isamaa (National Fatherland
Party, or Pro Patria), right wing,
nationalist, free market; Estonian Reform
Party (ERP), freemarket; Centre Party
(CP), moderate nationalist (formerly the
Estonian Popular Front (EPF;
Rahvarinne); Estonian National
Independence Party (ENIP), radical
nationalist; Communist Party of Estonia
(CPE); Our Home is Estonia; Estonian
Social Democratic Party (ESDP) (last
three draw much of their support from
ethnic Russian community)
Armed forces 4,000 (1995); plus a
reserve militia of 6,000 and a paramilitary
border guard of 2,000
Conscription compulsory for 12 months
(men and women)
Death penalty retained and used for
ordinary crimes
Defence spend (% GDP) 5.3 (1995)
Education spend (% GNP) 5.8
(1993–94)

Economy and resources

Currency kroon
GDP ($ US) 5 billion (1994)
Real GDP per capita (PPP) ($ US)
4,294 (1994)
GDP growth rate 4.7% (1994); –9.2%
(1990–95)
Average annual inflation 48% (1994);
76.2% (1985–95)
Foreign debt ($ US) 309 million (1995)
Trading partners Finland, Russia,
Sweden, Germany, Latvia, the
Netherlands, Lithuania, UK, Japan
Resources oilshale, peat, phosphorite
ore, superphosphates
Industries machine building, electronics,
electrical engineering, textiles, fish and
food processing, consumer goods
Exports foodstuffs, animal products,
textiles, timber products, base metals,
mineral products, machinery. Principal
market: Finland 19.8% (1996)
Imports machinery and transport
equipment, food products, textiles,
mineral products. Principal source:
Finland 36.7 (1996)
Arable land 34% (1993)
Agricultural products wheat, rye,
barley, potatoes, other vegetables;
livestock rearing (cattle and pigs); dairy
farming

Population and society

Population 1,471,000 (1996e)
Population growth rate –0.6%
(1990–95); –0.3 (2000–05)
Population density (per sq km) 33
(1996e)
Urban population (% of total) 73 (1995)
Age distribution (% of total population)
<15 20.6%, 15–65 66.6%, >65 12.8%
(1995)
Ethnic distribution 62% Finno-Ugric
ethnic Estonians, 30% Russian, 3%
Ukrainian, 2% Belarusian, 1% Finnish
Languages Estonian (official), allied to
Finnish; Russian
Religions Lutheran, Russian Orthodox
Education (compulsory years) 9
Literacy rate 99% (men); 99% (women)
(1995e)
Labour force 8.7% agriculture, 35.7%
industry, 55.6% services (1994)
Unemployment 2.2% (1996)
Life expectancy 64 (men); 75 (women)
(1995–2000)
Child mortality rate (under 5, per 1,000
live births) 22 (1995)

Physicians 1 per 312 people (1993)
Hospital beds 1 per 105 people (1993)
TV sets (per 1,000 people) 383 (1995)
Radios (per 1,000 people) 491 (1995)

Transport

Airports international airports: Tallinn;
three domestic airports; total passenger
km: 92 mil (1994)
Railroads total length: 1,018 km/633 mi;
total passenger km: 537 mil (1994)
Roads total road network: 14,992 km/
9,316 mi, of which 54% paved (1995);
passenger cars: 226.4 per 1,000 people
(1994)

Chronology

1st century AD First independent state
formed.
9th century Invaded by Vikings.
13th century Tallinn, in the Danish-
controlled N, joined Hanseatic League, a
N European union of commercial towns;
Livonia, comprising S Estonia and Latvia,
came under control of German Teutonic
Knights and was converted to
Christianity.
1561 Sweden took control of N Estonia.
1629 Sweden took control of S Estonia
from Poland.
1721 Sweden ceded the country to
tsarist Russia.
late 19th century Estonian nationalist
movement developed in opposition to
Russian political and cultural repression
and German economic control.
1914 Occupied by German troops.
1918–19 Estonian nationalists, led by
Konstantin Pats, proclaimed and
achieved independence, despite efforts
by the Russian Red Army to regain
control.
1920s Land reforms and cultural
advances under democratic regime.
1934 Pats overthrew parliamentary
democracy in a quasi-fascist coup at a
time of economic depression; Baltic
Entente mutual defence pact signed with
Latvia and Lithuania.
1940 Estonia incorporated into Soviet
Union (USSR); 100,000 Estonians
deported to Siberia or killed.
1941–44 German occupation during
World War II.
1944 USSR regained control;
'Sovietization' followed, including
agricultural collectivization and
immigration of ethnic Russians.

late 1980s Beginnings of nationalist dissent, encouraged by *glasnost* initiative of reformist Soviet leader Mikhail Gorbachev.
1988 Popular Front (EPF) established to campaign for democracy. Sovereignty declaration issued by state assembly rejected by USSR as unconstitutional.
1989 Estonian replaced Russian as main language.
1990 CPE monopoly of power abolished; pro-independence candidates secured majority after multiparty elections; coalition government formed with EPF leader Edgar Savisaar as prime minister;

Arnold Rüütel became president. Prewar constitution partially restored.
1991 Independence achieved after attempted anti-Gorbachev coup in Moscow; CPE outlawed. Estonia joined United Nations.
1992 Savisaar resigned over food and energy shortages; Isamaa leader Lennart Meri became president and free-marketer Mart Laar prime minister.
1993 Joined Council of Europe; free-trade agreement with Latvia and Lithuania.
1994 Last Russian troops withdrawn. Radical economic-reform programme

introduced; controversial law on 'aliens' passed, requiring non-ethnic Estonians to apply for residency. Laar resigned.
1995 Former communists won largest number of seats in general election; left-of-centre coalition formed under Tiit Vahi.
1996 President Meri re-elected. Ruling coalition collapsed; Prime Minister Tiit Vahi continued with a minority government.
1997 Vahi, accused of corruption, resigned and was replaced by Mart Siimann. Estonia invited to begin European Union membership negotiations.

Practical information

Visa requirements UK: visa not required. USA: visa not required
Embassy in the UK 16 Hyde Park Gate, London SW7 5DG. Tel: (0171) 589 3428; fax: (0171) 589 3430
British embassy Kentmanni 20, EE-0100 Tallinn. Tel: (2) 313 353; fax: (2) 313 354
Embassy in the USA 2131 Massachusetts Avenue NW, Washington, DC 20008. Tel: (202) 588 0101; fax: (202) 789 0471

American embassy Kentmanni 20, Tallinn EE 0001. Tel: (6) 312 021; fax: (6) 312 025
Chamber of commerce Chamber of Commerce and Industry of the Republic of Estonia, Toom-Kooli Street 17, EE-0001 Tallinn. Tel: (2) 444 929; fax: (2) 443 656
Office hours 0830–1830 Mon–Fri
Banking hours 0930–1630 Mon–Fri
Time difference GMT +2
Chief tourist attractions historic towns of Tallinn and Tartu; nature reserves; coastal resorts
Major holidays 1 January, 24 February, 1 May, 23–24 June, 25–26 December; variable: Good Friday

---

Ethiopia Federal Democratic Republic of (formerly known as *Abyssinia*)

National name *Hebretesebawit Ityopia*
Area 1,096,900 sq km/423,513 sq mi
Capital Addis Ababa
Major towns/cities Jimma, Dire Dawa, Harar, Nazret, Dessie, Gonder, Mek'elē
Physical features a high plateau with central mountain range divided by Rift Valley; plains in E; source of Blue Nile River; Danakil and Ogaden deserts

Government

Head of state Negasso Ghidada from 1995
Head of government Meles Zenawi from 1995

Political system transition to democratic federal republic
Administrative divisions nine states and one metropolitan area
Political parties Ethiopian People's Revolutionary Democratic Front (EPRDF), nationalist, left of centre; Tigré People's Liberation Front (TPLF); Ethiopian People's Democratic Movement (EPDM); United Oromo Liberation Front, Islamic nationalist
Armed forces 120,000 (1995)
Conscription voluntary
Death penalty retained and used for ordinary crimes
Defence spend (% GDP) 2.1 (1995)
Education spend (% GNP) 5.1 (1992)
Health spend (% GDP) 2.3 (1990)

Economy and resources

Currency Ethiopian birr
GDP ($ US) 4.7 billion (1994)
Real GDP per capita (PPP) ($ US) 427 (1994)
GDP growth rate 4.8% (1994)
Average annual inflation 5.9% (1985–95e)
Foreign debt ($ US) 5.22 billion (1995)

Trading partners Germany, Saudi Arabia, USA, Japan, UK, Italy, France
Resources gold, salt, platinum, copper, potash. Reserves of petroleum have not been exploited
Industries food processing, petroleum refining, beverages, textiles
Exports coffee, hides and skins, petroleum products, fruit and vegetables. Principal market: Germany 31.7% (1994)
Imports machinery, aircraft and other vehicles, petroleum and petroleum products, basic manufactures, chemicals and related products. Principal source: Saudi Arabia 15% (1994)
Arable land 10.9% (1993)
Agricultural products coffee, teff (an indigenous grain), barley, maize, sorghum, sugar cane; livestock rearing (cattle and sheep) and livestock products (hides, skins, butter and ghee)

Population and society

Population 58,243,000 (1996e)
Population growth rate 3% (1990–95); 2.9% (2000–05)

Population density (per sq km) 53 (1996e)
Urban population (% of total) 13 (1995)
Age distribution (% of total population) <15 46.4%, 15–65 50.8%, >65 2.9% (1995)
Ethnic distribution over 70 different ethnic groups, the two main ones are the Galla (mainly in the E and S of the central plateau), who comprise about 40% of the population, and the Amhara and Tigré (largely in the central plateau itself), who constitute about 35%
Languages Amharic (official), Tigrinya, Orominga, Arabic
Religions Sunni Muslim, Christian (Ethiopian Orthodox Church, which has had its own patriarch since 1976) 40%, animist
Education (compulsory years) 6
Literacy rate 45% (men); 25% (women) (1995e)
Labour force 88.6% agriculture, 2% industry, 9.4% services (1995)
Unemployment 40.5% (1992e)
Life expectancy 48 (men); 52 (women) (1995–2000)
Child mortality rate (under 5, per 1,000 live births) 195 (1995)
Physicians 1 per 33,333 people (1991)
Hospital beds 1 per 4,035 people (1991)
TV sets (per 1,000 people) 4.4 (1995)
Radios (per 1,000 people) 193 (1995)

Transport

Airports international airports: Addis Ababa (Bole), Dire Dawa; over 40 small domestic airports or airfields; total passenger km: 1,607 mil (1994)
Railroads total length: 781 km/485 mi; total passenger km: 230 mil (1993)

Roads total road network: 28,360 km/17, 623 mi, of which 15% paved (1995e); passenger cars: 0.8 per 1,000 people (1995)

Chronology

1st–7th centuries AD Founded by Semitic immigrants from Saudi Arabia, the kingdom of Aksum and its capital, NW of Ādwa, flourished. It reached its peak in the 4th century when Coptic Christianity was introduced from Egypt.
7th century onwards Islam was spread by Arab conquerors.
11th century Emergence of independent Ethiopian kingdom of Abyssinia, which was to remain dominant for nine centuries.
late 15th century Abyssinia visited by Portuguese explorers.
1889 Abyssinia reunited by Menelik II.
1896 Invasion by Italy defeated by Menelik at Ādwa, who went on to annex Ogaden in the SE and areas to the W.
1916 Haile Selassie became regent.
1930 Haile Selassie became emperor.
1936 Conquered by Italy and incorporated in Italian East Africa.
1941 Return of Emperor Selassie after liberation by the British.
1952 Ethiopia federated with Eritrea.
1962 Eritrea annexed by Selassie; Eritrean People's Liberation front (EPLF) resistance movement began, a rebellion that was to continue for 30 years.
1963 First conference of Selassie-promoted Organization of African Unity (OAU) held in Addis Ababa.
1973–74 Severe famine in N Ethiopia; 200,000 died in Wallo province.
1974 Haile Selassie deposed and replaced by a military government led

by Gen Teferi Benti.
1977 Teferi Benti killed and replaced by Col Mengistu Haile Mariam. Somali forces ejected from the Somali-peopled Ogaden in the SE.
1977–79 'Red Terror' period in which Mengistu's single-party Marxist regime killed thousands of people and promoted collective farming; Tigré People's Liberation Front guerrillas began fighting for regional autonomy in the northern highlands.
1984 Workers' Party of Ethiopia (WPE) declared the only legal political party.
1985 Worst famine in more than a decade; Western aid sent and forcible internal resettlement programmes undertaken in Eritrea and Tigré in the N.
1987 Mengistu Mariam elected president under new constitution. New famine; food aid hindered by guerrillas.
1989 Coup attempt against Mengistu foiled. Peace talks with Eritrean rebels mediated by former US president Jimmy Carter.
1991 Mengistu overthrown; transitional government set up by opposing Ethiopian People's Revolutionary Democratic Front (EPRDF), headed by Meles Zenawi. EPLF took control over Eritrea. Famine gripped the country.
1993 Eritrean independence recognized after referendum; private farming and market sector encouraged by EPRDF government.
1994 New federal constitution adopted.
1995 Ruling EPRDF won majority of seats in first multiparty elections to a interim parliament. Negasso Ghidada chosen as president; Zenawi appointed premier.

Practical information

Visa requirements UK: visa required. USA: visa required
Embassy in the UK 17 Prince's Gate, London SW7 1PZ. Tel: (0171) 589 7212; fax: (0171) 584 7054
British embassy PO Box 858, Fikre Mariam Abatechan Street, Addis Ababa. Tel: (1) 612 354; fax: (1) 610 588
Embassy in the USA 2134 Kalorama Road NW, Washington, DC 20008. Tel: (202) 234 2281/2; fax: (202) 328 7950
American embassy Entoto Street, Addis Ababa. Tel: (1) 550 666; fax: (1) 552 191
Chamber of commerce Ethiopian Chamber of Commerce,

PO Box 517, Mexico Square, Addis Ababa. Tel: (1) 518 240; telex: 21213
Office hours 0800–1200 and 1300–1700 Mon–Fri
Banking hours 0800–1200 and 1300–1700 Mon–Thu; 0830–1130 and 1300–1700 Fri
Time difference GMT +3
Chief tourist attractions early Christian churches and monuments; ancient capitals of Gonder and Aksum; Blue Nile Falls; national parks of Semien and Bale Mountains
Major holidays 7, 19 January, 2 March, 6 April, 1 May, 12, 27 September; variable: Eid-ul-Adha, end of Ramadan, Ethiopian New Year (September), Prophet's Birthday, Ethiopian Good Friday and Easter

Fiji Republic of

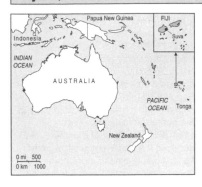

Area 18,333 sq km/7,078 sq mi
Capital Suva
Major towns/cities Lautoka, Nadi, Ba, Labasa
Major ports Lautoka and Levuka
Physical features comprises about 844 Melanesian and Polynesian islands and islets (about 100 inhabited), the largest being Viti Levu (10,429 sq km/4,028 sq mi) and Vanua Levu (5,556 sq km/2,146 sq mi); mountainous, volcanic, with tropical rainforest and grasslands; almost all islands surrounded by coral reefs; high volcanic peaks

Government

Head of state Ratu Sir Kamisese Mara from 1994
Head of government Col Sitiveni Rabuka from 1992
Political system democratic republic
Administrative divisions 14 provinces
Political parties National Federation Party (NFP), moderate left of centre, Indian; Fijian Labour Party (FLP), left of centre, Indian; United Front, Fijian; Fijian Political Party (FPP), Fijian centrist
Armed forces 3,900 (1995)
Conscription voluntary
Death penalty laws provide for the death penalty only for exceptional crimes such as crimes under military law or crimes committed in exceptional cricumstances such as wartime (last execution 1964)
Defence spend (% GDP) 1.5 (1995)
Education spend (% GNP) 5.4 (1993–94)
Health spend (% GDP) 1.3 (1994)

Economy and resources

Currency Fiji dollar
GDP ($ US) 1.84 billion (1994)
Real GDP per capita (PPP) ($ US) 5,763 (1994)

GDP growth rate 5.2% (1994)
Average annual inflation 4.9% (1985–95)
Foreign debt ($ US) 343 million (1991–93)
Trading partners Australia, New Zealand, Japan, UK, USA
Resources gold, silver, copper
Industries food processing (sugar, molasses, and copra), ready-made garments, animal feed, cigarettes, cement, tourism
Exports sugar, gold, fish and fish products, clothing, re-exported petroleum products, timber, ginger, molasses. Principal market: Australia 22.4% (1995)
Imports basic manufactured goods, machinery and transport equipment, food, mineral fuels. Principal source: Australia 39.2% (1995)
Arable land 9.9% (1993)
Agricultural products sugar cane, coconuts, ginger, rice, tobacco, cocoa; forestry (for timber)

Population and society

Population 797,000 (1996e)
Population growth rate 1.5% (1990–95); 1.5% (2000–05)
Population density (per sq km) 44 (1996e)
Urban population (% of total) 41 (1995)
Age distribution (% of total population) <15 34.6%, 15–65 61.5%, >65 3.8% (1995)
Ethnic distribution 48% Fijians (of Melanesian and Polynesian descent), 51% Asians
Languages English (official), Fijian, Hindi
Religions Methodist, Hindu, Muslim, Sikh
Education not compulsory
Literacy rate 94% (men); 89% (women) (1995e)
Labour force 34% of population: 46% agriculture, 15% industry, 39% services (1990)
Unemployment 5.6% (1993)
Life expectancy 71 (men); 75 (women) (1995–2000)
Child mortality rate (under 5, per 1,000 live births) 25 (1995)
Physicians 1 per 2,011 people (1992)
Hospital beds 1 per 417 people (1992)
TV sets (per 1,000 people) 18 (1995)
Radios (per 1,000 people) 612 (1995)

Transport

Airports international airports: Nadi; 16 domestic airports and airfields; total passenger km: 1,101 mil (1994)
Railroads no passenger railroad system; Fiji Sugar Cane Corporation operates a 595-km/370-mi railroad
Roads total road network: 3,370 km/2,094 mi, of which 49% paved (1995e); passenger cars: 39.7 per 1,000 people (1993e)

Chronology

c. 1500 BC Peopled by Polynesian and, later, by Melanesian settlers.
1643 The islands were visited for the first time by a European, the Dutch navigator Abel Tasman.
1830s Arrival of Western Christian missionaries.
1840s–50s Western Fiji came under dominance of a Christian convert prince, Cakobau, ruler of Bau islet, who proclaimed himself Tui Viti (King of Fiji), while the E was controlled by Ma'afu, a Christian prince from Tonga.
1857 British consul appointed, encouraging settlers from Australia and New Zealand to set up cotton farms in Fiji.
1874 Fiji became a British crown colony after deed of cession signed by King Cakobau.
1875–76 A third of the Fijian population wiped out by a measles epidemic; rebellion against British suppressed with the assitance of Fijian chiefs.
1877 Fiji became headquarters of the British Western Pacific High Commission (WPHC), which controlled other British protectorates in the Pacific region.
1879–1916 Indian labourers brought in, on ten-year indentured contracts, to work sugar plantations.
1904 Legislative Council formed, with elected Europeans and nominated Fijians, to advise the British governor.
1963 Legislative Council enlarged; women and Fijians were enfranchised. The predominantly Fijian Alliance Party (AP) formed.
1970 Independence achieved from Britain; Ratu Sir Kamisese Mara of the AP elected as first prime minister.
1973 Ratu Sir George Cakobau, great-grandson of the chief who had sworn allegiance to the British in 1874, became governor general.

1985 FLP formed by Timoci Bavadra, with trade-union backing.
1987 After general election had brought to power an Indian-dominated coalition led by Bavadra, Lt-Col Sitiveni Rabuka seized power after a military coup, and proclaimed a Fijian-dominated republic outside the Commonwealth.

1990 New constitution, favouring indigenous (Melanese) Fijians, introduced. Civilian rule re-established, with resignations from cabinet of military officers, but Rabuka remained as home affairs minister, with Mara as prime minister.
1992 General election produced coalition

government with Rabuka of the FPP as prime minister.
1993 President Ganilau died and was replaced by Ratu Sir Kamisese Mara.
1994 Rabuka and FPP re-elected.
1997 Fiji re-admitted to the Commonwealth.

Practical information

Visa requirements UK: visa not required. USA: visa not required
Embassy in the UK 34 Hyde Park Gate, London SW7 5DN. Tel: (0171) 839 2200; fax: (0171) 839 9050
British embassy PO Box 1355, Victoria House, 47 Gladstone Road, Suva. Tel: (679) 311 033; fax: (679) 301 406
Embassy in the USA Suite 240, 2233 Wisconsin Avenue NW, Washington, DC 20007. Tel: (202) 337 8320; fax: (202) 337 1996
American embassy 31 Loftus Street, Suva.

Tel: (679) 314 466; fax: (679) 300 081
Chamber of commerce Suva Chamber of Commerce, PO Box 337, 2nd Floor, GB Hari Building, 12 Pier Street, Suva. Tel: (679) 303 854; fax: (679) 300 475
Office hours 0800–1630 Mon–Fri (some businesses close 30 minutes earlier on Fri)
Banking hours 0930–1500 Mon–Thu; 0930–1600 Fri
Time difference GMT +12
Chief tourist attractions climate; scenery; fishing; diving
Major holidays 1 January, 12 October, 25–26 December; variable: Diwali, Good Friday, Easter Monday, Holy Saturday, Prophet's Birthday, August Bank Holiday, Queen's Birthday (June), Prince Charles's Birthday (November)

Finland Republic of

National name *Suomen Tasavalta*
Area 338,145 sq km/130,557 sq mi
Capital Helsinki (Helsingfors)
Major towns/cities Tampere, Turku, Espoo, Vantaa
Major ports Turku, Oulu
Physical features most of the country is forest, with low hills and about 60,000 lakes; one-third is within the Arctic Circle; archipelago in S includes Åland Islands; Helsinki is the most northerly national capital on the European continent. At the 70th parallel there is constant daylight for 73 days in summer and 51 days of uninterrupted night in winter.

Government

Head of state Martti Ahtisaari from 1994

Head of government Paavo Lipponen from 1995
Political system democratic republic
Administrative divisions 12 provinces
Political parties Finnish Social Democratic Party (SSDP), moderate left of centre; National Coalition Party (KOK), moderate right of centre; Finnish Centre Party (KESK), radical centrist, rural-oriented; Swedish People's Party (SFP), independent Swedish-oriented; Finnish Rural Party (SMP), farmers and small businesses; Left-Wing Alliance (VL), left wing
Armed forces 31,100 (1995)
Conscription up to 11 months, followed by refresher training of 40–100 days (before age 50)
Death penalty abolished 1972
Defence spend (% GDP) 2.0 (1995)
Education spend (% GNP) 8.4 (1993–94)
Health spend (% GDP) 7.0 (1993)

Economy and resources

Currency markka
GDP ($ US) 124 billion (1996)
Real GDP per capita (PPP) ($ US) 18,657 (1996)
GDP growth rate 3.9% (1996); –0.5% (1990–95)
Average annual inflation 1.2% (1996); 3.8% (1985–95)
Trading partners Germany, Sweden,

UK, USA, Russia, Denmark, Norway, the Netherlands
Resources copper ore, lead ore, gold, zinc ore, silver, peat, hydro power, forests
Industries food processing, paper and paper products, machinery, printing and publishing, wood products, metal products, shipbuilding, chemicals, clothing and footwear
Exports metal and engineering products, gold, paper and paper products, machinery, ships, wood and pulp, clothing and footwear, chemicals. Principal market: Germany 12.1% (1996)
Imports mineral fuels, machinery and transport equipment, food and live animals, chemical and related products, textiles, iron and steel. Principal source: Germany 15.1% (1996)
Arable land 9% (1993)
Agricultural products oats, sugar beet, potatoes, barley, hay; forestry and animal husbandry

Population and society

Population 5,126,000 (1996e)
Population growth rate 0.5% (1990–95); 0.3% (2000–05)
Population density (per sq km) 15 (1996e)
Urban population (% of total) 63 (1995)

Age distribution (% of total population)
<15 19.1%, 15–65 66.8%, >65 14.1%
(1995)
Ethnic distribution majority descended
from Russian inhabitants
Languages Finnish 93%, Swedish 6%
(both official); small Saami- and
Russian-speaking minorities
Religions Lutheran 90%, Orthodox 1%
Education (compulsory years) 9
Literacy rate 100% (men); 100%
(women) (1995e)
Labour force 52% of population: 8%
agriculture, 31% industry, 61% services
(1990)
Unemployment 15.8% (1996)
Life expectancy 73 (men); 80 (women)
(1995–2000)
Child mortality rate (under 5, per 1,000
live births) 5 (1995)
Physicians 1 per 345 people (1994)
Hospital beds 1 per 108 people
(1994)
TV sets (per 1,000 people) 519 (1995)
Radios (per 1,000 people) 1,008
(1995)

Transport

Airports international airports: Helsinki
(Vantaa); 20 domestic airports; total
passenger km: 6,720 mil (1994)
Railroads total length: 5,859 km/
3,641 mi; total passenger km: 3,037 mil
(1994)
Roads total road network: 77,722 km/
48,296 mi, of which 63% paved (1995);
passenger cars: 371 per 1,000 people
(1995)

Chronology

1st century Occupied by Finnic nomads
from Asia who drove out native Saami
(Lapps) to the far N.

12th–13th centuries Series of Swedish
crusades conquered Finns and
converted them to Christianity.
16th–17th centuries Finland was a
semi-autonomous Swedish duchy with
Swedish landowners ruling Finnish
peasants; Finland allowed relative
autonomy, becoming a grand duchy
1581.
1634 Finland fully incorporated into
Swedish kingdom.
1700–21 Great Northern War between
Sweden and Russia; half of Finnish
population died in famine and
epidemics.
1741–43 and 1788–90 Further Russo–
Swedish wars; much of the fighting took
place in Finland.
1808 Russia invaded Sweden (with
support of Napoleon).
1809 Finland ceded to Russia as grand
duchy with Russian tsar as grand duke;
Finns retained their own legal system
and Lutheran religion and were exempt
from Russian military service.
1812 Helsinki became capital of grand
duchy.
19th century Growing prosperity was
followed by rise of national feeling
among new Finnish middle class.
1904–05 Policies promoting
Russification of Finland provoked
national uprising; Russians imposed
military rule.
1917 Finland declared independence.
1918 Bitter civil war between Reds
(supported by Russian Bolsheviks) and
Whites (supported by Germany); Baron
Carl Gustaf Mannerheim led Whites to
victory.
1919 Republican constitution adopted
with Kaarlo Juho Ståhlberg as first
president.
1927 Land reform broke up big estates

and created many small peasant
farms.
1939–40 Winter War: USSR invaded
Finland after demand for military bases
was refused.
1940 Treaty of Moscow: Finland ceded
territory to USSR.
1941 Finland joined German attack on
USSR in hope of regaining lost
territory.
1944 Finland agreed separate
armistice with USSR; German troops
withdrawn.
1947 Finno-Soviet peace treaty: Finland
forced to cede 12% of its total area and
to pay $300 million in reparations.
1948 Finno-Soviet Pact of Friendship,
Cooperation, and Mutual Assistance
(YYA treaty): Finland pledged to repel
any attack on USSR through its
territories.
1950s Unstable centre-left coalitions
excluded communists from government
and adopted strict neutrality in foreign
affairs.
1955 Finland joined United Nations
(UN) and Nordic Council.
1956 Urho Kekkonen elected president.
General strike as a result of
unemployment and inflation.
1973 Trade agreements signed with
European Economic Community (EEC)
and Comecon.
1982 Mauno Koivisto elected
president.
1987 New coalition of Social Democrats
and conservatives formed.
1991 Big swing to Centre Party in
general election.
1994 Martti Ahtisaari (SSDP) elected
president.
1995 Finland joined European Union
(EU); Social Democrats won general
election.

Practical information

Visa requirements UK: visa not required. USA: visa not
required
Embassy in the UK 38 Chesham Place, London
SW1X 8HW. Tel: (0171) 235 9531; fax: (0171) 235 3680
British embassy Itäinen Puistotie 17, 00140 Helsinki.
Tel: (0) 661 293; fax: (0) 661 342
Embassy in the USA 3301 Massachusetts Avenue NW,
Washington, DC 20008. Tel: (202) 298 5800;
fax: (202) 298 6030
American embassy Itäinen Puistotie 14A, FIN-00140,
Helsinki. Tel: (0) 171 931; fax: (0) 174 681

Chamber of commerce Keskuskauppakamari (Central
Chamber of Commerce of Finland), PO Box 1000,
Fabianinkatu 14, 00101 Helsinki. Tel: (0) 650 133;
fax: (0) 650 303
Office hours 0800–1615 Mon–Fri
Banking hours 0915–1615 Mon–Fri
Time difference GMT +2
Chief tourist attractions scenery: forests, lakes (Europe's
largest inland water system)
Major holidays 1 January, 1 May, 31 Octobor, 1 November,
1, 24–26, 31 December; variable: Ascension Thursday, Good
Friday, Easter Monday, Midsummer Eve and Day (June),
Twelfthtide (January), Whitsuntide (May/June)

France French Republic

National name *République Française*
Area (including Corsica) 543,965 sq km/
210,024 sq mi
Capital Paris
Major towns/cities Lyon, Lille,
Bordeaux, Toulouse, Nantes, Strasbourg,
Montpellier, Saint-Etienne, Rennes,
Reims, Grenoble
Major ports Marseille, Nice, Le Havre
Physical features rivers Seine, Loire,
Garonne, Rhône; mountain ranges Alps,
Massif Central, Pyrenees, Jura, Vosges,
Cévennes; Auvergne mountain region;
Mont Blanc (4,810 m/15,781 ft);
Ardennes forest; Riviera; caves of
Dordogne with relics of early humans;
the island of Corsica
Territories Guadeloupe, French Guiana,
Martinique, Réunion, St Pierre and
Miquelon, Southern and Antarctic
Territories, New Caledonia, French
Polynesia, Wallis and Futuna, Mayotte

Government

Head of state Jacques Chirac from 1995
Head of government Lionel Jospin from
1997
Political system liberal democracy
Administrative divisions 22 regions
containing 96 departments, four
overseas departments, two territorial
collectivities, and four overseas territories
Political parties Rally for the Republic
(RPR), neo-Gaullist conservative; Union
for French Democracy (UDF), centre
right; Socialist Party (PS), left of centre;
Left Radical Movement (MRG), centre
left; French Communist Party (PCF),
Marxist-Leninist; National Front, far right;
Greens, fundamentalist-ecologist;
Génération Ecologie, pragmatic
ecologist; Movement for France, right
wing, anti-Maastricht

Armed forces 409,000; paramilitary
gendarmerie 93,400 (1995)
Death penalty abolished 1981
Defence spend (% GDP) 3.1 (1995)
Education spend (% GNP) 5.8
(1993–94)
Health spend (% GDP) 7.3 (1993)

Economy and resources

Currency franc
GDP ($ US) 1,540.1 billion (1996)
Real GDP per capita (PPP) ($ US)
20,534 (1996)
GDP growth rate 1.1% (1996); 1%
(1990–95)
Average annual inflation 1% (1996);
2.8% (1985–95)
Trading partners EU (principally
Germany, Italy, Benelux, UK); USA
Resources coal, petroleum, natural gas,
iron ore, copper, zinc, bauxite
Industries mining, quarrying, food
products, transport equipment, nonelectrical machinery, electrical machinery,
weapons, metals and metal products,
yarn and fabrics, wine, tourism, aircraft,
weapons
Exports machinery and transport
equipment, food and live animals,
beverages and tobacco, textile yarn,
fabrics and other basic manufactures,
clothing and accessories, perfumery and
cosmetics. Principal market: Germany
17.1% (1996)
Imports food and live animals, mineral
fuels, machinery and transport
equipment, chemicals and chemical
products, basic manufactures. Principal
source: Germany 17.4% (1996)
Arable land 33.1%
Agricultural products wheat, sugar
beet, maize, barley, vine fruits, potatoes,
fruit, vegetables; livestock and dairy
products

Population and society

Population 58,333,000 (1996e)
Population growth rate 0.4%
(1990–95); 0.2% (2000–05)
Population density (per sq km) 106
(1996e)
Urban population (% of total) 73 (1995)
Age distribution (% of total population)
<15 19.6%, 15–65 65.5%, >65 14.9%
(1995)
Ethnic distribution predominantly
French ethnic, of Celtic and Latin
descent; Basque minority in the SW; 7%
of the population are immigrants – a third

of these are from Algeria and Morocco
and live mainly in the Marseille Midi
region and in northern cities, 20%
originate from Portugal, and 10% each
from Italy and Spain
Languages French (regional languages
include Basque, Breton, Catalan, and
Provençal)
Religions Roman Catholic; also Muslim,
Protestant, and Jewish minorities
Education (compulsory years) 10
Literacy rate 100% (men); 100%
(women) (1995e)
Labour force 44% of population: 5%
agriculture, 29% industry, 66% services
(1990)
Unemployment 12.4% (1996)
Life expectancy 74 (men); 81 (women)
(1995–2000)
Child mortality rate (under 5, per 1,000
live births) 9 (1995)
Physicians 1 per 362 people (1993)
Hospital beds 1 per 106 people (1993)
TV sets (per 1,000 people) 599 (1995)
Radios (per 1,000 people) 895 (1995)

Transport

Airports international airports: Paris
(Orly, Roissy-Charles de Gaulle, Le
Bourget), Bordeaux (Merignac), Lille
(Lesquin), Lyon, Marseille, Nice,
Strasbourg, Toulouse (Blagnac); 45
domestic airports; total passenger km:
68,019 mil (1994)
Railroads total length: 34,322 km/21,328
mi; total passenger km: 58,930 mil (1994)
Roads total road network: 812,700 km/
505,012 mi (1995); passenger cars: 433
per 1,000 people (1995)

Chronology

5th century BC Celtic peoples invaded
the region.
58–51 BC Romans conquered Celts and
formed province of Gaul.
5th century AD Gaul overrun by Franks
and other Germanic tribes.
481–511 Frankish chief Clovis accepted
Christianity and formed a kingdom based
at Paris; under his successors, the
Merovingian dynasty, the kingdom
disintegrated.
751–68 Pepin the Short usurped the
Frankish throne, reunified the kingdom,
and founded the Carolingian dynasty.
768–814 Charlemagne conquered much
of W Europe and created the Holy
Roman Empire.

843 Treaty of Verdun divided the Holy Roman Empire into three, with the western portion corresponding to modern France.

9th–10th centuries Weak central government allowed the great nobles to become virtually independent.

987 Frankish crown passed to House of Capet; the Capets ruled the district around Paris, but were surrounded by vassals more powerful than themselves.

1180–1223 Philip II doubled the royal domain and tightened control over the nobles; the power of the Capets gradually extended with support of church and towns.

1328 When Charles IV died without an heir, Philip VI established the House of Valois.

1337 Start of the Hundred Years' War: Edward III of England disputed the Valois succession and claimed the throne. English won victories at Crécy 1346 and Agincourt 1415.

1429 Joan of Arc raised the siege of Orléans; Hundred Years' War ended with Charles VII expelling the English 1453.

1483 France annexed Burgundy and Brittany after Louis XI had restored royal power.

16th–17th centuries French kings fought the Habsburgs (of Holy Roman Empire and Spain) for supremacy in W Europe.

1562–98 Civil wars between nobles were fought under religious slogans, Catholic versus Protestant (or Huguenot).

1589–1610 Henry IV, first king of Bourbon dynasty, established peace, religious tolerance, and absolute monarchy.

1634–48 The ministers Richelieu and Mazarin, by intervening in the Thirty Years' War, secured Alsace and made France the leading power in Europe.

1701–14 War of the Spanish Succession: England, Austria, and allies checked expansionism of France under Louis XIV.

1756–63 Seven Years' War: France lost most of its colonies in India and Canada to Britain.

1789 French Revolution abolished absolute monarchy and feudalism; First Republic proclaimed and revolutionary wars began 1792.

1799 Napoleon Bonaparte seized power in coup; crowned himself emperor 1804; France conquered much of Europe.

1814 Defeat of France; restoration of Bourbon monarchy; comeback by Napoleon defeated at Waterloo 1815.

1830 Liberal revolution deposed Charles X in favour of his cousin Louis Philippe, the 'Citizen King'.

1848 Revolution established Second Republic; conflict between liberals and socialists; Louis Napoleon, nephew of Napoleon I, elected president.

1852 Louis Napoleon proclaimed Second Empire, taking title Napoleon III.

1870–71 Franco-Prussian War: France lost Alsace-Lorraine; Second Empire abolished; Paris Commune crushed; Third Republic founded.

late 19th century France colonized Indochina, much of N Africa, and S Pacific.

1914–18 France resisted German invasion in World War I; Alsace-Lorraine recovered 1919.

1936–37 Left-wing 'Popular Front' government of Léon Blum introduced many social reforms.

1939 France entered World War II.

1940 Germany invaded and occupied N France; Marshal Pétain formed right-wing puppet regime at Vichy; resistance maintained by Maquis and Free French; Germans occupied all France 1942.

1944 Allies liberated France; provisional government formed by Gen Charles de Gaulle, leader of Free French.

1946 Fourth Republic proclaimed.

1949 Became a member of NATO; withdrew from military command structure 1966.

1954 French withdrew from Indochina after eight years of war; start of guerrilla war against French rule in Algeria.

1957 France was a founder member of the European Economic Community.

1958 Algerian crisis caused collapse of Fourth Republic; de Gaulle took power, becoming president of the Fifth Republic 1959.

1962 Algeria achieved independence.

1968 'May events': revolutionary students rioted in Paris; general strike throughout France.

1981 François Mitterrand elected Fifth Republic's first socialist president.

1986–88 'Cohabitation' of socialist president with conservative prime minister; again 1993–95.

1995 Conservative Jacques Chirac elected president. Widespread condemnation of government's decision to resume nuclear tests in Pacific region.

1996 End to nuclear testing in S Pacific. Spending cuts agreed to meet European Monetary Union entry criteria. Unemployment at postwar high. Leader of Corsican separatist wing of outlawed National Liberation Front captured by police.

1997 General election called by President Chirac. Unexpected victory for Socialists; Lionel Jospin appointed prime minister.

Practical information

Visa requirements UK: visa not required. USA: visa not required

Embassy in the UK 58 Knightsbridge, London SW1X 7JT. Tel: (0171) 201 1000; fax: (0171) 201 1004

British embassy 35 rue du Faubourg St Honoré, 75383 Paris. Tel: (1) 4266 9142; fax: (1) 4266 9590

Embassy in the USA 4101 Reservoir Road NW, Washington, DC 20007. Tel: (202) 944 6000

American embassy 2 avenue Gabriel, 75382 Paris Cedex 08. Tel: (1) 4312 2222; fax: (1) 4266 9783

Chamber of commerce Chambre de Commerce et d'Industrie de Paris, 27 avenue de Friedland, 75382 Paris. Tel: (1) 4289 7000; fax: (1) 4289 7286

Office hours generally 0900–1200 and 1400–1800 Mon–Fri

Banking hours 0900–1200 and 1400–1600 Mon–Fri; some banks close on Mon. Banks close early (1200) on the day before a bank holiday; in rare cases, they may also close for all or part of the day after

Time difference GMT +1

Chief tourist attractions Paris, with its boulevards, historic buildings, art treasures, theatres, restaurants, and night clubs; resorts on Mediterranean and Atlantic coasts; many ancient towns; châteaux of the Loire valley; theme parks (Futuroscope and EuroDisney)

Major holidays 1 January, 1, 8 May, 14 July, 14, 15 August, 31 October, 1, 11 November, 24–25, 31 December; variable: Ascension Eve, Ascension Thusday, Good Friday, Easter Monday, Holy Saturday, Whit Holiday Eve, Whit Monday, Law of 20 December 1906, Law of 23 December 1904

Gabon Gabonese Republic

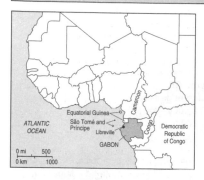

National name *République Gabonaise*
Area 267,667 sq km/103,346 sq mi
Capital Libreville
Major towns/cities Port-Gentil, Masuku
(Franceville), Lambaréné, Mouanda
Major ports Port-Gentil and Owendo
Physical features virtually the whole
country is tropical rainforest; narrow
coastal plain rising to hilly interior with
savanna in E and S; Ogooué River flows
N–W

Government

Head of state Omar Bongo from 1964
Head of government Paulin Obame-
Nguema from 1994
Political system emergent democracy
Administrative divisions nine provinces
Political parties Gabonese Democratic
Party (PDG), nationalist; Gabone
Progress Party (PGP), left of centre;
National Rally of Woodcutters (RNB), left
of centre
Armed forces 4,700 (1995) plus a
paramilitary force of 4,800
Conscription military service
Death penalty retained and used for
ordinary crimes
Defence spend (% GDP) 1.7 (1995)
Education spend (% GNP) 3.2
(1993–94)
Health spend (% GDP) 3.2 (1990)

Economy and resources

Currency franc CFA
GDP ($ US) 3.9 billion (1994)
Real GDP per capita (PPP) ($ US)
3,641 (1994)
GDP growth rate 1.3% (1994); –2.5%
(1990–95)
Average annual inflation 36.2% (1994);
4.8% (1985–95)
Foreign debt ($ US) 4.5 billion (1995)
Trading partners France, USA,
Germany, Spain, Japan, the Netherlands

Resources petroleum, natural gas,
manganese (one of world's foremost
producers and exporters), iron ore,
uranium, gold, niobium, talc, phosphates
Industries mining, food processing
(particularly sugar), petroleum refining,
processing of other minerals, timber
preparation, chemicals
Exports petroleum and petroleum
products, manganese, timber and wood
products, uranium. Principal market: USA
49.9% (1994)
Imports machinery and apparatus,
transport equipment, food products,
metals and metal products. Principal
source: France 39.8% (1994)
Arable land 1.1% (1993)
Agricultural products cassava, sugar
cane, cocoa, coffee, plantains, maize,
groundnuts, bananas, palm oil; forestry
(forests cover approximately 75% of the
land)

Population and society

Population 1,106,000 (1996e)
Population growth rate 2.8%
(1990–95); 2.5% (2000–05)
Population density (per sq km) 4
(1996e)
Urban population (% of total) 50 (1995)
Age distribution (% of total population)
<15 39.2%, 15–65 55.1%, >65 5.8%
(1995)
Ethnic distribution 40 Bantu peoples in
four main groupings: the Fang, Eshira,
Mbede, and Okande; there are also
Pygmies and about 10% Europeans
(mainly French)
Languages French (official), Bantu
Religions Roman Catholic, also Muslim,
animist
Education (compulsory years) 10
Literacy rate 73% (men); 48% (women)
(1995e)
Labour force 64.2% agriculture, 10.8%
industry, 25% services (1994)
Life expectancy 54 (men); 57 (women)
(1995–2000)
Child mortality rate (under 5, per 1,000
live births) 148 (1995)
Physicians 1 per 2,500 people (1991)
Hospital beds 1 per 230 people (1991)
TV sets (per 1,000 people) 46 (1995)
Radios (per 1,000 people) 181 (1995)

Transport

Airports international airports: Port-
Gentil, Masuku, Libreville; 65 public

domestic-services airfields; total
passenger km: 719 mi (1994)
Railroads total length: 668 km/415 mi;
total passenger journeys: 180,000 (1994)
Roads total road network: 7,633 km/
4,743 mi, of which 8.2% paved (1995e);
passenger cars: 17.4 per 1,000 people
(1995e)

Chronology

12th century Immigration of Bantu
speakers into an area previously peopled
by Pygmies.
1472 Gabon Estuary first visited by
Portuguese navigators, who named it
Gabao ('hooded cloak'), after the shape
of the coastal area.
17th–18th centuries Fang, from
Cameroon in N, and Omiene peoples
colonized the area, attracted by
presence in coastal areas of European
traders, who developed the ivory and
slave trades, which lasted until the mid-
19th century.
1839–42 Mpongwe coastal chiefs agreed
to transfer sovereignty to France;
Catholic and Protestant missionaries
attracted to the area.
1849 Libreville ('Free Town') formed by
slaves from a slave ship liberated by the
French.
1889 Became part of French Congo, with
Congo.
1910 Became part of French Equatorial
Africa, which also comprised Congo,
Chad, and Central African Republic.
1890s–1920s Human and natural
resources exploited by private
concessionary companies.
1940–44 Supported the 'Free French'
anti-Nazi cause during World War II.
1946 Became overseas territory within
the French Community, with its own
assembly.
1960 Independence achieved; Léon
M'ba, a Fang of the pro-French
Gabonese Democratic Block (BDG)
became the first president.
1964 Attempted military coup by
supporters of rival party foiled with
French help.
1967 M'ba died and was succeeded by
his protégé Albert Bernard Bongo, drawn
from the Teke community.
1968 One-party state established, with
BDG dissolved and replaced by
Gabonese Democratic Party (PDG).
1973 Bongo converted to Islam and
changed his first name to Omar, but

continued to follow pro-Western policy course and exploit rich mineral resources to increase prosperity.
1989 Coup attempt against Bongo defeated as economy deteriorated.

1990 PDG won first multiparty elections since 1964 amid allegations of ballot-rigging. French troops sent in to maintain order following antigovernment riots.
1993 National unity government formed,

including some opposition members.
1997 Paulin Obame-Nguema was reappointed prime minister after ruling Gabonese Democratic Party (PDG) won large assembly majority.

Practical information

Visa requirements UK: visa required. USA: visa required
Embassy for the UK 27 Elvaston Place, London SW7 5NL. Tel: (0171) 823 9986; fax: (0171) 584 0047
British embassy the British Embassy in Gabon closed in July 1991; all staff based in Yaoundé, Cameroon. The West African Department of the Foreign and Commonwealth Office is currently handling consular and commercial enquiries for Gabon; tel: (0171) 270 2516; fax: (0171) 270 3739
Embassy in the USA Suite 200, 2034 20th Street NW, Washington, DC 20009. Tel: (202) 797 1000; fax: (202) 332 0668

American embassy Boulevard de la Mer, Libreville. Tel: (241) 762 003/762 004/743 492; fax: (241) 745 507
Chamber of commerce Chambre de Commerce, d'Agriculture, d'Industrie et de Mines du Gabon, BP 2234, Libreville. Tel: (241) 722 064; fax: (241) 746 477
Office hours 0730–1200 and 1430–1800 Mon–Fri
Banking hours 0730–1130 and 1430–1630 Mon–Fri
Time difference GMT +1
Chief tourist attractions national parks; tropical vegetation
Major holidays 1 January, 12 March, 1 May, 17 August, 1 November, 25 December; variable: Eid-ul-Adha, Easter Monday, end of Ramadan, Whit Monday

---

Gambia, the Republic of

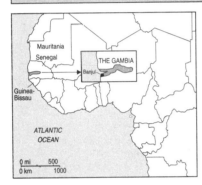

Area 10,402 sq km/4,016 sq mi
Capital Banjul
Major towns/cities Serekunda, Birkama, Bakau, Farafenni, Sukuta, Gunjur, Georgetown
Physical features consists of narrow strip of land along the River Gambia; river flanked by low hills

Government

Head of state and government (interim) Yahya Jameh from 1994
Political system transitional
Administrative divisions 35 districts, grouped into six Area Councils
Political parties Progressive People's Party (PPP), moderate centrist; National Convention Party (NCP), left of centre
Armed forces 800 (1995)
Conscription military service is mainly voluntary
Death penalty retains the death penalty for ordinary crimes but can be

considered abolitionist in practice (last execution 1981)
Defence spend (% GDP) 3.8 (1995)
Education spend (% GNP) 2.7 (1993–94)
Health spend (% GDP) 1.6 (1990)

Economy and resources

Currency dalasi
GDP ($ US) 4 million (1994)
Real GDP per capita (PPP) ($ US) 939 (1994)
GDP growth rate 6.2% (1994); 1.6% (1990–95)
Average annual inflation 1.7% (1994); 10.3% (1985–95e)
Foreign debt ($ US) 426 million (1995)
Trading partners UK, Belgium, Italy, Hong Kong, China, Japan
Resources ilmenite, zircon, rutile, petroleum (well discovered, but not exploited)
Industries food processing (fish, fish products, and vegetable oils), beverages, construction materials
Exports groundnuts and related products, cotton lint, fish and fish preparations, hides and skins. Principal market: UK 25% (1995)
Imports food and live animals, basic manufactures, machinery and transport equipment, mineral fuels and lubrications, miscellaneous manufactured articles, chemicals. Principal source: UK 14.3% (1995)
Arable land 15.9% (1993)
Agricultural products groundnuts,

cotton, rice, citrus fruits, avocados, sesame seed, millet, sorghum, maize; livestock rearing (cattle); fishing

Population and society

Population 1,141,000 (1996e)
Population growth rate 3.8% (1990–95); 2.4% (2000–05)
Population density (per sq km) 101 (1996e)
Urban population (% of total) 26 (1995)
Age distribution (% of total population) <15 41.3%, 15–65 55.8%, >65 2.9%
Ethnic distribution wide mix of ethnic groups, the largest is the Mandingo (about 40%); other main groups are the Fula, Wolof, Jola, and Serahuli
Languages English (official), Mandinka, Fula, and other local languages
Religions Muslim 90%, with animist and Christian minorities
Education free, but not compulsory
Literacy rate 53% (men); 25% (women) (1995e)
Labour force 50% of population: 79.6% agriculture, 4.2% industry, 16.2% services (1994)
Unemployment 26% (1994e)
Life expectancy 45 (men); 47 (women) (1995–2000)
Child mortality rate (under 5, per 1,000 live births) 110 (1995)
Physicians 1 per 14,530 people (1991)
TV sets (per 1,000 people) 3.2 (1995)
Radios (per 1,000 people) 164 (1995)

Transport

Airports international airport: Banjul (Yundum); total passenger km: 50 mil (1994)
Railroads none
Roads total road network: 2,640 km/1,640 mi, of which 35.3% paved (1995e); passenger cars: 7.9 per 1,000 people (1995e)

Chronology

13th century Wolof, Malinke (Mandingo), and Fulani tribes settled in the region from E and N.
14th century Became part of the great Muslim Mali Empire, which, centred to NE, also extended across Senegal, Mali, and S Mauritania.
1455 Gambia River first sighted by the Portuguese.
1663 and 1681 British and French established small settlements on the river at Fort James and Albreda.
1843 The Gambia became a British crown colony, administered with Sierra Leone until 1888.
1965 Independence achieved as a constitutional monarchy within the Commonwealth, with Dawda K Jawara of the People's Progressive Party (PPP) as prime minister at the head of a multiparty democracy.
1970 Became a republic, with Jawara as president.
1981 Attempted coup foiled with the help of Senegal.
1982 Formed with Senegal the Confederation of Senegambia, which involved integration of military forces, economic and monetary union, and coordinated foreign policy.
1994 Jawara ousted in military coup, and fled to Senegal; Yahya Jameh named acting head of state.
1995 Counter-coup attempt failed.
1996 Civilian constitution adopted.

Practical information

Visa requirements UK: visa not required for visits of up to 90 days. USA: visa required
Embassy in the UK 57 Kensington Court, London W8 5DG. Tel: (0171) 937 6316/7/8; fax: (0171) 937 9095
British embassy British High Commission, PO Box 507, 48 Atlantic Road, Fajara, Banjul. Tel: (220) 495 133/4; fax: (220) 496 134
Embassy in the USA Suite 1000, 1155 15th Street NW, Washington, DC 20005. Tel: (202) 785 1399, 1379, 1425; fax: (202) 785 1430

American embassy Fajara, Kairaba Avenue, Banjul. Tel: (220) 392 856/858, 391 970/971; fax: (220) 392 475
Chamber of commerce Gambia Chamber of Commerce and Industry, PO Box 33, 78 Wellington Street, Banjul. Tel: (220) 227 765
Office hours 0800–1600 Mon–Thu; 0800–1230 Fri and Sat
Banking hours 0800–1330 Mon–Thu; 0800–1100 Fri
Time difference GMT +/–0
Chief tourist attractions beaches; coastal resorts; birdlife
Major holidays 1 January, 1, 18 February, 1 May, 15 August, 25 December; variable: Eid-ul-Adha, Ashora, end of Ramadan (2 days), Good Friday, Prophet's Birthday

---

Georgia Republic of

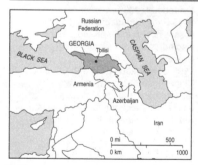

Area 69,700 sq km/26,911 sq mi
Capital Tbilisi
Major towns/cities Kutaisi, Rustavi, Batumi, Sukhumi
Physical features largely mountainous with a variety of landscape from the subtropical Black Sea shores to the ice and snow of the crest line of the Caucasus; chief rivers are Kura and Rioni

Government

Head of state Eduard Shevardnadze from 1992
Head of government Otar Patsatsia from 1993

Political system transitional
Political parties Citizens' Union of Georgia (CUG), nationalist, pro-Shevardnadze; National Democratic Party of Georgia (NDPG), nationalist; Round Table/Free Georgia Bloc, nationalist; Georgian Popular Front (GPF), moderate nationalist, prodemocratization; Georgian Communist Party (GCP); National Independence Party (NIP), ultranationalist; Front for the Reinstatement of Legitimate Power in Georgia, strong nationalist
Armed forces 20,000 (planned in 1996); 9,000 (1995); approximately 22,000 Russian troops were stationed in three military bases 1996
Conscription compulsory for two years
Death penalty retained and used for ordinary crimes
Defence spend (% GDP) 3.4 (1995)
Education spend (% GDP) 1.9% (1993–94)
Health spend 2.2% of total spend (1996)

Economy and resources

Currency lari
GDP ($ US) 2 billion (1994)
Real GDP per capita (PPP) ($ US) 1,585 (1994)
GDP growth rate 8% (1996); –26.9% (1990–95)
Average annual inflation 44.1% (1996); 310% (1985–95)
Foreign debt ($ US) 1.2 billion (1995)
Trading partners Russia, Turkey, Turkmenistan, Azerbaijan
Resources coal, manganese, barytes, clay, petroleum and natural gas deposits, iron and other ores, gold, agate, marble, alabaster, arsenic, tungsten, mercury
Industries metalworking, light industrial goods, motor cars, food processing, textiles (including silk), chemicals, construction materials
Exports metal products, machinery, tea, beverages. Principal market: Russia 29% (1996)
Imports mineral fuels, chemical and petroleum products, food products (mainly wheat and flour), light industrial products, beverages. Principal source: Russia 21% (1996)
Arable land 43% (1993)
Agricultural products grain, tea, citrus fruits, wine grapes, flowers, tobacco, almonds, sugar beet; sheep and goat farming; forest resources

Population and society

Population 5,442,000 (1996e)
Population growth rate 0.1% (1990–95);
0.4% (2000–05)
Population density (per sq km) 78
(1996e)
Urban population (% of total) 58 (1995)
Age distribution (% of total population)
<15 23.7%, 15–65 64.8%, >65 11.4%
(1995)
Ethnic distribution 70% ethnic Georgian,
8% Armenian, 7% ethnic Russian, 5%
Azeri, 3% Ossetian, 2% Abkhazian, and
2% Greek
Language Georgian
Religions Georgian Orthodox, also
Muslim
Education (compulsory years) 9
Literacy rate 99% (men); 99% (women)
(1995e)
Labour force 27.1% agriculture, 19.4%
industry, 53.5% services (1991)
Unemployment 2% (1993)
Life expectancy 70 (men); 78 (women)
(1995–2000)
Child mortality rate (under 5, per 1,000
live births) 26 (1995)
Physicians 1 per 200 people (1994)
Hospital beds 1 per 105 people (1994)
TV sets (per 1,000 people) 468 (1995)
Radios (per 1,000 people) 551 (1995)

Transport

Airports international airports: Tbilisi;
total passenger km: 283 mil (1994)
Railroads total length: 1,583 km/984 mi;
total passenger km: 1,003 mil (1993)
Roads total road network: 21,000 km/
13,049 mi, of which 93.5% paved (1995);
passenger cars: 82.4 per 1,000 people
(1995)

Chronology

4th century BC Georgian kingdom
founded.
1st century BC Part of the Roman Empire.
AD 337 Christianity adopted.
458 Tbilisi founded by King Vakhtang
Gorgasal.
mid-7th century Tbilisi brought under

Arab rule and renamed Tiflis.
1121 Tbilisi liberated by King David II the
Builder, of the Gagrationi dynasty, which
traced its ancestry to the biblical King
David. An empire was established across
the Caucasus region, remaining powerful
until Mongol onslaughts in the 13th and
14th centuries.
1555 W Georgia fell to Turkey and E
Georgia to Persia (Iran).
1783 Treaty of Georgievsk established
Russian dominance over Georgia.
1804–13 First Russo-Iranian war fought
largely over Georgia.
late 19th century Abolition of serfdom
and beginnings of industrialization, but
Georgian church suppressed.
1918 Independence established after
Russian Revolution.
1921 Invaded by Red Army; Soviet
republic established.
1922–36 Linked with Armenia and
Azerbaijan as the Transcaucasian
Federation.
1930s Rapid industrial development, but
resistance to agricultural collectivization
and violent political purges instituted by
the Georgian Soviet dictator Joseph
Stalin.
1936 Became separate republic within
the USSR.
early 1940s 200,000 Meskhetians
deported from S Georgia to Central Asia
on Stalin's orders.
1972 Drive against endemic corruption
launched by new Georgian Communist
Party (GCP) leader Eduard
Shevardnadze.
1977 Initiative Group for the Defence of
Human Rights formed by Zviad
Gamsakhurdia, a nationalist intellectual.
1978 Violent demonstrations by
nationalists in Tbilisi.
1981–88 Increasing demands for
autonomy encouraged from 1986 by the
glasnost initiative of the reformist Soviet
leader Mikhail Gorbachev.
1989 Formation of nationalist Georgian
Popular Front led the minority Abkhazian
and Ossetian communities in NW and
central N Georgia to demand secession,

provoking interethnic clashes. State of
emergency imposed in Abkhazia; 20 pro-
independence demonstrators massacred
in Tbilisi by Soviet troops; Georgian
sovereignty declared by parliament.
1990 Nationalist coalition triumphed in
elections and Gamsakhurdia became
president. GCP seceded from
Communist Party of USSR.
1991 Independence declared. GCP
outlawed and all relations with USSR
severed. Demonstrations against
increasingly dictatorial Gamsakhurdia;
state of emergency declared. Georgia
failed to join new Commonwealth of
Independent States (CIS) as civil war
raged.
1992 Gamsakhurdia fled to Armenia;
Shevardnadze, with military backing,
appointed interim president. Georgia
admitted into United Nations (UN).
Clashes continued in South Ossetia and
Abkhazia, where independence had been
declared.
1993 Conflict with Abkhazi separatists
intensified, forcing Shevardnadze to seek
Russian military help. Pro-Gamsakhurdia
revolt was put down by government
forces and Gamsakhurdia died.
1994 Georgia joined CIS. Military
cooperation pact signed with Russia.
Cease-fire agreed with Abkhazi
separatists; 2,500 Russian peacekeeping
troops deployed in region and
paramilitary groups disarmed. Inflation
exceeded 5,000% a year.
1995 Shevardnadze survived an
assassination attempt and was re-
elected; mass privatization programme
launched.
1996 Cooperation pact with European
Union signed as economic growth
resumed and monthly inflation fell to
below 3%. Elections to secessionist
Abkhazi parliament declared illegal by
Georgian government.
1997 New opposition party formed, Front
for the Reinstatement of Legitimate
Power in Georgia. Talks between
government and breakaway Abkhazi
government.

Practical information

Visa requirements UK: visa required. USA: visa required
Embassy in the UK 45 Avanmore Road, London W14.
Tel/fax: (0171) 603 5325
British embassy Sosiiskaya Naberzehnaya, Moscow 72. Tel:
(70095) 231 8511; fax: (70095) 233 3563
Embassy in the USA (temporary) Suite 424, 1511 K Street
NW, Washington, DC 20005. Tel: (202) 393 5959;
fax: (202) 393 6060
American embassy 25 Antoneli Street, Tbilisi 380026.
Tel: (8832) 989 967, 933 803; fax: (8832) 933 759

Chamber of commerce Chamber of Commerce and Industry of
Georgia, Prospekt I, Chavchavadze 11, 380079 Tbilisi.
Tel: (32) 230 045; fax: (32) 235 760
Office hours 0900–1300 and 1430–1700/1800
Banking hours 0930–1730 Mon–Fri
Time difference GMT +3
Chief tourist attractions mountain scenery; health spas with
mineral waters; waterfalls and caves
Major holidays 1, 19 January, 3, 26 May, 28 August, 14
October, 23 November; variable: Orthodox Christmas (January),
Orthodox Easter (March/April)

Germany Federal Republic of

National name *Bundesrepublik Deutschland*
Area 357,041 sq km/137,853 sq mi
Capital Berlin (government offices moving in phases from Bonn back to Berlin)
Major towns/cities Cologne, Hamburg, Munich, Essen, Frankfurt am Main, Dortmund, Stuttgart, Düsseldorf, Leipzig, Dresden, Bremen, Duisburg, Hannover
Major ports Hamburg, Kiel, Bremerhaven, Rostock
Physical features flat in N, mountainous in S with Alps; rivers Rhine, Weser, Elbe flow N, Danube flows SE, Oder, Neisse flow N along Polish frontier; many lakes, including Müritz; Black Forest, Harz Mountains, Erzgebirge (Ore Mountains), Bavarian Alps, Fichtelgebirge, Thüringer Forest

Government

Head of state Roman Herzog from 1994
Head of government Helmut Kohl from 1982
Political system liberal democratic federal republic
Administrative divisions 16 states
Political parties Christian Democratic Union (CDU), right of centre, 'social market'; Christian Social Union (CSU), right of centre; Social Democratic Party (SPD), left of centre; Free Democratic Party (FDP), liberal; Greens, environmentalist; Party of Democratic Socialism (PDS), reform-socialist (formerly Socialist Unity Party: SED)
Armed forces 340,000 (1995)
Conscription 10 months
Death penalty abolished in the Federal Republic of Germany 1949 and in the German Democratic Republic 1987
Defence spend (% GDP) 2.0 (1995)

Education spend (% GNP) 4.8 (1993–94)
Health spend (% GDP) 6.0 (1993)

Economy and resources

Currency Deutschmark
GDP ($ US) 2,353.2 billion (1996)
Real GDP per capita (PPP) ($ US) 21,116 (1996)
GDP growth rate 2.8% (1996); 1.9% (1994–95)
Average annual inflation 1.9% (1996)
Trading partners EU (particularly France, the Netherlands, and Ireland), USA, Japan, Switzerland
Resources lignite, hard coal, potash salts, crude oil, natural gas, iron ore, copper, timber, nickel, uranium
Industries mining, road vehicles, chemical products, transport equipment, nonelectrical machinery, metals and metal products, electrical machinery, electronic goods, cement, food and beverages
Exports road vehicles, electrical machinery, metals and metal products, textiles, chemicals. Principal market: France 10.9% (1996)
Imports road vehicles, electrical machinery, food and live animals, clothing and accessories, crude petroleum and petroleum products. Principal source: France 10.6% (1996)
Arable land 32.7% (1993)
Agricultural products potatoes, sugar beet, barley, wheat, maize, rapeseed, vine fruits; livestock (cattle, pigs, and poultry) and fishing

Population and society

Population 81,992,000 (1996e)
Population growth rate 0.6% (1990–95); –0.1% (2000–05)
Population density (per sq km) 230 (1996e)
Urban population (% of total) 87 (1995)
Age distribution (% of total population) <15 16.1%, 15–65 68.7%, >65 15.2% (1995)
Ethnic distribution predominantly Germanic; notable Danish and Slavonic ethnic minorities in the N; significant population of foreigners, including 1.9 million officially recognized *Gastarbeiter* ('guest workers'), predominantly Turks, Greeks, Italians, and Yugoslavs; by 1993 Germany had received more than 200,000 refugees fleeing the Yugoslav civil war

Language German
Religions Protestant (mainly Lutheran) 43%, Roman Catholic 36%
Education (compulsory years) 12
Literacy rate 100% (men); 100% (women) (1995e)
Labour force 50% of population: 4% agriculture, 38% industry, 58% services (1990)
Unemployment 9% (1996)
Life expectancy 74 (men); 80 (women) (1995–2000)
Child mortality rate (under 5, per 1,000 live births) 7 (1995)
Physicians 1 per 303 people (1994)
Hospital beds 1 per 129 people (1994)
TV sets (per 1,000 people) 564 (1995)
Radios (per 1,000 people) 944 (1995)

Transport

Airports international airports: Berlin-Tegel (Otto Lilienthal), Berlin-Schönefeld, Berlin-Tempelhof, Leipzig/Halle, Dresden (Klotsche), Bremen (Neuenland), Cologne, Düsseldorf (Lohausen), Frankfurt, Hamburg, Hannover (Langenhagen), Munich (Franz Joseph Strauss), Münster-Osnabrück, Nuremberg, Saarbrucken (Ensheim), Stuttgart (Echterdingen); several domestic airports; total passenger km: 56,903 mil (1994)
Railroads total length: 40,209 km/24,986 mi; total passenger km: 61,327 mil (1994)
Roads total road network: 650,700 km/404,345 mi, of which 99% paved (1995e); passenger cars: 494.8 per 1,000 people (1995)

Chronology

c. 1000 BC Germanic tribes from Scandinavia began to settle the region between the rivers Rhine, Elbe, and Danube.
AD 9 Romans tried and failed to conquer Germanic tribes.
5th century Germanic tribes plundered Rome, overran W Europe, and divided it into tribal kingdoms.
496 Clovis, King of the Franks, conquered the Alemanni tribe of western Germany.
772–804 After series of fierce wars, Charlemagne extended Frankish authority over Germany, subjugated Saxons, imposed Christianity, and took title of Holy Roman emperor.
843 Treaty of Verdun divided the Holy

Roman Empire into three, with E portion corresponding to modern Germany; local princes became virtually independent.
919 Henry the Fowler restored central authority and founded Saxon dynasty.
962 Otto the Great enlarged the kingdom and revived title of Holy Roman emperor.
1024–1254 Emperors of Salian and Hohenstaufen dynasties came into conflict with popes; frequent civil wars allowed German princes to regain independence.
12th century German expansion eastwards into lands between rivers Elbe and Oder.
13th–14th centuries Hanseatic League of allied German cities became a great commercial and naval power.
1438 Title of Holy Roman emperor became virtually hereditary in the Habsburg family of Austria.
1517 Martin Luther began the Reformation; Emperor Charles V tried to suppress Protestantism; civil war ensued.
1555 Peace of Augsburg: Charles V forced to accept that each German prince could choose religion of his own lands.
1618–48 Thirty Years' War: bitter conflict, partly religious, between certain German princes and emperor, with foreign intervention; the war wrecked the German economy and reduced the Holy Roman Empire to a name.
1701 Frederick I, Elector of Brandenburg, promoted to king of Prussia.
1740 Frederick the Great of Prussia seized Silesia from Austria and retained it through war of Austrian Succession (1740–48) and Seven Years' War (1756–63).
1772–95 Prussia joined Russia and Austria in the partition of Poland.
1792 Start of French Revolutionary

Wars, involving many German states, with much fighting on German soil.
1806 Holy Roman Empire abolished; France formed puppet Confederation of the Rhine in western Germany and defeated Prussia at Battle of Jena.
1813–15 National revival enabled Prussia to take part in defeat of Napoleon at battles of Leipzig and Waterloo.
1814–15 Congress of Vienna rewarded Prussia with Rhineland, Westphalia, and much of Saxony; loose German Confederation formed by 39 independent states.
1848–49 Liberal revolutions in many German states; Frankfurt assembly sought German unity; revolutions suppressed.
1862 Otto von Bismarck became prime minister of Prussia.
1866 Seven Weeks' War: Prussia defeated Austria, dissolved German Confederation, and established North German Confederation under Prussian leadership.
1870–71 Franco-Prussian War; S German states agreed to German unification; German Empire proclaimed, with king of Prussia as emperor and Bismarck as chancellor.
1890 Wilhelm II dismissed Bismarck and sought to make Germany a leading power in world politics.
1914 Germany encouraged Austrian attack on Serbia that started World War I; Germany invaded Belgium and France.
1918 Germany defeated; revolution overthrew monarchy.
1919 Treaty of Versailles: Germany lost land to France, Denmark, and Poland; demilitarization and reparations imposed; Weimar Republic proclaimed.
1922–23 Hyperinflation: in 1922, one dollar was worth 50 marks; in 1923, one dollar was worth 2.5 trillion marks.

1929 Start of economic slump caused mass unemployment and brought Germany close to revolution.
1933 Adolf Hitler, leader of Nazi Party, became chancellor.
1934 Hitler took title of *Führer* (leader), murdered rivals, and created one-party state with militaristic and racist ideology; rearmament reduced unemployment.
1938 Germany annexed Austria and Sudeten; occupied remainder of Czechoslovakia 1939.
1939 German invasion of Poland started World War II; Germany defeated France 1940, attacked USSR 1941, and pursued extermination of Jews.
1945 Germany defeated and deprived of its conquests; eastern lands transferred to Poland; USA, USSR, UK, and France established zones of occupation.
1948–49 Disputes between Western allies and USSR led to Soviet blockade of West Berlin.
1949 Partition of Germany: US, French, and British zones in West Germany became Federal Republic of Germany with Konrad Adenauer as chancellor; Soviet zone in East Germany became communist German Democratic Republic led by Walter Ulbricht.
1953 Uprising in East Berlin suppressed by Soviet troops.
1955 West Germany became a member of NATO; East Germany joined the Warsaw Pact.
1957 West Germany was a founder member of the European Economic Community.
1960s 'Economic miracle': West Germany achieved rapid growth and great prosperity.
1961 East Germany constructed Berlin Wall to prevent emigration to West Berlin (part of West Germany).
1969 Willy Brandt, Social Democratic Party chancellor of West Germany,

---

Practical information

Visa requirements UK: visa not required. USA: visa not required
Embassy in the UK 23 Belgrave Square, London SW1X 8PZ. Tel: (0171) 824 1300; fax: (0171) 824 1435
British embassy Friedrich-Ebert-Allée 77, 53113 Bonn. Tel: (228) 91670; fax: (228) 9167 331
Embassy in the USA 4645 Reservoir Road NW, Washington, DC 20007. Tel: (202) 298 4000; fax: (202) 298 4249
American embassy Deichmanns Aue 29, D-53179 Bonn. Tel: (228) 3391; fax: (228) 339 2663
Chamber of commerce Deutscher Industrie- und Handelstag (Association of German Chambers of Industry and

Commerce), Adenauerallée 148, 53113 Bonn. Tel: (228) 1040; fax: (228) 104 158
Office hours 0800–1600 Mon–Fri
Banking hours generally 0830–1300 and 1400/1430–1600 Mon–Fri; Thu until 1730 in main cities. Main branches do not close for lunch
Time difference GMT +1
Chief tourist attractions spas; summer and winter resorts; medieval towns and castles; Black Forest; Rhine Valley; North and Baltic Sea coasts; mountains of Thuringia and Bavaria and the Erzgebirge
Major holidays 1, 6 January, 1 May, 3 October, 1 November, 25–26 December; variable: Good Friday, Easter Monday, Ascension Thursday, Whit Monday, Corpus Christi, Assumption

sought better relations with USSR and East Germany.
1971 Erich Honecker succeeded Ulbricht as Communist Party leader, and became head of state 1976.
1972 Basic Treaty established relations between West Germany and East Germany as between foreign states.
1982 Helmut Kohl (Christian Democratic Union) became West German chancellor.

1989 Mass exodus of East Germans to West Germany via Hungary; Honecker replaced; East Germany opened frontiers, including Berlin Wall.
1990 Collapse of communist regime in East Germany; reunification of Germany with Kohl as chancellor.
1991 Maastricht Treaty: Germany took the lead in pressing for closer European integration.

1995 Unemployment reached postwar high of 3.8 million.
1996 Public-sector labour dispute over welfare reform plans and the worsening economy. Spending cuts agreed to meet European Monetary Union entry criteria.
1997 Unemployment reached record levels. Former East German leader Egon Krenz and two colleagues convicted of manslaughter.

Ghana Republic of (formerly the *Gold Coast*)

Area 238,305 sq km/92,009 sq mi
Capital Accra
Major towns/cities Kumasi, Tamale, Tema, Sekondi-Takoradi, Cape Coast, Sunyani, Koforidua, Ho, Yendi, Tarkwa, Wa, Bolgatanga
Major ports Sekondi, Tema
Physical features mostly tropical lowland plains; bisected by River Volta

Government

Head of state and government Jerry Rawlings from 1981
Political system emergent democracy
Administrative divisions ten regions
Political parties National Democratic Congress (NDC), centrist, progovernment; New Patriotic Party (NPP), left of centre
Armed forces 7,000 (1995); plus a paramilitary force of 5,000
Conscription military service is voluntary
Death penalty retained and used for ordinary crimes
Defence spend (% GDP) 1.2 (1995)
Education spend (% GNP) 3.1 (1993–94)
Health spend (% GDP) 1.7 (1990)

Economy and resources

Currency cedi
GDP ($ US) 5.4 billion (1994)

Real GDP per capita (PPP) ($ US) 1,960 (1994)
GDP growth rate 3.8% (1994); 4.3% (1990–95)
Average annual inflation 50% (1995); 28.4% (1985–95)
Foreign debt ($ US) 5.88 billion (1995)
Trading partners UK, USA, Germany, Nigeria, Japan, France
Resources diamonds, gold, manganese, bauxite
Industries food processing, textiles, vehicles, aluminium, cement, paper, chemicals, petroleum products, tourism
Exports gold, cocoa and related products, timber. Principal market: USA 14.6% (1995)
Imports raw materials, machinery and transport equipment, petroleum, food, basic manufactures. Principal source: UK 16.2% (1995)
Arable land 11.7% (1993)
Agricultural products cocoa (world's third-largest producer), coffee, bananas, oil palm, maize, rice, cassava, plantain, yams, coconuts, kola nuts, limes, shea nuts; forestry (timber production)

Population and society

Population 17,832,000 (1996e)
Population growth rate 3% (1990–95); 2.8% (2000–05)
Population density (per sq km) 75 (1996e)
Urban population (% of total) 36 (1995)
Age distribution (% of total population) <15 45.3%, 15–65 51.8%, >65 2.9% (1995)
Ethnic distribution over 75 ethnic groups; most significant are the Akan in the S and W (44%), the Mole-Dagbani in the N, the Ewe in the S, the Ga in the region of the capital city, and the Fanti in the coastal area
Languages English (official) and African languages

Religions Christian 62%, Muslim 16%, animist
Education (compulsory years) 9
Literacy rate 70% (men); 51% (women) (1995e)
Labour force 47% of population: 47.5% agriculture, 12.8% industry, 39.7% services (1994)
Unemployment 10% (1991)
Life expectancy 57 (men); 60 (women) (1995–2000)
Child mortality rate (under 5, per 1,000 live births) 130 (1995)
Physicians 1 per 20,375 people (1992)
TV sets (per 1,000 people) 92 (1995)
Radios (per 1,000 people) 231 (1995)

Transport

Airports international airport: Accra (Koteka); four domestic airports; total passenger km: 478 mil (1994)
Railroads total length: 953 km/592 mi; total passenger km: 277 mil (1991)
Roads total road network: 37,561 km/23,340 mi, of which 24.9% paved (1995e); passenger cars: 4.9 per 1,000 people (1995e)

Chronology

5th–12th century Ghana Empire (from which present-day country's name derives) flourished, with its centre 500 mi/800 km to the NW, in Mali.
13th century In coastal and forest areas Akan peoples founded first states.
15th century Gold-seeking Mande traders entered N Ghana from the NE, founding Dagomba and Mamprussi states; Portuguese navigators visited coastal region, naming it the 'Gold Coast', building a fort at Elmina, and slave trading began.
17th century Gonja kingdom founded in N by Mande speakers; Ga and Ewe states founded in the SE by immigrants from Nigeria; in central Ghana, controlling gold reserves around Kumasi,

the Ashanti, a branch of the Akans, founded what became the most powerful state in precolonial Ghana.
1618 British trading settlement established on Gold Coast.
18th–19th centuries Centralized Ashanti kingdom at its height, dominating between Komoe River in the W and Togo Mountains in the E and active in slave trade; Fante state powerful along coast in the S.
1874 Britain, after ousting the Danes and Dutch and defeating the Ashanti, made the Gold Coast (the southern provinces) a crown colony.
1898–1901 After three further military campaigns, Britain finally subdued and established protectorates over Ashanti and the northern territories.
early 20th century The colony developed into a major cocoa-exporting region.
1917 West Togoland, formerly German-

ruled, was administered with the Gold Coast as British Togoland.
1949 Campaign for independence launched by Kwame Nkrumah, who formed Convention People's Party (CPP) and became prime minister in 1952.
1957 Independence achieved, within the Commonwealth, as Ghana, which included British Togoland; Nkrumah became prime minister. Policy of 'African socialism' and nonalignment pursued.
1960 Became a republic, with Nkrumah as president.
1964 Ghana became a one-party state, dominated by the CCP, and developed links with communist bloc.
1966 Nkrumah deposed in military coup and replaced by Gen Joseph Ankrah; political prisoners released.
1969 Ankrah replaced by Gen Akwasi Afrifa, who initiated a return to civilian government.

1970 Edward Akufo-Addo elected president.
1972 Another coup placed Col Ignatius Acheampong at the head of a military government as economy deteriorated.
1978 Acheampong deposed in a bloodless coup led by Frederick Akuffo; another coup put Flight-Lt Jerry Rawlings, a populist soldier who launched a drive against corruption, in power.
1979 Return to civilian rule under Hilla Limann.
1981 Rawlings seized power again. All political parties banned.
1992 Pluralist constitution approved in referendum, lifting the ban on political parties. Rawlings won presidential elections.
1996 Rawlings re-elected. New Democratic Congress (NDC) won assembly majority.

Practical information

Visa requirements UK: visa required. USA: visa required
Embassy in the UK (education and visas) 104 Highgate Hill, London N6 5HE. Tel: (0181) 342 8686; fax: (0181) 342 8566; (tourist information) 102 Park Street, London W1Y 3RJ. Tel: (0171) 493 4901; fax: (0171) 629 1730
British embassy British High Commission, PO Box 296, Osu Link, off Gamel Abdul Nasser Avenue, Accra. Tel: (21) 221 665; fax: (21) 664 652
Embassy in the USA 3512 International Drive NW, Washington, DC 20008. Tel: (202) 686 4520; fax: (202) 686 4527
American embassy Ring Road East, East of Danquah

Circle, Accra. Tel: (21) 775 348; fax: (21) 775 747
Chamber of commerce Ghana National Chamber of Commerce, PO Box 2325, Accra. Tel: (21) 662 427; fax: (21) 662 210
Office hours 0800–1200 and 1400–1700 Mon–Fri
Banking hours 0830–1400 Mon–Thu and 0830–1500 Fri. A few city branches are open 0830–1200 Sat
Time difference GMT +/–0
Chief tourist attractions game reserves; beaches; traditional festivals; old castles and trading posts
Major holidays 1 January, 6 March, 1 May, 4 June, 1 July, 25–26, 31 December; variable: Good Friday, Easter Monday, Holy Saturday

Greece Hellenic Republic

National name *Elliniki Dimokratia*
Area 131,957 sq km/50,948 sq mi
Capital Athens
Major towns/cities Thessaloníki,

Piraeus, Patras, Irákleion, Larissa, Volos
Major ports Piraeus, Thessaloníki, Patras, Irákleion
Physical features mountainous (Mount Olympus); a large number of islands, notably Crete, Corfu, and Rhodes, and Cyclades and Ionian Islands

Government

Head of state Costis Stephanopoulos from 1995
Head of government Costis Simitis from 1996
Political system democratic republic
Administrative divisions 13 regions divided into 51 departments
Political parties Panhellenic Socialist Movement (PASOK), nationalist, democratic socialist; New Democracy Party (ND), centre right; Democratic

Renewal (DIANA), centrist; Communist Party (KJKE), left wing; Political Spring, moderate, left of centre
Armed forces 171,300; gendarmerie 26,500; National Guard 35,000 (1995)
Conscription 19–24 months
Death penalty abolished 1993
Defence spend (% GDP) 4.6 (1995)
Education spend (% GNP) 3 (1993–94)
Health spend (% GDP) 4.3 (1993)

Economy and resources

Currency drachma
GDP ($ US) 122.8 billion (1996)
Real GDP per capita (PPP) ($ US) 12,694 (1996)
GDP growth rate 2.2% (1996); 1.1% (1990–95)

Average annual inflation 5.4% (1996); 15.1% (1985–95)
Trading partners Germany, Italy, France, the Netherlands, USA, UK
Resources bauxite, nickel, iron pyrites, magnetite, asbestos, marble, salt, chromite, lignite
Industries food products, metals and metal products, textiles, petroleum refining, machinery and transport equipment, tourism, wine
Exports fruit and vegetables, clothing, mineral fuels and lubricants, textiles, iron and steel, aluminium and aluminium alloys. Principal market: Germany 27.7% (1995)
Imports petroleum and petroleum products, machinery and transport equipment, food and live animals, chemicals and chemical products. Principal source: Germany 17.9% (1995)
Arable land 18.3% (1993)
Agricultural products fruit and vegetables, cereals, sugar beet, tobacco, olives; livestock and dairy products

Population and society

Population 10,490,000 (1996e)
Population growth rate 0.4% (1990–95); 0% (2000–05)
Population density (per sq km) 79 (1996e)
Urban population (% of total) 65 (1995)
Age distribution (% of total population) <15 16.7%, 15–65 67.4%, >65 15.9% (1995)
Ethnic distribution predominantly Greek; main minorities are Turks, Slavs, and Albanians
Languages Greek (official), Macedonian (100,000–200,000 est)
Religions Greek Orthodox; also Roman Catholic
Education (compulsory years) 9
Literacy rate 98% (men); 89% (women) (1995e)
Labour force 42% of population: 23% agriculture, 27% industry, 50% services (1990)
Unemployment 8.8% (1995)
Life expectancy 76 (men); 81 (women) (1995–2000)
Child mortality rate (under 5, per 1,000 live births) 10 (1995)
Physicians 1 per 308 people (1991)
Hospital beds 1 per 198 people (1991)
TV sets (per 1,000 people) 220 (1995)
Radios (per 1,000 people) 430 (1995)

Transport

Airports international airports: Athens (Athinai), Iráklion/Crete, Thessaloníki (Micra), Corfu (Kerkira), Rhodes (Paradisi); 25 domestic airports, of which 14 are also international; total passenger km: 8,429 mil (1994)
Railroads total length: 2,474 km/1,537 mi; total passenger km: 1,599 mil (1994)
Roads total road network: 116,440 km/ 72,356 mi, of which 91.7% paved (1995e); passenger cars: 210 per 1,000 people (1995)

Chronology

c. 2000–1200 BC Mycenaean civilization flourished.
c. 1500–1100 BC Central Greece and Peloponnese invaded by tribes of Achaeans, Aeolians, Ionians, and Dorians.
c. 1000–500 BC Rise of the Greek city states; Greek colonies established around the shores of the Mediterranean.
c. 490–404 BC Ancient Greek culture reached its zenith in the democratic city state of Athens.
357–338 BC Philip II of Macedon won supremacy over Greece; cities fought to regain and preserve independence.
146 BC Roman Empire defeated Macedon and annexed Greece.
476 AD Western Roman Empire ended; Eastern Empire continued as Byzantine Empire, based at Constantinople, with essentially Greek culture.
1204 Crusaders partitioned Byzantine Empire; Athens, Achaea, and Thessaloniki came under Frankish rulers.
late 14th century–1461 Ottoman Turks conquered mainland Greece and captured Constantinople 1453; Greek language and culture preserved by Orthodox Church.
1685 Venetians captured Peloponnese; regained by Turks 1715.
late 18th century Beginnings of Greek nationalism among émigrés and merchant class.
1814 *Philike Hetairia* ('Friendly Society') formed by revolutionary Greek nationalists in Odessa.
1821 *Philike Hetairia* raised Peloponnese brigands in revolt against Turks; War of Independence ensued.
1827 Battle of Navarino: Britain, France, and Russia intervened to destroy Turkish fleet; Count Ioannis Kapodistrias elected president of Greece.
1829 Treaty of Adrianople: under Russian pressure, Turkey recognized independence of small Greek state.
1832 Great Powers elected Otto of Bavaria as king of Greece.

1843 Coup forced King Otto to grant a constitution.
1862 Mutiny and rebellion led King Otto to abdicate.
1863 George of Denmark became king of the Hellenes.
1864 Britain transferred Ionian islands to Greece.
1881 Following Treaty of Berlin 1878, Greece was allowed to annex Thessaly and part of Epirus.
late 19th century Politics dominated by Kharilaos Trikoupis, who emphasized economic development, and Theodoros Deliyiannis, who emphasized territorial expansion.
1897 Greco-Turkish War ended in Greek defeat.
1908 Cretan assembly led by Eleutherios Venizelos proclaimed union with Greece.
1910 Venizelos became prime minister and introduced financial, military, and constitutional reforms.
1912–13 Balkan Wars: Greece annexed a large area of Epirus and Macedonia.
1916 'National Schism': Venizelos formed rebel pro-Allied government while royalists remained neutral.
1917–18 Greek forces fought on Allied side in World War I.
1919–22 Greek invasion of Asia Minor; after Turkish victory, a million refugees came to Greece.
1924 Republic declared amid great political instability.
1935 Greek monarchy restored with George II.
1936 Gen Ioannia Metaxas established right-wing dictatorship.
1940 Greece successfully repelled Italian invasion.
1941–44 German occupation of Greece; rival monarchist and communist resistance groups operated from 1942.
1946–49 Civil war: communists defeated by monarchists with military aid from Britain and USA.
1952 Became a member of NATO.
1967 'Greek Colonels' seized power under George Papadopoulos; political activity banned; King Constantine II exiled.
1973 Republic proclaimed with Papadopoulos as president.
1974 Cyprus crisis caused downfall of military regime; Constantine Karamanlis returned from exile to form Government of National Salvation and restore democracy.
1981 Andreas Papandreou elected Greece's first socialist prime minister;

Greece entered the European Community.
1989–93 Election defeat of Panhellenic Socialist Movement (PASOK) followed by unstable coalition governments.
1993 PASOK returned to power.
1996 Costis Simitis succeeded Papandreou as prime minister. PASOK retained its majority in the general election.
1997 Direct talks with Turkey.

Practical information

Visa requirements UK: visa not required. USA: visa not required
Embassy in the UK Embassy of the Hellenic Republic, 1A Holland Park, London W11 3TP. Tel: (0171) 221 6467; fax: (0171) 243 3202
British embassy Odos Ploutarchon 1, 106 75 Athens. Tel: (1) 723 6211/9; fax: (1) 724 1872
Embassy in the USA 2221 Massachusetts Avenue NW, Washington, DC 20008. Tel: (202) 939 5800; fax: (202) 939 5824
American embassy 91 Vasilissis Sophias Boulevard, 10160 Athens. Tel: (1) 721 2951, 8401; fax: (1) 645 6282

Chamber of commerce Athens Chamber of Commerce, Odos Akademias 7, 106 71 Athens. Tel: (1) 360 2411; fax: (1) 360 7897
Office hours 0800–1430 and 1730–1730 Mon–Fri
Banking hours 0800–1400 Mon–Fri. Many banks on larger islands stay open in the afternoon and some during the evening to offer currency-exchange facilities during the tourist season
Time difference GMT +2
Chief tourist attractions Aegean islands; historical and archaeological remains – palace of Knossos on Crete, Delphi, the Acropolis in Athens; climate
Major holidays 1, 6 January, 25 March, 1 May, 15 August, 28 October, 25–26 December; variable: Monday in Lent, Good Friday, Easter Monday, Whit Monday

---

Grenada

Area (including the southern Grenadine Islands, notably Carriacou and Petit Martinique) 340 sq km/131 sq mi
Capital St George's
Major towns/cities Grenville, Sauteurs, Victoria, Hillsborough (Carriacou)
Physical features southernmost of the Windward Islands; mountainous; Grand-Anse beach; Annandale Falls; the Great Pool volcanic crater

Government

Head of state Elizabeth II from 1974, represented by governor general Reginald Palmer from 1992
Head of government Keith Mitchell from 1995
Political system emergent democracy
Administrative divisions six parishes
Political parties Grenada United Labour Party (GULP), nationalist, left of centre; National Democratic Congress (NDC), centrist; National Party (TNP), centrist
Armed forces no standing army; 730-strong regional security unit (1995)
Death penalty retained and used for ordinary crimes

Economy and resources

Currency Eastern Caribbean dollar
GDP ($ US) 172 million (1994)
Real GDP per capita (PPP) ($ US) 5,137 (1994)
GDP growth rate 0.9% (1994)
Average annual inflation 2.6% (1994); 5.3% (1985–95)
Foreign debt ($ US) 139.2 million (1993)
Trading partners USA, UK, Trinidad and Tobago, the Netherlands, Germany
Industries agricultural products (nutmeg oil distillation), rum, beer, soft drinks, cigarettes, clothing, tourism
Exports cocoa, bananas, cocoa, mace, fresh fruit. Principal market: UK, USA, France 18.5% each (1995)
Imports foodstuffs, mineral fuels, machinery and transport equipment, basic manufactures, beverages, tobacco. Principal source: USA 30% (1995)
Arable land 32.4% (1993)
Agricultural products cocoa, bananas, nutmeg (world's second-largest producer), and mace, sugar cane, fresh fruit and vegetables; livestock productions (for domestic use); fishing

Population and society

Population 92,000 (1996e)
Population growth rate 0.3% (1990–95)
Population density (per sq km) 269 (1996e)
Urban population (% of total) 25 (1992)
Age distribution (% of total population) <15 35.2%, 15–65 58.2%, >65 6.6% (1993)
Ethnic distribution majority is of black African descent
Languages English (official); some French-African patois spoken
Religions Roman Catholic 53%, Anglican, Seventh Day Adventist, Pentecostal
Education (compulsory years) 11
Literacy rate 85% (1994e)
Labour force 19.8% agriculture, 24.5% industry, 55.7% services (1989)
Unemployment 40% (1995e)
Life expectancy 68 (men); 73 (women) (1996e)
Child mortality rate (under 5, per 1,000 live births) 33 (1995)
Physicians 1 per 1,428 people (1991)
Hospital beds 1 per 196 people (1991)
TV sets (per 1,000 people) 348 (1995)
Radios (per 1,000 people) 598 (1995)

Transport

Airports international airports: St George's (Point Salines); total passengers landed: 82,320 (1993)
Railroads none
Roads total road network: 1,020 km/634 mi, of which 61.2% paved (1995e)

Chronology

1498 Sighted by the explorer Christopher Columbus; Spanish named it Grenada since its hills were reminiscent of the Andalusian city.
1650 Colonized by French settlers from Martinique, who faced resistance from the local Carib Indian community armed with poison arrows, before the defeated Caribs performed a mass suicide.
1783 Ceded to Britain as a colony by the Treaty of Versailles; black African slaves imported to work cotton, sugar, and tobacco plantations.
1795 Abortive rebellion against British rule led by Julien Fedon, a black planter inspired by the ideas of the French Revolution.
1834 Slavery abolished.
1950 Left-wing Grenada United Labour Party (GULP) founded by trade union leader Eric Gairy.

1951 Universal adult suffrage granted and GULP elected to power in a nonautonomous local assembly.
1958–62 Part of the Federation of the West Indies.
1967 Internal self-government achieved.
1974 Independence achieved within the Commonwealth, with Gairy as prime minister.
1979 Autocratic Gairy removed in bloodless coup led by left-wing Maurice Bishop of the New Jewel Movement; constitution suspended.
1982 Relations with the USA and Britain deteriorated as ties with Cuba and the USSR strengthened.
1983 After attempts to improve relations with the USA, Bishop was overthrown by left-wing opponents, precipitating military coup by Gen Hudson Austin. Bishop and three colleagues executed. USA invaded, accompanied by troops

from other E Caribbean countries; there were 250 fatalities. Austin arrested and 1974 constitution reinstated.
1984 Newly formed centre-left New National Party (NNP) won general election and its leader, Herbert Blaize, became prime minister.
1989 Blaize replaced as leader of NNP, but remained as head of government.
1991 Inconclusive general election; Nicholas Braithwaite of the centrist National Democratic Congress (NDC) became prime minister. Windward Islands confederation proposed.
1995 Brathwaite retired and was succeeded as prime minister by the new NDC leader, George Brizan. General election won by NNP, led by Keith Mitchell. A plague of pink mealy bugs caused damage to crops estimated at $60 million, depriving 15,000 farmers of an income.

Practical information

Visa requirements UK: visa not required. USA: visa not required
Embassy in the UK 1 Collingham Gardens, London SW5 0HW. Tel: (0171) 373 7809; fax: (0171) 370 7040
British embassy British High Commission, 14 Church Street, St George's. Tel: 440 3222; fax: 440 4939
Embassy in the USA 1701 New Hampshire Avenue NW, Washington, DC 20009. Tel: (202) 265 2561
American embassy Point Salines, Saint George's. Tel: (809) 444 1173–8; fax: (809) 444 4820

Chamber of commerce Grenada Chamber of Industry and Commerce, PO Box 129, Decaul Building, Mount Gay, St George's. Tel: 440 2937; fax: 440 6627
Office hours 0800–1200 and 1300–1600 Mon–Fri
Banking hours 0800–1400 Mon–Thu; 0800–1300 and 1400–1700 Fri
Time difference GMT –4
Chief tourist attractions white sandy beaches; mountainous interior; rainforest
Major holidays 1–2 January, 7 February, 1 May, 3–4 August, 25 October, 25–26 December; variable: Corpus Christi, Good Friday, Easter Monday, Whit Monday

Guatemala Republic of

National name *República de Guatemala*
Area 108,889 sq km/42,042 sq mi
Capital Guatemala City
Major towns/cities Quezaltenango, Escuintla, Puerto Barrios (naval base), Retalhuleu, Chiquimula
Physical features mountainous; narrow coastal plains; limestone tropical plateau in N; frequent earthquakes

Government

Head of state and government Alvaro Arzú from 1996
Political system democratic republic
Administrative divisions 22 departments
Political parties Guatemalan Christian Democratic Party (PDCG), Christian, centre left; Centre Party (UCN), centrist; Revolutionary Party (PR), radical; Movement of National Liberation (MLN), extreme right wing; Democratic Institutional Party (PID), moderate conservative; Solidarity and Action Movement (MAS), right of centre; Guatemalan Republican Front (FRG), right wing; National Advancement Party (PAN), right of centre; Social Democratic Party (PSD), right of centre
Armed forces 44,200 (1995); plus paramilitary forces of 12,300
Conscription selective conscription for 30 months

Death penalty retained and used for ordinary crimes
Defence spend (% GDP) 1.4 (1995)
Education spend (% GNP) 1.6 (1993–94)
Health spend (% GDP) 2.1 (1990)

Economy and resources

Currency quetzal
GDP ($ US) 12.9 billion (1994)
Real GDP per capita (PPP) ($ US) 3,208 (1994)
GDP growth rate 4% (1994); 4.0% (1990–95)
Average annual inflation 14% (1994); 18.6% (1985–95)
Foreign debt ($ US) 3.3 billion (1995)
Trading partners USA, El Salvador, Mexico, Costa Rica, Venezuela, Germany, Japan, Honduras
Resources petroleum, antimony, gold, silver, nickel, lead, iron, tungsten
Industries food processing, textiles, pharmaceuticals, chemicals, tobacco,

nonmetallic minerals, sugar, electrical goods, tourism
Exports coffee, bananas, sugar, cardamoms, shellfish, tobacco. Principal market: USA 36.6% (1996)
Imports raw materials and intermediate goods for industry, consumer goods, mineral fuels and lubricants. Principal source: USA 43.9% (1996)
Arable land 12.2% (1993)
Agricultural products coffee, sugar cane, bananas, cardamoms, cotton; one of the largest sources of essential oils (citronella and lemon grass); livestock rearing; fishing (chiefly shrimp); forestry (mahogany and cedar)

Population and society

Population 10,928,000 (1996e)
Population growth rate 2.9% (1990–95); 2.7% (2000–05)
Population density (per sq km) 100 (1996e)
Urban population (% of total) 41 (1995)
Age distribution (% of total population) <15 44.3%, 15–65 52.2%, >65 3.5% (1995)
Ethnic distribution two main ethnic groups: Native Americans and ladinos (others, including Europeans, black Africans, and mestizos). Native Americans are descended from the highland Mayas
Languages Spanish (official); 45% speak Mayan languages
Religions Roman Catholic 70%, Protestant 30%
Education (compulsory years) 6
Literacy rate 63% (men); 47% (women) (1995e)
Labour force 35% of population (1990): 48% agriculture, 23% industry, 29% services (1993)
Unemployment 6.1% (1993)
Life expectancy 65 (men); 70 (women) (1995–2000)
Child mortality rate (under 5, per 1,000 live births) 67 (1995)
Physicians 1 per 4,200 people (1991)

TV sets (per 1,000 people) 56 (1995)
Radios (per 1,000 people) 71 (1995)

Transport

Airports international airport: Guatemala City (La Aurora); over 380 airstrips serving internal travel; total passenger km: 411 mil (1994)
Railroads total length: 782 km/486 mi; total passenger km: 12,531 mil (1991)
Roads total road network: 12,795 km/ 7,951 mi, of which 27.5% paved (1995e); passenger cars: 9.5 per 1,000 people (1993e)

Chronology

c. AD 250–900 Part of culturally advanced Maya civilization.
1524 Conquered by the Spanish adventurer Pedro de Alvarado and became a Spanish colony.
1821 Independence achieved from Spain, joining Mexico initially.
1823 Became part of United Provinces (Federation) of Central America, also embracing Costa Rica, El Salvador, Honduras, and Nicaragua.
1839 Achieved full independence.
1844–65 Rafael Carrera held power as president.
1873–85 The country was modernized on liberal lines by President Justo Rufino Barrios, the army was built up, and coffee growing introduced.
1944 Juan José Arevalo became president, ending a period of rule by dictators. Socialist programme of reform instituted by Arevalo and his successor, from 1951, Col Jacobo Arbenz Guzman, including establishing a social security system and redistributing land expropriated from large estates to landless peasants.
1954 Col Carlos Castillo Armas became president in US-backed coup, after United Fruit Company plantations had been nationalized by Arbenz. Land reform halted.

1963 Castillo assassinated and military coup made Col Enrique Peralta president.
1966 Cesar Méndez elected president as civilian rule restored.
1970s More than 50,000 died in a spate of political violence as the military regime sought to liquidate left-wing dissidents.
1970 Carlos Araña elected president, with military back in power.
1976 Earthquake killed 27,000 and left more than 1 million homeless.
1981 Growth of antigovernment guerrilla movement. Death squads and soldiers killed an estimated 11,000 civilians during the year.
1982 Right-wing army coup installed Gen Ríos Montt as head of junta and then as president, determined to fight corruption and end violence.
1983 Montt removed in coup led by Gen Mejía Victores, who declared amnesty for the guerrillas.
1985 New constitution adopted; PDCG won congressional elections; Marco Vinicio Cerezo Arevalo became civilian president.
1989 Coup attempt against Cerezo foiled. Over 100,000 people killed and 40,000 reported missing since 1980.
1991 Jorge Serrano Elías of MAS elected president. Diplomatic relations established with Belize, which Guatemala had long claimed.
1993 President Serrano deposed after attempting to impose authoritarian regime; Ramiro de Leon Carpio, a human-rights ombudsman, elected president by assembly.
1994 Peace talks held with Guatemalan Revolutionary National Unity (URNG) rebels. Right-wing parties secured a majority in congress after elections.
1995 Government criticized by USA and United Nations for widespread human-rights abuses. First cease-fire by rebels in 30 years.
1996 Alvaro Arzú elected president. Peace agreement ended 36-year war.

Practical information

Visa requirements UK: visa required for business visits and tourist visits of over 90 days. USA: visa not required for a stay of up to 90 days
Embassy in the UK 13 Fawcett Street, London SW10 9HN. Tel: (0171) 351 3042; fax: (0171) 376 5708
British embassy British Embassy, 7th Floor, Edificio Centro Financiero, Tower Two, 7a Avenida 5–10, Zona 4, Guatemala City. Tel: (2) 321 601/2/4; fax: (2) 341 904
Embassy in the USA 2220 R Street NW, Washington, DC 20008. Tel: (202) 745 4952/3/4; fax: (202) 745 1908
American embassy 7-01 Avenida de la Reforma, Zone 10, Guatemala City. Tel: (2) 311 541; fax: (2) 318 885

Chamber of commerce Cámara de Comercio de Guatemala, 10a Calle 3–80, Zona 1, Guatemala City. Tel: (2) 82681; fax: (2) 514 197
Office hours 0800–1800 Mon–Fri; 0800–1200 Sat
Banking hours 1000–1500 Mon–Thu; 1000–1800 Fri
Time difference GMT –6
Chief tourist attractions mountainous and densely forested landscape; Mayan temples and ruins at Tikal, Palenque, and Kamihal Juyú; Guatemala City, with its archaeological and historical museums
Major holidays 1 January, 1 May, 30 June, 1 July, 15 September, 12, 20 October, 1 November, 24–25, 31 December; variable: Good Friday, Holy Thursday, Holy Saturday

Guinea Republic of

National name *République de Guinée*
Area 245,857 sq km/94,925 sq mi
Capital Conakry
Major towns/cities Labé, Nzérékoré, Kankan, Kindia
Physical features flat coastal plain with mountainous interior; sources of rivers Niger, Gambia, and Senegal; forest in SE; Fouta Djallon, area of sandstone plateaux, cut by deep valleys

Government

Head of state and government Lansana Conté from 1984
Political system emergent democratic republic
Administrative divisions 34 provinces (including Conakry)
Political parties Party of Unity and Progress (PUP), centrist; Rally of the Guinean People (RPG), left of centre; Union of the New Republic (UNR), left of centre; Party for Renewal and Progress (PRP), left of centre
Armed forces 9,700 (1995); plus paramilitary forces of 9,600
Conscription military service is compulsory for two years
Death penalty retained and used for ordinary crimes
Defence spend (% GDP) 1.4 (1995)
Education spend (% GNP) 2.2 (1993)
Health spend (% GDP) 2.3 (1990)

Economy and resources

Currency Guinean franc
GDP ($ US) 3.4 billion (1994)
Real GDP per capita (PPP) ($ US) 1,103 (1994)
GDP growth rate 4% (1994); 3.8% (1990–95)
Average annual inflation 16.8% (1985–95e)
Foreign debt ($ US) 3.24 billion (1995)

Trading partners France, USA, Belgium, Hong Kong, Spain, Ireland, Côte d'Ivoire
Resources bauxite (world's top exporter of bauxite and second-largest producer of bauxite ore), alumina, diamonds, gold, granite, iron ore, uranium, nickel, cobalt, platinum
Industries processing of agricultural products, cement, beer, soft drinks, cigarettes
Exports bauxite, alumina, diamonds, coffee. Principal market: USA 16.1% (1995)
Imports foodstuffs, mineral fuels, semi-manufactured goods, consumer goods, textiles and clothing, machinery and transport equipment. Principal source: France 23.3% (1995)
Arable land 2.5% (1993)
Agricultural products cassava, millet, rice, fruits, oil palm, groundnuts, coffee, vegetables, sweet potatoes, yams, maize; livestock rearing (cattle); fishing; forestry

Population and society

Population 7,518,000 (1996e)
Population growth rate 3% (1990–95); 2.9% (2000–05)
Population density (per sq km) 31 (1996e)
Urban population (% of total) 30 (1995)
Age distribution (% of total population) <15 47.1%, 15–65 50.3%, >65 2.6% (1995)
Ethnic distribution 24 ethnic groups, including the Malinke, Peul, and Soussou
Languages French (official), African languages (of which eight are official)
Religions Muslim 95%, Christian
Education (compulsory years) 6
Literacy rate 35% (men); 13% (women) (1995e)
Labour force 49% of population: 87% agriculture, 2% industry, 11% services (1990)
Life expectancy 46 (men); 47 (women) (1995–2000)
Child mortality rate (under 5, per 1,000 live births) 219 (1995)
Physicians 1 per 7,692 people (1991)
Hospital beds 1 per 1,701 people (1990)
TV sets (per 1,000 people) 8.8 (1995)
Radios (per 1,000 people) 44 (1995)

Transport

Airports international airport: Conakry; eight domestic airports; total passenger km: 33 mil (1994)
Railroads total length: 662 km/411 mi;

total passenger km: 41 mil (1991)
Roads total road network: 30,270 km/ 18,810 mi, of which 16.4% paved (1995e); passenger cars: 2 per 1,000 people (1995e)

Chronology

c. AD 900 The Susi people, a community related to the Malinke, immigrated from NE, pushing the indigenous Baga towards the Atlantic coast.
13th century Susi kingdoms established, extending their influence to the coast; NE Guinea was part of Muslim Mali Empire, centred to NE.
mid-15th century Portuguese traders visited the coast and later developed trade in slaves and ivory.
1849 French protectorate established over coastal region around Nunez River, which was administered with Senegal.
1890 Separate Rivières du Sud colony formed.
1895 Renamed French Guinea, the colony became part of French West Africa.
1946 French Guinea became an overseas territory of France.
1958 Full independence from France achieved as Guinea after referendum rejected remaining within French Community; Sékou Touré of the Democratic Party of Guinea (PDG) elected president.
1960s and 1970s Touré established socialist one-party state, leading to deterioration in economy as 200,000 fled abroad.
1979 Strong opposition to Touré's rigid Marxist policies forced him to accept return to mixed economy and legalize private enterprise.
1984 Touré died. Bloodless military coup brought Col Lansana Conté to power; PDG outlawed, political prisoners released; market-centred economic reforms.
1985 Attempted coup against Conté while he was out of the country was foiled by loyal troops.
1991 Antigovernment general strike and mass protests.
1992 Constitution amended to allow for multiparty politics.
1993 Conté narrowly re-elected in first direct presidential election.
1995 Assembly elections won by Conté's supporters.
1996 Attempted military coup thwarted.

Practical information

Visa requirements UK: visa required. USA: visa required
Embassy for the UK 51 rue de la Faisanderie, 75016 Paris, France. Tel: (1) 4704 8148; fax: (1) 4704 5765
British embassy British Consulate, BP 834, Conakry. (All staff based in Dakar, Senegal.) Tel: (224) 442 959; fax: (224) 414 215
Embassy in the USA 2112 Leroy Place NW, Washington, DC 20008. Tel: (202) 483 9420; fax: (202) 483 8688
American embassy Rue KA 038, Conakry.

Tel: (224) 411 520, 411 521, 411 523; fax: (224) 441 522
Chamber of commerce Chambre de Commerce, d'Industrie et d'Agriculture de Guinée, BP 545, Conakry. Tel: (224) 444 495; telex: 609
Office hours 0800–1630 Mon–Thu; 0800–1300 Fri
Banking hours 0830–1230 and 1430–1630 Mon–Fri
Time difference GMT +/–0
Major holidays 1 January, 3 April, 1 May, 15 August, 2 October, 1 November, 25 December; variable: Eid-ul-Adha, Easter Monday, end of Ramadan, Prophet's Birthday

Guinea-Bissau Republic of (formerly *Portuguese Guinea*)

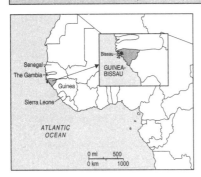

National name *República da Guiné-Bissau*
Area 36,125 sq km/13,947 sq mi
Capital Bissau (main port)
Major towns/cities Mansôa, São Domingos, Bolama/Bijagós, Catio, Buba, Butata, Farim, Cacine
Physical features flat coastal plain rising to savanna in E

Government

Head of state João Bernardo Vieira from 1980
Head of government Carlos Correia from 1997
Political system emergent democracy
Administrative divisions eight regions
Political parties African Party for the Independence of Portuguese Guinea and Cape Verde (PAIGC), nationalist socialist; Party for Social Renovation (PRS), left of centre; Guinea-Bissau Resistance–Bafata Movement (PRGB-MB), centrist
Armed forces 7,200 (1995); plus paramilitary gendarmerie of 2,000
Conscription selective conscription
Death penalty abolished 1993
Defence spend (% GDP) 3 (1995)

Education spend (% GNP) 2.8 (1990)
Health spend (% GDP) 1.3 (1990)

Economy and resources

Currency Guinean peso
GDP ($ US) 200 million (1994)
Real GDP per capita (PPP) ($ US) 793 (1994)
GDP growth rate 6.9% (1994); 3.5% (1990–95)
Average annual inflation 45.4% (1995); 62.8% (1985–95)
Foreign debt ($ US) 894 million (1995)
Trading partners Spain, Thailand, India, Portugal, Côte d'Ivoire, the Netherlands, Japan
Resources bauxite, phosphate, petroleum (largely unexploited)
Industries food processing, brewing, cotton processing, fish and timber processing
Exports cashew nuts, palm kernels, groundnuts, fish and shrimp, timber. Principal market: Spain 38% (1995)
Imports foodstuffs, machinery and transport equipment, fuels, construction materials. Principal source: Thailand 26.6% (1995)
Arable land 8.3% (1993)
Agricultural products groundnuts, sugar cane, plantains, palm kernels, rice, coconuts, millet, sorghum, maize, cashew nuts; fishing; forest resources

Population and society

Population 1,091,000 (1996e)
Population growth rate 2.1% (1990–95); 2.1% (2000–05)
Population density (per sq km) 30 (1996e)
Urban population (% of total) 22 (1995)
Age distribution (% of total population) <15 41.7%, 15–65 54.2%, >65 4.1% (1995)

Ethnic distribution majority originated in Africa, and comprises five main ethnic groups: the Balante in the central region, the Fulani in the N, the Malinke in the northern central area, and the Mandyako and Pepel near the coast
Languages Portuguese (official); Crioulo (Cape Verdean dialect of Portuguese), African languages
Religions animist 65%, Muslim 38%, Christian 5% (mainly Roman Catholic)
Education (compulsory years) 6
Literacy rate 50% (men); 24% (women) (1995e)
Labour force 48% of population: 85% agriculture, 2% industry, 13% services (1990)
Unemployment 5.1% (1992)
Life expectancy 44 (men); 47 (women) (1995–2000)
Child mortality rate (under 5, per 1,000 live births) 227 (1995)
Physicians 1 per 7,473 person (1991)
Hospital beds 1 per 741 people (1993)
Radios (per 1,000 people) 42 (1995)

Transport

Airports international airport: Bissau (Bissalanca); ten domestic airports; total passenger km: 10 mil (1994)
Railroads none
Roads total road network: 4,350 km/ 2,703 mi, of which 10.2% paved (1995e); passenger cars: 5.4 per 1,000 people (1995e)

Chronology

10th century Known as Gabu, became a tributary kingdom of the Mali Empire to NE.
1446 Portuguese arrived, establishing nominal control over coastal areas and capturing slaves to send to Cape Verde.
1546 Gabu kingdom became independent of Mali and survived until 1867.

1879 Portugal, which had formerly administered the area with Cape Verde islands, created the separate colony of Portuguese Guinea.
by 1915 The interior had been subjugated by the Portuguese.
1956 African Party for the Independence of Portuguese Guinea and Cape Verde (PAIGC) formed to campaign for independence from Portugal.
1961 The PAIGC began to wage a guerrilla campaign against Portuguese rule.

1973 Independence was declared in the two-thirds of the country that had fallen under the control of the PAIGC; heavy losses sustained by Portuguese troops who tried to put down the uprising.
1974 Independence separately from Cape Verde accepted by Portugal, with Luiz Cabral (PAIGC) president.
1980 Cabral deposed, and João Vieira became chair of a council of revolution.
1981 PAIGC confirmed as the only legal

party, with Vieira as its secretary general; Cape Verde decided not to form a union.
1984 New constitution made Vieira head of both government and state.
1991 Other parties legalized in response to public pressure.
1994 PAIGC secured a clear assembly majority and Vieira narrowly won first multiparty presidential elections.
1997 Carlos Correia appointed prime minister.

Practical information

Visa requirements UK: visa required. USA: visa required
Embassy in the UK Consulate General of the Republic of Guinea-Bissau, 8 Palace Gate, London W8 4RP.
Tel: (0171) 589 5253; fax: (0171) 589 9590
British embassy British Consulate, Maregro Int., CP 100, Bissau. (All staff based in Dakar, Senegal.)
Tel: (245) 201 224; fax: (245) 201 265
Embassy in the USA 918 16th Street NW, Mezzanine Suite,

Washington, DC 20006. Tel: (202) 872 4222; fax: (202) 872 4226
American embassy Bairro de Penha, Bissau.
Tel: (245) 252 273/4/5/6; fax: (245) 252 282
Chamber of commerce Associacão Comercial e Industrial e Agricola da Guiné-Bissau, Bissau. Tel/fax: (245) 201 602
Banking hours 0730–1430 Mon–Fri
Time difference GMT +/–0
Major holidays 1, 20 January, 8 February, 8 March, 1 May, 3 August, 12, 24 September, 14 November, 25 December

---

Guyana Cooperative Republic of

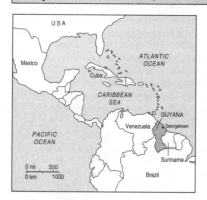

Area 214,969 sq km/82,999 sq mi
Capital Georgetown (and port)
Major towns/cities Linden, New Amsterdam, Rose Hall, Corriverton
Major ports New Amsterdam
Physical features coastal plain rises into rolling highlands with savanna in S; mostly tropical rainforest; Mount Roraima; Kaietur National Park, including Kaietur Falls on the Potaro (tributary of Essequibo) 250 m/821 ft

Government

Head of state Samuel Hinds from 1997
Head of government Samuel Hinds from 1992
Political system democratic republic

Administrative divisions ten regions
Political parties People's National Congress (PNC), Afro-Guyanan, nationalist socialist; People's Progressive Party (PPP), Indian-based, left wing
Armed forces 1,600 (1995); plus a paramilitary force of 1,500
Conscription military service is voluntary
Death penalty retained and used for ordinary crimes
Defence spend (% GDP) 1.1 (1995)
Education spend (% GNP) 5.0 (1993–94)

Economy and resources

Currency Guyana dollar
GDP ($ US) 540 million (1994e)
Real GDP per capita (PPP) ($ US) 2,730 (1994)
GDP growth rate 8.5% (1994)
Average annual inflation 8.1% (1995); 51.1% (1985–95)
Foreign debt ($ US) 1.76 billion (1991–93)
Trading partners USA, Canada, UK, Trinidad and Tobago, Italy, France, Japan
Resources gold, diamonds, bauxite, copper, tungsten, iron, nickel, quartz, molybdenum
Industries agro-processing (sugar, rice, coconuts, and timber), mining, rum, pharmaceuticals, textiles

Exports sugar, bauxite, alumina, rice, gold, rum, timber, molasses, shrimp. Principal market: Canada 24.9% (1995)
Imports mineral fuels and lubricants, machinery, capital goods, consumer goods. Principal source: USA 30.8% (1995)
Arable land 2.2% (1993)
Agricultural products sugar cane, rice, coffee, cocoa, coconuts, copra, tobacco, fruit and vegetables; forestry (timber production; approximately 76% of total land area was forested 1993)

Population and society

Population 838,000 (1996e)
Population growth rate 0.9% (1990–95); 1.1% (2000–05)
Population density (per sq km) 4 (1996e)
Urban population (% of total) 36 (1995)
Age distribution (% of total population) <15 32.2%, 15–65 63.7%, >65 4% (1995)
Ethnic distribution about 51% descended from settlers from the subcontinent of India; about 43% Afro-Indian; small minorities of Native Americans, Chinese, and Europeans
Languages English (official), Hindi, Native American languages
Religions Hindu 54%, Christian 27%, Sunni Muslim 15%

Education (compulsory years) 10
Literacy rate 98% (men); 97% (women) (1995e)
Labour force 40% of population (1990): 27% agriculture, 26% industry, 47% services (1993)
Unemployment 13.5% (1991)
Life expectancy 65 (men); 70 (women) (1995–2000)
Child mortality rate (under 5, per 1,000 live births) 59 (1995)
Physicians 1 per 3,360 people (1991)
TV sets (per 1,000 people) 48 (1995)
Radios (per 1,000 people) 646 (1995)

Transport

Airports international airport: Georgetown (Timehri); the larger settlements in the interior have airstrips serving domestic flights; total passenger km: 224 mil (1994)
Railroads none
Roads total road network: 7,820 km/ 4,859 mi, of which 7.3% paved (1995e); passenger cars: 30 per 1,000 people (1993e)

Chronology

1498 The explorer Christopher Columbus sighted Guyana, whose name, 'land of many waters', was derived from a local Native American word.
c. 1620 Settled by Dutch West India Company, who established armed bases and brought in slaves from Africa.
1814 After period of French rule, Britain occupied Guyana during the Napoleonic Wars and purchased Demerara, Berbice, and Essequibo.
1831 Became British colony under name of British Guiana.
1834 Slavery was abolished, resulting in an influx of indentured labourers from India and China to work on sugar plantations.
1860 Settlement of the Rupununi Savanna commenced.
1860s Gold was discovered.
1899 International arbitration tribunal found in favour of British Guiana in a long-running dispute with Venezuela over lands W of Essequibo River.
1953 Assembly elections won by left-wing People's Progressive Party (PPP), drawing most support from the Indian community; Britain suspended constitution and installed interim administration, fearing communist takeover.
1961 Internal self-government granted; Cheddi Jagan (PPP) became prime minister.
1964 PNC leader Forbes Burnham led PPP–PNC coalition; racial violence between the Asian- and African-descended communities.
1966 Independence achieved from Britain as Guyana, with Burnham as prime minister.
1970 Guyana became a republic within the Commonwealth, with Raymond Arthur Chung as president; Burnham remained as prime minister.
1980 Burnham became first executive president under new constitution, which ended the three-year boycott of parliament by the PPP.
1985 Burnham died; succeeded by Desmond Hoyte (PNC), as economy deteriorated.
1992 PPP had decisive victory in first completely free assembly elections for 20 years; Cheddi Jagan became president; privatization programme launched.
1997 Samuel Hinds became president on the death of Cheddi Jagan.

Practical information

Visa requirements UK: visa not required. USA: visa not required
Embassy in the UK 3 Palace Court, Bayswater Road, London W2 4LP. Tel: (0171) 229 7684; fax: (0171) 727 9809
British embassy British High Commission, PO Box 10849, 44 Main Street, Georgetown. Tel: (2) 65881–4; fax: (2) 53555
Embassy in the USA 2490 Tracy Place NW, Washington, DC 20008. Tel: (202) 265 6900/1
American embassy 99–100 Young and Duke Streets, Kingston, Georgetown. Tel: (2) 54900–9, 57960–9; fax: (2) 58497

Chamber of commerce Georgetown Chamber of Commerce and Industry, PO Box 10110, 156 Waterloo Street, Cumminsburg, Georgetown. Tel: (2) 63519
Office hours 0800–1200 and 1300–1630 Mon–Fri
Banking hours 0800–1200 Mon–Thu; 0800–1200 and 1530–1700 Fri
Time difference GMT –3
Chief tourist attractions scenery – Kaieteur Falls along Potaro River
Major holidays 1 January, 23 February, 1 May, 1 August, 25–26 December; variable: Eid-ul-Adha, Diwali, Good Friday, Easter Monday, Prophet's Birthday, Phagwah (March), Caribbean (July)

Haiti Republic of

National name *République d'Haïti*
Area 27,750 sq km/10,714 sq mi
Capital Port-au-Prince
Major towns/cities Cap-Haïtien, Gonaïves, Les Cayes, Port-de-Paix, Jérémie, Jacmée, St Marc
Physical features mainly mountainous and tropical; occupies western third of Hispaniola Island in Caribbean Sea

Government

Head of state René Preval from 1995
Head of government Claudette Werleigh from 1995
Political system transitional
Administrative divisions nine departments
Political parties National Front for Change and Democracy (FNCD), left of centre; Lavalas Political Organization, populist
Armed forces 7,300 (1994); armed forces effectively dissolved 1995 following restoration of civilian rule 1994; a 4,000-strong civilian police force has been formed

Conscription military service is voluntary
Death penalty abolished 1987
Defence spend (% GDP) 2.1 (1995)
Education spend (% GNP) 1.4 (1993–94)
Health spend (% GDP) 3.2 (1990)

Economy and resources

Currency gourde
GDP ($ US) 1.6 billion (1994)
Real GDP per capita (PPP) ($ US) 896 (1994)
GDP growth rate –13.2% (1994); –6.5% (1990–95)
Average annual inflation 42.6% (1994); 14.7% (1985–95)
Foreign debt ($ US) 807 million (1995)
Trading partners USA, the Netherlands, Antilles, France, Italy, Germany, Japan, UK
Resources marble, limestone, calcareous clay, unexploited copper and gold deposits
Industries food processing, metal products, machinery, textiles, chemicals, clothing, toys, electronic and electrical equipment, tourism; much of industry closed down during the international embargo imposed by the UN after Aristide was deposed 1991
Exports manufactured articles, coffee, essential oils, sisal. Principal market: USA 73.5% (1995)
Imports food and live animals, mineral fuels and lubricants, textiles, machinery, chemicals, pharmaceuticals, raw materials, vehicles. Principal source: USA 65% (1995)
Arable land 20.2% (1993)
Agricultural products coffee, sugar cane, rice, maize, sorghum, cocoa, sisal, sweet potatoes, bananas, cotton

Population and society

Population 7,259,000 (1996e)
Population growth rate 2% (1990–95); 2.1% (2000–05)
Population density (per sq km) 262 (1996e)
Urban population (% of total) 32 (1995)
Age distribution (% of total population) <15 40.2%, 15–65 55.9%, >65 3.9% (1995)
Ethnic distribution about 95% black African descent, the remainder are mulattos or Europeans
Languages French (official, spoken by literate 10% minority), Creole (official)

Religions Christian 95% (of which 80% are Roman Catholic), voodoo 4%
Education (compulsory years) 6
Literacy rate 59% (men); 47% (women) (1995e)
Labour force 45% of population: 68% agriculture, 9% industry, 23% services (1990)
Unemployment 12.7% (1994)
Life expectancy 57 (men); 60 (women) (1995–2000)
Child mortality rate (under 5, per 1,000 live births) 124 (1995)
Physicians 1 per 7,143 people (1991)
Hospital beds 1 per 1,420 people (1991)
TV sets (per 1,000 people) 4.8 (1995)
Radios (per 1,000 people) 53 (1995)

Transport

Airports international airport: Port-au-Prince (Mais Gaté); one domestic airport (Cap-Haïtien) and four smaller airfields
Railroads none
Roads total road network: 4,080 km/ 2,535 mi, of which 24.2% paved (1995e); passenger cars: 4.7 per 1,000 people (1993e)

Chronology

14th century Settled by Carib Indians, who followed an earlier wave of Arawak Indian immigration.
1492 The first landing place of the explorer Christopher Columbus in the New World, who named the island Hispaniola ('Little Spain').
1496 At Santo Domingo, now in the Dominican Republic to the E, the Spanish established the first European settlement in the Western hemisphere, which became capital of all Spanish colonies in America.
first half of 16th century A third of a million Arawaks and Caribs died, as a result of enslavement and exposure to European diseases; black African slaves were consequently brought in to work the island's gold and silver mines, which were swiftly exhausted.
1697 Spain ceded western third of Hispaniola to France, which became known as Haiti, but kept the E, which was known as Santo Domingo (the Dominican Republic).
1804 Independence achieved after uprising against French colonial rule led by the former slave Toussaint l'Ouverture, who died in prison 1803,

and Jean-Jacques Dessalines.
1818–43 Ruled by Jean-Pierre Boyer, who excluded the blacks from power.
1821 Santo Domingo fell under the control of Haiti until 1844.
1847–59 Blacks reasserted themselves under President Faustin Soulouque.
1915 Haiti invaded by USA as a result of political instability caused by black-mulatto friction; remained under US control until 1934.
1956 Dr François Duvalier (Papa Doc), a voodoo physician, seized power in military coup and was elected president one year later.
1964 Duvalier pronounced himself president for life, establishing a dictatorship based around a personal militia, the Tonton Macoutes.
1971 Duvalier died, succeeded by his son Jean-Claude (Baby Doc); thousands murdered during Duvalier era.
1986 Duvalier deposed and fled the country; replaced by Lt-Gen Henri Namphy as head of a governing council.
1988 Leslie Manigat became president, but was ousted in military coup by Brig-Gen Prosper Avril, who installed a civilian government under military control.
1989 Coup attempt against Avril foiled; US aid resumed.
1990 Left-wing Catholic priest Jean-Bertrand Aristide elected president.
1991 Aristide overthrown in military coup led by Brig-Gen Raoul Cedras. Sanctions imposed by Organization of American States (OAS) and USA.
1993 United Nations (UN) embargo imposed. Aristide's return blocked by military.
1994 Threat of US invasion led to regime recognizing Aristide as president, under agreement brokered by former US president Jimmy Carter. US troops landed peacefully; Cedras relinquished power and withdrew to Panama; Aristide returned.
1995 UN peacekeepers drafted in to replace US troops. Assembly elections won by Aristide's supporters. René Preval elected to replace Aristide as president.
1996 Peaceful handover of power to Preval.
1997 Prime Minister Smarth resigned, following a series of strikes and protests.

Honduras Republic of

National name *República de Honduras*
Area 112,100 sq km/43,281 sq mi
Capital Tegucigalpa
Major towns/cities San Pedro Sula, La Ceiba, El Progreso, Choluteca, Juticalpa, Danlí
Major ports La Ceiba, Puerto Cortés
Physical features narrow tropical coastal plain with mountainous interior, Bay Islands, Caribbean reefs

Government

Head of state and government Carlos Roberto Reina Idiaquez from 1993
Political system democratic republic
Administrative divisions 18 departments
Political parties Liberal Party of Honduras (PLH), centre left; National Party of Honduras (PNH), right wing
Armed forces 18,800 (1995); plus paramilitary forces numbering 5,500
Conscription military service is voluntary (conscription abolished 1995)
Death penalty abolished 1956
Defence spend (% GDP) 1.3 (1995)

Education spend (% GNP) 4 (1994)
Health spend (% GDP) 2.9 (1990)

Economy and resources

Currency lempira
GDP ($ US) 3.3 billion (1994)
Real GDP per capita (PPP) ($ US) 2,050 (1994)
GDP growth rate –1.4% (1994); 3.5% (1990–95)
Average annual inflation 26.8% (1995); 14.2% (1985–95)
Foreign debt ($ US) 4.41 billion (1994)
Trading partners USA, Guatemala, Japan, El Salvador, Germany, Belgium, UK
Resources lead, zinc, silver, gold, tin, iron, copper, antimony
Industries food processing, petroleum refining, cement, beverages, wood products, chemical products, textiles, beer, rum
Exports bananas, lobsters and prawns, zinc, meat. Principal market: USA 68.5% (1995)
Imports machinery, appliances and electrical equipment, mineral fuels and lubricants, chemical products, consumer goods. Principal source: USA 55.5% (1995)
Arable land 15% (1993)
Agricultural products coffee, bananas, maize, sorghum, plantains, beans, rice, sugar cane, citrus fruits; fishing (notably shellfish); livestock rearing (cattle); timber production

Population and society

Population 5,816,000 (1996e)
Population growth rate 3% (1990–95); 2.5% (2000–05)

Population density (per sq km) 52 (1996e)
Urban population (% of total) 44 (1995)
Age distribution (% of total population) <15 43.8%, 15–65 53.1%, >65 3.1% (1995)
Ethnic distribution about 90% of mixed Native American and Spanish descent (known as ladinos or mestizos); there are also Salvadorean, Guatemalan, American, and European minorities
Languages Spanish (official); English, Native American languages
Religion Roman Catholic
Education (compulsory years) 6
Literacy rate 75% (men); 71% (women) (1995e)
Labour force 34% of population: 43.5% agriculture, 19.2% industry, 37.3% services (1994)
Unemployment 40% (1994e)
Life expectancy 68 (men); 72 (women) (1995–2000)
Child mortality rate (under 5, per 1,000 live births) 38 (1995)
Physicians 1 per 1,266 people (1991)
Hospital beds 1 per 994 people (1995)
TV sets (per 1,000 people) 88 (1995)
Radios (per 1,000 people) 409 (1995)

Transport

Airports international airports: Tegucigalpa (Toncontín), San Pedro Sula, Roatún, La Ceiba; over 30 smaller airports serving domestic flights; total passenger km: 323 mil (1994)
Railroads total length: 939 km/583 mi; passenger journeys: 705,200 (1991)
Roads total road network: 15,100 km/ 9,383 mi, of which 20.2% paved (1995e); passenger cars: 4.7 per 1,000 people (1993e)

Chronology

c. AD 250–900 Part of culturally advanced Maya civilization.
1502 Visited by Christopher Columbus, who named the country Honduras ('depths') after the deep waters off the N coast.
1525 Colonized by Spain, who founded the town of Trujillo, but met with fierce resistance from the Native American population.
17th century onwards The northern 'Mosquito Coast' fell under the control of British buccaneers, as the Spanish concentrated on the inland area, with a British protectorate being established over the coast until 1860.
1821 Achieved independence from Spain and became part of Mexico.
1823 Became part of United Provinces (Federation) of Central America, also embracing Costa Rica, El Salvador, Guatemala, and Nicaragua, with the Honduran liberal Gen Francisco Morazan president of the Federation from 1830.
1838 Achieved full independence when the federation dissolved.

1880 Capital transferred from Comayagua to Tegucigalpa.
later 19th–early 20th centuries The USA's economic involvement significant, with banana production, which provided two-thirds of exports in 1913, being controlled by the United Fruit Company; political instability, with frequent changes of constitution and military coups.
1925 Brief civil war.
1932–49 Under a right-wing National Party (PNH) dictatorship, led by Gen Tiburcio Carias Andino.
1963–74 Following a series of military coups, Gen Oswaldo López Arelano held power, before resigning after allegedly accepting bribes from a US company.
1969 Brief 'Football War' with El Salvador, which attacked Honduras at the time of a football competition between the two states, following evictions of thousands of Salvadoran illegal immigrants from Honduras.
1980 First civilian government in more than a century elected, with Dr Roberto Suazo of the centrist Liberal Party (PLH) as president, but the commander in chief of the army, Gen Gustavo Alvárez,

retained considerable power.
1983 Close involvement with the USA in providing naval and air bases and allowing Nicaraguan counter-revolutionaries ('Contras') to operate from Honduras.
1984 Alvarez ousted in coup led by junior officers led by Gen Walter López Reyes, resulting in policy review towards USA and Nicaragua.
1986 José Azcona del Hoyo (PLH) elected president after electoral law changed, making Suazo ineligible for presidency, and despite receiving fewer votes than his opponent.
1989 Government and opposition declared support for Central American peace plan to demobilize Nicaraguan Contras (thought to number 55,000 with their dependents) based in Honduras. PNH won assembly elections; its leader, Rafael Leonardo Callejas Romero, elected president.
1992 Border dispute with El Salvador dating from 1861 finally resolved.
1993 PLH, under Carlos Roberto Reina Idiaquez, won assembly and presidential elections.

Practical information

Visa requirements UK: visa not required with full British passport. USA: visa not required
Embassy in the UK 115 Gloucester Place, London W1H 3PJ. Tel: (0171) 486 4880; fax: (0171) 486 4550
British embassy Apartado Postal 290, Edificio Palmira, 3° Piso, Colonia Palmira, Tegucigalpa. Tel: (504) 325 429; fax: (504) 325 480
Embassy in the USA 3007 Tilden Street NW, Washington, DC 20008. Tel: (202) 966 7702, 2604, 5008, 4596; fax: (202) 966 9751
American embassy Avenida La Paz, Apartado Postal No. 3453, Tegucigalpa. Tel: (504) 369 320, 385 114; fax: (504) 369 037

Chamber of commerce Federación de Cámaras de Comercio e Industrias de Honduras, Apartado Postal 3393, Edificio Castañito 2° Nivel, 6a Avenida, Colonia Los Castaños, Tegucigalpa. Tel: (504) 326 083; fax: (504) 321 870
Office hours 0800–1200 and 1400–1700 Mon–Fri; 0800–1100 Sat
Banking hours 0900–1500 Mon–Fri; some branches 0900–1100 Sat
Time difference GMT –6
Chief tourist attractions Mayan ruins at Copán; beaches on northern coast; fishing and boating in Trujillo Bay and Lake Yojoa, near San Pedro
Major holidays 1 January, 14 April, 1 May, 15 September, 3, 12, 21 October, 25, 31 December; variable: Good Friday, Holy Thursday

Hungary Republic of

National name *Magyar Köztársaság*
Area 93,032 sq km/35,919 sq mi
Capital Budapest
Major towns/cities Miskolc, Debrecen, Szeged, Pécs, Gyor, Nyiregyháza, Székesfehérvár, Kecskemét
Physical features Great Hungarian Plain covers eastern half of country; Bakony Forest, Lake Balaton, and Transdanubian Highlands in the W; rivers Danube, Tisza, and Raba; more than 500 thermal springs

Government

Head of state Arpád Göncz from 1990
Head of government Gyula Horn from 1994
Political system emergent democratic republic
Administrative divisions 19 counties and the capital city (with 22 districts)
Political parties over 50, including Hungarian Socialist Party (HSP), reform-socialist; Alliance of Free Democrats (AFD), centrist, radical free market;

Hungarian Democratic Forum (MDF), nationalist, centre right; Independent Smallholders Party (ISP), right of centre, agrarian; Christian Democratic People's Party (KDNP), right of centre; Federation of Young Democrats, liberal, anticommunist
Armed forces 71,000 (1995)
Conscription 12 months (men aged 18–23)
Death penalty abolished 1990
Defence spend (% GDP) 1.4 (1995)
Education spend (% GNP) 6.3 (1994)
Health spend (% GDP) 6 (1991)

Economy and resources

Currency forint
GDP ($ US) 41.4 billion (1994)
Real GDP per capita (PPP) ($ US) 6,437 (1994)
GDP growth rate 1% (1996); −1% (1990–95)
Average annual inflation 26.8% (1995); 19.9% (1985–95)
Foreign debt ($ US) 31.25 billion (1995)
Trading partners Germany, CIS countries, Italy, Austria, USA
Resources lignite, brown coal, natural gas, petroleum, bauxite, hard coal
Industries food and beverages, tobacco, steel, chemicals, petroleum and plastics, engineering, transport equipment, pharmaceuticals, textiles, cement
Exports raw materials, semi-finished products, industrial consumer goods, food and agricultural products, transport equipment. Principal market: Germany 29% (1996)
Imports mineral fuels, raw materials, semi-finished products, transport equipment, food products, consumer goods. Principal source: Germany 23.6% (1996)
Arable land 54% (1993)
Agricultural products wheat, maize, sugar beet, barley, potatoes, sunflowers, grapes; livestock and dairy products

Population and society

Population 10,049,000 (1996e)
Population growth rate −0.5% (1990–95); −0.3% (2000–05)
Population density (per sq km) 108 (1996e)
Urban population (% of total) 65 (1995)
Age distribution (% of total population) <15 18.1%, 15–65 67.9%, >65 14% (1995)

Ethnic distribution 93% indigenous Hungarian, or Magyar; there is a large Romany community of around 600,000; other ethnic minorities include Germans, Croats, Romanians, Slovaks, Serbs, and Slovenes
Languages Hungarian (or Magyar), one of the few languages of Europe with non-Indo-European origins; it is grouped with Finnish, Estonian, and others in the Finno-Ugric family
Religions Roman Catholic 67%, Calvinist 20%, other Christian denominations, Jewish
Education (compulsory years) 10
Literacy rate 99% (men); 99% (women) (1995e)
Labour force 46% of population: 15% agriculture, 38% industry, 55% services (1990)
Unemployment 11% (1996)
Life expectancy 65 (men); 74 (women) (1995–2000)
Child mortality rate (under 5, per 1,000 live births) 14 (1995)
Physicians 1 per 241 people (1994)
Hospital beds 1 per 101 people (1994)
TV sets (per 1,000 people) 433 (1995)
Radios (per 1,000 people) 643 (1995)

Transport

Airports international airport: Budapest (Ferihegy); six domestic airports; total passenger km: 1,653 mil (1994)
Railroads total length: 7,707 km/ 4,789 mi; total passenger km: 8,508 mil (1994)
Roads total road network: 158,633 km/ 98,575 mi, of which 44.1% paved (1995); passenger cars: 220 per 1,000 people (1995)

Chronology

1st century AD Region formed part of the Roman Empire.
4th century Germanic tribes overran central Europe.
c. 445 Attila the Hun established a short-lived empire, including Hungarian nomads living far to the E.
c. 680 Hungarians settled between the Don and Dniepr rivers under Khazar rule.
9th century Hungarians invaded central Europe; ten tribes united under Árpád, chief of the Magyar tribe, who conquered the area corresponding to modern Hungary 896.
10th century Hungarians colonized Transylvania and raided their neighbours for plunder and slaves.

955 Battle of Lech: Germans led by Otto the Great defeated Hungarians.
1001 St Stephen founded Hungarian kingdom to replace tribal organization and converted Hungarians to Christianity.
12th century Hungary became a major power when King Béla III won temporary supremacy over the Balkans.
1308–86 Angevin dynasty ruled after Arpádian line died out.
1456 Battle of Belgrade: János Hunyadi defeated Ottoman Turks and saved Hungary from invasion.
1458–90 Under Mátyás I Corvinus, Hungary enjoyed military success and cultural renaissance.
1526 Battle of Mohács: Turks under Suleiman the Magnificent decisively defeated Hungarians.
16th century Partition of Hungary between Turkey, Austria, and semi-autonomous Transylvania.
1699 Treaty of Karlowitz: Austrians expelled the Turks from Hungary, which was reunified under Habsburg rule.
1707 Prince Ferenc Rákóczi II led uprising against Austrians, who promised to respect Hungarian constitution 1711.
1780–90 Joseph II's attempts to impose uniform administration throughout Austrian Empire provoked nationalist reaction among Hungarian nobility.
early 19th century 'National Revival' movement led by Count Stephen Széchenyi and Lajos Kossuth.
1848 Hungarian Revolution: nationalists proclaimed self-government; Croat minority resisted Hungarian rule.
1849 Kossuth repudiated Habsburg monarchy; Austrians crushed revolution with Russian support.
1867 Austria conceded equality to Hungary within the dual monarchy of Austria-Hungary.
1918 Austria-Hungary collapsed in military defeat; Count Mihály Károlyi proclaimed Hungarian Republic.
1919 Communists took power under Béla Kun; Romanians invaded; Admiral Miklós Horthy overthrew Béla Kun.
1920 Treaty of Trianon: Hungary lost 72% of its territory to Czechoslovakia, Romania, and Yugoslavia; Horthy restored Kingdom of Hungary with himself as regent.
1921 Count István Bethlen became prime minister of authoritarian aristocratic regime.

1938–41 Diplomatic collaboration with Germany allowed Hungary to regain territories lost 1920; Hungary declared war on USSR in alliance with Germany 1941.
1944 Germany occupied Hungary and installed Nazi regime.
1945 USSR 'liberated' Hungary; Smallholders' Party won free elections, but communists led by Mátyás Rákosi took over by stages 1946–49.
1947 Peace treaty restored 1920 frontiers.
1949 Hungary became a Soviet-style dictatorship; Rákosi pursued Stalinist policies of collectivization and police terror.

1956 Hungarian uprising: anti-Soviet demonstrations led prime minister Imre Nagy to propose democratic reforms and neutrality; USSR invaded, crushed dissent, and installed János Kádár as communist leader.
1961 Kádár began to introduce pragmatic liberal reforms of a limited kind.
1988 Károly Grosz replaced Kádár and accelerated reform; Hungarian Democratic Forum formed by opposition groups.
1989 Communist dictatorship dismantled; transitional constitution restored multiparty democracy; opening of border with Austria destroyed the

'Iron Curtain'.
1990 Elections won by centre-right coalition led by József Antall, who pursued radical free-market reforms.
1991 Withdrawal of Soviet forces completed.
1994 Gyula Horn, the leader of the ex-communist Hungarian Socialist Party, became prime minister, pledging to continue reform policies.
1996 Friendship treaty with Slovak Republic signed. Cooperation treaty with Romania.
1997 Hungary invited to join NATO and to begin negotiations for membership of the European Union.

Practical information

Visa requirements UK: visa not required. USA: visa not required
Embassy in the UK 35 Eaton Place, London SW1X 8BY. Tel: (0171) 235 4048; fax: (0171) 823 1348
British embassy Harmincad Utca 6, 1051 Budapest. Tel: (1) 266 2888; fax: (1) 266 0907
Embassy in the USA 3910 Shoemaker Street NW, Washington, DC 20008. Tel: (202) 362 6730; fax: (202) 966 8135
American embassy V Szabadsag Ter 12, Budapest. Tel: (1) 267 4400, 269 9331; fax: (1) 269 9326

Chamber of commerce Magyar Kereskedelmi és Iparkamara (Hungarian Chamber of Commerce and Industry), PO Box 106, H-1389 Budapest. Tel: (1) 153 3333; fax: (1) 153 1285
Office hours 0800–1630 Mon–Fri
Banking hours 0900–1400 Mon–Fri
Time difference GMT +1
Chief tourist attractions boating and fishing on Lake Balaton; Budapest and other historical cities; Budapest has thermal springs feeding swimming pools equipped with modern physiotherapy facilities
Major holidays 1 January, 15 March, 1 May, 20 August, 23 October, 25–26 December; variable: Easter Monday

Iceland Republic of

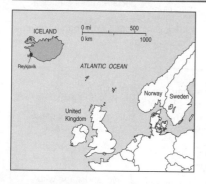

National name *Lýdveldid Ísland*
Area 103,000 sq km/39,768 sq mi
Capital Reykjavík
Major towns/cities Akureyri, Akranes, Kópavogur, Hafnerfjördur, Vestmannaeyjar
Physical features warmed by the Gulf Stream; glaciers and lava fields cover 75% of the country; active volcanoes (Hekla was once thought the gateway to

Hell), geysers, hot springs, and new islands created offshore (Surtsey in 1963); subterranean hot water heats 85% of Iceland's homes; Sidujokull glacier moving at 100 metres a day

Government
Head of state Olafur Ragner Grimsson from 1996
Head of government Davíd Oddsson from 1991
Political system democratic republic
Administrative divisions 23 counties within eight districts
Political parties Independence Party (IP), right of centre; Progressive Party (PP), radical socialist; People's Alliance (PA), socialist; Social Democratic Party (SDP), moderate, left of centre; Citizens' Party, centrist; Women's Alliance, women- and family-oriented
Armed forces no defence forces of its own; US forces under NATO are stationed there: 2,500 military

personnel and a 130-strong coastguard (1995)
Death penalty abolished 1928
Education spend (% GNP) 5.4 (1993–94)
Health spend (% GDP) 6.9 (1993)

Economy and resources
Currency krona
GDP ($ US) 7.3 billion (1996)
Real GDP per capita (PPP) ($ US) 23,434 (1996)
GDP growth rate 4.2% (1996); 2% (1994–95)
Average annual inflation 2.5% (1996); 11.8% (1985–95)
Trading partners EU (principally Germany, UK, and Denmark), Norway, USA, Japan
Resources aluminium, diatomite, hydroelectric and thermal power, fish
Industries mining, fish processing, processed aluminium, fertilizer, construction, cement

Exports fish products, aluminium, ferrosilicon, diatomite, fertilizer, animal products. Principal market: UK 19.3% (1995)
Imports machinery and transport equipment, motor vehicles, petroleum and petroleum products, foodstuffs, textiles. Principal source: Germany 11.4% (1995)
Arable land 0.1% (1993)
Agricultural products hay, potatoes, turnips; fishing industry, dairy products and livestock (lamb)

Population and society

Population 271,000 (1996e)
Population growth rate 1.1% (1990–95); 0.9% (2000–05)
Population density (per sq km) 3 (1996e)
Urban population (% of total) 92 (1995)
Age distribution (% of total population) <15 24.5%, 15–65 64.3%, >65 11.2% (1995)
Ethnic distribution most of the population is descended from Norwegians and Celts
Languages Icelandic, the most archaic Scandinavian language
Religion Evangelical Lutheran
Education (compulsory years) 9
Literacy rate 99% (men); 99% (women) (1995e)
Labour force 56% of population: 11% agriculture, 27% industry, 62% services (1990)
Unemployment 4.4% (1996)
Life expectancy 76 (men); 81 (women) (1995–2000)

Child mortality rate (under 5, per 1,000 live births) 5 (1995)
Physicians 1 per 334 people (1993)
Hospital beds 1 per 68 people (1991)
TV sets (per 1,000 people) 353 (1995)
Radios (per 1,000 people) 799 (1995)

Transport

Airports international airport: Keflavik (45 km/28 mi southwest of Reykjavík); ten major domestic airports, 12 local airports; total passenger km: 2,297 mil (1994)
Railroads none
Roads total road network: 12,378 km/ 7,692 mi, of which 24.8% paved (1995); passenger cars: 445 per 1,000 people (1995)

Chronology

7th century Iceland discovered by Irish seafarers.
874 First Norse settler, Ingólfr Arnarson, founded a small colony at Reykjavík.
c. 900 Norse settlers came in larger numbers, mainly from Norway.
930 Settlers established an annual parliament, the Althing, to make laws and resolve disputes.
985 Eric the Red left Iceland to found a settlement in Greenland.
1000 Icelanders adopted Christianity.
1263 Icelanders recognized authority of the king of Norway after brief civil war.
1397 Norway and Iceland united with Denmark and Sweden under a single monarch.
15th century Norway and Iceland were increasingly treated as appendages of

Denmark, especially after Sweden seceded in 1449.
1602 Denmark introduced a monopoly on Icelandic trade.
1783 Poisonous volcanic eruption caused great loss of life.
1814 Norway passed to the Swedish crown; Iceland remained under Danish rule.
1845 Althing re-established in modernized form.
1854 Danish monopoly on trade abolished.
1874 New constitution gave Iceland limited autonomy.
1918 Iceland achieved full self-government under the Danish crown.
1940 British forces occupied Iceland after Germany invaded Denmark; US troops took over 1941.
1944 Iceland became an independent republic under President Sveinn Björnsson.
1949 Became a member of NATO.
1953 Joined the Nordic Council.
1958 Introduction of exclusive 19-km/ 12-mi fishing limit led to first 'Cod War', when Icelandic patrol boats clashed with British fishing boats.
1972–73 Iceland extended its fishing limit 80 km/50 mi; renewed confrontation with Britain.
1975–76 Further extension of fishing limit to 341 km/200 mi caused third 'Cod War' with the UK.
1980 Vigdis Finnbogadóttir became the first woman president of Iceland.
1985 Iceland declared itself a nuclear-free zone.
1992 Iceland defied world ban to resume whaling industry.

Practical information

Visa requirements UK: visa not required. USA: visa not required
Embassy in the UK 1 Eaton Terrace, London SW1W 8EY. Tel: (0171) 730 5131/2; fax: (0171) 730 1683
British embassy PO Box 460, Laufásvegur 49, 101 Reykjavík. Tel: (354) 551 5883/4; fax: (354) 552 7940
Embassy in the USA Suite 1200, 1156 15th Street NW, Washington, DC 20005. Tel: (202) 265 6653–5; fax: (202) 265 6656
American embassy Laufasvegur 21, Reykjavík. Tel: (354) 562 9100; fax: (354) 562 9139
Chamber of commerce Verslunarrád Islands (Chamber of

Commerce), Hús verslunarinnar, 103 Reykjavík. Tel: (354) 588 6666; fax: (354) 568 6564
Office hours 0900–1700 Mon–Fri. Most offices are closed Sat; some firms close down completely for a three-week holiday, usually in July
Banking hours 0915–1600 Mon–Fri
Time difference GMT +/–0
Chief tourist attractions rugged volcanic landscape with geysers
Major holidays 1 January, 1 May, 17 June, 25–26 December; variable: Ascension Thursday, Good Friday, Easter Monday, Holy Thursday, First Day of Summer, August Holiday Monday

India Republic of

National name Hindi *Bharat*
Area 3,166,829 sq km/1,222,713 sq mi
Capital Delhi
Major towns/cities Bombay, Calcutta,
Chennai (Madras), Bangalore,
Hyderabad, Ahmadabad, Kanpur, Pune,
Nagpur, Bhopal, Jaipur, Lucknow, Surat
Major ports Calcutta, Bombay, Chennai
(Madras)
Physical features Himalaya mountains
on N border; plains around rivers
Ganges, Indus, Brahmaputra; Deccan
peninsula S of the Narmada River forms
plateau between Western and Eastern
Ghats mountain ranges; desert in W;
Andaman and Nicobar Islands,
Lakshadweep (Laccadive Islands)

Government

Head of state Kocheril Raman
Narayanan from 1997
Head of government Inder Kumar
Gujral from 1997
Political system liberal democratic
federal republic
Administrative divisions 25 states and
seven centrally administered union
territories
Political parties All India Congress
Committee, or Congress, cross-caste
and cross-religion coalition, left of centre;
Janata Dal (People's Party), secular, left
of centre; Bharatiya Janata Party (BJP),
radical right wing, Hindu-chauvinist;
Communist Party of India (CPI), Marxist-
Leninist; Communist Party of India-
Marxist (CPI–M), West Bengal–based
moderate socialist
Armed forces 11,450,000 (1995)
Conscription none, although all citizens
are constitutionally obliged to perform
national service when called upon

Death penalty limited to exceptional
circumstances, such as political
assassinations. Method: hanging
Defence spend (% GDP) 2.5 (1995)
Education spend (% GNP) 3.8
(1993–94)
Health spend (% GDP) 6.0 (1990)

Economy and resources

Currency rupee
GDP ($ US) 293.6 billion (1994)
Real GDP per capita (PPP) ($ US)
1,348 (1994)
GDP growth rate 6.3% (1994); 4.6%
(1990–95)
Average annual inflation 10.2% (1994);
9.8% (1985–95)
Foreign debt ($ US) 93.8 billion (1995)
Trading partners USA, CIS, UK,
Germany
Resources coal, iron ore, copper ore,
bauxite, chromite, gold, manganese ore,
zinc, lead, limestone, crude oil, natural
gas, diamonds
Industries mining (including coal, iron
and manganese ores, diamonds, and
gold), manufacturing (iron and steel,
mineral oils, shipbuilding, chemical
products, road transport, cotton cloth,
sugar, petroleum refining products)
Exports tea (world's largest producer),
coffee, fish, iron and steel, leather,
textiles, clothing, polished diamonds,
handmade carpets, engineering goods,
chemicals. Principal market: USA 17.4%
(1995–96)
Imports nonelectrical machinery, mineral
fuels and lubricants, pearls, precious and
semiprecious stones, chemicals,
transport equipment. Principal source:
USA 10.5% (1995–96)
Arable land 50.5% (1993)
Agricultural products cotton, tea,
wheat, rice, coffee, cashew nuts, jute,
spices, sugar cane, oil seeds

Population and society

Population 994,580,000 (1996e)
Population growth rate 1.9%
(1990–95); 1.6% (2000–05)
Population density (per sq km) 287
(1996e)
Urban population (% of total) 27 (1995)
Age distribution (% of total population)
<15 35.2%, 15–65 60.2%, >65 4.6%
(1995)
Ethnic distribution 72% of Indo-Aryan
descent; 25% (predominantly in the S)
Dravidian; 3% Mongoloid

Languages Hindi, English, and 17 other
official languages: Assamese, Bengali,
Gujarati, Kannada, Kashmiri, Konkani,
Malayalam, Manipur, Marathi, Nepali,
Oriya, Punjabi, Sanskrit, Sindhi, Tamil,
Telugu, Urdu; more than 1,650 dialects
Religions Hindu 83%, Sunni Muslim
11%, Christian 2.5%, Sikh 2%
Education (compulsory years) 8
Literacy rate 62% (men); 34% (women)
(1995e)
Labour force 43% of population: 64%
agriculture, 16% industry, 20% services
(1990)
Unemployment 9.1%
Life expectancy 63 (men); 63 (women)
(1995–2000)
Child mortality rate (under 5, per 1,000
live births) 115 (1995)
Physicians 1 per 2,564 people (1991)
Hospital beds 1 per 1,364 people (1993)
TV sets (per 1,000 people) 51 (1995)
Radios (per 1,000 people) 81 (1995)

Transport

Airports international airports:
Ahmadabad, Bombay, Calcutta, Delhi
(Indira Gandhi), Goa, Hyderabad, Madras,
Thiruvanathapuram; over 70 domestic
airports; total passenger km: 17,581 mil
(1994)
Railroads total length: 62,660 km/38,937
mi; total passenger km: 310,620 mil
(1994–95)
Roads total road network: 2,009,600
km/1,248,765 mi, of which 50.1% paved
(1995e); passenger cars: 3 per 1,000
people (1995e)

Chronology

c. 2500–1500 BC The earliest Indian
civilization evolved in the Indus Valley with
the city states of Harappa and Mohenjo
Daro.
c. 1500–1200 BC Aryan peoples from the
NW overran N India and the Deccan;
Brahmanism (a form of Hinduism)
developed.
321 BC Chandragupta, founder of the
Mauryan dynasty, began to unite N India
in a Hindu Empire.
268–232 BC Mauryan Empire reached its
height under Asoka, who ruled two-thirds
of India from his capital Pataliputra.
c. 180 BC Shunga dynasty replaced the
Mauryans; Hindu Empire began to break
up into smaller kingdoms.
AD 320–480 Gupta dynasty reunified N
India.

c. 500 Raiding Huns from central Asia destroyed the Gupta dynasty; India reverted to many warring kingdoms.

11th–12th centuries Rajput princes of N India faced repeated Muslim invasions by Arabs, Turks, and Afghans, and in 1206 the first Muslim dynasty was established at Delhi.

14th–16th centuries Muslim rule extended over N India and the Deccan; S remained independent under the Hindu Vijayanagar dynasty.

1498 Explorer Vasco da Gama reached India, followed by Portuguese, Dutch, French, and English traders.

1526 Last Muslim invasion: Zahir ud-din Muhammad (Babur) defeated the sultan of Delhi at Battle of Panipat and established the Mogul Empire, which was consolidated by Akbar the Great (1556–1605).

1600 East India Company founded by English merchants, who settled in Madras, Bombay, and Calcutta.

17th century Mogul Empire reached its zenith under Jahangir (1605–27), Shah Jehan (1628–58), and Aurangzeb (1658–1707).

1739 Persian king Nadir Shah invaded India and destroyed Mogul prestige; British and French supported rival Indian princes in subsequent internal wars.

1757 Battle of Plassey: Robert Clive defeated Siraj al-Daulah, nawab of Bengal; Bengal came under control of British East India Company.

1772–85 Warren Hastings, British governor general of Bengal, raised Indian army and pursued expansionist policies.

early 19th century British took control (directly or indirectly) throughout India by defeating powerful Indian states in a series of regional wars.

1858 'Indian Mutiny': mutiny in Bengal army erupted into widespread anti-British revolt; rebels sought to restore powers of Mogul emperor.

1858 British defeated the rebels; East India Company dissolved; India came under the British crown.

1885 Indian National Congress founded in Bombay as focus for nationalism.

1909 Morley–Minto Reforms: Indians received right to elect members of Legislative Councils; Hindus and Muslims formed separate electorates.

1919 British forces killed 379 Indian demonstrators at Amritsar; India Act (Montagu–Chelmsford Reforms) conceded a measure of provincial self-government.

1920–22 Mohandas Gandhi won control of the Indian National Congress, which launched campaign of civil disobedience in support of demand for complete self-rule.

1935 India Act provided for Indian control of federal legislature, with defence and external affairs remaining the viceroy's responsibility.

1940 Muslim League called for India to be partitioned along religious lines.

1947 British India partitioned into two independent dominions of India (mainly Hindu) and Pakistan (mainly Muslim) amid bloody riots; Jawaharlal Nehru of Congress Party became prime minister.

1950 India became a republic within the Commonwealth.

1962 India lost brief border war with China; retained Kashmir in war with Pakistan 1965.

1966 Indira Gandhi, daughter of Nehru, became prime minister.

1971 India defeated Pakistan in war and helped East Pakistan become independent as Bangladesh.

1975 Found guilty of electoral corruption, Mrs Gandhi declared state of emergency and arrested opponents.

1977–79 Janata Party formed government under Morarji Desai.

1980 Mrs Gandhi, heading Congress Party splinter group, Congress (I) ('I' for Indira), returned to power.

1984 Troops cleared Sikh separatists from the Golden Temple, Amritsar; Mrs Gandhi assassinated by Sikh bodyguards; her son Rajiv Gandhi became prime minister.

1989 After financial scandals, Congress ('I' was removed after Mrs Gandhi's assassination) lost elections; V P Singh formed Janata Dal minority government.

1990 Direct rule imposed on Jammu and Kashmir after upsurge in Muslim separatist violence; rising interethnic and religious conflict in Punjab and elsewhere.

1991 Rajiv Gandhi assassinated during election campaign; P V Narasimha Rao formed minority Congress government.

1992 Destruction of mosque at Ayodhya, N India, by Hindu extremists resulted in widespread violence.

1996 H D Deve Gowda became prime minister of a coalition government. Madras renamed Chennai. Rao resigned as Congress Party president and was replaced by Sitaram Kesri. Direct central rule imposed on Uttar Pradesh after inconclusive assembly elections.

1997 Sikh Akali Dal party and BNP successful in state elections. United Front government cut taxes in pro-business budget. Deve Gowda's government defeated in a confidence vote. United Front government reformed and led by Inder Kumar Gujral. Kocheril Raman Narayanan became first 'untouchable' to be elected president. It was announced that former prime minister Rao would face corruption charges. Discussions began to normalize relations with Pakistan.

Practical information

Visa requirements UK: visa required. USA: visa required
Embassy in the UK Office of the High Commissioner for India, India House, Aldwych, London WC2B 4NA. Tel: (0171) 836 8484; fax: (0171) 836 4331
British embassy British High Commission, Shanti Path, Chanakyapuri, New Delhi 110021. Tel: (11) 687 2161; fax: (11) 687 2882
Embassy in the USA 2107 Massachusetts Avenue NW, Washington, DC 20008. (Embassy located at 2536 Massachusetts Avenue NW, Washington, DC 20008.) Tel: (202) 939 7000

American embassy Shanti Path, Chanakyapuri, New Delhi 110021. Tel: (11) 600 651; fax: (11) 687 2028
Chamber of commerce India Exchange, 4 India Exchange Place, Calcutta 700001. Tel: (33) 220 3243; fax: (33) 220 4495
Office hours 0930–1730 Mon–Fri; 0930–1300 Sat
Banking hours 1000–1400 Mon–Fri; 1000–1200 Sat
Time difference GMT +5.5
Chief tourist attractions historic palaces, forts, and temples; Taj Mahal; varied scenery; wildlife
Major holidays 1 (some states), 26 January, 1 May (some states), 30 June, 15 August, 2 October, 25, 31 December; variable: New Year (Parsi, some states)

Indonesia Republic of

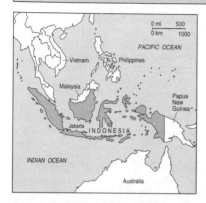

National name *Republik Indonesia*
Area 1,904,569 sq km/735,354 sq mi
Capital Jakarta
Major towns/cities Surabaya, Bandung, Yogyakarta (Java), Medan, Semarang (Java), Banda Aceh, Palembang (Sumatra), Ujung Pandang (Sulawesi), Denpasar (Bali), Kupang (Timor), Padang, Malang
Major ports Tanjung Priok, Surabaya, Semarang (Java), Ujung Pandang (Sulawesi)
Physical features comprises 13,677 tropical islands (over 6,000 of them are inhabited): the Greater Sundas (including Java, Madura, Sumatra, Sulawesi, and Kalimantan [part of Borneo]), the Lesser Sunda Islands/Nusa Tenggara (including Bali, Lombok, Sumbawa, Flores, Sumba, Alor, Lomblen, Timor, Roti, and Savu), Maluku/Moluccas (over 1,000 islands including Ambon, Ternate, Tidore, Tanimbar, and Halmahera), and Irian Jaya (part of New Guinea); over half the country is tropical rainforest; it has the largest expanse of peatlands in the tropics (17–27 million hectares). A million hectares of pristine swamp forest is to be drained in central Kalimantan; President Suharto endorsed the project 1996 without environmental assessment

Government

Head of state and government T N J Suharto from 1967
Political system authoritarian nationalist republic
Administrative divisions 27 provinces
Political parties Sekber Golkar, ruling military-bureaucrat-farmers' party; United Development Party (PPP), moderate Islamic; Indonesian Democratic Party (PDI), nationalist Christian

Armed forces 274,500; paramilitary and part-time auxiliary forces 1.67 million (1995)
Conscription 2 years (selective)
Death penalty retained and used for ordinary crimes
Defence spend (% GDP) 1.6 (1995)
Education spend (% GNP) 1.3 (1993–94)
Health spend (% GDP) 0.7 (1990)

Economy and resources

Currency rupiah
GDP ($ US) 174.6 billion (1994)
Real GDP per capita (PPP) ($ US) 3,740 (1994)
GDP growth rate 7.3% (1994); 7.6% (1990–95)
Average annual inflation 9.6% (1994); 8.8% (1985–95)
Foreign debt ($ US) 107.8 billion (1995)
Trading partners Japan, Singapore, USA, Hong Kong, Australia, Germany, the Netherlands
Resources petroleum (principal producer of petroleum in the Far East), natural gas, bauxite, nickel (world's third-largest producer), copper, tin (world's second-largest producer), gold, coal, forests
Industries petroleum refining, food processing, textiles, wood products, tobacco, chemicals, fertilizers, rubber, cement
Exports petroleum and petroleum products, natural and manufactured gas, textiles, rubber, palm oil, wood and wood products, electrical and electronic products, coffee, fishery products, coal, copper, tin, pepper, tea. Principal market: Japan 27.1% (1995)
Imports machinery, transport and electrical equipment, manufactured goods, chemical and mineral products. Principal source: Japan 22.7% (1995)
Arable land 9.9% (1993)
Agricultural products rice, cassava, maize, coffee, spices, tea, cocoa, tobacco, sugar cane, sweet potatoes, palm, rubber, coconuts, nutmeg; fishing

Population and society

Population 200,453,000 (1996e)
Population growth rate 1.6% (1990–95); 1.3% (2000–05)
Population density (per sq km) 105 (1996e)
Urban population (% of total) 35% (1995)

Age distribution (% of total population) <15 33%, 15–65 62.7%, >65 4.3% (1995)
Ethnic distribution comprises more than 300 ethnic groups, the majority of which are of Malay descent; important Malay communities include Javanese (about one-third of the population), Sundanese (7%), and Madurese (3%); the largest non-Malay community is the Chinese (2%); substantial numbers of Indians, Melanesians, Micronesians, and Arabs
Languages Bahasa Indonesia (official), closely related to Malay; there are 583 regional languages and dialects; Javanese is the most widely spoken local language. Dutch is also spoken
Religions Muslim 88%, Christian 10%, Buddhist and Hindu 2% (the continued spread of Christianity, together with an Islamic revival, have led to greater religious tensions)
Education (compulsory years) 6
Literacy rate 84% (men); 68% (women) (1995e)
Labour force 44% of population: 55% agriculture, 14% industry, 31% services (1990)
Unemployment 2.8% (1993)
Life expectancy 63 (men); 67 (women) (1995–2000)
Child mortality rate (under 5, per 1,000 live births) 75 (1995)
Physicians 1 per 7,143 people (1992)
Hospital beds 1 per 1,648 people (1992)
TV sets (per 1,000 people) 66 (1995)
Radios (per 1,000 people) 149 (1995)

Transport

Airports international airports: Jakarta (Sukarno-Hatta), Irian Jaya (Frans Kaisepo), Bali (Ngurah Rai), Surabaya, Manado (Sam Ratulangi); over 60 domestic airports; total passenger km: 21,166 mil (1994)
Railroads total length: 6,583 km/ 4,091 mi; total passenger km: 13,610 mil (1994)
Roads total road network: 378,000 km/ 234,889 mi, of which 45.5% paved (1995e); passenger cars: 10.2 per 1,000 people (1995e)

Chronology

3000–500 BC Immigrants from S China displaced original Melanesian population.

6th century AD Start of Indian cultural influence; small Hindu and Buddhist kingdoms developed.

8th century Buddhist maritime empire of Srivijaya expanded to include all Sumatra and Malay peninsula.

13th century Islam introduced to Sumatra by Arab merchants; spread throughout archipelago over next 300 years.

14th century Eastern Javanese kingdom of Majapahit destroyed Srivijaya and dominated the region.

c. 1520 Empire of Majapahit disintegrated; Javanese nobles fled to Bali.

16th century Portuguese merchants broke Muslim monopoly of spice trade.

1602 Dutch East India Company founded; it displaced the Portuguese and monopolized trade with the Spice Islands.

1619 Dutch East India Company captured port of Jakarta in Java and renamed it Batavia.

17th century Dutch introduced coffee plants and established informal control over central Java through divide-and-rule policy among local potentates.

1749 After frequent military intervention, the Dutch East India Company obtained formal sovereignty over Mataram.

1799 The Netherlands took over interests of bankrupt Dutch East India Company.

1808 French forces occupied Java; British expelled them 1811 and returned Java to the Netherlands 1816.

1824 Anglo-Dutch Treaty: Britain recognized entire Indonesian archipelago as Dutch sphere of influence.

1825–30 Java War: Prince Dipo Negoro led unsuccessful revolt against Dutch rule; further revolt 1894–96.

19th century Dutch formalized control over Java and conquered other islands; cultivation of coffee and sugar under tight official control made the Netherlands Indies one of the richest colonies in the world.

1901 Dutch introduced 'Ethical Policy' supposed to advance local interests.

1908 Dutch completed conquest of Bali.

1927 Communist revolts suppressed; Achmed Sukarno founded Indonesian Nationalist Party (PNI) to unite diverse anti-Dutch elements.

1929 Dutch imprisoned Sukarno and tried to suppress PNI.

1942–45 Japanese occupation; PNI installed as anti-Western puppet government.

1945 When Japan surrendered, President Sukarno declared an independent republic, but Dutch set about restoring colonial rule by force.

1947 Dutch 'police action': all-out attack on Java and Sumatra conquered two-thirds of the republic.

1949 Under US pressure, Dutch agreed to transfer sovereignty of the Netherlands Indies (except Dutch New Guinea or Irian Jaya) to the Republic of the United States of Indonesia.

1950 President Sukarno abolished federalism and proclaimed unitary Republic of Indonesia dominated by Java; revolts in Sumatra and South Moluccas.

1959 To combat severe political instability, Sukarno imposed authoritarian 'guided democracy'.

1963 The Netherlands ceded Irian Jaya to Indonesia.

1963–66 Indonesia tried to break up Malaysia by means of blockade and guerrilla attacks.

1965–66 Clashes between communists and army; Gen Raden Suharto imposed emergency administration and massacred up to 700,000 alleged communists.

1968 Suharto formally replaced Sukarno as president and proclaimed 'New Order' under strict military rule.

1970s Rising oil exports brought significant agricultural and industrial growth.

1975 Indonesia invaded East Timor when Portuguese rule collapsed; 200,000 died in ensuing war.

1986 After suppressing revolt on Irian Jaya, Suharto introduced a transmigration programme to settle 65,000 Javanese there and on outer islands.

1991 Democracy Forum launched to promote political dialogue.

1993 President Suharto re-elected for sixth consecutive term.

1994 Sukarno's daughter Megawati Sukarnoputri elected head of opposition party PDI.

1996 Megawati ousted by rival faction within PDI (aided by Suharto); government crackdown on opponents, including PDI supporters.

1997 Hundreds killed in ethnic riots in west Kalimantan province. PRD banned from general election and its leader, Budiman Sudjatmiko, imprisoned for subversion. Golkar Party won landslide victory in assembly elections.

Practical information

Visa requirements UK: visa not required. USA: visa not required

Embassy in the UK 38 Grosvenor Square, London W1X 9AD. Tel: (0171) 499 7661; fax: (0171) 491 4993

British embassy Jalan mil H Thamrin 75, Jakarta 10310. Tel: (21) 330 904; fax: (21) 314 1824

Embassy in the USA 2020 Massachusetts Avenue NW, Washington, DC 20036. Tel: (202) 775 5200; fax: (202) 775 5365

American embassy Medan Merdeka Selatan 5, Jakarta. Tel: (21) 360 360; fax: (21) 386 2259

Chamber of commerce Indonesian Chamber of Commerce and Industry, 3rd–5th Floors, Chandra Building, Jalan mil H Thamrin 20, Jakarta 10350. Tel: (21) 324 000; fax: (21) 310 6098

Office hours 0800–1600 or 0900–1700 Mon–Fri

Banking hours 0800–1500 Mon–Fri

Time difference GMT +7/9

Chief tourist attractions Java, with its temples and volcanic scenery; Bali, with its Hindu-Buddhist temples and religious festivals; Lombok, Sumatra, and Celebes

Major holidays 1 January, 17 August, 25 December; variable: Ascension Thursday, Eid-ul-Adha, end of Ramadan (2 days), Good Friday, New Year (Icaka, March), New Year (Muslim), Prophet's Birthday, Ascension of the Prophet (March/April), Waisak (May)

Iran Islamic Republic of (formerly *Persia*)

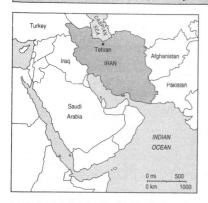

National name *Jomhori-e-Islami-e-Irân*
Area 1,648,000 sq km/636,292 sq mi
Capital Tehran
Major towns/cities Esfahan, Mashhad, Tabriz, Shiraz, Ahvaz, Bakhtaran, Qom, Kara
Major ports Abadan
Physical features plateau surrounded by mountains, including Elburz and Zagros; Lake Rezayeh; Dasht-e-Kavir desert; occupies islands of Abu Musa, Greater Tunb and Lesser Tunb in the Gulf

Government

Head of state and government Seyyed Mohammad Khatami from 1997
Leader of the Islamic Revolution Seyed Ali Khamenei from 1989
Political system authoritarian Islamic republic
Administrative divisions 25 provinces
Political parties none officially recognized
Armed forces 513,000 (1995); plus 350,000 army reserves
Conscription military service is compulsory for two years
Death penalty retained and used for ordinary crimes
Defence spend (% GDP) 3.9 (1995)
Education spend (% GNP) 5.9 (1993–94)
Health spend (% GDP) 1.5 (1990)

Economy and resources

Currency rial
GDP ($ US) 63.7 billion (1994)
Real GDP per capita (PPP) ($ US) 5,766 (1994)
GDP growth rate −1% (1994); 4.2% (1990–95)
Average annual inflation 40% (1995); 24.2% (1985–95)
Foreign debt ($ US) 22.7 billion (1994)

Trading partners Germany, Japan, UK, Italy, United Arab Emirates, Turkey
Resources petroleum, natural gas, coal, magnetite, gypsum, iron ore, copper, chromite, salt, bauxite, decorative stone
Industries mining, petroleum refining, textiles, food processing, transport equipment
Exports crude petroleum and petroleum products, agricultural goods, metal ores. Principal market: Japan 13.8% (1995)
Imports machinery and motor vehicles, paper, textiles, iron and steel and mineral products, chemicals and chemical products. Principal source: Germany 14.7% (1995)
Arable land 10.1% (1993)
Agricultural products wheat, barley, sugar beet, sugar cane, rice, fruit, tobacco, livestock (cattle, sheep, and chickens) for meat and wool production

Population and society

Population 69,975,000 (1996e)
Population growth rate 2.7% (1990–95); 2.5% (2000–05)
Population density (per sq km) 42 (1996e)
Urban population (% of total) 59 (1995)
Age distribution (% of total population) <15 43.5%, 15–65 52.6%, >65 3.9% (1995)
Ethnic distribution about 63% of Persian origin, 18% Turkic, 13% other Iranian, 3% Kurdish, and 3% Arabic
Languages Farsi (official), Kurdish, Turkish, Arabic, English, French
Religions Shi'ite Muslim (official) 94%, Sunni Muslim, Zoroastrian, Christian, Jewish, Baha'i
Education (compulsory years) 5
Literacy rate 89% (men); 43% (women) (1995e)
Labour force 29% of population: 39% agriculture, 23% industry, 39% services (1990)
Unemployment 10% (1993e)
Life expectancy 69 (men); 70 (women) (1995–2000)
Child mortality rate (under 5, per 1,000 live births) 40 (1995)
Physicians 1 per 3,125 people (1990)
Hospital beds 1 per 747 people (1992)
TV sets (per 1,000 people) 63 (1995)
Radios (per 1,000 people) 228 (1995)

Transport

Airports international airports: Tehran (Mehrabad), Abadan, Esfahan; over 20 domestic airports; total passenger km: 5,238 mil (1994)
Railroads total length: 5,093 km/3,165 mi; total passenger km: 6,422 mil (1993)
Roads total road network: 158,000 km/ 98,181 mi, of which 59.1% paved (1995e); passenger cars: 24.2 per 1,000 people (1994e)

Chronology

c. 2000 BC Migration from southern Russia of Aryans, from whom Persians claim descent.
612 The Medes, from NW Iran, destroyed Iraq-based Assyrian Empire to the W and established their own empire which extended into central Anatolia (Turkey-in-Asia).
550 BC Cyrus the Great overthrew Medes' empire and founded First Persian Empire, the Achaemenid, conquering much of Asia Minor, including Babylonia (Palestine and Syria) in 539 BC. Expansion continued into Afghanistan under Darius I, who ruled 521–486 BC.
499–449 BC The Persian Wars with Greece ended Persian domination of the ancient world.
330 BC Collapse of Achaemenid Empire following defeat by Alexander the Great of Macedon.
AD 224 Sassanian Persian Empire founded by Ardashir, with its capital at Ctesiphon, in the NE.
637 Sassanian Empire destroyed by Muslim Arabs at battle of Qadisiya; Islam replaced Zoroastrianism.
750–1258 Dominated by the Persianized Abbasid dynasty, who reigned as caliphs (Islamic civil and religious leaders), with a capital in Baghdad (Iraq).
1380s Conquered by the Mongol leader, Tamerlane.
1501 Emergence of Safavids; the arts and architecture flourished, particularly under Abbas I, 'the Great', who ruled 1588–1629.
1736 The Safavids were deposed by the warrior Nadir Shah Afshar, who ruled until 1747.
1790 Rise of the Qajars, who transferred the capital from Esfahan in central Iran to Tehran, further N.
19th century Increasing influence in the N of tsarist Russia, which took Georgia and much of Armenia 1801–28. Britain exercised influence in the S and E, and fought Iran 1856–57 over claims to Herat (W Afghanistan).

1906 Parliamentary constitution adopted after a brief revolution.

1925 Weak and corrupt Qajar dynasty overthrown, with some British official help, in a coup by Col Reza Khan, a nationalist Iranian Cossack military officer, who was crowned shah ('king of kings'), with the title Reza Shah Pahlavi.

1920s onwards Economic modernization, Westernization, and secularization programme launched, which proved unpopular with traditionalist elements.

1935 Name changed from Persia to Iran.

1941 Owing to his pro-German sentiments, Pahlavi Shah was forced to abdicate during World War II by Allied occupation forces and was succeeded by his son Mohammad Reza Pahlavi, who continued the modernization programme.

1946 British, US, and Soviet occupation forces left Iran.

1951 Oilfields nationalized by radical prime minister Muhammad Mossadeq as anti-British and US sentiment increased.

1953 Mossadeq deposed, the nationalization plan changed, and the US-backed shah, Muhammad Reza Shah Pahlavi, took full control of the government.

1963 Hundreds of protesters, who demanded the release of the arrested fundamentalist Shi'ite Muslim leader Ayatollah Ruhollah Khomeini, were killed by troops.

1970s Spiralling world oil prices brought rapid economic expansion.

1975 Shah introduced single-party system.

1977 Mysterious death in An Najaf of Mustafa, eldest son of the exiled Ayatollah Ruhollah Khomeini, sparked demonstrations by theology students, which were suppressed with the loss of six lives.

1978 Opposition to the shah organized from France by Ayatollah Ruhollah Khomeini, who demanded a return to the principles of Islam. Hundreds of demonstrators were killed by troops in Jaleh Square, Tehran.

1979 Amid mounting demonstrations by students and clerics, the shah left the country; Khomeini returned to create a nonparty theocratic Islamic state. Revolutionaries seized 66 US hostages at embassy in Tehran; US economic boycott.

1980 Iraq invaded Iran, provoking a bitter war; death of exiled shah.

1981 US hostages released.

1985–87 Fighting intensified in Iran–Iraq War, with heavy loss of life.

1988 Cease-fire in the war; talks with Iraq began.

1989 Khomeini issued a fatwa (public order) for the death of British writer Salman Rushdie for blasphemy against Islam. On Khomeini's death, Ayatollah Ali Khamenei was elected interim Leader of the Revolution; the speaker of Iranian parliament Hashemi Rafsanjani was elected president.

1990 Generous peace terms with Iraq accepted to close Iran–Iraq war.

1991 Nearly one million Kurds arrived from NW Iraq, fleeing persecution by Saddam Hussein after the Gulf War between Iraq and UN forces.

1993 President Rafsanjani re-elected, but with a smaller margin; free-market economic reforms introduced.

1996 Rafsanjani supporters won assembly elections.

1997 Moderate politician Seyyed Mohammad Khatami elected president.

Practical information

Visa requirements UK: visa required. USA: visa required

Embassy in the UK 16 Prince's Gate, London SW7 1PT. Tel: (0171) 584 8101; fax: (0171) 589 4440

British embassy PO Box 11365–4474, 143 Ferdowsi Avenue, Tehran 11344. Tel: (21) 675 011; fax: (21) 678 021

Embassy in the USA Iran has no diplomatic representation in the USA. It has an Interests Section in the Pakistani embassy: Iranian Interests Section, Pakistani Embassy, 2209 Wisconsin Avenue NW, Washington, DC 20007. Tel: (202) 965 4990

American embassy the USA has no diplomatic representation in Iran; protecting power in Iran is Switzerland

Chamber of commerce Iran Chamber of Commerce,

Industries and Mines, 254 Taleghani Avenue, Tehran. Tel: (21) 836 0319; fax: (21) 882 5111

Office hours 0800–1600 Sat–Wed

Banking hours 0900–1600 Sat–Wed; 0900–1200 Thu

Time difference GMT +3.5

Chief tourist attractions wealth of historical sites, notably Esfahan, Tabriz, Rasht, Persepolis, and Susa

Major holidays 11 February, 20–25 March, 1–2 April, 5 June; variable: Eid-ul-Adha, Ashora, end of Ramadan, Prophet's Birthday, Prophet's Mission (April), Birth of the Twelfth Imam (April/May), Martyrdom of Imam Ali (May), Death of Imam Jaffar Sadegh (June/July), Birth of Imam Reza (July), Id-E-Gihadir (August), Death of the Prophet and Martyrdom of Imam Hassan (October/November)

Iraq Republic of

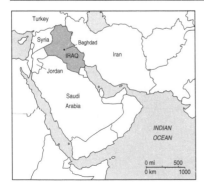

National name *al Jumhouriya al 'Iraqia*

Area 434,924 sq km/167,924 sq mi

Capital Baghdad

Major towns/cities Mosul, Basra, Kirkuk, Hilla, Najaf, Nasiriya

Major ports Basra and Um Qass closed from 1980

Physical features mountains in N, desert in W; wide valley of rivers Tigris and Euphrates running NW–SE; canal linking Baghdad and Persian Gulf opened 1992

Government

Head of state and government Saddam Hussein al-Tikriti from 1979

Political system one-party socialist republic

Administrative divisions 18 governates

Political party Arab Ba'ath Socialist Party, nationalist socialist

Armed forces 382,500 (1995)

Conscription military service is compulsory for 18–24 months; it is waived on the payment of the equivalent of $800

Death penalty retained and used for ordinary crimes
Defence spend (% GDP) 14.8 (1995)
Education spend (% GNP) 4.6 (1988)

Economy and resources

Currency Iraqi dinar
GDP ($ US) 57.7 billion (1994e)
Real GDP per capita (PPP) ($ US) 3,159 (1994)
GDP growth rate 0% (1994)
Average annual inflation 300% (1994e)
Foreign debt ($ US) 82.9 billion (1993)
Trading partners Jordan, Brazil, Turkey, Japan, the Netherlands, Spain, UK, France
Resources petroleum, natural gas, sulphur, phosphates
Industries chemical, petroleum, coal, rubber and plastic products, food processing, nonmetallic minerals, textiles, mining
Exports crude petroleum (accounting for more than 98% of total export earnings (1980–89), dates and other dried fruits. Principal market: Jordan 95% (1995)
Imports machinery and transport equipment, basic manufactured articles, cereals and other foodstuffs, iron and steel, military goods. Principal source: Jordan 48.7% (1995)
Arable land 12% (1993)
Agricultural products dates, wheat, barley, maize, sugar beet, sugar cane, melons, rice; livestock rearing (notably production of eggs and poultry meat)

Population and society

Population 20,607,000 (1996e)
Population growth rate 2.5% (1990–95); 2.8% (2000–05)
Population density (per sq km) 47 (1996e)
Urban population (% of total) 75 (1995)
Age distribution (% of total population) <15 43.6%, 15–65 53.2%, >65 3% (1995)
Ethnic distribution about 79% Arab, 16% Kurdish (mainly in the NE), 3% Persian, 2% Turkish
Languages Arabic (official); Kurdish, Assyrian, Armenian
Religions Shi'ite Muslim 60%, Sunni Muslim 37%, Christian 3%
Education (compulsory years) 6
Literacy rate 77% (men); 49% (women) (1995e)
Labour force 26% of population: 16% agriculture, 18% industry, 66% services

Life expectancy 67 (men); 70 (women) (1995–2000)
Child mortality rate (under 5, per 1,000 live births) 71 (1995)
Physicians 1 per 1,930 people (1991)
Hospital beds 1 per 576 people (1991)
TV sets (per 1,000 people) 80 (1995)
Radios (per 1,000 people) 224 (1995)

Transport

Airports international airports: Baghdad (Saddam), Basra, Bamerui; at least three domestic airports (many civilian airports sustained heavy damage during the 1991 Gulf War); total passenger km: 35 mil (1992)
Railroads total length: 2,389 km/1,485 mi; total passenger km: 1,566 mil (1993)
Roads total road network: 46,500 km/ 28,895 mi, of which 86% paved (1995e); passenger cars: 33.6 per 1,000 people (1993e)

Chronology

c. 3400 BC The world's oldest civilization, the Sumerian, arose in the land between the rivers Euphrates and Tigris, known as lower Mesopotamia, which lies in the heart of modern Iraq. Its cities included Lagash, Eridu, Uruk, Kish, and Ur.
c. 2350 BC The confederation of Sumerian city-states was forged into an empire by the Akkadian leader Sargon.
7th century BC In northern Mesopotamia, the Assyrian Empire, based around the River Tigris and formerly dominated by Sumeria and Euphrates-centred Babylonia, created a vast empire covering much of the Middle East.
612 BC The Assyrian capital of Nineveh was destroyed by Babylon and Mede (in NW Iran).
c. 550 BC Mesopotamia came under Persian control.
AD 114 Conquered by the Romans.
266 Came under the rule of the Persian-based Sassanians.
637 Sassanian Empire destroyed by Muslim Arabs at battle of Qadisiya, in southern Iraq; Islam spread.
750–1258 Dominated by Abbasid dynasty, who reigned as caliphs (Islamic civil and religious leaders) in Baghdad.
1258 Baghdad invaded and burned by Tatars.
1401 Baghdad destroyed by Mongol ruler Tamerlane.
1533 Annexed by Suleiman the Magnificent, becoming part of the Ottoman Empire until the 20th century,

despite recurrent anti-Ottoman insurrections.
1916 Occupied by Britain during World War I.
1920 Iraq became a British League of Nations protectorate.
1921 Hashemite dynasty established, with Faisal I installed by Britain as king.
1932 Independence achieved from British protectorate status, with Gen Nuri-el Said as prime minister.
1941–45 Occupied by Britain during World War II.
1955 Signed the Baghdad Pact collective security treaty with the UK, Iran, Pakistan, and Turkey.
1958 Monarchy overthrown in military-led revolution, in which King Faisal was assassinated; Iraq became a republic; joined Jordan in an Arab Federation; withdrew from Baghdad Pact as left-wing military regime assumed power.
1963 Joint socialist-nationalist Ba'athist-military coup headed by Col Salem Aref and backed by US Central Intelligence Agency; reign of terror launched against the left.
1968 Ba'athist military coup put Maj-Gen Ahmed Hassan al-Bakr in power.
1979 Al-Bakr replaced by Saddam Hussein of the Arab Ba'ath Socialist Party.
1980 War between Iraq and Iran broke out.
1985–87 Fighting intensified, with heavy loss of life.
1988 Cease-fire; talks began with Iran. Iraq used chemical weapons against Kurdish rebels seeking greater autonomy in the NW.
1989 Unsuccessful coup against President Hussein; Iraq successfully launched ballistic test missile.
1990 Peace treaty favouring Iran agreed. Iraq invaded and annexed Kuwait in Aug. US forces massed in Saudi Arabia at request of King Fahd. United Nations (UN) ordered Iraqi withdrawal and imposed total trade ban; further UN resolution sanctioned force. All foreign hostages released.
1991 US-led Allied forces launched aerial assault on Iraq and destroyed country's infrastructure; land–sea–air offensive to free Kuwait successful. Uprisings of Kurds and Shi'ites brutally suppressed by surviving Iraqi troops. Allied troops established 'safe havens' for Kurds in N prior to withdrawal, and left rapid-reaction force near Turkish border.
1992 UN imposed 'no-fly zone' over S Iraq to protect Shi'ites.

1993 Iraqi incursions into 'no-fly zone' prompted US-led alliance aircraft to bomb 'strategic' targets in Iraq. Continued persecution of Shi'ites in the S.
1994 Iraq renounced claim to Kuwait, but failed to fulfil other conditions required for lifting of UN sanctions.

1995 UN sanctions extended. Two of Saddam Hussein's top military aides and sons-in-law defected to Jordan. Hussein elected (uncontested) in closely monitored presidential election.
1996 Iraqi-backed attacks on Kurds prompted US retaliation; air strikes

destroyed Iraqi military bases in S. Hussein's sons-in-law shot dead in Baghdad. Dec: UN allowed Iraq to export a limited amount of oil to pay for food and medical supplies. Assassination attempt on Hussein's eldest son.

Practical information

Visa requirements UK: visa required. USA: visa required
Embassy in the UK Iraq has no diplomatic representation in the UK. The Embassy of the Hashemite Kingdom of Jordan deals with enquiries relating to Iraq: Iraq Interests Section, 21 Queen's Gate, London SW7 5JG. Tel: (0171) 584 7141/6; fax: (0171) 584 7716
British embassy the UK has no diplomatic representation in Iraq
Embassy in the USA Iraq has no diplomatic representation in the USA, but has an Interests Section in the Algerian embassy: Iraqi Interests Section, Algerian Embassy, 1801 P Street NW, Washington, DC 20036. Tel: (202) 483 7500; fax: (202) 462 5066

American embassy the USA has no diplomatic representation in Iraq, but has an Interests Section in the Polish embassy in Baghdad, which is in the Masbah Quarter (opposite the Foreign Ministry Club), PO Box 2447 Alwiyah, Baghdad. Tel: (1) 719 6138/9, 718 1840, 719 3791; telex 212287
Chamber of commerce Federation of Iraqi Chambers of Commerce, Mustansir Street, Baghdad. Tel: (1) 888 6111
Office hours 0800–1400 Sat–Wed; 0800–1300 Thu
Banking hours 0800–1200 Sat–Wed; 0800–1100 Thu; banks close at 1000 during Ramadan
Time difference GMT +3
Major holidays 1, 6 January, 8 February, 21 March, 1 May, 14, 17 July; variable: Eid-ul-Adha (4 days), Ashora, end of Ramadan (3 days), New Year (Muslim), Prophet's Birthday

---

Ireland, Republic of

National name *Eire*
Area 70,282 sq km/27,135 sq mi
Capital Dublin
Major towns/cities Cork, Limerick, Galway, Waterford, Wexford
Major ports Cork, Dun Laoghaire, Limerick, Waterford, Galway
Physical features central plateau surrounded by hills; rivers Shannon, Liffey, Boyne; Bog of Allen; Macgillicuddy's Reeks, Wicklow Mountains; Lough Corrib, lakes of Killarney; Galway Bay and Aran Islands

Government

Head of state Mary McAleese from 1997

Head of government Bertie Ahern from 1997
Political system democratic republic
Administrative divisions 26 counties within four provinces
Political parties Fianna Fáil (Soldiers of Destiny), moderate centre right; Fine Gael (Irish Tribe or United Ireland Party), moderate centre left; Labour Party, moderate left of centre; Progressive Democrats, radical free-enterprise
Armed forces 13,000 (1995)
Death penalty abolished 1990
Defence spend (% GDP) 1.2 (1994)
Education spend (% GNP) 6.4 (1993–94)
Health spend (% GDP) 5.1 (1993)

Economy and resources

Currency Irish pound (punt Eireannach)
GDP ($ US) 69.6 billion (1996)
Real GDP per capita (PPP) ($ US) 18,784 (1996)
GDP growth rate 6.5% (1996); 4.7% (1990–95)
Average annual inflation 1.8% (1996); 2.5% (1985–95)
Trading partners UK, USA, Germany, France
Resources lead, zinc, peat, limestone, gypsum, petroleum, natural gas, copper, silver
Industries textiles, machinery, chemicals, electronics, motor vehicle manufacturing and assembly, food

processing, beer, tourism
Exports beef and dairy products, live animals, machinery and transport equipment, electronic goods, chemicals. Principal market: UK 25.4% (1995)
Imports petroleum products, machinery and transport equipment, chemicals, foodstuffs, animal feed, textiles and clothing. Principal source: UK 35.6% (1995)
Arable land 13.1% (1993)
Agricultural products barley, potatoes, sugar beet, wheat, oats; livestock (cattle) and dairy products

Population and society

Population 3,554,000 (1996e)
Population growth rate 0.3% (1990–95); 0.4% (2000–05)
Population density (per sq km) 51 (1996e)
Urban population (% of total) 58 (1995)
Age distribution (% of total population) <15 24.4%, 15–65 64.3%, >65 11.2% (1995)
Ethnic distribution most of the population has Celtic origins
Languages Irish Gaelic and English (both official)
Religions Roman Catholic 95%, Church of Ireland, other Protestant denominations
Education (compulsory years) 9
Literacy rate 99% (men); 99% (women) (1995e)

Labour force 37% of population: 14% agriculture, 29% industry, 57% services (1990)
Unemployment 11.8% (1996)
Life expectancy 73 (men); 79 (women) (1995–2000)
Child mortality rate (under 5, per 1,000 live births) 7 (1995)
Physicians 1 per 431 people (1995)
Hospital beds 1 per 262 people (1995)
TV sets (per 1,000 people) 409 (1995)
Radios (per 1,000 people) 649 (1995)

Transport

Airports international airports: Dublin, Shannon, Cork, Knock (Horan), Galway; five domestic airports; total passenger km: 4,920 mil (1994)
Railroads total length: 1,967 km/1,222 mi; total passenger km: 1,102 mil (1994)
Roads total road network: 92,430 km/ 57,436 mi, of which 94% paved (1995e); passenger cars: 270.3 per 1,000 people (1995e)

Chronology

3rd century BC The Gaels, a Celtic people, invaded Ireland and formed about 150 small kingdoms.
AD c. 432 St Patrick introduced Christianity.
5th–9th centuries Irish Church remained a centre of culture and scholarship.
9th–11th centuries The Vikings raided Ireland until defeated by High King Brian Boru at Clontarf 1014.
12th–13th centuries Anglo-Norman adventurers conquered much of Ireland, but no central government was formed and many became assimilated.
14th–15th centuries Irish chieftains recovered their lands, restricting English rule to the Pale around Dublin.
1536 Henry VIII of England made ineffectual efforts to impose the Protestant Reformation on Ireland.
1541 Irish Parliament recognized Henry

VIII as king of Ireland; Henry gave peerages to Irish chieftains.
1579 English suppressed Desmond rebellion, confiscated rebel lands, and tried to 'plant' them with English settlers.
1610 James I established plantation of Ulster with Protestant settlers from England and Scotland.
1641 Catholic Irish rebelled against English rule; Oliver Cromwell brutally reasserted English control 1649–50; Irish landowners evicted and replaced with English landowners.
1689–91 Williamite War: following the 'Glorious Revolution', the Catholic Irish unsuccessfully supported James II against Protestant William III in civil war. Penal laws barred Catholics from obtaining wealth and power.
1720 Act passed declaring British Parliament's right to legislate for Ireland.
1739–41 Famine killed one-third of population of 1.5 million.
1782 Protestant landlords led by Henry Grattan secured end of restrictions on Irish trade and parliament.
1798 British suppressed revolt by Society of United Irishmen (with French support) led by Wolfe Tone.
1800 Act of Union abolished Irish parliament and created United Kingdom of Great Britain and Ireland, effective 1801.
1829 Daniel O'Connell secured Catholic Emancipation Act, which permitted Catholics to enter parliament.
1846–51 Potato famine reduced population by 20% through starvation and emigration.
1870 Land Act increased security for tenants but failed to halt agrarian disorder; Isaac Butt formed political party to campaign for Irish Home Rule (devolution).
1885 Home Rulers, led by Charles Stewart Parnell, held balance of power in parliament; first Home Rule Bill rejected 1886; second Home Rule Bill defeated 1893.

1905 Arthur Griffith founded the nationalist movement Sinn Féin ('Ourselves Alone').
1914 Ireland came close to civil war as Ulster prepared to resist implementation of Home Rule Act (postponed because of World War I).
1916 Easter Rising: nationalists proclaimed a republic in Dublin; British crushed revolt and executed 15 leaders.
1919 Sinn Féin MPs formed Irish parliament in Dublin in defiance of British government.
1919–21 Irish Republican Army (IRA) waged guerrilla war against British forces.
1921 Anglo-Irish Treaty partitioned Ireland; N Ireland (Ulster) remained part of the United Kingdom; S Ireland won full internal self-government with dominion status.
1922 Irish Free State proclaimed; IRA split over Anglo-Irish Treaty led to civil war 1922–23.
1932 Anti-Treaty party, Fianna Fáil, came to power under Éamonn de Valéra.
1937 New constitution established Eire (Gaelic name for Ireland) as a sovereign state and refused to acknowledge partition.
1949 After remaining neutral in World War II, Eire left the Commonwealth and became the Republic of Ireland.
1973 Ireland joined European Economic Community.
1985 Anglo-Irish Agreement gave the Republic of Ireland a consultative role, but no powers, in the government of Northern Ireland.
1990 Mary Robinson became the first woman president of Ireland.
1993 Downing Street Declaration: joint Anglo-Irish peace proposal for Northern Ireland issued.
1994 Cease-fires announced by Catholic and Protestant paramilitaries in Northern Ireland.
1995 Ulster framework peace document issued.
1997 Fianna Fáil leader Bertie Ahern became prime minister.

Practical information

Visa requirements UK: visa not required. USA: visa not required
Embassy in the UK 17 Grosvenor Place, London SW1X 7HR. Tel: (0171) 235 2171; fax: (0171) 245 6961
British embassy 31–33 Merrion Road, Dublin 4. Tel: (1) 269 5211; fax: (1) 283 8423
Embassy in the USA 2234 Massachusetts Avenue NW, Washington, DC 20008. Tel: (202) 462 3939
American embassy 42 Elgin Road, Ballsbridge, Dublin. Tel: (1) 668 8777; fax: (1) 668 9946

Chamber of commerce Chambers of Commerce of Ireland, 22 Merrion Square, Dublin 2. Tel: (1) 661 2888; fax: (1) 661 2811
Office hours 0900–1700 Mon–Fri
Banking hours 1000–1600 Mon–Fri
Time difference GMT +/–0
Chief tourist attractions scenery, notably the Killarney lakes and the west coast; Dublin, with its many literary associations and famous pub life
Major holidays 1 January, 17 March, 25–26 December; variable: Good Friday, Easter Monday, June Holiday, August Holiday, October Holiday, Christmas Holiday

Israel State of

National name *Medinat Israel*
Area 20,800 sq km/8,030 sq mi (as at 1949 armistice)
Capital Jerusalem (not recognized by United Nations)
Major towns/cities Tel Aviv-Yafo, Haifa, Bat-Yam, Holon, Ramat Gan, Petach Tikva, Rishon Leziyyon, Beersheba
Major ports Tel Aviv-Yafo, Haifa, 'Akko (formerly Acre), Eilat
Physical features coastal plain of Sharon between Haifa and Tel Aviv noted since ancient times for its fertility; central mountains of Galilee, Samaria, and Judea; Dead Sea, Lake Tiberias, and River Jordan Rift Valley along the E are below sea level; Negev Desert in the S; Israel occupies Golan Heights, West Bank, East Jerusalem, and Gaza Strip (the last was awarded limited autonomy, with West Bank town of Jericho, 1993)

Government

Head of state Ezer Weizman from 1993
Head of government Binyamin Netanyahu from 1996
Political system democratic republic
Administrative divisions six districts
Political parties Israel Labour Party, moderate, left of centre; Consolidation Party (Likud), right of centre; Meretz (Vitality), left-of-centre alliance
Armed forces 172,000; reserves of 602,000 (1995)
Conscription voluntary for Christians, Circassians, and Muslims; compulsory for Jews and Druzes (men 36 months, women 21 months)
Death penalty exceptional crimes only; last execution 1962
Defence spend (% GDP) 9.2 (1995)

Education spend (% GNP) 6 (1993–94)
Health spend (% GDP) 1.9 (1993)

Economy and resources

Currency shekel
GDP ($ US) 78 billion (1994)
Real GDP per capita (PPP) ($ US) 16,023 (1994)
GDP growth rate 7.1% (1995); 6.4% (1990–95)
Average annual inflation 10.1% (1995); 17.1% (1985–95)
Trading partners USA, UK, Germany, Belgium, Italy, Japan, Switzerland
Resources potash, bromides, magnesium, sulphur, copper ore, gold, salt, petroleum, natural gas
Industries food processing, beverages, tobacco, electrical machinery, chemicals, petroleum and coal products, metal products, diamond polishing, transport equipment, tourism
Exports citrus fruits, worked diamonds, machinery and parts, military hardware, food products, chemical products, textiles and clothing. Principal market: USA 30.1% (1995)
Imports machinery and parts, rough diamonds, chemicals and related products, crude petroleum and petroleum products, motor vehicles. Principal source: USA 18.6% (1995)
Arable land 17% (1993)
Agricultural products citrus fruits, vegetables, potatoes, wheat, melons, pumpkins, avocados; poultry and fish production

Population and society

Population 5,664,000 (1996e)
Population growth rate 3.8% (1990–95); 1.3% (2000–05)
Population density (per sq km) 269 (1996e)
Urban population (% of total) 91 (1995)
Age distribution (% of total population) <15 29.1%, 15–65 61.4%, >65 9.5% (1995)
Ethnic distribution around 85% of the population is Jewish, the majority of the remainder Arab. Under the Law of Return 1950, 'every Jew shall be entitled to come to Israel as an immigrant'; those from the East and Eastern Europe are Ashkenazim, and those from Mediterranean Europe

(Spain, Portugal, Italy, France, Greece) and Arab N Africa are Sephardim (over 50% of the population is now of Sephardic descent); an Israeli-born Jew is a Sabra
Languages Hebrew and Arabic (official); English, Yiddish, European and W Asian languages
Religions Israel is a secular state, but the predominant faith is Judaism 85%; also Sunni Muslim, Christian, and Druse
Education (compulsory years) 11
Literacy rate 97% (men); 93% (women) (1995e)
Labour force 39% of population: 4% agriculture, 29% industry, 67% services (1990)
Unemployment 7.2% (1994)
Life expectancy 75 (men); 79 (women) (1995–2000)
Child mortality rate (under 5, per 1,000 live births) 9 (1995)
Physicians 1 per 350 people (1991)
Hospital beds 1 per 152 people (1994)
TV sets (per 1,000 people) 290 (1995)
Radios (per 1,000 people) 489 (1995)

Transport

Airports international airports: Tel Aviv (Ben Gurion), Eilat; domestic airports in all major cities; total passenger km: 9,662 mil (1994)
Railroads total length: 530 km/329 mi; total passenger km: 238 mil (1994)
Roads total road network: 14,700 km/ 9,135 mi, of which 100% paved (1995); passenger cars: 200 per 1,000 people (1995)

Chronology

c. 2000 BC Abraham, father of the Jewish people, is believed to have come to Palestine from Mesopotamia.
c. 1225 BC Moses led the Jews out of slavery in Egypt towards the promised land of Palestine.
11th century BC Saul established a Jewish kingdom in Palestine; developed by kings David and Solomon.
586 BC Jews defeated by Babylon and deported; many returned to Palestine 539 BC.
333 BC Alexander the Great of Macedonia conquered the entire region.
3rd century BC Control of Palestine contested by Ptolemies of Egypt and Seleucids of Syria.

142 BC Jewish independence restored after Maccabean revolt.
63 BC Palestine fell to the Roman Empire.
70 AD Romans crushed the Zealot rebellion and destroyed Jerusalem; start of dispersion of Jews (diaspora).
614 Persians took Jerusalem from Byzantine Empire.
637 Muslim Arabs conquered Palestine.
1099 First Crusade captured Jerusalem; Christian kingdom lasted a century before falling to sultans of Egypt.
1517 Palestine conquered by the Ottoman Turks.
1897 Theodor Herzl organized the First Zionist Congress at Basel to publicize Jewish claims to Palestine.
1917 The Balfour Declaration: Britain expressed support for the creation of a Jewish National Home in Palestine.
1918 British forces expelled the Turks from Palestine, which became a British League of Nations mandate 1920.
1929 Severe communal violence around Jerusalem caused by Arab alarm at doubling of Jewish population in ten years.
1933 Jewish riots in protest at British attempts to restrict Jewish immigration.
1937 The Peel Report, recommending partition, accepted by most Jews but rejected by Arabs; open warfare ensued 1937–38.
1939 Britain postponed independence plans on account of World War II, and increased military presence.
1946 Resumption of terrorist violence; Jewish extremists blew up British headquarters in Jerusalem.
1947 United Nations (UN) voted for partition of Palestine.

1948 Britain withdrew; Independent State of Israel proclaimed with David Ben-Gurion as prime minister; Israel repulsed invasion by Arab nations; many Palestinian Arabs settled in refugee camps in the Gaza Strip and West Bank.
1952 Col Gamal Nasser of Egypt stepped up blockade of Israeli ports and support of Arab guerrillas in Gaza.
1956 War between Israel and Egypt; Israeli invasion of Gaza and Sinai followed by withdrawal 1957.
1963 Levi Eshkol succeeded Ben-Gurion as prime minister.
1964 Palestine Liberation Organization (PLO) founded to unite Palestinian Arabs with the aim of overthrowing the state of Israel.
1967 Israel defeated Egypt, Syria, and Jordan in the Six-Day War; Gaza, West Bank, E Jerusalem, Sinai, and Golan Heights captured.
1969 Golda Meir (Labour) elected prime minister; Yassir Arafat became chair of the PLO; escalation of terrorism and border raids.
1973 Yom Kippur War: Israel repulsed surprise attack by Egypt and Syria.
1974 Golda Meir succeeded by Yitzhak Rabin.
1977 Right-wing Likud bloc took office under Menachem Begin; President Anwar Sadat of Egypt began peace initiative.
1979 Camp David talks ended with signing of peace treaty between Israel and Egypt; Israel withdrew from Sinai.
1980 United Jerusalem declared capital of Israel.

1982 Israeli forces invaded S Lebanon to drive out PLO guerrillas; occupation continued until 1985.
1985 Labour and Likud formed coalition government led by Shimon Peres 1985–86 and Yitzhak Shamir 1986–90.
1988 Israeli handling of Palestinian uprising (Intifada) in occupied territories provoked international criticism.
1990 Shamir headed Likud government following the breakup of the coalition; PLO formally recognized the state of Israel.
1991 Iraq launched missile attacks on Israel during Gulf War; Middle East peace talks began in Madrid.
1992 Labour government elected under Yitzhak Rabin.
1993 Rabin and Arafat signed peace accord; Israel granted limited autonomy to Gaza Strip and Jericho.
1994 Arafat became head of autonomous Palestinian authority in Gaza and Jericho; peace agreement between Israel and Jordan.
1995 Rabin assassinated by Jewish opponent of peace accord; Peres became prime minister.
1996 Likud government elected under Binyamin Netanyahu, critic of peace accord. Revival of communal violence; peace process threatened. The opening of a 2,000-year-old tunnel near the Al Aqsa mosque in Jerusalem in Sept provoked renewed Palestinian–Israeli conflict.
1997 Israeli schoolgirls killed by Jordanian soldier. Jewish settlement in E Jerusalem widely condemned. Netanyahu's government investigated for corruption. Suicide bombs by Hamas in Jerusalem.

Practical information

Visa requirements UK: visa not required. USA: visa not required
Embassy in the UK 2 Palace Green, London W8 4QB. Tel: (0171) 957 9500; fax: (0171) 957 9555
British embassy 192 Rehov Hayarkon, Tel Aviv 63405. Tel: (3) 524 9171/8; fax: (3) 524 3313
Embassy in the USA 3514 International Drive NW, Washington, DC 20008. Tel: (202) 364 5500; fax: (202) 364 5610
American embassy 71 Hayarkon Street, Tel Aviv. Tel: (3) 519 7575; fax: (3) 517 3227
Chamber of commerce Federation of Israeli Chambers of Commerce, PO Box 20027, 84 Hahashmonaim Street, Tel Aviv 67011. Tel: (3) 563 1010; fax: (3) 561 9025

Office hours 0800–1300 and 1500–1800 Sun–Thu (November–May); 0730–1430 Sun–Thu (June–October)
Banking hours 0830–1230 and 1600–1730 Mon, Tue, and Thu; 0830–1230 Wed; 0830–1200 Fri
Time difference GMT +2
Chief tourist attractions resorts along Mediterranean coast, Red Sea coast (Eilat), and Dead Sea; ancient city of Jerusalem, with its four quarters (Armenian, Christian, Jewish, and Muslim), its many sites include Temple Mount, the Cathedral of St James, Dome of the Rock, Al Aqsa Mosque, and Church of the Holy Sepulchre
Major holidays 1 January, 14 May; variable: New Year (Jewish, September/October), Purim (March), first day of Passover (April), last day of Passover (April), Pentecost (June), Fast of Av (August), Yom Kippur (October), Feast of Tabernacles (October, 2 days)

Italy Republic of

National name *Repubblica Italiana*
Area 301,300 sq km/116,331 sq mi
Capital Rome
Major towns/cities Milan, Naples, Turin, Palermo, Genoa, Bologna
Major ports Naples, Genoa, Palermo, Bari, Catania, Trieste
Physical features mountainous (Maritime Alps, Dolomites, Apennines) with narrow coastal lowlands; continental Europe's only active volcanoes: Vesuvius, Etna, Stromboli; rivers Po, Adige, Arno, Tiber, Rubicon; islands of Sicily, Sardinia, Elba, Capri, Ischia, Lipari, Pantelleria; lakes Como, Maggiore, Garda

Government

Head of state Oscar Luigi Scalfaro from 1992
Head of government Romano Prodi from 1996
Political system democratic republic
Administrative divisions 94 provinces within 20 regions (of which five have a greater degree of autonomy)
Political parties Forza Italia (Go Italy!), free market, right of centre; Northern League (LN), Milan-based, federalist, right of centre; National Alliance (AN), neofascist; Italian Popular Party (PPI), Catholic, centrist; Italian Renewal Party, centrist; Democratic Party of the Left (PDS), pro-European, moderate left wing (ex-communist); Italian Socialist Party (PSI), moderate socialist; Italian Republican Party (PRI), social democratic, left of centre; Democratic Alliance (AD), moderate left of centre; Christian Democratic Centre (CCD), Christian, centrist; Olive Tree alliance, centre left; Panella List, radical liberal; Union of the Democratic Centre (UDC), right of centre; Pact for Italy, reformist;

Communist Refoundation (RC), Marxist; Verdi, environmentalist; La Rete (the Network), anti-Mafia
Armed forces 329,000 (1995)
Conscription 12 months
Death penalty abolished 1994
Defence spend (% GDP) 1.8 (1995)
Education spend (% GNP) 5.2 (1993–94)
Health spend (% GDP) 6.2 (1993)

Economy and resources

Currency lira
GDP ($ US) 1,207.7 billion (1996)
Real GDP per capita (PPP) ($ US) 19,950 (1996)
GDP growth rate –0.4% (1996); 1% (1990–95)
Average annual inflation 3.9% (1996); 6% (1985–95)
Trading partners EU (principally Germany, France, and UK), USA
Resources lignite, lead, zinc, mercury, potash, sulphur, fluorspar, bauxite, marble, petroleum, natural gas, fish
Industries machinery and machine tools, textiles, leather, footwear, food and beverages, steel, motor vehicles, chemical products, wine, tourism
Exports machinery and transport equipment, textiles, clothing, footwear, wine (leading producer and exporter), metals and metal products, chemicals, wood, paper and rubber goods. Principal market: Germany 18.7% (1995)
Imports mineral fuels and lubricants, machinery and transport equipment, chemical products, foodstuffs, metal products. Principal source: Germany 19.1% (1995)
Arable land 30% (1993)
Agricultural products sugar beet, grapes, wheat, maize, tomatoes, olives, citrus fruits, vegetables; fishing

Population and society

Population 57,226,000 (1996e)
Population growth rate 0.1% (1990–95); –0.2% (2000–05)
Population density (per sq km) 190 (1996e)
Urban population (% of total) 67% (1995)
Age distribution (% of total population) <15 15.1%, 15–65 68.9%, >65 16% (1995)
Ethnic distribution mainly Italian; some minorities of German origin
Languages Italian; German, French, Slovene, and Albanian minorities
Religion Roman Catholic 100% (state religion)

Education (compulsory years) 8
Literacy rate 98% (men); 96% (women) (1995e)
Labour force 43% of the population: 9% agriculture, 31% industry, 60% services (1990)
Unemployment 12% (1996)
Life expectancy 75 (men); 81 (women) (1995–2000)
Child mortality rate (under 5, per 1,000 live births) 8 (1995)
Physicians 1 per 192 people (1993)
Hospital beds 1 per 158 people (1993)
TV sets (per 1,000 people) 446 (1995)
Radios (per 1,000 people) 822 (1995)

Transport

Airports international airports: Bologna (G Marconi), Genoa (Cristoforo Colombo), Milan (Linate and Malpensa), Naples (Capodichino), Palermo (Punta Rais), Pisa (Galileo Galilei), Rome (Leonardo da Vinci and Ciampino), Turin, Venice (Marco Polo); over 30 domestic airports; total passenger km: 31,738 mil (1994)
Railroads total length: 15,942 km/9,906 mi; total passenger km: 50,000 mil (1995)
Roads total road network: 314,360 km/195,343 mi, of which 100% paved (1995e); passenger cars: 552.4 per 1,000 people (1995e)

Chronology

4th and 3rd centuries BC Italian peninsula united under Roman rule.
AD 476 End of Western Roman Empire.
568 Invaded by Lombards.
756 Papal States created in central Italy.
800 Charlemagne united Italy and Germany in Holy Roman Empire.
12th and 13th centuries Papacy and Holy Roman Empire contended for political supremacy; papal power reached its peak under Innocent III (1198–1216).
1183 Cities of Lombard League (founded 1164) became independent.
14th century Beginnings of Renaissance in N Italy.
15th century Most of Italy ruled by five rival states: the city-states of Milan, Florence, and Venice; the Papal States; and the Kingdom of Naples.
1494 Charles VIII of France invaded Italy.
1529–59 Spanish Habsburgs secured dominance in Italy.
17th century Italy effectively part of Spanish Empire; economic and cultural decline.
1713 Treaty of Utrecht gave political

control of most of Italy to Austrian Habsburgs.
1796–1814 France conquered Italy, setting up satellite states and introducing principles of French Revolution.
1815 Old regimes largely restored; Italy divided between Austria, Papal States, Naples, Sardinia, and four duchies.
1831 Giuseppe Mazzini founded 'Young Italy' movement with aim of creating unified republic.
1848–49 Liberal revolutions occurred throughout Italy; reversed everywhere except Sardinia, which became centre of nationalism under leadership of Count Camillo di Cavour.
1859 France and Sardinia forcibly expelled Austrians from Lombardy.
1860 Sardinia annexed duchies and Papal States (except Rome); Giuseppe Garibaldi overthrew Neapolitan monarchy.
1861 Victor Emmanuel II of Sardinia proclaimed king of Italy in Turin.
1866 Italy gained Venetia after defeat of Austria by Prussia.
1870 Italian forces occupied Rome in defiance of pope, completing unification of Italy.
1882 Italy joined Germany and Austria-Hungary in Triple Alliance.

1896 Attempt to conquer Ethiopia defeated at Battle of Adowa.
1900 King Umberto I assassinated by an anarchist.
1912 Annexation of Libya and Dodecanese after Italo-Turkish War.
1915 Italy entered World War I on side of Allies.
1919 Peace treaties awarded Trentino, South Tyrol, and Trieste to Italy.
1922 Mussolini established fascist dictatorship following period of strikes and agrarian revolts.
1935–36 Conquest of Ethiopia.
1939 Invasion of Albania.
1940 Italy entered World War II as ally of Germany.
1943 Allies invaded southern Italy; Mussolini removed from power; Germans occupied northern and central Italy.
1945 Allies completed liberation.
1946 Monarchy replaced by republic.
1947 Peace treaty stripped Italy of its colonies.
1948 New constitution adopted; Christian Democrats emerged as main party of government in political system marked by ministerial instability.
1957 Italy became a founder member of European Economic Community (EEC).

1963 Creation of first of long series of fragile centre-left coalition governments.
1976 Communists attempt to join coalition, the 'historic compromise', rejected by Christian Democrats.
1978 Christian Democrat Aldo Moro, architect of historic compromise, murdered by Red Brigade guerrillas infiltrated by Western intelligence agents.
1983–87 Bettino Craxi, Italy's first Socialist prime minister, led coalition; economy improved.
1993 Major political crisis triggered by exposure of government corruption and Mafia links; governing parties discredited; new electoral system replaced proportional representation with 75% majority voting.
1994 Media tycoon Silvio Berlusconi created new party, Forza Italia, and formed right-wing coalition.
1995 Lamberto Dini headed nonparty government of 'experts'.
1996 Olive Tree Alliance won general election; Romano Prodi became prime minister.
1997 Prodi survived parliamentary vote of censure.

Practical information

Visa requirements UK: visa not required. USA: visa not required
Embassy in the UK 14 Three Kings Yard, Davies Street, London W1Y 2EH. Tel: (0171) 312 2000; fax: (0171) 312 2230
British embassy Via XX Settembre 80A, 00187 Rome. Tel: (6) 482 5551; fax: (6) 487 3324
Embassy in the USA 1601 Fuller Street NW, Washington, DC 20009. Tel: (202) 328 5500; fax: (202) 483 2187
American embassy Via Veneto 119/A, 00187 Rome. Tel: (6) 46741; fax: (6) 488 2672
Chamber of commerce Unione Italiana delle Camere di

Commercio, Industria, Artigianato e Agricoltura, Piazza Sallustio 21, 00187 Rome. Tel: (6) 47041; telex: 622 327
Office hours 0900–1300 and 1400–1800 Mon–Fri
Banking hours generally 0830–1330 and 1530–1930 Mon–Fri
Time difference GMT +1
Chief tourist attractions Alpine and Mediterranean scenery; ancient Greek and Roman archaeological remains; medieval, Renaissance, and Baroque churches (including St Peter's, Rome); Renaissance towns and palaces; museums; art galleries; opera houses
Major holidays 1, 6 January, 25 April, 1 May, 14 August (mid-August holiday, 2 days), 1 November, 8, 25–26 December; variable: Easter Monday

---

Jamaica

Area 10,957 sq km/4,230 sq mi
Capital Kingston
Major towns/cities Montego Bay, Spanish Town, St Andrew, Portmore, May Pen
Physical features mountainous tropical island; Blue Mountains (so called because of the haze over them)

Government

Head of state Elizabeth II from 1962, represented by governor general Howard Felix Hanlan Cooke from 1991
Head of government Percival Patterson

from 1992
Political system constitutional monarchy
Administrative divisions 13 parishes
Political parties Jamaica Labour Party (JLP), moderate, centrist; People's National Party (PNP), left of centre; National Democratic Union (NDM), centrist
Armed forces 3,320 (1995)
Conscription military service is voluntary
Death penalty retained and used for ordinary crimes
Defence spend (% GDP) 0.6 (1995)

Education spend (% GNP) 4.2 (1994)
Health spend (% GDP) 2.9 (1990)

Economy and resources

Currency Jamaican dollar
GDP ($ US) 4.2 billion (1994)
Real GDP per capita (PPP) ($ US)
3,816 (1994)
GDP growth rate 0.8% (1994); 2.9%
(1990–95)
Average annual inflation 15.8%
(1995); 28.3% (1985–95)
Foreign debt ($ US) 4.3 billion (1995)
Trading partners USA, UK, Mexico,
Venezuela, Germany, Canada, Norway
Resources bauxite (one of world's
major producers), marble, gypsum,
silica, clay
Industries mining and quarrying,
bauxite processing, food processing,
petroleum refining, clothing, cement,
glass, tourism
Exports bauxite, alumina, gypsum,
sugar, bananas, garments, rum.
Principal market: USA 45.4% (1995)
Imports mineral fuels, machinery and
transport equipment, basic manufactures,
chemicals, food and live animals,
miscellaneous manufactured articles.
Principal source: USA 58% (1995)
Arable land 14.1% (1993)
Agricultural products sugar cane,
bananas, citrus fruit, coffee, cocoa,
coconuts; livestock rearing (goats,
cattle, and pigs)

Population and society

Population 2,491,000 (1996e)
Population growth rate 0.7%
(1990–95); 1% (2000–05)
Population density (per sq km) 227
(1996e)
Urban population (% of total) 54
(1995)

Age distribution (% of total population)
<15 30.8%, 15–65 62.6%, >65 6.6%
(1995)
Ethnic distribution nearly 80% of
African descent; about 15% of mixed
African-European origin. There are also
Chinese, Indian, and European
minorities
Language English, Jamaican creole
Religions Protestant 70%, Rastafarian
Education (compulsory years) 6
Literacy rate 98% (men); 99% (women)
(1995e)
Labour force 49% of population: 25%
agriculture, 23% industry, 52% services
(1990)
Unemployment 15.7% (1992)
Life expectancy 72 (men); 77 (women)
(1995–2000)
Child mortality rate (under 5, per 1,000
live births) 13 (1995)
Physicians 1 per 6,045 people (1992)
Hospital beds 1 per 463 people (1993)
TV sets (per 1,000 people) 162 (1995)
Radios (per 1,000 people) 438 (1995)

Transport

Airports international airports: Kingston
(Norman Manley), Montego Bay (Donald
Sangster); four domestic airports; total
passenger km: 1,430 mil (1994)
Railroads total length: 272 km/169 mi;
total passenger km: 1.2 mil (1992)
Roads total road network: 18,600 km/
11,558 mi, of which 70.6% paved
(1995e); passenger cars: 42.1 per 1,000
people (1993e)

Chronology

c. AD 900 Settled by Arawak Indians,
who gave the island the name Jamaica
('well watered').
1494 The explorer Christopher
Columbus reached Jamaica.

1509 Occupied by Spanish; much of the
Arawak community died from exposure
to European diseases; black African
slaves were brought in to work the
sugar plantations.
1655 Captured by Britain and became
its most valuable Caribbean colony.
1838 Slavery abolished.
1870 Banana plantations established as
sugar cane industry declined in face of
competition from European beet sugar.
1938 Serious riots during the economic
depression and, as a sign of growing
political awareness, the People's
National Party (PNP) was formed by
Norman Manley.
1944 First constitution adopted.
1958–62 Part of West Indies Federation.
1959 Internal self-government granted.
1962 Independence achieved within the
Commonwealth, with Alexander
Bustamante of the centre-right Jamaica
Labour Party (JLP) as prime minister.
1967 JLP re-elected under Hugh
Shearer.
1972 Michael Manley of the PNP
became prime minister and pursued a
policy of economic self-reliance.
1980 JLP elected, with Edward Seaga
as prime minister, following violent
election campaign.
1981 Diplomatic links with Cuba
severed; free-market economic
programme pursued.
1983 JLP won all 60 seats in the
general election.
1988 Island badly damaged by
Hurricane Gilbert.
1989 PNP won a landslide victory with a
newly moderate Manley returning as
prime minister.
1992 Manley retired; succeeded by
Percival Patterson.
1993 PNP increased its majority in
general election.

Practical information

Visa requirements UK: visa not required. USA: visa not
required
Embassy in the UK 1–2 Prince Consort Road, London SW7
2BZ. Tel: (0171) 823 9911; fax: (0171) 589 5154
British embassy British High Commission, PO Box 575,
Trafalgar Road, Kingston 10. Tel: (809) 926 9050;
fax: (809) 929 7869
Embassy in the USA 1520 New Hampshire Avenue NW,
Washington, DC 20036. Tel: (202) 452 0660;
fax: (202) 452 0081
American embassy Jamaica Mutual Life Center, 2 Oxford

Road, 3rd floor, Kingston. Tel: (809) 929 4850–9;
fax: (809) 926 6743
Chamber of commerce PO Box 172, 7–8 East Parade,
Kingston. Tel: (809) 922 0150; fax: (809) 924 9056
Office hours 0830–1630/1700 Mon–Fri
Banking hours 0900–1400 Mon–Thu; 0900–1500 Fri
Time difference GMT –5
Chief tourist attractions climate; beaches; mountains;
historic buildings
Major holidays 1 January, 23 May, 5 August, 20 October,
25–26 December; variable: Ash Wednesday, Good Friday,
Easter Monday

Japan

National name *Nippon*
Area 377,535 sq km/145,766 sq mi
Capital Tokyo
Major towns/cities Yokohama, Osaka,
Nagoya, Fukuoka, Kitakyushu, Kyoto,
Sapporo, Kobe, Kawasaki, Hiroshima
Major ports Osaka, Nagoya, Yokohama,
Kobe
Physical features mountainous,
volcanic (Mount Fuji, volcanic Mount
Aso, Japan Alps); comprises over 1,000
Islands, the largest of which are
Hokkaido, Honshu, Kyushu, and Shikoku

Government

Head of state (figurehead) Emperor
Akihito (Heisei) from 1989
Head of government Ryūtarō
Hashimoto from 1996
Political system liberal democracy
Administrative divisions 47 prefectures
Political parties Liberal Democratic
Party (LDP), right of centre; Shinshinto
(New Frontier Party) opposition coalition,
centrist reformist; Social Democratic
Party of Japan (SDPJ, former Socialist
Party), left of centre but moving towards
centre; Shinto Sakigake (New Party
Harbinger), right of centre; Japanese
Communist Party (JCP), socialist;
Democratic Party of Japan (DPJ),
Sakigake and SDPJ dissidents
Armed forces self-defence forces:
240,000; US forces stationed there:
44,800 (1995)
Death penalty retained and used for
ordinary crimes
Defence spend (% GDP) 1.1 (1995)
Education spend (% GNP) 4.7
(1993–94)
Health spend (% GDP) 5.2 (1993)

Economy and resources

Currency yen
GDP ($ US) 4,599.7 billion (1996)

Real GDP per capita (PPP) ($ US)
22,863 (1996)
GDP growth rate 2.6% (1996); 1%
(1990–95)
Average annual inflation 0.3% (1996);
1.4% (1985–95)
Trading partners USA, China, Australia,
South Korea, Indonesia, Germany,
Taiwan, Hong Kong
Resources coal, iron, zinc, copper,
natural gas, fish
Industries motor vehicles, steel,
machinery, electrical and electronic
equipment, chemicals, textiles
Exports motor vehicles, electronic goods
and components, chemicals, iron and
steel products, scientific and optical
equipment. Principal market: USA 27.2%
(1996)
Imports mineral fuels, foodstuffs, live
animals, bauxite, iron ore, copper ore,
coking coal, chemicals, textiles, wood.
Principal source: USA 22.7% (1996)
Arable land 10.7% (1993)
Agricultural products rice, potatoes,
cabbages, sugar cane, sugar beet, citrus
fruit; one of the world's leading fishing
nations (8 million tonnes in 1993)

Population and society

Population 125,351,000 (1996e)
Population growth rate 0.3%
(1990–95); 0.1% (2000–05)
Population density (per sq km) 332
(1996e)
Urban population (% of total) 78 (1995)
Age distribution (% of total population)
<15 16.2%, 15–65 69.6%, >65 14.1%
(1995)
Ethnic distribution more than 99% of
Japanese descent; Ainu (aboriginal
people of Japan) in N Japan (Hokkaido,
Kuril Islands)
Languages Japanese; also Ainu
Religions Shinto, Buddhist (often
combined), Christian
Education (compulsory years) 9
Literacy rate 99% (men); 99% (women)
(1995e)
Labour force 52% of population: 7%
agriculture, 34% industry, 59% services
(1990)
Unemployment 3.4% (1996)
Life expectancy 77 (men); 83 (women)
(1995–2000)
Child mortality rate (under 5, per 1,000
live births) 6 (1995)
Physicians 1 per 542 people (1994)
Hospital beds 1 per 75 people (1994)

TV sets (per 1,000 people) 684 (1995)
Radios (per 1,000 people) 916 (1995)

Transport

Airports international airports: Tokyo
(Narita), Fukuoka, Kagoshima, Kansai,
Nagoya, Osaka; one principal domestic
services airport (Haneda), smaller
airports cover connections between
major towns and islands; total passenger
km: 118,011 mil (1994)
Railroads total length: 38,125 km/23,690
mi; total passenger km: 402,513 mil
(1994)
Roads total road network: 1,144,360
km/711,105 mi, of which 74% paved
(1995e); passenger cars: 360.3 per
1,000 people (1995e)

Chronology

660 BC According to legend, Jimmu
Tenno, descendent of the Sun goddess,
became the first emperor of Japan.
c. 400 AD The Yamato, one of many
warring clans, unified central Japan;
Yamato chiefs are the likely ancestors of
the imperial family.
5th–6th centuries Writing,
Confucianism, and Buddhism spread to
Japan from China and Korea.
646 Start of the Taika Reform: Emperor
Kōtoku organized central government on
the Chinese model.
794 Heian became imperial capital; later
called Kyoto.
858 Imperial court fell under control of
the Fujiwara clan, who reduced the
emperor to a figurehead.
11th century Central government grew
ineffectual; real power exercised by great
landowners (daimyo) with private armies
of samurai.
1185 Minamoto clan seized power under
Yoritomo, who established military rule.
1192 Emperor gave Yoritomo the title of
shogun (general); the shogun ruled in the
name of the emperor.
1274 Mongol conqueror Kublai Khan
attempted to invade Japan, making a
second attempt 1281; each time Japan
was saved by a typhoon.
1336 Warlord Takauji Ashikaga overthrew
the Minamoto shogunate; emperor
recognized Ashikaga shogunate 1338.
16th century Power of Ashikagas
declined; constant civil war.
1543 Portuguese sailors were the first
Europeans to reach Japan; followed by
Spanish, Dutch, and English traders.

1549 Spanish missionary St Francis Xavier began to preach Roman Catholic faith in Japan.

1585–98 Warlord Hideyoshi took power and attempted to conquer Korea 1592 and 1597.

1603 Ieyasu Tokugawa founded new shogunate at Edo, reformed administration, and suppressed Christianity.

1630s Japan adopted policy of isolation: all travel forbidden and all foreigners expelled except small colony of Dutch traders in Nagasaki harbour.

1853 USA sent warships to Edo with demand that Japan open diplomatic and trade relations; Japan conceded 1854.

1867 Revolt by isolationist nobles overthrew the Tokugawa shogunate.

1868 Emperor Mutsuhito assumed full powers, adopted the regal era name *Meiji* ('enlightened rule'), moved imperial capital from Kyoto to Edo (renamed Tokyo), and launched policy of swift Westernization.

1894–95 Sino-Japanese War: Japan expelled Chinese from Korea.

1902 Japan entered a defensive alliance with Britain; ended 1921.

1904–05 Russo-Japanese War: Japan drove Russians from Manchuria and Korea; Korea annexed 1910.

1914 Japan entered World War I and occupied German possessions in Far East.

1923 Earthquake destroyed much of Tokyo and Yokohama.

1931 Japan invaded Chinese province of Manchuria and created puppet state of Manchukuo; Japanese government came under control of military and extreme nationalists.

1937 Japan resumed invasion of China.

1940 After Germany defeated France, Japan occupied French Indochina.

1941 Japan attacked US fleet at Pearl Harbor; USA and Britain declared war on Japan.

1942 Japanese conquered Thailand, Burma, Malaya, Dutch East Indies, Philippines, and northern New Guinea.

1945 USA dropped atomic bombs on Hiroshima and Nagasaki; Japan surrendered; US general Douglas MacArthur headed Allied occupation administration.

1947 MacArthur supervised introduction of democratic 'Peace Constitution', accompanied by demilitarization and land reform.

1952 Occupation ended.

1955 Liberal Democratic Party (LDP) founded with support of leading businesspeople.

1956 Japan admitted to United Nations.

1950s–70s Rapid economic development; growth of manufacturing exports led to great prosperity.

1993 Economic recession and financial scandals brought downfall of LDP government in general election. Coalition government formed.

1995 Earthquake devastated Kobe.

1996 General election produced inconclusive result; minority LDP government subsequently formed. New party, the Taiyōtō (Sun Party) formed by former prime minister Tsutomu Hata.

1997 Ryūtarō Hashimoto's new government pledged itself to different economic policies. Hashimoto reelected LDP president. Financial crash after bank failures.

Practical information

Visa requirements UK: visa not required. USA: visa not required for a stay of up to 90 days

Embassy in the UK 101–104 Piccadilly, London W1V 9FN. Tel: (0171) 465 6500; fax: (0171) 491 9348

British embassy No. 1 Ichiban-cho, Chiyoda-ku, Tokyo 102. Tel: (3) 3265 5511; fax: (3) 5275 3164

Embassy in the USA 2520 Massachusetts Avenue NW, Washington, DC 20008. Tel: (202) 939 6700; fax: (202) 328 2187

American embassy 10-5, Akasaka 1-chome, Minato-ku, Tokyo 107. Tel: (3) 3224 5000; fax: (3) 3505 1862

Chamber of commerce 2nd Floor, Salisbury House, 29 Finsbury Circus, London EC2M 5QQ. Tel: (0171) 628 0069; fax: (0171) 628 0248. Nippon Shoko Kaigi-sho, 3-2-2, Marunouchi, Chiyoda-ku, Tokyo 10. Tel: (3) 3283 7851

Office hours 0900–1700 Mon–Fri

Banking hours 0900–1500 Mon–Fri

Time difference GMT +9

Chief tourist attractions ancient capital of Kyoto; Buddhist and Shinto temples; pagodas; forests and mountains; classical kabuki theatre; traditional festivals

Major holidays 1–3, 15 January, 11 February, 21 March, 29 April, 3, 5 May, 15, 23 September, 10 October, 3, 23 November

---

Jordan Hashemite Kingdom of

National name *Al Mamlaka al Urduniya al Hashemiyah*

Area 89,206 sq km/34,442 sq mi (West Bank 5,879 sq km/2,269 sq mi)

Capital Amman

Major towns/cities Zarqa, Irbid, Saet, Ma'an

Major ports Aqaba

Physical features desert plateau in E; Rift Valley separates E and W banks of the River Jordan

Government

Head of state King Hussein ibn Tal

Abdulla el Hashim from 1952

Head of government Abdul-Karim Kabariti from 1996

Political system constitutional monarchy

Administrative divisions eight governates

Political parties independent groups loyal to the king predominate; of the 21 parties registered since 1992, the most significant is the Islamic Action Front (IAF), Islamic fundamentalist

Armed forces 98,600 (1995); plus paramilitary forces of more than 200,000

Conscription selective

Death penalty retained and used for ordinary crimes
Defence spend (% GDP) 6.7 (1995)
Education spend (% GNP) 3.8 (1993–94)
Health spend (% GDP) 1.8 (1990)

Economy and resources

Currency Jordanian dinar
GDP ($ US) 6.1 billion (1994)
Real GDP per capita (PPP) ($ US) 4,187 (1994)
GDP growth rate 5.7% (1994); 8.2% (1990–95)
Average annual inflation 3% (1995); 7.1% (1985–95e)
Foreign debt ($ US) 7.94 billion (1995)
Trading partners Iraq, India, Saudi Arabia, Germany, Italy, UK, USA, Japan
Resources phosphates, potash, shale
Industries mining and quarrying, petroleum refining, chemical products, alcoholic drinks, food products, phosphate, cement, potash, tourism
Exports phosphate, potash, fertilizers, foodstuffs, pharmaceuticals, fruit and vegetables, cement. Principal market: Iraq 18.9% (1995)
Imports food and live animals, basic manufactures, mineral fuels, machinery and transport equipment. Principal source: Iraq 12.2% (1995)
Arable land 3.5% (1993)
Agricultural products wheat, barley, maize, tobacco, vegetables, fruits, nuts; livestock rearing (sheep and goats)

Population and society

Population 5,581,000 (1996e)
Population growth rate 4.9% (1990–95); 3% (2000–05)
Population density (per sq km) 57 (1996e)
Urban population (% of total) 71 (1995)
Age distribution (% of total population) <15 43.3%, 15–65 54%, >65 2.7% (1995)
Ethnic distribution majority of Arab descent; small Circassian, Armenian, and Kurdish minorities
Languages Arabic (official), English
Religions Sunni Muslim 80%, Christian 8%
Education (compulsory years) 10
Literacy rate 75% (men); 70% (women) (1995e)
Labour force 27% of population: 15% agriculture, 23% industry, 61% services (1990)
Unemployment 25% (1992e)
Life expectancy 68 (men); 72 (women)

(1995–2000)
Child mortality rate (under 5, per 1,000 live births) 25 (1995)
Physicians 1 per 825 people (1994)
Hospital beds 1 per 749 people (1994)
TV sets (per 1,000 people) 80 (1995)
Radios (per 1,000 people) 251 (1995)

Transport

Airports international airports: Amman (charter flights only), Zizya (Queen Alia, 30 km south of Amman), Aqaba; internal flights operate between Amman and Aqaba; total passenger km: 4,155 mil (1994)
Railroads total length: 788 km/490 mi; total passenger km: 2 mil (1994)
Roads total road network: 6,750 km/ 4,194 mi, of which 100% paved (1995e); passenger cars: 35 per 1,000 people (1993)

Chronology

13th century BC Oldest known 'states' of Jordan, including Gideon, Ammon, Moab, and Edom, established.
c. 1000 BC East Jordan was part of kingdom of Israel, under David and Solomon.
4th century BC SE Jordan occupied by the independent Arabic-speaking Nabataeans.
64 BC Conquered by Romans and became part of province of Arabia.
AD 636 Became largely Muslim after the Byzantine forces of Emperor Heraclius were defeated by Arab armies at battle of Yarmuk, in N Jordan.
1099–1187 Part of the Latin Kingdom established by the Crusaders in Jerusalem.
from early 16th century Part of Turkish Ottoman Empire, administered from Damascus.
1920 Trans-Jordan (the area E of the River Jordan) and Palestine (which includes the West Bank) were placed under British administration by a League of Nations mandate.
1923 Trans-Jordan was separated from Palestine and recognized by Britain as a substantially independent state under the rule of Emir Abdullah ibn Hussein, a member of the Hashemite dynasty of Arabia.
1946 Trans-Jordan achieved independence from Britain, with Abd Allah as king; name changed to Jordan.
1948 British mandate for Palestine expired, leading to fighting between

Arabs and Jews, who each claimed the area.
1950 Jordan annexed West Bank; 400,000 Palestinian refugees flooded into Jordan, putting pressure on the economy.
1951 King Abdullah assassinated in Jerusalem; succeeded by his son King Talal.
1952 Partially democratic constitution introduced.
1953 Hussein ibn Tal Abdulla el Hashim officially became king of Jordan, after his father, King Talal, stepped down.
1958 Jordan and Iraq formed Arab Federation that ended when the Iraqi monarchy was deposed.
1967 Israel defeated Egypt, Syria, and Jordan in the Arab–Israeli Six-Day War, and captured and occupied the West Bank, including Arab Jerusalem. Martial law imposed.
1970–71 Jordanians moved against the increasingly radicalized Palestine Liberation Organization (PLO), which had launched guerrilla raids on Israel from Jordanian territory, resulting in bloody civil war, before PLO leadership fled abroad.
1976 Lower house dissolved, political parties banned, elections postponed until further notice.
1980 Jordan emerged as important ally of Iraq in its war against Iran, an ally of Syria, with whom Jordan's relations were tense.
1982 Hussein tried to mediate in Arab–Israeli conflict, following the Israeli invasion of Lebanon.
1984 Women voted for the first time; parliament recalled.
1985 Hussein and PLO leader Yassir Arafat put forward framework for Middle East peace settlement. Secret meeting between Hussein and Israeli prime minister.
1988 Hussein announced willingness to cease administering the West Bank as part of Jordan, passing responsibility to the PLO, and the suspension of parliament.
1989 Prime Minister Zaid al-Rifai resigned; Hussein promised new parliamentary elections. Riots over price increases of up to 50% following fall in oil revenues. First parliamentary elections for 22 years; Muslim Brotherhood won 25 of 80 seats but exiled from government; martial law lifted.
1990 Hussein unsuccessfully tried to mediate after Iraq's invasion of Kuwait.

Huge refugee problems as thousands fled to Jordan from Kuwait and Iraq.
1991 24 years of martial law ended; ban on political parties lifted; remained neutral during the Gulf War involving

Saddam Hussein's Iraq.
1993 Candidates loyal to Hussein won majority in parliamentary elections; several leading Islamic fundamentalists lost their seats.

1994 Economic cooperation pact singed with PLO. Peace treaty signed with Israel, ending 46-year-old 'state of war'.
1996 Abdul-Karim Kabariti appointed prime minister.

Practical information

Visa requirements UK: visa required. USA: visa required
Embassy in the UK 6 Upper Phillimore Gardens, London W8 7HB. Tel: (0171) 937 3685; fax: (0171) 937 8795
British embassy PO Box 87, Abdoun, Amman. Tel: (6) 823 100; fax: (6) 813 759
Embassy in the USA 3504 International Drive NW, Washington, DC 20008. Tel: (202) 966 2664; fax: (202) 966 3110
American embassy Jabel Amman, Amman. Tel: (6) 820 101; fax: (6) 820 159

Chamber of commerce Amman Chamber of Commerce, PO Box 287, Amman. Tel: (6) 666 151; telex: 21543
Office hours 0900–1700 Sat, Wed, and Thu
Banking hours 0830–1230 and 1530–1730 Sat–Thu; generally 0830–1000 during Ramadan
Time difference GMT +2
Chief tourist attractions ancient cities of Petra and Jerash
Major holidays 1 January, 1, 25 May, 10 June, 11 August, 14 November, 25 December; variable: Eid-ul-Adha (4 days), first day of Ramadan, end of Ramadan (4 days), New Year (Muslim), Prophet's Birthday

---

Kazakhstan Republic of

National name *Kazak Respublikasy*
Area 2,717,300 sq km/1,049,150 sq mi
Capital Almaty (until 2000; then Akmola)
Major towns/cities Karaganda, Pavlodar, Semipalatinsk, Petropavlovsk, Chimkent
Physical features Caspian and Aral seas, Lake Balkhash; Steppe region; natural gas and oil deposits in the Caspian Sea

Government

Head of state Nursultan Nazarbayev from 1990
Head of government Nurlan Balgimbayev from 1997
Political system authoritarian nationalist
Administrative divisions 19 provinces
Political parties Congress of People's Unity of Kazakhstan, moderate, centrist; People's Congress of Kazakhstan, moderate, ethnic; Socialist Party of

Kazakhstan (SPK), left wing; Republican Party, right-of-centre coalition
Armed forces 40,000 (1995)
Death penalty retained and used for ordinary crimes
Defence spend (% GDP) 3 (1995)
Education spend (% GNP) 5.4 (1993–94)
Health spend (% GDP) 4.9 (1994e)

Economy and resources

Currency tenge
GDP ($ US) 18 billion (1994)
Real GDP per capita (PPP) ($ US) 3,284 (1994)
GDP growth rate −8.9% (1995); −11.9% (1990–95)
Average annual inflation 39.1% (1996); 307.3% (1985–95e)
Foreign debt ($ US) 3.7 billion (1995)
Trading partners Russia and other CIS nations, Germany, the Netherlands, Switzerland, Czech Republic, Italy
Resources petroleum, natural gas, coal, bauxite, chromium, copper, iron ore, lead, titanium, magnesium, tungsten, molybdenum, gold, silver, manganese
Industries metal processing, heavy engineering, mining and quarrying, chemicals, fuel, power, machine-building, textiles, food processing, household appliances
Exports ferrous and non-ferrous metals, mineral products (including petroleum and petroleum products), chemicals. Principal market: Russia 42.1% (1995)
Imports energy products and electricity, machinery and transport equipment, chemicals. Principal source: Russia 46.2% (1995)

Arable land 13%
Agricultural products fruits, sugar beet, vegetables, potatoes, cotton, cereals; livestock rearing (particularly sheep); karakul and astrakhan wool

Population and society

Population 16,820,000 (1996e)
Population growth rate 0.5% (1990–95); 0.8% (2000–05)
Population density (per sq km) 6 (1996e)
Urban population (% of total) 60 (1995)
Age distribution (% of total population) <15 29.8%, 15–65 63.2%, >65 7% (1995)
Ethnic distribution 40% of Kazakh descent, 38% ethnic Russian, 6% German, 5% Ukranian, 2% Uzbek, and 2% Tatar
Languages Kazakh (official), related to Turkish; Russian
Religion Sunni Muslim
Education (compulsory years) 11
Literacy rate 97.5% (men); 97.5% (women) (1995e)
Labour force 24% agriculture, 20.4% industry, 55.6% services (1992)
Unemployment 3.5% (1996)
Life expectancy 67 (men); 75 (women) (1995–2000)
Child mortality rate (under 5, per 1,000 live births) 47 (1995)
Physicians 1 per 254 people (1994)
Hospital beds 1 per 75 people (1994)
TV sets (per 1,000 people) 256 (1995)
Radios (per 1,000 people) 384 (1995)

Transport

Airports international airports: Almaty, Aktau, Atyrau; 18 domestic airports; total passenger km: 1,787 mil (1994)

Railroads total length: 13,826 km/8,591 mi; total passenger km: 17,362 mil (1994)
Roads total road network: 158,655 km/ 98,588 mi, of which 68.4% paved (1995e); passenger cars: 59.8 per 1,000 people (1995e)

Chronology

early Christian era Settled by Mongol and Turkic tribes.
8th century Spread of Islam.
10th century Southward migration into E Kazakhstan of Kazakh tribes, displaced from Mongolia by the Mongols.
13th–14th centuries Part of Mongol Empire.
late 15th century Kazakhs emerged as distinct ethnic group from Kazakh Orda tribal confederation.
early 17th century The nomadic, cattle-breeding Kazakhs split into smaller groups, united in the three Large, Middle, and Lesser Hordes (federations), led by khans (chiefs).
1731–42 Faced by attacks from the E by Oirot Mongols, protection was sought from the Russian tsars, and Russian control was gradually established.
1822–48 Conquest by tsarist Russia completed; khans deposed. Large-scale Russian and Ukrainian peasant

settlement of the steppes after the abolition of serfdom in Russia in 1861.
1887 Alma-Alta (now Almaty), established 1854 as a fortified trading centre and captured by the Russians 1865, destroyed by earthquake.
1916 150,000 killed as anti-Russian rebellion brutally repressed.
1917 Bolshevik coup in Russia followed by outbreak of civil war in Kazakhstan.
1920 Autonomous republic in USSR.
early 1930s More than 1 million died of starvation during campaign to collectivize agriculture.
1936 Joined USSR and became a full union republic.
early 1940s Volga Germans deported to the republic by Soviet dictator Joseph Stalin.
1954–56 Part of Soviet leader Nikita Khrushchev's ambitious 'Virgin Lands' agricultural extension programme; large influx of Russian settlers made Kazakhs a minority in their own republic.
1986 Nationalist riots in Alma-Alta (now Almaty) after reformist Soviet leader Mikhail Gorbachev ousted local communist leader and installed an ethnic Russian.
1989 Nursultan Nazarbayev, a reformist and mild nationalist, became leader of

Kazakh Communist Party (KCP) and instituted economic and cultural reform programmes, encouraging foreign inward investment.
1990 Nazarbayev became head of state; economic sovereignty declared.
1991 Nazarbayev condemned attempted anti-Gorbachev coup in Moscow; KCP abolished. Joined new Commonwealth of Independent States, formed at Almaty; independence recognized by USA.
1992 Admitted into United Nations and Conference on Security and Cooperation in Europe (CSCE; now the Organization on Security and Cooperation in Europe, OSCE).
1993 Presidential power increased by new constitution. Privatization programme launched; Kazakhstan ratified START-1 (disarmament treaty) and the Nuclear Non-Proliferation Treaty.
1994 Economic, social, and military union with Kyrgyzstan and Uzbekistan.
1995 Economic and military cooperation pact with Russia. Achieved nuclear-free status. Nazarbayev's popular mandate reratified in national referendum.
1996 Agreement signed with Kyrgyzstan and Uzbekistan to form single economic market.
1997 Nurlan Balgimbayev was appointed prime minister.

Practical information

Visa requirements UK: visa required. USA: visa required
Embassy in the UK 3 Warren Mews, London W1P 5DJ. Tel/fax: (0171) 387 1047
British embassy 173 Furmanova Street, Almaty. Tel: (3272) 506 191; fax: (3272) 506 260
Embassy in the USA (temporary) 3421 Massachusetts Avenue, NW, Washington, DC 20008. Tel: (202) 333 4504/5/6/7; fax: (202) 333 4509
American embassy 99/97 Furmanova Street, 480012

Almaty. Tel: (3272) 633 905, 631 375, 632 426; fax: (3272) 632 942
Chamber of commerce Chamber of Commerce and Industry of Kazakhstan, pr. Ablaikhana 93/95, 480091 Almaty. Tel: (3272) 621 446; fax: (3272) 620 594
Office hours 0900–1200/1300 and 1300/1400–1800 Mon–Fri
Banking hours 0930–1300 and 1400–1730 Mon–Fri
Time difference GMT +6
Major holidays 1, 28 January, 8, 22 March, 1, 9 May, 25 October, 31 December

---

Kenya Republic of

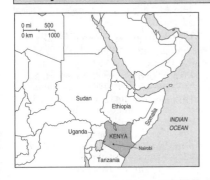

National name *Jamhuri ya Kenya*
Area 582,600 sq km/224,941 sq mi
Capital Nairobi
Major towns/cities Mombasa, Kisumu, Nakuru, Eldoret, Nyeri
Major ports Mombasa
Physical features mountains and highlands in W and centre; coastal plain in S; arid interior and tropical coast; semi-desert in N; Great Rift Valley, Mount Kenya, Lake Nakuru (salt lake with world's largest colony of flamingos), Lake Turkana (Rudolf)

Government

Head of state and government Daniel arap Moi from 1978
Political system authoritarian nationalist
Administrative divisions seven provinces and the Nairobi municipality
Political parties Kenya African National Union (KANU), nationalist, centrist; Forum for the Restoration of Democracy–Kenya (FORD–Kenya), left of centre; Forum for the Restoration of Democracy–Asili (FORD–Asili), left of

centre; Democratic Party (DP), centrist;
Safina, centrist
Armed forces 24,200; paramilitary force
5,000 (1995)
Death penalty retained and used for
ordinary crimes
Defence spend (% GDP) 2.3 (1995)
Education spend (% GNP) 6.8
(1993–94)
Health spend (% GDP) 2.7 (1990)

Economy and resources

Currency Kenya shilling
GDP ($ US) 6.9 billion (1994)
Real GDP per capita (PPP) ($ US)
1,404 (1994)
GDP growth rate 3% (1994); 1.4%
(1990–95)
Average annual inflation 28.8%
(1994); 13% (1985–95)
Foreign debt ($ US) 7.4 billion (1995)
Trading partners Uganda, UK,
Tanzania, Germany, Japan, United Arab
Emirates
Resources soda ash, fluorspar, salt,
limestone, rubies, gold, vermiculite,
diatonite, garnets
Industries food processing, petroleum
refining and petroleum products, textiles
and clothing, leather products,
chemicals, cement, paper and paper
products, beverages, tobacco, ceramics,
rubber and metal products, vehicle
assembly, tourism
Exports coffee, tea, petroleum
products, soda ash, horticultural
products. Principal market: Uganda
15.8% (1995)
Imports crude petroleum, motor
vehicles, industrial machinery, iron and
steel, chemicals, basic manufactures.
Principal source: UK 12.6% (1995)
Arable land 6.9% (1993)
Agricultural products coffee, tea,
maize, wheat, sisal, sugar cane,
pineapples, cotton, horticulture; dairy
products

Population and society

Population 27,799,000 (1996e)
Population growth rate 3.6%
(1990–95); 3% (2000–05)
Population density (per sq km) 48
(1996e)
Urban population (% of total) 28
(1995)
Age distribution (% of total population)
<15 47.7%, 15–65 49.4%, >65 2.9%
(1995)
Ethnic distribution main ethnic groups
are the Kikuyu (about 21%), the Luhya

(14%), the Luo (13%), the Kalenjin
(11%), the Kamba (11%), the Kisii (6%),
and the Meru (5%); there are also
Asian, Arab, and European minorities
Languages Kiswahili (official), English;
there are many local dialects
Religions Roman Catholic, Protestant,
Muslim, traditional tribal religions
Education (years) 8 (not compulsory,
but free)
Literacy rate 86% (men); 70% (women)
(1995e)
Labour force 48% of population: 80%
agriculture, 7% industry, 13% services
(1990)
Unemployment 16% (1992e)
Life expectancy 57 (men); 61 (women)
(1995–2000)
Child mortality rate (under 5, per 1,000
live births) 90 (1995)
Physicians 1 per 6,430 people (1994)
Hospital beds 1 per 786 people (1994)
TV sets (per 1,000 people) 18 (1995)
Radios (per 1,000 people) 96 (1995)

Transport

Airports international airports:
Mombasa (Moi), Nairobi (Jomo
Kenyatta), Eldoret (opening date of
1997 delayed); three domestic airports;
total passenger km: 1,737 mil (1994)
Railroads total length: 2,740 km/1,702
mi; total passenger km: 464 mil (1994)
Roads total road network: 63,663 km/
39,560 mi, of which 14% paved (1995);
passenger cars: 11 per 1,000 people
(1995e)

Chronology

8th century Arab traders began to
settle along coast of E Africa.
16th century Portuguese defeated
coastal states and exerted spasmodic
control over them.
18th century Sultan of Oman
reasserted Arab overlordship of E
African coast, making it subordinate to
Zanzibar.
19th century Europeans, closely
followed by Christian missionaries,
began to explore inland.
1887 British East African Company
leased area of coastal territory from
sultan of Zanzibar.
1895 Britain claimed large inland region
as East African Protectorate.
1903 Railway from Mombasa to Uganda
built using Indian labourers, many of
whom settled in the area; British and
South African settlers began to farm
highlands.

1920 East African Protectorate became
crown colony of Kenya, with legislative
council elected by white settlers (and by
Indians and Arabs soon afterwards).
1923 Britain rejected demand for
internal self-government by white
settlers.
1944 First African appointment to
legislative council; Kenyan African Union
(KAU) founded to campaign for African
rights.
1947 Jomo Kenyatta became leader of
KAU, which was dominated by Kikuyu
tribe.
1952 Mau Mau (Kikuyu secret society)
began terrorist campaign to drive white
settlers from tribal lands; Mau Mau
largely suppressed by 1954 but state of
emergency lasted for eight years.
1953 Kenyatta charged with
management of Mau Mau activities and
imprisoned by the British.
1956 Africans allowed to elect members
of legislative council on restricted
franchise.
1959 Kenyatta released from prison, but
exiled to N Kenya.
1960 Britain announced plans to
prepare Kenya for majority African rule.
1961 Kenyatta allowed to return to help
negotiate Kenya's independence.
1963 Kenya achieved independence
with Kenyatta as prime minister.
1964 Kenya became a republic with
Kenyatta as president.
1967 East African Community (EAC)
formed by Kenya, Tanzania, and
Uganda to retain customs union
inherited from colonial period.
1969 Kenya became one-party state
under Kenyan African National Union
(KANU).
1977 Political and economic disputes
led to collapse of EAC.
1978 Death of President Kenyatta;
succeeded by Daniel arap Moi.
1984 Violent clashes between
government troops and ethnic Somali
population at Wajir.
1989 Moi announced release of political
prisoners.
1991 Multiparty system conceded after
Oginga Odinga launched opposition
group.
1992 Moi re-elected in multiparty
elections amid allegations of fraud.
1995 New Centrist party, Safina, formed
by palaeoanthropologist Richard
Leakey.
1997 Demonstrations calling for
democratic reform. Constitutional
refoms adopted.

Practical information

Visa requirements UK: visa not required. USA: visa required
Embassy in the UK 45 Portland Place, London W1N 4AS.
Tel: (0171) 636 2371/5; fax: (0171) 323 6717
British embassy British High Commission, PO Box 30465,
Bruce House, Standard Street, Nairobi. Tel: (2) 335 944;
fax: (2) 333 196
Embassy in the USA 2249 R Street NW, Washington, DC
20008. Tel: (202) 387 6101; fax: (202) 462 3829
American embassy corner of Moi Avenue and Hailé
Sélassie Avenue, Nairobi. Tel: (2) 334 141; fax: (2) 340 838
Chamber of commerce Kenya National Chamber of
Commerce and Industry, PO Box 47024, Ufanisi House,

Hailé Sélassie Avenue, Nairobi. Tel: (2) 334 413
Office hours 0800–1300 and 1400–1700 Mon–Fri; in
Mombasa offices usually open and close a half hour earlier
Banking hours 0900–1500 Mon–Fri; 0900–1100 on the first
and last Sat of every month
Time difference GMT +3
Chief tourist attractions wildlife – 25 national parks and 23
game reserves, notably the Rift Valley, containing Aberdare
National Park, overlooked by Mount Kenya, which also has a
national park; Indian Ocean coast
Major holidays 1 January, 1 May, 1 June, 10, 20 October,
12, 25–26 December; variable: Good Friday, Easter Monday,
end of Ramadan

Kiribati Republic of (formerly part of the Gilbert and Ellice Islands)

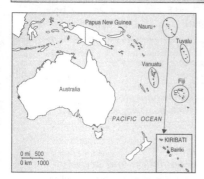

National name *Ribaberikin Kiribati*
Area 717 sq km/276 sq mi
Capital Bairiki (on Tarawa Atoll) (and port)
Towns pricipal atolls: North Tarawa,
Gilbert group, Abaiang, Tabiteuea
Major ports Betio (on Tarawa)
Physical features comprises 33 Pacific
coral islands: the Kiribati (Gilbert),
Rawaki (Phoenix), Banaba (Ocean
Island), and three of the Line Islands
including Kiritimati (Christmas Island);
island groups crossed by Equator and
International Date Line

Government

Head of state and government
Teburoro Tito from 1994
Political system liberal democracy
Political parties Maneaban Te Mauri
(MTM), dominant faction; National
Progressive Party (NPP), former
governing faction 1979–94
Armed forces no standing army
Death penalty abolished 1979
Education spend (% GNP) 6.5 (1991)

Economy and resources

Currency Australian dollar

GDP ($ US) 68 million (1995e)
Real GDP per capita (PPP) ($ US) 860
(1995e)
GDP growth rate 2.6% (1995e)
Average annual inflation 2.9% (1994);
3.8% (1985–95)
Foreign debt ($ US) 21 million (1993)
Trading partners Australia, Bangladesh,
Japan, Fiji, USA, France, New Zealand,
China
Resources phosphate, salt
Industries handicrafts, coconut-based
products, soap, foods, furniture, leather
goods, garments, tourism
Exports copra, fish, seaweed, bananas,
breadfruit, taro. Principal market:
Bangladesh 67% (1993)
Imports foodstuffs, machinery and
transport equipment, mineral fuels, basic
manufactures. Principal source: Australia
(1993)
Arable land 50.7% (1994)
Agricultural products copra, coconuts,
bananas, screw-pine, papaya, breadfruit;
livestock rearing (pigs and chickens);
fishing and seaweed cultivation

Population and society

Population 80,000 (1996e)
Population growth rate 1.7% (1990–95)
Population density (per sq km) 110
(1996e)
Urban population (% of total) 35.7
(1995)
Age distribution (% of total population)
<15 38.1%, 15–65 55.9%, >65 6%
(1992)
Ethnic distribution predominantly
Micronesian, with a Polynesian minority;
also European and Chinese minorities
Language English (official), Gilbertese
Religions Roman Catholic, Protestant

(Congregationalist)
Education (compulsory years) 9
Literacy rate 90% (men); 90%(women)
(1993e)
Unemployment 2.8% (1990)
Life expectancy 51 (men); 56 (women)
(1992)
Child mortality rate (under 5, per 1,000
live births) 98.4 (1994)
Physicians 1 per 4,685 people (1991)
Hospital beds 1 per 265 people (1991)
TV sets (per 1,000 people) 9 (1995)
Radios (per 1,000 people) 212 (1995)

Transport

Airports international airports: South
Tarawa (Bonikri), Kiritimati Island
(Cassidy), Butaritari Island (Antekana),
Kanton Island, Tabuaeran Island; 15
domestic airports; total passenger km:
10 mil (1994)
Railroads none
Roads total road network: about 640 km/
398 mi, of which 483 km/300 mi is
suitable for vehicles

Chronology

1st millenium BC Settled by
Austronesian-speaking peoples.
1606 Visited by Spanish explorers.
late 18th century Visited by British naval
officers.
1857 Christian mission established.
1892 Gilbert (Kiribati) and Ellice (Tuvalu)
Islands proclaimed a British protectorate.
1916–39 Uninhabited Phoenix Islands,
Christmas Island, Ocean Island, and Line
Island (Banaba) added to colony.
1942–43 Occupied by Japanese, it was
the scene of fierce fighting with US
troops.

late 1950s UK tested nuclear weapons on Christmas Island (Kiritimati).
1958 Christmas Island transferred to Australia.
1963 Legislative council established.
1974 Legislative council replaced by an elected House of Assembly.
1975 The mainly Melanesian-populated Ellice Islands separated to become Tuvalu.

1977 The predominantly Micronesian-populated Gilbert Islands granted internal self-government.
1979 Independence achieved within the Commonwealth, as the Republic of Kiribati, with Ieremia Tabai as president.
1985 Kiribati's first political party, the opposition Christian Democrats, formed.

1991 Tabai re-elected but not allowed under constitution to serve further term; Teatao Teannaki won run-off presidential election.
1994 Government resigned, after losing vote of confidence. Ruling National Progressive Party (NPP) defeated in general election. Teburoro Tito elected president.

Practical information

Visa requirements UK: visa not required for a stay of up to 28 days. USA: visa required
Embassy in the UK Consulate of Kiribati, Faith House, 7 Tufton Street, London SW1P 3QN. Tel: (0171) 222 6952; fax: (0171) 976 7180
British embassy the British High Commission in Suva (see Fiji) deals with enquiries relating to Kiribati
Embassy in the USA Kiribati does not have an embassy in the USA

American embassy the USA does not have an embassy in Kiribati; the ambassador to Fiji is accredited to Kiribati
Chamber of commerce none
Office hours 0800–1230 and 1330–1615 Mon–Fri
Banking hours 0930–1500 Mon–Fri
Time difference GMT –10/–11
Chief tourist attractions remoteness; game-fishing; ecotourism, particularly birdwatching
Major holidays 1 January, 12 June (3 days), 25–26 December; variable: Good Friday, Easter Monday, Holy Saturday, Youth (August)

Korea, North People's Democratic Republic of

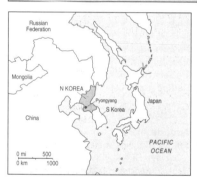

National name *Chosun Minchu-chui Inmin Konghwa-guk*
Area 120,538 sq km/46,539 sq mi
Capital Pyongyang
Major towns/cities Hamhung, Chongjin, Nampo, Wonsan, Sinuiji
Physical features wide coastal plain in W rising to mountains cut by deep valleys in interior

Government

Head of state Kim Jong Il from 1994
Head of government Hong Song Nam from 1997
Political system communism
Administrative divisions three cities and nine provinces
Political parties Korean Workers' Party (KWP), Marxist-Leninist (leads Democratic Front for the Reunification of the Fatherland, including Korean Social

Democratic Party and Chondoist Chongu Party)
Armed forces 1,128,000 (1995)
Conscription conscription is selective for 3–10 years
Death penalty retained and used for ordinary crimes
Defence spend (% GDP) 25.2% (1995)

Economy and resources

Currency won
GDP ($ US) 21.5 billion (1995e)
Real GDP per capita (PPP) ($ US) 920 (1995e)
GDP growth rate –5% (1995e)
Average annual inflation N/A
Foreign debt ($ US) 10.3 billion (1993e)
Trading partners China, Japan, CIS, South Korea, Germany, Italy, Hong Kong, Iran
Resources coal, iron, lead, copper, zinc, tin, silver, gold, magnesite (has 40–50% of world's deposits of magnesite)
Industries mining, metallurgy, electricity, machine-building, textiles, cement, chemicals, cotton, silk and rayon weaving, foods
Exports base metals, textiles, vegetable products, machinery and equipment. Principal market: Japan 27.9% (1995e)
Imports petroleum and petroleum products, machinery and equipment, grain, coal, foodstuffs. Principal source: China 32.6% (1995e)
Arable land 14.1% (1993)

Agricultural products rice, maize, sweet potatoes, soya beans; livestock rearing (cattle and pigs); forestry; fishing

Population and society

Population 22,466,000 (1996e)
Population growth rate 1.9% (1990–95); 1.3% (2000–05)
Population density (per sq km) 186 (1996e)
Urban population (% of total) 61 (1995)
Age distribution (% of total population) <15 29.1%, 15–65 66.3%, >65 4.6% (1995)
Ethnic distribution entirely Korean, with the exception of a 50,000 Chinese minority
Language Korean
Religions Chondoist, Buddhist, Christian, traditional beliefs
Education (compulsory years) 10
Literacy rate 99% (men); 99%(women) (1995e)
Labour force 50% of population: 38% agriculture, 31% industry, 31% services (1990)
Life expectancy 69 (men); 75 (women) (1995–2000)
Child mortality rate (under 5, per 1,000 live births) 30 (1995)
Physicians 1 per 370 people (1993)
TV sets (per 1,000 people) 48 (1995)
Radios (per 1,000 people) 136 (1995)

Transport

Airports international airport: Pyongyang (Sunan); two domestic airports (which foreigners are not allowed to use); total passenger km: 197 mil (1994)
Railroads total length: 8,000 km/4,971 mi; total passenger km: 3,400 mil (1993)
Roads total road network: 30,600 km/ 19,015 mi, of which 6.3% paved (1995e)

Chronology

2333 BC Legendary founding of Korean state by Tangun dynasty.
1122 BC–4TH century AD Period of Chinese Kija dynasty.
668–1000 Peninsula unified by Buddhist Shilla kingdom, with capital at Kyongju.
1392–1910 Period of Chosun, or Yi, dynasty, during which Korea became a vassal of China and Confucianism became dominant intellectual force.
1910 Korea formally annexed by Japan.
1920s and 1930s Heavy industries developed in the coal-rich N, with Koreans forcibly conscripted as low-paid labourers; suppression of Korean culture led to development of resistance movement.

1945 Russian and US troops entered Korea at the end of World War II, forced surrender of Japanese, and divided the country in two at the 38th parallel. Soviet troops occupied North Korea.
1946 Soviet-backed provisional government installed, dominated by Moscow-trained Korean communists, including Kim Il Sung; radical programme of land reform and nationalization launched.
1948 Democratic People's Republic of Korea declared after pro-USA Republic of Korea founded in the S; Soviet troops withdrew.
1950 North Korea invaded South Korea to unite the nation, beginning the Korean War.
1953 Armistice agreed to end Korean War, which had involved US participation on the side of South Korea, and Chinese on that of North Korea. The war ended in stalemate, at a cost of 2 million lives.
1961 Friendship and mutual assistance treaty signed with China.
1972 New constitution, with executive president, adopted. Talks with South Korea about possible reunification.

1983 Four South Korean cabinet ministers assassinated in Rangoon, Burma (Myanmar), by North Korean army officers.
1985 Improved relations with the Soviet Union (USSR).
1990 Diplomatic contacts with South Korea and Japan suggested a thaw in North Korea's relations with rest of world.
1991 Became a member of the United Nations. Signed nonaggression agreement with South Korea.
1992 Signed Nuclear Safeguards Agreement, allowing international inspection of nuclear facilities. Also signed pact with South Korea for mutual inspection of nuclear facilities.
1994 Kim Il Sung died; succeeded by his son, Kim Jong Il. Agreement to halt nuclear-development programme in return for US aid, resulting in easing of 44-year-old US trade embargo.
1996 US aid sought in the face of severe famine; rice imported from South Korea. Floods caused near-famine conditions; food aid provided by UN.
1997 Kang Song San replaced as prime minister by Hong Song Nam. Grave food shortages revealed.

Practical information

Visa requirements UK: visa required. USA: visa required
Embassy for the UK General Delegation of the DPRK, 104 boulevard Bineau, 92200 Neuilly-sur-Seine, France. Tel: (1) 4745 1797; fax: (1) 4738 1250
British embassy the UK has no diplomatic representation in North Korea
Embassy in the USA North Korea has no diplomatic representation in the USA; North Korea has a Permanent Mission to the UN in New York

American embassy the USA has no diplomatic representation in North Korea
Chamber of commerce DPRK Committee for the Promotion of External Economic Cooperation, Jungsongdong, Central District, Pyongyang. Tel: (2) 33974; fax: (2) 814 498
Time difference GMT +9
Chief tourist attractions tourism is permitted only in officially accompanied parties
Major holidays 1 January, 16 February, 8 March, 15 April, 9 September, 10 October, 27 December

---

Korea, South Republic of Korea

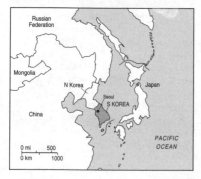

National name *Daehan Min-kuk*
Area 98,799 sq km/38,146 sq mi

Capital Seoul
Major towns/cities Pusan, Taegu, Inchon, Kwangju, Taejon
Major ports Pusan, Inchon
Physical features southern end of a mountainous peninsula separating the Sea of Japan from the Yellow Sea

Government

Head of state Kim Young Sam from 1993
Head of government Koh Kun from 1997
Political system emergent democracy
Administrative divisions nine provinces and six cities with provincial status
Political parties New Korea Party (NKP, formerly Democratic Liberal Party (DLP)),

right of centre; National Congress for New Politics (NCNP), centre left; Democratic Party (DP), left of centre; New Democratic Party (NDP), centrist, pro-private enterprise; United Liberal Democratic Party (ULD), ultra-conservative, pro-private enterprise
Armed forces 633,000 (1995)
Conscription 26 months (army); 30 months (navy and air force)
Death penalty retained and used for ordinary crimes
Defence spend (% GDP) 3.4 (1995)
Education spend (% GNP) 4.5 (1993–94)
Health spend (% GDP) 2.7 (1990)

Economy and resources

Currency won
GDP ($ US) 376.5 billion (1994)
Real GDP per capita (PPP) ($ US) 10,656 (1994)
GDP growth rate 8.4% (1994); 7.2% (1990–95)
Average annual inflation 6.2% (1994); 6.8% (1985–95)
Foreign debt ($ US) 54.5 billion (1994)
Trading partners USA, Japan, Germany, Saudi Arabia, Australia, Hong Kong, Singapore, China
Resources coal, iron ore, tungsten, gold, molybdenum, graphite, fluorite, natural gas, hydroelectric power, fish
Industries electrical machinery, transport equipment (principally motor vehicles and shipbuilding), chemical products, textiles and clothing, iron and steel, electronics equipment, food processing, tourism
Exports electrical machinery, textiles, clothing, footwear, telecommunications and sound equipment, chemical products, ships ('Invisible export' – overseas construction work). Principal market: USA 16.7% (1996)
Imports machinery and transport equipment (especially electrical machinery), petroleum and petroleum products, grain and foodstuffs, steel, chemical products, basic manufactures. Principal source: USA 22.2% (1996)
Arable land 19% (1993)
Agricultural products rice, maize, barley, potatoes, sweet potatoes, fruit; livestock (pigs and cattle)

Population and society

Population 45,314,000 (1996e)
Population growth rate 1% (1990–95); 0.8% (2000–05)
Population density (per sq km) 458 (1996e)
Urban population (% of total) 81 (1995)
Age distribution (% of total population) <15 37.1%, 15–65 57.1%, >65 5.8% (1995)
Ethnic distribution with the exception of a small Nationalist Chinese minority, the population is almost entirely of Korean descent
Language Korean
Religions Shamanist, Buddhist, Confucian, Protestant, Roman Catholic
Education (compulsory years) 9
Literacy rate 99% (men); 93% (women) (1995e)
Labour force 46% of population: 18% agriculture, 35% industry, 47% services

(1990)
Unemployment 2% (1996)
Life expectancy 69 (men); 76 (women) (1995–2000)
Child mortality rate (under 5, per 1,000 live births) 9 (1995)
Physicians 1 per 888 people (1993)
Hospital beds 1 per 389 people (1993)
TV sets (per 1,000 people) 334 (1995)
Radios (per 1,000 people) 1,024 (1995)

Transport

Airports international airports: Seoul (Kimpo), Pusan (Kim Hae), Cheju; three principal domestic airports; total passenger km: 39,579 mil (1994)
Railroads total length: 3,081 km/1,915 mi; total passenger km: 31,912 mil (1994)
Roads total road network: 74,235 km/46,130 mi, of which 76% paved (1995); passenger cars: 134 per 1,000 people (1995)

Chronology

2333 BC Traditional date of founding of Korean state by Tangun (mythical son from union of bear-woman and god).
1122 BC Ancient texts record founding of kingdom in Korea by Chinese nobleman Kija.
194 BC NW Korea united under warlord, Wiman.
108 BC Korea conquered by Chinese.
1st–7th centuries AD Three Korean kingdoms – Koguryo, Paekche, and Silla – competed for supremacy.
668 Korean peninsula unified by Buddhist Silla kingdom; culture combining Chinese and Korean elements flourished.
935 Silla dynasty overthrown by Wang Kon of Koguryo, who founded Koryo dynasty in its place.
1258 Korea accepted overlordship of Mongol Yüan Empire.
1392 Yi dynasty founded by Gen Yi Song-gye, vassal of Chinese Ming Empire; Confucianism replaced Buddhism as official creed; extreme conservatism characterized Korean society.
1592 and 1597 Japanese invasions repulsed by Korea.
1636 Manchu invasion forced Korea to sever ties with Ming dynasty.
18th–19th centuries Korea resisted change in political and economic life and rejected contact with Europeans.
1864 Attempts to reform government and strengthen army by Taewongun (who

ruled in name of his son, King Kojong); converts to Christianity persecuted.
1873 Taewongun forced to cede power to Queen Min; reforms reversed; government authority collapsed.
1882 Chinese occupied Seoul and installed governor.
1894–95 Sino-Japanese War: Japan forced China to recognize independence of Korea; Korea fell to Japanese influence.
1896 Fearing for his life, King Kojong sought protection of Russian legation.
1904–05 Russo-Japanese War: Japan ended Russian influence in Korea.
1910 Korea formally annexed by Japan; Japanese settlers introduced modern industry and agriculture; Korean language banned.
1919 'Samil' nationalist movement suppressed by Japanese.
1945 After defeat of Japan in World War II, Russia occupied regions of Korea N of 38th parallel (demarcation line agreed at Yalta Conference) and US occupied regions S of it.
1948 USSR refused to permit United Nations (UN) supervision of elections in N zone; S zone became independent as Republic of Korea, with Syngman Rhee as president.
1950 North Korea invaded South Korea; UN forces (mainly from USA) intervened to defend South Korea; China intervened in support of North Korea.
1953 Korean War ended with armistice which restored 38th parallel; no peace treaty agreed and US troops remained in South Korea.
1960 President Syngman Rhee forced to resign by student-led protests against corruption and fraudulent elections.
1961 Military coup placed Gen Park Chung Hee in power; major programme of industrial development began.
1972 Martial law imposed; presidential powers increased.
1979 President Park assassinated; interim government of President Choi Kyu-Hah introduced liberalizing reforms.
1979 Gen Chun Doo Hwan assumed power after anti-government riots; Korea emerged as leading shipbuilding nation and exporter of electronic goods.
1987 Constitution made more democratic as a result of Liberal pressure; ruling Democratic Justice Party (DJP) candidate Roh Tae Woo elected president amid allegations of fraud.
1988 Olympic Games held in Seoul.

1991 Large-scale anti-government protests forcibly suppressed; South Korea joined UN.
1992 South Korea established diplomatic relations with China; Kim Young Sam elected president.

1994 US military presence stepped up in response to perceived threat from North Korea.
1996 Roh Tae Woo and Chun Doo Hwan charged with treason for alleged role in massacre of demonstrators 1980.

1997 South Korea admitted to OECD. Prison sentences on former presidents Roh Tae Woo and Chun Doo Hwan upheld on appeal. Koh Kun appointed prime minister.

Practical information

Visa requirements UK: visa not required for a stay of up to 90 days. USA: visa not required
Embassy in the UK 4 Palace Gate, London W8 5NF. Tel: (0171) 581 0247; fax: (0171) 581 8076
British embassy 4 Chung-dong, Chung-ku, Seoul 100. Tel: (2) 735 7341/3; fax: (2) 733 8368
Embassy in the USA 2450 Massachusetts Avenue NW, Washington, DC 20008. Tel: (202) 939 5600, 524 9273
American embassy 82 Sejong-Ro, Chongro-ku, Seoul. Tel: (2) 397 4114; fax: (2) 738 8845

Chamber of commerce Korean Chamber of Commerce and Industry, PO Box 25, 45 4-ka, Namdaemun-no, Chung-ku, Seoul 100.Tel: (2) 316 3114; fax: (2) 757 9475
Office hours 0830–1800 Mon–Fri; 0900–1300 Sat
Banking hours 0930–1630 Mon–Fri; 0930–1330 Sat
Time difference GMT +9
Chief tourist attractions historic sites; mountain scenery; Cheju Island is a popular resort
Major holidays 1–3 January, 1, 10 March, 5 May, 6 June, 17 July, 15 August, 1, 3, 9 October, 25 December; variable: New Year (Chinese, January/February), Lord Buddha's Birthday (May), Moon Festival (September/October)

Kuwait State of

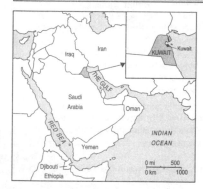

National name *Dowlat al Kuwait*
Area 17,819 sq km/6,879 sq mi
Capital Kuwait (also chief port)
Major towns/cities as-Salimiya, Hawalli, Faranawiya, Abraq Kheetan, Jahra, Ahmadi, Fahaheel
Physical features hot desert; islands of Failaka, Bubiyan, and Warba at NE corner of Arabian Peninsula

Government

Head of state Sheikh Jabir al-Ahmad al-Jabir as-Sabah from 1977
Head of government Crown Prince Sheikh Saad al-Abdullah as-Salinas as-Sabah from 1978
Political system absolute monarchy
Administrative divisions five governates
Political parties none
Armed forces 16,600 (1995)
Conscription compulsory for two years
Death penalty retained and used for ordinary crimes

Defence spend (% GDP) 11.8 (1995)
Education spend (% GNP) 5.6 (1993–94)
Health spend (% GDP) 3.5 (1994)

Economy and resources

Currency Kuwaiti dinar
GDP ($ US) 26.7 billion (1995)
Real GDP per capita (PPP) ($ US) 21,630 (1995)
GDP growth rate –4% (1994); 12.2% (1990–95)
Average annual inflation 4.5% (1995); –0.5 (1985–95)
Trading partners USA, Japan, Germany, France, Saudi Arabia, United Arab Emirates, India, UK, Italy
Resources petroleum, natural gas, mineral water
Industries petroleum refining, petrochemicals, food processing, gases, construction
Exports petroleum and petroleum products (accounted for more than 93% of export revenue 1994), chemical fertilizer, gas (natural and manufactured), basic manufactures. Principal market: Japan 23.5% (1996)
Imports machinery and transport equipment, basic manufactures (especially iron, steel, and textiles) and other manufactured goods, live animals and food. Principal source: USA 16.3% (1996)
Arable land 0.3% (1993)
Agricultural products melons, tomatoes, cucumbers, onions; livestock rearing (poultry); fishing

Population and society

Population 1,687,000 (1996e)
Population growth rate –6.5% (1990–95); 2.5% (2000–05)
Population density (per sq km) 95 (1996e)
Urban population (% of total) 97 (1995)
Age distribution (% of total population) <15 39.8%, 15–65 58.5%, >65 1.7% (1995)
Ethnic distribution about 42% Kuwaiti, 40% non-Kuwaiti Arab, 5% Indian and Pakistani, 4% Iranian
Languages Arabic (official) 78%, Kurdish 10%, Farsi 4%, English
Religions Sunni Muslim, Shi'ite Muslim, Christian
Education (compulsory years) 8
Literacy rate 61% (men); 67% (women) (1995e)
Labour force 42% of population: 1% agriculture, 25% industry, 74% services (1990)
Unemployment 0.5% (1995e)
Life expectancy 74 (men); 78 (women) (1995–2000)
Child mortality rate (under 5, per 1,000 live births) 14 (1995)
Physicians 1 per 581 people (1993)
Hospital beds 1 per 350 people (1993)
TV sets (per 1,000 people) 370 (1995)
Radios (per 1,000 people) 473 (1995)

Transport

Airports international airports: Kuwait City; total passenger km: 4,509 mil (1994)

Railroads none
Roads total road network: 4,360 km/
2,709 mi, of which 80.5% paved (1995e);
passenger cars: 358.7 per 1,000 people
(1993e)

Chronology

c. 3000 BC Archaeological evidence
suggests that coastal parts of Kuwait may
have been part of a commercial
civilization contemporary with the
Sumerian, based in Mesopotamia (the
Tigris and Euphrates valley area of Iraq).
c. 323 BC Visited by Greek colonists at
time of Alexander the Great.
7th century AD Islam introduced.
late 16th century Fell under nominal
control of the Turkish Ottoman Empire.
1710 Control was assumed by the Utab, a
member of the Anaza tribal confederation
in N Arabia, and Kuwait city was founded,
soon developing from a fishing village into
an important port.
1756 Autonomous sheikdom of Kuwait
founded by Abd Rahman of the al-Sabah
family, a branch of the Utab.
1776 British East India Company set up a
base in the Gulf.
1899 Concerned at the potential threat of
growing Ottoman and German influence,

Britain signed a treaty with Kuwait,
establishing a self-governing protectorate
in which the emir received an annual
subsidy from Britain in return for agreeing
not to alienate any territory to a foreign
power.
1914 Britain recognized Kuwait as an
'independent government under British
protection'.
1922–33 Agreement on frontiers with Iraq,
to the N, and Nejd (later Saudi Arabia) to
the SW.
1938 Oil discovered; large-scale
exploitation after World War II transformed
the economy.
1961 Full independence achieved from
Britain, with Sheik Abdullah al-Salem al-
Sabah as emir. Attempted Iraqi invasion
discouraged by dispatch of British troops
to the Gulf.
1962 Constitution introduced, with
franchise restricted to 10% of the
population.
1965 Sheik Abdullah died; succeeded by
his brother, Sheik Sabah al-Salem al-
Sabah.
1977 Sheik Sabah died; succeeded by
Crown Prince Jabir. National Assembly
dissolved.
1981 National Assembly was
reconstituted.

1983 Shi'ite guerrillas bombed targets in
Kuwait; 17 arrested.
1986 National assembly dissolved.
1987 Kuwaiti oil tankers reflagged,
received US Navy protection; missile
attacks by Iran.
1988 Aircraft hijacked by pro-Iranian
Shi'ites demanding release of convicted
guerrillas; Kuwait refused.
1989 Two of the convicted guerrillas
released.
1990 Prodemocracy demonstrations
suppressed. Kuwait annexed by Iraq in
Aug, causing extensive damage to
property and environment. Emir set up
government in exile in Saudi Arabia.
1991 US-led coalition forces defeated
Iraqi forces in Kuwait during the Gulf War.
New government omitted any opposition
representatives.
1992 Reconstituted national assembly
elected, with opposition nominees,
including Islamic candidates, winning
majority of seats.
1993 Incursions by Iraq into Kuwait
repelled by US-led air strikes on Iraqi
military sites.
1994 Massing of Iraqi troops on Kuwait
border prompted US-led response. Iraqi
president Saddam Hussein publicly
renounced claim to Kuwait.

Practical information

Visa requirements UK: visa required. USA: visa required
Embassy in the UK 45–46 Queen's Gate, London
SW7 5HR. Tel: (0171) 589 4533; fax: (0171) 589 7183
British embassy PO Box 2, Arabian Gulf Street, 13001 Safat,
Kuwait City. Tel: (965) 240 3324/5/6; fax: (965) 240 7395
Embassy in the USA 2940 Tilden Street NW, Washington,
DC 20008. Tel: (202) 966 0702; fax: (202) 966 0517
American embassy Bneid al-Gar (opposite Kuwait
International Hotel), Kuwait City. Tel: 242 4151–9;
fax: 244 2855

Chamber of commerce Kuwait Chamber of Commerce and
Industry, PO Box 775, Chamber's Building, Ali as-Salem
Street, 13008 Safat, Kuwait City. Tel: (965) 243 3864; fax:
(965) 240 4110
Office hours 0700–1400 Sat–Wed (winter); 0730–1400
Sat–Wed (summer)
Banking hours 0800–1200 Sun–Thu
Time difference GMT +3
Major holidays 1 January, 25 February (3 days); variable:
Eid-ul-Adha (3 days), end of Ramadan (3 days), New Year
(Muslim), Prophet's Birthday, Ascension of the Prophet
(March/April), Standing on Mount Arafat (August)

Kyrgyzstan Republic of

National name *Kyrgyz Respublikasy*
Area 198,500 sq km/76,640 sq mi
Capital Bishkek (formerly Frunze)
Major towns/cities Osh, Przhevalsk,
Kyzyl-Kiya, Tokmak, Djalal-Abad
Physical features mountainous, an
extension of the Tian Shan range

Government

Head of state Askar Akayev from 1990
Head of government Apas Jumagulov
from 1993
Political system emergent democracy
Administrative divisions six provinces

Political parties Party of Communists of
Kyrgyzstan (banned 1991–92); Ata
Meken, Kyrgyz-nationalist; Erkin
Kyrgyzstan, Kyrgyz-nationalist; Social
Democratic Party, nationalist, pro-Akayev;
Democratic Movement of Kyrgyzstan,
nationalist reformist
Armed forces 7,000 (1995)
Conscription compulsory for 12–18
months
Death penalty retained and used for
ordinary crimes
Defence spend (% GDP) 3.5 (1995)
Education spend (% GNP) 6.5 (1994)

Health spend (% GDP) 3.2 (1994e)

Economy and resources

Currency som
GDP ($ US) 3 billion (1994)
Real GDP per capita (PPP) ($ US) 1,930 (1994)
GDP growth rate –6.7% (1995)
Average annual inflation 31.9% (1995); 172.3% (1985–95e)
Foreign debt ($ US) 610 million (1995)
Trading partners Russia, Kazakhstan, Uzbekistan, Turkey, China, UK, Cuba, Ukraine
Resources petroleum, natural gas, coal, gold, tin, mercury, antimony, zinc, tungsten, uranium
Industries metallurgy, machinery, electronics and instruments, textiles, food processing (particularly sugar refining), mining
Exports wool, cotton yarn, tobacco, electric power, electronic and engineering products, non-ferrous metallurgy, food and beverages. Principal market: Kazakhstan 28% (1994)
Imports petroleum, natural gas, engineering products, food products. Principal source: Russia 22% (1994)
Arable land 54% (1993)
Agricultural products grain, potatoes, grapes, cotton, tobacco, sugar beet, hemp, kenat, kendyr, medicinal plants; livestock rearing (sheep, cattle, goats, yaks, and horses) is the mainstay of agricultural activity

Population and society

Population 4,469,000 (1996e)
Population growth rate 1.7% (1990–95); 1.5% (2000–05)
Population density (per sq km) 23 (1996e)
Urban population (% of total) 39 (1995)
Age distribution (% of total population) <15 37.1%, 15–65 57.1%, >65 5.8% (1995)
Ethnic distribution 53% ethnic Kyrgyz, 22% Russian, 13% Uzbek, 3% Ukrainian, and 2% German

Language Kyrgyz, a Turkic language
Religion Sunni Muslim
Education (compulsory years) 9
Literacy rate 97% (men); 97% (women) (1995e)
Labour force 43% agriculture, 21% industry, 36% services (1994)
Unemployment 4.4% (1996)
Life expectancy 67 (men); 74 (women) (1995–2000)
Child mortality rate (under 5, per 1,000 live births) 54 (1995)
Physicians 1 per 337 people (1994)
Hospital beds 1 per 101 people (1994)
TV sets (per 1,000 people) 34 (1995)
Radios (per 1,000 people) 114 (1995)

Transport

Airports international airports: Bishkek (Bishkek Manas), Osh; three domestic airports; total passenger km: 568 mil (1994)
Railroads total length: 376 km/234 mi; passengers carried: 2.3 mil (1993)
Roads total road network: 18,560 km/ 11,533 mi, of which 68.4% paved (1995e); passenger cars: 35.9 per 1,000 people (1995e)

Chronology

8th century Spread of Islam.
10th century onwards Southward migration of Kyrgyz people from upper Yenisey River region to Tian-Shan region; accelerated following rise of Mongol Empire in 13th century.
13th–14th centuries Part of Mongol Empire.
1685 Came under control of Mongol Oirots following centuries of Turkic rule.
1758 Kyrgyz people became nominal subjects of Chinese Empire, following Oirots' defeat by Chinese rulers, the Manchus.
early 19th century Came under suzerainty of Khanate (chieftaincy) of Kokand, to the W.
1864–76 Incorporated into tsarist Russian Empire.
1916–17 Many Kyrgyz migrated to China

after Russian suppression of rebellion in Central Asia and outbreak of civil war following 1917 October Revolution in Russia, with local armed guerrillas (*basmachi*) resisting Bolshevik Red Army.
1917–1924 Part of independent Turkestan republic.
1920s Land reforms resulted in settlement of many formerly nomadic Kyrgyz; literacy and education improved.
1924 Became autonomous republic within USSR.
1930s Agricultural collectivization programme provoked *basmachi* resistance and local 'nationalist communists' were purged from Kyrgyz Communist Party (KCP).
1936 Became full union republic within USSR.
1990 State of emergency imposed in Bishkek after ethnic clashes. Askar Akayev, a reform communist, chosen as president.
1991 Akayev condemned attempted coup in Moscow against the reformist Mikhail Gorbachev; Kyrgyzstan joined new Commonwealth of Independent States (CIS); independence recognized by USA.
1992 Joined the United Nations and Conference on Security and Cooperation in Europe (CSCE; now the Organization on Security and Cooperation in Europe, OSCE). Market-centred economic reform programme instituted.
1994 National referenda overwhelmingly supported Akayev's presidency. Joined Central Asian Union, with Kazakhstan and Uzbekistan.
1995 Pro-Akayev independents successful in elections to a new bicameral legislature.
1996 Constitutional amendment increased powers of president. Agreement with Kazakhstan and Uzbekistan to create single economic market.
1997 Private ownership of land legalized but privatization programme suspended. Agreement on border controls with Russia.

Practical information

Visa requirements UK: visa not required. USA: visa not required
Embassy for the UK 32 rue de Châtelain, 1050 Brussels, Belgium. Tel: (2) 627 1916; fax: (2) 627 1900
British embassy the British Embassy in Almaty (see Kazakhstan) deals with enquiries relating to Kyrgyzstan
Embassy in the USA (temporary) Suite 706, 1511 K Street NW, Washington, DC 20005. Tel: (202) 347 3732; fax: (202) 347 3718
American embassy Erkindik Prospekt 66, Bishkek 720002.

Tel: (3312) 222 920/777/631/473; fax: (3312) 223 551
Chamber of commerce Kyrgyz Chamber of Commerce and Industry, Kievskaya 107, 720001 Bishkek. Tel: (3312) 210 574; fax: (3312) 210 575
Office hours 0900–1800 Mon–Sat
Banking hours usually 0930–1730 Mon–Fri
Time difference GMT +5
Chief tourist attractions tourist facilities are limited – the country is visited mostly by mountaineers; spectacular and largely unspoilt mountain scenery; great crater lake of Issyk-Kul; several historical and cultural sites
Major holidays 1, 7 January, 8, 21 March, 1, 9 May, 31 August

Laos Lao People's Democratic Republic

National name *Saathiaranagroat Prachhathippatay Prachhachhon Lao*
Area 236,790 sq km/91,424 sq mi
Capital Vientiane
Major towns/cities Louangphrabang (the former royal capital), Pakse, Savannakhet
Physical features landlocked state with high mountains in E; Mekong River in W; rainforest covers nearly 60% of land

Government

Head of state Nouhak Phoumsavan from 1992
Head of government General Khamtay Siphandon from1991
Political system communist, one-party state
Administrative divisions 17 provinces
Political party Lao People's Revolutionary Party (LPRP, the only legal party)
Armed forces 37,000 (1995)
Conscription military service is compulsory for a minimum of 18 months
Death penalty retained and used for ordinary crimes
Defence spend (% GDP) 4.2 (1995)
Education spend (% GNP) 2.3 (1993–94)
Health spend (% GDP) 1 (1990)

Economy and resources

Currency new kip
GDP ($ US) 1.5 billion (1994)
Real GDP per capita (PPP) ($ US) 2,484 (1994)
GDP growth rate 8.4% (1994)
Average annual inflation 19.6% (1995); 22.6 (1985–95e)
Foreign debt ($ US) 2.16 billion (1995)

Trading partners Thailand, Japan, Germany, France, China, Italy
Resources coal, tin, gypsum, baryte, lead, zinc, nickel, potash, iron ore; small quantities of gold, silver, and precious stones
Industries processing of agricultural produce, sawmilling, textiles and garments, handicrafts, basic consumer goods
Exports timber, textiles and garments, motorcycles, electricity, coffee, tin, gypsum. Principal market: Thailand 20.8% (1994)
Imports food (particularly rice and sugar), mineral fuels, machinery and transport equipment, cement, cotton yarn. Principal source: Thailand 48.5% (1994)
Arable land 3.3% (1993)
Agricultural products rice, maize, tobacco, cotton, coffee, sugar cane, cassava, potatoes; sweet potatoes; livestock rearing (pigs, poultry, and cattle); fishing; forest resources including valuable wood such as Teruk (logging suspended 1991 to preserve the forest area); opium is produced but its manufacture is controlled by the state

Population and society

Population 5,035,000 (1996e)
Population growth rate 3% (1990–95); 2.6% (2000–05)
Population density (per sq km) 21 (1996e)
Urban population (% of total) 22 (1995)
Age distribution (% of total population) <15 44.8%, 15–65 52.2%, >65 3% (1995)
Ethnic distribution 60% Laotian, predominantly Lao Lum, 35% hill dwellers, and 5% Vietnamese and Chinese
Languages Lao (official), French, English
Religions Theravāda Buddhist 85%, animist beliefs among mountain dwellers
Education (compulsory years) 5
Literacy rate 92% (men); 76% (women) (1995e)
Labour force 50% of population: 78% agriculture, 6% industry, 16% services (1990)
Unemployment 3% (1993)
Life expectancy 52 (men); 55 (women) (1995–2000)
Child mortality rate (under 5, per 1,000 live births) 134 (1995)

Physicians 1 per 4,545 person (1991)
Hospital beds 1 per 363 people (1991)
TV sets (per 1,000 people) 9 (1995)
Radios (per 1,000 people) 129 (1995)

Transport

Airports international airports: Vientiane (Wattai); three domestic airports; total passenger km: 209 mil (1994)
Railroads none
Roads total road network: 18,153 km/ 11,280 mi, of which 13.8% paved (1995); passenger cars: 3.6 per 1,000 people (1995e)

Chronology

c. 2000–500 BC Early Bronze Age civilizations in central Mekong River and Plain of Jars regions.
5th–8th centuries Occupied by immigrants from S China.
8th century onwards Theravāda Buddhism spread by Mon monks.
9th–13th centuries Part of the sophisticated Khmer Empire, centred on Angkor in Cambodia.
12th century Small independent principalities, notably Louangphrabang, established by Lao invaders from Thailand and Yunnan, S China; they adopted Buddhism.
14th century United by King Fa Ngum; the first independent Laotian state, Lan Xang, formed. It was to dominate for four centuries, broken only by a period of Burmese rule 1574–1637.
17th century First visited by Europeans.
1713 The Lan Xang kingdom split into three separate kingdoms, Louangphrabang, Vientiane, and Champassac, which became tributaries of Siam (Thailand) from the late 18th century.
1893–1945 Laos was a French protectorate, comprising the three principalities of Louangphrabang, Vientiane, and Champassac.
1945 Temporarily occupied by Japan.
1946 Retaken by France, despite opposition by the Chinese-backed Lao Issara (Free Laos) nationalist movement.
1950 Granted semi-autonomy in French Union, as an associated state under the constitutional monarchy of the king of Louangphrabang.
1954 Independence achieved from France under the Geneva Agreements, but civil war broke out between a

moderate royalist faction of the Lao Issara, led by Prince Souvanna Phouma, and the communist Chinese-backed Pathet Lao (Land of the Lao) led by Prince Souphanouvong (Souvanna's half-brother).

1957 Coalition government, headed by Souvanna Phouma, established by Vientiane Agreement.

1959 Savang Vatthana became king.

1960 Right-wing pro-Western government seized power, headed by Prince Boun Gum.

1962 Geneva Agreement established new coalition government, led by Souvanna Phouma, but civil war continued, the Pathet Lao receiving backing from the North Vietnamese, and Souvanna Phouma from the USA.

1973 Vientiane cease-fire agreement divided the country between the communists and the Souvanna Phouma regime and brought the withdrawal of US, Thai, and North Vietnamese forces.

1975 Communists seized power; republic proclaimed, with Prince Souphanouvong as head of state and the Communist Party leader Kaysone Phomvihane as the controlling prime minister.

1979 Food shortages and the flight of 250,000 refugees to Thailand led to an easing of the drive towards nationalization and agricultural collectivization.

1985 Greater economic liberalization received encouragement from the Soviet Union's reformist leader Mikhail Gorbachev.

1989 First assembly elections since communist takeover; Vietnamese troops withdrawn from the country.

1991 Kaysone Phomvihane was elected president and the army commander General Khamtay Siphandon became prime minister. Security and cooperation pact signed with Thailand, and agreement reached on phased repatriation of Laotian refugees.

1992 Phomvihane died; replaced as president by Nouhak Phoumsavan.

1995 The US lifted its 20-year aid embargo.

1996 Military tightened its grip on political affairs; but inward investment and private enterprise continued to be encouraged, fuelling economic expansion.

1997 Membership of Association of South East Asian Nations (ASEAN) announced.

Practical information

Visa requirements UK: visa required. USA: visa required
Embassy for the UK 74 avenue Raymond Poincaré, 75116 Paris, France. Tel: (1) 4553 0298; fax: (1) 4727 5789
British embassy Laos has no diplomatic representation in the UK; the British Embassy in Bangkok (see Thailand) deals with enquiries relating to Laos
Embassy in the USA 2222 S Street NW, Washington, DC 20008. Tel: (202) 332 6416/7; fax: (202) 332 4923
American embassy Rue Bartholonie, BP 114, Vientiane.

Tel: (21) 212 581/2/5; fax: (21) 212 584
Chamber of commerce Lao National Chamber of Commerce and Industry, BP 4596, rue Phonsay, Vientiane. Tel: (21) 412 392; fax: (21) 414 383
Office hours 0800–1200 and 1400–1700 Mon–Fri; 0800–1200 Sat
Banking hours 0900–1630 Mon–Fri
Time difference GMT +7
Chief tourist attractions spectacular scenery; ancient pagodas and temples; wildlife
Major holidays 24 January, 13–15 April, 1 May, 2 December

Latvia Republic of

National name *Latvijas Republika*
Area 63,700 sq km/24,594 sq mi
Capital Riga
Major towns/cities Daugavpils, Leipāja, Jurmala, Jelgava, Ventspils
Major ports Ventspils, Leipāja
Physical features wooded lowland (highest point 312 m/1,024 ft), marshes, lakes; 472 km/293 mi of coastline; mild climate

Government

Head of state Guntis Ulmanis from 1993
Head of government Guntar Krasts from 1997
Political system emergent democratic republic
Administrative divisions 26 districts and seven municipalities
Political parties Latvian Way, right of centre; Latvian National and Conservative Party (LNNK), right wing, nationalist; Economic-Political Union (formerly known as Harmony for Latvia and Rebirth of the National Economy), centrist; Ravnopravie (Equal Rights), centrist; For the Fatherland and Freedom (FFF), extreme nationalist; Latvian Peasants' Union (LZS), rural based, centre left; Union of Christian Democrats, centre right; Democratic Centre Party, centrist; Movement for Latvia, pro-Russian, populist; Master in Your Own Home (Saimnieks), ex-communist, populist; Latvian National Party of Reforms, right of centre nationalist coalition

Armed forces 7,000 (1995)
Conscription compulsory for 18 months
Death penalty retained and used for ordinary crimes
Defence spend (% GDP) 3.2 (1995)
Education spend (% GNP) 6.4 (1994)

Economy and resources

Currency lat
GDP ($ US) 6 billion (1994)
Real GDP per capita (PPP) ($ US) 3,332 (1994)
GDP growth rate 1.5% (1996); −13.7% (1990–95)
Average annual inflation 18% (1996); 73.2% (1985–95)
Foreign debt ($ US) 462 million (1995)
Trading partners Russia, Germany, Lithuania, Finland, Sweden, Estonia
Resources peat, gypsum, dolomite, limestone, amber, gravel, sand
Industries food processing, machinery and equipment (major producer of electric railway passenger cars and long-distance

telephone exchanges), chemicals and chemical products, sawn timber, paper and woollen goods

Exports timber and timber products, textiles, food and agricultural products, machinery and electrical equipment, metal industry products. Principal market: Russia 22.8% (1996)

Imports mineral fuels and products, machinery and electrical equipment, chemical industry products. Principal source: Russia 20.2% (1996)

Arable land 41% (1993)

Agricultural products oats, barley, rye, potatoes, flax; cattle and dairy farming and pig breeding are the chief agricultural occupations

Population and society

Population 2,504,000 (1996e)

Population growth rate –0.9% (1990–95); –0.5% (2000–05)

Population density (per sq km) 39 (1996e)

Urban population (% of total) 73 (1995)

Age distribution (% of total population) <15 20.6%, 15–65 66.1%, >65 13.3% (1995)

Ethnic distribution 53% of Latvian ethnic descent, 34% ethnic Russian, 4% Belarusian, 3% Ukrainian, 2% Polish, 1% Lithuanian

Language Latvian

Religions Lutheran, Roman Catholic, Russian Orthodox

Education (compulsory years) 9

Literacy rate 99% (men); 99% (women) (1995e)

Labour force 19.5% agriculture, 28.5% industry, 52% services (1993)

Unemployment 7% (1996)

Life expectancy 63 (men); 75 (women) (1995–2000)

Child mortality rate (under 5, per 1,000 live births) 26 (1995)

Physicians 1 per 293 people (1994)

Hospital beds 1 per 84 people (1994)

TV sets (per 1,000 people) 477 (1995)

Radios (per 1,000 people) 678 (1995)

Transport

Airports international airports: Riga

(Spilva), Jelgava; total passenger km: 145 mil (1994)

Railroads total length: 2,703 km/1,680 mi; total passenger km: 1,794 mil (1994)

Roads total road network: 60,046 km/ 37,313 mi, of which 38.3% paved (1995); passenger cars: 132.7 per 1,000 people (1995)

Chronology

9th–10th centuries Invaded by Vikings and Russians.

13th century Conquered by crusading German Teutonic Knights, who named the area Livonia and converted population to Christianity; Riga joined Hanseatic League, a N European union of commercial towns.

1520s Lutheranism established as a result of the Reformation.

16th–17th centuries Successively under Polish, Lithuanian, and Swedish rule.

1721 Tsarist Russia took control.

1819 Serfdom abolished.

1900s Emergence of independence movement.

1914–18 Under partial German occupation during World War I.

1918–19 Independence proclaimed and achieved after Russian Red Army troops expelled by German, Polish, and Latvian forces.

1920s Land reforms introduced by Farmers' Union government of Karlis Ulmanis.

1934 Democracy overthrown and, at time of economic depression, Ulmanis established autocratic regime; Baltic Entente mutual defence pact with Estonia and Lithuania.

1940 Incorporated into Soviet Union (USSR) as constituent republic, following secret German–Soviet agreement.

1941–44 Occupied by Germany.

1944 USSR regained control; mass deportations of Latvians to Central Asia, followed by immigration of ethnic Russians; agricultural collectivization.

1960s and 1970s Extreme repression of Latvian cultural and literary life.

1980s Nationalist dissent began to grow, influenced by the Polish Solidarity

movement and Mikhail Gorbachev's *glasnost* ('openness') initiative in the USSR.

1988 Latvian Popular Front established to campaign for independence. Prewar flag readopted; official status given to Latvian language.

1989 Latvian parliament passed sovereignty declaration.

1990 Popular Front secured majority in local elections and its leader, Ivan Godmanir, became prime minister. Latvian Communist Party split into pro-independence and pro-Moscow wings. Entered 'transitional period of independence'; Baltic Council reformed.

1991 Soviet troops briefly seized key installations in Riga. Overwhelming vote for independence in referendum. Full independence achieved following failure of anti-Gorbachev coup attempt in Moscow; CP outlawed. Joined United Nations (UN); market-centred economic reform programme instituted.

1992 Curbing of rights of noncitizens prompted Russia to request minority protection by UN.

1993 Right-of-centre Latvian Way won most seats in general election, and Valdis Birkavs became premier; free-trade agreement with Estonia and Lithuania.

1994 Last Russian troops departed. Birkavs replaced by Maris Gailis; economic growth resumed.

1995 Trade and cooperation agreement signed with European Union (EU). General election produced 'hung parliament', in which extremist parties received most support. Latvia applied officially for EU membership. Independent Andris Skele became prime minister.

1996 Guntis Ulmanis re-elected president. Finance minister and deputy prime minister resigned from eight-party coalition.

1997 New political party formed, Latvian National Party of Reforms. Prime Minister Skele replaced by Guntar Krasts.

Practical information

Visa requirements UK: visa not required. USA: visa required

Embassy in the UK 45 Nottingham Place, London W1M 3FE. Tel: (0171) 312 0040; fax: (0171) 312 0042

British embassy Alunana iela 5, LV-1010 Riga. Tel: (371) 782 8126; fax: (371) 733 8132

Embassy in the USA 4325 17th Street NW, Washington, DC 20011. Tel: (202) 726 8213/4; fax: (202) 726 6785

American embassy Raina Boulevard 7, LV-1510 Riga. Tel: (371) 210 005; fax: (371) 226 530

Chamber of commerce Latvian Chamber of Commerce and Industry, Brivibas bulvaris 21, LV-1849 Riga. Tel: (371) 722 5595; fax: (371) 782 0092

Office hours 0830–1730 Mon–Fri

Banking hours 1000–1800 Mon–Fri

Time difference GMT +2

Chief tourist attractions historic centre of Riga, with medieval and Art Nouveau architecture; extensive beaches on Baltic coast; Gauja National Park; winter-sports facilities at Sigulda

Major holidays 1 January, 1 May, 23–24 June, 18 November, 25–26 December; variable: Good Friday

Lebanon Republic of

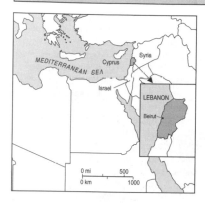

National name *Jumhouria al-Lubnaniya*
Area 10,452 sq km/4,035 sq mi
Capital Beirut (and port)
Major towns/cities Tripoli, Zahlé, Baabda, Baalbek, Jezzine
Major ports Tripoli, Tyre, Sidon, Jounie
Physical features narrow coastal plain; fertile Bekka valley running N–S between Lebanon and Anti-Lebanon mountain ranges

Government

Head of state Elias Hrawi from 1989
Head of government Rafik al-Hariri from 1992
Political system emergent democratic republic
Administrative divisions six governates
Political parties Phalangist Party, Christian, radical, nationalist; Progressive Socialist Party (PSP), Druse, moderate, socialist; National Liberal Party (NLP), Maronite, centre left; National Bloc, Maronite, moderate; Lebanese Communist Party (PCL), nationalist, communist; Parliamentary Democratic Front, Sunni Muslim, centrist
Armed forces 44,300 (1995); in 1995 there were 30,000 Syrian troops and the pro-Israeli South Lebanese army numbered 2,500
Conscription compulsory for 12 months
Death penalty retained and used for ordinary crimes
Defence spend (% GDP) 5.3 (1995)
Education spend (% GNP) 1.5 (1994)

Economy and resources

Currency Lebanese pound
GDP ($ US) 10.31 billion (1994)
Real GDP per capita (PPP) ($ US) 4,863 (1994)

GDP growth rate 8.5% (1994)
Average annual inflation 12% (1994); 45.8% (1985–95e)
Foreign debt ($ US) 3 billion (1995)
Trading partners United Arab Emirates, Italy, Saudi Arabia, Syria, Germany, USA, France, Kuwait, Jordan
Resources there are no commercially viable mineral deposits; small reserves of lignite and iron ore
Industries food processing, petroleum refining, textiles, furniture and woodworking, paper and paper products
Exports paper products, textiles, fruit and vegetables, jewellery. Principal market: UAE 28.7% (1995)
Imports electrical equipment, vehicles, petroleum, metals, machinery, consumer goods. Principal source: Italy 13% (1995)
Arable land 20.8% (1993)
Agricultural products citrus fruits, potatoes, melons, apples, grapes (viticulture is significant), wheat, sugar beet, olives, bananas; livestock rearing (goats and sheep); although illegal, hashish is an important export crop

Population and society

Population 3,084,000 (1996e)
Population growth rate 3.3% (1990–95); 1.5% (2000–05)
Population density (per sq km) 297 (1996e)
Urban population (% of total) 87 (1995)
Age distribution (% of total population) <15 34.1%, 15–65 60.4%, >65 5.5% (1995)
Ethnic distribution about 90% Arab, with Armenian, Assyrian, Jewish, Turkish, and Greek minorities
Languages Arabic (official), French, Armenian, English
Religions Muslim 58% (Shiite 35%, Sunni 23%), Christian 27% (mainly Maronite), Druse 3%; other Christian denominations including Orthodox, Armenian, and Roman Catholic
Education not compulsory
Literacy rate 88% (men); 73% (women) (1995e)
Labour force 31% of population: 7% agriculture, 31% industry, 62% services (1990)
Unemployment 35% (1993e)
Life expectancy 68 (men); 72 (women) (1995–2000)
Child mortality rate (under 5, per 1,000 live births) 40 (1995)
Physicians 1 per 413 people (1991)

Hospital beds 1 per 284 people (1991)
TV sets (per 1,000 people) 366 (1995)
Radios (per 1,000 people) 891 (1995)

Transport

Airports international airports: Beirut (Khaldeh); most major cities have domestic airports; total passenger km: 1,588 mil (1994)
Railroads total length: 222 km/138 mi
Roads total road network: 6,359 km/3,951 mi, of which 95% paved (1995); passenger cars: 733.8 per 1,000 people (1995)

Chronology

5th century BC–1ST century AD Part of the E Mediterranean Phoenician Empire.
1st century Came under Roman rule; Christianity introduced.
635 Islam introduced by Arab tribes, who settled in S Lebanon.
11th century Druse faith developed by local Muslims.
1516 Became part of the Turkish Ottoman Empire.
1860 Massacre of thousands of Christian Maronites by the Muslim Druse led to French intervention.
1920–41 Administered by French under League of Nations mandate.
1943 Independence achieved as a republic, with constitution that enshrined Christian and Muslim power-sharing.
1945 Joined Arab League.
1948–49 Lebanon joined first Arab war against Israel; Palestinian refugees settled in S.
1958 Revolt by radical Muslims opposed to pro-Western policies of Christian president, Camille Chamoun.
1964 Palestine Liberation Organization (PLO) founded in Beirut.
1967 More Palestinian refugees settled in Lebanon following Arab–Israeli war.
1971 PLO expelled from Jordan; established headquarters in Lebanon.
1975 Outbreak of civil war between conservative Christians and leftist Muslims backed by PLO.
1976 Cease-fire agreed; Syrian-dominated Arab deterrent force formed to keep the peace, but considered by Christians as an occupying force.
1978 Israel launched limited invasion of S Lebanon in search of PLO guerrillas. International United Nations

peacekeeping force unable to prevent further fighting.
1979 Part of S Lebanon declared an 'independent free Lebanon' by right-wing army officer.
1982 Bachir Gemayel, a Maronite Christian, elected president but assassinated; he was succeeded by his brother Amin Gemayel. Israel again invaded Lebanon. Palestinians withdrew from Beirut under supervision of international peacekeeping force; PLO moved its headquarters to Tunis.
1983 Agreement reached for withdrawal of Syrian and Israeli troops but abrogated under Syrian pressure; intense fighting between Christian Phalangists and Muslim Druse militias.
1984 Most of international peacekeeping force withdrawn. Radical Muslim militia took control of W Beirut.

1985 Lebanon in chaos; many foreigners taken hostage and Israeli troops withdrawn.
1987 Syrian troops sent into Beirut.
1988 Agreement on Christian successor to Gemayel failed and Gen Michel Aoun appointed to head caretaker military government; Premier Selim el-Hoss set up rival government; threat of partition hung over country.
1989 Gen Aoun declared 'war of liberation' against Syrian occupation; Arab League-sponsored talks resulted in cease-fire and revised constitution recognizing Muslim majority; René Mouhawad assassinated after 17 days as president; Maronite Christian Elias Hrawi named as successor; Aoun occupied presidential palace, rejecting constitution.
1990 Release of Western hostages

began. Gen Aoun, crushed by Syrians, surrendered and legitimate government was restored.
1991 Government extended control to the whole country. Treaty of cooperation with Syria signed.
1992 Remaining Western hostages released. Pro-Syrian administration re-elected with Rafik al-Hariri as prime minister after many Christians boycotted general election.
1993 Israel launched attacks against Shia fundamentalist Hezbollah strongholds in S Lebanon before USA and Syria brokered agreement to avoid use of force.
1996 Israel launched a rocket attack on S Lebanon, in response to Hezbollah activity. USA, Israel, Syria, and Lebanon attempted to broker new cease-fire.

Practical information

Visa requirements UK: visa required. USA: visa required
Embassy in the UK 21 Kensington Palace Gardens, London W8 4QH. (0171) 229 7265; fax: (0171) 243 1699
British embassy British Embassy in West Beirut, Shamma Building, Raoucheh, Ras Beirut. Tel: (1) 812 849; telex: 20465
Embassy in the USA 2560 28th Street NW, Washington, DC 20008. Tel: (202) 939 6300; fax: (202) 939 6324
American embassy Antelias, Beirut. Tel: (1) 402 200, 403 300, 406 650, 406 651, 426 183, 417 774, 889 926; fax: (1) 407 112
Chamber of commerce Beirut Chamber of Commerce and

Industry, PO Box 11-1801, Sanayeh, Beirut. Tel: (1) 349 530; fax: (1) 865 802
Office hours 0800–1300 Mon–Sat (June–October); 0830–1230 and 1500–1800 Mon–Fri; 0830–1230 Sat (November–May)
Banking hours 0800–1400 Mon–Sat
Time difference GMT +2
Chief tourist attractions sunny climate; scenery; historic sites
Major holidays 1 January, 9 February, 1 May, 15 August, 1, 22 November, 25 December; variable: Eid-ul-Adha (3 days), Ashora, Good Friday, Easter Monday, end of Ramadan (3 days), New Year (Muslim), Prophet's Birthday

---

Lesotho Kingdom of

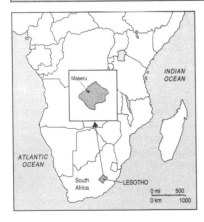

Area 30,355 sq km/11,720 sq mi
Capital Maseru
Major towns/cities Qacha's Nek,

Teyateyaneng, Mafeteng, Hlotse, Roma, Quthing
Physical features mountainous with plateaux, forming part of South Africa's chief watershed

Government

Head of state King Letsie III from 1996
Head of government Ntsu Mokhehle from 1993
Political system constitutional monarchy
Administrative divisions ten districts
Political parties Basotho National Party (BNP), traditionalist, nationalist, right of centre; Basutoland Congress Party (BCP), left of centre
Armed forces 2,000 (1995)
Conscription military service is voluntary

Death penalty retained and used for ordinary crimes
Defence spend (% GDP) 5.5 (1995)
Education spend (% GNP) 4.8 (1993–94)
Health spend (% GDP) 1.2 (1990)

Economy and resources

Currency loti
GDP ($ US) 0.9 billion (1994)
Real GDP per capita (PPP) ($ US) 1,109 (1994)
GDP growth rate 11.9% (1994); 7.5% (1990–95)
Average annual inflation 8.4% (1994); 13.6% (1985–95)
Foreign debt ($ US) 659 million (1995)
Trading partners SACU (South African Customs Union) members: Lesotho, Botswana, Swaziland, Namibia, and

South Africa); Taiwan, Hong Kong, USA, Canada, Italy, and other EU countries
Resources diamonds, uranium, lead, iron ore; believed to have petroleum deposits
Industries food products and beverages, textiles and clothing, mining, baskets, furniture; approximately 35% of Lesotho's adult male labour force was employed in South African mines 1995
Exports clothing, footwear, furniture, food and live animals (cattle), hides, wool and mohair, baskets. Principal market: SACU 51.4% (1994)
Imports food and live animals, machinery and transport equipment, electricity, petroleum products. Principal source: SACU 81.8% (1994)
Arable land 10.5% (1993)
Agricultural products maize, wheat, sorghum, asparagus, peas, and other vegetables; livestock rearing (sheep, goats, and cattle)

Population and society

Population 2,078,000 (1996e)
Population growth rate 2.7% (1990–95); 2.6% (2000–05)
Population density (per sq km) 68 (1996e)
Urban population (% of total) 23 (1995)
Age distribution (% of total population) <15 42.1%, 15–65 53.9%, >65 4% (1995)
Ethnic distribution almost entirely Bantus (of Southern Sotho) or Basotho
Languages Sesotho, English (official), Zulu, Xhosa
Religions Protestant 42%, Roman Catholic 38%, indigenous beliefs
Education (compulsory years) 7
Literacy rate 62% (men); 84% (women) (1995e)
Labour force 76.3% agriculture, 11.1%

industry, 12.6% services (1994e)
Unemployment 50% (1993e)
Life expectancy 61 (men); 66 (women) (1995–2000)
Child mortality rate (under 5, per 1,000 live births) 154 (1995)
Physicians 1 per 14,306 people (1993)
Hospital beds 1 per 789 people (1992)
TV sets (per 1,000 people) 12 (1995)
Radios (per 1,000 people) 37 (1995)

Transport

Airports international airports: Maseru (Moshoeshoe I); 40 airstrips, of which 14 receive charter and regular scheduled air services; total passenger km: 9 mil (1994)
Railroads total length: 2.6 km/1.6 mi (a branch line connecting Maseru with the Bloemfontein – Natal line at Marseilles)
Roads total road network: 4,955 km/3,079 mi, of which 17.9% paved (1995); passenger cars: 5.3 per 1,000 people (1995e)

Chronology

18th century Formerly inhabited by nomadic hunter-gatherer San, Zulu-speaking Ngunis, and Sotho-speaking peoples settled in the region.
1820s Under the name of Basutoland, Sotho nation founded by Moshoeshoe I, who united the people to repulse Zulu attacks from S.
1843 Moshoeshoe I negotiated British protection as tension with South African Boers increased.
1868 Became British territory, administered by Cape Colony (in South Africa) from 1871.
1884 Became British crown colony, after revolt against Cape Colony control; Basuto chiefs allowed to govern according to custom and tradition, but

rich agricultural land W of the Caledon river was lost to South Africa.
1900s Served as a migrant labour reserve for South Africa's mines and farms.
1952 Left-of-centre Basutoland African Congress, later Congress Party (BCP), founded by Ntsu Mokhehle to campaign for self rule.
1966 Independence achieved within Commonwealth, as Kingdom of Lesotho, with Moshoeshoe II as king and Chief Leabua Jonathan of conservative Basotho National Party (BNP) as prime minister.
1970 State of emergency declared; king briefly forced into exile after attempting to increase his authority.
1973 State of emergency lifted; BNP won majority of seats in general election.
1975 Members of ruling party attacked by South African-backed guerrillas, who opposed African National Congress (ANC) guerrillas using Lesotho as a base.
1986 South Africa imposed border blockade, forcing deportation of 60 ANC members. Gen Lekhanya ousted Chief Jonathan in a coup.
1990 Lekhanya replaced in coup by Col Elias Ramaema; Moshoeshoe II dethroned and replaced by son, as King Letsie III.
1993 Free multiparty elections ended military rule; Ntsu Mokhehle (BCP) became prime minister.
1994 Fighting between rival army factions ended by peace deal, brokered by Organization of African Unity.
1995 Letsie abdicated to restore King Moshoeshoe II to the throne.
1996 King Moshoeshoe II killed in car accident; King Letsie III restored to throne.

Practical information

Visa requirements UK: visa not required for visits of up to 30 days. USA: visa required
Embassy in the UK 7 Chesham Place, Belgravia, London SW1 8HN. Tel: (0171) 235 5686; fax: (0171) 235 5023
British embassy British High Commission, PO Box Ms 521, Maseru 100. Tel: (266) 313 961; fax: (266) 310 120
Embassy in the USA 2511 Massachusetts Avenue NW, Washington, DC 20008. Tel: (202) 797 5533–6; fax: (202) 234 6815
American embassy address N/A, Maseru (mailing address: PO Box 333, Maseru 100, Lesotho). Tel: (266) 312 666;

fax: (266) 310 116
Chamber of commerce Lesotho Chamber of Commerce and Industry, PO Box 79, Maseru 100. Tel: (266) 323 482
Office hours 0800–1245 and 1400–1630 Mon–Fri; 0800–1300 Sat
Banking hours 0830–1530 Mon, Tue, Thu, and Fri; 0830–1300 Wed; 0830–1100 Sat
Time difference GMT +2
Chief tourist attractions mountain scenery
Major holidays 1 January, 12, 21 March, 2 May, 4 October, 25–26 December; variable: Ascension Thursday, Good Friday, Easter Monday, Family (July), National Sports (October)

Liberia Republic of

Area 111,370 sq km/42,999 sq mi
Capital Monrovia (and port)
Major towns/cities Bensonville,
Saniquillie, Gbarnga, Voinjama,
Buchanan
Major ports Buchanan, Greenville
Physical features forested highlands;
swampy tropical coast where six rivers
enter the sea

Government

Head of state and government Ruth
Perry from 1996
Political system emergent democratic
republic
Administrative divisions 13 counties
Political parties National Democratic
Party of Liberia (NDPL), nationalist, left
of centre; National Patriotic Front of
Liberia (NPFL), left of centre; United
Democratic Movement of Liberia for
Democracy (Ulimo), left of centre
Armed forces 21,000 (1995); ULIMO
(12,000) and NPFL (8,000) forces
controlled most of the country; the
ECOWAS peacekeeping force number
approximately 7,300 late 1995
Conscription military service is
voluntary
Death penalty retained and used for
ordinary crimes
Defence spend (% GDP) 3.2 (1995)
Education spend (% GNP) 2.7 (1988)
Health spend (% GDP) 3.5 (1990)

Economy and resources

Currency Liberian dollar
GDP ($ US) 2.3 billion (1994e)
Real GDP per capita (PPP) ($ US) 800
(1994e)
GDP growth rate 0% (1994e)
Average annual inflation 50% (1994e);
4.6% (1980–89)
Foreign debt ($ US) 1.74 billion (1993)
Trading partners Belgium/Luxembourg,

Japan, USA, Germany, the Netherlands,
Italy, France
Resources iron ore, diamonds, gold,
barytes, kyanite
Industries beverages (soft drinks and
beer), mineral products, chemicals,
tobacco and other agricultural products,
cement, mining, rubber, furniture, bricks,
plastics
Exports iron ore, rubber, timber, coffee,
cocoa, palm-kernel oil, diamonds, gold.
Principal market: Belgium/Luxembourg
56.3% (1994e)
Imports machinery and transport
equipment, mineral fuels, rice, basic
manufactures, food and live animals.
Principal source: Japan 37.2% (1994e)
Arable land 3.8% (1993)
Agricultural products rice, cassava,
coffee, citrus fruits, cocoa, palm kernels,
sugar cane; timber production; rubber
plantation

Population and society

Population 2,245,000 (1996e)
Population growth rate 3.3%
(1990–95); 3.1% (2000–05)
Population density (per sq km) 20
(1996e)
Urban population (% of total) 45
(1995)
Age distribution (% of total population)
<15 46%, 15–65 50.4%, >65 3.7%
(1995)
Ethnic distribution 95% indigenous
peoples, including the Kpelle, Bassa,
Gio, Kru, Grebo, Mano, Krahn, Gola,
Ghandi, Loma, Kissi, Vai, and Bella; 5%
descended from repatriated US slaves
Languages English (official), over 20
Niger-Congo languages
Religions animist, Sunni Muslim,
Christian
Education (compulsory years) 9
Literacy rate 50% (men); 29% (women)
(1995e)
Labour force 41% of population: 72%
agriculture, 6% industry, 22% services
(1990)
Unemployment 80% (1995e)
Life expectancy 56 (men); 59 (women)
(1995–2000)
Child mortality rate (under 5, per 1,000
live births) 216 (1995)
TV sets (per 1,000 people) 26 (1995)
Radios (per 1,000 people) 318 (1995)

Transport

Airports international airports: Monrovia

(Robertsfield and Spriggs Payne);
regular services operate from Monrovia
to major towns (most air services have
been suspended since 1992); total
passenger km: 7 mil (1992)
Railroads total length: 490 km/304 mi.
The railways were originally constructed
for iron-ore transport; after several years
of civil war, there is no report that any of
them are still in operation
Roads total road network: 10,300 km/
6,400 mi, of which 6.1% paved (1995e);
passenger cars: 3.1 per 1,000 people
(1995e)

Chronology

1821 Purchased by philanthropic
American Colonization Society and
turned into settlement for liberated black
slaves from southern USA.
1847 Recognized as an independent
republic.
1869 The True Whig Party founded,
which was to dominate politics for more
than a century, providing all presidents.
1926 Large concession sold to
Firestone Rubber Company as foreign
indebtedness increased.
1944 William Tubman, descendant of
US slaves, elected president.
1971 Tubman died; succeeded by
William Tolbert.
1980 Tolbert assassinated in military
coup led by Sgt Samuel Doe, who
banned political parties and launched
anticorruption drive.
1984 New constitution approved in
referendum. National Democratic Party
(NDPL) founded by Doe as political
parties relegalized.
1985 Doe and the NDPL won decisive
victories in allegedly rigged elections.
1990 Doe killed as bloody civil war
broke out, involving Charles Taylor and
Gen Hezekiah Bowen, who led rival
rebel armies, the National Patriotic Front
(NPFL) and the Armed Forces of Liberia
(AFL). War left 150,000 dead and
2 million homeless. West African
peacekeeping force drafted in. Amos
Sawyer, with NPFL backing, became
interim head of government.
1992 Monrovia under siege by Taylor's
rebel forces as fighting continued.
1993 Peace agreement signed under
OAU–UN auspices, but soon
collapsed.
1995 Ghanaian-backed peace proposals
accepted by rebel factions; interim

Council of State established, comprising leaders of three main rebel factions and chaired by Wilton Sankawulo.

1996 Renewed fighting in capital; USA began evacuation of foreigners. Peace plan reached in talks convened by the

Economic Community of West African States (ECOWAS); Ruth Perry became Liberia's first female head of state.

Practical information

Visa requirements UK: visa required. USA: visa required
Embassy in the UK 2 Pembridge Place, London W2 4XB. Tel: (0171) 221 1036
British embassy the British High Commission in Abidjan (see Ivory Coast) deals with enquiries relating to Liberia
Embassy in the USA 5201 16th Street NW, Washington, DC 20011. Tel: (202) 723 0437
American embassy 111 United Nations Drive, Monrovia. Tel: (231) 226 370; fax: (231) 226 148

Chamber of commerce PO Box 92, Monrovia. Tel: (231) 223 738; telex: 44211
Office hours 0800–1200 and 1400–1600 Mon–Fri
Banking hours 0900–1200 Mon–Thu; 0800–1400 Fri
Time difference GMT +/–0
Chief tourist attractions sandy beaches along Atlantic coast; mountain scenery
Major holidays 1 January, 11 February, 15 March, 12 April, 14 May, 26 July, 24 August, 29 November, 25 December; variable: Decoration (March), National Fast and Prayer (April), Thanksgiving (November)

Libya Great Socialist People's Libyan Arab Republic

National name *Jamahiriya al-Arabiya al-Libya al-Shabiya al-Ishtirakiya al-Uzma*
Area 1,759,540 sq km/679,358 sq mi
Capital Tripoli
Towns and cities Benghazi, Misurata, Az-Zaiwa, Tobruk, Ajdabiya, Derna
Major ports Benghazi, Misurata, Az-Zaiwa, Tobruk, Ajdabiya, Derna
Physical features flat to undulating plains with plateaux and depressions stretch S from the Mediterranean coast to an extremely dry desert interior

Government

Head of state and government Moamer al-Khaddhafi from 1969
Political system one-party socialist state
Administrative divisions 25 municipalities
Political party Arab Socialist Union (ASU), radical, left wing
Armed forces 80,000 (1995)
Conscription conscription is selective for two years
Death penalty retained and used for ordinary crimes

Defence spend (% GDP) 5.5 (1995)
Education spend (% GNP) 9.6 (1986); N/A (1993–94)

Economy and resources

Currency Libyan dinar
GDP ($ US) 32.8 billion (1994e)
Real GDP per capita (PPP) ($ US) 6,125 (1994)
GDP growth rate –4.5% (1994)
Average annual inflation 45% (1995e); 0.2% (1980–93)
Foreign debt ($ US) 4.2 billion (1996e)
Trading partners Italy, Germany, Greece, Spain, UK, France, Turkey, Morocco, the Netherlands
Resources petroleum, natural gas, iron ore, potassium, magnesium, sulphur, gypsum
Industries petroleum refining, processing of agricultural products, cement and other building materials, fish processing and canning, textiles, clothing and footwear
Exports crude petroleum (accounted for 94% of 1991 export earnings), chemicals and related products. Principal market: Italy 39.8% (1995)
Imports machinery and transport equipment, basic manufactures, food and live animals, miscellaneous manufactured articles. Principal source: Italy 21.7% (1995)
Arable land 1% (1993)
Agricultural products barley, wheat, grapes, olives, dates; livestock rearing (sheep, goats, and camels); fishing

Population and society

Population 5,593,000 (1996e)
Population growth rate 3.5% (1990–95); 3.2% (2000–05)

Population density (per sq km) 3 (1996e)
Urban population (% of total) 86 (1995)
Age distribution (% of total population) <15 45.4%, 15–65 52%, >65 2.6% (1995)
Ethnic distribution majority are of Berber and Arab origin, with a small number of Tebou and Touareg nomads and semi-nomads, mainly in S
Language Arabic
Religion Sunni Muslim
Education (compulsory years) 9
Literacy rate 75% (men); 50% (women) (1995e)
Labour force 29% of population: 18% agriculture, 31% industry, 51% services (1990)
Unemployment 30% (1995e)
Life expectancy 64 (men); 68 (women) (1995–2000)
Child mortality rate (under 5, per 1,000 live births) 63 (1995)
Physicians 1 per 962 people (1991)
TV sets (per 1,000 people) 102 (1995)
Radios (per 1,000 people) 231 (1995)

Transport

Airports international airports: Tripoli, Benghazi (Benina), Sebhah (international civilian links with Libya have been suspended since April 1992, in accordance with a UN Security Council Resolution of March 1992); seven domestic airports; total passenger km: 425 mil (1994)
Railroads none
Roads total road network: 81,600 km/ 50,706 mi, of which 57.1% paved (1995e); passenger cars: 110 per 1,000 people (1995e)

Chronology

7th century BC Tripolitania, in western Libya, was settled by Phoenicians, who founded Tripoli; it became an eastern province of Carthaginian kingdom, which was centred on Tunis to the W.

4th century BC Cyrenaica, in eastern Libya, colonized by Greeks, who called it Libya.

74 BC Became a Roman province, with Tripolitania part of Africa Nova province and Cyrenaica combined with Crete as a province.

19 BC The desert region of Fezzan (Phazzania), inhabited by Garmante people, was conquered by Rome.

6th century AD Came under control of Byzantine Empire.

7th century Conquered by Arabs, who spread Islam: Egypt ruled Cyrenaica and Morrocan Berber Almohads controlled Tripolitania.

mid-16th century Became part of Turkish Ottoman Empire, who combined the three ancient regions into one regency in Tripoli.

1711 Karamanli (Qaramanli) dynasty established virtual independence from Ottomans.

1835 Ottoman control reasserted.

1911–12 Conquered by Italy.

1920s Resistance to Italian rule by Sanusi order and Umar al-Mukhtar.

1934 Colony named Libya.

1942 Italians ousted, and area divided into three provinces: Fezzan (under French control), Cyrenaica, and Tripolitania (under British control).

1951 Achieved independence as United Kingdom of Libya, under King Idris, former Amir of Cyrenaica and leader of Sanusi order.

1959 Discovery of oil transformed economy, but also led to unsettling social changes.

1969 King deposed in military coup led by Col Moamer al-Khaddhafi. Revolution Command Council set up and Arab Socialist Union (ASU) proclaimed the only legal party in a new puritanical Islamic-socialist republic which sought Pan-Arab unity.

1970s Economic activity collectivized, oil industry nationalized, opposition suppressed by Khaddhafi's revolutionary regime.

1972 Proposed federation of Libya, Syria, and Egypt abandoned.

1980 Proposed merger with Syria abandoned. Libyan troops began fighting in northern Chad.

1986 US bombed Khaddhafi's headquarters, following allegations of his complicity in terrorist activities.

1988 Diplomatic relations with Chad restored; political prisoners freed; economy liberalized.

1989 US navy shot down two Libyan planes; reconciliation with Egypt.

1992 Khaddhafi under international pressure to extradite suspected Lockerbie and UTA (Union de Transports Aériens) bombers for trial outside Libya. United Nations sanctions imposed; several countries severed diplomatic and air links with Libya.

1995 Antigovernment campaign of violence by Islamicists. Hundreds of Palestinians and thousands of foreign workers expelled.

Practical information

Visa requirements UK: visa required. USA: visa required

Embassy for the UK British Interests Section, c/o Embassy of the Italian Republic, PO Box 4206, Sharia Uahran 1, Tripoli. Tel: (21) 333 1191; telex: 20296 (a/b BRITEMB LY)

British embassy c/o Permanent Mission of the Socialist People's Libyan Arab Jamahiriya to the United Nations, 309–315 East 48th Street, New York, NY 10017, USA. Tel: (212) 752 5775; fax: (212) 593 4787. Paris Libyan People's Bureau. Tel: (1) 4720 1970

Embassy in the USA Libya does not have an embassy in the USA

American embassy the USA suspended all embassy activities in Tripoli on 2 May 1980

Chamber of commerce Tripoli Chamber of Commerce, Industry and Agriculture, PO Box 2321, Sharia al-Fatah September, Tripoli. Tel: (21) 333 3755; telex: 20181

Office hours generally 0700–1400 Sat–Wed

Banking hours 0800–1200 Sat–Wed (winter); 0800–1200 Sat–Thu and 1600–1700 Sat and Wed (summer)

Time difference GMT +1

Chief tourist attractions Tripoli, with its beaches and annual International Fair; the ancient Roman towns of Leptis Magna, Sabratha, and Cyrene

Major holidays 2, 8, 28 March, 11 June, 23 July, 1 September, 7 October; variable: Eid-ul-Adha (4 days), end of Ramadan (3 days), Prophet's Birthday

Liechtenstein Principality of

National name *Fürstentum Liechtenstein*

Area 160 sq km/62 sq mi

Capital Vaduz

Major towns/cities Balzers, Schaan, Ruggell, Triesen, Eschen

Physical features landlocked Alpine; includes part of Rhine Valley in W

Government

Head of state Prince Hans Adam II from 1989

Head of government Mario Frick from 1993

Political system constitutional monarchy

Administrative divisions 11 communes

Political parties Patriotic Union (VU), conservative; Progressive Citizens' Party (FBP), conservative

Armed forces no standing army since 1868; there is a police force of 59 men and 19 auxiliaries

Conscription in an emergency Liechtensteiners under the age of 60 are liable to military service

Death penalty abolished 1987 (last execution 1785)

Economy and resources

Currency Swiss franc

GDP ($ US) 1.52 billion (1994)
Real GDP per capita (PPP) ($ US) 23,200 (1992)
GDP growth rate −0.1% (1994)
Average annual inflation 0.9% (1994)
Trading partners Switzerland and other EFTA countries, EU countries
Resources hydro power
Industries small machinery, textiles, ceramics, chemicals, furniture, precision instruments, pharmaceutical products, heating appliances, financial services, tourism
Exports small machinery, artificial teeth and other material for dentistry, stamps, precision instruments, ceramics. Principal market: Switzerland 14% (1994)
Imports machinery and transport equipment, foodstuffs, textiles, metal goods. Principal source: Switzerland
Arable land 25% (1993)
Agricultural products maize, potatoes; cattle rearing and dairy farming

Population and society

Population 31,000 (1996e)
Population growth rate 1.4% (1990–95)
Population density (per sq km) 195 (1996e)
Urban population (% of total) 21 (1995)
Age distribution (% of total population) <15 19.8%, 15–65 69.4%, >65 10.8% (1990)
Ethnic distribution indigenous population of Alemannic origin; one-third of the population are foreign-born resident workers
Languages German (official); an Alemannic dialect is also spoken
Religions Roman Catholic (87%), Protestant
Education (compulsory years) 8
Literacy rate 99% (men); 99% (women) (1995e)
Labour force 1.7% agriculture, 47.6% industry, 50.7% services (1994)
Unemployment 1% (1994)
Life expectancy 78 (men); 83 (women) (1995–2000)
Child mortality rate (under 5, per 1,000 live births) 0.03 (1993)
TV sets (per 1,000 people) 339 (1995)
Radios (per 1,000 people) 665 (1995)

Transport

Airports international airports: none, the nearest is at Zürich, Switzerland
Railroads total length: 18.5 km/11.5 mi
Roads total road network: 250 km/ 155 mi; passenger cars: 614 per 1,000 people (1995)

Chronology

c. AD 500 Settled by Germanic-speaking Alemanni tribe.
1342 Became sovereign state.
1434 Present boundaries established.
1719 Former independent lordships of Schellenberg and Vaduz were united by Princes of Liechtenstein to form present state.
1815–66 A member of German Confederation.
1868 Abolished standing armed forces.
1871 Liechtenstein was only German principality to stay outside newly formed German Empire.
1918 Patriotic Union (VU) party founded, drawing most support from the mountainous S.
1919 Switzerland replaced Austria as foreign representative of Liechtenstein.
1921 Adopted Swiss currency; constitution created a parliament.
1923 United with Switzerland in customs and monetary union.
1938 Prince Franz Josef II came to power.
1970 After 42 years as main governing party, northern-based Progressive Citizens' Party (FBP) defeated by VU which, except for 1974–78, became dominant force in politics.
1978 Joined Council of Europe.
1984 Prince Franz Josef II handed over power to Crown Prince Hans Adam. Vote extended to women in national elections.
1989 Prince Franz Josef II died; succeeded by Hans Adam II.
1990 Became a member of United Nations.
1991 Became seventh member of European Free Trade Association.
1993 Mario Frick of VU became Europe's youngest head of government, aged 28, after two general elections.
1997 Mario Frick and ruling VU-FBP government retained power after general election. FBP withdrew from coalition.

Practical information

Visa requirements UK: visa not required. USA: visa not required
Embassy in the UK Liechtenstein is generally represented overseas by Switzerland
British embassy enquiries relating to Liechtenstein are dealt with by the British Consulate General, Dufourstrasse 56, CH-8008 Zürich, Switzerland. Tel: (1) 261 1520–6; fax: (1) 252 8351
Embassy in the USA Liechtenstein does not have an embassy in the USA, but is represented by the Swiss embassy in routine diplomatic matters
American embassy the USA does not have an embassy in Liechtenstein, but the US Consul General at Zürich, Switzerland has consular accreditation in Vaduz
Chamber of commerce Liechtenstein Industrie-und – Handeslkammer (Chamber of Industry and Commerce), Postfach 232, Josef Rheinberger-Strasse 11, FL-9490 Vaduz. Tel: (4175) 232 2744; fax: (4175) 233 1503
Office hours generally 0800–1200 and 1400–1800 Mon–Fri
Banking hours 0800–1630 Mon–Fri
Time difference GMT +1
Chief tourist attractions alpine setting; postal museum; Prince's castle; National Museum and State Art Collection at Vaduz
Major holidays 1, 6 January, 2 February, 19 March, 1 May, 15 August, 1 November, 8, 24–26, 31 December; variable: Ascension Thursday, Carnival, Corpus Christi, Good Friday, Easter Monday, Whit Monday

Lithuania Republic of

National name *Lietuvos Respublika*
Area 65,200 sq km/25,173 sq mi
Capital Vilnius
Major towns/cities Kaunas, Klaipeda, Siauliai, Panevezys
Physical features central lowlands with gentle hills in W and higher terrain in SE; 25% forested; some 3,000 small lakes, marshes, and complex sandy coastline; river Nemen

Government

Head of state Algirdas Brazauskas from 1993
Head of government Gediminas Vagnorius from 1996
Political system emergent democracy
Administrative divisions 12 regions
Political parties Lithuanian Democratic Labour Party (LDLP), reform-socialist (ex-communist); Homeland Union–Lithuanian Conservatives (Tevynes Santara), right of centre, nationalist; Christian Democratic Party of Lithuania, centre right; Lithuanian Social Democratic Party, left of centre
Armed forces 5,000 (1995)
Conscription military service is compulsory for 12 months
Death penalty retained and used for ordinary crimes
Defence spend (% GDP) 2.4 (1995)
Education spend (% GNP) 4.2 (1994)
Health spend (% GDP) 3.2 (1994)

Economy and resources

Currency litas
GDP ($ US) 5 billion (1994)
Real GDP per capita (PPP) ($ US) 4,011 (1994)
GDP growth rate 1% (1996); –9.7% (1990–95)
Average annual inflation 24.2% (1996); 151% (1985–95e)

Foreign debt ($ US) 802 million (1995)
Trading partners Russia, Germany, Belarus, Latvia, Ukraine, Poland, Italy, the Netherlands
Resources small deposits of petroleum, natural gas, peat, limestone, gravel, clay, sand
Industries petroleum refining and petroleum products, cast iron and steel, textiles, mineral fertilizers, fur coats, refrigerators, TV sets, bicycles, paper
Exports textiles, machinery and equipment, non-precious metals, animal products, timber. Principal market: Russia 23.8 (1996)
Imports petroleum and natural gas products, machinery and transport equipment, chemicals, fertilizers, consumer goods. Principal source: Russia 29.1% (1996)
Arable land 46% (1993)
Agricultural products cereals, sugar beet, potatoes, vegetables; livestock rearing and dairy farming (animal husbandry accounted for more than 50% of the value of total agricultural production 1992)

Population and society

Population 3,728,000 (1996e)
Population growth rate –0.1% (1990–95); 0.1% (2000–05)
Population density (per sq km) 57 (1996e)
Urban population (% of total) 72 (1995)
Age distribution (% of total population) <15 21.9%, 15–65 66%, >65 12.2% (1995)
Ethnic distribution 80% Lithuanian ethnic descent, 9% ethnic Russian, 7% Polish, 2% Belarusian, 1% Ukrainian
Language Lithuanian (official)
Religions predominantly Roman Catholic; Lithuanian Lutheran Church
Education (compulsory years) 9
Literacy rate 98% (men); 98% (women) (1995e)
Labour force 19.6% agriculture, 38% industry, 42.4% services (1992)
Unemployment 7.1% (1996)
Life expectancy 65 (men); 76 (women) (1995–2000)
Child mortality rate (under 5, per 1,000 live births) 19 (1995)
Physicians 1 per 247 people (1994)
Hospital beds 1 per 89 people (1995)
TV sets (per 1,000 people) 415 (1995)
Radios (per 1,000 people) 401 (1995)

Transport

Airports international airports: Vilnius, Kaunas, Siauliai; few domestic flights; total passenger km: 241 mil (1994)
Railroads total length: 2,007 km/1,247 mi; total passenger km: 1,574 mil (1994)
Roads total road network: 61,442 km/ 38,180 mi, of which 86.4% paved (1995); passenger cars: 193.6 per 1,000 people (1995)

Chronology

late 12th century Became a separate nation.
1230 Mindaugas united Lithuanian tribes to resist attempted invasions by German and Livonian Teutonic Knights, and adopted Christianity.
14th century Strong Grand Duchy formed by Gediminas, founder of Vilnius and Jogaila dynasty, and his son, Algirdas; absorbing Ruthenian territories to E and S, it stretched from the Baltic to the Black Sea and E, nearly reaching Moscow.
1410 Led by Duke Vytautas, and in alliance with Poland, the Teutonic Knights were defeated decisively at Battle of Tannenberg.
1569 Joined Poland in a confederation, under the Union of Lublin, in which Poland had the upper hand and Lithuanian upper classes were Polonized.
1795 Came under control of Tsarist Russia, following partition of Poland; 'Lithuania Minor' (Kaliningrad) fell to Germany.
1831 and 1863 Failed revolts for independence.
1880s Development of organized nationalist movement.
1914–18 Occupied by German troops during World War I.
1918–19 Independence declared and, after uprising against attempted imposition of Soviet Union (USSR) control, was achieved as a democratic republic.
1920–39 Province and city of Vilnius occupied by Poles.
1926 Democracy overthrown in authoritarian coup by Antanas Smetona, who became president.
1934 Baltic Entente mutual-defence pact signed with Estonia and Latvia.
1939–40 Secret German–Soviet agreement brought most of Lithuania

under Soviet influence as a constituent republic.

1941 Lithuania revolted and established own government, but during World War II Germany again occupied the country and 210,000, mainly Jews, were killed.

1944 USSR resumed rule.

1944–52 Lithuanian guerrillas fought USSR, which persecuted the Catholic Church, collectivized agriculture, and deported half a million Balts to Siberia.

1972 Demonstrations against Soviet government.

1980s Growth in nationalist dissent, influenced by Polish Solidarity movement and glasnost ('openness') initiative of reformist Soviet leader Mikhail Gorbachev.

1988 Popular Front, the Sajudis, formed

to campaign for increased autonomy; parliament declared Lithuanian the state language and readopted the flag of interwar republic.

1989 Communist Party (CP) split into pro-Moscow and nationalist wings, and lost local monopoly of power; over 1 million took part in nationalist demonstrations.

1990 Nationalist Sajudis won elections; their leader, Vytautas Landsbergis, became president; unilateral declaration of independence rejected by USSR, who imposed an economic blockade.

1991 Soviet paratroopers briefly occupied key buildings in Vilnius, killing 13; CP outlawed; independence recognized by USSR and Western nations and admitted into United Nations.

1992 Ex-communist Democratic Labour Party (LDLP) won majority in parliamentary elections as economic restructuring caused contraction in GDP.

1993 LDLP leader Algirdas Brazauskas elected president, and Adolfas Slezevicius became prime minister. Free-trade agreement with other Baltic states. Last Russian troops departed.

1994 Friendship and cooperation treaty with Poland.

1994 Trade and cooperation agreement with European Union.

1996 Slezevicius resigned over banking scandal; replaced by Laurynas Stankevicius. New conservative coalition formed, led by Gediminas Vagnorius.

Practical information

Visa requirements UK: visa not required for a stay of up to 90 days. USA: visa not required for a stay of up to 90 days

Embassy in the UK 17 Essex Villas, London W8 7BP. Tel: (0171) 938 2481; fax: (0171) 938 3329

British embassy PO Box 863, Anta Kalnio 2, 2055 Vilnius. Tel: (2) 222 070; fax: (2) 357 579

Embassy in the USA 2622 16th Street NW, Washington, DC 20009. Tel: (202) 234 5860, 2639; fax: (202) 328 0466

American embassy Akmenu 6, Vilnius 2600.

Tel: (8) 973 0000, 227 224; fax: (8) 670 6084

Chamber of commerce Association of Lithuanian Chambers of Commerce and Industry, Kudirkos 18, 2600 Vilnius. Tel: (2) 222 630; fax: (2) 222 621

Office hours 0900–1300 and 1400–1800 Mon–Fri

Time difference GMT +2

Chief tourist attractions historic cities of Vilnius, Klaipeda, Kaunas, and Trakai; coastal resorts such as Palanga and Kursiu Nerija; picturesque countryside

Major holidays 1 January, 16 February, 5 May, 6 July, 1 November, 25–26 December; variable: Easter Monday

---

Luxembourg Grand Duchy of

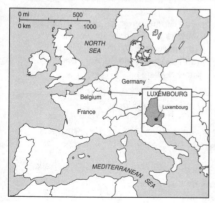

National name *Grand-Duché de Luxembourg*

Area 2,586 sq km/998 sq mi

Capital Luxembourg

Major towns/cities Esch-Alzette, Differdange, Dudelange, Petange

Physical features on the river Moselle; part of the Ardennes (Oesling) forest in N

Government

Head of state Grand Duke Jean from 1964

Head of government Jean-Claude Juncker from 1995

Political system liberal democracy

Administrative divisions 12 cantons

Political parties Christian Social Party (PCS), moderate, left of centre; Luxembourg Socialist Workers' Party (POSL), moderate, socialist; Democratic Party (PD), centre left; Communist Party of Luxembourg, pro-European left wing

Armed forces 1,000 (1995); gendarmerie 560

Death penalty abolished 1979

Defence spend (% GDP) 0.9 (1995)

Education spend (% GNP) 3.1 (1993–94)

Health spend (% GDP) 6.3 (1993)

Economy and resources

Currency Luxembourg franc

GDP ($ US) 17.5 billion (1996)

Real GDP per capita (PPP) ($ US) 32,665 (1996)

GDP growth rate 2.1% (1996); 3.7% (1994–95)

Average annual inflation 1.4% (1996); 4.7% (1985–95)

Trading partners EU (principally Belgium, Germany, and France)

Resources iron ore

Industries steel and rolled steel products, chemicals, rubber and plastic products, metal and machinery products, paper and printing products, food products, financial services

Exports base metals and manufactures,

mechanical and electrical equipment, rubber and related products, plastics, textiles and clothing. Principal market: Germany 28.2% (1993)
Imports machinery and electrical apparatus, transport equipment, mineral products. Principal source: Belgium 38.1% (1993)
Arable land 27%
Agricultural products maize, roots and tubers, wheat, forage crops, grapes; livestock rearing and dairy farming

Population and society

Population 412,000 (1996e)
Population growth rate 1.3% (1990–95)
Population density (per sq km) 160 (1996e)
Urban population (% of total) 89.1 (1995)
Age distribution (% of total population) <15 17%, 15–65 69%, >65 14% (1994)
Ethnic distribution majority descended from the Moselle Franks
Languages French, German, local Letzeburgesch (all official)
Religion Roman Catholic
Education (compulsory years) 9
Literacy rate 99% (1995e)
Labour force 43% of population: 4% agriculture, 27% industry, 69% services (1990)
Unemployment 3.4% (1995)
Life expectancy 73 (men); 80 (women) (1995–2000)
Child mortality rate (under 5, per 1,000 live births) 8.5 (1992)
Physicians 1 per 469 people (1994)
Hospital beds 1 per 87 people (1994)
TV sets (per 1,000 people) 381 (1995)
Radios (per 1,000 people) 639 (1995)

Transport

Airports international airports: Luxembourg (Findel); no domestic airports; total passenger km: 361 mil (1994)
Railroads total length: 275 km/171 mi; total passenger km: 282 mil (1991); international passenger km: 46 mil (1995)
Roads total road network: 5,137 km/3,192 mi, of which 99% paved (1995); passenger cars: 563.3 per 1,000 people (1995)

Chronology

963 Luxembourg became autonomous within Holy Roman Empire under Siegfried, Count of Ardennes.
1060 Conrad, descendent of Siegfried, took the title Count of Luxembourg.
1354 Emperor Charles IV promoted Luxembourg to status of duchy.
1441 Luxembourg ceded to dukes of Burgundy.
1482 Luxembourg came under Habsburg control.
1555 Luxembourg became part of Spanish Netherlands on division of Habsburg domains.
1684–97 Much of Luxembourg occupied by France.
1713 Treaty of Utrecht transferred Spanish Netherlands to Austria.
1797 Conquered by revolutionary France.
1815 Congress of Vienna made Luxembourg a grand duchy, under King William of the Netherlands.
1830 Most of Luxembourg supported Belgian revolt against the Netherlands.
1839 Western part of Luxembourg assigned to Belgium.
1842 Luxembourg entered the Zollverein (German customs union).

1867 Treaty of London confirmed independence and neutrality of Luxembourg to allay French fears about possible inclusion in a unified Germany.
1870s Development of iron and steel industry.
1890 Link with Dutch crown ended on accession of Queen Wilhelmina, since Luxembourg's law of succession did not permit a woman to rule; Adolphe of Nassau-Weilburg became grand duke.
1912 Revised law of succession allowed Marie-Adelaide to become grand duchess.
1914–18 Occupied by Germany.
1919 Plebiscite overwhelmingly favoured continued independence; Marie-Adelaide abdicated after allegations of collaboration with Germany; succeeded by Grand Duchess Charlotte.
1921 Entered into close economic links with Belgium.
1940 Invaded by Germany.
1942–44 Annexed by Germany.
1948 Luxembourg formed Benelux customs union with Belgium and the Netherlands.
1949 Luxembourg became founding member of North Atlantic Treaty Organization (NATO).
1958 Luxembourg became founding member of European Economic Community (EEC).
1964 Grand Duchess Charlotte abdicated in favour of her son Jean.
1974–79 Christian Social Party outside governing coalition for first time since 1919.
1994 Former premier Jacques Santer became president of European Commission (EC).
1995 Jean-Claude Juncker became prime minister.

Practical information

Visa requirements UK: visa not required. USA: visa not required for a stay of up to 90 days
Embassy in the UK 27 Wilton Crescent, London SW1X 8SD. Tel: (0171) 235 6961; fax: (0171) 235 9734
British embassy 14 boulevard Roosevelt, L-2450 Luxembourg-Ville. Tel: (352) 229 864/5/6; fax: (352) 229 867
Embassy in the USA 2200 Massachusetts Avenue NW, Washington, DC 20008. Tel: (202) 265 4171; fax: (202) 328 8270
American embassy 22 boulevard Emmanuel-Servais, 2535 Luxembourg-Ville. Tel: (352) 460 123; fax: (352) 461 401
Chamber of commerce 7 rue Alcide de Gasperi, L-2981

Luxembourg-Kirchberg. Tel: (352) 435 853; fax: (352) 438 326
Office hours generally 0830–1200 and 1400–1800 Mon–Fri
Banking hours generally 0900–1200 and 1330–1630 Mon–Fri
Time difference GMT +1
Chief tourist attractions Luxembourg-Ville, with its historic monuments and many cultural events; medieval castles (Clerf, Esch/Sauer, Vianden, Wietz); Benedictine abbey at Echternach; thermal centre at Mandorf-les-Bains; footpaths and hiking trails
Major holidays 1 January, 1 May, 23 June, 15 August, 1–2 November, 25–26, 31 December; variable: Ascension Thursday, Easter Monday, Whit Monday, Shrove Monday

Macedonia Former Yugoslav Republic of (official international name); Republic of Macedon (official internal name)

National name *Republika Makedonija*
Area 25,700 sq km/9,922 sq mi
Capital Skopje
Major towns/cities Bitolj, Prilep,
Kumanovo, Tetovo
Physical features mountainous; rivers:
Struma, Vardar; lakes: Ohrid, Prespa,
Scutari; partly Mediterranean climate with
hot summers

Government

Head of state (acting) Stojan Andov
from 1995
Head of government Branko
Crvenkovski from 1992
Political system emergent democracy
Administrative divisions 34 communes
Political parties Socialist Party (SP);
Social Democratic Alliance of Macedonia
(SM) bloc, left of centre; Party for
Democratic Prosperity (PDP), ethnic
Albanian, left of centre; Internal
Macedonian Revolutionary
Organization–Democratic Party for
Macedonian National Unity
(VMRO–DPMNE), radical nationalist;
Democratic Party of Macedonia (DPM),
nationalist, free market
Armed forces 10,450 (1996); plus
paramilitary force of 7,500; UN
peacekeeping force (UNPREDEP)
numbered 1,150 1995
Conscription military service is
compulsory for nine months
Death penalty laws do not provide for
the death penalty for any crime
Education spend (% GNP) 5.6
(1993–94)

Economy and resources

Currency Macedonian denar
GDP ($ US) 2 billion (1994)

Real GDP per capita (PPP) ($ US)
3,965 (1994)
GDP growth rate 3% (1996); –40%
(1989–93)
Average annual inflation 16% (1995)
Foreign debt ($ US) 1.21 billion (1995)
Trading partners Bulgaria, Yugoslavia,
Germany, Russia, Italy, Slovenia,
Croatia, USA, Turkey, the Netherlands
Resources coal, iron, zinc, chromium,
manganese, lead, copper, nickel, silver,
gold
Industries metallurgy, chemicals,
textiles, buses, refrigerators, detergents,
medicines, wood pulp, wine
Exports manufactured goods, machinery
and transport equipment, miscellaneous
manufactured articles, sugar beet,
vegetables, cheese, lamb, tobacco.
Principal market: Bulgaria 20% (1994)
Imports mineral fuels and lubricants,
manufactured goods, machinery and
transport equipment, food and live
animals, chemicals. Principal source:
Yugoslavia 23% (1994)
Arable land 26% (1993)
Agricultural products rice, wheat,
barley, sugar beet, fruit and vegetables,
tobacco, sunflowers, potatoes, grapes
(wine industry is important); livestock
rearing and dairy farming

Population and society

Population 2,174,000 (1996e)
Population growth rate 1.1%
(1990–95); 0.7% (2000–05)
Population density (per sq km) 85
(1996e)
Urban population (% of total) 60 (1995)
Age distribution (% of total population)
<15 24.4%, 15–65 67.5%, >65 8.2%
(1995)
Ethnic distribution 66% Macedonian
ethnic descent, 22% ethnic Albanian, 5%
Turkish, 3% Romanian, 2% Serb, and
2% Muslim, comprising Macedonian
Slavs who converted to Islam during the
Ottoman era, and are known as Pomaks.
This ethnic breakdown is disputed by
Macedonia's ethnic Albanian population,
who claim that they form 40% of the
population, and seek autonomy and by
ethnic Serbs, who claim that they form
11.5%
Language Macedonian, closely allied to
Bulgarian and written in Cyrillic
Religions Christian, mainly Orthodox;
Muslim 2.5%
Education (compulsory years) 8

Literacy rate 94% (1995e)
Labour force 8.6% agriculture, 48.7%
industry, 42.7% services (1994)
Unemployment 21% (1995e)
Life expectancy 70 (men); 76 (women)
(1995–2000)
Child mortality rate (under 5, per 1,000
live births) 24 (1994)
Physicians 1 per 479 people (1994)
Hospital beds 1 per 200 people (1994)
TV sets (per 1,000 people) 166 (1994)
Radios (per 1,000 people) 182 (1994)

Transport

Airports international airports: Skopje,
Ohrid; domestic services between Skopje
and Ohrid; total passenger km: 319 mil
(1994)
Railroads total length: 699 km/434 mi;
passengers carried: 1.25 mil (1994)
Roads total road network: 8,532 km/
5,302 mi, of which 63.3% paved (1995);
passenger cars: 147.6 per 1,000 people
(1995)

Chronology

4th century BC Part of ancient great
kingdom of Macedonia, which included N
Greece and SW Bulgaria and, under
Alexander the Great, conquered a vast
empire; Thessaloniki founded.
146 BC Macedonia became a province of
the Roman Empire.
395 AD On the division of the Roman
Empire, came under the control of
Byzantine Empire, with its capital at
Constantinople.
6th century Settled by Slavs, who later
converted to Christianity.
9th–14th centuries Under successive
rule by Bulgars, Byzantium, and Serbia.
1371 Became part of Islamic Ottoman
Empire.
late 19th century The 'Internal
Macedonian Revolutionary Organization',
through terrorism, sought to provoke
Great Power intervention against Turks.
1912–13 After First Balkan War,
partitioned between Bulgaria, Greece,
and the area that constitutes the current
republic of Serbia.
1918 Serbian part included in what was
to become Yugoslavia; Serbian imposed
as official language.
1941–44 Occupied by Bulgaria.
1945 Created a republic within Yugoslav
Socialist Federation.
1967 The Orthodox Macedonian
archbishopric of Skopje, forcibly

abolished 200 years earlier by the Turks, was restored.
1980 Rise of nationalism after death of Yugoslav leader Tito.
1990 Multiparty elections produced inconclusive result.
1991 Kiro Gligorov, a pragmatic former communist, became president. Referendum supported independence.
1992 Independence declared, and

accepted by Serbia/Yugoslavia, but international recognition withheld because of objections to name by Greece.
1993 Sovereignty recognized by UK and Albania; won United Nations membership under provisional name of Former Yugoslav Republic of Macedonia; Greece blocked full European Union (EU) recognition.
1994 Independence recognized by USA;

trade embargo imposed by Greece, causing severe economic damage.
1995 Independence recognized by Greece; trade embargo lifted. President Gligorov survived assassination attempt.
1997 Plans to reduce strength of UN Preventive Deployment Force (UNPREDEP) were abandoned. Government announced compensation for public's losses in failed investment schemes.

Practical information

Visa requirements UK: visa not required. USA: visa required
Embassy in the UK 10 Harcourt House, 19A Cavendish Square, London W1M 9AD. Tel: (0171) 499 5152; fax (0171) 499 2864
British embassy Office of the British Government Representative, Ul VeljkoVlahovic 26, 91000 Skopje. Tel: (91) 116 772; fax: (91) 117 005
Embassy in the USA 3050 K Street, NW, Suite 210,

Washington, DC 20007. Tel: (202) 337 3063; fax: (202) 337 3093
American embassy Ul 27 Mart No. 5, 9100 Skopje. Tel: (91) 116 180; fax: (91) 117 103
Chamber of commerce Economic Chamber of Macedonia, PO Box 324, Dimitrie Cupovski 13, 91000 Skopje. Tel: (91) 233 215; fax: (91) 116 210
Office hours 0700/0800–1500/1600 Mon–Fri
Time difference GMT +1
Chief tourist attractions mountain scenery
Major holidays 1–2 January, 1–2 May, 2 August, 11 October

Madagascar Democratic Republic of

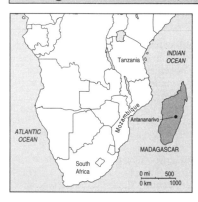

National name *Repoblika Demokratika n`i Madagaskar*
Area 587,041 sq km/226,656 sq mi
Capital Antananarivo
Major towns/cities Antsirabe, Mahajanga, Fianarantsoa, Toamasina, Ambatondrazaka
Major ports Toamasina, Antsiranana, Toliary, Mahajanga
Physical features temperate central highlands; humid valleys and tropical coastal plains; arid in S

Government

Head of state Didier Ratsiraka from 1996
Head of government Pascal Rakotomavo from 1997
Political system emergent democratic republic

Administrative divisions six provinces
Political parties National Front for the Defence of the Malagasy Socialist Revolution (FNDR), left-of-centre coalition; Comité des Forces Vives, pro-Zafy, left-of-centre coalition
Armed forces 21,000 (1995); plus paramilitary gendarmerie of 7,500
Conscription military service is compulsory for 18 months
Death penalty retains the death penalty for ordinary crimes but can be considered abolitionist in practice (last known execution 1958)
Defence spend (% GDP) 1.1 (1995)
Education spend (% GDP) 1.9 (1993–94)
Health spend (% GDP) 1.3 (1990)

Economy and resources

Currency Malagasy franc
GDP ($ US) 1.9 billion (1994)
Real GDP per capita (PPP) ($ US) 694 (1994)
GDP growth rate 0% (1994); 2.5% (1990–95)
Average annual inflation 47.2% (1995); 17.9% (1985–95)
Foreign debt ($ US) 4.3 billion (1995)
Trading partners France, Japan, Germany, USA
Resources graphite, chromite, mica, titanium ore, small quantities of precious stones, bauxite and coal deposits, petroleum reserves

Industries food products, textiles and clothing, beverages, chemical products, cement, fertilizers, pharmaceuticals
Exports coffee, shrimps, cloves, vanilla, petroleum products, chromium, cotton fabrics. Principal market: France 29.2% (1995)
Imports minerals (crude petroleum), chemicals, machinery, vehicles and parts, metal products, electrical equipment. Principal source: France 31.8% (1995)
Arable land 5.3% (1993)
Agricultural products rice, cassava, mangoes, bananas, potatoes, sugar cane, seed cotton, sisal, vanilla, cloves, coconuts, tropical fruits; cattle-farming; sea-fishing

Population and society

Population 15,353,000 (1996e)
Population growth rate 3.2% (1990–95); 3.1% (2000–05)
Population density (per sq km) 26 (1996e)
Urban population (% of total) 27 (1995)
Age distribution (% of total population) <15 46.1%, 15–65 51.1%, >65 2.8% (1995)
Ethnic distribution 18 main Malagasy tribes of Malaysian–Polynesian origin; also French, Chinese, Indians, Pakistanis, and Comorans
Languages Malagasy (official); French, English

Religions traditional beliefs, Roman Catholic, Protestant
Education (compulsory years) 5
Literacy rate 88% (men); 73% (women) (1995e)
Labour force 48% of population: 78% agriculture, 7% industry, 15% services (1990)
Life expectancy 58 (men); 61 (women) (1995–2000)
Child mortality rate (under 5, per 1,000 live births) 164 (1995)
Physicians 1 per 8,333 people (1991)
Hospital beds 1 per 1,153 people (1990)
TV sets (per 1,000 people) 20 (1995)
Radios (per 1,000 people) 192 (1995)

Transport

Airports international airports: Antananarivo (Ivato), Mahajunga (Amborovi); two domestic airports and 57 airfields open to public air traffic; total passenger km: 567 mil (1994)
Railroads total length: 1,054 km/655 mi; total passenger km: 60 mil (1994)
Roads total road network: 49,837 km/30,969 mi, of which 11.5% paved (1995); passenger cars: 4 per 1,000 people (1995e)

Chronology

c. 6th–10th centuries AD Settled by migrant Indonesians.
1500 First visited by European navigators.
17th century Development of Merina and Sakalava kingdoms in the central highlands and W coast.
1642–74 France established a coastal settlement at Fort-Dauphin, which they abandoned after a massacre by local inhabitants.
late 18th–early 19th century Merinas, united by their ruler Andrianampoinimerina, became dominant kingdom; court converted to Christianity.
1861 Ban on Christianity (imposed 1828) and entry of Europeans lifted by Merina king, Radama II.
1885 Became French protectorate.
1895 Merina army defeated by French and became a colony; slavery abolished.
1942–43 British troops invaded to overthrow French administration allied to the pro-Nazi Germany Vichy regime and install anti-Nazi Free French government.
1947–48 Nationalist uprising brutally suppressed by French.
1960 Independence achieved from France, with Philibert Tsiranana, the leader of the Social Democratic Party (PSD), as president.
1972 Merina-dominated army overthrew Tsiranana's government, dominated by the cotier (coastal tribes), as economy deteriorated.
1975 Martial law imposed; new one-party state Marxist constitution adopted, with Lt-Commander Didier Ratsiraka as president.
1978 More than 1,000 people killed in race riots in Majunga city in NW.
1980 Ratsiraka abandoned Marxist experiment, which had involved nationalization and severing ties with France.
1983 Ratsiraka re-elected, despite strong opposition from radical socialist movement under Monja Jaona.
1990 Political opposition legalized; 36 new parties created.
1991 Antigovernment demonstrations. Ratsiraka formed new unity government, which included opposition members.
1992 Constitutional reform approved by referendum.
1993 Albert Zafy elected president and pro-Zafy left-of-centre coalition won majority in multiparty assembly elections.
1995 Referendum backed appointment of prime minister by president, rather than assembly.
1996 Norbert Ratsirahonana became prime minister and then interim president upon parliament's removal of Zafy. Didier Ratsiraka elected president.
1997 Pascal Rakotomavo appointed prime minister.

Practical information

Visa requirements UK: visa required. USA: visa required
Embassy in the UK Consulate of the Republic of Madagascar, 16 Lanark Mansions, Pennard Road, London W12 8DT. Tel: (0181) 746 0133; fax: (0181) 746 0134
British embassy BP 167, 1er Etage, Immeuble 'Ny Havana', Cité de 67 Ha, 101 Antananarivo. Tel: (2) 27749; fax: (2) 26690
Embassy in the USA 2374 Massachusetts Avenue NW, Washington, DC 20008. Tel: (202) 265 5525/6
American embassy 14–16 rue Rainitovo, Antsahavola, Antananarivo. Tel: (2) 21257, 20089, 20718; fax: (2) 234 539
Chamber of commerce Fédération des Chambres de Commerce, d'Industrie et d'Agriculture de Madagascar, BP 166, 20 rue Colbert, 101 Antananarivo. Tel: (2) 21567
Banking hours 0800–1100 and 1400–1600 Mon–Fri
Time difference GMT +3
Chief tourist attractions unspoilt scenery; unusual wildlife; much of Madagascar's flora and fauna is unique to the island – there are 3,000 endemic species of butterfly
Major holidays 1 January, 29 March, 1 May, 26 June, 15 August, 1 November, 25, 30 December; variable: Ascension Thursday, Good Friday, Easter Monday, Whit Monday

---

Malawi Republic of (formerly *Nyasaland*)

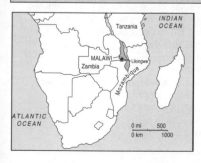

National name *Malawi*
Area 118,000 sq km/45,559 sq mi
Capital Lilongwe
Major towns/cities Blantyre, Lilongwe, Mzuzu, Zomba
Physical features landlocked narrow plateau with rolling plains; mountainous W of Lake Nyasa

Government

Head of state and government Bakili Muluzi from 1994

Political system emergent democratic republic
Administrative divisions three regions, subdivided into 24 districts
Political parties Malawi Congress Party (MCP), multiracial, right wing; United Democratic Front (UDF), left of centre; Alliance for Democracy (AFORD), left of centre
Armed forces 8,200 (1996)
Conscription military service is voluntary

Death penalty retained and used for ordinary crimes
Defence spend (% GDP) 1.2 (1995)
Education spend (% GNP) 3.3 (1992); N/A (1993–94)
Health spend (% GDP) 2.9 (1990)

Economy and resources

Currency Malawi kwacha
GDP ($ US) 1.3 million (1994)
Real GDP per capita (PPP) ($ US) 694 (1994)
GDP growth rate −12% (1994); 0.7% (1990–95)
Average annual inflation 34.7% (1994); 22% (1985–95)
Foreign debt ($ US) 2.14 billion (1995)
Trading partners South Africa, UK, Japan, Germany, the Netherlands
Resources marble, coal, gemstones, bauxite and graphite deposits, reserves of phosphates, uranium, glass sands, asbestos, vermiculite
Industries food products, chemical products, textiles, beverages, cement
Exports tobacco, tea, sugar, cotton, groundnuts. Principal market: South Africa 13.8% (1995)
Imports petroleum products, fertilizers, coal, machinery and transport equipment, miscellaneous manufactured articles. Principal source: South Africa 34.4% (1995)
Arable land 14.1% (1993)
Agricultural products maize, cassava, groundnuts, pulses, tobacco, tea, sugar cane

Population and society

Population 9,845,000 (1996e)
Population growth rate 3.5% (1990–95); 2% (2000–05)
Population density (per sq km) 83 (1996e)
Urban population (% of total) 14 (1995)
Age distribution (% of total population) <15 46.7%, 15–65 50.5%, >65 2.7% (1995)
Ethnic distribution almost all indigenous Africans, divided into numerous ethnic groups, such as the Chewa, Nyanja, Tumbuka, Yao, Lomwe, Sena, Tonga, and Ngoni. There are also Asian and European minorities
Languages English, Chichewa (both official)
Religions Christian 75%, Muslim 20%
Education (compulsory years) 8
Literacy rate 52% (men); 31% (women) (1995e)
Labour force 87% agriculture, 5% industry, 8% services (1990)
Unemployment 1.3% (1989)
Life expectancy 44 (men); 45 (women) (1995–2000)
Child mortality rate (under 5, per 1,000 live births) 219 (1995)
Physicians 1 per 33,330 people (1991)
Hospital beds 1 per 612 people (1993)
Radios (per 1,000 people) 256 (1995)

Transport

Airports international airports: Lilongwe (Kamuzu), Blantyre (Chileka); three domestic airports; total passenger km: 289 mil (1994)
Railroads total length: 797 km/495 mi; total passenger km: 19 mil (1994)
Roads total road network: 27,880 km/ 17,325 mi, of which 18.4% paved (1995e); passenger cars: 2.2 per 1,000 people (1995e)

Chronology

1st–4th centuries AD Immigration by Bantu-speaking peoples.
1480 Foundation of Maravi (Malawi) Confederacy, which covered much of central and southern Malawi and lasted into the 17th century.
1530 First visited by the Portuguese.
1600 Ngonde kingdom founded in northern Malawi by immigrants from Tanzania.
18th century Chikulamayembe state founded by immigrants from E of Lake Nyasa; slave trade flourished and Islam introduced in some areas.
mid-19th century Swahili-speaking Ngoni peoples, from South Africa, and Yao entered the region, dominating settled agriculturalists; Christianity introduced by missionaries, such as David Livingstone.
1891 Became British protectorate of Nyasaland; cash crops, particularly coffee, introduced.
1915 Violent uprising, led by Rev John Chilembwe, against white settlers who had moved into the fertile S, taking land from local population.
1953 Became part of white-dominated Central African Federation, which included South Rhodesia (Zimbabwe) and North Rhodesia (Zambia).
1958 Dr Hastings Kamuzu Banda returned to the country after working abroad for 40 years and became head of conservative-nationalist Nyasaland/Malawi Congress Party (MCP), which spearheaded campaign for independence.
1963 Central African Federation dissolved.
1964 Independence achieved, within Commonwealth, as Malawi, with Banda as prime minister.
1966 Became one-party republic, with Banda as president.
1967 Banda became pariah of Black Africa by recognizing racist, white-only republic of South Africa.
1971 Banda made president for life.
1970s Reports of human-rights violations and murder of Banda's opponents.
1980s Economy began to deteriorate after nearly two decades of expansion.
1986–89 Influx of nearly a million refugees from Mozambique.
1992 Calls for multiparty politics. Countrywide industrial riots caused many fatalities. Western aid suspended over human-rights violations.
1993 Referendum overwhelmingly supported ending of one-party rule.
1994 New multiparty constitution adopted. Bakili Muluzi, of the United Democratic Front (UDF), elected president in first free elections for 30 years. Inconclusive assembly elections.
1995 Banda and former minister of state John Tembo charged with conspiring to murder four political opponents 1983, but were cleared.

Practical information

Visa requirements UK: visa not required. USA: visa not required
Embassy in the UK 33 Grosvenor Street, London W1X 0DE. Tel: (0171) 491 4172/7; fax: (0171) 491 9916
British embassy British High Commission, PO Box 30042, Lingadzi House, Lilongwe 3. Tel: (265) 782 400; fax: (265) 782 657
Embassy in the USA 2408 Massachusetts Avenue NW, Washington, DC 20008. Tel: (202) 797 1007
American embassy address N/A, in new capital city development area in Lilongwe. Tel: (265) 783 166; fax: (265) 780 471
Chamber of commerce Associated Chambers of Commerce and Industry of Malawi, PO Box 258, Chichiri Trade Fair Grounds, Blantyre. Tel: (265) 671 988; fax: (265) 671 147
Office hours 0730–1700 Mon–Fri
Banking hours 0800–1300 Mon–Fri
Time difference GMT +2
Chief tourist attractions beaches on Lake Malawi; varied scenery; big game; excellent climate
Major holidays 1 January, 3 March, 14 May, 6 July, 17 October, 22, 25–26 December; variable: Good Friday, Easter Monday, Holy Saturday

Malaysia Federation of (FOM)

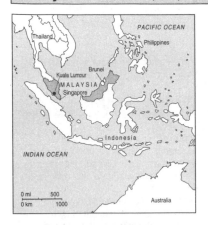

National name *Persekutuan Tanah Malaysia*
Area 329,759 sq km/127,319 sq mi
Capital Kuala Lumpur
Major towns/cities Johor Baharu, Ipoh, George Town (Penang), Kuala Trengganu, Kuala Baharu, Petalong Jaya, Kelang, Kuching in Sarawak, Kota Kinabalu in Sabah
Major ports Kelang
Physical features comprises peninsular Malaysia (the nine Malay states – Johore, Kedah, Kelantan, Negri Sembilan, Pahang, Perak, Perlis, Selangor, Trengganu – plus Malacca and Penang); states of Sabah and Sarawak and federal territory of Kuala Lumpur; 75% tropical rainforest; central mountain range (Mount Kinabalu, the highest peak in SE Asia); swamps in E; Niah caves (Sarawak)

Government

Head of state Jaafar bin Abd al-Rahman from 1994
Head of government Mahathir bin Mohamed from 1981
Political system liberal democracy
Administrative divisions 13 states
Political parties New United Malays' National Organization (UMNO Baru), Malay-oriented nationalist; Malaysian Chinese Association (MCA), Chinese-oriented, conservative; Gerakan Party, Chinese-oriented, socialist; Malaysian Indian Congress (MIC), Indian-oriented; Democratic Action Party (DAP), multiracial but Chinese-dominated, left of centre; Pan-Malayan Islamic Party (PAS), Islamic; Semangat '46 (Spirit of 1946), moderate, multiracial
Armed forces 114,500; reserve force 58,300; paramilitary force 186,000 (1995)

Death penalty retained and used for ordinary crimes
Defence spend (% GDP) 4.5 (1995)
Education spend (% GNP) 4.4 (1994)
Health spend (% GDP) 1.3 (1990)

Economy and resources

Currency ringgit
GDP ($ US) 70.6 billion (1994)
Real GDP per capita (PPP) ($ US) 8,865 (1994)
GDP growth rate 9.2% (1994); 8.7% (1990–95)
Average annual inflation 3.7% (1994); 3.3% (1985–95)
Foreign debt ($ US) 34.35 billion (1995)
Trading partners Japan, USA, Singapore, Taiwan, UK and other EU countries
Resources tin, bauxite, copper, iron ore, petroleum, natural gas, forests
Industries electrical and electronic appliances (particularly radio and TV receivers), food processing, rubber products, industrial chemicals, wood products, petroleum refinery, motor vehicles, tourism
Exports palm oil, rubber, crude petroleum, machinery and transport equipment, timber, tin, textiles, electronic goods. Principal market: USA 20.7% (1995)
Imports machinery and transport equipment, chemicals, foodstuffs, crude petroleum, consumer goods. Principal source: Japan 27.3% (1995)
Arable land 3.2% (1993)
Agricultural products rice, cocoa, palm, rubber, pepper, coconuts, tea, pineapples

Population and society

Population 20,581,000 (1996e)
Population growth rate 2.4% (1990–95); 1.7% (2000–05)
Population density (per sq km) 62 (1996e)
Urban population (% of total) 54 (1995)
Age distribution (% of total population) <15 38%, 15–65 58.1%, >65 3.9% (1995)
Ethnic distribution 58% of the population is Malay, four-fifths of whom live in rural areas; 32% is Chinese, four-fifths of whom are in towns; 9% is Indian, mainly Tamil
Languages Malay (official), English, Chinese, Tamil, Iban
Religions Muslim (official), Buddhist, Hindu, local beliefs

Education (compulsory years) 11
Literacy rate 86% (men); 70% (women) (1995e)
Labour force 39% of population: 27% agriculture, 23% industry, 50% services (1990)
Unemployment 2.9% (1994)
Life expectancy 70 (men); 74 (women) (1995–2000)
Child mortality rate (under 5, per 1,000 live births) 13 (1995)
Physicians 1 per 2,397 people (1992)
Hospital beds 1 per 592 people (1994)
TV sets (per 1,000 people) 164 (1995)
Radios (per 1,000 people) 432 (1995)

Transport

Airports international airports: Kuala Lumpur (Subang), Penang (Bayan Lepas), Kota Kinabalu, Kuching; 15 domestic airports; total passenger km: 20,335 mil (1994)
Railroads total length: 1,882 km/1,169 mi; total passenger km: 1,367 mil (1994)
Roads total road network: 93,975 km/ 58,396 mi, of which 75% paved (1995e); passenger cars: 130.2 per 1,000 people (1995)

Chronology

1st century AD Peoples of Malay peninsula influenced by Indian culture and Buddhism.
8th–13th centuries Malay peninsula formed part of Buddhist Srivijaya Empire based in Sumatra.
14th century Siam (Thailand) expanded to included most of Malay peninsula.
1403 Muslim traders founded port of Malacca, which became a great commercial centre, encouraging spread of Islam.
1511 Portuguese attacked and captured Malacca.
1641 Portuguese ousted from Malacca by Dutch after seven-year blockade.
1786 British East India Company established a trading post on island of Penang.
1795–1815 Britain occupied Dutch colonies after France conquered the Netherlands.
1819 Stamford Raffles of East India Company obtained Singapore from Sultan of Johore.
1824 Anglo-Dutch Treaty ceded Malacca to Britain in return for territory in Sumatra.

1826 British possessions of Singapore, Penang, and Malacca formed Straits Settlements, ruled by governor of Bengal; ports prospered and expanded.
1840 Sultan of Brunei gave Sarawak to James Brooke, whose family ruled it as an independent state until 1946.
1851 Responsibility for Straits Settlements assumed by governor general of India.
1858 British government, through India Office, took over administration of Straits Settlements.
1867 Straits Settlements became crown colony of British Empire.
1874 British protectorates established over four Malay states of Perak, Salangor, Pahang, and Negri Sembilan, which federated 1896.
1888 Britain declared protectorate over N Borneo (Sabah).
late 19th century Millions of Chinese and thousands of Indians migrated to Malaya to work in tin mines and on rubber plantations.
1909–14 Britain assumed indirect rule

over five northern Malay states after agreement with Siam (Thailand).
1941–45 Japanese occupation.
1946 United Malay National Organization (UMNO) founded to oppose British plans for centralized Union of Malaya.
1948 Britain federated nine Malay states with Penang and Malacca to form single colony of Federation of Malaya.
1948–60 Malayan emergency: British forces suppressed insurrection by communist guerrillas.
1957 Federation of Malaya became independent with Prince Abdul Rahman (leader of UMNO) as prime minister.
1963 Federation of Malaya combined with Singapore, Sarawak, and Sabah to form Federation of Malaysia.
1963–66 'The Confrontation' – guerrillas supported by Indonesia opposed federation with intermittent warfare.
1965 Singapore withdrew from Federation of Malaysia.
1968 Philippines claimed sovereignty over Sabah.
1969 Malay resentment of Chinese

economic dominance resulted in race riots in Kuala Lumpur.
1971 *Bumiputra* policies which favoured ethnic Malays in education and employment introduced by Tun Abul Razak of UMNO.
1981 Mahathir bin Muhammad (UMNO) became prime minister; government increasingly dominated by Muslim Malays.
1987 Malay–Chinese relations deteriorated; over 100 opposition activists arrested.
1988 UMNO split over Mahathir's leadership style; his supporters formed UMNO Baru (New UMNO); his critics formed Semangat '46, a new multiracial party 1989.
1991 Launch of economic development policy aimed at 7% annual growth.
1996 Semangat '46 rejoined UMNO Baru, which remained under Mahathir's leadership.
1997 Deputy prime minister Anwar Ibrahim acting head of government during Mahathir's sabbatical. Currency allowed to float.

Practical information

Visa requirements UK: visa not required. USA: visa not required
Embassy in the UK 45 Belgrave Square, London SW1X 8QT. Tel: (0171) 235 8033; fax: (0171) 235 5161
British embassy British High Commission, PO Box 11030, 185 Jalan Ampang, 50450 Kuala Lumpur. Tel: (3) 248 2122; fax: (3) 248 0880
Embassy in the USA 2401 Massachusetts Avenue NW, Washington, DC 20008. Tel: (202) 328 2700; fax: (202) 483 7661
American embassy 376 Jalan Tun Razak, 50400 Kuala Lumpur. Tel: (3) 248 9011; fax: (3) 242 2207
Chamber of commerce Malaysian International Chamber of

Commerce and Industry, PO Box 12921, Wisma Damansara, 10th Floor, Jalah Semantan, 50792 Kuala Lumpur. Tel: (3) 254 2677; fax: (3) 255 4946
Office hours vary between Peninsular Malaysia and East Malaysia; generally 0830–1200/1300 and 1400/1500–1600/1730 Mon–Fri; 0830–1200 Sat
Banking hours 1000–1500 Mon–Fri; 0930–1130 Sat
Time difference GMT +8
Chief tourist attractions cultures of the country's many ethnic groups; tranquil beaches backed by dense rainforest
Major holidays 1 January (in some states), 1 May, 3 June, 31 August, 25 December; variable: Eid-ul Adha, Diwali (in most states), end of Ramadan (2 days), New Year (Chinese, January/February, most states), New Year (Muslim), Prophet's Birthday, Wesak (most states), several local festivals

Maldives Republic of the

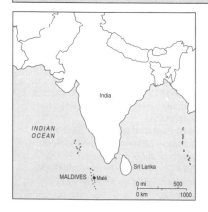

National name *Divehi Raajjeyge Jumhooriyaa*
Area 298 sq km/115 sq mi
Capital Malé
Major towns/cities Seenu, Kurehdhu, Kunfunadhoo, Dhiggiri, Anthimatha
Physical features comprises 1,196 coral islands, grouped into 12 clusters of atolls, largely flat, none bigger than 13 sq km/5 sq mi, average elevation 1.8 m/6 ft, 203 are inhabited

Government

Head of state and government Maumoon Abd al-Gayoom from 1978

Political system authoritarian nationalist
Administrative divisions 20 districts
Political parties none; candidates elected on basis of personal influence and clan loyalties
Armed forces no standing army
Death penalty retains the death penalty for ordinary crimes but can be considered abolitionist in practice (last known execution 1952)
Education spend (% GNP) 8.1 (1993–94)
Health spend (% GDP) 5 (1990)

Economy and resources

Currency rufiya
GDP ($ US) 390 million (1994e)
Real GDP per capita (PPP) ($ US) 1,560 (1994e)
GDP growth rate 6.6% (1994)
Average annual inflation 16.5% (1994); 9.2% (1985–95e)
Foreign debt ($ US) 162 million (1994)
Trading partners UK, Singapore, USA, India, Sri Lanka, Thailand, Germany, Japan
Resources coral (mining was banned as a measure against the encroachment of the sea)
Industries fish canning, clothing, soft-drink bottling, shipping, lacquer work, shell craft, tourism
Exports marine products (tuna bonito ('Maldive Fish'), clothing. Principal market: UK 26% (1995)
Imports consumer manufactured goods, petroleum products, food, intermediate and capital goods. Principal source: Singapore 27.4% (1995)
Arable land 10% (1993)
Agricultural products coconuts, maize, cassava, sweet potatoes, chillies; fishing (the Maldives' second largest source of foreign exchange after tourism 1995)

Population and society

Population 263,000 (1996e)
Population growth rate 3.3% (1990–95)
Population density (per sq km) 884 (1996e)
Urban population (% of total) 33 (1995)
Age distribution (% of total population) <15 47%, 15–65 50%, >65 3% (1994)

Ethnic distribution four main groups: Dravidian in the northern islands, Arab in the middle islands, Sinhalese in the southern islands, and African
Languages Divehi (Sinhalese dialect), English
Religion Sunni Muslim
Education not compulsory
Literacy rate 93% (men); 93% (women) (1995e)
Labour force 41% of population: 32% agriculture, 31% industry, 37% services (1990)
Unemployment 1.6% (1985)
Life expectancy 66 (men); 63 (women) (1995–2000)
Child mortality rate (under 5, per 1,000 live births) 78 (1994)
Physicians 1 per 6,057 people (1992)
Hospital beds 1 per 1,218 people (1992)
TV sets (per 1,000 people) 26 (1995)
Radios (per 1,000 people) 118 (1995)

Transport

Airports international airports: Malé, Gan; total passenger km: 7 mil (1994)
Railroads none
Roads total road network: 9.6 km/6 mi; passenger cars: 3.4 per 1,000 people (1992)

Chronology

12th century AD Islam introduced by seafaring Arabs, who displaced the indigenous Dravidian population.
14th century Ad-Din sultanate established.
1558–73 Under Portuguese rule.
1645 Became a dependency of Ceylon (Sri Lanka), which was ruled by the Dutch until 1796 and then by the British, with Sinhalese and Indian colonies being established.
1887 Became internally self-governing British protectorate, which remained a dependency of Sri Lanka until 1948.
1932 Formerly hereditary, the sultanate became an elected position when Maldives' first constitution was introduced.
1953 Maldive Islands became a republic within the Commonwealth, as the ad-Din sultanate was abolished.
1954 Sultan restored.
1959–60 Secessionist rebellion in Suvadiva (Huvadu) and Addu southern atolls.
1965 Achieved full independence outside Commonwealth.
1968 Sultan deposed after referendum; republic reinstated with Ibrahim Nasir as president.
1975 Closure of British airforce staging post on southern island of Gan led to substantial loss in income.
1978 The autocratic Nasir retired; replaced by Maumoon Abd al-Gayoom.
1980s Economic growth boosted by rapid development of tourist industry.
1982 Rejoined Commonwealth.
1985 Became founder member of South Asian Association for Regional Cooperation.
1986 The High Court sentenced exiled Nasir in absentia to 25 years' banishment on charges of embezzlement of public funds, but pardon was granted two years later.
1988 Coup attempt by Sri Lankan mercenaries, thought to have the backing of former president Nasir, foiled by Indian paratroops.

Practical information

Visa requirements UK: visa required. USA: visa required
Embassy in the UK Honorary Tourism Representative for the Maldives Republic in the UK, Toni the Maldive Lady, 3 Esher House, 11 Edith Terrace, London SW10 0TH. Tel: (0171) 352 2246; fax: (0171) 351 3382
British embassy the British High Commission in Colombo (see Sri Lanka) deals with enquiries relating to the Maldives
Embassy in the USA the Maldives does not have an embassy in the USA, but has a Permanent Mission to the UN in New York
American embassy the USA does not have an embassy in the Maldives; the US Ambassador to Sri Lanka is accredited to the Maldives and makes periodic visits there
Chamber of commerce State Trading Organisation, STO Building, 7 Haveeree Higun, Malé 20-02. Tel: (960) 323 279; fax: (960) 325 218
Office hours 0730–1330 Sat–Thu
Banking hours 0900–1300 Sun–Thu
Time difference GMT +5
Chief tourist attractions white sandy beaches; multi-coloured coral formations; water and underwater sports/activities
Major holidays 1 January, 26 July (2 days), 11 November (2 days); variable: Eid-ul-Adha (4 days), end of Ramadan (3 days), New Year (Muslim), Prophet's Birthday, first day of Ramadan (2 days), Huravee (February), Martyrs (April), National (October/November, 2 days)

Mali Republic of

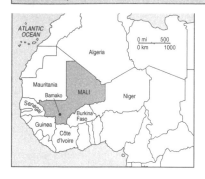

National name *République du Mali*
Area 1,240,142 sq km/478,818 sq mi
Capital Bamako
Major towns/cities Mopti, Kayes,
Ségou, Timbuktu, Sikasso
Physical features landlocked state with
river Niger and savanna in S; part of the
Sahara in N; hills in NE; Senegal River
and its branches irrigate the SW

Government

Head of state Alpha Oumar Konare from
1992
Head of government Ibrahim Boubaker
Keita from 1994
Political system emergent democratic
republic
Administrative divisions capital district
of Bamako and eight regions
Political parties Alliance for Democracy
in Mali (ADEMA), left of centre; National
Committee for Democratic Initiative
(CNID), centre left; Assembly for
Democracy and Progress (RDP), left of
centre; Civic Society and the Democracy
and Progress Party (PDP), left of centre;
Malian People's Democratic Union
(UDPM), nationalist socialist
Armed forces 7,400 (1995); plus
paramilitary forces numbering 7,800
Conscription selective conscription for
two years
Death penalty retains the death penalty
for ordinary crimes but can be
considered abolitionist in practice (last
execution 1980)
Defence spend (% GDP) 2.4 (1995)
Education spend (% GNP) 2.1 (1993–94)
Health spend (% GDP) 2.8 (1990)

Economy and resources

Currency franc CFA
GDP ($ US) 1.9 billion (1994)
Real GDP per capita (PPP) ($ US) 543
(1994)

GDP growth rate 2.4% (1994); 2.5%
(1990–95)
Average annual inflation 28% (1994);
151.9% (1985–95)
Foreign debt ($ US) 3.06 billion (1995)
Trading partners Côte d'Ivoire,
Thailand, CIS countries, Belgium,
France, China, Ireland, Senegal
Resources iron ore, uranium, diamonds,
bauxite, manganese, copper, lithium,
gold
Industries food processing, cotton
processing, textiles, clothes, cement,
pharmaceuticals
Exports cotton, livestock, gold,
miscellaneous manufactured articles.
Principal market: Thailand 18.5% (1995)
Imports machinery and transport
equipment, food products, petroleum
products, other raw materials, chemicals,
miscellaneous manufactured articles.
Principal source: Côte d'Ivoire 22%
(1995)
Arable land 2% (1993)
Agricultural products seed cotton,
cotton lint, groundnuts, millet, sugar
cane, rice, sorghum, sweet potatoes,
mangoes, vegetables; livestock rearing
(cattle, sheep, and goats); fishing

Population and society

Population 11,134,000 (1996e)
Population growth rate 3.2%
(1990–95); 2.9% (2000–05)
Population density (per sq km) 9
(1996e)
Urban population (% of total) 27 (1995)
Age distribution (% of total population)
<15 47.4%, 15–65 50%, >65 2.5%
(1995)
Ethnic distribution around 50% belong
to the Mande group, including the
Bambara, Malinke, and Sarakole; other
significant groups include the Fulani,
Minianka, Senutu, Songhai, and the
nomadic Tuareg in the N
Languages French (official), Bambara
Religions Sunni Muslim 90%, animist,
Christian
Literacy rate 41% (men); 24% (women)
(1995e)
Labour force 50% of population: 86%
agriculture, 2% industry, 12% services
(1990)
Life expectancy 46 (men); 50 (women)
(1995–2000)
Child mortality rate (under 5, per 1,000
live births) 210 (1995)
Physicians 1 per 20,000 people (1991)

Hospital beds 1 per 2,623 people
(1990)
TV sets (per 1,000 people) 1.9 (1995)
Radios (per 1,000 people) 46 (1995)

Transport

Airports international airports: Bamako
(Senou), Mopti; ten domestic airports;
total passenger km: 215 mil (1994)
Railroads total length: 641 km/398 mi;
total passenger km: 846 mil (1993)
Roads total road network: 14,776 km/
9,182 mi, of which 12% paved (1995);
passenger cars: 2.8 per 1,000 people
(1995e)

Chronology

5th–13th centuries Ghana Empire
founded by agriculturist Soninke people,
based on the Saharan gold trade for
which Timbuktu became an important
centre. At its height in the 11th century it
covered much of the western Sahel,
comprising parts of present-day Mali,
Senegal, and Mauritania. Wars with
Muslim Berber tribes from the N led to its
downfall. Its capital was at Kumbi, 125
mi/200 km N of Bamako, in SE
Mauritania.
13th–15th centuries Ghana Empire
superseded by Muslim Mali Empire of
Malinke (Mandingo) people of SW, from
which Mali derives its name. At its peak,
under Mansa Musa in the 14th century, it
covered parts of Mali, Senegal, Gambia,
and S Mauritania.
15th–16th centuries Muslim Songhai
Empire, centred around Timbuktu and
Gao, superseded Mali Empire. Under
Sonni Ali Ber, who ruled 1464–92, it
covered Mali, Senegal, Gambia, and
parts of Mauritania, Niger, and Nigeria,
and included a professional army and
civil service.
1591 Songhai Empire destroyed by
Moroccan Berbers, under Ahmad al-
Mansur, who launched an invasion to
take over western Sudanese gold trade
and took control over Timbuktu.
18th–19th centuries Niger valley region
was divided between the nomadic
Tuareg, in the area around Gao in the
NE, and the Fulani and Bambara
kingdoms, around Macina and Bambara
in the centre and SW.
late 18th century Western Mali visited
by Scottish explorer Mungo Park.
mid-19th century The Islamic Tukolor,
as part of a jihad (holy war) conquered

much of western Mali, including Fulani and Bambara kingdoms, while in the S, Samori Ture, a Muslim Malinke (Mandingo) warrior, created a small empire.

1880–95 Region conquered by French, who overcame Tukolor and Samori resistance to establish colony of French Sudan.

1904 Became part of federation of French West Africa.

1946 French Sudan became an overseas territory within the French Union, with its own territorial assembly and representation in the French parliament; the pro-autonomy Sudanese Union and Sudanese Progressive Parties founded in Bamako.

1959 With Senegal, formed the Federation of Mali.

1960 Separated from Senegal and became independent Republic of Mali, with Modibo Keita, an authoritarian socialist of the Sudanese Union party, as president.

1968 Keita replaced in army coup by Lt Moussa Traoré, as economy deteriorated: constitution suspended and political activity banned.

1974 New constitution made Mali a one-party state, dominated by Traoré's nationalistic socialist Malian People's Democratic Union (UDPM), formed 1976.

1979 More than a dozen killed after a student strike was crushed.

1985 Five-day conflict with Burkina Faso over long-standing border dispute; mediated by International Court of Justice.

late 1980s Closer ties developed with

the West and free-market economic policies pursued, including privatization, as Soviet influence waned.

1991 Violent demonstrations and strikes against one-party rule led to 150 deaths; Traoré ousted in a coup led by Lt-Col Amadou Toumani Toure.

1992 Referendum endorsed new democratic constitution. The opposition Alliance for Democracy in Mali (ADEMA) won multiparty elections; Alpha Oumar Konare elected president. Coalition government formed. Peace pact signed with Tuareg rebels fighting in N Mali for greater autonomy.

1993–94 Student unrest forced two changes of prime minister. Ex-president Traoré sentenced to death for his role in suppressing the 1991 riots.

1997 President Konare re-elected.

Practical information

Visa requirements UK: visa required. USA: visa required
Embassy for the UK 487 avenue Molière, B-1060 Brussels, Belgium. Tel: (2) 345 7432; fax: (2) 344 5700
British embassy British Consulate, BP 1598, Plan International, Bamako. Tel: (223) 230 583; fax: (223) 228 143
Embassy in the USA 2130 R Street NW, Washington, DC 20008. Tel: (202) 332 2249, 939 8950
American embassy rue Rochester NY and rue Mohamed V, Bamako. Tel: (223) 225 470; fax: (223) 223 712
Chamber of commerce Chambre de Commerce et d'Industrie de Mali, BP 46, place de la Liberté, Bamako.

Tel: (223) 225 036; fax: (223) 222 120
Office hours 0730–1230 and 1300–1600 Mon–Thu; 0730–1230 and 1430–1730 Fri
Banking hours 0730–1200 and 1315–1500 Mon–Thu; 0730–1230 Fri
Time difference GMT +/–0
Chief tourist attractions cultural heritage, including the historic town of Timbuktu, with its 13th–15th-century mosques; oases along the ancient trans-Sahara camel route
Major holidays 1, 20 January, 1, 25 May, 22 September, 19 November, 25 December; variable: Eid-ul-Adha, end of Ramadan, Prophet's Birthday, Prophet's Baptism (November)

Malta Republic of

National name *Repubblika Ta'Malta*
Area 320 sq km/124 sq mi
Capital Valletta (and port)
Major towns/cities Rabat, Birkirkara, Qormi, Sliema, Zetjun, Zabor
Major ports Marsaxlokk, Valletta
Physical features includes islands of

Gozo 67 sq km/26 sq mi and Comino 3 sq km/1 sq mi

Government

Head of state Mifsud Bonnici from 1994
Head of government Edward Fenech Adami from 1987
Political system liberal democracy
Administrative divisions 67 local councils
Political parties Malta Labour Party (MLP), moderate, left of centre; Nationalist Party (PN), Christian, centrist, pro-European
Armed forces 2,000 (1995)
Conscription military service is voluntary
Death penalty laws provide for the death penalty only for exceptional crimes such as crimes under military law or crimes committed in exceptional circumstances such as wartime (last execution 1943)

Defence spend (% GDP) 1.1 (1995)
Education spend (% GNP) 5.1 (1993–94)

Economy and resources

Currency Maltese lira
GDP ($ US) 2.6 billion (1994)
Real GDP per capita (PPP) ($ US) 13,009 (1994)
GDP growth rate 5.1% (1994)
Average annual inflation 4% (1995); 2.9% (1985–95e)
Foreign debt ($ US) 806.6 million (1994)
Trading partners Italy, Germany, UK, USA, France, Libya, the Netherlands
Resources stone, sand; offshore petroleum reserves were under exploration 1988–95
Industries transport equipment and machinery, food and beverages, textiles and clothing, chemicals, ship repair and shipbuilding, tourism

Exports machinery and transport equipment, manufactured articles (including clothing), beverages, chemicals, tobacco. Principal market: Italy 37.5% 1994

Imports machinery and transport equipment, basic manufactures (including textile yarn and fabrics), food and live animals, mineral fuels. Principal source: Italy 26.5% (1994)

Arable land 37.5% (1993)

Agricultural products potatoes, tomatoes, peaches, plums, nectarines, apricots, melons, strawberries, wheat, barley; livestock rearing (cattle, pigs, and poultry) and livestock products (chicken eggs, pork, and dairy products)

Population and society

Population 369,000 (1996e)
Population growth rate 0.7% (1990–95)
Population density (per sq km) 1,168 (1996e)
Urban population (% of total) 89 (1995)
Age distribution (% of total population) <15 22%, 15–65 67%, >65 11% (1994)
Ethnic distribution essentially European, supposedly originated from ancient North African kingdom of Carthage
Languages Maltese, English (both official)
Religion Roman Catholic 98%
Education (compulsory years) 10
Literacy rate 86% (men); 86% (women) (1995e)
Labour force 2.5% agriculture, 34% industry, 63.5% services (1992)
Unemployment 3.5% (1995)
Life expectancy 75 (men); 79 (women) (1995–2000)

Child mortality rate (under 5, per 1,000 live births) 9 (1995)
Physicians 1 per 406 people (1995)
Hospital beds 1 per 172 people (1995)
TV sets (per 1,000 people) 749 (1995)
Radios (per 1,000 people) 545 (1995)

Transport

Airports international airports: Luga (Malta, 8 km/5 mi from Valetta); helicopter service between Malta and Gozo; total passenger km: 1,821 mil (1994)
Railroads none
Roads total road network: 1,604 km/ 997 mi, of which 94% paved; passenger cars: 442 per 1,000 people (1994)

Chronology

7th century BC Invaded and subjugated by Carthaginians from North Africa.
218 BC Came under Roman control.
AD 60 Converted to Christianity by the apostle Paul, who was shipwrecked.
395 On division of Roman Empire, became part of Eastern (Byzantine) portion, dominated by Constantinople.
870 Came under Arab rule.
1091 Arabs defeated by Norman Count Roger I of Sicily; Roman Catholic Church re-established.
1530 Handed over by Holy Roman Emperor Charles V to religious military order, the Hospitallers (Knights of St John of Jerusalem).
1798–1802 Briefly occupied by French.
1814 Annexed to Britain by Treaty of Paris on condition that Roman Catholic Church was maintained and Maltese Declaration of Rights honoured.

later 19th century–early 20th century Became vital British naval base, with famous dockyard that developed as island's economic mainstay.
1942 Awarded George Cross for valour in resisting severe Italian aerial attacks during World War II.
1947 Achieved self-government.
1955 Dom Mintoff of left-of-centre Malta Labour Party (MLP) became prime minister.
1956 Referendum approved MLP's proposal for integration with UK. Plebiscite opposed and boycotted by right-of-centre Nationalist Party (PN).
1958 MLP rejected final British integration proposal.
1962 PN elected, with Dr Giorgio Borg Olivier as prime minister.
1964 Independence achieved from Britain, within Commonwealth. Ten-year defence and economic-aid treaty with UK signed.
1971 Mintoff adopted policy of nonalignment and declared 1964 treaty invalid; negotiations began for leasing NATO base in Malta.
1972 Seven-year NATO agreement signed.
1974 Became a republic.
1979 British military base closed; closer links established with communist and Arab states, including Libya.
1984 Mintoff retired; replaced by Karmenu Mifsud Bonnici as prime minister and MLP leader.
1987 Edward Fenech Adami (PN) narrowly elected prime minister; he adopted a more pro-European and pro-American policy stance than preceding administration.
1990 Formal application made for European Community membership.
1994 Mifsud Bonnici elected president.

Practical information

Visa requirements UK: visa not required. USA: visa not required
Embassy in the UK Malta House, 36–38 Piccadilly, London W1V 0PP. Tel: (0171) 292 4800; fax: (0171) 734 1832
British embassy British High Commission, PO Box 506, 7 St Anne Street, Floriana, Valetta. Tel: (356) 233 134; fax: (356) 242 001
Embassy in the USA 2017 Connecticut Avenue NW, Washington, DC 20008. Tel: (202) 462 3611/2; fax: (202) 387 5470
American embassy 2nd Floor, Development House, St Anne Street, Floriana, Malta. Tel: (356) 235 960; fax: (356) 243 229

Chamber of commerce Exchange Building, Republic Street, Valetta VLT 05. Tel: (356) 247 233; fax: (356) 245 223
Office hours 0830–1245 and 1430–1730 Mon–Fri; 0830–1200 Sat
Banking hours 0800–1200 Mon–Thu; 0800–1200 and 1430–1600 Fri; 0800–1130 Sat
Time difference GMT +1
Chief tourist attractions fine climate; sandy beaches and rocky coves; Blue Lagoon of Comino; prehistoric temples and Ta' Plnh church of Gozo; Valetta, with its 16th-century churches, palaces, hospitals, and aqueducts, and its yachting centre
Major holidays 1 January, 31 March, 1 May, 15 August, 13, 25 December; variable: Good Friday

Marshall Islands Republic of the (RMI)

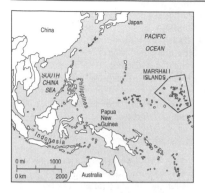

Area 181 sq km/69 sq mi
Capital Dalap-Uliga-Darrit (on Majuro atoll)
Major towns/cities Ebeye (the only other town)
Physical features comprises the Ratak and Ralik island chains in the W Pacific, which together form an archipelago of 31 coral atolls, 5 islands, and 1,152 islets

Government

Head of state and government Imata Kabua from 1997
Political system liberal democracy
Political parties no organized party system, but in 1991 an opposition grouping, the Ralik Ratak Democratic Party, was founded to oppose the ruling group
Armed forces the USA maintains a military presence on the Kwajalein Atoll (the Compact of Free Association gave the USA responsibility for defence in return for US assistance)
Death penalty abolished 1991
Education spend (% GDP) 6 (1994)

Economy and resources

Currency US dollar
GDP ($ US) 94 million (1995e)

Real GDP per capita (PPP) ($ US) 1,680 (1995e)
GDP growth rate 1.5% (1995e)
Average annual inflation 4% (1995e); 5.4% (1985–95e)
Foreign debt ($ US) 170 million (1994)
Trading partners USA, Japan, Australia
Resources phosphates
Industries processing of agricultural products, handicrafts, fish products and canning, tourism
Exports coconut products, trochus shells, copra, handicrafts, fish, live animals. Principal market: USA
Imports foodstuffs, beverages and tobacco, building materials, machinery and transport equipment, mineral fuels, chemicals. Principal source: USA
Agricultural products coconuts, tomatoes, melons, breadfruit, cassava, sweet potatoes, copra; fishing; seaweed and pearl oyster cultivation developed during first half of 1990s

Population and society

Population 57,000 (1996e)
Population growth rate 2.9% (1990–95)
Population density (per sq km) 313 (1996e)
Urban population (% of total) 69.1 (1995)
Ethnic distribution 97% Marshallese, of predominantly Micronesian descent
Language Marshallese, English (both official)
Religions Christian (mainly Protestant) and Baha'i
Education (compulsory years) 8
Literacy rate 91% (men); 90% (women) (1994e)
Labour force 26.1% agriculture, 9.5% industry, 64.4% services (1989)
Unemployment 16% (1991e)
Life expectancy 62 (men); 65 (women) (1995)
Child mortality rate (under 5, per 1,000 live births) 48 (1994)

Physicians 1 per 2,631 people (1990)
Hospital beds 1 per 926 people (1990)
TV sets (per 1,000 people) 52 (1992)

Transport

Airports international airports: Majuro; ten domestic airports; total passenger km: 41 mil (1994)
Railroads none

Chronology

after c. 1000 BC Micronesians first settled the islands.
1529 Visited by Spanish navigator Miguel de Saavedra and thereafter came under Spanish influence.
1875 Spanish rule formally declared in face of increasing encroachment by German traders.
1885 German protectorate established.
1914 Seized by Japan on the outbreak of World War I.
1920–44 Administered under League of Nations mandate by Japan and vigorously colonized.
1944 Japanese removed after heavy fighting with US troops during World War II.
1946–63 Eniwetok and Bikini atolls used for US atom-bomb tests; islanders later demanded rehabilitation and compensation for the damage.
1947 Became part of United Nations (UN) Pacific Islands Trust Territory, administered by USA.
1979 Amata Kabua elected president as internal self-government established.
1986 Compact of Free Association with USA granted islands self-government, with USA retaining responsibility for defence and security until 2001.
1990 UN trust status terminated.
1991 Independence agreed with Kabua as president; UN membership granted.
1996 Death of President Amata Kabua.
1997 Imata Kabua elected president.

Practical information

Visa requirements UK: visa required. USA: visa required
Embassy in the UK none; enquiries relating to the Marshall Islands are dealt with by the Marshall Islands Visitors Authority, PO Box 1727, Ministry of Resources and Development, Majuro 96960. Tel: (692) 625 3206; fax: (692) 625 3218
British embassy none
Embassy in the USA 2433 Massachusetts Avenue NW, Washington, DC 20008. Tel: (202) 234 5414; fax: (202) 232 3236

American embassy Oceanside, Long Island, Majuro. Tel: (692) 247 4011; fax: (692) 247 4012
Chamber of commerce Majuro Chamber of Commerce, Majuro 96960. Tel: (692) 625 3051; fax: (692) 625 3343
Office hours 0800–1700 Mon–Fri
Banking hours generally 1000–1500 Mon–Thu; 1000–1800 Fri
Time difference GMT +12
Chief tourist attractions sandy beaches; coral atolls; tropical vegetation
Major holidays 1 January, 1 March, 1 May, 1 July, 21 October, 17 November, 4, 25 December

Mauritania Islamic Republic of

National name *République Islamique Arabe et Africaine de Mauritanie*
Area 1,030,700 sq km/397,953 sq mi
Capital Nouakchott (port)
Major towns/cities Nouâdhibou, Kaédi, Zouerate, Kiffa, Rosso, Atar
Major ports Nouâdhibou
Physical features valley of river Senegal in S; remainder arid and flat

Government

Head of state Maaoya Sid'Ahmed Ould Taya from 1984
Head of government Cheik el Avia Ould Muhammad Khouna from 1996
Political system emergent democratic republic
Administrative divisions 12 regions
Political parties Democratic and Social Republican Party (PRDS), centre left, militarist; Rally for Democracy and National Unity (RDNU), centrist; Mauritian Renewal Party (MPR), centrist; Umma, Islamic fundamentalist
Armed forces 15,700 (1995); plus paramilitary force of around 5,000
Conscription military service is by authorized conscription for two years
Death penalty retained and used for ordinary crimes
Defence spend (% GDP) 1.9 (1995)
Education spend (% GNP) 4.0 (1994)
Health spend (% GDP) 5.5 (1990)

Economy and resources

Currency ouguiya
GDP ($ US) 1 billion (1994)
Real GDP per capita (PPP) ($ US) 1,593 (1994)
GDP growth rate 4.6% (1994), 4% (1990–95)
Average annual inflation 14.5% (1994); 6.9% (1985–95)
Foreign debt ($ US) 2.5 billion (1995)
Trading partners Japan, France, Spain,

Italy, Belgium, Germany
Resources copper, gold, iron ore, gypsum, phosphates, sulphur, peat
Industries fish products, cheese and butter, processing of minerals (including imported petroleum), mining
Exports fish and fish products, iron ore. Principal market: Japan 27.2% (1995)
Imports machinery and transport equipment, foodstuffs, consumer goods, building materials, mineral fuels. Principal source: France 23.9% (1995)
Arable land 0.2% (1993)
Agricultural products millet, sorghum, dates, maize, rice, pulses, groundnuts, sweet potatoes; livestock rearing (the principal occupation of rural population); fishing (providing 56% of export earnings 1993). Only 1% of Mauritania receives enough rain to grow crops

Population and society

Population 2,333,000 (1996e)
Population growth rate 2.5% (1990–95); 2.5% (2000–05)
Population density (per sq km) 2 (1996e)
Urban population (% of total) 54 (1995)
Age distribution (% of total population) <15 43.1%, 15–65 53.7%, >65 3.2% (1995)
Ethnic distribution over 80% of the population is of Moorish or Moorish-black origin; about 18% is black African (concentrated in the S); there is a small European minority
Languages French and Hasaniya Arabic (both official), African languages including Pulaar, Soninke, and Wolof
Religion Sunni Muslim
Education not compulsory
Literacy rate 47% (men); 21% (women) (1995e)
Labour force 46% of population: 55% agriculture, 10% industry, 34% services (1990)
Unemployment 20% (1991e)
Life expectancy 52 (men); 55 (women) (1995–2000)
Child mortality rate (under 5, per 1,000 live births) 195 (1995)
Physicians 1 per 11,316 people (1994)
Hospital beds 1 per 1,311 people (1990)
TV sets (per 1,000 people) 25 (1995)
Radios (per 1,000 people) 150 (1995)

Transport

Airports international airports: Nouakchott, Nouâdhibou; six domestic

airports; total passenger km: 289 mil (1994)
Railroads total length: 704 km/437 mi; the principal traffic is iron ore; passenger traffic is negligible
Roads total road network: 7,600 km/4,723 mi, of which 11.2% paved (1995e); passenger cars: 7.4 per 1,000 people (1995e)

Chronology

early Christian era A Roman province with the name Mauritania, after the Mauri, its Berber inhabitants who became active in the long-distance salt trade.
7th–11th centuries Eastern Mauritania was incorporated in the larger Ghana Empire, centred on Mali to the E, but with its capital at Kumbi in SE Mauritania. The Berbers were reduced to vassals and converted to Islam in the 8th century.
11th–12th centuries The area's Sanhadja Berber inhabitants, linked to the Morocco-based Almoravid Empire, destroyed the Ghana Empire and spread Islam among neighbouring peoples.
13th–15th centuries SE Mauritania formed part of Muslim Mali Empire, which extended to E and S.
1441 Coast visited by Portuguese, who founded port of Arguin and captured Africans to sell as slaves.
15th–16th centuries Eastern Mauritania formed part of Muslim Songhai Empire, which spread across western Sahel, and Arab tribes migrated into the area.
1817 Senegal Treaty recognized coastal region (formerly disputed by European nations) as French sphere of influence.
1903 Formally became French protectorate.
1920 Became French colony, within French West Africa.
1960 Independence achieved, with Moktar Ould Daddah, leader of Mauritanian People's Party (PPM), as president. New capital built at Nouakchott.
1968 Underlying tensions between agriculturalist black population of S and economically dominant semi-nomadic Arabo-Berber peoples, or Moors, of desert N became more acute after Arabic was made an official language (with French).
1976 Western Sahara, to the NW, ceded by Spain to Mauritania and Morocco.

Mauritania occupied the southern area and Morocco the mineral-rich N. Polisario Front formed in Sahara to resist this occupation and guerrilla war broke out, with the Polisario receiving backing from Algeria and Libya.
1978 Daddah deposed in bloodless coup; replaced by Col Mohamed Khouna Ould Haidalla in military government.
1979 Peace accord signed with Polisario Front in Algiers, in which Mauritania, crippled by cost of military struggle over a largely uninhabited area, renounced

claims to southern Western Sahara (Tiris el Gharbia region) and recognized Polisario regime; diplomatic relations restored with Algeria.
1981 Diplomatic relations with Morocco broken after it annexed southern Western Sahara.
1984 Haidalla overthrown by Col Maaoya Sid'Ahmed Ould Taya.
1985 Relations with Morocco restored.
1989 Violent clashes in Mauritania and Senegal between Moors and black Africans, chiefly of Senegalese origins;

over 50,000 Senegalese expelled.
1991 Amnesty for political prisoners. Calls for resignation of President Taya. Political parties legalized and new multiparty constitution approved in referendum.
1992 First multiparty elections largely boycotted by opposition; Taya and his Social Democratic Republican Party (DSRP) re-elected. Diplomatic relations with Senegal resumed.
1996 Cheikh el Avia Ould Muhammad Khouna appointed prime minister.

Practical information

Visa requirements UK: visa required. USA: visa required
Embassy in the UK Honorary Consulate of the Islamic Republic of Mauritania, 140 Bow Common Lane, London E3 4BH. Tel: (0181) 980 4382; fax: (0181) 980 2232
British embassy the British Embassy in Rabat (see Morocco) deals with enquiries relating to Mauritania
Embassy in the USA 2129 Leroy Place NW, Washington, DC 20008. Tel: (202) 232 5700
American embassy address N/A, Nouakchott. Tel: (222) 52660/3; fax: (222) 51592

Chamber of commerce Chambre de Commerce, d'Agriculture, d'Elevage, d'Industrie et des Mines de Mauritanie, BP 215 Nouakchott. Tel: (222) 52214; telex: 581
Office hours 0800–1500 Sat–Wed; 0800–1300 Thu
Banking hours 0700–1500 Sun–Thu
Time difference GMT +/–0
Chief tourist attractions game reserves; national parks; historic sites, several of which have been listed by UNESCO under its World Heritage programme
Major holidays 1 January, 1, 25 May, 10 July, 28 November; variable: Eid-ul-Adha, end of Ramadan, New Year (Muslim), Prophet's Birthday

---

Mauritius Republic of

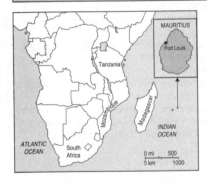

Area 1,865 sq km/720 sq mi; the island of Rodrigues is part of Mauritius; there are several small island dependencies
Capital Port Louis (port)
Major towns/cities Beau Bassin-Rose Hill, Curepipe, Quatre Bornes, Vacoas-Phoenix
Physical features mountainous, volcanic island surrounded by coral reefs

Government

Head of state Cassam Uteem from 1992
Head of government Navim Ramgoolam from 1995
Political system liberal democratic republic

Administrative divisions five municipalities and four district councils
Political parties Mauritius Socialist Movement (MSM), moderate socialist-republican; Mauritius Labour Party (MLP), democratic socialist, Hindu-oriented; Mauritius Social Democratic Party (PMSD), conservative, Francophile; Mauritius Militant Movement (MMM), Marxist-republican; Organization of Rodriguan People (OPR), left of centre
Armed forces no standing defence forces; 1,300-strong police mobile unit (1995)
Death penalty abolished 1995
Defence spend (% GDP) 0.5 (1995)
Education spend (% GNP) 3.6 (1993)
Health spend (% GDP) 2 (1990)

Economy and resources

Currency Mauritian rupee
GDP ($ US) 3.4 billion (1994)
Real GDP per capita (PPP) ($ US) 13,172 (1994)
GDP growth rate 5.1% (1994); 4.9% (1990–95)
Average annual inflation 5.8% (1996); 8.8% (1985–95)
Foreign debt ($ US) 1.8 billion (1995)
Trading partners UK, France, South

Africa, India, Australia, Germany
Industries textiles and clothing, footwear and other leather products, food products, diamond cutting, jewellery, electrical components, chemical products, furniture, tourism
Exports raw sugar, clothing, tea, molasses, jewellery. Principal market: UK 34% (1995)
Imports textile yarn and fabrics, petroleum products, industrial machinery, motor vehicles, manufactured goods. Principal source: France 19.9% (1995)
Arable land 49% (1993)
Agricultural products sugar cane, tea, tobacco, potatoes, maize; poultry farming; fishing; forest resources

Population and society

Population 1,129,000 (1996e)
Population growth rate 1.1% (1990–95); 1.1% (2000–05)
Population density (per sq km) 553 (1996e)
Urban population (% of total) 41 (1995)
Age distribution (% of total population) <15 27.7%, 15–65 66.4%, >65 5.8% (1995)
Ethnic distribution five principal ethnic groups: French, black Africans, Indians,

Chinese, and Mulattos (or Creoles).
Indo-Mauritians predominate, constituting
67% of the population, followed by
Creoles (29%), Sino-Mauritians (3.5%),
and Europeans (0.5%)
Languages English (official), French,
Creole, Indian languages
Religions Hindu, Christian (mainly
Roman Catholic), Muslim
Education (compulsory years) 7
Literacy rate 87% (men); 78% (women)
(1995e)
Labour force 15.7% agriculture, 43.7%
industry, 40.6% services (1992)
Unemployment 7.1% (1994)
Life expectancy 68 (men); 75 (women)
(1995–2000)
Child mortality rate (under 5, per 1,000
live births) 23 (1995)
Physicians 1 per 1,000 people (1993)
Hospital beds 1 per 350 people (1993)
TV sets (per 1,000 people) 222 (1995)
Radios (per 1,000 people) 367 (1995)

Transport

Airports international airport: Plaisance

(Sir Seewoosagur Ramgoolam, 48 km/
30 mi southeast of Port Louis); two
domestic airports; total passenger km:
2,972 mil (1994)
Railroads none
Roads total road network: 1,877 km/
1,166 mi, of which 93% paved (1995);
passenger cars: 56.3 per 1,000 people
(1995e)

Chronology

1598 Previously uninhabited, the island
was discovered by the Dutch and named
after Prince Morris of Nassau.
1710 Dutch colonists withdrew.
1721 Reoccupied by French East India
Company, who renamed it Ile de France,
and established sugar cane and tobacco
plantations worked by imported African
slaves.
1814 Ceded to Britain by Treaty of Paris.
1835 Slavery abolished; indentured
Indian and Chinese labourers imported
to work the sugar-cane plantations,
which were later hit by competition from
beet sugar.

1903 Formerly administered with
Seychelles, it became a single colony.
1936 Mauritius Labour Party (MLP)
founded, drawing strong support from
sugar workers.
1957 Internal self-government granted.
1968 Independence achieved from
Britain within Commonwealth, with
Seewoosagur Ramgoolam as centrist
Indian-dominated MLP as prime minister.
1971 State of emergency temporarily
imposed as a result of industrial unrest.
1982 Aneerood Jugnauth, of the
moderate socialist Mauritius Socialist
Movement (MSM) became prime
minister, pledging a programme of
nonalignment, nationalization, and the
creation of a republic.
1992 Mauritius became a republic, within
the Commonwealth, with Cassam Uteem
elected president.
1995 MLP and cross-community
Mauritian Militant Movement (MMM)
coalition won landslide election victory;
Navim Ramgoolam (MLP) became prime
minister.

Practical information

Visa requirements UK: visa not required. USA: visa not
required
Embassy in the UK 32/33 Elvaston Place, London
SW7 5NW. Tel: (0171) 581 0294; fax: (0171) 823 8437
British embassy British High Commission, PO Box 186, Les
Cascades Building, Edith Cavell Street, Port Louis.
Tel: (230) 211 1361; fax: (230) 211 1369
Embassy in the USA Suite 441, 4301 Connecticut Avenue
NW, Washington, DC 20008. Tel: (202) 244 1491/2;
fax: (202) 966 0983
American embassy 4th Floor, Rogers House, John Kennedy
Street, Port Louis. Tel: (230) 208 2347, 208 2354, 208

9763–9767; fax: (230) 208 9534
Chamber of commerce Mauritius Chamber of Commerce
and Industry, 3 Royal Street, Port Louis. Tel: (230) 208 3301;
fax: (230) 208 0076
Office hours 0900–1600 Mon–Fri; 0900–1200 Sat (some
offices only)
Banking hours 0930–1430 Mon–Fri; 0900–1130 Sat (except
Bank of Mauritius)
Time difference GMT +4
Chief tourist attractions fine scenery and beaches; pleasant
climate; blend of cultures
Major holidays 1–2 January, 12 March, 1 May, 1 November,
25 December; variable: Eid-ul-Adha, Diwali, end of Ramadan,
Prophet's Birthday, Chinese Spring Festival (February)

Mexico United States of

National name *Estados Unidos
Mexicanos*
Area 1,958,201 sq km/756,061 sq mi
Capital Mexico City
Major towns/cities Guadalajara,
Monterrey, Puebla, Netzahualcóyotl,
Ciudad Juárez, Tijuana
Major ports 49 ocean ports
Physical features partly arid central
highlands; Sierra Madre mountain ranges
E and W; tropical coastal plains;
volcanoes, including Popocatepetl; Rio
Grande

Government

Head of state and government Ernesto
Zedillo Ponce de Leon from 1994
Political system federal democratic
republic
Administrative divisions 31 states and
a Federal District
Political parties Institutional
Revolutionary Party (PRI), moderate, left
wing; National Action Party (PAN),
moderate, Christian, centre right; Party of
the Democratic Revolution (PRD), centre
left

Armed forces 175,000; rural defence militia of 14,000 (1995)
Conscription one year, part-time (conscripts selected by lottery)
Death penalty only for exceptional crimes; last execution 1937
Defence spend (% GDP) 0.9 (1995)
Education spend (% GNP) 5.8 (1993–94)
Health spend (% GDP) 1.6 (1990)

Economy and resources

Currency Mexican peso
GDP ($ US) 334.2 billion (1996)
Real GDP per capita (PPP) ($ US) 7,744 (1996)
GDP growth rate 5% (1996); 1.1% (1990–95)
Average annual inflation 34.2% (1996); 36.7% (1985–95)
Foreign debt ($ US) 165.74 billion (1995)
Trading partners USA, Japan, Spain, France, Germany, Brazil, Canada
Resources petroleum, natural gas, zinc, salt, silver, copper, coal, mercury, manganese, phosphates, uranium, strontium sulphide
Industries motor vehicles, food processing, iron and steel, chemicals, beverages, electrical machinery, electronic goods, petroleum refining, cement, metals and metal products, tourism
Exports petroleum and petroleum products, engines and spare parts for motor vehicles, motor vehicles, electrical and electronic goods, fresh and preserved vegetables, coffee, cotton. Principal market: USA 83.9% (1996)
Imports motor vehicle chassis, industrial machinery and equipment, iron and steel, telecommunications apparatus, organic chemicals, cereals and cereal preparations, petroleum and petroleum products. Principal source: USA 75.5% (1996)
Arable land 11.8%
Agricultural products maize, wheat, sorghum, barley, rice, beans, potatoes, coffee, cotton, sugar cane, fruit and vegetables; livestock raising and fisheries

Population and society

Population 92,718,000 (1996e)
Population growth rate 2.1% (1990–95); 1.5% (2000–05)
Population density (per sq km) 47 (1996e)
Urban population (% of total) 75 (1995)

Age distribution (% of total population) <15 35.9%, 15–65 59.9%, >65 4.2% (1995)
Ethnic distribution around 60% mestizo (mixed Native American and Spanish descent), 30% Native Americans, remainder mainly of European origin
Languages Spanish (official); Nahuatl, Maya, Zapoteco, Mixteco, Otomi
Religion Roman Catholic
Education (compulsory years) 6
Literacy rate 89% (men); 85% (women) (1995e)
Labour force 37% of population: 28% agriculture, 24% industry, 48% services (1990)
Unemployment 5.5% (1996)
Life expectancy 69 (men); 75 (women) (1995–2000)
Child mortality rate (under 5, per 1,000 live births) 32 (1995)
Physicians 1 per 889 people (1994)
Hospital beds 1 per 1,230 people (1992)
TV sets (per 1,000 people) 219 (1995)
Radios (per 1,000 people) 263 (1995)

Transport

Airports international airports: Mexico City (Benito Juárez), Guadalajara (Miguel Hidalgo), Acapulco (General Juan N Alvarez), Monterrey (General Mariano Escobeno), and 40 others; 39 domestic airports; total passenger km: 23,521 mil (1994)
Railroads total length: 20,596 km/12,798 mi; total passenger km: 1,855 mil (1994)
Roads total road network: 249,520 km/155,052 mi, of which 37.3% paved (1995e); passenger cars: 93.2 per 1,000 people (1995e)

Chronology

c. 2600 BC Mayan civilization originated in Yucatán peninsula.
1000–500 BC Zapotec civilization developed around Monte Albán in S Mexico.
4th–10th centuries AD Mayan Empire at its height.
10th–12th centuries Toltecs ruled much of Mexico from their capital at Tula.
12th century Aztecs migrated south into valley of Mexico.
c. 1325 Aztecs began building their capital Tenochtitlán on site of present-day Mexico City.
15th century Montezuma I built up Aztec Empire in central Mexico.
1519–21 Hernán Cortes conquered Aztec Empire and secured Mexico for Spain.

1520 Montezuma II, last king of the Aztecs, killed.
1535 Mexico became Spanish viceroyalty of New Spain; plantations and mining developed with Indian labour.
1519–1607 Indigenous population reduced from 21 million to 1 million, due mainly to lack of resistance to diseases transported from Old World.
1810 Father Miguel Hidalgo led unsuccessful revolt against Spanish.
1821 Independence proclaimed by Augustín de Iturbide with support of Church and landowners.
1822 Iturbide overthrew provisional government and proclaimed himself Emperor Augustín I.
1824 Federal republic established amid continuing public disorder.
1824–55 Military rule of Antonio López de Santa Anna, who imposed stability (he became president 1833).
1846–48 Mexican War: Mexico lost California and New Mexico to USA.
1848 Revolt of Mayan Indians suppressed.
1855 Benito Juárez aided overthrow of Santa Anna's dictatorship.
1857–60 Sweeping liberal reforms and anti-clerical legislation introduced by Juárez led to civil war with conservatives.
1861 Mexico suspended payment on foreign debt leading to French military intervention; Juárez resisted with US support.
1864 Supported by conservatives, France installed Archduke Maximilian of Austria as emperor of Mexico.
1867 Maximilian shot by republicans as French troops withdrew; Juárez resumed presidency.
1872 Death of Juárez.
1876 Gen Porfirio Diaz established dictatorship; Mexican economy modernized through foreign investment.
1911 Revolution overthrew Diaz; liberal president Francisco Madero introduced radical land reform and labour legislation but political disorder increased.
1914 and 1916–17 US military intervened to quell disorder.
1917 New constitution, designed to ensure permanent democracy, adopted with US encouragement.
1924–35 Government dominated by anti-clerical Gen Plutarco Calles, who introduced further social reforms.
1929 Foundation of National Revolutionary Party (PRFN).
1938 President Lázaro Cárdenas nationalized all foreign-owned oil wells in face of US opposition.

1942 Mexico declared war on Germany and Japan (and so regained US favour).
1946 PRFN renamed PRI.
1946–52 Miguel Alemán first of succession of authoritarian PRI presidents to seek moderation and stability rather than further radical reform.
1960s Rapid industrial growth partly financed by borrowing.
1976 Discovery of huge oil reserves in SE state of Chiapas; oil production tripled in six years.
1982 Falling oil prices caused grave financial crisis; Mexico defaulted on debt.
1985 Earthquake in Mexico City killed thousands.
1994 Uprising in Chiapas by Zapatista National Liberation Army (EZLN), seeking rights for Mayan Indian population; Mexico formed North American Free Trade Area with USA and Canada.
1995 Government agreed to offer greater autonomy to Mayan Indians in Chiapas.
1996 Short-lived peace talks with EZLN; violent attacks against government by new leftist Popular Revolutionary Army (EPR) increased.
1997 PRI lost its assembly majority. PRI leader resigned. Civilian counterpart to the Zapatista rebels formed, the Zapatista National Liberation Front (FZLN).

Practical information

Visa requirements UK: visa (tourist card) required. USA: visa (tourist card) required
Embassy in the UK 42 Hertford Street, London W1Y 7TF. Tel: (0171) 499 8586; fax: (0171) 495 4053
British embassy Apartado 96 bis, Rió Lerma 71, Colonia Cuauhtémoc, 06500 Mexico Distrito Federal. Tel: (5) 207 2089; fax: (5) 207 7672
Embassy in the USA 1911 Pennsylvania Avenue NW, Washington, DC 20006. Tel: (202) 728 1600
American embassy Paseo de la Reforma 305, Colonia Cuauhtémoc, 06500 Mexico, Distrito Federal. Tel: (5) 211 0042; fax: (5) 511 9980, 208 3373
Chamber of commerce Confederacíon de Cámaras Nacionales de Comercio, Servicios y Turismo, Apartado 113 bis, 2° y 3°, Balderas 144, Centro Curuhtémoc, 06079 Mexico Distrito Federal. Tel: (5) 709 1559; fax: (5) 709 1152
Office hours vary considerably; usually 0900–1600 Mon–Fri
Banking hours 0900–1330 Mon–Fri; some banks open Sat afternoon
Time difference GMT –6/–8
Chief tourist attractions coastal scenery; volcanoes; Sierra Nevada (Sierra Madre) mountain range; Mayan and Aztec monuments and remains; Spanish colonial churches and other buildings
Major holidays 1 January, 5 February, 21 March, 1, 5 May, 1, 16 September, 12 October, 2, 20 November, 12, 25, 31 December; variable: Holy Thursday, Good Friday

---

Micronesia Federated States of (FSM)

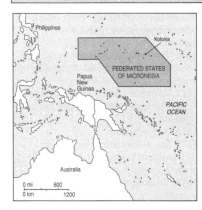

Area 700 sq km/270 sq mi
Capital Kolonia, in Pohnpei state
Major towns/cities Weno, in Chuuk state; Lelu, in Kosrae state
Major ports Teketik, Lepukos, Okak
Physical features an archipelago of 607 equatorial, volcanic islands in the W Pacific

Government

Head of state and government Bailey Olter from 1991
Political system democratic federal state

Administrative divisions four states
Political parties no formally organized political parties
Armed forces USA is responsible for country's defence
Death penalty laws do not provide for the death penalty for any crime

Economy and resources

Currency US dollar
GDP ($ US) 205 million (1994e)
Real GDP per capita (PPP) ($ US) 1,700 (1994e)
GDP growth rate 1.4% (1994e)
Average annual inflation 4% (1994e); 4.5% (1985–95e)
Trading partners USA, Japan
Industries food processing (coconut products), tourism
Exports copra, pepper, fish
Imports manufactured goods, machinery and transport equipment, mineral fuels
Agricultural products mainly subsistence farming; coconuts, cassava, sweet potatoes, breadfruit, bananas, copra, citrus fruits, taro, peppers; fishing

Population and society

Population 126,000 (1996e)
Population growth rate 2.8% (1990–95)
Population density (per sq km) 180 (1996e)
Urban population (% of total) 27.6 (1995)
Ethnic distribution main ethnic groups are the Trukese (41%) and Pohnpeian (26%), both Micronesian
Languages English (official) and eight local languages
Religion Christianity (mainly Roman Catholic in Yap state, Protestant elsewhere)
Education (compulsory years) 8
Literacy rate 91% (men); 88% (women) (1980e)
Labour force 48% agriculture, 6% industry, 46% services (1990)
Unemployment 13.5% (1990)
Life expectancy 68 (men); 72 (women) (1995–2000)
Child mortality rate (under 5, per 1,000 live births) 37 (1994)
Physicians 1 per 2,380 people (1993)
Hospital beds 1 per 365 people (1993)
TV sets (per 1,000 people) 12 (1993)
Radios (per 1,000 people) 16 (1993)

Transport

Airports international airports: Pohnpei (5 km/3 mi from Kolonia), Chuuk, Yap, Kosrae; domestic services also operate between these airports
Railroads none
Roads total road network: 235 km/146 mi, of which 79.3% paved (1995e)

Chronology

c. 1000 BC Micronesians first settled the islands.
1525 Portuguese navigators first visited Yap and Ulithi islands in the Carolines (Micronesia).
later 16th century Fell under Spanish influence.

1874 Spanish rule formally declared in face of increasing encroachment by German traders.
1885 Yap seized by German naval forces, but restored to Spain after arbitration by Pope Leo XIII on condition that Germany was allowed freedom of trade.
1899 Purchased for $4.5 million by Germany from Spain, after the latter's defeat in the Spanish–American War.
1914 Occupied by Japan on outbreak of World War I.
1919 Administered under League of Nations mandate by Japan, and vigorously colonized.
1944 Occupied by USA after Japanese forces defeated in World War II.

1947 Administered by USA as part of the United Nations (UN) Trust Territory of the Pacific Islands, under the name of the Federated States of Micronesia (FSM).
1979 Constitution adopted, establishing a federal system for its four constituent states (Yap, Chuuk, Pohnpei, and Kosrae) and internal self-government.
1986 Compact of Free Association entered into with USA, granting the islands self-government with USA retaining responsibility for defence and security until 2001.
1990 UN trust status terminated.
1991 Independence agreed, with Bailey Olter as president. Entered into UN membership.

Practical information

Visa requirements UK: visa not required for a stay of up to 30 days. USA: visa not required
Embassy in the UK Micronesia has no diplomatic representation in the UK; the Department of Trade and Industry has a Pacific Islands Desk. Tel: (0171) 215 4760; fax: (0171) 215 4398
British embassy the UK has no diplomatic representation in Micronesia
Embassy in the USA 1725 N Street NW, Washington, DC 20036. Tel: (202) 223 4383; fax: (202) 223 4391
American embassy address N/A, Kolonia.

Tel: (691) 320 2187; fax: (691) 320 2186
Chamber of commerce Resources and Development Department, Pohnpei 96941. Tel: (691) 320 5133. Resources and Development Department, Chuuk 96942. Tel: (691) 330 2552; fax: (691) 330 4194
Time difference GMT +10 (Chuuk and Yap); +11 (Kosrae and Pohnpei)
Chief tourist attractions excellent conditions for scuba-diving (notably in Chuuk Lagoon); ancient ruined city of Nan Madol on Pohnpei; World War II battle sites and relics (many underwater)
Major holidays 1 January, 10 May, 24 October, 3 November, 25 December (some variations from island to island)

Moldova Republic of

National name *Republica Moldoveneasca*
Area 33,700 sq km/13,011 sq mi
Capital Chisinău (Kishinev)
Major towns/cities Tiraspol, Beltsy, Bendery
Physical features hilly land lying largely between the rivers Prut and Dniester; N Moldova comprises the level plain of the Beltsy Steppe and uplands; the climate is warm and moderately continental

Government

Head of state Petru Lucinschi from 1997
Head of government Ion Cebuc from 1997
Political system emergent democracy
Administrative divisions 38 districts, four municipalities, and two autonomous territorial units – Gauguz (Gagauzi Yeri) and Transdniestr (status of latter was under dispute 1996)
Political parties Agrarian Democratic Party (ADP), nationalist, centrist; Socialist Party and Yedinstvo/Unity Movement, reform-socialist; Peasants and Intellectuals, Romanian nationalist; Christian Democratic Popular Front (CDPF), Romanian nationalist; Gagauz-Khalky (GKPM; Gagauz People's Movement), Gagauz separatist
Armed forces 12,000 (1995)
Conscription military service is compulsory for up to 18 months
Death penalty abolished 1995
Defence spend (% GDP) 3.7 (1995)
Education spend (% GNP) 5.2 (1994)
Health spend (% GDP) 6.4 (1995e)

Economy and resources

Currency leu
GDP ($ US) 4 billion (1994)
Real GDP per capita (PPP) ($ US) 1,576 (1994)
GDP growth rate 1.5% (1996)
Average annual inflation 21% (1996); 32.4% (1980–93)
Foreign debt ($ US) 691 million (1995)
Trading partners CIS countries (Russia and Ukraine), Romania, Germany, Bulgaria, USA
Resources lignite, phosphorites, gypsum, building materials; petroleum and natural gas deposits discovered early 1990s were not yet exploited 1996
Industries food processing, wine, tobacco, metalworking, light industry,

machine building, cement, textiles, footwear
Exports food and agricultural products, machinery and equipment, textiles, clothing. Principal market: Russia 59.9% (1996)
Imports mineral fuels, energy and mineral products, mechanical engineering products, foodstuffs, chemicals, textiles, clothing. Principal source: Russia 28% (1996)
Arable land 79% (1993)
Agricultural products grain, sugar beet, potatoes, vegetables, wine grapes and other fruit, tobacco; livestock products (milk, pork, and beef)

Population and society

Population 4,444,000 (1996e)
Population growth rate 0.3% (1990–95); 0.5% (2000–05)
Population density (per sq km) 132 (1996e)
Urban population (% of total) 52 (1995)
Age distribution (% of total population) <15 26.4%, 15–65 64.4%, >65 9.3% (1995)
Ethnic distribution 65% ethnic Moldovan (Romanian), 14% Ukrainian, 13% ethnic Russian, 4% Gagauzi, 2% Bulgarian, 2% Jewish
Language Moldovan
Religion Russian Orthodox
Education (compulsory years) 11
Literacy rate 98.9% (men); 98.9% (women) (1995e)
Labour force 43.3% agriculture, 26% industry, 30.7% services (1992)
Unemployment 1.5% (1996); 'hidden unemployment' is considerably higher
Life expectancy 64 (men); 72 (women) (1995–2000)
Child mortality rate (under 5, per 1,000 live births) 34 (1995)
Physicians 1 per 258 people (1994)
Hospital beds 1 per 82 people (1994)
TV sets (per 1,000 people) 273 (1995)
Radios (per 1,000 people) 699 (1995)

Transport

Airports international airports: Chisinău; no domestic services; total passenger km: 1,078 mil (1994)
Railroads total length: 1,328km/825 mi; total passenger km: 1,661 mil (1994)
Roads total road network: 12,259 km/7,618 mi, of which 87.2% paved (1995); passenger cars: 46.1 per 1,000 people (1995)

Chronology

AD 106 The current area covered by Moldova, which lies chiefly between the Prut river, bordering Romania in the W, and the Dniestr river, with Ukraine in the E, was conquered by the Roman Emperor Trajan and became part of the Roman province of Dacia. It was known in earlier times as Bessarabia.
mid-14th century Formed part of an independent Moldovan principality, which included areas, such as Bukovina to the W, that are now part of Romania.
late 15th century Under Stephen IV 'the Great' the principality reached the height of its power.
16th century Became a tributary of the Ottoman Turks.
1774–75 Moldovan principality, though continuing to recognize Turkish overlordship, was placed under Russian protectorship; Bukovina was lost to Austria.
1812 Bessarabia ceded to tsarist Russia.
1856 Remainder of Moldovan principality became largely independent of Turkish control.
1859 Moldovan Assembly voted to unite with Wallachia, to the SW, to form state of Romania, ruled by Prince Alexandru Ion Cuza. State became fully independent 1878.
1918 Following Russian Revolution, Bessarabia was seized and incorporated within Romania.
1924 Moldovan autonomous Soviet Socialist Republic (SSR) created, as part of Soviet Union, comprising territory E of

Dniestr river.
1940 Romania returned Bessarabia, E of Prut River, to Soviet Union, which divided it between Moldovan SSR and Ukraine, with Trans-Dniestr region transferred from Ukraine to Moldova.
1941 Moldovan SSR occupied by Romania and its wartime ally Germany.
1944 Red Army reconquered Bessarabia.
1946–47 Widespread famine as agriculture was collectivized; rich farmers and intellectuals liquidated.
1950 Immigration by settlers from Russia and Ukraine as industries were developed.
late 1980s Upsurge in Moldovan nationalism, encouraged by *glasnost* initiative of reformist Soviet leader Mikhail Gorbachev.
1988 Moldovan Movement in Support of Perestroika (economic restructuring) campaigned for accelerated political reform.
1989 Nationalist demonstrations in Kishinev (now Chisinău. Moldovan Popular Front (MPF) founded; Moldovan made state language. Campaigns for autonomy among ethnic Russians, strongest in industrialized Trans-Dniestr region, and Turkish-speaking but Orthodox Christian Gagauz minority in SW.
1990 MPF polled strongly in parliamentary elections and Mircea Snegur, a reform-nationalist communist, became president. Economic and political sovereignty declared.
1991 Independence declared and Communist Party outlawed after conservative coup in Moscow against Gorbachev; joined Commonwealth of Independent States (CIS). Insurrection in Trans-Dniestr region.
1992 Admitted into United Nations and the Conference on Security and Cooperation in Europe; peace agreement signed with Russia to end civil war in Trans-Dniestr, giving special status to the region. MPF-dominated government fell;

Practical information

Visa requirements UK: visa required. USA: visa required
Embassy in the UK 219 Marsh Wall, Isle of Dogs, London E14 9PD. Tel: (0171) 538 8600; fax: (0171) 538 5967
British embassy the British Embassy in Moscow (see Russian Federation) deals with enquiries relating to Moldova
Embassy in the USA Suites 329, 333, 1511 K Street NW, Washington, DC 20005. Tel: (202) 783 3012; fax: (202) 783 3342

American embassy Strada Alexei Mateevich 103, Chisinău 277014. Tel: (2) 233 772; fax: (2) 233 044
Chamber of commerce Chamber of Commerce and Industry of the Republic of Moldova, 28 Emineskou, 277012 Chisinău. Tel: (2) 221 552; fax: (2) 233 810
Time difference GMT +2
Major holidays 1, 7–8 January, 8 March, 9 May, 27, 31 August; variable: Mertsishor (Spring Festival, first week in March), Good Friday, Easter Monday

'Government of national accord' formed, headed by Andrei Sangheli and dominated by ADP.
1993 New currency, the leu, introduced. Privatization programme launched and closer ties established with Russia.

1994 Parliamentary elections won by ADP. Plebiscite rejected nationalist demands for merger with Romania. Russia agreed to withdraw Trans-Dniestr troops by 1997.
1995 Joined Council of Europe; economic growth resumed.

1996 Petru Lucinschi elected president. Dnestr region president Igor Smirnov re-elected.
1997 Ion Cebuc appointed prime minister. New centrist party formed, supporting President Lusinschi. Major party realignments.

Monaco Principality of

National name *Principauté de Monaco*
Area 1.95 sq km/0.75 sq mi
Capital Monaco-Ville
Major towns/cities Monte Carlo, La Condamine; heliport Fontvieille
Physical features steep and rugged; surrounded landwards by French territory; being expanded by filling in the sea

Government

Head of state Prince Rainier III from 1949
Head of government Paul Dijoud from 1994
Political system constitutional monarchy under French protectorate
Administrative divisions four districts
Political parties no formal parties, but lists of candidates: Liste Campora, moderate, centrist; Liste Medecin, moderate, centrist
Armed forces no standing defence forces; defence is the responsibility of France
Death penalty abolished 1962
Education spend (% GNP) 5.6 (1992)

Economy and resources

Currency French franc
GDP ($ US) 788 million (1994e)
Real GDP per capita (PPP) ($ US) 25,000 (1994e)
GDP growth rate N/A

Trading partners full customs integration with France (for external trade figures, see France)
Industries chemicals, pharmaceuticals, plastics, microelectronics, electrical goods, paper, textiles and clothing, gambling, banking and finance, real estate, tourism (which provided an estimated 25% of total government revenue 1991)
Imports largely dependent on imports from France
Agricultural products no agricultural land; some fish farming

Population and society

Population 32,000 (1996e)
Population growth rate 1.2% (1990–95)
Population density (per sq km) 32,097 (1996e)
Urban population (% of total) 100 (1995)
Age distribution (% of total population) <15 11.9%, 15–65 65.6%, >65 22.5% (1990)
Ethnic distribution 58% French; 19% Monegasque
Languages French (official); English, Italian
Religion Roman Catholic
Education (compulsory years) 10
Literacy rate 99% (men); 99% (women) (1995e)
Unemployment 2.2% (1994e)
Life expectancy 74 (men); 83 (women) (1995)
Child mortality rate (under 5, per 1,000 live births) 7 (1994)
Physicians 1 per 254 people (1994)
TV sets (per 1,000 people) 750 (1995)
Radios (per 1,000 people) 1,019 (1995)

Transport

Airports international airports: none – helicopter services link the principality with the nearest airport, Nice (Nice-Côte d'Azur); total passenger km: 1 mil (1994)
Railroads total length: 1.7 km/1 mi (operated by French state railways)

Roads total road network: 43 km/ 27 mi, of which 100% paved (1995); passenger cars: 691.1 per 1,000 people (1995)

Chronology

1191 The Genoese took control of Monaco, which had formerly been part of the Holy Roman Empire.
1297 Came under the rule of the Grimaldi dynasty, the current ruling family, who initially allied themselves to the French.
1524–1641 Came under Spanish protection.
1793 Annexed by France during French Revolutionary Wars. One member of ruling family was guillotined; the rest imprisoned.
1815 Placed under protection of Sardinia.
1848 The towns of Menton and Roquebrune, which had formed the greater part of the principality, seceded and later became part of France.
1861 Franco-Monagesque treaty restored Monaco's independence under French protection; casino built.
1865 Customs union established with France.
1918 France given veto over succession to throne and established that if reigning prince dies without a male heir, Monaco is to be incorporated into France.
1941–45 Occupied successively by Italians and Germans during World War II.
1949 Prince Rainier III ascended the throne.
1956 Prince Rainier married US actress Grace Kelly.
1958 Birth of male heir, Prince Albert.
1959 Constitution of 1911 suspended and National Council dissolved.
1962 New, more liberal constitution adopted and National Council restored.
1982 Princess Grace died in car accident.
1993 Joined United Nations.

Practical information

Visa requirements UK: visa not required. USA: visa not required
Embassy in the UK Embassy and Consulate General, 4 Cromwell Place, London SW7 2JE. Tel: (0171) 225 2679; fax: (0171) 581 8161
British embassy British Consulate, BP 265, 33 boulevard Princesse Charlotte, MC-98005, Monaco, Cedex. Tel: 9350 9966; fax: 9350 1447
Embassy in the USA Monaco does not have an embassy in the USA
American embassy the USA does not have an embassy in Monaco; the US Consul General in Marseille (France) is accredited to Monaco

Chamber of commerce Conseil Economique, 8 rue Louis Notari, MC-98000, Monaco, Cedex. Tel: 9330 2082; fax: 9350 0596
Office hours 0900–1200 and 1400–1800 Mon–Fri
Banking hours 0900–1200 and 1400–1630 Mon–Fri
Time difference GMT +1
Chief tourist attractions dramatic scenery; Mediterranean climate; 13th-century Palais du Prince; numerous entertainment facilities, including casinos, Jardin Exotique, Musée Océanographique, world championship Grand Prix motor race and annual car rally at Monte Carlo
Major holidays 1, 27 January, 1, 8 May, 14 July, 15 August, 3 September, 1, 11, 19 November, 8, 25 December; variable: Easter Monday, Whit Monday

Mongolia State of (*Outer Mongolia* until 1924; *People's Republic of Mongolia* until 1991)

National name *Mongol Uls*
Area 1,565,000 sq km/604,246 sq mi
Capital Ulaanbaatar (Ulan Bator)
Major towns/cities Darhan, Choybalsan, Erdenet
Physical features high plateau with desert and steppe (grasslands); Altai Mountains in SW; salt lakes; part of Gobi desert in SE; contains both the world's southernmost permafrost and northernmost desert

Government

Head of state Natsagiyn Bagabandi from 1997
Head of government Mendsayhany Enhsayhan from 1996
Political system emergent democracy
Administrative divisions 18 provinces and three municipalities
Political parties Mongolian People's Revolutionary Party (MPRP), reform-socialist (ex-communist); Mongolian National Democratic Party (MNDP), traditionalist, promarket economy; Union

Coalition (UC, comprising the MNPD and the Social Democratic Party (SDP)), democratic, promarket economy
Armed forces 21,100 (1995); plus a paramilitary force of around 10,000
Conscription military service is compulsory for 12 months
Death penalty retained and used for ordinary crimes
Defence spend (% GDP) 2.4 (1995)
Education spend (% GNP) 5.2 (1994)
Health spend (% GDP) 1.6 (1995e)

Economy and resources

Currency tugrik
GDP ($ US) 700 million (1994)
Real GDP per capita (PPP) ($ US) 3,766 (1994)
GDP growth rate 2.1% (1994); –3.3% (1990–95)
Average annual inflation 53% (1995); 51.6% (1985–95)
Foreign debt ($ US) 512 million (1995)
Trading partners Russia, China, Japan, Kazakhstan, South Korea, Germany, USA
Resources copper, nickel, zinc, molybdenum, phosphorites, tungsten, tin, fluorospar, gold, lead; reserves of petroleum discovered 1994
Industries mostly small-scale; food products, copper and molybdenum concentrates, cement, lime, wood and metal-worked products, beverages, leather articles
Exports minerals and metals (primarily copper concentrate), consumer goods, foodstuffs, agricultural products. Principal market: Japan 18.7% (1995)
Imports engineering goods, mineral fuels and products, industrial consumer

goods, foodstuffs. Principal source: Russia 52% (1995)
Arable land 0.9% (1993)
Agricultural products wheat, oats, barley, potatoes, vegetables; animal herding (particularly cattle rearing) is country's main economic activity (there were 28.6 million cattle, sheep, goats, horses, and camels 1995)

Population and society

Population 2,515,000 (1996e)
Population growth rate 2% (1990–95); 1.9% (2000–05)
Population density (per sq km) 2 (1996e)
Urban population (% of total) 61 (1995)
Age distribution (% of total population) <15 38%, 15–65 58.5%, >65 3.4% (1995)
Ethnic distribution 90% Mongol, 4% Kazakh, 2% Chinese, and 2% Russian
Languages Khalkha Mongolian (official); Chinese, Russian, and Turkic languages
Religion officially none (Tibetan Buddhist Lamaism suppressed in 1930s)
Education (compulsory years) 8
Literacy rate 88% (men); 76% (women) (1995e)
Labour force 43% agriculture, 16% industry, 41% services (1995)
Unemployment 8.5% (1994)
Life expectancy 64 (men); 67 (women) (1995–2000)
Child mortality rate (under 5, per 1,000 live births) 74 (1995)
Physicians 1 per 389 people (1991)
Hospital beds 1 per 83 people (1992)
TV sets (per 1,000 people) 45 (1995)
Radios (per 1,000 people) 134 (1995)

Transport

Airports international airports: Ulaanbaatar (Buyant Ukha); six domestic airports; total passenger km: 491 mil (1994)
Railroads total length: 2,052 km/1,275 mi; total passenger km: 681 mil (1995)
Roads total road network: 11,180 km/ 6,947 mi, of which 11% paved (1995e); passenger cars: 9.1 per 1,000 people (1995e)

Chronology

AD **1206** Nomadic Mongol tribes united by Genghis Khan to form nucleus of vast Mongol Empire which, stretching across central Asia, reached its zenith under Genghis Khan's grandson, Kublai Khan.
late 17th century Conquered by China to become province of Outer Mongolia.
1911 Independence proclaimed by Mongolian nationalists after Chinese 'republican revolution'; Tsarist Russia helped Mongolia to secure autonomy, under a traditionalist Buddhist monarchy in the form of a reincarnated lama.
1915 Chinese sovereignty reasserted.
1921 Chinese rule overthrown with Soviet help.
1924 People's Republic proclaimed on death of king, when the monarchy was abolished; defeudalization programme launched, entailing collectivization of agriculture and suppression of Lama Buddhism.
1932 Armed antigovernment uprising suppressed with Soviet assistance; 100,000 killed in political purges.
1946 China recognized Mongolia's independence.
1952 Death of Marshal Horloogiyn Choybalsan, the dominant force in the ruling communist Mongolian People's Revolutionary Party (MPRP) since 1939.
1958 Yumjaagiyn Tsedenbal became dominant figure in MPRP and country.
1962 Joined Comecon.
1966 20-year friendship, cooperation, and mutual-assistance pact signed with Soviet Union (USSR). Relations with China deteriorated.
1984 Tsedenbal, the effective leader, retired; replaced by Jambyn Batmunkh.
1987 Reduction in number of Soviet troops; Mongolia's external contacts broadened. Tolerance of traditional social customs encouraged nationalist revival.
1989 Further Soviet troop reductions.
1990 Demonstrations and democratization campaign launched, influenced by events in E Europe; Batmunkh resigned and charged with corruption. Ex-communist MPRP elected in first free multiparty elections; Punsalmaagiyn Ochirbat indirectly elected president. Mongolian script readopted.
1991 Massive privatization programme launched. GDP declined by 10%. Ochirbat resigned from MPRP in wake of anti-Gorbachev attempted coup in USSR.
1992 MPRP returned to power in assembly elections held under new, non-communist constitution. Economic situation worsened; GDP again declined by 10%.
1993 Ochirbat won first direct presidential elections.
1996 Economy showed signs of revival. Union Coalition won assembly elections, defeating MPRP and ending 75 years of communist rule. Defence cooperation agreement signed with USA. Mendsayhany Enhsayhan became prime minister.
1997 Ex-communist Natsagiyn Bagabandi elected MPRP chairman. Economic 'shock therapy' programme, supervised by IMF and World Bank, created unemployment and made government unpopular. Bagabandi elected president. Mongolia first country to abolish all taxes and tariffs on trade.

Practical information

Visa requirements UK: visa required. USA: visa required
Embassy in the UK 7 Kensington Court, London W8 5DL. Tel: (0171) 937 0150; fax: (0171) 937 1117
British embassy PO Box 703, 30 Enkh Taivny Gudammzh, Ulaanbaatar 13. Tel: (1) 358 133; fax: (1) 358 036
Embassy in the USA 2833 mil Street NW, Washington, DC 20007. Tel: (202) 333 7117; fax: (202) 298 9227
American embassy inner north side of the Big Ring, just west of the Selbe Gol, Ulaanbaatar. Tel: (1) 329 095/606; fax: (1) 320 776

Chamber of commerce Mongolian Chamber of Commerce and Industry, Sambuugiyn Gudamj 11, Ulaanbaatar 38. Tel: (1) 324 620; telex: 79336
Office hours 0900–1800 Mon–Fri; 0900–1500 Sat
Banking hours 1000–1500 Mon–Fri
Time difference GMT +8
Chief tourist attractions spectacular scenery, including Gobi Desert and Altai chain; wildlife; historical relics; tourism is relatively undeveloped
Major holidays 1–2 January, 8 March, 1 May, 1 June, 10 July (3 days), 7 November; variable: Tsagaan (Lunar New Year, January/February, 2 days)

Morocco Kingdom of

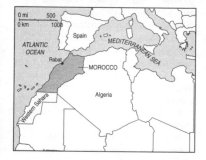

National name *al-Mamlaka al-Maghrebia*
Area 458,730 sq km/177,115 sq mi (excluding Western Sahara)
Capital Rabat
Major towns/cities Casablanca, Marrakesh, Fez, Oujda, Kenitra, Tetouan, Meknès
Major ports Casablanca, Tangier, Agadir
Physical features mountain ranges, including the Atlas Mountains NE–SW; fertile coastal plains in W

Government

Head of state Hassan II from 1961
Head of government Abd al-Latif Filali from 1994
Political system constitutional monarchy
Administrative divisions 49 provinces and prefectures with seven economic regions
Political parties Constitutional Union (UC), right wing; National Rally of Independents (RNI), royalist; Popular Movement (MP), moderate, centrist;

Istiqlal, nationalist, centrist; Socialist Union of Popular Forces (USFP), progressive socialist; National Democratic Party (PND), moderate, nationalist
Armed forces 195,500; paramilitary forces of 42,000 (1995)
Conscription 18 months
Death penalty retained and used for ordinary crimes
Defence spend (% GDP) 4.3 (1995)
Education spend (% GNP) 4.8 (1994)
Health spend (% GDP) 0.9 (1990)

Economy and resources

Currency dirham (DH)
GDP ($ US) 30.8 billion (1994)
Real GDP per capita (PPP) ($ US) 3,681 (1994)
GDP growth rate 11.8% (1994); 1.2% (1990–95)
Average annual inflation 5.1 % (1994); 4.8% (1985–95)
Foreign debt ($ US) 32.4 billion (1995)
Trading partners France, Spain, USA, Japan, UK, Italy, Iran
Resources phosphate rock and phosphoric acid, coal, iron ore, barytes, lead, copper, manganese, zinc, petroleum, natural gas, fish
Industries phosphate products (chiefly fertilizers), petroleum refining, food processing, textiles, clothing, leather goods, paper and paper products, tourism
Exports phosphates and phosphoric acid, mineral products, seafoods and seafood products, citrus fruit, tobacco, clothing, hosiery. Principal market: France 29.7% (1995)
Imports crude petroleum, raw materials, wheat, chemicals, sawn wood, consumer goods. Principal source: France 21.8% (1995)
Arable land 20.7%
Agricultural products wheat, barley, sugar beet, citrus fruits, tomatoes, potatoes; fishing (seafoods)

Population and society

Population 27,021,000 (1996e)
Population growth rate 2.1% (1990–95); 1.6% (2000–05)
Population density (per sq km) 61 (1996e)
Urban population (% of total) 48 (1995)
Age distribution (% of total population) <15 36.1%, 15–65 59.8%, >65 4.1% (1995)
Ethnic distribution majority indigenous Berbers; sizeable Jewish minority
Languages Arabic (official) 75%; Berber 25%, French, Spanish
Religion Sunni Muslim
Education (compulsory years) 6

Literacy rate 61% (men); 38% (women) (1995e)
Labour force 38% of population: 45% agriculture, 25% industry, 31% services (1990)
Unemployment 16% (1994)
Life expectancy 64 (men); 68 (women) (1995–2000)
Child mortality rate (under 5, per 1,000 live births) 75 (1995)
Physicians 1 per 3,790 people (1994)
Hospital beds 1 per 1,168 people (1994)
TV sets (per 1,000 people) 94 (1995)
Radios (per 1,000 people) 226 (1995)

Transport

Airports international airports: Casablanca (Mohammed V), Rabat (Salé), Tangier (Boukhalef Sohahel), Agadir (Al Massira), Fez (Sais), Marrakesh, Oujda, Al-Hocina el-Aaiun, Ouarzazate; domestic services operate between these; total passenger km: 4,573 mil (1994)
Railroads total length: 1,907 km/1,185 mi; total passenger km: 1,881 mil (1994)
Roads total road network: 60,513 km/37,603 mi, of which 50.3% paved (1995); passenger cars: 38.8 per 1,000 people (1995e)

Chronology

10th–3rd centuries BC Phoenicians from Tyre settled along N coast.
1st century AD NW Africa became Roman province of Mauritania.
5th–6th centuries Invaded by Vandals and Visigoths.
682 Start of Arab conquest, followed by spread of Islam.
8th century King Idris I established small Arab kingdom.
1056–1146 The Almoravids, a Berber dynasty based at Marrakesh, built an empire embracing Morocco and parts of Algeria and Spain.
1122–1268 After a civil war, the Almohads, a rival Berber dynasty, overthrew the Almoravids; Almohads extended empire but later lost most of Spain.
1258–1358 Beni Merin dynasty supplanted Almohads.
14th century Moroccan Empire fragmented into separate kingdoms, based in Fez and Marrakesh.
15th century Spain and Portugal occupied Moroccan ports; expulsion of Muslims from Spain 1492.
16th century Saadian dynasty restored unity of Morocco and resisted Turkish

invasion.
1649 Foundation of current Alaouite dynasty of sultans; Morocco remained independent and isolated kingdom.
1856 Under British pressure, sultan opened Morocco to European commerce.
1860 Spain invaded Morocco, which was forced to cede the SW region of Ifni.
1905 Major international crisis caused by German objections to increasing French influence in Morocco.
1911 Agadir Crisis: further German objections to French imperialism in Morocco overcome by territorial compensation in central Africa.
1912 Morocco divided into French and Spanish protectorates; sultan reduced to puppet ruler.
1921 Moroccan rebels, the Riffs, led by Abd el-Krim, defeated large Spanish force at Anual.
1923 City of Tangier separated from Spanish Morocco and made a neutral international zone.
1926 French forces crushed Riff revolt.
1944 Nationalist party, Istiqlal, founded to campaign for full independence.
1948 Consultative assemblies introduced.
1953–55 Serious anti-French riots.
1956 French and Spanish forces withdrew; Morocco regained effective independence under Sultan Muhammad V, who took title of king 1957.
1961 Muhammad V succeeded by Hassan II.
1962 First constitution adopted; replaced 1970 and 1972.
1965–77 King Hassan suspended constitution and ruled by decree.
1969 Spanish overseas province of Ifni returned to Morocco.
1975 Spain withdrew from Western Sahara, leaving Morocco and Mauritania to divide it between themselves.
1976 Polisario Front, supported by Algeria, began guerrilla war in Western Sahara with aim of securing its independence as Sahrahwi Arab Democratic Republic.
1979 Mauritania withdrew from its portion of Western Sahara, which Morocco annexed after major battles with Polisario.
1984 Morocco signed mutual defence with Libya, which had previously supported Polisario.
1991 UN-sponsored cease-fire came into effect in Western Sahara.
1992 Constitution amended in attempt to increase influence of parliament.
1994 Abd-al Latif Filali became prime minister.
1996 New two-chamber assembly approved.

Practical information

Visa requirements UK: visa not required. USA: visa not required
Embassy in the UK 49 Queen's Gate Gardens, London SW7 5NE. Tel: (0171) 581 5001–4; fax: (0171) 225 3862
British embassy BP 45, 17 boulevard de la Tour Hassan, Rabat. Tel: (7) 720 905/6; fax: (7) 704 531
Embassy in the USA 1601 21st Street NW, Washington, DC 20009. Tel: (202) 462 7979–7982; fax: (202) 265 0161
American embassy 2 avenue de Marrakesh, Rabat. Tel: (7) 762 265; fax: (7) 765 661
Chamber of commerce La Fédération des Chambres de Commerce et de l'Industrie du Maroc, 6 rue d'Erfoud, Rabat-

Agdal. Tel: (7) 767 078; fax: (7) 767 076
Office hours generally 0830–1200 and 1430–1830 Mon–Fri (September–July, except Ramadan); 0900–1500/1600 Mon–Fri (Ramadan and July–early September)
Banking hours 0830–1130 and 1430–1700 Mon–Fri (winter); 0800–1530 Mon–Fri (summer) (hours may vary during Ramadan)
Time difference GMT +/–0
Chief tourist attractions sunny climate; ancient sites and cities (notably Marrakesh , Fez, Meknès, Rabat); spectacular scenery; resorts on Atlantic and Mediterranean coasts
Major holidays 1 January, 3 March, 1, 23 May, 9 July, 14 August, 6, 18 November; variable: Eid-ul-Adha (2 days), end of Ramadan (2 days), New Year (Muslim), Prophet's Birthday

Mozambique People's Republic of

National name *República Popular de Moçambique*
Area 799,380 sq km/308,640 sq mi
Capital Maputo (and chief port)
Major towns/cities Beira, Nampula, Nacala, Chimoio
Major ports Beira, Nacala, Quelimane
Physical features mostly flat tropical lowland; mountains in W; rivers Zambezi and Limpopo

Government

Head of state Joaquim Alberto Chissano from 1986
Head of government Pascoal Mocumbi from 1994
Political system emergent democratic republic
Administrative divisions 10 provinces
Political parties National Front for the Liberation of Mozambique (Frelimo), free market; Renamo, or Mozambique National Resistance (MNR), former rebel movement, right of centre
Armed forces 12,000 (1995)

Conscription early 1996 government was seeking to reintroduce compulsory military service, which had been suspended under the General Peace Accord
Death penalty abolished 1990
Defence spend (% GDP) 3.7 (1995)
Education spend (% GNP) 6.2 (1992)
Health spend (% GDP) 4.4 (1990)

Economy and resources

Currency metical
GDP ($ US) 1.5 billion (1994)
Real GDP per capita (PPP) ($ US) 986 (1994)
GDP growth rate 5% (1994); 7.1% (1990–95)
Average annual inflation 52.5% (1994); 52.2% (1985–95)
Foreign debt ($ US) 5.8 billion (1995)
Trading partners Spain, South Africa, USA, Japan, Italy, India, Zimbabwe, Portugal, France
Resources coal, salt, bauxite, graphite; reserves of iron ore, gold, precious and semi-precious stones, marble, natural gas (all largely unexploited 1996)
Industries food products, steel, engineering, textiles and clothing, beverages, tobacco, chemical products
Exports shrimps and other crustaceans, cashew nuts, raw cotton, sugar, copra, lobsters. Principal market: Spain 16.1% (1995)
Imports foodstuffs, capital goods, crude petroleum and petroleum products, machinery and spare parts, chemicals. Principal source: South African 51.7% (1995)
Arable land 4% (1993)
Agricultural products cassava, maize, bananas, rice, groundnuts, copra,

cashew nuts, cotton, sugar cane; fishing (shrimps, prawns, and lobsters) is principal export activity (42% of export earnings 1994); forest resources (eucalyptus, pine, and rare hardwoods)

Population and society

Population 17,796,000 (1996e)
Population growth rate 2.4% (1990–95); 2.8% (2000–05)
Population density (per sq km) 22 (1996e)
Urban population (% of total) 34 (1995)
Age distribution (% of total population) <15 44.7%, 15–65 52%, >65 3.2% (1995)
Ethnic distribution the majority belong to local groups, the largest being the Makua-Lomue, who comprise about 38% of the population; the other significant group is the Tsonga (24%)
Languages Portuguese (official); 16 African languages
Religions animist, Roman Catholic, Muslim
Education (compulsory years) 7
Literacy rate 64% (men); 37% (women) (1995e)
Labour force 53% of population: 83% agriculture, 8% industry, 9% services (1990)
Unemployment 50% (1990e)
Life expectancy 45 (men); 48 (women) (1995–2000)
Child mortality rate (under 5, per 1,000 live births) 275 (1995)
Physicians 1 per 37,141 people (1991)
Hospital beds 1 per 1,205 people (1993)
TV sets (per 1,000 people) 3.5 (1995)
Radios (per 1,000 people) 38 (1995)

Transport

Airports international airports: Maputo

(Mavalane), Beira, Nampula; five domestic airports; total passenger km: 443 mil (1994)
Railroads total length: 3,131 km/1,946 mi; passengers carried: 0.9 mil (1994)
Roads total road network: 29,810 km/ 18,524 mi, of which 18.6% paved (1995e); passenger cars: 4.2 per 1,000 people (1995)

Chronology

1st–4th centuries AD Bantu-speaking peoples settled in Mozambique.
8th–15th century Arab gold traders established independent city-states on coast.
1498 Portuguese navigator Vasco da Gama was the first European visitor; at this time the most important local power was the Maravi kingdom of the Mwene Matapa peoples, who controlled much of the Zambezi basin.
1626 The Mwene Matapa formally recognized Portuguese sovereignty. Portuguese soldiers set up private agricultural estates and used slave labour to exploit gold and ivory resources.
late 17th century Portuguese temporarily pushed S of Zambezi by the ascendant Rozwi kingdom.
1752 First Portuguese colonial governor

appointed; slave trade outlawed.
late 19th century Concessions given by Portugal to private companies to develop and administer parts of Mozambique.
1930 Colonial Act established more centralized Portuguese rule, ending concessions to monopolistic companies and forging closer integration with Lisbon.
1951 Became an overseas province of Portugal and, economically, a cheap labour reserve for South Africa's mines.
1962 Frelimo (National Front for the Liberation of Mozambique) established in exile in Tanzania by Marxist guerrillas, including Samora Machel, to fight for independence.
1964 Fighting broke out between Frelimo forces and Portuguese troops, starting a ten-year liberation war; Portugal despatched 70,000 troops to Mozambique.
1969 Eduardo Mondlane, leader of Frelimo, was assassinated.
1975 Following revolution in Portugal, independence achieved as a socialist republic, with Machel as president, Joaquim Chissano as prime minister, and Frelimo as sole legal party; Portuguese settlers left the country. Lourenço Marques renamed Maputo. Key enterprises nationalized.

1977 Renamo resistance group formed, with covert backing of South Africa.
1979 Machel encouraged Patriotic Front guerrillas in Rhodesia to accept Lancaster House Agreement, creating Zimbabwe.
1983 Good relations restored with Western powers.
1984 Nkomati Accord of nonaggression signed with South Africa.
1986 Machel killed in air crash near South African border; succeeded by Chissano.
1988 Tanzanian troops withdrawn from Mozambique.
1989 Renamo continued attacks on government facilities and civilians.
1990 One-party rule officially ended, and Frelimo abandoned Marxist–Leninism and embraced market economy.
1992 Peace accord signed with Renamo.
1993 Price riots in Maputo as IMF-promoted reforms to restructure the economy devastated by war and drought were implemented.
1994 Demobilization of contending armies completed. Chissano and Frelimo re-elected in first multiparty elections; Renamo (now a political party) agreed to cooperate with government.
1995 Mozambique admitted to Commonwealth.

Practical information

Visa requirements UK: visa required. USA: visa required
Embassy in the UK 21 Fitzroy Square, London W1P 5HJ. Tel: (0171) 383 3800; fax: (0171) 383 3801
British embassy Caixa Postal 55, Avenida Vladimir I Léuine 310, Maputo. Tel: (1) 420 111/2/5/6/7; fax: (1) 421 666
Embassy in the USA Suite 570, 1990 mil Street NW, Washington, DC 20036. Tel: (202) 293 7146. fax: (202) 835 0245
American embassy Avenida Kenneth Kaunda 193, Maputo. Tel: (1) 492 797; fax: (1) 490 114
Chamber of commerce Câmara de Comércio de

Mozambique, CP 1836, Rua Mateus Sansão Mutemba 452, Maputo. Tel: (1) 491 970; telex: 6498
Office hours 0730–1200 and 1400–1730 Mon–Fri; 0800–1330 Sat
Banking hours 0745–1115 Mon–Fri
Time difference GMT +2
Chief tourist attractions Indian Ocean coastline with beaches bordered by lagoons, coral reefs, and strings of islands (travel within Mozambique can be dangerous due to risk of armed robbery and unexploded landmines)
Major holidays 1 January, 3 February, 7 April, 1 May, 25 June, 7, 25 September, 25 December

---

Myanmar Union of (formerly *Burma*, until 1989)

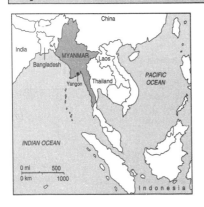

National name *Thammada Myanmar Naingngandaw*
Area 676,577 sq km/261,226 sq mi
Capital Yangon (formerly Rangoon) (and chief port)
Major towns/cities Mandalay, Mawlamyine, Bago, Bassein, Taunggyi, Sittwe, Manywa
Physical features over half is rainforest; rivers Irrawaddy and Chindwin in central lowlands ringed by mountains in N, W, and E

Government

Head of state and government Than

Shwe from 1992
Political system military republic
Administrative divisions seven states and seven divisions
Political parties National Unity Party (NUP), military-socialist ruling party; National League for Democracy (NLD), pluralist opposition grouping
Armed forces 286,000 (1995); plus two paramilitary units totalling 85,000
Conscription military service is voluntary
Death penalty retained and used for ordinary crimes
Defence spend (% GDP) 6.2 (1995)

Education spend (% GNP) 2.4 (1992);
N/A (1993–94)
Health spend (% GDP) 0.8 (1990)

Economy and resources

Currency kyat
GDP ($ US) 79.2 billion (1994)
Real GDP per capita (PPP) ($ US) 600
(1994)
GDP growth rate 6.8% (1994); 5.7%
(1990–95)
Average annual inflation 22.4%
(1985–95e)
Foreign debt ($ US) 6.5 billion (1994)
Trading partners China, Singapore,
India, Japan, Malaysia, Hong Kong
Resources natural gas, petroleum, zinc,
tin, copper, tungsten, coal, lead, gems,
silver, gold
Industries food processing, beverages,
cement, fertilizers, plywood, petroleum
refining, textiles, paper, motor cars,
tractors, bicycles
Exports teak, rice, pulses and beans,
rubber, hardwood, base metals, gems,
cement. Principal market: Singapore
12.9% (1995)
Imports raw materials, machinery and
transport equipment, tools and spares,
construction materials, chemicals,
consumer goods. Principal source: China
31.3% (1995)
Arable land 14.9 (1993)
Agricultural products rice, sugar cane,
maize, groundnuts, pulses, rubber,
tobacco; fishing; forest resources (teak
and hardwood) – teak is frequently felled
illegally and smuggled into Thailand;
cultured pearls and oyster shells are part
of aquacultural fish production

Population and society

Population 45,922,000 (1996e)
Population growth rate 2.1%
(1990–95); 1.9% (2000–05)
Population density (per sq km) 68
(1996e)
Urban population (% of total) 26 (1995)
Age distribution (% of total population)
<15 37.4%, 15–65 58.5%, >65 4.1%
(1995)
Ethnic distribution Burmans, who
predominate in the fertile central river
valley and southern coastal and delta
regions, constitute the ethnic majority,
comprising 72% of the total population.
Out of more than 100 minority
communities, the most important are the
Karen (7%), Shan (6%), Indians (6%),
Chinese (3%), Kachin (2%), and Chin
(2%). The indigenous minority

communities, who predominate in
mountainous border regions, show
considerable hostility towards the
culturally and politically dominant
Burmans, undermining national unity
Languages Burmese (official), English
Religions Hinayāna Buddhist 85%,
animist, Christian, Muslim
Education (compulsory years) 5
Literacy rate 89% (men); 72% (women)
(1995e)
Labour force 68.7% agriculture, 9.8%
industry, 21.5% services (1994)
Unemployment 2.1% (1994e)
Life expectancy 59 (men); 62 (women)
(1995–2000)
Child mortality rate (under 5, per 1,000
live births) 150 (1995)
Physicians 1 per 3,554 people (1994)
Hospital beds 1 per 1,571 people
(1994)
TV sets (per 1,000 people) 5.1 (1995)
Radios (per 1,000 people) 89 (1995)

Transport

Airports international airports: Yangon
(Mingaladon); 21 domestic airports; total
passenger km: 140 mil (1994)
Railroads total length: 4,621 km/2,871
mi; total passenger km: 4,390 mil (1994)
Roads total road network: 27,600 km/
17,151 mi, of which 12.1% paved
(1995e); passenger cars: 0.6 per 1,000
people (1993e)

Chronology

3rd century BC Sittoung valley settled by
Mons; Buddhism introduced by
missionaries from India.
3rd century AD Arrival of Burmans from
Tibet.
1057 First Burmese Empire established
by King Anawrahta, who conquered
Thaton, established a capital inland at
Pagan, and adopted Theravāda
Buddhism.
1287 Pagan sacked by Mongols.
1531 Founding of Toungoo dynasty,
which survived until the mid-18th century.
1755 Nation reunited by Alaungpaya,
with port of Rangoon as capital.
1824–26 First Anglo-Burmese war
resulted in Arakan coastal strip, between
Chittagong and Cape Negrais, being
ceded to British India.
1852 Following defeat in second Anglo-
Burmese war, Lower Burma, including
Rangoon, was annexed by British.
1886 Upper Burma ceded to British after
defeat of Thibaw in third Anglo-Burmese
war; British united Burma, which was

administered as a province of British
India.
1886–96 Guerrilla warfare waged
against British in northern Burma.
early 20th century Burma developed
as major rice, teak and, later, oil
exporter, drawing in immigrant labourers
and traders from India and China.
1937 Became British crown colony in
Commonwealth, with a degree of
internal self-government.
1942 Invaded and occupied by Japan,
who installed anti-British nationalist
puppet government headed by Ba Maw.
1945 Liberated from Japanese control
by British, assisted by nationalists Aung
San and U Nu, formerly ministers in
puppet government, who had formed
the socialist Anti Fascist People's
Freedom League (AFPFL).
1947 Assassination of Aung San and six
members of interim government by
political opponents.
1948 Independence achieved from
Britain as Burma, with U Nu as prime
minister. Left Commonwealth. Quasi-
federal state established.
1958–60 Administered by emergency
government, formed by army chief of
staff Gen Ne Win.
1962 Gen Ne Win reassumed power in
left-wing army coup; he proceeded to
abolish federal system and follow
'Burmese Way to Socialism', involving
sweeping nationalization and
international isolation, which crippled
the economy.
1973–74 Adopted presidential-style
'civilian' constitution.
1975 Opposition National Democratic
Front formed by regionally-based
minority groups, who mounted guerrilla
insurgencies.
1987 Student demonstrations in
Rangoon as food shortages
worsened.
1988 Government resigned after violent
student demonstrations and workers'
riots. Gen Saw Maung seized power in
military coup believed to have been
organized by the ousted Ne Win; over
2,000 killed.
1989 Martial law declared; thousands
arrested including advocates of
democracy and human rights. Country
renamed Myanmar and capital
Yangon.
1990 Landslide victory for opposition
National League for Democracy (NLD)
in general election ignored by military
junta; NLD leaders U Nu and Suu Kyi,
the daughter of Aung San, placed under

house arrest. Breakaway opposition group formed 'parallel government'.
1991 Martial law and human-rights abuses continued. Government crackdown on Karen ethnic rebels in SE. Suu Kyi, still imprisoned, awarded Nobel Peace Prize. Pogrom against Muslim community in Arakan province in SW Myanmar. Western countries imposed sanctions.
1992 Saw Maung replaced by Than

Shwe. Several political prisoners liberated. Martial law lifted, but restrictions on political freedom remained.
1993 Cease-fire agreed with Kachin rebels in NE.
1995 Karen rebels forced to flee to Thailand after further military crackdown. Suu Kyi released from house arrest, but her appointment as NLD leader declared illegal. NLD

boycotted constitutional convention.
1996 Karen rebels agreed to peace talks. Suu Kyi held first party congress since her release; 200 supporters detained by government. Major demonstrations in support of Suu Kyi.
1997 Admission to Association of South East Asian Nations (ASEAN) granted, despite US sanctions for human-rights abuses. Currency under threat from speculators.

Practical information

Visa requirements UK: visa required. USA: visa required
Embassy in the UK 19a Charles Street, Berkeley Square, London W1X 8ER. Tel: (0171) 629 6966; fax: (0171) 629 4169
British embassy PO Box 638, 80 Strand Road, Yangon. Tel: (1) 95300; fax: (1) 89566
Embassy in the USA 2300 S Street NW, Washington, DC 20008. Tel: (202) 332 9044/5
American embassy 581 Merchant Street, Rangoon (GPO 521). Tel: (1) 82055, 82182 (operator assistance required); fax: (1) 80409
Chamber of commerce Myanmar Foreign Trade Bank, PO

Box 203, 80–86 Maha Bandoola Garden Street, Yangon. Tel: (1) 83129; fax: (1) 89585
Office hours 0930–1630 Mon–Fri
Banking hours 1000–1400 Mon–Fri
Time difference GMT +6.5
Chief tourist attractions palaces; Buddhist temples and shrines in Yangon, Mandalay, Taunggyi, and Pagan (notably Yangon's ancient Sule, Botataung, and Shwedagon pagodas); Indian Ocean coast; mountainous interior
Major holidays 4 January, 12 February, 2, 27 March, 1 April, 1 May, 19 July, 1 October, 25 December; variable: New Year (Burmese), Thingyan (April, 4 days), end of Buddhist Lent (Oct), Full Moon days

---

Namibia Republic of (formerly *South West Africa*)

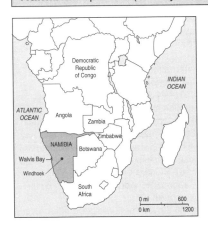

Area 824,300 sq km/318,262 sq mi
Capital Windhoek
Major towns/cities Swakopmund, Rehoboth, Rundu
Major ports Walvis Bay
Physical features mainly desert (Namib and Kalahari); Orange River; Caprivi Strip links Namibia to Zambezi River; includes the enclave of Walvis Bay (area 1,120 sq km/432 sq mi)

Government

Head of state Sam Nujoma from 1990

Head of government Hage Geingob from 1990
Political system democratic republic
Administrative divisions 13 regions
Political parties South West Africa People's Organization (SWAPO), socialist Ovambo-oriented; Democratic Turnhalle Alliance (DTA), moderate, multiracial coalition; United Democratic Front (UDF), disaffected ex-SWAPO members; National Christian Action (ACN), white conservative
Armed forces 8,100 (1995)
Conscription military service is voluntary
Death penalty abolished 1990
Defence spend (% GDP) 2.7 (1995)
Education spend (% GNP) 8.7 (1993/94)
Health spend (% GDP) 5 (1990)

Economy and resources

Currency Namibia dollar
GDP ($ US) 2.9 billion (1994)
Real GDP per capita (PPP) ($ US) 4,027 (1994)
GDP growth rate 5.4% (1994); 3.8% (1990–95)
Average annual inflation 10.8% (1994); 10.5% (1985–95)

Foreign debt ($ US) 4.7 billion (1993)
Trading partners South Africa, UK, Japan, Germany, France, USA
Resources uranium, copper, lead, zinc, silver, tin, gold, salt, semi-precious stones, diamonds (one of the world's leading producers of gem diamonds), hydrocarbons, lithium, manganese, tungsten, cadmium, vanadium
Industries food processing (fish), mining and quarrying, metal and wooden products, brewing, meat processing, chemicals, textiles, cement, leather shoes
Exports diamonds, fish and fish products, live animals and meat, uranium, karakul pelts. Principal market: UK 37% (1994)
Imports food and live animals, beverages, tobacco, transport equipment, mineral fuels, chemicals, electrical and other machinery. Principal source: South Africa 85% (1994)
Arable land 0.8% (1993)
Agricultural products wheat, maize, sunflower seed, sorghum, vegetables (crop farming is greatly limited by scarcity of water and poor rainfall); fishing; principal agricultural activity is livestock rearing (cattle, sheep, and goats); beef and karakul sheepskin are also produced

Population and society

Population 1,575,000 (1996e)
Population growth rate 2.7%
(1990–95); 2.5% (2000–05)
Population density (per sq km) 2
(1996e)
Urban population (% of total) 37 (1995)
Age distribution (% of total population)
<15 41.9%, 15–65 54.4%, >65 3.7%
(1995)
Ethnic distribution 85% black African,
of which 51% belong to the Ovambo
tribe; the remainder includes the pastoral
Nama and hunter-gatherer groups. There
is a 6% white minority
Languages English (official), Afrikaans,
German, indigenous languages
Religions mainly Christian (Lutheran,
Roman Catholic, Dutch Reformed
Church, Anglican)
Education (compulsory years) 7
Literacy rate N/A
Labour force 42% of population: 49%
agriculture, 15% industry, 36% services
(1990)
Unemployment 38% (1995e)
Life expectancy 60 (men); 63 (women)
(1995–2000)
Child mortality rate (under 5, per 1,000
live births) 78 (1995)
Physicians 1 per 4,321 people (1992)
Hospital beds 1 per 232 people (1992)
TV sets (per 1,000 people) 25 (1995)
Radios (per 1,000 people) 140 (1995)

Transport

Airports international airports: Windhoek;
all major towns have domestic airports or
landing strips; total passenger km: 751 mil
(1994)
Railroads total length: 2,382 km/1,480
mi; total passenger km: 35 mil (1994)
Roads total road network: 40,450 km/
25,136 mi, of which 13.1% paved
(1995e); passenger cars: 42.3 per 1,000
people (1995e)

Chronology

1480s Coast visited by European
explorers.
16th century Bantu-speaking Herero
migrated into NW and Ovambo settled in
northernmost areas.
1840s Rhenish Missionary Society began
to spread German influence; Jonkar
Afrikaner conquest state dominant in
southern Namibia.
1884 Germany annexed most of the area,
calling it South West Africa, with Britain
incorporating a small enclave around
Walvis Bay in the Cape Colony of South
Africa.
1892 German farmers arrived to settle in
the region.
1903–04 Uprisings by the long-settled
Nama (Khoikhoi) and Herero peoples
brutally repressed by Germans, with over
half the local communities slaughtered.
1908 Discovery of diamonds led to a
larger influx of Europeans.
1915 German colony invaded and seized
by South Africa during World War I and
the Ovambo, in the N, were conquered.
1920 Administered by South Africa, under
League of Nations mandate.
1946 Full incorporation in South Africa
refused by United Nations (UN).
1949 White voters in South West Africa
given representation in the South African
parliament.
1958 South West Africa People's
Organization (SWAPO) formed to
campaign for racial equality and full
independence.
1960 Radical wing of SWAPO, led by
Sam Nujoma, forced into exile.
1964 UN voted to end South Africa's
mandate, but South Africa refused to
relinquish control or soften its policies
towards the economically disenfranchised
black majority.
1966 South Africa's apartheid laws
extended to the country; 60% of land was
allocated to whites, who formed 10% of
the population.

1968 South West Africa redesignated
Namibia by UN; SWAPO, drawing strong
support from the Ovambo people of the
N, began armed guerrilla struggle against
South African rule, establishing People's
Liberation Army of Namibia (PLAN).
1971 Prolonged general strike by black
Namibian contract workers.
1973 UN recognized SWAPO as the
'authentic representative of the Namibian
people'.
1975–76 Establishment of new Marxist
regime in independent Angola
strengthened position of SWAPO guerrilla
movement, but also led to increased
military involvement of South Africa in the
region.
1978 UN Security Council Resolution 435
for the granting of full independence
accepted by South Africa and then
rescinded.
1983 Direct rule reimposed by Pretoria
after the resignation of the Democratic
Turnhalle Alliance (DTA), a conservative
administration dominated by whites.
1985 South Africa installed new puppet
administration, the Transitional
Government of National Unity (TGNU),
which tried to reform apartheid system,
but was not recognized by UN.
1988 Peace talks between South Africa,
Angola, and Cuba led to agreement on
troop withdrawals and full independence
for Namibia.
1989 UN peacekeeping force stationed to
oversee free elections to assembly to
draft new constitution; SWAPO won the
elections.
1990 Liberal multiparty constitution
adopted; independence achieved. Sam
Nujoma, SWAPO's former guerrilla leader,
elected president. Joined Commonwealth.
1993 South Africa, with its new multiracial
government, relinquished claim to Walvis
Bay sovereignty. Namibia dollar launched
with South African rand parity.
1994 SWAPO won assembly elections;
Nujoma re-elected president.

Practical information

Visa requirements UK: visa not required. USA: visa not
required
Embassy in the UK 6 Chandos Street, London W1M 0LQ.
Tel: (0171) 636 6244; fax: (0171) 637 5694
British embassy British High Commission, PO Box 22202,
116 Robert Mugabe Avenue, Windhoek. Tel: (61) 223 022;
fax: (61) 228 895
Embassy in the USA 1605 New Hampshire Avenue NW,
Washington, DC 20009. Tel: (202) 986 0540;
fax:(202) 986 0443
American embassy Ausplan Building, 14 Lossen St,

Windhoek. Tel: (61) 221 601; fax: (61) 229 792
Chamber of commerce Namibia National Chamber of
Commerce and Industry, PO Box 9355, Windhoek. Tel: (61)
228 809; fax: (61) 228 009
Office hours 0800–1700 Mon–Fri
Banking hours 0900–1530 Mon–Fri; 0830–1100 Sat
Time difference GMT +1
Chief tourist attractions game parks; nature reserves
(notably the Etosha National Park and Game Reserve); the
government is promoting the development of ecotourism
Major holidays 1 January, 21 March, 1, 4, 16, 25 May,
26 August, 10, 25–26 December; variable: Good Friday,
Easter Monday

Nauru Republic of

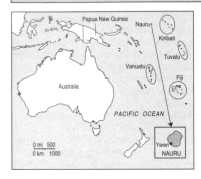

National name *Naoero*
Area 21 sq km/8.1 sq mi
Capital (seat of government) Yaren
District
Physical features tropical coral island in
SW Pacific; plateau encircled by coral
cliffs and sandy beaches

Government

Head of state and government Kinza
Klodimar from 1997
Political system liberal democracy
Administrative divisions 14 districts
Political parties candidates are
traditionally elected as independents,
grouped into pro- and antigovernment
factions; Democratic Party of Nauru
(DPN), only formal political party,
antigovernment
Armed forces no standing army;
Australia is responsible for Nauru's
defence
Death penalty retains the death penalty
for ordinary crimes but can be considered
abolitionist in practice (no executions
since independence)

Economy and resources

Currency Australian dollar
GDP ($ US) 100 million (1993e)
Real GDP per capita (PPP) ($ US)
10,000 (1993e)
Average annual inflation –3.6% (1993)
Trading partners Australia, New Zealand,
Philippines, Japan

Resources phosphates
Industries phosphate mining, financial
services
Exports phosphates. Principal market:
Australia
Imports food and live animals, building
construction materials, petroleum,
machinery, medical supplies. Principal
source: Australia
Agricultural products small-scale
production; coconuts, bananas,
pineapples, screw-pines, livestock rearing
(pigs and chickens); almost all the
country's requirements (including most of
its drinking water) are imported

Population and society

Population 11,000 (1996e)
Population growth rate 2.6% (1990–95)
Population density (per sq km) 510
(1996e)
Urban population (% of total) 100 (1995)
Ethnic distribution about 87% of
European origin (mostly British), about 9%
Maori, and about 2% Pacific Islander
Languages Nauruan (official), English
Religions Protestant, Roman Catholic
Education (compulsory years) 10
Literacy rate 99% (men); 99% (women)
(1994e)
Life expectancy N/A
Child mortality rate (under 5, per 1,000
live births) 40 (1994)
Physicians 1 per 700 people (1990)
Radios (per 1,000 people) 580 (1995)

Transport

Airports international airports: Nauru
Island; total passenger km: 206 mil (1994)
Railroads total length: 5.2 km/3.2 mi
serving the phosphate works (1996)
Roads total road network: 28 km/17 mi,
of which 79.3% paved (1995e)

Chronology

1798 British whaler Capt John Fearn first
visited Nauru and named it 'Pleasant
Island'.
1830s–80s The island was a haven for
white runaway convicts and deserters.

1888 Annexed by Germany at the request
of German settlers who sought protection
from local clan unrest.
1899 Phosphate deposits discovered;
mining began eight years later, with
indentured Chinese labourers brought in
to work British Australian-owned mines.
1914 Occupied by Australia on outbreak
of World War I.
1920 Administered by Australia on behalf
of itself, New Zealand, and the UK until
independence, except 1942–43, when
occupied by Japan, and two-thirds of the
population were deported briefly to
Micronesia.
1951 Local Government Council set up to
replace Council of Chiefs.
1956 Hammer DeRoburt became head
chief of Nauru.
1968 Independence achieved, with
'special member' British Commonwealth
status. Hammer DeRoburt elected
president.
1976 Bernard Dowiyogo elected president
as criticism of DeRoburt's personal style
of government mounted.
1978 DeRoburt re-elected.
1986 DeRoburt briefly replaced as
president by opposition leader Kennan
Adeang.
1987 Adeang established Democratic
Party of Nauru.
1989 DeRoburt replaced by Kenas Aroi,
who was later succeeded by Dowiyogo.
1992 DeRoburt died.
1994 Australia agreed to out-of-court
settlement of A$107 million, payable over
20 years, for environmental damage
caused by phosphate mining which had
left 80% of land agriculturally barren.
1995 Lagumot Harris replaced Dowiyogo
as president.
1996 President Harris replaced by
Bernard Dowiyogo, following general
election.
1997 President Dowiyogo defeated in
confidence motion. Kinza Klodimar
became president after new general
election; new cabinet included former
presidents Dowiyogo and Kennan Adeang.

Practical information

Visa requirements UK: visa required. USA: visa required
Embassy in the UK Nauru Government Office, 3 Chesham
Street, London SW1X 8ND. Tel: (0171) 235 6911; fax: (0171)
235 7423
British embassy the British Embassy in Suva (see Fiji) deals
with enquiries relating to Nauru
Embassy in the USA Nauru does not have an embassy in
the USA

American embassy the USA does not have an embassy in
Nauru; the US Ambassador to Fiji is accredited to Nauru
Chamber of commerce Central Bank of Nauru, PO Box 289,
Nauru. Tel: 444 3238; fax: 444 3203
Time difference GMT +12
Chief tourist attractions beautiful beaches interspersed by
coral pinnacles
Major holidays 1, 31 January, 17 May, 1 July, 27 October,
25–26 December; variable: Good Friday, Easter Monday,
Easter Tuesday

Nepal Kingdom of

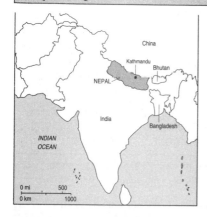

National name *Nepal Adhirajya*
Area 147,181 sq km/56,826 sq mi
Capital Kathmandu
Major towns/cities Pátan, Moráng, Bhádgáon, Biratnagar, Lalitpur, Bhaktapur, Pokhara
Physical features descends from the Himalayan mountain range in N through foothills to the river Ganges plain in S; Mount Everest, Mount Kanchenjunga

Government

Head of state King Birendra Bir Bikram Shah Dev from 1972
Head of government Lokendra Bahadur Chand from 1997
Political system constitutional monarchy
Administrative divisions 14 zones
Political parties Nepali Congress Party (NCP), left of centre; United Nepal Communist Party (UNCP; Unified Marxist–Leninist), left wing; Rashtriya Prajatantra Party (RPP), monarchist
Armed forces 35,000 (1995)
Conscription military service is voluntary
Death penalty laws provide for the death penalty only for exceptional crimes such as crimes under military law or crimes committed in exceptional circumstances such as wartime (last execution 1979)
Defence spend (% GDP) 1 (1995)
Education spend (% GNP) 2.9 (1993/94)
Health spend (% GDP) 2.2 (1990)

Economy and resources

Currency Nepalese rupee
GDP ($ US) 4 billion (1994)
Real GDP per capita (PPP) ($ US) 1,137 (1994)
GDP growth rate 11.1% (1994); 5.1% (1990–95)
Average annual inflation 8.9% (1994); 11.6% (1985–95)

Foreign debt ($ US) 2.4 billion (1995)
Trading partners Germany, Thailand, India, Japan, Singapore, USA, Switzerland
Resources lignite, talcum, magnesite, limestone, copper, cobalt
Industries bricks and tiles, carpets, clothing, paper, cotton fabrics, cement, leather, jute goods, electrical cable, soap, edible oils, sugar, tourism
Exports woollen carpets, clothing, hides and skins, food grains, jute, timber, oil seeds, ghee, potatoes, medicinal herbs, cattle. Principal market: Germany 38.7% (1995)
Imports basic manufactures, machinery and transport equipment, chemicals, pharmaceuticals. Principal source: Thailand 10.3% (1995)
Arable land 16.5% (1993)
Agricultural products rice, maize, wheat, sugar cane, millet, potatoes, barley, tobacco, cardamoms, fruits, oil seeds; livestock rearing (cattle and pigs)

Population and society

Population 22,021,000 (1996e)
Population growth rate 2.6% (1990–95); 2.4% (2000–05)
Population density (per sq km) 156 (1996e)
Urban population (% of total) 14 (1995)
Age distribution (% of total population) <15 42.4%, 15–65 54.2%, >65 3.4% (1995)
Ethnic distribution 80% of Indo-Nepalese origin, including the Gurkhas, Paharis, Newars, and Tharus; 20% of Tibeto-Nepalese descent (concentrated in the N and E)
Languages Nepali (official); 20 dialects spoken
Religions Hindu 90%; Buddhist, Muslim, Christian
Education (compulsory years) 5
Literacy rate 38% (men); 13% (women) (1995e)
Labour force 47% of population: 93% agriculture, 1% industry, 6% services (1991)
Unemployment 4.9% (1990)
Life expectancy 57 (men); 57 (women) (1995–2000)
Child mortality rate (under 5, per 1,000 live births) 114 (1995)
Physicians 1 per 16,288 people (1992)
Hospital beds 1 per 4,235 people (1992)
TV sets (per 1,000 people) 5.1 (1995)
Radios (per 1,000 people) 36 (1995)

Transport

Airports international airports: Kathmandu (Tribhuvan); 37 domestic airports and airfields; total passenger km: 812 mil (1994)
Railroads total length: 101 km/63 mi; total passenger km: 18,044 mil (1994)
Roads total road network: 7,550 km/4,692 mi, of which 41.4% paved (1995e)

Chronology

8th century BC Kathmandu Valley occupied by Ahirs (shepherd kings), Tibeto-Burman migrants from N India.
c. 563 BC In Lumbini in far S, Prince Siddhartha Gautama, the historic Buddha, was born.
AD 300 Licchavis dynasty immigrated from India and introduced caste system.
13th–16th centuries Dominated by Malla dynasty, great patrons of the arts.
1768 Nepal emerged as unified kingdom after ruler of the principality of the Gurkhas in the W, King Prithwi Narayan Shah, conquered Kathmandu Valley.
1792 Nepal's expansion halted by defeat at the hands of Chinese in Tibet; commercial treaty signed with Britain.
1815–16 Anglo-Nepali 'Gurkha War'; Nepal became British-dependent buffer state with British resident stationed in Kathmandu.
1846 Fell under sway of Rana family, who became hereditary chief ministers, dominating powerless monarchy and isolating Nepal from outside world.
1923 Full independence formally recognized by Britain.
1951 Monarchy restored to power and Ranas overthrown in 'palace revolution' supported by Nepali Congress Party (NCP).
1959 Constitution created elected legislature.
1960–61 Parliament dissolved by King Mahendra; political parties banned after NCP's pro-India socialist leader B P Koirala became prime minister.
1962 New constitution provided for tiered, traditional system of indirectly elected local councils (*panchayats*) and an appointed prime minister.
1972 King Mahendra died; succeeded by his son, King Birendra Bikram Shah Dev.
1980 Constitutional referendum held following popular agitation led by B P Koirala resulted in introduction of direct, but nonparty, elections to National Assembly.

1983 Overthrow of monarch-supported prime minister by directly elected deputies to National Assembly.
1986 New assembly elections returned majority opposed to *panchayat* system of partyless government.
1988 Strict curbs placed on opposition activity; over 100 supporters of banned NCP arrested; censorship imposed.
1989 Border blockade imposed by India during treaty dispute.
1990 *Panchayat* system collapsed after mass NCP-led violent prodemocracy demonstrations; new democratic constitution introduced, and ban on political parties lifted.
1991 Nepali Congress Party, led by Girija Prasad Koirala, won general election.
1992 Communists led antigovernment demonstrations in Kathmandu and Pátan.
1994 Koirala's government defeated on 'no-confidence' motion; parliament dissolved. After new elections, minority communist government formed under Man Mohan Adhikari.
1995 Parliament dissolved by King Birendra at Prime Minister Adhikari's request; fresh elections called but Supreme Court ruled the move unconstitutional. Sher Bahadur Deuba (NCP) became prime minister.
1997 Prime Minister Deuba defeated in vote of confidence. New coalition formed, led by right-wing Rastriya Prajatantra Party under Prime Minister Lokendra Bahadur Chand. UCPN successes in local elections.

Practical information

Visa requirements UK: visa required. USA: visa required
Embassy in the UK 12a Kensington Palace Gardens, London W8 4QV. Tel: (0171) 229 1594; fax: (0171) 792 9861
British embassy PO Box 106, Lainchaur, Kathmandu. Tel: (1) 410 583; fax: (1) 411 789
Embassy in the USA 2131 Leroy Place NW, Washington, DC 20008. Tel: (202) 667 4550
American embassy Pani Pokhari, Kathmandu. Tel: (1) 411 179; fax: (1) 419 963
Chamber of commerce PO Box 198, Chamber Bhavan, Kantipath, Kathmandu. Tel: (1) 222 890; fax: (1) 229 998
Office hours 1000–1700 Sun–Fri (summer); 1000–1600 Sun–Fri (winter)
Banking hours 1000–1450 Sun–Thu; 1000–1230 Fri
Time difference GMT +5.5
Chief tourist attractions Lumbini, birthplace of Buddha; the Himalayas, including Mount Everest, the world's highest peak; the lake city of Pokhara; wildlife includes tigers, leopards, elephants, buffalo, and gaur
Major holidays 11 January, 19 February, 8 November, 16, 29 December; variable: New Year (Sinhala/Tamil, April), Maha Shivarata (February/March)

Netherlands, the Kingdom of (popularly referred to as *Holland*)

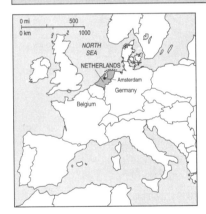

National name *Koninkrijk der Nederlanden*
Area 41,863 sq km/16,163 sq mi
Capital Amsterdam
Major towns/cities Rotterdam, The Hague (seat of government), Utrecht, Eindhoven, Groningen, Tilburg, Maastricht, Haarlem, Apeldoorn, Nijmegen, Enschede
Major ports Rotterdam
Physical features flat coastal lowland; rivers Rhine, Schelde, Maas; Frisian Islands
Territories Aruba, Netherlands Antilles (Caribbean)

Government

Head of state Queen Beatrix Wilhelmina Armgard from 1980
Head of government Wim Kok from 1994
Political system constitutional monarchy
Administrative divisions 12 provinces
Political parties Christian Democratic Appeal (CDA), Christian, right of centre; Labour Party (PvdA), democratic socialist, left of centre; People's Party for Freedom and Democracy (VVD), liberal, free enterprise; Democrats 66 (D66), ecologist, centrist; Political Reformed Party (SGP), moderate Calvinist; Evangelical Political Federation (RPF), radical Calvinist; Reformed Political Association (GPV), fundamentalist Calvinist; Green Left, ecologist; General League of the Elderly (AOV), pensioner-oriented
Armed forces 74,000 (1995)
Death penalty abolished 1982
Defence spend (% GDP) 2.2 (1995)
Education spend (% GNP) 5.5 (1993/94)
Health spend (% GDP) 6.8 (1993)

Economy and resources

Currency guilder
GDP ($ US) 392.4 billion (1996)
Real GDP per capita (PPP) ($ US) 20,626 (1996)
GDP growth rate 2.1% (1996); 1.8% (1990–95)
Average annual inflation 2.3% (1996); 1.7% (1985–95)
Trading partners EU (principally Germany, Benelux, UK, France, and Italy), USA
Resources petroleum, natural gas
Industries electrical machinery, metal products, food processing, electronic equipment, chemicals, rubber and plastic products, petroleum refining, dairy farming, horticulture, diamond cutting
Exports machinery and transport equipment, foodstuffs, live animals, petroleum and petroleum products, natural gas, chemicals, plants and cut flowers, plant-derived products. Principal market: Germany 28.6% (1995)
Imports electrical machinery, cars and other vehicles, mineral fuels, metals and metal products, plastics, paper and cardboard, clothing and accessories. Principal source: Germany 23.4% (1995)
Arable land 24.3% (1993)
Agricultural products sugar beet, potatoes, wheat, barley, flax, fruit, vegetables, flowers; dairy farming

Population and society

Population 15,575,000 (1996e)
Population growth rate 0.7% (1990–95); 0.3% (2000–05)

Population density (per sq km) 381 (1996e)
Urban population (% of total) 89 (1995)
Age distribution (% of total population) <15 18.4%, 15–65 68.4%, >65 13.2% (1995)
Ethnic distribution primarily Germanic, with some Gallo-Celtic mixtures; sizeable Indonesian and Surinamese minorities
Language Dutch
Religions Roman Catholic, Dutch Reformed Church
Education (compulsory years) 11
Literacy rate 99% (men); 99% (women) (1995e)
Labour force 46% of population: 5% agriculture, 26% industry, 70% services (1990)
Unemployment 6.3% (1996)
Life expectancy 75 (men); 81 (women) (1995–2000)
Child mortality rate (under 5, per 1,000 live births) 8 (1995)
Physicians 1 per 394 people (1994)
Hospital beds 1 per 255 people (1995)
TV sets (per 1,000 people) 497 (1995)
Radios (per 1,000 people) 937 (1995)

Transport

Airports international airports: Amsterdam (Schipol), Rotterdam (Zestienhoven), Eindhoven (Welschap), Maastricht (Beck), Groningen (Eelde), Enschede (Twente); domestic services operate between these; total passenger km: 42,435 mil (1994)
Railroads total length: 2,739 km/1,702 mi; total passenger km: 14,439 mil (1994)
Roads total road network: 120,800 km/ 75,065 mi, of which 90% paved (1995); passenger cars: 363.4 per 1,000 people (1995)

Chronology

55 BC Julius Caesar brought lands S of Rhine under Roman rule.
4th century AD Region overrun by Franks and Saxons.
7th–8th centuries Franks subdued

Saxons N of Rhine and imposed Christianity.
843–12th centuries Division of Holy Roman Empire: the Netherlands repeatedly partitioned, not falling clearly into either French or German kingdoms.
12th–14th centuries Local feudal lords, led by count of Holland and bishop of Utrecht, became practically independent; Dutch towns became prosperous trading centres, usually ruled by small groups of merchants.
15th century Low Countries (Holland, Belgium, and Flanders) came under rule of dukes of Burgundy.
1477 Low Countries passed by marriage to Habsburgs.
1555 The Netherlands passed to Spain upon division of Habsburg domains.
1568 Dutch rebelled under leadership of William the Silent, Prince of Orange, and fought a long war of independence.
1579 Union of Utrecht: seven northern rebel provinces formed United Provinces.
17th century 'Golden Age': Dutch led world in trade, art, and science, and founded colonies in East and West Indies, primarily through Dutch East India Company, founded 1602.
1648 Treaty of Westphalia: United Provinces finally recognized as independent Dutch Republic.
1652–54 Commercial and colonial rivalries led to naval war with England.
1652–72 Johann de Witt ruled Dutch Republic as premier after conflict between republicans and House of Orange.
1665–67 Second Anglo-Dutch war.
1672–74 Third Anglo-Dutch war.
1672 William of Orange became stadholder (ruling as chief magistrate) of the Dutch Republic, an office which became hereditary in the Orange family.
1672–78 The Netherlands fought to prevent domination by King Louis XIV of France.
1688–97 and 1701–13 War with France resumed.
18th century Exhausted by war, the

Netherlands ceased to be a Great Power.
1795 Revolutionary France conquered the Netherlands and established Batavian Republic.
1806 Napoleon made his brother Louis king of Holland.
1810 France annexed the Netherlands.
1815 Northern and southern Netherlands (Holland and Belgium) unified as Kingdom of the Netherlands under King William I of Orange, who also became grand duke of Luxembourg.
1830 Southern Netherlands rebelled and declared independence as Belgium.
1848 Liberal constitution adopted.
1890 Queen Wilhelmina succeeded to throne; dynastic link with Luxembourg broken.
1894–96 Dutch suppressed colonial revolt in Java.
1914–18 The Netherlands neutral during World War I.
1940–45 Occupied by Germany during World War II.
1948 The Netherlands formed Benelux customs union with Belgium and Luxembourg; Queen Wilhelmina abdicated in favour of her daughter Juliana.
1949 Became founding member of North Atlantic Treaty Organization (NATO); most of Dutch East Indies became independent as Indonesia after four years of war.
1953 Dykes breached by storm; nearly two thousand people and tens of thousands of cattle died in flood.
1954 Remaining Dutch colonies achieved internal self-government.
1958 The Netherlands became founding member of European Economic Community (EEC).
1963 Dutch colony of Western New Guinea ceded to Indonesia.
1975 Dutch Guiana became independent as Suriname.
1980 Queen Juliana abdicated in favour of her daughter Beatrix.
1994 Following inconclusive general election, three-party coalition formed under PvdA leader Wim Kok.

Practical information

Visa requirements UK: visa not required. USA: visa not required
Embassy in the UK 38 Hyde Park Gate, London SW7 5DP. Tel: (0171) 584 5040; fax: (0171) 581 3458
British embassy Lange Voorhout 10, 2514 ED The Hague. Tel: (70) 364 5800; fax: (70) 427 0345
Embassy in the USA (temporary) 4200 Wisconsin Avenue NW, Washington, DC 20016. Tel: (202) 244 5300; fax: (202) 362 3430
American embassy Lange Voorhout 102, 2514 EJ The Hague. Tel: (70) 310 9209; fax: (70) 361 4688

Chamber of commerce The Hague Chamber of Commerce and Industry, Konigskade 30, 2596 AA The Hague. Tel: (70) 328 7100; fax: (70) 324 0684
Office hours 0830–1700 Mon–Fri
Banking hours 0900–1600 Mon–Fri
Time difference GMT +1
Chief tourist attractions the lively, cosmopolitan city of Amsterdam, with its museums and historical buildings; old towns; canals; the bulb fields in spring; art galleries; modern architecture; outlying islands
Major holidays 1 January, 30 April, 5 May, 25–26 December; variable: Ascension Thursday, Good Friday, Easter Monday, Whit Monday

New Zealand Dominion of

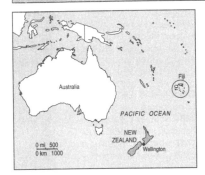

Area 268,680 sq km/103,737 sq mi
Capital Wellington (and port)
Major towns/cities Auckland, Hamilton, Palmerston North, Christchurch, Dunedin, Napier-Hastings
Major ports Auckland
Physical features comprises North Island, South Island, Stewart Island, Chatham Islands, and minor islands; mainly mountainous; Ruapehu in North Island, 2,797 m/9,180 ft, highest of three active volcanoes; geysers and hot springs of Rotorua district; Lake Taupo (616 sq km/238 sq mi), source of Waikato River; Kaingaroa state forest. In South Island are Southern Alps and Canterbury Plains
Territories Tokelau (three atolls transferred 1926 from former Gilbert and Ellice Islands colony); Niue Island (one of the Cook Islands, separately administered from 1903: chief town Alafi); Cook Islands are internally self-governing but share common citizenship with New Zealand; Ross Dependency in Antarctica

Government

Head of state Queen Elizabeth II from 1952, represented by governor general Catherine Tizard from 1990
Head of government Jenny Shipley from 1997
Political system constitutional monarchy
Administrative divisions 93 counties, 12 regions, and 6 territorial authorities
Political parties Labour Party, moderate, left of centre; New Zealand National Party, free enterprise, centre right; Alliance Party bloc, left of centre, ecologists; New Zealand First Party (NZFP), centrist; United New Zealand Party (UNZ), centrist
Armed forces 10,000; 2,650 regular reserves and 5,200 territorial reserves (1995)

Death penalty abolished 1989
Defence spend (% GDP) 1.7 (1995)
Education spend (% GNP) 7.3 (1993/94)
Health spend (% GDP) 5.9 (1993)

Economy and resources

Currency New Zealand dollar
GDP ($ US) 65.1 billion (1996)
Real GDP per capita (PPP) ($ US) 17,264 (1996)
GDP growth rate 1.2% (1996); 3.6% (1990–95)
Average annual inflation 1.1% (1996); 3.9% (1985–95)
Trading partners Australia, USA, Japan, UK
Resources coal, clay, limestone, dolomite, natural gas, hydroelectric power, pumice, iron ore, gold, forests
Industries food processing, machinery, textiles and clothing, fishery, wood and wood products, paper and paper products, metal products; farming, particularly livestock and dairying, cropping, fruit growing, horticulture
Exports meat, dairy products, wool, fish, timber and wood products, fruit and vegetables, aluminium, machinery. Principal market: Australia 20.3% (1995)
Imports machinery and mechanical appliances, vehicles and aircraft, petroleum, fertilizer, consumer goods. Principal source: Australia 23.5% (1995)
Arable land 9% (1993)
Agricultural products barley, wheat, maize, fodder crops, exotic timber, fruit (kiwi fruit and apples); livestock and dairy farming

Population and society

Population 3,602,000 (1996e)
Population growth rate 1.2% (1990–95); 0.8% (2000–05)
Population density (per sq km) 13 (1996e)
Urban population (% of total) 86 (1995)
Age distribution (% of total population) <15 23.4%, 15–65 65.3%, >65 11.3% (1995)
Ethnic distribution around 87% of European origin, 9% Maori, 2% Pacific Islander
Languages English (official), Maori
Religion Christian
Education (compulsory years) 11
Literacy rate 99% (men); 99% (women) (1995e)
Labour force 48% of population: 10%

agriculture, 25% industry, 65% services (1990)
Unemployment 6.1% (1996)
Life expectancy 73 (men); 79 (women) (1995–2000)
Child mortality rate (under 5, per 1,000 live births) 9 (1995)
Physicians 1 per 298 people (1994)
Hospital beds 1 per 141 people (1994)
TV sets (per 1,000 people) 514 (1995)
Radios (per 1,000 people) 997 (1995)

Transport

Airports international airports: Auckland (Mangere), Christchurch, Wellington (Rongotai); 32 domestic airports; total passenger km: 16,946 mil (1994)
Railroads total length: 3,973 km/2,469 mi; total passengers carried: 10.6 mil (1995)
Roads total road network: 92,100 km/ 57,230 mi, of which 58% paved (1995e); passenger cars: 462.6 per 1,000 people (1995e)

Chronology

1642 Dutch explorer Abel Tasman reached New Zealand but indigenous Maoris prevented him from going ashore.
1769 English explorer James Cook surveyed coastline of islands.
1773 and 1777 Cook again explored coast.
1815 First British missionaries arrived in New Zealand.
1826 New Zealand Company founded in London to establish settlement.
1839 New Zealand Company relaunched, after initial failure, by Edward Gibbon Wakefield.
1840 Treaty of Waitangi: Maoris accepted British sovereignty; colonization began and large-scale sheep farming developed.
1845–47 Maori revolt against loss of land.
1851 Became separate colony (was originally part of Australian colony of New South Wales).
1852 Colony procured constitution after dissolution of New Zealand Company; self-government fully implemented 1856.
1860–72 Second Maori revolt led to concessions, including representation in parliament.
1891 New Zealand took part in Australasian Federal Convention in Sydney but rejected idea of joining Australian Commonwealth.

1893 Became first country to give women the right to vote in parliamentary elections.
1898 Liberal government under Richard Seddon introduced pioneering old-age pension scheme.
1899–1902 Volunteers from New Zealand fought alongside imperial forces in Boer War.
1907 New Zealand achieved dominion status within British Empire.
1912–25 Government of Reform Party, led by William Massey, reflected interests of North Island farmers and strongly supported imperial unity.
1914–18 130,000 New Zealanders fought for British Empire in World War I.
1916 Labour Party of New Zealand established.

1931 Statute of Westminster affirmed equality of status between Britain and dominions, effectively granting independence to New Zealand.
1935–49 Labour governments of Michael Savage and Peter Fraser introduced social reforms and encouraged state intervention in industry.
1936 Liberal Party merged with Reform Party to create National Party.
1939–45 New Zealand troops fought in World War II, notably in Crete, N Africa, and Italy.
1947 Parliament confirmed independence of New Zealand within British Commonwealth.
1951 New Zealand joined Australia and USA in ANZUS Pacific security treaty.

1965–72 New Zealand contingent took part in Vietnam War.
1973 British entry into European Economic Community (EEC) forced New Zealand to seek closer trading relations with Australia.
1985 Non-nuclear military policy led to disagreements with France and USA.
1986 USA suspended defence obligations to New Zealand after it banned entry of US warships.
1988 Free-trade agreement signed with Australia.
1991 Alliance Party formed to challenge two-party system.
1992 Ban on entry of US warships lifted.
1996 Inconclusive general election result; coalition formed, led by Jim Bolger.

Practical information

Visa requirements UK: visa not required. USA: visa not required
Embassy in the UK New Zealand House, 80 Haymarket, London SW1Y 4TQ. Tel: (0171) 930 8422; fax: (0171) 839 4580
British embassy British High Commission, PO Box 1818, 44 Hill Street, Wellington 1. Tel: (4) 472 6049; fax: (4) 471 1974
Embassy in the USA 37 Observatory Circle NW, Washington, DC 20008. Tel: (202) 328 4800
American embassy 29 Fitzherbert Terrace, Thorndon, Wellington. Tel: (4) 472 2068; fax: (4) 472 3537

Chamber of commerce New Zealand Chambers of Commerce and Industry, PO Box 1590, 9th Floor, 109 Featherston Street, Wellington. Tel: (4) 472 2725; fax: (4) 471 1767
Office hours 0900–1700 Mon–Fri
Banking hours 0900–1630 Mon–Fri
Time difference GMT +12
Chief tourist attractions famous for its trout- and deep-sea fishing and generally idyllic setting, including beaches, hot springs; mountains, lakes, and forests
Major holidays 1, 2 January, 6 February, 25 April, 25–26 December; variable: Good Friday, Easter Monday, Queen's Birthday (June), Labour (October)

Nicaragua Republic of

National name *República de Nicaragua*
Area 127,849 sq km/49,362 sq mi
Capital Managua
Major towns/cities León, Chinandega, Masaya, Granada
Major ports Corinto, Puerto Cabezas, El Bluff

Physical features narrow Pacific coastal plain separated from broad Atlantic coastal plain by volcanic mountains and lakes Managua and Nicaragua; one of world's most active earthquake regions

Government

Head of state and government Arnoldo Aleman from 1996
Political system emergent democracy
Administrative divisions 16 departments
Political parties Sandinista National Liberation Front (FSLN), Marxist–Leninist; Opposition Political Alliance (APO, formerly National Opposition Union: UNO), loose US-backed coalition
Armed forces 12,000 (1995)
Conscription military service is voluntary (since 1990)
Death penalty abolished 1979
Defence spend (% GDP) 1.8 (1995)
Education spend (% GNP) 3.7 (1994)
Health spend (% GDP) 6.7 (1990)

Economy and resources

Currency cordoba
GDP ($ US) 1.8 billion (1994)
Real GDP per capita (PPP) ($ US) 1,580 (1994)
GDP growth rate 2.5% (1994); 1.1% (1990–95)
Average annual inflation 13% (1995); 963.7% (1985–95)
Foreign debt ($ US) 9.3 billion (1994)
Trading partners USA, Germany, Japan, Canada, Cuba, Costa Rica, Venezuela
Resources gold, silver, copper, lead, antimony, zinc, iron, limestone, gypsum, marble, bentonite
Industries food products, beverages, petroleum refining, chemicals, metallic products, processed leather, cement
Exports coffee, meat, cotton, sugar, seafood, bananas, chemical products. Principal market: USA 46.7% (1995)
Imports machinery and transport

equipment, food and live animals,
consumer goods, mineral fuels and
lubricants, basic manufactures,
chemicals and related products.
Principal source: USA 26.3% (1995)
Arable land 8.5% (1993)
Agricultural products coffee, cotton,
sugar cane, bananas, maize, rice,
beans, green tobacco; livestock rearing
(cattle and pigs); fishing; forest
resources

Population and society

Population 4,238,000 (1996e)
Population growth rate 3.7%
(1990–95); 2.8% (2000–05)
Population density (per sq km) 33
(1996e)
Urban population (% of total) 63
(1995)
Age distribution (% of total population)
<15 46%, 15–65 50.9%, >65 3.1%
(1995)
Ethnic distribution over 70% of mixed
Indian, Spanish, and African origin;
about 9% African; 5% Indian
Languages Spanish (official), Indian,
English
Religion Roman Catholic 95%
Education (compulsory years) 6
Literacy rate 64% (men); 66% (women)
(1995e)
Labour force 34% of population: 28%
agriculture, 26% industry, 46% services
(1990)
Unemployment 15% (1992)
Life expectancy 67 (men); 70 (women)
(1995–2000)
Child mortality rate (under 5, per 1,000
live births) 60 (1995)
Physicians 1 per 1,566 people (1993)
Hospital beds 1 per 856 people
(1993)
TV sets (per 1,000 people) 73 (1995)
Radios (per 1,000 people) 280 (1995)

Transport

Airports international airports: Managua
(Augusto Cesar Sandino); total
passenger km: 72 mil (1994)
Railroads total length: 287 km/178 mi;
freight services reported withdrawn
1994
Roads total road network: 17,146 km/
10,655 mi, of which 10% paved (1995);
passenger cars: 17.5 per 1,000 people
(1995)

Chronology

10th century AD Indians from Mexico
and Mesoamerica migrated to
Nicaragua's Pacific lowlands.
1522 Visited by Spanish explorer Gil
Gonzalez de Avila, who named the area
Nicaragua after local Indian chief,
Nicarao.
1523–24 Colonized by the Spanish,
under Francisco Hernandez de Cordoba,
who was attracted by local gold deposits
and founded cities of Granada and León.
17th–18th centuries British were
dominant force on Caribbean side of
Nicaragua, while Spain controlled Pacific
lowlands.
1821 Independence achieved from
Spain; Nicaragua was initially part of
Mexican Empire.
1823 Became part of United Provinces
(Federation) of Central America, also
embracing Costa Rica, El Salvador,
Guatemala, and Honduras.
1838 Became fully independent when it
seceded from the Federation.
1857–93 Ruled by succession of
Conservative Party governments.
1860 The British ceded control over
Caribbean ('Mosquito') Coast to
Nicaragua.
1893 Liberal Party leader, José Santos
Zelaya, deposed Conservative president
and established dictatorship which lasted

until overthrown by US marines in 1909.
1912–25 At Nicaraguan government's
request, with political situation
deteriorating, USA established military
bases and stationed marines.
1927–33 Re-stationed US marines faced
opposition from anti-American guerrilla
group led by Augusto César Sandino,
who was assassinated 1934 on the
orders of the commander of the US-
trained National Guard, Gen Anastasio
Somoza Garcia.
1937 Gen Somoza elected president;
start of near-dictatorial rule by Somoza
family, which amassed huge personal
fortune.
1956 Gen Somoza assassinated and
succeeded as president by his elder son,
Luis Somoza Debayle.
1961 Left-wing Sandinista National
Liberation Front (FSLN) formed to fight
Somoza regime.
1967 Luis Somoza died and was
succeeded as president by his brother
Anastasio Somoza Debayle, who headed
an even more oppressive regime.
1978 Nicaraguan Revolution: Pedro
Joaquin Chamorro, a popular publisher
and leader of anti-Somoza Democratic
Liberation Union (UDEL), was
assassinated, sparking general strike
and mass movement in which moderates
joined with FSLN to overthrow Somoza
regime.
1979 Somoza government ousted by
FSLN after military offensive.
1980 Anastasio Somoza assassinated in
Paraguay; FSLN junta took power in
Managua, headed by Daniel Ortega
Saavedra; lands held by Somozas were
nationalized and farming cooperatives
established.
1982 Subversive activity against
government by right-wing Contra
guerrillas promoted by USA and

Practical information

Visa requirements UK: visa not required for a stay of up to
90 days. USA: visa not required for a stay of up to 90 days
Embassy in the UK 2nd Floor, 36 Upper Brook Street,
London W1Y 1PE. Tel: (0171) 409 2536; fax: (0171) 409
2593
British embassy Apartado A-169, El Reparto 'Los Robles',
Primera Etapa, Entrada principal de la Carretera a Massaya,
4a Casa a Mano Derecha, Managua. Tel: (2) 780 014;
fax: (2) 784 085
Embassy in the USA 1627 New Hampshire Avenue NW,
Washington, DC 20009. Tel: (202) 939 6570
American embassy Kilometer 4.5 Carretera Sur, Managua.

Tel: (2) 666 010–013, 666 015–18, 666 026/7, 666 032/3; fax:
(2) 669 074
Chamber of commerce Cámara de Comercio de Nicaragua,
Apartado 135, Frente a Lotería Popular, C C Managua JR.
Tel: (2) 670 718
Office hours 0800–1600 Mon–Fri
Banking hours 0800–1600 Mon–Fri; 0830–1130 Sat
Time difference GMT –6
Chief tourist attractions Lake Nicaragua, with its 310
beautiful islands; the Momotombo volcano; the Corn Islands
(Islas de Maiz) in the Caribbean, fringed with white coral and
palm trees
Major holidays 1 January, 1 May, 19 July, 14–15 September,
8, 25 December; variable: Good Friday, Holy Thursday

attacking from bases in Honduras. State of emergency declared.
1984 US troops mined Nicaraguan harbours. Action condemned by World Court 1986 and $17 billion in reparations ordered. FSLN won assembly elections.
1985 Denunciation of Sandinista government by US president Ronald Reagan, who vowed to 'remove it' and imposed US trade embargo.

1987 Central American peace agreement cosigned by Nicaraguan leaders.
1988 Peace agreement failed. Nicaragua held talks with Contra rebel leaders. Hurricane left 180,000 people homeless.
1989 Demobilization of rebels and release of former Somozan supporters; cease-fire ended but economy in ruins after Contra war; 60% unemployment.
1990 FSLN defeated by right-of-centre

National Opposition Union (UNO), a US-backed coalition; Violeta Barrios de Chamorro, widow of the murdered Pedro Joaquin Chamorro, elected president. Antigovernment riots.
1992 Around 16,000 made homeless by earthquake.
1994 Peace accord with remaining Contra rebels.
1996 Right-wing candidate Arnoldo Aleman won presidential elections.

Niger Republic of

National name *République du Niger*
Area 1,186,408 sq km/458,072 sq mi
Capital Niamey
Major towns/cities Zinder, Maradi, Tahoua, Agadez, Birui N'Konui
Physical features desert plains between hills in N and savanna in S; river Niger in SW, Lake Chad in SE

Government

Head of state Ibrahim Barre Mainassara from 1996
Head of government Amadou Boubacar Cisse from 1997
Political system transitional
Administrative divisions seven regions and the municipality of Niamey
Political parties National Movement for a Development Society (MNSD–Nassara), left of centre; Alliance of the Forces for Change (AFC), left-of-centre coalition; Party for Democracy and Socialism–Tarayya (PNDS–Tarayya), left of centre
Armed forces 5,300 (1995); plus paramilitary forces of 5,400
Conscription conscription is selective for two years
Death penalty retains the death penalty for ordinary crimes but can be considered abolitionist in practice (last known execution 1976)
Defence spend (% GDP) 0.9 (1995)

Education spend (% GNP) 3.1 (1993/94)
Health spend (% GDP) 3.4 (1990)

Economy and resources

Currency franc CFA
GDP ($ US) 1.5 billion (1994)
Real GDP per capita (PPP) ($ US) 787 (1994)
GDP growth rate 2.6% (1994); 0.5% (1990–95)
Average annual inflation 9.2% (1995); 1.3% (1985–95)
Foreign debt ($ US) 1.63 billion (1995)
Trading partners France, Nigeria, Japan, USA, Côte d'Ivoire, Spain
Resources uranium (one of world's leading producers), phosphates, gypsum, coal, cassiterite, tin, salt, gold; deposits of other minerals (including petroleum, iron ore, copper, lead, diamonds, and tungsten) have been confirmed
Industries processing of agricultural products, textiles, furniture, chemicals, brewing, cement
Exports uranium ore, live animals, hides and skins, cow-peas, cotton. Principal market: EU 75.2% (1994)
Imports machinery and transport equipment, miscellaneous manufactured articles, cereals, chemicals, refined petroleum products. Principal source: EU 33% (1994)
Arable land 2.8% (1993)
Agricultural products millet, maize, sorghum, groundnuts, cassava, sugar cane, sweet potatoes, cotton; livestock rearing (cattle and sheep) is especially important among the nomadic population; agricultural production is dependent upon adequate rainfall

Population and society

Population 9,465,000 (1996e)
Population growth rate 3.4% (1990–95); 3.2% (2000–05)

Population density (per sq km) 7 (1996e)
Urban population (% of total) 17 (1995)
Age distribution (% of total population) <15 48.4%, 15–65 49.2%, >65 2.4% (1995)
Ethnic distribution three ethnic groups make up over 75% of the population: the Hausa (mainly in central areas and the S), Djerma-Songhai (SW), and Beriberi-Manga (E); there is also a significant number of the mainly nomadic Fulani people, and the Tuareg in the N
Languages French (official), Hausa, Djerma, and other minority languages
Religions Sunni Muslim; also Christian, and traditional animist beliefs
Education (compulsory years) 8
Literacy rate 40% (men); 17% (women) (1995e)
Labour force 49% of population: 90% agriculture, 4% industry, 6% services
Unemployment 20.9% (1991)
Life expectancy 47 (men); 50 (women) (1995–2000)
Child mortality rate (under 5, per 1,000 live births) 320 (1995)
Physicians 1 per 48,000 people (1992)
TV sets (per 1,000 people) 11 (1995)
Radios (per 1,000 people) 68 (1995)

Transport

Airports international airports: Niamey, Agadez; four major domestic airports; total passenger km: 215 mil (1994)
Railroads none
Roads total road network: 9,863 km/6,129 mi, of which 7.9% paved (1995); passenger cars: 4 per 1,000 people (1995e)

Chronology

10th–13th centuries Kanem-Bornu Empire flourished in SE, near Lake Chad, spreading Islam from the 11th century.

15th century Tuareg sultanate of Agades dominant in N.
17th century Songhai-speaking Djerma established an empire on Niger river.
18th century Powerful Gobir kingdom founded by Hausa people, who had migrated from S in 14th century.
late 18th–early 19th centuries Visited by European explorers, including the Scottish explorer, Mungo Park; Sultanate of Sokoto formed by Islamic revivalist Fulani, who had defeated the Hausa in a jihad (holy war).
1890s French conquered region and ended local slave trade.
1904 Became part of French West Africa, although Tuareg resistance continued until 1922.
1946 Became French overseas territory, with its own territorial assembly and representation in French Parliament.
1958 Became autonomous republic within French community.

1960 Achieved full independence; Hamani Diori of Niger Progressive Party (NPP) elected president, but maintained close ties with France.
1971 Uranium production commenced.
1974 Diori ousted in army coup led by Lt-Col Seyni Kountché after long Sahel drought had led to civil disorder; military government launched drive against corruption.
1977 Cooperation agreement signed with France.
1984 Partial privatization of state firms as a result of further drought and increased government indebtedness as world uranium prices slumped.
1987 Kountché died; replaced by Gen Ali Saibu.
1989 Ali Saibu elected president without opposition.
1991 Saibu stripped of executive powers, and transitional government formed amid student and industrial unrest.

1992 Transitional government collapsed amid economic problems and ethnic unrest among secessionist-minded Tuareg in N. Referendum approved of new multiparty constitution.
1993 Alliance of the Forces for Change (AFC) left-of-centre coalition won absolute majority in assembly elections. Mahamane Ousmane, a Muslim Hausa, elected president in first free presidential election.
1994 Peace agreement with northern Tuareg.
1995 AFC coalition won general election with reduced majority.
1996 President Ousmane ousted in military coup led by Ibrahim Barre Mainassara. Civilian government restored with Boukary Adji as premier; Mainassara formally elected president amidst claims of electoral fraud.
1997 Amadou Boubacar Cisse appointed prime minister.

Practical information

Visa requirements UK: visa required. USA: visa required
Embassy for the UK 154 rue du Longchamps, 75116 Paris, France. Tel: (1) 4504 8060; fax: (1) 4504 6226
British embassy Honorary British Vice-Consulate, BP 11168, Niamey. Tel: (227) 732 015/539
Embassy in the USA 2204 R Street NW, Washington, DC 20008. Tel: (202) 483 4224–7
American embassy rue des Ambassades, Niamey. Tel: (227) 722 661–4; fax: (227) 733 167
Chamber of commerce Chambre de Commerce, d'Agriculture, d'Industrie et d'Artisanat du Niger, BP 209,

place de la Concertation, Niamey. Tel: (227) 732 210; telex: 5242
Office hours 0730–1230 and 1530–1830 Mon–Fri; 0730–1230 Sat
Banking hours 0800–1100 and 1600–1700 Mon–Fri
Time difference GMT +1
Chief tourist attractions the Aïr and Ténéré Nature Reserve, covering 77,000 sq km/29,730 sq mi; Agadez, surrounded by green valleys and hot springs, and still a major terminus for trans-Saharan caravans
Major holidays 1 January, 15 April, 1 May, 3 August, 18, 25 December; variable: Eid-ul-Adha, end of Ramadan, Prophet's Birthday

---

Nigeria Federal Republic of

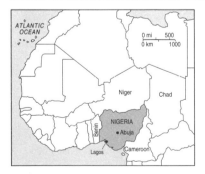

Area 923,773 sq km/356,668 sq mi
Capital Abuja
Major towns/cities Ibadan, Lagos, Ogbomosho, Kano, Oshogbo, Ilorin, Abeokuta, Zaria, Ouitsha, Iwo, Kaduna

Major ports Lagos, Port Harcourt, Warri, Calabar
Physical features arid savanna in N; tropical rainforest in S, with mangrove swamps along coast; river Niger forms wide delta; mountains in SE

Government

Head of state and government General Sani Abacha from 1993
Political system military republic
Administrative divisions 30 states and a Federal Capital Territory
Political parties Social Democratic Party (SDP), left of centre; National Republican Convention (NRC), right of centre (all parties dissolved on resumption of military rule 1992)
Armed forces 77,100 (1995)
Death penalty retained and used for

ordinary crimes
Defence spend (% GDP) 2.9 (1995)
Education spend (% GNP) 1.3 (1993/94)
Health spend (% GDP) 1.2 (1990)

Economy and resources

Currency naira
GDP ($ US) 35.2 billion (1994)
Real GDP per capita (PPP) ($ US) 1,351 (1994)
GDP growth rate 1.3% (1994); 1.6% (1990–95)
Average annual inflation 57% (1994); 33% (1985–95)
Foreign debt ($ US) 35 billion (1995)
Trading partners USA, UK, Germany, France, Spain, the Netherlands, Italy
Resources petroleum, natural gas,

coal, tin, iron ore, uranium, limestone, marble, forest
Industries food processing, brewing, petroleum refinery, iron and steel, motor vehicles (using imported components), textiles, cigarettes, footwear, pharmaceuticals, pulp and paper, cement
Exports petroleum, cocoa beans, rubber, palm products, urea and ammonia, fish. Principal market: USA 39.4% (1995)
Imports machinery and transport equipment, basic manufactures, cereals, chemicals, foodstuffs. Principal source: UK 13.4% (1995)
Arable land 32.3% (1993)
Agricultural products cocoa, groundnuts, oil palm, rubber, rice, maize, taro, yams, cassava, sorghum, millet, plantains; livestock (principally goats, sheep, cattle, and poultry) and fisheries

Population and society

Population 115,020,000 (1996e)
Population growth rate 3% (1990–95); 2.7% (2000–05)
Population density (per sq km) 125 (1996e)
Urban population (% of total) 39 (1995)
Age distribution (% of total population) <15 46.5%, 15–65 51.7%, >65 2.8% (1995)
Ethnic distribution over 250 tribal groups; major tribes include the Hausa and Fulani in N, Yoruba in S, and Ibo in E
Languages English (official), Hausa, Ibo, Yoruba
Religions Sunni Muslim 50% (in N), Christian 40% (in S), local religions 10%
Education (compulsory years) 6
Literacy rate 62% (men); 39% (women) (1995e)
Labour force 40% of population: 43% agriculture, 7% industry, 50% services (1990)
Unemployment 3.4% (1992)
Life expectancy 51 (men); 54 (women) (1995–2000)

Child mortality rate (under 5, per 1,000 live births) 191 (1995)
Physicians 1 per 5,882 people (1991)
Hospital beds 1 per 916 people (1991)
TV sets (per 1,000 people) 55 (1995)
Radios (per 1,000 people) 197 (1995)

Transport

Airports international airports: Lagos (Murtala Mohammed), Kano, Abuja, Port Harcourt, Calabar; 14 domestic airports; total passenger km: 985 mil (1994)
Railroads total length: 3,557 km/2,210 mi; total passenger km: 555 mil (1993)
Roads total road network: 32,810 km/20,388 mi, of which 82.6% paved (1995e); passenger cars: 5.3 per 1,000 people (1995e)

Chronology

4th century BC–2nd century AD Highly organized Nok culture flourished in N Nigeria.
9th century NE Nigeria became part of empire of Kanem-Bornu, based around Lake Chad.
11th century Creation of Hausa states, including Kano and Katsina.
13th century Arab merchants introduced Islam in N.
15th century Empire of Benin at its height in S; first contact with European traders.
17th century Oyo Empire dominant in SW; development of slave trade in Niger delta.
1804–17 Islamic Fulani (or Sokoto) Empire established in N.
1861 British traders procured Lagos; spread of Christian missionary activity in S.
1884–1904 Britain occupied most of Nigeria by stages.
1914 N and S protectorates united; growth of railway network and trade.
1946 Nigerians allowed a limited role in decision-making in three regional councils (N, W, and E).

1951 Introduction of elected representation led to formation of three regional political parties.
1954 New constitution increased powers of regions.
1958 Oil discovered in SE.
1960 Achieved independence from Britain, within Commonwealth; breakdown of law and order amid growing ethnic and regional conflict.
1963 Became a republic, with Nnamdi Azikiwe as president.
1966 Gen Aguiyi-Ironsi of Ibo tribe seized power and imposed unitary government; massacre of Ibo by Hausa in N; Gen Gowon seized power and restored federalism.
1967 Conflict over oil revenues led to secession of eastern region as independent Ibo state of Biafra; ensuing civil war claimed up to a million lives.
1970 Surrender of Biafra and end of civil war; development of oil industry financed more effective central government.
1975 Gowon ousted in military coup; second coup put Gen Olusegun Obasanjo in power.
1979 Civilian rule restored under President Shehu Shagari.
1983 Bloodless coup staged by Maj-Gen Muhammadu Buhari; economy suffered as a result of falling oil prices.
1985 Buhari replaced by Maj-Gen Ibrahim Babangida; Islamic northerners dominant in regime.
1989 Ban on political activity lifted; two official non-regional political parties created.
1992 Multiparty elections won by Babangida's SDP.
1993 Moshood Abiola (SDP) won first free presidential election; results suspended. Gen Sani Abacha restored military rule and dissolved political parties.
1995 Commonwealth membership suspended in protest at human-rights abuses by military regime.

Practical information

Visa requirements UK: visa required. USA: visa required
Embassy in the UK Nigeria House, 9 Northumberland Avenue, London WC2N 5BX. Tel: (0171) 839 1244; fax: (0171) 839 8746
British embassy British High Commission, Private Mail Bag 12136, 11 Eleke Crescent, Victoria Island, Lagos. Tel: (1) 619 531; fax: (1) 666 909
Embassy in the USA 1333 16th Street NW, Washington, DC 20036. Tel: (202) 986 8400
American embassy 2 Eleke Crescent, Lagos. Tel: (1) 261 0097; fax: (1) 261 0257

Chamber of commerce The Nigerian Association of Chambers of Commerce, Industry, Mines and Agriculture; Private Mail Bag 12816; 15a Ikorodu Road, Maryland, Lagos. Tel: (1) 496 4737; telex 21368
Office hours 0730–1530 Mon–Fri
Banking hours 0800–1500 Mon; 0800–1330 Tue–Fri
Time difference GMT +1
Chief tourist attractions fine coastal scenery; dense forests; rich diversity of arts
Major holidays 1 January, 1 May, 1 October, 25–26 December; variable: Eid-ul-Adha (2 days), end of Ramadan (2 days), Good Friday, Easter Monday, Prophet's Birthday

Norway Kingdom of

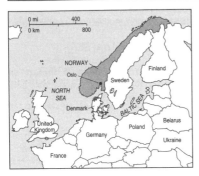

National name *Kongeriket Norge*
Area 387,000 sq km/149,420 sq mi
(includes Svalbard and Jan Mayen)
Capital Oslo
Major towns/cities Bergen, Trondheim,
Stavanger, Kristiansand, Drammen
Physical features mountainous with
fertile valleys and deeply indented coast;
forests cover 25%; extends N of Arctic
Circle
Territories dependencies in the Arctic
(Svalbard and Jan Mayen) and in
Antarctica (Bouvet and Peter I Island, and
Queen Maud Land)

Government

Head of state Harald V from 1991
Head of government Kjell Magne
Bondevik from 1997
Political system constitutional monarchy
Administrative divisions 19 counties
Political parties Norwegian Labour Party
(DNA), moderate left of centre;
Conservative Party, progressive, right of
centre; Christian People's Party (KrF),
Christian, centre left; Centre Party (Sp),
left of centre, rural-oriented; Progress
Party (FrP), right wing, populist
Armed forces 30,000 (1995); Home
Guard 79,000 (1995); fast mobilization
reserve 282,000 (1995)
Conscription 12 months, with 4–5
refresher training periods
Death penalty abolished 1979
Defence spend (% GDP) 2.6 (1995)
Education spend (% GNP) 9.2 (1993/94)
Health spend (% GDP) 7.6 (1993)

Economy and resources

Currency Norwegian krone
GDP ($ US) 156.2 billion (1996)
Real GDP per capita (PPP) ($ US)
24,169 (1996)
GDP growth rate 0.4% (1996); 3.5%
(1990–95)
Average annual inflation 2.2% (1996);
3.1% (1985–95)

Trading partners EU (principally UK and
Sweden), USA, Japan
Resources petroleum, natural gas, iron
ore, iron pyrites, copper, lead, zinc, forests
Industries mining, fishery, food
processing, non-electrical machinery,
metals and metal products, paper
products, printing and publishing,
shipbuilding, chemicals
Exports petroleum, natural gas, fish
products, non-ferrous metals, wood pulp
and paper. Principal market: UK 19.8%
(1995)
Imports machinery and transport
equipment, chemicals, clothing, fuels and
lubricants, iron and steel, office machines
and computers, telecommunications and
sound apparatus and equipment. Principal
source: Sweden 15.4% (1995)
Arable land 2.7% (1993)
Agricultural products wheat, barley,
oats, potatoes, fruit; fishing industry,
including fish farming

Population and society

Population 4,348,000 (1996e)
Population growth rate 0.5% (1990–95);
0.3% (2000–05)
Population density (per sq km) 13
(1996e)
Urban population (% of total) 73 (1995)
Age distribution (% of total population)
<15 19.5%, 15–65 64.7%, >65 15.9%
(1995)
Ethnic distribution majority of Nordic
descent; Saami minority in far N
Languages Norwegian (official); there are
Saami- (Lapp) and Finnish-speaking
minorities
Religion Evangelical Lutheran (endowed
by state)
Education (compulsory years) 9
Literacy rate 99% (men); 99% (women)
(1995e)
Labour force 50% of population: 6%
agriculture, 25% industry, 68% services
(1990)
Unemployment 4.9% (1996)
Life expectancy 74 (men); 81 (women)
(1995–2000)
Child mortality rate (under 5, per 1,000
live births) 8 (1995)
Physicians 1 per 300 people (1994)
Hospital beds 1 per 184 people (1994)
TV sets (per 1,000 people) 433 (1995)
Radios (per 1,000 people) 808 (1995)

Transport

Airports international airports: Oslo
(Fornebu), Stavanger (Sola), Bergen
(Flesland); 54 domestic airports with

scheduled services; total passenger km:
7,663 mil (1994)
Railroads total length: 4,023 km/2,500
mi; total passenger km: 2,381 mil (1995)
Roads total road network: 90,261 km/
56,088 mi, of which 73.5% paved (1995);
passenger cars: 385.6 per 1,000 people
(1995)

Chronology

5th century First small kingdoms
established by Goths.
c. 900 Harald Fairhair created united
Norwegian kingdom; it dissolved after his
death.
8th–11th centuries Vikings from Norway
raided and settled in many parts of
Europe.
c. 1016–28 Olav II (St Olav) reunited the
kingdom and introduced Christianity.
1217–63 Haakon VI established royal
authority over nobles and church and
made monarchy hereditary.
1263 Iceland submitted to authority of
king of Norway.
1397 Union of Kalmar: Norway,
Denmark, and Sweden united under a
single monarch.
15th century Norway, the weakest of the
three kingdoms, was increasingly treated
as an appendage of Denmark.
1523 Secession of Sweden further
undermined Norway's status.
16th century Introduction of sawmill
precipitated development of timber
industry and growth of export trade.
1661 Denmark restored formal equality
of status to Norway as a twin kingdom.
18th century Norwegian merchants
profited from foreign wars which
increased demand for naval supplies.
1814 Treaty of Kiel: Denmark ceded
Norway (minus Iceland) to Sweden;
Norway retained its own parliament but
cabinet appointed by king of Sweden.
19th century Economic decline followed
slump in timber trade due to Canadian
competition; expansion of merchant navy
and whaling industry.
1837 Democratic local government
introduced.
1884 Achieved internal self-government
when king of Sweden made Norwegian
cabinet accountable to Norwegian
parliament.
1895 Start of constitutional dispute over
control of foreign policy: Norway's
demand for a separate consular service
refused by Sweden.
1905 Union with Sweden dissolved;
Norway achieved independence under
King Haakon VII.

1907 Norway became first European country to grant women the right to vote in parliamentary elections.
early 20th century Development of industry based on hydroelectric power; long period of Liberal government committed to neutrality and moderate social reform.
1935 First Labour government took office.
1940–45 German occupation with Vidkun Quisling as puppet leader.
1945–65 Labour governments introduced economic planning and permanent price controls.

1949 Became a founding member of North Atlantic Treaty Organization (NATO).
1952 Joined Nordic Council.
1957 Olaf V succeeded his father King Haakon VII.
1960 Joined European Free Trade Association (EFTA).
1972 National referendum rejected membership of European Economic Community (EEC).
1975 Export of North Sea oil began.
1981 Gro Harlem Brundtland (Labour) became Norway's first woman prime minister.

1982 Kare Willoch formed first Conservative government since 1928.
1986 Falling oil prices caused recession; Labour re-elected under Brundtland.
1991 Olaf V succeeded by his son Harald V.
1994 National referendum rejected membership of European Union (formerly EC).
1996 Brundtland resigned; succeeded by Thorbjoern Jagland.
1997 Jagland failed to win decisive majority in general election.

Practical information

Visa requirements UK: visa not required. USA: visa not required
Embassy in the UK 25 Belgrave Square, London SW1X 8QD. Tel: (0171) 235 7151; fax: (0171)245 6993
British embassy Thomas Heftyesgate 8, 0244 Oslo 2. Tel: (22) 552 400; fax: (22) 434 005
Embassy in the USA 2720 34th Street NW, Washington, DC 20008. Tel: (202) 333 6000; fax: (202) 337 0870
American embassy Drammensveien 18, 0244 Oslo. Tel: (22) 448 550; fax: (22) 443 363

Chamber of commerce Norwegian Trade Council, Drammensveien 40, 0243 Oslo. Tel: (22) 926 300; fax: (22) 926 400
Office hours 0800–1600 Mon–Fri
Banking hours 0900–1700 Mon–Thu in major cities and 0900–1530 Fri
Time difference GMT +1
Chief tourist attractions rugged landscape with fjords, forests, lakes, and rivers; winter sports
Major holidays 1 January, 1, 17 May, 25–26 December; variable: Ascension Thursday, Good Friday, Easter Monday, Holy Thursday, Whit Monday

---

Oman Sultanate of

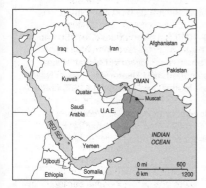

National name *Saltanat `Uman*
Area 272,000 sq km/105,019 sq mi
Capital Muscat
Major towns/cities Salalah, Ibri, Sohar, Al-Buraimi, Nizwa
Major ports Mina Qaboos, Mina Raysut
Physical features mountains to N and S of a high arid plateau; fertile coastal strip; Jebel Akhdar highlands; Kuria Muria Islands

Government

Head of state and government Qaboos bin Said from 1970
Political system absolute monarchy
Administrative divisions eight regional

governates and 59 districts
Political parties none
Armed forces 43,500 (1995)
Conscription military service is voluntary
Death penalty retained and used for ordinary crimes
Defence spend (% GDP) 15.1 (1995)
Education spend (% GNP) 4.0 (1994)
Health spend (% GDP) 2.1 (1990)

Economy and resources

Currency Omani rial
GDP ($ US) 11.6 billion (1994)
Real GDP per capita (PPP) ($ US) 10,078 (1994)
GDP growth rate 3.5% (1994); 6% (1990–95)
Average annual inflation −1.3% (1995); −0.2 (1985–95)
Foreign debt ($ US) 3.1 billion (1995)
Trading partners United Arab Emirates, Japan, South Korea, China
Resources petroleum, natural gas, copper, chromite, gold, salt, marble, gypsum, limestone
Industries mining, petroleum refining, cement, construction materials, copper smelting, food processing, chemicals, textiles
Exports petroleum, metals and metal goods, textiles, animals and products.

Principal market: Japan 32.2% (1995)
Imports machinery and transport equipment, basic manufactures, food and live animals, beverages, tobacco. Principal source: UAE 24.8% (1995)
Arable land 0.1% (1993)
Agricultural products dates, tomatoes, limes, alfalfa, mangoes, melons, bananas, coconuts, cucumbers, onions, peppers, frankincense (agricultural production is mainly at subsistence level); livestock; fishing

Population and society

Population 2,302,000 (1996e)
Population growth rate 4.2% (1990–95); 3.7% (2000–05)
Population density (per sq km) 11 (1996e)
Urban population (% of total) 13 (1995)
Age distribution (% of total population) <15 47.5%, 15–65 49.9%, >65 2.6% (1995)
Ethnic distribution predominantly Arab, with substantial Iranian, Baluchi, Indo-Pakistani, and East African minorities
Languages Arabic (official); English, Urdu, other Indian languages
Religions Ibadhi Muslim 75%, Sunni Muslim, Shi'ite Muslim, Hindu
Education not compulsory

Literacy rate 52% (men); 34% (women) (1994e)
Labour force 9.4% agriculture, 27.8% industry, 62.8% services (1993)
Unemployment 11.9% (1993)
Life expectancy 69 (men); 73 (women) (1995–2000)
Child mortality rate (under 5, per 1,000 live births) 25 (1995)
Physicians 1 per 1,265 people (1994)
Hospital beds 1 per 442 people (1994)
TV sets (per 1,000 people) 657 (1995)
Radios (per 1,000 people) 580 (1995)

Transport

Airports international airports: Muscat (Seeb), Salalah; domestic services operate between these; total passenger km: 2,439 mil (1994)
Railroads none
Roads total road network: 30,830 km/ 19,158 mi of which 22% paved (1995e); passenger cars: 95.8 per 1,000 people (1995)

Chronology

c. 3000 BC Archaeological evidence suggests Oman may have been the semilegendary Magan, a thriving seafaring state at the time of the Sumerian Civilization of Mesopotamia (the Tigris and Euphrates region of Iraq).
9th century BC Migration of Arab clans to Oman, notably the Qahtan family from SW Arabia and the Nizar from NW Arabia, between whom rivalry has continued.
4th century BC–AD 800 North Oman under Persian control.
AD 630 Converted to Islam.
751 Julanda ibn Masud was elected imam (spiritual leader); Oman remained under imam rule until 1154.
1151 Dynasty established by Banu Nabhan.
1428 Dynastic rule came under challenge from the imams.
1507 Coastal area, including port city of Muscat, fell under Portuguese control.
1650 Portuguese ousted by Sultan ibn Sayf, a powerful Ya'ariba leader.
early 18th century Civil war between the Hinawis (descendents of the Qahtan) and the Ghafiris (descendents of the Nizar).
1749 Independent Sultanate of Muscat and Oman established by Ahmad ibn Said, founder of the Al Bu Said dynasty that still rules Oman.
first half of 19th century Muscat and

Oman was most powerful state in Arabia, ruling Zanzibar until 1861, and coastal parts of Persia, Kenya, and Pakistan; came under British protection.
1951 The Sultanate of Muscat and Oman achieved full independence from Britain. Treaty of Friendship with Britain signed.
1964 Discovery of oil led to transformation of undeveloped kingdom into modern state.
1970 After 38 years' rule, Sultan Said bin Taimur replaced in bloodless coup by his son Qaboos bin Said. Name changed to Sultanate of Oman and modernization programme launched.
1975 Left-wing rebels in Dhofar in the S, who had been supported by South Yemen, defeated with UK military assistance, ending a ten-year insurrection.
1981 Consultative Council set up; Oman played key role in establishment of six-member Gulf Cooperation Council.
1982 Memorandum of Understanding with UK signed, providing for regular consultation on international issues.
1991 Joined US-led coalition opposing Iraq's occupation of Kuwait.
1994 Proposal to allow women members of parliament.

Practical information

Visa requirements UK: visa required. USA: visa required
Embassy in the UK 167 Queen's Gate, London SW7 5HE. Tel: (0171) 225 0001; fax: (0171) 589 2505
British embassy PO Box 300, 113 Muscat. Tel: (968) 693 077; fax: (968) 693 087
Embassy in the USA 2535 Belmont Road, NW, Washington, DC 20008. Tel: (202) 387 1980/1/2; fax: (202) 745 4933
American embassy address N/A, Muscat (mailing address: PO Box 202, Code No. 115, Medinat Qaboos, Muscat). Tel: (968) 698 989; fax: (968) 699 779
Chamber of commerce Oman Chamber of Commerce and

Industry, PO Box 1400, 112 Ruwi. Tel: (968) 707 684; fax: (968) 708 497
Office hours 0830–1300 and 1600–1900 Sat–Wed; 0800–1300 Thu
Banking hours 0800–1200 Sat–Wed and 0800–1130 Thu
Time difference GMT +4
Chief tourist attractions the old towns of Muscat, Nizwa (ancient capital of the interior), and Dhofar; the forts of Nakhl, Rustaq, and Al-Hazm – tourism was introduced 1985 and is strictly controlled
Major holidays 18 November (2 days), 31 December; variable: Eid-ul-Adha (5 days), end of Ramadan (4 days), New Year (Muslim), Prophet's Birthday, Lailat al-Miraj (March/April)

Pakistan Islamic Republic of

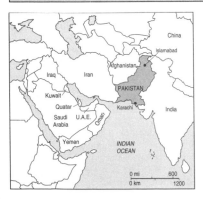

National name Islami Jamhuriya e Pakistan
Area 796,100 sq km/307,374 sq mi; one-third of Kashmir under Pakistani control
Capital Islamabad
Major towns/cities Lahore, Rawalpindi, Faisalabad, Karachi, Hyderabad, Multan, Peshawar, Gujranwala, Sialkot, Sargodha, Quetta, Islamabad
Major ports Karachi, Port Qasim
Physical features fertile Indus plain in E, Baluchistan plateau in W, mountains in N and NW; the 'five rivers' (Indus, Jhelum, Chenab, Ravi, and Sutlej) feed

the world's largest irrigation system; K2 mountain; Khyber Pass

Government

Head of state Farooq Leghari from 1993
Head of government Nawaz Sharif from 1997
Political system emergent democracy
Administrative divisions four provinces, the Federal Capital Territory, and the federally administered tribal areas
Political parties Islamic Democratic Alliance (IDA), conservative; Pakistan

People's Party (PPP), moderate, Islamic, socialist; Pakistan Muslim League (PML), Islamic conservative (contains pro- and antigovernment factions); Pakistan Islamic Front (PIF), Islamic fundamentalist, right wing; Awami National Party (ANP), left wing; National Democratic Alliance (NDA) bloc, left of centre; Mohajir National Movement (MQM), Sind-based *mohajir* settlers (Muslims previously living in India); Movement for Justice, reformative, anti-corruption

Armed forces 587,000; paramilitary forces 275,000 (1995)

Death penalty retained and used for ordinary crimes

Defence spend (% GDP) 6.5 (1995)

Education spend (% GNP) 2.7 (1993/94)

Health spend (% GDP) 1.8 (1990)

Economy and resources

Currency Pakistan rupee

GDP ($ US) 52 billion (1994)

Real GDP per capita (PPP) ($ US) 2,154 (1994)

GDP growth rate 3.1% (1994); 4.6% (1990–95)

Average annual inflation 12.5% (1994); 9.3% (1985–95)

Foreign debt ($ US) 30.15 billion (1995)

Trading partners Japan, USA, Germany, UK, Saudi Arabia

Resources iron ore, natural gas, limestone, rock salt, gypsum, silica, coal, petroleum, graphite, copper, manganese, chromite

Industries textiles (principally cotton), food processing, petroleum refining, leather production, soda ash, sulphuric acid, bicycles

Exports cotton, textiles, petroleum and petroleum products, clothing and accessories, leather, rice, food and live animals. Principal market: USA 15% (1995)

Imports machinery and transport equipment, mineral fuels and lubricants, chemicals and related products, edible oil. Principal source: Japan 10.7% (1995)

Arable land 26.1% (1993)

Agricultural products cotton, rice, wheat, maize, sugar cane

Population and society

Population 139,973,000 (1996e)

Population growth rate 2.8% (1990–95); 2.7% (2000–05)

Population density (per sq km) 156 (1996e)

Urban population (% of total) 35 (1995)

Age distribution (% of total population) <15 44.3%, 15–65 52.7%, >65 3% (1995)

Ethnic distribution four principal, regionally based, antagonistic communities: Punjabis in the Punjab; Sindhis in Sind; Baluchis in Baluchistan; and the Pathans (Pushtans) in the Northwest Frontier Province

Languages Urdu (official); English, Punjabi, Sindhi, Pashto, Baluchi, other local dialects

Religions Sunni Muslim 75%, Shi'ite Muslim 20%; also Hindu, Christian, Parsee, Buddhist

Education (years) 5–12 (not compulsory, but free)

Literacy rate 47% (men); 21% (women) (1995e)

Labour force 35% of population: 52% agriculture, 19% industry, 30% services (1990)

Unemployment 10% (1991e)

Life expectancy 63 (men); 65 (women) (1995–2000)

Child mortality rate (under 5, per 1,000 live births) 137 (1995)

Physicians 1 per 1,929 people (1993)

Hospital beds 1 per 1,534 people (1993)

TV sets (per 1,000 people) 20 (1995)

Radios (per 1,000 people) 92 (1995)

Transport

Airports international airports: Karachi (Civil), Lahore, Islamabad, Peshawar, Quetta, Rawalpindi; 30 domestic airports; total passenger km: 1,400 mil (1994)

Railroads total length: 8,163 km/5,072 mi; total passenger km: 18,044 mil (1994)

Roads total road network: 216,564 km/ 134,573 mi, of which 54% paved (1995); passenger cars: 4.3 per 1,000 people (1995)

Chronology

2500–1600 BC The area was the site of the Indus Valley civilization, a sophisticated, city-based ancient culture.

327 BC Invaded by Alexander the Great of Macedonia.

1st–2nd centuries North Pakistan was the heartland of the Kusana Empire, formed by invaders from Central Asia.

8th century First Muslim conquests, in Baluchistan and Sind, followed by increasing immigration by Muslims from the W, from the 10th century.

1206 Establishment of Delhi Sultanate, stretching from NW Pakistan and across northern India.

16th century Sikh religion developed in Punjab.

16th–17th centuries Lahore served intermittently as a capital city for the Mogul Empire, which stretched across the northern half of the Indian subcontinent.

1843–49 Sind and Punjab annexed by British and incorporated within empire of 'British India'.

late 19th century Major canal irrigation projects in West Punjab and the northern Indus Valley drew in settlers from the E, as wheat and cotton production expanded.

1933 The name 'Pakistan' (Urdu for 'Pure Nation') invented by Choudhary Rahmat Ali, as Muslims within British India began to campaign for the establishment of an independent Muslim territory that would embrace the four provinces of Sind, Baluchistan, Punjab, and the Northwest Frontier.

1940 The All-India Muslim League (established 1906), led by Karachi-born Muhammad Ali Jinnah, endorsed the concept of a separate nation for Muslims in the Lahore Resolution.

1947 Independence achieved from Britain, as dominion within the Commonwealth. Pakistan, which included East Bengal, a Muslim-dominated province more than 1,600 km/1,000 mi from Punjab, was formed following the partition of British India. Large-scale and violent cross-border migrations of Muslims, Hindus, and Sikhs followed, and a brief border war with India over disputed Kashmir.

1948 Jinnah, the country's first governor general, died.

1956 Proclaimed a republic.

1958 Military rule imposed by Gen Ayub Khan.

1965 Border war with India over disputed territory of Kashmir.

1969 Power transferred to Gen Yahya Khan following strikes and riots.

1970 General election produced clear majority in East Pakistan for pro-autonomy Awami League, led by Sheikh Mujibur Rahman, and in West Pakistan for Islamic socialist Pakistan People's Party (PPP), led by Zulfiqar Ali Bhutto.

1971 East Pakistan secured independence, as Bangladesh, following a civil war in which it received decisive military support from India. Power was transferred from the military to the populist Bhutto in Pakistan.

1977 Bhutto overthrown in military coup by Gen Zia ul-Haq following months of

civil unrest; martial law imposed.
1979 Bhutto executed for alleged murder; tight political restrictions imposed by Zia regime.
1980 3 million refugees fled to Northwest Frontier Province and Baluchistan as a result of Soviet invasion of Afghanistan.
1981 Broad-based Opposition Movement for the Restoration of Democracy formed. Islamization process pushed forward by government.
1985 Martial law and ban on political parties lifted.
1986 Agitation for free elections launched by Benazir Bhutto, the daughter of Zulfiqar Ali Bhutto.
1988 Islamic legal code, the Shari'a,

introduced; Zia killed in military plane crash. Benazir Bhutto became prime minister after the now centrist PPP won the general election.
1989 Tension with India increased by outbreaks of civil war in Kashmir. Pakistan rejoined the Commonwealth, which it had left in 1972.
1990 Bhutto dismissed as prime minister by President Ghulam Ishaq Khan on charges of incompetence and corruption. The conservative Islamic Democratic Alliance (IDA), led by Nawaz Sharif, won general election and launched a privatization and economic deregulation programme.
1993 Khan and Sharif resigned, ending

months of political stalemate and unrest; Benazir Bhutto and PPP re-elected. Farooq Leghari (PPP) elected president.
1994 Escalation in regional sectarian violence between Shiah and Sunni Muslims, centred in Karachi.
1996 Justice Movement formed by former cricket captain Imran Khan. Benazir Bhutto dismissed by Leghari amid allegations of corruption and mismanagement. Meraj Khalid appointed interim prime minister.
1997 Landslide victory for right-of-centre Pakistan Muslim League in general election, returning Nawaz Sharif to power as prime minister. Discussions began to normalize relations with India.

Practical information

Visa requirements UK: visa required. USA: visa required
Embassy in the UK 40 Lowndes Square, London SW1X 9JN. Tel: (0171) 235 2044
British embassy British High Commission, PO Box 1122, Diplomatic Enclave, Ramna 5, Islamabad. Tel: (51) 822 131/5; fax: (51) 823 439
Embassy in the USA 2315 Massachusetts Avenue NW, Washington, DC 20008. Tel: (202) 939 6200; fax: (202) 387 0484
American embassy Diplomatic Enclave, Ramna 5, Islamabad. Tel: (51) 826 161–179; fax: (51) 214 222
Chamber of commerce Chamber of Commerce and Industry,

PO Box 4833, Talpur Road, Karachi. Tel: (21) 241 0814; fax: (21) 242 7315
Office hours 0900–1700 Sat–Thu
Banking hours 0900–1300 and 1500–2000 Sun–Thu (some banks open on Sat)
Time difference GMT +5
Chief tourist attractions Himalayan scenery; fine climate; mountaineering; trekking; winter sports; archaeological remains and historic buildings
Major holidays 23 March, 1 May, 1 July, 14 August, 6, 11 September, 9 November, 25, 31 December; variable: Eid-ul-Adha (3 days), Ashora (2 days), end of Ramadan (3 days), Prophet's Birthday, first day of Ramadan

---

Palau Republic of (also known as *Belau*)

Area 508 sq km/196 sq mi
Capital Koror (on Koror Island)
Major towns/cities Melekeiok, Garusuun, Malakal
Physical features more than 350 (mostly uninhabited) islands, islets, and atolls in the W Pacific; warm, humid climate, susceptible to typhoons

Government

Head of state and government Kuniwo Nakamura from 1992
Political system liberal democracy
Administrative divisions 16 states
Political parties there are no formally organized political parties
Armed forces no defence forces of its own; under the Compact of Free Association, the USA is responsible for the defence of Palau; two US military bases operate on the islands
Death penalty laws do not provide for the death penalty for any crime

Economy and resources

Currency US dollar
GDP ($ US) 81.8 million (1994e)
Real GDP per capita (PPP) ($ US) 5,000 (1994e)
Average annual inflation N/A
Foreign debt ($ US) 100 million (1990)
Trading partners USA, UK, Japan

Industries processing of agricultural products, fish products, handicrafts, tourism
Exports copra, coconut oil, handicrafts, trochus, tuna
Imports food and live animals, crude materials, mineral fuels, beverages, tobacco, chemicals, basic manufactures, machinery and transport equipment
Agricultural products coconuts, cassava, bananas, sweet potatoes; farming and fishing are mainly on a subsistence level; fishing licences are sold to foreign fleets including those of the USA, Taiwan, Japan, and the Philippines

Population and society

Population 17,000 (1996e)
Population growth rate 2.3% (1990–95)
Population density (per sq km) 37 (1996e)
Urban population (% of total) 70.6 (1995)

Ethnic distribution predominantly
Micronesian
Languages Palauan and English
Religion Christian, principally Roman
Catholic
Education (compulsory years) 8
Literacy rate 92% (1980)
Unemployment 20% (1988e)
Life expectancy 68 (men); 74 (women)
(1994)
Child mortality rate (under 5, per 1,000
live births) 35 (1995)
Physicians 1 per 1,512 people (1990)
Hospital beds 1 per 216 people (1990)
TV sets (per 1,000 people) 51 (1985)

Transport

Airports international airports: Koror
(Palau International, on Babelthaup
Island, near Koror Island); two domestic
airfields
Railroads none
Roads total road network: 61 km/38 mi,
of which 41% paved (many routes are
inaccessible to ordinary traffic)

Chronology

c. 1000 BC Micronesians first settled the
islands.
1543 First visited by Spanish navigator
Ruy Lopez de Villalobos.
16th century Colonized by Spain.
later 16th century Fell under Spanish
influence.
1899 Purchased from Spain by Germany.
1914 Occupied by Japan at the outbreak
of World War I.
1920 Administered by Japan under
League of Nations mandate.
1944 Occupied by USA after Japanese
removed during World War II.
1947 Became part of United Nations
(UN) Pacific Islands Trust Territory,
administered by USA.
1981 Acquired autonomy as the Republic
of Belau (Palau) under a constitution
which prohibited the entry, storage, or
disposal of nuclear or biological
weapons.
1982 Compact of Free Association
signed with USA, providing for the right
to maintain US military facilities in return
for economic aid. However, the compact
could not come into force since it
contradicted the constitution, which could
only be amended by a 75% vote in
favour.
1985 President Haruo Remeliik
assassinated; succeeded by Lazarus
Salii.
1988 President Salii committed suicide
and was succeeded by Ngiratkel Etpison.
1992 Kuniwo Nakamura elected
president.
1993 Referendum approved
constitutional amendment allowing
implementation of Compact of Free
Association with USA.
1994 Independence achieved; UN
membership granted.

Practical information

Visa requirements UK: visa not required for a stay of up to 30
days. USA: visa not required for a stay of up to 30 days
Embassy in the UK Palau has no diplomatic representation in
the UK; the UK Department of Trade and Industry has a
Pacific Islands Desk. Tel: (0171) 215 4760; fax: (0171) 215
4398
British embassy the UK has no diplomatic representation in
Palau
Embassy in the USA 2000 L Street NW, Suite 407,
Washington, DC 20036. Tel: (202) 452 6814; fax: (202) 452
6281

American embassy address N/A, Koror (mailing address: PO
Box 6028, Republic of Palau 96940). Tel: (680) 488 2920,
2990; fax: (680) 488 2911
Chamber of commerce Palau Visitors Authority, PO Box
6028, Koror 96940. Tel: (680) 488 2920; fax: (680) 488 2911
Office hours generally 0730–1130 and 1230–1630 Mon–Fri
Banking hours 1000–1500 Mon–Thu; 1000–1800 Fri
Time difference GMT +9
Chief tourist attractions rich marine environment; the myriad
Rock Islands, known as the Floating Garden Islands
Major holidays 1 January, 15 March, 5 May, 1 June, 9 July, 5
September, 24 October, 24 November, 25 December

Panama Republic of

National name *República de Panamá*
Area 77,100 sq km/29,768 sq mi
Capital Panamá (Panama City)
Major towns/cities San Miguelito,
Colón, David, La Chorrera, Santiago,
Chitré
Major ports Colón, Cristóbal, Balboa
Physical features coastal plains and
mountainous interior; tropical rainforest in
E and NW; Archipelago de las Perlas in
Gulf of Panama; Panama Canal

Government

Head of state and government Ernesto
Pérez Balladares from 1994
Political system emergent democratic
republic
Administrative divisions nine provinces
and one special territory (San Blas)
Political parties Democratic
Revolutionary Party (PRD), right wing;
Arnulfista Party (PA), left of centre;
Authentic Liberal Party (PLA), left of
centre; Nationalist Liberal Republican
Movement (MOLIRENA), right of centre;
Papa Ego Movement (MPE), moderate,
centre left
Armed forces army abolished by
National Assembly (1994); paramilitary
forces numbered 11,800 (1995); National
Maritime and National Air Services each
numbered 400 (1995)
Conscription military service is voluntary
Death penalty laws do not provide for
the death penalty for any crime (last
known execution 1903)
Defence spend (% GDP) 1.3 (1995)
Education spend (% GNP) 5.0 (1994)

Economy and resources

Currency balboa
GDP ($ US) 7 billion (1994)

Real GDP per capita (PPP) ($ US) 6,104 (1994)
GDP growth rate 4.7% (1994); 6.3% (1990–95)
Average annual inflation 1.3% (1994); 1.7% (1985–95)
Foreign debt ($ US) 7.18 billion (1995)
Trading partners USA, Japan, Costa Rica, Ecuador, Germany, Venezuela, Italy
Resources limestone, clay, salt; deposits of coal, copper, and molybdenum have been discovered
Industries food processing, petroleum refining and petroleum products, chemicals, paper and paper products, beverages, textiles and clothing, plastic products, light assembly, tourism
Exports bananas, shrimps and lobsters, sugar, clothing, coffee. Principal market: USA 41.9% (1995)
Imports machinery and transport equipment, petroleum and mineral products, chemicals and chemical products, electrical and electronic equipment, foodstuffs. Principal source: USA 39.1% (1995)
Arable land 6.6% (1993)
Agricultural products rice, maize, dry beans, bananas, sugar cane, coffee, oranges, mangoes, cocoa; cattle rearing; tropical timber; fishing (particularly shrimps for export)

Population and society

Population 2,677,000 (1996e)
Population growth rate 1.9% (1990–95); 1.4% (2000–05)
Population density (per sq km) 35 (1996e)
Urban population (% of total) 53 (1995)
Age distribution (% of total population) <15 33.4%, 15–65 61.4%, >65 5.2% (1995)
Ethnic distribution about 70% mestizos (of Spanish–American and American–Indian descent), 14% West Indian, 10% white American or European, and 6% Indian
Languages Spanish (official), English
Religion Roman Catholic
Education (compulsory years) 8
Literacy rate 88% (men); 88% (women) (1995e)
Labour force 39% of population: 26% agriculture, 16% industry, 58% services (1990)
Unemployment 12.5% (1994e)
Life expectancy 72 (men); 76 (women) (1995–2000)
Child mortality rate (under 5, per 1,000 live births) 20 (1995)
Physicians 1 per 844 people (1990)
Hospital beds 1 per 300 people (1990)
TV sets (per 1,000 people) 175 (1995)
Radios (per 1,000 people) 228 (1995)

Transport

Airports international airports: Panama City (Tocumen); two domestic airports; total passenger km: 405 mil (1994)
Railroads total length: 583 km/362 mi; total passenger km: 51,250 mil (1994)
Roads total road network: 10,792 km/6,706 mi, of which 33.5% paved (1995e); passenger cars: 65.3 per 1,000 people (1993e)

Chronology

1502 Visited by Spanish explorer Rodrigo de Bastidas, at which time it was inhabited by Cuna, Choco, Guaymi, and other Indian groups.
1513 Spanish conquistador Vasco Núñez de Balboa explored Pacific Ocean from Darien isthmus; he was made governor of Panama (meaning 'abundance of fish'), but was later executed as a result of Spanish court intrigue.
1519 Spanish city established at Panama, which became part of the Spanish viceroyalty of New Andalucia (later New Granada).
1572–95 and 1668–71 Spanish settlements sacked by British buccaneers Francis Drake and Henry Morgan.
1821 Achieved independence from Spain; joined confederacy of Gran Colombia, which included Colombia, Venezuela, Ecuador, Peru, and Bolivia.
1830 Gran Colombia split up and Panama became part of Colombia.
1846 Treaty signed with USA, allowing it to construct a railway across the isthmus.
1880s French attempt to build a Panama canal connecting the Atlantic and Pacific Oceans failed as a result of financial difficulties and the death of 22,000 workers from yellow fever and malaria.
1903 Full independence achieved with US help on separation from Colombia; USA bought rights to build Panama Canal, and were given control of a 10-mile strip, the Canal Zone, in perpetuity.
1914 Panama Canal opened.
1939 Panama's status as a US protectorate was terminated by mutual agreement.
1968–81 Military rule of Gen Omar Torrijos Herrera, leader of the National Guard, who deposed the elected president and launched a costly programme of economic modernization.
1977 USA–Panama treaties transferred the canal to Panama (effective from 2000), with the USA guaranteeing protection and annual payment.
1984 Nicolás Ardito Barletta of the right-wing Democratic Revolutionary Party (PRD) elected president by narrow margin.
1985 Barletta resigned; replaced by Eric Arturo del Valle, to the dissatisfaction of the USA.
1987 Gen Manuel Noriega (head of the National Guard and effective ruler since 1983) resisted calls for his removal,

---

Practical information

Visa requirements UK: visa not required (business visitors need a business visa). USA: visa required
Embassy in the UK 48 Park Street, London W1Y 3PD. Tel: (0171) 493 4646; fax: (0171) 493 4333
British embassy Apartado 889, Zona 1, 4th and 5th Floors, Torre Banco Sur, Calle 53 Este, Panamà 1. Tel: (2) 690 866; fax: (2) 230 730
Embassy in the USA 2862 McGill Terrace NW, Washington, DC 20008. Tel: (202) 483 1407
American embassy Avenida Balboa and Calle 38, Apartado 6959, Panamá 5. Tel: (2) 227 1377; fax: (2) 227 1964

Chamber of commerce Cámara de Comercio, Industrias y Agricultura de Panamá, Apartado 74, Edificio Comosa, Avenida Samuel Lewis, Planta Baja, Panamá 1. Tel: (2) 271 233; fax: (2) 274 186
Office hours 0800–1200 and 1400–1700 Mon–Fri
Banking hours 0800–1330 Mon–Fri; 0830–1200 Sat
Time difference GMT –5
Chief tourist attractions Panamá; ruins of Portobelo; San Blas Islands, off the Atlantic coast; 800 sandy tropical islands in Gulf of Panama
Major holidays 1, 9 January, 1 May, 11–12 October, 3–4, 28 November, 8, 25 December; variable: Carnival (2 days), Good Friday

despite suspension of US military and economic aid.

1988 Del Valle replaced by Manuel Solis Palma after trying to oust Noriega. Noriega, charged with drug smuggling by the USA, declared a state of emergency after the coup against him failed.

1989 Assembly elections declared invalid when won by opposition. 'State of war'

with USA announced, and US invasion (codenamed 'Operation Just Cause') deposed Noriega; 4,000 Panamanians died in the fighting. Guillermo Endara, who had won earlier elections, was installed as president in Dec.

1991 Attempted antigovernment coup foiled. Constitutional reforms approved by assembly, including abolition of

standing army; privatization programme introduced.

1992 Noriega found guilty of drug offences and given 40-year prison sentence in USA. Referendum rejected proposed constitutional reforms.

1994 Ernesto Pérez Balladares (PRD) elected president. Constitution amended by assembly; army formally abolished.

Papua New Guinea

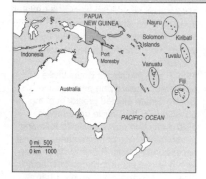

Area 462,840 sq km/178,702 sq mi
Capital Port Moresby (on E New Guinea) (also port)
Major towns/cities Lae, Madang, Arawa, Wewak, Goroka, Rabaul, Mount Hagen
Major ports Rabaul
Physical features mountainous; swamps and plains; monsoon climate; tropical islands of New Ireland, New Britain, and Bougainville; Admiralty Islands, D'Entrecasteaux Islands, and Louisiade Archipelago; active volcanoes Vulcan and Tavurvur

Government

Head of state Queen Elizabeth II, represented by governor general Wiwa Korowi from 1991
Head of government Bill Skate from 1997
Political system liberal democracy
Administrative divisions 19 provinces and the National Capital District
Political parties Papua New Guinea Party (Pangu Pati: PP), urban- and coastal-oriented nationalist; People's Democratic Movement (PDM), 1985 breakaway from the PP; National Party (NP), highlands-based, conservative; Melanesian Alliance (MA), Bougainville-based, pro-autonomy, left of centre; People's Progress Party (PPP), conservative; People's Action Party

(PAP), right of centre
Armed forces 3,800 (1995)
Conscription military service is voluntary
Death penalty retains the death penalty for ordinary crimes but can be considered abolitionist in practice (last execution 1950)
Defence spend (% GDP) 1.3 (1995)
Education spend (% GNP) 6.3 (1993e)
Health spend (% GDP) 2.8 (1990)

Economy and resources

Currency kina
GDP ($ US) 5.4 billion (1994)
Real GDP per capita (PPP) ($ US) 2,821 (1994)
GDP growth rate 3.5% (1994); 9.3% (1990–95)
Average annual inflation 4.6% (1985–95)
Foreign debt ($ US) 2.4 billion (1995)
Trading partners Australia, Japan, USA, Singapore, Germany, South Korea, UK
Resources copper, gold, silver; deposits of chromite, cobalt, nickel, quartz; substantial reserves of petroleum and natural gas (petroleum production began 1992)
Industries food processing, beverages, tobacco, timber products, metal products, machinery and transport equipment, fish canning
Exports gold, copper ore and concentrates, crude petroleum, timber, coffee beans, coconut and copra products. Principal market: Australia 32.5% (1995)
Imports machinery and transport equipment, manufactured goods, food and live animals, miscellaneous manufactured articles, chemicals, mineral fuels. Principal source: Australia 51.6% (1995)
Arable land 0.1% (1993)
Agricultural products coffee, cocoa, coconuts, pineapples, palm oil, rubber, tea, pyrethrum, peanuts, spices,

potatoes, maize, taro, bananas, rice, sago, sweet potatoes; livestock; poultry; fishing; timber production

Population and society

Population 4,400,000 (1996e)
Population growth rate 2.3% (1990–95); 2.1% (2000–05)
Population density (per sq km) 10 (1996e)
Urban population (% of total) 16% (1995)
Age distribution (% of total population) <15 39.5%, 15–65 57.5%, >65 2.9% (1995)
Ethnic distribution mainly Melanesian, particularly in coastal areas; inland (on New Guinea and larger islands), Papuans predominate. On the outer archipelagos and islands, mixed Micronese-Melanesians are found. A small Chinese minority also exists
Languages English (official); pidgin English, 715 local languages
Religions Protestant, Roman Catholic, local faiths
Education not compulsory
Literacy rate 65% (men); 38% (women) (1995e)
Labour force 49% of population: 79% agriculture, 7% industry, 14% services (1990)
Life expectancy 57 (men); 59 (women) (1995–2000)
Child mortality rate (under 5, per 1,000 live births) 95 (1995)
Physicians 1 per 12,870 people (1991)
Hospital beds 1 per 245 people (1991)
TV sets (per 1,000 people) 3.5 (1995)
Radios (per 1,000 people) 77 (1995)

Transport

Airports international airports: Port Moresby (Jackson); 177 domestic airports and airstrips with scheduled services; total passenger km: 837 mil (1994)
Railroads none

Roads total road network: 19,400 km/ 12,055 mi, of which 3.4% paved (1995e); passenger cars: 7.5 per 1,000 people (1993e)

Chronology

c. 3000 BC New settlement of Austronesian (Melanesian) immigrants.
1526 Visited by Portuguese navigator Jorge de Menezes, who named the main island the Ilhos dos Papua after the 'frizzled' hair of the inhabitants.
1545 Spanish navigator Ynigo Ortis de Retez gave the island the name of New Guinea, as a result of a supposed resemblance of the peoples with those of the Guinea coast of Africa.
17th century Regularly visited by Dutch merchants.
1828 Dutch East India Company incorporated western part of New Guinea into Netherlands East Indies (becoming Irian Jaya, in Indonesia).
1884 NE New Guinea annexed by Germany; SE claimed by Britain.
1870s Visits by Western missionaries and traders increased.
1890s Copra plantations developed in German New Guinea.
1906 Britain transferred its rights to

Australia, which renamed the lands Papua.
1914 German New Guinea occupied by Australia at outbreak of World War I; from the merged territories Papua New Guinea was formed.
1920–42 Held as League of Nations mandate by Australia.
1942–45 Occupied by Japan, who lost 150,000 troops resisting Allied counterattack.
1947 Held as United Nations Trust Territory by Australia.
1951 Legislative Council established.
1964 Elected House of Assembly formed.
1967 Pangu Party (Pangu Pati; PP) formed to campaign for home rule.
1975 Independence achieved from Australia, within Commonwealth, with Michael Somare (PP) as prime minister.
1980 Sir Julius Chan of People's Progress Party (PPP) became prime minister.
1982 Somare returned to power.
1985 Somare challenged by deputy prime minister Paias Wingti, who later left the PP and formed the People's Democratic Movement (PDM); he became head of a five-party coalition government.
1988 Wingti defeated on no-confidence

vote; replaced by Rabbie Namaliu (PP), heading coalition government. Joined Solomon Islands and Vanuatu to form Spearhead Group, aiming to preserve Melanesian cultural traditions.
1989 State of emergency imposed on copper-rich Bougainville in response to separatist violence.
1990 Bougainville Revolutionary Army (BRA) issued unilateral declaration of independence.
1991 Economic boom as gold production doubled.
1992 Wingti appointed premier, heading a three-party coalition.
1994 Wingti replaced as premier by Sir Julius Chan. Short-lived peace agreement with BRA.
1996 Prime minister of Bougainville murdered, jeopardizing peace process. Gerard Sinato elected president of the transitional Bougainville government.
1997 Army and police mutinied following government's use of mercenaries against secessionist rebels. Prime Minister Chan forced to resign but returned after being cleared of corruption charges. Chan's coalition polled badly in general election; Bill Skate (PDM) appointed prime minister.

Practical information

Visa requirements UK: visa required. USA: visa required
Embassy in the UK 14 Waterloo Place, London SW1Y 4AR. Tel: (0171) 930 0922/7; fax: (0171) 930 0828
British embassy British High Commission, PO Box 4778, Kiroki Street, Waigani, Boroko, Port Moresby. Tel: (675) 325 1677; fax: (675) 325 3547
Embassy in the USA 3rd floor, 1615 New Hampshire Avenue NW, Washington, DC 20009. Tel: (202) 745 3680; fax: (202) 745 3679
American embassy Douglas Street, Port Moresby. Tel: (675) 321 1455; fax: (675) 321 3423
Chamber of commerce Papua New Guinea Chamber of

Commerce and Industry, PO Box 1621, Port Moresby. Tel: (675) 213 057; fax: (675) 214 203
Office hours 0800–1630 Mon–Fri
Banking hours 0900–1500 Mon–Thu; 0900–1700 Fri
Time difference GMT +10
Chief tourist attractions spectacular scenery; the greatest variety of ecosystems in the South Pacific; abundant wildlife – birds include 38 species of birds of paradise, also the megapode and cassowary; two-thirds of the world's orchid species come from Papua New Guinea
Major holidays 1 January, 15 August, 16 September, 25–26 December; variable: Good Friday, Easter Monday, Holy Saturday, Queen's Birthday (June), Remembrance (July)

Paraguay Republic of

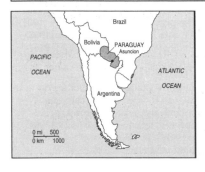

National name *República del Paraguay*
Area 406,752 sq km/157,046 sq mi
Capital Asunción (and port)
Major towns/cities Ciudad del Este, Pedro Juan Caballero, San Lorenzo, Fernando de la Mora, Lambare, Concepción, Villartica, Encaración
Major ports Concepción
Physical features low marshy plain and marshlands; divided by Paraguay River; Paraná River forms SE boundary

Government

Head of state and government Juan Carlos Wasmosy from 1993
Political system emergent democratic republic
Administrative divisions 17 departments
Political parties National Republican Association (Colorado Party), right of centre; Authentic Radical Liberal Party (PLRA), centrist; National Encounter, right of centre; Radical Liberal Party

(PLR), centrist; Liberal Party (PL), centrist
Armed forces 20,300 (1995)
Conscription 12 months (army); 24 months (navy)
Death penalty retains the death penalty only for exceptional crimes such as crimes under military law or crimes committed in exceptional circumstances such as wartime (last execution 1928)
Defence spend (% GDP) 1.4 (1995)
Education spend (% GNP) 2.7 (1994)
Health spend (% GDP) 1.2 (1990)

Economy and resources

Currency guaraní
GDP ($ US) 7.8 billion (1994)
Real GDP per capita (PPP) ($ US) 3,531 (1994)
GDP growth rate 3.5% (1994); 3.1% (1990–95)
Average annual inflation 10.5% (1995); 24.9 (1985–95)
Foreign debt ($ US) 2.3 billion (1995)
Trading partners Brazil, Argentina, the Netherlands, Japan, USA, France, UK
Resources gypsum, kaolin, limestone, salt; deposits (not commercially exploited) of bauxite, iron ore, copper, manganese, uranium; deposits of natural gas discovered 1994; exploration for petroleum deposits ongoing mid-1990s
Industries food processing, beverages, tobacco, wood and wood products, textiles (cotton), clothing, leather, chemicals, metal products, machinery
Exports soya beans (and other oil seeds), cotton, timber and wood manufactures, hides and skins, meat. Principal market: Brazil 46.5% (1996)
Imports machinery, vehicles and parts, mineral fuels and lubricants, beverages, tobacco, chemicals, foodstuffs. Principal source: Brazil 23.7% (1996)
Arable land 5.4% (1993)

Agricultural products cassava, soya beans, maize, cotton, wheat, rice, tobacco, sugar cane, 'yerba maté' (strongly flavoured tea); livestock rearing; forest resources

Population and society

Population 4,957,000 (1996e)
Population growth rate 2.8% (1990–95); 2.3% (2000–05)
Population density (per sq km) 12 (1996e)
Urban population (% of total) 53 (1995)
Age distribution (% of total population) <15 40.3%, 15–65 55.9%, >65 3.8% (1995)
Ethnic distribution predominantly mixed-race mestizos; less than 5% Spanish or Indian
Languages Spanish 6% (official), Guaraní 90%
Religions Roman Catholic (official religion); Mennonite, Anglican
Education (compulsory years) 6
Literacy rate 92% (men); 88% (women) (1995e)
Labour force 45.2% agriculture, 22.5% industry, 32.3% services (1994)
Unemployment 9% (1993)
Life expectancy 69 (men); 73 (women) (1995–2000)
Child mortality rate (under 5, per 1,000 live births) 34 (1995)
Physicians 1 per 1,235 people (1990)
Hospital beds 1 per 856 people (1990)
TV sets (per 1,000 people) 93 (1995)
Radios (per 1,000 people) 180 (1995)

Transport

Airports international airports: Asunción (Silvio Pettirossi), Ciudad del Este (Guaraní); three domestic airports; total passenger km: 1,235 mil (1994)
Railroads total length: 441 km/274 mi; total passenger km: 1 mil (1994)

Roads total road network: 28,900 km/ 17,958 mi, of which 9.4% paved (1995e); passenger cars: 15.2 per 1,000 people (1993e)

Chronology

1526 Visited by Italian navigator Sebastian Cabot, who travelled up Paraná river; at this time the E of the country had long been inhabited by Guaraní-speaking Amerindians, who gave the country its name, which means 'land with an important river'.
1537 Spanish made an alliance with Guaraní Indians against hostile Chaco Indians, enabling them to colonize interior plains; Asunción founded by Spanish.
1609 Jesuits arrived from Spain to convert local population to Roman Catholicism and administer the country.
1767 Jesuit missionaries expelled.
1776 Formerly part of Spanish Viceroyalty of Peru, which covered much of South America, became part of Viceroyalty of La Plata, with capital at Buenos Aires (Argentina).
1808 With Spanish monarchy overthrown by Napoleon Bonaparte, La Plata Viceroyalty became autonomous, but Paraguayans revolted against rule from Buenos Aires.
1811 Independence achieved from Spain.
1814 Under dictator Gen José Gaspar Rodriguez Francia ('El Supremo'), Paraguay became an isolated state.
1840 Francia was succeeded by his nephew, Carlos Antonio Lopez, who opened country to foreign trade and whose son, Francisco Solano Lopez, as president from 1862, built up powerful army.
1865–70 War with Argentina, Brazil, and Uruguay over access to sea; more than

---

Practical information

Visa requirements UK: visa not required. USA: visa not required
Embassy in the UK Braemar Lodge, Cornwall Gardens, London SW7 4AQ. Tel: (0171) 937 1253; fax: (0171) 937 5687
British embassy Casilla 404, Calle Presidente Franco 706, Asunción. Tel: (21) 444 472; fax: (21) 446 385
Embassy in the USA 2400 Massachusetts Avenue NW, Washington, DC 20008. Tel: (202) 483 6960/1/2; fax: (202) 234 4508
American embassy 1776 Avenida Mariscal Lopez, Casilla

Postal 402, Asunción. Tel: (21) 213 715; fax: (21) 213 728
Chamber of commerce Cámara y Bolsa de Comercio, Estrella 540, Asunción. Tel: (21) 493 321; fax: (21) 440 817
Office hours 0800–1200 and 1500–1730/1900 Mon–Fri
Banking hours 0845–1215 Mon–Fri
Time difference GMT –3/4
Chief tourist attractions the Iguaçu Falls; the sparsely populated Gran Chaco; Asunción (La Encaración church, the Pantheon of Heroes)
Major holidays 1 January, 3 February, 1 March, 1, 14–15 May, 12 June, 15, 25 August, 29 September, 12 October, 1 November, 8, 25, 31 December; variable: Corpus Christi, Good Friday, Holy Thursday

half the population died and 150,000 sq km/58,000 sq mi of territory lost; President Lopez killed.

later 1880s Conservative Colorado Party and Liberal Party founded.

1912 Liberal leader Edvard Schaerer came to power, ending decades of political instability.

1932–35 Territory in W won from Bolivia during Chaco War (settled by arbitration 1938).

1940–48 Presidency of autocratic Gen Higinio Morínigo.

1948–54 Political instability; six different presidents.

1954 Gen Alfredo Stroessner seized power in coup. He ruled as a ruthless autocrat, suppressing civil liberties; received initial US backing as economy expanded.

1989 Stroessner ousted in coup led by Gen Andrés Rodríguez. Rodríguez

elected president; right-of-centre military-backed Colorado Party won assembly elections.

1992 New democratic constitution adopted.

1993 Colorado Party won most seats in first free multiparty elections, but no overall majority; its candidate, Juan Carlos Wasmosy, won first free presidential elections.

Peru Republic of

National name *República del Perú*
Area 1,285,200 sq km/496,216 sq mi
Capital Lima
Major towns/cities Arequipa, Iquitos, Chiclayo, Trujillo, Cuzco, Piura, Chimbote
Major ports Callao, Chimbote, Salaverry
Physical features Andes mountains NW–SE cover 27% of Peru, separating Amazon river-basin jungle in NE from coastal plain in W; desert along coast N–S (Atacama Desert); Lake Titicaca

Government

Head of state Alberto Fujimori from 1990
Head of government to be announced
Political system democratic republic
Administrative divisions 24 departments and the constitutional province of Callao
Political parties American Popular Revolutionary Alliance (APRA), moderate, left wing; United Left (IU), left wing; Change 90 (Cambio 90), centrist; New Majority (Nueva Mayoria), centrist; Popular Christian Party (PPC), right of centre; Liberal Party (PL), right wing
Armed forces 115,000 (1995); plus paramilitary police forces numbering 60,000

Conscription conscription is selective for two years
Death penalty retains the death penalty only for exceptional crimes such as crimes under military law or crimes committed in exceptional circumstances such as wartime (last execution 1979)
Defence spend (% GDP) 1.6 (1995)
Education spend (% GNP) 3.5 (1992); N/A (1993/94)
Health spend (% GDP) 1.9 (199)

Economy and resources

Currency nuevo sol
GDP ($ US) 50.1 billion (1994)
Real GDP per capita (PPP) ($ US) 3,645 (1994)
GDP growth rate 12.9% (1994)
Average annual inflation 21.2% (1996); 398.5% (1985–95)
Foreign debt ($ US) 30.8 billion (1995)
Trading partners USA, Japan, UK, Germany, Italy, China, Argentina, Brazil, Colombia
Resources lead, copper, iron, silver, zinc (world's fourth-largest producer), petroleum
Industries food processing, textiles and clothing, petroleum refining, metals and metal products, chemicals, machinery and transport equipment, beverages, tourism
Exports copper, fishmeal, zinc, gold, refined petroleum products. Principal market: USA 20.9% (1995)
Imports machinery and transport equipment, basic foodstuffs, basic manufactures, chemicals, mineral fuels, consumer goods. Principal source: USA 27.6% (1995)
Arable land 2.6%
Agricultural products potatoes, wheat, seed cotton, coffee, rice, maize, beans, sugar cane; fishing (particularly for South American pilchard and *anchovetta*)

Population and society

Population 23,944,000 (1996e)
Population growth rate 1.9% (1990–95); 1.7% (2000–05)
Population density (per sq km) 19 (1996e)
Urban population (% of total) 72 (1995)
Age distribution (% of total population) <15 35.1%, 15–65 60.8%, >65 4.1% (1995)
Ethnic distribution about 45% South American Indian, 37% mestizo, 15% European, and 3% African
Languages Spanish, Quechua (both official), Aymara
Religion Roman Catholic (state religion)
Education (compulsory years) 11
Literacy rate 92% (men); 88% (women) (1995e)
Labour force 33% agriculture, 16.9% industry, 53.1% services (1992)
Unemployment 9.4% (1994e)
Life expectancy 66 (men); 69 (women) (1995–2000)
Child mortality rate (under 5, per 1,000 live births) 55 (1995)
Physicians 1 per 1,031 people (1991)
Hospital beds 1 per 825 people (1992)
TV sets (per 1,000 people) 106 (1995)
Radios (per 1,000 people) 259 (1995)

Transport

Airports international airports: Lima (Jorge Chávez), Iquitos (Colonel Francisco Secada Vignetta), Cuzco (Velasco Astete), Arequipa (Rodríguez Ballón); 27 domestic airports; total passenger km: 2,601 mil (1994)
Railroads total length: 3,661 km/2,275 mi; total passenger km: 241 mil (1994)
Roads total road network: 71,400 km/44,368 mi, of which 10.9% paved (1995e); passenger cars: 62 per 1,000 people (1993e)

Chronology

4000 BC Evidence of early settled agriculture in Chicama Valley.

AD 700–1100 Period of Wari Empire, first expansionist militarized empire in Andes.

1200 Manco Capac became first emperor of South American Indian Quechua-speaking Incas, who established a growing and sophisticated empire centred on the Andean city of Cuzco, and believed their ruler was descended from the Sun.

late 15th century At its zenith, Inca Empire stretched from Quito in Ecuador to beyond Santiago in S Chile. It superseded Chimu civilization, which had flourished in Peru 1250–1470.

1532–33 Incas defeated by Spanish conquistadores, led by Francisco Pizarro. King Atahualpa killed. Empire came under Spanish rule, as part of Viceroyalty of Peru, with capital in Lima, founded 1535.

1541 Pizarro assassinated as rivalries broke out among conquistadores.

1780 Tupac Amaru, who claimed to be descended from last Inca chieftain, led failed native revolt against Spanish.

1810 Peru became headquarters for Spanish government as European settlers rebelled elsewhere in Spanish America.

1820–22 Fight for liberation from Spanish rule led by Gen José de San Martín and Army of Andes which, after freeing Argentina and Chile, invaded S Peru.

1824 Became last colony in Central and South America to achieve independence from Spain after attacks from N by Field Marshal Sucre, acting for freedom fighter Simón Bolívar.

1836–39 Failed attempts at union with Bolivia.

1845–62 Economic progress under rule of Gen Ramón Castilla.

1849–74 Around 80,000–100,000 Chinese labourers arrived in Peru to fill menial jobs such as collecting guano.

1866 Victorious naval war fought with Spain.

1879–83 Pacific War fought in alliance with Bolivia and Chile over nitrate fields of the Atacama Desert in the S; three provinces along coastal S lost to Chile.

1902 Boundary dispute with Bolivia settled.

mid–1920s After several decades of civilian government, series of right-wing dictatorships held power.

1927 Boundary dispute with Colombia settled.

1929 Tacna province, lost to Chile 1880, was returned.

1941 Brief war with Ecuador secured Amazonian territory.

1945 Civilian government, dominated by left-of-centre American Popular Revolutionary Alliance (APRA, formed 1924), came to power after free elections.

1948 Army coup installed military government led by Gen Manuel Odría, who remained in power until 1956.

1963 Return to civilian rule, with centrist Fernando Belaúnde Terry as president.

1968 Return of military government in bloodless coup by Gen Juan Velasco Alvarado, following industrial unrest. Populist land reform programme introduced.

1975 Velasco replaced, in a bloodless coup, by Gen Morales Bermúdez.

1980 Return to civilian rule, with Fernando Belaúnde as president; agrarian and industrial reforms pursued. Sendero Luminoso ('Shining Path') Maoist guerrilla group active.

1981 Boundary dispute with Ecuador renewed.

1985 Belaúnde succeeded by Social Democrat Alan García Pérez, who launched campaign to remove military and police 'old guard'.

1987 President García delayed nationalization of Peru's banks after vigorous campaign against the proposal.

1988 García pressured to seek help from International Monetary Fund (IMF) as economy deteriorated. Sendero Luminoso increased campaign of violence.

1990 Right-of-centre Alberto Fujimori, the son of Japanese immigrants, defeated ex-communist writer Vargas Llosa in presidential elections. Assassination attempt on president failed. Inflation 400%; privatization programme launched.

1992 Fujimori allied himself with the army and suspended constitution, provoking international criticism. Sendero Luminoso leader arrested and sentenced to life imprisonment after 'show trial'. New single-chamber legislature elected.

1993 New constitution adopted, enabling Fujimori to seek re-election.

1994 Fujimori removed his wife as First Lady on the grounds of disloyalty; 6,000 Sendero Luminoso guerrillas surrendered to the authorities.

1995 Border dispute with Ecuador resolved after armed clashes. Fujimori re-elected to second term. Controversial amnesty granted to those previously convicted of human-rights abuses.

1996 Prime Minister Dante Cordova resigned in protest against rapid pace of market reform. Hostages held in Japanese embassy by Marxist Tupac Amaru Revolutionary Movement (MRTA) guerrillas.

1997 Hostage siege successfully ended.

Practical information

Visa requirements UK: visa not required for a stay of up to 90 days. USA: visa not required for a stay of up to 90 days

Embassy in the UK 52 Sloane Street, London SW1X 9SP. Tel: (0171) 235 1917; fax: (0171) 235 4463

British embassy PO Box 854, Natalio Sanchez 125, Edificio El Pacifico, Pisos 11/12, Plaza Washington, Lima 100. Tel: (1) 433 5032; fax: (1) 433 4738

Embassy in the USA 1700 Massachusetts Avenue NW, Washington, DC 20036. Tel: (202) 833 9860–9; fax: (202) 659 8124

American embassy Avenida Encalada, Cuadra 17, Monterrico, Lima. Tel: (12) 211 202; fax: (12) 213 543

Chamber of commerce Confederación de Cámaras de Comercio y Producción del Perú, Avenida Gregorio Escobedo 398, Lima 11. Tel: (1) 463 3434; fax: (1) 463 2820

Office hours 0900–1700 Mon–Fri

Banking hours 0930–1600 Mon–Fri (some banks open 0930–1230 Sat)

Time difference GMT –5

Chief tourist attractions Lima, with its Spanish colonial architecture; Cuzco, with its pre-Inca and Inca remains, notably Machu Picchu; Lake Titicaca; Amazon rainforest in NE

Major holidays 1 January, 1 May, 29–30 June, 28 July (2 days), 30 August, 8 October, 1 November, 8, 25, 31 December; variable: Good Friday, Holy Thursday

Philippines Republic of the

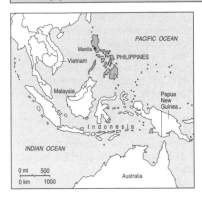

National name *Republika ng Pilipinas*
Area 300,000 sq km/115,830 sq mi
Capital Manila (on Luzon) (and chief port)
Major towns/cities Quezon City (on Luzon), Davao, Caloocan, Cebu, Zamboanga
Major ports Cebu, Davao (on Mindanao), Iloilo, Zamboanga (on Mindanao)
Physical features comprises over 7,000 islands; volcanic mountain ranges traverse main chain N–S; 50% still forested. The largest islands are Luzon 108,172 sq km/41,754 sq mi and Mindanao 94,227 sq km/36,372 sq mi; others include Samar, Negros, Palawan, Panay, Mindoro, Leyte, Cebu, and the Sulu group; Pinatubo volcano (1,759 m/5,770 ft); Mindanao has active volcano Apo (2,954 m/9,690 ft) and mountainous rainforest

Government

Head of state and government Fidel Ramos from 1992
Political system emergent democracy
Administrative divisions 15 regions (two of which are autonomous)
Political parties Laban ng Demokratikong Pilipino (Democratic Filipino Struggle Party; LDP–DFSP), centrist, liberal-democrat coalition; Lakas ng Edsa (National Union of Christian Democrats; LNE–NUCD), centrist; Liberal Party, centrist; Nationalist Party (Nacionalista), right wing; New Society Movement (NSM; Kilusan Bagong Lipunan), conservative, pro-Marcos; National Democratic Front, left-wing umbrella grouping, including the Communist Party of the Philippines (CPP); Mindanao Alliance, island-based decentralist body

Armed forces 106,500 (1995); reserve forces 131,000; paramilitary forces around 60,000 (1994)
Death penalty retained in law, but considered abolitionist in practice; last execution 1976
Defence spend (% GDP) 1.6 (1995)
Education spend (% GNP) 2.4 (1993/94)
Health spend (% GDP) 1.0 (1990)

Economy and resources

Currency peso
GDP ($ US) 64.2 billion (1994)
Real GDP per capita (PPP) ($ US) 2,681 (1994)
GDP growth rate 4.3% (1994); 1% (1990–95)
Average annual inflation 9.3% (1994); 9.8% (1985–95)
Foreign debt ($ US) 39.4 billion (1995)
Trading partners Japan, USA, Singapore, Taiwan, South Korea, Hong Kong
Resources copper ore, gold, silver, chromium, nickel, coal, crude petroleum, natural gas, forests
Industries food processing, petroleum refining, textiles, chemical products, pharmaceuticals, electrical machinery (mainly telecommunications equipment), metals and metal products, tourism
Exports electronic products (notably semiconductors and microcircuits), garments, agricultural products (particularly fruit and seafood), woodcraft and furniture, lumber, chemicals, coconut oil. Principal market: USA 35.3% (1995)
Imports machinery and transport equipment, mineral fuels, basic manufactures, food and live animals, textile yarns, base metals, cereals and cereal preparations. Principal source: Japan 22.4% (1995)
Arable land 18.4% (1993)
Agricultural products rice, maize, cassava, coconuts, sugar cane, bananas, pineapples; livestock (chiefly pigs, buffaloes, goats, and poultry) and fisheries

Population and society

Population 69,282,000 (1996e)
Population growth rate 2.1% (1990–95); 1.8% (2000–05)
Population density (per sq km) 231 (1996e)
Urban population (% of total) 54 (1995)
Age distribution (% of total population)

<15 38.3%, 15–65 58.3%, >65 3.4% (1995)
Ethnic distribution comprises more than 50 ethnic communities, although 95% of the population is designated 'Filipino', an Indo-Polynesian ethnic grouping
Languages Tagalog (Filipino, official); English and Spanish; Cebuano, Ilocano, and more than 70 other indigenous languages
Religions mainly Roman Catholic; Protestant, Muslim, local religions
Education (compulsory years) 6
Literacy rate 90% (men); 89% (women) (1995e)
Labour force 40% of population: 46% agriculture, 15% industry, 39% services (1990)
Unemployment 8.9% (1993)
Life expectancy 67 (men); 70 (women) (1995–2000)
Child mortality rate (under 5, per 1,000 live births) 53 (1995)
Physicians 1 per 853 people (1993)
Hospital beds 1 per 804 people (1993)
TV sets (per 1,000 people) 49 (1995)
Radios (per 1,000 people) 147 (1995)

Transport

Airports international airports: Manila (Ninoy Aquino), Cebu (Mactan), Laoag City, Davao, Zamboanga, Puerto Princesa City, Subic Bay, Freeport; comprehensive internal services; total passenger km: 13,977 mil (1994)
Railroads total length: 897 km/577 mi (of which 492 km/306 mi in operation); total passenger km: 164 mil (1995)
Roads total road network: 204,200 km/126,890 mi (1995e), of which around 14% paved (1996); passenger cars: 8.7 per 1,000 people (1995e)

Chronology

14th century Traders from Malay peninsula introduced Islam and created Muslim principalities of Manila and Jolo.
1521 Portuguese navigator Ferdinand Magellan reached the islands, but was killed in battle with islanders.
1536 Philippines named after Charles V's con (later Philip II of Spain) by Spanish navigator Ruy López de Villalobos.
1565 Philippines conquered by Spanish army led by Miguel López de Lagazpi.
1571 Manila was made capital of the colony, which was part of the viceroyalty of Mexico.

17th century Spanish missionaries converted much of lowland population to Roman Catholicism.

1762–63 British occupied Manila.

1834 End of Spanish monopoly on trade; British and American merchants bought sugar and tobacco.

1896–97 Emilio Aguinaldo led revolt against Spanish rule.

1898 Spanish-American War: US navy destroyed Spanish fleet in Manila Bay; Aguinaldo declared independence, but Spain ceded Philippines to USA.

1898–1901 Nationalist uprising suppressed by US troops; 200,000 Filipinos killed.

1907 Americans set up elected legislative assembly.

1916 Bicameral legislature introduced on US model.

1935 Philippines gained internal self-government with Manuel Quezon as president.

1942–45 Occupied by Japan.

1946 Philippines achieved independence from USA under President Manuel Roxas; USA retained military bases and supplied economic aid.

1957–61 'Filipino First' policy introduced by President Carlos García to reduce economic power of Americans and Chinese; official corruption increased.

1965 Ferdinand Marcos elected president.

1972 Marcos declared martial law and ended freedom of press; economic development financed by foreign loans, of which large sums were diverted by Marcos for personal use.

1981 Martial law officially ended but Marcos retained sweeping emergency powers, ostensibly needed to combat long-running Muslim and communist insurgencies.

1983 Opposition leader Benigno Aquino murdered at Manila airport while surrounded by government troops.

1986 Marcos falsified election results. Corazon Aquino (widow of Benigno Aquino) used 'people's power' to force Marcos to flee country.

1987 'Freedom constitution' adopted; Aquino's People's Power won congressional elections.

1989 State of emergency declared after sixth coup attempt suppressed with US aid.

1991 Philippine senate called for withdrawal of US forces; US renewal of Subic Bay naval base lease rejected.

1992 Fidel Ramos elected to succeed Aquino; 'Rainbow Coalition' government formed.

1995 Imelda Marcos (widow of Ferdinand Marcos) elected to House of Representatives while on bail from prison.

1996 LDP withdrew from coalition. Peace agreement between government and Moro National Liberation Front (MNLF) after 25 years of civil unrest on Mindanao.

1997 Preliminary peace talks between government and Muslim secessionist Moro Islamic Liberation Front (MILF). Major changes in political parties. Supreme Court rejected proposal to allow second presidential term.

Practical information

Visa requirements UK: visa not required for a stay of up to 21 days. USA: visa not required for a stay of up to 21 days

Embassy in the UK 9a Palace Green, London W8 4QE. Tel: (0171) 937 1600; fax: (0171) 937 2925

British embassy 15th–17th Floors, LV Locsin Building, 6752 Ayala Avenue, Makati, Metro Manila 1226. Tel: (2) 816 7116; fax: (2) 819 7206

Embassy in the USA 1600 Massachusetts Avenue NW, Washington, DC 20036. Tel: (202) 467 9300; fax: (202) 328 7614

American embassy 1201 Roxas Boulevard, Ermita Manila 1000. Tel: (2) 521 7116; fax: (2) 522 4361

Chamber of commerce Philippine Chamber of Commerce and Industry, Ground Floor, CCP Complex, Roxas Boulevard, Makati, Metro Manila 2801. Tel: (2) 833 8591; fax: (2) 816 1946

Office hours usually 0800–1200 and 1300–1700 Mon–Fri; some offices open 0800–1200 Sat

Banking hours 0900–1600 Mon–Fri

Time difference GMT +8

Chief tourist attractions thousands of islands and islets, some ringed by coral reefs; Mindanao; the Visayas Islands

Major holidays 1 January, 1 May, 12 June, 4 July, 1, 30 November, 25, 30–31 December; variable: Good Friday, Holy Thursday

---

Poland Republic of

National name *Rzeczpospolita Polska*

Area 312,683 sq km/120,726 sq mi

Capital Warsaw

Major towns/cities Lódý, Kraków (Cracow), Wrocław (Breslau), Poznań (Posen), Gdańsk (Danzig), Szczecin (Stettin), Katowice (Kattowitz), Bydgoszcz (Bromberg), Lublin

Major ports Gdańsk (Danzig), Szczecin (Stettin), Gdynia (Gdingen)

Physical features part of the great plain of Europe; Vistula, Oder, and Neisse rivers; Sudeten, Tatra, and Carpathian mountains on S frontier

Government

Head of state Alexander Kwaśniewski from 1995

Head of government Jerzy Buzek from 1997

Political system emergent democratic republic

Administrative divisions 49 voivodships (or provinces)

Political parties Democratic Left Alliance (SLD), reform socialist (ex-communist); Polish Peasant Party (PSL), moderate, agrarian; Freedom Union (UW), moderate, centrist; Labour Union (UP), left wing; Non-Party Bloc in

Support of Reforms (BBWR), Christian Democrat, right of centre, pro-Wałesa; Confederation for an Independent Poland (KPN), right wing
Armed forces 279,000 (1995)
Conscription military service is compulsory
Death penalty retained and used for ordinary crimes
Defence spend (% GDP) 2.5 (1995)
Education spend (% GNP) 5.5 (1993/94)
Health spend (% GDP) 4.5 (1994)

Economy and resources

Currency zloty
GDP ($ US) 93 billion (1994)
Real GDP per capita (PPP) ($ US) 5,002 (1994)
GDP growth rate 6% (1996); 2.4% (1990–95)
Average annual inflation 19.9% (1996); 91.8% (1985–95)
Foreign debt ($ US) 42.3 billion (1995)
Trading partners Germany, the Netherlands, Russia, Italy, UK, France, USA
Resources coal (world's fifth-largest producer), copper, sulphur, silver, petroleum and natural gas reserves
Industries machinery and transport equipment, food products, metals, chemicals, beverages, tobacco, textiles and clothing, petroleum refining, wood and paper products, tourism
Exports machinery and transport equipment, textiles, chemicals, coal, coke, copper, sulphur, steel, food and agricultural products, clothing and leather products, wood and paper products. Principal market: Germany 38.3% (1995)
Imports electro-engineering products, fuels and power (notably crude petroleum and natural gas), textiles, food products, iron ore, fertilizers. Principal source: Germany 26.6% (1995)
Arable land 61% (1993)
Agricultural products wheat, rye, barley, oats, maize, potatoes, sugar beet; livestock rearing; forest resources

Population and society

Population 38,601,000 (1996e)
Population growth rate 0.1% (1990–95); 0.3% (2000–05)
Population density (per sq km) 119 (1996e)
Urban population (% of total) 65 (1995)
Age distribution (% of total population) <15 22.9%, 15–65 66.1%, >65 11% (1995)

Ethnic distribution 98% ethnic Western-Slav ethnic Poles; small ethnic German, Ukrainian, and Belarusian minorities
Languages Polish (official), German
Religion Roman Catholic 95%
Education (compulsory years) 8
Literacy rate 99% (men); 99% (women) (1995e)
Labour force 25.8% agriculture, 31.6% industry, 42.6% services (1993)
Unemployment 16.4% (1994); 13.5% (1996)
Life expectancy 67 (men); 76 (women) (1995–2000)
Child mortality rate (under 5, per 1,000 live births) 16 (1995)
Physicians 1 per 440 people (1994)
Hospital beds 1 per 179 people (1994)
TV sets (per 1,000 people) 311 (1995)
Radios (per 1,000 people) 454 (1995)

Transport

Airports international airports: Warsaw (Okecie), Kraków (Balice), Wrocław (Strachowice), Gdańsk; four domestic airports; total passenger km: 3,690 mil (1994)
Railroads total length: 24,313 km/15,108 mi; total passenger km: 27,610 mil (1994)
Roads total road network: 372,479 km/231,458 mi, of which 65.3% paved (1995); passenger cars: 194.7 per 1,000 people (1995)

Chronology

966 Polish Slavic tribes under Mieszko I, leader of Piast dynasty, adopted Christianity and united region around Poznań to form first Polish state.
1241 Devastated by Mongols.
13th–14th centuries German and Jewish refugees settled among Slav population.
1386 Jagellion dynasty came to power: golden age for Polish culture.
1569 Poland united with Lithuania to become largest state in Europe.
1572 Jagellion dynasty became distinct; future kings were elected by nobility and gentry, who formed 10% of the population.
mid-17th century Defeat in war against Russia, Sweden, and Brandenburg (in Germany) set in a process of irreversible decline.
1772–95 Partitioned between Russia, which ruled the NE; Prussia, the W, including Pomerania; and Austria in the south-centre, including Galicia, where there was greatest autonomy.

1815 After Congress of Vienna, Russian eastern portion of Poland re-established as kingdom within Russian Empire.
1830 and 1863 Uprisings against repressive Russian rule.
1892 Nationalist Polish Socialist Party (PPS) founded.
1918 Independent Polish republic established after World War I, with Marshal Jozef Pilsudski, founder of the PPS, elected president.
1919–21 Abortive advance into Lithuania and Ukraine.
1926 Pilsudski seized full power in coup and established autocratic regime.
1935 On Pilsudski's death, military regime held power under Marshal Smigly-Rydz.
1939 Invaded by Germany; W Poland incorporated into Nazi Reich (state) and the rest became a German colony; 6 million Poles – half of them Jews – were slaughtered in the next five years.
1944–45 Liberated from Nazi rule by Soviet Union's Red Army; boundaries redrawn westwards at Potsdam Conference. One half of 'old Poland', 180,000 sq km/70,000 sq mi in the E, was lost to the Soviet Union; 100,000 sq km/ 40,000 sq mi of ex-German territory in Silesia, along the Oder and Neisse rivers, was added, shifting the state 240 km/150 mi westwards; millions of Germans were expelled.
1947 Communist people's republic proclaimed after manipulated election.
1949 Joined Comecon.
early 1950s Harsh Stalinist rule under communist leader Boleslaw Bierut: nationalization; rural collectivization; persecution of Catholic Church members.
1955 Joined Warsaw Pact defence organization.
1956 Poznań strikes and riots. The moderate Wladyslaw Gomułka installed as Polish United Workers' Party (PUWP) leader.
1960s Private farming reintroduced and Catholicism tolerated.
1970 Gomułka replaced by Edward Gierek after Gdańsk riots against food price rises.
1970s Poland heavily indebted to foreign creditors after failed attempt to boost economic growth.
1980 Solidarity, led by Lech Wałęsa, emerged as free trade union following Gdańsk disturbances.
1981 Martial law imposed by Gen Wojciech Jaruzelski, trade-union activity banned and Solidarity leaders and supporters arrested.

1983 Martial law ended.
1984 Amnesty for 35,000 political prisoners.
1988 Solidarity-led strikes and demonstrations for pay increases. Reform-communist Mieczysław Rakowski became prime minister.
1989 Agreement to relegalize Solidarity, allow opposition parties, and adopt a more democratic constitution, after round-table talks involving Solidarity, the Communist Party, and the Catholic Church. Widespread success for Solidarity in first open elections for 40 years; noncommunist 'grand coalition' government formed, headed by Tadeusz Mazowiecki of Solidarity; economic austerity and free-market restructuring programme began.
1990 PUWP dissolved and re-formed as Democratic Left Alliance (SLD). Wałesa

was elected president and Jan Bielecki became prime minister.
1991 Shock-therapy economic restructuring programme, including large-scale privatization, produced sharp fall in living standards and rise in unemployment rate to 11%. Unpopular Bielecki resigned and, after inconclusive elections, Jan Olszewski formed fragile centre-right coalition government.
1992 Political instability continued, with Waldemar Pawlak, of centre-left Polish Peasant Party (PSL), and Hanna Suchocka, of centrist Democratic Union, successively replacing Olszewski as prime minister.
1993 Economy became first in Central Europe to grow since collapse of communism. After new elections, Pawlak formed coalition government with ex-communist SLD, which pledged

to continue to build market-based economy and seek early entry into European Union.
1994 Joined NATO 'partnership for peace' programme; last Russian troops left Poland.
1995 Ex-communist Jozef Oleksy replaced Pawlak as prime minister. Wałesa narrowly defeated by Alexander Kwasniewski, leader of the SLD, in presidential election.
1996 Oleksy resigned as prime minister amid allegations of spying for Russia's secret service; replaced by Wlodzimierz Cimoszewicz.
1997 Speeding-up of structural reform and privatization. Gdansk shipyard closed. New constitution approved. Poland invited to join NATO and begin negotiations to join European Union.

Practical information

Visa requirements UK: visa not required for a stay of up to six months. USA: visa not required
Embassy in the UK 47 Portland Place, London W1N 3AG. Tel: (0171) 580 4324/9; fax: (0171) 323 4018
British embassy Aleje Róz 1, 00-556 Warsaw. Tel: (22) 628 1001–5; fax: (22) 217 161
Embassy in the USA 2640 16th Street NW, Washington, DC 20009. Tel: (202) 234 3800–2; fax: (202) 328 6271
American embassy Aleje Ujazdowskie 29/31, Warsaw. Tel: (2) 628 3041; fax: (2) 628 8298

Chamber of commerce Krajowa Izba Gospodarcza (Polish Chamber of Commerce), PO Box 361, Trebacka 4, 00-077 Warsaw. Tel: (22) 260 221; fax: (22) 274 673
Office hours 0700–1600 Mon–Fri
Banking hours 0800–1800 Mon–Fri
Time difference GMT +1
Chief tourist attractions historic cities of Gdańsk, Wrocław, Kraków, and Warsaw; numerous health and climatic resorts; mountain and forest scenery
Major holidays 1 January, 1, 3, 9 May, 15 August, 1, 11 November, 25–26 December; variable: Corpus Christi, Easter Monday

---

Portugal Republic of

National name *República Portuguesa*
Area 92,000 sq km/35,521 sq mi (including the Azores and Madeira)
Capital Lisbon
Major towns/cities Porto, Coimbra, Amadora, Setúbal, Guarde, Portalegre
Major ports Porto, Setúbal

Physical features mountainous in the N (Serra da Estrêla mountains); plains in the S; rivers Minho, Douro, Tagus (Tejo), Guadiana

Government

Head of state Jorge Sampaio from 1996
Head of government Antonio Guterres from 1995
Political system democratic republic
Administrative divisions 18 districts and two autonomous regions
Political parties Social Democratic Party (PSD), moderate left of centre; Socialist Party (PS), centre left; People's Party (PP), right wing, anti-European integration
Armed forces 54,000 (1995)
Conscription 4–18 months
Death penalty abolished 1976
Defence spend (% GDP) 2.9 (1995)

Education spend (% GNP) 5.4 (1993/94)
Health spend (% GDP) 4.1 (1993)

Economy and resources

Currency escudo
GDP ($ US) 104 billion (1996)
Real GDP per capita (PPP) ($ US) 13,059 (1996)
GDP growth rate 2.8% (1996); 0.8%(1990–95)
Average annual inflation 3.1% (1996); 11.2% (1985–95)
Trading partners EU (principally Spain, Germany, and France)
Resources limestone, granite, marble, iron, tungsten, copper, pyrites, gold, uranium, coal, forests
Industries textiles and clothing, footwear, paper pulp, cork items (world's largest producer of cork), chemicals, petroleum refining, fish processing,

viticulture, electrical appliances, ceramics, tourism

Exports textiles, clothing, footwear, pulp and waste paper, wood and cork manufactures, tinned fish, electrical equipment, wine, refined petroleum. Principal market: Germany 21.6% (1995)

Imports foodstuffs, machinery and transport equipment, crude petroleum, natural gas, textile yarn, coal, rubber, plastics, tobacco. Principal source: Spain 20.8% (1995)

Arable land 25.5% (1993)

Agricultural products wheat, maize, rice, potatoes, tomatoes, grapes, olives, fruit; fishing (1993 sardine catch was the world's largest at 89,914 tonnes/88,494 tons)

Population and society

Population 9,808,000 (1996e)

Population growth rate –0.1% (1990–95); 0% (2000–05)

Population density (per sq km) 106 (1996e)

Urban population (% of total) 36 (1995)

Age distribution (% of total population) <15 18.8%, 15–65 67%, >65 14.1% (1995)

Ethnic distribution most of the population is descended from Caucasoid peoples who inhabited the whole of the Iberian peninsula in classical and pre-classical times; there are a number of minorities from Portugal's overseas possessions and former possessions

Language Portuguese

Religion Roman Catholic 97%

Education (compulsory years) 9

Literacy rate 89% (men); 81% (women) (1995e)

Labour force 49% of population: 18% agriculture, 34% industry, 48% services (1990)

Unemployment 7.3% (1996)

Life expectancy 72 (men); 79 (women) (1995–2000)

Child mortality rate (under 5, per 1,000 live births) 11 (1995)

Physicians 1 per 343 people (1993)

Hospital beds 1 per 255 people (1993)

TV sets (per 1,000 people) 326 (1995)

Radios (per 1,000 people) 245 (1995)

Transport

Airports international airports: Lisbon (Portela de Sacavem), Faro, Oporto (Oporto Sá Carneiro), Madeira (Funchal), Azores (Santa Maria), São Miguel; domestic services operate between these; total passenger km: 7,880 mil (1994)

Railroads total length: 3,072 km/1,909 mi; total passenger km: 5,149 mil (1994)

Roads total road network: 68,732 km/ 42,710 mi, of which 87% paved (1995); passenger cars: 242.2 per 1,000 people (1994)

Chronology

2nd century BC Romans conquered Iberian peninsula.

5th century AD Iberia overrun by Vandals and Visigoths after fall of Roman Empire.

711 Visigoth kingdom overthrown by Muslims invading from N Africa.

997–1064 Christians resettled northern area, which came under rule of Léon and Castile.

1139 Afonso I, son of Henry of Burgundy, defeated Muslims; the area became an independent kingdom.

1340 Final Muslim invasion defeated.

1373 Anglo-Portuguese alliance signed.

15th century Age of exploration: Portuguese mariners surveyed coast of Africa, opened sea route to India (Vasco da Gama), and reached Brazil (Pedro Cabral).

16th century 'Golden Age': Portugal flourished as commercial and colonial power.

1580 Philip II of Spain took throne of Portugal.

1640 Spanish rule overthrown in bloodless coup; Duke of Braganza proclaimed as King John IV.

1668 Spain recognized Portuguese independence.

1755 Lisbon devastated by earthquake.

1755–77 Politics dominated by chief minister Sebastiao de Carlvalho, Marquis of Pombal, who introduced secular education and promoted trade.

1807 Napoleonic France invaded Portugal; Portuguese court fled to Brazil.

1807–11 In the Peninsular War British forces played leading part in liberating Portugal from French.

1820 Liberal revolution forced King John VI to return from Brazil and accept constitutional government.

1822 Brazil declared independence; first Portuguese constitution adopted.

1826 First constitution replaced by more conservative one.

1828 Dom Miguel blocked succession of his niece, Queen Maria, and declared himself absolute monarch; civil war ensued between liberals and conservatives.

1834 Queen Maria regained throne with British, French, and Brazilian help; constitutional government restored.

1840s Severe disputes between supporters of radical 1822 constitution and more conservative 1826 constitution.

1851 'Regeneration' to promote order and economic growth launched by Duke of Saldanha after coup.

late 19th century Government faced severe financial difficulties; rise of socialist, anarchist, and republican parties.

1908 Assassination of King Carlos I.

1910 Portugal became republic after three-day insurrection forced King Manuel II to flee.

1911 New regime adopted liberal constitution, but republic proved unstable, violent, and corrupt.

1916–18 Portugal fought in World War I on Allied side.

1926–51 Popular military coup installed Gen António de Fragoso Carmona as president.

1928 António de Oliveira Salazar became finance minister and introduced successful reforms.

1932 Salazar became prime minister with dictatorial powers.

1933 Authoritarian 'Estado Novo' ('New State') constitution adopted; living conditions improved, but Salazar resisted political change at home and in colonies.

1949 Portugal became founding member of North Atlantic Treaty Organization (NATO).

1968 Salazar retired; succeeded by Marcello Caetano.

1974 Army seized power to end stalemate situation in African colonial wars; Gen Antó Ribeiro de Spínola became president; succeeded by Gen Francisco da Costa Gomes.

1975 Portuguese colonies achieved independence; Gomes narrowly averted communist coup.

1976 First free elections in 50 years resulted in minority government under socialist leader Mario Soares; Gen António Ramahlo Eanes won presidency.

1980 Francisco Balsemão (PSD) formed centre-party coalition.

1986 Soares became first civilian president in 60 years; Portugal joined European Community (EC).

1989 Social Democrat government started to dismantle socialist economy and privatize major industries.

1996 Jorge Sampaio (PS) elected president.

Practical information

Visa requirements UK: visa not required for a stay of up to three months. USA: visa not required for a stay of up to two months
Embassy in the UK 11 Belgrave Square, London SW1X 8PP. Tel: (0171) 235 5331/4; fax: (0171) 245 1287
British embassy Rua de São Bernardo 33, 1200 Lisbon. Tel: (1) 396 1191; fax: (1) 397 6768
Embassy in the USA 2125 Kalorama Road NW, Washington, DC 20008. Tel: (202) 328 8610; fax: (202) 462 3726
American embassy Avenida das Forcas Armadas, 1600 Lisbon. Tel: (1) 726 6600, 6659, 8670, 8880; fax: (1) 726 9109

Chamber of commerce Confederação do Comércio Português, Rua dos Correeiros 79, 1° Andar, 1100 Lisbon. Tel: (1) 301 0192; fax: (1) 301 0626
Office hours 0900–1300 and 1500–1900 Mon–Fri
Banking hours generally 0830–1500 Mon–Fri
Time difference GMT +/–0
Chief tourist attractions mild climate; historic town of Lisbon; summer resorts in the Algarve; winter resorts on Madeira and the Azores
Major holidays 1 January, 25 April, 10 June, 15 August, 5 October, 1 November, 1, 8, 24–25 December; variable: Carnival, Corpus Christi, Good Friday

Qatar State of

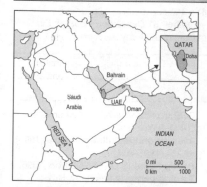

National name *Dawlat Qatar*
Area 11,400 sq km/4,401 sq mi
Capital Doha (and chief port)
Major towns/cities Dukhan, centre of oil production; Halul, terminal for offshore oilfields; Umm Said, Ruwais, Wakra, Al-Khour
Physical features mostly flat desert with salt flats in S

Government

Head of state and government Sheik Hamad bin Khalifa al-Thani from 1995
Political system absolute monarchy
Administrative divisions nine municipalities
Political parties none
Armed forces 11,100 (1995)
Conscription military service is voluntary
Death penalty retained and used for ordinary crimes
Defence spend (% GDP) 4.4 (1995)
Education spend (% GNP) 3.2 (1993)
Health spend (% GDP) 3.1 (1990)

Economy and resources

Currency Qatari riyal
GDP ($ US) 7.17 billion (1994)

Real GDP per capita (PPP) ($ US) 18,403 (1994)
GDP growth rate −4.1% (1994)
Average annual inflation 2.7% (1995)
Foreign debt ($ US) 1.5 billion (1993e)
Trading partners Japan, Italy, USA, UK, Germany, France, Saudi Arabia, Spain
Resources petroleum, natural gas, water resources
Industries petroleum refining and petroleum products, industrial chemicals, iron and steel, flour, cement, concrete, plastics, paint
Exports petroleum. Principal market: Japan 54.3% (1995)
Imports machinery and transport equipment, basic manufactures, food and live animals, miscellaneous manufactured articles, chemicals. Principal source: Italy 15.5% (1995)
Arable land 0.6% (1993)
Agricultural products cereals, vegetables, fruits (especially dates); livestock rearing; fishing

Population and society

Population 558,000 (1996e)
Population growth rate 2.5% (1990–95)
Population density (per sq km) 51 (1996e)
Urban population (% of total) 91 (1995)
Ethnic composition only about 25% of the population are indigenous Qataris; 40% are Arabs, and the others Pakistanis, Indians, and Iranians
Languages Arabic (official); English
Religion Sunni Muslim
Education not compulsory
Literacy rate 78% (men); 78% (women) (1995e)
Labour force 57% of population: 3% agriculture, 32% industry, 65% services (1990)

Unemployment dependent on immigrant workers – shortage of indigenous labour
Life expectancy 70 (men); 75 (women) (1995–2000)
Child mortality rate (under 5, per 1,000 live births) 23 (1995)
Physicians 1 per 681 people (1993)
Hospital beds 1 per 484 people (1993)
TV sets (per 1,000 people) 401 (1995)
Radios (per 1,000 people) 438 (1995)

Transport

Airports international airports: Doha; total passenger km: 2,439 mil (1994)
Railroads none
Roads total road network: 1,210 km/752 mi, of which 90% paved (1995e); passenger cars: 233.7 per 1,000 people (1993e)

Chronology

7th century AD Islam introduced.
8th century Developed into important trading centre during time of Abbasid Empire.
1783 The al-Khalifa family, who had migrated to NE Qatar from W and N of the Arabian Peninsula, foiled Persian invasion and moved their headquarters to Bahrain Island, while continuing to rule the area of Qatar.
1867–68 After the Bahrain-based al-Khalifa had suppressed a revolt by their Qatari subjects, destroying the town of Doha, Britain intervened and installed Muhammad ibn Thani al-Thani, from the leading family of Qatar, as the ruling sheik (or emir). A British Resident was given power to arbitrate disputes with Qatar's neighbours.
1871–1914 Nominally part of Turkish Ottoman Empire, although in 1893 sheik's forces inflicted a defeat on Ottomans.

1916 Qatar became British protectorate after treaty signed with Sheik Adbullah al-Thani.
1949 Oil production began at onshore Dukhan field in W.
1960 Sheik Ahmad al-Thani became new emir.
1968 Britain's announcement that it would remove its forces from the Persian Gulf by 1971 led Qatar to make an

abortive attempt to arrange a federation of Gulf states.
1970 Constitution adopted, confirming emirate as absolute monarchy.
1971 Independence achieved from Britain.
1972 Emir Sheik Ahmad replaced in bloodless coup by his cousin, the Crown Prince and prime minister Sheik Khalifa ibn Hamad al-Thani.

1991 Forces joined United Nations coalition in Gulf War against Iraq.
1995 Sheik Khalifa ousted by his son Crown Prince Sheik Hamad bin Khalifa al-Thani.
1996 Announcement of plans to introduce democracy were followed by an assassination attempt on Sheik Hamad.

Practical information

Visa requirements UK: visa not required for a stay of up to 30 days. USA: visa required
Embassy in the UK 1 South Audley Street, London W1Y 5DQ. Tel: (0171) 493 2200; fax: (0171) 493 3894
British embassy PO Box 3, Doha. Tel: (974) 421 991; fax: (974) 438 692
Embassy in the USA Suite 1180, 600 New Hampshire Avenue NW, Washington, DC 20037. Tel: (202) 338 0111

American embassy 149 Armed Bin Ali Street, Fariq Bin Omran (opposite the television station), Doha. Tel: (974) 864 701/2/3; fax: (974) 861 669
Chamber of commerce PO Box 402, Doha. Tel: (974) 425 131; fax: (974) 425 186
Office hours 0730–1230 and 1430–1800 Sat–Thu
Banking hours 0730–1130 Sat–Thu
Time difference GMT +3
Major holidays 3 September, 31 December; variable: Eid-ul-Adha (4 days), end of Ramadan (4 days)

Romania

National name *România*
Area 237,500 sq km/91,698 sq mi
Capital Bucharest
Major towns/cities Braşov, Timişoara, Cluj-Napoca, Iaşl, Constanţa, Galaţi, Craiova, Ploieşti
Major ports Galaţi, Constanţa, Brăila
Physical features mountains surrounding a plateau, with river plains S and E. Carpathian Mountains, Transylvanian Alps; river Danube; Black Sea coast; mineral springs

Government

Head of state Emil Constantinescu from 1996
Head of government Victor Ciorbea from 1996

Political system emergent democratic republic
Administrative divisions 41 counties
Political parties Democratic Convention of Romania (DCR), centre-right coalition; Social Democratic Union (SDU), reformist; Social Democracy Party of Romania (PSDR), social democrat; Romanian National Unity Party (RNUP), Romanian nationalist, right wing, anti-Hungarian; Greater Romania Party (Romania Mare), far right, ultranationalist, anti-Semitic; Democratic Party–National Salvation Front (DP–NSF), promarket; National Salvation Front (NSF), centre left; Hungarian Democratic Union of Romania (HDUR), ethnic Hungarian; Christian Democratic–National Peasants' Party (CD–PNC), centre right, promarket; Socialist Labour Party (SLP), ex-communist
Armed forces 217,000 (1995)
Conscription military service is compulsory for 12–18 months
Death penalty abolished 1989
Defence spend (% GDP) 3.1 (1995)
Education spend (% GNP) 3.1 (1994)
Health spend (% GDP) 4.8 (1994)

Economy and resources

Currency leu
GDP ($ US) 30 billion (1994)
Real GDP per capita (PPP) ($ US) 4,037 (1994)

GDP growth rate 7.1% (1995); −1.4% (1990–95)
Average annual inflation 32.3% (1995); 69.1% (1985–95)
Foreign debt ($ US) 6.65 billion (1995)
Trading partners Germany, Russia, Italy, USA, France, Iran, China, Turkey
Resources brown coal, hard coal, iron ore, salt, bauxite, copper, lead, zinc, methane gas, petroleum (reserves expected to be exhausted by mid to late 1990s)
Industries metallurgy, mechanical engineering, chemical products, timber and wood products, textiles and clothing, food processing
Exports base metals and metallic articles, textiles and clothing, machinery and equipment, mineral products, foodstuffs. Principal market: Germany 17.9% (1996)
Imports mineral products, machinery and mechanical appliances, textiles, motor cars. Principal source: Germany 17.1% (1996)
Arable land 64% (1993)
Agricultural products wheat, maize, potatoes, sugar beet, barley, apples, grapes, sunflower seeds; wine production; forestry; fish breeding

Population and society

Population 22,655,000 (1996e)
Population growth rate −0.3% (1990–95); −0.2% (2000–05)

Population density (per sq km) 95 (1996e)

Urban population (% of total) 55 (1995)

Age distribution (% of total population) <15 20.4%, 15–65 67.7%, >65 11.8% (1995)

Ethnic distribution 89% non-Slavic ethnic Romanian; substantial Hungarian, German, and Serbian minorities

Languages Romanian (official), Hungarian, German

Religion mainly Romanian Orthodox

Education (compulsory years) 8

Literacy rate 97% (men); 97% (women) (1995e)

Labour force 35.9% agriculture, 35.8% industry, 28.3% services (1993)

Unemployment 7.8% (1996)

Life expectancy 67 (men); 73 (women) (1995–2000)

Child mortality rate (under 5, per 1,000 live births) 29 (1995)

Physicians 1 per 561 people (1995)

Hospital beds 1 per 131 people (1995)

TV sets (per 1,000 people) 220 (1995)

Radios (per 1,000 people) 211 (1995)

Transport

Airports international airports: Bucharest (Otopeni), Constanţa (Mihail Kogāiniceanu), Timişoara, Arad; 12 domestic airports; total passenger km: 2,584 mil (1994)

Railroads total length: 11,365 km/7,062 mi; total passenger km: 18,313 mil (1994)

Roads total road network: 153,170 km/ 95,180 mi, of which 51% paved (1995); passenger cars: 96.9 per 1,000 people (1995)

Chronology

106 Formed heartland of ancient region of Dacia, which was conquered by Roman Emperor Trajan and became a province of Roman Empire; Christianity introduced.

275 Taken from Rome by invading Goths, a Germanic people.

4th–10th centuries Invaded by successive waves of Huns, Avars, Bulgars, Magyars, and Mongols.

c. 1000 Transylvania, in N, became an autonomous province under Hungarian crown.

mid-14th century Two Romanian principalities emerged, Wallachia in S, around Bucharest, and Moldova in NE.

15th–16th centuries The formerly autonomous principalities of Wallachia, Moldova, and Transylvania became tributaries to Ottoman Turks, despite peasant uprisings and resistance from Vlad Tepes ('the Impaler'), ruling prince of Wallachia.

late 17th century Transylvania conquered by Austrian Habsburgs.

1829 Wallachia and Moldova brought under tsarist Russian suzerainty.

1859 Under Prince Alexandru Ion Cuza, Moldova and Wallachia united to form Romanian state.

1878 Romania's independence recognized by Great Powers in Congress of Berlin.

1881 Became kingdom under Carol I.

1916–18 Fought on Triple Entente side (Britain, France, and Russia) during World War I; acquired Transylvania and Bukovina, in N, from dismembered Austro-Hungarian Empire, and Bessarabia, in E, from Russia. This made it largest state in Balkans.

1930 To counter growing popularity of fascist and antisemitic 'Iron Guard' mass movement, King Carol II abolished democratic institutions and established dictatorship.

1940 Forced to surrender Bessarabia and N Bukovina, adjoining Black Sea, to Soviet Union, and N Transylvania to Hungary; King Carol II abdicated, handing over effective power to Gen Ion Antonescu, who signed Axis Pact with Germany.

1941–44 Fought on German side against Soviet Union; thousands of Jews massacred.

1944 Antonescu ousted; Romania joined war against Germany.

1945 Occupied by Soviet Union; communist-dominated government installed.

1947 Paris Peace Treaty reclaimed Transylvania for Romania, but lost S Dobruja to Bulgaria and N Bukovina and Bessarabia to Soviet Union; King Michael, son of Carol II, abdicated and People's Republic proclaimed.

1948–49 New Soviet-style constitution; joined Comecon; nationalization and agricultural collectivization.

1955 Romania joined Warsaw Pact.

1958 Soviet occupation forces removed.

1965 Nicolae Ceausescu replaced Gheorghe Gheorghiu-Dej as Romanian Communist Party leader, and pursued foreign policy autonomous of Moscow, refusing to participate in Warsaw Pact manoeuvres.

1975 Ceausescu made president.

1985–86 Winters of austerity and power cuts as Ceausescu refused to liberalize the economy.

1987 Workers' demonstrations against austerity programme brutally crushed at Brasov.

1988–89 Relations with Hungary deteriorated over 'systematization programme', designed to forcibly resettle ethnic Hungarians in Transylvania.

1989 Bloody overthrow of Ceausescu regime in 'Christmas Revolution'; Ceausescu and wife tried and executed; estimated 10,000 dead in civil war.

Practical information

Visa requirements UK: visa required. USA: visa not required for a stay of up to 30 days

Embassy in the UK Arundel House, 4 Palace Green, London W8 4QD. Tel: (0171) 937 9666/8; fax: (0171) 937 8069

British embassy Strada Jules Michelet 24, 70154 Bucharest. Tel: (1) 312 0305; fax: (1) 312 0229

Embassy in the USA 1607 23rd Street NW, Washington, DC 20008. Tel: (202) 332 4846, 4848, 4851; fax: (202) 232 4748

American embassy Strada Tudor Arghezi 7–9, Bucharest.

Tel: (1) 210 0149, 4042; fax: (1) 210 0395

Chamber of commerce Chamber of Commerce and Industry of Romania, Boulevard Nicolae Balcescu 22, 79502 Bucharest. Tel: (1) 615 4703; fax: (1) 312 2091

Office hours 0700–1530 Mon–Fri

Banking hours 0900–1200 Mon–Fri; 1300–1500 Mon–Fri (currency exchange only)

Time difference GMT +2

Chief tourist attractions Black Sea resorts (including Mangalia, Mamaia, and Eforie); Carpathian Mountains; Danube delta

Major holidays 1–2 January, 15 April, 1 May, 1, 25–26 December

Power assumed by NSF, headed by Ion Iliescu.

1990 Securitate secret police replaced by new Romanian Intelligence Service; Eastern Orthodox Church and private farming re-legalized; systematization programme abandoned.

1991 Privatization law passed. Prime minister Petre Roman resigned following riots by striking miners; succeeded by

Theodor Stolojan heading a new cross-party coalition government.

1992 NSF split; Iliescu re-elected president; Nicolai Vacaroiu appointed prime minister of minority coalition government.

1994 Military cooperation pact with Bulgaria. Far-right parties brought into governing coalition.

1996 Signs of economic growth;

parliamentary elections won by DCR who formed coalition government with SDU; Emil Constantinescu of Democratic Convention elected president; Victor Ciorbea appointed prime minister.

1997 Economic 'shock therapy' reform programme and drive against corruption announced. Sharp increase in inflation. Former King Michael returned from exile.

Russian Federation (formerly to 1991 *Russian Soviet Federal Socialist Republic (RSFSR)*)

National name *Rossiskaya Federatsiya*

Area 17,075,400 sq km/6,592,811 sq mi

Capital Moscow

Major towns/cities St Petersburg (Leningrad), Nizhniy Novgorod (Gorky), Rostov-na-Donu, Samara (Kuibyshev), Tver (Kalinin), Volgograd, Vyatka (Kirov), Ekaterinburg (Sverdlovsk), Novosibirsk, Chelyabinsk, Kazan, Omsk, Perm, Ufa

Physical features fertile Black Earth district; extensive forests; the Ural Mountains with large mineral resources; Lake Baikal, world's deepest lake

Government

Head of state Boris Yeltsin from 1991

Head of government Viktor Chernomyrdin from 1992

Political system emergent democracy

Administrative divisions 21 republics, 6 territories, 49 provinces, 10 autonomous areas, two cities with federal status, and one autonomous region

Political parties Russia is Our Home, centrist; Party of Unity and Accord (PRUA), moderate reformist; Communist Party of the Russian Federation (CPRF), left wing, conservative (ex-communist); Agrarian Party, rural-based, centrist; Liberal Democratic Party, far right,

ultranationalist; Congress of Russian Communities, populist, nationalist; Russia's Choice, reformist, centre right; Yabloko, gradualist free market; Russian Social Democratic People's Party (Derzhava), communist-nationalist; Patriotic Popular Union of Russia (PPUR), communist-led; Russian People's Republican Party (RPRP)

Armed forces 1,520,000; paramilitary forces of 280,000 (1995)

Conscription two years

Death penalty retained and used for ordinary crimes

Defence spend (% GDP) 7.4 (1995)

Education spend (% GNP) 4.4 (1993/94)

Health spend (% GDP) 2.9 (1992)

Economy and resources

Currency rouble

GDP ($ US) 377 billion (1994)

Real GDP per capita (PPP) ($ US) 4,828 (1994)

GDP growth rate –4% (1995); –9.8% (1990–95)

Average annual inflation 47.6% (1996); 148.9% (1985–95)

Foreign debt ($ US) 120.4 billion (1995)

Trading partners CIS republics, Germany, UK, China, USA, Japan, Italy

Resources petroleum, natural gas, coal, peat, copper (world's fourth-largest producer), iron ore, lead, aluminium, phosphate rock, nickel, manganese, gold, diamonds, platinum, zinc, tin

Industries cast iron, steel, rolled iron, synthetic fibres, soap, cellulose, paper, cement, machinery and transport equipment, glass, bricks, food processing, confectionery

Exports mineral fuels, ferrous and non-ferrous metals and derivatives, precious stones, chemical products, machinery and transport equipment, weapons, timber and paper products. Principal market: Ukraine 9% (1996)

Imports machinery and transport equipment, grain and foodstuffs, chemical products, textiles, clothing, footwear, pharmaceuticals, metals. Principal source: Ukraine 14% (1996)

Arable land 8% (1993)

Agricultural products grain, potatoes, flax, sunflower seed, vegetables, fruit and berries, tea; livestock and dairy farming

Population and society

Population 148,146,000 (1996e)

Population growth rate –0.1% (1990–95); –0.2% (2000–05)

Population density (per sq km) 9 (1996e)

Urban population (% of total) 76 (1995)

Age distribution (% of total population) <15 21.1%, 15–65 66.9%, >65 12.1% (1995)

Ethnic distribution predominantly ethnic Russian (eastern Slav); significant Tatar, Ukranian, Chuvash, Belarusian, Bashkir, and Chechen minorities

Language Russian

Religion traditionally Russian Orthodox

Education (compulsory years) 9

Literacy rate 99% (men); 99% (women) (1995e)

Labour force 52% of population: 14% agriculture, 42% industry, 45% services (1990)

Unemployment 3.5% (1996)

Life expectancy 62 (men); 74 (women) (1995–2000)

Child mortality rate (under 5, per 1,000 live births) 30 (1995)

Physicians 1 per 222 people (1994)

Hospital beds 1 per 78 people (1994)

TV sets (per 1,000 people) 377 (1995)

Radios (per 1,000 people) 340 (1995)

Transport

Airports international airports: Moscow (Sheremetyevo), St Petersburg (Pulkovo); six principal domestic airports

operate services to all major cities; total passenger km: 65,144 mil (1994)
Railroads total length: 91,116 km/56,619 mi; total passenger km: 228,000 mil (1995)
Roads total road network: 949,000 km/ 589,709 mi, of which 78.8% paved (1995); passenger cars: 91.1 per 1,000 people (1993e)

Chronology

9th–10th centuries Viking chieftains established own rule in Novgorod, Kiev, and other cities.
10th–12th centuries Kiev temporarily united Russian peoples into its empire. Christianity introduced from Constantinople 988.
13th century Mongols (Golden Horde) overran the southern steppes 1223, compelling Russian princes to pay tribute.
14th century Belarusia and Ukraine came under Polish rule.
1462–1505 Ivan the Great, grand duke of Muscovy, threw off Mongol yoke and united lands in NW.
1547–84 Ivan the Terrible assumed title of tsar and conquered Kazan and Astrakhan; colonization of Siberia began.
1613 First Romanov tsar, Michael, elected after period of chaos.
1667 Following Cossack revolt, E Ukraine reunited with Russia.
1682–1725 Peter the Great modernized the bureaucracy and army; he founded a navy and a new capital, St Petersburg, introduced Western education, and wrested the Baltic seaboard from Sweden. By 1700 colonization of Siberia had reached the Pacific.
1762–96 Catherine the Great annexed the Crimea and part of Poland and recovered W Ukraine and Belarusia.
1798–1814 Russia intervened in Revolutionary and Napoleonic Wars (1798–1801, 1805–07); repelled Napoleon, and took part in his overthrow (1812–14).
1827–29 Russian attempts to dominate Balkans led to war with Turkey.
1853–56 Crimean War.
1856–64 Caucasian War of conquest completed annexation of N Caucasus, causing more than a million people to emigrate.
1858–60 Treaties of Aigun 1858 and Peking 1860 imposed on China, annexing territories N of the Amur and E of the Ussuri rivers; Vladivostok founded on Pacific coast.

1861 Serfdom abolished (on terms unfavourable to peasants). Rapid growth of industry followed, a working-class movement developed, and revolutionary ideas spread, culminating in assassination of Alexander II 1881.
1877–78 Russo-Turkish War
1898 Social Democratic Party founded by Russian Marxists; split into Bolshevik and Menshevik factions 1903.
1904–05 Russo-Japanese War caused by Russian expansion in Manchuria.
1905 A revolution, though suppressed, forced tsar to accept parliament (Duma) with limited powers.
1914 Russo-Austrian rivalry in Balkans was a major cause of outbreak of World War I; Russia fought in alliance with France and Britain.
1917 Russian Revolution: tsar abdicated, provisional government established; Bolsheviks seized power under Vladimir Lenin.
1918 Treaty of Brest-Litovsk ended war with Germany; murder of former tsar; Russian Empire collapsed; Finland, Poland, and Baltic States seceded.
1918–22 Civil War between Red Army, led by Leon Trotsky, and White Russian forces with foreign support; Red Army ultimately victorious; control regained over Ukraine, Caucasus, and Central Asia.
1922 Former Russian Empire renamed Union of Soviet Socialist Republics.
1924 Death of Lenin.
1928 Joseph Stalin emerged as absolute ruler after ousting Trotsky.
1928–33 First Five-Year Plan collectivized agriculture by force; millions died in famine.
1936–38 The Great Terror: Stalin executed his critics and imprisoned millions of people on false charges of treason and sabotage.
1939 Nazi-Soviet nonaggression pact; USSR invaded eastern Poland and attacked Finland.
1940 USSR annexed Baltic States.
1941–45 'Great Patriotic War' against Germany ended with Soviet domination of eastern Europe and led to 'Cold War' with USA and its allies.
1949 Council for Mutual Economic Assistance (Comecon) created to supervise trade in Soviet bloc.
1953 Stalin died; 'collective leadership' in power.
1955 Warsaw Pact created.
1956 Nikita Khrushchev made 'secret speech' criticizing Stalin; USSR invaded Hungary.

1957–58 Khrushchev ousted his rivals and became effective leader, introducing limited reforms.
1960 Rift between USSR and Communist China.
1962 Cuban missile crisis: Soviet nuclear missiles installed in Cuba but removed after ultimatum from USA.
1964 Khrushchev ousted by new 'collective leadership' headed by Leonid Brezhnev and Alexei Kosygin.
1968 USSR and allies invaded Czechoslovakia.
1970s 'Détente' with USA and western Europe.
1979 USSR invaded Afghanistan; fighting continued until Soviet withdrawal ten years later.
1982 Brezhnev died; Uri Andropov became leader.
1984 Andropov died; Konstantin Chernenko became leader.
1985 Chernenko died; Mikhail Gorbachev became leader and announced wide-ranging reform programme (*perestroika*).
1986 Chernobyl nuclear disaster.
1988 Special All-Union Party Congress approved radical constitutional changes and market reforms; start of open nationalist unrest in Caucasus and Baltic republics.
1989 Multi-candidate elections held in move towards 'socialist democracy'; collapse of Soviet satellite regimes in eastern Europe; end of Cold War.
1990 Anti-communists and nationalists polled strongly in multi-party local elections; Baltic and Caucasian republics defied central government; Boris Yeltsin became president of Russian Federation and left Communist Party.
1991 Unsuccessful coup by hardline communists; republics declared independence; dissolution of communist rule in Russian Federation; USSR replaced by loose Commonwealth of Independent States (CIS).
1992 Russia assumed former USSR seat on United Nations (UN) Security Council; new constitution devised; end of price controls.
1993 Power struggle between Yeltsin and Congress of People's Deputies; congress dissolved; attempted coup foiled; new parliament elected.
1994 Russia joined North Atlantic Treaty Organization (NATO) 'Partnership for Peace'; Russian forces invaded breakaway republic of Chechnya.
1995 Bloody civil war in Chechnya continued.

1996 Re-election of President Yeltsin. Peace plan and final withdrawal of Russian troops from Chechnya. 1997 Peace treaty with Chechnya signed. Yeltsin agreed to expansion of NATO into central Europe, and signed agreement on cooperation with NATO. Russia gained effective admission to G-7 group. World Bank loan and International Monetary Fund (IMF) credit agreed in return for continuing economic reforms.

Practical information

Visa requirements UK: visa required. USA: visa required
Embassy in the UK 13 Kensington Palace Gardens, London W8 4QX. Tel: (0171) 229 3628; fax: (0171) 727 8625
British embassy Sofiyskaya Naberezhnaya 14, Moscow 72. Tel: (095) 956 7200; fax: (095) 956 7420
Embassy in the USA 2650 Wisconsin Avenue NW, Washington, DC 20007. Tel: (202) 298 5700–4; fax: (202) 298 5735
American embassy Novinskiy Bul'var 19/23, Moscow. Tel: (095) 252 2451–9; fax: (095) 956 4261
Chamber of commerce Chamber of Commerce and Industry of the Russian Federation, Ulitsa Ilynka 6, 103684 Moscow. Tel: (095) 925 3581
Office hours 0900–1800/1900 Mon–Fri
Banking hours 0930–1730 Mon–Fri

Time difference GMT +2–12
Chief tourist attractions historic cities of Moscow and St Petersburg, with their cathedrals, fortresses, and art treasures – the Hermitage in St Petersburg has one of the world's largest art collections; the Great Palace at Petrodvorets (formerly Peterhof); Trans-Siberian Railway; the Tver region is famed for its rivers, lakes, reservoirs, and other waterways; the Yaroslavl region has several historic towns including Yaroslavl and Uglich; the Nizhegorodskaya region has the medieval cities of Nizhny Novgorod and Gordets, Vladimir, and Novgorod, one of Russia's oldest and grandest cities, with its famous early churches; the country's landscape includes forests, lakes, marshes, and pasture, with a rich variety of wildlife and geological formations including the volcanoes of Kamchatka and the cave formations near Archangelsk
Major holidays 1, 7 January, 8 March, 15 April, 1–2, 9 May, 12 June, 22 August, 7 November

Rwanda Republic of

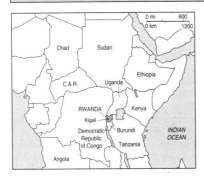

National name *Republika y'u Rwanda*
Area 26,338 sq km/10,169 sq mi
Capital Kigali
Major towns/cities Butare, Ruhengeri, Gisenyi
Physical features high savanna and hills, with volcanic mountains in NW; part of lake Kivu; highest peak Mount Karisimbi 4,507 m/14,792 ft; Kagera River (whose headwaters are the source of the Nile)

Government

Head of state Pasteur Bizimungu from 1994
Head of government Pierre Celestin Rwigema from 1995

Political system transitional
Administrative divisions 10 prefectures
Political parties National Revolutionary Development Movement (MRND), nationalist-socialist, Hutu-oriented; Social Democratic Party (PSD), left of centre; Christian Democratic Party (PDC), Christian, centrist; Republican Democratic Movement (MDR), Hutu nationalist; Liberal Party (PL), moderate centrist; Rwanda Patriotic Front (FPR), Tutsi-led but claims to be multiethnic
Armed forces 40,000 (1995)
Conscription military service is voluntary
Death penalty retains the death penalty for ordinary crimes but can be considered abolitionist in practice (last execution 1982)
Defence spend (% GDP) 4.4 (1995)
Education spend (% GNP) 3.8 (1992); N/A (1993/94)
Health spend (% GDP) 1.9 (1990)

Economy and resources

Currency Rwanda franc
GDP ($ US) 0.6 billion (1994)
Real GDP per capita (PPP) ($ US) 352 (1994)
GDP growth rate 25% (1995e); –12.8% (1990–95)

Average annual inflation 22% (1995e); 10.4% (1985–95)
Foreign debt ($ US) 1 billion (1995)
Trading partners Brazil, Kenya, Belgium, Germany, the Netherlands, South Africa, France, UK
Resources cassiterite (a tin-bearing ore), wolframite (a tungsten-bearing ore), natural gas, gold, columbo-tantalite, beryl
Industries food processing, beverages, tobacco, mining, chemicals, rubber and plastic products, metals and metal products, machinery
Exports coffee, tea, tin ores and concentrates, pyrethrum, quinquina. Principal market: Brazil 45.5% (1995)
Imports food, clothing, mineral fuels and lubricants, construction materials, transport equipment, machinery, tools, consumer goods. Principal source: Kenya 19.3% (1995)
Arable land 44.4% (1993)
Agricultural products sweet potatoes, cassava, dry beans, sorghum, plantains, coffee, tea, pyrethrum; livestock rearing (long-horned Ankole cattle and goats)

Population and society

Population 5,397,000 (1996e)
Population growth rate 2.6% (1990–95); 2.5% (2000–05)

Population density (per sq km) 205 (1996e)
Urban population (% of total) 6 (1995)
Age distribution (% of total population) <15 46%, 15–65 51.5%, >65 2.5% (1995)
Ethnic distribution about 84% belong to the Hutu tribe, most of the remainder being Tutsis; there are also Twa and Pygmy minorities
Languages Kinyarwanda, French (official); Kiswahili
Religions Roman Catholic 54%, animist 23%, Protestant 12%, Muslim 9%
Education (compulsory years) 7
Literacy rate 64% (men); 37% (women) (1995e)
Labour force 52% of population: 92% agriculture, 3% industry, 5% services (1990)
Life expectancy 45 (men); 48 (women) (1995–2000)
Child mortality rate (under 5, per 1,000 live births) 139 (1995)
Physicians 1 per 25,000 people (1991)
Hospital beds 1 per 675 people (1990)
Radios (per 1,000 people) 101 (1995)

Transport

Airports international airports: Kigali (Kanombe), Kamembe; four domestic airfields; total passenger km: 2 mil (1994)
Railroads none
Roads total road network: 14,565 km/ 9,051 mi, of which 9.9% paved (1995e); passenger cars: 1.3 per 1,000 people (1995e)

Chronology

10th century onwards Hutu peoples settled in region formerly inhabited by hunter-gatherer Twa Pygmies, becoming peasant farmers.
14th century onwards Majority Hutu community came under dominance of cattle-owning Tutsi peoples, immigrants from the E, who became a semi-aristocracy and established control through land and cattle contracts.
15th century Ruganzu Bwimba, a Tutsi leader, founded kingdom near Kigali.
17th century Central Rwanda and outlying Hutu communities subdued by Tutsi mwami (king) Ruganzu Ndori.
late 19th century Under the great Tutsi king, Kigeri Rwabugiri, a unified state with a centralized military structure was established.
1890 Known as Ruandi, the Tutsi kingdom, along with neighbouring Burundi, came under nominal German control, as Ruanda-Urundi.
1916 Occupied by Belgium, during World War I.
1923 Belgium granted League of Nations mandate to administer Ruanda-Urundi; they were to rule 'indirectly' through Tutsi chiefs.
1959 Interethnic warfare between Hutu and Tutsi, forcing mwami (king) Kigeri V into exile.
1961 Republic proclaimed after mwami deposed.
1962 Independence from Belgium achieved as Rwanda, with Hutu Grégoire Kayibanda as president; many Tutsis left the country.
1963 20,000 killed in interethnic clashes, after Tutsis exiled in Burundi had launched a raid.
1973 Kayibanda ousted in military coup led by Hutu Maj-Gen Juvenal Habyarimana; this was caused by resentment of Tutsis, who held some key government posts.
1981 Elections created civilian legislation, but dominated by Hutu socialist National Revolutionary Development Movement (MRND), in a one-party state.
1988 Hutu refugees from Burundi massacres streamed into Rwanda.
1990 Government attacked by Rwanda Patriotic Front (FPR), a Tutsi refugee military-political organization based in Uganda, which controlled parts of N Rwanda.
1992 Peace accord with FPR.
1993 United Nations mission sent to monitor peace agreement.
1994 President Habyarimana and Burundian Hutu president Ntaryamira killed in air crash; involvement of FPR suspected. Half a million killed in ensuing civil war, with many Tutsi massacred by Hutu death squads and exodus of 2 million refugees to neighbouring countries. Government fled as FPR forces closed in. French peacekeeping troops established 'safe zone' in SW. Interim coalition government installed, with moderate Hutu and FPR leader, Pasteur Bizimungu, as president.
1995 War-crimes tribunal opened. Government human-rights abuses reported.
1996 Rwanda and Zaire (Congo) on brink of war after Tutsi killings of Hutu in Zaire. Massive Hutu refugee crisis narrowly averted as thousands allowed to return to Rwanda.
1997 Tutsi killings by Hutus.

Practical information

Visa requirements UK: visa required. USA: visa required
Embassy in the UK 42 Aylmer Road, London N2. Tel/fax: (0171) 347 6967
British embassy the British Embassy in Kampala (see Uganda) deals with enquiries relating to Rwanda; British Consulate, BP 356, Avenue Paul VI, Kigali. Tel: 75219 or 75905; telex: 509 (a/b 09 RWANDEX RW)
Embassy in the USA 1714 New Hampshire Avenue NW, Washington, DC 20009. Tel: (202) 232 2882; fax: (202) 232 4544
American embassy Boulevard de la Révolution, Kigali. Tel: (250) 75601/2/3, 72126, 77147; fax: (250) 72128
Chamber of commerce Chambre de Commerce et de l'Industrie du Rwanda, BP 319, Kigali.
Office hours 0800–1600 Mon–Fri; 0800–1200 Sat
Banking hours 0800–1200 and 1400–1800 Mon–Fri; 0800–1300 Sat
Time difference GMT +2
Chief tourist attractions are advised against all but essential travel to Rwanda; random violence and robbery continue
Major holidays 1, 28 January, 1 May, 1, 5 July, 1, 15 August, 25 September, 26 October, 1 November, 1, 8, 24–25 December; variable: Carnival, Corpus Christi, Good Friday

St Kitts and Nevis (or St Christopher and Nevis) Federation of

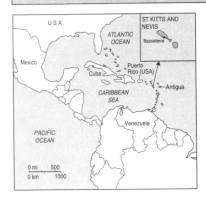

Area 269 sq km/103 sq mi (St Kitts 176 sq km/67 sq mi, Nevis 93 sq km/36 sq mi)
Capital Basseterre (on St Kitts) (and port)
Major towns/cities Charlestown (largest on Nevis), Newcastle, Sandy Point Town, Dieppe Bay Town
Physical features both islands are volcanic; fertile plains on coast; black beaches

Government

Head of state Queen Elizabeth II from 1983, represented by governor general Clement Arrindell from 1983
Head of government Denzil Douglas from 1995
Political system federal constitutional monarchy
Administrative divisions 14 parishes
Political parties People's Action Movement (PAM), centre right; Nevis Reformation Party (NRP), Nevis-separatist, centrist; Labour Party (SKLP), moderate left of centre
Armed forces army disbanded 1981 and absorbed by Volunteer Defence Force; participates in US-sponsored Regional Security System established 1982
Death penalty retained and used for ordinary crimes
Education spend (% GNP) 2.7 (1993)
Health spend (% GDP) 3.4 (1990)

Economy and resources

Currency East Caribbean dollar
GDP ($ US) 220 million (1995e)
Real GDP per capita (PPP) ($ US) 9,380 (1995e)
GDP growth rate 3.4% (1995)
Average annual inflation 2.9% (1995); 5.5% (1985–95)
Foreign debt ($ US) 45.8 million (1994)

Trading partners USA, UK, Trinidad and Tobago, St Vincent and the Grenadines, Canada, Barbados
Industries electronic equipment, food and beverage processing (principally sugar and cane spirit), clothing, footwear, tourism
Exports sugar, manufactures, postage stamps; sugar and sugar products accounted for approximately 40% of export earnings 1992. Principal market: UK 48.7% (1992)
Imports foodstuffs, basic manufactures, machinery, mineral fuels. Principal source: USA 38.7% (1992)
Arable land 22.2% (1993)
Agricultural products sugar cane, coconuts, yams, sweet potatoes, groundnuts, sweet peppers, carrots, cabbages, bananas, cotton; fishing

Population and society

Population 41,000 (1996e)
Population growth rate –0.3 (1990–95)
Population density (per sq km) 158 (1996e)
Urban population (% of total) 42.4 (1995)
Age distribution (% of total population) <15 30%, 15–65 55%, >65 15% (1992)
Ethnic distribution almost entirely of African descent
Language English (official)
Religions Anglican 36%, Methodist 32%, other Protestant 8%, Roman Catholic 10%
Education (compulsory years) 12
Literacy rate 98% (men); 86% (women) (1993e)
Labour force 29.6% agriculture, 24.3% industry, 48.8% services (1985)
Unemployment 4.3% (1995e)
Life expectancy 66 (men); 72 (women) (1995e)
Child mortality rate (under 5, per 1,000 live births) 40 (1995)
Physicians 1 per 2,200 people (1991)
Hospital beds 1 per 158 people (1991)
TV sets (per 1,000 people) 244 (1994)
Radios (per 1,000 people) 668 (1995)

Transport

Airports international airports: Basseterre (Golden Rock), Charlestown on Nevis (Newcastle Airfield); domestic services operate between these
Railroads total length: 36 km/22 mi (serving sugar plantations)
Roads total road network: 310 km/193 mi,

of which 42.5% paved (1995e); passenger cars: 167 per 1,000 people (1993e)

Chronology

1493 Visited by the explorer Christopher Columbus, after whom the main island is named, but for next two centuries the islands were left in the possession of the indigenous Caribs.
1623 and 1628 St Kitts and Nevis islands successively settled by British as their first Caribbean colony, with 2,000 Caribs brutally massacred in 1626.
1783 In the Treaty of Versailles France, which had long disputed British possession, rescinded its claims to the islands, on which sugar cane plantations developed, worked by imported African slaves.
1816 Anguilla was joined politically to the two islands.
1834 Abolition of slavery.
1871–1956 Part of the Leeward Islands Federation.
1932 Centre-left Labour Party founded to campaign for independence.
1937 Internal self-government granted.
1952 Universal adult suffrage granted.
1958–62 Part of the Federation of the West Indies.
1967 St Kitts, Nevis, and Anguilla achieved internal self-government, within the British Commonwealth, with Robert Bradshaw, Labour Party leader, as prime minister.
1970 NRP formed, calling for separation for Nevis.
1971 Anguilla returned to being a British dependency after rebelling against domination by St Kitts.
1978 Bradshaw died; succeeded by Paul Southwell.
1979 Southwell died; succeeded by Lee L Moore.
1980 People's Action Movement (PAM) and NRP centrist coalition government, led by Kennedy Simmonds, formed after inconclusive general election.
1983 Full independence achieved within the Commonwealth.
1993 Simmonds continued in office despite strong criticism of his leadership. Antigovernment demonstrations followed inconclusive general election.
1994 Three-week state of emergency imposed after violent antigovernment riots by Labour Party supporters in Basseterre.
1995 Labour Party won general election; Denzil Douglas became prime minister.

Practical information

Visa requirements UK: visa not required. USA: visa not required
Embassy in the UK High Commission for Eastern Caribbean States, 10 Kensington Court, London W8 5DL. Tel: (0171) 937 9522; fax: (0171) 937 5514
British embassy the British High Commission in St John's (see Antigua and Barbuda) deals with enquiries relating to St Kitts and Nevis
Embassy in the USA 3216 New Mexico Avenue NW, Washington, DC 20016. Tel: (202) 686 2636; fax: (202) 686 5740
American embassy the US does not have an embassy in St Kitts and Nevis; US interests are monitored by the embassy in Bridgetown, Barbados

Chamber of commerce St Kitts and Nevis Chamber of Industry and Commerce, PO Box 332, South Square Street, Basseterre. Tel: (809) 465 2980; fax: (809) 465 4490
Office hours 0800–1200 and 1300–1600 Mon–Fri
Banking hours 0800–1500 Mon–Thu; 0800–1500/1700 Fri and 0830–1100 Sat
Time difference GMT –4
Chief tourist attractions coral beaches on St Kitts' north and west coasts; coconut forests; spectacular mountain scenery on Nevis; St Kitts' historical Brimstone Hill Fort and associations with Lord Nelson and Alexander Hamilton
Major holidays 1 January, 19 September, 25–26, 31 December; variable: Good Friday, Easter Monday, Whit Monday, Labour (May), Queen's Birthday (June), August Monday

St Lucia

Area 617 sq km/238 sq mi
Capital Castries
Major towns/cities Soufrière, Vieux-Fort, Laborie
Major ports Vieux-Fort
Physical features mountainous island with fertile valleys; mainly tropical forest; volcanic peaks; Gros and Petit Pitons

Government

Head of state Queen Elizabeth II from 1979, represented by governor general Stanislaus A James from 1992
Head of government Kenny Anthony from 1997
Political system constitutional monarchy
Administrative divisions eight regions
Political parties United Workers' Party (UWP), moderate left of centre; St Lucia Labour Party (SLP), moderate left of centre; Progressive Labour Party (PLP), moderate left of centre
Armed forces none; participates in the US-sponsored Regional Security System

established 1982; police force numbers around 300
Death penalty retained and used for ordinary crimes
Education spend (% GNP) 5.2 (1992); N/A (1993/94)

Economy and resources

Currency East Caribbean dollar
GDP ($ US) 513 million (1994)
Real GDP per capita (PPP) ($ US) 6,182 (1994)
GDP growth rate 2.2% (1994)
Average annual inflation 5.9% (1995); 3.2% (1985–95e)
Foreign debt ($ US) 114.7 million (1994)
Trading partners USA, UK, Trinidad and Tobago (and other CARICOM member states), Japan, Canada, Italy
Resources geothermal energy
Industries processing of agricultural products (principally coconut oil, meal, and copra), clothing, rum, beer, and other beverages, plastics, paper and packaging, electronic assembly, tourism
Exports bananas, coconut oil, cocoa beans, copra, beverages, tobacco, miscellaneous articles. Principal market: USA 26.3% (1993)
Imports machinery and transport equipment, foodstuffs, basic manufactures, mineral fuels. Principal source: USA 36.2% (1993)
Arable land 8.1% (1993)
Agricultural products bananas, cocoa, coconuts, mangoes, citrus fruits, spices, breadfruit

Population and society

Population 144,000 (1996e)

Population growth rate 1.4% (1990–95)
Population density (per sq km) 232 (1996e)
Urban population (% of total) 48.1 (1995)
Age distribution (% of total population) <15 41.3%, 15–65 52.7%, >65 6% (1992)
Ethnic distribution great majority of African descent
Languages English; French patois
Religion Roman Catholic 90%
Education (compulsory years) 10
Literacy rate 82% (men); 79%(women) (1993e)
Labour force 24% agriculture, 13.6% industry, 62.4% services (1991)
Unemployment 20% (1993e)
Life expectancy 68 (men); 75 (women) (1995e)
Child mortality rate (under 5, per 1,000 live births) 22 (1995)
Physicians 1 per 2,125 people (1993)
Hospital beds 1 per 313 people (1993)
TV sets (per 1,000 people) 211 (1995)
Radios (per 1,000 people) 765 (1995)

Transport

Airports international airports: Castries (Vigie), Vieux Fort (Hewanorra); domestic flights operate between these; aircraft arrivals: 42,436 (1993)
Railroads none
Roads total road network: 1,185 km/ 736 mi, of which 5.1% paved (1995e); passenger cars: 843.5 per 1,000 people (1995e)

Chronology

1502 Sighted by the explorer Christopher

Columbus on St Lucia's day but not settled for more than a century due to hostility of the island's Carib Indian inhabitants.

1635 Settled by French, who brought in slaves to work sugar cane plantations as Carib community was annihilated.

1814 Ceded to Britain as a crown colony, following Treaty of Paris; black African slaves brought in to work sugar cane plantations.

1834 Slavery abolished.

1860s A major coal warehousing centre until the switch to oil and diesel fuels in 1930s.

1871–1956 Part of Leeward Islands Federation.

1951 Universal adult suffrage granted.

1967 Acquired internal self-government as a West Indies associated state.

1979 Independence achieved within Commonwealth with John Compton, leader of United Workers' Party (UWP), as prime minister; Compton was replaced by Allan Louisy, leader of the St Lucia Labour Party (SLP), following elections.

1981 Louisy resigned; replaced by Winston Cenac.

1982 Compton returned to power at head of UWP government.

1991 Integration with other Windward Islands (Dominica, Grenada, and St Vincent) proposed.

1993 Unrest and strikes by farmers and agricultural workers as a result of depressed prices for the chief cash crop, bananas.

1997 SLP won general election; Kenny Anthony appointed prime minister.

Practical information

Visa requirements UK: visa not required. USA: visa not required

Embassy in the UK High Commission for Eastern Caribbean States, 10 Kensington Court, London W8 5DL. Tel: (0171) 937 9522; fax: (0171) 937 5514

British embassy British High Commission, PO Box 227, Derek Walcott Square, Castries. Tel: (809) 452 2484; fax: (809) 453 1543

Embassy in the USA 3216 New Mexico Avenue NW, Washington, DC 20016. Tel: (202) 364 6792–5; fax: (202) 364 6728

American embassy the USA does not have an embassy in Saint Lucia; the ambassador to Saint Lucia resides in Bridgetown, Barbados

Chamber of commerce St Lucia Chamber of Commerce, Industry and Agriculture, PO Box 482, Micond Street, Castries. Tel: (809) 452 3165; fax: (809) 453 6907

Office hours 0800–1600 Mon–Fri

Banking hours generally 0800–1500 Mon–Thu; 0800–1700 Fri (some banks open 0800–1200 Sat)

Time difference GMT –4

Chief tourist attractions tropical climate; sandy beaches; mountain scenery; rich birdlife; historical sites; sulphur baths at Soufrière

Major holidays 1–2 January, 22 February, 1 May, 13, 25–26 December; variable: Carnival, Corpus Christi, Good Friday, Easter Monday, Whit Monday, Emancipation (August), Thanksgiving (October)

St Vincent and the Grenadines

Area 388 sq km/149 sq mi, including islets of the Northern Grenadines 43 sq km/17 sq mi

Capital Kingstown

Major towns/cities Georgetown, Châteaubelair, Layon, Baronallie

Physical features volcanic mountains, thickly forested; La Soufrière volcano

Government

Head of state Queen Elizabeth II from 1979, represented by governor general David Jack from 1989

Head of government James Mitchell from 1984

Political system constitutional monarchy

Administrative divisions six parishes

Political parties New Democratic Party (NDP), right of centre; St Vincent Labour Party (SVLP), moderate left of centre

Armed forces none – police force only; participates in the US-sponsored Regional Security System established 1982

Death penalty retained and used for ordinary crimes

Education spend (% GNP) 6.7 (1993/94)

Health spend (% GDP) 4.4 (1990)

Economy and resources

Currency East Caribbean dollar

GDP ($ US) 256.6 million (1994)

Real GDP per capita (PPP) ($ US) 5,650 (1994)

GDP growth rate 3.8% (1995)

Average annual inflation 2.4% (1995); 3.6% (1985–95)

Foreign debt ($ US) 118.2 million (1994)

Trading partners USA, UK, Trinidad and Tobago, Antigua and Barbuda, Barbados, Canada, Japan, St Lucia

Industries clothing, assembly of electronic equipment, processing of agricultural products (including brewing, flour milling, rum distillation, dairy products), industrial gases, plastics, tourism

Exports bananas, eddoes, dasheen, sweet potatoes, flour, ginger, tannias, plantains. Principal market: UK 32% (1994)

Imports basic manufactures, machinery and transport equipment, food and live animals, mineral fuels, chemicals, miscellaneous manufactured articles. Principal source: USA 36.1% (1994)

Arable land bananas, cocoa, citrus fruits, mangoes, avocado pears, guavas, sugar cane, vegetables, spices; world's leading producer of arrowroot starch; fishing

Population and society

Population 113,000 (1996e)

Population growth rate 0.9% (1990–95)

Population density (per sq km) 290 (1996e)

Urban population (% of total) 47 (1995)
Age distribution (% of total population)
<15 34.6%, 15–65 59.8%, >65 5.6%
(1992)
Ethnic distribution largely of African
origin; most of the original indigenous
Caribs have disappeared
Languages English; French patois
Religions Anglican, Methodist, Roman
Catholic
Education not compulsory
Literacy rate 92% (men); 86% (women)
(1993e)
Labour force 25.1% agriculture, 21.1%
industry, 53.8% services (1991)
Unemployment 20% (1991)
Life expectancy 70 (men); 75 (women)
(1995e)
Child mortality rate (under 5, per 1,000
live births) 23 (1995)
Physicians 1 per 4,037 people (1992)
Hospital beds 1 per 213 people (1991)

TV sets (per 1,000 people) 158 (1995)
Radios (per 1,000 people) 670 (1995)

Transport

Airports international airports:
Kingstown (E T Joshua); four domestic
airports
Railroads none
Roads total road network: 1,020 km/634
mi, of which 30.6% paved (1995e)

Chronology

1498 Main island visited by the explorer
Christopher Columbus on St Vincent's
day.
17th–18th centuries Possession
disputed by France and Britain, with
fierce resistance from the indigenous
Carib community.
1783 Recognized as British crown colony
by Treaty of Versailles.

1795–97 Carib uprising, with French
support, resulted in deportation of 5,000
to Belize and Honduras.
1834 Slavery abolished.
1902 Over 2,000 killed by the eruption of
La Soufrière volcano.
1951 Universal adult suffrage granted.
1958–62 Part of West Indies Federation.
1969 Achieved internal self-government.
1979 Achieved full independence within
Commonwealth, with Milton Cato of
centre-left St Vincent Labour Party
(SVLP) as prime minister.
1981 General strike against new
industrial-relations legislation at a time of
economic recession.
1984 James Mitchell, of the centre-right
New Democratic Party (NDP), replaced
Cato as prime minister.
1991 Integration with other Windward
Islands (Dominica, Grenada, and
St Lucia) proposed.

Practical information

Visa requirements UK: visa not required. USA: visa not
required
Embassy in the UK High Commission for East Caribbean
States, 10 Kensington Court, London W8 5DL.
Tel: (0171) 937 9522; fax: (0171) 937 5514
British embassy British High Commission, PO Box 132,
Granby Street, Kingstown. Tel: (809) 457 1701/2; fax: (809)
456 2720
Embassy in the USA 1717 Massachusetts Avenue NW,
Suite 102, Washington, DC 20036. Tel: (202) 462 7806,
7846; fax: (202) 462 7807
American embassy the USA does not have an embassy in

St Vincent and the Grenadines; the ambassador to St
Vincent and the Grenadines resides in Bridgetown, Barbados
Chamber of commerce St Vincent and the Grenadines
Chamber of Industry and Commerce, PO Box 134, Halifax
Street, Kingstown. Tel: (809) 457 1464; fax: (809) 456 2944
Office hours generally 0800–1600 Mon–Fri
Banking hours 0800–1500 Mon–Thu; 0800–1700 Fri
Time difference GMT –4
Chief tourist attractions famous white beaches, clear
waters, lush vegetation; excellent yachting facilities
Major holidays 1, 22 January, 27 October, 25–26 December;
variable: Carnival (July), Good Friday, Easter Monday, Whit
Monday, Labour (May), Caricom (July), Emancipation
(August)

Samoa Independent State of

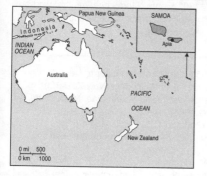

National name *Malotutu'atasi o Samoa
i Sisifo*
Area 2,830 sq km/1,092 sq mi
Capital Apia (on Upolu island) (and chief
port)

Major towns/cities Lalomanu, Falevai,
Tuasivi, Falealupo
Physical features comprises South
Pacific islands of Savai'i and Upolu, with
two smaller tropical islands and
uninhabited islets; mountain ranges on
main islands; coral reefs; over half forested

Government

Head of state King Malietoa Tanumafili II
from 1962
Head of government Tofilau Eti Alesana
from 1988
Political system liberal democracy
Administrative divisions 11 districts
Political parties Human Rights
Protection Party (HRPP), led by Tofilau
Eti Alesana; Samoa Democratic Party
(SDP), led by Le Tagaloa Pita; Samoa

National Development Party (SNDP), led
by Tupuola Taisi Efi and Va'ai Kolone. All
'parties' are personality-based groupings
Armed forces no standing defence
forces; under Treaty of Friendship signed
with New Zealand 1962, the latter acts
as sole agent in Samoa's dealings with
other countries and international
organizations
Death penalty retains the death penalty
for ordinary crimes, but can be
considered abolitionist in practice
Education spend (% GNP) 4.2
(1993/94)
Health spend (% GDP) 5.6 (1990)

Economy and resources

Currency tala, or Samoa dollar
GDP ($ US) 415 million (1995e)

Real GDP per capita (PPP) ($ US)
1,900 (1995e)
GDP growth rate 9.6% (1995e)
Average annual inflation 1% (1995);
10.6% (1985–95e)
Foreign debt ($ US) 154.8 million (1994)
Trading partners New Zealand,
Australia, Fiji, American Samoa, Japan,
USA
Industries coconut-based products,
timber, light engineering, construction
materials, beer, cigarettes, clothing,
leather goods, wire, tourism
Exports coconut cream, beer, cigarettes,
taro, copra, cocoa, bananas, timber.
Principal market: New Zealand 45.5%
(1994)
Imports food and live animals,
machinery and transport equipment,
mineral fuel, clothing and other
manufactured goods. Principal source:
New Zealand 37.3% (1994)
Arable land 19.4% (1993)
Agricultural products coconuts, taro,
copra, bananas, papayas, mangoes,
pineapples, cocoa, taamu, breadfruit,
maize, yams, passion fruit; livestock
rearing (pigs, cattle, poultry, and goats) is
important for local consumption; forest
resources provide an important export
commodity (47% of land was forest and
woodland early 1990s)

Population and society

Population 166,000 (1996e)
Population growth rate 1.1% (1990–95)
Population density (per sq km) 59
(1996e)
Urban population (% of total) 21 (1995)
Age distribution (% of total population)
<15 47%, 15–65 50%, >65 3% (1994)
Ethnic distribution 90% of Samoan
(Polynesian) origin; 10% Euronesian
(mixed European and Polynesian)
Languages English, Samoan (official)

Religions Congregationalist; also
Roman Catholic, Methodist
Education not compulsory
Literacy rate 92% (men); 88% (women)
(1994e)
Labour force 58% agriculture (1990)
Life expectancy 68 (men); 71 (women)
(1995–2000)
Child mortality rate (under 5, per 1,000
live births) 54 (1995)
Physicians 1 per 3,665 people (1992)
Hospital beds 1 per 250 people (1991)
TV sets (per 1,000 people) 41 (1995)
Radios (per 1,000 people) 485 (1995)

Transport

Airports international airports: Apia
(Faleolo); two domestic airstrips
Railroads none
Roads total road network: 781 km/
485 mi, of which 42% paved (1995);
passenger cars: 30 per 1,000 people
(1993e)

Chronology

c. 1000 BC Settled by Polynesians from
Tonga.
AD 950–1250 Ruled by Tongan invaders;
the Matai (chiefly) system was
developed.
15th century United under the Samoan
Queen Salamasina.
1722 Visited by Dutch traders.
1768 Visted by the French navigator
Louis Antoine de Bougainville.
1830 Christian mission established and
islanders were soon converted to
Christianity.
1887–89 Samoan rebellion against
German attempt to depose paramount
ruler and install its own puppet regime.
1889 Under the terms of the Act of
Berlin, Germany took control of the nine
islands of Western Samoa, while the
USA was granted American Samoa, and

Britain Tonga and the Solomon Islands.
1900s More than 2,000 Chinese brought
in to work coconut plantations.
1914 Occupied by New Zealand on the
outbreak of World War I.
1918 Nearly a quarter of the population
died in an influenza epidemic.
1920s Development of nationalist
movement, the Mau, which resorted to
civil disobedience.
1920–61 Administered by New Zealand
under League of Nations and, later,
United Nations mandate.
1959 Local government established,
headed by chief minister Fiame Mata'afa
Mulinu'u.
1961 Referendum favoured
independence.
1962 Independence achieved within
Commonwealth, with Mata'afa as prime
minister, a position he retained (apart
from a short break 1970–73) until his
death in 1975.
1976 Tupuola Taisi Efi became first
nonroyal prime minister.
1982 Va'ai Kolone, the head of the
opposition Human Rights Protection
Party (HRPP), became prime minister,
but was forced to resign over charges of
electoral malpractice. The new HRPP
leader, Tofilau Eti Alesana, became prime
minister.
1985 Tofilau Eti Alesana resigned after
opposition to budget; head of state
invited Va'ai Kolone to lead the
government.
1988 Elections produced hung
parliament, with first Tupuola Efi as prime
minister and then Tofilau Eti Alesana.
1990 Universal adult suffrage introduced
and power of Matai (elected clan
leaders) reduced.
1991 Fiame Naome became first woman
in cabinet; major damage caused by
'Cyclone Val'.

Practical information

Visa requirements UK: visa not required. USA: visa not
required
Embassy for the UK avenue Franklin D Roosevelt 123,
B-1050 Brussels, Belgium. Tel: (2) 660 8454;
fax: (2) 675 0336
British embassy Office of the Honorary British
Representative, c/o Kruse Va'ai and Barlow, PO Box 2029,
Apia. Tel: (685) 21895, fax: (685) 21407
Embassy in the USA 820 Second Avenue, Suite 800, New
York, NY 10017. Tel: (212) 599 6196/7; fax: (212) 599 0797
American embassy 5th floor, Beach Road, Apia. Tel: (685)

21631; fax: (685) 22030 (the US ambassador to New
Zealand and Samoa resides in Wellington, New Zealand)
Chamber of commerce c/o Pacific Forum Line, Matantu-tai,
PO Box 655, Apia. Tel: (685) 20345
Office hours 0800–1200 and 1300–1630 Mon–Fri
Banking hours 0900–1500 Mon–Fri; some banks open
0830–1130 Sat
Time difference GMT –11
Chief tourist attractions pleasant climate; spectacular
scenery
Major holidays 1–2 January, 25 April, 1 June (3 days), 12
October, 25–26 December; variable: Good Friday, Easter
Monday, Holy Saturday

San Marino Most Serene Republic of

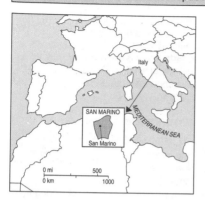

National name *Serenissima Repubblica di San Marino*
Area 61 sq km/24 sq mi
Capital San Marino
Major towns/cities Serravalle (industrial centre), Faetano, Fiorentino, Monte Giardino
Physical features the slope of Mount Titano

Government

Head of state and government two captains regent, elected for a six-month period
Political system direct democracy
Administrative divisions nine districts
Political parties San Marino Christian Democrat Party (PDCS), Christian centrist; Progressive Democratic Party (PDP) (formerly the Communist Party: PCS), moderate left wing; Socialist Party (PS), left of centre
Armed forces voluntary military forces and a paramilitary gendarmerie
Conscription military service is not compulsory, but all citizens between the ages of 15 and 55 may be enlisted in certain circumstances to defend the state
Death penalty abolished 1865

Economy and resources

Currency Italian lira
GDP ($ US) 480 million (1993e)
Real GDP per capita (PPP) ($ US) 20,100 (1993e)
GDP growth rate 2.4% (1993e)
Average annual inflation 5.5% (1993)
Trading partners maintains customs union with Italy (for trade data see Italy)
Resources limestone and other building stone
Industries cement, synthetic rubber, leather, textiles, ceramics, tiles, wine, chemicals, olive oil, tourism, postage stamps
Exports wood machinery, chemicals, wine, olive oil, textiles, tiles, ceramics, varnishes, building stone, lime, chestnuts, hides. Principal market: Italy
Imports consumer goods, raw materials, energy supply. Principal source: Italy
Arable land 17% (1993)
Agricultural products wheat, barley, maize, grapes, olives, fruit, vegetables; viticulture; dairy farming

Population and society

Population 25,000 (1996e)
Population growth rate 1.5% (1990–95)
Population density (per sq km) 415 (1996e)
Urban population (% of total) 94.2 (1995)
Age distribution (% of total population) <15 17.7%, 15–65 69.5%, >65 12.8% (1990)
Ethnic distribution predominantly Italian
Language Italian
Religion Roman Catholic 95%
Education (compulsory years) 8
Literacy rate 98% (men); 98% (women) (1995e)
Labour force 1.6% agriculture, 43% industry, 55.1% services (1995)

Unemployment 4.5% (1994)
Life expectancy 75 (men); 81 (women) (1995e)
Child mortality rate (under 5, per 1,000 live births) 6 (1994)
Physicians 1 per 405 people (1990)
Hospital beds 1 per 163 people (1990)
TV sets (per 1,000 people) 360 (1995)
Radios (per 1,000 people) 600 (1995)

Transport

Airports international airports: none (the closest are at Rimini and Bologna, in Italy; a bus service connects San Marino with Rimini)
Railroads none
Roads total road network: 237 km/147 mi

Chronology

c. AD 301 Founded as a republic (the world's oldest surviving) by St Marinus and a group of Christians who settled there to escape persecution.
12th century Self-governing commune.
1600 Statutes (constitution) provided for a parliamentary form of government, based around the Great and General Council.
1815 Independent status of the republic recognized by the Congress of Vienna.
1862 Treaty with Italy signed; independence recognized under Italy's protection.
1945–57 Communist–Socialist administration in power, eventually ousted in a bloodless 'revolution'.
1957–86 Governed by a series of left-wing and centre-left coalitions.
1971 Treaty with Italy renewed.
1986 Formation of Communist and centre-right Christian Democrat (PDCS) 'grand coalition'.
1992 Joined the United Nations. PDCS withdrew from 'grand coalition' to form alliance with Socialist Party.

Practical information

Visa requirements UK: visa not required. USA: visa not required
Embassy in the UK San Marino has no diplomatic representation in the UK; the UK Department of Trade and Industry has an Italy desk. Tel: (0171) 215 4385; fax (0171) 215 4711
British embassy British Consulate, Lungarno Corsini 2, 50123 Florence, Italy. Tel: (55) 284 133; fax: (55) 219 112
Embassy in the USA San Marino does not have an embassy in the USA

American embassy the USA does not have an embassy in San Marino; the US Consul General in Florence, Italy is accredited to San Marino
Office hours see Italy
Banking hours see Italy
Time difference GMT +1
Chief tourist attractions mild climate; varied scenery; well preserved medieval architecture
Major holidays 1, 6 January, 5 February, 25 March, 1 May, 28 July, 1 August, 3 September, 1 October, 1–2 November, 8, 25–26 December; variable: Corpus Christi, Easter Monday

São Tomé and Príncipe Democratic Republic of

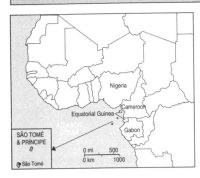

National name *República Democrática de São Tomé e Príncipe*
Area 1,000 sq km/386 sq mi
Capital São Tomé
Major towns/cities São António, Santana, Porto-Alegre
Physical features comprises two main islands and several smaller ones, all volcanic; thickly forested and fertile

Government

Head of state Miguel Trovoada from 1991
Head of government Carlos da Graca from 1994
Political system emergent democratic republic
Administrative divisions two provinces
Political parties Movement for the Liberation of São Tomé e Príncipe–Social Democratic Party (MLSTP–PSD), nationalist socialist; Democratic Convergence Party–Reflection Group (PCD–GR), moderate left of centre; Independent Democratic Action (ADI), centrist
Armed forces no proper army; reorganization of island's armed forces (estimated at 900) and police into two separate police forces (one for public order, the other for criminal investigations) was initiated 1992
Death penalty abolished 1990
Education spend (% GNP) 4.3 (1986); N/A (1993/94)

Economy and resources

Currency dobra
GDP ($ US) 138 million (1994e)
Real GDP per capita (PPP) ($ US) 980 (1994e)
GDP growth rate 1.5% (1994e)
Average annual inflation 38% (1994e); 40.1% (1985–95)

Foreign debt ($ US) 165 million (1995)
Trading partners Portugal, the Netherlands, Germany, Spain, Belgium, France, Japan, Angola
Industries agricultural and timber processing, soft drinks, soap, textiles, beer, bricks, ceramics, shirts
Exports cocoa, copra, coffee, bananas, palm oil. Principal market: the Netherlands 75.7% (1995)
Imports capital goods, food and live animals (of which 60.7% were donations 1994), petroleum and petroleum products. Principal source: Portugal 32.2% (1995)
Arable land 1% (1993)
Agricultural products cocoa, coconuts, copra, bananas, palm oil, cassava, sweet potatoes, yams, coffee; fishing; forest resources (75% of land area was forest and woodland early 1990s)

Population and society

Population 135,100 (1996e)
Population growth rate 2.2% (1990–95)
Population density (per sq km) 140 (1996e)
Urban population (% of total) 46.7 (1995)
Age distribution (% of total population) <15 46.4%, 15–65 38.8%, >65 4.8% (1992)
Ethnic distribution predominantly African
Languages Portuguese (official); Fang (a Bantu language)
Religions Roman Catholic 80%, animist
Education (compulsory years) 4
Literacy rate 85% (men); 62% women (1991e)
Labour force 39.9% agriculture, 13.6% industry, 46.5% services (1991)
Unemployment 38% (1995)
Life expectancy 67 (men); 73 (women) (1994e)
Child mortality rate (under 5, per 1,000 live births) 81 (1995)
Physicians 1 per 1,780 people (1992)
Hospital beds 1 per 214 people (1992)
TV sets 162 (1994)
Radios (per 1,000 people) 271 (1995)

Transport

Airports international airports: São

Tomé; one domestic airport (Príncipe); total passenger km: 8 mil (1994)
Railroads none
Roads total road network: 310 km/ 193 mi, of which 68% paved (1995e); passenger cars: 29.5 per 1,000 people (1995e)

Chronology

1471 First visited by the Portuguese, who imported convicts and slaves to work on sugar plantations in the formerly uninhabited islands.
1522 Became a province of Portugal.
1530 Slaves successfully revolted, forcing plantation owners to flee to Brazil; thereafter became a key staging post for Congo-Americas slave trade.
19th century Forced contract labour used to work coffee and cocoa plantations.
1953 More than 1,000 striking plantation workers gunned down by Portuguese troops.
1960 First political party formed, the forerunner of the socialist-nationalist Movement for the Liberation of São Tomé e Príncipe (MLSTP).
1974 Military coup in Portugal led to strikes, demonstrations, and army mutiny in São Tomé; thousands of Portuguese settlers fled the country.
1975 Independence achieved, with Manuel Pinto da Costa (MLSTP) as president; close links developed with communist bloc, and plantations nationalized.
1984 Formally declared a nonaligned state as economy deteriorated.
1988 Coup attempt against da Costa foiled by Angolan and East European troops.
1990 Influenced by collapse of communism in Eastern Europe, MLSTP abandoned Marxism; new pluralist constitution approved in referendum.
1991 In first multiparty elections, the ruling MLSTP lost its majority and the independent Miguel Trovoada, MLSTP prime minister before 1978, was elected president.
1994 MLSTP returned to power with Carlos da Graca as prime minister.
1995 Abortive coup by junior army officers; unemployment at 38% and foreign indebtedness $165 million.

Saudi Arabia Kingdom of

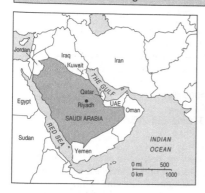

National name *Mamlaka al-'Arabiya as-Sa'udiya*
Area 2,200,518 sq km/849,619 sq mi
Capital Riyadh
Major towns/cities Jiddah, Mecca, Medina, Taif, Dammam, Hufuf
Major ports Jiddah, Dammam, Jubail, Jizan, Yanbu
Physical features desert, sloping to the Persian Gulf from a height of 2,750 m/ 9,000 ft in the W

Government

Head of state and government King Fahd Ibn Abdul Aziz from 1996
Political system absolute monarchy
Administrative divisions 13 provinces
Political parties none
Armed forces 162,500 (1995); paramilitary forces 10,500; National Guard 77,000
Death penalty retained and used for ordinary crimes
Defence spend (% GDP) 10.6 (1995)
Education spend (% GNP) 6.4 (1992); N/A (1993/94)
Health spend (% GDP) 3.1 (1990)

Economy and resources

Currency rial
GDP ($ US) 117.2 billion (1994)
Real GDP per capita (PPP) ($ US) 9,338 (1994)
GDP growth rate 0% (1994); 1.7% (1990–95)
Average annual inflation 5% (1995); 2.7% (1985–95)
Trading partners USA, Japan, Germany, South Korea, France, Italy, Singapore, the Netherlands
Resources petroleum, natural gas, iron ore, limestone, gypsum, marble, clay, salt, gold, uranium, copper, fish
Industries petroleum and petroleum

products, urea and ammonia fertilizers, steel, plastics, cement
Exports crude and refined petroleum, petrochemicals, wheat. Principal market: Japan 17.6% (1995)
Imports machinery and transport equipment, foodstuffs, beverages, tobacco, chemicals and chemical products, base metals and metal manufactures, textiles and clothing. Principal source: USA 21.4% (1995)
Arable land 2% (1993)
Agricultural products wheat, barley, sorghum, millet, tomatoes, dates, watermelons, grapes; livestock (chiefly poultry) and dairy products

Population and society

Population 18,836,000 (1996e)
Population growth rate 2.2% (1990–95); 3.1% (2000–05)
Population density (per sq km) 9 (1996e)
Urban population (% of total) 80 (1995)
Age distribution (% of total population) <15 41.9%, 15–65 55.4%, >65 2.7% (1995)
Ethnic distribution around 90% Arab; 10% Afro-Asian
Language Arabic
Religions Sunni Muslim; there is a Shi'ite minority
Literacy rate 73% (men); 48% (women) (1995e)
Labour force 34% of population: 19% agriculture, 20% industry, 61% services (1990)
Life expectancy 70 (men); 73 (women) (1995–2000)
Child mortality rate (under 5, per 1,000 live births) 34 (1995)
Physicians 1 per 636 people (1994)
Hospital beds 1 per 491 people (1994)
TV sets (per 1,000 people) 257 (1995)
Radios (per 1,000 people) 291 (1995)

Transport

Airports international airports: Riyadh (King Khaled), Dhahran (Al Khobar), Jiddah (King Abdul Aziz); 20 domestic airports; total passenger km: 18,250 mil (1994)
Railroads total length: 1,390 km/864 mi; total passenger km: 139 mil (1993)
Roads total road network: 159,000 km/ 98,803 mi, of which 42.7% paved (1995e); passenger cars: 98.7 per 1,000 people (1995e)

Chronology

622 Muhammad began to unite Arabs in Muslim faith.
7th–8th centuries Muslim Empire expanded, ultimately stretching from India to Spain, with Arabia itself being relegated to a subordinate part.
12th century Decline of Muslim Empire; Arabia grew isolated and internal divisions multiplied.
13th century Mameluke sultans of Egypt became nominal overlords of Hejaz in W Arabia.
1517 Hejaz became a nominal part of Ottoman Empire after Turks conquered Egypt.
18th century Al Saud family united tribes of Nejd in central Arabia in support of the Wahhabi religious movement.
c.1830 The Al Saud established Riyadh as the Wahhabi capital.
c.1870 Turks took effective control of Hejaz and also Hasa on Persian Gulf.
late 19th century Rival Wahhabi dynasty of Ibn Rashid became leaders of Nejd.
1902 Ibn Saud organized Bedouin revolt and regained Riyadh.
1913 Ibn Saud completed the reconquest of Hasa from Turks.
1915 Britain recognized Ibn Saud as emir of Nejd and Hasa.
1916–18 British-backed revolt, under aegis of Sharif Hussein of Mecca, expelled Turks from Arabia.
1919–25 Ibn Saud fought and defeated Sharif Hussein and took control of Hejaz.
1926 Proclamation of Ibn Saud as king of Hejaz and Nejd.
1932 Hejaz and Nejd renamed the United Kingdom of Saudi Arabia.
1933 Saudi Arabia allowed American-owned Standard Oil Company to prospect for oil, which was discovered in Hasa 1938.
1939–45 Although officially neutral in World War II, Saudi Arabia received subsidies from USA and Britain.
1940s Commercial exploitation of oil began, bringing great prosperity.
1953 Ibn Saud died; succeeded by his eldest son, Saud.
1964 King Saud forced to abdicate; succeeded by his brother, Faisal.
1975 King Faisal assassinated; succeeded by his half-brother, Khalid.
1982 King Khalid died; succeeded by his brother, Fahd.
1987 Rioting by Iranian pilgrims caused 400 deaths in Mecca and breach in diplomatic relations with Iran.

1990 Iraqi troops invaded Kuwait and massed on Saudi Arabian border, prompting King Fahd to call for assistance from US and UK forces.
1991 Saudi Arabia fought on Allied side against Iraq in Gulf War.
1992 Under international pressure to move towards democracy, King Fahd formed a 'consultative council' to assist in government of kingdom.

1995 King Fahd suffered a stroke and transferred power to Crown Prince Abdullah.
1996 King Fahd resumed power.

Practical information

Visa requirements UK: visa required. USA: visa required
Embassy in the UK 30 Charles Street, London W1X 7PH. Tel: (0171) 917 3000; fax: (0171) 917 3330
British embassy PO Box 94351, Riyadh 11693. Tel: (1) 488 0077; fax: (1) 488 2373
Embassy in the USA 601 New Hampshire Avenue NW, Washington, DC 20037. Tel: (202) 342 3800
American embassy Collector Road M, Diplomatic Quarter, Riyadh 11693. Tel: (1) 488 3800; fax: (1) 488 7360
Chamber of commerce Riyadh Chamber of Commerce and

Industry, PO Box 596, Riyadh 11421. Tel: (1) 404 0044; fax: (1) 402 1103
Office hours 0900–1300 and 1630–2000 Sat–Thu (2000–0100 during Ramadan)
Banking hours 0830–1200 and 1700–1900 Sat–Wed; 0830–1200 Thu
Time difference GMT +3
Chief tourist attractions the holy cities of Medina, Jiddah, and Mecca – notably Mecca's Al-Harram Mosque and large bazaars, and Medina's numerous mosques and Islamic monuments
Major holidays 23 September; variable: Eid-ul-Adha (7 days), end of Ramadan (4 days)

Senegal Republic of

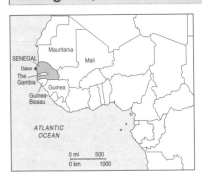

National name *République du Sénégal*
Area 196,200 sq km/75,752 sq mi
Capital Dakar (and chief port)
Major towns/cities Thiès, Kaolack, Saint-Louis, Ziguinchor, Diourbel
Physical features plains rising to hills in SE; swamp and tropical forest in SW; river Senegal; The Gambia forms an enclave within Senegal

Government

Head of state Abdou Diouf from 1981
Head of government Habib Thiam from 1993
Political system emergent socialist democratic republic
Administrative divisions ten regions
Political parties Senegalese Socialist Party (PS), democratic socialist; Senegalese Democratic Party (PDS), centrist
Armed forces 13,400 (1995)

Conscription military services is by selective conscription for two years
Death penalty retains the death penalty for ordinary crimes but can be considered abolitionist in practice (last execution 1967)
Defence spend (% GDP) 1.9 (1995)
Education spend (% GNP) 4.4 (1993)
Health spend (% GDP) 2.3 (1990)

Economy and resources

Currency franc CFA
GDP ($ US) 3.9 billion (1994)
Real GDP per capita (PPP) ($ US) 1,596 (1994)
GDP growth rate 2% (1994); 1.9% (1990–95)
Average annual inflation 7.9% (1995); 3.7% (1985–95)
Foreign debt ($ US) 3.8 billion (1995)
Trading partners France, India, Italy, USA, Mali, Côte d'Ivoire, Nigeria, Thailand
Resources calcium phosphates, aluminium phosphates, salt, natural gas; offshore deposits of petroleum to be developed
Industries food processing (principally fish, groundnuts, palm oil, and sugar), mining, cement, artificial fertilizer, chemicals, textiles, petroleum refining (imported petroleum), tourism
Exports fresh and processed fish, refined petroleum products, chemicals, groundnuts and related products, calcium phosphates and related products.

Principal market: France 30% (1995)
Imports food and live animals, machinery and transport equipment, mineral fuels and lubricants (mainly crude petroleum), basic manufactures, chemicals. Principal source: France 37.8% (1995)
Arable land 11.8% (1993)
Agricultural products groundnuts, cotton, millet, sorghum, rice, maize, cassava, vegetables; fishing

Population and society

Population 8,532,000 (1996e)
Population growth rate 2.5% (1990–95); 2.6% (2000–05)
Population density (per sq km) 43 (1996e)
Urban population (% of total) 42 (1995)
Age distribution (% of total population) <15 44.6%, 15–65 52.5%, >65 2.9% (1995)
Ethnic distribution the Wolof group are the most numerous, comprising about 36% of the population; the Fulani comprise about 21%; the Serer 19%; the Diola 7%; and the Mandingo 6%
Languages French (official); Wolof
Religion mainly Sunni Muslim
Education (compulsory years) 6
Literacy rate 52% (men); 25% (women) (1995e)
Labour force 45% of population: 77% agriculture, 8% industry, 16% services (1990)
Unemployment 10.2% (1993)

Life expectancy 50 (men); 52 (women) (1995–2000)
Child mortality rate (under 5, per 1,000 live births) 110 (1995)
Physicians 1 per 16,667 people (1991)
Hospital beds 1 per 1,698 people (1991)
TV sets (per 1,000 people) 38 (1995)
Radios (per 1,000 people) 120 (1995)

Transport

Airports international airports: Dakar (Dakar-Yoff); three domestic airports and 12 smaller airfields; total passenger km: 224 mil (1994)
Railroads total length: 904 km/562 mi; total passenger km: 173 mil (1991)
Roads total road network: 14,580 km/ 9,060 mi, of which 28.9% paved (1995e); passenger cars: 9.7 per 1,000 people (1995e)

Chronology

10th–11th centuries Links established with N Africa; the Tukolor community was converted to Islam.

1445 First visited by Portuguese explorers.
1659 French founded Saint-Louis as a colony.
17th–18th centuries Export trades in slaves, gums, ivory, and gold developed by European traders.
1854–65 Interior occupied by French · under their imperialist governor, Louis Faidherbe, who checked the expansion of the Islamic Tukulor Empire; Dakar founded.
1902 Became territory of French West Africa.
1946 Became French overseas territory, with own territorial assembly and representation in French parliament.
1948 Leopold Sedar Senghor founded Senegalese Democratic Bloc to campaign for independence.
1959 Formed Federation of Mali with French Sudan.
1960 Achieved independence and withdrew from federation. Senghor, leader of socialist Senegalese

Progressive Union (UPS), became president.
1966 UPS declared only legal party.
1974 Pluralist system re-established.
1976 UPS reconstituted as Socialist Party (PS). Prime Minister Abdou Diouf nominated as Senghor's successor.
1980 Senghor resigned; succeeded by Diouf. Troops sent to defend The Gambia against suspected Libyan invasion.
1981 Military help again sent to The Gambia to thwart coup attempt.
1982 Confederation of Senegambia came into effect.
1983 Diouf re-elected. Post of prime minister abolished.
1989 Diplomatic links with Mauritania severed after 450 died in violent clashes; over 50,000 people repatriated from both countries. Senegambia federation abandoned.
1992 Post of prime minister reinstated. Diplomatic links with Mauritania re-established.
1993 Assembly and presidential elections won by ruling PS.

Practical information

Visa requirements UK: visa not required. USA: visa not required
Embassy in the UK 11 Phillimore Gardens, London W8 7QG. Tel: (0171) 937 0925/6; fax: (0171) 937 8130
British embassy BP 6025, 20 rue du Docteur Guillet, Dakar. Tel: (221) 237 392; fax: (221) 232 766
Embassy in the USA 2112 Wyoming Avenue NW, Washington, DC 20008. Tel: (202) 234 0540/1
American embassy avenue Jean XXIII at the corner of avenue Kleber, Dakar. Tel: (221) 234 296, 233 424; fax: (221) 222 991
Chamber of commerce Chambre de Commerce et

d'Industrie et d'Agriculture de la Région de Dakar, BP 118, 1 place de l'Indépendance, Dakar. Tel: (221) 237 189; telex: 61112
Office hours 0800–1200 and 1430–1800 Mon–Fri; 0800–1200 Sat
Banking hours 0800–1115 and 1430–1630 Mon–Fri
Time difference GMT +/–0
Chief tourist attractions fine beaches; six national parks; the island of Gorée, near Dakar, a former centre for the slave trade
Major holidays 1 January, 1 February, 4 April, 1 May, 15 August, 1 November, 25 December; variable: Eid-ul-Adha, Easter Monday, end of Ramadan, New Year (Muslim), Prophet's Birthday, Whit Monday

Seychelles Republic of

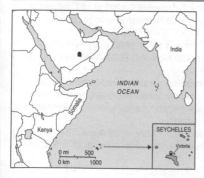

Area 453 sq km/174 sq mi
Capital Victoria (on Mahé island) (and chief port)
Major towns/cities Cascade, Port Glaud, Misere
Physical features comprises two distinct island groups: one, the Granitic group, concentrated, the other, the Outer or Coralline group, widely scattered; totals over 100 islands and islets

Government

Head of state and government

France-Albert René from 1977
Political system emergent democracy
Administrative divisions 23 districts
Political parties Seychelles People's Progressive Front (SPPF), nationalist socialist; Democratic Party (DP), left of centre
Armed forces 300 (1996); plus a coastguard numbering 500 (1995); plus 1,000-strong national guard
Conscription military service is voluntary
Death penalty retains death penalty

only for exceptional crimes such as crimes under military law or crimes committed in exceptional circumstances such as wartime
Defence spend (% GDP) 3.9 (1995)
Education spend (% GNP) 7.4 (1993/94)
Health spend (% GDP) 3.8 (1994e)

Economy and resources

Currency Seychelles rupee
GDP ($ US) 474.6 million (1994e)
Real GDP per capita (PPP) ($ US) 7,891 (1994)
GDP growth rate –3% (1994)
Average annual inflation 1.9% (1994); 3.3% (1985–95)
Foreign debt ($ US) 170.1 million (1994)
Trading partners UK, Singapore, Bahrain, South Africa, France, USA, Réunion, Japan
Resources guano; natural gas and metal deposits were being explored mid-1990s
Industries food processing (including cinnamon, coconuts, and tuna canning), beer and soft drinks, petroleum refining, cigarettes, paper, metals, chemicals, wood products, paints, tourism
Exports fresh and frozen fish, canned tuna, shark fins, cinnamon bark, refined petroleum products. Principal market: UK 16.6% (1995)
Imports machinery and transport equipment, food and live animals, petroleum and petroleum products, chemicals, basic manufactures. Principal source: Singapore 24.7% (1995)
Arable land 2.2% (1993)
Agricultural products coconuts, copra, cinnamon bark, tea, patchouli, vanilla, limes, sweet potatoes, cassava, yams, sugar cane, bananas; poultry meat and

egg production are important for local consumption; fishing

Population and society

Population 74,000 (1996e)
Population growth rate 1.1% (1990–95)
Population density (per sq km) 163 (1996e)
Urban population (% of total) 54.5 (1994)
Age distribution (% of total population) <15 36.8%, 15–65 56.8%, >65 6.4% (1992)
Ethnic distribution predominantly Creole (of mixed African and European descent); small European minority (mostly French and British)
Languages creole (Asian, African, European mixture) 95%, English, French (all official)
Religion Roman Catholic
Education (compulsory years) 9
Literacy rate 86% (men); 82% (women) (1994e)
Labour force 9.9% agriculture, 18.8% industry, 71.3% services (1989)
Unemployment 8.3% (1993)
Life expectancy 69 (men); 78 (women) (1994e)
Child mortality rate (under 5, per 1,000 live births) 20 (1995)
Physicians 1 per 1,032 people (1993)
Hospital beds 1 per 170 people (1993)
TV sets (per 1,000 people) 137 (1995)
Radios (per 1,000 people) 548 (1995)

Transport

Airports international airports: Mahé Island (Seychelles); five domestic airports; total passenger km: 685 mil (1994)
Railroads none
Roads total road network: 270 km/168 mi, of which 62.8% paved (1995e);

passenger cars: 90.7 per 1,000 people (1995e)

Chronology

early 16 century First sighted by European navigators.
1744 Became French colony.
1756 Claimed as French possession and named after an influential French family.
1770s French colonists brought African slaves to settle the previously uninhabited islands; plantations established.
1794 Captured by British during French Revolutionary Wars.
1814 Ceded by France to Britain; incorporated as dependency of Mauritius.
1835 Slavery abolished by British, leading to influx of liberated slaves from Mauritius and Chinese and Indian immigrants.
1903 Became British crown colony, separate from Mauritius.
1963–64 First political parties formed.
1976 Independence achieved from Britain as republic within Commonwealth, with a moderate, James Mancham, of the centre-right Seychelles Democratic Party (SDP) as president.
1977 More radical France-Albert René ousted Mancham in armed bloodless coup and took over presidency; white settlers emigrated.
1979 Nationalistic socialist Seychelles People's Progressive Front (SPPF) became sole legal party under new constitution; became nonaligned state.
1981 Attempted coup by South African mercenaries thwarted.
1991 Multiparty politics promised.
1993 New multiparty constitution adopted. René defeated Mancham, who had returned from exile, in competitive presidential elections; the SPPF won parliamentary elections.

Practical information

Visa requirements UK: visa not required. USA: visa not required
Embassy in the UK 2nd Floor, Eros House, 111 Baker Street, London W1M 1FE. Tel: (0171) 224 1660; fax: (0171) 487 5756
British embassy British High Commission, PO Box 161, 3rd Floor, Victoria House, Victoria, Mahé. Tel: (248) 225 225; fax: (248) 225 127
Embassy in the USA (temporary) 820 Second Avenue, Suite 900F, New York, NY 10017. Tel: (212) 687 9766/7; fax: (212) 922 9177
American embassy 4th Floor, Victoria House, Box 251,

Victoria, Mahé. Tel: (248) 225 256; fax: (248) 225 189
Chamber of commerce Seychelles Chamber of Commerce and Industry, PO Box 443, 38 Premier Building, Victoria, Mahé. Tel: (248) 223 812
Office hours 0800–1200 and 1300–1600 Mon–Fri
Banking hours 0830–1430 Mon–Fri; 0830–1100 Sat
Time difference GMT +4
Chief tourist attractions fine coral beaches; lush tropical vegetation; mountain scenery; rainforest; many unique plant and animal species; national parks and reserves; Aldabra, the largest atoll in the world
Major holidays 1–2 January, 1 May, 5, 29 June, 15 August, 1 November, 8, 25 December; variable: Corpus Christi, Good Friday, Holy Saturday

Sierra Leone Republic of

Area 71,740 sq km/27,698 sq mi
Capital Freetown
Major towns/cities Koidu, Bo, Kenema, Makeni
Major ports Bonthe-Sherbro
Physical features mountains in E; hills and forest; coastal mangrove swamps

Government

Head of state and government Johnny Paul Koroma from 1997
Political system transitional
Administrative divisions four provinces
Political parties All People's Congress (APC), moderate socialist; United Front of Political Movements (UNIFORM), centre left. Party political activity suspended from 1992
Armed forces 6,200 (1996)
Conscription military service is voluntary
Death penalty retained and used for ordinary crimes
Defence spend (% GDP) 5.7 (1995)
Education spend (% GNP) 1.4 (1992); N/A (1993–94)
Health spend (% GDP) 1.7 (1990)

Economy and resources

Currency leone
GDP ($ US) 800 million (1994)
Real GDP per capita (PPP) ($ US) 643 (1994)
GDP growth rate –4% (1994)
Average annual inflation 23.9% (1994); 61.5% (1985–95)
Foreign debt ($ US) 1.2 billion (1995)
Trading partners Belgium/Luxembourg, UK, USA, the Netherlands, Nigeria, Germany
Resources gold, diamonds, bauxite, rutile (titanium dioxide)
Industries palm oil and other agro-based industries, rice mills, textiles, mining, sawn timber, furniture making
Exports rutile, diamonds, bauxite, gold, coffee, cocoa beans. Principal market: Belgium/Luxembourg 42% (1995)
Imports machinery and transport

equipment, food and live animals, basic manufactures, chemicals, miscellaneous manufactured articles. Principal source: UK 18.7% (1995)
Arable land 8% (1993)
Agricultural products rice, cassava, palm oil, coffee, cocoa, bananas; cattle production

Population and society

Population 4,297,000 (1996e)
Population growth rate 2.4% (1990–95); 2.3% (2000–05)
Population density (per sq km) 60 (1996e)
Urban population (% of total) 36 (1995)
Age distribution (% of total population) <15 44.2%, 15–65 52.8%, >65 3% (1995)
Ethnic distribution 18 ethnic groups, 3 of which (the Mende, Tenne, and Limbe) comprise almost 70% of the population
Languages English (official), Krio (a creole language)
Religions animist 52%, Muslim 39%, Protestant 6%, Roman Catholic 2% (1980e)
Education not compulsory
Literacy rate 31% (men); 11% (women) (1995e)
Labour force 37% of population: 67% agriculture, 15% industry, 17% services (1990)
Unemployment 12% (1990)
Life expectancy 40 (men); 43 (women) (1995–2000)
Child mortality rate (under 5, per 1,000 live births) 284 (1995)
Physicians 1 per 11,619 people (1990)
Hospital beds 1 per 873 people (1990)
TV sets (per 1,000 people) 12 (1995)
Radios (per 1,000 people) 250 (1995)

Transport

Airports international airports: Freetown (Lungi); six domestic airports; total passenger km: 66 mil (1994)
Railroads total length: 84 km/52 mi (unused since 1985)
Roads total road network: 11,674 km/ 7,254 mi, of which 11% paved (1995); passenger cars: 4.7 per 1,000 people (1995)

Chronology

15th century Mende, Temne, and Fulani peoples moved from Senegal into region formerly populated by Bulom, Krim, and Gola peoples. The Portuguese, who named the area Serra Lyoa, established a coastal fort, trading manufactured goods for slaves and ivory.
17th century English trading posts

established on Bund and York islands.
1787–92 English abolitionists and philanthropists bought land to establish settlement for liberated and runaway African slaves (including 1,000 rescued from Canada), known as Freetown.
1808 Became a British colony and Freetown a base for British naval operations against slave trade, after parliament declared it illegal.
1896 Hinterland conquered and declared British protectorate.
1951 First political party, Sierra Leone People's Party (SLPP), formed by Dr Milton Margai, who became 'leader of government business', in 1953.
1961 Independence achieved within Commonwealth, with Margai as prime minister.
1964 Margai died; succeeded by his half-brother, Albert Margai.
1965 Free-trade area pact signed with Guinea, Liberia, and Ivory Coast.
1967 Election won by All People's Congress (APC), led by Siaka Stevens, but disputed by army, who set up National Reformation Council and forced governor general to leave the country.
1968 Army revolt brought back Stevens as prime minister.
1971 New constitution made Sierra Leone a republic, with Stevens as president.
1978 New constitution made APC the only legal party.
1985 Stevens retired; succeeded as president and APC leader by Maj-Gen Joseph Momoh.
1989 Attempted coup against President Momoh foiled.
1991 Referendum endorsed multiparty politics and new constitution. Liberian-based rebel group began guerrilla activities.
1992 President Momoh overthrown by military and party politics suspended as National Provisional Ruling Council established under Capt Valentine Strasser; 500,000 Liberians fled to Sierra Leone as a result of civil war.
1995 Ban on political parties lifted. Coup attempt foiled.
1996 Strasser overthrown by deputy, Julius Maada Bio, who was replaced as president by Ahmad Tejan Kabbah after multiparty elections.
1997 President Kabbah's civilian government ousted by mutinous troops in bloody coup. Maj Johnny Paul Koroma seized presidency; Revolutionary Council formed. Government attempt to regain control failed. UN Security Council voted to impose sanctions in an effort to condemn military junta.

Practical information

Visa requirements UK: visa required. USA: visa required
Embassy in the UK 33 Portland Place, London W1N 3AG. Tel: (0171) 636 6483/6; fax: (0171) 323 3159
British embassy British High Commission, Standard Chartered Bank Building, Lightfoot-Boston Street, Freetown. Tel: (232) 223 961/5; telex: 3235 (a/b 3235 UKREP SL)
Embassy in the USA 1701 19th Street NW, Washington, DC 20009. Tel: (202) 939 9261
American embassy Corner of Walpole and Siaka Stevens Streets, Freetown. Tel: (232) 226 481–5; fax: (232) 225 471

Chamber of commerce Sierra Leone Chamber of Commerce, Industry and Agriculture, PO Box 502, 5th Floor, Guma Building, Lamina, Sankoh Street, Freetown. Tel: (232) 226 305; fax: (232) 228 005
Office hours 0800–1200 and 1400–1645 Mon–Fri
Banking hours 0800–1330 Mon–Thu; 0800–1400 Fri
Time difference GMT +/–0
Chief tourist attractions mountains; game reserves; coastline
Major holidays 1 January, 19 April, 25–26 December; variable: Eid-ul-Adha, end of Ramadan, Good Friday, Easter Monday, Prophet's Birthday

Singapore Republic of

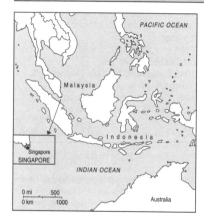

Area 622 sq km/240 sq mi
Capital Singapore City
Major towns/cities Jurong, Changi
Physical features comprises Singapore Island, low and flat, and 57 small islands; Singapore Island is joined to the mainland by causeway across Strait of Johore

Government

Head of state Ong Teng Cheong from 1993
Head of government Goh Chok Tong from 1990
Political system liberal democracy with strict limits on dissent
Administrative divisions five districts
Political parties People's Action Party (PAP), conservative, free market, multi-ethnic; Workers' Party (WP), socialist; Singapore Democratic Party (SDP), liberal pluralist
Armed forces 53,900; 210,000 reserves (1995)
Conscription two years
Death penalty retained and used for ordinary crimes

Defence spend (% GDP) 5.9 (1995)
Education spend (% GNP) 2.4 (1994)
Health spend (% GDP) 1.1 (1990)

Economy and resources

Currency Singapore dollar
GDP ($ US) 68.9 billion (1994)
Real GDP per capita (PPP) ($ US) 20,987 (1994)
GDP growth rate 10.1% (1994); 8.7% (1990–95)
Average annual inflation 3.9% (1985–95)
Trading partners Japan, USA, Malaysia, Hong Kong, Thailand
Resources granite
Industries electrical machinery (particularly radios and televisions), petroleum refining and petroleum products, transport equipment (especially shipbuilding), chemicals, metal products, machinery, food processing, clothing, finance and business services
Exports electrical and nonelectrical machinery, transport equipment, petroleum products, chemicals, rubber, foodstuffs, clothing, metal products, iron and steel, orchids and other plants, aquarium fish. Principal market: USA 18.4% (1996)
Imports electrical and nonelectrical equipment, crude petroleum, transport equipment, chemicals, food and live animals, textiles, scientific and optical instruments, paper and paper products. Principal source: Japan 18.2% (1996)
Arable land 1.6% (1993)
Agricultural products vegetables, plants, orchids; poultry and fish production

Population and society

Population 3,384,000 (1996e)
Population growth rate 1% (1990–95);

0.6% (2000–05)
Population density (per sq km) 5,476 (1996e)
Urban population (% of total) 100 (1995)
Age distribution (% of total population) <15 22.7%, 15–65 70.5%, >65 6.7% (1995)
Ethnic distribution 77% of Chinese ethnic descent, predominantly Hokkien, Teochew, and Cantonese; 15% Malay; 7% Indian, chiefly Tamil
Languages Malay (national tongue), Chinese, Tamil, English (all official)
Religions Buddhist, Taoist, Muslim, Hindu, Christian
Education (compulsory years) 6
Literacy rate 93% (men); 79% (women) (1995e)
Labour force 49% of population: 0% agriculture, 36% industry, 64% services (1990)
Unemployment 2.6% (1994)
Life expectancy 74 (men); 79 (women) (1995–2000)
Child mortality rate (under 5, per 1,000 live births) 6 (1995)
Physicians 1 per 709 people (1994)
Hospital beds 1 per 351 people (1994)
TV sets (per 1,000 people) 361 (1995)
Radios (per 1,000 people) 601 (1995)

Transport

Airports international airports: Singapore (Changi); total passenger km: 44,947 mil (1994)
Railroads total length: 26 km/16 mi
Roads total road network: 2,972 km/ 1,847 mi, of which 97.3% paved (1995); passenger cars: 115.7 per 1,000 people (1995)

Chronology

12th century First trading settlement established on Singapore Island.

14th century Settlement destroyed, probably by Javanese Empire of Mahapahit.
1819 Stamford Raffles of British East India Company obtained Singapore from sultan of Johore.
1826 Straits Settlements formed from British possessions of Singapore, Penang, and Malacca ruled by governor of Bengal.
1832 Singapore became capital of Straits Settlements; the port prospered, attracting Chinese and Indian immigrants.
1851 Responsibility for Straits Settlements fell to governor general of India.
1858 British government, through the India Office, took over administration of Straits Settlements.
1867 Straits Settlements became crown colony of British Empire.

1922 Singapore chosen as principal British military base in Far East.
1942 Japan captured Singapore, taking 70,000 British and Australian prisoners.
1945 British rule restored after defeat of Japan.
1946 Singapore became separate crown colony.
1959 Internal self-government achieved as State of Singapore with Lee Kuan Yew (PAP) as prime minister.
1960s Rapid development as leading commercial and financial centre.
1963 Singapore combined with Federation of Malaya, Sabah, and Sarawak to form Federation of Malaysia.
1965 Became independent republic after withdrawing from Federation of Malaysia in protest at alleged discrimination against ethnic Chinese.

1971 Last remaining British military bases closed.
1984 Two opposition members elected to national assembly for first time.
1986 Opposition leader convicted of perjury and prohibited from standing for election.
1988 Ruling PAP won all but one of available assembly seats; increasingly authoritarian rule.
1990 Lee Kuan Yew retired from premiership after 31 years; succeeded by Goh Chok Tong.
1992 Lee Kuan Yew surrendered PAP leadership to Goh Chok Tong.
1993 Ong Teng Cheong elected president with increased powers.
1996 Constitutional change introduced, allowing better representation of minority races.
1997 PAP, led by Prime Minister Goh Chok Tong, won general election.

Practical information

Visa requirements UK: visa not required. USA: visa not required
Embassy in the UK 9 Wilton Cresscent, London SW1X 8SA. Tel: (0171) 235 8315; fax: (0171) 245 6583
British embassy British High Commission, Tanglin Road, Singapore 1024. Tel: (65) 473 9333; fax: (65) 475 2320
Embassy in the USA 3501 International Place NW, Washington, DC 20008. Tel: (202) 537 3100; fax: (202) 537 0876
American embassy 30 Hill Street, Singapore 0617. Tel: (65) 338 0251; fax: (65) 338 4550

Chamber of commerce Singapore International Chamber of Commerce, 10-001 John Hancock Tower, 6 Raffles Quay, Singapore 0104. Tel: (65) 224 1255; fax: (65) 224 2785
Banking hours 1000–1500 Mon–Fri; 1100–1600 Sat
Time difference GMT +8
Chief tourist attractions blend of cultures; excellent shopping facilities; Singapore City, with its Tiger Balm Gardens, Sultan Mosque, Buddhist temples, House of Jade, bird park, botanical gardens, and national museum
Major holidays 1 January, 1 May, 9 August, 25 December; variable: Eid-ul-Adha, Diwali, end of Ramadan, Good Friday, New Year (Chinese, January/February, 2 days), Vesak

---

Slovak Republic Slovak Republic

National name *Slovenská Republika*
Area 49,035 sq km/18,932 sq mi
Capital Bratislava
Major towns/cities Košice, Nitra, Prešov, Banská Bystrica, Žilina, Trnava
Physical features Western range of Carpathian Mountains, including Tatra and Beskids in N; Danube plain in S; numerous lakes and mineral springs

Government

Head of state Michal Kovak from 1993
Head of government Vladimir Meciar from 1994
Political system emergent democracy
Administrative divisions four regions
Political parties Movement for a Democratic Slovakia (MDS), centre left, nationalist-populist; Democratic Union of Slovakia (DUS), centrist; Christian Democratic Movement (KSDH), right of centre; Slovak National Party (SNP), nationalist; Party of the Democratic Left (PDL), reform socialist, (ex-communist); Association of Workers of Slovakia, left wing; Hungarian Coalition, ethnic Hungarian
Armed forces 47,000 (1995)
Conscription military service is compulsory for 18 months
Death penalty abolished 1990
Defence spend (% GDP) 2.8 (1995)
Education spend (% GNP) 4.3 (1994)
Health spend (% GDP) 5.9 (1991)

Economy and resources

Currency Slovak koruna (based on Czechoslovak koruna)
GDP ($ US) 12 billion (1994)
Real GDP per capita (PPP) ($ US) 6,389 (1994)
GDP growth rate 6.9% (1996); −2.8% (1990–95)
Average annual inflation 5.8% (1996); 10.4% (1985–95e)
Foreign debt ($ US) 5.7 billion (1995)

Trading partners Czech Republic, Germany, Russia, Austria, Hungary, Italy
Resources brown coal, lignite, copper, zinc, lead, iron ore, magnesite
Industries chemicals, pharmaceuticals, heavy engineering, munitions, mining, textiles, clothing, glass, leather, footwear, construction materials, televisions, transport equipment (cars, lorries, and motorcycles)
Exports basic manufactures, machinery and transport equipment, miscellaneous manufactured articles. Principal market: Czech Republic 35.2% (1995)
Imports machinery and transport equipment, mineral fuels and lubricants, basic manufactures, chemicals and related products. Principal source: Czech Republic 27.5% (1995)
Arable land 51% (1993)
Agricultural products wheat and other grains, sugar beet, potatoes and other vegetables; livestock rearing (cattle, pigs, and poultry)

Population and society

Population 5,347,000 (1996e)
Population growth rate 0.4% (1990–95); 0.4% (2000–05)
Population density (per sq km) 109 (1996e)
Urban population (% of total) 59 (1995)
Age distribution (% of total population) <15 22.9%, 15–65 66.3%, >65 10.8% (1995)
Ethnic distribution 87% ethnic Slovak, 11% ethnic Hungarian (Magyar); small Czech, Moravian, Silesian, and Romany communities
Language Slovak (official)
Religions Roman Catholic (over 50%), Lutheran, Reformist, Orthodox
Education (compulsory years) 9
Literacy rate 99% (men); 99% (women) (1995e)
Labour force 12.1% agriculture, 39.8%

industry, 48.1% services (1993)
Unemployment 13.1% (1995); 12.6% (1996)
Life expectancy 67 (men); 75 (women) (1995–2000)
Child mortality rate (under 5, per 1,000 live births) 15 (1995)
Physicians 1 per 287 people (1993)
Hospital beds 1 per 127 people (1993)
TV sets (per 1,000 people) 476 (1995)
Radios (per 1,000 people) 570 (1995)

Transport

Airports international airports: Bratislava (M R Stefanik), Poprad-Tatry, Košice, Piešt'any, Sliač; domestic services to most major cities; total passenger km: 12 mil (1994)
Railroads total length: 3,665 km/2,277 mi; total passenger km: 44 mil (1993)
Roads total road network: 17,868 km/ 11,103 mi, of which 98.8% paved (1995); passenger cars: 189.2 per 1,000 people (1995)

Chronology

9th century Part of kingdom of Greater Moravia, in Czech lands to W, founded by Slavic Prince Sviatopluk; Christianity adopted.
906 Came under Magyar (Hungarian) domination and adopted Roman Catholicism.
1526 Came under Austrian Habsburg rule.
1867 With creation of dual Austro-Hungarian monarchy, came under separate Hungarian rule; policy of forced Magyarization stimulated a revival of Slovak national consciousness.
1918 Austro-Hungarian Empire dismembered; Slovaks joined Czechs to form independent state of Czechoslovakia. Slovak-born Tomas Masaryk remained president until 1935, but political and economic power became

concentrated in Czech lands.
1939 Germany annexed Czechoslovakia, which became Axis puppet state under the Slovak autonomist leader Monsignor Jozef Tiso; Jews persecuted.
1944 Popular revolt against German rule ('Slovak Uprising').
1945 Liberated from German rule by Soviet troops; Czechoslovakia re-established.
1948 Communists assumed power in Czechoslovakia.
1950s Heavy industry introduced into previously rural Slovakia; Slovak nationalism and Catholic Church forcibly suppressed.
1968–69 'Prague Spring' political reforms introduced by Slovak-born Communist Party leader Alexander Dubček; Warsaw Pact forces invaded Czechoslovakia to stamp out reforms; Slovak Socialist Republic, with autonomy over local affairs, created under new federal constitution; Slovak-born Gustáv Husák became Communist Party leader in Czechoslovakia.
1989 Prodemocracy demonstrations in Bratislava; new political parties, including centre-left People Against Violence (PAV), formed and later legalized; Communist Party stripped of powers; new government formed, with ex-dissident playwright Václav Havel as president.
1990 Slovak nationalists polled strongly in multiparty elections, with Vladimir Meciar (PAV) becoming prime minister.
1991 Increasing Slovak separatism, as economy deteriorated with exposure to market forces. Meciar formed PAV splinter group, Movement for a Democratic Slovakia (HZDS), pledging greater autonomy for Slovakia. Pro-Meciar rallies in Bratislava followed his dismissal.
1992 Meciar returned to power following electoral victory for HZDS. Slovak

---

Practical information

Visa requirements UK: visa not required. USA: visa not required
Embassy in the UK 25 Kensington Palace Gardens, London W8 4QY. Tel: (0171) 243 0803; fax: (0171) 727 5824
British embassy Grösslingova 35, 811 09 Bratislava. Tel: (7) 364 420; fax: (7) 364 396
Embassy in the USA (temporary) Suite 380, 2201 Wisconsin Avenue NW, Washington, DC 20007. Tel: (202) 965 5161; fax: (202) 965 5166
American embassy Hviezdoslavovo Namestie 4, 811 02 Bratislava. Tel: (7) 533 0861, 3338; fax: (7) 533 5439

Chamber of commerce Slovak Chamber of Commerce and Industry, Gorkéno 9, 816 03 Bratislava. Tel: (7) 362 787; fax: (7) 362 222
Office hours 0800–1600 Mon–Fri
Banking hours generally 0800–1700 Mon–Fri
Time difference GMT +1
Chief tourist attractions ski resorts in the High and Low Tatras and other mountain regions; historic towns, including Bratislava, Košice, Nitra, and Bardejov; numerous castles and mansions; over 20 spa resorts with thermal and mineral springs
Major holidays 1, 6 January, 1 May, 5 July, 29 August, 1, 15 September, 1 November, 24–26 December; variable: Good Friday, Easter Monday

parliament's declaration of sovereignty led to Havel's resignation; 'velvet divorce' agreement on separate Czech and Slovak states established a free-trade customs union.
1993 Slovak Republic entered United Nations and Council of Europe as sovereign state, with Meciar as prime minister and Michal Kovac, formerly of HZDS, as president.

1994 Joined NATO's 'Partnership for Peace' programme. Meciar ousted on no-confidence vote, but later returned after new elections, heading 'red-brown' coalition government that included ultranationalists and socialists.
1995 Second wave of mass privatization postponed; Slovak made sole official language; Treaty of Friendship and Cooperation signed with Hungary,

easing tensions among Hungarian minority community.
1996 Anti-Meciar coalition formed, the Slovak Democratic Coalition, comprising five opposition parties.
1997 Referendum on NATO membership and direct presidential elections declared invalid after government caused confusion over voting papers.

Slovenia Republic of

National name *Republika Slovenija*
Area 20,251 sq km/7,818 sq mi
Capital Ljubljana
Major towns/cities Maribor, Kranj, Celji, Velenje, Koper (Capodistria)
Major ports Koper
Physical features mountainous; Sava and Drava rivers

Government

Head of state Milan Kučan from 1990
Head of government Janez Drnovšek from 1992
Political system emergent democracy
Administrative divisions 62 districts
Political parties Slovenian Christian Democrats (SKD), right of centre; Slovenian People's Party (SPP), conservative; Liberal Democratic Party of Slovenia (LDS), centrist; Slovenian Nationalist Party (SNS), right-wing nationalist; Democratic Party of Slovenia (LDP), left of centre; United List of Social Democrats (ZLSD) left of centre, ex-communist
Armed forces 8,000 (1995); plus reserve forces of 70,000 and a paramilitary police force of 4,500
Conscription military service is compulsory for seven months
Death penalty abolished 1989

Defence spend (% GDP) 1.5% (1995)
Education spend (% GNP) 5.6% (1994)

Economy and resources

Currency tolar
GDP ($ US) 14 billion (1994)
Real GDP per capita (PPP) ($ US) 10,404 (1994)
GDP growth rate 3.1% (1996)
Average annual inflation 10.7% (1996)
Foreign debt ($ US) 3.5 million (1995)
Trading partners Germany, Italy, Croatia, France, Austria, former USSR, USA
Resources coal, lead, zinc; small reserves/deposits of natural gas, petroleum, salt, uranium
Industries metallurgy, furniture making, sports equipment, electrical equipment, food processing, textiles, paper and paper products, chemicals, wood and wood products
Exports raw materials, semi-finished goods, machinery, electric motors, transport equipment, foodstuffs, clothing, pharmaceuticals, cosmetics. Principal market: Germany 30.7% (1996)
Imports machinery and transport equipment, raw materials, semi-finished goods, foodstuffs, chemicals, miscellaneous manufactured articles, mineral fuels and lubricants. Principal source: Germany 21.7% (1996)
Arable land 15% (1993)
Agricultural products wheat, maize, sugar beet, potatoes, cabbage, fruits (especially grapes); forest resources (approximately 45% of total land area was forest 1994)

Population and society

Population 1,924,000 (1996e)
Population growth rate 0.3% (1990–95); –0.1% (2000–05)
Population density (per sq km) 95 (1996e)

Urban population (% of total) 64 (1995)
Age distribution (% of total population) <15 18.3%, 15–65 69.2%, >65 12.4% (1995)
Ethnic distribution 98% of Slovene origin, 3% ethnic Croat, 2% Serb
Language Slovene, resembling Serbo-Croat, written in Roman characters
Religion Roman Catholic
Education (compulsory years) 8
Literacy rate 96% (men); 96% (women) (1995e)
Labour force 11.5% agriculture, 42.3% industry, 46.2% services (1994)
Unemployment 13.9% (1996)
Life expectancy 69 (men); 78 (women) (1995–2000)
Child mortality rate (under 5, per 1,000 live births) 8 (1995)
Physicians 1 per 481 people (1995)
Hospital beds 1 per 171 people (1995)
TV sets (per 1,000 people) 327 (1995)
Radios (per 1,000 people) 384 (1995)

Transport

Airports international airports: Ljubljana (Brnik), Maribor, Portorož; two domestic airports; total passenger km: 329 mil (1994)
Railroads total length: 1,201 km/746 mi; total passenger km: 566 mil (1993)
Roads total road network: 14,760 km/ 9,172 mi, of which 80% paved (1995); passenger cars: 351 per 1,000 people (1995)

Chronology

1st century BC Came under Roman rule.
AD 395 In division of Roman Empire, stayed in W, along with Croatia and Bosnia.
6th century Settled by the Slovene South Slavs.
7th century Adopted Christianity as Roman Catholics.
8th–9th centuries Under successive rule of Franks and dukes of Bavaria.

907–55 Came under Hungarian domination.
1335 Absorbed in Austro-Hungarian Habsburg Empire, as part of Austrian crownlands of Carniola, Styria, and Carinthia.
1848 Slovene struggle for independence began.
1918 On collapse of Habsburg Empire, Slovenia united with Serbia, Croatia, and Montenegro to form the 'Kingdom of Serbs, Croats and Slovenes', under Serbian Karageorgevic dynasty.
1929 Kingdom became known as Yugoslavia.
1941–45 Occupied by Nazi Germany and Italy during World War II; anti-Nazi Slovene Liberation Front formed and

became allies of Marshal Tito's communist-led Partisans.
1945 Became constituent republic of Yugoslav Socialist Federal Republic.
mid-1980s Slovenian Communist Party liberalized itself and agreed to free elections. Yugoslav counterintelligence (KOV) began repression.
1989 Constitution changed to allow secession from federation.
1990 Nationalist Democratic Opposition of Slovenia (DEMOS) coalition secured victory in first multiparty parliamentary elections; Milan Kučan, a reform communist, became president. Sovereignty declared. Independence overwhelmingly approved in referendum.

1991 Seceded from Yugoslav federation, along with Croatia; 100 killed after Yugoslav federal army intervened; cease-fire brokered by European Community (EC) brought withdrawal of Yugoslav army.
1992 Janez Drnovšek, a centrist Liberal Democrat, appointed prime minister; independence recognized by EC and USA. Admitted into United Nations. Liberal Democrats and Christian Democrats won assembly elections.
1996 Governing coalition weakened by withdrawal of ZLSD. LDS failed to win overall majority in assembly elections.
1997 New government formed by ruling LDS, led by Prime Minister Janez Drnovsek.

Practical information

Visa requirements UK: visa not required. USA: visa not required
Embassy in the UK Suite 1, Cavendish Court, 11–15 Wigmore Street, London W1H 9LA. Tel: (0171) 495 7775; fax: (0171) 495 7776
British embassy 4th Floor, Trg Republike 3, 61000 Ljubljana. Tel: (61) 125 7191; fax: (61) 125 0174
Embassy in the USA 1525 New Hampshire Avenue NW, Washington, DC 20036. Tel: (202) 667 5363; fax: (202) 667 4563
American embassy Prazakova 4, 1000 Ljubljana; Tel: (386) 61 301 427; fax: (386) 61 301 401

Chamber of commerce Chamber of Economy of Slovenia, Slovenska 41, 61000 Ljubljana. Tel: (61) 125 0122; fax: (61) 219 536
Office hours 0700–1500 Mon–Fri
Banking hours 0800–1800 Mon–Fri
Time difference GMT +1
Chief tourist attractions Alps in N; Mediterranean beaches; Karst limestone regions, with more than 6,000 caves; Ljubljana, with its castle, cathedral, Tivoli sports park, fairs, and festivals
Major holidays 1–2 January, 8 February, 27 April, 1–2 May, 25 June, 15 August, 31 October, 1 November, 25–26 December; variable: Good Friday, Easter Monday

Solomon Islands

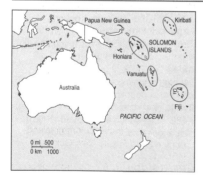

Area 27,600 sq km/10,656 sq mi
Capital Honiara (on Guadalcanal) (and port)
Major towns/cities Gizo, Kieta, Auki
Major ports Yandina
Physical features comprises all but the northernmost islands (which belong to Papua New Guinea) of a Melanesian archipelago stretching nearly 1,500 km/

900 mi. The largest is Guadalcanal (area 6,500 sq km/2,510 sq mi); others are Malaita, San Cristobal, New Georgia, Santa Isabel, Choiseul; mainly mountainous and forested

Government

Head of state Queen Elizabeth II, represented by governor general Moses Pitakaka from 1994
Head of government Solomon Malamoni from 1994
Political system constitutional monarchy
Administrative divisions seven provinces and a capital territory
Political parties Group for National Unity and Reconciliation (GNUR), centrist coalition; National Coalition Partners (NCP), broad-based coalition; People's Progressive Party (PPP); People's Alliance Party (PAP)
Armed forces no standing army; 80-strong marine wing of police force (1995)

Death penalty laws do not provide for the death penalty for any crime
Education spend (% GNP) 4.2 (1993/94)
Health spend (% GDP) 5 (1990)

Economy and resources

Currency Solomon Island dollar
GDP ($ US) 218 million (1994e)
Real GDP per capita (PPP) ($ US) 2,310 (1994e)
GDP growth rate 5.2% (1994)
Average annual inflation 13.6% (1994); 11.7% (1985–95)
Foreign debt ($ US) 196 million (1993)
Trading partners Australia, Japan, UK, New Zealand, Singapore, South Korea
Resources bauxite, phosphates, gold, silver, copper, lead, zinc, cobalt, asbestos, nickel
Industries food processing (mainly palm oil and rice milling, fish, and coconut-based products), saw milling, logging,

tobacco, furniture, handicrafts, boats, clothing, tourism
Exports timber, fish products, oil palm products, copra, cocoa, coconut oil. Principal market: Japan 41.1% (1994)
Imports rice, machinery and transport equipment, meat preparations, refined sugar, mineral fuels, basic manufactures, construction materials. Principal source: Australia 37.2% (1994)
Arable land 2% (1993)
Agricultural products coconuts, cocoa, rice, cassava, sweet potatoes, yam, taro, banana, palm oil; livestock rearing (pigs and cattle); fishing, sea shells, and seaweed farming; forestry

Population and society

Population 391,000 (1996e)
Population growth rate 3.3% (1990–95); 3.1% (2000–05)
Population density (per sq km) 14 (1996e)
Urban population (% of total) 17 (1995)
Age distribution (% of total population) <15 44.2%, 15–65 52.9%, >65 2.9% (1995)
Ethnic distribution 93% Melanesian, 4% Polynesian, 1.5% Micronesian, 0.7% European, 0.2% Chinese
Languages English (official); there are some 120 Melanesian dialects spoken by 85% of the population, and Papuan and Polynesian languages
Religions Anglican, Roman Catholic, South Sea Evangelical, other Protestant
Education not compulsory
Literacy rate 60% (men); 60% (women) (1994e)
Labour force 27.4% agriculture, 13.7% industry, 58.9% services (1993)
Life expectancy 70 (men); 74 (women) (1995–2000)
Child mortality rate (under 5, per 1,000 live births) 31 (1995)

Physicians 1 per 5,190 people (1991)
Hospital beds 1 per 193 people (1990)
TV sets (per 1,000 people) 6.1 (1995)
Radios (per 1,000 people) 122 (1995)

Transport

Airports international airport: Honiara (Henderson); 26 domestic airports; total passenger km: 5 mil (1994)
Railroads none
Roads total road network: 1,330 km/826 mi, of which 2.4% paved (1995e)

Chronology

1568 The islands, rumoured in South America to be the legendary gold-rich 'Islands of Solomon', were first sighted by Spanish navigator Alvaro de Mendana, journeying from Peru.
1595 and 1606 Unsuccessful Spanish efforts to settle the islands, which had long been peopled by Melanesians.
later 18th century Visited again by Europeans.
1840s Christian missions established.
1870s Development of copra export trade and shipment of islanders to work on sugar cane plantations in Australia and Fiji.
1886 Northern Solomon Islands became German protectorate.
1893 Southern Solomon Islands placed under British protection.
1899 Germany ceded Solomon Islands possessions to Britain in return for British recognition of its claims to Western Samoa.
1900 Unified British Solomon Islands Protectorate formed and placed under jurisdiction of Western Pacific High Commission (WPHC), with its headquarters in Fiji.
1942–43 Occupied by Japan. Site of fierce fighting, especially on Guadalcanal, which was recaptured by US forces, with the loss of 21,000 Japanese and 5,000

US troops.
1943–50 Development of Marching Rule (Ma'asina Ruru) cargo cult populist movement on Malaita island, campaigning for self-rule.
1945 Headquarters of WPHC moved to Honiara.
1960 Legislative and executive councils established by constitution.
1974 Became substantially self-governing, with Solomon Mamaloni of centre-left People's Progressive Party (PPP) as chief minister.
1976 Became fully self-governing, with Peter Kenilorea of right-of-centre Solomon Islands United Party (SIUPA) as chief minister.
1978 Independence achieved from Britain within Commonwealth, with Kenilorea as prime minister.
1981 Mamaloni (PPP) became prime minister, pledging to decentralize power.
1984 Kenilorea returned to power, heading coalition government.
1986 Kenilorea resigned after allegations of corruption; replaced by his deputy, Ezekiel Alebua.
1988 Kenilorea elected deputy prime minister. Joined Vanuatu and Papua New Guinea to form Spearhead Group, aiming to preserve Melanesian cultural traditions.
1989 Mamaloni, now leader of People's Alliance Party (PAP), appointed prime minister.
1990 Mamaloni resigned as PAP party leader, but continued as head of a government of national unity, which included Kenilorea as foreign minister.
1993 New Mamaloni-led coalition won largest number of seats in general election, but Francis Billy Hilly, an independent politician, appointed prime minister.
1994 Billy Hilly resigned; Mamaloni returned to power.

Practical information

Visa requirements UK: visa not required. USA: visa not required
Embassy for the UK BP 3, avenue de l'Yser 13, B-1040 Brussels, Belgium. Tel: (2) 732 7082; fax: (2) 732 6885; Solomon Islands Honorary Consulate, 19 Springfield Road, London SW19 7AL. Tel: (0181) 296 6232; fax: (0181) 946 1744
British embassy British High Commission, PO Box 676, Telekom House, Mendana Avenue, Honiara. Tel: (677) 21705/6; fax: (677) 20765
Embassy in the USA the Solomon Islands do not have an embassy in the USA; the ambassador to the USA traditionally

resides in Honiara, Solomon Islands
American embassy the US embassy in the Solomon Islands closed July 1993; the ambassador to Papua New Guinea is accredited to the Solomon Islands
Chamber of commerce PO Box 64, Honiara. Tel: (677) 22960
Office hours 0800–1200 and 1300–1630 Mon–Fri; 0730–1200 Sat
Banking hours 0830–1500 Mon–Fri
Time difference GMT +11
Chief tourist attractions tourism restricted by relative inaccessibility of country and inadequacy of tourist facilities
Major holidays 1 January, 7 July, 25–26 December; variable: Good Friday, Easter Monday, Holy Saturday, Whit Monday, Queen's Birthday (June)

Somalia Somali Democratic Republic

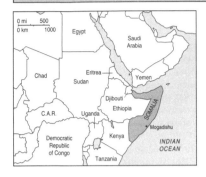

National name *Jamhuriyadda Dimugradiga ee Soomaliya*
Area 637,700 sq km/246,215 sq mi
Capital Mogadishu (and port)
Major towns/cities Hargeysa, Berbera, Kismayo, Marka
Major ports Berbera, Marka, Kismayo
Physical features mainly flat, with hills in N

Government

Head of state and government (interim) Hussein Aidid from 1996
Political system transitional
Administrative divisions 18 regions
Political parties parties are mainly clan-based and include the United Somali Congress (USC), Hawiye clan; Somali Patriotic Movement (SPM), Darod clan; Somali Southern Democratic Front (SSDF), Majertein clan; Somali Democratic Alliance (SDA), Gadabursi clan; United Somali Front (USF), Issa clan; Somali National Movement (SNM) based in self-proclaimed Somaliland Republic
Armed forces following breakdown of government 1991 there were no national armed forces; police force of 8,000 formed 1994; UN withdrawal 1995
Death penalty retained and used for ordinary crimes
Education spend (% GNP) 0.5 (1985); N/A (1993/94)
Health spend (% GDP) 0.9 (1990)

Economy and resources

Currency Somali shilling
GDP ($ US) 3.6 billion (1995e)
Real GDP per capita (PPP) ($ US) 650 (1995e)
GDP growth rate 2% (1995e)
Average annual inflation N/A
Foreign debt ($ US) 2.5 billion (1991–93)

Trading partners Saudi Arabia, Kenya, Italy, USA, UK, Germany, Ethiopia
Resources chromium, coal, salt, tin, zinc, copper, gypsum, manganese, iron ore, uranium, gold, silver; deposits of petroleum and natural gas have been discovered but remain unexploited
Industries food processing (especially sugar refining), textiles, petroleum refining, processing of hides and skins
Exports livestock, skins and hides, bananas, fish and fish products, myrrh. Principal market: Saudi Arabia 47.6% (1992)
Imports petroleum, fertilizers, foodstuffs, machinery and parts, manufacturing raw materials. Principal source: Italy 30% (1991)
Arable land 1.6% (1993)
Agricultural products bananas, sugar cane, maize, sorghum, grapefruit, seed cotton; agriculture is based on livestock rearing (cattle, sheep, goats, and camels) – 80% of the population depend on this activity

Population and society

Population 9,822,000 (1996e)
Population growth rate 1.3% (1990–95); 3% (2000–05)
Population density (per sq km) 15 (1996e)
Urban population (% of total) 26 (1995)
Age distribution (% of total population) <15 47.5%, 15–65 49.8%, >65 2.7% (1995)
Ethnic distribution 98% indigenous Somali (about 84% Hamitic and 14% Bantu); population is divided into around 100 clans
Languages Somali, Arabic (both official), Italian, English
Religion Sunni Muslim
Education (compulsory years) 8
Literacy rate 36% (men); 14% (women) (1995e)
Labour force 44% of population: 75% agriculture, 8% industry, 16% services (1990)
Life expectancy 47 (men); 51 (women) (1995–2000)
Child mortality rate (under 5, per 1,000 live births) 211 (1995)
Physicians 1 per 5,691 people (1990)
Hospital beds 1 per 897 people (1990)
TV sets (per 1,000 people) 13 (1995)
Radios (per 1,000 people) 42 (1995)

Transport

Airports international airports: Mogadishu, Berbera; seven domestic airports and airfields; passengers carried: 46,000 (1991)
Railroads none
Roads total road network: 23,000 km/14,292 mi, of which 12.2% paved (1995e); passenger cars: 0.2 per 1,000 people (1995e)

Chronology

8th–10th centuries Arab ancestors of Somali clan families migrated to the region and introduced Sunni Islam; coastal trading cities, including Mogadishu, were formed by Arabian immigrants and developed into sultanates.
11th–14th century Southward and westward movement of Somalis and Islamization of Christian Ethiopian interior.
early 16th century Portuguese contacts with coastal region.
1820s First British contacts with N Somalia.
1884–87 British protectorate of Somaliland established in N.
1889 Italian protectorate of Somalia established in S.
1927 Italian Somalia became a colony and part of Italian East Africa from 1936.
1941 Italian Somalia occupied by Britain during World War II.
1943 Somali Youth League (SYL) formed as nationalist party.
1950 Italy resumed control over Italian Somalia under UN trusteeship.
1960 Independence achieved from Italy and Britain as Somalia, with Aden Abdullah Osman as president.
1963 Border dispute with Kenya; diplomatic relations broken with Britain for five years.
1967 Dr Abdirashid Ali Shermarke (SYL) became president.
1969 President Ibrahim Egal assassinated in army coup led by Maj-Gen Muhammad Siad Barre; constitution suspended, political parties banned, Supreme Revolutionary Council set up, and socialist-Islamic state formed.
1972 20,000 died in severe drought.
1978 Defeated in eight-month war with Ethiopia fought on behalf of Somali guerrillas in Ogaden to the SW. Armed insurrection began in N and hundreds of thousands became refugees.

1979 New constitution for socialist one-party state dominated by Somali Revolutionary Socialist Party (SRSP).
1982 Antigovernment Ethiopian-backed Somali National Movement (SNM) formed in N. Oppressive countermeasures by government.
late 1980s Guerrilla activity increased in N as civil war intensified.
1991 Mogadishu captured by rebels; Barre fled; Ali Mahdi Muhammad named president; free elections promised.

Secession of NE Somalia, as Somaliland Republic, announced but not recognized internationally.
1992 Widespread famine. Western food-aid convoys hijacked by 'warlords'. United Nations peacekeeping troops, led by US Marines, sent in to protect relief operations.
1993 Leaders of armed factions (excepting Somaliland-based faction) agreed to federal system of government. US-led UN forces destroyed headquarters

of warlord Gen Muhammad Farah Aidid after killing of Pakistani peacekeepers.
1994 Ali Mahdi Muhammad and Aidid signed truce. Majority of Western peacekeeping troops withdrawn, but clan-based fighting continued.
1995 Last UN peacekeepers withdrawn.
1996 Aidid killed in renewed faction fighting; his son Hussein Aidid succeeded him, as interim president.
1997 Peace agreement signed between USC and breakaway USC-SNA.

Practical Information

Visa requirements UK: visa required. USA: visa required
Embassy in the UK no diplomatic representation at present
British embassy all staff have been withdrawn for the present; the British Embassy in Addis Ababa (see Ethiopia) deals with enquiries relating to Somalia
Embassy in the USA Somalia does not have an embassy in the USA (operations ceased on 8 May 1991)
American embassy the USA does not have an embassy in Somalia; US interests are represented by the US Embassy in

Nairobi at Moi Avenue and Hailé Sélassie Avenue; mailing address: PO Box 30137, Unit 64100, Nairobi; APO AE 09831. Tel: (2) 334 141; fax: (2) 340 838
Office hours 0800–1400 Sat–Thu
Banking hours 0800–1130 Sat–Thu
Time difference GMT +3
Chief tourist attractions beaches protected by a coral reef, among the longest in the world
Major holidays 1 January, 1 May, 26 June, 1 July, 21 October (2 days); variable: Eid-ul-Adha (2 days), end of Ramadan (2 days), Prophet's Birthday

---

South Africa Republic of

National name *Republiek van Suid-Afrika*
Area 1,222,081 sq km/471,845 sq mi
Capital Cape Town (legislative) (and port), Pretoria (administrative), Bloemfontein (judicial)
Major towns/cities Johannesburg, Durban, Port Elizabeth, Vereeniging, East London, Pietermaritzburg, Kimberley
Major ports Durban, Port Elizabeth, East London
Physical features southern end of large plateau, fringed by mountains and lowland coastal margin; Drakensberg

Mountains, Table Mountain; Limpopo and Orange rivers
Territories Marion Island and Prince Edward Island in the Antarctic

Government

Head of state and government Nelson Mandela from 1994
Political system liberal democracy
Administrative divisions nine provinces
Political parties African National Congress (ANC), left of centre; National Party (NP), right of centre; Inkatha Freedom Party (IFP), centrist, multiracial (formerly Zulu nationalist); Freedom Front (FF), right wing; Democratic Party (DP), moderate, centre left, multiracial; Pan-Africanist Congress (PAC), black, left wing; African Christian Democratic Party (ACDP), Christian, right of centre
Armed forces 136,900 (1995)
Conscription none
Death penalty for exceptional crimes only (from 1995)
Defence spend (% GDP) 2.9 (1995)
Education spend (% GNP) 7.1 (1993/94)
Health spend (% GDP) 3.2 (1990)

Economy and resources

Currency rand
GDP ($ US) 121.9 billion (1994)

Real GDP per capita ($ US) 4,291 (1994)
GDP growth rate 2.3% (1994); 0.6% (1990–95)
Average annual inflation 9% (1994); 13.7% (1985–95)
Trading partners Germany, Italy, UK, USA, Japan, Switzerland
Resources gold (world's largest producer), coal, platinum, iron ore, diamonds, chromium, manganese, limestone, asbestos, fluorspar, uranium, copper, lead, zinc, petroleum, natural gas
Industries chemicals, petroleum and coal products, gold, diamonds, food processing, transport equipment, iron and steel, metal products, machinery, fertilizers, textiles, paper and paper products, clothing, wood and cork products
Exports metals and metal products, gold, precious and semiprecious stones, mineral products and chemicals, natural cultured pearls, machinery and mechanical appliances, wool, maize, fruit, sugar. Principal market: Italy 7.8% (1995)
Imports machinery and electrical equipment, transport equipment, chemical products, mechanical appliances, textiles and clothing,

vegetable products, wood, pulp, paper and paper products. Principal source: Germany 15.9% (1995)

Arable land 10.1% (1993)

Agricultural products maize, sugar cane, sorghum, fruits, wheat, groundnuts, grapes, vegetables; livestock rearing, wool production

Population and society

Population 38,000,000 (1996e)

Population growth rate 2.2% (1990–95); 2.1% (2000–05)

Population density (per sq km) 35 (1996e)

Urban population (% of total) 51 (1995)

Age distribution (% of total population) <15 37.3%, 15–65 58.3%, >65 4.4% (1995)

Ethnic distribution 77% of the population is black African, 12% white (of European descent), 9% of mixed African–European descent, and 2% Asian.

Languages English and Afrikaans (both official); main African languages: Xhosa, Zulu, and Sesotho (all official)

Religions Dutch Reformed Church and other Christian denominations, Hindu, Muslim

Education (compulsory years) 10

Literacy rate 81% (men); 81% (women) (1995e)

Labour force 39% of population: 14% agriculture, 32% industry, 55% services (1990)

Unemployment 29% (early 1995)

Life expectancy 62 (men); 68 (women) (1995–2000)

Child mortality rate (under 5, per 1,000 live births) 67 (1995)

Physicians 1 per 1,528 people (1994)

Hospital beds 1 per 269 people (1994)

TV sets (per 1,000 people) 109 (1995)

Radios (per 1,000 people) 316 (1995)

Transport

Airports international airports: Cape Town (D F Malan), Durban (Louis Botha), Johannesburg (Jan Smuts); six domestic airports, 212 public aerodromes; total passenger km: 12,352 mil (1994)

Railroads total length: 21,595 km/ 13,419 mi; total passenger km: 71,573 mil (1993)

Roads total road network: 182,580 km/ 114,112 mi, of which 32.8% paved (1995e); passenger cars: 96 per 1,000 people (1995e)

Chronology

1652 Dutch East India Company established colony at Cape Town as a port of call.

1795 Britain occupied Cape after France conquered the Netherlands.

1814 Britain bought Cape Town and hinterland from the Netherlands for £6 million.

1820s Zulu people established military kingdom under Shaka.

1836–38 The Great Trek: 10,000 Dutch settlers (known as Boers, meaning 'farmers') migrated north to escape British rule.

1843 Britain established colony of Natal on E coast.

1852–54 Britain recognized Boer republics of Transvaal and Orange Free State.

1872 The Cape became self-governing colony within British Empire.

1877 Britain annexed Transvaal.

1879 Zulu War: Britain destroyed power of Zulus.

1881 First Boer War: Transvaal Boers defeated British at Majuba Hill and regained independence.

1886 Disovery of gold on Witwatersrand attracted many migrant miners (uitlanders) to Transvaal, which denied them full citizenship.

1895 Jameson Raid: uitlanders, backed by Cecil Rhodes, tried to overthrow President Paul Kruger of Transvaal.

1899–1902 Second South African War (also known as Boer War): dispute over rights of uitlanders led to conflict which ended with British annexation of Boer republics.

1907 Britain granted internal self-government to Transvaal and Orange Free State on whites-only franchise.

1910 Cape Colony, Natal, Transvaal, and Orange Free State formed Union of South Africa, with Louis Botha as prime minister.

1912 Gen Barry Hertzog founded (Boer) Nationalist Party; ANC formed to campaign for rights of black majority.

1914 Boer revolt in Orange Free State suppressed; South African troops fought for British Empire in World War I.

1919 Jan Smuts succeeded Botha as premier; South West Africa (Namibia) became South African mandate.

1924 Hertzog became prime minister, aiming to sharpen racial segregation and loosen ties with British Empire.

1939–45 Smuts led South Africa into World War II despite neutralism of Hertzog; South African troops fought with Allies in Middle East, East Africa, and Italy.

1948 Policy of apartheid ('separateness') adopted when National Party (NP) took power under Daniel Malan; continued by his successors Johannes Strijdom 1954–58, Hendrik Verwoerd 1958–66, B J Vorster 1966–78, and P J Botha 1978–89.

1950 Entire population classified by race; Group Areas Act segregated blacks and whites; ANC responded with campaign of civil disobedience.

1960 70 black demonstrators killed at Sharpville; ANC banned.

1961 South Africa left Commonwealth and became republic.

1964 ANC leader Nelson Mandela sentenced to life imprisonment.

1967 Terrorism Act introduced indefinite detention without trial.

1970s Over 3 million people forcibly resettled in black 'homelands'.

1976 Over 600 killed in clashes between black protesters and security forces in Soweto.

1984 New constitution gave segregated representation to coloureds and Asians, but continued to exclude blacks.

1985 Growth of violence in black townships led to proclamation of state of emergency.

1986 USA and Commonwealth imposed limited economic sanctions against South Africa.

1989 F W de Klerk succeeded P W Botha as president; public facilities desegregated; many ANC activists released.

1990 Ban on ANC lifted; Mandela released; talks began between government and ANC; daily average of 35 murders; Namibia became independent.

1991 De Klerk repealed remaining apartheid laws; sanctions lifted; severe fighting between ANC and Zulu Inkatha movement.

1993 Interim majority rule constitution adopted; de Klerk and Mandela agreed to form government of national unity after free elections.

1994 ANC victory in first nonracial elections; Mandela became president; Commonwealth membership restored.

1996 De Klerk withdrew NP from coalition after new constitution failed to provide for power-sharing after 1999.

1997 New constitution signed by President Mandela. F W de Klerk announced his retirement from politics.

Practical information

Visa requirements UK: visa not required. USA: visa not required

Embassy in the UK South Africa House, Trafalgar Square, London WC2N 5DP. Tel: (0171) 930 4488; fax: (0171) 451 7284

British embassy British High Commission, 255 Hill Street, Arcadia, Pretoria 0002. Tel: (12) 433 121; fax: (12) 433 207

Embassy in the USA 3051 Massachusetts Avenue NW, Washington, DC 20008. Tel: (202) 232 4400

American embassy 877 Pretorius Street, Arcadia 0083.

Tel: (12) 342 1048; fax: (12) 342 2244

Chamber of commerce South African Chamber of Business, PO Box 91267, Auckland Park 20006. Tel: (11) 482 2524; fax: (11) 726 1344

Office hours 0830–1630 Mon–Fri

Banking hours 0830–1530 Mon–Fri; 0800–1130 Sat

Time difference GMT +2

Chief tourist attractions fine climate; varied scenery; wildlife reserves

Major holidays 1 January, 21 March, 27 April, 1 May, 16 June, 9 August , 24 September, 16, 25–26 December; variable: Good Friday

Spain Kingdom of

National name *Reino de España*
Area 504,750 sq km/194,883 sq mi
Capital Madrid
Major towns/cities Barcelona, Valencia, Zaragoza, Seville, Málaga, Bilbao, Las Palmas de Gran Canarias, Murcia, Córdoba, Palma de Mallorca, Granada
Major ports Barcelona, Valencia, Cartagena, Málaga, Cádiz, Vigo, Santander, Bilbao
Physical features central plateau with mountain ranges, lowlands in S; rivers Ebro, Douro, Tagus, Guadiana, Guadalquivir; Iberian Plateau (Meseta); Pyrenees, Cantabrian Mountains, Andalusian Mountains, Sierra Nevada
Territories Balearic and Canary Islands; in N Africa: Ceuta, Melilla, Alhucemas, Chafarinas Is, Peñón de Vélez

Government

Head of state King Juan Carlos I from 1975
Head of government José Maria Aznar from 1996
Political system constitutional monarchy
Administrative divisions 17 autonomous regions (contain 50 provinces)

Political parties Socialist Workers' Party (PSOE), democratic socialist; Popular Party (PP), centre right
Armed forces 206,000 (1995)
Conscription nine months
Death penalty abolished 1995
Defence spend (% GDP) 1.5 (1995)
Education spend (% GNP) 4.7 (1993/94)
Health spend (% GDP) 5.7 (1993)

Economy and resources

Currency peseta
GDP ($ US) 581.6 billion (1996)
Real GDP per capita (PPP) ($ US) 14,794 (1996)
GDP growth rate 2.9% (1996); 1.1% (1990–95)
Average annual inflation 3.6% (1996); 6.3% (1985–95)
Trading partners EU (principally France, Germany, Italy, and UK), USA, Japan
Resources coal, lignite, anthracite, copper, iron, zinc, uranium, potassium salts
Industries machinery, motor vehicles, textiles, footwear, chemicals, electrical appliances, wine, olive oil, fishery products, steel, cement, tourism
Exports motor vehicles, machinery and electrical equipment, vegetable products, metals and their manufactures, foodstuffs. Principal market: France 20.5% (1995)
Imports machinery and transport equipment, electrical equipment, petroleum and petroleum products, chemicals, consumer goods. Principal source: France 17.1% (1995)
Arable land 29.7% (1993)
Agricultural products barley, wheat, sugar beet, vegetables, citrus fruit, grapes, olives; fishing (one of world's largest fishing fleets)

Population and society

Population 39,674,000 (1996e)
Population growth rate 0.2% (1990–95); 0% (2000–05)
Population density (per sq km) 79 (1996e)
Urban population (% of total) 76 (1995)
Age distribution (% of total population) <15 16.5%, 15–65 68.6%, >65 14.9% (1995)
Ethnic distribution mostly of Moorish, Roman, and Carthaginian descent
Languages Spanish (Castilian, official), Basque, Catalan, Galician
Religion Roman Catholic
Education (compulsory years) 10
Literacy rate 97% (men); 93% (women) (1995e)
Labour force 41% of population: 12% agriculture, 33% industry, 55% services (1990)
Unemployment 22.1% (1996)
Life expectancy 75 (men); 81 (women) (1995–2000)
Child mortality rate (under 5, per 1,000 live births) 9 (1995)
Physicians 1 per 246 people (1994)
Hospital beds 1 per 229 people (1994)
TV sets (per 1,000 people) 404 (1995)
Radios (per 1,000 people) 314 (1995)

Transport

Airports international airports: Alicante (Altet), Barcelona (del Prat), Bilbao, Tenerife (2), Madrid (Barajas), Málaga, Santiago de Compostela, Gerona, Gran Canaria, Lanzarote, Palma de Mallorca, Mahon, Valladolid, Seville, Valencia, Zarragoza; domestic services to all major towns; total passenger km: 26,654 mil (1994)

Railroads total length: 15,372 km/ 9,552 mi; total passenger km: 16,044 mil (1995)
Roads total road network: 343,197 km/ 213,263 mi, of which 99% paved (1995); passenger cars: 351.3 per 1,000 people (1995)

Chronology

2nd century BC Roman conquest of the Iberian peninsula, which became the province of Hispania.
5th century AD After the fall of the Roman Empire, Iberia was overrun by Vandals and Visigoths.
711 Muslims invaded from N Africa and overthrew Visigoth kingdom.
9th century Christians in northern Spain formed kingdoms of Asturias, Aragón, Navarre, and Léon, and county of Castile.
10th century Abd-al-Rahman III established caliphate of Córdoba; Muslim culture at its height in Spain.
1230 Léon and Castile united under Ferdinand III, who drove the Muslims from most of southern Spain.
14th century Spain consisted of Christian kingdoms of Castile, Aragón, and Navarre, and the Muslim emirate of Granada.
1469 Marriage of Ferdinand of Aragón and Isabella of Castile; kingdoms united on their accession 1479.
1492 Conquest of Granada ended Muslim rule in Spain.
1494 Treaty of Tordesillas; Spain and Portugal divided newly discovered America; Spain became a world power.
1519–56 Emperor Charles V was both King of Spain and Archduke of Austria;

he also ruled Naples, Sicily, and the Low Countries; Habsburgs dominant in Europe.
1555 Charles V divided his domains between Spain and Austria before retiring; Spain retained the Low Countries and southern Italy as well as South American colonies.
1568 Dutch rebelled against Spanish rule; Spain recognized independence of Dutch Republic 1648.
1580 Philip II of Spain inherited the throne of Portugal, where Spanish rule lasted until 1640.
1588 The Spanish Armada: attempt to invade England defeated.
17th century Spanish power declined amid wars, corruption, inflation, and loss of civil and religious freedom.
1701–14 War of the Spanish Succession: allied powers fought France to prevent Philip of Bourbon inheriting throne of Spain.
1713–14 Treaties of Utrecht and Rastat: Bourbon dynasty recognized, but Spain lost Gibraltar, southern Italy, and Spanish Netherlands.
1793 Spain declared war on revolutionary France; reduced to a French client state 1795.
1808 Napoleon installed his brother Joseph as King of Spain.
1808–14 Peninsular War: British forces played a large part in liberating Spain and restoring Bourbon dynasty.
1810–30 Spain lost control of its South American colonies.
1833–39 Carlist civil war: Don Carlos (backed by conservatives) unsuccessfully contested the succession of his niece Isabella II (backed by liberals).

1870 Offer of Spanish throne to Leopold of Hohenzollern-Sigmaringen sparked Franco-Prussian War.
1873–74 First republic ended by military coup which restored Bourbon dynasty with Alfonso XII.
1898 Spanish-Amercian War: Spain lost Cuba and Philippines.
1923–30 Dictatorship of General Primo de Rivera with support of Alfonso XIII.
1931 Proclamation of Second Republic, initially dominated by anticlerical radicals and socialists.
1933 Moderates and Catholics won elections; insurrection by socialists and Catalans 1934.
1936 Left-wing Popular Front narrowly won fresh elections; General Francisco Franco launched military rebellion.
1936–39 Spanish Civil War: Nationalists (with significant Italian and German support) defeated Republicans (with limited Soviet support); Franco became dictator of nationalist-fascist regime.
1941 Though officially neutral in World War II, Spain sent 40,000 troops to fight USSR.
1955 Spain admitted to the United Nations (UN).
1975 Death of Franco; succeeded by King Juan Carlos I.
1978 Referendum endorsed democratic constitution.
1982 Socialists took office under Felipe González; Spain joined the North Atlantic Treaty Organization (NATO); Basque separatist organization (ETA) stepped up terrorist campaign.
1986 Spain joined the European Economic Community (EEC).
1996 José Maria Aznar formed a minority PP government.

Practical information

Visa requirements UK: visa not required. USA: visa not required
Embassy in the UK 24 Belgrave Square, London SW1X 8SB. Tel: (0171) 235 5555/6/7; fax: (0171) 235 9905
British embassy Calle de Fernando el Santo 16, 28010 Madrid. Tel: (1) 319 0200, fax: (1) 319 0423
Embassy in the USA 2375 Pennsylvania Avenue NW, Washington, DC 20037. Tel: (202) 452 0100, 728 2340; fax: (202) 833 5670
American embassy Serrano 75, 28006 Madrid. Tel: (1) 577 4000, 2301; fax: (1) 577 5735
Chamber of commerce Consejo Superior de Cámaras Officiales de Comercio, Industria y Navigación de España, Calle Claudio Coello 19, 1°, 28001 Madrid.

Tel: (1) 575 3400; fax: (1) 435 2392
Office hours 0800–1500, or 0900–1300 and 1600/1630–1900/1930 Mon–Fri
Banking hours 0900–1400 Mon–Fri; 0900–1300 Sat (except during summer)
Time difference GMT +1
Chief tourist attractions climate; beaches; mountain scenery; winter resorts on the Canary Islands; many cities of historical interest, including Madrid, Seville, Córdoba, Barcelona, and Valencia, with their cathedrals, churches, palaces, fortresses, and museums
Major holidays 1, 6 January, 19 March (most areas), 1 May, 25 July, 15 August, 12 October, 1 November, 8, 25 December; variable: Corpus Christi, Good Friday, Holy Saturday, Holy Thursday

Sri Lanka Democratic Socialist Republic of (formerly to 1972 *Ceylon*)

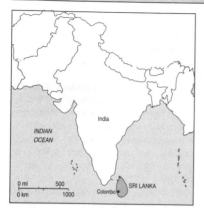

National name *Sri Lanka Prajathanthrika Samajawadi Janarajaya*
Area 65,610 sq km/25,332 sq mi
Capital Colombo (and chief port)
Major towns/cities Kandy, Dehiwala-Mount Lavinia, Moratuwa, Jaffna, Kotte, Kandy
Major ports Jaffna, Galle, Negombo, Trincomalee
Physical features flat in N and around coast; hills and mountains in S and central interior

Government

Head of state Chandrika Bandaranaike Kumaratunga from 1994
Head of government Sirimavo Bandaranaike from 1994
Political system liberal democratic republic
Administrative divisions nine provinces, 25 districts
Political parties United National Party (UNP), right of centre; Sri Lanka Freedom Party (SLFP), left of centre; Democratic United National Front (DUNF), centre left; Tamil United Liberation Front (TULF), Tamil autonomy (banned from 1983); Eelam People's Revolutionary Liberation Front (EPRLF), Indian-backed Tamil-secessionist 'Tamil Tigers'; People's Liberation Front (JVP), Sinhalese-chauvinist, left wing (banned 1971–77 and 1983–88)
Armed forces 125,300 (1995); plus paramilitary forces numbering around 110,200
Conscription military service is voluntary

Death penalty retains the death penalty for ordinary crimes but can be considered abolitionist in practice (last execution 1976)
Defence spend (% GDP) 4.9 (1995)
Education spend (% GNP) 3.7 (1994)
Health spend (% GDP) 1.5 (1993)

Economy and resources

Currency Sri Lankan rupee
GDP ($ US) 11.7 billion (1994)
Real GDP per capita (PPP) ($ US) 3,277 (1994)
GDP growth rate 5.6% (1994); 4.8% (1990–95)
Average annual inflation 7.6% (1995); 11.1% (1985–95)
Foreign debt ($ US) 8.23 million (1995)
Trading partners Japan, USA, Germany, UK, India, Malaysia, Singapore, Hong Kong, Taiwan, China, Iran
Resources gemstones, graphite, iron ore, monazite, rutile, uranium, iemenite sands, limestone, salt, clay
Industries food processing, textiles, clothing, petroleum refining, leather goods, chemicals, rubber, plastics, tourism
Exports clothing and textiles, tea (world's largest exporter and third-largest producer), precious and semi-precious stones, coconuts and coconut products, rubber. Principal market: USA 34% (1996)
Imports machinery and transport equipment, petroleum, food and live animals, beverages, construction materials. Principal source: India 10.4% (1996)
Arable land 14.2% (1993)
Agricultural products rice, tea, rubber, coconuts; livestock rearing (cattle, buffaloes, pigs, and poultry); fishing

Population and society

Population 18,100,000 (1996e)
Population growth rate 1.3% (1990–95); 1.1% (2000–05)
Population density (per sq km) 276 (1996e)
Urban population (% of total) 22 (1995)
Age distribution (% of total population) <15 30.7%, 15–65 63.5%, >65 5.8% (1995)
Ethnic distribution 73% Sinhalese, 19% Tamil, and 7% Moors or Muslims

(concentrated in E); the Tamil community is divided between the long-settled 'Sri Lankan Tamils' (11% of the population), who reside in northern and eastern coastal areas, and the more recent immigrant 'Indian Tamils' (8%), who settled in the Kandyan highlands during the 19th and 20th centuries
Languages Sinhala, Tamil, English
Religions Buddhist 69%, Hindu 15%, Muslim 8%, Christian 7%
Education (compulsory years) 10
Literacy rate 93% (men); 83% (women) (1995e)
Labour force 42.6% agriculture, 11.7% industry, 45.7% services (1993)
Unemployment 13.6% (1994)
Life expectancy 71 (men); 75 (women) (1995–2000)
Child mortality rate (under 5, per 1,000 live births) 19 (1995)
Physicians 1 per 5,203 people (1992)
Hospital beds 1 per 362 people (1992)
TV sets (per 1,000 people) 51 (1995)
Radios (per 1,000 people) 206 (1995)

Transport

Airports international airports: Colombo (Katunayake); five domestic airports; total passenger km: 3,683 mil (1994)
Railroads total length: 1,484 km/922 mi; total passenger km: 3,265 mil (1994)
Roads total road network: 102,600 km/63,756 mi, of which 39% paved (1995e); passenger cars: 12.3 per 1,000 people (1995e)

Chronology

c. 550 BC Arrival of the Sinhalese, led by Vijaya, from N India, displacing long-settled Veddas.
5th century BC Sinhalese kingdom of Anuradhapura founded by King Pandukabaya.
c. 250–210 BC Buddhism, brought from India, became established in Sri Lanka.
AD 992 Downfall of Anuradhapura kingdom, defeated by South Indian Colas.
1070 Overthrow of Colas by Vijayabahu I and establishment of the Sinhalese kingdom of Polonnaruva, which survived for more than two centuries before a number of regional states arose.

late 15th century Kingdom of Kandy established in central highlands.

1505 Arrival of Portuguese navigator Lorenço de Almeida, attracted by spice trade developed by Arab merchants who had called the island Serendip.

1597–1618 Portuguese controlled most of Sri Lanka, with the exception of Kandy.

1658 Dutch conquest of Portuguese territories.

1795–98 British conquest of Dutch territories.

1802 Treaty of Amiens recognized island as British colony of Ceylon.

1815 British won control of Kandy, becoming first European power to rule whole island.

1830s Immigration of S Indian Hindu Tamil labourers to work central coffee plantations.

1880s Tea and rubber become chief cash crops after blight ended production of coffee.

1919 Formation of the Ceylon National Congress to campaign for self rule; increasing conflicts between Sinhalese majority community and Tamil minority.

1931 Universal adult suffrage introduced for elected legislature and executive council in which power was shared with British.

1948 Ceylon achieved independence from Britain within Commonwealth, with Don Senanayake of conservative United National Party (UNP) as prime minister.

1949 Indian Tamils disenfranchised.

1952 Death of Don Senanayake, who was succeeded as prime minister by his son, Dudley.

1956 Sinhala established as official language; Solomon Bandaranaike became prime minister.

1959 Bandaranaike assassinated.

1960 Sirimavo Bandaranaike, the widow of Solomon, won general election and formed SLFP government, which nationalized oil industry.

1965 General election won by UNP; Dudley Senanayake became prime minister.

1970 Sirimavo Bandaranaike returned to power as prime minister, leading United Front government.

1971 Sinhalese Marxist uprising, led by students and People's Liberation Army (JVP).

1972 Socialist Republic of Sri Lanka proclaimed; Buddhism given 'foremost place' in new state, antagonizing Tamils.

1976 Tamil United Liberation Front formed to fight for independent Tamil state ('Eelam') in N and E Sri Lanka.

1978 Presidential constitution adopted by new free-market government headed by Junius Jayawardene of UNP.

1983 Ethnic riots as Tamil guerrilla violence escalated; state of emergency imposed; more than 1,000 Tamils killed by Sinhalese mobs.

1987 President Jayawardene and Indian prime minister Rajiv Gandhi signed Colombo Accord aimed at creating new provincial councils, disarming Tamil militants ('Tamil Tigers'), and stationing 7,000-strong Indian Peace Keeping Force. Violence continued despite cease-fire policed by Indian troops.

1988 Left-wing JVP guerrillas campaigned against Indo-Sri Lankan peace pact. Prime Minister Ranasinghe Premadasa elected president.

1989 Dingiri Banda Wijetunga became prime minister. Leaders of Tamil Tigers and banned Sinhala extremist JVP assassinated.

1990 Indian peacekeeping force withdrawn. Violence continued, with death toll exceeding 1,000 per month.

1991 Defence minister Ranjan Wijeratne assassinated; Sri Lankan army killed 2,552 Tamil Tigers at Elephant Pass in northern Jaffna region. Impeachment motion against President Premadasa failed. A new party, Democratic National United Front (DUNF), formed by former members of UNP.

1992 Several hundred Tamil Tiger rebels killed in army offensive, code-named 'Strike Force Two'.

1993 DUNF leader and President Premadasa assassinated by Tamil Tiger terrorists; succeeded by Dingiri Banda Wijetunge.

1994 UNP narrowly defeated in general election; Chandrika Kumaratunga became prime minister of SLFP-led left-of-centre coalition. Peace talks opened with Tamil Tigers. Kumaratunga elected first female president; her mother, Sirimavo Bandaranaike, became prime minister.

1995 Renewed bombing campaign by Tamil Tigers. Major offensive drove out Tamil Tigers from Jaffna city.

1996 State of emergency extended nationwide after Tamils bombed capital. Government forces launched new major offensive against Tamil Tigers.

1997 Major offensive launched against Tamil separatists.

Practical information

Visa requirements UK: visa only required by business visitors. USA: visa only required by business visitors

Embassy in the UK 13 Hyde Park Gardens, London W2 2LU. Tel: (0171) 262 1841; fax: (0171) 262 7970

British embassy PO Box 1433, 190 Galle Road, Kollupitiya, Colombo 3. Tel: (1) 437 336; fax: (1) 430 308

Embassy in the USA 2148 Wyoming Avenue NW, Washington, DC 20008. Tel: (202) 483 4025–8; fax: (202) 232 7181

American embassy 210 Galle Road, Colombo 3. Tel: (1) 448 007; fax: (1) 437 345

Chamber of commerce Federation of Chambers of Commerce and Industry of Sri Lanka, 29 Gregory's Road, Colombo 7. Tel: (1) 698 225; fax: (1) 699 530

Office hours 0830/0900–1615/1700 Mon–Fri

Banking hours 0900–1300 Mon and Sat; 0900–1500 Tue–Fri

Time difference GMT +5.5

Chief tourist attractions Buddhist festivals and ancient monuments; scenery

Major holidays 14 January, 4 February, 1, 22 May, 30 June, 25, 31 December; variable: Eid-ul-Adha, Diwali, end of Ramadan, Good Friday, New Year (Sinhala/Tamil, April), Prophet's Birthday, Maha Sivarathri (February/March), Full Moon (monthly)

Sudan Democratic Republic of

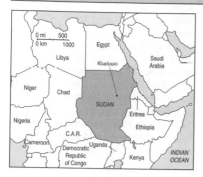

National name *Jamhuryat es-Sudan*
Area 2,505,800 sq km/967,489 sq mi
Capital Khartoum
Major towns/cities Omdurman, Port Sudan, Juba, Wadi Medani, al-Obeid, Kassala, Atbara, al-Qadarif, Kosti
Major ports Port Sudan
Physical features fertile Nile valley separates Libyan Desert in W from high rocky Nubian Desert in E

Government

Head of state and government General Omar Hassan Ahmed al-Bashir from 1989
Political system military republic
Administrative divisions 26 states
Political parties officially banned from 1989, but an influential grouping is the fundamentalist National Islamic Front
Armed forces 118,500 (1995)
Conscription military service is compulsory for three years
Death penalty retained and used for ordinary crimes
Defence spend (% GDP) 4.3 (1995)
Education spend (% GNP) 4 (1985); N/A (1993/94)
Health spend (% GDP) 0.5 (1990)

Economy and resources

Currency Sudanese dinar
GDP ($ US) 17.2 billion (1994)
Real GDP per capita (PPP) ($ US) 1,084 (1994)
GDP growth rate 2% (1994)
Average annual inflation 83.2% (1995); 63.2% (1985–95e)
Foreign debt ($ US) 17.7 billion (1994)
Trading partners Saudi Arabia, Libya, Thailand, Italy, Germany, UK, China, Japan
Resources petroleum, marble, mica, chromite, gypsum, gold, graphite, sulphur, iron, manganese, zinc, fluorspar,

talc, limestone, dolomite, pumice
Industries food processing (especially sugar refining), textiles, cement, petroleum refining, hides and skins
Exports cotton, sesame seed, gum arabic, sorghum, livestock, hides and skins. Principal market: Saudi Arabia 16.6% (1995)
Imports basic manufacture, crude materials (mainly petroleum and petroleum products), foodstuffs, machinery and equipment. Principal source: Libya 17.6% (1995)
Arable land 5.2% (1993)
Agricultural products sorghum, sugar cane, groundnuts, cotton, millet, wheat, sesame, fruits; livestock rearing (cattle, sheep, goats, and poultry)

Population and society

Population 27,291,000 (1996e)
Population growth rate 2.7% (1990–95); 2.6% (2000–05)
Population density (per sq km) 11 (1996e)
Urban population (% of total) 25 (1995)
Age distribution (% of total population) <15 43.8%, 15–65 53.3%, >65 2.9% (1995)
Ethnic distribution over 50 ethnic groups and almost 600 subgroups; the population is broadly distributed between Arabs in the N and black Africans in the S
Languages Arabic 51% (official), local languages
Religions Sunni Muslim; also animist and Christian
Education (compulsory years) 6
Literacy rate 43% (men); 12% (women) (1995e)
Labour force 36% of population: 69% agriculture, 8% industry, 22% services (1990)
Unemployment 30% (1993e)
Life expectancy 54 (men); 56 (women) (1995–2000)
Child mortality rate (under 5, per 1,000 live births) 115 (1995)
Physicians 1 per 8,979 people (1990)
Hospital beds 1 per 1,193 people (1990)
TV sets (per 1,000 people) 84 (1995)
Radios (per 1,000 people) 270 (1995)

Transport

Airports international airports: Khartoum (civil); 20 domestic airports; total passenger km: 615 mil (1994)
Railroads total length: 4,764 km/2,960

mi; total passenger km: 1,183 mil (1993)
Roads total road network: 11,610 km/ 7,214 mi, of which 36.2% paved (1995e); passenger cars: 8.6 per 1,000 people (1995e)

Chronology

c. 600 BC–AD 350 Meroë, near Khartoum, was capital of the Nubian Empire, which covered S Egypt and N Sudan.
6th century Converted to Coptic Christianity.
7th century Islam first introduced by Arab invaders, but did not spread widely until the 15th century.
16th–18th centuries Arab-African Fur and Fung Empires established in central and northern Sudan.
1820 Invaded by Muhammad Ali and brought under Egyptian control.
1881–85 Revolt led to capture of Khartoum by Sheik Muhammad Ahmed, a self-proclaimed Mahdi ('messiah'), and the killing of British general Charles Gordon.
1898 Anglo-Egyptian offensive led by Lord Kitchener subdued Mahdi revolt at Battle of Omdurman in which 20,000 Sudanese died.
1899 Sudan administered as Anglo-Egyptian condominium.
1923 White Flag League formed by Sudanese nationalists in N; British instituted policy of reducing contact between northern and southern Sudan, with the aim that S would eventually become part of federation of eastern African states.
1955 Civil war between the dominant Arab Muslim N and black African Christian and animist S broke out.
1956 Sudan achieved independence from Britain and Egypt as a republic.
1958 Military coup replaced civilian government with Supreme Council of the Armed Forces.
1964 Civilian rule reinstated after October Revolution of student demonstrations.
1969 Coup led by Col Gaafar Mohammed al-Nimeri abolished political institutions and concentrated power in a leftist Revolutionary Command Council.
1971 Nimeri confirmed as president and the Sudanese Socialist Union (SSU) declared the only legal party by a new constitution.

1972 Plans to form Federation of Arab Republics, comprising Sudan, Egypt, and Syria, abandoned due to internal opposition. To end 17-year-long civil war, Nimeri agreed to give S greater autonomy.
1974 National assembly established.
1980 Country reorganized into six regions, each with own assembly and effective autonomy.
1983 Shari'a (Islamic law) imposed. Sudan People's Liberation Movement (SPLM) formed in S as civil war broke out again.
1985 Nimeri deposed in a bloodless coup led by Gen Swar al-Dahab following industrial unrest in N. State of emergency declared.
1986 Coalition government formed after general election, with Sadiq al-Mahdi, great-grandson of the Mahdi, as prime minister.
1987 Virtual civil war with Sudan People's Liberation Army (SPLA), military wing of SPLM; drought and famine in S and refugee influx from Ethiopa and Chad.
1988 Peace pact signed with SPLA, but fighting continued.
1989 Al-Mahdi overthrown in coup led by Islamic fundamentalist Gen Omar Hassan Ahmed el-Bashir. All political activity suspended.
1991 Federal system introduced, with division of country into nine states as civil war continued.
1995 SPLA faction leaders agreed to cease-fire, but fighting continued.
1996 First presidential and parliamentary elections held since coup of 1989.
1997 Treaty signed between Sudan's Islamic government and four southern rebel groups.

Practical information

Visa requirements UK: visa required. USA: visa required
Embassy in the UK 3 Cleveland Row, St James Street, London SW1A 1DD. Tel: (0171) 839 8080; fax: (0171) 839 7560
British embassy PO Box 801, Street 10, off Sharia Al Baladiya, Khartoum East. Tel: (11) 770 769; telex: 22189 (a/b PRDRM SD)
Embassy in the USA 2210 Massachusetts Avenue NW, Washington, DC 20008. Tel: (202) 338 8565–70; fax: (202) 667 2406
American embassy operations in Khartoum were suspended in February 1996; staff have relocated to Nairobi, Kenya, and operate out of the US Embassy there; the embassy is located at the corner of Moi Avenue and Hailé Sélassie Avenue; mailing address: PO Box 30137, Unit 64100, APO AE 09831. Tel: (2) 334 141; fax: (2) 340 838
Chamber of commerce PO Box 81, Khartoum. Tel: (11) 72346
Office hours 0800–1430 Sat–Thu
Banking hours 0830–1200 Sat–Thu
Time difference GMT +2
Major holidays 1 January, 3 March, 6 April, 25 December; variable: Eid-ul-Adha (5 days), end of Ramadan (5 days), New Year (Muslim), Prophet's Birthday, Sham al-Naseem (April/May)

Suriname Republic of (formerly *Dutch Guiana*)

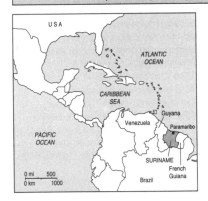

National name *Republiek Suriname*
Area 163,820 sq km/63,250 sq mi
Capital Paramaribo
Major towns/cities Nieuw Nickerie, Moengo, Pontoetoe, Brokopondo, Nieuw Amsterdam
Physical features hilly and forested, with flat and narrow coastal plain; Suriname River

Government

Head of state Jules Wijdenbosch from 1996
Head of government to be announced
Political system emergent democratic republic
Administrative divisions ten districts
Political parties New Front (NF), alliance of four left-of-centre parties: Party for National Unity and Solidarity (KTPI), Suriname National Party (NPS), Progressive Reform Party (VHP), Suriname Labour Party (SPA); National Democratic Party (NDP), left of centre; Democratic Alternative 1991 (DA '91), alliance of three left-of-centre parties
Armed forces 1,800 (1995)
Conscription military service is voluntary
Death penalty retains the death penalty for ordinary crimes but can be considered abolitionist in practice (last execution 1982)

Defence spend (% GDP) 3.9 (1995)
Education spend (% GNP) 3.6 (1993/94)
Health spend (% GDP) 5.7 (1990)

Economy and resources

Currency Suriname guilder
GDP ($ US) 1.3 billion (1995e)
Real GDP per capita (PPP) ($ US) 2,950 (1995e)
GDP growth rate 4% (1995e)
Average annual inflation 62% (1995); 48.5% (1985–95)
Foreign debt ($ US) 68.2 million (1995)
Trading partners USA, Norway, Trinidad and Tobago, the Netherlands, Netherlands Antilles, Brazil, Japan
Resources petroleum, bauxite (one of the world's leading producers), iron ore, copper, manganese, nickel, platinum, gold, kaolin
Industries bauxite refining and smelting, food processing, beverages,

cigarettes, wood products, chemical products, cement

Exports alumina, aluminium, shrimps, bananas, plantains, rice, wood and wood products. Principal market: Norway 26% (1996)

Imports raw materials and semi-manufactured goods, mineral fuels and lubricants, investment goods, foodstuffs, cars and motorcycles, textiles. Principal source: USA 42.4% (1996)

Arable land 0.3% (1993)

Agricultural products rice, citrus fruits, bananas, plantains, vegetables, coconuts, cassava, root crops, sugar cane; forest resources; commercial fishing

Population and society

Population 432,900 (1996e)

Population growth rate 1.1% (1990–95)

Population density (per sq km) 3 (1996e)

Urban population (% of total) 50 (1995)

Age distribution (% of total population) <15 35%, 15–65 60%, >65 5% (1995)

Ethnic distribution a wide ethnic composition, including Creoles, East Indians, Indonesians, Africans, Native Americans, Europeans, and Chinese

Languages Dutch (official), Sranan (creole), English, Hindi, Javanese, Chinese. Spanish is the main working language

Religions Christian, Hindu, Muslim

Education (compulsory years) 11

Literacy rate 95% (men); 95% (women) (1994e)

Labour force 20% agriculture, 20% industry, 60% services (1992)

Unemployment 16.3% (1993)

Life expectancy 69 (men); 74 (women)

(1995–2000)

Child mortality rate (under 5, per 1,000 live births) 32 (1995)

Physicians 1 per 1,605 people (1994)

Hospital beds 1 per 290 people (1994)

TV sets (per 1,000 people) 141 (1995)

Radios (per 1,000 people) 679 (1995)

Transport

Airports international airport: Paramaribo (Johan A Pengel); one domestic airport and 35 airstrips; total passenger km: 541 mil (1994)

Railroads total length: 301 km/187 mi (private freight railways)

Roads total road network: 4,470 km/2,778 mi, of which 26% paved (1995); passenger cars: 108.5 per 1,000 people (1995e)

Chronology

AD 1593 Visited and claimed by Spanish explorers; the name Suriname derived from the country's earliest inhabitants, the Surinen, who were driven out by other Amerindians in the 16th century.

1602 Dutch settlements established.

1651 British colony founded by settlers sent from Barbados.

1667 Became a Dutch colony, received in exchange for New Amsterdam (New York) by Treaty of Breda.

1682 Coffee and sugar cane plantations introduced, worked by imported African slaves.

1795–1802 and 1804–16 Under British rule.

1863 Slavery abolished and indentured labourers brought in from China, India, and Java.

1915 Bauxite discovered and gradually became main export.

1954 Achieved internal self-government as Dutch Guiana.

1958–69 Politics dominated by Johan Pengel, charismatic leader of the mainly Creole Suriname National Party (NPS).

1975 Independence achieved, with Dr Johan Ferrier as president and Henck Arron (NPS) as prime minister; 40% of population emigrated to the Netherlands.

1980 Arron's government overthrown in army coup; Ferrier refused to recognize military regime; appointed Dr Henk Chin A Sen of the Nationalist Republican Party (PNR) to lead civilian administration. Army replaced Ferrier with Dr Chin A Sen.

1982 Army, led by Lt Col Desi Bouterse, seized power, setting up a Revolutionary People's Front; economic aid from the Netherlands and US cut off after opposition leaders, charged with plotting a coup, were executed.

1985 Ban on political activities lifted.

1986 Antigovernment rebels brought economic chaos to Suriname.

1988 Ramsewak Shankar of the combined opposition parties elected president under new constitution.

1989 Bouterse rejected peace accord reached by President Shankar with guerrilla insurgents, the Bush Negro (descendents of escaped slaves) maroons, and vowed to continue fighting.

1990 Shankar deposed in army coup engineered by Bouterse.

1991 Johan Kraag (NPS) became interim president. New Front opposition alliance won assembly majority. Ronald Venetiaan elected civilian president.

1992 Peace accord reached with guerrilla groups.

1996 General election result inconclusive.

Practical information

Visa requirements UK: visa not required. USA: visa required

Embassy for the UK Alexander Gogelweg 2, 2517 JH The Hague, The Netherlands. Tel: (70) 365 0844; fax: (70) 361 7445

British embassy British Honorary Consulate, c/o VSH United Buildings, PO Box 1860, Van't Hogerhuysstraat 9–11, Paramaribo. Tel: (597) 472 870; fax: (597) 475 515

Embassy in the USA Suite 108, 4301 Connecticut Avenue NW, Washington, DC 20008. Tel: (202) 244 7488, 7490/1/2; fax: (202) 244 5878

American embassy Dr Sophie Redmondstraat 129, Paramaribo. Tel: (597) 472 900, 477 881, 476 459;

fax: (597) 420 800

Chamber of commerce Suriname Chamber of Commerce and Industry, PO Box 149, Dr J C de Mirandasstraat 10, Paramaribo. Tel: (597) 473 527; fax: (597) 474 779

Office hours 0700–1500 Mon–Thu; 0700–1430 Fri

Banking hours 0730–1400 Mon–Fri

Time difference GMT –3.5

Chief tourist attractions numerous historical sites; varied cultural activities; unspoiled interior with varied flora and fauna; 13 nature reserves and 1 nature park

Major holidays 1 January, 25 February, 1 May, 1 July, 25 November, 25–26 December; variable: Good Friday, Easter Monday, end of Ramadan, Holi (March)

Swaziland Kingdom of

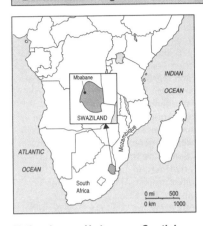

National name *Umbuso we Swatini*
Area 17,400 sq km/6,718 sq mi
Capital Mbabane
Major towns/cities Manzini, Big Bend,
Mhlume, Havelock Mine, Nhlangano
Physical features central valley;
mountains in W (Highveld); plateau in
E (Lowveld and Lubombo plateau)

Government

Head of state King Mswati III from 1986
Head of government Barnabas Sibusiso
Dlamini from 1997
Political system transitional absolute
monarchy
Administrative divisions four regions
Political parties Imbokodvo National
Movement (INM), nationalist monarchist;
Swaziland United Front (SUF), left of
centre; Swaziland Progressive Party
(SPP), left of centre; People's United
Democratic Movement, left of centre
Armed forces 127,280 (1995)
Conscription military service is
compulsory for two years
Death penalty retained and used for
ordinary crimes
Defence spend (% GDP) 2.5 (1993e)
Education spend (% GNP) 6.8
(1993/94)
Health spend (% GDP) 1.1 (1990)

Economy and resources

Currency lilangeni
GDP ($ US) 98.8 billion (1994e)
Real GDP per capita (PPP) ($ US) 2,841
(1994e)
GDP growth rate –3% (1994)
Average annual inflation 14.7% (1995);
11.7% (1985–95)
Foreign debt ($ US) 23.7 billion (1994)
Trading partners South Africa, UK, the
Netherlands, Switzerland, France

Resources coal, asbestos, diamonds,
gold, tin, kaolin, iron ore, talc, pyrophyllite,
silica
Industries food processing, paper,
textiles, wood products, beverages, metal
products
Exports sugar, wood pulp, cotton yarn,
canned fruits, asbestos, coal, diamonds,
gold. Principal market: South Africa 32%
(1994)
Imports machinery and transport
equipment, minerals, fuels and lubricants,
manufactured items, food and live
animals. Principal source: South Africa
83.3% (1994)
Arable land 10.8% (1993)
Agricultural products sugar cane,
cotton, citrus fruits, pineapples, maize,
sorghum, tobacco, tomatoes, rice;
livestock rearing (cattle and goats);
commercial forestry

Population and society

Population 881,000 (1996e)
Population growth rate 2.8% (1990–95);
2.6% (2000–05)
Population density (per sq km) 51
(1996e)
Urban population (% of total) 31 (1995)
Age distribution (% of total population)
<15 43%, 15–65 54.4%, >65 2.7% (1995)
Ethnic distribution about 90%
indigenous African, comprising the Swazi,
Zulu, Tonga, and Shangaan peoples;
there are European and Afro-European
(Eurafrican) minorities numbering around
22,000
Languages Swazi, English (both official)
Religions Christian, animist
Education (compulsory years) 7
Literacy rate 76% (men); 73% (women)
(1995e)
Labour force 34% of population: 39%
agriculture, 22% industry, 38% services
(1990)
Unemployment 30% (1994e)
Life expectancy 58 (men); 62 (women)
(1995–2000)
Child mortality rate (under 5, per 1,000
live births) 107 (1995)
Physicians 1 per 9,091 people (1991)
Hospital beds 1 per 423 people (1991)
TV sets (per 1,000 people) 21 (1995)
Radios (per 1,000 people) 163 (1995)

Transport

Airports international airport: Manzini
(Matsapha); total passenger km: 48 mil
(1994)
Railroads total length: 301 km/187 mi
(freight)

Roads total road network: 3,825 km/
2,377 mi, of which 32% paved (1995e);
passenger cars: 29.2 per 1,000 people
(1995e)

Chronology

late 16th century King Ngwane II
crossed Lubombo mountains from the E
and settled in SE Swaziland; his
successors established a strong
centralized Swazi kingdom, dominating
the long-settled Nguni and Sothi peoples.
mid-19th century Swazi nation was ruled
by the warrior King Mswati who, at the
height of his power, controlled an area
three times the size of the present-day
state.
1882 Gold was discovered in the NW,
attracting European fortune hunters, who
coerced Swazi rulers into granting land
concessions.
1894 Came under joint rule of Britain and
the Boer republic of Transvaal.
1903 Following the South African War,
Swaziland became a special British
protectorate, or High Commission territory,
against South Africa's wishes.
1922 King Sobhuza II succeeded to the
Swazi throne.
1968 Independence achieved within the
Commonwealth, as the Kingdom of
Swaziland, with King (or Ngwenyama)
Sobhuza II as head of state.
1973 The king suspended the
constitution, banned political activity, and
assumed absolute powers after the
opposition deputies had been elected to
parliament.
1977 King announced substitution of
traditional tribal communities (*tinkhundla*)
for the parliamentary system, arguing it
was more suited to Swazi values.
1982 King Sobhuza died; his place was
taken by one of his wives, Queen
Dzeliwe, until his son, Prince
Makhosetive, reached the age of 21.
1983 Queen Dzeliwe ousted by a younger
wife, Queen Ntombi, as real power
passed to the prime minister, Prince
Bhekimpi Dlamini.
1984 After royal power struggle, it was
announced that the crown prince would
become king at 18.
1986 Crown prince formally invested as
King Mswati III.
1993 Direct elections of *tinkhundla*
candidates held for the first time; Prince
Jameson Mbilini Dlamini appointed
premier.
1996 Prince Dlamini dismissed without a
successor being named.

Practical information

Visa requirements UK: visa not required. USA: visa not required
Embassy in the UK 20 Buckingham Street, London SW1E 6LB. Tel: (0171) 630 6611; fax: (0171) 630 6564
British embassy British High Commission, Allister Miller Street, Private Bag, Mbabane. Tel: (268) 42581; fax: (268) 42585
Embassy in the USA 3400 International Drive NW, Washington, DC 20008. Tel: (202) 362 6683/5; fax: (202) 244 8059
American embassy Central Bank Building, Warner Street,

Mbabane. Tel: (268) 46441–5; fax: (268) 45959
Chamber of commerce Swaziland Chamber of Commerce and Industry, PO Box 72, Mbabane. Tel: (268) 44408; fax: (268) 45442
Office hours 0800–1300 and 1400–1700 Mon–Fri; 0800–1300 Sat
Banking hours 0830–1430 Mon–Fri; 0830–1100 Sat
Time difference GMT +2
Chief tourist attractions magnificent mountain scenery; game reserves
Major holidays 1 January, 25 April, 22 July, 6 September, 24 October, 25–26 December; variable: Ascension Thursday, Good Friday, Easter Monday, Commonwealth (March)

Sweden Kingdom of

National name *Konungariket Sverige*
Area 450,000 sq km/173,745 sq mi
Capital Stockholm (and port)
Major towns/cities Göteborg, Malmö, Uppsala, Norrköping, Våsterås, Linköping, Orebro, Jönköping, Helsingborg, Borås
Major ports Helsingborg, Malmö, Göteborg
Physical features mountains in W; plains in S; thickly forested; more than 20,000 islands off the Stockholm coast; lakes, including Vånern, Våttern, Målaren, and Hjålmaren

Government

Head of state King Carl XVI Gustaf from 1973
Head of government Goran Persson from 1996
Political system constitutional monarchy
Administrative divisions 24 counties
Political parties Christian Democratic Community Party (KdS), Christian,

centrist; Left Party (Vp), European, Marxist; Social Democratic Labour Party (SAP), moderate, left of centre; Moderate Party (M), right of centre; Liberal Party (Fp), centre left; Centre Party (C), centrist; Ecology Party (MpG), ecological; New Democracy (NG), right wing, populist
Armed forces 64,000 (1995)
Conscription 7–15 months (army and navy); 8–12 months (air force)
Death penalty abolished 1972
Defence spend (% GDP) 2.9 (1995)
Education spend (% GNP) 8.4 (1993/94)
Health spend (% GDP) 6.2 (1993)

Economy and resources

Currency Swedish krona
GDP ($ US) 250.3 billion (1996)
Real GDP per capita (PPP) ($ US) 19,117 (1996)
GDP growth rate 1.7% (1996); –0.1% (1990–95)
Average annual inflation 0.6% (1996); 5.5% (1985–95)
Trading partners Germany, UK, Norway, USA, Denmark, France
Resources iron ore, uranium, copper, lead, zinc, silver, hydroelectric power, forests
Industries motor vehicles, foodstuffs, machinery, precision equipment, iron and steel, metal products, wood products, chemicals, shipbuilding, electrical goods
Exports forestry products (wood, pulp, and paper), machinery, motor vehicles, power-generating non-electrical machinery, chemicals, iron and steel.

Principal market: Germany 11.7% (1996)
Imports machinery and transport equipment, chemicals, mineral fuels and lubricants, textiles, clothing, footwear, food and live animals. Principal source: Germany 18.7% (1996)
Arable land 6.2% (1993)
Agricultural products barley, wheat, oats, potatoes, sugar beet, tame hay, oil seed; livestock and dairy products

Population and society

Population 8,819,000 (1996e)
Population growth rate 0.5% (1990–95); 0.3% (2000–05)
Population density (per sq km) 20 (1996e)
Urban population (% of total) 83 (1995)
Age distribution (% of total population) <15 19%, 15–65 63.7%, >65 17.3% (1995)
Ethnic distribution predominantly of Teutonic descent, with small Saami (Lapp), Finnish, and German minorities
Languages Swedish; there are Finnish- and Saami-speaking minorities
Religion Evangelical Lutheran (established national church)
Education (compulsory years) 9
Literacy rate 99% (men); 99% (women) (1995e)
Labour force 54% of population: 4% agriculture, 30% industry, 66% services (1990)
Unemployment 10% (1996)
Life expectancy 76 (men); 82 (women) (1995–2000)

Child mortality rate (under 5, per 1,000 live births) 5 (1995)
Physicians 1 per 393 people (1994)
Hospital beds 1 per 193 people (1994)
TV sets (per 1,000 people) 478 (1995)
Radios (per 1,000 people) 882 (1995)

Transport

Airports international airports: Stockholm (Arlanda), Göteborg (Landvetter), Malmö (Sturup); over 30 domestic airports; total passenger km: 1,064 mil (1994)
Railroads total length: 11,269 km/ 7,003 mi; total passenger km: 5,975 mil (1993)
Roads total road network: 136,233 km/ 84,655 mi, of which 76% paved (1995); passenger cars: 410.9 per 1,000 people (1995)

Chronology

8th century Kingdom of the Svear, based near Uppsala, extended its rule across much of southern Sweden.
9th–11th centuries Swedish Vikings raided and settled along the rivers of Russia.
c. 1000 Olaf Skötkonung, king of the Svear, adopted Christianity and united much of Sweden (except S and W coasts, which remained Danish until 17th century).
11th–13th centuries Sweden existed as isolated kingdom under the Stenkil, Sverker, and Folkung dynasties; series of crusades incorporated Finland.
1397 Union of Kalmar: Sweden, Denmark, and Norway united under a single monarch; Sweden effectively ruled by succession of regents.
1448 Breach with Denmark: Sweden alone elected Charles VIII as king.

1523 Gustavus Vasa, leader of insurgents, became king of fully independent Sweden.
1527 Swedish Reformation: Gustavus confiscated Church property and encouraged Lutherans.
1544 Swedish crown became hereditary in House of Vasa.
1592–1604 Sigismund Vasa, a Catholic, was king of both Sweden and Poland until ousted from Swedish throne by his Lutheran uncle Charles IX.
17th century Sweden, a great military power under Gustavus Adolphus 1611–32, Charles X 1654–60, and Charles XI 1660–97, fought lengthy wars with Denmark, Russia, Poland, and Holy Roman Empire.
1709 Battle of Poltava: Russians inflicted major defeat on Swedes under Charles XII.
1720 Limited monarchy established; political power passed to Riksdag (parliament) dominated by nobles.
1721 Great Northern War ended with Sweden losing nearly all its conquests of the previous century.
1741–43 Sweden defeated in disastrous war with Russia; further conflict 1788–90.
1771–92 Gustavus III increased royal power and introduced wide-ranging reforms; assassinated at a masked ball.
1809 Russian invaders annexed Finland; Swedish nobles staged coup and restored powers of Riksdag.
1810 Napoleonic marshal, Jean-Baptiste Bernadotte, elected crown prince of Sweden, as Charles XIII had no heir.
1812 Bernadotte allied Sweden with Russia against France.
1814 Treaty of Kiel: Sweden obtained Norway from Denmark.

1818–44 Bernadotte reigned in Sweden as Charles XIV John.
1846 Free enterprise established by abolition of trade guilds and monopolies.
1866 Series of liberal reforms culminated in new two-chambered Riksdag dominated by bureaucrats and farmers.
late 19th century Development of large-scale forestry and iron-ore industry; neutrality adopted in foreign affairs.
1905 Union with Norway dissolved.
1907 Adoption of proportional representation and universal suffrage.
1920s Economic boom transformed Sweden from an agricultural to an industrial economy.
1932 Social Democrat government of Per Halbin Hansson introduced radical public-works programme to combat trade slump.
1940–43 Under duress, neutral Sweden permitted limited transit of German forces through its territory.
1946–69 Social Democrat government of Tage Erlander developed comprehensive welfare state.
1959 Sweden joined European Free Trade Association.
1969–76 Social Democratic Party in power, under Prime Minister Olaf Palme.
1971 Constitution amended to create single-chamber Riksdag.
1975 Remaining constitutional powers of monarch removed.
1976–82 Centre-right government of Thorbjörn Fälldin ended 44 years of Social Democrat dominance.
1982 Palme regained premiership; assassinated 1986.
1995 Sweden became a member of European Union.

Practical information

Visa requirements UK: visa not required. USA: visa not required
Embassy in the UK 11 Montagu Place, London W1H 2AL. Tel: (0171) 917 6400; fax: (0171) 724 4174
British embassy PO Box 27819, Skarpögatan 6–8, 115 93 Stockholm. Tel: (8) 671 9000; fax: (8) 662 9989
Embassy in the USA 1501 mil Street NW, Washington, DC 20005. Tel: (202) 467 2600; fax: (202) 467 2699
American embassy Strandvagen 101, S-115 89 Stockholm. Tel: (8) 783 5300; fax: (8) 661 1964
Chamber of commerce Federation of Swedish Commerce

and Trade, PO Box 5512, Grevgatan 34, 114 85 Stockholm. Tel: (8) 666 1100; fax: (8) 662 7457
Office hours flexible, with lunch break 1200–1300
Banking hours generally 0930–1500 Mon–Fri
Time difference GMT +1
Chief tourist attractions varied landscape – mountains N of the Arctic Circle; white sandy beaches in the S, lakes, waterfalls, and forests; Stockholm, with its modern architecture and cultural activities
Major holidays 1, 6 January, 1 May, 1 November, 24–26, 31 December; variable: Ascension Thursday, Good Friday, Easter Monday, Whit Monday, Midsummer Eve and Day (June)

Switzerland Swiss Confederation

National name German *Schweiz*, French *Suisse*, Romansch *Svizra*
Area 41,300 sq km/15,945 sq mi
Capital Bern (Berne)
Major towns/cities Zürich, Geneva, Basel, Lausanne, Luzern, St Gallen, Winterthur
Major ports river port Basel (on the Rhine)
Physical features most mountainous country in Europe (Alps and Jura mountains); highest peak Dufourspitze 4,634 m/15,203 ft in Apennines

Government

Head of state and government Arnold Koller from 1997
Government federal democratic republic
Administrative divisions 20 cantons and six demi-cantons
Political parties Radical Democratic Party (FDP/PRD), radical, centre left; Social Democratic Party (SP/PS), moderate, left of centre; Christian Democratic People's Party (CVP/PDC), Christian, moderate, centrist; Swiss People's Party (SVP/UDC), centre left; Liberal Party (LPS/PLS), federalist, right of centre; Green Party (GPS/PES), ecological
Armed forces 31,000 (1995)
Conscription 17 weeks' recruit training, followed by refresher training of varying length according to age
Death penalty abolished 1992
Defence spend (% GDP) 1.9 (1995)
Education spend (% GNP) 5.6 (1993/94)
Health spend (% GDP) 6.8 (1993)

Economy and resources

Currency Swiss franc
GDP ($ US) 293.4 billion (1996)

Real GDP per capita (PPP) ($ US) 25,141 (1996)
GDP growth rate −0.7% (1996); 0.1% (1990–95)
Average annual inflation 0.5% (1996), 3.4% (1985–95)
Trading partners EU (principally Germany, France, Italy, and UK), USA, Japan
Resources salt, hydroelectric power, forest
Industries heavy engineering, machinery, precision engineering (clocks and watches), jewellery, textiles, chocolate, dairy products, cigarettes, footwear, wine, international finance and insurance services, tourism
Exports machinery and equipment, pharmaceutical and chemical products, foodstuffs, precision instruments, clocks and watches, metal products. Principal market: Germany 23.3% (1996)
Imports machinery, motor vehicles, agricultural and forestry products, construction material, fuels and lubricants, chemicals, textiles and clothing. Principal source: Germany 32.8% (1996)
Arable land 9.6% (1993)
Agricultural products sugar beet, potatoes, wheat, apples, pears, tobacco, grapes; livestock and dairy products, notably cheese

Population and society

Population 7,224,000 (1996e)
Population growth rate 1.1% (1990–95); 0.5% (2000–05)
Population density (per sq km) 175 (1996e)
Urban population (% of total) 61 (1995)
Age distribution (% of total population) <15 17.7%, 15–65 68.1%, >65 14.2% (1995)
Ethnic distribution majority of Alpine descent; sizeable Nordic element
Languages German 64%, French 19%, Italian 8%, Romansch 0.6% (all official)
Religions Roman Catholic 50%, Protestant 48%
Education (compulsory years) 8–9 (depending on canton)
Literacy rate 99% (men); 99% (women) (1995e)
Labour force 53% of population: 6% agriculture, 35% industry, 60% services (1990)
Unemployment 3.3% (1996)

Life expectancy 75 (men); 82 (women) (1995–2000)
Child mortality rate (under 5, per 1,000 live births) 7 (1995)
Physicians 1 per 288 people (1992)
Hospital beds 1 per 597 people (1993)
TV sets (per 1,000 people) 419 (1995)
Radios (per 1,000 people) 851 (1995)

Transport

Airports international airports: Zürich (Kloten), Geneva, Bern (Belp), Basel (Basel-Mulhouse); domestic services operate between these; total passenger km: 18,858 mil (1994)
Railroads total length: 5,208 km/3,236 mi; total passenger km: 13,836 mil (1994)
Roads total road network: 71,055 km/44,154 mi (1995); passenger cars: 457 per 1,000 people (1995)

Chronology

58 BC Celtic Helvetii tribe submitted to Roman authority after defeat by Julius Caesar.
4th century AD Region overrun by Germanic tribes, Burgundians, and Alemannians.
7th century Formed part of Frankish kingdom and embraced Christianity.
9th century Included in Charlemagne's Holy Roman Empire.
12th century Many autonomous feudal holdings developed as power of Holy Roman Empire declined.
13th century Habsburgs became dominant as overlords of eastern Switzerland.
1291 Cantons of Schwyz, Uri, and Lower Unterwalden formed Everlasting League, a loose confederation to resist Habsburg control.
1315 Battle of Morgarten: Swiss Confederation defeated Habsburgs.
14th century Luzern, Zürich, Basel, and other cantons joined Swiss Confederation, which became independent of Habsburgs.
1523–29 Zürich, Bern, and Basel accepted Reformation but rural cantons remained Roman Catholic.
1648 Treaty of Westphalia recognized Swiss independence from Holy Roman Empire.
1798 French invasion established Helvetic Republic, a puppet state with centralized government.
1803 Napoleon's Act of Mediation restored considerable autonomy to cantons.

1814 End of French domination; Switzerland reverted to loose confederation of sovereign cantons with a weak federal parliament.
1815 Great Powers recognized 'Perpetual Neutrality' of Switzerland.
1845 Seven Catholic cantons founded Sonderbund league to resist any strengthening of central government by Liberals.
1847 Federal troops defeated Sonderbund in brief civil war.

1848 New constitution introduced greater centralization; Bern chosen as capital.
1874 Powers of federal government increased; principle of referendum introduced.
late 19th century Development of industry, railways, and tourism led to growing prosperity.
1920 League of Nations selected Geneva as its headquarters.
1923 Switzerland formed customs union with Liechtenstein.

1960 Joined European Free Trade Association (EFTA).
1971 Women gained right to vote in federal elections.
1986 Referendum rejected proposal for membership of United Nations (UN).
1992 Closer ties with European Community (EC) rejected in national referendum.
1996 Jean-Paul Delamuraz became president.
1997 Arnold Koller elected president.

Practical information

Visa requirements UK: visa not required. USA: visa not required
Embassy in the UK 16–18 Montagu Place, London W1H 2BQ. Tel: (0171) 616 6000; fax: (0171) 724 7001
British embassy Thunstrasse 50, CH-3005 Bern 15. Tel: (31) 352 5021/6; fax: (31) 352 0583
Embassy in the USA 2900 Cathedral Avenue NW, Washington, DC 20008. Tel: (202) 745 7900; fax: (202) 387 2564
American embassy Jubilaeumstrasse 93, 3005 Bern. Tel: (31) 357 7011; fax: (31) 357 7344

Chamber of commerce Schweizerischer Handels- und Industrie-Verein (Swiss Federation of Commerce and Industry), PO Box 690, Mainaustrasse 49, CH-8034 Zürich. Tel: (1) 382 2323; fax: (1) 382 2332
Office hours 0800–1200 and 1400–1700 Mon–Fri
Banking hours 0830–1630 Mon–Fri
Time difference GMT +1
Chief tourist attractions the Alps; lakes and lake resorts; walking; mountaineering; winter sports
Major holidays 1 January, 1, 15 August (many cantons), 1 November (many cantons), 24–26 December; variable: Ascension Thursday, Corpus Christi (many cantons), Good Friday, Easter Monday, Whit Monday; many local holidays

Syria Syrian Arab Republic

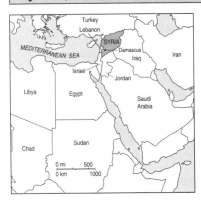

National name *al-Jamhuriya al-Arabya as-Suriya*
Area 185,200 sq km/71,505 sq mi
Capital Damascus
Major towns/cities Aleppo, Homs, Latakia, Hama
Major ports Latakia
Physical features mountains alternate with fertile plains and desert areas; Euphrates River

Government

Head of state and government Hafez al-Assad from 1971
Political system socialist republic

Administrative divisions 14 administrative districts
Political parties National Progressive Front (NPF), pro-Arab, socialist coalition, including the Communist Party of Syria, the Arab Socialist Party, the Arab Socialist Unionist Party, the Syrian Arab Socialist Union Party, the Ba'ath Arab Socialist Party
Armed forces 423,000; reserve forces 400,000; paramilitary forces 8,000 (1995)
Conscription 30 months
Death penalty retained and used for ordinary crimes
Defence spend (% GDP) 6.8 (1995)
Education spend (% GNP) 4.2 (1992); N/A (1993/94)
Health spend (% GDP) 0.4 (1990)

Economy and resources

Currency Syrian pound
GDP ($ US) 16.8 billion (1995)
Real GDP per capita (PPP) ($ US) 5,397 (1994)
GDP growth rate 5.8% (1995e); –0.6% (1990–95)
Average annual inflation 22% (1995); 15.8% (1985–95)
Foreign debt ($ US) 21.3 billion (1995)
Trading partners Germany, Italy, France, Lebanon, Japan, UK, Romania, Belgium
Resources petroleum, natural gas, iron ore, phosphates, salt, gypsum, sodium chloride, bitumen
Industries petroleum and petroleum products, coal, rubber and plastic products, textiles, clothing, leather products, tobacco, processed food
Exports crude petroleum, textiles, vegetables, fruit, raw cotton, natural phosphate. Principal market: Germany 16.7% (1995)
Imports crude petroleum, wheat, base metals, metal products, foodstuffs, machinery, motor vehicles. Principal source: Italy 8.6% (1995)
Arable land 27.6% (1993)
Agricultural products cotton, wheat, barley, maize, olives, lentils, sugar beet, fruit, vegetables; livestock (principally sheep and goats)

Population and society

Population 14,574,000 (1996e)
Population growth rate 3.4% (1990–95); 3.2% (2000–05)
Population density (per sq km) 79 (1996e)
Urban population (% of total) 52 (1995)

Age distribution (% of total population) <15 47.3%, 15–65 49.9%, >65 2.8% (1995)

Ethnic distribution predominantly Arab, with many differences in language and regional affiliations

Languages Arabic 89% (official); Kurdish 6%, Armenian 3%

Religions Sunni Muslim 90%; other Islamic sects, Christian

Education (compulsory years) 6

Literacy rate 53% (men); 51% (women) (1995e)

Labour force 28% of population: 33% agriculture, 24% industry, 43% services (1990)

Life expectancy 67 (men); 71 (women) (1995–2000)

Child mortality rate (under 5, per 1,000 live births) 36 (1995)

Physicians 1 per 969 people (1994)

Hospital beds 1 per 918 people (1994)

TV sets (per 1,000 people) 67 (1995)

Radios (per 1,000 people) 264 (1995)

Transport

Airports international airports: Damascus, Aleppo (Nejrab), Latakia (chartered flights); four domestic airports; total passenger km: 820 mil (1994)

Railroads total length: 1,998 km/1,242 mi; total passenger km: 769 mil (1994)

Roads total road network: 39,243 km/ 24,386 mi, of which 71% paved (1995); passenger cars: 9 per 1,000 people (1995e)

Chronology

c.1750 BC Syria became part of Babylonian Empire; during the next millennium it was successively conquered by Hittites, Assyrians, Chaldeans, and Persians.

333 BC Alexander the Great of Macedonia conquered Persia and Syria.

301 BC Seleucus I, one of the generals of Alexander the Great, founded kingdom of Syria, which the Seleucid dynasty ruled for over 200 years.

64 BC Syria became part of Roman Empire.

4th century AD After division of Roman Empire, Syria came under Byzantine rule.

634 Arabs conquered most of Syria and introduced Islam.

661–750 Damascus was capital of Muslim Empire.

1055 Seljuk Turks overran Syria.

1095–99 First Crusade established Latin states on Syrian coast.

13th century Mameluke sultans of Egypt took control.

1516 Ottoman Turks conquered Syria.

1831 Egyptians led by Mehemet Ali drove out Turks.

1840 Turkish rule restored; Syria opened up to European trade.

late 19th century French firms built ports, roads, and railways in Syria.

1916 Sykes-Picot Agreement: secret Anglo-French deal to partition Turkish Empire allotted Syria to France.

1918 British expelled Turks with help of Arab revolt.

1919 Syrian national congress called for independence under Emir Faisal and opposed transfer to French rule.

1920 Syria became League of Nations protectorate, administered by France.

1925 People's Party founded to campaign for independence and national unity; insurrection by Druse religious sect against French control.

1936 France promised independence within three years, but martial law imposed 1939.

1941 British forces ousted Vichy French regime in Damascus and occupied Syria in conjunction with Free French.

1944 Syrian independence proclaimed but French military resisted transfer of power.

1946 Syria achieved effective independence when French forces withdrew.

1948–49 Arab–Israeli War: Syria joined unsuccessful invasion of newly independent Israel.

1958 Syria and Egypt merged to form United Arab Republic (UAR).

1959 USSR agreed to give financial and technical aid to Syria.

1961 Syria seceded from UAR.

1964 Ba'ath Socialist Party established military dictatorship.

1967 Six-Day War: Syria lost Golan Heights to Israel.

1970–71 Syria invaded Jordan in support of Palestinian guerrillas.

1970 Hafez al-Assad staged coup; elected president 1971.

1973 Yom Kippur War: Syrian attack on Israel repulsed.

1976 Start of Syrian military intervention in Lebanese civil war.

1978 Syria opposed peace deal between Egypt and Israel.

1986 Britain broke off diplomatic relations, accusing Syria of involvement in international terrorism.

1990 Diplomatic links with Britain restored.

1991 Syria contributed troops to US-led coalition in Gulf War against Iraq. US Middle East peace plan approved by Assad.

1994 Israel offered partial withdrawal from Golan Heights in return for peace, but Syria remained sceptical.

1995 Security framework agreement with Israel.

1997 President Assad reported ill.

Practical information

Visa requirements UK: visa required. USA: visa required

Embassy in the UK 8 Belgrave Square, London SW1X 8PH. Tel: (0171) 245 9012; fax: (0171) 235 4621

British embassy PO Box 37, Quarter Malki, 11 rue Mohammed Kurd Ali, Immeuble Kotob, Damascus. Tel: (11) 712 561/2/3; fax: (11) 713 592

Embassy in the USA 2215 Wyoming Avenue NW, Washington, DC 20008. Tel: (202) 232 6313; fax: (202) 234 9548

American embassy Abou Roumaneh, Al-Mansur Street No. 2, Damascus. Tel: (11) 333 2814, 333 0788, 332 0783; fax: (11) 224 7938

Chamber of commerce Federation of Syrian Chambers of Commerce, PO Box 5909, rue Mousa Ben Nousair, Damascus. Tel: (11) 333 7344; fax: (11) 333127

Office hours 0830–1430 Sat–Thu (Christian firms generally open Mon–Sat)

Banking hours 0800–1400 Sat–Thu (banks tend to close early on Thu)

Time difference GMT +2

Chief tourist attractions antiquities of Damascus and Palmyra; bazaars; Mediterranean coastline; mountains

Major holidays 1 January, 8 March, 17 April, 1, 6 May, 23 July, 1 September, 6 October, 25 December; variable: Eid-ul-Adha (3 days), end of Ramadan (4 days), Easter Sunday, New Year (Muslim), Prophet's Birthday

Taiwan Republic of China

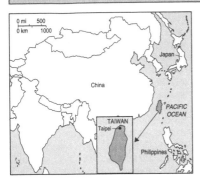

National name *Chung Hua Min Kuo*
Area 36,179 sq km/13,968 sq mi
Capital Taipei
Major towns/cities Kaohsiung,
Taichung, Tainan, Panchiao, Yunlin
Major ports Kaohsiung, Keelung
Physical features island (formerly
Formosa) off People's Republic of China;
mountainous, with lowlands in W;
Penghu (Pescadores), Jinmen
(Quemoy), Mazu (Matsu) islands

Government

Head of state Lee Teng-hui from 1988
Head of government Vincent Siew from
1997
Political system emergent democracy
Administrative divisions 16 counties,
five municipalities, and two special
municipalities (Taipei and Kaohsiung)
Political parties Nationalist Party of
China (Kuomintang: KMT),
anticommunist, Chinese nationalist;
Democratic Progressive Party (DPP),
centrist-pluralist, proself-determination
grouping; Workers' Party (Kuntang), left
of centre
Armed forces 376,000 (1995); plus
paramilitary forces numbering 26,700
and reserves totalling 1,657,500
Conscription military service is
compulsory for two years
Death penalty retained and used for
ordinary crimes
Defence spend (% GDP) 5 (1995)
Education spend (% GDP) 2.5 (1994)

Economy and resources

Currency New Taiwan dollar
GDP ($ US) 241.9 billion (1994)
Real GDP per capita (PPP) ($ US)
11,900 (1994)
GDP growth rate 6% (1995)
Average annual inflation 3.7% (1995)

Foreign debt ($ US) 3.1 billion (1994)
Trading partners USA, Japan, Hong
Kong, Germany, Singapore, South
Korea, Australia, China
Resources coal, copper, marble,
dolomite; small reserves of petroleum
and natural gas
Industries electronics, plastic and rubber
goods, textiles and clothing, base metals,
vehicles, aircraft, ships, footwear,
cement, fertilizers, paper
Exports electronic products, base metals
and metal articles, textiles and clothing,
machinery, information and
communication products, plastic and
rubber products, vehicles and transport
equipment, footwear, headwear,
umbrellas, toys, games, sports
equipment. Principal market: USA 23.3%
(1996)
Imports machinery and transport
equipment, basic manufactures,
chemicals, base metals and metal
articles, minerals, textile products, crude
petroleum, plastics, precision
instruments, clocks and watches, musical
instruments. Principal source: Japan
27.2% (1996)
Arable land 24% (1993)
Agricultural products rice, tea,
bananas, pineapples, sugar cane, maize,
sweet potatoes, soya beans, peanuts;
fishing; forest resources

Population and society

Population 21,465,900 (1996e)
Population growth rate 0.9% (1994)
Population density (per sq km) 589
(1994)
Urban population (% of total) 75 (1994)
Age distribution (% of total population)
<15 29.6%, 15–65 62.2%, >65 8.2%
(1992)
Ethnic distribution 98% Han Chinese
and 2% aboriginal by descent; around
87% are Taiwan-born and 13% are
'mainlanders'
Languages Mandarin Chinese (official);
Taiwan, Hakka dialects
Religions officially atheist; Taoist,
Confucian, Buddhist, Christian
Education (compulsory years) 9
Literacy rate 95% (men); 93% (women)
(1995e)
Labour force 10.9% agriculture, 39.2%
industry, 49.9% services (1994)
Unemployment 2.1% (1995)
Life expectancy 72 (men); 78 (women)
(1995)

Child mortality rate (under 5, per 1,000
live births) 6 (1994)
Physicians 1 per 878 people (1995);
3,030 doctors of traditional Chinese
medicine (1995)
Hospital beds 1 per 192 people (1995)
TV sets (per 1,000 people) 235 (1994)
Radios (per 1,000 people) 744 (1994)

Transport

Airports international airports: Taipei
(Chaing Kai-shek), Kaohsiung; 14
domestic airports; total passenger km:
38,247 mil (1995)
Railroads total length: 1,108 km/689 mi;
total passenger km: 9,489 mil (1995)
Roads total road network: 19,584 km/
12,169 mi, of which 87.4% paved (1995);
passenger cars: 184.8 per 1,000 people
(1995)

Chronology

7th century AD Island occupied by
aboriginal community of Malayan
descent; immigration of Chinese from
mainland began, but remained limited
before 15th century.
1517 Sighted by Portuguese vessels en
route to Japan and named Ilha Formosa
('beautiful island').
1624 Occupied and controlled by Dutch.
1662 Dutch defeated by Chinese Ming
general, Cheng Ch'eng-kung (Koxinga),
whose family came to rule Formosa for a
short period.
1683 Annexed by China's rulers, the
Manchu Qing.
1786 Major rebellion against Chinese
rule.
1860 Ports opened to Western trade.
1895 Ceded 'in perpetuity' to Japan
under Treaty of Shominoseki at end of
Sino-Japanese war.
1945 Recovered by China's Nationalist
Kuomintang (Guomindang) government
at end of World War II.
1947 Rebellion against Chinese rule
brutally suppressed.
1949 Flight of Nationalist government,
led by Generalissimo Chiang Kai-shek,
to Taiwan after Chinese communist
revolution. They retained the designation
of Republic of China (ROC), claiming to
be the legitimate government for all
China, and were recognized by USA and
United Nations (UN).
1950s onwards Rapid economic growth
as Taiwan became successful export-
orientated Newly Industrializing Country

(NIC) and land was redistributed from the gentry 'to-the-tiller'.

1954 US–Taiwanese mutual defence treaty.

1971 Expulsion from UN as USA adopted new policy of détente towards communist China.

1972 Commencement of legislature elections as programme of gradual democratization and Taiwanization launched by mainlander-dominated Kuomintang.

1975 President Chiang Kai-shek died; replaced as Kuomintang leader by his son, Chiang Ching-kuo.

1979 USA severed diplomatic relations and annulled 1954 security pact.

1986 Centrist Democratic Progressive Party (DPP) formed as opposition to nationalist Kuomintang.

1987 Martial law lifted; opposition parties legalized; press restrictions lifted.

1988 President Chiang Ching-kuo died; replaced by Taiwanese-born Lee Teng-hui.

1990 Chinese-born Kuomintang members became minority in parliament.

1991 President Lee Teng-hui declared

end to civil war with China. Constitution amended. Kuomintang won landslide victory in elections to new National Assembly, the 'superparliament'.

1993 Cooperation pact with China signed.

1995 Ruling Kuomintang retained majority in working assembly (Legislative Yuan) by slim margin.

1996 Lee Teng-hui elected president in first-ever Chinese democratic election.

1997 Government narrowly survived no-confidence motion. Vincent Siew became prime minister.

Practical information

Visa requirements UK: visa not required for a stay of up to 14 days. USA: visa not required for a stay of up to 14 days
Embassy in the UK Taipei Representative Office in the UK, 50 Grosvenor Gardens, London SW1W 0EB. Tel: (0171) 396 9152; fax: (0171) 396 9151
British embassy the UK has no diplomatic representation in Taiwan
Embassy in the USA none; unofficial commercial and cultural relations with the USA are maintained through a private instrumentality, the Taipei Economic and Cultural Representative Office (TECRO), with headquarters in Taipei and offices in Washington and ten other US cities
American embassy none; unofficial commercial and cultural relations with Taiwan are maintained through a private institution, the American Institute in Taiwan (AIT), which has offices in Taipei at 7, Lane 134, Hsin Yi Road, Section 3,

tel: (2) 709 2000, fax: (2) 702 7675, and in Kaohsiung at 2 Chung Cheng 3d Road, tel: (7) 224 0154–7, fax: (7) 223 8237, and the American Trade Center at Room 3207, International Trade Building, Taipei World Trade Center, 333 Keelung Road Section 1, Taipei 10548, tel: (2) 720 1550
Chamber of commerce General Chamber of Commerce, 6th Floor, 390 Flushing South Road, Section 1, Taipei. Tel: (2) 701 2671; fax: (2) 755 5493
Office hours 0830–1730 Mon–Fri; 0830–1230 Sat
Banking hours 0900–1530 Mon–Fri; 0900–1230 Sat
Time difference GMT +8
Chief tourist attractions island scenery; festivals; ancient art treasures
Major holidays 1–3 January, 29 March, 5 April, 1 July, 28 September, 10, 25, 31 October, 12 November, 25 December; variable: New Year (Chinese, January/February, 3 days), Dragon Boat Festival (June), Mid-Autumn Festival (September/October)

Tajikistan Republic of

National name *Respublika i Tojikiston*
Area 143,100 sq km/55,250 sq mi
Capital Dushanbe
Major towns/cities Khodzhent (formerly Leninabad), Kurgan-Tyube, Kulyab
Physical features mountainous, more

than half of its territory lying above 3,000 m/10,000 ft; huge mountain glaciers, which are the source of many rapid rivers

Government

Head of state Imamali Rakhmanov from 1994
Head of government Yahya Azimov from 1996
Political system authoritarian nationalist
Administrative divisions two provinces and one autonomous region (Gornyi Badakhstan)
Political parties Communist Party of Tajikistan (CPT), pro-Rakhmanov; Democratic Party of Tajikistan (DP), anticommunist (banned from 1993); Party of Popular Unity and Justice, anticommunist
Armed forces 3,000 (1995); paramilitary forces (mainly Russian) around 16,500; CIS forces 12,000

Death penalty retained and used for ordinary crimes
Defence spend (% GDP) 6.9 (1995)
Education spend (% GNP) 9.5 (1993/94)

Economy and resources

Currencies Tajik and Russian rouble
GDP ($ US) 2 billion (1994)
Real GDP per capita (PPP) ($ US) 1,117 (1994)
GDP growth rate 16.7% (1996); −18.1% (1990–95)
Average annual inflation 65% (1996); 146.6% (1985–95)
Foreign debt ($ US) 730 million (1995)
Trading partners Uzbekistan, the Netherlands, Switzerland, Russia, UK
Resources coal, aluminium, lead, zinc, iron, tin, uranium, radium, arsenic, bismuth, gold, mica, asbestos, lapis lazuli; small reserves of petroleum and natural gas

Industries mining, aluminium production, engineering, food processing, textiles (including silk), carpet making, clothing, footwear, fertilizers

Exports aluminium, cotton lint. Principal market: the Netherlands 34.1% (1995)

Imports industrial products and machinery (principally for aluminium plants), unprocessed agricultural products, food and beverages, petroleum and chemical products, consumer goods. Principal source: Uzbekistan 31.5% (1995)

Population and society

Population 5,935,000 (1996e)

Population growth rate 2.9% (1990–95); 2.5% (2000–05)

Population density (per sq km) 41 (1996e)

Urban population (% of total) 32 (1995)

Age distribution (% of total population) <15 43.1%, 15–65 52.6%, >65 4.3% (1995)

Ethnic distribution 62% ethnic Tajik, 24% Uzbek, 8% ethnic Russian, 1% Tatar, 1% Kyrgyz, and 1% Ukrainian

Language Tajik (official), similar to Farsi (Persian)

Religion Sunni Muslim

Education (compulsory years) 9

Literacy rate 97% (men); 97% (women) (1995e)

Labour force 51.2% agriculture, 18.1% industry, 30.7% services (1993)

Unemployment 2.5% (1996)

Life expectancy 69 (men); 74 (women) (1995–2000)

Child mortality rate (under 5, per 1,000 live births) 79 (1995)

Physicians 1 per 442 people (1994)

Hospital beds 1 per 96 people (1994)

TV sets (per 1,000 people) 19 (1994)

Transport

Airports international airport: Dushanbe; three domestic airports; total passenger km: 2,231 mil (1994)

Railroads total length: 511 km/318 mi; total passenger km: 103 mil (1992)

Roads total road network: 13,600 km/ 8,451 mi, of which 82.7% paved (1995e); passenger cars: 0.2 per 1,000 people (1995e)

Chronology

c. 330 Formed an eastern part of empire of Alexander the Great of Macedonia.

8th century Tajiks established as distinct ethnic group, with semi-independent territories under the tutelage of the Uzbeks, to the W; spread of Islam.

13th century Conquered by Genghis Khan and became part of Mongol Empire.

1860–1900 Northern Tajikistan came under tsarist Russian rule, while the S was annexed by Emirate of Bukhara, to the W.

1917–18 Attempts to establish Soviet control after Bolshevik revolution in Russia resisted initially by armed guerrillas (basmachi).

1921 Became part of Turkestan Soviet Socialist Autonomous Republic.

1924 Tajik Autonomous Soviet Socialist Republic formed.

1929 Became constituent republic of Soviet Union (USSR).

1930s Stalinist era of collectivization led to widespread repression of Tajiks.

1978 13,000 participated in anti-Russian riots.

late 1980s Resurgence in Tajik consciousness, stimulated by the *glasnost* initiative of Soviet leader Mikhail Gorbachev.

1989 Rastokhez ('Revival') Popular Front established and Tajik declared state language. New mosques constructed.

1990 Violent interethnic Tajik–Armenian clashes in Dushanbe; state of emergency imposed.

1991 President Kakhar Makhkamov, local communist leader since 1985, forced to resign after supporting failed anti-Gorbachev coup in Moscow. Independence declared. Rakhman Nabiyev, communist leader 1982–85, elected president. Joined new Commonwealth of Independent States (CIS).

1992 Joined Muslim Economic Cooperation Organization, the Conference on Security and Cooperation in Europe (CSCE; now the Organization on Security and Cooperation in Europe, OSCE), and United Nations. Violent demonstrations by Islamic and prodemocracy groups forced Nabiyev to resign. Civil war between pro- and anti-Nabiyev forces claimed 20,000 lives, made 600,000 refugees, and wrecked the economy. Imamali Rakhmanov, a communist sympathetic to Nabiyev, took over as head of state.

1993 Nabiyev and his militia ally, Sangak Safarov, died. Government forces regained control of most of the country. CIS peacekeeping forces drafted in to patrol border with Afghanistan, the base of pro-Islamic rebels.

1994 Cease-fire agreed. Rakhmanov popularly elected president under new constitution.

1995 Parliamentary elections won by Rakhmanov's supporters. Renewed fighting on Afghan border.

1996 Pro-Islamic rebels captured towns in SW. UN-sponsored cease-fire between government and pro-Islamic rebels.

1997 Four-stage peace plan signed. President Rakhmanov seriously injured by grenade. Peace accord with Islamic rebel group, the United Tajik Opposition (UTO).

Practical information

Visa requirements UK: visa required. USA: visa required

Embassy in the UK Tajikistan has no diplomatic representation in the UK

British embassy the British Embassy in Tashkent (see Uzbekistan) deals with all enquiries relating to Tajikistan

Embassy in the USA Tajikistan does not have an embassy in the USA, but has a mission at the UN: 136 East 67th Street, New York, NY 10021. Tel: (212) 472 7645; fax: (212) 628 0252

American embassy interim chancery, Oktyabrskaya Hotel, 105A Prospect Rudaki, Dushanbe 734001. Tel: (3772) 210

356; telex; 20116

Chamber of commerce Chamber of Commerce and Industry, Ulitsa Mazayeva 21, Dushanbe 7340012. Tel: (3772) 279 519

Office hours 0900–1800 Mon–Fri

Banking hours 0900–1730 Mon–Fri

Time difference GMT +5

Chief tourist attractions spectacular mountain scenery; sites of historical interest in the Ferghana Valley, notably the city of Khojand

Major holidays 1 January, 8, 21 March, 9 May, 9 September, 14 October; variable: end of Ramadan

Tanzania United Republic of

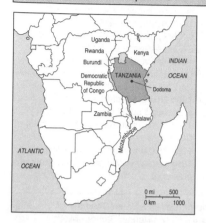

National name *Jamhuri ya Muungano wa Tanzania*
Area 945,000 sq km/364,864 sq mi
Capital Dodoma (since 1983)
Major towns/cities Zanzibar Town, Mwanza, Tabora, Mbeya, Tanga
Major ports (former capital) Dar es Salaam
Physical features central plateau; lakes in N and W; coastal plains; lakes Victoria, Tanganyika, and Nyasa; half the country is forested; comprises islands of Zanzibar and Pemba; Mount Kilimanjaro, 5,895 m/19,340 ft, the highest peak in Africa; Olduvai Gorge; Ngorongoro Crater, 14.5 km/9 mi across, 762 m/2,500 ft deep

Government

Head of state Benjamin Mkapa from 1995
Head of government Cleoopa Msuya from 1994
Political system emergent democracy
Administrative divisions 25 administrative regions
Political parties Revolutionary Party of Tanzania (CCM), African, socialist; Civic Party (Chama Cha Wananchi), left of centre; Tanzania People's Party (TPP), left of centre; Democratic Party (DP), left of centre; Zanzibar United Front (Kamahuru), Zanzibar-based, centrist
Armed forces 34,600; citizen's militia of 80,000 (1995)
Conscription two years
Death penalty retained and used for ordinary crimes
Defence spend (% GDP) 2.7 (1995)
Education spend (% GNP) 5.0 (1993/94)
Health spend (% GDP) 3.2 (1990)

Economy and resources

Currency Tanzanian shilling
GDP ($ US) 3.4 billion (1994)
Real GDP per capita (PPP) ($ US) 656 (1994)
GDP growth rate 3.5% (1994); 3.2% (1990–95)
Average annual inflation 35% (1994); 32.3% (1985–95)
Foreign debt ($ US) 7.3 billion (1995)
Trading partners UK, Germany, Japan, India, the Netherlands, Belgium, Italy, Oman
Resources diamonds, other gemstones, gold, salt, phosphates, coal, gypsum, tin, kaolin (exploration for petroleum in progress)
Industries food processing, textiles, cigarette production, pulp and paper, petroleum refining, diamonds, cement, brewing, fertilizers, clothing, footwear, pharmaceuticals, electrical goods, metalworking, vehicle assembly
Exports coffee beans, raw cotton, tobacco, tea, cloves, cashew nuts, minerals, petroleum products. Principal market: Germany 9.2% (1995)
Imports machinery and transport equipment, crude petroleum and petroleum products, construction materials, foodstuffs, consumer goods. Principal source: UK 9.6% (1995)
Arable land 3.2% (1993)
Agricultural products coffee, cotton, tobacco, cloves, tea, cashew nuts, sisal, pyrethrum, sugar cane, coconuts, cardamoms

Population and society

Population 30,799,000 (1996e)
Population growth rate 3% (1990–95); 2.6% (2000–05)
Population density (per sq km) 33 (1996e)
Urban population (% of total) 24% (1995)
Age distribution (% of total population) <15 45.9%, 15–65 51.6%, >65 2.6% (1995)
Ethnic distribution 99% of the population are Africans, ethnically classified as Bantus, and distributed among over 130 tribes; main tribes are Bantu, Vilotic, Nilo-Hamitic, Khoisan, and Iraqwi
Languages Kiswahili, English (both official)
Religions Muslim, Christian, traditional religions

Education (compulsory years) 7
Literacy rate 79% (men); 54% (women) (1995e)
Labour force 52% of population: 84% agriculture, 5% industry, 11% services (1990)
Life expectancy 50 (men); 53 (women) (1995–2000)
Child mortality rate (under 5, per 1,000 live births) 160 (1995)
Physicians 1 per 23,053 people (1991)
Hospital beds 1 per 1,062 people (1991)
TV sets (per 1,000 people) 2.3 (1995)
Radios (per 1,000 people) 276 (1995)

Transport

Airports international airports: Dar es Salaam, Kilimanjaro, Zanzibar; 50 domestic airports and landing strips; total passenger km: 165 mil (1994)
Railroads total length: 3,569 km/2,218 mi; total passenger km: 990 mil (1992)
Roads total road network: 88,100 km/54,745 mi, of which 4.2% paved (1995e); passenger cars: 0.9 per 1,000 people (1995e)

Chronology

8th century Growth of city states along coast after settlement by Arabs from Oman.
1499 Portuguese navigator Vasco da Gama visited island of Zanzibar.
16th century Portuguese occupied Zanzibar, defeated coastal states, and exerted spasmodic control over them.
1699 Portuguese ousted from Zanzibar by Arabs of Oman.
18th century Sultan of Oman reasserted Arab overlordship of E African coast, which became subordinate to Zanzibar.
1744–1837 Revolt of ruler of Mombasa against Oman spanned 93 years until final victory of Oman.
1822 Moresby Treaty: Britain recognized regional dominance of Zanzibar, but protested against slave trade.
1840 Sultan Seyyid bin Sultan moved his capital from Oman to Zanzibar; trade in slaves and ivory flourished.
1861 Sultanates of Zanzibar and Oman separated on death of Seyyid.
19th century Europeans started to explore inland, closely followed by Christian missionaries.
1884 German Colonization Society began to acquire territory on mainland in defiance of Zanzibar.

1890 Britain obtained protectorate over Zanzibar, abolished slave trade, and recognized German claims to mainland.
1897 German East Africa formally established as colony.
1905–06 Maji Maji revolt suppressed by German troops.
1916 Conquest of German East Africa by British and South African forces, led by Gen Jan Smuts.
1919 Most of German East Africa became British League of Nations mandate of Tanganyika.
1946 Britain continued to govern Tanganyika as United Nations (UN) trusteeship.

1954 Julius Nyerere organized the Tanganyikan African National Union (TANU) to campaign for independence.
1961 Tanganyika achieved independence from Britain with Nyerere as prime minister.
1962 Tanganyika became republic under President Nyerere.
1963 Zanzibar achieved independence.
1964 Arab-dominated sultanate of Zanzibar overthrown by Afro-Shirazi Party in violent revolution; Zanzibar merged with Tanganyika to form United Republic of Tanzania.
1967 East African Community (EAC) formed by Tanzania, Kenya, and Uganda

to retain customs union formed in colonial period; Arusha Declaration by Nyerere pledged to build socialist state.
1977 Revolutionary Party of Tanzania (CCM) proclaimed as only legal party; EAC dissolved.
1979 Tanzanian troops intervened in Uganda to help overthrow President Idi Amin.
1985 Nyerere retired as president; succeeded by Ali Hassan Mwinyi.
1990 Nyerere surrendered leadership of CCM to Mwinyi.
1992 Multiparty politics permitted.
1995 Benjamin Mkapa of CCM elected president.

Practical information

Visa requirements UK: visa required. USA: visa required
Embassy in the UK 43 Hertford Street, London W1Y 8D8. Tel: (0171) 499 8951; fax: (0171) 499 8954
British embassy British High Commission, PO Box 9200, Hifadhi House, Samora Avenue, Dar es Salaam. Tel: (51) 46300/4; fax: (51) 46301
Embassy in the USA 2139 R Street NW, Washington, DC 20008. Tel: (202) 939 6125; fax: (202) 797 7408
American embassy 36 Laibon Road (off Bagamoyo Road), Dar es Salaam. Tel: (51) 66010–5; fax: (51) 66701

Chamber of commerce Dar es Salaam Chamber of Commerce, PO Box 41, Kelvin House, Samora Machel Avenue, Dar es Salaam. Tel: (51) 21893
Office hours 0730–1430 Mon–Fri
Banking hours 0830–1600 Mon–Fri; 0830–1300 Sat
Time difference GMT +3
Chief tourist attractions national parks and game and forest reserves comprise one-third of the country; beaches and coral reefs along the Indian Ocean coast
Major holidays 1, 12 January, 5 February, 1 May, 7 July, 9, 25 December; variable: Eid-ul-Adha, Good Friday, Easter Monday, end of Ramadan (2 days), Prophet's Birthday

---

Thailand Kingdom of

National name *Prathet Thai* or *Muang Thai*
Area 513,115 sq km/198,113 sq mi
Capital Bangkok (and chief port)
Major towns/cities Chiangmai, Hat Yai, Khon Kaen, Songkhla, Chon Buri, Nakhon Si Thammarat, Lampang, Phitsannlok, Ratchasima
Major ports Nakhon Sawan
Physical features mountainous, semi-arid plateau in NE, fertile central region,

tropical isthmus in S; rivers Chao Phraya, Mekong, and Salween

Government

Head of state King Bhumibol Adulyadej from 1946
Head of government Chavalit Yongchaiyudh from 1996
Political system military-controlled emergent democracy
Administrative divisions 76 provinces
Political parties Democrat Party (DP), centre left; Thai Nation (Chart Thai), right wing, pro-private enterprise; New Aspiration Party (NAP), centrist; Palang Dharma Party (PDP), anti-corruption, Buddhist; Social Action Party (SAP), moderate, conservative; Chart Pattana (National Development), conservative
Armed forces 259,000 (1995)
Conscription two years
Death penalty retained and used for ordinary crimes
Defence spend (% GDP) 2.5 (1995)
Education spend (% GNP) 3.8 (1993/94)
Health spend (% GDP) 1.1 (1990)

Economy and resources

Currency baht
GDP ($ US) 143.2 billion (1994)
Real GDP per capita (PPP) ($ US) 7,104 (1994)
GDP growth rate 8.6% (1995); 8.4% (1990–95)
Average annual inflation 5.7% (1995); 5% (1985–95)
Foreign debt ($ US) 56.8 billion (1995)
Trading partners Japan, USA, Singapore, Germany, Taiwan, Hong Kong
Resources tin ore, lignite, gypsum, antimony, manganese, copper, tungsten, lead, gold, zinc, silver, rubies, sapphires, natural gas, petroleum, fish
Industries textiles and clothing, electronics, electrical goods, cement, petroleum refining, sugar refining, motor vehicles, agricultural products, beverages, tobacco, metals and metal products, plastics, furniture, tourism
Exports textiles and clothing, electronic goods, rice, rubber, gemstones, sugar, cassava (tapioca), fish (especially prawns), machinery and manufactures,

chemicals. Principal market: USA 17.8% (1995)
Imports petroleum and petroleum products, machinery, chemicals, iron and steel, consumer goods. Principal source: Japan 30.6% (1995)
Arable land 34.3% (1993)
Agricultural products rice, cassava, rubber, sugar cane, maize, kenat (a jutelike fibre), tobacco, coconuts; fishing (especially prawns) and livestock (mainly buffaloes, cattle, pigs, and poultry)

Population and society

Population 58,703,000 (1996e)
Population growth rate 1.1% (1990–95); 0.9% (2000–05)
Population density (per sq km) 114 (1996e)
Urban population (% of total) 20% (1995)
Age distribution (% of total population) <15 28.3%, 15–65 66.7%, >65 5% (1995)
Ethnic distribution 75% of the population is of Thai descent; 14% ethnic Chinese, one-third of whom live in Bangkok; Thai Malays constitute the next largest minority, followed by hill tribes; a substantial Kampuchean (Khmer) refugee community resides in border camps
Languages Thai and Chinese (both official); Lao, Chinese, Malay, Khmer
Religion Buddhist
Education (compulsory years) 6
Literacy rate 96% (men); 90% (women) (1995e)
Labour force 57% of population: 64% agriculture, 14% industry, 22% services (1990)
Unemployment 3.2% (1993)
Life expectancy 65 (men); 72 (women) (1995–2000)
Child mortality rate (under 5, per 1,000 live births) 32 (1995)
Physicians 1 per 4,354 people (1992)
Hospital beds 1 per 701 people (1992)
TV sets (per 1,000 people) 189 (1995)
Radios (per 1,000 people) 189 (1995)

Transport

Airports international airports: Bangkok (Don Muang), Chiangmai, Phuket, Hat Yai, U-tapao; domestic services to all major towns; total passenger km: 25,242 mil (1994)
Railroads total length: 3,865 km/

2,402 mi; total passenger km: 14,496 mil (1994)
Roads total road network: 62,000 km/ 38,527 mi, of which 97.4 paved (1995e); passenger cars: 24 per 1,000 people (1995e)

Chronology

13th century Siamese (Thai) people migrated south and settled in valley of Chao Phraya river in Khmer Empire.
1238 Siamese ousted Khmer governors and formed new kingdom based at Sukhothai.
14th and 15th centuries Siamese expanded at expense of declining Khmer Empire.
1350 Siamese capital moved to Ayatthaya (which also became name of kingdom).
1511 Portuguese traders first reached Siam.
1569 Conquest of Ayatthaya by Burmese ended years of rivalry and conflict.
1589 Siamese regained independence under King Naresuan.
17th century Foreign trade under royal monopoly developed with Chinese, Japanese, and Europeans.
1690s Siam expelled European military advisers and missionaries and adopted policy of isolation.
1767 Burmese invaders destroyed city of Ayatthaya, massacred ruling families, and withdrew, leaving Siam in a state of anarchy.
1782 Reunification of Siam after civil war under Gen Phraya Chakri, who founded new capital at Bangkok and proclaimed himself King Rama I.
1824–51 King Rama III reopened Siam to European diplomats and missionaries.
1851–68 King Mongkut employed European advisers to help modernize government, legal system, and army.
1856 Royal monopoly on foreign trade ended.
1868–1910 King Chulalongkorn continued modernization and developed railway network using Chinese immigrant labour; Siam became major exporter of rice.
1896 Anglo-French agreement recognized Siam as independent buffer state between British Burma and French Indo-China.
1932 Bloodless coup forced King Rama VII to grant a constitution with mixed civilian-military government.

1939 Siam changed its name to Thailand (briefly reverting to Siam 1945–49).
1941 Japanese invaded; Thailand became puppet ally of Japan under Field Marshal Phibun Songkhram.
1945 Japanese withdrawal; Thailand compelled to return territory taken from Laos, Cambodia, and Malaya.
1946 King Ananda Mahidol assassinated.
1947 Phibun regained power in military coup, reducing monarch to figurehead; Thailand adopted strongly pro-American foreign policy.
1955 Political parties and free speech introduced.
1957 State of emergency declared; Phibun deposed in bloodless coup; military dictatorship continued under Gen Sarit Thanarat (1957–63) and Gen Thanom Kittikachorn (1963–73).
1967–72 Thai troops fought in alliance with USA in Vietnam War.
1973 Military government overthrown by student riots.
1974 Adoption of democratic constitution, followed by civilian coalition government.
1976 Military reassumed control in response to mounting strikes and political violence.
1978 Gen Kriangsak Chomanan introduced constitution with mixed civilian–military government.
1980 Gen Prem Tinsulanonda assumed power.
1983 Prem relinquished army office to head civilian government; martial law maintained.
1988 Chatichai Choonhavan succeeded Prem as prime minister.
1991 Military coup imposed new military-oriented constitution despite mass protests.
1992 General election produced five-party coalition; riots forced Prime Minister Suchinda Kraprayoon to flee; Chuan Leekpai formed new coalition government.
1995 Ruling coalition collapsed; Banharn Silpa-archa appointed premier.
1996 Banharn resigned; general election resulted in new six-party coalition led by Chavalit Yongchaiyudh.
1997 Major financial crisis led to floating of currency. Austerity rescue plan agreed with International Monetary Fund (IMF).

Practical information

Visa requirements UK: visa not required. USA: visa not required
Embassy in the UK 1/3 Yorkshire House, Grosvenor Crescent, London SW1X 7ET. Tel: (0171) 371 7621; fax: (0171) 235 9808
British embassy Wireless Road, Bangkok 10200. Tel: (2) 253 0191; fax: (2) 255 8619
Embassy in the USA 1024 Wisconsin Avenue NW, Washington, DC 20007. Tel: (202) 944 3600; fax: (202) 944 3611

American embassy 95 Wireless Road, Bangkok. Tel: (2) 252 5040; fax: (2) 254 2990
Chamber of commerce 150 Thanon Rajbopit, Bangkok 10200. Tel: (2) 225 0086; fax: (2) 225 3372
Office hours 0800–1700 Mon–Fri
Banking hours 0830–1530 Mon–Fri
Time difference GMT +7
Chief tourist attractions temples, pagodas, palaces; islands
Major holidays 1 January, 6, 13 April, 1, 5 May, 1 July, 12 August, 23 October, 5, 10, 31 December; variable: end of Ramadan, Makha Bucha (February), Visakha Bucha (May), Buddhist Lent (July)

Togo Republic of (formerly *Togoland*)

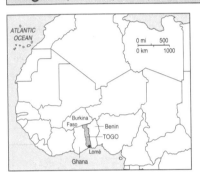

National name *République Togolaise*
Area 56,800 sq km/21,930 sq mi
Capital Lomé
Major towns/cities Sokodé, Kpalimé, Kara, Atakpamé, Bassar, Tsévié
Physical features two savanna plains, divided by range of hills NE–SW; coastal lagoons and marsh; Mono Tableland, Oti Plateau, Oti River

Government

Head of state Etienne Gnassingbé Eyadéma from 1967
Head of government Kwasi Klutse from 1996
Political system emergent democracy
Administrative divisions five regions
Political parties Rally of the Togolese People (RPT), nationalist, centrist; Action Committee for Renewal (CAR), left of centre; Togolese Union for Democracy (UTD), left of centre
Armed forces 7,000 (1995)
Conscription military service is by selective conscription for two years
Death penalty retains the death penalty for ordinary crimes, but can be considered abolitionist in practice
Defence spend (% GDP) 2.5 (1995)
Education spend (% GNP) 6.1

(1993/94)
Health spend (% GDP) 2.5 (1990)

Economy and resources

Currency franc CFA
GDP ($ US) 1 billion (1994)
Real GDP per capita (PPP) ($ US) 1,109 (1994)
GDP growth rate 16.3% (1994); –3.4% (1990–95)
Average annual inflation 15.1% (1995); 3% (1985–95e)
Foreign debt ($ US) 1.5 billion (1995)
Trading partners Canada, Ghana, France, Nigeria, Mexico, the Netherlands, Japan, USA, Spain
Resources phosphates, limestone, marble, deposits of iron ore, manganese, chromite, peat; exploration for petroleum and uranium was under way in the early 1990s
Industries processing of phosphates, steel rolling, cement, textiles, processing of agricultural products, beer, soft drinks
Exports phosphates (mainly calcium phosphates), ginned cotton, green coffee, cocoa beans. Principal market: Canada 9.2% (1995)
Imports machinery and transport equipment, cotton yarn and fabrics, cigarettes, antibiotics, food (especially cereals) and live animals, chemicals, refined petroleum products, beverages. Principal source: Ghana 17.3% (1995)
Arable land 36.5% (1993)
Agricultural products cotton, cocoa, coffee, oil palm, yams, cassava, maize, millet, sorghum

Population and society

Population 4,201,000 (1996e)
Population growth rate 3.2% (1990–95); 2.9% (2000–05)

Population density (per sq km) 74 (1996e)
Urban population (% of total) 31 (1995)
Age distribution (% of total population) <15 45.7%, 15–65 51.1%, >65 3.2% (1995)
Ethnic distribution predominantly of Sudanese Hamitic origin in the N, and black African in the S; they are distributed among 37 different ethnic groups. There are also European, Syrian, and Lebanese minorities
Languages French (official), Ewe, Kabre, Gurma
Religions animist, Catholic, Muslim, Protestant
Education (compulsory years) 6
Literacy rate 56% (men); 31% (women) (1995e)
Labour force 42% of population: 66% agriculture, 10% industry, 24% services (1990)
Unemployment 2.5% (1989e)
Life expectancy 55 (men); 59 (women) (1995–2000)
Child mortality rate (under 5, per 1,000 live births) 128 (1995)
Physicians 1 per 13,059 people (1991)
Hospital beds 1 per 626 people (1991)
TV sets (per 1,000 people) 12 (1995)
Radios (per 1,000 people) 215 (1995)

Transport

Airports international airports: Lomé, Niamtougou; four domestic airports and several smaller airfields; total passenger km: 215 mil (1994)
Railroads total length: 525 km/326 mi; total passenger km: 10 mil (1993e)
Roads total road network: 7,519 km/ 4,672 mi, of which 31.6% paved (1995); passenger cars: 18.5 per 1,000 people (1995)

Chronology

15th–17th centuries Formerly dominated by Kwa peoples in SW and Gur-speaking Votaic peoples in N, Ewe clans immigrated from Nigeria and the Ane (Mina) from Ghana and Ivory Coast.
18th century Coastal area held by Danes.
1847 Arrival of German missionaries.
1884–1914 Togoland was a German protectorate until captured by Anglo-French forces; cocoa and cotton plantations developed, using forced labour.
1922 Divided between Britain and France under League of Nations mandate.
1946 Continued under United Nations trusteeship.
1957 British Togoland, comprising one-third of the area and situated in the W, integrated with Ghana, following a plebiscite.
1960 French Togoland, situated in the E,

achieved independence from France as Republic of Togo with Sylvanus Olympio, leader of United Togolese (UP) party, as head of state.
1963 Olympio killed in a military coup. His brother-in-law, Nicolas Grunitzky, became president.
1967 Grunitzky replaced by Lt-Gen Etienne Gnassingbé Eyadéma in bloodless coup; political parties banned.
1969 Assembly of the Togolese People (RPT) formed by Eyadéma as sole legal political party.
1975 EEC Lomé convention signed in Lomé, establishing trade links with developing countries.
1977 Assassination plot against Eyadéma, allegedly involving Olympio family, thwarted.
1979 Eyadéma returned in election. Further EEC Lomé convention signed.
1986 Attempted coup failed and situation stabilized with help of French troops.
1990 Violent antigovernment

demonstrations in Lomé suppressed with casualties; Eyadéma relegalized political parties.
1991 Gilchrist Olympio returned from exile. Eyadéma was forced to call a national conference which limited the president's powers, and elected Joseph Kokou Koffigoh head of interim government. Three attempts by Eyadéma's troops to unseat government failed.
1992 Strikes in S Togo; Olympio was attacked by soldiers and fled to France. Overwhelming referendum support for multiparty politics. New constitution adopted.
1993 Eyadéma won first multiparty presidential elections amid widespread opposition.
1994 Antigovernment coup foiled. Opposition CAR polled strongly in assembly elections. Eyadéma appointed Edem Kodjo of the minority UTD as prime minister.
1996 Kwasi Klutse appointed prime minister.

Practical information

Visa requirements UK: visa not required. USA: visa not required
Embassy in the UK 8 rue Alfred Roll, 75017 Paris, France. Tel: (1) 4380 1213; fax: (1) 4380 9071
British embassy British Honorary Consulate, BP 20050, British School of Lomé, Lomé. Tel: (228) 264 606; fax: (228) 214 989
Embassy in the USA 2208 Massachusetts Avenue NW, Washington, DC 20008. Tel: (202) 234 4212; fax: (202) 232 3190
American embassy rue Pelletier Caventou and Rue Vauban,

Lomé. Tel: (228) 217 717, 212 991–994; fax: (228) 217 952
Chamber of commerce Chambre de Commerce, d'Agriculture et d'Industrie du Togo, BP 360, angle avenue de la Présidence, Lomé. Tel: (228) 217 065; fax: (228) 214 730
Office hours 0700–1730 Mon–Fri
Banking hours 0800–1600 Mon–Fri
Time difference GMT +/–0
Chief tourist attractions long sandy beaches shaded by palm trees along the coast between Lomé and Cotonou (Benin)
Major holidays 1, 13, 24 January, 24, 27 April, 1 May, 15 August, 1 November, 25 December; variable: Ascension Thursday, Eid-ul-Adha, end of Ramadan

---

Tonga Kingdom of (or *Friendly Islands*)

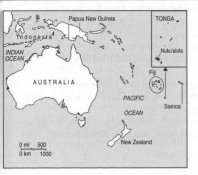

National name *Pule'anga Fakatu'i 'o Tonga*
Area 750 sq km/289 sq mi
Capital Nuku'alofa (on Tongatapu Island)
Major towns/cities Pangai, Neiafu
Physical features three groups of islands in SW Pacific, mostly coral formations, but actively volcanic in W; of the 170 islands in the Tonga group, 36 are inhabited

Government

Head of state King Taufa'ahau Tupou IV from 1965

Head of government Baron Vaea from 1991
Political system constitutional monarchy
Administrative divisions five divisions comprising 23 districts
Political parties legally none, but one prodemocracy grouping, the People's Party
Armed forces 125-strong naval force (1995)
Conscription military service is voluntary

Death penalty retains the death penalty for ordinary crimes, but can be considered abolitionist in practice (last execution 1982)
Education spend (% GNP) 4.8 (1992)
Health spend (% GDP) 4.1 (1991e)

Economy and resources

Currency Tongan dollar or pa'anga
GDP ($ US) 228 million (1995e)
Real GDP per capita (PPP) ($ US) 2,160 (1995e)
GDP growth rate −1.6% (1995)
Average annual inflation 1.4% (1995); 7.9% (1985–95e)
Foreign debt ($ US) 64.4 million (1994)
Trading partners New Zealand, Japan, Australia, Fiji, USA, UK
Industries concrete blocks, small excavators, clothing, coconut oil, furniture, handicrafts, sports equipment (including small boats), brewing, sandalwood processing, tourism
Exports vanilla beans, pumpkins, coconut oil and other coconut products, watermelons, knitted clothes, cassava, yams, sweet potatoes, footwear. Principal market: Japan 48% (1995)
Imports foodstuffs, basic manufactures, machinery and transport equipment, mineral fuels. Principal source: New Zealand 38% (1995)
Arable land 25% (1993)
Agricultural products coconuts, copra, cassava, vanilla, pumpkins, yams, taro, sweet potatoes, watermelons, tomatoes, lemons and limes, oranges, groundnuts, breadfruit; livestock rearing (pigs, goats, poultry, and cattle); fishing

Population and society

Population 98,000 (1996e)

Population growth rate 0.4% (1990–95)
Population density (per sq km) 132 (1996e)
Urban population (% of total) 41.1 (1995)
Age distribution (% of total population) <15 39.6%, 15–65 54.7%, >65 5.7% (1992)
Ethnic distribution 98% of Tongan ethnic origin, a Polynesian group with a small mixture of Melanesian; the remainder is European and part-European
Languages Tongan (official); English
Religion Free Wesleyan Church
Education (compulsory years) 8
Literacy rate 95% (men); 89% (women) (1994e)
Labour force 38.1% agriculture, 20.6% industry, 41.3% (1990)
Unemployment 4.2% (1990)
Life expectancy 67 (men); 71 (women) (1996e)
Infant mortality rate (per 1,000 live births) 20 (1994)
Physicians 1 per 2,325 people (1991)
Hospital beds 1 per 286 people (1991)
TV sets (per 1,000 people) 16 (1995)
Radios (per 1,000 people) 571 (1995)

Transport

Airports international airports: Fua'amotu (15 km/9 mi from Nuku'alofa); five domestic airstrips; total passenger km: 11 mil (1994)
Railroads none
Roads total road network: 674 km/ 419 mi, of which 27% paved (1995); passenger cars: 11.1 per 1,000 people (1995)

Chronology

c. 1000 BC Settled by Polynesian

immigrants from Fiji.
c. AD 950 The legendary Aho'eitu became the first hereditary Tongan king (Tu'i Tonga).
13th–14th centuries Tu'i Tonga kingdom at the height of its power.
1643 Visited by the Dutch navigator, Abel Tasman.
1773 Islands visited by British navigator Capt James Cook, who named them the 'Friendly Islands'.
1826 Methodist mission established.
1831 Tongan dynasty founded by a Christian convert and chief of Ha'apai, Prince Taufa'ahau Tupou, who became king 14 years later.
1845–93 Reign of King George Tupou I, during which the country was reunited after half a century of civil war; Christianity was spread and a modern constitution adopted 1875.
1900 Friendship ('Protectorate') treaty signed between King George Tupou II and Britain, establishing British control over defence and foreign affairs, but leaving internal political affairs under Tongan control.
1918 Queen Salote Tupou III ascended the throne.
1965 Queen Salote died; succeeded by her son, King Taufa'ahau Tupou IV, who had been prime minister since 1949.
1970 Independence from Britain, but remained within Commonwealth.
1993 Six prodemocracy candidates elected. Calls for reform of absolutist power.
1996 Prodemocracy movement led by People's Party won a majority of the 'commoner' seats in legislative assembly. Prodemocracy campaigner Akilisis Pohiva released after a month's imprisonment.

Practical information

Visa requirements UK: visa required (issued on arrival). USA: visa required (issued on arrival)
Embassy in the UK 36 Molyneux Street, London W1H 6AB. Tel: (0171) 724 5828; fax: (0171) 723 9074
British embassy British High Commission, PO Box 56, Vuna Road, Nuku'alofa. Tel: (676) 21020/1; fax: (676) 24109
Embassy in the USA Tonga does not have an embassy in the USA; the ambassador resides in London
American embassy the USA does not have an embassy in Tonga; the ambassador to Fiji is accredited to Tonga

Chamber of commerce Office of the Minister of Labour, Commerce and Industries, PO Box 110, Nuku'alofa. Tel/fax: (676) 23688
Office hours 0830–1630 Mon–Fri; 0800–1200 Sat
Banking hours 0930–1530 Mon–Fri; 0830–1130 Sat
Time difference GMT +13
Chief tourist attractions mild climate; scenic beauty; beautiful beaches; high volcanic and low coral forms give the islands a unique character
Major holidays 1 January, 25 April, 5 May, 4 June, 4 July, 4 November, 4, 25–26 December; variable: Good Friday, Easter Monday

Trinidad and Tobago Republic of

Area 5,130 sq km/1,980 sq mi including smaller islands (Trinidad 4,828 sq km/ 1,864 sq mi and Tobago 300 sq km/115 sq mi)
Capital Port of Spain (and port)
Major towns/cities San Fernando, Arima, Point Fortin
Major ports Scarborough, Point Lisas
Physical features comprises two main islands and some smaller ones in Caribbean Sea; coastal swamps and hills E–W

Government

Head of state Noor Hassanali from 1987
Head of government Basdeo Panday from 1995
Political system democratic republic
Administrative divisions nine counties, two municipalities, and three borough corporations, plus the island of Tobago
Political parties National Alliance for Reconstruction (NAR), nationalist, left of centre; People's National Movement (PNM), nationalist, moderate, centrist; United National Congress (UNC), left of centre; Movement for Social Transformation (Motion), left of centre
Armed forces 2,100 (1995); plus a paramilitary force of 4,800
Conscription military service is voluntary
Death penalty retained and used for ordinary crimes
Defence spend (% GDP) 1.3 (1995)
Education spend (% GNP) 4.1 (1994)
Health spend (% GDP) 2.6 (1990)

Economy and resources

Currency Trinidad and Tobago dollar
GDP ($ US) 4.8 billion (1994)
Real GDP per capita (PPP) ($ US) 9,124 (1994)

GDP growth rate 4.7% (1994); 1% (1990–95)
Average annual inflation 5.6% (1995); 6.8% (1985–95)
Foreign debt ($ US) 2.5 million (1995)
Trading partners USA, Venezuela, UK, Germany, Canada, Barbados, Jamaica, Guyana, Netherlands Antilles
Resources petroleum, natural gas, asphalt (world's largest deposits of natural asphalt)
Industries petroleum refining, food processing, iron and steel, beverages, chemicals, cement, beer, cigarettes, motor vehicles, paper, printing and publishing, tourism (third-largest source of foreign exchange)
Exports mineral fuels and lubricants, chemicals, basic manufactures, food. Principal market: USA 42.9% (1995)
Imports machinery and transport equipment, manufactured goods, mineral fuel products, food and live animals, chemicals. Principal source: USA 49.9% (1995)
Arable land 14.6% (1993)
Agricultural products sugar cane, coffee, cocoa, citrus fruits; fishing

Population and society

Population 1,297,000 (1996e)
Population growth rate 1.1% (1990–95); 1.1% (2000–05)
Population density (per sq km) 253 (1996e)
Urban population (% of total) 72 (1995)
Age distribution (% of total population) <15 32.3%, 15–65 62%, >65 5.7% (1995)
Ethnic distribution the two main ethnic groups are Africans and East Indians; there are also European, Afro-European, and Chinese minorities. The original Carib population has largely disappeared
Languages English (official); Hindi, French, Spanish
Religions Roman Catholic, Anglican, Hindu, Muslim
Education (compulsory years) 7
Literacy rate 97% (men); 95% (women) (1995e)
Labour force 12.4% agriculture, 25.4% industry, 62.2% services (1994)
Unemployment 18.4 (1994e)
Life expectancy 71 (men); 75 (women) (1995–2000)
Child mortality rate (under 5, per 1,000 live births) 18 (1995)
Physicians 1 per 1,113 people (1994)

Hospital beds 1 per 279 people (1994)
TV sets (per 1,000 people) 322 (1995)
Radios (per 1,000 people) 505 (1995)

Transport

Airports international airports: Port of Spain, Trinidad (Piarco), Crown Point (near Scarborough, Tobago); domestic services between these; total passenger km: 4,112 mil (1994)
Railroads railway service discontinued 1968
Roads total road network: 8,160 km/ 5,071 mi, of which 51% paved (1995e); passenger cars: 95.7 per 1,000 people (1993e)

Chronology

1498 Visited by the explorer Christopher Columbus, who named Trinidad after the three peaks at its SE tip and Tobago after the local form of tobacco pipe. Carib and Arawak Indians comprised the indigenous community.
1532 Trinidad colonized by Spain.
1630s Tobago settled by Dutch, who introduced sugar-cane growing.
1797 Trinidad captured by Britain and ceded by Spain five years later under Treaty of Amiens.
1814 Tobago ceded to Britain by France.
1834 Abolition of slavery resulted in indentured labourers being brought in from India, rather than Africa, to work sugar plantations.
1889 Trinidad and Tobago amalgamated as British colony.
1956 The People's National Movement (PNM) founded by Eric Williams, a moderate nationalist.
1958–62 Part of West Indies Federation.
1959 Achieved internal self-government, with Williams as chief minister.
1962 Independence achieved within Commonwealth, with Williams as prime minister.
1970 Army mutiny and violent Black Power riots directed against minority East Indian population; state of emergency imposed for two years.
1976 Became a republic, with former governor general Ellis Clarke as president and Williams as prime minister.
1981 Williams died; succeeded by George Chambers.
1986 Tobago-based National Alliance for Reconstruction (NAR), headed by Arthur Robinson, won general election.
1987 Noor Hassanali became president.

1990 Attempted antigovernment coup by Islamic fundamentalists foiled.
1991 General election victory for PNM, with Patrick Manning as prime minister.
1995 United National Congress (UNC), a breakaway from the NAR rooted in the Indian community, and PNM tied in general election; UNC–NAR coalition formed, led by Basdeo Panday.

Practical information

Visa requirements UK: visa not required for a stay of up to three months. USA: visa not required for a stay of up to three months
Embassy in the UK 42 Belgrave Square, London SW1X 8NT. Tel: (0171) 245 9351; fax: (0171) 823 1065
British embassy British High Commission, PO Box 778, 19 Clair Avenue, St Clair, Port of Spain. Tel: (809) 622 2748; fax: (809) 622 4555
Embassy in the USA 1708 Massachusetts Avenue NW, Washington, DC 20036. Tel: (202) 467 6490; fax: (202) 785 3130
American embassy 15 Queen's Park West, Port of Spain.

Tel: (809) 622 6372–6, 6176; fax: (809) 628 5462
Chamber of commerce Trinidad and Tobago Chamber of Industry and Commerce, PO Box 499, Room 950–952, Hilton Hotel, Port of Spain. Tel: (809) 627 4461; fax: (809) 627 4376
Office hours 0800–1600 Mon–Fri
Banking hours 0900–1400 Mon–Thu; 0900–1200 and 1500–1700 Fri
Time difference GMT –4
Chief tourist attractions sunny climate; attractive coastline (especially Tobago); the annual pre-Lenten carnival
Major holidays 1 January, 19 June, 1, 31 August, 24 September, 25–26 December; variable: Corpus Christi, Good Friday, Easter Monday, Whit Monday

---

Tunisia Tunisian Republic

National name *al-Jumhuriya at-Tunisiya*
Area 164,150 sq km/63,378 sq mi
Capital Tunis (and chief port)
Major towns/cities Sfax, Ariana, Bizerte, Djerba, Gabès, Sousse, Kairouan, Bardo, La Goulette
Major ports Sfax, Sousse, Bizerte
Physical features arable and forested land in N graduates towards desert in S; fertile island of Jerba, linked to mainland by causeway (identified with island of lotus-eaters); Shott el Jerid salt lakes

Government

Head of state Zine el-Abidine Ben Ali from 1987
Head of government Hamed Karoui from 1989
Political system emergent democratic republic
Administrative divisions 23 governates
Political parties Constitutional Democratic Rally (RCD), nationalist, moderate, socialist; Popular Unity Movement (MUP), radical, left of centre;

Democratic Socialists Movement (MDS), left of centre; Renovation Movement (MR), reformed communists
Armed forces 35,500 (1995); plus paramilitary forces numbering 23,000
Conscription military service is by selective conscription for 12 months
Death penalty retained and used for ordinary crimes
Defence spend (% GDP) 2 (1995)
Education spend (% GNP) 6.3 (1993/94)
Health spend (% GDP) 3.3 (1990)

Economy and resources

Currency Tunisian dinar
GDP ($ US) 15.8 billion (1994)
Real GDP per capita (PPP) ($ US) 5,319 (1994)
GDP growth rate 2.4% (1995); 3.9% (1990–95)
Average annual inflation 6.3% (1995); 6% (1985–95)
Foreign debt ($ US) 10 billion (1995)
Trading partners France, Italy, Germany, Belgium, USA, Spain, the Netherlands, UK, Libya, Japan
Resources petroleum, natural gas, phosphates, iron, zinc, lead, aluminium fluoride, fluorspar, sea salt
Industries processing of agricultural and mineral products (including superphosphate and phosphoric acid), textiles and clothing, machinery, chemicals, paper, wood, motor vehicles, radio and television sets, tourism
Exports textiles and clothing, crude petroleum, phosphates and fertilizers, olive oil, fruit, leather and shoes, fishery products, machinery and electrical appliances. Principal market: France 28% (1995)
Imports machinery, textiles, food (mainly

cereals, dairy produce, meat, and sugar) and live animals, petroleum and petroleum products. Principal source: France: 25.6% (1995)
Arable land 18.3 (1993)
Agricultural products wheat, barley, olives, citrus fruits, dates, almonds, grapes, melons, apples, apricots and other fruits, chickpeas, sugar beet, tobacco; fishing

Population and society

Population 9,156,000 (1996e)
Population growth rate 1.9% (1990–95); 1.5% (2000–05)
Population density (per sq km) 56 (1996e)
Urban population (% of total) 57 (1995)
Age distribution (% of total population) <15 34.9%, 15–65 60.7%, >65 4.4% (1995)
Ethnic distribution about 10% of the population is Arab; the remainder are of Berber-Arab descent. There are small Jewish and French communities
Languages Arabic (official); French
Religions Sunni Muslim; Jewish, Christian
Education (compulsory years) 9
Literacy rate 74% (men); 56% (women) (1995e)
Labour force 21.6% agriculture, 34.4% industry, 44% services (1994)
Unemployment 15% (1995e)
Life expectancy 68 (men); 71 (women) (1995–2000)
Child mortality rate (under 5, per 1,000 live births) 37 (1995)
Physicians 1 per 1,822 people (1991)
Hospital beds 1 per 492 people (1991)
TV sets (per 1,000 people) 89 (1995)
Radios (per 1,000 people) 200 (1995)

Transport

Airports international airports: Tunis (Carthage), Monastir (Skanes), Djerba (Melita), Sfax, Tozeur (Nefta), Tabarka; domestic services operate between these; total passenger km: 1,977 mil (1994) **Railroads** total longth: 2,162 km/1,343 mi; total passenger km: 1,038 mil (1994) **Roads** total road network: 22,490 km/ 13,975 mi, of which 78.8% paved (1995e); passenger cars: 27.9 per 1,000 people (1995e)

Chronology

814 BC Phoenician emigrants from Tyre, in Lebanon, founded Carthage, near modern Tunis, as a trading post. By 6th century BC Carthaginian kingdom dominated western Mediterranean.
146 BC Carthage destroyed by Punic Wars with Rome, which began 264 BC; Carthage became part of Rome's African province.
AD 533 Came under control of Byzantine Empire.
7th century Invaded by Arabs, who introduced Islam. Succession of Islamic dynasties followed, including Aghlabids (9th century), Fatimids (10th century), and

Almohads (12th century).
1574 Became part of Islamic Turkish Ottoman Empire and a base for 'Barbary Pirates' who operated against European shipping until 19th century.
1705 Husayn Bey founded local dynasty, which held power under rule of Ottomans.
early 19th century Ahmad Bey launched programme of economic modernization, which was to nearly bankrupt the country.
1881 Became French protectorate, with bey retaining local power.
1920 Destour (Constitution) Party, named after original Tunisian constitution of 1861, founded to campaign for equal Tunisian participation in French-dominated government.
1934 Habib Bourguiba founded radical splinter party, the Neo-Destour Party, to spearhead nationalist movement.
1942–43 Brief German occupation during World War II.
1956 Independence achieved as monarchy under bey, with Bourguiba as prime minister.
1957 Bey deposed; Tunisia became one-party republic with Bourguiba as president.
1975 Bourguiba made president for life.
1979 Headquarters for Arab League

moved to Tunis after Egypt signed Camp David Accords with Israel.
1981 Multiparty elections held, as a sign of political liberalization, but were won by Bourguiba's Destourian Socialist Party (DSP).
1982 Allowed Palestine Liberation Organization (PLO) to use Tunis for its headquarters.
1985 Diplomatic relations with Libya severed; Israel attacked PLO headquarters.
1987 Zine el-Abidine Ben Ali, new prime minister, declared Bourguiba (now aged 84) incompetent for government and seized power as president.
1988 2,000 political prisoners freed; privatization initiative. Diplomatic relations with Libya restored. DSP renamed RCD.
1990 Arab League's headquarters returned to Cairo, Egypt.
1991 Opposition to US actions during Gulf War. Crackdown on religious fundamentalists; Renaissance Party banned.
1992 Western criticism of human-rights transgressions.
1994 Ben Ali and RCD re-elected. PLO transferred headquarters to Gaza City in Palestine.

Practical information

Visa requirements UK: visa not required. USA: visa not required
Embassy in the UK 29 Prince's Gate, London SW7 1QG. Tel: (0171) 584 8117; fax: (0171) 225 2884
British embassy 5 place de la Victoire, Tunis. Tel: (1) 341 444; fax: (1) 354 877
Embassy in the USA 1515 Massachusetts Avenue NW, Washington, DC 20005. Tel: (202) 862 1850
American embassy 144 avenue de la Liberté, 1002 Tunis-Belvedere. Tel: (1) 782 566; fax: (1) 789 719
Chamber of commerce Chambre de Commerce et d'Industrie de Tunis, 1 rue des Entrepreneurs, 1000 Tunis.

Tel: (1) 242 872; fax: (1) 354 744
Office hours 0800–1230 and 1430–1800 Mon–Fri; 0800–1200 Sat (winter); 0800–1300 Mon–Sat (summer)
Banking hours 0730–1100 Mon–Fri (summer); 0800–1100 and 1400–1615 Mon–Thu; 0800–1130 and 1300–1515 Fri (winter)
Time difference GMT +1
Chief tourist attractions Moorish architecture; Roman remains; the ancient Phoenician city of Carthage; sandy beaches
Major holidays 1, 18 January, 20 March, 9 April, 1 May, 1–2 June, 25 July, 3, 13 August, 3 September, 15 October; variable: Eid-ul-Adha (2 days), end of Ramadan (2 days), New Year (Muslim), Prophet's Birthday

---

Turkey Republic of

National name *Türkiye Cumhuriyeti*
Area 779,500 sq km/300,964 sq mi
Capital Ankara
Major towns/cities Istanbul, Izmir, Adana, Bursa, Antakya, Gaziantep, Konya, Mersin, Kayseri, Edirne, Antalya
Major ports Istanbul and Izmir
Physical features central plateau surrounded by mountains, partly in Europe (Thrace) and partly in Asia (Anatolia); Bosporus and Dardanelles; Mount Ararat (highest peak Great Ararat, 5,137 m/16,854 ft); Taurus Mountains in SW (highest peak Kaldi Dag, 3,734 m/

12,255 ft); sources of rivers Euphrates and Tigris in E

Government

Head of state Suleiman Demirel from 1993
Head of government Mesut Yilmaz from 1997
Political system democratic republic
Administrative divisions 73 provinces
Political parties Motherland Party (ANAP), Islamic, nationalist, right of centre; Republican People's Party (CHP), centre left; True Path Party

(DYP), centre right, pro-Western; Welfare Party (Refah), Islamic fundamentalist
Armed forces 507,800 (1995)
Conscription 18 months
Death penalty retained for ordinary crimes, but considered abolitionist in practice; last execution 1984
Defence spend (% GDP) 3.6 (1995)
Education spend (% GNP) 2.9 (1994)
Health spend (% GDP) 1.5 (1990)

Economy and resources

Currency Turkish lira
GDP ($ US) 182.6 billion (1996)
Real GDP per capita (PPP) ($ US) 6,103 (1996)
GDP growth rate 7.4% (1996); 3.2% (1990–95)
Average annual inflation 85.2% (1996); 64.6% (1985–95)
Foreign debt ($ US) 73.6 billion (1995)
Trading partners Germany, USA, Italy, France, Saudi Arabia, UK
Resources chromium, copper, mercury, antimony, borax, coal, petroleum, natural gas, iron ore, salt
Industries textiles, food processing, petroleum refining, coal, iron and steel, industrial chemicals, tourism
Exports textiles and clothing, agricultural products and foodstuffs (including figs, nuts, and dried fruit), tobacco, leather, glass, refined petroleum and petroleum products. Principal market: Germany 23.3% (1995)
Imports machinery, construction material, motor vehicles, consumer goods, crude petroleum, iron and steel, chemical products, fertilizer, livestock. Principal source: Germany 15.5% (1995)
Arable land 31.4% (1993)
Agricultural products barley, wheat, maize, sunflower and other oilseeds, sugar beet, potatoes, tea (world's fifth-largest producer), olives, fruits, tobacco

Population and society

Population 61,797,000 (1996e)
Population growth rate 2% (1990–95); 1.5% (2000–05)
Population density (per sq km) 79 (1996e)
Urban population (% of total) 69 (1995)
Age distribution (% of total population) <15 33.9%, 15–65 61.1%, >65 5% (1995)
Ethnic distribution over 90% of the population are Turks, although only about 5% are of Turkic or Western Mongoloid descent; most are descended from earlier conquerors, such as the Greeks

Languages Turkish (official); Kurdish, Arabic
Religions Sunni Muslim; Orthodox, Armenian churches
Education (compulsory years) 5
Literacy rate 90% (men); 71% (women) (1995e)
Labour force 45% of population: 53% agriculture, 18% industry, 29% services (1990)
Unemployment 6.9% (1996)
Life expectancy 67 (men); 71 (women) (1995–2000)
Child mortality rate (under 5, per 1,000 live births) 50 (1995)
Physicians 1 per 1,176 people (1991)
Hospital beds 1 per 452 people (1991)
TV sets (per 1,000 people) 189 (1995)
Radios (per 1,000 people) 164 (1995)

Transport

Airports international airports: Ankara (Esenboga), Istanbul (Atatürk), Izmir (Adnan Menderes), Adana, Trabzon, Dalaman, Antalya; 15 domestic airports; total passenger km: 8,576 mil (1994)
Railroads total length: 10,386 km/6,454 mi; total passenger km: 6,335 mil (1994)
Roads total road network: 381,300 km/ 236,940 mi, of which 23% paved (1995); passenger cars: 51.7 per 1,000 people (1995)

Chronology

1st century BC Asia Minor became part of Roman Empire, later passing to Byzantine Empire.
6th century AD Turkic peoples spread from Mongolia into Turkestan, where they adopted Islam.
1055 Seljuk Turks captured Baghdad; their leader Tughrul took title of sultan.
1071 Battle of Manzikert: Seljuk Turks defeated Byzantines and conquered Asia Minor.
13th century Ottoman Turks, driven west by Mongols, became vassals of Seljuk Turks.
c. 1299 Osman I founded small Ottoman kingdom, which quickly displaced Seljuks to include all Asia Minor.
1354 Ottoman Turks captured Gallipoli and began their conquests in Europe.
1389 Battle of Kossovo: Turks defeated Serbs to take control of most of Balkan peninsula.
1453 Constantinople, capital of Byzantine Empire, fell to the Turks; became capital of Ottoman Empire as Istanbul.

16th century Ottoman Empire reached its zenith under Suleiman the Magnificent 1520–66; Turks conquered Egypt, Syria, Arabia, Mesopotamia, Tripoli, Cyprus, and most of Hungary.
1683 Failure of Siege of Vienna marked start of decline of Ottoman Empire.
1699 Treaty of Karlowitz: Turks forced out of Hungary by Austrians.
1774 Treaty of Kuchuk Kainarji: Russia drove Turks from Crimea and won the right to intervene on behalf of Christian subjects of the sultan.
19th century 'The Eastern Question': Ottoman weakness caused intense rivalry between great Powers to shape future of Near East.
1821–29 Greek war of independence: Greeks defeated Turks with help of Russia, Britain, and France.
1854–56 Crimean War: Britain and France fought to defend Ottoman Empire from further pressure by Russians.
1877–78 Russo-Turkish War ended with Treaty of Berlin and withdrawal of Turks from Bulgaria.
1908 Young Turk revolution forced sultan to grant constitution; start of political modernization.
1911–12 Italo-Turkish War: Turkey lost Tripoli (Libya).
1912–13 Balkan War: Greece, Serbia, and Bulgaria expelled Turks from Macedonia and Albania.
1914 Ottoman Empire entered World War I on German side.
1919 Following Turkish defeat, Mustapha Kemal launched nationalist revolt to resist foreign encroachments.
1920 Treaty of Sèvres partitioned Ottoman Empire, leaving no part of Turkey fully independent.
1922 Kemal, having defied Allies, expelled Greeks, French, and Italians from Asia Minor; sultanate abolished.
1923 Treaty of Lausanne recognized Turkish independence; secular republic established by Kemal, who imposed rapid Westernization.
1935 Kemal adopted surname Atatürk ('Father of the Turks').
1938 Death of Kemal Atatürk; succeeded as president by Ismet Inönü.
1950 First free elections won by opposition Democratic Party; Adnan Menderes became prime minister.
1952 Turkey became a member of NATO.
1960 Military coup led by Gen Cemal Gürsel deposed Menderes, who was executed 1961.
1961 Inönü returned as prime minister;

politics dominated by the issue of Cyprus.
1965 Justice Party came to power under
Suleyman Demirel.
1971–73 Prompted by strikes and student
unrest, army imposed military rule.
1974 Turkey invaded northern Cyprus.
1980–83 Political violence led to further

military rule.
1984 Kurds began guerrilla war in quest
for greater autonomy.
1989 Application to join European
Community rejected.
1990–91 Turkey joined UN coalition
against Iraq in Gulf War.

1995 Turkish offensives against Kurdish
bases in N Iraq; Islamicist Welfare Party
won largest number of seats in general
election.
1997 Plans agreed for curbing of Muslim
fundamentalism. Mesut Yilmaz appointed
prime minister.

Practical information

Visa requirements UK: visa not required for a stay of up to
three months. USA: visa not required for a stay of up to three
months
Embassy in the UK 43 Belgrave Square, London
SW1X 8PA. Tel: (0171) 393 0202; fax: (0171) 393 0066
British embassy Senit Ersan Caddesi 46/A, Cankaya,
Ankara. Tel: (312) 468 6230; fax: (312) 468 3214
Embassy in the USA 1714 Massachusetts Avenue NW,
Washington, DC 20036. Tel: (202) 659 8200
American embassy 110 Ataturk Boulevard, Ankara.
Tel: (312) 468 6110; fax: (312) 467 0019
Chamber of commerce Union of Chambers of Commerce,

Industry, Maritime Commerce and Commodity Exchanges of
Turkey, Atatürk Bul 149, Bakanhliklar, 06640, Ankara.
Tel: (312) 417 7700; fax: (312) 418 3568
Office hours 0830–1200 and 1300–1730 Mon–Fri
Banking hours 0830–1200 and 1300–1700 Mon–Fri
Time difference GMT +3
Chief tourist attractions sunny climate; fine beaches;
ancient monuments; historic Istanbul, with its 15th-century
Topkapi Palace, 6th-century Hagia Sophia basilica, Blue
Mosque, mosque of Suleiman the Magnificent, covered
bazaars, and Roman cisterns
Major holidays 1 January, 23 April, 19 May, 30 August,
29 October; variable: Eid-ul-Adha (4 days), end of Ramadan
(3 days)

Turkmenistan Republic of

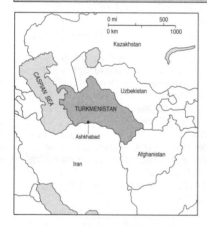

Area 488,100 sq km/188,455 sq mi
Capital Ashkhabad
Major towns/cities Chardzhov, Mary
(Merv), Nebit-Dag, Krasnovodsk
Major ports Turkmenbashi
Physical about 90% of land is desert
including the Kara Kum 'Black Sands'
desert (area 310,800 sq km/120,000
sq mi)

Government

Head of state and government
Saparmurad Niyazov from 1991
Political system authoritarian nationalist
Administrative divisions five regions
Political parties Democratic Party of
Turkmenistan, ex-communist, pro-

Niyazov; Turkmen Popular Front
(Agzybirlik), nationalist
Armed forces 11,000 (1995)
Conscription military service is
compulsory for 18 months
Death penalty retained and used for
ordinary crimes
Defence spend (% GDP) 1.9 (1995)
Education spend (% GNP) 7.9 (1993/94)

Economy and resources

Currency manat
GDP ($ US) 5 billion (1994)
Real GDP per capita (PPP) ($ US)
3,469 (1994)
GDP growth rate –3% (1996); –10.6%
(1990–95)
Average annual inflation 992% (1996);
381.4% (1985–95)
Foreign debt ($ US) 418 million (1994)
Trading partners Germany, Ukraine,
Russia, Armenia, Azerbaijan, Turkey,
Switzerland, Italy
Resources petroleum, natural gas, coal,
sulphur, magnesium, iodine-bromine,
sodium sulphate and different types of
salt
Industries mining, petroleum refining,
energy generation, textiles, chemicals,
cement, mineral fertilizer, footwear
Exports natural gas, cotton yarn, electric
energy, petroleum and petroleum
products. Principal market: Germany
11.4% (1995)
Imports machinery and metalwork, light

industrial products, processed food,
agricultural products. Principal source:
Germany 25.4% (1995)

Population and society

Population 4,155,000 (1996e)
Population growth rate 2.3%
(1990–95); 1.9% (2000–05)
Population density (per sq km) 9
(1996e)
Urban population (% of total) 45
(1995)
Age distribution (% of total population)
<15 39.5%, 15–65 56.4%, >65 4.2%
(1995)
Ethnic distribution 72% ethnic
Turkmen, 10% ethnic Russian, 9%
Uzbek, 3% Kazakh, 1% Ukrainian
Language West Turkic, closely related
to Turkish
Religion Sunni Muslim
Education (compulsory years) 9
Literacy rate 98% (1995e)
Labour force 43.4% agriculture, 20.8%
industry, 35.8% services (1993)
Unemployment 2.5% (1992e)
Life expectancy 64 (men); 70 (women)
(1995–2000)
Child mortality rate (under 5, per 1,000
live births) 85 (1995)
Physicians 1 per 311 people (1994)
Hospital beds 1 per 95 people (1994)
TV sets (per 1,000 people) 180 (1995)
Radios (per 1,000 people) 81 (1995)

Transport

Airports international airports:
Ashkhabad; three domestic airports; total
passenger km: 1,562 mil (1994)
Railroads total length: 2,187 km/1,359
mi; total passenger km: 21 mil (1993)
Roads total road network: 23,500 km/
14,603 mi, of which 81.2% paved
(1995e)

Chronology

6th century BC Part of Persian Empire
of Cyrus the Great.
4th century BC Part of empire of
Alexander the Great of Macedonia.
7th century Spread of Islam into
Transcaspian region, followed by Arab
rule from 8th century.
10th–13th centuries Immigration from
NE by nomadic Oghuz Seljuk and
Mongol tribes, whose Turkic-speaking
descendants now dominate the country;
conquest by Genghis Khan.
16th century Came under dominance
of Persia, to the S.
1869–81 Fell under control of tsarist

Russia after 150,000 Turkmen were
killed in Battle of Gok Tepe 1881;
became part of Russia's Turkestan
Governor-Generalship.
1916 Turkmen revolted violently against
Russian rule; autonomous Transcaspian
government formed after Russian
Revolution of 1917.
1919 Brought back under Russian
control following invasion by the Soviet
Red Army.
1921 Part of Turkestan Soviet Socialist
Autonomous Republic.
1925 Became constituent republic of
USSR.
1920s–30s Soviet programme of
agricultural collectivization and
secularization provoked sporadic
guerrilla resistance and popular
uprisings.
1960–67 Lenin Kara-Kum Canal built,
leading to dramatic expansion in cotton
production in previously semidesert
region.
1985 Saparmurad Niyazov replaced
Muhammad Gapusov, local communist
leader since 1971, whose regime had

been viewed as corrupt.
1989 Stimulated by *glasnost* initiative of
reformist Soviet leader Mikhail
Gorbachev, Agzybirlik 'popular front'
formed by Turkmen intellectuals.
1990 Economic and political sovereignty
declared. Niyazov elected state
president.
1991 Niyazov initially supported
attempted anti-Gorbachev coup in
Moscow. Independence was later
declared; joined new Commonwealth of
Independent States (CIS).
1992 Joined Muslim Economic
Cooperation Organization and United
Nations; new constitution adopted.
1993 New currency, manat, introduced
and programme of cautious economic
reform introduced, with foreign
investment in country's huge oil and gas
reserves encouraged; but economy
contracted to 1995.
1994 Nationwide referendum
overwhelmingly backed Niyazov's
presidency. Ex-communists won most
seats in parliamentary elections.
1997 Private land ownership legalized.

Practical information

Visa requirements UK: visa required. USA: visa required
Embassy in the UK Turkmenistan has no diplomatic
representation in the UK; the Department of Trade and
Industry has a desk which deals with enquiries relating to
Turkmenistan. Tel: (0171) 215 8427; fax: (0171) 215 4817
British embassy the UK has no diplomatic representation in
Turkmenistan
Embassy in the USA 1511 K Street NW, Suite 412,
Washington, DC 20005. Tel: (202) 737 4800;
fax: (202) 737 1152

American embassy 9 Pushkin Street, Ashkhabad. Tel:
(3632) 350 042/5/6, tie line 962 0000; fax: (3632) 511 305
Chamber of commerce Commission for International
Economic Affairs of the Office of the President of
Turkmenistan, Ulitsa Kemine 92, Ashkhabad 744000. Tel:
(3632) 298 770; fax: (3632) 297 524
Time difference GMT +5
Chief tourist attractions ruins of the 12th-century Seljuk
capital at Merv (now Mary); hot springs at Bacharden, on the
Iranian border; the bazaar at Ashkhabad
Major holidays 1, 12 January, 19, 22 February, 8 March, 29
April, 9, 18 May, 27–28 October

Tuvalu South West Pacific State of (formerly *Ellice Islands*)

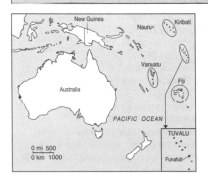

Area 25 sq km/9.6 sq mi
Capital Fongafale (on Funafuti atoll)
Major towns/cities Vaitupu, Niutao,
Nanumea
Physical features nine low coral atolls
forming a chain of 579 km/650 mi in the
SW Pacific

Government

Head of state Queen Elizabeth II from
1978, represented by governor general
Tulaga Manuella from 1994
Head of government Bikenibeu Paeniu

from 1996
Political system liberal democracy
Administrative divisions one town
council and seven island councils
Political parties none; members are
elected to parliament as independents
Armed forces no standing defence
force
Death penalty laws do not provide for
the death penalty for any crime

Economy and resources

Currency Australian dollar

GDP ($ US) 8 million (1995e)
Real GDP per capita (PPP) ($ US) 800
(1995e)
GDP growth rate N/A
Average annual inflation 3.9
(1985–93)
Foreign debt ($ US) 6 million (1993)
Trading partners Australia, Fiji, New
Zealand, UK
Industries processing of agricultural
products (principally coconuts), soap,
handicrafts, tourism; a large source of
income is from Tuvaluans working
abroad, especially in the phosphate
industry on Nauru
Exports copra. Principal market:
Australia
Imports food and live animals,
beverages, tobacco, consumer goods,
machinery and transport equipment,
mineral fuels. Principal source: Australia
Agricultural products coconuts, pulaka,
taro, papayas, screw-pine (pandanus),
bananas; livestock rearing (pigs, poultry,
and goats); honey production and fishing
supplement basic subsistence; fishing is
largely unexploited, although Japan,
Taiwan, and South Korea have been
granted licences to fish since the late
1980s

Population and society

Population 10,000 (1996e)
Population growth rate 1.4% (1990–95)
Population density (per sq km) 372
(1996e)
Urban population (% of total) 46.2
(1995)

Ethnic distribution almost entirely of
Polynesian origin, maintaining close ties
with Samoans and Tokelauans to the S
and E
Languages Tuvaluan, English
Religions Christian (mainly Protestant)
Education (compulsory years) 9
Literacy rate N/A
Life expectancy 63 (men); 65 (women)
(1995)
Child mortality rate (under 5, per 1,000
live births) 28 (1994)
Physicians 1 per 2,743 people (1990)
Hospital beds 1 per 229 people
(1990)
Radios (per 1,000 people) 320 (1995)

Transport

Airports international airport: Funafuti;
no internal air service
Railroads none
Roads total road network: 8 km/5 mi
(1995e)

Chronology

c. 300 BC First settled by Polynesian
peoples.
16th century Invaded and occupied by
Samoans.
1765 Islands first reached by
Europeans.
1850–75 Population decimated by
European slave traders capturing
Tuvaluans to work in South America and
by exposure to European diseases.
1856 The four southern islands,
including Funafuti, claimed by USA.
1865 Christian mission established.

1877 Came under control of British
Western Pacific High Commission
(WPHC), with its headquarters in Fiji.
1892 Known as the Ellice Islands, they
were joined with Gilbert Islands (now
Kiribati) to form British protectorate.
1916 Gilbert and Ellice Islands colony
formed.
1942–43 Became base for US airforce
operations when Japan occupied Gilbert
Islands during World War II.
1975 Following referendum, the
predominantly Melanesian-peopled
Ellice Islands, fearing domination by
Micronesian-peopled Gilbert Islands in
an independent state, were granted
separate status.
1978 Independence achieved within
Commonwealth, with Toaripi Lauti as
prime minister; reverted to former name
Tuvalu ('eight standing together').
1979 The USA signed friendship treaty,
relinquishing its claim to the four
southern atolls in return for continued
access to military bases.
1981 Dr Tomasi Puapua became
premier after Louti implicated in alleged
investment scandal.
1986 Islanders rejected proposal for
republican status.
1989 Bikenibeu Paeniu became prime
minister.
1993 Kamuta Laatasi became prime
minister.
1995 Union flag removed from national
flag, presaging move towards republican
status.
1996 Bikenibeu Paeniu appointed prime
minister.

Practical information

Visa requirements UK: visa not required. USA: visa required
Embassy for the UK Honorary Consulate General of Tuvalu,
Klövensteenweg 115A, 22559 Hamburg, Germany. Tel: (40)
810 580; fax: (40) 811 016
British embassy the British Embassy in Suva (see Fiji) deals
with enquiries relating to Tuvalu
Embassy in the USA Tuvalu does not have an embassy in
the USA
American embassy the USA does not have an embassy in
Tuvalu

Chamber of commerce Development Bank of Tuvalu, PO
Box 9, Vaiaku, Funafuti. Tel: (688) 20198; telex: 4800
Office hours 0730–1615 Mon–Thu and 0730–1245 Fri
Banking hours 0930–1300 Mon–Thu; 0830–1200 Fri
Time difference GMT +12
Chief tourist attractions Funafuti lagoon; sandy beaches;
development of tourism has been limited due to Tuvalu's
remote location and lack of amenities
Major holidays 1 January, 4 March, 15 June, 5 August,
1–2 October, 14 November, 25–26 December; variable:
Good Friday, Easter Monday

Uganda Republic of

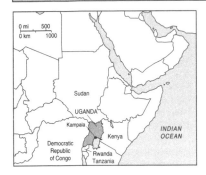

Area 236,600 sq km/91,351 sq mi
Capital Kampala
Major towns/cities Jinja, Mbale, Entebbe, Masaka, Bugembe
Physical features plateau with mountains in W (Ruwenzori Range, with Mount Margherita, 5,110 m/16,765 ft); forest and grassland; 18% is lakes, rivers, and wetlands (Owen Falls on White Nile where it leaves Lake Victoria; Lake Albert in W); arid in NE

Government

Head of state Yoweri Museveni from 1986
Head of government Kinti Musoke from 1994
Political system emergent democratic republic
Administrative divisions 38 districts within four regions
Political parties National Resistance Movement (NRM), left of centre; Democratic Party (DP), centre left; Conservative Party (CP), centre right; Uganda People's Congress (UPC), left of centre; Uganda Freedom Movement (UFM), left of centre. From 1986, political parties were forced to suspend activities
Armed forces 50,000 (1995)
Conscription military service is voluntary
Death penalty retained and used for ordinary crimes
Defence spend (% GDP) 2.6 (1995)
Education spend (% GNP) 1.9 (1993/94)
Health spend (% GDP) 1.6 (1990)

Economy and resources

Currency Uganda new shilling
GDP ($ US) 4 billion (1994)
Real GDP per capita (PPP) ($ US) 1,370 (1994)
GDP growth rate 8.5% (1995); 6.6% (1990–95)

Average annual inflation 5% (1995); 65.5% (1985–95e)
Foreign debt ($ US) 3.5 billion (1995)
Trading partners Kenya, Spain, UK, Germany, the Netherlands, USA, France
Resources copper, apatite, limestone; believed to possess the world's second-largest deposit of gold (hitherto unexploited); also reserves of magnetite, tin, tungsten, beryllium, bismuth, asbestos, graphite
Industries processing of agricultural products, brewing, vehicle assembly, textiles, cement, soap, fertilizers, footwear, metal products, paints, batteries, matches
Exports coffee, cotton, tea, tobacco, oil seeds and oleaginous fruit; hides and skins, textiles. Principal market: Spain 22.8% (1995)
Imports machinery and transport equipment, basic manufactures, petroleum and petroleum products, chemicals, miscellaneous manufactured articles, iron and steel. Principal source: Kenya 26.2% (1995)
Arable land 28.7% (1993)
Agricultural products coffee, cotton, tea, maize, tobacco, sugar cane, cocoa, horticulture, plantains, cassava, sweet potatoes, millet, sorghum, beans, groundnuts, rice; livestock rearing (cattle, goats, sheep, and poultry); freshwater fishing

Population and society

Population 20,256,000 (1996e)
Population growth rate 3.4% (1990–95); 2.7% (2000–05)
Population density (per sq km) 86 (1996e)
Urban population (% of total) 13 (1995)
Age distribution (% of total population) <15 48.8%, 15–65 48.8%, >65 2.4% (1995)
Ethnic distribution about 40 different peoples concentrated into four main groups; the Bantu (the most numerous), Eastern Nilotic, Western Nilotic, and Central Sudanic; there are also Rwandan, Sudanese, Zairean, and Kenyan minorities
Languages English (official), Kiswahili, Bantu and Nilotic languages
Religions Christian 50%, animist 40%, Muslim 10%
Education not compulsory
Literacy rate 62% (men); 45% (women) (1995e)

Labour force 51% of population: 85% agriculture, 5% industry, 11% services (1990)
Life expectancy 42 (men); 44 (women) (1995–2000)
Child mortality rate (under 5, per 1,000 live births) 185 (1995)
Physicians 1 per 23,688 people (1991)
Hospital beds 1 per 823 people (1991)
TV sets (per 1,000 people) 13 (1995)
Radios (per 1,000 people) 117 (1995)

Transport

Airports international airports: Entebbe; domestic services operate to all major towns; total passenger km: 52 mil (1994)
Railroads total length: 1,241 km/771 mi; passengers carried: 221,000 (1994)
Roads total road network: 26,800 km/ 16,654 mi, of which 7.7% paved (1995e); passenger cars: 1.2 per 1,000 people (1995e)

Chronology

16th century Bunyoro kingdom founded by immigrants from SE Sudan.
17th century Rise of kingdom of Buganda people, which became particularly powerful from 17th century.
mid-19th century Arabs, trading ivory and slaves, reached Uganda; first visits by European explorers and Christian missionaries.
1885–87 Uganda Martyrs: Christians persecuted by Buganda ruler, Mwanga.
1890 Royal Charter granted to British East African Company, a trading company whose agent, Frederick Lugard, concluded treaties with local rulers, including the Buganda and the western states of Ankole and Toro.
1894 British protectorate established, with Buganda retaining some autonomy under its traditional prince (Kabaka) and other resistance being crushed.
1904 Cotton growing introduced by Buganda peasants.
1958 Internal self-government granted.
1962 Independence achieved from Britain, within Commonwealth, with Milton Obote of Uganda People's Congress (UPC) as prime minister.
1963 Proclaimed federal republic with King Mutesa II (of Buganda) as president and Obote as prime minister.
1966 King Mutesa, who opposed creation of one-party state, ousted in coup led by Obote, who ended federal status and became executive president.

1969 All opposition parties banned after assassination attempt on Obote; key enterprises nationalized.

1971 Obote overthrown in army coup led by Maj-Gen Idi Amin Dada; constitution suspended and ruthlessly dictatorial regime established; nearly 49,000 Ugandan Asians expelled; over 300,000 opponents of regime killed.

1976 Relations with Kenya strained by Amin's claims to parts of Kenya.

1979 After annexing part of Tanzania, Amin forced to leave country by opponents backed by Tanzanian troops. Provisional government set up with Yusuf Lule as initial president and then Godfrey Binaisa.

1978–79 Fighting broke out against Tanzanian troops.

1980 Binaisa overthrown by army. Elections held and Milton Obote returned to power.

1985 After opposition by pro-Lule National Resistance Army (NRA), and indiscipline in army, Obote ousted by Gen Tito Okello; constitution suspended; power-sharing agreement entered into with NRA leader Yoweri Museveni.

1986 Museveni became president, heading broad-based coalition government.

1993 King of Buganda reinstated as formal monarch, in the person of Ronald Muwenda Mutebi II.

1996 Landslide victory won by Museveni in first direct presidential elections.

Practical information

Visa requirements UK: visa not required. USA: visa not required

Embassy in the UK Uganda House, 58–59 Trafalgar Square, London WC2N 5DX. Tel: (0171) 839 5783; fax: (0171) 839 8925

British embassy British High Commission, PO Box 7070, 101–12 Parliament Avenue, Kampala. Tel: (41) 257 301/4; telex: 61202 (a/b UKREP KAMPALA)

Embassy in the USA 5911 16th Street NW, Washington, DC 20011. Tel: (202) 726 7100/1/2, 0416; fax: (202) 726 1727

American embassy address: Parliament Avenue, Kampala. Tel: (41) 259 792/3/5; fax: (41) 259 794

Chamber of commerce Uganda Investment Authority, PO Box 7418, Investment Center, Kampala Road, Kampala. Tel: (41) 234 105; fax: (41) 242 903

Office hours 0800–1230 and 1400–1630 Mon–Fri

Banking hours 0830–1400 Mon–Fri

Time difference GMT +3

Chief tourist attractions good year-round climate; lakes; forests; wildlife; varied scenery includes tropical forest and tea plantations on the slopes of the snow-capped Ruwenzori Mountains and the arid plains of the Karamoja

Major holidays 1 January, 1 April, 1 May, 9 October, 25–26 December; variable: Good Friday, Easter Monday, Holy Saturday, end of Ramadan

---

Ukraine

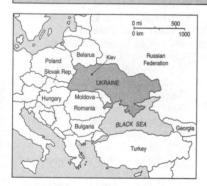

Area 603,700 sq km/233,088 sq mi
Capital Kiev
Major towns/cities Kharkov, Donetsk, Dnepropetrovsk, Lugansk (Voroshilovgrad), Lviv (Lvov), Mariupol (Zhdanov), Krivoy Rog, Zaporozhye, Odessa
Physical features Russian plain; Carpathian and Crimean Mountains; rivers: Dnieper (with the Dnieper dam 1932), Donetz, Bug

Government

Head of state Leonid Kuchma from 1994
Head of government Valery Pustovoitenko from 1997
Political system emergent democracy
Administrative divisions 24 provinces and one semi-autonomous region (Crimea)
Political parties Ukrainian Communist Party (UCP), left wing, anti-nationalist (banned 1991–93); Peasants' Party of the Ukraine (PPU), conservative agrarian; Ukrainian Socialist Party (SPU), left wing, anti-nationalist; Ukrainian People's Movement (Rukh), Ukrainian Republican Party (URP), Congress of Ukrainian Nationalists (CUN), and Democratic Party of Ukraine (DPU) – all moderate nationalist; Social Democratic Party of Ukraine (SDPU), federalist
Armed forces 453,000 (1995)
Conscription 18 months (males over 18)
Death penalty moratorium placed on executions since 1991 as condition for application to join Council of Europe (joined 1995). Despite continued demands by Council to uphold moratorium, executions have continued
Defence spend (% GDP) 3 (1995)
Education spend (% GNP) 6.8 (1994)
Health spend (% GDP) 3.3 (1991)

Economy and resources

Currency hryvna
GDP ($ US) 91 billion (1994)
Real GDP per capita (PPP) ($ US) 2,718 (1994)
GDP growth rate –10% (1996); –14.3% (1990–95)
Average annual inflation 80% (1996); 362.5% (1985–95e)
Foreign debt ($ US) 8.4 billion (1995)
Trading partners Russia, Belarus, China, Moldova, Turkmenistan, USA, Switzerland, Germany
Resources coal, iron ore (world's fifth-largest producer), crude oil, natural gas, salt, chemicals, brown coal, alabaster, gypsum
Industries metallurgy, mechanical engineering, chemicals, machinery products
Exports grain, coal, oil, various minerals. Principal market: Russia 38.7% (1996)
Imports mineral fuels, machine-building components, chemicals and chemical products. Principal source: Russia 48% (1996)
Arable land 55.2% (1993)
Agricultural products wheat, buckwheat, sugar beet, potatoes, fruit

and vegetables, sunflowers, cotton, flax, tobacco, hops; animal husbandry accounts for more than 50% of agricultural activity

Population and society

Population 51,608,000 (1996e)
Population growth rate −0.1% (1990–95); −0.2% (1993–2000)
Population density (per sq km) 85 (1996e)
Urban population (% of total) 70 (1995)
Age distribution (% of total population) <15 20.1%, 15–65 65.9%, >65 14% (1995)
Ethnic distribution 73% of the population is of Ukrainian descent; 22% ethnic Russian; 1% Jewish; 1% Belarusian
Language Ukrainian (a Slavonic language)
Religions traditionally Ukrainian Orthodox; also Ukrainian Catholic
Education (compulsory years) 8 (7–15 age limit)
Literacy rate 99% (men); 99% (women) (1995e)
Labour force 50% of population: 20% agriculture, 40% industry, 40% services (1990)
Unemployment 0.6% (1995)
Life expectancy 64 (men); 74 (women) (1995–2000)
Child mortality rate (under 5, per 1,000 live births) 24 (1995)
Physicians 1 per 226 people (1994)
Hospital beds 1 per 77 people (1994)
TV sets (per 1,000 people) 339 (1995)
Radios (per 1,000 people) 856 (1995)

Transport

Airports international airports: Kiev (Borispol); four principal domestic airports; total passenger km: 1,294 mil (1994)
Railroads total length: 22,564 km/14,021 mi; total passenger km: 70,882 mil (1994)
Roads total road network: 172,257 km/ 107,040 ml, of which 94.8% paved

(1995); passenger cars: 85.2 per 1,000 people (1995e)

Chronology

9th century Rus' people established state centred on Kiev and adopted Eastern Orthodox Christianity 988.
1199 Reunification of southern Rus' lands, after period of fragmentation, under Prince Daniel of Galicia-Volhynia.
13th century Mongol-Tatar Golden Horde sacked Kiev and destroyed Rus' state.
14th century Poland annexed Galicia; Lithuania absorbed Volhynia and expelled Tatars; Ukraine peasants became serfs of Polish and Lithuanian nobles.
1569 Poland and Lithuania formed single state; clergy of Ukraine formed Uniate Church, which recognized papal authority but retained Orthodox rites, to avoid Catholic persecution.
16th and 17th centuries Runaway serfs known as Cossacks ('outlaws') formed autonomous community in eastern borderlands.
1648 Cossack revolt led by Gen Bogdan Khmelnitsky drove out Poles from central Ukraine; Khmelnitsky accepted Russian protectorate 1654.
1660–90 'Epoch of Ruins': Ukraine devastated by civil war and invasions by Russians, Poles, and Turks; Poland regained W Ukraine.
1687 Gen Ivan Mazepa entered into alliance with Sweden in effort to regain Cossack autonomy from Russia.
1709 Battle of Poltava: Russian victory over Swedes ended hopes of Cossack independence.
1772–95 Partition of Poland: Austria annexed Galicia, Russian annexations included Volhynia.
1846–47 Attempt to promote Ukrainian national culture through formation of Cyril and Methodius Society.
1899 Revolutionary Ukrainian Party founded.
1917 Revolutionary parliament (Rada),

proclaimed Ukrainian autonomy within a federal Russia.
1918 Ukraine declared full independence; civil war ensued between Rada (backed by Germans) and Reds (backed by Russian Bolsheviks).
1919 Galicia united with Ukraine; conflict escalated between Ukrainian nationalists, Bolsheviks, anarchists, White Russians, and Poles.
1921 Treaty of Riga: Russia and Poland partitioned Ukraine.
1921–22 Several million people perished in famine.
1922 Ukrainian Soviet Socialist Republic (Ukrainian SSR) became part of Union of Soviet Socialist Republics (USSR).
1932–33 Enforced collectivization of agriculture caused another catastrophic famine with more than 7.5 million deaths.
1939 USSR annexed E Poland and added Galicia-Volhynia to Ukrainian SSR.
1940 USSR seized N Bukhovina from Romania and added it to Ukrainian SSR.
1941–44 Germany occupied Ukraine; many Ukrainians collaborated; millions of Ukrainians and Ukrainian Jews enslaved and exterminated by Nazis.
1945 USSR annexed Ruthenia from Czechoslovakia and added it to Ukrainian SSR, which became a nominal member of United Nations (UN).
1946 Uniate Church forcibly merged with Russian Orthodox Church.
1954 Crimea transferred from Russian Federation to Ukrainian SSR.
1986 Major environmental disaster caused by explosion of nuclear reactor at Chernobyl, N of Kiev.
1989 Rukh (nationalist movement) established as political party; ban on Uniate Church lifted.
1990 Ukraine declared sovereignty under President Leonid Kravchuk, leader of the CP.
1991 Ukraine declared independence from USSR; President Kravchuk left CP; Ukraine joined newly formed

---

Practical information

Visa requirements UK: visa required. USA: visa required
Embassy in the UK 78 Kensington Park Road, London W11 2PL. Tel: (0171) 727 6312; fax: (0171) 792 1708
British embassy vul Desyatinna 9, 252025 Kiev. Tel: (044) 228 0504; fax: (044) 228 3972
Embassy in the USA 3350 M Street NW, Washington, DC 20007. Tel: (202) 333 0606; fax: (202) 333 0817
American embassy 10 Yuria Kotsyubinskovo, 252053 Kiev 53. Tel: (44) 244 7345; fax: (44) 244 7350

Chamber of commerce Chamber of Commerce and Industry, vul Velyka Zhytomyrska 33, 254655 Kiev. Tel: (044) 212 2911; fax: (044) 212 3353
Office hours 0900–1800 (lunch breaks tend to last at least 1 hr 30 mins)
Time difference GMT +2
Chief tourist attractions popular Black Sea resorts, including Odessa and Yalta; the Crimean peninsula; cities of historical interest, including Kiev and Odessa
Major holidays 1, 7 January, 8 March, 1–2, 9 May, 24 August

Commonwealth of Independent States (CIS).
1992 Crimean sovereignty declared but then rescinded.
1994 Election gains for radical nationalists in W Ukraine and Russian unionists in E Ukraine; Leonid Kuchma succeeded

Kravchuk as president.
1996 New constitution replaced Soviet system, making presidency stronger; remaining nuclear warheads returned to Russia for destruction; new currency introduced.
1997 New government appointments

made to speed economic reform. Treaty of friendship with Russia signed, solving issue of Russian Black Sea fleet. Prime Minister Lazarenko replaced by Valery Pustovoitenko. Loan of $750 million from International Monetary Fund (IMF) approved.

United Arab Emirates (UAE) federation of the emirates of Abu Dhabi, Ajman, Dubai, Fujairah, Ras al Khaimah, Sharjah, Umm al Qaiwain

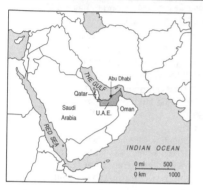

National name *Ittihad al-Imarat al-Arabiyah*
Area 83,657 sq km/32,299 sq mi
Capital Abu Dhabi
Major towns/cities Dubai, Sharjah, Ras al-Khaimah, Ajman, Fujairah
Major ports Dubai
Physical features desert and flat coastal plain; mountains in E

Government

Head of state and government Sheik Zayed bin Sultan al-Nahayan of Abu Dhabi from 1971
Supreme council of rulers *Abu Dhabi* Sheik Zayed bin Sultan al-Nahayan, president (1966); *Ajman* Sheik Humaid bin Rashid al-Nuami (1981); *Dubai* Sheik Maktoum bin Rashid al-Maktoum (1990); *Fujairah* Sheik Hamad bin Muhammad al-Sharqi (1974); *Ras al Khaimah* Sheik Saqr bin Muhammad al-Quasimi (1948); *Sharjah* Sheik Sultan bin Muhammad al-Quasimi (1972); *Umm al Qaiwain* Sheik Rashid bin Ahmad al-Mu'alla (1981)
Political system absolutism
Administrative divisions seven emirates
Political parties none
Armed forces 70,000 (1995)
Conscription military service is voluntary
Death penalty retained and used for ordinary crimes

Defence spend (% GDP) 4.8 (1995)
Education spend (% GNP) 1.8 (1993)
Health spend (% GDP) 1.8 (1994)

Economy and resources

Currency UAE dirham
GDP ($ US) 35.4 billion (1994)
Real GDP per capita (PPP) ($ US) 16,000 (1994)
GDP growth rate 1.8% (1995)
Average annual inflation 5% (1995)
Trading partners Japan, USA, UK, Germany, South Korea, France, Thailand, Italy, India
Resources petroleum and natural gas
Industries petroleum production and refining, gas handling, petrochemicals and other petroleum products, aluminium products, cable, cement, chemicals, fertilizers, rolled steel, plastics, tools, clothing
Exports crude petroleum, natural gas, re-exports (mainly machinery and transport equipment). Principal market: Japan 38% (1995)
Imports machinery and transport equipment, food and live animals, fuels and lubricants, chemicals, basic manufactures. Principal source: Japan 8.6% (1995)
Arable land 0.3% (1993)
Agricultural products dates, tomatoes, aubergines, other vegetables and fruits; livestock rearing; fishing

Population and society

Population 2,260,000 (1996e)
Population growth rate 2.6% (1990–95); 1.8% (2000–05)
Population density (per sq km) 27 (1996e)
Urban population (% of total) 84 (1995)
Age distribution (% of total population) <15 31.3%, 15–65 67%, >65 1.7% (1995)
Ethnic distribution 75% Iranians, Indians, and Pakistanis; about 25% Arabs
Languages Arabic (official), Farsi, Hindi,

Urdu, English
Religions Muslim 96%; Christian, Hindu
Education (compulsory years) 6
Literacy rate 78% (men); 78% (women) (1995e)
Labour force 51% of population: 8% agriculture, 27% industry, 65% services (1990); 93% of workforce were non-UAE nationals (1992e)
Life expectancy 74 (men); 77 (women) (1995–2000)
Child mortality rate (under 5, per 1,000 live births) 19 (1995)
Physicians 1 per 715 people (1993)
Hospital beds 1 per 497 people (1993)
TV sets (per 1,000 people) 104 (1995)
Radios (per 1,000 people) 271 (1995)

Transport

Airports international airports: Abu Dhabi (Nadia), Dubai, Ras al-Khaimah, Sharjah, Fujairah; domestic services operate between Abu Dhabi and Dubai; total passenger km: 1,225 mil (1994)
Railroads none
Roads total road network: 4,750 km/ 2,952 mi, of which 100% paved (1995e); passenger cars: 11.4 per 1,000 people (1995e)

Chronology

7th century AD Islam introduced.
early 16th century Portuguese established trading contacts with Persian Gulf states.
18th century Rise of trade and seafaring among Qawasim and Bani Yas, respectively in Ras al-Khaimah and Sharjah in N and Abu Dhabi and Dubai in desert of S. Emirates' current ruling families are descended from these peoples.
early 19th century Britain signed treaties ('truces') with local rulers, ensuring that British shipping through the Gulf was free from 'pirate' attacks and bringing Emirates under British protection.
1892 Trucial Sheiks signed Exclusive

Agreements with Britain, agreeing not to cede, sell, or mortgage territory to another power.

1952 Trucial Council established by seven sheikdoms of Abu Dhabi, Ajman, Dubai, Fujairah, Ras al Khaimah, Sharjah, and Umm al Qawain, with a view to later forming a federation.

1958 Large-scale exploitation of oil reserves led to rapid economic progress.

1968 Britain's announcement that it would remove its forces from the Persian Gulf by 1971 led to abortive attempt to arrange federation between seven Trucial States and Bahrain and Qatar.

1971 Bahrain and Qatar ceded from Federation of Arab Emirates, which was dissolved. Six Trucial States formed United Arab Emirates, with ruler of Abu Dhabi, Sheik Zayed, as president. Provisional constitution adopted.

1972 Seventh state, Ras al Khaimah, joined federation.

1976 Sheik Zayed threatened to relinquish presidency unless progress towards centralization became more rapid.

1985 Diplomatic and economic links with Soviet Union and China established.

1987 Diplomatic relations with Egypt restored.

1990–91 Iraqi invasion of Kuwait opposed; UAE troops fought as part of United Nations coalition.

1991 Bank of Commerce and Credit International (BCCI), controlled by Abu Dhabi's ruler, collapsed at cost to the UAE of $10 billion.

1992 Border dispute with Iran.

1994 Abu Dhabi agreed to pay BCCI creditors $1.8 billion.

Practical information

Visa requirements UK: visa not required for a stay of up to 30 days. USA: visa required
Embassy in the UK 30 Prince's Gate, London SW7 1PT. Tel: (0171) 581 1281; fax: (0171) 581 9616
British embassy PO Box 248, Abu Dhabi. Tel: (2) 326 600; fax: (2) 341 744
Embassy in the USA Suite 600, 3000 K Street NW, Washington, DC 20007. Tel: (202) 338 6500
American embassy Al-Sudan Street, Abu Dhabi. Tel: (2) 436 691/2; fax: (2) 434 771
Chamber of commerce Dubai Chamber of Commerce and Industry, PO Box 1457, Diera, Dubai. Tel: (4) 221 181;

fax: (4) 211 646
Office hours 0800–1300 and 1600–1900 Sat–Wed and 0800–1200 Thu
Banking hours 0800–1200 Sat–Wed and 0800–1100 Thu in Abu Dhabi (0800–1200 Thu in the Northern States). Some are also open 1600–1730
Time difference GMT +4
Chief tourist attractions Dubai, popularly known as the 'Pearl of the Gulf', with its 16 km/10 mi deep-water creek
Major holidays 1 January, 6 August, 2 December (2 days); variable: Eid-ul-Adha (3 days), end of Ramadan (4 days), New Year (Muslim), Prophet's Birthday, Lailat al-Miraj (March/April)

United Kingdom of Great Britain and Northern Ireland (UK)

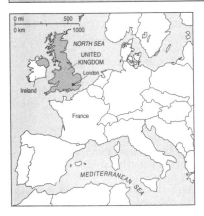

Area 244,100 sq km/94,247 sq mi
Capital London
Major towns/cities Birmingham, Glasgow, Leeds, Sheffield, Liverpool, Manchester, Edinburgh, Bradford, Bristol, Coventry, Belfast, Newcastle upon Tyne, Cardiff
Major ports London, Grimsby, Southampton, Liverpool
Physical features became separated from European continent about 6000 BC;

rolling landscape, increasingly mountainous towards the N, with Grampian Mountains in Scotland, Pennines in N England, Cambrian Mountains in Wales; rivers include Thames, Severn, and Spey
Territories Anguilla, Bermuda, British Antarctic Territory, British Indian Ocean Territory, British Virgin Islands, Cayman Islands, Falkland Islands, Gibraltar, Montserrat, Pitcairn Islands, St Helena and Dependencies (Ascension, Tristan da Cunha), Turks and Caicos Islands. The Channel Islands and the Isle of Man are not part of the UK but are direct dependencies of the crown

Government

Head of state Queen Elizabeth II from 1952
Head of government Tony Blair from 1997
Political system liberal democracy
Administrative divisions England: 35 non-metropolitan counties, 7 metropolitan counties, 65 unitary authorities (as of Oct 1997; local government changes ongoing through 1998); Scotland: 9 regions, 29 unitary authorities, and 3 island authorities (from 1996); Wales: 9 counties and 22 unitary authorities/county boroughs (from 1996); Northern Ireland: 26 districts within 6 geographical counties
Political parties Conservative and Unionist Party, right of centre; Labour Party, moderate left of centre; Social and Liberal Democrats, centre left; Scottish National Party (SNP), Scottish nationalist; Plaid Cymru (Welsh Nationalist Party), Welsh nationalist; Official Ulster Unionist Party (OUP), Democratic Unionist Party (DUP), Ulster People's Unionist Party (UPUP), all Northern Ireland right of centre, in favour of remaining part of United Kingdom; Social Democratic Labour Party (SDLP), Northern Ireland, moderate left of centre; Green Party, ecological
Armed forces 240,000 (1995)
Death penalty abolished for ordinary crimes 1973; laws provide for the death penalty for exceptional crimes only; last execution 1964
Defence spend (% GDP) 3.1 (1995)
Education spend (% GNP) 5.4 (1993/94)
Health spend (% GDP) 5.9 (1993)

Economy and resources

Currency pound sterling (£)
GDP ($ US) 1,145.8 billion (1996)
Real GDP per capita (PPP) ($ US) 18,616 (1996)
GDP growth rate 2.3% (1996); 1.4% (1990–95)
Average annual inflation 3.3% (1996); 5.1% (1985–95)
Trading partners Germany, USA, France, the Netherlands, Japan
Resources coal, limestone, crude petroleum, natural gas, tin, iron, salt, sand and gravel
Industries machinery and transport equipment, steel, metals and metal products, food processing, shipbuilding, aircraft, petroleum and gas extraction, electronics and communications, chemicals and chemical products, business and financial services, tourism
Exports industrial and electrical machinery, automatic data-processing equipment, motor vehicles, petroleum, chemicals, finished and semi-finished manufactured products, agricultural products and foodstuffs. Principal market: Germany 12% (1996)
Imports industrial and electrical machinery, motor vehicles, food and live animals, petroleum, automatic data processing equipment, consumer goods, textiles, paper, paper board. Principal source: Germany 14.1% (1996)
Arable land 24.8% (1993)
Agricultural products wheat, barley, potatoes, sugar beet, fruit, vegetables; livestock rearing (chiefly poultry and cattle), animal products, fishing

Population and society

Population 58,144,000 (1996e)
Population growth rate 0.3% (1990–95); 0.2% (2000–05)
Population density (per sq km) 238 (1996e)
Urban population (% of total) 89 (1995)
Age distribution (% of total population) <15 19.6%, 15–65 65%, >65 15.5% (1995)
Ethnic distribution 81.5% English; 9.6% Scots; 2.4% Irish; 1.9% Welsh; 2% West Indian, Asian, and African
Languages English, Welsh, Gaelic
Religions Church of England (established Church); other Protestant denominations, Roman Catholic, Muslim, Jewish, Hindu, Sikh
Education (compulsory years) 11
Literacy rate 99% (men); 99% (women) (1995e)

Labour force 50% of population: 2% agriculture, 29% industry, 69% services (1990)
Unemployment 8.2% (1996)
Life expectancy 75 (men); 79 (women) (1995–2000)
Child mortality rate (under 5, per 1,000 live births) 7 (1995)
Physicians 1 per 629 people (1993)
Hospital beds 1 per 205 people (1993)
TV sets (per 1,000 people) 448 (1995)
Radios (per 1,000 people) 1,433 (1995)

Transport

Airports international airports: London (Heathrow, Gatwick, London City, Stansted, Luton), Birmingham, Manchester, Newcastle, Bristol, Cardiff, Norwich, Derby, Edinburgh, Glasgow, Leeds/Bradford, Liverpool, Southampton; 22 domestic airports; total passenger km: 139,088 mil (1994)
Railroads total length: 37,849 km/23,519 mi; total passenger km: 29,210 mil (1995)
Roads total road network: 367,000 km/228,054 mi, of which 100% paved (1995); passenger cars: 365.8 per 1,000 people (1995e)

Chronology

c. 400–200 BC British Isles conquered by Celts.
55–54 BC Romans led by Julius Caesar raided Britain.
AD 43–60 Romans conquered England and Wales, which formed the province of Britannia; Picts stopped them penetrating further N.
5th–7th centuries After Romans withdrew, Anglo-Saxons overran most of England and formed kingdoms, including Wessex, Northumbria, and Mercia; Wales was stronghold of Celts.
500 The Scots, a Gaelic-speaking tribe from Ireland, settled in the kingdom of Dalriada (Argyll).
5th–6th centuries British Isles converted to Christianity.
829 King Egbert of Wessex accepted as overlord of all England.
c. 843 Kenneth McAlpin unified Scots and Picts to become first king of Scotland.
9th–11th centuries Vikings raided British Isles, conquering N and E England and N Scotland.
1066 Normans led by William I defeated Anglo-Saxons at Battle of Hastings and conquered England.
12th–13th centuries Anglo-Norman adventurers conquered much of Ireland, but effective English rule remained limited to area around Dublin.

1215 King John of England forced to sign Magna Carta, which placed limits on royal powers.
1265 Simon de Montfort summoned the first English parliament in which the towns were represented.
1284 Edward I of England invaded Scotland; Scots defeated English at Battle of Stirling Bridge 1297.
1314 Robert the Bruce led Scots to victory over English at Battle of Bannockburn; England recognized Scottish independence 1328.
1455–85 Wars of the Roses: House of York and House of Lancaster disputed English throne.
1513 Battle of Flodden: Scots defeated by English; James IV of Scotland killed.
1529 Henry VIII founded Church of England after break with Rome; Reformation effective in England and Wales, but not in Ireland.
1536–43 Acts of Union united Wales with England, with one law, one parliament, and one official language.
1541 Irish parliament recognized Henry VIII of England as king of Ireland.
1557 First Covenant established Protestant faith in Scotland.
1603 Union of crowns: James VI of Scotland became James I of England also.
1607 First successful English colony in Virginia marked start of three centuries of overseas expansion.
1610 James I established plantation of Ulster in Northern Ireland with Protestant settlers from England and Scotland.
1642–52 English Civil War between king and Parliament, with Scottish intervention and Irish rebellion, resulted in victory for Parliament.
1649 Execution of Charles I; Oliver Cromwell appointed Lord Protector 1653; monarchy restored 1660.
1689 'Glorious Revolution' confirmed power of Parliament; replacement of James II by William III resisted by Scottish Highlanders and Catholic Irish.
1707 Act of Union between England and Scotland created United Kingdom of Great Britain, governed by a single parliament.
1721–42 Cabinet government developed under Robert Walpole, in effect the first prime minister.
1745 'The Forty-Five': rebellion of Scottish Highlanders in support of Jacobite pretender to throne; defeated 1746.
c. 1760–1850 Industrial Revolution: Britain became the first industrial nation in the world.
1775–83 American Revolution: Britain lost

13 American colonies; empire continued to expand in Canada, India, and Australia.
1793–1815 Britain at war with revolutionary France, except for 1802–03.
1800 Act of Union created United Kingdom of Great Britain and Ireland, governed by a single parliament; effective 1801.
1832 Great Reform Act extended franchise; further extensions 1867, 1884, 1918, and 1928.
1846 Repeal of Corn Laws reflected shift of power from landowners to industrialists.
1870 Home Rule Party formed to campaign for restoration of separate Irish parliament.
1880–90s Rapid expansion of British Empire in Africa.
1906–14 Liberal governments introduced social reforms and curbed power of House of Lords.
1914–18 United Kingdom played leading part in World War I; British Empire expanded in Middle East.
1919–21 Anglo-Irish war ended with secession of S Ireland as Irish Free State; Ulster remained within United Kingdom of Great Britain and Northern Ireland with some powers devolved to Northern Irish parliament.
1924 First Labour government led by Ramsay MacDonald.
1926 General Strike arose from coal dispute. Equality of status recognized between United Kingdom and Dominions of British Commonwealth.
1931 National Government coalition formed to face economic crisis; unemployment reached 3 million.
1939–45 United Kingdom played a leading part in World War II.
1945 First Scottish Nationalist MP elected; first Welsh Nationalist MP 1966.
1945–51 Labour government of Clement Attlee created welfare state and nationalized major industries.
1947–71 Decolonization brought about end of British Empire.
1969 Start of Troubles in Northern Ireland; Northern Irish Parliament suspended 1972.
1973 UK joined European Economic Community.
1979 Referenda failed to approve devolution of power to Scottish and Welsh assemblies.
1979–90 Conservative government of Margaret Thatcher pursued radical free-market economic policies.
1982 Unemployment over 3 million. Falklands War.
1991 British troops took part in US-led war against Iraq under United Nations umbrella. Severe economic recession and unemployment.
1993 Peace proposal for Northern Ireland, the Downing Street Declaration, issued jointly with Irish government.
1994 Irish Republican Army and Protestant paramilitary declared cease-fire in Northern Ireland.
1996 IRA renewed bombing campaign in London. Conservative Party's majority in House of Commons reduced to one seat.
1997 Labour Party won landslide victory in general election. Tony Blair became prime minister. Blair launched new Anglo-Irish peace initiative; IRA declared a cease-fire. Princess Diana killed in car crash. Breakaway nationalist group exploded a bomb in Northern Ireland.

Practical information

Visa requirements USA: visa not required
Embassy in the USA 3100 Massachusetts Avenue NW, Washington, DC 20008. Tel: (202) 462 1340; fax: (202) 898 4255
American embassy 24/31 Grosvenor Square, London, W1A 1AE. Tel: (0171) 499 9000; fax: (0171) 409 1637
Chamber of commerce Association of British Chambers of Commerce, 9 Tufton Street, London SW1P 3QB. Tel: (0171) 222 1555; fax: (0171) 799 2202
Office hours 0900/0930–1700/1730 Mon–Fri
Banking hours 0930–1530/1630 Mon–Fri (some banks open Sat morning)
Time difference GMT +/–0
Chief tourist attractions London, with its many historic monumments, cathedrals, churches, palaces, parks, and museums; historic towns, including York, Bath, Edinburgh, Oxford, and Cambridge; the Lake District in the NW; the mountains of N Wales; varied coastline includes sandy beaches, cliffs, and the fjord-like inlets of NW Scotland
Major holidays 1 January, 25–26 December; variable: Good Friday, Easter Monday (not Scotland), Early May, Late May and Summer (August) Bank Holidays; Northern Ireland also has 17 March, 29 December; Scotland has 2 January

United States of America

Area 9,372,615 sq km/3,618,766 sq mi
Capital Washington, DC
Major towns/cities New York, Los Angeles, Chicago, Philadelphia, Detroit, San Francisco, Washington, Dallas, San Diego, San Antonio, Houston, Boston, Baltimore, Phoenix, Indianapolis, Memphis, Honolulu, San José
Physical features topography and vegetation from tropical (Hawaii) to arctic (Alaska); mountain ranges parallel with E and W coasts; the Rocky Mountains separate rivers emptying into the Pacific from those flowing into the Gulf of Mexico; Great Lakes in N; rivers include Hudson, Mississippi, Missouri, Colorado, Columbia, Snake, Rio Grande, Ohio
Territories the commonwealths of Puerto Rico and Northern Marianas; Guam, the US Virgin Islands, American Samoa, Wake Island, Midway Islands, and Johnston and Sand Islands

Government

Head of state and government Bill Clinton from 1993
Political system liberal democracy
Administrative divisions 50 states
Political parties Democratic Party, liberal centre; Republican Party, centre right
Armed forces 1,547,000 (1995)

Death penalty retained and used for ordinary crimes
Defence spend (% GDP) 3.8 (1995)
Education spend (% GNP) 5.5 (1993/94)
Health spend (% GDP) 6.2 (1993)

Economy and resources

Currency US dollar
GDP ($ US) 7,341.9 billion (1996)
Real GDP per capita (PPP) ($ US) 27,655 (1996)
GDP growth rate 2.8% (1996); 2.6% (1990–95)
Average annual inflation 2.9% (1996); 3.2% (1985–95)
Trading partners Canada, Japan, Mexico, EU (principally UK and Germany)
Resources coal, copper (world's second-largest producer), iron, bauxite, mercury, silver, gold, nickel, zinc (world's fifth-largest producer), tungsten, uranium, phosphate, petroleum, natural gas, timber
Industries machinery, petroleum refining and products, food processing, motor vehicles, pig iron and steel, chemical products, electrical goods, metal products, printing and publishing, fertilizers, cement
Exports machinery, motor vehicles, agricultural products and foodstuffs, aircraft, weapons, chemicals, electronics. Principal market: Canada 22% (1996)
Imports machinery and transport equipment, crude and partly refined petroleum, office machinery, textiles and clothing. Principal source: Canada 19.8% (1996)
Arable land 18.9% (1993)
Agricultural products hay, potatoes, maize, wheat, barley, oats, sugar beet, soya beans, citrus and other fruit, cotton, tobacco; livestock (principally cattle, pigs, and poultry)

Population and society

Population 269,444,000 (1996e)
Population growth rate 1% (1990–95); 0.8% (2000–05)
Population density (per sq km) 29 (1996e)
Urban population (% of total) 76 (1995)
Age distribution (% of total population) <15 22%, 15–65 65.3%, >65 12.6% (1995)
Ethnic distribution approximately

three-quarters of the population are of European origin, including 29% who trace their descent from Britain and Ireland, 8% from Germany, 5% from Italy, and 3% each from Scandinavia and Poland; 12% are African-Americans, 8% Hispanic, and 3% Asian and Pacific islander; African-Americans form 30% of the population of the states of the 'Deep South', namely Alabama, Georgia, Louisiana, Mississippi, and South Carolina; Asians are most concentrated in California
Languages English, Spanish
Religions Christian 86.5% (Roman Catholic 26%, Baptist 19%, Methodist 8%, Lutheran 5%); Jewish 1.8%; Muslim 0.5%; Buddhist and Hindu less than 0.5%
Education (compulsory years) 10
Literacy rate 99% (men); 99% (women) (1995e)
Labour force 50% of population: 3% agriculture, 26% industry, 71% services (1990)
Unemployment 5.4% (1996)
Life expectancy 73 (men); 80 (women) (1995–2000)
Child mortality rate (under 5, per 1,000 live births) 10 (1995)
Physicians 1 per 398 people (1994)
Hospital beds 1 per 230 people (1994)
TV sets (per 1,000 people) 805 (1995)
Radios (per 1,000 people) 2,093 (1995)

Transport

Airports international airports: Anchorage, Atlanta (Hartsfield), Baltimore (Baltimore/Washington), Boston (Logan), Chicago (O'Hare), Cincinnati (Northern Kentucky), Cleveland (Hopkins), Dallas/Fort Worth, Denver (Stapleton), Detroit Metropolitan, Honolulu, Houston Intercontinental, Kansas City, Las Vegas (McCarran), Los Angeles, Miami, Minneapolis/St Paul, New Orleans, New York (John F Kennedy, La Guardia, Newark), Orlando, Philadelphia, Phoenix (Sky Harbor), Pittsburgh, Portland, St Louis (Lambert), Salt Lake City, San Diego (Lindbergh Field), San Francisco, Seattle-Tacoma, Tampa, Washington, DC (Dulles, National); about 800 domestic airports; total passenger km: 822,152 mil (1994)
Railroads total length: 225,000 km/ 139,815 mi; total passenger km: 9,529 mil (1994)
Roads total road network: 6,238,500

km/ 3,876,604 mi, of which 60% paved (1995e); passenger cars: 562.8 per 1,000 people (1995e)

Chronology

c.15,000 BC First evidence of human occupation in North America.
1513 Ponce de Léon of Spain explored Florida in search of the Fountain of Youth; Francisco Coronado explored SW region of North America 1540–42.
1565 Spanish founded St Augustine (Florida), the first permanent European settlement in N America.
1585 Sir Walter Raleigh tried to establish English colony on Roanoke Island in what he called Virginia.
1607 English colonists founded Jamestown, Virginia, and began growing tobacco.
1620 The Pilgrim Fathers founded Plymouth Colony (near Cape Cod); other English Puritans followed them to New England.
1624 Dutch formed colony of New Netherlands; Swedes formed New Sweden 1638; both taken by England 1664.
17th–18th centuries Millions of Africans were sold into slavery on American cotton and tobacco plantations.
1733 Georgia became thirteenth British colony on E coast.
1763 British victory over France in Seven Years' War secured territory as far W as Mississippi River.
1765 British first attempted to levy tax in American colonies with Stamp Act; protest forced repeal in 1767.
1773 'Boston Tea Party': colonists boarded ships and threw cargoes of tea into sea in protest at import duty.
1774 British closed Boston harbour and billeted troops in Massachusetts; colonists formed First Continental Congress.
1775 American Revolution: colonies raised Continental Army led by George Washington to fight against British rule.
1776 American colonies declared independence; France and Spain supported them in war with Britain.
1781 Americans defeated British at Battle of Yorktown; rebel states formed loose confederation, codified in Articles of Confederation.
1783 Treaty of Paris: Britain accepted loss of colonies.
1787 'Founding Fathers' devised new constitution for United States of

America.

1789 Washington elected first president of USA.

1791 Bill of Rights guaranteed individual freedom.

1803 Louisiana Purchase: France sold former Spanish lands between Mississippi River and Rocky Mountains to USA.

1812–14 War with Britain arose from dispute over blockade rights during Napoleonic Wars.

1819 USA bought Florida from Spain.

19th centuries Mass immigration from Europe; settlers moved westwards, crushing Indian resistance and claiming 'manifest destiny' of USA to control North America. By end of century, number of states in the Union had increased from 17 to 45.

1846–48 Mexican War: Mexico ceded vast territory to USA.

1854 Kansas–Nebraska Act heightened controversy over slavery in southern states; abolitionists formed Republican Party.

1860 Abraham Lincoln (Republican) elected president.

1861 Civil war broke out after 11 southern states, wishing to retain slavery, seceded from USA and formed Confederate States of America under Jefferson Davis.

1865 USA defeated Confederacy; slavery abolished; President Lincoln assassinated.

1867 Alaska bought from Russia.

1869 Railway linked E and W coasts; rapid growth of industry and agriculture 1870–1920 made USA very rich.

1876 Sioux Indians defeated US troops at Little Big Horn; Indians finally defeated at Wounded Knee 1890.

1898 Spanish–American War: USA gained Puerto Rico and Guam; also Philippines (until 1946) and Cuba (until 1901); USA annexed Hawaii.

1913 16th amendment to constitution gave federal government power to levy income tax.

1917–18 USA intervened in World War I; President Woodrow Wilson took leading part in peace negotiations 1919, but USA rejected membership of League of Nations.

1920 Women received right to vote; sale of alcohol prohibited, until 1933.

1924 Native Americans made citizens of USA by Congress.

1929 'Wall Street Crash': stock market collapse led to Great Depression with 13 million unemployed by 1933.

1933 President Franklin Roosevelt launched 'New Deal' with public works to alleviate Depression.

1941 Japanese attacked US fleet at Pearl Harbor, Hawaii; USA declared war on Japan; Germany declared war on USA, which henceforth played a leading part in World War II.

1945 USA ended war in Pacific by dropping two atomic bombs on Hiroshima and Nagasaki, Japan.

1947 'Truman Doctrine' pledged US aid for nations threatened by communism; start of Cold War between USA and USSR.

1950–53 US forces engaged in Korean War.

1954 Racial segregation in schools deemed unconstitutional; start of campaign to secure civil rights for black Americans.

1962 Cuban missile crisis: USA forced USSR to withdraw nuclear weapons from Cuba.

1963 President John F Kennedy assassinated.

1964–68 President Lyndon Johnson introduced 'Great Society' programme of civil-rights and welfare measures.

1961–75 USA involved in Vietnam War.

1969 US astronaut Neil Armstrong was first person on Moon.

1974 'Watergate' scandal: evidence of domestic political espionage compelled President Richard Nixon to resign.

1979–80 Iran held US diplomats hostage, humiliating President Jimmy Carter.

1981–89 Tax-cutting policies of President Ronald Reagan led to large federal budget deficit.

1986 'Irangate' scandal: secret US arms sales to Iran illegally funded Contra guerrillas in Nicaragua.

1990 President George Bush declared end to Cold War.

1991 Gulf War: USA played leading part in expelling Iraqi forces from Kuwait.

1992 Democrat Bill Clinton won presidential elections; his running mate Al Gore became vice president.

1996 Clinton re-elected. US missile attacks on Iraq in response to Hussein's incursions into Kurdish safe havens. Final composition of House of Representatives confirmed. Public criticism brought about tightening of Democratic Party funding.

1997 Clinton made major changes to government personnel for second term. Budget deal agreed between President and Congress. Reform in welfare law brought substantial drop in number of people receiving welfare.

Practical information

Visa requirements UK: visa not required for a stay of up to 90 days

Embassy in the UK 24 Grosvenor Square, London W1A 1AE, Tel: (0171) 499 9000; fax: (0171) 629 9124

British embassy 3100 Massachusetts Avenue, NW, Washington, DC 20008. Tel: (202) 462 1340; fax: (202) 898 4255

Chamber of commerce 1615 H Street, NW, Washington, DC 20062-0001. Tel: (202) 659 6000; fax: (202) 463 5836

Office hours 0900–1730 Mon–Fri

Banking hours variable, but generally 0900–1500 Mon–Fri

Time difference GMT –5–11

Chief tourist attractions many cities of interest, including New York, with its skyscrapers, Washington, DC, with its monuments, Boston, San Francisco, and New Orleans; enormous diversity of geographical features – the Rocky Mountains, the Everglades of Florida, the Grand Canyon; hundreds of national parks, historical parks, and reserves, including Redwood, Yosemite, and Death Valley (all in California); Disneyland (California) and Walt Disney World (Florida)

Major holidays 1 January, 4 July, 12 October (not all states), 11 November, 25 December; variable: Martin Luther King's birthday (January, not all states), George Washington's birthday (February), Memorial (May), Labor (first Mon in September), Columbus (October), Thanksgiving (last Thu in November); much local variation

Uruguay Oriental Republic of

National name *República Oriental del Uruguay*
Area 176,200 sq km/68,030 sq mi
Capital Montevideo
Major towns/cities Salto, Paysandú, Las Piedras
Physical features grassy plains (pampas) and low hills; rivers Negro, Uruguay, Río de la Plata

Government

Head of state and government Julio Maria Sanguinetti from 1994
Political system democratic republic
Administrative divisions 19 departments
Political parties Colorado Party (PC), progressive, centre left; National (Blanco) Party (PN), traditionalist, right of centre; New Space (NE), moderate, left wing; Progressive Encounter (EP), left wing
Armed forces 25,600 (1995); plus paramilitary forces of 1,200
Conscription military service is voluntary
Death penalty abolished 1907
Defence spend (% GDP) 2.6 (1995)
Education spend (% GNP) 2.5 (1994)
Health spend (% GDP) 2.5 (1990)

Economy and resources

Currency Uruguayan peso
GDP ($ US) 15.5 billion (1994)
Real GDP per capita (PPP) ($ US) 6,752 (1994)
GDP growth rate −2.4% (1995); 4% (1990–95)
Average annual inflation 42.2% (1995); 70.5% (1985–95)
Foreign debt ($ US) 5.3 billion (1995)
Trading partners Brazil, Argentina, USA,

Italy, Germany, Spain, China
Resources small-scale extraction of building materials, industrial minerals, semi-precious stones; gold deposits are being developed
Industries food processing, textiles and clothing, beverages, cement, chemicals, light engineering and transport equipment, leather products
Exports textiles, meat (chiefly beef), live animals and by-products (mainly hides and leather products), cereals, footwear. Principal market: Brazil 34.6% (1996)
Imports machinery and appliances, transport equipment, chemical products, petroleum and petroleum products, agricultural products. Principal source: Brazil 26.1% (1996)
Arable land 7.1% (1993)
Agricultural products rice, sugar cane, sugar beet, wheat, potatoes, barley, maize, sorghum; livestock rearing (sheep and cattle) is traditionally country's major economic activity – exports of animals, meat, skins, and hides accounted for 36.6% of total export revenue (1994)

Population and society

Population 3,204,000 (1996e)
Population growth rate 0.6% (1990–95); 0.6% (2000–05)
Population density (per sq km) 18 (1996e)
Urban population (% of total) 90 (1995)
Age distribution (% of total population) <15 24.4%, 15–65 63.3%, >65 12.3% (1995)
Ethnic distribution predominantly of European descent: about 54% Spanish, 22% Italian, with minorities from other European countries
Language Spanish (official)
Religions mainly Roman Catholic
Education (compulsory years) 6
Literacy rate 97% (men); 96% (women) (1995e)
Labour force 15% agriculture, 18% industry, 67% services (1993)
Unemployment 10.5% (1995e)
Life expectancy 70 (men); 76 (women) (1995–2000)
Child mortality rate (under 5, per 1,000 live births) 21 (1995)
Physicians 1 per 515 people (1990)
Hospital beds 1 per 136 people (1990)
TV sets (per 1,000 people) 235 (1995)
Radios (per 1,000 people) 609 (1995)

Transport

Airports international airport: Montevideo (Carrasco); seven domestic airports; total passenger km: 645 mil (1994)
Railroads total length: 2,073 km/1,288 mi (passenger service withdrawn 1988, partially resumed 1993)
Roads total road network: 50,900 km/ 31,629 mi, of which 13.7% paved (1995e); passenger cars: 73 per 1,000 people (1993e)

Chronology

1516 Río de la Plata visited by Spanish navigator Juan Diaz de Solis, who was killed by native Charrua Amerindians. This discouraged European settlement for more than a century.
1680 Portuguese from Brazil founded Nova Colonia do Sacramento on Río de la Plata estuary.
1726 Spanish established fortress at Montevideo and wrested control over Uruguay from Portugal, with much of the Amerindian population being killed.
1776 Became part of Viceroyalty of La Plata, with capital at Buenos Aires.
1808 With Spanish monarchy overthrown by Napoleon Bonaparte, La Plata Viceroyalty became autonomous, but Montevideo remained loyal to Spanish Crown and rebelled against Buenos Aires control.
1815 Dictator José Gervasio Artigas overthrew Spanish and Buenos Aires control.
1820 Artigas ousted by Brazil, which disputed control of Uruguay with Argentina.
1825 Independence declared after fight led by Juan Antonio Lavalleja.
1828 Independence recognized by country's neighbours.
1836 Civil war between Reds and Whites, after which Colorado and Blanco parties were named.
1840 Merino sheep introduced by British traders, who later established meat processing factories for export trade.
1865–70 Fought successfully alongside Argentina and Brazil in war against Paraguay.
1903 After period of military rule, José Battle y Ordonez, a progressive from centre-left Colorado Party, became president. As president 1903–07 and 1911–15, he gave women the franchise and created an advanced welfare state

as a successful ranching economy developed.

1930 First constitution adopted, but period of military dictatorship followed during Depression period.

1958 After 93 years out of power, right-of-centre Blanco Party returned to power.

1967 Colorado Party in power, with Jorge Pacheco Areco as president. Period of labour unrest and urban guerrilla activity by left-wing Tupamaros.

1972 Juan María Bordaberry Arocena of Colorado Party became president.

1973 Parliament dissolved and Bordaberry shared power with military dictatorship, which crushed Tupamaros and banned left-wing groups.

1976 Bordaberry deposed by army; Dr Aparicio Méndez Manfredini became president.

1981 Gen Grigorio Alvárez Armellino became new military ruler.

1984 Violent antigovernment protests after ten years of repressive rule and deteriorating economy.

1985 Agreement reached between army and political leaders for return to constitutional government and freeing of political prisoners. Colorado Party won general election; Dr Julio María Sanguinetti became president.

1986 Government of national accord established under President Sanguinetti.

1989 Luis Alberto Lacalle Herrera of Blanco Party elected president.

1992 Public voted against privatization in national referendum.

1994 Colorado candidate Julio Maria Sanguinetti elected president.

Practical information

Visa requirements UK: visa not required. USA: visa not required

Embassy in the UK 2nd Floor, 140 Brompton Road, London SW3 1HY. Tel: (0171) 584 8192; fax: (0171) 581 9585

British embassy PO Box 16024, Calle Marco Bruto 1073, 1130 Montevideo. Tel: (2) 623 630; fax: (2) 627 815

Embassy in the USA 1918 F Street NW, Washington, DC 20006. Tel: (202) 331 1313–6

American embassy Lauro Muller 1776, Montevideo. Tel: (2) 236 061, 487 777; fax: (2) 488 611

Chamber of commerce Cámara Nacional de Comercio, Edificio de la Bolsa de Comercio, Misiones 1400, Casilla 1000, 11000 Montevideo. Tel: (2) 961 277; fax: (2) 961 243

Office hours 0830–1200 and 1430–1830/1900 Mon–Fri

Banking hours 1330–1730 Mon–Fri (summer); 1300–1700 Mon–Fri (winter)

Time difference GMT –3

Chief tourist attractions sandy beaches; forests; tropical swamps on the coast; variety of flora and fauna

Major holidays 1 January, 19 April, 1, 18 May, 19 June, 18 July, 25 August, 12 October, 2 November, 25 December; variable: Carnival (2 days), Good Friday, Holy Thursday, Mon–Wed of Holy Week

---

Uzbekistan Republic of

National name *Ozbekistan Respublikasy*

Area 447,400 sq km/172,741 sq mi

Capital Tashkent

Major towns/cities Samarkand, Bukhara, Namangan, Andizhan

Physical features oases in deserts; rivers: Amu Darya, Syr Darya; Ferghana Valley; rich in mineral deposits

Government

Head of state Islam Karimov from 1990

Head of government Otkir Sultonov from 1995

Political system authoritarian nationalist

Administrative divisions 12 regions and one autonomous republic (Karakalpakstan)

Political parties People's Democratic Party of Uzbekistan (PDP), reform socialist (ex-communist); Fatherland Progress Party (FP; Vatan Taraqioti), pro-private enterprise; Erk (Freedom Democratic Party), mixed economy; Social Democratic Party of Uzbekistan, pro-Islamic; National Revival Democratic Party, centrist, intelligentsia-led

Armed forces 25,000 (1995)

Conscription military service is compulsory for 18 months

Death penalty retained and used for ordinary crimes

Defence spend (% GDP) 3.6 (1995)

Education spend (% GNP) 11 (1993/94)

Economy and resources

Currency som

GDP ($ US) 22 billion (1994)

Real GDP per capita (PPP) ($ US) 2,438 (1994)

GDP growth rate 1.6% (1996); –4.4% (1990–95)

Average annual inflation 64% (1996); 239% (1985–95e)

Foreign debt ($ US) 1.6 billion (1995)

Trading partners CIS nations (principally Russia, Tajikistan, and Kazakhstan), Switzerland, Czech Republic, the Netherlands

Resources petroleum, natural gas, coal, gold (world's seventh-largest producer), silver, uranium (world's fourth-largest producer), copper, lead, zinc, tungsten

Industries processing of agricultural and mineral raw materials, agricultural machinery, chemical products, metallurgy, cement, mineral fertilizer, paper, textiles, footwear, electrical appliances

Exports cotton fibre, textiles, machinery, food and energy products, gold. Principal market: Russia 22.3% (1996)

Imports machinery, light industrial goods, food and raw materials. Principal source: Russia 24.9% (1996)

Arable land 63% (1993)

Agricultural products cotton (among the world's five largest producers), grain, potatoes, vegetables, fruit and berries; livestock rearing; silkworm breeding

Population and society

Population 23,209,000 (1996e)
Population growth rate 2.2% (1990–95); 1.9% (2000–05)
Population density (per sq km) 50 (1994)
Urban population (% of total) 41 (1995)
Age distribution (% of total population) <15 39.9%, 15–65 55.6%, >65 4.4% (1995)
Ethnic distribution 71% Uzbek, 8% ethnic Russian, 4% Tajik, 3% Kazakh, 2% Tatar
Language Uzbek, a Turkic language
Religion Sunni Muslim
Education (compulsory years) 9
Literacy rate 97% (men); 96% (women) (1995e)
Labour force 43.4% agriculture, 21.3% industry, 35.3% services (1992)
Unemployment 0.4% (1996)
Life expectancy 68 (men); 73 (women) (1995–2000)
Child mortality rate (under 5, per 1,000 live births) 62 (1995)
Physicians 1 per 284 people (1994)
Hospital beds 1 per 106 people (1994)
TV sets (per 1,000 people) 191 (1995)
Radios (per 1,000 people) 81 (1995)

Transport

Airports international airport: Tashkent; eight domestic airports; total passenger km: 4,855 mil (1994)
Railroads total length: 3,380 km/2,100 mi; total passenger km: 59 mil (1993)
Roads total road network: 80,000 km/ 49,712 mi, of which 87.2% paved (1995e)

Chronology

6th century BC Part of Persian Empire of Cyrus the Great.
4th century BC Part of empire of Alexander the Great of Macedonia.
1st century BC Samarkand (Maracanda) developed as transit point on strategic Silk Road trading route between China and Europe.
7th century City of Tashkent founded; spread of Islam.
12th century Tashkent taken by Turks; Khorezem (Khiva), in NW, became centre of large Central Asian polity, stretching from Caspian Sea to Samarkand in the E.
13th–14th centuries Conquered by Genghis Khan and became part of Mongol Empire, with Samarkand serving as capital for Tamerlane.
18th–19th centuries Dominated by independent emirates and khanates (chiefdoms) of Bukhara in SW, Kokand in E, and Samarkand in centre.
1865–67 Tashkent was taken by Russia and made capital of Governor-Generalship of Turkestan.
1868–76 Tsarist Russia annexed emirate of Bukhara (1868); and khanates of Samarkand (1868), Khiva (1873), and Kokand (1876).
1917 Following Bolshevik revolution in Russia, Tashkent soviet ('people's council') established, which deposed the emir of Bukhara and other khans 1920.
1918–22 Mosques closed and Muslim clergy persecuted as part of secularization drive by new communist rulers, despite nationalist guerrilla (basmachi) resistance.
1921 Part of Turkestan Soviet Socialist Autonomous Republic.
1925 Became constituent republic of USSR.
1930s Skilled ethnic Russians immigrated into urban centres as industries developed.
1944 About 160,000 Meskhetian Turks forcibly transported from their native Georgia to Uzbekistan by Soviet dictator Joseph Stalin.
1950s–80s Major irrigation projects stimulated cotton production, but led to desiccation of Aral Sea.
late 1980s Upsurge in Islamic consciousness stimulated by *glasnost* initiative of Soviet Union's reformist leader Mikhail Gorbachev.
1989 Birlik ('Unity'), nationalist movement, formed. Violent attacks on Meskhetian and other minority communities in Ferghana Valley.
1990 Economic and political sovereignty declared by increasingly nationalist UCP, led by Islam Karimov, who became president.
1991 Attempted anti-Gorbachev coup by conservatives in Moscow initially supported by President Karimov. Independence declared. Joined new Commonwealth of Independent States (CIS); Karimov directly elected president.
1992 Violent food riots in Tashkent. Joined Economic Cooperation Organization and United Nations. New constitution adopted.
1993 Crackdown on Islamic fundamentalists as economy deteriorated.
1994 Economic, military, and social union formed with Kazakhstan and Kyrgyzstan. Economic integration treaty signed with Russia. Links with Turkey strengthened and foreign inward investment encouraged.
1995 Ruling PDP (formerly UCP) won general election, from which opposition was banned from participating. Karimov's tenure extended for further five-year term by national plebiscite.
1996 Agreement with Kazakhstan and Kyrgyzstan to create single economic market.
1997 New law governing political parties.

Practical information

Visa requirements UK: visa required. USA: visa required
Embassy in the UK 72 Wigmore Street, London W1H 9DL. Tel: (0171) 935 1899; fax: (0171) 935 9554
British embassy 6 Murtazayeva Street, Tashkent 700084. Tel: (3712) 345 652; fax: (873) 340 465
Embassy in the USA (temporary) Suites 619 and 623, 1511 K Street NW, Washington, DC 20005. Tel: (202) 638 4266/7; fax: (202) 638 4268
American embassy 82 Chilanzarskaya, Tashkent. Tel: (3712) 771 407/081, 776 986; fax: (3712) 891 335

Chamber of commerce Tashkent International Business Centre, Ulitsa Pushkina 17, Tashkent. Tel: (3712) 323 231; fax: (3712) 334 414
Office hours 0900–1700 Mon–Fri
Banking hours 0900–1700 Mon–Fri
Time difference GMT +5
Chief tourist attractions over 4,000 historical monuments, largely associated with the ancient 'Silk Route'; many historical sites and cities, including Samarkand (Tamerlane's capital), Bukhara, and Khiva
Major holidays 1–2 January, 8, 21 March, 1 September, 8 December

Vanuatu Republic of

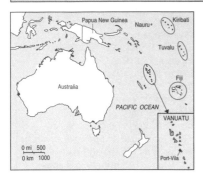

National name *Ripablik blong Vanuatu*
Area 14,800 sq km/5,714 sq mi
Capital Port-Vila (on Efate) (and port)
Major towns/cities Luganville (on Espíritu Santo)
Major ports Santo
Physical features comprises around 70 inhabited islands, including Espíritu Santo, Malekula, and Efate; densely forested, mountainous; three active volcanoes; cyclones on average twice a year

Government

Head of state Jean Marie Leye from 1994
Head of government Serge Vohor from 1996
Political system democratic republic
Administrative divisions six provincial authorities
Political parties Union of Moderate Parties (UMP), Francophone centrist; National United Party (NUP), formed by Walter Lini; Vanua'aku Pati (VP), Anglophone centrist; Melanesian Progressive Party (MPP), Melanesian centrist; Fren Melanesian Party
Armed forces no standing defence force; paramilitary force of around 300; police naval service of around 50 (1995)
Death penalty laws do not provide for the death penalty for any crime
Education spend (% GNP) 4.8 (1993/94)
Health spend (% GDP) 2.9 (1990)

Economy and resources

Currency vatu
GDP ($ US) 198.9 million (1994e)
Real GDP per capita (PPP) ($ US) 2,276 (1994)
GDP growth rate 3.2% (1995)
Average annual inflation 2.2% (1995); 5.5% (1985–95)

Foreign debt ($ US) 237 million (1994)
Trading partners Japan, Australia, the Netherlands, New Zealand, New Caledonia, France
Resources manganese; gold, copper, and large deposits of petroleum have been discovered but have hitherto remained unexploited
Industries processing of agricultural products (chiefly copra, meat canning, fish freezing, saw milling), soft drinks, building materials, furniture, aluminium, tourism, offshore banking, shipping registry
Exports copra, beef, timber, cocoa, shells. Principal market: Japan 24.1% (1995)
Imports machinery and transport equipment, food and live animals, basic manufactures, miscellaneous manufactured articles, mineral fuels, chemicals, beverages, tobacco. Principal source: Japan 35.4% (1995)
Arable land 1.6% (1993)
Agricultural products coconuts and copra, cocoa, coffee, yams, taro, cassava, breadfruit, squash and other vegetables, bananas; livestock rearing (cattle, pigs, goats, and poultry); forest resources

Population and society

Population 174,000 (1996e)
Population growth rate 2.5% (1990–95)
Population density (per sq km) 14 (1996e)
Urban population (% of total) 19.3 (1995)
Age distribution (% of total population) <15 45.6%, 15–65 50.4%, >65 4% (1990)
Ethnic distribution 95% Melanesian, 3% European or mixed European, 2% Vietnamese, Chinese, or other Pacific islanders
Languages Bislama 82%, English, French (all official)
Religions Christian 80%, animist
Education (compulsory years) 6
Literacy rate 54% (men); 23% (women) (1995e)
Labour force 68% agriculture, 8% industry, 24% services (1990)
Life expectancy 66 (men); 70 (women) (1995–2000)
Child mortality rate (under 5, per 1,000 live births) 58 (1995)
Physicians 1 per 7,147 people (1990)
Hospital beds 1 per 393 people (1990)

TV sets (per 1,000 people) 13 (1995)
Radios (per 1,000 people) 296 (1995)

Transport

Airports international airports: Port-Vila (Banerfield); 28 domestic airports and airstrips; total passenger km: 143 mil (1994)
Railroads none
Roads total road network: 1,050 km/652 mi, of which 23.8% paved (1995e); passenger cars: 24.7 per 1,000 people (1993e)

Chronology

1606 First visited by Portuguese navigator Pedro Fernandez de Queiras, who named the islands Espíritu Santo.
1774 Visited by British navigator Capt James Cook, who named them the New Hebrides, after the Scottish islands.
1830s European merchants attracted to islands by sandalwood trade. Christian missionaries arrived, but many were attacked by the indigenous Melanesians who, in turn, were ravaged by exposure to European diseases.
later 19th century Britain and France disputed control; islanders were shipped to Australia, Fiji, Samoa, and New Caledonia to work as plantation labourers.
1906 Islands jointly administered by France and Britain as the Condominium of the New Hebrides.
1963 Indigenous Na-Griamel (NG) political grouping formed on Espíritu Santo to campaign against European acquisition of more than a third of the land area.
1975 Representative assembly established following pressure from the VP, formed 1972 by English-speaking Melanesian Protestants.
1978 Government of national unity formed, with Father Gerard Leymang as chief minister.
1980 Revolt on the island of Espíritu Santo by French settlers and pro-NG plantation workers delayed independence but it was achieved within the Commonwealth, with George Kalkoa (adopted name Sokomanu) as president and left-of-centre Father Walter Lini (VP) as prime minister.
1988 Dismissal of Lini by Sokomanu led to Sokomanu's arrest for treason. Lini reinstated.

1989 Sokomanu succeeded as president by Fred Timakata.
1991 Lini voted out by party members; replaced by Donald Kalpokas. General election produced coalition government of the Francophone Union of Moderate Parties (UMP) and Lini's new National United Party (NUP) under Maxime Carlot Korman.

1993 Cyclone caused extensive damage.
1994 Timakata succeeded as president by Jean Marie Leye.
1995 Governing UMP–NUP coalition won general election, but Serge Vohor, of VP-dominated Unity Front, became prime minister.
1996 Vohor briefly replaced by Maxime

Carlot Korman, but Vohor returned to power leading new coalition after Carlot government implicated in financial scandal. MFT expelled from governing coalition and replaced by Vanua'aku Party, led by Donald Kalpokas.
1997 Prime Minister Vohor formed new coalition.

Practical information

Visa requirements UK: visa not required. USA: visa not required
Embassy in the UK Vanuatu has no diplomatic representation in the UK; the UK Department of Trade and Industry has a Pacific Islands Desk. Tel: (0171) 215 4985; fax: (0171) 215 4398
British embassy British High Commission, PO Box 567, KPMG House, rue Pasteur, Port-Vila. Tel: (678) 23100; fax: (678) 23651
Embassy in the USA Vanuatu does not have an embassy in the USA

American embassy the USA does not have an embassy in Vanuatu; the ambassador to Papua New Guinea is accredited to Vanuatu
Chamber of commerce PO Box 189, Port-Vila. Tel/fax: (678) 23255
Office hours 0730–1130 and 1330–1630 Mon–Fri
Banking hours generally 0830–1500 Mon–Fri (some banks close for lunch at midday)
Time difference GMT +11
Chief tourist attractions unspoilt landscape
Major holidays 1 January, 5 March, 1 May, 30 July 15 August, 25–26 December; variable: Ascension, Good Friday, Easter Monday, Constitution (October), Unity (November)

Vatican City State

National name *Stato della Città del Vaticano*
Area 0.4 sq km/0.2 sq mi
Physical features forms an enclave in the heart of Rome, Italy

Government

Head of state John Paul II from 1978
Head of government Cardinal Sebastiano Baggio
Political system absolute Catholicism
Death penalty abolished 1969

Economy and resources

Currency Vatican City lira; Italian lira
GDP see Italy
Real GDP per capita (PPP) see Italy
Industries the Vatican has three main

sources of income: the Istituto per le Opere di Religione, 'Peter's pence' (voluntary contributions), and interest on investments managed by the Administration of the Patrimony of the Holy See

Population and society

Population 1,000 (1996e)
Population density (per sq km) 2,273 (1996e)
Urban population (% of total) 100 (1995)
Languages Latin (official), Italian
Religions Roman Catholic
Life expectancy see Italy
Literacy rate see Italy

Transport

Airports international airports: one heliport serves visiting heads of state and Vatican officials; the closest international airport is Rome (see Italy)
Railroads total length: 862 m/2,828 ft (a small railway carrying supplies and goods into the Vatican from Italy)

Chronology

AD **64** Death of St Peter, a Christian martyr who, by legend, was killed in Rome and became regarded as the first bishop of Rome. The Pope, as head of the Roman Catholic Church, is viewed as

the spiritual descendent of St Peter.
756 The Pope became temporal ruler of the Papal States, which stretched across central Italy, centred around Rome.
11th–13th centuries Under Gregory VII and Innocent III the papacy enjoyed its greatest temporal power.
1377 After seven decades in which the papacy was based in Avignon (France), Rome once again became the headquarters for the Pope, with the Vatican Palace becoming the official residence.
1860 Umbria, Marche, and much of Emilia Romagna which, along with Lazio formed the Papal States, were annexed by the new unified Italian state.
1870 First Vatican Council defined as a matter of faith the absolute primacy of the Pope and the infallibility of his pronouncements on 'matters of faith and morals'.
1870–71 French forces, which had been protecting the Pope, were withdrawn, allowing Italian nationalist forces to capture Rome, which became the capital of Italy; Pope Pius IX retreated into the Vatican Palace, from which no Pope was to emerge until 1929.
1929 Lateran Agreement, signed by the Italian fascist leader Benito Mussolini and Pope Pius XI, restored full sovereign jurisdiction over the Vatican City State to the bishopric of Rome (Holy See) and

declared the new state to be a neutral and inviolable territory.
1947 New Italian constitution confirmed the sovereignty of the Vatican City State.

1962 Second Vatican Council called by Pope John XXIII.
1978 John Paul II became the first non-Italian pope for more than 400 years.

1985 New concordat signed under which Roman Catholicism ceased to be Italy's state religion.
1992 Relations with East European states restored.

Practical information

Visa requirements see Italy. There is free access to certain areas, including St Peter's Church and Square, the Vatican Museum, and Vatican Gardens; special permission is required to visit all other areas
Embassy in the UK Apostolic Nunciature, 54 Parkside, London SW19 5NE. Tel: (0181) 946 1410; fax: (0181) 947 2494
British embassy Via Condotti 91, 00187 Rome. Tel: (6) 678 9462; fax: (6) 994 0684
Embassy in the USA Apostolic Nunciature, 3339 Massachusetts Avenue, Washington, DC 20008–3687.

Tel: (202) 333 7121; fax: (202) 337 4036
American embassy Via Veneto 119/a, 00187 Rome. Tel: (6) 46 741; fax (6) 488 2672
Chamber of commerce Prefecture of the Economic Affairs of the Holy See, Palazzo delle Congregazioni, Largo del Colonnato 3, 00193 Rome. Tel: (6) 6988 4263; fax: (6) 6988 5011
Time difference GMT +1
Chief tourist attractions St Peter's Church; St Peter's Square; Vatican Museum; the Pope's Sunday blessing
Major holidays see Italy

Venezuela Republic of

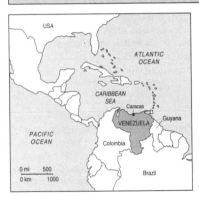

National name *República de Venezuela*
Area 912,100 sq km/352,161 sq mi
Capital Caracas
Major towns/cities Maracaibo, Maracay, Barquisimeto, Valencia, Ciudad Guayana, San Cristóbal
Major ports Maracaibo
Physical features Andes Mountains and Lake Maracaibo in NW; central plains (llanos); delta of river Orinoco in E; Guiana Highlands in SE

Government

Head of state and government Rafael Caldera Rodriguez from 1993
Political system federal democratic republic
Administrative divisions 20 states, two federal territories, one federal district, and 72 federal dependencies
Political parties Democratic Action Party (AD), moderate left of centre; Christian Social Party (COPEI), Christian, centre right; National Convergence (CN), broad coalition

grouping; Movement towards Socialism (MAS), left of centre; Radical Cause (LCR), left wing
Armed forces 46,000 (1995)
Conscription military service is by selective conscription for 30 months
Death penalty abolished 1863
Defence spend (% GDP) 1.1 (1995)
Education spend (% GNP) 5.1 (1993/94)
Health spend (% GDP) 2 (1990)

Economy and resources

Currency bolívar
GDP ($ US) 58.3 billion (1994)
Real GDP per capita (PPP) ($ US) 8,120 (1994)
GDP growth rate 3.4% (1995); 2.4% (1990–95)
Average annual inflation 59.9% (1995); 37.6% (1985–95)
Foreign debt ($ US) 35.8 billion (1995)
Trading partners USA, Japan, Germany, Italy, the Netherlands, Antilles, Colombia, Brazil
Resources petroleum, natural gas, aluminium, iron ore, coal, diamonds, gold, zinc, copper, silver, lead, phosphates, manganese, titanium
Industries refined petroleum products, metals (mainly aluminium, steel and pig-iron), food products, chemicals, fertilizers, cement, paper, vehicles
Exports petroleum and petroleum products, metals (mainly aluminium and iron ore), natural gas, chemicals, basic manufactures, motor vehicles and parts. Principal market: USA 49.2% (1995)
Imports machinery and transport equipment, chemicals, food and live animals, basic manufactures, crude

materials. Principal source: USA 42.1% (1995)
Arable land 3.5% (1993)
Agricultural products coffee, cocoa, sugar cane, bananas, maize, rice, plantains, oranges, sorghum, cassava, wheat, tobacco, cotton, beans, sisal; livestock rearing (cattle)

Population and society

Population 22,311,000 (1996e)
Population growth rate 2.3% (1990–95); 1.8% (2000–05)
Population density (per sq km) 24 (1996e)
Urban population (% of total) 93 (1995)
Age distribution (% of total population) <15 36.2%, 15–65 59.7%, >65 4.1% (1995)
Ethnic distribution 67% mestizos (of Spanish-American and American-Indian descent), 21% Europeans, 10% Africans, 2% Indians
Languages Spanish (official), Indian languages 2%
Religions Roman Catholic
Education (compulsory years) 10
Literacy rate 87% (men); 86% (women) (1995e)
Labour force 9.7% agriculture, 26.3% industry, 64% services (1993)
Unemployment 10.7% (1995)
Life expectancy 70 (men); 76 (women) (1995–2000)
Child mortality rate (under 5, per 1,000 live births) 24 (1995)
Physicians 1 per 577 people (1992)
Hospital beds 1 per 384 people (1992)
TV sets (per 1,000 people) 169 (1995)
Radios (per 1,000 people) 458 (1995)

Transport

Airports international airports: Caracas (Simón Bolívar), Cabello, Maracaibo; domestic services operate to most large towns; total passenger km: 6,426 mil (1994)
Railroads total length: 336 km/209 mi; total passenger km: 31 mil (1994)
Roads total road network: 82,700 km/ 51,390 mi, of which 39.3% paved (1995e); passenger cars: 73.4 per 1,000 people (1993e)

Chronology

1st millenium BC Beginnings of settled agriculture.
AD 1498–99 Visited by Christopher Columbus and Alonso de Ojeda, at which time the principal indigenous Indian communities were the Caribs, Arawaks, and Chibchas; it was named Venezuela ('little Venice') since the coastal Indians lived in stilted thatched houses.
1521 Spanish settlement established on the NE coast and was ruled by Spain from Santo Domingo (Dominican Republic).
1567 Caracas founded by Diego de Losada.
1739 Became part of newly created Spanish Viceroyalty of New Granada, with capital at Bogotá (Colombia), but, lacking gold mines, retained great autonomy.
1749 First rebellion against Spanish colonial rule.
1806 Rebellion against Spain led by Francisco Miranda.
1811–12 First Venezuelan Republic declared by patriots, taking advantage

of Napoleon Bonaparte's invasion of Spain, but Spanish Royalist forces re-established their authority.
1813–14 The Venezuelan, Simón Bolívar, 'El Libertador' (the Liberator), created another briefly independent republic, before being forced to withdraw to Colombia.
1821 After battle of Carabobo, Venezuelan independence achieved within Republic of Gran Colombia (which also comprised Colombia, Ecuador, and Panama).
1829 Became separate state of Venezuela after leaving Republic of Gran Colombia.
1830–48 Gen José Antonio Páez, the first of a series of caudillos (military leaders), established political stability.
1870–88 Antonio Guzmán Blanco ruled as benevolent liberal–conservative dictator, modernizing infrastructure and developing agriculture (notably coffee) and education.
1899 International arbitration tribunal found in favour of British Guiana (Guyana) in long-running dispute over border with Venezuela.
1902 Ports blockaded by British, Italian, and German navies as a result of Venezuela's failure to repay loans.
1908–35 Harsh rule of dictator Juan Vicente Gómez, during which period Venezuela became world's largest exporter of oil, which had been discovered in 1910.
1947 First truly democratic elections held, but the new president, Rómulo Gallegos, was removed within eight months by the military in the person of Col Marcos Pérez Jimenez.
1958 Overthrow of Perez and

establishment of an enduring civilian democracy, headed by left-wing Romulo Betancourt of Democratic Action Party (AD).
1964 Dr Raúl Leoni (AD) became president in first-ever constitutional handover of civilian power.
1969 Dr Rafael Caldera Rodríguez, of centre-right Christian Social Party (COPEI), became president.
1974 Carlos Andrés Pérez (AD) became president, with economy remaining buoyant through oil revenues. Oil and iron industries nationalized.
1979 Dr Luis Herrera (COPEI) became president.
1984 Dr Jaime Lusinchi (AD) became president; social pact established between government, trade unions, and business; national debt rescheduled as oil revenues plummetted.
1987 Widespread social unrest triggered by inflation; student demonstrators shot by police.
1989 Carlos Andrés Pérez (AD) elected president. Economic austerity programme enforced by a loan of $4.3 billion from International Monetary Fund. Price increases triggered riots known as 'Caracazo'; 300 people killed. Martial law declared. General strike followed. Elections boycotted by opposition groups.
1992 Attempted antigovernment coups failed, at a cost of 120 lives.
1993 Pérez resigned, accused of corruption; Ramon José Velasquez succeeded him as interim head of state. Former president Dr Rafael Caldera (COMEI) re-elected.
1996 Pérez found guilty on corruption charges and imprisoned.

Practical information

Visa requirements UK: visa not required. USA: visa not required
Embassy in the UK 1 Cromwell Road, London SW7 2HW. Tel: (0171) 584 4206/7; fax: (0171) 589 8887
British embassy Apartado 1246, Edificio Torre Las Mercedes, 3°, Avenida la Estancia, Chuao, Caracas 1060. Tel: (2) 993 4111; fax: (2) 993 9989
Embassy in the USA 1099 30th Street NW, Washington, DC 20007. Tel: (202) 342 2214
American embassy Calle F con Calle Suapure, Colinas de Valle Arriba, Caracas 1060. Tel: (2) 977 2011; fax: (2) 977 0843

Chamber of commerce Federación Venezolana de Cámaras y Associaciones de Comercio y Producción, Apartado 2568, Edificio Fedecámaras, 5°, Avenida El Empalme, Urb El Bosque, Caracas. Tel: (2) 731 1711; fax: (2) 731 0220
Office hours 0800–1800 Mon–Fri (there is a long midday break)
Banking hours 0830–1130 and 1400–1630 Mon–Fri
Time difference GMT –4
Major holidays 1, 6 January, 19 March, 19 April, 1 May, 24, 29 June, 5, 24 July, 15 August, 12 October, 1 November, 8, 25 December; variable: Ascension Thursday, Carnival (2 days), Corpus Christi, Good Friday, Holy Thursday

Vietnam Socialist Republic of

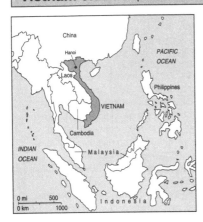

National name *Công Hòa Xã Hôi Chu Nghĩa Viêt Nam*
Area 329,600 sq km/127,258 sq mi
Capital Hanoi
Major towns/cities Ho Chi Minh City (formerly Saigon), Haiphong, Da Nang, Can Tho, Nha Trang, Nam Dinh
Major ports Ho Chi Minh City (formerly Saigon), Da Nang, Haiphong
Physical features Red River and Mekong deltas, centre of cultivation and population; tropical rainforest; mountainous in N and NW

Government

Head of state Le Duc Anh from 1992
Head of government Vo Van Kiet from 1991
Political system communism
Administrative divisions 53 provinces within seven regions
Political party Communist Party
Armed forces 572,000 (1995); plus paramilitary forces numbering 4–5 million
Conscription military service is compulsory for two years
Death penalty retained and used for ordinary crimes
Defence spend (% GDP) 4.3 (1995)
Education spend (% GNP) 2.7 (1994)
Health spend (% GDP) 1.1 (1990)

Economy and resources

Currency dong
GDP ($ US) 15.6 billion (1994)
Real GDP per capita (PPP) ($ US) 1,208 (1994)
GDP growth rate 9.5% (1995); 8.3% (1990–95)
Average annual inflation 17% (1995); 88.3% (1985–95)
Foreign debt ($ US) 26.5 billion (1995)

Trading partners Singapore, Japan, Hong Kong, France, Germany, South Korea
Resources petroleum, coal, tin, zinc, iron, antimony, chromium, phosphate, apatite, bauxite
Industries food processing, chemicals, machinery, textiles, beer, glass and glassware, cigarettes, crude steel, cement, fertilizers, tourism (steady growth in early 1990s)
Exports rice (leading exporter), crude petroleum, coal, coffee, marine products, handicrafts, light industrial goods, rubber, nuts, tea, garments, tin. Principal market: Japan 28.5% (1995)
Imports petroleum products, machinery and spare parts, steel, artificial fertilizers, basic manufactures, consumer goods. Principal source: Singapore 17% (1995)
Arable land 16.6% (1993)
Agricultural products rice (world's fifth-largest producer), coffee, tea, rubber, cotton, groundnuts, sugar cane, coconuts; livestock rearing; fishing

Population and society

Population 75,181,000 (1996e)
Population growth rate 2.2% (1990–95); 1.9% (2000–05)
Population density (per sq km) 227 (1996e)
Urban population (% of total) 21 (1995)
Age distribution (% of total population) <15 37.5%, 15–65 57.7%, >65 4.9% (1995)
Ethnic distribution 88% Viet (also known as Kinh), 2% Chinese, 2% Khmer, 8% consists of more than 50 minority nationalities, including the Hmong, Meo, Muong, Nung, Tay, Thai, and Tho tribal groups
Languages Vietnamese (official); French, English, Khmer, Chinese, local languages
Religions Taoist, Buddhist, Roman Catholic
Education (compulsory years) 5
Literacy rate 92% (men); 84% (women) (1995e)
Labour force 73% agriculture, 13.3% industry, 13.7% services (1994)
Unemployment 7% (1994e)
Life expectancy 65 (men); 70 (women) (1995–2000)
Child mortality rate (under 5, per 1,000 live births) 45 (1995)
Physicians 1 per 3,140 people (1991)
Hospital beds 1 per 573 people (1991)

TV sets (per 1,000 people) 43 (1995)
Radios (per 1,000 people) 106 (1995)

Transport

Airports international airports: Hanoi (Noi Bai), Ho Chi Minh City (Tan Son Nhat); seven domestic airports; total passenger km: 209 mil (1994)
Railroads total length: 2,605 km/1,619 mi; total passenger km: 1,834 mil (1993)
Roads total road network: 106,048 km/ 65,898 mi, of which 25.9% paved (1995)

Chronology

300 BC Rise of Dong Son culture.
111 BC Came under Chinese rule.
1st–6th centuries AD Southern Mekong delta region controlled by independent Indianized Funan kingdom.
939 Chinese overthrown by Ngo Quyen at battle of Bach Dang River; first Vietnamese dynasty founded.
11th century Theravāda Buddhism promoted.
15th century North and South Vietnam united, as kingdom of Champa in the S was destroyed 1471.
16th century Contacts with French missionaries and European traders as political power became decentralized.
early 19th century Under Emperor Nguyen Anh authority was briefly recentralized.
1858–84 Conquered by France and divided into protectorates of Tonkin (North Vietnam) and Annam (South Vietnam).
1887 Became part of French Indo-China Union, which included Cambodia and Laos.
late 19th–early 20th century Development of colonial economy based in S on rubber and rice, drawing migrant labourers from N.
1930 Indochinese Communist Party (ICP) formed by Ho Chi Minh to fight for independence.
1941 Occupied by Japanese during World War II; ICP formed Vietminh as guerrilla resistance force designed to overthrow Japanese-installed puppet regime headed by Bao Dai, Emperor of Annam.
1945 Japanese removed from Vietnam at end of World War II; Vietminh, led by Ho Chi Minh, in control of much of the country, declared independence.
1946 Vietminh war began against French, who tried to reassert colonial control and set up noncommunist state in S 1949.

1954 France decisively defeated at Dien Bien Phu. Vietnam divided along 17th parallel between communist-controlled N and US-backed S.

1963 Ngo Dinh Diem, leader of South Vietnam, overthrown in military coup by Lt-Gen Nguyen Van Thieu.

1964 US combat troops entered Vietnam War as N Vietnamese army began to attack S and allegedly attacked US destroyers in the Tonkin Gulf.

1969 Death of Ho Chi Minh, who was succeeded as Communist Party leader by Le Duan. US forces, which numbered 545,000 at their peak, gradually began to be withdrawn from Vietnam as a result of domestic opposition to the rising casualty toll.

1973 Paris cease-fire agreement provided for withdrawal of US troops and release of US prisoners of war.

1975 Saigon captured by North Vietnam, violating Paris Agreements.

1976 Socialist Republic of Vietnam proclaimed. Hundreds of thousands of southerners became political prisoners; many more fled abroad. Collectivization extended to S.

1978 Diplomatic relations severed with China. Admission into Comecon. Vietnamese invasion of Cambodia.

1979 Sino-Vietnamese 17-day border war; 700,000 Chinese and middle-class Vietnamese fled abroad as refugee 'boat people'.

1986 Death of Le Duan and retirement of 'old guard' leaders; pragmatic Nguyen Van Linh became Communist Party leader and encouraged the private sector through *doi moi* ('renovation') initiative.

1987–88 Over 10,000 political prisoners released.

1989 Troops fully withdrawn from Cambodia.

1991 Economic reformer Vo Van Kiet replaced Do Muoi as prime minister. Cambodia peace agreement signed. Relations with China normalized.

1992 New constitution adopted, guaranteeing economic freedoms. Conservative Le Duc Anh elected president. Relations with South Korea normalized.

1994 US 30-year-old trade embargo removed.

1995 Full diplomatic relations re-established with USA. Became full member of ASEAN.

1996 Economic upturn gained pace.

1997 Diplomatic relations with USA restored.

Practical information

Visa requirements UK: visa required. USA: visa required
Embassy in the UK 12–14 Victoria Road, London W8 5RD. Tel: (0171) 937 1912; fax: (0171) 937 6108
British embassy 16 Pho Ly Thuong Kiet, Hanoi. Tel: (4) 252 349; fax: (4) 265 762
Embassy in the USA 1233 20th Street NW, Washington, DC 20036, Suite 501. Tel: (202) 861 0737; fax: (202) 861 0917
American embassy 7 Lang Ha Road, Ba Dinh District, Hanoi. Tel: (4) 431 500; fax: (4) 350 484

Chamber of commerce Vietcochamber (Chamber of Industry and Commerce of Vietnam), 33 Ba Trieu, Hanoi. Tel: (4) 253 023; fax: (4) 256 446
Office hours 0730–1200 and 1300–1630 Mon–Sat
Time difference GMT +7
Chief tourist attractions Hanoi, with its 11th-century Temple of Literature, Mot Cot Pagoda, 3rd-century Co Loa citadel, and museums (many historical sites were destroyed by war); tropical rainforest
Major holidays 1 January, 30 April, 1 May, 1–2 September; variable: Têt, Lunar New Year (January/February, 3 days)

Yemen Republic of

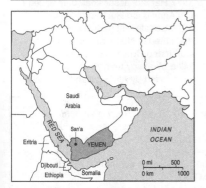

National name *Jamhuriya al Yamaniya*
Area 531,900 sq km/205,366 sq mi
Capital San'a
Major towns/cities Aden, Ta'izz, Al Mukalla, Hodeida, Ibb, Dhamar
Major ports Aden
Physical features hot, moist coastal plain, rising to plateau and desert

Government

Head of state Ali Abdullah Saleh from 1990
Head of government Farag Said Ben Ghanem from 1997
Political system emergent democratic republic
Administrative divisions 17 governates
Political parties General People's Congress (GPC), left of centre; Yemen Socialist Party (YSP), left wing; Yemen Reform Group (al-Islah), Islamic, right of centre; National Opposition Front, left of centre
Armed forces 39,500 (1995); plus paramilitary forces numbering at least 30,000
Conscription military service is compulsory for two years
Death penalty retained and used for ordinary crimes
Defence spend (% GDP) 3.9 (1995)

Education spend (% GNP) 5.8 (1990)
Health spend (% GDP) 1.5 (1990)

Economy and resources

Currency riyal (North); dinar (South), both legal currency throughout the country
GDP ($ US) 18.17 billion (1994e)
Real GDP per capita (PPP) ($ US) 805 (1994)
GDP growth rate 1% (1995)
Average annual inflation 55% (1995)
Foreign debt ($ US) 6.2 billion (1995)
Trading partners China, United Arab Emirates, USA, Saudi Arabia, Japan, UK, Germany
Resources petroleum, natural gas, gypsum, salt; deposits of copper, gold, lead, zinc, molybdenum
Industries petroleum refining and petroleum products, building materials, food processing, beverages, tobacco,

chemical products, textiles, leather goods, metal goods
Exports petroleum and petroleum products, cotton, basic manufactures, clothing, live animals, hides and skins, fish, rice, coffee. Principal market: China 23.4% (1995)
Imports textiles and other manufactured consumer goods, petroleum products, sugar, grain, flour, other foodstuffs, cement, machinery, chemicals. Principal source: UAE 14.2% (1995)
Arable land 2.6% (1993)
Agricultural products sorghum, sesame, millet, potatoes, tomatoes, cotton, wheat, grapes, watermelons, coffee, alfalfa, dates, bananas; livestock rearing; fishing

Population and society

Population 15,678,000 (1996e)
Population growth rate 5% (1990–95); 3.1% (2000–05)
Population density (per sq km) 30 (1996e)
Urban population (% of total) 34 (1995)
Age distribution (% of total population) <15 46.7%, 15–65 50.9%, >65 2.4% (1995)
Ethnic distribution predominantly Arab
Language Arabic
Religions Sunni Muslim 63%, Shi'ite Muslim 37%
Education (compulsory years): 6 (North); 8 (South)
Literacy rate 53% (men); 26% (women) (1995e)
Labour force 30% of population: 61% agriculture, 17% industry, 22% services (1990)
Unemployment 36% (1993)
Life expectancy 52 (men); 52 (women) (1995–2000)
Child mortality rate (under 5, per 1,000 live births) 110 (1995)
Physicians 1 per 4,763 people (1992)

Hospital beds 1 per 1,691 people (1992)
TV sets (per 1,000 people) 28 (1995)
Radios (per 1,000 people) 43 (1995)

Transport

Airports international airports: Sana'a (El-Rahaba), Ta'izz (al-Jahad), Hodeida, Aden (Khormaksar), Mukalla (Riyan), Seybun; domestic services operate between these; total passenger km: 1,183 mil (1994)
Railroads none
Roads total road network: 64,605 km/ 40,146 mi, of which 7.9% paved (1995); passenger cars: 14 per 1,000 people (1995)

Chronology

1st millenium BC South Yemen (Aden) divided between economically advanced Qataban and Hadramawt kingdoms.
c. 5th century BC Qataban fell to the Sabaeans (Shebans) of North Yemen (Sana).
c. 100 BC–AD 525 All of Yemen became part of Himyarite kingdom.
AD 628 Islam introduced.
1174–1229 Under control of Egyptian Ayyubids.
1229–1451 'Golden age' for arts and sciences under the Rasulids, who had served as governors of Yemen under the Ayyubids.
1538 North Yemen came under control of Turkish Ottoman Empire.
1636 Ottomans left North Yemen and power fell into hands of Yemeni Imams, based on local Zaydi tribes, who also held South Yemen until 1735.
1839 Aden became a British territory. Port developed into important ship refuelling station after opening of Suez Canal 1869; protectorate was gradually established over 23 Sultanates inland.

1870s The Ottomans re-established control over North Yemen.
1918 North Yemen became independent, with Imam Yahya from Hamid al-Din family as king.
1937 Aden became British crown colony.
1948 Imam Yahya assassinated by exiled Free Yemenis nationalist movement, but uprising was crushed by his son, Imam Ahmad.
1959 Federation of South Arabia formed by Britain between city of Aden and feudal Sultanates (Aden Protectorate).
1962 Military coup on death of Imam Ahmad; North Yemen declared Yemen Arab Republic (YAR), with Abdullah al-Sallal as president. Civil war broke out between royalists (supported by Saudi Arabia) and republicans (supported by Egypt).
1963 Armed rebellion by National Liberation Front (NLF) began against British rule in Aden.
1967 Civil war ended with republicans victorious. Sallal deposed and replaced by Republican Council. The Independent People's Republic of South Yemen formed after British withdrawal from Aden. Many fled to N as repressive communist NLF regime took over in S.
1970 People's Republic of South Yemen renamed People's Democratic Republic of Yemen.
1971–72 War between South Yemen and YAR; union agreement brokered by Arab League signed but not kept.
1974 The pro-Saudi Col Ibrahim al-Hamadi seized power in North Yemen; Military Command Council set up.
1977 Hamadi assassinated; replaced by Col Ahmed ibn Hussein al-Ghashmi.
1978 Constituent people's assembly appointed in North Yemen and Military Command Council dissolved. Ghashmi killed by envoy from South Yemen; succeeded by Ali Abdullah Saleh. War

---

Practical information

Visa requirements UK: visa required. USA: visa required
Embassy in the UK 57 Cromwell Road, London SW7 2ED. Tel: (0171) 584 6607; fax: (0171) 589 3350
British embassy PO Box 1287, 129 Haddah Road, Sana'a. Tel: (1) 215 630; fax: (1) 263 059
Embassy in the USA Suite 705, 2600 Virginia Avenue NW, Washington, DC 20037. Tel: (202) 965 4760/1; fax: (202) 337 2017
American embassy Dhahr Himyar Zone, Sheraton Hotel District, Sana'a Tel: (1) 238843–52; fax: (1) 251 563
Chamber of commerce Federation of Chambers of

Commerce, PO Box 16992, Sana'a. Tel: (1) 221 765; telex: 2229
Office hours 0800–1230 and 1600–1900 Mon–Wed; 0800–1100 Thu
Banking hours 0800–1200 Sat–Wed; 0800–1130 Thu
Time difference GMT +3
Chief tourist attractions sandy beaches along coastal plains; Hadramaut mountain range; Aden; Sana's old city, with its medieval mosques and other buildings; hillside villages of Kawkaban, Thulla, and Shiban
Major holidays 1 May, 26 September; variable: Eid-ul-Adha (5 days), end of Ramadan (4 days), New Year (Muslim), Prophet's Birthday

broke out again between two Yemens. South Yemen president deposed and executed; Yemen Socialist Party (YSP) formed in S by communists.
1979 Cease-fire agreed with commitment to future union.
1980 YSP leader Ali Nasser Muhammad became head of state in South Yemen.
1986 Civil war in South Yemen; autocratic Ali Nasser dismissed. New administration formed under more moderate Haydar Abu Bakr al-Attas, who was committed to negotiating union with N as a result of deteriorating economy in S.
1989 Draft multiparty constitution for single Yemen state published.
1990 Border between two Yemens opened; countries formally united 22 May as Republic of Yemen.
1991 New constitution approved; Yemen opposed US-led operations against Iraq in Gulf War.
1992 Anti-government riots.
1993 Saleh's General People's Congress (GPC) won most seats in general election but no overall majority; five-member presidential council elected, including Saleh as president, YSP leader Ali Salim al-Baidh as vice president, and Bakr al-Attas as prime minister.
1994 Fighting erupted between northern forces, led by President Saleh, and southern forces, led by Vice President al-Baidh, as southern Yemen announced its secession. Saleh inflicted crushing defeat on al-Baidh and new GPC coalition appointed.
1997 GPC election victory. Farag Said Ben Ghanem appointed prime minister.

Yugoslavia Federal Republic of

National name *Federativna Republika Jugoslavija*
Area 58,300 sq km/22,509 sq mi
Capital Belgrade
Major towns/cities Priština, Novi Sad, Niš, Rijeka, Kragujevac, Podgorica (formerly Titograd), Subotica
Physical features federation of republics of Serbia and Montenegro and two former autonomous provinces, Kosovo and Vojvodina

Government

Head of state Slobodan Milošević from 1997
Head of government Radoje Kontic from 1993
Political system socialist pluralist republic
Administrative divisions 29 districts
Political parties Socialist Party of Serbia (SPS), Serb nationalist, reform socialist (ex-communist); Montenegrin Social Democratic Party (SDPCG), federalist, reform socialist (ex-communist); Serbian Radical Party (SRS), Serb nationalist, extreme right wing; People's Assembly Party, Christian democrat, centrist; Democratic Party (DS), moderate nationalist; Democratic Party of Serbia (DSS), moderate nationalist; Democratic Community of Vojvodina Hungarians (DZVM), ethnic Hungarian; Democratic Party of Albanians/Party of Democratic Action (DPA/PDA), ethnic Albanian; New Socialist Party of Montenegro (NSPM), left of centre
Armed forces 126,500 (1995)
Conscription military service is compulsory for 12–15 months; voluntary military service for women introduced 1983
Death penalty retained and used for ordinary crimes
Defence spend (% GDP) 22.1 (1995)
Education spend (% GNP) 6.1 (1992; former Yugoslavia)

Economy and resources

Currency new Yugoslav dinar
GDP ($ US) 15.9 billion (1995e)
Real GDP per capita (PPP) ($ US) 4,400 (1995e)
GDP growth rate 4% (1995e)
Average annual inflation 120% (1995e)
Foreign debt ($ US) 10.5 billion (1995e)
Trading partners Germany, CIS nations, Italy, USA, Macedonia
Resources petroleum, natural gas, coal, copper ore, bauxite, iron ore, lead, zinc
Industries crude steel, pig-iron, steel castings, cement, machines, passenger cars, electrical appliances, artificial fertilizers, plastics, bicycles, textiles and clothing
Exports basic manufactures, machinery and transport equipment, clothing, miscellaneous manufactured articles, food and live animals. Principal market: developed countries 40.2% (1996)
Imports machinery and transport equipment, electrical goods, agricultural produce, mineral fuels and lubricants, basic manufactures, foodstuffs, chemicals. Principal source: developed countries 51.7% (1996)
Arable land 30% (1993)
Agricultural products maize, sugar beet, wheat, potatoes, grapes, plums, soya beans, vegetables; livestock production declined 1991–95

Population and society

Population 10,294,000 (1996e)
Population growth rate 1.3% (1990–95); 0.4% (2000–05)
Population density (per sq km) 101 (1996e)
Urban population (% of total) 57 (1995)
Age distribution (% of total population) <15 22%, 15–65 66.6%, >65 11.4% (1995)
Ethnic distribution according to the 1991 census, 62% of the population of the rump federal republic is ethnic Serb, 17% Albanian, 5% Montenegrin, 3% 'Yugoslav', and 3% Muslim. Serbs predominate in the republic of Serbia, where they form (excluding the autonomous areas of Kosovo and Vojvodina) 85% of the population; in Vojvodina they comprise 55% of the population. Albanians constitute 77% of the population of Kosovo; Montenegrins comprise 69% of the population of the republic of Montenegro; and Muslims predominate in the Sandzak region, which straddles the Serbian and Montenegrin borders. Since 1992 an influx of Serb refugees from Bosnia and Kosovo has increased the proportion of Serbs in Serbia, while many ethnic Hungarians have left Vojvodina, and an estimated 500,000 Albanians have left Kosovo

Languages Serbo-Croatian; Albanian (in Kosovo)
Religions Serbian and Montenegrin Orthodox; Muslim in S Serbia
Education (compulsory years) 8
Literacy rate 97% (men); 88% (women) (1995e)
Labour force 6% agriculture, 41% industry, 53% services (1993e)
Unemployment 23.8% (1994)
Life expectancy 70 (men); 75 (women) (1995–2000)
Infant mortality rate (per 1,000 live births) 23 (1995)
Physicians 1 per 506 people (1993)
Hospital beds 1 per 183 people (1993)
TV sets (per 1,000 people) 190 (1995)
Radios (per 1,000 people) 141 (1995)

Transport

Airports international airports: Belgrade (Surcin), Podgorica; three domestic airports; total passenger km: 3,443 mil (1991)
Railroads total length: 3,987 km/2,478 mi; total passenger km: 2,525 mil (1994)
Roads total road network: 47,000 km/29,206 mi, of which 59.7% paved (1995e)

Chronology

3rd century BC Serbia (then known as Moesia Superior) conquered by Romans; empire was extended to Belgrade centuries later by Emperor Augustus.
6th century AD Slavic tribes, including Serbs, Croats, and Slovenes, crossed river Danube and settled in Balkan Peninsula.
879 Serbs converted to Orthodox Church by Sts Cyril and Methodius.
mid-10th–11th centuries Serbia broke free briefly from Byzantine Empire to establish independent state.
1217 Independent Serbian kingdom re-established, reaching its height in mid-14th century under Stefan Dushan, when it controlled much of Albania and northern Greece.
1389 Serbian army defeated by Ottoman Turks at Battle of Kosovo; area became Turkish *pashalik* (province). Montenegro in SW survived as sovereign principality. Croatia and Slovenia in NW became part of Habsburg Empire.
18th century Vojvodina enjoyed protection from the Austrian Habsburgs.
1815 Uprisings against Turkish rule secured autonomy for Serbia.
1878 Independence achieved as Kingdom of Serbia, after Turks defeated

by Russians in war over Bulgaria.
1912–13 During Balkan Wars, Serbia expanded its territory at expense of Turkey and Bulgaria.
1918 Joined Croatia and Slovenia, formerly under Austrian Habsburg control, to form Kingdom of Serbs, Croats, and Slovenes under Serbian Peter Karageorgevic (Peter I); Montenegro's citizens voted to depose their ruler, King Nicholas, and join the union.
1929 New name of Yugoslavia ('Land of the Southern Slavs') adopted; Serbian-dominated military dictatorship established by King Alexander I as opposition mounted from Croatian federalists.
1934 Alexander I assassinated by a Macedonian with Croatian terrorist links; his young son Peter II succeeded, with Paul, his uncle, as regent; Nazi Germany and fascist Italy increased their influence.
1941 Following coup by pro-Allied air-force officers, Nazi Germany invaded. Peter II fled to England. Armed resistance to German rule began, spearheaded by pro-royalist, Serbian-based Chetniks ('Army of the Fatherland'), led by Gen Draza Mihailović, and communist Partisans ('National Liberation Army'), led by Marshal Tito. An estimated 900,000 Yugoslavs died in the war, including more than 400,000 Serbs and 200,000 Croats.
1943 Provisional government formed by Tito at liberated Jajce in Bosnia.
1945 Yugoslav Federal People's Republic formed under leadership of Tito; communist constitution introduced.
1948 Split with Soviet Union after Tito objected to Soviet 'hegemonism'; expelled from Cominform.
1953 Workers' self-management principle enshrined in constitution and private farming supported; Tito became president.
1961 Nonaligned movement formed under Yugoslavia's leadership.
1971 In response to mounting separatist demands in Croatia, new system of collective and rotating leadership introduced.
1980 Tito died; collective leadership assumed power.
1981–82 Armed forces suppressed demonstrations in Kosovo province, S Serbia, by Albanians demanding full republic status.
1986 Slobodan Milošević, a populist-nationalist hardliner who had the

ambition of creating a 'Greater Serbia', became leader of communist party in the Serbian republic.
1988 Economic difficulties: 1,800 strikes, 250% inflation, 20% unemployment. Ethnic unrest in Montenegro and Vojvodina, and separatist demands in rich NW republics of Croatia and Slovenia; 'market socialist' reform package, encouraging private sector, inward investment, and liberalizing prices combined with austerity wage freeze.
1989 Reformist Croatian Ante Marković became prime minister. Ethnic riots in Kosovo province against Serbian attempt to end autonomous status of Kosovo and Vojvodina; at least 30 were killed and a state of emergency imposed.
1990 Multiparty systems established in republics; Kosovo and Vojvodina stripped of autonomy. In Croatia, Slovenia, Bosnia, and Macedonia elections bought to power new non-communist governments seeking a looser confederation.
1991 Demonstrations against Serbian president Slobodan Milošević in Belgrade crushed violently by riot police and tanks. Slovenia and Croatia declared independence, resulting in clashes between federal and republican armies; Slovenia accepted peace pact sponsored by European Community, but fighting intensified in Croatia, where Serb militias controlled over one-third of the republic; Federal President Stipe Mesic and Prime Minister Markovic resigned.
1992 EC-brokered cease-fire in Croatia; EC and USA recognized Slovenia's and Croatia's independence. Bosnia-Herzegovina and Macedonia declared independence. Bosnia-Herzegovina recognized as independent by EC and USA. New Federal Republic of Yugoslavia (FRY) proclaimed by Serbia and Montenegro but not recognized externally. International sanctions imposed. UN membership suspended. Ethnic Albanians proclaimed new 'Republic of Kosovo', but it was not recognized.
1993 Pro-Milošević Zoran Lilic became Yugoslav president. Antigovernment rioting in Belgrade. Macedonia recognized as independent under name of Former Yugoslav Republic of Macedonia. Economy severely damaged by international sanctions.
1994 Border blockade imposed by Yugoslavia against Bosnian Serbs; sanctions eased as a result.

1995 Serbia played key role in US-brokered Dayton peace accord for Bosnia-Herzegovina and accepted separate existence of Bosnia and Croatia. US economic sanctions against Serbia lifted.
1996 Diplomatic relations restored between Serbia and Croatia. UN sanctions against Serbia lifted. Allies of Milošević successful in parliamentary elections. Full diplomatic relations established with Bosnia-Herzegovina. Ruling party won assembly elections. Mounting opposition to Milošević's government, following its refusal to accept opposition victories in municipal elections.
1997 Serbian parliament passed legislation recognizing the elections, thus ending opposition demonstrations. Slobodan Milošević elected president.

Practical information

Visa requirements UK: visa required. USA: visa required
Embassy in the UK 5–7 Lexham Gardens, London W8 5JJ. Tel: (0171) 370 6105; fax: (0171) 370 3838
British embassy Ulica Generala Zdanova 46, 11000 Belgrade. Tel: (1) 645 055; fax: (1) 659 651
Embassy in the USA 2410 California Street NW, Washington, DC 20008. Tel: (202) 462 6566
American embassy mailing address: Unit 1310, APO AE 09213-1310. Tel: (11) 645 655; fax: (11) 645 332
Chamber of commerce Chamber of Economy of Serbia, Ulica Generala Zdanova 13–15, 11000 Belgrade. Tel: (1) 340 611; fax: (1) 330 949. Chamber of Economy of Montenegro, Novaka Miloseva 29/II, 81000 Podgorica. Tel: (81) 31071; fax: (81) 34926
Office hours 0700–1430 Mon–Fri
Banking hours 0700–1500 Mon–Fri
Time difference GMT +1
Chief tourist attractions Montenegro's Adriatic coastline and its great lake of Scutari; varied scenery – rich alpine valleys, rolling green hills, bare, rocky gorges, thick forests, limestone mountains
Major holidays 1–2 January, 1–2 May, 4, 7 (Serbia only), 13 (Montenegro only) July, 29–30 November; Orthodox Christian holidays may also be celebrated throughout much of the region

---

Zambia Republic of (formerly *Northern Rhodesia*)

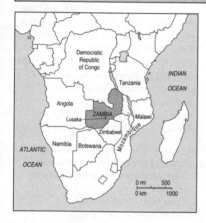

Area 752,600 sq km/290,578 sq mi
Capital Lusaka
Major towns/cities Kitwe, Ndola, Kabwe, Mufulira, Chingola, Luanshya, Livingstone
Physical features forested plateau cut through by rivers; Zambezi River, Victoria Falls, Kariba Dam

Government

Head of state and government Frederick Chiluba from 1991
Political system emergent democratic republic
Administrative divisions nine provinces

Political parties United National Independence Party (UNIP), African socialist; Movement for Multiparty Democracy (MMD), moderate, left of centre; Multiracial Party (MRP), moderate, left of centre, multiracial; National Democratic Alliance (NADA), left of centre; Democratic Party (DP), left of centre
Armed forces 21,600 (1995); plus paramilitary forces of 1,400
Conscription military service is voluntary
Death penalty retained and used for ordinary crimes
Defence spend (% GDP) 1.9 (1995)
Education spend (% GNP) 2.6 (1993/94)
Health spend (% GDP) 2.2 (1990)

Economy and resources

Currency Zambian kwacha
GDP ($ US) 3.5 billion (1994)
Real GDP per capita (PPP) ($ US) 962 (1994)
GDP growth rate –3.9% (1995); –0.2% (1990–95)
Average annual inflation 31.7% (1995); 91.6% (1985–95)
Foreign debt ($ US) 6.3 billion (1995)
Trading partners South Africa, Japan, UK, Germany, France, Thailand, India
Resources copper (world's fourth-largest producer), cobalt, zinc, lead, coal, gold, emeralds, amethysts and other gemstones, limestone, selenium
Industries metallurgy (smelting and refining of copper and other metals), food canning, fertilizers, explosives, textiles, bottles, bricks, copper wire, batteries
Exports copper, zinc, lead, cobalt, tobacco. Principal market: Japan 16% (1995)
Imports machinery and transport equipment, mineral fuels, lubricants, electricity, basic manufactures, chemicals, food and live animals. Principal source: South Africa 33.1% (1995)
Arable land 7% (1993)
Agricultural products maize, sugar cane, seed cotton, tobacco, groundnuts, wheat, rice, beans, cassava, millet, sorghum, sunflower seeds, horticulture; cattle rearing

Population and society

Population 8,275,000 (1996e)
Population growth rate 3% (1990–95); 2.4% (2000–05)
Population density (per sq km) 11 (1996e)
Urban population (% of total) 43 (1995)
Age distribution (% of total population)

<15 47.4%, 15–65 50.2%, >65 2.4% (1995)

Ethnic distribution over 95% indigenous Africans, belonging to more than 70 different ethnic groups, including the Bantu-Botatwe and the Bemba

Languages English (official); Bantu languages

Religions Christian, animist, Hindu, Muslim

Education (compulsory years) 7

Literacy rate 81% (men); 65% (women) (1995e)

Labour force 42% of population: 75% agriculture, 8% industry, 17% services (1990)

Life expectancy 45 (men); 47 (women) (1995–2000)

Child mortality rate (under 5, per 1,000 live births) 203 (1995)

Physicians 1 per 7,929 people (1991)

Hospital beds 1 per 562 people (1991)

TV sets (per 1,000 people) 32 (1995)

Radios (per 1,000 people) 99 (1995)

Transport

Airports international airports: Lusaka; over 127 domestic airports, aerodromes, and airstrips; total passenger km: 428 mil (1994)

Railroads total length: 1,289 km/801 mi; total passenger km: 268 mil (1990)

Roads total road network: 38,898 km/24,171 mi, of which 18.3% paved

(1995e); passenger cars: 14.3 per 1,000 people (1995e)

Chronology

16th century Immigration of peoples from Luba and Lunda Empires of Zaire, to the NW, who set up small kingdoms.

late 18th century Visited by Portuguese explorers.

19th century Instability with immigration of Ngoni from E, Kololo from W, establishment of Bemba kingdom in N, and slave-trading activities of Portuguese and Arabs from E Africa.

1851 Visited by British missionary and explorer David Livingstone.

1889 As Northern Rhodesia, came under administration of British South Africa Company of Cecil Rhodes, and became involved in copper mining, especially from 1920s.

1924 Became a British protectorate.

1948 Northern Rhodesia African Congress (NRAC) formed by black Africans to campaign for self-rule.

1953 Became part of Central African Federation, which included South Rhodesia (Zimbabwe) and Nyasaland (Malawi).

1960 UNIP formed by Kenneth Kaunda as breakaway from NRAC, as African socialist body to campaign for independence and dissolution of Federation dominated by South Rhodesia's white minority.

1963 Federation dissolved; internal self-government achieved.

1964 Independence achieved within Commonwealth as Republic of Zambia with Kaunda of the UNIP as president.

later 1960s Key enterprises brought under state control.

1972 UNIP declared only legal party.

1975 Opening of Tan-Zam railway from Zambian copperbelt, 322 mi/200 km N of Lusaka, to port of Dar es Salaam in Tanzania. This reduced Zambia's dependence on rail route via Rhodesia for its exports.

1976 Zambia declared support for Patriotic Front (PF) guerrillas fighting to topple white-dominated regime in Rhodesia (Zimbabwe).

1980 Unsuccessful South African-promoted coup against President Kaunda; relations with Zimbabwe improved when PF came to power.

1985 Kaunda elected chair of African Front Line States.

1991 New multiparty constitution adopted. MMD won landslide election victory, and its leader Frederick Chiluba became president in what was the first democratic change of government in English-speaking black Africa.

1993 State of emergency declared after rumours of planned anti-government coup, privatization programme launched.

1996 Kaunda barred from future elections; President Chiluba re-elected.

Practical information

Visa requirements UK: visa not required. USA: visa required

Embassy in the UK 2 Palace Gate, London W8 5NG. Tel: (0171) 589 6655; fax: (0171) 581 1353

British embassy British High Commission, PO Box 50050, Independence Avenue, 15101 Ridgeway, Lusaka. Tel: (1) 251 133; fax: (1) 253 798

Embassy in the USA 2419 Massachusetts Avenue NW, Washington, DC 20008. Tel: (202) 265 9717/8/9; fax: (202) 332 0826

American embassy corner of Independence Avenue and United Nations Avenue, Lusaka. Tel: (1) 250 955, 252 230; fax: (1) 252 225

Chamber of commerce Ministry of Commerce, Trade and Industry, PO Box 31968, Kwacha Annex, Cairo Road, Lusaka. Tel: (1) 228 301; fax: (1) 226 727

Office hours 0800–1300 and 1400–1700 Mon–Fri

Banking hours 0815–1430 Mon–Fri

Time difference GMT +2

Chief tourist attractions unspoilt scenery; wildlife; 19 national parks, including the magnificent Luangava and Kafue National Parks, which have some of the most prolific animal populations in Africa; Victoria Falls

Major holidays 1 January, 1, 25 May, 24 October, 25 December; variable: Good Friday, Holy Saturday, Youth (March), Heroes (July), Unity (July), Farmers (August)

Zimbabwe Republic of (formerly *Southern Rhodesia)*

Area 390,300 sq km/150,694 sq mi
Capital Harare
Major towns/cities Bulawayo, Gweru,
Kwekwe, Mutare, Hwange, Chitungwiza
Physical features high plateau with
central high veld and mountains in E;
rivers Zambezi, Limpopo; Victoria Falls

Government

Head of state and government Robert
Mugabe from 1987
Political system effectively one-party
socialist republic
Administrative divisions eight
provinces and two cities with provincial
status
Political parties Zimbabwe African
National Union–Patriotic Front
(ZANU–PF), African socialist; opposition
parties exist but none have mounted
serious challenge to ruling party
Armed forces 45,000 (1995);
paramilitary police force 19,500; national
militia 1,000
Death penalty retained and used for
ordinary crimes
Defence spend (% GDP) 4.2 (1995)
Education spend (% GNP) 8.3
(1993/94)
Health spend (% GDP) 3.2 (1990)

Economy and resources

Currency Zimbabwe dollar
GDP ($ US) 5.4 billion (1994)
Real GDP per capita (PPP) ($ US)
2,196 (1994)
GDP growth rate 7.4% (1994); 1.0%
(1990–95)
Average annual inflation 22.2% (1994);
20.9% (1985–95)
Foreign debt ($ US) 4.9 billion (1995)
Trading partners South Africa, UK,

Germany, Japan, USA
Resources gold, nickel, asbestos, coal,
chromium, copper, silver, emeralds,
lithium, tin, iron ore, cobalt
Industries metal products, food
processing, textiles, furniture and other
wood products, chemicals, fertilizers
Exports tobacco, metals and metal
alloys, textiles and clothing, cotton lint.
Principal market: South Africa 13.5%
(1995)
Imports machinery and transport
equipment, basic manufactures, mineral
fuels, chemicals, foodstuffs. Principal
source: South Africa 40.9% (1995)
Arable land 7% (1993)
Agricultural products tobacco, maize,
cotton, coffee, sugar cane, wheat, soya
beans, groundnuts, horticulture; livestock
(cattle)

Population and society

Population 11,439,000 (1996e)
Population growth rate 2.6%
(1990–95); 2% (2000–05)
Population density (per sq km) 29
(1996e)
Urban population (% of total) 32 (1995)
Age distribution (% of total population)
<15 44.1%, 15–65 53.1%, >65 2.8%
(1995)
Ethnic distribution four distinct ethnic
groups: indigenous Africans, who
account for about 95% of the population,
Europeans (mainly British), who account
for about 3.5%, and Afro-Europeans and
Asians, who each comprise about 0.5%
Languages English (official), Shona,
Sindebele
Religions Christian, Muslim, Hindu,
animist
Education (compulsory years) 8
Literacy rate 74% (men); 60% (women)
(1995e)
Labour force 46% of population: 68%
agriculture, 8% industry, 24% services
(1990)
Unemployment 44% (1993)
Life expectancy 50 (men); 52 (women)
(1995–2000)
Child mortality rate (under 5, per 1,000
live births) 74 (1995)
Physicians 1 per 7,692 people (1991)
TV sets (per 1,000 people) 29 (1995)
Radios (per 1,000 people) 89 (1995)

Transport

Airports international airports: Harare,
Bulowayo, Victoria Falls; domestic air

services operate between most of the
larger towns; total passenger km: 666 mil
(1994)
Railroads total length: 2,759 km/1,714
mi; total passenger km: 545,977 mil
(1995)
Roads total road network: 91,810 km/
57,051 mi, of which 19% paved (1995e);
passenger cars: 40.1 per 1,000 people
(1995e)

Chronology

13th century Shona people settled
Mashonaland (E Zimbabwe), erecting
stone buildings (hence name Zimbabwe,
'stone house').
15th century Shona Empire reached its
greatest extent.
16th–17th centuries Portuguese settlers
developed trade with Shona states and
achieved influence over kingdom of
Mwanamutapa in N Zimbabwe 1629.
1837 Ndebele (or Matabele) people
settled in SW Zimbabwe after being
driven north from Transvaal by Boers;
Shona defeated by Ndebele led by King
Mzilikazi who formed military empire
based at Bulawayo.
1870 King Lobengula succeeded King
Mzilikazi.
1889 Cecil Rhodes' British South Africa
Company (BSA Co) obtained exclusive
rights to exploit mineral resources in
Lobengula's domains.
1890 Creation of white colony in
Mashonaland and founding of Salisbury
(Harare) by Leander Starr Jameson,
associate of Rhodes.
1893 Matabele War: Jameson defeated
Lobengula; white settlers took control of
country.
1895 Matabeleland, Mashonaland, and
Zambia named Rhodesia after Cecil
Rhodes.
1896 Matabele revolt suppressed.
1898 Southern Rhodesia (Zimbabwe)
became British protectorate administered
by BSA Co; farming, mining, and
railways developed.
1922 Union with South Africa rejected by
referendum among white settlers.
1923 Southern Rhodesia became self-
governing colony; Africans progressively
disenfranchised.
1933–53 Prime Minister Godfrey Huggins
(later Lord Malvern) pursued 'White
Rhodesia' policy of racial segregation.
1950s Immigration doubled white
population to around 250,000, while

indigenous African population stood at around 6 million.

1953 Southern Rhodesia formed part of Federation of Rhodesia and Nyasaland.

1961 Zimbabwe African People's Union (ZAPU) formed with Joshua Nkomo as leader; declared illegal a year later.

1962 Rhodesia Front party of Winston Field took power in Southern Rhodesia, pledging to preserve white rule.

1963 Federation of Rhodesia and Nyasaland dissolved as Zambia and Malawi moved towards independence; Zimbabwe African National Union (ZANU) formed, with Robert Mugabe as secretary; declared illegal a year later.

1964 Ian Smith became prime minister; he rejected British terms for independence which required moves towards black majority rule; Nkomo and Mugabe imprisoned.

1965 Smith made unilateral declaration of independence (UDI); Britain broke off all relations.

1966–68 United Nations (UN) imposed economic sanctions on Rhodesia, which still received help from South Africa and Portugal.

1969 Rhodesia declared itself a republic.

1972 Britain rejected draft independence agreement as unacceptable to African population.

1974 Nkomo and Mugabe released and jointly formed Patriotic Front to fight Smith regime in mounting civil war.

1975 Geneva Conference between British, Smith regime, and African nationalists failed to reach agreement.

1978 At height of civil war, whites were leaving Rhodesia at rate of 1,000 per month.

1979 Rhodesia became Zimbabwe-Rhodesia with new 'majority' constitution which nevertheless retained special rights for whites; Bishop Abel Muzorewa became premier; Mugabe and Nkomo rejected settlement; Lancaster House

Agreement temporarily restored Rhodesia to British rule.

1980 Zimbabwe achieved independence from Britain with full transition to African majority rule; Mugabe became prime minister with Rev Canaan Banana as president.

1981 Rift between Mugabe (ZANU-PF) and Nkomo (ZAPU); Nkomo dismissed from cabinet 1982.

1984 ZANU-PF party congress agreed to principle of one-party state.

1987 Mugabe combined posts of head of state and prime minister as executive president; Nkomo became vice president.

1989 ZANU-PF and ZAPU formally merged; Zimbabwe Unity Movement founded by Edgar Tekere to oppose one-party state.

1992 United Party formed to oppose ZANU-PF. Mugabe declared drought and famine a national disaster.

1996 Mugabe re-elected president.

Practical information

Visa requirements UK: visa not required. USA: visa not required

Embassy in the UK Zimbabwe House, 429 Strand, London WC2R 0SA. Tel: (0171) 836 7755; (0171) 379 1167

British embassy British High Commission, PO Box 4490, Stanley House, Jason Moyo Avenue, Harare. Tel: (4) 793 781; fax: (4) 728 380

Embassy in the USA 1608 New Hampshire Avenue NW, Washington, DC 20009. Tel: (202) 332 7100; fax: (202) 483 9326

American embassy 172 Herbert Chitepo Avenue, Harare. Tel: (4) 794 521; fax: (4) 796 488

Chamber of commerce Zimbabwe National Chambers of Commerce, PO Box 1934, Equity House, Rezende Street, Harare. Tel: (4) 753 444; fax: (4) 753 450

Office hours 0800–1630 Mon–Fri

Banking hours 0800–1500 Mon, Tue, Thu, Fri; 0800–1300 Wed; 0800–1130 Sat

Time difference GMT +2

Chief tourist attractions Victoria Falls; Kariba Dam; mountain scenery, including Mount Inyanganai; some of southern Africa's best wildlife parks, notably Hwange, Matapos, and Nyanga national parks; ruins of old Zimbabwe, near Fort Victoria; World's View in the Matapos Hills

Major holidays 1 January, 18–19 April, 1, 25 May, 11 August (2 days), 25–26 December; variable: Good Friday, Easter Monday

Gazetteer

Aachen (French *Aix-la-Chapelle*) German cathedral city and spa in the administrative region (German *Land*) of North Rhine–Westphalia, 64 km/40 mi SW of Cologne; population (1993) 246,100. It has thriving electronic, glass, and rubber industries, and is one of Germany's principal railway junctions. Aachen was the Roman *Aquisgranum* and was the site of baths in the 1st century AD. Charlemagne was born and buried in Aachen, and founded the cathedral 796. The Holy Roman Emperors were crowned here 813–1531.

Aalborg Alternative form of ◊Ålborg, a port in Denmark.

Aalen Industrial city in the *Land* of Baden-Württemberg, Germany, on the river Köcher, 65 km/40 mi E of Stuttgart; population (1994) 67,000. Textiles, iron, and optical goods are manufactured. Aalen was one of the city-states of the Holy Roman Empire until 1802.

Aalesund Alternative form of ◊Ålesund, a town in Norway.

Aalst (French *Alost*) Industrial town (brewing, textiles) in East Flanders, Belgium, on the river Dender 24 km/15 mi NW of Brussels; population (1993 est) 76,500.

Aarau Commune and capital of the Swiss canton of Aargau, on the river Aar, 35 km/22 mi W of Zürich; population (1995) 15,900. Silk, leather, cotton goods, and mathematical instruments are made in the town.

Aargau (French *Argovie*) Canton of N Switzerland; area 1,404 sq km/542 sq mi; population (1995) 528,900. Taking its name from the river Aar flowing through it, the canton is bounded on the N by the Rhine and on the S by the canton of Lucerne. The main towns are Aarau (the capital), Baden, and Brugg. The majority of the population of Aargau live in the fertile lowlands, and work in agriculture (dairy and mixed farming, fruit growing, and cattle breeding).

Aarhus Alternative form of ◊Århus, a port in Denmark.

Abacos or **Abaco Islands** Group of islands in the N Bahamas, comprising Great Abaco – population (1990) 10,100 – Little Abaco, and a number of keys (small, low-lying islands of sand and coral fragments); area 963 sq km/372 sq mi. The largest town in the group is Marsh Harbour on Great Abaco, and the largest town on Little Abaco is Fox Town. Tourism is an important industry.

Abadan Iranian oil port on the E side of the Shatt-al-Arab waterway; population (1991) 84,800. Abadan is the chief refinery and shipping centre for Iran's oil industry, nationalized 1951. This measure was the beginning of the worldwide movement by oil-producing countries to assume control of profits from their own resources. Oil installations were badly damaged during the Iran–Iraq war 1980–88.

Abakan Coal-mining city and capital of Khakass autonomous republic in the Krasnoyarsk territory of the Russian Federation, in W Siberia; population (1992) 158,000.

Abana Alternative form of the river ◊Amana, now the Barada.

Abbeville Town in N France in the Somme *département*, 19 km/12 mi inland from the mouth of the river Somme; population (1990) 24,500.

Abdera Town in ancient Thrace on the Aegean Sea (now in ruins); the birthplace of the philosopher Democritus and the sophist Protagoras. Its inhabitants had a reputation for stupidity, and 'Abderite' became a term for a simpleton. The site is occupied by the modern town of Avdhira, Greece.

Abeokuta Agricultural trade centre in Nigeria, W Africa, on the Ogun River, 103 km/64 mi N of Lagos; population (1992 est) 386,800.

Aberbrothock Another name for ◊Arbroath, a town in Scotland.

Aberdare (Welsh *Aberdâr*) Town in Rhondda Cynon Taff, Wales; industries include electrical cables and light engineering; population (1982 est) 38,000.

Aberdeen City and seaport on the E coast of Scotland, administrative headquarters of Aberdeen City unitary authority and of Aberdeenshire. Industries include agricultural machinery, paper, knitwear, carpets, and textiles; fishing; ship-building; granite-quarrying; and engineering. There are shore-based maintenance and service depots for the North Sea oil rigs. Aberdeen is Scotland's third-largest city and its biggest resort. It is Scotland's main centre for offshire oil exploration.

Aberdeen City Unitary authority in E Scotland created 1996 from part of the former Grampian region; population (1996) 219,100; area 184 sq km/71 sq mi.

Aberdeenshire Unitary authority in NE Scotland. A former county, it was merged 1975–96 into Grampian Region; administrative headquarters Aberdeen; population (1996) 226,500; area 6,289 sq km/2,428 sq mi. Industries include oil and gas, papermaking, whisky distilling, farming, beef, fishing, seafood, tourism (skiing at Aviemore). The area includes the Cairngorm Mountains and Balmoral Castle. The Braemar Highland Games are held here.

Aberfan Former coal-mining village in Merthyr Tydfil unitary authority, Wales. Coal waste from a slag heap overwhelmed a school and houses 1966; of 144 dead, 116 were children.

Aberystwyth Resort and university town in Ceredigion, Wales, on Cardigan Bay; population (1991) 11,150. The Welsh Plant Breeding Station and National Library of Wales are here.

Abidjan Port and former capital (until 1983) of the Republic of Côte d'Ivoire, W Africa; population of metroplitan area (1990) 2,500,000. Products include coffee, palm oil, cocoa, and timber (mahogany). Yamoussoukro became the new capital 1983, but was not internationally recognized as such until 1992.

Abilene Town in Kansas, USA, on the Smoky Hill River; population (1990) 6,240. Industries include the manufacture of aircraft and missile components and oil-field equipment.

Abilene City in central Texas, USA, SW of Fort Worth; seat of Taylor County; population (1992) 108,100. It is a centre for oil-drilling equipment. Abilene was founded 1881 as the terminus for the Texas and Pacific Railroad.

Abingdon Town in Oxfordshire, England, on the Thames 10 km/6 mi S of Oxford; population (1991) 35,200. The abbey was founded 675 but was largely destroyed at the Dissolution; remains include Checker Hall, restored as an Elizabethan-type theatre, and the 15th century gateway.

Abkhazia Autonomous republic in Georgia, situated on the Black Sea
capital Sukhumi
area 8,600 sq km/3,320 sq mi
industries tin, fruit, tobacco, tea
population (1990) 537,500
history From 1989 the region was the scene of secessionist activity on the part of the minority Muslim Abkhazi community, culminating in the republic's declaration of independence 1992. Georgian troops invaded and took control Aug 1992, but secessionists subsequently gained control of the N half of the republic. In Oct 1993 they took the region's capital, Sukhumi, as well as much of the republic's remaining territory. A cease-fire was agreed 1994. Many ethnic Georgians fled Abkhazia during the four-year war, which claimed around 30,000 lives.

Åbo Swedish name for ◊Turku, a port in SW Finland.

Abomey Town in Benin, W Africa; population (1982) 54,500. It was once the capital of the kingdom of Dahomey, which flourished in the 17th–19th centuries, and had a mud-built defence wall 10 km/6 mi in circumference.

Abruzzi Mountainous region of S central Italy, comprising the provinces of L'Aquila, Chieti, Pescara, and Teramo; area 10,794 sq km/4,168 sq mi; population (1995) 1,267,700; capital L'Aquila. Gran Sasso d'Italia, 2,914 m/9,564 ft, is the highest point of the ◊Apennines.

Abu Dhabi Sheikdom in SW Asia, on the Persian Gulf, capital of the United Arab Emirates; area 67,350 sq km/ 26,000 sq mi; population (1985) 670,100. Formerly under British protection, it has been ruled since 1971 by Sheik Sultan Zayed bin al-Nahayan, who is also president of the Supreme Council of Rulers of the United Arab Emirates.

Abuja Capital of Nigeria (formally designated as such 1982, although not officially recognized until 1992); population of Federal Capital District (1991) 378,700; population of city alone (1992 est) 305,900. Shaped like a crescent, the city was designed by Japanese architect Kenzo Tange; it began construction 1976 as a replacement for Lagos.

Abu Musa Small island in the Persian Gulf. Formerly owned by the ruler of Sharjah, it was forcibly occupied by Iran 1971.

Abu Simbel or *Ibsambul* Site of two ancient temples cut into the rock on the banks of the Nile in S Egypt during the reign of Ramses II, commemorating him and his wife Nefertari. The temples were moved in sections 1966–67 and rebuilt 60 m/200 ft above their original location before the site was flooded by the waters of the Aswan High Dam.

Abydos Ancient city in Upper Egypt, cult centre of Osiris and burial place of the kings of the 1st and 2nd dynasties. There are remains from all periods. The well-preserved Great Temple of Seti I, dating from about 1300 BC, contains the 'Table of Abydos', a list of all the kings preceding Seti, which is of great historical importance.

Abyssinia Former name of Ethiopia.

Acadia (French *Acadie*) Name given to ◊Nova Scotia by French settlers 1604, from which the term Cajun derives.

Acapulco or *Acapulco de Juarez* Port and holiday resort in S Mexico; population (1990) 593,200. There is deep-sea fishing, and tropical products are exported. Acapulco was founded 1550 and was Mexico's major Pacific coast port until about 1815.

Accra Capital and port of Ghana; population (1988 est) 949,100. The port trades in cacao, gold, and timber. Industries include engineering, brewing, and food processing. Osu (Christiansborg) Castle is the presidential residence.

Accrington Industrial town (textiles, engineering, brick manufacturing) in Lancashire, England; population (1991) 36,500.

Achaea or *Achaia* In ancient Greece, an area of the N Peloponnese. The *Achaeans* were the predominant society during the Mycenaean period and are said by Homer to have taken part in the siege of Troy. The larger Roman province of Achaea was created after the defeat of the Achaean League 146 BC; it included all mainland Greece S of a line drawn from the Ambracian to the Maliac Gulf.

Achelous (Greek *Akheloos*) River in Greece, 219 km/136 mi long. It rises in the ◊Pindus Mountains and flows S into the Ionian Sea, cutting through deep gorges to a swampy delta near the Echinades Islands. The Kremasta hydroelectricity scheme on the Achelous started operation in 1965 and is now also the centre of an irrigation scheme supplying water to farms on the plain of Thessaly.

Achill Island or *Eagle Island* Largest of the Irish islands, off County Mayo; area 148 sq km/57 sq mi.

Aconcagua, Cerro Extinct volcano in the Argentine Andes; the highest peak in the Americas, 6,960 m/22,834 ft. It was first climbed by Edward Fitzgerald's expedition 1897.

Acre Former name of the Israeli seaport of ◊Akko.

ACT Abbreviation for ◊Australian Capital Territory.

Adana Capital of Adana (Seyhan) province, S Turkey; population (1990) 916,150. It is a major cotton-growing centre and Turkey's fourth-largest city.

Addis Ababa or *Addis Abeba* Capital of Ethiopia; population (1992) 2,213,000. It was founded 1887 by Menelik, chief of Shoa, who ascended the throne of Ethiopia 1889. His former residence, Menelik Palace, is now occupied by the government.

Adelaide Capital and industrial city of South Australia; population (1993) 1,071,100. Industries include oil refining, shipbuilding, and the manufacture of electrical goods and cars. Grain, wool, fruit, and wine are exported. Founded 1836, Adelaide was named after William IV's queen. It is a fine example of town planning, with residential districts separated from commercial areas by a 'green belt', one of the earliest examples of its kind, developed by William Light (1786–1839). The business district of the city is situated on the river Torrens, which is dammed to form Adelaide's water supply. Impressive streets include King William Street and North Terrace, and fine buildings include Parliament House, Government House, the Anglican cathedral of St Peter, and Roman Catholic cathedral, two universities, the state observatory, and the museum and art gallery.

Adélie Land (French *Terre Adélie*) Region of Antarctica between 136° and 142° E, which is about 140 km/87 mi long, mountainous, covered in snow and ice, and inhabited only by a research team. It covers an area of 432,000 sq km/166,800 sq mi. It was claimed for France 1840.

Adelsberg German name for Postojna, a town in Slovenia.

Aden (Arabic *'Adan*) Main port and commercial centre of Yemen, on a rocky peninsula at the SW corner of Arabia, commanding the entrance to the Red Sea; population (1995) 562,000. The city's economy is based on oil refining, fishing, and shipping. A British territory from 1839, Aden became part of independent South Yemen 1967; it was the capital of South Yemen until 1990.

Adige Second longest river (after the Po) in Italy, 410 km/255 mi in length. It crosses the Lombardy Plain and enters the Adriatic just N of the Po delta.

Adirondacks Mountainous area in NE New York State, USA, rising to 1,629 m/5,344 ft at Mount Marcy; the source of the Hudson and Ausable rivers. Adirondacks is named after a Native American people, and has beautiful scenery and good sports facilities.

Adjaria Autonomous republic in Georgia; area 3,000 sq km/ 1,160 sq mi; population (1990) 382,000; capital Batum. Products include tea, lemons, grapes, bamboo, and eucalyptus. The population is Sunni Muslim.

Admiralty Islands Group of small islands in the SW Pacific, part of Papua New Guinea; population (1980) 25,000. The main island is Manus. Exports are copra and pearls. The islands became a German protectorate 1884 and an Australian mandate 1920.

Adour River in SW France; length 335 km/208 mi. The Adour rises in the Hautes-Pyrénées and flows through the *départements* of Gers and Landes to the Bay of Biscay, near Bayonne.

Adowa Alternative form of ◊Ādwa, the former capital of Ethiopia.

Adriatic Sea Large arm of the Mediterranean Sea, lying NW to SE between the Italian and the Balkan peninsulas. The W shore is Italian; the E includes Croatia, Montenegro, and Albania, with a small strip of coastline owned by Slovenia. Bosnia has 20 km/12 mi of coastline, but no port. The sea is about 805 km/500 mi long, and its area is 135,250 sq km/52,220 sq mi.

Ādwa or *Adowa* or *Aduwa* Former capital of Ethiopia until 1889 when Addis Ababa became the new capital. It lies

about 180 km/110 mi SW of Massawa, Eritrea at an altitude of 1,910 m/6,270 ft; population (1984) 20,000.

Adygeya Autonomous republic of SW Russian Federation, in Krasnodar territory
area 7,600 sq km/2,934 sq mi
capital Maikop
physical extends from the Kuban River to the foothills of the Caucasus; mostly plain, with rich soil
industries timber, woodworking, food processing, engineering, cattle breeding, agriculture, flowers (especially Crimean roses and lavender)
population (1995) 451,000.

Aegean Islands Islands of the Aegean Sea, but more specifically a region of Greece comprising the Dodecanese islands, the Cyclades islands, Lesvos, Samos, and Chios; area 9,122 sq km/3,523 sq mi; population (1991) 460,800.

Aegean Sea Branch of the Mediterranean between Greece and Turkey; the Dardanelles connect it with the Sea of Marmara. The numerous islands in the Aegean Sea include Crete, the Cyclades, the Sporades, and the Dodecanese. There is political tension between Greece and Turkey over sea limits claimed by Greece around such islands as Lesvos, Chios, Samos, and Kos.

Aegina (Greek *Aíyna* or *Aíyina*) Greek island in the Gulf of Aegina about 32 km/20 mi SW of Piraeus; area 83 sq km/ 32 sq mi; population (1981) 11,100.

Aeolian Islands Another name for the ◊Lipari Islands.

Afars and the Issas, French Territory of the Former French territory that became the Republic of Djibouti 1977.

Africa Second largest of the five continents. Africa is connected with Asia by the isthmus of Suez, and separated from Europe by the Mediterranean Sea. The name Africa was first given by the Romans to their African provinces with the city of Carthage, and it has since been extended to the whole continent.
area 30,097,000 sq km/11,620,451 sq mi (three times the area of Europe)
largest cities (population over 1 million) Cairo, Algiers, Lagos, Kinshasa, Abidjan, Cape Town, Nairobi, Casablanca, El Gîza, Addis Ababa, Luanda, Dar es Salaam, Ibadan, Mogadishu, Maputo, Johannesburg, Harare, Alexandria, Antananarivo, Rabat, Dakar, Durban, East Rand, Pretoria, Tunis, Kinshasa
features Great Rift Valley, containing most of the great lakes of E Africa (except Lake Victoria); Atlas Mountains in the NW; Drakensberg mountain range in the SE; Sahara Desert (world's largest desert) in the N; Namib, Kalahari, and Great Karoo deserts in the S; Nile, Congo/Zaïre, Niger, Zambezi, Limpopo, Volta, and Orange rivers
physical dominated by a uniform central plateau comprising a S tableland with a mean altitude of 1,070 m/ 3,000 ft that falls northwards to a lower elevated plain with a mean altitude of 400 m/1,300 ft. Although there are no great alpine regions or extensive coastal plains, Africa has a mean altitude of 610 m/2,000 ft, two times greater than Europe. The highest points are Mount Kilimanjaro 5,895 m/ 19,340 ft, and Mount

Kenya 5,200 m/17,058 ft; the lowest point is Lake Assal in Djibouti −153 m/−502 ft. Compared with other continents, Africa has few broad estuaries or inlets and therefore has proportionately the shortest coastline (24,000 km/15,000 mi). The geographical extremities of the continental mainland are Cape Hafun in the E, Cape Almadies in the W, Ras Ben Sekka in the N, and Cape Agulhas in the S. The Sahel is a narrow belt of savanna and scrub forest which covers 700 million hectares/1.7 billion acres of W and central Africa; 75% of the continent lies within the tropics.

Africa, Horn of Projection constituted by Somalia and adjacent territories.

Afsluitdijk Dyke in the Netherlands, separating the North Sea from the ◊IJsselmeer. The dyke is 30 km/19 mi long and extends from Den Oever in the province of North Holland to Friesland. Construction of the dyke was completed in 1932.

Agadir Resort and seaport in S Morocco, near the mouth of the river Sus; population (1990, urban area) 439,000. It was rebuilt after being destroyed by an earthquake 1960.

Agaña Capital of Guam, in the W Pacific; population (1990) 1,139. It is a US naval base and administrative centre of the island, bordered by residential Agana Heights and Apra Harbor.

Agen French town, capital of the *département* of Lot-et-Garonne, 120 km/75 mi SE of Bordeaux, on the river Garonne; population (1990) 32,200. It has chemical industries, and a long tradition of making preserved fruit, especially prunes.

Agra City of Uttar Pradesh, India, on the river Yamuna, 160 km/100 mi SE of Delhi; population (1991) 892,000. A commercial and university centre, it was the capital of the Mogul empire 1566–69 and 1601–58, from which period the Taj Mahal dates.

Agrigento Town in Sicily, known for Greek temples; population (1990) 56,660.

Agrigento Province of Italy, in SW ◊Sicily; capital Agrigento; area 3,041 sq km/1,174 sq mi; population (1992) 177,200. The ancient Greeks called it Akrangas, the Romans Agrigentum, and its name until 1927 was Girgenti.

Agrinion Town in Greece in the department of Aetolia and Acarnania, Central Greece and Euboea region, 29 km/18 mi N of Missolonghi; population (1993) 40,000. It is at the centre of a tobacco- and currant-producing region.

Aguascalientes City in central Mexico, and capital of a state of the same name; population (1990) 479,700. It has hot mineral springs.

Aguascalientes State of central Mexico; area 5,589 sq km/2,157 sq mi; population (1995 est) 862,300. Its capital is Aguascalientes. The main occupations are cereal production and cattle-raising.

Agulhas, Cape Southernmost cape in Africa. In 1852 the British troopship *Birkenhead* sank off the cape with the loss of over 400 lives.

Ahaggar or *Hoggar* Mountainous plateau of the central Sahara, Algeria, whose highest point, Tahat, at 2,918 m/9,576 ft, lies between Algiers and the mouth of the Niger. It is the home of the formerly nomadic Tuareg.

Ahlen City in the *Land* of North Rhine–Westphalia, Germany, 96 km/60 mi NE of Düsseldorf; population (1994) 55,600. The principal industries are textiles, coal mining, and metalworking.

Ahmadabad or *Ahmedabad* City in India; population (1991) 3,298,000. It is a cotton-manufacturing centre, and has many sacred buildings of the Hindu, Muslim, and Jain faiths.

Ahmadnagar City in Maharashtra, India, 195 km/120 mi E of Bombay, on the left bank of the river Sina; population (1991) 222,000. It is a centre of cotton trade and manufacture.

Ahváz Industrial capital of the province of Khuzestan, on the river Karun, W Iran; population (1991) 725,000. The ancient city was rebuilt in the 3rd century AD; it became a prosperous city in the 20th century after the discovery of oil.

Ahvenanmaa Finnish name of ◊Åland Islands.

Aigues-Mortes Town in the *département* of Gard, S France; population (1990) 5,200. In the Middle Ages it was an important port, from which its founder, Louis IX, twice sailed for the Crusades. Its ancient walls remain, and tourism is the mainstay of the economy. The town is now 5 km/3 mi from the Mediterranean coast.

Ailsa Craig Rocky islet in the Firth of Clyde, Scotland, about 16 km/10 mi off the coast of South Ayrshire, opposite Girvan. Ailsa Craig rock is used in the manufacture of curling stones. It is a breeding ground for birds and home to around 250,000 puffins.

Ain River of E central France, giving its name to a *département*; length 190 km/118 mi. Rising in the Jura Mountains, it flows S into the Rhône.

Ain *Département* in the ◊Rhône-Alpes region of France; area 5,756 sq km/2,222 sq mi; population (1990) 235,200. It is bounded in the W by the river Saône and in the S by the river Rhône. It takes its name from the river Ain, which rises in the *département* in the Jura Mountains and flows S through steep gorges into the Rhône. On the N and W plains cereals, fruit, and vegetables are grown. Livestock is bred, including poultry. The S region is swampy. There are vineyards in the valleys of the Jura Mountains in the E. The region has hydroelectric schemes and a plastics industry. Principal towns include Bourg-en-Bresse (the capital), Belley, Gex, and Nantua.

Aintab Syrian name (until 1922) of ◊Gaziantep, a city in Turkey.

Aisne River of N France, giving its name to a *département*; length 282 km/175 mi.

Aisne *Département* in the ◊Picardy region of France; area 7,378 sq km/2,849 sq mi; population (1990) 264,300. It is generally flat, wooded in the N and undulating in the S. Aisne is an agricultural *département*, producing cereals, potatoes, sugar beet, vines, and livestock. About half the workforce (1997) are employed in the service sector and 35% in manufacturing industries, producing precision tools and electrical appliances. Three rivers flow through the region: the Marne, Oise, and Aisne. The principal towns are Laon (the capital), St-Quentin, and Soissons.

Aix-en-Provence   City in the *département* of Bouches-du-Rhône, France, 29 km/18 mi N of Marseille; population (1990) 126,800. It is the capital of Provence and dates from Roman times.

Aix-la-Chapelle   French name of ◊Aachen, an ancient city in Germany.

Aix-les-Bains   Spa with hot springs in the *département* of Savoie, France, near Lake Bourget, 13 km/8 mi N of Chambéry; population (1990) 24,800.

Ajaccio   Capital and second largest port of Corsica; population (1990) 59,300. Founded by the Genoese 1492, it was the birthplace of Napoleon; it has been French since 1768.

Ajman   Smallest of the seven states that make up the United Arab Emirates; area 250 sq km/96 sq mi; population (1985) 64,318.

Ajmer   City in Rajasthan, India; population (1991) 402,000. Situated in a deep valley in the Aravalli Mountains, it is a commercial and industrial centre, notably of cotton manufacture. It has many ancient remains, including a Jain temple.

AK   Abbreviation for the state of ◊Alaska, USA.

Akaba   Alternative transliteration of ◊Aqaba, a gulf of the Red Sea.

Akheloos   Greek name for the ◊Achelous, a river in Greece.

Akko   formerly *Acre* Seaport in NW Israel, situated on the Mediterranean Sea; population (1994) 45,300. Taken by the Crusaders 1104, it was captured by Saladin 1187 and retaken by Richard the Lionheart 1191. Napoleon failed in a siege 1799. British field marshal Allenby captured the port 1918. From being part of British mandated Palestine, it became part of Israel 1948.

Akmola   formerly *Tselinograd* Commercial and industrial city in N Kazakhstan, on the river Ishim, situated at a railway junction; population (1990) 281,000. It produces agricultural machinery, textiles, and chemicals. It has been the capital of Kazakhstan since 1995, replacing ◊Almaty.

Akola   City in Maharashtra, India, near the Purnar; population (1991) 328,000. It is a major cotton and grain centre.

Akranes   Town on Faxa Bay, Iceland, in the county of Vesturland, N of Reykjavik. It is a trading and fishing centre with a cement factory using offshore shell deposits for lime.

Akron   (Greek 'summit') City in Ohio, USA, on the Cuyahoga River, 56 km/35 mi SE of Cleveland; population (1992) 223,600. Known as the 'Rubber Capital of the World', it is home to the headquarters of several tyre and rubber companies, although production there had ended by 1982. Akron was first settled 1807.

Akrotiri   Peninsula on the S coast of Cyprus; it has a British military base.

Aksai Chin   Part of Himalayan Kashmir lying to the E of the Karakoram range. It is occupied by China but claimed by India.

Aktyubinsk   Industrial city (chemicals, metals, electrical equipment) in Kazakhstan; population (1990) 267,000. Established 1869, it expanded after the opening of the Trans-Caspian railway 1905. It is the capital of Aktyubinsk Oblast.

AL   Abbreviation for the state of ◊Alabama, USA.

Alabama   State in S USA; nicknamed Heart of Dixie/Camellia State
area   134,700 sq km/51,994 sq mi
capital   Montgomery
towns and cities   Birmingham, Mobile, Huntsville, Tuscaloosa
physical   the state comprises the Cumberland Plateau in the N with the Appalachian Mountains; the Black Belt, or Canebrake, cotton-growing country in the centre; and S of this, the coastal plain of Piny Woods. The Alabama River (the largest in the state) and the Tennessee River flow through the state
features   Fort Morgan (dating from the early 1800s) on Pleasure Island in the Gulf of Mexico; De Soto Caverns, onyx caves used as a Native American burial ground 2,000 years ago; Mobile, with Fort Conde (a restored 1711 fort), pre-Civil War mansions, and Mardi Gras celebrations (the first Mardi Gras in the USA took place here); Birmingham, with the Birmingham Civil Rights Institute (1992) and the Jazz Hall of Fame; Montgomery, with pre-Civil War houses, the White House of the Confederacy (1835), and the Alabama Shakespeare Festival; Battleship Park, with USS *Alabama* and the submarine USS *Drum* from World War II; Tuskegee University, a centre for the study of black history; US Space Camp, with NASA laboratories and shuttle test sites, at Huntsville
industries   cotton (still important though no longer prime crop); soya beans, peanuts, wood products, coal, livestock, poultry, iron, chemicals, textiles, paper
population   (1995) 4,253,000
famous people   Hank Aaron, Tallulah Bankhead, Nat King Cole, W C Handy, Helen Keller, Joe Louis, Willie Mays, Jesse Owens, Leroy 'Satchel' Paige, George C Wallace, Booker T Washington, Hank Williams
history   first settled by the French in the early 18th century, it was ceded to Britain 1763, passed to the USA 1783, and became a state 1819. It was one of the Confederate States in the American Civil War, and Montgomery was the first capital of the Confederacy. Birmingham became the South's leading industrial centre in the late 19th century. Alabama was in the forefront of the civil-rights movement in the 1950s and 1960s: Martin Luther King led a successful boycott of segregated Montgomery buses 1955; school integration began in the early 1960s despite the opposition of Governor George C Wallace; the 1965 Selma march resulted in federal voting-rights legislation.

Åland Islands   (Finnish *Ahvenanmaa* 'land of waters') Group of some 6,000 islands in the Baltic Sea, at the S extremity of the Gulf of Bothnia; area 1,481 sq km/572 sq mi; population (1992) 25,000. Only 80 are inhabited; the largest island, Åland, has a small town, Mariehamn. The main sectors of the island economy are tourism, agriculture, and shipping.

Alania (formerly *North Ossetia*) autonomous republic of SW Russian Federation. A new constitution was adopted 1994 and the republic took its former name of Alania
area 8,000 sq km/3,088 sq mi
capital Vladikavkaz (formerly Ordzhonikidze)
physical in the Caucasus, between the Russian Federation and Georgia
industries mining and metallurgy, maize processing, timber and woodworking, textiles, building materials, distilleries, food processing
population (1995) 659,000.

Alaska Largest state of the USA, on the NW extremity of North America, separated from the lower 48 states by British Columbia; nicknamed Mainland State Last Frontier; territories include ◊Aleutian Islands
total area 1,531,100 sq km/591,005 sq mi
land area 1,478,457 sq km/570,833 sq mi
capital Juneau
towns and cities Anchorage, Fairbanks, Fort Yukon, Holy Cross, Nome
physical much of Alaska is mountainous and includes Mount McKinley (Denali), 6,194 m/20,322 ft, the highest peak in North America, surrounded by Denali national park. Caribou (descended from 2,000 reindeer imported from Siberia in early 1900s) thrive in the Arctic tundra, and elsewhere there are extensive forests
features Denali national park (2.4 million ha/6 million acres) with Mount McKinley and Wonder Lake; Glacier Bay national park, a marine reserve; Katmai national park, a volcanic area, including Mount Katmai, which erupted 1912 and formed the Valley of Ten Thousand Smokes; the Arctic Wildlife Range; Tongass national forest; Wrangell-St Alias national park, the largest in the USA; Kenai Fjords national park; Little Diomede Island, only 4 km/2.5 mi from the Russian Big Diomede; hot springs N of Fairbanks; Aleutian Islands; Yukon River; remains of Russian settlements, including the Russian Bishop's House in Sitka, capital of Russian America until the sale of Alaska in 1867; Ketchikan, with collections of totem poles at Totem Bight state historical park and Totem Heritage Center; gold rush town of Nome; Skagway historic district; St Nicholas Russian Orthodox Church (1894), Juneau; Alaska State Museum, Juneau; Anchorage Museum of History and Art; Living Museum of the Arctic, Kotzebue; University of Alaska near Fairbanks
products oil, natural gas, coal, copper, iron, gold, tin, fur, salmon fisheries and canneries, lumber
population (1995) 603,600; including Native Americans, Aleuts, and Inuits
history various groups of Indians crossed the Bering land bridge about 15,000 years ago; the Inuit began to settle the Arctic coast from Siberia about 2000 BC; the Aleuts settled the Aleutian archipelago about 1000 BC. The first European to visit Alaska was Vitus Bering in 1741. Alaska was a Russian colony from 1744 until purchased by the USA in 1867 for $7,200,000; gold was discovered five years later. It became a state in 1959. A Congressional act of 1980 gave environmental protection to 42 million ha/104 million acres. Valuable mineral resources have been exploited from 1968, especially in the Prudhoe Bay area to the SE of Point Barrow. An oil pipeline (1977) runs from Prudhoe Bay to the port of Valdez. Oilspill from a tanker in Prince William Sound caused great environmental damage in 1989. Under construction is an underground natural-gas pipeline to Chicago and San Francisco.

Alaska Highway Road that runs from Dawson Creek, British Columbia, to Fairbanks, Alaska (2,450 km/1,522 mi). It was built 1942 as a supply route for US military forces in Alaska. The highway, which runs along the E edge of the Rocky Mountains, is paved in Alaska but mostly gravel-surfaced in Canada.

Álava Province of N Spain in the ◊Basque Country autonomous community; capital ◊Vitoria; area 3,046 sq km/1,176 sq mi; population (1995) 282,900. Largest and most southerly of the Basque provinces, it includes part of the Cantabrian Mountains, and tributaries of the river Ebro, including the Zadora. The mountains are wooded and rich in minerals. Products include cereals, flax, hemp, fruit, oil, and wine.

Alba Gaelic name for Scotland.

Albacete Market town in the province of the same name, SE Spain; population (1994) 141,000. Once famous for cutlery, it now produces clothes and footwear.

Albacete Province of SE Spain in S ◊Castilla–La Mancha autonomous community; capital Albacete; area 14,864 sq km/5,739 sq mi; population (1995) 361,300. It is a tableland, hilly in places with fertile valleys and plains. The main industries are stock-raising and agriculture.

Alba Iulia (German *Karlsburg*) City on the river Mures, W central Romania; population (1992) 71,300. It was founded by the Romans in the 2nd century AD. The Romanian kings were crowned here, Michael the Brave (1601), and the kings of modern Romania until World War II.

Albany Port in Western Australia, population (1991) 11,200. It suffered from the initial development of ◊Fremantle, but has grown with the greater exploitation of the surrounding area. The *Albany Doctor* is a cooling breeze from the sea, rising in the afternoon.

Albany City on the Flint River, Georgia, USA, SE of Columbus; seat of Dougherty County; population (1992) 79,600. It is a commercial centre for the production of pecans and peanuts, chemicals, lumber, and other industrial products. Albany was founded 1836 and was an important cotton market in the 19th century.

Albany Capital of New York State, USA, situated on the W bank of the Hudson River, about 225 km/140 mi N of New York City; population (1992) 99,700. Albany, a deepwater port, began as the Dutch trading post Fort Nassau 1614. It was renamed Albany 1664 when the English took control. The completion of the Erie Canal 1825 fostered its economic development.

al-Basrah Arabic name for the Iranian port of ◊Basra.

Albemarle Sound Large inlet of the Atlantic Ocean on the coast of North Carolina, E USA. It is crossed by the Intracoastal Waterway and is 88 km/55 mi long and 8–24 km/5–15 mi wide.

Alberta Province of W Canada

area 661,190 sq km/255,285 sq mi

capital Edmonton

towns and cities Calgary, Lethbridge, Medicine Hat, Red Deer

physical Rocky Mountains; dry, treeless prairie in the centre and S; towards the N this merges into a zone of poplar, then mixed forest. The valley of the Peace River is the most northerly farming land in Canada (except for Inuit pastures), and there are good grazing lands in the foothills of the Rockies. National parks are Banff, Elk Island, Jasper, Waterton Lake, and Wood Buffalo; Waterton Glacier International Peace Park (partly in Montana) is a World Heritage Site

features annual Calgary stampede; extensive dinosaur finds near Drumheller

industries coal; wheat, barley, oats, sugar beet in the S; more than a million head of cattle; oil and natural gas; an oil pipeline extends from Edmonton to Lake Superior; the McMurray district has deposits of bituminous sands to the SW of Lake Athabasca, which become economic to work at times of high world fuel prices; lumbering is important; Alberta has the largest coal resources in Canada, the principal mines being near Edmonton and at Anthracite, Mountain Park, Lethbridge, and Canmore

population (1995 est) 2,656,000

history in the 17th century much of its area was part of a grant to the Hudson's Bay Company for the fur trade, and the first trading posts were established in the late 18th century. The grant was bought by Canada 1869, and Alberta became a province 1905. After an oil strike in 1947, Alberta became a major oil and gas producer.

Albert Canal Canal, 128 km/80 mi long, designed as part of Belgium's frontier defences; it also links the industrial basin of Liège with the port of Antwerp. It was built 1930–39 and named after Albert I, King of Belgium 1909–34.

Albert, Lake Lake on the border of Uganda and the Democratic Republic of Congo (formerly Zaire) in the Great ◊Rift Valley; area 4,275 sq km/ 1,650 sq mi. The first European to see it was the British explorer Samuel Baker, who named it Lake Albert after the Prince Consort. It was renamed 1973 by the former Zaire's President Mobutu after himself.

Albertville Resort town at the entrance to the Val d'Arly in the *département* of Savoie, SE France; population (1981) 17,500. It was the scene of the 1992 Winter Olympics.

Albi Chief town in Tarn *département*, Midi-Pyrénées, SW France, on the river Tarn, 72 km/45 mi NE of Toulouse; population (1990) 48,700. It was the centre of the Albigensian heresy and the birthplace of the artist H R Toulouse-Lautrec. It has a 13th-century cathedral.

Ålborg Port in Denmark 32 km/20 mi inland from the Kattegat, on the S shore of the Limfjord; population (1995) 159,000. One of Denmark's oldest cities, it has a castle and the Budolfi cathedral (named after the English St Botolph), dating mainly from about 1400. It is the capital of Nordjylland county in Jylland (Jutland); the port is linked to Nørresundby on the N side of the fjord by a tunnel built 1969.

Albufeira Fishing village and resort on the Algarve coast of S Portugal, 43 km/27 mi W of Faro; it is known as the St Tropez of the Algarve. There are Moorish remains.

Albuquerque Largest city of New Mexico, USA, situated E of the Rio Grande, in the Pueblo district; population (1992) 398,500. It is a resort and industrial centre, specializing in electronic products and aerospace equipment. Founded 1706, it was named after Afonso de Albuquerque.

Albury-Wodonga Twin town on the New South Wales–Victoria border, Australia; population (1991) 23,600. It was planned to relieve overspill from Melbourne and Sydney, and produces car components.

Alcalá de Henares Town in the autonomous community of Madrid, Spain, on the river Henares; population (1995) 166,900. Its university, founded in 1510, was moved to Madrid in 1836. It is a centre for research and development. Miguel de Cervantes, author of *Don Quixote de la Mancha*, was born here.

Alcántara (Arabic 'the bridge') Town in the province of Cáceres, W Spain, situated on a rocky height above the river Tagus; population (1995) 2,000. The town is named after its six-arched Roman bridge, built in AD 105, which is 204 m/669 ft long and 40 m/131 ft high.

Alcatraz Small island in San Francisco Bay, California, USA. Its fortress was a military prison 1886–1934 and then a federal penitentiary until closed 1963. The dangerous tides allowed few successful escapes.

Alcázar de San Juan Town in the province of Ciudad Real, central Spain, on the plain of La Mancha; population (1995) 26,700. It is an important rail junction and has a large wine trade.

Alcoy Town in the province of Alicante, E Spain, on the river Serpis; population (1995) 64,000. Products include textiles, paper, and machinery. During an annual festival here, a mock battle is staged between Moors and Christians.

Aldabra Islands High limestone island group in the Seychelles, some 420 km/260 mi NW of Madagascar; area 154 sq km/59 sq mi. A nature reserve since 1976, it has rare plants and animals, including the giant tortoise.

Aldeburgh Small town and coastal resort in Suffolk, England; population (1991) 2,700. It is the site of the Aldeburgh Festival, annual music festival founded by the English composer Benjamin Britten, and is also the home of the Britten–Pears School for Advanced Musical Studies.

Alderney Third largest of the ◊Channel Islands, with its capital at St Anne's; area 8 sq km/3 sq mi; population (1991) 2,300. It gives its name to a breed of cattle, better known as the Guernsey. It exports early potatoes.

Aldershot Town in Hampshire, England, SW of London; population (1991) 51,400. It has a military camp and barracks dating from 1854.

Aleksandrovsk Former name (to 1921) of ◊Zaporozhye, a city in Ukraine.

Alençon Capital of the Orne *département* of France, situated in a rich agricultural plain to the SE of Caen; population (1990) 31,100. Lace, now a declining industry, was once a major product.

Alentejo Region of E central Portugal divided into the districts of Alto Alentejo and Baixo Alentejo. The chief towns are Evora, Neja, and Portalegre.

Aleppo (Syrian *Halab*) Ancient city in NW Syria; population (1993) 1,494,000. There has been a settlement on the site for at least 4,000 years.

Alès French town in the *département* of Gard, 45 km/ 28 mi SW of Nîmes, on the river Gardon in the foothills of the Cévennes; population (1990) 42,300. Its high-technology industries make it an important industrial centre; silk, glass, and metal goods are also manufactured.

Alessandria Town in N Italy on the river Tanaro. It was founded 1168 by Pope Alexander III as a defence against Frederick I Barbarossa.

Alessandria Province of N Italy in SE ◊Piedmont region; capital Alessandria; area 3,565 sq km/1,377 sq mi.

Ålesund or *Aalesund* Coastal town in Møre og Romsdal county, W Norway; population (1995) 37,100. It is the main centre of the Norwegian herring-fishing industry. The town is built on five islands, linked by bridges.

Aletsch Most extensive glacier in Europe, 23.6 km/14.7 mi long, beginning on the S slopes of the Jungfrau in the Bernese Alps, Switzerland.

Aleutian Islands Volcanic island chain in the N Pacific, stretching 1,200 mi/1,900 km SW of Alaska, of which it forms part; population 6,000 Aleuts (most of whom belong to the Orthodox Church), plus a large US military establishment. There are 14 large and more than 100 small islands running along the Aleutian Trench. The islands are mountainous, barren, and treeless; they are ice-free all year but are often foggy, with only about 25 days of sunshine recorded annually.

Alexander Archipelago Group of over a thousand islands in the Gulf of Alaska, off the coast S of Juneau in SE Alaska, USA. The chief products are timber, fish, and fur. The largest islands in the group are Baranof Island, Prince of Wales, Chichagof, Admiralty, Kuin, Kupreanof, and Revillagigedo, which are densely forested. The principal towns are Ketchikan (on Revillagigedo Island) and Sitka (on Baranof Island).

Alexandretta Former name (to 1939) of ◊Iskenderun, a port in S Turkey.

Alexandria or *El Iskandariya* City, chief port, and second-largest city of Egypt, situated between the Mediterranean and Lake Maryut; population (1994 est) 3,419,000. It is linked by canal with the Nile and is an industrial city (oil refining, gas processing, and cotton and grain trading). Founded 331 BC by Alexander the Great, Alexandria was the capital of Egypt for over 1,000 years.

Alexandria City in central Louisiana, USA, on the Red River, NW of Baton Rouge; seat of Rapides parish; population (1990) 49,200. It is a centre for livestock, meatpacking, and timber. Founded in 1810, Alexandria was an important river port until the Civil War.

Alföld (Great Plain of Hungary) Large area of flat open land in Hungary, between the river Danube and the Carpathian Mountains. Cereals, vines, tobacco, hemp, and flax are produced, and livestock is reared. The plain occupies about half the area of Hungary, with small areas in Romania, Croatia, and Yugoslavia. The Great Alföld (Hungarian *Nagyalföld*) is the central plain; the Little Alföld (Hungarian *Kisalföld*) is in NW Hungary, NW of the Transcaucasian highlands.

Algarve (Arabic *al-gharb* 'the west') Ancient kingdom in S Portugal, the modern district of Faro, a popular holiday resort; population (1991) 341,400. Industries include agriculture, fishing, wine, mining, and tourism. The Algarve began to be wrested from the Moors in the 12th century and was united with Portugal as a kingdom 1253.

Algeciras Port in S Spain, to the W of Gibraltar across the Bay of Algeciras; population (1994) 104,000. Founded by the Moors 713, it was taken from them by Alfonso XI of Castile 1344.

Algiers (Arabic *al-Jazair*; French *Alger*) Capital of Algeria, situated on the narrow coastal plain between the Atlas Mountains and the Mediterranean; population (1995) 2,168,000.

Algoa Bay Broad and shallow inlet in Eastern Cape Province, South Africa, where the Portuguese explorer Bartolomeu Diaz landed after rounding the Cape 1488.

Alicante City and seaport in E Spain on the Mediterranean Sea, 123 km/77 mi S of Valencia; population (1994) 275,000. It is the commercial port for Madrid, exporting wine, olive oil, and fruit; there are manufacturing industries.

Alicante Province of SE Spain in S Valencia autonomous community; capital Alicante; area 5,864 sq km/2,264 sq mi; population (1995) 1,363,800. Its W coastline is on the Mediterranean Sea. Products include cereals, olives, fruit, and vines; silkworms are reared.

Aligarh City in Uttar Pradesh, N central India; population (1991) 480,000. Industries include agricultural manufacturing and processing, engineering, and textiles. The city is also named *Koil*; Aligarh is the name of a nearby fort.

Al Khalil Arabic name for ◊Hebron in the Israeli-occupied West Bank.

Alkmaar Town in the province of North Holland, Netherlands, 32 km/20 mi NW of Amsterdam; population (1996) 93,100. Alkmaar is situated on the North Holland Canal and is intersected by a network of canals. The town has a Gothic church, built 1470–1512, and a Gothic town hall, and holds a large weekly cheese market.

al Kūt (or *Kūt-al-Imāra*) City in Iraq, on the river Tigris; population (1987) 183,000. It is a grain market and carpet-manufacturing centre. In World War I it was under siege by Turkish forces from Dec 1915 to April 1916, when the joint British and Indian garrison surrendered.

Allahabad ('city of god') Historic city in Uttar Pradesh state, NE India, 580 km/360 mi SE of Delhi, on the Yamuna River where it meets the Ganges and the mythical Seraswati River; population (1991) 806,000. A Hindu religious event, the festival of the jar of nectar of immortality (Khumbh Mela), is held here every 12 years with the participants washing away sin and sickness by bathing in the rivers.

Allegheny Mountains Range over 800 km/500 mi long extending from Pennsylvania to Virginia, USA, rising to more than 1,500 m/4,900 ft and averaging 750 m/2,500 ft. The mountains are a source of timber, coal, iron, and limestone. They initially hindered W migration, the first settlement to the W being Marietta 1788.

Allen, Bog of Wetland E of the river Shannon in the Republic of Ireland, comprising some 958 sq km/370 sq mi of the counties of Offaly, Leix, and Kildare; the country's main source of peat fuel.

Allen, Lough Lake in County Leitrim, Republic of Ireland, on the upper course of the river Shannon. It is 11 km/7 mi long and 5 km/3 mi broad.

Allentown City in E Pennsylvania, USA, on the Lehigh River, just NW of Philadelphia; population (1992) 106,400. It is an industrial centre for textiles, machinery, and electronic equipment. It was founded 1762 as Northampton, and renamed Allentown 1838. During the American Revolution it was a centre for munitions production.

Allier River in central France, a tributary of the Loire; it is 565 km/350 mi long and gives its name to a *département*. Vichy is the chief town on the Allier.

Allier *Département* in the ◊Auvergne region of central France; area 7,340 sq km/2,835 sq mi; population (1990) 358,326. The principal rivers are the ◊Allier, the Cher, and the Loire (which forms the E boundary of the *département*). Allier is primarily agricultural, though manufactured goods produced here include cutlery, glass, and textiles. The departmental capital is ◊Moulins; other important urban centres are the spa town of Vichy, Montluçon, and Lapalisse.

Almaden Mining town in Ciudad Real province, Castilla-La Mancha, central Spain; population (1981) 9,700. It has the world's largest supply of mercury, worked since the 4th century BC.

Al Manamah Capital and free trade port of Bahrain, on Bahrain Island; population (1991) 137,000. It handles oil and entrepôt trade.

Almaty *Vernyi* (to 1921); *Alma-Ata* (to 1994) Former capital of Kazakhstan; population (1991) 1,151,300. Industries include engineering, printing, tobacco processing, textile manufacturing, and leather products. Established 1854 as a military fortress and trading centre, the town was destroyed by an earthquake 1887.

Almelo Town in the province of Overijssel, Netherlands, 45 km/28 mi SE of Zwolle; population (1996) 65,300. Almelo is situated on the Overijssel Canal, and has textile mills.

Almere New town in the polder of S Flevoland, Netherlands, which started receiving its first inhabitants in 1976; population (1996) 112,900. Together with Lelystad, Almere acts an overspill commuter suburb for the N Randstad, particularly Amsterdam.

Almería Spanish city, chief town of a province of the same name on the Mediterranean; population (1994) 167,000. The province is famous for its white grapes, and in the Sierra Nevada are rich mineral deposits.

Almería Province of S Spain in E ◊Andalusia autonomous community; capital Almería; area 8,777 sq km/3,388 sq mi; population (1995) 493,100. Products include cereals, fruit, and wine. The province has rich deposits of copper, iron, silver, lead, and mercury. It was formerly part of the kingdom of Granada.

Al Mukalla Seaport capital of the Hadhramaut coastal region of S Yemen; on the Gulf of Aden 480 km/300 mi E of Aden; population (1995 est) 154,400.

Al Mukha or *Mocha* Seaport of N Yemen near the mouth of the Red Sea, once famed for its coffee exports; population about 8,000.

Alost French name for the Belgian town of ◊Aalst.

Alpes-de-Haute-Provence *Département* in the ◊Provence-Alpes-Côte d'Azur region of France; area 6,944 sq km/2,681 sq mi; population (1990) 64,300. It is situated in the Alps, and winter sports are important to the economy. The main rivers are the Durance and the Verdon. Forestry and livestock farming are the main occupations in the uplands, and the growing of vines, fruit, potatoes, and olives in the valleys. The principal towns are Digne (the capital), Barcelonnette, and Castellane.

Alpes-Maritimes *Département* in the ◊Provence-Alpes-Côte d'Azur region of France; area 4,292 sq km/1,657 sq mi; population (1990) 457,000. Bordered on the E and NE by Italy, it has a coastline on the Ligurian Sea in the S and surrounds the principality of Monaco. The N boundary is formed by the Maritime Alps, from which several mountain spurs run S. The main river is the Var. There are many mineral springs in the region. Tourism is the main industry, with resorts on the coast, the Côte d'Azur, including ◊Nice (the capital), Antibes, Menton, and Cannes. Flowers, fruit, and early vegetables are grown and there are olive-oil, perfume, and metal industries. On the coast there is fishing for tuna and sardines. The main towns are Nice and ◊Grasse.

Alps Mountain chain, the barrier between N Italy and France, Germany and Austria. Skiing and summer tourism is important. Skiing is damaging the Alpine environment; high forest is cut down to create pistes, increasing the risk of avalanches. Acid rain is destroying trees.

Peaks include Mont Blanc, the highest at 4,809 m/15,777 ft, first climbed by Jacques Balmat and Michel Paccard 1786; Matterhorn in the Pennine Alps, 4,479 m/14,694 ft, first climbed by Edward Whymper 1865 (four of the party of seven were killed when a rope broke during their descent); Eiger in the Bernese Alps/Oberland, 3,970 m/13,030 ft, with a near-vertical rock wall on the N face, first climbed 1858; Jungfrau, 4,166 m/13,673 ft; and Finsteraarhorn 4,275 m/14,027 ft.

Passes include Brenner, the lowest, Austria/Italy; Great St Bernard, one of the highest, 2,472 m/8,113 ft, Italy/Switzerland (by which Napoleon marched into Italy 1800); Little St Bernard, Italy/France (which Hannibal is thought to have used); and St Gotthard, S Switzerland, which field marshal A V Suvorov used when ordered by the tsar to withdraw his troops from Italy. All have been superseded by all-weather road/rail tunnels. The Alps extend down the Adriatic coast into Slovenia with the Julian and Dinaric Alps.

Alps, Australian Highest area of the E Highlands in Victoria/New South Wales, Australia, noted for winter sports. They include the Snowy Mountains and Mount Kosciusko, Australia's highest mountain, 2,229 m/7,316 ft, first noted by Polish-born Paul Strzelecki 1829 and named after a Polish hero Tadeusz Kościuszho.

Alps, Southern Range of mountains running the entire length of South Island, New Zealand. They are forested to the W, with scanty scrub to the E. The highest point is Mount Cook, 3,764 m/12,349 ft. Scenic features include gorges, glaciers, lakes, and waterfalls. Among its lakes are those at the S end of the range: Manapouri, Te Anau, and the largest, Wakatipu, 83 km/52 mi long, which lies about 300 m/1,000 ft above sea level and has a depth of 378 m/1,242 ft.

Als (German *Alsen*) Danish island in Little Belt, Baltic Sea, off the coast of Slesvig; area 310 km sq/120 sq mi. The island, about 30 km/19 mi long and 5–20 km/3–12 mi wide, is part of the county of Sønderborg. Since 1930 it has been connected with mainland Denmark by a bridge across Als Sound. A number of engineering and systems-engineering companies are located here. Sønderborg is the principal town.

Alsace Region of France; area 8,280 sq km/3,197 sq mi; population (1990) 1,624,400. It consists of the *départements* of Bas-Rhin and Haut-Rhin, and its capital is Strasbourg.

Alsace-Lorraine Area of NE France, lying W of the river Rhine. It forms the French regions of ♭Alsace and ♭Lorraine. The former iron and steel industries are being replaced by electronics, chemicals, and precision engineering. The German dialect spoken does not have equal rights with French, and there is autonomist sentiment.

Alsen German name for the Danish Island of ♭Als.

Altai Autonomous republic of S Russian Federation, in Altai territory
area 92,600 sq km/35,740 sq mi
capital Gorno-Altaisk
physical in the foothills of the Altai Mountains, bordered in the S by Mongolia and China; forested mountains and high plateaux
industries gold, mercury, and coal mining, timber, chemicals, dairying, cattle breeding
population (1992) 198,000.

Altai Territory of the Russian Federation, in SW Siberia; area 261,700 sq km/101,043 sq mi; capital Barnaul; population (1991 est) 2,851,000. Industries include mining, light engineering, chemicals, and timber. Altai was colonized by the Russians from the 18th century.

Altai Mountains Mountain system of Kazakhstan, W Siberian Russia, W Mongolia, and N China. It is divided into two parts, the Russian Altai, which includes the highest peak, Mount Belukha, 4,506 m/14,783 ft, and the Mongolian or Great Altai.

Altamaha River in Georgia, SE USA; length 220 km/136 mi. It is formed by the junction of the Oconee and Ocmulgee and flows SE into the Altamaha Sound at Darien.

Altamira Amazonian city in the state of Pará, NE Brazil, situated at the junction of the Trans-Amazonian Highway with the Xingu River, 700 km/400 mi SW of Belém; population (1991) 157,900. In 1989 a protest by Brazilian Indians and environmentalists against the building of six dams focused world attention on the devastation of the Amazon rainforest.

Altdorf Capital of the Swiss canton Uri at the head of Lake Lucerne, Switzerland; population 9,000. It was the scene of the legendary exploits of William Tell.

Altiplano Upland plateau of the Andes of South America, stretching from S Peru to NW Argentina. The height of the Altiplano is 3,000–4,000 m/10,000–13,000 ft.

Altmühl River in Bavaria, Germany; length 166 km/103 mi. The Altmühl rises near Rothenburg, and flows in a mainly southeasterly direction to the river ♭Danube.

Alton City in W Illinois, USA, on the Mississippi River, just NE of St Louis, Missouri; population (1990) 32,900. Alton is an industrial centre with flour mills and oil refineries. The city was founded 1817 and became a busy river port.

Altoona City in S central Pennsylvania, USA, in the Allegheny Mountains, NW of Harrisburg; population (1992) 52,500. It is a railroad manufacturing and repair centre, and there is coal mining. Altoona was founded 1849 as a base for railway building. The first steel railroad tracks in the USA were laid from Pittsburgh to Altoona.

Älvsborg County of SW Sweden, between Lake Vänern and the Skagerrak; area 12,742 sq km/4,920 sq mi; population (1995) 159,000. The region has poor soils and is largely forested. Industry is concentrated around Borås, supplied by hydroelectric power from the Göta River. Its capital is Vänersborg.

Alwar City in Rajasthan, India, chief town of the district (formerly princely state) of the same name; population (1991) 211,000. It has fine palaces, temples, and tombs. Flour milling and trade in cotton goods and millet are major occupations.

Alzira Town in the province of Valencia, E Spain; population (1995) 41,100. Built on the site of the Roman town of Saetabicula, it has a 14th-century bridge, a Gothic church, and several old mansions. It is the centre of a rich orange-growing district.

Amagasaki Industrial city on the NW outskirts of Osaka, Honshu island, Japan; population (1994) 487,000.

Amalfi Port 39 km/24 mi SE of Naples, Italy, situated at the foot of Monte Cerrato, on the Gulf of Salerno; population 7,000. For 700 years it was an independent republic. It is an ancient archiepiscopal see (seat of an archbishop) and has a Romanesque cathedral.

Amana or *Abana* One of the biblical 'rivers of Damascus', now the Barada, the Greek Chrysorrhoas.

Amarillo City in the Texas panhandle, USA; population (1992) 161,100. The centre of the world's largest cattle-producing area, it processes the live animal into frozen supermarket packets in a single continuous operation on an assembly line. Industries include oil, farming, copper refining, and the manufacture of helicopters. There is a large helium plant. It is also a centre for assembly of nuclear warheads. Amarillo was founded 1887 as a railway construction base.

Amazon (Indian *Amossona* 'destroyer of boats') South American river, the world's second longest, 6,570 km/4,083 mi, and the largest in volume of water. Its main headstreams, the Marañón and the Ucayali, rise in central Peru and unite to flow E across Brazil for about 4,000 km/ 2,500 mi. It has 48,280 km/30,000 mi of navigable waterways, draining 7,000,000 sq km/2,750,000 sq mi, nearly half the South American landmass. It reaches the Atlantic on the Equator, its estuary 80 km/50 mi wide, discharging a volume of water so immense that 64 km/40 mi out to sea, fresh water remains at the surface. The Amazon basin covers 7.5 million sq km/3 million sq mi, of which 5 million sq km/ 2 million sq mi is tropical forest containing 30% of all known plant and animal species (80,000 known species of trees, 3,000 known species of land vertebrates, 2,000 freshwater fish). It is the wettest region on Earth; average rainfall 2.54 m/ 8.3 ft a year.

Amazon

Amazonia Those regions of Brazil, Colombia, Ecuador, Peru, and Bolivia lying within the basin of the Amazon River.

Ambala or *Umballa* City and railway junction in N India, situated 176 km/110 mi NW of Delhi; population (1991) 140,050. Food processing, flour milling, and cotton ginning are the foremost industries. It is an archaeological site with prehistoric artefacts.

Amberg City in Bavaria, Germany, 153 km/95 mi N of Munich; population (1993) 43,700. Iron has been worked in the city since the 14th century. Other industries include extraction of brown coal (lignite) and brewing. Amberg has medieval walls, a castle, and several old churches, including the 15th-century Gothic St Martins-kirche.

Amboise French town in the *département* of Indre-et-Loire, on the river Loire, 25 km/16 mi E of Tours; population (1990) 11,500. Agricultural machinery and textiles are manufactured; tourism is important. Its château, one of the finest of the Loire châteaux, rises on a terrace above the river, and was a residence of the Valois dynasty. Other buildings in the town include a 12th-century church.

Ambon or *Amboina* Small island in Maluku, Republic of Indonesia; population (1990) 206,300. The town of Ambon, formerly a historic centre of Dutch influence, has shipyards and is a port for trade in spices. It is a popular diving centre for tourists.

America Western hemisphere of the Earth, containing the continents of ◊North America and ◊South America, with ◊Central America in between. This great landmass extends from the Arctic to the Antarctic, from beyond 75° N to past 55° S. The area is about 42,000,000 sq km/16,000,000 sq mi, and the estimated population is over 500 million. Politically, it consists of 36 nations and US, British, French, and Dutch dependencies.

American Samoa See ◊Samoa, American.

Amersfoort City in the Netherlands, 19 km/12 mi NE of Utrecht; population (1993) 106,900. Industries include brewing, chemicals, and light engineering.

Amherst Town in W Massachusetts, NE USA; population (1990) 35,200. Amherst College and the University of Massachusetts are located here. The poet Emily Dickinson was born, lived, and died in Amherst.

Amiens Ancient city of NE France at the confluence of the rivers Somme and Avre; capital of Somme *département* main town of the Picardy region and centre of a market-gardening region irrigated by canals; population (1990) 136,200. It has a magnificent Gothic cathedral with a spire 113 m/370 ft high and gave its name to the battles of Aug 1918, when British field marshal Douglas Haig launched his victorious offensive in World War I.

Amman Capital and chief industrial centre of Jordan; population (1994 est) 1,300,000. It is a major communications centre, linking historic trade routes across the Middle East.

Amoy Former (until 1979) name of ◊Xiamen.

Amritsar Industrial city in the Punjab, India; population (1991) 709,000. It is the holy city of Sikhism, with the Guru Nanak University (named after the first Sikh guru), and the Golden Temple. The city was the scene of the Amritsar

Massacre 1919, when the British general Dyer ordered troops to fire on a crowd agitating for self-government; 379 were killed and 1,200 wounded. In 1984, Indian prime minister Indira Gandhi was assassinated in reprisal by Sikh extremists wanting an independent Sikh state in Punjab. The whole of Punjab was put under presidential control 1987 following riots.

Amsterdam Capital of the Netherlands; population (1994) 724,100. Canals cut through the city link it with the North Sea and the Rhine, and as a Dutch port it is second only to Rotterdam. Industries include shipbuilding, printing, food processing, banking, and insurance. Art galleries include the Rijksmuseum, Stedelijk, Vincent van Gogh Museum, and the Rembrandt house. Notable also are the Royal Palace 1655 and the Anne Frank house.

The city developed out of a fishing village at the mouth of the Amstel; became part of Holland 1317; and passed to the duke of Burgundy 1428. It was freed from Spanish domination 1579. After the golden age of the 17th century it declined in maritime importance. It was occupied by the Germans during World War II.

Amu Darya formerly *Oxus* River in central Asia, flowing 2,540 km/1,578 mi from the ◊Pamirs to the ◊Aral Sea.

Amur River in E Asia. Formed by the Argun and Shilka rivers, the Amur enters the Sea of Okhotsk. At its mouth at Nikolevsk it is 16 km/10 mi wide. For much of its course of over 4,416 km/2,744 mi it forms, together with its tributary, the Ussuri, the boundary between Russia and China.

Anaconda Town in Montana, USA; population (1990) 10,278. The city was founded as Copperopolis 1883 by the Anaconda Copper Mining Company, and was incorporated as Anaconda 1888; at one time it had the world's largest copper smelter (closed 1980). The town is 1,615 m/5,300 ft above sea level and 42 km/26 mi NW of Butte.

Anaheim City in SW California, USA, SE of Los Angeles; industries include electronic and farm equipment and processed foods; population (1992) 274,200. Disneyland amusement park is here. Anaheim was settled by German immigrants 1858 as a wine-producing community.

Anahuac (Aztec 'near the water') Geographical region of Mexico. The name was originally applied by the Aztecs to their kingdom, but is now used to describe the whole of the central Mexican plateau, and more specifically the plateau-valley around Mexico City.

Anatolia (Turkish *Anadolu*) Asian part of Turkey, consisting of a mountainous peninsula with the Black Sea to the N, the Aegean Sea to the W, and the Mediterranean Sea to the S.

Anchorage Port and largest city of Alaska, USA, at the head of Cook Inlet; population (1992) 245,900. It is an important centre of administration, communication, and commerce. Oil and gas extraction and fish canning are also important to the local economy. Anchorage was founded 1914.

Ancona Italian city and naval base on the Adriatic Sea, capital of Marche region; population (1992) 100,700. It has a Romanesque cathedral and a former palace of the popes.

Ancona Province of E Italy in central Le ◊Marche region; capital Ancona; area 1,981 sq km/765 sq mi; population (1992) 437,600.

Andalusia (Spanish *Andalucía*) Fertile autonomous region of S Spain, including the provinces of Almería, Cádiz, Córdoba, Granada, Huelva, Jaén, Málaga, and Seville; area 87,300 sq km/33,698 sq mi; population (1991) 6,940,500. Málaga, Cádiz, and Algeciras are the chief ports and industrial centres. The ◊Costa del Sol on the S coast has many tourist resorts, including Marbella and Torremolinos.

Andaman and Nicobar Islands Two groups of islands in the Bay of Bengal, between India and Myanmar, forming a Union Territory of the Republic of India; capital Port Blair; area 8,249 sq km/3,185 sq mi; population (1994 est) 322,000. The economy is based on fishing, timber, rubber, fruit, nuts, coffee, and rice.

Anderlecht Town SW of Brussels, Belgium. Anderlecht has an important cattle market, and is known internationally for its football team; population (1991) 87,900.

Andermatt Village in the Swiss canton of Uri, some 25 km/16 mi S of Altdorf; population (1995) 1,400. It is a tourist and winter-sports centre in the upper Reuss valley (altitude 1,432m/4,690 ft), and is situated at the junction of the roads leading to the Furka Pass and the ◊St Gotthard Pass.

Andernach City in the *Land* of Rhineland-Palatinate, Germany, on the river Rhine, 17 km/10 mi NW of Koblenz; population (1994) 30,000. Its manufacturing industries include chemicals and cement. Pumice stone is mined in the surrounding region. Andernach is a tourist centre.

Anderson City in E central Indiana, USA, NE of Indianapolis; seat of Madison County; population (1992) 60,400.

Andes Great mountain system or *cordillera* that forms the W fringe of South America, extending through some 67° of latitude and the republics of Colombia, Venezuela, Ecuador, Peru, Bolivia, Chile, and Argentina. The mountains exceed 3,600 m/12,000 ft for half their length of 6,500 km/4,000 mi.

Andhra Pradesh State in E central India
area 275,045 sq km/106,195 sq mi
capital Hyderabad
towns and cities Secunderabad, Visakhapatnam, Vijayawada, Kakinda, Guntur, Nellore
industries rice, sugar cane, tobacco, groundnuts, cotton
population (1994 est) 71,800,000
language Telugu, Urdu, Tamil
history formed 1953 from the Telegu-speaking areas of Madras, and enlarged 1956 from the former Hyderabad state.

Andros Greek island, most northerly of the ◊Cyclades; area 383 sq km/147 sq mi. It is 40 km/25 mi long, 12 km/7.5 mi wide, mountainous, and produces wine. The principal town, Andros, is situated on the E coast.

Androscoggin River in N New Hampshire and Maine, NE USA; length 280 km/175 mi. The river rises in the White

Mountains and subsequently joins the Kennebec S of Augusta, just before the Kennebec enters the sea.

Aneto, Pico Highest peak of the Pyrenees mountains, rising to 3,404 m/11,168 ft in the Spanish province of Huesca.

Angel Falls Highest waterfalls in the world, on the river Caroní in the tropical rainforest of Bolívar Region, Venezuela; total height 979 m/3,212 ft. They were named after the aviator and prospector James Angel who flew over the falls and crash-landed nearby 1935.

Angeln Region in NE ◊Schleswig-Holstein, Germany, said to be the original home of the Angles, who invaded Britain in the 6th–7th centuries.

Ångermanland Region in Våsternorrland county, N Sweden. The river Ångerman, over 320 km/199 mi in length, flows through the region to the Gulf of Bothnia. It is a wild and picturesque country. There is agriculture in rural areas; the main town is Hårnösand, at the mouth of the river, with manufacturing and service industries.

Angers Ancient French city, capital of Maine-et-Loire *département*, on the river Maine; population (1990) 146,100. Products include electrical machinery and Cointreau liqueur. It has a 12th–13th-century cathedral and castle and was formerly the capital of the duchy and province of Anjou.

Angkor Site of the ancient capital of the Khmer Empire in NW Cambodia, N of Tonle Sap. The remains date mainly from the 10th–12th centuries AD, and comprise temples originally dedicated to the Hindu gods, shrines associated with Theravāda Buddhism, and royal palaces. Many are grouped within the enclosure called *Angkor Thom*, but the great temple of *Angkor Wat* (early 12th century) lies outside.

Anglesey (Welsh *Ynys Môn*) Island and unitary authority off the NW coast of Wales; administrative headquarters Llangefri; population (1996) 71,100; area 720 sq km/278 sq mi. It is separated from the mainland by the Menai Straits, which are crossed by the Britannia tubular railway bridge and Telford's suspension bridge, constructed 1819–26 but since rebuilt.

Angora Former name of the Turkish capital ◊Ankara.

Angostura Former name of ◊Ciudad Bolívar, a port in Venezuela.

Angoulême French town, capital of the *département* of Charente, on the Charente River; population (1990) 46,100. It has a cathedral, and a castle and paper mills dating from the 16th century.

Anguilla Island in the E Caribbean
area 160 sq km/62 sq mi
capital The Valley
features white coral-sand beaches; 80% of its coral reef has been lost through tourism (pollution and souvenir sales)
exports lobster, salt
currency Eastern Caribbean dollar
population (1992) 8,960
language English, Creole

Anguilla

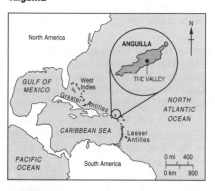

government from 1982, governor, executive council, and legislative house of assembly

history a British colony from 1650, Anguilla was long associated with St Kitts and Nevis but revolted against alleged domination by the larger island and seceded 1967. A small British force restored order 1969, and Anguilla retained a special position at its own request; since 1980 it has been a separate dependency of the UK.

Angus Unitary authority on the E coast of Scotland. A former county, it was part of Tayside Region 1975–96; administrative headquarters Forfar; population (1996) 111,300; area 2,184 sq km/843 sq mi.

Anhui or *Anhwei* Province of E China, watered by the Chang Jiang (Yangtze River)
area 139,900 sq km/54,015 sq mi
capital Hefei
industries cereals in the N; cotton, rice, tea in the S
population (1990) 52,290,000.

Ankara formerly *Angora* Capital of Turkey; population (1990) 2,559,500. Industries include cement, textiles, and leather products. It replaced Istanbul (then in Allied occupation) as capital 1923.

Annaba formerly *Bône* Seaport in Algeria; population (1989) 348,000. The name means 'city of jujube trees'. There are metallurgical industries, and iron ore and phosphates are exported.

An Najaf City near the Euphrates in Iraq, 144 km/90 mi S of Baghdad; population (1987) 309,000. The tomb of Ali, son-in-law of Muhammad, is a Shi'ite Muslim shrine.

Annapolis Seaport and capital of Maryland, USA; population (1992) 34,100. Founded 1694 as the capital of colonial Maryland, it was named after Princess (later Queen) Anne 1697.

Annapolis Royal Town in W Nova Scotia, Canada, on the Bay of Fundy; population (1991) 650. Annapolis Royal was founded by the French in 1605 under the name of Port Royal, the oldest French settlement in Canada. It was ceded to Britain in 1713, and was given the name Annapolis Royal after Queen Anne of England (ruled 1702–14). It was the capital of Nova Scotia until 1750.

Annapurna Mountain 8,075 m/26,502 ft in the Himalayas, Nepal. The N face was first climbed by a French expedition (Maurice Herzog) 1950 and the S by a British team 1970.

Ann Arbor City in SE Michigan, USA, W of Dearborn and Detroit, on the Huron River; seat of Washtenaw County; population (1992) 109,800. It is a centre for medical, aeronautical, nuclear, and chemical research, and the site of the University of Michigan (1837). Ann Arbor was founded 1824.

Annecy Capital of the *département* of Haute-Savoie, SE France, at the N end of Lake Annecy; population (1990) 51,100. It has some light industry, including precision instruments, and is a tourist resort.

Anniston City in E Alabama, USA, NE of Birmingham; seat of Calhoun County; population (1990) 26,600. Lying in the foothills of the Appalachian Mountains, Anniston is the site of iron mines; its industries include iron products as well as textiles and chemicals. Anniston was founded 1872.

Annobón formerly (1973–79) *Pagalu* Island in Equatorial Guinea; area 17 sq km/7 sq mi; population (1983) 2,000. Its inhabitants are descended from slaves of the Portuguese and still speak a Portuguese patois. It was Portuguese from the end of the 5th century until it was ceded to Spain 1778.

Ansbach formerly *Anspach* City in Bavaria, Germany, 150 km/93 mi N of Munich, on the river Rezat; population (1993) 39,000. The city manufactures machinery and electrical goods. From 1460 to 1791 Ansbach was the seat of the margraves of Ansbach, and from 1791 to 1806 it belonged to Prussia. The city has a 15th-century church and examples of Baroque architecture, including the castle.

Anshan Chinese city in Liaoning province, 89 km/55 mi SE of Shenyang (Mukden); population (1991) 1,390,000. The iron and steel centre started here 1918, was expanded by the Japanese, dismantled by the Russians, and restored by the Communist government of China. It produces 6 million tonnes of steel annually.

Antakya or *Hatay* City in SE Turkey, site of the ancient Antioch; population (1990) 124,000.

Antalya Mediterranean port on the W coast of Turkey and capital of a province of the same name; population (1990) 378,200. The port trades in grain and timber. Industries include canning and flour milling. It is a popular coastal resort.

Antananarivo formerly *Tananarive* Capital of Madagascar, on the interior plateau, with a rail link to Tamatave; population (1993) 1,053,000. Industries include food processing, leather goods, and clothing.

Antarctica Continent surrounding the South Pole, arbitrarily defined as the region lying S of the Antarctic Circle. Occupying 10% of the world's surface, Antarctica contains 90% of the world's ice, representing 90% of its fresh water
area 13,900,000 sq km/5,400,000 sq mi
features Mount Erebus on Ross Island is the world's southernmost active volcano; the Ross Ice Shelf is formed by several glaciers coalescing in the Ross Sea

physical formed of two blocs of rock with an area of about 8 million sq km/3 million sq mi, Antarctica is covered by a cap of ice that flows slowly towards its 22,400 km/14,000 mi coastline, reaching the sea in high ice cliffs. The most southerly shores are near the 78th parallel in the Ross and Weddell seas. E Antarctica is a massive bloc of ancient rocks that surface in the Transantarctic Mountains of Victoria Land, much of it over 3,000 m/10,000 ft high. Separated by a deep channel, W Antarctica is characterized by the mountainous regions of Graham Land, the Antarctic Peninsula, Palmer Land, and Ellsworth Land; the highest peak is Vinson Massif (5,140 m/16,863 ft).

In 1996 the British Antarctic Survey discovered a 14,000 sq km/5,400 sq mi freshwater lake, Lake Vostok, 4,000 m/1,312 ft beneath the Antarctic ice. The ice sheet acts as an insulating layer and its pressure melts lower regions of ice, enabling the lake to persist at subzero temperatures. The lake is believed to be about 5 million years old and may contain unique microorganisms.

Antarctic Ocean Popular name for the reaches of the Atlantic, Indian, and Pacific oceans extending S of the Antarctic Circle (66° 32'S). The term is not used by the International Hydrographic Bureau.

Antarctic Peninsula Mountainous peninsula of W Antarctica extending 1,930 km/1,200 mi N toward South America; originally named *Palmer Land* after a US navigator, Captain Nathaniel Palmer, who was the first to explore the region 1820. It was claimed by Britain 1832, Argentina 1940, and Chile 1942. Its name was changed to the Antarctic Peninsula 1964.

Antep Former name (until 1992) of ◊Gaziantep, Turkey.

Antibes Resort, which includes Juan les Pins, on the French Riviera, in the *département* of Alpes Maritimes; population (1990) 70,600. There is a Picasso collection in the 17th-century castle museum.

Anticosti Island Island in the Gulf of St Lawrence, part of Quebec, E Canada; length 225 km/140 mi; width 48 km/30 mi; population (1991) 264. The island was discovered by the French navigator Jacques Cartier 1534.

Anti-Lebanon or *Antilibanus* Mountain range on the Lebanese-Syrian border, including Mount Hermon, 2,800 m/ 9,200 ft. It is separated from the Lebanon Mountains by the Bekaa Valley.

Antilles Group of West Indian islands, divided N–S into the *Greater Antilles* (Cuba, Jamaica, Haiti–Dominican Republic, Puerto Rico) and *Lesser Antilles*, subdivided into the Leeward Islands (Virgin Islands, St Kitts and Nevis, Antigua and Barbuda, Anguilla, Montserrat, and Guadeloupe) and the Windward Islands (Dominica, Martinique, St Lucia, St Vincent and the Grenadines, Barbados, and Grenada).

Antioch Ancient capital of the Greek kingdom of Syria, founded 300 BC by Seleucus I and famed for its splendour and luxury. The site is now occupied by the Turkish town of ◊Antakya.

Antofagasta Port of N Chile, capital of the region of Antofagasta; population (1992) 226,750. The area of the region is 125,300 sq km/48,366 sq mi; its population (1982) 341,000. Nitrates from the Atacama Desert are exported.

Antrim County of Northern Ireland
area 2,830 sq km/1,092 sq mi
towns and cities Belfast (county town), Larne (port), Antrim
features ◊Giant's Causeway, a World Heritage site, of natural hexagonal basalt columns on the N coast, which, according to legend, was built to enable the giants to cross between Ireland and Scotland; peat bogs; Antrim borders Lough Neagh, and is separated from Scotland by the North Channel, 30 km/20 mi wide
industries potatoes, oats, linen, synthetic textiles, flax, shipbuilding. Manufacture of man-made fibres has largely replaced traditional linen production
population (1995 est) 707,000.

Antwerp (Flemish *Antwerpen*, French *Anvers*) Port in Belgium on the river Schelde, capital of the province of Antwerp; population (1995) 459,000. One of the world's busiest ports, it has shipbuilding, oil-refining, petrochemical, textile, and diamond-cutting industries. The home of the artist Rubens is preserved, and many of his works are in the Gothic cathedral.

Antwerp Province of Belgium, bounded to the N and NE by the Netherlands, to the S by Brabant, to the SE by Limbourg, and to the SW by East Flanders; area 2,859 sq km/1,104 sq mi; population (1995) 1,628,700.

Anuradhapura Ancient holy city in Sri Lanka; population (district, 1993 est) 741,000. It was the capital of the Sinhalese kings of Sri Lanka 5th century BC–8th century AD; rediscovered in the mid-19th century. Sacred in Buddhism, it claims a Bo tree descended from the one under which the Buddha became enlightened.

Anvers French form of ◊Antwerp, a province in N Belgium.

Anyang City in Henan province, E China; population (1990) 420,000. It was the capital of the Shang dynasty (13th–12th centuries BC). Rich archaeological remains have been uncovered since the 1930s.

Antilles

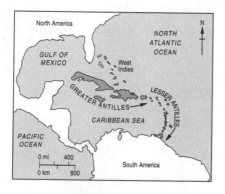

Anzhero-Sudzhensk City in the Russian Federation, in W Siberia, 80 km/50 mi N of Kemerovo in the Kuznetsk basin; population (1990) 108,000. Its chief industry is coal mining.

Anzin Suburb of the French town of ◊Valenciennes, in the *département* of Nord, on the river Schelde. It was an important coalmining centre, but its chief industries are now manufacturing machinery and metal industries.

Anzio Seaport and resort on the W coast of Italy, 53 km/33 mi SE of Rome; population (1984) 25,000. It is the site of the Roman town of Antium, birthplace of the emperor Nero.

Aomori Port at the head of Mutsu Bay, on the N coast of Honshu Island, Japan; 40 km/25 mi NE of Hirosaki; population (1994) 293,000.

Aosta Italian city, 79 km/49 mi NW of Turin; population (1990 est) 36,100. It is the capital of ◊Valle d'Aosta (French-speaking) autonomous region, and has extensive Roman remains.

Aosta Province of NW Italy in ◊Valle d'Aosta region; capital Aosta; area 3,263 sq km/1,260 sq mi; population (1992) 116,600.

Aotearoa (Maori 'long daylight') Maori name for New Zealand, reflecting its difference in latitude from their Pacific homeland.

Aozou Strip Disputed territory 100 km/60 mi wide on the Chad–Libya frontier, occupied by Libya 1973, part of Chad according to an International Court of Justice ruling 1994. Lying to the N of the Tibesti massif, the area is rich in uranium and other minerals.

Apeldoorn Commercial city in Gelderland province, E central Netherlands; population (1994) 149,500. Het Loo, which is situated nearby, has been the summer residence of the Dutch royal family since the time of William of Orange.

Apennines Chain of mountains stretching the length of the Italian peninsula. A continuation of the Maritime Alps, from Genoa it swings across the peninsula to Ancona on the E coast, and then back to the W coast and into the 'toe' of Italy. The system is continued over the Strait of Messina along the N Sicilian coast, then across the Mediterranean Sea in a series of islands to the Atlas Mountains of N Africa. The highest peak is Gran Sasso d'Italia at 2,914 m/9,560 ft.

Apia Capital and port of Samoa, on the N coast of Upolu Island, in the W Pacific; population (1986) 32,200. It was the final home of the writer Robert Louis Stevenson 1888–94, who is buried on Mount Vaea.

Apo, Mount Active volcano and highest peak in the Philippines, rising to 2,954 m/9,692 ft on the island of Mindanao.

Apostle Islands Group of 22 islands in SW Lake Superior in Wisconsin, N central USA; they total about 518 sq km/200 sq mi. The largest and only commercially developed island is Madeline Island. The picturesque islands are designated a national lakeshore, popular with campers, tourists, and outdoors enthusiasts.

Appalachia Region of E USA, corresponding roughly to the area covered by the Appalachian Mountains. Stretching from the Gulf of St Lawrence to central Alabama, the region consists of 373 counties in 11 states, and is isolated and physically fragmented.

Appalachian Mountains Mountain system of E North America, stretching about 2,400 km/1,500 mi from Alabama to Quebec, composed of ancient eroded rocks and rounded peaks. The chain includes the Allegheny, Catskill, and Blue Ridge Mountains, the last-named having the highest peak, Mount Mitchell, 2,045 m/6,712 ft. The E edge has a fall line to the coastal plain where Philadelphia, Baltimore, and Washington stand. The Appalachians are heavily forested and have deposits of coal and other minerals.

Appenzell Village and capital of the Inner Rhodes part of the canton of Appenzell, Switzerland, on the river Sitter, 10 km/6 mi SE of St Gallen; population (1995) 5,500. The village produces embroidery work and cheese.

Appenzell Canton in NE Switzerland, enclosed within the canton of St Gallen; area 415 sq km/160 sq mi. Appenzell is subdivided into the regions of *Outer Rhodes* (capital Herisau) and *Inner Rhodes* (population (1996) 14,800; capital Appenzell). Textiles are manufactured in Outer Rhodes, whereas Inner Rhodes is mainly agricultural. The highest point in the canton is Mount Santis (2,500 m/8,202 ft), which is surmounted by an observatory.

Appleton City in E central Wisconsin, USA, NW of Oshkosh, on the Fox River; seat of Outagamie County; population (1992) 68,500. It is a manufacturing centre for paper products. It was founded 1847 and claims to have the world's first hydroelectric plant, built 1882.

Apulia English form of ◊Puglia, a region of Italy.

Aqaba or *Akaba,* **Gulf of** Gulf extending for 160 km/100 mi between the Negev and the Red Sea; its coastline is uninhabited except at its head, where the frontiers of Israel, Egypt, Jordan, and Saudi Arabia converge. The two ports of Elat (Israeli 'Elath') and Aqaba, Jordan's only port, are situated here. A border crossing near the two ports was opened 1994, for non-Israelis and non-Jordanians, to encourage the E Mediterannean tourist industry.

Aquitaine Region of SW France; capital Bordeaux; area 41,308 sq km/15,949 sq mi; population (1990) 2,795,800. It comprises the *départements* of Dordogne, Gironde, Landes, Lot-et-Garonne, and Pyrénées-Atlantiques. Red wines (Margaux, St Julien) are produced in the Médoc district, bordering the Gironde. Aquitaine was an English possession 1152–1453.

AR Abbreviation for the state of ◊Arkansas, USA.

Arab Emirates See United Arab Emirates.

Arabia Peninsula between the Persian Gulf and the Red Sea, in SW Asia; area 2,600,000 sq km/1,000,000 sq mi. The peninsula contains the world's richest gas reserves and half the world's oil reserves. It comprises the states of Bahrain, Kuwait, Oman, Qatar, Saudi Arabia, the United Arab Emirates, and Yemen.

Arabian Gulf Another name for the ◊Persian Gulf.

Arabian Sea Northwestern branch of the ◊Indian Ocean.

Arad Romanian city on the river Mures, 160 km/100 mi NE of Belgrade; population (1993) 189,000. It is a major trading centre with many industries.

Arafāt also called *Jabal al-Rahma* 'the mount of mercy' Hill and plain about 24 km/15 mi E and about 19 km/12 mi SW of Mecca. The hill is granite and rises to 61 m/200 ft; it is also called Jebel al-Rahma. The most important ceremony of the Muslim pilgrimage, or hajj, occurs on this hill.

Arafura Sea Area of the Pacific Ocean between N Australia and Indonesia, bounded by the Timor Sea in the W and the Coral Sea in the E. It is 1,290 km/800 mi long and 560 km/350 mi wide.

Aragón Autonomous region of NE Spain including the provinces of Huesca, Teruel, and Zaragoza; area 47,700 sq km/18,412 sq mi; population (1991) 1,188,800. Its capital is Zaragoza, and products include almonds, figs, grapes, and olives. Aragón was an independent kingdom 1035–1479.

Aragón River in N Spain; length 130 km/80 mi. Rising in the Pyrenees, it flows SW through the provinces of Huesca and Zaragoza, and the autonomous community of Navarre, where it joins the river ◊Ebro.

Arakan State of Myanmar (formerly Burma) on the Bay of Bengal coast, some 645 km/400 mi long and strewn with islands; population (1983) 2,046,000. The chief town is Sittwe. It is bounded along its E side by the Arakan Yoma, a mountain range rising to 3,000 m/10,000 ft. The ancient kingdom of Arakan was conquered by Burma 1785.

Aral Sea Inland sea divided between Kazakhstan and Uzbekistan, the world's fourth largest lake; former area 64,500 sq km/24,903 sq mi, but decreasing. Water from its tributaries, the Amu Darya and Syr Darya, has been diverted for irrigation and city use, and the sea is disappearing, with long-term consequences for the climate.

Aran Islands Three rocky islands (Inishmore, Inishmaan, Inisheer) in the mouth of Galway Bay, Republic of Ireland;

Aral Sea

population approximately 4,600. The capital is Kilronan. J M Synge used the language of the islands in his plays.

Aranjuez Spanish town on the river Tagus, 40 km/ 25 mi SE of Madrid; population (1991) 35,900. The palace was a royal residence for centuries.

Ararat Wheat and wool centre in NW Victoria, Australia; population (1986) 8,000. It is a former gold-mining town.

Ararat, Mount Double-peaked mountain in Turkey near the Iranian border; Great Ararat, at 5,137 m/16,854 ft, is the highest mountain in Turkey.

Aras (ancient *Araxes*) River rising in NE Turkey and flowing E through Armenia and Azerbaijan to the Caspian Sea; length 1,100 km/660 mi.

Araxes Any of several rivers: (1) in Armenia and Azerbaijan, the modern ◊Aras; (2) in Persia, which flowed into a salt lake not far below the town of Persepolis, which stood on its banks; (3) the Araxes or Khabur in Mesopotamia, mentioned by the Greek historian Xenophon, which is around 200 mi/320 km long, rises in SE Turkey, and flows generally S through NE Syria to enter the Euphrates River; (4) the Araxes mentioned by Herodotus, which is probably the Iaxartes or the Oxus.

Arbīl *or Irbīl* Kurdish capital city, in a province of the same name in N Iraq; population (1985) 334,000. Occupied since Assyrian times, it was the site of a battle 331 BC at which Alexander the Great defeated the Persians under Darius III. In 1974 Arbīl became the capital of a Kurdish autonomous region set up by the Iraqi government. It was captured by the Kurdish Democratic Party 1996 with the help of Saddam Hussein.

Arbroath (or *Aberbrothock*) Fishing town in Angus, on the E coast of Scotland; population (1991) 23,500. In 1320 the Scottish Parliament asserted Scotland's independence here in a letter to the pope. There are engineering, sailmaking, and knitwear industries. The town is famous for its smoked haddock (Arbroath smokies).

Arcadia (Greek *Arkadhia*) Central plateau and department of S Greece; area 4,419 sq km/1,706 sq mi; population (1991) 103,800. Tripolis is the capital town.

Archangel (Russian *Arkhangel'sk*) Port in N Russian Federation; population (1994) 407,000. It is the chief timber-exporting port of Russia. Formerly blocked by ice for half the year, it has been kept open constantly since 1979 by ice-breakers. Archangel was made an open port by Boris Godunov and was of prime importance until Peter the Great built St Petersburg.

Archipelago de las Perlas or *Pearl Islands* Group of some 180 islands in the Gulf of Panama, Central America. The main islands are San Miguel (the largest), San José, and Pedro González. The main industries are pearl fishing and sea angling.

Arctic, The That part of the N hemisphere surrounding the North Pole; arbitrarily defined as the region lying N of the Arctic Circle (66° 32′N) or N of the tree line. There is no Arctic continent; the greater part of the region comprises the Arctic Ocean, which is the world's smallest ocean. Arctic climate, fauna, and flora extend over the islands and N edges of continental land masses that surround the Arctic Ocean (Svalbard, Iceland, Greenland, Siberia, Scandinavia, Alaska, and Canada)

area 36,000,000 sq km/14,000,000 sq mi

physical pack-ice floating on the Arctic Ocean occupies almost the entire region between the North Pole and the coasts of North America and Eurasia, covering an area that ranges in diameter from 3,000 km/1,900 mi to 4,000 km/ 2,500 mi. The pack-ice reaches a maximum extent in Feb when its outer limit (influenced by the cold Labrador Current and the warm Gulf Stream) varies from 50°N along the coast of Labrador to 75°N in the Barents Sea N of Scandinavia. In spring the pack-ice begins to break up into ice floes which are carried by the S-flowing Greenland Current to the Atlantic Ocean. Arctic ice is at its minimum area in Aug. The greatest concentration of icebergs in Arctic regions is found in Baffin Bay. They are derived from the glaciers of W Greenland, then carried along Baffin Bay and down into the N Atlantic where they melt off Labrador and Newfoundland.

Arctic Ocean Ocean surrounding the North Pole; area 13,224 sq km/5,105,700 sq mi. Because of the Siberian and North American rivers flowing into it, it has comparatively low salinity and freezes readily.

Ardabil or *Ardebil* City in NW Iran, near the frontier with Azerbaijan; population (1991) 311,000. Ardabil exports dried fruits, carpets, and rugs.

Ardèche River in SE France, a tributary of the Rhône. Near Vallon it flows under the Pont d'Arc, a natural bridge. It gives its name to a *département*.

Ardèche *Département* in the ◊Rhône-Alpes region of France; area 5,523 sq km/2,132 sq mi; population (1990) 135,900. The area is mountainous, containing part of the Vivarais mountain range in the W. The river Ardèche flows through the SE of the *département*. Cereals, vines, chestnuts, mushrooms, and olives are produced. Coal and iron are mined. The principal towns are Privas (the capital), Largentière, and Tournon.

Arden, Forest of Former forest region of N Warwickshire, England, the setting for William Shakespeare's play *As You Like It*.

Ardennes Wooded plateau in NE France, SE Belgium, and N Luxembourg, cut through by the river Meuse; also a *département* of ◊Champagne-Ardenne. There was heavy fighting here in World Wars I and II.

Ardennes *Département* in the Champagne-Ardennes region of France, bordering on Belgium; area 5,218 sq km/ 2,105 sq mi; population (1990) 146,300. It is wooded and hilly: the Forest of Ardennes covers about one-third of the *département*. The W and the valleys of the rivers Aisne and Meuse are fertile. Livestock farming and cereal production are important. There is a nuclear power station, car manufacture, and a growing service sector. Principal towns are Charleville-Mézières (the capital), ◊Sedan, Vouziers, and Rethel.

Arequipa City in Peru at the base of the volcano El Misti; population (1993) 619,200. Founded by Pizarro 1540 on the site of an ancient Inca city, it is the cultural focus of S Peru and a busy commercial centre (soap, textiles).

Arezzo Town in the Tuscan region of Italy; 80 km/50 mi SE of Florence; population (1990) 91,600. The writers Petrarch and Aretino were born here. It is a mining town and also trades in textiles, olive oil, and antiques. There is a fresco series by Renaissance painter Piero della Francesca.

Arezzo Province of N Italy in central ◊Tuscany region; capital Arezzo; area 3,232 sq km/1,248 sq mi; population (1992) 314,600.

Argentan French town in the *département* of Orne, Normandy, on the river Orne; population (1990) 17,000. The town is a centre for horse-breeding and leather production.

Argenteuil Industrial NW suburb of Paris, France, on the river Seine; population (1990) 94,200.

Argovie French name of ◊Aargau, a canton in N Switzerland.

Argyll and Bute Unitary authority in W Scotland created 1996 from part of the former Strathclyde region; administrative headquarters Lochgilphead; population (1996) 89,300; area 4,001 sq km/1,545 sq mi. The area includes Loch Lomond.

Argyllshire Former county on the W coast of Scotland, including many of the Western Isles, which was for the most part merged in Strathclyde Region 1975–96.

Århus or *Aarhus* Second largest city of Denmark, on the E coast overlooking the Kattegat; population (1995) 277,500. It is the capital of Århus county in Jylland (Jutland) and a shipping and commercial centre.

Ariana formerly *Aequum Tuticum* Italian town in Campania, NE of Avellino. It was originally a Samnite town.

Arica Port in Chile; population (1992) 169,200. Much of Bolivia's trade passes through it, and there is contention over the use of Arica by Bolivia to allow access to the Pacific Ocean. It is Chile's northernmost city. Drilling began on large porphyry copper deposit nearby 1993.

Ariège River in S France, a tributary of the Garonne, which rises in the Pyrenees; length 170 km/106 mi. It gives its name to a *département*.

Ariège *Département* in the Midi-Pyrénées region of France: area 4,890 sq km/1,888 sq mi; population (1990) 136,600. Spurs of the Pyrenees mountains cover a large part of the *département* and there are many fertile valleys. In the E flows the river Ariège, and in the W, the Salat, both tributaries of the Garonne. Cereals, vines, vegetables, potatoes, and hemp are produced, and livestock is farmed. Iron, zinc, manganese, and bauxite are mined, and there are chemical, metallurgical, textile, and paper industries. The principal towns are Foix (the capital), Pamiers, and St-Girons.

Arizona State in SW USA; nicknamed Grand Canyon State/Apache State
area 294,100 sq km/113,523 sq mi
capital Phoenix

towns and cities Tucson, Scottsdale, Tempe, Mesa, Glendale, Flagstaff
physical Colorado Plateau in the N and E, desert basins and mountains in the S and W; the Grand Canyon (a World Heritage Site), the rock gorge through which the Colorado River flows, 350 km/217 mi long, 6–28 km/4–18 mi wide, and up to over 1.6 km/1 mi deep; Monument Valley; Saguaro national monument, with huge saguaro cactus, Tucson; Petrified Forest and the Painted Desert; Organ Pipe Cactus national monument park; Coconino national forest; Sunset Crater Volcano
features Arizona–Sonora Desert Museum, Tucson; Canyon de Chelly, with ruins of ancient Anasazi North Native American peoples, and rock paintings; Navajo national monument, the largest ruin in Arizona, abandoned before 1300; Walnut Canyon national monument, site of 14th-century Anasazi cliff dwellings; Wupatki national monument; Casa Grande Ruins national monument; Mission San Xavier del Bac; Tombstone, site of the gunfight at the OK Corral, commemorated in Tombstone Courthouse state historic park, and Boot Hill Graveyard; Bisbee, former mining boom town; Navaho Nation Museum, Window Rock; Taliesin West, Scottsdale, the home of Frank Lloyd Wright; old London Bridge (moved 1971 to the tourist resort of Lake Havasu City)
industries cotton under irrigation, livestock, copper, molybdenum, silver, electronics, aircraft
population (1995) 4,217,900; including 5.6% Native Americans (Navajo, Hopi, Apache), who by treaty own 25% of the state
famous people Cochise, Wyatt Earp, Geronimo, Barry Goldwater, Zane Grey, Percival Lowell, Frank Lloyd Wright
history part of New Spain 1752; part of Mexico 1824; passed to the USA after the Mexican War 1848; territory 1863; statehood achieved 1912.

Arkansas State in S central USA; nicknamed Land of Opportunity/Bear State
area 137,800 sq km/53,191 sq mi
capital Little Rock
towns and cities Fort Smith, Pine Bluff, Fayetteville
physical Ozark Mountains with Ozark national forest and plateau in the W, lowlands in the E; Arkansas, Mississippi, and Buffalo rivers; Felsenthal national wildlife refuge; Ouachita national forest; many lakes
features Hot Springs, a spa town with renovated Art Deco hotels, including the Arlington, with Hot Springs national park, and the boyhood home of President Bill Clinton; Hope, the birthplace of President Clinton, with Old Washington historic state park (the state capital during the Civil War), and Hope Watermelon Festival; Arkansas Post, the first European settlement in French Louisiana; Fort Smith national historic site; Prairie Grove Battlefield Park; Shiloh historic district and museum; Eureka Springs, a 19th-century spa town in the Ozark Mountains; Little Rock, with the Old State House (1830s), the Quapaw Quarter (a restored 19th-century neighbourhood, with the Villa Marre 1881), Arkansas Territorial Reservation (a group of 14 buildings from the early 1800s), and the Arkansas Arts Center

industries cotton, soya beans, rice, oil, natural gas, bauxite, timber, processed foods

population (1995) 2,483,800

famous people Johnny Cash, Bill Clinton, J William Fulbright, Douglas MacArthur, Winthrop Rockefeller

history explored by Hernando de Soto 1541; European settlers 1648, who traded with local Native Americans; part of Louisiana Purchase 1803; statehood achieved 1836.

Arlberg Mountain range in the Austrian ◊Alps, extending from the province of Tirol into ◊Vorarlberg. A road link between the two provinces passes through the Arlberg Pass (altitude 1,793 m/5,882 ft); nearby, a railway tunnel more than 10 km/6 mi long (highest point 1,310 m/4,298 ft) has been in use since 1884.

Arles Town in Bouches-du-Rhône *département*, SE France, on the left bank of the Rhône; population (1990) 52,600. It is an important fruit- and vine-growing district. Roman relics include an amphitheatre for 25,000 spectators. The cathedral of St Trophime is a notable Romanesque structure. The painter Van Gogh lived here 1888–89, during which period he painted some of his major works.

Arlington City in N Texas, USA, located between Dallas and Fort Worth; population (1992) 275,900. Industries include machinery, paper products, steel, car assembly, rubber, and chemicals. Arlington was first settled 1843 on a Native American site, and the city was laid out 1876 and named after the Confederate general Robert E Lee's Virginia home.

Arlington County in Virginia, USA, and suburb of Washington DC; population (1990) 170,900. It is the site of the National Cemetery for the dead of the US wars. The grounds were first used as a military cemetery 1864 during the American Civil War. The Unknown Soldier of both world wars, President John F Kennedy, and his brother Robert Kennedy are all buried there.

Arlon Capital of the province of Luxembourg in SE Belgium. Arlon is one of the oldest settlements in Belgium, and was a trading centre in Roman times. Trade is now conducted from the town in corn, ironware, tobacco, and crockery.

Armagh County of Northern Ireland

area 1,250 sq km/483 sq mi

towns and cities Armagh (county town), Lurgan, Portadown, Keady

features smallest county of Northern Ireland; flat in the N, with many bogs; low hills in the S; the rivers Bann and Blackwater, flowing into Lough Neagh, and the Callan tributary of the Blackwater

industries chiefly agricultural: apples, potatoes, flax; linen manufacture; milling; light engineering; concrete; potato crisps

population (1981) 119,000.

Armagh City in County Armagh, Northern Ireland; population (1991) 14,300. Industries include textiles (its chief product), linen manufacture, engineering, whiskey, shoes, optical instruments, chemicals, and food processing. It

became the religious centre of Ireland in the 5th century when St Patrick was made archbishop. For 700 years it was the seat of the kings of Ulster. It is the seat of both the Roman Catholic and Anglican archbishops of Ireland, who each bear the title 'Archbishop of Armagh and Primate of All Ireland'.

Armagnac Former district in S France, a part of Gascony, now included in the *département* of Gers. It has rich, fertile soil, produces wine, and gives its name to a brandy (armagnac). The capital of Armagnac was Auch.

Armentières Town in N France on the Lys River; population (1990) 26,200. The song 'Mademoiselle from Armentières' originated during World War I, when the town was held by the British and was a popular rest centre for British troops. The town was flattened by German bombardment during the spring offensive of 1918 and subsequently rebuilt.

Armidale Town in New South Wales, Australia; population (1985) 21,500. The University of New England is here, and mansions of the squatters (early settlers) survive.

Arnhem City in the Netherlands, on the Rhine SE of Utrecht; population (1993) 133,300. It produces salt, chemicals, and pharmaceuticals.

Arnhem Land Plateau of the central peninsula in Northern Territory, Australia. It is named after a Dutch ship which dropped anchor here 1618. The chief town is Nhulunbuy. It is the largest of the Aboriginal reserves, and a traditional way of life is maintained, now threatened by mineral exploitation.

Arno Italian river 240 km/150 mi long, rising in the Apennines, and flowing westwards to the Mediterranean Sea. Florence and Pisa stand on its banks. A flood 1966 damaged virtually every Renaissance landmark in Florence.

Aroostook River in NE North America; length 225 km/140 mi. It rises to the N of Maine, and flows into the Saint John River in New Brunswick, Canada. Its valley forms a boundary area between the USA and Canada.

Arosa Swiss winter-sports resort (altitude 1,830 m/6,003 ft) in the canton of ◊Graubünden, 30 km/19 mi SE of Chur; population (1995) 2,600.

Arran Large mountainous island in the Firth of Clyde, in North Ayrshire, Scotland; area 427 sq km/165 sq mi; population (1991) 4,474. It is popular as a holiday resort. The chief town is Brodick.

Arras French town on the Scarpe River NE of Paris; population (1990) 42,700. It is the capital of Pas-de-Calais *département*, and was formerly known for tapestry. It was the birthplace of the French revolutionary leader M Robespierre.

Arta Town and department in the ◊Epirus region of Greece; area (department) 1,612 sq km/622 sq mi; population (town) (1993) 80,500. It derives its name from the river Arakhthos, on which it stands and which formed the boundary between Greece and Turkey until 1912. Its chief industries are woollen and cotton textiles, embroidery, and leather-working. The town has a Byzantine castle and a medieval bridge.

Arthur's Pass Road-rail link across the Southern Alps, New Zealand, at 926 m/3,038 ft, linking Christchurch with Greymouth.

Arthur's Seat Hill of volcanic origin, Edinburgh, Scotland; height 251 m/823 ft. It is only fancifully linked with King Arthur.

Aruba Island in the Caribbean, the westernmost of the Lesser Antilles; an overseas territory of the Netherlands
area 193 sq km/75 sq mi
population (1991) 68,900 (half of Indian descent)
language Dutch (official), Papiamento (a Creole language)
economy based largely on tourism
history Part of the Dutch West Indies from 1828, and part of the Netherlands Antilles from 1845, Aruba obtained separate status from the other Netherlands Antilles 1986 and has full internal autonomy. It was due to become fully independent 1996, but a 1990 agreement deleted references to eventual independence.

Arunachal Pradesh State of India, in the Himalayas on the borders of Tibet and Myanmar
area 83,743 sq km/32,333 sq mi
capital Itanagar
industries rubber, coffee, spices, fruit, timber
population (1994 est) 965,000; over 80 ethnic groups
language 50 different dialects
history formerly part of the state of Assam, it became a state of India 1987.

Arundel Town in West Sussex, England, on the river Arun; population (1991) 3,300. It has a magnificent castle (much restored and rebuilt), the seat of the Duke of Norfolk and Earl of Arundel, Earl Marshal of England.

Arvand River Iranian name for the ◊Shatt-al-Arab waterway.

Arvida City in Quebec, Canada; population (1990) 21,800. The town grew up around the large aluminium smelting plant erected by the Aluminium Company of Canada in 1926, sited here to take advantage of the hydroelectric developments on the ◊Saguenay.

Aryana Ancient name of Afghanistan.

Asante Alternative form of ◊Ashanti, a region of Ghana.

Ascension British island of volcanic origin in the S Atlantic, a dependency of ◊St Helena since 1922; area 88 sq km/34 sq mi; population (1993) 1,117 (excluding military personnel). The chief settlement is Georgetown.

Aschaffenburg City in Bavaria, Germany, on the river Main, 40 km/25 mi SE of Frankfurt am Main; population (1993) 65,200. Aschaffenburg is a river port and holiday resort. Its main industries are metalworking and the manufacture of clothing and paper. The city stands on the site of a former Roman fortress. The Renaissance castle of Johannisburg was once the residence of the archbishops of Mainz.

Ascoli Piceno Province of central Italy in Le ◊Marche region; capital Ascoli Piceno (population (1990) 52,600); area 2,088 sq km/806 sq mi; population (1992) 361,800.

Ascot Village in Berkshire, England 9.5 km/6 mi SW of Windsor. Queen Anne established the racecourse on Ascot Heath 1711, and the Royal Ascot meeting is a social as well as a sporting event. Horse races include the Gold Cup, Ascot Stakes, Coventry Stakes, and King George VI and Queen Elizabeth Stakes.

Ashanti or *Asante* Region of Ghana, W Africa; area 25,100 sq km/9,700 sq mi; population (1984) 2,089,683. Kumasi is the capital. Most Ashanti are cultivators and the main crop is cocoa, but the region is also noted for its metalwork and textiles. For more than 200 years Ashanti was an independent kingdom.

Ashby-de-la-Zouch Market town in Leicestershire, England, 26 km/16 mi NW of Leicester; population (1991) 11,000. It is the centre of an agricultural area. It was named after the La Zouche family who built the 15th-century castle, where Mary Queen of Scots was imprisoned 1569. The castle features in Walter Scott's novel *Ivanhoe* 1819.

Ashdod Deep-water port of Israel, on the Mediterranean 32 km/20 mi S of Tel-Aviv, which it superseded 1965; population (1994) 120,100. It stands on the site of the ancient Philistine stronghold of Ashkelon.

Asheville Textile town in the Blue Ridge Mountains of North Carolina, USA; population (1992) 62,800. Asheville was first settled 1794. It has the 19th-century Biltmore mansion, home of millionaire George W Vanderbilt, and the birthplace and home of the writer Thomas Wolfe.

Ashford Market town in Kent, England, on the river Stour, SW of Canterbury; population (1991) 52,000. It expanded in the 1980s as a new commercial and industrial centre (railway works, light engineering, brewing) for SE England, and has continued to expand because of the Channel Tunnel.

Ashgabat formerly *Ashkhabad* Capital of Turkmenistan; population (1990) 407,000. The spelling was changed 1992 to reflect the Turkmen origin of the name. Industries include glass, carpets ('Bukhara' carpets are made here), and cotton; the spectacular natural setting has been used by the filmmaking industry.

Ashland City in NE Kentucky, USA, on the Ohio River, E of Louisville; population (1990) 23,600. Industries include chemicals, coal, oil, limestone, coke, petroleum products, steel, clothing, and leather goods. Ashland was settled 1786. It developed as an iron and steel centre.

Ashmore and Cartier Islands Group of uninhabited Australian islands comprising Middle, East, and West Islands (the Ashmores), and Cartier Island, in the Indian Ocean, about 190 km/120 mi off the NW coast of Australia; area 5 sq km/2 sq mi. They were transferred to the authority of Australia by Britain 1931. Formerly administered as part of the Northern Territory, they became a separate territory 1978. West Ashmore has an automated weather station. Ashmore reef was declared a national nature reserve 1983.

Ashtabula   City and port on Lake Erie, in Ohio, midwestern USA; population (1990) 21,800. It has steel, leather, and agricultural processing industries.

Ashton under Lyne   Town in Greater Manchester, England; population (1994 est) 177,000. Industries include rubber, textiles, tobacco, light engineering, plastics, leather goods, footwear, and cotton milling.

Asia   Largest of the continents, occupying one-third of the total land surface of the world. The origin of the name is unknown, though it seems probable that it was at first used with a restricted local application, gradually extended to the whole continent.

area   44,000,000 sq km/17,000,000 sq mi

largest cities   (population over 5 million) Tokyo, Shanghai, Osaka, Beijing, Seoul, Calcutta, Bombay, Jakarta, Bangkok, Tehran, Hong Kong, Delhi, Tianjin, Karachi

features   Mount Everest, at 8,848 m/29,029 ft is the world's highest mountain; the Dead Sea at −400 m/−1,312 ft is the world's lowest point below sea level; rivers (over 3,200 km/ 2,000 mi) include Chiang Jiang (Yangtze), Huang He (Yellow River), Ob-Irtysh, Amur, Lena, Mekong, Yenisey; lakes (over 18,000 sq km/7,000 sq mi) include the Caspian Sea (the largest lake in the world), the Aral Sea, Lake Baikal (largest freshwater lake in Eurasia), Balkhash; deserts include the Gobi, Takla Makan, Syrian Desert, Arabian Desert, Negev

physical   lying in the E hemisphere, Asia extends from the Arctic Circle to just over 10° S of the Equator. The Asian mainland, which forms the greater part of the Eurasian continent, lies entirely in the N hemisphere and stretches from Cape Chelyubinsk at its N extremity to Cape Piai at the S tip of the Malay Peninsula. From Dezhneva Cape in the E, the mainland extends W over more than 165° longitude to Cape Baba in Turkey.

Asia Minor   Historical name for ◊Anatolia, the Asian part of Turkey.

Asian Republics, Central   See ◊Central Asian Republics.

Asmara   or *Asmera* Capital of Eritrea; 64 km/40 mi SW of Massawa on the Red Sea; population (1991) 367,100. Products include beer, clothes, and textiles. It has a naval school. The population is half Christian and half Muslim.

Asnières   Northwestern suburb of Paris, France, on the left bank of the river Seine; population (1990) 72,200. It is a boating centre and pleasure resort.

Aspen   Town in W central Colorado, on the Roaring Fork River, lying at an altitude of 2,417 m/7,930 ft; population (1991) 3,700. Established as a silver-mining town in the 1880s, Aspen now offers winter skiing and summer river rafting and is a cultural centre with an annual music festival.

Assam   State of NE India
area   78,438 sq km/30,285 sq mi
capital   Dispur
towns and cities   Guwahati, Dibrugarh, Silchar

industries   half of India's tea is grown and half its oil produced here; rice, jute, sugar, cotton, coal, petrochemicals, paper, cement

population   (1994 est) 24,200,000, including 12 million Assamese (Hindus), 5 million Bengalis (chiefly Muslim immigrants from Bangladesh), Nepalis, and 2 million indigenous people (Christian and traditional religions)

language   Assamese

history   a thriving region from 1000 BC; Assam migrants came from China and Myanmar (Burma). After Burmese invasion 1826, Britain took control and made Assam a separate province 1874; it was included in the Dominion of India, except for most of the Muslim district of Silhet, which went to Pakistan 1947. Ethnic unrest started in the 1960s when Assamese was declared the official language. After protests, the Gara, Khasi, and Jainitia tribal hill districts became the state of Meghalaya 1971; the Mizo hill district became the Union Territory of Mizoram 1972. There were massacres of Muslim Bengalis by Hindus 1983. In 1987 members of the Bodo ethnic group began fighting for a separate homeland. In the early 1990s the Marxist-militant United Liberation Front of Assam (ULFA), which had extorted payments from tea-exporting companies, spearheaded a campaign of separatist terrorist violence. Between November 1990 and March 1991 the ULFA was reportedly involved in 97 killings, mainly of Congress I politicians.

Assen   Capital of the province of Drenthe, Netherlands, 25 km/16 mi S of Groningen; population (1996) 53,300.

Assiniboine   River in Saskatchewan and Manitoba, S Canada; length about 1,070 km/665 mi. It rises in SE Saskatchewan and joins the Red River of the North at Winnipeg.

Assisi   Town in Umbria, Italy, 19 km/12 mi SE of Perugia; population (1989 est) 24,600. St Francis was born here and is buried in the Franciscan monastery, completed 1253. The churches of St Francis are adorned with frescoes by Giotto, Cimabue, and others. The town was severly damaged by two earthquakes which hit Italy in September 1997.

Assiut   Alternative transliteration of ◊Asyut, a city in Egypt.

Assuan   Alternative transliteration of ◊Aswan, a city in Egypt.

Assy   Plateau in Haute-Savoie, E France, 1,000 m/3,280 ft above sea level. The area has numerous sanatoriums. The church of Notre Dame de Toute Grâce, begun 1937 and consecrated 1950, is adorned with works by Braque, Chagall, Matisse, Derain, Rouault, and other artists.

Asti   Town in Piedmont, SE of Turin, Italy; population (district, 1992) 208,400. Asti province is famed for its sparkling wine. Other products include chemicals, textiles, and glass.

Asti   Province of N Italy in central ◊Piedmont region; capital Asti; area 1,510 sq km/583 sq mi; population (1992) 208,300.

Astrakhan   City in the Russian Federation, on the delta of the river Volga, capital of Astrakhan region; population

(1994) 512,000. In ancient times a Tatar capital, it became Russian 1556. It is the chief port for the Caspian fisheries.

Asturias Autonomous region of N Spain; area 10,600 sq km/4,092 sq mi; population (1991) 1,093,900. Half of Spain's coal comes from the mines of Asturias. Agricultural produce includes maize, fruit, and livestock. Oviedo and Gijón are the main industrial towns.

Asunción Capital and port of Paraguay, on the Paraguay River; population (1992) 502,400 (metropolitan area 637,700). It produces textiles, footwear, and food products.

Aswan Winter resort in Upper Egypt; population (1991) 215,000. It is near the ◊Aswan High Dam, built 1960–70, which keeps the level of the Nile constant throughout the year without flooding. It produces steel and textiles.

Aswan High Dam Major rock-fill dam across the Nile near Aswan, Egypt. It is 111 m/364 ft high and 3,600 m/11,815 ft long, with a volume of 42,600,000 cubic metres/55,809,000 cubic yards. Financed by the USSR, construction of the dam began 1960 and was completed 1970. It has the capacity to generate 2,100 megawatts of electricity.

Asyut Commercial centre in Upper Egypt, near the Nile, 322 km/200 mi S of Cairo; population (1992) 321,000. An ancient Graeco-Egyptian city, it has many tombs of 11th- and 12th-dynasty nobles.

Atacama Desert Desert in N Chile; area about 80,000 sq km/31,000 sq mi. There are mountains inland, and the coastal area is rainless and barren. The desert has silver and copper mines, and extensive nitrate deposits. The world's largest and most powerful telescope is being built at the Cerro Paranal Space Observatory, for the European Southern Observatory.

Atatürk Dam Dam on the river Euphrates, in the province of Gaziantep, S Turkey, completed 1989. The lake, 550 km/340 mi SE of Ankara, covers 815 sq km/315 sq mi (when full, it holds four times the annual flow of the Euphrates). In 1990 it was filled for the first time, submerging 25 villages, all of whose 55,000 inhabitants were relocated.

Athabasca Lake and river in Alberta and Saskatchewan, Canada, with large tar-sand deposits (source of the hydrocarbon mixture 'heavy oil') to the SW of the lake.

Athens (Greek *Athinai*) Capital city of Greece and of ancient Attica; population (1991) 784,100, metropolitan area (1991) 3,096,800. Situated 8 km/5 mi NE of its port of Piraeus on the Gulf of Aegina, it is built around the rocky hills of the Acropolis 169 m/555 ft and the Areopagus 112 m/368 ft, and is overlooked from the NE by the hill of Lycabettus, 277 m/ 909 ft high. It lies in the S of the central plain of Attica, watered by the mountain streams of Cephissus and Ilissus. It has less green space than any other European capital (4%) and severe air and noise pollution.

Athens City in NE Georgia, USA, on the Oconee River, NE of Atlanta; seat of Clarke County; population (1990) 45,700. Industries include cotton and electrical products. It was founded 1801 as seat of the University of Georgia (chartered 1785).

Athos Mountainous peninsula on the Macedonian coast of Greece. Its peak is 2,033 m/6,672 ft high. The promontory is occupied by a group of 20 Orthodox monasteries, inhabited by some 3,000 monks and lay brothers. A council of representatives from the monasteries runs the affairs of the peninsula as a self-governing republic under the protection of the Greek government.

Atlanta Capital and largest city of Georgia, USA, in the foothills of the Blue Ridge Mountains; population (1992) 394,850, metropolitan area (1992) 3,143,000. It is the headquarters of Coca-Cola, and there are Ford and Lockheed motor-vehicle and aircraft assembly plants. The CNN Center, headquarters of Cable News Network, is here. Originally named Terminus, Atlanta was settled 1837; the name was changed to Atlanta 1845. Atlanta hosted the 1996 Olympic Games.

Atlantic City Seaside resort on Absecon Island, New Jersey; population (1990) 38,000. Formerly a family resort, Atlantic City has become a centre for casino gambling, which was legalized 1978.

Atlantic Ocean Ocean lying between Europe and Africa to the E and the Americas to the W, probably named after the legendary island continent of Atlantis; area of basin 86,557,000 sq km/33,420,000 sq mi; including the Arctic Ocean and Antarctic seas, 106,200,000 sq km/41,000,000 sq mi. The average depth is 3,575 m/11,730 ft; greatest depth the Milwaukee Depth in the Puerto Rico Trench 8,648 m/ 28,374 ft. The *Mid-Atlantic Ridge*, of which the Azores, Ascension, St Helena, and Tristan da Cunha form part, divides it from N to S. Lava welling up from this central area annually increases the distance between South America and Africa. The North Atlantic is the saltiest of the main oceans and has the largest tidal range.

Atlas Mountains Mountain system of NW Africa, stretching 2,400 km/1,500 mi from the Atlantic coast of Morocco to the Gulf of Gabes, Tunisia, and lying between the Mediterranean on the N and the Sahara on the S. The highest peak is Mount Toubkal 4,167 m/13,670 ft.

Attica (Greek *Attiki*) Region of Greece comprising Athens and the district around it; area 3,381 sq km/1,305 sq mi; population (1991) 3,522,800. It is renowned for its language, art, and philosophical thought in Classical times. It is a prefecture of modern Greece with Athens as its capital.

Attleboro City in SE Massachusetts, USA, NW of New Bedford; population (1990) 38,400. Industries include jewellery, tools, silver products, electronics, and paper goods. Attleboro was settled 1669 and incorporated 1694.

Attock City in Punjab province, E Pakistan, near Rawalpindi; capital of Attock district; population (1981) 40,000. Under British rule, it was known as *Campbellpore*.

Aube River of NE France, a tributary of the Seine, length 248 km/155 mi; it gives its name to a *département*.

Aube *Département* in the ◊Champagne-Ardenne region of NE France; area 6,002 sq km/2,318 sq mi; population (1990) 289,466. The E part of Aube is drained by the River ◊Aube, and its W part by the Seine. It is at the centre of the

Champagne wine-producing region. The principal towns are the capital, ◊Troyes, Bar-sur-Aube, and Nogent-sur-Seine. Industry is based on the quarrying of chalk, potter's clay, building stone, and limestone, and on cotton-spinning and weaving.

Auburn City in SW Maine, USA, on the Androscoggin River, W of Lewiston; seat of Androscoggin County; population (1990) 24,300. Industries include shoes, textiles, poultry, livestock, and bricks. Auburn was first settled 1786.

Aubusson Town in the *département* of Creuse, France. Its carpet and tapestry industries date from the 15th century.

Auch Capital of the French *département* of Gers, on the river Gers: population (1990) 25,000. It has footwear industries and trade in brandy, horses, and poultry. Auch is the seat of an archbishop, and has a Gothic cathedral.

Auckland Largest city in New Zealand, situated in N North Island; population (1993) 910,200. It fills the isthmus that separates its two harbours (Waitemata and Manukau), and its suburbs spread N across the Harbour Bridge. It is the country's chief port and leading industrial centre, having iron and steel plants, engineering, car assembly, textiles, food processing, sugar refining, and brewing. There was a small whaling settlement on the site in the 1830s, and Auckland was officially founded as New Zealand's capital 1840, remaining so until 1865. The university was founded 1882.

Auckland Islands Six uninhabited volcanic islands 480 km/300 mi S of South Island, New Zealand; area 60 sq km/23 sq mi.

Aude River in SE France, 210 km/130 mi long; it gives its name to a *département*. Carcassonne is the main town through which it passes.

Audenarde French form of ◊Oudenaarde, a town in Belgium.

Augrabies Falls Waterfalls in the Orange River, Northern Cape Province, South Africa; height 148 m/480 ft.

Augsburg Industrial city in Bavaria, Germany, at the confluence of the Wertach and Lech rivers, 52 km/32 mi NW of Munich; population (1993) 265,000. It is named after the Roman emperor Augustus, who founded it 15 BC.

Augusta City in E central Georgia, USA, on the Savannah River on the South Carolina border; seat of Richmond County; population (1990) 44,600. Industries include textiles and other cotton products and building materials. Established 1736 as Fort Augusta, an Indian trading post, it was the site of several battles during the American Revolution and served as Georgia's capital 1786–95.

Augusta Capital of Maine, USA, located in the SW part of the state, on the Kennebec River, NE of Lewiston and Auburn; population (1992) 21,800. Industries include cotton, timber, and textiles. Augusta was first settled 1754, and incorporated as Harrington 1797 and later the same year as Augusta. Industrialization followed the damming of the Kennebec River 1837.

Augustów Town in Białystok province, Poland, on the

Augustów canal between the rivers Vistula and Neman, 80 km/50 mi N of Białystok; population 20,000. Industries include wood, leather, and flour.

Aurich Town in the *Land* of Lower Saxony, Germany, on the Ems–Jade canal, 188 km/117 mi NW of Hannover; population (1994) 5,000. Electrical goods, clothing, and food are manufactured. Until 1744 Aurich was the seat of the rulers of East Friesland; the district then passed to Prussia.

Aurillac Capital of the French *département* of Cantal, on the river Jordanne; population (1990) 33,000. It has a livestock market. Historically, Aurillac was important for its monastic school.

Aurora City in NE Illinois, USA, on the Fox River, W of Chicago; population (1992) 105,900. Industries include transportation equipment, glass, and chemicals. Aurora was founded as a trading post 1834 and was a pioneer in the use of electric streetlights.

Auschwitz (Polish *Oświęcim*) Town near Kraków in Poland, the site of one of the largest Nazi concentration camps in World War II.

Aust-Agder County of S Norway, bordering the ◊Skagerrak arm of the North Sea; area 9,212 sq km/3,557 sq mi; population (1995) 100,200. Nickel and iron ore are mined in the area. Horticulture and forestry are the main sources of income. The county town is Arendal.

Austin Capital of Texas, on the Colorado River; population (1992) 492,300. It is a centre for electronic and scientific research, and is the home of the University of Texas. Austin was founded 1838 and developed as a stop on the Chisholm cattle-drive trail in the 1860s.

Australasia and Oceania Two geographical terms: *Australasia* is applied somewhat loosely to the islands of the South Pacific, including Australia, New Zealand, and their adjacent islands, while *Oceania* is a general or collective name for the groups of islands in the S and central Pacific Ocean, comprising all those intervening between the SE shores of Asia and the W shores of America. The 10,000 or more Pacific Islands offer a great diversity of environments, from almost barren, waterless coral atolls to vast, continental islands.
area 8,500,000 sq km/3,300,000 sq mi (land area)
largest cities (population over 500,000) Sydney, Melbourne, Brisbane, Perth, Adelaide, Auckland
features the Challenger Deep in the Mariana Trench –11,034 m/–36,201 ft is the greatest known depth of sea in the world; Ayers Rock in Northern Territory, Australia, is the world's largest monolith; the Great Barrier Reef is the longest coral reef in the world; Mount Kosciusko 2,229 m/7,316 ft in New South Wales is the highest peak in Australia; Mount Cook 3,764 m/12,349 ft is the highest peak in New Zealand
physical Oceania can be broadly divided into groups of volcanic and coral islands on the basis of the ethnic origins of their inhabitants: Micronesia (Guam, Kiribati, Mariana, Marshall, Caroline Islands), Melanesia (Papua New Guinea, Vanuatu, New Caledonia, Fiji, Solomon Islands) and

Polynesia (Tonga, Samoa, Line Islands, Tuvalu, French Polynesia, Pitcairn); the highest point is Jaya, Papua New Guinea 5,030 m/16,502 ft; the lowest point is Lake Eyre, South Australia –16 m/–52 ft; the longest river is the Murray in SE Australia 2,590 km/1,609 mi; Australia is the largest island in the world. Most of the small islands are coral atolls, though some are of volcanic origin.

Australian Antarctic Territory Islands and territories S of 60° S, between 160° and 45° E longitude, excluding Adélie Land; area 6,044,000 sq km/2,333,590 sq mi of land and 75,800 sq km/29,259 sq mi of ice shelf. The population on the Antarctic continent is limited to research personnel.

Australian Capital Territory Territory ceded to Australia by New South Wales 1911 to provide the site of ◊Canberra, with its port at Jervis Bay, ceded 1915; area 2,400 sq km/926 sq mi; population (1994) 304,100.

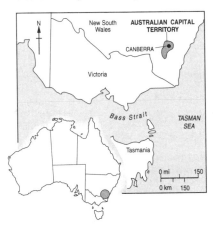

Australian Capital Territory

Austral Islands Alternative name for ◊Tubuai Islands, part of ◊French Polynesia.

Autun French town in the *département* of Saône-et-Loire, 80 km/50 mi NW of Mâcon, on the river Arroux; population (1990) 23,000. It has metallurgical, furniture, and oil-shale industries; tourism is important. Roman remains include a pyramid, a theatre, and two gates. There is also a cathedral, mainly of the 12th century.

Auvergne Ancient province of central France and modern region comprising the *départements* of Allier, Cantal, Haute-Loire, and Puy-de-Dôme; capital Clermont-Ferrand; area 26,013 sq km/10,044 sq mi; population (1990) 1,321,200. It is a mountainous area, composed chiefly of volcanic rocks in several masses. Industries include cattle, wheat, wine, and cheese.

history a Roman province, it was named after the ancient Gallic Avenni tribe whose leader, Vercingetorix, led a revolt against the Romans 52 BC. In the 14th century the Auvergne was divided into a duchy, dauphiny, and countship. The duchy and dauphiny were united by the dukes of Bourbon

before being confiscated by Francis I 1527. The countship united with France 1615.

Auxerre Capital of Yonne *département*, France, 170 km/106 mi SE of Paris, on the river Yonne; population (1990) 40,600. The Gothic cathedral, founded 1215, has exceptional sculptures and stained glass.

Avellino Province of S Italy in central ◊Campania region; capital Avellino (population (1990) 55,800); area 2,802 sq km/1,082 sq mi; population (1992) 440,100.

Avenches Commune of Switzerland situated in a detached part of the canton of Vaud, 30 km/19 mi E of Bern; population (1995) 2,600. It was the ancient capital of ◊Helvetia.

Avernus Circular lake, near Naples, Italy. Because it formerly gave off fumes that killed birds, it was thought by the Romans to be the entrance to the lower world.

Aveyron River in S France; length 250 km/155 mi. The Aveyron rises in the Lozère *département* and flows through Aveyron and Tarn-et-Garonne *départements* to join the river ◊Garonne near Moissac.

Aveyron *Département* in the Midi-Pyrénées region of France; area 8,734 sq km/3,372 sq mi; population (1990) 138,400. The region is mountainous with the rivers Lot, Tarn, and Aveyron flowing through it. In the N it is penetrated by spurs of the Cantal mountains, and in the S by spurs of the Cévennes. The land is used primarily for stock rearing, but some cereals, vines, tobacco, and fruit trees are cultivated. Textiles, iron, and cheese are manufactured. Hydroelectric plants provide some power for the region. The principal towns are Rodez (the capital), Millau, and Villefranche-de-Rouergue.

Aviemore Winter sports centre, in the Highlands, Scotland, SE of Inverness among the Cairngorm Mountains.

Avignon City in Provence, France, capital of Vaucluse *département*, on the river Rhône NW of Marseilles; population (1990) 89,400. An important Gallic and Roman city, it has a 12th-century bridge (only half still standing), a 13th-century cathedral, 14th-century walls, and the Palais des Papes, built during the residence here of the popes, comprised of Le Palais Vieux (1334–42) to the N, and Le Palais Nouveau (1342–52) to the S. Avignon was papal property 1348–1791.

Ávila City in Spain, 90 km/56 mi NW of Madrid; population (1986) 45,000. It is the capital of a province of the same name. It has the remains of a Moorish castle, a Gothic cathedral, and the convent and church of St Teresa, who was born here. The medieval town walls are among the best preserved in Europe.

Ávila Province of W central Spain in S Castilla-León autonomous community; capital Ávila; area 8,047 sq km/3,107 sq mi; population (1995) 176,800. It is mountainous with fertile valleys. Cattle is raised, and timber, cereals, olives, and chestnuts are produced.

Avilés Town in the autonomous community of ◊Asturias, N Spain; population (1995) 88,500. There are coal and copper mines nearby, and industries include iron and steel, zinc, aluminium, and glass.

Avon Former county of SW England, formed 1974 from the city and county of Bristol and parts of NE Somerset and SW Gloucestershire. It was abolished 1996 when the unitary authorities of Bristol, Bath and North East Somerset, North Somerset, and South Gloucestershire were created.

Avon Any of several rivers in England and Scotland. The Avon in Warwickshire is associated with Shakespeare.

Avranches French town in the *département* of Manche, Normandy; population (1990) 9,500. Situated on a hill, the town overlooks the estuary of the river Sée. Horse breeding, leatherwork, and fishing are the main industries.

Awash River that rises to the S of Addis Ababa in Ethiopia and flows NE to Lake Abba on the frontier with Djibouti; length 800 km/500 mi. Although deep inside present-day Ethiopia, the Awash River was considered by Somalis to mark the E limit of Ethiopian sovereignty prior to the colonial division of Somaliland in the 19th century.

Awe Longest (37 km/23 mi) of the Scottish freshwater lochs, in Argyll and Bute, SE of Oban. It is drained by the river Awe into Loch Etive.

Axholme, Isle of Area of 2,000 ha/5,000 acres in North Lincolnshire, England, bounded by the Trent, Don, Idle, and Torne rivers, where a form of 'medieval' open-field strip farming is still practised. The largest village, Epworth, is the birthplace of the Methodist John Wesley.

Ayacucho Capital of a province of the same name in the Andean Mountains of central Peru; population (1993) 105,900. The last great battle against Spanish troops in the war of independence was fought near here Dec 1824.

Ayers Rock (Aboriginal *Uluru*) Vast ovate mass of pinkish rock in Northern Territory, Australia; 335 m/1,110 ft high and 9 km/6 mi around. For the Aboriginals, whose paintings decorate its caves, it has magical significance.

Ayot St Lawrence Village in Hertfordshire, England, where Shaw's Corner (home of the playwright George Bernard Shaw) is preserved.

Ayr Town in South Ayrshire, SW Scotland, at the mouth of the river Ayr; population (1991) 48,000. Auld Bridge was built in the 5th century, the New Bridge 1788 (rebuilt 1879). Ayr has associations with Robert Burns. Industries include fishing, machinery, woollens, silicon chips, and aircraft.

Ayrshire Former county of SW Scotland, with a 113 km/70 mi coastline on the Firth of Clyde. From 1975–1996 the major part was merged into Strathclyde Region.

AZ Abbreviation for the state of ◊Arizona, USA.

Azerbaijan, Iranian Two provinces of NW Iran, *Eastern Azerbaijan* (capital Tabriz), population (1991) 3,278,700, and *Western Azerbaijan* (capital Orúmiyeh), population (1991) 2,284,200. Azerbaijanis in Iran, as in the Republic of Azerbaijan, are mainly Shi'ite Muslim ethnic Turks, descendants of followers of the Khans from the Mongol Empire.

Azores Group of nine islands in the N Atlantic, belonging to Portugal; area 2,247 sq km/867 sq mi; population (1991) 237,800. They are outlying peaks of the Mid-Atlantic Ridge and are volcanic in origin. The capital is Ponta Delgada on the main island, São Miguel.

Azov (Russian *Azovskoye More*) Inland sea of Europe forming a gulf in the NE of the Black Sea, between Ukraine and Russia; area 37,555 sq km/14,500 sq mi. Principal ports include Rostov-na-Donu, Kerch, and Taganrog. Azov is a good source of freshwater fish.

Baabda Capital of the province of Jebel Lubnan in central Lebanon, SE of Beirut. It is the site of the country's presidential palace.

Babalegi Industrial township in North-West Province, South Africa, established 1969. It is 40 km/25 mi from Pretoria.

Bāb el Mandab Strait that joins the Red Sea and the Gulf of Aden, and separates Arabia and Africa. The name, meaning 'gate of tears', refers to its currents.

Babi Yar Ravine near Kiev, Ukraine, where more than 100,000 people (80,000 Jews; the others were Poles, Russians, and Ukrainians) were killed by the Nazis 1941. The site was ignored until the Soviet poet E Yevtushenko wrote a poem called 'Babi Yar' 1961 in protest at plans for a sports centre on the site.

Babruysk City in Belarus, on the Beresina River; population (1990) 223,000. Industries include timber, machinery, tyres, and chemicals.

Bacău Industrial city in Romania, 250 km/155 mi NE of Bucharest, on the river Bistrita; population (1993) 207,000. It is the capital of Bacău county, a leading oil-producing region.

Badajoz City in Extremadura, Spain, on the Portuguese frontier; population (1994) 130,000. It has a 13th-century cathedral and ruins of a Moorish castle. Badajoz has often been besieged and was stormed by the Duke of Wellington 1812 with the loss of 5,000 British troops.

Badajoz Province of W Spain in S ◊Extremadura autonomous community; capital Badajoz; area 21,657 sq km/ 8,362 sq mi; population (1995) 675,600.

Bad Ems or *Ems* Town and spa in the Rhineland-Palatinate, Germany, on the river Lahn, 17 km/10 mi S of Koblenz; population (1994) 10,200. The peak years of the spa were 1875–1914.

Baden Town in Aargau canton, Switzerland, near Zurich; at an altitude of 388 m/1,273 ft; population (1990) 14,780. Its hot sulphur springs and mineral waters have been visited since Roman times.

Baden-Baden Black Forest spa in Baden-Württemberg, Germany; population (1991) 52,500. Fashionable in the 19th century, it is now a conference centre.

Baden-bei-Wien Austrian spa town in the province of Lower Austria, 25 km/16 mi S of Vienna; population (1995) 23,500. It has sulphur springs, and was known to the Romans as Aquae Panoniae.

Baden-Württemberg Administrative region (German *Land*) of Germany
area 35,752 sq km/13,804 sq mi
capital Stuttgart
towns and cities Mannheim, Karlsruhe, Freiburg, Heidelberg, Heilbronn, Pforzheim, Ulm
physical Black Forest; Rhine boundary S and W; source of the river Danube
industries wine, jewellery, watches, clocks, musical instruments, textiles, chemicals, iron, steel, electrical equipment, surgical instruments
population (1995) 10,319,400
history formed 1952 (following a plebiscite) by the merger of the *Länder* Baden, Württemberg-Baden, and Württemberg-Hohenzollern.

Bad Godesburg Southeastern suburb of ◊Bonn, Germany, formerly a spa, and the meeting place of Chamberlain and Hitler before the Munich Agreement 1938.

Bad Hersfeld City and spa for liver and diabetic cures in Hessen, Germany, on the river Fulda, 115 km/71 mi NE of Wiesbaden; population (1994) 31,200. Textiles (Trevira), cables, and carpets are manufactured here. Festival plays are held annually in Bad Hersfeld's 11th-century abbey church.

Bad Kreuznach City and spa in Germany; see Kreuznach.

Bad Nauheim Town and spa in Germany; see Nauheim.

Baeza Town in the province of Jaén, S Spain; population (1995) 15,900. It was a flourishing city under the Moors, but was sacked 1228 by the Castilians. There is a Gothic cathedral and several fine churches. The town had a university 1533–1807.

Baffin Island Island in the Northwest Territories, Canada
area 507,450 sq km/195,875 sq mi
features largest island in the Canadian Arctic; mountains rise above 2,000 m/6,000 ft, and there are several large lakes. The northernmost part of the strait separating Baffin Island from Greenland forms Baffin Bay, the S end is Davis Strait.
It is named after William Baffin, who carried out research here 1614 during his search for the ◊Northwest Passage.

Baghdad Historic city and capital of Iraq, on the river Tigris; population (1987) 3,850,000. Industries include oil refining, distilling, tanning, tobacco processing, and the manufacture of textiles and cement. Founded 762, it became Iraq's capital 1921. During the Gulf War 1991, the UN coalition forces bombed it in repeated air raids and destroyed much of the city.

Bago or *Pegu* City in S Myanmar on the river Pegu, NE of Yangon; population (1983) 254,762. It was founded 573 and was once an important seaport. It is the site of the celebrated Shwemawdaw pagoda, 99 m/324 ft high and said to contain two of the Buddha's hairs. It was almost completely destroyed by an earthquake 1930 and was rebuilt after World War II. The town also contains the statue of the Reclining Buddha, 55 m/181 ft long.

Baguio Summer resort on Luzon island in the Philippines, 200 km/125 mi N of Manila, 1,370 m/4,500 ft above sea level; population (1990) 156,000. It is the official summer residence of the Philippine president.

Bahawalpur City in the Punjab, Pakistan; population (1981) 178,000. Once the capital of a former state of Bahawalpur, it is now an industrial city producing textiles and soap. It has a university, established 1975.

Bahia State of E Brazil
area 561,026 sq km/216,556 sq mi
capital Salvador
physical low coastal plain rising to central plateau in W, crossed by São Francisco River
industries oil, chemicals, agriculture, sugar cane, tobacco, cotton, cacao; industrial diamonds are mined
population (1991) 11,868,000.

Bahía Blanca Port in S Argentina, on the river Naposta, 5 km/3 mi from its mouth; population (1991) 271,500. It is a major distribution centre for wool and food processing. The naval base of Puerto Belgrano is here.

Baia Mare Industrial town and capital of Maramures county, N Romania, 100 km/63 mi N of Cluj Napoca; population (1993) 150,000. Chemicals, metals, machinery, food, and fertilizers are produced. The nearby area is rich in ores containing gold, silver, copper, lead, zinc, and uranium.

Baikal, Lake (Russian *Baykal Ozero*) Freshwater lake in S Siberia, Russia, the largest in Asia, and the eighth largest in the world (area 31,499 sq km/12,162 sq mi); also the deepest in the world (up to 1,640 m/5,700 ft). Fed by more than 300 rivers, it is drained only by the Lower Angara. It has sturgeon fisheries and is rich in fauna.

Baile Atha Cliath Official Gaelic name of ◊Dublin, capital of the Republic of Ireland, from 1922.

Bailén Town in the province of Jaén, S Spain; population (1995) 17,800. During the Peninsular War, the French suffered their first serious reverse against the Spaniards here in 1808.

Bailleul French town in the *département* of Nord, 25 km/16 mi NW of Lille. The chief industries are the manufacture of linen and lace. The town hall dates from the 15th century. The town was largely destroyed during World War I and was rebuilt.

Baja Market town in S Hungary, near the river Danube, 96 km/60 mi SW of Kecskemét. Industries include engineering, chemicals and textiles.

Baja California Mountainous peninsula that forms the twin NW states of Lower (Spanish *baja*) California, Mexico; ◊Baja California Norte in the N, and ◊Baja California Sur in the S.

Baja California Norte State of NW Mexico, occupying the N part of Baja California peninsula between the Gulf of California and the Pacific; area 70,113 sq km/27,071 sq mi; population (1995 est) 2,108,100. Its capital is Mexicali. The main occupations are fishing, and mining for silver, gold, lead, copper, iron ore, and kaolin.

Baja California Sur State of NW Mexico, occupying the S part of the Baja California peninsula between the Gulf of California and the Pacific; area 73,677 sq km/28,447 sq mi; population (1995 est) 375,450. Its capital is La Paz. The main products are cotton, olives, and sugar cane. There are fish packing plants, salt works, and copper mines. It attracts many US tourists for fishing, whale-watching (grey whales winter here), swimming, and sunbathing.

Bakersfield City in S California, USA, NE of Santa Barbara, on the Kern River; the seat of Kern County; population (1992) 188,000. It has featured oil wells and oil products since oil was first discovered there 1899.

Bakhtaran formerly (until 1980) *Kermanshah* Capital of Bakhtaran province, NW Iran; population (1986) 624,100. The province (area 23,700 sq km/9,148 sq mi; population 1,463,000) is on the Iraqi border and is mainly inhabited by Kurds. Industries include oil refining, carpets, and textiles.

Bakony Mountains or *Bakony Forest*, (German *Bakonyer Wald)* Wooded range in Hungary, N of Lake Balaton and SW of Budapest. It is an outlying section of the E ◊Alps, separated from the Carpathian Mountains by the river Danube. The highest point is Köris-hegy (704 m/2,347 ft). The mountains hold mineral resources (bauxite, manganese, coal), and the S-facing slopes are suitable for vineyards. The chief town is the historic Veszprém.

Baku Capital city of the Republic of Azerbaijan, industrial port (oil refining) on the Caspian Sea; population (1993) 1,700,000. It is a major oil centre and is linked by pipelines with Batumi on the Black Sea. In January 1990 there were violent clashes between the Azeri majority and the Armenian minority, and Soviet troops were sent to the region; over 13,000 Armenians subsequently fled from the city. In March 1992, opposition political forces sponsored protests in the city that led to the resignation of President Mutalibov.

Bala Lake (Welsh *Llyn Tegid)* Lake in Gwynedd, N Wales, about 6.4 km/4 mi long and 1.6 km/1 mi wide. Bala Lake has a unique primitive species of fish, the gwyniad (a form of whitefish), a protected species from 1988.

Balaton, Lake (German *Plattensee)* Lake in W Hungary, S of the Bakony Mountains. It is the largest freshwater lake in central Europe, 77 km/48 mi long and covering 635 sq km/ 245 sq mi. Its waters drain into the river Danube. Vineyards cover the hilly N shores, but the S shore is generally flat. Fruit and wine are produced in the surrounding region, and there are numerous lakeside holiday resorts.

Bâle French form of Basle or ◊Basel, a city in Switzerland.

Balearic Islands (Spanish *Baleares)* Group of Mediterranean islands forming an autonomous region of Spain; including ◊Mallorca, ◊Menorca, ◊Ibiza, Cabrera, and Formentera
area 5,000 sq km/1,930 sq mi
capital Palma de Mallorca
industries figs, olives, oranges, wine, brandy, coal, iron, slate; tourism is crucial

Balearic Islands

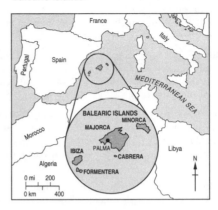

population (1991) 709,100
history a Roman colony from 123 BC, the Balearic Islands were an independent Moorish kingdom 1009–1232; they were conquered by Aragón 1343.

Bali Island of Indonesia, E of Java, one of the Sunda Islands; area 5,800 sq km/2,240 sq mi; population (1990) 2,777,800. The capital is Denpasar. The island features volcanic mountains. Industries include gold and silver work, woodcarving, weaving, copra, salt, coffee, and tourism, with 1 million tourists a year (1990); arts include Balinese dancing, music, and drama. Bali's Hindu culture goes back to the 7th century; the Dutch gained control of the island by 1908.

Balikesir City in NW Turkey, capital of Aydin province; population (1990) 170,600. There are silver mines nearby.

Balikpapan Port in Indonesia, on the E coast of S Kalimantan, Borneo; population (urban area, 1990 est) 1,200,000. It is an oil-refining centre.

Bali Strait Narrow strait between the two islands of Bali and Java, Indonesia. On 19–20 February 1942 it was the scene of a naval action between Japanese and Dutch forces that served to delay slightly the Japanese invasion of Java.

Balkan Mountains (Bulgarian *Stara Planina*, ancient *Haemus)* Range of mountains in central Europe, extending 603 km/377 mi E–W through central Bulgaria from the Black Sea to Yugoslavia, about 25–40 km/16–25 mi in breadth. The highest peak is Mount Botev (2,376 m/7,920 ft). Its chief crossing, the Šipka Pass, runs from Veliko Turnovo S to Kazanlúk.

Balkans (Turkish 'mountains') Peninsula of SE Europe, stretching into Slovenia between the Adriatic and Aegean seas, comprising Albania, Bosnia-Herzegovina, Bulgaria, Croatia, Greece, Romania, the part of Turkey in Europe, and Yugoslavia. It is joined to the rest of Europe by an isthmus 1,200 km/750 mi wide between Rijeka on the W and the mouth of the Danube on the Black Sea to the E. Ethnic diversity and interfighting have made the Balkans a byword for political dissention.

Balkhash City on the N shore of Lake Balkhash in Kazakhstan; population (1985) 112,000. It was founded 1928. Chief industries include copper mining and salt extraction.

Balkhash Salt lake in Kazakhstan; area 18,421 sq km/ 7,112 sq mi. It is 600 km/375 mi long and receives several rivers, but has no outlet. It is very shallow and is frozen throughout the winter.

Ballarat Town in Victoria, Australia; population (1993) 81,200. It was founded in the 1851 gold rush, and the mining village and workings have been restored for tourists. The Eureka Stockade miners' revolt took place here 1854.

Ballinasloe Town in Galway, Republic of Ireland; population (1991) 5,800. Industries include limestone quarrying, footwear, bonemeal, and electrical equipment. The annual horse fair in October is the largest in Ireland.

Balmoral Castle Residence of the British royal family in Scotland on the river Dee, 10.5 km/61/2 mi NE of Braemar, Grampian region. The castle is dominated by a square tower and circular turret rising 30 m/100 ft. It was rebuilt 1853–55 by Prince Albert, who bought the estate in 1852.

Baltic Exchange (in full the Baltic Mercantile and Shipping Exchange) Market in London mainly for the chartering of freight. Most of the world's chartering of freight is carried out here, where cargo space on ships and aeroplanes is bought and sold. It originated in the 17th century when merchants and ships' captains met in coffee houses to organize cargoes, and was concentrated in the Baltic coffee house 1810. It was destroyed by an IRA bomb 1992.

Baltic Sea Large shallow arm of the North Sea, extending NE from the narrow Skagerrak and Kattegat, between Sweden and Denmark, to the Gulf of Bothnia between Sweden and Finland. Its coastline is 8,000 km/5,000 mi long, and its area, including the gulfs of Riga, Finland, and Bothnia, is 382,000 sq km/147,500 sq mi. Its shoreline is shared by Denmark, Germany, Poland, the Baltic States, Russia, Finland, and Sweden.

Baltic Sea

Baltic States Collective name for the states of Estonia, Latvia, and Lithuania, former constituent republics of the USSR (from 1940). They regained independence Sept 1991.

Baltimore Industrial port and largest city in Maryland, USA, on the W shore of Chesapeake Bay, NE of Washington DC; population (1992) 726,100; metropolitan area (1992) 2,434,000. Industries include shipbuilding, oil refining, food processing, and the manufacture of steel, chemicals, and aerospace equipment. Baltimore dates from 1729 and was incorporated 1797. It is the seat of Johns Hopkins University.

Baltistan Region in the Karakoram range of NE Kashmir, held by Pakistan since 1949. It is the home of Balti Muslims of Tibetan origin. The chief town is Skardu, but Ghyari is of greater significance to Muslims as the site of a mosque built by Sayyid Ali Hamadani, a Persian who brought the Shia Muslim religion to Baltistan in the 14th century.

Baluchistan Mountainous desert area, comprising a province of Pakistan, part of the Iranian province of Sistán and Balúchestan, and a small area of Afghanistan. The Pakistani province has an area of 347,200 sq km/134,019 sq mi and a population (1993 est) of 6,520,000; its capital is Quetta. Sistán and Balúchestan has an area of 181,600 sq km/70,098 sq mi and a population (1986) of 1,197,000; its capital is Zahedan. The port of Gwadar in Pakistan is strategically important, situated on the Indian Ocean and the Strait of Hormuz. The common religion of the Baluch (or Baluchi) people is Islam, and they speak Baluchi, a member of the Iranian branch of the Indo-European language family. In the drier areas they make use of tents, moving when it becomes too arid. Although they practise nomadic pastoralism, many are settled agriculturalists.

Bamako Capital and port of Mali on the river Niger; population (1992) 746,000. It produces pharmaceuticals, chemicals, textiles, tobacco, and metal products.

Bamberg City in Bavaria, Germany, on the river Regnitz; population (1985) 70,400. The economy is based on engineering and the production of textiles, carpets, and electrical goods. It has an early 13th-century Romanesque cathedral.

Banaba formerly *Ocean Island* Island in the Republic of Kiribati.

Banaras Alternative transliteration of ◊Varanasi, a holy Hindu city in Uttar Pradesh, India.

Banbury Town in Oxfordshire, England, on the river Cherwell; population (1991) 39,900. Industries include car components, electrical goods, aluminium, food processing, and printing. The *Banbury Cross* of the nursery rhyme was destroyed by the Puritans 1602, but replaced 1858. *Banbury cakes* are criss-cross pastry cases with a mince-pie-style filling.

Banca Alternative form of the Indonesian island ◊Bangka.

Bandar-e 'Abbas Port and winter resort in Iran on the Strait of Hormuz, Persian Gulf; population (1991) 250,000.

Formerly called Gombroon, it was renamed and made prosperous by Shah Abbas I (1571–1629). It is a naval base.

Bandar Seri Begawan (formerly (until 1970) *Brunei Town*)Capital and largest town of Brunei, 14 km/9 mi from the mouth of the Brunei River; population (1992) 55,000. Industries include oil refining and construction.

Bandar Shah Port in Iran on the Caspian Sea, and N terminus of the Trans-Iranian railway.

Bandung Commercial city and capital of Jawa Barat (West Java) province on the island of Java, Indonesia; population (1990) 2,026,900. Bandung is the third-largest city in Indonesia and was the administrative centre when the country was the Netherlands East Indies.

Banff Resort in Alberta, Canada, 100 km/62 mi NW of Calgary; population (1991) 5,700. It is a centre for Banff National Park (Canada's first, founded 1885) in the Rocky Mountains. Industries include brewing and iron founding.

Banffshire Former county of NE Scotland, from 1975–96 in Grampian Region; now in Aberdeenshire.

Bangalore Capital of Karnataka state, S India; population (1991) 4,087,000. Industries include electronics, aircraft and machine-tools construction, and coffee.

Banghazi Alternative form of ◊Benghazi, Libya.

Bangka or *Banka* or *Banca* Indonesian island off the E coast of Sumatra; area 12,000 sq km/4,600 sq mi. The capital is Pangkalpinang. It is one of the world's largest producers of tin.

Bangkok (Thai *Krung Thep* 'City of Angels') Capital and port of Thailand, on the river Chao Phraya; population (1993) 5,572,700. Products include paper, ceramics, cement, textiles, aircraft, and silk. It is the headquarters of the Southeast Asia Treaty Organization (SEATO).

Bangor Resort town in County Down, N Ireland, on the shore of Belfast Lough; population 52,400 (1991). It is the site of a famous missionary abbey of the Celtic church founded by St Comgall 555 and sacked by the Danes in the 9th century. The abbey was the home of St Columbanus and St Gall. Bangor's Seafront Developers Scheme includes the largest marina in Ireland.

Bangor Cathedral city in Gwynedd, N Wales, on the Menai Strait; population (1981) 12,300. The cathedral was begun 1495. Industries include chemicals, electrical goods, and engineering. Slate from Penrhyn quarries is exported.

Bangui Capital and port of the Central African Republic, on the river Ubangi; population (1988) 597,000. Industries include beer, cigarettes, office machinery, and timber and metal products.

Banja Luka 'Baths of St Luke' Town in Bosnia-Herzegovina, situated on the river Vrbas; population (1991) 143,000. It is a commercial and manufacturing centre. The town dates from Roman times. It has a spa, is the seat of Roman Catholic and Orthodox bishops, and has several mosques. It lies at the centre of Bosnian Serb territory.

Banjarmasin River port in Indonesia, on the island of Borneo; capital of Kalimantan Selatan province; population (1990) 443,700. It exports rubber, timber, and precious stones.

Banjul Capital and chief port of Gambia, on an island at the mouth of the river Gambia; population of urban area (1993) 228,200; city (1993) 42,300. Established 1816 as a settlement for freed slaves, it was known as Bathurst until 1973.

Banka Alternative form of ◊Bangka, an Indonesian island.

Banská-Bystrica (German *Neusohl*, Hungarian *Beszterczebanya*) Industrial town (textiles) in the Slovak Republic, on the river Hron, 160 km/100 mi NE of Bratislava; population (1991) 177,600. It is the capital of the Central Slovakia region, and has Gothic churches.

Baranof Island Island in the Alexander Archipelago in the Gulf of Alaska, SE Alaska; area 4,162 sq km/1,607 sq mi. The chief town on the island is the fishing and naval port of Sitka. Fishing and timber are important industries.

Barbican, the Arts and residential complex in the City of London. The Barbican Arts Centre (1982) contains theatres, cinemas, and exhibition and concert halls. The architects were Powell, Chamberlin, and Bon.

Barbuda One of the islands that form the state of Antigua and Barbuda.

Barcelona Capital, industrial city (textiles, engineering, chemicals), and port of Cataluña, NE Spain; population (1994) 1,631,000. As the chief centre of anarchism and Catalunian nationalism, it was prominent in the overthrow of the monarchy 1931 and was the last city of the republic to surrender to Franco 1939. In 1992 the city hosted the Summer Olympics.

Barcelona Province of NE Spain in W ◊Cataluña autonomous community; capital Barcelona; area 7,733 sq km/2,986 sq mi; population (1991) 4,654,400. It has a heavily urbanized coastline on the Mediterranean Sea. The N and centre of the province contain spurs of the Pyrenean mountain range. Agricultural products include fruit, wine, and olives.

Bardsey Island (Welsh *Ynys Enlli*) Former pilgrimage centre in Gwynedd, Wales, with a 6th-century ruined abbey.

Bareilly Industrial city in Uttar Pradesh, India; population (1991) 591,000. It was a Mogul capital 1657 and at the centre of the Indian Mutiny 1857.

Barents Sea Section of the E ◊Arctic Ocean which has oil and gas reserves. In World War II, the *Battle of the Barents Sea* 30 Dec 1942 was a humiliating defeat for the German Navy.

Bari Capital of Puglia region, S Italy, and industrial port on the Adriatic Sea; population (1992) 342,100. It is the site of Italy's first nuclear power station; the part of the town known as Tecnopolis is the Italian equivalent of ◊Silicon Valley.

Bari Province of SE Italy in ◊Puglia region; capital Bari; area 5,128 sq km/1,980 sq mi; population (1992) 1,535,700.

Barisal River port and capital city of Barisal region, S Bangladesh; population (1991) 173,000. It trades in jute, rice, fish, and oilseed.

Barking and Dagenham Outer London borough of E Greater London
features 15th–16th-century St Margaret's Church; Barking Abbey, with its 15th-century tower; Cross Keys Inn at Dagenham (about 1500); Quaker burial ground where Elizabeth Fry is buried
industries paint; telephone cables; pharmaceuticals
population (1991) 143,700.

Barkly Tableland Large-scale, open-range, cattle-raising area in Northern Territory and Queensland, Australia.

Bar-le-Duc French town, capital of the *département* of Meuse, on the river Ornain, and on the Marne–Rhine canal; population (1990) 18,600. The chief industries are the manufacture of hosiery and metal goods. Once capital of the duchy of Bar, the town has many old churches and mansions and the remains of the ducal palace.

Barletta Industrial port on the Adriatic Sea, Italy; population (1990) 88,200. It produces chemicals and soap; as an agriculture centre it trades in wine and fruit. There is a Romanesque cathedral built 1150 and a 13th-century castle.

Barnaul Industrial city in the Russian Federation, in S central Siberia, capital of Altai Territory; population (1994) 596,000. Industries include engineering, textiles, and timber. Founded 1738, it developed alongside the Turkestan–Siberian railway.

Barnet Outer London borough of NW Greater London. It includes the district of Hendon
features site of the Battle of Barnet 1471 in one of the Wars of the Roses; Lawrence Campe almshouses 1612; Hadley Woods; department for newspapers and periodicals of the British Library at Colindale; Metropolitan Police Training Centre and Royal Air Force Battle of Britain and Bomber Command museums in Hendon; Hampstead Garden Suburb
population (1991) 293,600.

Barnsley Town in South Yorkshire, England; population (1991) 220,900. It is an industrial town (iron and steel, glass, paper, carpets, cakes (Lyons) sports equipment (Dunlop-Slazenger) clothing,) on one of Britain's richest coal fields (the coal industry is in decline).

Baroda Former name of ◊Vadodara, a city in Gujarat, India.

Barossa Valley Wine-growing area in the Lofty mountain ranges, South Australia.

Barquisimeto Capital of Lara state, NW Venezuela; population (1990) 625,450; metropolitan area (1990) 745,400. It is the centre of a coffee-growing area and trades in coffee, cacao, sugar, and rum. Industries include flour milling, tanning, textiles, leather goods, biscuits, and cement.

Barra Southernmost island of the larger Outer Hebrides, Scotland; area 90 sq km/35 sq mi; population (1991) 1,250. It is separated from South Uist by the Sound of Barra. The main town is Castlebay. The main industries are fishing and tourism.

Barrancabermeja Port and oil-refining centre on the Magdalena River in the department of Santander, NE Colombia; population (1985) 137,000. It is a major outlet for oil from the De Mares fields, which are linked by pipeline to Cartagena on the Caribbean coast.

Barranquilla Seaport in N Colombia, on the Magdalena River; population (1994) 1,049,000. Products include chemicals, tobacco, textiles, furniture, and footwear.

Barren Lands/Grounds Tundra region of Canada, W of Hudson Bay.

Barrow Northernmost town in the USA, at Point Barrow, Alaska; the world's largest Inuit settlement; population (1990) 3,500. There is oil at nearby Prudhoe Bay, and the US Naval Research Laboratory is in the vicinity. Barrow developed as a whaling centre about 1900.

Barrow-in-Furness Port in Cumbria, England; population (1991) 73,100. Industries include shipbuilding, the manufacture of nuclear submarines, and those industries associated with offshore gasfields. Features include the ruins of Furness Abbey (1124).

Barrow Island Arid island and wildlife sanctuary in the Indian Ocean, between the Monte Bello Islands and the NW coast of Western Australia; area 202 sq km/78 sq mi. Its chief settlement is Wapet Camp.

Barry (Welsh *Y Barri*) Port and administrative head-quarters of Vale of Glamorgan, Wales; population (1991) 49,900. With *Barry Island*, it is a holiday resort.

Basel or *Basle* (French *Bâle*) Financial, commercial, and industrial city (dyes, vitamins, agrochemicals, dietary products, genetic products) in Switzerland; population (1994) 179,600. Basel was a strong military station under the Romans. In 1501 it joined the Swiss confederation and later developed as a centre for the Reformation.

Basel (French *Bâle*) or *Basle* Canton of Switzerland, divided into two half-cantons: Basel-Stadt (area 37 sq km/14 sq mi; population (1995) 195,800) and Basel-Land (area 428 sq km/ 165 sq mi; population (1995) 252,300; capital Liestal). Outside the city, the canton is primarily agricultural land, with fruit growing, dairy farming, and cattle breeding the main economic activities.

Bashkortostan (formerly Bashkiria) Autonomous republic of the Russian Federation
area 143,600 sq km/55,430 sq mi
capital Ufa
physical Ural Mountains on the E
industries minerals, oil, natural gas
population (1995) 4,080,000
language Russian, Bashkir.

Basildon Industrial town in Essex, England; population (1994 est) 101,000. It was designated a new town 1949 from several townships to accommodate overspill population from London. Industries include chemicals, clothing, printing, engineering, and tobacco.

Basilicata Mountainous region of S Italy, comprising the provinces of Potenza and Matera; area 9,992 sq km/ 3,858 sq mi; population (1995) 610,700. Its capital is Potenza. It was the Roman province of Lucania.

Basingstoke Industrial town (light engineering, scientific instruments, medical equipment, leather goods, agricultural machinery, electronics, printing, publishing) in Hampshire, England, 72 km/45 mi SW of London; population (1991) 77,800. It is the headquarters of the Automobile Association and Sun Life Insurance.

Basle Alternative form of ◊Basel, a city in Switzerland.

Basque Country (Basque *Euskal Herria*) Homeland of the Basque people in the W Pyrenees, divided by the Franco-Spanish border. The Spanish Basque Country (Spanish *País Vasco*) is an autonomous region (created 1979) of central N Spain, comprising the provinces of Vizcaya, Alava, and Guipúzcoa (Basque *Bizkaia, Araba*, and *Gipuzkoa*); area 7,300 sq km/2,818 sq mi; population (1991) 2,104,000. The French Basque Country (French *Pays Basque*) is the area occupied by Basques in the *département* of Pyrénées-Atlantiques. It is estimated that there are about 170,000 Basques in France. To Basque nationalists *Euskal Herria* also includes the autonomous Spanish province of Navarre.

Basque Provinces See ◊Basque Country.

Basra (Arabic *al-Basrah*) Principal port in Iraq, in the Shatt-al-Arab delta, 97 km/60 mi from the Persian Gulf, founded in the 7th century; population (1991) 850,000. Exports include wool, oil, cereal, and dates. Aerial bombing during the 1991 Gulf War destroyed much of the town's infrastructure and the port. A Shi'ite rebellion March 1991 was crushed by the Iraqi army, causing further death and destruction.

Bas-Rhin *Département* in the Alsace region of France, situated on the Rhine and the German frontier; area 4,787 sq km/1,848 sq mi; population (1990) 489,600. In the W are the Vosges mountains, covered with forests of beech and fir trees. The central plains are very fertile, producing cereals, tobacco, hops, beets, and fruit. Livestock is also farmed. Vines are grown on the hill slopes. The *département* has oil and manufacturing industries such as machinery, textiles, chemicals, and pottery. The principal towns are ◊Strasbourg (the capital), Haguenau, Molsheim, Saverne, Sélestat, and Wissembourg.

Bassein Port in Myanmar (formerly *Burma*), in the Irrawaddy delta, 125 km/78 mi from the sea; population (1983) 355,588. Bassein was founded in the 13th century.

Basse-Normandie or *Lower Normandy* Coastal region of NW France lying between Haute-Normandie and Brittany (Bretagne). It includes the *départements* of Calvados, Manche, and Orne; area 17,589 sq km/6,791 sq mi; population (1990) 1,391,300. Its capital is Caen. Apart from stock farming, dairy farming, and textiles, the area produces Calvados (apple brandy).

Basse-Terre Main island of the French West Indian island group of Guadeloupe; area 848 sq km/327 sq mi; population (1991) 149,900. It has an active volcano, Grande Soufrière, rising to 1,484 m/4,870 ft.

Basse-Terre Port on Basse-Terre, one of the Leeward Islands; population (1988) 14,000. It is the capital of the French overseas *département* of Guadeloupe.

Basseterre Capital and port of St Kitts and Nevis, in the Leeward Islands; population (1990 est) 15,000. Industries include data processing, rum, clothes, and electrical components.

Bass Rock Islet in the Firth of Forth, Scotland, about 107 m/350 ft high, with a lighthouse. It is a seabird sanctuary.

Bass Strait Channel between Australia and Tasmania, named after British explorer George Bass; oil was discovered here in the 1960s.

Bastia (Italian *bastiglia* 'fortress') Port and commercial centre in NE Corsica, France; capital of the *département* of Haute-Corse; population (1990) 38,700. Founded by the Genoese 1380, it was the capital of Corsica until 1811. There are several fine churches.

Basutoland Former name (to 1966) for Lesotho, a kingdom in S Africa.

Bataan Peninsula in Luzon, the Philippines, which was defended against the Japanese in World War II by US and Filipino troops under General MacArthur 1 Jan–9 April 1942. MacArthur was evacuated, but some 67,000 Allied prisoners died on the *Bataan Death March* to camps in the interior.

Batavia Former name (to 1949) for ◊Jakarta, capital of Indonesia on the island of Java.

Bath Historic city and administrative headquarters of Bath and North East Somerset unitary authority; population (1991) 78,700. Industries include printing, plastics, and engineering.

features Hot springs; the ruins of the baths after which it is named, as well as a great temple, are the finest Roman remains in Britain. Excavations 1979 revealed thousands of coins and 'curses', offered at a place which was thought to be the link between the upper and lower worlds. The Gothic Bath Abbey has an unusually decorated W front and fan vaulting. There is much 18th-century architecture, notably the Royal Crescent by John Wood. The Assembly Rooms 1771 were destroyed in an air raid 1942 but reconstructed 1963. The Bath Festival Orchestra is based here. The city of Bath is a World Heritage site.

history The Roman spa town of Aquae Sulis ('waters of Sul' – the British goddess of wisdom) was built in the first 20 years after the Roman invasion. In medieval times the hot springs were crown property, administered by the church, but the city was transformed in the 18th century to a fashionable spa, presided over by 'Beau' Nash. At his home here the astronomer William Herschel discovered Uranus 1781. Visitors included the novelists Tobias Smollett, Henry Fielding, and Jane Austen.

Bath and North East Somerset Unitary authority in SW England created 1996 from part of the former county of

Avon; administrative headquarters Bristol; population (1996) 158,700; area 351 sq km/136 sq mi.

Bathurst Town in New South Wales, on the Macquarie River, Australia; population (1991) 24,700. It dates from the 1851 gold rush.

Bathurst Port in New Brunswick, Canada, at the mouth of the Nepisiguit River; population (1991) 15,900. Industries include copper and zinc mining; products include paper and timber. It was founded by the French 1619 and called Nepisiguit. It became British 1755 and was renamed in the 1820s.

Bathurst Former name (to 1973) of ◊Banjul, the capital of the Gambia.

Baton Rouge Deep-water port on the Mississippi River, USA, the capital of Louisiana; population (1992) 224,700. Industries include oil refining, petrochemicals, and iron. The port has become one of the nation's largest. Baton Rouge was settled 1719 and was, successively, under French, British, Spanish, French, and Spanish rule before the residents rebelled against Spain 1819 and joined it to the USA.

Battersea District of the Inner London borough of Wandsworth on the S bank of the Thames. It has a park (including a funfair 1951–74), Battersea Dogs' Home (opened 1860) for strays, and Battersea Power Station (1937, designed by Sir Giles Gilbert Scott, with an Art Deco interior), closed 1983. A listed building from 1980, plans were approved 1996 for its conversion into a leisure complex.

Battle Town in Sussex, England, named after the Battle of Hastings, which took place here. There are remains of an abbey founded by William the Conqueror.

Battle Creek City in S Michigan, USA, directly E of Kalamazoo; population (1992) 54,400. It was settled 1831 and became a flour and woollen mill centre. It became known as the cereal capital of the world after J H Kellogg, W K Kellogg, and C W Post established dry cereal and grain factories here. Battle Creek was also a station on the Underground Railroad.

Batumi Black Sea port and capital of the autonomous republic of Adzhar, in Georgia; population (1991) 138,000. Main industries include oil refining, food canning, engineering, clothing, drug factories. There is a shipyard.

Bavaria (German *Bayern*) Administrative region (German *Land*) of Germany
area 70,551 sq km/27,240 sq mi
capital Munich
towns and cities Nürnberg, Augsburg, Würzburg, Regensburg
features largest of the German *Länder*; forms the Danube basin; festivals at Bayreuth and Oberammergau
industries beer, electronics, electrical engineering, optics, cars, aerospace, chemicals, plastics, oil refining, textiles, glass, toys
population (1995) 11,993,500
famous people Lucas Cranach, Franz Josef Strauss, Richard Strauss
religion 70% Roman Catholic, 26% Protestant

history the last king, Ludwig III, abdicated 1918, and Bavaria declared itself a republic.

Bay City Industrial city in Michigan, USA, on the Saginaw River; population (1990) 38,900. Industries include ship-building and engineering.

Bayern German name for ◊Bavaria, a region of Germany.

Bayeux Town in Normandy, N France. Its museum houses the Bayeux Tapestry. There is a 13th-century Gothic cathedral.

Bay of Pigs Inlet on the S coast of Cuba about 145 km/90 mi SW of Havana. It was the site of an unsuccessful invasion attempt by 1,500 US-sponsored Cuban exiles 17–20 April 1961; 1,173 were taken prisoner.

Bayonne River port in SW France; population (1990) 41,800. It trades in timber, steel, fertilizer, and brandy. It is a centre of Basque life. The bayonet was invented here.

Bayonne City in NE New Jersey, NE USA; population (1990) 61,400. A 510-m/1,673-ft bridge connects the city with Staten Island, New York City. Bayonne has large oil refineries connected by pipeline to the oilfields of SW USA; it has docks, a US Navy terminal, supply depots, and a wide variety of industries, including chemicals and textiles.

Bayreuth Town in Bavaria, S Germany, where opera festivals are held every summer; population (1991) 72,800. It was the home of composer Richard Wagner, and the Wagner theatre was established 1876 as a performing centre for his operas.

Bayview Hamlet near Brownsville, Texas, USA, the site of a tent city, erected 1989, for the detention of Central American immigrants filing invalid claims for political asylum.

Beachy Head (French *Béveziers*) Chalk headland (162 m/532 ft high) on the S coast of England, between Seaford and Eastbourne in Sussex, the E end of the South Downs. The lighthouse off the shore is 38 m/125 ft high.

Beaconsfield Town in Buckinghamshire, England; 37 km/23 mi WNW of London; population (1991) 12,300. It has associations with Benjamin Disraeli (created Earl of Beaconsfield 1876), political theorist Edmund Burke, and the poet Edmund Waller.

Beagle Channel Channel to the S of Tierra del Fuego, South America, named after the ship of Charles Darwin's voyage. Three islands at its E end, with krill and oil reserves within their 322 km/200 mi territorial waters, and the dependent sector of the Antarctic with its resources, were disputed between Argentina and Chile and awarded to Chile 1985.

Bearn Former province of France, now included in the *département* of Pyrénées-Atlantiques. Its capital was Pau.

Beas River in Himachal Pradesh, India, an upper tributary of the Sutlej, which in turn joins the Indus. It is one of the five rivers that give the Punjab its name. The ancient *Hyphasis*, it marked the limit of the invasion of India by Alexander the Great.

Beauce District of central France; area about 7,000 sq km/ 2,700 sq mi. It includes parts of the *départements* of Eure-et-Loir, Loir-et-Cher, and Loire. Beauce is a very fertile wheat-growing region. The principal town is ◊Chartres.

Beaufort Sea Section of the Arctic Ocean off Alaska and Canada, named after Francis Beaufort. Oil drilling is allowed only in the winter months because the sea is the breeding and migration route of bowhead whales, the staple diet of the local Inuit people.

Beaulieu Village in Hampshire, England, 9 km/6 mi SW of Southampton. The former abbey is the home of Lord Montagu of Beaulieu and has the Montagu Museum of vintage cars.

Beauly Firth Arm of the North Sea cutting into Scotland N of Inverness, spanned by Kessock Bridge 1982.

Beaumont City and port in SE Texas, USA, on the Neches River, NE of Houston; seat of Jefferson County; population (1992) 115,500. It is an oil-processing centre for the surrounding oil fields and a shipping point via the Sabine–Neches canal to the Gulf of Mexico; other industries include shipbuilding and paper production.

Beaune City SW of Dijon, France; population (1990) 22,100. It is the centre of the Burgundian wine trade, and has a wine museum. Other products include agricultural equipment and mustard.

Beauvais City 76 km/47 mi NW of Paris, France; population (1990) 56,300. It is a trading centre for fruit, dairy produce, and agricultural machinery. Beauvais has a Gothic cathedral, the tallest in France (68 m/223 ft), and is renowned for tapestries (which are now made at the Gobelins factory, Paris).

Bebington Town on Merseyside, England, on the Wirral Peninsula; population (1991) 60,100. Industries include oil, soap, engineering, and chemicals. *Port Sunlight* is a model housing estate originally built 1888 for workers at Lever Brothers (now Unilever) soap and margarine factory.

Becej Town in Vojvodina province, N Serbia, Yugoslavia, on the Marshal Tito canal; population (1991) 26,600. It has mineral springs and is a commercial and agricultural centre.

Bechuanaland Former name (to 1966) of Botswana.

Bedford Administrative headquarters of Bedfordshire, England, on the river Ouse; population (1991) 73,900. Industries include agricultural machinery, airships, diesel engines, pumps, foodstuffs, bricks, communications systems, and electronic equipment. John Bunyan wrote *The Pilgrim's Progress* (1678) while imprisoned here.

Bedfordshire County of S central England
area 1,192 sq km/460 mi
towns and cities Bedford (administrative headquarters), Dunstable
features low lying with Chiltern Hills in the SW; Whipsnade Zoo 1931, near Dunstable, a zoological park (200 ha) belonging to the London Zoological Society; Woburn Abbey, seat of the duke of Bedford
industries cereals, vegetables, agricultural machinery,

electrical goods, cement, clay, chalk, sand, gravel, packaging, motor vehicles, clutches and brakes for motor vehicles. Agriculture is important, especially wheat and barley. It has one of the world's largest brickworks
population (1995 est) 373,000
famous people John Bunyan, John Howard, Joseph Paxton.

Bedloe's Island Former name (until 1956) of ◊Liberty Island, an island in New York harbour, USA, S of Manhattan Island.

Beds Abbreviation for ◊Bedfordshire.

Beemster Polder in the province of North Holland, Netherlands, 20 km/12 mi N of Amsterdam; population (1996) 8,100. The land was reclaimed in the 17th century from the Zuider Zee (see ◊IJsselmeer).

Beersheba Industrial city in Israel; population (1994) 147,900. It is the chief centre of the Negev Desert and has been a settlement from the Stone Age.

Beijing or *Peking* Capital of China; part of its NE border is formed by the Great Wall of China; population (1993) 6,560,000. The municipality of Beijing has an area of 17,800 sq km/6,873 sq mi and a population (1994) of 12,000,000. Industries include textiles, petrochemicals, steel, and engineering.

Beira Port at the mouth of the River Pungwe, Mozambique; population (1990) 299,300. It exports minerals, cotton, and food products. A railway through the *Beira Corridor* links the port with Zimbabwe.

Beirut or *Beyrouth* Capital and port of Lebanon, devastated by civil war in the 1970s and 1980s, when it was occupied by armies of neighbouring countries; population (1993) 1,200,000. Beirut dates back to at least 1400 BC. Before the civil war the city was an international financial and educational centre.

Bejaia formerly *Bougie* Port in Algeria, 193 km/120 mi E of Algiers; population (1989) 124,000. It is linked by pipeline with oil wells at Hassi Messaoud. It exports wood and hides.

Béjar Town in the province of Salamanca, W Spain; population (1995) 17,200. It is situated on a high ridge and has a 13th-century church, and a 16th-century palace belonging to the dukes of Béjar. The town is an important textile centre.

Bekaa, the or *El Beqa'a* Governorate of E Lebanon separated from Syria by the Anti-Lebanon Mountains. Zahlé and the ancient city of Baalbek are the chief settlements. The Bekaa Valley was of strategic importance in the Syrian struggle for control of N Lebanon. In the early 1980s the valley was penetrated by Shia Muslims who established an extremist Hezbollah stronghold with the support of Iranian Revolutionary Guards.

Békéscsaba Town in SE Hungary, near the river Körös, 177 km/111 mi SE of Budapest. It is the capital of Békés county, an agricultural district of the Alföld (Great Plain). Industries include textiles and food processing. Turks destroyed a settlement on this site in the 16th century, and the present town was founded by Slovaks in the 18th century.

Belau Former name for the Republic of Palau.

Belém Port and naval base in N Brazil; population (1991) 1,235,600 (metropolitan area 1,620,600). The chief trade centre of the Amazon basin, it is also known as Pará, the name of the state of which it is capital. It was founded about 1615 as Santa Maria de Belém do Grãs Pará.

Belfast City and industrial port in County Antrim and County Down, Northern Ireland, at the mouth of the river Lagan on Belfast Lough; the capital of Northern Ireland since 1920. It is the county town of County Antrim. Since 1968 the city has been heavily damaged by civil disturbances, until the peace accord 1994.
population (1994 est) 290,000 (Protestants form the majority in E Belfast, Catholics in the W)
industries shipbuilding, engineering, electronics, aircraft, textiles, tobacco, linen, rope, aircraft components, and fertilizers
features 19th-century City Hall; Stormont (site of N Ireland parliament 1932 until suspended 1972); Waterfront Hall, opened 1997

Belfort Town in NE France; population (1990) 51,900. It is in the strategic *Belfort Gap* between the Vosges and Jura mountains and is the capital of the *département* of Territoire de Belfort. Industries include chemicals, engineering, plastics, and textiles.

Belfort, Territoire de *Département* in the ◊Franche-Comté region of E France; area 610 sq km/236 sq mi; population (1990) 134,313. Situated in the narrow area of lowland between the ◊Vosges and ◊Jura mountains, it is the smallest such administrative area in France, outside the suburban *départements* around Paris. The capital, and only major town, is ◊Belfort.

Belgaum City in Karnataka, S India; population (1991) 402,000. The main industry is cotton manufacture. It is known for its Jain temples.

Belgian Congo Former name (1908–60) of the Democratic Republic of the Congo; known (1960–97) as Zaire.

Belgrade (Serbo-Croatian *Beograd*) Capital of Yugoslavia and Serbia, and Danube river port linked with the port of Bar on the Adriatic Sea; population (1991) 1,168,500. Industries include light engineering, food processing, textiles, pharmaceuticals, and electrical goods.

Belgravia Residential district of W central London, laid out in squares by Thomas Cubitt (1788–1855) 1825–30, and bounded to the N by Knightsbridge.

Belitung or *Billitonin* Indonesian island in the Java Sea, between Borneo and Sumatra, one of the Sunda Islands; area 4,830 sq km/1,860 sq mi. The chief port is Tanjungpandan. Tin mining is the chief industry.

Belize Chief port of Belize, and capital until 1970; population (1991) 44,000. After the city was destroyed by a hurricane 1961 it was decided to move the capital inland, to Belmopan.

Belle Isle, Strait of Channel between Newfoundland and Labrador, NE Canada, forming an entrance to the Gulf of St Lawrence from the Atlantic Ocean. The channel is about

130 km/81 mi long and 16–30 km/10–19 mi wide. During the winter months it is often blocked with ice.

Belleville City in SW Illinois, USA, SE of East St Louis; seat of St Clair County; population (1990) 42,800. Industries include coal, beer, furnaces and boilers, and clothing. Belleville was founded 1814.

Bellingham City and port in NW Washington, USA, just S of the Canadian border, on Bellingham Bay in the Strait of Georgia; population (1992) 55,300. It is a port of entry for the logging and paper industry; there are also shipbuilding and food processing industries. Bellingham was settled 1852, and became a staging area for the Frazer River gold rush 1857–58.

Bellingshausen Sea Section of the S Pacific off the Antarctic coast. It is named after the Estonian explorer Fabian Gottlieb von Bellingshausen.

Bellinzona Town in Switzerland on the river Ticino, 16 km/ 10 mi from Lake Maggiore; capital of Ticino canton; population (1990) 16,900. It is a traffic centre for the St Gotthard Pass, and also a tourist centre.

Belluno Province of NE Italy in ◊Veneto region; capital Belluno (population (1990) 35,900); area 3,680 sq km/1,421 sq mi; population (1992) 212,000. The town of Belluno is on the river Piave.

Belmopan Capital of Belize from 1970; population (1991) 3,558. It replaced Belize city as the administrative centre of the country.

Belo Horizonte Industrial city (steel, engineering, textiles) in SE Brazil, capital of the fast-developing state of Minas Gerais; population (1991) 2,103,300 (metropolitan area 4,620,600). Built in the 1890s, it was Brazil's first planned modern city.

Beloit City in SE Wisconsin, USA, on the Rock River, SE of Madison; population (1994 est) 36,600. Industries include electrical, papermaking, and woodworking machinery, shoes, generators, and diesel engines. Beloit was settled 1837 by the New England Emigrating Company.

Benares Alternative transliteration of ◊Varanasi, a holy Hindu city in Uttar Pradesh, India.

Bendigo City in Victoria, Australia, about 120 km/75 mi NW of Melbourne; population (1993) 71,300. Founded 1851 at the start of a gold rush, the city takes its name from the pugilist William Thompson (1811–1889), known as 'Bendigo'.

Benevento Historic town in Campania, S Italy; population (1990) 64,700. It is known for the production of Strega liqueur.

Benevento Province of S Italy in NE ◊Campania region; capital Benevento; area 2,062 sq km/796 sq mi; population (1992) 293,100.

Bengal, Bay of Part of the Indian Ocean lying between the E coast of India and the W coast of Myanmar (Burma) and the Malay Peninsula. The Irrawaddy, Ganges, and

Brahmaputra rivers flow into the bay. The principal islands are to be found in the Andaman and Nicobar groups.

Benghazi or *Banghazi* Historic city and industrial port in N Libya on the Gulf of Sirte; population (1984) 485,000. It was controlled by Turkey between the 16th century and 1911, and by Italy 1911–42; it was a major naval supply base during World War II.

Benguela Port in Angola, SW Africa; population province (1983) 155,000. It was founded 1617. Its railway runs inland to the copper mines of the Democratic Republic of Congo (formerly Zaire) and Zambia, but is in limited use because of landmines remaining from the Angolan civil war.

Benidorm Fishing village and popular tourist resort on the Mediterranean Costa Blanca, in Alicante province, E Spain; population (1991) 74,900.

Benin Former African kingdom 1200–1897, now a province of Nigeria. It reached the height of its power in the 14th–17th centuries when it ruled the area between the Niger Delta and Lagos.

Ben Nevis Highest mountain in the British Isles (1,343 m/ 4,406 ft), in the Grampian Mountains, Scotland.

Benoni City in Gauteng Province, South Africa, 27 km/ 17 mi E of Johannesburg; population (1991) 114,000. It was founded 1903 as a gold-mining centre.

Bensberg Suburb of ◊Cologne in North Rhine– Westphalia, Germany. It is the home of Interatom, an atomic research centre. Machinery, pharmaceutical products, and chemicals are produced.

Bentiu Oil-rich region to the W of the White Nile, in the Upper Nile province of S Sudan.

Benton Harbor City in SW Michigan, USA, NE of Chicago, Illinois, which is across Lake Michigan; population (1990) 12,820. Industries include iron and other metal products and food processing. A religious sect, House of David, was established here 1903.

Benue River in Nigeria, largest tributary of the river Niger; it is navigable for most of its length of 1,400 km/870 mi.

Beograd Serbo-Croatian form of ◊Belgrade, the capital of Yugoslavia.

Berat Town in Albania, capital of Berat district, on the river Osum; population (1990) 43,800. It is thought to be the site of the ancient Greek Antipatria, and was named Berat in the 14th century. The Stalin oil field is 11 km/7 mi to the N.

Berbera Seaport in Somalia, with the only sheltered harbour on the S side of the Gulf of Aden; population (1987) 65,000. It is in a strategic position on the oil route and has a deep-sea port completed 1969. It was under British control 1884–1960.

Berdichev City in W Ukraine, 48 km/30 mi S of Zhitomir; population (1980) 60,000. Industries include engineering and food processing.

Berdyansk City and port on the Berdyansk Gulf of the Sea of Azov, in SE Ukraine; population (1992) 137,000.

Berezniki City in the Russian Federation, on the Kama River N of Perm, in the Urals; population (1992) 199,000. It was formed 1932 by the amalgamation of several older towns. Industries include chemicals and paper.

Bergamo City in Lombardy, Italy, 48 km/30 mi NE of Milan; population (1992) 115,100. Industries include silk and metal. The Academia Carrara holds a fine collection of paintings.

Bergamo Province of N Italy in central ◊Lombardy region; capital Bergamo; area 2,760 sq km/1,068 sq mi; population (1992) 936,100.

Bergen Industrial port (shipbuilding, engineering, fishing) in SW Norway; population (1994) 195,000. Founded 1070, Bergen was a member of the Hanseatic League.

Bergen-op-Zoom Fishing port in the SW Netherlands; population (1991) 46,900. It produces chemicals, cigarettes, and precision goods.

Bergerac French market town in the *département* of Dordogne, on the river Dordogne; population (1990) 28,000. It is the centre of the French tobacco-growing area, and trades also in truffles, wine, and maize. It has distilleries and spinning mills. Bergerac was a Huguenot religious stronghold.

Bergisch Gladbach Industrial city (paper, metal products) in North Rhine–Westphalia, Germany; population (1991) 104,000.

Bering Sea Section of the N Pacific between Alaska and Siberia, from the Aleutian Islands N to the Bering Strait.

Bering Strait Strait between Alaska and Siberia, linking the N Pacific and Arctic oceans.

Berkeley City on San Francisco Bay in California; population (1992) 101,100. It is the site of a branch of the University of California, with nuclear research at the Lawrence Berkeley Laboratory. Berkeley was settled 1853.

Berks Abbreviation for *Berkshire*.

Berkshire or *Royal Berkshire* County of S central England. The county of Berkshire will be abolished in April 1998, and split into 6 unitary authorities.
area 1,260 sq km/486 sq mi
towns and cities Reading (administrative headquarters), Eton, Slough, Maidenhead, Ascot, Bracknell, Newbury, Windsor, Wokingham
features rivers Thames and Kennet; Inkpen Beacon, 297 m/ 975 ft; Bagshot Heath; Ridgeway Path, walkers' path (partly prehistoric) running from Wiltshire across the Berkshire Downs into Hertfordshire; Windsor Forest and Windsor Castle; Eton College; Royal Military Academy at Sandhurst; atomic-weapons research establishment at Aldermaston; the former main UK base for US cruise missiles at Greenham Common, Newbury
industries general agricultural and horticultural goods, electronics, plastics, pharmaceuticals, engineering, paints, biscuits, pigs, poultry, barley, dairy products
population (1994) 769,200
famous people William Laud, Jethro Tull, Stanley Spencer.

Berkshire Hills Upland district of W Massachusetts, NE USA. The mountains lie to the W of the Connecticut River and are a continuation of the Green Mountains of Vermont; they are part of the Appalachian Mountains. The highest point is Greylock (1,065 m/3,494 ft). As part of the Appalachian Trail, the area is a popular resort.

Berlin Industrial city (machine tools, electrical goods, paper, printing) and capital of the Federal Republic of Germany; area 889 sq km/343 sq mi; population (1995) 3,471,400. After the division of Germany 1949, East Berlin became the capital of East Germany and Bonn was made the provisional capital of West Germany. The *Berlin Wall* divided the city from 1961 until it was dismantled 1989. Following reunification East and West Berlin were once more reunited as the 16th *Land* (administrative region) of the Federal Republic (1990).

Bermuda

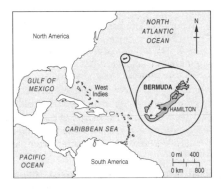

Bermuda British colony in the NW Atlantic Ocean
area 54 sq km/21 sq mi
capital and chief port Hamilton
features consists of about 150 small islands, of which 20 are inhabited, linked by bridges and causeways; Britain's oldest colony
industries Easter lilies, pharmaceuticals; tourism, banking, and insurance are important
currency Bermuda dollar
population (1994) 60,500
language English
religion Christian
government under the constitution of 1968, Bermuda is a fully self-governing British colony, with a governor (Lord Waddington from 1992), senate, and elected House of Assembly (premier from 1997 Pamela Gordon, United Bermuda Party)
history the islands were named after Juan de Bermudez, who visited them 1515, and were settled by British colonists 1609. It is Britain's oldest colony, officially taken by the crown 1684. Indian and African slaves were transported from 1616 and soon outnumbered the white settlers. Racial violence 1977 led to intervention, at the request of the government, by British troops. A 1995 referendum rejected independence.

Bermuda Triangle Sea area bounded by Bermuda, Florida, and Puerto Rico, which gained the nickname 'Deadly Bermuda Triangle' 1964 when it was suggested that unexplained disappearances of ships and aircraft were exceptionally frequent there. Analysis of the data has not confirmed the idea.

Bern (French *Berne*) Capital of Switzerland and of Bern canton, in W Switzerland on the Aare River; population (1994) 134,100; canton (1994 est) 943,600. It was founded 1191, and made a free imperial city by Frederick II 1218. It joined the Swiss confederation 1353 and became the capital 1848. Industries include textiles, chocolate, pharmaceuticals, and light metal and electrical goods.

Bern (French *Berne*) Canton of W Switzerland; area 6,887 sq km/2,659 sq mi; population (1995) 942,000. Bern is the country's second largest and second most populous canton. Tourism is an important industry in this picturesque region; among the peaks of the Bernese Oberland to the SE are the ◊Finsteraarhorn, ◊Jungfrau, ◊Eiger, and Schreckhorn; lakes in the canton include Thun, Brienz, and Bienne (see ◊Biel).

Bernese Alps or *Bernese Oberland* Mountainous area in the S of Bern canton. It includes the ◊Jungfrau, ◊Eiger, and ◊Finsteraarhorn peaks. Interlaken is the chief town.

Bernkastel-Kues Town in the Rhineland-Palatinate, Germany, 50 km/31 mi NE of Trier; population (1993) 111,200. It is a wine-growing and tourist centre on the river Moselle, and holds a wine festival each Sept.

Berre, Etang de Saltwater lagoon in the French *département* of Bouches-du-Rhône, W of ◊Marseilles; area 155 sq km/60 sq mi. It is joined to the Mediterranean by the Martigues canal and the Rove tunnel. The port and industrial development at Fos is located to the W of the lagoon.

Berry Former province of central France, now divided into the *départements* of Indre, Cher, and parts of Creuse, Nièvre, and Allier. It passed to the crown in 1100, and became a duchy in 1360. Its capital was ◊Bourges.

Berwickshire Former county of SE Scotland, a district of Borders Region from 1975–96, now part of Scottish Borders unitary authority.

Berwick-upon-Tweed Town in Northumberland, NE England, at the mouth of the Tweed, 5 km/3 mi SE of the Scottish border; population (1991) 13,500. It is a fishing port. Other industries include iron foundries, foodstuffs, fertilizers, tweeds, knitwear, and agricultural engineering. Three bridges cross the Tweed: the Old Bridge 1611–34 with 15 arches, the Royal Border railway bridge 1850 constructed by Robert Stephenson, and the Royal Tweed Bridge 1928. Held alternately by England and Scotland for centuries, Berwick was made a neutral town 1551; it was attached to Northumberland 1885.

Besançon City on the river Doubs, France; population (1990) 119,200. It is the capital of Franche-Comté. The first factory to produce artificial fibres was established here 1890. Industries include textiles and clock-making. It has fortifications by Vauban, Roman remains, and a Gothic cathedral. The writer Victor Hugo and the Lumière brothers, inventors of cinematography, were born here.

Bessarabia Region in SE Europe, divided between Moldova and Ukraine. Bessarabia was annexed by Russia 1812, but broke away at the Russian Revolution to join Romania. The cession was confirmed by the Allies, but not by Russia, in a Paris treaty of 1920; the USSR reoccupied it 1940 and divided it between the Moldavian and Ukrainian republics (now independent Moldova and Ukraine). Romania recognized the position in the 1947 peace treaty.

Bessemer Industrial city in Jefferson County, Alabama, SE USA, 25 km/16 mi SW of Birmingham; population (1990) 33,500. Situated close to rich coal and iron deposits, Bessemer was planned for steel production. Today, chemical and railway-car manufacturing are important. The town is named after Henry Bessemer, the inventor of the Bessemer process of steelmaking.

Beszterczebanya Hungarian name for ◊Banská-Bystrica, a town in the Slovak Republic.

Bethlehem (Hebrew *Beit-Lahm*) Town on the W bank of the river Jordan, S of Jerusalem; population about 20,000. It was occupied by Israel 1967. In the Bible it is mentioned as the birthplace of King David and Jesus, and in 326 AD the Church of the Nativity was built over the grotto said to be the birthplace of Jesus.

Bethlehem City in E Pennsylvania, USA; population (1992) 72,400. Its former steel industry has been replaced by high technology. Bethlehem was founded 1741 by Moravian missionaries from Germany.

Béthune Town in N France, W of Lille; population (1990) 25,200. Industries include textiles, machinery, and tyres.

Betuwe District of the Netherlands, situated between the rivers Waal and Rhine, in the province of ◊Gelderland. It is very fertile and contains many orchards.

Betws-y-coed Village in Conwy, N Wales. It is a tourist centre. There are waterfalls nearby.

Beuthen German name for ◊Bytom, a town in Poland.

Beveland, North and South Two islands in the Scheldt river estuary, the Netherlands. They are part of the ◊Zeeland Islands, of which South Beveland is the largest and most fertile. Railways built on dykes connect this island with Walcheren and the mainland.

Beverly Hills Residential city and a part of greater Los Angeles, California, USA; population (1990) 31,900. It is known as the home of Hollywood film stars.

Béveziers French name for ◊Beachy Head, England.

Bexhill-on-Sea Seaside resort in E Sussex, England, SW of Hastings; population (1991) 38,900.

Bexley Outer borough of SE Greater London. It includes the suburbs of Crayford, Erith, Sidcup
features 16th-century Hall Palace; Red House (1859), home of William Morris 1860–65; 18th-century Danson Park, with grounds landscaped by 'Capability' Brown
industries armaments manufacture (important since the 19th century at Crayford, site of Vickers Factory)
population (1991) 215,600.

Beynouth Alternative name for ◊Beirut, Lebanon.

Béziers City in Languedoc-Roussillon, S France; population (1990) 72,300. It is a centre of the wine trade. It was once a Roman station and was the site of a massacre 1209 in the Albigensian Crusade.

Bhagalpur City in the state of Bihar, N India, on the river Ganges; population (1991) 253,000. It manufactures silk and textiles. Several Jain temples are here.

Bhamo Town in Myanmar (Burma), near the Chinese frontier, on the Irrawaddy River. It is the inland limit of steam navigation and is mainly a trading centre.

Bharat Hindi name for India.

Bhatgaon or *Bhadgaon* or *Bhaktapur* Town in Nepal, 11 km/7 mi SE of Kathmandu; population (1991) 61,100. It has been a religious centre since the 9th century; there is a palace.

Bhavnagar Port in Gujarat, NW India, in the Kathiawar peninsula; population (1991) 404,000. It is a centre for textile industry. It was capital of the former Rajput princely state of Bhavnagar.

Bhopal Industrial city (textiles, chemicals, electrical goods, jewellery) and capital of Madhya Pradesh, central India; population (1991) 1,064,000. Nearby Bhimbetka Caves, discovered 1973, have the world's largest collection of prehistoric paintings, about 10,000 years old. In 1984 some 2,600 people died from an escape of the poisonous gas methyl isocyanate from a factory owned by US company Union Carbide; another 300,000 suffer from long-term health problems.

Bhubaneshwar City in NE India; capital of Orissa state; population (1991) 412,000. Utkal University was founded 1843. A place of pilgrimage and centre of Siva worship, it has temples of the 6th–12th centuries. Tourism is important.

Biafra, Bight of or *Bight of Bonny* Area of sea off the coasts of Nigeria and Cameroon.

Białystok City in E Poland; capital of Białystok region; population (1993) 273,300. Industries include textiles, chemicals, and tools. Founded 1310, the city belonged to Prussia 1795–1807 and to Russia 1807–1919.

Biarritz Town on the Bay of Biscay, France, near the Spanish border; population (1990) 28,900. A seaside resort and spa town, it was popularized by Queen Victoria and Edward VII.

Biberach an der Riss City in the *Land* of Baden-Württemberg, Germany, on the river Riss, 85 km/53 mi SE of Stuttgart; population (1993) 170,900. The city has machinery, chemical, and pharmaceutical industries. Biberach was one of the city-states of the Holy Roman Empire. It has medieval towers and gates, old mansions, and a 13th–18th-century church.

Biel (French *Bienne*) Town in NW Switzerland; population (1990) 52,700. Its main industries include engineering, scientific instruments, and watch-making.

Bielefeld City in North Rhine–Westphalia, Germany, 55 km/34 mi E of Münster; population (1993) 324,400.

Industries include textiles, drinks, chemicals, machinery, and motorcycles.

Bielitz German name for ◊Bielsko-Biała, a town in Poland.

Bielostok Russian form of ◊Białystok, a city in Poland.

Bielsko-Biała (German *Bielitz*) Industrial town (woollen textiles, engineering, chemicals) in Katowice province, Poland, on the river Biała, 47 km/29 mi S of Katowice.

Bienne French form of ◊Biel, a town in Switzerland.

Bighorn Mountains Range of the ◊Rocky Mountains lying principally in N Wyoming, USA, to the E of the Bighorn River. The range runs NW to SE for nearly 200 km/125 mi, and has a number of summits over 3,000 m/9,800 ft, culminating in Cloud Peak, 4,019 m/13,186 ft. At the N end of the range, in the Crow Reservation in SE Montana, is the site of the Battle of Little Bighorn 1876. The foothills are used for livestock grazing and irrigated agriculture. The mountains are a popular visitor destination.

Bihac Town in Bosnia-Herzegovina, on the river Una; population (1991) 71,000. It was under Turkish rule 1592–1878, and has many old buildings, including a mosque that was formerly a Gothic church. Bihac was designated a 'safe haven' by the United Nations 1993.

Bihar or *Behar* State of NE India
area 173,877 sq km/67,134 sq mi
capital Patna
features river Ganges in the N, Rajmahal Hills in the S
industries copper, iron, coal, rice, jute, sugar cane, grain, oilseed, tobacco, potatoes; 40% of India's mineral production
language Hindi, Bihari
population (1994 est) 93,080,000
famous people Chandragupta, Asoka
history the ancient kingdom of Magadha roughly corresponded to central and S Bihar. Many Bihari people were massacred as a result of their protest at the establishment of Bangladesh 1971. Elections were postponed and direct rule imposed after public disturbances 1995.

Bikaner City in Rajasthan, N India; population (1991) 415,000. Once capital of the Rajput state of Bikaner, it is now a centre for carpet-weaving.

Bikini Atoll Atoll in the Marshall Islands, W Pacific, where the USA carried out 23 atomic- and hydrogen-bomb tests (some underwater) 1946–58.

Bilbao Industrial port (iron and steel, chemicals, cement, food) in N Spain, capital of Biscay province; population (1994) 372,000. Work began 1993 on the Guggenheim Museum Bilbao.

Billings City in S central Montana, USA, on the N shore of the Yellowstone River; seat of Yellowstone County; population (1992) 84,000. It is a centre for transporting livestock and animal products and for vegetable and grain processing. Nearby, to the SE, is Bighorn Native American reservation where the Battle of the Little Bighorn took place 1876.

Billingsgate Chief London wholesale fish market, formerly (from the 9th century) near London Bridge. It re-

opened 1982 at the new Billingsgate market, West India Dock, Isle of Dogs.

Billiton Alternative name for the Indonesian island of ◊Belitung.

Biloxi Port in Mississippi, USA; population (1990) 46,300. Chief occupations include tourism and seafood canning. Named after a local people, Biloxi was founded 1719 by the French.

Bingen City in the Rhineland-Palatinate, Germany, on the river Rhine, 32 km/20 mi W of Mainz; population (1994) 23,900. Bingen is a centre for tourism and has a long history of wine trading.

Binghamton City in S central New York State, USA, where the Chenango River meets the Susquehanna River; population (1992) 52,050. Industries include electronic, computer, and camera equipment and textiles. Johnson City and Endicott, directly to the W on the Susquehanna River, form the Triple Cities with Binghamton. Binghamton was first settled 1787 on the site of an Iroquois village, and laid out 1800.

Bío-Bío Longest river in Chile; length 370 km/230 mi from its source in the Andes to its mouth on the Pacific. The name is an Araucanian term meaning 'much water'.

Bioko Island in the Bight of Biafra, W Africa, part of Equatorial Guinea; area 2,017 sq km/786 sq mi; products include coffee and cacao; population (1983) 57,200. Formerly a Spanish possession, as *Fernando Póo*, it was known 1973–79 as *Macías Nguema Bijogo*.

Bipontium Roman name for ◊Zweibrücken, a town in Germany.

Birkenhead Seaport in Merseyside, England, on the Mersey estuary opposite Liverpool; population (1994 est) 218,000. Chief industries include engineering and flour milling. The rail Mersey Tunnel 1886 and road Queensway Tunnel 1934 link Birkenhead with Liverpool.

Bîrlad Town in Vaslui county, E Romania, on the river Bîlad, 100 km/63 mi NW of Galati (Galatz). Industries include soap and candles. An annual horse fair is held in the town.

Birmingham Industrial city in the West Midlands, second largest city of the UK; population (1994 est) 1,220,000, metropolitan area 2,632,000. It is an important manufacturing and commercial centre. Industries include engineering, motor vehicles, machine tools, aerospace control systems, plastics, chemicals, food, chocolates, jewellery, tyres, glass, cars, and guns.

Birmingham Commercial and industrial city (iron, steel, chemicals, building materials, computers, cotton textiles) and largest city in Alabama, USA; population (1992) 265,000. Birmingham was settled 1813, and the city founded 1871.

Birobijan Town in Khabarovsk Territory, E Russian Federation, near the Chinese border; population (1994) 217,800. Industries include sawmills and clothing. It was capital of the Jewish Autonomous Region of Birobijan 1928–51.

Biscay, Bay of Bay of the Atlantic Ocean between N Spain and W France, known for rough seas and exceptionally high tides.

Bishkek (formerly *Pishpek* until 1926, and *Frunze* 1926–92) Capital of Kyrgyzstan; population (1991 est) 641,400. It produces textiles, farm machinery, metal goods, and tobacco.

Biskra Oasis town in Algeria on the edge of the Sahara Desert; population (1987) 128,300.

Bismarck Capital of North Dakota, USA, on the Missouri River in Burleigh County, in the S part of the state; population (1992) 51,300. It is a shipping point for the region's agricultural and livestock products from surrounding farms and for oil products from nearby oil wells. Serving as the capital of the Dakota Territory from 1883, it remained the capital when North Dakota became a state 1889. Named after German chancellor Otto von Bismarck, it was the terminus of the heavily German-funded Northern Pacific Railroad.

Bismarck Archipelago

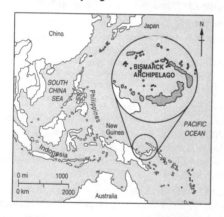

Bismarck Archipelago Group of over 200 islands in the SW Pacific Ocean, part of Papua New Guinea; area 49,660 sq km/19,200 sq mi. The largest island is New Britain.

Bissau Capital and chief port of Guinea-Bissau, on an island at the mouth of the Geba River; population (1992) 145,000. Originally a fortified slave-trading centre, Bissau became a free port 1869, with industries including agricultural processing and fishing.

Bitola or *Bitolj*, (Turkish *Monastir*) Town in the Former Yugoslav Republic of Macedonia, in the strategic Monastir Gap, at the junction of the main N–S and E–W roads through the S Balkans; population (1994) 75,400. Agricultural produce, tobacco, and wool are traded, and textiles and filigree work manufactured. Held by the Turks (under whom it was known as Monastir) from 1382, it was taken by the Serbs 1912 during the First Balkan War. Retaken by Bulgaria 1915, it was again taken by the Allies Nov 1916.

Bitterroot Mountains Range of mountains forming part of the boundary between Idaho and Montana, NW USA; maximum altitude 3,000 m/9,840 ft. The range is an outlying part of the ◊Rocky Mountains, branching off S where the main range turns E through Montana. The mountains are part of the Bitterroot national forest.

Bizerte or *Bizerta* Port in Tunisia, N Africa; population (1994) 98,900. Chief industries include fishing, oil refining, and metal works.

Björneborg Swedish name of ◊Pori, a town in Finland.

Blackburn Industrial city in Lancashire, England, on the Leeds–Liverpool canal, 32 km/20 mi NW of Manchester; population (1991) 106,000. Historically it was a centre of the textile industry. It will be a unitary authority from April 1998. Textiles, electronics, paint, paper, tufted carpets, and compact discs are produced, and there are other high-tech industries.

Black Country Central area of England, to the W and N of Birmingham. Heavily industrialized, it gained its name in the 19th century from its belching chimneys and mining spoil. Antipollution laws have changed its aspect, and coal mining in the region ceased 1968.

Black Forest (German *Schwarzwald*) Mountainous region of coniferous forest in Baden-Württemberg, W Germany. Bounded to the W and S by the Rhine, which separates it from the Vosges, it has an area of 4,660 sq km/ 1,800 sq mi and rises to 1,493 m/4,905 ft in the Feldberg. Parts of the forest have recently been affected by acid rain.

Blackheath Suburb of London, lying S of Greenwich Park on the London–Dover road. It falls within the Greater London boroughs of ◊Greenwich and ◊Lewisham and takes its name from the common, where Wat Tyler encamped during the 1381 Peasants' Revolt. It developed as a residential suburb from the late 18th century.

Black Hills Mountains in the Dakotas and Wyoming, USA. They occupy about 15,500 sq km/6,000 sq mi and rise to 2,207 m/7,242 ft at Harney Peak, South Dakota. The Black Hills include a national forest and Mount ◊Rushmore, which has the visages of four presidents carved on a cliff face. Gold, discovered in 1874, is still mined here.

Black Mountain Ridge of hills in the Brecon Beacons National Park in Carmarthenshire and Powys, S Wales, stretching 19 km/12 mi N from Swansea. The hills are composed of limestone and red sandstone.

Black Mountains Upland massif with cliffs and steepsided valleys in Powys and Monmouthshire, SE Wales, lying to the W of ◊Offa's Dyke. The highest peak is Waun Fach (811 m/2,660 ft).

Black Mountains Mountain range in W North Carolina, E USA. They are part of the ◊Appalachian Mountains, the highest point being Mount Mitchell (2,037 m/6,683 ft), and lie within the Pisgah national forest.

Black National State Area in the Republic of South Africa set aside, 1971–94, for development towards self-government by black Africans, in accordance with apartheid.

Before 1980 these areas were known as *black homelands* or *bantustans*. Making up less than 14% of the country, they tended to be situated in arid areas (though some had mineral wealth), often in scattered blocks. Those that achieved nominal independence were Transkei 1976, Bophuthatswana 1977, Venda 1979, and Ciskei 1981. They were not recognized outside South Africa because of their racial basis.

Blackpool Seaside resort in Lancashire, England, 45 km/ 28 mi N of Liverpool; population (1994 est) 156,000. It will be a unitary authority from April 1998.

Black Sea (Russian *Chernoye More*) Inland sea in SE Europe, linked with the seas of Azov and Marmara, and via the Dardanelles strait with the Mediterranean. Uranium deposits beneath it are among the world's largest. About 90% of the water is polluted, mainly by agricultural fertilizers.

Black Sea

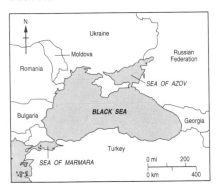

Blackwall Tunnel Road tunnel under the river Thames, London, linking the Bugsby Marshes (S) with the top end of the Isle of Dogs (N). The northbound tunnel, 7,056 km/ 4,410 ft long with an internal diameter of 7.2 m/24 ft, was built 1891–97 to a design by Alexander Binnie; the southbound tunnel, 4,592 km/2,870 ft long with an internal diameter of 8.25 m/27.5 ft, was built 1960–67 to a design by Mott, Hay, and Anderson.

Blaenau Gwent Unitary authority in S Wales created 1996 from part of the former county of Gwent; administrative headquarters Ebbw Vale; population 73,000 (1996); area 109 sq km/42 sq mi. The area no longer depends on coal, iron, and steel industries, and former industrial land is being redeveloped. The Brecon Beacons National Park is here.

Blagoevgrad Town in Sofia region, SW Bulgaria, near the river Struma, 77 km/48 mi SW of Sofia; population (1990) 86,200. It is a commercial centre and health resort. The town was built on the ruins of the ancient Thracian town of Scaptopara (founded 3rd century BC).

Blankenberghe Seaside resort on the coast of the province of West Flanders, Belgium, 21 km/13 mi NE of Ostend. The town has fishing and shipbuilding industries.

Blantyre Chief industrial and commercial centre of Malawi, in the Shire highlands; population (1993) 399,000. It

produces tea, coffee, rubber, tobacco, textiles, and wood products.

Blekinge Coastal county of SE Sweden on the Baltic Sea; area 3,365 sq km/1,299 sq mi; population (1990) 149,600. The land is low-lying with small lakes and rivers. Intensively cultivated, it is known as the 'garden of Sweden'. The chief town is Karlskrona.

Blenheim Centre of a sheep-grazing area in the NE of South Island, New Zealand; population (1986) 18,300.

Bloemfontein Capital of the ◊Free State (formerly Orange Free State) and judicial capital of the Republic of South Africa; population (1991) 300,150. Founded 1846, the city produces canned fruit, glassware, furniture, plastics, and railway engineering.

Blois Town on the river Loire in central France; population (1990) 51,500. It has a château partly dating from the 13th century.

Bloomington City in central Illinois, USA, SE of Peoria; seat of McLean County; population (1992) 54,100. It is in the middle of a rich farming and livestock area. Bloomington was settled 1822 and the town laid out 1831.

Bloomington City in S central Indiana, USA, SW of Indianapolis; seat of Monroe County; population (1992) 61,500. It is an exporter of limestone from nearby quarries. It is also a centre for the manufacture of electrical products and lifts. Indiana University (1820) is located here. Bloomington was laid out 1818.

Bloomsbury Area in the borough of Camden, London, a series of squares between Gower Street and High Holborn. It contains London University, the British Museum (1759), and the Royal Academy of Dramatic Arts. Between the world wars it was the home of the Bloomsbury Group of writers and artists.

Bludenz Austrian town in the province of Vorarlberg, on the river Ill 40 km/25 mi S of Bregenz; population (1995) 13,600. It has a 16th-century church and a Renaissance castle, and is a tourist resort.

Bluefields One of three major port facilities on the E coast of Nicaragua, situated on an inlet of the Caribbean Sea; population (1990 est) 18,000.

Blue Mountains Part of the ◊Great Dividing Range, New South Wales, Australia, ranging 600–1,100 m/2,000–3,600 ft and blocking Sydney from the interior until the crossing 1813 by surveyor William Lawson, Gregory Blaxland, and William Wentworth.

Blue Mountains Mountain range in NE Oregon and SE Washington, USA. The average elevation of the range is 2,000 m/6,500 ft; the highest peak is Rock Creek Butte (2,775 m/9,105 ft). The mountains are the source of tributaries to the Columbia River. Densely forested, the mountains are used for stock grazing and some lumbering. They are also popular with outdoors enthusiasts.

Blue Mountains Range of mountains in Jamaica. The Blue Mountain Peak is 2,256 m/7,402 ft, the highest mountain on the island. The altitude of this system, whose main chain extends from E to W, varies between 1,524 m/5,000 ft and 2,134 m/7,000 ft. Coffee is grown in the valleys, and the mountains are a popular tourist destination.

Blue Nile (Arabic *Bahr el Azraq*) River rising in the mountains of Ethiopia. Flowing W then N for 2,000 km/ 1,250 mi, it eventually meets the White Nile at Khartoum. Some 80% of Sudan's electricity is provided by hydroelectric schemes at Roseires and Sennar.

Blue Ridge Mountains Range extending from West Virginia to Georgia, USA, and including Mount Mitchell 2,045 m/6,712 ft; part of the ◊Appalachian Mountains.

Bobigny Capital of Seine-St-Denis *département*, France; population (1990) 44,700.

Bóbr (German *Bober*) River in Poland, a tributary of the river ◊Oder; length 267 km/167 mi. It rises at the SE edge of the Karkonosze mountains and flows N to join the Oder near Krosno.

Boca Raton City in SE Florida, USA, on the Atlantic Ocean, N of Miami; population (1992) 64,300. Although it is mainly a resort and residential area, there is some light industry.

Bocholt City in the *Land* of North Rhine–Westphalia, Germany, 69 km/43 mi NW of Düsseldorf, near the Dutch border; population (1994) 70,200. The town's industries include textiles and engineering. Bocholt has a Renaissance *Rathaus* (town hall) and a 15th-century church.

Bochum City in the Ruhr district in North Rhine–Westphalia, Germany; population (1993) 400,700. Industries include metallurgy, vehicles, and chemicals.

Bodensee German name for Lake ◊Constance, N of the Alps.

Bodmin Market town in Cornwall, England, 48 km/30 mi from Plymouth; population (1991) 12,500. It is the centre of a farming area. *Bodmin Moor* to the NE is a granite upland, culminating in Brown Willy 419 m/1,375 ft.

Bognor Regis Seaside resort in West Sussex, England, 105 km/66 mi SW of London; population (1991) 56,700. It owes the Regis part of its name to the convalescent visit by King George V 1929.

Bogotá Capital of Colombia, South America; 2,640 m/ 8,660 ft above sea level on the edge of the plateau of the E Cordillera; population (1994) 5,132,000. Main industries are textiles, chemicals, food processing, and tobacco.

Bohemia Area of the Czech Republic, a fertile plateau drained by the Elbe and Vltava rivers. It is rich in mineral resources, including uranium, coal, lignite, iron ore, silver, and graphite. The main cities are Prague and Plzeň. The name Bohemia derives from the Celtic Boii, its earliest known inhabitants.

Bohemian Forest (German *Böhmer Wald*, Czech *Český Les*) Wooded mountain range, a S extension of the Bohemian massif, stretching over 200 km/125 mi from Bavaria, Germany, to the SW Czech Republic. The river Vltava, rising in the Czech Republic, cuts deeply through the rugged and sparsely populated terrain. The highest point in Bavaria is the Gross Arber (1,457 m/4,856 ft) and in the Czech Republic, the Plechý Plöchenstein (1,378 m/4,593 ft).

Bohn Former name of ◊Annaba, a port in Algeria.

Bois de Boulogne Large park in ◊Paris, France, to the W of the city, bordered by the Seine. It was enclosed in about 1800, and was given to the city by Napoleon III in 1852. In it are the racecourses of Auteuil and Longchamp, zoological and botanical gardens, and fine drives, especially the fashionable Allée de Longchamp.

Boise Capital of Idaho, USA, located in the W part of the state, on the Boise River in the W foothills of the Rocky Mountains; population (1992) 135,500. It serves as a centre for the farm and livestock products of the region and has meat-packing and food-processing industries; steel and lumber products are also manufactured. It was founded during the Idaho gold rush of 1862 and served as territorial capital 1864–90, when Idaho became a state.

Bois-le-Duc French form of ◊'s-Hertogenbosch, a town in North Brabant, the Netherlands.

Bokhara Variant spelling of ◊Bukhara, a city in Uzbekistan.

Bolesławiec (German *Bunzlau*) Town in Wrocław province, Poland, on the river Bóbr, 103 km/64 mi W of Wrocław. Pottery has been produced since the 16th century, and copper is mined locally.

Bologna Industrial city and capital of Emilia-Romagna, Italy, 80 km/50 mi N of Florence; population (1992) 401,300. It was the site of an Etruscan town, later of a Roman colony, and became a republic in the 12th century. It came under papal rule 1506 and was united with Italy 1860.

Bologna Province of N Italy in central ◊Emilia-Romagna region; capital Bologna; area 3,700 sq km/1,429 sq mi; population (1992) 907,400.

Bolton Town in Greater Manchester, England, 18 km/11 mi NW of Manchester; population (1994 est) 210,000. Industries include engineering, chemicals, textiles, and the manufacture of missiles. It was a former cotton-spinning town. The first Lord Leverhulme was born here, as was Samuel Crompton, inventor of the spinning mule in 1779.

Bolzano (German *Bozen*) City in Italy, in Trentino-Alto Adige region on the river Isarco in the Alps; population (1990) 100,000. Bolzano belonged to Austria until 1919. Its inhabitants are mostly German-speaking.

Bolzano (German *Bozen*) Province of N Italy in ◊Trentino–Alto Adige autonomous region; capital Bolzano; area 7,400 sq km/2,857 sq mi; population (1992) 442,500.

Boma Port in the Democratic Republic of Congo (formerly Zaire), on the estuary of the river Congo/Zaire 88 km/55 mi from the Atlantic; population (1991 est) 246,200. The oldest European settlement in the Democratic Republic of Congo, it was a centre of the slave trade, and capital of the Belgian Congo until 1927.

Bombay Industrial port (textiles, engineering, pharmaceuticals, diamonds), commercial centre, and capital of Maharashtra, W India; population (1994) 14,500,000. It is the centre of the Hindi film industry.

Bonanza Creek   Valley in Yukon, NW Canada. The valley has rich gold deposits, and opens into the ◊Klondike River near Dawson City. A rich strike here in 1896 triggered the Klondike gold rush.

Bône   Former name of ◊Annaba, a port in Algeria.

Bonin and Volcano Islands   Japanese islands in the Pacific, N of the Marianas and 1,300 km/800 mi E of the Ryukyu Islands. They were under US control 1945–68. The *Bonin Islands* (Japanese *Ogasawara Gunto*) number 27 (in three groups), the largest being Chichijima: area 104 sq km/40 sq mi, population (1991) 2,430. The *Volcano Islands* (Japanese *Kazan Retto*) number three, including ◊Iwo Jima, scene of some of the fiercest fighting of World War II; total area 28 sq km/11 sq mi. They have no civilian population, but a 200-strong maritime self-defence force and a 100-strong air self-defence force are stationed there.

Bonn   Industrial city (chemicals, textiles, plastics, aluminium) in North Rhine–Westphalia in the Federal Republic of Germany, 18 km/15 mi SE of Cologne, on the left bank of the Rhine; population (1993) 297,900. It was the seat of government of West Germany 1949–90 and of the Federal Republic of Germany from 1990.

Bonneville Salt Flats   Bed of a prehistoric lake in Utah, USA, of which the Great Salt Lake is the surviving remnant. The flats, near the Nevada border, have been used to set many land speed records.

Bonny, Bight of   Alternate name for the Bight of ◊Biafra.

Bootle   Seaport in Merseyside, England, adjoining Liverpool; population (1991) 65,500.

Bophuthatswana   (Republic of) Former independent Black National State within South Africa, independent from 1977 (although not recognized by the United Nations) until 1994 when it was re-integrated into South Africa in North West Province, Free State (formerly Orange Free State), and Mpumalanga (formerly Eastern Transvaal) after rioting broke out in the run-up to the first multiracial elections.

Boppard   Town in the Rhineland-Palatinate, Germany, on the left bank of the Rhine, 20 km/12 mi S of Koblenz; population (1994) 16,100. It is the centre of a wine-growing area.

Bora-Bora   One of the 14 Society Islands of French Polynesia; situated 225 km/140 mi NW of Tahiti; area 39 sq km/15 sq mi; population (1977) 2,500. Exports include mother-of-pearl, fruit, and tobacco.

Borås   City in SW Sweden; population (1992) 102,800. Chief industries include textiles and engineering.

Bordeaux   Port on the river Garonne, capital of Aquitaine, SW France, a centre for the wine trade, oil refining, and aeronautics and space industries; population (1990) 213,300. Bordeaux was under the English crown for three centuries until 1453. In 1870, 1914, and 1940 the French government was moved here because of German invasion.

Borders   Former region of Scotland, replaced in 1996 by Scottish Borders unitary authority.

Borinage   Coal-mining district of Belgium, lying S and W of Mons, in the province of ◊Hainaut.

Borlänge   Town in SE Kopparberg county, central Sweden, on the W river Dal; population (1995) 48,500. It is an important steel and paper-mill centre.

Borneo   Third-largest island in the world, one of the Sunda Islands in the W Pacific; area 744,100 sq km/287,300 sq mi. It comprises the Malaysian territories of ◊Sabah and ◊Sarawak; Brunei; and, occupying by far the largest part, the Indonesian territory of ◊Kalimantan. It is mountainous and densely forested. In coastal areas the people of Borneo are mainly of Malaysian origin, with a few Chinese, and the interior is inhabited by the indigenous Dyaks. It was formerly under both Dutch and British colonial influence until Sarawak was formed 1841.

Bornholm   Danish island in the Baltic Sea, 35 km/22 mi SE of the nearest point of the Swedish coast; it constitutes a county of the same name
area   587 sq km/227 sq mi
capital   Rönne
population   (1993) 45,200.

Borobudur   Site of a Buddhist shrine near ◊Yogyakarta, Indonesia.

Bosna   River in Bosnia-Herzegovina, 257 km/160 mi long. It rises S of Sarajevo, and flows N to join the Sava.

Bosporus   (Turkish *Karadeniz Boğazı*) Strait 27 km/17 mi long, joining the Black Sea with the Sea of Marmara and forming part of the water division between Europe and Asia. Istanbul stands on its W side. The Bosporus Bridge 1973, 1,621 m/5,320 ft, links Istanbul and Anatolia (the Asian part of Turkey). In 1988 a second bridge across the straits was opened, linking Asia and Europe.

Boston   Seaport and market town in Lincolnshire, England, on the river Witham; population (1991) 34,600. St Botolph's is England's largest parish church, and its tower 'Boston stump' is a landmark for sailors.

Boston   Industrial port and commercial centre, capital of Massachusetts, USA, on Massachusetts Bay; population (1992) 551,700; metropolitan area (1992) 5,439,000. Its economy is dominated by financial and health services and government. It is also a publishing and academic centre. The subway system (begun 1897) was the first in the USA. Boston was founded by Puritans 1630 and has played an important role in American history.

Boston was a centre of opposition to British trade restrictions, culminating in the Boston Tea Party 1773. After the first shots of the American Revolution 1775 at nearby Lexington and Concord, the Battle of Bunker Hill was fought outside the city; the British withdrew 1776. In the 19th century, Boston became the metropolis of New England. Urban redevelopment and the growth of service industries have compensated for the city's industrial decline.

Features include the Freedom trail (2.4 km/1.5 mi) which covers 16 sites connected with the American Revolution; Old Granary Burial Ground; and the Bunker Hill Monument. Notable museums are the Museum of Fine Arts, the Isabella Stewart Gardner Museum, and the Museum of Science. The John F Kennedy Library and Museum are in South Boston. Among the 64 colleges and universities in the Boston area are Harvard University (1636), the oldest in the country, and Massachusetts Institute of Technology (MIIT).

Botany Bay   Inlet on the E coast of Australia, 8 km/5 mi S of Sydney, New South Wales. Chosen 1787 as the site for a penal colony, it proved unsuitable. Sydney now stands on the site of the former settlement. The name Botany Bay continued to be popularly used for any convict settlement in Australia.

Bottrop   City in North Rhine–Westphalia, Germany; population (1991) 118,800.

Bouches-du-Rhône   *Département* in the Provence-Alpes-Côte d'Azur region in France, containing the delta of the river ◊Rhône; area 5,112 sq km/1,974 sq mi; population (1990) 851,200. The W portion, known as the ◊Camargue, is a low-lying plain, and in the N and E the Alpes Maritimes slope down to the Rhône basin. Between the mountains and the sea is an arid plain called La Crau. The sea coast is indented and has many lagoons. The amount of arable land is small, though some cereals are grown. Olives are grown extensively in the NE, and there is livestock farming, particularly horses and cattle. Lignite and bauxite are found, and salt is mined. There are heavy industries, especially petrochemicals, in ◊Marseille (the capital). The other chief towns are Aix-en-Provence and Arles.

Bougainville   Island province of Papua New Guinea; largest of the Solomon Islands archipelago
area   10,620 sq km/4,100 sq mi
capital   Kieta
environment   waste from the Paguna workings, one of the world's largest copper mines, owned by Australian company CRA Minerals, has devastated the island's environment (according to rebel government sources 1992), silting up the streams of the Jaba River system and contaminating the water with dangerous heavy metals. In 1989, the Paguna workings produced nearly 49 million tonnes of ore and nearly 50 tonnes of waste
industries   copper, gold, and silver
population   (1994) 160,000
history   named after the French navigator Bougainville who arrived 1768. It was occupied by the Japanese during World War II from March 1942 until liberated by US troops 1943 and then held by the Australians until the end of the war. In 1976 Bougainville became a province (with substantial autonomy) of Papua New Guinea. A state of emergency was declared 1989 after secessionist violence. In 1990 the secessionist Bougainville Revolutionary Army took control of the island, declaring it independent; government troops regained control 1992. A peace agreement 1994 set up four neutral zones occupied by the Pacific peacekeeping force (from Fiji, Tonga, and Vanuatu).

Bougie   Former name (to 1962) of ◊Bejaia, a port in Algeria.

Boukra   or *Bou Kraa* Principal phosphate-mining centre of Western Sahara, linked by conveyor belt to the Atlantic coast near Laâyoune.

Boulder   City in N central Colorado, USA, NW of Denver, in the E foothills of the Rocky Mountains; population (1992) 85,600. The site of the University of Colorado (1876) and a centre of scientific research, especially space research, it also has agriculture, mining, and tourism. Boulder was first settled by miners 1858, and incorporated 1871.

Boulogne-sur-Mer   Town on the English Channel in the *département* of Pas-de-Calais, France; population (1990) 44,200. Industries include oil refining, food processing, and fishing. It is also a ferry port (connecting with Dover and Folkestone) and seaside resort. Boulogne was a medieval countship, but became part of France 1477.

Boulonnais   Former division of France, now in the *département* of Pas-de-Calais.

Boundary Peak   Highest mountain in Nevada, USA, rising to 4,006 m/13,143 ft on the Nevada–California frontier.

Bourbon   Former name (1649–1815) of the French island of ◊Réunion, in the Indian Ocean.

Bourg (-en-Bresse)   Capital of the French *département* of Ain, on the river Reyssouze, 75 km/47 mi W of Geneva; population 43,700. There is trade in horses, cattle, poultry, grains, and copper goods. The suburb of Brou has a 16th-century church, containing royal tombs and stained glass.

Bourges   City in central France, 200 km/125 mi S of Paris; population (1990) 78,800. Industries include aircraft, engineering, and tyres. It has a 13th-century Gothic cathedral and notable art collections.

Bourget, Lac du   Lake in the *département* of Savoie, France, near Aix-les-Bains. It is 17 km/11 mi long and about 3 km/2 mi wide.

Bourgogne   French name of ◊Burgundy, a region of E France.

Bournemouth   Seaside resort and unitary authority in S England; population (1994) 160,900; area 46 sq km/18 sq mi. It was part of the county of Dorset to 1997. Industries include communications systems (Siemens), insurance, banking, and finance. The International Conference Centre is here.

Bouvet Island   Uninhabited island in the S Atlantic Ocean, a dependency of Norway since 1930; area 48 sq km/19 sq mi. Discovered by the French captain Jacques Bouvet 1738, it was made the subject of a claim by Britain 1825, but this was waived in Norway's favour 1928.

Boyne   River in the Republic of Ireland. Rising in the Bog of Allen in County Kildare, it flows 110 km/69 mi NE to the Irish Sea near Drogheda. The Battle of the Boyne was fought at Oldbridge near the mouth of the river 1690.

Boyoma Falls   Series of seven cataracts in under 100 km/60 mi in the Lualaba (upper Congo/Zaïre River) above Kisangani, central Africa. They have a total drop of over 60 m/200 ft.

Bozen   German form of ◊Bolzano, a city in Italy.

Brabant   (Flemish *Braband*) Former duchy of W Europe, comprising the Dutch province of ◊North Brabant and the Belgian provinces of Brabant and Antwerp. They were divided when Belgium became independent 1830. The present-day Belgian Brabant is comprised of two provinces: Flemish Brabant (capital Leuven), with an area of 2,106 sq km/813 sq mi and a population of 995,300 (1995); and Wallern Brabant (capital Wavre), with an area of 1,091 sq km/421 sq mi and a population of 336,500 (1995).

Bracknell New town in Berkshire, England, SE of Reading, founded 1949; population (1991 est) 93,800. Bracknell Forest will become a unitary authority in April 1998. The headquarters of the Meteorological Office are here, and Bracknell (with Washington DC) is one of the two global area forecasting centres of upper-level winds and temperatures for the world's airlines. Industries include engineering, clothing, and furniture.

Bradenton City in W Florida, USA, on the S shores of Tampa Bay, SW of Tampa; seat of Manatee County; population (1990) 43,800. The Spanish explorer Hernando de Soto landed nearby 1539, but the first permanent settlement dates from 1854.

Bradford Industrial city (engineering, chemicals, machine tools, electronics, printing) in West Yorkshire, England, 14 km/9 mi W of Leeds; population (1994 est) 357,000. Industries also include financial services and it is the main city for wool textiles in the UK.

Braemar Village in Grampian, Scotland, where the most celebrated of the Highland Games, the *Braemar Gathering*, takes place on the first Saturday in September.

Braga City in N Portugal 48 km/30 mi NE of Porto; population (1987) 63,000. Industries include textiles, electrical goods, and vehicle manufacture. It has a 12th-century cathedral, and the archbishop is primate of the Iberian peninsula. As *Bracara Augusta* it was capital of the Roman province Lusitania.

Bragança Capital of a province of the same name in NE Portugal, 176 km/110 mi NE of Porto; population (1991) 16,500. It was the original family seat of the House of Braganza, which ruled Portugal 1640–1910.

Brahmaputra River in Asia 2,736 km/1,700 mi long, a tributary of the Ganges.

Brăila Port in Romania on the river Danube; 170 km/106 mi from its mouth; population (1993) 236,000. It is a naval base. Industries include the manufacture of artificial fibres, iron and steel, machinery, and paper. It was controlled by the Ottoman Empire 1544–1828.

Brandenburg Administrative region (German *Land*) of Germany
area 29,479 sq km/11,382 sq mi
capital Potsdam
towns and cities Cottbus, Brandenburg, Frankfurt-an-der-Oder
industries iron and steel, paper, pulp, metal products, semiconductors
population (1995) 2,542,000
history The Hohenzollern rulers who took control of Brandenburg 1415 later acquired the powerful duchy of Prussia and became emperors of Germany. At the end of World War II, Brandenburg lost over 12,950 sq km/5,000 sq mi of territory when Poland advanced its frontier to the line of the Oder and Neisse rivers. The remainder, which became a region of East Germany, was divided 1952 into the districts of Frankfurt-an-der-Oder, Potsdam, and Cottbus. When Germany was reunited 1990, Brandenburg reappeared as a state of the Federal Republic.

Brandenburg Town in Germany, on the river Havel; 60 km/36 mi W of Berlin; population (1991) 88,800. Industries include textiles, cars, and aircraft. It has a 12th-century cathedral.

Brandon Town in Manitoba, Canada, situated on the Assiniboine River, approximately 211 km/131 mi W of Winnipeg; population (1991) 38,600. The town is in one of the most richly cultivated parts of the province, wheat being the chief crop. It is an important centre for research and development in agricultural techniques and agricultural genetics. It is Manitoba's second-largest town and a booming tourist centre.

Brandywine Creek Stream rising in Chester County, Pennsylvania, E USA; length 32 km/20 mi. It rises in SE Pennsylvania and flows into the Christina River, and finally into the Delaware at Wilmington. It was the site of a significant battle 1777 in the American War of Independence, and gives its name to a widespread marine and alluvial terrace.

Brasília Capital of Brazil from 1960, 1,000 m/3,000 ft above sea level; population (1991) 1,601,100. The main area of employment is in government service.

Braşov formerly (1948–56) *Oreşul Stalin*, (Hungarian *Brassó*, German *Krondstadt*) Industrial city (machine tools, industrial equipment, chemicals, cement, woollens) in central Romania at the foot of the Transylvanian Alps; population (1993) 324,000. It belonged to Hungary until 1920.

Bratislava (German *Pressburg*) Industrial port (engineering, chemicals, oil refining) and capital of the Slovak Republic, on the river Danube; population (1991) 441,500. It was the capital of Hungary (as Pozsony) 1526–1784 and capital of Slovakia (within Czechoslovakia) until 1993.

Braunau am Inn Austrian town in the province of Upper Austria, situated on the border with the German *Land* of Bavaria, 92 km/57 mi W of Linz; population (1995) 17,600. Braunau was the birthplace of the Nazi leader Adolf Hitler. The town contains several Gothic churches, and in its industrial suburb has the largest aluminium plant in Austria.

Braunschweig German form of ◊Brunswick, a city in Lower Saxony, Germany.

Brazzaville Capital of the Republic of the Congo (Congo-Brazzaville), industrial port (foundries, railway repairs, shipbuilding, shoes, soap, furniture, bricks) on the river Congo/Zaïre, opposite Kinshasa; population (1992) 938,000. There is a cathedral 1892 and the Pasteur Institute 1908. It stands on Pool Malebo (Stanley Pool).

Brcko Town in Serbian Bosnia-Herzegovina, on the river Sava; population (1991) 87,300. It grew up around a Turkish fort, and is the centre of a rich agricultural region.

Brecknockshire or *Breconshire* (Welsh *Sir Frycheiniog*)

Former county of Wales, merged into ◊Powys 1974–1996, now part of Powys unitary authority.

Breda City in North Brabant, the Netherlands; population (1994) 129,100. It was here that Charles II of England made the declaration that paved the way for his restoration 1660.

Bregenz Capital of the Austrian province of ◊Vorarlberg, at the E end of Lake Constance; population (1995) 27,500. It is a tourist resort, trades in agricultural produce, and has textile, chemicals, and woodworking industries. The Romans called it Brigantium. Part of the 13th-century walls remain, and the church is partly 11th century. A music festival is held annually in the city.

Breisach Town in Baden-Württemberg, Germany, on a hill overlooking the river Rhine, 25 km/15 mi W of Freiburg im Breisgau; population (1994) 11,800. The centre of the Baden wine-growing region, Breisach contains Europe's largest wine cellars, with a capacity of 80 million litres. In the Middle Ages, it was an important stronghold.

Breisgau Region in SW Germany between the river Rhine and the Black Forest, now part of the *Land* of ◊Baden-Württemberg; its principal towns are ◊Freiburg im Breisgau and Breisach.

Breizh Celtic name for ◊Brittany, a region of France.

Bremen Industrial port in Germany, on the river Weser 69 km/43 mi from the open sea; population (1993) 552,700. Industries include iron, steel, oil refining, chemicals, aircraft, cars, and shipbuilding. The Bremer Vulkan Shipyards closed 1996.

Bremen Administrative region (German *Land*) of Germany, consisting of the cities of Bremen and Bremerhaven; area 404 sq km/156 sq mi; population (1995 est) 679,800.

Bremerhaven formerly (until 1947) *Wesermünde* Port at the mouth of the river Weser in the *Land* of Bremen, Germany; population (1991) 130,900. Industries include fishing and shipbuilding. It serves as an outport for Bremen.

Bremerton City in W Washington, USA, SW of Seattle and NW of Tacoma, on an inlet of Puget Sound; population (1990) 38,100. It serves as a port for the area's fish, dairy, and lumber products. Tourism is also important to the economy. Bremerton was laid out 1899.

Brenner Pass Lowest of the Alpine passes, 1,370 m/4,495 ft; it leads from Trentino–Alto Adige, Italy, to the Austrian Tirol, and is 19 km/12 mi long.

Brent Outer borough of NW Greater London. It includes the suburbs of Wembley and Willesden
features Wembley Stadium (1923); a new National Sports Stadium is to be built at Wembley, designed by Sir Norman Foster; former State Cinema in Willesden (1937), the largest cinema in Europe when built; Brent Cross shopping centre (1976), first regional shopping centre in Europe
population (1991) 243,000.

Brescia (ancient *Brixia*) Historic and industrial city (textiles, engineering, firearms, metal products) in N Italy, 84 km/52 mi E of Milan; population (1992) 192,900. It has medieval walls and two cathedrals (12th and 17th century).

Brescia Province of N Italy in central ◊Lombardy region; capital Brescia; area 4,760 sq km/1,838 sq mi; population (1992) 1,047,600.

Breslau German name of ◊Wrocław, a city in Poland.

Bresse Former district of France, once part of ◊Burgundy, situated E of the river Saône. Bourges was the capital.

Brest City in Belarus, on the river Bug and the Polish frontier; population (1991) 277,000. It was in Poland (*Brześć nad Bugiem*) until 1795 and again 1921–39. In World War I, the Russian truce with Germany, the *Treaty of Brest-Litovsk* (an older Russian name of the city), was signed here March 1918.

Brest Naval base and industrial port (electronics, engineering, chemicals) on *Rade de Brest* (Brest Roads), a great bay at the W extremity of Brittany, France; population (1990) 201,500. Occupied as a U-boat base by the Germans 1940–44, the city was destroyed by Allied bombing and rebuilt.

Bretagne French form of ◊Brittany, a region of NW France.

Brevent, Mont Mountain of the Pennine Alps, in the *département* of Haute-Savoie, France. It rises above the valley of Chamonix. From its summit (altitude 2,525 m/8,282 ft) there is a fine view of ◊Mont Blanc.

Briançon French town on the river Durance, in the *département* of Hautes-Alpes; population (1990) 35,600. It has a trade in *craie de Briançon* (French chalk) and cheese. The highest town in Europe, it is a tourist resort – the older part of the town, strongly fortified by the 17th-century military engineer Vauban, is over 1,200 m/3,900 ft above sea level.

Bridgend Unitary authority in S Wales created 1996 from part of the former county of Mid Glamorgan; population (1996) 128,300; area 40 sq km/15 sq mi. Industries include civil engineering and chocolate manufacture.

Bridgeport City in Connecticut, USA, on Long Island Sound; population (1992) 137,000. Industries include metal goods, electrical appliances, and aircraft, but many factories closed in the 1970s. Bridgeport was settled 1639 and incorporated 1800.

Bridgeton City in SW New Jersey, USA, at the head of the Cohansey River; seat of Cumberland County; population (1990) 18,900. Industries include food processing, glassmaking, clothing, and dairy products. Bridgeton was founded 1686.

Bridgetown Port and capital of Barbados; population (1990) 6,700. Sugar is exported through the nearby deepwater port. Bridgetown was founded 1628.

Bridgwater Market town and port in Somerset, England, on the river Parret NE of Taunton; population (1991) 34,600. Industries include bricks, furniture, engineering, wire rope, fibre fabrics, cellophane, footwear, plastics, and electrical goods. The site of the Battle of Sedgemoor is 5 km/3 mi to the SE.

Brie District of N France, lying between the rivers Seine and Marne; area 6,500 sq km/2,510 sq mi. The district is divided into two parts: West Brie, now absorbed into ◊Ile-de-France region, and East Brie, formerly the county of Meaux. The district gives its name to a type of cheese.

Brieg German name for Brzeg, a town in Poland.

Brienz Commune in the canton of Bern, Switzerland, 52 km/32 mi SE of Bern; population (1995) 125. Brienz is the centre of the Bernese Oberland woodcarving industry and also manufactures violins. It is situated NE of *Lake Brienz*, at the foot of the *Brienzergrat* mountain range. The lake is 14 km/9 mi long and 5 km/3 mi wide, and lies in the valley of the river Aar.

Brighton Seaside resort and administrative headquarters of Brighton and Hove unitary authority, on the S coast of England; it was part of the county of East Sussex to 1997; population (1994 est) 155,000. It has Regency architecture and the Royal Pavilion 1782 in Oriental style. There are two piers and an aquarium.

Brighton and Hove Unitary authority in S England created 1997; administrative headquarters Brighton; population (1994) 248,000; area 84 sq km/32 sq mi.

Brindisi (ancient *Brundisium*) Port and naval base on the Adriatic Sea, in Puglia, on the heel of Italy; population (district, 1992) 412,600. Industries include food processing and petrochemicals. It is one of the oldest Mediterranean ports, at the end of the Appian Way from Rome. The poet Virgil died here 19 BC.

Brindisi Province of SE Italy in E ◊Puglia region; capital Brindisi; area 1,836 sq km/709 sq mi; population (1992) 412,000.

Brisbane Industrial port (brewing, engineering, tanning, tobacco, shoes; oil pipeline from Moonie), capital of Queensland, E Australia, near the mouth of Brisbane River, dredged to carry ocean-going ships; population (1993) 1,421,600.

Bristol City in central Connecticut, USA, SW of Hartford; population (1992) 64,100. Products include clocks, tools, and machinery parts. Known as the clockmaking capital of the USA, the city has the American Clock and Watch Museum. Bristol was first settled 1727.

Bristol Industrial port and unitary authority in SW England, created 1996 from part of the former county of Avon; population (1996) 374,300; area 109 sq km/42 sq mi. The old docks have been redeveloped for housing, industry, yachting facilities, and the National Lifeboat Museum. Further developments include a new city centre, with Brunel's Temple Meads railway station at its focus, and a weir across the Avon nearby to improve the waterside environment. Industries include aircraft engines, engineering, microelectronics, tobacco, chemicals, paper, printing, soap, metal refining, chocolate, banking, and insurance.

Bristol City located in Virginia and Tennessee (the border runs through the centre of the city), USA, NE of Knoxville; population (1990) 23,400 (Tennessee), 18,400 (Virginia). This dual city is divided politically, but constitutes one unit economically. Industries include lumber, steel, office machines, pharmaceuticals, missile parts, and textiles.

Bristol Bay Arm of the Bering Sea in the N Pacific, lying to the N of the peninsula of Aleutia. The name is also applied to the empty, lake-strewn area of Alaska on the N shore of the bay. The bay's shallowness limits navigation.

Britain Island off the NW coast of Europe, one of the British Isles. It comprises England, Scotland, and Wales (together officially known as ◊Great Britain), and is part of the United Kingdom. The name is derived from the Roman name Britannia, which in turn is derived from the ancient Celtic name of the inhabitants, *Bryttas*.

British Antarctic Territory British dependent territory created 1962 and comprising all British territories S of latitude 60° S and between 20° and 80° W longitude: the South Orkney Islands, the South Shetland Islands, the Antarctic Peninsula and all adjacent lands, and Coats Land, extending to the South Pole; total land area 1,810,000 sq km/700,000 sq mi; population (exclusively scientific personnel) about 300.

British Columbia Province of Canada on the Pacific Ocean

area 947,800 sq km/365,946 sq mi

capital Victoria

towns and cities Vancouver, Prince George, Kamloops, Kelowna, Surrey

physical Rocky Mountains and Coast Range; deeply indented coast; rivers include the Fraser and Columbia; over 80 lakes; Tatshensini Provincial Park; more than half the land is forested

industries fruit and vegetables; timber and wood products; fish; coal, copper, iron, lead; oil and natural gas; hydro-electricity

population (1995 est) 3,529,000

history Captain Cook explored the coast 1778; a British colony was founded on Vancouver Island 1849, and the gold rush of 1858 extended settlement to the mainland; it became a province 1871. In 1885 the Canadian Pacific Railroad linking British Columbia to the E coast was completed.

British Colombia

British Honduras   Former name (to 1973) of ◊Belize.

British Indian Ocean Territory   British colony in the Indian Ocean directly administered by the Foreign and Commonwealth Office. It consists of the Chagos Archipelago some 1,900 km/1,200 mi NE of Mauritius
area   60 sq km/23 sq mi
features   lagoons; US naval and air base on Diego Garcia
industries   copra, salt fish, tortoiseshell
population   There is no permanent population.
history   purchased 1965 for $3 million by Britain from Mauritius to provide a joint US/UK base. The islands of Aldabra, Farquhar, and Desroches, some 485 km/300 mi N of Madagascar, originally formed part of the British Indian Ocean Territory but were returned to the administration of the Seychelles 1976.

British Isles   Group of islands off the NW coast of Europe, consisting of Great Britain (England, Wales, and Scotland), Ireland, the Channel Islands, the Orkney and Shetland islands, the Isle of Man, and many other islands that are included in various counties, such as the Isle of Wight, Scilly Isles, Lundy Island, and the Inner and Outer Hebrides. The islands are divided from Europe by the North Sea, Strait of Dover, and the English Channel, and face the Atlantic to the W.

British Virgin Islands   Part of the ◊Virgin Islands group in the West Indies.

Brittany   (French *Bretagne*, Breton *Breiz*) Region of NW France in the Breton peninsula between the Bay of Biscay and the English Channel; area 27,208 sq km/10,505 sq mi; capital Rennes; population (1990) 2,795,600. A farming region, it includes the *départements* of Côtes-d'Armor, Finistère, Ille-et-Vilaine, and Morbihan.
history   Brittany was the Gallo-Roman province of Armorica after being conquered by Julius Caesar 56 BC. It was devastated by Norsemen after the Roman withdrawal. Established under the name of Brittany in the 5th century AD by Celts fleeing the Anglo-Saxon invasion of Britain, it became a strong, expansionist state that maintained its cultural and political independence despite pressure from the Carolingians, Normans, and Capetians. In 1171, the duchy of Brittany was inherited by Geoffrey, son of Henry II of England, and remained in the Angevin dynasty's possession until 1203, when Geoffrey's son Arthur was murdered by King John, and the title passed to the Capetian Peter of Dreux. Under the Angevins, feudalism was introduced, and French influence increased under the Capetians. By 1547 it had been formally annexed by France, and the Breton language was banned in education. A separatist movement developed after World War II, and there has been guerrilla activity.

Brive (-la-Gaillarde)   French town in the *département* of Corrèze, on the river Corrèze; population (1990) 53,000. It manufactures shoes, textiles, and paper, and has a metal-processing industry. There is trade in chestnuts, wine, and truffles. It was known to the Romans as Brive Curretiae and has a 12th-century church.

Brno   (German *Brünn*) Industrial city (chemicals, arms, textiles, machinery) in the Czech Republic; population (1993) 390,000. Now the second largest city in the Czech Republic, Brno was formerly the capital of the Austrian crown land of Moravia.

Broads, Norfolk   Area of navigable lakes and rivers in England; see ◊Norfolk Broads.

Brocken   Highest peak of the Harz Mountains (1,142 m/ 3,746 ft) in Germany. On 30 April (Walpurgis night), witches are said to gather here.

Brockton   City in SW Massachusetts, USA, S of Boston; population (1992) 89,200. Industries include footwear, tools, and electronic equipment. Brockton was built on land sold by Native Americans in 1649 to Myles Standish and John Alden, which became part of the Plymouth colony. It was part of Bridgewater until renamed 1874.

Broken Hill   Mining town in New South Wales, Australia; population (1981) 27,000. It is the base of the Royal Flying Doctor Service.

Broken Hill   Former name (to 1967) of ◊Kabwe, a city in Zambia.

Bromberg   German name of ◊Bydgoszcz, a town in Poland.

Bromley   Outer borough of SE Greater London
features   Crystal Palace, re-erected at Sydenham 1854 and burned down 1936, site now partly occupied by the National Sports Centre; 13th-century parish church of SS Peter and Paul; 17th-century Bromley College; chalk caves and tunnels at Chislehurst; Keston Common has a Roman cemetery and traces of a Roman villa; Holwood Park contains 'Caesar's Camp', the site of a British encampment with earthworks dating from c. 200 BC. It is the best surviving field monument in Greater London.
population   (1991) 290,600
famous people   William Pitt, H G Wells, W G Grace.

Bronx, the   Borough of New York City, USA, NE of the Harlem River; area 109 sq km/42 sq mi; population (1990) 1,169,000. It is largely residential. The New York Zoological Society and Gardens are here, popularly called the Bronx Zoo and the Bronx Botanical Gardens.

Brooklyn   Borough of New York City, USA, occupying the SW end of Long Island. It is linked to Manhattan Island by the Brooklyn–Battery Tunnel, the Brooklyn Bridge 1883, the Williamsburg and the Manhattan bridges, and to Staten Island by the Verrazano-Narrows Bridge 1964. There are more than 60 parks, of which Prospect is the largest. There is also a museum, botanical garden, and a beach and amusement area at Coney Island.

Browns Ferry   Site of a nuclear power station on the Alabama River, central Alabama, USA. A nuclear accident 1975 resulted in the closure of the plant for 18 months. This incident marked the beginning of widespread disenchantment with nuclear power in the USA.

Brownsville   City in S Texas, USA, on the Rio Grande just before it flows into the Gulf of Mexico, S of Corpus Christi and N of Matamoros, Mexico; seat of Cameron County; population (1992) 105,750. It is a port of entry to the USA; industries include chemicals and food products; tourism is also important. Originally Fort Taylor 1846, it was an important Confederate port during the Civil War.

Bruay-la-Buissiere (formerly *Bruay-en-Artois*) French town in the *département* of Pas-de-Calais; population (1990) 25,500.

Bruchsal City in Baden-Württemberg, Germany, 20 km/ 12 mi NW of Karlsruhe; population (1994) 40,100. Bruchsal is an important railway junction and has metallurgical, chemical, paper, and textile industries.

Bruck an der Mur Town in the Austrian province of Styria, 40 km/25 mi NW of Graz. It has a number of old buildings, and manufactures iron and steel, paper, and cables.

Bruges (Flemish *Brugge*) Historic city in NW Belgium; capital of W Flanders province, 16 km/10 mi from the North Sea, with which it is connected by canal; population (1995) 116,000. Bruges was the capital of medieval ◊Flanders and was the chief European wool manufacturing town as well as its chief market. The contemporary port handles coal, iron ore, oil, and fish; local industries include lace, textiles, paint, steel, beer, furniture, and motors.

Brugg Town in the canton of Aargau, Switzerland, 45 km/ 28 mi W of Basel; population (1995) 9,200.

Brugge Flemish form of ◊Bruges, a city in Belgium.

Brühl City in North Rhine–Westphalia, Germany, 12 km/ 7 mi SW of Cologne, and administratively a suburb of ◊Bonn; population (1994) 43,400. Manufactures include food, iron, chemicals, and paper.

Brunei Town Former name (to 1970) of ◊Bandar Seri Begawan, the capital of Brunei.

Brünn German form of ◊Brno, a city in the Czech Republic.

Brunswick (German *Braunschweig*) Industrial city (chemical engineering, precision engineering, food processing) in Lower Saxony, Germany; population (1993) 257,800. Brunswick was one of the chief cities of N Germany in the Middle Ages and a member of the Hanseatic League. It was capital of the duchy of Brunswick from 1671.

Brunswick (German *Braunschweig*) Former independent duchy, a republic from 1918, which is now part of ◊Lower Saxony, Germany.

Brusa Alternative form of ◊Bursa, a city in Turkey.

Brussels (Flemish *Brussel*, French *Bruxelles*) Capital of Belgium, industrial city (lace, textiles, machinery, and chemicals); population (1995) 952,000 (80% French-speaking, the suburbs Flemish-speaking). It is the headquarters of the European Union (EU) and since 1967 of the international secretariat of NATO. First settled in the 6th century, and a city from 1312, Brussels became the capital of the Spanish Netherlands 1530 and of Belgium 1830.

It has fine buildings including the 13th-century church of Sainte Gudule; the Hôtel de Ville, Maison du Roi, and others in the Grande Place; the royal palace. The Musées Royaux des Beaux-Arts de Belgique hold a large art collection. The bronze fountain statue of a tiny naked boy urinating, the

Manneken Pis (1388) is to be found here. Brussels is also the site of the world's largest cinema complex, with 24 film theatres.

Brüx German name for Most, a town in the Czech Republic.

Bruxelles French form of ◊Brussels, the capital of Belgium.

Bryan City in E Texas, USA, NW of Houston; seat of Brazos County; population (1992) 56,550. Its industries include the manufacture of cotton gins.

Bryansk City in W central Russian Federation, SW of Moscow on the river Desna; population (1994) 460,000. Industries include sawmills, textiles, and steel.

Brzeg (German *Brieg*) Industrial town (chemicals, electrical goods) in Opole province, Poland, on the river Oder, 43 km/27 mi NW of Opole; population (1990) 5,400.

Brześć nad Bugiem Polish name of ◊Brest, a city in Belarus.

Bubiyan Uninhabited island off Kuwait, occupied by Iraq 1990; area about 1,000 sq km/380 sq mi. On 28 Feb 1991, following Allied success in the Gulf War, Iraqi troops were withdrawn.

Bucaramanga Industrial and commercial city (coffee, tobacco, cacao, cotton) in N central Colombia; population (1992) 350,000. It was founded by the Spanish 1622.

Bucharest (Romanian *Bucureşti*) Capital and largest city of Romania; population (1993) 2,343,800. The conurbation of Bucharest district has an area of 1,520 sq km/ 587 sq mi. It was originally a citadel built by Vlad the Impaler to stop the advance of the Ottoman invasion in the 14th century. Bucharest became the capital of the princes of Wallachia 1698 and of Romania 1861. Savage fighting took place in the city during Romania's 1989 revolution.

Buckingham Market town in Buckinghamshire, England, on the river Ouse; population (1991) 10,200. University College was established 1974, and was given a royal charter as the University of Buckingham 1983.

Buckinghamshire County of SE central England
area 1,565 sq km/604 sq mi
towns and cities Aylesbury (administrative headquarters), Buckingham, High Wycombe, Beaconsfield, Olney
features Chiltern Hills; Chequers (country seat of the prime minister); Burnham Beeches and the church of the poet Gray's 'Elegy' at Stoke Poges; Cliveden, a country house designed by Charles Barry (now a hotel, it was once the home of Nancy, Lady Astor); Bletchley Park, home of World War II code-breaking activities, now used as a training post for GCHQ (Britain's electronic surveillance centre); homes of the poets William Cowper at Olney and John Milton at Chalfont St Giles, and of the Tory prime minister Disraeli at Hughenden; Stowe gardens
products furniture, chiefly beech; agricultural goods including barley, wheat, oats, sheep, cattle, poultry, pigs
population (1997 est) 468,700
famous people John Hampden, Edmund Waller, William Herschel, George Gilbert Scott, Ben Nicholson.

Bucks Abbreviation for ◊Buckinghamshire.

Budapest Capital of Hungary, industrial city (chemicals, textiles) on the river Danube; population (1993 est) 2,009,000. The site of a Roman outpost in the 1st century AD, Buda was the seat of Magyar kings from the 14th century. It was later occupied by the Turks, and was under Habsburg rule from the end of the 17th century. Buda, on the right bank of the Danube, became the Hungarian capital 1867 and was joined with Pest, on the left bank, 1872.

Budějovice A town in the Czech Republic; see ◊České Budějovice.

Budweis German form of ◊České Budějovice, a town in the Czech Republic.

Buenos Aires Capital and industrial city and port of Argentina, on the S bank of the Río de la Plata; population (1992 est) 11,662,050. Its main exports are grain, beef, and wool.

Buffalo Industrial port in New York State, USA, at the E end of Lake Erie; population (1992) 323,300; metropolitan area (1992) 1,194,000. It is linked with New York City by the New York State Barge Canal, and is an important port, especially as a centre for trade between the USA and Canada. Settled in 1780, Buffalo was burned by the British during the War of 1812 but was soon rebuilt and flourished with the completion of the Erie Canal 1825. An industrial city, Buffalo was hard hit by the closing of steel mills and auto factories in the late 1970s and early 1980s.

Bug Name of two rivers in E Europe: the *West Bug* rises in SW Ukraine and flows to the Vistula, length 768 km/480 mi, and the *South Bug* rises in W Ukraine and flows to the Black Sea, length 853 km/530 mi.

Buganda Either of two provinces (North and South Buganda) of Uganda, home of the Baganda people and formerly a kingdom from the 17th century. The former *kabaka* or king, Edward Mutesa II (1924–1969), was the first president of independent Uganda 1962–66. He was deposed as monarch 1966. His son Ronald Mutebi (1955–) is *sabataka* (head of the Baganda clans) and from 1993 (when the monarchy was restored) also king.

Bujumbura Capital of Burundi; population (1994 est) 300,000. Formerly called *Usumbura* (until 1962), it was founded 1899 by German colonists. The university was established 1960.

Bukavu Port in E Democratic Republic of Congo (formerly Zaire), on Lake Kivu; population (1991 est) 209,600. Mining is the chief industry. Called *Costermansville* until 1966, it is the capital of Kivu region.

Bukhara or *Bokhara* Central city in Uzbekistan; population (1990) 228,000. It is the capital of Bukhara region, which has given its name to carpets (made in Ashgabat). It is an Islamic centre, with a Muslim theological training centre. An ancient city in central Asia, it was formerly the capital of the independent emirate of Bukhara, annexed to Russia 1868.

Bukharest Alternative form of ◊Bucharest, the capital of Romania.

Bukovina Region in SE Europe, divided between the Ukraine and Romania. It covers 10,500 sq km/4,050 sq mi. Part of Moldavia during the Turkish regime, it was ceded by the Ottoman Empire to Austria 1777, becoming a duchy of the Dual Monarchy 1867–1918; then it was included in Romania. N Bukovina was ceded to the USSR 1940 and included in Ukraine as the region of Chernovtsy; the cession was confirmed by the peace treaty 1947, but the question of its return has been raised by Romania. The part of Bukovina remaining in Romania became the district of Suceava.

Bulawayo Industrial city and railway junction in Zimbabwe; population (1992) 620,900. It lies at an altitude of 1,355 m/4,450 ft on the river Matsheumlope, a tributary of the Zambezi, and was founded on the site of the kraal (enclosed village), burned down 1893, of the Matabele chief, Lobenguela. It produces cement and agricultural and electrical equipment. The former capital of Matabeleland, Bulawayo developed with the exploitation of gold mines in the neighbourhood.

Bunzlau German name for Bolesławiec, a town in Poland.

Burgas Black Sea port and resort in Bulgaria; population (1990) 204,900.

Burgdorf (French *Berthoud*) Commune in the canton of Bern, Switzerland, on the river Emme, 18 km/11 mi NE of Bern; population (1995) 14,500. It has silk and clothmaking industries and a trade in cheese. In the castle at Burgdorf, the educational reformer Johann Heinrich Pestalozzi established his first school 1798–1804.

Burgenland Province of SE Austria, extending S from the Danube along the W border of the Hungarian plain; area 3,965 sq km/1,531 sq mi; population (1995) 274,334. It is a largely agricultural region adjoining the Neusiedler See, and produces timber, fruit, sugar, wine, lignite, antimony, and limestone. Its capital is Eisenstadt.

Burgess Shale Site Site of fossil-bearing rock formations created 530 million years ago by a mud slide, in Yoho National Park, British Columbia, Canada. The shales in this corner of the Rocky Mountains contain more than 120 species of marine invertebrate fossils.

Burgos City in Castilla-León, Spain, 217 km/135 mi N of Madrid; population (1994) 166,000. It produces textiles, motor parts, and chemicals. It was capital of the old kingdom of Castile, and the national hero El Cid is buried in the cathedral, built 1221–1567 and regarded as one of the most important examples of Gothic architecture in Europe.

Burgos Province of N central Spain in NW Castilla-León autonomous community; capital Burgos; area 14,268 sq km/ 5,509 sq mi; population (1995) 360,700. It is a tableland with a severe climate and barren soil, crossed by ranges of high mountains and the Ebro and Duero rivers. Main industries include agriculture, forestry, and sheepraising.

Burgundy (French *Bourgogne*) Modern region and former duchy of France that includes the *départements* of Côte-d'Or,

Nièvre, Saône-et-Loire, and Yonne; area 31,582 sq km/ 12,194 sq mi; population (1990) 1,609,700. Its capital is Dijon.

Burlington City in N central North Carolina, USA, NW of Durham; population (1990) 39,500. Industries include textiles, chemicals, furniture, and agricultural products. It was incorporated 1866 as Company Shops, and renamed 1887.

Burlington City in NW Vermont, USA, on the E shore of Lake Champlain; seat of Chittenden County; population (1990) 39,100. It is a port of entry to the USA; industries include computer parts, steel, marble, lumber, dairy products, and tourism. It was settled 1773, and was a naval base during the War of 1812.

Burnley Town in Lancashire, England, 19 km/12 mi NE of Blackburn; population (1989 est) 85,400. Formerly a cotton-manufacturing town, its industries include light engineering, textiles, aerospace equipment, and vehicle components.

Bursa or *Brusa* City in NW Turkey, with a port at Mudania; population (1990) 834,600. It was the capital of the Ottoman Empire 1326–1423.

Burton upon Trent Town in Staffordshire, England, NE of Birmingham; population (1991) 60,500. Industries include brewing, tyres, engineering, food processing, and rubber products. It is a former cotton-spinning town. The Benedictine monks of Burton Abbey (founded 1002) began its tradition of brewing in the 11th century.

Bury City in Greater Manchester, England, on the river Irwell, 16 km/10 mi N of central Manchester; population (1991) 62,600. It is a textile town, concentrating on cotton spinning and weaving. Other industries include chemicals, engineering, textile machinery, felt, paint, printing, and paper making.

Buryatia Autonomous republic of the Russian Federation, in East Siberia
area 351,300 sq km/135,600 sq mi
capital Ulan-Ude
physical bounded S by Mongolia, W by Lake Baikal; mountainous and forested
industries coal, timber, building materials, fish, sheep, cattle
population (1992) 1,059,000

Bury St Edmunds Market town in Suffolk, England, on the river Lark; population (1991) 31,200. Industries include brewing, sugar beet refining, electronic equipment, cameras, lamps, and confectionery. It was named after St Edmund, and there are remains of a large Benedictine abbey founded 1020.

Buskerud County of SE Norway; area 14,855 sq km/ 5,736 sq mi; population (1995) 229,400. The rivers Lågen and Drammen flow through Buskerud into Oslofjord. There are mountains and lakes in the NE, but the E of the county is chiefly agricultural; fruit and corn are grown. Paper and pulp mills are the main industries along the Drammen. The principal town, which stands on the river, is also called Drammen.

Bute Island and resort in the Firth of Clyde, Scotland; area 120 sq km/46 sq mi. The chief town is Rothesay. There is

farming and tourism. It is separated from the mainland in the N by a winding channel, the *Kyles of Bute*. With Arran and the adjacent islands it comprised the former county of Bute, merged 1975–96 into Strathclyde Region. It is now part of Argyll and Bute unitary authority.

Butte Mining town in Montana, USA, in the Rocky Mountains; population (1990) 33,900. Butte was founded 1864 during a rush for gold, soon exhausted; copper was found some 20 years later on what was called 'the richest hill on earth'.

Buxton Former spa town in Derbyshire, England; population (1991) 19,900. Known from Roman times for its hot springs, it is today a source for bottled mineral water and a tourist centre. It has a restored Edwardian opera house and an annual opera festival.

Buzău Capital of Buzău county, Romania, on the river Buzău, 68 km/43 mi NE of Bucharest; population (1993) 149,000. It is a market town at the centre of a cereal and livestock region, trading in grain, timber, and petroleum, and produces metalwork and wire. Buzău has a 12th-century bishop's palace and a 15th-century cathedral.

Buzzards Bay Large inlet (48 km/30 mi long, 8–15 km/ 5–9 mi wide) of the Atlantic Ocean on the SE coast of Massachusetts, USA. New Bedford stands on the bay at the mouth of the Acushnet River, which falls, with other small streams, into the bay. The bay is enclosed on the S side by the Elizabeth Islands.

Bydgoszcz Industrial river port in N Poland, 105 km/ 65 mi NE of Poznań on the river Warta; population (1993) 383,600. As *Bromberg* it was under Prussian control 1772–1919.

Byelorussia See Belarus.

Bytom (German *Beuthen*) Mining town in Katowice province, Poland, 13 km/8 mi NW of Katowice; population (1990) 231,200. The district is a large source of coal, lead, and zinc, mined since medieval times, and has engineering industries. Formerly in Upper Silesia, Bytom remained German after the plebiscite of 1921 but was incorporated to Poland 1945.

CA Abbreviation for the state of ◊California, USA.

Cabinda or *Kabinda* African coastal enclave, a province of Angola; area 7,770 sq km/3,000 sq mi; population (1992 est) 152,100. The capital is Cabinda. There are oil reserves. Attached to Angola 1886, the enclave has made claims to independence.

Cáceres Capital of the province of Cáceres, W Spain; population (1995) 81,000. Built on a hill, the old part of the town, surrounded by Roman and Moorish walls, is preserved as a national monument. It has many churches and towers, and medieval and Renaissance mansions. Products include textiles, soap, and leather goods. Agriculture is important.

Cáceres Province of W Spain in ◊Extremadura autonomous community; capital Cáceres; area 19,961 sq km/7,707 sq mi; population (1995) 424,900. Bordered on the W by

Portugal, it lies largely in the basin of the river Tagus. Main products include wool, oil, ham, and red sausages (*embutidos*).

Cádiz Spanish city and naval base, capital and seaport of the province of Cádiz, standing on Cádiz Bay, an inlet of the Atlantic, 103 km/64 mi S of Seville; population (1994) 155,000. After the discovery of the Americas 1492, Cádiz became one of Europe's most vital trade ports. The English adventurer Francis Drake burned a Spanish fleet here 1587 to prevent the sailing of the Armada.

Cádiz Province of S Spain in SW ◊Andalusia autonomous community; capital Cádiz; area 7,324 sq km/2,828 sq mi; population (1995) 1,127,600. It borders in the S both the Atlantic Ocean and the Mediterranean Sea, and is separated from N Africa by the Strait of Gibraltar. The province produces sherry.

Caen Capital of Calvados *département*, Normandy, France, on the river Orne; population (1990) 115,600. It is a business centre, with ironworks and electric and electronic industries; Caen building stone has a fine reputation. In World War II Caen was one of the main objectives of the D-Day landings and was finally captured by British forces 9 July 1944 after five weeks' fighting, during which it was badly damaged.

Caerleon Small town in Newport unitary authority, Wales, on the river Usk, 5 km/3 mi NE of Newport. It stands on the site of the Roman fortress of Isca. There is a Legionary Museum and remains of an amphitheatre.

Caernarfon or *Caernarvon* Administrative headquarters of Gwynedd, N Wales, situated on the SW shore of the Menai Strait; population (1991) 9,700.

Caernarvonshire (Welsh *Sir Gaernarfon*) Former county of N Wales, merged in ◊Gwynedd 1974–96.

Caerphilly (Welsh *Caerffili*) Market town in S Wales, 11 km/7 mi N of Cardiff; population (1991) 35,900. The castle was built by Edward I. The town gives its name to mild Caerphilly cheese.

Caerphilly Unitary authority in S Wales created 1996 from parts of the former counties of Mid Glamorgan and Gwent; administrative headquarters Hengoed; population (1996) 172,000; area 270 sq km/104 sq mi.

Cagliari Capital and port of Sardinia, Italy, on the Gulf of Cagliari; population (1992) 180,300.

Cagliari Province of Italy in S ◊Sardinia; capital Cagliari; area 9,298 sq km/3,590 sq mi; population (1981) 727,200.

Cagnes-sur-Mer City SW of Nice, France; capital of the *département* of Alpes-Maritimes; population (1990) 41,300.

Cahora Bassa Hydroelectric project in Africa, created as a result of the damming of the Zambezi River to form a reservoir 230 km/144 mi long in W Mozambique.

Cahors French town, capital of the *département* of Lot, 100 km/62 mi N of Toulouse, on the river Lot; population (1990) 20,800. The town's main industries are the manufacture of leather and pottery. It is the centre of a wine-producing area.

Cairngorm Mountains Granite mountain group in Scotland, N part of the ◊Grampian Mountains. The central range includes four out of five of Britain's highest mountains.

Cairns Seaport of NE Queensland, Australia; population (1991 est) 86,200. Its chief industry is the export of sugar and timber; tourism is important.

Cairo (Egyptian *Misr*, Arabic *El Qahira*) Capital of Egypt, on the E bank of the river Nile, 32 km/20 mi north of the site of the ancient city of ◊Memphis; the largest city in Africa and in the Middle East; population (1994) 9,400,000; metropolitan area (1994 est) 13,000,000. An earthquake in a suburb of the city Oct 1992 left over 500 dead.

El Fustat (Old Cairo) was founded by Arabs about AD 642, Al Qahira about 1000 by the Fatimid ruler Gowhar. Cairo was the capital of the Ayyubid dynasty, one of whose sultans, Saladin, built the Citadel, which contains the impresive 19th-century Muhammad Ali mosque, in the late 1100s. Under the Mamelukes 1250–1517 the city prospered, but declined in the 16th century after conquest by the Turks. It became the capital of the virtually autonomous kingdom of Egypt established by Mehmet Ali 1805. During World War II it was the headquarters of the Allied forces in north Africa.

Cairo is a leading administrative and commercial centre, and the semi-official newspaper *al Ahram* is an influential voice in the Arab world. Industries include the manufacture of textiles, cement, vegetable oils, and beer. At Helwan, 24 km/15 mi to the S, an industrial centre is developing, with iron and steelworks powered by electricity from the Aswan High Dam. There are two secular universities: Cairo University (1908) and Ein Shams (1950).

Calabar Port and capital of Cross River State, SE Nigeria, on the Cross River, 64 km/40 mi from the Atlantic Ocean; population (1992 est) 157,800. Rubber, timber, and vegetable oils are exported. It was a centre of the slave trade in the 18th and 19th centuries.

Calabria Mountainous earthquake region occupying the 'toe' of Italy, comprising the provinces of Catanzaro, Cosenza, and Reggio; capital Catanzaro; area 15,080 sq km/5,822 sq mi; population (1995) 2,076,100. Reggio is the industrial centre.

Calahorra Town in the autonomous community of La Rioja, N Spain; population (1995) 19,300. Its ancient Roman name is Calagurris.

Calais Port in Pas-de-Calais *département*, N France; population (1990) 75,800. Taken by England's Edward III 1347, it was saved from destruction by the personal surrender of the burghers of Calais, commemorated in Auguste Rodin's sculpture; the French retook it 1558. In World War II, following German occupation May 1940–Oct 1944, it was surrendered to the Canadians.

Calais, Pas de French name for the Strait of ◊Dover.

Călăraşi Capital of Călăraşi county, Romania, on the river Borcea (a tributary of the Danube), 96 km/60 mi SE of

Bucharest; population (1993) 78,500. It is a market town, chiefly trading in timber and wheat.

Calatayud (Arabic *Kalut Ayub* 'Ayub's castle') Market town in the province of Zaragoza, Spain; population (1995) 17,300. Founded by the Moors, it has a collegiate church, originally a mosque, and a 12th-century church of the Knights of Jerusalem. Calatayud also has rock dwellings. The ruins of the Roman town of Bibilis are 3 km/ 2 mi to the E.

Calatrava la Vieja Fortress in the province of Ciudad Real, Spain, on the river Guadiana in the district of Campos de Calatrava. During the Middle Ages it was considered the key defence of the Sierra Morena. It was taken from the Moors in 1147, and a Cistercian order of soldier monks, the Knights of Calatrava, was founded here in 1158.

Calcutta City in India, on the river Hooghly, the western-most mouth of the river Ganges, some 130 km/80 mi N of the Bay of Bengal. Calcutta is the capital of West Bengal; population (1994) 11,500,000. It is chiefly a commercial and industrial centre (engineering, shipbuilding, jute, and other textiles), and was the seat of government of British India 1773–1912. There is severe air pollution.

Caldey Island or *Caldy Island* (Welsh *Ynys Bŷr*) Island in Carmarthen Bay off the coast of Pembrokeshire, Wales, near Tenby, separated from the mainland by Caldey Sound. It has been inhabited by Celtic monks since the 6th century. A monastery, built by Anglican Benedictines 1906, is now occupied by Belgian Trappist monks. There is a small village and a lighthouse.

Caledonian Canal Waterway in NW Scotland, 98 km/ 61 mi long, linking the Atlantic and the North Sea. Of its total length only a 37 km/23 mi stretch is artificial, the rest being composed of lochs Lochy, Oich, and Ness. The canal was built by Thomas Telford 1803–23.

Calgary City in S Alberta, SW Canada, on the E of the Rocky Mountains, at the junction of the Bow and Elbow rivers; population (1991) 710,700. It is the largest city in Alberta and the regional capital of the S part of the province. Calgary was founded in 1875 and grew rapidly with the growth of the petroleum industry. Other industries include tourism, agriculture, petrochemicals, and service industries.

Cali City in SW Colombia, in the Cauca Valley 975 m/ 3,200 ft above sea level; population (1994) 1,687,000. Cali was founded 1536. It has textile, sugar, and engineering industries, and is the commercial centre of a rich farming area.

California Pacific-coast state of the USA; nicknamed the Golden State (originally because of its gold mines, more recently because of its orange groves and sunshine)
area 411,100 sq km/158,685 sq mi
capital Sacramento
cities Los Angeles, San Diego, San Francisco, San Jose, Fresno
physical Sierra Nevada, including Yosemite and Sequoia national parks (the former a World Heritage Site), Lake Tahoe, Mount Whitney (4,418 m/14,500 ft, the highest mountain in the lower 48 states); the Coast Range; Death Valley (86 m/282 ft below sea level, the lowest point in the Western hemisphere); Colorado and Mojave deserts; Monterey Peninsula; Salton Sea; the San Andreas fault; huge, offshore underwater volcanoes with tops 5 mi/8 km across; Yosemite Falls (739 m/2,425 ft), the highest water-fall in North America; redwood trees in several state parks, including Redwood national park (a World Heritage Site), Humboldt Redwoods state park, and the Avenue of the Giants; Joshua Tree national monument; Lava Beds nation-al monument; Point Reyes national seashore; Point Lobos State Reserve, with sea lions; Big Sur, coastline S of Carmel; Anza-Borrego Desert state park
features Spanish missions, including Carmel Mission (1770), Mission San Luis Obispo de Tolosa (1772), Mission San Luis Rey (1798), and La Purisma Concepcion Mission, Lompoc; gold-rush towns, including Downieville; Marshall Gold Discovery state historic park; Fort Ross, established 1812 by the Russian-American Company; Hearst Castle, built by newspaper proprietor William Randolph Hearst (begun 1919); Monterey, with the Custom House (1827) and Cannery Row; J Paul Getty Museum, Malibu; California Institute of Technology (Caltech); University of California at Berkeley, centre of student protest in the 1960s; University of California at Los Angeles (UCLA); Stanford University at Palo Alto; Hollywood, with Universal Studios, Sunset Strip, and Beverly Hills; San Diego Wild Animal Park; Napa Valley wine country; Orange County, with Disneyland; homes of celebrities at Malibu and Palm Beach
products leading agricultural state with fruit (peaches, citrus, grapes in the valley of the San Joaquin and Sacramento rivers), nuts, wheat, vegetables, cotton, and rice, all mostly grown by irrigation, the water being car-ried by concrete-lined canals to the Central and Imperial valleys; beef cattle; timber; fish; oil; natural gas; aerospace technology; electronics (Silicon Valley); food processing; films and television programmes; great reserves of energy (geothermal) in the hot water that lies beneath much of the state
population (1995) 31,589,200, the most populous state of the USA
famous people Luther Burbank, Walt Disney, William Randolph Hearst, Jack London, Marilyn Monroe, Richard Nixon, Ronald Reagan, John Steinbeck
history colonized by Spain 1769; ceded to the USA after the Mexican War 1848; became a state 1850. The discovery of gold in the Sierra Nevada Jan 1848 was followed by the gold rush 1849–56.

California, Gulf of Gulf on the Pacific coast of Mexico, separating the mainland of Mexico from the peninsula of ◊Baja California. It is 1,125 km/700 mi long and 80–210 km/ 50–130 ml wide. The chief ports on the gulf are Guaymas on the mainland and La Paz on the peninsula. The Colorado River reaches the sea at the gulf.

California, Lower British name for ◊Baja California.

Calisia Ancient name of ◊Kalisz, a town in Poland.

Callao Chief commercial and fishing port of Peru, 12 km/ 7 mi SW of Lima; population (1993) 369,800. Founded 1537, it was destroyed by an earthquake 1746. It is Peru's main naval base, and produces fertilizers.

Calpe Name of ◊Gibraltar in ancient Phoenician and Carthaginian times.

Caltanissetta City in Sicily, Italy, 96 km/60 mi SE of Palermo; population (1981) 61,146. It is the centre of the island's sulphur industry. It has a Baroque cathedral.

Caltanissetta Province of Italy in central ◊Sicily; capital Caltanissetta; area 2,106 sq km/813 sq mi; population (1992) 278,500.

Calvados French brandy distilled from apple cider, named after the *département* in the Basse-Normandie region of NW France where it is produced.

Calvados Maritime *département* in the NW region of ◊Basse-Normandie, France; area 5,536 sq km/2,137 sq mi; population (1990) 619,235. Calvados is best known for the local brandy of the same name, which is distilled from cider apples grown in the extensive orchards of the Pays d'Auge, E of the departmental capital of ◊Caen. Other major towns are ◊Bayeux, ◊Lisieux, and the holiday resort of ◊Deauville.

Calvi Seaport of NW Corsica, 72 km/45 mi N of Ajaccio, in the *département* of Haute Corse. The town's main industries are tourism and wine. It was founded in 1268, and was an important Genoese stronghold.

Camagüey City in Cuba; population (1990 est) 283,000. It is the capital of Camagüey province in the centre of the island. Founded about 1514, it was the capital of the Spanish West Indies during the 19th century. It has a 17th-century cathedral.

Camargue Marshy area of the ◊Rhône delta, S of Arles, France; about 780 sq km/300 sq mi. Black bulls and white horses are bred here, and the nature reserve, which is known for its bird life, forms the S part.

Camborne-Redruth Town in Cornwall, 16 km/10 mi SW of Truro, England; population (1985) 18,500. Part of a former tin-mining area, its present-day industries include engineering and milk production. The only surviving tin mine is at South Crofty, near Camborne. There is a School of Metalliferous Mining.

Cambrai Chief city of Nord *département*, France, on the river Escaut (Schelde); population (1990) 34,200. Industries include light textiles (cambric is named after the town) and confectionery. The *Peace of Cambrai* or Ladies' Peace (1529) was concluded on behalf of Francis I of France by his mother Louise of Savoy and on behalf of Charles V by his aunt Margaret of Austria.

Cambridge City in England, on the river Cam (a river sometimes called by its earlier name, Granta), 80 km/50 mi N of London; population (1994 est) 117,000. It is the administrative headquarters of Cambridgeshire. The present-day city is centred on Cambridge University (founded 12th century), some of whose outstanding buildings, including King's College Chapel, back onto the river. Industries

include the manufacture of scientific instruments, radios, electronics, paper, flour milling, fertilizers, printing, and publishing.

Cambridge City in Massachusetts, USA; population (1992) 93,550. Industries include paper and publishing. Harvard University (1636) and the Massachusetts Institute of Technology (1861) are here. Cambridge was first settled 1630.

Cambridgeshire County of E England. Peterborough is to become a unitary authority in April 1998.
area 3,410 sq km/1,316 sq mi
towns and cities Cambridge (administrative headquarters), Ely, Huntingdon, Peterborough
features fens; flat with very fertile, fenland soil; rivers: Ouse, Cam, Nene; Isle of Ely; Cambridge University; at RAF Molesworth, near Huntingdon, Britain's second cruise missile base was deactivated Jan 1989
products mainly agricultural, including cereals, fruit and vegetables; industries include electronics, food processing, and mechanical engineering; scientific and pharmaceutical research establishments
population (1994) 686,900
famous people Oliver Cromwell, Octavia Hill, John Maynard Keynes.

Cambs Abbreviation for ◊Cambridgeshire, an English county.

Camden Inner borough of NW Greater London. It includes the districts of ◊Bloomsbury, Fitzrovia, ◊Hampstead, Highgate, Holborn, and Somerton
features St Pancras station (1868), chosen 1994 as the international terminal for the high-speed rail link between the Channel Tunnel and London; Highgate Cemetery (1839), burial place of George Eliot, Michael Faraday, Karl Marx, and Herbert Spencer; new British Library; Inns of Court; Hatton Garden, centre of the diamond trade; the London Silver Vaults; Camden lock street market; Hampstead Heath; the Roundhouse, Chalk Farm (1846), a former engine shed, to be converted into the British Architectural Library; Kenwood; British Museum
population (1991) 170,400
famous people Francis Bacon, John Betjeman; Charles Dickens and A E Housman were residents; the early 20th-century Camden Town Group of artists, centred around Walter Sickert, was based here

Camden Industrial city of New Jersey, USA, on the Delaware River; population (1992) 86,900. The city is linked with Philadelphia, Pennsylvania, by the Benjamin Franklin suspension bridge (1926). The Campbells Soup Company factory opened here 1869.

Campagna Romana Lowland stretch of the Italian peninsula, including and surrounding the city of Rome. Lying between the Tyrrhenian Sea and the Sabine Hills to the NE, and the Alban Hills to the SE, it is drained by the lower course of the river Tiber and a number of small streams, most of which dry up in the summer. Prosperous in Roman times, it later became virtually derelict through overgrazing, lack of water, and the arrival in the area of the malaria-carrying *Anopheles* mosquito. Extensive land reclamation and drainage in the 19th and 20th centuries restored its usefulness.

Campania Agricultural region (wheat, citrus, wine, vegetables, tobacco) of S Italy, including the volcano ◊Vesuvius; area 13,595 sq km/5,249 sq mi; population (1995) 5,745,800. The capital is ◊Naples; industrial centres include Benevento, Caserta, and Salerno. There are ancient sites at Pompeii, Herculaneum, and Paestum.

Campeche, Bay of Southwestern area of the Gulf of Mexico, site of a major oil-pollution disaster from the field off Yucatán peninsula 1979.

Campeche State of SE Mexico; area 51,833 sq km/20,013 sq mi; population (1995 est) 642,100. Its capital is Campeche. Timber is the main product.

Campinas City of São Paulo, Brazil, situated on the central plateau; population (1991) 960,000. It is a coffee-trading centre. There are also metallurgical and food industries, sugar refining, and textiles.

Campobasso Capital of Molise region, Italy, about 190 km/120 mi SE of Rome; population (1991) 51,300. It has a high reputation for its cutlery.

Campobasso Province of S central Italy in ◊Molise region; capital Campobasso; area 2,909 sq km/1,123 sq mi; population (1992) 239,200.

Cam Ranh Port in S Vietnam; population (1989) 114,000. In the Vietnam War it was a US base; it later became a staging complex for the Soviet Pacific fleet.

Camrose City in Alberta, Canada, 110 km/68 mi SE of Edmonton; population (1991) 13,400. It is the centre of an extensive farming area.

Canary Islands (Spanish *Canarias*) Group of volcanic islands 100 km/60 mi off the NW coast of Africa, forming the Spanish provinces of Las Palmas and Santa Cruz de Tenerife; area 7,300 sq km/2,818 sq mi; population (1991) 1,493,800. The chief centres are Santa Cruz on Tenerife (which also has the highest peak in extracontinental Spain, Pico de Teide, 3,713 m/12,186 ft), and Las Palmas on Gran Canaria. The province of Santa Cruz comprises Tenerife, Palma, Gomera, and Hierro; the province of Las Palmas comprises Gran Canaria, Lanzarote, and Fuerteventura. There are also six uninhabited islets. The Northern Hemisphere Observatory (1981) is on the island of La Palma. Observation conditions are exceptionally good because there is no moisture, no artificial-light pollution, and little natural airglow.

Canary Wharf 4.5 million-sq ft office development on the Isle of Dogs in London's ◊Docklands, the first phase of which was completed 1992, along with the foundations for a further 8 million sq ft. The complex of offices, surrounding landscaped squares, is best known for its central skyscraper, the second tallest in Europe at 244 m/800 ft.

Canberra Capital of Australia (since 1908), situated in the Australian Capital Territory, enclosed within New South Wales, on a tributary of the Murrumbidgee River;

Canary Islands

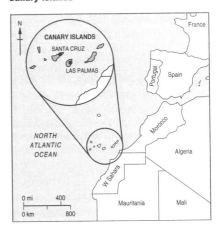

area (Australian Capital Territory including the port at Jervis Bay) 2,432 sq km/939 sq mi; population (1993) 324,600. It contains the Parliament House (first used by the Commonwealth Parliament 1927), the Australian National University (1946), the Canberra School of Music (1965), and the National War Memorial. The site for the new city was selected 1908, located between Sydney and Melbourne, rivals to be capital of the new country. The city was named Canberra 1913 and was designed by the architect Walter Burley Griffin. Parliament first convened there 1927, but the city's development was slow until after World War II. The new Parliament House was opened 1988.

Cancún Resort in Yucatán, Mexico, created on a barrier island 1974 by the Mexican government to boost tourism; population around 30,000 (almost all involved in the tourist industry). It is Mexico's most popular tourist destination, with beaches, a coral reef, and a lagoon.

Candia Italian name for the Greek island of ◊Crete. Also, formerly the name of Crete's largest city, ◊Irákleion, founded about AD 824.

Canea (Greek *Chaniá* or *Khaniá*) City on the NW coast of Crete, capital until 1971, when it was replaced by Irákleion; population (1991) 65,500. It was founded 1252 by the Venetians and is surrounded by a wall. Vegetable oils, soap, and leather are exported. Heavy fighting took place here during World War II, after the landing of German parachutists May 1941.

Cangas de Onís Market town in the autonomous community of ◊Asturias, N Spain; population (1995) 6,500. Its many Roman remains include a bridge. The town was proclaimed the capital of Christian Spain in the 8th century.

Cannes Resort in Alpes-Maritimes *département*, S France; population (1990) 69,400. A prestigious film festival is held here annually. Formerly only a small seaport, in 1834 it attracted the patronage of Lord Brougham and other distinguished visitors and soon became a fashionable holiday resort. A new town (La Bocca) grew up facing the Mediterranean.

Canso Strait Channel between Nova Scotia and Cape Breton Island, E Canada, 27 km/17 mi long and 4 km/2.5 mi wide. A causeway 1,375 m/1,504 yd long and 25 m/27 yd wide links Cape Breton Island to the mainland by road and railway. The *Canso Canal* allows shipping to pass through the causeway. Port Hawkesbury at the E end of the strait has a pulp and paper mill, a large oil refinery, making use of the deep-water access for supertankers, a thermal power station, and a heavy-water plant.

Cantabria Autonomous region of N Spain; area 5,300 sq km/2,046 sq mi; population (1991) 527,300. The capital is Santander. From the coastline on the Bay of Biscay it rises to the Cantabrian Mountains. Mining is the major industry.

Cantabrian Mountains (Spanish *Cordillera Cantabrica*) Mountain range running along the N coast of Spain, reaching 2,648 m/8,688 ft in the Picos de Europa massif. The mountains contain coal and iron deposits.

Cantal Volcanic mountain range in central France, which gives its name to Cantal *département*. The highest point is the Plomb du Cantal, 1,858 m/6,096 ft.

Cantal *Département* in the ◊Auvergne region of central France; area 5,741 sq km/2,217 sq mi; population (1990) 158,761. Cantal takes its name from the mountain range in the region. The principal towns are Aurillac (the capital), Mauriac, and St-Flour. Agriculture is the main economic activity; cattle are reared, and rye, potatoes, and chestnuts are grown. A hard cheese named after the *département* is produced.

Canterbury Historic cathedral city in Kent, England, on the river Stour, 100 km/62 mi SE of London; population (1991) 36,500. In 597 King Ethelbert welcomed Augustine's mission to England here, and the city has since been the metropolis of the Anglican Communion and seat of the archbishop of Canterbury. The cathedral was begun in the 11th century. Canterbury Cathedral, St Augustine's Abbey, and St Martin's Church are a World Heritage site.

Canterbury Plains Area of rich grassland between the mountains and the sea on the E coast of South Island, New Zealand; area 10,000 sq km/4,000 sq mi. Canterbury lamb is produced here.

Canton Alternative spelling of Kwangchow or ◊Guangzhou, a city in China.

Canton City in NE Ohio, USA, SE of Akron; seat of Stark County; population (1992) 84,800. Its products include office equipment, ceramics, and steel. The home of President William McKinley is here, as is the Football Hall of Fame. The town was laid out 1805.

Cape Breton Island Island forming the N part of the province of Nova Scotia, Canada; area 10,282 sq km/3,970 sq mi; population (1991) 120,100. Bisected by a waterway, it has road and rail links with the mainland across the Strait of Canso. It has coal resources and steelworks, and

there has been substantial development in the strait area, with docks, oil refineries, and newsprint production from local timber. In the N, the surface rises to 550 m/1,800 ft at North Cape, and the coast has many fine harbours. There are cod fisheries. The climate is mild and very moist. The chief towns are Sydney and Glace Bay. The first British colony was established 1629 but was driven out by the French. In 1763 Cape Breton Island was ceded to Britain and attached to Nova Scotia 1763–84 and from 1820.

Cape Byron Eastern extremity of Australia, in New South Wales, just S of the border with Queensland.

Cape Coast Port of Ghana, W Africa, 130 km/80 mi W of Accra; population (1984) 57,200. It has been superseded as the main port since 1962 by Tema. The town was first established by the Portuguese in the 16th century.

Cape Cod Hook-shaped peninsula in SE Massachusetts, USA, 100 km/60 mi long and 1.6–32 km/1–20 mi wide. Its beaches and woods make it a popular tourist area. It is separated from the rest of the state by the Cape Cod Canal. The islands of Martha's Vineyard and Nantucket are just S of the cape. Basque and Norse fisherfolk are believed to have visited Cape Cod before the English Pilgrims landed at Princetown 1620.

Cape Horn Southernmost point of South America, in the Chilean part of the archipelago of ◊Tierra del Fuego; notorious for gales and heavy seas. It was named 1616 by Dutch explorer Willem Schouten (1580–1625) after his birthplace (Hoorn).

Cape of Good Hope South African headland forming a peninsula between Table Bay and False Bay, Cape Town. The first European to sail around it was Bartolomeu Diaz 1488. Formerly named Cape of Storms, it was given its present name by King John II of Portugal.

Cape Province (Afrikaans *Kaapprovinsie*) Former province of the Republic of South Africa to 1994, now divided into Western, Eastern, and Northern Cape Provinces. It was named after the Cape of Good Hope. Dutch traders established the first European settlement on the Cape 1652, but it was taken by the British 1795, after the French Revolutionary armies had occupied the Netherlands, and was sold to Britain for £6 million 1814. The Cape achieved self-government 1872. It was an original province of the Union 1910.

Cape Town (Afrikaans *Kaapstad*) Port and oldest city (founded 1652) in South Africa, situated in the SW on Table Bay; population (1991) 2,350,200 (urban area). Industries include horticulture and trade in wool, wine, fruit, grain, and oil. It is the legislative capital of the Republic of South Africa and capital of ◊Western Cape province.

Cape Wrath (Norse *huaf* 'point of turning') Headland at the NW extremity of Scotland, extending 159 m/523 ft into the Atlantic Ocean. Its lighthouse dates from 1828.

Cape York Peninsula, the northernmost point (10° 41' S) of the Australian mainland, named by Capt James Cook

1770. The peninsula is about 800 km/500 mi long and 640 km/400 mi wide at its junction with the mainland. Its barrenness deterred early Dutch explorers, although the S is being developed for cattle (Brahmin type). In the N there are large bauxite deposits.

Caporetto Former name of ◊Kobarid, a village in Slovenia.

Capri Italian island at the S entrance of the Bay of Naples; 32 km/20 mi S of Naples; area 13 sq km/5 sq mi. It has two towns, Capri and Anacapri, a profusion of flowers, beautiful scenery, and an ideal climate. The Blue Grotto on the N coast is an important tourist attraction.

Caprivi Strip Northeastern part of Namibia, a narrow strip between Angola and Botswana, giving the country access to the Zambezi River.

Capua Italian town in Caserta province on the Volturno River, in a fertile plain N of Naples; population (1990) 19,500. There was heavy fighting here 1943 during World War II, which almost destroyed the Romanesque cathedral.

Caracas Chief city and capital of Venezuela, situated on the slopes of the Andes Mountains, 13 km/8 mi S of its port La Guaira on the Caribbean coast; population of metropolitan area (1990) 1,824,900 (Federal District 2,265,900). It is now a large industrial and commercial centre, notably for oil companies, developed since the 1950s.

Carcassonne City in SW France, capital of Aude *département*, on the river Aude, which divides it into the ancient and modern town; population (1990) 45,000. Its medieval fortifications (restored) are the finest in France.

Cardiff Unitary authority in S Wales created 1996 from part of the former county of South Glamorgan; population 306,500 (1996); area 139 sq km/54 sq mi.

Cardiff (Welsh *Caerdydd*) Seaport and capital of Wales (from 1955) and administrative headquarters of Cardiff unitary authority, at the mouth of the Taff, Rhymney, and Ely rivers; population (1994 est) 290,000. Industries include car components, flour milling, ship repairs, electrical goods, paper, and cigars; there are also high-tech industries.

Cardiganshire (Welsh *Ceredigion* or *Sir Aberteifi*) Former county of W Wales. It was merged, together with Pembrokeshire and Carmarthenshire, into Dyfed 1974–96; now part of Ceredigion.

Caribbean Sea Western part of the Atlantic Ocean between the S coast of North America and the N coasts of South America. Central America is to the W and the West Indies are the islands within the sea, which is about 2,740 km/1,700 mi long and 650–1,500 km/400–900 mi wide. It is from here that the Gulf Stream turns towards Europe.

Carinthia (German *Kärnten*) Federal province of Alpine SE Austria, bordering Italy and Slovenia in the S; area 9,533 sq km/3,681 sq mi; population (1995) 560,994. The capital is Klagenfurt. It was an independent duchy from 976 and a possession of the Habsburg dynasty 1276–1918.

Carisbrooke Village SW of Newport, Isle of Wight, England. Charles I was imprisoned in its castle 1647–48.

Carlisle City in Cumbria, NW England, situated on the river Eden at the W end of Hadrian's Wall, administrative centre of the county; population (1991) 99,800. It is a leading railway centre; textiles, engineering, metal goods, and biscuit making are the chief industries. It was the Roman *Luguvalium*. There is a Norman cathedral and a castle. The bishopric dates from 1133.

Carlisle City in S Pennsylvania, USA, in the Cumberland Valley, SW of Harrisburg; seat of Cumberland County; population (1990) 18,400. Industries include electronics and steel products. The city was laid out 1751. Its fort was a base during the French and Indian Wars (part of the Seven Years' War).

Carlow County of the Republic of Ireland, in the province of Leinster; county town Carlow; area 900 sq km/347 sq mi; population (1996 est) 41,600. Mostly flat except for mountains in the S, the land is fertile, and well suited to dairy farming. Products include barley, wheat, and sugar beet.

Carmarthenshire (Welsh *Sir Gaerfyrddin*) Unitary authority in S Wales. A former county, it was part of Dyfed 1975–96; administrative headquarters Carmarthen; population (1996) 68,900; area 2,390 sq km/923 sq mi.
features Museum of the Woollen Inudstry at Dre-Fach Felindre; village of Laugharne (home of Dylan Thomas); Black Mountain; industrial port of Llanelli.

Carnarvon Alternative spelling of ◊Caernarfon, a town in Wales.

Carnatic Region of SE India, in Madras state. It is situated between the Eastern Ghats and the Coromandel coast and was formerly a leading trading centre.

Carolina Either of two separate states of the USA; see ◊North Carolina and ◊South Carolina.

Caroline Islands Scattered archipelago in Micronesia, Pacific Ocean, consisting of over 500 coral islets; area 1,200 sq km/463 sq mi. The chief islands are Ponape, Kusai, and Truk in the E group, and Yap and Palau in the W group.

Carpathian Mountains Central European mountain system, forming a semicircle through Slovakia– Poland– Ukraine–Moldova–Romania, 1,450 km/900 mi long. The central *Tatra Mountains* on the Slovak–Polish frontier include the highest peak, Gerlachovka, 2,663 m/8,737 ft.

Carpentaria, Gulf of Shallow gulf opening out of the Arafura Sea, N of Australia. It was discovered by the Dutch navigator Abel Tasman 1606 and named 1623 in honour of Pieter Carpentier, governor general of the Dutch East Indies.

Carpentras French town in the *département* of Vaucluse, on the river Auzun, and on the *Carpentras Canal*, 21 km/ 13 mi NE of Avignon; population (1990) 24,200. It has a textile industry, tourism, and an important market for fruit and vegetables. Carpentras has a late Gothic church (1405–1519), an 18th-century synagogue, and an 18th-century aqueduct. There is also a Roman triumphal arch.

Carrara Town in Tuscany, Italy, 60 km/37 mi NW of Livorno; population (1990) 68,500. It is known for its quarries of fine white marble, which were worked by the Romans, abandoned in the 5th century, and came into use again with the revival of sculpture and architecture in the 12th century.

Carrickfergus Seaport on Belfast Lough, County Antrim, Northern Ireland; population (1991) 32,750. There is some light industry. The remains of the castle, built 1180, house two museums.

Carse of Gowrie Fertile lowland plain bordering the Firth of Tay, Scotland. It is 24 km/15 mi long, and is one of the country's most productive agricultural areas, including soft fruit. William III landed here before the Battle of the Boyne, 1690.

Carson City Capital of Nevada, USA; population (1992) 42,800. Settled as a trading post 1851, it was named after the frontier guide Kit Carson 1858. It flourished as a boom town after the discovery of the nearby Comstock silver-ore lode 1859.

Cartagena or *Cartagena de los Indes* Port, industrial centre, and capital of the department of Bolívar, NW Colombia; population (1994) 726,000. Plastics and chemicals are produced here.

Cartagena City in the province of Murcia, Spain, on the Mediterranean coast; population (1994) 180,000. It is a seaport and naval base. It was founded as *Carthago Nova* about 225 BC by the Carthaginian Hasdrubal, son-in-law of Hamilcar Barca. It continued to flourish under the Romans and the Moors and was conquered by the Spanish 1269. It has a 13th-century cathedral and Roman remains.

Casablanca (Arabic *Dar el-Beida*) Port, commercial and industrial centre on the Atlantic coast of Morocco; population (1990, urban area) 3,079,000. It trades in fish, phosphates, and manganese. The Great Hassan II Mosque, completed 1989, is the world's largest; it is built on a platform (40,000 sq m/430,000 sq ft) jutting out over the Atlantic, with walls 60 m/200 ft high, topped by a hydraulic sliding roof, and a minaret 175 m/574 ft high.

Cascade Range Volcanic mountains in the W USA and Canada, extending 1,120 km/700 mi from N California through Oregon and Washington to the Fraser River. They include Mount St Helens and Mount Rainier (the highest peak, 4,392 m/14,408 ft), which is noteworthy for its glaciers. The mountains are the most active in the USA, excluding Alaska and Hawaii.

Cascais Fishing port and resort town on the Costa do Sol, 25 km/16 mi W of Lisbon, Portugal; population (1991) 19,500. The 17th-century citadel is the summer palace of the president. There is local fishing and canning; tourism is important.

Caserta Town in S Italy 33 km/21 mi NE of Naples; population (town, 1990) 69,300; (district, 1992) 823,600. It trades in chemicals, olive oil, wine, and grain. The base for Garibaldi's campaigns in the 19th century, it was the Allied headquarters in Italy 1943–45, and the German forces sur-

rendered to field marshal H Alexander here 1945.

Caserta Province of S Italy in W central ◊Campania region; capital Caserta; area 2,639 sq km/1,019 sq mi; population (1992) 239,200. The province was formerly called Terra di Lavoro.

Caspe Town in the province of Zaragoza, NW Spain, near the confluence of the Guadalope and Ebro Rivers; population (1995) 8,200. Its castle was the scene of the *Compromise of Caspe* in 1410, when the delegates of Aragón, Catalonia, and Valencia chose Ferdinand of Antequera as king Ferdinand I of Aragón.

Casper City in E central Wyoming, USA, on the North Platte River, NW of Cheyenne; seat of Natrona County; population (1990) 46,700. The largest city in Wyoming, it serves as the marketing centre for the region's livestock and petroleum products. It developed around Fort Caspar on a pioneer crossing on the Oregon Trail, and was founded as a town 1888.

Caspian Sea World's largest inland sea, divided between Iran, Azerbaijan, Russia, Kazakhstan, and Turkmenistan; area about 370,990 sq km/143,239 sq mi, with a maximum depth of 1,000 m/3,250 ft. The chief ports are Astrakhan and Baku. Drainage in the N and damming of the Volga and Ural rivers for hydroelectric power left the sea approximately 28 m/92 ft below sea level. In June 1991 opening of sluices in the dams caused the water level to rise dramatically, threatening towns and industrial areas.

Caspian Sea

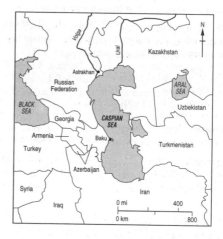

Cassel Alternative spelling of ◊Kassel, an industrial town in Germany.

Cassino Town in S Italy, 80 km/50 mi NW of Naples, at the foot of Monte Cassino; population (1990) 34,600. It was the scene of heavy fighting during World War II 1944, as it was a key position blocking the Allied advance to Rome, and most of the town was destroyed. It was rebuilt 1.5 km/1 mi to the N. The abbey on the summit of Monte Cassino, founded by St Benedict 529, was rebuilt 1956 to repair the damage caused by the Allied bombardment during World War II.

Castel Gandolfo Village in Italy 24 km/15 mi SE of Rome, named after a castle that once stood on the site. There is a 17th-century palace, built by Pope Urban VIII, which is still used by the pope as a summer residence.

Castellón Province of E Spain in N Valencia autonomous community; capital Castellón de la Plana; area 6,679 sq km/ 2,579 sq mi; population (1995) 464,700. Its E coastline is on the Mediterranean Sea. It is fertile and populous on the coastal plains, through which the river Mijares runs, but barren in the hilly districts of the interior. Products include oranges, cereals, olives, and almonds.

Castellón de la Plana Port in Spain, facing the Mediterranean to the E; population (1994) 139,000. It is the capital of Castellón province and is the centre of an orange-growing district.

Castilla–La Mancha Autonomous region of central Spain; area 79,200 sq km/30,571 sq mi; population (1991) 1,658,400. It includes the provinces of Albacete, Ciudad Real, Cuenca, Guadalajara, and Toledo. Irrigated land produces grain and chickpeas, and merino sheep graze here.

Castilla la Nueva Former region of central Spain. Extending S from the Castilian sierras in the form of a plateau, with an average height of 900 m/3,000 ft and a harsh climate, it included the provinces of Ciudad Real, Cuenca, Guadalajara, Madrid, and Toledo.

Castilla la Vieja Former region of N central Spain, called Vieja ('Old') because it was the first part of Castile to be recovered from the Moors. It included the provinces of Ávila, Burgos, Logroño, Santander, Segovia, and Soria, and extended N from the Castilian sierras in the form of an elevated plateau, with an average height of 850 m/2,800 ft.

Castilla–León Autonomous region of central Spain; area 94,100 sq km/36,323 sq mi; population (1991) 2,545,900. It includes the provinces of Ávila, Burgos, León, Palencia, Salamanca, Segovia, Soria, Valladolid, and Zamora. Irrigated land produces wheat and rye. Cattle, sheep, and fighting bulls are bred in the uplands.

Castleford Town in West Yorkshire, England, at the confluence of the rivers Aire and Calder, 15 km/10 mi SE of Leeds; population (1991) 36,000. Originally a coal-mining town, present-day industries include chemicals, glass, and earthenware products. The town stands on the site of Roman *Lagentium*.

Castres French town in the *département* of Tarn, on the river Agout; population (1990) 47,000. Its main industries include textiles, metals, pottery, and mechanical and electrical goods. It grew up around a 7th-century Benedictine abbey. In the 16th century it was a Huguenot religious stronghold.

Castries Port and capital of St Lucia, on the NW coast of the island in the Caribbean; population (1992) 53,900. It produces textiles, chemicals, tobacco, and wood and rubber products.

Cataluña or *Catalonia* (Catalan *Catalunya*) Autonomous region of NE Spain; area 31,900 sq km/12,313 sq mi; population (1991) 6,059,500. It includes Barcelona (the capital), Gerona, Lérida, and Tarragona. Industries include wool and cotton textiles; hydroelectric power is produced.

Catania Industrial port in Sicily, just S of Mount Etna; population (1992) 329,900. It exports local sulphur; there are also shipbuilding and textile industries.

Catania Province of Italy in E ◊Sicily; capital Catania; area 3,553 sq km/1,372 sq mi; population (1992) 1,040,800.

Catanzaro Province of S Italy in central ◊Calabria region; capital Catanzaro (population (1990) 103,800); area 5,325 sq km/2,056 sq mi; population (1992) 742,900.

Catskills US mountain range, mainly in SE New York State, W of the Hudson River; the highest point is Slide Mountain, 1,281 m/4,204 ft.

Catterick Village near Richmond in North Yorkshire, England, where there is a large military camp.

Caucasus Series of mountain ranges between the Caspian and Black seas, in the republics of Russia, Georgia, Armenia, and Azerbaijan; 1,200 km/750 mi long. The highest peak is Elbrus, 5,633 m/18,480 ft. The N Caucasus region is home to some 40 different ethnic groups.

Cauvery or *Kaveri* River of S India, rising in the W Ghats and flowing 765 km/475 mi SE to meet the Bay of Bengal in a wide delta. It has been a major source of hydroelectric power since 1902 when India's first hydropower plant was built on the river.

Caux Former French district corresponding to that of the modern ◊Le Havre, ◊Dieppe, and Yvetot. Its name is derived from the chalk soil of the region.

Cavan County of the Republic of Ireland, in the province of Ulster; county town Cavan; area 1,890 sq km/729 sq mi; population (1996 est) 52,900. The river Erne divides it into a narrow, mostly low-lying peninsula, 30 km/20 mi long, between Leitrim and Fermanagh, and an E section of wild and bare hill country. The soil is generally poor and the climate moist and cold. The chief towns are Cavan, population about 3,000; Kilmore, seat of Roman Catholic and Protestant bishoprics; and Virginia.

Cavite Town and port of the Philippine Republic; 13 km/ 8 mi S of Manila; population (1990) 106,000. It is the capital of Cavite province, Luzon. It was in Japanese hands Dec 1941–Feb 1945. After the Philippines achieved independence 1946, the US Seventh Fleet continued to use the naval base.

Cawnpore Former spelling of ◊Kanpur, a city in India.

Cayenne Capital and chief port of French Guiana, on Cayenne Island, NE South America, at the mouth of the river Cayenne; population (1990) 41,700. The main occupation is shrimping.

Cayman Islands British island group in the West Indies
area 260 sq km/100 sq mi
capital George Town (on Grand Cayman)
features comprises three low-lying islands: Grand Cayman, Cayman Brac, and Little Cayman

Cayman Islands

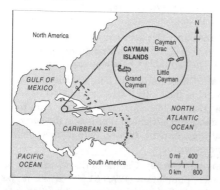

government governor, executive council, and legislative assembly

exports seawhip coral, a source of prostaglandins; shrimps; honey; jewellery

currency Cayman Island dollar

population (1993 est) 31,150 (mostly on Grand Cayman)

language English

history first reached by Chrisopher Columbus 1503; acquired by Britain following the Treaty of Madrid 1670; became a dependency of Jamaica 1863. In 1959 the islands became a separate crown colony, although the inhabitants chose to remain British. From that date, changes in legislation attracted foreign banks and the Caymans are now an international financial centre and tax haven as well as a tourist resort, with emphasis on scuba diving.

Cebu Chief city and port of the island of Cebu in the Philippines; population (1990) 610,400; area of the island 5,086 sq km/1,964 sq mi. The oldest city of the Philippines, Cebu was founded as San Miguel 1565 and became the capital of the Spanish Philippines.

Cedar Falls City in NE Iowa, USA, on the Cedar River, W of Waterloo; population (1990) 35,000. Industries include farm and other heavy equipment, rotary pumps, and tools. Settled 1845, it was an important port.

Cedar Rapids City in E Iowa, USA; population (1992) 112,000. It produces communications equipment, construction machinery, and processed foods. Cedar Rapids was settled 1837, incorporated 1849, and became an important grain and livestock market.

Cegléd Town in Pest county, Hungary, 72 km/45 mi SE of Budapest. It is a trading centre for agricultural and market-garden produce, and has distillery, flour, and brick industries.

Celebes English name for ◊Sulawesi, an island of Indonesia.

Celje Town in Slovenia, on the river Savinja; population (1991) 40,200. It is a zinc-smelting and metallurgical centre. It was founded by the Romans as Claudia Celea, and retains its medieval walls.

Celle or *Zelle* City in Lower Saxony, Germany, on the river Aller, 35 km/22 mi NE of Hannover; population (1994)

177,500. The city has a stud farm founded 1735, and manufactures dyes, foodstuffs, furniture, leather, and electrical goods. The city dates from 1292.

Celtic Sea Sea area bounded by Wales, Ireland, and SW England; the name is commonly used by workers in the oil industry to avoid nationalist significance. The Celtic Sea is separated from the Irish Sea by St George's Channel.

Central Former region of Scotland; replaced in 1996 by Clackmannanshire, Falkirk, and Stirling unitary authorities.

Central America The part of the Americas that links Mexico with the Isthmus of Panama, comprising Belize, Costa Rica, El Salvador, Guatemala, Honduras, Nicaragua, and Panama. It is also an isthmus, crossed by mountains that form part of the Cordilleras, rising to a maximum height of 4,220 m/ 13,845 ft. There are numerous active volcanoes. Central America is about 523,000 sq km/200,000 sq mi in area and has a population (1980) estimated at 22,700,000, mostly Indians or mestizos (of mixed white-Indian ancestry). Tropical agricultural products and other basic commodities and raw materials are exported.

Central Asian Republics Group of five republics: Kazakhstan, Kyrgyzstan, Tajikistan, Turkmenistan, and Uzbekistan. They were part of the USSR until their independence was recognized 1991. They comprise a large part of the geographical region of ◊Turkestan and are the home of large numbers of Muslims.

Central Lowlands One of the three geographical divisions of Scotland, occupying the fertile and densely populated plain that lies between two geological fault lines, which run nearly parallel NE–SW across Scotland from Stonehaven to Dumbarton and from Dunbar to Girvan.

Central Mount Stuart Flat-topped mountain 844 m/ 2,770 ft high, at approximately the central point of Australia.

Central Provinces and Berar Former British province of India, now part of ◊Madhya Pradesh.

Centre Region of N central France; area 39,151 sq km/ 15,116 sq mi; population (1990) 2,371,000. Centre includes the *départements* of Cher, Eure-et-Loir, Indre, Indre-et-Loire, Loire-et-Cher, and Loiret. Its capital is Orléans.

Centre, the Region of central Australia, including the tourist area between the Musgrave and MacDonnell ranges which contains Ayers Rock and Lake Amadeus.

Centre, Canal du Canal in the *département* of Saône-et-Loire, France, joining the rivers ◊Saône and ◊Loire. The canal is 120 km/75 mi long, stretching from Chalon-sur-Saône to Digoin, and serves the industrial region of Le Creusot and Montceau-les-Mines. It was constructed in 1781.

Cephalonia English form of ◊Kefallinia, the largest of the Ionian Islands, off the W coast of Greece.

Cephisus (Greek *Kifisos*) River in Greece, rising on Mount Parnes and flowing S through olive groves W of Athens into the Bay of Phaleron, E of Piraeus.

Ceram Alternative form of ◊Seram, an Indonesian island.

Ceará Alternative name for ◊Fortaleza, Brazil.

Ceredigion Unitary authority in SW Wales created 1996 from part of the former county of Dyfed; administrative headquarters Aberaeron; population (1996) 68,900; area 1,793 sq km/692 sq mi. Part of the Cambrian Mountains are here, including Plynlimon Fawr (752 m/2,468 ft).

Cernăuti Romanian form of ◊Chernivtsi, a city in Ukraine.

České Budějovice (German *Budweis*) Town in the Czech Republic, on the river Vltava; population (1991) 123,400. It is a commercial and industrial centre for S Bohemia, producing beer, timber, and metal products.

Český Les Czech name of the Bohemian Forest, a wooded mountain range in central Europe.

Český Těšin Industrial town (coal, textiles) of N Moravia, in the Czech Republic, on the river Olše, 25 km/16 mi SE of Ostrava; population (1991) 28,700. The river marks the border with Poland, dividing the town from the Polish town of Cieszyn.

Cetinje Town in Montenegro, Yugoslavia, 19 km/12 mi SE of Kotor; population (1981) 20,213. Founded 1484 by Ivan the Black, it was capital of Montenegro until 1918. It has a palace built by Nicholas, the last king of Montenegro.

Ceuta Spanish seaport and military base in Morocco, N Africa, 27 km/17 mi S of Gibraltar and overlooking the Mediterranean approaches to the Straits of Gibraltar; area 18 sq km/7 sq mi; population (1991) 67,600. It trades in petrol products.

Cévennes Series of mountain ranges on the S, SE, and E borders of the Central Plateau of France. The highest peak is Mount Mézenc, 1,754 m/5,755 ft.

Ceylon Former name (to 1972) of Sri Lanka.

Chablis White burgundy wine produced near the town of the same name in the Yonne *département* of central France.

Chaco Province of Argentina; area 99,633 sq km/38,458 sq mi; population (1991) 838,300. Its capital is Resistencia, in the SE. The chief crop is cotton, and there is forestry.

Chad, Lake Lake on the NE boundary of Nigeria, the most significant body of water in the Sahel. It once varied in extent between rainy and dry seasons from 26,000 sq km/ 10,000 sq mi to 10,400 sq km/4,000 sq mi, but a series of droughts 1979–89 reduced its area by 80%. The S Chad irrigation project used the lake waters to irrigate the surrounding desert, but the 4,000 km/2,500 mi of canals dug for the project are now permanently dry because of the shrinking size of the lake (on average 16,310 sq km/6,297 sq mi). The Lake Chad basin is being jointly developed for oil and natron by Cameroon, Chad, Niger, and Nigeria, though commercial oil production is not yet under way.

Chagos Archipelago Island group in the Indian Ocean; area 60 sq km/23 sq mi. Formerly a dependency of Mauritius, it now forms the ◊British Indian Ocean Territory. The chief island is Diego Garcia, now a US-British strategic base.

Chaillot District of ◊Paris, France, on the N bank of the Seine, opposite the Eiffel Tower. In 1878 the Palais du Trocadero was built here for an exhibition. It was reconstructed as the *Palais de Chaillot* for an international exhibition in 1937.

Chalatenango Department on the N frontier of El Salvador; area 2,507 sq km/968 sq mi; population (1992) 180,600. The capital is Chalatenango.

Chalcis (Greek *Khalkis*) Main town of the Greek island of Euboea, in the Central Greece and Euboea region; population (1990) 50,000. Chalcis is an important trading centre for dairy and agricultural produce; the harbour exports mineral ores, cement, timber, wines, olives, and imports coal and other fuels.

Châlons-sur-Marne Capital of the *département* of Marne, NE France; population (1990) 51,500. It is a market town and trades mainly in champagne. Tradition has it that Attila was defeated in his attempt to invade France at the *Battle of Châlons* 451 by the Roman general Aëtius and the Visigoth Theodoric.

Chalon-sur-Saône Town in the *département* of Saône-et-Loire, France, on the river Saône and the Canal du Centre; population (1990) 56,300. It has mechanical and electrical engineering and chemical industries.

Chambéry Former capital of Savoy, now capital of Savoie *département*, France; population (1990) 55,600. It is the seat of an archbishopric and has some industry; it is also a holiday and health resort. The town gives its name to a French vermouth.

Chambord French château of the Renaissance period, situated in the *département* of Loir-et-Cher, 19 km/12 mi E of Blois. The castle was begun by Francis I in 1519, and was completed by his successors. It has many turrets and gables, and stands in a walled park.

Chamonix-Mont-Blanc French village and holiday resort in the *département* of Haute-Savoie, on the river Arve, 65 km/40 mi SE of Geneva; population (1990) 10,000; altitude about 1,000 m/ 3,400 ft. It is in a scenic, narrow valley at the foot of Mont Blanc in the French Alps. The most commonly used approach to ◊Mont Blanc, it is a mountaineering and winter-sports centre. It was the site of the first Winter Olympics 1924.

Champagne-Ardenne Region of NE France; area 25,606 sq km/9,886 sq mi; population (1990) 1,347,900. Its capital is Reims, and it comprises the *départements* of Ardennes, Aube, Marne, and Haute-Marne. It has sheep and dairy farming and vineyards.

Champaign City in E central Illinois, USA, directly W of Urbana; population (1992) 64,350. Industries include electronic equipment, academic clothing, and air-conditioning equipment. Together with Urbana, it is the site of the University of Illinois. The city was incorporated 1857.

Champlain, Lake Lake in NE USA (extending some 10km/ 6 mi into Canada) on the New York–Vermont border; length 201 km/125 mi; area 692 sq km/430 sq mi. It is linked by canal to the St Lawrence and Hudson rivers.

Chancellorsville Site in Virginia, USA, in Spotsylvania

County, between Richmond and Washington, 16 km/10 mi W of Fredericksburg. It was the scene of a battle in the American Civil War 1863, when General 'Stonewall' Jackson was fatally wounded and General Hooker was defeated by the Confederate army under Robert E Lee. The site lies within the Fredericksburg and Spotsylvania National Military Park.

Chandannagar ('city of sandalwood') City on the river Hooghly, India, in the state of West Bengal; population (1991) 120,400. Formerly a French settlement, it was ceded to India by treaty 1952.

Chandigarh City of N India, in the foothills of the Himalayas; population (1991) 511,000. It is also a union territory; area 114 sq km/44 sq mi; population (1994 est) 725,000. Planned by the architect Le Corbusier, the city was inaugurated 1953 to replace Lahore (capital of British Punjab), which went to Pakistan under partition 1947. Since 1966, when Chandigarh became a Union Territory, it has been the capital city of both Haryana and Punjab, pending the construction of a new capital for the former.

Changchiakow Alternative transcription of ◊Zhangjiakou, a trading centre in China.

Changchun Industrial city and capital of Jilin province, China; population (1993) 2,400,000. Machinery and motor vehicles are manufactured. It is also the centre of an agricultural district.

Chang Jiang or *Yangtze Kiang* Longest river of China, flowing about 6,300 km/3,915 mi from Tibet to the Yellow Sea. It is a main commercial waterway. Work began on the Three Gorges Dam on the river Dec 1994.

Chang Jiang

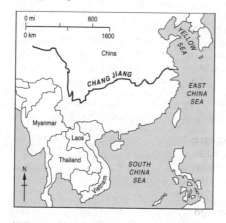

Changsha Port on the river Xiang (or Hsiang), capital of Hunan province, China; population (1993) 1,480,000. It trades in rice, tea, timber, and nonferrous metals; works antimony, lead, and silver; and produces chemicals, electronics, porcelain, and embroideries.

Chaniá Alternative name for the Greek town of ◊Canea.

Channel Country Area of SW Queensland, Australia, in which channels such as Cooper's Creek (where explorers

Robert Burke and William Wills died 1861) are cut by intermittent rivers. Summer rains supply rich grass for cattle, and there are the 'beef roads', down which herds are taken in linked trucks for slaughter.

Channel, English See ◊English Channel.

Channel Islands Group of islands in the English Channel, off the NW coast of France; they are a possession of the British crown. They comprise the islands of Jersey, Guernsey, Alderney, Great and Little Sark, with the lesser Herm, Brechou, Jethou, and Lihou.

Channel Islands

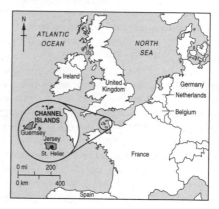

Channel Tunnel Tunnel built beneath the English Channel, linking Britain with mainland Europe. It comprises twin rail tunnels, 50 km/31 mi long and 7.3 m/24 ft in diameter, located 40 m/130 ft beneath the seabed. Construction began 1987, and the French and English sections were linked Dec 1990. It was officially opened 6 May 1994. The shuttle train service, Le Shuttle, opened to lorries May 1994 and to cars Dec 1994. The tunnel's high-speed train service, Eurostar, linking London to Paris and Brussels, opened Nov 1994.

Chantilly Town in Oise *département*, France, NE of Paris. It is the centre of French horseracing and was the headquarters of the French military chief Joseph Joffre 1914–17. It formerly produced lace and porcelain.

Chao Phraya Chief river (formerly Menam) of Thailand, flowing 1,200 km/750 mi into the Bight of Bangkok, an inlet of the Gulf of Thailand.

Charente French river, rising in Haute-Vienne *département* and flowing past Angoulême and Cognac into the Bay of Biscay below Rochefort. It is 360 km/225 mi long. Its wide estuary is much silted up. It gives its name to two *départements*, Charente and Charente-Maritime (formerly Charente-Inférieure).

Charente *Département* in the ◊Poitou-Charentes region of France; area 5,952 sq km/2,298 sq mi; population (1990) 176,300. The rivers Vienne and Dronne flow through it, the latter forming the S boundary. The countryside is undulating, crossed by the low spurs of the Limousin, Guyenne, and Poitou hills. There are extensive areas of forest and heathland. The *département* is predominantly agricultural, growing cereals, potatoes, beet, hemp, flax, and truffles, but the most important product is the brandy made from grapes grown in the Charente basin. Industries include the manufacture of paper, textiles, chemicals, and metals. The principal towns are Angoulême (the capital), Cognac, and Confolens.

Charente-Maritime *Département* in the ◊Poitou-Charentes region of France, including the islands of Ré and Oléron; area 6,848 sq km/2,644 sq mi; population (1990) 271,400. The rivers Charente, Boutonne, Sèvre-Niortaise, Touvre, and Gironde flow through the region. Cereals, vines, sugar beet, potatoes, hemp, and fruit are grown, and livestock is reared. Industries include the production of brandy, iron, chemicals, and salt. The principal towns are ◊La Rochelle (the capital), ◊Rochefort, and Saintes.

Charing Cross District in Westminster, London, around Charing Cross railway station. It derives its name from the site of the last of 12 stone crosses erected by Edward I 1290 at the resting-places of the coffin of his queen, Eleanor. The present cross was designed by A S Barry 1865.

Charleroi City in Belgium on the river Sambre, Hainault province; population (1995) 206,000. Its coal industry declined in the 1970s; other industries include steel, electronics and electrical engineering, pharmaceuticals, glass, and cement.

Charleston Capital and chief city of West Virginia, USA, on the Kanawha River; population (1992) 57,100. It is the centre of a region that produces coal, natural gas, salt, clay, timber, and oil, and it is a chemical-producing centre. Charleston developed from a fort built 1788 and became an important salt centre in the early 19th century.

Charleston Main port and city of South Carolina, USA; population (1992) 81,300. Industries include textiles, clothing, and paper products. A nuclear-submarine naval base and an air-force base are nearby. The city dates from 1670, and there are many historic houses and fine gardens.

Charleville-Mézières French town, capital of the *département* of Ardennes, situated on a bend in the river Meuse; population (1990) 58,000. Industries include machine tools and hardware.

Charlotte City in North Carolina, USA, on the border with South Carolina; population (1992) 416,300; metropolitan area (1992) 1,212,000. Industries include data processing, textiles, chemicals, machinery, and food products. Settled around 1750, it was the gold-mining centre of the country until gold was discovered in California 1849. Charlotte enjoyed rapid growth in the 1970s and is the largest city in the state.

Charlotte Amalie Capital, tourist resort, and free port of the US Virgin Islands, on the island of St Thomas; population (1990) 12,331. Boatbuilding and rum distilling are among the economic activities. It was founded 1672 by the Danish West India Company.

Charlottesville City in central Virginia, USA, in the Blue Ridge mountain foothills, NW of Richmond, on the Rivanna River; seat of Albemarle County; population (1990) 40,300. Tourism is important, and some textiles are manufactured. Charlottesville is the site of the University of Virginia, established 1819 by Thomas Jefferson. Jefferson's home, Monticello, is nearby, as is President James Monroe's home, Ash Lawn.

Charlottetown Capital of Prince Edward Island, Canada; population (1991) 15,400. The city trades in textiles, fish, timber, vegetables, and dairy produce. It was founded by French settlers in the 1720s.

Chartres Capital of the *département* of Eure-et-Loir, NW France, 96 km/59 mi SW of Paris, on the river Eure; population (1990) 41,850. The city is an agricultural centre for the fertile Plaine de la Beauce. Its cathedral of Notre Dame, completed about 1240, is a masterpiece of Gothic architecture.

Châteauroux French town, capital of the *département* of Indre, on the river Indre; population (1990) 52,900. The town manufactures textiles, agricultural machinery, foodstuffs, and tobacco. Châteauroux is named after a 10th-century château built by Raoul of Deols. The present château was built in the 15th century. Situated close to the Loire valley, the town attracts tourists.

Chatellerault French town in the *département* of Vienne, on the river Vienne, 35 km/22 mi NE of Poitiers; population (1990) 35,000. It manufactures small arms, cutlery, and preserves, and has a distillery. The town has a 15th-century château, two 12th-century churches, and a number of historic houses.

Chatham City in Ontario, E Canada, on the Thames River, 19 km/12 mi from its mouth, 103 km/64 mi SW of London and 290 km/180 mi W of Toronto; population (1991) 43,600. It is the centre of a large natural gas field, and also has hydroelectric power. The chief products are natural gas, fruit and dairy products, and metal products. Before the American Civil War Chatham was the N terminus of the Underground Railroad for escaped slaves.

Chatham Town in Kent, England, on the river Medway; population (1991) 71,700. As a focus of revival for the whole Medway area, The Royal Dockyard 1588–1984 was from 1985 converted to an industrial area, marina, and museum, with part of the dockyard being preserved as the Chatham Historic Dockyard. Industries include navigation equipment, cement, and electronics.

Chatham Islands Two Pacific islands (Chatham and Pitt), forming a county of South Island, New Zealand; area 960 sq km/371 sq mi; population (1991) 769. The chief settlement is Waitangi.

Chattahoochee River in W Georgia, SE USA; length 700km/435 mi. Its source is in the Blue Ridge Mountains. Flowing through Atlanta, the river forms part of the W boundary between Georgia, Alabama, and Florida on the W, and after joining the Flint River at Lake Seminole becomes the Apalachicola. It is navigable from Columbus to its mouth.

Chattanooga City in Tennessee, USA, on the Tennessee River; population (1992) 152,900. It is the focus of the Tennessee Valley Authority area. Developed as a salt-trading centre after 1835, it now produces chemicals, textiles, and metal products. Chattanooga was laid out 1838 after Cherokee Native Americans were removed from the area. Union forces captured it from the Confederacy 1863.

Chaux-de-Fonds, La Industrial commune in the canton of Neuchâtel, Switzerland; population (1995) 37,400. It is situated at an altitude of 990 m/3,248 ft in the Jura Mountains, 14 km/9 mi NW of the town of Neuchâtel. It is a centre of the watchmaking industry, and has a school for the engraving and enamelling of watch cases.

Cheapside Street running from St Paul's Cathedral to Poultry, in the City of London, England. It was the scene of the 13th-century 'Cheap', a permanent fair and general market. Christopher Wren's church of St Mary-le-Bow in Cheapside has the Bow Bells.

Cheb (German *Eger*) Industrial town (textiles) in W Bohemia, in the Czech Republic, on the river Ohře near the German border, 145 km/91 mi W of Prague; population (1991) 31,800. The town has a 13th-century church and was formerly a strategic fortress.

Chechnya or *Chechenia* Breakaway part of the former Russian autonomous republic of Checheno-Ingush on the N slopes of the Caucasus Mountains; official name *Noxcijn Republika Ickeriy* from 1994
area 16,064 sq km/6,202 sq mi
capital Grozny
industries oil extraction (at one of the largest Russian oilfields), engineering, chemicals, building materials, timber
population (1995) 904,000
religion Muslim.

Cheddar Market town in Somerset, England, where Cheddar cheese was first produced. It is part of an agricultural area. Nearby are Cheddar Gorge (a limestone gorge) and caves with stalactites and stalagmites. In 1962 excavation revealed the site of a Saxon palace.

Chefoo Former name of ◊Yantai, a port in China.

Chekiang Alternative transcription of ◊Zhejiang, a province of China.

Chełm (Russian *Kholm*) Industrial town (metals, bricks, cement, food processing) in Lublin province, Poland, 64 km/40 mi E of Lublin; population (1990) 66,400.

Chelmsford Market town in Essex, England, 48 km/30 mi NE of London; population (1991) 97,500. It is the administrative headquarters of the county, with radio, electrical, engineering, agricultural-machinery, flour-milling, and brewing industries. It was the Roman *Caesaromagus*.

Chelsea Historic area of the Royal Borough of Kensington and Chelsea, London, immediately N of the Thames where it is crossed by the Albert and Chelsea bridges.

Cheltenham Spa town at the foot of the Cotswold Hills, Gloucestershire, England; population (1991) 91,300. There are annual literary and music festivals, a racecourse (the Cheltenham Gold Cup is held annually), and Cheltenham College (founded 1854). The town has light industries including aerospace electronics and food processing (Kraft). It is the headquarters of Gulf Oil.

Chelyabinsk Industrial city and capital of Chelyabinsk region, in the Russian Federation, in the S Ural Mountains; population (1994) 1,125,000. It has iron and engineering works and makes chemicals, motor vehicles, and aircraft. Waste from the plutonium plant makes it possibly the most radioactive place in the world.

Chemnitz Industrial city (engineering, textiles, chemicals) in Saxony, Federal Republic of Germany, on the river Chemnitz, 65 km/40 mi SE of Leipzig; population (1993) 282,000. As a former district capital of East Germany it was named *Karl-Marx-Stadt* 1953–90.

Chemulpo Former name for ◊Inchon, port and summer resort on the W coast of South Korea.

Chenab Tributary of the river ◊Indus, in India and Pakistan.

Chengchow Alternative transcription of ◊Zhengzhou, the capital of Henan province, China.

Chengde or *Chengteh* City in Hebei province, China, NE of Beijing; population (1990) 247,000. It is a market town for agricultural and forestry products. It was the summer residence of the Manchu rulers and has an 18th-century palace and temples. As *Jehol*, it was capital of a former province of the same name.

Chengdu or *Chengtu* Ancient city, capital of Sichuan province, China; population (1993) 2,670,000. It is a busy rail junction and has railway workshops, and textile, electronics, and engineering industries. It has well-preserved temples.

Chennai formerly (to 1996) *Madras* Industrial port (cotton, cement, chemicals, iron, and steel) and capital of Tamil Nadu, India, on the Bay of Bengal; population (1991) 5,361,000. Fort St George 1639 remains from the East India Company when Chennai was the chief port on the E coast. Chennai was occupied by the French 1746–48 and shelled by the German ship *Emden* 1914, the only place in India attacked in World War I.

Chenonceaux French Renaissance château in the *département* of Indre-et-Loire, E of ◊Tours, on the river Cher. The building was begun in 1515 by Thomas Bohier, a tax collector. In 1560 a long gallery, which crosses the river Cher, was added by Philibert Delorme. The château, confiscated by Francis I in 1535, was given by Henry II to Diane de Poitiers, from whom it was forcibly taken by Catherine de Medici in exchange for the château of Chaumont. Chenonceaux later belonged to the Vendôme and Bourbon-Condé families. It is now open to the public.

Chepstow (Welsh *Casgwent*) Market town in Monmouthshire, Wales, on the river Wye. The high tides, sometimes 15 m/50 ft above low level, are the highest in Britain. There is a Norman castle, and the ruins of Tintern Abbey are 6.5 km/4 mi to the N. There are light industries, farming, and tourism.

Cher French river that rises in Creuse *département* and flows into the river Loire below Tours, length 355 km/220 mi. It gives its name to a *département*.

Cher *Département* in the ◊Centre region of France; area 7,227 sq km/2,790 sq mi; population (1990) 157,100. The landscape is generally level and wooded. It is a fertile agricultural region, producing corn, vines, fruit trees, sugar beet, hemp, and flax, and there is livestock farming. The principal towns are ◊Bourges (the capital) and St-Amand-Mont-Rond.

Cherbourg French port and naval station at the N end of the Cotentin peninsula, in Manche *département*; population (1990) 28,800. There is an institute for studies in nuclear warfare, and large shipbuilding yards.

Cherepovets Iron and steel city in W Russian Federation, on the Volga-Baltic waterway; population (1994) 319,000. It was originally a tax-exempt settlement.

Chernihiv City and port on the river Desna in N Ukraine; population (1992) 311,000. Lumbering, textiles, chemicals, distilling, and food-canning are among its industries. It has an 11th-century cathedral.

Chernivtsi City in W Ukraine; population (1992) 261,000. Industries include textiles, clothing, and machinery. It has formerly been called *Czernowitz* (before 1918), *Cernăuti* (1918–40, when it was part of Romania), and *Chrenovitsy* (1940–44).

Chernobyl Town in N Ukraine; site of a nuclear power station. In April 1986 two huge explosions destroyed a central reactor, breaching the 1,000-tonne roof. In the immediate vicinity of Chernobyl, 31 people died (all firemen or workers at the plant) and 135,000 were permanently evacuated. It has been estimated that there will be an additional 20,000–40,000 deaths from cancer in the following 60 years; 600,000 are officially classified as at risk. According to WHO figures of 1995, the incidence of thyroid cancer in children has increased 200-fold in Belarus as a result of fallout from the disaster.

Ches. Abbreviation for ◊Cheshire, an English county.

Chesapeake Bay Largest of the inlets on the Atlantic coast of the USA, bordered by Maryland and Virginia. It is about 320 km/200 mi in length and 6–64 km/4–40 mi in width.

Cheshire County of NW England. Halton and Warrington will become unitary authorities in April 1998.
area 2,320 sq km/896 sq mi
towns and cities Chester (administrative headquarters), Warrington, Crewe, Widnes, Macclesfield, Congleton
features chiefly a fertile plain, with the Pennines in the E; rivers: Mersey, Dee, Weaver; salt mines and geologically rich former copper workings at Alderley Edge (in use from

Roman times until the 1920s); Little Moreton Hall; discovery of Lindow Man, the first 'bogman' to be found in mainland Britain, dating from around 500 BC; Museum of the Chemical Industry on Spike Island; Quarry Bank Mill at Styal is a cotton-industry museum
industries textiles, chemicals, dairy products, aerospace industry, salt, pharmaceuticals, vehicles
famous people the novelist Elizabeth Gaskell lived at Knutsford (the locale of **Cranford**); Charles Dodgson (Lewis Carroll)
population (1994) 975,600.

Chesil Bank Shingle bank extending 19 km/11 mi along the coast of Dorset, England, from Abbotsbury to the Isle of Portland.

Chester City in Cheshire, England, on the river Dee 26 km/16 mi S of Liverpool; population (1991) 115,000. It is the administrative headquarters of Cheshire. There are engineering, aerospace (airbus), metallurgical, and clothing industries, and car components are manufactured. It was a Roman legionary fortress *Deva* and there are many Roman remains, and a medieval town centre. It is the only English city to retain its city walls (3 km/2 mi long) intact. The cathedral dates from the 11th century but was restored 1876. The church of St John the Baptist is a well-known example of early Norman architecture. The 'Rows' are covered arcades dating from the Middle Ages.

Chester Port city in Pennsylvania, NE USA, lying on the N bank of the Delaware River, midway between Philadelphia and Wilmington; population (1990) 41,900. Originally settled by Swedes, it was once the seat of the state's government. Industries include chemicals and paper.

Chesterfield Market town of Derbyshire, England, near the Peak District National Park, 40 km/25 mi N of Derby, on the Rother River; population (1991) 71,900. Industries include iron founding, chemicals, pottery, engineering, and glass. It is the burial place of the engineer George Stephenson. All Saints' Church is renowned for its crooked spire.

Cheviot Hills Range of hills 56 km/35 mi long, mainly in Northumberland, forming the border between England and Scotland for some 48 km/30 mi. The highest point is the Cheviot, 816 m/2,676 ft. For centuries the area was a battleground between the English and the Scots. It gives its name to a breed of sheep.

Cheyenne Capital of Wyoming, USA, located in the SE part of the state, just N of the Colorado border in the foothills of the Laramie Mountains; population (1992) 51,900. An agricultural and transportation centre, its industries include iron, steel, chemicals, electrical goods, machinery, meat packing, and food processing. Tourism is also important to the economy. Cheyenne was settled 1867 when the Union Pacific Railroad arrived.

Chiang Mai Alternative name for ◊Chiengmai, a town in Thailand.

Chiapas Southernmost state of Mexico, on the border of Guatemala; area 73,887 sq km/28,528 sq mi; population

(1995 est) 3,606,800. Its capital is Tuxtla Gutíerrez. The main occupation is farming, producing fruit, coffee, cotton, and hardwoods.

Chiba Industrial city (paper, steel, textiles) in Kanton region, E Honshu Island, Japan, 40 km/25 mi W of Tokyo; population (1994) 839,000.

Chicago (Ojibway 'wild onion place') Financial and industrial city in Illinois, USA, on Lake Michigan. It is the third largest US city; population (1992) 2,768,500; metropolitan area (1992) 8,410,000. Industries include iron, steel, chemicals, electrical goods, machinery, meatpacking and food processing, publishing, and fabricated metals. The once famous stockyards are now closed. Chicago grew from a village in the mid-19th century. The world's first skyscraper was built here 1885 and some of the world's tallest skyscrapers, including the tallest, the Sears Tower at 443 m/1,454 ft, are in Chicago.

Chichester City and market town in West Sussex; 111 km/69 mi SW of London, near Chichester Harbour; population (1991) 26,600. It is the administrative headquarters of West Sussex. Chichester was a Roman township (*Noviomagus Regnensium*), and the remains of the Roman palace built around AD 80 at nearby Fishbourne are unique outside Italy. There is a cathedral consecrated 1108, later much rebuilt and restored, and the Chichester Festival Theatre (1962). The town lies in an agricultural area.

Chickahominy River in Virginia, E USA, a tributary of the James River, which it joins 35 km/22 mi S of Richmond; length 110 km/70 mi. During the American Civil War many battles took place near the river, including in 1862 the battles of Fair Oaks, Mechanicsville, Gaines' Mill, Savage's Station, and White Oak Swamp, and in 1864 the Battle of Cold Harbor.

Chiclayo Capital of Lambayeque department, NW Peru; population (1993) 411,500. At the centre of an agricultural area, its industries include rice milling, cotton ginning, brewing, and tanning.

Chico City in N California, USA, NW of Sacramento; population (1990) 40,000. Situated in the fertile Sacramento Valley, a farming region, it includes food processing and lumber products among its industries. It was founded 1860.

Chiengmai or *Chiang Mai* City in N Thailand; population (1993) 161,500. There is a trade in teak and lac (as shellac, a resin used in varnishes and polishes) and many handicraft industries. It is the former capital of the Lan Na Thai kingdom.

Chieti Province of S central Italy in ◊Abruzzi region; capital Chieti (population (1990) 57,500); area 2,590 sq km/1,000 sq mi; population (1992) 383,200.

Chignecto Bay and isthmus between Nova Scotia and New Brunswick, Canada, which forms the N extremity of the Bay of Fundy.

Chihuahua Capital of Chihuahua state, Mexico, 1,285 km/800 mi NW of Mexico City; population (1990) 530,800.

It was founded 1707. It is the centre of a mining district and has textile mills.

Chihuahua State of N Mexico, the largest in Mexico; area 247,087 sq km/95,400 sq mi; population (1995 est) 2,793,000. Its capital is Chihuahua. The main occupations are farming and mining.

Chiltern Hills Range of chalk hills extending for some 72 km/45 mi in a curve from a point N of Reading to the Suffolk border. Coombe Hill, near Wendover, 260 m/852 ft high, is the highest point.

Chimbote Largest fishing port in Peru; population (1993) 297,000. Sugar and fish products are exported; other industries include iron and steel.

China Sea Area of the Pacific Ocean bordered by China, Vietnam, Borneo, the Philippines, and Japan. Various groups of small islands and shoals, including the Paracels, 500 km/300 mi E of Vietnam, have been disputed by China and other powers because they lie in oil-rich areas.

Chinghai Alternative transcription of ◊Qinghai, a province of China.

Chinon French town in the *département* of Indre-et-Loire, on the river Vienne; population (1990) 9,000. It is the centre of a wine-producing area, and there is a nuclear power plant nearby at Avoine. On a hill above the town are the ruins of a large stronghold, which is three castles combined as one. Clovis I took the town from the Visigoths. In the Middle Ages it belonged to the Plantagenets, but was lost by Philip II of France to Henry II of England, who died here 1189.

Chios (Greek *Khios*) One of the ◊Aegean Islands in Greece, 13 km/8 mi off the W coast of Turkey at the entrance to the Gulf of Smyrna; area 830 sq km/320 sq mi; population (1993) 50,200. The island is 50 km/31 mi long and 12–25 km/8–16 mi wide. Grapes, oranges, lemons, figs, olives, aniseed, and tobacco are grown. The capital of the island is also called Chios.

Chisinău (Russian *Kishinev*) Capital of Moldova, situated in a rich agricultural area; population (1992) 667,000. It is a commercial and cultural centre; industries include cement, food processing, tobacco, and textiles.

Chita City in E Siberia, on the Chita River; population (1994) 367,000. It is on the Trans-Siberian railway, and has chemical and engineering works and coal mines.

Chittagong City and port in Bangladesh, 16 km/10 mi from the mouth of the Karnaphuli River, on the Bay of Bengal; population (1991) 1,364,000. Industries include steel, engineering, chemicals, and textiles.

Chittagong Hill Tracts Area of SE Bangladesh. There is conflict between Muslim Bengali settlers and the mainly Buddhist indigenous peoples, collectively known as Jumma. Most of the ethnic peoples of Bangladesh (12 linguistic groups) live here. Non-Jumma settlers increased from 6% 1951 to 45% 1983, and thousands of Jumma fled to India. Some 30,000 fled across the border 1986.

Chkalov Former name (1938–57) of ♢Orenburg, a town in the Russian Federation.

Chomutov (German *Komotau*) Industrial town (engineering, coal) in N Bohemia, the Czech Republic, at the foot of the Erzgebirge, 80 km/50 mi NW of Prague; population (1991) 53,200.

Chongjin Port and capital of North Hamgyong province on the NE coast of North Korea; population (1984) 754,000. Timber, iron, and textiles are exported; there is steel, pig-iron, and fish processing.

Chongqing or *Chungking*, also known as *Pahsien* City in Sichuan province, China, that stands at the confluence of the ♢Chang Jiang and Jialing Jiang rivers; population (1993) 3,780,000. Industries include iron, steel, chemicals, synthetic rubber, and textiles.

Chorzów Industrial town in Katowice province, Upper Silesia, S Poland, 6 km/4 mi NW of Katowice; population (1990) 131,900. It is a centre for coal, iron, steel, chemicals (nitrates), and engineering.

Christchurch City on South Island, New Zealand, 11 km/7 mi from the mouth of the Avon River; population (1993) 312,600, urban area 306,900. It is the principal city of the Canterbury plains and the seat of the University of Canterbury. Industries include fertilizers and chemicals, canning and meat processing, rail workshops, and shoes.

Christchurch Resort town in Dorset, S England, adjoining Bournemouth at the junction of the Stour and Avon rivers; population (1991) 36,400. Light industries include plastics and electronics. There is a Norman and Early English priory church.

Christiania Former name of the Norwegian capital of ♢Oslo (1624–1924), after King Christian IV who replanned it after a fire 1624.

Christmas Island Island in the Indian Ocean, 360 km/224 mi S of Java; area 135 sq km/52 sq mi; population (1994 est) 2,500. Found to be uninhabited when reached by Capt W Mynars on Christmas Day 1643, it was annexed by Britain 1888, occupied by Japan 1942–45, and transferred to Australia 1958. After a referendum 1984, it was included in Northern Territory. Its phosphate mine was closed 1987. Tourism and casinos are being developed.

Christmas Island Former name of ♢Kiritimati, an island in Kiribati, in the central Pacific.

Chrzanów Coal-mining town in Katowice province, Poland, 40 km/25 mi NW of Kraków; population (1990) 10,100.

Chubu Mountainous coastal region of central Honshu Island, Japan; area 66,776 sq km/25,782 sq mi; population (1995) 21,400,000. The chief city is Nagoya.

Chufu Alternative transcription of ♢Qufu, a city in Shandong province, China.

Chugoku SW region of Honshu Island, Japan; area 31,908 sq km/12,320 sq mi; population (1995) 7,775,000. The chief city is ♢Hiroshima.

Chukchi Sea Part of the Arctic Ocean, situated N of the Bering Strait between Asia and North America.

Chungking Alternative transcription of ♢Chongqing, a city in Sichuan province, China.

Chur (French *Coire*, Italian *Coira*, Romansch *Cuera*) Capital of the canton of ♢Graubünden, Switzerland, in the valley of the upper Rhine; population (1995) 30,100. The Roman Catholic cathedral of St Lucius was begun 1178.

Churchill Town in the province of Manitoba, Canada, situated on Hudson Bay; population (1991) 1,143. Although the port is ice-free only three months a year, Churchill handles about 500,000 tonnes of grain annually, as well as fuel oil and bulk cargo. It is a major centre for Arctic research, health programmes, and education. The Hudson's Bay Company established a post here and named it after Lord Churchill (later 1st duke of Marlborough).

Churchill Falls Waterfalls on the Churchill River, the longest river in Labrador, E Canada, situated about 400 km/249 mi from the mouth of the river. They fall 75 m/245 ft. A power plant at the falls supplies hydroelectric power, much of which is transmitted from the province to other parts of Canada and the USA.

Chuvashia Autonomous republic of W Russian Federation.
area 18,300 sq km/7,066 sq mi
capital Cheboksary
physical W of Volga River, 560 km/350 mi E of Moscow; Chuvash Plateau
industries lumbering, grain farming, electrical and engineering industries, phosphate, and limestone
population (1995) 1,361,000

Cicero Industrial city in NE Illinois, USA, 11 km/7 mi W of Chicago; population (1990) 67,400. It has large telephone, radio, and electrical equipment plants.

Cienfuegos Port and naval base in Cuba; population (1990 est) 123,600. It trades in sugar, fruit, and tobacco. It was founded 1819, destroyed by a storm 1825, and rebuilt.

Cilicia Ancient region of Asia Minor, now forming part of Turkey, situated between the Taurus Mountains and the Mediterranean. Access from the N across the Taurus range is through the *Cilician Gates*, a strategic pass that has been used for centuries as part of a trade route linking Europe and the Middle East.

Cincinnati City and port in Ohio, USA, on the Ohio River; population (1992) 364,300; metropolitan area (1992) 1,865,000. Chief industries include machinery, clothing, furniture making, wine, chemicals, and meatpacking. Founded 1788, Cincinnati became a city 1819. It attracted large numbers of European immigrants, particularly Germans, during the 19th century.

Circassia Former name of an area of the N Caucasus, the dominant principality until c. 1700, ceded to Russia by Turkey 1829 and now part of the Karachay-Cherkess region of Russia.

Cirencester Market town in Gloucestershire, England, in the Cotswolds; population (1991) 15,200. Industries include engineering and the manufacture of electrical goods. It was the second-largest town in Roman Britain (*Corinium Dobunnorum*), and has an amphitheatre which seated 8,000, and the Corinium Museum. The Royal Agricultural College is here.

Ciskei Republic of; former independent Black National State within South Africa, independent from 1981 (but not recognized by the United Nations) until 1994 when it was re-integrated into South Africa, in Eastern Cape Province. The region covers an area of 7,700 sq km/2,974 sq mi, and produces wheat, sorghum, sunflower, vegetables, timber, metal products, leather, and textiles. It was one of two homelands of the Xhosa people created by South Africa, the other being Transkei; Xhosa is spoken here.

Citeaux Abbey in the *département* of Côte-d'Or, NE of Beaune, France. Here the monastic order of Cistercians was founded in 1098.

Citlaltépetl (Aztec 'star mountain') Dormant volcano, the highest mountain in Mexico at 5,700 m/18,700 ft, N of the city of Orizaba (after which it is sometimes named). It last erupted 1687.

Ciudad Bolívar formerly (1824–49) *Angostura* Capital of Bolívar state, SE Venezuela, and river port on the river Orinoco, 400 km/250 mi from its mouth; population (1990) 225,800. Gold is mined in the vicinity. The city is linked with Soledad across the river by the Angostura Bridge (1967), the first to span the Orinoco.

Ciudad Guayana City in Venezuela, on the S bank of the river Orinoco, population (1990) 524,000. Main industries include iron and steel. The city was formed by the union of Puerto Ordaz and San Felix, and has been opened to ocean-going ships by dredging.

Ciudad Juárez City on the Rio Grande, in Chihuahua, N Mexico, on the US border; population (1990) 797,650. It is a centre for cotton.

Ciudad Real City of central Spain, 170 km/105 mi S of Madrid; population (1991) 59,400. It is the capital of Ciudad Real province. It trades in livestock and produces textiles and pharmaceuticals. Its chief feature is a huge Gothic cathedral.

Ciudad Real Province of central Spain in S ♢Castilla–La Mancha autonomous community; capital Ciudad Real; area 19,748 sq km/7,625 sq mi; population (1995) 490,600.

Ciudad Rodrigo Town in the province of Salamanca, W Spain, on a hill above the river Agueda; population (1995) 15,700. It was taken by the English in 1706, during the War of the Spanish Succession, and again in 1812, during the Peninsular War, by the Duke of Wellington; he was subsequently created duke of Ciudad Rodrigo. Products include leather, soap, and pottery.

Ciudad Trujillo Former name (1936–61) of ♢Santo Domingo, capital city and seaport of the Dominican Republic.

Civitavecchia Ancient port on the W coast of Italy, in Lazio region, 64 km/40 mi NW of Rome; population (1990) 51,200. Industries include fishing and the manufacture of cement and calcium carbide.

Clackmannanshire Unitary authority in central Scotland, bordering the Firth of Forth. A former county, it was a district of Central Region 1975–1996; administrative headquarters Alloa; population (1996) 47,700; area 161 sq km/62 sq mi.

Clacton-on-Sea Seaside resort in Essex, England; 19 km/12 mi SE of Colchester; population (1991) 45,100. The 16th-century St Osyth's priory is nearby.

Clare County on the W coast of the Republic of Ireland, in the province of Munster; county town Ennis; area 3,190 sq km/1,231 sq mi; population (1996 est) 93,900.

Clarksville City in N Tennessee, USA, at the confluence of the Cumberland and Red rivers, NW of Nashville; population (1992) 84,400. Industries include tobacco products, clothing, air-conditioning and heating equipment, rubber, and cheese. Beef and dairy cattle are raised in the area. Clarksville was settled 1784 and developed as an important river port in the 19th century.

Clearwater City in W central Florida, USA, on the Gulf of Mexico, NW of St Petersburg; seat of Pinellas County; population (1992) 98,100. Industries include tourism, citrus fruits, fishing, electronics, and flowers. It was settled in the 1840s.

Cleethorpes Seaside resort in North East Lincolnshire, NE England, on the Humber estuary; population (1987 est) 35,500. Fishing is important to the local economy.

Clermont-Ferrand City, capital of Puy-de-Dôme *département*, in the Auvergne region of France; population (1990) 140,200. It is a centre for agriculture, and its rubber industry is the largest in France.

Cleveland Former county of NE England, formed 1974 from parts of Durham and NE Yorkshire. It was abolished 1996 when the unitary authorities of Hartlepool, Middlesborough, Redcar and Cleveland, and Stockton-on-Tees were created.

Cluj-Napoca (German *Klausenberg*) City in Transylvania, Romania, located on the river Somes; population (1993) 322,000. It is a communications centre for Romania and the Hungarian plain. Industries include machine tools, furniture, and knitwear.

Cluny Town in Saône-et-Loire *département*, France, on the river Grosne; population (1982) 4,500. Its abbey, now in ruins, was the foundation house 910–1790 of the Cluniac order, originally a reformed branch of the Benedictines. Cluny was once a lace-making centre; it has a large cattle market.

Clutha Longest river in South Island, New Zealand, 322 km/201 mi long. It rises in the Southern Alps, has hydroelectric installations, and flows to meet the sea near Kaitangata.

Clwyd Former county of N Wales, 1974–96, now divided between Conwy, Denbighshire, Flintshire, Powys, and Wrexham unitary authorities.

Clyde River in central Scotland; 170 km/103 mi long. The Firth of Clyde and Firth of Forth are linked by the Forth and

Clyde Canal, 56 km/35 mi long. The shipbuilding yards have declined in recent years.

Clydebank Town on the river Clyde, part of the City of Glasgow unitary authority, Scotland, 10 km/6 mi NW of Glasgow; population (1991) 29,200. At the John Brown yard, liners such as the *Queen Elizabeth II* were built. Shipbuilding is now in decline.

CO Abbreviation for the state of ◊Colorado, USA.

Coahuila State of NE Mexico, on the border of Texas, USA; area 151,571 sq km/58,522 sq mi; population (1995 est) 2,172,100. Its capital is Saltillo. The main occupations are farming, and mining for coal, copper, silver, and lead. Cotton is grown in the W.

Coast Ranges Mountain system in North America, extending from the Coast Mountains of Alaska and British Columbia, through Washington, Oregon, and California, to Baja California in NW Mexico, and running almost parallel to the Pacific coast. The mountains of the Coast Ranges are very irregular in height and geological structure, with some peaks rising to 2,000 m/6,600 ft. In some places, especially the S, the mountains are almost bare, while in other places they are densely covered with forests. To the S, the ranges are subject to occasional earthquakes.

Coatbridge Town in North Lanarkshire, Scotland; 13 km/8 mi E of Glasgow; population (1991) 43,600. Coal and iron are mined nearby. Industries include iron, ore, steel, engineering, and metallurgical industries.

Cobh Seaport and market town on Great Island, Republic of Ireland; in the estuary of the Lee, County Cork; population (1991) 6,200. Cobh was formerly a port of call for transatlantic steamers. The town was known as Cove of Cork until 1849 and Queenstown until 1922.

Coblenz Alternative spelling of the German city ◊Koblenz.

Coburg Town in Bavaria, Germany, on the river Itz, 80 km/50 mi SE of Gotha; population (1991) 44,700. Industries include machinery, toys, and porcelain. Formerly the capital of the duchy of Coburg, it was part of Saxe-Coburg-Gotha 1826–1918, and a residence of its dukes.

Cochabamba City in central Bolivia, SE of La Paz; population (1992) 404,100. Its altitude is 2,550 m/8,370 ft; it is a centre of agricultural trading and oil refining.

Cochin Present-day region and former princely state lying W of the Anamalai hills in S India. It was part of Travancore-Cochin from 1949 until merged into Kerala 1956.

Cochin Seaport in Kerala state, India, on the Malabar coast; population (1991) 564,000. It is a fishing port, naval training base, and an industrial centre with oil refineries; ropes and clothing are also manufactured here. It exports coir, copra, tea, and spices. Vasco da Gama established a Portuguese factory at Cochin 1502, and St Francis Xavier made it a missionary centre 1530. The Dutch held Cochin from 1663 to 1795, when it was taken by the English.

Cochin-China Region of SE Asia. With Cambodia it formed part of the ancient Khmer empire. In the 17th–18th centuries it was conquered by Annam. Together with Cambodia it became, 1863–67, the first part of the Indochinese peninsula to be occupied by France. Since 1949 it has been part of Vietnam.

Cocos Islands or *Keeling Islands* Group of 27 small coral islands in the Indian Ocean, about 2,770 km/1,720 mi NW of Perth, Australia; area 14 sq km/5.5 sq mi; population (1994) 593. They are owned by Australia.

Cody Resort town in NW Wyoming, USA, on the Shoshone River, situated at the entrance to Yellowstone National Park; population (1990) 7,897. It was founded by William F Cody ('Buffalo Bill') 1901.

Cognac Town in Charente *département*, France, 40 km/25 mi W of Angoulême. Situated in a vine-growing district, Cognac has given its name to a brandy. Bottles, corks, barrels, and crates are manufactured here.

Coimbatore City in Tamil Nadu, S India, on the Noyil River; population (1991) 816,000. It has textile industries and the Indian Air Force Administrative College.

Coimbra City in Portugal, on the Mondego River, 32 km/19 mi from the sea; population (1987 est) 74,600. It produces fabrics, paper, pottery, and biscuits. There is a 12th-century Romanesque cathedral incorporating part of an older mosque, and a university, founded in Lisbon 1290 and transferred to Coimbra 1537. Coimbra was the capital of Portugal 1139–1385.

Colchester City and river port in Essex, E England, on the river Colne; 80 km/50 mi NE of London; population (1991 est) 87,500. In an agricultural area, it is a market centre with clothing manufacture and engineering and printing works. It is famous for its oysters.

history Claiming to be the oldest town in England (the Roman *Camulodunum*), Colchester dates from the time of Cymbeline (c. AD 10–43). It became a colony of Roman ex-soldiers AD 50, it was the first Roman capital of Britain and one of the most prosperous towns in Roman Britain despite its burning by Boudicca (Boadicea) 61. Most of the Roman walls remain, as well as ruins of the Norman castle, and St Botolph's priory. Holly Tree Mansion (1718) is a museum of 18th-and 19th-century social life.

Colima State of SW Mexico, on the Pacific; area 5,455 sq km/2,106 sq mi; population (1995 est) 487,300. Its capital is Colima. The main occupation is farming.

College Station City in E central Texas, USA, NW of Houston, adjoining the city of Bryan; population (1992) 55,700. Texas A & M (Agricultural and Mechanical) University is here; the city grew up around the college, founded 1876.

Colmar Capital of Haut-Rhin *département*, France, between the river Rhine and the Vosges Mountains; population (1990) 64,900. It is the centre of a wine-growing and market-gardening area. Industries include engineering, food processing, and textiles. The church of St Martin is 13th–14th century, and the former Dominican monastery, now the Unterlinden Museum, contains a Grünewald altarpiece.

Cologne (German *Köln*) Industrial and commercial port in North Rhine–Westphalia, Germany, on the left bank of the Rhine, 35 km/22 mi SE of Düsseldorf; population (1993) 961,600. To the N is the Ruhr coalfield, on which many of Cologne's industries are based. Cologne is an important transshipment centre. The famous Gothic cathedral was begun in the 13th century, but its towers were not completed until 1850. Cologne suffered severely during World War II; 85% of the city was destroyed.

Colombes Suburb of Paris, France; population (1990) 79,100. It is the capital of Hauts-de-Seine *département*. Tyres, electronic equipment, and chemicals are manufactured.

Colombey-les-Deux-Eglises (French 'Colombey with the two churches') Village in Haute-Marne, France, where General de Gaulle lived and was buried; population (1981) 700.

Colombo Capital and principal seaport of Sri Lanka, on the W coast near the mouth of the Kelani River; population (1993) 2,026,000. It trades in tea, rubber, andcacao. It has iron- and steelworks and an oil refinery.

Colón Second largest city in Panama, at the Caribbean end of the Panama Canal; population (1990) 140,900. It has a special economic zone (created 1948) used by foreign companies to avoid taxes on completed products in their home countries; $2 billion worth of goods passed through the zone in 1987, from dozens of countries and 600 companies.

Colón, Archipiélago de Official name of the ◊Galápagos Islands.

Colorado River in North America, rising in the Rocky Mountains and flowing 2,333 km/1,450 mi to the Gulf of California through Colorado, Utah, Arizona (including the Grand Canyon), and N Mexico. The many dams along its course, including Hoover and Glen Canyon, provide power and irrigation water, but have destroyed wildlife and scenery, and very little water now reaches the sea. To the W of the river in SE California is the Colorado Desert, an arid area of 5,000 sq km/2,000 sq mi.

Colorado State of the W central USA; nicknamed Centennial State
area 269,700 sq km/104,104 sq mi
capital Denver
towns and cities Colorado Springs, Aurora, Lakewood, Fort Collins, Greeley, Pueblo, Boulder
physical Great Plains in the E; the main ranges of the Rocky Mountains, with peaks over 4,000 m/14,000 ft; high plateaus of the Colorado Basin in the W; Pike's Peak; Colorado River; Garden of the Gods (natural sandstone sculptures); Dinosaur and Great Sand Dunes national monuments
features Rocky Mountains Royal Gorge (the Grand Canyon of Colorado), carved by the Arkansas River, has the world's highest suspension bridge; Mesa Verde national park (a World Heritage Site), with prehistoric cliff dwellings of the Anasazi Native Americans; La Junta adobe trading fort (1833); goldmining ghost towns; 19th-century towns, including Breckenridge, Durango (a railroad town), Leadville (1878) and Silverton (silver-mining towns);

Denver, with Denver Art Museum, containing a collection of Native American art, and the capitol building with its gold dome (1894); Colorado Springs, with the US Air Force Academy, the US Olympic Center, and the Pro Rodeo Hall of Fame and Museum of the American Cowboy; University of Colorado, Boulder; Aspen Music Festival; ski resorts, including Vail (the largest ski mountain in North America), Aspen, and Steamboat Springs
products cereals, meat and dairy products, oil, coal, molybdenum, uranium, iron, steel, machinery
population (1995) 3,746,600
famous people Jack Dempsey, Douglas Fairbanks
history first visited by Spanish explorers in the 16th century; claimed for Spain 1706; E portion passed to the USA 1803 as part of the Louisiana Purchase, the rest 1845 and 1848 as a result of the Mexican War. It attracted fur traders, and Denver was founded following the discovery of gold 1858. Colorado became a state 1876. The discovery of silver ore 1877 made Leadville the silver capital of America. Irrigated agriculture, ranching, tourism and outdoor sports, energy development, and the establishment of military bases fuelled rapid growth after World War II.

Colorado Springs City in Colorado, USA, 120 km/75 mi SE of Denver; population (1992) 295,800. At an altitude of about 1,800 m/6,000 ft, and surrounded by magnificent scenery, it was founded as a health resort 1871. A gold strike at nearby Cripple Creek 1892 aided its growth.

Columbia City in central Missouri, USA, NE of Jefferson City, seat of Boone County; population (1992) 73,100. It was laid out 1821 and is the site of Stephens College for women 1833 and the University of Missouri 1853, the first university W of the Mississippi River.

Columbia River in W North America, over 1,950 km/1,218 mi long; it rises in British Columbia, Canada, and flows through Washington State, USA, to the Pacific below Astoria. It is harnessed for irrigation and power by the Grand Coulee and other great dams. It was listed 1994 as in danger of ecological collapse, along with its tributary the Snake River.

Columbia Capital of South Carolina, USA, on the Congaree River; population (1992) 98,800. Manufacturing includes textiles, plastics, electrical goods, fertilizers, and hosiery, but the chief product is fuel assemblies for nuclear reactors. Columbia was laid out as the state capital 1786. It was burned by Union troops 1865, near the close of the Civil War.

Columbus City in W central Georgia, USA, SW of Macon, across the Chattahoochee River from Phenix City, Alabama; seat of Muscogee County; population (1992) 185,700. It is one of the largest textile centres in the South; other industries include processed food, machinery, iron and steel, and peanuts. It is a distribution centre for surrounding farmlands, and lies just N of the US Army infantry base Fort Benning. Founded 1827, it became an important cotton port.

Columbus Capital of Ohio, USA, on the rivers Scioto and Olentangy; population (1992) 643,000; metropolitan area

(1992) 1,394,000. It has coalfield and natural gas resources nearby; its industries include the manufacture of cars, aircraft, space equipment, missiles, and electrical goods. Columbus was founded 1812, became the state capital 1816, and developed as an important transport centre.

Colwyn Bay (Welsh *Bae Colwyn*) Seaside town in Conwy, N Wales, known as the 'garden resort of Wales'; population (1991) 29,900.

Communism Peak Alternative form of Pik ◊Kommunizma, the highest mountain in the ◊Pamirs.

Como City in Lombardy, Italy, on Lake Como at the foot of the Alps; population (1981) 95,500. Motorcycles, glass, silk, and furniture are produced here. The river Adda flows N–S through the lake, and the shores are extremely beautiful. Como has a marble cathedral, built 1396–1732, and is a tourist resort.

Como Province of N Italy in W ◊Lombardy region; capital Como; area 2,070 sq km/799 sq mi; population (1992) 798,300.

Comodoro Rivadavia Port in Patagonia, SE Argentina; population (1991) 124,000. Argentina's main oilfields and natural gas are nearby.

Comorin, Cape Southernmost cape of the Indian subcontinent, in Tamil Nadu, where the Indian Ocean, Bay of Bengal, and Arabian Sea meet.

Compiègne Town in Oise *département*, France, on the river Oise near its confluence with the river Aisne; population (1990) 44,700. It has an enormous château, built by Louis XV. The armistices of 1918 and 1940 were signed (the latter by Hitler and Pétain) in a railway coach in the forest of Compiègne.

Comstock Lode Silver mine in W Nevada, W USA, discovered in 1857. It was one of the largest silver deposits ever discovered, and contributed to the development of Nevada as an important mining area. Virginia City was established adjacent to the mines in 1859 and was once the largest city in Nevada, before the flooding of the richest deposits brought about a rapid decline in the 1880s.

Comtat Venaissin Historic district of S France, which now forms part of the *département* of ◊Vaucluse. It lay between Mont Ventoux and the rivers Rhône and Durance; its capital was Carpentras. Ceded by Philip III (the Bold) of France to the pope in 1274, Comtat Venaissin remained papal territory until 1791, when it was annexed by France.

Conakry Capital and chief port of the Republic of Guinea; population (1992) 950,000. It is on the island of Tumbo, linked with the mainland by a causeway and by rail with Kankan, 480 km/300 mi to the NE. Bauxite and iron ore are mined nearby.

Concarneau Seaport in the *département* of Finistère, France, 20 km/12 mi SE of Quimper; population (1990) 20,000. It is a centre of the sardine, mackerel, and tuna fisheries, and there are boatyards. The old town, which is surrounded by ramparts, dates from the 14th century; it lies on an island near the bay of La Forét, while the newer portion, St-Croix, is on the opposite shore.

Concepción City in Chile, near the mouth of the river Bió-Bió; population (1992) 330,400. It is the capital of the province of Concepción. It is in a rich agricultural district and is also an industrial centre for coal, steel, paper, and textiles.

Concord Town in Massachusetts, USA, now a suburb of Boston; population (1990) 17,300. Concord was settled 1635 and was the site of the first battle of the American Revolution, 19 April 1775. The writers Ralph Waldo Emerson, Henry David Thoreau, Nathaniel Hawthorne, and Louisa May Alcott lived here.

Concord Capital of New Hampshire, USA, in the S central part of the state, on the Merrimack River, N of Manchester; population (1992) 35,600. Industries include granite, leather goods, electrical equipment, printed products, and wood products. The town was settled 1727 and was named Rumford until 1765.

Coney Island Seaside resort on a peninsula in Brooklyn, in the SW of Long Island, New York, USA. It has been popular for ocean bathing and its amusement parks since the 1840s.

Congo Former name (1960–71) of the Democratic Republic of Congo (Zaire). Also the name of the Republic of the Congo (Congo-Brazzaville).

Congo/Zaïre River Second-longest river in Africa, rising near the Zambia–Congo (Zaire) border (and known as the *Lualaba River* in the upper reaches) and flowing 4,374 km/2,718 mi to the Atlantic Ocean, running in a great curve that crosses the equator twice, and discharging a volume of water second only to the Amazon. The chief tributaries are the Ubangi, Sangha, and Kasai.

Connacht or *Connaught* Province of the Republic of Ireland, comprising the counties of Galway, Leitrim, Mayo, Roscommon, and Sligo; area 17,130 sq km/6,612 sq mi; population (1991) 422,900. The chief towns are Galway, Roscommon, Castlebar, Sligo, and Carrick-on-Shannon. Mainly lowland, it is agricultural and stock-raising country, with poor land in the W.

Connecticut State in New England, USA; nicknamed Constitution State/Nutmeg State
area 13,000 sq km/5,018 sq mi
capital Hartford
towns and cities Bridgeport, New Haven, Waterbury
physical highlands in the NW; Connecticut River and valley; Housatonic Valley; Litchfield Hills
features Mystic Seaport, the largest maritime museum in the USA, a replica of a 19th-century shipbuilding town; Litchfield village; Stonington; Mark Twain House, Hartford; Old Lyme, with Florence Griswold House Museum (1817), once the home of the Old Lyme Art Colony; Monte Cristo Cottage, New London, summer home of Eugene O'Neill; Prudence Crandall School, Canterbury, New England's first school for black girls, founded 1833, now a museum; Baldwin Museum of Connecticut History, Hartford, with a collection of Colt revolvers; US Naval Submarine base at Groton, with the *Nautilus* memorial (the *Nautilus*, the

world's first nuclear-powered submarine, was launched here 1954, and is now permanently berthed and open to visitors); Barnum Museum, Bridgeport, with a model of P T Barnum's three-ring circus; Noah Webster house and museum, Hartford, the birthplace of the author of the American Dictionary; Yale University (1701); Trinity College, Hartford (1823); Wesleyan University (1831); US Coastguard Academy, New London; American Shakespeare Theatre, Stratford

products dairy, poultry, and market-garden products; tobacco, watches, clocks, silverware, helicopters, jet engines, nuclear submarines, hardware and locks, electrical and electronic equipment, guns and ammunition, optical instruments. Hartford is the centre of the nation's insurance industry

population (1995) 3,274,700

famous people Phineas T Barnum, George Bush, Katharine Hepburn, Charles Ives, Eugene O'Neill, Wallace Stevens, Harriet Beecher Stowe, Mark Twain, Eli Whitney, Benedict Arnold, Jonathan Edwards, Nathan Hale, Edward H Land

history Dutch navigator Adriaen Block was the first European to record the area 1614, and in 1633 Dutch colonists built a trading post near modern Hartford but it soon was settled by Puritan colonists from Massachusetts 1635. It was one of the original 13 colonies and became a state 1788. It prospered in the 19th century from shipbuilding, whaling, and growing industry. In the 20th century it became an important supplier of military equipment. Connecticut is second to Alaska among states in personal income per capita. Many of New York City's most affluent residential suburbs are in SW Connecticut.

Connellsville Town in Fayette County, SW Pennsylvania, USA; population (1994 est) 9,200. At one time it was the source of the bulk of the supply of coke required by the steel-manufacturing industry of Pittsburgh.

Connemara Western part of County Galway, Republic of Ireland, an area of rocky coastline and mountainous scenery. There is fishing and tourism.

Constance (German *Konstanz*) Town in Baden-Württemberg, Germany, on the section of the river Rhine joining Lake Constance and Lake Untersee; population (1989 est) 70,000. Suburbs stretch across the frontier into Switzerland. Constance has clothing, machinery, and chemical factories, and printing works.

Constance, Lake (German *Bodensee*) Lake bounded by Germany, Austria, and Switzerland, through which the river Rhine flows; area 530 sq km/200 sq mi.

Constanta Chief Romanian port on the Black Sea, capital of Constanta region, and second largest city of Romania; population (1993) 349,000. It has refineries, shipbuilding yards, and food factories.

Constantine City in NE Algeria; population (1989) 449,000. Products include carpets and leather goods. It was one of the chief towns of the Roman province of Numidia, but declined and was ruined, then restored 313 by Constantine the Great, whose name it bears. It was subse-

quently ruled by Vandals, Arabs, and Turks and was captured by the French 1837.

Contadora Panamanian island of the Pearl Islands group in the Gulf of Panama.

Conwy Unitary authority in N Wales created 1996 from parts of the former counties of Clwyd and Gwynedd; administrative headquarters Conwy; population 113,000 (1996); area 1,107 sq km/427 sq mi. Tourism is important, with the Snowdonia National Park, and a coastline of sandy beaches, including the seaside resort of Colwyn Bay.

Conwy Port in Wales and administrative headquarters of Conwy unitary authority, on the river Conwy; population (1991) 3,600. It was known until 1972 by the anglicized form *Conway*. Still surrounded by walls, Conwy has the ruins of a castle rebuilt by Edward I 1284.

Coober Pedy (native Australian 'white man in a hole') Town in the Great Central Desert, Australia; 700 km/ 437 mi NW of Adelaide, S Australia; population (1976) 1,900. Opals were discovered 1915, and are mined amid a moonscape of diggings in temperatures up to 60°C/140°F.

Cooch Behar Former princely state in India, merged into ◊West Bengal 1950.

Cookham-on-Thames Village in Berkshire, England. The artist Stanley Spencer lived here for many years and a memorial gallery of his work was opened 1962.

Cook Islands Group of six large and a number of smaller Polynesian islands 2,600 km/1,600 mi NE of Auckland, New Zealand; area 290 sq km/112 sq mi; population (1991) 19,000. Their main products include fruit, copra, and crafts. They became a self-governing overseas territory of New Zealand 1965.

Cook, Mount Highest point, 3,764 m/12,353 ft, of the Southern Alps, a range of mountains running through New Zealand.

Cook Strait Strait dividing North Island and South Island, New Zealand. A submarine cable carries electricity from South to North Island.

Cooper Creek River, often dry, in ◊Channel Country, SW Queensland, Australia. It is 1,420 km/880 mi long. The explorers Burke and Wills died here 1861.

Coorg or *Kurg* Mountainous district of the state of Karnataka in the Western Ghats of India. Formerly the princely state of Coorg, it was merged in ◊Karnataka 1956.

Copán Site of the town Santa Rosa de Copán in W Honduras; population (1991) 21,200. The nearby site of a Mayan city, including a temple and pyramids, was bought by John Stephens of the USA in the 1830s for $50.

Copenhagen (Danish *København*) Capital of Denmark, on the islands of Zealand and Amager; population (1995) 1,353,300 (including suburbs).

Coral Sea (or *Solomon Sea*) Part of the ◊Pacific Ocean bounded by NE Australia, New Guinea, the Solomon Islands, Vanuatu, and New Caledonia. It contains numerous coral islands and reefs. The Coral Sea Islands are a territory of Australia; they comprise scattered reefs and islands over an area of about 1,000,000 sq km/386,000 sq mi. They are uninhabited except for a meteorological station on Willis Island. The ◊Great Barrier Reef lies along its W edge, just off the E coast of Australia.

Corby Town in Northamptonshire, England; population (1991) 49,100. It developed in the 1930s from a village to a new town through the establishment of a steel-making industry. The steelworks closed 1979 and it is now an enterprise zone producing plastics. Industries also include steel tube manufacturing and electronics.

Cordilleras, the Mountainous W section of North America, with the Rocky Mountains and the coastal ranges parallel to the contact between the North American and the Pacific plates.

Córdoba Province of S Spain in N ◊Andalusia autonomous community; capital ◊Córdoba; area 13,719 sq km/5,297 sq mi; population (1995) 782,200. The river Guadalquivir and its tributaries (Guadiato, Bembezar, and Guadajoz) run through the province, which also includes part of the Sierra Morena mountain range. Main products include cereals, vines, olives, fruit, and beans; lead, copper, and coal; horses and cattle are raised here.

Córdoba Capital of Córdoba province, Spain, on the river Guadalquivir; population (1994) 316,000. Paper, textiles, and copper products are manufactured here. It has many Moorish remains, including the mosque, now a cathedral, founded by 'Abd-ar-Rahman I 785, which is one of the largest Christian churches in the world. Córdoba was probably founded by the Carthaginians; it was held by the Moors 711–1236.

Córdoba City in central Argentina, on the Río Primero; population (1992 est) 1,179,400. It is the capital of Córdoba province. Main industries include cement, glass, textiles, and vehicles. Founded 1573, it has a university founded 1613, a military aviation college, an observatory, and a cathedral.

Corfe Castle Village in the Isle of Purbeck, Dorset, S England, built around the ruins of a Norman castle destroyed in the Civil War. Industries include electronics and oil; tourism is important.

Corfu (Greek *Kérkyra*) Northernmost and second largest of the Ionian islands of Greece, off the coast of Epirus in the Ionian Sea; area 1,072 sq km/414 sq mi; population (1991) 105,000. Its businesses include tourism, fruit, olive oil, and textiles. Its largest town is the port of Corfu (Kérkyra), population (1991) 36,900. Corfu was colonized by the Corinthians about 700 BC. Venice held it 1386–1797, Britain 1815–64.

Corinth (Greek *Kórinthos*) Port in Greece, on the isthmus connecting the Peloponnese with the mainland; population (1981) 22,650. The rocky isthmus is bisected by the 6.5 km/4 mi Corinth canal, opened 1893. The site of the ancient city-state of Corinth lies 7 km/4.5 mi SW of the port.

Corinth (Greek *Korinthia*) Department of Greece, in the ◊Peloponnese region, bordering the isthmus of Corinth;

area 2,279 sq km/880 sq mi; population (1993) 156,600. The area is a coastal lowland with a broad alluvial plain. Its main crops are grapes, cereals, and olives. It is one of the richest agricultural areas in Greece. Its capital is Corinth.

Cork Largest county of the Republic of Ireland, in the province of Munster; county town Cork; area 7,460 sq km/2,880 sq mi; population (1996 est) 420,300. It is agricultural, but there is also some copper and manganese mining, marble quarrying, and river and sea fishing. Natural gas and oil fields are found off the S coast at Kinsale.

Cork City and seaport of County Cork, on the river Lee, at the head of the long inlet of Cork harbour; population (1991) 127,000. Cork is the second port of the Republic of Ireland. The lower section of the harbour can berth liners, and the city has distilleries, shipyards, and iron foundries. Other industries include tanning, food processing, and brewing. St Finbarr's 7th-century monastery was the original foundation of Cork. It was eventually settled by Danes who were dispossessed by the English 1172.

Corn Belt Agricultural region of North America, S and W of the Great Lakes. This fertile area lies within the states of Indiana, Illinois, Iowa, parts of South Dakota and Nebraska, and a small part of W Ohio, USA, and SW Ontario, Canada. The agricultural operation in the area integrates corn production and livestock rearing: corn and supplementary crops are intensively produced and fed to the livestock in the region (cattle and pigs). Soya beans are also grown extensively in the area.

Corner Brook Second-largest city in W Newfoundland, Canada, on the Humber estuary; population (1991) 22,400. The city includes large newsprint plants and also has cement, gypsum, and plasterboard industries. It is also a service centre for the W part of the island.

Corniche (French 'mountain ledge') *La Grande* (Great) *Corniche* is a road with superb alpine and coastal scenery, built between Nice and Menton, S France, by Napoleon; it rises to 520 m/1,700 ft. *La Moyenne* (Middle) and *la Petite* (Little) *Corniche* are supplementary parallel roads, the latter being nearest the coast.

Cornouaille District in Brittany, France, in the *département* of ◊Finistère; the chief town is ◊Quimper. Many parts of the district are barren and rocky; in others, there is livestock and dairy farming, and vegetables are grown.

Cornwall City in E Ontario, Canada, 88 km/55 mi SE of Ottawa, at the foot of the long Sault Rapids of the St Lawrence River; population (1991) 47,100. The city lies on the main line of the Canadian National Railway, and on the Canadian Pacific and New York Central railways. Industries include textile and chemical plants, furniture, pulp and paper, and there is a large power plant in the city. Cornwall was founded in 1784 by United Empire Loyalists, and became a town in 1848.

Cornwall County in SW England including the Isles of ◊Scilly (Scillies)
area (excluding Scillies) 3,550 sq km/1,370 sq mi
towns and cities Truro (administrative headquarters),

Camborne, Launceston; resorts of Bude, Falmouth, Newquay, Penzance, St Ives

features Bodmin Moor (including Brown Willy 419 m/ 1,375 ft); Land's End peninsula; St Michael's Mount; rivers Tamar, Fowey, Fal, Camel; Poldhu, site of first transatlantic radio signal 1901; the Stannary or Tinners' Parliament has six members from each of the four Stannary towns: Losthwithiel, Launceston, Helston, and Truro; Tate Gallery; St Ives; the Mineral Tramways Project aims to preserve the mining landscape, once the centre of the world's hard-rock mining industry

industries electronics; spring flowers; dairy farming; market gardening; tin (mined since the Bronze Age, some workings renewed 1960s, though the industry has all but disappeared); kaolin (St Austell); fish

population (1994) 479,600

famous people John Betjeman, Humphry Davy, Daphne Du Maurier, William Golding

history the Stannary, established in the 11th century, ceased to meet 1752 but its powers were never rescinded at Westminster, and it was revived 1974 as a separatist movement.

Coromandel Coast East coast of Tamil Nadu, India, between the Kistma river delta in the N and Point Calimere in the S.

Coromandel Peninsula Peninsula on North Island, New Zealand, E of Auckland.

Corpus Christi City and port in SE Texas, USA, on the Gulf of Mexico at the mouth of the river Nueces, SE of San Antonio; seat of Nueces County; population (1992) 266,400. Its main industries are oil refining and shipping, commercial fishing, and the processing and shipping of agricultural products. Corpus Christi was originally a small trading post.

Corregidor Island fortress off the Bataan Peninsula at the mouth of Manila Bay, Luzon, the Philippines. On 6 May 1942, Japanese forces captured Corregidor and its 10,000 US and Filipino defenders, completing their conquest of the Philippines. US forces recaptured Corregidor in a combined air and sea operation 6 Feb 1945.

Corrèze River of central France flowing 89 km/55 mi from the Plateau des Millevaches, past Tulle, capital of Corrèze *département* (to which it gives its name), to join the Vézère River. It is used for generating electricity at Bar, 9.5 km/6 mi NW of Tulle.

Corrèze *Département* in the Limousin region of France, area 5,860 sq km/2,263 sq mi; population (1990) 115,800. The region is tableland, with hills in the NE, and is broken up by fertile river valleys. The chief rivers are the Dordogne, Vézère, and Corrèze. The main agricultural activity is the raising of cattle, pigs, and poultry. Industries include the manufacture of metals, textiles, leather, and food. There is an important hydroelectric power station at Bort-les-Orgues. The principal towns are Tulle (the capital), Brive, and Ussel.

Corrientes City and river port of Argentina, on the

Paraná River; population (1991) 267,700. Capital of Corrientes province, it is in a stock-raising district. Industries include tanning, sawmilling, and textiles.

Corse French name for ◊Corsica.

Corse-du-Sud *Département* covering the S half of the French island of Corsica; area 4,014 sq km/1,550 sq mi; population (1990) 118,515. Together with Haute-Corse, it comprises the administrative region of ◊Corsica. The border with the N *département* runs for the most part along the central mountain spine of the island; peaks over 2,000 m/ 6,500 ft in Corse-du-Sud include Monte d'Oro (2,391 m/7,844 ft) and L'Incudine (2,136 m/7,008 ft). Sheep and goats are grazed on this mainly rocky, infertile terrain, while olives, olive oil, and wine (from the lower slopes) are the principal agricultural produce. The island's capital, ◊Ajaccio, on the W coast, is also the departmental capital; other towns include Sartène, Sari-d'Orcino, Vico, and Piana.

Corsica (French *Corse*) Island region of France, in the Mediterranean off the W coast of Italy, N of Sardinia; it comprises the *départements* of Haute Corse and Corse du Sud

area 8,680 sq km/3,351 sq mi

capital Ajaccio (port)

physical mountainous; maquis vegetation (drought-tolerant shrubs such as cork oak and myrtle)

features maquis vegetation. Corsica's mountain bandits were eradicated 1931, but the tradition of the vendetta or blood feud lingers. The island is the main base of the Foreign Legion

government its special status involves a 61-member regional parliament with the power to scrutinize French National Assembly bills applicable to the island and propose amendments

products wine, olive oil

population (1990) 250,400, including just under 50% native Corsicans. There are about 400,000 *émigrés*, mostly in Mexico and Central America, who return to retire

language French (official); the majority speak Corsican, an Italian dialect

famous people Napoleon Bonaparte.

Corsica

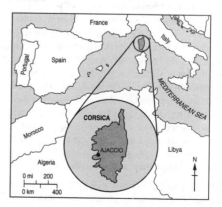

Cortona Town in Tuscany, N Italy, 22 km/13 mi SE of Arezzo; population (1981) 22,000. It is one of Europe's oldest cities, encircled by walls built by the Etruscans, and has a medieval castle and an 11th-century cathedral.

Coruña or *Corunna* City in the extreme NW of Spain; population (1991) 251,300. It is the capital of Coruña province. Industry is centred on the fisheries; tobacco, sugar refining, and textiles are also important. The Armada sailed from Coruña 1588, and the town was sacked by Francis Drake 1589.

Cos Alternative spelling of ◊Kos, a Greek island.

Cosenza Town in Calabria, S Italy, at the junction of the rivers Crati and Busento; population (1989) 105,300. It is the capital of Cosenza province and is an archiepiscopal see. Alaric, king of the Visigoths, is buried here.

Cosenza Province of S Italy in N ◊Calabria region; capital Cosenza; area 6,650 sq km/2,567 sq mi; population (1992) 752,000.

Cossyra Ancient name for ◊Pantelleria, Italian island in the Mediterranean.

Costa Blanca (Spanish 'White Coast') Mediterranean coastline of Alicante and Murcia provinces, E Spain. The chief ports are Alicante and Cartagena; popular resorts include Benidorm and Torrevieja.

Costa Brava (Spanish 'Wild Coast') Mediterranean coastline of NE Spain, stretching from Port-Bou on the French border southwards to Blanes, NE of Barcelona. It is noted for its irregular rocky coastline, small fishing villages, and resorts such as Puerto de la Selva, Palafrugell, Playa de Aro, and Lloret del Mar.

Costa del Sol (Spanish 'Coast of the Sun') Mediterranean coastline of Andalucia, S Spain, stretching for nearly 300 km/190 mi from Algeciras to Almeria. Málaga is the principal port and Marbella, Torremolinos, and Nerja are the chief tourist resorts.

Côte d'Azur Mediterranean coast from Menton to St Tropez, France, renowned for its beaches; it is part of the region ◊Provence-Alpes-Côte d'Azur.

Côte d'Or *Département* in the ◊Bourgogne region of France; area 8,765 sq km/3,384 sq mi; population (1990) 240,500. A chain of hills known as the Plateau de Langres runs through the centre of the *département*; in the S is the Côte d'Or chain. The river Seine rises in Châtillonnais, a densely wooded NW district. Other rivers of the region are the Rhône and the Loire. A canal 150 km/93 mi long connects the Saône with the Yonne. The plains and valleys are fertile, and there is rich pastureland. The main wealth of the region lies in its vineyards where Burgundy wines are produced. Other products are wheat, barley, potatoes, hops, and some tobacco. Sheep and cattle rearing takes place in the W districts. Iron and coal are mined, and there are chemical, metallurgical, food, and service industries. The principal towns are ◊Dijon (the capital), ◊Beaune, and Montbard.

Cotentin District of N France, forming part of the *département* of Manche. Cap de la Hague is on its jagged N coast.

Its chief town is ◊Cherbourg. Cotentin has apple orchards and dairy production. It is an economic growth area, with dockyards at Cherbourg and a nuclear power station at Flamanville and a nuclear waste-treatment plant at Beaumont-Hague.

Côtes d'Armor Maritime *département* in the ◊Brittany region of France (formerly Côtes-du-Nord); area 6,877 sq km/ 2,655 sq mi; population (1990) 540,000. Off the steep, rocky coast lie Bréhat and other small islands. Côtes d'Armor is an undulating plateau, with three ranges of hills in the S. On the high lands the soil is poor, but along the coast it has been improved by seaweed and sand. Wheat, oats, flax, potatoes, apples, and plums are grown; the *département* is the nation's leading producer of pork and poultry; and there is horse breeding. Slate, lime, and china clay are found, and there are flour mills, tanneries, ironworks, and shipyards. The fishing industry is of great importance; scallions are caught in St-Brieuc bay. The principal towns are St-Brieuc (the capital), ◊Dinan, Guingamp, and Lannion.

Cotonou Chief port and largest city of Benin, on the Bight of Benin; population (1994) 537,000. Palm products and timber are exported. Although not the official capital, it is the seat of the president, and the main centre of commerce and politics.

Cotopaxi (Quechua 'shining peak') Active volcano, situated to the S of Quito in Ecuador. It is 5,897 m/19,347 ft high and was first climbed 1872.

Cotswold Hills or *Cotswolds* Range of hills in Gloucestershire, South Gloucestershire, and Bath and North East Somerset, England, 80 km/50 mi long, between Bath and Chipping Camden. They rise to 333 m/1,086 ft at Cleeve Cloud, near Cheltenham, but average about 200 m/600 ft. The area is known for its picturesque villages, built with the local honey-coloured stone.

Cottbus Industrial city (textiles, carpets, glassware) in the *Land* of Brandenburg, Germany; population (1991) 123,300. It was formerly the capital of the East German district of Cottbus 1952–90.

Cottian Alps Part of the main chain of the ◊Alps, lying on the borders of France and Italy. The Cottian Alps extend from the Graian Alps on the N to the Maritime Alps on the S, and form a division of the W Alps, distinct from the Dauphiné Alps to the W. The range has more than 30 peaks exceeding 3,300 m/10,827 ft, of which the most important are Monte Viso (3,841 m/12,602 ft), Aiguille de Scolette (3,505 m/11,499 ft), Aiguille de Chambeyron (3,400 m/ 11,155 ft), Rognosa d'Etache (3,385 m/11,106 ft), Dents d'Ambin (3,382 m/11,096 ft), Rochebrune (3,324 m/10,905 ft), and Rognosa di Sestrières (3,279 m/10,758 ft).

Council Bluffs City and capital of Pottawattamie County, SW Iowa, USA, on the Missouri River opposite Omaha, Nebraska; population (1990) 54,300. It became the E terminus of the Union Pacific Railroad in 1859. It has an agricultural economy, though the railway has stimulated some industrial development.

Courland (German *Kurland*) Baltic province of Latvia. In early medieval times it was inhabited by the pagan Cours (or Curonians). By 1230 the area had been conquered by the bishop of Riga, assisted by a small military order called the Sword Brothers. Following the Sword Brothers' defeat by pagans from neighbouring Lithuania 1236, a larger military order, the Teutonic Knights, set up an independent state in the region and found a long campaign against the Lithuanians and Prussians.

Courtrai (Flemish *Kortrijk*) Town in Belgium on the river Lys, in West Flanders; population (1993 est) 76,300. It is connected by canal with the coast, and by river and canal with Antwerp and Brussels. It has a large textile industry, including damask, linens, and lace.

Covent Garden London square (named from the convent garden once on the site) laid out by Inigo Jones 1631. The buildings that formerly housed London's fruit and vegetable market (moved to Nine Elms, Wandsworth 1973) have been adapted for shops and restaurants. The Royal Opera House, also housing the Royal Ballet, is here; also the London Transport Museum.

Coventry Industrial city in West Midlands, England; population (1994 est) 303,000. Industries include cars, electronic equipment, machine tools, agricultural machinery, man-made fibres, aerospace components, telecommunications equipment, engineering, and coal mining.

Covington Town in Kentucky, USA, on the Ohio River opposite ◊Cincinnati; population (1990) 43,300. It has tobacco and meatpacking plants, breweries, distilleries, and foundries, and forms a part of the Cincinnati metropolitan area. It is linked to Cincinnati by the John A Roebling Suspension Bridge.

Cowes Seaport and resort on the N coast of the Isle of Wight, England, on the Medina estuary, opposite Southampton Water; population (1981) 19,600. It is the headquarters of the Royal Yacht Squadron, which holds the annual Cowes Regatta. There are maritime industries including boat building, marine engineering, hovercraft construction, and radar industries. In East Cowes is Osborne House, once a residence of Queen Victoria, now used as a museum.

Cracow English form of ◊Kraków, a Polish city.

Craigavon City in Armagh county, Northern Ireland; population (1990 est) 62,000. It was created and designated a New Town from 1965 by the merging of Lurgan and Portadown and named after James Craig (Viscount Craigavon), the first prime minister of Northern Ireland (1921–40).

Craiova City in S Romania, near the river Jiu; population (1992) 303,500. Industries include electrical engineering, food processing, textiles, fertilizers, and farm machinery.

Crater Lake Lake in the crater which forms the remains of Mount Mazama in SW Oregon, USA.

Crau, La Area in the *département* of Bouches-du-Rhône, France. Composed of ancient depositional fans of the rivers ◊Rhône and Durance, it was a stony desert, used primarily for the raising of sheep. Irrigation from the the Craponne and Langlade canals has developed part of the region into a prosperous agricultural district.

Crawley Town in West Sussex, England, NE of Horsham; population (1981) 73,000. It was chartered by King John 1202 and developed as a new town from 1947. Industries include plastics, light engineering, electronics, pharmaceuticals, furniture, and printing. London's Gatwick Airport is to the N.

Creil Suburb of ◊Paris, France, in the *département* of Oise, on the river Oise; population (1990) 32,500. It is an important railway junction, and manufactures rolling stock, machinery, chemicals, pottery, and glass. It has a 12th–15th-century church.

Cremona City in Lombardy, Italy, on the river Po, 72 km/45 mi SE of Milan; population (1990) 75,200. It is the capital of Cremona province. Once a violin-making centre, it now produces food products and textiles. It has a 12th-century cathedral.

Cremona Province of N Italy in S ◊Lombardy; capital Cremona; area 1,772 sq km/684 sq mi; population (1992) 328,300.

Crete (Greek *Kríti*) Largest Greek island in the E Mediterranean Sea, 100 km/62 mi SE of mainland Greece
area 8,378 sq km/3,234 sq mi
capital Irákleion (Heraklion)
towns and cities Chaniá (Canea), Rethymnon, Aghios Nikolaos
products citrus fruit, olives, wine
population (1991) 536,900
language Cretan dialect of Greek
history it has remains of the Minoan civilization 3000–1400 BC, and was successively under Roman, Byzantine, Venetian, and Turkish rule. The island was annexed by Greece 1913.

Crete

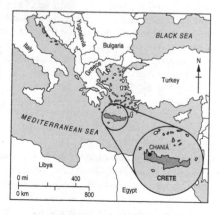

Creuse River in central France flowing 255 km/158 mi generally N from the Plateau des Millevaches to the Vienne River. It traverses Creuse *département*, to which it gives its name.

Creuse *Département* in the ◊Limousin region of France; area 5,559 sq km/2,146 sq mi; population (1990) 66,800. The river Creuse flows through the region, which is mountainous and has thin, unproductive soil. In the S hills there is good pasture land. Stock-rearing is important, but potatoes and some cereals are also produced. There are a few coal mines, and some gold is present in the region. Carpets and textiles are manufactured. The principal towns are Guéret (the capital) and ◊Aubusson.

Creusot, Le French town in the *département* of Saône-et-Loire, 65 km/40 mi NW of Mâcon; population (1990) 29,200. It is a coal-mining centre and has neighbouring iron-ore mines. There are numerous metal and engineering works, including the manufacture of armaments and nuclear reactors.

Crewe Town in Cheshire, England; population (1991) 63,400. It owed its growth to its position as a railway junction; the chief construction workshops of British Rail are here. It is the centre of the dairy industry, providing cattle breeding, management, and animal health services. Other occupations include chemical works, clothing factories, and vehicle manufacture (Rolls Royce cars).

Crimea Northern peninsula on the Black Sea, an autonomous republic of Ukraine; formerly a region (1954–91)
area 27,000 sq km/10,425 sq mi
capital Simferopol
towns and cities Sevastopol, Yalta
features mainly steppe, but S coast is a holiday resort; home of the Black Sea fleet (ownership of which has been the source of a dispute between Russia and Ukraine)
products iron, oil
population (1991 est) 2,549,800 (65% Russian, 25% Ukranian, despite return of 150,000 Tatars since 1989)
history Crimea was under Turkish rule 1475–1774; a subsequent brief independence was ended by Russian annexation 1783. Crimea was the republic of Taurida 1917–20 and the Crimean Autonomous Soviet Republic from 1920 until occupied by Germany 1942–44. It was then reduced to a region, its Tatar people being deported to Uzbekistan for collaboration. In 1954 Khrushchev made Crimea part of Ukraine. Although the Tatar people were exonerated 1967 and some were allowed to return, others were forcibly re-exiled 1979. A drift back to their former homeland began 1987 and a federal ruling 1988 confirmed their right to residency. Since 1991 the Crimea has sought to gain independence from the Ukraine; the latter has resisted all secessionist moves. A 1994 referendum in Crimea supported demands for greater autonomy and closer links with Russia.

Crimmitschau Town in the *Land* of ◊Saxony, Germany, on the river Pleisse, 37 km/23 mi W of Chemnitz; population (1996) 24,000. It has wool- and silk-weaving mills and engineering industries.

Crisul Romanian name for the ◊Körös, a river in Romania and Hungary.

Croagh Patrick Holy mountain rising to 765 m/2,510 ft in County Mayo, W Ireland, one of the three national places of pilgrimage in Ireland (with Lough Derg and Knock). An annual pilgrimage on the last Sunday of July commemorates St Patrick who fasted there for the 40 days of Lent 440 AD.

Croydon Outer borough of S Greater London. It includes the suburbs of Purley and Coulsdon.
features 11th-century Addington Palace, former residence of archbishops of Canterbury; Whitgift School, founded 1599 by John Whitgift, a resident of the borough; Whitgift's 16th-century almshouses; Surrey Street market (dating from the 13th century); Fairfield Halls (1962), including Ashcroft Theatre, Fairfield Hall, and Arnhem Gallery; largest office centre in South of England (outside central London)
industries pharmaceuticals, electronics, engineering, foodstuffs
population (1991) 313,500.

Crozet Archipelago Volcanic islands in the S Indian Ocean at almost equal distances from each other between the Cape of Good Hope and Kerguelen Islands; area 500 sq km/193 sq mi. The Crozet Archipelago is a French overseas territory administered under a special statute as part of the French Southern and Antarctic Territories. The names of the main islands are Possession, East, and Penguin. Sixteen islands are uninhabited and the rest are home mainly to scientific missions.

CT Abbreviation for state of ◊Connecticut, USA.

Cubango The Okavango River (see ◊Okavango Delta) in Angola, Africa. For part of its length it forms the border between Angola and Namibia. At the W end of the Caprivi Strip it crosses into Namibia and is known as the Kavango River; it becomes known as the Okavango when it enters Botswana.

Cúcuta Capital of Norte de Santander department, NE Colombia; population (1994) 470,000. It is situated in a tax-free zone close to the Venezuelan border, and trades in coffee, tobacco, and cattle. It was a focal point of the independence movement and meeting place of the first Constituent Congress 1821.

Cuenca Province of central Spain in NW ◊Castilla–La Mancha autonomous community; capital Cuenca; area 17,060 sq km/6,587 sq mi; population (1995) 207,500. In general a dry plateau, it has fertile river valleys and a mountainous region, the *Serranía de Cuenca*, which contains large coniferous forests.

Cuenca City in Castilla–La Mancha, Spain, 135 km/84 mi SE of Madrid, at the confluence of the rivers Júcar and Huécar; population (1991) 45,800. It is the capital of Cuenca province. It has a 13th-century cathedral.

Cuenca City in S Ecuador; population (1991) 193,000. It is the capital of Azuay province. Industries include chemicals, food processing, agricultural machinery, flour milling, tyres, panama hats, and textiles. It was founded by the Spanish 1557, and is a commercial centre trading in cinchona bark, sugar cane, and cereals.

Cuiaba City in Brazil, on the river Cuiaba; population (1991) 389,000. It is the capital of Mato Grosso state. Gold and diamonds are worked nearby. It is a distribution centre for cattle, hides, and dried meat.

Culham Village near Oxford, England; site of JET (Joint European Torus), a nuclear fusion research establishment. It is also the site of the UK centre for thermonuclear research.

Culiacán (Spanish *Culiacán Rosales*) Capital of Sinaloa state, NW Mexico, on the Culiacán River; population (1990) 415,000. It trades in vegetables and textiles. It was founded 1599.

Cumberland Former county in NW England, part of Cumbria from 1974.

Cumberland City in NW Maryland, USA, in the Allegheny Mountains, on the Potomac River, directly S of Johnstown, Pennsylvania; seat of Allegheny County; population (1990) 23,700. Its industries include the mining and shipping of coal, sheet metal, iron products, and tyres. It was first an Indian village and then a trading post and fort before it was incorporated 1815.

Cumberland Gap Pass cut by the Cumberland River through the Cumberland Mountains range of the Appalachian Mountains, between SW Virginia and SE Kentucky, E USA, at an altitude of 518 m/1,700 ft. This route was followed by the pioneer Daniel Boone, who drove his Wilderness Trail through the mountains into Kentucky, paving the way for the early settlers migrating to the W. Its position gave it strategic importance during the time of the American Civil War and it was held alternately by the Confederates and the Union forces. The area is now a national historical park.

Cumbernauld New town in North Lanarkshire, Scotland, 18 km/11 mi from Glasgow; population (1991) 48,800. It was founded 1956 to take in city overspill. In 1966 it won a prize as the world's best-designed community.

Cumbria County of NW England, created 1974 from Cumberland, Westmorland, and parts of NW Lancashire and NW Yorkshire
area 6,810 sq km/2,629 sq mi
towns and cities Carlisle (administrative headquarters), Barrow, Kendal, Whitehaven, Workington, Penrith
features Lake District National Park, including Scafell Pike 978 m/3,210 ft, the highest mountain in England; Helvellyn 950 m/3,118 ft; Lake Windermere, the largest lake in England, 17 km/10.5 mi long, 1.6 km/1 mi wide; other lakes (Derwentwater, Ullswater); Grizedale Forest sculpture project; Furness peninsula; permission granted 1992 to build fifteen 24 m/80 ft-high wind generators; nuclear stations at Calder Hall (the world's first nuclear power station, 1956) and Sellafield (formerly Windscale); British Nuclear Fuels THORP nuclear reprocessing plant began operating 1994
products the traditional coal, iron, and steel industries of the coast towns have been replaced by newer industries including chemicals, plastics, marine engineering, and electronics; in the N and E there is dairying, and West Cumberland Farmers is the country's largest agricultural cooperative; shipbuilding at Barrow-in-Furness (nuclear submarines and warships)
population (1994) 490,200.

Cunene or *Kunene* River rising near Nova Lisboa in W central Angola. It flows S to the frontier with Namibia, then W to the Atlantic Ocean; length 250 km/150 mi.

Cuneo Province of N Italy in SW ◊Piedmont region; capital Cuneo (population (1990) 55,800); area 6,902 sq km/2,665 sq mi; population (1992) 547,700.

Curaçao Island in the West Indies, one of the ◊Netherlands Antilles; area 444 sq km/171 sq mi; population (1993 est) 146,800. The principal industry, dating from 1918, is the refining of Venezuelan petroleum. Curaçao was colonized by Spain 1527, annexed by the Dutch West India Company 1634, and gave its name from 1924 to the group of islands renamed the Netherlands Antilles 1948. Its capital is the port of Willemstad.

Curitiba City in Brazil, on the Curitiba River; population (1991) 1,248,300 (metropolitan area 2,319,500). The capital of Paraná state, it dates from 1654 and makes paper, furniture, textiles, and chemicals. Coffee, timber, and maté (a beverage) are exported.

Curragh, the Horse-racing course on the Curragh plain in County Kildare, Republic of Ireland, where all five Irish Classic races are run. At one time used for hurdle races, it is now used for flat racing only. It is also the site of the national stud.

Curtea de Arges City in Arges county, Romania, on the river Arges, a tributary of the Danube, 25 km/15 mi NW of Piteşti. Its cathedral dates from the 16th century. The town was capital of Wallachia 1330–83.

Cuttack City and river port in E India, on the Mahanadi River delta; population (1991) 403,000. It was the capital of Orissa state until 1950. The old fort (Kataka) from which the city takes its name is in ruins.

Cuxhaven Seaport in Germany on the S side of the Elbe estuary, at its entrance into the North Sea; population (1986) 56,100. It acts as an outport for Hamburg.

Cuzco City in S Peru, capital of Cuzco department, in the Andes Mountains, over 3,350 m/11,000 ft above sea level and 560 km/350 mi SE of Lima; population (1993) 255,600. It was founded in c. AD 1200 as the ancient capital of the Inca empire and was captured by the Spanish conqueror Francisco Pizarro 1533.

Cwmbran (Welsh 'Vale of the Crow') Town and administrative headquarters of Monmouth-shire in SE Wales, on the Afon Lywel, a tributary of the river Usk; population (1991) 46,000. It was established 1949 to provide a focus for new industrial growth in a depressed area, producing scientific instruments, car components, nylon, and biscuits. There are also engineering and electrical industries.

Cyclades (Greek *Kikládhes*) Group of about 200 Greek islands in the Aegean Sea, lying between mainland Greece and Turkey; area 2,579 sq km/996 sq mi; population (1991) 95,100. They include Andros, Melos, Paros, Naxos, and Siros, on which is the capital Hermoupolis.

Cymru Welsh name for ◊Wales.

Częstochowa City in Poland, on the river Vistula, 193 km/ 120 mi SW of Warsaw; population (1993) 258,700. It produces iron goods, chemicals, paper, and cement. The basilica of Jasna Góra is a centre for Catholic pilgrims (it contains the painting known as the Black Madonna).

Dabrowa Górnicza Industrial city in Katowice province, Poland, 25 km/16 mi E of Katowice. At the centre of a coal basin, it also produces iron, zinc, and steel. It became Prussian 1795, part of Russian Poland 1815, and was ceded to Poland 1919.

Dacca Alternative name for ◊Dhaka, the capital of Bangladesh.

Dachau Site of a Nazi concentration camp during World War II, in Bavaria, Germany. The first such camp to be set up, it opened 1933 and functioned as a detention and forced labour camp until liberated 1945.

Dadra and Nagar Haveli Since 1961, a union territory of W India; capital Silvassa; area 491 sq km/190 sq mi; population (1994 est) 153,000. It was formerly part of Portuguese Daman. It produces rice, wheat, and millet. 40% of the total area is forest. Since 1985 there has been a moratorium on commercial felling.

Dagestan Autonomous republic of S Russian Federation
area 50,300 sq km/19,421 sq mi
capital Makhachkala
physical E of the Caucasus, bordering the Caspian Sea. Mountainous, with deep valleys
industries engineering, oil, chemicals, woodworking, textiles, and agriculture (wheat and grapes), sheep farming, and cattle breeding
population (1995) 2,067,000.

Dairen Former name for the Chinese port of Dalian, part of ◊Lüda.

Dakar Capital and chief port (with artificial harbour) of Senegal; population (1992 est) 1,729,800. It is an industrial centre, and there is a university, established 1957.

Dakhla Port in Western Sahara; population (1982) 17,800. First established as a Spanish trading port 1476, it was known as *Villa Cisneros*.

Dakota See ◊North Dakota and ◊South Dakota.

Dal (Swedish *Dalaålv*) River in SE Sweden, length 400 km/ 249 mi. It is formed by the confluence of the Österdalålv and Västerdalålv (East and West Dal), and enters the Gulf of Bothnia about 95 km/60 mi from Uppsala.

Dales or *Yorkshire Dales* Series of river valleys in N England, running E from the Pennines in West Yorkshire; a National Park was established 1954. The principal valleys are Airedale, Nidderdale, Swaledale, Teesdale, Wensleydale, and Wharfedale. The three main peaks are Ingleborough, Whernside, and Pen-y-Ghent. The Dales are highly scenic and popular with walkers and potholers; dry stone walls and barns are regular features of the landscape.

Dalian Industrial port (engineering, chemicals, textiles, oil refining, shipbuilding, food processing) in Liaoning, China,

on Liaodong Peninsula, facing the Yellow Sea; population (1986) 4,500,000. It comprises the naval base of Lüshun (known under 19th-century Russian occupation as Port Arthur) and the commercial port of Dalian (formerly Talien/Dairen).

Dallas Commercial city on the Trinity River, in Texas, USA; population (1992) 1,022,500, metropolitan area (with Fort Worth) 4,215,000. Dallas is a cultural centre, with a symphony orchestra, opera, ballet, and theatre. Industries include banking, insurance, oil, aviation, aerospace, and electronics. Dallas has a football team, the Dallas Cowboys; The Cotton Bowl annual football game is played in Dallas. Dallas–Fort Worth Regional Airport (opened 1973) is one of the world's largest. The city was founded 1841.

Dalmatia Region divided between Croatia, Montenegro in Yugoslavia, and Bosnia-Herzegovina. The capital is Split. It lies along the E shore of the Adriatic Sea and includes a number of islands. The interior is mountainous. Important products are wine, olives, and fish. Notable towns in addition to the capital are Zadar, Sibenik, and Dubrovnik.
history Dalmatia became Austrian 1815 and by the treaty of Rapallo 1920 became part of the kingdom of the Serbs, Croats, and Slovenes (Yugoslavia from 1931), except for the town of Zadar (Zara) and the island of Lastovo (Lagosta), which, with neighbouring islets, were given to Italy until transferred to Yugoslavia 1947.

Daman Part of the Union Territory of Daman and Diu, W India.

Daman and Diu Union territory of W India; area 112 sq km/43 sq mi; capital Daman; population (1994 est) 111,000. *Daman* has an area of 72 sq km/28 sq mi. The port and capital, Daman, is on the W coast, 160 km/100 mi N of Bombay. The economy is based on tourism and fishing. *Diu* is an island off the Kathiawar peninsula with an area of 40 sq km/15 sq mi. The main town is also called Diu. The economy is based on tourism, coconuts, pearl millet, and salt.
history Daman was seized by Portugal 1531 and ceded to Portugal by the Shah of Gujarat 1539; Diu was captured by the Portuguese 1534. Both areas were annexed by India 1961 and were part of the Union Territory of Goa, Daman, and Diu until ◊Goa became a separate state 1987.

Damaraland Central region of Namibia, home of the nomadic Bantu-speaking Herero. Damaraland lies between the Namib and Kalahari deserts and is largely grassland.

Damascus (Arabic *Dimashq*) Capital of Syria, on the river Barada, SE of Beirut; population (1993) 1,497,000. It produces silk, wood products, and brass and copperware. Said to be the oldest continuously inhabited city in the world, Damascus was an ancient city even in Old Testament times. Most notable of the old buildings is the Great Mosque, completed as a Christian church in the 5th century.

Damietta or *Dumyat* Town in Egypt at the mouth of the river Nile; population (1991) 113,000. Cotton goods are produced.

Damme In the Middle Ages, the port for ◊Bruges, in the province of West Flanders, Belgium. Damme is now a village some 8 km/5 mi NE of that city.

Damodar Indian river flowing 560 km/350 mi from Chota Nagpur plateau in Bihar, through Bihar and West Bengal states to join the ◊Hooghly River 40 km/25 mi SW of Calcutta. The Damodar Valley is an industrial centre with a hydroelectric project, combined with irrigation works.

Da Nang Port city (formerly Tourane) of S Vietnam, 80 km/50 mi SE of Hué; population (1989) 370,600. Following the reunion of North and South Vietnam, the major part of the population was dispersed 1976 to rural areas.

Danbury City in SW Connecticut, USA, NW of Bridgeport; population (1992) 65,300. Settled 1685, Danbury was burned by the British 1777 during the Revolution. Since 1780 it has been a centre for the manufacturing of hats; newer industries include electronics, publishing, chemicals, and furniture. It has the headquarters of the Union Carbide corporation.

Danube (German *Donau*) Second longest of European rivers, rising on the E slopes of the Black Forest, and flowing 2,858 km/1,776 mi across Europe to enter the Black Sea in Romania by a swampy delta.

Danube

Danville City in S Virginia, USA, just above the North Carolina border, on the Dan River, SE of Roanoke; seat of Averett County; population (1992) 53,600. Danville is situated in a tobacco-growing area. Industries include tobacco processing and marketing and the manufacture of tools, textiles, and building materials. Danville was chartered 1793.

Danzig German name for the Polish port of ◊Gdańsk.

Dardanelles (ancient name *Hellespont*, Turkish name *Canakkale Boğazi*) Turkish strait connecting the Sea of Marmara with the Aegean Sea; its shores are formed by the Gallipoli peninsula on the NW and the mainland of Anatolia on the SE. It is 75 km/47 mi long and 5–6 km/3–4 mi wide.

Dar el-Beida Arabic name for the port of ◊Casablanca, Morocco.

Dar es Salaam (Arabic 'haven of peace') Chief seaport in Tanzania, on the Indian Ocean, and capital of Tanzania until its replacement by ◊Dodoma 1974; population (1988) 1,361,000.

Darfur Former province in the W of the Republic of Sudan; area 196,555 sq km/75,920 sq mi; population (1983) 3,093,699. The capital was El Fasher (population 30,000). The area is a vast rolling plain. It produces gum arabic, and there is also some stock raising. Darfur was an independent sultanate until conquered by Egypt 1874. It was divided into three federal states 1994: Northern Darfur, Southern Darfur, and Western Darfur.

Darhan or *Darkhan* Industrial town in Mongolia, near the border with Russia; population (1991) 90,000. Industries include the manufacture of cement and bricks, and to the S is Erdenet, where copper and molybdenum are mined.

Darien Former name for the Panama isthmus as a whole, and still the name of an E province of Panama; area 16,803 sq km/6,490 sq mi; population (1990) 43,800. The *Gulf of Darien*, part of the Caribbean Sea, lies between Panama and Colombia. The *Darien Gap* is the complex of swamp, jungle, and ravines, which long prevented the linking of the North and South American sections of the Pan-American Highway, stretching about 300 km/200 mi between Canitas, Panama, and Chigorodo, Colombia. At the Colombian end is the Great Atrato Swamp, 60 km/35 mi across and over 300 m/1,000 ft deep. The final link across the Darien Gap has still not been completed, because of lack of capital, engineering obstacles, and political problems.

The *Darien Expedition* was a Scottish attempt to colonize the isthmus 1698–99, which failed disastrously owing to the climate and Spanish hostility. The British Trans-Americas Expedition, led by John Blashford-Snell, made the first motorized crossing 1972.

Darjiling or *Darjeeling* Town and health resort in West Bengal, India; situated 2,150 m/7,000 ft above sea level, on the S slopes of the Himalayas; population (1981) 57,600. It is

Dardanelles

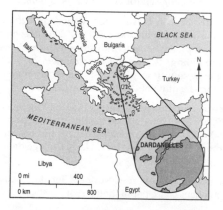

connected by rail with Calcutta, 595 km/370 mi to the S. It is the centre of a tea-producing district.

Darling River in SE Australia, a tributary of the river Murray, which it joins at Wentworth. It is 3,075 km/1,910 mi long, and its waters are conserved in Menindee Lake (155 sq km/60 sq mi) and others nearby. The name comes from Sir Ralph Darling (1775–1858), governor of New South Wales 1825–31. The *Darling Range*, a ridge in W Australia, has a highest point of about 582 m/1,669 ft.

Darlington Industrial town and unitary authority in NE England on the river Skerne, near its junction with the river Tees; population (1996) 100,600; area 197 sq km/76 sq mi. It was part of the county of Durham to 1997. It has coal and ironstone mines; there is heavy engineering. Darlington produces iron and steel goods, knitting wool, and textiles. The world's first passenger railway was opened between Darlington and Stockton 27 Sept 1825.

Darmstadt City in the *Land* of Hessen, Germany, 29 km/18 mi S of Frankfurt-am-Main; population (1993) 140,900. Industries include iron founding and the manufacture of chemicals, plastics, and electronics. It is a centre of the European space industry. It has a ducal palace and a technical university.

Dartford Industrial town in Kent, England, 27 km/17 mi SE of London; population (1991) 28,400. Cement, chemicals, paper, and pharmaceuticals are manufactured. The Dartford Tunnel (1963) runs under the Thames to Purfleet, Essex. Congestion in the tunnel was relieved 1991 by the opening of the Queen Elizabeth II bridge.

Dartmoor Plateau of SW Devon, England, over 1,000 sq km/400 sq mi in extent, of which half is some 300 m/1,000 ft above sea level. Most of Dartmoor is a National Park. The moor is noted for its wild aspect, and rugged blocks of granite, or 'tors', crown its higher points. The highest are *Yes Tor* 618 m/2,028 ft and *High Willhays* 621 m/2,039 ft. Devon's chief rivers have their sources on Dartmoor. There are numerous prehistoric remains. Near Hemerdon there are tungsten reserves.

Dartmoor Prison, opened 1809 originally to house French prisoners-of-war during the Napoleonic Wars, is at Princetown in the centre of the moor, 11 km/7 mi E of Tavistock. It is still used for category B prisoners.

Dartmouth Port in Nova Scotia, Canada, on the NE of Halifax harbour; population (1991) 67,800. It is virtually part of the capital city itself. Industries include oil refining and shipbuilding. It was the headquarters of a Quaker whaling company from 1784, and was incorporated 1873. The Bedford Institute of Oceanography is nearby.

Dartmouth English seaport at the mouth of the river Dart; 43 km/27 mi E of Plymouth, on the Devon coast; population (1996 est) 6,000. It is a centre for yachting and has an excellent harbour. The Britannia Royal Naval College dates from 1905.

Darwin Capital and port in Northern Territory, Australia, in NW Arnhem Land; population (1993) 77,900. It serves the uranium mining site at Rum Jungle to the S. Destroyed 1974 by a cyclone, the city was rebuilt on the same site.

Dasht-e-Kavir or *Dasht-i-Davir* Salt desert SE of Tehran, Iran; US forces landed here 1980 in an abortive mission to rescue hostages held at the American Embassy in Tehran.

Daugavpils (Russian *Dvinsk*) City in Latvia on the river Daugava (W Dvina); population (1995) 120,000. A fortress of the Livonian Knights 1278, it became the capital of Polish Livonia (former independent region until 1583, comprising most of present-day Latvia and Estonia). Industries include timber, textiles, engineering, and food products.

Daulaghiri Mountain in the ◊Himalayas, NW of Pokhara, Nepal; it rises to 8,172 m/2,681 ft.

Davao City in the Philippine Republic, at the mouth of the Davao River on the island of Mindanao; population (1990) 849,900. It is the capital of Davao province. It is the centre of a fertile district and trades in pearls, copra, rice, and corn.

Davenport City in SE Iowa, USA, S of Dubuque, directly across from Rock Island, Illinois, on the Mississippi River; seat of Scott County; population (1992) 97,500. Davao forms the 'Quad Cities' metropolitan area with the Illinois cities of Rock Island, Moline, and East Moline. Industries include aluminium, agriculture, and machinery parts. It was the site of the first railway bridge across the Mississippi, built 1856.

Daventry Town in Northamptonshire, England, 19 km/12 mi W of Northampton; population (1991) 18,000. Because of its central position, it became the site of the BBC high-power radio transmitter 1925. Originally specializing in footwear manufacture, it received London and Birmingham overspill from the 1950s, and developed varied light industries.

Davos Town in an Alpine valley in Grisons canton, Switzerland 1,559 m/5,115 ft above sea level; population (1990) 10,400. It is recognized as a health resort and as a winter sports centre.

Dawson Town in Canada, capital until 1953 of ◊Yukon Territory, at the junction of the Yukon and Klondike rivers; population (1991) 2,000. It was founded 1896, at the time of the Klondike gold rush.

Dawson Creek Town in British Columbia, Canada; population (1991) 11,000. It is the SE terminus of the Alaska Highway. The town was laid out 1919 and grew after completion of the Alaska Highway during World War II.

Dayton City in Ohio, USA; population (1992) 183,200. It produces precision machinery, household appliances, and electrical equipment. It has an aeronautical research centre and was the home of aviators Wilbur and Orville Wright. It is the centre of an agricultural region.

Daytona Beach City on the Atlantic coast of Florida, USA; population (1992) 64,600. Economic activities include printing, commercial fishing, and manufacture of electronic equipment and metal products. It is also a resort. The Daytona International Speedway for motor racing is here.

DE   Abbreviation for ◊Delaware, a state of the USA.

Dead Sea   Large lake, partly in Israel and partly in Jordan, lying 400 m/1,312 ft below sea level; it is the lowest surface point on earth; area 1,020 sq km/394 sq mi. The chief river entering it is the Jordan; it has no outlet and the water is very salty. It is not, however, completely dead. *Dunaliella parva*, a single-celled green alga, and a group of halophilic (salt-loving) Archaea live in it.

Dead Sea

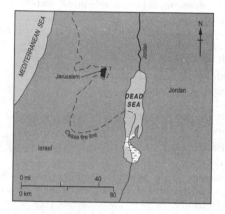

Deal   Port and resort on the E coast of Kent, England; population (1989 est) 27,000. It was one of the Cinque Ports. Julius Caesar is said to have landed here 55 BC. The castle was built by Henry VIII and houses the town museum.

Dearborn   City in Michigan, USA, on the Rouge River 16 km/10 mi SW of Detroit; population (1992) 88,300. Settled 1795, it was the birthplace and home of Henry Ford, who built his first car factory here. Motor-vehicle manufacturing is still the main industry. Dearborn also makes aircraft parts, steel, and bricks.

Death Valley   Depression 225 km/140 mi long and 6–26 km/ 4–16 mi wide in SE California, USA. At 86 m/282 ft below sea level, it is the lowest point in North America. Bordering mountains rise to 3,000 m/10,000 ft. It is one of the world's hottest and driest places, with temperatures sometimes exceeding 51.7°C/125°F and an annual rainfall of less than 5 cm/2 in. Borax, iron ore, tungsten, gypsum, and salts are extracted.

Deauville   Holiday resort of Normandy in the Calvados *département*, France, on the English Channel and at the mouth of the Touques, opposite Trouville; population (1989 est) 4,800.

Debrecen   Second largest city in Hungary, 193 km/120 mi E of Budapest, in the Great Plain (◊Alföld) region; population (1995) 211,000. It produces tobacco, agricultural machinery, and pharmaceuticals. Lajos Kossuth declared Hungary independent of the Habsburgs here 1849. It is a commercial centre and has a university founded 1912.

Decatur   City in central Illinois, USA, on Lake Decatur; population (1992) 84,300. It has engineering, food process-

ing, and plastics industries. It was founded 1829 and named after the US naval hero Stephen Decatur.

Decazeville   French town in the *département* of Aveyron, 30 km/19 mi NW of Rodez; population (1990) 8,800. It was the centre of the old Aveyron coalfield, and has ironworks, chemical factories, and cement works.

Deccan   Triangular tableland in E India, stretching between the Vindhya Hills in the N, and the Western and Eastern Ghats in the S.

Děčín   (German *Tetschen*) River port in N Bohemia, in the Czech Republic, on the river Elbe opposite Podmoklý near the German border, 72 km/45 mi N of Prague; population (1991) 55,100. Manufactures include chemicals, textiles, and paper.

Dee   River in Aberdeenshire, Scotland; length 139 km/87 mi. From its source in the Cairngorm Mountains, it flows E into the North Sea at Aberdeen (by an artificial channel). It is noted for salmon fishing.

Dehra Dun   City in Uttar Pradesh, India; population (1991) 367,000. It is the capital of Dehra Dun district. It has a military academy, a forest research institute, and a Sikh temple built 1699.

Delaware   River flowing through the states of New York, Pennsylvania, New Jersey, and Delaware, USA; length 650 km/450 mi. It serves as a state boundary along much of its course.

Delaware   State in NE USA; nicknamed First State/Diamond State
area   5,300 sq km/2,046 sq mi
capital   Dover
towns and cities   Wilmington, Newark
physical   divided into two physical areas, one hilly and wooded, the other gently undulating; Delaware River; Atlantic beaches, including Rehoboth Beach; Bombay Hook and Prime Hook national wildlife refuges, with waterfowl, in marshland
features   one of the most industrialized states; headquarters of the Du Pont chemical firm; the Piedmont; New Castle, the restored colonial capital, site of William Penn's first landing in North America, with New Castle Courthouse and the George Read II House (1797); Wilmington, the first permanent settlement in the Delaware Valley (1638), with Old Swedes Church (1698) and Hendrickson House Museum (1690), Kalmar Nyckel Shipyard Museum, and Delaware Art Museum; Henry Francis du Pont Winterthur Museum and Gardens, with a collection of American furniture and decorative arts; Hagley Museum, a museum of the development of American manufacturing and the history of the Du Pont Company, with preserved early Du Pont mills; Colonial buildings in Dover, laid out 1722; the University of Delaware
industries   dairy, poultry, and market-garden produce; chemicals, motor vehicles, and textiles
population   (1995) 717,200
famous people   Du Pont family, J P Marquand

history the first settlers were Dutch 1631 and Swedes 1638, but in 1664 the area was captured by the British and transferred to William Penn. A separate colony from 1704, it fought in the American Revolution as a state 1776, was one of the original 13 states, and was the first state to ratify the US Constitution 7 Dec 1787. In 1802 the Du Pont gunpowder mill was established near Wilmington. Completion of the Philadelphia–Baltimore railroad line 1838, through Wilmington, fostered development. Delaware was important as a chemical centre by the early 1900s. Two auto-assembly plants and an oil refinery were built after World War II.

Delft Town in South Holland province, the Netherlands, on the Schie Canal, 14 km/9 mi NW of Rotterdam; population (1994) 91,900. It is known worldwide for its pottery and porcelain; other industries include electronic equipment and cables. There is a technical university (1863). The Dutch nationalist leader William the Silent was murdered here 1584. It is the birthplace of the artist Jan Vermeer.

Delhi Capital of India, comprising the walled city of *Old Delhi* (built 1639), situated on the W bank of the river Yamuna, and *New Delhi* to the S, largely designed by English architect Edwin Lutyens and chosen to replace Calcutta as the seat of government 1912 (completed 1929; officially inaugurated 1931). Delhi is the administrative centre of the state of Delhi and India's largest commercial and communications centre; population (1991) 8,375,000. Traditional handicrafts have been revived, including hand-woven textiles and jewellery.

Delhi Union Territory of the Republic of India from 1956; capital Delhi; area 1,483 sq km/573 sq mi; population (1994) 10,865. It produces grain, sugar cane, fruit, and vegetables.

Delos Greek island, smallest in the ◊Cyclades group, in the SW Aegean Sea; area about 5 sq km/2 sq mi. The great temple of Apollo (4th century BC) is still standing.

Delray Beach City in SE Florida, USA, on the Atlantic Ocean, N of Fort Lauderdale; population (1990) 47,200. A tourist resort, it also relies economically on the motor-vehicle industry and the cultivation of flowers. It was laid out 1896.

Delta Plan Sea-defence and land-reclamation project carried out in ◊Zeeland in the SW Netherlands, and completed 1986. It was designed to control tidal flow in the deltas of the rivers Maas (see ◊Meuse) and Rijn (see ◊Rhine). The plan was conceived after the region suffered catastrophic flooding in 1953.

Demerara River in Guyana, 215 mi/346 km long, rising in the centre of the country and entering the Atlantic Ocean at Georgetown. It gives its name to the country's chief sugar cane growing area, after which Demerara sugar is named.

Denain French town in the *département* of Nord, 40 km/25 mi SE of Lille, on the river Scheldt. Denain has coalmines and metal industries. During the War of the Spanish Succession, it was the site of the decisive victory of the French forces under Marshal Villars (1653–1734) over the Austrian forces led by Prince Eugène in July 1712.

Denbighshire (Welsh *Sir Ddinbych*) Unitary authority in N Wales; administrative headquarters Ruthin; population 91,000 (1996); area 844 sq km/326 sq mi. A former county, it was largely merged 1974–96, together with Flint and part of Merioneth, into Clwyd; a small area along the W border was included in Gwynedd. Main features include the Clwydian range of mountains with Offa's Dyke along the main ridge; Denbigh, Chirk, and Rhuddlan castles; and seaside resorts of Rhyl and Prestatyn. Leading industries are tourism and agriculture.

Dender River in Belgium; length 88 km/55 mi. The Dender rises in the province of Hainaut; it joins the Scheldt at Dendermonde, after passing Ath, Grammont, Ninove, and Alost, and is navigable from its junction with the Scheldt to Ath.

Dendermonde (French *Termonde*) Town in the Belgian province of East Flanders, 25 km/16 mi E of Ghent, strategically located near the confluence of the rivers Dender and Scheldt. Dendermonde has a 15th-century Gothic cathedral. A carnival is held in the town in May.

Den Haag Dutch form of The ◊Hague, a city in the Netherlands.

Den Helder Port in North Holland province, the Netherlands, 65 km/40 mi N of Amsterdam, on the entrance to the North Holland Canal from the North Sea; population (1993) 61,100. It is a fishing port and naval base.

Dénia Town in the province of ◊Alicante, E Spain, on the Mediterranean coast; population (1995) 27,700. Founded by the Phoenicians, it was important in Roman times; under the Moors its population was 50,000.

Denison City in NE Texas, USA, near the Red River and the Oklahoma border, N of Dallas; population (1990) 21,500. A distribution centre for grain and dairy products, its industries include textiles, wood products, and food processing.

Denpasar Capital town of Bali in the Lesser Sunda Islands of Indonesia; population (urban area, 1990 est) 3,370,000. Industries include food processing, machinery, papermaking and printing, and handicrafts. There is a university (1962) and, housed in the temple and palace, a museum of Balinese art.

Denver City and capital of Colorado, USA, on the South Platte River, on the W edge of the Great Plains, near the foothills of the Rocky Mountains; population (1992) 483,900; Denver–Boulder metropolitan area (1992) 2,089,000. At 1,609 m/5,280 ft above sea level, it is known as 'Mile High City'. It was first settled 1858 following the discovery of gold.

Deptford District in SE London, in the Greater London borough of ◊Lewisham, on the river Thames W of Greenwich. It was a major royal naval dockyard 1513–1869, established by Henry VIII to build the flagship *Great Harry*. Now mainly residential, its industries include engineering and chemicals.

Derby Industrial city and unitary authority in N central England; population (1996) 218,800; area 87 sq km/30 sq mi. Products include Rolls-Royce cars and aero engines,

Toyota cars, train repair workshops, chemicals, paper, textiles, plastics, and electrical, mining, and engineering equipment. There is also a sugar refining industry. The museum collections of Royal Crown Derby china, the Rolls-Royce collection of aero engines, and the Derby Playhouse are here.

Derbyshire County of N central England
area 2,550 sq km/984 sq mi
towns and cities Matlock (administrative headquarters), Chesterfield, Ilkeston
features Peak District National Park (including Kinder Scout 636 m/2,088 ft); rivers: Derwent, Dove, Rother, Trent; Chatsworth House, Bakewell (seat of the Duke of Devonshire); Haddon Hall
industries cereals; dairy and sheep farming; textiles; Toyota cars at Burnaston; quarrying; heavy engineering; there have been pit and factory closures, but the area is being redeveloped, and there are large reserves of fluorite
population (1995 est) 726,000
famous people Samuel Richardson, Thomas Cook, Marquess Curzon of Kedleston.

Derg, Lough Lake in County Donegal, NW Ireland. The island (Station Island or St Patrick's Purgatory) is the country's leading place of pilgrimage. Associated with St Patrick, a monastery flourished here from early times.

Derry One of four districts in the county of Londonderry, Northern Ireland; population (1991) 99,000. The name is also commonly used in the Republic of Ireland for the city and county of Londonderry.

Derwent River in North Yorkshire, NE England; length 112 km/70 mi. Rising in the North Yorkshire moors, it joins the river Ouse SE of Selby.

Des Moines Capital city of Iowa, USA, on the Des Moines River, a tributary of the Mississippi; population (1992) 194,500. It is a major road, railway, and air centre. Industries include printing, banking, insurance, and food processing. Fort Des Moines was founded 1843 and the surrounding settlement was incorporated as the city of Des Moines 1851; it became the state capital 1857.

Dessau City in the state of Saxony-Anhalt, Germany, on the river Mulde, 115 km/70 mi SW of Berlin; population (1991) 95,100. It is the former capital of Anhalt duchy and state. It manufactures chemicals, machinery, and chocolate and was the site of the Junkers aeroplane works. The Bauhaus school of art was based in Dessau 1925–33.

Detmold City and region of ◊North Rhine–Westphalia, Germany, on the river Werre, 25 km/15 mi SE of Bielefeld; population (1994) 72,600 (city). It is a tourist centre and has furniture and metallurgical industries. Detmold was formerly the capital of the principality of Lippe. The city has a Renaissance castle and a medieval church.

Detroit Industrial city and port in Michigan, USA, situated on Detroit River; population (1992) 1,012,100, metropolitan area 5,246,000. It has the headquarters of Ford, Chrysler, and General Motors, hence its nickname, Motown (from

'motor town'). Its baseball team is the Detroit Tigers. The city began as a trading post 1701.

Detskoe Selo (Russian 'children's village') former name (1917–37) of ◊Tsarskoe Selo, near St Petersburg.

Deûle River in the *départements* of Pas-de-Calais and Nord, France; length 68 km/42 mi. It is a tributary of the Lys, which unites with the Scheldt in Belgium. Rising near Carency, the Deûle flows past Lille and Quesnoy, joining the main river near Deûlément.

Deuxponts French name for ◊Zweibrücken, a town in Germany.

Deux-Sèvres *Département* in the ◊Poitou-Charentes region of France; area 6,004 sq km/2,318 sq mi; population (1990) 346,300. The rivers Sèvre-Niortaise and the Sèvre-Nantaise flow through the *département*. In the N, centre, and W the land is marshy, though parts have been drained. The S is a limestone plain. Cereals, sugar beet, and vines are produced. Horses, cattle, and a particular breed of mule are raised and there is much wildfowl. There are some textile industries. The principal towns are Niort (the capital), Bressuire, and Parthenay.

Deventer Town in Overijssel province, the Netherlands, on the river Ijssel, 45 km/28 mi S of the IJsselmeer lake; population (1993) 68,500. It is an agricultural and transport centre and produces carpets, precision equipment, and packaging machinery.

Devil's Island (French *Ile du Diable*) Smallest of the Iles du Salut, off French Guiana, 43 km/27 mi NW of Cayenne. The group of islands was collectively and popularly known by the name Devil's Island and formed a penal colony notorious for its terrible conditions.

Devil's Marbles Area of granite boulders, S of Tennant Creek, off the Stuart Highway in Northern Territory, Australia.

Devizes Historic market town in Wiltshire, England; population (1991) 13,200. It was formerly known for its trade in cloth, but is now a centre for brewing, engineering, and food processing. Special features include ancient earthworks and the shattered remains of a Norman castle stormed by Oliver Cromwell 1645.

Devon or *Devonshire* County of SW England; Plymouth and Torbay will become unitary authorities in April 1998.
area 6,720 sq km/2,594 sq mi
towns and cities Exeter (administrative headquarters), Plymouth; resorts: Paignton, Torquay, Teignmouth, and Ilfracombe
features rivers: Dart, Exe, Tamar; National Parks: Dartmoor, Exmoor; Lundy bird sanctuary and marine nature reserve in the Bristol Channel
industries mainly agricultural, with sheep and dairy farming and beef cattle; cider and clotted cream; kaolin in the S; Honiton lace; Dartington glass; carpets (Axminster); quarrying; fishing
population (1994) 1,053,400
famous people Francis Drake, John Hawkins, Charles Kingsley, Robert F Scott.

Dhahran Oil town in E Saudi Arabia, near the Gulf Coast; it was used as a military base during the Gulf War 1991.

Dhaka or *Dacca* Capital of Bangladesh from 1971, in Dhaka region, W of the river Meghna; population (1991) 3,397,200. It trades in jute, oilseed, sugar, and tea and produces textiles, chemicals, glass, and metal products.

Dhaulagiri Mountain in the ◊Himalayas of W central Nepal, rising to 8,172 m/26,811 ft.

Dhofar Mountainous W province of Oman, on the border with Yemen; population (1982) 40,000. South Yemen supported left-wing guerrilla activity here against the Oman government in the 1970s, while Britain and Iran supported the government's military operations. The guerillas were defeated 1975. The capital is Salalah, which has a port at Rasut.

Diego Garcia Island in the ◊Chagos Archipelago, Indian Ocean, named after its Portuguese discoverer 1532; see ◊British Indian Ocean Territory. It houses a joint US–British electronic monitoring and strategic post.

Dieppe Channel port at the mouth of the river Arques, Seine-Maritime *département*, N France; population (1990) 36,600. There are ferry services from its harbour to Newhaven and elsewhere; industries include fishing, shipbuilding, and pharmaceuticals.

Digne Capital of the French *département* of Alpes-de-Haute-Provence, in the Bléone valley; population (1990) 17,400. Perfume is produced and fruit processed. It has a cathedral (15th–19th centuries) and a Romanesque church. There are sulphur springs 3 km/2 mi to the E.

Dijon City in Côte-d'Or *département*, E central France, capital of Burgundy region; population (1990) 151,600. As well as metallurgical, chemical, and other industries, it has a wine trade and is famed for its mustard.

Dillingen Town in the Saarland, Germany, on the river Saar, 24 km/15 mi NW of Saarbrücken; population (1994) 22,100. Dillingen is a railway junction and its principal industries are steelmaking, engineering, and chemicals.

Dinan Town in Côtes-d'Armor *département*, N France, on the river Rance; population (1989 est) 14,200. The river is harnessed for tidal hydroelectric power.

Dinant Ancient town in Namur province, Belgium, on the river Meuse; population (1991) 12,100. It is a tourist centre for the Ardennes.

Dinaric Alps Extension of the European ◊Alps that runs parallel to the E Adriatic coast, stretching from Slovenia along the frontier between Croatia and Bosnia-Herzegovina into W Yugoslavia and N Albania. The highest peak is Durmitor at 2,522 m/8,274 ft.

Dinkelsbühl Town in Bavaria, Germany, on the river Wörnitz, 141 km/88 mi NW of Munich; population (1994) 11,400. One of the city-states of the Holy Roman Empire, Dinkelsbühl has extensive medieval fortifications, including town walls, towers, and a moat, a late Gothic church (1448–99), many half-timbered medieval houses, and a former castle of the Teutonic Knights.

Dinosaur Provincial Park Provincial park in Alberta, Canada, with one of the world's richest fossil beds. Lying 142 km/90 mi from the town of Drumheller, it comprises a valley, some 3 km/2 mi wide and over 120 m/394 ft deep, through which the Red Deer River runs. Dinosaur skeletons have been found here, as well as petrified oyster shells filled with pure white crystal, fish impressions, and evidence of tropical vegetation. They were deposited 70 million years ago. About 60 varieties of prehistoric reptiles have been found, preserved by quicksands. The park is a World Heritage Site.

Dinslaken City in North Rhine–Westphalia, Germany, close to the right bank of the river Rhine, 18 km/11 mi N of Duisburg; population (1994) 68,100. Iron, steel, and shoe-making industries predominate. Each summer, an international jazz festival is held in Dinslaken.

Diomede Two islands off the tip of the Seward peninsula, Alaska. *Little Diomede* (6.2 sq km/2.4 sq mi) belongs to the USA and is only 3.9 km/2.4 mi from *Big Diomede* (29.3 sq km/11.3 sq mi), owned by Russia. They were first sighted by the Danish navigator Vitus Bering 1728.

Dismal Swamp Large marsh situated in SE Virginia and NE North Carolina, USA; area about 2,000 sq km/750 sq mi. Many trees grow in the marsh, mostly cypress, black gum, pine, and cedar. The area is gradually being reclaimed and canals have been cut through it, the longest of which is the *Dismal Swamp Canal* (length 35 km/22 mi), which connects ◊Chesapeake Bay and Albermarle Sound.

District of Columbia Federal district of the USA, see ◊Washington DC.

Dithmarschen or *Ditmarsh* District of Germany in the *Land* of ◊Schleswig-Holstein; population (1994) 133,000. It is a low-lying, partly marshy area on the W coast between the estuary of the Elbe and the river Eider. The largest town in the area is Heide.

Diu Island off the Kathiawar peninsula, NW India, part of the Union Territory of ◊Daman and Diu.

Diyarbakir Town in Asiatic Turkey, on the river Tigris. It has a trade in gold and silver filigree work, copper, wool, and mohair, and manufactures textiles and leather goods. The population grew from 381,000 in 1900 to 1.5 million in 1995 because of the influx of Kurds evicted from homes in SE Turkey.

Djakarta Variant spelling of ◊Jakarta, the capital of Indonesia.

Djibouti Chief port and capital of the Republic of Djibouti, on a peninsula 240 km/149 mi SW of Aden and 565 km/351 mi NE of Addis Ababa; population (1995) 383,000.

Dnieper or *Dnepr* River rising in the Smolensk region of the Russian Federation and flowing S through Belarus and Ukraine to enter the Black Sea near Kherson; total length 2,285 km/1,420 mi.

Dniprodzerzhinsk Port in Ukraine, on the river Dnieper, 48 km/30 mi NW of Dnipropetrovsk; population (1992) 286,000. It produces chemicals, iron, and steel.

Dnipropetrovsk (Russian *Dnepropetrovsk*) City in Ukraine, on the right bank of the river Dnieper; population (1992) 1,190,000. It is the centre of a major industrial region, with iron, steel, chemical, and engineering industries. It is linked with the Dnieper Dam, 60 km/37 mi downstream.

Dobruja District in the Balkans, bounded N and W by the Danube and E by the Black Sea. It is low-lying, partly marshland, partly fertile steppe land. Constanta is the chief town. Dobruja was divided between Romania and Bulgaria 1878. In 1913, after the second Balkan War, Bulgaria ceded its part to Romania but received it back 1940, a cession confirmed by the peace treaty of 1947.

Docklands Urban development area E of St Katherine's Dock, London, occupying the site of the former Wapping and Limehouse docks, the Isle of Dogs, and Royal Docks. It comprises 2,226 hectares/5,550 acres of former wharves, warehouses, and wasteland. Plans for its redevelopment were set in motion 1981 and by 1993 over 13,000 private housing units had been built, including terraced houses at Maconochies Wharf, Isle of Dogs. Distinguished buildings include the Tidal Basin Pumping Station in Royal Docks, designed by Richard Rogers, and the printing plant for the Financial Times, designed by Nicholas Grimshaw. The Limehouse Link motorway and tunnel, linking Tower Hill and Canary Wharf, opened 1993. The tallest building is the ◊Canary Wharf tower. Docklands is served by the London City airport (Stolport) and the Docklands Light Railway (DLR).

Dodecanese (Greek *Dhodhekánisos* 'twelve islands') Group of islands in the Aegean Sea; area 1,028 sq m/2,663 sq km; population (1991) 162,400. Once Turkish, the islands were Italian 1912–47, when they were ceded to Greece. They include ◊Rhodes and ◊Kos. Chief products include fruit, olives, and sponges.

Dodge City City in SW Kansas, USA, on the Arkansas River; population (1990) 21,100. Farm and livestock-handling machinery are manufactured here. It was an important cattle-trading centre 1865–85, in the days of the Wild West.

Dodoma Capital (replacing Dar es Salaam 1974) of Tanzania; 1,132 m/3,713 ft above sea level; population (1988) 203,800. It is a centre of communications, linked by rail with Dar es Salaam and Kigoma on Lake Tanganyika, and by road with Kenya to the N and Zambia and Malawi to the S.

Dogger Bank Submerged sandbank in the North Sea, about 115 km/70 mi off the coast of Yorkshire, England. In places the water is only 11 m/36 ft deep, but the general depth is 18–36 m/60–120 ft; it is a well-known fishing ground.

Dogs, Isle of District of E London, England, part of the Greater London borough of ◊Tower Hamlets.

Doha (Arabic *Ad Dawhah*) Capital and chief port of Qatar; population (1992) 243,000. Industries include oil refining, refrigeration plants, engineering, and food processing. It is the centre of vocational training for all the Persian Gulf states.

Doi Inthanon Highest mountain in Thailand, rising to 2,595 m/8,513 ft SW of Chiang Mai in NW Thailand.

Dole French town in the *département* of Jura, on the river Doubs and the Rhine–Rhône canal; population (1990)

Dodecanese

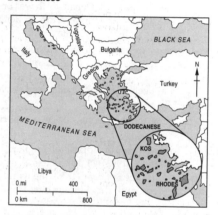

26,000. Situated on a vine-clad slope, it faces the heights of the forest of Chaux. The town has iron and copper foundries. Other industries include the manufacture of machines and chemicals. Its Roman name was Dola Sequanorum, and it was the capital of the former province of ◊Franche-Comté before being displaced by Besançon.

Dolgellau (formerly *Dolgelly*) Market town at the foot of Cader Idris in Gwynedd, Wales, on the river Wnion; population (1991) 2,400. The town is also a tourist centre. Nearby are the Gwynfynydd ('White Mountain') and Clogau gold-mines; a nugget from the latter has supplied gold for the wedding rings of royal brides since 1923.

Domremy-La-Pucelle French village in the *département* of Vosges, birthplace of Joan of Arc. It lies on the W bank of the river Meuse, 50 km/31 mi SW of Nancy; population (1990)

Dnieper

200. The house where she was born is preserved as a national memorial, and a basilica (1881) stands on the alleged spot where she first heard voices.

Don River in the Russian Federation, rising to the S of Moscow and entering the NE extremity of the Sea of Azov; length 1,900 km/1,180 mi. In its lower reaches the Don is 1.5 km/1 mi wide, and for about four months of the year it is closed by ice. Its upper course is linked with the river Volga by a canal.

Doñana National Park Park area of wetlands on the Guadalquivir delta, S Spain. It is one of the most important wildlife sanctuaries in W Europe. More than 200 bird species, over half Europe's total, are found here, including the griffin vulture, marbled teal, and the extremely rare Andalusian hemiphode. In the 1990s the park was threatened by falling water levels caused by 30 dams along the Guadalquivir river.

Donastia-San Sebastián Port and resort in the Basque Country, Spain; population (1994) 178,000. It was formerly the summer residence of the Spanish court.

Donau German name for the river ◊Danube.

Donauwörth Town in Bavaria, Germany, at the confluence of the rivers Danube (Donau) and Wörnitz, 40 km/25 mi N of Augsburg; population (1994) 17,700. Machinery and aircraft parts are manufactured. Donauwörth was one of the city-states of the Holy Roman Empire. A former Benedictine abbey in the Baroque style stands in the town.

Donawitz-Leoben Industrial town in the province of Styria, Austria, on the river Mur, 44 km/27 mi NW of Graz. Donawitz stands on the left bank of the river, Leoben on the right; the town has been a centre of mining and steelmaking since the mid-19th century.

Donbas Acronym for the ◊Donets Basin, a coal-rich area in Ukraine.

Doncaster Town in South Yorkshire, England, on the river Don; population (1991) 71,600. It has a racecourse; famous races here are the St Leger (1776), the world's oldest classic race, in Sept and the Lincolnshire Handicap in March.

Donegal Mountainous county in Ulster province in the NW of the Republic of Ireland, surrounded on three sides by the Atlantic Ocean; area 4,830 sq km/1,864 sq mi; county town Lifford; population (1996 est) 129,400. The market town and port of Donegal is at the head of Donegal Bay in the SW. Commercial activities include sheep and cattle raising, tweed and linen manufacture, and some deep-sea fishing. The river Erne hydroelectric project (1952) involved the building of large power stations at Ballyshannon.

Donets River rising in the Kursk region of the Russian Federation and flowing 1,080 km/670 mi through Ukraine to join the river Don 100 km/60 mi E of Rostov; see also ◊Donets Basin.

Donets Basin (abbreviated to *Donbas*) Area in Ukraine, situated in the bend formed by the rivers Don and Donets, which holds one of Europe's richest coalfields, together with salt, mercury, and lead.

Donetsk formerly (1872–1924) *Yuzovka* City in Ukraine; capital of Donetsk region, situated in the Donets Basin, a major coal-mining area, 600 km/372 mi SE of Kiev; population (1992) 1,121,000. It has blast furnaces, rolling mills, and other heavy industries.

Dongola Town in the Northern Province of the Sudan, above the third cataract on the river Nile. It was founded about 1812 to replace *Old Dongola*, 120 km/75 mi upriver, which was destroyed by the Mamelukes. Old Dongola, a trading centre on a caravan route, was the capital of the Christian kingdom of Nubia between the 6th and 14th centuries.

Dongting Lake in Hunan province, China; area 10,000 sq km/4,000 sq mi.

Donnybrook Former village, now part of Dublin, Republic of Ireland, notorious until 1855 for riotous fairs.

Dorchester Market town in Dorset, England, on the river Frome, N of Weymouth; population (1991) 15,000. It is the administrative centre for the county. The hill-fort Maiden Castle to the SW was occupied as a settlement from about 2000 BC. The novelist Thomas Hardy was born nearby.

Dordogne River in SW France, rising in Puy-de-Dôme *département* and flowing 490 km/300 mi to join the river Garonne 23 km/14 mi N of Bordeaux. It gives its name to a *département* and is a major source of hydroelectric power.

Dordogne *Département* in the ◊Aquitaine region of France; area 9,183 sq km/3,546 sq mi; population (1990) 386,900. The land is hilly and wooded, with fertile valleys in the centre and marshes in the E. There are numerous vineyards on the hill slopes. Chestnuts, truffles, wheat, maize, tobacco, and potatoes are grown. Industries include distilling, and the manufacture of leather goods and textiles. The principal towns are ◊Périgueux (the capital), Bergerac, Sarlat, and Nantran.

Dordrecht or *Dort* River port on an island in the Maas, South Holland, the Netherlands, 19 km/12 mi SE of Rotterdam; population (1994) 113,400, metropolitan area of Dordrecht-Zwijndrecht 214,000. It has shipbuilding yards and makes heavy machinery, plastics, and chemicals.

Dore, Monts Group of volcanic peaks in the *département* of Puy-de-Dôme, France, part of the Auvergne system. The highest point is the Puy-de-Sancy (1,886 m/6,188 ft).

Dornbirn Austrian town in the province of Vorarlberg, 10 km/6 mi S of Bregenz and near Lake Constance; population (1995) 40,900. There are iron, chemical, brewing, and textile industries in the town.

Dorpat German name for the Estonian city of ◊Tartu.

Dorset County of SW England
area 2,541 sq km/981 sq mi
towns and cities Dorchester (administrative headquarters), Shaftesbury, Sherborne; resorts: Lyme Regis, Weymouth
features Chesil Bank, a shingle bank along the coast 19 km/11 mi long; Isle of Purbeck, a peninsula where china clay and Purbeck 'marble' are quarried, and which includes

Corfe Castle and the holiday resort of Swanage; Dorset Downs; Cranborne Chase; rivers Frome and Stour; Maiden Castle; Tank Museum at Royal Armoured Corps Centre, Bovington, where the cottage of the soldier and writer T E Lawrence is a museum; Canford Heath, the home of some of Britain's rarest breeding birds and reptiles (including the nightjar, Dartford warbler, sand lizard, and smooth snake) **industries** Wytch Farm is the largest onshore oilfield in the UK; production at Wareham onshore oilfield started 1991 **population** (1994 est) 374,800
famous people Anthony Ashley Cooper, Thomas Love Peacock, Thomas Hardy.

Dorsten City in North Rhine–Westphalia, Germany, on the river Lippe, 50 km/31 mi NE of Düsseldorf; population (1994) 80,400. It has a large coal mine and a gasworks, together with factories producing wire, chemicals, carpets, and furniture.

Dort Another name for ◊Dordrecht, a port in the Netherlands.

Dortmund City and industrial centre in the ◊Ruhr, in North Rhine–Westphalia, Germany, 58 km/36 mi NE of Düsseldorf; population (1993) 602,400. It is the largest mining town of the Westphalian coalfield and the S terminus of the Dortmund–Ems Canal. The enlargement of the Wesel–Datteln Canal 1989, connecting Dortmund to the Rhine River, allows barges to travel between Dortmund and Rotterdam in the Netherlands. Industries include iron, steel, construction machinery, engineering, and brewing.

Dortmund–Ems Canal Canal in Germany connecting the country's principal industrial region – the ◊Ruhr – with the North Sea port of ◊Emden. The canal is 271 km/168 mi long, and the principal town on its route is Münster.

Dothan City in the SE corner of Alabama, USA, SE of Montgomery; seat of Houston County; population (1992) 54,800. Its industries include fertilizer, clothing, furniture, vegetable oils, and hosiery. It is an agricultural and livestock marketing centre. Dothan was settled 1858 and renamed 1911. The National Peanut Festival is held here every Oct.

Douai Town in Nord *département*, France, on the river Scarpe; population (1990) 44,200. It has coal mines, iron foundries, and breweries. An English Roman Catholic college was founded here 1568 by English Catholics in exile. The Douai-Reims Bible, published 1582–1610, influenced the translators of the King James Version.

Douala or *Duala* Chief port and industrial centre (aluminium, chemicals, textiles, pulp) of Cameroon, on the Wouri river estuary; population (1991) 884,000. Known as Kamerunstadt until 1907, it was capital of German Cameroon, which became a German protectorate in 1884, 1885–1901.

Douarnenez French fishing town in the *département* of Finistère; population (1990) 17,000. The sardine and mackerel fisheries are important, and 20% of the world's tuna is landed here (1997). Other industries include boat-building, net- and ropemaking.

Doubs River in France and Switzerland, rising in the Jura Mountains and flowing 430 km/265 mi to join the river Saône. It gives its name to a *département*.

Doubs *Département* in the ◊Franche-Comté region of France; area 5,228 sq km/2,019 sq mi; population (1990) 485,200. It falls naturally into three regions. The plains between the rivers Ognon and Doubs are very fertile, producing wheat, oats, and other cereals, as well as vegetables, hemp, fruits, and vines. The central plateau is mostly used as grazing land for cattle. The mountainous districts, crossed by four parallel spurs of the Jura, are thickly wooded. The main manufacturing industries are machinery, textiles, clocks and watches, hardware, food, and wine. There are rock-salt deposits in the region, and building stone is quarried. The principal towns are ◊Besançon (the capital), Montbéliard, and Pontarlier.

Douglas Capital of the Isle of Man in the Irish Sea; population (1991) 22,200. It is a holiday resort and terminus of shipping routes to and from Fleetwood and Liverpool; banking and financial services are important.

Dounreay Former experimental nuclear reactor site on the N coast of Scotland in the Highland unitary authority, 12 km/7 mi W of Thurso. It was the site of the world's first fast breeder nuclear reactor in 1962–77, when an explosion contaminated beaches. It has since been linked to the high incidence of childhood leukaemia in the area. A second reactor opened in 1974 and continued until the site was decommissioned in 1994 and replaced with a nuclear reprocessing plant. A 1996 survey by the UK Atomic Energy Authority found 1,500 patches of radioactive contamination. There was a plutonium leak Sept in 1996 into the sea. One of its reprocessing plants had to be temporarily shut down.

A sodium treatment plant at Dounreay was closed down by the Scottish Environment Agency (SEPA) in 1997 due to concerns that it was discharging excessive radioactive waste.

Douro (Spanish *Duero*) River rising in N central Spain and flowing through N Portugal to the Atlantic at Porto; length 800 km/500 mi. Navigation at the river mouth is hindered by sand bars. There are hydroelectric installations. Vineyards (port and Mateus rosé) are irrigated with water from the river.

Dover Capital of Delaware, USA, located in the central part of the state, on the St Jones River, S of Wilmington; population (1992) 28,200. Industries include synthetic materials, adhesives, latex, resins, chemicals, food products, and space equipment. It is an agricultural trade centre and was laid out 1717.

Dover City in SE New Hampshire, USA, on the Cocheco River, NW of Portsmouth; seat of Strafford County; population (1990) 25,000. Industries include lumber, electronics, rubber, and aluminium products. Dover was settled 1623 and suffered attacks by Native Americans, including one in 1689.

Dover Market town and seaport on the SE coast of Kent, England; population (1991) 34,200. It is Britain's nearest point to mainland Europe, being only 34 km/21 mi from Calais, France. As England's principal cross-channel port, Dover's development has been chiefly due to the cross-channel traffic, which includes train, ferry, hovercraft, and other services. It was one of the original Cinque Ports. Industries include electronics. Under Roman rule, Dover (*Dubris*) was at the end of Watling Street, and the beacon or 'lighthouse' in the grounds of the Norman castle dates from about 50 AD, making it one of the oldest buildings in Britain.

Dover, Strait of (French *Pas-de-Calais*) Stretch of water separating England from France, and connecting the English Channel with the North Sea. It is about 35 km/22 mi long and 34 km/21 mi wide at its narrowest part. It is one of the world's busiest sea lanes.

Down County of SE Northern Ireland
area 2,470 sq km/953 sq mi
towns and cities Downpatrick (county town), Bangor (seaside resort)
features Mourne Mountains; Strangford sea lough
industries agriculture, linen, potatoes, oats, light manufacturing, plastics, high technology and computer companies
population (1981) 339,200.

Downs, the Roadstead (partly sheltered anchorage) off E Kent, England, between Deal and the Goodwin Sands. Several 17th-century naval battles took place here, including a defeat of Spain by the Dutch 1639.

Downs, North and South Two lines of chalk hills in SE England; see ◊North Downs and ◊South Downs.

Draguignan French town in the *département* of Var, 65 km/40 mi NE of Toulon, on the river Nartuby; population (1990) 29,600. It has leather and textile industries, and a large US military cemetery from World War II.

Drakensberg (Afrikaans 'dragon's mountain') Mountain range in South Africa (Sesuto name *Quathlamba*), on the boundary of Lesotho and the Free State with KwaZulu-Natal. Its highest point is Thabane Ntlenyana, 3,482 m/11,424 ft, near which is Natal National Park.

Drama Town and department of NW Greece, in the ◊Macedonia region; population (1993) 102,000. It is a centre for the Greek tobacco trade, and has commercial, administrative, and strategic importance. There are also food-processing factories.

Drammen Town and port in SE Norway, on the Drammen Fjord, a branch of the Oslo Fjord; population (1990) 51,900. There are engineering, water power equipment, food processing, and brewing industries; paper and wood pulp are manufactured and shipped from here.

Drava or *Drave*, (German *Drau*) River in central Europe, the second largest tributary on the right bank of the ◊Danube; length 720 km/447 mi. The Drava rises in E Tirol and flows in a generally southeasterly direction through Austria and Slovenia to join the Danube 21 km/13 mi E of Osijek. For part of its course, the river forms the boundary between Croatia and Hungary.

Drenthe Low-lying N province of the Netherlands
area 2,660 sq km/1,027 sq mi
capital Assen
cities Emmen, Hoogeveen
physical fenland and moors; well-drained clay and peat soils
industries livestock, arable crops, horticulture, petroleum
population (1995 est) 454,900
history governed in the Middle Ages by provincial nobles and by bishops of Utrecht, Drenthe was eventually acquired by Charles V of Spain 1536. It developed following land drainage initiated in the mid-18th century and was established as a separate province of the Netherlands 1796.

Dresden Capital of the *Land* of Saxony, Germany; population (1993) 480,500. Industries include chemicals, machinery, glassware, and musical instruments. It was one of the most beautiful German cities until its devastation by Allied fire-bombing 1945. Dresden county has an area of 6,740 sq km/2,602 sq mi and a population of 1,772,000.

Drin River in Albania; length 300 km/186 mi. It is formed by the confluence at Kukes of the Black Drin, which rises in Lake ◊Ohrid, and the White Drin, which rises in the Albanian Alps. The Drin flows into the Adriatic Sea.

Drina River in Yugoslavia, 402 km/250 mi long. It rises at the frontier of Montenegro, at the junction of the rivers Tara and Diva, and flows N along the border between Bosnia and Serbia to join the river Sava 105 km/65 mi W of Belgrade.

Drogheda Seaport near the mouth of the river Boyne, County Louth, Republic of Ireland. The port trades in cattle and textiles; industries include chemicals, foodstuffs, brewing, linen, cotton, and engineering. In 1649 the town was stormed by Oliver Cromwell, who massacred most of the garrison. In 1690 Drogheda surrendered to William III after the Battle of the Boyne.

Drôme River in France, rising in Dauphiné Pre-Alps and flowing NW for 101 km/63 mi to join the river Rhône below Livron. It gives its name to a *département*.

Drôme *Département* in the ◊Rhône-Alpes region of SE France area 6,525 sq km/2,519 sq mi; population (1990) 414,546. Drôme extends from the wide and fertile Rhône valley in the W to the edge of the Cottian Alps (Alpes du Dauphiné) in the E. The chief products are maize, potatoes, buckwheat, mulberries, fruit, truffles, and wine (including Hermitage and Crozes-Hermitage). There are electrical, aerospace, chemical, foodstuffs, and paper industries. Silk and leather are also produced here. The capital is ◊Valence; other towns of importance are Die, Nyons, ◊Montélimar, Crest, and Romans-sur-Isère.

Dubai One of the United Arab Emirates.

Dublin (Gaelic *Baile Atha Cliath*) Capital and port on the E coast of the Republic of Ireland, at the mouth of the river Liffey, facing the Irish Sea; population (1991) 478,400, Greater Dublin, including Dún Laoghaire (1986 est) 921,000. It is the site of one of the world's largest breweries (Guinness); other industries include textiles, pharmaceuticals, electrical goods, whisky distilling, glass, food processing, and machine tools.

Dublin County in the Republic of Ireland, in Leinster province, facing the Irish Sea; county town Dublin; area 920 sq km/355 sq mi; population (1996 est) 1,056,700. It is mostly level and low-lying, but rises in the S to 753 m/2,471 ft in Kippure, part of the Wicklow Mountains. The river Liffey enters Dublin Bay. Dublin, the capital of the Republic of Ireland, and Dún Laoghaire are the two major towns.

Dubna Town in the Russian Federation, 40 km/25 mi W of Tula; population (1985) 61,000. It is a metal-working centre, and has the Volga Nuclear Physics Centre.

Dubrovnik (Italian *Ragusa*) City and port in Croatia on the Adriatic coast; population (1991) 49,700. It manufactures cheese, liqueurs, silk, and leather.

Dubuque City in E central Iowa, USA, NE of Iowa City, just across the Mississippi River from the Wisconsin–Illinois border; population (1992) 58,600. An important port, it has shipbuilding and agricultural marketing facilities; industries include meatpacking, lumber, metals, and machinery.

Dudley Town NW of Birmingham, West Midlands, England; population (1994 est) 141,000. Industries include light engineering, glass, and clothing manufacture. There is a 13th-century castle and the Black Country Museum.

Dufourspitze Second highest of the alpine peaks, 4,634 m/15,203 ft high. It is the highest peak in the Monte Rosa group of the Pennine Alps on the Swiss-Italian frontier.

Duisburg River port and industrial city in North Rhine–Westphalia, Germany, at the confluence of the Rhine and Ruhr rivers; population (1993) 538,100. It is the largest inland river port in Europe. Heavy industries include oil refining and the production of steel and machinery.

Dukeries Area of estates in Nottinghamshire, England, with magnificent stately homes, few now surviving. Thoresby Hall, said to be the largest house in England (about 365 rooms), was sold as a hotel 1989 and the contents dispersed.

Duluth Port in the USA on Lake Superior, by the mouth of the St Louis River, Minnesota; population (1992) 85,400. It manufactures steel, flour, timber, and dairy produce. The westernmost port on the St Lawrence Seaway, it trades in iron ore, grain, coal, oil, and timber. Permanent settlement on what had been a fur-trading post began 1852. The town was laid out 1856.

Dulwich District of the Greater London borough of Southwark. It contains Dulwich College (founded 1619 by Edward Alleyn, an Elizabethan actor); the Horniman Museum (1901), with a fine ethnological collection; Dulwich Picture Gallery (1814), England's oldest public picture gallery (designed by John Soane, rebuilt 1953 after being bombed during World War II); Dulwich Park; and Dulwich Village.

Dumbarton Administrative headquarters of West Dunbartonshire, Scotland; population (1991) 22,000.

Industries include marine engineering, whisky distilling, and electronics.

Dumfries Administrative headquarters of Dumfries and Galloway unitary authority, Scotland; population (1991) 32,100. It is situated on the river Nith. Industries include knitwear, plastics, light engineering, and textiles.

Dumfries and Galloway Unitary authority in S Scotland; former Region 1975–96; administrative headquarters Dumfries; population (1996) 147,800; area 6,394 sq km/2,468 sq mi.

towns and cities Dumfries (administrative headquarters)
features Solway Firth; Galloway Hills, setting of John Buchan's *The Thirty-Nine Steps*; Glen Trool National Park; Ruthwell Cross, a runic cross dating from about 800 in Ruthwell Parish Church
industries horses and cattle (for which the Galloway area was renowned), sheep, timber, agriculture
population (1991) 147,800
famous people Robert the Bruce, Robert Burns, Thomas Carlyle.

Dumfriesshire Former county of S Scotland, merged 1975–96 into Dumfries and Galloway Region.

Dumyat Alternate name for the Egyptian port of ◊Damietta.

Duna Hungarian name for the river ◊Danube.

Dunarea Romanian name for the river ◊Danube.

Dunbartonshire Former county of Scotland, bordering the N bank of the Clyde estuary, merged 1975–96 into Strathclyde Region.

Dundee City and unitary authority in E Scotland, on the N side of the Firth of Tay; population (1996) 155,000; area 65 sq km/25 sq mi. It is a fishing port, and an important shipping and rail centre. Industries include engineering, textiles, electronics, printing, and food processing.

Dunedin Port on Otago harbour, South Island, New Zealand; population (1993) 111,200. It is a road, rail, and air centre, with engineering and textile industries. The city was founded 1848 by members of the Free Church of Scotland. Its university was established 1869.

Dunfermline Industrial city near the Firth of Forth in Fife, Scotland; population (1991) 55,100. It is the site of the naval base of Rosyth; industries include engineering, electronics, and textiles. Many Scottish kings, including Robert the Bruce, are buried in Dunfermline Abbey. Dunfermline is the birthplace of the industrialist Andrew Carnegie.

Dungeness Shingle headland on the S coast of Kent, England. It has nuclear power stations, a lighthouse, and a bird sanctuary.

Dunkirk (French *Dunkerque*) Seaport on the N coast of France, in Nord *département*, on the Strait of Dover; population (1990) 71,100. Its harbour is one of the foremost in France, and it has widespread canal links with the rest of France and with Belgium; there is a ferry service to Ramsgate, England. Industries include oil refining, fishing, and the manufacture of textiles, machinery, and soap.

Dunkirk was close to the front line during much of World War I, and in World War II, 337,131 Allied troops (including about 110,000 French) were evacuated from the beaches as German forces approached.

Dún Laoghaire formerly *Kingstown* Port and suburb of Dublin, Republic of Ireland; population (1986 est) 54,700. It is a terminal for ferries to Britain, and there are fishing industries.

Dunmow, Little Village in Essex, England, scene every four years of the *Dunmow Flitch* trial (dating from 1111), in which a side of bacon is presented to any couple who 'will swear that they have not quarrelled nor repented of their marriage within a year and a day after its celebration'; they are judged by a jury whose members are all unmarried.

Dunstable Town in SW Bedfordshire, England, at the N end of the Chiltern Hills; 48 km/30 mi NW of London; population (1991) 49,700. Whipsnade Zoo is nearby. Industries include printing, paper, engineering, cement, and commercial vehicles.

Durance River in SE France; length 305 km/190 mi. It rises in the *département* of Hautes-Alpes, and flows SW past Briançon in a series of gorges. In its lower reaches it is canalized for irrigation purposes, and its course becomes northwesterly. It finally enters the river Rhône 5 km/3 mi below Avignon. Its chief tributary is the river Verdon.

Durango State of N Mexico; area 119,648 sq km/46,196 sq mi; population (1995 est) 1,431,000. Its capital is Victoria de Durango. The main occupations are farming and mining.

Durazzo Italian form of ◊Durrës, a port in Albania.

Durban Principal port of KwaZulu-Natal, South Africa, and second port of the republic; population (urban area, 1991) 1,137,400. It exports coal, maize, and wool; imports heavy machinery and mining equipment; and is also a holiday resort.

Düren City in North Rhine–Westphalia, Germany, on the river Ruhr, 51 km/32 mi SW of Düsseldorf; population (1994) 256,300. Metal goods, textiles, paper, and sugar are manufactured here. Düren dates from before AD 911.

Durham City and administrative headquarters of the county of Durham, England; population (1991) 80,700. Formerly a centre for the coal-mining industry (the last pit closed 1993), current industries include textiles, light engineering, carpets, and clothing. It has a Norman cathedral founded 995, where the remains of the theologian and historian Bede were transferred around 1020, and in 1370 encased and put in the Lady Chapel; the castle was built 1072 by William I and the university was founded 1832. Durham Cathedral and Castle is a World Heritage site.

Durham County of NE England
area 2,232 sq km/862 sq mi
towns and cities Durham (administrative headquarters), Peterlee, Newton Aycliffe
features Pennine Hills; rivers Wear and Tees; Beamish open-air industrial museum; site of one of Britain's richest coalfields (pits no longer functioning); Bowes Museum; Barnard Castle

industries sheep and dairy produce; clothing, chemicals. There are also iron and steel processing and light engineering industries. Consett Steel Works closed 1980.
population (1995 est) 492,900
famous people Elizabeth Barrett Browning, Anthony Eden.

Durham City in N central North Carolina, USA, NW of Raleigh; seat of Durham County; population (1992) 140,900. Tobacco is the main industry, and other products include precision instruments, textiles, furniture, and lumber. Durham was settled 1750 and developed around the tobacco industry in the 19th century, especially after the Duke factory opened 1874. Duke University (1924) is here.

Dürnstein or *Dürrenstein* Austrian village in the province of Lower Austria, on the river Danube, 7 km/4 mi W of Krems. It is overlooked by the ruins of a castle in which the English King Richard I was imprisoned 1192–93 after being captured on his return from the Third Crusade.

Durostorum Roman name for ◊Silistra, now a town in Bulgaria.

Durrës Chief port of Albania; population (1991) 86,900. It is a commercial and communications centre, with flour mills, soap and cigarette factories, distilleries, and an electronics plant. It was the capital of Albania 1912–21.

Dushanbe formerly (1929–69) *Stalinabad* Capital of Tajikistan, 160 km/100 mi N of the Afghan frontier; population (1991) 582,000. It is a road, rail, and air centre. Industries include cotton mills, tanneries, meat-packing factories, and printing works. It is the seat of Tajik state university.

Düsseldorf Industrial city of Germany, on the right bank of the river Rhine, 26 km/16 mi NW of Cologne, capital of North Rhine–Westphalia; population (1993) 577,600. It is a river port and the commercial and financial centre of the Ruhr area, with food processing, brewing, agricultural machinery, textile, and chemical industries.

Dutch East Indies Former Dutch colony, which in 1945 became independent as Indonesia.

Dutch Guiana Former Dutch colony, which in 1975 became independent as Suriname.

Dvinsk Russian name for ◊Daugavpils, Latvia.

Dvůr Králové (German *Königinhof*) Town in E Bohemia, in the Czech Republic, on the river Elbe, 100 km/63 mi NE of Prague; population (1991) 17,000. Industries include brewing, milling, and textiles.

Dyfed Former county of SW Wales, 1974–96, now divided between Carmarthenshire, Ceredigion, and Pembroke-shire unitary authorities.

Dzerzhinsk City in the Russian Federation, on the Oka River, 32 km/20 mi W of Gorky; population (1994) 286,000. There are engineering, chemical, and timber industries.

Dzhambul City in S Kazakhstan, in a fruit-growing area NE of Tashkent; population (1990) 311,000. Industries include fruit canning, sugar refining, and the manufacture of phosphate fertilizers.

Dzierżoniów (German *Reichenbach*) Town in Wałbrzych province, Poland, 50 km/31mi SW of Wrocław; population

(1990) 9,900. Cotton textiles and electrical goods are manufactured, and grain and cattle traded. The town was founded in the 13th century.

Eagle Island Alternative form of ◊Achill Island, Ireland.

Ealing Outer borough of W Greater London
features 18th-century Pitshanger Manor; Gunnersbury House and Gunnersbury Park, both Regency-style houses; Ealing Studios (1931), the first British sound-film studios ('Ealing comedies' became a noted genre in British filmmaking); Hoover factory (1932), Art Deco; there is a large Asian population in Southall
industries engineering, chemicals
population (1991) 283,600
famous people Spencer Perceval was resident in Ealing 1801–12.

East Anglia Region of E England, formerly a Saxon kingdom, including Norfolk, Suffolk, and parts of Essex and Cambridgeshire. Norwich is the principal city of East Anglia. The Sainsbury Centre for Visual Arts, opened 1978, at the University of East Anglia, has a collection of ethnographic art and sculpture. East Anglian ports such as Harwich and Felixstowe have greatly developed as trade with the rest of Europe has increased.

East Ayrshire Unitary authority in SW Scotland created 1996 from part of the former Strathclyde region; administrative headquarters Kilmarnock; population (1996) 124,000; area 1,271 sq km/491 sq mi. Agriculture, dairy farming, sheep, and beef cattle are important. Industries include textiles, engineering, food and drink, and printing.

Eastbourne Seaside resort in East Sussex, SE England, 103 km/64 mi SE of London; population (1991) 81,400. The old town was developed in the early 19th century as a model of town planning, largely owing to the 7th duke of Devonshire. The modern town extends along the coast for 5 km/3 mi.

East Chicago City in NW Indiana, USA, on Lake Michigan; population (1992) 34,600. East Chicago forms part of the metropolitan area of Gary–Hammond–East Chicago and is on the S fringe of the ◊Chicago conurbation. The petrochemical industry is important to the local economy. Inland the city is enclosed by the territory of Gary and Hammond but on the lakeside reclamation has created the port of Indiana Harbor, one of the major ports of the Great Lakes.

East Dunbartonshire Unitary authority in central Scotland created 1996 from part of the former Strathclyde region; administrative headquarters Kirkintilloch; population (1996) 110,000; area 202 sq km/78 sq mi.

Easter Island or *Rapa Nui* Chilean island in the S Pacific Ocean, part of the Polynesian group, about 3,500 km/2,200 mi W of Chile; area about 166 sq km/64 sq mi; population (1985) 2,000. It was first reached by Europeans on Easter Sunday 1722. On it stand over 800 huge carved statues (*moai*) and the remains of boat-shaped stone houses, the work of Neolithic peoples from Polynesia. The chief centre is Hanga-Roa.

Eastern Cape Province of the Republic of South Africa

from 1994, formerly part of Cape Province
area 170,616 sq km/65,875 sq mi
capital Bisho
towns and cities East London, Port Elizabeth, Grahamstown
features includes the former independent homelands of the Transkei and the Ciskei; Little and Great Karoo; Drakensberg mountains; Orange River
industries motor manufacturing, textiles, sheep, citrus fruits
population (1995 est) 6,481,300
languages Xhosa 85%, Afrikaans 9%, English 3%

East Flanders (Flemish *Oost-Vlaanderen*) Province of Belgium, bounded by Antwerp to the E, Brabant to the SE, and West Flanders to the SW; area 2,970 sq km/1,147 sq mi; population (1992) 1,343,000. East Flanders includes the basin of the river Scheldt, and under skilful cultivation yields excellent crops, such as sugar beet, flax, and hops, especially in the Waes district, which was once barren marsh. There is also a substantial trade in flowers and textiles. The principal towns are ◊Ghent (the capital), Sint-Niklaas, Alost, Eekloo, Dendermonde, and Oudenaarde.

East Indies The Malay Archipelago; the Philippines are sometimes included. The term is also used to refer more generally to SE Asia.

East Kilbride Town in South Lanarkshire, Scotland; population (1991) 70,400. It was an old village, designated a new town 1947 to take overspill from Glasgow, 11 km/6 mi to the NE. It is the site of the National Engineering Laboratory. There are various light industries, including clothing, printing, electrical equipment, and electronics, and some engineering, including jet engines.

East London Port and resort on the SE coast of Eastern Cape Province, South Africa; population (urban area, 1991) 270,100. Founded 1846 as *Port Rex*, its name was changed to East London 1848. It has a good harbour, is the terminus of a railway from the interior, and is a leading wool-exporting port.

East Lothian Unitary authority in SE Scotland; administrative headquarters Haddington; population (1996) 85,500; area 681 sq km/263 sq mi. A former county, it merged with West Lothian and Midlothian 1975–96 in Lothian Region. Features include the Lammermuir Hills, Bass Rock in the Firth of Forth, noted for seabirds.

East Orange City in Essex County, New Jersey, NE USA, 20 km/12 mi W of New York City and adjoining Newark; population (1990) 73,600. Settled since 1666, it is primarily a residential area, although electronics is an important local industry.

East Renfrewshire Unitary authority in central Scotland created 1996 from part of the former Strathclyde region; administrative headquarters Giffnock; population (1996) 86,800; area 172 sq km/66 sq mi. There is farming and light industry.

East Riding of Yorkshire Unitary authority in N England created 1996 from part of the former county of Humberside; administrative headquarters Beverley; population (1996) 310,000; area 2,416 sq km/933 sq mi.

East River Tidal strait 26 km/16 mi long, running between Manhattan and the Bronx, and Long Island, in New York, USA. It links Long Island Sound with New York Bay and is also connected, via the Harlem River, with the Hudson River. There are docks and many bridges, including the Brooklyn Bridge.

East Siberian Sea Part of the ◊Arctic Ocean, off the N coast of Russia, between the New Siberian Islands and Chukchi Sea. The world's widest continental shelf, with an average width of nearly 650 km/404 mi, lies in the East Siberian Sea.

East St Louis City in SW Illinois, USA, on the Mississippi River, across from St Louis, Missouri; population (1990) 40,900. A centre for the processing of livestock; its other industries include steel, paint materials, and machinery. East St Louis started as a ferry station 1797, and was incorporated 1859. After the opening of the National Stock Yards in National City 1872, meatpacking became a major industry.

East Sussex County of SE England, created 1974, formerly part of Sussex
area 1,725 sq mi sq km/666 sq mi
towns and cities Lewes (administrative headquarters), Newhaven (cross-channel port), Eastbourne, Hastings, Bexhill, Winchelsea, Rye
features Beachy Head, highest headland on the S coast at 180 m/590 ft, the E end of the ◊South Downs; the Weald (including Ashdown Forest); Friston Forest; rivers: Ouse, Cuckmere, East Rother; Romney Marsh; the 'Long Man' chalk hill figure at Wilmington, near Eastbourne; Herstmonceux, with a 15th-century castle (conference and exhibition centre) and adjacent modern buildings, site of the Greenwich Royal Observatory 1958–90; other castles at Hastings, Lewes, Pevensey, and Bodiam; Battle Abbey and the site of the Battle of Hastings; Michelham Priory; Sheffield Park garden; University of Sussex at Falmer, near Brighton, founded 1961
industries electronics, gypsum, timber; light engineering; agricultural products, including cereals, hops, fruit, and vegetables
population (1995) 482,800
famous people former homes of Henry James at Rye, Rudyard Kipling at Burwash, Virginia Woolf at Rodmell.

East Timor Disputed territory on the island of ◊Timor in the Malay Archipelago, claimed by Indonesia as the province of Timor Timor; prior to 1975, it was a Portuguese colony for almost 460 years.
area 14,874 sq km/5,706 sq mi
capital Dili
industries coffee
population (1990) 747,750
history Following Portugal's withdrawal 1975, East Timor was left with a literacy rate of under 10% and no infrastructure. Civil war broke out and the left-wing Revolutionary Front of Independent East Timor (Fretilin) occupied the capital, calling for independence. In opposition, troops from neighbouring Indonesia invaded the territory, declaring

East Timor (*Loro Sae*) the 17th province of Indonesia July 1976 – a claim not recognized by the United Nations. (It had long been the aim of Indonesian military rulers to absorb the remaining colonial outposts in the East Indies.)

The war and its attendant famine are thought to have caused more than 100,000 deaths, but starvation had been alleviated by the mid-1980s, and the Indonesian government had built schools, roads, and hospitals. Fretilin guerrillas remained active protesting against the 'transmigration' of Indonesian Muslims into the predominantly Christian island. In Nov 1991 Indonesian troops fired on pro-independence demonstrators, killing 50. Between 100 and 200 unarmed protestors died in ensuing clashes. More than 1,000 Fretilin guerrillas were reported to have surrendered Nov 1992 following the capture of their leader, Jose Alexandre Gusmao. Indonesia announced plans to withdraw most of its troops from East Timor Aug 1993. The 1996 Nobel Peace Prize was awarded jointly to Bishop Carlos Belo, who had persistently denounced human-rights violations by Indonesian soldiers in East Timor, and Jorge Ramas-Horta, an exiled spokesman for the Fretilin Independence Movement.

Eau Claire City in W central Wisconsin, USA, N of LaCrosse, on the Chippewa River; seat of Eau Claire County; population (1992) 58,000. It is a processing and marketing centre for the region's dairy farmers. Industries include machine parts, electronics, printing, and brewing. Tourism is important to the economy. Eau Claire was settled in the 1840s.

Ebbw Vale (Welsh *Glyn Ebwy*) Town and administrative headquarters of Blaenau Gwent unitary authority, Wales; population (1991) 19,500. It was formerly a coal-mining town, with iron and steel industries which ended in the 1970s; tin-plate manufacture and engineering have continued. To the E is Blaenavon, where the Big Pit (no longer working) is a tourist attraction.

Ebro River in NE Spain, which rises in the Cantabrian Mountains and flows some 800 km/500 mi SE to meet the Mediterranean Sea SW of Barcelona. Zaragoza is on its course, and ocean-going ships can sail as far as Tortosa, 35 km/22 mi from its mouth. It is a major source of hydroelectric power.

Eccles Town near Manchester, England, 8 km/5 mi W of Manchester, on the river Irwell and Manchester Ship Canal; population (1991) 36,000. Industries include cotton textiles, machinery, and pharmaceuticals. Eccles cakes, rounded pastries with a dried fruit filling, originated here.

Echternach Town in the Grand Duchy of Luxembourg, situated on the river Sauer, 32 km/20 mi NE of the city of Luxembourg. It is a tourist centre and was largely rebuilt after World War II.

Écija Town in the province of Seville, S Spain; population (1995) 37,500. It lies in the centre of the fertile valley of the river Genil, a tributary of the Guadalquivir. Écija is called 'the frying pan of Andalusia' because of its intense summer heat. Shoes, food, and textiles are produced here.

Eckernförde Town in Schleswig-Holstein, Germany, 30 km/19 mi NW of Kiel; population (1994) 22,800. It was formerly a naval port, but is now a fishing port and holiday resort with optical and clothing industries.

Edam Town in the Netherlands on the river IJ, North Holland province. Founded as a customs post in the 13th century, Edam's prosperity in the 16th and 17th centuries was based upon its cheese trade; it is still famous today for its round cheeses covered in red wax.

Eddystone Rocks Rocks in the English Channel, 23 km/14 mi S of Plymouth. The lighthouse, built 1882, is the fourth on this exposed site.

Eden River in Cumbria, NW England; length 104 km/65 mi. From its source in the Pennines, it flows NW to enter the Solway Firth NW of Carlisle.

Edessa (Greek *Edhessa*) Town in Greece, capital of the department of Pella, W Macedonia, 77 km/48 mi NW of Thessaloniki. Industries are linked to nearby hydroelectric schemes; there are cotton and silk factories, and carpet manufacture. It is at the centre of a fertile agricultural area and there is food processing.

Edinburg City in SE Texas, USA, NW of Brownsville; seat of Hidalgo County; population (1990) 29,800. It is a shipping centre for the area's citrus fruit crops. It was founded 1907 as Chapin, and renamed 1911.

Edinburgh Capital of Scotland and unitary authority, near the S shores of the Firth of Forth; population (1996) 447,550; area 261 sq km/101 sq mi. Industries include printing, publishing, banking, insurance, chemical manufactures, electronics distilling, brewing. Edinburgh International Festival of Music and Drama, begun 1947, is the largest in the world. The university was established 1583.

Edirne Town in European Turkey, on the river Maritsa, about 225 km/140 mi NW of Istanbul; population (province, 1990) 404,600. Founded on the site of ancient Uscadama, it was formerly known as *Adrianople*, named after the Emperor Hadrian about AD 125.

Edmonton Capital of Alberta, Canada, on the North Saskatchewan River; population (1991) 616,700. It is the centre of an oil and mining area to the N and also an agricultural and dairying region. Manufactured goods include processed foods, petrochemicals, plastic and metal products, lumber, and clothing. Edmonton is on the Alaska Highway. Petroleum pipelines link Edmonton with Superior, Wisconsin, USA, and Vancouver, British Columbia. Fort Edmonton, a Hudson's Bay Company fur-trading post, was built in 1795.

Edmonton A locality, once a town, part of the London borough of Enfield. John Keats lived at Edmonton, and Charles Lamb lived and died here. The Bell Inn is referred to in William Cowper's poem 'John Gilpin'.

Edward, Lake Lake in Uganda, area 2,150 sq km/830 sq mi, at about 900 m/3,000 ft above sea level in the Albertine rift valley. It was known as Lake Idi *Amin Dada*, after President Amin of Uganda, 1973–79.

Eger German name for ◊Cheb, a town in the Czech Republic.

Eger (German *Erlau*) Capital of Heves county, N Hungary, in the Eger valley near the Mátra Mountains, 105 km/66 mi NE· of Budapest; population (1993) 63,400. Bull's Blood wine is produced here. The town is an agricultural trading centre, and a tourist base for mountain activities.

Egmont, Mount (Maori *Taranaki*) Symmetrical extinct volcano in North Island, New Zealand, situated S of New Plymouth; it is 2,517 m/8,260 ft high and lies within Mount Egmont National Park.

Ehrenbreitstein Suburb of ◊Koblenz in North Rhine–Westphalia, Germany, on the right bank of the river Rhine. Its fortress, situated on a rock 120 m/400 ft above the river, is believed to date from the time of the Roman emperor Julian (360–363).

Eider River in N Germany forming the boundary between the regions of Schleswig and Holstein. Its importance declined with the opening of the ◊Kiel Canal, with which it is connected.

Eiffel Tower Iron structure in Paris, France, just over 300 m/ 984 ft high. It was designed by Gustave Eiffel to demonstrate French engineering skills, and was erected 1887–89 in the Champ-de-Mars, on the S bank of the river Seine.

Eiger Mountain peak in the Swiss ◊Alps (3,970 m/13,030 ft), first climbed by Barrington 1858.

Eilat Alternative spelling of ◊Elat, a port in Israel.

Einbeck Town in Lower Saxony, Germany, 64 km/40 mi S of Hannover; population (1994) 29,400. Carpet manufacture and brewing are the town's main industries. Einbeck was a member of the Hanseatic League trade federation, and was the seat of the princes of Grubenhagen. The town has medieval walls and watchtowers and a number of historic buildings.

Eindhoven City in North Brabant province, the Netherlands, on the river Dommel; population (1995) 196,100. Industries include electrical and electronic equipment; Philips Electronics have their headquarters here.

Einsiedeln Commune in the canton of Schwyz, Switzerland, 33 km/21 mi SE of Zürich; population (1995) 11,700. Pilgrims visit a Benedictine abbey founded about 934 on the site of the cell of St Meinrad, who was murdered in 861.

Eire Former name (1937–48) of Southern Ireland, now the Republic of Ireland. In Gaelic the name Eire is also used to refer to the whole of Ireland.

Eisenach Industrial town (pottery, vehicles, machinery) in the state of Thuringia, Germany; population (1989 est) 48,800. Martin Luther made the first translation of the Bible into German in Wartburg Castle and the composer J S Bach was born here.

Eisenerz (German 'iron ore') Town in the Austrian province of ◊Styria, 26 km/16 mi NW of Donawitz-Leoben.

It is a mining town at the foot of the Erzberg (height 1,533 m/5,029 ft), with the largest opencast iron-ore mine in continental Europe. Mineral extraction has taken place here since the Iron Age.

Eisenhower, Mount Rocky Mountain peak in Alberta, Canada, included in Banff National Park; it is 2,862 m/9,390 ft.

Eisenstadt (Hungarian *Kishmarton*) Capital of the Austrian province of ◊Burgenland, 44 km/28 mi SE of Vienna, near the Neusiedlersee; population (1995) 12,000. Eisenstadt has a great castle, seat of the Esterházy de Galantha princes. The composer Joseph Haydn, who was *Kapellmeister* to the Esterházy family, lived in the town 1760–90. Eisenstadt is also the centre of a wine-growing region.

Ekaterinodar Pre-revolutionary name of Krasnodar, an industrial town in the Russian Federation.

Ekaterinoslav Pre-revolutionary name of ◊Dnipropetrovsk, the centre of an industrial region in the Ukraine.

El Aaiún Arabic name of ◊Laâyoune.

Elat or *Eilat* Port at the head of the Gulf of Aqaba, Israel's only outlet to the Red Sea; population (1994) 35,700. Founded 1948, on the site of the Biblical Elath, it is linked by road with Beersheba. There are copper mines and granite quarries nearby, and a major geophysical observatory, opened 1968, is 16 km/10 mi to the N.

Elba Island in the Mediterranean Sea, 10 km/6 mi off the W coast of Italy; area 223 sq km/86 sq mi; population (1981) 35,000. Iron ore is exported from the island's capital, Portoferraio, to the Italian mainland, and there is a fishing industry. The small uninhabited island of *Monte Cristo*, 40 km/25 mi to the S, supplied the title of Alexandre Dumas's hero in his historical romance *The Count of Monte Cristo* 1844. Elba was Napoleon's place of exile 1814–15.

Elbasan Town in Albania, capital of Elbasan district, on the right bank of the river Shkumbi; population (1990) 83,300. It is the centre of a fertile agricultural region and its industries include olive oil processing, soapmaking, and timber milling. It is a railway terminus. There is an oil refinery at Cerrik, to the SW.

Elbe One of the principal rivers of Germany, 1,166 km/725 mi long, rising on the S slopes of the Riesengebirge, Czech Republic, and flowing NW across the German plain to the North Sea.

El Bega'a Alternative name for the Lebanese government of ◊Bekaa.

Elberfeld German industrial town, merged with ◊Wuppertal 1929.

Elbeuf French town in the *département* of Seine-Maritime, on the river Seine; population (1990) 55,000. It has been one of the chief centres of the woollen industry in France since the 13th century. Elbeuf also has important car and chemical industries. The town was severely damaged during World War II.

Elbing German name for Elblag, a town and a river in Poland.

Elblag (German *Elbing*) River port in Gdańsk province, Poland, on the river Elblag near the SW end of the Vistula lagoon, 50 km/31 mi SE of Gdańsk; population (1990) 126,000. Industries include shipbuilding, engineering, and electrical products. Founded in the 13th century by settlers from Bremen and Lübeck, Elblâg became a member of the medieval Hanseatic League merchant confederation, trading with England. It belonged to Poland 1466–1772 and to German East Prussia until 1945.

Elbrus or *Elbruz* Highest mountain (5,642 m/18,510 ft) on the continent of Europe, in the Caucasus Mountains, Georgia.

Elburz Mountains Volcanic mountain range in NW Iran, close to the S shore of the Caspian Sea; the highest point is Mount Damavand at 5,670 m/18,602 ft.

Elche Town in the province of ◊Alicante, E Spain; population (1991) 192,500. Its large forest of palm trees, irrigated by canals, provides all Catholics in Spain with leaves for Palm Sunday. A unique religious mystery play is performed here each year on 14–15 Aug. Products include leather goods.

Elephanta Island in Bombay harbour, Maharashtra, India, some 8 km/5 mi from Bombay. The Temple Caves (6th century), cut out of solid rock, have sculptures of many Hindu deities 450–740. There was formerly a large stone elephant near the island's landing place.

El Faiyûm City in N Egypt, 90 km/56 mi SW of Cairo; population (1991) 244,000. It was a centre of prehistoric culture; the crocodile god Sobek was worshipped nearby, and realistic mummy portraits dating from the 1st–4th centuries AD were found in the area.

El Ferrol (full name *El Ferrol del Caudillo*) City and port in La Coruña province, on the NW coast of Spain; population (1991) 84,500. It is a naval base and has a deep, sheltered harbour and shipbuilding industries. It is the birthplace of the Spanish dictator Francisco Franco.

Elgin Administrative headquarters of Moray unitary authority, NE Scotland, on the river Lossie 8 km/5 mi S of its port of Lossiemouth on the S shore of the Moray Firth; population (1991) 19,000. There are sawmills and whisky distilleries. Gordonstoun public school is nearby. Elgin Cathedral, founded 1224, was destroyed 1390. The 13th-century Bishop's Palace at Spynie was restored 1994.

Elgin City in NE Illinois, USA, NW of Chicago, on the Fox River; population (1992) 81,100. Industries include electrical machinery and dairy products. Elgin was founded 1835.

Elis (Greek *Ilia*) Department of Greece and ancient country of the ◊Peloponnese region; bounded on the N by Achaea, on the E by Arcadia, on the S by Messenia, and on the W by the Ionian Sea; area 2,618 sq km/1,035 sq mi; population (1993) 181,700. The capital is Pyrgos.

Elisabethville Former name of ◊Lubumbashi, a town in the Democratic Republic of Congo (formerly Zaire).

Elizabeth City in NE New Jersey, USA; population (1992) 107,900. Established 1664, it was the first English settlement in New Jersey. It has car, sewing-machine, and tool factories; oil refineries; and chemical works.

Elizavetpol Former name of ◊Gyandzha, an industrial town in Azerbaijan.

El Khârga or *Kharijah* Oasis in the Western Desert of Egypt, known to the Romans, and from 1960 headquarters of the New Valley irrigation project. An area twice the size of Italy is watered from natural underground reservoirs.

Elkhart City in N Indiana, USA, E of South Bend, where the Elkhart River meets the St Joseph River; population (1990) 43,600. Its factories produce mobile homes, firefighting apparatus, recreational vehicles, pharmaceuticals, and musical instruments. Elkhart was laid out 1832.

Ellesmere Second largest island of the Canadian Arctic archipelago, Northwest Territories; area 212,687 sq km/82,097 sq mi. It is for the most part barren or glacier-covered.

Ellesmere Port Oil port and industrial town (petroleum products, cars, chemicals, car engines, paper, engineering) in Cheshire, England, on the river Mersey and the Manchester Ship Canal; population (1988 est) 79,700.

Ellice Islands Former name of Tuvalu, a group of islands in the W Pacific Ocean.

Ellis Island Island in New York Harbor, USA; area 11 hectares/27 acres. A former reception centre for steerage-class immigrants during the immigration waves between 1892 and 1943 (12 million people passed through it in the years 1892–1924), it was later used as a detention centre for non-residents without documentation, or for those who were being deported. It is a National Historic Site (1964) and has the Museum of Immigration (1989). In 1997, Ellis Island was listed as one of America's 11 Most Endangered Historic Places.

Ellwangen Town in Baden-Württemberg, Germany, on the river Jagst, 70 km/43 mi NE of Stuttgart; population (1994) 28,800. Batteries are manufactured here, and it is a garrison town. Ellwangen has a 12th-century Romanesque church with three towers, and on a hill overlooking the town is a medieval castle.

Elmira City in S central New York, USA, on the Chemung River, W of Binghamton, just below the Finger Lakes region; seat of Chemung County; population (1990) 33,700. It is the processing and marketing centre for the area's dairy and poultry farms. Other industries include business machinery, machine parts, aeroplanes, and fire engines. Elmira was settled 1788 and renamed 1828.

Elmshorn City in Schleswig-Holstein, Germany, 30 km/19 mi NW of Hamburg; population (1994) 46,600. There is agricultural processing, woodworking, and the production of fertilizers.

El Obeid Capital of Kordofan province, Sudan; population (1983) 140,000. Linked by rail with Khartoum, it is a market for cattle, gum arabic, and durra (Indian millet).

El Paso City in Texas, USA, at the base of the Franklin Mountains, on the Rio Grande, opposite the Mexican city of Ciudad Juárez; population (1992) 543,800. It is the centre of an agricultural and cattle-raising area, and there are electronics, food processing, packing, and leather industries, as well as oil refineries and industries based on local iron and copper mines. There are several military installations in the area.

Elsinore English form of ◊Helsingør, a port on the NE coast of Denmark.

Elster Name of two rivers in Germany. The *Weisse Elster* (White Elster) rises in the Czech Republic and, after a few kilometres, enters Germany to flow through Plauen, Gera, and Leipzig; length 193 km/121 mi. It joins the river Saale S of Halle.

The *Schwarze Elster* (Black Elster) flows 188 km/117 mi in a northwesterly direction to join the ◊Elbe near Wittenberg.

Ely City in Cambridgeshire, England, on the Great Ouse River 24 km/15 mi NE of Cambridge; population (1991) 10,300. Industries include sugar beet, paper, pottery, chemicals, plastics, and engineering. The 11th-century cathedral is one of the largest in England.

Elyria City in N Ohio, USA, on the Black River, W of Cleveland; seat of Lorain County; population (1992) 57,300. Industries include tools, electric motors, chromium hardware, chemicals, and motor vehicle parts. It was first settled 1817.

Emba River in Kazakhstan, 612 km/380 mi long, draining into the N part of the Caspian Sea.

Emden Port in Lower Saxony, Germany, at the mouth of the river Ems; population (1984) 51,000. It is a fishing port and an export outlet for the river ◊Ruhr, with which it is connected by the Dortmund–Ems Canal. There are oil refineries here.

Emi Koussi Highest point of the Tibesti massif in N Chad, rising to 3,415 m/11,204 ft.

Emilia-Romagna Region of N central Italy including much of the Po Valley; area 22,123 sq km/8,542 sq mi; population (1995) 3,922,600. The capital is Bologna; other towns include Reggio, Rimini, Parma, Ferrara, and Ravenna. Agricultural produce includes fruit, wine, sugar beet, beef, and dairy products; oil and natural gas resources have been developed in the Po Valley.

Emmental District in the valley of the Emme River, Berne, Switzerland, where a hard cheese of the same name has been made since the mid-15th century. The main town in Emmental is Langnau.

Emmerich City in North Rhine–Westphalia, Germany, 79 km/49 mi NW of Düsseldorf, on the right bank of the river Rhine close to the Dutch frontier; population (1994) 29,100. Food, chemicals, and machinery are manufactured. There is a long suspension bridge over the Rhine at Emmerich.

Ems Short form of ◊Bad Ems, a town in Germany.

Ems River in N Germany. It rises in the Teutoburger Wald, and flows across North Rhine–Westphalia and Lower Saxony to an inlet of the North Sea known as the Dollart.

Emsdetten Town in North Rhine–Westphalia, Germany, near the river Ems, 30 km/19 mi SW of Osnabrück; population (1994) 33,400. It is a centre for the manufacture of textiles. Emsdetten was formerly in the Prussian province of Westphalia.

Enewetak Atoll Atoll in the Marshall Islands, in the central Pacific Ocean; population (1988) 715. It was taken from Japan by the USA 1944, which made the island a naval base; 43 atomic tests were conducted there from 1947. The inhabitants were resettled at Ujelang, but insisted on returning home 1980. Despite the clearance of nuclear debris and radioactive soil to the islet of Runit, high radiation levels persisted.

Enfield Outer borough of NE Greater London. It includes the districts of ◊Edmonton and Southgate
features the royal hunting ground of Enfield Chase partly survives in the 'green belt'; early 17th-century Forty Hall; Lea Valley Regional Park, opened 1967
industries engineering (the Royal Small Arms factory, which closed 1989, produced the Enfield rifle), textiles, furniture, cement, electronics, metal, and plastic products
population (1991) 257,400.

Engadine Upper valley of the river Inn in Switzerland, a winter sports resort.

England Largest division of the United Kingdom.
area 130,357 sq km/50,318 sq mi
capital London
towns and cities Birmingham, Cambridge, Coventry, Leeds, Leicester, Manchester, Newcastle upon Tyne, Nottingham, Oxford, Sheffield, York; ports: Bristol, Dover, Felixstowe, Harwich, Liverpool, Portsmouth, Southampton
features variability of climate and diversity of scenery; among European countries, only the Netherlands is more densely populated
exports agricultural (cereals, rape, sugar beet, potatoes); meat and meat products; electronic (software) and telecommunications equipment (main centres Berkshire and Cambridge); scientific instruments; textiles and fashion goods; North Sea oil and gas, petrochemicals, pharmaceuticals, fertilizers; beer; china clay, pottery, porcelain, and glass; film and television programmes, and sound recordings. Tourism is important. There are worldwide banking and insurance interests
currency pound sterling
population (1993 est) 48,500,000
language English, with more than 100 minority languages
religion Christian, with the Church of England as the established church, 31,500,000, and various Protestant groups, of which the largest is the Methodist 1,400,000; Roman Catholic about 5,000,000; Muslim 900,000; Jewish 410,000; Sikh 175,000; Hindu 140,000
government returns 529 members to Parliament; a mixture of 2-tier and unitary local authorities, with 36 counties, six metropolitan counties (non-elected), and 27 unitary authorities; 19 more unitary authorities will be created in April 1998.

For *government* and *history*, see United Kingdom.

English Channel Stretch of water between England and France, leading in the W to the Atlantic Ocean, and in the E via the Strait of Dover to the North Sea; it is also known as *La Manche* (French 'the sleeve') from its shape. The ◊Channel Tunnel, opened 1994, runs between Folkestone, Kent, and Sangatte, W of Calais.

Enid City in N central Oklahoma, USA, N of Oklahoma City, seat of Garfield County; population (1990) 45,300. It is a processing and marketing centre for the surrounding region's poultry, cattle, dairy farms, and oil wells. Enid was founded 1893, when land in the Cherokee Strip region, which was originally put aside for Native American peoples, was opened to settlement by others.

Enkhuizen Town in the province of North Holland, the Netherlands, 45 km/28 mi NE of Amsterdam; population (1996) 16,200. Together with Hoorn, Enkhuizen was a thriving port in the 17th century. It has an open-air museum of reconstructed old buildings portraying life in former times on the ◊Zuider Zee.

Enna Province of Italy in central ◊Sicily; capital Enna (population (1990) 29,400); area 2,561 sq km/989 sq mi; population (1992) 186,400.

Ennis County town of County Clare, Republic of Ireland, on the river Fergus, 32 km/20 mi NW of Limerick; population (1981) 15,000. There are distilleries, flour mills, and furniture manufacturing.

Enniskillen County town of Fermanagh, Northern Ireland, between Upper and Lower Lough Erne; population (1991) 11,400. There is some light industry (engineering, food processing) and it has been designated for further industrial growth. A bomb exploded here at a Remembrance Day service Nov 1987, causing many casualties.

Enns River in Austria, a tributary of the ◊Danube; length 255 km/158 mi. The Enns rises S of Radstadt, 56 km/35 mi SE of Salzburg, and flows into the Danube near the town of Enns in Upper Austria. Its chief tributary is the Steier.

Enns Town in the province of Upper Austria, situated 17 km/10 mi SE of Linz, on the river Enns close to where it joins the Danube. A large hydroelectric plant supplies power to the steel mills at Linz. Enns was a prosperous commercial town in the Middle Ages.

Enschede Textile manufacturing centre in the province of Overijssel, the Netherlands; population (1995) 147,600, urban area of *Enschede-Hengelo* 250,000.

Entebbe City in Uganda, on the NW shore of Lake Victoria, 20 km/12 mi SW of Kampala, the capital; 1,136 m/ 3,728 ft above sea level; population (1991) 41,600. Founded 1893, it was the administrative centre of Uganda 1894–1962.

Enugu City in Nigeria, capital of Anambra state; population (1992 est) 286,100. It is a coal-mining centre, with steel and cement works, and is linked by rail with Port Harcourt.

Eperjes Hungarian name for Prešov, a town in the Slovak Republic.

Épernay Town in Marne *département*, Champagne-Ardenne region, France; population (1990) 27,700. Together with Reims, it is the centre of the champagne industry. Corks, casks, and bottles are manufactured alongside the production and storage of champagne.

Épinal Capital of Vosges *département*, on the river Moselle, France; population (1990) 39,500. A cotton-textile centre, it dates from the 10th century.

Epirus (Greek *Ipiros*, 'mainland') Region of NW Greece; area 9,200 sq km/3,551 sq mi; population (1991) 339,200. Its capital is Yannina, and it consists of the provinces (nomes) of Arta, Thesprotia, Yannina, and Preveza. There is livestock farming. It was part of an ancient Greek region by the same name: the N part was in Albania, the remainder in NW Greece.

Epping Forest Forest in Essex, SE England. Once part of the ancient forest of Waltham, it originally covered the whole of Essex.

Epsom Town in Surrey, England; population (with Ewell) (1991) 64,400. In the 17th century it was a spa producing Epsom salts. There is a racecourse, where the Derby and the Oaks horse races are held. The site of Henry VIII's palace of Nonsuch was excavated 1959.

Epupa Falls Waterfall on the river Cunene, on the Angola–Namibia border.

Erebus, Mount The world's southernmost active volcano, 3,794 m/12,452 ft high, on Ross Island, Antarctica.

Erfurt City in Germany on the river Gera, capital of the state of Thuringia; population (1993) 202,100. It is in a rich horticultural area, and its industries include textiles, typewriters, and electrical goods.

Erie City and port on the Pennsylvania bank of Lake Erie, USA; population (1992) 109,300. It has heavy industries and a trade in iron, grain, and freshwater fish. A French fort was built on the site 1753, and a permanent settlement was laid out 1795.

Erie Canal Canal in New York, USA, which connects Lake Erie N of Buffalo with the Hudson River at Albany and Troy; it passes through Utica, Syracuse, and Rochester. It is 45 m/148 ft broad and has an average depth of 3.6 m/12 ft. The canal was begun in 1817 and completed in 1825 at a cost of over $7 million. Together with the Champlain, Oswego, and Cayuga–Seneca canals, it constitutes the New York State Barge Canal System, 845 km/525 mi in length.

Erie, Lake Fourth largest of the Great Lakes of North America, connected to Lake Ontario by the Niagara River and bypassed by the Welland Canal; area 25,657 sq km/9,906 sq mi. It is an important component of the St Lawrence Seaway.

Erivan Alternative transliteration of ◊Yerevan, the capital of Armenia.

Erlangen Industrial city in Bavaria, Germany; population (1991) 102,400. Products include electrical equipment, textiles, glass, and beer.

Erlau German name for ◊Eger, a town in Hungary.

Ermoupolis Greek name for ◊Hermoupolis, a town in Greece.

Erzgebirge (German 'ore mountains') Mountain range on the border between Germany and the Czech Republic, where the rare metals uranium, cobalt, bismuth, arsenic, and antimony are mined. Some 145 km/90 mi long, its highest summit is Mount Klinovec (Keilberg), 1,244 m/4,080 ft, in the Czech Republic. In 1991, following the reunification of Germany, many uranium mines were closed and plans to clean up the heavily polluted region were formulated.

Erzurum Capital of Erzurum province, NE Turkey; population (1990) 297,500. It is a centre of agricultural trade and mining, and has a military base.

Esbjerg Port of Ribe county, Denmark, on the W coast of Jutland; population (1993) 82,300. It is the terminus of links with Sweden and the UK, and is a base for Danish North Sea oil exploration.

Esch (or *Esch-sur-Alzette*) Town in the Grand Duchy of Luxembourg, 17 km/11 mi SW of the city of Luxembourg; population (1991) 24,000. An important iron and steel industry is centred on Esch and towns in the surrounding canton.

Eschwege City in Hessen, Germany, on the river Werra, 40 km/25 mi SE of Kassel; population (1994) 22,800. Its location close to the border with the former country of East Germany led to the creation of several new industries during the 1950s, such as metallurgy and textiles.

Eschweiler City in North Rhine–Westphalia, Germany, 15 km/9 mi N of Aachen; population (1994) 56,200. It has opencast brown coal (lignite) mines, power stations, and plants producing machinery, sugar, food, and textiles.

Esfahan or *Isfahan* Industrial city (steel, textiles, carpets) in central Iran; population (1991) 1,127,000. It was the ancient capital (1598–1722) of Abbas I, and its features include the Great Square, Grand Mosque, and Hall of Forty Pillars.

Eskilstuna Town W of Stockholm, Sweden; population (1992) 89,600. It has iron foundries and steel and armament works; it was known in the 17th century for its swords and cutlery.

Eskisehir City in Turkey, 200 km/125 mi W of Ankara; population (1990) 415,800. Products include meerschaum, chromium, magnesite, cotton goods, tiles, and aircraft.

Espoo (Swedish *Esbo*) Town in S Uusimaa province of Finland, just W of Helsinki. Formerly a rural district, Espoo became a town in 1963; as a dormitory town for the capital, it saw rapid population growth and became the second largest city in Finland. The ancient coastal road from Turku to Vyborg runs through Espoo.

Esquipulas Pilgrimage city in Chiquimula department, SE Guatemala; seat of the 'Black Christ', which is a symbol of peace throughout Central America. In May 1986 five Central American presidents met here to discuss a plan for peace in the region.

Essen City in North Rhine–Westphalia, Germany; population (1993) 624,600. It is the administrative centre of the Ruhr region, situated between the rivers Emscher and Ruhr, and has textile, chemical, and electrical industries. Its 9th–14th-century minster is one of the oldest churches in Germany.

Essequibo Longest river in Guyana, South America, rising in the Guiana Highlands of S Guyana; length 1,014 km/630 mi. Part of the district of Essequibo, which lies to the W of the river, is claimed by Venezuela.

Essex County of SE England; Southend and Thurrock will become unitary authorities in April 1998
area 3,670 sq km/1,417 sq mi
towns and cities Chelmsford (administrative headquaters), Colchester; ports: Harwich, Tilbury; resorts: Southend-on-Sea, Clacton
features former royal hunting ground of Epping Forest (controlled from 1882 by the City of London); the marshy coastal headland of the Naze; since 1111 at Great Dunmow the Dunmow flitch (side of cured pork) can be claimed every four years by any couple proving to a jury they have not regretted their marriage within the year (winners are few); Stansted, London's third airport; new Roman Catholic cathedral at Brentwood (designed by Quinlan Terry) dedicated 1991
industries dairy products, cereals, fruit, sugar beet, oysters, cars
population (1994) 1,560,300.

Esslingen City in Baden-Württemberg, Germany, 16 km/10 mi SE of Stuttgart, on the river Neckar; population (1994) 489,500. Esslingen has electrical, automotive engineering, textile, and food industries. Esslingen was founded in the 8th century. There are several old churches, including the Frauenkirche 1321–1516, a former *Rathaus* (town hall) with a Renaissance façade, and a Baroque *Rathaus*.

Essonne *Département* in the ◊Ile-de-France region of France, situated to the S of Paris; area 1,811 sq km/699 sq mi; population (1990) 1,085,000. The rivers Orge and Essonne flow through the region, both tributaries of the Seine. Considerable woodland remains and agriculture is important. The *département* is crossed by major communications axes and now functions as an outer suburb for Paris. Multinational companies producing electronic and electrical equipment are located here. Chief towns are Evry (the capital), Corbeil-Essonnes, and Etampes.

Estoril Fashionable resort on the coast 20 km/13 mi W of Lisbon, Portugal; population (1981) 16,000. There is a Grand Prix motor-racing circuit.

Esztergom City on the Danube, NW of Budapest, Hungary; population about 32,000. It was the birthplace of St Stephen and the former ecclesiastical capital of Hungary, with a fine cathedral.

Etaples Fishing port and seaside resort on the Canche estuary, Pas de Calais *département*, France; population (1985) 11,500. During World War I it was a British base and hospital centre; a large military cemetery was also established which eventually contained some 12,000 graves.

Etna Volcano on the E coast of Sicily, 3,323 m/10,906 ft, the highest in Europe. About 90 eruptions have been recorded since 1800 BC, yet because of the rich soil, the cultivated zone on the lower slopes is densely populated, including the coastal town of Catania. The most recent eruption was in Dec 1985.

Eton Town in Berkshire, England, on the N bank of the river Thames, opposite Windsor; population (1991) 2,000. *Eton College* is one of the UK's oldest, largest, and most prestigious public (private and fee-paying) schools. It was founded 1440.

Euboea (Greek *Evvoia*) Mountainous island off the E coast of Greece, in the Aegean Sea; area 3,755 sq km/1,450 sq mi; about 177 km/110 mi long; population (1991) 209,100. Mount Delphi reaches 1,743 m/5,721 ft. The chief town, Khalkis, is connected by a bridge to the mainland.

Eugene City in W central Oregon, USA, S of Portland, on the Willamette River; population (1992) 116,000. It is a processing and shipping centre for agricultural products from the surrounding region; wood products are also manufactured. Eugene was settled 1846 and laid out 1852. It developed as an agricultural and lumbering centre. The University of Oregon (1872) is here.

Eupen Town in the province of ◊Liège, Belgium, 14 km/9 mi S of the German border city of Aachen. Eupen is predominantly German-speaking, having been part of Prussia (and thereafter the German Empire) from the early 19th century to the end of World War I.

Eupen-et-Malmédy Region of Belgium around the towns of Eupen and Malmédy. It was Prussian from 1814 until it became Belgian 1920 after a plebiscite; there was fierce fighting here in the German Ardennes offensive Dec 1944.

Euphrates (Arabic *Furat*) River, rising in E Turkey, flowing through Syria and Iraq and joining the river Tigris above Basra to form the river Shatt-al-Arab, at the head of the Persian/Arabian Gulf; 2,736 km/1,700 mi in length. The ancient cities of Babylon, Eridu, and Ur were situated along its course.

Eure River rising in Orne *département*, France, and flowing SE, then N, to the river Seine; length 115 km/70 mi. Chartres is on its banks. It gives its name to two *départements*, Eure and Eure-et-Loire.

Eure *Département* in the ◊Haute-Normandie region of France; area 6,004 sq km/2,318 sq mi; population (1990) 259,300. The territory of Eure is broken up by its rivers – the lower Seine and its tributaries Eure, Andelle, and Epte, and the Risle – into wooded plateaux. Its chief products are wheat, flax, and beetroot. Cattle and horses of pure Normandy stock are bred here. Industries include textiles and metallurgy. The principal town is Evreux.

Eure-et-Loir *Département* in the ◊Centre region of France; area 5,875 sq km/2,268 sq mi; population (1990) 396,600. The region lies SE of the *département* of Eure. The E part is a gently undulating plain, called La Beauce; the W, called the

Perche, is more diverse, with hills, forests, and numerous rivers. The chief river in the N is the Eure, in the S are the Loir and the Huisne. None is navigable except the Eure for a short distance. The Perche district has a slightly colder climate than La Beauce. Wheat and oats are the principal crops and apples are grown. Textiles and boots are manufactured and there are foundries. The principal towns are ◊Chartres (the capital), Dreux, Châteaudun, and Nogent-le-Rotrou.

Europe The second-smallest continent, occupying 8% of the Earth's surface

area 10,400,000 sq km/4,000,000 sq mi

largest cities (population over 1.5 million) Athens, Barcelona, Berlin, Birmingham, Bucharest, Budapest, Hamburg, Istanbul, Kharkov, Kiev, Lisbon, London, Madrid, Manchester, Milan, Moscow, Paris, Rome, St Petersburg, Vienna, Warsaw

features Mount Elbrus 5,642 m/18,510 ft in the Caucasus Mountains is the highest peak in Europe; Mont Blanc 4,807 m/15,772 ft is the highest peak in the Alps; lakes (over 5,100 sq km/2,000 sq mi) include Ladoga, Onega, Vånern; rivers (over 800 km/500 mi) include the Volga, Danube, Dnieper, Ural, Don, Pechora, Dniester, Rhine, Loire, Tagus, Ebro, Oder, Prut, Rhône

physical conventionally occupying that part of Eurasia to the W of the Ural Mountains, N of the Caucasus Mountains, and N of the Sea of Marmara, Europe lies entirely in the N hemisphere between 36° N and the Arctic Ocean. About two-thirds of the continent is a great plain which covers the whole of European Russia and spreads westwards through Poland to the Low Countries and the Bay of Biscay. To the N lie the Scandinavian highlands, rising to 2,472 m/8,110 ft at Glittertind in the Jotenheim range of Norway. To the S, a series of mountain ranges stretch E–W (Caucasus, Balkans, Carpathians, Apennines, Alps, Pyrenees, and Sierra Nevada). The most westerly point of the mainland is Cape Roca in Portugal; the most southerly location is Tarifa Point in Spain; the most northerly point on the mainland is Nordkynn in Norway.

Europoort Deep-sea port extension of ◊Rotterdam, the Netherlands. It is situated some 25 km/16 mi W of the city and covers more than 35 sq km/13.5 sq mi. Europoort contains facilities for handling bulk goods and crude oil imports, and was completed in 1968.

Euskal Herria Basque name for the ◊Basque Country.

Euskirchen City in North Rhine–Westphalia, Germany, 25 km/15 mi SW of Bonn; population (1994) 180,400. There are electrical and mechanical engineering factories, as well as glass and sugar manufacturers.

Evanston City on the shores of Lake Michigan, NE Illinois, USA, N of Chicago; population (1994) 73,400. Industries include paper products and chemicals.

Evansville Industrial city and port in SW Indiana, USA, on the Ohio River; population (1992) 127,600. Industries include pharmaceuticals and plastics. The community, which dates from 1812, grew after the 1853 completion of the Wabash and Erie canal linking the Ohio at Evansville with Lake Erie.

Everest, Mount (Chinese *Qomolungma* 'goddess mother of the snows/world'; Nepalese; *Sagarmatha* 'goddess of the universe') The world's highest mountain above sea level, in the Himalayas, on the China–Nepal frontier; height 8,848 m/29,029 ft. It was first climbed by New Zealand mountaineer Edmund Hillary and Sherpa Tenzing Norgay 1953. The expedition was led by Col John Hunt. More than 360 climbers have reached the summit; over 100 have died during the ascent.

Everett City and port in Washington, NW USA, 40 km/25 mi N of Seattle on Puget Sound; population (1992) 73,800. It has a fine harbour, beautiful scenery, and timber mills. A Boeing aircraft plant is nearby.

Everglades Area of swamps, marsh, and lakes in S Florida, USA; area 7,000 sq km/2,700 sq mi. Formed by overflow of Lake Okeechobee after heavy rains, it is one of the wildest areas in the USA, with distinctive plant and animal life. The only human residents are several hundred Seminole, a Native American people. A national park covers the S tip of the Everglades.

Evesham Town in Hereford and Worcester, England, on the river Avon SE of Worcester; population (1990 est) 18,000. Fruit and vegetables are grown in the fertile *Vale of Evesham*. In the Battle of Evesham, 4 Aug 1265, during the Barons' Wars, Edward, Prince of Wales, defeated Simon de Montfort, who was killed.

Evreux Capital of Eure *département*, situated in the Iton River valley, in NW France; population (1990) 51,500. It produces pharmaceuticals, rubber, and textiles; there are also printing and electronic companies.

Evvoia Greek name for the island of ◊Euboea.

Exeter City, administrative headquarters of Devon, England, on the river Exe; population (1994 est) 107,000. It was founded by the Romans as *Isca Dumnoniorum* and has medieval, Georgian, and Regency architecture, including a cathedral (1280–1369) and a market centre. Agricultural machinery, pharmaceuticals, textiles, leather goods, and metal products are manufactured here.

Exmoor Moorland in Devon and Somerset, England, forming (with the coast from Minehead to Combe Martin) a National Park since 1954. It includes Dunkery Beacon, 520 m/1,707 ft, and the Doone Valley.

Exmouth Resort town (sailing centre) and port in Devon, SW England, at the mouth of the river Exe; population (1991) 28,400. There are engineering industries. The port was permanently closed to commercial vessels 1989.

Extremadura Autonomous region of W Spain including the provinces of Badajoz and Cáceres; area 41,600 sq km/16,058 sq mi; population (1991) 1,061,900. Irrigated land is used for growing wheat; the remainder is either oak forest or used for pig or sheep grazing.

Eyre, Lake Australia's largest lake, in central South Australia, which frequently runs dry, becoming a salt marsh in dry seasons; area up to 9,000 sq km/3,500 sq mi. It is the continent's lowest point, 16 m/52 ft below sea level.

Eyre Peninsula Peninsula in South Australia, which includes the iron and steel city of Whyalla. Over 50% of the iron used in Australia's steel industry is mined at Iron Knob; the only seal colony on mainland Australia is at Point Labatt.

Faenza City on the river Lamone in Ravenna province, Emilia-Romagna, Italy; population (1989 est) 54,100. It has many medieval remains, including the 15th-century walls. It gave its name to faience pottery, tin-glazed earthenware first produced here.

Faeroe Islands or *Faeroes* Alternative spelling of the ◊Faroe Islands, in the N Atlantic.

Fagatogo Seat of government of American ◊Samoa, situated on Pago Pago Harbour, Tutuila Island; population (1980) 30,124 (no current population figures available).

Fairbanks Town in central Alaska, situated on the Chena Slough, a tributary of the Tanana River; population (1990) 30,800. Founded 1902, it became a gold-mining and fur-trading centre and the terminus of the Alaska Railroad and the Pan-American Highway.

Fairfield City in W central California, USA, SW of Sacramento; seat of Solano County; population (1992) 82,200. It is a trading centre for the area's fruits, grains, and dairy products. It was founded 1859.

Faisalabad City in Punjab province, Pakistan, 120 km/ 75 mi W of Lahore; population (1981) 1,092,000. It trades in grain, cotton, and textiles.

Faizabad City in Uttar Pradesh, N India; population (1991) 178,000. It lies at the head of navigation of the river Ghaghara and has sugar refineries and an agricultural trade.

Falaise Town 32 km/20 mi SE of Caen, in Normandy, France; population (1982) 8,820. It is a market centre, manufacturing cotton and leather goods and trading in livestock and cheese. The 12th–13th-century castle was that of the first dukes of Normandy, and William the Conqueror was born here 1027.

Falkirk Unitary authority in central Scotland created 1996 from part of the former Central region; population (1996) 142,500; area 294 sq km/114 sq mi; administrative headquarters Falkirk. There are chemical and petroleum industries at the port of Grangemouth. Other industries include the manufacture of buses, bookbinding, paper-making, soft drinks, toffees, and castings. The Scottish Railway Preservation Society is at Bo'ness.

Falkirk Administrative headquarters of Falkirk unitary authority, Scotland, 37 km/23 mi W of Edinburgh; population (1991) 35,600. A former iron-founding centre, Falkirk has brewing, distilling, tanning, chemical, printing, aluminium-rolling, and bus-building industries. Edward I defeated the Scots here 1298, and Bonnie Prince Charlie defeated the English army here 1746.

Falkland Islands (Argentine *Islas Malvinas*) British crown colony in the S Atlantic, 300 miles E of the Straits of Magellan

area 12,173 sq km/4,700 sq mi, made up of two main islands: East Falkland 6,760 sq km/2,610 sq mi, and West Falkland 5,413 sq km/2,090 sq mi

capital Stanley; new port facilities opened 1984, Mount Pleasant airport 1985

features in addition to the two main islands, there are about 200 small islands, all with wild scenery and rich bird life; Mount Usborne (705 m/2,312 ft); moorland

industries wool, alginates (used as dyes and as a food additive) from seaweed beds, fishing (especially squid)

population (1991) 2,120.

Falkland Islands

Fall River City and port in Massachusetts; population (1992) 91,100. It stands at the mouth of the Taunton River, over the Little Fall River, which gave it its name. Textiles and clothing, rubber, paper, and plastics are among the goods produced. The city was founded 1656 and was one of the nation's most important textile-mill centres in the 19th century.

Falmouth Port on the S coast of Cornwall, England, on the estuary of the river Fal; population (1981) 18,500. There are ship-repairing and marine engineering industries.

Falster Danish island off the S coast of Sjaelland in the Baltic Sea; area 518 sq km/200 sq mi; part of the county of Storstrøm. Falster is 48 km/20 mi long and 3–20 km/2–12 mi wide. It is joined to Sjaelland and Lolland, an island to the W, by bridges. The soil is fertile, the climate milder and sunnier than in the rest of Denmark, and the white sandy beaches attract holidaymakers. The principal town is Nyköbing.

Falun Capital of Kopparberg county in S Sweden, on Lake Runn; population (1995) 55,100. It grew up around a copper mine established in the 13th century. The main industries are now chemical production and timber processing. Falun is an international skiing centre.

Famagusta Seaport on the E coast of Cyprus, in the Turkish Republic of Northern Cyprus; population (1985)

19,500. It was the chief port of the island until the Turkish invasion 1974.

Fao or *Faw* Oil port on a peninsula at the mouth of the Shatt-al-Arab in Iraq. Iran launched a major offensive against Iraq 1986, capturing Fao for two years.

Farakka Barrage across the river ◊Ganges in India 18 km/ 11 mi from the border with Bangladesh, built by India in 1974 to control the flow of the Ganges and divert water into the Hooghy River to improve its navigability. It is a source of conflict between the two countries, as the Ganges water is needed by Bangladesh.

Far East Geographical term for all Asia E of the Indian subcontinent.

Fareham Town in Hampshire, England, 10 km/6 mi NW of Portsmouth; population (1994 est) 102,000. Bricks, ceramics, chemicals, and rope are made and there is engineering and boat building as well as varied light industries, including scientific instruments and horticulture.

Fargo City in SE North Dakota, USA, across the Red River from Moorhead, Minnesota; seat of Cass County; population (1992) 77,100. The largest city in the state, it is a centre for processing and distributing agricultural products and farm machinery, and meatpacking. Chemicals and building materials are also manufactured. It was founded 1871 by the Northern Pacific Railway, and named after W G Fargo of Wells, Fargo and Company.

Farnborough Town in Hampshire, England, N of Aldershot; population (1991) 52,500. Farnborough is the birthplace of aeronautical research and experimental work is carried out at the Royal Aircraft Establishment. Aeronautical displays are given at the biennial air show. The mansion of Farnborough Hill was occupied by Napoleon III and the Empress Eugénie, and she, her husband, and her son, are buried in a mausoleum at the Roman Catholic church she built.

Farne Islands Rocky island group in the North Sea, off Northumberland, England. The islands are a sanctuary for birds and grey seals.

Farnham Town in Surrey, England, on the river Wey; population (1985 est) 20,900. The parish church was once part of Waverley Abbey (1128), the first Cistercian house in England; Walter Scott named his first novel after the abbey.

Faroe Islands or *Faeroe Islands* or *Faeroes* (Danish *Faerøerne* 'Sheep Islands') Island group (18 out of 22 inhabited) in the N Atlantic, between the Shetland Islands and Iceland, forming an outlying part of Denmark
area 1,399 sq km/540 sq mi; largest islands are Strømø, Østerø, Vagø, Suderø, Sandø, and Bordø
capital Thorshavn on Strømø, population (1992) 14,600
industries fish, crafted goods
currency Danish krone
population (1992 est) 46,800
language Faeroese, Danish
government since 1948 the islands have had full self-government; they do not belong to the European Union
history first settled by Norsemen in the 9th century, the Faroes were a Norwegian province 1380–1709. Their parliament was restored 1852. They withdrew from the European Free Trade Association 1972.

Fars Province of SW Iran, comprising fertile valleys among mountain ranges running NW–SE; population (1991) 3,543,800; area 133,300 sq km/51,487 sq mi. The capital is Shiraz, and there are imposing ruins of Cyrus the Great's city of Parargardae and of Persepolis.

Fayetteville City in the NW corner of Arkansas, USA, SE of Fort Smith; seat of Washington County; population (1990) 42,100. It is an agricultural trading centre. Its main industry is poultry processing; others include lumber, clothing, and tools. The University of Arkansas (1871) is here.

Fayetteville City in S central North Carolina, USA, on the Cape Fear River, S of Durham and Chapel Hill and SW of Raleigh; population (1992) 76,650. Its industries include processing of the area's agricultural products, tools, textiles, and lumber. It was first settled 1739 and later named after the French revolutionary Marquis de Lafayette.

Feather River in California, SW USA; length 128 km/ 80 mi. Rising in the Sierra Nevada, it joins the ◊Sacramento River about 29 km/18 mi N of Sacramento. It is a major supplier for the main California water project. It was one of the rivers that yielded placer gold from alluvial deposits in the California gold rush. It is navigable to Marysville, and supplies water to a rich agricultural area.

Fécamp Seaport and resort of France, NE of Le Havre, in the *département* of Seine Maritime; industries include shipbuilding and fishing; population (1990) 21,100. Benedictine liqueur was first produced here in the early 16th century.

Fehmarn German island in the Baltic Sea, belonging to the *Land* of ◊Schleswig-Holstein and covering an area of 185 sq km/71 sq mi; population (1991) 11,800. Fehmarn is separated from the Danish island of Laaland by the *Fehmarn Belt*. It has mostly grazing land and farmland growing wheat, barley, and rape. The sandy beaches are a holiday destination. The principal town is Burg.

Feldkirch Town in the Austrian province of Vorarlberg, on the river Ill near the Liechtenstein border. It has a castle and a Gothic church. There are textile, timber, and paper industries.

Felixstowe Port and resort opposite Harwich in Suffolk, England, between the Orwell and Deben estuaries; population (1981) 21,000. It is Britain's busiest container port, and also has ferry services to Gothenburg, Rotterdam, and Zeebrugge.

Fens, the Level, low-lying tracts of land in E England, W and S of the Wash, about 115 km/70 mi N–S and 55 km/ 34 mi E–W. They fall within the counties of Lincolnshire, Cambridgeshire, and Norfolk, consisting of a huge area, formerly a bay of the North Sea, but now crossed by numerous drainage canals and forming some of the most productive agricultural land in Britain. The peat portion of the Fens is known as the *Bedford Level*.

Ferghana City in Uzbekistan, in the fertile Ferghana Valley; population (1990) 183,000. It is the capital of the major cotton- and fruit-growing Ferghana region; nearby are petroleum fields. The *Ferghana Valley* is divided between the republics of Uzbekistan, Kyrgyzstan, and Tajikistan, causing interethnic violence among Uzbek, Meskhetian, and Kyrgyz communities. An afforestation project is under way in the valley to prevent sand drifts.

Fermanagh County of Northern Ireland
area 1,680 sq km/648 sq mi
towns and cities Enniskillen (county town), Lisnaskea, Irvinestown
features in the centre is a broad trough of low-lying land, in which lie Upper and Lower Lough Erne
industries mainly agricultural; livestock, potatoes, tweeds, clothing, cotton thread, food processing, light engineering, china, tourism, electronics
population (1991) 50,000.

Fernando Póo Former name (to 1973) of the island of ◊Bioko, part of Equatorial Guinea.

Ferrara Industrial city and archbishopric in Emilia-Romagna region, N Italy, on a branch of the Po delta 52 km/32 mi W of the Adriatic Sea; population (1992) 137,100. There are chemical industries and textile manufacturers. It became a powerful city state in the 13th century.

Ferrara Province of Italy in NE ◊Emilia-Romagna region; capital Ferrara; area 2,631 sq km/1,016 sq mi; population (1992) 359,600.

Ferrol Alternative name for ◊El Ferrol, a city and port in Spain.

Fertile Crescent Region of the Middle East stretching from the Persian Gulf to the Nile Valley, and including the Euphrates and Tigris rivers. It was the birthplace of several ancient empires, including those of Sumer, Assyria, and Persia.

Fertö tó Hungarian name for the ◊Neusiedler See, a lake in Austria and Hungary.

Fès or *Fez* Former capital of Morocco 808–1062, 1296–1548, and 1662–1912, in a valley N of the Great Atlas Mountains, 160 km/100 mi E of Rabat; population (1990) 735,000; urban area (1990) 735,000. Textiles, carpets, and leather are manufactured, and the *fez*, a brimless hat worn in S and E Mediterranean countries, is traditionally said to have originated here. Kairwan Islamic University dates from 859; a second university was founded 1961.

Fezzan Former province of Libya, a desert region with many oases, and with rock paintings from about 3000 BC. It was captured from Italy 1942, and placed under French control until 1951 when it became a province of the newly independent United Kingdom of Libya. It was split into smaller divisions 1963.

Fichtelgebirge Chain of mountains in Bavaria, Germany, on the border with the Czech Republic. The highest peak is the *Schneeberg*, 1,051 m/3,448 ft. There are granite quarries, uranium mining, china and glass industries, and forestry.

Fiesole Resort town 6 km/4 mi NE of Florence, Italy, with many Etruscan and Roman relics; population (1971) 14,400. The Romanesque cathedral was completed 1028.

Fife Unitary authority in E Scotland; former Region 1975–96; administrative headquarters Glenrothes; population (1996) 351,200; area 1,340 sq km/517 sq mi. Towns and cities include Dunfermline, St Andrews, Kirkcaldy, and Cupar. Fife faces the North Sea and Firth of Forth. Features include the Lomond Hills in the NW (the only high land); rivers Eden and Leven; Rosyth naval base and dockyard (used for nuclear submarine refits) on N shore of the Firth of Forth; Tentsmuir, possibly the earliest settled site in Scotland. The ancient palace of the Stuarts was at Falkland, and eight Scottish kings are buried at Dunfermline. Industries include agriculture (potatoes, cereals, sugar beet), electronics, petrochemicals (Mossmorran), light engineering, aluminium refining, coal mining, and fishing.

Figueras Town in Cataluña, NE Spain; population (1991) 33,450. It was the home of the Surrealist painter Salvador Dalí. The Salvador Dalí museum, opened 1974, was designed by the artist.

Fingal's Cave Cave on the island of Staffa, Inner Hebrides, Scotland. It is lined with natural basalt columns, and is 60 m/200 ft long and 20 m/65 ft high. Fingal, based on the Irish hero Finn Mac Cumhaill, was the leading character in Macpherson's Ossianic forgeries. Visited by the German Romantic composer Felix Mendelssohn 1829, the cave was the inspiration of his *Hebrides* overture, otherwise known as *Fingal's Cave.*

Finistère (Latin *finis terrae* 'land's end') *Département* of ◊Brittany, NW France, occupying a headland with the English Channel to the N and the Bay of Biscay to the S; area 7,030 sq km/2,714 mi; population (1990) 838,700. The administrative centre is Quimper; Brest and Douarnenez are the chief towns. Inland there is heathland and fertile valleys; the Arrée and Black mountains run E–W. Horses and cattle are raised, and there is agriculture and seasonal fishing.

Finisterre, Cape (Latin *finis terrae* 'land's end') Promontory in the extreme NW of Spain.

Finland, Gulf of Eastern arm of the ◊Baltic Sea, separating Finland from Estonia.

Finnmark County of Norway, in the extreme N; area 48,650 sq km/1,878 sq mi; population (1995) 76,500. It is part of ◊Lapland. The coast is rocky and the interior barren and mountainous. Fishing is the main industry. The chief towns are the fishing ports of ◊Hammerfest, Vardø, and Vadsø, and the iron-mining town of Kirkenes, not far from the border with Russia.

Finsteraarhorn Highest mountain, 4,274 m/14,020 ft, in the Bernese Alps, Switzerland.

Firenze Italian form of ◊Florence, a city in Italy.

Firenze Province of N central Italy in N ◊Tuscany region; capital ◊Florence; area 3,880 sq km/1,498 sq mi; population (1992) 1,182,100.

Fishguard (Welsh *Abergwaun*) Seaport on an inlet on the S side of Fishguard Bay, Pembrokeshire, SW Wales; population about 5,000. There is a ferry service to Rosslare in the Republic of Ireland.

Fitchburg City in N Massachusetts, USA, on the Nashua River, N of Worcester; population (1990) 41,200. Industries include paper, textiles, furniture, clothing, and foundry products. Fitchburg was settled 1740 on the Mohawk Trail, and became a textile-manufacturing town.

FL Abbreviation for ◊Florida, a state of the USA.

Flagstaff City in Arizona, USA, 400 km/249 mi N of Phoenix; population (1990) 45,900. The largest city in N central Arizona, Flagstaff is the railway and livestock-market centre for the surrounding region, and has timber mills which use the local yellow pine. The Lowell Observatory (1894) is here. Situated 129 km/80 mi S of the Grand Canyon, Flagstaff is a centre of tourism, and there are local ski resorts.

Flanders Region of the Low Countries that in the 8th and 9th centuries extended from Calais to the Schelde and is now covered by the Belgian provinces of Oost Vlaanderen and West Vlaanderen (East and West Flanders), the French *département* of Nord, and part of the Dutch province of Zeeland. The language is Flemish. East Flanders, capital Ghent, has an area of 3,000 sq km/1,158 sq mi and a population (1995) of 1,349,400. West Flanders, capital Bruges, has an area of 3,100 sq km/1,197 sq mi and a population (1995) of 1,121,100.

Fleet Street Street in London, England (named after the subterranean river Fleet), traditionally the centre of British journalism. It runs from Temple Bar eastwards to Ludgate Circus. With adjoining streets it contained the offices and printing works of many leading British newspapers until the mid-1980s, when most moved to sites farther from the centre of London.

Fleetwood Port and seaside resort in Lancashire, England, at the mouth of the river Wyre; population (1981) 24,500. The fishing industry has declined, but the port still handles timber, petroleum, and chemicals.

Flensburg Port on the E coast of Schleswig-Holstein, Germany, with shipyards and breweries; population (1991) 87,200. Rum and smoked eels are specialities.

Fleurus Town in the province of Hainaut, Belgium, 11 km/7 mi NW of Charleroi. It was the site of three important battles: in 1622 during the Thirty Years' War, in 1690 during the Nine Years' War, and in 1794 during the French Revolutionary Wars.

Flevoland (formerly *IJsselmeerpolders*) Low-lying province of the Netherlands, created 1986.
area 1,410 sq km/544 sq mi
capital Lelystad
towns and cities Dronten, Almere
population (1995 est) 262,300
history established 1986 out of land reclaimed from the IJsselmeer 1950–68.

Flint City in Michigan, USA, on the Flint River, 90 km/56 mi NW of Detroit; population (1992) 139,300. Car manufacturing is the chief industry but it is declining. Flint was founded as a trading post 1819 and laid out 1836. In 1886 the Durant-Dort Carriage Company was founded here to build horse-drawn carriages. The General Motors Company, founded 1908, was based here.

Flintshire (Welsh *Sir y Fflint*) Unitary authority in N Wales. A former county, it was part of Clwyd 1974–96; administrative headquarters Mold; population (1996) 144,000; area 437 sq km/167 sq mi. Greenfield Valley was in the forefront of the Industrial Revolution before the advent of steam, and now has a museum of industrial archaeology.

Florence (Italian *Firenze*) Capital of ◊Tuscany, N Italy, 88 km/55 mi from the mouth of the river Arno; population (1992) 397,400. It has printing, engineering, and optical industries; many crafts, including leather, gold and silver work, and embroidery; and its art and architecture attract large numbers of tourists. Notable medieval and Renaissance citizens included the writers Dante and Boccaccio, and the artists Giotto, Leonardo da Vinci, and Michelangelo.

Florence City in NW Alabama, USA, on the Tennessee River near the Tennessee Valley Authority's Wilson Dam, NW of Birmingham; seat of Lauderdale County; population (1990) 36,400. Industries include agricultural and poultry products, building materials, lumber, and fertilizers.

Florence City in NE South Carolina, USA, NW of Myrtle Beach; seat of Florence County; population (1990) 29,800. It is a centre of the trucking industry, serving as a terminus for many companies. Other industries include dairy products, fertilizers, film, furniture, machined goods, and clothing. Florence developed in the 1950s as a railway junction.

Florianópolis Seaport and resort on Santa Caterina Island, Brazil; population (1991) 256,000. It is linked to the mainland by two bridges, one of which is the largest expansion bridge in Brazil.

Florida Southeasternmost state of the USA; mainly a peninsula jutting into the Atlantic, which it separates from the Gulf of Mexico; nicknamed Sunshine State/Everglade state.
area 152,000 sq km/58,672 sq mi
capital Tallahassee
towns and cities Miami, Tampa, Jacksonville
physical 50% forested; lakes (including Okeechobee 1,800 sq km/695 sq mi); low-lying, mostly less than 30 m/100 ft above sea level; Biscayne national park, a marine park with a living coral reef 320 km/200 mi long; Apalachia, Ocala, and Oscoela national forests; the Florida Keys, 31 islands between the Atlantic Ocean and the Gulf of Mexico, including Key Largo, with Crocodile Lakes national wildlife refuge; Tampa Bay; Everglades national park (a World Heritage Site, 5,000 sq km/1,930 sq mi), with birdlife, mangrove and cypress forests, alligators
features Fort Lauderdale; St Augustine, the oldest city in the USA; the Spanish fortress, Castillo de San Marcos national monument; Penascola (1559) with Spanish colonial buildings; Key West, with 19th-century buildings; Talla-

hassee, with pre–Civil War plantation mansions; John and Mable Ringling Museum of Art, Sarasota; Miami, with Art Deco district; Elgin Air Force Base; John F Kennedy Space Center, Cape Canaveral; Palm Beach island resort; beach resorts on Gulf and on Atlantic; Daytona International Speedway; Walt Disney World, and Epcot (Experimental Prototype Community of Tomorrow) Center; Universal Studios Florida; fishing at Destin

industries citrus fruits, melons, vegetables, fish, shellfish, phosphates, chemicals, electrical and electronic equipment, aircraft, fabricated metals

population (1995) 14,165,600, one of the fastest-growing of the states; including 12% Hispanic (especially Cuban) and 13.6% African-American

famous people Chris Evert, Henry Flagler, James Weldon Johnson, Sidney Poitier, Philip Randolph, Joseph Stilwell

history discovered by Ponce de Leon and under Spanish rule from 1513 until its cession to England 1763; returned to Spain 1783 and purchased by the USA 1819, becoming a state 1845. It grew rapidly in the early 1920s, stimulated by feverish land speculation. Despite the 1926 collapse of the boom, migration continued, especially of retired people from the North. After World War II, resorts, agriculture, and industry grew in importance. The space centre at Cape Canaveral also contributed to the state economy. More recently, Florida has become a banking centre, a development often partially attributed to the sizable inflow of cash derived from the traffic in illegal drugs from Latin America. Because of its proximity to Caribbean nations, the state became a haven for refugees from such countries as Cuba and Haiti.

Hurricane Andrew ravaged S Florida and Louisiana 1993, killing 13 and making 250,000 people homeless.

Florida Keys Series of small coral islands that curve over 240 km/150 mi SW from the S tip of Florida. The most important are Key Largo and Key West (with a US naval and air station); they depend on fishing and tourism. A causeway links the keys to the mainland. Key West is the largest settlement.

Flow Country Wilderness and wildlife habitat in Caithness and Sunderland districts, Highland unitary authority, N Scotland. Under threat from commercial afforestation, it consists of treeless peat bog and various lochs, which are home to many rare plants and wading birds.

Flushing English form of ◊Vlissingen, a port in the Netherlands.

Focşani Capital of Vrancea county, Romania; 200 km/125 mi NE of Bucharest; population (1993) 101,400. It is a commercial centre, with trade along the river Milcov, which joins the river Siret, to Galaţi. An Austro-Russian alliance defeated the Turks at Focşani 1789, during a sustained offensive against the Ottoman Empire in the Balkans.

Foggia City of Puglia region, S Italy; population (1992) 155,700. The cathedral, dating from about 1170, was rebuilt after an earthquake 1731. Natural gas is found nearby.

Foggia Province of SE Italy in NW ◊Puglia region; capital Foggia; area 7,185 sq km/2,774 sq mi; population (1992)

696,900. It was formerly named Capitanata and was a province of the Kingdom of Naples.

Föhr One of the North Frisian Islands in the North Sea, belonging to Germany, off the W coast of ◊Schleswig-Holstein; population (1991) 8,200. Föhr covers an area of 82 sq km/31 sq mi. Fishing is the main occupation, with oysters being exported to the German mainland. The main town, Wyk, is also a health resort. In autumn, wildfowl mass in great numbers on the island.

Folkestone Port and holiday resort on the SE coast of Kent, England, 10 km/6 mi SW of Dover; population (1991) 45,600. It was one of the Cinque Ports. There are ferry and hovercraft services to and from Boulogne, and the Channel Tunnel terminal is here. It is the birthplace of the physician William Harvey.

Fond du Lac City in W Wisconsin, USA, at the S end of Lake Winnebago, 88 km/55 mi NW of Milwaukee; population (1990) 37,800. Industries include dairy farming and tourism. It manufactures precision tools, machinery, and motor-vehicle parts.

Fontainebleau Town to the SE of Paris, in Seine-et-Marne *département*. The château was built by François I in the 16th century. Mme de Montespan lived here in the reign of Louis XIV, and Mme du Barry in that of Louis XV. Napoleon signed his abdication here 1814. Nearby is the village of Barbizon, the haunt of several 19th-century painters (known as the Barbizon School).

Foochow Alternative transcription of ◊Fuzhou, a port and capital of Fujian province, SE China.

Forbach French town in the *département* of Moselle, 50 km/31 mi E of Metz; population (1990) 30,000. There is a paper mill and woodworking, and the town is emerging as a sporting and cultural centre.

Forchheim City in Bavaria, Germany, on the Rhein–Main–Donau canal, 31 km/19 mi N of Nürnberg; population (1994) 108,900. Textiles, dyes, chocolate, paper, and optical goods are manufactured. In the early Middle Ages Forchheim was an important city of the Holy Roman Empire.

Foreland, North and South Headlands on the Kent coast, England. *North Foreland*, with one lighthouse, lies 4 km/2.5 mi E of Margate; *South Foreland*, with two, lies 4.8 km/3 mi NE of Dover.

Forez, Monts du Mountain range in France, part of the Auvergne range in the Auvergne region, lying between the rivers Allier and Loire. The highest peak is Pierre sur Haute (1,640 m/5,381 ft).

Forfarshire Former name (to 1928) of ◊Angus.

Forlì City and market centre in Emilia-Romagna region, NE Italy, S of Ravenna; population (1992) 109,100. Felt, majolica, and paper are manufactured.

Forlì Province of N central Italy in SE ◊Emilia-Romagna region; capital Forlì; area 2,912 sq km/1,124 sq mi; population (1992) 609,400.

Formentera Smallest inhabited island in the Spanish Balearic Islands, lying S of Ibiza; area 93 sq km/36 sq mi. The chief town is San Francisco Javier and the main port is La Sabina. The main industry is tourism.

Formentor, Cape Northern extremity of ◊Mallorca, in the Balearic Islands of the W Mediterranean Sea.

Fortaleza (also called *Ceará*) Industrial port in NE Brazil and capital of Ceará state; population (1991) 1,708,700 (metropolitan area 2,357,100). It has textile, flour-milling, and sugar-refining industries.

Fort Collins City in N Colorado, USA, on the Cache de la Poudre River, NE of Boulder; seat of Larimer County; population (1992) 93,300. It is the processing and marketing centre for the surrounding agricultural area. Industries include engines, cement, plastics, film, and prefabricated metal buildings. The city was established as a fort 1864 for the protection of travellers on the Overland Trail.

Fort-de-France Capital, chief commercial centre, and port of Martinique, West Indies, at the mouth of the Madame River; population (1990) 101,500. It trades in sugar, rum, and cacao.

Fort Duquesne Former French fort and trading post established in 1754 on the site where ◊Pittsburgh, Pennsylvania, USA, now stands. In 1758 British forces under General Forbes destroyed the French fort, replaced it with Fort Pitt (named after William Pitt, prime minister of Britain at the time), and established the town of Pittsburgh.

Forth River in SE Scotland, with its headstreams rising on the NE slopes of Ben Lomond. It flows approximately 72 km/45 mi to Kincardine where the *Firth of Forth* begins. The Firth is approximately 80 km/50 mi long, and is 26 km/16 mi wide where it joins the North Sea.

Fort Lamy Former name of ◊N'djamena, the capital of Chad.

Fort Lauderdale City in SE coastal Florida, USA, just N of Miami; seat of Broward County; population (1992) 148,500. The city's main industry is tourism. Channels for boating cross the city, Atlantic Ocean beaches line it on the E, and deep-water Port Everglades to the S allows ocean-going vessels to dock. A fort was built here 1837 during the Seminole War.

Fort Myers City in SW Florida, USA, on the Caloosahatchee River, SE of St Petersburg; seat of Lee County; population (1990) 45,200. It is a shipping centre for its fish, fruit, and vegetable products. Tourism is also an important industry. The surrender of Holatto-Micco, the last Seminole chief, took place here 1858.

Fort Pierce City in E central Florida, USA, where the Indian River flows into the Atlantic Ocean; seat of St Lucie County; population (1990) 36,800. It is a transport centre for the fruit and vegetable crops of the surrounding area. Fishing and tourism are significant industries. The fort was built 1838–42, and settlement began in the 1860s.

Fort Smith City in W Arkansas, USA, on the Arkansas River where it crosses the Oklahoma–Arkansas border, SW of Fayetteville; population (1992) 73,950. It is the site of coal and natural-gas mines; industries include furniture, cars, paper, plastics, and metals. Fort Smith national historic site is here: the fort was built 1817, and the town laid out 1821.

Fort Walton Beach City in the NW panhandle of Florida, USA, on the Gulf of Mexico, E of Pensacola; population (1990) 21,500. It is a centre for tourism, fishing, and yachting.

Fort Wayne Town in NE Indiana, USA; population (1992) 173,700. Industries include electrical goods, electronics, and farm machinery. A fort was built here against the Native Americans 1794 by General Anthony Wayne (1745–1796).

Fort Worth City in NE Texas, USA; population (1992) 454,400. Manufactured products include aerospace equipment, motor vehicles, and refined petroleum. It is also a grain and railway centre serving the S USA. Fort Worth developed from an army post 1849 and was a stop on the Chisholm cattle trail. The arrival of the railroad 1876 fostered economic development that was furthered by the discovery of oil nearby in 1920.

Fos-sur-Mer Harbour and medieval township near Marseille, France, forming the S focus of a direct Rhône–Rhine route to the North Sea.

Fougères French town in the *département* of Ille-et-Vilaine, 48 km/30 mi NE of Rennes; population (1990) 23,100. There is a 12th-century castle with 13 towers, and the 15th-century walls still stand. Footwear, metal goods, cloth, and glass are manufactured; tourism is important.

Fou-Liang Former name of ◊Jingdezhen, a town in China.

Foveaux Strait Stretch of water between the extreme S of South Island, New Zealand, and Stewart Island, New Zealand. It is a fishing area and produces a considerable oyster catch.

Fowey Port and resort in Cornwall, England, near the mouth of the Fowey estuary; population, with ◊St Austell (1988 est) 2,600. It is an outlet for the Cornish china clay mining industry.

Fox River in Wisconsin, USA; length 285 km/177 mi. It rises in the lake area to the N of Madison and is connected by the Portage Canal with the Wisconsin River; it continues NE to Lake Winnebago at Oshkosh and beyond this to Green Bay. In its lower course it provides water for an important industrial area specializing in papermaking.

Fox River in SE Wisconsin and NE Illinois, USA; length 225 km/139 mi. Rising in Washington County, it flows in a southerly direction through Waukesha and Fox Lake, then on to Elgin and Aurora, before turning SW to meet the Illinois River at Ottawa, Illinois. It flows though an important manufacturing and agricultural region.

Foyle Sea lough on the N coast of Ireland, traversed by the frontier of Northern Ireland and the Irish Republic.

Franche-Comté Region of E France; area 16,202 sq km/6,256 sq mi; population (1990) 1,097,400. Its capital is Besançon, and it includes the *départements* of Doubs, Jura, Haute Saône, and Territoire de Belfort. In the mountainous Jura, there is farming and forestry, and elsewhere there are engineering and plastics industries.

Frankenthal City in the Rhineland-Palatinate, Germany, 7 km/4 mi NW of Ludwigshafen; population (1994) 47,000. Frankenthal is situated a short distance from the left bank of the river Rhine, with which it is connected by canal. Leather, cork, metals, and fertilizers are manufactured.

Frankenwald Mountainous district of Germany, situated principally in NE ◊Bavaria. The Frankenwald is an undulating plateau some 610 m/2,000 ft above sea level and just NW of the Fichtelgebirge mountain range.

Frankfort Capital of Kentucky, USA, located in the N central part of the state, on the Kentucky River, E of Louisville; population (1990) 26,000. Industries include bourbon (whisky), electronic equipment, furniture, and footwear. Frankfort was founded 1786 and became the capital of Kentucky 1792.

Frankfurt am Main City in Hessen, Germany, 72 km/45 mi NE of Mannheim; population (1993) 663,600. It is a commercial and banking centre, with electrical and machine industries, and an inland port on the river Main. An international book fair is held here annually.

Frankfurt-an-der-Oder Industrial town in the state of Brandenburg, Germany, 80 km/50 mi SE of Berlin; population (1991) 85,400. It was the former capital of the East German district of Frankfurt 1952–90. It is linked by the river Oder and its canals to the rivers Vistula and Elbe. Industries include semiconductors, chemicals, engineering, paper, and leather.

Franklin District of ◊Northwest Territories, Canada; area 1,422,550 sq km/549,250 sq mi. Fur trapping is important to the economy.

Franz Josef Land (Russian *Zemlya Frantsa Iosifa*) Archipelago of over 85 islands in the Arctic Ocean, E of Spitsbergen and NW of Novaya Zemlya, Russia; area 20,720 sq km/8,000 sq mi. There are scientific stations on the islands.

Fraser River in British Columbia, Canada. It rises in the Yellowhead Pass of the Rockies and flows NW, then S, then W to the Strait of Georgia. It is 1,370 km/850 mi long and rich in salmon.

Frauenfeld Capital of the canton of Thurgau, Switzerland, on the river Murg 34 km/21 mi NE of Zürich; population (1995) 20,400. Products manufactured in the town are cottons, silks, woollens, and iron and aluminium goods. Frauenfeld has a 10th-century castle.

Fray Bentos River port in Uruguay; population (1985) 20,000. Linked by a bridge over the Uruguay with Puerto Unzué in Argentina (1976), it is known for meat-packing, particularly of corned beef.

Fredericksburg City in Spotsylvania County, Virginia, E USA, situated on the Rappahannock River, about 88 km/55 mi S of Washington; population (1994 est) 22,200. Fredericksburg serves an agricultural region and has light manufacturing. During the American Civil War it was the scene of four significant battles 1862–64: Fredericksburg, Chancellorsville, Wilderness, and the Spotsylvania Courthouse. The battlefields lie W of the city, within the Fredericksburg and Spotsylvania National Military Park.

Fredericton Capital of New Brunswick, Canada, on the St John River; population (1991) 45,400. It was known as St Anne's Point until 1785, when it was named after Prince Frederick, second son of George III.

Fredrikstad Norwegian port at the mouth of the river Glomma, on the Oslo Fjord; population (1991) 26,500. It is a centre of the timber trade and has shipyards; there are also canning, paint, porcelain, and plastic industries.

Free State (formerly Orange Free State) Province of the Republic of South Africa
area 127,993 sq km/49,405 sq mi
capital Bloemfontein
towns and cities Springfontein, Kroonstad, Bethlehem, Harrismith, Koffiefontein
features plain of the High Veld; Lesotho forms an enclave on the KwaZulu-Natal and Eastern Province border; Orange River; Vaal River
industries grain, wool, cattle, gold, oil from coal, cement, pharmaceuticals
population (1995 est) 2,782,500; 82% ethnic Africans
languages Sotho 56%, Afrikaans 14%, Xhosa 9%
history original settlements from 1810 were complemented by the Great Trek, and the state was recognized by Britain as independent 1854. Following the South African, or Boer, War 1899–1902, it was annexed by Britain as the Orange River Colony until it entered the union as a province 1910.

Freetown Capital of Sierra Leone, W Africa; population (1992) 505,000. It has a naval station and a harbour. Industries include cement, plastics, footwear, oil refining, and food production. Platinum, chromite, rutile, diamonds, and gold are traded. It was founded as a settlement for freed slaves in the 1790s.

Freiburg im Breisgau Industrial city (pharmaceuticals, precision instruments) in Baden-Württemberg, Germany; population (1993) 196,700. It has a university and a 12th-century cathedral.

Freising City in Bavaria, Germany, on the river Isar, 32 km/20 mi NE of Munich; population (1994) 138,500. Freising has one of the oldest breweries in the world, dating from 1040. Other industries include light engineering. There is a cathedral (1161–1205) and a former Benedictine abbey (now a school of agriculture and brewing).

Fréjus French town in the *département* of Var, 25 km/16 mi SW of Cannes; population (1990) 45,100. It stands on a hill above an alluvial plain 2 km/1 mi from the Mediterranean. It was founded by Caesar and has Roman remains, including an amphitheatre, baths, and aqueduct; the harbour built by Augustus has been silted up by the river Argens. The Gothic cathedral has a 5th-century baptistry. There are cork, olive oil, and wine industries; tourism is important.

Fremantle Chief port of Western Australia, at the mouth of the Swan River, SW of ◊Perth; population (1991) 23,800. It has shipbuilding yards, sawmills, and iron foundries and exports wheat, fruit, wool, and timber. It was founded as a penal settlement 1829. The America's Cup yacht race was held here 1987.

French Antarctica *French Southern and Antarctic Territories* Territory created 1955; area 10,100 sq km/3,900 sq mi; population about 200 research scientists. It includes Adélie Land on the Antarctic continent, the Kerguelen and Crozet archipelagos, and St Paul and Nouvelle Amsterdam islands in the S seas. It is administered from Paris.

French Guiana (French *Guyane Française*) French overseas *département* from 1946, and administrative region from 1974, on the N coast of South America, bounded W by Suriname and E and S by Brazil
area 83,500 sq km/32,230 sq mi
capital Cayenne
towns and cities St Laurent
features Eurospace rocket launch pad at Kourou; Îles du Salut, which include ◊Devil's Island
industries timber, shrimps, gold
currency franc
population (1990) 114,800
language 90% Creole, French, Native American
famous people Alfred Dreyfus
history first settled by France 1604, the territory became a French possession 1817; penal colonies, including Devil's Island, were established from 1852; by 1945 the shipments of convicts from France ceased.

French Guiana

French Polynesia French Overseas Territory in the S Pacific, consisting of five archipelagos: Windward Islands, Leeward Islands (the two island groups comprising the ◊Society Islands), ◊Tuamotu Archipelago (including ◊Gambier Islands), ◊Tubuai Islands, and ◊Marquesas Islands
total area 3,940 sq km/1,521 sq mi
capital Papeete on Tahiti
industries cultivated pearls, coconut oil, vanilla; tourism is important
population (1994) 216,600
languages Tahitian (official), French
government the French government is represented by a

high commissioner (Paul Roncière). It is administered by a Council of Ministers, with a president elected by the Territorial Assembly from its own members; two deputies are returned to the National Assembly in France and one senator to the Senate
history first visited by Europeans 1595; French protectorate 1843; annexed to France 1880–82; became an Overseas Territory, changing its name from French Oceania 1958; self-governing 1977. Following demands for independence in ◊New Caledonia 1984–85, agitation increased also in Polynesia.

French Somaliland Former name (to 1967) of ◊Djibouti, in E Africa.

French Sudan Former name (1898–1959) of Mali.

French West Africa Group of French colonies administered from Dakar 1895–1958. They are now Senegal, Mauritania, Sudan, Burkina Faso, Guinea, Niger, Côte d'Ivoire, and Benin.

Fresno City in central California, USA, SE of San Jose, seat of Fresno County; population (1992) 376,100. It is the processing and marketing centre for the fruits and vegetables of the San Joaquin Valley. Industries include glass, machinery, fertilizers, and vending machines. Fresno was settled 1872, originally a stop on the Central Pacific Railroad.

Fribourg (German *Freiburg*) City in W Switzerland, on the river Sarine, capital of the canton of Fribourg; population (1989 est) 35,000. It is renowned for its food products, such as the cheese of the Gruyère district.

Fribourg (German *Freiburg*) Swiss canton situated in the SW of the country; area 1,670 sq km/639 sq mi; population (1995) 224,600. It lies in the foothills of the Alps, the highest point being 2,395 m/7,858 ft. The chief rivers in the canton are La Broye and La Sarine.

Friedrichshafen City in Baden-Württemberg, Germany, on the NE shore of Lake Constance, 115 km/71 mi SE of Stuttgart; population (1994) 56,200. The town is a resort and conference centre, and has car and aerospace industries.

Friendly Islands Another name for Tonga, a country in the Pacific.

Friesland Maritime province of the N Netherlands, which includes the Frisian Islands and land that is still being reclaimed from the former Zuyder Zee; the inhabitants of the province are called Frisians
area 3,400 sq km/1,312 sq mi
capital Leeuwarden
towns and cities Drachten, Harlingen, Sneek, Heerenveen
features sailing is popular; the *Elfstedentocht* (skating race on canals through 11 towns) is held in very cold winters
industries livestock (Friesian cattle originated here; black Friesian horses), dairy products, small boats
population (1995 est) 609,600
history ruled as a county of the Holy Roman Empire during the Middle Ages, Friesland passed to Saxony 1498 and, after a revolt, to Charles V of Spain. In 1579 it subscribed to the Treaty of Utrecht, opposing Spanish rule. In 1748 its

stadholder, Prince William IV of Orange, became stadholder of all the United Provinces of the Netherlands.

Frisian Islands Chain of low-lying islands 5–32 km/ 3–20 mi off the NW coasts of the Netherlands and Germany, with a northerly extension off the W coast of Denmark. They were formed by the sinking of the intervening land. *Texel* is the largest and westernmost island, at the S end of the chain.

Friuli-Venezia Giulia Autonomous agricultural and wine-growing region of NE Italy, bordered to the E by Slovenia; area 7,846 sq km/3,029 sq mi; population (1995) 1,191,200. Cities include Udine (the capital), Gorizia, Pordenone, and Trieste.

Frosinone Province of central Italy in SE ◊Lazio region; capital Frosinone (population (1990) 47,800); area 3,240 sq km/1,251 sq mi; population (1992) 481,100.

Frunze Former name (1926–91) of ◊Bishkek in Kyrgyzstan. Prior to 1926 it was called Pishpek.

Fuenterrabia Fishing town in the province of Guipúzcoa, N Spain, on the Bay of Biscay and the French frontier; population (1995) 14,000. Once an important fortress, it has the remains of a castle from the 12th–16th centuries. The town is now a fashionable holiday resort.

Fujairah or *Fujayrah* One of the seven constituent member states of the United Arab Emirates; area 1,150 sq km/ 450 sq mi; population (1985) 54,000.

Fuji, Mount or *Fuji Yama* Japanese volcano and highest peak, on Honshu Island, near Tokyo; height 3,778 m/12,400 ft. Extinct since 1707, it has a Shinto shrine and a weather station on its summit. Fuji has long been revered for its picturesque cone-shaped crater peak, and figures prominently in Japanese art, literature, and religion.

Fujian or *Fukien* Province of SE China, bordering Taiwan Strait, opposite Taiwan
area 123,100 sq km/47,528 sq mi
capital Fuzhou
physical dramatic mountainous coastline
features being developed for tourists; designated as a pace-setting province for modernization 1980
industries steel rolling, electrical goods, sugar, rice, special aromatic teas, tobacco, timber, fruit
population (1990) 30,048,000.

Fukien Alternative transcription of ◊Fujian, a province of SE China.

Fukuoka formerly *Najime* Japanese industrial port on the NW coast of Kyushu Island; population (1994) 1,221,000. It produces chemicals, textiles, paper, and metal goods.

Fukushima City in the N of Honshu Island, Japan; population (1994) 281,000. It has a silk industry. It is the capital of Fukushima prefecture.

Fukuyama Port in the SW of Honshu Island, Japan, at the mouth of the Ashida River; population (1994) 373,000. Exports include cotton and rubber.

Fulda City in Hessen, Germany, on the river Fulda, 82 km/ 51 mi NE of Frankfurt am Main; population (1994) 60,100. The city produces textiles, carpets, and rubber. Fulda dates from the Middle Ages, and was made a city 1157. St Michael's Chapel 818 is the second oldest church in Germany. The river Fulda rises in Bavaria.

Funabashi City in Kanto region, Honshu Island, E of Tokyo, Japan; population (1994) 531,000.

Funafuti Atoll consisting of 30 islets in the W Pacific, port and capital of the state of Tuvalu; area 2.8 sq km/1.1 sq mi; population (1995 est) 2,865.

Funchal Capital and chief port of the Portuguese island of Madeira, on the S coast; population (1987) 44,100. Tourism and Madeira wine are the main industries.

Fundy, Bay of Canadian Atlantic inlet between New Brunswick and Nova Scotia, with a rapid tidal rise and fall of 18 m/60 ft (harnessed for electricity since 1984). In summer, fog increases the dangers to shipping.

Fünen German form of ◊Fyn, an island forming part of Denmark.

Fünfkirchen (German 'Five Churches') German name for ◊Pécs, a town in SW Hungary.

Furness Peninsula in England, formerly a detached N portion of Lancashire, separated from the main part by Morecambe Bay. In 1974 it was included in the new county of ◊Cumbria. Barrow is its ship-building and industrial centre.

Fürstenfeldbruck City in Bavaria, Germany, 22 km/14 mi W of Munich; population (1994) 185,300. Clothing manufacture is the town's main industry. Fürstenfeldbruck has a number of Baroque churches.

Fürth Town in Bavaria, Germany, adjoining Nürnberg; population (1991) 105,300. It has electrical, chemical, textile, and toy industries.

Fushun Coal-mining and oil-refining centre in Liaoning province, China, 40 km/25 mi E of Shenyang; population (1993) 1,350,000. It has aluminium, steel, and chemical works.

Fuzhou or *Foochow* Industrial port and capital of Fujian province, on Min River in SE China; population (1993) 1,290,000. It is a centre for shipbuilding and steel production; rice, sugar, tea, and fruit pass through the port. There are joint foreign and Chinese factories.

Fyn (German *Fünen*) Island forming part of Denmark and lying between the mainland and Zealand; capital Odense; area 2,976 sq km/1,149 sq mi; population (1995) 467,700.

GA Abbreviation for the state of ◊Georgia, USA.

Gabcikovo Dam Hydroelectric dam on the river Danube, at the point where it crosses the frontier between Hungary and the Slovak Republic. A treaty agreeing to its construction was signed by Hungary and Czechoslovakia 1977, but work was suspended 1989 after Hungary withdrew its support for a scheme to divert water from the river. Czechoslovakia resumed work 1991, despite warnings from scientists and environmentalists that the scheme would destroy valuable wetlands in the Danube valley.

Gabès Port in E Tunisia; population (1994) 98,900. Fertilizers and dates are exported. The town stands on the site of the Roman town of *Tacapae*.

Gaborone Capital of Botswana, mainly an administrative and government-service centre; population (1991) 133,500. The University of Botswana (1976) is here. The city developed after it replaced Mafikeng as the country's capital 1965.

Gabrovo Industrial town (textiles) in Lovech region, central Bulgaria, on the N slopes of the Balkan Mountains, 55 km/34 mi NW of Stara Zagora; population (1990) 88,100.

Gadsden City in NE Alabama, USA, on the Coosa River, SE of Huntsville; seat of Etowah County; population (1990) 42,500. It is a distribution centre for the area's livestock, poultry, and dairy products. Industries include manganese, bauxite, coal, timber, steel, rubber products, electrical machinery parts, and farm equipment.

The city was founded 1846, and renamed 1853 after James Gadsden, who negotiated the Gadsden Purchase of territory from Mexico.

Gafsa Oasis town in central Tunisia, centre of a phosphate-mining area; population (1984) 60,900.

Gainesville City in N Florida, USA, SW of Jacksonville; seat of Alachua County; population (1992) 86,800. Its industries include electronic parts, concrete, and wooden products. The University of Florida (1901) is here. The city developed around a trading post founded 1832.

Gainsborough Market town in Lincolnshire, England; population (1991) 19,700. It is an agricultural marketing centre with flour mills and the manufacture of agricultural machinery. It stands on the river Trent, which periodically rises in a tidal wave, the 'eagre'.

Galápagos Islands (official name *Archipiélago de Colón*) group of 12 large and several hundred smaller islands in the Pacific about 500 miles from the mainland, belonging to Ecuador; area 7,800 sq km/3,000 sq mi; population (1990) 9,800. The capital is San Cristóbal. The islands are a nature reserve; their unique fauna (including giant tortoises, iguanas, penguins, flightless cormorants, and Darwin's finches, which inspired Charles Darwin to formulate the principle of evolution by natural selection) is under threat from introduced species. The main industry is tuna and lobster fishing.

Galaţi (German *Galatz*) Port on the river Danube in Romania; population (1993) 324,000. Industries include shipbuilding, iron, steel, textiles, food processing, and cosmetics.

Galdhøpiggen Mountain in the Jotunheim range, Norway, 2,469 m/8,100 ft. It is counted as second to ◊Glittertind, 2,472 m/8,110 ft (with glacier ice), although without ice and snow Galdhøpiggen is the higher of the two.

Galicia Region of central Europe, extending from the N slopes of the Carpathian Mountains to the Romanian border. Once part of the Austrian Empire, it was included in Poland after World War I and divided 1945 between Poland and the USSR.

Galicia Mountainous but fertile autonomous region of NW Spain, formerly an independent kingdom; area 29,400 sq km/11,348 sq mi; population (1991) 2,731,700. It includes La Coruña, Lugo, Orense, and Pontevedra. Industries include the mining of tungsten and tin, and fishing; Galicia has the largest fishing fleet in the European Union. The language is similar to Portuguese.

Gallipoli Port in European Turkey, giving its name to the peninsula (ancient name *Chersonesus*) on which it stands. In World War I, an unsuccessful attempt was made Feb 1915–Jan 1916 by Allied troops to force their way through the Dardanelles and link up with Russia. The campaign was fought mainly by Australian and New Zealand forces, who suffered heavy losses.

Gällivare Iron-mining town above the Arctic Circle in Norrbotten county, N Sweden; population (1991) 22,400.

Galloway Ancient area of SW Scotland, now part of Dumfries and Galloway.

Galveston Gulf of Mexico port on Galveston Island in Texas, USA; population (1992) 59,600. It exports cotton, petroleum, wheat, and timber and has chemical works and petroleum refineries. Fishing is important, and the city has long been a resort for the island's sandy beaches. The city dates from an 1817 settlement by the pirate Jean Lafitte. In the 19th century it was a major port, and many historic homes remain.

Galway County on the W coast of the Republic of Ireland, in the province of Connacht; county town Galway; area 5,940 sq km/2,293 sq mi; population (1996 est) 188,600. Towns include Ballinasloe, Tuam, Clifden, and Loughrea (near which deposits of lead, zinc, and copper were found 1959).

Galway Fishing port and county town of County Galway, Republic of Ireland; population (1991) 50,800. It produces textiles and chemicals, and there is salmon and eel fishing. University College is part of the national university, and Galway Theatre stages Irish Gaelic plays.

Gambia River in W Africa, 1,000 km/620 mi long, which gives its name to The Gambia. It rises in Guinea and flows W along the country to the Atlantic Ocean.

Gambier Islands Island group, part of ◊French Polynesia, administered with the ◊Tuamotu Archipelago; area 36 sq km/14 sq mi; population (1988) 582. It includes four coral islands and many small islets. The main island is Mangareva, with its town Rikitea.

Gandia Seaport in the province of Valencia, E Spain, on the Mediterranean coast; population (1995) 58,100. It has an old college, once a university, a Gothic church, and the palace of the dukes of Gandia. Exports include oranges, raisins, onions, and wine.

Gandzha Former name (until 1804 and 1918–35) of ◊Gyandzha in Azerbaijan.

Ganges

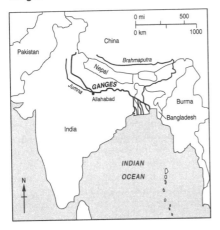

Ganges (Hindi *Ganga*) Major river of India and Bangladesh; length 2,510 km/1,560 mi. It is the most sacred river for Hindus.

Gannet Peak The highest peak in Wyoming, USA, rising to 4,207 m/13,804 ft. It is in the Rocky Mountains.

Gansu or *Kansu* Province of NW China
area 530,000 sq km/204,633 sq mi
capital Lanzhou
features subject to earthquakes; the 'Silk Road' (now a motor road) passed through it in the Middle Ages, carrying trade to central Asia
industries coal, oil, hydroelectric power from the Huang He (Yellow) River
population (1990) 22,930,020, including many Muslims.

Gaoxiong Mainland Chinese form of ◊Kaohsiung, a port in Taiwan.

Gap French town, capital of the *département* of Hautes-Alpes. It stands 750 m/2,461 ft above sea level, and is the seat of a bishop. There is a trade in timber and livestock.

Garching Town N of Munich, Germany, site of a nuclear research centre.

Gard French river, 133 km/83 mi long, a tributary of the Rhône, which it joins above Beaucaire. It gives its name to Gard *département* in Languedoc-Roussillon region.

Gard *Département* in the ◊Languedoc-Roussillon region of France; area 5,848 sq km/2,258 sq mi; population (1990) 585,400. It has a short coastline on the Mediterranean, and flowing through it is the river Rhône and its tributaries the Cèze, the Ardèche, and the Gard. In the NW are ridges of the Cévennes mountains, of which Mont Aigoual is the highest at 1,560 m/5,118 ft. In the S the land is low-lying with marshy plains yielding salt. The Garrigues range in the SW are limestone hills. The *département* suffers from the cold, dry mistral wind that blows across parts of S France. Olives, vines, mulberries (for silkworms), fruit, and cereals are produced in great quantities, and cattle are raised. There is much mineral wealth, including coal, iron, lignite, copper,

asphalt, zinc, and lead, and there are metallurgical, silk, leather, and oil industries. The principal towns are ◊Nîmes (the capital), Alès, and Le Vigan.

Garda, Lake Largest lake in Italy; situated on the border between the regions of Lombardia and Veneto; area 370 sq km/143 sq mi.

Garden Grove City in S California, USA, 50 km/31 mi SE of the centre of Los Angeles; population (1994 est) 228. It is the site of the impressive Crystal Cathedral.

Garden of the Gods District of Colorado, W USA, 10 km/6 mi NW of Colorado Springs. The district contains formations of eroded red sandstone, some of which resemble cathedral spires. The area is a popular tourist destination.

Gard, Pont du Roman aqueduct in France, crossing the river Gard 26 km/16 mi W of Avignon. It is 275 m/902 ft long and 49 m/161 ft high, with three tiers of arches. Built by Marcus Agrippa in 19 BC to bring water to Nîmes, it is now a tourist attraction.

Garmisch-Partenkirchen Town in Bavaria, Germany, located at the confluence of the Loisach and Partnach rivers and close to the Austrian border, 94 km/58 mi S of Munich; population (1994) 85,400. Nearby is the peak known as the Zugspitze (2,963 m/9,721 ft); Garmisch-Partenkirchen is a major Alpine skiing resort and health centre, and hosted the 1936 Winter Olympics.

Garonne River in SW France, rising on the Spanish side of the Pyrenees and flowing to the ◊Gironde estuary; length 560 km/350 mi.

Gary City in NW Indiana, USA; population (1992) 116,700. It contains the steel and cement works of the US Steel Corporation and was named after E H Gary (1846–1927), its chair. Cutbacks in steel production in the mid–late 20th century left the city economically depressed.

Gaspé Peninsula Mountainous peninsula in SE Quebec, Canada; area 29,500 sq km/11,390 sq mi. It has fishing and lumbering industries.

Gastein Valley in the Austrian province of ◊Salzburg, about 60 km/37 mi S of the town of Salzburg in the N foothills of the Hohe Tauern Alpine range. *Badgastein* is an international spa, with *Bad Hofgastein* higher up the valley. The valley's scenic beauty attracts tourists.

Gastonia City in SW North Carolina, USA, directly W of Charlotte; seat of Gaston County; population (1992) 57,100. Its most important industry is textiles. It was the site of a violent labour strike 1929.

Gateshead Port in Tyne and Wear, NE England; population (1994 est) 127,000. It is situated on the S bank of the river Tyne, opposite Newcastle upon Tyne. Formerly a port for the Tyne coalfields and a railway workshop centre, present-day industries include engineering, chemicals, glass, paint, plastics, clothing, printing, and rubber.

Gâtinais Former district of France, SE of Paris, now comprising the greater part of the *départements* of Seine-et-Marne and Loiret. It is crossed by the river Loing, and the land is low-lying and swampy.

Gatwick Site of Gatwick Airport, West Sussex, England, constructed 1956–58. One of London's three international airports, it is situated 42 km/26 mi S from London's city centre.

Gauteng (Sotho for 'Place of Gold') Province of the Republic of South Africa from 1994, known as Pretoria-Witwatersrand-Vereeniging before 1995.

area 18,760 sq km/7,243 sq mi

capital Johannesburg

towns and cities Pretoria, Vereeniging, Krugersdorp, Benoni, Germiston

features Vaal River

industries gold mining, coal, iron and steel, uranium, chemicals, railway workshops, tobacco, maize

population (1995 est) 7,048,300

languages Afrikaans 20%, Zulu 18%, English 15%.

Gåvle Seaport and capital of Gåvleborg county, Sweden, on the Gulf of Bothnia; population (1995) 90,600. The town is situated at the mouth of the river Gåvle, 150 km/93 mi NW of Stockholm, and is spread over the riverbanks and two islands. Shipbuilding, textiles, machinery, and pottery are the main industries. The chief exports are iron goods, timber, and wood pulp.

Gaya Ancient city in Bihar state, NE India; population (1991) 294,000. It is a centre of pilgrimage for Buddhists and Hindus with many temples and shrines; there is a tourist centre. A bo tree at Buddh Gaya is said to be a direct descendant of the original tree under which the Buddha sat.

Gaza Capital of the Gaza Strip, once a Philistine city; population (1980 est) 120,000.

Gazankulu Former Black National State in the former Transvaal Province, South Africa, with self-governing status from 1971; population (1985) 497,200. It is now in Northern Province.

Gaza Strip Strip of land on the Mediterranean sea, occupied by Israel 1967–94 when responsibility for its administration was transferred to the Palestine Liberation Organization; capital Gaza; area 363 sq km/140 sq mi; population (1994) 724,500, mainly Palestinians, plus about 2,500 Israeli settlers. Agriculture is the main activity, producing citrus fruits, wheat, and olives.

Gaziantep Turkish city 185 km/115 mi NE of Adana; population (1990) 603,400. It has textile and tanning industries. Until 1922 it was known as *Antep* or *Aintab*.

Gdańsk (German *Danzig*) Polish port; population (1993) 466,500. Oil is refined, and textiles, televisions, and fertilizers are produced. In the 1980s there were repeated antigovernment strikes at the Lenin shipyards whose many workshops were subsequently closed 1996 because of economic difficulties.

Gdynia Port in N Poland; population (1990) 251,500. It was established 1920 to give newly constituted Poland a sea outlet to replace lost ◊Gdańsk. It has a naval base and shipyards and is now part of the 'Tri-city', which includes Sopot and Gdańsk.

Geelong Industrial port in S Victoria, Australia; population (1993) 151,900. In addition to oil refining and trade in grain, it produces aluminium, motor vehicles, textiles, glass, and fertilizers.

Geislingen an der Steige City in Baden-Württemberg, Germany, 53 km/33 mi SE of Stuttgart; population (1994) 28,400. Geislingen is a manufacturing centre for metal and cotton goods, and has traditional craft industries such as glasswork and woodcarving. Many of its medieval buildings survive, including a late Gothic church.

Gelderland (English *Guelders*) Province of the E Netherlands

area 5,020 sq km/1,938 sq mi

capital Arnhem

towns and cities Apeldoorn, Nijmegen, Ede

industries livestock, textiles, electrical goods

population (1995 est) 1,864,700

history in the Middle Ages Gelderland was divided into Upper Gelderland (Roermond in N Limburg) and Lower Gelderland (Nijmegen, Arnhem, Zutphen). These territories were inherited by Charles V of Spain, but when the revolt against Spanish rule reached a climax 1579, Lower Gelderland joined the United Provinces of the Netherlands.

Geleen Town in the province of Limburg, the Netherlands, 15 km/9 mi NE of Maastricht; population (1996) 33,900. Geleen once manufactured goods associated with by-products of coal from the nearby coalfield, but its main industries are now concerned with petroleum by-products and natural gas production.

Gelsenkirchen Industrial city in the ◊Ruhr, in North Rhine–Westphalia, Germany, 25 km/15 mi W of Dortmund; population (1993) 294,800. It has iron, steel, chemical, and glass industries.

Geneva (French *Genève*) Swiss city, capital of Geneva canton, on the shore of Lake Geneva; population (1994 est) city 174,400; canton 391,100. It is a point of convergence of natural routes and is a cultural and commercial centre. Industries include the manufacture of watches, scientific and optical instruments, foodstuffs, jewellery, and musical boxes. CERN, the particle physics research organization, is here.

Geneva (French *Genève*; German *Genf*) Canton in SW Switzerland, bounded by Lake Geneva, the canton of Vaud, and France; area 282 sq km/108 sq mi; population (1995) 395,500. It lies in the ◊Rhône valley between the S Jura Mountains and the foothills of the Alps. The canton was admitted into the Swiss Confederation in 1815.

Geneva, Lake (French *Lac Léman*) Largest of the central European lakes, between Switzerland and France; area 580 sq km/225 sq mi.

Genk Town in the province of Limbourg, Belgium, 14 km/9 mi E of Hasselt. The town's chief employer is the Ford Motor Company, which has a car-assembly plant here. The Limbourg coalfield provides employment in Genk and surrounding villages, but the mining industry has been in decline since the 1960s and there is high unemployment in the area.

Gennesaret, Lake of   Another name for Lake ◊Tiberias (Sea of Galilee) in N Israel.

Genoa   (Italian *Genova*) Historic city in NW Italy, capital of Liguria; population (1992) 667,600. It is Italy's largest port; industries include oil refining, chemicals, engineering, and textiles.

Genoa   (Italian *Genova*) Province of NW Italy in central ◊Liguria region; capital Genoa; area 1,831 sq km/707 sq mi; population (1992) 944,200.

George, Lake   Lake in NE New York State, USA, 64 km/40 mi N of Saratoga in the Adirondack Mountains, connected with Lake Champlain by Ticonderoga Creek. It has beautiful scenery, and the town of Lake George is a popular summer resort.

George Town   or *Penang* Chief port of the Federation of Malaysia, and capital of Penang, on the island of Penang; population (1991) 219,000. It produces textiles and toys.

Georgetown   District of ◊Washington DC, USA, situated about 3 km/2 mi NW of the White House. It has many colonial buildings and is a popular residential section of the capital.

Georgetown   Capital and port of Guyana, situated at the mouth of the Demerara River on the Caribbean coast; population (1992) 200,000. There is food processing and shrimp fishing.

Georgia   State in SE USA; nicknamed Empire State of the South/Peach State
area   152,600 sq km/58,904 sq mi
capital   Atlanta
towns and cities   Columbus, Savannah, Macon
physical   Okefenokee Swamp national wildlife refuge (1,700 sq km/656 sq mi); Golden Isles, including Cumberland Island national seashore; Chattahoochee national forest
features   St Simons Island (with Fort Frederica national monument), Sea Island, and Jekyll Island, including Jekyll Island Club historic district, with the mansions built by wealthy families such as the Rockefellers and the Vanderbilts; Savannah (founded 1733), with a 4-sq-km/2.5-sq-mi historic district with town squares and over 1,000 restored houses, including Regency houses designed by William Jay (Owens Thomas House, 1817, and Telfair mansion and art museum, 1819), Juliette Gordon Low Girl Scout National Center (birthplace of Daisy Low, founder of the Girl Scouts of the USA), Isaiah Davenport House (1815), Olde Pink House (1771), King-Tisdall Cottage (a museum of black history and culture), and the site of the Siege of Savannah (1779); Atlanta, site of the 1996 Olympic Games, with Martin Luther King Jr national historic district (including Martin Luther King's birthplace and Ebenezer Baptist Church), Stone Mountain Park (with the world's largest sculpture memorial, to the Confederate war heroes), the CNN Center, and the World of Coca-Cola; Andersonville national historic site, site of the National Prisoners of War

Museum; Fort Jackson on Salter's Island, the oldest colonial fort in the state; Nennesaw Mountain national battlefield; Calloway Gardens, Pine Mountain, with the Cecil B Day Butterfly Center, the largest glass-enclosed tropical butterfly conservatory in North America
industries   poultry, livestock, tobacco, maize, peanuts, cotton, soya beans, china clay, crushed granite, textiles, carpets, aircraft, paper products
population   (1995) 7,200,900; 27% African-American
famous people   Jim Bowie; Erskine Caldwell; Jimmy Carter; Ray Charles; Ty Cobb; Joel Chandler Harris; Bobby Jones; Martin Luther King Jr; Carson McCullers; Margaret Mitchell; James Oglethorpe; Jackie Robinson
history   explored 1540 by Hernando de Soto; claimed by the British and named after George II of England; founded 1733 as a colony for the industrious poor by James Oglethorpe, a philanthropist; one of the original 13 states of the USA it joined the union 1788. In 1864, during the Civil War, General W T Sherman's Union troops cut a wide swath of destruction as they marched from Atlanta to the sea. The state benefited after World War II from the growth of Atlanta as the financial and transportation centre of the SE USA.

Georgian Bay   Bay in Ontario, Canada, forming the NE section of Lake Huron, the second largest of the Great Lakes of North America; it is divided from the lake by Manitoulin Island and the Bruce Peninsula of Ontario; length 160 km/100 mi; width 80 km/50 mi. About 30 islands at the S end form the Georgian Bay national park. The area is a popular tourist destination.

Georgia, Strait of   Strait in British Columbia, Canada, separating Vancouver Island from the mainland; length about 400 km/250 mi. It is about 80 km/50 mi broad at its widest part, but narrows considerably towards the N, where it merges into Johnstone Strait and Queen Charlotte Strait. It meets the Pacific Ocean at Juan De Fuca Strait in the S.

Gera   Industrial city (textiles, electronics) in the *Land* of Thuringia, Germany, on the White Elster River; population (1991) 126,500. It was the former capital of the East German district of Gera 1952–90.

German Ocean   German name for the ◊North Sea.

Germantown   Suburb of NW ◊Philadelphia, Pennsylvania, USA. Once an independent town, it was founded in 1683 by 13 Mennonite families from Germany, led by Francis Pastorius. In the War of Independence George Washington was defeated by the British at the Battle of Germantown in Oct 1777.

Germiston   City in the Gauteng Province, South Africa; population (1991) 134,000. Industries include gold refining, chemicals, steel, and textiles.

Gerona   Town in Cataluña, NE Spain, capital of Gerona province; population (1991) 66,900. Industries include textiles and chemicals. There are ferry links with Ibiza, Barcelona, and Málaga.

Gerona Province of NE Spain in E ◊Cataluña autonomous community; capital Gerona; area 5,887 sq km/ 2,273 sq mi; population (1995) 542,000. The province lies at the E end of the Pyrenees, with its coastline on the Mediterranean Sea. The rivers Ter and Fluvia flow through the province, which encompasses mountain ranges, the plain of El Ampurdan, and the Costa Brava. It has coal, copper, lead, and iron resources. Products include textiles, paper, cork, leather, cement, and cured fish. Tourism is also important.

Gers River in France, 178 km/110 mi in length; it rises in the Lannemezan Plateau and flows N to join the river Garonne 8 km/5 mi above Agen. It gives its name to a *département* in Midi-Pyrénées region.

Gers *Département* in the ◊Midi-Pyrénées region of SW France; area 6,254 km/2,416 sq mi; population (1990) 175,360. It contains sections of the foothills of the Pyrenees and is drained by many rivers, including the Gers, Baise, Save, and Gimone. Vines are extensively grown, primarily for distillation into Armagnac brandy. Cereals, vegetables, fruit, and tobacco are also produced. Stock raising (horses, cattle, and poultry) is important. The principal towns are Auch (the capital), Condom, and Mirande.

Gethsemane Site of the garden where Judas Iscariot, according to the New Testament, betrayed Jesus. It is on the Mount of Olives, E of Jerusalem. When Jerusalem was divided between Israel and Jordan 1948, Gethsemane fell within Jordanian territory.

Gettysburg Site of one of the decisive battles of the American Civil War: a Confederate defeat by Union forces 1–3 July 1863, at Gettysburg, Pennsylvania, 80 km/50 mi NW of Baltimore. The site is now a national cemetery, at the dedication of which President Lincoln delivered the Gettysburg Address 19 Nov 1863.

Gezira, El Plain in the Republic of Sudan, between the Blue and White Nile rivers. The cultivation of cotton, sorghum, wheat, and groundnuts is made possible by irrigation.

Ghaghara or *Gogra* River in N India, a tributary of the ◊Ganges. It rises in Tibet and flows through Nepal and the state of Uttar Pradesh; length 1,000 km/620 mi.

Ghats, Eastern and Western Twin mountain ranges in S India, E and W of the central plateau; a few peaks reach about 3,000 m/9,800 ft. The name is a European misnomer, the Indian word *ghat* meaning 'pass', not 'mountain'.

Ghent (Flemish *Gent*, French *Gand*) City and port in East Flanders, NW Belgium; population (1995) 227,000. Industries include textiles, chemicals, electronics, metallurgy, and motor-vehicle manufacturing. The cathedral of St Bavon (12th–14th centuries) has paintings by van Eyck and Rubens.

Giant's Causeway Stretch of basalt columns forming a headland on the N coast of Antrim, Northern Ireland. It was formed by an outflow of lava in Tertiary times that has solidified in polygonal columns.

Gibraltar British dependency, situated on a narrow rocky

Gibraltar

promontory in S Spain, the *Rock of Gibraltar*.
area 6.5 sq km/2.5 sq mi
features strategic naval and air base, with NATO underground headquarters and communications centre; colony of Barbary apes; the frontier zone is adjoined by the Spanish port of La Línea
exports mainly a trading centre for the import and re-export of goods
population (1993) 29,000
history captured from Spain 1704 by English admiral George Rooke (1650–1709), it was ceded to Britain under the Treaty of Utrecht 1713. A referendum 1967 confirmed the wish of the people to remain in association with the UK, but Spain continues to claim sovereignty and closed the border 1969–85. In 1991, UK ground troops were withdrawn but navy and airforce units remained.

Gibraltar, Strait of Strait between N Africa and Spain, with the Rock of Gibraltar to the N side and Jebel Musa to the S, the so-called Pillars of Hercules.

Gibson Desert Desert in central Western Australia, between the Great Sandy Desert to the N and the Great Victoria Desert in the S; area 220,000 sq km/85,000 sq mi.

Giessen Manufacturing town (machine tools, rubber, leather, tobacco) on the river Lahn, Hessen, Germany; population (1984) 71,800. Its university was established 1605.

Gijón Port on the Bay of Biscay, Oviedo province, N Spain; population (1994) 270,000. It produces iron, steel, chemicals, and oil; it is an outlet for the coal mines of Asturias and is a major fishing and shipbuilding centre.

Gilbert and Ellice Islands Former British colony in the Pacific, known since independence 1978 as the countries of Tuvalu and Kiribati.

Gilgit Mountainous region on the NW frontier of Kashmir, under the rule of Pakistan; area 38,021 sq km/ 14,676 sq mi. It is drained by the Gilgit and Indus rivers. The region's town, Gilgit, was formerly a Buddhist centre.

Gilly Town in the Belgian province of Hainaut, Belgium, 2 km/1 mi E of Charleroi. The chief industries are iron and copper foundries, brewing and distilling. It also has important coal mines.

Gippsland Lakes Series of shallow lagoons on the coast of Victoria, Australia. The main ones are Wellington, Victoria and King (broadly interconnected), and Reeve.

Girgenti Former name (to 1927) of ◊Agrigento, a town in Italy.

Gironde Navigable estuary 80 km/50 mi long, formed by the mouths of the ◊Garonne, length 580 km/360 mi, and ◊Dordogne rivers, in SW France. The Lot, length 480 km/ 300 mi, is a tributary of the Garonne.

Gironde *Département* in the ◊Aquitaine region of France; area 10,000 sq km/3,861 sq mi; population (1990) 1,214,400. It is fertile in the E but marshy and covered with pine woods in the W. The woods are separated from the sea by sand dunes, which extend for 120 km/75 mi along the coast. The great wine-producing district of Médoc lies along the W bank of the Gironde estuary. Cereals, fruit, tobacco, and vegetables are grown, and livestock is farmed. Turpentine, pitch, and charcoal are obtained from the pine forests. The principal towns are ◊Bordeaux (the capital), Blaye, Langon, Lesparre, and Libourne.

Gisborne Port on the E coast of North Island, New Zealand, exporting dairy products, wool and meat; population (1993) 31,500.

Giurgiu (Bulgarian *Giurgevo*) Border town and capital of Giurgiu county, Romania, on the left bank of the river Danube, opposite Bulgarian Ruse, 64 km/40 mi SW of Bucharest; population (1995) 72,300. It is a centre of commerce between Romania and Bulgaria, trading in chemicals, petroleum, timber, salt, and grain, and has large sawmills.

Gîza, El or *al-Jizah* Site of the Great Pyramids and Sphinx; a suburb of ◊Cairo, Egypt; population (1992) 2,144,000. It has textile and film industries.

Glace Bay Port on Cape Breton Island, Nova Scotia, Canada; population (1991) 19,500. It was the centre of a coal-mining area, but fishing and fish processing are now more important. The inventor Guglielmo Marconi sent a transatlantic wireless message from here 1902.

Glacier National Park National park in the Selkirk Mountains, British Columbia, Canada, established 1930 (although a much smaller area was designated in 1886); area 1,350 sq km/521 sq mi.

Gladbeck City in North Rhine–Westphalia, Germany, 40 km/25 mi NE of Düsseldorf; population (1994) 80,000. It has coal, metal, and electrical industries.

Glamorgan (Welsh *Morgannwg*) Three counties of S Wales – ◊Mid Glamorgan, ◊South Glamorgan, and ◊West Glamorgan – created 1974 from the former county of Glamorganshire. All are on the Bristol Channel. In 1996 Mid Glamorgan was divided amongst Rhondda Cynon Taff, Merthyr Tydfil, Bridgend, and Vale of Glamorgan; South Glamorgan was divided amongst Cardiff and Vale of Glamorgan; and West Glamorgan was divided into Neath Port Talbot and Swansea.

Glarus Capital of the Swiss canton of Glarus, situated on the river Linth at the foot of the Glärnisch Massif (height 2,700 m/8,858 ft); population (1995) 5,600.

Glarus Canton in E Switzerland; area 684 sq km/264 sq mi; population (1995) 39,400. Glarus contains part of the valley of the river Linth and is extremely mountainous, its highest point being Mount Tödi (3,623 m/11,886 ft). Relatively isolated, the canton has remained mainly agricultural, with stock-rearing the principal occupation.

Glasgow City and unitary authority in central Scotland
population (1996) 618,400
area 177 sq km/68 sq mi
industries engineering; chemicals; printing; whisky distilling and blending; brewing; electronics; textiles; shipbuilding (Kvaerner-Govan and Yarrow shipyards)
history founded 6th century by St Mungo; 18th century tobacco trade with New World; 19th century Industrial Revolution, shipbuilding.

Glastonbury Market town in Somerset, England, on the river Brue; population (1991) 7,750. There is light industry and tourism. Nearby are two excavated lake villages thought to have been occupied for about 150 years before the Romans came to Britain. *Glastonbury Tor*, a hill with a ruined church tower, rises to 159 m/522 ft.

Glatz German name for ◊Kłodzko, a town in Poland.

Glencoe Glen in NW Scotland, where members of the Macdonald clan were massacred on 13 Feb 1692. John Campbell, Earl of Breadalbane, was the chief instigator. It is now a winter sports area.

Gleneagles Glen in Perth and Kinross, Scotland, famous for its golf course and for the *Gleneagles Agreement*, formulated 1977 at the Gleneagles Hotel by Commonwealth heads of government, that 'every practical step (should be taken) to discourage contact or competition by their nationals' with South Africa, in opposition to apartheid.

Glenrothes Town and administrative headquarters of Fife, Scotland, 10 km/6 mi N of Kirkcaldy, designated a new town from 1948; population (1991) 38,650. Industries include electronics, plastics, food processing, timber, and paper.

Glens Falls City in E central New York, USA, N of Albany and S of lakes George and Champlain; population (1990) 15,000. It is situated in Warren County by a waterfall in the Hudson River. Its industries include clothing, paper, machinery parts, insurance, and tourism. The site was developed in the 1760s by Quakers, who built timber, paper, and textile mills.

Glittertind Highest mountain in Norway, rising to 2,472 m/ 8,110 ft (including glacier ice) in the Jotunheim range. Glittertind is measured as the highest mountain, but if the measurement was exclusive of ice and snow Galdhøpiggen would be the highest, at 2,469 m/8,100 ft.

Gliwice City in Katowice region, S Poland, formerly in German Silesia; population (1990) 214,200. It has coal-mining, iron, steel, and electrical industries. It is connected to the river Oder by the Gliwice Canal.

Glomma River in Norway, 570 km/350 mi long. The largest river in Scandinavia, it flows into the Skagerrak (an arm of the North Sea) at Fredrikstad.

Glos Abbreviation for ◊Gloucestershire, an English county.

Gloucester City, port, and administrative headquarters of Gloucestershire, England; population (1994 est) 102,000. Industries include the manufacture of aircraft components, agricultural machinery, match-making, financial and insurance companies. There was a Roman colony (*Glevum*) here at the end of the 1st century AD. The 11th–14th-century cathedral has a Norman nucleus and additions in every style of Gothic.

Gloucester City in NE Massachusetts, USA, on Cape Ann, NE of Boston; population (1990) 28,700. A fishing port, its industries include tourism and fish processing, especially lobster, whiting, and cod. Gloucester was first settled 1623.

Gloucestershire County of SW England
area 2,640 sq km/1,019 sq mi
towns and cities Gloucester (administrative headquarters), Stroud, Cheltenham, Tewkesbury, Cirencester
features Cotswold Hills; river Severn and tributaries; Berkeley Castle, where Edward II was murdered; Prinknash Abbey, where pottery is made; Cotswold Farm Park, near Stow-on-the-Wold, which has rare and ancient breeds of farm animals; Tewkesbury Abbey, with early 12th-century nave
industries cereals, fruit, dairy products; engineering; timber; aerospace industry (Dowty)
population (1994) 549,500.

Gmünd Short form of Schwäbisch-Gmünd, a town in Germany.

Gmunden Town in the province of Upper Austria, 57 km/35 mi SW of Linz, at the top of Lake Traun in the Salzkammergut. Gmunden is a popular tourist resort. There are salt mines close to the town.

Gniezno Industrial town and commercial centre in Poznań province, Poland, 48 km/30 mi E of Poznań ; population (1990) 70,400. Industries include machinery, chemicals, and food processing, and cattle are traded. Gniezno is where the Polish state is said to have been founded; its archbishopric, the first in Poland, was established in 1000 by the Holy Roman emperor Otto III, and Polish kings were crowned here until 1320.

Goa State of India
area 3,702 sq km/1,429 sq mi
capital Panaji
population (1994 est) 1,235,000
features Portuguese colonial architecture; church with remains of St Francis Xavier
industries rice, pulses, cashew nuts, coconuts, ragi (a cereal), iron ore, tourism
history captured by the Portuguese 1510; the inland area was added in the 18th century. Goa was incorporated into India as a union territory with ◊Daman and Diu 1961 and became a state 1987.

Gobi Vast desert region of Central Asia in the independent state of Mongolia, and Inner Mongolia, China. It covers an area of 1,295,000 sq km/500,000 sq mi and lies on a high plateau 900–1,500 m/2,950–4,920 ft above sea level. It is mainly rocky, with shifting sands, and salt marshes at lower levels. It is sparsely populated, mainly by nomadic herders. It is rich in fossil remains of extinct species, and stone-age implements.

Godalming Town in Surrey, SE England; population (1991) 20,600. Industries include light engineering and textiles. The writer Aldous Huxley lived here.

Godavari River in central India, flowing from the Western Ghats to the Bay of Bengal; length 1,450 km/900 mi. It is sacred to Hindus.

Göding German name for ◊Hodonín, a town in the Czech Republic.

Godthaab (Greenlandic *Nuuk*) Capital and largest town of Greenland; population (1993) 12,200. It is a storage centre for oil and gas, and the chief industry is fish processing.

Goes Town in the province of Zeeland, the Netherlands, situated on the island of South Beveland, 22 km/14 mi E of Middelburg; population (1996) 34,000. There is a 16th-century Gothic basilica and a town hall restored in 1771.

Gogra Alternative transcription of the river ◊Ghaghara in India.

Golan Heights (Arabic *Jawlan*) Plateau on the Syrian border with Israel, bitterly contested in the Arab–Israeli Wars and annexed by Israel 14 Dec 1981. In the 1996 peace talks Syria insisted that Israel withdraw from the Golan Heights, following its capture 1967.

Gold Coast Former name for Ghana, but historically the W coast of Africa from Cape Three Points to the Volta River, where alluvial gold is washed down. Portuguese and French navigators visited this coast in the 14th century, and a British trading settlement developed into the colony of the Gold Coast 1618. With its dependencies of Ashanti and Northern Territories plus the trusteeship territory of Togoland, it became Ghana 1957. The name is also used for many coastal resort areas – for example, in Florida, USA.

Gold Coast Resort region on the E coast of Australia, stretching 32 km/20 mi along the coast of Queensland and New South Wales S of Brisbane; population (1991) 279,600.

Golden Gate Strait in California, USA, linking San Francisco Bay with the Pacific, spanned by a suspension bridge that was completed 1937. The longest span is 1,280 m/4,200 ft.

Gonder Town in Ethiopia about 2,300 m/7,500 ft above sea level and 40 km/25 mi N of Lake Tana; population (1992) 156,000. It is the capital of a region by the same name. Cattle, grain, and seed are traded. It was the capital of Ethiopia 1632–1855.

Goodwin Sands Sandbanks off the coast of Kent, England, exposed at low tide, and famous for wrecks. According to legend, they are the remains of the island of Lomea, owned by Earl Godwin in the 11th century.

Goose Bay Settlement at the head of Lake Melville on the Labrador coast of Newfoundland, Canada. A Canadian airforce base is on land claimed by the indigenous Innu (or Montagnais-Naskapi) people, who call themselves a sovereign nation (in 1989 they numbered 9,500). In World War II Goose Bay was used as a staging post by US and Canadian troops on their way to Europe. Until 1975 it was used by the US Air Force as a low-level-flying base, and the NATO military base here still trains jet pilots in low-level flying.

Göppingen City in Baden-Württemberg, Germany, on the river Fils, 40 km/25 mi E of Stuttgart; population (1994) 254,200. It has a 15th-century church and a 16th-century castle. There are mineral springs and metal, textile, chemical, and tanning industries.

Gorakhpur City in Uttar Pradesh, N India, situated on the Rapti River, at the centre of an agricultural region producing cotton, rice, and grain; population (1991) 506,000.

Gorgonzola Town NE of Milan in Lombardy, Italy; population (1971 est) 13,000. It is famous for its blue-veined cheese. Bel Paese is also made here.

Gorinchem Town in the province of South Holland, Netherlands, 37 km/23 mi SE of Rotterdam; population (1996) 32,000. Gorinchem is sited at a major junction of inland waterway routes.

Gorizia Town in Friuli-Venezia-Giulia region, N Italy, on the Isonzo, SE of Udine; population (1981) 41,500. Industries include textiles, furniture, and paper. It has a 16th-century castle, and was a cultural centre during Habsburg rule.

Gorizia Province of NE Italy in E ◊Friuli-Venezia Giulia region; capital Gorizia; area 472 sq km/182 sq mi; population (1992) 138,100.

Gorky (Russian *Gor'kiy*) Name 1932–90 of ◊Nizhniy-Novgorod, a city in central Russia.

Görlitz Manufacturing town (rolling stock) in the state of Saxony, Germany; population (1981) 81,000.

Gorlovka Industrial city (coal mining, chemicals, engineering) on the ◊Donets Basin coalfield, Ukraine; population (1990) 338,000.

Gorzów Wielkopolski (German *Landsberg-an-der-Warthe*) Industrial town (chemicals, metals, textiles) in Zielona Góra province, Poland, on the river Warta, 57 km/36 mi N of Zielona Góra; population (1990) 124,300. The town, with its 13th-century church, was founded by German settlers 1257, but was assigned to Poland after World War II.

Goshen City in N Indiana, USA, on the Elkhart River, SE of South Bend; seat of Elkhart County; population (1990) 23,700. It is situated in an agricultural area and serves as a market town. Industries include steel, rubber, electrical, and building products.

Goslar City in Lower Saxony, Germany, on the N side of the Harz Mountains, 76 km/47 mi SE of Hannover; population (1994) 162,200. Goslar is a diversified industrial city and a tourist centre for the Harz Mountains. In the Middle Ages, it was an important town and imperial residence; the imperial palace remains.

Gosport Naval base opposite ◊Portsmouth, Hampshire, England; population (1991) 75,000. Industries include chemicals, plastics, engineering, and yacht building.

Göta River in S Sweden; length 109 km/67 mi. It flows from Lake Vänern to the Kattegat, which separates Denmark from Sweden. The river divides at the town of Kungålv, the S branch passing Göteborg. It is navigable; the Trollhättan Canal was constructed to avoid the Trollhåtta Falls near the river's source.

Göteborg (German *Gothenburg*) Port and industrial city (ships, vehicles, chemicals) on the W coast of Sweden, at the mouth of the Göta River; population (1994 est) 444,600. It is Sweden's second largest city and is linked with Stockholm by the Göta Canal (built 1832).

Gotha Town in Thuringia, Germany, former capital of the duchy of Saxe-Coburg-Gotha; population (1989 est) 57,200. It has a castle and two observatories; pottery, soap, textiles, precision instruments, and aircraft are manufactured here.

Gothenburg German form of ◊Göteborg, a city in Sweden.

Gotland Swedish island in the Baltic Sea; area 3,140 sq km/1,212 sq mi; population (1994 est) 58,200. The capital is Visby. Its products are mainly agricultural (sheep and cattle), and there is tourism. It was an area of dispute between Sweden and Denmark but became part of Sweden 1645.

Göttingen City in Lower Saxony, Germany; population (1991) 124,000. Industries include printing, publishing, precision instruments, and chemicals. Its university was founded by George II of England 1734.

Gouda Town in South Holland province, W Netherlands; population (1993) 68,600. It stands at the confluence of the rivers Gouwe and IJssel. It is known for its round, flat cheeses and dairy products; stoneware and candles are also produced.

Goulburn Town in New South Wales, Australia, SW of Sydney; population (1983) 22,500. It is an agricultural centre, and manufactures bricks, tiles, and pottery.

Gower Peninsula (Welsh *Penrhyn Gwyr*) Peninsula in Swansea unitary authority, S Wales, extending into the Bristol Channel. There is tourism on the S coast; the N is marshy.

Grafton Town in New South Wales, Australia, S of Brisbane; population (1985) 17,600. Industries include sugar, timber, and dairy products.

Graham Land Mountainous peninsula in Antarctica, formerly a dependency of the Falkland Islands, and from 1962 part of the ◊British Antarctic Territory. It was discovered by John Biscoe 1832 and until 1934 was thought to be an archipelago.

Grahamstown Town in Eastern Cape Province, South Africa; population (1991) 19,800. It is the seat of Rhodes University, established 1951, founded 1904 as Rhodes University College.

Grampian Former Region of Scotland to 1996; replaced by Aberdeen City and Aberdeenshire unitary authorities.

Grampian Mountains Range that separates the Highlands from the Lowlands of Scotland. It includes **Ben Nevis**, the highest mountain in the British Isles at 1,340 m/4,406 ft, and the Cairngorm Mountains, which include **Ben Macdhui** 1,309 m/4,296 ft. The region includes Aviemore, a winter holiday and sports centre.

Grampians Western end of Australia's E highlands, in Victoria; the highest peak is Mount William, 1,167 m/3,829 ft.

Granada Former Moorish kingdom in S Spain, roughly coextensive with the present provinces of Granada, Almería, and Málaga. It grew up around the city of Granada, founded by the Moors in the 8th century, and until 1236 was part of the territory of the caliph of Córdoba. In 1492 it was taken by Ferdinand II and Isabella, and incorporated in the new Spanish kingdom. With the capture of Granada, the Moorish power in Spain was finally extinguished; the last Moorish king, Boabdil, went into exile.

Granada Nicaraguan city on the NW shore of Lake Nicaragua; population (1985) 89,000. It has shipyards and manufactures sugar, soap, clothing, and furniture. Founded 1523, it is the oldest city in Nicaragua.

Granada Province of S Spain in central ◊Andalusia autonomous community; capital Granada; area 12,530 sq m/4,838 sq mi; population (1995) 841,800. Its physical features include the snow-capped Sierra Nevada, a hot Mediterranean coastal plain, and a fertile elevated inland plain. The river Guadalquivir and its tributaries flow through the province. Products include textiles, brandy, and sugar. There are large mineral deposits.

Granada City in the Sierra Nevada in Andalusia, S Spain; population (1994) 271,000. It produces textiles, soap, and paper. The *Alhambra*, a fortified hilltop palace, was built in the 13th and 14th centuries by the Moorish kings.

Gran Canaria One of the chief ◊Canary Islands, in the Spanish province of Las Palmas; capital ◊Las Palmas; area 1,533 sq km/592 sq mi. It is fertile, of volcanic origin with deep valleys, and its peaks reach 1,980 m/6,495 ft.

Gran Chaco Large lowland plain in N Argentina, W Paraguay, and SE Bolivia; area 650,000 sq km/251,000 sq mi. It consists of swamps, forests (a source of quebracho timber), and grasslands, and there is cattle-raising.

Grand Canal (Chinese *Da Yune*) The world's longest canal. It is 1,600 km/1,000 mi long and runs N from Hangzhou to Tianjin, China; it is 30–61 m/100–200 ft wide, and reaches depths of over 1.5 km/1 mi. The earliest section was completed 486 BC; the central section linking the Chiang Jiang (Yangtse-Kiang) and Huang He (Yellow) rivers was built AD 605–610; and the N section was built AD 1282–92, during the reign of Kublai Khan.

Grand Canyon Gorge of multicoloured rock strata cut by and containing the Colorado River, N Arizona, USA. It is 350 km/217 mi long, 6–29 km/4–18 mi wide, and reaches depths of over 1.7 km/1.1 mi. It was made a national park 1919, and is a World Heritage Site. Millions of tourists visit the canyon each year.

Grand Falls Town in Newfoundland, NW of St John's, Canada; population (1991) 6,100. It is the site of large paper and pulp mills, and is a base for hunting and fishing. Grand Falls developed around a newspaper and pulp mill built 1905.

Grand Forks City in E central North Dakota, USA, on the Minnesota border, on the Red River, N of Fargo; seat of Grand Forks County; population (1990) 49,400. It serves the surrounding agricultural area; most of its industries, such as food-processing mills and fertilizer plants, are associated with agriculture. A fur-trading post, founded 1801, it was permanently settled 1871. The University of North Dakota 1883 is located here.

Grand Rapids City in W Michigan, USA, on the Grand River; population (1992) 191,200. It produces furniture, motor bodies, plumbing fixtures, and electrical goods. A fur-trading post was founded here 1826, and the furniture industry developed in the 1840s.

Grand Teton Highest point of the Teton mountain range, NW Wyoming, USA, rising to 4,197 m/13,770 ft. Grand Teton National Park was established 1929.

Granite City City in SW Illinois, USA, across the Mississippi River from St Louis, Missouri; population (1990) 32,800. An industrial city with its own port on the Chain of Rocks Canal, it manufactures steel products, car frames, and building materials. It was founded 1891 when a graniteware factory was built.

Grantham Market town in SE Lincolnshire, England; population (1991) 33,200. It is an agricultural centre, dating from Saxon times; other industries include engineering, sausages, and pastries. The former UK prime minister Margaret Thatcher was born here.

Grasmere English lake and village in the Lake District, Cumbria, associated with many writers. William Wordsworth and his sister Dorothy lived at Dove Cottage (now a museum) 1799–1808, Thomas de Quincey later made his home in the same house, and both Samuel Coleridge and Wordsworth are buried in the churchyard of St Oswald's.

Grasse Town near Cannes, SE France; population (1990) 42,100. It is the centre of a perfume-manufacturing region, and flowers are grown on a large scale for this purpose.

Graubünden (French *Grisons*) Swiss canton, the largest in Switzerland; area 7,106 sq km/2,743 sq mi; population (1990) 170,400. The inner valleys are the highest in Europe, and the main sources of the river Rhine rise here. It also includes the resort of Davos and, in the Upper Engadine, St Moritz. The capital is Chur. Romansch is still widely spoken. Graubünden entered the Swiss Confederation 1803.

Graudenz German name for ◊Grudziądz, a town in Poland.

Gravesend Town on the river Thames, Kent, SE England, linked by ferry with Tilbury opposite; population (1991) 51,400. Industries include electrical goods, engineering, printing, and paper-making.

Graz Capital of Styria province, and second-largest city in Austria; population (1991) 237,800. Industries include engineering, chemicals, iron, steel, and automobile manufacturing. It has a 15th-century cathedral and a university founded 1573. Lippizaner horses are bred near here.

Great Australian Bight Broad bay of the Indian Ocean in S Australia, notorious for storms. It was discovered by a Dutch navigator, Captain Thyssen, 1627.

Great Barrier Reef Chain of coral reefs and islands about 2,000 km/1,250 mi long, off the E coast of Queensland, Australia, at a distance of 15–45 km/10–30 mi. It is made up of 3,000 individual reefs, and is believed to be the world's largest living organism. The Great Barrier Reef is an immense natural breakwater, the coral rock forming a structure larger than all human-made structures on Earth combined. It used to be thought that it was between 3 and 4 million years old, because of its proximity to the coral reefs of Papua New Guinea, which have been dated as being that old. However, new research (1997) indicated that the Great Barrier Reef only began to grow between 300,000 and 400,000 years ago, when the sea level was high. Therefore, the formation of the reef is now thought to be a recent geological event.

Great Basin Large arid region of W USA, which includes nearly all Nevada, Utah, and parts of Oregon and California, and lies between the Sierra Nevada mountain range in California on the W and the Wasatch Mountains on the E. Mountains run from N to S of it, and rise to a height of 1,220 m/4,003 ft above the plateau. The soil is fertile where irrigation is possible, but the hills are barren. It has numerous lakes, including the Great Salt Lake, Lake Utah, Lake Sevier, Lake Walker, and Lake Carson. The mountains are rich in minerals, especially silver ore.

Great Bear Lake Lake on the Arctic Circle, in the Northwest Territories, Canada; area 31,316 sq km/12,091 sq mi.

Great Britain Official name for ◊England, ◊Scotland, and ◊Wales, and the adjacent islands (except the Channel Islands and the Isle of Man) from 1603, when the English and Scottish crowns were united under James I of England (James VI of Scotland). With Northern ◊Ireland it forms the United Kingdom.

Great Dividing Range E Australian mountain range, extending 3,700 km/2,300 mi N–S from Cape York Peninsula, Queensland, to Victoria. It includes the Carnarvon Range, Queensland, which has many Aboriginal cave paintings, the Blue Mountains in New South Wales, and the Australian Alps.

Great Falls City in central Montana, USA, on the Missouri River, NE of Helena; seat of Cascade County; population (1992) 55,100. Its main industries are involved with the processing of copper and zinc from nearby mines. The processing of agricultural products and oil refining is also important. The city is named after nearby waterfalls, first discovered 1805 by Meriwether Lewis and William Clark.

Great Lake Australia's largest freshwater lake, 1,030 m/3,380 ft above sea level, in Tasmania; area 114 sq km/44 sq mi. It is used for hydroelectric power and is a tourist attraction.

Great Lakes Series of five freshwater lakes along the US-Canadian border: Superior, Michigan, Huron, Erie, and Ontario; total area 245,000 sq km/94,600 sq mi. Interconnecting canals make the lakes navigable by large ships, and they are drained by the ◊St Lawrence River. The whole forms the St Lawrence Seaway. They are said to contain 20% of the world's surface fresh water.

Great Lakes

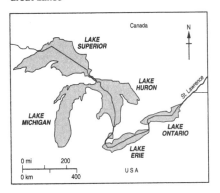

Great Plain of Hungary Alternative name for the ◊Alföld region in Hungary.

Great Plains Semi-arid region to the E of the Rocky Mountains, USA, stretching as far as the 100th meridian of longitude through Oklahoma, Kansas, Nebraska, and the Dakotas. The plains, which cover one-fifth of the USA, extend from Texas in the S over 2,400 km/1,500 mi N to Canada. Ranching and wheat farming have resulted in overuse of water resources to such an extent that available farmland has been reduced by erosion.

Great Rift Valley Longest 'split' in the Earth's surface; see ◊Rift Valley, Great.

Great Salt Lake Lake in NW Utah, USA, 18 km/11 mi NW of Salt Lake City. It is 130 km/81 mi long and 80 km/50 mi wide, with an area of approximately 4,145 sq km/1,600 sq mi (although it fluctuates greatly in size). It lies some 1,280 m/4,200 ft above sea level, and is situated in the E part of the Great Basin near the foot of the Wasatch Mountains. The lake is generally 5 m/16 ft deep but its depth, like its area, fluctuates greatly. The lake is fed by the Bear, Weber, and Jordan rivers, but it has no outlet (other than evaporation). It is the second most saline body of water in the world (after the Dead Sea); the manufacture of salt is an important industry. It is a popular bathing resort.

Great Sandy Desert Desert in N Western Australia; 338,500 sq km/150,000 sq mi. It is also the name of an arid region in S Oregon, USA.

Great Slave Lake Lake in the Northwest Territories, Canada; area 28,560 sq km/11,027 sq mi. It is the deepest lake (615 m/2,020 ft) in North America.

Great Yarmouth Alternative name for the resort and port of ◊Yarmouth in Norfolk, England.

Greeley City in N Colorado, USA, at the point where the Cache de Poudre River flows into the South Platte River, NE of Boulder; population (1992) 61,800. Greeley is a distribution centre for the surrounding agricultural area, and its main industry is the processing of sugar beet. The city was founded 1870 as Union Colony, a cooperative agricultural enterprise, and was renamed after the publisher Horace Greeley, one of its founders.

Green Bay City in NE Wisconsin, USA, where the Little Fox River flows into Green Bay on Lake Michigan; seat of Brown County; population (1992) 100,000. It is a port of entry to the USA through the St Lawrence Seaway and serves as a distribution centre. Industries include paper and food products. Green Bay was first settled 1634.

Greenland (Greenlandic *Kalaallit Nunaat*) World's largest island, lying between the North Atlantic and Arctic Oceans E of North America
area 2,175,600 sq km/840,000 sq mi
capital Godthaab (Greenlandic *Nuuk*) on the W coast
features the whole of the interior is covered by a vast ice sheet (the remnant of the last glaciation, part of the N polar icecap); the island has an important role strategically and in civil aviation, and shares military responsibilities with the USA; there are lead and cryolite deposits, and offshore oil is being explored
economy fishing and fish-processing
population (1993) 55,100; Inuit (Ammassalik Eskimoan), Danish, and other European
language Greenlandic (Ammassalik Eskimoan)
history Greenland was discovered in about 982 by Eric the Red, who founded colonies on the W coast soon after Inuit from the North American Arctic had made their way to Greenland. Christianity was introduced to the Vikings in about 1000. In 1261 the Viking colonies accepted Norwegian

Greenland

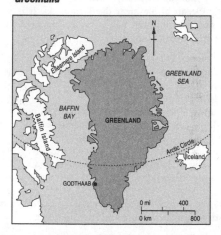

sovereignty, but early in the 15th century all communication with Europe ceased, and by the 16th century the colonies had died out, but the Inuit had moved on to the E coast. It became a Danish colony in the 18th century, and following a referendum in 1979 was granted full internal self-government in 1981.

Greenland Sea Area of the ◊Arctic Ocean between Spitsbergen and Greenland, and N of the Norwegian Sea.

Green Mountains Mountain range in Vermont, NE USA, representing a N extension of the ◊Appalachian Mountains. The highest peak in the range is Mount Mansfield (1,339 m/4,393 ft). The area's popularity for skiing has led to erosion problems. The Green Mountain national forest was created 1932 to protect the environment.

Greenock Port and administrative headquarters of Inverclyde, W Scotland, on the S shore of the Firth of Clyde; population (1991) 50,000. Industries include shipbuilding, engineering, electronics, chemicals, and sugar refining. It is the birthplace of the engineer and inventor James Watt.

Green River River in Wyoming and Utah, USA; length 1,160 km/721 mi. It is one of the two rivers that ultimately form the Colorado River (the other is the San Juan). It rises in the Wind River Mountains in W Wyoming and flows S through the canyons of E Utah before joining the Colorado River. Navigation is almost impossible.

Greensboro City in N central North Carolina, USA, W of Durham; seat of Guilford County; population (1992) 190,000. It has textile, chemical, and tobacco industries. Many schools are located here, including Guilford College (1834) and the University of North Carolina at Greensboro (1891). The city was founded 1808 and named after General Nathanael Greene, commander of the American forces in the Battle of Guilford Courthouse 1781, which was fought nearby.

Greenville City in NW South Carolina, USA, on the Reedy River, near the foothills of the Blue Ridge Mountains, SW of Spartanburg; seat of Greenville County; population (1990) 44,900. It is known as a major textile manufacturing centre. Other industries include lumber and chemicals. Settled in the 1760s, Greenville was chartered 1831.

Greenwich Outer London borough of SE Greater London. It includes the districts of ◊Woolwich and Eltham.

Greenwich Town on the coast of Connecticut, NE USA, situated on Long Island Sound, about 56 km/35 mi NE of New York; population (1991) 58,500. It is a residential area with many recreation facilities.

Greifswald Town in the *Land* of ◊Mecklenburg–West Pomerania, Germany, on the river Ryck, 84 km/52 mi E of Rostock. Its university dates from 1456. The town's chief industries are fish-preserving and the manufacture of machinery and chemicals. There are many medieval houses and a 13th-century church.

Greiz Town in the *Land* of ◊Thuringia, Germany, on the river Weisse Elster at the mouth of the Göltzsch, 26 km/16 mi S of Gera. Textiles, paper, and chemicals are manufactured. Until 1918 it was the capital of one of the Reuss principalities, and has two palaces.

Grenadines Chain of about 600 small islands in the Caribbean Sea, part of the group known as the Windward Islands. They are divided between St Vincent and Grenada.

Grenoble Alpine city in the Isère *département*, Rhône-Alpes region, SE France; population (1990) 154,000. Industries include engineering, nuclear research, hydroelectric power, computers, technology, chemicals, plastics, and gloves.

Grimsby Fishing port and administrative headquarters of North East Lincolnshire, England; population (1991) 90,500. It declined in the 1970s when Icelandic waters were closed to British fishing fleets.

Grindelwald Valley and town in the canton of Bern, Switzerland, in the ◊Bernese Alps; altitude 1,040 m/3,412 ft; population (1995) 4,100. Grindelwald is a popular sports resort in both summer and winter. The towering N face of the Eiger dominates the town.

Gris Nez Cape in the *département* of Pas-de-Calais, France, and the point on the French coast nearest to Britain. It is opposite Dover and midway between Calais and Boulogne. Gris Nez has a lighthouse.

Grisons French name for the Swiss canton of ◊Graubünden.

Groningen Most northerly province of the Netherlands, on the Ems estuary and including the innermost W Friesian Islands; area 2,350 sq km/907 sq mi; population (1995 est) 558,000; capital Groningen. Other towns and cities are Hoogezand-Sappemeer, Stadskanaal, Veendam, Delfzijl, and Winschoten. Industries include natural gas, arable farming, dairy produce, sheep, and horses.

Groningen Capital of Groningen province in the Netherlands; population (1996) 170,100. Groningen is the most important town in the N Netherlands; its position as a centre for trade is promoted by its canal connections with the Dollart (the basin of the river Ems) and the IJsselmeer. Linen, woollens, and tobacco are produced, and there is boat-building. The University of Groningen was founded 1614.

Grosseto Province of N central Italy in S ◊Tuscany region; capital Grosseto (population (1990) 71,400); area 4,496 sq km/1,736 sq mi; population (1992) 216,800.

Grossglockner Highest mountain in Austria, rising to 3,797 m/12,457 ft in the Hohe Tauern range of the Tirol Alps.

Grozny Capital of Chechnya and of the former Russian republic of Checheno-Ingush; population (1992) 388,000. Situated on the Sunzha River, it was founded 1818 as a Cossack fortress. Large-scale oil production began 1893 and it became a major oil centre with pipelines to the Caspian Sea at Makhachkala and the Black Sea at Tuapse. Half its residential areas were damaged beyond repair and its infrastructure destroyed by Russian bombing 1994–95.

Grudziądz (German *Graudenz*) Town in Toruń province, Poland, on the river Vistula, 64 km/40 mi NE of Bydgoszcz;

population (1990) 81,700. Manufactures include chemicals, machinery, and glass, and timber and agricultural produce are traded. The town has a castle of the Teutonic Knights (a German Christian military order), and was part of Prussia 1772–1920.

Grünberg German name for ◊Zielona Góra, a town in Poland.

Gruyère District in Fribourg canton, W Switzerland, renowned for its pale yellow cheese with large holes. Gruyère centres on the Saane Valley. Bulle is the present-day capital, Gruyères the historic capital. In addition to cheese production, cattle are raised and chocolate is made here.

Guadalajara Industrial city (textiles, glass, soap, pottery), capital of Jalisco state, W Mexico; population (1990) 2,847,000. It is a key communications centre. It has a 16th–17th-century cathedral, the Governor's Palace, and an orphanage with murals by the Mexican painter José Orozco (1883–1949).

Guadalajara Province of central Spain in N ◊Castilla–La Mancha autonomous community; capital Guadalajara; area 12,194 sq km/4,708 sq mi; population (1995) 155,900. It is largely on the plateau NE of Madrid. The river Tagus and its tributaries (Henares and Tajuna) flow through it. The river valleys are fertile, but in general the province is unproductive. There are some silver deposits. There was severe fighting here during the Spanish Civil War 1936–39.

Guadalaviar River in W Spain, rising in the Sierra de Albarracín in the province of Teruel; length 320 km/199 mi. It flows E to the town of Teruel, from which point it is usually called the Turia, then curves S to the Mediterranean Sea near Valencia. It is important for irrigation.

Guadalcanal Largest of the Solomon Islands; area 6,500 sq km/2,510 sq mi; population (1991) 60,700. Gold, copra, and rubber are produced. During World War II it was the scene of a battle for control of the area that was won by US forces after six months of fighting.

Guadalquivir (Arabic Wadi al-Kebir) River in S Spain, rising in the E of Jaén province; length 600 km/373 mi. It flows by Baeza, Andújar, Córdoba, and Seville, to the Atlantic Ocean at Sanlúcar de Barrameda. It is navigable below Seville, although it has to be canalized. It is very important for irrigation.

Guadeloupe Island group in the Leeward Islands, West Indies, an overseas *département* of France. The main islands are Basse-Terre and Grande-Terre.
area 1,705 sq km/658 sq mi
chief town The chief town and seat of government is Basse-Terre (on the island of the same name), population (1988) 14,000.
population (1990) 387,000 (77% mulatto, 10% black, and 10% mestizo). The people of St Barthélemy and Les Saintes are mainly descended from 17th century Norman and Breton settlers
languages French (official); Creole (the main language)
industries sugar refining and rum distilling

Guadiana River in Spain and Portugal; length 800 km/ 497 mi. Its headstream is the river Záncara, which rises in the central Spanish province of Cuenca. Near the Záncara are the Ojos del Guadiana lagoons, frequented by wildfowl. The Guadiana flows W to Badajoz, then S, weaving across the Spanish-Portuguese border to the Atlantic Ocean at Ayamonte.

Guam Largest of the ◊Mariana Islands in the W Pacific, an unincorporated territory of the USA
area 540 sq km/208 sq mi
capital Agaña
towns and cities Apra (port), Tamuning
features major US air and naval base, much used in the Vietnam War; tropical, with much rain
industries sweet potatoes, fish; tourism is important
currency US dollar
population (1992) 140,200
language English, Chamorro (basically Malay-Polynesian)
religion 96% Roman Catholic
government popularly elected governor (Joseph F Ada from 1991) and single-chamber legislature
history claimed by Magellan for Spain 1521. The indigenous population of Chamorros dwindled from 80,000 in 1668 to 1,500 in 1783, partly as a result of infectious disease, partly as a result of Spanish brutality. Guam was captured by the USA 1898 in the Spanish-American War. It was occupied by Japan as an air and naval base 1941–44. Guam achieved full US citizenship and self-government from 1950. It became the headquarters of the US Pacific Strategic Air Command 1954 and is also central command for all US naval operations in the W Pacific, with 21,000 US military personnel (1991) and storage of nuclear weapons. A referendum 1982 favoured the status of a commonwealth, in association with the USA. The USA spends $750 million a year on its military presence in Guam.

Guangdong or *Kwantung* Province of S China
area 231,400 sq km/89,343 sq mi
capital Guangzhou
features tropical climate; Hainan, Leizhou peninsula; Hong Kong; the foreign enclave of Macau in the Pearl River delta
industries rice, sugar, tobacco, minerals, fish
population (1990) 63,210,000.

Guangxi Zhuang or *Kwangsi Chuang* Autonomous region in S China
area 220,400 sq km/85,096 sq mi
capital Nanning
industries rice, sugar, fruit
population (1990) 42,246,000, including the Zhuang people, allied to the Thai, who form China's largest ethnic minority.

Guangzhou or *Kwangchow* or *Canton* Capital of Guangdong province, S China; population (1993) 3,560,000. Industries include shipbuilding, engineering, chemicals, and textiles.

Guanajuato State of central Mexico; area 30,589 sq km/ 11,810 sq mi; population (1995 est) 4,393,200. Its capital is Guanajuato. The main occupation is mining for silver, gold, zinc, copper, mercury, and lead.

Guantánamo Capital of a province of the same name in SE Cuba; population (1990 est) 200,400. It is a trading centre in a fertile agricultural region producing sugar. Iron, copper, chromium, and manganese are mined nearby. There is a US naval base, for which the Cuban government has refused to accept rent since 1959.

Guatemala Capital of Guatemala; population (1990 est) 1,675,600. It produces textiles, tyres, footwear, and cement. It was founded 1776 when its predecessor (Antigua) was destroyed in an earthquake. It was severely damaged by another earthquake 1976.

Guavio Dam Hydroelectric rockfill dam in central Colombia, opened 1990. It is the highest in South America, 245 m/804 ft, and has a generating capacity of 1,600 megawatts.

Guayaquil Largest city and chief port of Ecuador near the mouth of the Guayas river; population (1990) 1,508,000. The economic centre of Ecuador and the capital of Guayas province, Guayaquil manufactures machinery and consumer goods, processes food, and refines petroleum. It was founded 1537 by the Spanish explorer Francisco de Orellana. The port exports bananas, cacao, and coffee.

Guben Town in the *Land* of ◊Brandenburg, Germany, on the left bank of the river Neisse, 35 km/22 mi NE of Cottbus. Since the expansion of Poland's W border in 1945 the part of the town on the right bank of the river has formed a separate town in Poland called *Gubin*. There are brown coal (lignite) mines and a textile industry.

Guelders English name for ◊Gelderland, a province of the Netherlands.

Guelph Industrial town and agricultural centre in SE Ontario, Canada, on the Speed River; population (1991) 88,000. Industries include food processing, electrical goods, and pharmaceuticals. The town was founded 1827 by John Galt, a Scottish novelist, and named after the family name of the royal house of Hanover.

Guernica Town in the ◊Basque province of Vizcaya, N Spain; population (1989) 16,400. Here the Castilian kings formerly swore to respect the rights of the Basques. It was almost completely destroyed 1937 by German bombers aiding General Franco in the Spanish Civil War and rebuilt 1946. The bombing inspired a painting by Pablo Picasso and a play by dramatist Fernando Arrabal.

Guernsey Second largest of the ◊Channel Islands; area 63 sq km/24.3 sq mi; population (1991) 58,900. The capital is St Peter Port. Products include electronics, tomatoes, flowers, and butterflies; from 1975 it has been a major financial centre. Guernsey cattle, which are a distinctive pale fawn colour and give rich, creamy milk, originated here.

Guerrero State of SW Mexico, on the Pacific; area 63,794 sq km/24,631 sq mi; population (1995 est) 2,915,500. Its capital is Chilpancingo. The main occupation is farming, producing cereals, cotton, sugar-cane, and coffee.

Guiana NE part of South America that includes ◊French Guiana, Guyana, and Suriname.

Guildford City in Surrey, S England, on the river Wey; population (1991) 66,000. It has a ruined Norman castle, a cathedral (founded 1936 and completed 1961), and the University of Surrey (1966). There is a cattle market, and industries include flour-milling, plastics, engineering, vehicles, and pharmaceuticals. The Yvonne Arnaud Theatre opened 1965.

Guilin or *Kweilin* Principal tourist city of S China, on the Li River, Guangxi province; population (1990) 364,000. The dramatic limestone mountains are a tourist attraction.

Guinea, Gulf of Part of the Atlantic Ocean off the coast of W Africa between Cape Palmas, Liberia, and Cap Lopez, Gabon. It includes the coastal features of the Bight of Benin and the Bight of Bonny. The rivers Volta, Niger, and Ogooué flow into it.

Guipúzcoa Province of N Spain in N ◊Basque Country autonomous community; capital San Sebastián; area 1,997 sq km/771 sq mi; population (1995) 684,100. The smallest of the three Basque provinces, situated on the Bay of Biscay and the French border. It is densely populated. There are numerous mineral springs and some zinc deposits. Main products include textiles, chemicals, glass, paper, metal, and leather goods. Stock-raising and fishing are important.

Guiyang or *Kweiyang* Capital and industrial city of Guizhou province, S China; population (1993) 1,070,000. Industries include metals and machinery.

Guizhou or *Kweichow* Province of S China
area 174,000 sq km/67,164 sq mi
capital Guiyang
industries rice, maize, nonferrous minerals
population (1990) 32,181,000.

Gujarat or *Gujerat* State of W India, formed from N and W Bombay State 1960
area 196,024 sq km/75,685 sq mi
capital Gandhinagar
features heavily industrialized; includes most of the Rann of Kutch; the Gir Forest (the last home of the wild Asian lion); Karjan Dam under construction
industries cotton, petrochemicals, oil, gas, rice, textiles, fishing, coal, limestone
language Gujarati (Gujerati), Hindi
population (1994 est) 44,235,000.

Gujranwala City in Punjab province, Pakistan; population (1981) 597,000. It is a centre of grain trading. The city is a former Sikh capital and the birthplace of Sikh leader Ranjit Singh (1780–1839).

Gujrat City in Punjab province, E Pakistan, N of Lahore; products include cotton, pottery, brassware, and furniture; population (1981) 154,000. It occupies the site of a fort built 1580 by the Moghul ruler Akbar. Gujrat was the scene of the final battle between the British and the Sikhs in the Sikh Wars 1845–49; the British subsequently annexed the Punjab.

Gulfport City in SE Mississippi, USA, on the Gulf of Mexico, W of Biloxi and E of New Orleans, Louisiana; seat of Harrison County and a port of entry to the USA; population (1990) 40,700. It is a major shipping point for lumber, cotton, and food products. With an artificially created sandy beach 45 km/28 mi long, it is an important resort. Gulfport was founded 1887 as a railway terminus.

Gulf States Oil-rich countries sharing the coastline of the ◊Persian Gulf (Bahrain, Iran, Iraq, Kuwait, Oman, Qatar, Saudi Arabia, and the United Arab Emirates). In the USA, the term refers to those states bordering the Gulf of Mexico (Alabama, Florida, Louisiana, Mississippi, and Texas).

Güns German name for ◊Kőszeg, a town in Hungary.

Güstrow Town in the *Land* of ◊Mecklenburg–West Pomerania, Germany, 60 km/37 mi NE of Schwerin, on the river Nebel. Metal goods are manufactured. Güstrow was 1621–1695 the capital of the Duchy of Mecklenburg-Güstrow.

Gütersloh City in North Rhine–Westphalia, Germany, 135 km/84 mi NE of Düsseldorf; population (1996) 324,300. It has electronic, textile, and publishing industries, and a large NATO airbase.

Gwalior City in Madhya Pradesh, India; population (1991) 691,000. Industries include textiles, flour, oilseed milling, and the manufacture of pottery and footwear. It was formerly a small princely state and has Jain and Hindu monuments.

Gwent Former county of S Wales, 1974–96, now divided between Blaenau Gwent, Caerphilly, Monmouthshire, Newport, and Torfaen unitary authorities.

Gwynedd Unitary authority in NW Wales, created 1996 from part of the former county of Gwynedd; administrative headquarters Caenarfon; population (1996) 116,000; area 2,546 sq km/983 sq mi.

Gyandzha City in Azerbaijan, the former capital; industries include cottons, woollens, and processed foods; population (1990) 281,000. It was known as *Elizavetpol* 1804–1918, *Gandzha* before 1804 and again 1918–35, and *Kirovabad* 1935–89.

Győr Industrial city (steel, vehicles, textiles, foodstuffs) in NW Hungary, near the frontier with the Slovak Republic; population (1993) 131,000.

Gyumri formerly (until 1990) *Leninakan*; also *Kumayri* City in Armenia, 40 km/25 m NW of Yerevan; population (1994) 120,000. Industries include textiles and engineering. It was founded 1837 as a fortress called Alexandropol. The city was virtually destroyed by an earthquake 1926 and again 1988.

Haarlem Industrial city and capital of the province of North Holland, the Netherlands, 20 km/12 mi W of Amsterdam; population (1994) 150,200. At Velsea to the N a road-rail tunnel runs under the North Sea Canal, linking North and South Holland. Industries include chemicals, pharmaceuticals, textiles, and printing. Haarlem is in an area of flowering bulbs and has a 15th–16th-century cathedral and a Frans Hals museum.

Haarlem, Lake (Dutch *Haarlemmermeer*) Area of land in the province of North Holland, the Netherlands, reclaimed 1840–53 from a lake. It lies between Amsterdam, Haarlem, and Leiden, and covers some 180 sq km/69 sq mi. The international airport of Schiphol is sited in this area.

Hackney Inner borough of N central Greater London. It includes the districts of Shoreditch, Hoxton, and Stoke Newington
features Hackney Downs and Hackney Marsh, formerly the haunt of highwaymen, now a leisure area; The Theatre, Shoreditch, site of England's first theatre 1576; the Geffrye Museum of the domestic arts; early 16th-century Sutton House, housing the Early Music Centre; Spitalfields market, moved here 1991. The *hackney carriage*, a carriage for hire that was originally horse-drawn, is so named because horses were bred here in the 14th century
famous people Richard Burbage, Daniel Defoe, Kate Greenaway, Joseph Priestley (the discoverer of oxygen), Mary Wollstencraft
population (1991) 181,200.

Haddington Agricultural market town and administrative headquarters of East Lothian, Scotland, on the river Tyne, 16 km/10 mi SW of Dunbar; population (1991) 8,800. The Protestant reformer John Knox was born here.

Hadhramaut District of Yemen, which was formerly ruled by Arab chiefs in protective relations with Britain. A remote plateau region at 1,400 m/4,500 ft, it was for a long time unknown to westerners and later attracted such travellers as Harry St John Philby and Freya Stark. Cereals, tobacco, and dates are grown by settled farmers, and there are nomadic Bedouin. The chief town is Al Mukalla.

Haemus Ancient name for the ◊Balkan Mountains in central Europe.

Hagen Industrial city in the Ruhr, North Rhine–Westphalia, Germany, at the confluence of the Ennepe and Volme rivers; population (1991) 214,100. It produces iron, steel, textiles, paper, and food products.

Hagerstown City in NW Maryland, USA, on Antietam Creek, NW of Baltimore and just S of the Pennsylvania border; population (1990) 35,400. Industries include engine and missile parts and furniture. The city was laid out 1762. During the Civil War it was a centre of fighting.

Hague, The (Dutch *'s-Gravenhage* or *Den Haag*) Capital of the province of South Holland and seat of the Netherlands government, linked by canal with Rotterdam and Amsterdam; population (1994) 445,300.

Hague, Cape La Cape in France at the NW end of the Cotentin peninsula, in the *département* of Manche. It lies between Cherbourg and the island of Alderney, facing the English Channel (La Manche).

Haguenau French town in the *département* of Bas-Rhin, on the river Moder, in the *Haguenau forest*. In 1154 it became a

town and in 1257 it was made a free imperial city. Haguenau has two old churches, dating from the 13th and 14th centuries. It manufactures carpets, machinery, oil, and leather goods, and has a hop market.

Haifa Port in NE Israel, at the foot of Mount Carmel; population (1994) 246,700. Industries include oil refining and chemicals. It is the capital of a district of the same name.

Hainan Island in the South China Sea; area 34,000 sq km/13,127 sq mi; population (1990) 6,420,000. The capital is Haikou. In 1987 Hainan was designated a Special Economic Zone; in 1988 it was separated from Guangdong and made a new province. It is China's second-largest island.

Hainaut Industrial province of SW Belgium; capital Mons; area 3,800 sq km/1,467 sq mi; population (1995) 1,286,600. It produces coal, iron, and steel.

Haiphong Industrial port in N Vietnam; population (1989) 456,000. Among its industries are shipbuilding and the making of cement, plastics, phosphates, and textiles.

Hakodate Port in Hokkaido, Japan; population (1994) 301,000. It was the earliest port opened to the West after the period of isolation, 1854.

Halab Arabic name of ◊Aleppo, a city in Syria.

Halabja Kurdish town near the Iran border in Sulaymaniyah province, NE Iraq. In Aug 1988 international attention was focused on the town when Iraqi planes dropped poison gas, killing 5,000 of its inhabitants.

Halberstadt Town in the *Land* of ◊Saxony-Anhalt, Germany, in the foothills of the Harz Mountains, 48 km/30 mi SW of Magdeburg. Textiles, chemicals, rubber goods, and paper are manufactured. Halberstadt has a cathedral (13th–17th centuries) and a 14th-century town hall.

Halifax Capital of Nova Scotia, E Canada's main port; population (1991) 321,000. Its industries include oil refining and food processing. There are six military bases in Halifax and it is a centre of oceanography. It was founded by British settlers 1749.

Halifax Woollen textile town in West Yorkshire, England, on the river Calder; population (1991) 91,100. The cloth trade dates from the 15th century. Present-day industries include textiles, carpets, clothing, and engineering.

Halland County of SW Sweden on the Kattegat arm of the North Sea, opposite Denmark; area 4,930 sq km/1,903 sq mi; population (1990) 244,400. It is a low-lying coastal region of heaths and ridges; the W coast has long sandy beaches. Its capital is Halmstad.

Halle Industrial city (salt, chemicals, lignite) on the river Saale, in the *Land* of Saxony-Anhalt, Germany; population (1993) 398,100. It was the capital of the East German district of Halle 1952–90.

Halle (French *Hal*) Town in the province of Brabant, Belgium, on the river Senne, 16 km/10 mi S of Brussels. The chief products are paper, sugar, and chicory. The basilica of Notre Dame dates from the 14th century.

Hallein Town in the Austrian province of Salzburg, on the river Salzach, 12 km/7 mi S of the town of Salzburg. It is a tourist resort, and has marble, paper, and rayon industries. A large salt mine, worked since the Bronze Age, is now open to the public.

Halmstad Seaport and capital of Halland county in SW Sweden; population (1996) 54,200. It is situated at the mouth of the river Nissa, on the E shore of the Kattegat. The town manufactures beer, wood pulp, jute, and paper. The chief exports are granite, timber, and butter.

Hamadán City in NW Iran on the site of Ecbatana, capital of the Medes (an ancient Indo-European people); population (1991) 350,000. Carpets and rugs are traded. The tomb of the Arab philosopher and physician Avicenna is here.

Hamamatsu Industrial city (textiles, chemicals, motorcycles) in Chubu region, central Honshu Island, Japan; population (1994) 550,000.

Hambledon Village in SE Hampshire, England. The first cricket club was founded here 1750.

Hamburg Largest inland port of Europe, in Germany, on the river Elbe; population (1993) 1,701,600. Industries include oil, chemicals, electronics, and cosmetics.

Hamburg Administrative region (German *Land*) of Germany
area 755 sq km/292 sq mi
capital Hamburg
features comprises the city and surrounding districts; there is a university, established 1919, and the Hamburg Schauspielhaus is one of Germany's leading theatres
industries refined oil, chemicals, electrical goods, ships, processed food
population (1995) 1,705,900
religion 74% Protestant, 8% Roman Catholic
history in 1510 the emperor Maximilian I made Hamburg a free imperial city, and in 1871 it became a state of the German Empire.

Häme Province of SW central Finland; area 18,387 sq km/7,099 sq mi. Häme is chiefly agricultural, and has many lakes. Its capital is Hämeenlinna, and Tampere is the largest town.

Hämeenlinna (Swedish *Tavastehus*) Capital of Häme province, S central Finland; population (1995) 44,900. It is 100 km/62 mi NW of Helsinki, on Lake Vanajavesi. It has a 13th-century castle.

Hameln (English form *Hamelin*) Town in Lower Saxony, Germany; population (1984) 56,300. Old buildings include the *Rattenhaus* (rat-catcher's house). Hameln is the setting for the Pied Piper legend.

Hamersley Range Range of hills above the Hamersley Plateau, Western Australia, with coloured rocks and river gorges, as well as iron reserves.

Hamilton Capital (since 1815) of Bermuda, on Bermuda Island; population about (1994) 1,100. It has a deep-sea harbour.

Hamilton Port in Ontario, Canada; population (1991) 318,500; metropolitan area 599,800. Linked with Lake Ontario by the Burlington Canal, it has a hydroelectric plant and steel, heavy machinery, electrical, chemical, and textile industries. It lies at the centre of a fruit-growing district. Hamilton was settled 1778 by United Empire Loyalists from the American colonies.

Hamilton Industrial and university city on North Island, New Zealand, on Waikato River; population (1993) 151,800. It trades in forestry, horticulture, and dairy-farming products. Waikato University was established here 1964.

Hamilton City in the SW corner of Ohio, USA, on the Great Miami River, NW of Cincinnati; seat of Butler County; population (1992) 63,800. Its industries include livestock processing, metal products, paper, and building materials. Hamilton was laid out 1794.

Hamilton Administrative headquarters of South Lanarkshire, Scotland; population (1991) 50,000. Industries include textiles, electronics, and engineering.

Hamm Industrial city in North Rhine–Westphalia, Germany; population (1991) 180,300. There are coal mines and chemical and engineering industries.

Hammerfest Fishing port in NW Norway, the northernmost town in Europe; population (1991) 6,900.

Hammersmith and Fulham Inner borough of W central Greater London, N of the Thames
features Hammersmith Terrace, 18th-century houses on riverside; Parish Church of St Paul (1631); Lyric Theatre (1890); Fulham Palace, residence of the bishops of London from the 12th century until 1973, it is one of the best medieval domestic sites in London, with buildings dating from the 15th century; Riverside studios; Olympia exhibition centre (1884); 18th-century Hurlingham Club; White City Stadium; Wormwood Scrubbs prison
famous people Leigh Hunt; Ouida and Henri Gaudier-Brzeska were residents
population (1991) 136,500.

Hammond City in the NW corner of Indiana, USA, on the Calumet River, just S of Chicago, Illinois; population (1992) 84,250. It is a major transportation centre, connecting to Lake Michigan via the Calumet Canal. Industries include soap, cereal products, publishing, railroad equipment, and transportation facilities for the city's surrounding steel plants and oil refineries. It was founded 1869 by George Hammond, a pioneer in the transportation of refrigerated beef.

Hampshire County of S England
area 3,770 sq km/1,455 sq mi
towns and cities Winchester (administrative headquarters), Southampton, Portsmouth, Gosport
features New Forest, area 373 sq km/144 sq mi, a Saxon royal hunting ground; the river Test, which has trout fishing; the river Itchen; Hampshire Basin, where Britain has onshore and offshore oil; Danebury, 2,500-year-old Celtic hillfort; Beaulieu (including National Motor Museum); Broadlands (home of Lord Mountbatten); Highclere castle

(home of the Earl of Carnarvon, with gardens by 'Capability' Brown); Hambledon, where the first cricket club was founded 1750; site of the Roman town of Silchester, the only one in Britain known in such detail; Jane Austen's cottage 1809–17 is a museum; naval bases at Portsmouth and Gosport; Twyford Down section of the M3 motorway was completed 1994 despite protests
industries agricultural including watercress growing; oil from refineries at Fawley; chemicals, pharmaceuticals, brewing, aeronautics, perfume, electronics, shipbuilding
population (1995) 1,213,600
famous people Gilbert White, Jane Austen, Charles Dickens.

Hampstead District in the Greater London borough of ◊Camden. It is the site of Primrose Hill, Hampstead Heath, and Parliament Hill (on which Boudicca is said to have been buried in a barrow); Hampstead Garden suburb was begun 1907. Notable buildings include Kenwood (about 1616, remodelled by Robert Adam 1764), containing the Iveagh Bequest of paintings; Fenton House (1693), with a large collection of early keyboard instruments; and Keats House (1815–16), home of the poet John Keats, now a museum. John Constable is buried in the churchyard. Many famous people lived here, including Martin Frobisher, John Galsworthy, Edward Elgar, Ramsay Macdonald, and Anna Pavlova.

Hanau City in Hessen, Germany, at the confluence of the rivers Kinzig and the Main, 18 km/11 mi E of Frankfurt am Main; population (1994) 88,900. Hanau has jewellery and diamond-cutting trades, rubber and stainless steel production.

Hangzhou or *Hangchow* Port and capital of Zhejiang province, China; population (1993) 1,740,000. It has jute, steel, chemical, tea, and silk industries. Hangzhou has fine landscaped gardens and was the capital of China 1127–1278 under the Sung dynasty.

Hanley One of the old Staffordshire pottery towns in England, now part of ◊Stoke-on-Trent. It is the birthplace of footballer Stanley Matthews.

Hannibal Town in Missouri, USA, population (1990) 18,000. It is a centre for railway and river traffic and trades in agricultural and dairy products, cement, steel, and metal goods. It was settled 1819; Mark Twain lived here as a boy and made it the setting for his novel *The Adventures of Huckleberry Finn*.

Hannover Industrial city, capital of Lower Saxony, Germany; population (1993) 525,300. Industries include machinery, vehicles, electrical goods, rubber, textiles, and oil refining.

Hanoi Capital of Vietnam, on the Red River; population (1989) 1,088,900. Central Hanoi has one of the highest population densities in the world: 1,300 people per hectare/3,250 per acre. Industries include textiles, paper, and engineering.

Hants Abbreviation for ◊Hampshire, an English county.

Hanyang Former Chinese city, now merged in ◊Wuhan, in Hubei province.

Haora or *Howrah* City of West Bengal, India, on the right bank of the river Hooghly, opposite Calcutta; population (1981) 742,298. The capital of Haora district, it has jute and cotton factories; rice, flour, and saw mills; chemical factories; and engineering works. Haora suspension bridge, opened 1943, spans the river.

Harare formerly (until 1980) *Salisbury* Capital of Zimbabwe, on the Mashonaland plateau, about 1,525 m/5,000 ft above sea level; population (1992) 1,184,200. It is the centre of a rich farming area (tobacco and maize), with metallurgical and food processing industries.

Harbin or *Haerhpin* or *Pinkiang* Port on the Songhua River, NE China, capital of Heilongjiang province; population (1993) 3,100,000. Industries include metallurgy, machinery, paper, food processing, and sugar refining, and it is a major rail junction. Harbin was developed by Russian settlers after Russia was granted trading rights here 1896, and more Russians arrived as refugees after the October Revolution 1917. In World War II, it was the key objective of the Soviet invasion of Manchuria Aug 1945.

Harderwijk Port in the province of Gelderland, the Netherlands, on the SE shore of the ◊IJsselmeer, 50 km/31 mi E of Amsterdam; population (1996) 37,400. Herring curing is the chief industry.

Hardwar City in Uttar Pradesh, India, on the right bank of the river Ganges; population (1991) 147,300. The name means 'door of Hari' (or Vishnu). It is one of the holy places of the Hindu religion and a pilgrimage centre. The *Kumbhmela* festival, held every 12th year in honour of the god Siva, attracts about 1 million pilgrims.

Harfleur Port in NW France; population (1985) 9,700. It was important in medieval times, but was later superseded by ◊Le Havre.

Hargeysa Trading centre (meat, livestock, skins) in NW Somalia; population (1988) 400,000.

Haringey Inner borough of N Greater London. It includes the suburbs of Wood Green, Tottenham, Hornsey, and Harringey
features Bruce Castle, Tottenham, an Elizabethan manor house (said to stand on the site of an earlier castle built by Robert the Bruce's father); Alexandra Palace (1873), with park; Finsbury Park (1869), one of the earliest municipal parks
industry light industry
population (1991) 202,200
famous people Rowland Hill.

Harlech Town in Gwynedd, N Wales; population (1991) 1,230. The castle, now in ruins, was built by the English king Edward I 1283–89. It was captured by the Welsh chieftain Owen Glendower 1404–08 and by the Yorkists in the Wars of the Roses 1468. Harlech is now a centre for visiting Snowdonia National Park.

Harlem Commercial and residential district of NE Manhattan, New York City, USA. The principal thoroughfare, 125th Street, runs E–W between the Hudson River and the East River. Originally a Dutch settlement 1658, Harlem developed as a black ghetto after World War I. Harlem's heyday was in the 1920s, when it established its reputation as the intellectual, cultural, and entertainment centre of black America. It is known as a centre for music, particularly jazz. The Apollo Theatre 1934–84 was one of many influential music venues. The Dance Theater and Theater of Harlem are also here.

Harlingen City in the SE corner of Texas, USA, S of Corpus Christi and just N of the Mexican border; population (1992) 52,000. Connected to the Rio Grande by an intracoastal waterway, it serves as the processing and marketing area for the lower Rio Grande Valley. Industries include citrus fruit processing and cotton products.

Harlingen Port in the province of Friesland, the Netherlands, situated 25 km/16 mi SW of Leeuwarden, on the Waddenzee; population (1996) 15,200. Harlingen is intersected by numerous canals, has an excellent harbour, and exports dairy products, potatoes, and meat. The town was inundated by floods in 1134 and in 1566, before a dyke was constructed for its protection.

Harper's Ferry Village in W Virginia, USA, where the Potomac and Shenandoah rivers meet. In 1859 antislavery leader John Brown seized the federal government's arsenal here, an action that helped precipitate the Civil War.

Harris Southern part of ◊Lewis, in the Outer ◊Hebrides Islands off Scotland; area 500 sq km/193 sq mi; population (1971) 2,900. It is joined to Lewis by a narrow isthmus. Harris tweeds are produced here.

Harrisburg Capital city of Pennsylvania, USA, located in the S central part of the state, on the Susquehanna River; seat of Dauphin County; population (1992) 53,400. Industries include steel, railroad equipment, food processing, printing and publishing, and clothing. The city was laid out 1785, and became the state capital 1812.

Harrogate Resort and spa in North Yorkshire, England; population (1991) 66,200. There is a US communications station at Menwith Hill.

Harrow Outer London borough of NW Greater London
features Harrow School (1571)
population (1991) 200,100
famous people R B Sheridan, Charles Kingsley, Robert Ballantyne, Matthew Arnold, Anthony Trollope.

Hartford Capital city of Connecticut, USA, located in the N central part of the state, on the Connecticut River, NE of Waterbury; population (1992) 132,000; metropolitan area (1992) 1,156,000. The 'insurance capital of the nation', Hartford is the base of over 40 insurance companies. Other industries include firearms, office equipment, and tools. Hartford was first settled 1635 by Puritans from the Massachusetts Bay Colony.

Hartlepool Unitary authority in NE England created 1996 from part of the former county of Cleveland; administrative

headquarters Hartlepool; population (1996) 90,400; area 94 sq km/36 sq mi. There are metal industries and engineering. The author Compton Mackenzie was born here.

Hartz Mountains Range running N–S in Tasmania, Australia, with two remarkable peaks: Hartz Mountain (1,254 m/4,113 ft) and Adamsons Peak (1,224 m/4,017 ft).

Harwich Seaport in Essex, England; with ferry services to Scandinavia and NW Europe; population (1988 est) 15,500. Reclamation of Bathside Bay mudflats is making it a rival, as a port, to Felixstowe.

Haryana State of NW India, formed 1966
area 44,212 sq km/17,070 sq mi
capital Chandigarh
features part of the Ganges plain; a centre of Hinduism
industries sugar, cotton, oilseed, textiles, cement, iron ore, rice, pulses.
population (1994 est) 17,925,000
language Hindi.

Harz Mountains Most northerly mountain range in Germany, situated between the rivers Weser and ◊Elbe and covering a total area of around 2,030 sq km/784 sq mi. The highest peak in the Harz Mountains – a popular area for recreation and designated a nature park – is the ◊Brocken (1,143 m/3,750 ft).

Haskovo Alternative name for ◊Khaskovo, a town and region of Bulgaria.

Hasselt Capital of the Belgian province of ◊Limbourg. The town manufactures linen fabrics and tobacco, and has gin distilleries.

Hastings Resort in East Sussex, England, on the English Channel; population (1991) 80,800. William the Conqueror landed at Pevensey and defeated Harold at the Battle of Hastings 1066. The chief of the Cinque Ports, it has ruins of a Norman castle. As a port, it declined in importance as the harbour silted up; present-day industries include scientific instruments, plastics, engineering, electronics, and clothing. The Hastings Premier, England's leading international chess tournament, is held here every January.

Hatay Alternative name for the Turkish town of ◊Antakya.

Hatfield Town in Hertfordshire, England, 8 km/5 mi E of St Albans; population (1991) 31,100. Designated a new town 1948, it has light engineering industries. It was the site of the 12th-century palace of the bishops of Ely, which was seized by Henry VIII and inhabited by Edward VI and Elizabeth I before their accession. James I gave the palace in part exchange to Robert Cecil, 1st Earl of Salisbury, who replaced it 1611 with the existing Jacobean mansion, Hatfield House.

Hatteras Cape on the coast of North Carolina, where the waters of the N Atlantic meet the Gulf Stream, causing great turbulence; more than 700 shipwrecks are said to have occurred here, and it is nicknamed 'the Graveyard of the Atlantic'. Cape Hatteras National Seashore has both natural and historical interest, including a lighthouse and sea life typical of both the temperate and tropical zones.

Haugesund Seaport in Rogaland county, S Norway, 58 km/36 mi NW of the town of Stavanger; population

(1995) 29,200. It has important fisheries and a large merchant fleet.

Haute-Corse *Département* comprising the N half of the French island of Corsica; area 4,666 sq km/1,801 sq mi; population (1990) 131,520. Together with Corse-du-Sud, it makes up the administrative region of ◊Corsica. The highest peak on the island, Monte Cinto (2,710 m/8,891 ft) is located here; other peaks over 2,000 m/c.6,500 ft in Haute-Corse include Monte Rotondo (2,625 m/8,612 ft) and Col de Vergio (2,329 m/7,641 ft). Wine, olives, and olive oil are produced. The departmental capital is the port of ◊Bastia on the NE coast; other significant towns are Calvi, Corte, Calenzana, Ile-Rousse and St Florent.

Haute-Garonne *Département* in the ◊Midi-Pyrénées region of France; area 6,300 sq km/2,432 sq mi; population (1990) 925,900. The S is mountainous, containing some of the highest peaks of the Pyrenees, including Mont Perdiguère (3,219 m/10,561 ft). The valleys are very fertile. The centre of the *département* is a hilly plateau. The chief river is the Garonne, and the Canal du Midi and the Canal Latéral à la Garonne cross the N of the *département*. Vines, cereals, fruit, and potatoes are cultivated, and livestock raised. There are chemical, metallurgical, paper, foodstuff, engineering, aeronautical, and leather industries, and tourism. The principal towns are ◊Toulouse (the capital), Muret, and St-Gaudens; Luchon is a resort for winter sports.

Haute-Loire *Département* in the Auvergne region of France; area 4,965 sq km/1,917 sq mi; population (1990) 207,000. Situated on the central plateau of France, it is crossed by four mountain ranges, running N to S: the Vivarais and its continuation, the Boutières; the Massif du Megal; the Velay mountains; and the Margeride mountains. The chief rivers are the Loire, with its tributaries the Borne and the Lignon, and the Allier. In the river valleys fruit trees and vines are cultivated. In the rest of the *département* the principal industries are the raising of stock and forestry. The main towns are Le Puy (the capital), Brioude, and Yssingeaux.

Haute-Marne *Département* ◊Champagne-Ardenne region of NE France; area 6,215 sq km/2,400 sq mi; population (1990) 204,577. Haute-Marne is extensively forested. The soil is mostly poor, but cereals and vines are cultivated in places. There are iron-ore mines and mineral springs. The principal towns are the departmental capital, Chaumont, Langres, and St-Dizier.

Haute-Normandie or *Upper Normandy* Coastal region of NW France lying between Basse-Normandie and Picardy and bisected by the river Seine; area 12,317 sq km/4,756 sq mi; population (1990) 1,737,200. It comprises the *départements* of Eure and Seine-Maritime; its capital is Rouen. Ports include Dieppe and Fécamp. The area has many beech forests.

Hautes-Alpes *Département* in the ◊Provence-Alpes-Côte d'Azur region of France, bordered on the E by Italy; area 5,520 sq km/2,131 sq mi; population (1990) 56,100. The region is situated in the Alps; in the E are the slopes of the Cottian Alps. The main river is the Durance. The chief

sources of income are livestock farming, cultivation of vines, fruit, and vegetables, and tourism, especially winter sports. The principal towns are Gap (the capital) and Briançon.

Haute-Saône *Département* in the ◊Franche-Comté region of France; area 5,343 km sq/2,063 mi sq; population (1990) 230,300. The land is mainly a plateau, gradually descending from the Vosges mountains in the N (highest point, Ballon de Servance, 1,182 m/3,900 ft) towards the S, and intersected by many valleys. The chief rivers are the Saône and its tributaries, the Coney, Lanterne, Durgeon, and Ognon. There is much forest, and wheat, oats, rye, vegetables, and tobacco are grown. Some wine is produced. The principal towns are Vesoul (the capital) and Lure.

Haute-Savoie *Département* in the ◊Rhône-Alpes region of France; area 4,391 sq km/1,695 sq mi; population (1990) 568,800. The land is mountainous – the *département* includes ◊Mont Blanc. The chief rivers are the Arve, Dranse, Ussel, and Fier, tributaries of the Rhône. Much of the land is forested. Cereals and hardy root crops are grown, and on the lower slopes orchard fruits, vines, and tobacco. There is dairy production, particularly cheese. The most fertile district is in the N and NW. Industry is limited, but includes textiles, watches and clocks. Tourist come both summer and winter. The principal towns are ◊Annecy (the capital), Bonneville, Thonon, and St-Julien.

Hautes-Pyrénées *Département* in the ◊Midi-Pyrénées region of France on the Spanish frontier; area 4,507 sq km/1,740 sq mi; population (1990) 224,900. The S part is very mountainous; the hills gradually descend to a plain in the N. In the NE lies the desolate plateau of Lannemezan. The chief rivers are the Adour, with its tributaries the Arros and Gave de Pau; the Garonne is on the SE frontier. There is much forest, and wheat, maize, vines, tobacco, flax, and chestnuts are grown. Marble and slate are quarried, lignite, zinc, manganese, and lead are found, and there are mineral springs. There are aeronautical, armament, chemical, and engineering industries, and tourism is important, especially in ski resorts such as Val Louron, Peyragudes, and Cauterets Lys. The principal towns are ◊Tarbes (the capital), Argelés-Gazost, and Bagnères-de-Bigorre.

Haute-Vienne *Département* in the ◊Limousin region of central France; area 5,512 sq km/2,129 sq mi; population (1990) 353,914. Haute-Vienne is extremely hilly; the River Vienne flows between the Marche hills in the centre of the *département* and the Limousin hills in the S. Some cereals and hemp are grown, and there is widespread breeding of livestock. Minerals exploited in the area include uranium, wolfram, manganese, and kaolin. There are important porcelain, leather, paper, and textile industries. The principal towns are ◊Limoges (the capital), Bellac, and Rochechouart.

Haut-Rhin *Département* in the Alsace region of France; area 3,522 sq km/1,360 sq mi; population (1990) 952,600. The Rhine is the E boundary of the *département*, which is fertile and densely wooded. Cereals, vines, and hops are grown. Textiles, machinery, and food are manufactured, and there are potash mines and factories. The principal towns are ◊Colmar (the capital) and Mulhouse.

Hauts-de-Seine *Département* in the ◊Ile-de-France region of N France; area 175 sq km/68 sq mi; population (1990) 1,390,592. Situated to the W of Paris, Hauts-de-Seine is made up of the outer W and NW suburbs of the capital. Here, major new residential estates have been built to replace older housing. Many manufacturing industries are sited within the *département*, including a major automobile factory (Renault) at Billancourt on the Seine, and a fine porcelain works at Sèvres. There are extensive wooded areas, including the Forêt de Meudon and the Parc de St-Cloud; the capital is Nanterren. Fast road and railway links connect Hauts-de-Seine to central Paris.

Havana Capital and port of Cuba, on the NW coast of the island; population (1990) 2,096,100. Products include cigars and tobacco, sugar, coffee, and fruit. The palace of the Spanish governors and the stronghold of La Fuerza (1583) survive.

Havel River in E Germany; length 346 km/215 mi. The Havel rises in a small lake 9 km/6 mi NW of Neustrelitz. It flows S to Berlin and then W past Potsdam and Rathenow to join the Elbe 29 km/18 mi SE of Wittenberg. To the W of Berlin the Havel passes through a series of lakes, one of which bears the river's name. At this point it is also joined by the river Spree; via the Oder–Spree Canal, traffic from the Havel can reach the river Oder on Germany's border with Poland.

Haverhill City in NE Massachusetts, USA, on the Merrimac River, N of Boston; population (1992) 52,200. Products include paints, chemicals, machine tools, and shoes. It was founded 1640, and the poet John Greenleaf Whittier lived here.

Havering Outer London borough of NE Greater London. It includes the districts of Hornchurch and Romford
features 15th-century Church House, Romford; St Andrew's church, the only church in England to have a bull's head and horns instead of a cross at the E end; site of a small medieval palace, known as The Bower, at Havering atte Bower; this was the official residence of queens of England until 1620, after which time it fell into decay and was sold during the Commonwealth; the present Bower House was built 1729; some of the grounds of the medieval palace survive as Havering Country Park
population (1991) 229,500.

Havířov Town in N Moravia, in the Czech Republic, 12 km/8 mi SE of Ostrava; population (1991) 86,300. The town was built 1955 on the Silesian coalfield.

Havre, Le See ◊Le Havre, a port in France.

Hawaii Pacific state of the USA; nicknamed Aloha State
area 16,800 sq km/6,485 sq mi
capital Honolulu on Oahu
towns and cities Hilo
physical Hawaii consists of a chain of some 20 volcanic islands, of which the chief are:
(1) *Hawaii* (or Big Island), with Hawaii Volcanoes national park (a World Heritage Site), including Mauna Kea (4,201 m/13,788 ft), the world's highest island mountain; Mauna Loa (4,170 m/13,686 ft), the world's largest active volcanic crater; and Kilauea, the world's most active volcano; Kau Desert; the Waipio Valley with waterfalls
(2) *Maui*, the second largest of the islands, with Haleakala national park;
(3) *Oahu*, the third largest, with Waikiki beach;
(4) *Kauai*, with Waimea Canyon (1,097 m/3,600 ft deep, 3.2 km/2 mi wide, and 16 km/10 mi long);
(5) *Molokai*
features (1) Hawaii: Mauna Kea has telescopes that make Hawaii a world centre for astronomy; Honokaa (where the first macadamia trees were planted 1881); Puukohola national historic site (temples built 1791); Hulihea Palace (the king's summer residence, 1880s); (2) Maui has the Alexander and Baldwin Sugar Museum; Wailuku historical district; Lahaina (with a banyan tree planted 1873); (3) Oahu, the most populated of the islands, and the most popular with tourists, includes Honolulu, with the Mission House Museum (home of the first US missionaries, dating from the 1820s), Kawaiahao Church (1842), Iolani Palace (1882, the only royal palace in the USA), Aliiolani Hale (the old judiciary building), Honolulu Hale (1929, the City Hall), the Honolulu Academy of Arts, and Pearl Harbor naval base, including the USS *Arizona* Pearl Harbor Memorial; (4) Kauai, a former plantation town, has Waioli Mission (founded 1837 at Hanalei); (5) Molokai, a leper colony until 1888, has the Meyer Sugar Mill (1878) and the Kalaupapa national historic park. Surfing originated in ancient Hawaii.
industries sugar, coffee, pineapples, flowers, clothing; tourism is the chief source of income
population (1995) 1,186,800 (34% European, 25% Japanese, 14% Filipino, 12% Hawaiian, 6% Chinese)
famous people James Michener
history a Polynesian kingdom from the 6th century, the islands were united as one kingdom in the late 18th century. The whaling industry was important in the 19th century. Because of US, British, and French rivalry over the islands, Kamehameha III placed Hawaii under US protection 1851. Under the Reciprocity Treaty imposed 1887, in exchange for duty-free sugar transport, Pearl Harbor was ceded to the USA, who established a naval base there. Republican forces overthrew the monarchy 1893 (for which the USA officially apologized 1993), and the republican government agreed to annexation by the USA 1898. It became a US territory 1900, and the 50th state of the Union 1959. Japan's air attack on Pearl Harbor 7 Dec 1941 crippled the US Pacific fleet and turned the territory into an armed camp, under martial law, for the remainder of the war.

Hawarden (Welsh *Penarlâg*) Town in Flintshire, N Wales. The Liberal politician William Gladstone lived at Hawarden Castle for many years, and founded St Deiniol's theological library in Hawarden.

Hawkesbury River in New South Wales, Australia; length 480 km/300 mi. It rises in the Great Dividing Range and reaches the Tasman Sea at Broken Bay. It is a major source of Sydney's water.

Hay-on-Wye (Welsh *Y Gelli*) Town in Powys, Wales, on the S bank of the river Wye, known as the 'town of books' because of the huge secondhand bookshop started there 1961 by Richard Booth; it was followed by others.

Heard Island and McDonald Islands Group of islands forming an Australian external territory in the S Indian Ocean, about 4,000 km/2,500 mi SW of Fremantle; area 410 sq km/158 sq mi. They were discovered 1833, annexed by Britain 1910, and transferred to Australia 1947. They are unpopulated. *Heard Island*, 42 km/26 mi by 19 km/12 mi, is glacier-covered, although the volcanic mountain *Big Ben* (2,742 m/9,000 ft) is still active. A weather station was built 1947. *Shag Island* is 8 km/5 mi to the N and the craggy McDonalds are 42 km/26 mi to the W.

Heathrow Major international airport to the W of London in the Greater London borough of Hounslow, approximately 24 km/14 mi from the city centre. Opened 1946, it is one of the world's busiest airports, with four terminals. It was linked with the London underground system 1977. It was the target of three mortar attacks by the Irish Republican Army (IRA) March 1994, all of which failed to detonate.

Hebei or *Hopei* or *Hupei* Province of N China
area 202,700 sq km/78,262 sq mi
capital Shijiazhuang
features includes special municipalities of Beijing and Tianjin
industries cereals, textiles, iron, steel
population (1990) 60,280,000.

Hebrides Group of more than 500 islands (fewer than 100 inhabited) off W Scotland; total area 2,900 sq km/1,120 sq mi. The Hebrides were settled by Scandinavians during the 6th to 9th centuries and passed under Norwegian rule from about 890 to 1266.

Hebron (Arabic *Al Khalil*) Town on the West Bank of the Jordan, occupied by Israel 1967; population (1996) 120,500. It has been a front-line position in the confrontation between Israelis and Arabs in the Intifada. In 1994 the Hebron mosque was the scene of a massacre in which 39 Palestinians were shot dead by an Israeli settler while at morning prayer. Within the mosque is the traditional site of the tombs of Abraham, Isaac, and Jacob. In Sept 1995 Israel and the PLO signed an accord stating that Israeli troops would hand over Hebron to Palestinian authority by March 1996, but that an Israeli military presence would be deployed to protect it. The city was to be divided into three zones, one administered by Palestine, one by Israel, and one jointly. The subsequent delay in Israeli withdrawal from the town created serious tensions between the communities throughout 1996, jeopardizing the Middle East peace process.

Heerlen Town in the province of Limburg, the Netherlands, 21 km/13 mi NE of Maastricht; population (1996) 95,900. Heerlen is an important industrial centre. The Thermen Museum incorporates the excavations of a Roman bath complex.

Hefei or *Hofei* Capital of Anhui province, China; population (1993) 1,110,000. Products include textiles, chemicals, and steel.

Heidelberg City on the S bank of the river Neckar, 19 km/12 mi SE of Mannheim, in Baden-Württemberg, Germany; population (1993) 139,900. Heidelberg University, the oldest in Germany, was established 1386. The city is overlooked by the ruins of its 13th–17th-century castle, 100 m/330 ft above the river.

Heidenheim City in Baden-Württemberg, Germany, on the river Brenz, 68 km/42 mi E of Stuttgart; population (1994) 136,600. There are machinery, metal, and textile industries. Heidenheim is built on a rocky outcrop and has an 11th-century castle (Hellenstein).

Heilbronn River port in Baden-Württemberg, Germany, on the river Neckar, N of Stuttgart; population (1990) 116,200. It trades extensively in wine.

Heilongjiang or *Heilungkiang* Province of NE China, in Manchuria
area 463,600 sq km/178,996 sq mi
capital Harbin
features China's largest oilfield, near Anda
industries cereals, gold, coal, copper, zinc, lead, cobalt
population (1990) 34,770,000.

Heilsbronn Town in Bavaria, Germany, 25 km/15 mi SW of Nuremberg; population (1994) 8,900. Heilsbronn has a Romanesque basilica, part of a Cistercian abbey (1132–1578) founded by Bishop Otto; several members of the Hohenzollern royal family are buried here.

Hejaz Province of Saudi Arabia, on the Red Sea. A former independent kingdom, it merged 1932 with Nejd to form Saudi Arabia; population (1985 est) 3,043,200. The capital is Mecca.

Helena Capital of Montana, USA, located in the W central part of the state, near the Big Belt Mountains, S of the Missouri River; population (1992) 24,600. Industries include agricultural products, machine parts, ceramics, paints, sheet metal, and chemicals. It was settled after gold was discovered 1864, and became the state capital 1889.

Heligoland Island in the North Sea, one of the North Frisian Islands; area 0.6 sq km/0.2 sq mi. It is administered by the state of Schleswig-Holstein, Germany, having been ceded to Germany by Britain 1890 in exchange for ◊Zanzibar. It was used as a naval base in both world wars.

Hellespont Former name of the ◊Dardanelles, the strait that separates Europe from Asia.

Hell Gate Channel between Manhattan Island, Long Island, and the mainland of New York State, USA, which links New York's East River with Long Island Sound. It received its name from early Dutch navigators, who found its waters treacherous; there was a whirlpool here, and wrecks were frequent. It is today bridged by the Hell Gate Bridge (railway) and the Triborough Bridge (road).

Helmand Longest river in Afghanistan. Rising in the Hindu Kush, W of Kabul, it flows SW for 1,125 km/703 mi before entering the marshland surrounding Lake Saberi on the Iranian frontier.

Helmond Town in the province of North Brabant, the Netherlands, 13 km/8 mi NE of Eindhoven; population (1996) 75,300. The town has textile and engineering industries.

Helmstedt City in Lower Saxony, Germany, 36 km/22 mi E of Brunswick; population (1994) 26,900. Textiles, machinery, soap, and margarine are manufactured, and brown coal (lignite) is mined in the area. Helmstedt dates from the Middle Ages.

Helsingborg (Swedish *Hälsingborg*) Port in SW Sweden, linked by ferry with Helsingør across Øre Sound; population (1994) 113,400. Industries include copper smelting, rubber and chemical manufacture, and sugar refining.

Helsingør (English *Elsinore*) Port in NE Denmark; population (1993) 56,700. It is linked by ferry with Helsingborg across Øre Sound; Shakespeare made it the scene of *Hamlet*.

Helsinki (Swedish *Helsingfors*) Capital and port of Finland; population (1994) 516,000. Industries include shipbuilding, engineering, and textiles. The port is kept open by icebreakers in winter.

Helvellyn Peak of the English Lake District in ◊Cumbria, 950 m/3,118 ft high.

Helvetia Region, corresponding to W Switzerland, occupied by the Celtic Helvetii 1st century BC–5th century AD. In 58 BC Caesar repulsed their invasion of S Gaul at Bibracte (near Autun) and Helvetia became subject to Rome. *Helvetian* is another word for Swiss.

Hemel Hempstead Town in Hertfordshire, England, designated a new town 1946; population (1991) 79,200. Industries include manufacture of paper, electrical goods, and office equipment.

Henan or *Honan* Province of E central China
area 167,000 sq km/64,479 sq mi
capital Zhengzhou
features river plains of the Huang He (Yellow River); ruins of Xibo, the 16th-century BC capital of the Shang dynasty, were discovered here in the 1980s
industries cereals, cotton
population (1990) 86,140,000.

Hendon Residential district in the Greater London borough of ◊Barnet. The Metropolitan Police Detective Training and Motor Driving schools are here, and the RAF Museum (1972) includes the Battle of Britain Museum (1980).

Hengelo Town in the province of Overijssel, the Netherlands, 8 km/5 mi NW of Enschede; population (1996) 8,400. There are large diesel-engine and cotton industries, in addition to dyeing, brewing, and railway engineering. The town centre was severely damaged during World War II.

Henley-on-Thames Town in Oxfordshire, England; population (1984) 11,000. The Royal Regatta, held here annually since 1839, is in July; Henley Management College, established 1946, was the first in Europe.

Henzada Alternative name for ◊Hinthada.

Heraklion Alternative name for ◊Irákleion, a Greek port.

Herat Capital of Herat province, and the largest city in W Afghanistan, on the N banks of the Hari Rud River; population (1988) 177,000. A principal road junction, it was a great city in ancient and medieval times.

Hérault River in S France, 160 km/100 mi long, rising in the Cévennes Mountains and flowing into the Gulf of Lyons near Agde. It gives its name to a *département*.

Hérault *Département* in the ◊Languedoc-Roussillon region of S France; area 6,112 sq km/2,360 sq mi; population (1990) 795,142. Hérault is on the Golfe du Lion, and its coastline comprises a series of long lagoons separated from the land by narrow strips of land. The area is drained by the rivers Aude, Orb, and Hérault. Wine is produced extensively, cereals, fruit trees, and vegetables are grown, and silkworms are reared. Iron, bauxite, and salt are also found. The chief manufactures are chemicals and textiles. The main towns are the capital ◊Montpellier, ◊Béziers, and Lodève.

Hercules, Pillars of Rocks (at Gibraltar and Ceuta) which guard the W entrance to the Mediterranean Sea.

Hereford Town in the county of Hereford and Worcester, on the river Wye, England; population (1991) 50,200. Products include cider, beer, cattle, leather goods, metal goods, and chemicals. The cathedral, which was begun 1079, contains a *Mappa Mundi* ('map of the world' about 1314), a medieval map of the world. An appeal was launched 1988 and the money was raised to restore and preserve the map. Hereford has the largest chained library in the world.

Hereford and Worcester County of W central England, created 1974 from the counties of Herefordshire and Worcestershire. The county will be abolished in April 1998 and split into the unitary authority of Heredfordshire (with pre-1974 boundaries) and the two-tier county of Worcestershire
area 3,930 sq km/1,517 sq mi
towns and cities Worcester (administrative headquarters), Hereford, Kidderminster, Evesham, Ross-on-Wye, Ledbury
features rivers: Wye, Severn; Malvern Hills (high point Worcester Beacon, 425 m/1,395 ft) and Black Mountains; fertile Vale of Evesham; Droitwich, once a Victorian spa, reopened its baths 1985 (the town lies over a subterranean brine reservoir); Three Choirs Festival
industries mainly agricultural: apples, pears, cider, hops, vegetables, Hereford cattle; carpets; porcelain; some chemicals; salt; food processing; engineering; car accessories
population (1994) 699,900
famous people William Langland, Edward Elgar, A E Housman, John Masefield, David Garrick.

Herford City in the *Land* of North Rhine–Westphalia, Germany, on the rivers Werre and Aa, 15 km/9 mi N of Bielefeld; population (1994) 248,300. Furniture, carpets, and metal goods are manufactured here. Herford was once a member of the Hanseatic League medieval trade federation.

Herisau Commune in the canton of Appenzell, Switzerland, and capital of the half-canton of Outer Rhodes,

10 km/6 mi SW of St Gallen; population (1995) 16,200. Herisau has an old belltower and town hall. Cotton goods and embroidery are produced here.

Hermon, Mount (Arabic *Jebel esh-Sheikh*) Snow-topped mountain, 2,814 m/9,232 ft high, on the Syria–Lebanon border. According to tradition, Jesus was transfigured here.

Hermoupolis (Greek *Ermoupolis*) Port and capital of Syros Island, Greece, and capital of the ◊Cyclades department. It is the only industrial town in the Cyclades; cotton and Turkish delight are manufactured, and there are ship-repairing yards. It was at one time the chief port of Greece, but declined with the growth of Piraeus in the late 19th century.

Herne Industrial city in North Rhine–Westphalia, Germany; population (1991) 179,100. Industries include civil engineering, coal mining, construction, and chemicals.

Herne Bay Seaside resort in Kent, SE England, 11 km/ 7 mi N of Canterbury; population (1985 est) 27,800.

Herrnhut Town in the *Land* of ◊Saxony-Anhalt, Germany, 72 km/45 mi SE of Dresden. The settlement was founded as the headquarters of the Moravian Church in 1721 by Count Nikolaus Ludwig von Zinzendorf; adherents of this evangelical strain of Protestantism were popularly known as *Herrnhüter*.

Herstal Town in the province of Liège, Belgium, a suburb of the city of ◊Liège, on the river Meuse. Herstal has a small-arms factory, a cannon foundry, and coal-mines, and manufactures iron and steel. It is the reputed birthplace of Pepin the Short and his son Charlemagne.

Herstmonceux or *Hurstmonceux* Village 11 km/7 mi N of Eastbourne, East Sussex, England. From 1958 the Royal Greenwich Observatory was here, alongside the 15th-century castle. The Observatory moved to Cambridge 1990, but its fine antique telescopes remained as the centrepiece of a proposed scientific theme park. The Isaac Newton telescope was moved to the Canary Islands 1979.

Hertford Administrative headquarters of Hertfordshire, SE England, on the river Lea; population (1989 est) 25,000. There are brewing, printing, brush manufacturing, engineering, and brick industries.

Hertfordshire County of SE England
area 1,630 sq km/629 sq mi
towns and cities Hertford (administrative headquarters), St Albans, Watford, Hatfield, Hemel Hempstead, Bishop's Stortford, Letchworth (the first garden city, followed by Welwyn 1919 and Stevenage 1947)
features rivers: Lea, Stort, Colne; part of the Chiltern Hills; Hatfield House; Knebworth House (home of Lord Lytton); Brocket Hall (home of Palmerston and Melbourne); home of G B Shaw at Ayot St Lawrence; Berkhamsted Castle (Norman); Rothamsted agricultural experimental station
industries engineering, aircraft, electrical goods, paper and printing; general agricultural goods; barley for brewing industry, dairy farming, market gardening, horticulture, tanning, computer electronics, plastics, pharmaceuticals
population (1994) 1,005,400

famous people Henry Bessemer, Cecil Rhodes, Graham Greene.

Hertogenbosch See ◊'s-Hertogenbosch, a city in the Netherlands.

Herts Abbreviation for ◊Hertfordshire, an English county.

Herzegovina or *Hercegovina* Part of Bosnia-Herzegovina (which was formerly, until 1991, a republic of Yugoslavia).

Hesse-Homburg Former landgraviate of Germany, composed of Bad Homburg on the right bank of the Rhine and Meisenheim on the left bank. The first of these regions is now part of the *Land* of ◊Hessen, while the latter is part of the ◊Rhineland-Palatinate.

Hessen Administrative region (German *Land*) of Germany
area 21,114 sq km/8,152 sq mi
capital Wiesbaden
towns and cities Frankfurt am Main, Kassel, Darmstadt, Offenbach am Main
features valleys of the rivers Rhine and Main; Taunus Mountains, rich in mineral springs, as at Homburg and Wiesbaden
industries wine, timber, chemicals, cars, electrical engineering, optical instruments
population (1995) 6,009,900
religion Protestant 61%, Roman Catholic 33%
history until 1945, Hessen was divided in two by a strip of Prussian territory, the S portion consisting of the valleys of the rivers Rhine and the Main, the N being dominated by the Vogelsberg Mountains (744 m/2,442 ft). Its capital was Darmstadt.

Hexham Town in Northumberland, England, 21 mi/ 34 km W of Newcastle upon Tyne. It is a centre of tourism for Hadrian's Wall (a World Heritage site), including Chesters Roman Fort, Housesteads Roman Fort, and Vindolanda (the remains of eight forts and settlements). Hexham Abbey dates from the 12th century.

HI Abbreviation for ◊Hawaii, a state of the USA.

Hialeah City in SE Florida, USA, just NW of Miami; population (1992) 191,700. Industries include clothing, furniture, plastics, and chemicals. Hialeah Park racetrack (1925) is a centre for horse racing. The city was settled 1910.

Hickory City in W central North Carolina, USA, in the foothills of the Blue Ridge Mountains, NW of Charlotte; population (1990) 28,300. The city's main industry is hosiery manufacture. Other products include rope, cotton, and wagons. It was founded 1874.

Hidalgo State of central Mexico; area 20,987 sq km/ 8,103 sq mi; population (1995 est) 2,111,800. Its capital is Pachuca de Soto. The main occupation is silver mining, producing two-thirds of Mexican silver. Gold, copper, and lead are also mined. Cereals, sugar-cane, cotton, coffee, and tobacco are produced.

Higashi-Osaka Industrial city (textiles, chemicals, engineering), an E suburb of Osaka, Kinki region, Honshu Island, Japan; population (1993) 496,000.

High Country In New Zealand, the generally mountainous land, many peaks rising to heights between 2,400–3,800 m/8,000–13,000 ft, most of which are on South Island. The lakes, fed by melting snow, are used for hydroelectric power, and it is a skiing, mountaineering, and tourist area.

Highland Unitary authority in N Scotland; former Region 1975–96; administrative headquarters Inverness; population (1996) 207,500; area 25,304 sq km/9,767 sq mi; area 26,100 sq km/10,077 sq mi. Towns and cities include Thurso and Wick. Highland comprises almost half the country of Scotland. The area includes the Grampian Mountains, Ben Nevis (highest peak in the UK), Loch Ness, the Caledonian Canal, Inner Hebrides, the Queen Mother's castle of Mey at Caithness, John O'Groats' House, Dounreay (site of Atomic Energy Authority's first experimental fast-breeder reactor and a nuclear processing plant, decommissioned 1994, and replaced by nuclear-waste reprocessing plant). Industries include oil services, winter sports, timber, livestock, grouse and deer hunting, salmon fishing, sheep farming, aluminium smelting, pulp and paper production, and distilling. Famous people from the area include Alexander Mackenzie and William Smith. Gaelic is spoken by 7.5 % of the population.

Highlands One of the three geographical divisions of Scotland, lying to the N of a geological fault line that stretches from Stonehaven in the North Sea to Dumbarton on the Clyde. It is a mountainous region of hard rocks, shallow infertile soils, and high rainfall.

High Point City in N central North Carolina, USA, SW of Greensboro; population (1992) 70,750. The furniture industry is very important to the economy; the Southern Furniture Market is held four times a year. Hosiery is also manufactured. High Point was settled by Quakers in the 1750s and laid out 1853.

High Wycombe Market town in Buckinghamshire, on the river Wye, England; population (1991) 71,700. Hughenden Manor, home of Benjamin Disraeli is here. RAF Strike Command has its underground headquarters (built 1984) beneath the Chiltern Hills nearby, a four-storey office block used as Joint Headquarters in the Gulf War 1991. Industries include the manufacture of furniture, paper, precision instruments, naval command systems, and clothing, and waste management.

Hildesheim Industrial city in Lower Saxony, Germany, linked to the Mittelland Canal; population (1993) 106,500. Products include electronics and hardware. A bishopric from the 9th century, Hildesheim became a free city of the Holy Roman Empire in the 13th century. It was under Prussian rule 1866–1945.

Hillingdon Outer borough of W Greater London. It includes the district of Uxbridge
features Cedar House (about 1850); Hillingdon parish workhouse (1747); Swakeleys, Jacobean mansion at Ickenham; Grand Union Canal; Heathrow airport (1946), built on the site of a Neolithic settlement

industries pharmaceuticals (Glaxo Wellcome at Uxbridge)
population (1991) 231,600.

Hilversum City in North Holland province of the Netherlands, 27 km/17 mi SE of Amsterdam; population (1994) 84,200. Besides being a summer resort, Hilversum is the main centre of Dutch broadcasting.

Himachal Pradesh State of NW India
area 55,673 sq km/21,495 sq mi
capital Shimla
features mainly agricultural state, one-third forested, with softwood timber industry
industries timber, grain, rice, fruit, seed potatoes
population (1994 est) 5,530,000; mainly Hindu
language Pahari, Hindi
history created as a union territory 1948, it became a full state 1971.

Himalaya Vast mountain system of central Asia, extending from the Indian states of Kashmir in the W to Assam in the E, covering the S part of Tibet, Nepal, Sikkim, and Bhutan. It is the highest mountain range in the world. The two highest peaks are Mount ◊Everest and ◊K2. Other peaks include ◊Kanchenjunga, Makalu, Annapurna, and Nanga Parbat, all over 8,000 m/26,000 ft.

Hinckley Market town in Leicestershire, England; population (1991) 40,600. Industries include engineering and the manufacture of footwear and hosiery.

Hindenburg German name 1915–45 of the Polish city of ◊Zabrze.

Hindu Kush Mountain range in central Asia, length 800 km/500 mi, greatest height Tirich Mir, 7,690 m/25,239 ft, in Pakistan. The narrow *Khyber Pass* (53 km/33 mi long) connects Pakistan with Afghanistan and was used by Babur and other invaders of India. The present road was built by the British in the Afghan Wars.

Hindustan ('land of the Hindus') the whole of India, but more specifically the plain of the Ganges and Yamuna rivers, or that part of India N of the Deccan.

Hinnoy Largest of the Lofoten Islands (see ◊Lofoten and Vesterålen) off the N coast of Norway. Hinnoy is Norway's largest island and lies within the Arctic Circle. It is mountainous and wooded; Moysalen (1,262 m/4,140 ft) is the highest peak. The main economic activities are fishing and tourism. Harstad, in the N of the island, is the most important town and port. There is a 13th-century church N of Harstad.

Hinthada City in S central Myanmar (Burma), on the Irrawaddy River; population (1980 est) 284,000. Products include rice and potatoes.

Hiroshima Industrial city and port on the S coast of Honshu Island, Japan, destroyed by the first wartime use of an atomic bomb 6 Aug 1945. The city has largely been rebuilt since the war; population (1994) 1,077,000.

Hirschberg German name of ◊Jelenia Góra, a town in Poland.

Hispaniola (Spanish 'little Spain') West Indian island, first landing place of Columbus in the New World, 6 December 1492; it is now divided into Haiti and the Dominican Republic.

Hitachi City on Honshu Island, Japan; population (1993) 202,100. The chief industry is the manufacture of electrical and electronic goods.

Hitchin Market town in Hertfordshire, England, 48 km/ 30 mi NW of London; population (1991) 32,200. Industries include engineering and flour milling, and parchment is manufactured.

Hjörring Town in Nordjylland county, N Denmark. An ancient town and commercial centre, it has three churches dating from the 13th century.

Hobart Capital and port of Tasmania, Australia; population (1994) 194,200. Products include zinc, textiles, and paper. Founded 1804 as a penal colony, it was named after Lord Hobart, then secretary of state for the colonies.

Hoboken City and port in NE New Jersey, USA, on the Hudson River opposite Manhattan; population (1990) 33,400. Industries include electronics, electrical equipment, and chemicals. The site was bought by the Dutch from Native Americans 1630. The first brewery in America was built here 1642.

Ho Chi Minh City (until 1976 *Saigon*) Chief port and industrial city of S Vietnam; population (1989) 3,169,100. Industries include shipbuilding, textiles, rubber, and food products. Saigon was the capital of the Republic of Vietnam (South Vietnam) from 1954 to 1976, when it was renamed.

Hodeida or *Al Hudaydah* Red Sea port of Yemen; population (1987) 155,110. It trades in coffee and spices.

Hódmezővásárhely Industrial town (textiles, machinery, wood, maiolica pottery) in SE Hungary, near the river Tizsa, 175 km/109 mi SE of Budapest. It lies in the rich agricultural district of the ◊Alföld (Great Plain).

Hodonín (German *Göding*) Town of S Moravia, in the Czech Republic, on the river Morava, 50 km/31 mi SE of Brno; population (1991) 39,700. It is the centre of a district that produces oil, gas, lignite, and wine. Industries include sugar refining and glassmaking. There is a Renaissance castle and a Baroque church.

Hof City in Bavaria, Germany, on the river Saale, in the foothills of the ◊Fichtelgebirge; population (1994) 52,700. It is an important railway junction.

Hofei Alternative transcription of ◊Hefei, a city in China.

Hoggar Alternative name of ◊Ahaggar, a plateau in the Sahara Desert.

Hohensalza German name for ◊Inowrocław, a town in Poland.

Hohenzollern Former province of Prussia, now part of the *Land* of ◊Baden-Württemberg. Its capital was Sigmaringen. It gave its name to the Hohenzollern emperors of Germany 1871–1918.

Hohhot or *Huhehot* City and capital of Inner Mongolia (Nei Mongol) autonomous region, China (see ◊Mongolia,

Inner); population (1993) 730,000. Industries include textiles, electronics, and dairy products. There are Lamaist monasteries and temples here.

Hokkaido formerly (until 1868) *Yezo* or *Ezo* Northernmost of the four main islands of Japan, separated from Honshu to the S by Tsugaru Strait and from Sakhalin to the N by Soya Strait; area 83, 451sq km/32,220 sq mi; population (1995) 5,692,000, including 16,000 Ainus. The capital is Sapporo. Natural resources include coal, mercury, manganese, oil and natural gas, timber, and fisheries. Coal mining and agriculture are the main industries.

Holland Popular name for the Netherlands; also two provinces of the Netherlands, see ◊North Holland and ◊South Holland.

Holland, parts of Former separate administrative county of SE Lincolnshire, England.

Hollywood District in the city of Los Angeles, California; the centre of the US film industry from 1911. It is the home of film studios such as Twentieth Century Fox, MGM, Paramount, Columbia Pictures, United Artists, Disney, and Warner Bros. Many film stars' homes are situated nearby in Beverly Hills and other communities adjacent to Hollywood.

Holyhead (Welsh *Caergybi*) Seaport on the N coast of Holyhead Island, off Anglesey, N Wales; population (1988 est) 13,000. Holyhead Island is linked by road and railway bridges with Anglesey, and there are regular sailings between Holyhead and Dublin.

Holy Island or *Lindisfarne* Island in the North Sea, area 10 sq km/4 sq mi, 3 km/2 mi off Northumberland, England, with which it is connected by a causeway. St Aidan founded a monastery here 635.

Holy Loch Western inlet of the Firth of Clyde, W Scotland. It had a US nuclear submarine base 1961–92. It is one of the dirtiest stretches of water in the world, and is to be cleaned up by the Ministry of Defence from 1997.

Holyoke City in SW Massachusetts, USA, on the Connecticut River, 11 km/7 mi N of ◊Springfield; population (1990) 43,700. The first town in America to manufacture paper, Holyoke also produces textiles, machinery, steel products, and electrical supplies. It is a part of the metropolitan area of Springfield–Holyoke.

Homburg or *Bad Homburg* Town and spa at the foot of the Taunus Mountains, Germany; population (1984) 41,800.

Home Counties The counties in close proximity to London, England: Hertfordshire, Essex, Kent, Surrey, Buckinghamshire, Berkshire, and formerly Middlesex.

Homs or *Lebda* or *Hims* City, capital of Homs district, W Syria, near the Orontes River; population (1993) 537,000. Silk, cereals, and fruit are produced in the area, and industries include silk textiles, oil refining, and jewellery. Zenobia, Queen of Palmyra, was defeated at Homs by the Roman emperor Aurelian 272.

Honan Alternative name of ◊Henan, a province of China.

Hondo Another name for ◊Honshu, an island of Japan.

Honfleur Seaport in the *département* of Calvados, France, on the S bank of the river Seine opposite Le Havre; population (1990) 10,000. It is a tourist resort and fishing and sailing port. A picturesque town, with a Gothic church of the 15th century built entirely of wood, it was visited by several Impressionist painters.

Hong Kong Special administrative region in the SE of China, comprising Hong Kong Island; the Kowloon Peninsula; many other islands, of which the largest is Lantau; and the mainland New Territories. A former British crown colony, it reverted to Chinese control July 1997
area 1,070 sq km/413 sq mi
capital Victoria (Hong Kong City)
towns and cities Kowloon, Tsuen Wan (in the New Territories)
features an enclave of Kwantung province, China, it has one of the world's finest natural harbours; Hong Kong Island is connected with Kowloon by undersea railway and ferries; a world financial centre, its stock market has four exchanges
environment world's most densely populated city; surrounding waters heavily polluted
exports textiles, clothing, electronic goods, clocks, watches, cameras, plastic products; a large proportion of the exports and imports of S China are transshipped here; tourism is important
population (1995 est) 6,189,800; 57% Hong Kong Chinese, most of the remainder refugees from the mainland
language English, Chinese
religion Confucianist, Buddhist, Taoist, with Muslim and Christian minorities
government Hong Kong is a special administrative region within China, with a chief executive, Tung Chee-hwa, from 1997. There is an executive council, which comprises a mixture of business and political figures, and an appointed legislative council. Until reversion to Chinese control July 1997 Hong Kong was a British dependency administered by a crown-appointed governor who presided over an unelected executive council, composed of 4 ex-officio and 11 nominated members, and a legislative council composed of 3 ex-officio members, 18 appointees, and 39 elected members (21 of these elected by constituencies each representing an occupational of professional group, and 18 directly elected by 9 geographical constituencies).
history formerly part of China, Hong Kong Island was occupied by Britain 1841, during the first of the Opium Wars, and ceded by China under the 1842 Treaty of Nanking. The Kowloon Peninsula was acquired under the 1860 Beijing (Peking) Convention and the New Territories secured on a 99-year lease from 1898. The colony, which developed into a major centre for Sino-British trade during the late 19th and early 20th centuries, was occupied by Japan 1941–45. The restored British administration promised, after 1946, to increase self-government. These plans were shelved, however, after the 1949 communist revolution in China. During the 1950s almost 1 million Chinese (predominantly Cantonese) refugees fled to Hong Kong. Immigration continued during the 1960s and 1970s, raising

Hong Kong

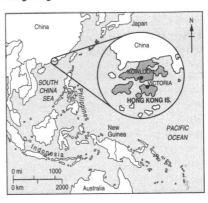

the colony's population from 1 million in 1946 to 5 million in 1980, leading to the imposition of strict border controls during the 1980s. From 1975, 160,000 Vietnamese boat people fled to Hong Kong; in 1991 some 61,000 remained. The UK government began forced repatriation 1989. Hong Kong's economy expanded rapidly during the corresponding period and the colony became one of Asia's major commercial, financial, and industrial centres, boasting the world's busiest container port from 1987. As the date (1997) for the termination of the New Territories' lease approached, negotiations on Hong Kong's future were opened between Britain and China 1982. These culminated 1984 in an agreement that Britain would transfer full sovereignty of the islands and New Territories to China 1997 in return for Chinese assurance that Hong Kong's social and economic freedom and capitalist lifestyle would be preserved for at least 50 years.

As plans for the transfer became more detailed, fears that China would exert more control than agreed led to tensions between the UK and China. Tung Chee-hwa, a Shanghai-born shipping magnate who had studied in Britain and the USA before running, with Chinese financial help, a large ocean fleet out of Taiwan and Hong Kong, was elected by a 400-member Chinese-established selection committee, to become the first chief executive (replacing the British-appointed governor) of the Hong Kong Special Administrative Region (HKSAR) when Hong Kong reverted to Chinese sovereignty in July 1997.

In Jan 1997 Tung announced that the new Executive Council would comprise a mixture of business and political figures with strong links with mainland China. In Feb 1997 the Chinese parliament voted to substantially dilute Hong Kong's bill of rights and freedoms of association and assembly after the July 1997 handover.

Honiara Port and capital of the Solomon Islands, on the NW coast of Guadalcanal Island, on the river Mataniko; population (1989) 33,750.

Honiton Market town in Devon, SW England, on the river Otter; population (1991) 7,850. Its handmade pillow-lace industry is undergoing a revival.

Honolulu (Hawaiian 'sheltered bay') Capital city and

port of Hawaii, on the S coast of Oahu; population (1992) 371,000. It is a holiday resort, because of its scenery and tropical vegetation, with some industry.

Honshu or *Hondo* Principal island of Japan. It lies between Hokkaido to the NE and Kyushu to the SW; area 230,966 sq km/89,176 sq mi, including 382 smaller islands; population (1995) 100,995,000. A chain of volcanic mountains runs along the island, which is subject to frequent earthquakes. The main cities are Tokyo, Yokohama, Osaka, Kobe, Nagoya, and Hiroshima.

Hooghly or *Hugli* River and city in West Bengal, India; population (1981) 125,193. The river is the W stream of the Ganges delta. The city is on the site of a factory set up by the East India Company 1640, which was moved to Calcutta, 40 km/25 mi downstream, 1686–90.

Hook of Holland (Dutch *Hoek van Holland* 'corner of Holland') Small peninsula and village in South Holland, the Netherlands; the terminus for ferry services with Harwich (Parkeston Quay), England.

Hoorn Town in the province of North Holland, the Netherlands, on the W coast of the IJsselmeer, 40 km/25 mi N of Amsterdam; population (1996) 62,100. It is a picturesque town with cheese and cattle markets, boatyards, and sawmills. Hoorn was a port on the ◊Zuider Zee in the 17th century, handling Baltic trade to the colonies, and held the headquarters of the Dutch East India Company, but the town declined in importance after the harbour silted up and the IJsselmeer was created.

Hoover Dam Highest concrete dam in the USA, 221 m/726 ft, on the Colorado River at the Arizona–Nevada border. It was constructed 1931–36. It was known as *Boulder Dam* 1933–47. The dam created Lake Mead. It has a hydroelectric power capacity of 1,300 megawatts.

Hopei Alternative transcription of ◊Hebei, a province of China.

Hopkinsville City in SW Kentucky, USA, SW of Louisville; population (1990) 29,800. It is a marketplace for tobacco and livestock.

Hordaland County of S Norway, on the Atlantic coast; area 15,650 sq km/604 sq mi; population (1995) 425,200. There are many islands off the coast. On the mainland, mountains dominate the landscape. Hardangervidda national park spills over into the adjoining counties of Buskerud and Telemark to the E. Hydroelectric development has created several industrial centres; fishing and farming are also important, and Hordaland is popular with tourists. The main town is ◊Bergen.

Horgen Suburb of ◊Zürich, Switzerland, on the W shore of Lake Zürich. It forms a commune in the canton of Zürich; population (1995) 16,500. It manufactures electronic machinery, cotton, and silk.

Hormuz or *Ormuz* Small island, area 41 sq km/16 sq mi, in the Strait of Hormuz, belonging to Iran. It is strategically important because oil tankers leaving the Persian Gulf for Japan and the West have to pass through the strait to reach the Arabian Sea.

Horsham Town and market centre on the river Arun, in West Sussex, England, 26 km/16 mi SE of Guildford; population (1991) 45,600. The public school Christ's Hospital is about 3 km/2 mi to the SW. The poet Percy Bysshe Shelley was born here.

Hortobágy Part of the Hungarian ◊Alföld (Great Plain), near Debrecen, containing the country's only remaining natural steppe lands (Hungarian *puszta*). Its damp pastureland is grazed by livestock.

Hot Springs Resort town in W central Arkansas, USA, 88 km/55 mi SW of Little Rock; population (1990) 32,500. It is situated in a narrow valley and contains 47 hot springs which produce over 3,785,000 l/1,000,000 gall of mineral water each day, with an average temperature of 62°C/143°F. The town is a popular spa and the springs are contained in a reservation now designated a national park (the only national park to fall within city limits).

Houma City in S Louisiana, USA, on the gulf intracoastal waterway, SW of New Orleans; population (1990) 30,500. Linked to the Gulf of Mexico by the Houma Navigation Canal, it is a supply centre for offshore oil rigs. Industries include shellfish processing and sugar refining. Houma developed as a fishing and fur port in the 19th century. It is the seat of Terrebonne parish.

Hounslow Outer borough of W Greater London. It includes the districts of Heston, Brentford, and Isleworth
features reputed site of Caesar's crossing of the Thames 54 BC at Brentford; Hounslow Heath, formerly the haunt of highwaymen; 16th-century Osterley Park, reconstructed by Robert Adam in the 1760s; 16th-century Syon House, seat of duke of Northumberland, where Lady Jane Grey was offered the crown 1553; the artist William Hogarth's House, Chiswick; Boston Manor House (1662); Chiswick House, Palladian villa designed by Richard Burlington 1725–29; site of London's first civil airport (1919)
population (1991) 204,400
famous people Thomas Gresham.

Housatonic River in New England, NE USA; length 238 km/148 mi. It rises in Berkshire County, Massachusetts, and flows generally southwards through Connecticut to enter Long Island Sound at Milford. It is used as a source of hydroelectric power.

Houston Port in Texas, USA; linked by the Houston Ship Canal to the Gulf of Mexico, in the Gulf Coastal Plain; population (1992) 1,690,200; metropolitan area (1992) 3,962,000. A major centre of finance and commerce, Houston is also one of the busiest US ports. Industrial products include refined petroleum, oil-field equipment, and petrochemicals, chief of which are synthetic rubber, plastics, insecticides, and fertilizers. Other products include iron and steel, electrical and electronic machinery, paper products, and milled rice. Houston was first settled 1826.

Hove Residential town and seaside resort in Brighton and Hove unitary authority, on the S coast of England; adjoining

Brighton to the W; population (1991) 67,600. It was one of the world's pioneering film-making centres at the turn of the century.

Hoyerswerda Town in the *Land* of ◊Brandenburg, Germany, 40 km/25 mi S of Cottbus. The town is dominated by a huge power-generating and lignite-processing complex, built to exploit the extensive opencast mining of brown coal in the area. Hoyerswerda also manufactures glass.

Hradec Králové (German *Königgrätz*) Capital of East Bohemia, in the Czech Republic, on the river Elbe, 100 km/63 mi E of Prague; population (1991) 98,900. It is an industrial town producing chemicals, photographic equipment, and textiles. The Gothic cathedral is partly 14th century.

Hrodna formerly *Grodno* Industrial city in Belarus, on the Nyoman (Neman) River; population (1991) 284,800. Part of Lithuania from 1376, it passed to Poland 1596, Russia 1795, Poland 1920, and the USSR 1939.

Huallaga River Tributary of the Marayon River in NE Peru. The upper reaches of the river valley are used for growing coca, a major source of the drug cocaine.

Huambo Town in central Angola; population (1995) 400,000. Founded 1912, it was known as *Nova Lisboa* ('New Lisbon') 1928–78. It is an agricultural centre. A battle here 1993 between MPLA (government forces) and UNITA (right-wing rebels) lasted 55 days and cost an estimated 13,500 lives; UNITA won. It fell to government forces 1994, and UNITA leader, Jonas Savimbi, fled. Huambo was the former headquarters of UNITA.

Huang He or *Hwang Ho* River in China; length 5,464 km/3,395 mi. It takes its name (meaning 'yellow river') from its muddy waters. Formerly known as 'China's sorrow' because of disastrous floods, it is now largely controlled through hydroelectric works and flood barriers.

Huangshan Mountains Mountain range in S Anhui province, China; the highest peak is Lotus Flower, 1,873 m/5,106 ft.

Huascaran, Nev de Extinct volcano in the Andes; the highest mountain in Peru, 6,768 m/22,205 ft.

Hubei or *Hupei* Province of central China, through which flow the river Chang Jiang and its tributary the Han Shui
area 187,500 sq km/72,394 sq mi
capital Wuhan
features high land in the W, the river Chang breaking through from Sichuan in gorges; elsewhere low-lying, fertile land; many lakes
industries beans, cereals, cotton, rice, vegetables, copper, gypsum, iron ore, phosphorus, salt
population (1990) 54,760,000.

Huddersfield Industrial town in West Yorkshire, on the river Colne, linked by canal with Manchester and other N England centres; population (1994 est) 139,000. A village in Anglo-Saxon times, it was a thriving centre of woollen manufacture by the end of the 18th century; industries now include dyestuffs, chemicals, electrical and mechanical engineering, wool textiles, prams, and carpets.

Hudson River of the NE USA; length 485 km/300 mi. It rises in the Adirondack Mountains and flows S, emptying into a bay of the Atlantic Ocean at New York City.

Hudson Bay Inland sea of NE Canada, linked with the Atlantic Ocean by *Hudson Strait* and with the Arctic Ocean by Foxe Channel; area 730,000 sq km/281,900 sq mi. It is named after Henry Hudson, who reached it 1610.

Hué City in central Vietnam, formerly capital of Annam, 13 km/8 mi from the China Sea; population (1989) 211,100. The Citadel, within which is the Imperial City enclosing the palace of the former emperor, lies to the W of the Old City on the N bank of the Huong (Perfume) River; the New City is on the S bank.

Huelva Port and capital of Huelva province, Andalusia, SW Spain, near the mouth of the river Odiel; population (1994) 145,000. Industries include shipbuilding, oil refining, fisheries, and trade in ores from Río Tinto. Columbus began and ended his voyage to America at nearby Palos de la Frontera.

Huelva Province of SW Spain in W ◊Andalusia autonomous community; capital Huelva; area 10,100 sq km/3,900 sq mi; population (1995) 458,700. It borders the Portuguese frontier to the W and the Atlantic Ocean to the S. Much of the province is occupied by spurs of the Sierra Morena mountain range. The rivers Tinto and Odiel, and tributaries of the Guadiana and Guadalquivir rivers flow through it; some districts are very fertile. There are rich deposits of iron and copper pyrites.

Huesca Capital of Huesca province in Aragón, N Spain; population (1991) 50,000. Industries include engineering and food processing. Among its buildings are a fine 13th-century cathedral and the former palace of the kings of Aragón.

Huesca Province of NE Spain in N ◊Aragón autonomous community; capital Huesca; area 15,672 sq km/6,051 sq mi; population (1995) 210,300. It borders the French frontier to the N and is very mountainous, containing the highest peak in the Pyrenees (Aneto, 3,405 m/11,171 ft).

Huhehot Former name of ◊Hohhot, a city in Inner Mongolia.

Hull Shortened name of ◊Kingston upon Hull, a city and unitary authority on the N bank of the Humber estuary, E England.

Hull City in S Quebec, E Canada, on the N shore of the Ottawa River opposite Ottawa; population (1991) 60,700. Its industries include pulp, paper, cement, clothing, timber, concrete blocks, and jewellery. There are four large electricity-generating stations within the city and its surroundings. Hull is the shopping centre for a prosperous farming community, and has a number of government offices.

Humber Estuary in NE England formed by the Ouse and Trent rivers, which meet E of Goole and flow 60 km/38 mi to enter the North Sea below Spurn Head. The main ports are Hull on the N side, and Grimsby on the S side. The *Humber Bridge* (1981) is the longest single-span suspension bridge in the world.

Humberside Former county of NE England, created 1974 out of N Lincolnshire and parts of the East and West Ridings of Yorkshire. It was abolished 1996 when the unitary authorities of East Riding of Yorkshire, Kingston upon Hull, North East Lincolnshire, and North Lincolnshire were created.

Humboldt River in Nevada, W USA; length 490 km/ 304 mi. It rises in NE Nevada, flows SW through the *Humboldt Lake*, and ends in the area of interior drainage known as the *Humboldt Sink*. It is used for irrigation.

Hunan Province of S central China
area 210,500 sq km/81,274 sq mi
capital Changsha
features Dongting Lake; farmhouse in Shaoshan village where Mao Zedong was born
industries rice, tea, tobacco, cotton; nonferrous minerals
population (1990) 60,660,000.

Hunedoara Industrial town in W Romania, 15 km/9 mi S of Deva (capital of Hunedoara county). It has a large iron and steel works fed by locally obtained ores. The Gothic castle dates from 1452.

Hunter River in New South Wales, Australia, which rises in the Mount Royal Range and flows into the Pacific Ocean near Newcastle, after a course of about 465 km/290 mi. Although the river is liable to flooding, the Hunter Valley has dairying and market gardening, and produces wines.

Huntingdon Town in Cambridgeshire, E England, on the river Ouse, 26 km/16 mi NW of Cambridge; population (1991) 15,600. It is a market town with a number of light industries, including furniture, plastics, brewing, knitwear, and printing. A bridge built 1332 connects Huntingdon with Godmanchester on the S bank of the river, and the two towns were united 1961. Samuel Pepys and Oliver Cromwell attended the grammar school founded 1565 in a 12th-century building, formerly part of the medieval hospital; it was opened 1962 as a Cromwell museum. The Environmental Information Centre was opened 1989.

Huntingdonshire Former English county, merged 1974 into a much enlarged Cambridgeshire.

Huntington City in W West Virginia, USA, across the Ohio River from Ohio, NW of Charleston; seat of Cabell County; population (1992) 54,100. It is an important transportation centre for coal mined to the S. Other industries include chemicals; metal, wood, and glass products; tobacco; and fruit processing. It was first settled 1796.

Huntsville City in NE Alabama; population (1992) 163,300. Manufactured products include textiles, electrical and electronic goods, metal products, chemicals, machinery, and cosmetics. Huntsville was settled 1805. During the Civil War, it was occupied and burned by Union troops.

Hunza Former princely state in NW Kashmir; area 10,101 sq km/3,900 sq mi; capital Baltit (also known as Hunza). It recognized the sovereignty of the Maharajah of Jammu and

Kashmir 1869, combined with the state of Nagar 1888, and became part of the Gilgit Agency 1889. Since 1948 it has been administered by Pakistan.

Hupei Alternative transcription of ◊Hubei, a province of China.

Huron Second largest of the Great Lakes of North America, on the US-Canadian border; area 59,547 sq km/22,991 sq mi. It includes Georgian Bay, Saginaw Bay, and Manitoulin Island.

Hurstmonceux Alternative spelling of ◊Herstmonceux, a village in East ◊Sussex.

Huşi Town in Vaslui county, E Romania, near the border with Moldova formed by the river Prut, 65 km/41 mi S of Iaşi; population (1995) 26,800. Wine is produced in the area.

Huy (Flemish *Hoei*) Town in the province of Liège, Belgium, on the river Meuse, about 27 km/17 mi SW of the city of ◊Liège. The town has distilleries and manufactures paper.

Hvannadalshnukur Highest peak in Iceland, rising to 2,119 m/6,952 ft in the SE of the country.

Hvar Capital of the island of Hvar, off the coast of Dalmatia, Croatia; population (1990) 3,600. It is a fortified town, with medieval walls and buildings, and has a 13th-century cathedral and a 17th-century theatre. It is a popular tourist resort.

Hwange formerly (until 1982) *Wankie* Coal-mining town in Zimbabwe; population (1992) Hwange Urban 42,600; Hwange Rural 72,200. Hwange National Park is nearby.

Hwang Ho Alternative transcription of ◊Huang He, a river in China.

Hydaspes Classical name of river ◊Jhelum, a river in Pakistan and Kashmir.

Hyde Park One of the largest open spaces in London, England. It occupies about 146 ha/350 acres in Westminster. It adjoins Kensington Gardens, and includes the Serpentine, a boating lake with a 'lido' for swimming. Rotten Row is a famous riding track in the park. Open-air meetings are held at Speakers' Corner. In 1851 the Great Exhibition was held here.

Hyderabad Capital city of the S central Indian state of ◊Andhra Pradesh, on the river Musi; population (1991) 4,280,000. Products include carpets, silks, and metal inlay work. It was formerly the capital of the state of Hyderabad. Buildings include the Jama Masjid mosque and Golconda fort.

Hyderabad City in Sind province, SE Pakistan; population (1981) 795,000. It produces gold, pottery, glass, and furniture. The third-largest city of Pakistan, it was founded 1768.

Hyères Town on the Côte d'Azur in the *département* of Var, S France; population (1990) 50,100. It has a mild climate, and is a winter health resort. Industries include olive-oil pressing and the export of violets, strawberries, and vegetables.

Hyphasis Classical name of the river ◊Beas, in India.

Hythe Seaside resort (one of the original Cinque Ports) in the Romney Marsh area of Kent, SE England; population (1981) 12,700. Industries include plastics and horticulture.

IA Abbreviation for ◊Iowa, a state of the USA.

Iaşi (German *Jassy*) City in NE Romania; population (1993) 328,000. It has chemical, machinery, electronic, and textile industries. It was the capital of the principality of Moldavia 1568–1889.

Ibadan City in SW Nigeria and capital of Oyo state; population (1992 est) 1,295,000. Industries include chemicals, electronics, plastics, and vehicles.

Ibagué Capital of Tolima department, W central Colombia; population (1994) 343,000. Leather goods and a local drink, Mistela, are produced here.

Iberia Name given by ancient Greek navigators to the Spanish peninsula, derived from the river Iberus (Ebro). Anthropologists have given the name *'Iberian'* to a Neolithic people, traces of whom are found in the Spanish peninsula, S France, the Canary Isles, Corsica, and part of North Africa.

Ibiza or *Iviza* One of the ◊Balearic Islands, a popular tourist resort; area 596 sq km/230 sq mi; population (1990 est) 71,000. The capital and port, also called Ibiza, has a cathedral.

Ibsambul Alternative name for ◊Abu Simbel.

Içel Another name for ◊Mersin, a city in Turkey.

Ichang Alternative form of ◊Yichang, a port in China.

Iconium City of ancient Turkey; see ◊Konya.

ID Abbreviation for ◊Idaho, a state of the USA.

Idaho State of NW USA; nicknamed Gem State
area 216,500 sq km/83,569 sq mi
capital Boise
towns and cities Pocatello, Idaho Falls
physical Rocky Mountains; Sawtooth Mountains, with peaks up to 11,800 feet; Snake River, which runs through Hell's Canyon (2,330 m/7,647 ft), the deepest gorge in North America; Shoshone Falls; Salmon River; Lava Hot Springs; Coeur d'Alene Lake, with a large population of ospreys
features the National Reactor Testing Station on the plains of Hell's Canyon's upper reaches; Nez Percé national historic park; Craters of the Moon national monument; Old Mission at Cataldo (1850), the oldest building in the state; Coeur d'Alene Native American reservation; EBR-1, the first nuclear reactor in the USA to generate usable amounts of electricity, now a national historic landmark; Soda Springs, with the only artificial geyser in the world; Sun Valley, the first ski resort in the USA (1935) and site of the world's first chair lifts
industries potatoes, wheat, livestock, timber, silver, lead, zinc, antimony
population (1995) 1,163,300
famous people Ezra Pound
history part of the Louisiana Purchase 1803; explored by Lewis and Clark 1805–06; the first non-natives to settle permanently were the Mormons 1860, the same year gold was

discovered. Settlement in the 1870s led to a series of battles between US forces and Native American tribes. Idaho became a state in 1890. The timber industry began 1906, and by World War I agriculture was a leading enterprise.

Idaho Falls City on the Snake River in SE Idaho, NW USA; population (1990) 43,900. It is a shipping centre for an agricultural area (potatoes and livestock), and industries include food processing and tourism. The waterfalls provide electric power and there is a US Atomic Energy Commission plant nearby.

Idi Amin Dada, Lake Former name (1973–79) of Lake ◊Edward in Uganda/Democratic Republic of Congo.

If Small French island in the Mediterranean about 3 km/2 mi off Marseille, with a castle, Château d'If, built about 1529. This was used as a state prison features in Alexandre Dumas's novel *The Count of Monte Cristo.*

Ifni Former Spanish overseas province in SW Morocco 1860–1969; area 1,920 sq km/740 sq mi. The chief town is Sidi Ifni.

Iglau German name of ◊Jihlava, a town in the Czech Republic.

Igls Winter sports resort in the Austrian Tyrol, near Innsbruck; it was the venue for the 1964 Winter Olympics.

Iguaçu Falls or *Iguassú Falls* Waterfall in South America, on the border between Brazil and Argentina. The falls lie 19 km/12 mi above the junction of the river Iguaçu with the Paraná. The falls are divided by forested rocky islands and form a spectacular tourist attraction. The water plunges in 275 falls, many of which have separate names. They have a height of 82 m/269 ft and a width of about 4 km/2.5 mi.

IJmuiden Port in the province of North Holland, the Netherlands, 10 km/6 mi NW of Haarlem. IJmuiden stands at the end of the North Sea Canal, a waterway leading to Amsterdam, of which it is an outport. There are fisheries and chemical industries.

IJssel River in the Netherlands; length 110 km/68 mi. The IJssel is the northernmost arm of the ◊Rhine delta, leaving the main stream near Arnhem and flowing N into the ◊IJsselmeer, 6 km/4 mi NW of Kampen. The river is navigable for its entire length.

IJssel, Hollandsche River in the Netherlands, a branch of the river Lek, connected by canal with the Oude Rijn (see ◊Rhine) at Utrecht; length 77 km/48 mi. It joins the Nieuwe Maas (see ◊Meuse) 4 km/2 mi E of Rotterdam.

IJsselmeer or *Ysselmeer* Lake in the Netherlands, area 1,217 sq km/470 sq mi. It was formed 1932 after the Zuider Zee was cut off from the North Sea by a dyke 32 km/20 mi long (the *Afsluitdijk*); it has been freshwater since 1944. The rivers Vecht, IJssel, and Zwatewater empty into the lake.

IJsselmonde Island in the province of ◊South Holland, Netherlands, situated between two branches of the river Maas (see ◊Meuse) – the Oude and Nieuwe Maas – opposite Rotterdam. It is 24 km/15 mi long and 8 km/5 mi wide. There is a small town of the same name on the island.

IL   Abbreviation for ◊Illinois, a state of the USA.

Ile-de-France   Region of N France; area 12,012 sq km/ 4,638 sq mi; population (1990) 10,660,600. It includes the French capital, Paris, and the towns of Versailles, Sèvres, and St-Cloud and comprises the *départements* of Essonne, Val-de-Marne, Val d'Oise, Ville de Paris, Seine-et-Marne, Hauts-de-Seine, Seine-Saint-Denis, and Yvelines. From here the early French kings extended their authority over the whole country.

Ile de la Tortue   (French *La Tortue* 'turtle') Island off the N coast of Haiti; area 180 sq km/69 sq mi. It was a pirate lair during the 17th century.

Ilfracombe   Resort on the N coast of Devon, SW England; population (1991) 10,400. There is a 14th-century chapel.

Ilia   Greek name for ◊Elis, a department of Greece.

Ilkeston   Town in SE Derbyshire, England; population (1991) 35,100. Part of a former coal-mining region, industries include plastics, iron founding, clothing, furnishings, and pipe-making.

Ilkley   Town in West Yorkshire, England, noted for nearby *Ilkley Moor*; population (1991) 13,500.

Ille   French river 45 km/28 mi long, which rises in Lake Boulet and enters the Vilaine at Rennes. It gives its name to the *département* of Ille-et-Vilaine in Brittany.

Ille-et-Vilaine   *Département* in the ◊Brittany region of France, bordering Mont-Saint-Michel bay and the English Channel; area 6,758 sq km/2,609 sq mi; population (1990) 799,200. Ille-et-Vilaine is bounded in the W by the *départements* of Côtes-d'Armor and Morbihan, in the S by Loire-Atlantique, and in the E and NE by Mayenne and Manche. The rivers Ille and Vilaine flow from the N and E, uniting at Rennes. Wheat, barley, flax, and potatoes are among the chief crops. The oysters of Cancale are exported, and fishing grounds off the coast are exploited. The principal industries are footwear (Fougères), cars, electronics, and leatherwork (Rennes). Mineral resources include granite (around Fougères), slate, and lead at Bruz. The principal towns are ◊Rennes (the capital), Fougères, Redon, and the ports of St-Servan and St-Malo.

Illimani   Highest peak in the Bolivian Andes, rising to 6,402 m/21,004 ft E of the city of La Paz.

Illinois   Midwestern state of the USA; nicknamed Prairie State/Inland Empire/Land of Lincoln; became a state 1818
area   146,100 sq km/56,395 sq mi
capital   Springfield
cities   Chicago, Rockford, Peoria, Decatur, Aurora
physical   Lake Michigan; the Mississippi, Illinois, Ohio, and Rock rivers; prairies; Shawnee national forest
features   Cahokia Mounds, the largest group of prehistoric earthworks in the USA (a World Heritage Site); Nauvoo, founded 1839 by the Mormons, and their point of departure 1846 on the trek that led them to Utah; Abraham Lincoln's home in Springfield; Abraham Lincoln national historic park; Galena, a lead-mining town dating from the 1820s, with pre–Civil War buildings, including the Dowling House (1826), the Belvedere Mansion and Gardens (1857), and the Ulysses S Grant House (1860); Chicago, with the Art Institute of Chicago, the Museum of Science and Industry, the Sears Tower (the world's tallest building 1974, 443 m/1,454 ft high), and the Rookery (1886) with a lobby designed by Frank Lloyd Wright 1905; Frank Lloyd Wright's home and studio, Oak Park; Ernest Hemingway's boyhood home, Oak Park; the Dana Thomas House, Springfield, designed by Frank Lloyd Wright 1903; gambling casinos on replicas of 19th-century Mississippi paddle boats
industries   soya beans, cereals, meat and dairy products, machinery, electrical and electronic equipment
population   (1995) 11,829,900
famous people   Jane Addams, Frances Cabrini, Clarence Darrow, Ernest Hemingway, Jesse Jackson, Abraham Lincoln, Edgar Lee Masters, Ronald Reagan, Carl Sandburg, Louis Sullivan, Frank Lloyd Wright.

Ilmenau   Town in the *Land* of ◊Thuringia, Germany, on the river Ilm in the Thuringian Forest, 19 km/12 mi NE of Suhl; population (1996) 26,300. It is a health resort in a fluorspar-mining area, and was frequented by Goethe, who wrote his play *Iphigenia auf Tauris* here.

Ilorin   Capital of Kwara state, Nigeria; population (1992 est) 430,600. It trades in tobacco and wood products.

Imatra Falls   Stretch of water in SE Finland on the river Vuoksi, near the border with the Russian Federation, a short distance after the river leaves Lake Saimaa. The falls drop 24 m/79 ft and were harnessed for hydroelectric power in the 1920s, but are released during the tourist season.

Imbros   (Turkish *Imroz*) Island in the Aegean Sea; area 280 sq km/108 sq mi. Occupied by Greece in World War I, it became Turkish under the Treaty of Lausanne 1923.

Immingham   Town on the river Humber, Humberside, NE England; population (1981) 11,500. It is a bulk cargo handling port, with petrochemical works and oil refineries. It exports chemicals, iron and steel, and petroleum products.

Imperia   Province of NW Italy in W ◊Liguria region; capital Imperia (population (1990) 41,300); area 1,155 sq km/446 sq mi; population (1992) 215,200.

Imphal   Capital of Manipur state on the Manipur River, India; population (1991) 201,000; a communications and trade centre (tobacco, sugar, fruit). It was besieged March–June 1944, when Japan invaded Assam, but held out with the help of supplies dropped by air.

Imroz   Turkish form of ◊Imbros, an island in the Aegean Sea.

IN   Abbreviation for ◊Indiana, a state of the USA.

Inari, Lake   Lake in the extreme N of Finland, in the province of Lappi; area 1,153 sq km/445 sq mi. It is rich in fish and contains more than 3,000 islands. The small town of Inari on the shore of the lake is a centre of the Saami culture of Lapland and the seat of the Finnish Saami parliament.

Inchon formerly *Chemulpo* Chief port of Seoul, South Korea; population (1990) 1,818,300. It produces steel and textiles.

Independence City in W Missouri, USA; population (1992) 112,700. Industries include steel, Portland cement, petroleum refining, and flour milling.

Settled 1827, it was the starting point for the Santa Fe, Oregon, and California trails, and later for wagon trains to the gold mines in California. President Harry S Truman was raised here, and it is the site of the Truman Library and Museum.

Indiana State of the midwest USA; nicknamed Hoosier State; became a state 1816

area 93,700 sq km/36,168 sq mi

capital Indianapolis

cities Fort Wayne, Gary, Evansville, South Bend

physical Ohio and Wabash rivers; Wyandotte Cavern; Indiana Dunes national lakeshore, on Lake Michigan

features Vincennes, the oldest community in the state; Indianapolis, the scene of the Indianapolis 500 car race, with the Indianapolis Motor Speedway Hall of Fame Museum; Abraham Lincoln boyhood national memorial; New Harmony, Robert Owen's utopian community; Amish country; the inhabitants of the state are known as Hoosiers

industries maize, pigs, soya beans, limestone, machinery, electrical goods, coal, steel, iron, chemicals

population (1995) 5,803,500

famous people Hoagy Carmichael, Eugene V Debs, Theodore Dreiser, Michael Jackson, Cole Porter, J Dan Quayle, Booth Tarkington, Kurt Vonnegut, Wilbur Wright.

Indianapolis Capital and largest city of Indiana, on the White River; population (1992) 746,500; metropolitan area (1992) 1,424,000. It is an industrial centre and venue of the Indianapolis 500 car race. Indianapolis was founded 1821 and became the state capital 1825.

Indian Ocean Ocean between Africa and Australia, with India to the N, and the S boundary being an arbitrary line from Cape Agulhas to S Tasmania; area 73,427,500 sq km/ 28,350,500 sq mi; average depth 3,840 m/12,598 ft. The greatest depth is the Java Trench 7,725 m/25,353 ft.

Indochina Name given by the French to their colonies in Southeast Asia: Cambodia, Laos, and Vietnam, which became independent after World War II.

Indore City in Madhya Pradesh, India; population (1991) 1,092,000. A former capital of the princely state of Indore, it now produces cotton, chemicals, and furniture.

Indre River rising in the Auvergne Mountains, France, and flowing NW for 260 km/165 mi to join the Loire below Tours. It gives its name to the *départements* of Indre and Indre-et-Loire.

Indre *Département* in the ◊Centre region of France; area 6,777 sq km/2,617 sq mi; population (1990) 237,687. It is drained by the rivers ◊Indre and Creuse. The chief cash crops grown here are cereals, beet, and vegetables. Vines and fruit trees are also widely cultivated. Poultry and sheep

are raised, especially in the Champagne district. The chief manufactures are textiles, paper, leather goods, and pottery. The principal towns are Châteauroux, the departmental capital, Le Blanc, La Châtre, and Issoudun.

Indre-et-Loire *Département* in the ◊Centre region of France; area 6,124 sq km/2,364 sq mi; population (1990) 529,800. The river Loire and its tributaries, principally the Indre, Cher, and Vienne, flow through the *département*. The chief districts of the Indre-et-Loire are the Gâtine, a plateau of woods and plains N of the Loire; the Champagne, a chain of vine-clad slopes between the Cher and the Indre; the Veron, a district of orchards and vines between the Loire and the Vienne; the unproductive plateau of Sainte-Maure; and the marshy district of Breune. The chief products are wine (Vouvray and Mont Louis), wheat, barley, and fruit. There is some textile and paper manufacturing. The châteaux in the Loire valley attract tourists. The principal towns are ◊Tours (the capital), Chinon, and Loches.

Indus River in Asia, rising in Tibet and flowing 2,897 km/ 1,800 mi to the Arabian Sea. In 1960 the use of its waters, including those of its five tributaries, was divided between India (rivers Ravi, Beas, Sutlej) and Pakistan (rivers Indus, Jhelum, Chenab).

Ingelheim am Rhein Town in the Rhineland-Palatinate, Germany, 18 km/11 mi W of Mainz; population (1994) 21,200. Ingelheim is the centre of a wine-producing district specializing in red wines. The upper town (Oberingelheim) has an ancient fortress and a medieval church, while the lower town (Niederingelheim) contains the remains of a palace of Charlemagne.

Ingolstadt City in Bavaria, Germany, 69 km/43 mi NW of Munich; population (1994) 110,900. Cars are manufactured in the city and oil, supplied by pipeline from the Italian ports of Genoa and Trieste, is refined here. Ingolstadt is on the river Danube, which was diverted to pass the town in 1363.

Ingushetia Autonomous republic of the Russian Federation, on the N slopes of the Caucasus mountains

area 3,236 sq km/1,249 sq mi

capital Nazran

industries farming and cattle-raising; petroleum drilling

population (1995) 280,000

religion Muslim

Inhambane Seaport on the SE coast of Mozambique, 370 km/231 mi NE of Maputo; population (1980) 56,000.

Inland Sea (Japanese *Seto Naikai*) Arm of the Pacific Ocean, 390 km/240 mi long, almost enclosed by the Japanese islands of Honshu, Kyushu, and Shikoku. It has about 300 small islands.

Inn River in S central Europe, tributary of the Danube. Rising in the Swiss Alps, it flows 507 km/317 mi NE through Austria and into Bavaria, Germany, where it meets the Danube at Passau.

Innsbruck Capital of Tirol state, W Austria; population (1991) 118,100. It is a tourist and winter sports centre and a route junction for the Brenner Pass. The 1964 and 1976 Winter Olympics were held here.

Inowrocław (German *Hohensalza*) Spa town in Bydgoszcz province, Poland, 45 km/28 mi S of Bydgoszcz; population (1990) 76,600. Industries include engineering, glass, sugar, and brass; and salt and gypsum are mined in the district. The town was part of Prussia 1772–1919.

Interlaken Chief town of the Bernese Alps, on the river Aar between lakes Brienz and Thun, Switzerland; population (1990 est) 15,000. The site was first occupied 1130 by a monastery, suppressed 1528.

International Petroleum Exchange Commodity market in the City of London that trades in petroleum. It was established 1980.

Intracoastal Waterway Water route running from the US-Mexican border at Brownsville, Texas, along the Gulf of Mexico and Atlantic coasts to New York; length 4,800 km/2,983 mi. It is an important shipping route. The main cargoes transported are petroleum products and chemicals.

Invercargill City on the S coast of South Island, New Zealand; population (1993) 51,700. It has sawmills and meatpacking and aluminium-smelting plants.

Inverclyde Unitary authority in W Scotland created 1996 from part of the former Strathclyde region; administrative headquarters Greenock; population (1996) 90,000; area 157 sq km/60 sq mi.

Inverness Town in the Highland unitary authority, Scotland, at the head of the Moray Firth, lying in a sheltered site at the mouth of the river Ness; population (1991) 41,200. It is a tourist centre with tweed, tanning, engineering, distilling, iron-founding, boat-building, and electronics industries. Until 1975 it was the county town of Inverness-shire.

Inverness-shire Largest of the former Scottish counties, it was merged into Highland Region 1975–1996, and is now part of the Highland unitary authority.

Inyangani Highest peak in Zimbabwe, rising to 2,593 m/8,507 ft near the Mozambique frontier in NE Zimbabwe.

Inyokern Village in the Mojave Desert, California, USA, 72 km/45 mi NW of Mojave. It is the site of a US naval ordnance test station, founded 1944, carrying out research in rocket flight and propulsion.

Ioannina Town in Greece, capital of Ioannina department, on the shore of Lake Ioannina, about 80 km/50 mi from the sea and 480 m/1,575 ft above sea level, opposite the island of Corfu. It has a tanning and fur-dressing industry.

IOM Abbreviation for *Isle of* ◊Man, an island in the Irish Sea.

Iona Island in the Inner Hebrides; area 850 hectares/2,100 acres. A centre of early Christianity, it is the site of a monastery founded 563 by St Columba. It later became a burial ground for Irish, Scottish, and Norwegian kings. It has a 13th-century abbey.

Ionian Islands (Greek *Ionioi Nisoi*) Island group off the W coast of Greece; area 860 sq km/332 sq mi; population (1991) 191,000. A British protectorate from 1815 until their cession to Greece 1864, they include Cephalonia (Greek Kefallínia); Corfu (Kérkyra), a Venetian possession 1386–1797; Cythera (Kíthira); Ithaca (Itháki), the traditional home of Odysseus; Leukas (Levkás); Paxos (Paxoí); and Zante (Zákynthos).

Ionian Sea Part of the Mediterranean Sea that lies between Italy and Greece, to the S of the Adriatic Sea, and containing the Ionian Islands.

IOW Abbreviation for *Isle of* ◊Wight, an island and unitary authority off the coast of S England.

Iowa State of the midwest USA; nicknamed Hawkeye State/Corn State
area 145,800 sq km/56,279 sq mi
capital Des Moines
towns and cities Cedar Rapids, Davenport, Sioux City
physical Mississippi River; prairies; Iowa Lakes
features 90% of land farmed; Effigy Mounds national monument, with prehistoric Native American burial ground; the Amana colonies, seven villages founded by German-Swiss immigrants in the 19th century as a utopian religious community (ended 1932); Herbert Hoover birthplace, library, and museum near West Branch; Czech Village, museum, and immigrant home, Cedar Rapids; Des Moines, with Post-Modern state historical building of Iowa, Court Avenue District with 19th-century commercial buildings and warehouses, Sherman Hill historic district with Victorian houses, and Living History Farms; Victorian river merchants' houses at Dubuque; Museum of Art, Cedar Rapids, with a collection of paintings by Grant Wood; Grant Wood Gallery, Davenport; casino riverboat gambling, including the President Riverboat Casino, Davenport; the US presidential race starts at Des Moines with the Iowa Caucuses
industries cereals, soya beans, pigs and cattle, chemicals, farm machinery, electrical goods, hardwood lumber, minerals
population (1995) 2,841,800
famous people Bix Beiderbecke, Buffalo Bill, Herbert Hoover, Glenn Miller, Lillian Russell, Grant Wood
history Iowa was part of the Louisiana Purchase 1803. Native Americans of the Sauk and Fox peoples were forced to cede their lands 1832 in what is now E Iowa. Because of its rich topsoil, Iowa quickly attracted settlers and became a state 1846. The economy remains based on agriculture; the state usually leads all others in the production of corn, soybeans, and hogs.

Iowa City City in E Iowa, USA, on the Iowa River, S of Cedar Rapids, seat of Johnson County; population (1992) 59,300. It is a distribution centre for the area's agricultural products. Other industries include printed matter and building materials. The University of Iowa (1847) is here. Iowa City was founded 1839. The Old Capitol (1840) is on the university campus. The state capital was moved to Des Moines 1857.

Ipoh Capital of Perak state, Peninsular Malaysia; population (1991) 383,000. The economy is based on tin mining.

Ipswich River port on the Orwell estuary, administrative headquarters of Suffolk, England; population (1994 est)

115,000. Industries include engineering, printing, brewing, flour-milling, and the manufacture of textiles, plastics, electrical goods, fertilizers, and tobacco; British Telecom laboratories are here. Ipswich was an important wool port in the 16th century.

Iquique City and seaport in N Chile, capital of the province of Tarapaca; population (1992) 152,700. It is on the edge of Atacama Desert and is rainless, so water has to be piped in. It exports sodium nitrate from its desert region. Industries include fishing, sugar, and oil refining.

Iquitos River port on the Amazon, in Peru, also a tourist centre for the rainforest; population (1993) 274,800.

Irákleion or *Heraklion* Chief commercial port and capital city of Crete, Greece; population (1991) 117,200. There is a ferry link to Piraeus on the mainland. The archaeological museum contains a fine collection of antiquities from the island.

Irbīl Alternative name for the Kurdish capital city ◊Arbīl.

Ireland One of the British Isles, lying to the W of Great Britain, from which it is separated by the Irish Sea. It comprises the provinces of Ulster, Leinster, Munster, and Connacht, and is divided into the Republic of Ireland (which occupies the S, centre, and NW of the island) and Northern ◊Ireland (which occupies the NE corner and forms part of the United Kingdom).

Ireland, Northern Constituent part of the United Kingdom
area 13,460 sq km/5,196 sq mi
capital Belfast
towns and cities Londonderry, Enniskillen, Omagh, Newry, Armagh, Coleraine
features Mourne Mountains, Belfast Lough and Lough Neagh; Giant's Causeway; comprises the six counties (Antrim, Armagh, Down, Fermanagh, Londonderry, and Tyrone) that form part of Ireland's northernmost province of Ulster
exports engineering, shipbuilding, textile machinery, aircraft components; linen and synthetic textiles; processed foods, especially dairy and poultry products; rubber products, chemicals
currency pound sterling
population (1993 est) 1,632,000
language English; 5.3% Irish-speaking
religion Protestant 51%, Roman Catholic 38%
famous people Viscount Montgomery, Lord Alanbrooke
government direct rule from the UK since 1973. Northern Ireland is entitled to send 18 members to the Westminster Parliament. Local government: 26 district councils The province costs the UK government £3 billion annually.
history The creation of Northern Ireland dates from 1921 when the Irish Free State (subsequently the Republic of Ireland) was established separately from the mainly Protestant counties of Ulster (six out of nine), which were given limited self-government but continued to send members to the House of Commons. Spasmodic outbreaks of violence by the Irish Republican Army (IRA) occurred, but only in 1968–69 were there serious disturbances arising

from Protestant political dominance and discrimination against the Roman Catholic minority in employment and housing. British troops were sent 1969 to restore peace and protect Catholics, but disturbances continued and in 1972 the parliament at Stormont superseded by direct rule from Westminster.

Under the Anglo-Irish Agreement 1985, the Republic of Ireland was given a consultative role in the government of Northern Ireland, but agreed that there should be no change in its status except by majority consent. The agreement was approved by Parliament, but all 12 Ulster members gave up their seats, so that by-elections could be fought as a form of 'referendum' on the views of the province itself. A similar boycotting of the Northern Ireland Assembly led to its dissolution 1986 by the UK government.

Direct negotiations between the British government and the main Northern Ireland parties 1993 resulted in a joint peace proposal, the Downing Street Declaration. In August 1994 the Provisional IRA announced a unilateral cease-fire; this was broken in February 1996 when two bombs exploded in London.

Irian Jaya Western portion of the island of New Guinea, province of Indonesia
area 420,000 sq km/162,000 sq mi
capital Jayapura
industries copper, palm oil
population (1990) 1,648,700
history part of the Dutch East Indies 1828 as Western New Guinea; retained by the Netherlands after Indonesian independence 1949 but ceded to Indonesia 1963 by the United Nations and remained part of Indonesia by an 'Act of Free Choice' 1969. In the 1980s, 283,500 hectares/700,000 acres were given over to Indonesia's controversial transmigration programme for the resettlement of farming families from overcrowded Java, causing destruction of rainforests and displacing indigenous people. In 1989 Indonesia began construction of a space launching pad on the island of Biak, near the equator, where the Earth's atmosphere is least thick.

Irish Sea Arm of the N Atlantic Ocean separating England and Wales from Ireland; area 88,550 sq km/4,200 sq mi. It joins the Atlantic to the S by St George's Channel and to the N by the North Channel.

Irkutsk City in S Siberian Russia; population (1994) 632,000. It produces coal, iron, steel, and machine tools. Founded 1652, it began to grow after the Trans-Siberian railway reached it 1898.

Ironbridge Gorge Site, near Telford New Town, Shropshire, England, of the Iron Bridge (1779), one of the first and most striking products of the Industrial Revolution in Britain: it is now part of an open-air museum of industrial archaeology. Ironbridge Gorge is a World Heritage site.

Iron Gate (Romanian *Portile de Fier*) Narrow gorge, interrupted by rapids, in Romania. A hydroelectric scheme undertaken 1964–70 by Romania and Yugoslavia transformed this section of the river Danube into a lake 145 km/90 mi long and eliminated the rapids as a navigation hazard. Before flooding, in 1965, an archaeological survey revealed Europe's oldest urban settlement, *Lepenski Vir.*

Irrawaddy (Myanmar *Ayeryarwady*) Chief river of Myan-mar (Burma), flowing roughly N–S for 2,152 km/1,337 mi across the centre of the country into the Bay of Bengal. Its sources are the Mali and N'mai rivers; its chief tributaries are the Chindwin and Shweli.

Irvine Administrative headquarters of North Ayrshire, W Scotland, designated a 'new town' 1966; population (1991) 33,000. It overlooks the Isle of Arran, and is a holiday resort. Industries include engineering and pharmaceuticals.

Isar River in Austria and Germany, a tributary of the ◊Danube; length 364 km/226 mi. It rises in the Austrian Tyrol and flows N through Bavaria and its capital Munich to join the Danube near Deggendorf.

Ischia Volcanic island about 26 km/16 mi SW of Naples, Italy, in the Tyrrhenian Sea; population (1985) 26,000. It has mineral springs (known to the Romans) and beautiful scenery, and is a holiday resort.

Ischl or *Bad Ischl* Austrian town in the province of Upper Austria, at the confluence of the rivers Traun and Ischl. Ischl is the main town of the Salzkammergut, has saline springs, and is a tourist and health resort.

Ise City SE of Kyoto, on Honshu Island, Japan; population (1990) 104,200. It is the site of the most sacred Shinto shrine, dedicated to the sun-goddess Amaterasu, rebuilt every 20 years in the form of a perfect thatched house of the 7th century BC and containing the octagonal mirror of the goddess.

Isère River in SE France, 290 km/180 mi long, a tributary of the Rhône. It gives its name to the *département* of Isère.

Isère *Département* in the ◊Rhône-Alpes region of France, lying E of the river Rhône; area 7,474 sq km/2,886 sq mi; population (1990) 1,016,700. The river Isère and its tributaries the Drac and Romanche flow through the *département*. In the SE the land is heavily wooded and mountainous, including the ranges of Grande-Chartreuse and Vercors. In the NE the land is lower, but generally infertile except in the river valleys. Some wheat, potatoes, tobacco, and hemp are grown and livestock is reared. In the Isère river valley wine is produced. Coal, iron, and lead are found and hydroelectric power is well developed. There are metallurgical, chemical, textile, and paper industries. The principal towns are ◊Grenoble (the capital), La Tour-du-Pin, and Vienne.

Iserlohn City in the *Land* of North Rhine–Westphalia, Germany, 20 km/12 mi E of Hagen; population (1994) 98,600. In the Middle Ages armour was manufactured here. Textiles, steelmaking, and electronic goods are now the main industries.

Isernia Province of S central Italy in ◊Molise region; capital Isernia (population (1990) 21,800); area 1,529 sq km/590 sq mi; population (1992) 92,000.

Isfahan Alternative form for the Iranian city of ◊Esfahan.

Isis Local name for the river ◊Thames around Oxford.

Iskandariya Arabic name for the Egyptian port of ◊Alexandria.

Iskenderun Port, naval base, and steel-manufacturing town in Turkey; population (1990) 176,000. It was founded by Alexander the Great 333 BC and called *Alexandretta* until 1939.

Islamabad Capital of Pakistan from 1967, in the Potwar district, at the foot of the Margala Hills and immediately NW of Rawalpindi; population (1981) 201,000. The city was designed by Constantinos Doxiadis in the 1960s. The Federal Capital Territory of Islamabad has an area of 907 sq km/350 sq mi and a population (1985) of 379,000.

Islay Southernmost island of the Inner Hebrides, on the W coast of Scotland, in Argyll and Bute, separated from Jura by the Sound of Islay; area 610 sq km/235 sq mi; population (1991) 3,500. The principal towns are Bowmore and Port Ellen. It produces malt whisky, and its wildlife includes eagles and rare wintering geese. A wave-power electricity-generating station opened 1991 near Portnahaven on the Rinns of Islay.

Isle of Ely Former county of England, in East Anglia. It was merged with Cambridgeshire 1965.

Isle of Man See ◊Man, Isle of.

Isle of Wight See ◊Wight, Isle of.

Islington Inner borough of N Greater London. It includes the suburbs of Finsbury, Barnsbury, and Holloway
features Sadler's Wells music hall, built 1638 when Clerkenwell springs were exploited and Islington Spa became famous; present Sadler's Wells theatre (1927–31), where opera and ballet companies were established under direction of Lilian Baylis; 16th-century St John's Gate at Clerkenwell; 17th-century houses at Newington Green; 18th- and 19th-century squares and terraces in Canonbury, Highbury, and Barnsbury; Wesley's Chapel (1777, restored 1978), with museum of Methodism and John Wesley's house; Regents canal, with tunnel 886 m/2,910 ft long; Tower Theatre (1952) in early 16th-century Canonbury Tower; Kings Head, pioneer of public-house theatres in the late 1960s; Almeida Theatre; Packington estate; Business Design Centre; Chapel Market; Pentonville and Holloway prisons; Camden Passage (antiques centre)
population (1991) 164,700
famous people Duncan Grant, Vanessa Bell, George Weedon Grossmith, Basil Spence, Yehudi Menuhin, and Tony Blair all lived here.

Isma'iliya City in NE Egypt; population (1994) 400,000. It was founded 1863 as the headquarters for construction of the Suez Canal and was named after the Khedive Ismail.

Isonzo ancient *Sontius* River in Yugoslavia and Italy, which rises in the Julian Alps, and flows on a winding course S past Gorizia to the Adriatic; length 134 km/83 mi. It is deep and rapid, and has a rich alluvial plain.

Israel Ancient kingdom of N ◊Palestine, formed after the death of Solomon by Jewish peoples seceding from the rule of his son Rehoboam and electing Jeroboam as their leader.

Istanbul City and chief seaport of Turkey; population (1990) urban area 6,407,200; city 6,293,400. It produces textiles, tobacco, cement, glass, and leather. Founded as *Byzantium* about 660 BC, it was renamed *Constantinople* AD 330 and was the capital of the Byzantine Empire until captured by the Turks 1453. As *Istamboul* it was capital of the Ottoman Empire until 1922. Notable features include the harbour of the Golden Horn; Hagia Sophia (Emperor Justinian's church of the Holy Wisdom, 537, now a mosque); Sultan Ahmet Mosque, known as the Blue Mosque, from its tiles; Topkapi Palace of the Sultans, with a harem of 400 rooms (now a museum). The Selimye Barracks in the suburb of *Usküdar* (Scutari) was used as a hospital in the Crimean War; the rooms used by Florence Nightingale, with her personal possessions, are preserved as a museum.

Itaipu Reservoir World's largest hydroelectric plant, situated on the Paraná River, SW Brazil. A joint Brazilian-Paraguayan venture, it came into operation 1984; it supplies hydroelectricity to a wide area.

Italian Somaliland Former Italian trust territory on the Somali coast of Africa extending to 502,300 sq km/194,999 sq mi. Established 1892, it was extended 1925 with the acquisition of Jubaland from Kenya; administered from Mogadishu; under British rule 1941–50. Thereafter it reverted to Italian authority before uniting with British Somaliland 1960 to form the independent state of Somalia.

Ithaca (Greek *Itháki*) Greek island in the Ionian Sea, area 93 sq km/36 sq mi. Important in pre-Classical Greece, Ithaca was (in Homer's poem) the birthplace of Odysseus, though this is sometimes identified with the island of Leukas (some archaeologists have equated ancient Ithaca with Leukas rather than modern Ithaca).

Itzehoe Seaport in Schleswig-Holstein, Germany, 60 km/ 37 mi NW of Hamburg; population (1994) 34,200. Cement, pumps, nets, and paper are manufactured in the city. There is an abbey (13th–17th centuries) and a Baroque church.

Ivanovo Capital of Ivanovo region, Russia, 240 km/150 mi NE of Moscow; population (1994) 476,000. Industries include textiles, chemicals, and engineering.

Iviza Alternative spelling of ◊Ibiza, one of the ◊Balearic Islands.

Iwo Jima Largest of the Japanese Volcano Islands in the W Pacific Ocean, 1,222 km/760 mi S of Tokyo; area 21 sq km/ 8 sq mi. Annexed by Japan 1891, it was captured by the USA 1945 after fierce fighting. It was returned to Japan 1968.

Izhevsk Industrial city in central Russian Federation, capital of Udmurt Autonomous Republic; population (1994) 653,000. Industries include steel, agricultural machinery, machine tools, and armaments. It was founded 1760.

Izmir (formerly *Smyrna*) Port and naval base in Turkey; population (1990) 1,757,400. Products include steel, electronics, and plastics. The largest annual trade fair in the Middle East is held here. It is the headquarters of North Atlantic Treaty Organization SE Command.

Jabalpur or *Jubbulpore* Industrial city near the Narbarda River in Madhya Pradesh, India; population (1991) 742,000. Products include textiles, oil, bauxite, and armaments.

Jablonec Town in the Czech Republic, on the river Neisse, NE of Prague; population (1991) 45,900. It has had a glass industry since the 14th century.

Jackson City in S Michigan, USA, on the Grand River, S of Lansing; seat of Jackson County; population (1990) 37,400. Its industries include motor-vehicle and aircraft parts, tools, plastics, and air-conditioning equipment. It was settled 1829 at the meeting place of various Native American trails, and named after President Andrew Jackson.

Jackson Largest city and capital of Mississippi, on the Pearl River; population (1992) 196,200. It produces furniture, cottonseed oil, and iron and steel castings, and owes its prosperity to the discovery of gas fields to the S in the 1930s. Named after Andrew Jackson, later president, it dates from 1821 and was virtually destroyed by Union troops 1863, during the American Civil War. Educational institutions include Jackson State University, Millsaps College, and the University of Mississippi Medical Centre.

Jacksonville Port, resort, and commercial centre in NE Florida, USA; population (1992) 661,200. The port has naval installations and ship-repair yards. To the N the Cross-Florida Barge Canal links the Atlantic with the Gulf of Mexico. Manufactured goods include wood and paper products, chemicals, and processed food. Jacksonville dates from 1816. Among the educational institutions are Jacksonville University and the University of North Florida. French Huguenots built a short-lived settlement 1564, but the site of the present city was not settled until 1816. Much of the city was destroyed by Union troops in the Civil War 1861–65, and there was a destructive fire 1901. The city absorbed most of Duval County 1968, greatly increasing its area and population.

Jacobabad City in Sind province, SE Pakistan, 400 km/ 250 mi NE of Karachi; population (1981) 80,000. Founded by General John Jacob as a frontier post, the city now trades in wheat, rice, and millet. It has a low annual rainfall (about 5 cm/2 in) and temperatures are among the highest in the Indian subcontinent – up to 53°C/127°F.

Jadar Small river in NW Serbia, a tributary of the Drina, joining it SW of Belgrade. By their success at the battles of Jadar and Sabac in 1914 the Serbs stopped the Austrian armies invading Serbia from N and W and compelled the Austrians to abandon the invasion.

Jaén Capital of Jaén province, S Spain, on the river Guadalbullon; population (1994) 113,000. It has remains of its Moorish walls and citadel.

Jaén Province of S Spain in NE ◊Andalusia autonomous community; capital Jaén; area 13,480 sq km/5,205 sq mi;

population (1995) 666,800. The rivers Guadalquivir and Segura flow through the province, and it is mountainous in the S. Lead is mined here, and products include cereals, oil, fruit, and wine.

Jaffa (biblical name *Joppa*) Port in W Israel, part of ◊Tel Aviv-Yafo from 1950.

Jaffna Capital of Jaffna district, Northern Province, Sri Lanka; population (1990) 129,000. It was the focal point of Hindu Tamil nationalism and the scene of recurring riots during the 1980s.

Jaipur Capital of Rajasthan, India; population (1991) 1,458,000. It was formerly the capital of the state of Jaipur, which was merged with Rajasthan 1949. Products include textiles and metal products.

Jajce Town in Bosnia-Herzegovina, at the confluence of the rivers Pliva and Vrbas; population (1991) 44,900. There are leather and textile industries and hydroelectric installations nearby. In the 15th century it was the capital of the kingdom of Bosnia, and here the last king was put to death by the Turks in 1463.

Jakarta or *Djakarta* formerly until 1949 *Batavia* Capital of Indonesia on the NW coast of Java; population (1993) 9,000,000. Industries include textiles, chemicals, and plastics; a canal links it with its port of Tanjung Priok where rubber, oil, tin, coffee, tea, and palm oil are among its exports; also a tourist centre. Respiratory-tract infections caused by air pollution account for 12.6% of deaths annually. Jakarta was founded by Dutch traders 1619.

Jalalabad Capital of Nangarhar province, E Afghanistan, on the road from Kabul to Peshawar in Pakistan; population (1988 est) 55,000 (numbers swelled to over 1 million during the civil war). The city was besieged by mujaheddin rebels after the withdrawal of Soviet troops from Afghanistan 1989.

Jalisco State of Mexico, on the Pacific; area 80,137 sq km/ 30,941 sq mi; population (1995 est) 5,990,100. Its capital is Guadalajara. It is an important mining centre, and cereals, tobacco, sugar-cane, and cotton are farmed.

Jambol Alternative form of Yambol, a town in Bulgaria.

James River River in Virginia, E USA; length 547 km/ 340 mi. It rises in the Allegheny Mountains in W Virginia and flows across the state, through Richmond, and into Chesapeake Bay, the largest of the inlets on the Atlantic coast of the USA. It is navigable to Richmond. The chief tributaries are the Chickahominy and the Appomattox.

Jammu Winter capital of the state of Jammu and Kashmir, India; population (1991) 206,000. It stands on the river Tavi and was linked to India's rail system 1972.

Jammu and Kashmir State of N India
area 222,236 sq km/85,805 sq mi
capital Jammu (winter); Srinagar (summer)
towns and cities Leh
industries timber, grain, rice, fruit, silk, carpets

population (1994) 8,435,000 (Indian-occupied territory)
history part of the Mogul Empire from 1586, Jammu came under the control of Gulab Singh 1820. In 1947 Jammu was attacked by Pakistan and chose to become part of the new state of India. Dispute over the area caused further hostilities 1971 between India and Pakistan (ended by the Simla agreement 1972). Since then, separatist agitation has developed, complicating the territorial dispute between India and Pakistan. There are currently 150,000 Indian troops stationed in Kashmir, where Muslim separatists have been in revolt against the Indian authorities since 1990, claiming thousands of lives. In Oct 1996 the National Congress Party, which aims to retain the state within India, won the first local elections to be held since the separatist violence broke out 1990.

Jamnagar City in Gujarat, India, on the Gulf of Kutch, SW of Ahmadabad; population (1991) 342,000. Its port is at Bedi.

Jamshedpur City in Bihar, India; population (1991) 461,000. It was built 1909 and takes its name from the industrialist Jamsheedji Tata who founded the Tata iron and steel works here and in Bombay.

Jämtland County of central Sweden; area 51,800 sq km/ 20,000 sq mi; population (1990) 133,400. It has lakes, wild mountains, and a central core of fertile agricultural lowland where dairying is important. Its chief town is Östersund.

Janesville City in S Wisconsin, USA, on the Rock River, SE of Madison; seat of Rock County; population (1992) 54,300. Industries include cars and car parts, building materials, and electronic equipment. It is a processing and marketing centre for the area's agricultural products. Janesville was settled 1835.

Jan Mayen Norwegian volcanic island in the Arctic Ocean, between Greenland and Norway; area 380 sq km/ 147 sq mi. It is named after a Dutchman who visited it about 1610, and was annexed by Norway 1929.

Japan, Sea of Sea separating Japan from the mainland of Asia.

Jarosław Town in Przemyśl province, Poland, on the river San, 48 km/30 mi E of Rzeszów; population (1990) 41,200. Industries include building materials, flour, confectionery, and timber. The town was founded in the 11th century by Iaroslav, Grand Duke of Kiev, and was part of Austria 1772–1919.

Jarrow Town in Tyne and Wear, NE England, on the S bank of the Tyne, 10 km/6 mi E of Newcastle and connected with the N bank by the Tyne Tunnel (1967); population (1991) 29,300. The Venerable Bede lived in a monastery here in the early 8th century. In 1933 the closure of Palmer's shipyard in Jarrow prompted the unemployed to march to London, a landmark event of the Depression. Present-day industries include chemicals, oil, iron and steel.

Jasper National Park National park in the Rocky Mountains, N Alberta, Canada, established in 1907; area 10,900 sq km/4,207 sq mi. The park is much used for skiing, and the town of Jasper, about 1,075 m/3,527 ft above sea level, is a tourist centre.

Jassy German name for the Romanian city of ◊Iasi.

Jászberény Town in central Hungary, on the river Zagyva, 50 km/31 mi NW of Szolnok; population (1993) 29,000. Industries are diverse, and trade includes cereals, wine, and livestock. It was formerly the centre of the nomadic Jazygians, descendants of the Alares who settled here in the 13th century.

Java or *Jawa* Most populated island of Indonesia, situated between Sumatra and Bali
area (with the island of Madura) 126,600 sq km/48,900 sq mi
capital Jakarta (also capital of Indonesia)
towns ports include Surabaya and Semarang; Bandung
physical about half the island is under cultivation, the rest being thickly forested. Mountains and sea breezes keep temperatures down, but humidity is high, with heavy rainfall from Dec to March
features a chain of mountains, some of which are volcanic, runs along the centre, rising to 2,750 m/9,000 ft. The highest mountain, Semeru (3,676 m/12,060 ft), is in the E
industries rice, coffee, cocoa, tea, sugar, rubber, quinine, teak, petroleum, textiles
population (with Madura; 1990) 107,581,300, including people of Javanese, Sundanese, and Madurese origin, with differing languages
religion predominantly Muslim
history fossilized early human remains (*Homo erectus*) were discovered 1891–92. In central Java there are ruins of magnificent Buddhist monuments and of the Sivaite temple in Prambanan. The island's last Hindu kingdom, Majapahit, was destroyed about 1520 and followed by a number of short-lived Javanese kingdoms. The Dutch East India company founded a factory 1610. Britain took over during the Napoleonic period, 1811–16, and Java then reverted to Dutch control. Occupied by Japan 1942–45, Java then became part of the republic of Indonesia.

Jedburgh Small town in the Scottish Borders unitary authority, SE Scotland, on Jed Water; population (1991) 4,100. It has the remains of a 12th-century abbey.

Jedda Alternative spelling for the Saudi Arabian port ◊Jiddah.

Jefferson City Capital of Missouri, USA, located in the central part of the state, W of St Louis, on the Missouri River; population (1992) 37,100. Industries include agricultural products, shoes, electrical appliances, and cosmetics. Jefferson City was founded 1821 as the state capital.

Jehol Former name for the city of ◊Chengde in NE Hebei province, N China.

Jelenia Góra (German *Hirschberg*) Capital of Jelenia Góra province, Poland, on the river Bóbr at the foot of the Karkonosze mountains, 96 km/60 mi W of Wrocław; population (1990) 93,400. Textiles, chemicals, and optical lenses are manufactured. The town dates from the 14th century, passing from Bohemia to Prussia 1741, and to Poland 1945.

Jelgava or *Jalgava* formerly (until 1917) *Mitau* Town in W Latvia, an inland port on the Lielupe River, 48 km/30 mi S of Riga; population (1991) 74,500. Industries include textiles and sugar-refining. The town was founded 1265 by Teutonic knights. It was the capital of the former Russian province of Courland.

Jemappes Town in the province of Hainaut, Belgium, 5 km/3 mi W of Mons. There are rich coal mines and glass, porcelain, crystal, iron, and chemical works. At Jemappes, in 1792, a French revolutionary army under General Dumouriez defeated the Austrians, thus gaining control of what is now Belgium.

Jena Town SE of Weimar, in the *Land* of Thuringia, Germany, population (1993) 100,400. Industries include the Zeiss firm of optical instrument makers, founded 1846. Here in 1806 Napoleon defeated the Prussians, and Schiller and Hegel taught at the university, which dates from 1558.

Jerez de la Frontera City in Andalusia, SW Spain; population (1994) 190,000. It is famed for sherry, the fortified wine to which it gave its name.

Jericho Town in Jordan, N of the Dead Sea, occupied by Israel 1967–94 when responsibility for its administration was transferred to the Palestine Liberation Organization (PLO). Jericho was settled by 8000 BC, and by 6000 BC had become a walled city with 2,000 inhabitants. In the Old Testament it was the first Canaanite stronghold captured by the Israelites, and its walls, according to the Book of Joshua, fell to the blast of Joshua's trumpets. Successive archaeological excavations since 1907 show that the walls of the city were destroyed many times.

Jersey Largest of the ◊Channel Islands; capital St Helier; area 117 sq km/45 sq mi; population (1991) 58,900. It is governed by a lieutenant governor, representing the English crown, and an assembly. Jersey cattle were originally bred here. Jersey gave its name to a woollen garment

Jersey City City of NE New Jersey, USA; population (1992) 228,600. It faces Manhattan Island, to which it is connected by tunnels. A former port, it is now an industrial centre. The area was settled by Dutch trappers 1618, settled permanently 1660, and became British 1674.

Jerusalem Ancient city of Palestine, divided 1948 between Jordan and the new republic of Israel; area (pre-1967) 37.5 sq km/14.5 sq mi, (post-1967) 108 sq km/42 sq mi, including areas of the West Bank; population (1992) 544,200 (70% Israelis, 30% Palestinians). In 1950 the W New City was proclaimed as the Israeli capital, and, having captured from Jordan the E Old City 1967, Israel affirmed 1980 that the united city was the country's capital; the United Nations does not recognize East Jerusalem as part of Israel, and regards Tel Aviv as the capital.

Jervis Bay Deep bay on the coast of New South Wales, Australia, 145 km/90 mi SW of Sydney. The federal government in 1915 acquired 73 sq km/28 sq mi here to create a port for ◊Canberra. It forms part of the Australian

Capital Territory and is the site of the Royal Australian Naval College.

Jewish Autonomous Region Part of the Khabarovsk Territory, in the Russian Federation, in E Siberia, on the river Amur; capital Birobijan; area 36,000 sq km/13,900 sq mi; population (1994) 217,800. Industries include textiles, leather, metallurgy, light engineering, agriculture, and timber. It was established as a Jewish National District 1928 and became an Autonomous Region 1934 but became only nominally Jewish after the Stalinist purges 1936–47 and 1948–49.

Jhansi City in Uttar Pradesh, NE India, 286 km/178 mi SW of Lucknow; population (1991) 313,000. It is a railway and road junction and a market centre. It was founded 1613, and was the scene of a massacre of British civilians 1857.

Jhelum River rising in Kashmir and flowing into Pakistan; length about 720 km/450 mi. The Mangla Dam 1967, one of the world's largest earth-filled dams, stores flood waters for irrigation and hydroelectricity. The Jhelum is one of the five rivers that give Punjab its name and was known in the ancient world as the *Hydaspes*, on whose banks Alexander the Great won a battle 326 BC.

Jiangsu or *Kiangsu* Province on the coast of E China
area 102,200 sq km/39,459 sq mi
capital Nanjing
features the swampy mouth of the river Chang Jiang; the special municipality of Shanghai
industries cereals, rice, tea, cotton, soya beans, fish, silk, ceramics, textiles, coal, iron, copper, cement
population (1990) 68,170,000
history Jiangsu was originally part of the Wu kingdom, and Wu is still a traditional local name for the province. Jiangsu's capture by Japan 1937 was an important step in that country's attempt to conquer China.

Jiangxi or *Kiangsi* Province of SE China
area 164,800 sq km/63,629 sq mi
capital Nanchang
industries rice, tea, cotton, tobacco, porcelain, coal, tungsten, uranium
population (1990) 38,280,000
history the province was Mao Zedong's original base in the first phase of the Communist struggle against the Nationalists.

Jibuti Variant spelling of Djibouti, a republic of NE Africa.

Jiddah or *Jedda* Port in Hejaz, Saudi Arabia, on the E shore of the Red Sea; population (1991 est) 1,500,000. Industries include cement, steel, and oil refining. Pilgrims pass through here on their way to Mecca.

Jihlava (German *Iglau*) Town in E Bohemia, in the Czech Republic, on the river Jihlava, 140 km/87 mi SE of Prague; population (1991) 52,300. Trade is mainly agricultural, and industries include textiles and engineering. Silver deposits were mined from the 8th century; the town being prosperous as a royal mint in the Middle Ages. There are many historic buildings.

Jilin or *Kirin* Province of NE China in central Manchuria
area 187,000 sq km/72,201 sq mi
capital Changchun
population (1990) 25,150,000.

Jinan or *Tsinan* City and capital of Shandong province, China; population (1993) 2,050,000. It has food-processing and textile industries.

Jingdezhen or *Chingtechen* or *Fou-liang* Town in Jiangxi, China; population (1991) 281,000. Ming blue-and-white china was produced here, the name of the clay (kaolin) coming from Kaoling, a hill E of Jingdezhen; some of the best Chinese porcelain is still made here.

Jinja Town in Busoga Province, Uganda, on the Victoria Nile E of Kampala; population (1991) 61,000. Nearby is the Owen Falls Dam (1954).

Jinsha Jiang River that rises in SW China and forms the ◊Chang Jiang (Yangtze Kiang) at Yibin.

Jodhpur City in Rajasthan, India, formerly capital of Jodhpur princely state, founded 1459 by Rao Jodha; population (1991) 668,000. It is a market centre and has the training college of the Indian air force, an 18th-century Mogul palace, and a red sandstone fort. A style of riding breeches is named after it.

Jogjakarta Alternative spelling of ◊Yogyakarta, a city in Indonesia.

Johannesburg Largest city of South Africa, situated on the Witwatersrand River in Gauteng Province; population (urban area, 1991) 1,916,100. It is the centre of a large gold-mining industry; other industries include engineering works, meat-chilling plants, and clothing factories

John o' Groats Village in NE Highland unitary authority, Scotland, about 3 km/2 mi W of Duncansby Head, proverbially Britain's northernmost point. It is named after the Dutchman John de Groot, who built a house there in the 16th century.

Johnson City City in NE Tennessee, USA, just below the Virginia border, in the Appalachian Mountains NE of Knoxville; population (1992) 50,400. Industries include tobacco, furniture, building materials, metals, textiles, and food processing. It was first settled 1857.

Johnston Atoll Coral island in the mid-Pacific, lying between the Marshall Islands and Hawaii; area 2.8 sq km/1.1 sq mi. The island is only 2.4 m/8 ft above sea level and subject to hurricanes and tidal waves. It has the status of a National Wildlife Refuge but was contaminated by fallout from nuclear weapons testing 1962, and has since 1971 been used as a repository for chemical weapons left over from the Korean and Vietnam wars. An unincorporated territory of the USA, it is administered by the US Defense Nuclear Agency (DNA).

Johnstown City in SW Pennsylvania, USA, on the Conemaugh River, E of Pittsburgh; population (1990) 28,100. Industries include steel, coal and coal by-products, chemicals, building materials, and clothing. Johnstown was the victim of disastrous floods 1889. The city was founded 1800 by Joseph Johns, a Swiss Mennonite. It became an important steelmaking centre.

Johor State in S Peninsular Malaysia; capital Johor Baharu; area 19,000 sq km/7,334 sq mi; population (1993) 2,106,700. The southernmost point of mainland Asia, it is joined to Singapore by a causeway. It is mainly forested, with swamps. There is bauxite and iron.

Joliet City in NE Illinois, USA, on the Des Plaines River, SW of Chicago; seat of Will County; population (1992) 78,900. It is a centre for barge traffic. Industries include building materials, chemicals, oil refining, heavy construction machinery, and paper. The city was settled 1833 and named after the explorer Louis Joliet, who visited the site 1673. Limestone from Joliet was used throughout the Midwest.

Jönköping Town at the S end of Lake Vättern, Sweden; population (1994 est) 114,800. It is an industrial centre in an agricultural and forestry region.

Joplin City in SW Missouri, USA, W of Springfield; population (1990) 41,000. Industries include zinc and lead smelting, leather goods, and furniture. It was founded 1871.

Joppa Ancient name of ◊Jaffa, a port in W Israel.

Jordan River rising on Mount Hermon, Syria, at 550 m/ 1,800 ft above sea level and flowing S for about 320 km/ 200 mi via the Sea of Galilee to the Dead Sea, 390 m/1,290 ft below sea level. It occupies the N part of the Great Rift Valley; its upper course forms the boundary of Israel with Syria and the kingdom of Jordan; its lower course runs through Jordan; the West Bank has been occupied by Israel since 1967.

Jotunheim Mountainous region of S Norway, containing the highest mountains in Scandinavia, Glittertind (2,472 m/8,110 ft) and Galdhøpiggen (2,469 m/8,100 ft). In Norse mythology it is the home of the giants.

Jounie Port on the Mediterranean coast of Lebanon, 15 km/9 mi N of Beirut. It was the centre of an anti-Syrian enclave during the civil war.

Juan Fernández Islands Three small volcanic Pacific islands 360 miles from Valparaiso, belonging to Chile; almost uninhabited. The largest is Más-a-Tierra (also sometimes called Juan Fernández Island), where Alexander Selkirk was marooned 1704–09. The islands were named after the Spanish navigator who reached them 1563.

Juba Capital of Southern Region, Sudan Republic; situated on the left bank of the White Nile, at the head of navigation above Khartoum, 1,200 km/750 mi to the N; population (1990 est) 100,000

Juba River in E Africa, formed at Dolo, Ethiopia, by the junction of the Ganale Dorya and Dawa rivers. It flows S

for about 885 km/550 mi through the Somalia (of which its valley is the most productive area) into the Indian Ocean.

Jubbulpore Alternative name for the city of ◊Jabalpur in India.

Jugoslavia Alternative spelling of Yugoslavia.

Jülich Town in North Rhine–Westphalia, Germany, 44 km/ 27 mi SW of Düsseldorf; population (1994) 31,800. Paper and sugar industries provide the town's main employment. Jülich, the ancient Juliacum, was once the seat of the dukes of Aix-la-Chapelle (◊Aachen). It was a strong fortress town in the 17th century.

Jumna Alternative name for the ◊Yamuna river in India.

Juneau Ice-free port and state capital of Alaska, USA, on Gastineau Channel in the S Alaska panhandle; population (1992) 28,400. Juneau is the commercial and distribution centre for the fur-trading and mining of the panhandle region; also important are salmon fishing, fish processing, and lumbering. Settled 1880 by gold prospectors, Juneau was named the capital 1900.

Jungfrau (German 'maiden') Mountain in the Bernese Alps, Switzerland; 4,166 m/ 13,669 ft high. A railway ascends to the plateau of the Jungfraujoch, 3,456 m/11,340 ft, where there is a winter-sports centre.

Jura Island of the Inner Hebrides; area 380 sq km/ 147 sq mi; population (1991) 196. It is separated from Scotland by the Sound of Jura. The whirlpool Corryvreckan (Gaelic 'Brecan's cauldron') is off the N coast.

Jura *Département* in the ◊Franche-Comté region of France; area 5,007 sq km/1,933 sq mi; population (1990) 249,100. It is bordered in the E by Switzerland. The greater part of the *département* is occupied by the Jura Mountains, but there is a plain in the W. The chief rivers are the Doubs and the Ain. Some cereals and sugar beet are grown, sheep and horses are raised, and wine is produced. There are metallurgical, paper, furniture, food, and watchmaking industries and hydroelectric schemes. The principal towns are Lons-le-Saunier (the capital), Dole, and St-Claude.

Jura Mountains Series of parallel mountain ranges running SW–NE along the French-Swiss frontier between the rivers Rhône and Rhine, a distance of 250 km/156 mi. The highest peak is *Crête de la Neige*, 1,723 m/5,650 ft

Jutland (Danish *Jylland*) Peninsula of N Europe; area 29,500 sq km/11,400 sq mi. It is separated from Norway by the Skagerrak and from Sweden by the Kattegat, with the North Sea to the W. The larger N part belongs to Denmark, the S part to Germany.

Jylland Danish name for the mainland of Denmark, the N section of the Jutland peninsula. The chief towns are Ålborg, Århus, Esbjerg, Fredericia, Horsens, Kolding, Randers, and Vejle.

K2 or *Chogori* Second highest mountain above sea level, 8,611 m/28,251 ft, in the Karakoram range, in a disputed region of Pakistan. It was first climbed 1954 by an Italian expedition.

Kabardino-Balkaria Autonomous republic of SW Russian Federation.
area 12,500 sq km/4,826 sq mi
capital Nalchik
physical N Caucasus Mountains
industries ore-mining, timber, engineering, coal, food processing, timer, grain, livestock breeding, dairy farming, wine growing
population (1995) 790,000

Kabinda Part of Angola; see ◊Cabinda.

Kabul Capital of Afghanistan, 2,100 m/6,900 ft above sea level, on the river Kabul; population (1993 est) 700,000. Products include textiles, plastics, leather, and glass. It commands the strategic routes to Pakistan via the ◊Khyber Pass.

Kabwe City in central Zambia (formerly *Broken Hill*); population (1990) 167,000. It is a mining centre (copper and cadmium); lead and zinc were also mined until June 1994.

Kaduna City in N Nigeria, on the Kaduna River, capital of Kaduna State; population (1992 est) 309,600. It is a market centre for grain and cotton; industries include textiles, cars, timber, pottery, and oil refining.

Kafue River in central Zambia, a tributary of the Zambezi, 965 km/600 mi long. The upper reaches of the river form part of the Kafue national park (1951). Kafue town, 44 km/27 mi S of Lusaka, population (1980) 35,000, is the centre of Zambia's heavy industry. A hydroelectric power station opened 1972 on the lower Kafue river at Kafue Gorge; its 600,000-kilowatt generating facility was expanded to 900,000 in the late 1970s by the construction of a storage dam upstream.

Kagoshima Industrial city (Satsumayaki porcelain) and port on Kyushu Island, SW Japan; population (1994) 534,000.

Kaieteur Falls Waterfall on the river Potaro, a tributary of the Essequibo, Guyana. At 250 m/822 ft, it is five times as high as Niagara Falls.

Kaifeng Former capital of China, 907–1127, and of Honan province; population (1990) 508,000. It has lost its importance because of the silting-up of the nearby Huang He River.

Kaikouras Double range of mountains in the NE of South Island, New Zealand, separated by the Clarence River, and reaching 2,885 m/9,465 ft.

Kaingaroa Forest NE of Lake Taupo in North Island, New Zealand, one of the world's largest planted forests.

Kairouan Muslim holy city in Tunisia, N Africa, S of Tunis; population (1994) 102,600. It is a centre of carpet production. The city, said to have been founded AD 617, ranks after Mecca and Medina as a place of pilgrimage.

Kaiserslautern Industrial city (textiles, cars) in Germany, in the Rhineland-Palatinate, 48 km/30 mi W of Mannheim; population (1991) 101,500. It dates from 882; the castle from which it takes its name was built by Frederick Barbarossa 1152 and destroyed by the French 1703.

Kakadu National park E of Darwin in the Alligator Rivers Region of Arnhem Land, Northern Territory, Australia. Established 1979, it overlies one of the richest uranium deposits in the world. As a result of this, the park has become the focal point of controversy between conservationists and mining interests.

Kalahari Desert Arid to semi-arid desert area forming most of Botswana and extending into Namibia, Zimbabwe, and South Africa; area about 582,800 sq km/225,000 sq mi. The only permanent river, the Okavango, flows into a delta in the NW forming marshes rich in wildlife. Its inhabitants are the nomadic Kung.

Kalamazoo (American Indian 'boiling pot') City in SW Michigan, on the Kalamazoo River, SW of Lansing; seat of Kalamazoo County; population (1992) 81,250. Its industries include the processing of the area's agricultural products, car and transportation machinery parts, chemicals, and metal and paper products. Kalamazoo was settled 1829 on the site of a fur-trading post. The paper industry has been important since 1874. Celery was particularly grown in the area.

Kalgan City in NE China, now known as ◊Zhangjiakou.

Kalgoorlie Town in Western Australia, 545 km/340 mi NE of Perth, amalgamated with Boulder 1966; population (1991) 26,100. Gold has been mined here since 1893.

Kalimantan Province of the republic of Indonesia occupying part of the island of Borneo; area 543,900 sq km/210,000 sq mi; population (urban area, 1990 est) 9,100,000. The land is mostly low-lying, with mountains in the N. Towns and cities include Banjarmasin and Balikpapan. Industries include petroleum, rubber, coffee, copra, pepper, and timber.

Kalinin Former name (1932–91) of ◊Tver, a city in Russia.

Kaliningrad formerly *Königsberg* Baltic naval base in W Russia; population (1994) 415,000. Industries include engineering and paper. It was the capital of East Prussia until the latter was divided between the USSR and Poland 1945 under the Potsdam Agreement, when it was renamed in honour of President Kalinin.

Kalisz ancient *Calisia* Industrial town, capital of Kalisz province, Poland, on the river Prosna, 109 km/68 mi SE of Poznań; population (1990) 106,100. It has been a major textile producer since the Middle Ages. Other industries include metal goods, embroidery, and food processing, and lignite is mined in the district.

Kalmar Port on the SE coast of Sweden; population (1992) 56,900. Industries include paper, matches, and the Orrefors glassworks.

Kalmykia Autonomous republic of central Russian Federation.
area 76,100 sq km/29,382 sq mi
capital Elista
physical on Caspian Sea
industries mainly agricultural, including cattle breeding

and the production of fodder crops, fishing, canning **population** (1995) 320,000.

Kaluga City in central Russian Federation, on the river Oka, 160 km/100 mi SW of Moscow, capital of Kaluga region; population (1994) 345,000. Industries include hydro-electric installations and engineering works, telephone equipment, chemicals, and measuring devices.

Kamakura City on Honshu Island, Japan, near Tokyo; population (1990) 174,300. It was the seat of the first shogu-nate 1192–1333, which established the rule of the samurai class, and the Hachimangu Shrine is dedicated to the gods of war; the 13th-century statue of Buddha (Daibutsu) is 13 m/43 ft high. From the 19th century, artists and writers (for example, the novelist Kawabata) settled here.

Kamara'n Island in the Red Sea, formerly belonging to South Yemen, and occupied by North Yemen 1972. It was included in the territory of the Yemen Republic formed 1990; area 180 sq km/70 sq mi.

Kamchatka Mountainous peninsula separating the Bering Sea and Sea of Okhotsk, forming (together with the Chukchi and Koryak national districts) a region of the Russian Federation, in E Siberia. Its capital, Petropavlovsk, is the only town; agriculture is possible only in the S. Most of the inhabitants are fishers and hunters.

Kamenz Town in the *Land* of ◊Saxony, Germany, on the river Schwarze Elster, 56 km/35 mi NE of Dresden. It has textile and glass industries. The Enlightenment thinker Gotthold Ephraim Lessing was born here.

Kamet Himalayan mountain 7,756 m/25,447 ft high on the Tibet–India border.

Kamienna Góra (German *Landeshut*) Industrial town (coal, textiles, engineering) in Jelenia Góra province, Poland, on the river Bóbr at the foot of the Karkonosze mountains, 64 km/40 mi SW of Wrocław; population (1990) 23,500. Formerly in Lower Silesia, the town was the scene of two battles between Prussian and Austrian troops: the Prussians were victorious 1745, defeated 1760. The town became part of Poland 1945.

Kamloops City in S British Columbia, Canada, on the Thompson tributary of the Fraser River and the Trans-Canada Highway; population (1991) 67,100. Originally established as a fur-trading post in 1812, it is the distribut-ing centre of a timber-processing and ranching district, and a junction on the Canadian Pacific Railway. Tourism (fish-ing, windsurfing, sailing, and mountain tours) has become important.

Kampala Capital of Uganda, on Lake Victoria; population (1991) 773,000. It is linked by rail with Mombasa. Products include tea, coffee, textiles, fruit, and vegetables.

Kampen Town on the river IJssel, in the province of Overijssel, the Netherlands, 14 km/9 mi NW of Zwolle; population (1996) 32,400. The chief products are machinery, blankets, and cigars. Kampen was a member of the medieval Hanseatic League.

Kampuchea Former name (1975–89) of Cambodia.

Kanagawa Port on the E coast of Honshu, Japan, where US emissary Matthew Perry negotiated with the Japanese in 1854. The resultant trade agreement was one of the unequal treaties. Kanagawa was the site of the first US legation but was superseded by nearby Yokohama as a treaty port. Kanagawa is also the name of a prefecture adjoining Tokyo.

Kananga Chief city of Kasai Occidental region, W central Democratic Republic of Congo (formerly Zaire), on the Lulua River; population (1991 est) 371,900. It was known as *Luluabourg* until 1966.

Kanawha River of West Virginia, USA; length 156 km/97 mi. Rising in the Blue Ridge Mountains, North Carolina, in its upper course it is called the New River. It flows NW through the Allegheny Mountains to the Ohio River at Point Pleasant, Mason County, West Virginia. For much of its course the Kanawha and its tributaries are incised into the coal field of the Allegheny plateau. Owing to the natural gas in the valley and the nearby salt deposits, the region is an important chemical manufacturing area, centred on Charleston.

Kanazawa Industrial city (textiles and porcelain) on Honshu Island, in Chubu region, Japan, 160 km/100 mi NNW of Nagoya; population (1994) 433,000. Kanazawa was a feudal castle town from the 16th century and has a num-ber of old samurai residences.

Kanchenjunga (or *Kanchenjunga*) Himalayan mountain on the Nepal– Sikkim border, 8,586 m/28,170 ft high, 120 km/75 mi SE of Mount Everest. The name means 'five trea-sure houses of the great snows'. Kanchenjunga was first climbed by a British expedition 1955.

Kandahar City in Afghanistan, 450 km/280 mi SW of Kabul, capital of Kandahar province and a trading centre, with wool and cotton factories; population (1988) 225,500. It is surrounded by a mud wall 8 m/25 ft high. When Afghanistan became independent 1747, Kandahar was its first capital.

Kandy City in central Sri Lanka, on the Mahaweli River; capital of a district of the same name; population (1990) 104,000. Products include tea. One of the most sacred Buddhist shrines, the Dalada Maligawa, is situated in Kandy; it contains an alleged tooth of the Buddha.

Ka Ngwane Former black homeland in Mpumalanga Province, South Africa.

Kankakee City in NE Illinois, on the Kankakee River, S of Chicago; seat of Kankakee County; population (1990) 27,600. It is a distribution centre for corn. Industries also include building materials, furniture, pharmaceuticals, and farm machinery. It was founded in the 1850s.

Kano Capital of Kano state in N Nigeria, trade centre of an irrigated area; population (1992 est) 699,900. Products include bicycles, glass, furniture, textiles, and chemicals. Founded about 1000 BC, Kano is a walled city, with New Kano extending beyond the walls.

Kanpur formerly *Cawnpore* Capital of Kanpur district, Uttar Pradesh, India, SW of Lucknow, on the river Ganges; a commercial and industrial centre (cotton, wool, jute, chemicals, plastics, iron, steel); population (1991) 2,029,900.

Kansas State in central USA; nicknamed Sunflower State/Jayhawkes
area 213,200 sq km/82,295 sq mi
capital Topeka
cities Kansas City, Wichita, Overland Park
physical Great Plains; Cimarron national grassland; Kansas and Arkansas rivers
features Fort Scott national historic site (built 1840s); Fort Larned national historic site, a restored prairie fort built 1868 to protect travellers on the Santa Fe Trail; the Santa Fe Trail Center at Larned; Kansas City, with the Shawnee Methodist Mission (begun 1839 as a school to teach English to Native Americans), and Mahaffie Farmstead Stagecoach Stop; Dodge City, once 'cowboy capital of the world', with the capitol (1866) and historic Ward-Meade Park; the Eisenhower Center, with the president's boyhood home, at Abilene; Wichita, known as the air capital of the world because of its importance as an aircraft production centre; Pony Express station, Hannover; Wichita Cowtown, a frontier-era reproduction; Kansas Cosmosphere and Space Center; it was the first state to prohibit alcohol (1880), and prohibition was not lifted until 1948.
industries wheat, cattle, coal, petroleum, natural gas, aircraft, minerals
population (1995) 2,565,300
famous people Amelia Earhart; Dwight D Eisenhower; William Inge; Buster Keaton; Carry Nation; Charlie Parker, Damon Runyon
history explored by Francisco de Coronado for Spain 1541 and Robert de la Salle for France 1682; ceded to the USA 1803 as part of the Louisiana Purchase, it joined the union 1861.

Kansas City Twin city in the USA at the confluence of the Missouri and Kansas rivers, partly in Kansas and partly in Missouri; population (1992) of Kansas City (Kansas) 146,500, Kansas City (Missouri) 431,550. It is a market and agricultural distribution centre and one of the chief livestock centres of the USA. Kansas City, Missouri, has car assembly plants and Kansas City, Kansas, has the majority of offices.

Kansu Alternative spelling for the Chinese province ◊Gansu.

Kanto Flat, densely populated region of E Honshu Island, Japan; area 32,418 sq km/12,517 sq mi; population (1995) 1,423,800. The chief city is Tokyo.

Kanton and Enderbury Two atolls in the Phoenix group, which forms part of the Republic of Kiribati. They were a UK-US condominium (joint rule) 1939–80. There are US aviation, radar, and tracking stations here.

Kaohsiung City and port on the W coast of Taiwan; population (1992) 1,396,400. Industries include aluminium ware, fertilizers, cement, oil refineries, iron and steel works, shipyards, and food processing. Kaohsiung began to develop as a commercial port after 1858; its industrial development came about while it was occupied by Japan, as Takaō 1895–1945.

Kapfenburg Town in the S Austrian province of Styria, just to the NE of Bruck an der Mur. A fortified town since the 12th century, it has had an ironworks since the 15th century. Kapfenburg has important steelworks, and also manufactures materials, chemicals, and electronic equipment.

Kaposvár Capital of Somogy county, SW Hungary, on the river Kapos, 188 km/117 mi SW of Budapest; population (1993) 71,100. Industries include engineering, textiles, and food processing.

Kappel Village in the Swiss canton of Zürich, 7 km/4 mi N of Zug; population (1995) 846. The religious reformer Ulrich Zwingli was killed in battle here in 1531, while engaged in a struggle against those Swiss cantons that had not accepted the Protestant Reformation.

Kara Bogaz Gol Shallow gulf of the Caspian Sea, Turkmenistan; area 20,000 sq km/8,000 sq mi. Rich deposits of sodium chloride, sulphates, and other salts have formed by evaporation.

Karachai-Cherkessia Autonomous republic of SW Russian Federation, part of Stavropol territory
area 14,100 sq km/5,444 sq mi
capital Cherkessk
physical in the Caucasus Mountains; densely forested
industries ore-mining, chemical and woodworking industries, livestock breeding, grain; tourism is important
population (1995) 436,000.

Karachi Largest city and chief seaport of Pakistan, and capital of Sind province, NW of the Indus delta; population (1996) approximately 10 million; 4 million live in squatter settlements. Industries include engineering, chemicals, plastics, and textiles. It was the capital of Pakistan 1947–59.

Karafuto Japanese name for ◊Sakhalin Island.

Karaganda Industrial city (coal, copper, tungsten, manganese) in Kazakhstan, linked by canal with the Irtysh River; capital of Karaganda region; population (1991) 1,339,900.

Karaikal Small port in India, 250 km/155 mi S of Madras, at the mouth of the right branch of the Cauvery delta. On a tract of land acquired by the French 1739, it was transferred to India 1954, confirmed by treaty 1956. It is part of the Union Territory of ◊Pondicherry.

Kara-Kalpak Autonomous republic of Uzbekistan
area 158,000 sq km/61,000 sq mi
capital Nukus
towns and cities Munyak
industries cotton, rice, wheat, fish, wine, leather goods
population (1990) 1,244,700 (Kara-Kalpaks, Uzbeks, Kazakhs)
history named after the Kara-Kalpak ('black hood') people who live S of the Sea of Aral and were conquered by Russia

1867. An autonomous Kara-Kalpak region was formed 1926 within Kazakhstan, transferred to the Soviet republic 1930, made a republic 1932, and attached to Uzbekistan 1936.

Karakoram Mountain range in central Asia, divided among China, Pakistan, and India. Peaks include K2, Masharbrum, Gasharbrum, and Mustagh Tower. *Ladakh* subsidiary range is in NE Kashmir on the Tibetan border.

Karakoram Highway Road constructed by China and Pakistan and completed 1978; it runs 800 km/500 mi from Havelian (NW of Rawalpindi), via ♢Gilgit in Kashmir and the Khunjerab Pass (4,800 m/16,000 ft) to ♢Kashi in China.

Karakorum Ruined capital of Mongol ruler Genghis Khan, SW of Ulaanbaatar in Mongolia.

Kara-Kum Sandy desert occupying most of Turkmenistan; area about 310,800 sq km/120,000 sq mi. It is crossed by the Caspian railway.

Kara Sea (Russian *Kavaskoye More*) Part of the Arctic Ocean off the N coast of the Russian Federation, bounded to the NW by the island of Novaya Zemlya and to the NE by Severnaya Zemlya. Novy Port on the Gulf of Ob is the chief port, and the Yenisey River also flows into it.

Karbala or *Kerbala* Holy city of the Shi'ite Muslims, 96 km/60 mi SW of Baghdad, Iraq; population (1987) 296,700. Karbala is built on the site of the battlefield where Husein, son of Ali and Fatima, was killed 680 while defending his succession to the khalifate; his tomb in the city is visited every year by many pilgrims.

Kardhitsa Town in Thessaly, central Greece, capital of Kardhitsa department; population (1991 est) 30,000. It is an administrative and market centre for an agricultural region, trading in cereals, cotton, sheep, wool, hides, tobacco, and dairy products.

Karelia Autonomous republic of NW Russian Federation
area 172,400 sq km/66,564 sq mi
capital Petrozavodsk
physical mainly forested
industries fishing, timber, chemicals, coal
population (1995) 789,000.

Karelian Isthmus Strip of land between Lake Ladoga and the Gulf of Finland, in the Russian Federation, with St Petersburg at the S extremity and Vyborg at the N. Finland ceded it to the USSR 1940–41 and from 1947.

Kargopol Town on the left bank of the Onega River, NW Russia; population (1980) 1,200. It developed with the salt trade from about the 14th century and has several outstanding 17th-century churches, notably the Church of St Vladimir (1653) and the Blagoveshchenie Church (1682–92). The town gives its name to the hunting and fishing Kargopol culture, which flourished in the area during the late Mesolithic and Neolithic periods.

Kariba Dam Concrete dam on the Zambezi River, on the Zambia–Zimbabwe border, about 386 km/240 mi downstream from the Victoria Falls, constructed 1955–60 to supply power to both countries. The dam crosses Kariba Gorge, and the reservoir, Lake Kariba, has important fisheries.

Karl-Marx-Stadt Former name (1953–90) of ♢Chemnitz, a city in Germany.

Karlovy Vary (German *Karlsbad*) Spa in the Bohemian Forest, Czech Republic, celebrated from the 14th century for its alkaline thermal springs; population (1991) 56,300.

Karlsburg German name for the Romanian town of ♢Alba Iulia.

Karlsruhe Industrial city (nuclear research, oil refining) in Baden-Württemberg, Germany; population (1993) 278,500.

Karlstad Capital of Vårmland county, S Sweden; population (1995) 79,500. It stands at the N end of Lake Vånern at the mouth of the river Klar. Karlstad has metal and clothing factories and a racetrack. On the nearby island is Skoghatt, Europe's largest integrated timber plant.

Karnak Village of modern Egypt, on the E bank of the river Nile, that gives its name to the temple of Ammon (constructed by Seti I and Ramses I) around which the major part of the ancient city of Thebes was built. An avenue of rams leads to ♢Luxor.

Karnataka formerly (until 1973) *Mysore* State in SW India
area 191,791 sq km/74,051 sq mi
capital Bangalore
industries mainly agricultural; minerals include manganese, chromite, India's only sources of gold and silver, sandalwood processing
population (1994) 48,150,000
language Kannada
famous people Hyder Ali, Tipu Sultan.

Kärnten German name for ♢Carinthia, a province of Austria.

Karroo Two areas of semi-desert in Eastern Cape Province, South Africa, divided into the *Great Karroo* and *Little Karroo* by the Swartberg Mountains. The two Karroos together have an area of about 260,000 sq km/100,000 sq mi.

Karviná Industrial town of NE Moravia, in the Czech Republic, on the Polish border 15 km/9 mi E of Ostrava; population (1991) 68,400. The town is situated on the Silesian coalfield and produces high-grade coal, chemicals, and iron.

Kasai River that rises in Angola and forms the frontier with the Democratic Republic of Congo (formerly Zaire) before entering Congo and joining the Congo/Zaïre River, of which it is the chief tributary. It is 2,100 km/1,300 mi long and is rich in alluvial diamonds.

Kashi formerly *Kashgar* Oasis city in Xinjiang Uyghur autonomous region, China, on the river Kaxgar He. It is the capital of Kashi district, which adjoins the Kirghiz and Tadzik republics, Afghanistan, and Jammu and Kashmir; population (1990) 175,000. It is a trading centre, the Chinese terminus of the ♢Karakoram Highway, and a focus of Muslim culture.

Kashmir Pakistan-occupied area, 30,445 sq mi/78,900 sq km, in the NW of the former state of Kashmir, now ♢Jammu and Kashmir. Azad ('free') Kashmir in the W has its own legislative assembly based in Muzaffarabad while

Gilgit and Baltistan regions to the N and E are governed directly by Pakistan. The ◊Northern Areas are claimed by India and Pakistan

population 1,500,000

towns and cities Gilgit, Skardu

features W Himalayan peak Nanga Parbat 8,126 m/ 26,660 ft, Karakoram Pass, Indus River, Baltoro Glacier.

Kassel Industrial city (engineering, chemicals, electronics) in Hessen, Germany, on the river Fulda; population (1991) 196,800. There is the spectacular Wilhelmshöhe mountain park, and the Grimm Museum commemorates the compilers of fairy tales who lived here.

Kastoria Town in Macedonia, Greece, capital of Kastoria department, situated S of Florina on the small Kastoria lake. The town dates back 2,500 years but flourished mainly in the 17th and 18th centuries as a fur-trading centre. It is an administrative centre and a resort, and there is commercial fishing.

Katanga formerly (until 1993) *Shaba* Region of the Democratic Republic of Congo (formerly Zaire); area 496,965 sq km/191,828 sq mi; population (1991 est) 5,207,000. Its main town is Lubumbashi (formerly Elisabethville).

Kathiawar Peninsula on the W coast of India. Formerly occupied by a number of princely states, all Kathiawar (60,723 sq km/23,445 sq mi) had been included in Bombay state by 1956 but was transferred to Gujarat 1960. Mahatma Gandhi was born in Kathiawar at Porbandar.

Kathmandu or *Katmandu* Capital of Nepal; population (1991) 419,100. Founded in the 8th century on an ancient pilgrim and trade route from India to Tibet and China, it has a royal palace, Buddhist temples, monasteries, and a tourist centre.

Katmai Active volcano in Alaska, USA, 2,046 m/6,715 ft. Its eruption 1912 created the 'Valley of Ten Thousand Smokes'. Katmai national park, area 6,922 sq mi/17,928 sq km, was designated 1980.

Katowice Industrial city (anthracite, iron and coal mining, iron foundries, smelting works, machine shops) in Upper Silesia, S Poland; population (1993) 366,900.

Kattegat Sea passage between Denmark and Sweden. It is about 240 km/150 mi long and 135 km/85 mi wide at its broadest point.

Kaufbeuren City in Bavaria, Germany, on the river Wertach, 28 km/17 mi SW of Munich; population (1994) 42,600. It has glass, jewellery, electronic, and timber industries. Kaufbeuren was one of the city-states of the Holy Roman Empire, and has two Gothic churches.

Kaunas formerly (until 1917) *Kovno* Industrial river port (textiles, chemicals, agricultural machinery) in Lithuania, on the Niemen (Neman) River; population (1995) 415,000. It was the capital of Lithuania 1910–40.

Kavalla Town in NE Greece, capital of Kavalla department, built on a promontory. Its port handles 6% of Greek trade. Exports include tobacco and manganese, and imports include fertilizers, wheat, and timber. There are flour and rice mills. The town was a member of the Attica Naval League in 478–463 BC and was later a Roman naval base.

Kawasaki Industrial city (iron, steel, shipbuilding, chemicals, textiles) on Honshu Island, Japan; population (1994) 1,171,000.

Kayah State. Division of Myanmar (formerly Burma), area 11,900 sq km/4,600 sq mi, formed 1954 from the Karenni states (Kantarrawaddy, Bawlake, and Kyebogyi) and inhabited mainly by the Karen people. Kayah State has a measure of autonomy.

Kayseri (ancient name *Caesarea Mazaca*) Capital of Kayseri province, central Turkey; population (1990) 421,400. It produces textiles, carpets, and tiles. In Roman times it was capital of the province of Cappadocia.

Kazan Capital of Tatarstan, central Russian Federation, on the river Volga; population (1994) 1,092,000. It is a transport, commercial, and industrial centre (engineering, oil refining, petrochemicals, textiles, large fur trade). Formerly the capital of a Tatar khanate, Kazan was captured by Ivan IV 'the Terrible' 1552.

Kebnekaise Highest peak in Sweden, rising to 2,111 m/ 6,926 ft in the Kolen range, W of the town of Kiruna.

Kecskemét City in Hungary, situated on the Hungarian plain SE of Budapest; population (1993 est) 105,000. It is a trading centre of an agricultural region.

Kedah State in NW Peninsular Malaysia; capital Alor Setar; area 9,400 sq km/3,628 sq mi; population (1993) 1,412,000. Products include rice, rubber, tapioca, tin, and tungsten. Kedah was transferred by Siam (Thailand) to Britain 1909, and was one of the Unfederated Malay States until 1948.

Keeling Islands Another name for the ◊Cocos Islands, an Australian territory.

Keelung or *Chi-lung* Industrial port (shipbuilding, chemicals, fertilizer) on the N coast of Taiwan, 24 km/15 mi NE of Taipei; population (1993) 363,000.

Keewatin Eastern district of Northwest Territories, Canada, including the islands in Hudson and James bays

area 590,935 sq km/228,160 sq mi

towns and cities (trading posts) Chesterfield Inlet, Eskimo Point, and Coral Harbour (site of an air base set up during World War II)

physical upland plateau in the N, the S low and level, covering the greater part of the Arctic prairies of Canada; numerous lakes

industries furs (trapping is main occupation)

population (1991) 5,800

history Keewatin District formed 1876, under the administration of Manitoba; it was transferred to Northwest Territories 1905, and in 1912 lost land S of 60° N to Manitoba and Ontario.

Kefallinia (English *Cephalonia*) Largest of the Ionian Islands off the W coast of Greece; area 935 sq km/360 sq mi; population (1981) 31,300. It was devastated by an earthquake 1953 that destroyed the capital Argostolion.

Keflavík Fishing port in Iceland, 35 km/22 mi SW of Reykjavik; population (1990) 7,500. Its international airport was built during World War II by US forces (who called it Meeks Field). Keflavik became a NATO base 1951.

Keighley Industrial town on the river Aire, NW of Bradford in West Yorkshire, England; population (1991) 49,600. Haworth, home of the Brontë family of writers, is now part of Keighley. Industries include woollens and worsteds, textile machinery, and machine tools.

Kelang formerly (until 1971) *Port Swettenham* Malaysian rubber port on the Strait of Malacca, 40 km/25 mi SW of Kuala Lumpur; population (1980) 192,080.

Kelantan State in NE Peninsular Malaysia; capital Kota Baharu; area 14,900 sq km/5,751 sq mi; population (1993) 1,221,700. It produces rice, rubber, copra, tin, manganese, and gold. Kelantan was transferred by Siam (Thailand) to Britain 1909 and until 1948 was one of the Unfederated Malay States.

Kemerovo Coal-mining city in the Russian Federation, in W Siberia, centre of Kuznetz coal basin; population (1994) 513,000. It has chemical and metallurgical industries. It was formed out of the villages of Kemerovo and Shcheglovisk, and was known 1918–32 as *Shcheglovisk*.

Kempen (French *Campine*) Region of NE Belgium stretching between the rivers Scheldt and Meuse to the N of the Dyle and the Demer. It is an area of flat, sandy moorland. Hasselt, Herentals, and Turnhout are the chief towns.

Kempten City in Bavaria, Germany, on the river Iller, 104 km/65 mi SW of Munich; population (1994) 61,400. The city is a market centre specializing in dairy products, and there are textile, paper, and precision engineering industries. Kempten contains a Baroque church, a Gothic *Rathaus* (town hall), and the former palace of the abbot-princes of the old imperial city.

Kendal Town in Cumbria, England, on the river Kent; population (1991) 25,500. It is an industrial centre (light industry, agricultural machinery, footwear, and, since the 14th century, wool) and tourist centre for visitors to the ◊Lake District. Kendal mint cake comes from here. It is the birthplace of Catherine Parr.

Kenilworth Town in Warwickshire, England; population (1986 est) 21,400. The Norman castle, celebrated in Walter Scott's novel *Kenilworth*, became a royal residence (Edward II relinquished his crown here 1327). It was enlarged by John of Gaunt and later by the Earl of Leicester, who entertained Elizabeth I here 1575, but was dismantled after the Civil War. Industries include tanning, and motor and agricultural engineering.

Kennewick City in SE Washington, USA, on the Columbia River, SE of Seattle; population (1990) 42,200. Dams built on the Columbia and Snake rivers provide irrigation for the area's grape, sugar beet, alfalfa, and corn crops. The city was laid out 1892.

Kenosha (Indian 'pike' or 'pickerel') City and port in the SE corner of Wisconsin, USA, on Lake Michigan, SE of Milwaukee, seat of Kenosha County; population (1992) 83,500. Its industries include food-processing equipment, fertilizers, motor vehicles, textiles and clothing, and food products. It was founded 1835.

Kensington and Chelsea Inner borough of central Greater London

features Holland House (about 1606) and Holland Park; Camden House (about 1612); Kensington Palace, Jacobean house redesigned by Christopher Wren for William and Mary 1689; Kensington Gardens, with statue of Peter Pan; Leighton House (1866); Imperial College of Science and Technology (1907); Kensington and Chelsea Town Hall (1976) designed by Basil Spence; museums – Victoria and Albert, Natural History, Science, and Geology; Royal College of Music; Royal College of Art; annual Notting Hill Carnival, held each August, is the largest street carnival in Europe

famous people William Wilberforce lived here

population (1991) 138,400.

Kent County of SE England, known as the 'garden of England'; Rochester and Gillingham will join to become the new unitary authority of the Medway Towns in April 1998

area 3,730 sq km/1,440 sq mi

towns and cities Maidstone (administrative headquarters), Canterbury, Dover, Chatham, Rochester, Sheerness, Tunbridge Wells; resorts: Folkestone, Margate, Ramsgate

features the North Downs; rivers: Thames, Darent, Medway, Stour (traditionally, a 'man of Kent' comes from E of the Medway and a 'Kentish man' from W Kent); New Ash Green, a new town; Romney Marsh; the Isles of Grain, Sheppey (on which is the resort of Sheerness, formerly a royal dockyard), and Thanet; Weald (agricultural area); Leeds Castle (converted to a palace by Henry VIII); Ightham Mote; Hever Castle (where Henry VIII courted Anne Boleyn); Chartwell (Churchill's country home), Knole, Sissinghurst Castle and gardens; the Brogdale Experimental Horticulture Station at Faversham has the world's finest collection of apple and other fruit trees; the former RAF Manston became Kent International Airport 1989

industries hops, apples, soft fruit, cement, paper, oil refining, shipbuilding. The East Kent coalfield ceased production 1989

population (1994) 1,546,300

famous people Christopher Marlowe, Edward Heath.

Kentucky State in S central USA; nicknamed Bluegrass State

area 104,700 sq km/40,414 sq mi

capital Frankfort

towns and cities Louisville, Lexington, Owensboro, Covington, Bowling Green

physical Ohio and Kentucky rivers; Cumberland Gap national park; the bluegrass country; Daniel Boone national forest; Red River Gorge; Breaks Interstate Park; Mammoth Cave national park (main cave 6.5 km/4 mi long, up to 38 m/125 ft high, where Native American councils were once held), a World Heritage Site

features racehorse breeding, with over 400 horse farms, including Calumet, Spendthrift, Normany; the mansion at

Manchester said to be the inspiration for Tara in M Mitchell's *Gone with the Wind*; parks landscaped by Frederick Law Olmsted, including Shawnee Park; Abraham Lincoln's birthplace at Hodgenville; Shaker Village of Pleasant Hill, Harrodsburg; Louisville, with 19th-century cast-iron architecture in West Main Street (including the Hart Block, 1884), Jefferson County Courthouse (1835), the Cathedral of the Assumption (1849–52), Farmington (1810, designed by Thomas Jefferson), the Cherokee Triangle (large houses built 1870–1910), the American Life and Accident Building (1973, designed by Mies van der Rohe), the Humana Building (1985), and the Kentucky Derby Museum; Bardstown, the Colonial mansion visited by Stephen Foster 1852, site of his song 'My Old Kentucky Home'; Gratz Park historic district in Lexington, with two houses from 1814; Transylvania University (1780), the first college to be founded W of the Alleghenies; the Kentucky Derby, run at Churchill Downs, Louisville; Fort Knox, the US gold bullion depository; Maker's Mark Distillery; Jim Beam American Outpost Museum

industries tobacco, cereals, textiles, coal, whisky, horses, transport vehicles

population (1995) 3,860,200

famous people Muhammad Ali, Daniel Boone, Louis D Brandeis, Kit Carson, Henry Clay, D W Griffith, Thomas Hunt Morgan, Harland 'Colonel' Sanders, Robert Penn Warren

history Kentucky was the first region W of the Alleghenies settled by American pioneers. James Harrod founded Harrodsburg 1774; in 1775 Daniel Boone, who blazed his Wilderness Trail 1767, founded Boonesboro. Originally part of Virginia, Kentucky became a state 1792. Badly divided over the slavery question, the state was racked by guerrilla warfare and partisan feuds during the Civil War.

Kenya, Mount or *Kirinyaga* Extinct volcano from which Kenya takes its name, 5,199 m/17,057 ft; the first European to climb it was Halford Mackinder 1899.

Kerala State of SW India, formed 1956 from the former princely states of Travancore and Cochin

area 38,863 sq km/15,005 sq mi

capital Trivandrum

features most densely populated, and most literate (60%), state of India; strong religious and caste divisions make it politically unstable

industries tea, coffee, rice, oilseed, rubber, textiles, chemicals, electrical goods, fish

population (1994 est) 30,555,000

language Kannada, Malayalam, Tamil.

Kerbala Alternative form for the city of ◊Karbala.

Kerch Port in the Crimea, Ukraine, at the E end of *Kerch peninsula*, an iron-producing area; population (1990) 176,000. Built on the site of an ancient Greek settlement, Kerch belonged to Russia from 1783.

Kerguelen Islands or *Desolation Islands* Volcanic archipelago in the Indian Ocean, part of the French Southern and Antarctic Territories; area 7,215 km/2,787 sq mi. It was discovered 1772 by the Breton navigator Yves de Kerguelen and annexed by France 1949. Uninhabited except for scientists (centre for joint study of geomagnetism with Russia), the islands support a unique wild cabbage containing a pungent oil.

Kerkrade Town in the province of Limburg, the Netherlands, 24 km/15 mi NE of Maastricht, near the border with Germany; population (1996) 52,700. Kerkrade forms the centre of an industrial region. The town was founded 1104.

Kérkyra Greek form of ◊Corfu, an island in the Ionian Sea.

Kermadec Islands Volcanic group, a dependency of New Zealand since 1887; area 30 sq km/12 sq mi. They are uninhabited except for a meteorological station on the largest island, Raoul.

Kerman City in Kerman province SE Iran; population (1991) 312,000. It is a centre for the mining of copper and precious metals.

Kermanshah Former name (to 1980) of ◊Bakhtaran in NW Iran.

Kernow Celtic name for ◊Cornwall, an English county.

Kerry County of the Republic of Ireland, W of Cork, in the province of Munster; county town Tralee; area 4,700 sq km/1,814 sq mi; population (1996 est) 125,900. Low lying in the N, to the S are the highest mountains in Ireland, including Carrantuohill (part of ◊Macgillycuddy's Reeks), the highest peak in Ireland at 1,041 m/3,417 ft. The W coastline is deeply indented and there are many rivers and lakes, notable of which are the Lakes of Killarney. Industries include engineering, woollens, shoes, cutlery, fishing, farming; tourism is important.

Keski-Suomi Province in S central Finland; area 16,430 sq km/6,344 sq mi; population (1995) 130,000. The land is low-lying with many interconnected lakes. Farming and timber are the main industries and the area is popular with holidaymakers. The capital, Jyväskylä, is the fourth-biggest commercial centre in Finland.

Kesteven, Parts of Area of SW Lincolnshire, England, formerly an administrative unit with county offices at Sleaford 1888–1974.

Keweenaw Peninsula Part of the upper peninsula of Michigan, USA, curving 95 km/50 mi into Lake Superior, largest of the Great Lakes of North America. Formerly very rich in copper, it is now primarily a resort area; other industries include timber processing, farming, and commercial fishing.

Key West Town at the tip of the Florida peninsula, USA; population (1990) 24,800. It was incorporated 1828 and is the southernmost town in the continental USA. As a tourist resort, it was popularized by the novelist Ernest Hemingway.

Khabarovsk Industrial city (oil refining, saw milling, meat packing) in the Russian Federation, in SE Siberia; population (1994) 609,000.

Khabarovsk Territory of the Russian Federation, in SE Siberia, bordering the Sea of Okhotsk and drained by the

Amur River; area 824,600 sq km/318,501 sq mi; population (1985) 1,728,000. The capital is Khabarovsk. Mineral resources include gold, coal, and iron ore.

Khajurāho Town in Madhya Pradesh, central India, former capital of the Candella monarchs, and site of 35 sandstone temples – Jain, Buddhist, and Hindu – built in the 10th and 11th centuries. The temples are covered inside and out with erotic relief sculptures symbolizing mystic union with the deity. The Parshvanatha Temple about 950–70 has the finest array, providing outstanding examples of medieval Hindu art as well as some of the world's most sensual images.

Khakassia Autonomous republic of central Russian Federation, in Krasnoyarsk territory
area 61,900 sq km/23,900 sq mi
capital Abakan
physical includes the Minusinsk River basin
industries coal and ore mining, timber, woodworking, sheep and goat farming
population (1995) 584,000

Khalkis Greek name for ◊Chalcis, a town on the island of Euboea in Greece.

Khaniá Alternative name for ◊Chaniá, a port in Crete.

Khardung Pass Road linking the Indian town of Leh with the high-altitude military outpost on the Siachen Glacier at an altitude of 5,401 m/17,730 ft in the Karakoram range, Kashmir. It is thought to be the highest road in the world.

Kharg Island Small island in the Persian Gulf used by Iran as a deep-water oil terminal. Between 1982 and 1988 Kharg Island came under frequent attack during the Iran–Iraq War.

Kharkov Capital of the Kharkov region, E Ukraine, 400 km/250 mi E of Kiev; population (1992) 1,622,000. It is a railway junction and industrial city (engineering, tractors), close to the Donets Basin coalfield and Krivoy Rog iron mines. Kharkov was founded 1654 as a fortress town.

Khartoum Capital and trading centre of Sudan, at the junction of the Blue and White Nile; population (1983) 561,000, and of Khartoum North, across the Blue Nile, 341,000. ◊Omdurman is also a suburb of Khartoum, giving the urban area a population of over 1.3 million.

Khaskovo or *Haskovo* Capital of Khaskovo region, S Bulgaria, on a tributary of the river Maritsa, 56 km/35 mi SE of Plovdiv; population (1990) 117,400. Industries include textiles and tobacco. The town was founded by Turks in the 14th century.

Kherson Port in S Ukraine, on the river Dnieper, capital of Kherson region; population (1992) 368,000. Industries include shipbuilding, soap, and tobacco manufacture. Kherson was founded 1778 by army commander Potemkin as the first Russian naval base on the Black Sea.

Khios Greek name for ◊Chios, an island and town in Greece.

Khmer Republic Former name (1970–76) of Cambodia.

Kholm Russian name for Chełm, a town in Poland.

Khorramshahr Former port and oil-refining centre in Iran, on the Shatt-al-Arab River and linked by bridge to the island of Abadan. It was completely destroyed in the 1980s in the Iran–Iraq War.

Khulna Capital of Khulna region, SW Bangladesh, situated close to the Ganges delta; population (1991) 545,800. Industry includes shipbuilding and textiles; it trades in jute, rice, salt, sugar, and oilseed.

Khuzestan Province of SW Iran, which includes the chief Iranian oil resources; population (1991) 3,175,900. Cities include Ahvaz (capital) and the ports of Abadan and Khuninshahr. There have been calls for Sunni Muslim autonomy, under the name Arabistan.

Khyber Pass Pass 53 km/33 mi long through the mountain range that separates Pakistan from Afghanistan. The Khyber Pass was used by invaders of India. The present road was constructed by the British during the Afghan Wars.

Kiangsi Alternative spelling of ◊Jiangxi, a province of China.

Kiangsu Alternative spelling of ◊Jiangsu, a province of China.

Kicking Horse Pass Pass in the ◊Rocky Mountains, between British Columbia and Alberta, W Canada, 56 km/35 mi NW of Banff. With an altitude of 1,627 m/5,338 ft, it is the highest point on the Canadian Pacific Railway. It lies in the Banff–Yoho national parks.

Kidderminster Market town in the West Midlands of England, on the river Stour; population (1991) 54,600. It has a carpet industry dating from about 1735. Other industries include woollen and worsted yarn, textile machinery, rocket motors, sugar beet, tin-plating, and chemicals.

Kiel Baltic port (fishing, shipbuilding, electronics, engineering) in Germany; capital of Schleswig-Holstein; population (1993) 249,100. Kiel Week in June is a yachting meeting.

Kiel Canal formerly *Kaiser Wilhelm Canal* Waterway 98.7 km/61 mi long that connects the Baltic with the North Sea. Built by Germany in the years before World War I, the canal allowed the German navy to move from Baltic bases to the open sea without travelling through international waters, although it was also of value to commercial traffic. It was declared an international waterway by the Versailles Treaty 1919.

Kielce City in central Poland, NE of Kraków; population (1991) 214,200. It is an industrial rail junction (chemicals, metals).

Kiev Capital of Ukraine, industrial centre (chemicals, clothing, leatherwork), on the confluence of the Desna and Dnieper rivers; population (1992) 2,643,000. It was the capital of Russia in the Middle Ages.

Kifisos Greek name for the ◊Cephisus, a river in Greece.

Kigali Capital of Rwanda, central Africa, 80 km/50 mi E of Lake Kivu; population (1993) 234,500. Products include coffee, tea, hides, shoes, paints, and varnishes; there is tin mining. Much of the city's infrastructure has been damaged in Rwanda's civil war.

Kigoma Town and port on the E shore of Lake Tanganyika, Tanzania, at the W terminal of the railway from Dar es Salaam; population (1978) 50,044. It trades in timber, cotton, and tobacco.

Kikinda Town in Serbia, Yugoslavia, in the fertile region of Vojvodina; population (1990) 43,000. It is a railway junction, has a trade in wheat and fruit, and lies on a natural-gas field.

Kildare County of the Republic of Ireland, in the province of Leinster; county town Naas; area 1,690 sq km/652 sq mi; population (1996 est) 134,900. It is wet and boggy in the N and includes part of the Bog of Allen; the village of Maynooth, with a training college for Roman Catholic priests; and the Curragh, a plain that is the site of the national stud and headquarters of Irish horse racing at Tully. Products include oats, barley, potatoes, and cattle.

Kilimanjaro Volcano in Tanzania, the highest mountain in Africa, 5,895 m/19,340 ft.

Kilkenny County of the Republic of Ireland, in the province of Leinster; county town Kilkenny; area 2,060 sq km/795 sq mi; population (1996 est) 75,200. It has the rivers Nore, Suir, and Barrow. Industries include coal mining, clothing, footwear, brewing, and agricultural activities such as cattle rearing and dairy farming.

Killarney Market town in County Kerry, Republic of Ireland; population (1991) 7,300. A famous beauty spot in Ireland, it has ◊Macgillycuddy's Reeks (a range of mountains) and the Lakes of Killarney to the SW. Industries include hosiery and container cranes.

Killeen City in central Texas, S of Fort Worth and N of Austin; population (1992) 66,600. Although some concrete is produced here, the economy relies heavily on the nearby army base, Fort Hood, established 1942. The town was laid out 1882.

Kilmarnock Administrative headquarters of East Ayrshire, Scotland, 32 km/20 mi SW of Glasgow; population (1991) 44,300. Industries include carpets, agricultural machinery, woollens, lace, footwear, earthenware, and whisky; Robert Burns's first book of poems was published here 1786.

Kimberley Diamond site in Western Australia, found 1978–79, estimated to have 5% of the world's known gem-quality stones and 50% of its industrial diamonds.

Kimberley Diamond-mining capital city of Northern Cape Province, South Africa, 153 km/95 mi NW of Bloemfontein; population (1991) 167,100. Its mines have been controlled by De Beers Consolidated Mines since 1887.

Kincardineshire Former county of E Scotland, merged 1975–96 into Grampian Region; now in Aberdeenshire.

King's County Older name of ◊Offaly, an Irish county.

King's Lynn Port and market town at the mouth of the Great Ouse River, Norfolk, E England; population (1991) 41,300. A thriving port in medieval times, it was called Lynn

until its name was changed by Henry VIII. Industries include food canning, sugar beet refining, brewing, fishing, and engineering.

Kingsport City in NE Tennessee, USA, on the Holston River, NE of Knoxville, near the Virginia border; population (1990) 36,400. Products include plastics, chemicals, textiles, paper and printing, and cement. Fort Patrick Henry, built here 1776, protected the Wilderness Road.

Kingston Town in E Ontario, Canada, on Lake Ontario; population (1991) 56,600. Industries include shipbuilding yards, engineering works, and grain elevators. It grew from 1782 around the French Fort Frontenac, was captured by the English 1748, and renamed in honour of George III.

Kingston Capital and principal port of Jamaica, West Indies, the cultural and commercial centre of the island; population (1991) 587,800 (metropolitan area). Founded 1693, Kingston became the capital of Jamaica 1872.

Kingston upon Hull City, port, and unitary authority on the N bank of the Humber estuary, E England, where the river Hull flows into it; population (1996) 265,000; area 71 sq km/27 sq mi. It is linked with the S bank of the estuary by the Humber Bridge, the world's longest single-span suspension bridge. Industries include fish processing, vegetable oils, flour milling, electrical goods, textiles, paint, pharmaceuticals, chemicals, caravans, aircraft, sawmilling, paper, marine engineering, and food processing.

Kingston upon Thames Outer borough of SW Greater London; administrative headquarters of Surrey
features seven Saxon kings, from Edward the Elder in 900 to Ethelred the Unready in 979, were crowned at Kingston, their coronation stone is preserved here, set with seven silver pennies; oldest of the three Royal Boroughs of England, with ancient right to elect own High Steward and Recorder; Kingston Grammar School, founded by Elizabeth I 1561
industries aviation, chemicals, engineering, plastics, printing, refrigeration
population (1991) 133,000.

Kingstown Former name for ◊Dún Laoghaire, a port near Dublin, Ireland.

Kingstown Capital and principal port of St Vincent and the Grenadines, West Indies, in the SW of the island of St Vincent; population (1991) 26,200.

King-Te-Chen Alternative spelling of ◊Jingdezhen, a city in China.

Kinki Region of S Honshu Island, Japan; population (1995) 22,468,000. It has an area of 33,094 sq km/12,778 sq mi. The chief city is Osaka.

Kinshasa formerly *Léopoldville* Capital of the Democratic Republic of Congo (formerly Zaire) on the Congo/Zaïre River, 400 km/250 mi inland from the port of Matadi; population (1991 est) 3,804,000. Industries include chemicals, textiles, engineering, food processing, and furniture. It was founded by the explorer Henry Stanley 1887.

Kirchheim unter Teck City in Baden-Württemberg, Germany, 25 km/15 mi SE of Stuttgart; population (1994)

38,000. There are textile and steel industries. The town's full name derives from its position beneath the fortress of Teck.

Kirghizia Alternative form of Kyrgyzstan, a country in central Asia.

Kirin Alternative name for ◊Jilin, a Chinese province.

Kirinyaga Alternative name of Mount ◊Kenya.

Kiritimati formerly *Christmas Island* Island in Kiribati, in the central Pacific; one of the Line Islands.

Kirkcaldy Seaport on the Firth of Forth, Fife, Scotland; population (1991) 47,200. Industries include floor coverings, paper, coarse textiles, and whisky. It is the birthplace of the economist Adam Smith and the architect Robert Adam.

Kirkcudbright Former county of S Scotland, merged 1975–96 into Dumfries and Galloway Region; now part of Dumfries and Galloway unitary authority.

Kirkenes Town in Finnmark, N Norway, near the border with the Russian Federation, on the shore of Varanger Fjord. Kirkenes is a port for the shipment of iron ore from the nearby Syd-Varanger mines, the largest mines in Norway.

Kirkuk City in NE Iraq; population (1987) 418,600. It is the centre of a major oilfield. Formerly it was served by several pipelines providing outlets to Lebanon, Syria, and other countries, but closures caused by the Iran–Iraq War left only the pipeline to Turkey operational. 100,000 Kurds were expelled 1991.

Kirkwall Administrative headquarters and port of the Orkney Islands, Scotland, on the N coast of the largest island, Mainland; population (1991) 6,700. The Norse cathedral of St Magnus dates from 1137.

Kirov formerly (until 1934) *Vyatka* City NE of Nizhniy-Novgorod, on the river Vyatka, central Russian Federation; population (1994) 491,000. It is a rail and industrial centre for rolling stock, tyres, clothing, toys, and machine tools.

Kirovabad Former name of ◊Gyandzha, a city in Azerbaijan.

Kirovograd City in central Ukraine; population (1992) 280,000. Manufacturing includes agricultural machinery and food processing. The city is on a lignite field. It was known as *Yelizavetgrad* until 1924 and *Zinovyevsk* 1924–36.

Kirriemuir Market town in Angus, Scotland, called 'Thrums' in James Barrie's novels; it is his birthplace.

Kiruna Town in Swedish Lapland; population 30,000. In area it is the largest town in the world. It includes vast iron-ore fields; most of the mining is opencast. The iron ore is transported to the Norwegian seaport of Narvik by rail, and to the Swedish Baltic port of Luleå, which is closed by ice in winter. The mines in the Kiruna area produce 25 million tonnes of iron ore a year.

Kisangani (formerly (until 1966) *Stanleyville*) City in NE Democratic Republic of Congo (formerly Zaire), on the upper Congo/Zaïre River, below Stanley Falls; population (1991 est) 373,400. It is a communications centre.

Kishinev Russian name for ◊Chisinău, the capital of Moldova.

Kiskunfélegyháza Market town on the Great Plain (Alföld) of Hungary, 26 km/16 mi S of Kecskemét; population (1993) 33,900. Cereals, fruit, wine, tobacco, and livestock are traded from the surrounding rich agricultural district. The town was destroyed by the Turks in the 17th century but rebuilt 1743.

Kitakyushu Industrial port city (coal, steel, chemicals, cotton thread, plate glass, alcohol) in Japan, on the Hibiki Sea, N Kyushu Island, formed 1963 by the amalgamation of Moji, Kokura, Tobata, Yawata, and Wakamatsu; population (1994) 1,015,000. A tunnel (1942) links it with Honshu.

Kitchener City in SW Ontario, Canada; population (1991) 168,300, metropolitan area (with Waterloo) 356,000. Manufacturing includes agricultural machinery and tyres. Settled by Germans from Pennsylvania in the 1800s, it was known as Berlin until 1916.

Kitimat Port near Prince Rupert, British Columbia, Canada; population (1991) 11,300. It has one of the world's largest aluminium smelters, powered by the Kemano hydroelectric scheme and was founded 1953.

Kitwe Commercial centre for the Zambian copperbelt; population (1990) 338,000. To the S are Zambia's emerald mines.

Kitzbühel Winter-sports resort in the Austrian Tirol, NE of Innsbruck; population (1985) 9,000.

Kivu Lake in the Great Rift Valley between the Democratic Republic of Congo (formerly Zaire) and Rwanda, about 105 km/65 mi long. The chief port is Bukavu.

Kladno Industrial town (coal, iron, steel, engineering) in central Bohemia, in the Czech Republic, 25 km/16 mi W of Prague; population (1991) 71,700.

Klagenfurt Capital of the Austrian province of ◊Carinthia, on a tributary of the river Drava near the Slovenian border. The city has iron, chemical, textile, leather, machinery, and tobacco industries, and hosts an annual trade fair. It has a Renaissance cathedral and several old churches.

Klaipeda formerly *Memel* Port in Lithuania, on the Baltic coast at the mouth of the river Dane; population (1995) 203,000. Industries include shipbuilding and iron foundries; it trades in timber, grain, and fish. It was founded on the site of a local fortress 1252 as the castle of Memelburg by the Teutonic Knights, joined the Hanseatic League soon after, and has changed hands among Sweden, Russia, and Germany. Lithuania annexed Klaipeda 1923, and after German occupation 1939–45 it was restored to Soviet Lithuania 1945–91.

Kłodzko (German *Glatz*) Town in Wałbrzych province, Poland, on the river Nysa, 80 km/50 mi S of Wrocław; population (1990) 30,400. Textiles and machinery are manufactured. Lying at the S edge of the Sudeten Mountains, near the Czech border, Kłodzko was part of German Lower Silesia until 1945.

Klondike Gold-mining area in ◊Yukon, Canada, named after the river valley where gold was found 1896. About 30,000 people moved to the area during the following few months.

Klosterneuburg Suburb of ◊Vienna, Austria, in the province of Lower Austria. It lies on the N edge of the metropolitan area, on the slopes of the Wienerwald. An Augustinian abbey was founded here in 1106. The town produces wine and pharmaceuticals.

Klosters Fashionable Alpine skiing resort (altitude 1,191 m/3,908 ft) in Grisons canton, E Switzerland, on the river Landquart, 10 km/6 mi NE of Davos. To the East, Kloster Pass leads to Austria.

Knaresborough Market town in North Yorkshire, England, 6 km/4 mi NE of Harrogate; population (1991) 13,400. It has a castle dating from about 1070.

Knock Village in County Mayo, W Ireland, known for its church shrine (the Basilica of Our Lady, *Queen of Ireland*), one of three national places of pilgrimage (with Lough Derg and Croagh Patrick). On 21 August 1879 it was the scene of an alleged apparition of the Virgin Mary, St Joseph, and St John to a group of about 14 people. Pope John Paul II (the first pope to set foot on Irish soil) celebrated Mass for the Sick here 100 years later, 1979.

Knokke-Heist Fashionable resort town on the coast of West Flanders, Belgium, NE of Blankenberge; population (1991) 31,700. The fishing village of Knokke merged with the residential suburb of Het Zoute 1880 and, as the town developed, other villages were absorbed. It has a casino and one of the largest golf courses in Europe.

Knoxville City in E Tennessee, USA; population (1992) 167,300. It is the centre of a mining and agricultural region, and the administrative headquarters of the ◊Tennessee Valley Authority. The University of Tennessee (1794) is here, and Oak Ridge National Laboratory, one of the world's largest nuclear research facilities, is nearby. Settlement began 1786, and it was the first state capital (1796–1812; 1817–19).

Knutsford Town in Cheshire, England; population (1990 est) 14,000. There is engineering, and chemicals and scientific instruments are produced. The novelist Elizabeth Gaskell, who lived in Knutsford for 22 years and is buried here, chose it as the setting for her novel *Cranford*.

Kobarid formerly *Caporetto* Village on the river Isonzo in NW Slovenia. Originally in Hungary, it was in Italy from 1918, and in 1947 became Kobarid. During World War I, German-Austrian troops heavily defeated Italian forces here Oct 1917 in the *Battle of Caporetto*, the town's former name.

Kobe Deep-water port in S Honshu, Japan; population (1994) 1,479,000. It originated as a treaty port 1868–99 (for foreigners exempt from Japanese law). *Port Island*, an artificial island of 5 sq km/2 sq mi in Kobe harbour, was created 1960–68 from the rock of nearby mountains. It was one of the world's largest construction projects, and is now a residential and recreation area with a luxury hotel, amusement park, and conference centres. It is linked to the city by a driverless, computerized monorail.

København Danish name for ◊Copenhagen, the capital of Denmark.

Koblenz City in the Rhineland-Palatinate, Germany, at the junction of the rivers Rhine and Mosel; population (1993) 109,900. The city dates from Roman times. It is a centre of communications and the wine trade, with industries (shoes, cigars, paper).

Kodiak Island off the S coast of Alaska; area 9,505 sq km/3,670 sq mi. It is the home of the Kodiak bear, the world's largest bear. The town of Kodiak is one of the largest US fishing ports (mainly salmon).

Koil Alternative name for the city of ◊Aligarh, India.

Kokand Oasis city in Uzbekistan; population (1990) 176,000. It was the capital of Kokand khanate when annexed by Russia 1876. Industries include fertilizers, cotton, and silk.

Kokomo City in N central Indiana, USA, on Wildcat Creek, N of Indianapolis and SW of Fort Wayne; seat of Howard County; population (1990) 45,000. The city's industries produce car, radio, and plumbing parts; steel and wire; and electrical machinery. Kokomo was settled 1844, and expanded after the discovery of natural gas 1886. The first car to use petrol was invented and tested here 1893.

Koko Nor Mongolian form of ◊Qinghai, a province of China.

Kola Peninsula (Russian *Kol'skiy Poluostrov*) Peninsula in the N Russian Federation, bounded S and E by the White Sea and N by the Barents Sea; area 129,500 sq km/50,000 sq mi; population 1.3 million (of whom 2,000 are Saami). Kola is coterminous with Murmansk region. Apatite and other minerals are exported.

Kolberg German name for ◊Kołobrzeg, a town in Poland.

Kolchugino Former name (to 1925) of ◊Leninsk-Kuznetsky, a town in Russia.

Kolhapur Industrial city and film production centre in Maharashtra, India; population (1991) 417,000. It is also an ancient Buddhist site and a centre of pilgrimage.

Kolín River port in central Bohemia, in the Czech Republic, on the Elbe, 25 km/16 mi E of Prague; population (1991) 31,600. It is a railway junction; industries include chemicals, petroleum refining, and engineering. During the Seven Years' War, the Austrians defeated the Prussians at Kolín 1757, forcing them out of Bohemia.

Köln German form of ◊Cologne, a city in Germany.

Kołobrzeg (German *Kolberg*) Industrial port (shipyards) and seaside resort in Koszalin province, Poland, at the mouth of the river Parsęta on the Baltic Sea, 40 km/25 mi W of Koszalin; population (1990) 45,400. The town dates from the Middle Ages but was almost destroyed in World War II.

Kolwezi Mining town (copper and cobalt) in Shaba province, SE Democratic Republic of Congo (Zaire); population (1991 est) 544,500. In 1978 former police of the province invaded from Angola and massacred some 650 of the inhabitants.

Komárno (German *Komorn*, Hungarian *Komárom*) River port and border town in SW Slovak Republic, at the confluence of the rivers Váh and Danube; population (1991) 37,400. Textile manufacturing and shipbuilding are its chief industries. Formerly a strategic stronghold, until 1920 the port was part of Hungarian Komárom on the S bank; it remains connected by bridge.

Komi Autonomous republic of N central Russian Federation
area 415,900 sq km/160,579 sq mi
capital Syktyvkar
physical in basin of the Pechora River
industries livestock breeding, coal, oil, timber, gas, asphalt, building materials
population (1995) 1,202,000

Kommunizma, Pik or *Communism Peak* Highest mountain in the ◊Pamirs, a mountain range in Tajikistan; 7,495 m/24,599 ft. As part of the former USSR, it was known as *Mount Garmo* until 1933 and *Mount Stalin* 1933–62.

Komorn German name for ◊Komárno, a town in the Slovak Republic.

Komotau German name for ◊Chomutov, a town in the Czech Republic.

Kongur Shan Mountain peak in China, 7,719 m/25,325 ft high, part of the Pamir range (see ◊Pamirs). The 1981 expedition that first reached the summit was led by British climber Chris Bonington.

Königgratz German name for ◊Hradec Králové, a town in the Czech Republic.

Königinhof German name for ◊Dvúr Králové, a town in the Czech Republic.

Königsberg Former name of ◊Kaliningrad, a port in Russia.

Königswinter Town in North Rhine–Westphalia, Germany, on the river Rhine, 68 km/42 mi SE of Düsseldorf; population (1994) 36,600. It is virtually a suburb of ◊Bonn. Situated in the picturesque Siebengebirge area, Königswinter is a centre for leisure activities and tourism.

Konstanz German form of ◊Constance, a city in Germany.

Konya (Roman *Iconium*) City in SW central Turkey; population (1990) 513,300. Carpets and silks are made here, and the city contains the monastery of the dancing dervishes.

Koper Seaport in Slovenia, on the Istrian peninsula, 15 km/9 mi SW of Trieste; population (1991) 24,100. It stands on an island in the Gulf of Trieste and is connected with the mainland by a causeway. The town has saltworks and vehicle production, and trades in fish, oil, and wine. It was the capital of Istria 1278–1797, under Venetian and Genoan rule.

Korce Town and district of Albania, near the Greek border; population (1990) 65,400 (town); 218,200 (district). It is an industrial and commercial centre producing textiles and leather within the country's chief wheat-growing region. Korce is the principal town of S Albania.

Korcula Yugoslav island in the Adriatic Sea, part of the Dalmatian archipelago; area 277 sq km/107 sq mi; population (1995) 8,200. The principal town, also called Korcula, has a 15th-century cathedral.

Kordofan Former province of central Sudan, known as the 'White Land'; area 146,990 sq km/56,752 sq mi; population (1983) 3,093,300. It was divided 1994 into three new federal states: North, South, and West Kordofan (or Kurdofan). Although it has never been an independent state, it has a character of its own. It is mainly undulating plain, with acacia scrub producing gum arabic, marketed in the chief town ◊El Obeid. Formerly a rich agricultural region, it is threatened by desertification.

Korea Peninsula in E Asia, divided into N and S; see Korea, North, and Korea, South.

Korinthia Greek name for ◊Corinth, a department of Greece.

Korinthos Greek form of ◊Corinth, a port in Greece.

Körös (Romanian *Crisul*) River in Romania and Hungary, a tributary of the ◊Tisza; length 560 km/350 mi. It rises in the Bihor Mountains in three headstreams, which unite in the E Alföld (Great Plain of Hungary) before joining the Tisza at Csongrád. The length after the headstreams meet is about 193 km/120 mi.

Kortrijk Flemish form of ◊Courtrai, a town in Belgium.

Kos or *Cos* Fertile Greek island, one of the Dodecanese, in the Aegean Sea; area 287 sq km/111 sq mi. It gives its name to the Cos lettuce.

Kosciusko Highest mountain in Australia (2,229 m/7,316 ft), in New South Wales.

Košice City in the Slovak Republic; population (1991) 234,800 (92% Magyar-speaking). It has a textile industry and is a road centre. Košice was in Hungary until 1920 and 1938–45.

Kosovo or *Kossovo* Autonomous region 1945–1990 of S Serbia; capital Priština; area 10,900 sq km/4,207 sq mi; population (1991) 2,012,500, consisting of about 210,000 Serbs and about 1.8 million Albanians. Products include wine, nickel, lead, and zinc. Since it is largely inhabited by Albanians and bordering on Albania, there have been demands for unification with that country, while in the late 1980s Serbians agitated for Kosovo to be merged with the rest of Serbia. A state of emergency was declared Feb 1990 after fighting broke out between ethnic Albanians, police, and Kosovo Serbs. The parliament and government were dissolved July 1990 and the Serbian parliament formally annexed Kosovo Sept 1990.

Koszalin (German *Koslin*) Capital of Koszalin province, Poland, near the Baltic Sea coast, 200 km/125 mi N of Poznań; population (1990) 108,700. Industries include engineering, electronics, wood, and food processing.

Köszeg (German *Güns*) Town in Vas county, Hungary, near the Austrian border crossing, 17 km/11 mi N of Szom-bathely. Industries include textiles, flour, and distilling. The town has many 18th-century buildings and historic monuments.

Kota Baharu Capital of Kelantan, Malaysia; population (1991) 220,000. The local economy centres on fishing; there is also batik craft work.

Kota Kinabalu formerly (until 1968) *Jesselton* Capital and port in Sabah, Malaysia; population (1991) 208,000. Exports include rubber and timber. Originally named after Sir Charles Jessel of the Chartered Company which rebuilt the town, it is now named after Mount Kinabulu.

Köthen Town in the *Land* of ◊Saxony-Anhalt, Germany, 29 km/18 mi N of Halle. Sugar and textile industries are the main employers. The town was formerly the capital of the Duchy of Anhalt-Köthen, and the ducal palace is preserved.

Kotka Seaport in the S Finnish province of Kymi on the Gulf of Finland; population (1995) 56,000. Situated on two islands at the mouth of the river Kymi, it is a centre of the pulp and timber trade and the chief port for the exports and imports of E Finland.

Kotor Port in Montenegro, Yugoslavia, at the head of the Gulf of Kotor; population (1991) 36,700. It has been a naval base since Roman times. The town is situated at the foot of a cliff, facing the 32 km/20 mi gulf, surrounded by mountains.

Kottbus Alternative spelling of ◊Cottbus, a city in Germany.

Kourou River in French Guiana.

Kourou Second-largest town of French Guiana, NW of Cayenne, site of the Guiana Space Centre of the European Space Agency; population (1996) 20,000 (20% of the total population of French Guiana).

Kovno Russian form of ◊Kaunas, a port in Lithuania.

Kowloon Peninsula on the SE coast of China, formerly an administrative area of ◊Hong Kong. The city of Kowloon is a residential area. It is connected by rail to Canton.

Kragujevać Garrison city and former capital (1818–39) of Serbia, Yugoslavia; population (1991) 146,600.

Krajina Region on the frontier between Croatia and Bosnia-Herzegovina; the chief town is Knin. Dominated by Serbs, the region proclaimed itself an autonomous Serbian province after Croatia declared its independence from Yugoslavia 1991. Krajina was the scene of intense inter-ethnic fighting during the civil war in Croatia 1991–92 and, following the cease-fire Jan 1992, 10,000 UN troops were deployed here and in E and W Slavonia.

Krakatoa (Indonesian *Krakatau*) Volcanic island in Sunda Strait, Indonesia, that erupted 1883, causing 36,000 deaths on Java and Sumatra by the tidal waves that followed. The island is now uninhabited.

Kraków or *Cracow* City in Poland, on the river Vistula; population (1993) 751,300. It is an industrial centre producing railway wagons, paper, chemicals, and tobacco. It was capital of Poland about 1300–1595.

Kramatorsk Industrial city in E Ukraine, in the Donets Basin, N of Donetsk; population (1990) 199,000. Industries include coal-mining machinery, steel, ceramics, and railway repairs.

Krasnodar formerly (until 1920) *Ekaterinodar* Industrial city at the head of navigation of the river Kuban, in SW Russian Federation; population (1994) 638,000. It is linked by pipeline with the Caspian oilfields.

Krasnodar Territory of the SW Russian Federation, in the N Caucasus Mountains, adjacent to the Black Sea; area 83,600 sq km/32,290 sq mi; population (1991 est) 5,174,800. The capital is Krasnodar. In addition to stock rearing and the production of grain, rice, fruit, and tobacco, oil is refined.

Krasnoyarsk Industrial city (locomotives, paper, timber, cement, gold refining, and a large hydroelectric works) in the Russian Federation, in central Siberia; population (1994) 914,000. There is an early-warning and space-tracking radar phased array at nearby Abalakova.

Krasnoyarsk Territory of the Russian Federation in central Siberia stretching N to the Arctic Ocean; area 2,401,600 sq km/927,617 sq mi; population (1985) 3,430,000. The capital is Krasnoyarsk. It is drained by the Yenisey River. Mineral resources include gold, graphite, coal, iron ore, and uranium.

Krefeld Industrial city near the river Rhine; 52 km/32 mi NW of Cologne, in North Rhine–Westphalia, Germany; population (1993) 249,200. Industries include chemicals, textiles, and machinery. It is situated on the Westphalian coalfield.

Kremenchuk Industrial city on the river Dnieper, in central Ukraine; population (1992) 245,000. Manufacturing includes road-building machinery, railway wagons, and processed food.

Krems Austrian town in the province of Lower Austria, on the river Danube. It has a 13th-century Dominican church (now a museum). There is a trade in wine and fruit and the town manufactures preserves.

Kreuznach or *Bad Kreuznach* City and spa in the Rhineland-Palatinate, Germany, on the river Nahe, 15 km/9 mi S of Bingen; population (1994) 154,700. It is a wine-growing centre, and has optical and leather industries. Kreuznach was founded in Celtic times and the castle dates from the 14th century.

Kristiansand Seaport on the S coast of Norway; population (1995) 69,300. It is the county town of Vest-Agder, close to the Skagerrak arm of the North Sea. The third port of Norway, it is 280 km/174 mi SW of Oslo by sea. There are textile, timber, electrometallurgical, and electrochemical factories.

Kristianstad Capital of Kristianstad county, Sweden; population (1995) 27,000. It is situated E of Hålsingborg, 22 km/14 mi from the Baltic coast. Textiles are manufactured. There is a 17th-century church.

Krivoy Rog or *Kryvyy Rih* (Russian 'crooked horn') City in central Ukraine, 130 km/80 mi SW of Dnipropetrovsk; population (1992) 729,000. The surrounding district is rich in iron ore, and there is a metallurgical industry.

Kronoberg County of S Sweden; area 9,840 sq km/3,799 sq mi; population (1990) 174,100. The region is a mixture of rolling plateaux, woods, and extensive marshland. Industries include timber, glass, and paper production. The capital is Våxjö.

Kruger National Park Game reserve in Mpumalanga Province, South Africa, between the Limpopo and Crocodile rivers; it has an area of about 20,720 sq km/8,000 sq mi. The Sabie Game Reserve was established 1898 by President Kruger, and the park declared 1926.

Krugersdorp Mining city in the Witwatersrand district, Gauteng Province, South Africa; population (1985) 122,000. Manganese, uranium, and gold are mined.

Krusevac Town in Serbia, Yugoslavia, on the river Morava. It manufactures wine, tobacco, and munitions. Before 1389 it was the capital of the Serbian princes.

KS Abbreviation for ◊Kansas, a state of the USA.

Kuala Lumpur Capital of the Federation of Malaysia; area 240 sq km/93 sq mi; population (1991) 1,145,000. The city developed after 1873 with the expansion of tin and rubber trading; these are now its main industries. Formerly within the state of Selangor, of which it was also the capital, it was created a federal territory 1974.

Kuban River in E Europe, rising in Georgia and flowing through Russia to the Sea of Azov; length 906 km/563 mi.

Kuching Capital and port of Sarawak state, E Malaysia, on the Sarawak River; population (1991) 148,000.

Kufra Group of oases in the Libyan Desert, North Africa, SE of Tripoli. By the 1970s the vast underground reservoirs were being used for irrigation.

Kuibyshev or *Kuybyshev* former name (1935–91) of ◊Samara, Russia.

Kulmbach City in Bavaria, Germany, on the river Main, in the foothills of the ◊Fichtelgebirge, 20 km/12 mi NW of Bayreuth; population (1994) 77,800. It has breweries, and a massive 13th-century Hohenzollern fortress.

Kumamoto City on Kyushu Island, Japan, 80 km/50 mi E of Nagasaki; population (1994) 628,000. A military stronghold until the 19th century, the city is now a centre for fishing, food processing, and textile industries.

Kumasi Second largest city in Ghana, W Africa, capital of Ashanti region, with trade in cocoa, rubber, and cattle; its market is one of the largest in W Africa; population (1988 est) 385,200.

Kumayri Alternative spelling of ◊Gyumri, a city in Armenia

Kunlun Shan Mountain range on the edge of the great Tibetan plateau, China; 4,000 km/2,500 mi E–W; highest peak Muztag (7,282 m/23,900 ft).

Kunming formerly *Yunnan* Capital of Yunnan province, China, on Lake Dian Chi, about 2,000 m/6,500 ft above sea level; population (1993) 1,450,000. Industries include chem-

icals, textiles, and copper smelted with nearby hydroelectric power.

Kuopio Capital of Kuopio province in E central Finland. It produces timber, matches, and flour, and has distilleries. Situated on Lake Kallavesi, it is a tourist and sports centre. The town was founded 1782 by Gustavus III of Sweden, and has a university.

Kurdistan or *Kordestan* Hilly region in SW Asia near Mount Ararat, where the borders of Iran, Iraq, Syria, Turkey, Armenia, and Azerbaijan meet; area 193,000 sq km/74,600 sq mi; total population around 18 million. It is the home of the Kurds and the area over which Kurdish nationalists have traditionally fought to win sovereignty. Also the name of a NW Iranian province, covering 25,000 sq km/9,650 sq mi, population (1991) 1,233,500.

Kure Naval base and port 32 km/20 mi SE of Hiroshima, on the S coast of Honshu Island, Japan; population (1990) 216,700. Industries include shipyards and engineering works.

Kuria Muria Islands Group of five islands in the Arabian Sea, off the S coast of Oman; area 72 sq km/28 sq mi.

Kuril Islands or *Kuriles* Chain of about 50 small islands stretching from the NE of Hokkaido, Japan, to the S of Kamchatka, Russia; area 14,765 sq km/5,700 sq mi; population (1990) 25,000. Some of them are of volcanic origin. Two of the Kurils (Etorofu and Kunashiri) are claimed by both Japan and Russia; they are of strategic importance and also have mineral deposits.

Kursk Capital city of Kursk region of W Russian Federation; population (1994) 439,000. Industries include chemicals, machinery, alcohol, and tobacco. It dates from the 9th century.

Kūt-al-Imāra Alternative term for ◊al Kūt, a city in Iraq.

Kutch, Rann of Salt-marsh area in Gujarat state, India, that forms two shallow lakes (the *Great Rann* and the *Little Rann*) in the wet season and is a salt-covered desert in the dry. It takes its name from the former princely state of Kutch, which it adjoined. An international tribunal 1968 awarded 90% of the Rann of Kutch to India and 10% (about 800 sq km/300 sq mi) to Pakistan, the latter comprising almost all the elevated area above water the year round.

Kutno Town in Płock province, Poland, on the river Ochnia, 53 km/33 mi N of Łódź; population (1990) 123,400. Lignite is mined in the district, and industries include engineering, cement, soap, sugar, and flour production. It is a railway junction.

Kuwait (Arabic *Al Kuwayt*) formerly *Qurein* Chief port and capital of the state of Kuwait, on the S shore of Kuwait Bay; population (1993) 31,200. Kuwait is a banking and investment centre. It was heavily damaged during the Gulf War.

Kuznetsk Basin or *Kuzbas* Industrial area in Kemorovo region, in the Russian Federation, in E Siberia, lying on the Tom River N of the Altai Mountains; development began in the 1930s. It takes its name from the old town of Kuznetsk.

Kwa Ndebele Former black homeland in former Transvaal Province, South Africa; now partly in Mpumalanga and partly in Gauteng.

Kwangchow Alternative transliteration of ◊Guangzhou, a city in China.

Kwangju or *Kwangchu* Capital of South Cholla province, SW South Korea; population (1990) 1,144,700. It is at the centre of a rice-growing region. A museum in the city houses a large collection of Chinese porcelain dredged up 1976 after lying for over 600 years on the ocean floor.

Kwangsi-Chuang Alternative transliteration of ◊Guangxi, a region of China.

Kwangtung Alternative transliteration of ◊Guangdong, a province of China.

KwaZulu Former black homeland in former Natal Province, South Africa. In 1994 it became part of ◊KwaZulu-Natal Province. It achieved self-governing status 1971. In 1994 it was placed under a state of emergency in the run-up to the first multiracial elections, after mounting violence by the Zulu-based Inkatha party threatened to destabilize the election process. Homelands were to disappear progressively under the 1993 nonracial constitution, but Inkatha's leader (and the homeland's chief minister), Mangosuthu Buthelezi, won substantial concessions for KwaZulu prior to agreeing to participate in the elections.

KwaZulu-Natal Province of the Republic of South Africa, formed from the former province of Natal and the former independent homeland of KwaZulu

area 91,481 sq km/35,321 sq mi

capital Pietermaritzburg

towns and cities Durban, Richards Bay

features Ndumu Game Reserve; Kosi Bay Nature Reserve; Sodwana Bay National Park; Maple Lane Nature Reserve; St Lucia National Park, which extends from coral reefs of the Indian Ocean N of Umfolozi River (whales, dolphins, turtles, crayfish), over forested sandhills to inland grasslands and swamps of Lake St Lucia, 324 sq km/125 sq mi (reedbuck, buffalo, crocodiles, hippopotami, black rhinos, cheetahs, pelicans, flamingos, storks); it is under threat from titanium mining

industries oil refining, coal, iron and steel, sugar, maize, fruit, black wattle, maize, tobacco, vegetables

population (1995 est) 8,713,100; 75% Zulu

languages Zulu 80%, English 15%, Afrikaans 2%.

Kweichow Alternative transliteration of ◊Guizhou, a province of China.

Kweilin Alternative transliteration of ◊Guilin, a city in China.

Kwidzyń (German *Marienwerder*) Town in Elblâg province, Poland, near the river Vistula, 72 km/45 mi S of Gdańsk. The town was founded by the Teutonic Knights in 1233 in East Prussia. It was a medieval stronghold (a German Christian military order) and a catholic bisporic. It was assigned to Poland 1945.

KY Abbreviation for ◊Kentucky, a state of the USA.

Kymi Province in SE Finland, bordered to the E by the

Russian Federation, to the N by Mikkeli province, and to the S by the Gulf of Finland; area 10,736 sq km/4,145 sq mi. It is forested, with many lakes, including part of Lake Saimaa. Timber is the main industry and there is a hydroelectric power station at Imatra Falls. Kouvola is the capital; principal towns include the port of Kotka on the Gulf of Finland.

Kyoga Lake in central Uganda; area 4,425 sq km/1,709 sq mi. The Victoria Nile River passes through it.

Kyoto Former capital of Japan 794–1868 (when the capital was changed to Tokyo) on Honshu Island, linked by canal with Biwa Lake; population (1994) 1,391,000. Industries include electrical, chemical, and machinery plants; silk weaving; and the manufacture of porcelain, bronze, and lacquerware.

Kyrenia Port in Turkish-occupied Cyprus, about 20 km/12 mi N of Nicosia; population (1985) 7,000. The Turkish army landed at Kyrenia during the 1976 invasion, and the town was temporarily evacuated.

Kyushu Southernmost of the main islands of Japan, separated from Shikoku and Honshu islands by Bungo Channel and Suo Bay, but connected to Honshu by bridge and rail tunnel

area 42,154 sq km/16,276 sq mi, including about 370 small islands

capital Nagasaki

cities Fukuoka, Kumamoto, Kagoshima

physical mountainous, volcanic, with subtropical climate

features the active volcano Aso-take (1,592 m/5,225 ft), with the world's largest crater

industries coal, gold, silver, iron, tin, rice, tea, timber

population (1995) 13,424,000.

Kyustendil Town with hot springs in SW Bulgaria, SW of Sofia; population about 25,000.

Kyzyl-Kum Desert in Kazakhstan and Uzbekistan, between the Sur-Darya and Amu-Darya rivers; area about 259,000 sq km/100,000 sq mi. It is being reclaimed for cultivation by irrigation and protective tree planting.

LA Abbreviation for ◊Louisiana, a state of the USA; ◊Los Angeles, a city in California, USA.

Laâyoune (Arabic *El Aaiún*) Capital of Western Sahara; population (1982) 97,000. It has expanded from a population of 25,000 in 1970 as a result of Moroccan investment (Morocco lays claim to Western Sahara).

Labrador Area of NE Canada, part of the province of Newfoundland, lying between Ungava Bay on the NW, the Atlantic Ocean on the E, and the Strait of Belle Isle on the SE; area 266,060 sq km/102,699 sq mi; population (1991) 30,000. It consists primarily of a gently sloping plateau with an irregular coastline of numerous bays, fjords, inlets, and cliffs (60–120 m/200–400 ft high). Industries include fisheries, timber and pulp, and many minerals. Hydroelectric resources include Churchill Falls on Churchill River, where one of the world's largest underground power houses is situated. There is a Canadian air force base at ◊Goose Bay

Labuan Flat, wooded island off NW Borneo, a Federal Territory of East Malaysia; area 100 sq km/39 sq mi; population (1990) 54,300. Its chief town and port is Victoria, population 3,200. Labuan was ceded to Great Britain 1846, and from 1963 it was included in Sabah, a state of the Federation of Malaysia.

Laccadive, Minicoy, and Amindivi Islands Former name of the Indian island group ◊Lakshadweep.

La Ceiba Chief Atlantic port of Honduras; population (1991) 77,100. It exports fruit, especially bananas and pineapples.

Lachine City in Quebec, Canada, on Lake St Louis, 11 km/7 mi SW of Montréal; population (1991) 35,300. Steel bridges, wire, electrical apparatus, motors and equipment, and engines are manufactured. There is a canal link with Montréal, circumventing the *Lachine Rapids* of the St Lawrence River and forming part of the St Lawrence Seaway, which allows ocean-going vessels to navigate from Montréal to the Great Lakes.

Lachlan River that rises in the Blue Mountains, Australia; a tributary of the Murrumbidgee; length 1,485 km/920 mi.

La Condamine Commune of Monaco, SW of Monte Carlo. It is a seaside resort.

La Coruña Province of NW Spain in W ◊Galicia autonomous community; capital La Coruña; area 7,899 sq km/3,050 sq mi; population (1995) 1,136,300. Situated on the Atlantic coast, it includes Cape Finisterre, the most westerly point in Spain. Agriculture and industry are well developed, and the province is rich in minerals.

La Crosse City in SW Wisconsin, USA, at the confluence of the Black, La Crosse, and Mississippi rivers, NW of Madison; seat of La Crosse County; population (1992) 51,350. The processing and marketing centre for the area's agricultural products, it also manufactures plastics, rubber products, and electrical machinery.

The city began as a French trading post 1841 and grew as a lumber town. It was named Prairie La Crosse after the Native American game of lacrosse.

Ladakh Subsidiary range of the ◊Karakoram Mountains and district of NE Kashmir, India, on the border of Tibet; chief town Leh. After China occupied Tibet 1951, it made claims on the area.

Ladoga (Russian *Ladozhskoye Ozero*) Largest lake on the continent of Europe, in the Russian Federation, just NE of St Petersburg; area 17,695sq km/6,832 sq mi. It receives the waters of several rivers, including the Svir, which drains Lake Onega and runs to the Gulf of Finland by the river Neva.

Ladrones Spanish name (meaning 'thieves') of the ◊Mariana Islands.

Ladysmith Town in province of KwaZulu-Natal (formerly Natal), South Africa, 185 km/115 mi NW of Durban, near the Klip; population (1989 est) 56,600. It was besieged by the Boers, 2 Nov 1899–28 Feb 1900, during the South African War. Ladysmith was named in honour of the wife of Henry Smith, a British soldier and colonial administrator.

Lafayette City in W central Indiana, USA, on the Wabash River, NW of Indianapolis, seat of Tippecanoe County; pop-

ulation (1990) 43,760. A distribution centre for the area's agricultural products, its industries also include building materials, chemicals, wire, pharmaceuticals, and motor-vehicle parts. It was laid out 1825.

Lafayette City in S Louisiana, USA, on the Vermilion River, W of New Orleans and SW of Baton Rouge; seat of Lafayette parish; population (1992) 97,400. Its economy centres around the area's oil industry. Settled by Acadians from Nova Scotia in the late 1700s, Lafayette is in the heart of the area of Louisiana that is associated with French-speaking Cajuns.

Lagos Chief port and former capital of Nigeria, located at the W end of an island in a lagoon and linked by bridges with the mainland via Iddo Island; population (1992 est) 1,347,000. Industries include chemicals, metal products, and fish. Its surrounding waters are heavily polluted. One of the most important slaving ports, Lagos was bombarded and occupied by the British 1851, becoming the colony of Lagos 1862. Abuja was designated the new capital 1982 (officially recognized as such 1992).

Lahn River in Germany, a tributary of the ◊Rhine; length 217 km/135 mi. It rises in the Rothaargebirge, 15 km/9 mi E of Siegen, and flows to join the Rhine 9 km/6 mi S of Koblenz. The main cities on its banks are Marburg, Giessen, Wetzlar, and Limburg.

Lahore Capital of the province of Punjab and second city of Pakistan; population (1981) 2,920,000. Industries include engineering, textiles, carpets, and chemicals. It is associated with the Mogul rulers Akbar, Jahangir, and Aurangzeb, whose capital it was in the 16th and 17th centuries.

Lahti Town in S Finland, in SE Häme province; population (1995) 100,000. Timber, furniture, and domestic appliances are manufactured. It is a winter-sports resort with a huge ski jump.

Laibach German name of ◊Ljubljana, capital of Slovenia.

Lake Charles City in SW Louisiana, USA, on the Calcasieu River, SW of Baton Rouge, seat of Calcasieu parish; population (1992) 71,100. It is a port of entry on the Gulf of Mexico via a deep-water channel in the Calcasieu River. Most of the city's industries are related to the area's oil and gas resources and major crop, rice. It was settled 1781.

Lake District Region in Cumbria, England; area 1,800 sq km/700 sq mi. It contains the principal English lakes, which are separated by wild uplands rising to many peaks, including Scafell Pike (978 m/3,210 ft), the highest peak in England.

Lake Havasu City City in Arizona, USA, founded 1963 as a tourist resort. Old London Bridge was transported and reconstructed here 1971.

Lakeland City in W central Florida, USA, NE of Tampa and SW of Orlando, in the lake region and citrus belt; population (1992) 72,600. It serves as a centre for the area's citrus products, but its economy depends mainly on its reputation as a winter resort. It was founded 1883.

Lake of the Woods Lake in SW Ontario, Canada, on the border between Canada and the USA, extending into the province of Manitoba, Canada, and the state of Minnesota, USA; it lies between Lake Winnipeg and Lake Superior; area 4,860 sq km/1,876 sq mi. Its waters are 25 m/82 ft deep. The chief river flowing into the lake is the Rainy River, from the E.

Lakshadweep Group of 36 coral islands, 10 inhabited, in the Indian Ocean, 32 km/12 mi off the Malabar coast, forming a Union Territory of the Republic of India; area 32 sq km/12 sq mi; population (1994 est) 56,000. The administrative headquarters are on Kavaratti Island. Products include coir, copra, and fish. The religion is Muslim. The first Western visitor was Vasco da Gama 1499. The islands were British from 1877 until Indian independence (1947) and were created a Union Territory 1956. Formerly known as the *Laccadive, Minicoy, and Amindivi Islands,* they were renamed Lakshadweep 1973.

La Laguna Town in the ◊Canary Islands, in the Spanish province of Santa Cruz de Tenerife; population (1995) 127,700. Formerly the capital of Tenerife, it has fine streets of balconied houses, a cathedral, and a university.

La Línea Town and port on the isthmus of Algeciras Bay, S Spain, adjoining the frontier zone with Gibraltar; population (1991) 58,200.

La Louvière Town in the province of Hainaut, Belgium, 18 km/11 mi E of Mons. It has collieries, blast furnaces, and stone, lime, and moulding-clay quarries. The chief manufactures are iron, steel, glass, ceramics, and fireproof products.

La Mancha (Arabic *al mansha* 'the dry land') Former province of Spain, now part of the autonomous region of ◊Castilla–La Mancha. The fictional travels of Cervantes's *Don Quixote de la Mancha* 1605 begin here.

Lambeth Inner borough of S central Greater London. It includes the districts of Waterloo, Kennington, Clapham, Stockwell, and Brixton
features Lambeth Palace, chief residence of the archbishop of Canterbury since 1200, with brick Tudor gatehouse (1495); Tradescant museum of gardening history; the ◊South Bank, including Royal Festival Hall, Hayward Gallery, National Theatre, the Art Deco Oxo Wharf Tower (1928) now converted into mixed-use development; the Oval (headquarters of Surrey County Cricket Club from 1846) at Kennington, where the first England–Australia test match was played 1880; Old Vic theatre (1816–18); Brixton Prison; Anti-Slavery Archive in Brixton; Channel Tunnel rail terminal at Waterloo; London Aquarium opened 1997 in part of converted County Hall
population (1991) 244,800.

Lammermuir Hills Range of hills dividing East Lothian and Scottish Borders, Scotland, running from Gala Water to St Abb's Head. The highest point is Meikle Says Law (533 m/1,750 ft).

Lamu Island off the E coast of Kenya, 200 km/124 mi NE of Mombasa; population (1991 est) 12,000. The chief centre, Lamu, was formerly the focal point of a coastal city-state,

trading in ivory, cowries, spices, tortoiseshell, oil seed, and grain. The island's economy declined following the abolition of slavery 1907, but in recent years tourism has developed alongside traditional crafts such as dhow building.

Lanark Town in South Lanarkshire, Scotland; population (1991) 8,900. William Wallace once lived here, and later returned to burn the town and kill the English sheriff. *New Lanark* to the S was founded as a cotton-spinning centre and 'model community' by Robert Owen and Richard Arkwright at the end of the 18th century, with the aim of providing decent conditions for workers and their families.

Lanarkshire Former county of S Scotland, merged 1975–96 into Strathclyde Region; now part of North Lanarkshire and South Lanarkshire.

Lancashire County of NW England; Blackburn and Blackpool will become unitary authorities in April 1998
area 3,040 sq km/1,173 sq mi
towns and cities Preston (administrative headquarters), which forms part of Central Lancashire New Town from 1970 (together with Fulwood, Bamber Bridge, Leyland, and Chorley); Lancaster, Accrington, Blackburn, Burnley; ports Fleetwood and Heysham; seaside resorts Blackpool, Morecambe, and Southport
features the river Ribble; the Pennines; the Forest of Bowland (moors and farming valleys); Pendle Hill
industries formerly a world centre of cotton manufacture, now replaced with high-technology aerospace, nuclear fuels, and electronics industries. There is dairy farming and market gardening
population (1994) 1,424,000.

Lancaster City in Lancashire, England, on the river Lune; population (1991) 125,600. It was the former county town of Lancashire (now Preston). Industries include paper, furniture, plastics, chemicals, textiles, and floor coverings. A castle here, which incorporates Roman work, was captured by Cromwell during the Civil War. The Ruskin Library (1996) at the University of Lancaster houses a collection of works by John Ruskin.

Lancaster City in Pennsylvania, USA, 115 km/70 mi W of Philadelphia; population (1992) 57,200. It produces textiles and electrical goods. It was capital of the USA briefly 1777, and was the state capital 1799–1812.

Lanchow Alternative transcription of ◊Lanzhou, a city in China.

Lancs Abbreviation for ◊Lancashire, an English county.

Landau in der Pfalz City in the Rhineland-Palatinate, Germany, 35 km/22 mi NW of Karlsruhe; population (1994) 39,400. There are two Gothic churches. Landau is in the central Pfälzerwald and is a centre of trade in fruit, tobacco, and wine.

Landes Sandy, low-lying area in SW France, along the Bay of Biscay, about 12,950 sq km/5,000 sq mi in extent. Formerly covered with furze and heath, it has in many parts been planted with pine and oak forests. It gives its name to a *département* and extends into the *départements* of Gironde and Lot-et-Garonne. There is a testing range for rockets and missiles at Biscarosse, 72 km/45 mi SW of Bordeaux. There is an oilfield at Parentis-en-Born.

Landes *Département* in the ◊Aquitaine region of France, on the Bay of Biscay; area 9,236 sq km/3,566 sq mi; population (1990) 311,900. It is divided into two parts by the river Adour. The N part includes three-fifths of the *département* and is composed of tracts of heath and sand, interspersed with forests of pines and cork trees and numerous marshes, which gradually drain into the shallow lagoons that fringe the sea coast. The S part is hilly and covered with oak plantations and vineyards. The Adour valley has agriculture and food industries. Oil is drilled at Parentis. There are mineral springs at Dax, and rock salt is obtained there. The principal towns are Mont-de-Marsan (the capital) and Dax.

Landeshut German name of ◊Kamienna Góra, a town in Poland.

Landsberg Town in Bavaria, Germany, on the river Lech, 36 km/22 mi S of Augsburg; population (1994) 98,000. The town has a number of Gothic and Rococo churches.

Landsberg-an-der-Warthe German name for ◊Gorzów Wielkopolski, a town in Poland.

Land's End Promontory of W Cornwall, 15 km/9 mi WSW of Penzance, the westernmost point of England.

Landshut City in Bavaria, Germany, on the river Isar, 61 km/38 mi NE of Munich; population (1994) 59,400. Snuff, chocolate, beer, dyes, paints, and machinery are manufactured here. In the 14th century Landshut was the seat of the dukes of Bavaria-Landshut. There are several Gothic and Renaissance churches, a 14th-century *Rathaus* (town hall), and a Renaissance palace.

Landskrona Town and port in Sweden, on the ◊Sound, 32 km/20 mi N of Malmö; population (1990) 36,300. Industries include shipyards, machinery, chemicals, and sugar refining. Carl XI defeated the Danes off Landskrona 1677.

Langeland (English *Long Island*) Danish island in the Great Belt channel between the islands of Fyn and Lolland. It is 50 km/31 mi long and very narrow. Chief exports are corn, timber, dairy produce, and fish. The beaches attract holidaymakers. Rudkøbing on the W coast is the chief town.

Languedoc Former province of S France, bounded by the river Rhône, the Mediterranean Sea, and the regions of Guienne and Gascony.

Languedoc, Canal du Alternative name for the *Canal du Midi* (see ◊Midi, Canal du), a waterway in France.

Languedoc-Roussillon Region of S France, comprising the *départements* of Aude, Gard, Hérault, Lozère, and Pyrénées-Orientales; area 27,376 sq km/10,570 sq mi; population (1990) 114,900. Its capital is Montpellier, and products include fruit, vegetables, wine, and cheese.

Lansing Capital of Michigan, USA, at the confluence of the Grand and Red Cedar rivers; population (1992) 126,700. Manufacturing includes motor vehicles, diesel engines, and pumps. General Motors automobile plants are here, and Michigan State University is in the adjoining city of East Lansing. Lansing was settled in the 1840s and has been the state capital since 1847.

Lanzarote Most easterly of the Spanish Canary Islands; area 795 sq km/307 sq mi; capital Arrecife. The desertlike volcanic landscape is dominated by the Montañas de Fuego ('Mountains of Fire') with more than 300 volcanic cones.

Lanzhou or *Lanchow* Capital of Gansu province, China, on the river Huang He, 190 km/120 mi S of the Great Wall; population (1993) 1,320,000. Industries include oil refining, chemicals, fertilizers, and synthetic rubber.

Laois or *Laoighis* County of the Republic of Ireland, in the province of Leinster; county town Port Laoise; area 1,720 sq km/664 sq mi; population (1996 est) 52,800. It was formerly known as **Queen's County**. It is flat, except for the Slieve Bloom Mountains in the NW, and there are many bogs. Industries include sugar beet, dairy products, woollens, and agricultural machinery.

Laon Capital of Aisne *département*, Picardie, N France; 120 km/75 mi NE of Paris; population (1990) 28,700. It was the capital of France and a royal residence until the 10th century. It has a 12th-century cathedral.

La Palma One of the Spanish Canary Islands; see ◊Palma, La.

La Pampa Province in Argentina, characterized by the plains of the E pampas and salt marshes; population (1991) 260,000; area 143,400 sq km/55,367 sq mi; capital Santa Rosa. Industries include stock raising.

La Paz Capital city of Bolivia, in Murillo province, 3,800 m/12,400 ft above sea level; population (1992) 711,000 (metropolitan area 1,126,000). It is in a canyon formed by the La Paz river, and is the world's highest capital city. Products include textiles and copper. It has been the seat of government since 1898, but Sucre is the legal capital and seat of the judiciary.

Lapland Region of Europe within the Arctic Circle in Norway, Sweden, Finland, and the Kola Peninsula of NW Russia, without political definition. Its chief resources are chromium, copper, iron, timber, hydroelectric power, and tourism. The indigenous population are the Saami (formerly known as Lapps), 10% of which are nomadic, the remainder living mostly in coastal settlements. Lapland has low temperatures, with three months' continuous daylight in summer and three months' continuous darkness in winter. There is summer agriculture.

La Plata Capital of Buenos Aires province, Argentina; population (1991) 542,600; metropolitan area (1992 est) 676,100. Industries include meat packing and petroleum refining. It was founded 1882.

la Plata, Río de Estuary in South America; see ◊Plata, Río de la.

Lappi Northernmost province of Finland, encompassing Finnish ◊Lapland; area (excluding water) 93,860 sq km/ 36,329 sq mi. It lies within the Arctic Circle, and snow covers the ground Oct–May. Forestry, farming, and hydroelectricity are important in the economy, and it is fast developing into a tourist area. The administrative centre is ◊Rovaniemi. The town of Kemi at the top of the Gulf of Bothnia has lumber and pulp mills, and is a timber-shipping centre.

Laptev Sea Part of the Arctic Ocean off the N coast of Russia between Taimyr Peninsula and New Siberian Island.

L'Aquila Province of central Italy in NW ◊Abruzzi region; capital L'Aquila (population (1990) 67,800); area 5,035 sq km/1,944 sq mi; population (1992) 298,300.

Laramie Town in Wyoming, USA, on the Laramie Plains, a plateau 2,300 m/7,500 ft above sea level, bounded N and E by the Laramie Mountains; population (1990) 26,680. The *Laramie River*, on which it stands, is linked with the Missouri via the Platte. It is a commercial and transport centre for a ranching and lumber-producing area; its manufactures include cement and wood products. On the overland trail and Pony Express route, Fort Laramie, built 1834, features in the legend of the west. A rail line came through 1868, and Laramie was incorporated 1874.

Larderello Site in the Tuscan hills, NE Italy, where the sulphur springs were used by the Romans for baths and exploited for boric acid in the 18th–19th centuries. Since 1904 they have been used to generate electricity; the water reaches 220°C/396°F.

Laredo City on the Rio Grande, Texas, USA; population (1992) 136,500. Industries include oil refining and metal processing. Laredo was founded 1755. *Nuevo Laredo*, Mexico, on the opposite bank, is a textile centre; population (1990) 201,300. It was considered part of Laredo until the international border was established 1848. There is much cross-border trade.

La Rioja Region of N Spain; area 5,000 sq km/1,930 sq mi; population (1991) 263,400. The river Ebro passes through the region, but it is a tributary of the Río Oja, which gives its name to the region. The capital is Logroño. La Rioja is known for its red and white oaked wines.

Lárisa Town in Thessaly, Greece, S of Mount Olympus; population (1991) 113,400. Industries include textiles and agricultural produce.

Larne Seaport of County Antrim, Northern Ireland, on Lough Larne, terminus of sea routes to Stranraer, Liverpool, Dublin, and other places; population (1991) 17,500.

La Rochelle Fishing port in W France; population (1990) 73,700. It is the capital of Charente-Maritime *département*. Industries include shipbuilding, chemicals, and motor vehicles. A Huguenot stronghold, it was taken by Cardinal Richelieu in the siege of 1627–28.

La Roche-sur-Yon Capital of the French *département* of Vendée. It is situated on a plateau overlooking the Yon valley. The town was purpose-built by Napoleon I in 1804, on the site of the old fortress of La Roche, and was called first Napoleon-Vendée and later Bourbon-Vendée. It is a market town and horse-breeding centre, and has flour mills.

Las Alpujarras Mountainous district in the province of Granada, S Spain, lying to the S of the Sierra Nevada mountain range. In its fertile valleys, the Moors sought to retain their independence after the fall of Granada in 1492.

Las Cruces City in S New Mexico, on the Rio Grande, N of the Mexican border; population (1990) 62,120. It is a processing centre for the area's crops, such as pecans, cotton, and vegetables. White Sands Missile Range is nearby.

Lashio Town in N Myanmar (Burma), about 200 km/125 mi NE of Mandalay. The Burma Road to Kunming in China, constructed 1938, starts here.

Las Palmas or *Las Palmas de Gran Canaria* Tourist resort on the NE coast of Gran Canaria, Canary Islands; population (1994) 372,000. Products include sugar and bananas.

Las Palmas Province of Spain in the ◊Canary Islands autonomous community, comprising the islands of Gran Canaria, Lanzarote, and Fuerteventura; population (1995) 844,100.

La Spezia Port in NW Italy, chief Italian naval base; population (1992) 100,500. Industries include shipbuilding, engineering, electrical goods, and textiles. The English poet Percy Bysshe Shelley drowned in the Gulf of Spezia.

La Spezia Province of NW Italy in E ◊Liguria region; capital La Spezia; area 880 sq km/340 sq mi; population (1992) 226,600.

Las Vegas City in Nevada, USA, with many nightclubs and gambling casinos; population (1992) 295,500. Las Vegas entertains millions of visitors each year and is an important convention centre. Founded 1855 in a ranching area, the modern community developed with the coming of the railroad 1905. The first casino hotel opened 1947. Las Vegas is the easiest place to get married in the USA, with numerous chapels along the Strip (main street) and hotel chapels.

Latakia or *Lattakia* Port with tobacco industries in NW Syria; population (1993) 293,000.

Latina Province of Italy in SE ◊Lazio region; capital Latina (population (1990) 103,600); area 2,250 sq km/869 sq mi; population (1992) 478,800.

Latin America Large territory in the Western hemisphere S of the USA, consisting of Mexico, Central America, South America, and the West Indies. The main languages spoken are Spanish, Portuguese, and French.

Laugharne (Welsh *Talacharn*) Village at the mouth of the river Taf, Carmarthenshire, Wales. The home of the poet Dylan Thomas, it features in his work 'Under Milk Wood'.

Launceston Port in NE Tasmania, Australia, on the Tamar River; population (1991) 93,350. Founded 1805, its industries include woollen blanket weaving, sawmilling, engineering, furniture and pottery making, and railway workshops.

Laurahutte German name for ◊Siemianowice Śląskie, a town in Poland.

Lausanne Resort and capital of Vaud canton, W Switzerland, above the N shore of Lake Geneva; population (1990) 123,200. Industries include chocolate, scientific instruments, and publishing. There is a cathedral 1275 and university 1537. An Olympic Museum opened 1993.

Lauterbrunnen Commune and resort in the Swiss canton of Bern, 10 km/6 mi SE of Interlaken, in the ◊Bernese Alps; population (1995) 3,000. Lacemaking is an important industry.

La Vendée French river; see ◊Vendée, La.

Lawrence City in NE Kansas, USA, on the Kansas River between Topeka to the W and Kansas City to the E; seat of Douglas County; population (1992) 67,800. Its main industries are food processing and chemicals. Lawrence was founded 1854 by antislavery campaigners, who wanted to make Kansas a nonslavery state.

Lawrence Town in Massachusetts, USA; population (1992) 65,500. Industries include textiles, clothing, paper, and radio equipment. The town was established 1845 to utilize power from the Merrimack Rapids on a site first settled 1655.

Lawton City in SW Oklahoma, USA, on Cache Creek, SW of Oklahoma City, seat of Comanche County; population (1992) 87,200. Processing the area's agricultural products is the city's main industry. Fort Sill, an army base, is to the N. The site was settled by Native Americans 1869. The city was founded 1901 near the fort.

Lazio (Roman *Latium*) Region of W central Italy; area 17,203 sq km/6,642 sq mi; capital Rome; population (1995 est) 5,193,200. Products include olives, wine, chemicals, pharmaceuticals, and textiles. Home of the Latins from the 10th century BC, it was dominated by the Romans from the 4th century BC.

Lea River that rises N of Luton, Bedfordshire, England, and joins the river Thames at Blackwall; length 74 km/46 mi. It is the source of much of London's water supply.

Leamington officially *Royal Leamington Spa* Town and health resort in the West Midlands, England, on the river Leam, adjoining Warwick; population (1991) 55,400. The Royal Pump Room offers spa treatment. The first tennis club started here 1872. Industries include engineering.

Leatherhead Town in Surrey, England, SW of London, on the river Mole at the foot of the North Downs; population (1991) 42,900. It has industrial research stations, the Thorndike Theatre (1968), and the Royal School for the Blind (1799). Industries include engineering and electrical goods.

Leavenworth City in Kansas, central USA, on the Missouri River, 32 km/20 mi NW of Kansas City; population (1991) 38,800. Leavenworth was one of the chief river ports and fitting-out centres in the 19th-century colonization of the USA. It is now popular with outdoors enthusiasts. Fort Leavenworth is nearby.

Lebanon City in SE Pennsylvania, USA, NE of Harrisburg, seat of Lebanon County; population (1990) 24,800. Industries include iron and steel products, textiles, clothing, and chemicals. It was settled by German immigrants in the 1720s, and the city laid out 1756. Because of the nearby iron mines, it developed as an iron centre.

Lebda Former name of ◊Homs, a city in Syria.

Lebowa Former black homeland in former Transvaal Province, South Africa, now in Northern Transvaal. It achieved self-governing status 1972.

Lecce Province of SE Italy in E ◊Puglia region; capital Lecce (population (1990) 102,300); area 2,758 sq km/1,065 sq mi; population (1992) 806,700.

Lech River in Austria and Germany; length 270 km/168 mi. The Lech rises in the Lechtaler Alps in the province of Vorarlberg, and flows N across the W Tirol, past Augsburg, to join the ◊Danube E of Donauwörth.

Leeds Industrial city in West Yorkshire, England, on the river Aire; population (1994 est) 529,000. Industries include engineering, printing, chemicals, glass, woollens, clothing, plastics, paper, metal goods, and leather goods. Notable buildings include the Town Hall designed by Cuthbert Brodrick, Leeds University (1904), the Art Gallery (1844), Temple Newsam museum (early 16th century, altered about 1630), and the Cistercian Abbey of Kirkstall (1147). It is a centre of communications where roads, rail, and canal (to Liverpool and Goole) meet.

Leer City and river port in Lower Saxony, Germany, at the confluence of the rivers Ems and Leda, 175 km/108 mi NW of Hannover; population (1994) 152,100. There are foodstuff, textile, and typewriter assembly industries here. The city has an old castle and churches.

Leeuwarden City in the Netherlands, on the Ee River; population (1993) 86,800. It is the capital of Friesland province. A marketing centre, it also makes gold and silver ware. After the draining of the Middelzee fenlands, the town changed from a port to an agricultural market town. Notable buildings include the palace of the stadholders of Friesland and the church of St Jacob.

Leeward Islands (1) group of islands, part of the ◊Society Islands, in ◊French Polynesia, S Pacific; (2) general term for the N half of the Lesser ◊Antilles in the West Indies; (3) former British colony in the West Indies (1871–1956) comprising Antigua, Montserrat, St Kitts and Nevis, Anguilla, and the Virgin Islands.

Leghorn Former English name for the Italian port ◊Livorno.

Legnica (German *Liegnitz*) Capital of Legnica province, Poland, 64 km/40 mi W of Wrocław; population (1990) 105,200. Lead is refined from local mines, and cables, textiles, and chemicals are manufactured. Formerly in Lower Silesia, it was the capital of the Duchy of Liegnitz 1163–1675, passing to the Habsburg family before joining Prussia 1742 and then Poland 1945.

Leh Capital of Ladakh region, E Kashmir, India, situated E of the river Indus, 240 km/150 mi E of Srinagar. Leh is the nearest supply base to the Indian army outpost on the Siachen Glacier.

Le Havre Industrial port (engineering, chemicals, oil refining) in Normandy, NW France, on the river Seine; population (1990) 197,200. It is the largest port in Europe, and has transatlantic passenger links.

Lehigh River in E central Pennsylvania, E USA, a tributary of the ◊Delaware; length 193 km/120 mi. It rises in the Pocono Mountains; its lower valley is an industrial area and is occupied by the towns of Allentown, Bethlehem, and Easton, where more than 1,000 industrial plants manufacture a wide range of products. Lehigh meets the Delaware at Easton.

Leicester Industrial city and unitary authority in central England, on the river Soar; it is also the administrative headquarters of Leicestershire; population (1996 est) 270,500; area 73 sq km/28 sq mi. It was part of the county of Leicestershire to 1997. Industries include food processing, hosiery, footwear, knitwear, engineering, electronics, printing, and plastics.

Leicestershire County of central England
area 2,084 sq km/804 sq mi
towns and cities Leicester (administrative headquarters), Loughborough, Melton Mowbray, Market Harborough
features river Soar; Rutland district (formerly England's smallest county, with Oakham as its county town); Rutland Water, one of Europe's largest reservoirs; Charnwood Forest; Vale of Belvoir (under which are large coal deposits)
industries horses, cattle, sheep, dairy products, coal, Stilton cheese, hosiery, footwear, bell founding
population (1996) 592,700
famous people Titus Oates, Thomas Babington Macaulay, C P Snow
history Richard III was defeated by Henry VII at the Battle of Bosworth 1485.

Leics Abbreviation for ◊Leicestershire, an English county.

Leiden or *Leyden* City in South Holland province, the Netherlands; population (1994) 114,900. Industries include textiles and cigars. It has been a printing centre since 1580, with a university established 1575. It is linked by canal to Haarlem, Amsterdam, and Rotterdam. The painters Rembrandt and Jan Steen were born here.

Leie Alternative name for the river ◊Lys of France and Belgium.

Leinster Southeastern province of the Republic of Ireland, comprising the counties of Carlow, Dublin, Kildare, Kilkenny, Laois, Longford, Louth, Meath, Offaly, Westmeath, Wexford, and Wicklow; area 19,630 sq km/7,577 sq mi; capital Dublin; population (1991) 1,860,000.

Leipzig City in W Saxony, Germany, 145 km/90 mi SW of Berlin; population (1993) 494,200. Products include furs, leather goods, cloth, glass, cars, and musical instruments.

Leith Port in City of Edinburgh unitary authority, Scotland, S of the Firth of Forth, incorporated in Edinburgh 1920. Leith was granted to Edinburgh as its port by Roberte Bruce 1329.

Leitrim County of the Republic of Ireland, in the province of Connacht, bounded NW by Donegal Bay; county town Carrick-on-Shannon; area 1,530 sq km/590 sq mi; population (1996 est) 25,000. The rivers Shannon, Bonet, Drowes, and Duff run through it. Industries include potatoes, cattle, linen, woollens, pottery, coal, iron, lead, sheep, and oats.

Leix Former spelling, used 1922–35, of ◊Laois, a county of Ireland.

Lelystad New town in the NW of East Flevoland; population (1996) 60,600. Having been rapidly populated by overspill from Amsterdam and surrounding conurbations, Lelystad serves mainly as a dormitory town for these cities. Some light industry has developed locally and the town is the main service centre for the S ◊IJsselmeer polder region.

Léman, Lac French name for Lake ◊Geneva, in Switzerland.

Le Mans Industrial city in Sarthe *département*, W France; population (1990) 148,500, conurbation 191,000. It has a motor-racing circuit where the annual endurance 24-hour race (established 1923) for sports cars and their prototypes is held.

Lemberg German name of ◊Lviv, a city in Ukraine.

Lemnos (Greek *Límnos*) Greek island in the N of the Aegean Sea
area 476 sq km/184 sq mi
towns Kastron, Mudros
physical of volcanic origin, rising to 430 m/1,411 ft
industries mulberries and other fruit, tobacco, sheep
population (1981) 15,700.

Lena Longest river in Asiatic Russia, 4,400 km/2,734 mi, with numerous tributaries. Its source is near Lake Baikal, and it empties into the Arctic Ocean through a delta 400 km/240 mi wide. It is ice-covered for half the year.

Leninakan Former name (to 1990) of ◊Gyumri, a town in Armenia.

Leningrad Former name (1924–91) of the Russian city ◊St Petersburg.

Leninsk-Kuznetsky Town in Kemerovo region, in the Russian Federation, in Siberia, on the Inya River, 320 km/200 mi SE of Tomsk; population (1990) 134,000. It is a mining centre in the Kuznetsk Basin, with a large iron and steel works; coal, iron, manganese, other metals, and precious stones are mined in the area. Formerly *Kolchugino*, the town was renamed Leninsk-Kuznetsky 1925.

Lens Coal-mining town in Pas-de-Calais, France; population (1990) 35,300, conurbation 327,000. During World War I it was in German occupation and close to the front line Oct 1914–Oct 1918, when the town and its mines were so severely damaged that mining operations could not restart until 1921. In World War II it was occupied by Germany, May 1940–Sept 1944, but suffered less physical damage.

Leominster City in N central Massachusetts, USA, on the Nashua River, NE of Worcester; population (1990) 38,140. Industries include plastics, paper products, clothing, and chemicals. The site was bought from Native Americans 1701, and incorporated as a town 1740.

León Province of NW Spain in N Castilla-León autonomous community; capital León; area 15,467 sq km/5,972 sq mi; population (1995) 532,700. It is bounded by the Cantabrian Mountains in the N and W. The Montes de León in the W separate the basins of the rivers Duero and Miño. In the S and E are plains which form part of the Castilian plateau. Sheep-rearing and agriculture are important, and coal and iron are mined.

León City in Castilla-León, Spain; population (1994) 147,000. It was the capital of the kingdom of León from the 10th century until 1230, when it was merged with Castile.

León Industrial city (leather goods, footwear) in central Mexico; population (1990) 956,100.

León City in W Nicaragua; population (1991 est) 158,600. Industries include textiles and food processing. Founded 1524, it was the capital of Nicaragua until 1855.

Léopoldville Former name (to 1966) of ◊Kinshasa, a city in the Democratic Republic of Congo (formerly Zaire).

Le Puy Capital of Haute-Loire *département*, Auvergne, SE France; population (1990) 23,400. It is dramatically situated on a rocky plateau, and has a 12th-century cathedral.

Lérida (Catalan *Lleida*) Capital of Lérida province, N Spain, on the river Segre; 132 km/82 mi W of Barcelona; population (1994) 114,000. Industries include leather, paper, glass, and cloth. Lérida was captured by the Roman general Julius Caesar 49 BC. It has a palace of the kings of Aragón.

Lérida Province of NE Spain in NW ◊Cataluña autonomous community; capital Lérida; area 12,028 sq km/4,644 sq mi; population (1995) 360,400. It borders France and Andorra in the N, and stretches from the Pyrenees to the river Ebro. The lowlands have been irrigated by means of canals, and produce large quantities of fruit. Exports include wine, wool, and cattle. There are also textile industries.

Lérins, Iles de Group of four small islands in the Mediterranean, 4 km/2 mi S of Cannes, in the French *département* of Alpes-Maritimes. Alexandre Dumas's story 'The Man in the Iron Mask', from his book *Le Vicomte de Bragelonne* 1848–50, was set on the island of St-Marguerite. Marshal Bazaine was also confined there. St-Honorat has a 5th-century monastery.

Lerwick Port in Shetland, Scotland; population (1991) 7,300. It is the administrative headquarters of Shetland. Main occupations include fishing and oil supply services. Hand-knitted shawls are a speciality. A Viking tradition survives in the Jan festival of Up-Helly-Aa when a replica of a longship is burned.

Lesbos Alternative spelling of ◊Lesvos, an island in the Aegean Sea.

Leskovac Town in Serbia, Yugoslavia, on the river Veternica. It is the centre of the Yugoslav textile industry, and is a market town for hemp and other produce of the fertile surrounding district.

Lesser Sunda Islands or *Nusa Tenggara* Volcanic archipelago in Indonesia, including ◊Bali, ◊Lombok, and ◊Timor; area 73,144 sq km/28,241 sq mi. The islands form two provinces of Indonesia: *Nusa Tenggara Barat*, population (1990) 3,369,600; and *Nusa Tenggara Timur*, population (1990) 3,268,600.

Lesvos Greek island in the Aegean Sea, near the coast of Turkey
area 2,154 sq km/831 sq mi
capital Mytilene
industries olives, wine, grain
population (1991) 103,700
history ancient name Lesbos; an Aeolian settlement, the home of the poets Alcaeus and Sappho; conquered by the Turks from Genoa 1462; annexed to Greece 1913.

Leszno (German *Lissa*) Capital of Leszno province, Poland, 65 km/41 mi S of Poznań; population (1990) 58,300. It is an industrial town manufacturing rolling stock and machinery; lignite is mined locally.

Letchworth Town in Hertfordshire, England, 56 km/35 mi NW of London; population (1991) 31,400. It was founded 1903 as the first English garden city (built in a rural area, designed to combine the advantages of the town and the country). Industries include clothing, furniture, scientific instruments, light metal goods, rubber, and printing.

Lethbridge City in S Alberta, Canada, 200 km/120 mi S of Calgary; population (1991) 61,000. Lying in the foothills of the Rocky Mountains, on the Oldman River, it is the centre of a large agricultural area and irrigation network, and industries include vegetable canning and freezing, flour-milling, brewing, coal, gas, and oil production.

Le Touquet Resort in N France, at the mouth of the river Canche; it was fashionable in the 1920s–1930s.

Leukas or *Levkas* (Greek 'white land') One of the ◊Ionian Islands of Greece, 80 km/50 mi SE of Corfu; area 293 sq km/113 sq mi; population (1993) 21,400. The main products are olive oil, currants, and wine. The principal town, Leukas, at the NE corner, is capital of the Leukas department.

Leuven Flemish form of ◊Louvain, Belgium.

Levant Former name for the E Mediterranean region, or more specifically, the Mediterranean coastal regions of Turkey, Syria, Lebanon, and Israel.

Leven Town in Fife, Scotland, at the mouth of the river Leven, where it meets the Firth of Forth; population (1991) 8,300. It has timber, paper, and engineering industries.

Leven, Loch Lake in Perth and Kinross, Scotland; area 16 sq km/6 sq mi. It is drained by the river Leven, and has seven islands; Mary Queen of Scots was imprisoned 1567–68 on Castle Island. It has been a national nature reserve since 1964. Leven is also the name of a sea loch in Highland unitary authority, Scotland.

Leverkusen River port in North Rhine-Westphalia, Germany, 8 km/5 mi N of Cologne; population (1993) 161,900. It has iron, steel, and chemical industries.

Lewes Market town (administrative headquarters) in E Sussex, England, on the river Ouse; population (1991) 15,400. There is light engineering, brewing, and printing. The Glyndebourne Festival Opera is held nearby, and a new opera house was opened 1994. Simon de Montfort defeated Henry III here 1264; there is a house which once belonged to Anne of Cleves, and a castle. The town is known for its 5th Nov celebrations.

Lewis Largest island in the Outer Hebrides; area 2,220 sq km/857 sq mi; population (1991) 21,700. Its main town is Stornoway. It is separated from NW Scotland by the Minch. There are many lakes and peat moors.

Lewisham Inner borough of SE Greater London. It includes the suburbs of ◊Blackheath, Sydenham, Catford, and ◊Deptford
features Deptford shipbuilding yard (1512–1869); Armoury Mill produced steel for armour in the 16th century, musket barrels in the Napoleonic Wars, and gold and silver thread for Victorian uniforms
population (1991) 215,300
famous people birthplace of James Elroy Fletcher; home of Samuel Smiles, Arthur Sullivan, W G Grace, Ernest Dowson, Ernest Shackleton.

Lewiston City in SW Maine, USA, across the Andros-coggin River from Auburn; population (1990) 39,750. It has textile, shoe, and clothing industries. Bates College (1855) is here. The town was settled 1770.

Lexington or *Lexington–Fayette* Town in Kentucky, USA, centre of the bluegrass country; population (1992) 232,600. Racehorses are bred in the area, and races and shows are held. There is a tobacco market and the University of Kentucky (1865).

Lexington Town in Massachusetts, USA; population (1990) 28,970. Industries include printing and publishing. The Battle of Lexington and Concord, 19 April 1775, opened the American Revolution.

Leyden Alternative form of ◊Leiden, a city in the Netherlands.

Leyland Industrial town in Lancashire, England; population (1991) 37,300. Industries include motor vehicles, paint, and rubber. The headquarters of Leyland Trucks is here.

Lhasa ('the Forbidden City') Capital of the autonomous region of Tibet, China, at 5,000 m/16,400 ft; population (1992) 124,000. Products include handicrafts and light industry. The holy city of Lamaism, Lhasa was closed to Westerners until 1904, when members of a British expedition led by Col Francis E Younghusband visited the city. It was annexed with the rest of Tibet 1950–51 by China, and the spiritual and temporal head of state, the Dalai Lama, fled 1959 after a popular uprising against Chinese rule. Monasteries have been destroyed and monks killed, and an influx of Chinese settlers has generated resentment. In 1988

and 1989 nationalist demonstrators were shot by Chinese soldiers.

Liao River in NE China, frozen Dec–March; the main headstream rises in the mountains of Inner Mongolia and flows E, then S to the Gulf of Liaodong; length 1,450 km/900 mi.

Liaoning Province of NE China
area 151,000 sq km/58,301 sq mi
capital Shenyang
towns Anshan, Fushun, Liaoyang
features one of China's most heavily industrialized areas
industries cereals, coal, iron, salt, oil
population (1990) 39,980,000
history developed by Japan 1905–45, including the *Liaodong Peninsula*, whose ports had been conquered from the Russians.

Liaoyang Industrial city (engineering, textiles) in Liaoning province, China; population (1986) 1,612,000.

Libau German name of the Latvian port ◊Liepāja.

Liberec (German *Reichenberg*) Industrial town in N Bohemia, in the Czech Republic, on the river Neisse near the Polish and German borders; population (1991) 101,900. It has engineering works and manufactures chemicals, textiles, and glass.

Liberty Island Rocky island in New York Harbor, USA, the site since 1886 of the 92-m/302-ft Statue of Liberty. It is 40 sq km/15 sq mi, and lies 4 km/2.5 mi S of Manhattan Island, with which it is connected by ferry. Until 1956 the island was called Bedloe's Island, after Isaac Bedloe, who had bought it in the 17th century. It was taken over by New York in 1758 and given to the federal government in 1798.

Liberty, Statue of Monument on Liberty Island in New York harbour. The 92-m/302-ft statue was presented to the US people by the French and dedicated in 1886, marking the centenary of American Independence and commemorating the alliance between the USA and France during the War of Independence. The statue, by the French sculptor Frédéric-Auguste Bartholdi and designed by Gustave Eiffel, represents a woman holding a fiery torch in her upraised right hand and a tablet inscribed with '4 July 1776' (the date of American Independence) in her left. It was declared a national monument in 1924.

Libreville (French 'free town') Capital of Gabon, on the estuary of the river Gabon; population (1992) 352,000. Products include timber, oil, and minerals. It was founded 1849 as a refuge for slaves freed by the French. Since the 1970s the city has developed rapidly due to the oil trade.

Lichfield Town in the Trent Valley, Staffordshire, England; population (1987 est) 28,300. The cathedral, 13th–14th century, has three spires. The writer Samuel Johnson was born here.

Liège (Flemish *Luik*) Industrial city (weapons, textiles, paper, chemicals), capital of Liège province in Belgium, SE of Brussels, on the river Meuse; population (1995) 192,000. The province of Liège has an area of 3,900 sq km/1,505 sq mi and a population (1995) of 1,015,000.

Liegnitz German name for ◊Legnica, a town in Poland.

Lienz Chief town and market centre for the E ◊Tirol in Austria, situated on the river Drava. Lienz is a tourist resort with some manufacturing industry. It stands on the site of a former Illyrian settlement and Roman township.

Liepāja (German *Libau*) Naval and industrial port in Latvia; population (1995) 100,000. The Knights of Livonia founded Liepāja in the 13th century. Industries include steel, engineering, textiles, and chemicals.

Lier (French *Lierre*) Town in the province of Antwerp, Belgium, situated on the river Nethe near the city of Antwerp. The chief manufactures are shoes, lace, embroideries, instruments of brass, and cutlery. There are several medieval buildings.

Liffey River in the E Republic of Ireland, flowing from the Wicklow Mountains to Dublin Bay; length 80 km/50 mi.

Liguria Coastal region of NW Italy, which includes the resorts of the Italian Riviera, lying between the W Alps and the Mediterranean Gulf of Genoa. The region comprises the provinces of Genova, La Spezia, Imperia, and Savona, with a population (1995) of 1,663,700 and an area of 5,416 sq km/2,091 sq mi. Genoa is the chief city and port.

Lille (Flemish *Ryssel*) Industrial city (textiles, chemicals, engineering, distilling), capital of Nord-Pas-de-Calais, France, on the river Deûle; population (1990) 178,300, metropolitan area 936,000. The world's first entirely automatic underground system was opened here 1982. The Eurostar train stops here, at the new Eurolille station.

Lilongwe Capital of Malawi since 1975, on the Lilongwe River; population (1993) 268,000. Products include tobacco and textiles. Capital Hill, 5 km/3 mi from the old city, is the site of government buildings and offices.

Lima Capital of Peru, an industrial city (textiles, chemicals, glass, cement) on the Rimac River, with its port at Callao; population (1993) 5,706,100.

Lima City in NW Ohio, USA, on the Ottawa River, N of Dayton; seat of Allen County; population (1990) 45,550. Industries include motor vehicle and aircraft parts, heavy machinery, electrical products, and oil processing. Lima was laid out 1831 and became the centre of oil fields.

Limassol Port in S Cyprus in Akrotiri Bay; population (1993) 137,000. Products include cigarettes and wine. Richard I of England married Berengaria of Navarre here 1191. The town's population increased rapidly with the influx of Greek Cypriot refugees after the Turkish invasion 1974.

Limbourg Province of N Belgium, bounded N and E by the Netherlands
area 2,422 sq km/935 sq mi
population (1995) 771,600
capital Hasselt
towns Genk, Tongeren
industries sugar refining, food processing
physical river Demer; Kempen heathland in the N; rich coalfields; agriculture in the S

history The province was formerly part of the feudal duchy of Limburg (which was divided 1839 into today's Belgian and Dutch provinces).

Limburg Southernmost province of the Netherlands, on the river Maas (Meuse); capital Maastricht; area 2,170 sq km/838 sq mi; population (1995 est) 1,130,050. Industries include chemicals, cement, fertilizer; mixed arable farming and horticulture are also important. The former coal industry is still remembered at Kerkrade, alleged site of the first European coal mine. A monument marks the *Drielandenpunt*, where the Dutch, German, and Belgian borders meet.

Limburg an der Lahn City in the *Land* of Hessen, Germany, 35 km/22 mi NW of Wiesbaden. Limburg has a Romanesque cathedral with seven towers. Iron was formerly mined in the district and there are now machinery, textile, glass, and leather industries.

Limehouse District in E London; part of ◊Tower Hamlets. It takes its name from the kilns which preceded shipping as the main industry. In the 1890s it was the home of Chinese sailors working from the West India Docks. Bomb damage during World War II led to a decline in population, especially after closure of the docks.

Limerick County of the Republic of Ireland, in the province of Munster; county town Limerick; area 2,690 sq km/1,038 sq mi; population (1996 est) 177,900. The land is fertile, with hills in the S. Industries include dairy products, lace, and hydroelectric power.

Limerick County town of Limerick, Republic of Ireland, the main port of W Ireland, on the Shannon estuary; population (1991) 52,000. It was founded in the 12th century. Industries include flour milling, tanning, and brewing.

Limoges City and capital of Limousin, France; population (1990) 136,400. Fine enamels were made here in the medieval period, and it is the centre of the modern French porcelain industry. Other industries include textiles, electrical equipment, and metal goods. The city was sacked by the Black Prince, the eldest son of Edward III of England, 1370.

Limousin Former province and modern region of central France; area 16,942 sq km/6,541 sq mi; population (1990) 722,900. It consists of the *départements* of Corrèze, Creuse, and Haute-Vienne. The chief town is Limoges. A thinly populated and largely infertile region, it is crossed by the mountains of the Massif Central. Fruit and vegetables are produced in the more fertile lowlands. Kaolin is mined.

Limpopo River in SE Africa, rising in the Transvaal and reaching the Indian Ocean in Mozambique; length 1,600 km/1,000 mi.

Linares Town in the province of Jaén, S Spain; population (1995) 61,700. It has rich mines of lead and copper mixed with silver. Sheet lead, pipes, rope, vehicles, and explosives are manufactured. Nearby are the ruins of the Roman town of Castulo.

Lincoln Industrial city in Lincolnshire, England; population (1991) 82,000. Manufacturing includes excavators, cranes, gas turbines, radios, vehicle components, cattle feed, pharmaceuticals, power units for oil platforms, and cosmetics. Under the Romans it was the flourishing colony of *Lindum*, and in the Middle Ages it was a centre for the wool trade. Paulinus built a church here in the 7th century, and the 11th–15th-century cathedral has the earliest Gothic work in Britain. The 12th-century High Bridge is the oldest in Britain still to have buildings on it.

Lincoln Industrial city and capital of Nebraska, USA; population (1992) 197,500. Industries include engineering, pharmaceuticals, electronic and electrical equipment, and food processing. It was known as Lancaster until 1867, when it was renamed after Abraham Lincoln and designated the state capital.

Lincolnshire County of E England
area 5,890 sq km/2,274 sq mi
towns and cities Lincoln (administrative headquarters), Skegness
features Lincoln Wolds; marshy coastline; the Fens in the SE; rivers: Witham, Welland; 16th-century Burghley House; Belton House, a Restoration mansion; Gibralter Point National Nature Reserve
industries cattle, sheep, horses, cereals, flower bulbs, oil, vegetables
population (1994) 605,600
famous people Isaac Newton, John Wesley, Alfred Tennyson, Margaret Thatcher.

Lincs Abbreviation for ◊Lincolnshire, an English county.

Lindau City in Bavaria, Germany, built partly on a small island in Lake ◊Constance, but linked by road and rail to the NE shore; population (1994) 75,500. With many buildings from its rich medieval history, Lindau is a tourist resort and a principal port of call for lake traffic. The city produces electrical goods and rubber.

Lindisfarne Site of a monastery off the coast of Northumberland, England; see ◊Holy Island.

Line Islands Group of coral islands in the Pacific Ocean; population (1990) 4,800. Products include coconut and guano. Eight of the islands belong to Kiribati, and three (Palmyra, Jarvis, and Kingman Reef) are uninhabited dependencies of the USA.

Lingen City in Lower Saxony, Germany, on the river Ems, 65 km/40 mi NW of Münster; population (1994) 52,300. Lingen is a centre for oil refining and natural-gas production from local wells, and also contains chemical, steel, and clothing industries. One of Germany's largest nuclear power stations is located nearby.

Linköping Industrial town in SE Sweden; 172 km/107 mi SW of Stockholm; population (1994) 130,500. Industries include hosiery, aircraft and engines, and tobacco. It has a 12th-century cathedral.

Linlithgow Tourist centre in West Lothian, Scotland; population (1991) 11,900. Linlithgow Palace, now in ruins, was once a royal residence, and Mary Queen of Scots was born there.

Linlithgowshire Former name of the county of West Lothian, Scotland, which was part of Lothian Region 1975–96, and became West Lothian unitary authority.

Linz Capital of Upper Austria and industrial port (iron, steel, metalworking) on the river Danube in N Austria; population (1991) 203,000. It is associated with the composers Mozart and Bruckner.

Lion, Golfe du (English *Gulf of the Lion*) Bay of the Mediterranean stretching along the shore of S France from Toulon to the Spanish border, and named because of the roughness of its waters. The rivers Rhône, Aude, Orb, and Têt flow into it. The principal port is ◊Marseille.

Lipari Islands or *Aeolian Islands* Volcanic group of seven islands off NE Sicily, including *Lipari* (on which is the capital of the same name), *Stromboli* (active volcano 926 m/3,038 ft high), and *Vulcano* (also with an active volcano); area 114 sq km/44 sq mi. In Greek mythology, the god Aeolus kept the winds imprisoned in a cave on the Lipari Islands.

Lippe River of N Germany flowing into the river Rhine; length 230 km/147 mi; also a former German state, now part of North Rhine–Westphalia.

Lisbon (Portuguese *Lisboa*) City and capital of Portugal, in the SW of the country, on the tidal lake and estuary formed by the river Tagus; population (1987) 830,500. Industries include steel, textiles, chemicals, pottery, shipbuilding, and fishing. It has been the capital since 1260 and reached its peak of prosperity in the period of Portugal's empire during the 16th century. In 1755 an earthquake killed 60,000 people and destroyed much of the city.

Lisburn Cathedral city and market town in County Antrim, Northern Ireland, on the river Lagan; population (1991) 42,100. It produces linen and furniture. Huguenot immigrants began the linen industry 1694. The Irish Linen Centre is at Lisburn Museum.

Lisieux Town in Calvados *département*, France, SE of Caen; population (1990) 24,500. St Thérèse of Lisieux spent her religious life in the Carmelite convent here, and pilgrims visit her tomb.

Lissa German name for ◊Leszno, a town in Poland.

Litani River rising near Baalbek in the Anti-Lebanon Mountains of E Lebanon, 144 km/89 mi long. It flows NE–SW through the Bekka Valley, then E to the Mediterranean 8 km/5 mi N of Tyre. Israeli forces invaded Lebanon as far as the Litani River 1978.

Littlehampton Seaside resort in W Sussex, England, at the mouth of the river Arun, 16 km/10 mi SE of Chichester; population (1981) 22,000. There is light engineering and production of foodstuffs.

Little Rock Largest city and capital of Arkansas, USA; population (1992) 176,900. Products include metal goods, oil-field and electronic equipment, chemicals, clothing, and processed food. A French trading post was built here 1722, and in 1821 it became the territorial capital.

Liverpool City and seaport in Merseyside, NW England; population (1994 est) 664,000. Liverpool is the UK's chief Atlantic port with miles of specialized, mechanized quays on the river Mersey. Imports include crude oil, grain, ores, edible oils, timber, and containers. There are ferries to Ireland and the Isle of Man. Traditional industries, such as ship-repairing, have declined. Present-day industries include flour-milling, sugar refining, electrical engineering, food processing, chemicals, soap, margarine, tanning, and motor vehicles. The Mersey Tunnel (1886), rail tunnel, and Queensway Tunnel (1934) link Liverpool and Birkenhead. Kingsway Tunnel (1971) links Liverpool and Wallasey.

features Bluecoat Chambers (1717); Town Hall (1754); St George's Hall (1838–54), a fine example of Classical architecture; Anglican Cathedral, designed by George Gilbert Scott (begun 1904, completed 1980); Roman Catholic Metropolitan Cathedral of Christ the King, designed by Frederick Gibberd, consecrated 1967; the Tate Gallery in the N in former Albert Dock, opened 1987. The Walker Art Gallery (1877) and the Liverpool Philharmonic Orchestra, founded 1840 (became Royal LPO 1957), are here. The Grand National steeplechase takes place at Aintree. Outstanding buildings include Speke Hall, the classical St George's Hall 1854, the university, the Dock Offices, the Port of Liverpool building 1907, Royal Liver Building 1911, and Cunard Building 1916 on Pier Head. In the Canning Conservation Area, 600 Georgian and Victorian houses are being restored. The city has one of the finest public libraries in the country. Britain's first International Garden Festival was held here 1984. The Beatles were born here. The Liverpool Institute for the Performing Arts (opened 1995), the world's first university of pop music, occupies the old Liverpool Institute for Boys where former Beatles Paul McCartney and George Harrison went to school.

history Liverpool grew in importance during the 18th century as a centre of the slave trade, and until the early 20th century through the export of the textiles of Lancashire and Yorkshire.

Livingston Industrial new town, administrative headquarters of West Lothian, Scotland, established 1962; population (1991) 41,600. Industries include electronics, engineering, paper, steel, scientific instruments, and industrial research.

Livingstone formerly *Maramba* Town in Zambia; population (1989) 102,000. Founded 1905, it was named after the Scottish explorer David Livingstone, and was capital of N Rhodesia 1907–35. The Victoria Falls are nearby.

Livorno (formerly English *Leghorn*) Industrial port in W Italy; population (1992) 166,400. Industries include shipbuilding, distilling, and motor vehicles. A fortress town since the 12th century, it was developed by the Medici family. It has a naval academy and is also a resort.

Livorno Province of central Italy in W ◊Tuscany region; capital Livorno; area 1,220 sq km/471 sq mi; population (1992) 336,700.

Lizard Point Southernmost point of England in Cornwall. The coast is broken into small bays overlooked by two cliff lighthouses.

Ljubljana (German *Laibach*) Capital and industrial city (textiles, chemicals, paper, leather goods) of Slovenia, near the confluence of the rivers Ljubljanica and Sava; population (1991) 276,100. It has a nuclear research centre and is linked with S Austria by the Karawanken road tunnel under the Alps (1979–83).

Llanberis Village in Gwynedd, Wales, point of departure for the ascent of Mount Snowdon.

Llandaff (Welsh *Llandaf*) Town in South Wales, 5 km/3 mi NW of Cardiff, of which it forms part. The 12th-century cathedral, heavily restored, contains Jacob Epstein's sculpture *Christ in Majesty*.

Llandrindod Wells Spa and administrative headquarters of Powys, E Wales; population (1991) 4,400.

Llandudno Resort and touring centre for N Wales, in Gwynedd. Great Orme's Head is a spectacular limestone headland.

Llanelli formerly *Llanelly* Industrial port in Carmarthenshire, Wales; population (1991) 45,000. Industries include tin plate, copper smelting, chemicals, bricks, and lenses.

Llanfair P G Village in Anglesey, Wales; full name *Llanfairpwllgwyngyllgogerychwyrndrobwllllantysiliogogogoch* (St Mary's church in the hollow of the white hazel near the rapid whirlpool of St Tysillio's church, by the red cave), the longest place name in the UK.

Lleyn Peninsula (Welsh *Llŷn*) Peninsula in Gwynedd, N Wales, between Cardigan Bay and Caernarfon Bay. It includes the resort of Pwllheli. Bardsey Island at its tip is the traditional burial place of 20,000 saints.

Llyn Tegid Welsh name for the ◊Bala Lake.

Lobito Port in Angola; population (1983) 150,000. It is linked by rail with Beira in Mozambique, via the Democratic Republic of Congo (formerly Zaire) and Zambia copperbelt, though landmines from the Angolan civil war have left parts of the track unusable.

Locarno Health resort in the Ticino canton of Switzerland on the N shore of Lago Maggiore, W of Bellinzona; population (1990) 14,200. Formerly in the duchy of Milan, it was captured by the Swiss 1803.

Lochaber Wild mountainous district in Highland unitary authority, Scotland, including Ben Nevis, the highest mountain in the British Isles. Fort William is the chief town of the area. It is the site of large hydroelectric installations.

Loch Ness Scottish lake; see ◊Ness, Loch.

Locle, Le Commune in the canton of Neuchâtel, Switzerland, on the French border 55 km/34 mi from Bern; population (1995) 11,000. Watches have been made here since 1705; Le Locle rivals the nearby town of La-Chaux-de-Fonds as the centre of the Swiss watchmaking industry.

Lodi Town in Italy, 30 km/18 mi SE of Milan; population (1980) 46,000. It is a market centre for agricultural produce; fertilizers, agricultural machinery, and textiles are produced.

Napoleon's defeat of Austria at the *battle of Lodi* 1796 gave him control of Lombardy.

Łódź Industrial city (textiles, machinery, dyes) in central Poland, 120 km/75 mi SW of Warsaw; population (1993) 844,900.

Lofoten and Vesterålen Island group off NW Norway; area 4,530 sq km/1,750 sq mi. Hinnøy, in the Vesterålens, is the largest island of Norway. The surrounding waters are rich in cod and herring. The *Maelström*, a large whirlpool hazardous to ships, which gives its name to similar features elsewhere, occurs in one of the island channels.

Logan, Mount Mountain in SW Yukon Territory, Canada. With an altitude of 5,950 m/19,520 ft, it is the highest peak in Canada and the second-highest peak in North America (the highest being Mount McKinley in Alaska). Part of the St Elias Mountains, Mount Logan is in the Kluane national park, designated a World Heritage Site 1979.

Logroño Market town and capital of La Rioja, N Spain, on the river Ebro; population (1994) 125,000. It is the centre of a wine-producing region.

Loir French river, rising N of Illiers in the *département* of Eure-et-Loir and flowing SE, then SW to join the Sarthe near Angers; 310 km/500 mi. It gives its name to the *départements* of Loir-et-Cher and Eure-et-Loir.

Loire Longest river in France, rising in the Cévennes Mountains, at 1,350 m/4,430 ft and flowing for 1,050 km/ 650 mi first N then W until it reaches the Bay of Biscay at St Nazaire, passing Nevers, Orléans, Tours, and Nantes. It gives its name to the *départements* of Loire, Haute-Loire, Loire-Atlantique, Indre-et-Loire, Maine-et-Loire, and Saône-et-Loire. There are many châteaux and vineyards along its banks.

Loire *Département* in the ◊Rhône-Alpes region of SE France; area 4,773 sq km/1,843 sq mi; population (1990) 746,677. The *département* is largely mountainous, but the plains of Forez and Roanne provide good agricultural and pasture lands. Vines are grown in the Rhône valley. The main goods manufactured are glass, silk, cast steel, hardware, machinery, and cutlery. The principal towns are St-Étienne (the capital), and Roanne.

Loire-Atlantique Maritime *département* in the ◊Pays de la Loire region of France; area 6,893 sq km/2,661 sq mi; population (1990) 1,051,400. It lies between the Bay of Biscay on the W and Maine-et-Loire on the E. The land is flat, with the river Loire and its tributaries the Erdre and the Sevre, and the river Isac, a tributary of the Vilaine, flowing through it. Horses and cattle are bred in the *département*, and cereals, vines, flax, and fruit are cultivated. The chief manufactures are hemp, linen, paper, sugar, biscuits, and soap. There are foundries and shipyards at ◊Nantes (the capital) and ◊St-Nazaire, and oil refining and petrochemical industries. The other principal towns are Ancenis, and Châteaubriant.

Loire, Haute- *Département* in the Auvergne region of France; see ◊Haute-Loire.

Loire, Pays de la French planning region; see Pays de la Loire.

Loiret French river, 11 km/7 mi long, rising near Olivet and joining the Loire 8 km/5 mi below Orléans. It gives its name to Loiret *département*.

Loiret *Département* in the ◊Centre region of France; area 6,742 sq km/2,603 sq mi; population (1990) 580,700. There is a large forest around ◊Orléans. The Loire valley in the S, in spite of the occasional floods, is an important agricultural area, and wine, wheat, barley, sugar beet, vegetables, and fruit are produced. There are also rubber, iron, preserved foods, mechanical, electrical, and other industries. The châteaux at Sully-sur-Loire and Chilliers-aux-Bois attract tourists. The principal towns are Orléans (the capital), Montargis, and Pithiviers.

Loir-et-Cher *Département* in the ◊Centre region of France; area 6,314 sq km/2,438 sq mi; population (1990) 306,500. In the N flows the river Loir, in the centre the Loire, and in the S the Cher. A large part of the land is forested, but there are also rich agricultural districts in the river basins and on the fertile plateau of lower Beauce, which lies across the centre of the *département*. Cereals, vines, fruit trees, and vegetables are cultivated, and sheep and turkeys are raised. Manufacturing industries include food, chemicals, and pottery. Stone, alabaster, and flint are quarried. The châteaux of the Loire attract many tourists. The principal towns are ◊Blois (the capital), Romorantin, and Vendôme.

Loja Town in the province of Granada, S Spain, on the river Genil; population (1995) 21,900. It was one of the last strongholds of the Moors. Products include salt, textiles, paper, and cakes (*roscos*).

Lombardy (Italian *Lombardia*) Region of N Italy, including Lake Como; capital Milan; area 23,856 sq km/9,211 sq mi; population (1995) 8,910,500. It is the country's chief industrial area (chemicals, pharmaceuticals, engineering, textiles).

Lombok (Javanese 'chili pepper') Island of Indonesia, E of Java, one of the Sunda Islands; area 4,730 sq km/1,826 sq mi; population (1980) 1,957,000. The chief town is Mataram. It has a fertile plain between N and S mountain ranges. The island has become a popular tourist destination.

Lomé Capital and port of Togo; population (1990) 450,000. It is a centre for gold, silver, and marble crafts; industries include steel production and oil refining; phosphates are exported.

Lomond, Loch Largest freshwater Scottish lake, 37 km/ 21 mi long, area 70 sq km/27 sq mi. It is overlooked by the mountain *Ben Lomond* (973 m/3,192 ft) and is linked to the Clyde estuary.

Lompoc City in SW California, USA, near the Pacific Ocean, W of Santa Barbara; population (1990) 37,650. Industries include the processing of oil from the city's oil wells. It was founded 1874.

London City in SW Ontario, Canada, on the river

Thames, 160 km/100 mi SW of Toronto; population (1991) 303,200, metropolitan area 381,500. The centre of a farming district, it has tanneries, breweries, and factories making hosiery, radio and electrical equipment, leather, and shoes. It dates from 1826 and is the seat of the University of Western Ontario.

London Capital of England and the United Kingdom, on the river Thames; its metropolitan area, *Greater London*, has an area of 1,580 sq km/610 sq mi and population (1994 est) of 6,967,000 (larger metropolitan area about 9 million). The *City of London*, known as the 'square mile', area 274 hectares/677 acres, is the financial and commercial centre of the UK. Greater London (see ◊London, Greater) from 1965 comprises the City of London and 32 boroughs. London is the only major European capital without a strategic authority covering the whole area. Popular tourist attractions include the Tower of London, St Paul's Cathedral, Buckingham Palace, and Westminster Abbey.

history Roman *Londinium* was established soon after the Roman invasion AD 43; in the 2nd century London became a walled city; by the 11th century, it was the main city of England and gradually extended beyond the walls to link with the originally separate Westminster. Throughout the 19th century London was the largest city in the world (in population).

features The Tower of London, built by William the Conqueror on a Roman site, houses the crown jewels and the royal armouries; 15th-century Guildhall; the Monument (a column designed by Christopher Wren) marks the site in Pudding Lane where the Great Fire of 1666 began; Mansion House (residence of the lord mayor); Barbican arts and conference centre; Central Criminal Court (Old Bailey) and the Inner and Middle Temples; Covent Garden, once a vegetable market, is now a tourist shopping and entertainment area

architecture London contains buildings in all styles of English architecture since the 11th century. *Norman*: the White Tower, Tower of London; St Bartholomew's, Smithfield; the Temple Church *Gothic*: Westminster Abbey; Westminster Hall; Lambeth Palace; Southwark Cathedral *Tudor*: St James's Palace; Staple Inn *17th century*: Banqueting Hall, Whitehall (Inigo Jones); St Paul's; Kensington Palace; many City churches (all by Wren) *18th century*: Somerset House (Chambers); St Martin-in-the-Fields; Buckingham Palace *19th century*: British Museum (Neo-Classical); Houses of Parliament; Law Courts (Neo-Gothic); Westminster Cathedral (Byzantine style) *20th century*: Lloyd's of London.

London Commodity Exchange Company that provides services for commodity markets in non-metals, including cocoa, sugar, grain, coffee, petroleum, rubber, and wool.

Londonderry also known as *Derry* Historic city and port on the river Foyle, County Londonderry, Northern Ireland; population (1991) 95,400. Industries include textiles, chemicals, shirt manufacturing, and acetylene from naphtha.

features the Protestant cathedral of St Columba (1633); the Guildhall (rebuilt 1912), containing stained glass windows presented by livery companies of the City of London

history Londonderry dates from the foundation of a monastery by St Columba AD 546. James I of England granted the borough and surrounding land to the citizens of London. The Irish Society was formed to build and administer the city and a large colony of English Protestants was established. From 1688–89 the city was besieged by the armies of James II in the Siege of Londonderry.

Londonderry also known as *Derry* County of Northern Ireland

area 2,070 sq km/799 sq mi

towns and cities Londonderry (county town), Coleraine, Portstewart

features rivers Foyle, Bann, and Roe; borders Lough Neagh

industries mainly agricultural, but farming is hindered by the very heavy rainfall; flax, cattle, sheep, food processing, textiles, light engineering, salmon and eel fisheries, stone and lime quarrying, shirt manufacturing

population (1981) 187,000

famous people Joyce Cary.

London, Greater Metropolitan area of ◊London, England, comprising the City of London, which forms a self-governing enclave, and 32 surrounding boroughs; area 1,580 sq km/610 sq mi; population (1994) 6,679,700. The population of Inner London is 2,504,500 and that of Outer London 4,175,200. Certain powers were exercised over this whole area by the Greater London Council (GLC) 1974–86.

London Metal Exchange Commodity market for trade in metals, incorporated 1881. With the Commodity Exchange of New York, it is the world's most important for copper, nickel, and zinc. It also trades in futures, and organises the storage of metals. In 1993 $1 million million was traded on the London Metal Exchange.

Long Beach Port and industrial city in SW California, USA; population (1992) 438,800. Long Beach forms part of Greater ◊Los Angeles and adjoins the San Pedro harbour of Los Angeles. Manufactured goods include aircraft, ships, petroleum products, chemicals, fabricated metals, electronic equipment, and processed food; the city also has oil wells and a naval shipyard, and is a convention centre. Long Beach was laid out in the 1880s; the port was opened 1909. Oil was discovered 1921, and the aircraft industry dates from World War II.

Longchamp Pleasure resort and racecourse in Paris, France, in the Bois de Boulogne. It is on the site of a former nunnery founded 1260, suppressed 1790. Many horse races in France are run at Longchamp including the most prestigious open-age group race in Europe, the *Prix de L'Arc de Triomphe*, which attracts a top-quality field every October.

Longford County of the Republic of Ireland, in the province of Leinster; county town Longford; area 1,040 sq km/401 sq mi; population (1996 est) 30,100. It is low-lying with bogs and has the rivers Camlin, Inny, and Shannon (which forms its W boundary), and several lakes. Agricultural activities include stock rearing and the production of oats and potatoes.

Long Island Island E of Manhattan and SE of Connecticut, USA, separated from the mainland by Long Island Sound and the East River; 120 mi/193 km long by about 30 mi/48 km wide; area 1,400 sq mi/3,627 sq km; population (1990) 6,861,500. Long Island includes two boroughs of New York City (Queens and Brooklyn), John F Kennedy airport, suburbs and resorts.

Longmont City in N central Colorado, USA, in the Rocky Mountain foothills, S of Fort Collins and NE of Boulder; population (1992) 54,600. Industries include business machinery, sugar-beet refining, and recreational vehicles. The city was founded 1871.

Longview City in E Texas, USA, E of Dallas; seat of Gregg County; population (1992) 72,700. In the heart of the oil fields of E Texas, Longview's industries are mainly oil and natural gas processing. It was settled in the early 19th century and incorporated 1872. It was a trading centre for beef cattle, pigs, and horses.

Longwy French town in the *département* of Meurthe-et-Moselle, on the river Chier, near the border with Belgium and Luxembourg; population (1990) 15,600. It has a fortress built in the 17th century by the military engineer Vauban. Longwy is in an iron-mining district, and has metallurgical and pottery industries.

Lons-le-Saunier French town, capital of the *département* of Jura, 75 km/47 mi NW of Geneva, on the river Vallière; population (1990) 20,000. It is a tourist centre, and has been known as a spa since the 4th century. There are a number of 18th-century houses and two medieval churches. Wines and salt are produced, and there is microtechnology industry and a trade in cheese, horses, and cattle.

Lop Nor Series of shallow salt lakes with shifting boundaries in the Taklimakan Shamo (desert) in Xinjiang Uyghur, NW China. Marco Polo, the Venetian traveller, visited Lop Nor, then a single lake of considerable extent, about 1273. The area is used for atomic tests.

Lorain City in N central Ohio, USA, on Lake Erie, NW of Akron and SW of Cleveland; population (1992) 71,500. An important Great Lakes port, it has shipbuilding yards and manufactures cars and heavy construction equipment. It was settled 1807 and incorported 1836.

Lorca Town in the province of Murcia, SE Spain; population (1995) 69,700. It has ancient walls, a Moorish castle, several Baroque churches, and mansions. Lorca lies in a very fertile district; its products include chemicals, textiles, and porcelain, and there are iron, silver, and sulphur mines.

Lord Howe Island Volcanic island and dependency of New South Wales, Australia, 700 km/435 mi NE of Sydney; area 15 sq km/6 sq mi; population (1989) 320. It is a tourist resort and heritage area because of its scenery and wildlife. The woodhen is a bird found only here.

Lorestan Alternative form of ◊Luristan, a province of Iran.

Loreto Town in the Marche region of central Italy; population (1990) 10,650. The town allegedly holds the Virgin Mary's house, carried there by angels from Nazareth; hence Our Lady of Loreto is the patron saint of aviators.

Lorient Commercial and naval port in Brittany, NW France; population (1990) 61,600. Industries include fishing and shipbuilding.

Lorraine Region of NE France in the upper reaches of the Meuse and Moselle rivers; bounded N by Belgium, Luxembourg, and Germany and E by Alsace; area 23,547 sq km/9,091 sq mi; population (1990) 2,305,700. It comprises the *départements* of Meurthe-et-Moselle, Meuse, Moselle, and Vosges, and its capital is Nancy. There are deposits of coal, iron ore, and salt; grain, fruit, and livestock are farmed. In 1871 the region was ceded to Germany as part of Alsace-Lorraine. The whole area saw heavy fighting in World War I.

Los Angeles City and port in SW California, USA; population (1994) 12,200,000; metropolitan area of Los Angeles–Long Beach (1992) 15,048,000. Industries include aerospace, electronics, motor vehicles, chemicals, clothing, printing, and food processing. Los Angeles was established as a Spanish settlement 1781, and grew in the 20th century with the film industry and the provision of water. Features include Hollywood, centre of the film industry since 1911; the Hollywood Bowl concert arena; observatories at Mount Wilson and Mount Palomar; Disneyland; the Huntingdon Art Gallery and Library; and the J Paul Getty Museum of Art (a re-creation of a Roman villa) housing the Classical collection, the rest of its exhibits being housed in the enlarged John Paul Getty Centre across the town in Brentwood.

Los Angeles was a farming region with orange groves until the early 20th century, when it annexed neighbouring communities and acquired distant water supplies, a deep-water port, and the film industry. In the 1920s large petroleum deposits were found in the area. The aircraft industry, with its need for year-round flying weather, developed here soon after and grew rapidly during World War II. There were serious interethnic riots in the Watts district 1965. In 1992 five days of riots, resulting in more than 50 deaths and extensive damage, followed a judge's acquittal of four white police officers charged with the beating of a black motorist. In Jan 1994 an earthquake (6.6 on the Richter scale) struck the city, killing 61 people and displacing an estimated 25,000. Estimates of the damage ranged between $15 billion and $30 billion, with 45,000 homes damaged by the quake; of those, 15,000 were declared uninhabitable.

Greater Los Angeles comprises 86 towns, including Long Beach, Redondo Beach, Venice, Santa Monica, Burbank, Compton, Beverly Hills, Glendale, Pasadena, and Pomona. It covers 10,000 sq km/4,000 sq mi.

Lossiemouth Fishing port and resort in Moray, Scotland; population (1991) 7,200. The politician Ramsay MacDonald was born and buried here.

Lot *Département* in the ◊Midi-Pyrénées region of France; area 5,228 sq km/2,019 sq mi; population (1990) 156,000. The land is crossed from E to W by the river Lot and is highest in the NE. Wheat is the chief cereal, but maize, oats, and barley are also cultivated. Wine is the principal product, the most valued being that of Cahors, grown in the Lot valley. Large quantities of chestnuts come from the NE, and the *département* also produces potatoes, tobacco, and hemp. Clothmaking, tanning, brewing, tourism, and the making of agricultural instruments are among its other industries. The principal towns are Cahors (the capital), Figeac, and Gourdon.

Lot French river; see ◊Gironde.

Lot-et-Garonne *Département* in the ◊Aquitaine region of France; area 5,358 sq km/2,069 sq mi; population (1990) 306,000. Its surface, which consists mainly of wide plains, is crossed from E to W by the rivers Garonne and Lot. The valleys of these rivers are fertile, and the slopes of the low hills are covered with orchards and vineyards. Wheat, maize, and barley are also grown. Some iron ore is mined. The principal towns are Agen (the capital), Marmande, Nérac, and Villeneuve.

Lothian Former Region of Scotland to 1996; replaced by East Lothian, Midlothian, West Lothian, and City of Edinburgh unitary authorities.

Louangphrabang or *Louang Prabang* Buddhist religious centre in Laos, on the Mekong River at the head of river navigation; population (1985) 68,400. It was the capital of the kingdom of Louangphrabang, incorporated in Laos 1946, and the royal capital of Laos 1946–75.

Loughborough Industrial town in Leicestershire, England; population (1991) 46,900. Occupations include engineering, bell-founding, electrical goods, knitwear, footwear, hosiery, and pharmaceuticals.

Louisiana State in S USA; nicknamed Pelican State/Sugar State/Creole State
area 135,900 sq km/52,457 sq mi
capital Baton Rouge
towns and cities New Orleans, Shreveport, Lafayette, Lake Charles
physical Mississippi River
features Sabine Wildlife Refuge Tower; Cajun country (Acadiana), including St Martinville (the 18th-century 'Petit Paris', with the church of St Martin de Tours and the Petit Paris Museum), and Lafayette (40% of the population speak Cajun French); Poverty Point State Commemorative Area, with prehistoric Native American sites dating from 1800–500 BC; Natchitoches, the oldest permanent European settlement of the Louisiana Purchase; plantation mansions, many designed by Henry Howard, including Nottoway (1859, the largest plantation mansion in the South, with 64 rooms), Madewood, Destrahan Plantation (the oldest surviving plantation in the Mississippi Valley), Rosedown Plantation and Gardens (1835), and Magnolia Mound Plantation; New Orleans, the birthplace of Dixieland jazz, with Mardi Gras celebrations, the French Quarter (Vieux Carré) around Jackson Square (the site of the original colony founded 1718; the only surviving building is the Old Ursuline Convent, 1749), St Louis Cemetery No. 1 (1789), Louisiana State Museum, 1850s House, Beauregard-Keyes House (home of novelist Frances Parkinson Keyes), St Louis Cathedral (1794), the Voodoo Museum, and the Garden District with mid-19th-century estates; Jean Lafitte national historic park and preserve; Chalmette national historic park; old houses in St Francisville; the old state capitol, Baton Rouge (1849); Port Hudson State Commemorative Area, site of Civil War battle; Tulane University; Audubon State Commemorative Area, where John James Audubon executed most of his *Birds of America* paintings; the American Rose Center, headquarters of the American Rose Society at Shreveport
industries rice, cotton, sugar, oil, natural gas, chemicals, sulphur, fish and shellfish, salt, processed foods, petroleum products, timber, paper
population (1995) 4,342,300; including Cajuns, descendants of 18th-century religious exiles from Canada, who speak a French dialect
famous people Louis Armstrong, P G T Beauregard, Truman Capote, Lillian Hellman, Huey Long
history explored by the Spanish Piñeda 1519, Cabeza de Vaca 1528, and Hernando de Soto 1541 and by the French explorer Robert de la Salle 1662, who named it after Louis XIV and claimed it for France. It became Spanish 1762, then French 1800, then passed to the USA 1803 under the Louisiana Purchase; admitted to the Union as a state 1812, seceded 1861, re-admitted 1868.

Louisville Industrial city and river port on the Ohio River, Kentucky, USA; population (1992) 271,000. Industries include electrical goods, agricultural machinery, motor vehicles, tobacco, and whisky. It is the home of the Kentucky Fair and Exposition Center, and the Kentucky Derby. Louisville was founded 1778.

Lourdes Town in Midi-Pyrénées region, SW France, on the Gave de Pau River; population (1982) 18,000. Its Christian shrine to St Bernadette has a reputation for miraculous cures and Lourdes is an important Catholic pilgrimage centre. The young peasant girl Bernadette Soubirous was shown the healing springs of the Grotte de Massabielle by a vision of the Virgin Mary 1858.

Lourenço Marques Former name of ◊Maputo, the capital of Mozambique.

Louth Smallest county of the Republic of Ireland, in the province of Leinster; county town Dundalk; area 820 sq km/317 sq mi; population (1996 est) 92,200. It is low-lying. There is cattle-rearing, and oats and potatoes are grown.

Louvain (Flemish *Leuven*) Industrial town in Brabant province, central Belgium; population (1995 est) 87,200. Manufacturing includes fertilizers and food processing. Its university dates from 1425 and there is a Science City.

Loveland City in N central Colorado, USA, S of Fort Collins; population (1990) 37,350. It is a processing and marketing centre for the agricultural products of the area.

Tourism is important to the economy, and Rocky Mountain National Park is to the W. Loveland was founded 1877.

Low Countries   Region of Europe that consists of Belgium and the Netherlands, and usually includes Luxembourg.

Lowell   City in Massachusetts, USA; population (1992) 99,900. Industries include electronics, plastics, and chemicals. Lowell was a textile centre in the 19th century; a substantial part of the old city was designated a national park 1978 as a birthplace of the US industrial revolution. Wang Laboratories moved its headquarters here 1978.

Lower Austria   (German *Niederösterreich*) Largest province of Austria; drained by the river Danube; area 19,174 sq km/7,403 sq mi; population (1995) 1,518,254. Its capital is St Pölten. In addition to wine, sugar beet, and grain, there are reserves of oil. Manufactured products include textiles, chemicals, and metal goods.

Lower California   English name for ◊Baja California, Mexico.

Lower Saxony   (German *Niedersachsen*) Administrative region (German *Land*) of N Germany
area   47,606 sq km/18,381 sq mi
capital   Hannover
towns and cities   Brunswick, Osnabrück, Oldenburg, Göttingen, Wolfsburg, Salzgitter, Hildesheim
features   Lüneburg Heath
industries   cereals, cars, machinery, electrical engineering
population   (1995) 7,780,400
religion   75% Protestant, 20% Roman Catholic
history   formed 1946 from Hannover, Oldenburg, Brunswick, and Schaumburg-Lippe.

Lowestoft   Resort town and most easterly port in Britain, in Suffolk, England, 62 km/38 mi NE of Ipswich; population (1990 est) 58,000. There is fishing and fish processing, and radar and electrical equipment is produced. *Lowestoft Ness* is the most easterly point in England.

Lozère   *Département* in Languedoc-Roussillon region, S France. Occupying a section of the Cévennes Mountains, it rises in Finiels to 1,702 m/5,584 ft. The capital is ◊Mende.

Lualaba   Another name for the upper reaches of the river the Democratic Republic of Congo/Zaïre in Africa, as it flows N through the Democratic Republic of Congo (formerly Zaïre) from near the Zambian border.

Luanda   formerly *Loanda* Capital and industrial port (cotton, sugar, tobacco, timber, textiles, paper, oil) of Angola; population (1995) 2,250,000. Founded 1575, it became a Portuguese colonial administrative centre as well as an outlet for slaves transported to Brazil.

Lubbock   City in NW Texas, USA, S of Amarillo; seat of Lubbock County; population (1992) 187,900. Industries include heavy farm and construction machinery, cotton, sorghum, and mobile homes. It is an important cotton market. The rock-and-roll singer Buddy Holly was born here. Lubbock was founded 1890.

Lübeck   Seaport of Schleswig-Holstein, Germany, on the Baltic Sea, 60 km/37 mi NE of Hamburg; population (1993) 217,100. Industries include machinery, aeronautical and space equipment, steel, ironwork, ship-building and servicing, fish canning; Lübeck is known for its wine trade and its marzipan. Founded 1143, it has five Gothic churches and a cathedral dating from 1173. The Holstentor (1477) with its twin towers is the emblem of the city. Once head of the powerful Hanseatic League, it later lost much of its trade to Hamburg and Bremen, but improved canal and port facilities helped it to retain its position as a centre of Baltic trade. Lübeck was a free state of both the empire and the Weimar Republic.

Lublin   City in Poland, on the Bystrzyca River, 150 km/95 mi SE of Warsaw; population (1993) 352,500. Industries include textiles, engineering, aircraft, and electrical goods. A trading centre from the 10th century, it has an ancient citadel, a 16th-century cathedral, and a university (1918). A council of workers and peasants proclaimed Poland's independence at Lublin 1918, and a Russian-sponsored committee of national liberation, which proclaimed itself the provincial government of Poland at Lublin 31 Dec 1944, was recognized by Russia five days later.

Lubumbashi   formerly (until 1966) *Elizabethville* Town in the Democratic Republic of Congo (formerly Zaire), on the Lualaba River; population (1991 est) 739,100. It is the chief commercial centre of the Shaba copper-mining region.

Lucca   City in NW Italy; population (1981) 91,246. It was an independent republic from 1160 until its absorption into Tuscany 1847. The composer Giacomo Puccini was born here.

Lucca   Province of central Italy in NE ◊Tuscany region; capital Lucca; area 1,772 sq km/684 sq mi; population (1992) 376,900.

Lucerne   (German *Luzern*) Capital and tourist centre of Lucerne canton, Switzerland, on the river Reuss where it flows out of Lake Lucerne; population (1994) city 61,700, canton 337,700. It developed around a Benedictine monastery, established about 750, and owes its prosperity to its position on the St Gotthard road and railway.

Lucerne   (German *Luzern*) Canton in central Switzerland, in the N foothills of the Alps; area 1,494 sq km/577 sq mi; population (1995) 340,500. The city of Lucerne is the capital of the canton, which mainly comprises fertile pasture land yielding grain, flax, clover, potatoes, and dairy products. A wide range of manufactures are also produced. The canton is German-speaking.

Lucerne, Lake   (German *Vierwaldstättersee*) Scenic lake in central Switzerland; area 114 sq km/44 sq mi.

Lucknow   Capital and industrial city (engineering, chemicals, textiles, many handicrafts) of the state of Uttar Pradesh, India; population (1991) 1,669,200. During the Indian Mutiny against British rule, it was besieged 2 July–16 Nov 1857.

Lüda   or *Lü-ta* or *Hüta* Chinese port; see ◊Dalian.

Lüdenscheid   City in North Rhine–Westphalia, Germany, 55 km/34 mi E of Düsseldorf; population (1994) 81,200. It once belonged to the Hanseatic League trade federation, and its iron industries date from the Middle Ages. Today there are aluminium, machinery, and metallurgical industries in the town.

Lüderitz Port on Lüderitz Bay, Namibia; population (1990) 6,000. It is a centre for diamond-mining. The town, formerly a German possession, was named after a German merchant who acquired land here 1883.

Ludlow Market town in Shropshire, England, on the river Teme, near the Welsh border, 42 km/26 mi S of Shrewsbury; population (1990 est) 8,000. Industries include agricultural machinery, precision engineering, and clothing. Milton's masque *Comus* was first presented at Ludlow Castle 1634. There is a large Norman keep.

Ludwigsburg City in Baden-Württemberg, Germany, 14 km/9 mi N of Stuttgart; population (1994) 483,100. Ludwigsburg was once a porcelain centre, but its main manufactures are now machinery and toys. There are three castles.

Ludwigshafen am Rhein City and Rhine river port, Rhineland-Palatinate, Germany; population (1991) 165,400. Industries include chemicals, dyes, fertilizers, plastics, and textiles.

Lugano Resort town on Lake Lugano, Switzerland; population (1990) 26,000. Industries include engineering and clothing.

Lugano, Lake Lake partly in Italy, between lakes Maggiore and Como, and partly in Switzerland; area 49 sq km/19 sq mi.

Lugo Capital of the province of Lugo, NW Spain, on the river Miño; population (1995) 88,300. It is surrounded by massive Roman walls, now promenades, and has a cathedral dating partly from the 12th century. There are hot sulphur springs nearby, used since Roman times. It has an important meat industry.

Lugo Province of NW Spain in NE ◊Galicia autonomous community; capital Lugo; area 9,803 sq km/3,785 sq mi; population (1995) 386,400. Its N coastline is on the Bay of Biscay. The basins of the rivers Miño and its tributary the Sil, which run through Lugo, are very fertile.

Lugoj Market town in Timiş county, W Romania, on the river Timiş 56 km/35 mi E of Timişoara. Wine, fruit, and textiles are its chief commodities, and it is a railway junction.

Luhansk formerly (1935–58 and 1970–89) *Voroshilovgrad* Industrial city (locomotives, textiles, mining machinery) in Ukraine; population (1991) 504,000.

Luik Flemish name of ◊Liège, a city in Belgium.

Luleå Port in N Sweden, on the Gulf of Bothnia, at the mouth of the river Luleå; population (1992) 68,900. It is the capital of Norrbotten county. Exports include iron ore and timber in ice-free months.

Luleålv River in the N of Sweden; length 410 km/255 mi. It flows through the county of Norrbotten into the Gulf of Bothnia, entering the sea at Luleå.

Lund City in Malmöhus county, SW Sweden; 16 km/10 mi NE of Malmö; population (1994) 95,900. It has an 11th-century Romanesque cathedral and a university established 1666. The treaty of Lund was signed 1676 after Carl XI had defeated the Danes.

Lundy Island Rocky island at the entrance to the Bristol Channel; 19 km/12 mi NW of Hartland Point, Devon, England; area 9.6 sq km/3.7 sq mi; population (1975) 40. Formerly used by pirates and privateers as a lair, it is now a bird sanctuary and the first British Marine Nature Reserve (1986). It has Bronze and Iron Age field systems, which can be traced by their boundaries which stand up above the surface.

Lüneburg Town in Lower Saxony, Germany, on the river Ilmenau; population (1990 est) 61,000. Industries include chemicals, paper, and ironworks. It is a health resort.

Lüneburg Heath (German *Lüneburger Heide*) Area in Lower Saxony, Germany, between the Elbe and Aller rivers. It was here that more than a million German soldiers surrendered to British General Montgomery on 4 May 1945.

Lünen City in North Rhine–Westphalia, Germany, on the river Lippe, 15 km/9 mi N of Dortmund; population (1994) 90,700. It has coal mines, aluminium, copper, pharmaceutical, and leather industries.

Lunéville French town in the *département* of Meurthe-et-Moselle, 30 km/19 mi SE of Nancy, on the river Meurthe; population (1990) 25,400. Textiles, pottery, and railway carriages are made. The château of the dukes of Lorraine is now a museum.

Luoyang or *Loyang* Industrial city (machinery and tractors) in Henan province, China, S of the river Huang He; population (1992) 1,190,000. It was formerly the capital of China and an important Buddhist centre in the 5th and 6th centuries.

Luray Caverns Caves in Page County, N Virginia, USA. The caves are the largest in the state (26 sq km/10 sq mi), and their several chambers are covered with stalactite and stalagmite formations of many colours and shapes.

Luristan or *Lorestan* Mountainous province in W Iran; area 28,800 sq km/11,117 sq mi; population (1991) 1,501,800. The capital is Khorramabad. The province is inhabited by Lur tribes who live by their sheep and cattle. Excavation in the area has revealed a culture of the 8th–7th century BC with bronzes decorated with animal forms; its origins are uncertain.

Lusaka Capital of Zambia from 1964 (of Northern Rhodesia 1935–64), 370 km/230 mi NE of Livingstone; it is a commercial and agricultural centre (flour mills, tobacco factories, vehicle assembly, plastics, printing); population (1990) 982,000.

Lüshun-Dalien Constituent parts of ◊Lüda, a port in China.

Lusignan French town in the *département* of Vienne, 23 km/14 mi SW of Poitiers; population (1990) 10,400. It has a church of the 11th–15th centuries. The castle of Lusignan (now ruined) was founded, according to legend, by the fairy Melusina, who was also the protectress of the great feudal family of Lusignan, one branch of which ruled Cyprus and Jerusalem 1191–1489.

Lusitania Ancient area of the Iberian peninsula, roughly equivalent to Portugal. Conquered by Rome in 139 BC, the province of Lusitania rebelled periodically until it was finally conquered by Pompey 73–72 BC.

Lü-ta Alternative transcription of ◊Lüda, a port in China.

Luton Industrial city and unitary authority in S central England, 53 km/33 mi SW of Cambridge; population (1997) 181,400; area 43 sq km/17 sq mi. It was part of the county of Bedfordshire to 1997. Luton airport is a secondary airport for London. Manufacturing includes cars, chemicals, engineering components, electrical goods, ballbearings, as well as, traditionally, hats. The straw and fashion hat industry was responsible for Luton's prosperity in the 19th century.

Lützen Town in the *Land* of ◊Saxony-Anhalt, Germany, 29 km S of Halle. Lützen has an old castle, and sugar processing is the principal industry. It was the site of a battle 1632 in the Thirty Years' War and again in 1813 in the Napoleonic Wars.

Luxembourg Capital of the country of Luxembourg, on the Alzette and Petrusse rivers; population (1995) 76,000. The 16th-century Grand Ducal Palace, European Court of Justice, and European Parliament secretariat are situated here, but plenary sessions of the parliament are now held only in Strasbourg, France. Industries include steel, chemicals, textiles, and processed food.

Luxembourg Province of SE Belgium
area 4,400 sq km/1,698 sq mi
capital Arlon
towns and cities Bastogne, St Hubert, Bouillon
industries dairy products, iron and steel, tobacco
physical situated in the SE Ardennes and widely forested; rivers Ourthe, Semois, and Lesse
population (1995) 240,300
history formerly part of the Grand Duchy of Luxembourg, it became a Belgian province 1831.

Luxor (Arabic *al-Uqsur*) Small town in Egypt on the E bank of the river Nile; population (1992) 146,000. The ancient city of Thebes is on the W bank, with the temple of Luxor built by Amenhotep III (c. 1411–1375 BC) and the tombs of the pharaohs in the Valley of the Kings.

Luzern German name of ◊Lucerne, a city in Switzerland.

Luzon Largest island of the Philippines; area 104,688 sq km/40,420 sq mi; capital Quezon City; population (1970) 18,001,270. The chief city is Manila, capital of the Philippines. Industries include rice, timber, and minerals. It has US military bases.

Lviv (Russian *Lvov*, Polish *Lwów*) Capital and industrial city of Lviv region, Ukraine; population (1992) 807,000. Industries include textiles, metals, and engineering. The university was founded 1661. Lviv was formerly a trade centre on the Black Sea–Baltic route. Founded in the 13th century by a Galician prince (the name means 'city of Leo' or 'city of Lev'), it was Polish 1340–1772, Austrian 1772–1919, Polish 1919–39, and annexed by the USSR 1945.

It was the site of violent nationalist demonstrations Oct 1989, prior to Ukraine gaining independence 1991.

Lyme Regis Seaport and resort in Dorset, S England; population (1981) 3,500. The rebel duke of Monmouth, claimant to the English crown, landed here 1685. The Cobb (a massive stone pier) features in Jane Austen's *Persuasion* 1818 and John Fowles's *The French Lieutenant's Woman* 1969.

Lymington Port and yachting centre in Hampshire, S England; 8 km/5 mi SW of Southampton; population (1990 est) 15,000. It has a ferry link with the Isle of Wight.

Lynchburg City in S central Virginia, USA, on the James River, NE of Roanoke; population (1992) 66,100. Industries include clothing, paper and rubber products, and machine parts. It was settled 1757 by Quakers.

Lynn Industrial city in Massachusetts, USA, on Massachusetts Bay; population (1992) 78,650. Founded as Saugus 1629, it was renamed 1637 after King's Lynn, England.

Lynton and Lynmouth Twin resort towns on the N coast of Devon, SW England. The fishing village of Lynmouth is linked by an alpine road and cliff railway (1890) to Lynton, which lies 152 m/500 ft above at the top of a cliff. In Aug 1952, 22.5 cm/9 in of rainfall within 24 hours on nearby Exmoor caused disastrous flooding at Lynmouth, leaving 31 people dead and the harbour and over 100 buildings severely damaged. The harbour, a Rhenish tower, and much of the town were later rebuilt.

Lyon (English *Lyons*) Industrial city (textiles, chemicals, machinery, printing) and capital of Rhône *département*, Rhône-Alpes region, at the confluence of the rivers Rhône and Saône, 275 km/170 mi NW of Marseille; population (1990) 422,400, conurbation 1,221,000. It is the third largest city of France. Formerly a chief fortress, it was the ancient *Lugdunum*, taken by the Romans 43 BC.

Lyonnaise Former province of France, corresponding to the present *départements* of ◊Rhône, ◊Loire, and parts of Haute-Loire and Puy-de-Dôme. Originally autonomous, it was joined to the crown in 1312. The capital was ◊Lyon.

Lys or *Leie* River in France and Belgium; length 214 km/133 mi. It rises near Fruges in the Pas-de-Calais and flows past the towns of Aire, Armentières, and Courtrai, to join the Scheldt at Ghent.

Lytham St Annes Resort in Lancashire, England, on the river Ribble; 10 km/6 mi SE of Blackpool; population (1991) 40,900. It has a championship golf course.

MA Abbreviation for ◊Massachusetts, a state in the USA.

Maas Dutch or Flemish name for the river ◊Meuse.

Maastricht Industrial city (metallurgy, textiles, pottery) and capital of the province of Limburg, the Netherlands, on the river Maas, near the Dutch-Belgian frontier; population (1994) 118,100. Maastricht dates from Roman times. It was the site of the Maastricht summit Dec 1991.

McAllen City in S Texas, USA, just N of the Mexican border formed by the Rio Grande, SE of Laredo; population

(1992) 90,250. Industries include oil refining and the processing of agricultural products from the Rio Grande Valley. It is a US port of entry for Mexicans, and many of the city's inhabitants are Spanish-speaking. It is a winter resort. McAllen was founded 1905.

Macassar Another name for ◊Ujung Pandang, a port in Sulawesi, Indonesia.

Macau Portuguese possession on the S coast of China, about 65 km/40 mi W of Hong Kong, from which it is separated by the estuary of the Pearl River; it consists of a peninsula and the islands of Taipa and Colôane

area 17 sq km/7 sq mi
capital Macau, on the peninsula
features the peninsula is linked to Taipa by a bridge and to Colôane by a causeway, both 2 km/1 mi long
currency pataca
population (1994 est) 395,300
language Cantonese; Portuguese (official)
religion Buddhist, with 6% Catholic minority.

Macau

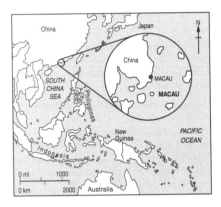

Macclesfield Industrial town in Cheshire, NW England, on the edge of the Pennines; population (1990 est) 69,000. Formerly the centre of the silk industry, present-day industries include textiles, light engineering, paper, pharmaceuticals (Zeneca) and plastics.

Macdonnell Ranges Mountain range in central Australia, Northern Territory, with the town of Alice Springs; highest peak Mount Zeil 1,510 m/4,955 ft.

Macedonia Ancient region of Greece, forming parts of modern Greece, Bulgaria, and the Former Yugoslav Republic of Macedonia. Macedonia gained control of Greece after Philip II's victory at Chaeronea 338 BC. His son, Alexander the Great, conquered a vast empire. Macedonia became a Roman province 146 BC.

Macedonia (Greek *Makedhonia*) Mountainous region of N Greece, part of the ancient country of Macedonia which was divided between Serbia, Bulgaria, and Greece after the Balkan Wars of 1912–13. Greek Macedonia is bounded W and N by Albania and the Former Yugoslav Republic of Macedonia; area 34,177 sq km/13,200 sq mi; population

(1991) 2,263,000. There are two regions, Macedonia Central, and Macedonia East and Thrace. The chief city is Thessaloniki. The Former Yugoslav Republic of Macedonia has refused to give up claims to the present Greek province of Macedonia, and has placed the star of Macedonia, symbol of the ancient Greek Kings of Macedonia, on its flag. Fertile valleys produce grain, olives, grapes, tobacco, and livestock. Mount Olympus rises to 2,918 m/9,570 ft on the border with Thessaly.

Maceió Industrial city (sugar, tobacco, textile, timber) in NE Brazil, capital of Alagaos state with its port at Jaraguá; population (1991) 699,800.

Macerata Province of E central Italy in central Le ◊Marche region; capital Macerata (population (1990) 43,500); area 2,775 sq km/1,071 sq mi; population (1992) 295,800.

Macgillycuddy's Reeks Range of mountains in SW Ireland lying W of Killarney, in County Kerry; Carrauntoohill 1,041 m/3,414 ft is the highest peak in Ireland.

Machu Picchu Ruined Inca city in Peru, built about AD 1500, NW of Cuzco, discovered 1911 by Hiram Bingham. It stands at the top of cliffs 300 m/1,000 ft high and contains the well-preserved remains of houses and temples.

Macias Nguema Former name (to 1979) of ◊Bioko, an island of Equatorial Guinea in the Bight of Biafra, W Africa.

Mackenzie River River in the Northwest Territories, Canada, flowing NW from Great Slave Lake to the Arctic Ocean; about 1,800 km/1,120 mi long. It is the main channel of the Finlay-Peace-Mackenzie system, 4,241 km/2,635 mi long.

Mackinac Island Island in the Straits of Mackinac, Michigan, USA, between Lake Michigan and Lake Huron; population (1990) 469. It lies just E of the bridge across the Straits of Mackinac; length 5 km/3 mi, width 3 km/2 mi. Visited by the French explorer Jean Nicolet in 1634–35, it became the chief fur-trading centre of a vast region. Fort Mackinac was built by the French army, but lost to the British. Under British rule from 1761 onwards, the island passed to the USA in 1783. The island is a popular tourist destination, though no private cars are allowed.

McKinley, Mount or *Denali* Peak in Alaska, USA, the highest in North America, 6,194 m/20,321 ft; named after US president William McKinley. It is in the ◊Rocky Mountains.

Mâcon Capital of the French *département* of Saône-et-Loire, on the river Saône, 72 km/45 mi N of Lyon; population (1990) 38,500. It produces wine. Mâcon dates from ancient Gaul, when it was known as *Matisco*. The French writer Alphonse Lamartine was born here.

Macon City in central Georgia, USA, on the Ocmulgee River, NE of Columbus; seat of Bibb County; population (1992) 107,300. An industrial city, Macon produces textiles, building materials, farm machinery, and chemicals; it processes fruits, pecans, and the special kaolin clay that is found nearby. It was originally settled 1806.

Macquarie Island Outlying Australian territorial possession, a Tasmanian dependency, some 1,370 km/850 mi SE of Hobart; area 170 sq km/65 sq mi; it is uninhabited except for an Australian government research station.

Madeira Group of islands forming an autonomous region of Portugal off the NW coast of Africa, about 420 km/260 mi N of the Canary Islands. Madeira, the largest, and Porto Santo are the only inhabited islands. The Desertas and Selvagens are uninhabited islets. Their mild climate makes them a year-round resort

area 796 sq km/308 sq mi

capital Funchal, on Madeira

physical Pico Ruivo, on Madeira, is the highest mountain at 1,861 m/6,106 ft

industries Madeira (a fortified wine), sugar cane, fruit, fish, handicrafts

population (1994 est) 256,000

history Portuguese from the 15th century; occupied by Britain 1801 and 1807–14. In 1980 Madeira gained partial autonomy but remains a Portuguese overseas territory.

Madeira

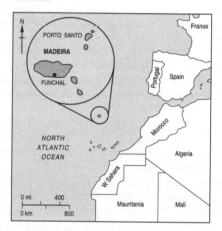

Madeira River of W Brazil; length 3,241 km/2,014 mi. It is formed by the rivers Beni and Mamoré, and flows NE to join the Amazon.

Madeleine, La French town in the *département* of Nord; population (1990) 21,800. It is a suburb of ◊Lille and has chemical and textile industries. Producer service industries now account for about 50% of economic activity.

Madhya Bharat State of India 1950–56. It was a union of 24 states of which Gwalior and ◊Indore were the most important. In 1956 Madhya Bharat was absorbed in ◊Madhya Pradesh.

Madhya Pradesh State of central India; the largest of the Indian states

area 443,446 sq km/171,215 sq mi

capital Bhopal

towns and cities Indore, Jabalpur, Gwalior, Durg-Bhilainagar, Raipur, Ujjain

industries cotton, oilseed, sugar, textiles, engineering, paper, aluminium, limestone, diamonds, steel

population (1994 est) 71,950,000

language Hindi

history formed 1950 from the former British province of Central Provinces and Berar and the princely states of Makrai and Chattisgarh; lost some SW districts 1956, including ◊Nagpur, and absorbed Bhopal, Madhya Bharat, and Vindhya Pradesh. In 1984 some 2,600 people died in ◊Bhopal from an escape of poisonous gas.

Madison Capital of Wisconsin, USA, 193 km/120 mi NW of Chicago, between lakes Mendota and Monona; population (1992) 195,200. Industries include agricultural machinery and medical equipment. The city was founded 1836 as the territorial capital and named after President James Madison.

Madras Former name, to 1996, of ◊Chennai, an industrial port and capital of the state of ◊Tamil Nadu, India.

Madras Former name of Tamil Nadu, a state of India.

Madrid Industrial city (leather, chemicals, furniture, tobacco, paper) and capital of Spain and of Madrid province; population (1994) 3,041,000. Built on an elevated plateau in the centre of the country, at 655 m/2,183 ft it is the highest capital city in Europe and has excesses of heat and cold. Madrid province has an area of 8,000 sq km/3,088 sq mi and a population of 4,855,000.

features The Real Academia de Bellas Artes (1752); the Prado museum (1785); the royal palace (1764), built for Philip V; the 15th century Retiro Park; the Plaza Mayor (1617–20); the Akalá Arch; and the basilica of San Francisco el Grande (1761–84).

history Madrid began as the Moorish city of Magerit. It was captured 1083 by King Alfonso VI of Castile. It remained a small provincial town until Philip II made it his capital 1561 because of its position at the centre of the Iberian peninsula. In 1808 there was an uprising against the occupation by Napoleon's troops. During the Spanish Civil War it was the centre of opposition to Franco, and was besieged by the Nationalists 1936–39.

Madrid Autonomous community and province of central Spain; area 8,000 sq km/3,088 sq mi; population (1995) 5,181,700. Bounded by the Sierra de Guadarrama mountains in the NW, and by the river Tagus in the SE, it is arid plateau country. It is crossed by several rivers, including the Jarama, a tributary of the Tagus. Products include fruit and vegetables, grown in the S; timber from the forests in the NE, and granite and gypsum from quarries in the mountains. El Escorial palace is in the NW.

Madura Island in Indonesia, off Surabaya, Java; one of the Sunda Islands.

Madurai City in Tamil Nadu, India; population (1991) 941,000. Founded in the 5th century BC, it is the site of the 16th–17th-century temple of Meenakshi. Industries include textiles (cotton) and brassware manufacturing.

Maeander Anglicized form of the ancient Greek name of the river ◊Menderes in Turkey.

Maestricht Alternative form of ◊Maastricht, a city in the Netherlands.

Mafikeng formerly (until 1980) *Mafeking* Town in North West Province (formerly the independent homeland of Bophuthatswana), South Africa. It was the capital of Bechuanaland, and the British officer Robert Baden-Powell held it under Boer siege 12 Oct 1899–17 May 1900.

Magadan Port for the gold mines in E Siberian Russia, off the N shore of the Sea of Okhotsk; population (1992) 164,000.

Magdeburg Industrial city (vehicles, paper, textiles, machinery) and capital of Saxony-Anhalt, Germany, on the river Elbe; population (1993) 272,400. A former capital of Saxony, Magdeburg became capital of Saxony-Anhalt on German reunification 1990. In 1938 the city was linked by canal with the Rhine and Ruhr rivers.

Magellan, Strait of Channel between South America and Tierra del Fuego, named after the Portuguese navigator Ferdinand Magellan. It is 595 km/370 mi long, and joins the Atlantic and Pacific oceans.

Maggiore, Lago Lake partly in Italy, partly in the Swiss canton of Ticino, with Locarno on its N shore, 63 km/39 mi long and up to 9 km/5.5 mi wide (area 212 sq km/82 sq mi), with fine scenery.

Maghreb Name for NW Africa (Arabic 'far West', 'sunset'). The Maghreb powers – Algeria, Libya, Morocco, Tunisia, and Western Sahara – agreed on economic coordination 1964–65, with Mauritania cooperating from 1970. In 1989 these countries formed an economic union known as the Arab Maghreb Union. Chad and Mali are sometimes included. Compare ◊Mashraq, the Arab countries of the E Mediterranean.

Magnitogorsk Industrial city (steel, motor vehicles, tractors, railway rolling stock) in Chelyabinsk region, in the Russian Federation, on the E slopes of the Ural Mountains; population (1994) 439,000. It was developed in the 1930s to work iron, manganese, bauxite, and other metals in the district.

Mahabad Kurdish town in Azerbaijan, W Iran; population (1983) 63,000. It formed the centre of a short-lived Kurdish republic (Jan–Dec 1946) before being reoccupied by the Iranians. In the 1980s Mahabad was the focal point of resistance by Iranian Kurds against the Islamic republic.

Maharashtra State in W central India
area 307,713 sq km/118,808 sq mi
capital Bombay
towns and cities Pune, Nagpur, Ulhasnagar, Sholapur, Nasik, Thana, Kolhapur, Aurangabad, Sangli, Amravati
features cave temples of Ajanta, containing 200 BC–7th century AD Buddhist murals and sculptures; Ellora cave temples 6th–9th century with Buddhist, Hindu, and Jain sculptures

industries cotton, rice, groundnuts, sugar, minerals
population (1994 est) 85,565,000
language Marathi 50%
religion Hindu 80%, Parsee, Jain, and Sikh minorities
history formed 1960 from the S part of the former Bombay state.

Mahé Chief island of the Seychelles.

Mahón or *Port Mahon* Capital and port of the Spanish island of Menorca; population (1991) 21,800. Probably founded by the Carthaginians, it was under British occupation 1708–56 and 1762–82.

Maidenhead Town in Berkshire, S England, 40 km/25 mi W of London, on the river Thames; population (1991) 59,600. It will join with Windsor to become a unitary authority in April 1998. Industries include computer software, plastics, pharmaceuticals, paper-making, electronics, and printing. It is a boating centre.

Maidstone Town in Kent, SE England, on the river Medway, administrative headquarters of the county; population (1991) 90,900. Industries include agricultural machinery and paper.

Maikop Capital of Adygeya autonomous Republic of the Russian Federation on the river Bielaia, with timber mills, distilleries, tanneries, and tobacco and furniture factories; population (1992) 149,000. Oilfields, discovered 1900, are linked by pipeline with Tuapse on the Black Sea.

Main River in central W Germany, 515 km/320 mi long, flowing through Frankfurt to join the river Rhine at Mainz. A canal links it with the Danube.

Maine Former province of W France. Since 1790 its territory has been divided between the *départements* of ◊Mayenne and Sarthe and parts of ◊Orne and Eure-et-Loir. Its capital was ◊Le Mans.

Maine Old French province bounded N by Normandy, W by Brittany, and S by Anjou. The modern *départements* of Sarthe and Mayenne approximately correspond to it.

Maine French river, 11 km/7 mi long, formed by the junction of the Mayenne and Sarthe; it enters the Loire below Angers, and gives its name to Maine-et-Loire *département*.

Maine Northeasternmost state of the USA, largest of the New England states; nicknamed Pine Tree State
area 86,200 sq km/33,273 sq mi
capital Augusta
towns and cities Portland, Lewiston, Bangor
physical Appalachian Mountains; 80% of the state is forested
features Kennebec and Penobscot rivers; 5,600 km/3,500 mi of coastline; Acadia national park, including Bar Harbor and Mount Desert Island, the first national park in E USA; Baxter state park, with Mount Katahdin (1,605 m/5,267 ft), the highest peak in the state, the N end of the Appalachian Trail; canoeing on the Allagush Wilderness Waterway; Moosehead Lake (190 sq km/120 sq mi), New England's largest lake; Sebago Lake; Penobscot Bay, with lobster fishing centred on Rockland; Roosevelt Campobello International Park, the summer home of President F D

Roosevelt; South Berwick, the site of the first permanent settlement in Maine (1631), with old houses including Sarah Orne Jewett House (1774); Artist's Covered Bridge, Newry (1872); Colonial York; Camden; Castine; Prout's Neck, the summer home of the artist Winslow Homer, with Portland Head Light; Paris Hill; Ogunquit, a 19th-century artists' colony; the Kennebunks, including Kennebunkport; Fort Kent (1839); Portland Museum of Art, with a 1983 wing designed by I M Pei, housing a collection of American art; Old Port Exchange, Portland, a renovated 19th-century waterfront area; Musical Wonder House, Wiscasset, with a collection of antique musical boxes and mechanical musical instruments; Maine Maritime Museum, Bath; Bowdoin College (1794); Norway, famous for the manufacture of snowshoes (Admiral Peary walked to the North Pole on Norway snowshoes); Perham's Mineral Store, West Paris; L L Bean store, Freeport; Kittery, with factory outlet stores; Poland Spring, source of famous mineral water

industries dairy and market garden produce, paper, pulp, timber, footwear, textiles, fish, lobster; tourism is important

population (1995) 1,241,400

famous people Henry Wadsworth Longfellow, Kate Douglas Wiggin, Edward Arlington Robinson, Edna St Vincent Millay

history permanently settled by the British from 1623; absorbed by Massachusetts 1691; became a state 1820.

Maine-et-Loire *Département* in the ◊Pays de la Loire region of France; area 7,130 sq km/2,753 sq mi; population (1990) 706,400. The river Loire crosses the *département* from E to W, and forms in its course several islands. The *département* is bounded in the N by the rivers Mayenne and Sarthe, in the E by Indre-et-Loir, in the S by Vienne, Deux-Sèvres, and Vendée, and in the W by Loire-Atlantique. Vines are grown in some parts of the *département* (Saumur, for example), and the fertile plains are used for growing cereals, hemp, and sugar beet, and for horticulture. There are computing, electronic, and car parts industries near Angers, the capital.

Mainz (French *Mayence*) Capital of Rhineland-Palatinate, Germany, on the Rhine, 37 km/23 mi WSW of Frankfurt-am-Main; population (1993) 185,200. In Roman times it was a fortified camp and became the capital of Germania Superior. Printing was possibly invented here about 1448 by Johann Gutenberg.

Majorca Alternative spelling of ◊Mallorca.

Makeyevka formerly (until 1931) *Dmitrievsk* Industrial city (coal, iron, steel, and chemicals) in the Donets Basin, SE Ukraine; population (1991) 424,000.

Makhachkala formerly (until 1922) *Port Petrovsk* Capital of Dagestan, Autonomous Republic of the Russian Federation, on the Caspian Sea, SE of Grozny, from which pipelines bring petroleum to Makhachkala's refineries; other industries include shipbuilding, meat packing, chemicals, matches, and cotton textiles; population (1994) 327,000.

Makó Town in Csongrád county, SE Hungary, on the river Mures, near the Romanian border, 15 km/9 mi E of Szeged;

population (1993) 26,700. The surrounding agricultural district specializes in onions.

Malabar Coast Coastal area of Karnataka and Kerala states, India, lying between the Arabian Sea and the Western Ghats; about 65 km/40 mi W–E, 725 km/450 mi N–S. A fertile area with heavy rains, it produces food grains, coconuts, rubber, spices; also teak, ebony, and other woods. Lagoons fringe the shore. A district of Tamil Nadu transferred 1956 to Kerala was formerly called the Malabar Coast.

Malabo Port and capital of Equatorial Guinea, on the island of Bioko; population (1992) 35,000. It was founded in the 1820s by the British as *Port Clarence*. Under Spanish rule it was known as *Santa Isabel* (until 1973).

Malacca or *Melaka* State of W Peninsular Malaysia; capital Malacca; area 1,700 sq km/656 sq mi; population (1993) 583,400 (about 70% Chinese). Products include rubber, tin, and wire. The town originated in the 13th century as a fishing village frequented by pirates, and later developed into a trading port. Portuguese from 1511, then Dutch from 1641, it was ceded to Britain 1824, becoming part of the Straits Settlements.

Malacca, Strait of Channel between Sumatra and the Malay Peninsula; length 965 km/600 mi; it narrows to less than 38 km/24 mi wide. It carries all shipping between the Indian Ocean and the South China Sea.

Málaga Industrial seaport (sugar refining, distilling, brewing, olive-oil pressing, shipbuilding) and holiday resort in Andalusia, Spain; capital of Málaga province on the Mediterranean; population (1994) 531,000. Founded by the Phoenicians and taken by the Moors 711, Málaga was capital of the Moorish kingdom of Malaga from the 13th century until captured 1487 by the Catholic monarchs Ferdinand and Isabella.

Málaga Province of S Spain in S ◊Andalusia autonomous community; capital Málaga; area 7,275 sq km/2,809 sq mi; population (1995) 1,225,000. Its S coastline is on the Mediterranean Sea. The province is mountainous, reaching 2,100 m/6,890 ft at some points. The lowlands, particularly the coastal plain, are very fertile, and products include oranges, melons, pomegranates, sugar cane, Malaga wine, and cotton.

Malagasy Republic Former name (1958–75) of Madagascar.

Malaspina Glacier Glacier in Alaska, USA, one of the world's largest ice sheets. It lies W of Yakutat Bay, NE Gulf of Alaska, and is part of the ◊St Elias Mountains glacier system, the most extensive outside the polar ice caps.

Malatya Capital of a province of the same name in E central Turkey, lying W of the river Euphrates; population (1990) 281,800.

Malawi, Lake Alternative name for Lake Nyasa (see ◊Nyasa, Lake).

Malay Peninsula Southern projection of the continent of Asia, lying between the Strait of Malacca, which divides it from Sumatra, and the China Sea. The N portion is partly in Myanmar (formerly Burma), partly in Thailand; the S forms part of Malaysia. The island of Singapore lies off its S extremity.

Malbork (German *Marienburg*) Town in Elblâg province, Poland, on the river Nogat, 40 km/25 mi SE of Gdańsk; population (1990) 39,600. Industries include timber and sugar refining. From 1309 to 1457 the Malbork Castle was the headquarters of the Grand Master of the Teutonic Knights (a German Christian military order).

Malé Capital and chief atoll of the Maldives in the Indian Ocean; population (1990) 55,100. It trades in copra, breadfruit, fish, and palm products; it is also a growing tourist centre.

Malines French name for ◊Mechelen, a city in Belgium.

Mallorca or *Majorca* Largest of the ◊Balearic Islands, belonging to Spain, in the W Mediterranean
area 3,640 sq km/1,405 sq mi
capital Palma
features the highest mountain is Puig Mayor, 1,445 m/4,741 ft
industries olives, figs, oranges, wine, brandy, timber, sheep; tourism is the mainstay of the economy
population (1990 est) 582,000
history captured 797 by the Moors, it became the kingdom of Mallorca 1276, and was united with Aragón 1343.

Malmédy Town in Liège, E Belgium, 40 km/25 mi S of Aachen, in the region of Eupen et Malmédy.

Malmesbury Market town in Wiltshire, England, on the river Avon. The parish church was formerly a Saxon abbey, founded in the 7th century, where Athelstan was buried. Its charter of 924 granted by Edward the Elder is one of the oldest in England. Its elaborate but decayed 12th-century S porch includes some of the finest pieces of Romanesque sculpture in Britain. The notable market cross dates from around 1490. Thomas Hobbes was born at nearby Westport; William of Malmesbury was a monk of the abbey, as was St Aldhelm.

Malmö Industrial port (shipbuilding, engineering, textiles) in SW Sweden, situated across the Øresund from Copenhagen, Denmark; population (1994 est) 242,700. Founded in the 12th century, Malmö is Sweden's third-largest city.

Malmöhus County of Sweden, the S part of the Skåne peninsula; area 4,847 sq km/1,871 sq mi; population (1990) 757,600. It is a very fertile district and is Sweden's principal sugar-beet-growing area. Malmö is the chief town and Sweden's third-largest city, and Lund is one of the oldest cities.

Maluku or *Moluccas* Group of Indonesian islands; area 74,500 sq km/28,764 sq mi; population (urban area, 1990 est) 1,856,000. The capital is Ambon, on Ambon. As the *Spice Islands*, they were formerly part of the Netherlands East Indies; the S Moluccas attempted secession from the newly created Indonesian republic from 1949; exiles continued agitation in the Netherlands.

Malvern English spa town in Hereford and Worcester, on the E side of the *Malvern Hills*, which extend for about 16 km/10 mi and have their high point in Worcester Beacon 425 m/1,395 ft; population (1991) 31,500. The *Malvern Festival* 1929–39, associated with the playwright G B Shaw and the composer Edward Elgar, was revived 1977. Elgar lived and was buried here.

Malvinas, Islas Argentine name for the ◊Falkland Islands.

Mammoth Cave Vast limestone cavern in Mammoth Cave National Park 1936, Kentucky, USA. The main cave is 6.5 km/4 mi long, and rises to a height of 38 m/125 ft; it is known for its stalactites and stalagmites. Native American councils were once held here.

Man. Abbreviation for ◊Manitoba, a Canadian province.

Manacor Town in SE Majorca, one of the Spanish ◊Balearic Islands; population (1995) 29,200. Products include shoes, handicraft souvenirs, and artificial pearls; tourism is important. At nearby Porto Cristo are the Caves of Drach ('the dragon') with stalactite and stalagmite formations, and one of the largest known subterranean lakes (Lake Martel).

Managua Capital and chief industrial city of Nicaragua, on the lake of the same name; population (1991 est) 615,000. It has twice been destroyed by earthquake and rebuilt, 1931 and 1972; it was also badly damaged during the civil war in the late 1970s.

Manaus Capital of Amazonas, Brazil, on the Río Negro, near its confluence with the Amazon; population (1991) 996,700. It can be reached by sea-going vessels, although it is 1,600 km/1,000 mi from the Atlantic. Formerly a centre of the rubber trade, it developed as a tourist centre in the 1970s.

Manawatu River in North Island, New Zealand, rising in the Ruahine Range. *Manawatu Plain* is a rich farming area, specializing in dairying and fat lamb production.

Mancha See ◊La Mancha, a former province of Spain.

Maluku

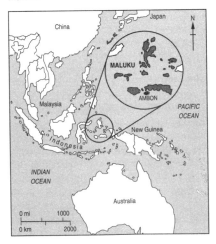

Manche, La French name for the ◊English Channel. It gives its name to a French *département*.

Manche Maritime *département* in the ◊Basse-Normandie region of France, facing the English Channel (La Manche); area 5,947 sq km/2,296 sq mi; population (1990) 480,900. It consists in part of the Cotentin peninsula, as far NW as Cape La Hague. In the SW is the bay of ◊Mont St Michel. Its principal towns are ◊St-Lô (the capital), Avranches, ◊Cherbourg, and Coutances. The chief products are grain, flax, hemp, beetroot, and fruit (especially apples for cider), and horses are reared. There are metal, textile, and service industries.

Manchester City in NW England, on the river Irwell, 50 km/31 mi E of Liverpool. It is a manufacturing (textile machinery, chemicals, rubber, engineering, electrical equipment, paper, printing, processed foods) and financial centre; population (1991) 404,900. It is linked by the Manchester Ship Canal, opened 1894, to the river Mersey and the sea.

Manchester Largest city in New Hampshire, NE USA; population (1994) 96,600. It is situated on the Merrimack River, 30 km/19 mi N of the New Hampshire–Massachusetts state line. First settled by Europeans in 1722, it was an important manufacturing town in the 19th century. Industries now include textiles, car accessories, and electrical goods.

Manchester, Greater Metropolitan county of NW England, created 1974; in 1986, most of the functions of the former county council were transferred to metropolitan district councils
area 1,290 sq km/498 sq mi
towns and cities Manchester, Bolton, Oldham, Rochdale, Salford, Stockport, and Wigan
features Manchester Ship Canal links it with the river Mersey and the sea; Old Trafford cricket ground at Stretford, and the football ground of Manchester United; a second terminal opened at Manchester Airport 1993
industries engineering, textiles, textile machinery, chemicals, plastics, electrical goods, electronic equipment, paper, printing, rubber, and asbestos
population (1994 est) 2,499,400
famous people John Dalton, James Joule, Emmeline Pankhurst, Gracie Fields, Anthony Burgess.

Mandalay Chief city of the Mandalay division of Myanmar (formerly Burma), on the river Irrawaddy, about 495 km/370 mi N of Yangon (Rangoon); population (1983) 533,000.

Manerplaw Remote town in the tropical forest of Karen state, SE Myanmar (Burma), near the border with Thailand. It is the headquarters of the ethnic Karen rebels.

Mangalore Industrial port (textiles, timber, food processing) at the mouth of the Netravati River in Karnataka, S India; population (1991) 273,000.

Manhattan Island 20 km/12.5 mi long and 4 km/2.5 mi wide, lying between the Hudson and East rivers and forming a borough of the city of ◊New York, USA. It includes the Wall Street business centre, Broadway and its theatres,

Carnegie Hall (1891), the World Trade Centre (1973), the Empire State Building (1931), the United Nations headquarters (1952), Madison Square Garden, and Central Park.

Manicouagan River in Quebec, Canada, flowing 485 km/301 mi S from Mushalagan and Manicouagan lakes to Baie Comeau on the St Lawrence River. Together with the Outardes River, which enters the St Lawrence E of Baie Comeau, the Manicouagan is the source of the largest hydroelectric power complex in Canada. It remains important for the transport of timber.

Manila Industrial port (textiles, tobacco, distilling, chemicals, shipbuilding) and capital of the Philippines, on the island of Luzon; population of the metropolitan area (including ◊Quezon City) 9,000,000 (1994); city (1990) 1,601,000.

Manipur State of NE India
area 22,327 sq km/8,620 sq mi
capital Imphal
features Loktak Lake; original Indian home of polo
industries grain, fruit, vegetables, sugar, textiles, cement, handloom weaving
population (1994 est) 2,010,000 (30% are hill tribes)
language Manipuri, English
religion Hindu 70%
history administered from the state of Assam until 1947 when it became a Union Territory. It became a state 1972.

Man, Isle of (Gaelic *Vannin, Ellan*) Island in the Irish Sea, a dependency of the British crown, but not part of the UK
area 570 sq km/220 sq mi
capital Douglas
towns and cities Ramsey, Peel, Castletown
features Snaefell 620 m/2,035 ft; annual TT (Tourist Trophy) motorcycle races, gambling casinos, Britain's first free port, tax haven; tailless Manx cat
industries light engineering products; agriculture, fishing, tourism, banking, and insurance are important
currency the island produces its own coins and notes in UK currency denominations
population (1991) 69,800

Man, Isle of

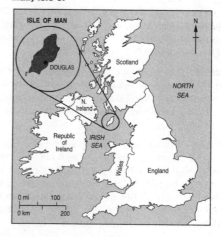

language English (Manx, nearer to Scottish than Irish Gaelic, has been almost extinct since the 1970s)

government crown-appointed lieutenant-governor, a legislative council, and the representative House of Keys, which together make up the Court of Tynwald, passing laws subject to the royal assent. Laws passed at Westminster only affect the island if specifically so provided

history Norwegian until 1266, when the island was ceded to Scotland; it came under UK administration 1765.

Manitoba Prairie province of Canada
area 649,950 sq km/250,946 sq mi
capital Winnipeg
physical lakes Winnipeg, Winnipegosis, and Manitoba (area 4,700 sq km/1,814 sq mi); 50% forested
exports grain, manufactured foods, beverages, machinery, furs, fish, nickel, zinc, copper, and the world's largest caesium deposits
population (1995 est) 1,105,000
history trading posts and forts were built here by fur traders in the 18th century. The first settlers were dispossessed Scottish Highlanders 1812. Known as the Red River settlement, it was administered by the Hudson's Bay Company until purchased by the new dominion of Canada 1869. This prompted the Riel Rebellion 1869–70. It was given the name Manitoba when it became a province 1870. The area of the province was extended 1881 and 1912.

Manitoba

Manitoba, Lake Lake in Manitoba province, Canada, which drains into Lake Winnipeg to the NE through the river Dauphin; area 4,700 sq km/1,800 sq mi.

Manizales City in the Central Cordillera in W Colombia 2,150 m/7,000 ft above sea level, centre of a coffee-growing area; population (1994) 333,000. It is linked with Mariquita by the world's longest overhead cable transport system, 72 km/45 mi long.

Mannheim Industrial city (heavy machinery, glass, earthenware, chemicals) on the Rhine in Baden-Württemberg, Germany; population (1993) 318,800. The modern symphony orchestra, with its balance of instruments and the vital role of the conductor, originated at Mannheim in the 18th century when the ruler of the Rhine Palatinate, Carl Theodor, assembled the finest players of his day.

Manresa Town in the province of Barcelona, NW Spain, on the river Cardoner; population (1995) 65,700. Products include cotton and tyres. It has a Gothic church and a 17th-century Baroque church, the latter adjoining the cave in which St Ignatius Loyola lived for some time following his conversion.

Mansfield Industrial town (textiles, shoes, machinery, chemicals, coal) in Nottinghamshire, England, on the river Maun, 22 km/14 mi N of Nottingham; population (1991) 71,900.

Mansfield Industrial city (car parts, steel and rubber products) in N central Ohio, USA, NE of Columbus, seat of Richland County; population (1992) 53,200. It is a winter-sports area. The town was laid out 1808.

Mansûra Industrial city (cotton) and capital of Dakahlia province, NE Egypt, on the Damietta branch of the river Nile; population (1991) 362,000. Mansûra was founded about 1220; St Louis IX, king of France, was imprisoned in the fortress 1250 while on a Crusade.

Mantes-la-Jolie French town in the *département* of Yvelines, on the river Seine; population (1990) 48,000. Paper, musical instruments, and bricks are manufactured here and it is a commuter town for Paris. Mantes was burnt in 1087 by William the Conqueror. It was formerly named Mantes-Gassicourt.

Mantua (Italian *Mantova*) Capital of Mantua province, Lombardy, Italy, on an island of a lagoon of the river Mincio, SW of Verona; industry (chemicals, brewing, printing); population (1990) 54,200. The poet Virgil was born near Mantua, which dates from Roman times; it has Gothic palaces and a cathedral founded in the 12th century.

Mantua (Italian *Mantova*) Province of N Italy in SE ◊Lombardy region; capital Mantua; area 2,340 sq km/903 sq mi; population (1992) 369,400.

Manzanares Town in the province of Ciudad Real, central Spain; population (1995) 18,300. Products include wine, saffron, and textiles. It has a castle, once the property of the marqués of Santillana.

Maputo formerly (until 1975) *Lourenço Marques* Capital of Mozambique, and Africa's second-largest port, on Delagoa Bay; population (1993 est) 2,000,000. Linked by rail with Zimbabwe and South Africa, it is a major outlet for minerals, steel, textiles, processed foods, and furniture.

Maracaibo Oil-exporting port in Venezuela, on the channel connecting Lake Maracaibo with the Gulf of Venezuela; population (1990) 1,207,500. It is the second-largest city in the country.

Maracaibo, Lake Lake in NW Venezuela; area 13,507 sq km/5,215 sq mi. Oil was discovered here 1917.

Maralinga Site in the S Australian desert about 1,000 km/620 mi N of Adelaide, used by the British government for nuclear testing between 1952 and 1963. Nine atomic explosions were conducted, resulting in the contamination of 3,000 sq km/1,200 sq mi of land. In 1993 the UK agreed to contribute 45% of the cost of cleaning the area. In 1994 the

Australian government agreed to compensate the Aborigines, who were removed from their traditional homelands before the tests started, and who can never return because of the contamination of the land.

Marbella Port and tourist resort on the Costa del Sol between Málaga and Algeciras in Andalucia, S Spain; population (1991) 80,645. There are three bullrings, a Moorish castle, and the remains of a medieval defensive wall.

Marburg Manufacturing town (chemicals, machinery, pottery) in Hessen, Germany, on the river Lahn, 80 km/50 mi N of Frankfurt-am-Main; population (1989 est) 71,400. The university was founded 1527 as a centre of Protestant teaching. Martin Luther and Ulrich Zwingli disputed on religion at Marburg 1529.

Marche Former province of central France, now divided into the *départements* of ◊Creuse and Haute-Vienne. It was originally a border district of the Duchy of Aquitaine, and was united to the French crown in 1527. Its capital was Guéret.

Marche, Le (English *the Marches*) Region of E central Italy consisting of the provinces of Ancona, Ascoli Piceno, Macerata, and Pesaro e Urbino; capital Ancona; area 9,694 sq km/3,743 sq mi; population (1995) 1,441,000.

Marches Boundary areas of England with Wales, and England with Scotland. In the Middle Ages these troubled frontier regions were held by lords of the Marches, sometimes called *marchiones* and later earls of March. The 1st Earl of March of the Welsh Marches was Roger de Mortimer (c. 1286–1330); of the Scottish Marches, Patrick Dunbar (died 1285).

Marcinelle Town in the province of Hainaut, Belgium, 3 km/2 mi SW of ◊Charleroi. It has coal mines and blast furnaces and manufactures steel goods and chemicals.

Marcq-en-Barœul French town in the *département* of Nord; population (1990) 38,600. It is a suburb of ◊Lille, part of the Lille–Roubaix–Tourcoing conglomeration, and situated on the river Marcq. Marcq-en-Barœul has metallurgical, textile, and food industries.

Margate Town and seaside resort on the N coast of Kent, SE England, on the Isle of Thanet; one of the original Cinque Ports; population (1991) 56,700. Industries include textiles and scientific instruments. It developed as a seaside resort at the end of the 18th century, and has a fine promenade and beach.

Mariana Islands or *Marianas* Archipelago in the NW Pacific, E of the Philippines, divided politically into ◊Guam (an unincorporated territory of the USA) and the ◊Northern Mariana Islands (a commonwealth of the USA with its own internal government).

Mariánské Lázně (German *Marienbad*) Spa town in the Czech Republic; population (1991) 15,400. An international reputation for its healthy waters was established before World War II. The water of its springs, which contains Glauber's salts, has been used medicinally since the 16th century.

Maribor (German *Marburg*) Town and resort on the river Drave in Slovenia, with a 12th-century cathedral and some industry (boots and shoes, railway rolling stock); population (1991) 108,100. Maribor dates from Roman times.

Mari El Autonomous republic of the Russian Federation
area 23,200 sq km/8,900 sq mi
capital Yoshkar-Ola
physical the Volga flows through the SW; 60% is forested; it is W of the Ural Mountains
industries timber, paper, grain, flax, potatoes, fruit
population (1995) 766,000

Marienbad German name of ◊Mariánské Lázně, a spa town in the Czech Republic.

Marienburg German name for ◊Malbork, a town in Poland.

Marienwerder (modern Polish ◊*Kwidzyń*) Town in Poland.

Marietta Industrial town (plastics, metal products, chemicals, and office equipment) in SE Ohio, USA; seat of Washington County; population (1990) 15,000. It lies where the Muskingum River flows into the Ohio River, SE of Columbus, and was the first permanent settlement (1788) in Ohio.

Maritsa (Greek *Hevros*; Turkish *Meric*) River rising in the Rhodope Mountains, Bulgaria, which forms the Greco-Turkish frontier before entering the Aegean Sea near Enez; length 440 km/275 mi.

Mariupol Industrial port (iron, steel) in E Ukraine, on the Sea of Azov; population (1991) 522,000. It was named *Zhdanov* 1948, in honour of Andrei Zhdanov (1896–1948), but reverted to its former name 1989 following the Communist Party's condemnation of Zhdanov as having been one of the chief organizers of the Stalinist mass repressions of the 1930s and 1940s.

Marlborough Market town in Wiltshire, England, on the river Kennet, 122 km/76 mi W of London; population (1991) 6,400. There is engineering, tanning, and tourism. It is the site of Marlborough College (1843), a public school.

Mariana Islands

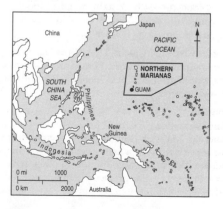

Marmara, Sea of Small inland sea separating Turkey in Europe from Turkey in Asia, connected through the Bosporus with the Black Sea, and through the Dardanelles with the Aegean; length 275 km/170 mi, breadth up to 80 km/50 mi.

Marne River in France which rises in the plateau of Langres and joins the Seine at Charenton near Paris; length 5,251 km/928 mi. It gives its name to the *départements* of Marne, Haute Marne, Seine-et-Marne, and Val de Marne; and to two battles of World War I.

Marne *Département* in the ◊Champagne-Ardenne region of France; area 8,163 sq km/3,152 sq mi; population (1990) 559,000. The river Marne crosses the *département* from SE to NW. The soil is very fertile in the S. The land is undulating in the centre of Marne, but level at the boundaries. In the dry and chalky soil of the N the best varieties of the Champagne vines are grown. Other industries include tanning, iron and copper founding, brewing, pottery, and tourism. The rearing of sheep is important, and woollen goods are manufactured. The principal towns are ◊Châlons-sur-Marne (the capital), Épernay, ◊Reims, Sainte-Menehould, and Vitry-le-François.

Maros Hungarian name for the Mures, a river in Romania and Hungary.

Marquesas Islands (French *Iles Marquises*) Island group in ◊French Polynesia, lying N of the Tuamotu Archipelago; area 1,270 sq km/490 sq mi; population (1988) 7,500. The administrative headquarters is Atuona on Hiva Oa. The islands were annexed by France 1842.

Marrakesh Historic city in Morocco in the foothills of the Atlas Mountains, about 210 km/130 mi S of Casablanca; population (1990) 665,000; urban area (1990) 665,000. It is a tourist centre, and has textile, leather, and food processing industries. Founded 1062, it has a medieval palace and mosques, and was formerly the capital of Morocco.

Marsala Port in W Sicily, Italy, notable for the sweet wine of the same name; population (1980) 85,000. The nationalist leader Giuseppe Garibaldi landed here 1860 at the start of his campaign to capture Sicily for Italy.

Marseille (English *Marseilles*) Chief seaport of France, industrial centre (chemicals, oil refining, metallurgy, shipbuilding, food processing), and capital of the *département* of Bouches-du-Rhône, on the Golfe du Lion, Mediterranean Sea; population (1990) 807,700.

Marshall City in NE Texas, USA, SE of Dallas and across the border from Shreveport, Louisiana; seat of Harrison County; population (1990) 23,700. Industries include food processing, cotton, clothing, building materials, vehicle parts, and chemicals. Marshall was founded 1841.

Martha's Vineyard Island 32 km/20 mi long off the coast of Cape Cod, Massachusetts, USA; chief town Edgartown. It is the former home of whaling captains, and now a summer resort. When the first English settlers arrived here 1642, they found wild grapes in abundance; hence the name.

Martigues French fishing town in the *département* of Bouches-du-Rhône; population (1990) 43,000. Martigues is situated on the Etang de Berre lagoon at its outlet to the Mediterranean, 29 km/18 mi NW of Marseilles. There are salt, cement, and vegetable-oil industries.

Martinique French island in the West Indies (Lesser Antilles)
area 1,079 sq km/417 sq mi
capital Fort-de-France
features several active volcanoes; Napoleon's empress Josephine was born in Martinique, and her childhood home is now a museum
industries sugar, cocoa, rum, bananas, pineapples
population (1990) 359,600
language French (official), Creole
history Martinique was reached by Spanish navigators 1493, became a French colony 1635, an overseas department 1946, and from 1974 also an administrative region of France.

Martinique

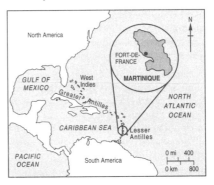

Martin's Hundred Plantation town established in Virginia, USA, 1619 and eliminated by a massacre by Native Americans three years later. Its remains, the earliest extensive trace of British colonization in America, were discovered 1970.

Mary Town in SE Turkmenistan, on the Murghab River; population (1985) 85,000. It is situated in a cotton-growing oasis in the Kara Kum Desert, near where Alexander the Great founded a city (*Merv*).

Maryborough Australian coastal and market town (grain, livestock) in SE Queensland; population (1988 est) 23,000. Industries include coal- and gold-mining, iron, and steel.

Maryborough Former name of ◊Port Laoise, the county town of County Laois in the Republic of Ireland. The name gradually went out of use during the 1950s.

Maryland State of E USA; nicknamed Old Line State/Free State
area 31,600 sq km/12,198 sq mi
capital Annapolis
cities Baltimore, Silver Spring, Dundalk, Bethesda
physical Chesapeake Bay, an inlet of the Atlantic Ocean; Assateague Island national seashore, a 60-km/37-mi barrier

island; Blackwater national wildlife refuge, marshland with Canada geese, ospreys, and bald eagles

features Chesapeake Bay Maritime Museum; the Piedmont region; Annapolis, a world yachting centre, with the Maryland State House (the only state capitol to have housed the US Congress), and the 40-block Colonial historic district; Baltimore, with the Inner Harbor area (renovated in the 1970s), the USF *Constellation* (1797, the first commissioned ship of the US Navy), the Walker Art Gallery, Baltimore Maritime Museum with the World War II submarine USS *Torsk*, Peale Museum, with paintings by Charles Wilson Peale (1814, the oldest museum in the USA), the B and O Railroad Museum, Star-Spangled Banner House, H L Mencken House, Edgar Allan Poe House, Babe Ruth's birthplace, and the Basilica of the Assumption (1812, the oldest Roman Catholic cathedral in the USA); horse racing (the Preakness Stakes at Baltimore); St Mary's City, settled 1634; Ocean City, an Atlantic resort; Columbia, a new city created in the mid-1960s; the US Naval Academy, Annapolis (1845); Johns Hopkins University, with a famous medical school, and the Peabody Institute for Music; St John's College, Annapolis (1784), the third oldest college in the USA; Fort Meade, a government electronic-listening centre; historic Fort McHenry

industries poultry, dairy products, machinery, steel, cars and parts, electric and electronic equipment, chemicals, fish and shellfish

population (1995) 5,042,400

famous people Stephen Decatur, Francis Scott Key, Edgar Allan Poe, Frederick Douglass, Harriet Tubman, Upton Sinclair, H L Mencken, Babe Ruth, Billie Holiday

history one of the original 13 states, first settled 1634; it became a state 1788. In 1608 John Smith explored Chesapeake Bay, but the colony of Maryland, awarded by royal grant 1632 to Lord Baltimore for the settlement of English Catholics, dates from 1634. It ratified the federal Constitution 1788. During the British bombardment of Fort McHenry in the War of 1812, Francis Scott Key wrote the poem 'The Star-Spangled Banner', which later became the lyrics to the US national anthem. Some Marylanders favoured secession during the Civil War, during which the state was largely occupied by Union troops because of its strategic location near Washington DC, and the Confederate armies three times invaded Maryland. In recent times the state has prospered from the growth of the federal government in nearby Washington and the redevelopment of Baltimore, whose port ranks second in handling foreign shipping. Between 1940 and 1980, Maryland's population more than tripled.

Maseru Capital of Lesotho, S Africa, on the Caledon River; population (1992 est) 367,000. Founded 1869, it is a centre for trade, light manufacturing, and food processing.

Mashhad or *Meshed* Holy city of the Shi'ites and industrial centre (carpets, textiles, leather goods) in NE Iran; population (1991) 1,759,000. It is the second-largest city in Iran.

Mashonaland Eastern Zimbabwe, the land of the Shona people, now divided into three administrative regions (Mashonaland East, Mashonaland Central, and Mashona-

land West). Granted to the British South Africa Company 1889, it was included in Southern Rhodesia 1923. The Zimbabwe ruins are here.

Mashraq (Arabic 'East') The Arab countries of the E Mediterranean: Egypt, Sudan, Jordan, Syria, and Lebanon. The term is contrasted with ◊Maghreb, comprising the Arab countries of NW Africa.

Masirah Island in the Arabian Sea, part of the sultanate of Oman, formerly used as an air staging post by British forces on their way to and from the Far East.

Mason–Dixon Line In the USA, the boundary line between Maryland and Pennsylvania (latitude 39° 43′ 26.3′ N), named after Charles Mason (1730–1787) and Jeremiah Dixon (died 1777), English astronomers and surveyors who surveyed it 1763–67. It is popularly seen as dividing the North from the South.

Massachusetts State of NE USA; nicknamed Bay State/ Old Colony

area 21,500 sq km/8,299 sq mi

capital Boston

towns and cities Worcester, Springfield, New Bedford, Brockton, Cambridge

physical the Berkshire Hills; Cape Cod national seashore

features the islands of Nantucket and Martha's Vineyard, former whaling ports; Cape Ann; Boston landmarks and the Freedom Trail; the town of Marblehead, founded 1629; Plymouth, with Mayflower II; Minute Man national historical park and battlefields of Lexington and Concord, with a replica of the Old North Bridge; Salem, site of 1690s witch trials; national historical park at Lowell, a 19th-century mill town; New Bedford Whaling Museum; Hancock Shaker Village; Norman Rockwell Museum, Stockbridge; Old Sturbridge Village, a re-creation of an early 19th-century farm village; historic Deerfield and Deerfield Academy; Amherst, with Amherst College and the Emily Dickinson homestead; Provincetown, with the Pilgrim Monument commemorating the landing of the Pilgrims 1620; Harvard University (Harvard College 1636), and Massachusetts Institute of Technology (MIT) in Cambridge; Williamstown, with Williams College (1793) and the Sterling and Francine Clark Art Institute; Mount Holyoake College (1837), the first women's college in the USA; Tanglewood Music Festival, summer home of the Boston Symphony Orchestra; Colby Museum of Art; the Museum of Fine Arts and the Isabella Stewart Gardner Museum, Boston; Woods Hole, Cape Cod, an international centre for marine research; National Basketball Hall of Fame, Springfield

industries electronic, communications, and optical equipment; precision instruments; nonelectrical machinery; fish; cranberries; dairy products

population (1995) 6,073,550

famous people Samuel Adams, Louis Brandeis, Emily Dickinson, Ralph Waldo Emerson, Robert Goddard, Nathaniel Hawthorne, Oliver Wendell Holmes, Winslow Homer, William James, John F Kennedy, Robert Lowell, Paul Revere, Henry Thoreau, Daniel Webster

history one of the original 13 states, it was first settled 1620 by the Pilgrims at Plymouth. After the Boston Tea Party 1773, the American Revolution began at Lexington and Concord 19 April 1775, and the British evacuated Boston the following year. Massachusetts became a state 1788.

Massa e Carrara Province of central Italy in NW ◊Tuscany region; capital Massa di Carrara; area 1,155 sq km/446 sq mi; population (1992) 200,100. The province was known as Apuania until 1945.

Massawa Chief port and naval base of Eritrea, on the Red Sea, with salt production and pearl fishing; population (1989) 19,400. It is one of the hottest inhabited places in the world, the temperature reaching 46°C/115°F in May. Massawa was an Italian possession 1885–1941.

Massif Central Mountainous plateau region of S central France; area 93,000 sq km/36,000 sq mi, highest peak Puy de Sancy, 1,886 m/6,188 ft. It is a source of hydroelectricity.

Masulipatnam or *Manchilipatnam*, also *Bandar* 'fish town' Indian seaport in Andhra Pradesh, at the mouth of the N branch of the river Kistna; population (1991) 159,000.

Matabeleland Western portion of Zimbabwe between the Zambezi and Limpopo rivers, inhabited by the Ndebele people
area 181,605 sq km/70,118 sq mi
towns and cities Bulawayo
features rich plains watered by tributaries of the Zambezi and Limpopo, with mineral resources
language Matabele
famous people Joshua Nkomo
history Matabeleland was granted to the British South Africa Company 1889 and occupied 1893 after attacks on white settlements in Mashonaland; in 1923 it was included in Southern Rhodesia. It is now divided into two administrative regions (Matabeleland North and Matabeleland South). Joshua Nkomo was accused of plotting to overthrow the post-independence government of Zimbabwe and then expelled from the cabinet 1981. Zimbabwe African People's Union (ZAPU) supporters, mostly drawn from the Ndebele people, began a loosely organized armed rebellion against the Zimbabwe African National Union (ZANU) government of Robert Mugabe. The insurgency was brought to an end April 1988, when a unity agreement was reached between ZANU and ZAPU and Nkomo was appointed minister of state in the office of vice president.

Matadi Chief port of the Democratic Republic of Congo (formerly Zaire) on the river Congo/Zaïre, 115 km/70 mi from its mouth, linked by oil pipelines with the capital Kinshasa; population (1991 est) 172,900.

Matanzas Industrial port (tanning, textiles, sugar) in NW Cuba; population (1990 est) 113,700. Founded 1693, it became a major centre of coffee, tobacco, and sugar production.

Matera Province of S Italy in E ◊Basilicata region; capital Matera (population (1990) 54,900); area 3,445 sq km/1,330 sq mi; population (1992) 208,900.

Matlock Spa town with warm springs, on the river Derwent, administrative headquarters of Derbyshire, England; population (1990 est) 15,000. Formerly known as a centre for hydropathic treatment, it manufactures textiles and high-tech products and caters for tourists.

Mato Grosso (Portuguese 'dense forest') Area of SW Brazil, now forming two states, with their capitals at Cuiaba and Campo Grande. The forests, now depleted, supplied rubber and rare timbers; diamonds and silver are mined.

Matsue City NW of Osaka on Honshu Island, Japan; population (1993) 145,000. It has remains of a castle, fine old tea houses, and the Izumo Grand Shrine (dating in its present form from 1744).

Matsuyama Largest city on Shikoku Island, Japan; population (1994) 456,000. Industries include agricultural machinery, textiles, and chemicals. There is a feudal fortress (1634).

Matterhorn (French *le Cervin*, Italian *il Cervino*) Mountain peak in the Alps on the Swiss-Italian border; 4,478 m/14,690 ft. It was first climbed 1865 by English mountaineer Edward Whymper (1840–1911); four members of his party of seven were killed when a rope broke during their descent.

Maubeuge French town in the *département* of Nord, on the river Sambre near the Belgian frontier; population (1990) 35,200. It has steel and engineering works, and manufactures mirrors. Maubeuge was fortified in the 17th century by the military engineer Vauban. It was besieged by German troops in 1870 in the Franco-Prussian War, and was the scene of heavy fighting in both world wars.

Maui Island in Hawaii, USA, in the central Pacific; area 1,885 sq km/728 sq mi; population (1990) 91,400. Maui is the second largest of the Hawaiian chain of islands and consists of two peninsulas divided by an isthmus of sand. The E peninsula contains the shield volcano of Haleakala, dormant since 1790, over 3,050 m/10,000 ft high and with a crater 30 km/19 mi in circumference. The chief towns are Lahaina, Wailuku, and Kahului. Maui is popular for its scenery, beaches, and resorts. Tourism is the main industry; fruit and flowers are grown.

Mauna Loa Active volcano rising to a height of 4,169 m/13,678 ft on the Pacific island of Hawaii; it has numerous craters, including the second-largest active crater in the world.

Mawlamyine Port and capital of Mon state in SE Myanmar, on the Salween estuary; population (1983) 202,967. There is sawmilling and rice milling, and rice and tea are exported.

Mayagüez Port in W Puerto Rico with needlework industry and a US agricultural experimental station; population (1990) 100,400.

Mayen City in the Rhineland-Palatinate, Germany, 30 km/19 mi W of Koblenz; population (1994) 202,400. It is the largest settlement in the remote and hilly Eifel region, which lies between the river Rhine and the German frontier with S Belgium and Luxembourg. There are carpet and paper industries in the city.

Mayence French name for the German city of ◊Mainz.

Mayenne *Département* of W France in Pays-de-Loire region, on the river Mayenne; area 5,212 sq km/2,033 sq mi; capital Laval; population (1990) 278,000. Industries include iron, slate, and paper.

Mayenne River in W France which gives its name to the *département* of Mayenne; length 200 km/125 mi. It rises in Orne, flows in a generally southerly direction through Mayenne and Maine-et-Loire, and joins the river Sarthe just above Angers to form the Maine.

Mayfair District of Westminster in London, England, vaguely defined as lying between Piccadilly and Oxford Street, and including Park Lane; formerly a fashionable residential district, but increasingly taken up by offices.

Maynooth Village in Kildare, Republic of Ireland, with a Roman Catholic training college for priests; population (1981) 3,388.

Mayo County of the Republic of Ireland, in the province of Connacht; county town Castlebar; area 5,400 sq km/ 2,084 sq mi; population (1996 est) 111,400. It has wild Atlantic coast scenery. Features include Lough Conn; Achill Island; Croagh Patrick 765 m/2,510 ft, the mountain where St Patrick spent the 40 days of Lent in 441, climbed by pilgrims on the last Sunday of July each year; and the village of Knock, where two women claimed a vision of the Virgin with two saints 1879, now a site of pilgrimage. Industries include sheep and cattle farming, salmon fishing, potatoes, oats, and pigs.

Mayotte (or *Mahore*) Island group of the Comoros, off the E coast of Africa, a *collectivité territoriale* of France by its own wish. The two main islands are Grande Terre and Petite Terre
area 374 sq km/144 sq mi
capital Dzaoudzi
industries coffee, copra, vanilla, fishing, cloves, cocoa, and ylang-ylang
language French, Swahili
population (1994 est) 109,600
history a French colony 1843–1914, and later, with the Comoros, an overseas territory of France. In 1974, Mayotte voted to remain a French dependency, and in the following year was accepted for membership to the United Nations (UN).

Mbabane Capital (since 1902) of Swaziland, 160 km/ 100 mi W of Maputo, in the Dalgeni Hills; population (1992) 42,000. Mining and tourism are important, and the University of Swaziland is here.

Mboma Another spelling of ◊Boma, a port in the Democratic Republic of Congo (formerly Zaire).

McKeesport City in Pennsylvania, NE USA, forming a part of the ◊Pittsburgh conurbation; population (1990) 26,000. It lies some 16 km/10 mi upstream on the Monongahela River from the centre of Pittsburgh, and shares Pittsburgh's iron and steel industry. The town developed in the 18th century as a fitting-out point for migrants embarking on the Ohio River for the W. Since the 1980s, steel-industry decline has created mass unemployment.

MD Abbreviation for ◊Maryland, a state of the USA.

ME Abbreviation for ◊Maine, a state of the USA.

Meath County of the Republic of Ireland, in the province of Leinster; county town Trim; area 2,340 sq km/903 sq mi; population (1996 est) 109,400. Tara Hill, 155 m/509 ft high, was the site of a palace and coronation place of many kings of Ireland (abandoned in the 6th century) and St Patrick preached here. Sheep, cattle, oats, and potatoes are produced.

Meaux French town in the *département* of Seine-et-Marne, 50 km/31 mi NE of Melun, on the river Marne; population (1990) 51,000. There is a 12th–16th-century cathedral and 15th-century ramparts built on Gallo-Roman foundations. The town has metal and chemical industries.

Mecca (Arabic *Makkah*) City in Saudi Arabia and, as birthplace of Muhammad, the holiest city of the Islamic world; population (1986) 618,000. In the centre of Mecca is the Great Mosque, in the courtyard of which is the Kaaba, the sacred shrine containing the black stone believed to have been given to Abraham by the angel Gabriel.

Mechelen (French *Malines*) Industrial city (furniture, carpets, textiles) and market-gardening centre in Antwerp province, N Belgium, which gave its name to Mechlin lace; population (1995 est) 75,700.

Mecklenburg Former (1934–45) state of NE Germany, consisting of the old grand duchies of *Mecklenburg-Schwerin* (area 13,157 sq km/5,079 sq mi; capital Schwerin) and *Mecklenburg-Strelitz* (area 2,926 sq km/ 1,130 sq mi; capital Neustrelitz). From 1952 to 1989, as part of East Germany, it was divided into the administrative districts (*Bezirke*) of Schwerin, Rostock, and Neubrandenburg. With German reunification, the name of the former state was revived in the *Land* of ◊Mecklenburg–West Pomerania.

Mecklenburg–West Pomerania (German *Mecklenburg-Vorpommern*) Administrative *Land* (state) of Germany
area 23,170 sq km/8,946 sq mi
capital Schwerin
towns and cities Rostock, Wismar, Stralsund, Neubrandenburg
products fish, ships, diesel engines, electronics, plastics, chalk
population (1995) 1,823,100
history the state was formerly the two grand duchies of Mecklenburg-Schwerin and Mecklenburg-Strelitz, which became free states of the Weimar Republic 1918–34, and were joined 1946 with part of Pomerania to form a region of East Germany. In 1952 it was split into the districts of Rostock, Schwerin, and Neubrandenburg. Following German reunification 1990, the districts were abolished and Mecklenburg–West Pomerania was reconstructed as one of the five new states of the Federal Republic.

Medan Seaport and economic centre of the island of Sumatra, Indonesia; population (1990) 1,885,000. It trades in rubber, tobacco, and palm oil.

Medellín Industrial city (textiles, chemicals, engineering, coffee) in the Central Cordillera, Colombia, 1,538 m/5,048 ft above sea level; population (1994) 1,608,000. It is the second city and main textile and gold and silver mining centre of Colombia, and the drug capital of South America. Other industries include coffee growing.

Medford City in SW Oregon, USA, S of Eugene; seat of Jackson County; population (1990) 47,000. It is a summer resort, and tourism is important to the economy. Other industries include processing of the area's timber, agricultural crops (pears), and dairy products. The town was founded 1883.

Medias Town in Sibiu county, central Romania, on the river Tirnava Mare, 40 km/25 mi N of Sibiu. Glass, leather goods, textiles, and chemicals are manufactured, there are engineering and food processing industries, and natural gas wells are found in the area.

Medicine Hat City in Alberta, Canada, 290 km/180 mi SE of Calgary; population (1991) 43,300. It lies on the Canadian Pacific Railway transcontinental main line and the Trans-Canada Highway. It was incorporated as a town in 1899 and became a city in 1907. The city's prosperity comes from its petrochemicals industry and intensive horticulture. It maintains Alberta's ranching tradition with its annual rodeo.

Medina (Arabic *Madinah*) Saudi Arabian city, about 355 km/220 mi N of Mecca; population (1986 est) 500,000. It is the second holiest city in the Islamic world, and is believed to contain the tomb of Muhammad. It produces grain and fruit.

Medina del Campo Town in the province of Valladolid, Spain; population (1995) 20,100. It is an important agricultural centre. It has medieval streets and an ancient castle, seat of the Castilian court during the 15th century.

Mediterranean Sea

Mediterranean Sea Inland sea separating Europe from N Africa, with Asia to the E; extreme length 3,700 km/ 2,300 mi; area 2,510,000 sq km/969,100 sq mi. It is linked to the Atlantic Ocean (at the Strait of Gibraltar), Red Sea, and Indian Ocean (by the Suez Canal), Black Sea (at the Dardanelles and Sea of Marmara). The main subdivisions are the Adriatic, Aegean, Ionian, and Tyrrhenian seas. It is highly polluted.

Médoc French district bordering the Gironde in Aquitaine region, N of Bordeaux. It is famed for its claret wines, Margaux and St Julien being two well-known names. Lesparre and Pauillac are the chief towns.

Medway River of SE England, rising in Sussex and flowing through Kent and the *Medway towns* (Chatham, Gillingham, Rochester) to Sheerness, where it enters the Thames; it is about 96 km/60 mi long. In local tradition it divides the 'Men of Kent', who live to the E, from the 'Kentish Men', who live to the W.

Meerut Industrial city (chemicals, soap, food processing) in Uttar Pradesh, N India; population (1991) 847,000. The Indian Mutiny began here 1857.

Meghalaya State of NE India
area 22,429 sq km/8,660 sq mi
capital Shillong
features mainly agricultural; comprises tribal hill districts
industries potatoes, cotton, jute, fruit, timber, mineral extraction (including 95% of India's sillimanite)
minerals coal, limestone, white clay, corundum, sillimanite
population (1994 est) 1,960,000, mainly Khasi, Jaintia, and Garo
religion Hindu 70%
language various.

Meissen Town in the *Land* of ◊Saxony, Germany, on the river Elbe, 22 km/14 mi NW of Dresden. The manufacture of so-called Dresden china moved here from Dresden 1710. Ceramics are still produced in the town from kaolin deposits nearby, and there are also engineering industries.

Mek'elē Capital of Tigré region, N Ethiopia; population (1992) 113,000. It trades in salt, incense, and resin.

Meknès (Spanish *Mequinez*) City in N Morocco, known for wine and carpetmaking; population (1990) 495,000; urban area (1990) 495,000. One of Morocco's four imperial cities, it was the capital until 1728, and is the site of the tomb of Sultan Moulay Ismail.

Mekong River rising as the Za Qu in Tibet and flowing to the South China Sea, through a vast delta (about 200,000 sq km/77,000 sq mi); length 4,180 km/2,597 mi. It is being

Mekong

developed for irrigation and hydroelectricity by Cambodia, Laos, Thailand, and Vietnam.

Melaka Malaysian form of ◊Malacca, a state of Peninsular Malaysia.

Melanesia Islands in the SW Pacific between Micronesia to the N and Polynesia to the E, embracing all the islands from the New Britain archipelago to Fiji.

Melanesia

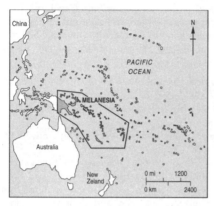

Melbourne Capital of Victoria, Australia, near the mouth of the river Yarra; population (1993) 3,189,200. Industries include engineering, shipbuilding, electronics, chemicals, food processing, clothing, and textiles. Founded 1835, it grew in the wake of the gold rushes, and was the seat of the Commonwealth government 1901–27. It is the country's second largest city, and was the site of the 1956 Olympic Games.

Melbourne Industrial city (food processing and electronic and aviation equipment) on the E coast of Florida, USA, on the Indian River, SE of Orlando; population (1992) 64,300. Aerospace industries and tourism are important because of its proximity to Cape Canaveral. The town was settled 1878.

Melilla Port and military base on the NE coast of Morocco; area 14 sq km/5 sq mi; population (1991) 56,600. It was captured by Spain 1496 and is still under Spanish rule. Also administered from Melilla are three other Spanish possessions: Peña ('rock') de Velez de la Gomera, Peña d'Alhucemas, and the Chaffarine Islands.

Melk Austrian town in the province of Lower Austria, on the river Danube. On a cliff 52 m/171 ft above the town stands a huge Benedictine abbey, one of the most magnificent Baroque buildings in the world.

Melos (modern Greek *Mílos*) Greek island in the Aegean, one of the Cyclades; area 155 sq km/60 sq mi. The sculpture of *Venus de Milo* was discovered here 1820 (now in the Louvre). The capital is Plaka.

Melrose Administrative headquarters of Scottish Borders, Scotland; population (1991) 2,300. The heart of Robert I the Bruce is buried here and the ruins of Melrose Abbey 1136 are commemorated in verse by Sir Walter Scott.

Melton Mowbray Market town in Leicestershire, England, on the river Eye; population (1991) 24,350. A fox-hunting

and horse-breeding centre, it has a large cattle market, and is also known for pork pies and Stilton cheeses. Britain's newest coalmine, Ashfordby Colliery, is here.

Melun French town, capital of the *département* of Seine-et-Marne; population (1990) 40,000. It is on the outskirts of the forest of Fontainebleau. Melun is an agricultural centre, manufactures glass, pottery, and sugar, and is also a commuter town for Paris. There are many old buildings, including a church dating from 1020.

Memel German name for ◊Klaipeda, a port in Lithuania.

Memmingen City in Bavaria, Germany, 106 km/66 mi SW of Munich; population (1994) 40,300. It is an agricultural centre with precision engineering and chemical industries. Formerly one of the city-states of the Holy Roman Empire.

Memphis Industrial port city (pharmaceuticals, food processing, cotton, timber, tobacco) on the Mississippi River, in Tennessee, USA; population (1992) 610,300. The French built a fort here 1739, but Memphis was not founded until 1819. Its musical history includes Beale Street, home of the blues composer W C Handy, and Graceland, home of Elvis Presley; its recording studios and record companies (Sun 1953–68, Stax 1960–75) made it a focus of the music industry.

Menai Strait (Welsh *Afon Menai*) Channel of the Irish Sea, dividing Anglesey from the Welsh mainland; about 22 km/14 mi long, up to 3 km/2 mi wide. It is crossed by Thomas Telford's suspension bridge 1826 (reconstructed 1940) and Robert Stephenson's tubular rail bridge 1850.

Menam Another name for the river ◊Chao Phraya, Thailand.

Mende Capital of the French *département* of Lozère, on the river Lot, 125 km/78 mi NW of Avignon; population (1990) 12,000. The town has a textile industry and a market. Mende is a bishopric, and its cathedral was begun in 1369 by Pope Urban V, who was born here. It is a base for tourists visiting the nearby Tarn Gorge and the Cévennes.

Menderes (Turkish *Büyük Menderes*) River in European Turkey, about 400 km/250 mi long, rising near Afyonkarahisar and flowing along a winding course into the Aegean Sea. The word 'meander' is derived from *maeander*, the ancient Greek name for the river.

Mendip Hills or *Mendips* Range of limestone hills in S England, stretching nearly 40 km/25 mi SE–NW from Wells in Somerset towards the Bristol Channel. There are many cliffs, scars, and caverns, notably *Cheddar Gorge*. The highest peak is *Blackdown* (326 m/1,068 ft).

Mendoza Capital of the Argentine province of the same name; population (1991) 121,700; metropolitan area (1992 est) 801,900. Founded 1561, it developed because of its position on the Trans-Andean railway; it lies at the centre of a wine-producing area.

Menin (Flemish *Menen*) Town in the province of West Flanders, Belgium, situated on the river Lys close to the French border. Goods from Menin tobacco, chicory, and soap. There are also textile and engineering industries.

Menindee Village and sheep centre on the Darling River in New South Wales, Australia. It is the centre of a scheme for conserving the waters of the Darling in *Menindee Lake* (155 sq km/60 sq mi) and other lakes nearby.

Menorca Second largest of the ◊Balearic Islands in the Mediterranean.

area 689 sq km/266 sq mi

capital Mahon

features megalithic remains; unique ecology; Makon is the largest natural port in the Mediterranean

industries leather goods; costume jewellery; cheese and dairy products; tourism is important

population (1990 est) 62,000.

Menton (Italian *Mentone*) Resort on the French Riviera, close to the Italian frontier; population (1990) 29,500. It belonged to the princes of Monaco from the 14th century until briefly independent 1848–60, when the citizens voted to merge with France.

Mequinez Spanish name for ◊Meknès, a town in Morocco.

Mer de Glace Glacier near Chamonix, France, running northwards from Mont Blanc between the precipices of the Chamonix Aiguilles on one side and the Drus and the Verte on the other. It is a tourist attraction.

Mérida Capital of Yucatán state, Mexico, a centre of the sisal industry; population (1990) 556,800. It was founded 1542, and has a cathedral 1598. Its port on the Gulf of Mexico is Progreso.

Mérida Town in the province of Badajoz, W Spain; population (1995) 52,500. It is the capital of ◊Extremadura autonomous community. Situated on the river Guadiana, it was founded by the Romans in 25 BC, and soon became one of the finest cities in the empire, and capital of ◊Lusitania.

Meriden Industrial city (plastics, silver, and electronics) in S central Connecticut, USA, E of Waterbury; population (1992) 58,600. The town was settled 1661. Pewter was produced here from 1794, and the International Silver Company established 1898.

Meridian County seat of Lauderdale County, E Mississippi, USA, 143 km/89 mi E of Jackson; population (1990) 41,000. It is an important centre for the cotton market and has cotton ginning and timber mills.

Merionethshire (Welsh *Sir Feirionnydd*) Former county of N Wales, included in the new county of Gwynedd 1974–96; now part of the unitary authority of Gwynedd.

Merrimack River of S New Hampshire, USA, rising in the White Mountains and flowing through N Massachusetts to the Atlantic Ocean; length 177 km/110 mi. With the river's many waterfalls and rapids supplying power for manufacturing, the Merrimack valley became one of the earliest industrial regions in North America, with many mill towns, including Lawrence and Lowell in Massachusetts. The river valley is now a tourist route.

Merseburg Town in the *Land* of ◊Saxony-Anhalt, Germany, on the river Saale, 14 km/9 mi S of Halle; population (1996) 42,000. Industries include engineering and paper, and there are lignite mines in the vicinity. Merseburg was capital of the Duchy of Saxe-Merseburg 1656–1736, and became part of the territory of Prussia in 1815. The town has a cathedral dating from the 11th–16th centuries.

Mersey River in NW England; length 112 km/70 mi. Formed by the confluence of the Goyt and Tame rivers at Stockport, it flows W to join the Irish Sea at Liverpool Bay. It is linked to the Manchester Ship Canal. It is polluted by industrial waste, sewage, and chemicals. In 1990 the British government announced plans to build a 1,800 m/5,907 ft barrage across the Mersey estuary to generate electricity from tides.

Merseyside Metropolitan county of NW England, created 1974; in 1986, most of the functions of the former county council were transferred to metropolitan district councils

area 650 sq km/251 sq mi

towns and cities Liverpool, Bootle, Birkenhead, St Helens, Wallasey, Southport

features river Mersey; Merseyside Innovation Centre (MIC), linked with Liverpool University and Polytechnic; Prescot Museum of clock- and watch-making; Speke Hall (Tudor), and Croxteth Hall and Country Park (a working country estate open to the public)

industries chemicals, electrical goods, vehicles, glass making

population (1994) 1,403,600

famous people George Stubbs, William Ewart Gladstone, the Beatles.

Mersin or *Içel* Turkish industrial free port (chrome, copper, textiles, oil refining); population (1990) 422,400.

Merthyr Tydfil Unitary authority in S Wales created 1996 from part of the former county of Mid Glamorgan; population (1996) 60,000; area 111 sq km/43 sq mi. The area has the largest land reclamation scheme in Europe, and includes part of the Brecon Beacons National Park.

Merthyr Tydfil Industrial town (light engineering, electrical goods) and administrative headquarters of Merthyr Tydfil unitary authority in S Wales, on the river Taff; population (1991) 39,500. It was formerly a centre of the Welsh coal and steel industries. It had the world's first steam railway 1804 and the largest ironworks in the world in the mid-19th century.

Merton Outer borough of SW Greater London. It includes the suburbs of ◊Wimbledon, Mitcham, and Morden

features Augustinian priory, founded 1114, where Thomas à Becket and Walter de Merton, founder of Merton College, Oxford, were educated (it was demolished at the dissolution and the stones used by Henry VIII to build Nonsuch Palace); Merton Place, where Admiral Nelson lived; Merton Park, laid out in the mid-19th century, claimed as the forerunner of garden suburbs; part of Wimbledon Common, includes Caesar's Camp – an Iron Age fort; All England Lawn Tennis Club (1877)

population (1991) 168,500.

Merwede Branch of the river ◊Meuse in the Netherlands.

Mesabi Range Low hills in Itasca and St Louis counties, Minnesota, USA, about 130 km/81 mi long. The district is important for the production of iron, but supplies of high-grade ore are gradually being exhausted. Lower-grade ores are treated nearby to remove impurities before being shipped to the blast furnaces of the Great Lakes region.

Mesa Verde (Spanish 'green table') Wooded clifftop in Colorado, USA, with Pueblo dwellings, called the Cliff Palace, built into its side. Dating from about 1000 BC, with 200 rooms and 23 circular ceremonial chambers (**kivas**), it had an estimated population of about 400 people and was probably a regional centre. Mesa Verde is a World Heritage Site.

Meshed Variant spelling of ◊Mashhad, a town in Iran.

Mesopotamia The land between the Tigris and Euphrates rivers, now part of Iraq. The civilizations of Sumer and Babylon flourished here. Sumer (3500 BC) may have been the earliest urban civilization.

Messenia (Greek *Messinia*) Department of Greece and country of ancient Greece in the ◊Peloponnese region, bounded on the E by Laconia, N by Elis and Arcadia, and surrounded on the E and W by the sea; area 2991 sq km/1154 sq mi; population (1993) 171,800. The capital is Kalamata.

Messina City and port in NE Sicily; population (1992) 232,900. It produces soap, olive oil, wine, and pasta. Originally an ancient Greek settlement (*Zancle*), it was taken first by Carthage and then by Rome. It was rebuilt after an earthquake 1908.

Messina Province of Italy in NE ◊Sicily; capital Messina; area 3,245 sq km/1,253 sq mi; population (1992) 649,200.

Messina, Strait of Channel in the central Mediterranean separating Sicily from mainland Italy; in Greek legend a monster (Charybdis), who devoured ships, lived in the whirlpool on the Sicilian side, and another (Scylla), who devoured sailors, in the rock on the Italian side. The classical hero Odysseus passed safely between them.

metropolitan county In England, a group of six counties established under the Local Government Act 1972 in the largest urban areas outside London: Tyne and Wear, South Yorkshire, Merseyside, West Midlands, Greater Manchester, and West Yorkshire. Their elected assemblies (county councils) were abolished 1986 when most of their responsibilities reverted to the metropolitan district councils.

Metz Industrial city (shoes, metal goods, tobacco) in Lorraine region, NE France, on the Moselle River; population (1990) 123,900. Part of the Holy Roman Empire 870–1552, it became one of the great frontier fortresses of France, and was in German hands 1871–1918.

Meurthe River rising in the Vosges Mountains in NE France and flowing NW to join the Moselle at Frouard, near Nancy; length 163 km/102 mi. It gives its name to the *département* of Meurthe-et-Moselle.

Meurthe-et-Moselle *Département* in the ◊Lorraine region of France; area 5,234 sq km/2,021 sq mi; population (1990) 712,600. The river Moselle and its tributaries, and the river Chiers, a tributary of the Meuse, flow through the *département*. Grand Rougimont in the Vosges mountains is the highest peak. The main industries include the manufacture of cast and sheet iron, iron and steel goods, and pottery and glass. Rock salt is found in abundance. Grapevines flourish, and cereals, potatoes, and hops are grown. The principal towns are ◊Nancy (the capital), Briey, Lunéville, and Toul.

Meuse (Dutch *Maas*) River flowing through France, Belgium, and the Netherlands; length 900 km/560 mi. It was an important line of battle in both world wars. It gives its name to a French *département*.

Meuse *Département* in the Lorraine region of France; area 6,220 sq km/2,402 sq mi; population (1990) 196,600. The rivers Meuse, Orne, and Chiers flow through the *département*. There are two N–S ridges of highlands: the Côtes de Meuse form the watershed between the rivers Seine and Rhine; and the Argonne is covered with oak forests. Cereals, potatoes, beets, and vines are grown, and livestock is raised. The principal industries are brewing and the manufacture of glass and tiles. The chief towns are Bar-le-Duc (the capital) and Verdun.

Mewar Another name for ◊Udaipur, a city in India.

Mexicali City in NW Mexico; population (1990) 601,900. It produces soap and cottonseed oil. The availability of cheap labour attracts many US companies (Hughes Aerospace, Rockwell International, and others).

Mexico (Spanish *Ciudad de México*) Capital, industrial (iron, steel, chemicals, textiles), and cultural centre of Mexico, 2,255 m/7,400 ft above sea level on the S edge of the central plateau; population (1994) 15,500,000. It is thought to be one of the world's most polluted cities because of its position in a volcanic basin 2,000 m/7,400 ft above sea level. Pollutants gather in the basin causing a smog cloud.

México State of central Mexico; area 21,461 sq km/8,286 sq mi; population (1995 est) 11,704,900. Its capital is Toluca de Lerdo. The main occupations are stock farming, agriculture, and mining.

mezzogiorno (Italian 'midday') Hot, impoverished area of S Italy, comprising six regions and the islands of Sardinia and Sicily. Agriculture is the chief mainstay of a generally poor economy; the main products are grains, vegetables, grapes, and olives. The region's economic, educational, and income levels are much lower than that of N Italy.

MI Abbreviation for ◊Michigan, a state of the USA.

Miami Industrial city (food processing, transportation and electronic equipment, clothing, and machinery) and port in Florida, USA; population (1992) 367,000. It is the hub of finance, trade, and air transport for the USA, Latin America, and the Caribbean. It is also a centre for oceanographic research. The first permanent settlement by people other than Native Americans dates from the 1870s. There has been an influx of immigrants from Cuba, Haiti, Mexico, and South America since 1959.

Michigan   State in N central USA; nicknamed Wolverine State/Great Lakes State
area   151,600 sq km/58,518 sq mi
capital   Lansing
cities   Detroit, Grand Rapids, Flint
physical   Great Lakes: Superior, Michigan, Huron, and Erie; Porcupine Mountains; Muskegon, Grand, St Joseph, and Kalamazoo rivers; over 50% forested; Isle Royale national park; the Upper Peninsula with Pictured Rocks national lakeshore and spectacular waterfalls; 94 state parks, including 23 in the Upper Peninsula; Lake Michigan shore, with the highest sand dunes outside the Sahara Desert in the Sleeping Bear Dunes national lakeshore
features   the Upper Peninsula is connected to the rest of the state since 1957 by the Mackinac Bridge (pronounced Mackinaw); resort towns including the artists' colony of Saugatuck, and the SS *Keewatin*, a passenger steamboat converted into a maritime museum; Mackinac Island, a Victorian village with no cars, including Old Fort Mackinac, a former British stronghold; the Keweenaw Peninsula, the source of much of the world's copper 1840s–1960s, with the Arcadian Copper Mine, Delaware Copper Mine, Coppertown USA, and the Victorian town of Callumat; Detroit, with the Detroit Institute of Art (1885), and the Henry Ford Museum and Greenfield Village at Dearborn; the Tulip Time Festival at Holland; the De Klomp Wooden Shoe and Delftware Factory, Holland; National Cherry Festival, Traverse City; National Music Camp, Interlochen; University of Michigan, Ann Arbor
products   motor vehicles and equipment; nonelectrical machinery; iron and steel; chemicals; pharmaceuticals; dairy products
population   (1995) 9,549,400
famous people   Edna Ferber, Gerald Ford, Henry Ford, Jimmy Hoffa, Iggy Pop, Diana Ross
history   temporary posts established in early 17th century by French explorers Etienne Brulé, Jacques Marquette, Louis Joliet, and Robert de la Salle; first settled 1668 at Sault Ste Marie; present-day Detroit settled 1701; passed to the British 1763 and to the USA 1796; statehood achieved 1837.

Michigan, Lake   Lake in N central USA, one of the Great Lakes; area 57,735 sq km/22,291 sq mi. Chicago and Milwaukee are its main ports. Lake Michigan is joined to Lake Huron by the Straits of Mackinac. Green Bay is the largest inlet.

Michoacán   State of Mexico, on the Pacific; area 59,864 sq km/23,113 sq mi; population (1995 est) 3,869,100. Its capital is Morelia. The main occupations are mining for silver, lead, and copper, and farming, producing cereals, rice, sugar-cane, and tobacco.

Micronesia, Federated States of   Group of islands in the Pacific Ocean lying N of ◊Melanesia, including the Federated States of Micronesia, Palau, Kiribati, the Mariana and Marshall Islands, Nauru, and Tuvalu.

Middelburg   Industrial town (engineering, tobacco, furniture) in the SW Netherlands, capital of Zeeland and a former Hanseatic town; population (1993) 40,100. Its town hall dates from the 15th century.

Middle East   Indeterminate area now usually taken to include the Balkan States, Egypt, and SW Asia. Until the 1940s, this area was generally called the Near East, and the term Middle East referred to the area from Iran to Burma (now Myanmar).

Middle Range   or *Middleback Range* Mountain range in the NE of Eyre Peninsula, South Australia, about 65 km/40 mi long, parallel with the W coast of Spencer Gulf. Iron deposits are mined at Iron Baron, Iron Knob, and Iron Monarch.

Middlesbrough   Industrial town, port and unitary authority, on the Tees, NE England; population (1997) 146,000; area 54 sq km/21 sq mi; commercial and cultural centre of the urban area formed by Stockton-on-Tees, Redcar, Billingham, Thornaby, and Eston. A transporter bridge (1911) across the river Tees has cable cars for passengers. Formerly a centre of heavy industry, it diversified its products in the 1960s. There are constructional, electronics, engineering, and shipbuilding industries, and iron, steel and chemicals are produced. It is the birthplace of the navigator Capt James Cook, of whom there is a museum. Teeside rivals Rotterdam as Europe's largest petrochemicals complex.

Middlesex   Former English county, absorbed by Greater London 1965. It was settled in the 6th century by Saxons, and its name comes from its position between the kingdoms of the East and West Saxons. Contained within the Thames basin, it provided good agricultural land before it was built over.

Middletown   City in S central Connecticut, USA, on the Connecticut River, S of Hartford; population (1990) 42,800. Industries include insurance, banking, vehicle parts, electronics, hardware, textiles, chemicals, and paper products. Wesleyan University (1831) is here. Middletown was settled 1650 on the site of a Native American village. It was an important seaport in the 18th and 19th centuries, and a base for trade in rum, slaves, and molasses between Africa and the West Indies.

Middletown   Industrial city (steel, paper products, and aircraft parts) in SW Ohio, USA, on the Miami River, N of Cincinnati; population (1990) 46,000. It was founded 1802.

Mid Glamorgan   (Welsh *Morgannwg Ganol*) Former county of S Wales, 1974–96, now divided between Rhonnda Cynon Taff, Merthyr Tydfil, Bridgend, and Vale of Glamorgan unitary authorities.

Midi, Canal du   or *Canal de Languedoc* Canal in the Languedoc-Roussillion region of France which connects the river Garonne with the Mediterranean; length 240 km/149 mi.

Midi-de-Bigorre, Pic du   Peak in the Pyrénées mountains, S France; 2,839 m/9,314 ft high. It is 10 km/6 mi S of Bagnères-de-Bigorre, almost on the Spanish frontier. Tourists come for recreation and winter sports.

Midi-Pyrénées Region of SW France, comprising the *départements* of Ariège, Aveyron, Haute-Garonne, Gers, Lot, Hautes-Pyrénées, Tarn, and Tarn-et-Garonne; capital Toulouse; area 45,348 sq km/17,509 sq mi; population (1990) 2,430,700. The region includes several spa towns (including Lourdes), winter resorts, and prehistoric caves; it produces fruit, wine, and livestock.

Midland Industrial city (chemicals and concrete) in central Michigan, USA, on the Tittabawassee River, NW of Saginaw; population (1990) 38,100. There are oil and gas wells. It was founded in the 1830s and developed as a centre of the chemical industry after the Dow Chemical Company was started 1888.

Midland City in W Texas, USA, halfway between Fort Worth and El Paso; population (1992) 95,200. The city's economy depends on the oil companies located here after the discovery of oil 1923. It lies in a cattle-ranching region, and was founded 1884.

Midlands Area of England corresponding roughly to the Anglo-Saxon kingdom of Mercia. The *E Midlands* comprises Derbyshire, Leicestershire, Northamptonshire, and Nottinghamshire. The *W Midlands* covers the metropolitan county of ◊West Midlands created from parts of Staffordshire, Warwickshire, and Worcestershire; and (often included) the *S Midlands* comprising Bedfordshire, Buckinghamshire, and Oxfordshire.

Midlothian Unitary authority in SE Scotland, S of the Firth of Forth. A former county, it was included 1975–96 in Lothian Region; administrative headquarters Dalkeith; population (1996) 79,900; area 355 sq km/137 sq mi. The area includes the Moorfoot Hills.

Midway Islands Two islands in the Pacific, 1,800 km/ 1,120 mi NW of Honolulu; area 5 sq km/2 sq mi. They were annexed by the USA 1867, and are now administered by the US Navy. The naval *Battle of Midway* 3–6 June 1942, between the USA and Japan, was a turning point in the Pacific in World War II; the US victory marked the end of Japanese expansion in the Pacific.

Midwest or *Middle West* Large area of the N central USA. It is loosely defined, but is generally taken to comprise the states of Illinois, Iowa, Wisconsin, Minnesota, Nebraska, Kansas, Missouri, North Dakota, and South Dakota and the portions of Montana, Wyoming, and Colorado that lie E of the Rocky Mountains. Ohio, Michigan, and Indiana are often variously included as well. Traditionally its economy is divided between agriculture and heavy industry. The main urban Midwest centre is Chicago. In the summer of 1993 the Midwest was devastated by floods, which left tens of thousands of people homeless.

Mikkeli Province of E central Finland; area 22,840 sq km/ 8,819 sq mi. More than one-third of the area is covered by lakes, with over 1,000 islands. The capital is also called Mikkeli.

Milan (Italian *Milano*) Industrial city (aircraft, cars, locomotives, textiles), financial and cultural centre, capital of Lombardy, and second largest city in Italy; population (1992) 1,358,600.

Milan Province of N Italy in W ◊Lombardy region; capital Milan; area 2,763 sq km/1,067 sq mi; population (1981) 4,038,700.

Mildura Town in NW Victoria, Australia, on the Murray River, with food-processing industries; population (1991) 23,200.

Mile End Area of the East End of London, England, in the district of Stepney, now part of the London borough of Tower Hamlets. Mile End Green (now Stepney Green) was the scene of Richard II's meeting with the rebel peasants 1381, and in later centuries was the exercise ground of the London 'trained bands', or militia.

Milford Industrial city (fabricated metal, writing pens, and electronics) in SW Connecticut, USA, situated by the Housatonic River and Long Island Sound, W of New Haven; population (1990) 49,900. The site was settled 1639.

Milford Haven (Welsh *Aberdaugleddau*) seaport in Pembrokeshire, SW Wales, on the estuary of the E and W Cleddau rivers; population (1991) 13,200. It has oil refineries, and a terminal for giant tankers linked by pipeline with Llandarcy, near Swansea. There is a fishing industry.

Milk River River in North America, a tributary of the ◊Missouri; length 1,175 km/730 mi. It rises in the Rocky Mountains, in NW Montana, and flows N and E into S Alberta, Canada, where it is used for irrigation. It then flows into Montana, where it joins the Missouri near Nashua.

Millau French town in the *département* of Aveyron, 50 km/31 mi S of Rodez, on the river Tarn; population (1990) 22,300. Its industries include the manufacture of gloves, leather goods, and furniture. There is a 14th–16th-century church and a Gothic belfry. In the 16th–17th centuries it was a Huguenot religious stronghold. It is close to the Tarn Gorge and other tourist sites.

Millville City in SW New Jersey, USA, on the Maurice River, SE of Philadelphia; population (1990) 26,000. Products include vegetables, poultry, and glass. Glassmaking became important in the 19th century.

Milton Keynes Industrial new town and unitary authority in S central England; population (1996) 198,600; area 310 sq km/120 sq mi. It was part of the county of Buckinghamshire to 1997. It was developed as a new town 1967 around the old village of the same name, following a grid design by Richard Llewelyn-Davies; it is the headquarters of the Open University (founded 1969). Industries include electronics, machine tools, clothing, and machinery.

Milwaukee Industrial port (meatpacking, brewing, engineering, machinery, electronic and electrical equipment, chemicals) in Wisconsin, USA, on Lake Michigan; population (1992) 617,000. The site was settled 1818 and drew a large influx of German immigrants, beginning in the 1840s.

Minas Gerais State in SE Brazil; centre of the country's iron ore, coal, diamond and gold mining industries; area 587,172 sq km/226,710 sq mi; capital Belo Horizonte; population (1991) 16,956,900.

Mindanao Second-largest island of the Philippines. The indigenous peoples are the Lumad and Moro; area 94,630 sq km/36,537 sq mi; population (1990) 14,298,250. Towns and cities include Davao and Zamboanga. Industries include pineapples, coffee, rice, coconut, rubber, hemp, timber, nickel, gold, steel, chemicals, and fertilizer. The island is mainly mountainous rainforest; the active volcano Apo reaches 2,954 m/9,600 ft, and the island is subject to severe earthquakes.

Minden Industrial town (tobacco, food processing) of North Rhine-Westphalia, Germany, on the river Weser; population (1985) 80,000. The French were defeated here 1759 by an allied army from Britain, Hannover, and Brunswick, commanded by the duke of Brunswick.

Mindoro Island of the Philippine Republic, S of Luzon
area 10,347 sq km/3,995 sq mi
towns and cities Calapan
features Mount Halcon 2,590 m/8,500 ft
population (1990) 832,600.

Minhow Name in use 1934–43 for ◊Fuzhou, a town in SE China.

Minneapolis City in Minnesota, USA, forming with St Paul the Twin Cities area; population (1992) 362,700; metropolitan area (1992) 2,618,000. It is at the head of navigation of the Mississippi River. Industries include food processing and the manufacture of machinery, electrical and electronic equipment, precision instruments, transport machinery, and metal and paper products. Minneapolis was incorporated as a village 1856.

Minnesota State in N midwest USA; nicknamed Gopher State/North Star State
area 218,700 sq km/84,418 sq mi
capital St Paul
towns and cities Minneapolis, Duluth, Bloomington, Rochester
physical more than 15,000 lakes; 260 km/160 mi of Lake Superior rocky shoreline; Voyageurs national park near the Canadian border, with 30 major lakes; headwaters of the Mississippi in Itasca state park; the Falls of St Anthony on the Mississippi River, and the Minnehaha Falls (mentioned by Longfellow in *The Song of Hiawatha*)
features Fort Snelling state park, with the fort built at the junction of the Mississippi and Minnesota rivers; Minneapolis, with the American Swedish Institute, the Walker Art Center with the Minneapolis Sculpture Garden (the largest outdoor urban sculpture garden in the USA); St Paul, with Summit Avenue (7.2 km/4.5 mi long, the longest stretch of residential Victorian architecture in the USA), including the James J Hill House (a Romanesque mansion), the Cathedral of St Paul, the state capitol (with a dome 68 m/223 ft high, the world's largest unsupported marble dome), the Alexander Ramsey House (1872), the Landmark Center (Romanesque Revival Old Federal Courts Buildings, 1902), and the carved onyx God of Peace statue by the Swedish sculptor Carl Milles (11 m/36 ft high); Soudan Underground Mine state park, with tours of Soudan Mine, the state's oldest iron mine, working until 1962; Hull-Rust Mahoning iron mine, the world's largest open-pit iron ore mine, at Hibbing; the Iron Range; the

United States Hockey Hall of Fame, Eveleth; Greyhound Origin Center at Hibbing, where the Greyhound bus system began; the Mayo Clinic, Rochester, including Maywood, former home of Dr Charles H Mayo
products cereals, soya beans, livestock, meat and dairy products, iron ore (about two-thirds of US output), non-electrical machinery, electronic equipment
population (1995) 4,609,500
famous people Bob Dylan, F Scott Fitzgerald, Hubert H Humphrey, Sinclair Lewis, Charles and William Mayo
history first European exploration, by French fur traders, in the 17th century; region claimed for France by Daniel Greysolon, Sieur Duluth, 1679; part E of Mississippi River ceded to Britain 1763 and to the USA 1783; part W of Mississippi passed to the USA under the Louisiana Purchase 1803; became a territory 1849; statehood achieved 1858.

Miño River of Spain and Portugal, rising in the Cantabrian Mountains, Spain; length 338 km/210 mi. It flows S through Lugo, then SW through ◊Orense and Portugal to the Atlantic Ocean. Its chief tributary is the river Sil.

Minsk or *Mensk* Industrial city (machinery, textiles, leather, computer industry) and capital of Belarus; population (1991) 1,633,600. Minsk dates from the 11th century and has in turn been held by Lithuania, Poland, Sweden, and Russia before Belarus became an independent republic 1991.

Miquelon Islands see ◊St Pierre and Miquelon

Mirpur District in SW Kashmir, Pakistan, between the Jhelum River and the Indian state of Jammu and Kashmir; capital Mirpur. Its products include cotton and grain.

Mirzapur City of Uttar Pradesh, India, on the river Ganges; a grain and cotton market, with bathing sites and temples on the river; population (1991) 169,000.

Mishawaka Industrial city (plastics, rubber, missiles, and vehicle and aircraft parts) in N central Indiana, USA, E of South Bend; population (1990) 42,600. The town was laid out 1833. It has a Flemish-speaking community as a result of Belgian immigration after World War II.

Miskolc Industrial city (iron, steel, textiles, furniture, paper) in NE Hungary, on the river Sajo, 145 km/90 mi NE of Budapest; population (1995 est) 182,000.

Misr Egyptian name for Egypt and for ◊Cairo.

Mission City in S Texas, USA, near the Rio Grande, W of McAllen; population (1990) 28,700. The economy is based on processing the area's citrus fruits and vegetables, and on nearby oil wells. The town was settled 1908 near a Franciscan Catholic mission.

Mississippi River in the USA, the main arm of the great river system draining the USA between the Appalachian and the Rocky mountains. The length of the Mississippi is 3,779 km/2,348 mi; with its tributary the Missouri 6,020 km/3,741 mi.

Mississippi

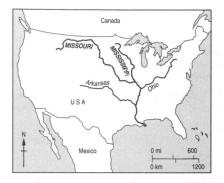

Mississippi State in SE USA; nicknamed Magnolia State/
Bayou State
area 123,600 sq km/47,710 sq mi
capital Jackson
towns and cities Biloxi, Meridian, Hattiesburg
physical Mississippi, Pearl, and Big Black rivers;
Mississippi Delta; Gulf Islands national seashore
features Jackson, with many Greek Revival buildings,
including the old capitol building from the 1830s (now the
State Historical Museum), City Hall (1847), the Mississippi
Governor's Mansion (1841), and Smith Robertson Museum
(formerly the first public school for black children in the
city, now a museum devoted to black life in the state);
Oxford, with Courthouse Square (including Lafayette
County Courthouse), Rowan Oak (1844, the home of
William Faulkner), and the Center for Study of Southern
Culture in Barnard Observatory (with the world's largest
blues archive); Natchez, with cotton plantation mansions
built in the first half of the 19th century, including Rosalie
(1823), Magnolia Hall (1858), Stanton Hall (1857), and
Longwood (1860, the largest octagonal house in the USA);
Vicksburg national military park (Civil War site); Port
Gibson, with the First Presbyterian Church (1859, with a
3.6-m/12-ft hand pointing up from the spire), restored
houses and churches on Church Street, including the
Disharoon House and Gage House (1830s) and Temple
Gemiluth Chassed (1892, a synagogue in the Byzantine
style); Grand Gulf Military Monument; Emerald Mound,
an Native American mound dating from c. 1300; Civil War
sites at Corinth; University of Mississippi (1848); Elvis
Presley's birthplace at Tupelo, with the Elvis Presley Park
and Elvis Presley Memorial Chapel; Natchez Trace
Parkway; the Biedenharn Candy Company, Vicksburg,
where Coca-Cola was first bottled 1894, now a Coca-Cola
museum
products cotton, rice, soya beans, chickens, fish and shellfish, lumber and wood products, petroleum and natural
gas, transportation equipment, chemicals
population (1995) 2,697,200
famous people Jefferson Davis, William Faulkner, John
Lee Hooker, Elvis Presley, Leontyne Price, Eudora Welty,
Tennessee Williams, Howlin' Wolf, Richard Wright
history first explored by Hernando de Soto for Spain 1540;

settled by the French 1699, the English 1763; ceded to USA
1798; statehood achieved 1817. After secession from the
Union during the Civil War, it was readmitted 1870.

Missolonghi (Greek *Mesolóngion*) Town in W central
Greece and Eubrea region, on the N shore of the Gulf of
Patras; population (1981) 10,200. It was several times under
siege by the Turks in the wars of 1822–26 and it was here
that the British poet Byron died.

Missoula City in Montana, NW USA, county seat of
Missoula County, on Clark Fork near the mouth of the
Bitterroot River, 153 km/95 mi NW of Helena; population
(1990) 42,900. The city's economy depends on its sawmills
and pastoral farming. It also has ski centres.

Missouri Major river in the central USA, a tributary of the
Mississippi, which it joins N of St Louis; length 3,726 km/
2,315 mi.

Missouri State in central USA; nicknamed Show Me
State/Bullion State
area 180,600 sq km/69,712 sq mi
capital Jefferson City
towns and cities St Louis, Kansas City, Springfield,
Independence
physical Ozark Mountains and the Lake of the Ozarks;
Missouri and Mississippi rivers; Mark Twain national forest
features St Louis, with the Gateway Arch (1966, 192 m/
630 ft high), in Jefferson National Expansion Memorial
Park, St Louis Art Museum, the Cathedral of St Louis, the
world headquarters of Anheuser-Busch (makers of
Budweiser beer), and the St Louis Cardinals Hall of Fame;
Wilson's Creek national battlefield; the Pony Express
national memorial, and the birthplace of Jesse James, in St
Joseph; Ste Genevieve, the oldest permanent settlement in
Missouri, with 18th-century Creole architecture; the
Carver national monument, the birthplace of George
Washington Carver; the Mark Twain home and museum,
Hannibal; Missouri Town 1855, in Blue Springs; Laura
Ingalls Wilder home, Mansfield; Harry S Truman library
and museum, and the Truman home, at Independence;
Fulton, site of Winston Churchill's 'Iron Curtain' speech
1946, with collection of Churchilliana in the Church of St
Mary the Virgin, Aldermanbury, bombed in London during World War II and reassembled at Fulton; Nelson-
Atkins Museum of Art, Kansas City, a fine collection of
Asian art; St Louis Symphony Orchestra; 'Bible Belt' centred on Springfield
products meat and other processed food, aerospace and
transport equipment, lead, zinc
population (1995) 5,323,500
famous people George Washington Carver, T S Eliot, Jesse
James, Joseph Pulitzer, Harry S Truman, Mark Twain
history explored by Hernando de Soto for Spain 1541;
acquired by the USA under the Louisiana Purchase 1803;
achieved statehood 1821, following the Missouri
Compromise of 1820.

Mitchell, Mount Highest peak in the Appalachian
Mountains, in E USA; height 2,037 m/6,683 ft. It is in the

Black Mountains range, 32 km/20 mi NE of Asheville, North Carolina. Its trees have been ravaged by acid rain.

Mitylene Alternative spelling of ◊Mytilene, a Greek town on the island of Lesvos.

Mizoram State of NE India
area 21,081 sq km/8,139 sq mi
capital Aizawl
products rice, hand-loom weaving
population (1994 est) 775,000
religion 84% Christian
history made a Union Territory 1972 from the Mizo Hills District of Assam. Rebels carried on a guerrilla war 1966–76, but 1976 acknowledged Mizoram as an integral part of India. It became a state 1986.

Mmabatho Capital of North West Province, South Africa; population (1991) 13,300. It is the location of ◊Sun City, a casino resort frequented by many white South Africans.

MN Abbreviation for ◊Minnesota, a state of the USA.

MO Abbreviation for ◊Missouri, a state of the USA.

Mobile Industrial city (meatpacking, paper, cement, clothing, chemicals) and only seaport in Alabama, USA; population (1992) 201,900. Founded 1702 by the French a little to the N of the present city, Mobile was capital of the French colony of Louisiana until 1763. It was then British until 1780, and Spanish to 1813.

Mobutu, Lake Alternate name of Lake ◊Albert in central Africa.

Moçambique Portuguese name for Mozambique.

Mocha Alternate form of ◊Al Mukha, Yemen.

Modena City in Emilia, Italy, capital of the province of Modena, 37 km/23 mi NW of Bologna; population (1992) 177,000. Products include vehicles, glass, pasta, and sausages. It has a 12th-century cathedral, a 17th-century ducal palace, and a university (1683), known for its medical and legal faculties.

Modena Province of N central Italy in central ◊Emilia-Romagna region; capital Modena; area 2,691 sq km/1,039 sq mi; population (1992) 605,900.

Modesto City in central California, USA, on the Tuolumne River, SE of San Francisco, on the fringes of the San Joaquin Valley; population (1992) 172,300. It is an agricultural centre for wine, apricots, melons, beans, peaches, and livestock. Modesto was founded 1870.

Mödling Suburb of the Austrian capital ◊Vienna, in the province of Lower Austria. Mödling, on the S edge of the Vienna metropolitan area, has some notable churches and a ruined castle. Shoes and metal goods are the main industries.

Mogadishu or *Mugdisho* Capital and chief port of Somalia; population (1987 est) 1,000,000. It is a centre for oil refining, food processing, and uranium mining. During the struggle to overthrow President Barre and the ensuing civil war 1991–92, much of the city was devastated and many thousands killed. In 1992 UN peacekeeping troops (including a large contingent of US Marines) were stationed in the

city to monitor a cease-fire and to protect relief operations. By 1994 troops were withdrawn.

Mogilev Industrial city (tractors, clothing, chemicals, furniture) in Belarus, on the river Dnieper, 193 km/120 mi E of Minsk; population (1991) 363,000. It was annexed by Russia from Sweden 1772. Belarus became an independent republic 1991.

Mogok Village in Myanmar (Burma), 114 km/71 mi N-NE of Mandalay, known for its ruby and sapphire mines.

Mohács River port in S Hungary, on the Danube, near the Croatian border, 37 km/23 mi E of Pécs; population (1993) 20,100. Coal is mined in the district. During the 16th and 17th centuries, two decisive battles were fought with the Ottoman Turks at the town.

Mohawk Main tributary of the ◊Hudson River in New York, USA; length 225 km/140 mi. It rises in the county of Oneida and joins the Hudson at Cohoes.

Mojave or *Mohave* **Desert** Arid region in S California, Nevada, Arizona and Utah, USA, part of the Great Basin; approximate area 65,000 sq km/25,000 sq mi.

Mold (Welsh *Yr Wyddgrug*) Market town and administrative headquarters of Flintshire, Wales, on the river Alyn; population (1991) 8,750. It has light industries. There are two theatres.

Moldau German name for the ◊Vltava, a river in the Czech Republic.

Moldavia Former principality in E Europe, on the river Danube, occupying an area divided today between Moldova and Romania. It was independent between the 14th and 16th centuries, when it became part of the Ottoman Empire. In 1861 Moldavia was united with its neighbouring principality Wallachia as Romania. In 1940 the E part, ◊Bessarabia, became part of the USSR, whereas the W part remained in Romania.

Moline Industrial city (farm implements, furniture, and metal products) in NW Illinois, USA, on the Mississippi River, W of Chicago; population (1990) 43,200. Moline was laid out 1843, and was a centre of plough production.

Molise Mainly agricultural region of S central Italy, comprising the provinces of Campobasso and Isernia; area 4,438 sq km/1,714 sq mi; population (1995) 332,200. Its capital is ◊Campobasso.

Molokai Mountainous island of Hawaii, USA, SE of Oahu
area 673 sq km/259 sq mi
features Kamakou 1,512 m/4,960 ft is the highest peak
population (1990) 6,700
history the island was the site of a leper colony organized 1873–89 by Belgian missionary Joseph De Veuster (Father Damien).

Molotov Former name of the port of ◊Perm in Russia.

Moluccas Another name for ◊Maluku, a group of Indonesian islands.

Mombasa Industrial port (oil refining, cement) and tourist resort in Kenya (the port also serves Uganda and

Tanzania), population (1989) 465,000. It stands on Mombasa Island and the adjacent mainland. Mombasa was founded by Arab traders in the 11th century and was an important centre for ivory and slave trading until the 16th century.

Møn Danish island lying between and to the E of Sjaelland and Falster; area 220 sq km/85 sq mi. It is 32 km/20 mi long and is divided from Sjaelland by Ulv Sound and from Falster by Gron Sound. It is the highest island point of Denmark after Bornholm, with precipitous limestone cliffs (150 m/492 ft high) on its E side; it has a lighthouse which is visible for 25 km/16 mi. The soil is chalky and fertile. Its chief town is Stege.

Mona Latin name for ◊Anglesey, an island off the coast of Wales.

Monadnock Mountain in New Hampshire, USA, 1,063 m/3,186 ft high. The term 'monadnock' is also used to mean any isolated hill or mountain.

Monaghan (Irish *Mhuineachain*) County of the Republic of Ireland, in the province of Ulster; county town Monaghan; area 1,290 sq km/498 sq mi; population (1996 est) 51,300. Products include cereals, linen, potatoes, and cattle. The county is low and rolling, and includes the rivers Finn and Blackwater.

Monastir Turkish name for the town of ◊Bitolj in the Former Yugoslav Republic of Macedonia.

Monastir Resort town on the Mediterranean coast of Tunisia, 18 km/11 mi S of Sousse. It is the birthplace of former president Habib Bourguiba and summer residence of the president of Tunisia.

Mönchengladbach Industrial city in North Rhine–Westphalia, Germany, on the river Niers near Düsseldorf; industries include textiles, machinery, paper; population (1993) 265,100. It is the NATO headquarters for N Europe.

Moncton City in SE New Brunswick, Canada, on the Petitcodiac River and the Trans-Canada Highway, 145 km/90 mi NE of St John; population (1991) 80,700. It is the regional headquarters of the Canadian National Railways, and a distribution centre for the maritime provinces and Newfoundland. Its industries include food processing and manufacture of paperboard and vehicle parts. There are oil wells and natural gas nearby.

Mongolia, Inner (Chinese *Nei Mongol*) Autonomous region of NE China from 1947
area 450,000 sq km/173,745 sq mi
capital Hohhot
features strategic frontier area with Russia; known for Mongol herders, now becoming settled farmers
physical grassland and desert
products cereals under irrigation; coal; reserves of rare earth oxides europium, and yttrium at Bayan Obo
population (1990) 21,110,000.

Monmouth (Welsh *Trefynwy*) Market town in Monmouthshire, Wales, at the confluence of the rivers Wye and Monnow; population (1991) 75,000. There is some light industry. Henry V was born in the now ruined castle.

Monmouthshire (Welsh *Sir Fynwy*) Unitary authority in SE Wales. A former county, from 1974–96 it was, minus a small strip on the border with Mid Glamorgan, the county of *Gwent*; administrative headquarters Cwmbran; population (1996) 80,400; area 851 sq km/328 sq mi. Features include the Wye Valley, Chepstow and Raglan castles, Tintern Abbey, and salmon and trout fishing.

Monongahela River in West Virginia and Pennsylvania, USA, formed by the junction of the Tygart and West Fork rivers. It flows 205 km/128 mi northwards to the Allegheny, which it joins at Pittsburgh, Pennsylvania, to form the ◊Ohio River. it is surrounded by the Monongahela national forest. Navigable by means of locks, it is also harnessed for hydroelectric power.

Monroe City in NE Louisiana, USA, on the Ouachita River, E of Shreveport; population (1992) 56,200. Industries include furniture, chemicals, paper, natural gas, and soya beans. It was founded 1785 by French settles.

Monrovia Capital and port of Liberia; population (1992) 490,000. Industries include rubber, cement, and petrol processing. Civil war damaged much of the infrastructure in and around Monrovia in the 1990s.

Mons (Flemish *Bergen*) Industrial city (coal mining, textiles, sugar) and capital of the province of Hainaut, Belgium; population (1995 est) 92,700. The military headquarters of NATO is at nearby Chièvres-Casteau.

Montana State in W USA, on the Canadian border; nicknamed Treasure State/Big Sky Country
area 318,100 sq km/147,143 sq mi
capital Helena
towns and cities Billings, Great Falls, Butte
physical mountainous forests in the W, rolling grasslands in the E; Missouri, Yellowstone, and Little Bighorn rivers; Glacier national park, on the Continental Divide; Waterton Glacier international peace park (a World Heritage Site); part of Yellowstone national park; Missouri Headwaters state park; National Bison Range; Flathead Lake, the largest freshwater lake W of the Mississippi; Madison Buffalo Jump state park, with a preserved cliff where the Plains Indians stampeded bison to their deaths
features Bannack, a frontier boom town, now a ghost town; Little Bighorn Battlefield national monument, the site of Custer's last stand, 1876; Big Hole national battlefield, the site of the battle between the US cavalry and the Nez Percé, 1877; Moss Mansion, Billings (1903); the Museum of the Plains Indians, Browning; gold rush mansions in Helena; C M Russell Museum, Great Falls, with works by the cowboy artist Charles Marion Russell; Our Lady of the Rockies, a 27-m/90-ft illuminated statue of the Virgin Mary on the Continental Divide, above Butte; hunting and ski resorts
products wheat (under irrigation), cattle, coal, copper, oil, natural gas, lumber, wood products
population (1995) 870,300
famous people Gary Cooper, Myrna Loy
history explored for France by Verendrye early 1740s;

passed to the USA 1803 in the Louisiana Purchase; first settled 1809; W Montana obtained from Britain in the Oregon Treaty 1846; influx of gold-seeking immigrants mid-19th century; fierce wars against the Native Americans 1867–77, which included 'Custer's last stand' at the Little Bighorn with the Sioux; achieved statehood 1889.

Montaubon Industrial town (porcelain, textiles) in the Midi-Pyrénées region, SW France, on the river Tarn; population about 51,200. The classical painter Jean Auguste Ingres was born here.

Montbéliard French town in the *département* of Doubs, 70 km/43 mi E of Besançon, on the Rhine and Rhône canal; population (1990) 33,600. Montbéliard has car industries. The former castle of the counts of Montbéliard, rebuilt in the 17th century, is a museum.

Mont Blanc (Italian *Monte Bianco*) Highest mountain in the ◊Alps, between France and Italy; height 4,807 m/ 15,772 ft. It was first climbed 1786 by Jacques Balmat and Michel Paccard of Chamonix.

Mont Cenis Pass in the Alps between Lyon, France, and Turin, Italy, at 2,082 m/6,831 ft.

Mont-de-Marsan French town, capital of the *département* of Landes, on the river Midouze; population (1990) 32,000. It has nursery gardens, and oil, wood, and resin industries.

Monte Bello Islands Group of uninhabited islands in the Indian Ocean, off the coast of W Australia. The British government used them as a nuclear test site in 1952 and 1956. They are now a marine park and conservation area: short visits are deemed safe though permanent residency is not.

Monte Carlo Town and luxury resort in the principality of Monaco, situated on a rocky promontory NE of Monaco town; population (1988 est) 28,000. It is known for its Casino (1878) designed by architect Charles Garnier, and the Monte Carlo car rally and Monaco Grand Prix.

Monte Cristo Small uninhabited island 40 km/25 mi S of Elba, in the Tyrrhenian Sea; its name supplied a title for the French novelist Alexandre Dumas's hero in *The Count of Monte Cristo* 1844.

Montego Bay Port and resort on the NW coast of Jamaica; population (1991) 83,400. The fine beaches and climate attract tourists.

Montélimar Town in Drôme district, France; known for the nougat to which its name is given; population (1990) 31,400.

Montenegro (Serbo-Croatian *Crna Gora*) Constituent republic of Yugoslavia
area 13,800 sq km/5,327 sq mi
capital Podgorica
towns and cities Cetinje
features smallest of the republics; Skadarsko Jezero (Lake Scutari) shared with Albania; Mount Lovćen (1,749 m/ 5,738 ft)

physical mountainous and karst region in SW; forests and grasslands in E
population (1991) 615,300, including c. 397,000 Montenegrins, 79,500 Muslims, and 39,500 Albanians
language Serbian variant of Serbo-Croat
religion Serbian Orthodox
famous people Milovan Djilas
history part of ◊Serbia from the late 12th century, it became independent (under Venetian protection) after Serbia was defeated by the Turks 1389. It was forced to accept Turkish suzerainty in the late 15th century, but was never completely subdued by Turkey. It was ruled by bishop princes until 1851, when a monarchy was founded, and became a sovereign principality under the Treaty of Berlin 1878. The monarch used the title of king from 1910. Montenegro participated in the Balkan Wars 1912 and 1913. It was overrun by Austria in World War I, and in 1918 voted after the deposition of King Nicholas to become part of Serbia. In 1946 Montenegro became a republic of Yugoslavia. In a referendum March 1992 Montengrins voted to remain part of the Yugoslav federation; the referendum was boycotted by Montenegro's Muslim and Albanian communities.

Monterey Fishing port on Monterey Bay in California, USA, once the state capital; population (1990) 32,000. It is the setting for John Steinbeck's novels *Cannery Row* 1945 and *Tortilla Flat* 1935, dealing with migrant fruit workers.

Monterrey Industrial city (iron, steel, textiles, chemicals, food processing) in NE Mexico; population (1990) 2,521,700. It was founded 1597.

Montevideo Capital and chief port (grain, meat products, hides) of Uruguay, on the Río de la Plata; population (1992) 1,383,700. Industries include meat packing, tanning, footwear, flour milling, and textiles.

Montgomery State capital of Alabama, USA, on the Alabama River; population (1992) 192,100. The present city dates from 1819, when two settlements were amalgamated. Montgomery was the capital of the Confederacy in the first months of the American Civil War. The 1955 Montgomery Bus Boycott was a landmark in the civil-rights campaign against segregation laws.

Montgomeryshire (Welsh *Sir Drefaldwyn*) Former county of N Wales, included in Powys 1974–96, now part of Powys unitary authority.

Montilla Town in the province of ◊Córdoba, S Spain; population (1995) 318,000. It gives its name to *amontillado*, a type of medium-dry sherry.

Montluçon French town in the *département* of Allier, on the river Cher; population (1990) 44,200. Industries in Montluçon include the manufacture of metals, chemicals, and rubber. On a hill above the town is a Bourbon castle, and there are many 15th–16th-century buildings in the town.

Montmartre District of Paris, France, dominated by the basilica of Sacré Coeur 1875. It is situated in the N of the city on a hill 120 m/400 ft. It is known for its nightlife and artistic associations and is a popular tourist site.

Montparnasse District of Paris, France, formerly frequented by artists and writers. It is situated in the W of the city. The Pasteur Institute is also here.

Montpelier Capital of Vermont, USA, in the Green Mountains in the central part of the state, on the Winooski River; population (1992) 8,250. Industries include granite, insurance, and tourism. It was settled 1787 and grew because of granite production.

Montpellier Industrial city (electronics, medical research, engineering, textiles, food processing, and a trade in wine and brandy), capital of ◊Languedoc-Roussillon, France; population (1990) 210,900. It is the birthplace of the philosopher Auguste Comte.

Montréal Inland port, industrial city (aircraft, chemicals, oil and petrochemicals, flour, sugar, brewing, meat packing) of Quebec, Canada, on Montréal Island at the junction of the Ottawa and St Lawrence rivers; population (1991) 1,017,700. The city dates from 1642.

Montreux Winter resort in W Switzerland on Lake Geneva; population (1990) 19,900. It is the site of the island rock fortress of Chillon, where François Bonivard (commemorated by the poet Byron), prior of the Abbey of St Victor, was imprisoned 1530–36 for his opposition to the duke of Savoy. At the annual television festival (first held 1961), the premier award is the *Golden Rose of Montreux*. A jazz festival is held every July.

Mont St Michel Islet off the coast of NW France converted to a peninsula by an artificial causeway; it has a Benedictine monastery, founded 708.

Montserrat Volcanic island in the West Indies, one of the Leeward group, a British crown colony; capital Plymouth; area 110 sq km/42 sq mi; population (1991) 11,957. Much destruction was caused by Hurricane Hugo in September 1989. The eruption of the Soufnère volcano in July 1997 buried Plymouth, the capital, under rock and ashes. Around 7,000 islanders were evacuated.

Montserrat (Spanish *monte serrado* 'serrated mountain') Isolated mountain in NE Spain, height 1,240 m/4,070 ft, so called because its uneven outline of eroded pinnacles resembles the edge of a saw.

Monza City in N Italy, known for its motor-racing circuit; population (1988) 123,000. Once the capital of the Lombards, it preserves the Iron Crown of Lombardy in the 13th-century cathedral. Umberto I was assassinated here.

Moonie Town in SE Queensland, W of Brisbane, the site of Australia's first commercial oil strike; oil was discovered 1961 and the oilfield was developed 1964; population (1981) under 200.

Moorhead City in W Minnesota, USA, on the Red River, opposite Fargo, North Dakota; population (1990) 32,300. The town was founded 1871.

Moose Jaw Town in S Saskatchewan, Canada, with grain elevators, extensive stockyards, petroleum refineries; population (1991) 33,600. It was founded 1882 as a rail terminus.

Moradabad Trading city in Uttar Pradesh, India, on the Ramganga River; population (1991) 444,000. It produces textiles and engraved brassware. It was founded 1625 by Rustan Khan, and the Great Mosque dates from 1631.

Moravia (Czech *Morava*) Area of central Europe, forming two regions of the Czech Republic:
South Moravia (Czech *Jihomoravský*)
area 15,030 sq km/5,802 sq mi
capital Brno
population (1991) 2,048,900
North Moravia (Czech *Severomoravský*)
area 11,070 sq km/4,273 sq mi
capital Ostrava
population (1991) 1,961,500
features (N and S) river Morava; 25% forested
products maize, grapes, wine in the S; wheat, barley, rye, flax, sugar beet in the N; coal and iron
history part of the Avar territory since the 6th century. In 874 the kingdom of Great Moravia was founded by the Slavic prince Sviatopluk, who ruled until 894. It was conquered by the Magyars 906, and became a fief of Bohemia 1029. It was passed to the Habsburgs 1526, and became an Austrian crown land 1849. It was incorporated in the new republic of Czechoslovakia 1918, forming a province until 1949. From 1960 it was divided into two administrative regions, North and South Moravia; part of the Czech Republic from 1993.

Moray Unitary authority in NE Scotland created 1996 from part of the former Grampian region. Administrative headquarters Elgin; population (1996) 85,000; area 2,217 sq km/856 sq mi.

Moray Firth North Sea inlet in Scotland, between Burghead (Moray) and Tarbat Ness (Highland), 38 km/15 mi wide at its entrance. The city of Inverness is situated at the head of the Firth.

Morayshire Former county of NE Scotland, divided 1975–96 between Highland Region and Grampian Region; now Moray unitary authority.

Morbihan, Gulf of (Breton 'little sea') Seawater lake in Brittany, W France, linked by a channel with the Bay of Biscay; area 104 sq km/40 sq mi. Morbihan gives its name to a *département*.

Mordovia Autonomous republic of central Russian Federation
area 26,200 sq km/10,100 sq mi
capital Saransk
physical river Sura on the E; forested in the W
industries sugar beet, grains, potatoes; sheep and dairy farming; timber, furniture, and textiles
population (1995) 959,000
language Russian, Mordvin

Morecambe Town and resort in Lancashire, England, on Morecambe Bay, conjoined with the port of Heysham, which has a ferry service to Ireland; joint population (1991) 46,700. Industries include shrimp fishing, clothing, plastics, and engineering.

Morecambe Bay Inlet of the Irish Sea, between the Furness Peninsula (Cumbria) and Lancashire, England, with shallow sands. There are oil wells, and natural gas 50 km/30 mi offshore.

Morelos State of central Mexico; area 4,941 sq km/1,908 sq mi; population (1995 est) 1,422,600. Its capital is Cuernavaca. The main occupation is farming, producing maize, rice, wheat, coffee, and sugar-cane.

Morlaix Seaport on the river Morlaix in Brittany, France, in the *département* of Finistère, 53 km/33 mi E of Brest; population (1990) 18,000. The main manufacturing industries are tobacco and paper. The surrounding country is an important vegetable-growing region. Many of the town's houses date from the 15th century. There is a marina for yachts.

Morón de la Frontera Town in the province of ◊Seville, S Spain; population (1995) 29,400. It has a Gothic castle and the ruins of a Moorish castle. There are mines, marble quarries, and mineral springs nearby. It is known for its cakes.

Moroni Capital of the Comoros Republic, on Njazidja (Grand Comore); population (1992) 22,000. It has a small natural harbour from which coffee, cacao, and vanilla are exported.

Moscow (Russian *Moskva*) Industrial city, capital of the Russian Federation and of the Moskva region, and formerly (1922–91) of the USSR, on the Moskva River 640 km/400 mi SE of St Petersburg; population (1994) 8,793,000. Its industries include machinery, electrical equipment, textiles, chemicals, and many food products.

Moselle or *Mosel* River in W Europe some 515 km/320 mi long; it rises in the Vosges Mountains, France, and is canalized from Thionville to its confluence with the ◊Rhine at Koblenz in Germany. It gives its name to the *départements* of Moselle and Meurthe-et-Moselle in France. Vineyards along the Moselle in Germany produce popular white wines.

Moselle *Département* in the ◊Lorraine region of France; area 6,213 sq km/2,399 sq mi; population (1990) 1,011,940. It has a boundary with Germany to the E, and with Luxembourg to the N and NE. The river Moselle flows through the *département*, which consists largely of a plateau. There are vineyards on the left bank; where soils are less fertile, drainage allows cultivation of barley, oats, and rye. The *département* has coal and iron mines and the manufacture of machinery, chemicals, and textiles. ◊Metz (the capital) has telecommunications industries; other towns are Boulay, Château-Salins, Forbach, Sarrebourg, Sarregue-mines, and Thionville.

Mosi-oa-tunya ('smoke that thunders') Local African name for the ◊Victoria Falls of the Zambezi River.

Moskva Russian name for ◊Moscow, the capital of the Russian Federation, and for the river on which the city stands.

Mosquito Coast Caribbean coast of Honduras and Nicaragua, characterized by swamp, lagoons, and tropical rainforest. The territory is inhabited by Miskito Indians, Garifunas, and Zambos. Between 1823 and 1860 Britain maintained a protectorate over the Mosquito Coast which was ruled by a succession of 'Mosquito Kings'.

Most (German *Brüx*) Industrial town (chemicals, lignite, metallurgy) in the NW Czech Republic, 77 km/48 mi NW of Prague; population (1991) 70,700. It has a 16th-century Gothic church. The town is situated in a coal-mining area at the foot of the Erzgebirge mountain range, on the small river Bída.

Mostaganem Industrial port (metal and cement) in NW Algeria, linked by pipeline with the natural gas fields at Hassi Messaoud; population (1987) 114,000. It was founded in the 11th century.

Mostar Industrial town (aluminium, tobacco) in Bosnia-Herzegovina, known for its grapes and wines; population (1991) 126,000. The E, mainly Muslim sector of the town was under siege by Bosnian Croat forces 1993–94.

Mosul Industrial city (cement, textiles) and oil centre in Iraq, on the right bank of the Tigris, opposite the site of ancient Nineveh; population (1987) 664,200.

Motherwell and Wishaw Industrial town and administrative headquarters of North Lanarkshire, Scotland, SE of Glasgow; population (1991) 60,500. The two burghs were amalgamated 1920. Formerly a coal-mining town, its industries include iron and engineering, although the Ravenscraig iron and steel works closed 1992.

Motril Town in the province of ◊Granada, S Spain; population (1995) 49,500. Situated in a valley, it has a port on the Mediterranean coast at Calahonda. Products include sugar cane, bananas, and flowers; resources include lead, iron, zinc, and copper.

Moulins Capital of the *département* of Allier, Auvergne, central France; main industries are cutlery, textiles, and glass; population (1990) 23,400. Moulins was capital of the old province of Bourbonnais 1368–1527.

Mount Isa Mining town (copper, lead, silver, zinc) in NW Queensland, Australia; population (1984) 25,000.

Mount Lofty Range Mountain range in SE South Australia; Mount Bryan at 934 m/3,064 ft is the highest peak.

Mount Vernon Village in Virginia, USA, on the Potomac River, where George Washington lived 1752–99 and was buried on the family estate, now a national monument.

Mouscron (Flemish *Moeskroen*) Town in the province of West Flanders, Belgium, 11 km/7 mi S of Courtrai, near the French border.

Mow Cop Site in England of an open-air religious gathering 31 May 1807 that is considered to be the start of Primitive Methodism. Mow Cop is a hill at the S end of the Pennines on the Cheshire–Staffordshire border and dominates the surrounding countryside. It remained a popular location for revivalist meetings.

Mpumalanga formerly *Eastern Transvaal* Province of the Republic of South Africa from 1994, formerly part of Transvaal province

area 81,816 sq km/31,589 sq mi
capital Nelspruit
features Limpopo River, Vaal River
industries farming, coal
population (1995 est) 3,007,100
languages Siswati, Zulu, Afrikaans

MS Abbreviation for ◊Mississippi, a state of the USA.

MT Abbreviation for ◊Montana, a state of the USA.

Mtwara Deepwater seaport in S Tanzania, on Mtwara Bay; population (1978) 48,500. It was opened 1954.

Mühlhausen Town in the *Land* of ◊Thuringia, Germany, on the river Unstrut, 48 km/30 mi NW of Erfurt. There are engineering and textile industries. The town dates from the Middle Ages.

Muir Glacier Large ice sheet in SE Alaska, USA, with 905 sq km/350 sq mi of surface area, discharging into Glacier Bay on the Pacific coast of SE Alaska. It was explored in 1880 by John Muir, a Scottish immigrant who spearheaded the conservation movement. Earthquake disturbances dislodged part of the glacier 1899. It lies within Glacier Bay national park.

Mukden Former name of ◊Shenyang, a city in China.

Mülheim an der Ruhr Industrial city in North Rhine–Westphalia, Germany, on the river Ruhr; population (1993) 177,400. Industries include iron and steel, building materials, and construction.

Mulhouse (German *Mülhausen*) Industrial city (textiles, engineering, electrical goods) in Haut-Rhin *département*, Alsace, E France; population (1990) 109,900.

Mull Second largest island of the Inner Hebrides, Scotland; area 950 sq km/367 sq mi; population (1991) 2,700. It is mountainous, and is separated from the mainland by the Sound of Mull. There is only one town, Tobermory. The economy is based on fishing, forestry, tourism, and some livestock.

Mullingar County town of County Westmeath, Republic of Ireland; population (1991) 30,300. It is a cattle market and trout-fishing centre.

Multan Industrial city (textiles, precision instruments, chemicals, pottery, jewellery) in Punjab province, central Pakistan, 205 km/190 mi SW of Lahore; population (1981) 732,000. It trades in grain, fruit, cotton, and wool. It is on a site inhabited since the time of Alexander the Great.

Mulu Mountainous region in N Borneo near the border with Sabah. Its limestone cave system, one of the largest in the world, was explored by a Royal Geographical Society Expedition 1978.

München German name of ◊Munich, a city in Germany.

Muncie City in E central Indiana, NE of Indianapolis, USA; population (1990) 71,000. Industries include vehicle parts, livestock, dairy products, steel forgings, and wire. It was founded 1827.

Munich (German *München*) Industrial city (brewing, printing, precision instruments, machinery, electrical goods, textiles), capital of Bavaria, Germany, on the river Isar; population (1993) 1,256,300.

Munster Southern province of the Republic of Ireland, comprising the counties of Clare, Cork, Kerry, Limerick, North and South Tipperary, and Waterford; area 24,140 sq km/9,318 sq mi; population (1991) 1,008,400.

Münster Industrial city (wire, cement, iron, brewing, and distilling) in North Rhine–Westphalia, NW Germany, formerly the capital of Westphalia; population (1993) 267,000. The Treaty of Westphalia was signed simultaneously here and at Osnabrück 1648, ending the Thirty Years' War.

Murcia Autonomous region of SE Spain; area 11,300 sq km/4,362 sq mi; population (1991) 1,045,600. It includes the cities Murcia and Cartagena, and produces esparto grass, lead, zinc, iron, and fruit.

Murcia Industrial city (silk, metal, glass, textiles, pharmaceuticals), capital of the Spanish province of Murcia, on the river Segura; population (1994) 342,000. Murcia was founded 825 on the site of a Roman colony by 'Abd-ar-Rahman II, caliph of Córdoba. It has a university and 14th-century cathedral.

Mures (Hungarian *Maros*) River in Romania and Hungary, rising in the Carpathian Mountains and flowing 725 km/453 mi to join the river ◊Tisza at Szeged in Hungary.

Murmansk Seaport in NW Russian Federation, on the Barents Sea; population (1994) 444,000. It is the largest city in the Arctic, Russia's most important fishing port, and the base of naval units and the icebreakers that keep the Northeast Passage open.

Murray Principal river of Australia, 2,575 km/1,600 mi long. It rises in the Australian Alps near Mount Kosciusko and flows W, forming the boundary between New South Wales and Victoria, and reaches the sea at Encounter Bay, South Australia. With its main tributary, the Darling, it is 3,750 km/2,330 mi long.

Murrumbidgee River of New South Wales, Australia; length 1,690 km/1,050 mi. It rises in the Australian Alps, flows N to the Burrinjuck reservoir, and then W to meet the river ◊Murray.

Muscat or *Masqat* Capital of Oman, E Arabia, adjoining the port of Matrah, which has a deep-water harbour; combined population (1993) 40,900. It produces natural gas and chemicals.

Muscat and Oman Former name of Oman, a country in the Middle East.

Musgrave Ranges Australian mountain ranges on the border between South Australia and the Northern Territory; the highest peak is Mount Woodruffe at 1,525 m/5,000 ft. The area is an Aboriginal reserve.

Muskegon City and port in W Michigan, USA, on the Muskegon River where it enters Lake Michigan, NW of Grand Rapids; population (1990) 40,300. Industries include heavy machinery, metal products, vehicle parts, and sporting goods. The town was laid out 1849 and became an important sawmill centre. It was rebuilt after a fire 1890.

Mustique Island in the Caribbean; see St Vincent and the Grenadines.

Mutare formerly (until 1982) *Umtali* Industrial town (vehicle assembly, engineering, tobacco, textiles, paper) in E Zimbabwe; population (1992) 131,800. It is the chief town of Manicaland province.

Mykolayiv formerly Nikolayev Port (with shipyards) and naval base on the Black Sea, Ukraine; population (1990) 508,000.

Mysore or *Maisur* Industrial city (engineering, silk) in ◊Karnataka, S India, some 130 km/80 mi SW of Bangalore; population (1991) 481,000.

Mytilene or *Mitylene* (modern Greek *Mytilíni*) Port, capital of the Greek island of Lesvos (to which the name Mytilene is sometimes applied) and a centre of sponge fishing; population (1991) 25,400.

Nablus Market town on the West Bank of the river Jordan, N of Jerusalem; the largest Palestinian town on the West Bank; population (1995) 130,000. Formerly Shechem, it was the ancient capital of Samaria, and a few Samaritans remain. Occupied by Israel since 1967, Israeli troops withdrew Dec 1995.

Nacala Seaport in Nampula province, N Mozambique; a major outlet for minerals; population (1990) 104,300. It is linked by rail with Malawi.

Naemen Flemish form of ◊Namur, a city in Belgium.

Nagaland state of NE India, bordering Myanmar (Burma) on the east
area 16,579 sq km/6,401 sq mi
capital Kohima
industries rice, tea, coffee, paper, sugar
population (1994 est) 1,410,000
history formerly part of Assam, the area was seized by Britain from Burma (now Myanmar) 1826. The British sent 18 expeditions against the Naga peoples in the north 1832–87. After India attained independence 1947, there was Naga guerrilla activity against the Indian government; the state of Nagaland was established 1963 in response to demands for self-government, but fighting continued sporadically. A peace accord was struck with the guerrillas 1975 but fighting resumed 1980. Charges of serious human-rights violations have been filed against Indian forces operating in the area. The Naga guerrillas have links with other rebel groups in NE India, but there is conflict between groups over protection money from the heroin trade, transport, and banking; by Aug 1993 they had forced the closure of 57 of the 63 bank branches in Nagaland and held hundreds of lorries to ransom on the Nagaland–Assam border.

Nagasaki Industrial port (coal, iron, shipbuilding) on Kyushu Island, Japan; population (1994) 438,000. Nagasaki was the only Japanese port open to European trade from the 16th century until 1859. An atom bomb was dropped on it by the USA 9 Aug 1945.

Nagorno-Karabakh (Russian 'mountainous Qarabagh') Autonomous region of Azerbaijan
area 4,400 sq km/1,700 sq mi
capital Xankâdi
industries cotton, grapes, wheat, silk
population (1990) 192,400 (77% Armenian, 22% Azeri), the Christian Armenians forming an enclave within the predominantly Shi'ite Muslim Azerbaijan
history The region formed part of Armenia until the 7th century, but was subsequently taken by the Arabs. An autonomous protectorate after the Russian Revolution 1917, it was annexed to Azerbaijan 1923 against the wishes of the largely Christian-Armenian population. From 1989, when the local council declared its intention to transfer control of the region to Armenia, the enclave was racked by fighting between local Armenian troops (reputedly backed by Armenia) and Azeri forces, both attempting to assert control. After a declaration of independence by the region's parliament Dec 1991, the conflict intensified and by June 1993 Armenian forces had overrun much of Nagorno-Karabakh. By Feb 1994, 18,000 Armenians and 5,000 Azeri were reported to have been killed in the conflict and one million people made refugees. By 1996, Nagorno-Karabakh was effectively an independent state.

Nagoya Industrial seaport (cars, textiles, clocks) on Honshu Island, Japan; population (1994) 2,091,000. It has a shogun fortress 1610 and a notable Shinto shrine, Atsuta Jingu.

Nagpur Industrial city (textiles, metals) in Maharashtra, India, on the river Pench; population (1991) 1,661,000. Nagpur was founded in the 18th century, and was the former capital of Berar and Madhya Pradesh states.

Naha Chief port on Okinawa Island, Japan; population (1994) 304,000. Industries include pottery and textiles; there is fishing.

Nahe River in Germany, a tributary of the ◊Rhine; length 115 km/71 mi. It rises in Saarland and flows NE to join the Rhine at Bingen. The Nahe valley produces white wines.

Nairnshire Former county of Scotland, included 1975–96 in the Highland Region; now part of the Highland unitary authority.

Nairobi Capital of Kenya, in the central highlands at 1,660 m/5,450 ft; population (1989) 1,346,000. It has light industry and food processing. It is the headquarters of the United Nations Environment Programme.

Nakhichevan Autonomous republic forming part of Azerbaijan; area 5,500 sq km/2,120 sq mi; population (1994) 315,000. Taken by Russia in 1828, it was annexed to Azerbaijan in 1924. Some 85% of the population are Muslim Azeris. Nakhichevan has been affected by the Armenia–Azerbaijan conflict; many Azeris have fled to Azerbaijan, and in Jan 1990 frontier posts and border fences with Iran were destroyed. In May 1992 Armenian forces made advances in the region, but Azeri forces soon regained control. The republic has sought independence from Azerbaijan.

Nakhodka   Pacific port in the Russian Federation, in E Siberia, on the Sea of Japan, E of Vladivostok; population (1990) 163,000. US-caught fish, especially pollock, is processed by Russian factory ships in a joint venture.

Nakuru, Lake   Salt lake in the Great Rift Valley, Kenya.

Namaqualand   or *Namaland* Near-desert area on the SW coast of Africa divided between Namibia and South Africa. *Great Namaqualand* is in Namibia, N of the Orange River; area 388,500 sq km/150,000 sq mi; sparsely populated by the Nama, a Khoikhoi people. *Little Namaqualand* is in Northern Cape Province, South Africa, S of the Orange River; area 52,000 sq km/20,000 sq mi; copper and diamonds are mined here.

Namib Desert   Coastal desert region in Namibia between the Kalahari Desert and the Atlantic Ocean. Its aridity is caused by the descent of dry air cooled by the cold Benguela current along the coast. The sand dunes of the Namib Desert are among the tallest in the world, reaching heights of 370 m/1,200 ft.

Nampo   formerly (until 1947) *Chinnampo* City on the W coast of North Korea, 40 km/25 mi SW of Pyongan; population (1984) 691,000.

Namur   (Flemish *Naemen*) Industrial city (cutlery, porcelain, paper, iron, steel), capital of the province of Namur, in S Belgium, at the confluence of the Sambre and Meuse rivers; population (1995) 105,000. It was a strategic location during both world wars and was occupied by Germany 1914–18. The province of Namur has an area of 3,700 sq km/1,428 sq mi and a population (1995) of 434,400.

Namur   (Flemish *Namen*) Province of Belgium, bounded N by Brabant, E by the provinces of Liège and Luxembourg, W by Hainaut, and S by France; area 3,660 sq km/1,402 sq mi; population (1992) 427,000. Its main cities are ◊Namur and Dinant, and its principal rivers the Meuse, the Sambre, and the Lesse. It is known as the gateway to the Ardennes.

Nanaimo   Former coal-mining centre of British Columbia, Canada, on the E coast of Vancouver Island; population (1991) 60,100. It was founded as a Hudson's Bay Company trading post and developed after the discovery of coal 1849; the last big coal mine closed 1960.

Nanchang   Industrial city (textiles, glass, porcelain, soap), capital of Jiangxi province, China, about 260 km/160 mi SE of Wuhan; population (1993) 1,420,000.

Nancy   Capital of the *département* of Meurthe-et-Moselle and of the region of Lorraine, France, on the Meurthe River 280 km/175 mi E of Paris; population (1990) 102,400. Nancy dates from the 11th century.

Nanda Devi   Peak in the Himalayas, Uttar Pradesh, N India; height 7,817 m/25,645 ft. Until Kanchenjunga was absorbed into India, Nanda Devi was the country's highest mountain.

Nanga Parbat   Peak in the Himalayan Karakoram Mountains of Kashmir; height 8,126 m/26,660 ft.

Nanjing   or *Nanking* Capital of Jiangsu province, China, 270 km/165 mi NW of Shanghai; centre of industry (engineering, shipbuilding, oil refining), commerce, and communications; population (1993) 2,430,000. The bridge 1968 over the river Chang Jiang is the longest in China at 6,705 m/22,000 ft.

Nanning   or *Yungning* Industrial river port, capital of Guangxi Zhuang autonomous region, China, on the You Jiang River; population (1993) 960,000. It was a supply town during the Vietnam War and the Sino-Vietnamese confrontation 1979.

Nanshan Islands   Chinese name for the ◊Spratly Islands.

Nantes   Industrial port in W France on the Loire River, capital of Pays de la Loire region; industries include oil, sugar refining, textiles, soap, and tobacco; population (1990) 252,000. It has a cathedral 1434–1884 and a castle founded 938.

Nantucket   Island and resort in Massachusetts, USA, S of Cape Cod, 120 sq km/46 sq mi. In the 18th–19th centuries, Nantucket was a whaling port; it is now a popular summer resort because of its excellent beaches. The island was discovered 1602, settled 1659 by Quakers, and became part of Massachusetts 1692.

Napa   City in NW California on the Napa River, NE of San Francisco on San Pablo Bay. It is a major trading centre for wine, produced in the surrounding Napa Valley vineyards; other products include fruit, clothing, steel pipe, and leather goods; population (1992) 63,300.

Napier   Wool port in Hawke Bay on the E coast of North Island, New Zealand; population of Napier-Hastings (1994 est) 110,200.

Naples   (Italian *Napoli*) Industrial port (shipbuilding, cars, textiles, paper, food processing) and capital of Campania, Italy, on the Tyrrhenian Sea; population (1992) 1,071,700. To the S is the Isle of Capri, and behind the city is Mount Vesuvius, with the ruins of Pompeii at its foot.

Naples   Province of S Italy in W ◊Campania region; capital Naples; area 1,170 sq km/452 sq mi; population (1992) 3,026,500.

Nara   City in Japan, in the S of Honshu Island, the capital of the country 710–84; population (1994) 355,000. It was the birthplace of Japanese art and literature and has ancient wooden temples.

Narbonne   City in Aude *département*, S France; population (1990) 47,100. It was the chief town of S Gaul in Roman times and a port in medieval times.

Narmada River   River that rises in the Maikala range in Madhya Pradesh state, central India, and flows 1,245 km/778 mi WSW to the Gulf of Khambat, an inlet of the Arabian Sea. Forming the traditional boundary between Hindustan and Deccan, the Narmada is a holy river of the Hindus.

Narragansett Bay   Atlantic inlet, Rhode Island, USA. Running inland for 45 km/28 mi, it encloses a number of islands. At the head of the bay is Providence, the state capital.

Narvik   Seaport in Nordland county, N Norway, on Ofot Fjord, exporting Swedish iron ore; population (1991) 18,600.

To secure this ore supply, Germany seized Narvik April 1940. British, French, Polish, and Norwegian forces recaptured the port but had to abandon it 10 June to cope with the worsening Allied situation elsewhere in Europe.

Nashua City in S New Hampshire, USA, on the Nashua River where it meets the Merrimack River, just N of the Massachusetts border; population (1992) 79,700. Industries include electronics, asbestos, chemicals, and glass products. Nashua was first settled 1656 and later became a textile-mill town.

Nashville Port on the Cumberland River and capital of Tennessee, USA; population (1992) 495,000. It is a banking and commercial centre, and has large printing, music-publishing, and recording industries. Nashville was settled 1779.

Nassau Capital and port of the Bahamas, on New Providence Island; population (1980) 135,000.

Natal Industrial seaport (textiles, salt refining) in Brazil on the Potengi river, capital of the state of Rio Grande do Norte; population (1991) 606,600. Natal was founded 1599 and became a city 1822.

Natal Former province of South Africa to 1994, bounded on the E by the Indian Ocean. In 1994 it became part of ◊KwaZulu-Natal Province.

Natchez City in Mississippi, on the E bluffs above the Mississippi River; population (1990) 19,400. The site was originally occupied by the Natchez Native American people. Before the Civil War it was a cotton-trading centre, and many houses from that period remain; Natchez continued to be important during the heyday of steamboat traffic.

Natron, Lake Salt and soda lake in the Great Rift Valley, Tanzania; length 56 km/35 mi, width 24 km/15 mi.

Natural Bridge Village in Virginia, USA, 185 km/115 mi W of Richmond. The nearby Cedar Creek is straddled by an arch of limestone 66 m/215 ft high and 27 m/90 ft wide.

Nauheim or *Bad Nauheim* Town and spa in Hessen, Germany, at the E end of the Taunus Mountains, 30 km/19 mi N of Frankfurt am Main; population (1994) 10,500. It has hot saline springs and medical research institutes.

Nauplia (Greek *Navplion*) Port of Greece, capital of the department of Argolis, at the N extremity of the Gulf of Argos, 11 km/7 mi SE of the town of Argos. Nauplia is one of the busiest ports of the ◊Peloponnese region, exporting dried and preserved fruit, vegetables, tobacco, and cotton. From 1824 to 1834 it was the capital of Greece.

Navarre (Spanish *Navarra*) Autonomous mountain region of N Spain, including Monte Adi 1,503 m/4,933 ft; area 10,400 sq km/4,014 sq mi; population (1992) 519,200. Its capital is Pamplona.

Náxos Island of Greece, the largest of the Cyclades, area 453 sq km/175 sq mi. Known since early times for its wine, it was a centre for the worship of Bacchus, who, according to Greek mythology, found the deserted Ariadne on its shore and married her.

Nayarit State of Mexico, on the Pacific; area 27,621 sq km/10,664 sq mi; population (1995 est) 896,000. Its capital is Tepic.

The main occupations are cattle-raising and farming, producing cereals, cotton, sugar-cane, coffee, and tobacco.

Nazareth Town in Galilee, N Israel, SE of Haifa; population about 64,000. According to the New Testament, it was the boyhood home of Jesus.

Nazca Town to the S of Lima, Peru, near a plateau that has geometric linear markings interspersed with giant outlines of birds and animals. The markings were made by American Indians, whose culture dates from the period 200 BC to AD 600, and their function is thought to be ritual rather than astronomical.

Naze, the Headland on the coast of Essex, England, S of the port of Harwich; also the English name for *Lindesnes*, a cape in S Norway.

NB Abbreviation for ◊New Brunswick, a Canadian province.

NC Abbreviation for ◊North Carolina, a state of the USA.

ND Abbreviation for ◊North Dakota, a state of the USA.

N'djamena formerly *Fort Larry* Capital of Chad, at the confluence of the Chari and Logone rivers, on the Cameroon border; population (1993) 531,000. Industries include cotton textiles and meat packing.

Ndola Mining centre and chief city of the Copperbelt province of central Zambia; population (1990) 376,000.

NE Abbreviation for ◊Nebraska, a state of the USA; ◊New England, the NE USA.

Neagh, Lough Lake in Northern Ireland, 25 km/15 mi W of Belfast; area 396 sq km/153 sq mi. It is the largest lake in the British Isles and is famous for eel fishing.

Near East Term used until the 1940s to describe the area of the Balkan states, Egypt, and SW Asia, now known as the ◊Middle East.

Neath (Welsh *Castell-nedd*) Town in North Port Talbot, Wales, near the mouth of the river Neath; population (1991) 46,000. The Roman fort of Nidum was discovered nearby 1949; there are also remains of a Norman castle and abbey.

Neath Port Talbot Unitary authority in S Wales created 1996 from part of the former county of West Glamorgan; administrative headquarters Port Talbot; population (1996) 139,400; area 442 sq km/171 sq mi. Port Talbot is an industrial port. The Roman fort of Nidum is near Neath.

Nebraska State in central USA; nicknamed Cornhusker State/Beef State
area 200,400 sq km/77,354 sq mi
capital Lincoln
towns and cities Omaha, Grand Island, North Platte
physical Rocky Mountain foothills; tributaries of the Missouri; prairies; Mission River; Platte River, with the Platte River Whooping Crane Habitat; Nebraska national forest
features a 206-km/128-mi stretch of the Oregon Trail, including Scotts Bluff national monument, Chimney Rock national historic site, and Courthouse and Jail Rocks; Buffalo Bill Ranch state historical park; Willa Cather Historical Center and Cather Memorial Prairie, Red Cloud;

Homestead national monument; Boys Town, founded 1917 for homeless boys; Fremont and Elkhorn Valley Railroad; Strategic Air Command Museum, Bellevue

industries cereals, livestock, processed foods, fertilizers, oil, natural gas

population (1995) 1,637,100

famous people Fred Astaire, William Jennings Bryan, Johnny Carson, Willa Cather, Henry Fonda, Harold Lloyd, Malcolm X

history exploited by French fur traders in the early 1700s; ceded to Spain by France 1763; retroceded to France 1801; part of the Louisiana Purchase 1803; explored by Meriwether Lewis and William Clark 1804–06; first settlement at Bellevue 1823; became a territory 1854 and a state 1867 after the Union Pacific began its transcontinental railroad at Omaha 1865.

Neckar German river, a tributary of the ◊Rhine; length 377 km/234 mi. From its source on the E slopes of the Black Forest, the Neckar winds NW past Tübingen, Stuttgart, Heilbronn, and Heidelberg, to join the Rhine at Mannheim. It is navigable as far as Plochingen.

Needles, the Group of rocks in the sea near the Isle of ◊Wight, S England.

Neenah City in E Wisconsin, USA, on the Fox River near Lake Winnebago, N of Oshkosh; population (1990) 23,200. To the E is Menasha, with which it forms one community. It is a processing and marketing centre for the area's agricultural products, and the paper industry is important. Neenah was settled 1835.

Negev Desert in S Israel that tapers to the port of Elat. It is fertile under irrigation, and minerals include oil and copper.

Negri Sembilan State of S Peninsular Malaysia; area 6,646 sq km/2,565 sq mi; population (1993) 723,900. It is mainly mountainous; products include rice and rubber. The capital is Seremban.

Negro, Río River in South America, rising in E Colombia and joining the Amazon at Manáus, Brazil; length 2,250 km/1,400 mi.

Nei Mongol Chinese name for Inner ◊Mongolia, a region of China.

Neisse Alternative name for ◊Nysa, a river and an industrial town in Poland.

Nejd Region of central Arabia consisting chiefly of desert; area about 2,072,000 sq km/800,000 sq mi. It forms part of the kingdom of Saudi Arabia and is inhabited by Bedouins. The capital is Riyadh.

Neretva River in Bosnia-Herzegovina and Croatia, one of the few sizeable rivers flowing to the Adriatic Sea; length 210 km/130 mi. Rising near Mount Zelengora in Herzegovina, it flows NW and then SW to the sea.

Ness, Loch Lake in the Highland unitary authority, Scotland, forming part of the Caledonian Canal; 36 km/22.5 mi long, 229 m/754 ft deep. There have been unconfirmed reports of a *Loch Ness monster* since the 15th century.

Netherlands Antilles Two groups of Caribbean islands, overseas territories of the Netherlands with full internal autonomy, comprising ◊Curaçao and Bonaire off the coast of Venezuela (◊Aruba is considered separately), and St Eustatius, Saba, and the S part of St Maarten in the Leeward Islands, 800 km/500 mi to the NE

area 797 sq km/308 sq mi

capital Willemstad on Curaçao

industries oil from Venezuela refined here; tourism is important; rum; small manufacturing industries

language Dutch (official), Papiamento, English

population (1993 est) 197,100.

Netherlands East Indies Former name (1798–1945) of Indonesia.

Netzahualcóyotl Mexican city lying to the S of Lake Texcoco, forming a suburb to the NE of Mexico City; population (1980) 1,341,200.

Neubrandenburg Former district of East Germany which, since 1990, has been absorbed into the state of Mecklenburg–West Pomerania, Germany.

Neubrandenburg Town in the *Land* of ◊Brandenburg, Germany, on the river Tollense, 113 km/70 mi N of Berlin; population (1991) 87,900. Between 1359 and 1471 Neubrandenburg was capital of the Duchy of Mecklenburg-Stargard.

Neuchâtel (German *Neuenburg*) Capital of Neuchâtel canton in NW Switzerland, on Lake Neuchâtel, W of Berne; population (1990) 32,800. It has a Horological (clock) Research Laboratory.

Neuchâtel Canton in the W of Switzerland, between Lake Neuchâtel and the French frontier; area 797 sq km/308 sq mi; population (1995) 165,300. Neuchâtel lies in the midst of the ◊Jura Mountains, four ranges of which traverse the canton, running NE–SW. The speciality of the canton is watchmaking; the chief centres of this industry are La Chaux-de-Fonds and Le Locle. Neuchâtel joined the Swiss Confederation in 1815.

Neumünster City in Schleswig-Holstein, Germany, 31 km/19 mi SW of Kiel; population (1994) 82,000. Metallurgy, electrical equipment, textiles and clothing are the main industries. The town was founded in 1142.

Neunkirchen City in the Saarland, Germany, on the river Blies, 19 km/12 mi NE of Saarbrücken; population (1994) 150,200. It is a coal-mining centre and has important iron and steel, chemical, and textile industries.

Netherlans Antilles

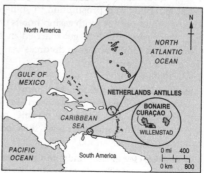

Neunkirchen am Steinfeld Austrian town in the province of Lower Austria, on the river Schwarza, 55 km/34 mi SW of Vienna. The town has iron and textile industries.

Neusalz German name for ◊Nowa Sól, a town in Poland.

Neusiedler See (Hungarian *Fertö Tó*) Shallow lake in E Austria and NW Hungary, SE of Vienna; area 152 sq km/60 sq mi; it is the only steppe lake in Europe.

Neusohl German name for ◊Banská-Bystrica, a town in the Slovak Republic.

Neuss Industrial city in North Rhine–Westphalia, Germany; population (1991) 148,000.

Neustadt German name for ◊Wejherowo, a town in Poland.

Neustadt an der Weinstrasse formerly *Neustadt an der Haardt* City in the Rhineland-Palatinate, Germany, situated at the foot of the Haardtberge, 71 km/44 mi SW of Mainz; population (1994) 53,900. The wine-trading centre of the largest wine-producing region in Germany, Neustadt also manufactures concrete, metal goods, paper, and textiles. There is a 14th-century church.

Neustrelitz Town in the *Land* of ◊Mecklenburg–West Pomerania, Germany, 24 km/15 mi S of Neubrandenburg. It was formerly the capital of the Grand Duchy of Mecklenburg-Strelitz, and contains the ducal palace. Neustrelitz has a number of engineering industries.

Nevada State in W USA; nicknamed Silver State/Sagebrush State/Battleborn State
area 286,400 sq km/110,550 sq mi
capital Carson City
towns and cities Las Vegas, Reno
physical Mojave Desert; lakes: Tahoe, Pyramid, Mead; mountains and plateaus alternating with valleys; plutonium and other radioactive materials are leaking out through cracks in the rocks around an underground nuclear-weapons testing site, and ground water and wild animals near the site have been found to be contaminated
features the most arid state; Great Basin national park, with Wheeler Peak (3,981 m/13,061 ft), and the Lehman Caves; Red Rock Canyon; Hoover Dam and Lake Mead (the largest artificial lake in the W hemisphere); Valley of Fire state park, with Pueblo Indian rock drawings and brightly coloured rock formations; Virginia City national historic district; legal gambling and prostitution in some counties; Las Vegas, a gambling resort, with casino hotels on the Las Vegas Strip, the easiest place to get married in the USA; Reno, known for gambling and easy divorces
industries mercury, barite, gold
population (1995) 1,530,100
history explored by Kit Carson and John C Fremont 1843–45; ceded to the USA after the Mexican War 1848; first permanent settlement and Mormon trading post 1848. Discovery of silver (the Comstock Lode) 1858 led to rapid population growth and statehood 1864.

Nevers Industrial city in Burgundy, central France, at the meeting of the Loire and Nièvre rivers; capital of the former province of Nivernais and the modern *département* of Nièvre; population (1990) 43,900.

New Amsterdam Town in Guyana, on the river Berbice, founded by the Dutch; population (1980) 25,000. It is the centre of the agricultural area, producing rice and sugar cane. Also a former name (1624–64) of ◊New York.

Newark Market town in Nottinghamshire, England, on the river Trent; population (1991) 35,100. It has the ruins of a 12th-century castle in which King John died. The British Horological Institute is based here. Industries include engineering, agricultural machinery, brewing, and building materials.

Newark Largest city (industrial and commercial) of New Jersey, USA; population (1992) 267,850. Industries include electrical equipment, machinery, chemicals, paints, canned meats. The city dates from 1666, when a settlement called Milford was made on the site.

New Bedford City in SE Massachusetts, USA, on the Acushnet River near Buzzards Bay, S of Boston; population (1992) 96,900. Industries include electronics, rubber and metal products, and fishing. During the 1800s it was a prosperous whaling town.

New Britain City in central Connecticut, USA, SW of Hartford and NE of Waterbury; population (1992) 72,900. Long an industrial city, its industries include tools, hardware, and household appliances. It was settled 1686 as the Great Swamp. Metalworking was important in the 18th century.

New Britain Largest island in the ◊Bismarck Archipelago, part of Papua New Guinea; capital Rabaul; population (1990) 312,000. Two volcanoes erupted Sept 1994, covering Rabaul in ash and mud, but there were no deaths. The previous eruption was 1937.

New Brunswick Maritime province of E Canada
area 73,440 sq km/28,355 sq mi
capital Fredericton
towns and cities St John, Moncton
physical Grand Lake, St John River; Bay of Fundy
features Fort Beauséjour
industries cereals, wood, paper, fish, lead, zinc, copper, oil, natural gas
population (1995 est) 738,000

New Brunswick

history first reached by Europeans (Jacques Cartier) 1534; explored by Samuel de Champlain 1604; remained a French colony as part of Nova Scotia until ceded to England 1713. After the American Revolution many United Empire Loyalists settled here, and it became a province of the Dominion of Canada 1867.

Newbury Market town in Berkshire, England; population (1991) 33,300. It will become a unitary authority in April 1998. It has a racecourse and training stables, and electronic, chemical, plastics and engineering industries.

New Caledonia Island group in the S Pacific, a French overseas territory between Australia and the Fiji Islands
area 18,576 sq km/7,170 sq mi
capital Nouméa
physical fertile, surrounded by a barrier reef
industries nickel (the world's third-largest producer), chrome, iron
currency CFP franc
population (1989) 164,200 (45% Kanak (Melanesian), 33% European, 7% Wallisian, 5% Vietnamese and Indonesian, 3% Polynesian)
language French (official)
religion Roman Catholic 60%, Protestant 30%
history New Caledonia was visited by Captain Cook 1774 and became French 1853. It has been a French Overseas Territory since 1958. A general strike to gain local control of nickel mines 1974 was defeated. In 1981 the French socialist government promised moves towards independence. The 1985 elections resulted in control of most regions by Kanaks, but not the majority of seats. In 1986 the French conservative government reversed the reforms. The Kanaks boycotted a referendum Sept 1987 and a majority were in favour of remaining a French dependency. In 1988 New Caledonia was divided into three autonomous provinces. In 1989 the leader of the Socialist National Liberation front (the most prominent separatist group), Jean-Marie Tjibaou, was murdered. A referendum on full independence is scheduled for 1998. The French high commissioner is Didier Cultiaux.

Newcastle Industrial port (iron, steel, chemicals, textiles, ships) in New South Wales, Australia; population (1993) 454,800. Coal was discovered nearby 1796. A penal settlement was founded 1804.

Newcastle-under-Lyme Industrial town (electronics, ceramics, bricks and tiles, clothing, paper, machinery) in Staffordshire, England; population (1991) 73,700.

Newcastle upon Tyne City in NE England on the river Tyne opposite Gateshead; population (1994 est) 274,000. It is the administrative centre of Tyne and Wear and regional centre of NE England. It is a centre for retail, commerce, communications, and the arts. The University of Newcastle was founded 1963, and the University of Northumbria 1992.
industries engineering (including offshore technology); food processing; brewing; electronics. Only 1% of the workforce is now in heavy industry, 80% are in the public or service sectors.

New Delhi City adjacent to Old Delhi on the Yamuna River in the Union Territory of Delhi, N India; population (1991) 301,000. It is the administrative centre of Delhi, and was designated capital of India by the British 1911. Largely designed by British architect Edwin Lutyens, New Delhi was officially inaugurated after its completion 1931. Chemicals, textiles, machine tools, electrical goods, and footwear are produced.

New England District of N New South Wales, Australia, especially the tableland area of Glen Innes and Armidale.

New England Region of NE USA, comprising the states of Maine, New Hampshire, Vermont, Massachusetts, Rhode Island, and Connecticut. It is a geographic region rather than a political entity, with an area of 172,681 sq km/66,672 sq mi. Boston is the principal urban centre of the region, and Harvard and Yale are its major universities. New England was originally settled by Pilgrims and Puritans from England.

New Forest Ancient forest in ◊Hampshire, S England. Its legal boundary encloses 38,000 ha (1995), of which 8,400 ha is enclosed plantation, and 20,000 ha is common land, including ancient woodland, heath, grassland, and bog. At least 46 rare plants are found in the New Forest, as well as more than half of Britain's species of butterflies, moths, and beetles.

Newfoundland Canadian province on the Atlantic Ocean
area 405,720 sq km/156,648 sq mi
capital St John's
towns and cities Corner Brook, Gander
physical Newfoundland island and ◊Labrador on the mainland on the other side of the Straits of Belle Isle; rocky
features Grand Banks section of the continental shelf rich in cod; home of the Newfoundland and Labrador dogs
industries newsprint, fish products, hydroelectric power, iron, copper, zinc, uranium, offshore oil
population (1995 est) 570,000
history colonized by Vikings about AD 1000; Newfoundland was reached by the English, under the Italian navigator Giovanni Caboto, 1497. It was the first English colony, established 1583. French settlements were made and British sovereignty was not recognized until 1713; France retained the offshore islands of St Pierre and Miquelon. Internal self-government was achieved 1855. In 1934, as Newfoundland had fallen into financial difficulties, administration was vested in a governor and a special commission. A 1948 ref-

Newfoundland

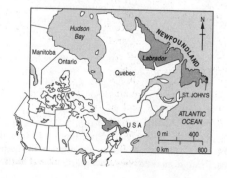

erendum favoured federation with Canada and the province joined Canada 1949.

New Glasgow Town in Nova Scotia, Canada, on East River, 16 km/10 mi SE of the seaport of Pictou; population (1991) 9,900. The town manufactures railway and heavy machinery and paper products. Some working coalmines remain in the surrounding region.

New Guinea Island in the SW Pacific, N of Australia, comprising Papua New Guinea and the Indonesian province of Irian Jaya; total area about 800,000 sq km/ 309,000 sq mi. Part of the Dutch East Indies from 1828, West Irian was ceded by the United Nations to Indonesia 1963.

Newham Inner borough of E Greater London, N of the river Thames. It includes the districts of East and West Ham and the N part of Woolwich

features site of former Royal Docks: Victoria (1855), Albert (1880), and King George V (1921); post-war tower blocks (collapse of Ronan Point 1968 led to official enquiry); Stratford has been chosen as an International Passenger Station for the Channel Tunnel Rail Link

population (1991) 200,200

famous people Dick Turpin, Gerard Manley Hopkins

history From 1671 onwards the borough was associated with the Quakers – from 1704 there was a meeting house in Plaistow, which the Gurneys, Frys, and Barclays attended; it was closed 1924.

New Hampshire State in NE USA; nicknamed Granite State

area 24,000 sq km/9,264 sq mi

capital Concord

towns and cities Manchester, Nashua

physical the Connecticut River, forming the boundary with Vermont; the White Mountains, the highest mountains in New England, including Mount Washington (1,917 m/6,288 ft), and the Old Man of the Mountains, a rocky formation resembling the profile of a man, above Profile Lake, Franconia Notch; Mount Monadnock; 29 km/18 mi of sea coast, and Great Bay estuary; Lake Winnipesaukee, with over 200 inhabited islands; over 80% forested

features Mount Washington's cog railway (1869), the world's first mountain-climbing railway; Hampton Beach, with a 5-km/3-mi boardwalk; whale watching; Isle of Shoals, with a religious conference centre on Star Island, and the home of 19th-century poet Celia Thaxter on Appledore Island; ski and tourist resorts; Odiorne Point state park, Rye, site of the first settlement; Fort Constitution at Newcastle, a British fort raided by rebels 1774 who used the stolen gunpowder against the British at the Battle of Bunker Hill; Strawbery Banke, Portsmouth, an outdoor museum of over 40 historic buildings; Exeter, settled 1638, the colonial capital during the American Revolution, with 18th- and 19th-century houses, Gilman Garrison House (about 1690), and Phillips Exeter Academy (founded 1781); Dartmouth College (1769), at Hannover, with murals by the Mexican artist José Clemente Orozco in the Baker Memorial Library; farm at Derry, home of the poet Robert Frost; home of Mary Baker Eddy, founder of Christian Science, at Concord; Cathedral of the Pines, Rindge, an outdoor cathedral dedicated to the war

dead; Currier Gallery of Art, Manchester; Saint Gaudens national historic site, Cornish; MacDowell Colony at Peterborough, founded 1907 for writers and composers; the earliest presidential primaries; the only state with no state income tax or sales tax

industries dairy, poultry, fruits, and vegetables; electrical and other machinery; pulp and paper

population (1995) 1,148,300

famous people Mary Baker Eddy, Robert Frost

history settled as a fishing colony near Rye and Dover 1623; separated from Massachusetts colony 1679. As leaders in the Revolutionary cause, its leaders received the honour of being the first to declare independence from Britain 4 July 1776. It became a state 1788, one of the original 13 states.

New Harmony Town in SW Indiana, midwestern USA, on the Wabash River, 35 km/22 mi NW of Evansville; population (1990) 846. It was settled in 1815 by the German Harmonist George Rapp and his followers. They sold the land in 1824 to the British social reformer Robert Owen, who renamed it New Harmony and tried, with about 1,000 settlers, to establish a cooperative community. It is now an agricultural trading centre.

Newhaven Port in E Sussex, SE England, at the mouth of the river Ouse, with container facilities and cross-Channel services to Dieppe, France; population (1991) 11,200.

New Haven City and port in Connecticut, USA, on Long Island Sound; population (1992) 124,000. *Yale University*, third oldest in the USA, was founded here 1701 and named after Elihu Yale (1648–1721), an early benefactor. New Haven was founded 1683 by English Protestants.

New Hebrides Former name (to 1980) of Vanuatu, a country in the S Pacific.

New Jersey State in NE USA; nicknamed Garden State

area 20,200 sq km/7,797 sq mi

capital Trenton

towns and cities Newark, Jersey City, Paterson, Elizabeth

physical Hudson River; about 200 km/125 mi of Jersey Shore

features the most densely populated state in the USA; the Jersey Shore has gambling casinos, amusement piers, and the boardwalk (the first elevated wooden walkway in USA, 1870) in Atlantic City, and the Victorian beach resort of Cape May, the state's oldest resort; Delaware Water Gap National Recreation Area; Palisades along W bank of the Hudson River; Morristown national historic park, commemorating the winters of 1777 and 1779–80 spent there by George Washington and his army; Edison national historic site, Menlo Park; Wharton State Forest, with Batsto state historic site, a restoration of an early 19th-century ironworking and glassmaking community; Walt Whitman House, Camden; Princeton Battle Monument; Princeton University (1746), with the Institute for Advanced Study; Rutgers University; Educational Testing Service; Bell Laboratories; Paterson (1791), the first planned industrial community in the USA; Garden State Arts Center (1968) in Monmouth County; the Meadowlands stadium; Statue of Liberty national monument (shared with New York)

industries fruits and vegetables, fish and shellfish, chemicals, pharmaceuticals, soaps and cleansers, transport equipment, petroleum refining
population (1995) 7,945,300
famous people Stephen Crane, Thomas Edison, Allen Ginsberg, Thomas Paine, Paul Robeson, Frank Sinatra, Bruce Springsteen, Woodrow Wilson
history colonized in the 17th century by the Dutch (New Netherlands); ceded to England 1664; became a state 1787. It was one of the original 13 states.

New London Port city in SE Connecticut, USA, on Long Island Sound at the mouth of the Thames River; population (1990) 28,500. Industries include submarine production, pharmaceuticals, and chemicals. Tourism is also important. Settled 1646 as part of the Massachusetts Bay Colony, it served as a privateering base during the American Revolution and a whaling centre during the 1800s.

Newlyn Seaport near Penzance, Cornwall, England, which gave its name to the *Newlyn School* of artists 1880–90, including Stanhope Forbes (1857–1947). The Ordnance Survey relates heights in the UK to mean sea level here.

Newmarket Town in Suffolk, E England, a centre for horse racing since James I's reign, notably the 1,000 and 2,000 Guineas, the Cambridgeshire, and the Cesarewitch. It is the headquarters of the Jockey Club, and a bookmaker who is 'warned off Newmarket Heath' is banned from all British racecourses. The National Horseracing Museum (1983) and the National Stud are here. Products include caravans and electronic equipment.

New Mexico State in SW USA; nicknamed Land of Enchantment/Sunshine State
area 315,000 sq km/121,590 sq mi
capital Santa Fe
towns and cities Albuquerque, Las Cruces, Roswell
physical more than 75% of the area lies over 1,200 m/ 3,900 ft above sea level; Great Plains; Rocky Mountains; Rio Grande; Carlsbad Caverns national park (a World Heritage Site)
features Aztec ruins; Navaho and Hopi Native American reservations; White Sands and Gila Cliff Dwellings national monuments; Chaco Culture national historic park (a World Heritage Site), with remains of pueblos, including Pueblo Bonito, the largest prehistoric Native American dwelling excavated in the SW, dating from the 12th century; Native American pueblos around Santa Fe and Albuquerque; Fort Sumner State Monument; Petroglyph national monument, with over 17,000 ancient rock drawings; Pecos national historic park; Albuquerque, dating from 1706, with San Felipe de Neri church, and the Indian Pueblo Cultural Center, with the largest collection of Native American arts and crafts in the SW; Santa Fe, with Spanish mission-style architecture, the pueblo-style Palace of the Governors, St Francis Cathedral, museums of Native American arts, the Institute of American Indian Arts, and San Miguel Mission (1625), the oldest church still in use in the USA; Taos Pueblo (a World Heritage Site), home of the Tiwa-speaking Native Americans, one of the oldest communities in the USA; Taos

art centre; Kit Carson home and museum, Taos; Ranchos de Taos, with San Francisco de Asis Church, an early mission church; Los Alamos National Laboratory, an atomic and space research centre; White Sands Missile Range (also used by space shuttle); Kiowa Ranch, site of the writer D H Lawrence's stay in the Sangre de Cristos Mountains; Santa Fe Opera Company, which performs in an outdoor theatre in the Sangre de Cristo Mountains
products uranium, potash, copper, oil, natural gas, petroleum and coal products; sheep farming; cotton; pecans; vegetables
population (1995) 1,685,400
famous people Billy the Kid, Kit Carson, Georgia O'Keeffe
history explored by Francisco de Coronado for Spain 1540–42; Spanish settlement 1598 on the Rio Grande; Santa Fe founded 1610; most of New Mexico ceded to the USA by Mexico 1848; became a state 1912. The first atomic bomb, a test device, was exploded in the desert near Alamogordo 16 July 1945. Oil and gas development and tourism now contribute to the state economy.

New Orleans Commercial and manufacturing city (refined petroleum and petrochemicals) and port on the Mississippi River, linked to the Gulf of Mexico, in Louisiana, USA; population (1992) 489,600; metropolitan area (1992) 1,303,000. It was settled by the French 1718. New Orleans is regarded as the traditional birthplace of jazz, which is thought to have started in Congo Square, developing out of the singing and voodoo rhythms popular with the large gatherings of slaves which took place during the 18th and 19th centuries.

New Plymouth Port on the W coast of North Island, New Zealand; population (1993) 49,100. It lies at the centre of a dairy-farming region; Taranaki gas fields are nearby.

Newport (Welsh *Casnewydd*) Unitary authority in S Wales created 1996 from part of the former county of Gwent; population (1996) 133,300; area 190 sq km/73 sq mi. The river Wye runs through the area. The Legionary Museum is at Caerleon, and a Roman amphitheatre. There are important steelworks, and telephone systems are manufactured.

Newport (Welsh *Casnewydd*) Seaport and administrative headquarters of Newport unitary authority, Wales, on the river Usk, NW of Bristol; population (1994 est) 111,000. There is a steelworks at nearby Llanwern, and a high-tech complex at Cleppa Park. Other industries include engineering, chemicals, fertilizers, aluminium, and electronics.

Newport River port, capital of the Isle of Wight, England; population (1991) 20,600. Charles I was imprisoned in nearby Carisbrooke Castle.

Newport News Industrial city (engineering, shipbuilding) and port of SE Virginia, USA, at the mouth of the James River; population (1992) 177,300. With neighbouring Chesapeake, Norfolk, and Portsmouth, it forms the Port of Hampton Roads, one of the chief US ports. It is the site of one of the world's largest shipyards. The site was settled by Irish colonists 1621.

New Providence Principal island of the Bahamas in the West Indies; area 150 sq km/58 sq mi; population (1990)

171,500. The island is about 34 km/21 mi long from E to W, and 11 km/7 mi wide from N to S. The island's principal city is Nassau, the capital and chief port of the Bahamas. The local economy centres on agriculture, fishing, rum, and tourism.

New Rochelle Residential suburb of New York, USA, on Long Island Sound; population (1992) 67,600.

New South Wales State of SE Australia
area 801,600 sq km/309,500 sq mi
capital Sydney
towns and cities Newcastle, Wollongong, Broken Hill
physical Great Dividing Range (including Blue Mountains) and part of the Australian Alps (including Snowy Mountains and Mount Kosciusko); Riverina district, irrigated by the Murray-Darling-Murrumbidgee river system; other main rivers Lachlan, Macquarie-Bogan, Hawkesbury, Hunter, Macleay, and Clarence
features a radio telescope at Parkes; Siding Spring Mountain 859 m/2,817 ft, NW of Sydney, with telescopes that can observe the central sector of the Galaxy. ◊Canberra forms an enclave within the state, and New South Wales administers the dependency of ◊Lord Howe Island
products cereals, fruit, sugar, tobacco, wool, meat, hides and skins, gold, silver, copper, tin, zinc, coal; hydroelectric power from the Snowy River
population (1994) 5,997,400; 60% in Sydney
history called New Wales by English explorer Capt Cook, who landed at Botany Bay 1770 and thought that the coastline resembled that of Wales. It was a convict settlement 1788–1850; opened to free settlement by 1819; achieved self-government 1856; and became a state of the Commonwealth of Australia 1901. Since 1973 there has been decentralization to counteract the pull of Sydney, and the New England and Riverina districts have separatist movements. .

New South Wales

Newton Aycliffe Town in Durham, England, on the river Skerne; population (1991) 25,100. It was designated a new town 1947.

New Westminster City in British Columbia, Canada, at the mouth of the Fraser River, 25 km/15 mi SE of

Vancouver; population (1991) 43,600. It was the capital of the colony of British Columbia 1859–66. After development of the docks 1921, it became one of Canada's main ports.

New World The Americas, so called by the first Europeans who reached them. The term also describes animals and plants of the W hemisphere.

New York Largest city in the USA, industrial port (printing, publishing, clothing), cultural, financial, and commercial centre, in S New York State, at the junction of the Hudson and East rivers and including New York Bay. It comprises the boroughs of the Bronx, Brooklyn, Manhattan, Queens, and Staten Island; population (1994) 16,300,000. New York is also known as the Big Apple. The Dutch established a settlement on Manhattan 1624, New Amsterdam. The Statue of Liberty stands on Liberty Island in the inner harbour of New York Bay. Manhattan skyscrapers include the twin towers of the World Trade Center (412 m/1,350 ft), the Art Deco Empire State Building (381m/1,250 ft), and the Chrysler Building; the headquarters of the United Nations is also here. There are a number of art galleries, among them the Frick Collection, the Metropolitan Museum of Art, the Museum of Modern Art, and the Guggenheim, designed by Frank Lloyd Wright. Columbia University (1754) is one of a number of institutions of higher education. Central Park is the largest park.

New York State in NE USA; nicknamed Empire State
area 127,200 sq km/49,099 sq mi
capital Albany
towns and cities New York, Buffalo, Rochester, Yonkers, Syracuse
physical mountains: Adirondacks, Catskills; lakes: Champlain, Placid, Erie, Ontario; rivers: Mohawk, Hudson, St Lawrence (with Thousand Islands); Niagara Falls; Long Island; New York Bay; Fire Island national seashore; Hudson Valley; Finger Lakes
features New York City; Erie Canal; Lake Placid, site of 1980 Winter Olympics; Long Island; Fort Ticonderoga; Franklin Delano Roosevelt national historic site and Roosevelt Library, Hyde Park; home of Theodore Roosevelt, Oyster Bay; Seneca Falls, site of women's-rights convention 1848; Mount Lebanon Shaker village; colleges: Columbia University (1745), Cornell University, Vassar College, New York University, Colgate, CUNY, SUNY, Renssalaer Polytech, Pratt, Juilliard, and the Eastman School of Music; West Point Military Academy (1801); the world's largest museum of photography, in George Eastman House, home of the founder of Eastman Kodak Company, in Rochester; Corning Museum of Glass; the National Baseball Hall of Fame, Cooperstown; Saratoga Springs, with medicinal springs, National Museum of Dance, and Performing Arts Centre (summer home of the Philadelphia Orchestra and the New York City Ballet); United Nations headquarters
products dairy products, apples, clothing, periodical and book printing and publishing, electronic components and accessories, office machines and computers, communications equipment, motor vehicles and equipment, pharmaceuticals, aircraft and parts

population (1995) 18,136,100
famous people Aaron Burr, Grover Cleveland, James Fenimore Cooper, George Gershwin, Alexander Hamilton, Fiorello La Guardia, Washington Irving, Henry James, Herman Melville, Arthur Miller, Nelson Rockefeller, Franklin D Roosevelt, Theodore Roosevelt, Peter Stuyvesant, Walt Whitman
history explored by the Italian navigator Giovanni da Verrazano for France 1524; explored by Samuel de Champlain for France and Henry Hudson for the Netherlands 1609; colonized by the Dutch from 1614; first permanent settlement at Albany (Fort Orange) 1624; Manhattan Island purchased by Peter Minuit 1625; New Amsterdam annexed by the English 1664. The first constitution was adopted 1788, when New York became one of the original 13 states. By 1810 New York was the most populous of the states, a rank it maintained until the 1960s. The Erie Canal, completed 1825, fostered commerce by providing a link between the Atlantic and the Great Lakes. After the Civil War, New York was transformed from a chiefly agricultural state to an industrial giant. By 1970, however, the state was suffering economic decline, particularly in manufacturing. But it remains an important industrial state, and in New York City it contains the commercial, financial (Wall Street), and cultural capital of the country.

NF Abbreviation for ◊Newfoundland, a Canadian province.

Ngorongoro Crater Crater in the Tanzanian section of the African Great ◊Rift Valley notable for its large numbers of wildebeest, gazelle, and zebra. It has a predator density of 30 kg per sq km, including cheetahs, hunting dogs, jackals, leopards, and lions.

NH Abbreviation for ◊New Hampshire, a state of the USA.

Niagara Falls City in S Ontario, Canada, on the W bank of the Niagara River, beside the Niagara Falls; population (1991) 75,400. Manufactures include chemicals, fertilizers, paper goods, and machinery. There is an important hydroelectric power plant and tourism is a major industry.

Niagara Falls City in New York State, NE USA, on the E bank of the Niagara River at the Niagara Falls, 30 km/19 mi NW of Buffalo; population (1990) 61,800. It is linked with the city of Niagara Falls, Canada, by the Rainbow Bridge (1941). Niagara Falls has chemical, engineering, aircraft, and metallurgical industries. It has an important hydroelectric power plant and it is a major tourist centre.

Niagara Falls Two waterfalls on the Niagara River, on the Canada–USA border, between lakes Erie and Ontario and separated by Goat Island. The *American Falls* are 51 m/167 ft high, 330 m/1,080 ft wide; *Horseshoe Falls*, in Canada, are 49 m/160 ft high, 790 m/2,600 ft across.

Niamey River port and capital of Niger; population (1988) 398,000. It produces textiles, chemicals, pharmaceuticals, and foodstuffs.

Nicaragua, Lake Lake in Nicaragua, the largest in Central America; area 8,250 sq km/3,185 sq mi.

Nice City on the French Riviera; population (1990) 345,700. Founded in the 3rd century BC, it repeatedly changed hands between France and the Duchy of Savoy from the 14th to the 19th century. In 1860 it was finally transferred to France.

Nicobar Islands Group of Indian islands, part of the Union Territory of ◊Andaman and Nicobar Islands.

Nicosia (Greek *Lefkosia*, Turkish *Lefkosha*) Capital of Cyprus, with leather, textile, and pottery industries; population (1993) 177,000. Nicosia was the residence of Lusignan kings of Cyprus 1192–1475. The Venetians, who took Cyprus 1489, surrounded Nicosia with a high wall, which still exists; the city fell to the Turks 1571. It was again partly taken by the Turks in the invasion 1974.

Niederösterreich German name for the federal state of ◊Lower Austria.

Niedersachsen German name for the federal state of ◊Lower Saxony, Germany.

Nieuwpoort (French *Nieuport*) Port in the Belgian province of West Flanders, 34 km/21 mi W of Bruges. It stands on the river Yser (Ijzer), about 3 km/2 mi above its mouth, and at the junction of several canals.

Nièvre River in central France, rising near Varzy and flowing 40 km/25 mi S to join the river Loire at Nevers; it gives its name to a *département*.

Nièvre *Département* in the ◊Burgundy region of central France; area 6,836 sq km/2,639 sq mi; population (1990) 233,528. It contains the basins of the rivers ◊Loire and ◊Seine. Forests cover large areas of Nièvre; farmland is largely devoted to rearing cattle, sheep, and horses. The chief crops are oats, wheat, and potatoes. Vines are grown in the Loire valley and in the neighbourhood of Clamecy; the white wines of Pouilly (notably, Pouilly Fumé) are famous. Coal is mined around Decize, and the chief manufactures are iron and steel, at Guérigny, Fourchambault, and Imphy. The principal towns are ◊Nevers (the capital), Château-Chinon, Clamecy, and Cosne.

Niger Third-longest river in Africa, 4,100 km/2,548 mi. It rises in the highlands bordering Sierra Leone and Guinea, flows NE through Mali, then SE through Niger and Nigeria to an inland delta on the Gulf of Guinea. It is sluggish and frequently floods its banks. It was explored by the Scotsman Mungo Park 1795–96.

Niigata Industrial port (textiles, metals, oil refining, chemicals) in Chubu region, Honshu Island, Japan; population (1994) 479,000.

Nijmegen Industrial city (brewery, electrical engineering, leather, tobacco) in the E Netherlands, on the Waal River; population (1994) 147,000. The Roman *Noviomagus*, Nijmegen was a free city of the Holy Roman Empire and a member of the Hanseatic League.

Nikopol Town in Lovech region, N Bulgaria, on the S bank of the river Danube, 37 km/23 mi NE of Pleven; population

6,000. In 1396 King Sigismund of Hungary was defeated at Nikopol by the Turks under Bajazet I, sultan of the Ottoman empire 1389–1403.

Nile River in Africa, the world's longest, 6,695 km/4,160 mi. The *Blue Nile* rises in Lake Tana, Ethiopia, the *White Nile* at Lake Victoria, and they join at Khartoum, Sudan. The river enters the Mediterranean Sea at a vast delta in N Egypt.

Nile

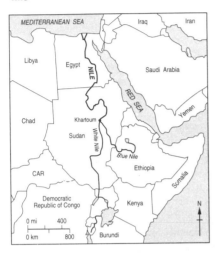

Nîmes Capital of Gard *département*, Languedoc-Roussillon, S France; population (1990) 133,600. Roman remains include an amphitheatre dating from the 2nd century and the Pont du Gard (aqueduct). The city gives its name to the cloth known as denim (*de Nîmes*).

Ningbo or *Ningpo* Port and special economic zone in Zhejiang province, E China; industries include fishing, shipbuilding, and high-tech equipment; population (1993) 1,070,000. Already a centre of foreign trade under the Tang dynasty (618–907), it was one of the original treaty ports 1842.

Ningxia or *Ningxia Hui* Autonomous region (formerly *Ninghsia-Hui*) of NW China
area 170,000 sq km/65,637 sq mi
capital Yinchuan
physical desert plateau
products cereals and rice under irrigation; coal
population (1990) 4,655,000.

Niort Capital of the French *département* of Deux-Sèvres, on the river Sèvre-Niortaise, 125 km/78 mi SE of Nantes; population (1990) 60,000. The main industries are the manufacture of footwear, gloves, and brushes; angelica is processed. Two towers of the 12th–13th-century fortress are preserved.

Nipigon, Lake Lake in SW Ontario, Canada; area 4,848 sq km/1,872 sq mi. It has 1,300 km/808 mi of shoreline and lies 55 km/34 mi N of Lake Superior in a forest reserve of over 18,130 sq km/7,000 sq mi. It is 112 km/70 mi long and 80 km/50 mi wide, is very deep and contains over 1,000

islands. The Nipigon River flows out of the lake and flows into Lake Superior. It supplies hydroelectric power to the region. The lake is known for its scenery and its wild surroundings.

Nippon English transliteration of the Japanese name for Japan.

Nis Town in Serbia, Yugoslavia, on the river Nisava; population (1991) 175,400. It is an important road and rail junction and has chemical and agricultural foodstuff industries.

Niterói or *Nictheroy* Port and resort city in Brazil on the E shore of Guanabara Bay, linked by bridge and ferry with Rio de Janeiro; population (1991) 455,200. Industries include shipbuilding, manufacture of metal goods, textiles, and matches.

Niue Coral island in the S Pacific, W of the Cook Islands; overseas territory of New Zealand
area 260 sq km/100 sq mi
towns and cities port Alofi
head of government Frank Lui
products coconuts, passion fruit, honey, taro, handicrafts, limes
population (1993) 2,300; 12,000 Niueans live in New Zealand
languages English and Niuean (official)
environment low water table; only 11–12% of the land can be cultivated
history inhabited by warriors who stopped English explorer Capt Cook from landing 1774; Christian missionaries arrived 1846; British protectorate 1900; annexed by New Zealand 1901; attained self-government in free association with New Zealand (with which there is common citizenship) 1974.

Nivernais Former province of central France, nearly corresponding to the present *département* of ◊Nièvre. It was formerly a duchy, with Nevers as its capital. Louis XIV joined it to the crown in 1669. The *canal of Nivernais*, constructed 1784–1842, connects the Loire and Yonne rivers.

Nizhnevartovsk City in Tyumen region, in the Russian Federation, in N Siberia; population (1994) 241,000. The oilfield discovered 1965 at nearby Lake Samotlor is one of the largest in the world, and there are natural gas fields to the N. Poor technology prevented their efficient exploitation until the 1990s.

Nizhniy-Novgorod formerly (1932–90) *Gorky* City in central Russian Federation; population (1990) 1,443,000. Cars, locomotives, and aircraft are manufactured here. The town was founded 1221 and annexed by Moscow in 1329.

NJ Abbreviation for ◊New Jersey, a state of the USA.

NM Abbreviation for ◊New Mexico, a state of the USA.

Nootka Sound Harbour on the Pacific coast of Canada, lying behind Nootka Island on the W coast of Vancouver Island, British Columbia. Nootka Sound, Barclay Sound on the SW coast of Vancouver, and Quatseenough Sound on the NW coast all have inlets into the heart of Vancouver Island.

Nord *Département* in the ◊Nord-Pas-de-Calais region of France, bordered in the N by Belgium; area 5,738 sq km/2,215 sq mi; population (1990) 2,533,500. The Flanders Canals system connects the rivers Sambre, Esceaut, Scarpe, Lys, Deûle, and Yser. Nord is one of the major industrial regions of France, with textile and metallurgical plants. Wheat, oats, sugar beet, potatoes, and vegetables are grown in the irrigated soil. The principal towns include ◊Lille (the capital), Roubaix, Tourcoing, Dunkirk, and Valenciennes.

Nordhausen Town in the *Land* of ◊Thuringia, Germany, in the foothills of the S Harz Mountains, 79 km/49 mi NW of Erfurt; population (1996) 47,000. The area has potash mines, and there are engineering, textile, and oil-refining industries. Nordhausen was a free city of the Holy Roman Empire 1253–1803.

Nord-Pas-de-Calais Region of N France; area 12,414 sq km/4,793 sq mi; population (1990) 3,965,100. Its capital is Lille, and it consists of the *départements* of Nord and Pas-de-Calais.

Nore, the Sandbank at the mouth of the river Thames, England; site of the first lightship 1732.

Norfolk County of E England
area 5,360 sq km/2,069 sq mi
towns and cities Norwich (administrative headquarters), King's Lynn; resorts: Great Yarmouth, Cromer, Hunstanton
features low-lying with the Fens in the W and the ◊Norfolk Broads in the E; rivers: Ouse, Yare, Bure, Waveney; Halvergate Marshes wildlife area; traditional reed thatching; Grime's Graves (Neolithic flint mines); shrine of Our Lady of Walsingham, a medieval and present-day centre of pilgrimage; Blickling Hall (Jacobean); residence of Elizabeth II at Sandringham (built 1869–71)
products cereals, turnips, sugar beets, turkeys, geese; offshore natural gas; fishing centred on Great Yarmouth
population (1996) 768,500.

Norfolk Seaport in SE Virginia, USA, on the Atlantic Ocean at the mouth of the James and Elizabeth rivers; population (1992) 253,800. It is the headquarters of the US Navy's Atlantic fleet, and the home of 22 other Navy commands. Industries include shipbuilding, chemicals, and motor-vehicle assembly. Norfolk was laid out in 1682.

Norfolk Broads Area of some 12 interlinked freshwater lakes in E England, created about 600 years ago by the digging-out of peat deposits; the lakes are used for boating and fishing. Chemical pollution has destroyed much of the wildlife.

Norfolk Island Pacific island territory of Australia, S of New Caledonia
area 40 sq km/15.5 sq mi
products citrus fruit, bananas; tourist industry
population (1994) 1,800
history reached by English explorer Capt Cook 1774; settled 1856 by descendants of the mutineers of the *Bounty* from ◊Pitcairn Island; Australian territory from 1914; largely self-governing from 1979.

Norilsk World's northernmost industrial city (nickel, cobalt, platinum, selenium, tellurium, gold, silver) in the Russian Federation, in Siberia; population (1992) 260,000. The permafrost is 300 m/1,000 ft deep, and the winter temperature may reach –55°C/–67°F.

Normal City in central Illinois, USA, NE of Bloomington; population (1990) 40,000. It is a marketing centre for the livestock and grains produced in the surrounding area. Illinois State University is here.

Normandy Former duchy of NW France now divided into two regions: ◊Haute-Normandie and ◊Basse-Normandie. Normandy was named after the Viking Norsemen (Normans), the people who conquered and settled in the area in the 9th century. As a French duchy it reached its peak under William the Conqueror and was renowned for its centres of learning established by Lanfranc and St Anselm. Normandy was united with England 1100–35. England and France fought over it during the Hundred Years' War, England finally losing it 1449 to Charles VII. In World War II the Normandy beaches were the site of the Allied invasion on D-day, 6 June 1944.

Norrköping Town and port in Sweden in the county of Östergötland, 180 km/112 mi SW of Stockholm, on both banks of the river Motala; population (1995) 123,800. There are paper, textile, engineering, and timber mills as well as shipyards.

Norrland The northernmost region of Sweden. The term is traditional rather than administrative.

Northallerton Market town, administrative headquarters of North Yorkshire, England; industries include tanning, flour-milling, trailer-manufacturing, and light engineering; population (1991) 13,800.

North America Third largest of the continents (including Greenland and Central America), and over twice the size of Europe
area 24,000,000 sq km/9,400,000 sq mi
largest cities (population over 1 million) Mexico City, New York, Chicago, Toronto, Los Angeles, Montréal, Guadalajara, Monterrey, Philadelphia, Houston, Guatemala City, Vancouver, Detroit, San Diego, Dallas
features Lake Superior (the largest body of fresh water in the world); Grand Canyon on the Colorado River; Redwood National Park, California, has some of the world's tallest trees; San Andreas Fault, California; deserts: Death Valley, Mojave, Sonoran; rivers (over 1,600 km/1,000 mi) include Mississippi, Missouri, Mackenzie, Rio Grande, Yukon, Arkansas, Colorado, Saskatchewan-Bow, Columbia, Red, Peace, Snake
physical occupying the N part of the landmass of the W hemisphere between the Arctic Ocean and the tropical SE tip of the isthmus that joins Central America to South America; the northernmost point on the mainland is the tip of Boothia Peninsula in the Canadian Arctic; the northernmost point on adjacent islands is Cape Morris Jesup on Greenland; the most westerly point on the mainland is Cape Prince of Wales, Alaska; the most westerly point on adjacent islands is Attu Island in the Aleutians; the most easterly point on the mainland lies on the SE coast of Labrador; the highest point is Mount McKinley, Alaska, 6,194 m/20,321 ft;

the lowest point is Badwater in Death Valley –86 m/–282 ft.

Perhaps the most dominating characteristic is the W cordillera running parallel to the coast from Alaska to Panama; it is called the ◊Rocky Mountains in the USA and Canada and its continuation into Mexico is called the ◊Sierra Madre. The cordillera is a series of ranges divided by intermontane plateaus and takes up about one-third of the continental area.

To the E of the cordillera lie the Great Plains, the agricultural heartland of North America, which descend in a series of steps to the depressions occupied by the ◊Great Lakes in the E and the Gulf of Mexico coastal lowlands in the SE. The Plains are characterized by treeless expanses crossed by broad, shallow river valleys. To the N and E of the region lie the Laurentian Highlands of Canada, an ancient plateau or shield area. Glaciation has deeply affected its landscape. In the E are the Appalachian Mountains, flanked by the narrow coastal plain which widens further S. Erosion here has created a line of planed crests, or terraces, at altitudes between 300–1,200 m/985–3,935 ft. This has also formed a ridge-and-valley topography which was an early barrier to continental penetration. The Fall Line is the abrupt junction of plateau and coastal plain in the E.

Northampton Administrative centre of Northamptonshire, England, on the river Nene; population (1994 est) 175,000. Boots and shoes (of which there is a museum) are still made, but engineering has superseded them as the chief industry; other industries include food processing, brewing, the manufacture of shoe machinery, cosmetics, leather goods, and motor car accessories. It was designated a new town 1968.

Northamptonshire County of central England
area 2,370 sq km/915 sq mi
towns and cities Northampton (administrative headquarters), Kettering
features rivers Welland and Nene; Canons Ashby, Tudor house, home of the Drydens for 400 years; churches with broached spires
industries cereals, cattle, sugar beet, shoemaking, food processing, printing, engineering
population (1994) 594,800
famous people Richard III, Robert Browne, John Dryden
history The site of the victory of Oliver Cromwell at the Battle of Naseby 1645.

Northants Abbreviation for ◊Northamptonshire, an English County.

North Ayrshire Unitary authority in W Scotland created 1996 from part of the former Strathclyde region; administrative headquarters Irvine; population (1996) 139,200; area 878 sq km/339 sq mi.

North Brabant (Dutch *Noord Brabant*) Southern province of the Netherlands, lying between the Maas River (Meuse) and Belgium
area 4,940 sq km/1,907 sq mi
capital 's-Hertogenbosch
towns and cities Breda, Eindhoven, Tilburg

population (1995 est) 2,276,200
physical former heathland is now under mixed farming
industries brewing, engineering, microelectronics, textile manufacture.

North Cape (Norwegian *Nordkapp*) Cape in the Norwegian county of Finnmark; the most northerly point of Europe.

North Carolina State in E USA; nicknamed Tar Heel State/Old North State
area 136,400 sq km/52,650 sq mi
capital Raleigh
towns and cities Charlotte, Greensboro, Winston-Salem
physical Great Smoky Mountain national park; Blue Ridge Mountains, with Blowing Rock (1,200 m/4,000 ft); Cape Hatteras national seashore, with marshland and sandy beaches; Cape Lookout national seashore
features Cape Hatteras Lighthouse, 63 m/208 ft, the tallest in the USA; the Piedmont; Ocracoke Island, with Ocracoke Lighthouse (1823); Fort Raleigh national historic site, Roanoke Island, site of the first English colony, 1587; Edenton, with the Cupola House and Gardens (about 1725), Chowan County Courthouse (1767), and St Paul's Church; Tryon Palace, New Bern (the Colonial capitol, dating from the 1770s); USS *North Carolina* Battleship Memorial, Wilmington; Biltmore Estate Gardens, Asheville, the 1890s home of George Vanderbilt, a 225-room French Renaissance style chateau designed by Richard Morris Hunt, with gardens landscaped by Frederick Law Olmsted; the Wright Brothers national memorial, Kill Devil Hills, the site of Wilbur and Orville Wright's first powered flight from the sand dunes at Kitty Hawk; Carl Sandburg home national historic site; University of North Carolina (the Chapel Hill campus, founded 1795, was the first state university in the USA); Duke University
industries tobacco, corn, soya beans, livestock, poultry, textiles, clothing, cigarettes, furniture, chemicals, machinery; tourism
population (1995) 7,195,100
famous people Billy Graham, O Henry, Jesse Jackson, Carl Sandburg, Thomas Wolfe
history after England's Roanoke Island colony was unsuccessful 1585 and 1587, permanent settlement was made 1663; it was one of the original 13 states 1789.

Northd Abbreviation for ◊Northumberland, an English county.

North Dakota State in N USA; nicknamed Peace Garden State
area 183,100 sq km/70,677 sq mi
capital Bismarck
towns and cities Fargo, Grand Forks, Minot
physical Red River Valley; Missouri River; the Badlands, so called because the pioneers had great difficulty in crossing them, with Theodore Roosevelt national park, and Painted Canyon; Lake Sakakawea; Devils Lake, breeding ground for migratory waterfowl; Pembina Gorge
features Garrison Dam power plant on the Missouri River; the geographical centre of North America at Rugby; Knife

River Native American villages national historic site; frontier forts, including Fort Buford (1866), where the Sioux leader Sitting Bull was imprisoned, and Fort Abercrombie; Fort Abraham Lincoln state park, including Custer House; Bismarck, with Art Deco state capitol, and the Victorian former Governor's Mansion; International Peace Garden, on Canadian border; 90% of the land is cultivated

industries cereals, meat products, farm equipment, oil, coal

population (1995) 641,400

famous people Maxwell Anderson, Louis L'Amour

history explored by La Verendrye's French Canadian expedition 1738–40; acquired by the USA partly in the Louisiana Purchase 1803 and partly by treaty with Britain 1813. The earliest settlement was Pembina 1812, by Scottish and Irish families, and North Dakota became a state 1889, attracting many German and Norwegian settlers.

North Downs Line of chalk hills in SE England, running from Salisbury Plain across Hampshire, Surrey, and Kent to the cliffs of South Foreland. They face the ◊South Downs across the Weald of Kent and Sussex and are much used for sheep pasture.

North-East Frontier Agency Former name (to 1972) for ◊Arunachal Pradesh, a territory of India.

North-East India Area of India (Meghalaya, Assam, Mizoram, Tripura, Manipur, Nagaland, and Arunachal Pradesh) linked with the rest of India only by a narrow corridor. There is opposition to immigration from Bangladesh and the rest of India, and demand for secession.

North East Lincolnshire Unitary authority in E England created 1996 from part of the former county of Humberside; administrative headquarters Grimsby; population (1996 est) 164,000; area 192 sq km/74 sq mi. The area includes the deep water ports of Grimsby and Immingham. Industries include fishing and fish processing (based on Grimsby), tourism (Cleethorpes), and chemicals.

Northeast Passage Sea route from the N Atlantic, around Asia, to the N Pacific, pioneered by Swedish explorer Nils Nordenskjöld 1878–79 and developed by the USSR in settling N Siberia from 1935. Russia owns offshore islands and claims it as an internal waterway; the USA claims that it is international.

Northern Areas Districts N of Azad Kashmir, directly administered by Pakistan but not merged with it. India and Pakistan-held Azad Kashmir each claim them as part of disputed Kashmir. They include Baltistan, Gilgit, Skardu, and Hunza (an independent principality for 900 years until 1974).

Northern Cape Province of the Republic of South Africa from 1994, formerly part of Cape Province, including the former independent homeland of Venda

area 363,389 sq km/140,305 sq mi

capital Kimberley

features largest and most sparsely populated province

industries diamonds, iron, manganese, asbestos, cotton

population (1995 est) 742,000

languages Afrikaans 65%, Setswana (Tswana) 22%, Xhosa 4%

Northern Ireland See ◊Ireland, Northern.

Northern Mariana Islands Archipelago in the NW Pacific, with ◊Guam known collectively as the Mariana Islands. The Northern Marianas are a commonwealth in union with the USA.

area 471 sq km/182 sq mi

capital Garapan on Saipan

physical 16 islands and atolls extending 560 km/350 mi N of Guam

political system liberal democracy

political parties Democratic Party, centre-left; Republican Party, right of centre; Territorial Party, nationalist

currency US dollar

population (1995 est) 47,200

language English

religion mainly Roman Catholicism

history came under Spanish control 1565; sold to Germany 1899; came under Japanese control 1914 and Japanese rule under a League of Nations mandate 1921. Taken by US marines in World War II, the islands became a UN Trust Territory administered by the USA 1947 and a US commonwealth territory 1978. Granted internal self-government and full US citizenship 1986. UN Trusteeship status ended 22 Dec 1990.

Northern Province formerly *Northern Transvaal* Province of the Republic of South Africa from 1994, formerly part of Transvaal

area 119,606 sq km/46,180 sq mi

capital Pietersburg

industries copper, asbestos, iron, diamonds, wheat, maize, tobacco, groundnuts, tourism. Many men in rural areas are migrant workers in Gauteng province

population (1995 est) 5,397,200

languages Sepedi (North Sotho) 56%, Shangaan 22%, Venda 12%

Northern Rhodesia Former name (to 1964) of Zambia, a country in Africa.

Northern Territory Territory of Australia

area 1,346,200 sq km/519,767 sq mi

Northern Territory

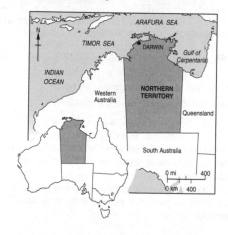

capital Darwin (chief port)

towns and cities Alice Springs

features mainly within the tropics, although with wide range of temperature; very low rainfall, but artesian bores are used; Macdonnell Ranges (Mount Zeil 1,510 m/4,956 ft); ◊Cocos and ◊Christmas Islands included in the territory 1984; 50,000–60,000-year-old rock paintings of animals, birds, and fish in Kakadu National Park

industries beef cattle, prawns, bauxite (Gove), gold and copper (Tennant Creek), uranium (Ranger)

population (1994) 173,900

government there is an administrator and a legislative assembly, and the territory is also represented in the federal parliament

history originally part of New South Wales, it was annexed 1863 to South Australia but from 1911 until 1978 (when self-government was introduced) was under the control of the Commonwealth of Australia government. Mineral discoveries on land occupied by Aborigines led to a royalty agreement 1979.

Northern Transvaal Former name of ◊Northern Province, a province of the Republic of South Africa.

North Holland (Dutch *Noord Holland*) Low-lying coastal province of the Netherlands occupying the peninsula jutting northward between the North Sea and the IJsselmeer

area 2,670 sq km/1,031 sq mi

population (1995 est) 2,463,600

capital Haarlem

towns and cities Amsterdam, Hilversum, Den Helder, the cheese centres Alkmaar and Edam

physical most of the province is below sea level, protected from the sea by a series of sand dunes and artificial dykes

products flower bulbs, grain, and vegetables

history once part of the former county of Holland that was divided into two provinces (North and South) 1840.

North Island Smaller of the two main islands of New Zealand, with an area of 114,669 sq km/44,274 sq mi.

North Korea See Korea, North.

North Lanarkshire Unitary authority in central Scotland created 1996 from part of the former Strathclyde region; administrative headquarters Motherwell; population (1996) 326,750; area 466 sq km/180 sq mi.

North Lincolnshire Unitary authority in E England created 1996 from part of the former county of Humberside; administrative headquarters Scunthorpe; population (1996 est) 153,000; area 850 sq km/328 sq mi. There are oil refineries, and steel and metal industries.

North Ossetia Former name for ◊Alania.

North Platte River in Colorado and Wyoming, USA; length 1,094 km/680 mi. In Nebraska it unites with the South Platte River to form the Platte River. The North Platte rises in N central Colorado in the Medicine Bow, Park, and Rabbits Ear ranges. It flows N into Wyoming, bending SE before turning westwards into Nebraska. Its waters are used as part of a power, irrigation, and flood-control project.

North Pole The N point where an imaginary line penetrates the Earth's surface by the axis about which it revolves; see also ◊Arctic.

North Rhine–Westphalia (German *Nordrhein-Westfalen*) Administrative region (*Land*) of Germany

area 34,077 sq km/13,157 sq mi

capital Düsseldorf

towns and cities Cologne, Essen, Dortmund, Duisburg, Bochum, Wuppertal, Bielefeld, Bonn, Gelsenkirchen, Münster, Mönchengladbach

features valley of the Rhine; Ruhr industrial district

industries iron, steel, coal, lignite, electrical goods, fertilizers, synthetic textiles

population (1995) 17,893,000

religion 53% Roman Catholic, 42% Protestant.

North Sea Sea to the E of Britain and bounded by the coasts of Belgium, the Netherlands, Germany, Denmark, and Norway; part of the Atlantic Ocean; area 427,000 sq km/164,900 sq mi; average depth 94 m/308 ft, greatest depth 660 m/2,165 ft. In the NE it joins the Norwegian Sea, and in the S it meets the Strait of Dover. It has 300 oil platforms, 10,000 km/6,200 mi of gas pipeline (gas was discovered 1965), and fisheries (especially mackerel and herring).

North Shields Industrial town and fishing port in Tyne and Wear, NE England, 7 mi/11 km E of Newcastle upon Tyne; it is part of the Tyneside urban area, on the N bank of the river Tyne; population (1981) 41,600. It is the birthplace of the steam trawler.

North Somerset Unitary authority in SW England created 1996 from part of the former county of Avon; administrative headquarters Weston-super-Mare; population (1996) 177,000; area 372 sq km/144 sq mi.

North Uist Island of the Outer Hebrides, Scotland. Lochmaddy is the main port of entry. It produces tweeds and seaweed, and crofting is practised.

Northumberland County of N England

area 5,030 sq km/1,942 sq mi

towns and cities Morpeth (administrative headquarters), Berwick-upon-Tweed, Hexham

features Cheviot Hills; rivers: Tweed, upper Tyne; Northumberland National Park in the W; ◊Holy Island; the ◊Farne island group; part of Hadrian's Wall (a World Heritage site) and Housestead's Fort; Alnwick and Bamburgh castles; Thomas Bewick museum; large moorland areas are used for military manoeuvres; Longstone Lighthouse from which Grace Darling rowed to the rescue is no longer inhabited, the crew having been replaced by an automatic light; wild white cattle of Chillingham; Kielder Water (1982), the largest artificial lake in N Europe

industries sheep, fishing

population (1996) 307,700

famous people Thomas Bewick, Grace Darling, Jack and Bobby Charlton.

Northumberland Strait Strait in E Canada separating ◊Prince Edward Island from Nova Scotia and New Brunswick; length 210 km/130 mi, width 15–50 km/9–31 mi.

North West Province of the Republic of South Africa from 1994
area 118,710 sq km/45,834 sq mi
capital Mmabatho
features includes part of the former independent homeland of Bophuthatswana
industries platinum, chrome, iron, groundnuts
population (1995 est) 3,351,800
languages Setswana (Tswana) 63%, Xhosa 14%, Sesotho (Sotho) 8%

North-West Frontier Province Province of Pakistan; capital Peshawar; area 74,500 sq km/28,757 sq mi; population (1993 est) 20,090,000. It was a province of British India 1901–47. It includes the strategic Khyber Pass, the site of constant struggle between the British Raj and the Pathan warriors. In the 1980s it had to accommodate a stream of refugees from neighbouring Afghanistan.

Northwest Passage Atlantic–Pacific sea route around the N of Canada. Canada, which owns offshore islands, claims it as an internal waterway; the USA insists that it is an international waterway and sent an icebreaker through without permission 1985.

Northwest Territories Territory of Canada
area 3,426,320 sq km/1,322,902 sq mi
capital Yellowknife
physical extends into the Arctic Circle, to Hudson's Bay in the E, and in the W to the edge of the Canadian Shield; Mackenzie River; lakes: Great Slave, Great Bear; Miles Canyon
products oil, natural gas, zinc, lead, gold, tungsten, silver
population (1995 est) 62,000
history the area was the N part of Rupert's Land, bought by the Canadian government from the Hudson's Bay Company 1869. An act of 1952 placed the Northwest Territories under a commissioner acting in Ottawa under the Ministry of Northern Affairs and Natural Resources. In 1990 territorial control of over 350,000 sq km/135,000 sq mi of the Northwest Territories was given to the Inuit, and in 1992 the creation of an Inuit autonomous homeland, Nunavut, was agreed in a regional referendum.

Northwest Territories

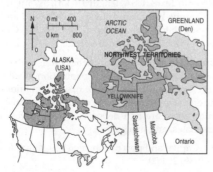

North Yorkshire County of NE England, created 1974 from most of the North Riding and parts of East and West Ridings of Yorkshire
area 8,320 sq km/3,212 sq mi

towns and cities Northallerton (administrative head-quarters); resorts: Harrogate, Scarborough, Whitby
features England's largest county; including part of the Pennines, the Vale of York, and the Cleveland Hills and North Yorkshire Moors, which form a national park (within which is Fylingdales radar station to give early warning – 4 minutes – of nuclear attack); Rievaulx Abbey; Yorkshire Dales National Park (including Swaledale, Wensleydale, and Bolton Abbey in Wharfedale); rivers: Derwent, Ouse; Fountains Abbey near Ripon, with Studley Royal Gardens (a World Heritage site); Castle Howard, designed by Vanbrugh, has Britain's largest collection of 18th–20th-century costume; largest accessible cavern in Britain, the Battlefield Chamber, Ingleton
industries cereals, wool and meat from sheep, dairy products, coal, electrical goods, footwear, clothing, vehicles, plastics, foodstuffs, high technology industries, light industry
population (1995) 556,200
famous people Alcuin, Guy Fawkes, W H Auden.

Norwalk City in SW Connecticut, USA, on the Norwalk River where it flows into Long Island Sound, NE of Stamford; population (1992) 78,500. Industries include electronic equipment, clothing, hardware, and furniture. It was settled 1640. the main industry used to be the manufacture of hats.

Norwegian Sea Part of the ◊Arctic Ocean.

Norwich Cathedral city in Norfolk, E England, on the river Wensum; administrative headquarters of Norfolk; population (1994 est) 130,000. Industries include financial services, shoes, clothing, chemicals, confectionery, engineering, printing, and insurance. It has a Norman castle, a 15th-century Guildhall, 32 medieval churches, Tudor houses, and a Georgian Assembly House. Its City Hall dates from 1938; the Castle Mall Shopping Centre was completed 1993. It is the largest medieval walled city in England.

Norwich City in SE Connecticut, USA, at the confluence of the Yantic and Quinebaug rivers that form the Thames River, N of New London; seat of New London County; population (1990) 37,400. Industries include leather, paper, and metal products; electronic equipment; and clothing. It was settled 1659; in the 1700s it was a shipping and shipbuilding centre.

Nottingham Industrial city (engineering, coal mining, bicycles, textiles, knitwear, pharmaceuticals, tobacco, lace, electronics) and administrative headquarters of Nottinghamshire, England; it will become a unitary authority in April 1998; population (1994 est) 285,000. Nottingham was founded by the Danes. The English Civil War began here 1642. Nottingham is famous for the Goose Fair held in October.

Nottinghamshire County of central England; Nottingham City will become a unitary authority in April 1998
area 2,160 sq km/834 sq mi
towns and cities Nottingham (administrative headquarters), Mansfield, Worksop, Newark
features river Trent; the remaining areas of Sherwood Forest (home of Robin Hood), formerly a royal hunting ground, are included in the 'Dukeries'; Cresswell Crags

(remains of prehistoric humans); D H Lawrence commemorative walk from Eastwood (where he lived) to Old Brinsley Colliery

industries cereals, cattle, sheep, light engineering, footwear, limestone, coal mining, ironstone, oil, cigarettes, tanning, furniture, pharmaceuticals, typewriters, gypsum, gravel. There are many orchards, and there is market gardening

population (1995) 1,030,900

famous people William Booth, D H Lawrence, Alan Sillitoe.

Notts Abbreviation for ◊Nottinghamshire.

Nouakchott Capital of Mauritania, 270 mi/435 km NE of Dakar, Senegal; population (1992) 600,000. It is the largest city in the Sahara. Products include salt, cement, and insecticides. Exports include copper, petroleum, and phosphates.

Nouméa Port and capital on the SW coast of New Caledonia; population (1992) 65,000.

Nova Lisboa Former name (1928–73) for ◊Huambo, a town in Angola.

Novara Province of N Italy in NE ◊Piedmont region; capital Novara (population (1990) 103,300); area 3,595 sq km/1,388 sq mi; population (1992) 497,500.

Nova Scotia Maritime province of E Canada
area 55,490 sq km/21,425 sq mi
capital Halifax (chief port)
towns and cities Dartmouth, Sydney, Annapolis Royal
physical comprising a peninsula with a highly indented coastline extending SE from New Brunswick into the Atlantic Ocean, and ◊Cape Breton Island which is linked to the mainland by the Canso Causeway
features Cabot Trail (Cape Breton Island); Alexander Graham Bell Museum; Fortress Louisbourg; Fort Anne (oldest historic building in Canada); Strait of Canso Superport, the largest deep-water harbour on the Atlantic coast of North America
industries coal, gypsum, dairy products, poultry, fruit, forest products, fish products (including scallop and lobster)
population (1995 est) 918,000
history Nova Scotia was visited by the Italian navigator Giovanni Caboto 1497. A French settlement was established 1604, but expelled 1613 by English colonists from Virginia. The name of the colony was changed from Acadia to Nova Scotia 1621. England and France contended for possession of

Nova Scotia

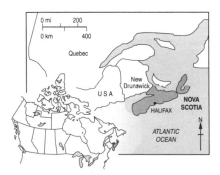

the territory until Nova Scotia (which then included present-day New Brunswick and Prince Edward Island) was ceded to Britain 1713; Cape Breton Island remained French until 1763. Nova Scotia was one of the four original provinces of the Dominion of Canada.

Novaya Zemlya (Russian 'new land') Arctic island group off NE Russian Federation; area 81,279 sq km/31,394 sq mi; population, a few Samoyed. It is rich in birds, seals, and walrus.

Novgorod Industrial city (chemicals, engineering, clothing, brewing) on the Volkhov River, NW Russian Federation; a major trading city in medieval times; population (1994) 233,000.

Novi Sad Industrial and commercial city (pottery and cotton), capital of the autonomous province of Vojvodina in N Serbia, Yugoslavia, on the river Danube; population (1991) 179,600. Products include leather, textiles, and tobacco.

Novokuznetsk Industrial city (steel, aluminium, chemicals) in the Kuznetsk Basin, S central Russian Federation; population (1994) 593,000. It was called *Stalinsk* 1932–61.

Novorossiisk Black Sea port and industrial city (cement, metallurgy, food processing) in the Russian Federation; population (1990) 188,000.

Novosibirsk Industrial city (engineering, textiles, chemicals, food processing) in the Russian Federation, in W Siberia, on the Ob River; population (1994) 1,418,000. Winter lasts eight months here.

Nowa Huta Industrial suburb of Kraków, Poland, on the Vistula River. It is the centre of the country's steel industry.

Nowa Sól (German *Neusalz*) River port in Zielona Góra province, Poland, on the river Oder, 21 km/13 mi SE of Zielona Góra; population (1990) 43,300. Paper, textiles, and metal goods are manufactured.

NS Abbreviation for ◊Nova Scotia, a Canadian province.

NSW Abbreviation for ◊New South Wales, an Australian state.

Nueces River in Texas, USA; length 510 km/317 mi. It rises in Edwards County, W of San Antonio, and flows S and SE, finally emerging into Corpus Christi Bay, in the Gulf of Mexico. It is an important source of irrigation.

Nuevo León State of NE Mexico, on the border of the USA; area 64,555 sq km/24,925 sq mi; population (1995 est) 3,549,200. Its capital is Monterrey. The main occupations are cattle raising and farming, producing cereals, sugar-cane, cotton, and fruit. There are rich deposits of gold, silver, lead, copper, phosphates, and manganese.

Nuku'alofa Capital and port of Tonga on Tongatapu Island; population (1989) 29,000.

Nullarbor Plain (Latin *nullus arbor* 'no tree') Arid coastal plateau area divided between Western and South Australia; there is a network of caves beneath it. Atom-bomb experiments were carried out in the 1950s at Maralinga, an area in the NE bordering on the Great Victoria Desert.

Nunavut (Inuit 'our land') Semi-autonomous Inuit homeland in Northwest Territories, Canada, extending over approximately 1,994,300 sq km/770,000 sq mi in the present regions of Baffin, Keewatin, and Kitikmat. In a regional plebiscite 1992, its creation in 1999 was approved by a narrow majority, after representatives of the Inuit had negotiated hunting and fishing rights in the area. A final land-claims agreement, signed 1993 on Baffin Island (proposed capital of Nunavut), gave the Inuit outright ownership of 353,610 sq km/136,493 sq mi of the land, and mineral rights to 36,257 sq km/13,995 sq mi. Of Nunavut's population of 26,000, all but 3,900 are Inuit.

Nuneaton Market town in Warwickshire, central England, on the river Anker, NE of Coventry; industries include ceramics, tiles, bricks, textiles, engineering, and electronics; population (1991) 66,700.

Nuoro Province of Italy in central ◊Sardinia; capital Nuoro (population (1990) 38,100); area 7,273 sq km/2,808 sq mi; population (1992) 272,900.

Nürnberg Industrial city (electrical and other machinery, precision instruments, textiles, toys) in Bavaria, Germany; population (1993) 499,800. From 1933 the Nürnberg rallies were held here, and in 1945 the Nürnberg trials of war criminals.

Nuuk Greenlandic for ◊Godthaab, the capital of Greenland.

NV Abbreviation for ◊Nevada, a state of the USA.

NY Abbreviation for ◊New York, a city and state of the USA.

Nyasa, Lake or *Lake Malawi* African lake, bordered by Malawi, Tanzania, and Mozambique, formed in a section of the Great ◊Rift Valley. It is about 500 m/1,650 ft above sea level and 560 km/350 mi long, with an area of 28,867 sq km/11,146 sq mi and a depth of 700 m, making it the 9th biggest lake in the world. It is intermittently drained to the S by the river Shire into the Zambezi.

Nyasaland Former name (to 1964) for Malawi.

Nyíregyháza Market town in E Hungary; population (1993 est) 115,000. It trades in tobacco and vegetables.

Nyon Commune in the canton of Vaud, Switzerland, on the W shore of Lake Geneva, about 20 km/12 mi N of Geneva; population (1995) 15,400. Nyon produces fine porcelain and lies at the junction of the Geneva–Lausanne railway line and a line running into France. Nyon was the site of the Roman colony of Julia Equestris.

Nysa (German *Neisse*) Industrial town (machinery, food processing) in Opole province, S Poland, on the river Nysa, 48 km/30 mi SW of Opole. It was capital of a principality of the bishops of Breslau (now Wrocław) 1198–1810, and part of German Upper Silesia until 1945.

Nysa (German *Neisse*) Two rivers in central Europe, tributaries of the ◊Oder.

The *Nysa Łżycka* (German *Lausitzer Neisse*) rises near Liberec in the N Czech Republic and flows 257 km/160 mi northwards along the German-Polish frontier to join the ◊Oder SE of Frankfurt-an-der-Oder.

The *Nysa Kłodzka* (German *Glatzer Neisse*) rises in the Sudeten Mountains on the Czech-Polish frontier and flows 193 km/120 mi NE to join the Oder NW of Opole.

NZ Abbreviation for New Zealand.

Oahu Island of Hawaii, USA, in the N Pacific
area 1,525 sq km/589 sq mi
towns and cities Honolulu (state capital)
physical formed by two extinct volcanoes
features Waikiki beach; Pearl Harbor naval base; Diamond Head; punchbowl craters
industries sugar, pineapples; tourism is a major industry
population (1990 est) 850,000.

Oakland Industrial port (vehicles, textiles, chemicals, food processing, shipbuilding) in California, USA, on the E coast of San Francisco Bay; population (1992) 373,200. It is linked by bridge (1936) with San Francisco. The community was laid out 1852 and became a terminus of the first transcontinental railroad 1869. It was damaged by earthquake 1989.

Oak Ridge Town in Tennessee, E USA, on the Clinch River, with the Oak Ridge National Laboratory (1943), which manufactures plutonium for nuclear weapons; population (1990) 27,300. The community was founded 1942 as part of the Manhattan Project to develop an atomic bomb; by the end of World War II its population was more than 75,000. Ownership of the community passed to the residents in the late 1950s.

Oaxaca State of S Mexico, on the Pacific; area 95,364 sq km/36,820 sq mi; population (1995 est) 3,224,300. Its capital is Oaxaca de Juárez. The main occupation is farming, producing cereals, rice, coffee, sugar-cane, cotton, tobacco, and fruit. There are rubber plantations and large mineral deposits.

Oaxaca de Juárez Capital of the state Oaxaca in the Sierra Madre del Sur mountain range, Mexico; population (1990) 212,900. Industries include food processing, textiles, and handicrafts.

Ob River in Asian Russia, flowing 3,380 km/2,100 mi from the Altai Mountains through the W Siberian Plain to the Gulf of Ob in the Arctic Ocean. With its main tributary, the *Irtysh*, it is 5,410 km/3,362 mi long.

Ob

Oban Seaport and resort in Argyll and Bute, W Scotland; population (1991) 8,200.

Obeid, El See ◊El Obeid, a city in Sudan.

Oberhausen Industrial (metals, machinery, plastics, chemicals) and coal-mining city in the Ruhr Valley, North Rhine–Westphalia, Germany; population (1993) 226,300.

Oberösterreich German name for the federal state of ◊Upper Austria.

Ocala City in N central Florida, USA, SE of Gainesville; seat of Marion County; population (1990) 42,000. It is a marketing and shipping centre for the citrus, poultry, cotton, and tobacco products grown in the surrounding area. Tourism is also vital to the economy. The town grew up around Fort King, built 1827.

Oceania The groups of islands in the S and central Pacific Ocean, comprising all those intervening between the SE shores of Asia and the W shores of America. See ◊Australasia and Oceania.

Ocean Island Former name for ◊Banaba, an island belonging to Kiribati.

Ocussi Ambeno Port on the N coast of Indonesian West Timor, until 1975 an exclave of the Portuguese colony of East Timor. The port is an outlet for rice, copra, and sandalwood.

Ödenburg German name for ◊Sopron, a town in Hungary.

Odense Industrial port (shipbuilding, electrical goods, glass, textiles) on the island of Fyn, Denmark; population (1993) 180,800. It is the birthplace of Hans Christian Andersen.

Odenwald Mountainous region of SW Germany, stretching across parts of ◊Hessen, ◊Baden-Württemberg, and ◊Bavaria. The Odenwald lies S of the river Main. The chief peaks are Katzenbuckel (626 m/2,053 ft), Neunkircher Hohe (605 m/1,982 ft), and the Krahberg (600 m/1,968 ft). The region is densely forested, with many old castles.

Oder (Polish *Odra*) European river flowing N from the Czech Republic to the Baltic Sea (the Nysa River is a tributary); length 885 km/550 mi.

Odessa Seaport in Ukraine, on the Black Sea, capital of Odessa region; population (1992) 1,096,000. Products include chemicals, pharmaceuticals, and machinery. Occupied by Germany 1941–44, it suffered severe damage under the Soviet-scorched earth policy and from German destruction.

Odessa City in W Texas, USA, SW of Big Springs; seat of Ector County; population (1992) 93,800. Industries include petroleum products; it is also a livestock processing and shipping centre. It was founded 1886 and grew up among the oilfields located here.

Offaly County of the Republic of Ireland, in the province of Leinster, between Galway on the W and Kildare on the E; county town Tullamore; area 2,000 sq km/772 sq mi; population (1996 est) 59,100. It is low-lying, with part of the Bog of Allen to the N.

Offa's Dyke Defensive earthwork dyke along the Welsh border, of which there are remains from the mouth of the river Dee to that of the river Severn. It was built about AD 785 by King Offa of Mercia, England, and represents the boundary secured by his wars with Wales.

Offenbach City in Hessen, Germany, on the river Main, 10 km/6 mi E of Frankfurt; population (1994) 116,600. Offenbach produces leather goods and artificial fibres, and there are engineering industries.

Offenburg City in Baden-Württemberg, Germany, on the river Kinzig, 14 km/9 mi from its junction with the Rhine, 96 km/60 mi SW of Stuttgart; population (1994) 327,000. It is the centre of a fruit- and wine-growing district, but also has electrical and mechanical engineering factories.

Ogaden Desert region in Harar province, SE Ethiopia, that borders on Somalia. It is a desert plateau, rising to 1,000 m/3,280 ft, inhabited mainly by Somali nomads practising arid farming.

Ogallala Aquifer The largest source of groundwater in the USA, stretching from S South Dakota to NW Texas. The overexploitation of this water resource resulted in the loss of more than 18% of the irrigated farmland of Oklahoma and Texas in the period 1940–90.

Ogbomosho City and commercial centre in W Nigeria, 80 km/50 mi NE of Ibadan; population (1992 est) 660,600.

Ogden City in N Utah, USA, on the Weber and Ogden rivers, N of Salt Lake City; population (1992) 66,200. It is a railway, trading, and military supply centre; Hill Air Force Base is nearby. Tourism is also important to the economy. Ogden was laid out 1850.

Ogun State of SW Nigeria; area 16,762 sq km/6,474 sq mi; capital Abeokuta; population (1991) 2,338,600.

OH Abbreviation for the state of ◊Ohio, USA.

Ohio River in the USA, 1,580 km/980 mi long; it is formed by the union of the Allegheny and Monongahela at Pittsburgh, Pennsylvania, and flows SW until it joins the river Mississippi at Cairo, Illinois.

Ohio State in N central USA; nicknamed Buckeye State; became a state 1803
area 107,100 sq km/41,341 sq mi
capital Columbus
towns and cities Cleveland, Cincinnati, Dayton, Akron, Toledo, Youngstown, Canton
physical Lake Erie; Ohio River
features Serpent Mound, a 1.3-m/4-ft embankment, 405 m/1,330 ft long and about 5 m/18 ft across, built by Hopewell American Indians in the 2nd–1st centuries BC; Mound City Group, 23 prehistoric mounds, a burial ground of the Hopewell American Indians; Perry's Victory and International Peace Memorial, the site of Perry's naval victory over the British in the war of 1812, with views into Canada; Cleveland, with the Old Arcade (1890), the Cleveland Museum of Art, and the Rock and Roll Hall of Fame and Museum (1995); Cincinnati, with the William Howard Taft birthplace, Cincinnati Art Museum, Museum

Center at Union Terminal, the Carew Tower, and Omni Netherland Plaza Hotel; Columbus, a centre for banking and insurance, with German Village (built by 19th-century immigrants); Dayton, with the Wright Brothers Bicycle Shop and the Wright Memorial, and the US Air Force Museum; the National Afro-American Museum and Cultural Center, Canton; Oberlin College (1833), the first coeducational college in the USA; the Cleveland Orchestra; the Cincinnati Symphony Orchestra; the Neil Armstrong Air and Space Museum; the Pro Football Hall of Fame, Canton

industries coal, cereals, livestock, dairy foods, machinery, chemicals, steel, motor vehicles, automotive and aircraft parts, rubber products, office equipment, refined petroleum

population (1995) 11,150,500

famous people Sherwood Anderson, Neil Armstrong, Hart Crane, Thomas Edison, James Garfield, John Glenn, Ulysses S Grant, Zane Grey, Warren Harding, Benjamin Harrison, William H Harrison, Rutherford B Hayes, William McKinley, Paul Newman, Jesse Owens, John D Rockefeller, William T Sherman, William H Taft, James Thurber, Orville and Wilbur Wright.

Ohrid Town in Macedonia, Yugoslavia, near the Albanian border, situated on the shore of Lake Ohrid. It is on the site of an ancient Greek colony and is said to be the oldest town in Yugoslavia. Its buildings include a 10th-century fortress and an 11th-century church. Sts Cyril and Methodius, creators of the Slavonic alphabet, are believed to have worked here.

Ohrid, Lake Lake on the frontier between Albania and the Former Yugoslav Republic of Macedonia; area 350 sq km/135 sq mi.

Oise European river that rises in the Ardennes plateau, Belgium, and flows SW through France for 300 km/186 mi to join the Seine about 65 km/40 mi below Paris. It gives its name to a French *département* in Picardy.

Oise *Département* in the ◊Picardy region of N France; area 5,860 sq km/2,263 sq mi; population (1990) 726,869. The main rivers are the Oise and the Aisne. Fruit and dairy produce are among the area's agricultural produce. Principal towns are the capital ◊Beauvais, ◊Compiègne, Creil, and Senlis. The town of ◊Chantilly, with its famous château and racecourse, is in the S of the *département*.

OK Abbreviation for the state of ◊Oklahoma, USA.

Okavango Delta Marshy area in NW Botswana covering about 20,000 km/7,722 sq mi, fed by the *Okavango River*, which rises in Angola and flows SE about 1,600 km/1,000 mi. It is an important area for wildlife.

Okayama Industrial port (textiles, cotton) in the SW of Honshu Island, Japan; population (1994) 598,000.

Okeechobee Lake in the N Everglades, Florida, USA; 65 km/40 mi long and 40 km/25 mi wide. It is the largest lake in the S USA, about 1,800 sq km/700 sq mi.

Okefenokee Swamp in SE Georgia and NE Florida, USA, rich in alligators, bears, deer, and birds. Much of its 1,700 sq km/660 sq mi forms a natural wildlife refuge. It is drained by the St Marys and Suwannee rivers.

Okhotsk, Sea of Arm of the N Pacific Ocean between the Kamchatka Peninsula and Sakhalin and bordered to the S by the Kuril Islands; area 937,000 sq km/361,700 sq mi. It is free of ice only in summer, and is often fogbound.

Okinawa Group of islands, forming part of the Japanese ◊Ryukyu Islands in the W Pacific; the largest island is Okinawa

area 2,265 sq km/875 sq mi

capital Naha

features Okinawa, the largest island of the group (area 1,176 sq km/453 sq mi; population (1990) 105,852), has a large US military base

population (1995) 1,274,000

history virtually all buildings were destroyed in World War II. The principal island, Okinawa, was captured by the USA in the *Battle of Okinawa* 1 April–21 June 1945, with 47,000 US casualties (12,000 dead) and 60,000 Japanese (only a few hundred survived as prisoners). During the invasion over 150,000 Okinawans, mainly civilians, died; many were massacred by Japanese forces. The island was returned to Japan 1972.

Oklahoma State in S central USA; nicknamed Sooner State

area 181,100 sq km/69,905 sq mi

capital Oklahoma City

towns and cities Tulsa, Lawton, Norman, Enid

physical Arkansas, Red, and Canadian rivers; Wichita Mountains Wildlife Refuge; Ouachita national forest; Tallgrass Prairie Reserve; Grand Lake o'the Cherokees; Salt Plains national wildlife refuge, with whooping cranes and bald eagles

features a large Native American population, mainly in the E, as a result of the 19th-century displacement of Native Americans to the Indian Territory; Fort Sill Military Reservation (1869), where Geronimo died 1909; Tahlequah, headquarters of the Cherokee Nation, site of signing of the Cherokee constitution 1839, with the Cherokee National Museum; Anadarko, with the Southern Plains Indian Museum and Craft Centre, the National Hall of Fame for Native Americans, and Indian City USA; Spiro Mounds Archaeological state park, with the remains of earth mounds lived in by the Spiro 900–1400; Guthrie; Dog Iron Ranch and Will Rogers Birthplace; Will Rogers Memorial; Oklahoma City, including the Oklahoma state capitol (with oil wells in its grounds), Harn Homestead and 1889er Museum, and the National Cowboy Hall of Fame and Western Heritage Center; Tulsa, with art deco architecture from the 1920s, and the Gilcrease Museum (with a collection of Native American art); Bartlesville, with the Frank Phillips home (1909) and the Price Tower (1956, designed by Frank Lloyd Wright); Woolacre Museum, a wildlife reserve with a museum of the West

industries cereals, peanuts, cotton, livestock, oil, natural gas, helium, machinery and other metal products

population (1995) 3,277,700

famous people John Berryman, Ralph Ellison, Woody Guthrie, Mickey Mantle, Will Rogers, Jim Thorpe

history explored for Spain by Francisco de Coronado 1541;

most acquired by the USA from France with the Louisiana Purchase 1803. The W Panhandle became US territory when Texas was annexed 1845. It was divided into Indian Territory and Oklahoma Territory 1890, part of which was thrown open to settlers with lotteries and other hurried distribution of land. Together with what remained of Indian Territory, it became a state 1907.

Oklahoma City Industrial city (oil refining, machinery, aircraft, telephone equipment), capital of Oklahoma, USA, on the Canadian River; population (1992) 454,000. On 22 April 1889, a tent city of nearly 10,000 inhabitants was set up overnight as the area was opened to settlement. In 1910 Oklahoma City became the state capital. It was the site of a right-wing terrorist bomb attack 1995.

Öland Swedish island in the Baltic, separated from S Sweden by Kalmar Sound, though connected by a bridge; area 1,344 sq km/519 sq mi. The island is 136 km/85 mi long but only 16 km/10 mi at its broadest. It is wooded in parts, and has good pasture for cattle. There are fisheries all round the coast, but tourism is becoming the most important source of income. Borgholm, on the W coast, is the capital and only town; population (1995) 11,900.

Oldenburg Industrial city in Lower Saxony, Germany, on the river Hunte; population (1991) 145,200. It is linked by river and canal to the Ems and Wieser rivers.

Oldham Industrial town in Greater Manchester, England; population (1994 est) 176,000. Industries include textiles and textile machinery, plastics, electrical goods, and electronic equipment. It was traditionally a cotton-spinning town.

Olduvai Gorge Deep cleft in the Serengeti steppe, Tanzania, where Louis and Mary Leakey found prehistoric stone tools in the 1930s. They discovered Pleistocene remains of prehumans and gigantic animals 1958–59. The gorge has given its name to the *Olduvai culture*, a simple stone-tool culture of prehistoric hominids, dating from 2–0.5 million years ago.

Old World The continents of the E hemisphere, so called because they were familiar to Europeans before the Americas. The term is also used as an adjective to describe animals and plants that live in the E hemisphere.

Oléron, Ile d' Island in the Atlantic Ocean, off the SW coast of France and part of the *département* of Charente-Maritime; area 170 sq km/66 sq mi. Its greatest length is 29 km/18 mi and breadth 11 km/7 mi. The island produces corn and wine; salt is collected from the salt marshes, and fishing and tourism are important. The principal towns are St-Pierre and Le Château d'Oléron.

Olmos Small town on the edge of the Sechura Desert, NW Peru.

Olney Small town in Buckinghamshire, England, where every Shrove Tuesday local women run a pancake race.

Olomouc Industrial city in the Czech Republic, at the confluence of the Bystrice and Morava rivers; population (1991) 105,700. Industries include sugar refining, brewing, and metal goods.

Olsztyn formerly *Allenstein* Industrial town in NE Poland, at the centre of the Mazurian Lakes region; population (1990) 162,900. It was founded 1334 and was formerly in East Prussia.

Olt River in S Romania, rising in the Carpathian Mountains and flowing through Transylvania to join the ◊Danube near Turnu Măgurele, after a distance of 560 km/350 mi.

Olten Commune in the canton of Solothurn, Switzerland, on the river Aar, 34 km/21 mi SE of Basel; population (1995) 17,100. Olten contains the main workshops of the Swiss federal railway, and also manufactures electrical apparatus, car parts, and textiles.

Olympia Capital of Washington, USA, located in the W central part of the state, on the Deschutes River near Puget Sound; population (1992) 36,800. It is a deep-water port; fishing, lumber, and tourism are important to the economy. It was laid out 1851 as Smithfield, and renamed for the Olympic Mountains.

Olympus (Greek *Olimbos*) Mountain in N Thessaly, Greece, 2,918 m/9,577 ft high. In ancient Greece it was considered the home of the gods.

Omagh Town in County Tyrone, Northern Ireland, on the river Strule, 48 km/30 mi S of Londonderry; population (1991) 17,300. Industries include dairy produce, footwear, and engineering; there is salmon fishing and it is a tourist centre.

Omaha City in E Nebraska, USA, on the Missouri River; population (1992) 339,700. It is a livestock-market centre, with food-processing and meat-packing industries. Omaha was laid out in 1854. Its location at the E terminus of the Union Pacific Railroad (1869) spurred economic growth.

Omdurman City in Sudan, on the White Nile, a suburb of Khartoum; population (1983) 526,000. It was the residence of the Sudanese sheik known as the Mahdi 1884–98.

Omsk Industrial city (agricultural and other machinery, food processing, sawmills, oil refining) in the Russian Federation, capital of Omsk region, W Siberia; population (1994) 1,161,000. Its oil refineries are linked with Tuimazy in Bashkortostan by a 1,600-km/1,000-mi pipeline.

Onega, Lake (Russian *Onezhskoe Ozero*) Second-largest lake in Europe, NE of St Petersburg, partly in Karelia, in the Russian Federation; area 9,600 sq km/3,710 sq mi. The *Onega Canal*, along its S shore, is part of the Mariinsk system linking St Petersburg with the river Volga.

Oneida Town in New York State, USA, named after the Oneida people (a nation of the Iroquois confederacy). The town was founded 1834. From 1848 the *Oneida Community*, a religious sect, practised a form of 'complex marriage' until its dissolution 1879.

Ont. Abbreviation for ◊Ontario, a Canadian province.

Ontario Province of central Canada
area 1,068,580 sq km/412,579 sq mi
capital Toronto
towns and cities Hamilton, Ottawa (federal capital),

Ontario

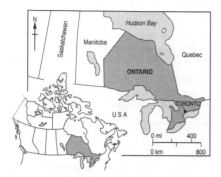

London, Windsor, Kitchener, St Catharines, Oshawa, Thunder Bay, Sudbury
physical Niagara Falls
features Black Creek Pioneer Village; Sainte-Marie among the Hurons, a Roman Catholic mission (1639–49); richest, chief manufacturing, most populated, and leading cultural province of English-speaking Canada
industries nickel, iron, gold, forest products, motor vehicles, iron, steel, paper, chemicals, copper, uranium
population (1995 est) 10,768,000
history first explored by the French in the 17th century, it came under British control 1763 (Treaty of Paris). An attempt 1841 to form a merged province with French-speaking Quebec failed, and Ontario became a separate province of Canada 1867. Under the protectionist policies of the new federal government, Ontario gradually became industrialized and urban. Since World War II, more than 2 million immigrants, chiefly from Europe, have settled in Ontario.

Ontario, Lake Smallest and easternmost of the Great Lakes, on the US-Canadian border; area 19,010 sq km/ 7,340 sq mi. It is connected to Lake Erie by the Welland Canal and the Niagara River, and drains into the St Lawrence River. Its main port is Toronto.

Oostende Flemish form (meaning 'E end') of ◊Ostend.

Opole Industrial town in S Poland, on the river Oder; population (1990) 128,400. It is an agricultural centre; industries include textiles, chemicals, and cement.

Oporto English form of ◊Porto, a city in Portugal.

OR Abbreviation for ◊Oregon, a state of the USA.

Oradea or *Oradea-Mare* Industrial city in Romania, on the river Crişul Repede; population (1993) 222,000. Industries include agricultural machinery, chemicals, non-ferrous metallurgy, leather goods, printing, glass, textiles, clothing, and brewing.

Oran (Arabic *Wahran*) Seaport in Algeria; population (1989) 664,000. Products include iron, textiles, footwear, and processed food; the port trades in grain, wool, vegetables, and native esparto grass.

Orange Town in New South Wales, Australia, 200 km/ 125 mi NW of Sydney; population (1987) 32,500. There is a woollen-textile industry based on local sheep flocks, and fruit is grown.

Orange Town in France, N of Avignon; population (1990) 28,100. It has the remains of a Roman theatre and arch. It was a medieval principality from which came the European royal house of Orange.

Orange River in South Africa, rising on the Mont aux Sources in Lesotho and flowing W to the Atlantic Ocean; length 2,092 km/1,300 mi. It runs along the S boundary of the Free State Province (formerly Orange Free State). Water from the Orange is diverted via the Orange-Fish River Tunnel (1975) to irrigate the semi-arid Eastern Cape Province. It was named 1779 after William of Orange.

Orange County Metropolitan area of S California, USA; area 2,075 sq km/801 sq mi; it adjoins Los Angeles County; population (1996) 2,636,900. Industries include aerospace and electronics. Oranges and strawberries are grown. Disneyland is here, and Santa Ana is the chief town.

Oraşul Stalin Former name (1948–56) of the Romanian town ◊Braşov.

Ordzhonikidze Former name (1954–91) of ◊Vladikavkaz, the capital of Alania (formerly North Ossetia) in SW Russia.

Oregon State in NW USA, on the Pacific coast; nicknamed Beaver State/Sunset State
area 251,500 sq km/97,079 sq mi
capital Salem
towns and cities Portland, Eugene
physical Columbia and Snake rivers; the fertile Willamette River valley; Crater Lake national park (the deepest lake in the USA, 589 m/1,933 ft), formed as a result of the eruption of Mount Mazama; Newberry national volcanic monument; Oregon Caves national monument; Cascade Mountains; Pacific coast; Mount Hood national forest (Mount Hood 3,427 m/11,245 ft)
features vineyards; High Desert Museum, Bend, with a living exhibit of plants and animals native to the arid region of the Pacific Northwest; Portland, with Yamhill and Skidmore national historic districts, End of the Trail Interpretative Center (the history of the Oregon Trail), the McLoughlin historic district, with Victorian buildings, including the John McLoughlin House national historic site (1846), Pittock Mansion (1909), Portland Art Museum, Chinatown, Forest Park (the largest urban wilderness in the USA), and Washington Park Rose Garden and Japanese Garden; Fort Clatsop national memorial, commemorating the first sight of the Pacific by Meriwether Lewis and William Clark 1805; Hoover-Minthorne House (1881), the boyhood home of President Herbert Hoover; Willamette University, Salem (1842), the oldest college in the West; Reed College (1909); the Oregon Shakespeare Festival, Ashland
industries wheat, livestock, timber, electronics
population (1995) 3,140,600
famous people Chief Joseph, Ursula LeGuin, Linus Pauling, John Reed
history coast sighted by Spanish and English sailors 16th–17th centuries; part of coastline charted by James Cook

1778 on his search for the Northwest Passage; claimed for the USA 1792 by Robert Gray, whose ship *Columbia* sailed into the river now named for it; explored by Meriwether Lewis and William Clark 1805; Astoria, John Jacob Astor's fur depot, founded at the mouth of the Columbia 1811; boundary between US settlers and the Hudson's Bay Company fixed 1846 by Oregon Treaty. Oregon Territory included Washington until 1853; Oregon achieved statehood 1859.

Orel Industrial city in the Russian Federation, capital of Orel region, on the river Oka, 320 km/200 mi SW of Moscow; population (1994) 346,000. Industries include engineering, textiles, and foodstuffs.

Orem City in N central Utah, USA, SE of Salt Lake City; population (1990) 67,500. It was settled by Mormons 1861. Industries include electronics and steel.

Orenburg City in S central Russian Federation, on the Ural River; population (1994) 558,000. It is a trading and mining centre and capital of Orenburg region. It dates from the early 18th century and was called *Chkalov* 1938–57 in honour of Soviet aviator Valeri Chkalov (1904–1938).

Orense Town in NW Galicia, Spain, on the river Miño; population (1994) 109,000. It produces textiles, furniture, food products, and metal goods.

Orense Province of NW Spain in SW ◊Galicia autonomous community; capital Orense; area 7,278 sq km/2,810 sq mi; population (1995) 364,500. Its S border is on the Portuguese frontier. The province is mountainous, with fertile valleys through which the river Miño and its tributary the Sil run.

Øresund Strait between Sweden and Denmark; in English it is called the ◊Sound.

Orihuela Town in the province of ◊Alicante, SE Spain; population (1995) 52,000. Situated on the river Segura, in a fertile, irrigated region, it trades in oranges, wine, and oil; textiles are manufactured. It has a much-restored 14th-century cathedral, and a 17th-century college.

Orinoco River in N South America, flowing for about 2,559 km/1,590 mi through Venezuela and forming for about 320 km/200 mi the boundary with Colombia; tributaries include the Guaviare, Meta, Apure, Ventuari, Caura, and Caroni. It is navigable by large steamers for 1,125 km/700 mi from its Atlantic delta; rapids obstruct the upper river.

Orissa State of NE India
area 155,707 sq km/60,118 sq mi
capital Bhubaneshwar
towns and cities Cuttack, Rourkela
features mainly agricultural; Chilka Lake with fisheries and game; temple of Jagannath or Juggernaut at Puri
industries rice, wheat, oilseed, sugar, timber, chromite (95% of India's output), dolomite, graphite, iron
population (1994 est) 33,795,000
language Oriya (official)
religion 90% Hindu
history administered by the British 1803–1912 as a subdivision of Bengal, it joined with Bihar to become a

province. In 1936 Orissa became a separate province, and in 1948–49 its area was almost doubled before its designation as a state 1950.

Oristano Province of Italy in S ◊Sardinia; capital Oristano (population (1990) 32,800); area 2,631 sq km/1,016 sq mi; population (1992) 157,100.

Orizaba Industrial city (brewing, paper, and textiles) and resort in Veracruz state, Mexico; population (1990) 114,000. An earthquake severely damaged it 1973.

Orizaba Spanish name for ◊Citlaltépetl, a mountain in Mexico.

Orkney Causeway or *Churchill Barriers* Construction in N Scotland put up in World War II, completed 1943, joining four of the Orkney Islands. It was built to protect the British fleet from intrusion through the E entrances to Scapa Flow. The Orkney Causeway links the E mainland with the islands of Lambholm, Glimsholm, Burray, and South Ronaldsay.

Orkney Islands Island group off the NE coast of Scotland
area 970 sq km/375 sq mi
towns and cities Kirkwall (administrative headquarters), on Mainland (Pomona)
features comprises about 90 islands and islets, low-lying and treeless; mild climate owing to the Gulf Stream; Skara Brae, a well-preserved Neolithic village on Mainland. On the island of Hoy is an isolated stack known as the Old Man of Hoy. The population, long falling, has in recent years risen as the islands' remoteness from the rest of the world attracts new settlers. Scapa Flow, between Mainland and Hoy, was a naval base in both world wars, and the German fleet scuttled itself here 21 June 1919; there is an oil terminal at Flotta
industries fishing and farming, beef cattle, poultry, fish curing, woollen weaving, wind power (Burgar Hill has the world's most productive wind-powered generator; a 300 KW wind turbine with blades 60 m/197 ft diameter, capable of producing 20% of the islands' energy needs), distilling, boat-building
population (1996) 19,600
famous people Edwin Muir, John Rae
history The population is of Scandinavian descent. Harald I (Fairhair) of Norway conquered the islands 876; they were pledged to James III of Scotland 1468 for the dowry of Margaret of Denmark and annexed by Scotland (the dowry unpaid) 1472.

Orkneys, South Islands in the British Antarctic Territory; see ◊South Orkney Islands.

Orlando Industrial city in Florida, USA; population (1992) 174,200. It is a winter resort and tourist centre, with Walt Disney World and the Epcot Center nearby. Electronic and aerospace equipment are manufactured in the city, and citrus fruit products are processed here. Educational institutions include the University of Central Florida. Orlando was settled 1843.

Orléanais Former province of France, called *Pagus Aurelianensis* by the Romans. It corresponded to the present *départements* of Loiret, Loir-et-Cher, and Eure-et-Loir, and parts of Nièvre and the former Seine-et-Oise. The capital was Orléans.

Orléans Industrial city of France, on the river Loire; 115 km/70 mi SW of Paris; population (1990) 108,000. It is the capital of Loiret *département*. Industries include engineering and food processing.

Orly Suburb of Paris in the *département* of Val-de-Marne; population (1990) 21,800. Orly international airport is the busiest in France.

Ormuz Alternative name for the Iranian island of ◊Hormuz.

Orne French river rising E of Sées and flowing NW, then NE to the English Channel below Caen; 152 km/94 mi long. A ship canal runs alongside it from Caen to the sea at Ouistreham. The Orne gives its name to a *département* in Normandy; population (1990) 293,200.

Orne *Département* in the ◊Basse-Normandie region of France; area 6,100 sq km/2,355 sq mi; population (1990) 294,000. It comprises two distinct physical regions: the W consisting of rugged hills and extensive forests, with patches of pasture, and the E with fertile valleys and extensive rich pasture lands and orchards. Horses and cattle are reared in the *département*, and dairy produce (including cheese from the village of Camembert) is exported. Electrical appliances, car parts, and chemicals are the principal manufactured products. The main towns are ◊Alençon (the capital) and Argentan.

Orontes (Arabic *'Asi*) River flowing from Lebanon through Syria and Turkey to the Mediterranean Sea and used mainly for irrigation; length 400 km/250 mi.

Orsk Industrial city in S central Russian Federation, at the junction of the Or and Ural rivers; population (1990) 271,000. Industries include mining, oil refining, locomotives, and aluminium. Its refineries are fed by a pipeline from Guriev. The town was originally a fortress.

Orvieto Town in Umbria, Italy, NE of Lake Bolsena, population (1990) 22,600. Built on the site of *Volsinii*, an Etruscan town destroyed by the Romans 280 BC, Orvieto has many Etruscan remains. The name is from Latin **Urbs Vetus** meaning 'old town'.

Osaka Industrial port (iron, steel, shipbuilding, chemicals, textiles) on Honshu Island, Japan; population (1994) 2,481,000. It is the oldest city of Japan and was at times the seat of government in the 4th–8th centuries.

Oshkosh City in E central Wisconsin, USA, where the Fox River flows into Lake Winnebago, NW of Milwaukee; seat of Winnebago County; population (1992) 56,300. Industries include clothing, machinery, lumber, and electronics. Oshkosh was settled 1836.

Oshogbo City and trading centre in W Nigeria, 200 km/125 mi NE of Lagos; population (1992 est) 441,600. It is the capital of Osun State. It developed as a trading centre after the arrival of the railway 1906. It trades in cocoa and palm oil. The main industry is cotton-weaving.

Osijek (German *Esseg*) Industrial port in Croatia, on the river Drava; population (1991) 104,800. Industries include textiles, chemicals, and electrical goods.

Oslo Capital and industrial port (textiles, engineering, timber) of Norway; population (1991) 461,600. The first recorded settlement was made in the 11th century by Harald III Hardrada, but after a fire 1624, it was entirely replanned by Christian IV and renamed *Christiania* 1624–1924.

Osnabrück Industrial city in Lower Saxony, Germany; 115 km/71 mi W of Hannover; population (1993) 167,500. Industries include engineering, iron, steel, textiles, clothing, paper, and food processing. The Treaty of Westphalia was signed at Osnabrück and Münster 1648, ending the Thirty Years' War.

Ossa Mountain in Thessaly, Greece; height 1,978 m/6,490 ft. In mythology, two of Poseidon's giant sons were said to have tried to dislodge the gods from Olympus by piling nearby Mount Pelion on top of Ossa to scale the great mountain.

Ossa, Mount The highest peak on the island of Tasmania, Australia; height 1,617 m/5,250 ft.

Ossetia Region in the Caucasus, on the border between Russia and Georgia. It is inhabited by the Ossets, who speak the Iranian language Ossetic, and who were conquered by the Russians 1802. Some live in ◊Alania (formerly North Ossetia), an autonomous republic in the SW Russian Federation. The rest live in ◊South Ossetia, an autonomous region of the Georgian republic. The region has been the scene of Osset–Georgian interethnic conflict since 1989. More than 100,000 Ossets from South Ossetia moved to Alania 1989–92, in turn causing the Ingush there to flee to Ingushetia.

Ostend (Flemish *Oostende*) Seaport and pleasure resort in W Flanders, Belgium; 108 km/67 mi NW of Brussels; population (1995 est) 68,900. There are large docks, and the Belgian fishing fleet has its headquarters here. There are ferry links to Dover and Folkestone, England. It was occupied by the Germans 1914–18 and developed as an important naval base.

Östergötland County of S Sweden, containing several lakes, lying between Lake Vättern and the Baltic Sea; area 11,048 sq km/4,266 sq mi; population (1990) 395,600. It is a fertile agricultural area, interspersed with lakes, waterways, and forests. There are iron and copper mines. The chief town is Norrköping.

Östersund Chief town of Jämtland county, Sweden; population (1995) 59,700. Situated on Lake Storsjön, it is an important service and military centre.

Ostia Ancient Roman town near the mouth of the Tiber. Founded about 330 BC, it was the port of Rome and had become a major commercial centre by the 2nd century AD. It was abandoned in the 9th century. The present-day seaside resort *Ostia Mare* is situated nearby.

Ostmark Name given to Austria by the German Nazi government, after the country had been incorporated into Greater Germany in 1938. The designation originated during the reign of Charlemagne, when the region served as a frontier of the German Empire against the Slavs.

Ostrava Industrial city (iron works, furnaces, coal, chemicals) in the Czech Republic, capital of Severomoravský region, NE of Brno; population (1991) 327,600.

Oswestry Market town in Shropshire, England; population (1991) 15,600. Industries include agricultural machinery and plastics. It is named after St Oswald, killed here 642.

Oświęcim Polish town, formerly ◊Auschwitz.

Otago Peninsula Peninsula and coastal plain on South Island, New Zealand, constituting a district; area 64,230 sq km/25,220 sq mi; chief cities include Dunedin and Invercargill.

Otaru Fishing port on the W coast of Hokkaido Island, Japan; industries include fish processing, paper, sake; population (1993) 161,000.

Otranto Seaport in Puglia, Italy, on the *Strait of Otranto*; population (1981) 5,000. It has Greek and Roman remains, a ruined castle (the inspiration for Horace Walpole's novel *The Castle of Otranto* 1764), and a cathedral begun 1080. The port is linked by ferry with the island of Corfu.

Ottawa Capital of Canada, in E Ontario, on the hills overlooking the Ottawa River and divided by the Rideau Canal into the Upper (W) and Lower (E) towns; population (1991) 314,000, metropolitan area (with adjoining Hull, Quebec) 920,900. Industries include timber, pulp and paper, engineering, food processing, and publishing. It was founded 1826–32 as Bytown, in honour of John By (1781–1836), whose army engineers were building the Rideau Canal. It was renamed 1854 after the Outaouac Indians. Features include the National Museum, National Art Gallery, Observatory, Rideau Hall (the governor general's residence), and the National Arts Centre 1969 (with an orchestra and English/French theatre). In 1858 it was chosen by Queen Victoria as the country's capital.

Ottawa River in E Canada; length 1,271 km/790 mi. It rises in the Laurentian plateau and flows E through S Quebec and into the ◊St Lawrence River near Montréal. During its course it widens into numerous large lakes, and is fed by many tributaries. Hydroelectric schemes along its course supply energy for Quebec and Ontario.

Otztal Alps Range of the Alps in Italy and Austria, rising to 3,774 m/12,382 ft at Wildspitze, Austria's second highest peak.

Ouachita River or *Washita* River in Arkansas and Louisiana, S USA; length 973 km/605 mi. It rises in the Ouachita Mountains in SW Arkansas and flows SE across the state into Louisiana, where it enters the ◊Red River.

Ouagadougou Capital and industrial centre of Burkina Faso; population (1991 est) 634,000. Products include textiles, vegetable oil, beverages, and soap. The city has the palace of Moro Naba, emperor of the Mossi people, a neo-

Romanesque cathedral, and a central avenue called the Champs Elysées.

Oudenaarde Town of E Flanders, W Belgium, on the River Schelde, 28 km/18 mi SSW of Ghent; population (1991) 27,200. It is a centre of tapestry-making and carpet-weaving.

Oudh Region of N India, now part of Uttar Pradesh. An independent kingdom before it fell under Mogul rule, Oudh regained independence 1732–1856, when it was annexed by Britain. Its capital was Lucknow, centre of the Indian Mutiny 1857–58. In 1877 it was joined with Agra, from 1902 as the United Provinces of Agra and Oudh, renamed Uttar Pradesh 1950.

Ouessant French form of ◊Ushant, an island W of Brittany.

Oujda Industrial and commercial city (lead and coal mining) in N Morocco, near the border with Algeria; population (urban area, 1990) 661,000. It trades in wool, grain, and fruit.

Oulu (Swedish *Uleåborg*) Industrial port (sawmills, tanneries, shipyards) in W Finland, on the Gulf of Bothnia; population (1992) 103,500. It was originally a Swedish fortress 1375.

Oulu Northern province of Finland; area 56,706 sq km/ 21,894 sq mi. It consists of the Laponia plateau (300–360 m/ 984 ft–1,181 ft), the fertile lowlands of Ostrobothnia on the Gulf of Bothnia, and the plateaux of Suomenselkä and Kajaani (450–500 m/1,476 ft–1,640 ft).

Ourthe River in Belgium, tributary of the ◊Meuse; length 185 km/115 mi, of which 57 km/35 mi are navigable. It is formed in the Ardennes by the confluence of the East and West Ourthe, both rising in the province of Luxembourg. The river joins the Meuse near the city of Liège.

Ouse (Celtic 'water') Any of several British rivers: The *Great Ouse* rises in Northamptonshire and winds its way across 250 km/160 mi to enter the Wash N of King's Lynn. A large sluice across the Great Ouse, near King's Lynn, was built as part of extensive flood-control works 1959. The *Little Ouse* flows for 38 km/ 24 mi along part of the Norfolk–Suffolk border and is a tributary of the Great Ouse. The Yorkshire *Ouse* is formed by the junction of the Ure and Swale near Boroughbridge and joins the river Trent to form the Humber. The Sussex *Ouse* rises between Horsham and Cuckfield and flows through the South Downs to enter the English Channel at Newhaven.

Ovamboland Region of N Namibia stretching along the Namibia–Angola frontier; the scene of conflict between SWAPO guerrillas and South African forces in the 1970s and 1980s.

Ovens River River in Victoria, Australia, a tributary of the Murray.

Overijssel Province of the E central Netherlands, containing the rivers rivers IJssel and Vecht; area 3,340 sq km/1,289 sq mi; population (1995 est) 1,050,400. Its capital is Zwolle; other towns and cities include Enschede, Hengelo, Deventer. Its industries are livestock, dairy products, and textiles.

Oviedo Industrial city (textiles, metal goods, pharmaceuticals, matches, chocolate, sugar) and capital of Asturias region, Spain, 25 km/16 mi S of the Bay of Biscay; population (1994) 202,000.

Owen Falls Waterfall in Uganda on the White Nile, 4 km/ 2.5 mi below the point at which the river leaves Lake Victoria. A dam, built 1949–60, provides hydroelectricity for Uganda and Kenya and helps to control the flood waters.

Owensboro City in NW Kentucky, USA, on the Ohio River, SW of Louisville; seat of Davies County; population (1992) 53,400. Industries include bourbon (whisky), electronics, tobacco, and steel. The town was laid out 1816.

Oxford University city and administrative centre of Oxfordshire in S central England, at the confluence of the rivers Thames (called the Isis around Oxford) and Cherwell; population (1994 est) 121,000. Oxford University has 36 colleges, the oldest being University College (1249). Other features include the Divinity School and Duke Humphrey's Library (1488), now part of the Bodleian Library. Industries include motor vehicles at Cowley, steel products, electrical goods, paper, publishing, and English language schools. Tourism is important.

The town was first occupied in Saxon times as a fording point, and is first mentioned in written records in the Anglo-Saxon Chronicle of 912. The University of Oxford, the oldest in England, is first mentioned in the 12th century, when its growth was encouraged by the influx of English students expelled from Paris 1167. During the Civil War, the university supported the Royalist cause while the city declared for Parliament. Oxford became the headquarters of the king and court 1642, but yielded to the Parliamentary commander in chief, General Fairfax, 1646. By the beginning of the 20th century, the city had experienced rapid expansion and industrialization, and printing and publishing industries had become firmly established. In the 1920s the English industrial magnate William Morris (1877–1963), later Lord Nuffield, began a motor-car industry at Cowley, just outside the city, which became the headquarters of the Austin-Rover group.

Oxfordshire County of S central England
area 2,610 sq km/1,007 sq mi
towns and cities Oxford (administrative headquarters), Abingdon, Banbury, Henley-on-Thames, Witney, Woodstock
features river Thames and tributaries; Cotswolds and Chiltern Hills; Vale of the White Horse (chalk hill figure at Uffington, 114 m/374 ft long); Oxford University; Blenheim Palace (a World Heritage site), Woodstock (started 1705 by Vanbrugh with help from Nicholas Hawksmoor, completed 1722), with landscaped grounds by 'Capability' Brown; early 14th-century Broughton Castle; Rousham Park (1635), remodelled by William Kent 1738–40, with landscaped garden; Ditchley Park, designed by James Gibbs 1720; Europe's major fusion project JET (Joint European Torus) at the UK Atomic Energy Authority's fusion laboratories at Culham; The Manor House, Kelmscott (country house of William Morris, leader of the Arts and Crafts movement)

industries cereals, cars, paper, bricks, cement, medical electronic equipment (Oxford Instruments), dairy farming, high technology industries, aluminium, sheep, publishing, nuclear research at Harwell nuclear research establishment run by AEA Technology, providing scientific services (nuclear and non-nuclear) and products and consultancy to governments and industries throughout the world
population (1994) 590,200
famous people William Davenant, Flora Thompson, Winston Churchill, William Morris (founder of Morris Motors Ltd, and of Nuffield College, Oxford 1937).

Oxnard City in SW California, USA, NW of Los Angeles; population (1992) 144,800. Industries include paper products, aircraft parts, and oil refining. Oxnard was founded 1898 and developed around a sugar-beet factory.

Oxus Ancient name of ◊Amu Darya, a river in Central Asia.

Ozark Mountains Area in the USA (shared by Arkansas, Illinois, Kansas, Mississippi, Oklahoma) of ridges, valleys, and streams; highest point only 700 m/2,300 ft; area 130,000 sq km/50,000 sq mi. This heavily forested region between the Missouri and Arkansas rivers has agriculture and lead and zinc mines.

PA Abbreviation for the state of ◊Pennsylvania, USA.

Paarl Town on the Great Berg River, Western Cape Province, South Africa; population (1991) 73,400. It is the centre of a wine-producing area, 50 km/31 mi NE of Cape Town. Nelson Mandela served the last days of his imprisonment at the Victor Vester prison near here.

Pabianice Industrial town (textiles, chemicals, machinery) in Łódź province, Poland, 13 km/8 mi SW of Łódź; population (1990) 75,200.

Pacaraima Mountains Mountain range along the Brazil-Venezuela frontier, extending into Guyana; length 620 km/ 385 mi; highest point *Mount Roraima*, a plateau about 50 sq km/20 sq mi, 2,810 m/9,222 ft above sea level, surrounded by cliffs 300 m/1,000 ft high, at the conjunction of the three countries. Formed 300 million years ago, it has unique fauna and flora, because of its isolation, consisting only of grasses, bushes, flowers, insects, and small amphibians.

Pacific Islands Former (1947–90) United Nations trust territory in the W Pacific captured from Japan during World War II. The territory comprised over 2,000 islands and atolls and was assigned to the USA 1947. The islands were divided into four governmental units: the *Northern Mariana Islands* (except Guam) which became a self-governing commonwealth in union with the USA 1975 (inhabitants granted US citizenship 1986); the Marshall Islands, the Federated States of Micronesia, and the Republic of Palau (formerly also known as Belau) became self-governing 1979–80, signing agreements of free association with the USA 1986. In December 1990 the United Nations Security Council voted to dissolve its trusteeship over the islands with the exception of Palau. The Marshall Islands and the Federated States of Micronesia were granted UN membership 1991.

Pacific Ocean World's largest ocean, extending from Antarctica to the Bering Strait; area 166,242,000 sq km/ 64,186,300 sq mi; average depth 3,939 m/12,925 ft; greatest depth of any ocean 11,034 m/36,210 ft in the Mariana Trench.

Padang Port on the W coast of Sumatra, Indonesia; population (1990) 477,300. The Dutch secured trading rights here 1663. The port trades in copra, coffee, and rubber.

Paderborn Market town in North Rhine–Westphalia, Germany; population (1991) 126,000. Industries include leather goods, metal products, and precision instruments. It was the seat of a bishopric in Charlemagne's time and later became a member of the Hanseatic League.

Padua (Italian *Padova*) City in N Italy, 45 km/28 mi W of Venice; population (1992) 213,700. The astronomer Galileo Galilei taught at the university, founded 1222.

Padua (Italian *Padova*) Province of NE Italy in SE ◊Veneto region; capital Padua; area 2,142 sq km/827 sq mi; population (1992) 822,200.

Paducah City in W Kentucky, SE USA, near the border with Illinois, 137 km/85 mi SW of Evansville, Indiana; population (1990) 27,300. Situated at the confluence of the Ohio and Tennessee rivers, it is a centre for tobacco, agriculture, and coal. It is also a centre of rail, river, and air transport. Growth has been generated by federal energy-production projects.

Pagalu Former name (1973–79) of ◊Annobón, an island in Equatorial Guinea.

Pago Pago Chief port and capital of American Samoa on the island of Tutuila; population (1990) 4,000. Formerly a naval coaling station, it was acquired by the USA under a commercial treaty with the local king 1872, and was a US naval base until 1951. It exports tinned tuna.

Pahang State of E Peninsular Malaysia; capital Kuantan; area 36,000 sq km/13,896 sq mi; population (1993) 1,056,100. It is mountainous and forested and produces rubber, tin, gold, and timber. There is a port at Tanjung Gelang. Pahang is ruled by a sultan.

Pahsien Alternative name of ◊Chongqing, a port in SW China.

Paisley Administrative headquarters of Renfrewshire, Scotland, part of the Clydeside urban area; population (1991) 75,500. Industries include textiles, thread, and pharmaceuticals. It was an important centre for the manufacture of textiles, especially the woollen Paisley shawl, with a pattern based on the shape of a palm shoot. The Paisley Museum and Art Gallery includes a collection of shawls. The 12th-century abbey was rebuilt after the battle of Bannockburn 1314.

Paldiski Small, ice-free port in Estonia; 40 km/25 mi W of Tallinn at the entrance to the Gulf of Finland. It was built by Tsar Peter I the Great as a Russian naval base, and later became a Soviet submarine base.

Palembang Oil-refining city in Indonesia, capital of S Sumatra province; population (1990) 1,084,500. Products include rubber and palm oil. Palembang was the capital of a sultanate when the Dutch established a trading station here 1616.

Palencia Capital of the province of Palencia, N Spain, on the river Carrión; population (1995) 79,900. Industries include rolling stock, agricultural machinery, textiles, pottery, and soap; it has a bell foundry. There is a Gothic cathedral, begun in 1321, which contains paintings by El Greco and Zurbarán. The first university in Spain was founded here in 1208, but was transferred to Salamanca later in the same century.

Palencia Province of N Spain in ◊Castilla–León autonomous community; capital Palencia; area 8,029 sq km/3,100 sq mi; population (1995) 186,000. It is situated on a high plateau, S of the Cantabrian Mountains, and has a severe climate. It includes the fertile valleys of the river Carrión and other tributaries of the river Duero. Products include wool, grain, wine, and honey.

Palermo Capital and seaport of Sicily; population (1992) 696,700. Industries include shipbuilding, steel, glass, and chemicals. It was founded by the Phoenicians in the 8th century BC.

Palermo Province of Italy in NW ◊Sicily; capital Palermo; area 5,017 sq km/1,937 sq mi; population (1992) 1,227,900.

Palestine (Arabic *Falastin* 'Philistine') Historic geographical area at the E end of the Mediterranean sea, also known as the Holy Land because of its historic and symbolic importance for Jews, Christians, and Muslims. Early settlers included the Canaanites, Hebrews, and Philistines. Over the centuries it became part of the Egyptian, Assyrian, Babylonian, Macedonian, Ptolemaic, Seleucid, Roman, Byzantine, Arab, and Ottoman empires. Today, it comprises parts of modern Israel, and Jordan.

Palk Strait Channel separating SE India from the island of Sri Lanka; it is 53 km/33 mi at the widest point.

Palma One of the Canary Islands, Spain
area 730 sq km/282 sq mi
capital Santa Cruz de la Palma
features forested
industries wine, fruit, honey, silk; tourism is important
population (1981) 77,000.

Palma de Mallorca Industrial port (textiles, cement, paper, pottery), resort, and capital of the Balearic Islands, Spain, on Mallorca; population (1994) 322,000. Palma was founded 276 BC as a Roman colony. It has a Gothic cathedral, begun 1229.

Palmas, Las Port in the Canary Islands; see ◊Las Palmas.

Palm Beach Luxurious winter resort in Florida, USA, on an island between Lake Worth and the Atlantic; population (1990) 9,800. Palm Beach was settled in the 1870s.

Palmerston North Town on the SW coast of North Island, New Zealand; population (1993) 74,100. Industries include textiles, dairy produce, and electrical goods.

Palm Springs   Resort and spa in S California, USA, about 160 km/100 mi E of Los Angeles; population (1990) 40,200.

Palmyra   Coral atoll 1,600 km/1,000 mi SW of Hawaii, in the Line Islands, S Pacific, purchased by the USA from a Hawaiian family 1979 for the storage of highly radioactive nuclear waste from 1986.

Palmyra   Ancient city and oasis in the desert of Syria, about 240 km/150 mi NE of Damascus. Palmyra, the biblical *Tadmor*, was flourishing by about 300 BC. It was destroyed AD 272 after Queen Zenobia had led a revolt against the Romans. Extensive temple ruins exist, and on the site is a town called Tadmor.

Palo Alto   City in California, USA, situated SE of San Francisco at one end of the high-tech region known as Silicon Valley; population (1992) 56,200. It is the site of Stanford University. Palo Alto was founded 1891.

Pamir   Central Asian plateau mainly in Tajikistan, but extending into China and Afghanistan, traversed by mountain ranges. Its highest peak is Kommunizma Pik (Communism Peak 7,495 m/24,600 ft) in the Akademiya Nauk range.

Pampas   Flat, treeless, Argentine plains, lying between the Andes Mountains and the Atlantic Ocean and rising gradually from the coast to the lower slopes of the mountains. The E Pampas contain large cattle ranches and the flax- and grain-growing area of Argentina; the W Pampas are arid and unproductive.

Pamplona   Industrial city (wine, leather, shoes, textiles) in Navarre, N Spain, on the Arga River; population (1994) 182,000. A pre-Roman town, it was rebuilt by Pompey 68 BC, captured by the Visigoths 476, sacked by Charlemagne 778, became the capital of Navarre, and was taken by the Duke of Wellington in the Peninsular War 1813. An annual running of bulls takes place in the streets in July as part of the fiesta of San Fermín, a local patron saint.

Panama   Capital of the Republic of Panama, near the Pacific end of the Panama Canal; population (1990) 584,800. Products include chemicals, plastics, and clothing. An earlier Panama, to the NE, founded 1519, was destroyed 1671, and the city was founded on the present site 1673.

Panama Canal   Canal across the Panama isthmus in Central America, connecting the Pacific and Atlantic oceans; length 80 km/50 mi, with 12 locks. Built by the USA 1904–14 after an unsuccessful attempt by the French, it was formally opened 1920. The *Panama Canal Zone* was acquired 'in perpetuity' by the USA 1903, comprising land extending about 5 km/3 mi on either side of the canal. The zone passed to Panama 1979, and control of the canal itself was ceded to Panama by the USA Jan 1990 under the terms of the Panama Canal Treaty 1977. The Canal Zone has several US military bases.

Pan-American Highway   Road linking the USA with Central and South America; length 25,300 km/15,700 mi. Starting from the US-Canadian frontier (where it links with the Alaska Highway), it runs through San Francisco, Los Angeles, and Mexico City to Panama City, then down the W side of South America to Valparaiso, Chile, where it crosses the Andes and goes to Buenos Aires, Argentina. The road was first planned 1923, and work began 1928. Completion of the final section, across the Darien Gap, will lead to a major ecological transformation of the region.

Panay   One of the Philippine islands, lying between Mindoro and Negros; area 11,515 sq km/4,446 sq mi. The capital is Iloilo. Industries include rice, sugar, pineapples, bananas, copra, and copper. The island is mountainous, reaching 2,215 m/7,265 ft in Madiaás. It was seized by Spain 1569, and occupied by Japan 1942–45.

Panipat, Battles of   Three decisive battles in the vicinity of this Indian town, about 120 km/75 mi N of Delhi: 1526, when Babur, great-grandson of the Mongol conqueror Tamerlane, defeated the emperor of Delhi and founded the Mogul empire; 1556, won by his descendant Akbar; 1761, when the Marathas were defeated by Ahmad Shah Durrani of Afghanistan.

Panjshir Valley   Valley of the river Panjshir, which rises in the Panjshir range to the N of Kabul, E Afghanistan. It was the chief centre of mujaheddin rebel resistance against the Soviet-backed Najibullah government in the 1980s.

Pantanal   Large area of swampland in the Mato Grosso of SW Brazil, occupying 220,000 sq km/84,975 sq mi in the upper reaches of the Paraguay River; one of the world's great wildlife refuges of which 1,370 sq km/530 sq mi were designated a national park 1981.

Pantelleria   Volcanic island in the Mediterranean, 100 km/62 mi SW of Sicily and part of that region of Italy
area   115 sq km/45 sq mi
towns   Pantelleria
industries   sheep, fruit, olives, capers
population   (1981) 7,800
history   Pantelleria has drystone dwellings dating from prehistoric times. The Romans called it *Cossyra* and sent people into exile there. Strategically placed, the island has been the site of many battles. It was strongly fortified by Mussolini in World War II but surrendered to the Allies 11 June 1943.

Papeete   Capital and port of French Polynesia on the NW coast of Tahiti; population (1992) 24,200. Products include vanilla, copra, and mother-of-pearl.

Paphos   Resort town on the SW coast of Cyprus; population (1992 est) 32,600. It was the capital of Cyprus in Roman times and the legendary birthplace of the goddess Aphrodite, who rose out of the sea.

Papua   Original name of the island of New Guinea, but latterly its SE section, now part of Papua New Guinea.

Pará   State of N Brazil; alternative name of the Brazilian port ◊Belém.

Paracel Islands   (Chinese *Xisha*; Vietnamese *Hoang Sa*) Group of about 130 small islands in the South China Sea.

Paramaribo   Port and capital of Suriname, South America,

24 km/15 mi from the sea on the river Suriname; population (1993 est) 201,100. Products include coffee, fruit, timber, and bauxite.

Paraná Industrial port (flour mills, meat canneries) and capital of Entre Rios province in E Argentina, on the Paraná River, 560 km/350 mi NW of Buenos Aires; population (1991) 276,000.

Paraná River in South America, formed by the confluence of the Río Grande and Paranaiba; the Paraguay joins it at Corrientes, and it flows into the Río de la Plata with the Uruguay; length 3,943 km/2,450 mi. It is used for hydroelectric power by Argentina, Brazil, and Paraguay.

Pardubice (German *Pardubitz*) Industrial market town of E Bohemia, in the central Czech Republic, on the river Elbe, 94 km/59 mi E of Prague; population (1991) 94,900.

Paris Port and capital of France, on the river Seine; *département* in the Île de France region; area 105 sq km/40.5 sq mi; population (1994) 9,400,000. It is the core of a highly centralized national administration. Products include metal, leather, and luxury goods and chemicals, glass, and tobacco. During World War I Paris suffered from air raids and bombardment, and in World War II it was occupied by German troops June 1940–Aug 1944. The German commandant, General Cholitz, ignored Hitler's order to defend Paris at all costs to avoid causing large-scale damage to the city. Large-scale architectural projects of note were again undertaken during the presidency of François Mitterrand 1981–95.

Churches include Notre Dame cathedral built 1163–1250; the Invalides, housing the tomb of Napoleon; and the 19th-century basilica of Sacré-Coeur. The former palace of the Louvre (with its glass pyramid entrance by I M Pei 1989) is one of the world's major art galleries; the Musée d'Orsay 1986 has Impressionist and other paintings from the period 1848–1914; the Pompidou Centre (Beaubourg) 1977 exhibits modern art. Other landmarks are the Tuileries Gardens, the Place de la Concorde, the Eiffel Tower and the Champs-Elysées avenue leading to the Arc de Triomphe. Euro Disney opened 1992.

Paris-Plage Resort in Nord-Pas-de-Calais region, N France, adjoining Le Touquet.

Paris, Ville de French *département* comprising the central districts of the city of ◊Paris, part of the ◊Ile-de-France region; area 105 sq km/40.5 sq mi; population (1990) 2,151,245.

Parkersburg City in NW West Virginia, USA, where the Little Kanawha River flows into the Ohio River, N of Charleston; population (1990) 33,900.

Parma City in Emilia-Romagna, N Italy; population (1992) 170,600. Industries include food processing, textiles, and engineering. Founded by the Etruscans, it was the capital of the duchy of Parma 1545–1860. It has given its name to Parmesan cheese.

Parma Province of N central Italy in NW ◊Emilia-Romagna region; capital Parma; area 3,450 sq km/1,332 sq mi; population (1992) 391,500.

Parnassus Mountain in central Greece, height 2,457 m/8,200 ft, revered by the ancient Greeks as the abode of Apollo and the Muses. The sacred site of Delphi lies on its S flank.

Parramatta River inlet, W arm of Sydney Harbour, New South Wales, Australia. It is 24 km/15 mi long and is lined with industrial suburbs of Sydney: Balmain, Drummoyne, Concord, Parramatta, Ermington and Rydalmere, Ryde, and Hunter's Hill.

Parry Islands Group of islands in the Canadian Arctic, W of Baffin Bay and N of Lancaster Sound, Viscount Melville Sound, and Barrow Strait. The Parry Islands (a subgroup of the Queen Elizabeth Islands) include Bathurst Island, Melville Island, Cornwallis Island, and Prince Patrick Island. They are covered with tundra and are uninhabited.

Pasadena City in SW California, USA, part of Greater ◊Los Angeles; population (1992) 132,600. Products include electronic equipment and precision instruments. Farmers from Indiana founded a settlement here 1874.

Pascagoula City in SE Mississippi, USA, at the mouth of the Pascagoula River, E of Biloxi; population (1990) 25,900. Industries include fishing, shipbuilding, paper, petroleum, and chemicals.

Pasco City and river port in SE Washington, USA, on the Columbia River, seat of Franklin County; population (1990) 20,300. It was founded 1880.

Pas-de-Calais *Département* in the ◊Nord-Pas-de-Calais region of France, with a coastline on the Strait of Dover; area 6,639 sq km/2,563 sq mi; population (1990) 694,700. The *département* was the scene of severe fighting in both world wars. The principal towns are Arras (the capital), Béthune, Boulogne-Sur-Mer, St-Omer, Calais, and Lens.

Passaic City in NW New Jersey, USA, on the Passaic River, N of Jersey City; population (1992) 57,000. Products include television cables, chemicals, plastics, pharmaceuticals, and clothing.

Passamaquoddy Bay Deeply indented inlet of the Bay of Fundy, between Maine, USA, and SE New Brunswick, Canada.

Passau Town in SE Bavaria, Germany, at the junction of the rivers Inn and Ilz with the Danube.

Patagonia Southernmost region of Argentina, S of latitude 40° S, with sheep farming, and coal and oil resources. It has an area of about 673,000 sq km/260,000 sq mi. Uranium ore deposit was found in 1993. Sighted by Ferdinand Magellan 1520, it was claimed by both Argentina and Chile until divided between them 1881.

Paterson City of NE New Jersey, USA, on the Passaic River; population (1990) 140,900. It is part of the industrial and residential conurbation of Paterson–Clifton–Passaic. First settled 1771 by American revolutionaries, Paterson developed as an important centre of the textile industry owing to the water power available from the Passaic Falls. It produces machinery and chemicals, and attracts visitors to the falls.

Patiala City in E Punjab, India; population (1991) 269,000. Industries include textiles and metalwork.

Patmos Greek island in the Aegean Sea, one of the Dodecanese; the chief town is Hora. St John is said to have written the New Testament Book of Revelation while in exile here.

Patna Capital of Bihar state, India, on the river Ganges; population (1991) 917,000. It has remains of a hall built by the emperor Asoka in the 3rd century BC, when it was called Pataliputra.

Patras (Greek *Pátrai*) Industrial city (hydroelectric installations, textiles, paper) in the NW Peloponnese region, Greece, on the Gulf of Patras; population (1991) 155,200. The ancient *Patrai*, it is the only one of the 12 cities of the ancient Greek province of ◊Achaea to survive.

Pau Industrial city (electrochemical and metallurgical products) and resort, capital of Pyrénées-Atlantiques *département* in Aquitaine, SW France, near the Spanish border; population (1990) 83,900. It is the centre of the Basque area of France, and the site of fierce guerrilla activity.

Pavia Province of N Italy in SW ◊Lombardy region; capital Pavia (population (1990) 80,100); area 2,966 sq km/1,145 sq mi; population (1992) 190,500.

Pawtucket City in NE Rhode Island, USA, on the Blackstone River, NE of Providence; population (1992) 72,000. Industries include textiles, thread, machinery, and metal and glass products. Pawtucket was settled 1671 and became an ironmongery centre. It was the home of the first US water-powered cotton mill 1790.

Paysandú City in Uruguay, capital of Paysandú department, on the river Uruguay; population (1985) 74,000. Tinned meat is the main product. The city dates from 1772 and is linked by a bridge built 1976 with Puerto Colón in Argentina.

Pays de la Loire Agricultural region of W France, comprising the *départements* of Loire-Atlantique, Maine-et-Loire, Mayenne, Sarthe, and Vendée; capital ◊Nantes; area 32,082 sq km/12,387 sq mi; population (1990) 3,059,200. Industries include shipbuilding and wine production.

Peace River formed in British Columbia, Canada, by the union at Finlay Forks of the Finlay and Parsnip rivers and flowing through the Rocky Mountains and across Alberta to join the river Slave just N of Lake Athabasca; length 1,600 km/1,000 mi.

Peak District Tableland of the S Pennines in NW Derbyshire, England. It is a tourist region and a national park (1951). The highest point is Kinder Scout, 636 m/2,088 ft.

Pec Town in Serbia, Yugoslavia, in the autonomous region of Kosovo. It is on the river Bistrica, at the foot of Mount Koprivnik. Pec is a busy commercial town. In the Middle Ages it was the seat of the Serbian patriarchs; the great monastery complex in which they resided remains.

Pechenga (Finnish *Petsamo*) Ice-free fishing port near Murmansk, NW Russian Federation, on the Barents Sea.

Russia ceded Pechenga to Finland 1920 but recovered it under the 1947 peace treaty.

Pechora River in N Russia, rising in the N Urals. It transports coal, timber, and furs (June–Sept) to the Barents Sea, 1,800 km/1,125 mi to the N. In 1994 it was polluted by an oil spill from a leaking pipeline near Vsinski in the Komi region.

Pecos River in S USA; length 1,490 km/926 mi. It rises in the Sangre de Cristo Mountains in NE New Mexico, and flows SE through Texas, to join the ◊Rio Grande, 55 km/34 mi NW of Del Rio. Its principal importance is as a source of irrigation.

Pécs City in SW Hungary, the centre of a coal-mining area on the Croatian frontier; population (1995 est) 163,000. Industries include metal, leather, and wine. The town dates from Roman times and was under Turkish rule 1543–1686.

Peeblesshire Former county of S Scotland, included from 1975–96 in Borders Region; now in Scottish Borders.

Peel Fishing port in the Isle of Man, UK, 19 km/12 mi NW of Douglas.

Pegu Alternative name of the city of ◊Bago, Myanmar.

Peine City in Lower Saxony, Germany, 35 km/22 mi SE of Hannover; population (1994) 125,800. Oil and gas deposits in the vicinity are exploited and the city also has a steelworks.

Peiping Name (meaning 'N peace') 1928–49 of ◊Beijing in China.

Peipus, Lake (Estonian *Peipsi*, Russian *Chudskoye*) Lake forming the boundary between Estonia and Pskov' oblast', an administrative region of Russia. The lake's area is 3,555 sq km/1,373 sq mi. Its chief outlet is the Narva River. Aleksander Nevski defeated the Teutonic Knights on its frozen surface 1242.

Peking Alternative transcription of ◊Beijing, the capital of China.

Pelée, Mont Volcano on the island of Martinique in the West Indies; height 1,350 m/4,428 ft. It destroyed the town of St Pierre during its eruption 1902.

Pelion Mountain in Thessaly, Greece, near Mount Ossa; height 1,548 m/5,079 ft. In Greek mythology it was the home of the centaurs, creatures half-human and half-horse.

Peloponnese (Greek *Peloponnesos*) Peninsula forming the S part of Greece; area 21,549 sq km/8,318 sq mi; population (1991) 1,077,000. It is joined to the mainland by the narrow isthmus of Corinth and is divided into the nomes (administrative areas) of Argolis, Arcadia, Achaea, Elis, Corinth, Lakonia, and Messenia, representing its seven ancient states. It is divided into two regions; Greece West (including Achaea and Elis), and Peloponnese (including Argolis, Arcadia, Corinth, Lakonia, and Messenia).

Pemba Island Coral island in the Indian Ocean, 48 km/30 mi NE of Zanzibar, and forming with it part of Tanzania **area** 984 sq km/380 sq mi

capital Chake Chake
industries cloves, copra
population (1988) 265,000.

Pembroke (Welsh *Penfro*) Seaport and engineering centre in Pembrokeshire, Wales; population (1991) 8,650. Henry VII was born in Pembroke Castle.

Pembrokeshire (Welsh *Sir Benfro*) Unitary authority in SW Wales. A former county, from 1974–96 it was part of the new county of Dyfed; administrative headquarters Haverfordwest; population (1996) 117,700; area 1,588 sq km/613 sq mi. The area includes the Pembrokeshire Coast National Park and there is an oil refinery at Milford Haven.

Penang (Malay *Pulau Pinang*) State in W Peninsular Malaysia, formed of *Penang Island*, Province Wellesley, and the Dindings on the mainland; area 1,030 sq km/398 sq mi; capital Penang (George Town); population (1993) 1,141,500. Penang Island was bought by Britain from the ruler of Kedah 1785; Province Wellesley was acquired 1800.

Penarlâg Welsh name of ◊Hawarden, a town in Clwyd, Wales.

Pennines, The Mountain system, 'the backbone of England', broken by a gap through which the river Aire flows to the E and the Ribble to the W; length (Scottish border to the Peaks in Derbyshire) 400 km/250 mi. It is the watershed for the main rivers of NE England. The rocks are carboniferous limestone and millstone grit, the land high moorland and fell.

Pennsylvania State in NE USA; nicknamed Keystone State
area 117,400 sq km/45,316 sq mi
capital Harrisburg
towns and cities Philadelphia, Pittsburgh, Erie, Allentown, Scranton
physical Allegheny Mountains; Ohio, Susquehanna, and Delaware rivers; Allegheny national forest; the Poconos, a mountainous wilderness on the Delaware River
features Poconos resort region; Pennsylvania Dutch country (the name comes from Deutsch, meaning German), settled in the 18th century by German immigrants escaping religious persecution, and the home of sects, including the Amish in Lancaster County; Hans Herr House (1719), former Mennonite meeting place, the best example of early German architecture in North America; Hopewell Furnace, a reconstruction of an 18th-century ironworks; Independence national historic park, Philadelphia; Valley Forge national historic park; Gettysburg national military park, site of the Civil War battle 1863; Eisenhower national historic site; University of Pennsylvania; Carnegie Mellon Institute; University of Pittsburgh; Andy Warhol museum, Pittsburgh; Bryn Mawr College (1880); Swarthmore College (1864); Curtis Institute of Music; Philadelphia Orchestra; Philadelphia Museum of Art; Hershey, the 'Chocolate Town', founded by Milton S Hershey 1903, including Hersheypark and Hershey's Chocolate World
industries hay, cereals, mushrooms, cattle, poultry, dairy products, cement, coal, steel, petroleum products, pharma-

ceuticals, motor vehicles and equipment, electronic components, textiles
population (1995) 12,071,800
famous people Marian Anderson, Andrew Carnegie, Stephen Foster, Benjamin Franklin, Robert Fulton, Martha Graham, George C Marshall, Robert E Peary, Benjamin Rush, Gertrude Stein, John Updike, Andy Warhol
history disputed by Sweden, the Netherlands, and England early 17th century; granted to Quaker William Penn 1682 by English King Charles II, after the 1664 capture of New Netherlands. The Declaration of Independence was proclaimed in Philadelphia, and many important Revolutionary War battles were fought here 1777–78. One of the original 13 states (1787), Pennsylvania was a leader in both agriculture and industry. The Battle of Gettysburg 1863 was a turning point in the Civil War for the Union cause. Until 1920, Pennsylvania was dominant in oil, coal, iron, steel, and textile production, but it already was losing its industrial lead when the Great Depression struck; by 1933, 37% of the workforce was unemployed. Some areas never fully recovered, and the state now looks to agriculture, service-related industries, trade, and tourism for economic growth.

There was a breakdown at the Three Mile Island nuclear reactor plant in Harrisburg 1979.

Pensacola Port in NW Florida, USA, on the Gulf of Mexico, with a large naval air-training station; population (1992) 59,800. Industries include chemicals, synthetic fibres, and paper. Pensacola developed around a Spanish fort in the 18th century.

Pentland Firth Channel separating the Orkney Islands from N Scotland.

Penza Industrial city (sawmills, bicycles, watches, calculating machines, textiles) in W central Russian Federation, capital of Penza region, 560 km/350 mi SE of Moscow, at the junction of the Penza and Sura rivers; population (1992) 551,000. It was founded as a fort 1663.

Penzance Seaport for the Scilly Isles and resort in Cornwall, SW England, on Mount's Bay; population (1991) 19,700. It now incorporates the seaport of ◊Newlyn. It is known as the 'Cornish Riviera'. Early fruit, flowers, and vegetables are produced.

Peoria City in central Illinois, USA, on the Illinois River; a transport, mining, and agricultural centre; population (1992) 114,000. Fort Crève Coeur was built here by the French explorer Robert de la Salle 1680 and became a trading centre. The first US settlers arrived 1818, and the town was known as Fort Clark until 1825.

Perak State of W Peninsular Malaysia; capital Ipoh; area 21,000 sq km/8,106 sq mi; population (1993) 2,222,400. It produces tin and rubber. The government is a sultanate. The other principal city is Taiping.

Pereira Capital of Risaralda department, central Colombia, situated at an altitude of 1,463 m/4,800 ft, overlooking the fertile Cauca Valley, W of Bogotá; population

(1994) 347,000. Founded 1863, the city has developed into a centre for the national coffee and cattle industries.

Périgueux Capital of Dordogne *département*, Aquitaine, France, on the river Isle, 127 km/79 mi ENE of Bordeaux; population (1990) 32,800. It is a trading centre for wine and truffles. The cathedral, dating from 984, was reconstructed in the mid 19th century, and is Byzantine in style.

Perim Island in the strait of Bāb al Mandab, the S entrance to the Red Sea; part of Yemen; area 13 sq km/5 sq mi.

Perlis Border state of Peninsular Malaysia, NW Malaysia; capital Kangar; area 800 sq km/309 sq mi; population (1993) 187,600. It produces rubber, rice, coconuts, and tin. Perlis is ruled by a raja. It was transferred by Siam (Thaland) to Britain 1909.

Perm Industrial city (shipbuilding, oil refining, aircraft, chemicals, sawmills), and capital of Perm region, N Russian Federation, on the Kama near the Ural Mountains; population (1994) 1,086,000. It was called Molotov 1940–57.

Pernambuco State of NE Brazil, on the Atlantic coast; area 98,281 sq km/37,946 sq mi; population (1991) 7,122,500. The capital is Recife (former name Pernambuco). There are highlands, and the coast is low and humid. Cotton, sugar and tropical fruit are produced.

Pernik Industrial city (coal mining, steel, glassware) in W Bulgaria, 25 km/16 mi SW of Sofia; population (1990) 121,000.

Perpignan Market town (olives, fruit, wine), resort, and capital of the Pyrénées-Orientales *département* of France, just off the Mediterranean coast, near the Spanish border; population (1990) 108,000. Overlooking Perpignan is the castle of the counts of Roussillon.

Persian Gulf or *Arabian Gulf* Large shallow inlet of the Arabian Sea; area 23,000 sq km/88,800 sq mi. It divides the Arabian peninsula from Iran and is linked by the Strait of Hormuz and the Gulf of Oman to the Arabian Sea. Oilfields surround it in the Gulf States of Bahrain, Iran, Iraq, Kuwait, Oman, Qatar, Saudi Arabia, and the United Arab Emirates.

Perth Capital of Western Australia, with its port at nearby Fremantle on the Swan River; population (1993) 1,221,200. Industries include textiles, cement, furniture, vehicles, and oil refining. It was founded 1829 and expanded after gold was discovered at Kalgoorlie 1893. It is the commercial and cultural centre of the state, and the headquarters of the Royal Perth Yacht Club, from which the America's Cup challenge was staged 1987.

Perth Industrial town and administrative headquarters of Perth and Kinross, E Scotland, on the river Tay; population (1991) 41,500. It was the capital of Scotland from the 12th century until James I of Scotland was assassinated here 1437. Industries include dyeing, textiles, whisky distilling, and carpets.

Perth and Kinross Unitary authority in central Scotland created 1996 from part of the former Tayside region ; administrative headquarters Perth; population (1996) 131,800; area

5,328 sq km/2,058 sq mi. Natural features include the Sidlaw Hills and Lochs Tay and Rannoch. Soft fruit is grown in the Carse of Gowrie.

Perthshire Former inland county of central Scotland, of which the major part was included in Tayside Region 1975–96, the SW part being included in Central Region; now mostly in Perth and Kinross unitary authority.

Perugia Capital of Umbria, Italy, 520 m/1,700 ft above the river Tiber, about 137 km/85 mi N of Rome; population (1992) 146,200. Its industries include textiles, liqueurs, and chocolate. One of the 12 cities of the ancient country of Etruria, it surrendered to Rome 309 BC. There is a university, founded 1276; a municipal palace, built 1281; and a 15th-century cathedral.

Perugia Province of central Italy in N ◊Umbria region; capital Perugia; area 6,335 sq km/2,446 sq mi; population (1992) 590,200.

Pesaro e Urbino Province of E central Italy in N Le ◊Marche region; capital Pesaro (population (1990) 90,300); area 2,893 sq km/1,117 sq mi; population (1992) 336,100. Pesaro is a resort on the Adriatic coast.

Pescadores (Chinese *Penghu*) Group of about 60 islands off Taiwan, of which they form a dependency; area 130 sq km/50 sq mi.

Pescara City in Abruzzi, E Italy, at the mouth of the Pescara River, on the Adriatic coast; population (1992) 121,400. Hydroelectric installations supply Rome with electricity. It is linked by ferry to Split in Croatia.

Pescara Province of S central Italy in E ◊Abruzzi region; capital Pescara; area 1,225 sq km/473 sq mi; population (1992) 290,000.

Peshawar Capital of North-West Frontier Province, Pakistan, 18 km/11 mi E of the Khyber Pass; population (1981) 555,000. Products include textiles, leather, and copper.

Petaluma City in NW California, USA, N of San Francisco, on the Petaluma River; population (1990) 43,200. It is an agricultural centre for poultry and dairy products. It was founded 1852.

Peterborough City in Cambridgeshire, England, on the river Nene. It will become a unitary authority in April 1998. It is noted for its 12th-century cathedral; population (1994 est) 139,000, one of the fastest growing cities in Europe. It has an advanced electronics industry. Nearby Flag Fen disclosed 1985 a well-preserved Bronze Age settlement of 660 BC.

Peterborough City in Ontario, Canada, on the Otonabee River, 113 km/70 mi NE of Toronto and 45 km/28 mi N of Lake Ontario; population (1991) 68,400. Peterborough is the chief commercial centre for central Ontario. It has a large cereal mill and electrical-goods plant and also manufactures marine equipment. The world's largest deposit of nepheline, used in the manufacture of glass, is mined N of the city, and the refined product is shipped to the glass industry round the world. The surrounding lake district area attracts tourists.

Peterhead Industrial seaport (fishing, fish-curing, light engineering, whisky distilling, woollens) in Aberdeenshire, Scotland, 54 km/33 mi NE of Aberdeen; population (1991) 18,700. It was a former whaling port. James Edward Stuart, the Old Pretender, landed here 1715. The harbour is used by service industries for North Sea oil. It is the most easterly town in Scotland, built of locally quarried pink granite.

Peter I Island Uninhabited island in the Bellingshausen Sea, Antarctica, belonging to Norway since 1931; area 180 sq km/69 sq mi.

Peterlee Town in County Durham, England, designated a new town 1948; population (1991) 31,100. It was named after Peter Lee, first Labour chair of a county council. Industries include transport equipment, textiles, and engineering.

Petersburg City in SE Virginia, USA, on the Appomattox River, S of Richmond; population (1990) 38,400. Industries include tobacco products, textiles, leather products, boat building, and chemicals. It was established 1748 on the site of Fort Henry (1645), and was the site of American Revolution and Civil War battles.

Petra (Arabic *Wadi Musa*) Ancient city carved out of the red rock at a site in Jordan, on the E slopes of the Wadi el Araba, 90 km/56 mi S of the Dead Sea. An Edomite stronghold and capital of the Nabataeans in the 2nd century, it was captured by the Roman emperor Trajan 106 and destroyed by the Arabs in the 7th century. It was forgotten in Europe until 1812 when the Swiss traveller Johann Ludwig Burckhardt (1784–1817) came across it.

Petrograd Former name (1914–24) of ◊St Petersburg, a city in Russia.

Petropavlovsk Industrial city (flour, agricultural machinery, leather) in N Kazakhstan, on the Ishim River, the Trans-Siberian railway, and the Transkazakh line, opened 1953; population (1990) 245,000. A former caravan station, it was founded as a Russian fortress 1782.

Petropavlovsk formerly *Petropavlovsk-Kamchatskiy* Pacific seaport and naval base on the E coast of the Kamchatka peninsula, Russian Federation; population (1990) 271,000.

Petrópolis Hill resort in SE Brazil, founded by Pedro II; population (1991) 294,200. Industries include textiles and brewing.

Petrovsk Former name (to 1921) of the Russian port ◊Makhachkala.

Petrozavodsk Industrial city (metal goods, cement, prefabricated houses, sawmills), and capital of the autonomous republic of Karelia, Russian Federation, on the W shore of Lake Onega; population (1991) 279,000. Peter the Great established the township 1703 as an ironworking centre; it was named Petrozavodsk 1777.

Petsamo Finnish name of the Russian port ◊Pechenga.

Pevensey English village in East Sussex, 8 km/5 mi NE of Eastbourne, the site of the Norman king William the Conqueror's landing 1066. The walls remain of the Roman fortress of Anderida, later a Norman castle, which was prepared against German invasion in World War II.

Pforzheim City in Baden-Württemberg, Germany, 26 km/16 mi SE of Karlsruhe; there are goldsmith industries; population (1991) 115,500. It was a Roman settlement, and the residence of the margraves (princes) of Baden 1300–1565.

Philadelphia 'the city of brotherly love' Industrial city and financial centre, and the world's largest freshwater port, on the Delaware River at the junction of the Schuykill River, in Pennsylvania, USA; population (1992) 1,552,600; metropolitan area (1992) 5,939,000. Industries include refined oil, chemicals, textiles, processed food, printing and publishing, and transportation equipment. It was founded 1682, and was the first capital of the USA 1790–1800.

Philae Island in the river Nile, Egypt, above the first rapids, famed for the beauty of its temple of Isis (founded about 350 BC and in use until the 6th century AD). In 1977 the temple was re-erected on the nearby island of Agilkia above the flooding caused by the Aswan Dam.

Philippeville Former name (to 1962) of the Algerian port of ◊Skikda.

Phnom Penh Capital of Cambodia, on the Mekong River, 210 km/130 mi NW of Saigon; population (1994) 920,000. Industries include textiles and food-processing. It has been Cambodia's capital since the 15th century, and has royal palaces, museums, and pagodas.

Phoenix Capital of Arizona, USA; industrial city (steel, aluminium, electrical goods, food processing) and tourist centre on the Salt River; population (1992) 1,012,200. Settled 1886, Phoenix became the territorial capital 1889 and the state capital 1912. The completion of a dam 1912 provided the water and power needed for economic development.

Phoenix Islands Group of eight islands in the South Pacific, included in Kiribati; total land area 18 sq km/11 sq mi. Drought has rendered them all uninhabitable, and there is no permanent population.

Piacenza Industrial city (agricultural machinery, textiles, pottery) in Emilia-Romagna, N Italy, on the river Po, 65 km/40 mi SE of Milan; population (1992) 102,200. The Roman *Placentia*, Piacenza dates from 218 BC and has a 12th-century cathedral.

Piacenza Province of N central Italy in NW ◊Emilia-Romagna region; capital Piacenza; area 2,600 sq km/1,004 sq mi; population (1992) 267,700.

Piatra-Neamț Capital of Neamț county, E Romania, on the river Bistrița, at the foot of the Carpathian Mountains, 97 km/61 mi W of Iași; population (1993) 125,200. It is a market town, trading chiefly in timber. Piatra-Neamț has textile, foodprocessing, paper, and oil refining industries, and is also a centre of folk culture.

Picardy (French *Picardie*) Region of N France, including Aisne, Oise, and Somme *départements*; area 19,399 sq km/7,490 sq mi; population (1990) 1,810,700. Its industries include chemicals and metals. Main cities include ◊Amiens (the capital), Compiègne, and Beauvais.

Picton Small port at the NE extremity of South Island, New Zealand, with a ferry to Wellington, North Island.

Pictou Seaport in Nova Scotia, Canada, 135 km/84 mi NE of Halifax; population (1991) 4,100. It is situated in a fertile district, with extensive coal mines and steel mills. Coal, timber, fish, and lobster are exported, ships are built and repaired, and there is a foundry. Pictou is an important N port for the Gulf of St Lawrence and overseas trade. The port was settled by Scots 1773.

Piedmont (Italian *Piemonte*) Region of N Italy, bordering Switzerland to the N and France to the W, and surrounded, except to the E, by the Alps and the Apennines; area 25,399 sq km/9,807 sq mi; population (1995) 4,298,000. Its capital is Turin, and towns include Alessandria, Asti, Vercelli, and Novara. It also includes the fertile Po river valley. Products include fruit, grain, cattle, cars, and textiles. The movement for the unification of Italy started in the 19th century in Piedmont, under the house of Savoy.

Pierre Capital of South Dakota, USA, located in the central part of the state, on the Missouri River, near the geographical centre of North America; population (1992) 12,900. Industries include tourism and grain and dairy products. As Fort Pierre in the early 1800s, it served as a fur-trading post; in the late 1800s it was a supply centre for gold miners.

Pietermaritzburg Industrial city (footwear, furniture, aluminium, rubber, brewing) in South Africa. Capital of KwaZulu-Natal Province; population (1991) 228,500. Founded 1838 by Boer trekkers from the Cape, it was named after their leaders, Piet Retief and Gert Maritz, who were killed by Zulus.

Pikes Peak Mountain in the Rampart of the Rocky Mountains, Colorado, USA; height 4,300 m/14,110 ft. It has commanding views, accessible by cog railway and road. Pikes Peak was discovered 1806 by Zebulon Pike and first scaled 1820.

Pik Pobedy Highest peak in the ◊Tian Shan mountain range on the Kyrgyz-Chinese border, at 7,439 m/24,406 ft.

Piła (German *Schneidemühl*) Capital of Piła province, Poland, on the river Gwda, a tributary of the Noteć, 77 km/48 mi N of Poznań; population (1990) 72,300. Machinery and glass are manufactured, and livestock and timber traded. It is a railway junction. Until 1945 it was in German Pomerania.

Pilsen German form of ◊Plzeň, a city in the Czech Republic.

Pinatubo, Mount Active volcano on Luzon Island, the Philippines, 88 km/55 mi N of Manila. Dormant for 600 years, it erupted June 1991, killing 343 people and leaving as many as 200,000 homeless. Surrounding rice fields were covered with 3 m/10 ft of volcanic ash.

Pindus Mountains (Greek *Pindhos Oros*) Range in NW Greece and Albania, between Epirus and Thessaly; highest point Smolikas, 2,633 m/8,638 ft.

Pine Bluff City and port in SE Arkansas, USA, on the Arkansas River, SE of Little Rock, seat of Jefferson County; population (1992) 57,700. Industries include paper, cotton, grain, and furniture. It was settled 1819 as a trading post.

Piotrków Trybunalski Capital of Piotrków province, Poland, 42 km/26 mi S of Łódź. It is an industrial town producing textiles, chemicals, machinery, and glass. In the 10th–17th centuries it was the seat of a royal tribunal and Polish parliament.

Piraeus Port of both ancient and modern Athens and main port of Greece, on the Gulf of Aegina; population (1991) 169,600. Constructed as the port of Athens about 493 BC, it was linked with that city by the Long Walls, a fortification protecting the approaches to Athens comprising three walls built 496–456 BC. After the destruction of Athens by Sulla 86 BC, Piraeus declined. Piraeus is now an industrial suburb of Athens.

Piran Seaport in Slovenia, on a promontory on the S side of the Gulf of Trieste, 72 km/45 mi NW of Rijeka; population (1991) 4,700. It is an old Venetian town with medieval buildings, including churches.

Pirmasens City in the Rhineland-Palatinate, Germany, 45 km/28 mi E of Saarbrücken; population (1994) 48,700. It is the centre of the German boot- and shoe-manufacturing industry.

Pirna Town in the *Land* of ◊Saxony, Germany, on the river Elbe, 18 km/11 mi SE of Dresden. The town is a health resort, and has paper and textile industries.

Pirot Town in Serbia, Yugoslavia, on the river Nisava. It is the centre for the produce of the fertile plain of Pirot, and has a carpet industry.

Pisa City in Tuscany, Italy; population (1991) 101,000. It has an 11th–12th-century cathedral. Its famous campanile, the Leaning Tower of Pisa (repaired 1990), is 55 m/180 ft high and about 5 m/16.5 ft out of perpendicular. It has foundations only about 3 m/10 ft deep.

Pisa Province of N central Italy in NE ◊Tuscany region; capital Pisa; area 2,447 sq km/945 sq mi; population (1992) 385,100.

Pistoia City in Tuscany, Italy, 16 km/10 mi NW of Florence; population (district, 1992) 265,200. Industries include steel, small arms, paper, pasta, and olive oil. Pistoia was the site of the Roman rebel Catiline's defeat 62 BC. It is surrounded by walls (1302) and has a 12th-century cathedral.

Pistoia Province of N central Italy in N ◊Tuscany region; capital Pistoia; area 966 sq km/373 sq mi; population (1992) 264,800.

Pitcairn Islands British colony in Polynesia, 5,300 km/3,300 mi NE of New Zealand
area 27 sq km/10 sq mi
capital Adamstown

features the uninhabited Henderson Islands, an unspoiled coral atoll with a rare ecology, and tiny Ducie and Oeno islands, annexed by Britain 1902
industries fruit and souvenirs to passing ships
population (1994) 56
language English
government the governor is the British high commissioner in New Zealand
history settled 1790 by nine mutineers from the British ship the *Bounty* together with some Tahitians; their occupation remained unknown until 1808.

Pitești Capital of Argeş county, Romania, 120 km/75 mi NW of Bucharest; population (1993) 182,900. It is situated on an oil- and gasfield and has developed associated industries; it also produces wine, textiles, machinery, motor vehicles, leather, shoes, chemicals, and has food processing.

Pittsburgh Industrial city (machinery, chemicals) in the NE USA and the nation's largest inland port, where the Allegheny and Monongahela rivers join to form the Ohio River in Pennsylvania; population (1992) 366,850; metropolitan area (1992) 2,406,000.

Pittsfield City in W central Massachusetts, USA, on the Housatonic River, just E of the New York border; population (1990) 48,600. Industries include electronics and tourism. It was settled in the 1740s and incorporated 1761, and named after the British political leader William Pitt.

Piura Capital of the department of the same name in the arid NW of Peru, situated on the Piura River, 160 km/100 mi SW of Punta Pariñas; population (1993) 278,000. It is the westernmost point in South America and was founded 1532 by the Spanish conquistadors left behind by Francisco Pizarro. Cotton is grown in the surrounding area.

Plata, Río de la (or *River Plate*) Estuary in South America into which the rivers Paraná, Iguazú, and Uruguay flow; length 320 km/200 mi and width up to 240 km/150 mi. The basin drains much of Argentina, Bolivia, Brazil, Uruguay, and Paraguay, which all cooperate in its development. Buenos Aires is in its estuary.

Platte River in Nebraska, central USA; length 500 km/310 mi. It is formed at North Platte, Nebraska, USA, by the confluence of the North Platte and South Platte rivers and flows mainly E to join the ◊Missouri River 25 km/16 mi S of Omaha. The three Platte rivers contain many dams for flood control and irrigation. They are unnavigable, but the W trails to Oregon and California followed them in the mid-19th century.

Plattensee German name for Lake ◊Balaton in Hungary.

Plauen Town in the *Land* of ◊Saxony, Germany, 68 km/42 mi SW of Chemnitz. It is situated on the river Weisse Elster, at the foot of the ◊Erzgebirge; population (1996) 67,300. Its textile industry dates from the 15th century, and it also has steel and engineering industries.

Plenty, Bay of Broad inlet on the NE coast of North Island, New Zealand, with the port of Tauranga. One of the canoes of the celebrated second Maori migration landed here about 1350.

Pleven Industrial city (textiles, machinery, ceramics) in N Bulgaria; population (1990) 168,000. In the Russo-Turkish War 1877, Pleven surrendered to the Russians after a siege of five months.

Płock (Russian *Plotsk*) Capital of Płock province, Poland, 96 km/60 mi W of Warsaw, on the river Vistula; population (1990) 123,400. The city has oil refineries and petrochemical works. The 12th-century cathedral contains the tombs of Polish kings.

Ploiești Industrial city (textiles, paper, petrochemicals; oil centre) in SE Romania; population (1993) 254,000.

Plovdiv Industrial city (textiles, chemicals, leather, tobacco) in Bulgaria, on the river Maritsa; population (1991) 379,000. Conquered by Philip of Macedonia in the 4th century BC, it was known as *Philippopolis* ('Philip's city'). It was capital of Roman Thrace.

Plymouth City and seaport in Devon, England, at the mouth of the river Plym, with dockyard, barracks, and a naval base at Devonport; it will become a unitary authority in April 1998; population (1994 est) 257,000. There are marine industries; clothing, radio equipment, and processed foods are produced. The Devonport dockyard is used for the refitting of nuclear submarines. The city rises N of the Hoe headland where tradition has it that Francis Drake played bowls as the Spanish Armada approached 1588. The *Mayflower* Pilgrims sailed from here 1620.

Plymouth Town in E Massachusetts, NE USA, situated on ◊Cape Cod about 55 km/34 mi SE of Boston; population (1990) 45,600. Founded by the Pilgrims in 1620, it was the first settlement by Europeans in New England. There are several handsome churches and a hall with Pilgrim relics and historical paintings. Of great cultural significance to the American people, Plymouth attracts many tourists.

Plynlimon Mountain in Powys, Wales, with three summits; the highest is 752 m/2,468 ft.

Plzeň (German *Pilsen*) Industrial city (heavy machinery, cars, beer) in the Czech Republic, at the confluence of the Radbuza and Mze rivers, capital of Západočeský (West Bohemia) region; 84 km/52 mi SW of Prague; population (1991) 173,100.

Pnom Penh Alternative form of ◊Phnom Penh, the capital of Cambodia.

Po Longest river in Italy, flowing from the Cottian Alps to the Adriatic Sea; length 668 km/415 mi. Its valley is fertile and contains natural gas. The river is heavily polluted with nitrates, phosphates, and arsenic.

Pocatello City in SE Idaho, USA, on Portneuf River, near the American Falls reservoir, and 314 km/195 mi E of Boise; population (1994 est) 49,600. It is the second-largest city in Idaho, a railway centre, and a wholesale trade and shipping point for the surrounding agricultural area.

Podgorica formerly (1946–92) *Titograd* Capital of Montenegro, Yugoslavia; population (1993 est) 135,000. Industries include metalworking, furniture-making, and tobacco. It was damaged in World War II and after rebuilding was renamed in honour of Marshal Tito; it reverted to its original name with the collapse of communism. It was the birthplace of the Roman emperor Diocletian.

Podolsk Industrial city (oil refining, machinery, cables, cement, ceramics) in the Russian Federation, 40 km/25 mi SW of Moscow; population (1990) 209,000.

Pointe-Noire Chief port of the Republic of the Congo, formerly (1950–58) the capital; population (1992) 576,000. Industries include oil refining, shipbuilding, potash processing, and food exporting.

Poitiers Capital of Poitou-Charentes, W France; population (1990) 82,500. Products include chemicals and clothing. The Merovingian king Clovis defeated the Visigoths under Alaric here 507; Charles Martel stemmed the Saracen advance 732, and Edward the Black Prince of England defeated the French 1356.

Poitou-Charentes Region of W central France, comprising the *départements* of Charente, Charente-Maritime, Deux-Sèvres, and Vienne; area 25,809 sq km/9,965 sq mi; population (1990) 1,595,100. Its capital is Poitiers. Industries include dairy products, wheat, chemicals, and metal goods; brandy is made at Cognac.

Poltava Industrial city (machinery, foodstuffs, clothing) in Ukraine, capital of Poltava region, on the river Vorskla; population (1992) 324,000. Peter the Great defeated Charles XII of Sweden here 1709.

Polynesia Islands of Oceania E of 170° E latitude, including Hawaii, Kiribati, Tuvalu, Fiji, Tonga, Tokelau, Samoa, Cook Islands, and French Polynesia.

Polynesia

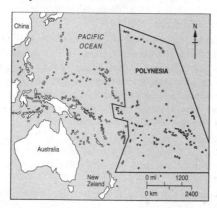

Pomerania (Polish *Pomorze*, German *Pommern*) Region along the S shore of the Baltic Sea, including the island of Rügen, divided between Poland and (W of the Oder–Neisse line) East Germany 1945–90, and the Federal Republic of Germany after reunification 1990. The chief port is Gdańsk. It was formerly a province of Germany.

Pomfret Old form of ◊Pontefract, a town in West Yorkshire, England.

Pommern German form of ◊Pomerania, a region of N Europe, now largely in Poland.

Pomorze Polish form of ◊Pomerania, a region of N Europe, now largely in Poland.

Pompano Beach City in SE Florida, USA, N of Fort Lauderdale, on the Atlantic Ocean; population (1992) 72,900. Tourism, fruit processing, and fishing are important to the economy. The town was settled about 1900.

Ponce Major city and industrial port (iron, textiles, sugar, rum) in S Puerto Rico, population (1990) 187,750. The settlement, established in the late 17th century, was named after the Spanish explorer Juan Ponce de León.

Pondicherry Union territory of SE India; area 492 sq km/190 sq mi; population (1994 est) 894,000. Its capital is Pondicherry, and products include rice, peanuts, cotton, and sugar. Pondicherry was founded by the French 1674 and changed hands several times among the French, Dutch, and British before being returned to France 1814 at the close of the Napoleonic Wars. Together with Karaikal, Yanam, and Mahé (on the Malabar Coast) it formed a French colony until 1954 when all were transferred to the government of India; since 1962 they have formed the Union Territory of Pondicherry. Languages spoken include French, English, Tamil, Telegu, and Malayalam.

Ponta Delgada Port, resort, and chief commercial centre of the Portuguese ◊Azores Islands, on São Miguel; population (1981) 22,200.

Pontefract Town in Wakefield borough, West Yorkshire, N England, 34 km/21 mi SW of York; population (1991) 28,400. Industries include coal, market gardening, and confectionery (liquorice Pontefract cakes). Features include the remains of the Norman castle where Richard II was murdered 1399.

Pontevedra Capital of the province of Pontevedra, NW Spain, at the mouth of the river Lerez; population (1995) 77,300. It has a naval radio station, and products include agricultural ones, wine, textiles, and pottery. There is a 16th-century Gothic cathedral, and a 13th-century episcopal palace.

Pontevedra Province of NW Spain in ◊Galicia autonomous community; capital Pontevedra; area 4,478 sq km/1,729 sq mi; population (1995) 937,800. It has a deeply indented coastline on the Atlantic Ocean, and is separated from Portugal by the river Miño. The province is mountainous and heavily populated. Its chief port is Vigo. Agriculture and fishing are important.

Pontiac City in Michigan, USA, 38 km/24 mi NW of Detroit, a centre of motor manufacturing; population (1992) 69,350.

Pontine Marshes Former malarial marshes in the Lazio region of Italy, near the coast 40 km/25 mi SE of Rome. Roman attempts to drain them were unsuccessful, and it was not until 1926, under Mussolini's administration, that they were brought into cultivation. Products include cereals, fruit and wine, and sugar beet.

Pontypool (Welsh *Pontypwl*) Industrial town and administrative headquarters of Torfaen unitary authority, SE Wales, on the Afon Llwyd, 15 km/9 mi N of Newport; population (1991) 35,600. Products include iron and steel goods, tinplate, glass, synthetic textiles, and scientific instruments.

Pontypridd Industrial town (chain and cable works, iron and brass founding, chemicals, light industry on the Treforest trading estate) in Rhonnda Cynon Taff, S Wales; population (1990 est) 33,600.

Poole Industrial town (chemicals, engineering, boat building, packaging materials, confectionery, pottery from local clay), unitary authority, and yachting centre and port on Poole Harbour, S England, 8 km/5 mi W of Bournemouth; population (1996) 138,100; area 64 sq km/25 sq mi; it was part of the county of Dorset to 1997.

Pool Malebo Lake on the border between the Congo Republic and the Democratic Republic of Congo, formed by a widening of the Congo/Zaïre River, 560 km/350 mi from its mouth.

Poona Former English spelling of ◊Pune, a city in India; after independence 1947 the form Poona was gradually superseded by Pune.

Popocatépetl (Aztec 'smoking mountain') Volcano in central Mexico, 50 km/30 mi SE of Mexico City; 5,340 m/17,526 ft. It last erupted 1920.

Pordenone Province of NE Italy in W ◊Friuli-Venezia Giulia region; capital Pordenone (population (1990) 50,200); area 2,273 sq km/878 sq mi; population (1992) 275,400.

Pori (Swedish *Björneborg*) Ice-free industrial port (nickel and copper refining, sawmills, paper, textiles) in the Gulf of Bothnia, SW Finland; population (1992) 76,300. A deep-water harbour was opened 1985.

Port Adelaide Industrial port (cement, chemicals) in South Australia, on Gulf St Vincent, 11 km/7 mi NW of Adelaide; population (1985) 37,000.

Port Arthur Former name (to 1905) of the port and naval base of Lüshun in NE China, now part of ◊Lüda.

Port Arthur Industrial deep-water port (oil refining, shipbuilding, brass, chemicals) in Texas, USA, 24 km/15 mi SE of Beaumont; population (1992) 59,700. Founded 1895, it gained importance with the discovery of petroleum near Beaumont 1901.

Port Augusta Port (trading in wool and grain) in South Australia, at the head of Spencer Gulf, NNW of Adelaide; population (1994) 14,600. It is a base for the Royal Flying Doctor Service.

Port-au-Prince Capital and industrial port (sugar, rum, textiles, plastics) of Haiti; population (1992) 1,255,100.

Port Darwin Port serving Darwin, the capital of Northern Territory, Australia.

Port Elizabeth Industrial port (engineering, steel, food processing) in Eastern Cape Province, South Africa, about 710 km/440 mi E of Cape Town on Algoa Bay; population (urban area, 1991) 853,200.

Porterville City in S central California, USA, N of Bakersfield; population (1990) 29,600. Industries include citrus fruits and olive oil.

Port Harcourt Port (trading in coal, palm oil, and groundnuts) and capital of Rivers state in SE Nigeria, on the river Bonny in the Niger delta; population (1992 est) 371,000. It is also an industrial centre producing refined mineral oil, sheet aluminium, tyres, and paints.

Portland Industrial port and largest city of Maine, USA, on Casco Bay, SE of Sebago Lake; population (1992) 62,800. Portland was first settled 1632.

Portland Industrial port and capital of Multnomah County, NW Oregon, USA; on the Columbia River, 173 km/108 mi from the sea, at its confluence with the Willamette River; population (1992) 445,500. Industries include aluminium, paper, timber, lumber machinery, and electronics. Portland was settled 1829 on an early Native American site, and laid out 1844. The city grew rapidly because of its position on the Oregon Trail.

Portland, Isle of Rocky peninsula in Dorset, S England, joined to the mainland by the bank of shingle, ◊Chesil Bank. It is Europe's largest man-made harbour. Portland Castle was built by Henry VIII 1520; the naval base (founded 1845) closed 1995; the Naval Air Station will close 1999; building stone is still quarried. Portland stone was used for St Paul's Cathedral, London.

Port Laoise or *Portlaoighise*, formerly *Maryborough* County town of County Laois, Republic of Ireland, 80 km/50 mi WSW of Dublin; population (1990 est) 9,500. It has woollen, flour-milling, and malting industries, and is the site of a top-security prison.

Port Louis Capital of Mauritius, on the island's NW coast; population (1993) 144,250. Exports include sugar, textiles, and electronic goods.

Port Mahón or *Maó* Port serving the capital Mahón on the Spanish island of Menorca (second in size of the Balearic Islands, after Mallorca). The largest natural port in the Mediterranean, Mahón was occupied and colonized by the great seafaring powers of antiquity (the Phoenicians and the Romans), and later by the Dutch, the French, and the English during the 17th–19th centuries.

Portmeirion Holiday resort in Gwynedd, Wales, built by the architect Clough Williams-Ellis in Italianate fantasy style; it was the setting of the 1967 cult television series *The Prisoner*.

Port Moresby Capital and port of Papua New Guinea, on the S coast of New Guinea; population (1990) 193,200. The port trades in coffee, copper, gold, copra, palm oil, and timber.

Porto (English *Oporto*) Industrial city (textiles, leather, pottery) in Portugal, on the river Douro, 5 km/3 mi from its mouth; population (1987) 350,000. It exports port wine; the suburb Vila Nova de Gaia on the S bank of the Douro is known for its port lodges.

Pôrto Alegre Port and capital of Rio Grande do Sul state, S Brazil; population (1991) 1,254,600 (metropolitan area

3,757,500). It is a freshwater port for ocean-going vessels and is Brazil's major commercial centre.

Port-of-Spain Port and capital of Trinidad and Tobago, on the island of Trinidad; population (1990) 58,400. It has a cathedral (1813–28) and the San Andres Fort (1785).

Porto-Novo Capital of Benin, W Africa; population (1994) 179,000. It was a former Portuguese centre for the slave and tobacco trade with Brazil and became a French protectorate 1863.

Porto Rico Former name (to 1932) of ◊Puerto Rico, a US island in the Caribbean.

Port Phillip Bay Inlet off Bass Strait, Victoria, Australia, on which the city of Melbourne stands.

Port Pirie Industrial port (smelting of ores from the Broken Hill mines, and chemicals) in South Australia; population (1994) 14,700.

Port Rashid Port serving ◊Dubai in the United Arab Emirates.

Port Royal Former capital of Jamaica, at the entrance to Kingston harbour.

Port Said Port in Egypt, on reclaimed land at the N end of the ◊Suez Canal; population (1994) 526,000. During the 1967 Arab-Israeli War the city was damaged and the canal blocked; Port Said was evacuated by 1969 but by 1975 had been largely reconstructed.

Portsmouth Port in Rockingham County, SE New Hampshire, USA, on the estuary of the Piscataqua River; the state's only seaport; population (1990) 25,900. Founded 1623, Portsmouth was the state capital 1679–1775.

Portsmouth City, naval port, and unitary authority in S England, opposite the Isle of Wight; population (1996) 189,300; area 42 sq km/16 sq mi. It was part of the county of Hampshire to 1997. The naval dockyard was closed 1981 although some naval facilities remain. It is a continental ferry port. There are high-technology and manufacturing industries, including aircraft engineering, electronics, shipbuilding, and ship maintenance.

Portsmouth Port and independent city in SE Virginia, USA, on the Elizabeth River, seat of a US navy yard and training centre; population (1992) 104,400. Manufactured goods include electronic equipment, chemicals, clothing, and processed food. Portsmouth was founded 1752.

Port Sunlight Model village built 1888 by W H Lever (1851–1925) for workers at the Lever Brothers (now Unilever) soap factory on the Wirral Peninsula at Birkenhead, near Liverpool, NW England. Designed for a population of 3,000, and covering an area of 353 ha/130 acres, it includes an art gallery, church, library, and social hall. It is now a part of Bebington, Merseyside.

Port Swettenham Former name of ◊Kelang, a port in Peninsular Malaysia.

Port Talbot Industrial port (tinplate, chemicals, and steel strip mill) on the Bristol Channel and administrative headquarters of Neath Port Talbot, Wales; population (1991) 37,600. The port accommodates bulk carriers of iron ore.

Portuguese East Africa Former name (to 1975) of Mozambique in SE Africa.

Portuguese Guinea Former name (to 1974) of Guinea-Bissau in W Africa.

Portuguese West Africa Former name (to 1975) of Angola in SW Africa.

Port-Vila Port and capital of Vanuatu, on the SW of Efate Island; population (1989) 19,400.

Posen German name for ◊Poznań, a city in Poland.

Postojna (German *Adelsberg*) Town in Slovenia, in the district of Carniola; population (1991) 8,200. Here the underground river Pivka enters the caves of Postojna, which are filled with dramatically shaped stalactites and stalagmites. The river contains the blind salamander *Proteus anguinus*.

Potchefstroom Oldest town in the former Transvaal, South Africa, on the river Mooi, founded by Boers (descendants of Dutch settlers) trekking from the Cape 1838. It is the centre of a large cattle-rearing area.

Potenza Province of S Italy in W ◊Basilicata region; capital Potenza (population (1990) 68,500); area 6,805 sq km/2,627 sq mi; population (1992) 401,500.

Potomac River in West Virginia, Virginia, and Maryland states, USA, rising in the Allegheny Mountains, and flowing SE through Washington DC, into Chesapeake Bay. It is formed by the junction of the N Potomac, about 153 km/95 mi long, and S Potomac, about 209 km/130 mi long, and is itself 459 km/285 mi long.

Potosí City in SW Bolivia; on the Cerro de Potosí slopes at 4,020 m/13,189 ft; it is one of the highest cities in the world; population (1992) 112,300. It was founded by Spaniards 1545. Silver, tin, lead, and copper are mined here; during the 17th and 18th centuries it was the chief silver-mining town and foremost city in South America, but it is now mainly tin that is mined.

Potsdam Capital of the *Land* of Brandenburg, Germany, on the river Havel SW of Berlin; population (1993) 139,500. Products include textiles, pharmaceuticals, and electrical goods. A leading garrison town and Prussian military centre, Potsdam was restored to its position of capital of Brandenburg with the reunification of Germany 1990. The New Palace 1763–70 and Sans Souci were both built by Frederick the Great, and Hitler's Third Reich was proclaimed in the garrison church 21 March 1933. The Potsdam Conference took place here 1945.

Poughkeepsie City in SE New York, USA, on the Hudson River, N of New York City; population (1990) 28,900. Products include chemicals, ball bearings, and cough drops. Vassar College is here. Settled by the Dutch 1687, Poughkeepsie was the temporary capital of New York 1717.

Poverty Bay Inlet on the E coast of North Island, New Zealand, on which the port of Gisborne stands. The English explorer Capt James Cook made his first landing here 1769.

Powys Unitary authority in central Wales, created 1996 from the former county of Powys; administrative headquarters Llandrindod Wells; population (1996) 123,600; area

5,179 sq km/1,999 sq mi. Features include the Brecon Beacons National Park, the Black Mountains, the rivers Wye and Severn, which both rise on Plynlimon in Dyfed, Lake Vyrnwy, an artificial reservoir supplying Liverpool and Birmingham. There is an alternative technology centre near Machynlleth (Celtica). Industries include agriculture, dairy cattle, sheep, and tourism. Welsh is spoken by 20% of the population.

Poznań (German *Posen*) Industrial city (machinery, aircraft, beer) in W Poland; population (1993) 590,000. Founded 970, it achieved town status 1253 and passed to Prussia 1793; it was restored to Poland 1919.

Pozsony Hungarian name for ◊Bratislava, capital of Hungary 1526–1784.

Pozzuoli Port in Campania, S Italy, W of Naples; population (1981) 71,000. It is shaken by some 25 earth-quakes a day, 60% of its buildings are uninhabitable, and an eventual major disaster seems inevitable.

Prague (Czech *Praha*) City and capital of the Czech Republic on the river Vltava; population (1993) 1,217,300. Industries include cars, aircraft, chemicals, paper and printing, clothing, brewing, and food processing. It was the capital of Czechoslovakia 1918–93.

Praia Port and capital of the Republic of Cape Verde, on the island of São Tiago (Santiago); population (1990) 61,700. Industries include fishing and shipping.

prairie The central North American plain, formerly grass-covered, extending over most of the region between the Rocky Mountains on the W and the Great Lakes and Ohio River on the E.

Prato Industrial city producing woollens in Tuscany, central Italy; population (1992) 166,100. The 12th-century cathedral has works of art by Donatello, Filippo Lippi, and Andrea della Robbia.

Prešov (Hungarian *Eperjes*) Town in E Slovak Republic, on the river Torysa, 36 km/22 mi N of Košice; population (1991) 87,800. Machinery is manufactured and agricultural produce traded from the surrounding area. The town was granted a royal charter in 1374 and has many Renaissance and Baroque houses and churches.

Pressburg German name of ◊Bratislava, the capital of the Slovak Republic.

Preston Industrial town (textiles, chemicals, electrical goods, aircraft, plastics, engineering), and administrative headquarters of Lancashire, NW England, on the river Ribble, 34 km/21 mi S of Lancaster; population (1991) 126,100. Oliver Cromwell defeated the Royalists at Preston 1648. It is the birthplace of Richard Arkwright, inventor of cotton-spinning machinery, and was a centre of the cotton industry in the 18th century.

Prestwick Town in South Ayrshire, SW Scotland; population (1991) 13,700. Industries include engineering and aerospace engineering. The international airport is linked with a free port.

Pretoria City in Gauteng Province, South Africa; administrative capital of the Union of South Africa from 1910 and capital of Transvaal Province 1860–1994; population (1991) 1,080,200. Industries include engineering, chemicals, iron, and steel. Founded 1855, it was named after Boer leader Andries Pretorius (1799–1853).

Preveza Port and department of ◊Epirus, Greece, at the entrance to the Gulf of Arta; area (department) 1,086 sq km/419 sq mi; population (1991) 58,900 (department). Preveza is the third largest town of the Epirus region. The main port for the Arta agricultural plain area, it trades in coal, oil, textiles, and agricultural products. The town was founded in the 3rd century BC.

Pribilof Islands Group of four islands in the Bering Sea, of volcanic origin, 320 km/200 mi SW of Bristol Bay, Alaska, USA. Named after Gerasim Pribilov, who reached them 1786, they were sold by Russia to the USA 1867 with Alaska, of which they form part. They were made a fur-seal reservation 1868.

Příbram Mining town in central Bohemia, the Czech Republic, 53 km/33 mi SW of Prague; population (1991) 36,900. Silver has been worked here since 1330; other metals now also mined are lead, zinc, barium, and antimony.

Primorye Territory of the Russian Federation, in SE Siberia, on the Sea of Japan; capital Vladivostok; area 165,900 sq km/64,079 sq mi; population (1985) 2,136,000. Timber and coal are produced.

Prince Albert City in Saskatchewan, Canada, on the North Saskatchewan River and the Canadian Pacific Railway, 160 km/100 mi N of Saskatoon; population (1991) 34,200. The self-proclaimed 'Gateway to the North', it is the administrative centre of the provincial government for the N areas, a terminus for transport and communication into the forest, lake, and mining region of the N, and a trading centre. It is 65 km/40 mi from the Prince Albert national park (area 3,875 sq km/1,496 sq mi). The site of earlier fur-trading posts, the city was founded as a Presbyterian mission by James Nisbet in 1866.

Prince Edward Island Province of E Canada
area 5,660 sq km/2,185 sq mi
capital Charlottetown

Prince Edward Island

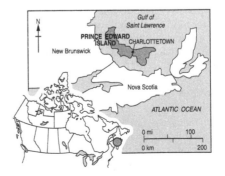

physical   Prince Edward Island National Park
features   Summerside Lobster Carnival
industries   potatoes, dairy products, lobsters, oysters, farm vehicles
population   (1995 est) 131,000
history   first recorded visit 1534 by the French explorer Jacques Cartier, who called it Isle St-Jean; settled by French; taken by British 1758; annexed to Nova Scotia 1763; separate colony 1769; renamed after Prince Edward of Kent, father of Queen Victoria 1798; settled by Scottish 1803; joined Confederation 1873.

Prince Rupert   Fishing port at the mouth of the Skeena River in British Columbia, Canada, on Kaien Island, W side of Tsimpsean peninsula; population (1991) 16,620.

Princeton   Borough in Mercer County, W central New Jersey, USA, 80 km/50 mi SW of New York; population (1990) 13,200. It is the seat of *Princeton University*, founded 1746 at Elizabethtown and moved to Princeton 1756. The borough was settled 1696 by Quakers and named Stony Brook; it was renamed 1724 to honour William III of Orange.

Princetown   Village on the W of Dartmoor, Devon, SW England, containing Dartmoor prison, opened 1809.

Prince William Sound   Channel in the Gulf of Alaska, extending 200 km/125 mi NW from Kayak Island. In March 1989 the oil tanker *Exxon Valdez* ran aground here, spilling 12 million gallons of crude oil in one of the world's greatest oil-pollution disasters.

Pripet   (Russian *Pripyat*) River in E Europe, a tributary of the river Dnieper, which it joins 80 km/50 mi above Kiev, Ukraine, after a course of about 800 km/500 mi. The *Pripet marshes* near Pinsk were of strategic importance in both World Wars.

Pristina   Capital of Kosovo autonomous province, S Serbia, Yugoslavia; population (1991) 108,000. Once capital of the medieval Serbian empire, it is now a trading centre.

Prizren   Town in Serbia, Yugoslavia, in the autonomous region of Kosovo. In the Middle Ages it was for a time the capital of the kingdom of Serbia. There are textile and glass industries, and the town is known for its silver filigree work and embroideries. It has a 14th-century church and an old fortress.

Prokopyevsk   Chief coal-mining city of the Kuzbas, in the Russian Federation, in Siberia, on the river Aba; population (1994) 266,000.

Provence-Alpes-Côte d'Azur   Region of SE France, comprising the *départements* of Alpes-de-Haute-Provence, Hautes-Alpes, Alpes-Maritimes, Bouches-du-Rhône, Var, and Vaucluse; area 31,400 sq km/12,123 sq mi; capital Marseille; population (1990) 4,257,900. The *Côte d'Azur*, on the Mediterranean, is a tourist centre. Provence was an independent kingdom in the 10th century, and the area still has its own language, Provençal.

Providence   Industrial seaport and capital of Rhode Island, USA, on Narragansett Bay and the Providence River,

27 mi/43 km from the Atlantic Ocean; the third largest city in New England; population (1992) 155,400. Providence was founded 1636, and was an important port in the West Indian trade and the American Revolution. It became the capital of the state 1900. The Rhode Island School of Design (1877) is here, one of the leading fine-arts colleges in the USA.

Provo   City in N central Utah, USA, on the Provo River, SE of Salt Lake City; seat of Utah County; population (1990) 86,800. Industries include iron and steel, food processing, and electronics. Brigham Young University is here. Provo was settled 1849 by Mormon missionaries.

Prudhoe Bay   Bay of the Arctic Ocean on the N coast (North Slope) of Alaska. An immense oil strike in the area in 1968 led to the construction of the 1,270-km/789-mi Trans-Alaska Pipeline, completed 1977, which carries oil from Prudhoe Bay to Valdez, on the S coast of Alaska.

Prut   River that rises in the Carpathian Mountains of SW Ukraine, and flows 900 km/565 mi to meet the Danube at Reni. For part of its course it follows the E frontier of Romania.

Przemyśl   Industrial city (timber, ceramics, flour milling, tanning, distilling, food processing, gas, engineering) in SE Poland; population (1991) 68,500.

Pskov   Industrial city (food processing, leather) in the Russian Federation, on the Velikaya River, SW of St Petersburg; population (1994) 207,000. Dating from 965, it was independent 1348–1510.

Puebla   Industrial city (textiles, sugar refining, metallurgy, hand-crafted pottery and tiles) and capital of Puebla state, S central Mexico; population (1990) 1,454,500. Founded 1535 as *Pueblo de los Angeles*, it was later renamed after General de Zaragoza, who defeated the French here 1862.

Puebla   State of central Mexico; area 33,919 sq km/13,096 sq mi; population (1995 est) 4,624,00. Its capital is Puebla. The main occupations are farming, producing maize, wheat, sugar-cane, and tobacco, and mining for gold, silver, and copper. There are many archaeological remains of the Pre-Columbian civilization.

Pueblo   City in S central Colorado, USA, on the Arkansas River, SE of Colorado Springs; population (1992) 98,600. Industries include steel, coal, lumber, livestock, and other agricultural products. Pueblo was laid out 1860.

Puerto de Santa María   Town in the province of Cádiz, S Spain, at the mouth of the river Guadalete, on the Atlantic Ocean; population (1995) 70,900. There is a large commerce in sherry. It has a Moorish castle and a baroque church.

Puertollano   Town in the province of Ciudad Real, central Spain; population (1995) 53,100. It is a busy refining and petrochemicals centre.

Puerto Rico   the Commonwealth of Easternmost island of the Greater Antilles, situated between the US Virgin Islands and the Dominican Republic
area   9,000 sq km/3,475 sq mi
capital   San Juan
towns and cities   ports Mayagüez, Ponce

features volcanic mountains run E–W; the islands of Vieques and Culebra belong to Puerto Rico
exports sugar, tobacco, rum, pineapples, textiles, plastics, chemicals, processed foods, vegetables, coffee
currency US dollar
population (1992 est) 3,336,000
language Spanish and English (official)
religion Roman Catholic
government under the constitution of 1952, similar to that of the USA, with a governor elected for four years, and a legislative assembly with a senate and house of representatives. Residents are US citizens, represented in US Congress by an elected Resident Commissioner with a seat in the House of Representatives
history visited 1493 by Columbus; annexed by Spain 1509; ceded to the USA after the Spanish-American War 1898; known as *Porto Rico* ('Rich Port') 1898–1932; achieved commonwealth status with local self-government 1952.

Puerto Sandino Major port on the Pacific W coast of Nicaragua, known as *Puerto Somoza* until 1979.

Puget Sound Inlet of the Pacific Ocean on the W coast of Washington State, USA.

Puglia (English *Apulia*) Region of Italy, the SE 'heel'; area 19,347 sq km/7,470 sq mi; capital Bari; population (1995) 4,075,800. Products include wheat, grapes, almonds, olives, and vegetables. The main industrial centre is Taranto.

Pula Commercial and naval port in W Croatia, on the Adriatic coast; population (1991) 62,400. A Roman naval base (*Colonia Pietas Julia*), it was seized by Venice 1148, passed to Austria 1815, to Italy 1919, to Yugoslavia 1947, and in 1991 became part of independent Croatia.

Pullman City in SE Washington, NW USA; population (1990) 23,500. It is a commercial and shipping centre for a grain, livestock, and poultry-producing region. The state college for science and agriculture is at Pullman and has played an important role in the development of new breeds and agricultural techniques for the NW region.

Pune formerly *Poona* City in Maharashtra, India; population (1991) 2,494,000. Products include chemicals, rice, sugar, cotton, paper, and jewellery. Industries include cars, trucks, scooters, and motorbikes; pumps, cables, machinery, arms and ammunitions, cutting tools, televisions, boilers, and generators.

Punjab State of NW India
area 50,400 sq km/19,454 sq mi
capital Chandigarh
towns and cities Amritsar, Jalandhar, Faridkot, Ludhiana
features mainly agricultural, crops chiefly under irrigation; longest life expectancy rates in India (59 for women, 64 for men); Harappa has ruins from the Indus Valley civilization 2500 to 1600 BC
industry wheat, rice, textiles, sewing machines, sugar
population (1994 est) 21,695,000
language Punjabi
religion 60% Sikh, 30% Hindu; there is friction between the two groups
history in 1919 unrest led to the Punjab riots.

Punjab State of NE Pakistan
area 205,344 sq km/79,263 sq mi
capital Chandigarh
features wheat cultivation (by irrigation)
population (1994) 21,695
language Punjabi, Urdu
religion Muslim.

Punta Arenas formerly *Magallanes* (Spanish 'sandy point') Seaport (trading in meat, wool, and oil) and sheep farming area in Chile, capital of Magallanes province, on Magellan Strait; population (1992) 113,700. It is the southernmost city in the world.

Purbeck, Isle of Peninsula in the county of Dorset, S England. Purbeck marble and china clay are obtained from the area, which includes Corfe Castle and Swanage.

Puri City in Orissa, E India; population (1991) 125,000. It has a statue of Jagganath or Vishnu, one of the three gods of Hinduism, dating from about 318, which is annually taken in procession on a large vehicle (hence the word 'juggernaut' used for a very large lorry). Devotees formerly threw themselves beneath its wheels.

Pusan or *Busan* Chief industrial port (textiles, rubber, salt, fishing) of Korea; population (1990) 3,797,600. It was invaded by the Japanese 1592 and opened to foreign trade 1883.

Puy-de-Dôme *Département* in the ◊Auvergne region of France; area 7,954 sq km/3,071 sq mi; population (1990) 598,900. Plateau and branches of the Cévennes and the Auvergne mountains occupy three-quarters of it, plain and valley the rest. The principal river is the Allier. The soil is, in general, light and poor; but the valley of Limagne is fertile throughout. The chief products are wheat, rye, flax, and fruit. The high pasturelands support large numbers of cattle. There are metalworking, aerospace, and motor-parts industries. The hot and cold mineral springs are a tourist attraction; among the most frequented are those of St-Myon and Châteldon. The principal towns are ◊Clermont-Ferrand (the capital), Ambert, Issoire, Riom, and Thiers.

Puy, Le See ◊Le Puy, a town in France.

Pwllheli Resort in Gwynedd, Wales, on Cardigan Bay; the Welsh National Party, Plaid Cymru, was founded here 1925.

Pyongyang Capital and industrial city (coal, iron, steel, textiles, chemicals) of North Korea; population (1984) 2,640,000.

Pyrenees (French *Pyrénées*; Spanish *Pirineos*) Mountain range in SW Europe between France and Spain; length about 435 km/270 mi; highest peak Aneto (French Néthon) 3,404 m/ 11,172 ft. Andorra is entirely within the range. Hydroelectric power has encouraged industrial development in the foothills.

Pyrénées-Atlantiques *Département* in the ◊Aquitaine region of France on the Spanish frontier; area 7,629 sq km/ 2,946 sq mi; population (1990) 578,800. The river Adour, fed by many mountain torrents, flows through the *département*. In the S are the peaks of the W Pyrénées, giving way to the wooded hills, the heathland, and the fertile valleys of the Basque country, and to the plateau of the NE. Wheat, maize, and vines are produced, and mules, horses, sheep, and pigs are raised, and there are agroindustries. Fishing is important, and there are hydroelectric installations, oil, natural gas, and a chemical waste treatment plant near Lacq. The tourist industry is well developed. The principal towns are ◊Pau (the capital), Bayonne, and Orolon.

Pyrénées, Hautes- *Département* in the Midi-Pyrénées region of France; see ◊Hautes-Pyrénées.

Pyrénées Orientales *Département* in the ◊Languedoc-Roussillon region of S France; area 4,086 sq km/1,578 sq mi; population (1990) 363,558. It comprises the W end of the Pyrenees, and is extremely mountainous, except for the plain of Roussillon in the E. The chief rivers are the Tet and the Tech. Vines, olives, vegetables, and fruit are grown, and livestock is raised. There are metallurgical and chemical industries, and a number of hydroelectric schemes. The principal towns are the departmental capital ◊Perpignan, Ceret, and Prades.

Qattara Depression Area of salt marsh in the Western Desert, Egypt, up to 134 m/440 ft 125 m/400 ft below sea level; area 20,000 sq km/7,500 sq mi. Its very soft sand, caused by seepage of groundwater, makes it virtually impassable to vehicles, and it protected the left flank of the Allied armies before and during the Second Battle of El Alamein 1942.

Qingdao or *Tsingtao* Industrial port (brewing) and summer resort in Shandong province, E China; population (1993) 2,240,000. It was a German colony 1898–1914. At the start of World War I it was captured by the Japanese who used it as a bargaining chip to force the Chinese to agree to their 'twenty-one demands' which were aimed at obtaining full control of Chinese economic and political affairs.

Qinghai *Chinghai*, or *Tsinghai* Province of NW China
area 721,000 sq km/278,378 sq mi
capital Xining
features mainly desert, with nomadic herders
industries oil, livestock, medical products
population (1990) 4,457,000; minorities include 900,000 Tibetans (mostly nomadic herders); Tibetan nationalists regard the province as being under colonial rule.

Qisarya Mediterranean port N of Tel Aviv-Yafo, Israel; there are underwater remains of Herod the Great's port of Caesarea.

QLD Abbreviation for ◊Queensland, an Australian state.

Qom or *Qum* Holy city of Shi'ite Muslims, in central Iran, 145 km/90 mi S of Tehran; population (1991) 681,000. The Islamic academy of Madresseh Faizieh 1920 became the headquarters of Ayatollah Khomeini.

Quai d'Orsay Part of the left bank of the river Seine in Paris, where the French Foreign Office and other government buildings are situated. The name has become synonymous with the Foreign Office itself.

Que. Abbreviation for ◊Quebec, a Canadian province.

Quebec or *Québec* Capital and industrial port (textiles, leather, timber, paper, printing, and publishing) of Quebec province, on the St Lawrence River, Canada; population (1991) 167,500, metropolitan area 645,600. A French colony 1608–1763, Quebec is a centre of French culture.

Quebec or *Québec* Province of E Canada
area 1,540,680 sq km/594,857 sq mi
capital Quebec
towns and cities Montréal, Laval, Sherbrooke, Verdun, Hull, Trois Rivières
features immense water-power resources (for example, the James Bay project)
industries iron, copper, gold, zinc, cereals, potatoes, paper, textiles, fish, maple syrup (70% of world's output)
population (1995 est) 7,134,000
language French (the only official language since 1974, although 17% speak English). Language laws 1989 prohibit the use of English on street signs
history known as New France 1534–1763; captured by the British and became province of Quebec 1763–90, Lower Canada 1791–1846, Canada East 1846–67; one of the original provinces 1867. In the 1960s nationalist feelings (despite existing safeguards for Quebec's French-derived civil law, customs, religion, and language) were encouraged by French president de Gaulle's exclamation '*Vive le Quebec libre*/Long live free Quebec' on a visit to the province, and led to the foundation of the Parti Québecois by René Lévesque 1968.

The Quebec Liberation Front (FLQ) separatists had conducted a bombing campaign in the 1960s and fomented an uprising 1970; Parti Québecois won power 1976; a referendum on 'sovereignty-association' (separation) was defeated 1980; however, a similar referendum, in 1995, was only narrowly rejected by 50.6% to 49.4%.

In 1982, when Canada severed its last legal ties with the UK, Quebec opposed the new Constitution Act as denying the province's claim to an absolute veto over constitutional change. The right of veto was proposed for all provinces of Canada 1987, but the agreement was not ratified by its 1990 deadline and support for Quebec's independence grew. In 1989 the Parti Québecois was defeated by the Liberal Party. Jacques Parizeau was succeeded as leader of the Parti Québecois by Lucien Bouchard Jan 1996.

Quebec

Quedlinburg Town in the *Land* of ◊Saxony-Anhalt, Germany, on the river Bode, on the NE edge of the Harz Mountains, 68 km/42 mi NW of Halle. Quedlinburg houses a research centre for plant biology, a horticultural industry, and manufactures machinery and chemicals. The town has many medieval buildings.

Queen Charlotte Islands Archipelago about 160 km/100 mi off the coast of British Columbia, W Canada, of which it forms part; area 9,790 sq km/3,780 sq mi; population 2,500. Graham and Moresby are the largest of about 150 islands. There are timber and fishing industries.

Queen Elizabeth Islands Group of islands in the Canadian Arctic, N of Lancaster and Viscount Melville Sounds. They include ◊Ellesmere, the northernmost island in the Canadian Arctic, Devon, Melville, Axel, Heiberg, Bathurst, Cornwallis, Prince Patrick, and the Ringnes Islands. They were named in 1954 after Queen Elizabeth II. There are virtually no indigenous inhabitants, but meteorological stations and Royal Canadian Mounted Police posts have been established in the area.

Queen Maud Land Region of Antarctica W of Enderby Land, between 20° W and 45° E longitude. It has been claimed by Norway since 1939.

Queens Borough and county at the W end of Long Island, New York City, USA; population (1996) 1,980,600. Queens is mainly residential.

Queen's County Former name (to 1920) of ◊Laois, a county in the Republic of Ireland.

Queensland State in NE Australia
area 1,727,200 sq km/666,872 sq mi
capital Brisbane
towns and cities Townsville, Toowoomba, Cairns
features Great Dividing Range, including Mount Bartle Frere 1,657 m/5,438 ft; Great Barrier Reef (collection of coral reefs and islands about 2,000 km/1,250 mi long, off the E coast); Gold Coast, 32 km/20 mi long, S of Brisbane; Mount Isa mining area; Sunshine Coast, a 100-km/60-mi stretch of coast N of Brisbane, between Rainbow Beach and Bribie

Queensland

Island, including the resorts of Noosa Heads, Coolum Beach, and Caloundra
industries sugar, pineapples, beef, cotton, wool, tobacco, copper, gold, silver, lead, zinc, coal, nickel, bauxite, uranium, natural gas
population (1994) 3,196,900
history part of New South Wales until 1859, when it became self-governing. In 1989 the ruling National Party was defeated after 32 years in power and replaced by the Labour Party, who maintained power in the 1992 elections.

Queenstown Former name (1849–1922) of ◊Cobh, a port in the Republic of Ireland.

Quemoy Island off the SE coast of China, and administered, along with the island of *Matsu*, by Taiwan. Quemoy: area 130 sq km/50 sq mi; population (1982) 57,847. Matsu: 44 sq km/17 sq mi; population (1982) 11,000. China claims Quemoy; the USA supported Taiwan until 1979, eight years after Taiwan had ceased to be a member of the United Nations. When the islands were shelled from the mainland 1960, the USA declared they would be defended if attacked. Since 1986 the Taiwanese government has encouraged the growth of tourism on Quemoy, and in 1992 ended 43 years of martial-law rule.

Querétaro State of central Mexico; area 11,769 sq km/4,544 sq mi; population (1995 est) 1,248,800. Its capital is Querétaro. The main occupations are farming, producing cereals and fruit, and mining for mercury and opals.

Quetta Summer resort and capital of Baluchistan, W Pakistan; population (1981) 281,000. It was linked to Shikarpur by a gas pipeline 1982.

Quezon City Former capital of the Philippines 1948–76, NE part of metropolitan ◊Manila (the present capital), on Luzon Island; population (1990) 1,166,800. It was named after the Philippines' first president, Manuel Luis Quezon (1878–1944).

Qufu or *Chufu* Town in Shandong province, China. Qufu was capital of the state of Lu during the Zhou dynasty (1066–221 BC). It is the birthplace of Kong Zi (Confucius) and the site of the Great Temple of Confucius. The tomb of Confucius is to the N of the temple.

Quiberon Peninsula and coastal town in Brittany, NW France; during the Seven Years' War, the British admiral Hawke defeated a French fleet (under the Marquis de Conflans) in Quiberon Bay 1759, wrecking French plans for an invasion of England and reasserting British command of the sea.

Quimper City in Brittany, NW France, on the river Odet; a centre for the manufacture of decorative pottery since the 16th century; population (1990) 62,500. There is a fine 15th-century Gothic cathedral.

Quincy City in E Massachusetts, NE USA, on Quincy Bay, 13 km/8 mi S of Boston; population (1990) 85,000. There are granite quarries. It was the birthplace of John Hancock, the first person to sign the Declaration of Independence in 1776, of John Adams, 2nd president of the USA, and of his son John Quincy Adams, 6th president of the USA. The first (horse-drawn) railroad in the USA was built here to haul granite.

Quintana Roo State of Mexico, on the ◊Yucatán Peninsula; area 50,350 sq km/19,440 sq mi; population (1995 est) 703,400. Its capital is Chetumal. The chief products are chicle and copra, and there is sponge and turtle fishing. Most of the inhabitants are descendents of Maya Indians, and there are important archaeological remains of the Pre-Columbian Mayan Empire.

Quito Capital and industrial city (textiles, chemicals, leather, gold, silver) of Ecuador, about 3,000 m/9,850 ft above sea level; population (1990) 1,101,000. It is on a plateau in the Andes, on the slopes of the volcano Pichincha, which last erupted 1666. It has a temperate climate all year round.

Qum Alternative spelling of ◊Qom, a city in Iran.

QwaQwa Former black homeland of South Africa in Orange Free State (now Free State).

Rabat Capital of Morocco, industrial port (cotton textiles, carpets, leather goods) on the Atlantic coast, 177 km/110 mi W of Fès; population (urban area, 1991) 519,000; Rabat-Salé 1,494,000. It is named after its original *ribat* or fortified monastery.

Rabaul Largest port of Papua New Guinea, on the volcanic island of New Britain, SW Pacific; one of the largest shipping centres for copra and coconut oil in the Pacific; population (1980) 14,954. It was destroyed by Allied bombing after its occupation by the Japanese in 1942, but was rebuilt.

Racibórz (German *Ratibor*) Industrial town in Katowice province, Poland, on the river Oder, 65 km/41 mi S of Opole; population (1990) 64,400. There are engineering, chemical, magnetite, and brewing industries. Until 1945 the town was part of German Upper Silesia; capital of a principality 1288–1532, and a duchy 1822–1918.

Racine City and port of entry in SW Wisconsin, USA, on the Root River where it flows into Lake Michigan; population (1992) 86,100. Industries include motor-vehicle parts, farm machinery, and wax products. It was founded 1834.

Radium Hill Mining site SW of Broken Hill, New South Wales, Australia, formerly a source of radium and uranium.

Radnorshire (Welsh *Sir Faesyfed*) Former border county of E Wales, included in new county of Powys 1974–96; now part of Powys unitary authority.

Radom Industrial city (flour-milling, brewing, tobacco, leather, bicycles, machinery; iron works) in Poland, 96 km/60 mi S of Warsaw; population (1993) 229,700. Radom became Austrian 1795, Russian 1825, and was returned to Poland 1919.

Ragusa Province of Italy in SE ◊Sicily; capital Ragusa; area 1,614 sq km/623 sq mi; population (1992) 290,700.

Ragusa Town in Sicily, Italy, 54 km/34 mi SW of Syracuse; there are textile industries; population (1981) 64,492. It stands over 450 m/1,500 ft above the river Ragusa, and there are ancient tombs in caves nearby.

Ragusa Italian name (to 1918) for the Croatian city of ◊Dubrovnik. Its English name was *Arrogosa*, from which the word 'argosy' is derived, because of the city's fame for its trading fleets while under Turkish rule in the 16th century.

Rainier, Mount Mountain in the ◊Cascade Range, Washington State, USA; 4,392 m/14,415 ft, crowned by 14 glaciers and carrying dense forests on its slopes. It is a quiescent volcano. Mount Rainier national park was dedicated 1899.

Rajasthan State of NW India
area 342,239 sq km/132,138 sq mi
capital Jaipur
features includes the larger part of the Thar Desert, where India's first nuclear test was carried out; in the SW is the Ranthambhor wildlife reserve, formerly the private hunting ground of the maharajahs of Jaipur, and rich in tiger, deer, antelope, wild boar, crocodile, and sloth bear
industries oilseed, cotton, sugar, asbestos, copper, textiles, cement, glass, gypsum, phosphate, silver
population (1994 est) 48,040,000
language Rajasthani, Hindi
religion 90% Hindu, 3% Muslim
history formed 1948; enlarged 1956.

Rajshahi Capital of Rajshahi region, W Bangladesh; population (1991) 299,700. It trades in timber and vegetable oil.

Raleigh Industrial city (food processing, electrical machinery, textiles) and capital of North Carolina, USA; population (1992) 220,500. The present site was named for the explorer Walter Raleigh, selected to be the state capital 1788, and laid out 1792.

Raleigh, Fort Site of the first English settlement in America, at the N end of Roanoke Island, North Carolina, USA, to which in 1585 English explorer Walter Raleigh sent 108 colonists from Plymouth, England, under his cousin Richard Grenville. In 1586 Francis Drake took the dissatisfied survivors back to England. The outline fortifications are preserved.

Ramat Gan Industrial city (textiles, food processing) in W Israel, NE of Tel Aviv; population (1992) 122,700. It was established 1921.

Rambouillet Town in the S of the forest of Rambouillet, SW of Paris, France; population (1990) 25,300. The former royal château is now the presidential summer residence. A breed of fine-fleeced sheep is named after the town.

Ramsgate Seaside resort, made popular by George IV, and cross-Channel port (ferry to Dunkirk, France and Ostend, Belgium) in the Isle of Thanet, Kent, SE England; population (1991) 37,900. There is a maritime museum. St Augustine is supposed to have landed here 597. The architect Pugin built his home here, and is buried in the church next door (St Augustine's). There is fishing and yachting.

Rance River in Brittany, NW France, rising in the *département* of Côtes-d'Armor, and flowing into the Gulf of St Malo. A dam built 1960–67 (with a lock for ships) uses the 13-m/44-ft tides to feed the world's first successful tidal power station.

Rand Shortened form of ◊Witwatersrand, a mountain ridge in Gauteng Province, South Africa.

Randers Seaport in Aarhus county, E Denmark, on the river Gudena. Randers has food-processing industries and manufactures agricultural machinery. There is a medieval monastery.

Randstad The main metropolitan region of the Netherlands, including the cities of ◊Amsterdam, The ◊Hague, ◊Rotterdam, and ◊Utrecht. The Randstad is an urbanized area forming a horseshoe-shaped zone around open countryside which is used for intensive agriculture.

Rangoon Former name (to 1989) of ◊Yangon, the capital of Myanmar (Burma).

Rantoul Town in E Illinois, USA, S of Chicago. It is a trading centre for agricultural products; population (1990) 17,200. Products include electronic equipment and motorcycle parts. It was settled 1854.

Rapallo Port and winter resort in Liguria, NW Italy, 24 km/15 mi SE of Genoa on the Gulf of Rapallo; population (1990 est) 30,000. Treaties were signed here 1920 (settling the common frontiers of Italy and Yugoslavia) and 1922 (cancelling German and Russian counterclaims for indemnities for World War I). German soldiers were also permitted to train in the USSR, in defiance of the Treaty of Versailles.

Rapa Nui Another name for ◊Easter Island, an island in the Pacific Ocean.

Rappahannock River in Virginia, USA, rising in the Blue Ridge Mountains; length 340 km/211 mi. It flows through Fredericksburg to Chesapeake Bay, parallel and to the S of the Potomac River. Some of the fiercest battles of the American Civil War took place along the Rappahannock and its tributary, the Rapidan.

Ras el Khaimah or *Ra's al Khaymah* Emirate on the Persian Gulf; area 1,690 sq km/652 sq mi; population (1985) 116,500. Products include oil, pharmaceuticals, and cement. It is one of the seven members of the United Arab Emirates.

Rastatt or *Rastadt* City in Baden-Württemberg, Germany, on the river Murg, 22 km W of Karlsruhe; population (1994) 222,300. Rastatt manufactures car parts, optical goods, televisions, and radios. The city has a Rococo palace and several old churches. The Treaty of Rastatt was signed here 1714 at the end of the War of the Spanish Succession.

Rathenow Town in the *Land* of ◊Brandenburg, Germany, on the river Havel, 72 km/45 mi W of Berlin; population (1996) 24,400. It manufactures optical and precision instruments and chemicals.

Rathlin Island Island off the N Irish coast, in Antrim; St Columba founded a church here in the 6th century, and in 1306 Robert the Bruce hid here after his defeat by the English at Methven.

Ratibor German name for ◊Racibórz, a town in Poland.

Ratisbon English name for the German city of ◊Regensburg.

Ratzeburg Town in Schleswig-Holstein, Germany, 24 km/ 15 mi S of Lübeck, and built partly on an island in Lake Ratzeburg; population (1994) 12,500. The town is a popular tourist resort, and has a Romanesque cathedral from 1154.

Ravenna Historical city and industrial port (petrochemical works) in Emilia-Romagna, Italy; population (1992) 137,100. It lies in a marshy plain and is known for its Byzantine churches with superb mosaics. Ravenna was a Roman port and naval station. It was capital of the W Roman emperors 404–93, of Theodoric the Great 493–526, and later of the Byzantine exarchs (bishops) 539–750. The British poet Byron lived for some months in Ravenna, home of Countess Guiccioli, during the years 1819–21.

Ravenna Province of N central Italy in E ◊Emilia-Romagna region; capital Ravenna; area 1,859 sq km/718 sq mi; population (1992) 350,300.

Ravensburg City in Baden-Württemberg, Germany, 116 km/72 mi SE of Stuttgart; population (1994) 260,000. Textiles and machinery are manufactured. The city has medieval towers and gates and is overlooked by the Veitsburg fortress, the birthplace of Henry the Lion.

Ravi River in the Indian subcontinent, a tributary of the ◊Indus. It rises in India, forms the boundary between India and Pakistan for some 110 km/70 mi, and enters Pakistan above Lahore, capital of Punjab province, on its 725-km/450-mi course. It is an important source of water for the Punjab irrigation canal system.

Rawalpindi City in Punjab province, Pakistan, in the foothills of the Himalayas; population (1981) 928,400. Industries include oil refining, iron, chemicals, and furniture.

Reading Industrial town (biscuits, brewing, boat building, engineering, printing, electronics) on the river Thames; administrative headquarters of Berkshire, England; it will become a unitary authority in April 1998; population (1994 est) 131,000. It is an agricultural and horticultural centre, and was extensively rebuilt after World War II. There is a 12th-century abbey where Henry I is buried.

Reading Industrial town (textiles, special steels) in E Pennsylvania, USA; population (1992) 79,000. Reading was laid out in 1748 and was an early iron- and steelmaking centre, connected by canal and rail to nearby anthracite mines.

Recife Industrial seaport (cotton textiles, sugar refining, fruit canning, flour milling) and naval base in Brazil; capital of Pernambuco state; population (1991) 1,335,700 (metropolitan area 2,921,700). It is situated at the mouth of the river Capibaribe, partly on an island and partly on a peninsula. It was founded 1504.

Recklinghausen Industrial city (coal, iron, chemicals, textiles, engineering) in North Rhine–Westphalia, Germany, 24 km/15 mi NW of Dortmund; population (1991) 126,000. It is said to have been founded by Charlemagne.

Redbridge Outer borough of NE Greater London. It includes the suburbs of Ilford, Wanstead, and Woodford, and parts of Chigwell and Dagenham

features takes its name from old Red Bridge over river Roding; Leper Hospital, founded about 1140, with 14th-century chapel and 18th-century almshouses; Valentines (1696); Friends Burial Ground, Wanstead; part of Epping Forest; Hainault Forest

industries light industry and manufacture of defence equipment

population (1991) 226,200

famous people William Penn, Richard Brinsley Sheridan, and Thomas Hood lived in Wanstead. Winston Churchill was member of Parliament for Woodford for 40 years.

Redcar and Cleveland Unitary authority in NE England created 1996 from part of the former county of Cleveland; administrative headquarters South Bank, Middlesbrough; population (1996) 144,000; area 240 sq km/93 sq mi. Europe's largest steel complex is at Redcar. Other industries include fabrics and chemicals. The area includes the North Yorkshire Moors.

Redditch Industrial town (needles, fishing tackle, springs, batteries, car and aircraft components, cycles, motorcycles, electrical equipment) in Hereford and Worcester, England; population (1991) 73,400. It was designated a new town 1964 to take Birmingham's overspill.

Redoubt, Mount Active volcanic peak rising to 3,140 m/ 10,197 ft, W of Cook inlet in S Alaska, USA. There were eruptions 1966 and 1989.

Red River or the *Red River of the South* Western tributary of the ◊Mississippi River 1,638 km/1,018 mi long; so called because of the reddish soil sediment it carries. The stretch that forms the Texas–Oklahoma border is called Tornado Alley because of the storms caused by the collision in spring of warm air from the Gulf of Mexico with cold fronts from the N. The largest city on the river is Shreveport, Louisiana.

Red River River in N Vietnam, 500 km/310 mi long, that flows into the Gulf of Tonkin. Its extensive delta is a main centre of population.

Red River of the North River in the USA and Canada; length 877 km/545 mi (770 km/440 mi in the USA). It rises in North Dakota and flows N, forming the boundary between Minnesota and North Dakota. It then flows through Manitoba, where it joins the Assiniboine River and flows into Lake Winnipeg.

Redruth Town in Cornwall, SW England, part of the combined town of ◊Camborne-Redruth.

Red Sea Submerged section of the Great ◊Rift Valley (2,000 km/1,200 mi long and up to 320 km/200 mi wide). Egypt, Sudan, Ethiopia, and Eritrea (in Africa) and Saudi Arabia (Asia) are on its shores.

Regensburg (English *Ratisbon*) City in Bavaria, Germany, on the river Danube at its confluence with the Regen, 100 km/63 mi NE of Munich; population (1993) 125,000. It has many medieval buildings, including a Gothic cathedral 1275–1530.

history Regensburg stands on the site of a Celtic settlement dating from 500 BC. It became the Roman *Castra Regina* AD 179, the capital of the Eastern Frankish Empire,

a free city 1245, and seat of the German *Diet* (parliament) 16th century–1806. It was included in Bavaria 1810.

Reggio di Calabria Industrial centre (farm machinery, olive oil, perfume) of Calabria, S Italy; population (1992) 177,600. It was founded by Greeks about 720 BC.

Reggio di Calabria Province of S Italy in S ◊Calabria region; capital Reggio di Calabria; area 3,185 sq km/1,230 sq mi; population (1992) 577,300.

Reggio nell'Emilia Chief city of the province of the same name in Emilia-Romagna region, N Italy; population (1992) 133,200. It was here in 1797 that the Congress of the cities of Emilia adopted the tricolour flag that was later to become the national flag of Italy.

Reggio nell'Emilia Province of N central Italy in central ◊Emilia-Romagna region; capital Reggio nell'Emilia; area 2,292 sq km/885 sq mi; population (1992) 421,700.

Regina Industrial city (oil refining, cement, steel, farm machinery, fertilizers), and capital of Saskatchewan, Canada; population (1991) 179,200. It was founded 1882 as Pile O'Bones, and renamed in honour of Queen Victoria of England.

Rehoboth Gebeit District of Namibia to the S of Windhoek; area 32,168 sq km/12,420 sq mi; chief town Rehoboth. The area is occupied by the Basters, a people of mixed European-Nama descent.

Reichenbach Town in the *Land* of ◊Saxony, Germany, 48 km/30 mi SW of Chemnitz, at the foot of the ◊Erzgebirge. Reichenbach has an important textile industry, and manufactures machinery and ceramics.

Reichenbach German name for ◊Dzierżoniów, a town in Poland.

Reichenberg German name for ◊Liberec, a town in the Czech Republic.

Reigate Town in Surrey, England, at the foot of the North Downs; population (1991 with Redhill) 47,600. With Redhill it forms a residential suburb of London.

Ré, Ile de French island off the shores of the *département* of Charente-Maritime, 10 km/6 mi W of La Rochelle; area 74 sq km/29 sq mi. It is level, with vineyards, early vegetables, orchards, cornfields, and oyster fisheries. Salt is collected from the salt marshes. St-Martin is the capital, fortified in the 17th century by Vauban. Since 1988, a 3-km/2-mi-long bridge has connected the island with the mainland. The Ile de Ré is a popular tourist destination, with a summer population (1994) of 100,000.

Reims (English *Rheims*) Capital of Champagne-Ardenne region, France; population (1990) 185,200. It is the centre of the champagne industry and has textile industries. It was known in Roman times as *Durocorturum*. From 987 all but six French kings were crowned here. Ceded to England 1420 under the Treaty of Troyes, it was retaken by Joan of Arc, who had Charles VII consecrated in the 13th-century cathedral. In World War II, the German High Command formally surrendered here to US general Eisenhower 7 May 1945.

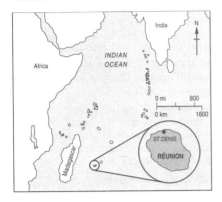

Réunion

Remagen Town in the Rhineland-Palatinate, Germany, on the left bank of the river Rhine, 25 km/15 mi SE of Bonn; population (1994) 16,300. Remagen is a tourist centre for the Middle Rhine.

Remscheid Industrial city in North Rhine–Westphalia, Germany, where stainless steel implements are manufactured; population (1991) 123,600.

Rendsburg City in Schleswig-Holstein, Germany, on the Kiel Canal, 40 km/25 mi W of Kiel; population (1994) 255,500. It has iron and steel and textile industries.

Renfrew Town on the Clyde, in Renfrewshire, Scotland, 8 km/5 mi NW of Glasgow; population (1991) 20,300. It was formerly the county town of Renfrewshire. Industries include the manufacture of steam generators and heavy equipment.

Renfrewshire Unitary authority in W central Scotland, bordering the Firth of Clyde area 261 sq km/101 sq mi; population (1996) 176,970; administrative headquarters Paisley. A former county, it was merged with the region of Strathclyde 1975–96 into Strathclyde Region. It is a major industrial area (engineering, computers, electronics, food and drink); agriculture is also important.

Rennes Industrial city (oil refining, chemicals, electronics, cars) and capital of Ille-et-Vilaine *département*, W France, at the confluence of the Ille and Vilaine, 56 km/35 mi SE of St Malo; population (1990) 203,500. It was the old capital of Brittany.

Reno City in Nevada, USA, known for gambling and easy divorces; population (1992) 139,900. Products include building materials and electronic equipment. Reno was settled 1858 and grew quickly with the discovery nearby of the Comstock Lode, a large gold and silver deposit. The transcontinental railroad reached Reno 1868.

Reşiţa Industrial town in W Romania, 73 km/46 mi SE of Timişoara. The town is situated at the foot of the S Carpathian Mountains. Metalworking is long-established in the region, and Reşiţa's iron- and steelworks uses local coal and ore.

Rethymnon (Greek *Rethimai*) Town and department in

◊Crete, Greece; population (1991) 69,300 (department). Its port is the outlet for produce from the surrounding agricultural area, and local industries include tanning, olive oil refining, and soap manufacturing. The town is surrounded by a Venetian wall, now in ruins, and a Venetian fort lies to the N.

Réunion formerly *Bourbon* French island of the Mascarenes group, in the Indian Ocean, 650 km/400 mi E of Madagascar and 180 km/110 mi SW of Mauritius
area 2,512 sq km/970 sq mi
capital St Denis
physical forested, rising in Piton de Neiges to 3,069 m/ 10,072 ft
features administers five uninhabited islands, also claimed by Madagascar
industries sugar, maize, vanilla, tobacco, rum
population (1995 est) 653,400
history explored by Portuguese (the first European visitors) 1513; annexed by Louis XIII of France 1642; overseas *département* of France 1946; overseas region 1972.

Reus Industrial city with an international airport in Cataluña, E Spain, 10 km/6 mi NW of Tarragona; population (1991) 87,700. Products include textiles, flowers, dried fruit, and vegetables. The architect Antonio Gaudí was born here.

Reutlingen City in Baden-Württemberg, Germany, 30 km/19 mi S of Stuttgart; population (1994) 270,000. The main industries are the manufacture of textiles, machinery, and leather, and the city is a centre for printing and publishing. It is sited on steep hill slopes, has old towers, walls, and houses, and a 13th-century Gothic church.

Reval Former name of the Estonian port of ◊Tallinn.

Reykjavík Capital (from 1918) and chief port of Iceland, on the SW coast; population (1994) 103,000. Fish processing is the main industry. Reykjavík is heated by underground mains fed by volcanic springs. It was a seat of Danish administration 1801–1918.

Rheims English version of ◊Reims, a city in France.

Rheingau District of ◊Hessen, Germany, on the right bank of the river Rhine, S of the Taunus Mountains, and extending from Rüdesheim to Wiesbaden. Many of the finest Rhine wines come from the region.

Rheinland-Pfalz German name for the ◊Rhineland-Palatinate region of Germany.

Rhine (German *Rhein*, French *Rhin*) European river rising in Switzerland and reaching the North Sea via Germany and the Netherlands; length 1,320 km/820 mi. Tributaries include the Moselle and the Ruhr. The Rhine is linked with the Mediterranean by the Rhine–Rhône Waterway, and with the Black Sea by the Rhine–Main–Danube Waterway.

Rhine and Marne Canal (French *Marne–Rhine Canal*) Canal in France, connecting the rivers ◊Rhine and ◊Marne, cut between 1838 and 1853. It is 360 km/224 mi long and runs from the Ill at Strasbourg to Vitry-le-François, crossing the rivers Meuse, Moselle, and Meurthe.

Rhineland-Palatinate (German *Rheinland-Pfalz*) Administrative region (German *Land*) of Germany
area 19,852 sq km/7,665 sq mi
capital Mainz
towns and cities Ludwigshafen, Koblenz, Trier, Worms
physical wooded mountain country, river valleys of Rhine and Moselle
industries wine (75% of German output), tobacco, chemicals, machinery, leather goods, pottery
population (1995) 3,983,300

Rhine–Rhône Canal Canal in France, uniting the two rivers after which it is named. It was cut between 1783 and 1834, and is nearly 350 km/217 mi long, running from the Saône, a tributary of the Rhône, to the Ill, near Strasbourg.

Rhin, Haut- *Département* in the Alsace region of France; see ◊Haut-Rhin.

Rhode Island Smallest state of the USA, in New England; nicknamed Little Rhody/Ocean State
area 3,100 sq km/1,197 sq mi
capital Providence
towns and cities Cranston, Newport, Woonsocket
physical Block Island; 640 km/400 mi of coastline
features Narragansett Bay, one of the greatest sailing centres in the world, home of America's Cup yacht races; Newport, with colonial waterfront and 19th-century mansions, the summer 'cottages' of the wealthiest families in America, including the Breakers (1895), built by Cornelius Vanderbilt II, Marble House (1892), and Chateau-sur-Mer (1851–52); Hammersmith Farm, the childhood summer home of Jacqueline Onassis Kennedy; the Friends Meeting House (1700), and the Touro Synagogue (1763), in Newport, both the oldest in the USA; Slater Mill historic site, Pawtucket; state capitol with marble dome, Providence; Narragansett Native American monument at Sprague Park; Charlestown, with Native American church and burial ground; US Naval War College and Museum, Newport; Brown University (1764); Rhode Island School of Design

Rhine

(1877); International Lawn Tennis Hall of Fame and Tennis Museum, Newport
industries electronics, machine tools, jewellery, textiles, silverware, rubber, and plastics. Agriculture is limited by the rocky terrain but is important in rural areas, the main crops being apples and potatoes. Rhode Island red hens were developed here from the 19th century
population (1995) 989,800
famous people George M Cohan, Anne Hutchinson, Matthew C Perry, Oliver Hazard Perry, Gilbert Stuart, Roger Williams
history founded 1636 by Roger Williams, exiled from Massachusetts Bay colony for religious dissent; one of the original 13 states, it joined the union 1790. The principle trends in the 19th century were industrialization, immigration, and urbanization. Rhode Island is highly industrialized and the second most densely populated state; it suffers from high unemployment, low-wage manufacturing industries, and susceptibility to recessions.

Rhodes (Greek *Ródhos*) Greek island, largest of the Dodecanese, in the E Aegean Sea
area 1,412 sq km/545 sq mi
capital Rhodes
industries grapes, olives
population (1981) 88,000
history settled by Greeks about 1000 BC; the Colossus of Rhodes (fell 224 BC) was one of the Seven Wonders of the World; held by the Knights Hospitallers of St John 1306–1522; taken from Turkish rule by the Italian occupation 1912; ceded to Greece 1947.

Rhodesia Former name of Zambia (Northern Rhodesia) and Zimbabwe (Southern Rhodesia), in S Africa.

Rhodope Mountains Range of mountains on the frontier between Greece and Bulgaria, rising to 2,925 m/9,497 ft at Musala.

Rhondda Industrial town in Rhonnda Cynon Taff, Wales; population (1991) 59,900. Light industries have replaced coal mining, formerly the main source of employment in the area. The closure of the Maerdy mine (opened 1875) in 1990 ended mining in the valley; Rhondda's coal powered 90% of the Royal Navy's ships in World War I. The Rhondda Heritage Park recreates a 1920s-style mining village for visitors.

Rhondda Cynon Taff Unitary authority in S Wales created 1996 from part of the former county of Mid Glamorgan; administrative headquarters Clydach Vale; population (1996) 232,600; area 440 sq km/170 sq mi. This was formerly an important coal mining area. The Royal Mint is at Llantrisant.

Rhône River of S Europe; length 810 km/500 mi. It rises in Switzerland and flows through Lake Geneva to Lyon in France, where at its confluence with the Saône the upper limit of navigation is reached. The river turns due S, passes Vienne and Avignon, and takes in the Isère and other tributaries. Near Arles it divides into the *Grand* and *Petit Rhône*, flowing respectively SE and SW into the Mediterranean W of Marseille. Here it forms a two-armed delta; the area between the tributaries is the marshy region known as the ◊Camargue.

Rhône *Département* in the ◊Rhône-Alpes region of France; area 3,215 sq km/1,241 sq mi; population (1990) 1,509,500. The river Rhône and its tributaries the Saône, Azergues, and Gier flow through the *département*. Moderate crops of cereals and potatoes grow on the rocky soil. The *département* produces wines (Juliénas, Côte-Rôtie, Moulin à-Vent). There are metallurgical, chemical, and textile industries around Lyon. The principal towns are ◊Lyon (the capital) and Villefranche.

Rhône-Alpes Region of E France in the upper reaches of the Rhône; area 43,698 sq km/16,872 sq mi; population (1992) 5,350,800. It consists of the *départements* of Ain, Ardèche, Drôme, Isère, Loire, Rhône, Savoie, and Haute-Savoie. The capital is Lyon. There are several wine-producing areas, including Chenas, Fleurie, and Beaujolais. Industrial products include chemicals, textiles, and motor vehicles.

Rhyl Seaside holiday resort in Denbighshire, N Wales; population (1991) 24,900. Products include furniture; tourism is important.

RI Abbreviation for the state of ◊Rhode Island, USA.

Ribble River in N England; length 120 km/75 mi. From its source in the Pennine hills, North Yorkshire, it flows S and SW past Preston, Lancashire, to join the Irish Sea.

Ribe Capital of Ribe county, on the W coast of Denmark. The river Ribe flows through the town, and dykes have been built to protect the town from flooding. The oldest city in Denmark, Ribe was an important port during the Middle Ages, and part of the medieval town still surrounds the cathedral.

Richborough (Roman *Rutupiae*) Former port in Kent, England; now marooned in salt marshes, it was militarily reactivated in both world wars.

Richland City in SE Washington, USA, on the Columbia River, NW of Walla Walla; population (1990) 33,300. It is a centre for research for the US Department of Energy and a major producer of plutonium for nuclear weapons. It grew as a residential community for employees of the Hanford Engineer Works that helped to develop the atomic bomb from 1943.

Richmond City and port in California, USA, N of Oakland on the E coast of San Francisco Bay; population (1990) 87,400. It is a manufacturing centre (aerospace components), with oil refineries, a motor-vehicle assembly plant, and shipyards.

Richmond Town in North Yorkshire, England; population (1991) 7,900. Its theatre was built 1788.

Richmond Industrial city and port on the James River and capital of Virginia, USA; population (1992) 202,300. It is a major tobacco market and distribution, commercial, and financial centre of the surrounding region. Its diversified manufactures include tobacco products, chemicals, paper and printing, and textiles. The first permanent colonial American settlement was established here 1637. Richmond was the capital of the Confederacy 1861–65, and several Civil War battles were fought nearby.

Richmond-upon-Thames Outer borough of SW Greater London, the only London borough with land on both sides of the river Thames. It includes the districts of Kew, Teddington, ◊Twickenham, and Hampton.

features Royal Botanic gardens, Kew; Richmond Park, 1,000 hectares/2470 acres, the largest urban park in Britain, enclosed by Charles I for hunting, with ancient oaks, deer, and White Lodge, home of the Royal Ballet School; Maids of Honour Row, Richmond (1724), terrace of four houses for maids of honour attending the princess of Wales; early 18th-century houses around Richmond green; gatehouse of former Richmond Palace; Richmond Theatre (1899); Garrick's Villa, Hampton, acquired by David Garrick 1754 and altered by Robert Adam; Old Court House, Hampton, last home of Christopher Wren; Faraday House, Hampton, home of Michael Faraday; Hampton Court Palace, begun by Thomas Wolsey in 1514; Bushy Park, acquired by Wolsey 1514, containing Bushey House, built 1665 and remodelled c. 1720, which now houses the National Physical Laboratory; highest tidal point of river Thames at Teddington; Ham House, Petersham (1610), with 17th-century garden; Twickenham Rugby football ground; Eel Pie Island, favourite for boating parties; Barnes Common; 18th- and 19th-century Barnes terrace, facing river Thames; Kneller Hall, Twickenham, is the home of the Royal Military School of Music
population (1991) 160,700
famous people Virginia and Leonard Woolf set up Hogarth Press here. Thomas Traherne and R D Blackmore lived in Teddington; Henry Fielding in Barnes.

Rideau Canal Canal in E Ontario, Canada; length 203 km/126 mi. It connects Ottawa with Kingston on Lake Ontario, by way of the Rideau River and lake, and by connections with the Mud Lake and Cataraqui River. The canal was built between 1826 and 1832. Never of great economic significance, it is used mainly by pleasure boats and tourists.

Riding from the old Norse 'thrithjungs' One of the three former administrative divisions of the county of Yorkshire until 1974: West Riding, North Riding, and East Riding; in 1974 they were reorganized into the counties of North Yorkshire and Humberside, and the metropolitan counties of West Yorkshire and South Yorkshire. In 1996 Humberside was abolished. The new unitary authority of the East Riding of Yorkshire was created, and the City and County of York was created from the S part of North Yorkshire, around York.

Riesa Town in the *Land* of ◊Saxony, Germany, on the river Elbe, 40 km/25 mi NW of Dresden. It is a river port, and has industries manufacturing steel, chemical, glass, tyres, and food.

Rieti Province of W central Italy in NE ◊Lazio region; capital Rieti (population (1990) 44,500); area 2,748 sq km/ 1,061 sq mi; population (1992) 146,100. The town of Ricti is on the river Velino.

Rif, Er Mountain range about 290 km/180 mi long on the Mediterranean seaboard of Morocco.

Rift Valley, Great Volcanic valley formed 10–20 million years ago by a crack in the Earth's crust and running about

8,000 km/5,000 mi from the Jordan Valley through the Red Sea to central Mozambique in SE Africa. It is marked by a series of lakes, including Lake Turkana (formerly Lake Rudolf), and volcanoes, such as Mount Kilimanjaro.

Riga   Capital and port of Latvia; population (1995) 840,000. Industries include engineering, brewing, food processing, and the manufacture of textiles and chipboard.

Rigi   Mountain in central Switzerland, between lakes Lauerz, Lucerne, and Zug; height 1,800 m/5,908 ft. The cogwheel train to the top was the first in Europe.

Rijeka   (Italian *Fiume*) Industrial port (oil refining, distilling, paper, tobacco, chemicals) in Croatia; population (1991) 168,000. It has changed hands many times and, after being seized by the Italian nationalist Gabriele D'Annunzio 1919, was annexed by Italy 1924. It was ceded back to Yugoslavia 1949; in 1991 it became part of newly independent Croatia.

Rimini   Industrial port (pasta, footwear, textiles, furniture) and holiday resort in Emilia-Romagna, Italy; population (1992) 129,900. Its name in Roman times was *Ariminum*, and it was the terminus of the Flaminian Way from Rome. In World War II it formed the E strongpoint of the German 'Gothic' defence line and was badly damaged in the severe fighting Sept 1944, when it was taken by the Allies.

Rineanna   Irish name of Shannon Airport, County Clare, in the Republic of Ireland.

Rio de Janeiro   Port and resort in E Brazil; population (1991) 5,480,800 (metropolitan area 10,389,400). Sugar Loaf Mountain stands at the entrance to the harbour. Rio was the capital of Brazil 1763–1960. The city is the capital of the state of Rio de Janeiro, which has a population of 13,267,100 (1987 est).

Río de Oro   Former district in the S of the province of Spanish Sahara. See ◊Western Sahara.

Rio Grande   River rising in the Rocky Mountains in S Colorado, USA, and flowing S to the Gulf of Mexico, where it is reduced to a trickle by irrigation demands on its upper reaches; length 3,058 km/1,900 mi. Its last 2,400 km/1,500 mi form the US-Mexican border (Mexican name *Río Bravo del Norte*).

Rio Grande do Norte   State of NE Brazil; area 53,000 sq km/20,460 sq mi; population (1991) 2,415,600. Its capital is Natal. Industries include agriculture and textiles; there is offshore oil.

Rio Grande do Sul   Most southerly state of Brazil, on the frontier with Argentina and Uruguay; area 282,184 sq km/108,993 sq mi; population (1991) 9,138,700. Its capital is Pôrto Alegre. Industries include agriculture and cattle, food processing, and textiles.

Rioja, La   See ◊La Rioja, a region of Spain.

Riom   Town on the river Ambène, in the Puy-de-Dôme *département* of central France. It was the scene in World War II of the 'war guilt' trials of several prominent Frenchmen by the Vichy government Feb–April 1942, including the former prime ministers Blum and Daladier.

Río Muni   The mainland portion of Equatorial Guinea.

Río Tinto   Town in Andalusia, Spain; population (1983) 8,400. Its copper mines, first exploited by the Phoenicians, are now almost worked out.

Ripon   City and market town in North Yorkshire, England, on the river Ure; population (1991) 13,800. There is a cathedral 1154–1520; and the nearby 12th-century ruins of Fountains Abbey are among the finest monastic ruins in Europe.

Riva del Garda   Town on Lake Garda, Italy, where the Prix Italia broadcasting festival has been held since 1948.

Riverina   District of New South Wales, Australia, between the Lachlan and Murray rivers, through which runs the Murrumbidgee. On fertile land, artificially irrigated from the three rivers, wool, wheat, and fruit are produced.

Riverside   City in California, USA, on the Santa Ana River, E of Los Angeles; population (1992) 238,600. It was founded 1870. It is the centre of a citrus-growing district and has a citrus research station; the seedless orange was developed at Riverside 1873.

Riviera   The Mediterranean coast of France and Italy from Marseille to La Spezia. The most exclusive stretch of the Riviera, with the finest climate, is the ◊Côte d'Azur, from Menton to St Tropez, which includes Monaco.

Riyadh   (Arabic *Ar Riyād*) Capital of Saudi Arabia and of the Central Province, formerly the sultanate of Nejd, in an oasis, connected by rail with Dammam on the Arabian Gulf; population (1994) 1,500,000.

Roanne   French town in the *département* of Loire, 75 km/47 mi NW of St-Etienne, on the river Loire and the Roanne canal; population (1990) 80,000. There are spinning and weaving mills.

Roanoke   (Native American 'shell money') Industrial city (railway repairs, chemicals, steel goods, furniture, textiles) in Virginia, USA, on the Roanoke River; population (1992) 96,800. It was settled 1740, chartered as Big Lick 1834 and renamed 1882. it was a small village until 1881 when the repair shops of the Virginia Railway were set up here, after which it developed rapidly.

Roanoke   River of Virginia and North Carolina, USA, formed by the Dan and Staunton rivers; length over 700 km/435 mi. It rises W of Roanoke in the Appalachian Mountains and flows across the Appalachian valley southeastwards into North Carolina, reaching the sea at the W end of Albemarle Sound, a large inlet on the coast of North Carolina.

Robben Island   Island in Table Bay, Cape Town, South Africa. It was used by the South African government to house political prisoners. Nelson Mandela was imprisoned here 1964–82.

Rochdale   Industrial town (textiles, machinery, asbestos) in Greater Manchester, England, on the river Roch 16 km/10 mi NE of Manchester; population (1994 est) 138,000. It was formerly an important cotton-spinning town. The so-called Rochdale Pioneers founded the first Co-operative Society in England, in Toad Lane, Rochdale, 1844. The singer Gracie Fields was born here and a theatre is named after her.

Rochefort Industrial port (metal goods, machinery) in W France, SE of La Rochelle and 15 km/9 mi from the mouth of the river Charente; population (1990) 26,900. The port dates from 1666 and it was from here that Napoleon embarked for Plymouth on the *Bellerophon* on his way to final exile 1815.

Rochelle, La See ◊La Rochelle, a port in W France.

Rochester Commercial centre with dairy and food-processing industries in Minnesota, USA; population (1992) 73,900. Rochester is the home of the Mayo Clinic, part of a medical centre established 1889. The community was settled 1854 and named for Rochester, New York.

Rochester Industrial city in New York, USA, on the Genesee River, S of Lake Ontario; population (1992) 234,200. Its manufactured products include photographic equipment and optical and other precision instruments. It was the birthplace of the Xerox copier, and the world headquarters of the Eastman Kodak Company are here. It was first settled 1812.

Rochester upon Medway City in Kent, England, on the Medway estuary; population (1991) 24,000. It will join with Gillingham to form the Medway Towns unitary authority in April 1998. It was a Roman town, *Durobrivae*. It has a 12th-century Norman castle keep (the largest in England), a 12th–15th-century cathedral, and many timbered buildings. The Dickens Centre 1982 commemorates the town's links with the novelist Charles Dickens, whose home was at Gad's Hill.

Rock River in Wisconsin and Illinois, USA; length 460 km/286 mi. It rises W of Fond du Lac in SE Wisconsin, and flows S and SW through Rockford and Rock Falls to the Mississippi River near Rock Island in NW Illinois. Its valley is an important industrial area and has small hydropower plants.

Rockall British islet in the Atlantic, 24 m/80 ft across and 22 m/65 ft high, part of the Hatton-Rockall bank, and 370 km/230 mi W of North Uist in the Hebrides. The bank is part of a fragment of Greenland that broke away 60 million years ago. It is in a potentially rich oil/gas area. A party of British marines landed 1955 formally to annex Rockall, but Denmark, Iceland, and Ireland challenge Britain's claims for mineral, oil, and fishing rights. The *Rockall Trough* between Rockall and Ireland, 250 km/155 mi wide and up to 3,000 m/10,000 ft deep, forms an ideal marine laboratory.

Rockford City in N Illinois, USA, on the Rock River, NW of Chicago; population (1992) 142,000. Industries include automotive parts, furniture, machine tools, and food products. Rockford was founded 1834.

Rockhampton Port in E Queensland, Australia, on the Fitzroy River; population (1994) 62,300. It is the centre of a beef-producing area.

Rock Hill City in N central South Carolina, USA, S of Charlotte, North Carolina; population (1990) 41,600. Industries include chemicals, textiles, and paper products. The town was established 1851.

Rock Island City in NW Illinois, USA, on the Mississippi River, W of Chicago; population (1990) 40,600. Industries include rubber and electronics. A US government arsenal is located here. The town was founded 1835.

Rocky Mountains or *Rockies* Largest North American mountain system. It extends from the junction with the Mexican plateau, N through the W central states of the USA, through Canada to the Alaskan border, and then forms part of the Continental Divide, which separates rivers draining into the Atlantic or Arctic oceans from those flowing toward the Pacific Ocean. Mount Elbert is the highest peak, 4,400 m/14,433 ft. Some geographers consider the Yukon and Alaska ranges part of the system, making the highest point Mount McKinley (Denali) 6,194 m/20,320 ft.

Ródhos Greek name for the island of ◊Rhodes.

Roermond Town in the province of ◊Limburg, Netherlands, on the river Maas (see ◊Meuse), 45 km/28 mi NE of Maastricht; population (1996) 43,800. The chief industries are the manufacture of cotton and woollen goods, tobacco, and dyeing. There is some fine carving in the 13th-century Romanesque Munsterkerk (minster).

Roeselare (French *Roulers*) Textile town in West Flanders province, NW Belgium; population (1993 est) 53,500. It was a major German base in World War I.

Rogers Pass Mountain pass in British Columbia, Canada, by which the Canadian Pacific Railway and the Trans-Canada Highway cross the Selkirk Mountains range of the Columbia Mountains; altitude 1,327 m/4,355 ft. It lies in the Glacier national park and is subject to severe avalanches.

Romagna Area of Italy on the Adriatic coast, under papal rule 1278–1860 and now part of the region of ◊Emilia-Romagna.

Roman Industrial town in W Romania, at the confluence of the rivers Moldavia and Siret, 55 km/34 mi SW of Iaşi; population (1993) 97,000. The main products are iron and steel, machinery, textiles, chemicals, and processed food. Coal and iron are mined nearby.

Romans-sur-Isère French town in the *département* of Drôme; population (1990) 60,000. It is situated on the river Isère, 18 km/11 mi NE of Valence. Romans has a 12th–13th-century church. The town is a tanning and leatherworking centre.

Rome Province of W central Italy in central ◊Lazio region; capital Rome; area 5,335 sq km/2,060 sq mi; population (1992) 3,766,100.

Rome (Italian *Roma*) Capital of Italy and of Lazio region, on the river Tiber, 27 km/17 mi from the Tyrrhenian Sea; population (1992) 2,723,300. Rome has few industries but it is an important cultural, road, and rail centre. East of the river are the seven hills on which Rome was originally built; to the west are the quarter of Trastevere, the residential quarters of the Prati, and the Vatican. Remains of the ancient city include the Colosseum, the Forum, and the Pantheon. The many churches of different periods include the five greater or patriarchal basilicas. The Vatican Palace, which adjoins St Peter's (San Pietro), the largest church in the world, is the residence of the pope. The city has numerous museums, including the vast papal collections (dating from the 15th century) of the Vatican, the Lateran museum, the Capitol, and the Thermae. The Sistine Chapel, with frescoes by Michelangelo, lies within the Vatican.

Rome City in central New York State, USA, on the Mohawk River, NW of Albany; population (1990) 44,400. Construction of the Erie Canal began here 1817.

Romney Marsh Stretch of drained marshland on the Kent coast, SE England, between Hythe and Rye. The seaward point is Dungeness. Romney Marsh was reclaimed in Roman times. *New Romney*, formed by the amalgamation of Romney, one of the original Cinque Ports, with Littlestone and Greatstone, is now more than a mile from the sea.

Romsey Market town in Hampshire, S England; population (1990 est) 14,700. Nearby Broadlands was the seat of Earl Mountbatten and Lord Palmerston.

Roncesvalles Village of N Spain, in the Pyrenees 8 km/5 mi S of the French border, the scene of the defeat of the rearguard of Charlemagne's army under Roland, who with the 12 peers of France was killed 778.

Ronda Town in the province of Málaga, S Spain; population (1995) 34,800. It stands on the edge of a rocky plateau, and is divided in two by a gorge 160 m/525 ft deep. Industries include horses, leather goods, and wine.

Rondônia State in NW Brazil; the centre of Amazonian tin and gold mining and of experiments in agricultural colonization; area 243,044 sq km/93,876 sq mi; population (1991) 1,132,700. The state is mainly rainforest. Its principal products are rubber and brazil nuts. Known as the Federal Territory of *Guaporé* until 1956, it became a state 1981.

Ronse (French *Renaix*) Town in the province of East Flanders, Belgium, 37 km/23 mi S of Ghent. It manufactures cotton and woollen goods, silk, thread, hats, and shoes. The church of St Hermes dates from the 11th century.

Roodepoort-Maraisburg Goldmining town in Gauteng Province, South Africa, 15 km/9 mi W of Johannesburg, at an altitude of 1,745 m/5,725 ft; population (1992) 163,000. Leander Starr Jameson and his followers surrendered here 1896 after an attempt to overthrow the government.

Roraima, Mount Mountain peak and plateau in the ◊Pacaraima mountain range in South America, rising to 2,810 m/9,222 ft on the Brazil–Guyana–Venezuela frontier.

Rosario Industrial river port (sugar refining, meat packing, maté processing) in Santa Fé province, Argentina, 280

km/175 mi NW of Buenos Aires, on the river Paraná; population (metropolitan area, 1992 est) 1,157,400. It was founded 1725.

Roscoff Port in N Brittany, France, with ferry links to Plymouth in England and to Cork in the Republic of Ireland; population (1982) 4,000.

Roscommon (originally Ros-Comain, 'wood around a monastery') County of the Republic of Ireland, in the province of Connacht; county town Roscommon; area 2,460 sq km/949 sq mi; population (1996 est) 51,900. It has rich pastures and is bounded on the E by the river Shannon, with lakes (Gara, Key, Allen) and bogs.

Roseau formerly *Charlotte Town* Capital of Dominica, West Indies, on the SW coast of the island; population (1981) 20,000.

Roseires, Er Port at the head of navigation of the Blue Nile in Sudan. A hydroelectric scheme here, together with one at Sennar, provides the country with 87% of its electrical power.

Rosenheim Industrial city in Bavaria, Germany, on the river Inn, 53 km/33 mi SE of Munich; population (1994) 58,600. Rosenheim has electronics, engineering, sports clothes, and shoe manufacturing industries.

Roskilde Port at the S end of Roskilde Fjord, Zealand, Denmark; population (1990) 49,100. It was the capital of the country from the 10th century until 1443.

Roskilde County in E Sjaelland, Denmark; area 890 sq km/344 sq mi; population (1990) 216,000. Largely urbanized, it adjoins the city of Copenhagen, which also influences its economic activity. The town of Roskilde, a former ancient capital of Denmark, lies at the head of Roskilde Bay.

Ross and Cromarty Former county of Scotland. In 1975 Lewis, in the Outer ◊Hebrides, became part of the ◊Western Isles. The mainland area was included in Highland Region to 1996; it is now part of the Highland unitary authority.

Ross Dependency All the Antarctic islands and territories between 160° E and 150° W longitude and S of 60° S latitude; it includes Edward VII Land, Ross Sea and its islands, and parts of Victoria Land. It is claimed by New Zealand.

Ross Island Either of two islands in Antarctica:
Ross Island in the Weddell Sea, discovered 1903 by the Swedish explorer Nils Nordenskjöld, area about 3,885 sq km/1,500 sq mi;
Ross Island in the Ross Sea, discovered 1841 by the British explorer James Ross, area about 6,475 sq km/2,500 sq mi, with the research stations Scott Base (New Zealand) and McMurdo (USA). Mount Erebus (3,794 m/12,520 ft) is the world's southernmost active volcano; its lake of molten lava may provide a window on the magma beneath the Earth's crust that fuels volcanoes.

Rosslare Port in County Wexford, Republic of Ireland, 15 km/9 mi SE of Wexford; population (1986) 700. It was founded by the English 1210 and has been the Irish terminus of the ferry route from Fishguard from 1906.

Ross Sea Antarctic inlet of the S Pacific. See also ◊Ross Dependency and ◊Ross Island.

Rostock Industrial port (electronics, fish processing, ship repair) in the *Land* of Mecklenburg–West Pomerania, Germany, on the river Warnow 13 km/8 mi S of the Baltic; population (1993) 239,700.

Rostov-na-Donu Industrial port (shipbuilding, tobacco, cars, locomotives, textiles) in the SW Russian Federation, capital of Rostov region, on the river Don, 23 km/14 mi E of the Sea of Azov; population (1994) 1,023,000. Rostov dates from 1761 and is linked by river and canal with Volgograd on the river Volga.

Rosyth Naval base and dockyard used for nuclear submarine refits, in Fife, Scotland, built 1909 on the N shore of the Firth of Forth. Its population was affected by defence cuts 1994. Decommissioned *Polaris* nuclear submarines are being stored here until underground storage facilities are ready in 2012.

Rota Port and naval base, 57 km/35 mi NW of Cádiz, Spain; population (1991) 27,100.

Rothenburg Town in Bavaria, Germany, 65 km/40 mi W of Nürnberg; population (1978) 13,000. It is known for its medieval buildings, churches, and walls.

Rotherham Industrial town (pottery, glass, iron and steel, brassware, machinery, coal) in South Yorkshire, England, on the river Don, NE of Sheffield; population (1994 est) 154,000.

Rotherhithe Tunnel Road tunnel extending 1,481 m/ 4,860 ft under the river Thames E of Wapping, London, connecting Rotherhithe with Shadwell. It was built 1904–08 to a design by Maurice Fitzmaurice (1861–1924). The top of the tunnel is 14.6 m/48 ft below the Trinity high-water mark to allow for the passage of large ships.

Rotorua Town with medicinal hot springs and other volcanic activity in North Island, New Zealand, near Lake Rotorua; population (1993) 54,200.

Rotterdam Industrial port in the Rhine-Maas delta of the Netherlands; the biggest oil-refining centre in the world, and one of its foremost ocean cargo ports. Other industries include brewing, distilling, shipbuilding, sugar and petroleum refining, margarine, and tobacco. It is linked by canal 1866–90 with the North Sea; population (1994) 598,500.

Roubaix Town in Nord *département*, N France, adjacent to Lille; population (1990) 98,200. It is a major centre of French woollen textile production.

Rouen Industrial port (cotton textiles, electronics, distilling, oil refining) on the river Seine, in Seine-Maritime *département*, central N France; population (1990) 105,500. Rouen was the capital of ◊Normandy from 912. Lost by King John 1204, it returned briefly to English possession 1419–49; Joan of Arc was burned in the square 1431. The novelist G Flaubert was born here, and the hospital where his father was chief surgeon is now a Flaubert museum.

Rouge River of SE Michigan, USA; length 95 km/60 mi. It rises in Oakland County, and flows 50 km/31 mi S and E through Dearborn and Detroit to the Detroit River at River Rouge City. The River Rouge Ford motor plant, with steelworks, is on its banks.

Roulers French name of ◊Roeselare, a town in Belgium.

Rovaniemi Capital of Lappi province, N Finland, and chief town of Finnish Lapland, situated just S of the Arctic Circle; population (1992) 34,300. After World War II the town was rebuilt by the architect Alvar Aalto, who laid out the main streets in the form of a reindeer's antlers.

Rovigo Province of NE Italy in SE ◊Veneto region; capital Rovigo (population (1990) 52,400); area 1,805 sq km/697 sq mi; population (1992) 247,600.

Roxburgh Former border county of Scotland, included 1975–96 in Borders Region; now part of Scottish Borders unitary authority.

RSFSR Abbreviation for ◊Russian Soviet Federal Socialist Republic, a republic of the former Soviet Union.

Ruahine Mountain range in North Island, New Zealand. It stretches NE from the Manawater Gorge to the headwaters of the Ngaruro River and lies within the 900 sq km/347 sq mi Ruahine State Forest Park designated 1976. The highest point is Mangaweka, 1,733 m/5,686 ft.

Ruanda Part of the former Belgian territory of Ruanda-Urundi until it achieved independence as Rwanda, a country in central Africa.

Ruapehu, Mount Volcano in New Zealand, SW of Lake Taupo; the highest peak in North Island, 2,797 m/9,175 ft.

Rub'al Khali (Arabic 'empty quarter') Vast sandy desert in S Saudi Arabia; area 647,500 sq km/250,000 sq mi. The British explorer Bertram Thomas (1892–1950) was the first European to cross it 1930–31.

Ruda Śląska Town in Silesia, Poland, with metallurgical industries, created 1959 by a merger of Ruda and Nowy Bytom; population (1989) 170,000. Silesia's oldest mine is nearby.

Rüdesheim Town in Hessen, Germany, 25 km/15 mi SW of Wiesbaden; population (1994) 10,300. It stands on the right bank of the river Rhine, opposite Bingen, and is in the region known as the Rheingau. The area produces wine and attracts tourists.

Rudolf, Lake Former name (to 1979) of Lake ◊Turkana in E Africa.

Rudolstadt Town in the *Land* of ◊Thuringia, Germany, in the Saale Valley, and lying at the NE edge of the Thuringian Forest, 56 km/35 mi SW of Gera. Porcelain and electrical equipment are manufactured.

Rugby Market town and railway junction in Warwickshire, England; population (1991) 61,100. Rugby School 1567 established its reputation under headmaster Thomas Arnold; it was described in Thomas Hughes' semi-autobiographical classic *Tom Brown's Schooldays*. Rugby football originated here. Industries include engineering and cement.

Rügen Baltic island in the state of Mecklenburg–West Pomerania, Germany; area 927 sq km/358 sq mi. It is a holiday centre, linked by causeway to the mainland; chief town Bergen, main port Sassnitz. As well as tourism, there is agriculture and fishing, and chalk is mined. Rügen was annexed by Denmark 1168, Pomerania 1325, Sweden 1648, and Prussia 1815.

Ruhr River in Germany; it rises in the Rothaargebirge mountains and flows W to join the Rhine at Duisburg. The *Ruhr Valley* (228 km/142 mi), a metropolitan industrial area (petrochemicals, cars, iron and steel at Duisburg and Dortmund), was formerly a coal-mining centre.

Rum or *Rhum* Island of the Inner Hebrides, Scotland, area 110 sq km/42 sq mi, a nature reserve from 1957. Askival is 810 m/2,658 ft high.

Rumania Alternative spelling of Romania.

Rumeila Oilfield straddling the frontier between Iraq and Kuwait. Kuwait's extraction of oil from this field was a contributory factor leading up to the Iraqi invasion of 1991 and the subsequent Gulf War 1992.

Rum Jungle Uranium-mining centre in the NW of Northern Territory, Australia.

Runcorn Industrial town (chemicals) in Cheshire, NW England, 24 km/15 mi up the Mersey estuary from Liverpool; population (1991) 64,200. Designated a new town 1964, it has received Merseyside overspill. There are chemical and brewing industries.

Rupert's Land Area of N Canada, of which Prince Rupert was the first governor. Granted to the Hudson's Bay Company 1670, it was later split among Quebec, Ontario, Manitoba, and the Northwest Territories.

Ruse (anglicized name *Ruschuk*) Danube port in Bulgaria, linked by rail and road bridge with Giurgiu in Romania; population (1991) 210,000.

Rushmore, Mount Mountain in the Black Hills, South Dakota, USA; height 1,890 m/6,203 ft. On its granite face are carved giant portrait heads of presidents George Washington, Thomas Jefferson, Abraham Lincoln, and Theodore Roosevelt. The sculptor was Gutzon Borglum, and he began the carving 1930.

Russia Originally the prerevolutionary Russian Empire (until 1917), now accurately restricted to the Russian Federation.

Russian Far East Geographical, not administrative, division of Asiatic Russia, on the Pacific coast. It includes the Amur, Lower Amur, Kamchatka, and Sakhalin regions, and Khabarovsk and Maritime territories.

Russian Soviet Federal Socialist Republic (RSFSR) The largest republic of the former Soviet Union; it became independent as the Russian Federation 1991.

Ruthenia or *Carpathian Ukraine* Region of central Europe, on the S slopes of the Carpathian Mountains, home of the Ruthenes or Russniaks. Dominated by Hungary from the 10th century, it was part of Austria-Hungary until World War I. In 1918 it was divided between Czechoslovakia,

Poland, and Romania; independent for a single day in 1938, it was immediately occupied by Hungary, captured by the USSR 1944 and incorporated 1945–47 (as the Transcarpathian Region) into Ukraine Republic, which became independent as Ukraine 1991.

Rutland Unitary authority in central England, formerly the smallest English county, part of ◊Leicestershire 1974–97; administrative headquarters Oakham; population (1997) 34,600; area 394 sq km/152 sq mi. Industries include engineering, cement, plastics, and clothing.

Ruwenzori Range Mountain range on the frontier between the Democratic Republic of Congo (formerly Zaire) and Uganda, rising to 5,119 m/16,794 ft at Mount Stanley. They are also known as the 'Mountains of the Moon'.

Ryazan Industrial city (agricultural machinery, leather, shoes) dating from the 13th century, capital of Ryazan region, W Russian Federation, on the river Oka SE of Moscow; population (1994) 526,000.

Rybinsk Port and industrial city (engineering) in the NW Russian Federation, on the river Volga, NE of Moscow; population (1994) 249,000. In 1984 it was renamed *Andropov*, commemorating the death that year of the president of the USSR. It reverted to its former name March 1989.

Rybnik Industrial town in Katowice province, SW Poland, near the Czech border and 48 km/30 mi SW of Katowice; population (1990) 144,000. There are coal mines and ironworks, and machine tools are manufactured. The town stands on the river Ruda, a tributary of the Oder.

Ryde English resort on the NE coast of the Isle of Wight, on the Solent opposite Portsmouth, with which there is ferry and hovercraft connection; population (1991) 20,500.

Rye Town in East Sussex, England; population (1991) 3,700. It was formerly a flourishing port (and one of the Cinque Ports), but silt washed down by the river Rother has left it 3 km/2 mi inland.

Ryukyu Islands Southernmost island group of Japan, stretching towards Taiwan and including Okinawa, Miyako, and Ishigaki
area 2,254 sq km/870 sq mi
capital Naha, on Okinawa
features 73 islands, some uninhabited; subject to typhoons
industries sugar, pineapples, fish
population (1985) 1,179,000
history originally an independent kingdom; ruled by China from the late 14th century until seized by Japan 1609 and controlled by the Satsuma feudal lords until 1868, when the Japanese government took over. Chinese claims to the islands were relinquished 1895. In World War II the islands were taken by the USA 1945 (see under ◊Okinawa); northernmost group, Oshima, restored to Japan 1953, the rest 1972.

Rzeszów Capital of Rzeszów province, SE Poland, on the river Wisłok, a tributary of the San, 145 km/90 mi E of Kraków; population (1990) 150,800. Industries include food processing, metallurgy, and machinery.

SA Abbreviation for ◊South Australia, an Australian state.

Saale River in E Germany; length 364 km/226 mi. It rises in the Fichtelgebirge and flows N past Jena and Halle to join the river ◊Elbe 26 km/16 mi SE of Magdeburg. The Saale is navigable for 160 km/100 mi to Naumburg.

Saalfeld Town in the *Land* of ◊Thuringia, Germany, on the river Saale, 58 km/36 mi SW of Gera; population (1996) 32,700. The district has iron-ore mines (silver was mined here in the 16th century), and there are machine-tool, textile, and electrical industries. Saalfeld was the capital of the Duchy of Saxe-Saalfeld 1680–1735. The town has a 13th-century friary (now a museum), a 14th-century church, and a 16th-century town hall.

Saar (French *Sarre*) River in W Europe; it rises in the Vosges Mountains in France, and flows 240 km/149 mi N to join the river Moselle in Germany. Its valley has many vineyards.

Saarbrücken City on the river Saar, and capital of the *Land* of Saarland, Germany; population (1991) 361,600. It is situated on a large coalfield, and is an industrial centre (engineering, optical equipment). It has been the capital of Saarland since 1919.

Saarland (French *Sarre*) Administrative region (German *Land*) of Germany
area 2,570 sq km/992 sq mi
capital Saarbrücken
features one-third forest; crossed NW–S by the river Saar
industries cereals and other crops; cattle, pigs, poultry. Former flourishing coal and steel industries survive only by government subsidy
population (1995) 1,084,400
history in 1919 the Saar district was administered by France under the auspices of the League of Nations; a plebiscite returned it to Germany 1935; Hitler gave it the name Saarbrücken. Part of the French zone of occupation 1945, it was included in the economic union with France 1947. It was returned to Germany 1957.

Sabac Town in Serbia, Yugoslavia, on the river Sava, the principal town of the province of Macva. It is a road and rail junction, and a river port which trades in agricultural produce. It produces heavy chemicals.

Sabadell City in the province of Barcelona, NE Spain, 16 km/10 mi N of Barcelona city; population (1995) 188,400. Industries include textiles, paper, agricultural produce, and oil.

Sabah Self-governing state of the federation of Malaysia, occupying NE Borneo, forming (with Sarawak) East Malaysia
area 73,613 sq km/28,415 sq mi
capital Kota Kinabalu (formerly Jesselton)
physical chiefly mountainous (highest peak Mount Kinabalu 4,098 m/13,450 ft) and forested
industries hardwoods (25% of the world's supplies), rubber, fish, cocoa, palm oil, copper, copra, and hemp
population (1990) 1,736,900, of which the Kadazans form the largest ethnic group at 30%; also included are 250,000 immigrants from Indonesia and the Philippines
language Malay (official) and English
religion Sunni Muslim and Christian (the Kadazans, among whom there is unrest about increasing Muslim dominance)
government consists of a constitutional head of state with a chief minister, cabinet, and legislative assembly
history in 1877–78 the sultan of Sulu made concessions to the North Borneo Company, which was eventually consolidated with Labuan as a British colony 1946, and became the state of Sabah within Malaysia 1963. The Philippines advanced territorial claims on Sabah 1962 and 1968 on the grounds that the original cession by the sultan was illegal, Spain having then been sovereign in the area.

Sachsen German form of ◊Saxony, a former kingdom and state of Germany.

Sacramento Industrial port and capital (since 1854) of California, USA, 130 km/80 mi NE of San Francisco; population (1992) 382,800; metropolitan area (1992) 1,563,000. It stands on the Sacramento River, which flows 615 km/382 mi through Sacramento Valley to San Francisco Bay. Industries include the manufacture of detergents and jet aircraft and food processing, including almonds, peaches, and pears. The city was founded as Fort Sutter 1848.

Sacramento River in N California, USA; length 615 km/382 mi. It rises close to Mount Shasta in the Cascade range, and flows SE to Sacramento, through the W part of the Sierra Nevada, and eventually into San Francisco Bay. The Shasta Dam on the upper Sacramento and the Keswick Dam provide flood control, power, and irrigation; the irrigated agricultural land is very productive. The river is navigable 412 km/256 mi to Red Bluff.

Safi Atlantic port in Tensift province, NW Morocco; population (1990) 398,000. It exports phosphates and has fertilizer plants, sardine factories, and boat-building yards.

Sagamihara City on the island of Honshu, Japan, with a large silkworm industry; population (1994) 552,000.

Sagan German name for Żagań, a town in Poland.

Sagarmatha Nepalese name for Mount ◊Everest, 'the Goddess of the Universe', and the official name of the 1,240-sq-km/476-sq-mi Himalayan national park established 1976.

Saginaw City and port in E Michigan, USA, on the Saginaw River, near Lake Huron, NW of Flint; population (1992) 70,700. Industries include automotive parts, metal products, salt, coal, and sugar beet. Saginaw developed as a fur-trading post from 1816 and was a lumber centre until the late 19th century.

Saguenay River in Quebec, Canada, used for hydro-electric power as it flows from Lac St Jean SE to the St Lawrence estuary; length 765 km/475 mi.

Sagunto Town in the province of Valencia, W Spain, on the river Palancia, 29 km/18 mi N of Valencia city; population (1995) 57,700. It has a large orange trade, steelworks, and exports Teruel iron ore from its port, 5 km/3 mi away on the Mediterranean coast. There are remains of a Roman theatre and circus, and it is overlooked by a citadel of Iberian, Roman, and Moorish origins.

Sahara Largest desert in the world, occupying 9,055,000 sq km/3,500,000 sq mi of N Africa from the Atlantic to the Nile, covering: W Egypt; part of W Sudan; large parts of Mauritania, Mali, Niger, and Chad; and S parts of Morocco, Algeria, Tunisia, and Libya. Small areas in Algeria and Tunisia are below sea level, but it is mainly a plateau with a central mountain system, including the Ahaggar Mountains in Algeria, the Aïr Massif in Niger, and the Tibesti Massif in Chad, of which the highest peak is Emi Koussi, 3,415 m/ 11,208 ft. The area of the Sahara expanded by 650,000 sq km/251,000 sq mi 1940–90, but reafforestation is being attempted in certain areas.

Sahel (Arabic *sahil* 'coast') Marginal area to the S of the Sahara, from Senegal to Somalia, which experiences desert-like conditions during periods of low rainfall. The desertification is partly due to climatic fluctuations but has also been caused by the pressures of a rapidly expanding population, which have led to overgrazing and the destruction of trees and scrub for fuelwood. In recent years many famines have taken place in the area.

Saida (ancient *Sidon*) Port in Lebanon; population (1991 est) 100,000. It stands at the end of the Trans-Arabian oil pipeline from Saudi Arabia. Sidon was the chief city of Phoenicia, a bitter rival of Tyre about 1400–701 BC, when it was conquered by Sennacherib. Later a Roman city, it was taken by the Arabs AD 637 and fought over during the Crusades.

Saigon Former name (to 1976) of ◊Ho Chi Minh City, Vietnam.

St Albans City in Hertfordshire, England, on the river Ver, 40 km/25 mi NW of London; population (1991) 80,400. There are the ruins of the Roman city of Verulamium on Watling Street. A Benedictine abbey was founded 793 in honour of St Alban, and it became a cathedral 1878. The Royal National Rose Society headquarters and gardens are in St Albans.

St-Amand-les-Eaux French town in the *département* of Nord, 35 km/22 mi SE of Lille, on the river Scarpe; population (1990) 16,900. St-Amand has been a centre of porcelain manufacture since the 18th century, and now also has metallurgical and textile industries. There are hot sulphur and calcium springs nearby, and a nature park in the vicinity is a resort area for the urban population of the Nord region.

St Andrews Town in Fife, Scotland, 19 km/12 mi SE of Dundee; population (1991) 11,100. Its university (1411) is the oldest in Scotland, and the Royal and Ancient Club (1754) is the ruling body of golf.

St Anthony, Falls of Waterfalls on the Mississippi River at Minneapolis, Minnesota, USA. The height of the falls is 15 m/50 ft. Harnessed by dams, the falls are today bypassed by the Upper St Anthony Lock, which enables river traffic to reach industrial areas of Minneapolis.

St Augustine Port and holiday resort in Florida, USA; population (1990) 11,700. Founded by the Spanish 1565, and the oldest permanent colonial settlement in the USA, it was burned by the English sea captain Francis Drake 1586 and

ceded to the USA 1821. It includes the oldest house (late 16th century) and oldest masonry fort (Castillo de San Marcos 1672) in the continental USA.

St Austell Market town in Cornwall, England, 22 km/ 14 mi NE of Truro; population (1991) 21,600 (with Fowey, with which it is administered). It is the centre of the china clay industry, which supplies the Staffordshire potteries.

St Bernard Passes Passes through the ◊Alps (the *Great St Bernard Pass* and *Little St Bernard Pass*).

St-Brieuc French town on St-Brieuc Bay in the *département* of Côtes d'Armor, 59 km/37 mi SW of St-Malo; population (1990) 48,000. It has a 13th–14th-century cathedral and many old houses; tourism is important. There are also iron- and steelworks. Agricultural implements and shoes are manufactured.

St-Cloud Town in the Ile de France region, France; population (1990) 28,700. The château of St-Cloud, linked with Marie Antoinette and Napoleon, was demolished 1781, but the park remains. It is the site of the Sèvres porcelain factory.

St David's (Welsh *Tyddewi*) Small city in Pembrokeshire, Wales. Its cathedral, founded by St David, was rebuilt 1180–1522.

St-Denis Industrial town, a N suburb of Paris, France; population (1990) 90,800. The French philosopher and theologian Peter Abelard was a monk at the 12th-century Gothic abbey, which contains many tombs of French kings.

St-Dizier French town in the *département* of Haute-Marne, on the river Marne. It has metallurgical industries and a brewery. It was besieged by the Holy Roman emperor Charles V in 1544, and was the scene of a victory of Napoleon in 1814.

St Elias Mountains Mountain range on the Alaska–Canada border. Its highest peak, Mount Logan 6,050 m/ 19,850 ft, is Canada's highest mountain.

Saint-Étienne City in S central France, capital of Loire *département*, Rhônes-Alpes region; population (1990) 201,600. Industries include the manufacture of aircraft engines, electronics, and chemicals, and it is the site of a school of mining, established 1816. In World War I, it was one of the principal French arsenals.

St Gall (German *Sankt Gallen*) Town in NE Switzerland; population (1990) 73,400. Industries include natural and synthetic textiles. It was founded in the 7th century by the Irish missionary St Gall, and the Benedictine abbey library has many medieval manuscripts.

St George's Port and capital of Grenada, on the SW coast; population (1989) 35,700. It was founded 1650 by the French.

St George's Channel Stretch of water between SW Wales and SE Ireland, linking the Irish Sea with the Atlantic Ocean. It is 160 km/100 mi long and 80–150 km/50–90 mi wide. It is also the name of a channel between New Britain and New Ireland, Papua New Guinea.

St-Germain-en-Laye Residential suburb on the W outskirts of ◊Paris, France, 100 m/328 ft above the river Seine, in the *département* of Yvelines; population (1990) 41,600. It is beside the forest of St-Germain, and is a popular tourist resort. The 16th-century royal château, incorporating part of an older structure, was occupied by James II of England from his banishment 1689 until his death 1701.

St Gotthard Pass Pass through the Swiss ◊Alps, at an altitude of 2,000 m/6,500 ft. A rail tunnel is planned, running 48 km/30 mi through the St Gotthard massif, to be built by 2010.

St Helena British island in the S Atlantic, 1,900 km/1,200 mi W of Africa, area 122 sq km/47 sq mi; population (1992) 5,700. Its capital is Jamestown, and it exports fish and timber. Ascension and Tristan da Cunha are dependencies.

St Helena

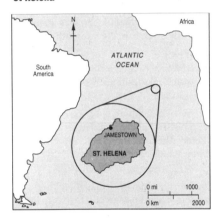

St Helens Town in Merseyside, England, 19 km/12 mi NE of Liverpool, and connected to the river Mersey by canal; population (1991) 175,300. It is a leading centre for the manufacture of sheet glass. Other industries include bricks and tiles, engineering, pharmaceuticals, and brewing.

St Helens, Mount Volcanic mountain in Washington State, USA. When it erupted 1980 after being quiescent since 1857, it devastated an area of 600 sq km/230 sq mi and its height was reduced from 2,950 m/9,682 ft to 2,560 m/8,402 ft.

St Helier Resort and capital of Jersey, Channel Islands; population (1991) 28,100. The 'States of Jersey', the island legislature, sits here in the *salle des états*.

St Ives Fishing port and resort in Cornwall; population (1991) 10,100. Its artists' colony, founded by Walter Sickert and James Whistler, later included Naum Gabo, Barbara Hepworth (a museum and sculpture gardens commemorate her), and Ben Nicholson. A branch of the Tate Gallery opened here 1993, displaying works of art from the Tate's collection by artists connected with St Ives.

Saint John Largest city of New Brunswick, Canada, on the Saint John River; population (1991) 75,000, metropolitan area 125,000. It is a fishing port and has shipbuilding, timber, fish processing, petroleum, refining, and textile indus-

tries. Founded by the French as Saint-Jean 1635, it was taken by the British 1758.

Saint John River in Maine, USA, and New Brunswick, E Canada, flowing into the Bay of Fundy at Saint John; length 673 km/420 mi. It flows from Maine to New Brunswick, forming the boundary between the USA for 130 km/81 mi. The principal tributaries are the Alagash, Aroostook, and Oromocto on the right bank, and the St Francis, Madawaska, Tobique, and Salmon on the left bank. The river produces hydroelectric power for New Brunswick.

St John's Port and capital of Antigua and Barbuda, on the NW coast of Antigua; population (1992) 38,000. It exports rum, cotton, and sugar.

St John's Capital and chief port of Newfoundland, Canada; population (1991) 95,800, metropolitan area 171,900. The main industry is fish processing; other products include textiles, fishing equipment, furniture, and machinery. The city was founded by the English navigator Humphrey Gilbert 1582.

St Johns River in Florida, USA; length 456 km/285 mi. Rising in Brevard County in E Florida, it flows N and at Jacksonville (24 km/15 mi from its mouth) turns E before reaching the Atlantic Ocean. It forms several large lakes. Much of the surrounding area consists of swamp, pine groves, or farmland. The river is used for commercial and recreational boats.

St John's Wood Residential suburb of NW London. It is the site of Lord's cricket ground, headquarters of the Marylebone Cricket Club (MCC).

St Joseph City in NW Missouri, USA, on the Missouri River, NW of Kansas City; population (1992) 71,900. Industries include food processing, dairy products, metal products, concrete, and steel. In the mid-1800s, it served as the E terminus for the Pony Express.

St Kilda Group of three mountainous islands, the most westerly of the Outer ◊Hebrides, 200 km/124 mi W of the Scottish mainland; area 16 sq km/6 sq mi. They were populated from prehistory until 1930, and now form a nature reserve belonging to the National Trust of Scotland. They have the world's largest colony of gannets, the oldest and largest colony of fulmars in the British Isles, and a large population of puffins. St Kilda is a World Heritage site.

St Lawrence River in E North America. From ports on the ◊Great Lakes it forms, with linking canals (which also give great hydroelectric capacity to the river), the St Lawrence Seaway for ocean-going ships, ending in the Gulf of St Lawrence. It is 745 mi/1,200 km long and is icebound for four months each year.

St Lawrence Seaway Deep-water channel and transport corridor in North America, connecting the St Lawrence River with the Great Lakes, allowing ocean-going vessels to navigate from the Atlantic Ocean to Lake Superior (3,769 km/2,342 mi). It was opened for navigation by the USA and Canada in 1959. Strictly the seaway is the section from

Montréal to Lake Ontario, but the name is applied generally to the whole system from the Atlantic to the Great Lakes. There are 78 ports on the seaway, which remains navigable for moderate-sized vessels for about 250 days a year.

St Leonards Seaside town near ◊Hastings, England.

St-Lô Market town in Normandy, France, on the river Vire; population (1990) 22,800. In World War II it was almost entirely destroyed 10–18 July 1944, when US forces captured it from the Germans.

St Louis City in Missouri, USA, on the Mississippi River; population (1992) 383,700; metropolitan area (1992) 2,519,000. Its products include aerospace equipment, aircraft, vehicles, chemicals, electrical goods, steel, and beer. Its central US location makes it a warehousing and distribution centre and a hub of rail, truck, and airline transport. Founded as a French trading post 1764, it passed to the USA 1803 under the Louisiana Purchase.

St-Malo Seaport and resort in the Ille-et-Vilaine *département*, W France, on the Rance estuary; population (1990) 49,300. It took its name from the Welshman Maclou, who was bishop here in about 640.

St Mary's River in Ontario, Canada and Michigan, USA; length 110 km/70 mi. It connects Lake Superior with Lake Huron, and flows through the twin ports of Sault Sainte Marie in Michigan and Ontario.

St Michael's Mount Island in Mount's Bay, Cornwall, England, linked to the mainland by a causeway.

St-Nazaire Industrial seaport in the Loire-Atlantique *département*, Pays de la Loire region, France; population (1990) 66,100. It stands at the mouth of the river Loire and in World War II was used as a German submarine base.

St-Omer Town in Pas-de-Calais *département*, France, 42 km/26 mi SE of Calais; population (1985) 15,500. In World War I it was the site of British general headquarters 1914–16.

Saintonge Former province of France, corresponding to part of the present *département* of Charente-Maritime. It was united to the French crown in 1372. The capital was Saintes.

St Paul Capital and industrial city of Minnesota, USA, adjacent to ◊Minneapolis; population (1992) 268,300. Industries include electronics, publishing and printing, chemicals, refined petroleum, machinery, and processed food. St Paul was settled 1838 on the site of Fort Snelling. It became the territorial capital 1849 and the state capital 1858.

St Peter Port Only town of Guernsey, Channel Islands; population (1991) 16,650.

St Petersburg Capital of the St Petersburg region, Russian Federation, at the head of the Gulf of Finland; population (1994) 4,883,000. Industries include shipbuilding, machinery, chemicals, and textiles. It was founded by Peter the Great 1703; played a crucial role in the October Revolution 1917; and was subject to a major German blockade 1941–44 during which nearly a million people died. It was renamed *Petrograd* 1914 and was called *Leningrad* 1924–91, when its original name was restored. Built on a low and swampy site, St Petersburg is split up by the mouths of the river Neva, which connects it with Lake Ladoga. The climate is severe. The city became a seaport when it was linked with the Baltic by a ship canal built 1875–93. It is also linked by canal and river with the Caspian and Black seas, and in 1975 a seaway connection was completed via lakes Onega and Ladoga with the White Sea near Belomorsk, allowing naval forces to reach the Barents Sea free of NATO surveillance.

St Petersburg Seaside resort and industrial city (space technology) in W Florida, USA; population (1992) 235,300. It lies across Tampa Bay from ◊Tampa. St Petersburg was first settled 1876, laid out 1884, and grew as a resort with the arrival of the railroad in the late 1880s.

St Pierre and Miquelon Territorial dependency of France, eight small islands off the S coast of Newfoundland, Canada
area St Pierre group 26 sq km/10 sq mi; Miquelon-Langlade group 216 sq km/83 sq mi
capital St Pierre
features the last surviving remnant of France's North American empire
industries fish
products cod; silver fox and mink are bred
currency French franc
population (1990) 6,400
language French
religion Roman Catholic
government French-appointed commissioner and elected local council; one representative in the National Assembly in France
history settled 17th century by Breton and Basque fisherfolk; French territory 1816–1976; overseas *département* until 1985; violent protests 1989 when France tried to impose its claim to a 320-km/200-mi fishing zone around the islands; Canada maintains that there is only a 19-km/12-mi zone.

St-Quentin Town on the river Somme, Picardie, N France; population (1990) 62,100. It was the site of a Prussian defeat of the French 1871 and was almost obliterated in World War I. Its traditional textile production has been replaced by chemicals and metalworks.

St-Servan-sur-Mer Seaport in the *département* of Ille-en-Vilaine, France, on the estuary of the river Rance. It is separated from the town of St-Malo by a creek 2 km/1.5 mi wide. Tourism and fishing are important industries.

St-Tropez Resort and fishing port on the French Côte d'Azur; population (1985) 6,250. It became popular as a resort in the 1960s.

St Vincent, Cape Cape of the Algarve region of SW Portugal off which England defeated the French and Spanish fleets 1797.

St Vincent, Gulf Inlet of the Southern Ocean on which Adelaide, South Australia, stands. It is named after Adam John Jervis, 1st Earl of St Vincent (1735–1823).

Sakai City on the island of Honshu, Japan; population (1994) 797,000. Industries include engineering, aluminium, and chemicals.

Sakha (formerly *Yakutia*) Autonomous republic of the Russian Federation, in Siberia
area 3,103,000 sq km/1,198,146 sq mi
capital Yakutsk
physical one of the world's coldest inhabited places; river Lena, the largest in Russia
industries furs, gold, natural gas, some agriculture in the S
population (1995) 1,036,000

Sakhalin (Japanese *Karafuto*) Island in the Pacific, N of Japan, that since 1947, with the Kurils, forms a region of Russia; capital Yuzhno-Sakhalinsk (Japanese *Toyohara*); area 76,400 sq km/29,500 sq mi; population (1981) 650,000, including aboriginal Ainu and Gilyaks. There are two parallel mountain ranges, rising to over 1,525 m/5,000 ft, which extend throughout its length, 965 km/600 mi.

Sakkara or *Saqqara* Village in Egypt, 16 km/10 mi S of Cairo, with 20 pyramids, of which the oldest (third dynasty) is the 'Step Pyramid' designed by Imhotep, whose own tomb here was the nucleus of the Aesklepieion, a centre of healing in the ancient world.

Salado Two rivers of Argentina, both rising in the Andes Mountains, and about 1,600 km/1,000 mi long. *Salado del Norte*, or *Juramento*, flows from the Andes to join the Paraná River; the *Salado del Sud*, or *Desaguadero*, joins the Colorado River and flows into the Atlantic S of Bahía Blanca.

Salamanca City in Castilla-León, W Spain, on the river Tormes, 260 km/162 mi NW of Madrid; population (1994) 167,000. It produces pharmaceuticals and wool. Its university was founded about 1230. It has a superbly designed square, the Plaza Mayor.

Salamanca Province of W central Spain in Castilla-León autonomous community; capital ◊Salamanca; area 12,336 sq km/4,763 sq mi; population (1995) 365,300. Bordered on the W by Portugal, it is in general a tableland. Products include cereals, oil, hemp, and wine. There are some mineral deposits.

Salamis Island off Piraeus, the port of ◊Athens, Greece; area 101 sq km/39 sq mi; population (1981) 19,000. The town of Salamis, on the W coast, is a naval station.

Salang Highway Main N–S route between Kabul, capital of Afghanistan, and Tajikistan; length 422 km/264 mi. The high-altitude *Salang Pass* and *Salang Tunnel* cross a natural break in the Hindu Kush Mountains about 100 km/60 mi N of Kabul. This supply route was a major target of the Mujaheddin resistance fighters during the Soviet occupation of Afghanistan.

Sale Town in Victoria, Australia, linked by canal via the Gippsland Lake to Bass Strait; population (1991) 13,900. It has benefited from the Strait deposits of oil and natural gas, and the brown coal to the S. The town was named after the British general Robert Sale (1782–1845).

Sale Residential suburb of Manchester, England; population (1991) 56,100.

Salem Industrial city (iron mining, textiles) in Tamil Nadu, India; population (1991) 367,000.

Salem City and manufacturing centre in Massachusetts, USA, 24 km/15 mi NE of Boston; population (1990) 38,100. It was settled 1626 and was the site of witch trials 1692, which ended in the execution of 19 people.

Salem City in NW Oregon, USA; population (1992) 112,000. It processes timber into wood products and has a fruit-and vegetable-canning industry. It was settled 1840–41 by Methodist missionaries, and became the territorial capital 1851 and state capital 1864.

Salerno Port in Campania, SW Italy, 48 km/30 mi SE of Naples; population (1992) 147,600. It was founded by the Romans about 194 BC, destroyed by Charlemagne, and sacked by Holy Roman Emperor Henry VI 1194. The temple ruins of the ancient Greek city of *Paestum*, with some of the earliest Greek paintings known, are nearby. Salerno has had a university (1150–1817, revived 1944) and medical school since medieval times.

Salerno Province of S Italy in ◊Campania region; capital Salerno; area 4,925 sq km/1,901 sq mi; population (1992) 1,069,400. It was formerly the Neapolitan province of Principato Citeriore.

Salford Industrial city in Greater Manchester, NW England, on the river Irwell and the Manchester Ship Canal; population (1994 est) 198,000. Industries include engineering, electrical goods, textiles, and chemicals. The artist L S Lowry painted here; a Lowry Centre is to be built.

Salgótarján Capital of Nógrád county in the N highlands of Hungary, near the border with the Slovak Republic, 80 km/50 mi N of Budapest; population (1993) 46,900. It is an industrial town with coalmining and the production of steel, glass, and agricultural machinery. It lies in the steep, wooded Tarján valley.

Salinas City in W central California, USA, S of San Jose; population (1992) 114,800. Fruits and vegetables, such as lettuce, are the economy's mainstay. Salinas was settled 1856.

Salisbury City and market town in Wiltshire, S England, 135 km/84 mi SW of London; population (1991) 39,300. Salisbury is an agricultural centre, and industries include brewing. The nearby Wilton Royal Carpet factory closed 1995. The cathedral of St Mary, built 1220–66, is an example of Early English architecture; its decorated spire 123 m/404 ft is the highest in England; its clock (1386) is one of the oldest still working. The cathedral library contains one of only four copies of the *Magna Carta*.

Salisbury Former name (to 1980) of ◊Harare, the capital of Zimbabwe.

Salisbury Plain Rolling plateau 775 sq km/300 sq mi between Salisbury and Devizes in Wiltshire, England. It rises to 235 m/770 ft in Westbury Down. Stonehenge stands on Salisbury Plain. For many years it has been a military training area.

Salonika English name for ◊Thessaloníki, a port in Greece.

Salop Abbreviation and former official name (1972–80) of ◊Shropshire, a county in England.

Salt Lake City Capital of Utah, USA, on the river Jordan, 18 km/11 mi SE of the Great Salt Lake; commercial centre and world capital of the Church of Jesus Christ of the Latter-day Saints (the Mormon Church); population (1992) 165,900. The Great Salt Lake is eight times saltier than the ocean, and is second only to the Dead Sea. Salt Lake City was chosen 1995 as the site for the 2002 Winter Olympic Games. It was founded 1847 by Brigham Young and a group of Mormons escaping religious persecution.

Salton Sea Brine lake in SE California, USA, area 650 sq km/250 sq mi, accidentally created in the early 20th century during irrigation works from the Colorado River. It is used to generate electricity.

Salvador Port and naval base, capital of Bahia state, NE Brazil, on the inner side of a peninsula separating Todos Santos Bay from the Atlantic Ocean; population (1991) 2,075,400 (metropolitan area 3,134,900). Products include cocoa, tobacco, and sugar. Founded 1510, it was the capital of Brazil 1549–1763.

Salvador, El Republic in Central America; see El Salvador.

Salween River rising in E Tibet and flowing 2,800 km/1,740 mi through Myanmar (Burma) to the Andaman Sea; it has many rapids.

Salzach River in Austria; length 225 km/140 mi. The Salzach rises in the Hohe Tauern Alpine range in E Tirol and flows N past Salzburg to the border with Germany before joining the ◊Inn 45 km/28 mi N of Salzburg.

Salzburg Capital of the state of Salzburg, W Austria, on the river Salzach; population (1991) 144,000. The city is dominated by the Hohensalzburg fortress. It is the seat of an archbishopric founded by St Boniface about 700 and has a 17th-century cathedral. Industries include stock rearing, dairy farming, forestry, and tourism. It is the birthplace of the composer Wolfgang Amadeus Mozart and an annual music festival has been held here since 1920. The Mozart Museum of Sound and Film opened 1991.

Salzburg Federal province of Austria; area 7,154 sq km/2,762 sq mi; population (1995) 506,850. Its capital is Salzburg.

Salzgitter City in Lower Saxony, Germany; population (1991) 115,000. Industries include iron and steel, shipbuilding, vehicles, and machine tools.

Salzkammergut Alpine district in the S of the province of ◊Upper Austria, extending into Styria and Salzburg; area 2,330 sq km/1,447 sq mi. The Salzkammergut is popular with tourists for its scenery of mountains and lakes, and the many sports and health resorts in the region include Ischl, Gmunden, and Hallstatt.

Samara Capital of Samara region, W central Russian Federation, and port at the junction of the rivers Samara and Volga, situated in the centre of the fertile middle Volga plain; population (1994) 1,223,000. Industries include aircraft, locomotives, cables, synthetic rubber, textiles, fertil-izers, petroleum refining, and quarrying. It was called *Kuibyshev* from 1935, reverting to its former name Jan 1991.

Samarkand City in E Uzbekistan, capital of Samarkand region, near the river Zerafshan, 217 km/135 mi E of Bukhara; population (1990) 370,000. Industries include cotton-ginning, silk manufacture, and engineering.

Samarra Ancient town in Iraq, on the river Tigris, 105 km/65 mi NW of Baghdad; population about 62,000. Founded 836 by the Abbasid caliph Motassim, it was the Abbasid capital until 892 and is a place of pilgrimage for Shi'ite Muslims. It is one of the largest archaeological sites in the world, and includes over 6,000 separate sites. The best preserved palace is Qasr al-Ashiq, built entirely of brick 878–882.

Sambre River of France and Belgium, which rises in the *département* of Aisne and flows 190 km/118 mi NE to join the ◊Meuse, of which it is the main tributary, at Namur. The towns of Landrecies and Maubeuge are on its banks in France; and Thuin, Charleroi, Châtelet, and Floreffe in Belgium. It is navigable for about 145 km/90 mi.

Samoa Volcanic island chain in the SW Pacific. It is divided into Samoa and American Samoa.

Samoa, American Group of islands 4,200 km/2,610 mi S of Hawaii, administered by the USA
area 200 sq km/77 sq mi
capital Pago Pago
physical five volcanic islands, including Tutuila, Tau, and Swain's Island, and two coral atolls; virgin rainforest; flying foxes
features national park (1988) includes prehistoric village of Saua
exports canned tuna, handicrafts, copra
currency US dollar
population (1993) 52,900
language Samoan and English
religion Christian
government as a non-self-governing territory of the USA, it is constitutionally an unincorporated territory of the USA, administered by the Department of the Interior
history the islands were acquired by the USA Dec 1899 by agreement with Britain and Germany under the Treaty of Berlin. A constitution was adopted 1960 and revised 1967. Around 85,000 American Samoans were living in the USA in 1990.

Samos Greek island in the Aegean Sea, off the W coast of Turkey; area 476 sq km/184 sq mi; capital Limén Vathéos; population (1991) 41,850. Mountainous but fertile, it produces wine (muscat) and olive oil. The mathematician Pythagoras was born here. The town of Teganion is on the site of the ancient city of Samos, which was destroyed by Darius I of Persia.

Samsun Black Sea port and capital of a province of the same name in N Turkey; situated at the mouth of the Murat River in a tobacco-growing area; population (1990) 303,900. It is the site of the ancient city of *Amisus*.

San River in Poland, rising in the Beskid Mountains and flowing 450 km/281 mi to the N, joining the ◊Vistula 6 km/4 mi NE of Sandomierz.

San'a Capital of Yemen, SW Arabia, 320 km/200 mi N of Aden; population (1995) 972,000. A walled city, with fine mosques and traditional architecture, it is rapidly being modernized. Weaving and jewellery are local handicrafts.

San Andreas fault Geological fault stretching for 1,125 km/700 mi NW–SE through the state of California, USA. It marks a conservative plate margin, where two plates slide past each other.

San Angelo City in W central Texas, USA, where the North and Middle Concho rivers meet, SW of Abilene; population (1992) 86,100. Industries include wool, food processing, oil, livestock, and clay products; it is an important wool and mohair centre. San Angelo was founded 1869.

San Antonio City in S Texas, USA; population (1992) 966,400. It is a commercial and financial centre; industries include aircraft maintenance, oil refining, and meatpacking. Founded 1718 as a Franciscan mission, it grew up round the site of the Alamo fort.

San Bernardino City in California, USA, 80 km/50 mi E of Los Angeles; population (1992) 172,000. Products include processed food, steel, and aerospace and electronic equipment. San Bernardino was named by Spanish missionaries who arrived 1810. A group of Mormons laid out the community in the 1850s.

San Bernardino Commune in the canton of Graubünden, Switzerland, 20 km/12 mi NW of the N Italian town of Chiavenna. It has mineral springs, and lies at the summit of the *San Bernardino Pass* (altitude 2,060 m/6,758 ft) on the road from Chur to Bellinzona.

San Cristóbal Capital of Tachira state, W Venezuela, near the Colombian border; population (1990) 220,700. It was founded by Spanish settlers 1561 and stands on the ◊Pan-American Highway. It is the centre of the coffee-growing region.

Sandhurst Small town in Berkshire, England. The Royal Military Academy (the British military officer training college), founded 1799, is nearby.

San Diego City and US naval air station, on the Pacific Ocean, and on the border of Mexico, in California, USA; population (1992) 1,148,900; metropolitan area (1992) 2,601,000. San Diego is linked to Tijuana, Mexico, by a 26-km/16-mi transit line (1981). It is an important fishing port. Manufacturing includes aerospace and electronic equipment, metal fabrication, printing and publishing, seafood canning, and shipbuilding. A Spanish mission and fort were established here 1769.

Sandomierz (Russian *Sandomir*) Market town in Tarnobrzeg province, Poland, on the left bank of the river Vistula, 80 km/50 mi E of Kielce. Large deposits of sulphur occur locally; industries include chemicals, glass, tanning, and food processing; and fruit is traded from the surrounding area. The 14th-century Gothic cathedral contains Byzantine-style frescoes.

Sandwich Resort and market town in Kent, England; population (1981) 4,200. It has many medieval buildings and was one of the original Cinque Ports, but recession of the sea has left the harbour useless since the 16th century. Industries include pharmaceutical research and manufacture (Pfizer).

Sandwich Islands Former name of ◊Hawaii, a group of islands in the Pacific Ocean.

Sandy Hook Narrow sandy peninsula between Sandy Hook Bay and the Atlantic Ocean, New Jersey, USA. It extends for 8 km/5 mi towards New York City. At the tip of the peninsula is Fort Hancock. Sandy Hook lighthouse (built 1763) is the oldest now in use in the USA. It is a Gateway national recreation area.

San Fernando Town in the province of Cádiz, S Spain; population (1995) 88,200. It is situated in an area of salt marshes, from which salt is produced. It has a naval school, an arsenal, and a meteorological observatory.

San Francisco Chief Pacific port on the tip of a peninsula in San Francisco Bay, in California, USA; population (1992) 728,900, metropolitan area of San Francisco and Oakland 3,686,600. The entrance to the bay was called the Golden Gate 1846, evoking the Golden Horn of Constantinople. The Golden Gate Strait was spanned 1937 by the world's second-longest single-span bridge, 1,280 m/4,200 ft. The strait gives access to San Francisco Bay. Manufactured goods include textiles, fabricated metal products, electrical equipment, petroleum products, chemicals, and pharmaceuticals. San Francisco is also a financial, trade, corporate, and diversified service centre; tourism is also important to its economy. A Spanish fort (the Presidio) and the San Francisco de Asis Mission were established here 1776. San Francisco has the largest Chinese community outside Asia.

San Francisco Peaks Group of mountains (the Humphreys, Agassiz, and Fremont peaks) in Arizona, SW USA. They rise above a plateau some 2,100 m/6,890 ft high, to an elevation of 3,851 m/12,633 ft. Their origin is volcanic. Situated just N of Flagstaff, they are used for tourism and lumbering, and include Sunset Crater Volcano national monument.

Sangre de Cristo Range of mountains in Colorado, central USA, part of the Rocky Mountains, with an altitude in places of over 4,260 m/13,976 ft. It extends for about 400 km/250 mi from NW to SE, and separates the river basins of the Rio Grande and the Arkansas.

San Joaquin River in California, SW USA; length 560 km/350 mi. It rises in the Sierra Nevada mountain range in E California, and flows SW and NW through the valley between the Sierra Nevada and the Coast Range to its junction with the Sacramento River. It irrigates a rich agricultural area.

San Jose Capital of Costa Rica; population (1991 est) 299,400. Products include coffee, cocoa, and sugar cane. It was founded 1737 and has been the capital since 1823.

San Jose City in Santa Clara Valley, California, USA; population (1992) 801,300. It is situated at one end of 'Silicon Valley', the site of many high-technology electronic firms turning out semiconductors and other computer components. There are also electrical, aerospace, missile, rubber, metal, and machine industries, and it is a commercial and transportation centre for orchard crops and wines produced in the area. San Jose was founded as a Spanish military supply base 1777 and served as the state capital 1849–51.

San Juan Capital of Puerto Rico; population (1990) 437,750. It is a port and industrial city. Products include chemicals, pharmaceuticals, machine tools, electronic equipment, textiles, plastics, and rum. San Juan was settled by Spanish colonists 1508 and founded as a city 1521; it remained under Spanish rule until 1898, when the island was ceded to the USA.

Sankt Polten Austrian town in the province of Lower Austria, 55 km/34 mi W of Vienna. Sankt Polten has many Baroque buildings. It has paper, textiles, and machinery industries.

Sanlúcar de Barrameda Resort town in the province of Cádiz, S Spain, at the mouth of the river Guadalquivir on the Atlantic coast; population (1995) 60,600. Exports include sherry. Christopher Columbus sailed from here on his third voyage to the New World, as did Ferdinand Magellan on his circumnavigation of the world. It has a 14th-century church and an old castle.

San Luis Potosí Silver-mining city and capital of San Luis Potosí state, central Mexico; population (1990) 525,700. Founded 1586 as a Franciscan mission, it became the colonial administrative headquarters and has fine buildings of the period.

San Luis Potosí State of central Mexico; area 62,848 sq km/24,266 sq mi; population (1995 est) 2,191,700. Its capital is San Luis Potosí. The main occupations are silver-mining, smelting and refining metal, and farming coffee and tobacco.

San Miguel de Tucumán Capital of Tucumán province, NW Argentina, on the Rio Sali, in the foothills of the Andes; population (1991) 473,000; metropolitan area (1992 est) 642,500. Industries include sugar mills and distilleries. Founded 1565, San Miguel de Tucumán was the site of the signing of the Argentine declaration of independence from Spain 1816.

San Pedro Sula Main industrial and commercial city in NW Honduras, the second-largest city in the country; population (1991 est) 325,900. It trades in bananas, coffee, sugar, and timber, and manufactures textiles, plastics, furniture, and cement.

San Roque Town in the province of Cádiz, S Spain, 11 km/7 mi N of Gibraltar; population (1995) 22,300. It was built by Spaniards from Gibraltar in 1704, after Gibraltar was taken by the English.

San Salvador Capital of El Salvador 48 km/30 mi from the Pacific Ocean, at the foot of San Salvador volcano (2,548 m/8,360 ft); population (1992) 422,600. Industries include food processing and textiles. Since its foundation 1525, it has suffered from several earthquakes.

Santa Ana City in S California, USA, 70 km/43 mi SE of Los Angeles; population (1990) 293,700. It is part of the metropolitan area of Anaheim–Santa Ana–Garden Grove.

Santa Ana Commercial city in NW El Salvador, the second-largest city in the country; population (1992) 202,300. It trades in coffee and sugar.

Santa Barbara City in S California, USA; population (1992) 85,100. Manufactures include aircraft and aerospace equipment, precision instruments, and electronic components, but the city is better known for its wealthy residents and as a resort. It is the site of a campus of the University of California. A Spanish presidio (military post) was established 1782, and a Franciscan mission (still in use) 1786.

Santa Cruz Capital of Santa Cruz department in E Bolivia, the second-largest city in the country; population (1992) 694,600. Sugar cane and cattle were the base of local industry until newly discovered oil and natural gas led to phenomenal growth.

Santa Cruz City in W central California at the N end of Monterey Bay, SW of San Jose; population (1990) 49,000. A division of the University of California is here. Industries include tourism, food processing (citrus fruit, cattle), fishing, electronics, and petroleum. There are many Spanish colonial-style buildings.

Santa Cruz de Tenerife Capital of Tenerife and of the Canary Islands; population (1994) 204,000. It is a fuelling port and cable centre. Industry also includes oil refining, pharmaceuticals, and trade in fruit. Santa Cruz was bombarded by the British admirals Blake 1657 and Nelson 1797 (the action in which he lost his arm).

Santa Cruz de Tenerife Province of Spain in the ◊Canary Islands autonomous community; capital Santa Cruz de Tenerife; area 3,209 sq km/1,239 sq mi; population (1995) 787,400. It includes the islands of Tenerife, Gomera, La Palma, and Hierro.

Santa Fé Capital of Santa Fé province, Argentina, on the Salado River 153 km/95 mi N of Rosario; population (1991) 395,000. It has shipyards and exports timber, cattle, and wool. It was founded 1573, and the 1853 constitution was adopted here.

Santa Fe Capital of New Mexico, USA, on the Santa Fe River in the Rio Grande Valley, 65 km/40 mi W of Las Vegas; population (1990) 55,900, many Spanish-speaking. The cultural capital of the Southwest, Santa Fe is home to many artists and has theatre and opera. Its chief industry is tourism; it also produces Native American jewellery and textiles. The city was founded by the Spanish 1610 on the site of a prehistoric Tiwa pueblo. Many wagons passed through on the Santa Fe Trail in the 19th century. The town was ceded to the USA 1848, and became the territorial capital 1851.

Santa Maria City in SW California, USA, NW of Santa Barbara; population (1992) 64,100. Industries include oil, food processing, and dairy products.

Santa Monica City in SW California, USA, 22 km/14 mi W of the centre of ◊Los Angeles; population (1990) 86,900. It has a beach and is a popular resort and residential area. The principal industry is now tourism, although specialized engineering and aircraft manufacturing are still important.

Santander Port on the Bay of Biscay, Cantabria, N Spain; population (1994) 195,000. Industries include chemicals, textiles, vehicles, and shipyards. It was sacked by the French marshal Nicolas Soult 1808 and was largely rebuilt after a fire 1941. Palaeolithic cave wall paintings of bison, wild boar, and deer were discovered at the nearby *Altamira* site 1879.

Santa Rosa City in NW California, USA, N of San Francisco; population (1992) 116,600. Industries include wine, fruit, chemicals, and clothing.

Santee River in South Carolina, USA, formed by the Congaree, Catawba, and Wateree rivers, which unite in Richland County, S of Columbia; length 866 km/538 mi. The Santee concrete dam (for hydroelectric power, navigation, and flood control) forms Lake Marion. The Cooper River is joined to the Santee River by a navigation canal built 1792–1800, and this connects with the Santee Catawba Waterway. It reaches the Atlantic at Santee Point, N of Charleston.

Santiago Capital of Chile, on the Mapocho River; population (1992) 4,385,500 (metropolitan area 5,180,800). Industries include textiles, chemicals, and food processing.

Santiago Second-largest city in the Dominican Republic; population (1991 est) 375,000. It is a processing and trading centre for sugar, coffee, and cacao.

Santiago de Compostela City in Galicia, Spain; population (1991) 105,500. The 11th-century cathedral was reputedly built over the grave of Sant Iago el Mayor (St James the Great), patron saint of Spain, and was a world-famous centre for medieval pilgrims.

Santiago de Cuba Port on the S coast of Cuba; population (1989) 405,400. Products include sugar, rum, and cigars.

Santo Domingo formerly *Ciudad Trujillo* Capital and chief sea port of the Dominican Republic; population (1991 est) 2,055,000. Founded 1496 by Bartolomeo, brother of Christopher Columbus, it is the oldest colonial city in the Americas. Its cathedral was built 1515–40.

Santos The world's leading coffee-exporting port, in SE Brazil, 72 km/45 mi SE of São Paulo; population (1991) 546,600. The Brazilian soccer player Pelé played here for many years.

Saône River in E France, rising in the Vosges Mountains and flowing 480 km/300 mi to join the Rhône at Lyon.

Saône-et-Loire *Département* in the Burgundy (Bourgogne) region of France; area 8,565 sq km/3,307 sq mi; population (1990) 560,000. The river Saône flows through the E of the *département*, and is connected by the Canal du Centre to the river Loire in the W. Wheat and oats grow on the plains, and the hilly district on the E bank of the Saône is a centre of the Burgundy wine trade. There is much industry around the coalfields of Autun and Montceau-les-Mines, and ironworks at Le Creusot. Cattle and poultry are bred in many parts. The principal towns are Mâcon (the capital), Autun, and Chalon-sur-Saône.

Saône, Haute- *Département* in the Franche-Comté region of France; see ◊Haute-Saône.

São Paulo City in Brazil, 72 km/45 mi NW of its port Santos; population (1992) 9,646,200 (metropolitan area 16,567,300). It is 900 m/3,000 ft above sea level, and 2° S of the Tropic of Capricorn. It is South America's leading industrial city, producing electronics, steel, and chemicals; it has meat-packing plants and is the centre of Brazil's coffee trade. It originated as a Jesuit mission 1554.

São Tomé Port and capital of São Tomé e Príncipe, on the NE coast of São Tomé island, Gulf of Guinea; population (1991) 43,400. It exports cocoa and coffee.

Sapporo Capital of ◊Hokkaido prefecture, Japan; population (1994) 1,719,000. Industries include rubber and food processing. It is a winter sports centre and was the site of the 1972 Winter Olympics. Giant figures are sculpted in ice at the annual snow festival.

Saragossa English spelling of ◊Zaragoza, a city in Spain.

Sarajevo Capital of Bosnia-Herzegovina; population (1991) 526,000. Industries include engineering, brewing, chemicals, carpets, and ceramics. A Bosnian, Gavrilo Princip, assassinated Archduke Franz Ferdinand here 1914, thereby precipitating World War I. From April 1992 the city was the target of a siege by Bosnian Serb forces in their fight to carve up the newly independent republic. A United Nations ultimatum and the threat of NATO bombing led to a cease-fire Feb 1994 and the effective end of the siege as Serbian heavy weaponry was withdrawn from the high points surrounding the city.

Sarasota City in SW Florida, USA, on the Gulf of Mexico, S of Tampa; population (1992) 50,900. It is a resort town specializing in food processing and electronics research. Saratoga was settled by Scots 1885.

Saratoga Springs City and spa in New York State, USA; population (1990) 25,000. In 1777 the British general John Burgoyne was defeated in two engagements nearby during the American Revolution. Horse racing is popular during the summer.

Saratov Industrial port (chemicals, oil refining) on the river Volga in W central Russian Federation; population (1994) 899,000. It was established in the 1590s as a fortress to protect the Volga trade route. The German population was deported 1941; an association of Volga Germans in Bonn is helping them to return.

Sarawak State of Malaysia, on the NW corner of the island of Borneo
area 124,400 sq km/48,018 sq mi
capital Kuching
physical mountainous; the rainforest, which may be 10 million years old, contains several thousand tree species. A third of all its plant species are endemic to Borneo. 30% of the forest was cut down 1963–89; timber is expected to run out by 2001

industries timber, oil, rice, pepper, rubber, coconuts, and natural gas

population (1991) 1,669,000; 24 ethnic groups make up almost half this number

history Sarawak was granted by the Sultan of Brunei to English soldier James Brooke 1841, who became 'Rajah of Sarawak'. It was a British protectorate from 1888 until captured by the Japanese in World War II. It was a crown colony 1946–63, when it became part of Malaysia.

Sardinia (Italian *Sardegna*) Mountainous island, special autonomous region of Italy; area 24,090 sq km/9,301 sq mi; population (1995) 1,659,500. Its capital is Cagliari, and it exports cork and petrochemicals. It is the second-largest Mediterranean island and includes Costa Smeralda (Emerald Coast) tourist area in the NE and *nuraghi* (fortified Bronze Age dwellings). After centuries of foreign rule, Sardinia became linked 1720 with Piedmont, and this dual kingdom became the basis of a united Italy 1861.

Sardinia

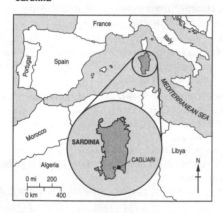

Sargans Town in the canton of St Gallen, Switzerland, 40 km/25 mi S of the city of St Gallen; population (1995) 4,800. Sargans stands at the junction of the Zürich–Chur and Zürich–Austria (Arlberg Express) railways. A medieval castle overlooks the town. Iron ore and manganese are mined nearby.

Sargasso Sea Part of the N Atlantic Ocean (between 40° and 80°W and 25° and 30°N) left static by circling ocean currents, and covered with floating weed *Sargassum natans*.

Sark One of the ◊Channel Islands, 10 km/6 mi E of Guernsey; area 5 sq km/2 sq mi; population (1991) 575. There is no town or village. It is divided into Great and Little Sark, linked by an isthmus, and is of great natural beauty. The Seigneurie of Sark was established by Elizabeth I, the ruler being known as Seigneur/Dame, and has its own parliament, the Chief Pleas. There is no income tax, divorce and cars are forbidden, and immigration is controlled.

Sarlat French town in the *département* of Dordogne, on the river Cuze; population (1990) 10,800. It has brandy, wine, and nut-oil industries. Sarlat is one of the most picturesque towns in France, with a medieval cathedral and 14th–16th-century buildings.

Sarnen Capital of Obwalden, Switzerland (W half of the canton of Unterwalden); population (1995) 8,900. It stands on the N shore of the Sarner See, 18 km/11 mi S of Lucerne.

Sarnia Town in Ontario, Canada, on the St Clair River, 80 km/50 mi W of London, on the Canada–USA border; population (1986) 49,000. It is the centre of a petrochemical industry. Oil was first discovered in this area in 1858, but it was only with the completion of the oil pipeline from Alberta that the great expansion of the refining and petrochemical industry began. The oil has served as a base for ammonia, ethylene, synthetic rubber, and insecticide plants.

Sarthe River in France; length 285 km/177 mi. It rises in the Orne *département* and flows S through the Sarthe *département* to join the ◊Loir upstream of Angers. Towns on its banks include Alençon, Le Mans, Sablé-sur-Sarthe, and Chateauneuf-sur-Sarthe. It is navigable from Le Mans.

Sarthe *Département* in the ◊Pays de la Loire region of France; area 6,210 sq km/2,398 sq mi; population (1990) 514,300. It is generally flat, with low ranges of hills in the N and NW, and is crossed N to SW by the river Sarthe. Cereals, potatoes, poultry, cider, and perry are produced and horses are bred. Iron, marble, slate, and limestone are found, and there are industries here connected with them. Hemp and linen are manufactured. The chief towns are ◊Le Mans (the capital), La Flèche, and Mamers.

Sarum Former settlement from which the modern city of ◊Salisbury, Wiltshire, England, developed.

Sasebo Seaport and naval base on the W coast of Kyushu Island, Japan; population (1994) 247,000.

Sask. Abbreviation for ◊Saskatchewan, a Canadian province.

Saskatchewan (Cree *Kis-is-ska-tche-wan* 'swift flowing') Province of W Canada

area 652,330 sq km/251,865 sq mi

capital Regina

towns Saskatoon, Moose Jaw, Prince Albert

physical prairies in the S; to the N, forests, lakes, and subarctic tundra; Prince Albert national park

Saskatchewan

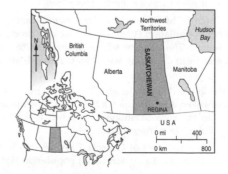

industries more than 60% of Canada's wheat; oil, natural gas, uranium, zinc, potash (world's largest reserves), copper, helium (the only W reserves outside the USA)

population (1995 est) 978,000

history once inhabited by Native Americans speaking Athabaskan, Algonquin, and Sioux languages, who depended on caribou and moose in the N and buffalo in the S. French trading posts established about 1750; owned by Hudson's Bay Company, first permanent settlement 1774; ceded to Canadian government 1870 as part of Northwest Territories; became a province 1905.

Saskatchewan (Cree *Kis-is-ska-tche-wan* 'swift flowing') River in Canada formed by two branches, N and S, both rising in W Alberta and meeting E of Prince Albert; length 1,939 km/1,205 mi. The island flows E to Lake Winnipeg, in S Manitoba, and then to Hudson Bay as the *Nelson River*. It has been dammed several times for irrigation purposes.

Saskatoon Largest city in Saskatchewan, Canada; population (1991) 186,100. It is the centre of a grain-producing area with agricultural industries, including meat packing and the manufacture of agricultural equipment. Other industries include chemicals, electronics, bio-technology, fibre optics, telecommunications, and potash mining. The University of Saskatchewan is here. Saskatoon was settled 1882.

Sassari Capital of the province of the same name, in the NW corner of Sardinia, Italy; population (1992) 122,000. Every May the town is the scene of the Sardinian Cavalcade, the greatest festival on the island.

Sassari Province of Italy in N ◊Sardinia region; capital Sassari; area 7,520 sq km/2,903 sq mi; population (1992) 455,600.

Satu Mare (Hungarian *Szatmar-Nemeti*) Capital of Satu Mare county, NW Romania, on the river Somes, near the Hungarian and Ukrainian borders, 174 km/109 mi NW of Cluj Napoca; population (1993) 131,400. Farm machinery, rolling stock, textiles, and processed food are manufactured, and the chief commodities are linen and wine.

Sault Ste Marie Twin industrial ports on the Canadian-US border, one in Ontario and one in Michigan; population (1991) 81,500 and (1990) 14,700, respectively. They stand at the falls (French *sault*) in St Mary's River, which links Lakes Superior and Huron. The falls are bypassed by canals. Industries include steel, pulp, and agricultural trade. A French Jesuit mission was established here 1669.

Saumur Town in Maine-et-Loire *département*, France, on the river Loire; population (1990) 31,900. The area produces sparkling wines. The cavalry school, founded 1768, has since 1942 also been a training school for the French armed forces.

Sava River in the Balkans; length 724 km/450 mi. It rises in the Karawanken Alps and flows SE across Slovenia and Croatia to join the river ◊Danube, of which it is the chief tributary, at Belgrade in Yugoslavia.

Savannah City and port of Georgia, USA, 29 km/18 mi from the mouth of the Savannah River; population (1992) 138,900. Manufactures include paper products, aircraft, transportation equipment, chemicals, and food products. Founded 1733, Savannah was the capital of Georgia 1754–86, and was the first city in the USA to be laid out in geometrically regular blocks.

Savannah River between Georgia and South Carolina, formed by the Tugaloo and Seneca rivers, which meet at Hartwell dam, Georgia; length 505 km/314 mi. It flows SE into Tybee Sound, 29 km/18 mi from Savannah in Georgia. The river is used for hydroelectric power and flood control.

Savoie *Département* in the ◊Rhône-Alpes region of France; area 6,035 sq km/2,330 sq mi; population (1990) 348,900. It is mountainous and wooded. Cereals and vines are cultivated in the valleys, and cattle, sheep, and horses are bred. Some coal, copper, and lead are found, and hydroelectric power is produced. There are textile and food manufactures, and an extensive tourist industry. The chief river is the Isère. The principal towns are ◊Chambéry (the capital), Albertville, and St-Jean-de-Maurienne.

Savoie, Haute- *Département* in the Rhône-Alpes region of France; see ◊Haute-Savoie.

Savona Province of NW Italy in central ◊Liguria region; capital Savona (population (1990) 69,000); area 1,545 sq km/596 sq mi; population (1992) 284,700. The town of Savona is a port on the Gulf of Genoa.

Saxony (German *Sachsen*) Administrative region (German *Land*) of Germany

area 18,412 sq km/7,109 sq mi

capital Dresden

towns Leipzig, Chemnitz, Zwickau

physical on the plain of the river Elbe N of the Erzgebirge mountain range

products electronics, textiles, vehicles, machinery, chemicals, coal

population (1995) 4,566,600

history conquered by Charlemagne 792, Saxony became a powerful medieval German duchy. The electors of Saxony were also kings of Poland 1697–1763. Saxony was part of East Germany 1946–90, forming a region with Anhalt.

Saxony-Anhalt Administrative region (German *Land*) of Germany

area 20,446 sq km/7,894 sq mi

capital Magdeburg

towns Halle, Dessau

industries chemicals, electronics, rolling stock, footwear, cereals, vegetables

population (1995) 2,738,900

history Anhalt became a duchy 1863 and a member of the North German Confederation 1866. Between 1946 and 1990 it was joined to the former Prussian province of Saxony as a region of East Germany.

Sayan Mountains Range in E Siberian Russia, on the Mongolian border; the highest peak is Munku Sardik 3,489 m/11,451 ft. The mountains have coal, gold, silver, graphite, and lead resources.

SC Abbreviation for the state of ◊South Carolina, USA.

Scafell Pike   Highest mountain in England, 978 m/3,210 ft. It is in Cumbria in the Lake District and is separated from Scafell (964 m/3,164 ft) by a ridge called Mickledore.

Scandinavia   Peninsula in NW Europe, comprising Norway and Sweden; politically and culturally it also includes Denmark, Iceland, the Faroe Islands, and Finland.

Scapa Flow   Expanse of sea in the Orkney Islands, Scotland, between Mainland and Hoy, until 1957 a base of the Royal Navy. It was the main base of the Grand Fleet during World War I and in 1919 was the scene of the scuttling of 71 surrendered German warships. It was abandoned as the main base for the fleet 1919 and operations transferred to Rosyth, but was reactivated as a base in World War II.

Scarabantia   Roman name for ◊Sopron, a town in Hungary.

Scarborough   Spa and holiday resort in North Yorkshire, England; population (1991) 38,800. A ruined Norman castle overlooks the town, which is a touring centre for the Yorkshire Moors.

Scarpe   River in France, rising in the Pas-de-Calais *département*. The Deule joins it near Arras, and from there, in a canal, it passes Douai to join the Scheldt near St-Amand.

Schaffhausen   Town in N Switzerland; population (1990) 34,200. Industries include the manufacture of watches, chemicals, and textiles. The Rhine falls here in a series of cascades 60 m/197 ft high.

Schaffhausen   Canton in N Switzerland, almost entirely surrounded by territory belonging to Germany; area 298 sq km/115 sq mi; population (1995) 7,062,400. The principal feature of this hilly region is the ◊Rhine valley, where the river falls in a series of cascades of up to 60 m/197 ft (the Rheinfall). Vine growing is the main agricultural activity.

Schässburg   German name for ◊Sighişoara, a town in Romania.

Schelde   (French *Escaut*) River rising in Aisne *département*, N France, and flowing 400 km/250 mi to join the North Sea S of Walcheren in the Netherlands. Antwerp is the chief town on the Schelde.

Schenectady   Industrial city on the Mohawk River, New York State, USA; population (1992) 65,400. It dates from 1662 and has long been a producer of electrical goods.

Scheveningen   Seaside resort and N suburb of The ◊Hague in the Netherlands. There is a ferry link with Great Yarmouth, England.

Schiedam   Port in Zuid-Holland province, SW Netherlands, on the river Meuse, 5 km/3 mi W of Rotterdam; population (1993) 71,900. It is famous for its gin.

Schleswig   (Danish *Slesvig*) Seaport in Schleswig-Holstein, Germany, at the W end of the 35 km/22 mi long Schlei inlet of the Baltic and 50 km/31 mi NW of Kiel; population (1994) 186,300. The city has food industries and is a tourist centre. Schleswig's cathedral dates partly from the 11th century.

Schleswig-Holstein   Administrative region (German *Land*) of Germany

area 15,770 sq km/6,089 sq mi
capital Kiel
towns Lübeck, Flensburg, Schleswig
features river Elbe, Kiel Canal, Heligoland
industries shipbuilding, mechanical and electrical engineering, food processing
population (1995) 2,725,500
religion 87% Protestant; 6% Catholic
history Schleswig (Danish *Slesvig*) and Holstein were two duchies held by the kings of Denmark from 1460, but did not form part of the kingdom; a number of the inhabitants were German, and Holstein was a member of the Confederation of the Rhine formed 1815. Possession of the duchies had long been disputed by Prussia, and when Frederick VII of Denmark died without an heir 1863, Prussia, supported by Austria, fought and defeated the Danes 1864, and in 1866 annexed the two duchies. A plebiscite held 1920 gave the N part of Schleswig to Denmark, which made it the province of Haderslev and Aabenraa; the rest, with Holstein, remained part of Germany.

Schmalkalden   Town in the *Land* of ◊Thuringia, Germany, on the river Schmalkalde, 22 km/14 mi NW of Suhl. There are iron-ore mines in the nearby hills of the Thuringian Forest, and the town has metal and glassmaking industries. Schmalkalden is also a spa.

Schneidemühl   German name for ◊Piła, a town in Poland.

Schönebeck   Town in the *Land* of ◊Saxony-Anhalt, Germany, on the river Elbe, 13 km/8 mi SE of Magdeburg. It has engineering and chemical industries.

Schuylkill   River in Pennsylvania, NE USA; length 210 km/130 mi. It rises in E central Pennsylvania, flows SE through the Blue Mountains, and past Reading to Philadelphia, where it joins the Delaware River.

Schwabisch-Gmünd   or *Gmünd* City in Baden-Württemberg, Germany, on the river Rems, 48 km/30 mi E of Stuttgart. It has produced gold and silverware since medieval times and it also manufactures watches, clothing, and metal goods. Schwabisch-Gmünd was one of the city-states of the Holy Roman Empire. It has an early 13th-century Romanesque basilica, and old houses and walls.

Schwarze Elster   or *Black Elster* River in E Germany; length 180 km/112 mi, of which 59 km/36 mi are navigable. The Schwarze Elster rises near Bautzen in Upper Lusatia, and flows in a generally northeasterly direction to join the river ◊Elbe near Wittenberg.

Schwarzwald   German name for the ◊Black Forest, a coniferous forest in Germany.

Schweinfurt   City in Bavaria, Germany, on the river Main, 100 km/62 mi E of Frankfurt am Main; population (1994) 55,500. Ballbearings, dyes, and fertilizers are manufactured. It has a harbour on the Rhein–Main–Donau Canal. Schweinfurt was one of the city-states of the Holy Roman Empire.

Schwerin   Capital of the *Land* of Mecklenburg–West Pomerania, Germany, on the W shore of the lake of

Schwerin; population (1993) 123,500. Products include machinery and chemicals. Formerly the capital of ◊Mecklenburg and earlier of the old republic of Mecklenburg–Schwerin, Schwerin became capital of Mecklenburg–West Pomerania with the reunification of Germany 1990.

Schwyz Capital of Schwyz canton, Switzerland; population (1990) 12,700. Schwyz was one of the three original cantons of the Swiss Confederation 1291, which gave its name to the whole country about 1450.

Scilly, Isles of or *Scilly Isles/Islands*, or *Scillies* Group of 140 islands and islets lying 40 km/25 mi SW of Land's End, England; administered by the Duchy of Cornwall; area 16 sq km/6.3 sq mi; population (1991) 2,050. The five inhabited islands are *St Mary's*, the largest, on which is Hugh Town, capital of the Scillies; *Tresco*, the second largest, with subtropical gardens; *St Martin's*, noted for beautiful shells; *St Agnes*; and *Bryher*.

Scone Site of ancient palace where most of the Scottish kings were crowned on the Stone of Destiny (now in the Coronation Chair at Westminster, London). The village of Scone is in Perth and Kinross, Scotland.

Scotland (Roman *Caledonia*) The northernmost part of Britain, formerly an independent country, now part of the UK
area 78,470 sq km/30,297 sq mi
capital Edinburgh
towns Glasgow, Dundee, Aberdeen
features the Highlands in the N (with the ◊Grampian Mountains); central Lowlands, including valleys of the Clyde and Forth, with most of the country's population and industries; Southern Uplands (including the ◊Lammermuir Hills); and islands of the Orkneys, Shetlands, and Western Isles; 8,000-year-old pinewood forests once covered 1,500,000 ha/3,706,500 acres, now reduced to 12,500 ha/30,900 acres. The 1995 Millennium Commission award is intended to fund the creation of the Millennium Forest, and double Scotland's forests
industry electronics, marine and aircraft engines, oil, natural gas, chemicals, textiles, clothing, printing, paper, food processing, tourism, whisky, coal, computer industries (Scotland's 'Silicon Glen' produces over 35 % of Europe's personal computers)
currency pound sterling
population (1993 est) 5,120,000
languages English; Scots, a lowland dialect (derived from Northumbrian Anglo-Saxon); Gaelic spoken by 1.3%, mainly in the Highlands
religions Presbyterian (Church of Scotland), Roman Catholic
famous people Robert the Bruce, Walter Scott, Robert Burns, Robert Louis Stevenson, Adam Smith
government Scotland sends 72 members to the UK Parliament at Westminster. The Local Government (Scotland) Bill 1994 abolished the two-tier system of local government. Since 1996 there have been 32 unitary authorities. There is a differing legal system to England. In a refer-

endum held Sept 1997, Scots voted in favour of the Scottish Parliament and devolution. The Scottish Parliament was backed by 75% of the electorate, and 63% agreed that it should habe tax-varying powers. Elections to the assembly were planned for spring 1999, with the Parliament coming into being in Edinburgh by the turn of the millenium.

Scottish Borders Unitary authority in SE Scotland created 1996 to replace the former Borders region; administrative headquarters Newton St Boswells; population (1996) 105,300; area 4,712 sq km/1,819 sq mi. Natural features include the river Tweed, and the Lammermuir, Pentland, and Moorfoot Hills. The novelist Sir Walter Scott lived at Abbotsford. Field Marshal Haig and Scott are buried at Dryburgh Abbey. Industries include electronics, timber, knitwear, and tweed.

Scranton Industrial city on the Lackawanna River, Pennsylvania, USA; population (1992) 79,700. Anthracite coal is mined nearby, but production has declined sharply, and the city now manufactures such products as electronic equipment, fabricated metal, clothing, plastic goods, and printed materials. Scranton was settled 1771 but developed chiefly with the erection of anthracite-fired furnaces 1840.

Scunthorpe Industrial town and administrative headquarters of North Lincolnshire, England, 39 km/24 mi W of Grimsby; population (1991) 76,000. It has one of Europe's largest iron and steel works, which has been greatly expanded with help from the European Union.

SD Abbreviation for ◊South Dakota, a state in the USA.

Seaham Seaport in Durham, England, 8 km/5 mi S of Sunderland; population (1991) 22,100. Coal mines and engineering were developed from the 19th century. The poet Byron married Anne Isabella Milbanke at Seaham Hall nearby.

Sea Islands Chain of islands lying off the coast of Georgia and South Carolina, SE USA. Sea Island cotton used to be the principal crop, but it was almost wiped out by the boll weevil. Rice and market-garden crops are grown on the low, marshy surface; fishing and tourism are also important.

Seaside City in W central California, USA, on the S shore of Monterey Bay, S of San Francisco; population (1990) 38,900. Industries include fruit processing.

Seattle Port on Lake Washington, USA; the largest city in the Pacific Northwest; population (1992) 519,600, metropolitan area with Everett (1990) 2,559,200. Industries include aerospace (it is the headquarters of the Boeing Company), timber, banking and insurance, paper industries, electronics (Microsoft is based in adjoining Redmond), and ocean science, and there is a large fishing fleet. Coffee has been an important product since the development of the Starbucks Company in the 1970s. The town was first settled 1851.

Sebastopol Alternative spelling of ◊Sevastopol, a port in Ukraine.

Secunderabad Northern suburb of Hyderabad city, Andhra Pradesh, India, separated from the rest of the city by the Hussain Sagar Lake; population (1981) 144,287.

Formerly a separate town, it was founded as a British army cantonment, with a parade ground where 7,000 troops could be exercised.

Sedan Town on the river Meuse, in Ardennes *département*, NE France; population (1990) 22,400. Industries include textiles and dyestuffs, the town's prosperity dates from the 16th–17th centuries, when it was a Huguenot centre. In 1870 Sedan was the scene of Napoleon III's surrender to Germany during the Franco-Prussian War. It was the focal point of the German advance into France 1940.

Seeland German form of ◊Sj´ælland, the main island of Denmark.

Segesvár Hungarian name for ◊Sighişoara, a town in Romania.

Segovia Town in Castilla-León, central Spain; population (1991) 58,000. Thread, fertilizer, and chemicals are produced. It has a Roman aqueduct with 118 arches in current use, and the Moorish alcázar (fortress) was the palace of the monarchs of Castile. Isabella of Castile was crowned here 1474.

Segovia Province of central Spain in Castilla-León autonomous community; capital Segovia; area 6,949 sq km/ 2,683 sq mi; population (1995) 149,700. Located N of Madrid, it is largely a plateau with fertile river valleys. Industries include grain, hemp, flax, and sheep-raising. There are granite and marble quarries.

Seikan Tunnel The world's longest underwater tunnel, opened 1988, linking the Japanese islands of Hokkaido and Honshu, which are separated by the Tsungaru Strait; length 51.7 km/32.3 mi.

Seine French river rising on the Langres plateau NW of Dijon, and flowing 774 km/472 mi NW to join the English Channel near Le Havre, passing through Paris and Rouen.

Seine-et-Marne *Département* in the ◊Ile-de-France region of France; area 5,916 sq km/2,284 sq mi; population (1990) 1,079,500. The rivers Seine and Marne, and their numerous tributaries, flow through the *département*. In the fertile level land between the rivers, wheat and vegetables are grown and cheese (especially Brie) manufactured. The S has a large wooded area, the forest of Fontainebleau. The principal towns are Melun (the capital), Meaux, and Provins.

Seine-et-Oise Former *département* in N France, formed of part of the Ile-de-France, and located W of Paris. Seven new *départements* were created from Seine and Seine-et-Oise in 1964: Paris, Hauts-de-Seine, Seine-St-Denis, Val-de-Marne, Yvelines, Val-d'Oise, and Essonne.

Seine-Maritime *Département* in the ◊Haute-Normandie region of France, bordering on the English Channel; area 6,354 sq km/2,453 sq mi; population (1990) 1,224,700. The broken plateau of the Pays de Caux, between the Channel and the river Seine, is well cultivated and the country to the E is wooded. Stock rearing is important, and dairy, apples, cider, flax, and fish are major products. The chief traditional industries are cotton manufacturing around ◊Rouen (the

capital), and woollen manufacturing at Elbeuf. There are metallurgical, chemical, and food-processing industries at Rouen and ◊Le Havre, which are also important ports, and the lower Seine valley is a focus for oil refining. Other principal towns are Dieppe and Fécamp.

Seine-St-Denis *Département* in the ◊Ile-de-France region of France to the NE of Paris; area 236 sq km/91 sq mi; population (1990) 1,381,200. It was created in the administrative reform of 1964. The *département* comprises the NE section of the Paris suburbs, with a large proportion of social housing. There are motor vehicle industries and office employment, but there is also intensive farming in the area. Seine-St-Denis is crossed by major road and rail links, and contains the Charles de Gaulle Airport at Roissy-en-France. The capital is Bobigny.

Sekondi-Takoradi Seaport of Ghana; population (1988 est) 103,700. The old port was founded by the Dutch in the 16th century. Takoradi has an artificial harbour, opened 1928, and railway engineering, boat-building, and cigarette manu-facturing industries.

Selangor State of the Federation of Malaysia; area 7,956 sq km/3,071 sq mi; population (1993 est) 1,981,200. It was under British protection from 1874 and was a federated state 1895–1946. The capital was transferred to Shah Alam from Kuala Lumpur 1973. Klang is the seat of the sultan and a centre for rubber-growing and tin-mining; Port Kelang (or Klang), formerly Port Swettenham, exports tin and rubber.

Selborne Village in Hampshire, S England, 8 km/5 mi SE of Alton. Gilbert White, author of *The Natural History of Selborne* 1789, was born here. The Selborne Society (founded 1885) promotes the study of wildlife.

Selby Town on the river Ouse, in the City and County of York, England; population (1991) 15,300. There is a 12th-century abbey church. The nearby *Selby coalfield*, discovered 1967, is the largest new coalfield in Europe. It consists of 2,000 million tonnes of pure coal; 5 mines produce 12 million tonnes a year. There are also sugar-beet refining, shipbuilding, paper, and chemical industries.

Selkirk Mountains Range of mountains in British Columbia, Canada, forming a subdivision of the Columbia Mountains. The range is bounded by the Columbia River on the E, W, and N. Mount Dawson (3,383 m/11,100 ft) is the highest peak, and there are others over 3,000 m/9,842 ft high. Rogers Pass lies in the range. A section of the mountains is contained within the Glacier National Park.

Selkirkshire Former inland county of Scotland, included in Borders Region 1975–96; now part of Scottish Borders unitary authority.

Sellafield Site of a nuclear power station on the coast of Cumbria, NW England. It was known as *Windscale* until 1971, when the management of the site was transferred from the UK Atomic Energy Authority to British Nuclear Fuels Ltd. It reprocesses more than 1,000 tonnes of spent fuel from nuclear reactors annually. The plant is the world's greatest discharger of radioactive waste: between 1968 and

1979, 180 kg/400 lb of plutonium was discharged into the Irish Sea.

Semarang Port in N Java, Indonesia; population (1990) 1,005,300. There is a shipbuilding industry, and exports include coffee, teak, sugar, tobacco, kapok, and petroleum from nearby oilfields.

Semipalatinsk Town in NE Kazakhstan, on the river Irtysh; population (1990) 339,000. It was founded 1718 as a Russian frontier post and moved to its present site 1776. Industries include meat-packing, tanning, and flour-milling, and the region produces nickel and chromium. The Kyzyl Kum atomic-weapon-testing ground is nearby.

Semois River in Belgium; length 190 km/118 mi. It rises near Arlon in the SE of the country and flows W through the provinces of Luxembourg and Namur to join the ◊Meuse above Montherme in France.

Sendai City in Tōhoku region, NE Honshu Island, Japan; population (1994) 928,000. Industries include metal goods (a metal museum was established 1975), electronics, textiles, pottery, and food processing. It was a feudal castle town from the 16th century.

Senegal River in W Africa, formed by the confluence of the Bafing and Bakhoy rivers and flowing 1,125 km/700 mi NW and W to join the Atlantic Ocean near St Louis, Senegal. In 1968 the Organization of Riparian States of the River Senegal (Guinea, Mali, Mauritania, and Senegal) was formed to develop the river valley, including a dam for hydroelectric power and irrigation at Joina Falls in Mali; its headquarters are in Dakar. The river gives its name to the Republic of Senegal.

Sennar Town about 260 km/160 mi SE of Khartoum, on the Blue Nile, Sudan Republic; population about 10,000. Nearby is the Sennar Dam 1926, part of the Gezira irrigation scheme.

Sens Town in Yonne *département*, Burgundy, France; population (1990) 27,800. Its 12th–16th-century cathedral is one of the earliest in the Gothic style in France.

Senta Town in Serbia, Yugoslavia, on the river Tisa, in the autonomous region of Vojvodina; population (1991) 22,800. It is a rail and road junction and a market centre.

Seoul or *Sŏul* Capital of South Korea (Republic of Korea), near the Han River, and with its chief port at Inchon; population (1994) 11,500,000. Industries include engineering, textiles, food processing, electrical and electronic equipment, chemicals, and machinery.

Seraing Industrial suburb of the city of ◊Liège, Belgium, on the river Meuse. The crystal works of Val-Saint-Lambert is situated in Seraing. It is ringed by decaying remnants of heavy industry.

Seram or *Ceram, Serang* Indonesian island in the Maluku (Moluccas) island group; area 17,142 sq km/6,621 sq mi. The principal town is Ambon, situated on a small island (also called Ambon) off the coast of Seram.

Serbia (Serbo-Croatian *Srbija*) Constituent republic of Yugoslavia, which includes Kosovo and Vojvodina
area 88,400 sq km/34,122 sq mi
capital Belgrade
physical fertile Danube plains in the N, mountainous in the S (Dinaric Alps, Sar Mountains, N Albanian Alps, Balkan Mountains); rivers Sava, Tisa, Morava
features includes the former autonomous provinces of ◊Kosovo, capital Priština, of which the predominantly Albanian population demands unification with Albania, and ◊Vojvodina, capital Novi Sad, largest town Subotica, with a predominantly Serbian population and a large Hungarian minority
population (1991) 9,791,400
language the Serbian variant of Serbo-Croatian
religion Serbian Orthodox
history The Serbs settled in the Balkans in the 7th century and became Christians in the 9th century. They were united as one kingdom in about 1169. After their defeat at Kosovo in 1389 they came under the domination of the Turks, who annexed Serbia in 1459. After a war with Turkey in 1876–78, Serbia became an independent kingdom.

The two Balkan Wars in 1912–13 greatly enlarged Serbia's territory at the expense of Turkey and Bulgaria. Serbia's designs on Bosnia-Herzegovina, backed by Russia, led to friction with Austria, culminating in the outbreak of war in 1914. Serbia was overrun in 1915–16 and was occupied until 1918, when it became the nucleus of the new kingdom of the Serbs, Croats, and Slovenes, and subsequently Yugoslavia. During World War II Serbia was under a puppet government set up by the Germans (94% of Serbian Jews were killed in 1941–44); after the war it became a constituent republic of Yugoslavia. The 1991 civil war in Yugoslavia arose from the Serbian nationalist government attempting the forcible annexation of Serb-dominated regions in Croatia. A ceasefire was agreed in Jan 1992. The European Union (EU) recognized Slovenia's and Croatia's independence in Jan 1992 and Bosnia-Herzegovina's in April 1992; this left Serbia dominating a greatly reduced 'rump' Yugoslavia.

Sergiyev Posad formerly (1930–92) *Zagorsk* Town 70 km/45 mi NE of Moscow in the Russian Federation; population (1990) 115,000. Paint, optical instruments, building materials, textiles, and furniture are produced. The Moscow Theological Academy is here. The town is the main centre of Orthodox Christianity in Russia.

Seringapatam Town in Karnataka, India, on an island in the Cauvery River. It was the capital of Mysore state 1610–1799, when it was taken from the sultan of Mysore, Tipu Sahib, by the British general Charles Cornwallis.

Serrai (Greek *Serres*) Town and department in ◊Macedonia region, N Greece; area (department) 3,987 sq km/1,539 sq mi; population (1991) 191,900 (department). It is the centre of a cotton-growing area, and has weaving and food industries. As the ancient Seris, it existed before 330 BC. It was occupied by the Turks between 1368 and 1912 and by the Bulgarians between 1913 and 1918.

Sète Town on the Mediterranean coast of France, in

Hérault *département*, SW of Montpellier; population (1990) 41,916. It is a seaport and handles fish, wine, brandy, and chemicals. It was founded 1666 as an outlet to the Canal du Midi.

Seto Naikai (Japanese 'inland sea') Narrow body of water almost enclosed by the Japanese islands of Honshu, Shikoku, and Kyushu. It is both a transport artery and a national park (1934) with 3,000 islands.

Sevastopol or *Sebastopol* Black Sea port, resort, and fortress in the Crimea, Ukraine; population (1992) 371,000. It was the base of the former Soviet Black Sea fleet. It also has shipyards and a wine-making industry. Founded by Catherine II 1784, it was successfully besieged by the English and French in the Crimean War (Oct 1854–Sept 1855), and in World War II by the Germans (Nov 1941–July 1942), but was retaken by Soviet forces 1944.

Sevenoaks Town in Kent, England. It lies 32 km/20 mi SE of London, population (1991) 24,500. Nearby are the 17th-century houses of Knole and Chevening. Most of its seven oak trees were blown down in the 1987 gale.

Severn River of Wales and England, rising on the NE side of Plynlimmon, N Wales, and flowing 338 km/210 mi through Shrewsbury, Worcester, and Gloucester to the Bristol Channel. It is the longest river in Great Britain. The *Severn bore* is a tidal wave up to 2 m/6 ft high.

Severn

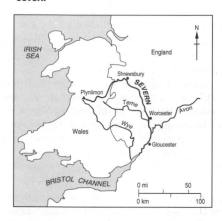

Severn Bridge Bridge linking England with S Wales across the Severn estuary, constructed 1961–66 at a cost of £8 million.

Seveso Town in Lombardy, Italy, site of a factory manufacturing the herbicide hexachlorophene. In 1976 one of its by-products, dioxin, escaped in a cloud that contaminated the area, resulting in severe skin disorders and deformed births. The town was evacuated for 16 months.

Seville (Spanish *Sevilla*) City in Andalusia, Spain, on the Guadalquivir River, 96 km/60 mi N of Cádiz; population (1994) 714,000. Products include machinery, spirits, porcelain, pharmaceuticals, silk, and tobacco.

Seville Province of S Spain in W ◊Andalusia autonomous community; capital Seville; area 14,001 sq km/5,406 sq mi; population (1995) 1,719,400. The river Guadalquivir and its tributaries Viar and Corbones flow through it. North and W of the Guadalquivir is part of the Sierra Morena mountain range; S and E of the river is a fertile plain. Main products include wheat, barley, silk, oil, wine, and fruit (particularly oranges). Cattle-raising is important. Copper, iron, and manganese are mined.

Sèvre Either of two French rivers from which the *département* of Deux Sèvres takes its name. The *Sèvre Nantaise* joins the Loire River at Nantes; the *Sèvre Niortaise* flows into the Bay of Biscay.

Sfax (Arabic *Safaqis*) Port and second-largest city in Tunisia; population (1994) 230,900. It is the capital of Sfax district, on the Gulf of Gabès, and lies about 240 km/150 mi SE of Tunis. Products include leather, soap, and carpets; there are also salt works and phosphate workings nearby. Exports include phosphates, fertilizers, olive oil, dates, almonds, esparto grass, and sponges.

SFSR Abbreviation for *Soviet Federal Socialist Republic*, administrative subdivision of the former USSR.

's-Gravenhage Dutch name for The ◊Hague.

Shaanxi or *Shensi* Province of NW China
area 195,800 sq km/75,598 sq mi
capital Xian
towns Yan'an
physical mountains; Huang He Valley, one of the earliest settled areas of China
industries iron, steel, mining, textiles, fruit, tea, rice, wheat
population (1990) 32,470,000.

Shache or *Yarkand* Walled city in the Xinjiang Uygur region of China, in an oasis of the Tarim Basin, on the caravan route to India and W Russia; population (1985) 100,000. It is a centre of Islamic culture.

Shaftesbury Market town and agricultural centre in Dorset, England, 30 km/19 mi SW of Salisbury; population (1991) 6,200. King Alfred is said to have founded an abbey on the site 880; Canute died at Shaftesbury 1035.

Shakhty Town in the Rostov region of the Russian Federation, 80 km/50 mi NE of Rostov; population (1990) 227,000. Industries include anthracite mining, stone quarrying, textiles, leather, and metal goods. It was known as *Aleksandrovsk Grushevskii* until 1921.

Shandong or *Shantung* Province of NE China
area 153,300 sq km/59,174 sq mi
capital Jinan
towns ports: Yantai, Weihai, Qingdao, Shigiusuo
features crossed by the Huang He River and the ◊Grand Canal; Shandong Peninsula
industries cereals, cotton, wild silk, varied minerals, wine
population (1990) 83,430,000.

Shanghai Port on the Huang-pu and Wusong rivers, Jiangsu province, China, 24 km/15 mi from the Chang Jiang estuary; population (1993) 8,760,000, the largest city in China. The municipality of Shanghai has an area of 5,800 sq km/2,239 sq mi and a population of 13,510,000, (1990). Industries include textiles, paper, chemicals, steel, agricultural machinery, precision instruments, shipbuilding, flour and vegetable oil milling, and oil refining. It handles about 50% of China's imports and exports.

Shannon Longest river in Ireland, rising in County Cavan and flowing 386 km/240 mi through loughs Allen and Ree and past Athlone, to reach the Atlantic Ocean through a wide estuary below Limerick. It is also the greatest source of electric power in the republic, with hydroelectric installations at and above Ardnacrusha, 5 km/3 mi N of Limerick.

Shantou or *Swatow* Port and industrial city in SE China; population (1990) 579,000. It was opened as a special foreign trade area 1979.

Shantung Alternative transliteration of the Chinese province of ◊Shandong.

Shanxi or *Shansi* or *Shensi* Province of NE China
area 157,100 sq km/60,656 sq mi
capital Taiyuan
towns Datong
features a drought-ridden plateau, partly surrounded by the Great Wall
industries coal, iron, fruit
population (1990) 28,180,000
history saw the outbreak of the Boxer Rebellion 1900.

Sharjah (or *Shariqah*) Third-largest of the seven member states of the United Arab Emirates, situated on the Arabian Gulf NE of Dubai; area 2,600 sq km/1,004 sq mi; population (1985) 269,000. Since 1952 it has included the small state of Kalba. In 1974 oil was discovered offshore. Industries include ship repair, cement, paint, and metal products.

Sharon Coastal plain in Israel between Haifa and Tel Aviv, and a sub-district of Central district; area 348 sq km/134 sq mi; population (1983) 190,400. It has been noted since ancient times for its fertility.

Sharon City in W Pennsylvania, USA, on the Shenango River, N of Pittsburgh, near the Ohio border; population (1990) 17,500. Industries include steel products and electronics. Sharon was settled 1802, and became a centre of the steel industry.

Sharpeville Black township in South Africa, 65 km/40 mi S of Johannesburg and N of Vereeniging; 69 people were killed here when police fired on a crowd of anti-apartheid demonstrators 21 March 1960.

Shasta, Mount Dormant volcano rising to a height of 4,317 m/14,162 ft in the Cascade Range, N California, USA.

Shatt-al-Arab (Persian *Arvand* 'river of Arabia') Waterway formed by the confluence of the rivers ◊Euphrates and ◊Tigris; length 190 km/120 mi to the Persian Gulf. Basra, Khorramshahr, and Abadan stand on it.

Sheba Ancient name for S Yemen (*Sha'abijah*). It was once renowned for gold and spices. According to the Old Testament, its queen visited Solomon; until 1975 the Ethiopian royal house traced its descent from their union.

Sheboygan City and port in E Wisconsin, USA, on Lake Michigan, N of Milwaukee; population (1992) 50,200. Industries include wood, food, plastic, and enamel products. It was established 1818 as a fur-trading post, and settled 1835. There were many German immigrants.

Sheerness Seaport and resort on the Isle of ◊Sheppey, Kent, England; population (1991) 11,700. Situated at the confluence of the rivers Thames and Medway, it was originally a fortress 1660, and was briefly held by the Dutch admiral de Ruyter 1667. It was a royal dockyard until 1960.

Sheffield Industrial city on the river Don, South Yorkshire, England; population (1994 est) 429,000. From the 12th century, iron smelting was the chief industry, and by the 14th century, Sheffield cutlery, silverware, and plate were made. During the Industrial Revolution the iron and steel industries developed rapidly. It now produces alloys and special steels, cutlery of all kinds, permanent magnets, drills, and precision tools. Other industries include electroplating, type-founding, and the manufacture of optical glass.

Shenandoah River in Virginia, USA, 89 km/55 mi long, a tributary of the Potomac, which it joins at Harper's Ferry, West Virginia.

Shensi Alternative transcription of the Chinese province of ◊Shanxi.

Shenyang formerly *Mukden* Industrial city and capital of Liaoning province, China; population (1993) 3,860,000. It was the capital of the Manchu emperors 1625–44; their tombs are nearby.

Shenzhen Special economic zone established 1980 opposite Hong Kong on the coast of Guangdong province, S China; population (1993) 2.4 million. Its status provided much of the driving force of its spectacular development in the 1980s when its population rose from 20,000 in 1980 to 600,000 in 1989. Part of the population is 'rotated': newcomers from other provinces return to their homes after a few years spent learning foreign business techniques.

Sheppey Island off the N coast of Kent, England; area 80 sq km/31 sq mi; population about 27,000. Situated at the mouth of the river Medway, it is linked with the mainland by Kingsferry road and rail bridge over the river Swale, completed 1960. The resort and port of Sheerness is here.

Sherbrooke Industrial city in S Quebec, Canada, at the junction of the Magog and St Francis rivers, 160 km/100 mi E of Montréal; population (1991) 76,400, metropolitan area 139,200. Paper, dairy, and leather products are manufactured, and a hydroelectric plant provides power. Sherbrooke is also an administrative centre.

Sherman City in NE Texas, USA, N of Dallas; population (1990) 31,600. It is a processing and shipping centre for agricultural products; textiles, electronics, and machinery are manufactured. It was founded in the 1840s.

's-Hertogenbosch or *Den Bosch* (French *Bois-le-Duc*) Capital of North Brabant province, the Netherlands, at the confluence of the Aa and Dommel rivers, 45 km/28 mi SE of Utrecht; population (1994) 95,400. It has a Gothic cathedral and was the birthplace of the painter Hieronymus Bosch.

Sherwood Forest Hilly stretch of parkland in W Nottinghamshire, England, area about 520 sq km/200 sq mi. Formerly a royal forest, it is associated with the legendary outlaw Robin Hood.

Shetland Islands Islands off the N coast of Scotland, beyond the Orkney Islands, an important centre of the North Sea oil industry

area 1,400 sq km/541 sq mi

towns Lerwick (administrative headquarters), on Mainland, largest of 19 inhabited islands

features over 100 islands including Muckle Flugga (latitude 60° 51' N) the northernmost of the British Isles

environment In 1993 the *Braer* ran aground on Shetland spilling 85,000 tonnes of oil. In Feb 1994, 50,000 birds, mostly guillemots and other fish-eating species, were washed up around the Islands. They appeared to have starved to death

industries processed fish, handknits from Fair Isle and Unst, miniature Shetland ponies, herring fishing, salmon farming, cattle and sheep farming; large oil and gas fields W of Shetland; Europe's largest oil port is Sullom Voe, Mainland; production at Foinaven oilfield, the first to be developed in Atlantic waters

population (1996) 22,500

language dialect derived from Norse, the islands having been a Norse dependency from the 9th century until 1472 when they were annexed by Scotland.

Shijiazhuang or *Shihchiachuang* City and major railway junction in Hebei province, China; population (1993) 1,210,000. Industries include textiles, chemicals, printing, and light engineering.

Shikoku Smallest of the four main islands of Japan, S of Honshu, E of Kyushu; area 18,798 sq km/7,258 sq mi; population (1995) 4,183,000; chief town Matsuyama. Products include rice, wheat, soya beans, sugar cane, orchard fruits, salt, and copper.

Shillelagh Village in County Wicklow, Republic of Ireland, which gives its name to a rough cudgel of oak or blackthorn. The district was once covered by the Shillelagh Wood, which supplied oak roofing for St Patrick's cathedral in Dublin.

Shillong Capital of Meghalaya state, NE India; population (1991) 222,000. It trades in rice, cotton, and fruit. It was the former capital of Assam.

Shimla Capital of Himachal Pradesh state, India, 2,300 m/7,500 ft above sea level, population (1991) 110,300. It was the summer administrative capital of British India 1864–1947.

Shimonoseki Seaport in the extreme SW of Honshu Island, Japan; population (1994) 255,000. It was opened to

foreign trade 1890. Industries include fishing, shipbuilding, engineering, textiles, and chemicals.

Shiraz Ancient walled city of S Iran, the capital of Fars province; population (1991) 965,000. It is known for its wines, carpets, silverwork, and for its many mosques.

Shire Highlands Upland area of S Malawi, E of the Shire River; height up to 1,750 m/5,800 ft. Tea and tobacco are grown.

Shizuoka Town in Chubo region, Honshu Island, Japan; population (1994) 471,000. Industries include metal and food processing, especially tea.

Shkodër (Italian *Scutari*) Town on the river Bojana, NW Albania, SE of Lake Scutari, 19 km/12 mi from the Adriatic Sea; population (1991) 83,700. Products include woollens and cement. During World War I it was occupied by Austria 1916–18, and during World War II by Italy.

Sholapur Town in Maharashtra state, India; population (1991) 604,000. Industries include textiles, leather goods, and chemicals.

Shreveport Port on the Red River, Louisiana, USA; population (1992) 196,600. Industries include oil, natural gas, steel, telephone equipment, glass, and timber. It was founded 1836 and named after Henry Shreeve, a riverboat captain who cleared a giant logjam. The discovery of oil nearby 1906 stimulated economic growth.

Shrewsbury Market town on the river Severn, Shropshire, England; population (1991) 90,900. It is the administrative headquarters of Shropshire. To the E is the site of the Roman city of *Viroconium* (larger than Pompeii). In the 5th century, as *Pengwern*, Shrewsbury was capital of the kingdom of Powys, which later became part of Mercia. The castle dates from 1070.

Shropshire County of W England. Sometimes abbreviated to *Salop*, it was officially known as such from 1974 until local protest reversed the decision 1980; The Wrekin will become a unitary authority in April 1998.

area 3,490 sq km/1,347 sq mi

towns Shrewsbury (administrative headquarters), Telford, Oswestry, Ludlow

features bisected, on the Welsh border, NW–SE by the river Severn; Ellesmere, the largest of several lakes; the Clee Hills rise to about 610 m/1,800 ft in the SW; Ironbridge Gorge open-air museum of industrial archaeology, with the Iron Bridge (1779), the world's first cast-iron bridge; Market Drayton is famous for its gingerbread, and Wem for its sweet peas

industries chiefly agricultural: sheep and cattle, cereals, sugar beet; it is the main iron-producing county in England; engineering

population (1997) 416,500

famous people Charles Darwin, A E Housman, Wilfred Owen, Gordon Richards

Shumen or *Šumen* Industrial city in Varna region, E Bulgaria, 80 km/50 mi W of Varna; population (1990) 126,300. Industries include metal and leather goods, beer, wine, and food processing. The Tombul Mosque built 1744 is the largest in Bulgaria. Founded in the 10th century on the site of a Roman fort, Shumen was a fortress town successively under Bulgarian, Byzantine, Turkish, and Russian rule.

Siachen Glacier Himalayan glacier at an altitude of 5,236 m/17,000 ft in the Karakoram Mountains of N Kashmir. Occupied by Indian forces 1984, the glacier has been the focal point of a territorial dispute between India and Pakistan since independence 1947.

Sialkot City in Punjab province, E Pakistan; population (1981) 302,000. Industries include the manufacture of surgical and sports goods, metalware, carpets, textiles, and leather goods.

Sian Alternative transliteration of ◊Xi'an, a city in China.

Sibenik Town in Croatia, on the Dalmatian coast, on the Gulf of Sibenik near the mouth of the river Krka; population (1991) 41,000. It is a naval base, has hydroelectric works, and exports bauxite, wood, wines, and marble. An old citadel overlooks the town, which has a 15th-century cathedral.

Siberia Asian region of Russia, extending from the Ural Mountains to the Pacific Ocean
area 12,050,000 sq km/4,650,000 sq mi
towns Novosibirsk, Omsk, Krasnoyarsk, Irkutsk
features long and extremely cold winters; the world's largest remaining native forests, covering about 5,000,000 sq km/1,930,000 sq mi, continue to be cut down; the world's largest cat, the Siberian tiger, although an endangered species, is hunted for its bones, which are used in traditional medicine
industries hydroelectric power from rivers Lena, Ob, and Yenisey; forestry; mineral resources, including gold, diamonds, oil, natural gas, iron, copper, nickel, cobalt.

Sibiu (German *Hermannstadt*; Hungarian *Nagyszeben*) Capital of Sibiu county, central Romania; population (1985) 177,000. The present city was founded by 12th century German colonists on the site of an earlier Roman settlement. It was the site of a battle during World War I when Romanian troops invaded Transylvania and were defeated by Austro-Hungarian forces.

Sichuan or *Szechwan* Province of central China
area 569,000 sq km/219,691 sq mi
capital Chengdu
towns Chongqing
features surrounded by mountains, it was the headquarters of the Nationalist government 1937–45, and China's nuclear research centres are here. It is China's most populous administrative area
industries rice, coal, oil, natural gas
population (1990) 106,370,000.

Sicily (Italian *Sicilia*) The largest Mediterranean island, an autonomous region of Italy; area 25,708 sq km/9,926 sq mi; population (1995) 5,082,700. Its capital is Palermo, and towns include the ports of Catania, Messina, Syracuse, and Marsala. It exports Marsala wine, olives, citrus, refined oil and petrochemicals, pharmaceuticals, potash, asphalt, and

marble. The region also includes the islands of ◊Lipari, Egadi, Ustica, and ◊Pantelleria. Etna, 3,323 m/10,906 ft high, is the highest volcano in Europe; its last major eruption was in 1971.

Sidi Barrani Coastal settlement in Egypt, about 370 km/230 mi W of Alexandria.

Sidi-Bel-Abbès Trading city in Algeria; population (1989) 186,000. Because of its strategic position, it was the headquarters of the French Foreign Legion until 1962.

Sidon Ancient name for the port of ◊Saida, Lebanon.

Siedlce Capital of Siedlce province, Poland, 90 km/56 mi E of Warsaw; population (1990) 72,000. It produces machinery, cement, glass, knitwear, and processed food, and is the chief trading centre for cattle and agricultural produce in the district. The town was founded in the 16th century.

Siegen City in North Rhine–Westphalia, Germany; population (1991) 110,000. There are iron and steel industries. It was once the seat of the Princes of Nassau-Orange and today is the cultural and economic centre of the Siegerland. The artist Rubens was born here.

Siemianowice Śląskie (German *Laurahutte*) Industrial town (coalmining, steel, iron) in Katowice province, Poland, 5 km/3 mi N of Katowice; population (1990) 81,100.

Siena City in Tuscany, Italy; population (1989 est) 58,400. Founded by the Etruscans, it has medieval sculpture including works in the 13th-century Gothic cathedral by Pisano and Donatello, and many examples of the Sienese school of painting that flourished from the 13th to the 16th centuries. The *Palio* ('banner', in reference to the prize) is a dramatic and dangerous horse race in the main square, held annually (2 July and 16 August) since the Middle Ages.

Siena Province of N central Italy in S ◊Tuscany region; capital Siena; area 3,820 sq km/1,475 sq mi; population (1992) 250,700.

Sierra Madre Chief mountain system of Mexico, consisting of three ranges, the Sierra Madre Oriental, the Sierra Madre del Sur, and the Sierra Madre Occidental, enclosing the central plateau of the country; highest Citlaltépetl 5,700 m/18,700 ft. The Sierra Madre del Sur ('of the S') runs along the SW Pacific coast.

Sierra Nevada Mountain range of S Spain; highest point Mulhacén 3,481 m/11,425 ft.

Sierra Nevada Mountain range in E California; highest point Mount Whitney 4,418 m/14,500 ft. The Sierra Nevada includes the King's Canyon, Sequoia, and Yosemite Valley national parks.

Sighişoara (German *Schässburg*, Hungarian *Segesvár*) Town in Mureş county, central Romania, on the river Tîrnava Mare, 72 km/45 mi NE of Sibiu; population (1993) 40,000. The town was founded in the 13th century by German colonists. It has an old citadel, walls, and towers, and several medieval churches.

Sigmaringen Town in Baden-Württemberg, Germany, on the river Danube, 75 km/47 mi S of Stuttgart; population (1994) 16,700. It was once the capital of the duchy of Hohenzollern-Sigmaringen. The castle in Sigmaringen contains art collections.

Si-Kiang Alternative transliteration of ◊Xi Jiang, a Chinese river.

Sikkim or *Denjong* State of NE India; formerly a protected state, it was absorbed by India 1975, the monarchy being abolished. China does not recognize India's sovereignty
area 7,096 sq km/2,740 sq mi
capital Gangtok
features Mount Kanchenjunga; wildlife including birds, butterflies, and orchids
industries rice, grain, tea, fruit, soya beans, carpets, cigarettes, lead, zinc, copper
population (1994 est) 444,000
language Bhutia, Lepecha, Khaskura (Nepali) – all official
religion Mahāyāna Buddhism, Hinduism
history ruled by the Namgyol dynasty from the 14th century to 1975, when the last chogyal, or king, was deposed. Allied to Britain 1886, Sikkim became a protectorate of India 1950 and a state of India 1975.

Silchester Archaeological site, a major town in Roman Britain. It is 10 km/6 mi N of Basingstoke, Hampshire.

Silicon Valley Nickname given to a region of S California, approximately 32 km/20 mi long, between Palo Alto and San Jose. It is the site of many high-technology electronic firms, whose prosperity is based on the silicon chip.

Silistra (Roman *Durostorum*, Turkish *Silistria*) Border town in NE Bulgaria, in Razgrad region, on the S bank of the river Danube, facing Romania, 110 km/69 mi from Varna; population (1990) 78,000. It is a river port with grain shipping. Founded as a Roman camp (Novae) in the 1st century AD, it became a major centre in the province of Moesia. The Turks captured and fortified the town during the early 15th century.

Sillein German name for ◊Žilina, a town in the Slovak Republic.

Simancas Town in the province of Valladolid, Spain, on the river Pisuerga; population (1995) 2,500. The national archives have been kept in its citadel since 1563.

Simcoe, Lake Lake in Ontario, Canada, between Lake Ontario and Georgian Bay; area 700 sq km/270 sq mi. It discharges into Lake Huron through the Severn River. It is a popular tourist destination.

Simferopol City in Ukraine; population (1992) 357,000. Industries include the manufacture of soap and tobacco. Simferopol is on the site of the Tatar town of *Ak-Mechet*, conquered by the Russians 1783 and renamed.

Similaun Glacier Glacier in the Tyrolean Alps on the Austria/Italy frontier. In 1991 the oldest intact human body was discovered here, having been preserved in ice for over 5,300 years.

Simplon (Italian *Sempione*) Alpine pass Switzerland–

Italy. The road was built by Napoleon 1800–05; the Simplon Tunnel, built in 1906, is 19.8 km/12.3 mi, one of Europe's longest.

Simpson Desert Desert area in Australia, chiefly in Northern Territory; area 145,000 sq km/56,000 sq mi. The desert was named after a president of the South Australian Geographical Society who financed its exploration.

Sinai Egyptian peninsula, at the head of the Red Sea; area 65,000 sq km/25,000 sq mi. Resources include oil, natural gas, manganese, and coal; irrigation water from the river Nile is carried under the Suez Canal.

Sinai, Mount (Arabic *Gebel Mûsa*) Mountain near the tip of the Sinai Peninsula; height 2,285 m/7,500 ft. According to the Old Testament this is where Moses received the Ten Commandments from God.

Sinaloa State of NW Mexico; area 58,092 sq km/22,429 sq mi; population (1995 est) 2,424,700. Its capital is Culiacán Rosales. The main occupations are farming and silver and gold mining.

Sind Province of SE Pakistan, mainly in the Indus delta
area 140,914 sq km/54,393 sq mi
capital and chief seaport Karachi
population (1993 est) 28,930,000
language 60% Sindi; others include Urdu, Punjabi, Baluchi, Pashto
features Sukkur Barrage, which enables water from the Indus River to be used for irrigation
history annexed 1843, it became a province of British India, and part of Pakistan on independence. There is agitation for its creation as a separate state, Sindhudesh.

Sindelfingen Town in Baden-Württemberg, Germany, 12 km/7 mi SW of Stuttgart; population (1994) 59,500. The town produces electronic equipment, computers (IBM), watches, and textiles. The motor-vehicle manufacturer Daimler Benz has had a factory in Sindelfingen since 1915.

Singapore Capital of Singapore, on the SE coast of the island of Singapore; population (1993) 2,874,000. Major industries include trade, shipping, banking, electronics, shipbuilding, and oil refining. Formerly a British colonial town, it was occupied by Japanese forces during World War II.

Sing Sing Name until 1901 of the village of *Ossining*, New York, USA, with a state prison of that name 1825–1969, when it was renamed the Ossining State Correctional Facility.

Sining Alternative transliteration of the city of ◊Xining in W central China.

Sinkiang-Uighur Alternative transliteration of ◊Xinjiang Uygur, an autonomous region of NW China.

Sinop or *Sinope* Ancient Black Sea port on the N coast of Asia Minor, founded as a Greek colony by Ionian settlers, probably in the late 7th century BC. It remained an important trading centre under successive Greek, Roman, and Byzantine rule.

Sint-Niklaas (French *St-Nicolas*) Town in the province of East Flanders, Belgium, 19 km/12 mi W of Antwerp. It manufactures woollen, cotton, and linen goods, carpets, pottery, bricks, and furniture. The marketplace in Sint-Niklaas, the Groote Markt, is the largest in the country. The municipal museum contains a collection of maps and globes made by the cartographer Gerardus Mercator.

Sint-Truiden (French *St-Trond*) Town in the province of Limbourg, Belgium, 17 km/11 mi SW of Hasselt. It has various manufacturing industries and is situated in a region (the Haspengouw) covered by extensive orchards. The town contains several ancient churches.

Sinuiju Capital of North Pyongan province, near the mouth of the Yalu River, North Korea; population (1984) 754,000. It was founded 1910.

Sion (German *Sitten*) Capital of the Swiss canton of Valais, lying in the valley of the river Rhône SE of Lake Geneva; population (1995) 26,100. It has three ruined castles, a 15th-century cathedral, and a 13th-century church. Sion is a market centre for the canton's vegetables, fruit, and wine.

Sioux City City in NW Iowa, USA, on the Missouri River, near Iowa's border with Nebraska and South Dakota; population (1992) 81,900. Industries include food processing, fabricated metals, fertilizer, and meatpacking. It is the head of navigation for the Missouri River. It was laid out 1848.

Sioux Falls Largest city in South Dakota, USA; population (1992) 105,600. Its industry (electrical goods and agricultural machinery) is powered by the Big Sioux River over the Sioux Falls 30 m/100 ft. Large stockyards, slaughterhouses, and meatpacking plants are also here. Sioux Falls was founded 1856 but was abandoned during the Sioux uprising of 1862. It was resettled with the establishment of Fort Dakota here 1865.

Sirte, Gulf of Gulf off the coast of Libya, on which the port of Benghazi stands. Access to the gulf waters has been a cause of dispute between Libya and the USA.

Sitka City and naval base on the W coast of Baranof Island in the Alexander Archipelago, facing Sitka Sound, in SE Alaska, USA; population (1990) 8,600. It was the chief town of Russian America 1804–67. Sitka is a trading and commercial centre and has fishing and timber-processing industries, as well as being a popular tourist destination.

Six Counties The six counties that form Northern Ireland: Antrim, Armagh, Down, Fermanagh, Londonderry, and Tyrone.

Sizewell Nuclear power station in Suffolk, England. Sizewell A, a Magnox nuclear power station, came into operation 1966. Sizewell B, Britain's first pressurized-water nuclear reactor (PWR) and the most advanced nuclear power station in the world, reached full load June 1995.

Sjælland or *Seeland* or *Zealand* Main island of Denmark, on which Copenhagen is situated; area 7,000 sq km/2,700 sq mi; population (1995) 2,157,700. It is low-lying with an irregular coastline. The chief industry is dairy farming.

Skagerrak Arm of the North Sea between the S coast of Norway and the N coast of Denmark. In May 1916 it was the scene of the inconclusive Battle of Jutland between British and German fleets.

Skagway City and ice-free port in SE Alaska, USA, 100 km/62 mi NW of Juneau at the head of Chilkoot Inlet of Lynn Canal; population (1990) 4,400. It is a trade and shipping centre for an interior mining area and the coastal terminus of the White Pass and Yukon railway; it is also a seaport and has an airport. It was founded 1897.

Skanderborg Town in Aarhus county, Jylland, Denmark, a tourist centre near the lakes Mosso and Silkeborg.

Skåne or *Scania* Area of S Sweden. It is a densely populated and fertile agricultural region, comprising the counties of Malmöhus and Kristianstad. Malmö and Hålsingborg are leading centres. It was under Danish rule until ceded to Sweden 1658.

Skegness Holiday resort on the coast of Lincolnshire, England; population (1991) 15,150. It was the site of the first Butlin holiday camp.

Skellefteå Town in Västerbotten county, N Sweden, on the river Skellefte, 16 km/10 mi from the sea; population (1995) 75,300. The town has grown considerably since the establishment of the Boliden mines with their rich variety of ores, including gold.

Skelmersdale Town in Lancashire, N England, W of Wigan; population (1991) 42,100. It was designated a new town 1961, with many light industries, including electronics, engineering, textiles, rubber, and glass. It received some of the overspill from Merseyside.

Skiddaw Mountain (930 m/3,052 ft) in Cumbria, England, in the Lake district, N of Keswick.

Skikda Trading port in Algeria; population (1989) 141,000. Products include wine, citrus, and vegetables. Industries include petrochemicals and oil-refining. It was founded by the French 1838 as *Philippeville* and renamed after independence 1962.

Skipton Industrial (engineering, textiles) town in North Yorkshire, England; population (1991) 13,600. There is an 11th-century castle.

Skopje Capital and industrial city of the Former Yugoslav Republic of Macedonia; population (1991) 563,300. Industries include iron, steel, chromium mining, and food processing.

Skye Largest island of the Inner Hebrides, off the W coast of Scotland; area 1,740 sq km/672 sq mi; population (1991) 8,900. It is separated from the mainland by the Sound of Sleat. The chief port is Portree. The economy is based on crofting, tourism, and livestock. The Skye Bridge, a privately financed toll bridge to the island, was completed 1995.

Skyros or *Skiros* Greek island, the largest of the N ◊Sporades; area 210 sq km/81 sq mi; population (1981) 2,750. It is known for its furniture and weaving. The English poet Rupert Brooke is buried here.

Slavkov Czech name of *Austerlitz*, a town in Moravia, Czech Republic.

Slavonia Region of E Croatia bounded by the Sava, Drava, and Danube rivers; Osijek is the largest town. E and W Slavonia declared themselves autonomous provinces of

Serbia following Croatia's declaration of independence from Yugoslavia 1991, and the region was the scene of fierce fighting between Croatian forces and Serb-dominated Yugoslav federal troops 1991–92. After the ceasefire 1992, 10,000 UN troops were deployed in E and W Slavonia and contested Krajina. Rebel Serbs in Croatia agreed Nov 1995 to return the region of E Slavonia to Croatian control.

Slavonski Brod Town in Croatia, on the left bank of the river Sava; population (1991) 55,600. It is an important rail and road junction, has oil and engineering works, and trades in wine and cereals. It has a Turkish citadel. Across the river is the twin town of *Bosanski Brod*.

Sligo County of the Republic of Ireland, in the province of Connacht, situated on the Atlantic coast of NW Ireland; area 1,800 sq km/694 sq mi; population (1996 est) 55,600. It is hilly. There is livestock and dairy farming.

Sliven Town in Burgas region, E Bulgaria, on the SE slopes of the Balkan Mountains, 64 km/40 mi NE of Stara Zagora. It is an agricultural centre with textile, carpet, and local coalmining industries. *Sliven Spa* lies about 11 km/7 mi to the SE.

Slough Industrial town (pharmaceuticals, electronics, engineering, chocolate manufacture) in Berkshire, England, near Windsor; it will become a unitary authority April 1998; population (1994 est) 105,000. The home of astronomer William Herschel is now a museum. The Trading Estate was the first of its kind to be established after World War I.

Słupsk (German *Stolp*) Capital of Słupsk province, Poland, on the river Słupia, 61 km/38 mi NE of Koszalin; population (1990) 101,200. It produces timber, footwear, furniture, chemicals, and has engineering industries. Until 1945 it was part of German Pomerania.

Smithfield Site of a meat market from 1868 and poultry and provision market from 1889, in the City of London, England. Formerly an open space, it was the scene of the murder of Wat Tyler, leader of the Peasants' Revolt 1381, and the execution of many Protestant martyrs in the 16th century. The annual Bartholomew Fair was held here 1614–1855.

Smolensk City on the river Dnieper, W Russian Federation; population (1994) 355,000. Industries include textiles, distilling, and flour milling. It was founded 882 as the chief town of a Slavic tribe and was captured by Napoleon 1812. German troops took the city 1941, and it was liberated by Soviet forces 1943. Nearby is Katyn Forest.

Smyrna Former name for ◊Izmir, Turkey.

Snaefell Highest mountain in the Isle of ◊Man, 620 m/ 2,035 ft.

Snake Tributary of the Columbia River, in NW USA; length 1,670 km/1,038 mi. It flows 65 km/40 mi through Hell's Canyon, one of the deepest gorges in the world.

Sneek Town in the province of Friesland, the Netherlands, 21 km/13 mi SW of Leeuwarden; population (1996) 29,900. It has a butter and cheese market and tobacco manufacturing. Formerly an important shipbuilding centre, Sneek is now a centre of the booming pleasure-boat indus-

try. Large regattas are held each August on the *Sneekermeer* to the E of the town.

Snowdon (Welsh *Y Wyddfa*) Highest mountain in Wales, 1,085 m/3,560 ft above sea level. It consists of a cluster of five peaks. At the foot of Snowdon are the Llanberis, Aberglaslyn, and Rhyd-ddu passes. A rack railway ascends to the summit from Llanberis. *Snowdonia*, the surrounding mountain range, was made a national park 1951. It covers 2,188 sq km/845 sq mi of mountain, lakes, and forest land.

Snowy Mountains Range in the Australian Alps, chiefly in New South Wales, near which the *Snowy River* rises; both river and mountains are known for a hydroelectric and irrigation system.

Sochi Seaside resort in S Russian Federation, on the Black Sea; population (1990) 339,000. In 1976 it became the world's first 'no smoking' city.

Society Islands (French *Archipel de la Société*) Archipelago in ◊French Polynesia, divided into the Windward Islands and the Leeward Islands; area 1,685 sq km/650 sq mi; population (1988) 162,600. The administrative headquarters is Papeete on ◊Tahiti. The *Windward Islands* (French *Iles du Vent*) have an area of 1,200 sq km/ 460 sq mi and a population (1988) of 140,300. They comprise Tahiti, Moorea (area 132 sq km/51 sq mi; population 7,000), Maio (or Tubuai Manu; 9 sq km/3.5 sq mi; population 200), and the smaller Tetiaroa and Mehetia. The *Leeward Islands* (French *Iles sous le Vent*) have an area of 404 sq km/156 sq mi and a population of 22,200 (1988). They comprise the volcanic islands of Raiatea (including the main town of Uturoa), Huahine, Bora-Bora, Maupiti, Tahaa, and four small atolls. Claimed by France 1768, the group became a French protectorate 1843 and a colony 1880.

Socotra Yemeni island in the Indian Ocean; capital Tamridah; area 3,500 sq km/1,351 sq mi. Under British protection from 1886, it became part of South Yemen 1967.

Söderhamn Seaport in Gåvleborg county, Sweden, near the mouth of the river Ljusne. There are sawmills, woodpulp and planing works and ironworks. The town has a large timber trade.

Södertälje Town in the county of Stockholm, E Sweden; population (1995) 82,400. It is a flourishing industrial town just W of the capital, with pharmaceutical, heavy vehicle construction, and engineering plants. *Södertälje Canal* connects Lake Mälaren with the Baltic.

Soest City in North Rhine–Westphalia, Germany, 50 km/ 31 mi E of Dortmund; population (1994) 294,800. Soest was an important member of the Hanseatic League medieval trade federation. Sugar refining is the principal industry. The town has several medieval churches, and is a tourist centre.

Sofia or *Sofiya* Capital of Bulgaria since 1878; population (1991) 1,221,000. Industries include textiles, rubber, machinery, and electrical equipment. It lies at the foot of the Vitosha Mountains.

Sogne Fjord Longest and deepest fjord in Norway, stretching 204 km/127 mi from inland Skjolden to its mouth on the W coast at Solund; it is 1,245 m/4,080 ft deep.

Soho District of central London, in the City of Westminster, which houses the offices of publishing, film, and recording companies; restaurants; nightclubs; and a decreasing number of sex shops.

Soissons Market town in Picardie region, N France; population (1990) 32,100. The chief industry is metallurgy. In 486 the Frankish king Clovis defeated the Gallo-Romans here, ending their rule in France. It has always been fortified as a barrier against invasion from the N and suffered great destruction in fighting around the town in the early part of World War I.

Sokoto Trading centre (cement, wood, leather) and capital of Sokoto state, NW Nigeria; population (1992 est) 185,500.

Sokoto State in Nigeria, established 1976; capital Sokoto; area 102,500 sq km/39,565 sq mi; population (1991) 4,392,400. It was a Fula sultanate from the 16th century until occupied by the British 1903.

Solbad Hall Town in the Austrian province of Tirol, on the river Inn some 7 km/4 mi E of Innsbruck. It is a spa with mineral springs, and the nearby salt mines are still worked. Brewing is a major industry.

Solent, the Channel between the coast of Hampshire, England, and the Isle of ◊Wight. It is now a yachting centre.

Solingen City in North Rhine–Westphalia, Germany; population (1991) 166,000. It was once a major producer of swords and today makes high-quality steel for razor blades and cutlery.

Solothurn Capital of the Swiss canton of the same name, on the river Aar, 30 km/19 mi N of Bern; population (1995) 15,400. It is an important railway junction; industries include electrical engineering and watchmaking.

Solothurn (French *Soleure*) Canton in NW Switzerland; area 791 sq km/305 sq mi; population (1997) 239,300. The canton stretches from Basel to Bern and is traversed by the foothills of the Jura Mountains. It is largely agricultural, but also has shoe, paper, cement, textile, watch, and engineering industries.

Solway Firth Inlet of the Irish Sea, formed by the estuaries of the rivers Eden and Esk, at the W end of the border between England and Scotland.

Somaliland Region of Somali-speaking peoples in E Africa including the former British Somaliland Protectorate (established 1887) and Italian Somaliland (made a colony 1927, conquered by Britain 1941, and administered by Britain until 1950) – which both became independent 1960 as the Somali Democratic Republic, the official name for Somalia – and former French Somaliland, which was established 1888, became known as the Territory of the Afars and Issas 1967, and became independent as Djibouti 1977.

Sombor Town in Serbia, Yugoslavia, in the autonomous region of Vojvodina; population (1991) 48,700. It is the centre of a rich agricultural district.

Somerset County of SW England
area 3,460 sq km/1,336 sq mi

towns Taunton (administrative headquarters); Wells, Bridgwater, Glastonbury, Yeovil
features rivers Avon, Parret, and Exe; marshy coastline on the Bristol Channel; Mendip Hills (including Cheddar Gorge and Wookey Hole, a series of limestone caves where Stone Age flint implements and bones of extinct animals have been found); Quantock Hills; Exmoor; Blackdown Hills
industries engineering, dairy products, cider, food processing, textiles, helicopters, stone quarrying, leather
population (1994) 477,900
famous people John Pym, Henry Fielding, Ernest Bevin.
history James II defeated the Duke of Monmouth at the Battle of Sedgemoor 1685.

Somme River in N France, on which Amiens and Abbeville stand; length 240 km/150 mi. It rises in Aisne *département* and flows W through Somme *département* to the English Channel.

Somme *Département* in the ◊Picardy region of France, with a short coastline on the English Channel; area 6,175 sq km/2,384 sq mi; population (1990) 549,100. It is crossed E to W by the river Somme. In general the land is level, a great plateau. Somme is an important agricultural area and produces cereals, sugar beet, apples, and livestock. The principal industries are textiles and chemicals, sugar refining, and distilling. The chief towns are ◊Amiens (the capital), ◊Abbeville, Montdidier, and Péronne.

Sondrio Province of N Italy in N ◊Lombardy region; capital Sondrio; area 3,215 sq km/1,241 sq mi; population (1992) 175,700.

Sonora State of NW Mexico, on the border of Arizona, USA, on the Gulf of California; area 184,934 sq km/71,403 sq mi; population (1995 est) 2,083,600. Its capital is Hermosillo. The main occupations are mining for silver, gold, lead, and zinc, and farming, producing sugar-cane, wheat, alfalfa, and rice.

Sontius Ancient name for the ◊Isonzo, a river in Yugoslavia and Italy.

Soochow Alternative transliteration of the Chinese city of ◊Suzhou.

Sopot (German *Zoppot*) Seaside resort and spa in Gdańsk province, Poland, 11 km/7 mi N of Gdańsk; population (1990) 46,700.

Sopron (German *Ödenburg*, Roman *Scarabantia*) Town in Györ-Sopron county, Hungary, near the Austrian border between the Neusiedler See and the E Alps, 77 km/48 mi W of Györ; population (1993) 56,100. Wine, textiles, and chemicals are produced. One of the best-preserved historic towns in Hungary, it attracts tourists.

Sorau German name for ◊Żary, a town in Poland.

Soria Capital of the province of Soria, N central Spain, on the river Duero; population (1995) 33,400. Products include food and timber. It has a Renaissance palace, several old churches, and a museum of objects from nearby Numantia.

Soria Province of N central Spain in Castilla-León autonomous community; capital Soria; area 10,287 sq km/

3,972 sq mi; population (1995) 94,500. It is an open, dry, generally infertile region, crossed by the upper waters of the river Duero. Products include timber, charcoal, salt, and asphalt.

Sorøy Norwegian island in the Norwegian Sea, off the NW coast of Norway, 17 km/10.5 mi W of Hammerfest, 450 km/280 mi N of the Arctic Circle; area 816 sq km/315 sq mi. The discovery of carved bas-relief images of reindeer, elk, bears, whales, birds, humans, and boats, believed to date from 7000 to 5000 BC, makes this the world's most northerly collection of rock art.

Sorrento Town on the Gulf of Naples, SW Italy; population (1981) 17,301. It has been a holiday resort since Roman times.

Sosnowiec Chief city of the Dąbrowa coal region in the Upper Silesian province of Katowice, S Poland; population (1990) 259,300.

Sound, the (Swedish and Danish *Øresund*) Strait dividing SW Sweden from Denmark and linking the ◊Kattegat strait and the Baltic Sea; length 113 km/70 mi; width between 5–60 km/3–37 mi.

Soûr (or *Tyre*) Town in SW Lebanon, about 80 km/50 mi S of Beirut, formerly a port until its harbour silted up; population (1991 est) 70,000. It stands on the site of the ancient city of the same name, a seaport of Phoenicia.

Sousse Port and commercial centre in NE Tunisia; population (1994) 125,000. It was founded by the Phoenicians and has Roman ruins.

South America Fourth largest of the continents, nearly twice as large as Europe (13% of the world's land surface), extending S from ◊Central America
area 17,864,000 sq km/ 6,900,000 sq mi
largest cities (population over 3.5 million) Buenos Aires, São Paulo, Rio de Janeiro, Bogotá, Santiago, Lima, Caracas
features Lake Titicaca (the world's highest navigable lake); La Paz (highest capital city in the world); Atacama Desert; Inca ruins at Machu Picchu; rivers include the Amazon (world's largest and second longest), Paraná, Madeira, São Francisco, Purus, Paraguay, Orinoco, Araguaia, Negro, Uruguay
physical occupying the S part of the landmass of the W hemisphere, the South American continent stretches from Point Gallinas on the Caribbean coast of Colombia to Cape Horn at the S tip of Horn Island, which lies adjacent to Tierra del Fuego; the most southerly point on the mainland is Cape Froward on the Brunswick peninsula, S Chile; at its maximum width (5,120 km/3,200 mi) the continent stretches from Point Pariñas, Peru, in the extreme W to Point Coqueiros, just N of Recife, Brazil, in the E; five-sixths of the continent lies in the S hemisphere and two-thirds within the tropics.

Southampton Seaport and unitary authority in S England, on Southampton Water; population (1997 est) 207,100; area 52 sq km/20 sq mi. It was part of the county of Hampshire to 1997. Industries include marine engineering, chemicals, plastics, flour-milling, cables, electrical goods,

tobacco, and financial services. It is a major passenger and container port. There is an oil refinery at Fawley.

South Arabia, Federation of Former grouping (1959–67) of Arab emirates and sheikdoms, joined by ◊Aden 1963. The W part of the area was claimed by Yemen, and sporadic fighting and terrorism from 1964 led to British withdrawal 1967 and the proclamation of the Republic of South Yemen.

South Australia State of the Commonwealth of Australia
area 984,377 sq km/380,070 sq mi
capital Adelaide (chief port)
towns Whyalla, Mount Gambier
features Murray Valley irrigated area, including winegrowing Barossa Valley; lakes: ◊Eyre, ◊Torrens; mountains: Mount Lofty, Musgrave, Flinders; parts of the ◊Nullarbor Plain, and Great Victoria and Simpson deserts; experimental rocket range in the arid N at Woomera
industries meat and wool (80% of area cattle and sheep grazing), wines and spirits, dried and canned fruit, iron (Middleback Range), coal (Leigh Creek), copper, uranium (Roxby Downs), oil and natural gas in the NE, lead, zinc, iron, opals, household and electrical goods, vehicles
population (1994) 1,463,200
history possibly known to the Dutch in the 16th century; surveyed by Dutch navigator Abel Tasman 1644; first European settlement 1834; province 1836; became a state 1901.

South Australia

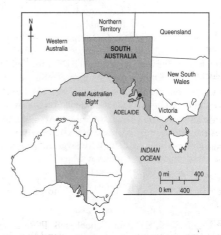

South Ayrshire Unitary authority in SW Scotland created 1996 from part of the former Strathclyde region; administrative headquarters Ayr; population (1996) 114,000; area 1,202 sq km/464 sq mi. Tourism and agriculture are important. Prestwick Airport is here. There are aerospace and high technology industries. Famous people: Robert Burns, Robert the Bruce.

South Bank Area of London S of the river Thames, between Waterloo Bridge and Hungerford Bridge. It was the site of the Festival of Britain 1951, and is now a cultural centre. Buildings include the Royal Festival Hall 1951 (Robert Matthew and Leslie Martin), the Queen Elizabeth

Hall and the Purcell Room 1967, the National Theatre 1976 (Denys Lasdun), the Hayward Gallery 1967, the National Film Theatre 1970, and the Museum of the Moving Image 1988, all connected by a series of walkways. It was announced 1991 that the Queen Elizabeth Hall was to be demolished to create a new South Bank Arts Centre. The South Bank Centre is to be refurbished by the architect Richard Rogers.

South Bend City on the St Joseph River, N Indiana, USA; population (1992) 105,900. Industries include the manufacture of agricultural machinery, cars, and aircraft equipment. The community developed around a fur-trading post established 1820, and was renamed 1830 for the bend in the river.

South Carolina State in SE USA; nicknamed Palmetto State; became a state 1788.
area 80,600 sq km/31,112 sq mi
capital Columbia
towns Charleston, Greenville-Spartanburg
physical large areas of woodland; subtropical climate in coastal areas; semitropical islands including Kiawah, Seabrook, and Isle of Palms; Frances Marion national forest
features the Grand Strand, a resort area with 89 km/55 mi of beach, including Huntington Beach and Myrtle Beach state parks, Pewley's Island, and Hilton Head Island; plantations, including Magnolia Plantation and Gardens (begun 1686, with a large collection of azaleas and camellias), Boone Hall Plantation (1681, with the original slave quarters), Hampton Plantation state park, and Hopsewee Plantation; Rice Museum at Georgetown, the centre of the rice plantation area; Charleston, with Greek Revival buildings (including St John's Lutheran Church 1817, Congregation Beth Elohim 1840, and the Edmonston-Alston House 1828), the French Huguenot Church (the only church in the USA still following the original Huguenot liturgy), Nathaniel Russell House (Adam style, 1808), Joseph Manigault Mansion (1803), St Michael's Episcopal Church (1761, modelled on the church of St Martin-in-the-Fields, London), the Gibbes Art Gallery, and the Charleston Museum (1773, the oldest city museum in the USA); Beaufort, established 1710, with large 18th- and 19th-century houses, including the John Mark Verdier House (1790) and the George Elliott House (1840); Cowpens national battlefield and Kings Mountain national military park, sites of British defeats; Fort Sumter national monument, where the first shot of the Civil War was fired 12 April 1861; St Helena Island, with the Penn School historic district and the York W Bailey Museum (the school was started during the Civil War as the first school for freed slaves in the South); Patriots Point, Mount Pleasant, the world's largest naval and maritime museum; Brookgreen Gardens, started 1931 on four former rice plantations, with the largest outdoor collection of US sculpture; Middleton Place, with the oldest landscape gardens in the USA (1741); the Spoleto Festival USA, founded 1977 by Gian Carlo Menotti as part of his Festival of Two Worlds
industries tobacco, soya beans, lumber, textiles, clothing, paper, wood pulp, chemicals, nonelectrical machinery, primary and fabricated metals
population (1995) 3,673,300

South Dakota State in W USA; nicknamed Coyote State/Sunshine State/Mount Rushmore State; became a state 1889
area 199,800 sq km/77,123 sq mi
capital Pierre
cities Sioux Falls, Rapid City, Aberdeen
physical Great Plains; Black Hills national forest; Badlands national park; the Missouri River; Wind Cave national park; Jewel Cave national monument; Custer state park
features in Black Hills, granite Mount Rushmore, on whose face giant relief portrait heads of former presidents Washington, Jefferson, Lincoln, and T Roosevelt are carved; Deadwood, a 19th-century gold-mining town, with legalized gambling; Wounded Knee Massacre Monument, in Pine Ridge Native American reservation; Sioux Indian Museum, Rapid City; Indian Museum of North America; Corn Palace (1892), Mitchell; Greek Revival state capitol (1910), Pierre; DeSmet, home of writer Laura Ingalls Wilder
industries cereals, hay, livestock, gold (second-largest US producer), meat products
population (1995) 729,000
famous people Crazy Horse, Sitting Bull, Ernest O Lawrence.

South Downs Line of chalk hills in SE England, running across Sussex to Beachy Head. They face the ◊North Downs and are used as sheep pasture.

South East Cape Southernmost point of Australia, in Tasmania.

Southend-on-Sea Resort in Essex, England, on the Thames estuary, the nearest seaside resort to London; population (1994 est) 171,000; it will become a unitary authority in April 1998. The shallow water of the Thames estuary enabled the building of a pier 2 km/1.25 mi long, the longest in the world.

Southern and Antarctic Territories French overseas territory created 1955. It comprises the islands of *St Paul* and *Amsterdam* (67 sq km/26 sq mi); the *Kerguelen* and *Crozet* Islands (7,515 sq km/2,901 sq mi); and *Adélie Land* on Antarctica (432,000 sq km/165,500 sq mi). All are uninhabited, except for research stations.

Southern Uplands One of the three geographical divisions of Scotland, occupying most of the hilly Scottish Borderland to the S of a geological fault line that stretches from Dunbar on the North Sea to Girvan on the Firth of Clyde. The Southern Uplands, largely formed by rocks of the Silurian and Ordovician age, are intersected by the broad valleys of the Nith and Tweed rivers.

South Georgia Island in the S Atlantic, a British crown colony administered, with the South Sandwich Islands, from the Falkland Islands by a commissioner; area 3,757 sq km/ 1,450 sq mi. The average temperature on the island is –2°C/28.4°F. There has been no permanent population since the whaling station was abandoned 1966. South Georgia lies 1,300 km/800 mi SE of the Falkland Islands, of which it was a dependency until 1985. The British Antarctic Survey has a station on nearby Bird Island.

South Glamorgan (Welsh *De Morgannwg*) Former county of S Wales, 1974–96, now divided between Cardiff and Vale of Glamorgan unitary authorities.

South Gloucestershire Unitary authority in SW England created 1996 from part of the former county of Avon; administrative headquarters Thornbury; population (1997 est) 220,000; area 497 sq km/192 sq mi.

South Holland (Dutch *Zuid Holland*) Low-lying coastal province of the Netherlands, between the provinces of North Holland and Zeeland

area 2,910 sq km/1,123 sq mi

capital The Hague

towns Rotterdam, Dordrecht, Leiden, Delft, Gouda

industries bulbs, horticulture, livestock, dairy products, chemicals, textiles

population (1995 est) 3,325,100

history once part of the former county of Holland, which was divided into two provinces 1840.

South Island Larger of the two main islands of New Zealand covering an area of 148,883 sq km/57,870 sq mi.

South Korea See Korea, South.

South Lanarkshire Unitary authority in S central Scotland created 1996 from part of the former Strathclyde region; administrative headquarters Hamilton; population (1996) 307,100; area 1,776 sq km/686 sq mi.

Southland Plain Plain on S South Island, New Zealand, on which Invercargill stands. It is an agricultural area with sheep and dairy farming.

South Orkney Islands Group of barren, uninhabited islands in ◊British Antarctic Territory, SE of Cape Horn; area 622 sq km/240 sq mi. They were discovered by the naval explorer Capt George Powell 1821. Argentina, which lays claim to the islands, maintained a scientific station here 1976–82.

South Ossetia Autonomous region of the Georgian republic; population (1990) 99,800; capital Tshkinvali, population (1989) 34,000.

South Platte River in Colorado and Nebraska, USA; length 711 km/422 mi. It rises near Mount Lincoln on the E side of the Rocky Mountains in central Colorado, and flows through Denver and then northwards to Nebraska, where it unites with the North Platte and forms the Platte River. It provides irrigation water for the N part of Colorado. Reservoirs and dams have been created for power, irrigation, and flood control.

South Sandwich Islands Actively volcanic uninhabited British Dependent Territory; area 337 sq km/130 sq mi. Along with ◊South Georgia, 750 km/470 mi to the NW, it is administered from the Falkland Islands. They were claimed by Capt Cook 1775 and named after his patron John Montagu, the 4th Earl of Sandwich. The islands were annexed by the UK 1908 and 1917. They were first formally claimed by Argentina 1948. In Dec 1976, 50 Argentine 'scientists' landed on Southern Thule and were removed June 1982. There is an ice-free port off Cumberland Bay. Over 21 million penguins breed on Zavadovski Island.

South Shetland Islands Archipelago of 12 uninhabited islands in the South Atlantic, forming part of ◊British Antarctic Territory; area 4,622 sq km/1,785 sq mi. The islands were discovered 1819 by William Smith.

South Shields Manufacturing port in Tyne and Wear, England, on the Tyne estuary, E of Gateshead; population (1991) 83,700. Products include electrical goods, cables, chemicals, and paint. The shipbuilding industry has disappeared.

South, the Historically, the states of the USA bounded on the N by the ◊Mason–Dixon Line, the Ohio River, and the E and N borders of Missouri, with an agrarian economy based on plantations worked by slaves, and which seceded from the Union 1861, beginning the American Civil War, as the Confederacy. The term is now loosely applied in a geographical and cultural sense, with Texas often regarded as part of the Southwest rather than the South.

South Uist Island in the Outer Hebrides, Scotland, separated from North Uist by the island of Benbecula. There is a guided-missile range here.

Southwark Inner borough of S Greater London. It includes the districts of Camberwell, ◊Dulwich, and Walworth. It is the oldest borough in London (after the City of London) and was the first to send representatives to Parliament.

features large Roman baths complex, about AD 120, and fine wall paintings have been excavated; Southwark Cathedral (1220), earliest Gothic church in London, with nave built in the 1890s (formerly a parish church, it became a cathedral 1905); inns and alehouses, including the Tabard Inn, where Chaucer's pilgrims met, and the George Inn (1677), the last galleried inn in London; formerly seven prisons, including the Clink and the Marshalsea; site of Globe Theatre (built on Bankside 1599 by Burbage, Shakespeare, and others, burned down 1613, rebuilt 1995); the International Shakespeare Globe Centre is planned to open 1999; Imperial War Museum; Dulwich Picture Gallery; Horniman Museum; Elephant and Castle public house, Walworth; Labour Party headquarters in Walworth Road; former Bankside power station to be transformed into the Tate Gallery of Modern Art (Swiss architects Herzog and de Meuron) with the help of a Millenium Award

population (1991) 218,500

famous people John Harvard (1607–1638), founder of Harvard College, Massachusetts, USA – he is commemorated in Harvard Chapel, Southwark Cathedral; Joseph Chamberlain.

South West Africa Former name (to 1968) of Namibia.

South Yorkshire Metropolitan county of NE England, created 1974; in 1986, most of the functions of the former county council were transferred to the metropolitan district councils

area 1,560 sq km/602 sq mi

towns Barnsley, Sheffield, Doncaster, Rotherham

features river Don; part of Peak District National Park; the 1995 Millennium Commission award will enable the Earth

Centre for environmental research to be built near Doncaster

industries metal work, coal, dairy, sheep, arable farming

population (1994) 1,262,600

famous people Ian Botham, Arthur Scargill.

Sovetsk Town on the river Niemen (Neman) in Kaliningrad region, W Russian Federation. Formerly in East Prussia, it was known as *Tilsit* until 1945. In 1807 Napoleon signed peace treaties with Prussia and Russia here.

Soviet Central Asia Former name (to 1991) of the ◊Central Asian Republics.

Soviet Far East Former name (to 1991) of a geographical division of Asiatic Russia, now known as the ◊Russian Far East.

Soviet Union Alternative name for the former Union of Soviet Socialist Republics (USSR).

Soweto (acronym for *South West Township*) Urban settlement in South Africa, SW of Johannesburg; population (1991) 597,000. It experienced civil unrest during the apartheid regime.

Spa Town in Liège province, Belgium; population (1991) 10,100. A health resort since the 14th century for its mineral springs, it has given its name to similar centres elsewhere.

Spaghetti Junction Nickname for a complex system of motorway flyovers and interchanges at Gravelly Hill, N Birmingham, in West Midlands, England.

Spalato Italian name for ◊Split, a port in Croatia.

Spalding Market town on the river Welland, in Lincolnshire, England; population (1991) 18,700. There are bulb farms and a flower festival in May.

Spanish Guinea Former name of the Republic of Equatorial Guinea.

Spanish Main Common term for the Caribbean Sea in the 16th–17th centuries, but more properly the South American mainland between the river Orinoco and Panama.

Spanish Sahara Former name for ◊Western Sahara.

Spanish Town Town in Middlesex county, Jamaica; population (1991) 92,400. Founded by Diego Columbus about 1525, it was the capital of Jamaica 1535–1871.

Spartanburg City in NW South Carolina, USA, NW of Columbia, in the foothills of the Blue Ridge Mountains; population (1990) 43,500. It is an agricultural centre. Its industries include food products, furniture, textiles, paper, and plumbing supplies. Spartanburg was established 1785.

Spey River in Highland, and Moray, Scotland, rising SE of Fort Augustus, and flowing 172 km/107 mi to the Moray Firth between Lossiemouth and Buckie. It has salmon fisheries at its mouth.

Speyer (English *Spires*) Ancient city on the Rhine, in Rhineland-Palatinate, Germany, 26 km/16 mi S of Mannheim; population (1991) 47,500. It was at the *Diet of Spires* 1529 that Protestantism received its name.

Spice Islands Former name of ◊Maluku, a group of islands in the Malay Archipelago.

Spitalfields District in the Greater London borough of ◊Tower Hamlets. It was once the home of Huguenot silk weavers.

Spithead Roadstead (partly sheltered anchorage) between the mainland of England and the Isle of ◊Wight. The name is often applied to the entire E area of the ◊Solent.

Spitsbergen Mountainous island with a deeply indented coastline in the Arctic Ocean, the main island in the Norwegian archipelago of ◊Svalbard, 657 km/408 mi N of Norway; area 39,043 sq km/15,075 sq mi. Fishing, hunting, and coal mining are the chief economic activities. The Norwegian Polar Research Institute operates an all-year scientific station on the W coast. Mount Newton rises to 1,713 m/5,620 ft.

Split (Italian *Spalato*) Port in Croatia, on the Adriatic coast; population (1991) 189,400. Industries include engineering, cement, and textiles. Split was bombed during 1991 as part of Yugoslavia's blockade of the Croatian coast.

Spokane City on the Spokane River, E Washington, USA; population (1992) 187,400. It is situated in a mining, timber, and rich agricultural area, and is the seat of Gonzaga University (1887). Spokane was incorporated 1881.

Spoleto Town in Umbria, central Italy; population (1985) 37,000. There is an annual opera and drama festival (June–July) established by Gian Carlo Menotti. It was a papal possession 1220–1860 and has Roman remains and medieval churches.

Sporades Greek island group in the Aegean Sea. The chief island of the *Northern Sporades* is ◊Skyros. The *Southern Sporades* are more usually referred to as the ◊Dodecanese.

Spratly Islands (Chinese *Nanshan Islands*) Disputed group of small islands, coral reefs, and sandbars dispersed over a distance of 965 km/600 mi in the South China Sea. The islands are of strategic importance, commanding the sea passage from Japan to Singapore, and in 1976 oil was discovered.

Spree River in E Germany; length 365 km/226 mi. The Spree rises on the borders of Bohemia and the *Land* of Saxony, and after flowing generally N and NW joins the river Havel to the W of Berlin, at Spandau. On its course, the Spree passes through Bautzen, Cottbus, and Berlin. A marshy area in its valley near Cottbus is called the *Spreewald*.

Springdale City in NW Arkansas, USA, NW of Little Rock; population (1990) 29,900. Industries include food and livestock processing.

Springfield Capital and agricultural and mining centre of Illinois, USA; population (1992) 106,400. Springfield was settled 1818 and became the state capital 1837. President Abraham Lincoln is buried here.

Springfield City in Massachusetts, USA; population (1992) 153,500. It was the site (1794–1968) of the US arsenal and armoury, known for the Springfield rifle. The community dates from 1636.

Springfield City and agricultural centre in Missouri, USA; population (1992) 145,400. Industries include electronic equipment and processed food. Springfield was settled 1829.

Springfield City in W Oregon, USA, on the Willamette River, E of Eugene; population (1990) 45,000. Industries include lumber, animal feeds, and agricultural products.

Springs City in Gauteng Province, South Africa, 40 km/ 25 mi E of Johannesburg; population (1991) 170,000. It is a mining centre, producing gold, coal, and uranium.

Srinagar Summer capital of the state of Jammu and Kashmir, India; population (1991) 595,000. It is a beautiful resort, intersected by waterways, and has carpet, papier mâché, and leather industries.

Stade City in Lower Saxony, Germany, 140 km/87 mi NW of Hannover; population (1994) 180,400. There are oil-refining, nuclear-power, chemical, and aluminium industries in this industrial growth area. The town was formerly a member of the medieval Hanseatic League trade federation.

Staffa Uninhabited island in the Inner Hebrides, W of Mull. It has a rugged coastline and many caves, including ◊Fingal's Cave.

Staffordshire County of W central England
area 2,623 sq km/1,012 sq mi
towns Stafford (administrative headquarters), Newcastle-under-Lyme
features largely flat; river Trent and its tributaries; Cannock Chase; Keele University 1962; Staffordshire bull terriers
industries china and earthenware in the Potteries and the upper Trent basin, especially Wedgwood; tractors and agricultural equipment (JCB, Uttoxeter); dairy farming; coal mining; electrical engineering
population (1996) 802,100
famous people Arnold Bennett, Peter de Wint, Robert Peel, Josiah Wedgwood.

Staffs Abbreviation for ◊Staffordshire, an English county.

Stalin Former name (1949–56) of the port of ◊Varna, Bulgaria.

Stalingrad Former name (1925–61) of the Russian city of ◊Volgograd.

Stalinsk Former name (1932–61) of the Russian city of ◊Novokuznetsk.

Stalowa Wola Industrial town in Rzeszów province, SE Poland, on the river San, 61 km/38 mi N of Rzeszów. Its steel mill was built in 1938 as part of a government policy to establish industrialization away from Poland's W frontier with Germany. The town has three electricity-generating stations.

Stamboul Old part of the Turkish city of ◊Istanbul, the area formerly known as Byzantium.

Stamford City in SW Connecticut, USA, on Long Island Sound, NE of New York City; population (1992) 107,600.

Industries include computers, hardware, rubber, plastics, and pharmaceuticals. There are many corporate headquarters here. Stamford was founded 1641.

Stanley Town on E Falkland, capital of the ◊Falkland Islands; population (1991) 1,557. After changing its name only once between 1843 and 1982, it was renamed five times in the space of six weeks during the Falklands War April–June 1982.

Stanley Falls Former name (to 1972) of ◊Boyoma Falls, on the Congo/Zaïre River.

Stanley Pool Former name (to 1972) of ◊Pool Malebo, on the Congo/Zaïre River.

Stanleyville Former name (to 1966) of the port of ◊Kisangani in the Democratic Republic of Congo (formerly Zaire).

Stansted London's third international airport, in Essex, England.

Stara Planina Bulgarian name for the ◊Balkan Mountains in central Europe.

Stara Zagora Town in Khaskovo region of central Bulgaria, S of the Shipka Pass through the Balkan Mountains; population (1990) 187,500. The chief industries are the production of chemicals and tobacco, and food processing. The town lies in a rose-growing area. Founded by the Romans, it became a major market centre under the Turks, and was ceded to Bulgaria 1877.

Stargard or *Stargard Szczeciński* Town in Szczecin province, Poland, on the river Ina, 36 km/22 mi E of Szczecin; population (1990) 71,000. Founded in the 12th century, it became a member of the medieval Hanseatic League trading confederation. It remained in German Pomerania until 1945; from 1648 as part of Brandenburg under the Treaty of Westphalia.

Stassfurt Town in the *Land* of ◊Saxony-Anhalt, Germany, on the river Bode, 29 km/18 mi S of Magdeburg. It has potash and magnetite deposits, and manufactures chemicals and machinery.

Staten Island Island in New York harbour, part of New York City, USA, comprising the county of Richmond and, since 1975, the borough of Staten Island; area 155 sq km/ 60 sq mi.

Stavanger Seaport and capital of Rogaland county, SW Norway, population (1994) 104,000. It has fish-canning, oil, and shipbuilding industries. It was founded in the 8th century and has a 12th-century cathedral.

Stavropol Territory of the Russian Federation, lying N of the Caucasus Mountains; area 80,600 sq km/31,128 sq mi; population (1991 est) 2,926,500. The capital is Stavropol. Irrigated land produces grain and sheep are also reared. There are natural gas deposits.

Stavropol formerly (1935–43) *Voroshilovsk* Town SE of Rostov, in the N Caucasus, SW Russian Federation; population (1994) 337,000. Founded 1777 as a fortress town, it is now a market centre for an agricultural area and makes agricultural machinery, textiles, and food products.

Steelville Town in Missouri, USA, on the edge of the Ozark Mountains; founded 1835 as a staging post. On completion of the 1990 census, it was calculated to be the demographic centre of the USA.

Steep Point The westernmost extremity of Australia, in Western Australia, NW of the Murchison River.

Steiermark German name for ◊Styria, a province of Austria.

Stellenbosch Town in Western Cape Province, South Africa; population (1991) 19,950. It is the centre of a wine-producing district. It was founded 1679, and is the oldest European settlement in South Africa after Cape Town.

Stendal Town in the *Land* of ◊Saxony-Anhalt, Germany, 56 km/35 mi NE of Magdeburg. There are metal, chemical, and food industries. In the second half of the 13th century Stendal was the capital of the area known as the Mark Brandenburg (Brandenburg Marches). The cathedral, begun in 1188, was rebuilt in the 14th century.

Stepney District of London, now part of the borough of ◊Tower Hamlets, N of the Thames, and E of the City of London.

Sterea Ellas-Evvoia Region of central Greece and Euboea, occupying the S part of the Greek mainland between the Ionian and Aegean seas and including the island of Euboea; area 24,391 sq km/9,421 sq mi; population (1991) 1,235,600. The chief city is Athens.

Stettin German name for the Polish city of ◊Szczecin.

Stettiner Haff German name for ◊Zalew Szczeciński, a lagoon in Poland and NE Germany.

Stettin Lagoon English name for ◊Zalew Szczeciński, a lagoon in Poland and NE Germany.

Steubenville City in E Ohio, USA, on the Ohio River, S of Youngstown, near the West Virginia border; population (1990) 22,100. Industries include steel, coal, paper, and chemicals. Originally Fort Steuben, it was built 1786 to protect government land agents from the Native Americans.

Stevenage Town in Hertfordshire, England, 45 km/28 mi N of London; population (1991) 76,100. Dating from medieval times, in 1946 Stevenage was the first place to be designated a new town (to accommodate overspill). Industries include aircraft manufacture, electrical and plastic goods, pharmaceuticals, missiles, space and satellites manufacturing centre of Matra Marconi Space Systems.

Stewart Island Volcanic island divided from South Island, New Zealand, by the Foveaux Strait; area 1,750 sq km/676 sq mi; population (1989 est) 450. Industries include farming, fishing, and granite quarrying. Oban is the main settlement.

St Gallen Capital of St Gallen canton, Switzerland, situated just S of Lake Constance. The town has an ancient abbey and a Baroque cathedral. St Gallen is also an industrial centre specializing in embroidered cotton textiles and nylon.

St Gallen (French *St Gall*) Canton in NE Switzerland; area 2,014 sq km/778 sq mi; population (1995) 442,300. It is mountainous in the S, near its border with Graubunden, but has gentler hills in the N region around Lake Constance. It entirely surrounds the canton of Appenzell. The chief industry is the manufacture of textiles. The main farming activity is dairying, supplemented by cattle-rearing on the Alpine pastures. There are numerous health and winter-sports resorts.

Stirling Unitary authority in central Scotland created 1996 from part of the former Central region; population (1996) 82,000; area 2,195 sq km/848 sq mi. Tourism is important because of the mountain scenery, including the Trossachs, and Lochs Lomond and Tay.

Stirling Administrative headquarters of Stirling unitary authority, Scotland, on the river Forth; population (1991) 30,500. Industries include the manufacture of agricultural machinery, textiles, chemicals, and carpets. Stirling is noted for its summer programme of historical theatre, the Scottish Wool Centre at Aberfoyle (opened 1993), showing the history of the wool and textile industries in Scotland. The castle, which guarded a key crossing of the river, predates the 12th century and was long a Scottish royal residence. William Wallace won a victory at Stirling bridge 1297. Edward II of England (in raising a Scottish siege of the town) went into battle at Bannockburn 1314 and was defeated by Robert I the Bruce.

Stirlingshire Former county of Scotland. From 1975–96 most of it was merged with Central Region, but a SW section, including Kilsyth, went to Strathclyde Region. It is now in Stirling unitary authority.

Stockholm Capital and industrial port of Sweden; population (1994 est) 703,600. It is built on a number of islands. Industries include engineering, brewing, electrical goods, paper, textiles, and pottery.

Stockholm County of E Sweden; area 6,503 sq km/2,510 sq mi; population (1990) 1,606,200. It surrounds the national capital of ◊Stockholm but is administratively separate. It is a fertile lowland region with many lakes. Small amounts of iron ore are mined in the NE, but the county's main industries are metallurgy and the manufacture of paper and electrical equipment.

Stockport Town in Greater Manchester, England; population (1994 est) 120,000. The rivers Tame and Goyt join here to form the Mersey. Industries include electronics, chemicals, engineering, textile and electrical machinery, hats, paper, plastics, and still some cotton textiles.

Stockton Industrial river port (agricultural machinery, food processing) on the San Joaquin River in California, USA; population (1992) 219,600. Stockton was founded as Tuleburg 1847 as a supply centre for the California gold rush, and renamed 1850.

Stockton-on-Tees Unitary authority in NE England created 1996 from part of the former county of Cleveland; population (1996 est) 176,600; area 200 sq km/77 sq mi. There are electronics industries at Billingham (Samsung).

Stockton-on-Tees Town and port and administrative headquarters of Stockton-on-Tees unitary authority, on the river Tees, NE England; population (1994 est) 157,000. There are ship-repairing, steel, and chemical industries, and it was the starting point for the world's first passenger railway 1825.

Stoke-on-Trent City and unitary authority in central England, on the river Trent; population (1996) 254,200; area 93 sq km/36 sq mi. It was part of the county of Staffordshire to 1997. It is the heart of the Potteries, a major ceramic centre, and the largest clay ware producer in the world. Other industries include steel, chemicals, engineering machinery, paper, and rubber. Pit closures 1992–93 have led to a decline in coal mining.

Stoke Poges Village in Buckinghamshire, England, 3 km/2 mi N of Slough, which inspired Thomas Gray to write his 'Elegy in a Country Churchyard'; the poet is buried here.

Stolp German name for ♦Słupsk, a town and province in Poland.

Stornoway Port on the island of Lewis in the Outer ♦Hebrides, Scotland; population (1991) 6,000. It is the administrative centre for the Western Isles. The economy is based on fishing, tourism, tweeds, and offshore oil. Stornoway was founded by James VI of Scotland (James I of England).

Stourbridge Market town in West Midlands, England, on the river Stour, SW of Birmingham; population (1991) 55,600. Industries include the manufacture of glass and bricks.

Straits Settlements Former province of the East India Company 1826–58, a British crown colony 1867–1946; it comprised Singapore, Malacca, Penang, Cocos Islands, Christmas Island, and Labuan.

Stranraer Port in Dumfries and Galloway, Scotland; population (1991) 11,300. There is a ferry service to Larne in Northern Ireland.

Strasbourg City on the river Ill, in Bas-Rhin *département*, capital of Alsace, France; population (1990) 255,900. Industries include car manufacture, tobacco, printing and publishing, and preserves. The Council of Europe meets here, and sessions of the European Parliament alternate between Strasbourg and Luxembourg.

Stratford Port and industrial town in SW Ontario, Canada; population (1991) 27,700. It is the site of a Shakespeare theatre festival.

Stratford-upon-Avon Market town on the river Avon, in Warwickshire, England; population (1991) 22,200. It is the birthplace of William Shakespeare and has the Royal Shakespeare Theatre 1932, the Swan Theatre, and The Other Place Theatre.

Strathclyde Former Region of Scotland to 1996; replaced by Argyll and Bute, East Ayrshire, East Dunbartonshire, East Renfrewshire, Glasgow City, Inverclyde, North Ayrshire, North Lanarkshire, South Ayrshire, South Lanarkshire, and West Dunbartonshire unitary authorities.

Stretford Town in Greater ♦Manchester, England; population (1991) 44,000. It includes the Old Trafford cricket ground. There are engineering, chemical, and textile industries.

Stromboli Italian island in the Tyrrhenian Sea, one of the ♦Lipari Islands; area 12 sq km/5 sq mi. It has an active volcano, 926 m/3,039 ft high. The island produces Malmsey wine and capers.

Strumica Town and district in the SE of the Former Yugoslav Republic of Macedonia, in the valley of the river Struma; population (1991 est) 90,000. It produces tobacco and other agricultural products.

Stuttgart Capital of Baden-Württemberg, on the river Neckar, Germany; population (1993) 598,000. Industries include the manufacture of vehicles and electrical goods, foodstuffs, textiles, papermaking and publishing; it is a fruit-growing and wine-producing centre. There are two universities. Stuttgart was founded in the 10th century.

Styria (German *Steiermark*) Alpine province of SE Austria; area 16,388 sq km/6,327 sq mi; population (1995) 1,206,317. Its capital is Graz, and its industries include iron, steel, lignite, vehicles, electrical goods, and engineering. An independent state from 1056 until it passed to the Habsburgs in the 13th century, it was annexed by Germany 1938.

Subotica Largest town in Vojvodina, NW Serbia, Yugoslavia; population (1991) 100,200. Industries include chemicals and electrical machinery.

Suceava Capital of Suceava county, N Romania; population (1993) 116,000. Industries include textiles and lumber. It was a former centre of pilgrimage and capital of Moldavia 1388–1564.

Sucre Legal capital and judicial seat of Bolivia; population (1992) 131,000. It stands on the central plateau at an altitude of 2,840 m/9,320 ft.

Sudbury City in Ontario, Canada; population (1991) 92,900, metropolitan area 157,400. A buried meteorite here yields 90% of the world's nickel.

Sudeten (Polish *Sudety*) Mountainous region in NE Bohemia, Czech Republic, extending eastwards along the border with Poland. Sudeten was annexed by Germany under the Munich Agreement 1938; it was returned to Czechoslovakia 1945. Germany and the Czech Republic sought to bury decades of mutual antagonism Jan 1997 by signing a joint declaration aimed at drawing a line under the vexed issue of the Sudetenland. Germany apologised for the suffering caused during the Nazi occupation. For their part, the Czechs expressed regret over the 'injustices' that took place during the expulsion of more than 2.5 million Sudetenland Germans after World War II. It took over two years to reach this agreement.

Suez (Arabic *El Suweis*) Port at the Red Sea terminus of the Suez Canal; population (1994) 458,000. Industries include oil refining and the manufacture of fertilizers. It was reconstructed 1979, after the Arab-Israeli Wars.

Suez Canal Artificial waterway, 160 km/100 mi long, from Port Said to Suez, linking the Mediterranean and Red seas, separating Africa from Asia, and providing the shortest eastwards sea route from Europe. The canal was opened 1869, nationalized 1956, blocked by Egypt during the Arab-Israeli War 1967, and not reopened until 1975.

Suffolk County of E England
area 3,800 sq km/1,467 sq mi
towns Ipswich (administrative headquarters), Bury St Edmunds, Lowestoft, Felixstowe
features undulating lowlands and flat coastline; rivers: Waveney, Alde, Deben, Orwell, Stour, Little Ouse; part of the Norfolk Broads; Minsmere marshland bird reserve, near Aldeburgh; the Sandlings (heathlands and birds); Sutton Hoo (7th-century ship burial); Sizewell B, Britain's first pressurized-water nuclear reactor plant, in operation 1995
industries cereals, sugar beet, timber, working horses (Suffolk punches), fertilizers, agricultural machinery, fishing, electronics, telecommunications research, printing, motor vehicle components, food processing, North Sea oil and gas exploration
population (1996) 649,500.

Sukkur or *Sakhar* Port in Sind province, Pakistan, on the river Indus; population (1981) 191,000. The Sukkur River–Lloyd Barrage 1928–32 lies to the W.

Sulawesi formerly *Celebes* Island in E Indonesia, one of the Sunda Islands; area (with dependent islands) 189,216 sq km/73,057 sq mi; population (1990) 12,520,700. It is mountainous and forested and produces copra and nickel.

Sulu Archipelago Group of about 870 islands off SW Mindanao in the Philippines, between the Sulawesi and Sulu seas; area 2,700 sq km/1,042 sq mi; population (1989) 12,507,700. The capital is Jolo, on the island (the largest) of the same name. Until 1940 the islands were an autonomous sultanate.

Sumatra or *Sumatera* Second-largest island of Indonesia, one of the Sunda Islands; area 473,600 sq km/182,800 sq mi; population (1990) 36,505,700. East of a longitudinal volcanic mountain range is a wide plain; both are heavily forested. Products include rubber, rice, tobacco, tea, timber, tin, and petroleum.

Šumen Alternative form for Shumen, a city in Bulgaria.

Sunbelt Popular name for a region of the USA, S of Washington DC, between the Pacific and Atlantic coasts, so called because of its climate. The largest city in the Sunbelt is Los Angeles.

Sunbury-on-Thames Market town and boating centre in Surrey, SE England, on the river Thames; population (1991) 27,400.

Sun City Holiday and casino resort in ◊Mmabatho, the capital of North West Province, South Africa.

Sunda Islands Islands W of Maluku (Moluccas), in the Malay Archipelago, the greater number belonging to Indonesia. They are so named because they lie largely on the Indonesian extension of the Sunda continental shelf. The *Greater Sundas* include Borneo, Java (including the small

island of Madura), Sumatra, Sulawesi, and Belitung. The *Lesser Sundas* (Indonesian *Nusa Tenggara*) are all Indonesian and include Bali, Lombok, Flores, Sumba, Sumbawa, and Timor.

Sunderland City and port in Tyne and Wear, NE England, at the mouth of the river Wear; population (1994 est) 176,000.

Sundsvall Port in E Sweden; population (1992) 94,300. It has oil, timber, and wood-pulp industries.

Sungari River in Manchuria, NE China, that joins the Amur River on the Siberian frontier; length 1,300 km/800 mi.

Sunshine Coast Chain of sandy beaches on the coast of Queensland, Australia, stretching for about 100 km/60 mi from Bribie Island, N of Brisbane, to Rainbow Beach. It includes the resorts of Noosa Heads and Caloundra.

Superior, Lake Largest and deepest of the ◊Great Lakes and the largest freshwater lake in the world; area 82,071 sq km/31,688 sq mi. It is bordered by the Canadian province of Ontario and the US states of Minnesota, Wisconsin, and Michigan. As the westernmost of the Great Lakes, Superior is at the W end of the St Lawrence Seaway.

Sur or *Soûr* Arabic name for the Lebanese port of Tyre.

Surabaya Port on the island of Java, Indonesia; population (1990) 2,421,000. It has oil refineries and shipyards and is a naval base.

Surat City in Gujarat, W India, at the mouth of the Tapti River; population (1991) 1,499,000. The chief industry is textiles. The first East India Company trading post in India was established here 1612.

Surrey County of S England
area 1,660 sq km/641 sq mi
towns Kingston upon Thames (administrative headquarters), Guildford, Woking, Reigate, Leatherhead
features rivers: Thames, Mole, Wey; hills: Box and Leith; North Downs; Runnymede, Thameside site of the signing of *Magna Carta*; Yehudi Menuhin School; Kew Palace and Royal Botanic Gardens
industries vegetables, agricultural products, service industries, horticulture, gravel
population (1994) 1,041,200
famous people John Galsworthy, Aldous Huxley, Laurence Olivier, Eric Clapton.

Surtsey Volcanic island 20 km/12 mi SW of Heimaey in the Westman Islands (Vestmannaeyjar) of Iceland. The island was created by an underwater volcanic eruption Nov 1963.

Susquehanna River rising in central New York State, USA, and flowing 715 km/444 mi to Chesapeake Bay. It is used for hydroelectric power. On the strength of its musical name, Samuel Coleridge planned to establish a communal settlement here with his fellow poet Robert Southey.

Sussex Former county of England, on the S coast, now divided into ◊East Sussex and ◊West Sussex.

Sutherlandshire Former county of N Scotland, included 1975–96 in Highland Region; now in Highland unitary authority.

Sutlej River in Pakistan, a tributary of the river ◊Indus; length 1,370 km/851 mi.

Sutton Outer borough of S Greater London
features probably a Saxon settlement in 6th and 7th centuries; site of Nonsuch Palace, built by Henry VIII, demolished in the 17th century; parish church of St Nicholas, rebuilt 1862; All Saints Church (1865); one of the first nursery schools in England, founded 1909; central library, opened 1975, one of the finest local libraries in Europe; large shopping mall, St Nicholas Centre, 1991
population (1991) 164,300
history Sutton expanded in the mid-19th century, after construction of a railway line, and became an early commuter town. It has remained a residential area.

Sutton Coldfield Residential part of the West Midlands conurbation around ◊Birmingham, England; population (1991) 106,000.

Sutton-in-Ashfield Town in Nottinghamshire, England; population (1990 est) 40,200. It has coal, hosiery, metal box, and plastics industries.

Suva Capital and industrial port of Fiji, on Viti Levu; population (1986) 69,700. It produces soap and coconut oil.

Suzhou or *Soochow* formerly 1912–49 *Wuhsien* City S of the Yangtze river delta and E of the ◊Grand Canal, in Jiangsu province, China; population (1990) 706,000. It has embroidery and jade-carving traditions and Shizilin and Zhuozheng gardens. The city dates from about 1000 BC, and the name Suzhou from the 7th century AD; it was reputedly visited by the Venetian Marco Polo.

Svalbard Norwegian archipelago in the Arctic Ocean. The main island is Spitsbergen; other islands include North East Land, Edge Island, Barents Island, and Prince Charles Foreland.

Svealand Central region of Sweden, historically the core of the country. The people of this area were the first to rise against the Danes in the 16th century.

Sverdlovsk Former name (1924–91) of the Russian town of ◊Yekaterinburg.

Swanage Town on the Isle of Purbeck, ◊Dorset, England.

Swansea Unitary authority in S Wales created 1996 from part of the former county of West Glamorgan; population (1996) 232,000; area 377 sq km/156 sq mi. The Gower Peninsula is an area of oustanding natural beauty. Industries include tinplate manufacturing and chemicals, and there are oil refineries.

Swansea (Welsh *Abertawe*) Port and administrative headquarters of Swansea unitary authority, S Wales, at the mouth of the river Tawe where it meets the Bristol Channel; population (1994 est) 172,000. It is the second-largest city in Wales. It has oil refineries, chemicals, metallurgical industries, tin plate manufacturing, and produces stained glass (since 1936).

Swatow Another name for the Chinese port of ◊Shantou.

Swindon Town and unitary authority in SW England, 124 km/77 mi W of London; population (1996) 170,000; area 230 sq km/89 sq mi; it was part of the county of Wiltshire to 1997. The site of a major railway engineering works 1841–1986 on the Great Western Railway, the town has diversified since 1950 into heavy engineering, electronics, electrical manufacture, and cars (Honda). Swindon Rail Works Ltd specializes in repair work for steam railway preservation societies. There is a railway museum. The White Horse of Uffington is nearby.

Sydney Capital and port of New South Wales, Australia; population (1993) 3,713,500. Industries include engineering, oil refining, electronics, scientific equipment, chemicals, clothing, and furniture. It is a financial centre, and has three universities. The 19th-century Museum of Applied Arts and Sciences is the most popular museum in Australia. It has been chosen as the site of the 2000 Olympic Games.

Syktyvkar Capital of the autonomous republic of Komi, N central Russia; population (1994) 227,000. Industries include timber, paper, and tanning. It was founded 1740 as a Russian colony.

Sylhet Capital of Sylhet region, NE Bangladesh; population (1991) 228,100. It is a tea-growing centre and also produces rice, jute, and sugar. There is natural gas nearby. It is the former capital of a Hindu kingdom and was conquered by Muslims in the 14th century. In the 1971 civil war, which led to the establishment of Bangladesh, it was the scene of heavy fighting.

Syracuse (Italian *Siracusa*) Province of Italy in ◊Sicily; capital Syracuse; area 2,108 sq km/804 sq mi; population (1992) 403,400.

Syracuse (Italian *Siracusa*) Industrial port (chemicals, salt) in E Sicily; population (1992) 126,800. It has a cathedral and remains of temples, aqueducts, catacombs, and an amphitheatre. Founded 734 BC by the Corinthians, it became a centre of Greek culture under the elder and younger Dionysius. After a three-year siege it was taken by Rome 212 BC. In AD 878 it was destroyed by the Arabs, and the rebuilt town came under Norman rule in the 11th century.

Syracuse Industrial city on Lake Onondaga, in New York State, USA; population (1992) 162,900. Industries include the manufacture of electrical and other machinery, paper, and food processing. There are canal links with the ◊Great Lakes and the Hudson and St Lawrence rivers. Syracuse was settled in the 1780s on the site of a former Iroquois capital and developed as a salt-mining centre.

Szatmar-Nemeti Hungarian name for ◊Satu Mare, a town in Romania.

Szczecin (German *Stettin*) Industrial (shipbuilding, fish processing, synthetic fibres, tools, iron) port on the river Oder, in NW Poland; population (1993) 414,200.

Szechwan Alternative spelling for the central Chinese province of ◊Sichuan.

Szeged Port on the river Tisza and capital of Csongrád county, S Hungary; population (1993 est) 179,000. The chief industry is textiles, and the port trades in timber and salt.

Székesfehérvár Industrial city (metal products) in W central Hungary; population (1993 est) 110,000. It is a market centre for wine, tobacco, and fruit.

Tabah or *Taba* Small area of disputed territory, 1 km/ 0.6 mi long, between Elat (Israel) to the E and the Sinai Desert (Egypt) to the W on the Red Sea. Under an Anglo-Egyptian-Turkish agreement 1906, the border ran through Tabah; under a British survey of 1915 headed by T E Lawrence (of Arabia), who made 'adjustments' allegedly under British government orders, it runs to the E. Taken by Israel 1967, Tabah was returned to Egypt 1989.

Tabasco State of SE Mexico, on the border of Guatemala; area 24,661 sq km/9,522 sq mi; population (1995 est) 1,748,700. Its capital is Villahermosa. The main occupations are livestock raising and farming, producing cacao, rice, sugar, coffee, and tobacco.

Table Bay Wide bay on the N coast of the Cape of Good Hope, South Africa, on which Cape Town stands. It is overlooked by Table Mountain.

Table Mountain Flat-topped mountain overlooking Table Bay and Cape Town on the coast of the Cape of Good Hope, South Africa. Its highest point is Maclear's Beacon, 1,087 m/ 3,566 ft. The flat summit of the mountain is often covered with cloud, known as the 'tablecloth'.

Tábor Industrial town (textiles, tobacco) of S Bohemia, in the Czech Republic, on the river Lužnice, 75 km/ 47 mi S of Prague; population (1991) 36,300. It was founded in 1420 as the military stronghold of a Hussite community of religious and political dissenters known as the Taborites.

Tabora Trading centre in W Tanzania; population (1988) 214,000. It was founded about 1820 by Arab traders of slaves and ivory.

Tabriz City in NW Iran; population (1991) 1,089,000. Industries include metal casting, carpets, cotton, and silk textiles.

Tacna City in S Peru; population (1993) 174,300. It is undergoing industrialization, and produces tobacco, cotton, sugar cane and sulphur. In 1880 Chile defeated a combined Peruvian-Bolivian army nearby and occupied Tacna until 1929.

Tacoma Port in Washington State, USA, on Puget Sound, 40 km/25 mi S of Seattle; population (1992) 183,900. It is a lumber and shipping centre, with fishing and boat-building industries. Other industries include primary metals, wood and paper products, chemicals, and processed foods. Founded 1868, the city developed after being chosen as the terminus of the North Pacific Railroad 1873.

Taegu Third-largest city in South Korea, situated between Seoul and Pusan; population (1990) 2,228,800. Nearby is the Haeinsa Temple, one of the country's largest monasteries and repository of the *Triptaka Koreana*, a collection of 80,000 wood blocks on which the Buddhist scriptures are carved. Grain, fruit, textiles, and tobacco are produced.

Taejon (Korean 'large rice paddy') Capital of South Chungchong province, central South Korea; population (1990) 1,062,100. Korea's tallest standing Buddha and oldest

wooden building are found NE of the city at Popchusa in the Mount Songnisan National Park.

Taganrog Port in the NE corner of the Sea of Azov, SW Russian Federation, W of Rostov; population (1994) 291,000. Industries include iron, steel, metal goods, aircraft, machinery, and shoes. A museum commemorates playwright Anton Chekhov, who was born here.

Tagus (Spanish *Tajo*, Portuguese *Tejo*) River rising in Aragón, Spain, and reaching the Atlantic Ocean at Lisbon, Portugal; length 1,007 km/626 mi. At Lisbon it is crossed by the April 25 (formerly Salazar) Bridge, so named in honour of the 1974 revolution. The *Tagus-Segura* irrigation scheme serves the rainless Murcia/Alicante region for early fruit and vegetable growing.

Tahiti Largest of the Society Islands, in ◊French Polynesia; area 1,042 sq km/402 sq mi; population (1988) 115,800. Its capital is Papeete. Tahiti was visited by Capt James Cook 1769 and by Admiral Bligh of the *Bounty* 1788. It came under French control 1843 and became a colony 1880.

Taipei or *Taibei* Capital and commercial centre of Taiwan; population (1995) 2,639,300. Industries include electronics, plastics, textiles, and machinery. The National Palace Museum 1965 houses the world's greatest collection of Chinese art, brought here from the mainland 1948.

T'ai Shan Sacred mountain of Chinese mythology, located in the province of Shandong; the greatest of five similar mountains, all closely associated with religious observances.

Taiyuan Capital of Shanxi province, on the river Fen He, NE China; population (1993) 1,680,000. Industries include iron, steel, agricultural machinery, and textiles. It is a walled city, founded in the 5th century AD, and is the seat of Shanxi University.

Ta'izz City in N Yemen, at the centre of a coffee-growing region; population (1986) 178,000. Cotton, leather, and jewellery are also produced.

Taj Mahal White marble mausoleum built 1630–53 on the river Yamuna near Agra, India. Erected by Shah Jahan to the memory of his favourite wife, it is a celebrated example of Indo-Islamic architecture, the fusion of Muslim and Hindu styles.

Tajo Spanish name for the river ◊Tagus.

Takao Japanese name for ◊Kaohsiung, a city on the W coast of Taiwan.

Takoradi Port in Ghana, administered with ◊Sekondi.

Talavera de la Reina Town in Castilla-Léon, central Spain, on the river Tagus, 120 km/75 mi SW of Madrid; population (1991) 68,600. It produces soap, pharmaceuticals, and textiles. Spanish and British forces defeated the French here in the Peninsular War 1809.

Talcahuano Port and chief naval base in Biobio region, Chile; population (1992) 246,600. Industries include oil refining and timber.

Talien Part of the port of ◊Lüda, China.

Tallahassee (Cree 'old town') Capital of Florida, USA; an agricultural and lumbering centre; population (1992) 130,400. It was a Native American settlement when the Spanish explorer Hernando de Soto arrived 1539. The site was chosen as the Florida territorial capital 1821.

Tallinn (German *Reval*) Naval port and capital of Estonia; population (1995) 435,000. Industries include electrical and oil-drilling machinery, textiles, and paper. Founded 1219, it was a member of the Hanseatic League; it passed to Sweden 1561 and to Russia 1750. Vyshgorod Castle (13th century) and other medieval buildings remain. It is a yachting centre.

Tamale Town in NE Ghana; population (1988 est) 151,100. It is a commercial centre, dealing in rice, cotton, and peanuts.

Tamar River flowing into Bass Strait, Tasmania, formed by the union of the North and South Esk; length 65 km/ 40 mi.

Tamar River rising in N Cornwall, England, and flowing to Plymouth Sound; for most of its 97 km/60 mi length it forms the Devon–Cornwall border.

Tamatave Former name (to 1979) for ◊Toamasina, the chief port of Madagascar.

Tamaulipas State of NE Mexico, on the Gulf of Mexico; area 79,829 sq km/30,821 sq mi; population (1995 est) 2,526,400. Its capital is Ciudad Victoria. The main occupations are farming for cotton, maize, beans, sugar-cane, and tobacco, and cattle-raising, fishing, and lumbering.

Tambov City in W central Russian Federation; population (1994) 313,000. Industries include engineering, flour milling, and the manufacture of rubber and synthetic chemicals.

Tamil Nadu formerly (until 1968) *Madras State* State of SE India
area 130,058 sq km/50,215 sq mi
capital Chennai
industries mainly industrial: cotton, textiles, silk, electrical machinery, tractors, rubber, sugar refining, tea, coffee, spices
population (1994 est) 58,840,000
language Tamil
history the present state was formed 1956. Tamil Nadu comprises part of the former British Madras presidency (later province) formed from areas taken from France and Tipu Sahib, the sultan of Mysore, in the 18th century, which became a state of the Republic of India 1950. The NE was detached to form Andhra Pradesh 1953; in 1956 other areas went to Kerala and Mysore (now Karnataka), and the Laccadive Islands (now Lakshadweep) became a separate union territory.

Tampa Port and resort on Tampa Bay in W Florida, USA; population (1992) 284,700. Industries include fruit and vegetable canning, shipbuilding, and the manufacture of fertilizers, clothing, beer, and cigars. Tampa was settled 1823, and a fort was built the next year, which was taken from Confederate forces by Union troops in the Civil War.

Tampere (Swedish *Tammerfors*) City in SW Finland; population (1994) 179,000, metropolitan area 258,000. Industries include textiles, paper, footwear, and turbines. It is the second-largest city in Finland.

Tampico Port on the Rio Pánuco, 10 km/6 mi from the Gulf of Mexico, in Tamaulipas state, Mexico; population (1990) 272,700. Industries include oil refining and fishing.

Tamworth Dairying centre with furniture industry in New South Wales, Australia, on the river Peel; population (1993 est) 33,800.

Tamworth Town in Staffordshire, England, on the river Tame, NE of Birmingham; population (1991) 70,100. Industries include engineering, paper, clothing, and brick and tile manufacturing.

Tana Lake in Ethiopia, 1,800 m/5,900 ft above sea level; area 3,600 sq km/1,390 sq mi. It is the source of the Blue Nile.

Tana River in Finnmark county, N Norway; length 400 km/ 249 mi. It is formed by the junction of the rivers Anar and Karas, and flows NE to enter the Arctic Ocean by Tana Fjord. For most of its length, Tana forms the Finnish-Norwegian border. Salmon are caught here.

Tananarive Former name for ◊Antananarivo, the capital of Madagascar.

Tanga Seaport and capital of Tanga region, NE Tanzania, on the Indian Ocean; population (1988) 187,600. The port trades in sisal, fruit, cocoa, tea, and fish.

Tanganyika Former state in E Africa, which now forms the mainland of Tanzania. A German colony 1884–1914, it was ceded to Britain 1919, first as League of Nations mandate, and from 1946 as UN Trust Territory. It gained independence 1961, and in 1964 united with Zanzibar to form Tanzania.

Tanganyika, Lake Lake 772 m/2,534 ft above sea level in the Great Rift Valley, East Africa, with the Democratic Republic of Congo (formerly Zaire) to the W, Zambia to the S, and Tanzania and Burundi to the E. It is about 645 km/400 mi long, with an area of about 32,880 sq km/12,695 sq mi, and is the deepest lake (1,435 m/4,710 ft) in Africa. The mountains around its shores rise to about 2,700 m/8,860 ft. The chief ports on the lake are Bujumbura (Burundi), Kigoma (Tanzania), and Kalémié (Congo).

Tangier or *Tangiers* or *Tanger* Port in N Morocco, on the Strait of Gibraltar; population (urban area, 1990) 420,000. It was a Phoenician trading centre in the 15th century BC. Captured by the Portuguese 1471, it passed to England 1662 as part of the dowry of Catherine of Braganza, but was abandoned 1684, and later became a lair of Barbary Coast pirates. From 1923 Tangier and a small surrounding enclave became an international zone, administered by Spain 1940–45. In 1956 it was transferred to independent Morocco and became a free port 1962.

Tangshan Industrial city in Hebei province, China; population (1990) 1,500,000. Almost destroyed by an earthquake 1976, with 242,000 killed, it was rebuilt on a new site. Coal seams were opened up under the old city.

Tannu-Tuva   Former independent republic in NE Asia; see ◊Tuva.

Taormina   Coastal resort in E Sicily, at the foot of Mount Etna; population (1985) 9,000. It has an ancient Greek theatre.

Tara Hill   Ancient religious and political centre in County Meath, S Ireland. It was the site of a palace and coronation place of many Irish kings, abandoned in the 6th century. St Patrick, patron saint of Ireland, preached here.

Taranaki   Peninsula in North Island, New Zealand, dominated by Mount Egmont; volcanic soil makes it a rich dairy-farming area, and cheese is manufactured here.

Taranto   Naval base and port in Puglia region, SE Italy; population (1992) 230,200. It is an important commercial centre, and its steelworks are part of the new industrial complex of S Italy. It was the site of the ancient Greek *Tarentum*, founded in the 8th century BC by Sparta, and was captured by the Romans 272 BC.

Taranto   Province of SE Italy in ◊Puglia region; capital Taranto; area 2,437 sq km/941 sq mi; population (1992) 589,500.

Tarawa   Port and capital of Kiribati; population (1990) 28,800. Mother-of-pearl and copra are exported.

Tarbes   Capital of Hautes-Pyrénées *département*, SW France, a tourist centre for the Pyrenees; population (1990) 50,200. It belonged to England 1360–1406.

Taree   Town in a dairying area of NE New South Wales, Australia; population (1989) 18,000.

Tarim Basin   (Chinese *Tarim Pendi*) Internal drainage area in Xinjiang Uygur province, NW China, between the Tien Shan and Kunlun mountains; area about 900,000 sq km/350,000 sq mi. It is crossed by the river Tarim He and includes the lake of Lop Nur. The Taklimakan desert lies to the S of the Tarim He.

Tarn   River in SW France, rising in the Cévennes Mountains and flowing 350 km/217 mi to the Garonne River. It cuts picturesque gorges in the limestone plateaux of the Lozère and Aveyron *départements*.

Tarn   *Département* in the ◊Midi-Pyrénées region of France; area 5,751 sq km/2,220 sq mi; population (1990) 343,300. The river Tarn and its tributary the Agout flow through the *département*. In the E and SE are the high plateaux of the Sidobre, in the W there is a fertile plain, and in the rest of the *département* there are small, wooded uplands. Cereals, vines, and vegetables are produced, and livestock are raised. There are agrofood and plastics industries. The principal towns are ◊Albi (the capital) and Castres.

Tarn-et-Garonne   *Département* in the ◊Midi-Pyrénées region of France; area 3,716 sq km/1,435 sq mi; population (1990) 200,400. It is an alluvial plain formed by the confluence of the rivers Garonne, Tarn, and Aveyron. There are some hills and the region is generally wooded. The *département* is predominantly agricultural. Cereals, fruit, vines, and truffles are produced, and sheep are raised. Tourists visit the medieval villages. The principal towns are Montauban (the capital) and Castelsarrasin.

Tarragona   Port in Cataluña, Spain; population (1994) 115,000. Industries include petrochemicals, pharmaceuticals, and electrical goods. It has a cathedral and Roman remains, including an aqueduct and amphitheatre.

Tarragona   Province of NE Spain in S ◊Cataluña autonomous community; capital Tarragona; area 6,283 sq km/2,426 sq mi; population (1995) 576,200. Its W coastline is on the Mediterranean Sea, and in the S is the delta of the river Ebro.

Tarrasa   City in Cataluña, NE Spain; population (1994) 161,000. Industries include textiles and fertilizers.

Tarsus   City in İçel province, SE Turkey, on the river Pamuk; population (1990) 168,700. Formerly the capital of the Roman province of Cilicia, it was the birthplace of St Paul.

Tartu   City in Estonia; population (1995) 105,000. Industries include engineering and food processing. Once a stronghold of the Teutonic Knights, it was taken by Russia 1558 and then held by Sweden and Poland but returned to Russian control 1704.

Tas.   Abbreviation for ◊Tasmania, an island off Australia.

Tashkent   Capital of Uzbekistan; population (1994) 2,100,000. Industries include the manufacture of mining machinery, chemicals, textiles, and leather goods. Founded in the 7th century, it was taken by the Turks in the 12th century and captured by Tamerlane 1361. In 1865 it was taken by the Russians. It was severely damaged by an earthquake 1966.

Tasmania   formerly (1642–1856) *Van Diemen's Land* Island off the S coast of Australia; a state of the Commonwealth of Australia
area   67,800 sq km/26,177 sq mi
capital   Hobart
towns and cities   Launceston (chief port)
features   an island state (including small islands in the Bass Strait, and Macquarie Island); Franklin River, a wilderness area saved from a hydroelectric scheme 1983, which also has a prehistoric site; unique fauna including the Tasmanian devil

Tasmania

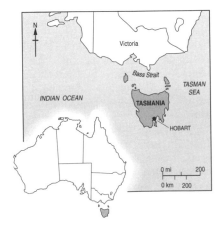

industries wool, dairy products, apples and other fruit, timber, iron, tin, coal, copper, silver

population (1994 est) 472,400

history the first European to visit here was Abel Tasman 1642; the last of the Tasmanian Aboriginals died 1876. Tasmania joined the Australian Commonwealth as a state 1901.

Tasman Sea Part of the ◊Pacific Ocean between SE Australia and NW New Zealand. It is named after the Dutch explorer Abel Tasman.

Tatarstan formerly *Tatar Autonomous Republic* Autonomous republic of E Russian Federation

area 68,000 sq km/26,255 sq mi

capital Kazan

physical in Volga River basin

industries oil, chemicals, textiles, timber

population (1995) 3,755,000

Tatra Mountains Range in central Europe, extending for about 65 km/40 mi along the Polish-Slovakian border; the highest part of the central ◊Carpathian Mountains.

Taunton Market town and administrative headquarters of Somerset, England; population (1991) 55,900. Industries include cider, leather, optical instruments, computer software, aeronautical instruments, precast concrete, and light engineering; there is a weekly cattle market. The Elizabethan hall survives, in which Judge Jeffreys held the Bloody Assizes 1685 after the Duke of Monmouth's rebellion.

Taunus Mountains Mountain range in Hessen, Germany; the Grosser Feldberg, 881 m/2,887 ft, is the highest peak in the Rhenish uplands. There are several mineral spas, including Wiesbaden, Bad Nauheim, and Bad Soden.

Taupo Largest lake in New Zealand, in a volcanic area of hot springs; area 620 sq km/239 sq mi. It is the source of the Waikato River.

Tauranga Port in North Island, New Zealand; population (1993) 73,800. It exports citrus fruit, dairy produce, and timber.

Taurus Mountains (Turkish *Toros Dağlari*) Mountain range in S Turkey, forming the S edge of the Anatolian plateau and rising to over 3,656 m/12,000 ft.

Tavistock Market town 24 km/15 mi N of Plymouth, Devon, England; population (1991) 10,200.

Tay Longest river in Scotland; length 189 km/118 mi. Rising in Stirling, it flows NE through Loch Tay, then E and SE past Perth to the Firth of Tay, crossed at Dundee by the Tay Bridge, before joining the North Sea. The Tay has salmon fisheries; its main tributaries are the Tummel, Isla, and Earn.

Tayside Former region of Scotland to 1996; replaced by Angus, Dundee City, and Perth and Kinross unitary authorities.

Tbilisi formerly *Tiflis* Capital of Georgia; industries include textiles, machinery, ceramics, and tobacco; population (1994 est) 1,300,000. Dating from the 5th century, it is a centre of Georgian culture, with fine medieval churches.

Anti-Russian demonstrations were quashed here by troops 1981 and 1989; the latter clash followed rejected demands for autonomy from the Abkhazia enclave, and resulted in 19 or more deaths from poison gas and 100 injured. In Dec 1991 at least 50 people were killed as well-armed opposition forces attempted to overthrow President Gamsakhurdia, eventually forcing him to flee.

Teddington Part of Twickenham, in the Greater London borough of ◊Richmond-upon-Thames; site of the National Physical Laboratory, established 1900.

Tees River flowing from the Pennines in Cumbria, England, to the North Sea via Tees Bay in ◊Cleveland; length 130 km/80 mi. It is polluted with industrial waste, sewage, and chemicals.

Teesside Industrial area at the mouth of the river Tees, NE England; population (1994 est) 323,000. Industries include high technology, plastics, petrochemicals, electronics, capital-intensive steelmaking, chemicals, an oil-fuel terminal, and the main North Sea natural-gas terminal. A gas-fired power station opened 1993, the largest combined heat and power plant in the world.

Tegucigalpa Capital of Honduras; population (1991 est) 670,100. Industries include textiles and food-processing. It was founded 1524 as a gold- and silver-mining centre.

Tehran Capital of Iran; population (1991) 6,476,000. Industries include textiles, chemicals, engineering, and tobacco. It was founded in the 12th century and made the capital 1788 by Muhammad Shah. Much of the city was rebuilt in the 1920s and 1930s. Tehran is the site of the Gulistan Palace (the former royal residence). There are three universities; the Shahyad Tower is a symbol of modern Iran.

Teignmouth Port and resort in S Devon, England, at the mouth of the river Teign; population (1991) 13,500.

Tejo Portuguese name for the river ◊Tagus.

Tel Aviv-Yafo or *Tel Aviv-Jaffa* City in Israel, on the Mediterranean coast; population (1994) 355,200. Industries include textiles, chemicals, sugar, printing, and publishing. Tel Aviv was founded 1909 as a Jewish residential area in the Arab town of Jaffa, with which it was combined 1949; their ports were superseded 1965 by Ashdod to the S. During the Gulf War 1991, Tel Aviv became a target for Iraqi missiles as part of Saddam Hussein's strategy to break up the Arab alliance against him. It is regarded by the UN as the capital of Israel.

Telemark County of Norway on the S coast; area 15,320 sq km/5,915 sq mi; population (1995) 163,200. It is a mountainous region with vast reserves of timber, commercially exploited. The Rjukan waterfall (126 m/413 ft) provides power for chemical works. Skien is the county capital.

Tema Port in Ghana; population (1988 est) 110,000. It has the largest artificial harbour in Africa, opened 1962, as well as oil refineries and a fishing industry.

Tempe, Vale of Valley in N Thessaly, Greece, renowned for its beautiful scenery. It was the traditional scene of Apollo's purification after the killing of the serpent Python, and of Daphne's metamorphosis.

Temple Industrial city (building materials, steel, furniture, railway supplies) in central Texas, USA, S of Waco; population (1990) 46,100. Temple was founded 1880.

Temuco Capital of Araucanía region, S Chile, situated to the N of the Lake District; population (1992) 240,900. Founded 1881, it is a market town for the Mapuche Indians and a centre for coal, steel, and textile production.

Tenerife Largest of the ◊Canary Islands, Spain; area 2,060 sq km/795 sq mi; population (1986) 759,400. *Santa Cruz* is the main town, and *Pico de Teide* is an active volcano.

Tennessee State in E central USA; nicknamed Volunteer State
area 109,200 sq km/42,151 sq mi
capital Nashville
towns and cities Memphis, Knoxville, Chattanooga, Clarksville
physical Great Smoky Mountains national park (a World Heritage Site); Cumberland River; Newfoundland Gap, with Clingmans Dome (2,024 m/6,643 ft), the highest point in the state; Lookout Mountain, Chattanooga
features Nashville, the capital of country music, with Opryland USA (*Grand Ole Opry*, the oldest radio show in the USA, started 1925, is broadcast from here), the Country Music Hall of Fame and Museum, RCA Studio B, the Parthenon in Centennial Park (a copy of the Parthenon in Athens), Belle Meade Mansion (a Greek Revival house and thoroughbred breeding estate, former site of the Iroquois, the oldest amateur steeplechase in the USA), Fort Nashborough (a recreation of the 1779 log fort), Historic Second Avenue Business District, Downtown Presbyterian Church (c. 1851, Egyptian Revival), the Hermitage (Andrew Jackson's mansion) and Andrew Jackson Center, and the Tennessee Botanical Garden at Cheekwood; Memphis, home of the blues, with the W C Handy Memphis home and museum, Sun Studio (the birthplace of rock and roll), Magevney House (1830s, the oldest building in the city), and Pyramid Arena (1991); the National Civil Rights Museum, site of the assassination of Martin Luther King Jr 1968; Shiloh national military park; Civil War battlefields at Chattanooga; Knoxville, with the Governor William Blount Mansion and the Armstrong-Lockett House (an 1834 farm mansion); Miss Mary Bobo's Boarding House (1867) at Lynchburg; the headquarters of the Tennessee Valley Authority, established 1933, the largest electricity-generating station in the USA, at Knoxville; Oak Ridge National Laboratory, founded 1943 as part of the Manhattan Project to develop an atomic bomb; Fisk University, Vanderbilt University, and Belmont College, in Nashville; Graceland, the estate of Elvis Presley; dogwood trees, especially in Knoxville
industries cereals, cotton, tobacco, soya beans, livestock, timber, coal, zinc, copper, chemicals
population (1995) 5,256,100
famous people Davy Crockett, David Farragut, Aretha Franklin, W C Handy, Cordell Hull, Andrew Jackson, Andrew Johnson, Dolly Parton, John Crowe Ransom, Bessie Smith
history settled by Europeans 1757; became a state 1796.

Tennessee was deeply divided in the Civil War; the battles of Shiloh, Murfreesboro, Chattanooga, and Nashville were fought here.

Teplice Industrial city (peat- and lignite-mining, glass, porcelain, cement, paper) and spa in N Bohemia, Czech Republic; population (1991) 127,800.

Teramo Province of S central Italy in ◊Abruzzi region; capital Teramo (population (1990) 52,500); area 1,947 sq km/752 sq mi; population (1992) 280,900.

Terengganu Alternative spelling of ◊Trengganu, a state in Peninsular Malaysia.

Terneuzen Port in the province of Zeeland, the Netherlands, on an arm of the river Scheldt, 45 km/28 mi NW of Antwerp, Belgium; population (1996) 35,100. Terneuzen is situated at the end of the 32-km/20-mi-long *Ghent–Terneuzen Canal*, on which are located iron and steelworks and other major industries.

Terni Industrial city in the valley of the river Nera, Umbria region, central Italy; population (1992) 108,000. The nearby Marmore Falls, the highest in Italy, were created by the Romans in order to drain the Rieti marshes.

Terni Province of central Italy in ◊Umbria region; capital ◊Terni; area 2,121 sq km/819 sq mi; population (1992) 223,000.

Terre Adélie French name for ◊Adélie Land, Antarctica.

Terre Haute City in W Indiana, USA, on the Wabash River; population (1992) 59,200. Industries include plastics, chemicals, and glass. Terre Haute was laid out 1816.

Teruel Province of E Spain in S ◊Aragón autonomous community; capital Teruel; area 14,802 sq km/5,715 sq mi; population (1995) 143,100. The rivers Guadalquivir and Turia flow through it.

Tethys Sea Sea that once separated Laurasia from Gondwanaland. It has now closed up to become the Mediterranean, the Black, the Caspian, and the Aral seas.

Tetschen German name for Děčín, a town in the Czech Republic.

Tetuán or *Tétouan* City in NE Morocco, near the Mediterranean coast, 64 km/40 mi SE of Tangier; population (urban area, 1990) 498,000. Products include textiles, leather, and soap. It was settled by Moorish exiles from Spain in the 16th century.

Texarkana Twin cities that straddle the Texas–Arkansas border, USA; population (1990) 22,600 (Texas), 31,700 (Arkansas). Industries include furniture, lumber, cotton, and sand and gravel. It was settled 1874.

Texas State in SW USA; nicknamed Lone Star State
area 691,200 sq km/266,803 sq mi
capital Austin
towns and cities Houston, Dallas–Fort Worth, San Antonio, El Paso, Corpus Christi, Lubbock
physical Rio Grande; Red River; arid Llano Estacado (Staked Plains); Big Bend national park in the Guadalupe Mountains, with canyons, the Chihuahuan Desert, and the

Chisos Mountains; Aransas national wildlife refuge, the principal wintering ground of the whooping crane; Padre Island national seashore; large pine forests in the E; Davy Crockett national forest

features Water Gardens Park, Fort Worth; Palo Duro Canyon state park, site of the last great battle with the Comanches; Mission Ysleta, the oldest Spanish mission in the SW; Presidio La Bahia, reconstructed 1749, a Spanish colonial fort in Goliad state historical park; San Jacinto monument and park; the Alamo, San Antonio, a monument to those who died 1836 while being besieged by the Mexican army; San Antonio, with Spanish missions, Spanish Governor's Palace, Victorian mansions, and the River Walk; Jefferson, on Big Cypress Bayou, including the Excelsior House, dating from the 1850s; Galveston, an island in the Gulf of Mexico, with Victorian buildings and ocean beaches; Lyndon B Johnson Space Center, Houston; Fredericksburg, founded in the 19th century by German immigrants, with strong German character; Bandera, a Polish community dating from 1855; Kimbell Art Museum, Fort Worth; buildings designed by I M Pei, including the First Interstate Bank Building, Dallas (1986), the Texas Commerce Tower, Houston, and the Morton H Meyerson Symphony Center, Dallas (1989); the Museum of Fine Arts, the Menil Collection, and the Rothko Chapel, Houston; Rice University; Texas Medical Center, Johnson City, with the birthplace of President Lyndon B Johnson, and the LBJ state historical park; Lyndon B Johnson library and museum, Austin; Dallas, the site of the assassination of President J F Kennedy 1963, with the Sixth Floor, an exhibit in the Texas School Book Depository; Kerrville, which reputedly enjoys the best climate in the USA

industries rice, cotton, sorghum, wheat, hay, livestock, shrimps, meat products, lumber, wood and paper products, petroleum (nearly one-third of US production), natural gas, sulphur, salt, uranium, chemicals, petrochemicals, nonelectrical machinery, fabricated metal products, transportation equipment, electric and electronic equipment

population (1995) 18,724,000

famous people James Bowie, George Bush, O Henry, Buddy Holly, Sam Houston, Howard Hughes, Lyndon Johnson, Janis Joplin, Katherine Anne Porter, Patrick Swayze, Tina Turner, Bob Wills

history settled by the Spanish 1682; part of Mexico 1821–36; Santa Anna massacred the Alamo garrison 1836, but was defeated by Sam Houston at San Jacinto the same year; Texas became an independent republic 1836–45, with Houston as president; in 1845 it became a state of the USA. Texas is the only state in the USA to have previously been an independent republic.

Texas City City and deep-water port in SE Texas, USA, on Galveston Bay, SE of Houston; population (1990) 40,800. Industries include tin, chemicals, oil, and grains.

Texel or *Tessel* Largest and southernmost of the ◊Frisian Islands, in North Holland province, the Netherlands; area 190 sq km/73 sq mi; population (1991) 12,700. Texel sheep are kept for their wool and cheese. The island is a good breeding ground for birds. Den Burg is the chief settlement.

Thames River in S England; length 338 km/210 mi. The longest river in England, it rises in the Cotswold Hills above Cirencester and is tidal as far as Teddington. Below London there is protection from flooding by means of the Thames Barrier (1982). The headstreams unite at Lechlade.

Thames, Firth of Inlet between Auckland and the Coromandel Peninsula, New Zealand.

Thames Tunnel Tunnel extending 365 m/1,200 ft under the river Thames, London, linking Rotherhithe with Wapping; the first underwater tunnel in the world. It was designed by Marc Isambard Brunel and was completed 1843. Originally intended as a road tunnel, it remained a pedestrian tunnel, for lack of funds, until the 1860s, when it was converted into a railway tunnel for the East London Railway. Today it carries underground trains.

Thanet, Isle of Northeast corner of Kent, England, bounded by the North Sea and the river Stour. It was an island until the 16th century, and includes the coastal resorts of Broadstairs, Margate, and Ramsgate.

Thar Desert or *Indian Desert* Desert on the borders of India and Pakistan; area about 250,000 sq km/96,500 sq mi.

Thessaloníki (English *Salonika*) Port in Macedonia, NE Greece, at the head of the Gulf of Thessaloníki; the second-largest city in Greece; population (1991) 378,000. Industries include textiles, shipbuilding, chemicals, brewing, and tanning. It was founded from Corinth by the Romans 315 BC as *Thessalonica* (to whose inhabitants St Paul addressed two epistles), captured by the Saracens AD 904 and by the Turks 1430, and restored to Greece 1912.

Thessaly (Greek *Thessalia*) Region of E central Greece, on the Aegean; area 13,904 sq km/5,367 sq mi; population (1991) 731,200. It is a major area of cereal production. It was an independent state in ancient Greece and later formed part of the Roman province of ◊Macedonia. It was Turkish from the 14th century until incorporated in Greece 1881.

Thetford Market town in Norfolk, England; population (1991) 20,100. It was an important Saxon town. There is light industry and printing. It is the birthplace of the political pamphleteer Thomas Paine.

Thetford Mines Site of the world's largest asbestos deposits, 80 km/50 mi S of Quebec, Canada; discovered 1876.

Thibodaux Town in SE Louisiana, USA, SW of New Orleans; population (1990) 14,000. It is an agricultural centre for sugar, dairy products, vegetables, and cotton. Thibodaux was founded 1750 as a river depot.

Thimphu Capital since 1962 of the Himalayan state of Bhutan; population (1993) 30,300. There is a 13th-century fortified monastery, Tashichoedzong, and the Memorial Charter to the Third King (1974).

Thionville (German *Diedenhofen*) Capital of the French *département* of Moselle, 25 km/16 mi N of Metz, on the river Moselle; population (1990) 41,500. It has large iron- and steelworks, and manufactures chemicals. Imperial Diets (meetings of the estates of the Holy Roman Empire) were held here in the 8th century.

Thousand Islands Group of about 1,700 islands in the upper St Lawrence River, on the border between Canada and the USA. Most of them are in Ontario, Canada; the rest are in the US state of New York. Some are in Canada's St Lawrence Islands National Park; many of the others are privately owned. The largest is Wolfe Island in Ontario, 127 sq km/49 sq mi. The islands are popular summer resorts.

Thrace (Greek *Thráki*) Ancient region of the Balkans, SE Europe, formed by parts of modern Greece and Bulgaria. It was held successively by the Greeks, Persians, Macedonians, and Romans.

Three Gorges Dam Dam being built to harness the power of the ◊Chang Jiang. It will create a reservoir 600 km/370 mi long and its turbines will have a 18,000 megawatt capacity (eight times the capacity of Egypt's Aswan Dam). Construction began December 1994. There is much concern about the project's environmental impact.

Three Mile Island Island in the Shenandoah River near Harrisburg, Pennsylvania, USA, site of a nuclear power station which was put out of action following a serious accident March 1979. Opposition to nuclear power in the USA was reinforced after this accident and safety standards reassessed.

Three Rivers English name for the Canadian port of ◊Trois Rivières.

Thule Greek and Roman name for the most northerly land known, originally used by the explorer Pytheas to refer to land he discovered six days after leaving the N coast of Britain. It has been identified with the Shetlands, the Orkneys, Iceland, and Scandinavia.

Thunder Bay City and port on Lake Superior, Ontario, Canada, formed by the union of Port Arthur and its twin city of Fort William to the S; industries include shipbuilding, timber, paper, wood pulp, and export of wheat; population (1991) 113,700.

Thuringia Administrative region (German *Land*) of Germany;
area 16,171 sq km/6,244 sq mi
capital Erfurt
towns and cities Weimar, Gera, Jena, Eisenach
industries machine tools, optical instruments, steel, vehicles, ceramics, electronics, glassware, timber
population (1995) 2,503,800
history an historic, densely forested region of Germany that became a province 1918 and a region of East Germany 1946. It was split into the districts of Erfurt, Gera, and Suhl 1952 but reconstituted as a state following German reunification 1990.

Thursday Island Island in Torres Strait, Queensland, Australia; area 4 sq km/1.5 sq mi; chief centre Port Kennedy. It is a centre of the pearl-fishing industry.

Thurso Port in the Highland unitary authority, Scotland; population (1991) 8,500. It is the mainland terminus of the steamer service to the Orkney Islands. The experimental nuclear reactor site of Dounreay to the W was closed down

1994, and replaced by a nuclear waste reprocessing plant.

Tianjin or *Tientsin* Port and industrial and commercial city in Hubei province, central China; population (1993) 4,970,000. The special municipality of Tianjin has an area of 4,000 sq km/1,544 sq mi and a population (1994) of 10,400,000. Its handmade silk and wool carpets are renowned. Dagan oilfield is nearby. Tianjin was opened to foreign trade 1860 and occupied by the Japanese 1937.

Tian Shan (Chinese *Tien Shan*) Mountain system in central Asia. ◊Pik Pobedy on the Xinjiang-Kyrgyz border is the highest peak at 7,440 m/24,415 ft.

Tiber (Italian *Tevere*) River in Italy on which Rome is built; length from its source in the Apennines to the Tyrrhenian Sea 400 km/250 mi.

Tiberias, Lake or *Lake of Gennesaret* or *Sea of Galilee* Lake in N Israel, 210 m/689 ft below sea level, into which the river ◊Jordan flows; area 170 sq km/66 sq mi. The first Israeli kibbutz (cooperative settlement) was founded nearby 1909.

Tibesti Range in the central Sahara, N Chad; the highest peak is ◊Emi Koussi at 3,415 m/11,208 ft.

Tibet Autonomous region of SW China (Pinyin form *Xizang*);
area 1,221,600 sq km/471,660 sq mi
capital Lhasa
features Tibet occupies a barren plateau bounded S and SW by the Himalayas and N by the Kunlun Mountains, traversed W to E by the Bukamagna, Karakoram, and other mountain ranges, and having an average elevation of 4,000–4,500 m/13,000–15,000 ft. The Sutlej, Brahmaputra, and Indus rivers rise in Tibet, which has numerous lakes, many of which are salty. The yak is the main domestic animal
government Tibet is an autonomous region of China, with its own People's Government and People's Congress. The controlling force in Tibet is the Communist Party of China, represented locally from 1985 by First Secretary Wu Jinghua. Tibetan nationalists regard the province as being under colonial rule. There is a government-in-exile in Dharmsala, Himachel Pradesh, India, where the Dalai Lama lives
industries wool, borax, salt, horn, musk, herbs, furs, gold, iron pyrites, lapis lazuli, mercury, textiles, chemicals, agricultural machinery. Tibet has the largest uranium reserves in the world: uranium processing and extraction is causing pollution and human and animal birth deformities
population (1993) 2,196,000; many Chinese have settled in Tibet; 2 million Tibetans live in China outside Tibet
religion traditionally Lamaist (a form of Mahāyāna Buddhism)
history Tibet was an independent kingdom from the 5th century AD. It came under nominal Chinese rule about 1700. From 1910–13 the capital, Lhasa, was occupied by Chinese troops, after which independence was re-established. China regained control 1951 when the historic ruler and religious leader, the Dalai Lama, was driven from the country and the monks (who formed 25% of the population) were forced out of the monasteries. The Chinese People's Liberation Army

(PLA) controlled Tibet 1951–59, although the Dalai Lama returned as nominal spiritual and temporal head of state. In 1959 a Tibetan uprising spread from bordering regions to Lhasa and was supported by Tibet's local government. The rebellion was suppressed by the PLA, prompting the Dalai Lama and 9,000 Tibetans to flee to India. The Chinese proceeded to dissolve the Tibet local government, abolish serfdom, collectivize agriculture, and suppress Lamaism. In 1965 Tibet became an autonomous region of China. Chinese rule continued to be resented, however, and the economy languished.

Tiel Town in the province of Gelderland, the Netherlands, on the river Waal, 30 km/19 mi E of Nijmegen; population (1996) 34,700. It is the centre of a fruit-growing district and has a large jam factory. In the Middle Ages Tiel was a member of the Hanseatic League.

Tienen (French *Tirlemont*) Town in the province of Brabant, Belgium, 40 km/25 mi E of Brussels, situated on the river Gette. It manufactures sugar from locally grown sugar beet, and has other industries. Tienen is thought to be of Roman origin. It was a busy market in the early Middle Ages.

Tien Shan Chinese form of ◊Tian Shan, a mountain system of central Asia.

Tientsin Alternative form of ◊Tianjin, an industrial city in NE China.

Tierra del Fuego Island group divided between Chile and Argentina. It is separated from the mainland of South America by the Strait of Magellan, and Cape Horn is at the southernmost point. The chief town, Ushuaia, Argentina, is the world's most southerly town. Industries include oil and sheep farming.

Tiflis Former name (to 1936) of the city of ◊Tbilisi in Georgia.

Tigré or *Tigray* Region in the N highlands of Ethiopia; area 65,900 sq km/25,444 sq mi. The chief town is Mek'elē. The region had an estimated population of 2.4 million in 1984, at a time when drought and famine were driving large numbers of people to fertile land in the S or into neighbouring Sudan. Since 1978 a guerrilla group known as the Tigré People's Liberation Front (TPLF) has been fighting for regional autonomy. In 1989 government troops were forced from the province, and the TPLF advanced towards Addis Ababa, playing a key role in the fall of the Ethiopian government May 1991.

Tigris (Arabic *Shatt Dijla*) River flowing through Turkey and Iraq (see also ◊Mesopotamia), joining the ◊Euphrates above Basra, where it forms the ◊Shatt-al-Arab; length 1,600 km/1,000 mi.

Tijuana City and resort in NW Mexico; population (1990) 742,700. It is known for horse races and casinos. ◊San Diego adjoins it across the US border.

Tilburg Town in the province of North Brabant, the Netherlands, 24 km/15 mi SW of 's Hertogenbosch; population (1996) 164,300. Tilburg is an industrial centre, manufacturing cloth, woollens and soap.

Tilbury Port in Essex, England, on the N bank of the Thames; population (1991) 11,700. Greatly extended 1976, it became London's largest container port. It dates from Roman times.

Tilsit Former name (to 1945) of the Russian town of ◊Sovetsk.

Timaru (Maori 'place of shelter') Industrial port and resort on South Island, New Zealand; population (1993) 27,100. Industries include flour milling, deep freezing, pottery, and brewing.

Timbuktu or *Tombouctou* Town in Mali; population about 20,500. A camel caravan centre on the fringe of the Sahara from the 11th century, it was taken over 1433 by the Tuareg nomads of the region, replacing the rule of the Mali. Since 1960 the area surrounding the town has become increasingly arid, and the former canal link with the river Niger is dry. Products include salt.

Timişoara Capital of Timiş county, W Romania; population (1993) 325,000. Industries include electrical engineering, chemicals, pharmaceuticals, textiles, food processing, metal, and footwear. The revolt against the Ceausescu regime began here Dec 1989 when demonstrators prevented the arrest and deportation of a popular Protestant minister who was promoting the rights of ethnic Hungarians. This soon led to large prodemocracy rallies.

Timor Largest and most easterly of the Lesser Sunda Islands, part of Indonesia; area 33,610 sq km/12,973 sq mi. Its indigenous people were the Atoni; successive migrants have included the Malay, Melanesian, Chinese, Arab, and Gujerati.

The Dutch were established in Kupang 1613, with the Portuguese in the N and E. Portugal established a colonial administration in Timor 1702, but the claim was disputed by the Dutch, as well as by the Timorese, who frequently rebelled. Timor was divided into *West Timor* and *East Timor* by treaties of 1859 and 1913 and subjected to Dutch and Portuguese control respectively; during World War II both parts were occupied by Japan. West Timor (capital Kupang) became part of Indonesia 1949. East Timor (capital Dili) comprises the enclave on the NW coast, and the islands of Atauro and Jaco. It was seized by Indonesia 1975, and became an Indonesian province 1976 (East Timor is the English name for the Indonesian province of Timor Timur). The annexation is not recognized by the United Nations, and guerrilla warfare by local people seeking independence continues. Since 1975 over 500,000 Timorese have been killed by Indonesian troops or have resettled in West Timor. Civilians demonstrating in Dili 1991 were massacred by Indonesian troops.

Products include coffee, maize, rice, and coconuts.

Tindouf Saharan oasis in the Aïn-Sefra region of Algeria, crossed by the Agadir–Dakar desert route. There are large iron deposits in the area. The oasis acted as a base for exiled Polisario guerrillas of Western Sahara.

Tintagel Village resort on the coast of N Cornwall, England. There are castle ruins, and legend has it that King Arthur was born and held court here.

Tipperary County of the Republic of Ireland, in the province of Munster, divided into North and South Ridings; county town Clonmel; area 4,260 sq km/1,644 sq mi; population (1996 est) 133,300. It includes part of the Golden Vale, a dairy-farming region. There is horse and greyhound breeding.

Tirana or *Tiranë* Capital (since 1920) of Albania; population (1991) 251,000. Industries include metallurgy, cotton textiles, soap, and cigarettes. It was founded in the early 17th century by Turks when part of the Ottoman Empire. Although the city is now largely composed of recent buildings, some older districts and mosques have been preserved.

Tîrgu Jiu Capital of Gorj county, SW Romania, near the river Jiu, 90 km/56 mi NW of Craiova; population (1993) 97,000. Large coal- and oilfields found locally, and timber trade, have encouraged its rapid growth since 1945.

Tîrgu Mureş City in Transylvania, Romania, on the river Mureş, 450 km/280 mi N of Bucharest; population (1993) 166,000. With a population comprising approximately equal numbers of ethnic Hungarians and Romanians, the city was the scene of rioting between the two groups following Hungarian demands for greater autonomy 1990.

Tirol Federal province of Austria; area 12,648 sq km/4,883 sq mi; population (1995) 658,312. Its capital is Innsbruck, and it produces diesel engines, optical instruments, and hydroelectric power. Tirol was formerly a province (from 1363) of the Austrian Empire, divided 1919 between Austria and Italy (see ◊Trentino–Alto Adige).

Tiruchchirappalli formerly *Trichinopoly* ('town of the sacred rock') City in Tamil Nadu, India; chief industries are cotton textiles, cigars, and gold and silver filigree; population (1991) 387,000. It is a place of pilgrimage and was the capital of Tamil kingdoms during the 10th to 17th centuries.

Tisa (Hungarian *Tisza*) Tributary of the river Danube, rising in Ukraine and flowing through Hungary to Yugoslavia; length 967 km/601 mi.

Titicaca, Lake Lake in the Andes, 3,810 m/12,500 ft above sea level and 1,220 m/4,000 ft above the tree line; area 8,300 sq km/3,200 sq mi, the largest lake in South America, and the world's highest navigable body of water. It is divided between Bolivia (port at Guaqui) and Peru (ports at Puno and Huancane). It has enormous edible frogs, and is one of the few places in the world where reed boats are still made (Lake Tana in Ethiopia is another).

Titograd Former name (1946–92) of ◊Podgorica, a city in Montenegro, Yugoslavia.

Titusville Town in E Florida, USA, on the Indian River, E of Orlando; population (1990) 39,400. Industries include aerospace, citrus fruits, and sport fishing. The Kennedy Space Center is nearby. Titusville was founded 1867.

Tivoli Town NE of Rome, Italy; population (1981) 52,000. It has remains of Hadrian's villa, with gardens; and the Villa d'Este, with Renaissance gardens laid out 1549 for Cardinal Ippolito d'Este.

Tlaxcala Smallest state of Mexico, in the centre; area 3,914 sq km/1,511 sq mi; population (1995 est) 883,600. Its capital is Tlaxcala. The main occupations are farming, producing vegetables, alfalfa, cereals, and maguey, and flour-milling and textile production.

Tlemcen (Roman *Pomaria*) City in NW Algeria; population (1989) 146,000. Carpets and leather goods are made, and there is a 12th-century mosque.

TN Abbreviation for the state of ◊Tennessee, USA.

Toamasina formerly (until 1979) *Tamatave* Port and coastal resort on the E coast of Madagascar; population (1990) 145,000. The country's principal port from which sugar, coffee, and tea are major exports.

Tobago Island in the West Indies; part of the republic of Trinidad and Tobago.

Tobolsk River port and lumber centre at the confluence of the Tobol and Irtysh rivers in N Tyumen, in the Russian Federation, in W Siberia; population (1985) 75,000. It was founded by Cossacks 1587; Tsar Nicholas II was exiled here 1917.

Tobruk Libyan port; population (1984) 94,000. Occupied by Italy 1911, it was taken by Britain 1941 during World War II, and unsuccessfully besieged by Axis forces April–Dec 1941. It was captured by Germany June 1942 after the retreat of the main British force to Egypt, and this precipitated the replacement of Auchinleck by Montgomery as British commander.

Togliatti or *Tolyatti*, formerly *Stavropol* Port on the river Volga, W central Russia; population (1994) 689,000. Industries include engineering and food processing. The city was relocated in the 1950s after a flood and renamed after the Italian communist Palmiro Togliatti.

Tōhoku Mountainous region of N Honshu Island, Japan; area 66,883 sq km/25,824 sq mi; population (1995) 9,834,000. Timber, fruit, fish, and livestock are produced. The chief city is Sendai. Aomori in the NE is linked to Hakodate on the island of Hokkaido by the *Seikan Tunnel*, the world's longest underwater tunnel.

Tokelau formerly *Union Islands* Overseas territory of New Zealand, 480 km/300 mi N of Samoa, comprising

Titicaca, Lake

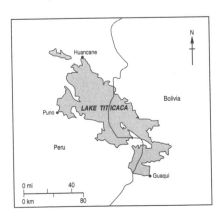

three coral atolls: Atafu, Fakaofo, and Nukunonu; area 10 sq km/4 sq mi; population (1991) 1,600.

Tokyo   Capital of Japan, on Honshu Island; population (1994) 7,874,000. It is Japan's main cultural and industrial centre (engineering, chemicals, textiles, electrical goods). Founded in the 16th century as *Yedo* (or *Edo*), it was renamed when the emperor moved his court here from Kyoto 1868. An earthquake 1923 killed 58,000 people and destroyed much of the city, which was again severely damaged by Allied bombing in World War II when 60% of Tokyo's housing was destroyed; US firebomb raids of 1945 were particularly destructive with over 100,000 people killed in just one night of bombing 9 March. The subsequent rebuilding has made it into one of the world's most modern cities.

Toledo   Province of central Spain in W Castilla-La Mancha autonomous community; capital Toledo; area 15,369 sq km/5,934 sq mi; population (1995) 515,400.

Toledo   City on the river Tagus, Castilla–La Mancha, central Spain; population (1982) 62,000. It was the capital of the Visigoth kingdom 534–711, then became a Moorish city, and was the Castilian capital 1085–1560.

Toledo   Port on Lake Erie, Ohio, USA, at the mouth of the Maumee River; population (1992) 329,300. Industries include food processing and the manufacture of vehicles, electrical goods, and glass. A French fort was built 1700, but permanent settlement did not begin until after the War of 1812.

Tomaszów Mazowiecki   Industrial town (woollen textiles, synthetic fibres) in Piotrków province, Poland, on the river Pilica, 47 km/29 mi S of Lódź; population (1990) 69,900.

Tomsk   City on the river Tom, in the Russian Federation, in W central Siberia; industries include synthetic fibres, timber, distilling, plastics, and electrical motors; population (1994) 496,000. It was formerly a gold-mining town and the administrative centre of much of Siberia.

Tønder   Former county in SW Jutland, Denmark, now part of Sonderjylland county; area 1,386 sq km/535 sq mi. The capital was Tønder. As part of ◊Schleswig-Holstein, the region belonged to Prussia and then Germany 1864–1920.

Tongariro   Volcanic peak at the centre of North Island, New Zealand. Considered sacred by the Maori, the mountain was presented to the government by chief Te Heuheu Tukino IV 1887. It was New Zealand's first national park and the fourth to be designated in the world.

Tongeren   (French *Tongres*) Town in the province of Limbourg, Belgium, 19 km/12 mi SE of Hasselt. Probably the oldest town in Belgium, Tongeren was known as Civitas Tongrorum under the Romans. Part of the Roman defensive wall can still be seen. The town also has a 15th-century church, a convent, and the Moerenpoort, a remnant of fortification from the 14th century. Tongeren is the site of a cattle market.

Tonkin   or *Tongking* Former region of Vietnam, on the China Sea; area 103,500 sq km/39,951 sq mi. Under Chinese rule from 111 BC, Tonkin became independent AD 939 and remained self-governing until the 19th century. A part of French Indochina 1885–1946, capital Hanoi, it was part of North Vietnam from 1954 and was merged into Vietnam after the Vietnam War.

Tonkin, Gulf of   Part of the South China Sea, with oil resources. China and Vietnam disagree over their respective territorial boundaries in the area.

Tonle Sap   or *Great Lake* Lake on a tributary of the ◊Mekong River, W Cambodia; area ranging from 2,600 sq km/1,000 sq mi to 6,500 sq km/2,500 sq mi at the height of the monsoon. During the June–Nov wet season it acts as a natural flood reservoir.

Toowoomba   Town and commercial and industrial centre (coal mining, iron working, engineering, clothing) in the Darling Downs, SE Queensland, Australia; population (1994) 89,500.

Topeka   Capital of Kansas, USA; population (1992) 120,300. It is a centre for agricultural trade, and its products include processed food, printed materials, and rubber and metal products. The community was founded 1854 by anti-slavery colonists and developed as a railway centre. It was made the state capital 1861.

Torbay   District in S Devon, England; population (1994 est) 128,000. It was created 1968 by the union of the seaside resorts of Paignton, Torquay, and Brixham.

Torfaen   Unitary authority in S Wales created 1996 from part of the former county of Gwent ; administrative headquarters Pontypool; population (1996) 90,700; area 98 sq km/38 sq mi. The old industries (iron and tinplate manufacturing, and coal mining) are gone. New industries include advanced electronics, and there are automotive and engineering companies.

Torgau   Town in Leipzig county, Saxony, Federal Republic of Germany; population 20,000. In 1760, during the Seven Years' War, Frederick II of Prussia defeated the Austrians nearby, and in World War II the US and Soviet forces first met here.

Torhout   (French *Thourhout*) Town in the province of West Flanders, Belgium, 19 km/12 mi SW of Bruges. The oldest town in Flanders, Torhout was once the chief cloth market of the country. The town still manufactures linen, and has a horse market.

Torino   Italian name for the city of ◊Turin.

Torness   Site of an advanced gas-cooled nuclear reactor 7 km/4.5 mi SW of Dunbar, East Lothian, Scotland. It started to generate power 1987.

Toronto   (Native American 'place of meeting') Port and capital of Ontario, Canada, on Lake Ontario; population (1991) 635,400, metropolitan area 3,893,000. It is Canada's main industrial and commercial centre (banking, shipbuilding, cars, farm machinery, food processing, publishing) and also a cultural centre, with theatres and a film industry. A French fort was established 1749, and the site became the provincial capital 1793; known until 1834 as York.

Torquay Resort in S Devon, England, part of the district of ◊Torbay. It is a sailing centre and has an annual regatta in August.

Torremolinos Tourist resort on the Costa del Sol between Málaga and Algeciras in Andalucia, S Spain; population (1991) 31,700. There is a wine museum and a modern congress and exhibition centre.

Torrens Salt lake 8 m/25 ft below sea level in E South Australia; area 5,800 sq km/2,239 sq mi. It is reduced to a marsh in dry weather.

Torreón Industrial and agricultural city in Coahuila state, N Mexico, on the river Nazas at an altitude of 1,127 m/ 3,700 ft; population (1990) 876,500. Before the arrival of the railway 1907 Torreón was the largest of the three Laguna cotton-district cities (with Gómez Palacio and Ciudad Lerdo). Since then it has developed as a major thoroughfare and commercial centre.

Torres Strait Channel separating New Guinea from Australia, with scattered reefs; width 130 km/80 mi. The first European to sail through it was the Spanish navigator Luis Vaez de Torres 1606.

Torres Vedras Town in Portugal, 40 km/25 mi N of Lisbon, where the fortifications known as the *lines of Torres Vedras* were built by the British commander Wellington in 1810, during the Peninsular War.

Toruń (German *Thorn*) Industrial river port (electronics, fertilizers, synthetic fibres) in N Poland, on the river Vistula; population (1991) 202,000. It was founded by the Teutonic Knights 1230 and is the birthplace of the astronomer Copernicus.

Toscana Italian name for the region of ◊Tuscany.

Tottenham District of the Greater London borough of ◊Haringey.

Toul French town in the *département* of Meurthe-et-Moselle, on the river Moselle and the Rhine–Marne Canal. Pottery is manufactured. The church of St-Étienne was built between 965 and 1496. Taken by the French from the Germans in 1552, Toul was finally ceded to France in 1648 under the Treaty of Westphalia.

Toulon Port and capital of Var *département*, SE France, on the Mediterranean Sea, 48 km/30 mi SE of Marseille; population (1990) 170,200. It is the chief Mediterranean naval station of France. Industries include oil refining, chemicals, furniture, and clothing. Toulon was the Roman *Telo Martius* and was made a port by Henry IV. It was occupied by the British 1793, and Napoleon first distinguished himself in driving them out. In World War II the French fleet was scuttled here to avoid its passing to German control.

Toulouse Capital of Haute-Garonne *département*, SW France, on the river Garonne, SE of Bordeaux; population (1990) 365,900. The chief industries are textiles and aircraft construction (Concorde was built here). It was the capital of the Visigoths and later of Aquitaine 781–843.

Touraine Former province of W central France, now part of the *départements* of Indre-et-Loire and Vienne; capital Tours.

Tourcoing Town in Nord *département*, France, part of metropolitan Lille; population (1990) 94,400. It is situated near the Belgian border, and has been a textile centre since the 12th century.

Tournai (Flemish *Doornik*) Town in Hainaut province, Belgium, on the river Schelde; population (1995 est) 68,100. Industries include carpets, cement, and leather. It stands on the site of a Roman relay post and has an 11th-century Romanesque cathedral.

Tours Industrial city (chemicals, textiles, machinery) and capital of the Indre-et-Loire *département*, W central France, on the river Loire; population (1990) 133,400. It has a 13th–15th-century cathedral. An ancient city and former capital of ◊Touraine, it was the site of the French defeat of the Arabs 732 under Charles Martel. Tours became the French capital for four days during World War II.

Tower Hamlets Inner borough of E Greater London. It includes the districts of Limehouse, Spitalfields, Bethnal Green, ◊Wapping, Poplar, Stepney, and the Isle of Dogs
features Tower of London; the Isle of Dogs bounded on three sides by the Thames; ◊Docklands redevelopment area (including ◊Canary Wharf); site of ◊Billingsgate fish market; Limehouse, the main centre of 18th- and 19th-century shipbuilding, which in the 1890s became a focal point for Chinese sailors working from West India Docks; Spitalfields, which derives its name from the priory and hospital of St Mary's Spital (1197), where silk weaving developed following the influx of Huguenot refugees to the area after 1685 (the industry collapsed mid-19th century); Spitalfields Market (fruit and vegetable market moved 1991) is being developed by Sir Norman Foster for Liffe (London International Financial Futures Exchange); Bethnal Green Museum of Childhood (1872); Victoria Park (1840s)
population (1991) 161,100
history Richard II met the Essex rebels at Mile End Green (now Stepney Green) during the Peasant's Revolt 1381. In the 17th century, the name Tower Hamlets referred to the E London military district of 21 hamlets from which the Lieutenant of the Tower of London had the right to muster militia.

Townsville Port on Cleveland Bay, N Queensland, Australia; population (1991) 116,200. It is the centre of a mining and agricultural area and exports meat, wool, sugar, and minerals, including gold and silver.

Trabzon formerly *Trebizond* Port on the Black Sea, NE Turkey, 355 km/220 mi SW of Batum; population (1990) 143,900. Its exports include fruit, tobacco, and hides.

Trail Mining centre in British Columbia, Canada, on the Columbia River; population (1991) 9,900. Industries include lead, zinc, copper, chemicals, fertilizers, food processing, and sawmilling.

Trans-Amazonian Highway or *Transamazonica* Road in Brazil, linking Recife in the E with the provinces of Rondonia, Amazonas, and Acre in the W.

Transcaucasia Geographical region S of the Caucasus Mountains, which includes Armenia, Azerbaijan, and Georgia. It formed the *Transcaucasian Republic* 1922, but was broken up 1936 into three separate Soviet republics. All three republics became independent 1991.

Trans-Dniester Region of NE Moldova, lying between the river Dniester and the Ukraine, largely inhabited by ethnic Slavs (Russians and Ukrainians). In Oct 1990, Slav separatists unilaterally declared a breakaway republic, fearing a resurgence of ethnic Romanian nationalism as Moldova moved toward independence. A state of emergency was declared Nov 1990. The violence escalated May 1992 in response to mounting fears of reunification with Romania and by July 1992 hundreds had died in the fighting. By Aug a cease-fire was in place and a Russian peacekeeping force reportedly deployed in the region.

Trans-jordan Part of the former Turkish Ottoman Empire and now part of Jordan (the present-day East Bank).

Transkei Former independent homeland Black National State within South Africa, part of Eastern Cape Province from 1994. It became self-governing 1963, and achieved full independence 1976. The largest of South Africa's homelands, it extended NW from the Great Kei River, on the coast of Cape Province, to the border of Natal. The region covers an area of 43,808 sq km/16,910 sq mi. Industries include livestock, coffee, tea, sugar, maize, and sorghum.

Trans-Siberian Railway The world's largest railway line, connecting the cities of European Russia with Omsk, Novosibirsk, Irkutsk, and Khabarovsk, and terminating at Vladivostok on the Pacific coast. It was built 1891–1905; from St Petersburg to Vladivostok is about 8,700 km/5,400 mi. A N line, 3,102 km/1,928 mi long, was completed 1984 after ten years' work.

Transvaal Former province of NE South Africa to 1994, when it was divided into Mpumalanga, Northern, and Gauteng Provinces. It borders Zimbabwe to the N. It was settled by *Voortrekkers*, Boers who left Cape Colony in the Great Trek from 1831. Independence was recognized by Britain 1852, until the settlers' difficulties with the conquered Zulus led to British annexation 1877. It was made a British colony after the South African War 1899–1902, and in 1910 became a province of the Union of South Africa.

Transylvania Mountainous area of central and NW Romania, bounded to the S by the Transylvanian Alps (an extension of the ◊Carpathian Mountains). Formerly a principality, with its capital at Cluj-Napoca, it was part of Hungary from about 1000 until its people voted to unite with Romania 1918. It is the home of the vampire legends. In a 1996 treaty Hungary renounced its claims on Transylvania.

Trapani Port and naval base in NW Sicily, about 48 km/30 mi N of Marsala; population (1990) 72,800. It trades in wine, salt, and fish.

Trapani Province of Italy in ◊Sicily; capital ◊Trapani; area 2,460 sq km/950 sq mi; population (1992) 428,000.

Trebizond Former English name of ◊Trabzon, a city in Turkey.

Treblinka Site of a Nazi concentration camp 80 km/50 mi NW of Warsaw. Jews from the Warsaw Ghetto were put to death here during World War II. The camp was closed down and dismantled in Nov 1943.

Trelleborg Town in Malmöhus county, Sweden; population (1995) 37,800. The southernmost Swedish town, Trelleborg prospered in the Middle Ages as a port and through herring fishing. It still has a coastal trade, and ferries run to Rostock, Travemünde, and Sassnitz in Germany. Trelleborg has sugar-refining, tyre, and other industries.

Trengganu or *Terengganu* State of E Peninsular Malaysia; capital Kuala Trengganu; area 13,000 sq km/5,018 sq mi; population (1993) 752,000. Its exports include copra, black pepper, tin, and tungsten; there are also fishing and offshore oil industries.

Trent Third longest river of England; length 275 km/170 mi. Rising in the S Pennines, it flows first S and then NE through the Midlands to the Humber estuary and out into the North Sea. It is navigable by barge for nearly 160 km/100 mi.

Trentino–Alto Adige Autonomous region of N Italy, comprising the provinces of Bolzano and Trento; capital Trento; chief towns Trento in the Italian-speaking S area, and Bolzano-Bozen in the N German-speaking area of South Tirol (the region was Austrian until ceded to Italy in the settlement following World War I 1919); area 13,613 sq km/5,256 sq mi; population (1995) 908,700.

Trento Capital of Trentino–Alto Adige region, Italy, on the Adige River; population (1992) 101,500. Industries include the manufacture of electrical goods and chemicals. The Council of Trent was held here 1545–63.

Trento Province of N Italy in ◊Trentino–Alto Adige region; capital ◊Trento; area 6,213 sq km/2,399 sq mi; population (1992) 451,300.

Trenton Capital and industrial city (metalworking, ceramics) of New Jersey, USA, on the Delaware River; population (1992) 87,800. It was first settled by Quakers 1679; George Washington defeated the British here 1776. It became the state capital 1790.

Tréport, Le Port and seaside resort on the English Channel, in the French *département* of Seine-Maritime; population (1990) 6,300. It has a 16th-century church and the ruins of an 11th-century abbey. It is separated by the river Bresle from Mer-le-Bains, which is in the *département* of Somme.

Trèves French name for ◊Trier, a city in Germany.

Treviso City in Veneto, NE Italy; population (1990) 83,900. Its industries include the manufacture of machinery and ceramics. The 11th-century cathedral has an altarpiece by Titian.

Treviso Province of NE Italy in ◊Veneto region; capital ◊Treviso; area 2,476 sq km/956 sq mi; population (1992) 746,000.

Tribal Areas, Federally Administered Part of the mountainous frontier of NW Pakistan with Afghanistan, comprising the districts of Malakand, Mohmand, Khyber, Kurram, and Waziristan, administered directly from Islamabad; area 27,219 sq km/10,507 sq mi; population (1985) 2,467,000. The chief towns are Wana, Razmak, and Miram Shah.

Trichinopoly Former name for ◊Tiruchchirappalli, a city in India.

Trier (French *Trèves*) City in Rhineland-Palatinate, Germany; population (1991) 98,800. It is a centre for the wine trade. Once the capital of the Treveri, a Celto-Germanic tribe, it became known as *Augusta Treverorum* under the Roman emperor Augustus about 15 BC and was the capital of an ecclesiastical principality during the 14th–18th centuries. Karl Marx was born here.

Trieste Port on the Adriatic coast, opposite Venice, in Friuli-Venezia-Giulia, Italy; population (1992) 228,400, including a large Slovene minority. It is the site of the International Centre for Theoretical Physics, established 1964. Trieste was under Austrian rule from 1382 (apart from Napoleonic occupation 1809–14) until transferred to Italy 1918. It was claimed after World War II by Yugoslavia; established as a Free Post 1947; the city and surrounding territory were divided 1954 between Italy and Yugoslavia. The territory is now part of Slovenia.

Trieste Province of NE Italy in ◊Friuli-Venezia Giulia region; capital ◊Trieste; area 210 sq km/81 sq mi; population (1992) 260,300.

Triglav Mountain in Slovenia, rising to 2,863 m/9,393 ft, the highest peak in the Julian Alps.

Trincomalee Port in NE Sri Lanka; population (district, 1993 est) 323,000. It was an early Tamil settlement, and a British naval base until 1957.

Trinidad Town in Beni region, N Bolivia, near the river Mamoré, 400 km/250 mi NE of La Paz; population (1980) 36,000. It is built on an artificial earth mound, above flood level, the work of a little-known early Native American people. Industries include sugar refining and alcohol distilling. It is also a commercial centre trading in rice, cotton, sugar cane, cattle, furs, and feathers.

Tripoli (Arabic *Tarabolus esh-sham*) Port in N Lebanon, 65 km/40 mi NE of Beirut; population (1991 est) 200,000. There is oil refining. It stands on the site of the Phoenician city of Oea.

Tripoli (Arabic *Tarabolus al-Gharb*) Capital and chief port of Libya, on the Mediterranean coast; population (1991 est) 1,000,000. Products include olive oil, fruit, fish, and textiles. Tripoli was founded about the 7th century BC by Phoenicians from Oea (now Tripoli in Lebanon). It was a base for Axis powers during World War II. In 1986 it was bombed by the US Air Force in retaliation for international guerrilla activity.

Tripolitania Former province of Libya, stretching from Cyrenaica in the E to Tunisia in the W. It came under Turkish rule in the 16th century; Italy captured it from Turkey 1912, and the British captured it from Italy 1942 and controlled it until it was incorporated into the newly independent United Kingdom of Libya, established 1951. In 1963 Tripolitania was subdivided into administrative divisions. Most of Libya's agricultural land is in Tripolitania, with principal crops including tomatoes, citrus fruits, wheat, barley, potatoes, olives, figs, apricots, and dates.

Tripura State of NE India since 1972, formerly a princely state, between Bangladesh and Assam
area 10,486 sq km/4,049 sq mi
capital Agartala
features agriculture on a rotation system in the rainforest, now being superseded by modern methods
industries rice, cotton, tea, sugar cane, steel, jute
population (1994 est) 3,055,000
language Bengali, Kokbarak
religion Hindu.

Tristan da Cunha Group of islands in the S Atlantic, part of the British dependency of ◊St Helena
area 110 sq km/42 sq mi
features comprises four islands: Tristan, Gough, Inaccessible, and Nightingale. Tristan consists of a single volcano 2,060 m/6,761 ft; it is an important meteorological and radio station
government administrator and island council
industries crayfish
currency pound sterling
population (1992) 295
language English
history the first European to visit the then uninhabited islands was the Portuguese admiral after whom they are named, 1506; they were annexed by Britain 1816. Believed to be extinct, the Tristan volcano erupted 1961 and the population was evacuated, but in 1963 they chose to return.

Trivandrum Capital of Kerala, SW India; population (1991) 524,000. It has chemical, textile, and rubber industries. Formerly the capital of the princely state of Travancore, it has many palaces, an old fort, and a shrine.

Trobriand Islands Group of coral islands in the Solomon Sea, forming part of the province of Milne Bay, Papua New Guinea; chief town Losuia; area 440 sq km/170 sq mi.

Trois Rivières (English *Three Rivers*) Port on the St Lawrence River, at the point where the St Maurice River enters the St Lawrence, Quebec, Canada; population (1991) 49,400, metropolitan area 136,300. The chief industry is the production of newsprint. It was founded by the French explorer Samuel de Champlain 1634.

Trollhättan Town in Älvsborg county, SW Sweden; population (1995) 52,500. The *Trollhätta Falls*, over 30 m/ 98 ft high, generate power for the surrounding factories. These include Saab car-assembly and engine works.

Troms County of N Norway; area 25,954 sq km/10,021 sq mi; population (1995) 151,200. It is predominantly mountainous, with many small islands; lack of road and rail communication hinders industrialization, and fishing is the chief activity. Tromsø is the capital.

Tromsø Fishing port and the largest town in NW Norway, on Tromsø Island; population (1991) 51,300. A church was founded here in the 13th century and the town grew up around it. It is used as a base for Arctic expeditions.

Trondheim Fishing port in Norway; population (1994) 134,000. It has canning, textile, margarine, and soap industries. It was the medieval capital of Norway, and Norwegian kings are crowned in the cathedral (1066–93). Trondheim was occupied by the Germans 1940–45.

Trossachs Woodland glen between lochs Katrine and Achray in Stirling unitary authority, Scotland, 3 km/2 mi long. Featured in the novels of Walter Scott, it has become a favoured tourist spot.

Trouville-sur-Mer French seaside resort in the *département* of Calvados; population (1990) 6,000. It is linked by a bridge across the river Touques with Deauville. It has a fishing trade, and there is some commercial traffic in the port.

Trowbridge Market town in Wiltshire, England, 12 km/7 mi SE of Bath; administrative headquarters of the county; population (1991) 29,300. Its industries include dairy produce, bacon, ham, brewing, and woollen manufacturing.

Troy City in E New York, USA, E of Albany on the E bank of the Hudson River; seat of Rensselear County, incorporated 1816; population (1992) 54,200. Industries include clothing, abrasives, metals, paper, car and railway parts, and processed foods.

Troyes Industrial city (textiles and food processing) in Champagne-Ardenne, NE France; population (1990) 60,800. It was the capital of the medieval province of Champagne. The *Treaty of Troyes* 1420 made Henry V of England heir to the French crown.

Trucial States Former name (to 1971) of the United Arab Emirates. It derives from the agreements made with Britain 1820 to ensure a truce in the area and to suppress piracy and slavery.

Trujillo City in NW Peru, with its port at Salaverry; population (1993) 509,300. Industries include engineering, copper, sugar milling, vehicle assembly and trade in agricultural produce.

Truk Group of about 55 volcanic islands surrounded by a coral reef in the E Caroline islands of the W Pacific, forming one of the four states of the Federated States of Micronesia. Fish and copra are the main products.

Truong Sa One of the ◊Spratly Islands in the South China Sea.

Truro Market town in Cornwall, England, and administrative headquarters of the county; population (1982) 16,000.

Tsaritsyn Former name (to 1925) of ◊Volgograd, a city in Russia.

Tsarskoe Selo (Russian 'the tsar's village') town NW of St Petersburg, in the Russian Federation; population (1985) 91,000. Founded by Peter the Great in 1708, it has a number of imperial summer palaces, restored after German troops devastated the town 1941–44. In the 1920s it was renamed

Detskoe Selo ('the children's village'), and from 1937 to the 1990s it was known as Pushkino, after the poet Aleksandr Pushkin, who was educated at the school that later became a museum commemorating him.

Tsavo National Park National park in SE Kenya, established 1948. One of the world's largest, it occupies 20,821 sq km/8,036 sq mi.

Tselinograd Former name of the Kazakh capital ◊Akmola.

Tsinan Alternative transliteration of ◊Jinan, the capital of Shandong province, E China.

Tsingtao Alternative transliteration of ◊Qingdao, a port in E China.

Tsumeb Principal mining centre (diamonds, copper, lead, zinc) of N Namibia, NW of Grootfontein; population (1990) 13,500.

Tsushima Japanese island between Korea and Japan in *Tsushima Strait*; area 702 sq km/271 sq mi; population (1990) 59,300. The Russian fleet was destroyed by the Japanese here 27 May 1905 in the Russo-Japanese War, and 12,000 Russians were killed. The chief settlement is Izuhara.

Tuamotu Archipelago Two parallel ranges of 78 atolls, part of ◊French Polynesia; area 690 sq km/266 sq mi; population (1988) 12,400, including the ◊Gambier Islands to the E. The atolls stretch 2,100 km/1,300 mi N and E of the Society Islands. The administrative headquarters is Apataki. The largest atoll is Rangiroa, the most significant is Hao; they produce pearl shell and copra. Mururoa and Fangataufa atolls to the SE have been a French nuclear test site since 1966. Spanish explorers landed 1606, and the islands were annexed by France 1881.

Tübingen Town in Baden-Württemberg, Germany, on the river Neckar, 30 km/19m S of Stuttgart; population (1985) 75,000. Industries include paper, textiles, and surgical instruments. The town dates from the 11th century; the university was established 1477.

Tubuai Islands or *Austral Islands* Chain of volcanic islands and reefs 1,300 km/800 mi long in ◊French Polynesia, S of the Society Islands; area 148 sq km/57 sq mi; population (1988) 6,500. The main settlement is Mataura on Tubuai. They were visited by Capt Cook 1777 and annexed by France 1880.

Tucson Resort city in the Sonora Desert in SE Arizona, USA; population (1992) 415,100. It stands 760 m/2,500 ft above sea level, and the Santa Catalina Mountains to the NE rise to about 2,750 m/9,000 ft. Industries include aircraft, electronics, and copper smelting. Tucson passed from Mexico to the USA 1853 and was the territorial capital 1867–77.

Tuileries Gardens in the centre of Paris, on the site of a former residence of the French sovereigns. There are two museums: L'Orangerie and Jeu de Paume. The gardens were planned by the landscape gardener André Le Nôtre.

Tula City in the Russian Federation, on the river Upa, 193 km/121 mi S of Moscow; population (1994) 535,000. Industries include engineering and metallurgy. It was the site of the government ordnance factory, founded 1712 by Peter the Great.

Tulare Town in S central California, USA, S of Fresno, in the San Joaquin Valley; population (1990) 33,200. Industries include food processing, wine, and dairy products. Tulare was built 1871 as a division headquarters for the Southern Pacific Railroad.

Tulle French town, capital of Corrèze *département* on the W edge of the Massif Central; population (1990) 17,200. The town was founded in the 7th century. Only a 12th-century nave and belfry remain of its ancient cathedral. Tulle is an industrial town with a government firearms factory. It gives its name to tulle, a fine silk net fabric which was once made in the region.

Tulsa City in NE Oklahoma, USA, on the Arkansas River, NE of Oklahoma City; population (1992) 375,300. It is an oil-producing and aerospace centre; other industries include mining, machinery, metals, and cement. Tulsa was settled by members of the Native American Creek people 1836.

Tunbridge Wells, Royal Spa town in Kent, SE England, with iron-rich springs discovered 1606; population (1991) 60,300. There is an expanding light industrial estate. The *Pantiles* or shopping parade (paved with tiles in the reign of Queen Anne), was a fashionable resort; the town has been named 'Royal' since 1909 after visits by Queen Victoria.

Tunbs, the Two islands in the Strait of Hormuz, formerly held by Ras al Khaimah and annexed from other Gulf states by Iran 1971; their return to their former owners was an Iraqi aim in the Iran-Iraq War.

Tungurahua Active volcano in the Andes of central Ecuador, the tenth highest peak in Ecuador; height 5,016 m/16,456 ft. Its last major eruption was in 1886.

Tunis Capital and chief port of Tunisia; population (1994) 674,100. Industries include chemicals and textiles. Founded by the Arabs, it was captured by the Turks 1533, then occupied by the French 1881 and by the Axis powers 1942–43. The ruins of ancient Carthage are to the NE.

Tunja Capital of the Andean department of Boyacá, E central Colombia; population (1992) 112,000. Formerly the seat of the Chibcha Indian kings, the Spanish built a city here 1539. In 1818 Simón Bolívar defeated Spanish Royalists near Tunja. Industries include agriculture and mining.

Turin (Italian *Torino*) Capital of Piedmont, NW Italy, on the river Po; population (1992) 952,700. Industries include iron, steel, cars, silk and other textiles, fashion goods, chocolate, and wine. There is a university, established 1404, and a 15th-century cathedral. Features include the Palazzo Reale (Royal Palace) 1646–58 and several gates to the city. It was the first capital of united Italy 1861–64.

Turin (Italian *Torino*) Province of N Italy in ◊Piedmont region; capital ◊Turin; area 6,830 sq km/2,637 sq mi; population (1992) 2,236,100.

Turkana, Lake formerly (until 1979) *Lake Rudolf* Lake in the Great Rift Valley, 375 m/1,230 ft above sea level, with its northernmost end in Ethiopia and the rest in Kenya; area

9,000 sq km/3,475 sq mi. It is saline, and shrinking by evaporation. Its shores were an early human hunting ground, and valuable remains have been found that are accurately datable because of undisturbed stratification.

Turkestan Area of central Asia divided among Kazakhstan, Kyrgyzstan, Tajikistan, Turkmenistan, Uzbekistan, Afghanistan, and China (part of Xinjiang Uygur).

Turks and Caicos Islands British crown colony in the West Indies, the SE archipelago of the Bahamas

area 430 sq km/166 sq mi

capital Cockburn Town on Grand Turk

features a group of 30 islands, of which six are inhabited. The largest is the uninhabited *Grand Caicos*; others include *Grand Turk* (1990 population 3,761), *South Caicos* (1,220), *Middle Caicos* (275), *North Caicos* (1,305), *Providenciales* (5,586), and *Salt Cay* (213); since 1982 the Turks and Caicos have developed as a tax haven

government governor, with executive and legislative councils (chief minister from 1993 Charles W Misick)

exports crayfish and conch (flesh and shell); tourism is important

currency US dollar

population (1990 est) 12,400, 90% of African descent

language English, French Creole

religion Christian

history uninhabited islands discovered by the Spanish 1512; they remained unoccupied until British settlers from Bermuda established a salt panning industry 1678. Secured by Britain 1766 against French and Spanish claims, the islands were a Jamaican dependency 1873–1962, and became a separate colony 1962.

Turku (Swedish *Åbo*) Port in SW Finland, near the mouth of the river Aura, on the Gulf of Bothnia; population (1992) 160,000. Industries include shipbuilding, engineering, textiles, and food processing. It was the capital of Finland until 1812.

Turnhout Town in the province of Antwerp, Belgium. It is the economic capital of the Kempen (Campine) region. Turnhout has a large paper industry; there are also printing works, iron foundries, mills, brick kilns, and manufactures of lace, pottery, and food.

Tuscaloosa City in W central Alabama, USA, on the Black Warrior River, SW of Birmingham; population (1992) 77,800. Industries include chemicals, tyres, paper, and lumber. It was originally founded by Creek Native Americans 1809.

Tuscany (Italian *Toscana*) Region of N central Italy, on the W coast; area 22,992 sq km/8,877 sq mi; population (1995 est) 3,526,000. Its capital is Florence, and cities include Pisa, Livorno, and Siena. The area is mainly agricultural, with many vineyards, such as in the Chianti hills; it also has lignite and iron mines and marble quarries (Carrara marble is from here). The Tuscan dialect has been adopted as the standard form of Italian. Tuscany was formerly the Roman *Etruria*, and was inhabited by Etruscans around 500 BC. In medieval times the area was divided into small states, united under Florentine rule during the 15th–16th centuries. It became part of united Italy 1861.

Tuva Autonomous republic (administrative unit) of the Russian Federation, in Siberia
area 170,500 sq km/65,830 sq mi
capital Kyzyl
physical basin of the Yenisey River
industries mining of gold, asbestos and cobalt; cattle farming
population (1995) 308,000

Tver formerly (1932–90) *Kalinin* City of NW Russian Federation, capital of Tver region, a transport centre on the river Volga, 160 km/100 mi NW of Moscow; population (1994) 454,000.

Tweed River rising in SW Scottish Borders, Scotland, and entering the North Sea at Berwick-upon-Tweed, Northumberland; length 156 km/97 mi. From Coldstream until near Berwick-upon-Tweed it forms the border between England and Scotland.

Twickenham District in the Greater London borough of ◊Richmond-upon-Thames. Twickenham Rugby football ground, headquarters of the Rugby Football Union, is here. Buildings include Marble Hill House (1723), a Palladian villa (home of the duchess of Suffolk, mistress of George II), and Horace Walpole's home Strawberry Hill (1748–77), an early example of the Gothic Revival style of architecture. The Royal Military School of Music is at Kneller Hall. Alexander Pope is buried in the church.

TX Abbreviation for the state of ◊Texas, USA.

Tyburn Stream in London, England, near which (at the junction of Oxford Street and Edgware Road) Tyburn gallows stood from the 12th century until 1783. The Tyburn now flows underground.

Tyler City in NE Texas, USA, SE of Dallas; population (1992) 76,900. Industries include oil, roses, vegetables, furniture, and plastics. There is an annual rose festival. Tyler was laid out 1846.

Tyne River of NE England formed by the union of the North Tyne (rising in the Cheviot Hills) and South Tyne (rising in Cumbria) near Hexham, Northumberland, and reaching the North Sea at Tynemouth; length 72 km/45 mi. Kielder Water (1980) in the North Tyne Valley is Europe's largest artificial lake, 12 km/7.5 mi long and 0.8 km/0.5 mi wide, and supplies the industries of Tyneside, Wearside, and Teesside.

Tyne and Wear Metropolitan county of NE England, created 1974; in 1986, most of the functions of the former county council were transferred to the metropolitan district councils
area 540 sq km/208 sq mi
towns and cities Newcastle upon Tyne (administrative headquarters), South Shields, North Shields, Gateshead, Sunderland
features bisected by the rivers Tyne and Wear; includes part of Hadrian's Wall; Newcastle and Gateshead, linked with each other and with the coast on both sides by the Tyne and Wear Metro (a light railway using existing suburban lines, extending 54 km/34 mi); Tyneside International Film Festival

industries once a centre of heavy industry, it is now being redeveloped and diversified; car manufacturing on Wearside, electronics, offshore technology (floating production vessels), automobile components, pharmaceuticals, computer science
population (1996) 1,095,200.

Tynemouth Port and resort in Tyne and Wear, England; population (1991) 17,400.

Tyrol Variant spelling of ◊Tirol, a state of Austria.

Tyrone County of Northern Ireland
area 3,160 sq km/1,220 sq mi
towns and cities Omagh (county town), Dungannon, Strabane, Cookstown
features rivers: Derg, Blackwater, Foyle; Lough Neagh; Sperrin Mountains
industries mainly agricultural: barley, flax, potatoes, turnips, cattle, sheep, brick making, linen, hosiery, shirts
population (1991) 158,500.

Tyrrhenian Sea Arm of the Mediterranean Sea surrounded by mainland Italy, Sicily, Sardinia, Corsica, and the Ligurian Sea. It is connected to the Ionian Sea through the Straits of Messina. Islands include Elba, Ustica, Capri, Stromboli, and the Lipari Islands.

Tyumen Oldest city in Siberia, in central Russian Federation (founded 1586), on the river Nitsa; population (1990) 487,000. Industries include oil refining, machine tools, and chemicals.

Tywi or *Towy* River in Carmarthenshire, SW Wales; length 108 km/68 mi. It rises in the Cambrian Mountains of central Wales, flowing SW to enter Carmarthen Bay.

Ubangi-Shari Former name (to 1958) of the Central African Republic.

Udaipur or *Mewar* Industrial city (cotton, grain) in Rajasthan, India, capital of the former princely state of Udaipur; population (1991) 308,000. It was founded 1568 and has several palaces (two on islands in a lake) and the Jagannath Hindu temple 1640.

Uddevalla Seaport in SW Sweden, in the county of Göteborg and Bohus; population (1995) 49,000. Industries include shipbuilding, chemicals, textiles, wood-pulp, and sugar refining.

Udine Industrial city (chemicals, textiles) NE of Venice, Italy; population (1990) 98,300. Udine was the capital of Friuli in the 13th century and passed to Venice 1420.

Udine Province of NE Italy in ◊Friuli-Venezia Giulia region; capital ◊Udine; area 4,864 sq km/1,878 sq mi; population (1992) 522,000.

Udmurtia (Russian *Udmurtskaya Oblast'*) Autonomous republic in central Russian Federation
area 42,100 sq km/16,255 sq mi
capital Izhevsk
physical in the foothills of the W Ural Mountains
industries timber, flax, potatoes, peat, quartz
population (1995) 1,641,000.

Ufa Industrial city (engineering, oil refining, petrochemicals, distilling, timber) and capital of Bashkortostan, central Russian Federation, on the river Bielaia, in the W Urals; population (1994) 1,092,000. It was founded by Russia 1574 as a fortress.

Uist Two small islands in the Outer ◊Hebrides, Scotland: North Uist and South Uist.

Ujiji Port on Lake Tanganyika, Tanzania, where Henry Stanley found David Livingstone 1871; population about 17,000. It was originally an Arab trading post for slaves and ivory.

Ujung Pandang formerly (until 1973) *Macassar* or *Makassar* Chief port (trading in coffee, rubber, copra, and spices) on Sulawesi, Indonesia, with fishing and food processing industries; population (1990) 913,200. It was established by Dutch traders 1607.

Ulaanbaatar or *Ulan Bator*, formerly until 1924 *Urga* Capital of the Mongolian Republic; a trading centre producing carpets, textiles, and vodka; population (1993) 600,500.

Ulan-Ude formerly (until 1934) *Verkhne-Udinsk* Industrial city (sawmills, cars, glass) and capital of the autonomous republic of Buryat in SE Russian Federation, on the river Ibla and the Trans-Siberian railway; population (1990) 359,000. It was founded as a Cossack settlement in the 1660s.

Uleåborg Swedish name for the Finnish port of ◊Oulu.

Ulm Industrial city (vehicles, agricultural machinery, precision instruments, textiles) in Baden-Württemberg, Germany, on the river Danube; population (1993) 114,700. Its Gothic cathedral with the highest stone spire ever built (161 m/528 ft) escaped damage in World War II when two-thirds of Ulm was destroyed. It was a free imperial city from the 14th century to 1802. The physicist and mathematician Albert Einstein was born here.

Ulsan Industrial city (vehicles, shipbuilding, oil refining, petrochemicals) in South Kyongsang province, SE South Korea; population (1990) 683,000.

Ulster Former kingdom in Northern Ireland, annexed by England 1461, from Jacobean times a centre of English, and later Scottish, settlement on land confiscated from its owners; divided 1921 into Northern Ireland (counties Antrim, Armagh, Down, Fermanagh, Londonderry, and Tyrone) and the Republic of Ireland (counties Cavan, Donegal, and Monaghan).

Ulundi Former capital of the former independent homeland KwaZulu in Natal, South Africa, now situated in KwaZulu-Natal Province. It was the capital of the Zulu kingdom and site of the battle that ended the Anglo-Zulu War July 1879. The defeated Zulu king, Cetewayo, was captured and banished to Cape Town. Ulundi was razed to the ground and Zululand annexed by the British.

Uluru see ◊Ayres Rock.

Umballa Alternative form of ◊Ambala, a city in India.

Umbria Mountainous region of Italy in the central Apennines, including the provinces of Perugia and Terni; area 8,456 sq km/3,265 sq mi; population (1995) 822,500. Its capital is Perugia, and the river Tiber rises in the region. Industries include wine, grain, olives, tobacco, textiles, chemicals, and metalworking. This is the home of the Umbrian school of artists, including Raphael.

Umeå Seaport and capital of Västerbotten county in NE Sweden on the Gulf of Bothnia at the mouth of the river Ume; population (1995) 101,300. Machinery, furniture, and wood pulp are manufactured here. It is the biggest city in N Sweden and a cultural centre. There is a ferry service to Vaasa in Finland.

Umm al Qaiwain One of the United Arab Emirates.

Umtali Former name (to 1982) for the town of ◊Mutare in Zimbabwe.

Umtata Former capital of the former black homeland of ◊Transkei, South Africa; population (1988 est) 45,000.

Ungava District in N Quebec and Labrador, Canada, E of Hudson Bay; area 911,110 sq km/351,780 sq mi. It has large deposits of iron ore.

United Arab Republic Union formed 1958, broken 1961, between Egypt and Syria. Egypt continued to use the name after the breach up until 1971.

United Provinces of Agra and Oudh Former province of British India, which formed the major part of the state of ◊Uttar Pradesh; see also ◊Agra, ◊Oudh.

Unzen Active volcano on the Shimbara peninsula, Kyushu Island, Japan, opposite the city of Kumamoto. Its eruption June 1991 led to the evacuation of 10,000 people.

Upper Austria (German *Oberösterreich*) Mountainous federal province of Austria, drained by the river Danube; area 11,980 sq km/4,625 sq mi; population (1995) 1,385,769. Its capital is Linz. In addition to wine, sugar beet, and grain, there are reserves of oil. Manufactured products include textiles, chemicals, and metal goods.

Upper Volta Former name (to 1984) of Burkina Faso.

Uppsala or *Upsala* City in Sweden, NW of Stockholm; population (1994) 181,200. Industries include engineering and pharmaceuticals. The university was founded 1477; there are Viking relics and a Gothic cathedral. The botanist Carolus Linnaeus lived here.

Uppsala or *Upsala* County of E central Sweden; area 5,325 sq km/2,056 sq mi; population (1990) 257,700. It is forested but is also a major agricultural region. Iron ore is mined locally. The main town is Uppsala, on the river Fyris.

Ural Mountains (Russian *Ural'skiy Khrebet*) Mountain system running from the Arctic Ocean to the Caspian Sea, traditionally separating Europe from Asia. The highest peak is Naradnaya, 1,894 m/6,214 ft. It has vast mineral wealth.

Urbana Industrial city (food processing, electronics, and metal products) in E central Illinois, USA, E of Springfield; population (1990) 36,300. The University of Illinois 1867 is here. Urbana was first settled 1822.

Urga Former name (to 1924) of ◊Ulaanbaatar, the capital of Mongolia.

Uri Canton of Switzerland on the SE of Lake Lucerne; area 1,075 sq km/415 sq mi; population (1995) 35,900. The capital is ◊Altdorf. The main river is the Reuss. Uri was founded 1291 and (together with Schwyz and Nidwalden) was one of the three original cantons of the Swiss Confederation. Forestry and tourism are the main industries.

Urumqi or *Urumchi* Industrial city and capital of Xinjiang Uygur autonomous region, China, at the N foot of the Tian Shan Mountains; population (1993) 1,110,000. It produces cotton textiles, cement, chemicals, iron, and steel.

Usedom Island (Polish *Uznam*) Island divided between Germany and Poland, lying between the Zalew Szczeciński lagoon and the Baltic Sea, off the mouth of the river Oder, covering an area of 440 sq km/1,139 sq mi. The chief town is the Polish Świnoujście, a bulk-cargo port and resort.

Ushant (French *Ouessant*) French island 18 km/11 mi W of Brittany, area 15 sq km/9 sq mi, off which the British admiral Richard Howe defeated the French navy 1794 on 'the Glorious First of June'. The chief town is Lampaul.

Ushuaia Southernmost town in the world, at the tip of Tierra del Fuego, Argentina, less than 1,000 km/620 mi from Antarctica; population (1991) 29,700. It is a free port and naval base. Industries include lumbering, sheep-rearing, and fishing.

Usküb Turkish name of ◊Skopje, the capital of the Former Yugoslav Republic of Macedonia.

Usküdar Suburb of Istanbul, Turkey; formerly a separate town, which under the name *Scutari* was the site of the hospital set up by Florence Nightingale during the Crimean War.

Ussuri River in E Asia, tributary of the Amur. Rising N of Vladivostok and joining the Amur S of Khabarovsk, it forms part of the border between the Russian Federation and the Chinese province of Heilongjiang. There were military clashes 1968–69 over the sovereignty of Damansky Island (Chenpao).

Ust-Kamenogorsk River port and chief centre of the nuclear industry in the Russian Federation, in the Altai Mountains, on the river Irtysh; population (1987) 321,000.

UT Abbreviation for ◊Utah, a state of the USA.

Utah State in W USA; nicknamed Beehive State/Mormon State
area 219,900 sq km/84,881 sq mi
capital Salt Lake City
towns and cities Provo, Ogden
physical Colorado Plateau to the E, mountains in centre, Great Basin to the W, Great Salt Lake; Great American Desert; Colorado river system; five national parks: the Arches, Bryce Canyon, Canyonlands, Capitol Reef, and Zion; the Uinta Mountains, Utah's tallest mountains (highest peak 4,123 m/13,528 ft); the Wasatch Mountains (over 3,300 m/11,000 ft); Great Salt Lake; Dinosaur national monument, with Dinosaur Quarry; Rainbow Bridge national monument; Natural Bridges national monument; Great Basin desert region; Green River

features Nine Mile Canyon, with rock carvings by the Fremont American Indians; Hovenweep national monument, with tower structures that may have been used by the Anasazi American Indians for making astronomical observations; Golden Spike national historic site, where the Union Pacific and Central Pacific railroads met 1869, completing the first transcontinental route; Bingham Canyon Copper Mine; Salt Lake City, based on Brigham Young's grid plan, with Temole Square, the Tabernacle (home of the Mormon Tabernacle Choir), the Family History Library (the largest collection of genealogical data in the world), the Beehive House (1854, Brigham Young's home), the Union Pacific Railroad Depot (1909), and the Utah state capitol (1915, a fine example of Renaissance Revival architecture, with murals depicting Utah's history added during the Depression); Brigham Young University; Monument Valley Tribal Park, a Navajo centre; Anasazi Indian village state park; Fremont Indian state park; Utah Shakespearean Festival, in an open-air replica of the Globe Theatre, at Cedar City; Intermountain Power Project, the world's largest coal-fired generating station; auto racing at Bonneville Salt Flats; Utah has the highest proportion of high-school graduates of any state
industries wool, gold, silver, copper, coal, salt, steel
population (1995) 1,951,400
famous people Brigham Young
history explored first by Franciscan friars for Spain 1776; Great Salt Lake discovered by US frontier scout Jim Bridger 1824; part of the area ceded by Mexico 1848; developed by Mormons, still by far the largest religious group in the state (70% 1996); territory 1850, but not admitted to statehood until 1896 because of Mormon reluctance to relinquish multiple marriage.

Utica Industrial city (engine parts, clothing) in central New York State, USA; population (1992) 66,850. Utica was an important textile centre from about 1850 to 1950. The first Woolworth store was opened here 1879. The settlement 1773 was on the site of an Iroquois centre and a British fort.

Utrecht Province of the Netherlands lying SE of Amsterdam, on the Kromme Rijn (Crooked Rhine); area 1,330 sq km/513 sq mi; capital Utrecht; population (1995) 1,063,500. Other towns and cities include Amersfoort, Zeist, Nieuwegeun, and Veenendaal. Industries are chemicals, livestock, textiles, and electrical goods.

Utrecht Capital of Utrecht province, Netherlands, on the river Oude Rijn (see ◊Rhine); 60 km/45 mi E of The Hague; population (1996) 234,800. The city's industries include textiles, carpets, pottery, chemicals, engineering, and printing. The city was important in the Middle Ages, and has a Gothic cathedral (1254–1517) with the highest church tower in the Netherlands. Utrecht's university was founded 1636.

Uttar Pradesh State of N India
area 294,411 sq km/113,672 sq mi
capital Lucknow
towns and cities Kanpur, Varanasi, Agra, Allahabad, Meerut
features most populous state; Himalayan peak Nanda Devi 7,817 m/25,655 ft

industries India's largest producer of grains; sugar, oil refining, textiles, leatherwork
population (1994 est) 150,695,000
famous people Indira Gandhi, Ravi Shankar
language Hindi
religion 80% Hindu, 15% Muslim
history formerly the heart of the Mogul Empire and generating point of the Indian Mutiny 1857 and subsequent opposition to British rule; see also ◊Agra and ◊Oudh. There are secessionist demands for a new hill state carved out of Uttar Pradesh.

Uusikaupunki (Swedish *Nystad*) Seaport of S Finland, on the Gulf of Bothnia 65 km/40 mi NW of Turku, in Turku ja Pori province.

Uusimaa (Swedish *Nyland*) Southern province of Finland on the Gulf of Finland; land area 9,859 sq km/3,807 sq mi. The land is low and flat with agriculture predominating; there is also some quarrying. The province includes Helsinki, the capital of Finland, and the new town of Tapiola.

Uznam Polish name for ◊Usedom Island, an island divided between Germany and Poland.

VA Abbreviation for the state of ◊Virginia, USA.

Vaal River in South Africa, the chief tributary of the Orange River. It rises in the Drakensberg mountain range and is 1,200 km/750 mi long.

Vaasa (Swedish *Vasa*) Capital of Vaasa province, W Finland. Situated on the Klemetso peninsula on the Gulf of Bothnia, this port is an important regional centre with food processing, engineering, textile, and chemical industries. Wheat is exported and there is a ferry service to Umeå in Sweden.

Vaasa Coastal province of W Finland on the Gulf of Bothnia; area 39,010 sq km/15,062 sq mi. It has flat, fertile farmland near the coast. The thickly forested interior has suffered severe economic decline, but timber is still produced.

Vadodara formerly (until 1976) *Baroda* Industrial city (metal goods, chemicals, jewellery, textiles) and rail junction in Gujarat, W India; population (1991) 1,115,000. Until 1947 it was capital of the princely state of Baroda. It has Lakshmi Vilas Palace, Pratap Vilas Palace (now the Railway Staff College), and several multi-level step wells (baoli).

Vaduz Capital of the European principality of Liechtenstein; industries include engineering and agricultural trade; population (1994 est) 5,067.

Váh (German *Waag*, Hungarian *Vág*) River in W Slovak Republic, a tributary of the ◊Danube; length 338 km/211 mi. It rises in the Carpathian Mountains and flows W, then S, to join the Danube near Komárno.

Valais (*German Wallis*) Canton of SW Switzerland, occupying the basin of the upper Rhône; area 5,231 sq km/2,019 sq mi; population (1995) 271,300. Its capital is Sion. Valais contains numerous high peaks, including the ◊Matterhorn

(4,478 m/14,691 ft), and glaciers; tourism is a major industry, and is catered for by many resorts and winter sports centres. The canton became part of the Swiss Confederation 1815.

Valdai Hills Small forested plateau in the Russian Federation, between St Petersburg and Moscow, where the Volga and W Dvina rivers rise. The Viking founders of the Russian state used it as a river route centre to reach the Baltic, Black, Caspian, and White seas. From the 15th century it was dominated by Moscow.

Val-de-Marne *Département* in the ◊Ile-de-France region of France, SE of Paris; area 244 sq km/94 sq mi; population (1990) 1,215,100. The *département* contains the confluence of the rivers Marne and Seine, and is largely urbanized. Employment is in manufacturing industries and offices, with many workers commuting to central Paris. Rural areas are used for intensive agriculture and for recreation. Val-de-Marne contains the Rungis wholesale market (replacing Les Halles in central Paris) and Orly airport. The capital is Créteil.

Valdivia Industrial port (shipbuilding, leather, beer, soap) and resort in Chile; population (1992) 122,400. It was founded 1552 by the Spanish conquistador Pedro de Valdivia (c. 1500–1554), conqueror of Chile.

Val-d'Oise *Département* in the ◊Ile-de-France region of France, NW of Paris and N of the confluence of the rivers Seine and Oise; area 1,248 sq km/482 sq mi; population (1990) 1,050,000. The plateaux of Vexin and the Plaine de France are bisected by the river Oise. Intensive agricultural production ranges from market gardening to large-scale arable cultivation. Important industries (metalworks, machinery, motor vehicles, high-tech and service industries) are located on the N margins of Paris and in the Oise valley. Major road, rail, and water routes cross the *département*, which functions increasingly as a part of greater Paris. The capital is the new city of Cergy-Pontoise.

Valence Market town and capital of Drôme *département*, SE France, on the river Rhône; population (1990) 65,000. Industries include electrical goods and components for aerospace. It is of pre-Roman origin and has a Romanesque cathedral consecrated 1095.

Valencia Province of W Spain in central Valencia autonomous community; capital Valencia; area 10,764 sq km/4,156 sq mi; population (1995) 2,200,300. Its E coastline is on the Mediterranean Sea. The rivers Guadalaviar and Júcar flow through it. The province is mountainous in the interior, and has a fertile, irrigated coastal plain. Products include oranges, olives, grapes, mulberries, figs, and rice.

Valencia Industrial city (wine, fruit, chemicals, textiles, ship repair) in Valencia region, E Spain; population (1991) 764,000. The Community of Valencia, consisting of Alicante, Castellón, and Valencia, has an area of 23,300 sq km/8,994 sq mi and a population of 3,772,000.

Valencia Industrial city (textiles, leather, sugar) and agricultural centre in Carabobo state, N Venezuela, on the

Cabriales River; population (1990) 903,100. It is 478 m/1,569 ft above sea level and was founded 1555.

Valencian Community Autonomous community of W Spain, comprising the provinces of Alicante, Castellón, and Valencia; capital ◊Valencia; area 23,307 sq km/8,999 sq mi; population (1995) 3,857,200.

Valenciennes Industrial town in Nord *département*, NE France, near the Belgian border, once known for its lace; population (1990) 39,300. It became French 1678.

Vale of Glamorgan Unitary authority in S Wales created 1996 from parts of the former counties of Mid Glamorgan and South Glamorgan; administrative headquarters Barry; population (1996) 119,500; area 337 sq km/130 sq mi. Barry is a major port. Agriculture and sheep farming are important.

Valladolid Industrial city (food processing, vehicles, textiles, engineering), and capital of Valladolid province, Spain; population (1994) 337,000.

Valladolid Province of Spain in central Castilla-León autonomous community; capital ◊Valladolid; area 8,200 sq km/3,166 sq mi; population (1995) 504,600. It is largely open country with the river Duero and its tributaries flowing through it. It is called the 'granary of Spain' and, besides cereals, produces fruit, oil, wine, and honey. Industries include textiles, metallurgy, and tanning.

Valle d'Aosta Autonomous region of NW Italy; area 3,262 sq km/1,259 sq mi; population (1995) 118,500, many of whom are French-speaking. It produces wine and livestock. Its capital is Aosta.

Vallejo Industrial city (fruit and flour processing and petroleum refining) in NW California, USA, on San Pablo Bay, NE of Berkeley; population (1992) 113,700. It was California's capital 1852–53.

Valletta Capital and port of Malta; population (1995) 9,129 (inner harbour area 102,600).

Valona Italian form of ◊Vlorë, a port in Albania.

Valparaíso Industrial port (sugar refining, textiles, chemicals) in Chile, on the Pacific Ocean; capital of Valparaíso province; population (1992) 276,700. Founded 1536, it was occupied by the English naval adventurers Francis Drake 1578 and John Hawkins 1595, pillaged by the Dutch 1600, and bombarded by Spain 1866; it has also suffered from earthquakes.

Van City in Turkey on a site on *Lake Van* that has been inhabited for more than 3,000 years; population (1990) 153,100. It is a commercial centre for a fruit- and grain-producing area.

Vancouver Industrial city (oil refining, engineering, shipbuilding, aircraft, timber, pulp and paper, textiles, fisheries) in Canada, its chief Pacific seaport, on the mainland of British Columbia; population (1991) 471,800, metropolitan area 1,602,500. It was settled by 1875, under the name of Granville, and was renamed when it became a city 1886, having been reached by the Canadian Pacific Railroad.

Vancouver City in SW Washington, USA, on the Columbia River, N of Portland, Oregon; population (1990) 46,400. It is a manufacturing and shipping centre for agriculture and timber. It began as a trading post for the Hudson's Bay Company 1825.

Vancouver Island Island off the W coast of Canada, part of British Columbia
area 32,136 sq km/12,404 sq mi
towns and cities Victoria, Nanaimo, Esquimalt (naval base)
industries coal, timber, fish
history visited by British explorer Captain Cook 1778; surveyed 1792 by Captain George Vancouver.

Van Diemen's Land Former name (1642–1855) of ◊Tasmania, Australia. It was named by Dutch navigator Abel Tasman after the governor general of the Dutch East Indies, Anthony van Diemen. The name Tasmania was used from the 1840s and became official 1855.

Vänern Largest lake in Sweden, area 5,550 sq km/2,140 sq mi. Karlstad, Vänersborg, Lidköping, and Mariestad are on its banks.

Vannes Seaport and capital of the French *département* of Morbihan; population (1990) 50,000. The industries include shipbuilding and tourism, and the manufacture of woollen fabrics, rope, tyres, and agricultural machinery. Medieval ramparts enclose the inner city, and there is a cathedral with a 16th-century chapel.

Vannin, Ellan Gaelic name for the Isle of ◊Man.

Var River in S France, rising in the Maritime Alps and flowing generally SE for 134 km/84 mi into the Mediterranean near Nice. It gives its name to a *département* in the Provence-Alpes-Côte d'Azur region.

Var *Département* in the ◊Provence-Alpes-Côte d'Azur region of France; area 6,000 sq km/2,317 sq mi; population (1990) 816,000. It has a much indented coastline on the Mediterranean. Var is generally hilly and wooded and the river Argens flows through it. Fruit, flowers, vines, and olives are produced in coastal districts; there are bauxite, lead, zinc, and salt deposits; there are engineering and chemical industries and furniture is made; tourism is important. The principal towns are ◊Toulon (the capital) and Draguignan. Resorts include ◊Hyères, Fréjus, and St-Raphaël.

Varanasi or *Benares* or *Banaras* Holy city of the Hindus in Uttar Pradesh, India, on the river Ganges; population (1991) 932,000. There are 1,500 golden shrines, and a 5 km/3 mi frontage to the Ganges with sacred stairways (ghats) for purification by bathing.

Varazdin Town in N Croatia, on the river Drava, near the Slovenian border; population (1991) 41,800. It has textile industries. It was a free city in the Middle Ages and its old fortifications remain.

Vardar River in the Balkans; length 322 km/200 mi. It rises W of Skopje in the Former Yugoslav Republic of Macedonia, and flows SE to the Aegean Sea near Thessaloniki, Greece.

Varese Province of N Italy in NW ◊Lombardy region; capital Varese (population (1990) 88,000); area 1,200 sq km/463 sq mi; population (1992) 798,600.

Varna Port in Bulgaria, on an inlet of the Black Sea; population (1991) 321,000. Industries include shipbuilding and the manufacture of chemicals.

Våsterås Capital of Våstmanland county in S central Sweden; population (1995) 123,700. It has engineering factories, chiefly electrical and metallurgical, and is Sweden's largest inland port. The town dates from the Middle Ages, and has a castle and a cathedral.

Vaucluse Mountain range in SE France, part of the Provence Alps, E of Avignon, rising to 1,242 m/4,075 ft. It gives its name to a *département*. The Italian poet Petrarch lived in the Vale of Vaucluse 1337–53.

Vaucluse *Département* in the ◊Provence-Alpes-Côte d'Azur region of SE France; area 3,566 sq km/1,377 sq mi; population (1990) 468,008. It is bordered on the W by the lower reaches of the River Rhône and on the S by the Durance. Vaucluse is drained by the rivers Eygues, Sorgue, Ouveze, and Coulon. It is known for its wines (including Châteauneuf-du-Pape) and its fruit. Olives, cereals, silk, and livestock are also produced. The chief industries are textiles, chemicals, and foodstuffs. The major towns are ◊Avignon (the capital), Carpentras, and Apt.

Vaud (German *Waadt*) Canton in SW Switzerland; area 3,211 sq km/1,240 sq mi; population (1995) 605,700. It is roughly triangular in shape, with its base formed by the N shore of Lake Geneva, and is traversed by the ◊Jura Mountains, which run SW–NE. Tourism is the most important industry, but Vaud is also Switzerland's premier vine-growing region. Wine, chocolate, tobacco, clocks, and milk products are among its principal manufactures. The capital of the canton is ◊Lausanne.

Veliko Turnovo (Romanian *Veliko Târnovo*) Historic town in Lovech region, N Bulgaria, in the gorge of the river Yantra on the N slopes of the Balkan Mountains, 193 km/121 mi NE of Sofia; population (1990) 99,900. Textiles are manufactured and agricultural produce traded from the surrounding area. The Shipka Pass runs S from the town to Kazanlúk. There are several medieval buildings.

Velsen Town in the province of North Holland, Netherlands, 24 km/15 mi NW of Amsterdam; population (1996) 65,500. Velsen lies opposite IJmuiden at the seaward end of the North Sea Canal, which leads to Amsterdam. There is a major iron and steelworks.

Venda Former Republic of; former independent homeland Black National State within South Africa, independent from 1979 (but not recognized by the United Nations) until 1994 when it was re-integrated into South Africa, in Northern Province. The region covers an area of 6,500 sq km/2,510 sq mi. Towns and cities include Makwarela, Makhade, and Sibasa; its main industries are coal, copper, graphite, and construction stone. Luvenda and English are spoken here.

Vendée La River in W France that rises near the village of La Châtaigneraie and flows 72 km/45 mi to join the Sèvre Niortaise 11 km/7 mi E of the Bay of Biscay.

Vendée, La Maritime *département* in the ◊Pays de la Loire region of W France; area 6,720 sq km/2,595 sq mi; population (1990) 509,845. The main cash crops grown here are wheat and sugar-beet. Vines are widely cultivated, and horses and cattle are bred. The principal towns are La Roche-sur-Yon (the capital), Fontenay-le-Comte, and Les-Sables-d'Olonne. The area was the scene of a royalist uprising against the French Revolution that began here in 1793 and was brutally suppressed.

Vendôme French town in the *département* of Loir-et-Cher, on the river Loir; population (1990) 18,500. Cheese and asparagus are produced in the vicinity. The church of the Trinity has a 12th-century belfry, and there is an 11th-century castle.

Venetia Roman name of that part of NE Italy which later became the republic of Venice, including the Veneto region.

Veneto Region of NE Italy, comprising the provinces of Belluno, Padova (Padua), Treviso, Rovigo, Venezia (Venice), and Vicenza; area 18,364 sq km/7,090 sq mi; population (1995) 1,122,300. Its capital is Venice, and towns include Padua, Verona, and Vicenza. The Veneto forms part of the N Italian plain, with the delta of the river Po; it includes part of the Alps and Dolomites, and Lake Garda. Products include cereals, fruit, vegetables, wine, chemicals, ships, and textiles.

Venice (Italian *Venezia*) City, port, and naval base on the NE coast of Italy; population (1992) 305,600. It is the capital of Veneto region. The old city is built on piles on low-lying islands in a salt-water lagoon, sheltered from the Adriatic Sea by the Lido and other small strips of land. There are about 150 canals crossed by some 400 bridges. Apart from tourism (it draws 8 million tourists a year), industries include glass, jewellery, textiles, and lace. Venice was an independent trading republic from the 10th century, ruled by a doge, or chief magistrate, and was one of the centres of the Italian Renaissance. It was renowned as a centre of early publishing; 15% of all printed books before 1500 were printed in Venice.

Venice Province of NE Italy in E ◊Veneto region; capital Venice; area 2,460 sq km/950 sq mi; population (1992) 819,600.

Venlo Town and railway junction in the province of Limburg, the Netherlands, on the river Maas (see ◊Meuse) and on the border with Germany; population (1996) 64,800. Industries include engineering and the manufacture of tobacco, paper, and electric lamps. Venlo was formerly a heavily fortified town.

Vent, Iles du French name for the Windward Islands, part of the ◊Society Islands in ◊French Polynesia. The Leeward Islands are known as the *Iles sous le Vent*.

Ventura City in SW California, USA, on the Pacific Ocean, NW of Los Angeles; population (1990) 92,600. Industries include oil and agricultural products, such as citrus fruits and lima beans. It was named after a Spanish mission, San Buenaventura, established 1782.

Veracruz Port (trading in coffee, tobacco, and vanilla) in E Mexico, on the Gulf of Mexico; population (1990) 328,600. Products include chemicals, sisal, and textiles. It was founded by the Spanish conquistador Hernán Cortés as Villa Nueva de la Vera Cruz ('new town of the true cross') on a nearby site 1519 and transferred to its present site 1599.

Veracruz State of E Mexico, on the Gulf of Mexico; area 72,815 sq km/28,114 sq mi; population (1995 est) 6,734,500. Its capital is Jalapa Enríquez. The main occupations are farming, producing cotton, rice, sugar-cane, coffee, maize, fruit, and tobacco, and manufacturing rubber and timber. There are oilfields on the coastal strip.

Vercelli Province of N Italy in NE ◊Piedmont region; capital Vercelli (population (1990) 50,200); area 3,005 sq km/1,160 sq mi; population (1992) 374,700.

Verden City in Lower Saxony, Germany, on the river Aller, 36 km/22 mi SE of Bremen; population (1994) 126,500. Verden is an important agricultural centre.

Vermont State in NE USA; nicknamed Green Mountain State
area 24,900 sq km/9,611 sq mi
capital Montpelier
towns and cities Burlington, Rutland, Barre
physical Green Mountain national forest, with brilliant autumn foliage; Mount Mansfield (1,339 m/4,393 ft), the highest peak in the state; Lake Champlain
features no large cities or industrial areas; covered bridges; Bennington, site of the Battle of Bennington 1777, with the Bennington Battle Monument and Bennington Museum, with paintings by Grandma Moses; Newfane, with Greek Revival courthouse; birthplace and family home of Calvin Coolidge at Plymouth; Woodstock (settled 1761), site of America's first ski tow (1934); Middlebury College (1800); Shelburne museum of the history of American life; State House, Montpelier; Marlboro Music Festival; Barre, the site of the world's largest granite quarry; Trapp Family Lodge, Stowe; winter sports
industries apples, maple syrup, dairy products, china clay, granite, marble, slate, business machines, paper and allied products; tourism is important
population (1995) 584,800
famous people Chester A Arthur, Calvin Coolidge, John Dewey
history explored by Samuel de Champlain from 1609; settled by the French 1666 and the English 1724; became a state 1791.

Vernyi Former name (to 1921) of ◊Almaty, Kazakhstan.

Veroia Town in the Macedonia region of Greece, capital of Emathia department. The abundant water supply attracted handicraft workers in the 18th and 19th centuries; now hydroelectric power supplies silk-spinning mills. The town is a commercial and communications centre for the region. It originated as the old Macedonian city of Berea.

Verona Industrial city (printing, paper, plastics, furniture, pasta) in Veneto, Italy, on the Adige River; population (1992) 255,500. It also trades in fruit and vegetables.

Verona Province of NE Italy in W ◊Veneto region; capital Verona; area 3,100 sq km/1,197 sq mi; population (1992) 789,900.

Versailles City in N France, capital of Les Yvelines *département*, on the outskirts of Paris; population (1990) 91,000. It grew up around the palace of Louis XIV, built 1661–87 on the site of Louis XIII's hunting lodge. Within the palace park are two small châteaux, Le Grand Trianon and Le Petit Trianon, built for Louis XIV (by Jules-Hardouin Mansart (1646–1708)) and Louis XV (by Jacques Gabriel 1698–1782) respectively. Versailles was France's seat of government 1682–1789.

Versecz Hungarian name for ◊Vršac, a town in Serbia, Yugoslavia.

Verviers Town in the Belgian province of Liège, on the river Vesdre, 21 km/13 mi E of the city of ◊Liège. Together with its suburb Ensival, it was one of the main centres of the Belgian woollen industry, using water from the Gileppe dam, 9 km/6 mi to the E. Other manufactures are soap, leather, footwear, chocolate, and chemicals.

Vestmannaeyjar Small group of islands off the S coast of Iceland. In 1973 volcanic eruption caused the population of 5,200 to be temporarily evacuated, and added 2.5 sq km/1 sq mi to the islands' area. Heimaey, the largest of the islands, is one of Iceland's chief fishing ports.

Vesuvius (Italian *Vesuvio*) Active volcano SE of Naples, Italy; height 1,277 m/4,190 ft. In AD 79 it destroyed the cities of Pompeii, Herculaneum, and Stabiae.

Veszprém (German *Weissbrunn*) Industrial town and commercial centre in W Hungary, 110 km/68 mi SW of Budapest; population (1993) 65,400. It is the capital of Veszprém county, on the river Séd, N of Lake Balaton in the Bakony Mountains, a major mining area. It has textile and oil plants, and trades in agricultural produce.

Vevey Tourist resort in the canton of Vaud, Switzerland, situated on Lake Geneva, 18 km/11 mi SE of Lausanne; population (1995) 15,700. The chief industries of the town are the manufacture of chocolate, machinery, and watches, and woodworking.

VI Abbreviation for *Virgin Islands*, in the West Indies; *Vancouver Island*, off the coast of Canada.

Via Mala Gorge in the canton of ◊Graubünden, Switzerland. It stands at the beginning of the Splügen Pass, is 6 km/4 mi long, and its sides rise to about 480 m/1,575 ft. A road high above the gorge has existed since Roman times.

Viborg Industrial town (brewing, engineering, textiles, tobacco) in Jutland, Denmark; population (1990) 39,400. It is also the Swedish name for ◊Vyborg, a port and naval base in Russia.

Vicenza City in Veneto region, NE Italy, capital of Veneto province, manufacturing textiles and musical instruments; population (1992) 107,500.

Vicenza Province of NE Italy in central ◊Veneto region; capital Vicenza; area 2,725 sq km/1,052 sq mi; population (1992) 750,300.

Vicksburg City and port in W Mississippi, USA, on the E bank of the Mississippi River; population (1990) 20,900. Industries include shipping and boat and vehicle building. It is a popular tourist destination because of its importance in the American Civil War, commemorated in the Vicksburg national military park, which encircles the city.

Victoria State of SE Australia

area 227,620 sq km/87,884 sq mi

capital Melbourne

towns and cities Geelong, Ballarat, Bendigo

physical part of the Great Dividing Range, running E–W and including the larger part of the Australian Alps; Gippsland lakes; shallow lagoons on the coast; the mallee shrub region

industries sheep, beef cattle, dairy products, tobacco, wheat, vines for wine and dried fruit, orchard fruits, vegetables, gold, brown coal (Latrobe Valley), oil and natural gas (Bass Strait)

population (1994) 4,475,500

history annexed for Britain by Capt Cook 1770; settled in the 1830s; after being part of New South Wales became a separate colony 1851, named after the queen; became a state 1901.

Victoria

Victoria Industrial port (shipbuilding, chemicals, clothing, furniture) on Vancouver Island, capital of British Columbia, Canada; population (1991) 21,200, metropolitan area 287,900. It was founded as Fort Victoria 1843 by the Hudson's Bay Company.

Victoria Port and capital of the republic of the Seychelles, tourist centre on NE coast of Mahé Island; population (1992) 30,000. Industries include copra, vanilla, guano, and cinnamon.

Victoria City in S Texas, USA, on the Guadalupe River, near the Gulf of Mexico; population (1990) 55,100. It is a transportation centre for oil, natural gas, chemicals, and dairy products. It was founded 1824 by Spanish settlers.

Victoria District of Hong Kong, rising to 554 m/1,800 ft at Victoria Park.

Victoria Falls or *Mosi-oa-tunya* (local name meaning 'smoke that thunders') Waterfall on the river Zambezi, on the Zambia– Zimbabwe border. The river is 1,700 m/5,580 ft wide and drops 120 m/400 ft to flow through a 30-m/100-ft wide gorge.

Victoria, Lake or *Victoria Nyanza* Largest lake in Africa; area over 69,463 sq km/26,820 sq mi; length 410 km/255 mi. It lies on the Equator at an altitude of 1,136 m/3,728 ft, bounded by Uganda, Kenya, and Tanzania. It is a source of the river Nile.

Victoria, Lake

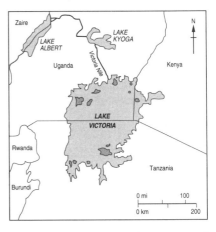

Vienna (German *Wien*) Capital of Austria, on the river Danube at the foot of the Wiener Wald (Vienna Woods); area 415 sq km/160 sq mi; population (1995) 1,592,596. Industries include engineering and the production of electrical goods and precision instruments.

Vienne River in France, rising in N Corrèze; length 350 km/217 mi. It flows N past Châtellerault, Limoges, and Chinon, to join the Loire 13 km/8 mi SE of Saumur. The river is navigable from Châtellerault.

Vienne French town in the *département* of Isère on the river Rhône, 26 km/16 mi S of Lyons; population (1990) 29,400. Vienne has woollen and metal manufacturing industries; tourism is important. The town's history goes back more than 2,000 years and there are Roman remains.

Vienne *Département* in the Poitou-Charentes region of France; area 6,984 sq km/2,697 sq mi; population (1990) 380,500. Vienne is flat and low-lying. The river Vienne and its tributary the Clain run through the *département*. Cereals, fruit, and some hemp are grown in the fertile soil, and stock is raised. Vienne contains numerous megalithic monuments. The principal towns are ◊Poitiers (the capital), Châtellerault, and Montmorillon.

Vientiane (Lao *Vieng Chan*) Capital and chief port of Laos on the Mekong River; population (1992) 449,000. Noted for its pagodas, canals, and houses on stilts, it is a trading centre for forest products and textiles. The Temple of the Heavy Buddha, the Pratuxai triumphal arch, and the Black Stupa are here. The Great Sacred Stupa to the NE of the city is the most important national monument in Laos.

Vigo Industrial port (oil refining, leather, paper, distilling) and naval station on Vigo Bay, Galicia, NW Spain; population (1994) 289,000.

Viipuri Finnish name of ◊Vyborg, a port and naval base formerly in Finland but now in Russia.

Vilaine River in France, rising in the Côtes-du-Nord *département*; length 225 km/140 mi. It flows through the *départements* of Ille-et-Vilaine and Morbihan to the Bay of Biscay. The towns on its banks include Vitré, Rennes, and Redon; the river is navigable from the Bay of Biscay to Rennes.

Villach Austrian city in the province of Carinthia, on the river Drava, 33 km/20 mi W of Klagenfurt. Villach has a spa with hot springs, is the centre of the timber trade with Italy, and has iron, paper, brewing, and lead industries. Villach has a 14th–15th-century church, a Renaissance town hall, and other old buildings, including a house once occupied by the medieval physician Paracelsus.

Vilnius Capital of Lithuania; population (1995) 576,000. Industries include engineering and the manufacture of textiles, chemicals, and foodstuffs.

Vilvoorde (French *Vilvorde*) Town in the province of Brabant, Belgium, 10 km/6 mi N of Brussels. The town has various manufacturing industries.

Vincennes City in SW Indiana, USA, on the border with Illinois, on the Wabash River, 80 km/50 mi N of Evansville; population (1990) 19,900. It is an agricultural and commercial centre with car-assembly and battery-manufacturing plants. Founded 1702, it is the oldest town in Indiana and the site of a French fort, taken in 1763 by the British and renamed Fort Sackville. Captured by General George Rogers Clark for the Americans during the American Revolution, it was ceded to the USA in 1783. It was the capital of the territory of Indiana 1800–1813.

Vincennes Suburb of E ◊Paris, France; population (1990) 43,000. The large castle was a royal residence and fortress in the Middle Ages, and was later a prison and a barracks. The area is now mainly residential, with tourism. The surrounding Bois de Vincennes parkland forms a recreation area for Parisians.

Vineland Industrial city (foundry products, glassware, chemicals, and vegetables) in SW New Jersey, USA, N of Millville; population (1992) 54,700. It was first settled 1861.

Vinson Massif Highest point in ◊Antarctica, rising to 5,140 m/16,863 ft in the Ellsworth Mountains.

Virginia State in E USA; nicknamed Old Dominion State/ Mother of Presidents; became a state 1788
area 105,600 sq km/40,762 sq mi
capital Richmond
towns and cities Norfolk, Virginia Beach, Newport News, Hampton, Chesapeake, Portsmouth

physical Blue Ridge Mountains, with the Shenandoah national park; Luray Caverns; George Washington and Jefferson national forests
features Jamestown Island, the site of the first permanent English settlement in North America (1607); Colonial Williamsburg, with craft workers and costumed guides, and buildings including the capitol and the governor's palace (1720), and the DeWitt Wallace Decorative Arts Gallery;

Yorktown Battlefield, the site of the last major battle of the American Revolution, 1781; Alexandria Old Town (established 1749), with 18th- and 19th-century redbrick buildings, including the boyhood home of Robert E Lee (1795), Lee-Fendall House (1785), Christ Church, Gadsby's Tavern Museum (1770), George Washington National Masonic Memorial, and the Torpedo Factory Art Center; Fredericksburg, with a 40-block national historic district, including Kenmore (1750s), home of George Washington's sister, the Hugh Mercer Apothecary Shop, and the James Monroe Museum and Memorial Library; old Richmond, with the Virginia state capitol (designed by Thomas Jefferson 1785), the Richmond national battlefield park, the Museum and White House of the Confederacy, and Agecroft Hall (a 15th-century house transported from Lancashire 1925);

Mount Vernon (1754), home of George Washington; Monticello (a World Heritage Site), Thomas Jefferson's house at Charlottesville, built 1769–1809, full of Jefferson's inventions; Woodlawn (1800) with the Pope-Leighey House (1940, designed by Frank Lloyd Wright) in its grounds; plantation houses, including Shirley (1723, the oldest in Virginia), Berkeley (1726, the home of President William Henry Harrison), Carter's Grove Plantation (1750), and Oatlands (1803); George Washington's birthplace national monument, Wakefield; Civil War battlefields, including Manassas (or Bull Ring) national battlefield park, Fredericksburg, and Spotsylvania national military park, and Petersburg national battlefield; Stratford Hall, the birthplace of Robert E Lee; Lexington, with the Lee Memorial Chapel and Museum, Virginia Military Institute (1839), Stonewall Jackson House, and the George C Marshall Museum; Appomattox Court House, the site of General Robert E Lee's surrender to General Ulysses S Grant 1865; Montpelier, home of President James Madison, and in the 20th century of the du Pont family; Staunton, with the Woodrow Wilson House, and the Museum of American Frontier Culture; Arlington national cemetery, the burial place of many US presidents, and veterans of 20th-century wars; Arlington House, the home of Robert E Lee; the College of William and Mary, Williamsburg (1693), the second oldest college in the USA; the University of Virginia (a World Heritage Site) in Charlottesville, designed and founded 1819 by Thomas Jefferson; Booker T Washington national monument (his birthplace, and a museum of life under slavery); Virginia Air and Space Museum, Hampton; US Naval Base, Norfolk; Loudon County horse farms. More US presidents have come from Virginia than from any other state
industries sweet potatoes, maize, tobacco, apples, peanuts, coal, ships, lorries, paper, chemicals, processed food, textiles

population (1995) 6,618,400
famous people Edgar Allan Poe, Booker T Washington.

Virginia Beach City and resort in SE Virginia, USA, on Chesapeake Bay, E of Norfolk; population (1992) 417,100. The colonists who settled Jamestown first landed here 1607.

Virginia City Town in W Nevada, USA, 40 km/25 mi E of Reno; population (1990) 900. The Comstock Lode (one of the largest silver and gold deposits ever found) was discovered in the area in 1857, and Virginia City was established adjacent to the mines in 1859. By 1880 its population is estimated to have reached 25,000, making it the largest city in Nevada. The town now exists chiefly as a popular tourist destination.

Virgin Islands Group of about 100 small islands, northernmost of the Leeward Islands in the Antilles, West Indies. Tourism is the main industry. They comprise the *US Virgin: Islands* St Thomas (with the capital, Charlotte Amalie), St Croix, St John, and about 50 small islets; area 350 sq km/135 sq mi; population (1990) 101,800; and the *British Virgin: Islands* Tortola (with the capital, Road Town), Virgin Gorda, Anegada, and Jost van Dykes, and about 40 islets (11 islands are inhabited); area 150 sq km/58 sq mi; population (1991) 16,100.

Virgin Islands

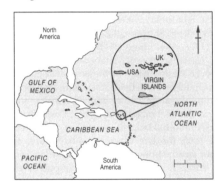

Visalia City in central California, USA, in the San Joaquin Valley, SE of Fresno; population (1992) 81,300. It is an agricultural centre for grapes, citrus fruits, and dairy products. Visalia was founded 1852.

Vistula (Polish *Wisła*) River in Poland that rises in the Carpathian Mountains and runs NW to the Baltic Sea at Gdańsk; length 1,090 km/677 mi. It is heavily polluted, carrying into the Baltic large quantities of industrial and agricultural waste, including phosphorus, oil, nitrogen, mercury, cadmium, and zinc.

Viterbo Province of W central Italy in NW ◊Lazio region; capital Viterbo (population (1990) 60,200); area 3,613 sq km/ 1,395 sq mi; population (1992) 279,900.

Vitoria Capital of Alava province, in the Basque country, N Spain; population (1994) 214,000. Products include motor vehicles, agricultural machinery, and furniture.

Vitsyebsk formerly (until 1992) Vitebsk Industrial city (glass, textiles, machine tools, shoes) in NE Belarus, on the Dvina River; population (1991) 369,200. Vitsyebsk dates from the 10th century.

Vittorio Veneto Industrial town (motorcycles, agricultural machinery, furniture, paper, textiles) in Veneto, NE Italy; population (1981) 30,000. It was the site of the final victory of Italy and its allies over Austria Oct 1918.

Vizcaya Basque form of ◊Biscay, a bay in the Atlantic Ocean off France and Spain. It is also the name of one of the three Spanish Basque provinces.

Vizcaya Province of N Spain in the ◊Basque Country autonomous community, on the Bay of Biscay; capital ◊Bilbao; area 2,209 sq km/853 sq mi; population (1995) 1,163,700. It is very rich in minerals, including deposits of iron, lead, copper, and zinc. Stock-raising, fishing, and agriculture are also important.

Vladikavkaz (formerly (1954–91) *Ordzhonikidze*) Capital of the autonomous republic of Alania (formerly North Ossetia), in the Russian Federation, on the river Terek in the Caucasus Mountains; population (1994) 311,000. Metal products, vehicles, and textiles are produced. Vladikavkaz was founded 1784 as a frontier fortress.

Vladivostok Port (naval and commercial) in the Russian Federation, in E Siberia, at the Amur Bay on the Pacific coast; population (1994) 637,000. It is kept open by icebreakers during winter. Industries include shipbuilding and the manufacture of precision instruments. There is a large Chinese population.

Vlissingen (English *Flushing*) port on Walcheren Island, Zeeland, the Netherlands; population (1993) 44,200. It stands at the entrance to the Schelde estuary, one of the principal sea routes into Europe. Industries include fishing, shipbuilding, and petrochemicals, and there is a ferry service to Harwich. Admiral de Ruyter was born at Vlissingen and is commemorated in the Jacobskerk.

Vlorë (Italian *Valona*) Port and capital of Vlorë province, SW Albania, population (1991) 76,000. A Turkish possession from 1464, it was the site of the declaration of independence by Albania 1912.

Vltava (German *Moldau*) River in the Czech Republic, rising in the Bohemian Forest and flowing 435 km/272 mi N to join the river ◊Elbe at Mělnik. It passes through České Budějovice and Prague.

Vojvodina Autonomous province in N Serbia, Yugoslavia, 1945–1990; area 21,500 sq km/8,299 sq mi; population (1991) 2,012,500, including 1,110,000 Serbs and 390,000 Hungarians, as well as Croat, Slovak, Romanian, and Ukrainian minorities. Its capital is Novi Sad. In Sept 1990 Serbia effectively stripped Vojvodina of its autonomous status, causing antigovernment and anticommunist riots in early 1991.

Volga Longest river in Europe; 3,685 km/2,290 mi, 3,540 km/2,200 mi of which are navigable. It drains most of the central and E parts of European Russia, rises in the

Volga

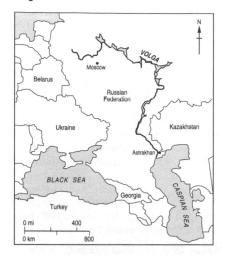

Valdai plateau, and flows into the Caspian Sea 88 km/55 mi below the city of Astrakhan.

Volgograd formerly (until 1925) *Tsaritsyn* and (1925–61) *Stalingrad* Industrial city (metal goods, machinery, sawmills, oil refining) in SW Russian Federation, on the river Volga; population (1994) 1,000,000.

Volta Main river in Ghana, about 1,600 km/1,000 mi long, with two main upper branches, the Black and White Volta. It has been dammed to provide power.

Volta, Upper Former name (to 1984) of Burkina Faso.

Vorarlberg 'in front of the Arlberg' Alpine federal province of W Austria draining into the river Rhine and Lake Constance; area 2,601 sq km/1,004 sq mi; population (1995) 343,109. Its capital is Bregenz. Industries include forestry and dairy farming.

Voronezh Industrial city (chemicals, construction machinery, electrical equipment) and capital of the Voronezh region of the Russian Federation, S of Moscow on the Voronezh River; population (1994) 905,000. There has been a town on the site since the 11th century.

Voroshilovgrad Former name (1935–58; 1970–89) of ◊Luhansk, a city in Ukraine.

Vosges Mountain range in E France, rising in the Ballon de Guebwiller to 1,422 m/4,667 ft and forming the W edge of the Rhine rift valley. It gives its name to a *département*.

Vosges *Département* in the ◊Lorraine region of NE France; area 7,424 sq km/2,866 sq mi; population (1990) 386,562. It is bordered on the E by the ◊Vosges mountains. The rivers ◊Moselle and Meuse have the largest drainage areas of any rivers in the region. Oats, wheat, and vines are cultivated, and cheese-making and cattle-grazing are important economic activities. Textile goods are the chief manufactures. The principal towns are ◊Épinal (the capital), St-Dié, Remiremont, and Neufchâteau.

Vostock, Lake A freshwater lake in ◊Antarctica.

Vratsa or *Vraca* Town in Mikhailovgrad region, NW Bulgaria, on the N slopes of the Balkan Mountains, 58 km/36 mi N of Sofia; population (1990) 102,800. Industries include chemicals and cement, and wine and agricultural produce are traded.

Vršac (Hungarian *Versecz*) Town in Serbia, Yugoslavia, in the autonomous region of Vojvodina; population (1991) 36,900. It produces wines and brandy. There is a cathedral.

VT Abbreviation for ◊Vermont, a state of the USA.

Vukovar River port in Croatia at the junction of the rivers Vuka and Danube, 32 km/20 mi SE of Osijek; population (1991) 44,600. Industries include foodstuffs manufacture, fishing, and agricultural trade. In 1991 the town resisted three months of siege by the Serb-dominated Yugoslav army before capitulating. It suffered the severest damage inflicted to any European city since the bombing of Dresden during World War II.

Vyborg (Finnish *Viipuri*) Port (trading in timber and wood products) and naval base in E Karelia, NW Russian Federation, on the Gulf of Finland, 112 km/70 mi NW of St Petersburg; population (1973) 51,000. Products include electrical equipment and agricultural machinery. Founded by the Swedes 1293, it was part of Finland until 1940.

WA Abbreviation for ◊Washington, a state of the USA; ◊Western Australia, an Australian state.

Waag German name for the Váh, a river in the Slovak Republic.

Waal River in the Netherlands; length 84 km/52 mi. The river ◊Rhine divides, 14 km/9 mi E of Nijmegen, into the Neder Rijn and the Waal, the latter becoming the Merwede at its confluence with the Maas (see ◊Meuse) 4 km/2 mi E of Gorinchem.

Wabash River of the USA; length 765 km/475 mi. It rises in W Ohio, flows W across Indiana, and then turns S, forming the boundary between Indiana and Illinois, before joining the Ohio River at the meeting point of Indiana, Illinois, and Kentucky.

Wachau The section of the ◊Danube valley that lies between the towns of Ybbs and Krems in N Austria; length 65 km/40 mi. The Wachau is a place of great natural beauty, with rocky crags, woods, vineyards, churches, and castles.

Waco City in E central Texas, USA, on the Brazos River, S of Fort Worth; population (1992) 104,000. It is an agricultural shipping centre for cotton, grain, and livestock; industries include aircraft parts, glass, cement, tyres, and textiles. Waco was founded 1849.

Waddenzee European estuarine area (tidal flats, salt marshes, islands, and inlets) N of the Netherlands, and W of Denmark; area 10,000 sq km/4,000 sq mi. It is the nursery for the North Sea fisheries, but the ecology is threatened by tourism and other development.

Wadi Halfa Frontier town in Sudan, NE Africa, on Lake Nuba (the Sudanese section of Lake Nasser, formed by the Nile dam at Aswan, Egypt, which partly flooded the archaeological sites here).

Wagga Wagga Agricultural town in SE New South Wales, Australia; population (1994 est) 56,700.

Waikato River on North Island, New Zealand, 355 km/ 220 mi long; Waikato is also the name of the dairy area the river traverses; chief town Hamilton.

Wairarapa Area of North Island, New Zealand, round *Lake Wairarapa*, specializing in lamb and dairy farming; population (1986) 39,600. The chief market centre is Masterton.

Wairau River in N South Island, New Zealand, flowing 170 km/105 mi NE to Cook Strait.

Waitaki River in SE South Island, New Zealand, that flows 215 km/135 mi to the Pacific Ocean. The Benmore hydro-electric installation has created an artificial lake.

Wakefield Industrial city (chemicals, machine tools, wool textiles), administrative headquarters of West Yorkshire, England, on the river Calder, S of Leeds; population (1991) 306,300. The Lancastrians defeated the Yorkists here 1460, during the Wars of the Roses. The National Coal Mining Museum for England is here.

Wake Island Small Pacific atoll comprising three islands 3,700 km/2,300 mi W of Hawaii, under US Air Force administration since 1972; area 8 sq km/3 sq mi. It was discovered by Captain William Wake 1841, annexed by the USA 1898, and uninhabited until 1935, when it was made an air staging point, with a garrison. It was occupied by Japan 1941–45.

Wałbrzych (German *Waldenburg*) Capital of Wałbrzych province, Poland, in the foothills of the Sudeten Mountains, 69 km/43 mi SW of Wrocław; population (1990) 141,000. The town has coal, iron, steel, and engineering industries, and produces chemicals, glass, and pottery. Until 1945 it was part of German Lower Silesia.

Walcheren Island in Zeeland province, the Netherlands, in the estuary of the river Schelde
area 200 sq km/80 sq mi
capital Middelburg
towns and cities Vlissingen (Flushing)
features flat and for the most part below sea level
industries dairy, sugar beet, and other root vegetables
history a British force seized Walcheren 1809; after 7,000 of the garrison of 15,000 had died of malaria, the remainder were withdrawn. It was flooded by deliberate breaching of the dykes to drive out the Germans 1944–45, and in 1953 by abnormally high tides.

Wales (Welsh *Cymru*) Principality of; constituent part of the UK, in the W between the British Channel and the Irish Sea
area 20,780 sq km/8,021 sq mi
capital Cardiff
towns and cities Swansea, Wrexham, Newport, Carmarthen
features Snowdonia Mountains (Snowdon 1,085 m/3,561 ft, the highest point in England and Wales) in the NW and

in the SE the Black Mountains, Brecon Beacons, and Black Forest ranges; rivers Severn, Wye, Usk, and Dee
industries traditional industries have declined, but varied modern and high-technology ventures are being developed. There are oil refineries and open-cast coal mining. The last deep coal mine in N Wales closed 1996. Wales has the largest concentration of Japanese-owned plants in the UK. It also has the highest density of sheep in the world and a dairy industry; tourism is important
currency pound sterling
population (1993 est) 2,906,000
language English, 19% Welsh-speaking
religion Nonconformist Protestant denominations; Roman Catholic minority
government returns 40 members to the UK Parliament; in April 1996, the 8 counties were replaced by 22 county and county borough unitary authorities. In 1997 a referendum approved devolution proposals by a narrow margin.

Walla Walla City in SE Washington, USA, lying near the S boundary of the state, in the centre of a wheat-producing area; population (1990) 26,500. It is a college and agricultural town, with onions the chief crop. It also has two military bases.

Wallis and Futuna Two island groups in the SW Pacific Ocean, an overseas territory of France; area 367 sq km/ 143 sq mi; population (1990) 13,700. They produce copra, yams and bananas. Discovered by European sailors in the 18th century, the islands became a French protectorate 1842 and an overseas territory 1961.

Wallsend Town in Tyne and Wear, NE England, on the river Tyne at the E end of Hadrian's Wall; population (1991) 45,300. Industries include engineering, floating oil production platforms for the North Sea, ship repairs, electronics, and transport equipment. The Swan Hunter shipyards were closed 1994 following the launch of the last ship to be built in the NE.

Wall Street The financial centre of the US on lower Manhattan Island in New York City. It is often synonymous with the New York Stock Exchange, which is housed there. The street was so named because of a stockade erected by the Dutch in 1653.

Walsall Industrial town (castings, tubes, electrical equipment, leather goods, machine tools, aircraft components, chemicals) in the West Midlands, England, 13 km/8 mi NW of Birmingham; population (1994 est) 115,000. Its art gallery contains the Garman–Ryan collection, over 350 paintings bequeathed by Kathleen Garman, Jacob Epstein's second wife, who was born in the town. Jerome K Jerome was born here.

Waltham Forest Outer borough of N Greater London. It includes the suburbs of Chingford, Leyton, and Walthamstow
features takes its name from former name for Epping Forest, referring to forest around Waltham Abbey; Lea Valley Regional Park (1967), including Walthamstow

Marshes; Water House, Walthamstow, home of William Morris, now the William Morris Gallery
population (1991) 212,000
famous people Martin Frobisher; Cardinal Wiseman lived in Leyton.

Walvis Bay Chief port serving Namibia, situated on the Atlantic Ocean, 275 km/171 mi WSW of Windhoek; population about 26,000. It is the only deep water harbour on the Namibian coast and has a fishing industry with allied trades. It was a detached part (area 1,100 sq km/425 sq mi) of Cape Province, South Africa, 1884–1993 (administered solely by South Africa 1922–92; from 1992 jointly by South Africa and Namibia). In 1993 South Africa waived its claim to sovereignty and control was passed to Namibia Feb 1994.

Wandsworth Inner borough of SW central Greater London
features made famous for hats in the 18th century by influx of Huguenot refugees who were skilled hatters (Roman cardinals ordered their hats from here); mills on river Wandle; Wandsworth Prison (1857); brewing industry (important since the 16th century); Battersea Park and Putney Heath are both in the borough; Battersea Power Station (1937, designed by Sir Giles Gilbert Scott).
industries light engineering, brewing, paint, candles, computers
population (1991) 252,400.

Wanganui Port (textiles, clothing) in SW North Island, New Zealand, at the mouth of the Wanganui River; population (1993) 44,600.

Wankie Former name (to 1982) of ◊Hwange, a town and national park in Zimbabwe.

Wapping District of the Greater London borough of ◊Tower Hamlets. The redevelopment of the London ◊Docklands began here 1969 with work on St Katherine Dock. From the mid-1980s it has been a centre of the newspaper industry.

Warnemünde Port and resort in the *Land* of ◊Mecklenburg–West Pomerania, Germany. Warnemünde stands on the Mecklenburg Bay in the Baltic Sea, and at the mouth of the river Warnow, 11 km/7 mi N of Rostock, for which it is the outport. A ferry service operates from here to the port of Gedser in Denmark.

Warner Robins City in central Georgia, USA, S of Macon; population (1990) 43,700. Industries include nuts, fruits, and aeroplane parts. It is the site of Robins Air Force base.

Warren Industrial city (steel and iron products, tools, and paint) in NE Ohio, USA, on the Mahoning River, NW of Youngstown; population (1992) 51,150. Warren was first settled 1799.

Warrington Industrial town (metal goods, chemicals, brewing, iron foundry, tanning, engineering, high technology industries) in Cheshire, NW England, on the river Mersey; it will become a unitary authority in April 1998; population (1994 est) 151,000. A trading centre since Roman times, it was designated a new town 1968. In 1993 bombs planted here by the Irish Republic Army (IRA) killed two

boys (one a three-year-old, believed to be the youngest victim of IRA violence in Britain) and wounded more than 50 others, causing national outrage.

Warrnambool Port near the mouth of Hopkins River, SW Victoria, Australia; population (1991) 23,900. A tourist centre, it also manufactures textiles and dairy products.

Warrumbungle Range (Aboriginal 'broken-up small mountains') Mountain range of volcanic origin in New South Wales, Australia. Siding Spring Mountain, 859 m/2,819 ft, is the site of an observatory; the Breadknife is a 90-m/300-ft high rock only 1.5 m/5 ft wide; the highest point is Mount Exmouth, 1,228 m/4,030 ft.

Warsaw (Polish *Warszawa*) Capital of Poland, on the river Vistula; population (1993) 1,653,300. Industries include engineering, food processing, printing, clothing, and pharmaceuticals.

Warta (German *Warthe*) River in Poland, rising about 48km/ 30 mi NW of Kraków, and flowing 790 km/494 mi to join the river ◊Oder at Kostrzyń on the W Polish border. Its chief tributaries are the Noteć and Prosna.

Warwick Market town, administrative headquarters of Warwickshire, England; population (1991) 22,500. Industries include carpets and engineering. Founded 914, it has many fine medieval buildings, including a 14th-century castle.

Warwickshire County of central England
area 1,980 sq km/764 sq mi
towns and cities Warwick (administrative headquarters), Royal Leamington Spa, Nuneaton, Rugby, Stratford-upon-Avon
features river Avon; Kenilworth and Warwick castles; remains of the 'Forest of Arden' (portrayed by Shakespeare in *As You Like It*); site of the Battle of Edgehill; annual Royal Agricultural Show held at Stoneleigh
industries mainly agricultural, engineering, textiles, motor industry
population (1994) 496,300
famous people William Shakespeare, George Eliot, Rupert Brooke.

Wasatch Mountains Range of the ◊Rocky Mountains in Utah and Idaho, USA. Largely pine-covered, they form the E margin of the Great Basin and contain at least four peaks over 3,350 m/11,000 ft high. The highest is Timpanogos Peak (3,660 m/12,000 ft). The Weber, Ogden, and Provo rivers flow through the range and it includes parts of Uinta and Wasatch national forests in Utah. Copper, lead, silver, and gold are mined near Provo and Salt Lake City, but tourism is also significant.

Wash, the Bay of the North Sea between Norfolk and Lincolnshire, England. The rivers Nene, Ouse, Welland, and Witham drain into the Wash. In 1992, 10,120 ha/25,000 acres of mudflats, marshes, and sand banks were designated a national nature reserve.

Washington Town on the river Wear, Tyne and Wear, NE England, designated a new town 1964; population (1991) 56,800. Industries include textiles, electronics, car assembly, chemicals, and electrical goods. Beamish Open-Air Museum is nearby.

Washington State in NW USA; nicknamed Evergreen State/Chinook state

area 176,700 sq km/68,206 sq mi

capital Olympia

towns and cities Seattle, Spokane, Tacoma

physical Columbia River; Cascade Range, with volcanic peaks in Mount Rainier national park (Mount Rainier 4,392 m/14,410 ft), North Cascades national park, and Mount St Helens national volcanic monument; Olympic Peninsula, with Olympic national forest and Dungeness national wildlife refuge; Mount Adams (3,867 m/12,688 ft)

features Whidbey Island, with Ebey's Landing national historic reserve and Couperville (founded 1852), and the San Juan Islands; Long Beach Peninsula, including Cape Disappointment Lighthouse (1856), Fort Canby State park, and Oysterville, established as an oystering town 1854; Seattle, with the Seattle Art Museum (1991, designed by Robert Venturi), the Klondike gold rush national historic park, the Seattle Center (built for the 1992 World Fair) and the Space Needle.

industries apples and other fruits, potatoes, livestock, fish, timber, processed food, wood products, paper and allied products, aircraft and aerospace equipment, aluminium, computer software

population (1995) 5,430,900 (including 1.4% Native Americans, mainly of the Yakima people)

famous people Bing Crosby, Jimi Hendrix, Mary McCarthy, Theodore Roethke

history explored by Spanish, British, and Americans in the 18th century; settled from 1811; became a territory 1853 and a state 1889.

Washington DC (District of Columbia) Capital city of the United States of America, on the Potomac River; the world's first planned national capital. It was named Washington DC to distinguish it from the state of Washington and because it is situated in, and coextensive with, the District of Columbia, an area of 180 sq km/69 sq mi within the city; population (1995) 554,300; metropolitan area, extending outside the District of Columbia 3,923,600 (1990). The first structures date from 1793. Notable buildings include the Pentagon, the White House, and the Supreme Court 1935. Washington houses much of the nation's historical and cultural wealth: it has one of the leading art galleries in the world, the National Gallery of Art 1941, and the Smithsonian Institution (founded 1846), the largest complex of museums in the world. Most of the cultural organizations of the USA maintain headquarters in Washington. Universities include Georgetown University 1789, George Washington University, and Howard University.

Washington, Mount Highest peak of the White Mountains, in N New Hampshire, USA. It is 1,917 m/6,288 ft high and can be ascended by a cog railway (opened 1869) and a road (1861). It is the highest peak in NE USA, and a popular tourist destination. There are a hotel and a meteorological station on the summit.

Waterbury City in W Connecticut, USA, on the Naugatuck River; population (1992) 106,900. Products include clocks, watches, brass and copper ware, and plastics. It was founded 1674.

Waterford County of the Republic of Ireland, in the province of Munster; county town Waterford; area 1,840 sq km/710 sq mi; population (1996 est) 94,600. It includes the rivers Suir and Blackwater, and the Comeragh and Monavallagh mountain ranges in the N and centre.

Waterford Port and county town of County Waterford, SE Republic of Ireland, on the river Suir; population (1991) 40,300. Handmade Waterford crystal glass (34% lead content instead of the normal 24%) was made here until 1851 and again from 1951.

Watford Industrial town (printing, engineering, and electronics) in Hertfordshire, SE England; population (1991) 74,600. It is a dormitory town for London.

Waukegan Industrial city and lake port in NE Illinois, USA, on Lake Michigan, 58 km/36 mi N of Chicago; population (1990) 69,400.

Waukesha City in SE Wisconsin, USA; population (1990) 37,100. It is situated on the Fox River in a dairying and former health-resort area 24 km/15 mi W of Milwaukee.

Wausau Industrial city in central Wisconsin, USA, on the Wisconsin River, NW of Green Bay; population (1990) 37,100. It was settled 1839 as a lumbering centre.

Waziristan Mountainous territory in Pakistan, on the border with Afghanistan, inhabited by Waziris and Mahsuds.

Weald, the (Old English 'forest') Area between the North and South Downs, England, once thickly wooded, and forming part of Kent, Sussex, Surrey, and Hampshire. It produces fruit, hops, and vegetables.

Wear River in NE England; length 107 km/67 mi. From its source in the Pennines it flows eastwards, past Durham to meet the North Sea at Sunderland.

Weddell Sea Arm of the S Atlantic Ocean that cuts into the Antarctic continent SE of Cape Horn; area 8,000,000 sq km/3,000,000 sq mi. Much of it is covered with thick pack ice for most of the year.

Weihai Commercial port (textiles, rubber articles, matches, soap, vegetable oils) in Shandong, China; population (1990) 129,000.

Weimar Town in the state of Thuringia, Germany, on the river Elm; population (1991) 59,100. Products include farm machinery and textiles. It was the capital of the grand duchy of Saxe-Weimar 1815–1918; in 1919 the German National Assembly drew up the constitution of the new Weimar Republic here. The writers Goethe, Schiller, and Herder and the composer Liszt lived in the town. The former concentration camp of Buchenwald is nearby.

Weirton Industrial city (coal, steel, chemicals, and cement) in West Virginia, USA, on the Ohio River, W of Pittsburgh; population (1990) 22,100.

Weissbrunn German name for ◊Veszprém, a town in Hungary.

Weissenfels Town in the *Land* of ◊Saxony-Anhalt, Germany, on the river Saale, 29 km/18 mi S of Halle. It has leather and engineering industries and lignite mining.

Wejherowo (German *Neustadt*) Industrial town (engineering, furniture, cement) in Gdańsk province, Poland, 40 km/25 mi NW of Gdańsk; population (1990) 46,200.

Welland Ship Canal Canadian waterway, part of the ◊St Lawrence Seaway, linking Lake Erie to Lake Ontario.

Wellington Capital and industrial port (woollen textiles, chemicals, soap, footwear, bricks) of New Zealand on North Island on the Cook Strait; population (1993) 326,900 (urban area). The harbour was sighted by Capt James Cook 1773.

Founded 1840 by Edward Gibbon Wakefield as the first settlement of the New Zealand Company, it has been the seat of government since 1865, when it replaced Auckland. Victoria University was founded 1897. A new assembly hall (designed by the British architect Basil Spence and popularly called 'the beehive' because of its shape) was opened 1977 alongside the original parliament building.

Wells Market and cathedral town in Somerset, SW England; population (1991) 9,800. The cathedral, built near the site of a Saxon church in the 12th and 13th centuries, has a W front with 386 carved figures. Wells was made the seat of a bishopric about 900 (Bath and Wells from 1244) and has a bishop's palace.

Wels Austrian town in the province of Upper Austria, on the river Traun, 25 km/16 mi SW of Linz. Wels has Baroque buildings, a 14th-century church, and the castle where the Holy Roman emperor Maximilian I died.

Welwyn Garden City Industrial town in Hertfordshire, England, 32 km/20 mi N of London; population (1991) 42,100. It was founded as a garden city 1919–20 by Ebenezer Howard, and designated a new town 1948.

Wembley District of the Greater London borough of Brent, site of Wembley Stadium, which was chosen 1997 as England's new National Sports Stadium, designed by Norman Foster. It will be completely rebuilt except for the famous 'twin towers'.

Wenzhou (or *Wenchow*) Industrial port (textiles, medicine) in Zhejiang, SE China; population (1990) 402,000. It was opened to foreign trade 1877 and is now a special economic zone.

Wernigerode Town in the *Land* of ◊Saxony-Anhalt, at the foot of the Harz Mountains, 64 km SW of Magdeburg. There are engineering and chemical industries. The town dates from the Middle Ages.

Wesel City in North Rhine–Westphalia, Germany, at the confluence of the rivers Rhine and Lippe, 38 km/24 mi N of Duisburg; population (1994) 462,600. Wesel was almost total-ly destroyed by bombing during World War II. The Gothic cathedral of St Willibrord dates from the 15th century.

Weser One of the largest rivers in Germany, formed by the junction of the Werra and Fulda; length 440 km/273 mi. From the junction at Münden, the river flows towards the North Sea. The lower reaches are canalized, and the river is navigable by large vessels as far as Bremerhaven, and by smaller vessels as far as Bremen.

Wesermünde Former name (to 1947) of ◊Bremerhaven, a port in Germany.

Wesseling Town in North Rhine–Westphalia, Germany, 12 km/7 mi S of Cologne, on the left bank of the Rhine; population (1994) 32,900.

West Bank Area (5,879 sq km/2,270 sq mi) on the W bank of the river Jordan; population (1994) 1,070,000. The West Bank was taken by the Jordanian army in 1948 at the end of the Arab-Israeli war that followed the creation of the state of Israel, and was captured by Israel during the Six-Day War (5–10 June 1967). The continuing Israeli occupation and settlement of the area created tensions with the Arab population and after 1987, as the Intifada (uprising) gained strength in the occupied territories, Israeli-military presence increased significantly. In Sept 1993 Israel signed a historic accord with the Palestine Liberation Organization, under which a phased withdrawal of Israeli troops was undertaken from the West Bank town of Jericho and responsibility for its administration transferred to the PLO in May 1994; self-rule arrangements for remaining Palestinian areas in the West Bank were agreed in Sept 1995. Israeli troops began their withdrawal from West Bank cities on schedule during 1995, but the town of Hebron was still occupied in late 1996, straining relations between Israel and Palestine. In June 1997 riots erupted in the West Bank and Gaza as an Egyptian mediation attempt met with no success.

West Bengal State of NE India
area 88,752 sq km/34,267 sq mi
capital Calcutta
towns and cities Asansol, Durgarpur
physical occupies the W part of the vast alluvial plain created by the rivers Ganges and Brahmaputra, with the Hooghly River; annual rainfall in excess of 250 cm/100 in
industries rice, jute, tea, coal, iron, steel, cars, locomotives, aluminium, fertilizers
population (1994 est) 73,600,000.

West Bromwich Industrial town (metalworking, springs, tubes) in West Midlands, England, NW of Birmingham; population (1991) 146,400.

West Dunbartonshire Unitary authority in W central Scotland created 1996 from part of the former Strathclyde region; administrative headquarters Dumbarton; population (1996) 97,800; area 155 sq km/60 sq mi. There are light manufacturing and service industries.

Western Australia State of Australia
area 2,525,500 sq km/975,095 sq mi
capital Perth

towns and cities main port Fremantle, Bunbury, Geraldton, Kalgoorlie-Boulder, Albany, Broome (old pearling port)

features largest state in Australia; Monte Bello Islands; rivers Fitzroy, Fortescue, Gascoyne, Murchison, Swan; NW coast subject to hurricanes (willy-willies); Lasseter's Reef; Nullarbor Plain; Gibson, Sandy, and Great Victoria deserts; old goldfields and ghost towns; karri and jarrah forests, and the Darling Range, in the SW; the Kimberleys in the N; wild flowers

industries wheat, fresh and dried fruit, meat and dairy products, natural gas (NW shelf) and oil (Canning Basin), iron (the Pilbara), copper, nickel, uranium, gold, diamonds, wine growing (in SW), lumbering, bauxite

population (1994) 1,715,300

history a short-lived convict settlement at King George Sound 1826; first non-convict settlement founded at Perth 1829 by Capt James Stirling (1791–1865); self-government 1890; became a state 1901.

Western Australia

Western Cape Province of the Republic of South Africa from 1994, formerly part of Cape Province

area 129,386 sq km/49,956 sq mi

capital Cape Town

towns and cities Simonstown, Stellenbosch

features Table Mountain (highest point McClear's Beacon 1,087 m/3,566 ft)

industries copper, fruit, wine, wheat, tobacco

population (1995 est) 3,721,200

languages Afrikaans 63%, English 20%, Xhosa 16%

Western Isles Island area of Scotland, comprising the Outer Hebrides (Lewis, Harris, North and South Uist, Benbecula, and Barra)

area 2,900 sq km/1,120 sq mi

towns and cities Stornoway on Lewis (administrative headquarters)

features divided from the mainland by the Minch channel; Callanish monolithic circles of the Stone Age on Lewis

industries Harris tweed, sheep, fish, cattle

population (1996) 27,800

famous people Flora MacDonald.

Western Provinces In Canada, the provinces of ◊Alberta, ◊British Columbia, ◊Manitoba, and ◊Saskatchewan.

Western Sahara formerly *Spanish Sahara* Disputed territory in NW Africa bounded to the N by Morocco, to the E and S by Mauritania, and to the W by the Atlantic Ocean

area 266,800 sq km/103,011 sq mi

capital Laâyoune (Arabic *El Aaiún*)

towns and cities Dhakla

features electrically monitored fortified wall enclosing the phosphate area

exports phosphates, iron ore

currency dirham

population (1993 est) 214,000; another estimated 196,000 live in refugee camps near Tindouf, SW Algeria. Ethnic composition: Sawrawis (traditionally nomadic herders)

language Arabic

religion Sunni Muslim

government administered by Morocco.

West Flanders (Flemish *West-Vlaanderen*) Most westerly province of Belgium, bounded on the E by the Netherlands and East Flanders, S by Hainaut and France, W by France, and NW by the North Sea for about 65 km/40 mi; area 3,232 sq km/1,247 sq mi; population (1992) 1,113,000. The land is extremely flat. The soil of the West Flanders polders is very productive; agriculture and cattle breeding are the chief occupations. Flax, hops, and tobacco are grown. Other industries include fishing, weaving, spinning, lacemaking, and bleaching. In the narrow belt of sand dunes along the coast lie seaside resorts, of which Ostend and Knokke-Heist are the most important. Other towns include the provincial capital ◊Bruges, Ypres, and the industrial centres of Courtrai, Mouscron, Roeselaere, Menin, and Izegem.

West Glamorgan (Welsh *Gorllewin Morgannwg*) Former county of SW Wales, 1974–96, now divided into Neath Port Talbot, and Swansea.

West Indies Archipelago of about 1,200 islands, dividing the Atlantic Ocean from the Gulf of Mexico and the Caribbean Sea. The islands are divided into: *Bahamas*; *Greater Antilles:* Cuba, Hispaniola (Haiti, Dominican Republic), Jamaica, and Puerto Rico; *Lesser Antilles*: Aruba, Netherlands Antilles, Trinidad and Tobago, the Windward Islands (Grenada, Barbados, St Vincent, St Lucia, Martinique, Dominica, Guadeloupe), the Leeward Islands (Montserrat, Antigua, St Kitts and Nevis, Barbuda, Anguilla, St Martin, British and US Virgin Islands), and many smaller islands.

West Irian Former name of ◊Irian Jaya, a province of Indonesia.

West Lothian Unitary authority in central Scotland, bordering the S shore of the Firth of Forth. A former county, it was part of Lothian Region 1975–96; administrative headquarters Livingston; population (1996) 147,900; area 475 sq km/183 sq mi. It was also known as Linlithgowshire.

Westman Islands Small group of islands off the S coast of Iceland; see ◊Vestmannaeyjar.

Westmeath County of the Republic of Ireland, in the province of Leinster; county town Mullingar; area 1,760 sq km/679 sq mi; population (1996 est) 63,200. There are the rivers Shannon, Inny, and Brosna, and the lakes Ree, Sheelin, and Ennell. It is low-lying, with much pasture. Cattle fattening is a prominent occupation. Agricultural and dairy products, limestone, and textiles are produced.

West Midlands Metropolitan county of central England, created 1974; in 1986, most of the functions of the former county council were transferred to the metropolitan district councils
area 900 sq km/347 sq mi
towns and cities Birmingham, Wolverhampton, Coventry, Walsall, Dudley, Solihull
industries industrial goods; coal mining; chemicals; machine tools; engineering; motor vehicles, including Land Rover at Solihull; aircraft components; electrical equipment; motor components; glass
population (1994) 2,551,700.

Westminster, City of Inner borough of central Greater London, on the N bank of the river Thames between Kensington and the City of London. It encompasses Bayswater, Belgravia, Mayfair, Paddington, Pimlico, Soho, St John's Wood, and Westminster; population (1994) 174,800

Westmorland Former county in the Lake District, England, part of Cumbria from 1974.

Weston-super-Mare Seaside resort and administrative headquarters of North Somerset, SW England, on the Bristol Channel; population (1991) 69,400. Industries include plastics and engineering.

West Palm Beach Town and resort on the SE coast of Florida, USA, on the lagoon Lake Worth, N of Miami; population (1992) 67,700. Industries include transistors, aircraft parts, building materials, and citrus fruits; tourism is important to the economy. It was settled 1880.

West Sussex County of S England, created 1974, formerly part of Sussex
area 1990 sq km/78 sq mi
towns and cities Chichester (administrative headquarters), Crawley, Horsham, Haywards Heath, Shoreham (port); resorts: Worthing, Littlehampton, Bognor Regis
features the Weald, South Downs; rivers Arun, West Rother, and Adur; Arundel and Bramber castles; Goodwood racecourse; Petworth House (17th century); Wakehurst Place, where the Royal Botanic Gardens, Kew, has additional grounds; the Weald and Downland Open Air Museum at Singleton; Fishbourne Palace, important Roman site, at Chichester
industries agricultural products, including cereals, root crops, dairy produce; electronics, light engineering
population (1994) 722,100
famous people Percy Bysshe Shelley, William Collins, Richard Cobden.

West Virginia State in E central USA; nicknamed Mountain State/Panhandle State; became a state 1863
area 62,900 sq km/24,279 sq mi
capital Charleston
towns and cities Huntington, Wheeling
physical Allegheny Mountains; Ohio River; Monongahela and George Washington national forests; Potomac Highlands
features Harpers Ferry national historic park, with view from Jefferson Rock over the confluence of the Potomac and Shenandoah rivers; Berkeley Springs state park, the country's first spa, frequented by George Washington; Lewisburg national historic district; Blennerhassett Island historic park and mansion; National Radio Astronomy Observatory, Green Bank; glassblowing factories; the highest state E of the Mississippi
industries apples, maize, poultry, dairy and meat products, coal, natural gas, oil, chemicals, synthetic fibres, plastics, steel, glass, pottery
population (1995) 1,828,100
famous people Pearl S Buck, Thomas 'Stonewall' Jackson, Walter Reuther, Cyrus Vance.

West Yorkshire Metropolitan county of NE England, created 1974; in 1986, most of the functions of the former county council were transferred to the metropolitan district councils
area 2,040 sq km/787 sq mi
towns and cities Wakefield, Leeds, Bradford, Halifax, Huddersfield
features Ilkley Moor, Haworth Moor, Haworth Parsonage; part of the Peak District National Park; British Library, Boston Spa (scientific, technical, and business documents)
industries woollen textiles; coal mining is in decline
population (1994) 2,013,700
famous people the Brontës, J B Priestley, Henry Moore, David Hockney.

Wetzlar City in Hessen, Germany, on the river Lahn, 54 km/33 mi NE of Wiesbaden; population (1994) 54,200. The Leitz camera and optical instruments industry is here; television sets and machinery are also manufactured. Wetzlar's abbey church dates from the 9th century.

Wexford County of the Republic of Ireland, in the province of Leinster; county town Wexford; 2,350 sq km/907 sq mi; population (1996 est) 104,300. The port of Rosslare has ferry links to England. Industries include fish, livestock, oats, barley, potatoes, cattle, agricultural machinery, and food processing. It was the first Irish county to be colonized from England 1169.

Wexford Seaport and county town of Wexford, Republic of Ireland, on the estuary of the river Slaney; population (1991) 9,500. Products include textiles, cheese, agricultural machinery, food processing, and motor vehicles. There is an annual opera festival in October. Wexford was founded by the Danes in the 9th century and devastated by Oliver Cromwell 1649.

Weymouth Seaport and resort in Dorset, S England; population (1991) 46,100. It is linked by ferry to France and the Channel Islands. Weymouth, dating from the 10th century, was the first place in England to suffer from the Black Death 1348. It was popularized as a bathing resort by George III.

Wheeling City in NW West Virginia, USA, on the Ohio River, SW of Pittsburgh, Pennsylvania; population (1990) 34,900. Industries include coal and natural-gas processing, iron and steel, textiles, glass, pottery, paper, and chemicals. Wheeling was settled 1769. Fort Henry, site of the last battle 1782 of the American Revolution, is here.

Whipsnade Zoo in Bedfordshire, England, 5 km/3 mi S of Dunstable, opened 1931, where wild animals and birds are bred and exhibited in conditions resembling their natural habitat.

Whitby Port and resort in North Yorkshire, England, on the North Sea coast; population (1991) 13,600. Industries include boat building, fishing, and plastics. Remains of a Benedictine abbey built 1078 survive on the site of the original foundation by St Hilda 657, which was destroyed by the Danes 867. Capt Cook's ship *Resolution* was built in Whitby, where he had served his apprenticeship, and he sailed from here on his voyage to the Pacific Ocean 1768; the Captain Cook Memorial Museum is here. Bram Stoker's *Dracula* (1897) was set here.

Whitehall Street in central London, England, between Trafalgar Square and the Houses of Parliament, with many government offices and the Cenotaph war memorial.

Whitehaven Town and port in Cumbria, NW England, on the Irish Sea coast; population (1991) 26,500. Industries include chemicals, printing, textiles, and food processing. Britain's first nuclear power station was sited at Calder Hall to the SE, where there is also a plant for reprocessing spent nuclear fuel at Sellafield.

Whitehorse Capital of Yukon Territory, Canada; population (1995 est) 22,900. Whitehorse is on the NW Highway. It was founded during the Klondike gold rush 1897–98, and replaced Dawson as capital 1953.

White Mountains Mountain range in New Hampshire, USA. Much of the area is high plateau country, from which rises the Presidential range culminating in Mount Washington (1,917 m/6,288 ft), the highest mountain in NE USA. The White Mountains are a northerly continuation of the ◊Appalachian Mountains. Tourism (particularly winter sports) and timber-processing are important.

White Russia English translation of Belarus.

White Sea (Russian *Beloye More*) Gulf of the Arctic Ocean, on which the port of Archangel stands. There is a warship construction base, including nuclear submarines, at Severodvinsk. The North Dvina and Onega rivers flow into it, and there are canal links with the Baltic, Black, and Caspian seas.

Whitney, Mount Peak of the ◊Sierra Nevada mountain range, S California, USA; height 4,418 m/14,495 ft. It is the highest peak in continental USA (excluding Alaska and Hawaii). It was named after Josiah Dwight Whitney, the first director of the California State Geological Service.

Whitstable Resort in Kent, SE England, at the mouth of the river Swale, noted for its oysters; population (1991) 28,900.

Whyalla Port and industrial city (iron and steel) in South Australia; population (1994) 24,650.

WI Abbreviation for ◊West Indies, an archipelago of islands between the Gulf of Mexico and the Caribbean Sea, and the Atlantic Ocean; ◊Wisconsin, a state of the USA.

Wichita Industrial city (oil refining, aircraft, motor vehicles) in S Kansas, USA; population (1992) 311,750. Wichita was founded about 1867. It became a stopover on the Chisholm cattle-driving trail; when the railroad arrived 1872, the city became a major cattle-shipping point. Petroleum was discovered nearby 1915, and aircraft manufacture began 1920.

Wichita Falls City in N Texas, USA, on the Wichita River, S of the Oklahoma border; population (1992) 95,000. It is an important petroleum-processing centre. Other industries include leather goods, textiles, foodstuffs, electronics, and pharmaceutical goods. Wichita Falls was founded 1876.

Wick Fishing port and industrial town (shipping, distilleries, knitwear, North Sea oil) in the Highland unitary authority, NE Scotland; population about 8,000. Air services to the Orkney and Shetland islands operate from here. An opera house at 15th-century Ackergill Tower opened 1994.

Wicklow County of the Republic of Ireland, in the province of Leinster; county town Wicklow; area 2,030 sq km/783 sq mi; population (1996 est) 102,400. It has the Wicklow Mountains, the rivers Slane and Liffey, and the coastal resort Bray. The village of Shillelagh gave its name to rough cudgels of oak or blackthorn made there. The main occupation is agriculture.

Wicklow Port and county town of County Wicklow, Republic of Ireland; population (1991) 5,800.

Wieliczka Town in Kraków province, Poland, 13 km/8 mi SE of Kraków; population (1990) 171,000. It stands in the foothills of the Carpathian Mountains. Vast salt deposits, mined since the 11th century, exist under the town.

Wien German name for ◊Vienna, the capital of Austria.

Wiener Neustadt Austrian city in the province of Lower Austria, 40 km/25 mi S of Vienna. Railway engines and cars are manufactured; other industries are brewing and leatherworking. Wiener Neustadt was the imperial seat under the Holy Roman emperor Frederick III. There are arcaded Gothic houses, the Romanesque and Gothic Liebfrauenkirche, and a castle in which Emperor Maximilian I was born; he is also buried here.

Wiesbaden Spa town and capital of Hessen, Germany, on the river Rhine 20 km/12 mi W of Frankfurt; population (1993) 269,600. Products include cement, plastics, wines, and spirits; most of the German sparkling wine cellars are in this area. Wiesbaden was the capital of the former duchy of Nassau from the 12th century until 1866.

Wigan Industrial town (food processing, engineering, paper, fibreglass, carpet tiles, package holidays) in Greater Manchester, NW England; population (1994 est) 100,000. The traditional coal and cotton industries have virtually disappeared.

The *Wigan Alps* are a recreation area with ski slopes and water sports created from industrial dereliction including colliery spoil heaps. *Wigan Pier* was made famous by the writer George Orwell in *The Road to Wigan Pier* 1932.

Wight, Isle of Island and unitary authority of S England; administrative headquarters Newport; population (1996) 130,000; area 380 sq km/147 sq mi. Resorts include Ryde, Sandown, Shanklin, and Ventnor. Features include the *Needles*, a group of pointed chalk rocks up to 30 m/100 ft high in the sea to the W; the *Solent*, the sea channel between Hampshire and the island (including the anchorage of *Spithead* opposite Portsmouth, used for naval reviews); *Cowes*, venue of Regatta Week and headquarters of the Royal Yacht Squadron; Osborne House, near Cowes, a home of Queen Victoria, for whom it was built 1845; Farringford, home of the poet Alfred Tennyson, near Freshwater. Agriculture, shipbuilding, and tourism are important. Industries also include the manufacture of aircraft components, electronics, plastics, and marine engineering. Famous people from the Isle of White include Robert Hooke and Thomas Arnold.

Wigtown Former county of SW Scotland extending to the Irish Sea, part of Dumfries and Galloway Region 1975–96; now part of Dumfries and Galloway unitary authority.

Wilhelmshaven North Sea industrial port, resort, and naval base in Lower Saxony, Germany, on Jade Bay; population (1983) 99,000. Products include chemicals, textiles, and machinery.

Wilkes Barre Industrial city (furniture, textiles, wire, tobacco products, and heavy machinery) in NE Pennsylvania, USA, on the Susquehanna River, SW of Scranton; population (1990) 47,500. It was first settled 1769.

Willamette River in Oregon, NW USA; length 480 km/298 mi. Following a course between the Coast Ranges and the Cascade Mountains, it flows N to join the Columbia River near Portland, and runs through a rich fruit and dairy area. A long growing season makes the Willamette valley ideal for vineyards and a wide variety of crops. Dams on its tributaries supply hydroelectric power and flood control.

Williamsburg Historic city in Virginia, USA; population (1990) 11,500. Founded 1632, capital of the colony of Virginia 1699–1779, much of it has been restored to its 18th-century appearance. The College of William and Mary (1693) is one of the oldest in the USA.

Williamsport Industrial city (electronics, plastics, metals, lumber, textiles, and aircraft parts) in N central Pennsylvania, USA, on the Susquehanna River, N of Harrisburg; population (1990) 31,900. It was founded 1795 and is the birthplace of Little League baseball (1939).

Wilmington Industrial port and largest city (chemicals, textiles, shipbuilding, iron and steel goods; headquarters of Du Pont enterprises) in Delaware, USA; population (1992) 72,400. Founded by Swedish settlers as Fort Christina 1638, it was taken from the Dutch and renamed by the British 1664.

Wilmington Port and industrial city (textiles, tobacco, lumber, and chemicals) in SE North Carolina, USA, on the Cape Fear River, near the Atlantic Ocean; population (1992) 59,500. Tourism is important to the economy. Wilmington was incorporated 1740. During the Civil War it was the last Confederate port to close, in 1865.

Wilton Market town in Wiltshire, S England, outside Salisbury; population (1991) 3,700. It manufactured carpets from the 16th century until 1995, when the Wilton Royal Carpet Factory closed. Wilton House, the seat of the earls of Pembroke, was built from designs by Holbein and Inigo Jones, and is associated with Sir Philip Sidney and Shakespeare.

Wilts Abbreviation for ◊Wiltshire, a county in England.

Wiltshire County of SW England
area 3,480 sq km/1,343 sq mi
towns and cities Trowbridge (administrative headquarters), Salisbury, Wilton
features Marlborough Downs; Savernake Forest; rivers: Kennet, Wylye, Salisbury and Bristol Avons; Salisbury Plain, a military training area used since Napoleonic times; Longleat House (Marquess of Bath); Wilton House (Earl of Pembroke); Stourhead, with 18th-century gardens; Neolithic Stonehenge, Avebury stone circle, Silbury Hill, West Kennet Long Barrow, finest example of a long barrow in Wiltshire, dating from the 3rd millennium BC; Stonehenge, Avebury, and associated sites are a World Heritage site
industries wheat, cattle, pig and sheep farming, rubber, engineering, clothing, brewing, electronics, computing, pharmaceuticals, plastics
population (1997 est) 424,600
famous people Christopher Wren, William Talbot, Isaac Pitman.

Wimbledon District of the Greater London borough of ◊Merton. The headquarters of the All-England Lawn Tennis and Croquet Club are here, and the Wimbledon Championships are played in June.

Winchester Cathedral city and administrative headquarters of Hampshire, on the river Itchen; population (1991) 36,100. Tourism is important, and there is also light industry. Originally a Roman town, Winchester was capital of the Anglo-Saxon kingdom of Wessex, and later of England. The cathedral is the longest medieval church in Europe and was remodelled from Norman-Romanesque to Perpendicular Gothic under the patronage of William of Wykeham (founder of Winchester College 1382), who is buried there, as are Saxon kings, St Swithun, and the writers Izaac Walton and Jane Austen.

Windermere Largest lake in England, in Cumbria, 17 km/10.5 mi long and 1.6 km/1 mi wide.

Windhoek Capital of Namibia; population (1992) 126,000. It is just N of the Tropic of Capricorn, 290 km/180 mi from the W coast.

Windscale Former name of ◊Sellafield, a nuclear power station in Cumbria, England.

Windsor Industrial lake port (car engines, pharmaceuticals, iron and steel goods, paint, bricks) in Ontario, SE Canada, opposite Detroit, Michigan, USA; population (1991) 191,400, metropolitan area 262,100. It was founded as a Hudson's Bay Company post 1853.

Windsor Town in Berkshire, S England, on the river Thames; population (1991) 30,100; it will join with Maidenhead to become a unitary authority in April 1998. It is the site of Windsor Castle, a royal residence, and Eton College (public school, 1540), and has a 17th-century guildhall designed by Christopher Wren.

Windward Islands Group of islands in the West Indies, forming part of the lesser ◊Antilles.

Winnipeg Capital and industrial city (processed foods, textiles, transportation, and transportation equipment) in Manitoba, Canada, on the Red River, S of Lake Winnipeg; population (1991) 616,800, metropolitan area 652,300. Established as Winnipeg 1870 on the site of earlier forts, the city expanded with the arrival of the Canadian Pacific Railroad 1881.

Winnipeg, Lake Lake in S Manitoba, Canada, draining much of the Canadian prairies; area 25,380 sq km/ 9,799 sq mi.

Winston-Salem Industrial city (tobacco products, textiles, clothing, and furniture) in N central North Carolina, USA, NE of Charlotte; population (1992) 144,800. It was created 1913 from two towns: Winston (founded 1849) and Salem (founded 1766).

Winter Haven City in central Florida, USA, E of Lakeland; a centre for the processing and shipping of citrus fruit and tomatoes; population (1990) 24,700. Other industries include tourism, cigars, and alcohol. Winter Haven was settled 1883.

Winterthur Swiss town and spa NE of Zürich; population (1994) 88,200. Manufacturing includes engines and textiles.

Wisconsin State in N central USA; nicknamed Badger State/America's Dairyland
area 145,500 sq km/56,163 sq mi
capital Madison
cities Milwaukee, Green Bay, Racine
physical Lakes Superior and Michigan, with Apostles Islands national lakeshore; Mississippi and Wisconsin rivers; Door Peninsula, with cherry trees; Wisconsin Dells
features Milwaukee, with the Milwaukee Art Museum, Kilbourntown House (1844), Iron Block Building (1860s), the Pabst Mansion (1893), Mitchell Park Conservatory, Annunciation Greek Orthodox Church (1961, designed by Frank Lloyd Wright), and the Allen Bradley Company clock (the largest four-faced clock in the world); Prairie du Chien (1673), including the Villa Louis Mansion (1870) with a fine collection of Victorian decorative arts; Old World Wisconsin, restored buildings depicting 19th- and 20th-century Wisconsin, in Southern Kettle Moraine State Forest; Spring Green, with Taliesin (1911), the home of Frank Lloyd

Wright, and the school of architecture started by him; Kohler, a planned village surrounding the factories of the plumbing fixtures manufacturer Kohler Company, including the Kohler Design Center and Waelderhaus (John M Kohler's home); House on the Rock, overlooking the Wyoming Valley, a re-creation of historic village streets (begun in the 1940s); Circus World Museum, Baraboo; University of Wisconsin (1849), including the Golda Meir Library, with the map collection of the American Geographical Society; American Players Theater, with an outdoor amphitheatre
industries leading US dairy state; maize, hay, industrial and agricultural machinery, engines and turbines, precision instruments, paper products, cars and lorries, plumbing equipment
population (1995) 5,122,900
famous people Edna Ferber, Harry Houdini, Joseph McCarthy, Spencer Tracy, Orson Welles, Thornton Wilder, Frank Lloyd Wright
history explored by Jean Nicolet for France 1634; originally settled near Ashland by the French; passed to Britain 1763; included in the USA 1783. Wisconsin became a territory 1836 and a state 1848.

Wisconsin River of Wisconsin, USA; length 700 km/ 435 mi. It rises in the lake area near the Michigan boundary, and flows SW to join the ◊Mississippi River, 80 km/50 mi S of La Crosse. The Portage Canal connects it with Fox River and Lake Michigan. There are many hydroelectric plants along its course, notably at Lake Wisconsin. It flows through the Wisconsin Dells, a scenic gorge.

Wismar German Baltic Sea port in the *Land* of ◊Mecklenburg–West Pomerania. The town's main employer is a large shipyard. Wismar became a member of the Hanseatic League in 1266, and was later ruled by Sweden, Denmark, and then Mecklenburg-Schwerin. It was heavily bombed during World War II, and was extensively rebuilt.

Witten City in North Rhine–Westphalia, Germany, on the Ruhr River; population (1993) 105,700. Industries include steel and chemicals.

Wittenberg Town in the state of Saxony-Anhalt, Germany, on the river Elbe, SW of Berlin; population (1989 est) 53,600. Wittenberg university was founded 1502, but transferred to Halle 1815. Luther preached in the Stadtkirche (in which he is buried), nailed his 95 theses to the door of the Schlosskirche 1517, and taught philosophy at the university. The artists Lucas Cranach, father and son, lived here.

Wittenberge Town in the *Land* of ◊Mecklenburg–West Pomerania, Germany, in the district of Schwerin, near the river Elbe, 72 km/45 mi S of Schwerin. It has textile, railway rolling-stock, and oil-refining industries.

Witwatersrand or *the Rand* (Afrikaans 'ridge of white water') Economic heartland of Gauteng Province, South Africa. Its reef, which stretches nearly 100 km/60 mi, produces over half the world's gold. Gold was first found here 1854. The chief city of the region is Johannesburg. Forming a watershed between the Vaal and the Olifant rivers, the Rand comprises a series of parallel ranges which extend 100 km/60 mi E–W and rise to 1,525–1,830 m/ 5,000–6,000 ft above sea level. Gold occurs in reefs that are mined at depths of up to 3,050 m/10,000 ft.

Włocławek Capital of Włocławek province, central Poland, on the river Vistula, 140 km/87 mi NW of Warsaw; population (1990) 122,100. It is a river port, and its chief industries are metalwork, paper, and food processing. Founded in the 11th century, it has a 14th-century cathedral.

Wolfenbüttel City in Lower Saxony, Germany, on the river Oker, 12 km/7 mi S of Brunswick; population (1994) 121,400. The chief industry is canning, but chemicals and musical instruments are also manufactured. Wolfenbüttel contains one of the most important research libraries in Germany. The town has some old churches and houses, and a castle (1570–1691).

Wolfsburg Town NE of Brunswick in Lower Saxony, Germany, chosen 1938 as the Volkswagen factory site; population (1993) 128,500.

Wollongong Industrial city (iron, steel) in New South Wales, Australia, 65 km/40 mi S of Sydney; population (1985, with Port Kembla) 238,000.

Wolverhampton Industrial town (metalworking, chemicals, tyres, aircraft, bicycles, locks and keys, engineering, commercial vehicles) in West Midlands, England, 20 km/12 mi NW of Birmingham; population (1994 est) 245,000. Europe's first power station fuelled by waste tyres opened here 1993.

Woolwich District in London, England, cut through by the river Thames, the N part being in the borough of ◊Newham and the S part in the borough of ◊Greenwich. The Thames Barrier (a flood barrier, constructed 1982) is here.

Woonsocket Industrial city (rubber, chemicals, woollen goods) in N Rhode Island, USA, on the Blackstone River, NW of Providence; population (1990) 43,900. Woonsocket was settled 1666. French is widely spoken, many inhabitants being descendants of French-Canadians.

Worcester Cathedral city with industries (shoes, Worcester sauce, Royal Worcester porcelain) in Hereford and Worcester, W central England, administrative headquarters of the county, on the river Severn; population (1991) 81,700. The cathedral dates from the 13th and 14th centuries. The birthplace of the composer Elgar at nearby Broadheath is a museum. At the *Battle of Worcester* 1651 Oliver Cromwell defeated Charles II.

Worcester Industrial port (textiles, engineering, printing) in central Massachusetts, USA, on the Blackstone River; population (1992) 163,400. It was permanently settled 1713.

Worcestershire Former Midland county of England, merged 1974 with Herefordshire in the new county of Hereford and Worcester, except for a small projection in the N, which went to West Midlands. Worcester was the county town. Worcestershire will become a county again in April 1998.

Worcs Abbreviation for ◊Worcestershire, a county in England.

Worksop Market and industrial town (coal, glass, chemicals, light engineering, food processing) in Nottinghamshire, central England, on the river Ryton; population (1991) 37,200. Mary Queen of Scots was imprisoned at Worksop Manor (burned 1761).

Worms Industrial town in Rhineland-Palatinate, Germany, on the river Rhine; population (1991) 77,400. The vineyards of the Liebfrauenkirche produced the original Liebfraumilch wine; it is now produced by many growers around Worms. The Protestant reformer Martin Luther appeared before the *Diet* (Assembly) *of Worms* 1521 and was declared an outlaw by the Roman Catholic church.

Worthing Seaside resort in West Sussex, England, at the foot of the South Downs; population (1991) 96,200. Industries include electronics, engineering, plastics, furniture, and horticulture. There are traces of prehistoric and Roman occupation in the vicinity. The headquarters of the English Bowling Association are at Worthing.

Wrexham (welsh *Wrecsam*) Unitary authority in NE Wales created 1996 from part of the former county of Clwyd; population (1996) 123,500; area 500 sq km/193 sq mi. Little traditional industry remains (ironmaking and coal mining). New industries include food manufacture, plastics, pharmaceuticals, and high technology industries. In Clywedog Valley there is beautiful countryside, and industrial archaeology.

Wrexham (Welsh *Wrecsam*) Administrative headquarters of Wrexham unitary authority, NE Wales, 19 km/12 mi SW of Chester; population (1991) 40,600. Industries include coal, electronics, pharmaceuticals, chemicals, cables, and metal goods. It is the seat of the Roman Catholic bishopric of Menevia (Wales). Elihu Yale, founder of Yale University, died in Wrexham and is buried in the 15th-century church of St Giles.

Wrocław formerly *Breslau* Industrial river port in Poland, on the river Oder; population (1993) 643,600. Industries include shipbuilding, engineering, textiles, and electronics. It was the capital of the German province of Lower Silesia until 1945.

Wuchang Former city in China; amalgamated with ◊Wuhan.

Wuhan River port and capital of Hubei province, China, at the confluence of the Han and Chang Jiang rivers, formed 1950 as one of China's greatest industrial areas by the amalgamation of Hankou, Hanyang, and Wuchang; population (1993) 3,860,000. It produces iron, steel, machine tools, textiles, and fertilizer.

Wuhsien Former name for ◊Suzhou, a city in China.

Wuppertal Industrial city in North Rhine–Westphalia, Germany, 32 km/20 mi E of Düsseldorf; population (1993) 387,700. Industries include textiles, plastics, brewing, and electronics. It was formed 1929 (named 1931) by uniting Elberfield (13th century) and Barmen (11th century).

Württemberg Former kingdom (1805–1918) in SW Germany that joined the German Reich 1870. Its capital was

Stuttgart. Divided 1946 between the administrative West German *Länder* of Württemberg-Baden and Württemberg-Hohenzollern, from 1952 it was part of the *Land* of ◊Baden-Württemberg.

Würzburg Industrial city (engineering, printing, wine, brewing) in NW Bavaria, Germany; population (1993) 129,200. The bishop's palace was decorated by the Italian Rococo painter Tiepolo.

WV Abbreviation for ◊West Virginia, a state of the USA.

WY Abbreviation for ◊Wyoming, a state of the USA.

Wye (Welsh *Gwy*) River in Wales and England; length 208 km/130 mi. It rises on Plynlimmon, NE Ceredigion, flows SE and E through Powys, and Hereford and Worcester, then follows the Gwent–Gloucestershire border before joining the river Severn S of Chepstow.

Wyoming State in W USA; nicknamed Equality State
area 253,400 sq km/97,812 sq mi
capital Cheyenne
cities Casper, Laramie
physical Rocky Mountains; Yellowstone national park (a World Heritage Site), the first national park in the USA (1872), with geysers (including Old Faithful), hot springs, and mud pots; Grand Teton national park; Bighorn Mountains; Gannett Peak (4,207 m/13,804 ft) in the Wind River Range, the highest peak in the state; Flaming George national park; Devils Tower national monument
features Jackson; Buffalo Bill Historical Center, Cody; state capitol, Cheyenne (1886); Wyoming Territorial Prison Park, Laramie; Fort Laramie (1834); University of Wyoming
industries oil, natural gas, sodium salts, coal, uranium, sheep, beef
population (1995) 480,200
famous people Buffalo Bill, Jackson Pollock
history acquired by the USA from France as part of the Louisiana Purchase 1803; Fort Laramie, a trading post, was settled 1834; women achieved the vote 1869; became a state 1890.

Xanten Town in North Rhine–Westphalia, Germany, near the left bank of the river Rhine, 50 km/31 mi NW of Düsseldorf; population (1994) 18,700. Its Gothic cathedral was begun 1190. Xanten is a tourist centre.

Xiamen formerly (until 1979) *Amoy* Port on Ku Lang Island in Fujian province, SE China; population (1993) 470,000. Industries include textiles, food products, and electronics. It was one of the original five treaty ports used for trade under foreign control 1842–1943 and a special export-trade zone from 1979.

Xi'an or *Sian* Industrial city and capital of Shaanxi province, China; population (1993) 2,360,000. It produces chemicals, electrical equipment, and fertilizers.

Xi Jiang or *Si-Kiang* River in China, that rises in Yunnan province and flows into the South China Sea; length 1,900 km/1,200 mi. Guangzhou lies on the N arm of its delta, and Hong Kong island at its mouth. The name means 'W river'.

Xingu Region in Pará, Brazil, crossed by branches of the Xingu River which flows for 1,900 km/1,200 mi to the Amazon Delta. In 1989 Xingu Indians protested at the creation of a vast, intrusive lake for the Babaquara and Kararao dams of the Altamira complex.

Xining or *Sining* Industrial city (chemicals, textiles, machinery, processed foods) and capital of Qinghai province, China, on the Xining River; population (1990) 552,000. For centuries it was a major trading centre on the caravan route to Tibet.

Xinjiang Uygur or *Sinkiang Uighur* Autonomous region of NW China
area 1,646,800 sq km/635,829 sq mi
capital Urumqi
features largest of Chinese administrative areas; Junggar Pendi (Dzungarian Basin) and Tarim Pendi (Tarim Basin, which includes ◊Lop Nor, China's nuclear testing ground, although the research centres were moved to the central province of Sichuan 1972) separated by the Tian Shan Mountains
industries cereals, cotton, fruit in valleys and oases; uranium, coal, iron, copper, tin, oil
population (1990) 15,156,000; the region has 13 recognized ethnic minorities, the largest being 6 million Uigurs (Muslim descendants of Turks)
religion 50% Muslim
history under Manchu rule from the 18th century. Large sections were ceded to Russia 1864 and 1881; China has raised the question of their return and regards the frontier between Xinjiang Uygur and Tajikistan, which runs for 480 km/ 300 mi, as undemarcated.

Xizang Chinese name for ◊Tibet, an autonomous region of SW China from 1965.

Xochimilco Lake about 11 km/7 mi SE of Mexico City, Mexico, which features floating gardens, all that remains of an ancient water-based agricultural system.

Yakima City in S central Washington, USA, on the Yakima River, SE of Seattle; population (1992) 58,450. It is an agricultural processing centre for sugar beet, apples, hops, and livestock, and produces cider and flour. It was incorporated 1883.

Yakutia (Russian *Yakutskaya*) Former name of ◊Sakha, an autonomous republic in the Russian Federation.

Yakutsk Capital of Sakha autonomous republic, Russian Federation (formerly Yakutia), on the river Lena; population (1994) 187,000. Industries include timber, tanning, and brick-making. It is the coldest point of the Arctic in NE Siberia, average winter temperature –50° C/–68° F, and has an institute for studying the permanently frozen soil area (permafrost). The lowest temperature ever recorded was in Yakutia, –70° C/–126° F.

Yalu River forming the N boundary between North Korea and Jilin and Liaoning provinces (Manchuria) in China; length 790 km/491 mi. It is only navigable near the mouth and is frozen Nov to March.

Yamal Peninsula Peninsula in NW Siberian Russia, with gas reserves estimated at 6 trillion cu m/212 trillion cu ft; supplies are piped to W Europe.

Yambol (Bulgarian *Jambol*) Town in Burgas region, E Bulgaria, on the river Tundzha, 25 km/16 mi from Sliven; population (1990) 98,900. It produces textiles, shoe machinery, and processed food. A stone mosque remains from its former Turkish rule.

Yamoussoukro Capital of Côte d'Ivoire; population (1990 est) 120,000. The economy is based on tourism and agricultural trade and production.

Yamuna or *Jumna* River in India, 1,385 km/860 mi in length, rising in the Himalayas, in Uttar Pradesh, and joining the river Ganges near Allahabad, where it forms a sacred bathing place. Agra and Delhi are also on its course.

Yan'an or *Yenan* District and industrial city in Shaanxi province, central China; population (1990) 113,000. The Long March ended here Jan 1937, and it was the communist headquarters 1936–47 (the caves in which Mao lived are preserved).

Yangon formerly (until 1989) *Rangoon* Capital and chief port of Myanmar (Burma) on the Yangon River, 32 km/20 mi from the Indian Ocean; population (1983) 2,459,000. Products include timber, oil, and rice. The city *Dagon* was founded on the site AD 746; it was given the name Rangoon (meaning 'end of conflict') by King Alaungpaya 1755.

Yangtze-Kiang Alternative transcription of ◊Chang Jiang, the longest river in China.

Yangzhou or *Yangchow* Canal port in Jiangsu province, E China, on the Chang Jiang River; population (1990) 313,000. Among its features are gardens and pavilions. It is an artistic centre for crafts, jade carving, and printing.

Yantai formerly *Chefoo* Ice-free port in Shandong province, E China; population (1990) 452,000. It is a special economic zone; its industries include tourism, wine, and fishing.

Yaoundé Capital of Cameroon, 210 km/130 mi E of the port of Douala; population (1991) 750,000. Industries include tourism, oil refining, food production, and textile manufacturing.

Yarkand Alternative name for ◊Shache, a city in China.

Yarmouth or *Great Yarmouth* Holiday resort and port in Norfolk, England, at the mouth of the river Yare; population (1991) 56,200. Formerly a herring-fishing port, it is now a base for North Sea oil and gas.

Yaroslavl Industrial city (textiles, rubber, paints, commercial vehicles) in W central Russian Federation, capital of Yaroslavl region, on the river Volga, 250 km/155 mi NE of Moscow; population (1994) 631,000.

Yazd or *Yezd* Silk-weaving city in central Iran, an oasis on a trade route and the capital of the province of Yazd; population (1991) 275,000.

Ybbs Austrian town in the province of Lower Austria, on the river Danube, 65 km/40 mi E of Linz. Ybbs lies at the W end of the Wachau area and has an ancient church and castle. Nearby, on the Danube, is the power station of Ybbs-Persenberg.

Yekaterinburg formerly (1924–91) *Sverdlovsk* Industrial city (copper, iron, platinum, engineering, and chemicals) in the Russian Federation in the E foothills of the Ural Mountains; population (1994) 1,347,000. Tsar Nicholas II and his family were murdered here 1918.

Yellowknife Capital of Northwest Territories, Canada, on the N shore of Great Slave Lake; population (1991) 15,200. It was founded 1935 when gold was discovered in the area and became the capital 1967.

Yellow River English name for the ◊Huang He River, China.

Yellow Sea Gulf of the Pacific Ocean between China and Korea; area 294,000 sq km/13,500 sq mi. It receives the Huang He (Yellow River) and Chang Jiang.

Yellowstone National Park Largest US nature reserve, established 1872, on a broad plateau in the Rocky Mountains, chiefly in NW Wyoming, but also in SW Montana and E Idaho; area 8,983 sq km/3,469 sq mi. The park contains more than 3,000 geysers and hot springs, including periodically erupting Old Faithful. It is a World Heritage Site and one of the world's greatest wildlife refuges. Much of the park was ravaged by forest fires 1988.

Yemen, North Former country in SW Asia. It was united with South Yemen 1990 as the Republic of Yemen.

Yemen, South Former country in SW Asia. It was united with North Yemen 1990 as the Republic of Yemen.

Yenan Alternative transcription of ◊Yan'an, a city in China.

Yenisey or *Yenisei* River in Asian Russia, rising in the Tuva region and flowing across the Siberian plain into the Arctic Ocean; length 4,100 km/2,548 mi.

Yerevan or *Erivan* Industrial city (tractor parts, machine tools, chemicals, bricks, bicycles, wine, fruit canning) and capital of Armenia, a few miles N of the Turkish border; population (1994) 1,200,000. It was founded in the 7th century and was alternately Turkish and Persian from the 15th century until ceded to Russia 1828. Armenia became an independent republic 1991.

Yezd Alternative name for the Iranian city of ◊Yazd.

Yezo Former name for ◊Hokkaido, the northernmost of the four main islands of Japan.

Yichang or *Ichang* Port at the head of navigation of the Chang Jiang River, Hubei province, China; population (1990) 372,000.

Yinchuan Capital of Ningxia autonomous region, NW China, on the Huang He River; population (1993) 430,000. It is a trading centre for the Ningxia plain, producing textiles and coal.

Ynys Enlli Welsh name for ◊Bardsey Island.

Ynys Môn Welsh name for the island of ◊Anglesey.

Yogyakarta City in Java, Indonesia, capital 1945–1949; population (1990) 412,400. The chief industries are batik textiles, handicrafts, and tourism. It is the cultural centre of the Javanese ethnic group.

Yokohama Japanese port on Tokyo Bay; population (1994) 3,265,000. Industries include shipbuilding, oil refining, engineering, textiles, glass, and clothing.

Yokosuka Japanese seaport and naval base (1884) on Tokyo Bay, S of Yokohama; population (1994) 437,000.

Yonkers City in Westchester County, New York, USA, on the Hudson River, just N of the Bronx, New York City; population (1992) 186,100. Products include machinery, processed foods, chemicals, clothing, and electric and electronic equipment. Yonkers was a Dutch settlement from about 1650.

Yonne French river, 290 km/180 mi long, rising in central France and flowing N into the Seine; it gives its name to a *département* in Burgundy region.

Yonne *Département* in the ◊Bourgogne region of France; area 7,424 sq km/2,830 sq mi; population (1990) 323,400. The river Yonne flows through it, and the land is mostly flat. The *département* is mainly agricultural, growing vines, cereals, sugar beet, and garden produce, and raising livestock. The principal towns are ◊Auxerre (the capital), and ◊Sens; Chablis is the centre of the wine-producing region.

York Unitary authority in NE England created 1996 from part of the county of North Yorkshire; population (1997 est) 174,800; area 271 sq km/105 sq mi.

York Cathedral and industrial city (scientific instruments, sugar, chocolate, and glass), and administrative headquarters of the City and County of York unitary authority, N England; population (1994 est) 107,000. Britain's last train-building factory closed Oct 1995. The city is visited by 3 million tourists a year.

features The Gothic York Minster contains medieval stained glass; the S transept was severely damaged by fire 1984, but has been restored. Much of the 14th-century city wall survives, with four gates or 'bars', as well as the medieval streets collectively known as the Shambles (after the slaughterhouse). The Jorvik Viking Centre, opened 1984 after excavation of a site at Coppergate, contains wooden remains of Viking houses. There are fine examples of 17th- to 18th-century domestic architecture; the Theatre Royal, site of a theatre since 1765; the Castle Museum; the National Railway Museum; and the university 1963.

history Traditionally the capital of the N of England, the city became from AD 71 the Roman fortress of *Eboracum*. Recent excavations of the Roman city have revealed the fortress, baths, and temples to Serapis and Mithras. The first bishop of York (Paulinus) was consecrated 627 in the wooden church that preceded York Minster. Paulinus baptized King Edwin there 627, and York was created an archbishopric 732. In the 10th century it was a Viking settlement. During the Middle Ages its commercial prosperity depended on the wool trade. An active Quaker element in the 18th and 19th centuries included the Rowntree family, who founded the chocolate factory.

York City in S Pennsylvania, USA, SE of Harrisburg; population (1990) 42,100. It is an agricultural processing centre for the area and manufactures paper products, building materials, and heavy machinery. The Articles of Confederation were adopted here during the Continental Congress 1777–78.

Yorks. Abbreviation for ◊Yorkshire, an English county.

Yorkshire Former county in NE England on the North Sea divided administratively into North, East, and West Ridings (thirds), but reorganized to form a number of new counties 1974: the major part of *Cleveland* and *Humberside*, *North Yorkshire*, *South Yorkshire*, and *West Yorkshire*. Small outlying areas also went to Durham, Cumbria, Lancashire, and Greater Manchester. In 1996 Cleveland and Humberside were abolished, and a number of unitary authorities were created to replace them.

Yorktown Historic town in SE Virginia, USA, on the York River. The last important battle of the American Revolution was fought here in 1781, when the British general Lord Charles Cornwallis surrendered to George Washington. It is now a popular tourist point.

Yosemite Area in the Sierra Nevada, E California, USA, a national park from 1890; area 3,079 sq km/1,189 sq mi. It includes Yosemite Gorge, Yosemite Falls (739 m/2,425 ft in three leaps) with many other lakes and waterfalls, and groves of giant sequoia trees. It is a World Heritage Site.

Youngstown Industrial city (fabricated metals) in E Ohio, USA, on the Mahoning River; population (1992) 94,400. Youngstown was laid out 1797.

Ypres (Flemish *Ieper*) Town in the province of West Flanders, Belgium, on the river Yperlee, 47 km/29 mi SW of Bruges. In the Middle Ages the town was a centre of the Flanders cloth trade, especially woollens, but the chief manufactures are now linen and biscuits. The Menin Gate 1927 is a memorial to the British and Commonwealth troops who lost their lives here in World War I.

Yser River of France and Belgium, rising 8 km/5 mi NE of St-Omer; length 79 km/49 mi. It flows eastwards across the *département* of Nord, turning gradually NW across Flanders, to the North Sea 3 km/2 mi NW of Nieuport. It connects several canals in Belgium.

Ysselmeer Alternative spelling of ◊IJsselmeer, a lake in the Netherlands.

Yuba City City in N central California, USA, on the Feather River, N of San Francisco; population (1990) 27,400. It is an agricultural trading centre for nuts, fruits, rice, and dairy products. It was laid out 1849 during the California gold rush.

Yucatán Peninsula in Central America, divided among Mexico, Belize, and Guatemala; area 180,000 sq km/70,000 sq mi. Tropical crops are grown. It is inhabited by Maya Indians and contains the remains of their civilization.

Yucatán State of SE Mexico; area 39,340 sq km/15,189 sq mi; population (1995 est) 1,555,700. Its capital is Mérida. The chief products are sisal fibre, hardwoods, sugar, tobacco, and maize. There are important Mayan ruins.

Yukon River River in North America, 3,185 km/1,979 mi long, flowing from Lake Tagish in Yukon Territory into Alaska, where it empties into the Bering Sea.

Yukon Territory   Territory of NW Canada
area   483,450 sq km/186,660 sq mi
capital   Whitehorse
towns and cities   Dawson, Mayo
physical   Yukon River; Mount Logan, at 6,050 m/19,850 ft the highest point in Canada
features   Klondike Gold Rush International Historical Park, which extends into Alaska
industries   gold, silver, lead, zinc, oil, natural gas, coal
population   (1995 est) 31,000
history   settlement dates from the gold rush 1896–1910, when 30,000 people moved to the ◊Klondike river valley (silver is now worked there). It became separate from the Northwest Territories 1898, with Dawson as the capital 1898–1951. Construction of the Alcan Highway during World War II helped provide the basis for further development.

Yungning   Alternative transcription of ◊Nanning, a Chinese port.

Yunnan   Province of SW China, adjoining Myanmar (Burma), Laos, and Vietnam
area   436,200 sq km/168,417 sq mi
capital   Kunming
physical   rivers: Chang Jiang, Salween, Mekong; crossed by the Burma Road; mountainous and well forested
industries   rice, tea, timber, wheat, cotton, rubber, tin, copper, lead, zinc, coal, salt
population   (1990) 36,973,000.

Yuzovka   Former name (1872–1924) for the town of ◊Donetsk, Ukraine, named after the Welshman John Hughes who established a metallurgical factory here in the 1870s.

Yvelines   *Département* in the ◊Ile-de-France region of France, W of Paris and largely S of the river Seine; area 2,270 sq km/876 sq mi; population (1990) 1,307,400. Connected to Paris by express underground, it houses commuters and its woodland is used for weekend recreation. There is also agriculture. The principal towns are ◊Versailles (the capital), Rambouillet, Mantes, and Poissy.

Yverdon   Commune and spa in the Swiss canton of Vaud, at the SW end of Lake Neuchâtel; population (1995) 23,200. Yverdon manufactures rolling stock and cigars. The town is built on the site of the Roman town of Eburodunum.

Zaandam   Industrial port (timber, paper) in North Holland province, the Netherlands, on the river Zaan, NW of Amsterdam, since 1974 included in the municipality of Zaanstad.

Zaanstad   Industrial town in W Netherlands which includes the port of Zaandam; population (1994) 132,500.

Zabrze   Industrial city (coal mining, iron, chemicals) in Silesia, S Poland; formerly (until 1945) the German town of Hindenburg; population (1991) 205,000.

Zacatecas   State of central Mexico; area 75,040 sq km/28,973 sq mi; population (1995 est) 1,336,300. The capital is Zacatecas. The main occupation is silver-mining.

Zadar   (Italian *Zara*) Port and resort in Croatia; population (1991) 76,300. The city was sacked by the army of the Fourth Crusade 1202, which led to the Crusade being excommunicated by Pope Innocent III. Zader was alternately held and lost by the Venetian republic from the 12th century until its seizure by Austria 1813. It was the capital of Dalmatia 1815–1918 and part of Italy 1920–47, when it became part of Yugoslavia; it now belongs to independent Croatia.

Żagań   (German *Sagan*) Industrial town (lignite mining, textiles) in Zielona Góra province, Poland, on the Bóbr river, 40 km/25 mi S of Zielona Góra; population (1990) 27,600. It has a 17th-century palace built by the German general Albrecht Wallenstein. Żagań was capital of a principality 1274–1472 and part of German Lower Silesia until 1945.

Zagorsk   Former name of ◊Sergiyev Posad, a town in the Russian Federation.

Zagreb   Industrial city (leather, linen, carpets, paper, and electrical goods) and capital of Croatia, on the Sava River; population (1991) 726,800. Zagreb was a Roman city (*Aemona*) and has a Gothic cathedral. Its university was founded 1874. The city was damaged by bombing Oct 1991 during the Croatian civil war.

Zaïre River   Former name of the Congo/Zaïre, the second-longest river in Africa.

Zaïre River

Zákynthos   or *Zante* Southernmost of the ◊Ionian Islands, Greece; area 410 sq km/158 sq mi; population (1981) 30,000. Products include olives, currants, grapes, and carpets.

Yukon

Zakopane Ski and health resort in the Tatra Mountains, Poland, at an altitude of 890 m/2,967 ft, in Nowy Sącz province, 80 km/50 mi S of Kraków. Mount Giewont (1,909 m/6,363 ft), popular with climbers, overlooks the town, which is Poland's main winter-sports centre.

Zalew Szczeciński (English *Stettin Lagoon*, German *Stettiner Haff*) Lagoon in Poland and NE Germany, 56 km/35 mi long, opening into the Bay of Pomerania in the Baltic Sea. It separates the politically divided island of Usedom (Uznam) and the Polish island of Wolin from the mainland. The river Oder enters the lagoon above Szczecin.

Zambezi River in central and SE Africa; length 2,650 km/1,647 mi from NW Zambia through Mozambique to the Indian Ocean, with a wide delta near Chinde. Major tributaries include the Kafue in Zambia. It is interrupted by rapids, and includes on the Zimbabwe–Zambia border the Victoria Falls (Mosi-oa-tunya) and Kariba Dam, which forms the reservoir of Lake Kariba with large fisheries.

Zamora Capital of the province of Zamora, NW Spain, on the river Duero; population (1995) 66,000. Products include textiles, pottery, and wine. It has a 12th-century Romanesque cathedral, a castle, and many old churches, walls, and houses.

Zamora Province of NW Spain in Castilla-León autonomous community; capital Zamora; area 10,559 sq km/4,077 sq mi; population (1995) 214,300. Its W border is on the Portuguese frontier. The river Duero and its tributaries flow through it. The sheep raised here produce much of Spain's merino wool.

Zante Alternative name for the Ionian island of ◊Zákynthos, Greece.

Zanzibar Island region of Tanzania
area 1,658 sq km/640 sq mi (80 km/50 mi long)
towns and cities Zanzibar
industries cloves, copra
population (1988) 375,500
history settled by Arab traders in the 7th century; occupied by the Portuguese in the 16th century; became a sultanate in the 17th century; under British protection 1890–1963. Together with the island of Pemba, some nearby islets, and a strip of mainland territory, it became a republic 1963. It merged with Tanganyika as Tanzania 1964.

Zaporozhye formerly (until 1921) *Aleksandrovsk* Industrial city (steel, chemicals, aluminium goods, pig iron, magnesium) in Ukraine, on the river Dnieper; capital of Zaporozhye region and site of the Dnieper Dam; population (1992) 898,000. It was occupied by Germany 1941–43.

Zara Italian name for ◊Zadar, a port on the Adriatic coast of Croatia.

Zaragoza (English *Saragossa*) Industrial city (iron, steel, chemicals, plastics, canned food, electrical goods) in Aragón, Spain; population (1994) 607,000. The medieval city walls and bridges over the river Ebro survive, and there is a 15th-century university.

Zaragoza Province of Spain in W ◊Aragón autonomous community; capital Zaragoza; area 17,195 sq km/6,639 sq mi; population (1995) 852,300. In general it is an open plain with extreme climates. The river Ebro and its tributaries (Jalón, Huerva, Arba) flow through it. The Pyrenees are to the N and W. Products include cereals, oil, wine, and livestock.

Żary (German *Sorau*) Industrial town (lignite, woollen textiles) in Zielona Góra province, W Poland, 45 km/28 mi SW of Zielona Góra; population (1990) 40,000. It had a medieval salt market. Until 1945 it was part of German Brandenburg; it was annexed to Saxony 1785 and to Prussia 1815.

Zealand Another name for ◊Sjælland, the main island of Denmark, and for ◊Zeeland, a province of the SW Netherlands.

Zeebrugge Small Belgian ferry port on the North Sea, linked to Bruges by a canal (built 1896–1907), 14 km/9 mi long. It was occupied by the Germans in World War I and developed as a major naval base. In March 1987 it was the scene of a disaster in which over 180 passengers lost their lives when the car ferry *Herald of Free Enterprise* put to sea from Zeebrugge with its car-loading doors still open.

Zeeland Province of the SW Netherlands, mostly below sea level; it is protected by a system of dykes; area 1,790 sq km/691 sq mi; capital Middelburg; population (1995) 365,800. Industries include cereals and potatoes.

Zeist Town in the Netherlands, a dormitory town for ◊Utrecht; population (1996) 59,200. It has some mixed manufacturing industry. Zeist is the Dutch headquarters of the Moravian Church.

Zelenograd City on the Skhodnia River, 37 km/23 mi NW of Moscow, in the Russian Federation; population (1992) 170,000. Construction began 1960 and Zelenpgrad achieved city status 1963. It is a centre for the microelectronics industry; construction materials and fruit and vegetables are also produced.

Zell am See Town and tourist resort in the Salzburg province of Austria, 55 km/34 mi SW of the city of Salzburg. Zell is situated on the W shore of a lake at the foot of a mountain, the Schmittenhöhe (height 1,968m/6,456 ft). Some copper is mined in the vicinity.

Zelle Alternative name for ◊Celle, a town in Germany.

Zenica Town in Bosnia-Herzegovina, 56 km/35 mi NW of Sarajevo. It lies on a brown-coal field and is the country's largest iron and steel town.

Zermatt Ski resort in the Valais canton, Switzerland, at the foot of the Matterhorn; population (1985) 3,700.

Zetland Official form until 1974 of the ◊Shetland Islands, a group of islands off N Scotland.

Zgierz Industrial town (chemicals, textiles, clothing) in Łódź province, central Poland, on the river Bzura, 11 km/7 mi N of Łódź; population (1990) 59,000.

Zgorzelec Industrial town (lignite, textiles) in Jelenia Góra province, W Poland, on the right bank of the river Nysa at the German border, 45 km/28 mi W of Wrocław; population (1990) 36,100. It was an E suburb of German Görlitz until 1945, and remains connected by bridge.

Zhangjiakou or *Changchiakow* Historic city and trade centre in Hebei province, China, 160 km/100 mi NW of Beijing, on the Great Wall; population (1990) 670,000. Zhangjiakou is on the border of Inner Mongolia (its Mongolian name is *Kalgan*, 'gate') and on the road and railway to Ulaanbaatar in Mongolia. It developed under the Manchu dynasty, and was the centre of the tea trade from China to Russia.

Zhdanov Former name (1948–89) of ◊Mariupol, a port in Ukraine.

Zhejiang or *Chekiang* Province of SE China
area 101,800 sq km/39,295 sq mi
capital Hangzhou
features smallest of the Chinese provinces; the base of the Song dynasty 12th–13th centuries; densely populated
industries rice, cotton, sugar, jute, maize; timber on the uplands
population (1990) 40,840,000.

Zhengzhou or *Chengchow* Industrial city (light engineering, cotton textiles, foods) and capital (from 1954) of Henan province, China, on the Huang He River; population (1993) 1,530,000.

Zhitomir Capital of Zhitomir region in W Ukraine, W of Kiev; population (1992) 299,000. It is a timber and grain centre and has furniture factories. Zhitomir dates from the 13th century.

Zhonghua Renmin Gonghe Guo Chinese for People's Republic of China.

Zian Alternative spelling of ◊Xi'an, a city in China.

Zielona Góra (German *Grünberg*) Capital of Zielona Góra province, W Poland, 117 km/73 mi SW of Poznań; population (1990) 114,100. Industries include metal, textile, and wine production, engineering, and food processing. The town became a commercial centre in the late Middle Ages. It has a 15th-century Gothic church and a 16th-century town hall.

Žilina (German *Sillein*, Hungarian *Zsolna*) Industrial town (textiles, paper) in N Slovak Republic, on the river Váh; population (1991) 83,900. The town is situated in the S foothills of the Carpathian Mountains.

Zittau Town in the *Land* of ◊Saxony, Germany, near the border with Poland and the Czech Republic, 77 km/48 mi SE of Dresden. It has textile and engineering industries.

Zlatoust Industrial city (metallurgy) in Chelyabinsk region, central Russian Federation, in the S Ural Mountains; population (1994) 206,000. It was founded 1754 as an iron- and copper-working settlement, destroyed 1774 by a peasant uprising, but developed as an armaments centre from the time of Napoleon's invasion of Russia.

Zlín formerly (1948–93) *Gottwaldov* Town in S Moravia, in the Czech Republic, 70 km/44 mi E of Brno; population (1991) 84,600. The shoe company Bata, founded here 1894, returned to Zlín 1989.

Znojmo (German *Znaim*) Town in Moravia, S Czech Republic, on the river Dyje near the Austrian border, 52 km/32 mi from Brno; population (1991) 39,900. Industries include pottery, footwear, sports equipment, and food processing. Znojmo is a historic town with a Romanesque monastery founded 1190.

Zoetermeer Town in the province of South Holland, the Netherlands; population (1996) 106,800. Zoetermeer was formerly a village in an agricultural region 14 km/9 mi E of The ◊Hague, but has developed into a dormitory town for the capital.

Zomba Former capital of Malawi, 32 km/20 mi W of Lake Shirwa; population (1987) 42,900. Industries included cement and fishing tackle. It was replaced by Lilongwe as capital 1975 but remains the university town.

Zoppot German name for ◊Sopot, a town in Poland.

Zrenjanin (formerly *Petrovgrad*) Town in Serbia, Yugoslavia, in the autonomous region of Vojvodina, 50 km/31 mi E of Novi Sad; population (1991) 81,300. Situated on the river Begej, it is a port and railway junction, and has chemical, food, soap, leather, and mechanical industries.

Zsolna Hungarian name for ◊Žilina, a town in the Slovak Republic.

Zug Capital of the Swiss canton of the same name, situated on Lake Zug 24 km/15 mi S of Zürich, at the foot of the Zugerberg (height 1,991 m/6,532 ft); population (1995) 22,800. Zug has factories manufacturing electrical equipment, metal goods, and textiles. There are some 16th-century Baroque buildings in the town.

Zug Canton in central Switzerland, the smallest such administrative division in the country; area 239 sq km/92 sq mi; population (1995) 92,400. The S and SE areas of Zug are mountainous. Lake Zug, with an area of 38 sq km/15 sq mi, lies partly in the canton and partly in Schwyz. Much fruit is grown, dairy farming is widespread, and industries include distilling and textile manufacture. Zug joined the Swiss Confederation in 1352.

Zuider Zee Former sea inlet in the NW Netherlands, closed off from the North Sea by a 32-km/20-mi dyke 1932; much of it has been reclaimed as land. The remaining lake is called the ◊IJsselmeer.

Zululand Region in KwaZulu Natal, South Africa, largely corresponding to the former Black National State ◊KwaZulu. The Zulus formed a powerful kingdom in the early 19th century under Shaka (died 1828) and built up an empire in Natal, displacing other peoples of S Africa. They were defeated by the British army at Ulundi 1879. Zululand became part of the British colony of Natal 1897.

Zürich Financial centre and industrial city (machinery, electrical goods, textiles) on Lake Zürich; population (1994) 353,400. Situated at the foot of the Alps, it is the capital of Zürich canton and the largest city in Switzerland.

Zürich Canton in NE Switzerland, bounded on the N by the river Rhine; area 1,729 sq km/668 sq mi; population (1996) 1,175,500. The greater part of Lake Zürich lies within its borders. Zürich is an industrialized canton, with much of Switzerland's heavy, electrical, and textile industry located here. It was the first canton to join the Swiss Confederation in 1351.

Zutphen Town in Gelderland province, the Netherlands; population (1993) 31,100.

Zweibrücken (French *Deuxponts*; Roman *Bipontium*) City in the Rhineland-Palatinate, Germany, 40 km/25 mi E of Saarbrücken; population (1994) 35,900. Machinery, footwear, and electrical equipment are produced. The former capital of the ancient duchy of Zweibrücken, it has a

15th-century church and some Baroque buildings. The city was largely rebuilt after World War II.

Zwickau Coal-mining and industrial town (vehicles, textiles) SW of Chemnitz in the state of Saxony, Germany, on the river Mulde; population (1991) 112,600. It was the birthplace of the composer Robert Schumann.

Zwolle Capital of Overijssel province, the Netherlands; a market town with brewing, distilling, butter-making, and other industries; population (1994) 99,100.

Appendices

Australia: States and Territories

(– = not applicable.)

State	Capital	Area		Population (1994)
		sq km	sq mi	
New South Wales	Sydney	801,600	309,500	5,997,400
Queensland	Brisbane	1,727,200	666,872	3,196,900
South Australia	Adelaide	984,377	380,070	1,463,200
Tasmania	Hobart	67,800	26,177	472,400
Victoria	Melbourne	227,620	87,884	4,475,500
Western Australia	Perth	2,525,500	975,095	1,715,300
Territories				
Northern Territory	Darwin	1,346,200	519,767	173,900
Australian Capital Territory	Canberra	2,400	926	304,100
External Territories				
Ashmore and Cartier Islands uninhabited	–	5	2	
Australian Antarctic Territory uninhabited except for scientific stations	–	6,044,000	2,333,590	
Christmas Island	–	135	52	2,500
Cocos (Keeling) Islands	–	14	5.5	593
Coral Sea Islands uninhabited except for scientific stations	*	–		
Heard Island and McDonald Islands uninhabited	–	410	158	
Norfolk Island	–	40	15.5	1,800 (1990)

* Sea area of Coral Sea Islands is 780,000 sq km/301,158 sq mi; land area of the islands is aproximately 2.6 sq km/1 sq mi.

Austria: Provinces

Province	Capital	Area		Population (1995)
		sq km	sq mi	
Burgenland	Eisenstadt	3,965	1,531	274,334
Carinthia	Klagenfurt	9,533	3,681	560,994
Lower Austria	St Pölten	19,174	7,403	1,518,254
Salzburg	Salzburg	7,154	2,762	506,850
Styria	Graz	16,388	6,327	1,206,317
Tirol	Innsbruck	12,648	4,883	658,312
Upper Austria	Linz	11,980	4,625	1,385,769
Vienna	Vienna	415	160	1,592,596
Vorarlberg	Bregenz	2,601	1,004	343,109

Canada: Provinces and Territories

Province	Capital	Area sq km	sq mi	Population (1994)
Alberta	Edmonton	661,190	255,285	2,656,000
British Columbia	Victoria	947,800	365,946	3,529,000
Manitoba	Winnipeg	649,950	250,946	1,105,000
New Brunswick	Fredericton	73,440	28,355	738,000
Newfoundland	St John's	405,720	156,648	570,000
Nova Scotia	Halifax	55,490	21,425	918,000
Ontario	Toronto	1,068,580	412,579	10,768,000
Prince Edward Island	Charlottetown	5,660	2,185	131,000
Quebec	Quebec	1,540,680	594,857	7,134,000
Saskatchewan	Regina	652,330	251,865	978,000

Territory

Territory	Capital	Area sq km	sq mi	Population (1994)
Northwest Territories	Yellowknife	3,426,320	1,322,902	62,000
Yukon Territory	Whitehorse	483,450	186,660	31,000

China: Provinces

(– = not applicable.)

Province	Alternative transcription	Capital	Area sq km	sq mi	Population (1990)
Anhui	Anhwei	Hefei	139,900	54,015	56,181,000
Fujian	Fukien	Fuzhou	123,100	47,528	30,048,000
Gansu	Kansu	Lanzhou	530,000	204,633	22,371,000
Guangdong	Kwantung	Guangzhou	231,400	89,343	62,829,000
Guizhou	Kweichow	Guiyang	174,000	67,181	32,392,000
Hainan	–	Haikou	34,000	13,127	6,420,000
Hebei	Hopei	Shijiazhuang	202,700	78,262	61,082,000
Heilongjiang	Heilungkiang	Harbin	463,600	178,996	35,215,000
Henan	Honan	Zhengzhou	167,000	64,479	85,510,000
Hubei	Hupei	Wuhan	187,500	72,394	53,969,000
Hunan	–	Changsha	210,500	81,274	60,660,000
Jiangsu	Kiangsu	Nanjing	102,200	39,459	67,057,000
Jiangxi	Kiangsi	Nanchang	164,800	63,629	37,710,000
Jilin	Kirin	Changchun	187,000	72,201	24,659,000
Liaoning	–	Shenyang	151,000	58,301	39,460,000
Qinghai	Tsinghai	Xining	721,000	278,378	4,457,000
Shaanxi	Shensi	Xian	195,800	75,598	32,882,000
Shandong	Shantung	Jinan	153,300	59,189	84,393,000
Shanxi	Shansi	Taiyuan	157,100	60,656	28,759,000
Sichuan	Szechwan	Chengdu	569,000	219,691	107,218,000
Yunnan	–	Kunming	436,200	168,417	36,973,000
Zhejiang	Chekiang	Hangzhou	101,800	39,305	41,446,000

Autonomous region

Province	Alternative transcription	Capital	Area sq km	sq mi	Population (1990)
Guangxi Zhuang	Kwangsi Chuang	Nanning	220,400	85,096	42,246,000
Nei Mongol	Inner Mongolia	Hohhot	450,000	173,745	21,457,000
Ningxia Hui	Ninghsia-Hui	Yinchuan	170,000	65,637	4,655,000
Xinjiang Uygur	Sinkiang Uighur	Urumqi	1,646,800	635,829	15,156,000
Xizang	Tibet	Lhasa	1,221,600	471,660	2,196,000

Municipality

Province	Alternative transcription	Capital	Area sq km	sq mi	Population (1990)
Beijing	Peking	–	17,800	6,873	10,870,000
Shanghai	–	–	5,800	2,239	13,510,000
Tianjin	Tientsin	–	4,000	1,544	8,830,000

England: Counties

Beginning in 1995, far-reaching local government changes took effect in England, based on recommendations of a government commission that was set up under the Local Government Act of 1992. The changes are being implemented in stages, and are to result in a combination of the existing two-tier structure with new single-tier (unitary) authorities. In 1995 and 1996, unitary authorities were introduced for the Isle of Wight, Avon, Cleveland, and Humberside (with the latter three being abolished as counties); the city of York, formerly in North Yorkshire, also became a unitary authority, with the rest of the county retaining the two-tier system. More counties underwent changes in 1997, with their main urban centres becoming unitary authorities and the rest of the county keeping the existing two-tier system. The changes were to continue through 1998.

The population figures are for the entire county, rather than the area administered by the county council. The land areas include the newly-separated unitary authorities, which still remain part of the county geographically.
(– = not applicable.)

County	Administrative headquarters	Area sq km	sq mi	Population (1994)
Bedfordshire	Bedford	1,240	478	547,300
[1]Berkshire	[2]Reading	1,260	486	769,200
Buckinghamshire	[3]Aylesbury	1,880	725	667,300
[4]Cambridgeshire	Cambridge	3,410	1,316	686,900
Cheshire	Chester	2,320	896	975,600
Cornwall	Truro	3,550	1,370	479,600
Cumbria	Carlisle	6,810	2,629	490,200
Derbyshire	[5]Matlock	2,550	984	726,000
[1]Devon	Exeter	6,720	2,594	1,053,400
Dorset	[6]Dorchester	2,650	1,023	673,200
Durham	[7]Durham	2,232	862	506,300
[4]East Sussex	[8]Lewes	1,795	693	730,100
[4]Essex	Chelmsford	3,670	1,417	1,560,300
Gloucestershire	Gloucester	2,640	1,019	549,500
Hampshire	[9]Winchester	3,770	1,455	1,622,000
[10]Hereford and Worcester	Worcester	3,930	1,517	699,900
Hertfordshire	Hertford	1,630	629	1,005,400
Kent	Maidstone	3,730	1,440	1,546,300
Lancashire	Preston	3,040	1,173	1,424,000
Leicestershire	[11]Leicester	2,084	804	592,700
[4]Lincolnshire	Lincoln	5,890	2,274	605,600
Norfolk	Norwich	5,360	2,069	768,500
Northamptonshire	Northampton	2,370	915	594,800
Northumberland	Morpeth	5,030	1,942	307,700
North Yorkshire	[12]Northallerton	8,320	3,212	556,200
[10]Nottinghamshire	Nottingham	2,160	834	1,030,900
Oxfordshire	Oxford	2,610	1,007	590,200
Shropshire	Shrewsbury	3,490	1,347	416,500
Somerset	Taunton	3,460	1,336	477,900
Staffordshire	[13]Stafford	2,720	1,050	1,046,900
[4]Suffolk	Ipswich	3,800	1,467	649,500
Surrey	Kingston upon Thames	1,660	641	1,041,200
Warwickshire	Warwick	1,980	764	496,300
West Sussex	Chichester	1,990	768	722,100
Wiltshire	[14]Trowbridge	3,480	1,343	594,000

[1]Metropolitan county[15]				Population (1991)
London, Greater[16]	–	1,580	610	6,679,700
Manchester, Greater	–	1,290	498	2,499,400
Merseyside	–	650	251	1,403,600
South Yorkshire	–	1,560	602	1,262,600
Tyne and Wear	–	540	208	1,095,200
West Midlands	–	900	347	2,551,700
West Yorkshire	–	2,040	787	2,013,700

[1] 1995 est.

[2] The county of Berkshire will be abolished in April 1998 and split into six unitary authorities.

[3] In April 1997, Milton Keynes became a separate unitary authority.

[4] 1997 est.

[5] In April 1997, Derby became a separate unitary authority.

[6] In April 1997, the boroughs of Bournemouth and Poole became a separate unitary authority.

[7] In April 1997, the borough of Darlington became a separate unitary authority.

[8] In April 1997, the boroughs of Brighton and Hove were combined into a separate unitary authority, Brighton and Hove.

[9] In April 1997, the cities of Southampton and Portsmouth became separate unitary authorities.

[10] 1996 est.

[11] In April 1997, the cities of Rutland and Leicester became separate unitary authorities.

[12] In April 1996, the citiy of York (and its environs) became separate unitary authority.

[13] In April 1997, Stoke-on-Trent became separate unitary authority.

[14] In April 1997, the town of Swindon (and its environs) became separate unitary authority.

[15] Most administrative functions of metropolitan counties reverted to metropolitan district councils from 1986.

[16] Former administrative region; most administrative functions of the Greater London Council (GLC) reverted to individual boroughs from 1986.

England: Local Government

Beginning in 1995, far-reaching local government changes took effect in England, based on recommendations of a government commission that was set up under the Local Government Act of 1992. The changes are being implemented in stages, and are to result in a combination of the existing two-tier structure with new single-tier (unitary) authorities. In 1995 and 1996, unitary authorities were introduced for the Isle of Wight, Avon, Cleveland, and Humberside (with the latter three being abolished as counties); the city of York, formerly in North Yorkshire, also became a unitary authority, with the rest of the county retaining the two-tier system. More counties underwent changes in 1997, with their main urban centres becoming unitary authorities and the rest of the county keeping the existing two-tier system. The changes were to continue through 1998.

England: Local Government Divisions

Local authority	Administrative headquarters	Area sq km	Area sq mi	Population (1994)
Bath and North East Somerset	Bristol	351	136	158,700
[1]Bedfordshire	Bedford	1,192	460	373,000
[2]Berkshire	[3]Reading	1,260	486	769,200
Bournemouth	Bournemouth	46	18	160,900
[2]Brighton and Hove	Brighton	84	32	248,000
[4]Bristol	Bristol	109	42	374,300
[1]Buckinghamshire	Aylesbury	1,565	604	468,700
[5]Cambridgeshire	Cambridge	3,410	1,316	686,900
Cheshire	Chester	2,320	896	975,600
Cornwall	Truro	3,550	1,370	479,600
Cumbria	Carlisle	6,810	2,629	490,200
Darlington	Darlington	197	76	100,600
[1]Derby City	Derby	87	30	218,800
[1]Derbyshire	Matlock	2,550	984	726,000
[2]Devon	Exeter	6,720	2,594	1,053,400
Dorset	Dorchester	2,541	981	374,800
[6]Durham	Durham	2,232	862	492,900
[2]East Riding of Yorkshire	Beverley	2,416	933	310,000
[1]East Sussex	Lewes	1,725	666	482,800
[4]Essex	Chelmsford	3,670	1,417	1,528,600
[7]Gloucestershire	Gloucester	2,640	1,019	549,500
Hampshire	Winchester	3,679	1,420	1,213,600
[4]Hartlepool	Hartlepool	94	36	90,400
[1]Hereford and Worcester	Worcester	3,930	1,517	699,900
Hertfordshire	Hertford	1,630	629	1,005,400
[1]Kent	Maidstone	3,730	1,440	1,546,300
Kingston upon Hull	Kingston upon Hull	71	27	265,000

[1]Lancashire	Preston	3,040	1,173	1,424,000
Leicester City	Leicester	73	28	270,500
[1]Leicestershire	Leicester	2,084	804	592,700
[4]Lincolnshire	Lincoln	5,890	2,274	605,600
London, Greater	London	1,580	610	6,679,700
[7]Luton	Luton	43	17	181,400
[8]Middlesbrough	Middlesbrough	54	21	146,000
[1]Milton Keynes	Milton Keynes	310	120	198,600
[1]Norfolk	Norwich	5,360	2,069	768,500
Northamptonshire	Northampton	2,370	915	594,800
North East Lincolnshire	Grimsby	192	74	164,000
[9]North Lincolnshire	Brigg	850	328	153,000
[1]North Somerset	Weston-super-Mare	372	144	177,000
[1]Northumberland	Morpeth	5,030	1,942	307,700
North Yorkshire	Northallerton	8,037	3,102	556,200
[4]Nottinghamshire	Nottingham	2,160	834	1,030,900
Oxfordshire	Oxford	2,610	1,007	590,200
Poole	Poole	64	25	138,100
[1]Portsmouth	Portsmouth	42	16	189,300
[1]Redcar and Cleveland	Middlesbrough	240	93	144,000
[1]Rutland	Oakham	394	152	34,600
[8]Shropshire	Shrewsbury	3,490	1,347	416,500
Somerset	Taunton	3,460	1,336	477,900
Southampton	Southampton	52	20	207,100
[5]South Gloucestershire	Bristol	497	192	220,000
[1]Staffordshire	Stafford	2,623	1,012	802,100
[4]Stockton-on-Tees	Stockton-on-Tees	200	77	176,600
[1]Stoke-on-Trent	Stoke-on-Trent	93	36	254,200
[1]Suffolk	Ipswich	3,800	1,467	649,500
Surrey	Kingston upon Thames	1,660	641	1,041,200
Swindon	Swindon	230	89	170,000
[1]Tyne and Wear	Newcastle upon Tyne	540	208	1,095,200
[7]Warwickshire	Warwick	1,980	764	496,300
West Sussex	Chichester	2,020	780	722,100
Wight, Isle of	Newport	380	147	130,000
[1]Wiltshire	Trowbridge	3,255	1,256	424,600
[5]York	York	271	105	174,800

Nonadministrative Metropolitan Counties

[6]Manchester, Greater	1,290	498	2,499,400
Merseyside	650	251	1,403,600
South Yorkshire	1,560	602	1,262,600
West Midlands	900	347	2,551,700
West Yorkshire	2,040	787	2,013,700

[1] 1996.

[2] 1995 est.

[3] Berkshire is to be abolished in April 1998 and split into six unitary authorities.

[4] 1995.

[5] 1997 est.

[6] 1994 est.

[7] 1991 est.

[8] 1997.

[9] 1996 est.

France: Regions and Départements

Region/département	Capital	Area sq km	sq mi	Population (1990)
Alsace	Strasbourg	8,280	3,197	1,624,400
Bas-Rhin	Strasbourg			
Haut-Rhin	Colmar			
Aquitaine	Bordeaux	41,308	15,949	2,795,800
Dordogne	Périgueux			
Gironde	Bordeaux			
Landes	Mont-de-Marsan			
Lot-et-Garonne	Agen			
Pyrénées-Atlantiques	Pau			
Auvergne	Clermont-Ferrand	26,013	10,044	1,321,200
Allier	Moulins			
Cantal	Aurillac			
Haute-Loire	Le Puy			
Puy-de-Dôme	Clermont-Ferrand			
Basse-Normandie	Caen	17,589	6,791	1,391,300
Calvados	Caen			
Manche	Saint-Lô			
Orne	Alençon			
Brittany (Bretagne)	Rennes	27,208	10,505	2,795,600
Côtes-d'Armor	St Brieuc			
Finistère	Quimper			
Ille-et-Vilaine	Rennes			
Morbihan	Vannes			
Burgundy (Bourgogne)	Dijon	31,582	12,194	1,609,700
Côte-d'Or	Dijon			
Nièvre	Nevers			
Saône-et-Loire	Mâcon			
Yonne	Auxerre			
Centre	Orléans	39,151	15,116	2,371,000
Cher	Bourges			
Eure-et-Loir	Chartres			
Indre	Châteauroux			
Indre-et-Loire	Tours			
Loir-et-Cher	Blois			
Loiret	Orléans			
Champagne-Ardenne	Reims	25,606	9,886	1,347,900
Ardennes	Charleville-Mézières			
Aube	Troyes			
Haute-Marne	Chaumont			
Marne	Châlons-sur-Marne			
Corsica	Ajaccio	8,680	3,351	250,400
Corse du Sud	Ajaccio			
Haute-Corse	Bastia			

France: Regions and Départements (continued)

Region/département	Capital	Area		Population (1990)
		sq km	sq mi	
Franche-Comté	Besançon	16,202	6,256	1,097,400
Doubs	Besançon			
Haute-Saône	Vesoul			
Jura	Lons-le-Saunier			
Territoire de Belfort	Belfort			
Haute-Normandie	Rouen	12,317	4,756	1,737,200
Eure	Evreux			
Seine-Maritime	Rouen			
Ile-de-France	Paris	12,012	4,638	10,660,600
Essonne	Evry			
Hauts-de-Seine	Nanterre			
Seine-et-Marne	Melun			
Seine-Saint-Denis	Bobigny			
Val-de-Marne	Créteil			
Val-d'Oise	Cergy-Pontoise			
Ville de Paris				
Yvelines	Versailles			
Languedoc-Roussillon	Montpellier	27,376	10,570	2,114,900
Aude	Carcassonne			
Gard	Nîmes			
Hérault	Montpellier			
Lozère	Mende			
Pyrénées-Orientales	Perpignan			
Limousin	Limoges	16,942	6,541	722,800
Corrèze	Tulle			
Creuse	Guéret			
Haute-Vienne	Limoges			
Lorraine	Metz	23,547	9,091	2,305,700
Meurthe-et-Moselle	Nancy			
Meuse	Bar-le-Duc			
Moselle	Metz			
Vosges	Épinal			
Midi-Pyrénées	Toulouse	45,348	17,509	2,430,700
Ariège	Foix			
Aveyron	Rodez			
Gers	Auch			
Haute-Garonne	Toulouse			
Hautes-Pyrénées	Tarbes			
Lot	Cahors			
Tarn	Albi			
Tarn-et-Garonne	Montauban			
Nord-Pas-de-Calais	Lille	12,414	4,793	3,965,100
Nord	Lille			
Pas-de-Calais	Arras			

France: Regions and Départements (continued)

Region/département	Capital	Area sq km	Area sq mi	Population (1990)
Pays de la Loire	Nantes	32,082	12,387	3,059,200
Loire-Atlantique	Nantes			
Maine-et-Loire	Angers			
Mayenne	Laval			
Sarthe	Le Mans			
Vendée	La Roche-sur-Yon			
Picardie	Amiens	19,399	7,490	1,810,700
Aisne	Laon			
Oise	Beauvais			
Somme	Amiens			
Poitou-Charentes	Poitiers	25,809	9,965	1,595,100
Charente	Angoulême			
Charente-Maritime	La Rochelle			
Deux-Sèvres	Niort			
Vienne	Poitiers			
Provence-Alpes-Côte d'Azur	Marseille	31,400	12,123	4,257,900
Alpes-de-Haute-Provence	Digne			
Alpes-Maritimes	Nice			
Bouches-du-Rhône	Marseille			
Hautes-Alpes	Gap			
Var	Toulon			
Vaucluse	Avignon			
Rhône-Alpes	Lyon	43,698	16,872	5,350,800
Ain	Bourg-en-Bresse			
Ardèche	Privas			
Drôme	Valence			
Haute-Savoie	Annecy			
Isère	Grenoble			
Loire	St Étienne			
Rhône	Lyon			
Savoie	Chambéry			

Germany: Administrative Regions

Administrative region	Capital	Area sq km	Area sq mi	Population (1995)
Baden-Württemberg	Stuttgart	35,752	13,804	10,319,400
Bavaria	Munich	70,551	27,240	11,993,500
Berlin	Berlin	889	343	3,471,400
Brandenburg	Potsdam	29,479	11,382	2,542,000
Bremen	Bremen	404	156	679,800
Hamburg	Hamburg	755	292	1,705,900
Hessen	Wiesbaden	21,114	8,152	6,009,900
Lower Saxony	Hannover	47,606	18,381	7,780,400
Mecklenburg–West Pomerania	Schwerin	23,170	8,946	1,823,100
North Rhine–Westphalia	Düsseldorf	34,077	13,157	17,893,000
Rhineland–Palatinate	Mainz	19,852	7,665	3,983,300
Saarland	Saarbrücken	2,570	992	1,084,400
Saxony	Dresden	18,412	7,109	4,566,600
Saxony–Anhalt	Magdeburg	20,446	7,894	2,738,900
Schleswig–Holstein	Kiel	15,770	6,089	2,725,500
Thuringia	Erfurt	16,171	6,244	2,503,800

India: States and Union Territories

State	Capital	Area		Population (1994 est)
		sq km	sq mi	
Andhra Pradesh	Hyderabad	275,045	106,195	71,800,000
Arunachal Pradesh	Itanagar	83,743	32,333	965,000
Assam	Dispur	78,438	30,285	24,200,000
Bihar	Patna	173,877	67,134	93,080,000
Goa	Panaji	3,702	1,429	1,235,000
Gujarat	Gandhinagar	196,024	75,685	44,235,000
Haryana	Chandigarh[2]	44,212	17,070	17,925,000
Himachal Pradesh	Shimla	55,673	21,495	5,530,000
Jammu and Kashmir	[1]Srinagar, Jammu	222,236	85,805	8,435,000
Karnataka	Bangalore	191,791	74,051	48,150,000
Kerala	Trivandrum	38,863	15,005	30,555,000
Madhya Pradesh	Bhopal	443,446	171,215	71,950,000
Maharashtra	Bombay	307,713	118,808	85,565,000
Manipur	Imphal	22,327	8,620	2,010,000
Meghalaya	Shillong	22,429	8,660	1,960,000
Mizoram	Aizawl	21,081	8,139	775,000
Nagaland	Kohima	16,579	6,401	1,410,000
Orissa	Bhubaneshwar	155,707	60,118	33,795,000
Punjab	Chandigarh[2]	5,362	2,070	21,695,000
Rajasthan	Jaipur	342,239	132,138	48,040,000
Sikkim	Gangtok	7096	2,740	444,000
Tamil Nadu	Madras	130,058	50,215	58,840,000
Tripura	Agartala	10,486	4,049	3,055,000
Uttar Pradesh	Lucknow	294,411	113,672	150,695,000
West Bengal	Calcutta	88,752	34,267	73,600,000

Union territory	Capital	Area		Population
		sq km	sq mi	
Andaman and Nicobar Islands	Port Blair	8,249	3,185	322,000
Chandigarh	Chandigarh	114	44	725,000
Dadra and Nagar Haveli	Silvassa	491	190	153,000
Daman and Diu	Daman	112	43	111,000
Delhi	Delhi	1,483	573	10,865,000
Lakshadweep	Kavaratti	32	12	56,000
Pondicherry	Pondicherry	492	190	894,000

[1]Includes area occupied by Pakistan and China.
[2]Joint state capital of Haryana and Punjab.

Republic of Ireland: Provinces and Counties

County	Administrative headquarters	Area		Population (1996 est)
		sq km	sq mi	
Ulster province				
Cavan	Cavan	1,890	729	52,900
Donegal	Lifford	4,830	1,864	129,400
Monaghan	Monaghan	1,290	498	51,300
Munster province				
Clare	Ennis	3,190	1,231	93,900
Cork	Cork	7,460	2,880	420,300
Kerry	Tralee	4,700	1,814	125,900
Limerick	Limerick	2,690	1,038	177,900

Republic of Ireland: Provinces and Counties (continued)

County	Administrative headquarters	Area sq km	Area sq mi	Population (1996 est)
Tipperary (N)	Nenagh	2,000	772	57,900
Tipperary (S)	Clonmel	2,260	872	75,400
Waterford	Waterford	1,840	710	94,600
Leinster province				
Carlow	Carlow	900	347	41,600
Dublin	Dublin	920	355	1,056,700
Kildare	Naas	1,690	652	134,900
Kilkenny	Kilkenny	2,060	795	75,200
Laois	Port Laoise	1,720	664	52,800
Longford	Longford	1,040	401	30,100
Louth	Dundalk	820	316	92,200
Meath	Trim	2,340	903	109,400
Offaly	Tullamore	2,000	772	59,100
Westmeath	Mullingar	1,760	679	63,200
Wexford	Wexford	2,350	907	104,300
Wicklow	Wicklow	2,030	783	102,400
Connacht (Connaught) province				
Galway	Galway	5,940	2,293	188,600
Leitrim	Carrick-on-Shannon	1,530	590	25,000
Mayo	Castlebar	5,400	2,084	111,400
Roscommon	Roscommon	2,460	949	51,900
Sligo	Sligo	1,800	694	55,600

Italy: Regions

Region	Capital	Area sq km	Area sq mi	Population (1995)
Abruzzi	L'Aquila	10,794	4,168	1,267,700
Basilicata	Potenza	9,992	3,858	610,700
Calabria	Catanzaro	15,080	5,822	2,076,100
Campania	Naples	13,595	5,249	5,745,800
Emilia-Romagna	Bologna	22,123	8,542	3,922,600
Friuli-Venezia Giulia	Udine	7,846	3,029	1,191,200
Lazio	Rome	17,203	6,642	5,193,200
Liguria	Genoa	5,416	2,091	1,663,700
Lombardy	Milan	23,856	9,211	8,910,500
Marche, Le	Ancona	9,694	3,743	1,441,000
Molise	Campobasso	4,438	1,714	332,200
Piedmont	Turin	25,399	9,807	4,298,000
Puglia	Bari	19,347	7,470	4,075,800
Sardinia	[1]Cagliari	24,090	9,301	1,659,500
Sicily	[1]Palermo	25,708	9,926	5,082,700
Trentino-Alto Adige	[1]Trento	13,613	5,256	908,700
Tuscany	Florence	22,992	8,877	3,526,000
Umbria	Perugia	8,456	3,265	822,500
Valle d'Aosta	[1]Aosta	3,262	1,259	118,500
Veneto	Venice	18,364	7,090	1,122,300

[1] Special autonomous regions.

Japan: Regions

Region	Chief city	Area		Population (1995)
		sq km	sq mi	
Chubu	Nagoya	66,776	25,782	21,400,000
Chugoku	Hiroshima	31,908	12,320	7,775,000
Hokkaido	Sapporo	83,451	32,220	5,692,000
Kanto	Tokyo	32,418	12,517	39,518,000
Kinki	Osaka	33,094	12,778	22,468,000
Kyushu	Nagasaki	42,154	16,276	13,424,000
Okinawa	Naha	2,265	875	1,274,000
Shikoku	Matsuyama	18,798	7,258	4,183,000
Tohuku	Sendai	66,883	25,824	9,834,000

Mexico: States

State	Capital	Area		Population (1995 est)
		sq km	sq mi	
Aguascalientes	Aguascalientes	5,589	2,157	862,300
Baja California Norte	Mexicali	70,113	27,071	2,108,100
Baja California Sur	La Paz	73,677	28,447	375,450
Campeche	Campeche	51,833	20,013	642,100
Chiapas	Tuxtla Gutiérrez	73,887	28,528	3,606,800
Chihuahua	Chihuahua	247,087	95,400	2,793,000
Coahuila	Saltillo	151,571	58,522	2,172,100
Colima	Colima	5,455	2,106	487,300
Durango	Victoria de Durango	119,648	46,196	1,431,000
Guanajuato	Guanajuato	30,589	11,810	4,393,200
Guerrero	Chilpancingo	63,794	24,631	2,915,500
Hidalgo	Pachuca de Soto	20,987	8,103	2,111,800
Jalisco	Guadalajara	80,137	30,941	5,990,100
México	Toluca de Lerdo	21,461	8,286	11,704,900
Michoacán	Morelia	59,864	23,113	3,869,100
Morelos	Cuernavaca	4,941	1,908	1,442,600
Nayarit	Tepic	27,621	10,664	896,000
Nuevo León	Monterrey	64,555	24,925	3,549,300
Oaxaca	Oaxaca de Juárez	95,364	36,820	3,224,300
Puebla	Puebla (de Zaragoza)	33,919	13,096	4,624,200
Querétaro	Querétaro	11,769	4,544	1,248,800
Quintana Roo	Chetumal	50,350	19,440	703,400
San Luis Potosí	San Luis Potosí	62,848	24,266	2,191,700
Sinaloa	Culiacán Rosales	58,092	22,429	2,424,700
Sonora	Hermosillo	184,934	71,403	2,083,600
Tabasco	Villahermosa	24,661	9,522	1,748,700
Tamaulipas	Ciudad Victoria	79,829	30,821	2,526,400
Tlaxcala	Tlaxcala	3,914	1,511	883,600
Veracruz	Jalapa Enríquez	72,815	28,114	6,734,500
Yucatán	Mérida	39,340	15,189	1,555,700
Zacatecas	Zacatecas	75,040	28,973	1,336,300

Russia: Republics

Republic	Capital	Area sq km	Area sq mi	Population (1995 est)
Adygeya	Maikop	7,600	2,934	451,000
Alania (or North Ossetia)	Vladikavkaz	8,000	3,089	659,000
Altai	Gorno-Altaisk	92,600	35,753	200,000
Bashkortostan	Ufa	143,600	55,444	4,080,000
Buryatia	Ulan-Ude	351,300	135,637	1,053,000
Chechnya	Grozny	16,064	6,202	904,000
Chuvashia	Cheboksary	18,300	7,066	1,361,000
Dagestan	Makhachkala	50,300	19,421	2,067,000
Ingushetia	Nazran	3,236	1,249	280,000
Kabardino-Balkaria	Nalchik	12,500	4,826	790,000
Kalmykia	Elista	76,100	29,382	320,000
Karachai-Cherkessia	Cherkessk	14,100	5,444	436,000
Karelia	Petrozavodsk	172,400	66,564	789,000
Khakassia	Abakan	61,900	23,900	584,000
Komi	Syktyvkar	415,900	160,579	1,202,000
Mari El	Yoshkar-Ola	23,200	8,958	766,000
Mordovia	Saransk	26,200	10,116	959,000
Sakha	Yakutsk	3,103,200	1,198,146	1,036,000
Tatarstan	Kazan	68,000	26,255	3,755,000
Tuva	Kyzyl	170,500	65,830	308,000
Udmurtia	Izhevsk	42,100	16,255	1,641,000

Scotland: Local Government

The Local Government (Scotland) Bill of 1994 abolished the two-tier system of local government. Since April 1996 there have been 32 unitary authorities.

Local authority	Administrative headquarters	Area sq km	Area sq mi	Population (1996)
Aberdeen City	Aberdeen	184	71	219,100
Aberdeenshire	Aberdeen	6,289	2,428	226,500
Angus	Forfar	2,184	843	111,300
Argyll and Bute	Lochgilphead	4,001	1,545	89,300
Clackmannanshire	Alloa	161	62	47,700
Dumfries and Galloway	Dumfries	6,394	2,468	147,800
Dundee City	Dundee	65	25	155,000
East Ayrshire	Kilmarnock	1,271	491	124,000
East Dunbartonshire	Kirkintilloch	202	78	110,000
East Lothian	Haddington	681	263	85,500
East Renfrewshire	Giffnock	172	66	86,800
Edinburgh, City of	Edinburgh	261	101	477,550
Falkirk	Falkirk	294	114	142,500
Fife	Glenrothes	1,340	517	351,200
Glasgow City	Glasgow	177	68	618,400
Highland	Inverness	25,304	9,767	207,500
Inverclyde	Greenock	157	60	90,000
Midlothian	Dalkeith	355	137	79,900
Moray	Elgin	2,217	856	85,000
North Ayrshire	Irvine	878	339	139,200
North Lanarkshire	Motherwell	466	180	326,750
Orkney Islands	Kirkwall	970	375	19,600
Perth and Kinross	Perth	5,328	2,058	131,800

Scotland: Local Government (continued)

Local authority	Administrative headquarters	Area sq km	sq mi	Population (1996)
Renfrewshire	Paisley	261	101	176,970
[1]Scottish Borders	Newtown St Boswells	4,712	1,819	105,300
Shetland Islands	Lerwick	1,400	541	22,500
South Ayrshire	Ayr	1,202	464	114,000
South Lanarkshire	Hamilton	1,776	686	307,100
Stirling	Stirling	2,195	848	82,000
West Dunbartonshire	Dumbarton	155	60	97,800
Western Isles	Stornoway	2,900	1,120	27,800
West Lothian	Livingston	475	183	147,900

[1] 1993 est.

United States of America: States

State	Nickname(s)	Abbreviation	Capital	Area sq km	sq mi	Population (1995)	Joined the union
Alabama	Heart of Dixie/Camellia State	AL	Montgomery	134,700	51,994	4,253,000	1819
Alaska	Mainland State/The Last Frontier	AK	Juneau	1,531,100	591,005	603,600	1959
Arizona	Grand Canyon State/Apache State	AZ	Phoenix	294,100	113,523	4,217,900	1912
Arkansas	Bear State/Land of Opportunity	AR	Little Rock	137,800	53,191	2,483,800	1836
California	Golden State	CA	Sacramento	411,100	158,685	31,589,200	1850
Colorado	Centennial State	CO	Denver	269,700	104,104	3,746,600	1876
Connecticut	Constitution State/Nutmeg State	CT	Hartford	13,000	5,018	3,274,700	1788
Delaware	First State/Diamond State	DE	Dover	5,300	2,046	717,200	1787
Florida	Sunshine State/Everglade State	FL	Tallahassee	152,000	58,672	14,165,600	1845
Georgia	Empire State of the South/Peach State	GA	Atlanta	152,600	58,904	7,200,900	1788
Hawaii	Aloha State	HI	Honolulu	16,800	6,485	1,186,800	1959
Idaho	Gem State	ID	Boise	216,500	83,569	1,163,300	1890
Illinois	Inland Empire/Prairie State/Land of Lincoln	IL	Springfield	146,100	56,395	11,829,900	1818
Indiana	Hoosier State	IN	Indianapolis	93,700	36,168	5,803,500	1816
Iowa	Hawkeye State/Corn State	IA	Des Moines	145,800	56,279	2,841,800	1846
Kansas	Sunflower State/Jayhawker State	KS	Topeka	213,200	82,295	2,565,300	1861
Kentucky	Bluegrass State	KY	Frankfort	104,700	40,414	3,860,200	1792
Louisiana	Pelican State/Sugar State/Creole State	LA	Baton Rouge	135,900	52,457	4,342,300	1812
Maine	Pine Tree State	ME	Augusta	86,200	33,273	1,241,400	1820
Maryland	Old Line State/Free State	MD	Annapolis	31,600	12,198	5,042,400	1788
Massachusetts	Bay State/Old Colony	MA	Boston	21,500	8,299	6,073,550	1788
Michigan	Great Lakes State/Wolverine State	MI	Lansing	151,600	58,518	9,549,400	1837
Minnesota	North Star State/Gopher State	MN	St Paul	218,700	84,418	4,609,500	1858
Mississippi	Magnolia State/Bayou State	MS	Jackson	123,600	47,710	2,697,200	1817
Missouri	Show Me State/Bullion State	MO	Jefferson City	180,600	69,712	5,323,500	1821
Montana	Treasure State/Big Sky Country	MT	Helena	381,200	147,143	870,300	1889
Nebraska	Cornhusker State/Beef State	NE	Lincoln	200,400	77,354	1,637,100	1867
Nevada	Sagebrush State/Silver State/Battleborn State	NV	Carson City	286,400	110,550	1,530,100	1864
New Hampshire	Granite State	NH	Concord	24,000	9,264	1,148,300	1788
New Jersey	Garden State	NJ	Trenton	20,200	7,797	7,945,300	1787
New Mexico	Land of Enchantment/Sunshine State	NM	Santa F	315,000	121,590	1,685,400	1912
New York	Empire State	NY	Albany	127,200	49,099	18,136,100	1788

United Kingdom and Ireland – county boundaries 1974–96

Districts of Northern Ireland

1 LARNE
2 CARRICKFERGUS
3 NEWTOWNABBEY
4 BELFAST
5 CASTLEREAGH
6 NORTH DOWN
7 ARDS
8 DOWN
9 LISBURN
10 ANTRIM
11 BALLYMENA
12 MOYLE
13 BALLYMONEY

14 COLERAINE
15 LIMAVADY
16 DERRY
17 STRABANE
18 MAGHERAFELT
19 COOKSTOWN
20 OMAGH
21 FERMANAGH
22 DUNGANNON
23 ARMAGH
24 CRAIGAVON
25 BANBRIDGE
26 NEWRY AND MOURNE

Counties of England and Wales

1 TYNE AND WEAR
2 CLEVELAND
3 WEST YORKSHIRE
4 SOUTH YORKSHIRE
5 GREATER MANCHESTER
6 MERSEYSIDE
7 NOTTINGHAMSHIRE
8 WEST MIDLANDS
9 WARWICKSHIRE
10 NORTHAMPTONSHIRE
11 BEDFORDSHIRE
12 BUCKINGHAMSHIRE
13 HERTFORDSHIRE
14 BERKSHIRE
15 WEST GLAMORGAN
16 MID GLAMORGAN
17 SOUTH GLAMORGAN

United Kingdom and Ireland – local government divisions 1997

England
1 DARLINGTON
2 HARTLEPOOL
3 STOCKTON-ON-TEES
4 MIDDLESBROUGH
5 REDCAR AND CLEVELAND
6 KINGSTON UPON HULL
7 NORTH EAST LINCOLNSHIRE
8 NORTH LINCOLNSHIRE
9 NOTTINGHAMSHIRE
10 DERBY CITY
11 DERBYSHIRE
12 SOUTH YORKSHIRE
13 WEST YORKSHIRE
14 GREATER MANCHESTER
15 MERSEYSIDE
16 STOKE-ON-TRENT
17 WEST MIDLANDS
18 WARWICKSHIRE
19 LEICESTER CITY
20 LEICESTERSHIRE
21 RUTLAND
22 NORTHAMPTONSHIRE
23 LUTON
24 BEDFORDSHIRE
25 HERTFORDSHIRE
26 MILTON KEYNES
27 BUCKINGHAMSHIRE
28 BERKSHIRE
29 SWINDON
30 BRISTOL
31 SOUTH GLOUCESTERSHIRE
32 BATH AND NE SOMERSET
33 NORTH SOMERSET
34 POOLE
35 BOURNEMOUTH
36 SOUTHAMPTON
37 PORTSMOUTH
38 BRIGHTON AND HOVE

Scotland
1 INVERCLYDE
2 WEST DUNBARTONSHIRE
3 RENFREWSHIRE
4 EAST RENFREWSHIRE
5 GLASGOW CITY
6 EAST DUNBARTONSHIRE
7 NORTH LANARKSHIRE
8 CLACKMANNANSHIRE
9 FALKIRK
10 WEST LOTHIAN
11 CITY OF EDINBURGH
12 MIDLOTHIAN
13 SOUTH LANARKSHIRE
14 EAST AYRSHIRE

Northern Ireland
1 LARNE
2 CARRICKFERGUS
3 NEWTOWNABBEY
4 BELFAST
5 CASTLEREAGH
6 NORTH DOWN
7 ARDS
8 DOWN
9 LISBURN
10 ANTRIM
11 BALLYMENA
12 MOYLE
13 BALLYMONEY
14 COLERAINE
15 LIMAVADY
16 DERRY
17 STRABANE
18 MAGHERAFELT
19 COOKSTOWN
20 OMAGH
21 FERMANAGH
22 DUNGANNON
23 ARMAGH
24 CRAIGAVON
25 BANBRIDGE
26 NEWRY AND MOURNE

Wales
1 SWANSEA
2 NEATH PORT TALBOT
3 BRIDGEND
4 RHONDDA CYNON TAFF
5 VALE OF GLAMORGAN
6 CARDIFF
7 CAERPHILLY
8 MERTHYR TYDFIL
9 BLAENAU GWENT
10 TORFAEN
11 NEWPORT
12 MONMOUTHSHIRE
13 DENBIGHSHIRE
14 WREXHAM
15 FLINTSHIRE

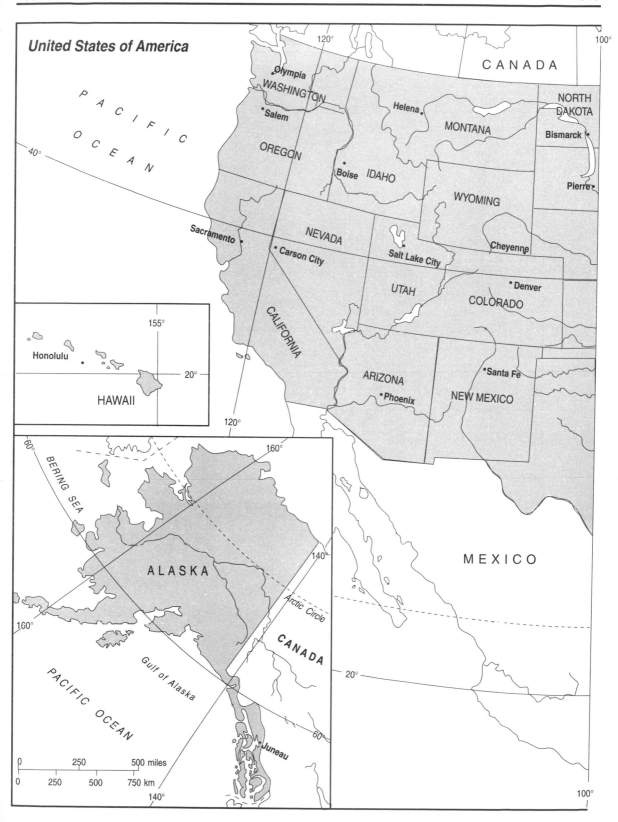

United States of America

PACIFIC OCEAN

40°

120°

100°

CANADA

Olympia
WASHINGTON
Salem

Helena
MONTANA

NORTH DAKOTA
Bismarck

OREGON

Boise
IDAHO

WYOMING

Pierre

Sacramento

NEVADA

Carson City

Salt Lake City

Cheyenne

Denver

UTAH

COLORADO

CALIFORNIA

ARIZONA

Phoenix

Santa Fe

NEW MEXICO

MEXICO

20°

155°

Honolulu

20°

HAWAII

120°

160°

60°
BERING SEA

ALASKA

140°

Arctic Circle

CANADA

160°

Gulf of Alaska

PACIFIC OCEAN

Juneau

60°

20°

0	250	500 miles
0	250	500	750 km

140°

100°

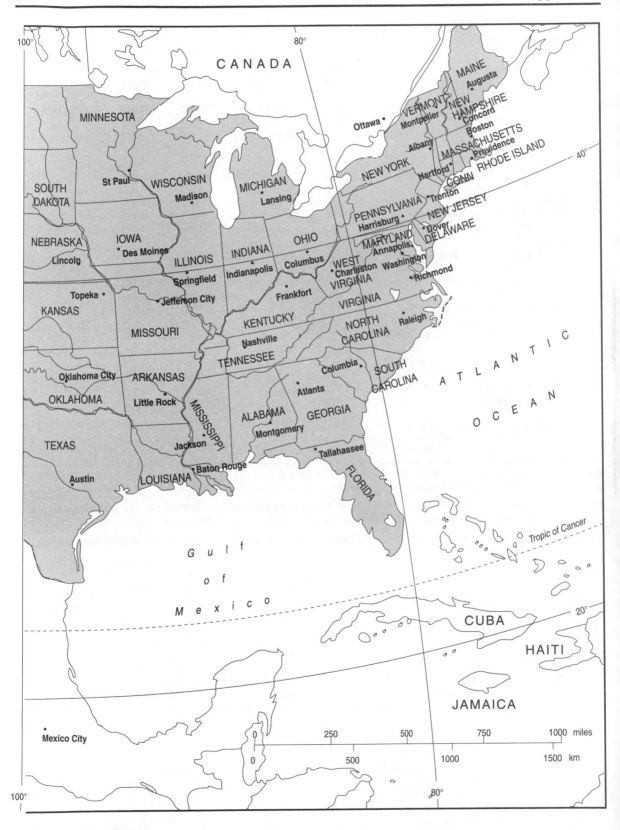

United States of America: States (continued)

State	Nickname(s)	Abbre-viation	Capital	Area sq km	Area sq mi	Population (1995)	Joined the union
North Carolina	Tar Heel State/Old North State	NC	Raleigh	136,400	52,650	7,195,100	1789
North Dakota	Peace Garden State	ND	Bismarck	183,100	70,677	641,400	1889
Ohio	Buckeye State	OH	Columbus	107,100	41,341	11,150,500	1803
Oklahoma	Sooner State	OK	Oklahoma City	181,100	69,905	3,277,700	1907
Oregon	Beaver State/Sunset State	OR	Salem	251,500	97,079	3,140,600	1859
Pennsylvania	Keystone State	PA	Harrisburg	117,400	45,316	12,071,800	1787
Rhode Island	Little Rhody/Ocean State	RI	Providence	3,100	1,197	989,800	1790
South Carolina	Palmetto State	SC	Columbia	80,600	31,112	3,673,300	1788
South Dakota	Coyote State/Mount Rushmore State/Sunshine State	SD	Pierre	199,800	77,123	729,000	1889
Tennessee	Volunteer State	TN	Nashville	109,200	42,151	5,256,100	1796
Texas	Lone Star State	TX	Austin	691,200	266,803	18,724,000	1845
Utah	Beehive State/Mormon State	UT	Salt Lake City	219,900	84,881	1,951,400	1896
Vermont	Green Mountain State	VT	Montpelier	24,900	9,611	584,800	1791
Virginia	Old Dominion State/Mother of Presidents	VA	Richmond	105,600	40,762	6,618,400	1788
Washington	Evergreen State/Chinook State	WA	Olympia	176,700	68,206	5,430,900	1889
West Virginia	Mountain State/Panhandle State	WV	Charleston	62,900	24,279	1,828,100	1863
Wisconsin	Badger State/America's Dairyland	WI	Madison	145,500	56,163	5,122,900	1848
Wyoming	Equality State	WY	Cheyenne	253,400	97,812	480,200	1890
District of Columbia (Federal District) established by Act of Congress 1790–91		DC	Washington	180	69	554,300	1791

Wales: Local Government

In April 1996 the eight counties of Wales – Clwyd, Dyfed, Gwent, Gwynned, Mid Glamorgan, Powys, South Glamorgan, and West Glamorgan – were replaced with 22 counties and county borough unitary authorities.

Local authority	Administrative headquarters	Local authorities	Administrative headquarters
Anglesey, Isle of	Llangefni	Merthyr Tydfil	Merthyr Tydfil
Blaenau Gwent	Ebbw Vale	Monmouthshire	Cwmbran
Bridgend	Bridgend	Neath Port Talbot	Port Talbot
Caerphilly	Hengoed	Newport	Newport
Cardiff	Cardiff	Pembrokeshire	Haverfordwest
Carmarthenshire	Carmarthen	Powys	Llandrindod Wells
Ceredigion	Aberaeron	Rhondda Cynon Taff	Clydach Vale
Conwy	Conwy	Swansea	Swansea
Denbighshire	Ruthin	Torfaen	Pontypool
Flintshire	Mold	Vale of Glamorgan	Barry
Gwynedd	Caernafon	Wrexham	Wrexham

World's Deepest Depressions

Depression	Location	Maximum depth below sea level	
		m	ft
Dead Sea	Israel/Jordan	400	1,312
Turfan Depression	Xinjiang, China	154	505
Lake Assal	Djibouti	153	502
Qattâra Depression	Egypt	133	436
Poloustrov Mangyshlak	Kazakhstan	131	430
Danakil Depression	Ethiopia	120	394
Death Valley	California, USA	86	282
Salton Sink	California, USA	71	233
Zapadnyy Chink Ustyurta	Kazakhstan	70	230
Priaspiyskaya Nizmennost	Russia/Kazakhstan	67	220
Ozera Sarykamysh	Uzbekistan/Kazakhstan	45	148
El Faiyûm	Egypt	44	144
Valdés Peninsula	Argentina	40	131

World's Largest Deserts

Desert	Location	Area	
		sq km	sq mi
Sahara	N Africa	9,065,000	3,500,000
Gobi	Mongolia/NE China	1,295,000	500,000
Patagonian	Argentina	673,000	260,000
Rub al-Khali	S Arabian peninsula	647,500	250,000
Kalahari	SW Africa	582,800	225,000
Chihuahuan	Mexico/SW USA	362,600	140,000
Taklimakan	N China	362,600	140,000
Great Sandy	NW Australia	338,500	150,000
Great Victoria	SW Australia	338,500	150,000
Kyzyl Kum	Uzbekistan/Kazakhstan	259,000	100,000
Thar	India/Pakistan	259,000	100,000
Sonoran	Mexico/SW USA	181,300	70,000
Simpson	Australia	103,600	40,000
Mojave	SW USA	65,000	25,000

[1] Desert areas are very approximate because clear physical boundaries may not occur.

Highest and Lowest Elevations, by Continent

Continent	Highest point	Height		Deepest depression	Depth below sea level	
		m	ft		m	ft
Africa	Mt Kilimanjaro, Tanzania	5,895	19,340	Lake Assal, Djibouti	153	502
Antarctica	Vinson Massif	5,140	16,863	Lake Vostok[1]	4,000	13,123
[1]Asia	Mt Everest, China–Nepal	8,848	29,029	Dead Sea, Israel/Jordan	400	1,312
Europe	Mt Elbrus, Russia	5,642	18,510	Caspian Sea, Azerbaijan/Russia/Kazakhstan/Turkmenistan/Iran	28	92
Oceania	Jaya, New Guinea	5,030	16,502	Lake Eyre, S Australia	16	52
North America	Mt McKinley (AK), USA	6,194	20,321	Death Valley (CA), USA	86	282
South America	Cerro Aconcagua, Argentina	6,960	22,834	Valdés Peninsula, Argentina	40	131

[1] Discovered by the British Antarctic Survey in 1996, the freshwater Lake Vostok lies beneath the ice sheets and covers an area of 14,000 sq km/5,400 sq mi.

World's Largest Islands

Island	Location	Area		Island	Location	Area	
		sq km	sq mi			sq km	sq mi
Greenland	N Atlantic	2,175,600	840,000	Newfoundland	NW Atlantic	108,860	42,030
New Guinea	SW Pacific	800,000	309,000	Luzon	W Pacific	104,688	40,420
Borneo	SW Pacific	744,100	287,300	Iceland	N Atlantic	103,000	39,768
Madagascar	Indian Ocean	587,041	226,657	Mindanao	W Pacific	94,630	36,537
Baffin	Canadian Arctic	507,450	195,875	Ireland (Northern Ireland and the Republic of Ireland)	N Atlantic	84,400	32,600
Sumatra	Indian Ocean	473,600	182,860				
Honshu	NW Pacific	230,966	89,176				
Great Britain	N Atlantic	218,078	84,200	Hokkaido	NW Pacific	83,515	32,245
Victoria	Canadian Arctic	217,206	83,896	Sakhalin	NW Pacific	76,400	29,500
Ellesmere	Canadian Arctic	196,160	75,767	Hispaniola – Dominican Republic and Haiti	Caribbean Sea	76,000	29,300
Sulawesi	Indian Ocean	189,216	73,057				
South Island, New Zealand	SW Pacific	149,883	57,870	Banks	Canadian Arctic	70,000	27,038
Java	Indian Ocean	126,602	48,900	Tasmania	SW Pacific	67,800	26,171
North Island, New Zealand	SW Pacific	114,669	44,274	Sri Lanka	Indian Ocean	64,600	24,900
Cuba	Caribbean Sea	110,860	42,803	Devon	Canadian Arctic	55,247	21,331

Largest Lakes of the World

Lake	Location	Area sq km	sq mi	Lake	Location	Area sq km	sq mi
Caspian Sea	Azerbaijan/Russia/ Kazakhstan/ Turkmenistan/Iran	370,990	143,239	Great Bear	Canada	31,316	12,091
				Nyasa (Malawi)	Malawi/Tanzania/ Mozambique	28,867	11,146
Superior	USA/Canada	82,071	31,688	Great Slave	Canada	28,560	11,027
Victoria	Tanzania/Kenya/Uganda	69,463	26,820	Erie	USA/Canada	25,657	9,906
Aral Sea	Kazakhstan/Uzbekistan	64,500	24,903	Winnipeg	Canada	25,380	9,799
Huron	USA/Canada	59,547	22,991	Ontario	USA/Canada	19,010	7,340
Michigan	USA	57,735	22,291	Balkhash	Kazakhstan	18,421	7,112
Tanganyika	Tanzania/Congo, Democratic Republic of/ Zambia/Burundi	32,880	12,695	Ladoga	Russia	17,695	6,832
				Chad	Chad/Cameroon/Nigeria	16,310	6,297
Baikal	Russia	31,499	12,162	Maracaibo	Venezuela	13,507	5,215

Latitude, Longitude, and Altitude of the World's Major Cities

City	Latitude°		Longitude°		Altitude m	ft
Adelaide, Australia	34	55 S	138	36 E	43	140
Algiers, Algeria	36	50 N	03	00 E	59	194
Almaty, Kazakhstan	43	16 N	76	53 E	775	2,543
Amsterdam, Netherlands	52	22 N	04	53 E	3	10
Ankara, Turkey	39	55 N	32	55 E	862	2,825
Asunción, Paraguay	25	15 S	57	40 W	139	456
Athens, Greece	37	58 N	23	43 E	92	300
Bangkok, Thailand	13	45 N	100	31 E	0	0
Barcelona, Spain	41	23 N	02	09 E	93	305
Beijing, China	39	56 N	116	24 E	183	600
Belfast, Northern Ireland	54	37 N	05	56 W	67	217
Belgrade, Yugoslavia	44	52 N	20	32 E	132	433
Berlin, Germany	52	31 N	13	25 E	34	110
Bogotá, Colombia	04	32 N	74	05 W	2,640	8,660
Bombay, India	18	58 N	72	50 E	8	27
Brussels, Belgium	50	52 N	04	22 E	100	328
Bucharest, Romania	44	25 N	26	07 E	92	302
Budapest, Hungary	47	30 N	19	05 E	139	456
Buenos Aires, Argentina	34	36 S	58	28 W	0	0
Cairo, Egypt	30	03 N	31	15 E	116	381
Cape Town, South Africa	33	55 S	18	22 E	17	56
Caracas, Venezuela	10	28 N	67	02 W	1,042	3,418
Copenhagen, Denmark	55	40 N	12	34 E	9	33
Dakar, Senegal	14	40 N	17	28 W	40	131
Delhi, India	28	35 N	77	12 E	218	714
Detroit (MI), USA	42	19 N	83	02 W	178	585
Djibouti, Djibouti	11	30 N	43	03 E	7	23
Dublin, Republic of Ireland	53	20 N	06	15 W	47	154
Edinburgh, Scotland	55	55 N	03	10 W	134	440
Frankfurt, Germany	50	07 N	08	41 E	103	338
Guatemala City, Guatemala	14	37 N	90	31 W	1,480	4,855
Havana, Cuba	23	08 N	82	23 W	24	80
Helsinki, Finland	60	10 N	25	00 E	46	151
Hong Kong	22	18 N	114	10 E	33	109
Istanbul, Turkey	41	06 N	29	03 E	114	374

Latitude, Longitude, and Altitude of the World's Major Cities (continued)

City	Latitude°		Longitude°		Altitude	
					m	ft
Jakarta, Indonesia	06	10 S	106	48 E	8	26
Jerusalem, Israel	31	46 N	35	14 E	762	2,500
Johannesburg, South Africa	26	12 S	28	05 E	1,750	5,740
Kabul, Afghanistan	34	30 N	69	13 E	1,827	5,955
Katmandu, Nepal	27	43 S	85	19 E	1,372	4,500
Karachi, Pakistan	24	48 N	66	59 E	4	13
Kiev, Ukraine	50	26 N	30	31 E	179	587
Kinshasa, Democratic Republic of Congo	04	18 S	15	17 E	322	1066
Lagos, Nigeria	06	27 N	03	24 E	3	10
La Paz, Bolivia	16	27 S	68	22 W	3,658	12,001
Lhasa, Tibet	29	40 N	91	07 E	3,685	12,090
Lima, Peru	12	00 S	77	02 W	120	394
Lisbon, Portugal	38	44 N	09	09 W	77	253
London, UK	51	32 N	00	05 W	75	245
Los Angeles (CA), USA	34	03 N	118	14 W	104	340
Madrid, Spain	40	26 N	03	42 W	660	2,165
Manila, Philippines	14	35 N	120	57 E	14	47
Mecca, Saudi Arabia	21	27 S	39	49 E	2,000	6,562
Melbourne, Australia	37	47 N	144	58 E	35	115
Mexico City, Mexico	19	24 N	99	09 W	2,239	7,347
Milan, Italy	45	27 S	09	10 E	121	397
Montevideo, Uruguay	34	53 N	56	10 W	22	72
Moscow, Russia	55	45 N	37	35 E	120	394
Nagasaki, Japan	32	48 S	129	57 E	133	436
Nairobi, Kenya	01	25 N	36	55 E	1,820	5,971
New Delhi, India	28	36 N	77	12 E	235	770
New York (NY), USA	40	45 N	73	59 W	17	55
Oslo, Norway	59	57 N	10	42 E	94	308
Ottawa, Canada	45	26 N	75	41 W	56	185
Panama City, Panama	08	58 N	79	32 W	0	0
Paris, France	48	52 N	02	20 E	92	300
Prague, Czech Republic	50	05 N	14	26 E	262	860
Quito, Ecuador	0	13 S	78	30 W	2,811	9,222
Reykjavík, Iceland	64	04 N	21	58 W	18	59
Rio de Janeiro, Brazil	22	43 S	43	13 W	9	30
Rome, Italy	41	53 N	12	30 E	29	95
St Petersburg, Russia	59	56 N	30	18 E	4	13
Santiago, Chile	33	27 S	70	40 W	1,500	4,921
Seoul, South Korea	37	34 N	127	00 E	10	34
Shanghai, China	31	10 N	121	28 E	7	23
Singapore	01	14 N	103	55 E	10	33
Sofia, Bulgaria	42	40 N	23	20 E	550	1,805
Stockholm, Sweden	59	17 N	18	03 E	44	144
Sydney, Australia	33	53 S	151	12 E	8	25
Tehran, Iran	35	40 N	51	26 E	1,110	3,937
Tokyo, Japan	35	42 N	139	46 E	9	30
Toronto, Canada	43	39 N	79	23 W	91	300
Tripoli, Libya	32	54 N	13	11 E	0	0
Vancouver, Canada	49	18 N	123	04 W	43	141
Vienna, Austria	48	14 N	16	20 E	203	666
Warsaw, Poland	52	15 N	21	00 E	110	360
Washington, DC, USA	38	53 N	77	00 W	8	25
Wellington, New Zealand	41	18 S	174	47 E	0	0
Zürich, Switzerland	47	21 N	08	31 E	493	1,618

World's Highest Mountains, with First Ascents

Mountain	Location	Height		Year of	Expedition nationality/leader
		m	ft	first ascent	
Everest	China/Nepal	8,848	29,029	1953	British/New Zealander (J Hunt)
K2	Kashmir/Jammu	8,611	28,251	1954	Italian (A Desio)
Kangchenjunga	India/Nepal	8,598	28,208	1955	British (C Evans; by way of SW face)
Lhotse	China/Nepal	8,511	27,923	1956	Swiss (E Reiss)
Yalung Kang (formerly Kangchenjunga West Peak)	India/Nepal	8,502	27,893	1973	Japanese (Y Ageta)
Kangchenjunga South Peak	India/Nepal	8,488	27,847	1978	Polish (W Wróż)
Makalu I	China/Nepal	8,481	27,824	1955	French (J Couzy)
Kangchenjunga Middle Peak	India/Nepal	8,475	27,805	1973	Polish (W Wróż)
Lhotse Shar	China/Nepal	8,383	27,503	1970	Austrian (S Mayerl)
Dhaulagiri	Nepal	8,172	26,811	1960	Swiss/Austrian (K Diemberger)
Manaslu	Nepal	8,156	26,759	1956	Japanese (T Imanishi)
Cho Oyu	China/Nepal	8,153	26,748	1954	Austrian (H Tichy)
Nanga Parbat	Kashmir/Jammu	8,126	26,660	1953	German (K M Herrligkoffer)
Annapurna I	Nepal	8,078	26,502	1950	French (M Herzog)
Gasherbrum I	Kashmir/Jammu	8,068	26,469	1958	American (P K Schoening; by the SW ridge)
Broad Peak	Kashmir/Jammu	8,047	26,401	1957	Austrian (M Schmuck)
Gasherbrum II	Kashmir/Jammu	8,034	26,358	1956	Austrian (S Larch; by the SW spur)
Gosainthan	China	8,012	26,286	1964	Chinese (195-strong team; accounts are inconclusive)
Broad Peak (Middle)	Kashmir/Jammu	8,000	26,246	1975	Polish (K Głazek)
Gasherbrum III	Kashmir/Jammu	7,952	26,089	1975	Polish (J Onyszkiewicz)
Annapurna II	Nepal	7,937	26,040	1960	British (C Bonington)
Gasherbrum IV	Kashmir/Jammu	7,923	25,994	1958	Italian (W Bonatti, C Mouri)
Gyachung Kang	Nepal	7,921	25,987	1964	Japanese (Y Kato, K Sakaizqwa)
Disteghil Shar	Kashmir	7,884	25,866	1960	Austrian (G Stärker, D Marchart)
Himalchuli	Nepal	7,864	25,800	1960	Japanese (M Harada, H Tanabe)
Nuptse	Nepal	7,841	25,725	1961	British (D Davis, C Bonington, L Brown)
Manaslu II	Nepal	7,835	25,705	1970	Japanese (H Watanabe, Lhakpa Tsering)
Masherbrum East	Kashmir	7,821	25,659	1960	Pakistani/American (G Bell, W Unsoeld)
Nanda Devi	India	7,817	25,646	1936	British (H W Tilman)
Chomo Lonzo	Nepal	7,815	25,639	1954	French (J Couzy, L Terry)

Oceans and Seas

Ocean/sea	Area		Average depth	
	sq km	sq mi	m	ft
Pacific Ocean	166,242,000	64,186,300	3,939	12,925
Atlantic Ocean	86,557,000	33,420,000	3,575	11,730
Indian Ocean	73,427,500	28,350,500	3,840	12,598
Arctic Ocean	13,224,000	5,105,700	1,038	3,407
South China Sea	2,975,000	1,148,500	1,464	4,802
Caribbean Sea	2,516,000	971,400	2,575	8,448
Mediterranean Sea	2,510,000	969,100	1,501	4,926
Bering Sea	2,261,000	873,000	1,491	4,893
Gulf of Mexico	1,508,000	582,100	1,614	5,297
Sea of Okhotsk	1,392,000	537,500	973	3,192
Sea of Japan	1,013,000	391,100	1,667	5,468
Hudson Bay	730,000	281,900	93	305
East China Sea	665,000	256,600	189	620
Andaman Sea	565,000	218,100	1,118	3,667
Black Sea	508,000	196,100	1,190	3,906
Red Sea	453,000	174,900	538	1,764

Oceans and Seas (continued)

Ocean/sea	Area		Average depth	
	sq km	sq mi	m	ft
North Sea	427,000	164,900	94	308
Baltic Sea	382,000	147,500	55	180
Yellow Sea	294,000	113,500	37	121
Persian Gulf	230,000	88,800	100	328
Gulf of St Lawrence	162,000	62,530	810	2,660
Gulf of California	153,000	59,100	724	2,375
English Channel	89,900	34,700	54	177
Irish Sea	88,550	34,200	60	197
Bass Strait	75,000	28,950	70	230

World's Longest Rivers

River	Location	Approximate length	
		km	mi
Nile	Africa	6,695	4,160
Amazon	South America	6,570	4,083
Chang Jiang (Yangtze)	China	6,300	3,915
Mississipi–Missouri–Red Rock	USA	6,020	3,741
Huang He (Yellow River)	China	5,464	3,395
Ob–Irtysh	China/Kazakhstan/Russia	5,410	3,362
Amur–Shilka	Asia	4,416	2,744
Lena	Russia	4,400	2,734
Congo–Zaire	Africa	4,374	2,718
Mackenzie–Peace–Finlay	Canada	4,241	2,635
Mekong	Asia	4,180	2,597
Niger	Africa	4,100	2,548
Yenisei	Russia	4,100	2,548
Paraná	Brazil	3,943	2,450
Mississippi	USA	3,779	2,348
Murray–Darling	Australia	3,751	2,331
Missouri	USA	3,726	2,315
Volga	Russia	3,685	2,290
Madeira	Brazil	3,241	2,014
Purus	Brazil	3,211	1,995
São Francisco	Brazil	3,199	1,988
Yukon	USA/Canada	3,185	1,979
Rio Grande	USA/Mexico	3,058	1,900
Indus	Tibet/Pakistan	2,897	1,800
Danube	Central and E Europe	2,858	1,776
Japura	Brazil	2,816	1,750
Salween	Myanmar/China	2,800	1,740
Brahmaputra	Asia	2,736	1,700
Euphrates	Iraq	2,736	1,700
Tocantins	Brazil	2,699	1,677
Zambezi	Africa	2,650	1,647
Orinoco	Venezuela	2,559	1,590
Paraguay	Paraguay	2,549	1,584
Amu Darya	Tajikistan/Turkmenistan/Uzbekistan	2,540	1,578
Ural	Russia/Kazakhstan	2,535	1,575
Kolyma	Russia	2,513	1,562
Ganges	India/Bangladesh	2,510	1,560
Arkansas	USA	2,344	1,459
Colorado	USA	2,333	1,450
Dnieper	Russia/Belarus/Ukraine	2,285	1,420
Syr Darya	Asia	2,205	1,370
Irrawaddy	Myanmar	2,152	1,337
Orange	South Africa	2,092	1,300

World's Highest Waterfalls

Waterfall	Location	Total drop	
		m	ft
Angel Falls	Venezuela	979	3,212
Yosemite Falls	USA	739	2,425
Mardalsfossen–South	Norway	655	2,149
Tugela Falls	South Africa	614	2,014
Cuquenan	Venezuela	610	2,000
Sutherland	New Zealand	580	1,903
Ribbon Fall, Yosemite	USA	491	1,612
Great Karamang River Falls	Guyana	488	1,600
Mardalsfossen–North	Norway	468	1,535
Della Falls	Canada	440	1,443
Gavarnie Falls	France	422	1,385
Skjeggedal	Norway	420	1,378
Glass Falls	Brazil	404	1,325
Krimml	Austria	400	1,312
Trummelbach Falls	Switzerland	400	1,312
Takkakaw Falls	Canada	366	1,200
Silver Strand Falls, Yosemite	USA	357	1,170
Wallaman Falls	Australia	346	1,137
Wollomombi	Australia	335	1,100
Cusiana River Falls	Colombia	300	984
Giessbach	Switzerland	300	984
Skykkjedalsfossen	Norway	300	984
Staubbach	Switzerland	300	984

The World's Largest Cities 1950–2015

Source: UN Department for Economic and Social Information

Rank	City	Population (millions)
1950		
1	New York (NY), USA	12.30
2	London, UK	8.70
3	Tokyo, Japan	6.90
4=	Paris, France	5.40
4=	Moscow, Russia	5.40
6=	Shanghai, China	5.30
6=	Essen, Germany	5.30
8	Buenos Aires, Argentina	5.00
9	Chicago (IL), USA	4.90
10	Calcutta, India	4.40
1980		
1	Tokyo, Japan	21.90
2	New York (NY), USA	15.60
3	Mexico City, Mexico	13.90
4	São Paulo, Brazil	12.10
5	Shanghai, China	11.70
6	Osaka, Japan	10.00
7	Buenos Aires, Argentina	9.90
8	Los Angeles (CA), USA	9.50
9=	Calcutta, India	9.00
9=	Beijing, China	9.00
1995		
1	Tokyo, Japan	26.84
2	São Paulo, Brazil	16.42
3	New York (NY), USA	16.33
4	Mexico City, Mexico	15.64
5	Bombay, India	15.09
6	Shanghai, China	15.08
7	Los Angeles (CA), USA	12.41
8	Beijing, China	12.36
9	Calcutta, India	11.67
10	Seoul, South Korea	11.64
2000		
1	Tokyo, Japan	27.90
2	Bombay, India	18.10
3	São Paulo, Brazil	17.80
4	Shanghai, China	17.20
5	New York (NY), USA	16.60
6	Mexico City, Mexico	16.40
7	Beijing, China	14.20
8	Jakarta, Indonesia	14.10
9	Lagos, Nigeria	13.50
10	Los Angeles (CA), USA	13.10
2010		
1	Tokyo, Japan	28.70
2	Bombay, India	24.30
3	Shanghai, China	21.50
4	Lagos, Nigeria	20.80
5	São Paulo, Brazil	20.10
6	Jakarta, Indonesia	19.20
7	Mexico City, Mexico	18.20
8	Beijing, China	17.80
9	Karachi, Pakistan	17.60
10	New York (NY), USA	17.30
2015		
1	Tokyo, Japan	28.70
2	Bombay, India	27.40
3	Lagos, Nigeria	24.40
4	Shanghai, China	23.40
5	Jakarta, Indonesia	21.20
6	São Paulo, Brazil	20.80
7	Karachi, Pakistan	20.60
8	Beijing, China	19.40
9	Dhaka, Bangladesh	19.00
10	Mexico City, Mexico	18.80

Largest Countries by Area

Rank	Country	Area	
		sq km	sq mi
1	Russia	17,075,500	6,591,100
2	Canada	9,970,610	3,849,674
3	China	9,571,300	3,695,479
4	USA	9,372,615	3,618,767
5	Brazil	8,511,965	3,285,618
6	Australia	7,682,300	2,966,136
7	India	3,166,829	1,222,396
8	Argentina	2,780,092	1,073,116
9	Kazakhstan	2,717,300	1,049,150
10	Sudan	2,505,800	967,489
11	Algeria	2,381,741	919,352
12	Congo, Democratic Republic of	2,344,900	905,366
13	Saudi Arabia	2,200,518	849,400
14	Mexico	1,958,201	756,198
15	Indonesia	1,904,569	735,354
16	Libya	1,759,540	679,182
17	Iran	1,648,000	636,128
18	Mongolia	1,565,000	604,480
19	Peru	1,285,200	496,216
20	Chad	1,284,000	495,621

Smallest Countries by Area

Rank	Country	Area	
		sq km	sq mi
1	Vatican City State	0.4	0.2
2	San Marino	61	24
3	Liechtenstein	160	62
4	Marshall Islands	181	70
5	St Kitts and Nevis	262	101
6	Maldives	298	115
7	Malta	320	124
8	Grenada	344	133
9	St Vincent and the Grenadines	388	150
10	Barbados	430	166
11	Antigua and Barbuda	441	170
12	Seychelles	453	175
13	Andorra	468	181
14	St Lucia	617	238
15	Singapore	622	240
16	Bahrain	688	266
17	Micronesia	700	270
18	Kiribati	717	277
19	Tonga	750	290
20	Dominica	751	290

Human Development Index

Source: UN Development Programme

The Human Development Index (HDI) is based on three indicators: longevity, as measured by life expectancy; educational attainment, as measured by a combination of adult literacy and combined primary, secondary, and tertiary enrolment ratios; and standard of living, as measured by real GDP per capita (PPP $).

Country	1993	1994
Industrialized Countries		
Canada	1	1
France	7	2
Norway	5	3
USA	2	4
Iceland	8	5
Netherlands	4	6
Japan	3	7
Finland	6	8
New Zealand	14	9
Sweden	9	10
Spain	10	11
Austria	13	12
Belgium	12	13
Australia	11	14
UK	16	15
Switzerland	15	16
Ireland, Republic of	19	17
Denmark	17	18
Germany	18	19
Greece	21	20
Developing Countries		
Hong Kong	22	22
Cyprus	23	24
Barbados	25	25
Singapore	34	26
Bahamas	26	28
Antigua and Barbuda	40	29
Chile	33	30
Korea, South	29	32
Costa Rica	31	33
Argentina	30	36
Uruguay	32	37
Brunei	36	38
Trinidad and Tobago	38	40
Dominica	65	41
Bahrain	39	43
United Arab Emirates	42	44
Panama	43	45
Fiji	47	46
Venezuela	44	47
St Kitts and Nevis	45	49

Estimated Populations of Indigenous Peoples

Source: World Directory of Minorities
© Minority Rights Group (edited and published by Minority Rights Group International, 1997, London, UK)
(Data for selected countries. Data from early-mid 1990s.)

Country/territory	Indigenous peoples	Estimated numbers (thousands)	% of total population
Australia	Aborigines	250	1.40
	Torres Strait Islanders	26	0.14
	South Sea Islanders	11	0.06
Bhutan	various	170	10.00
Bolivia	Aymara, Quechua, Chiquitano, Guaraní, Moxeño, and others	4,100	65.00
Cambodia	Cham and indigenous hill peoples	510	5.00
Canada	First Nations (including Huétis and Inuit)	1,000–1,200	3–4.10
Chile	Mapuche, Aymara, Rapanui, and others	990	7.00
Colombia	Arhuaco, Embera, Guambiano, Wayúu, Nukak, Kuna, Kogi, Paez, Zenu, and others	620	1.70
Costa Rica	various	25	0.78
El Salvador	Pipil, Pocoman, and Lenca	324–1,080	6–20.00
French Guiana	various (Maroons – no data)	4	3.60
Guatemala	Maya	5,782	59.00
	Garítuna	6	0.05
India	Adivasis (scheduled tribes)	69,000	7.50
	(including Nagas)	700	0.10
Indonesia	Batak	3,300	1.60
	Dayak	4,100	2.00
	Achnese	3,700	1.80
	Minangkabau	3,700	1.80
	Sundanese	30,500	15.00
	West Irians	1,200	0.60
Malaysia	Orang Asli	86	0.50
	Kadazan-Dusun	400	2.10
	Bajau	240	1.26
	Murut	64	0.34
	Dayak-Iban	570	3.00
	Malays	399	2.10
	Bidayuh	171	0.90
Mexico	56 indigenous peoples	10,000–20,000	10.8–23.80
Papua New Guinea	Bougainvilleans	159	4.00
Paraguay	Guaraní, Ayoreo, Toba-Maskoy, Aché, Sanapan, and others	95	2.30
Peru	Aguaruna, Ashaninka, Huambisa, Quechua, Aymara, and others	8,800	39.20
Philippines	various	2,050	3.00
Russia	Nenets	34	0.02
	Evenk	30	0.02
	Chukchi	15	0.01
	Koriaks	9	<0.01
Taiwan	Atayal, Bunun, Tsou, Paiwan, Rukai, Puyuma, Am, Yami, Saisiyat, and others	423	2.00
USA	Native Americans (including 240,000 Native Hawaiians and 80,000 Inuit and Alaska Natives)	1,960	0.79

Birth and Death Rates

Source: UN Population Division
(Data are for live births. Only selected countries are listed.)

1990–95

Country/region	Birth rate (per 1,000)	Death rate (per 1,000)
Africa		
Algeria	31	6
Angola	51	19
Burundi	46	20
Congo, Democratic Republic of	48	15
Côte d'Ivoire	39	13
Ethiopia	49	18
Ghana	40	12
Kenya	38	12
Lesotho	37	11
Nigeria	45	15
Sudan	35	14
Total	41	14
Asia		
Afghanistan	50	22
Bangladesh	27	11
China	18	7
India	27	10
Indonesia	25	8
Iran	38	7
Iraq	38	10
Japan	10	7
Korea, North	22	5
Korea, South	16	6
Pakistan	39	9
Philippines	31	6
Total	24	8
Europe		
France	13	9
Germany	10	12
Greece	10	10
Hungary	11	15
Russia	11	13
Sweden	14	11
UK	13	11
Total	11	11
Latin America		
Argentina	21	8
Bolivia	36	10
Brazil	22	7
Colombia	26	6
Cuba	15	7
Mexico	27	5
Venezuela	27	5
Total	25	7

Country/region	Birth rate (per 1,000)	Death rate (per 1,000)
North America		
Canada	14	7
USA	16	9
Total	15	9
Oceania		
Australia	15	7
New Zealand	17	8
Papua New Guinea	33	11
Total	19	8
World		
More developed regions	12	10
Less developed regions	27	9
Least developed regions	40	15
World total	24	9

Births to Teenage Mothers: Developing Countries

Source: UN Population Fund
(Data for women aged 15–19. The measure does not indicate the full dimensions of teen pregnancy as only live births are included in the numerator. Stillbirths and spontaneous or induced abortions are not reflected.)

1990–95

Rank	Country/territory	Number of births (per 1,000 women)
	Africa	
1	Guinea	241
2	Angola	236
3	Congo, Democratic Republic of	231
4	Liberia	230
5	Niger	219
6	Sierra Leone	212
7	Somalia	208
8	Mali	199
9	Equatorial Guinea	192
10	Guinea-Bissau	189
11	Uganda	180
Average		130
	Asia	
1	Afghanistan	153
2	Bangladesh	138
3	Saudi Arabia	124
4	Oman	122
5	India	116
6	Yemen	102
7	Iran	96
8	Pakistan	93
9	Nepal	92
10	Bhutan	86
Average		57

Rank	Country/territory	Number of births (per 1,000 women)	Rank	Country/territory	Number of births (per 1,000 women)
	Latin America and the Caribbean			**Oceania**	
1	Nicaragua	149	1	Solomon Islands	99
2	Honduras	127	2	Vanuatu	75
3	Guatemala	123	3	French Polynesia	73
4	Belize	117	4	Micronesia	65
5	El Salvador	105	5	New Caledonia	53
6	Venezuela	101	6	Polynesia	50
7	Jamaica	95	7	Fiji	46
8	Costa Rica	93	8	Melanesia	34
Average		78	**Average**		28

Births to Teenage Mothers: Developed Countries

1990–95 Country	Number of births (per 1,000 women)	Country	Number of births (per 1,000 women)
USA	64	Canada	27
Bulgaria	59	Portugal	25
Czech Republic	46	Austria	23
Slovak Republic	44	Greece	22
Ukraine	43	Australia	21
Yugoslavia	43	Israel	20
Hungary	41	Norway	19
Macedonia, Former Yugoslav Republic of	41	Ireland, Republic of	16
Romania	41	Finland	13
Moldova	38	Germany	13
Russia	37	Luxembourg	13
Latvia	35	Sweden	13
New Zealand	35	Malta	12
Estonia	34	Spain	12
Bosnia-Herzegovina	33	Belgium	10
UK	33	Denmark	10
Croatia	32	France	9
Lithuania	32	Italy	9
Slovenia	30	Netherlands	7
Iceland	29	Switzerland	5
Belarus	28	Japan	4
Poland	28		

Dependency Ratios

Source: UN Department for Economic and Social Information
(Dependency ratio is the ratio of the population under 15 and over 65 to the population aged 15–64.)

Region	Age	Dependency ratio per 100		
		1995	2025	2050
Africa				
Eastern Africa	0–14	91.2	64.5	36.5
	>65	5.5	5.5	9.9
Total		96.6	70.0	46.4
Northern Africa	0–14	67.9	40.8	32.6
	>65	6.7	10.1	18.9
Total		74.6	50.9	51.5
Southern Africa	0–14	65.6	43.7	33.4
	>65	7.4	10.0	17.5
Total		73.0	53.7	50.8
Western Africa	0–14	89.6	65.7	36.7
	>65	5.4	6.1	9.5
Total		95.1	71.8	46.1
Total	0–14	83.4	59.5	36.0
	>65	6.0	6.9	11.4
Total		89.4	66.4	47.4
Asia				
Eastern Asia	0–14	37.6	29.6	30.7
	>65	10.0	19.2	30.7
Total		47.6	48.8	61.4
South-central Asia	0–14	63.3	36.8	30.7
	>65	7.3	10.8	20.6
Total		70.6	47.6	51.3
Southeast Asia	0–14	57.1	35.1	31.4
	>65	7.0	11.5	22.6
Total		64.1	46.6	53.9
Western Asia	0–14	65.9	46.2	32.7
	>65	7.6	10.8	17.2
Total		73.5	57.0	49.9
Total	0–14	51.1	34.6	30.9
	>65	8.5	13.9	23.7
Total		59.6	48.4	54.7
Europe				
Eastern Europe	0–14	31.4	26.7	30.2
	>65	18.5	26.8	35.3
Total		49.9	53.5	65.5
Northern Europe	0–14	30.2	29.3	30.7
	>65	23.3	30.8	37.2
Total		53.5	60.0	67.9
Southern Europe	0–14	25.3	21.6	27.0
	>65	21.3	34.5	54.5
Total		46.6	56.1	81.5
Western Europe	0–14	26.2	24.4	28.4
	>65	22.1	35.4	47.1
Total		48.3	59.8	75.5

Region	Age	Dependency ratio per 100		
		1995	2025	2050
Total	0–14	28.7	25.5	29.3
	>65	20.6	30.9	41.7
Total		49.3	56.4	71.0
Latin America and the Caribbean				
Caribbean	0–14	48.3	38.5	32.9
	>65	10.2	16.3	25.0
Total		58.8	54.9	57.9
Central America	0–14	64.1	37.3	31.8
	>65	7.0	12.1	24.6
Total		71.1	49.4	56.3
South America	0–14	53.0	34.4	31.3
	>65	8.9	15.5	27.2
Total		61.8	49.9	58.5
Total	0–14	55.4	35.5	31.6
	>65	8.5	14.6	26.3
Total		63.9	50.1	57.8
Northern America				
Total	0–14	33.5	31.6	31.1
	>65	19.2	29.2	34.6
Total		52.7	60.7	65.7
Oceania				
Australia/New Zealand	0–14	32.8	30.7	30.9
	>65	17.4	27.0	37.2
Total		50.2	57.7	68.0
Total	0–14	40.4	34.6	31.6
	>65	14.8	21.3	29.6
Total		55.2	55.9	61.2
World				
[1]More developed regions	0–14	29.4	27.2	29.9
	>65	20.1	31.4	40.4
Total		49.5	58.6	70.3
[2]Less developed regions	0–14	57.0	39.7	32.3
	>65	7.7	12.1	20.4
Total		64.7	51.8	52.8
[3]Least developed countries	0–14	81.9	57.0	35.4
	>65	5.6	6.5	11.5
Total		87.5	63.5	46.9
Total	0–14	50.9	37.9	32.1
	>65	10.5	14.9	22.7
Total		61.4	52.8	54.7

[1] More developed regions comprise Northern America, Japan, Europe, and Australia and New Zealand.
[2] Less developed regions comprise all regions of Africa, Asia (excluding Japan), Latin America and the Caribbean, Melanesia, Micronesia, and Polynesia.
[3] Least developed countries according to standard UN designation.

Countries with the Fastest and Slowest Growing Populations

Source: UN Population Fund

1995–2000

Fastest Growing Populations			Slowest Growing Populations		
Rank	Country	Average population growth rate (%)	Rank	Country	Average population growth rate (%)
1	Afghanistan	5.6	1	Latvia	−0.7
2	Bosnia-Herzegovina	4.5	2	Estonia	−0.5
3	Oman	3.9	3=	Croatia	−0.3
4	Saudi Arabia	3.5	3=	Hungary	−0.3
5	Mozambique	3.4	3=	Yugoslavia	−0.3
6=	Angola	3.3	6=	Romania	−0.2
6=	Jordan	3.3	6=	Russia	−0.2
6=	Libya	3.3	6=	Ukraine	−0.2
6=	Niger	3.3	9=	Belarus	−0.1
6=	Syria	3.3	9=	Denmark	−0.1
11=	Côte d'Ivoire	3.2	11=	Germany	0.0
11=	Kuwait	3.2	11=	Italy	0.0
11=	Liberia	3.2	11=	Lithuania	0.0
11=	Yemen	3.2	11=	Portugal	0.0
15=	Madagascar	3.1	11=	Slovenia	0.0
15=	Nicaragua	3.1	16=	Czech Republic	0.1
15=	Somalia	3.1	16=	Spain	0.1
18=	Iraq	3.0	18=	Greece	0.2
18=	Mali	3.0	18=	Japan	0.2
18=	Togo	3.0	18=	Poland	0.2

World Population Growth, Major Areas

Source: UN Population Division

Region	1750	1800	1850	1900	1950	1994	2000	2050
Population Size (Millions)								
Africa	106	107	111	133	224	708	833	2,145
Asia	502	635	809	947	1,403	3,403	3,744	5,761
Europe	163	203	276	408	549	726	730	678
Latin America and the Caribbean	16	24	38	74	166	474	524	839
Northern America	2	7	26	82	166	290	306	839
Oceania	2	2	6	13	28	31	46	389
Total	791	978	1,262	1,650	2,520	5,630	6,168	9,857
% Distribution								
Africa	13.4	10.9	8.8	8.1	8.9	12.6	13.5	21.8
Asia	63.5	64.9	64.1	57.4	55.7	60.4	60.7	58.4
Europe	20.6	20.8	21.9	24.7	21.8	12.9	11.8	6.9
Latin America and the Caribbean	2.0	2.5	3.0	4.5	6.6	8.4	8.5	8.5
North America	0.3	0.7	2.1	5.0	6.6	5.2	5.0	3.9
Oceania	0.3	0.2	0.2	0.4	0.5	0.5	0.5	0.5

World Population Growth Rates and Percentage Increases

Source: UN Population Division

Region	Growth rate 1950–94	% increase	1950–94	1994–2050	1950–2050
Africa	2.62	217	202	858	
Asia	2.01	143	69	311	
Europe	0.64	32	–7	24	
Latin America and the Caribbean	2.38	186	77	406	
North America	1.27	75	34	134	
Oceania	1.74	123	64	265	

Urban Population Growth

Source: UN Population Division
(Table shows trends, size, and growth of urban population.)

Country/region	Level of urbanization Total number in millions			Urban population % annual growth rate			% of total population in urban settlements	
	1975	2000	2025	1975	2000	2025	1975–2000	2000–25
Africa								
Algeria	40.33	59.65	74.05	6.4	18.5	33.6	4.23	2.38
Angola	17.79	36.17	55.59	1.1	4.7	14.8	5.88	4.56
Cameroon	26.87	49.33	66.86	2.0	7.5	19.5	5.25	3.81
Congo, Democratic Republic of	29.50	31.03	49.82	6.8	15.8	52.1	3.35	4.76
Côte d'Ivoire	32.09	46.95	64.13	2.1	7.8	23.6	5.16	4.40
Egypt	43.45	46.36	62.20	16.8	32.0	60.5	2.57	2.54
Ghana	30.06	39.17	57.74	2.9	7.9	21.9	3.93	4.08
Kenya	12.92	31.76	51.48	1.7	10.3	32.6	7.05	4.59
Libya	60.95	88.35	92.75	1.5	5.6	11.9	5.32	3.00
Mozambique	8.62	41.07	61.09	0.9	7.8	21.5	8.62	4.05
Nigeria	23.38	43.29	61.64	14.6	55.7	146.9	5.34	3.88
Tanzania	10.08	28.20	48.25	1.6	9.6	30.3	7.17	4.60
Total	25.15	37.30	53.77	104.1	310.1	804.2	4.37	3.81
Asia								
Bangladesh	9.28	21.28	39.99	7.1	28.6	78.4	5.57	4.03
China	17.25	34.49	54.51	106.0	443.0	831.8	4.07	2.52
India	21.31	28.56	45.24	132.3	291.9	629.7	3.17	3.08
Indonesia	19.36	40.34	60.74	26.2	85.8	167.4	4.74	2.67
Iran	45.82	61.86	74.86	15.3	46.2	92.5	4.42	2.78
Japan	75.69	78.39	84.86	84.4	99.1	103.2	0.64	0.16
Korea, South	48.04	86.22	93.70	16.9	40.6	50.9	3.50	0.91
Pakistan	26.40	37.85	56.73	19.7	61.2	161.6	4.53	3.88
Philippines	35.56	59.01	74.26	15.3	44.0	77.6	4.23	2.27
Thailand	15.10	21.90	39.08	6.2	13.5	28.7	3.10	3.01
Total	24.62	37.68	54.81	592.3	1,407.8	2,718.4	3.46	2.63
Europe								
Total	67.07	75.14	83.22	453.4	548.4	597.6	0.76	0.34
Latin America								
Argentina	80.73	89.40	93.39	21.0	32.7	43.0	1.77	1.10
Bolivia	41.51	65.23	78.97	1.9	5.4	10.4	4.05	2.59
Brazil	61.15	81.21	88.94	66.0	141.9	204.8	3.06	1.47
Colombia	60.71	75.21	84.14	14.4	28.4	41.5	2.71	1.51

Country/region	Level of urbanization Total number in millions			Urban population % annual growth rate			% of total population in urban settlements	
	1975	2000	2025	1975	2000	2025	1975–2000	2000–25
Mexico	62.76	77.71	85.82	36.9	79.6	117.2	3.07	1.55
Paraguay	38.98	56.44	71.82	1.0	3.2	6.5	4.44	2.86
Peru	61.46	74.52	83.54	9.3	19.4	30.6	9.94	1.82
Venezuela	77.83	94.45	97.17	9.9	22.8	33.8	3.34	1.57
Total	61.32	76.61	84.67	196.2	401.1	600.9	2.86	1.61
Northern America								
Canada	75.61	77.16	83.67	17.5	23.9	32.0	1.24	1.16
USA	73.65	77.46	84.91	159.0	213.1	281.2	1.17	1.11
Total	73.85	77.44	84.78	176.7	237.2	313.3	1.18	1.11
Oceania								
Australia	85.92	84.69	88.59	11.9	16.3	21.8	1.24	1.18
New Zealand	82.78	87.20	91.64	2.5	3.3	4.0	1.00	0.81
Total	71.78	70.25	74.86	15.4	21.5	30.7	1.34	1.42
World								
More developed regions	69.84	76.52	83.98	729.3	904.2	1,040.0	0.86	0.56
Less developed regions	26.68	40.52	57.05	809.0	2,022.1	4,025.3	3.66	2.75
Total	37.73	47.52	61.07	1,538.3	2,926.4	5,065.3	2.57	2.19

Infant Mortality Rates and Female Fertility Rates

Source: UN Population Fund
Fertility rate is average number of children per woman. Only selected countries are listed.

1995–2000

Region	Country	Infant mortality rate	Fertility rate (per 1,000 births)
Africa			
Eastern Africa	Burundi	114	6.28
	Ethiopia	107	7.00
	Malawi	142	6.69
	Mozambique	110	6.06
	Somalia	112	7.00
	Zimbabwe	68	4.68
Total		99	6.05
Central Africa	Angola	124	6.69
	Cameroon	58	5.30
	Chad	115	5.51
	Gabon	85	5.40
Total		92	6.01
Northern Africa	Algeria	44	3.81
	Egypt	54	3.40
	Libya	56	5.92
	Sudan	71	4.61
Total		55	3.67
Southern Africa	Botswana	56	4.45
	Lesotho	72	4.86
	South Africa	48	3.81
Total		50	3.92

1995–2000

Region	Country	Infant mortality rate	Fertility rate (per 1,000 births)
Western Africa	Benin	84	5.83
	Guinea-Bissau	132	5.42
	Nigeria	77	5.97
	Sierra Leone	169	6.06
Total		90	5.95
Total in Africa		86	5.31
Asia			
Eastern Asia	China	38	1.80
	Japan	4	1.48
	Korea, South	9	1.65
	Mongolia	52	3.27
Total		35	1.78
South-central Asia	Afghanistan	154	6.90
	Bangladesh	78	3.14
	India	72	3.07
	Iran	39	4.77
	Pakistan	74	5.02
Total		72	3.42
Southeast Asia	Cambodia	102	4.50
	Philippines	35	3.62
	Singapore	5	1.79
	Thailand	30	1.74

1995–2000 Region	Country	Infant mortality rate	Fertility rate (per 1,000 births)
Western Asia	Azerbaijan	33	2.30
	Iraq	95	5.25
	Israel	7	2.75
	Turkey	44	2.50
	Yemen	80	7.60
Total		50	3.82
Total in Asia		56	2.65
Europe			
Eastern Europe	Czech Republic	9	1.40
	Poland	13	1.65
	Moldova	26	1.80
	Russia	19	1.35
	Ukraine	18	1.38
Total		17	1.41
Northern Europe	Denmark	7	1.82
	Estonia	12	1.30
	Ireland, Republic of	6	1.80
	Sweden	5	2.10
	UK	6	1.72
Total		6	1.73
Southern Europe	Albania	32	2.60
	Greece	8	1.38
	Italy	7	1.19
	Portugal	8	1.48
	Macedonia, Former Yugoslav Republic of	23	1.90
Total		10	1.34
Western Europe	Austria	6	1.42
	France	7	1.63
	Germany	6	1.30
	Switzerland	5	1.46
Total		6	1.46
Total in Europe		12	1.45

1995–2000 Region	Country	Infant mortality rate	Fertility rate (per 1,000 births)
Latin America and Caribbean			
Caribbean	Cuba	9	1.55
	Dominican Republic	34	2.80
	Haiti	82	4.60
	Martinique	7	2.00
Total		40	2.59
Central America	Costa Rica	12	2.95
	Mexico	31	2.75
	Nicaragua	44	3.85
	Panama	21	2.63
Total		33	3.04
South America	Argentina	22	2.62
	Bolivia	66	4.36
	Brazil	42	2.17
	Chile	13	2.44
	Peru	45	2.98
Total		36	2.51
Total in Latin America and the Caribbean		35	2.65
North America			
Northern America	Canada	6	1.61
	USA	7	1.96
Total		7	1.93
Oceania			
Oceania	Australia	6	1.89
	Fiji	20	2.76
	New Zealand	7	2.02
	Papua New Guinea	61	4.65
	Samoa	58	3.80
Total		24	2.46
World			
More developed regions		9	1.59
Less developed regions		62	3.08
Least developed countries		100	5.25
Total		57	2.79

World Life Expectancy at Birth

Source: UN Population Fund

1995–2000 Country	Life expectancy at birth Male	Female
Africa		
Algeria	67.5	70.3
Angola	44.9	48.1
Ethiopia	48.4	51.6
Ghana	56.2	59.9
Kenya	52.3	55.7
Madagascar	57.0	60.0
Mauritius	68.3	75.0
Nigeria	50.8	54.0
Rwanda	40.8	43.4
Sierra Leone	36.0	39.1
South Africa	62.3	68.3
Sudan	53.6	56.4
Tunisia	68.4	70.7
Uganda	40.4	42.3
Total	52.3	55.3
Asia		
Afghanistan	45.0	46.0
Bhutan	51.6	54.9
Cambodia	52.6	55.4
China	68.2	71.7
India	62.1	62.7
Iraq	66.9	63.9
Israel	75.7	79.5
Japan	76.9	82.9
Korea, North	68.9	75.1
Korea, South	68.8	76.0
Laos	52.0	55.0
Philippines	66.6	70.2
Singapore	75.1	79.5
Syria	66.7	71.2
Yemen	57.4	58.4
Total	64.8	67.7

1995–2000 Country	Life expectancy at birth Male	Female
Europe		
Austria	73.7	80.1
Croatia	68.1	76.5
Czech Republic	69.8	76.0
Estonia	63.9	75.0
Finland	73.0	80.1
France	74.6	82.9
Germany	73.4	79.9
Greece	75.5	80.6
Hungary	64.5	73.8
Ireland, Republic of	74.0	79.4
Italy	75.1	81.4
Norway	74.8	80.6
Romania	66.0	73.2
Sweden	76.2	80.8
Switzerland	75.3	81.8
UK	74.5	79.8
Total	68.3	77.0
Latin America and Caribbean		
Argentina	69.6	76.8
Bolivia	59.8	63.2
Brazil	63.4	71.2
Chile	72.3	78.3
Colombia	68.2	73.7
Costa Rica	74.5	79.2
Cuba	74.2	78.0
Dominican Republic	68.9	73.1
Guatemala	64.7	69.8
Haiti	52.8	56.0
Jamaica	72.4	76.8
Mexico	69.5	75.5
Nicaragua	65.8	70.6
Peru	65.9	70.9
Total	66.4	72.9

1995–2000 Country	Life expectancy at birth Male	Female
Northern America		
Canada	76.1	81.8
USA	73.4	80.1
Total	73.6	80.3
Oceania		
Australia	75.4	81.2
Micronesia	67.2	70.9
New Zealand	74.7	79.7
Papua New Guinea	57.2	58.7
Vanuatu	65.5	69.5
Total	71.5	76.4
Selected Countries of the Former USSR		
Armenia	67.2	74.0
Belarus	64.4	74.8
Georgia	68.5	76.7
Kazakstan	62.8	72.4
Russia	58.0	71.5
Turkmenistan	61.2	68.0
Ukraine	63.6	74.0
World		
More developed regions[1]	70.6	78.4
Less developed regions[2]	62.1	65.2
Least developed countries[3]	50.9	53.0
Total	63.4	67.7

[1] More developed regions comprise Northern America, Japan, Europe, and Australia and New Zealand.

[2] Less developed regions comprise all regions of Africa, Asia (excluding Japan), Latin America and the Caribbean, Melanesia, Micronesia, and Polynesia.

[3] Least developed countries according to standard UN designation.

World's Largest Countries, by Population Size

Source: UN Department for Economic and Social Information

Rank	Country	Population (millions)	% of world population	Rank	Country	Population (millions)	% of world population	Rank	Country	Population (millions)	% of world population
1996				**2015**				**2050**			
1	China	1,232	21.4	1	China	1,409	19.3	1	India	1,533	16.4
2	India	945	16.4	2	India	1,212	16.6	2	China	1,516	16.2
3	USA	269	4.7	3	USA	311	4.2	3	Pakistan	357	3.8
4	Indonesia	200	3.5	4	Indonesia	252	3.5	4	USA	348	3.7
5	Brazil	161	2.8	5	Pakistan	224	3.1	5	Nigeria	338	3.6
6	Russia	148	2.6	6	Brazil	200	2.7	6	Indonesia	318	3.4
7	Pakistan	140	2.4	7	Nigeria	191	2.6	7	Brazil	243	2.6
8	Japan	125	2.2	8	Bangladesh	163	2.2	8	Bangladesh	218	2.3
9	Bangladesh	120	2.1	9	Russia	138	1.9	9	Ethiopia	213	2.3
10	Nigeria	115	2.0	10	Japan	126	1.7	10	Iran	170	1.8

Refugees Worldwide

Source: UN High Commissioner for Refugees
The number of uprooted people around the world approached 50 million in 1997, including all estimated displaced within their own countries. One out of every 120 people on Earth has been forced into flight. The UN High Commissioner for Refugees (UNHCR) protects and assists more than 22 million people who have fled war or persecution.
(Data as of 1 January 1997. Figures in thousands. – = not applicable.)

Area	Refugees	Returnees	Others of concern	Internally displaced people	Total of concern to UNHCR
Africa	4,341	1,693	–	2,058	8,091
Asia	4,809	1,241	156	1,719	7,925
Europe	3,166	308	1,209	1,066	5,749
Latin America	88	70	–	11	169
North America	720	–	–	–	720
Oceania	750	–	–	–	75
Total	13,200	3,311	1,365	4,854	22,729

United Nations Membership	

The sovereign countries that are not UN members are Kiribati, Nauru, Switzerland, Taiwan, Tonga, Tuvalu, and Vatican City.

Country	Year of admission	Country	Year of admission	Country	Year of admission
Afghanistan	1946	Georgia	1992	Niger	1960
Albania	1955	Germany[2]	1973/1990	Nigeria	1960
Algeria	1962	Ghana	1957	Norway[1]	1945
Andorra	1993	Greece[1]	1945	Oman	1971
Angola	1976	Grenada	1974	Pakistan	1947
Antigua and Barbuda	1981	Guatemala[1]	1945	Palau	1994
Argentina[1]	1945	Guinea	1958	Panama[1]	1945
Armenia	1992	Guinea-Bissau	1974	Papua New Guinea	1975
Australia[1]	1945	Guyana	1966	Paraguay[1]	1945
Austria	1955	Haiti[1]	1945	Peru[1]	1945
Azerbaijan	1992	Honduras[1]	1945	Philippines[1]	1945
Bahamas	1973	Hungary	1955	Poland[1]	1945
Bahrain	1971	Iceland	1946	Portugal	1955
Bangladesh	1974	India[1]	1945	Qatar	1971
Barbados	1966	Indonesia	1950	Romania	1955
Belarus[1]	1945	Iran[1]	1945	Russia[3]	1945
Belgium[1]	1945	Iraq[1]	1945	Rwanda	1962
Belize	1981	Ireland, Republic of	1955	St Kitts and Nevis	1983
Benin	1960	Israel	1949	St Lucia	1979
Bhutan	1971	Italy	1955	St Vincent and the Grenadines	1980
Bolivia[1]	1945	Jamaica	1962	Samoa	1976
Bosnia-Herzegovina	1992	Japan	1956	San Marino	1992
Botswana	1966	Jordan	1955	São Tomé and Príncipe	1975
Brazil[1]	1945	Kazakhstan	1992	Saudi Arabia[1]	1945
Brunei	1984	Kenya	1963	Senegal	1960
Bulgaria	1955	Korea, North	1991	Seychelles	1976
Burkina Faso	1960	Korea, South	1991	Sierra Leone	1961
Burundi	1962	Kuwait	1963	Singapore	1965
Cambodia	1955	Kyrgyzstan	1992	Slovak Republic	1993
Cameroon	1960	Laos	1955	Slovenia	1992
Canada[1]	1945	Latvia	1991	Solomon Isles	1978
Cape Verde	1975	Lebanon[1]	1945	Somalia	1960
Central African Republic	1960	Lesotho	1966	South Africa[1]	1945
Chad	1960	Liberia[1]	1945	Spain	1955
Chile[1]	1945	Libya	1955	Sri Lanka	1955
China[1]	1945	Liechtenstein	1990	Sudan	1956
Colombia[1]	1945	Lithuania	1991	Suriname	1975
Comoros	1975	Luxembourg[1]	1945	Swaziland	1968
Congo, Democratic Republic of	1960	Macedonia, Former		Sweden	1946
Congo, Republic of the	1960	Yugoslav Republic of	1993	Syria[1]	1945
Costa Rica[1]	1945	Madagascar	1960	Tajikistan	1992
Côte d'Ivoire	1960	Malawi	1964	Tanzania	1961
Croatia	1992	Malaysia	1957	Thailand	1946
Cuba[1]	1945	Maldives	1965	Togo	1960
Cyprus	1960	Mali	1960	Trinidad and Tobago	1962
Czech Republic	1993	Malta	1964	Tunisia	1956
Denmark[1]	1945	Marshall Islands	1991	Turkey[1]	1945
Djibouti	1977	Mauritania	1961	Turkmenistan	1992
Dominica	1978	Mauritius	1968	Uganda	1962
Dominican Republic[1]	1945	Mexico[1]	1945	Ukraine[1]	1945
Ecuador[1]	1945	Micronesia	1991	United Arab Emirates	1971
Egypt[1]	1945	Moldova	1992	UK[1]	1945
El Salvador[1]	1945	Monaco	1993	USA[1]	1945
Equatorial Guinea	1968	Mongolia	1961	Uruguay[1]	1945
Eritrea	1993	Morocco	1956	Uzbekistan	1992
Estonia	1991	Mozambique	1975	Vanuatu	1981
Ethiopia[1]	1945	Myanmar	1948	Venezuela[1]	1945
Fiji	1970	Namibia	1990	Vietnam	1977
Finland	1955	Nepal	1955	Yemen[2]	1947
France[1]	1945	Netherlands[1]	1945	Yugoslavia[4]	1945
Gabon	1960	New Zealand[1]	1945	Zambia	1964
Gambia	1965	Nicaragua[1]	1945	Zimbabwe	1980

[1] Founder members.
[2] Represented by two countries until unification in 1990.

[3] Became a separate member upon the demise of the USSR which was a founder member in 1945.
[4] Founder member, but suspended from membership in 1993.